The 1996 Good Pub Guide

Edited by Alisdair Aird

Deputy Editor: Fiona May

Research Officer: Robert Unsworth
Editorial Research: Karen Fick

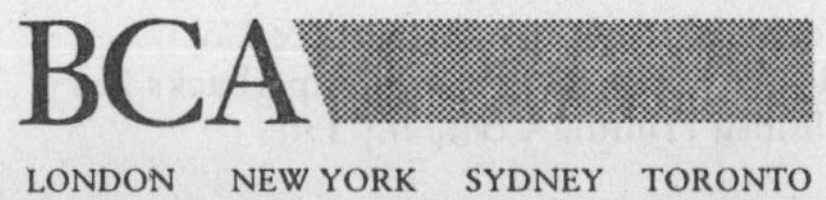

This edition first published in 1995 by BCA by arrangement with Vermilion, an imprint of Ebury Press

CN 3771

Typeset from author's disks by Clive Dorman & Co.
Printed and bound in Great Britain by BPC Paperbacks Ltd
A member of The British Printing Company Ltd

Contents

Introduction

Beer prices

Each year we compare what pubs charge for their beers with what those same pubs were charging a year before. This year there were 1,181 pubs in this direct price comparison. Our survey shows that, on average, this last year beer prices have increased by a whisker more than the overall rate of inflation – by 4.6%, against general inflation of 3.5% over the same period. Although not as good as last year (when beer prices rose almost exactly in line with inflation), it's still a much better performance than in previous years, when beer price increases tended to outstrip other prices by an outrageous margin. So it looks as though the regulations designed to weaken the monopoly power of the big national brewing combines are still helping to keep a lid on beer prices. Indeed, prices in pubs tied to the national brewers have if anything gone up slightly less this year than in other pubs. However, Scottish & Newcastle's takeover of Courage which is going ahead this year may change that. The merger gives the new group control over a quarter or more of the beer market. Our price survey shows that, as things are at the moment, Courage pubs (particularly those under the Inntrepreneur flag) are among the most expensive, and S & N pubs are significantly more expensive than average. It could go either way: the optimistic view is that combining the two brewers will allow production and marketing economies which will bring their prices down into line with other more competitive brewers; the pessimistic view is that the sheer size of the combination will give the new group so much monopoly power that it will become even more expensive. Obviously, we'll be watching developments with great interest.

Of the other big national brewers, it's worth noting that Carlsberg-Tetleys are close to S & N in the prices pubs supplied by them charge – nearly 10p a pint more than the national average. Whitbreads is a little cheaper than them, with its pubs charging around 5p more than average. Bass is the cheapest national brewer, with its pubs charging no more than the national average (and very much the same price as a typical free house).

We show below those breweries which came out cheapest of all in our survey. In each case we show how much on average you save in one of their tied pubs, compared with the typical pub tied to a big national brewer:

	saving per pint		saving per pint
Holts	55p	Timothy Taylors	26p
Clarks	31p	Sam Smiths	25p
Banks's/Hansons/ Camerons	29p	Hardys & Hansons	24p
		Lees	22p
Bathams	28p	Mitchells	21p
Hydes	28p	Donnington	21p
Batemans	26p	Robinsons	20p

All these are cheaper than typical prices charged by pubs which brew their own beers. Interestingly, Boddingtons (a big regional brewer which has given up brewing altogether and is supplied by Whitbreads) also comes into this group – charging an average 36p less in its pubs for Whitbreads-brewed beers than Whitbreads itself charges.

The most expensive part of Britain for drinks is now Surrey, where a pint of beer typically costs £1.75. It's nearly as expensive in the very centre of London (£1.73), but as London pubs a little outside the centre have held their prices down better than anywhere else in the country this year, the overall average for a London pint at £1.68 now makes it just a shade cheaper than in Sussex which now averages £1.69 – why oh why did we move the Guide offices from London to Sussex? Drinkers in Bucks, Kent and Hants are also paying well over the odds for their pint.

The cheapest area is the West Midlands, where a pint typically costs £1.34, and well below that in many pubs. So West Midlands drinkers are saving more than 40p a pint, compared with their Surrey counterparts. The other bargain areas (starting with the cheapest, and showing for each how much is saved in comparison with Surrey prices) are Lancs (saving 39p), Yorks and Notts (36p), Cheshire (35p), Herefs & Worcs (34p), Derbys, Staffs and Cumbria (33p), Northumbria (32p) and Shropshire (30p).

Beer quality

Some 270 pubs in this edition have qualified for our Beer Award, which marks those pubs looking after their beers exceptionally well, or keeping an unusually interesting range well. This is a marked increase on last year, suggesting that to attract customers more pubs are taking real care to offer a truly interesting range of well kept flavourful beers. Fewer readers than in the past have complained to us of poor beer quality, and one or two have commented specifically on the fact that the major brands of beer now seem to be almost universally well kept. Our inspection tours would confirm that this is the case. However, despite differences in strength and appearance between the major brands, it does seem that differences in flavour between them are becoming less marked. Is this just our memory, deluding us into the familiar feeling that the old days were better? Is our palate becoming dulled by age? Or are the big brewers deliberately reducing the amount of ullage in their beers, making them easier to keep in good condition in other words reducing complaints about poor beer quality, but at the expense of individuality of flavour?

Another trend worrying some readers is the southwards spread of the sparkler – the nozzle which increases the pressure and turbulence under which beer is forced through the dispenser, filling it with the tiny air bubbles which give a frothy head. In the North most people prefer their beer served that way, even though it brings the inconvenience that to get a full pint of liquid as opposed to froth you often have to take your glass back for a top-up (all brewers recommend their pubs to give such top-ups freely). Elsewhere, however, beer has always been served without this added creamy head. Faced with the sparkler invasion, the watchword for southerners should be that a creamy topping is ideal for Guinness and for strawberries, but not for beer.

Current superstars in the beer firmament are the Blackwood Arms at Littleworth Common (Bucks), the Old Ale House in Truro (Cornwall), the Watermill at Ings (Cumbria), the Alexandra in Derby, Old Crown in Shardlow and Derby Tup at Whittington Moor (Derbys), the Plough at Navestock (Essex), the Taps in Lytham (Lancs), the Rose & Crown at Hose (Leics), the Vane Arms in Sudborough (Midlands), the Market Hotel in Retford (Notts), the Richmond Arms at West Ashling (Sussex), the St Vincent Arms at Sutton upon Derwent, Tap & Spile in Wakefield and Tap & Spile in York (Yorks), the Athletic Arms in Edinburgh (Scotland) and the Star at Talybont on Usk (Wales). We choose Graham Titcombe of the Blackwood Arms at Littleworth Common (Bucks) as **Beer Man of the Year**: by the time this edition is published he may well have broken the UK record, with approaching 1,000 different beers served in a year.

Over three dozen of the pubs in this book brew their own beer, or are supplied by a brewery right beside them. Generally this is cheaper than the surrounding competition; often, it's exceptionally good. Those currently finding wide favour are the Cavendish Arms in Cartmel and Sun at Dent (Cumbria), the Burton Bridge at Burton on Trent (Derbys), the Tally Ho at Hatherleigh (Devon), the Flower Pots at Cheriton (Hants), the Brewers Arms at Snaith (Lincs), the Plough at Wistanstow (Shrops) and the White Horse at Trudoxhill (Somerset). Our choice as **Own Brew Pub of the Year** is the Cavendish Arms in Cartmel (Cumbria); the young brewmaster here, the landlord's son Nick Murray, has an exceptionally sure touch.

Whiskies

In Scotland it's easy to find pubs with a magnificent range of malt whiskies. More pubs south of the Border are taking the trouble to stock some interesting less well-known malts alongside the few widely promoted ones, and a few English pubs now have an exceptional range of whiskies. The best are to be found at the Cragg Lodge at Wormald Green (Yorks), which with over 1,000 has more than you will find anywhere else, and the Crown & Horns at East Ilsley (Berks), the Quayside in Falmouth (Cornwall), the King George IV at Eskdale Green (Cumbria), the Nobody Inn at Doddiscombsleigh (Devon), the Wight Mouse at Chale (Isle of Wight), the Bulls Head at Clipston (Midlands), the White Horse at Pulverbatch (Shrops), the Sandpiper at Leyburn and Pack Horse at Widdop (Yorks) and the Dinorben Arms at Bodfari (Wales) also stand out. For championing the malt whisky cause so far from the drink's home, with a grand choice of some 250 different malts, we choose the Nobody Inn at Doddiscombsleigh (Devon) as **Whisky Pub of the Year**.

The wine alternative

The wine tide has finally turned in British pubs. This is the first year that we've been able to say that it's now reasonable to expect decent wine in pubs – at least those that are main entries in this Guide. Just a few years ago, when our readers mentioned wine in their reports to us, it was usually to complain about how awful it was – a very poor choice, and badly kept. Now, that's changed. Even many of the more modest pubs now have a small but respectable wine list, and house wines that show some thought. It's become rare (rather than the rule it used to be) to see a dusty opened bottle of red languishing on a back shelf, or to be expected to drink a nasty warm sweetish oxidising white. In just the last year, we've been struck by a tremendous increase in the number of licensees taking a personal and informed interest in the wines they serve – and in the number of pubs with a really good choice of wines by the glass.

There are several reasons for the change. Starting with the customers, there's no doubt that most of us know and care more about wine choice and quality than we did just a few years ago. Women of all ages are going to pubs more than in the past (often for a meal), and we find that a high proportion choose wine rather than other drinks. As we've remarked in previous editions, there's been a massive swing to eating in pubs, and more recently to expecting good food – for many people, the natural accompaniment is a glass of wine. In a small way, our own intervention may have helped. Since the 1993 edition of this Guide, we have been marking with a wine glass symbol those pubs taking particular care over their wines; readers have been looking out for these Wine Award pubs, and we have evidence that licensees who have not been granted our Wine Award have been taking steps to qualify for one.

Then there's no doubt that licensees have seen the commercial sense in selling decent wines. At £1.50 for a 125ml glass, a 100% price mark-up still allows sound quality, with a very wide choice of respectable wines available wholesale at around £4.50 a bottle – a useful commercial weapon for publicans faced with the general decline in beer sales. Pubs offering this sort of value, as many in this Guide do, find customers willingly have a second glass; whereas pubs which still greedily follow the old system of charging the same sort of price for a glass of indifferent wine which a customer can get by the bottle from a supermarket for under twice as much are increasingly finding customers voting with their feet and simply walking out on such savage mark-ups. Finally, the technological revolution in keeping opened bottles of wine fresh – simple or sophisticated, from basic vacuum pumps up – has meant that pubs can safely offer as many different wines by the glass as they want, with virtually no risk of their going off. It's now surprisingly common for a pub to offer ten or more (at least three dozen pubs in this Guide), and we know of quite a few which offer 20 or more.

Most pubs still lag behind in the way they list and describe their wines. Even if the wines themselves are respectable, as far as the customer and bar staff is concerned it's just 'red' or 'white' or maybe 'medium dry white'. We believe all wines sold by the glass in pubs should certainly be listed as visibly as the beers and food, and preferably described in brief. In our experience and that of our readers, if a pub does not list and describe its wines in a way which gives confidence in their quality, red is generally a safer bet than white.

Pubs with a really exceptional range of wines by the glass, and a helpfully informative approach to choosing among them, are the Knife & Cleaver at Houghton Conquest (Beds), the Five Arrows in Waddesdon (Bucks), the Eagle in Cambridge and Pheasant at Keyston (Cambs), the Grosvenor Arms at Aldford (Cheshire), the Pandora near Mylor Bridge (Cornwall), the Cott at Dartington and Nobody Inn at Doddiscombsleigh (Devon), the Fox at Lower Oddington (Gloucs), the Red Lion at Boldre and Wykeham Arms in Winchester (Hants), the Rock at Tockholes (Lancs), the George in Stamford (Lincs), the Old Coach House at Ashby St Ledgers (Midlands), the Adam & Eve in Norwich and Rose & Crown at Snettisham (Norfolk), the Perch & Pike at South Stoke (Oxon), the Plough at Blackbrook (Surrey), the Angel at Hetton (Yorks) and the White Cross in Richmond (London). The Crown at Colkirk (Norfolk) will open any bottle from its main list for just a glass, and the Fox at Bramdean (Hants) has a similar sort of attitude. If it's rare bottles you're after, the Ancient Camp at Ruckhall (Herefs & Worcs) is well worth investigating.

From among these, we choose the Cott at Dartington (Devon) as our **Wine Pub of the Year.**

Pub food

Most pubs have kept the price of their main hot dishes virtually unchanged over the last year. In a sample of over 400 pubs' steak and kidney pies, we found that the average price increase was 2.7% – well below the general level of price increases. Food prices have held steadiest over the year (often falling in individual pubs) in Cornwall, Essex, Kent, Norfolk, Oxon, London, Scotland and the Channel Islands, though the cheapest places for pub food are London, the Isle of Wight, the Channel Islands, Lancashire, Cheshire, the Midlands generally (though prices are rising here much faster than elsewhere), and Derbys/Staffs. In all these places good hot pub main dishes can generally be had for under £5 – whereas in Hampshire, now the most expensive area for pub meals, it's more likely to be over £6.

In our view, £6 marks a sensible upper limit for the price of a decent middle-of-the-road pub main dish. It is quite possible for a pub to produce a comprehensive range of dishes profitably, using quality ingredients, within this limit. Good pubs can turn a profit on something more intricate or sophisticated for well under £8; only steaks and the more expensive fish can justify much more than that. A handful of pubs can justify prices higher than these levels on the grounds that their cooking is really first-class and is generally recognised to be so good that despite high prices it is good value. Excluding these special places, though, it makes sense to avoid pubs which charge more than the limits we have suggested.

A point to watch is that pubs have been putting up the price of some popular dishes disproportionately. The price of a ploughman's is rising nearly twice as quickly as most pub food. Oddly enough, it's in the North that it's become most expensive – in Cumbria, Northumbria and Yorkshire a ploughman's now tends to cost over rather than under £4. The excuse for pricing a ploughman's so high is generally a heap of unwanted miscellaneous greenery – substance rather than value, as lettuce leaves are among the cheapest 'fillers' around. For real ploughman's value, head for Manchester, where the Mark Addy, the Dukes 92 and particularly the Royal Oak in Didsbury heap your plate with enormous quantities of excellent cheeses, instead of a pile of rabbit-fodder hiding a tiny slice of cheese and a foil-wrapped packet of butter.

However, as we have said, the price of most pub food is holding remarkably steady. What's more, quality is decidedly on the up. Licensees are more than ever tracking down tip-top fresh local produce; it's now the norm in the Guide's foodier main entries. How it's used varies from the simplest homely cooking to immensely elaborate concoctions. Three notable trends have emerged this year. Fresh fish is more popular in pub cooking than we have ever known it before; what might have been thought unlikely ingredients – offal, rook, organic produce – are turning up more and more in country pubs; and Thai influences (lemon grass, fresh chillies and coriander, coconut and so forth) and recipes have made a deep and widespread impact on pub food. The Thai trend is more than just a passing fad. Beer (if not whisky or brandy) is what Thai people have traditionally drunk with food, and Thai textures and flavours, subtly aromatic and spicy, seem a perfect fit with British pub cuisine.

The more general use of fresh ingredients is a real help to the many people who have special diet needs, and the even greater number who don't want a full-sized helping. Pubs relying on freezer packs cannot modify their menus and recipes to suit individual customers; and if they do serve a smaller helping it means throwing away the rest of what was in the pack, so they can't really charge less for it. However, pubs using natural ingredients can change their cooking to suit you. In fact it's a good test of how accurate those sorely misused and rightly mistrusted words 'home-cooked' are. Try asking whether someone else you know could have a dish cooked with less salt, say, or whether they could have a smaller helping at a lower price. If you're met with a blank stare, then you can be pretty sure that that pub's 'home cooking' is limited to turning on the microwave. Or more directly, ask 'Is it home-made?' Pubs will always give you an honest answer, and – unlike 'home-cooked', which you should always be wary of – the words 'home-made' do mean what they say.

It used to be quite easy for us to choose a dining pub of the year – the general standard of pub cooking was such that a handful really stood out as exceptional. This year, the choice has been our most difficult ever. A great many pubs now offer really memorable meals out – combining excellent food with a most enjoyable atmosphere. Our final 'short list' is very long indeed: the Anchor at Sutton Gault (Cambridge), the Cholmondeley Arms near Bickley Moss (Cheshire), the Pheasant at Casterton, Queens Head at Tirril (a new entry) and Queens Head at Troutbeck (Cumbria), the New Inn at Coleford and Otter at Weston (Devon), the Green Man at Gosfield (Essex), the Sun at Bentworth and (new to the Guide) Dever Arms at Micheldever (Hants), the Roebuck at Brimfield, Bear & Ragged Staff at Bransford and Hunters Inn at Longdon (another new main entry, Herefs & Worcs), the George & Dragon at Watton at Stone (Herts), the Albion, an entirely new Faversham entry, and George at Newnham (Kent), the New Inn under its new licensees at Yealand Conyers (Lancs), the Martins Arms at Colston Bassett, Peacock at Redmile and another new entry the Bakers Arms at Thorpe Langton (Leics), the Bell at Monks Kirby, for its tapas (a new Midlands entry), the Chequers at Gedney Dyke (a new Lincs entry), the Hoste Arms at Burnham Market and Hare Arms at Stow Bardolph (Norfolk), the Boars Head at Ardington (yet another newcomer), Bear & Ragged Staff at Cumnor and Feathers in Woodstock (Oxon), the Globe at Appley and Rose & Crown at Stoke St Gregory (Somerset), the Brewers Arms at Rattlesden and Angel at Stoke by Nayland (Suffolk), the Woolpack at Elstead (Surrey), the Elsted Inn at Elstead, Griffin at Fletching, Crabtree at Lower Beeding and – yet another new entry – Horseguards at Tillington (Sussex), the new-entry George & Dragon at Rowde and Lamb at Semington (Wilts), the Three Hares at Bilbrough, Malt Shovel at Brearton (enterprising new licensees), Blue Lion at East Witton, Angel at Hetton and Wombwell Arms at Wass (Yorkshire), the Eagle in Farringdon St (London EC1), the Walnut Tree at Llandewi Skirrid (Wales), the Kilberry Inn at Kilberry and Wheatsheaf at Swinton (Scotland).

After racking our brains and our tastebuds, and sifting through readers' enthusiastic reports for the umpteenth time, we select as **Dining Pub of the Year** the Cholmondeley Arms near Bickley Moss in Cheshire.

As we've said, good fish cooking is an increasing highlight of the pub scene. Outstanding fish can be had at the Red Lion at Great Kingshill (a new Bucks entry), the Trinity Foot at Swavesey (Cambs), the Drewe Arms at Broadhembury, Anchor at Cockwood, Passage in Topsham and Start Bay at Torcross (Devon), Sankeys in Tunbridge Wells (Kent), the Red Lion at Icklingham and Pykkerel at Ixworth (Suffolk), the Half Moon at Kirdford and White Hart at Stopham (Sussex), the Crown at Portpatrick (Scotland), and the Vine Tree at Llangattock, Grapes at Maentwrog and Ferry at Pembroke Ferry (Wales). It's at the Drewe Arms at Broadhembury (Devon) that we've found the most perfectly cooked fresh fish: it is our **Fish Pub of the Year**.

Our **Vegetarian Pub of the Year** is the Drunken Duck at Barngates up above Hawkshead (Cumbria).

Our **Sandwich Pub of the Year** is the Three Acres at Shelley, a new Yorks entry; quite a grand dining pub which hasn't forgotten this humbler ingredient of the pub scene – a smashing enterprising choice.

The top pubs
For many people, there's nothing to beat a traditional unspoilt pub – no frills, maybe no food to speak of, lots of real character. Shining examples are the Bell at Aldworth and Pot Kiln at Frilsham (Berks), the Prince Albert at Frieth and (a new entry) Crown at Little Missenden (Bucks), the Free Press in Cambridge and Queens Head at Newton (Cambs), the White Lion at Barthomley (Cheshire), the Olde Gate at Brassington (Derbys), the Northmore Arms at Wonson (a new Devon entry), the Flitch of Bacon at Little Dunmow (a new Essex entry), the Boat at Ashleworth Quay (Gloucs), the White Horse near Petersfield and Harrow at Steep (Hants), the Fleece at Bretforton and Monkey House at Defford (Herefs & Worcs), the Adam & Eve in Norwich (Norfolk), the Falkland Arms at Great Tew (Oxon), the Rose & Crown at Huish Episcopi, Talbot at Mells (a new entry) and George at Norton St Philip (Somerset), the Yew Tree at Cauldon (Staffs), the Scarlett Arms at Walliswood (Surrey), Whitelocks in Leeds and the Farmers Arms at Muker (Yorks), and the Bow Bar in Edinburgh (Scotland). Among these, we choose Whitelocks in Leeds as **Town Pub of the Year**; and the Boat at Ashleworth Quay (Gloucs) as **Unspoilt Country Pub of the Year**.

We have already mentioned a number of new main entries which have given particular pleasure. Other specially rewarding finds are the Thatched Tavern at Cheapside (Berks), the Grosvenor Arms at Aldford (Cheshire), the Crown at Lanlivery (Cornwall), the Jolly Farmer at Locks Heath (Hants), the Lytton Arms at Knebworth (Herts), the Hunters at Longdon (Herefs & Worcs), the Eagle & Child at Bispham Green (Lancs), the White Swan at Harringworth (Midlands), the Talbot at Mells (Somerset), the Royal Oak at East Lavant (Sussex) and the White Cross in Richmond (London). From these we choose as **Newcomer of the Year** the Grosvenor Arms at Aldford (Cheshire).

The great majority of pubs in this Guide allow children inside, without making a great song and dance about it. To a few readers' delight, there are some which firmly exclude them – usually the smaller more old-fashioned places where people come for a quiet chat and a civilised drink. At the opposite end of the scale, an increasing number of pubs go all out to encourage families, with baby-changing facilities, good children's entertainment indoors and out, and special food deals for them. Whitbreads' growing chain of Brewers Fayre pubs is a good general example, including a fine one in the Coombe Cellars at Combeinteignhead (Devon). Other notable family pubs are the Barbridge Inn at Barbridge (Cheshire), the Wight Mouse at Chale (Isle of Wight), and the Old Coach House at Ashby St Ledgers (Midlands; living proof that it can be done without damaging or even dominating a pub's character). Of these, the Wight Mouse is **Family Pub of the Year**.

Pubs which are currently doing extremely well all round are the Trengilly Wartha near Costantine (Cornwall), the Royal Oak in Appleby, Masons Arms on Cartmel Fell, Britannia at Elterwater, Drunken Duck near Hawkshead, Shepherds at Melmerby, Queens Head at Tirril and Queens Head at Troutbeck (all Cumbria), the Roseland at Philleigh (Cornwall), the Cott at Dartington, Nobody Inn at Doddiscombsleigh, Castle at Lydford and Otter at Weston (all in Devon), the Fox at Corscombe (a new Dorset entry), the Sun at Bentworth and Wykeham Arms in Winchester (Hants), the Inn at Whitewell (Lancs), the Fox & Hounds at Great Wolford (Midlands), the Three Horseshoes at Warham (Norfolk), the Cook & Barker Arms at Newton on the Moor (Northumbria), the Falkland Arms at Great Tew (Oxon), the Unicorn in Ludlow (Shropshire), the Notley Arms at Monksilver (Somerset), the Angel in Lavenham and Crown in Southwold (Suffolk) and the White Hart at Ford (Wilts). Of these, the Queens Head at Troutbeck is our **1996 Pub of the Year**.

Some individual licensees stand out this year, for the warmly welcoming and happy atmosphere that they generate in their pubs: the Ross-Lowes of the Cholmondeley Arms near Bickley Moss (Cheshire), the Camerons of the Old Inn at St Breward (Cornwall), the Cheynes of the Royal Oak in Appleby and the

Coulthwaites of the Watermill at Ings (both Cumbria), Gerry McDonald of the Lantern Pike at Little Hayfield, Hayfield, the Lythgoes of the Packhorse at Little Longstone and the Taylors of the White Horse at Woolley Moor (all Derbys), the Greys of the Cott at Dartington (Devon), the Barretts of the Marquis of Lorne at Nettlecombe (Dorset), the Bektases of the Plough at Clifton Hampden (Oxon), and the Warings of the Wenlock Edge Inn on Wenlock Edge (Shrops). Ian and Anne Barrett, tenants of the Marquis of Lorne at Nettlecombe (Dorset), have made it such an enjoyable place in the short time since they reopened it for Palmers the Bridport brewery that they are our choice as 1996 Licensees of the Year.

Some grumbles

This year we asked a few dozen readers who visit pubs fairly often to let us know if anything general was causing them concern. We have already mentioned some of their worries – misuse of the words 'home-cooked', the increasing use of sparklers for serving beer, some unjustified pricing of drinks or food, lack of information about a pub's wines, for example. Apart from the nuisance of having to tolerate other people's smoke in some pubs, other points that cropped up were the inconvenience caused by pubs failing to show their opening hours clearly outside; the way that some pubs, shifting as they have had to do from the 1/6 gill spirits measure to the scarcely larger metric 25ml, have used the change as an unjustified excuse for increasing their spirits prices markedly; the way that a few pubs have the effrontery to make people having meals there share their tables with strangers; the practice in some pubs of charging more for a guest beer rather than less, even if the beer comes from a low-priced brewery.

All such worries fade into insignificance compared with two major concerns. Many people, ourselves included, deplore the way that perfectly good genuine pubs have their hearts ripped out, to be refitted in a standardised prettified fake-antique mock-olde-worlde way. One structural engineer even suggested to us that we should have a Wooden Pin Award to show those pubs where the antiquity is genuine (give-away clues to fakery include dead straight 'timber' beams ending in the middle of a lintel, timbers covering very long spans, and even join marks between the bottom and side edges of a 'beam'). Many other people are upset by unnecessary, unsuitable, repetitive, badly reproduced or over-loud piped music in pubs. One or two readers positively welcome the way that piped music drowns banal nearby conversations in otherwise quiet pubs. Most are reasonably happy with well reproduced individually chosen music if it more or less matches the style of the pub and the general mood of the customers at the time. But too many pubs seem instead to think of piped music as something to keep their staff happy – and for their customers, that's decidedly a turn-off.

What is a Good Pub?

The main entries in this book have been through a two-stage sifting process. First of all, some 2,000 regular correspondents keep in touch with us about the pubs they visit, and nearly double that number report occasionally. The present edition has used a total of around 34,000 reports from readers. This keeps us up-to-date about pubs included in previous editions – it's their alarm signals that warn us when a pub's standards have dropped (after a change of management, say), and it's their continuing approval that reassures us about keeping a pub as a main entry for another year. Very important, though, are the reports they send us on pubs we don't know at all. It's from these new discoveries that we make up a shortlist, to be considered for possible inclusion as new main entries. The more people that report favourably on a new pub, the more likely it is to win a place on this shortlist – especially if some of the reporters belong to our hard core of about five hundred trusted correspondents whose judgement we have learned to rely on. These are people who have each given us detailed comments on dozens of pubs, and shown that (when we ourselves know some of those pubs too) their judgement is closely in line with our own.

This brings us to the acid test. Each pub, before inclusion as a main entry, is inspected anonymously by the Editor, the Deputy Editor, or both. They have to find some special quality that would make strangers enjoy visiting it. What often marks the pub out for special attention is good value food (and that might mean anything from a well made sandwich, with good fresh ingredients at a low price, to imaginative cooking outclassing most restaurants in the area). Maybe the drinks are out of the ordinary (pubs with several hundred whiskies, with remarkable wine lists, with home-made country wines or good beer or cider made on the premises, with a wide range of well kept real ales or bottled beers from all over the world). Perhaps there's a special appeal about it as a place to stay, with good bedrooms and obliging service. Maybe it's the building itself (from centuries-old parts of monasteries to extravagant Victorian gin-palaces), or its surroundings (lovely countryside, attractive waterside, extensive well kept garden), or what's in it (charming furnishings, extraordinary collections of bric-a-brac).

Above all, though, what makes the good pub is its atmosphere – you should be able to feel at home there, and feel not just that *you're* glad you've come but that *they're* glad you've come.

It follows from this that a great many ordinary locals, perfectly good in their own right, don't earn a place in the book. What makes them attractive to their regular customers (an almost clubby chumminess) may even make strangers feel rather out-of-place.

Another important point is that there's not necessarily any link between charm and luxury – though we like our creature comforts as much as anyone. A basic unspoilt village tavern, with hard seats and a flagstone floor, may be worth travelling miles to find, while a deluxe pub-restaurant may not be worth crossing the street for. Landlords can't buy the Good Pub accolade by spending thousands on thickly padded banquettes, soft music and luxuriously shrimpy sauces for their steaks – they can only win it by having a genuinely personal concern for both their customers and their pub.

Using the *Guide*

THE COUNTIES
England has been split alphabetically into counties, mainly to make it easier for people scanning through the book to find pubs near them. Each chapter starts by picking out the pubs that are currently doing the best in the area, or are specially attractive for one reason or another.

Occasionally, counties have been grouped together into a single chapter, and metropolitan areas have been included in the counties around them – for example, Merseyside in Lancashire. When there's any risk of confusion, we have put a note about where to find a county at the place in the book where you'd probably look for it. But if in doubt, check the Contents.

Scotland and Wales have each been covered in single chapters, and London appears immediately before them at the end of England. Except in London (which is split into Central, North, South, West and East), pubs are listed alphabetically under the name of the town or village where they are. If the village is so small that you probably wouldn't find it on a road map, we've listed it under the name of the nearest sizeable village or town instead. The maps use the same town and village names, and additionally include a few big cities that don't have any listed pubs – for orientation.

We always list pubs in their true locations – so if a village is actually in Buckinghamshire that's where we list it, even if its postal address is via some town in Oxfordshire. Just once or twice, while the village itself is in one county the pub is just over the border in the next-door county. We then use the village county, not the pub one.

STARS ★
Specially good pubs are picked out with a star after their name. In a few cases, pubs have two stars: these are the aristocrats among pubs, really worth going out of your way to find. The stars do NOT signify extra luxury or specially good food – in fact some of the pubs which appeal most distinctively and strongly of all are decidedly basic in terms of food and surroundings. The detailed description of each pub shows what its special appeal is, and it's that that the stars refer to.

FOOD AND STAY AWARDS
The knife-and-fork rosette shows those pubs where food is quite outstanding. The bed symbol shows pubs which we know to be good as places to stay in – bearing in mind the price of the rooms (obviously you can't expect the same level of luxury at £15 a head as you'd get for £30 a head). Pubs with bedrooms are now mapped and are marked on the maps as a square.

This wine glass symbol marks out those pubs where wines are a cut above the usual run. This should mean that a glass of house wine will be at least palatable. The text of the entry will show whether you can expect much more than this.

The beer tankard symbol shows pubs where the quality of the beer is quite exceptional, or pubs which keep a particularly interesting range of beers in good condition.

£
This symbol picks out pubs where we have found decent snacks at £1.30 or less, or worthwhile main dishes at £3.50 or less.

RECOMMENDERS
At the end of each main entry we include the names of readers who have recently recommended that pub (unless they've asked us not to). Important note: the description of the pub and the comments on it are our own and *not* the

recommenders'; they are based on our own personal inspections and on later verification of facts with each pub. As some recommenders' names appear quite often, you can get an extra idea of what a pub is like by seeing which other pubs those recommenders have approved.

LUCKY DIPS

We've continued to raise the standard for entry to the Lucky Dip section at the end of each county chapter. This includes brief descriptions of pubs that have been recommended by readers, with the readers' names in brackets. As the flood of reports from readers has given so much solid information about so many pubs, we have been able to include only those which seem really worth trying. Where only one single reader has recommended a pub, we have now not included that pub in the list unless the reader's description makes the nature of the pub quite clear, and gives us good grounds for trusting that other readers would be glad to know of the pub. So with most, the descriptions reflect the balanced judgement of a number of different readers, increasingly backed up by similar reports on the same pubs from different readers in previous years (we do not name these readers). Many have been inspected by us. In these cases, LYM means the pub was in a previous edition of the *Guide*. The usual reason that it's no longer a main entry is that, although we've heard nothing really condemnatory about it, we've not had enough favourable reports to be sure that it's still ahead of the local competition. BB means that, although the pub has never been a main entry, we have inspected it, and found nothing against it. In both these cases, the description is our own; in others, it's based on the readers' reports.

Lucky Dip pubs marked with a ☆ are ones where the information we have (either from our own inspections or from trusted reader/reporters) suggests a firm recommendation. Roughly speaking, we'd say that these pubs are as much worth considering, at least for the virtues described for them, as many of the main entries themselves. Note that in the Dips we always commend food if we have information supporting a positive recommendation. So a bare mention that food is served shouldn't be taken to imply a recommendation of the food. The same is true of accommodation and so forth.

The Lucky Dips (particularly, of course, the starred ones) are under consideration for inspection for a future edition – so please let us have any comments you can make on them. You can use the report forms at the end of the book, the report card which should be included in it, or just write direct (no stamp needed if posted in the UK). Our address is *The Good Pub Guide*, FREEPOST TN1569, WADHURST, East Sussex TN5 7BR.

MAP REFERENCES

All pubs are given four-figure map references. On the main entries, it looks like this: SX5678 Map 1. Map 1 means that it's on the first map at the end of the book. SX means it's in the square labelled SX on that map. The first figure, 5, tells you to look along the grid at the top and bottom of the SX square for the figure 5. The *third* figure, 7, tells you to look down the grid at the side of the square to find the figure 7. Imaginary lines drawn down and across the square from these figures should intersect near the pub itself.

The second and fourth figures, the 6 and the 8, are for more precise pin-pointing, and are really for use with larger-scale maps such as road atlases or the Ordnance Survey 1:50,000 maps, which use exactly the same map reference system. On the relevant Ordnance Survey map, instead of finding the 5 marker on the top grid you'd find the 56 one; instead of the 7 on the side grid you'd look for the 78 marker. This makes it very easy to locate even the smallest village.

Where a pub is exceptionally difficult to find, we include a six-figure reference in the directions, such as OS Sheet 102 reference 654783. This refers to Sheet 102 of the Ordnance Survey 1:50,000 maps, which explain how to use the six-figure references to pin-point a pub to the nearest 100 metres.

MOTORWAY PUBS

If a pub is within four or five miles of a motorway junction, and reaching it doesn't involve much slow traffic, we give special directions for finding it from the motorway. And the Special Interest Lists at the end of the book include a list of these pubs, motorway by motorway.

PRICES AND OTHER FACTUAL DETAILS

The *Guide* went to press during the summer of 1995. As late as possible, each pub was sent a checking sheet to get up-to-date food, drink and bedroom prices and other factual information. In the last year, we've found that many pubs have held their food and accommodation prices almost unchanged. However there have been increases and we know that by summer 1996 there are bound to be more – to be prudent, you should probably allow around 5% extra by then. But if you find a significantly different price *please let us know.*

Breweries to which pubs are 'tied' are named at the beginning of the italic-print rubric after each main entry. That means the pub has to get most if not all of its drinks from that brewery. If the brewery is not an independent one but just part of a combine, we name the combine in brackets. Where a brewery no longer brews its own beers but gets them under contract from a different brewer, we name that brewer too. When the pub is tied, we have spelled out whether the landlord is a tenant, has the pub on a lease, or is a manager; tenants and leaseholders generally have considerably greater freedom to do things their own way, and in particular are allowed to buy drinks including a beer from sources other than their tied brewery.

Free houses are pubs not tied to a brewery, so in theory they can shop around to get the drinks their customers want, at the best prices they can find. But in practice many free houses have loans from the big brewers, on terms that bind them to sell those breweries' beers – indeed, about half of all the beer sold in free houses is supplied by the big national brewery combines to free houses that have these loan ties. So don't be too surprised to find that so-called free houses may be stocking a range of beers restricted to those from a single brewery.

Real ale is used by us to mean beer that has been maturing naturally in its cask. We do not count as real ale beer which has been pasteurised or filtered to remove its natural yeasts. If it is kept under a blanket of carbon dioxide to preserve it, we still generally mention it – as long as the pressure is too light for you to notice any extra fizz, it's hard to tell the difference. (For brevity, we use the expression 'under light blanket pressure' to cover such pubs; we do not include among them pubs where the blanket pressure is high enough to force the beer up from the cellar, as this does make it unnaturally fizzy.) If we say a pub has, for example, 'Whitbreads-related real ales', these may include not just beers brewed by the national company and its subsidiaries but also beers produced by independent breweries which the national company buys in bulk and distributes alongside its own.

Other drinks: we've also looked out particularly for pubs doing enterprising non-alcoholic drinks (including good tea or coffee), interesting spirits (especially malt whiskies), country wines (elderflower and the like) and good farm ciders. So many pubs now stock one of the main brands of draught cider that we normally mention cider only if the pub keeps quite a range, or one of the less common farm-made ciders.

Meals refers to what is sold in the bar, not in any separate restaurant. It means that pub sells food in its bar substantial enough to do as a proper meal – something you'd sit down to with knife and fork. It doesn't necessarily mean you can get three separate courses.

Snacks means sandwiches, ploughman's, pies and so forth, rather than pork scratchings or packets of crisps. We always mention sandwiches in the text if we know that a pub does them – if you don't see them mentioned, assume you can't get them.

The food listed in the description of each pub is an example of the sort of thing you'd find served in the bar on a normal day, and generally includes the dishes which are currently finding most favour with readers. We try to indicate any difference we know of between lunchtime and evening, and between summer and winter (on the whole stressing summer food more). In winter, many pubs tend to have a more restricted range, particularly of salads, and tend then to do more in the way of filled baked potatoes, casseroles and hot pies. We always mention barbecues if we know a pub does them. Food quality and variety may be affected by holidays –

particularly in a small pub, where the licensees do the cooking themselves (May and early June seems to be a popular time for licensees to take their holidays).

Any separate *restaurant* is mentioned. We also note any pubs which told us they'd be keeping their restaurant open into Sunday afternoons. But in general all comments on the type of food served, and in particular all the other details about meals and snacks at the end of each entry, relate to the pub food and not to the restaurant food.

Children's Certificates exist but in practice *Children* are allowed into at least some part of almost all the pubs included in this *Guide* (there are no legal restrictions on the movement of children over 14 in any pub, though only people over 18 may get alcohol). As we went to press, we asked the main-entry pubs a series of detailed questions about their rules. *Children welcome* means the pub has told us that it simply lets them come in, with no special restrictions. In other cases we report exactly what arrangements pubs say they make for children. However, we have to note that in readers' experience some pubs make restrictions which they haven't told us about (children only if eating, for example), and very occasionally pubs which have previously allowed children change their policy altogether, virtually excluding them. If you come across this, please let us know, so that we can clarify the information for the pub concerned in the next edition. Beware that if children are confined to the restaurant, they may be expected to have a full restaurant meal. Also, please note that a welcome for children does not necessarily mean a welcome for breast-feeding in public. Even if we don't mention children at all, it is worth asking: one or two pubs told us frankly that they do welcome children but don't want to advertise the fact, for fear of being penalised. All but one or two pubs (we mention these in the text) allow children in their garden or on their terrace, if they have one. Note that in Scotland the law allows children more freely into pubs so long as they are eating (and with an adult); there are moves afoot to follow suit in England and Wales. In the Lucky Dip entries we mention children only if readers have found either that they are allowed or that they are not allowed – the absence of any reference to children in a Dip entry means we don't know either way. This year a system of Children's Certificates has been introduced in England and Wales (Scotland already has such a system). This is supposed to smooth out inconsistencies over whether children are allowed in a particular pub. In practice so far, we've found that it has made virtually no difference. So we don't mention whether or not any individual pub has a Certificate. Instead, we say what the actual situation is in each pub.

Dogs, cats and other animals are mentioned in the text if we know either that they are likely to be present or that they are specifically excluded – we depend chiefly on readers and partly on our own inspections for this information.

Parking is not mentioned if you should normally be able to park outside the pub, or in a private car park, without difficulty. But if we know that parking space is limited or metered, we say so.

Telephone numbers are given for all pubs that are not ex-directory.

Opening hours are for summer weekdays; we say if we know of differences in winter, or on particular days of the week. In the country, many pubs may open rather later and close earlier than their details show unless there are plenty of customers around (if you come across this, please let us know – with details). Pubs are allowed to stay open all day Mondays to Saturdays from 11am (earlier if the area's licensing magistrates have permitted it) till 11pm. However, outside cities most English and Welsh pubs close during the afternoon. Scottish pubs are allowed to stay open until later at night, and the Government has said that it may introduce legislation to allow later opening in England and Wales too. We'd be very grateful to hear of any differences from the hours we quote. You are allowed 20 minutes' drinking-up time after the quoted hours – half an hour if you've been having a meal in the pub.

All day *Sunday* opening is now permitted for English and Welsh pubs, as well as Scottish ones. The law was changed in summer 1995, as we went to press.

Undoubtedly, it will be some time before all pubs settle into a firm pattern of what Sunday hours suit them. Spot checks with individual pubs suggest that at least for the time being their Sunday hours will be much the same as those we quote for their weekday opening. But if your Sunday depends on finding a particular pub open in mid-afternoon, ring them before you start your journey. For England and Wales, permitted hours for Sunday pub opening are 12-10.30, though pubs are allowed to open earlier (for instance to serve breakfast) so long as they don't serve alcohol. In Scotland, a few pubs close on Sundays (we specify those that we know of); most are open 12.30-2.30 and 6.30-11, and some stay open all day. In Wales, pubs in Dwyfor (from Porthmadog down through the Lleyn Peninsula) are not allowed to sell alcohol to non-residents on Sunday, and generally close then. If we know of a pub closing for any day of the week or part of the year, we say so. The few pubs which we say stay closed on Monday do open on bank holiday Mondays.

Bedroom prices normally include full English breakfasts (if these are available, which they usually are), VAT and any automatic service charge that we know about. If we give just one price, it is the total price for two people sharing a double or twin-bedded room for one night. Otherwise, prices before the / are for single occupancy, prices after it for double. A capital B against the price means that it includes a private bathroom, a capital S a private shower. As all this coding packs in quite a lot of information, some examples may help to explain it:

£30 on its own means that's the total bill for two people sharing a twin or double room without private bath; the pub has no rooms with private bath, and a single person might have to pay that full price

£30B means exactly the same – but all the rooms have private bath

£30(£35B) means rooms with private baths cost £5 extra

£18/£30(£35B) means the same as the last example, but also shows that there are single rooms for £18, none of which have private bathrooms

If there's a choice of rooms at different prices, we normally give the cheapest. If there are seasonal price variations, we give the summer price (the highest). This winter – 1995-96 – many inns, particularly in the country, will have special cheaper rates. And at other times, especially in holiday areas, you will often find prices cheaper if you stay for several nights. On weekends, inns that aren't in obvious weekending areas often have bargain rates for two- or three-night stays.

MEAL TIMES

Bar food is commonly served from 12-2 and 7-9, at least from Monday to Saturday (food service often stops a bit earlier on Sundays). If we don't give a time against the Meals and snacks note at the bottom of a main entry, that means that you should be able to get bar food at those times. However, we do spell out the times if we know that bar food service starts after 12.15 or after 7.15; if it stops before 2 or before 8.45; or if food is served for significantly longer than usual (say, till 2.30 or 9.45).

Though we note days when pubs have told us they don't do food, experience suggests that you should play safe on Sundays and check first with any pub before planning an expedition that depends on getting a meal there. Also, out-of-the-way pubs often cut down on cooking during the week, especially the early part of the week, if they're quiet – as they tend to be, except at holiday times. Please let us know if you find anything different from what we say!

NO SMOKING

We say in the text of each entry what if any provision a pub makes for non-smokers. Pubs setting aside at least some sort of no smoking area are also listed county by county in the Special Interest Lists at the back of the book. The Plough at Clifton Hampden (Oxon) and Free Press in Cambridge are completely no smoking.

CHANGES DURING THE YEAR – PLEASE TELL US

Changes are inevitable during the course of the year. Landlords change, and so do their policies. And, as we've said, not all returned our fact-checking sheets. We very much hope that you will find everything just as we say. But if you find anything different, please let us know, using the tear-out card in the middle of the book (which doesn't need an envelope), the report forms here, or just a letter. You don't need a stamp: the address is *The Good Pub Guide*, FREEPOST TN1569, WADHURST, East Sussex TN5 7BR.

Author's Acknowledgements

This book would not be possible without the unstinting help given to us by several thousand readers, reporting on pubs they visit: thanks to you all. Many have now been reporting for a good few years, often in marvellously helpful detail, and in some cases have now sent us several hundred reports – even a thousand or more. We rely heavily on this hugely generous help, all of it unpaid. Without it this book would be a mere shadow of what it has become. It owes its strength to these very generous readers.

For the exceptional help they've given us this last year, I'm specially grateful to Ian Phillips, Gwen and Peter Andrews, Roger Huggins, Tom McLean, Dave Irving, Ewan McCall, Richard Lewis, George Atkinson, Gordon, David Hanley, Peter and Audrey Dowsett, CMW, JJW, C J Westmoreland, Ann and Colin Hunt, John Wooll, Richard Houghton, Wayne Brindle, TBB, D C T and E A Frewer, Andy and Jill Kassube, Jenny and Michael Back, Marjorie and David Lamb, Thomas Nott, Dave Braisted, Jack and Philip Paxton, David and Shelia, Joan Olivier, Joy Heatherley, Jenny and Brian Seller, Susan and John Douglas, Tony and Louise Clarke, Stephen and Julie Brown, Lynn Sharpless and Bob Eardley, Colin Roberts, Colin Laffan, Basil Minson, John Fahy, Michael Butler, Karen and Graham Oddey, John Boylan, Andy Hazeldine, Andrew and Ruth Triggs, H K Dyson, Sue Holland and Dave Webster, John and Joan Nash, Mayur Shah, Derek and Sylvia Stephenson, Frank Cummins, Joan and Michel Hooper-Immins, Nick Wikeley, R J Walden, Ted George, M J Morgan, Neil and Anita Christopher, Alan Skull, Margaret and Nigel Dennis, Canon Kenneth Wills, HNJ, PEJ, Frank W Gadbois, Mr and Mrs A Plumb, Alan and Paula McCully, Brian and Anna Marsden, John and Christine Vittoe, Prof I H Rorison, Simon C Collett-Jones, Bob and Maggie Atherton, Tim and Sue Halstead, Graham Bush, John Evans, G Washington, Mr and Mrs F J Parmenter, Comus Elliott, Pat and Malcolm Rudlin, Mrs K Clapp, John Morley, Clive Gilbert, Don Kellaway and Angie Coles, Mike and Wendy Proctor, Neville Kenyon, Nick and Alison Dowson, Dorothee and Dennis Glover, Roger Bellingham, Rita Horridge, DWAJ, E G Parish, John Bowdler, John Fazakerley, Christopher Turner, Paul Silvestri and Jeanne Cross, Martin Jones, Jerry and Alison Oakes, Christopher Gallop, Meg and Colin Hamilton, Richard Dolphin, John C Baker, Mrs Pamela Goodwyn and Ron Gentry. Special thanks to our Channel Islands Inspectors, Steve and Carolyn Harvey.

Particular thanks too to the thousands of landlords, landladies and staff of Good Pubs who make life so enjoyable for us and our readers.

Alisdair Aird

England

Avon *see* Somerset

Bedfordshire *see* Cambridgeshire

Berkshire

In the Bell at Aldworth, Berkshire has one of Britain's finest country pubs, very popular indeed with readers. Other pubs currently doing particularly well here include the Pot Kiln at Frilsham, another unpretentious and timeless country pub, the Bull at Stanford Dingley (warmly friendly licensees, very good food), the friendly and very neatly kept Swan at Great Shefford (good food here too) and the stylish Water Rat at Marsh Benham (particularly good food these days: it's our Berkshire Dining Pub of the Year). It's worth noting that at the first three of these five top pubs drinks are much cheaper than in other Berkshire pubs; otherwise, this is an expensive area. A good crop of new entries, or pubs back in these pages after an absence, includes the very smartly rustic Thatched Tavern at Cheapside near Ascot, the welcoming and unaffected Fox & Hounds at Peasemore (off the beaten track but well worth a visit), and the Winterbourne Arms at Winterbourne (imaginative food beautifully presented). Particular changes to note include new licensees at the Ibex in Chaddleworth (fitting in well at this racehorse-country pub – they breed thoroughbreds), the Bull at Sonning (big changes on the accommodation side) and Rowbarge at Woolhampton; the handsome Royal Oak at Yattendon has a new manager. In the Lucky Dip section specially recommendable pubs (we have inspected almost all) include the Hinds Heads at Aldermaston and Bray, Pineapple at Brimpton Common, Crown at Burchetts Green, Inn on the Green at Cookham Dean, Bunk at Curridge, Swan at East Ilsley, Green Man at Hurst, Dundas Arms at Kintbury, both Knowl Hill entries, the Bridge at Paley Street, Sweeney & Todd in Reading, Little Angel at Remenham, Old Boot at Stanford Dingley, Duke of Edinburgh at Woodside and Rising Sun at Woolhampton. Good dips handy for the M4 are the Pheasant at Great Shefford, Fox at Hermitage, George at Holyport, Tally Ho at Hungerford Newtown and Five Bells at Wickham. The Swan at Inkpen, long a popular main entry, will be found in the Lucky Dip section this year: as we went to press its owner planned to sell it as a private house – but if it is still open, it's well worth a visit.

ALDWORTH SU5579 Map 2

Bell ★ £ 🍷 🍺

A329 Reading—Wallingford; left on to B4009 at Streatley

In the same family for over 200 years, this 14th-c country pub remains happily unaffected by its popularity – it is a wonderfully unspoilt, warmly friendly local, much loved by many of our readers. The cosy bar has benches around its panelled walls, a woodburning stove, beams in the shiny ochre ceiling, an ancient one-handed clock, and a glass-panelled hatch rather than a bar counter for service. The incredibly good value food is confined to hot crusty rolls (apart from winter home-made soup £1.95), filled with cheddar (80p), ham, brie, stilton or pâté such as wild mushroom and pork (90p), smoked salmon (£1.40), and salt beef or particularly good Devon crab in season (£1.50); salad basket and garlic dressing (£1.50). Very well kept and very cheap Arkells BBB and Kingsdown, Hook Norton Best and Morrells Bitter and Mild on handpump (they won't stock draught lager), and particularly good house wines. Darts, shove-ha'penny, dominoes, chess, and Aunt Sally. The quiet, old-fashioned garden is lovely in summer, and the pub is handy for the Ridgeway, so popular with walkers on Sundays. Occasional Morris dancing; Christmas mummers. *(Recommended by Stephen, Julie and Hayley Brown, John Melsher, Mr and Mrs J Brown, Mark Hydes, Liz, Wendy and Ian Phillips, Wayne Brindle, C A Hall, Tom McLean, Roger Huggins, Ewan McCall, Maysie Thompson, A T Langton, Dr Ian Crichton, John and Pam Smith, Jack and Philip Paxton, Mayur Shah, Iain McBride, J and P Maloney, Sheilah Openshaw, Ian and Nita Cooper, Michael Marlow)*

Free house ~ Licensee H E Macaulay ~ Real ale ~ Snacks (11-3, 6-11; not Mon) ~ (01635) 578272 ~ Well behaved children in tap room ~ Open 11-3, 6-11; closed Mon (open bank holidays), 25 Dec

CHADDLEWORTH SU4177 Map 2

Ibex 🍷

Off A338 Hungerford—Wantage and take second left after reaching summit of Downs; village is signpsted also, off B4494

The new licensees here are carrying on the racing tradition of the previous owner here – Mr and Mrs Froome breed thoroughbreds and own and have owned successful racehorses. The thoroughly traditional carpeted lounge has properly old-fashioned bench seating and refectory-style tables, a big log fire, paintings done by Mr Froome, and a good country atmosphere. The public bar has low settles, and darts, shove-ha'penny, cribbage, dominoes, and fruit machine; also, monthly quiz, golf society, race nights, and winter film evenings. Tables are set for evening meals in the sun lounge (and snug little dining room). Changing daily, the good bar food includes sandwiches, cheese and onion soup (£2.25), Ibex pie (£4.15), fish pie (£4.25), moussaka (£5.75), home-made steak and kidney pie or hotpot (£5.95), good steaks, and home-made puddings (£2.50). Well kept Bass, Morlands Old Speckled Hen, and Charles Wells Bombardier on handpump and summer drinks like pimms, sangria and fruit cups. Out on a sheltered lawn and on the floodlit terrace are some tables. This is very much a racing-country village: thatched cottages, narrow lanes, distant dog barks, signs saying 'Caution – Mares and Foals'. *(Recommended by HNJ, PEJ, Julie Peters, T R and B C Jenkins, Peter and Audrey Dowsett)*

Morlands ~ Lease: Sylvia and John Froome ~ Real ale ~ Meals and snacks (not winter Sun evenings) ~ Restaurant ~ (01488) 638311 ~ Children welcome ~ Open 11-11

CHEAPSIDE SU9469 Map 2

Thatched Tavern

Cheapside Road; off B383, which is itself off A332 and A329

No longer in fact thatched (slates now), but the name does conjure up an accurate image of the inside of the pub: polished flagstones, very low gnarled and nibbled beams, small windows with cheerful cottagey curtains, an old cast-iron range in a big inglenook with built-in wall benches snugly around it. But this is a discreetly upmarket version of olde England: the customers show how handy the pub is for the Guards Polo Club, nearby in Windsor Great Park (it's also well placed for walks around Virginia Water, with the Blacknest car park a mile or so down the road). Food is a main attraction here (bar food is served lunchtime only), with pretty red gingham tablecloths brightening up the longish carpeted back dining area, and a vast blackboard choice covering such dishes as sandwiches (from £1.50), home-made soup (£3.25), vegetarian dishes (from £5), home-made steak and kidney pudding (£9.50), slow-roasted half shoulder of lamb (£9.95), fish that's delivered daily like grilled cod or wild Tay salmon (from around £10.50), and lots of puddings such as fruit crumbles and bread and butter pudding (£3.75). Well kept Greene King IPA, Abbot and Sorcerer on handpump, friendly staff, spotless housekeeping, and no games or piped music. Rustic seats and tables are grouped on the sheltered back lawn, around a big old apple tree. *(Recommended by Mrs C Blake)*

Greene King ~ Licensees Robert King, Johnathan Michael Mee ~ Real ale ~ Bar meals and snacks lunchtime only ~ Restaurant ~ (01344) 20874 ~ Well behaved children welcome away from bar ~ Open 11.30-3, 6-11

CHIEVELEY SU4774 Map 2

Blue Boar

4 miles from M4 junction 13: A34 N towards Oxford, 200 yds left for Chieveley, then left at Wheatsheaf pub and straight on until T-junction with B4494; turn right to Wantage and pub is 500 yds on right; heading S on A34, don't take first sign to Chieveley

The three rambling rooms of the beamed bar in this thatched inn are furnished with high-backed settles, windsor chairs and polished tables, and decked out with a variety of heavy harness (including a massive collar); the left-hand room has a roaring log fire and a seat built into the sunny bow window. A lot of space is given over to eating the bar food, which includes soup, sandwiches, ploughman's, deep-fried mushrooms with garlic dip, speciality sausages (£4.95), half char-grilled chicken (£6.50), pies like beef in Guinness (£6.95), and puddings; there's a wider range in the civilised oak-panelled restaurant. Well kept Boddingtons, Gibbs Mew Bishops Finger, and Wadworths 6X on handpump; several malt whiskies; soft piped music. There are tables among tubs and flowerbeds on the rough front cobbles outside. Oliver Cromwell stayed here in 1644 on the eve of the Battle of Newbury. *(Recommended by Peter and Joy Heatherley, Gary Roberts, Ann Stubbs, Mayur Shah, Nigel Norman, Dave Braisted, B J Harding, Margaret Dyke, Mrs J Prior, Miss D P Barson, Gordon, Simon J Barber)*

Free house ~ Licensee Peter Ebsworth ~ Real ale ~ Meals and snacks ~ Restaurant (closed Sun) ~ (01635) 248236 ~ Children in eating area of bar ~ Open 11-3, 6-11 ~ Bedrooms: £45B/£52B

COOKHAM SU8884 Map 2

Bel & the Dragon

High Street; B4447 N of Maidenhead

Quietly civilised and restful, this fine old place has three peaceful rooms with pewter tankards hanging from heavy Tudor beams, deep leather chairs, old oak settles, and open fires (not always lit, even in cold weather); one room is no smoking. Service at the low zinc-topped bar counter is decorous and very much of the old school – and prices aren't cheap; well kept Brakspears PA tapped from the cask. A good choice of wines includes decent ports and champagne, and they have all the ingredients needed for proper cocktails, and freshly squeezed orange juice. There are often free home-made crisps, and bar food includes soup (£2.75), sandwiches (from £2.75), home-made quiche (£3.50), home-made cannelloni (£5), omelettes (from £5.25), home-made steak and kidney pie (£6.50), and home-made puddings (£2.50). In summer and good weather snacks are also served in the garden or on the back terrace. The inn has no car park and street parking can be very difficult. The Stanley Spencer Gallery is almost opposite. *(Recommended by Piotr Chodzko-Zajko, Nigel Norman, Nigel Wilkinson, Susan and John Douglas, Mr and Mrs G D Amos, Russell and Margaret Bathie, Martin and Karen Wake, Charles Bardswell)*

Free house ~ Licensee F E Stuber ~ Real ale ~ Meals and snacks (served throughout opening hours) ~ Restaurant (closed Sun evenings) ~ (01628) 521263 ~ Children welcome ~ Open 11-2.30, 6-10.30 (11 Sat)

COOKHAM DEAN SU8785 Map 2

Jolly Farmer

Off A308 N of Maidenhead, or from A4094 in Cookham take B4447 and fork right past Cookham Rise stn; can be reached from Marlow – fork left after bridge

Bustling with a jovial community atmosphere and a good mixed crowd, this part brick, part flint-faced village pub has small, happily traditional rooms with open fires; the middle room is the main bar serving well kept Courage Best and Wadworths 6X with guest beers such as Gales HSB, Morlands Old Speckled Hen or Youngs Special on handpump from a tiny counter, and at one end is the attractive dining room with its starched pink and white tablecloths. Bar food includes home-made soup (£1.95), filled french bread (£2.95), pan-fried sardines (£3.75), home-cooked gammon and two eggs (£3.75), home-made steak, kidney and ale pie or cheesy haddock and egg crumble (£5.95), Dutch calf's liver (£8.95), 8oz fillet steak (£12.95), and puddings (£2.75). It's quietest on weekday lunchtimes; dominoes, cribbage, shove-ha'penny, and piped music. You can eat outside at the picnic-tables in front of the pub, there's a terrace, and a big play area on the very long side lawn with swings, slides and a wendy house. The pub is attractively set just across the quiet lane from the little village green and church. *(Recommended by Martin and Karen Wake, Nigel Norman, Simon Collett-Jones, Mark Hydes, TBB, George Atkinson; more reports please)*

Free house ~ Licensees Simon and Tracey Peach ~ Real ale ~ Meals and snacks (not Sun evening or bank holiday evenings) ~ Restaurant (not Sun evening) ~ (01628) 482905 ~ Children in restaurant and eating area of bar ~ Open 11.30-3, 5.30(6 Sat)-11; closed 25 Dec pm

COOKHAM DEAN COMMON SU8785 Map 2

Uncle Toms Cabin

Hills Lane, Harding Green; village signposted off A308 Maidenhead—Marlow – keep on down past Post Office and village hall towards Cookham Rise and Cookham

Inside this pretty cream-washed cottage is a friendly series of 1930s-feeling, mainly carpeted little rooms with a chattily informal atmosphere, low beams and joists in the front ones, lots of shiny dark brown woodwork, and old-fashioned plush-cushioned wall seats, stools and so forth. Food includes french bread or granary rolls with a wide choice of good fillings such as brie with celery (£2.55), rare roast beef (£3.05), hot salt beef (£3.25) or bacon and onion (£3.35), filled baked potatoes (from £3.15), ploughman's, and home-made hot dishes from soup like chicken and leek (£2.50) through pizzas (£4.55), pasta with bacon and mushrooms (£5.25) and steak and Guinness pie (£5.75) to 8oz rump steak (£8.75), with a special such as chicken stuffed with banana and wrapped in bacon (£5.75), several puddings and children's dishes. Well kept Benskins Best and a weekly changing guest such as Adnams Broadside, Fullers London Pride or Shepherd Neame Spitfire on handpump, Addlestones cider, sensibly placed darts, cribbage. Piped music, if on, is well chosen and well reproduced (a small collection of framed golden discs runs from Judy Garland to Culture Club). Jess the fluffy black-and-white cat enjoys the winter coal fire and Oggie the busy black-and-white dog welcomes other dogs (who get a dog biscuit on arrival). There are picnic-table sets and a climbing frame in an attractive and sheltered back garden. *(Recommended by D Hayward, A Young, Nigel Norman; more reports please)*

Carlsberg Tetleys ~ Tenants Nick and Karen Ashman ~ Real ale ~ Meals and snacks (12-2, 7.30-10; half-hour later Sat/Sun lunchtime; not Sun evening) ~ (01628) 483339 ~ Well behaved children in eating area of bar ~ Open 11-3, 5.30-11

Post Office address codings confusingly give the impression that some pubs are in Berkshire, when they're really in Oxfordshire or Hampshire (which is where we list them).

CRAZIES HILL SU7980 Map 2

Horns

From A4, take Warren Row Road at Cockpole Green signpost just E of Knowl Hill, then past Warren Row follow Crazies Hill signposts; from Wargrave, take A321 towards Henley, then follow Crazies Hill signposts right at Shell garage, then left

Readers enjoy this little tiled whitewashed cottage very much and feel it is just as a proper pub should be – no jukebox or fruit machine, charming licensees, good home-made food, and a relaxed, informal atmosphere. The bars have exposed beams, open fires and stripped wooden tables and chairs, the barn room has been opened up to the roof like a medieval hall, and there's a huge boar's head on the wall. Bar food includes hot or cold filled rolls (from £1.50), crab salad (£4.65), honey-glazed bacon steaks, a pleasing late breakfast, and excellent liver and bacon, cumberland sausage or beef in ale (all £4.95); their half-helpings are a bargain, and on Friday and Saturday they serve brasserie-style food (bookings only); maybe summer Sunday barbecues. Well kept Brakspears PA, Mild, SB, Old and OBJ on handpump, lots of malt whiskies, and fresh orange juice. Darts, shove-ha'penny, dominoes and cribbage, and weekly live jazz/blues; the popular, young st bernard is called Queenie. Attractive three-acre garden. *(Recommended by Derek and Sylvia Stephenson, Ted and Jane Brown, Jane and Howard Appleton, Gordon, TBB, Roy Smylie, Simon Collett-Jones)*

Brakspears ~ Tenants David and Patsy Robinson ~ Real ale ~ Lunchtime meals and snacks (not Sun or Mon) ~ Restaurant (Fri and Sat evenings, bookings only) ~ (01734) 401416 ~ Children in converted barn attached to pub ~ Jazz/blues Mon evenings ~ Open 11-2.30(3 Sat), 5.30-11

EAST ILSLEY SU4981 Map 2

Crown & Horns

Just off A34, about 5 miles N of M4 junction 13

Racing prints and photographs on the walls of the four interesting beamed rooms in this friendly and busy old pub show that this is very much horse-training country; and the side bar may have locals watching the latest races on TV. The very wide range of regularly changing real ales, all reasonably priced, and typically including Bass, Fullers London Pride, Morlands Original and Old Master, Theakstons Old Peculier and Wadworths 6X, with guests like Brakspears or King & Barnes Festive on handpump. There is also an impressive collection of 170 whiskies from all over the world – Morocco, Korea, Japan, China, Spain and New Zealand. Good, interesting bar food includes sandwiches (from £1.60), home-made soup (£2.75), ploughman's (from £3.25), lasagne or liver and bacon casserole (£4.75), good game and venison pie in season (from £5.25), chicken breast with stilton and mushroom sauce or duck in a port and black cherry sauce (£7.25), steaks (from £7.95), and puddings such as home-made treacle tart (£2.45); quick, cheerful staff – even when busy. Skittle alley, darts, pool, bar billiards, shove-ha'penny, dominoes, cribbage, fruit machine, juke box and piped music. The pretty paved stable yard has tables under two chestnut trees. *(Recommended by J McMillan, Gordon, Wayne Brindle, Susie Northfield, Marjorie and David Lamb, HNJ, PEJ, Geraint Roberts, K R Waters, Tom McLean, Dayl Gallacher)*

Free house ~ Licensees Chris and Jane Bexx ~ Real ale ~ Meals and snacks (till 10pm) ~ (01635) 281205 ~ Children in eating area, restaurant and TV room ~ Open 11-3, 6-11; closed evening 25 Dec ~ Bedrooms: £30B/£405B

FRILSHAM SU5473 Map 2

Pot Kiln

From Yattendon take turning S, opposite church, follow first Frilsham signpost, but just after crossing motorway go straight on towards Bucklebury ignoring Frilsham signposted right; pub on right after about half a mile

In lovely countryside, this unpretentious, friendly pub has a really timeless feel – and although basic, it's not unsmart, with wooden floorboards and bare benches and pews; there's a good winter log fire, too. Beer is served from a hatch in the panelled entrance lobby – which has room for just one bar stool. Enjoyable, fairly simple food includes particularly good filled hot rolls, home-made soup (£2.20), a decent ploughman's (£3.25), vegetarian dishes such as good pâté and delicious lentil bake (from £3.55), excellent salmon and broccoli fishcake (£4.95), and daily specials such as steak in ale pie (£5.25) or venison steaks in red wine (£7.45); no chips, and vegetables are fresh. Rolls only on Sundays and Tuesdays. Well kept Arkells BBB, Morlands Original and Old Speckled Hen, and Morrells Mild on handpump. The public bar has darts, dominoes, shove-ha'penny and cribbage. The back room/dining room is no smoking. There are picnic-table sets in the big suntrap garden with good views of the woods and countryside. It's a good dog-walking area and they are allowed in public bar on a lead. *(Recommended by Jed and Virginia Brown, Tom McLean, Roger Huggins, Ewan McCall, Iain McBride, Samantha Hawkins, Mayur Shah, TBB, Lesley McEwen, Tracey Anderson, Gordon, Roger Byrne, Mick Simmons)*

Free house ~ Licensee Philip Gent ~ Real ale ~ Meals and snacks (until 9.45pm; limited food Sun and Tues) ~ (01635) 201366 ~ Well behaved children in eating area of bar ~ Folk music most Sun evenings ~ Open 12-2.30(3 Sat), 6.30-11

GREAT SHEFFORD SU3875 Map 2

Swan

2 miles from M4 junction 14; on A338 towards Wantage

Very neatly kept, inside and out, this friendly village pub seems to be going from strength to strength, and is popular with a good mix of people. The low-ceilinged rooms of the spacious bow-windowed lounge bar are attractively and comfortably furnished and have old photographs of the village and horse and jockey pictures on the walls, and the piped music is suitably unobtrusive; the public side has darts, cribbage, dominoes, pool, a fruit machine, and CD juke box. Very good food includes home-made soup (£2.25), salmon, cream cheese and chive terrine (£3.95), barbecue spare ribs (£4.95), vegetarian mixed bean burger (£5.50), chicken balti or beef, mushroom and Guinness pie (£6.95), local trout (£7.25), steaks using prime Angus beef (from £8.75), and daily specials. Well kept Butts Ale (from a micro-brewery in the village), Courage Best, Eldridge Pope Royal Oak, Wadworths 6X, and a guest beer on handpump; service is attentive and warmly friendly. In summer, it's lovely to sit in the relaxing garden with its sycamore and willow overhanging the ducks on the River Lambourn (the spic-and-span restaurant shares the same view). *(Recommended by R W Saunders, HNJ, PEJ, G and M Hollis, John and Shirley Dyson, H D Spottiswoode, J S M Sheldon)*

Courage ~ Managers Kevin Maul, Sue Jacobs ~ Real ale ~ Meals and snacks ~ Children in eating area of bar ~ Restaurant ~ (01488) 648271 ~ Open 11-2.30, 6-11; all day Sat and June-Sept

HAMSTEAD MARSHALL SU4165 Map 2

White Hart 🛏

Village signposted from A4 W of Newbury

The L-shaped bar in this pleasant country inn has red plush seats built into the bow windows, cushioned chairs around oak and other tables, a copper-topped bar counter, and a log fire open on both sides. Bar food – as you can see prices are on the high side – tends to concentrate on meals rather than snacks: home-made soups with home-made Italian bread (£3.20), pork liver and brandy pâté (£4.50), goat's cheese grilled with garlic and yoghurt (£5.50), various pasta dishes such as quadroni (mushroom and herb-stuffed ravioli with wild mushroom and cream sauce £7.50), fritelli (beef meatballs stuffed with mozzarella, braised in wine sauce, £8.90), cod fillet with creamy spinach sauce (£9.50), and puddings (£4.50); the food boards are attractively illustrated with Mrs Aromando's drawings. Badger Best and Wadworths 6X on handpump. No dogs (their own welsh setter's called Sam, and the pony's called Solo). The interesting walled garden is lovely in summer, and the quiet and comfortable beamed bedrooms are in a converted barn across the courtyard. *(Recommended by Verity Kemp, Richard Mills, Gordon, T R and B C Jenkins, Roger Byrne, JCW, Pippa Bobbett; more reports – especially on the food, please)*

Free house ~ Licensee Mr Nicola Aromando ~ Real ale ~ Meals and snacks (not Sun) ~ Partly no-smoking restaurant (not Sun) ~ (01488) 658201 ~ Children in eating area of bar and in restaurant ~ Open 12-2.30, 6-11; closed Sun, 25 and 26 Dec ~ Bedrooms: £40B/£60B

HARE HATCH SU8077 Map 2

Queen Victoria

Blakes Lane, The Holt; just N of A4 Reading—Maidenhead, 3 miles W of exit roundabout from A423(M) – keep your eyes skinned for the turning

Readers who have known – and enjoyed – this pub for many years are always glad to report that very little changes to spoil the buoyant, chatty atmosphere in this friendly local. The two low-beamed rooms are furnished with strong spindleback chairs, wall benches and window seats, and flowers on the tables, with decorations like a stuffed sparrowhawk and a delft shelf lined with beaujolais bottles; the tables on the right are no smoking. Popular bar food might include home-made soup (£1.50), sandwiches (from £1.60), sautéed chicken livers with bacon and granary toast (£3.35), sausages such as boar and apple, garlic or spicy (£4.50), Chinese chicken kebab with chilli dip (£4.60), prawn curry (£4.75), daily specials like hot fresh crab with brandy and parmesan cheese (£3.25), Mexican beef taco shells, smoked fish medley (from £4.20), and puddings (from £2.20); there's now a vegetarian menu (from £2.95), and vegetables are fresh. Well kept Brakspears PA, SB, Old and OBJ on handpump; shove-ha'penny, cribbage, dominoes, three dimensional noughts and crosses, fruit machine, and video game. There's a flower-filled covered terrace with tables and chairs, and a robust table or two in front by the car park. *(Recommended by Gordon, Ian Phillips, TBB, Andrew Brookes, D J and P M Taylor, S R Jordan)*

Brakspears ~ Tenant Ronald Rossington ~ Real ale ~ Meals and snacks (11.30-2.45, 6.30-10.45) ~ (01734) 402477 ~ Children welcome ~ Open 11-3, 5.30-11

HOLYPORT SU8977 Map 2

Belgian Arms

1½ miles from M4 junction 8/9; take A308(M) then at terminal roundabout follow Holyport signpost along A330 towards Bracknell; in village turn left on to big green, then left again at War Memorial shelter

Very handy for the M4, this homely pub has an L-shaped, low-ceilinged bar with framed postcards of Belgian military uniform and other good military prints on the walls, a china cupboard in one corner, a variety of chairs around a few small tables, and a winter log fire. Bar food includes sandwiches (from £1.20; the open prawn one at £3.75 is excellent, and the toasted 'special' is very well-liked: ham, cheese, sweetcorn, peppers, onion and mushroom £1.85), pizzas with different toppings (ham, cheese and pineapple is popular, from £3.25), home-cooked ham and eggs (£4.95), a range of daily specials such as good steak and kidney pie, lamb casserole in a plate-sized yorkshire pudding (£4.95), chicken tikka masala (£6.50), japanese-style breaded deep-fried prawns (£6.75), steaks (from £9.95), and puddings (from £2.50); you can also eat in the conservatory area. Well kept Brakspears PA, SB and in winter Old on handpump, and one or two good malts; friendly service. The charming garden has plenty of tables looking over the pond towards the village green, and a pen with a goat and hens. *(Recommended by TBB, Susan and John Douglas, Gary Roberts, Ann Stubbs, Mrs S Wright, Graham and Karen Oddey, Simon Collett-Jones, DJW, George Atkinson, Martin and Karen Wake)*

Brakspears ~ Tenant Alfred Morgan ~ Real ale ~ Meals and snacks (not Sun evening) ~ (01628) 34468 ~ Children in restaurant ~ Open 11-3, 5.30 (6 Sat)-11; closed evening 26 Dec

nr HURLEY SU8283 Map 2

Dew Drop

Just W of Hurley on A423 turn left (if coming from Maidenhead) up Honey Lane and keep going till get to T-junction, then turn right – the pub is down a right-hand turn-off at the first cluster of little houses

Mrs Morris has discovered a fine old inglenook fireplace in the simply furnished main bar here, and as we went to press it was being opened up. At each end of the room is another log fire (space is rather tight in the serving area) and quite a few golfing pictures, and at the back is a homely roughcast white room. The atmosphere is unchanging and friendly and the landlord has been here for over 20 years. Bar food includes filled french sticks (£1.75), ploughman's (£3.50), mushrooms on toast (£3.50), salads (from £3.50), gammon and eggs (£5.50), and puddings (£1.50). Well kept Brakspears PA and Old on handpump, and some good malt whiskies; darts. The wild sloping garden is attractive and there are tubs of bright flowers and a children's play area. Popular with dog owners. *(Recommended by Ian Phillips, Neil and Jenny Spink, Mark Hydes, Simon Collett-Jones; more reports please)*

Brakspears ~ Tenant Michael Morris ~ Real ale ~ Meals and snacks (not Sun evening or Mon) ~ Children in eating area of bar ~ (01628) 824327 ~ Open 11-2.30 (3 Sat), 6-11

MARSH BENHAM SU4267 Map 2

Water Rat

Village signposted from A4 W of Newbury

Berkshire Dining Pub of the Year

This old thatched pub is doing very well at the moment: once they've found it, people can't wait to go back. The garden is most attractive, the food and beer very good indeed, and service friendly and helpful. The comfortable, unpretentious bar has deeply carved Victorian gothick settles (and some older ones), and is attractively decorated with cheerful murals of *The Wind in the Willows* characters. All home-made, the bar food might include soup like cream of lettuce (£2.50), ciabatta bread with garlic, herbs and olive oil with sautéed field mushrooms (£3.95), smoked haddock marinated in cider with lemon grass and fresh lime (£4.25), duck breast with orange segments and plum sauce (£4.95), smoked salmon and mascarpone roulade (£5.75), lamb's liver and bacon (£8.90), wild mushroom and leek casserole in a brandy cream sauce (£9.50), seven or eight fresh fish dishes, and puddings such as white and dark chocolate terrine with a liqueur sauce or sticky toffee pudding (from £3.25); the restaurant is no smoking. Well kept Brakspears PA and SB, Shepherd Neame Spitfire, Theakstons XB and Wadworths 6X on handpump, lots of malt whiskies, and quite a few brandies. There are seats on the terrace or on the long lawns that slope down to water meadows and the River Kennet; there's a butterfly reserve, goldfish, and a play area with a climbing frame, sandpit and wooden playhouse for children. *(Recommended by Iain McBride, Samantha Hawkins, Gordon, Ian Phillips, J E Ellis, Roger Byrne, Betty Laker, Mr and Mrs D Pyatt, HNJ, PEJ, Neil Franklin)*

Free house ~ Licensee Ian Dodd ~ Real ale ~ Meals and snacks (12-2.30, 6-10) ~ Restaurant ~ (01635) 582017 ~ Children in eating area and in restaurant ~ Open 11-3, 6-11

Pubs staying open all afternoon are listed at the back of the book.

PEASEMORE SU4577 Map 2

Fox & Hounds ♀

Village signposted from B4494 Newbury—Wantage

Tucked away in a maze of roads, this unaffected pub has a nice countrified atmosphere and welcoming licensees. It's deep in horse-training country, and this is reflected inside by a full set of Somerville's entertaining Slipper's ABC of Fox-Hunting prints. On another stripped-brick wall there's a row of flat-capped fox masks. The two bars have brocaded stripped wall settles, chairs and stools around shiny wooden tables, a log-effect gas fire (open to both rooms), and piped music. Good bar food includes sandwiches, home-made soup (£1.50), home-made quiche (£3.95), home-made pies (£4.95), vegetarian dishes like chilli butterbean bake, spicy chicken in yoghurt (£6.95), steaks (from £6.95), home-made puudings such as baked jam roll or fruit crumble (£2), and daily specials. Well kept Greene King IPA, Abbot and Sorcerer on handpump, a good few malt whiskies, and a wide range of reasonably priced good wines. Sensibly placed darts, pool, dominoes, cribbage, fruit machine, discreet juke box, and piped music. From the picnic-table sets outside there are pleasant views of rolling fields – and on a clear day the view across to the high hills which form the Berkshire/Hampshire border about 20 miles southward, are marvellous. *(Recommended by HNJ, PEJ, Jeff Davies, Mr and Mrs Colquhoun)*

Free house ~ Licensees David and Loretta Smith ~ Real ale ~ Meals and snacks (till 10pm; not Mon) ~ Restaurant ~ (01635) 248252 ~ Children in restaurant and eating area of bar ~ Irish band or soul band Fri evening, monthly ~ Open 12-2.30(3 Sat), 6.30-11; closed Mon

SONNING SU7575 Map 2

Bull

Village signposted on A4 E of Reading; off B478, in village

New licensees have taken over this charming and unpretentious inn and are planning quite a few changes to the accommodation side. The pub part remains little changed and the two old-fashioned rooms have low ceilings and heavy beams, cosy alcoves, cushioned antique settles and low wooden chairs, and inglenook fireplaces. Well kept Gales Best, HSB and BBB on handpump and bar food such as good soup, filled french sticks (from £3.25), chilli con carne (£5.95), steak in Guinness pie (£6.95), salmon in filo pastry (£7.25) and steaks (from £8.50); piped music. The courtyard is particularly attractive in summer with tubs of flowers and a rose pergola resting under its wisteria-covered, black and white timbered walls – though at busy times it may be packed with cars. If you bear left through the ivy-clad churchyard opposite, then turn left along the bank of the river Thames, you come to a very pretty lock. *(Recommended by TBB, Roy Smylie, P J Caunt; more reports please)*

Gales ~ Tenants Mr and Mrs D Mason ~ Real ale ~ Lunchtime meals and snacks ~ Evening restaurant ~ (01734) 693901 ~ Children in restaurant ~ Open 10-2.30, 5.30-11~ Bedrooms undergoing major refurbishment as we went to press, so no prices available

STANFORD DINGLEY SU5771 Map 2

Bull

From M4 junction 12, W on A4, then right at roundabout on to A340 towards Pangbourne; first left to Bradfield, where left, then Stanford Dingley signposted on right

You can expect a warm and friendly welcome from the licensees in this attractive 15th-century pub – even when the place is busy. And the home-made bar food is very good as well: filled baked potatoes (from £1.85), delicious soups such as stilton or carrot and orange (from £2.20), ploughman's (from £2.75), good stilton and spinach filo parcels, tasty salmon and shrimp pancake or drunken fish pie (£4.95), tagliatelle with bacon, mushroom and wine sauce (£5.45), steaks (from £6.95), daily specials, and nice puddings. Under the dark beams in the middle of the tap room are two standing timbers hung with horse-brasses, firmly dividing the room into two parts. The main part is comfortably arranged with red-cushioned seats carved out of barrels, a window settle, wheelback chairs on the red quarry tiles, an old brick fireplace, and an old station clock; the other is similarly furnished but carpeted, and decorations include some corn dollies and a few old prints. The lounge bar has refectory-type tables and a very long oak pew and chairs on the rich persian rug on top of the polished wooden floor, half-panelled walls and a brick fireplace; a smaller area off this room has a shorter pew on the quarry tiles and quite a few musical instruments. Well kept (and very cheap for the area) Archers, Bass, and Brakspears on handpump, and interesting non alcoholic drinks such as elderflower pressé; quick, efficient service. Ring-the-bull, occasional classical or easy listening music. In front of the building are some big rustic tables and benches, and to the side is a small garden with a few more seats. *(Recommended by Bruce Greenfield, Werner Arend, Mayur Shah, M G Hart, Phil H Smith, Margaret Dyke, Gordon)*

Free house ~ Licensees Patrick and Trudi Langdon ~ Real ale ~ Meals and snacks (till 10pm; not Mon lunchtime) ~ (01734) 744409 ~ Children in saloon bar; not after 8.30pm; not Sat evening ~ Open 12-3, 7-11; closed Mon lunchtime – except bank hols

WALTHAM ST LAWRENCE SU8276 Map 2

Bell

In village centre

The lounge bar in this timbered black and white old pub has finely carved oak panelling, a good antique oak settle among more modern furniture, a log fire, and a pleasant atmosphere. The public bar has heavy beams, an attractive seat in the deep window recess, and well kept Adnams, Brakspears PA, Wadworths 6X and a guest beer every two weeks on handpump; lots of malt whiskies. Bar food includes soup (£1.75), ploughman's (from £3.45), filled baked potatoes (from £3.75), home-made pies like steak and kidney or chicken and asparagus (£4.95), sizzling cajun-style chicken (£5.95), gammon with two eggs (£6.95), and evening extras like rack of lamb (£8.50) or salmon steak (£8.75); the restaurant is no smoking. In summer, the hanging baskets in front of the building are very pretty, and the well kept back lawn (sheltered by a thatched barn and shaded by small trees and flowering shrubs) is very popular with walkers. The 'no children' policy is stricly enforced here. *(Recommended by Mayur Shah, Nick Holmes, Mark Hydes, Gordon, Amanda Hodges, Dawn and Phil Garside)*

Free house ~ Licensee S W Myers ~ Real ale ~ Meals and snacks (till 10pm; not Sun evening) ~ Restaurant ~ (01734) 341788 ~ Open 11.30-2.30(3 Sat), 6-11

WEST ILSLEY SU4782 Map 2

Harrow

Signposted at East Ilsley slip road off A34 Newbury—Abingdon

In a lovely spot with lots of nearby walks – the Ridgeway is just a mile away – this popular white tiled village pub has a big garden with picnic-table sets and other tables under cocktail parasols looking out over the duck pond and cricket green, a notable children's play area, and ducks, fowl, and a goat; the stubborn goose still sits in the road and refuses to budge for passing traffic. Inside, the open-plan bar has dark terracotta walls hung with many mainly Victorian prints and other ornaments, big turkey rugs on the floor, and a mix of antique oak tables, unpretentious old chairs, and a couple of more stately long settles; there's also an unusual stripped twin-seated high-backed settle between the log fire and the bow window. Good bar food includes granary rolls filled with hot sausage and home-made chutney or stilton, celery and apple (from £1.90), home-made soup (£2.75), ploughman's with British farmhouse cheeses (from £4.75), hazelnut and courgette bake with tomato sauce or wild rabbit pie (£5.25; you can take the pies home, too), lamb chop with rosemary gravy (£6.75), and home-made puddings like treacle tart or sticky toffee pudding (£2.75); children's helpings (and menu). The dining area is no smoking. Well kept Morlands Original and Old Speckled Hen, and a guest like Bass on handpump. Darts, fruit machine, piped music and quiz teams. *(Recommended by Mayur Shah, Guy Consterdine, J McMillan, Nigel Norman, Mrs C A Blake, Wayne Brindle, Christopher and Sharon Hayle, Bob Riley, HNJ, PEJ, I E and C A Prosser, John and Christine Simpson, George Atkinson, A T Langton, R C Morgan, Don Kellaway, Angie Coles, DAV, Pippa Bobbett, Marjorie and David Lamb, Mrs A Storm)*

Morlands ~ Lease: Mrs Heather Humphreys ~ Real ale ~ Meals and snacks (12-2.15, 6-9.15; not Sun evening Jan-Easter) ~ (01635) 281260 ~ Children welcome ~ Open 11-3, 6-11; closed 25 Dec pm

WINTERBOURNE SU4572 Map 2

Winterbourne Arms

3½ miles from M4 junction 13; village signposted from B4494 Newbury—Wantage

They seem to have struck a fine balance here between a country pub and a dining pub, though much emphasis is placed on the attractively presented, top quality food. This might include good soups such as stilton and celery or seafood chowder (£3.25), marinated herring fillets with a wholegrain mustard and dill dressing (£3.95), steamed steak and kidney pudding (£7.95), fillet of Scottish salmon with a chive cream sauce (£8.25), puddings like steamed treacle pudding or home-made ice cream in a brandy snap basket with soft fruit dressing (£3.25), British cheeses (£3.95), and vegetarian dishes. There's a pleasant old-fashioned atmosphere and decorations such as hop sways over the archways and doors, a collection of old irons around the fireplace, brass fire extinguishers, early prints and old photographs of the village, pretty dried flower arrangements, and a log fire; you can see the original bakers' ovens in the restaurant area, which was once a bakery. Dominoes, cribbage and unobtrusive piped classical music. Well kept Bass, Brakspears, Flowers Original, Fullers London Pride, or Wadworths 6X on handpump. The quiet road is slightly sunken between the pub's two lawns, and you can't actually see it from inside the bar – so the view from the big windows over the rolling fields is peaceful; there are picnic tables among the pretty flowering tubs and hanging baskets, a big weeping willow, and a children's play area with swings; nearby walks to Snelsmore and Donnington. *(Recommended by HNJ, PEJ, Anthony Fletcher, Gordon Tong, Trudi Pinkerton, Richard Robinson)*

Free house ~ Licensees Clive and Delia Saunders ~ Real ale ~ Meals and snacks (not Sun evening or Mon lunchtime) ~ Restaurant (not Sun evening) ~ (01635) 248200 ~ Children in eating area of bar ~ Open 11.30-2.30, 6-11; closed Mon lunchtime (except bank holidays)

WOOLHAMPTON SU5767 Map 2

Rowbarge

Turn S off A4 opposite the Angel (may be signposted Station)

New licensees have taken over this busy pub set by the Kennet & Avon canal. The beamed bar, adjoining panelled room and small snug are decorated with 80 brass blow lamps, cricketing mementoes and other bric-a-brac, and there's a no-smoking conservatory at the back of the building; piped music. Bar food now includes filled baked potatoes (£3.95), french bread filled with salmon and prawn (£4.95), vegetable bake (£5.95), home-made pies, and tagliatelle carbonara (£6.95). Well kept Courage Best, Brakspears SB, Fullers London Pride, Greene King Abbot and Wadworths 6X on handpump, and several malt whiskies; friendly service. The garden has a fishpond and lawns running down to the water. *(Recommended by Dr Ian Crichton, Simon Collett-Jones, John Hazel, Gordon; more reports on the new regime please)*

Free house ~ Licensee S J Hodgetts ~ Meals and snacks ~ Restaurant ~ (01734) 712213 ~ Children welcome ~ Open 11-2.30(3 Sat), 6-11; closed evening 25 Dec

YATTENDON SU5574 Map 2

Royal Oak ★

The Square; B4009 NE from Newbury; turn right at Hampstead Norreys, village signposted on left

The main reason for coming to this elegantly handsome inn is for its fine restaurant quality food: home-made soup (£3), ploughman's with home-made chutney (£3.95), moules marinières (£5), grilled prawns with aioli (£7.25), fish and chips (£7.75), braised veal with fresh herb stuffing and tagliatelle (£8.50), rump steak with herb butter (£11.50), and puddings like pear and almond tart, chocolate mousse or home-made ice-creams (£3.75); vegetables (£1.25). You must book a table for bar lunches. The comfortable lounge and prettily decorated panelled bar – it's through at the back – have a relaxed atmosphere, a marvellous winter log fire, and a mechanical wall clock behind the bar counter. Well kept Wychwood Dogs Bollocks, Fiddlers Elbow, and Dr Thirstys, Ruddles Best, and Wadworths 6X on handpump, a carefully chosen wine list, and home-made lemonade. The pleasant garden is primarily for the use of residents and restaurant guests, but is available on busy days for those in the bar. The attractive village is one of the few still owned privately, and the pub itself used to be the site of the Yattendon Revels. *(Recommended by G C Hackemer, Mayur Shah, Paul A Kitchener, Ralf Zeyssig, Gordon; more reports please)*

Free house ~ Manager Paul Marshall ~ Real ale ~ Meals and snacks (till 10pm) ~ No smoking restaurant (not Sun evenings) ~ (01635) 201325 ~ Children welcome ~ Open 11-3, 5.30-11 ~ Bedrooms: £70B/£85B

Lucky Dip

Besides the fully inspected pubs, you might like to try these Lucky Dips recommended to us and described by readers (if you do, please send us reports):

☆ **Aldermaston** [SU5965], *Hinds Head*: Subtly refurbished village inn with traditional interior, good home-cooked food inc oriental dishes (and special ones for diabetics if requested), friendly and obliging service (and friendly chunky black cat), well kept ales such as Courage Best and Fullers London Pride with a guest such as Morrells Varsity, children welcome (separate dining room with high chairs), superb enclosed garden; a good place to stay *(J Palka, Simon Collett-Jones, Sheilah Openshaw, BB)*

Aldworth [Haw Lane; B4009 towards Hampstead Norreys; SU5579], *Four Points*: Thatched family pub, long and low, with new licensees doing good generous plain food inc good value Sun roasts in long beamed room with lots of tables and big log fire; well kept Morlands ales, well kept garden with play area over road *(Gordon, Jenny and Michael Back, Mr and Mrs Richard Osborne, LYM)*

Ascot [London Rd; SU9268], *Wells*: Recently refurbished, with extended family room and big garden with play equipment; neat and tidy, with generous food *(Mayur Shah)*

☆ **Aston** [Ferry Lane; signed off A423 Henley—Maidenhead; SU7884], *Flower Pot*: Big unspoilt walkers' pub with great garden – views over meadows to cottages and far side of Thames; well kept Brakspears, reasonably priced food (no children's helpings), friendly young staff, bare-boards public bar, darts, unobtrusive piped music; popular Sun lunchtimes, handy for riverside strolls *(Mr and Mrs G D Amos, David Warrellow)*

☆ **Bagnor** [SU4569], *Blackbird*: Genuine country pub in lovely spot nr Watermill Theatre and River Lambourn, with clean and thoughtful decor, well varnished old sewing machine tables, cheerful chatty atmosphere, friendly locals, tables in pleasant side garden; efficient, friendly service, well kept ales such as Fullers London Pride, Marstons Pedigree, Ushers and Websters Yorkshire, wide range of well served straightforward food, quiet piped music *(TBB, HNJ, PEJ, Rona Murdoch)*

Beech Hill [Beech Hill Rd; SU6964], *Old Elm Tree*: Good views from friendly family-run pub with pleasant bar and adjoining restaurant, attentive service, good value food, well kept Brakspears *(David Betts, Dr Ian Crichton)*

☆ **Binfield** [B3034 Windsor rd; SU8471], *Stag & Hounds*: Comfortable 14th-c pub with low-beamed bars, open fires, antiques, brass, good value food in quite separate room from sandwiches up (menu spread over three blackboards), consistently affable landlord, free newspapers *(Gordon, Margaret Dyke, A M Pring)*

☆ **Binfield** [Terrace Rd North], *Victoria Arms*: Neat no-frills Fullers pub with good choice of seating areas, well kept real ales inc Chiswick, good reasonably priced bar food, children's room, summer barbecues in quiet garden *(G V Price, Martin Kay, Andrea*

Fowler, LYM)

Binfield, *Yorkshire Rose*: Country pub with delightful garden, conservatory, good value food *(Beverly Lagna)*

☆ **Bracknell** [Grenville Pl, High St; SU8769], *Old Manor*: Big open-plan Wetherspoons pub with usual good value food, sensibly priced real ales, no-smoking areas, good solid decor inc original oak beams; very useful for the M4/M25 short cut via M3 *(Dr Michael Smith, Peter and Lynn Brueton, T G Thomas)*

☆ **Bray** [2 miles from M4 junction 9; SU9079], *Hinds Head*: Increasingly popular 16th-c inn with lots of atmosphere in splendid old rooms, good reasonably priced bar food, Adnams, Brakspears and other real ales, welcoming fires, pleasant service, comfortable furnishings, more expensive upstairs restaurant; piped music *(Ian Phillips, TBB)*

☆ **Bray**, *Crown*: 14th-c pub with lots of low beams, timbers and panelling, leather seats, well kept Courage Best and Wadworths 6X on handpump, bar food, restaurant, attractive service, log fires; piped music, maybe karaoke Sun evening; well behaved children allowed, plenty of seating outside inc flagstoned vine arbour *(Richard Houghton, Nigel Norman, A Plumb, George Atkinson, Mr and Mrs P Smith, Simon Collett-Jones, LYM)*

Bray [Old Mill Lane], *Albion*: Limited choice of really good plain food in clean, friendly and comfortable L-shaped bar, conservatory restaurant *(TBB)*

☆ **Brimpton** [Brimpton Common; B3051, W of Heath End; SU5564], *Pineapple*: Friendly thatched and low-beamed country pub with stripped brick and timbering, tiled floor, solid rustic furnishings, open fire, snug and cosy atmosphere; helpful service, seven well kept Whitbreads-related ales, usual food noon-9, side games area, maybe piped pop music; lots of tables on sheltered lawn, play area; open all day; children in eating area *(Gordon, Simon Collett-Jones, Ian and Nita Cooper, LYM)*

☆ **Bucklebury** [Chapel Row; SU5570], *Blade Bone*: Comfortable pub, good reasonably priced food inc interesting specials and Sun lunches, pleasant service, conservatory; piped music in public bar; tables outside, play area *(W L G Watkins)*

☆ **Burchetts Green** [side rd between A4 and A404, nr Knowl Green; SU8381], *Crown*: Clean and comfortable, with friendly and efficient new management, some concentration on wide and quite sophisticated choice of good food, reasonable prices; good garden *(TBB, Lady Palmer)*

Cippenham [Stoneymeade; off A4 via Twinches Lane, by AEG factory; SU9480], *Earl of Cornwall*: Fairly new, in traditional style, on edge of trading estate and new housing; well kept Courage-related beers, plentiful cheap food *(Beryl and Terry Bryan)*

Compton [SU5279], *Swan*: Well modernised, with good food in comfortable lounge bar or restaurant; bedrooms *(Stan Edwards, Anne Cargill)*; *Red Lion*: Sadly this attractive country local has now closed *(BB)*

Cookham [formerly the White Hart; SU8884], *Spencers*: Pleasant ivy-clad exterior, good solid furniture, friendly service; piped music *(TBB)*

☆ **Cookham Dean** [OS Sheet 175 map reference 872853; SU8785], *Inn on the Green*: Inviting atmosphere, good solid furniture with attractive tables, unspoilt rambling layout, stripped beams, two-sided log fires, good genuine food inc delicious Swiss specialities, several real ales; occasional piped music may obtrude, and all too many of the well heeled local women who lunch here seem to be smokers; pleasant restaurant *(TBB, Prof Ron Leigh, Chris and Andy Crow)*

Cookham Rise [The Pound; B4447 Cookham—Maidenhead; SU8984], *Swan Uppers*: Flagstones, low beams, log fire, friendly management and good range of real ales in recently refurbished quaint and pleasant pub; bar food, unobtrusive piped music – Pavarotti etc; bedrooms *(Julian and Sarah Stanton, TBB, Thomas Neate, LYM)*

Cox Green [Cox Green Lane, nr M4 junction 9; SU8779], *Barley Mow*: Good atmosphere in cosy well cared-for pub with well kept beers, decent food, gardens front and back; live music Sat *(Andy Clarkson)*

☆ **Curridge** [3 miles from M4 junction 13: A34 towards Newbury, then first left to Curridge, Hermitage, and left into Curridge at Village Only sign – OS Sheet 174 map ref 492723; SU4871], *Bunk*: Good atmosphere in stylish dining pub with adventurous upmarket food (not Sun evening), smart stripped-wood tiled-floor bar on left, elegant stable-theme bistro on right with wooded-meadow views and conservatory; four well kept real ales, cheerful efficient service, tables in neat garden *(R C Watkins, Jim Reid, Bill Capper, Mrs C Layton, A T Langton, BB)*

Datchet [The Green; not far from M4 junction 5; SU9876], *Royal Stag*: Friendly and pleasant, with good value food, well kept Tetleys-related ales; bar partly panelled in claret case lids *(Mr and Mrs G D Amos, Ian Phillips, R Houghton)*

☆ **East Ilsley** [SU4981], *Swan*: Pleasant spick-and-span new-look interior, open-plan but comfortably divided and well spaced, with lots of interesting things to look at; generally quick food service, well kept Morlands ales, chatty helpful staff, rack of daily papers; children in eating area, good bedrooms *(Nick Wikeley, HNJ, PEJ, Wayne Brindle, J and P Maloney, Don Kellaway, Angie Coles, Alan Skull, Michael Sargent, LYM)*

Eton Wick [32 Eton Wick Rd; SU9478], *Pickwick*: Straightforward pub notable for its good authentic Malay food Weds and Sat evenings, slightly shorter menu at lunchtime – also English dishes; beautiful carpet, pleasant landlord, Youngs ales; maybe piped music *(Bill and Jane Rees, TBB)*

Fifield [formerly the White Hart; SU9076], *Fifield Inn*: Tidy, clean and spacious, with good garden in peaceful setting; newish licensees, quiet piped music, theme nights *(TBB)*

☆ **Great Shefford** [Shefford Woodland; less than ½ mile N of M4 junction 14 – B4000, just off A338; SU3875], *Pheasant*: Good relaxing motorway break, welcoming attentive service in four neat rooms, very wide choice of good food inc home-made dishes and Sun lunches, well kept Wadworths IPA and 6X, decent wines and coffee, open fires; public bar with games inc ring the bull; children welcome, attractive views from garden; under same ownership as Royal Oak at Wootton Rivers *(S J Edwards, Dr C E Morgan, LYM)*

☆ **Hampstead Norreys** [SU5276], *White Hart*: Spotless Morlands pub with low beams, partly tiled floor, wide range of reasonably priced hot and cold food inc children's, morning coffee, friendly atmosphere; darts, pool and fruit machine in second bar; back terrace and garden *(Joan Olivier)*

☆ **Hermitage** [Hampstead Norreys Rd; 2½ miles from M4 junction 13; SU5073], *Fox*: Useful motorway break with friendly young licensees, good attractively priced well presented bar food inc children's menu, well kept Courage-related ales, roaring log fire, attractive garden and terrace; service quick even when busy *(Mrs A Storm, Stephen, Julie and Hayley Brown, John R Ellis, LYM)*

☆ **Holyport** [The Green; 1½ miles from M4 junction 8/9 via A308(M)/A330; SU8977], *George*: Real home cooking inc good steak and kidney pie, roast beef, fresh veg; busily pubby low-ceilinged open-plan bar with bay window-seats and nice old fireplace, friendly efficient service, Courage real ales; maybe piped pop music; picnic-table sets outside, lovely village green *(TBB, Beryl and Terry Bryan)*

☆ **Hungerford** [Charnham St; 3 miles from M4 junction 14; town signposted at junction; SU3368], *Bear*: Civilised old-fashioned hotel bar with open fires, well kept real ales such as Wadworths 6X, pleasant service; decent food in bar (maybe via open-air passageway from kitchen) and comfortably unhurried restaurant; bedrooms comfortable and attractive *(Gordon, DGC, LYM)*

Hungerford [by Hungerford Common, E edge of town; SU3368], *Down Gate*: Prettily placed two-bar Arkells pub, friendly and relaxing, with good service, interesting bric-a-brac, tempting food in small deep-sunk room with open fire and a few small dining tables *(Gordon)*

☆ **Hungerford Newtown** [A338 a mile S of M4 junction 14; SU3571], *Tally Ho*: Roomy, friendly and enjoyable, with good well presented home-made food inc beautiful chips and puddings, well kept Wadworths and decent house wines, welcoming staff, plenty of room; children if eating *(Rona Murdoch, John and Wendy Trentham, A G Roby)*

Hurley [SU8283], *Black Boy*: Lots of flowers boxes and baskets, pleasant garden, friendly staff *(TBB)*; *Olde Bell*: Handsome timbered inn, civilised and old-fashioned, with some remarkable ancient features inc Norman doorway and window; fine gardens; restaurant, bedrooms *(Ian Phillips, LYM)*

☆ **Hurst** [Hinton Rd/Church Hill; SU7972], *Green Man*: Old-fashioned traditional low-ceilinged local, basic though comfortable furnishings with wooden seats and tables and cosy little areas, well kept Brakspears, bar food (not Mon evening), pub games, piped music; pleasant back garden *(Mike Davies, George Atkinson, Gordon, Dr Andrew Brookes, Roger and Valerie Hill)*

Hurst [opp church], *Castle*: Warm and cosy Morlands pub concentrating now on food; picnic tables overlooking bowling green – which, contrary to what we said in last edition, has no connection with pub *(Gordon)*

☆ **Inkpen** [Lower Inkpen; SU 3564], *Swan*: Rambling beamed pub with gentle decor, chintz and shiny woodwork, firmly recommended for its good atmosphere, well kept real ales such as Brakspears PA, Marstons Pedigree and Ringwood Fortyniner, and good genuine Singaporean food – but as we went to press it seemed likely if not certain to be sold as a private house before long *(LYM – news please)*

☆ **Kintbury** [SU3866], *Dundas Arms*: Clean and tidy with comfortably upmarket feel, lots of antique blue and white plates, bar food (not Mon evening or Sun) from sandwiches to good venison casserole and so forth, well kept real ales from smaller breweries, good wines by the glass and coffee, remarkable range of clarets and burgundies in evening restaurant, coolly professional staff; pleasant walks by Kennet & Avon Canal; children allowed; comfortable bedrooms opening on to secluded waterside terrace *(GB, Neil Franklin, L Walker, LYM)*

☆ **Knowl Hill** [A4 Reading—Maidenhead; SU8279], *Bird in Hand*: Relaxed civilised atmosphere and notable lunchtime cold buffet and other good home-made food in spacious and attractive beamed main bar which somehow largely manages to conceal its considerable age despite splendid log fire, cosy alcoves and much older side bar; well kept Brakspears and Fullers London Pride, wide choice of wines and other drinks, consistently good service, good side garden; no-smoking buffet area – where children allowed; bedrooms *(Simon Collett-Jones, Nigel Wilkinson, Mike Davies, Clifford Payton, LYM)*

☆ **Knowl Hill** [A4], *Seven Stars*: Simple old-fashioned relaxing place with good honest bar food from sandwiches to steaks at sensible prices, well kept Brakspears (full range), good choice of wines, a lot of panelling, roaring log fire, sleepy dog and cat; helpful professional service, fruit machine, flowers, big garden with summer barbecue *(TBB, Gordon, Nick and Alison Dowson, Mike & Heather Barnes, David and Gill Carrington, BB)*

Little Sandhurst [High St; SU8262], *Bird in Hand*: Friendly Morlands local nicely furnished with upholstered settles and polished tables; good freshly cooked food (so can be slow when busy), welcoming young licensees, Sun bar nibbles and raffle *(Margaret Dyke, Maureen Hobbs)*

☆ **Littlewick Green** [3¾ miles from M4 junction 9; A423(M) then left on to A4, from which village signposted on left; SU8379], *Cricketers*: Clean, attractive and neatly kept village pub opp cricket green, lots of cricketing pictures, decent food, good service, Brakspears and Flowers real ales; can be very quiet weekday lunchtimes *(Angela and Alan Dale, Clem Stephens, TBB, LYM)*

Maidenhead [Queen St; SU8783], *Hand & Flowers*: Very old building close to shopping area, well kept Brakspears, good atmosphere, pleasant landlord; limited lunchtime food, can be crowded weekday lunchtimes *(R Houghton)*

Newbury [SU4666], *Lock Stock & Barrel*: Spacious wood-floored curved bar with tables out on canalside terrace, friendly helpful servic, Fullers ales, bar food, coffee shop open all afternoon *(Tony Dickinson, George Atkinson)*; [West St], *Red Lion*: Good atmosphere, good choice of well kept Wadworths ales, friendly licensees *(Stephen Gennard)*

☆ **Old Windsor** [17 Crimp Hill, off B3021 – itself off A308/A328; SU9874], *Union*: Tidy L-shaped bar with interesting collection of nostalgic show-business photographs, real ales such as Courage, Everards and Flowers, bar food inc good baked potatoes and steaks and some more interesting dishes, good service even when very busy, woodburner in big fireplace, fruit machine; attractive copper-decorated restaurant, white plastic tables under cocktail parasols on sunny front terrace; comfortable bedrooms *(Ian Phillips, Mayur Shah, George Atkinson, BB)*

Old Windsor [Crimp Hill], *Oxford Blue*: Well kept beer, good food and atmosphere, interesting airline memorabilia *(Peter Catley)*

☆ **Paley Street** [3 miles SW of Bray; SU8675], *Bridge*: Memorable generous and reasonably priced home-made food in small beamed pub with pleasant dining room, welcoming young staff, several real ales; get there early on Sun or book; big garden *(Jeff and Rhoda Collins, G Medcalf, R J Purser)*

☆ **Reading** [10 Castle St, next to PO; SU7272], *Sweeney & Todd*: Food exceptional value esp dozens of different home-made pies, adventurous and generously served, such as hare and cherry, peach and pigeon; upstairs has several well kept changing real ales, downstairs is warren of small and cosy rooms and cubby holes; very busy lunchtime *(Chris Warne, Andy Cunningham, Susan and John Douglas)*

☆ **Reading** [Kennet Side], *Fishermans Cottage*: Fullers pub by lock on Kennet & Avon Canal, lovely big back garden, relaxed atmosphere, modern furnishings of character, pleasant stone snug behind woodburning range, light and airy conservatory; traditional pub lunches (very popular then), evening food inc Mexican, well kept ales, small choice of wines, quick pleasant service, small darts room *(Paul and Janet Giles, Martin Kay, Andrea Fowler)*

Reading [Chatham St], *Butler*: Horseshoe bar with particularly well kept Fullers, efficient service, usual food lunchtime and early evening *(Martin Kay, Andrea Fowler)*; [Kates Grove Lane – off A4 Pell St/Berkley Ave, next to flyover inner ring rd], *Hook & Tackle*: Real ale pub with pastiche traditional decor, often full of young people and loud music; good choice of beers, quick service, usual food, maybe smoky; outstanding twice-yearly beer festivals *(Mark and Diane Grist, Nick and Alison Dowson)*

☆ **Remenham** [A423, just over bridge E of Henley; SU7683], *Little Angel*: Bar snacks from sandwiches up and good if more expensive main meals in low-beamed dining pub with panelling and darkly bistroish decor, service very friendly and helpful even when busy; splendid range of wines by the glass, well kept Brakspears, back fish restaurant, floodlit terrace *(Brian and Anna Marsden, TBB, LYM)*

Riseley [SU7263], *Bull*: Good atmosphere, friendly staff and customers, good food inc gargantuan vegetarian dishes and huge steaks *(M O'Rourke)*

Shurlock Row [SU8374], *White Hart*: Attractive panelled pub, warm, comfortable and relaxing, with good if not cheap bar lunches, good range of Whitbreads-related ales, quietly attentive service; inglenook fireplace dividing bar from other rooms, old pictures and brasses, flying memorabilia *(Michael and Jenny Back, Gordon)*

☆ **Sindlesham** [Bearwood Rd; signposted Sindlesham from B3349; SU7769], *Walter Arms*: Three comfortable main rooms (one recently extended) each with a log fire, good range of reasonably priced food lunchtime and evening inc Suns, efficient service, no-smoking area, well kept Courage Best and Directors; very popular; tables outside; unpretentious bedrooms, good breakfasts *(Paul and Janet Giles, LYM)*

Slough [High St; SU9779], *Newt & Cucumber*: New pub with decent choice of real ales and sensibly priced food, pleasant outside area; can be busy with young people evenings (bouncers, loud music) *(Dave Kiely)*

☆ **Stanford Dingley** [SU5771], *Old Boot*: Good friendly atmosphere in comfortably busy country pub, beams, inglenook, old pews and other country furnishings, pleasant views from spacious and attractive suntrap garden, decent generous food, well kept Fullers Chiswick, ESB and London Pride, adjacent restaurant area; impressive lavatories, no dogs *(Angela and Alan Dale, Dr Ian Crichton, Nigel Wilkinson, TBB, Mary and Bob O'Hara, LYM)*

Sunningdale [A30 nr stn; SU9567], *Chequers*: Courage and Youngs real ales,

good value food, separate games room; small garden *(Tony and Wendy Hobden)*
Swallowfield [S of Reading – OS Sheet 175 map reference 735647; SU7364], *George & Dragon*: Old pub attractively modernised, good reasonably priced menu, welcoming young staff, broad appeal; surrounded by farmland *(D D Owen-Pawson)*
☆ **Theale** [Church St; SU6371], *Volunteer*: Well kept Fullers, nice wooden furniture, good choice of bar meals; children at reasonable times *(Martin Kay, Andrea Fowler, D and J Johnson)*
Theale [Church St], *Red Lion*: Particularly well kept real ales inc exemplary Bass, friendly English landlord with Norwegian wife, decent food, attractive prices *(Chris Wheway)*
☆ **Upper Basildon** [Aldworth Rd; SU5976], *Red Lion*: Small Victorian pub, welcoming and comfortable, with good interesting choice of real ales, good food in bar and restaurant inc fine range of home-made pies (even a vegan one), decent house wines, good young staff; no constraints on children *(Stan Edwards, Clifford Payton, Carolyn Lainbeer, KC)*
☆ **Wargrave** [High St; off A321 Henley—Twyford; SU7878], *Bull*: Quietly friendly and cottagey low-beamed pub popular for good food beyond the usual range, good value if not cheap; well kept Brakspears, good log fires, tables on pretty covered terrace; bedrooms *(S R Jordan, Gordon, Colin Pearson, LYM)*
Wexham [Wexham Rd; SU9981], *Plough*: Pleasant village pub with very good value food, friendly landlord *(B M Eshelby)*
☆ **Wickham** [3 miles from M4 junction 14, via A338, B4000; SU3971], *Five Bells*: Neatly kept and smartly simple racing-village inn dating from 16th century, with friendly licensees, big log fire, decent food inc some individual dishes, Courage-related real ales, garden with good play area; children in eating area, good value bedrooms *(HNJ, PEJ, LYM)*
Windsor [Thames St; SU9676], *Adam & Eve*: Small bustling pub by theatre, lots of thespian photographs, friendly courteous staff, juke box and fruit machines; occasional barbecues in little back yard *(Michael Fertig, LYM)*; [Datchet Rd – opp Riverside Stn, nr Castle], *Royal Oak*: Big and busy, with quick friendly service, red plush and panelling, some fine stained glass, good choice of reasonably priced bar food from big food servery in airy eating area, Marstons Pedigree and Wadworths 6X; white furniture on L-shaped terrace *(TBB, BB)*; [St Leonards Rd], *Trooper*: One-bar pub with pool table discreetly tucked away at back, limited range of Courage-related beers, cheap and cheerful food, charming faultless service; barbecues on terrace which seems much bigger than pub itself *(Ian Phillips)*; [Park St, off High St next to Mews], *Two Brewers*: Snug bars, interesting menu, relaxed and pleasant atmosphere *(Dave Braisted)*
Winkfield [Hatchet Lane – OS Sheet 175 map reference 922714; SU9271], *Olde Hatchet*: Attractive low-ceilinged pub, long and narrow, with appetising food and popular lower dining area *(Gordon)*; [A330, opp church], *White Hart*: Neatly modernised Tudor pub, very food-oriented, with ex-bakery bar and ex-courthouse restaurant; Courage real ale, sizeable garden *(TBB, Gordon, LYM)*
Winkfield Row [back rd outside village – OS Sheet 175 map reference 892713; SU8971], *Cricketers*: Doing well under newish licensees, with decent house wines, well kept Hook Norton and Whitbreads-related ales, sensible prices, and a real welcome for children – and dogs *(Mr and Mrs Damien Burke)*
☆ **Wokingham** [Gardeners Green, Honey Hill – OS Sheet 175 map reference 826668; SU8266], *Crooked Billet*: Well kept Brakspears in homely country pub, very busy weekends, with pews, tiles, brick serving counter, crooked black joists; big helpings of popular food, small no smoking restaurant area where children allowed, cosy local atmosphere; nice outside in summer *(D K Carter, Mrs C A Blake, Nick and Muriel Cox, Jeannette Campbell, P J Caunt, LYM)*
Wokingham, *Metropolitan*: Friendly High-St local, half-timbered, with two small bars, well kept Morlands *(Mike and Heather Barnes)*; [Peach St], *Redan*: Well kitted-out town pub with well kept Morlands beers, relaxed atmosphere, comfortable back garden; busy Sat nights *(Nick and Meriel Cox, Simon Minor)*; [Reading Rd], *Rifle Volunteer*: Friendly local with well kept ales, good lunchtime food, Sun quiz night; popular with young people weekends *(Ross Hannan)*; [222 London Rd], *Three Frogs*: Welcoming main-road local with sandwiches, ploughman's and usual hot dishes, Morlands and interesting guest ales *(Peter and Lynn Brueton, AMP)*
☆ **Woodside** [signed off A322 Windsor—Ascot; SU9270], *Duke of Edinburgh*: Pleasantly straightforward more or less open-plan pub with some attractive furnishings esp in Regency-style back room, cheery service, well kept Arkells 2B, 3B and Kingsdown, and big helpings of surprisingly good food (not Sun evening), inc a very wide and unusual range of fresh fish dishes; sensible prices, children welcome; maybe loudish piped music; some tables outside *(H F King, Beryl and Terry Bryan, Peter Ashcroft, Kim Turner, Nick Wikeley, R B Crail, BB)*
☆ **Woolhampton** [A4; SU5767], *Rising Sun*: Half a dozen or more well kept and interesting real ales and good welcoming atmosphere in plainly furnished pub with plentiful home-made food inc huge reasonably priced sandwiches, obliging service *(Eric J Locker, John Hazel, Rob and Helen Townsend, Gordon, Mark and Diane Grist, Roger Byrne, Phil H Smith, LYM)*

Buckinghamshire

Strong on food and on real character, many of Buckinghamshire's pubs, particularly in the Chilterns, have a great deal of charm. For food, we'd pick out the warmly friendly Seven Stars at Dinton, the Mole & Chicken at Easington (particularly good), the beautifully placed Walnut Tree at Fawley (our choice as Buckinghamshire Dining Pub of the Year), the Stag & Huntsman at Hambleden, the the very well run Pink & Lily near Lacey Green, the Greyhound at Marsh Gibbon (Thai food), the White Hart at Northend, the Red Lion at Princes Risborough, the Old Crown at Skirmett, and the Five Arrows at Waddesdon. Among new entries, the Hampden Arms at Great Hampden and Red Lion at Great Kingshill both have notably good food; the Old Ship at Cadmore End and Crown at Little Missenden are included for their warmth and character. Other pubs here currently doing very well include the remarkable Royal Standard of England at Forty Green, the chatty little Prince Albert at Frieth, the Blackwood Arms at Littleworth Common (an incredible roster of changing beers), and the pretty Bull & Butcher at Turville. This is not a cheap area; drinks prices are much higher than the national average, and the £2 pint has now reached Buckinghamshire. The Lucky Dip section is particularly strong in this county: we'd direct your attention specially to the Old Swan at Astwood, Greyhound in Beaconsfield, Fox at Ibstone, Rising Sun at Little Hampden, Angel in Long Crendon, Hit or Miss at Penn Street, Lone Tree at Thornborough, Brickmakers Arms on Wheelerend Common and Chequers on Wooburn Common, though all with stars stand comparison with many main entries.

nr AMERSHAM SU9495 Map 4

Queens Head

Whielden Gate; pub in sight just off A404, 1½ miles towards High Wycombe at Winchmore Hill turn-off; OS Sheet 165 map reference 941957

Unpretentious and friendly, this old brick and tile pub hopes to be redecorated by the time this book is published – and to have built a new outdoor eating area. The bar has low beams, traditional furnishings, horsebrasses, and lots of brass spigots; Monty the dalmatian may be wandering around. Flagstones surround the big inglenook fireplace (which still has the old-fashioned wooden built-in wall seat curving around right in beside the woodburning stove – with plenty of space under the seat for logs), a stuffed albino pheasant, old guns, and a good cigarette card collection. Home-made bar food – using home-grown vegetables from the garden – includes soup (£2.25), sweet pickled trout (£3), omelettes (£3.50), spinach and walnut pancakes (£4.75), pizzas (from £5; you can take them away as well), and venison pie (£6). Well kept Adnams, Ind Coope Burton, Morrells Graduate, and Marlow Rebellion on handpump; darts, shove-ha'penny, dominoes, cribbage, fruit machine, and piped music. The garden has swings, a climbing frame and slide, an aviary with cockatiels, a rabbit and a guinea pig in a large run, and bantams. *(Recommended by Ian Phillips, Gordon, Mr and Mrs G Arbib, Dr Jim Craig-Gray, Miles and Deborah Protter, B M Eshelby, AD, Mike Pugh, J S M Sheldon)*

Free house ~ Licensees Les and Mary Anne Robbins ~ Real ale ~ Meals and snacks (till 10pm; not Sun evening) ~ (01494) 725240 ~ Children in family room ~ Open 11-2.30(3 Sat), 5.30(6 Sat)-11

BEACONSFIELD SU9490 Map 2

Old Hare

A mile from M40 junction 2; 41 Aylesbury End, Old Beaconsfield

Popular with readers, this warmly friendly, bustling old pub has several rambling (and rather dimly-lit) cosy rooms. The ones by the odd-angled bar counter are decorated with prints of hares, photographs and prints of the pub, and to the right of the door an end room has a big, very high-backed antique settle and a serving hatch; a lighter room has a big inglenook with a copper hood. Good bar food includes home-made soup (£1.95), big filled baps and french bread (from £2.55), and daily specials like deep-fried brie (£3.95), chilli con carne (£4.95), steak in ale pie (£5.95), chicken curry madras (£5.50), a vegetarian dish, and 8oz rump steak (£8.95); every Wednesday they have a themed food day. Cheerfully helpful staff serve well kept Benskins Best, Ind Coope Burton and Tetleys plus a guest such as Marstons Pedigree on handpump; lots of malt whiskies, decent house wines, and good strong coffee; no machines or music. The big, sunny back garden has a terrace and lots of seating. *(Recommended by Steve Goodchild, Gordon, Ian and Colin Roe, A W Dickinson, Ian Phillips, N M Baleham, Simon Collett-Jones, G R Sharman, Roger and Valerie Hill, Ron and Sheila Corbett, Mark J Hydes, George Atkinson, T A Bryan, Dr Gerald W Barnett)*

Allied ~ Manager Peter Tye ~ Real ale ~ Meals and snacks (not Sun evening) ~ (01494) 673380 ~ Children in eating area of bar ~ Open 11-11; closed evening May 10 for annual street fair

BLEDLOW SP7702 Map 4

Lions of Bledlow

From B4009 from Chinnor towards Princes Risborough, the first right turn about 1 mile outside Chinnor goes straight to the pub; from the second, wider right turn, turn right through village

In the heart of the Chilterns with marvellous views, this mossy-tiled old pub has attractive low-beamed rooms – one with a woodburning stove – that are full of character. The inglenook bar has attractive oak stalls built into one partly panelled wall, more seats in a good bay window, and an antique settle resting on the deeply polished ancient tiles; log fires. Bar food includes home-made soup (£2), big filled cottage rolls (from £2.95), steak in Guinness pie (£5) and maybe daily specials such as chicken and ham pie (£4.75), roast chicken (£5.50) and grilled fresh fish (£7.50). Well kept Courage Best, Marstons Pedigree, John Smiths, and Wadworths 6X on handpump. One of the two cottagey side rooms has a video game, as well as dominoes and cribbage. A fair number of walkers from nearby Bledlow Ridge and the Chilterns come to the pub to enjoy the sheltered crazy-paved terrace and series of neatly kept small sloping lawns. *(Recommended by Gordon, Nigel Norman, Tony Dickinson, Jack and Philip Paxton, Tim and Ann Newell, Simon Collett-Jones)*

Free house ~ Licensee F J McKeown ~ Real ale ~ Meals and snacks (not Sun evening) ~ Restaurant (closed Sun evening) ~ (01844) 343345 ~ Children in eating areas of bar ~ Open 11-3, 6-11

BOLTER END SU7992 Map 4

Peacock

Just over 4 miles from M40 junction 5; A40 to Stokenchurch, then B482

The friendly licensees continue to run this busy pub with great enthusiasm – even after 16 years here. The brightly modernised bar has a rambling series of alcoves, a good log fire, and a cheerful atmosphere; the Old Darts bar is no smoking. And the home-made bar food is very good, too: ploughman's (from £3.25), pasta with spicy tomato and aubergine sauce (£3.95), spicy beef and bean chilli or cheesy mushroom pancakes (£4.25), steak and kidney pie (£5.50), local ham and chips (£5.95), poached fresh salmon (£6.95), and steaks (from £10.25; they only use Aberdeen Angus meat), plus three daily specials and a special pudding; their poultry is free-range, their air-dried ham, cheddar cheese and blue vinney comes from farms in Dorset, and fresh fish comes from Billingsgate on Fridays. Well kept ABC Bitter, Brakspears PA, Marstons Pedigree and Tetleys Bitter on handpump, decent wines including changing specials, freshly squeezed orange juice and elderflower pressé; darts, cribbage and dominoes. In summer there are seats around a low stone table and picnic table in the neatly kept garden. The 'no children' is strictly enforced here and there is no piped music. ***(Recommended by Sandra Iles, T A Bryan, Peter Plumridge, Dr Gerald W Barnett)***

Carlsberg Tetleys ~ Lease: Peter Hodges ~ Real ale ~ Meals and snacks (till 10pm; not Sun evening) ~ (01494) 881417 ~ Open 11.45-2.30, 6-11

BRILL SP6513 Map 4

Pheasant 🍷

Windmill Rd; village signposted from B4011 Bicester—Long Crendon

The licensees are hoping to build a large verandah onto the west wall of this 17th-c pub, which will enjoy the views of the windmill opposite – one of the oldest post windmills still in working order. There are also some picnic tables in the small, sheltered back garden. Inside, the quietly modernised and neatly kept beamed bar has been opened up, and refectory tables and windsor chairs have replaced the banquettes; there's a woodburning stove and a step up to a dining area which is decorated with attractively framed Alken hunting prints – and which also benefits from the view. Bar food now includes sandwiches, Greek salad with feta cheese and olives (£3.75), popular ploughman's (£3.95), moules marinières (£4.60), home-cooked ham (£4.75), tiger prawns in garlic butter or pasta with prawns and smoked salmon (£4.95), chicken breasts with a choice of five sauces (£6.95) and rump steak with a choice of seven sauces (£8.50). Well kept Tetleys and a guest such as Marstons Pedigree, locally-brewed Wychert Vale or Wadworths 6X on handpump, and seven good wines by the glass; piped music. No dogs (they have three golden retrievers themselves). The views are splendid, and it's said on a clear day that you can see nine counties from this hilltop. Roald Dahl used to drink here, and some of the tales the locals told him were worked into his short stories. ***(Recommended by K H Frostick, Bob and Maggie Atherton, Steve Goodchild, Ted George, Michael Sargent, Gordon, D A Edwards, Graham and Karen Oddey)***

Free house ~ Licensee Mike Carr ~ Real ale ~ Meals and snacks ~ Restaurant ~ (01844) 237104 ~ Children welcome ~ Open 11-3, 6-11; 11-11 summer Sats (maybe Suns, too); closed 25 and 26 Dec

CADMORE END SU7892 Map 4

Old Ship

B482 Stokenchurch—Marlow

Not to be missed if you're on this Chilterns road and like genuinely unspoilt country pubs: a tiled cottage huddled below the road, housing a tiny low-beamed two-room bar unchanged for decades. The furnishings are pretty basic – a couple of Formica-topped tables, leatherette wall benches and stools in the carpeted room on the right, and on the left scrubbed country tables, bench seating (one still has a hole for a game called five-farthings) bare boards and darts, shove-ha'penny, cribbage and dominoes. But what matters is the warmth of the landlady's cheerful welcome, the fine quality of the Brakspears PA, SB and Old tapped directly from casks down in the cellar, and the friendly unhurried atmosphere. Food is simple but decent and carefully prepared, with occasional special evenings such as a three-course Cajun supper: filled french bread (from £1.50; bacon, lettuce and tomato £2.15, steak £2.25), stilton mushrooms (£2.25), and chilli con carne (£3.50). There are white plastic tables out in a sheltered garden, and a play area for children (who are not allowed inside). Parking is on the other side of the road. *(Recommended by Gordon, Pete Baker)*

Brakspears ~ Tenants Thomas and Julie Chapman ~ Real ale ~ Meals and snacks (not Sun lunchtime) ~ (01494) 883496 ~ Open 11.30-3, 6-11

CHEDDINGTON SP9217 Map 4

Old Swan

58 High St

In summer, the outside of this mainly thatched old pub is attractively decorated with colourful hanging baskets and tubs, and there's a children's play area in the garden. Inside on the right, the quietly civilised bar rooms have old-fashioned plush dining chairs, a built-in wall bench, and a few tables with nice country-style chairs on the bare boards, a big inglenook with glass cabinets filled with brass on either side of it and quite a few horsebrasses, and little hunting prints on the walls. On the other side of the main door is a room with housekeepers' chairs on the rugs and quarry tiles and country plates on the walls, and a step up to a carpeted part with stripy wallpaper and pine furniture; TV. Bar food includes sandwiches and rolls (from £1.95), filled baked potatoes (from £2.35), ploughman's (from £2.65), nut cutlets (£4.40), gammon and egg (£4.90), home-made daily specials such as spicy pork and bean casserole, lots of puddings (£2.55), and children's menu (£2.90); the restaurant is no smoking. Well kept ABC Best, Greene King IPA, Ridgeway Bitter (from Tring), and Wadworths 6X on handpump, quite a few malt whiskies, and decent wines; very pleasant, efficient staff. Piped nostalgic pop, shove-ha'penny, table skittles, cribbage, darts, fruit machine, and trivia. *(Recommended by Mark and Caroline Thistlethwaite, Pat and Robert Wyatt, Maysie Thompson, The Shinkmans, Brian and Anna Marsden, Russell and Margaret Bathie, Marjorie and David Lamb)*

Ind Coope (Allied) ~ Lease: Paul Jarvis ~ Real ale ~ Meals and snacks (till 10pm) ~ Restaurant ~ (01296) 668226 ~ Children in eating area of bar and in restaurant ~ Occasional folk, jazz or theme nights ~ Open 11.30-2.30(3 winter Sats), 6-11; 11-11 Sat; closed evening 25 Dec

CHENIES TQ0198 Map 2

Red Lion

2 miles from M25 junction 18; A404 towards Amersham, then village signposted on right; Chesham Rd

Handy for Chenies Manor, this brick pub has an L-shaped bar with beige or plum-coloured cushions on the built-in wall benches by the front windows, wheelback chairs and plush stools around a mix of small tables, and photographs and prints of traction-engines, as well as advertising and other prints on the walls; there's also a small back snug and a dining room. Bar food includes soup (£2.25), salmon and tarragon pâté (£3.50), pasta with a mild curry and peanut sauce (£4.50), gammon with cabbage, red onion and potato hash (£5.50), popular lamb pie (from £5.95), pork rogan josh (£6.50), daily specials, and puddings such as apple pie or chocolate roulade (from £1.95); fresh vegetables, no chips. Well kept Benskins Best, Morrells Oxford, two local beers – Rebellion (from Marlow) and Ridgeway (from Tring) – and Wadworths 6X on handpump; no noisy games machines. The hanging baskets and window boxes are pretty in summer. *(Recommended by Kevin and Tracey Stephens, BKA, Gary Roberts, Ann Stubbs, A W Dickinson, Nigel Clifton, Bill Capper, June and Charles Samuel, J Slaughter)*

Free house ~ Licensees Heather and Mike Norris ~ Real ale ~ Meals and snacks (till 10pm) ~ (01923) 282722 ~ Open 11-2.30, 5.30-11; closed 25 Dec

DINTON SP7611 Map 4

Seven Stars

Stars Lane; follow Dinton signpost into New Road off A418 Aylesbury—Thame, near Gibraltar turn-off

It's well worth the effort it takes to find this pretty and warmly friendly old house. The characterful public bar (known as the Snug here) is notable for the two highly varnished ancient built-in settles facing each other across a table in front of the vast stone inglenook fireplace. The spotlessly kept lounge bar, with its beams, joists and growing numbers of old tools on the walls, is comfortably and simply modernised – and although these rooms are not large, there is a spacious and comfortable restaurant area. Well kept ABC, Tetleys and Wadworths 6X and occasional guest beer on handpump or tapped from the cask, and very good, popular home-cooked bar food that includes sandwiches (from £1.65; toasties 25p extra), filled baked potatoes (from £2.75), ploughman's, tasty ham and egg or quiche lorraine (all £3.75), vegetable lasagne (£4), boeuf bourguignon (£4.85), steaks (from £8.95), and good daily specials (from £4.75); summer barbecues, too. Darts and Aunt Sally. There are tables under cocktail parasols on the terrace, with more on the lawn of the pleasant sheltered garden. *(Recommended by Marjorie and David Lamb, H Hazzard, Gordon, John Fahy, Bill Capper, George Atkinson, Michael Sargent)*

Free house ~ Licensees Rainer and Sue Eccard ~ Real ale ~ Meals and snacks (not Sun or Tues evenings) ~ Restaurant (not Sun evening) ~ Children in eating area of bar and in restaurant ~ Aylesbury (01296) 748241 ~ Special theme evenings with live music ~ Open 12-3, 6-11; closed Tues evening

EASINGTON SP6810 Map 4

Mole & Chicken

From B4011 in Long Crendon follow Chearsley, Waddesdon signpost into Carters Lane opposite the Chandos Arms, then turn left into Chilton Road

Although this country dining pub is not really a place you'd come to just for a drink – virtually all the tables are set for meals – they do have well kept Hook Norton Best and Morlands Original and Old Speckled Hen on handpump, decent French house wines (and a good choice by the bottle), and 80 malt whiskies. Using good ingredients, the changing choice of food includes home-made soup (£2.50), a few starters that would do as a light lunch such as baked sweet pepper with mixed cheeses (£3.75), skewers of chicken and prawns with garlic bread (£3.95), or even home-grown asparagus (from £3.95), and very generously served main courses including interesting salads like ham and eggs or pasta with home-made pesto sauce (£5.95), duck and bacon salad with plum and red wine sauce or steak and kidney pie (£6.95), turkey breast strips with a blueberry and lemon sauce (£7.95), their speciality half shoulder of English lamb with honey, garlic and rosemary sauce (£9.95), char-grilled steaks (from £10.95), various fresh fish dishes, and puddings; it's essential to book. It's open-plan but excellently done so that all the different parts seem quite snug and self-contained without being cut off from what's going on. The beamed bar curves around the serving counter in a sort of S-shape – unusual, as is the decor of designed-and-painted floor, pink walls with lots of big antique prints, and even at lunchtime lit candles on the medley of tables to go with the nice mix of old chairs. Smiling young neatly dressed staff, a pleasant chatty and relaxed atmosphere with a good mix of different age-groups, unobtrusive piped music, good winter log fires, pistachio nuts and other nibbles on the counter; no dogs. There's a smallish garden with picnic tables under cocktail parasols, with an outside summer bar and lunchtime summer barbecues. *(Recommended by Hugh and Joyce Mellor, Brian White, Heather Couper, Karen and Graham Oddey, C A Hall, John Oddey, Michael Sargent)*

Free house ~ Licensee Johnny Chick ~ Real ale ~ Meals and snacks (till 10pm; all day Sun) ~ (01844) 208387 ~ Children welcome (until 9pm) ~ Open 11-3.30, 6-11; all day Sun

FAWLEY SU7586 Map 2

Walnut Tree

Village signposted off A4155 (then right at T-junction) and off B480, N of Henley

Buckinghamshire Dining Pub of the Year

In a lovely spot with the Chilterns all around, this well run dining pub is very popular for its good, often imaginative, food – which can be eaten in the attractively furnished bars, no-smoking conservatory, and restaurant: soup (£2.40), ploughman's (from £3.50), smoked salmon and trout terrine (£3.95), baked stuffed aubergine (£4.95), curry of the day (£5.25), steak and kidney pie (£5.75), hot ham and parsley sauce (£5.95), chicken oriental (£6.25), good rack of lamb with garlic crust, and puddings like sherry, lemon and ginger cheesecake, white chocolate ice cream or hot apple pie (£2.85). Well kept Brakspears PA and SB on handpump, and a good range of wines (including local English ones); attentive service. The big lawn around the front car park has some well spaced tables made from elm trees, with some seats in a covered terrace extension – and a hitching rail for riders. *(Recommended by Gwen and Peter Andrews, Leigh and Gillian Mellor, Piotr Chodzko-Zajko, Mike and Heather Barnes, Dave Carter, Jim Reid, Roger and Valerie Hill, Gordon)*

Brakspears ~ Tenant Ben Godbolt ~ Real ale ~ Meals and snacks ~ Restaurant ~ (01491) 638360 ~ Children in conservatory and in restaurant (must be over 5 in evening) ~ Open 12(11 Sat)-3, 6-11 ~ Bedrooms: £40S/£50S

FINGEST SU7791 Map 2

Chequers

Village signposted off B482 Marlow—Stokenchurch

Dating back 500 years, this white shuttered pub has several spotless old-fashioned rooms, warmed in winter by a huge log fire. The friendly central bar room has chairs of varying ages from ancient to modern, an 18th-c oak settle, and seats built into its black-painted wooden dado. On the walls are pistols, antique guns and swords, toby jugs, pewter mugs and decorative plates. A sunny lounge has comfortable easy chairs and french windows to the garden; there's also a small no-smoking room for eating. Very good, popular bar food includes sandwiches (from £1.60), soup (£2.95), ploughman's (from £3.75), seafood salad (£4.95), vegetarian dishes (from £4.95), roasts or liver and bacon (all £5.95), steak, kidney and mushroom pie (£6.50), freshly caught trout (£7.50), steaks (from £8.50), beef stroganoff (£10.50), and puddings like lovely banoffi pie or sherry trifle (£2.75); there's also a romantic restaurant, which you walk through part of the kitchen to get to. Well kept Brakspears PA, SB and Old Ale on handpump; dominoes, cribbage, backgammon. The big garden has lots of tables under cocktail parasols among flower beds and a view down the Hambleden valley; beyond this, quiet pastures slope up to beech woods. Over the road is a unique Norman twin-roofed church tower – probably the nave of the original church. *(Recommended by Leigh and Gillian Mellor, Susan and Alan Dominey, S Fazackerly, C Rowan, Jack and Philip Paxton, Nigel Norman, A Hill, Philip Brindle, Roger and Valerie Hill, Simon Collett-Jones, LM, John Waller, Andy Thwaites)*

Brakspears ~ Tenant Bryan Heasman ~ Real ale ~ Meals and snacks (till 10pm; not Sun evening) ~ Restaurant ~ (01491) 638335 ~ Children in eating area of bar and in restaurant ~ Open 11-3, 6-11; winter evening opening 7

FORD SP7709 Map 4

Dinton Hermit

Village signposted between A418 and B4009, SW of Aylesbury

Warmly welcoming and cosy, this tucked away country cottage has an attractively traditional partly tiled public bar on the left with scrubbed tables, a woodburning stove in its huge inglenook, and prints of a lady out hunting. The lounge on the right, with a log fire, has red plush banquettes along the cream walls and red leatherette chairs around polished tables, and red leatherette seats built into the stripped stone walls of a small room leading off. Mrs Tompkins cooks the good bar food, and at lunchtime (when they don't take reservations) this might include sandwiches (from £1.40), soup (£2), ploughman's (from £3), saucy mushrooms (£3.25), smoked haddock in mushroom and cheese sauce (£4.75), a vegetarian hotpot or kidneys in cognac sauce (£4.95), pancake with stilton and asparagus or curries (£5.75), and puddings such as home-made fruit pie or bread pudding (£2.50); in the evening (when you must book), dishes are slightly more expensive and include more grills and fish. Well kept ABC Best, Tetleys and Wadworths 6X on handpump. The sheltered and well planted garden opposite (they don't serve food out there in the evenings) has swings, a slide and a seesaw. ***(Recommended by Gordon, Karen and Graham Oddey, John Fahy, Michael Sargent)***

Free house ~ Licensees John and Jane Tompkins ~ Real ale ~ Meals and snacks (not Sun or Mon; not 2 wks in summer) ~ (01296) 748379 ~ Well behaved children welcome ~ Open 11-2.30, 6-11; closed Mon

FORTY GREEN SU9292 Map 4

Royal Standard of England

3½ miles from M40 junction 2, via A40 to Beaconsfield, then follow sign to Forty Green, off B474 ¾ mile N of New Beaconsfield

Full of history and interest, the rambling rooms in this ancient pub have huge black ship's timbers, finely carved old oak panelling, a massive settle apparently built to fit the curved transom of an Elizabethan ship, and roaring open fires and handsomely decorated iron firebacks; also, rifles, powder-flasks and bugles, lots of brass and copper, needlework samplers, ancient pewter and pottery tankards, and stained glass. Good bar food includes home-made soups (£2.70), sausages (£4.10), home-made pies such as chicken and mushroom, beef and oyster or venison in red wine (from £5.75), and good summer salads such as crab, salmon, prawn and cold pies (£6.75). Well kept Marstons Pedigree and Owd Rodger (the beer was originally brewed here, until the pub passed the recipe on to Marstons), Morlands Old Speckled Hen, and regular local guests on handpump; quite a few malt whiskies, several Irish ones, and fruit wines; friendly service. There are seats outside in a neatly hedged front rose garden, or in the shade of a tree. Perhaps at its best in winter when the summer crowds have gone. ***(Recommended by Heather Couper, A W Dickinson, Nigel Norman, Jack and Philip Paxton, Steve Goodchild, Mayur Shah, Chris Warne, W L G Watkins)***

Free house ~ Licensee Philip Eldridge ~ Real ale ~ Meals and snacks (till 10pm) ~ (01494) 673382 ~ Children in eating area of bar ~ Open 11-3, 5.30-11

FRIETH SU7990 Map 2

Prince Albert

Village signposted off B482 in Lane End; turn right towards Fingest just before village

A relaxing buzz of conversation fills this pretty little tiled cottage, standing alone in peaceful wooded countryside. On the left there are hop bines on the mantlebeam, and on the low black beams and joists, a leaded-light built-in wall cabinet of miniature bottles, brocaded cushions on high-backed settles (one with its back panelled in neat squares), and a big black stove in the brick inglenook with a bison's head looking out beside it, copper pots on top, and earthenware flagons in front. The slightly larger area on the right has more of a medley of chairs and a big log fire. Well kept Brakspears Bitter, Special, Mild, Old and OBJ on handpump; Georges Duboeuf house wines, decent whiskies on optic include Smiths Glenlivet and Jamesons, and elderflower pressé. There's an excellent assortment of generous fillings for hot granary bread rolls with salad (around £3.10), such as cheese and onion, giant sausage, black pudding and bacon or pastrami and cucumber, with a handful of robust hot dishes from ham and eggs to fried Japanese prawns. No music, but cribbage, dominoes and shove-ha'penny. The lovely dog is called Leo. A nicely planted informal side garden has views of woods and fields, and there are plenty of nearby walks. Please note, children are not allowed inside. *(Recommended by Jenny Sapp, Peter Hudson, Jack and Philip Paxton, Nigel Norman, Pete Baker, Andy Thwaites, Helen Hazzard, TBB, Pete Baker, Gordon)*

Brakspears ~ Licensee Frank Reynolds ~ Real ale ~ Meals and snacks (lunchtime only; not Sun) ~ (01494) 881683 ~ Open 11-3, 5.30-11

GREAT HAMPDEN SP8401 Map 4

Hampden Arms

Village signposted off A4010 S of Princes Risborough; OS Sheet 165 map reference 845015

The simple-looking exterior leaves you unprepared for this civilised and relaxed dining pub, with serious cooking, lots of fresh fish, and specials running to wild boar pie (£8.95), whole avocado filled with crab and baked with a Mornay sauce (£9.95), devilled diced supreme of chicken (£11.50), baked bass with prawns and almonds (£12.95) and even lobster and sirloin steak in a brandy and shallot sauce (£19.95): home-made soup (£2.75), croque monsieur (£3.75), home-made chicken and brandy pâté (£4.95), vegetable curry (£6.75), steak and mushroom pie (£7.25), home-cooked ham (£7.95), salmon and prawn crumble (£9.95), steaks (from £16.95), and puddings like treacle pudding (£2.95). A small corner bar has well kept Eldridge Pope Hardy Country, Greene King Abbot, Morlands Old Speckled Hen and Tetleys on handpump, Addlestones cider, and decent wines; service is quietly obliging. The cream-walled front room has broad dark tables, with a few aeroplane pictures and country prints; the back room has a slightly more rustic feel, with its pink-cushioned wall benches and big woodburning stove. There are tables out in the tree-sheltered garden; on the edge of Hampden Common, this has good walks nearby. *(Recommended by BKA, R A Buckler, Francis and Deirdre Gevers)*

Free house ~ Licensees Terry and Barbara Matthews ~ Real ale ~ Meals and snacks ~ (01494) 488255 ~ Children welcome ~ Open 12-2.30(3 Sat), 6-11

GREAT KINGSHILL SU8798 Map 4

Red Lion

A4128 N of High Wycombe

Another of those Chilterns specialities: a pub which seems at first sight like an unassuming local, but which turns out to concentrate on remarkably good cooking – in this case, to such an extent that it should almost be considered as a restaurant. Inside, the little brick and flint cottage certainly has the shiny brass wall lamps, decorative plates and simple furnishings of an unpretentious village pub, but the cooking is of an altogether higher order, and all the tables are set for dining, with proper tablecloths. The friendly Spanish landlord is the chef, and his speciality is fish and shellfish – a tremendous choice all fresh from Billingsgate, and very sensibly priced. Favourite examples include oysters (60p each), fresh calamares (£3.50), plaice (£5.50), fresh sardines (£6.50), skate (£7), sea bass (£9.50), and lobster thermidor (£12); the chips are freshly cut and good, and there's a bargain Sunday lunch. Ansells and Tetleys on handpump, good house wines, freshly squeezed orange juice. *(Recommended by Joseph Williams, Peter Saville, Cyril Brown)*

Benskins (Carlsberg Tetleys) ~ Tenant Pepe Cabrera ~ Real ale ~ Meals and snacks ~ Restaurant ~ (01494) 711262 ~ Open 12-3, 6-11; closed Sun evening, Mon

If you enjoy your visit to a pub, please tell the publican. They work extraordinarily long hours, and when people show their appreciation it makes it all seem worth while.

GREAT MISSENDEN SP8900 Map 4

Cross Keys

High St

Atmospheric and friendly, this old-fashioned little town pub is divided inside by wooden standing timbers. One half of the bar has old sewing machines on the window sill, collectors' postcards, bar and small brewery mirrors on the walls, horse bits and spigots and pewter mugs on the beams by the bar, and high wooden bar stools and an aged leather chair on the quarry tiles. The other has a bay window with a built-in seat overlooking the street, a couple of housekeepers' chairs in front of the big open fire, and a high-backed settle. Well kept Fullers Chiswick, London Pride, ESB on handpump and very cheap for the area. The large waitress-served eating room is attractively furnished with captain's chairs and iron tractor seats, traps and boxing gloves on some beams, and an old kitchen range in the brick fireplace. Bar food (with prices unchanged since last year) includes home-made soup (£2.25), 3-egg omelettes (£4.25), seafood pasta (£4.50), salad niçoise (£4.95), puddings like chocolate mousse or treacle tart (from £2.95), and specials such as smoked haddock in cheese sauce or or kidneys in madeira (from £5); good value set 3-course meals in the bistro (dinner £14.95). Cribbage, dominoes, shove-ha'penny, fruit machine, and piped music. The terrace at the back of the building has picnic tables with umbrellas – and you can eat out here, too. *(Recommended by Owen and Rosemary Warnock, Gordon, Wayne Brindle, George Atkinson, Martin Kay, Andrea Fowler; more reports please)*

Fullers ~ Tenants Martin and Freddie Ridler ~ Real ale ~ Lunchtime meals and snacks ~ Evening restaurant (not Sun evening but they do Sun lunch) ~ Well behaved children in restaurant ~ (01494) 865373 ~ Open 11-3, 5.30-11; closed 25 Dec

George

94 High St

The cosy two-roomed bar in this 15th-c inn has attractively moulded heavy beams, timbered walls decorated with prints, little alcoves (including one with an attractively carved box settle – just room for two – under a fine carved early 17th-c oak panel), and Staffordshire and other figurines over the big log fire. A snug inner room has a sofa, little settles and a smaller coal fire; shove-ha'penny. Bar food includes sandwiches (from £1.35), home-made soup (£2.25), filled baked potatoes (from £2.50), deep-fried crêpes (£3.50), ham and eggs (£4.25), and fresh pasta (vegetarian and meat, £4.95); huge Sunday roast (£6.25), and if you are staying, breakfasts are served until 11am. The restaurant is no smoking. Well kept Adnams, Wadworths 6X and two guests on handpump kept under light blanket pressure, sangria in summer, and mulled wine in winter; prompt and cheerful service. The garden area has tables and seats on the pea shingle at the back of the pub (in winter this area is used for extra parking). *(Recommended by Wayne Brindle, Peter Watkins, Pam Stanley, Graham and Karen Oddey, Dr D C Deeing, R J Saunders, Mark J Hydes, Nigel Norman)*

Greenalls ~ Tenants Guy and Sally Smith ~ Real ale ~ Snacks (served all day) and meals; not evenings 25 and 26 Dec ~ Restaurant ~ (01494) 862084 ~ Children in eating area of bar and in restaurant ~ Open 11-11; closed evenings 25 and 26 Dec ~ Bedrooms: /£60.95B

HAMBLEDEN SU7886 Map 2

Stag & Huntsman

Turn off A4155 (Henley—Marlow Rd) at Mill End, signposted to Hambleden; in a mile turn right into village centre

A new licensee has taken over this peaceful brick and flint house, and happily, things don't seem to have changed much. There's a bustling atmosphere in the compact L-shaped, half-panelled lounge bar with its low ceilings, large fireplace, and upholstered seating and wooden chairs on the carpet. The attractively simple public bar has darts, shove-ha'penny, dominoes, cribbage and a fruit machine, and there's a cosy snug at the front, too; piped music. A wide variety of good home-made bar food includes soup (£2.45), pâté (£3.25), ploughman's (from £3.30), creamy cauliflower and leek macaroni (£4.25), spinach enchilada or sausage and mash (£4.50), fresh salmon fishcakes (£5.45), steak, mushroom and ale pie (£5.50), marinated char-grilled chicken (£5.95), Scottish sirloin steak (£10.50), and puddings like bakewell tart, baked lemon cheesecake or chocolate mousse. Well kept Brakspears PA and SPA, Luxters Barn Ale, and Wadworths 6X on handpump, and good wines. The pub is set opposite the church in a particularly pretty Chilterns village and there's a spacious and neatly kept country garden. *(Recommended by TBB, Gwen and Peter Andrews, Francis and Deirdre Gevers, Frank Cummins, Barbara Houghton, Simon Collett-Jones)*

Free house ~ Licensees Hon Harry Smith and Andrew Fry ~ Real ale ~ Meals and snacks (not Sun evening) ~ Restaurant (not Sun evening) ~ (01491) 571227 ~ Children in eating area of bar and in restaurant ~ Open 11-2.30(3 in winter), 6-11; all day summer Sats; closed 25 Dec ~ Bedrooms: £38.50S/£48.50S

LACEY GREEN SP8201 Map 4

Pink & Lily

Parslow's Hillock; from A4010 High Wycombe—Princes Risborough follow Loosley signpost, and in that village follow Great Hampden, Great Missenden signpost; OS Sheet 165 map reference 826019

One reader, last here many years ago, was relieved to find the little taproom had been preserved very much as it used to be, with built in wall benches on the red flooring tiles, an old wooden ham-rack hanging from the ceiling and a broad inglenook with a low mantlepiece. Much of the building has been modernised and extended but has kept its warmly welcoming atmosphere and appeals to quite a cross-section of our readers – and Rupert Brooke liked it so much that he wrote about it at the start of one of his poems; the result is framed on the wall (and there's a room dedicated to him). The airy main bar has low pink plush seats, with more intimate side areas and an open fire, and there's a spanish-style extension with big arches and white garden furniture. Two open fires in winter. Very good home-made food includes sandwiches, filled baked potatoes (from £3), vegetarian curry (£3.75), chicken, bacon and stuffing or steak and kidney pies (£3.95), a roast of the day (£4.95), nice plaice fillet (£5.95), enjoyable pork chop in white wine, 8oz Scottish sirloin steak (£7.95), good home-made puddings like bakewell tart, sponges and tarts (£2.25), and daily specials; vegetables are fresh. The good range of well kept real ales on handpump includes Boddingtons, Brakspears PA, Chiltern Beechwood, Courage Directors, Flowers Original, Glenny Hobgoblin, Hook Norton, and Morlands Old Speckled Hen; six decent wines by the glass. Dominoes, cribbage and piped music. The big garden has lots of rustic tables and seats. *(Recommended by Dave Carter, Gordon, A W Dickinson, Alistair Ferguson, M E Wellington, Jack and Philip Paxton, Heather Couper, George Atkinson, Nigel Norman, N and J Strathdee, Simon Collett-Jones, Peter Watkins, Pam Stanley)*

Free house ~ Licensees Clive and Marion Mason ~ Real ale ~ Meals and snacks (not Sun evenings) ~ (01494) 488308 ~ Children over 5 if eating, in bottom bar only ~ Open 11.45(11 Sat)-3, 6-11

LEY HILL SP9802 Map 4

Swan

Village signposted from A416 in Chesham

The main bar in this cosy, old-fashioned pub has snugs and alcoves with cushioned window and wall seats, one of which is only just big enough for one person, low heavy black beams, black oak props, an old kitchen range, and collections of tobacco pipes and cricket bats. Popular bar food at lunchtime includes soup (£1.70), sandwiches (from £1.95; open sandwiches such as brie with apricot preserve £4.50), ploughman's (£3.50), filled baked potatoes (from £3.50), good vegetable chilli, fine steak and kidney or chicken, ham and mushroom pies (£4.75), and tortelloni ricotta or lamb and mango curry (£4.95), with evening dishes like plaice grilled with oranges and lemons (£6.95) and steaks with a choice of sauces (from £8.50); puddings like super chocolate mousse (from £2.50) and a thoughtful children's menu (from 55p for soup). The restaurant is no smoking. Well kept Benskins Best, Ind Coope Burton and Tetleys, and three weekly guest beers on handpump; cribbage, dominoes, trivia and piped music. On the front and back terraces and side lawn are picnic tables, as well as pretty hanging baskets, tubs of flowers and a climbing frame and adventure bridge, and opposite the pub are a cricket field and a common. *(Recommended by David Shillitoe, BKA, Dr Jim Craig-Gray, Roger and Valerie Hill, Wyn Churchill, J Slaughter, Helen Hazzard, Brian and Anna Marsden, Andrew Scarr)*

Benskins (Allied) ~ Managers Matthew and Theresa Lock ~ Real ale ~ Lunchtime bar meals and snacks ~ Evening restaurant ~ (01494) 783075 ~ Children in eating area of bar and in restaurant ~ Occasional jazz ~ Open 11-11; may close winter afternoons

LITTLE HORWOOD SP7930 Map 4

Shoulder of Mutton

Church St; back road 1 mile S of A421 Buckingham—Bletchley

Next to the quiet churchyard, this half-timbered partly thatched medieval pub is crowned by a striking arched chimney. Inside, the rambling and friendly T-shaped bar has a huge fireplace at one end with a woodburning stove, and is attractively but simply furnished with sturdy seats around chunky rustic tables on the quarry-tiles, and a showcase of china swans; the alsatian is called Benjamin and the black cat, Trouble. Well kept ABC Best and Flowers Original on handpump; shove-ha'penny, cribbage, dominoes, and fruit machine in the games area, piped music. Bar food includes sandwiches (from £1.80), basket meals (from £2.50), home-cooked ham and egg (£3.90), home-made steak and kidney pie (£5.20), curry (£5.90), steaks (from £8.50). French windows look out on the pleasant back garden where there are plenty of tables. From the north, the car park entrance is tricky. *(Recommended by John Hazel, Roger and Valerie Hill, John Honnor, Graham and Karen Oddey, Bob Riley)*

Pubmaster (Allied) ~ Tenant June Fessey ~ Real ale ~ Meals and snacks (not Sun evening, not Mon) ~ Restaurant (not Sun evening) ~ (01296) 712514 ~ Children in restaurant until 9pm ~ Open 11-2.30(3 Sat), 6-11; closed Mon lunchtime

LITTLE MISSENDEN SU9298 Map 4

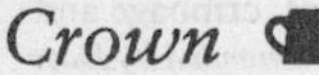

Crown

Crown Lane, SE end of village, which is signposted off A413 W of Amersham

This small brick cottage has been in the same family for 90 years – the present owners are the third generation. They couldn't be more obliging, and keep the place thoroughly traditional and sparkling clean, with its old red flooring tiles on the left, oak parquet on the right, built-in wall seats, studded red leatherette chairs, a few small tables, and a complete absence of music and machines. The atmosphere is very friendly and chatty, and the Bass, Eldridge Pope Hardy Country, Hook Norton Best, Marstons Pedigree and Morrells Varsity on handpump are kept particularly well; they also have farm ciders and decent malt whiskies. Bar food is simple but all home-made, majoring on a wide choice of generous very reasonably priced sandwiches; darts, shove-ha'penny, table skittles, cribbage, dominoes. There are picnic tables and other tables in an attractive sheltered garden behind. The village is pretty, with an interesting church.

(Recommended by DJW, Ron and Val Broom, Simon Collett-Jones, Julian and Sarah Stanton, Frank Daugherty)

Free house ~ Licensees Trevor and Carolyn How ~ Real ale ~ Snacks (not Sun) ~ (01494) 862571 ~ Open 11-2.30, 6-11

LITTLEWORTH COMMON SU9487 Map 2

Blackwood Arms

Common Lane; 3 m S of M40 junction 2: from A355 towards Slough, turn right at Littleworth Common sign, then sharp left into Common Lane after Jolly Woodman

During 1994, Mr Titcombe served 901 different real ales here (from independent brewers only) – which is probably a UK record; he is aiming for 1,000 now. On the six handpumps they may have up to 60 different beers a week such as Black Sheep Special, Clarks Festival, Hambleton Goldfields, Hop Back Summer Lightning, Mauldens Black Adder, Orkney Skull Splitter, Timothy Taylors Landlord and Woodfordes Nelson's Revenge; they also serve Belgian draught and bottled beers, a constantly changing farm cider, maybe a perry, and good choice of malt whiskies. Dominoes, cribbage. There's a friendly atmosphere (it does get crowded at weekends) and home-made food such as long rolls (from £1.75), traditional ploughman's or omelettes (£2.95), home-cured ham and egg or home-made steak in ale pie (£3.75), fillet of pork in a wine and apple sauce (£4.95), and steaks (from £6.95); Sunday roast lunch (£4.50); roaring winter log fire. The terrace has been extended and the garden lawn replanted; lots of country walks from here. *(Recommended by Dave Carter, G and M Stewart, TBB, Nick and Alison Dowson, Richard Houghton, Helen Hazzard, Bob and Maggie Atherton, Cindy and Chris Crow)*

Free house ~ Licensee Graham Titcombe ~ Real ale ~ Meals and snacks (12-2, 6-9.30) ~ (01753) 642169 ~ Children in eating area of bar ~ Open 11-2.30, 5.30-11; 11-11 Fri and Sat

MARLOW SU8586 Map 2

Hare & Hounds

Henley Rd (A4155 W)

New licensees have taken over this pretty and neatly kept ivy-clad cottage with its carefully refurbished inter-connecting rooms and cosy corners. There are comfortable armchairs, flowers on the tables, a log fire in the inglenook fireplace as well as two log-effect gas fires, and a big no-smoking area. Popular home-made food includes starters such as soup, duck and cointreau pâté or stilton mushrooms (from £2), and main courses like salmon and chickory, a daily pasta dish, seafood mornay, pork oriental and the house speciality – smoked chicken, bacon and croutons with salad and creamy dressing (from £7); the restaurant is partly no smoking. Well kept Boddingtons, Brakspears and Rebellion IPA (from the Rebellion Beer Company – a micro-brewery in Marlow), and good wines by the glass; piped music. There's a small garden. *(Recommended by T R and B C Jenkins, J S M Sheldon, Susan and John Douglas, Janet Pickles, Simon Collett-Jones, George Jonas, Andy Thwaites; more reports please)*

Whitbreads ~ Manager E M Surgeon ~ Real ale ~ Meals and snacks (till 10pm) ~ Restaurant ~ (01628) 483343 ~ Children welcome ~ Open 11-3, 5.30-11

MARSH GIBBON SP6423 Map 4

Greyhound

Back road about 4 miles E of Bicester; pub SW of village, towards A41 and Blackthorn

It's the good and very popular Thai food that draws readers to this friendly old stone pub. Attractively presented, there might be spring roll, spare ribs in a special sauce or chicken satay (£3.90), hot and sour Thai soup (£3.90 for one person, £7.50 for two), beef in oyster sauce (£6.20), fresh salmon with ginger in a black bean sauce or king prawn green curry (£7.20), and 8oz entrecote teriyaki (£8.50); half price for children. The pleasant bar is full of traditional charm, with stripped beams, comfortable heavy-armed seats, and tables on old Singer sewing machine bases. The walls are stripped back to golden-grey stone, unusual hexagonal floor tiles cover the floor, and there's a finely ornamented iron stove. Well kept Fullers London Pride, Greene King Abbot and IPA, Hook Norton Best, and McEwans 80/- on handpump; dominoes, cribbage, and classical piped music. A small but pretty front garden has picnic tables, and the more spacious one at the back has swings and a climbing frame tucked among the trees. *(Recommended by Karen and Graham Oddey, J McMillan, H O Dickinson, Paul and Maggie Baker, S Demont, T Barrow, N and J Strathdee)*

Free house ~ Licensee Richard Kaim ~ Real ale ~ Meals and snacks (till 10pm) ~ Thai restaurant ~ (01869) 277365 ~ Children over 6 allowed, if well behaved ~ Open 12-3, 6-11

MEDMENHAM SU8084 Map 2

Dog & Badger

A4155 Henley—Marlow

A short stroll from the Thames, this welcoming 14th-c stone and brick timbered pub has its history displayed on the wall. The long, busy low-beamed bar is comfortably modernised and neatly kept, with banquettes and stools around the tables, an open fire (as well as an illuminated oven), brasses, a crossbow on the ceiling, and soft lighting. Attractively presented bar food includes good home-made soup (£3.25), baps filled with chicken tikka, pâté and redcurrant sauce or cottage cheese and pineapple (£3.45), home-made pizza (£5.35), big filled baked potatoes (£5.55), sausage and egg (£5.65), mushroom, lamb or chicken balti (£6.25), Cajun chicken or good steak and kidney pie (£6.65), and puddings (£2.65); Sunday lunch (£9.75). Well kept Brakspears, Flowers Original, Fullers London Pride, and Wadworths 6X on handpump; darts, shove-ha'penny, dominoes, and unobtrusive piped pop music; prompt, pleasant service. A Roundhead cannon ball from the Civil War was found during restoration – it's on a shelf above a table in the restaurant area. *(Recommended by James Macrae, A Hill, Leigh and Gillian Mellor, Roger and Valerie Hill, S Brackenbury, TBB)*

Whitbreads ~ Lease: Bill Farrell ~ Real ale ~ Meals and snacks (till 10pm) ~ Restaurant ~ Henley-on-Thames (01491) 571362 ~ Children in small bar area and in restaurant ~ Open 11-3, 5.30-11

NORTHEND SU7392 Map 4

White Hart

On back road up escarpment from Watlington, past Christmas Common; or valley road off A4155 Henley—Marlow at Mill End, past Hambleden, Skirmett and Turville, then sharp left in Northend itself

In summer, after exploring the surrounding beechwoods, the lovely garden outside this cosy little 16th-c pub is a marvellous place to relax – there's a children's play area, too. Inside, you can expect a warm welcome from the friendly landlord and the quiet bar has good log fires (one in a vast fireplace), some panelling, very low handsomely carved oak beams, and comfortable window seats. Very good bar food – all home-made – includes soup (£2.50), ploughman's with home-made pickles (£3.95), vegetarian pasta (£5.50), stir-fried beef with pepper (£6.95), chicken in brie with a watercress sauce, roast duck with orange and grand marnier, daily specials like calf's liver and bacon and whole Dover sole, and home-made puddings. Well kept Brakspears PA, SB, Old and Mild on handpump, and a fair choice of wines. *(Recommended by Cicely Taylor, Dave Carter, Mr and Mrs A Atkinson, Gordon, Mrs R J Wyse, Dr Gerald W Barnett, Andy Thwaites)*

Brakspears ~ Tenant Andrew Hearn ~ Real ale ~ Meals and snacks (not Sun evening) ~ (01491) 638353 ~ Children in eating area of bar ~ Open 11.30-2.30, 6(6.30 winter)-11; closed 25 and 26 Dec

nr PRINCES RISBOROUGH SP8003 Map 4

Red Lion

Upper Icknield Way, Whiteleaf; village signposted off A4010 towards Aylesbury; OS Sheet 165 map reference 817040

With lovely views of thatched cottages across the quiet lane, this warmly friendly 17th-c pub has a fine local atmosphere in the well kept and pleasantly old-fashioned bar. There's a log fire, an alcove of antique winged settles, lots of sporting, coaching and ballooning prints on the walls, and quite a collection of antiques. Good bar food includes filled french bread (from £1.80), very tasty filled baked potatoes (from £2.60), double egg and chips (£2.75), a traditional ploughman's (from £4.15), home-made lasagne, steak and kidney pie or baltis (£4.95), chicken copycat (chicken topped with crabmeat, prawns and brolli with a hollandaise sauce £7.15), and weekday lunchtime home-made daily specials such as salmon, cod, prawn and mushroom pie (£6.15) or swordfish in Cajun spices (£6.95); popular Sunday lunch. Well kept Brakspears PA, Hook Norton Best, Morlands PA and Wadworths 6X on handpump; dominoes, cribbage and piped music. Outside there are tables in a small front lawn surrounded by colourful window boxes and hanging baskets, with more on a most attractive large back garden; the pub is close to Whiteleaf Fields (National Trust). ***(Recommended by Nigel Norman, Gordon, Marjorie and David Lamb, Owen and Rosemary Warnock, Steve Webb, Marianne Lantree, Bill Capper, Tom and Rosemary Hall, D Carter)***

Free house ~ Licensee Richard Howard ~ Real ale ~ Meals and snacks ~ Resaurant ~ (01844) 344476 ~ Children in restaurant ~ Open 11.30-3, 5.30 (6 Sat)-11 ~ Bedrooms: £29.50B/£39.50B

SKIRMETT SU7790 Map 2

Old Crown

High St; from A4155 NE of Henley take Hambleden turn and keep on; or from B482 Stokenchurch—Marlow take Turville turn and keep on

The emphasis in this early 18th-c village pub is almost wholly on the popular food: home-made soup (£3), home-made chicken liver pâté (£4.10), ploughman's (£4.25), filled baked potatoes (from £4.60), fresh seafood salad (starter £5.25, main course £10.50), stuffed aubergine (£7.50), lamb cutlets with rosemary and recurrant jelly (£9.65), fresh scallops in garlic and basil (£12.50), and roast duck in a port and orange sauce (£12.95); no pipes or cigars in the dining room. Well kept Brakspears PA and SB are tapped from casks in a still room, and served through a hatch. Of the three rooms, the small central room and larger one leading off have windsor chairs and tankards hanging from the beams, and the little no-smoking white-painted tap room has trestle tables and an old-fashioned settle; also, three open fires (two inglenooks), lots of beams, and over 700 bric-a-brac items, paintings, antiques, bottles and tools; dominoes, cribbage, and trivia. A sheltered front terrace has flower tubs, and old oak casks as seats; the pretty garden has picnic tables under cocktail parasols, and a fish pond. Note that children under 10 are not allowed and cigarettes and matches are not sold. There are two pub alsatians. ***(Recommended by TBB, Nigel Wilkinson, Wayne Brindle, Andy Thwaites, Susan and Alan Dominey, Roy and Pat Anstiss, Cyril S Brown, Nigel Norman, Mr and Mrs Tidy, A Hill, Jack and Philip Paxton, Karen and Graham Oddey, J R Whetton, Barbara Houghton)***

Brakspears ~ Tenants Peter and Liz Mumby ~ Real ale ~ Meals and snacks (not Mon, except bank hols) ~ Restaurant ~ (01491) 638435 ~ Open 11-2.30, 6-11; closed Mon except bank hols

TURVILLE SU7690 Map 2

Bull & Butcher

Valley road off A4155 Henley—Marlow at Mill End, past Hambleden and Skirmett

As this black-and-white timbered pub is so pretty (as is the village), it does get crowded at weekends and so perhaps might be best visited during the week. It's a fine place to finish a walk, and the attractive garden has tables on the lawn by fruit trees and a neatly umbrella-shaped hawthorn; good summer barbecues. Inside, the comfortable and atmospheric low-ceilinged bar is partly divided into two areas, with beams from ships seized in the Spanish Armada, cushioned wall settles, and an old-fashioned high-backed settle by one log fire. Good bar food includes smoked salmon pâté (£3.50), popular ploughman's, cumberland sausage (£5.25), beef in ale pie (£5.50), a range of balti curries (£6.95), steaks (from £8.50), and home-made puddings (£2.75). Well kept Brakspears PA, SB, Old, Mild and OBJ on handpump, and good house wines; darts, shove-ha'penny, dominoes, cribbage, and piped music. Once a month (Tuesday evenings) the MG car club meet here. *(Recommended by A Hill, Piotr Chodzko-Zajko, Jack and Philip Paxton, David Craine, Ann Reeder, Nigel Norman, Susan and Alan Dominey, Tina and David Woods-Taylor, Karen and Graham Oddey, Ron and Sheila Corbett, T R and B C Jenkins, Dave Carter, Gordon, David Warrellow)*

Brakspears ~ Tenant Nicholas Abbott ~ Real ale ~ Meals and snacks (till 10pm) ~ (01491) 638283 ~ Children in eating area of bar ~ Open 11-3, 6-11

WADDESDON SP7417 Map 4

Five Arrows

A41 NW of Aylesbury

Once inside this rather grand small hotel, owned by Lord Rothschild, there's a very relaxed and pleasantly informal atmosphere. The neat bar is an open-plan series of light and airy high-ceilinged rooms, most with solid upright pub furnishings on parquet flooring but one with comfortably worn-in armchairs and settees; there are also family portrait engravings, and lots of old estate-worker photographs. The bar counter is a handsome affair, carved with the five arrows of the Rothschild crest which symbolise the dispersal of the five founding sons of the international banking business. The regular bar menu includes staples such as sandwiches (from £2.95), burgers (£3.95) and salads like home-cooked ham or grilled goat's cheese (from £4.75), but the highlights tend to be found among the wide choice of daily-changing specials: carrot, coriander and cider soup (£2.95), brandied chicken liver parfait with an orange confit (£4.50), salad of Mediterranean vegetables (£4.25), Greek char-grilled chicken breast with a yoghurt, cucumber and garlic relish (£6.95), creole spiced lamb (£8.95), and good home-made puddings (£2.95). The formidable wine list naturally runs to Rothschild first-growth clarets as well as less well known Rothschild estate wines such as Los Vascos Chilean cabernet sauvignon. Well kept real ales – Chiltern Beechwood, Fullers London Pride and an unusual guest such as Archers Old Cobleigh on handpump, with Tring Old Icknield in a jacketed keg on the bar counter; other drinks including many malt whiskies are exemplary. Friendly efficient service, unobtrusive piped pop music. The sheltered back garden has attractively grouped wood and metal furnishings, with some weekend and bank holiday barbecues. *(Recommended by John and Christine Lowe, A McEwen, Iain McBride, J McMillan, JM, PM, Jennie Munro, Jim Wingate, Margaret and Ron Erlick, Richard Ames, C Fletcher)*

Free house ~ Licensees Julian Alexander-Worster, Fabia Bromovsky ~ Real ale ~ Meals and snacks ~ Restaurant ~ (01296) 651727 ~ Children welcome ~ Open 11.30-3, 6-11 ~ Bedrooms:£50B/£65B

If you see cars parked in the lane outside a country pub have left their lights on at night, leave yours on too: it's a sign that the police check up there.

WEST WYCOMBE SU8394 Map 4

George & Dragon

High St; A40 W of High Wycombe

This striking 15th-c building was being renovated as we went to press, though there won't be any significant changes – and the bedrooms were being refurbished, too. The comfortable and rambling main bar has a cheerful, bustling atmosphere as well as massive beams, sloping walls, and a big log fire; the magnificent oak staircase is said to be haunted by a wronged girl. The children's area is no smoking. Popular bar food includes home-made soup (£1.75), ploughman's (from £2.95), sandwiches (from £3.25; toasties from £1.50), herby mushrooms (£3.25), macaroni and broccoli cheese (£3.65), very good home-made pies like sole and grape, chicken and asparagus or duck, pigeon and orange pies (from £5.25), venison pasty with redcurrant sauce (£5.45), chicken masala (£5.75), 12oz sirloin steak (£9.95), and home-made puddings such as fresh fruit crumble or maple syrup and walnut tart (from £1.95). Courage Best and Directors and guests like Courage 1945 or Wadworths 6X on handpump, and quite a few malt whiskies. The arched and cobbled coach entry leads to a spacious, peaceful garden with picnic tables, a climbing frame and slides. It gets crowded at weekends – so it's best to get there early for a seat. Nearby you can visit West Wycombe Park with its fine furnishings and classical landscaped grounds. *(Recommended by James Macrae, TBB, Bob and Maggie Atherton, Tony Dickinson, Sue and Bob Ward, Nigel Norman, Piotr Chodzko-Zajko, Alan Skull, Simon Collett-Jones, Clifford Payton, Barbara Houghton, Dr Andrew Brookes, Barbara Hatfield, George Atkinson, Steve Webb, Marianne Lantree, Chris Warne)*

Courage ~ Lease: Philip Todd ~ Real ale ~ Meals and snacks (12-2, 6-9.30) ~ (01494) 464414 ~ Children in room set aside for them ~ Open 11-2.30, 5.30-11; 11-11 Sat; closed evenings 25 and 26 Dec ~ Bedrooms: £40B/£50B

WORMINGHALL SP6308 Map 4

Clifden Arms

4½ miles from M40 junction 8: B4011 to Oakley off A41 S of Bicester, then minor rd to Worminghall and Wheatley; or from Oxford bypass (A4142) take minor rd to Wheatley and Worminghall

Hanging from the heavy beams in the public bar of this particularly pretty cottage are lots of interesting bottles, brass powder-flasks, milk-yokes, black iron vices and tools; there's also a roaring log fire in the big fireplace, squint-timbered ochre walls, and old-fashioned seats. On the left, the beamed room has a second fire. Bar food includes sandwiches (from £1.65), filled baked potatoes (from £2.75), ploughman's or all day breakfast (£3.50), curries (from £4.50), potato, cheese and leek bake (£4.95), steak and kidney pie (£5.25), steaks (£10.95), and daily specials like liver and bacon (£5.75) or Belgian beef (£6.95). Well kept Adnams Broadside, Fullers ESB, Glenny Hobgoblin, Hook Norton and Morrells Varsity on handpump or tapped from the cask. Darts, shove-ha'penny, cribbage, dominoes and piped music. The lovely flower-filled garden has an ancient pump and a big children's play area with slides, log fort and so forth, and there are picnic tables in the orchard. The picturesque village has almshouses built in 1675, and the Norman church has a 15th-c tower and 14th-c chancel. Nearby Waterperry Gardens are worth a visit. *(Recommended by K H Frostick, Gordon, Wade and Jud Pollard, Michael Sargent, Marjorie and David Lamb, Martin Jones, Simon Collet-Jones)*

Free house ~ Licensee Michael Gilbert ~ Real ale ~ Meals and snacks (not Sun evening) ~ Restaurant ~ (01844) 339273 ~ Children welcome ~ Open 11.30-2.30(3 Sat), 6.30-11; winter evening opening 7

Children – if the details at the end of an entry don't mention them, you should assume that the pub does not allow them inside.

Lucky Dip

Besides the fully inspected pubs, you might like to try these Lucky Dips recommended to us and described by readers (if you do, please send us reports):

☆ **Adstock** [Main St (off A413); SP7330], *Old Thatched Inn*: Stylishly and comfortably done up, keeping beams, flagstones, open fires and cosy corners; sandwiches and ploughman's still, with well kept mainly Courage-related real ales, but some emphasis on more ambitious and expensive food; piped music; seats out in pleasant back arbour, children in restaurant and eating area *(Martin Janson, Cdr P Tailyour, Ian Phillips, Graham and Karen Oddey, John Fahy, Pat and Derek Westcott, Marjorie and David Lamb, Roger and Valerie Hill, LYM; more reports on current regime please)*

Adstock [Winslow Rd (A413)], *Folly*: Handy stop with very big garden and children's play equipment; spacious inside, with friendly chatty landlord, ABC ales, food inc good filled French bread; bedrooms *(George Atkinson)*

☆ *nr* **Adstock** [Verney Junction, Addington – OS Sheet 165 map reference 737274], *Verney Arms*: Good carefully presented bar food inc imaginative continental and spicy dishes in tucked-away country inn with homely collection of settees, motley furniture, pictures, memorabilia, lots of local books, games inc Scrabble; entertaining and welcoming landlord, friendly labrador, real ales such as Hook Norton Old Hookey; bedrooms *(George Atkinson, John Fahy)*

☆ **Akeley** [The Square; just off A413; SP7037], *Bull & Butcher*: Very good value lunchtime buffet (maybe only cold food; not Sun) inc wide range of help-yourself salads, several puddings, also evening steak bar (not Sun or Mon); three good fires in long open-plan beamed bar with red plush banquettes, well kept Fullers London Pride, Marstons Pedigree, Morlands Original and a guest beer, decent house wines, winter spiced wine, traditional games; children allowed in eating area, tables in attractive garden with notable flower beds and hanging baskets, occasional live entertainment; handy for Stowe Gardens *(Janet Pickles, Steve Goodchild, Michael Sargent, LYM)*

☆ **Amersham** [High St, Old Town (A413); SU9597], *Kings Arms*: Picture-postcard timbered building in charming street, lots of heavy beams and snug alcoves, big inglenook, high-backed antique settles and other quaint old furnishings among more standard stuff; low-priced bar food inc vegetarian, restaurant, pleasant service, well kept Tetleys-related and other ales, children in eating area; open all day, rather a young person's pub evening; nice garden *(Ian Phillips, E G Parish, LYM)*

Amersham [White Lion Rd, Amersham Common], *Pineapple*: Attractively refurbished, lots of pictures on pleasantly papered walls, comfortable seats, carpets; usual food done well inc lunchtime sandwiches and baked potatoes, Tetleys-related and changing guest ales, darts, piped music; tables on grass, separate play area *(Bill Capper)*

☆ **Aston Clinton** [SP8712], *Oak*: Attractively refurbished Fullers pub, big helpings of good food, decent wine list, no music or machines, obliging service *(Martin Kay, Andrea Fowler)*

☆ **Astwood** [off A422; SP9547], *Old Swan*: Attractive, clean, airy and spacious, giving invitingly up-to-date feel alongside traditional furnishings; well kept Courage-related and other real ales, wine or port by the jug, good bar food esp pies, warm cosy atmosphere, charming service; maybe home-made jams etc for sale, side garden bar *(Mr and Mrs J Brown, O J W Hunkin, Stephen G Brown, Nigel Norman, Mrs R Horridge, LYM)*

Aylesbury [Kingsbury Sq (A505); SP8213], *Hobgoblin*: Particularly well kept real ales; civilised and reasonably quiet lunchtime, lively evenings *(J Draper)*

☆ *nr* **Aylesbury** [Gibraltar; A418 some miles towards Thame, beyond Stone – OS Sheet 165 map reference 758108; SP7510], *Bottle & Glass*: Low-beamed thatched pub, still comfortably rambling after refurb with flame-effect fires and rustic ornamentation; wide choice of good imaginative food inc vegetarian dishes is the main draw, with warm friendly atmosphere and Tetleys and Wadworths 6X tapped from the cask, neat garden *(Michael Sargent, Gordon, LYM)*

☆ **Beaconsfield** [Windsor End; SU9490], *Greyhound*: Welcoming former licensees of the Old Hare doing very well in pleasant and cosy coaching inn: particularly good food in bar and back bistro-like restaurant, Courage-related and other ales, no piped music, rushed but friendly and attentive staff *(Dr Gerald W Barnett, Sally Barker, Dave Everitt)*

Beaconsfield [Aylesbury End, Old Beaconsfield], *Charles Dickens*: Good food inc good Sun roasts, well kept Marstons, very nice staff *(the Shinkmans)*

☆ **Bellingdon** [about 1½ miles NW of Chesham; SP9405], *Bull*: Concentration on good food – more meals than snacks – in friendly and pleasantly furnished pub with five real ales, decent wines by the glass, keen service; no piped music or machines *(Peter Saville, R C Hopton, Diana Bishop, LYM; more reports on current regime please)*

Bennett End [Radnage; SP7897], *Three Horseshoes*: Old beamed pub in pretty countryside, good traditional English food as well as Chinese and Indian dishes *(Henry*

Oliphant)
Bierton [SP8315], *Bell*: Good wide choice of food, good service; arrive early to get a seat *(J A Gardner)*
Botley [Tylers Hill Rd; narrow lane opp Hen & Chickens; SP9702], *Five Bells*: Friendly, quiet and cosy country local, well off the beaten track, with inglenook fireplaces, good range of well kept real ales, generous heartening home-made food, tables outside; well behaved children welcome *(Jan and Colin Roe, Adrian and Karen Bulley, Helen Hazzard, LYM)*
Bourne End [Hedsor Rd; SU8985], *Masons*: Popular bar lunches and well kept Fullers in friendly and cosy local with pleasantly simple furnishings inc good plain wooden tables; piped music, two pool tables in separate annexe, fruit machines and juke box; must book evening restaurant (not Mon); tables outside, but traffic noise *(Simon Collett-Jones, TBB, Dr Gerald Barnett, LYM)*
Brill [Windmill St; SP6513], *Sun*: Cosy and welcoming village pub, unpretentiously comfortable, with wide range of good food in bar and restaurant (butcher landlord), well kept beers *(N and J Strathdee)*
Bryants Bottom [4 miles N of High Wycombe, via Hughenden Valley off A4128; SU8599], *Gate*: Country pub with beamed and carpeted plush seated lounge spreading back from traditional little tiled front bar, very well prepared inexpensive food, well kept ales such as Bass, Greene King Abbot, Morlands Old Speckled Hen and Wadworths 6X, deep fireplace, no piped music, tables in safely fenced garden with cockatiels and play area; popular with walkers and cyclists *(Helen Hazzard, Nigel Norman, Bill Capper, Ian Phillips, BB)*
Burnham [High St; SU9381], *Garibaldi*: Two small plain bars with separate restaurant, varied and imaginative choice of good food, good friendly service *(G Otter)*
Cadmore End [B482 towards Stokenchurch; SU7892], *Blue Flag*: Wide choice of good interesting generous food at winning prices in old-fashioned beamed pub attached to small modern hotel, lots of proper big dining tables; well kept changing real ales, decent wines, good atmosphere, expert unobtrusive service, fascinating vintage MG pictures in side room; attractive little restaurant; bedrooms *(S J Patrick, DJW, Dr Gerald Barnett, D C Bail, BB)*
Calvert [off A41 Bicester—Aylesbury, towards Preston Bissett; SP6824], *Seven Stars*: Olde-worlde interior, good all-day food inc notable smoked mackerel sandwich, tables out on quiet lawn with flowerbeds; handy for Claydon House *(Mrs J Oakes)*
Chalfont St Giles [London Rd; SU9893], *Ivy House*: Well kept ales such as Brakspears, Fullers Mr Harry and Ushers on handpump, good range of food from soups and ploughman's to full meals, pleasant welcoming bar staff, coal-effect gas fire; piped pop music may obtrude *(P J Keen)*
☆ **Chalfont St Peter** [High St; SU9990], *Greyhound*: Spacious yet sometimes crowded traditional beamed bar with usefully long serving counter, well kept Courage-related and guest ales, good value food inc excellent soups, friendly staff, comfortable separate partly no smoking restaurant; open all day; bedrooms *(Nick and Alison Dowson, Gordon, Dr Andrew Brookes, Peter Watkins, Pam Stanley, Jan and Colin Roe, LYM)*
Chalfont St Peter, *White Hart*: Pleasantly refurbished character old low-ceilinged pub, said to be haunted; well kept Tetleys-related ales inc guest beer *(Nick and Alison Dowson)*
☆ **Chearsley** [SP7110], *Bell*: Thatched Fullers pub with single pleasant bar, very friendly welcome, good local food specials, summer barbecues *(Roger and Penny Gudge, Martin Kay, Andrea Fowler)*
☆ **Cheddington** [Station Rd; by stn, about a mile from village; SP9218], *Rosebery Arms*: Comfortable sofas by roaring log fire, pubbier seats by servery, old photographs on panelled walls, smart restaurant with no smoking area; good food from sandwiches to imaginative and original main courses, Charles Wells and guest ales, friendly service; maybe piped music; well spaced picnic tables on back lawn with play equipment and Wendy house *(Michael Sandy)*
☆ **Chesham** [Church St/Wey Lane; SP9501], *Queens Head*: Super local atmosphere, generous helpings of well cooked simple food and well kept Brakspears PA, SB and Old and Fullers London Pride in small, cosy and friendly pub next to River Chess, with sparkling brass, interesting pictures and paraphernalia, two coal fires, scrubbed tables, pleasant staff; tables in small courtyard *(David Wallington, Helen Hazzard, Jan and Colin Roe)*
☆ *nr* **Chesham** [Chesham Vale – back rd to Hawridge, Berkhamsted and Tring, off A416 as you leave centre], *Black Horse*: Friendly efficient service and big helpings of good value food inc lots of unusual home-made pies and sausages in quietly set and neatly extended country pub with black beams and joists, book-lined converted barn; well kept Tetleys-related and guest ales, lots of well spaced tables out on back grass *(Bill Capper, Helen Hazzard, Paul Coleman, LYM)*
☆ **Chicheley** [A422, quite handy for M1 junction 14; SP9045], *Chester Arms*: Wide choice of generous tasty home-made bar food from sandwiches up inc vegetarian dishes and children's helpings in cosy and pretty two-bar beamed pub with log fire, comfortable settles and chairs, friendly service, Greene King Abbot, darts, fruit machine, quiet piped music; sizeable evening restaurant, picnic tables in garden

(George Atkinson, Paul and Maggie Baker)

☆ **Colnbrook** [1¼ miles from M4 junction 5 via A4/B3378, then 'village only' rd; TQ0277], *Ostrich*: Striking Elizabethan pub, modernised but still giving feel of its long and entertaining history; good open fire, real ale and friendly service, though emphasis primarily on food side *(Dr Andrew Brookes, LYM)*

☆ **Denham** [¾ mile from M40 junction 1; follow Denham Village signs; TQ0486], *Swan*: Pretty pub in lovely village, quiet midweek lunchtime but pleasant busy atmosphere weekends, with helpful staff, real ales, wide choice of decent straightforward bar food inc good value Sun roast, comfortable seats, open fires, evening candlelight; big floodlit garden behind with play house *(Helen Hazzard, Bob and Maggie Atherton, Steve Goodchild)*

Denham, *Falcon*: Open-plan but cosy and traditional with inglenook fireside seats; well kept Marstons Pedigree and Morlands Old Speckled Hen, good lunchtime bar food, friendly welcome *(Mr and Mrs M J Martin, Mr and Mrs N Hazzard)*

☆ **Dorney** [Village Rd; SU9278], *Palmer Arms*: Friendly renovated village pub with wide choice of consistently good food inc fish and skillet dishes, decent wine list, interesting well kept real ales, friendly young staff; plenty of tables in pleasant garden behind *(C J Parsons, Nigel Norman, Simon Collett-Jones)*

Farnham Common [The Broadway; SU9684], *Foresters Arms*: Welcoming landlord and locals in relaxed and civilised dining pub with woodblock floor and panelling – feels like a cross between wine bar and pub; well kept Bass, Fullers and Highgate Mild at a price *(Simon Collett-Jones)*; [The Broadway], *Stag & Hounds*: Smart and comfortable open-plan refurbishment, very friendly service, well kept Greene King and guest beers, darts *(Richard Houghton)*; [Collins Wood Rd], *Yew Tree*: Well kept ales inc Morlands Old Speckled Hen, good choice of whiskies, friendly atmosphere, darts; good food inc stone cooking, separate dining room, reasonable prices *(Dr Jack A Frisch)*

☆ **Flackwell Heath** [3½ miles from M40 junction 4; A404 towards High Wycombe, 1st right to Flackwell Heath, right into Sheepridge Lane; SU8988], *Crooked Billet*: Old-fashioned 16th-c pub in lovely country setting, pleasant garden with quiet views, good value food, real ale *(Helen Hazzard, Colin Dear, BB)*

☆ **Frieth** [signed off B482 in Lane End; SU 7990], *Yew Tree*: This has long been a civilised place with several real ales, decent wines and other drinks, and good service; the Austrian landlord who gave it its special cachet and distinctive food has retired, and we know little yet of the new regime, though the pub now presents itself as more of a restaurant *(LYM; reports please)*

☆ **Gayhurst** [B526; SP8446], *Sir Francis Drake*: Good unusual home-made food in interesting Gothick traceried and pinnacled building, cosy and rather intimate inside; very friendly landlord, helpful staff, well kept real ales, good range of spirits; tables in small sheltered garden *(George Atkinson, LYM)*

Gerrards Cross [A40, E; TQ0087], *Apple Tree*: Pleasant little Beefeater with nice garden, surprisingly cosy atmosphere, Whitbreads-related ales, sensible prices *(Steve Goodchild)*

☆ **Great Brickhill** [Ivy Lane; SP9030], *Old Red Lion*: Back lawn with fabulous view over Buckinghamshire and beyond, pub itself (not that big) given over largely to tables for food (not winter Sun eves) from well filled crusty rolls to steaks and Sun roasts; decent house wines, well kept Whitbreads-related ales, maybe unobtrusive piped music; children in eating area *(Dr Paul Kitchener, Bob and Maggie Atherton, John Hazel, David and Mary Webb, Roger and Valerie Hill, KC, CW, JW, LYM)*

Great Horwood [B4033 N of Winslow; SP7731], *Swan*: Front lounge with inglenook fires and dining area, small back bar with pool, games machines and juke box, well prepared straightforward food using good ingredients, particularly well kept ales such as Bass, Greene King IPA, Jennings and Websters; side garden *(Karen and Graham Oddey)*

☆ **Great Kimble** [Risborough Rd (A4010); SP8206], *Bernard Arms*: Plush and popular upmarket pub with some nice prints, daily papers, wide choice of good imaginative bar food, four changing Tetleys-related and other ales, decent wines, good coffee, games room, well kept gardens, interesting food in restaurant; well equipped bedrooms *(J W Joseph, Mr and Mrs P W Reeve)*

☆ **Great Linford** [4½ miles from M1, junction 14; from Newport Pagnell take Wolverton Rd towards Stony Stratford; SP8542], *Black Horse*: Large rambling pub with good range of good value food inc pastas and help-yourself salads, well kept Tetleys-related and guest beers, friendly staff, good pubby atmosphere, upstairs restaurant; just below Grand Union Canal – drinks can be taken out on the towpath (good walks along here), and sizeable lawn with well spaced picnic tables and biggish play area; children allowed away from bar *(Bob Riley, John Fahy, LYM)*

☆ **Great Missenden** [London Rd; old London rd, E – beyond Abbey; SP8901], *Nags Head*: Wide choice of good quick straightforward food from sandwiches up in cosy creeper-covered small pub with well kept Tetleys-related and guest beers, big log fire, no piped music, picnic tables on back lawn *(John Waller)*

☆ **Haddenham** [Church End; SP7408], *Green Dragon*: Good helpings of home-cooked food and friendly relaxed atmosphere keep the regulars coming to this spacious pleasantly decorated 17th-c pub nr village green and duck pond; well kept real ales, decent house wines, attentive service, log fire, tables in quiet walled garden *(David Pither and others)*

Haversham [High St; SP8343], *Greyhound*: Pleasant 17th-c village pub in attractive countryside, some stripped stone and beams, Greene King IPA and Abbot, good choice of food, very quiet piped music; small garden with picnic tables and swing *(JJW, CMW)*

☆ **Hawridge** [The Vale; signed from A416 N of Chesham – OS Sheet 165 map reference 960050; SP9505], *Rose & Crown*: Newish licensees doing very good value two-course weekday lunches, also other more expensive well cooked food, in spaciously refurbished open-plan beamed bar, big log fire, peaceful country views from restaurant area, broad terrace with lawn dropping down beyond, play area; children allowed *(Peter Saville, Cyril S Brown, LYM)*

☆ **Hawridge Common** [off A416 N of Chesham; then towards Cholesbury; SP9505], *Full Moon*: Welcoming little country local with snugly comfortable low-beamed rambling bar and spacious common-edge lawn, good friendly service by cheerful young staff, good choice of reasonably priced food, wide choice of changing well kept real ales; children and dogs welcome *(Rhoda and Jeff Collins, Mark Belcher, S T Whitaker, LYM)*

☆ **Hedgerley** [SE of M40 junction 2; SU9686], *White Horse*: Welcoming old country local with particularly well kept ales tapped from the cask, Greene King IPA, Charles Wells Eagle and six others changing, relaxed atmosphere and very friendly service in charming small public bar; larger lounge rather dominated by bright food display unit (usual decent food inc good lunchtime sandwiches), occasional barbecues in pleasant and spacious back garden, lovely window boxes, occasional beer festivals; no children, can be very busy; quiet, pretty and immaculate village, good walks nearby *(Peter Whitehead, Richard Houghton, Nick and Alison Dowson, Helen Hazzard, Andrew Stephenson, D Irving, E McCall, R Huggins, T McLean)*

☆ **Hedgerley** [One Pin Lane, towards Gerrards X; OS Sheet 175 map reference 968863], *One Pin*: Unchanging family-run pub with friendly local atmosphere, Courage-related ales, log fires, decent food and well kept garden *(Nick and Alison Dowson, Jill Bickerton, Andy and Chris Crow)*

High Wycombe [Amersham Rd, Terriers; SU8792], *Beech Tree*: Well kept Courage Best and Directors and Wadworths 6X, cheerful staff even when busy; well equipped children's play area *(Tony Dickinson)*; [Frogmore (A4128)], *Bell*: Oak-beamed town-centre Fullers pub with good home-cooked food inc good value french bread with hot meat from roast of the day, well kept ale, friendly service; piped music *(Tony Dickinson, Martin Kay, Andrea Fowler)*

Hyde Heath [Hyde Heath Rd; village signposted off B485 Great Missenden—Chesham; SU9399], *Plough*: Prettily placed little pub with nicely presented reasonably priced food (not Sun evening or Mon), well kept Tetleys-related ales, open fires *(Jan and Colin Roe, LYM)*

☆ **Ibstone** [follow signs for Ibstone from M40; SU7593], *Fox*: Relaxed refuge from M40, generous helpings of decent bar food inc good sandwiches, children's dishes and home-made puddings, good value Sun lunches, well kept real ales such as Brakspears, Luxters Old Barn and Marlow Rebellion, good range of wines, nice decor, polite service, restaurant, pleasant garden, attractive countryside; can be busy on sunny days; comfortable bedrooms *(Derek and Sylvia Stephenson, LM, A W Dickinson, Sharon Hancock, Nigel Norman, David Wright, Wayne Brindle, John Watson, Mr and Mrs J W Allan, Mark Whitmore, Peter Watkins, Pam Stanley, Duncan Redpath, Marjorie and David Lamb, LYM)*

☆ **Ickford** [E of Thame; SP6407], *Rising Sun*: Pleasant and cosy low-beamed bar in pretty thatched local, reasonably priced hot and cold buffet, OAP discount, admirable starters, separate dining room; well kept ales maybe including Hancocks HB, decent wine *(A Y Drummond, Gordon)*

☆ **Iver** [TQ0381], *Gurkha*: Gurkha paintings and trophies in pleasant bar, spacious yet cosy and individual; consistently good generous home-cooked food, wide choice in big restaurant, over-60s club, friendly staff and locals *(N S Homes)*

Iver [Thorney Lane N], *Fox & Pheasant*: Lively local with pool, pinball, good karaoke Weds/Sun, lots of other activities, decent food, maybe free buffet late Sun; garden with good play area inc climbing frames, slides, maybe bouncy castle *(Phil Bicknell)*; [High St], *Swan*: Friendly cottagey local under new management, wide choice of food; piped music *(Helen Hazzard)*

☆ **Kingswood** [A41; SP6919], *Crooked Billet*: Welcoming and lively rambling pub with wide choice of decent food in bar and restaurant, Tetleys-related and other ales such as Hook Norton Best, Morlands Old Speckled Hen, Wadworths 6X, good service; can be busy; occasional special evenings eg medieval banquet *(Marjorie and David Lamb)*

Lavendon [High St (A428 Bedford—Northampton); SP9153], *Green Man*: Good food inc huge gorgeous puddings, not too expensive; lovely flower-filled terrace sheltered by pub's stone walls *(Meg and Colin Hamilton)*; [High St], *Horseshoe*: Comfortable village pub bright with hanging baskets and flower tubs, good meals, pleasant decor and service, well kept

Badger and Charles Wells Eagle *(Andy and Jill Kassube, Meg and Colin Hamilton)*

☆ **Little Hampden** [off back rd Gt Missenden—Stoke Mandeville, W of A413; SP8503], *Rising Sun*: Very popular dining pub with well kept ales such as Adnams, Brakspears, Hook Norton, Marstons Pedigree, decent house wine, food almost invariably very good, interesting and good value, service generally friendly and efficient; partly no smoking; attractive position in prime walking area – though walkers can feel out of place; children welcome, cl Sun evenings and Mon exc bank hols *(Nigel Norman, B D Jones, T A Bryan, Cyril S Brown, Mr and Mrs T F Marshall, Dave Carter, Susan and Alan Dominey, John Waller, Hazel Waller, Michael Sargent, M A and C R Starling, Piotr Chodzko-Zajko, Karen and Graham Oddey, LYM; more reports please)*

☆ **Little Kingshill** [Hare La; SU8999], *Full Moon*: Picturesque hidden-away pub doing well under friendly current management, huge helpings of reasonably priced food, constantly changing range of real ales, well kept attractive garden *(Dave Carter, J D T Andrews)*

☆ **Little Marlow** [Sheepridge Lane; off A4155 at Well End about two miles E of Marlow; SU8786], *Crooked Billet*: Warmly cosy and comfortable low-beamed pub with lovely little flower-filled front garden, good choice of lunchtime food (not Sun), separate eating area, friendly efficient service, well kept Brakspears and Whitbreads-related ales, pleasant views *(TBB, Richard Houghton)*

Little Marlow [Church Rd], *Kings Head*: Cosy and ancient flower-covered free house with emphasis on good food in lounge bar, separate genuine public bar, polite efficient service, five Whitbreads-related and other ales inc Wadworths *(Comus Elliott, Richard Houghton)*

☆ **Little Tingewick** [Mere Lane – off A421/B4031 SW of Buckingham; SP6432], *Red Lion*: Big divided bar and small dining area, well kept Fullers beers, wide choice of good bar food inc vegetarian, friendly staff, pleasant piped music *(George Atkinson, Martin Kay, Andrea Fowler)*

☆ **Long Crendon** [Bicester Rd (B4011); SP6808], *Angel*: Partly 17th-c, stylishly refurbished more as restaurant than pub, warm and clean, with good fresh well prepared generous food, esp fish; conservatory dining room, friendly young staff, well kept Brakspears and Marstons Pedigree *(Michael Sargent, Andy and Maureen Pickering)*

☆ **Long Crendon** [Bicester Rd (B4011)], *Chandos Arms*: Handsome thatched pub with pleasant low-beamed communicating bars, tasty well presented food, Whitbreads-related and other ales, log fire, lots of brass and copper, friendly efficient service *(Tim and Ann Newell, Andy and Maureen Pickering)*

☆ **Lower Hartwell** [Oxford Rd (A418); SP7913], *Bugle Horn*: Lovely rambling old pub, civilised and comfortable yet unspoilt, with polite friendly service, wide choice of food, big garden *(Gordon)*

☆ **Ludgershall** [off A41 Aylesbury—Bicester; SP6617], *Bull & Butcher*: Quiet little country pub with interesting china jugs hanging from beams, good range of meals in bar or back dining room (where children allowed), efficient friendly service, unobtrusive piped music, front lawn facing green *(N and J Strathdee)*

Maids Moreton [just off A413; SP7035], *Wheatsheaf*: Fairly recently pleasantly refurbished and rethatched free house, woodburner in new conservatory, cosy beamed original part, interesting choice of food, Whitbreads-related and other ales, friendly service, small enclosed garden; piped music, opens noon *(George Atkinson)*

☆ **Marlow** [St Peter St; first right off Station Rd from double roundabout; SU8586], *Two Brewers*: Reliably good food served promptly even when very busy in attractive and warmly welcoming low-beamed bar with shiny black woodwork, nautical pictures, gleaming brassware, Whitbreads-related real ales; sheltered back courtyard, glimpse of Thames from front benches; some concentration on restaurant (children allowed here if not too busy), piped music; good-sized car park – a special bonus here *(Mrs S Smith, TBB, MJH, Doug Hitchcock)*

Marlow [High St], *Chequers*: Attractive Brakspears pub with heavily beamed cosy front bars, friendly service, homely tables on pavement; bedrooms *(Gordon)*; [Quoiting Sq, Oxford Rd], *Clayton Arms*: Has been unusually welcoming and unspoilt, with well kept Brakspears, no music, machines or food; reports on new regime please *(Pete Baker)*; [Henley Rd (A4155 W)], *Hand & Flowers*: Olde-worlde pub very popular with its regulars for good well presented food in big sympathetically lit dining area leading off bar, pleasant staff, Morlands real ale *(Mark Hydes and others)*; [West St (A4155)], *Ship*: Fine collection of closely packed warship photographs and nautical equipment in low-beamed town local's small side-by-side bars, straightfoward bar lunches from sandwiches upwards, well kept Whitbreads-related real ales, good friendly service, piped music, tables on pleasant little back terrace, evening restaurant (children allowed here) *(John and Karen Day, TBB)*

Marlow Bottom [signed from Handy Cross roundabout off M40 junction 4; SU8486], *Three Horseshoes*: Family dining pub with welcoming landlord, pleasant fairly traditional interior, well kept Brakspears; maybe bouncy castle in garden *(Simon Collett-Jones)*

☆ **Marsworth** [Vicarage Rd; village signed off B489 Dunstable—Aylesbury; SP9214], *Red Lion*: Low-beamed partly thatched old pub with well kept real ales such as Bass, Hook

Norton Best and Wadworths 6X, decent wines, interesting good value food inc good vegetarian dishes, tiled-floor main bar with good atmosphere and simple unfussy traditional furnishings, two open fires and lively games area, steps up to cosy parlour; friendly service; tables in front, and in small sheltered back garden; provision for children; not far from impressive flight of canal locks *(Russell and Margaret Bathie, LYM)*

Mentmore [SP9119], *Stag*: Small civilised lounge bar with low oak tables, attractive fresh flower arrangements, open fire; restaurant and public bar leading off; good value well presented bar food from sandwiches to main dishes, with wider evening choice; well kept Charles Wells Eagle, polite well dressed staff, charming sloping garden *(Maysie Thompson, BB)*

Milton Keynes [Broughton Rd, Old Village; SP8938], *Swan*: Handsome and spacious dark-beamed thatched pub with pleasant dining area, inglenook fireplace, no smoking area; Boddingtons, Courage Best and Marstons Pedigree, vast choice of good generous if not cheap food inc vegetarian, attractive furnishings, friendly attentive service, maybe piped pop music; popular with businesspeople lunchtime, very busy Sun; picnic tables in back garden, footpaths to nearby lakes *(George Atkinson, Mary and David Webb, Prof John and Patricia White, Bob Riley)*

Milton Keynes [Newport Rd, Woolstone – off H6 via Pattison Lane; SP8738], *Barge*: Old beamed pub attractively set in untouched corner of an original village just off central Milton Keynes, with spacious tree-dotted lawns, modern conservatory, well kept Bass, sensibly priced usual food from big baguettes to enormous mixed grills; friendly staff, good food service *(George Atkinson)*; [also Newport Rd, Woolstone], *Cross Keys*: Pleasant old thatched and beamed pub, much extended with lots of rooms around central bar area, with jovial landlord, friendly service, well kept Charles Wells ales and a guest such as Arkells 3B, good range of food inc good home-made bread, pâté and sandwiches *(George Atkinson, John C Baker)*; [off Avebury Boulevard just below the Point, by garden centre], *Old Barn*: Theme pub with real fire and flagstones, usual food, Whitbreads-related ales; children welcome, with creche and toddlers' area; piped music *(George Atkinson)*; [Simpson, signed off H9; SP8836], *Plough*: Handy and friendly canalside pub with Charles Wells ales, food inc sensibly priced sandwiches and baked potatoes, carpeted lounge, dining area, games room, seats out between car park and canal; piped music *(George Atkinson)*

Moulsoe [Cranfield Rd; about a mile N of M1 junction 14; SP9041], *Carrington Arms*: Promising, as recently reopened by licensees who previously did well at the Black Horse, Woburn, Beds; food inc good if not cheap steaks (choose your own, priced by the ounce), veg extra *(V Green)*

Mursley [SP8128], *Green Man*: Very personable landlord, imaginative, varied good value food (not Sun-Weds eves), small pleasant dining room, reasonably priced house wines *(D C N Hudson)*

Naphill [SU8497], *Black Lion*: Good choice of food from sandwiches up in comfortable open-plan bar with aircraft pictures (Strike Command HQ nearby), and conservatory dining extension; Courage-related ales with a guest beer, fruit machine, maybe piped music, picnic tables in garden; has been open all day *(Nigel Norman, LYM)*

Olney [34 High St (A509); SP8851], *Two Brewers*: Very wide choice of popular food from good brie ploughman's to generous mixed grill, also Sun lunches, in big dining area with plenty of different-sized tables, well stocked bar, friendly prompt service; perhaps rather too many smokers on market day *(TGS)*

☆ **Penn Street** [SU9295], *Hit or Miss*: Some emphasis on good food from ploughman's to wide range of seafood inc lobster thermidor in comfortably modernised low-beamed three-room pub with own cricket ground, good cricket and chair-making memorabilia, welcoming landlord, quick pleasant service, well kept ales such as Brakspears, Fullers and Hook Norton, open fire, no piped music or machines, occasional live music; pleasant setting *(D G Clarke, Tony Dickinson, Dave Carter, H Hazzard, LYM)*

☆ **Penn Street**, *Squirrel*: Friendly and pubby, with good choice of home-cooked food at attractive prices, well kept Adnams, Bass and other ales, big garden opp cricket green; handy for lovely walks *(BH, Walter and Margaret Ingram)*

☆ **Preston Bisset** [signed from A421; SP6529], *Old Hat*: Quaint and homely village pub, basic but spotless; quiet and relaxed cottage-parlour atmosphere, with old pew, built-in wall settle, open fire – servery behind hatch-type bar looks more like granny's kitchen; well kept Hook Norton on handpump, no food, well behaved children if early; licensees and their dogs friendly and welcoming *(Pete Baker)*

Preston Bisset [Pound Lane], *White Hart*: Good food inc good fresh fish and some unusual dishes, real ale, good house wine, kind attractive service, good strong Irish coffee *(Martin Janson)*

☆ **Prestwood** [Wycombe Rd (A4128); SP8700], *Polecat*: Very well appointed dining pub with very wide choice of good interesting food, modest prices, very pleasant service, well kept Brakspears and Courage-related real ales, decent house wines; in fine old building with charming antique-style furniture, lots of stuffed animals and birds, soft piped classical music; nice big garden – handy for nice walks *(Dr Gerald W Barnett, Peter Neate, Nigel Norman, Rhoda and Jeff Collins)*

☆ **Skirmett** [SU7790], *Frog*: Country pub in attractive valley, good range of drinks inc local Luxters beer and Chiltern Valley wine, good reasonably priced home-cooked food using fresh ingredients, helpful cheerful service; a pleasant place to stay, with outstanding breakfasts *(Dagmar Junghanns, Colin Keane, Dave Carter)*

☆ **Speen** [Flowers Bottom Lane; road from village towards Lacey Green and Saunderton Stn – OS Sheet 165 map reference 835995; SU8399], *Old Plow*: Now restaurant not pub (they won't serve drinks unless you're eating, the bar's tiny compared with the dining room, and atmosphere's rather formal), but relaxing and charmingly cottagey, with good open fires, well kept Adnams and Brakspears, good food and wines (you can have just one course), fine service, children in eating area, pretty lawns, lovely countryside; closed Sun evening and Mon *(P Saville, Mrs Ailsa Wiggans, Francis and Deirdre Gevers, DJW, Andrew Scarr, LYM)*

☆ **Stewkley** [High St S, junction of Wing and Dunton rds; SP8526], *Carpenters Arms*: Very welcoming indeed, with big helpings of reasonably priced bar food, wide choice from sandwiches up, well kept ales inc Bass and Tetleys, friendly alsatian called Boon; bookcases in extended dining lounge, darts in jolly little public bar, subdued piped music *(Bill Capper, George Atkinson)*

☆ **Stoke Green** [a mile S of Stoke Poges; off B416 signposted Wexham and George Green – OS Sheet 175 map reference 986824; SU9882], *Red Lion*: Rambling layout with small room areas and interesting furnishings and decor giving plenty of atmosphere, usual bar food, well kept Bass and two guests such as Fullers or Wadworths, no-smoking room, tables outside, children welcome; summer barbecues; has been open all day Fri/Sat *(TBB, Dave Braisted, LYM; more reports on current management please)*

Stokenchurch [Oxford Rd; SU7695], *Charlie Bartholomews*: Stylishly modernised, very clean, with good food, well kept beers, family-style welcome *(Julian Bashford)*

☆ **Stony Stratford** [72 High St; SP7840], *Cock*: Quiet and comfortable old-fashioned hotel with handsome old oak settles in unchanging bar, good bar food served piping hot, very friendly service, well kept ales such as Hook Norton Best, Morlands Old Speckled Hen and Theakstons; bedrooms *(John and Joan Nash, LYM)*

Taplow [SU9082], *Feathers*: Modernised Millers Kitchen but still with a cosy welcoming feel; wide range of good individually prepared food, real ales *(Paul and Maggie Baker)*

☆ **The Lee** [Swan Bottom; back rd ¾ mile N of The Lee – OS Sheet 165 map reference 902055; SP8904], *Old Swan*: Four attractively furnished low-beamed interconnecting rooms, cooking-range log fire in inglenook, particularly well kept real ales inc interesting guests, decent wines, spacious and prettily planted back lawns with play area; food esp fish has been good – more reports on this aspect please *(JM, PM, LYM)*

☆ **Thornborough** [just off A421 4 miles E of Buckingham, outside village – pub name on OS165; SP7433], *Lone Tree*: Interesting quickly changing well kept beers such as Black Sheep and Cains Formidable, good choice of wines and good coffee in spotless long bar with old-fashioned tables and chairs, magazines and books in alcove, real fire in inglenook, polite service; wide choice of popular food, quiet piped music; garden with play area *(Tony Gilbert, A Morgan, George Atkinson, E J and M W Corrin, Marjorie and David Lamb, JJW, CMW)*

☆ **Twyford** [Galncott Rd; SP6626], *Seven Stars*: Pleasant and friendly beamed country pub popular for varied imaginative food in lounge bar and separate dining area, welcoming service, four well kept ales with two weekly changing guests, open fires, old farm tools, seats on pleasant lawn with animals for children *(Tim and Ann Newell, J McMillan, Karen and Graham Oddey, Dave Gabol)*

☆ **Wavendon** [not far from M1 junctions 13 and 14; SP9137], *Leathern Bottel*: Good friendly Charles Wells pub now very popular for good choice of decent food; good service, log fire *(K H Frostick, David and Mary Webb)*

☆ **Wendover** [High St; SP8607], *Red Lion*: Wide choice of good food inc Sun lunch in pleasant bustling refurbished oak-beamed bar and adjacent good value restaurant, several real ales such as Brakspears, Courage Directors and Hancocks HB, good wines, cheerful efficient service; walker-friendly – on Ridgeway Long Distance Path; comfortable bedrooms *(Neil and Anita Christopher, JM, PM, Mr and Mrs R Jacques)*

☆ **West Wycombe** [London Rd; SU8394], *Plough*: Welcoming snug beamed downstairs bar with good food, blazing corner log fire, pool table; upstairs lounge, restaurant, pretty little garden up behind *(IP)*

☆ **Weston Turville** [Church Lane; SP8510], *Chequers*: Wide choice of interesting food in flagstoned two-level bar and attractive and characterful beamed restaurant, particularly good range of wines and spirits, well kept Tetleys-related and other ales, open fire, stylish solid wooden furniture; tucked away in attractive part of village, some tables outside *(B D Jones, Michael Sargent)*

☆ **Weston Underwood** [off A509 at Olney; SP8650], *Cowpers Oak*: Charming old creeper-clad beamed pub with good value bar food in back restaurant area, friendly service, Hook Norton Best and Marstons Pedigree, tropical fish tank, games area with skittles and darts, unobtrusive piped music; tables in garden, attractive surroundings *(Maysie Thompson)*

☆ **Wheelerend Common** [just off A40; SU8093], *Brickmakers Arms*: Mellowed nicely to homely feel, with inglenook log fire, some exposed flintwork, panelling, low beams, elderly settees, kitchen and other tables, shelves of china; good changing food, upstairs dining room, decent range of beers and wines, welcoming efficient service; good play area in big garden, common opp for walks *(Gordon, Nigel Law)*

☆ **Whitchurch** [10 High St; A413 Aylesbury—Buckingham; SP 8020], *White Swan*: This friendly two-bar Fullers local has been a starred main entry until now, but the Tuckers who were such splendidly welcoming tenants with their cheerful good value food and well kept ales have now left, and we know nothing yet of the new regime; there's a rambling garden behind *(LYM; news please)*

☆ **Wooburn Common** [Kiln Lane, Widmoor; 2 miles from M40 junction 2 OS Sheet 175 map reference 910870; SU9187], *Chequers*: Authentic traditional feel in low-ceiling partly stripped-brick bar with lived-in sofas, tasteful dining room on left, real ales such as Eldridge Pope and Marlow ESB, open fire, bar food from attractively served choice of ploughman's to more upmarket blackboard dishes, popular restaurant; wrought-iron tables outside, hanging baskets, spacious garden away from road; cosy and attractive bedrooms furnished in stripped pine, good breakfasts *(Susan and John Douglas, Mark Percy, Mrs Lindsay Healey)*

☆ **Wooburn Common** [Wooburn Common Rd, about 3½ miles from M40; SU9387], *Royal Standard*: Busy pub with wide choice of good generous reasonably priced bar food, knowledgeable friendly staff, well kept Whitbreads-related beers, mix of old and brighter new decor with popular restaurant area; wide range of wines, tables outside; boules pitch behind *(Simon Collett-Jones, Andy and Chris Crow, LYM)*

☆ **Wooburn Green** [14 The Green; SU9188], *Red Cow*: Old beamed pub with open fires, snug atmosphere, very friendly staff, good atmosphere, appetising food *(H Kroll, Comus Elliott)*

Woughton on the Green [SP8737], *Olde Swan*: Pleasant old beamed pub in largely unspoilt village, friendly helpful staff, busy with Milton Keynes businessmen weekday lunchtimes *(George Atkinson)*

Bedroom prices normally include full English breakfast, VAT and any inclusive service charge that we know of. Prices before the '/' are for single rooms, after for two people in double or twin (B includes a private bath, S a private shower). If there is no '/', the prices are only for twin or double rooms (as far as we know there are no singles). If there is no B or S, as far as we know no rooms have private facilities.

Cambridgeshire and Bedfordshire

The cosy and individual Anchor at Sutton Gault shines out of readers' reports as currently the area's most rewarding pub: this year we award it a star, and choose it as Cambridgeshire Dining Pub of the Year. Bedfordshire's Dining Pub of the Year is the Knife & Cleaver at Houghton Conquest. Other pubs currently doing particularly well here include the nice old Eagle in Cambridge and the friendly no-smoking Free Press there, the Three Tuns at Fen Drayton (a fine all-rounder), the cheery Woodmans Cottage at Gorefield (amazing puddings), the charmingly set Old Ferry Boat near Holywell, the Three Horseshoes at Madingley (excellent food and wines) and the handsomely restored Bell at Stilton. This year we welcome to the main entries the happily pubby Black Bull at Godmanchester and (after a break) the Kings Head at Dullingham – a cosy dining pub with lots of vegetarian dishes. The Black Bull stands out for much lower drinks prices than usual in this area. Drinks prices here are otherwise rather higher than the national average, especially in the area's free houses. Pubs tied to Greene King, the regional brewer, have tended to hold their prices steadier than most this last year, and people have been enjoying the new seasonal beers introduced by Greene King. In the Lucky Dip section at the end of the chapter, pubs to note particularly include the Royal Oak at Barrington, Duke of Wellington at Bourn, Cock at Broom, White Swan at Conington, George & Dragon at Elsworth, Oliver Twist at Guyhirn, Pear Tree at Hildersham, Bell at Kennett, Rose & Crown at Ridgmont, White Horse at Swavesey, both Turvey entries and Tickell Arms at Whittlesford; we have inspected all of these except the Oliver Twist, and can firmly vouch for them.

BARNACK (Beds) TF0704 Map 5

Millstone

Millstone Lane; off B1443 SE Stamford; turn off School Lane near the Fox

The strongly traditional bar in this friendly village pub is very popular for good reliable food – so it's worth arriving early, even midweek lunchtime, to avoid waiting for a table. Dishes served by pleasant, attentive staff include lunchtime sandwiches, toasties and soup (from £1.95), prawn cocktail (£4.25), spare ribs (£3.50), lasagne or ocean pie (£5.95), Cajun chicken (£6.25), minted lamb bake (£6.50), stilton chicken (£7.95) and about three vegetarian dishes like vegetable tikka massala (£5.45) or leek and mushroom bake (£5.90); smaller portions for OAPs; usual children's menu; home-made puddings like sticky toffee or bread and butter pudding (from £1.95). All the food is freshly prepared so there might be a short delay at busy times. The excellently kept Adnams, Everards Old Original and Tiger and a good selection of guest beers on handpump draw plenty of praise from readers. There are also Gales Country wines, a good selection of malt whiskies and Scrumpy Jack. The atmospheric and comfortable timbered bar with high beams weighed down with lots of heavy harness is split into intimate areas. A little snug is decorated with the memorabilia of a former regular, including his medals from both World Wars. The snug and dining room are no smoking; piped music. *(Recommended by Stuart Earle, George Atkinson, Edward Storey, Eric Locker, John Baker, F J Robinson, Wayne Brindle, WHBM, John C Baker, Tom Evans, Richard Balls)*

Everards ~ Tenant Aubrey Sinclair-Ball ~ Real ale ~ Meals and snacks (11.30-2, 6.30(6 Fri and Sat)-9, not Sun eve) ~ Restaurant (not Sun eve) ~ (01780) 740296 ~ Well supervised children in eating areas ~ Open 11-2.30, 6(may open 5.30 summer)-11

BIDDENHAM (Beds) TL0249 Map 5

Three Tuns 

57 Main Road; village signposted from A428 just W of Bedford

The lively and bustling lounge of this prettily placed and welcoming thatched local has low beams and country paintings on the walls. The simple public bar has table skittles as well as darts, dominoes, and fruit machine. Good bar food (there may be a short wait on busy summer days) includes sandwiches (from £1.30), home-made soup (£1.40 – you can have it with a choice of any sandwich for £2.20), and pâté (£1.90), good, fresh ploughman's (£2.50), burgers (from £3), salads (£3.50), quiche or home-made chilli con carne (£4.20), seafood platter, home-made steak and kidney pie or chicken casserole (£5), and 8oz sirloin steak (£8); usual children's menu (£1.60). Very well kept Greene King IPA, Abbot and Rayments on handpump; cheerful, prompt service. The particularly attractive big garden is popular with families: it's very sheltered, there's a big terrace with lots of picnic tables, a very good separate children's play area has swings for all ages and a big proper wooden climbing frame, and doves and a dovecote. The village is pretty – especially in spring; piped music. *(Recommended by Michael Marlow, G and M Hollis, Ian Phillips, Piotr Chodzko-Zajko, Russell and Margaret Bathie, Bob and Maggie Atherton, L Walker, Klaus and Elizabeth Leist, Simon Cottrell, Dr and Mrs M Bailey, Wayne Brindle)*

Greene King ~ Tenant Alan Wilkins ~ Real ale ~ Meals and snacks (not Sun or Mon evenings) ~ (01234) 354847 ~ Children in small dining room ~ Open 11.30-2.30, 6-11

BOLNHURST (Beds) TL0859 Map 5

Olde Plough

B660 Bedford—Kimbolton

Under trees in the lovely garden with rustic seats and tables and a long crazy-paved terrace you can still see the remains of the moat that used to surround this pretty 500-year-old cottage. The spacious and comfortable carpeted lounge bar has a friendly relaxed atmosphere with black beams, little armchairs around low tables, a leather sofa and armchair, and a log fire in the big stone fireplace. On the walls are enlarged naughty postcards and watercolours for sale by a local artist. The landlady is a faith healer, holds local yoga lessons, and writes cheerful poems and philosophy which also appear on the pub walls. A dining room has seats around tables ingeniously salvaged from oak barn fittings; its wooden ceiling uses boards from a Bedford church. The public bar has a couple of refectory tables, settles and other seats on the flagstones, and a big woodburning stove; darts, pool, hood skittles, cribbage, dominoes and cards. The upstairs restaurant has old beams and polished tables. The same imaginative weekly changing menu is used in the upstairs restaurant (where there's a minimum charge of £10 per person) and bar; the food, nearly all home-made, is good value. It might include soup (£2.50), smoked fish pâté (£3.25), deep-fried prawns wrapped in filo pastry (£3.95), chicken, walnut and grapefruit salad (£4.25), steak, kidney and Guinness pie (£5.50), vegetarian risotto or smoked haddock and broccoli lasagne (£5.95), seafood pancake or chicken breast in creamy tarragon sauce (£6.95), fresh fillet of salmon with dill sauce (£7.95) and 8oz fillet steak (£11.95). There are also daily blackboard specials like vegetable curry or cottage pie (£3.95); puddings such as brûlée or crumble of the day or treacle tart (£2.95). Well kept Courage Directors, John Smiths Magnet and Ruddles Best on handpump, and summer specials such as kir royale and buck's fizz. The cats are called Blacky and Titch, the doberman Zeus and the other dog Lica – she likes to fall asleep under the tables; other dogs welcome. *(Recommended by Tom Saul, Michael Marlow, Mr and Mrs J Brown, John Fahy, B Eldridge, Stephen Brown, Mrs Cynthia Archer, Prof J V Wood)*

Free house ~ Licensee M J Horridge ~ Real ale ~ Meals and snacks (till 10 if busy) ~ Restaurant (Fri/Sat evenings and Sun lunch) ~ (01234) 376274 ~ Well behaved children welcome till 9pm ~ Open 12-2.30, 7-11; closed 25/26 Dec

BYTHORN (Cambs) TL0575 Map 5

White Hart

Village signposted just off A14 Kettering—Cambridge

The emphasis here is on the imaginative and very popular stylish bar and restaurant food. Starters (you choose them from the restaurant menu) might include home pickled salmon, quail eggs or chilled bouillabaisse salad (£4.50). Bar snacks include ploughman's with three cheeses (£4.95), toasted brie with bacon or angel-hair pasta with mushrooms (£5.95), leg of duck with soy sauce and ginger or game casserole (£6.95), crispy loin of pork or squid ink pasta with seafood (£7.50) and sirloin steak (£10); puddings from the restaurant menu include sticky toffee pudding, lemon tart, snow eggs (poached egg whites with orange flavoured custard) or chocolage orange pot. Behind the simple exterior there's an eclectic homely atmosphere and plenty to look at in the main bar and several linked smallish rooms. There's a big leather chesterfield, lots of silver teapots and so forth on a carved dresser and in a built-in cabinet, wing armchairs, attractive tables and an area with rugs on stripped boards, soft pale leather studded chairs and stools and a cosy log fire in a huge brick fireplace. There are cookery books and plenty of magazines for reading, not just decoration. Well kept Greene King IPA and Abbot on handpump; a good, no nonsense, well chosen wine list including four by the glass, free nuts and spicy sausages; pleasant staff and very hospitable professional licensees; no-smoking restaurant *(Recommended by Michael Sargent, Cdr Patrick Tailyour, Stephen, Julie and Hayley Brown, Rita Horridge, Mrs R Cotgreave)*

Free house ~ Licensees Bill and Pam Bennett ~ Real ale ~ Meals and snacks (till 10; not Sat eve) ~ Restaurant ~ Bythorn (01832) 710226 ~ Children welcome ~ Open 11-3, 6-11; closed Sun evening, all day Mon

CAMBRIDGE TL4658 Map 5

Anchor

Silver St

It's the lively atmosphere, the suntrap terrace marvellously set right by the River Cam (you can hire punts here) and straightforward inexpensive food that are the main draws here. Some readers enjoy the bustle and mix of foreign and local students and visitors, others have found the music and atmosphere too loud at times – it's particularly popular in the evening. The upstairs bar (part of which is no smoking) is pubby, with pews, wooden chairs and good riverside views. Downstairs, the cafe-bar (open all day) has enamel signs on the walls and a mix of interesting tables, settles, farmhouse chairs and hefty stools on the bare boards. Steps take you down to a similar though simpler flagstoned room, and french windows lead out to the terrace with picnic tables and some tubs of flowers. The generous helpings of bar food include sandwiches (from £1.95), ploughman's (from £3.10), salads (from £3.85) and daily specials like lasagne, steak and kidney pie and a vegetarian choice (£3.75), fish and chips (£3.85). Well kept Boddingtons, Flowers Original, Fullers London Pride, Greene King Abbot, Marstons Pedigree, Morlands Old Speckled Hen, Wadworths 6X, Whitbreads Castle Eden, one of Whitbreads' periodic special brews, and three changing guests on handpump; a good range of foreign bottled beers; cheerful young service, various trivia and fruit machines and a juke box. *(Recommended by John Fahy, J Brown, K Kennedy, Anthony Marriott, Wayne Brindle, Tom Smith, Paul Cartledge)*

Whitbreads ~ Manager Alastair Langton ~ Real ale ~ Meals and snacks (12-8, till 5 Fri and Sat, Sun 12-2.30) ~ (01223) 353554 ~ Children in eating area until 7 ~ Open 11-11

Eagle 🍷

Bene't Street

This fascinating and popular old stone-fronted 16th-c building was once Cambridge's most important coaching inn and is the town's most interesting pub. There's plenty of history to the five individually furnished superbly atmospheric rambling bars which still have many original features such as two fireplaces dating back to around 1600, two medieval mullioned windows, much of the original pine panelling, and the remains of two wall paintings, thought to be medieval. The high, dark red ceiling has been left unpainted since the war to preserve the signatures of British and American airmen worked in with with Zippo lighters, candle smoke and lipstick. The furniture is nicely old and creaky. Hidden behind sturdy wooden street gates is an attractive cobbled and galleried courtyard with heavy wooden seats and tables and pretty hanging baskets. The good value interesting bar food is well presented and includes vegetarian burgers (£3.75), hamburgers (£4), ploughman's (£4.25), steak and kidney pie, lasagne or chilli con carne (£4.50), breaded fillet of plaice (£4.95) and the chef's daily special; puddings are Dutch apple flan, toffee, pecan and apple pie and hot chocolate fudge cake (all £2.25). A neat little booklet lists up to 20 wines, sparkling wines and champagne by the glass which are presented from the bottle with a preservation system that ensures each is delivered in good condition, also jugs of Sangria and very well kept Greene King IPA, Abbot and Rayments on handpump. No noisy fruit machines or juke box but the licensee says he has trouble imposing his no smoking rule in one room; friendly service from well dressed staff. *(Recommended by John Wooll, G P Kernan, Anthony Marriott, Stephen and Julie Brown, Julian Holland, Helen McLagan, Tom Smith, Ian Phillips, Barry and Anne, Rita Horridge, Ben Regan)*

Greene King ~ Licensees Peter and Carol Hill ~ Real ale ~ Meals and snacks (12-2.30, 5.30-9; not Fri, Sat, Sun eve) ~ (01223) 301286 ~ Children in eating area of bar only ~ Open 11-11

Free Press

Prospect Row

Tucked away in a narrow street, this individual and unspoilt pub is one of the very few completely no-smoking ones we know about, it's also the only one we know of that's registered as a boat club, so they can display their collection of oars and rowing photographs with more legitimacy than most Cambridge pubs. The civilised traditional rooms are full of character and popular with locals; one room is served from a hatch. Very tasty and wholesome home-made bar food from a sensibly sized menu always includes two soups, one of which is always vegetarian, like carrot and coriander or stilton (£1.95), and hot dishes like chilli, leek crustade – the vegetarian food is delicious – pork and cider casserole, cheesy sausage pie, homity pie and many more (£3.95- £4.25) and a selection of cold dishes like chicken liver pâté and nut roast (£3.95) and game pie, minced lamb and garlic pie and chicken and bacon pie (£4.50); puddings like toffee apple tart or chocolate, cherry and marzipan cake (£1.90); get there early if you want a seat. Well kept Greene King IPA and Abbot on handpump, with a good selection of malt whiskies and freshly squeezed orange juice; iced coffee in hot weather; cards, cribbage and dominoes behind the bar. The long-serving licensees are particularly friendly, and their staff welcoming and efficient. The sheltered back garden is quite a sun trap, and home for some rabbits who have built their own burrows there; two friendly cats. *(Recommended by Helen McLagan,*

Frank Gadbois, Mike Beiley, Anthony Marriott, Amanda Dauncey, J Rudolf, JM, PM, Nigel and Sara Walker, Paul Cartledge, John and Marianne Cooper, Patricia and Tony Carroll)

Greene King ~ Lease Christopher Lloyd ~ Real ale ~ Meals and snacks (12-2, 6-8.30) ~ (01223) 68337 ~ Well behaved children welcome ~ Open 12-2.30, 6-11; closed 25 Dec evening, 26 Dec

Live & Let Live

40 Mawson Road; off Mill Road SE of centre

Well away from the town centre, this straightforward and comfortably busy pub is unpretentious and chatty with no machines or piped music. There's a relaxed atmosphere to the bare board and brickwork rooms with pale wood chairs around sturdy varnished pine tables, heavy timber baulks, coming-events posters at one end and lots of interesting old country bric-a-brac. Basic generous bar food, all home-made (you can see the comings and goings in the kitchen), includes sandwiches (from £1.30), ploughman's (from £3), chicken in wine sauce, chicken curry, chilli, garlic stuffed mushrooms and a few other things with chips, salads and peas (£3.50) and scampi (£3.95); puddings like chocolate fudge cake and apple pie (from £1.25). The eating area is no smoking and the low prices attract many graduate students. Friendly bar service, good table clearance; well kept Adnams, Banks & Taylor Dragonslayer, Everards Tiger, Morlands Old Speckled Hen, Shepherd Neame Bishops Finger and Wadworths Farmers Glory on handpump. ***(Recommended by K Kennedy, Anthony Marriott, Stephen Brown, Paul Cartledge; more reports please)***

Everards ~ Lease: Margaret Rose Holliday ~ Real ale ~ Meals and snacks (12-2, 6.30(7 Sun)-8.30) ~ (01223) 460261 ~ Children in eating area till 8.30 ~ Folk group Sun evening ~ Open 12-2.30, 6-11

Mill

Mill Lane

One of the main attractions here is the expanse of grass that runs down to a bend in the river Cam, and in summer it gets really busy (bar service can get a bit slow) with crowds sitting out in the sun drinking from plastic glasses. Eight handpumps serve a constantly changing range of real ales which might include Adnams, Black Sheep Bitter and Special, Daleside Bitter and Monkey Wrench, Marstons Pedigree or Nethergate Bitter, IPA and Growler. They get beers direct from local microbreweries, and have farm ciders and lots of English country wines. The chatty simple bars with a mixture of business and college customers have kitchen chairs, chunky stools, settles and a mix of wooden tables on bare boards and ancient quarry tiles; there are lots of display cases filled with clay pipes or brewery taps and slings, photographs of college games teams, and oars with names of past Pembroke College rowers; an open brick fireplace, too. Bar food includes sandwiches served in plastic wrappers, filled baked potatoes (£2.75), ploughman's (£3.80), chilli and lasagne (£3.95) and daily specials; fruit machine, piped pop music. The main place for hiring punts is next door. ***(Recommended by Terry Barlow, Anthony Marriott, K Kennedy, Julian Holland, Paul Cartledge, Dr and Mrs M Bailey)***

Pubmaster ~ Manager Peter Snellgrove ~ Real ale ~ Lunchtime meals and snacks (till 3) ~ (01223) 357026 ~ Children welcome in eating area of bar until 7pm if eating ~ Open 11-11

DULLINGHAM (Cambs) TL6357 Map 5

Kings Head

50 Station Road

This cosy dining pub has a peaceful old-fashioned atmosphere. It quickly fills up with people keen to enjoy the big helpings from a popular range of sophisticated freshly prepared bar food. Lots of the dishes are quite restauranty (chicken stilton at

£6.50, say), but there's still home-made soup (£1.95), home-made pâté (£3.25), filled baked potatoes (from £3.95), various omelettes (from £4.25), lasagne (£5.25), daily blackboard specials and a good few vegetarian dishes like mushroom and nut fettucine, three-bean chilli, wheat and walnut casserole and vegetable tikka massala; puddings from (£2.25) and lots of ice cream sundaes (from £2.25); usual children's menu (from £2.75). Very friendly and efficient staff serve well kept Ansells, Flowers IPA and Tetleys on handpump. The two pink-washed connecting carpeted rooms have small buttonback leatherette bucket seats, windsor chairs, some booths around sturdy wooden tables, hunting prints, and a coal fire at each end in winter. The family/function room across the yard is called the Loose Box. Under fairy lights on the grass above the car park there are sheltered seats, with more on a terrace overlooking the big sloping village green; there are also swings and an adventure playground. No dogs; one no-smoking room. *(Recommended by E A George, Stephen and Jean Curtis, Gwen and Peter Andrews, Frank Gadbois, Nigel and Sara Walker, John Fahy; more reports please)*

Pubmaster ~ Tenants Erich Kettenacker and Nigel Sampson ~ Real ale ~ Meals and snacks (till 10pm) ~ Restaurant ~ (01638) 507486 ~ Children in restaurant ~ Open 11-2.30, 6-11; closed 25, 26 Dec

DUXFORD (Cambs) TL4745 Map 5

John Barleycorn

Moorfield Rd; village signposted off A1301; pub at far end of village

The main attraction at this delightfully pretty thatched and shuttered mid-17th-c cottage is the quite restauranty food. The bar snack menu includes ploughman's (from £3.70), unusual open sandwiches such as hot black pudding with gooseberries (from £4.10), grilled sardines (£4.90), salads (from £6.50), Irish stew with parsley dumplings, spiced chilli beef (£6.90), venison, mushroom and vegetable pie (£7.20), smoked haddock with poached eggs (£7.40), chicken in sweet and sour sauce (£7.65), 8oz sirloin steak (£9) and puddings. It's best to book in the evenings. Well kept Greene King IPA under light blanket pressure; decent wines, a range of brandies, and mulled wine in winter. Service is reserved but courteous. The dimly lit relaxed bar is attractively furnished, with high-backed booth-type oak settles, some wheelback chairs and chunky country tables, and autumnal-coloured curtains to match the cushions. A couple of standing timbers and a brick pillar break up the room, and below a shotgun on the wall there's a raised brick fireplace with horsebrasses hung along the mantlebeam, as well as a mix of old prints, decorative plates (including game ones), photographs of the pub, brass lamps, a ship's clock and some scales, and horse bits and reins; dominoes and piped jazz. A small front terrace has delightful hanging baskets below the thatch, tubs and flowerbeds around picnic tables, and there are more tables in the colourful back garden surrounded by roses and flowering shrubs. There's also a converted barn with ancient timbers and some back-to-back seats, and an attractive brick barbecue and mini bar.
(Recommended by J F M West, Gary Roberts, Ann Stubbs, Ian Phillips, David Craine, Ann Reeder, Susan and Nigel Wilson, Martin and Pauline Richardson, RJH, I S Thomsom, Trevor P Scott, Brian and Jill Bond, Patricia and Tony Carroll, Paul Cartledge, Stephen, Julie and Hayley Brown, Gary Roberts, John and Shirley Dyson)

Greene King ~ Tenant Henry Sewell ~ Real ale ~ Meals and snacks (till 10pm) ~ (01223) 832699 ~ Open 12-11; closed 25, 26 Dec, 1 Jan

ELTISLEY (Cambs) TL2659 Map 5

Leeds Arms 🛏

The Green; village signposted off A428

The comfortable beamed bar of this straightforward tall white brick house overlooking the large peaceful village green is made up of two knocked-through rooms. There's a huge winter log fire with brass hunting horns, and decorative plates on the mantlepiece; this year the bar has been refurnished with dining tables and cushioned wheelback chairs. Down some steps a third room is dominated by tables with cushioned wheelback chairs. Nicely presented and sometimes unusual bar food includes home-made soup (£1.75), sandwiches (from £1.75), ploughman's or good spicy mushrooms (£2.75), seafood pancake (£3.50), lasagne (from £4.25), curries and vegetarian dishes (from £4.75), home-made steak and kidney pie (£5.50), steaks (from £9), and puddings such as lemon mousse or treacle tart (£2.20). Well kept Greene King IPA and Hook Norton Best or Charles Wells Bombardier under light blanket pressure; pleasant service; darts, dominoes, cribbage, trivia, a fruit machine sensibly set aside in an alcove, and piped music. The pleasant garden has swings, slides and picnic tables among the silver birches on the lawn. The bedrooms, plainly furnished but comfortable and well equipped, are in a separate block beyond the garden (you can hear road traffic from the ones at the back). *(Recommended by Wayne Brindle, P and D Carpenter, Fred Punter, C Fisher, Gwen and Peter Andrews)*

Free house ~ Licensee George Cottrell ~ Meals and snacks (12-2, 7-9.45) ~ Restaurant ~ (01480) 880283 ~ Children in eating area of bar and in restaurant only ~ Open 11.30-2.30, 6.30-11; closed 25 Dec ~ Bedrooms: £35B/£45B

ETTON (Cambs) TF1406 Map 5

Golden Pheasant

Village just off B1443, just E of Helpston level crossing; and will no doubt be signposted from near N end of new A15 Peterborough bypass

The comfortable homely bar in this tree-surrounded stone house has high-backed button-back maroon plush settles built against the walls and around the corners, an open fire, and prints on the walls; in the airy, glass-walled, no-smoking side room are some Lloyd Loom chairs around glass-topped cane tables. There are always seven very well kept changing real ales on handpump, such as Bass, Batemans XXXB, Boddingtons, Butcombe, Courage Directors, Greene King IPA, Hall & Woodhouse Tanglefoot, Timothy Taylors Landlord or Woodfordes Wherry, also lots of malt whiskies. Tasty bar food might include stilton chicken, minted lamb bake and duck with black cherries (£7.95), also cumberland sausage with Guinness gravy and vegetable-curry-filled yorkshire pudding. The stone-walled garden looks out across flat countryside; this year they've done quite a bit of work on it, including adding an adventure playground. There's an aviary with dozens of birds (golden pheasants, quail, cockatiels, rosella parakeets and budgerigars) and a big paddock. The golden labrador is called Bonnie. Pool, cribbage, dominoes, fruit machine, video game, and piped music. *(Recommended by John Baker, Wayne Brindle, Richard Balls; more reports please)*

Free house ~ Licensees Dennis and Hilary Wilson ~ Real ale ~ Meals and snacks (till 10pm) ~ Restaurant ~ (01733) 252387 ~ Children in eating area of bar, in restaurant and family room ~ Open 11-11

FEN DRAYTON (Cambs) TL3368 Map 5

Three Tuns

High Street; village signposted off A14 NW of Cambridge

There's a healthy mix of people drinking and dining at this pretty thatched village pub. The cosy, welcoming and unpretentious bar has heavy-set moulded Tudor beams and timbers and two inglenook fireplaces (one of which is usually alight). An interesting variety of seats includes cushioned settles, the timbered walls have big portraits, old photographs of local scenes, old local folk song sheets and brass plates, there's old crockery in a corner dresser, and they put out lots of fresh flowers. The popular well prepared bar food is good value – they haven't had a price rise for two years now. It includes sandwiches with a choice of brown, white or french bread (from £1.25), home-made soup (£1.80), home-made chicken liver and bacon pâté or Greek dips (£2.50), chicken satay or ploughman's (£3), salads (from £3.50), lasagne

(£4.25) or chicken curry (£4.50), gammon with pineapple (£5.50), chicken kiev (£6), and 8oz rump steak (£8); daily specials such as macaroni cheese (£3.50), a pie such as rabbit, bacon and apple or pigeon breast, bacon and black cherry or bobotie lamb (£4.75) and breast of chicken in garlic butter (£5); excellent vegetarian options and puddings like home-made apple pie and good treacle tart. Helpful staff serve Greene King IPA and Abbot and Rayments on handpump well kept under light blanket pressure, as well as a range of malt whiskies. Sensibly placed darts, shove-ha'penny, dominoes, cribbage and fruit machine. A well tended lawn at the back has tables under cocktail parasols, apple and flowering cherry trees, and some children's play equipment. The pub can get very crowded, so it's best to arrive early if you want to eat. *(Recommended by Dave Bundock, D Tapper, Maysie Thompson, Julian Holland, Gordon Theaker, Ian Phillips, Prof John and Mrs Patricia White, Wayne Brindle, S Brackenbury, Nigel Foster, Donald and Margaret Wood, Mr and Mrs Powell, Paul Cartledge)*

Greene King ~ Tenants Michael and Eileen Nugent ~ Meals and snacks (not evenings of 24/25 Dec or 1 Jan) ~ (01954) 230242 ~ Children in eating area of bar until 8pm ~ Open 11-2.30, 6.30-11; cl evening 25 Dec

FOWLMERE (Cambs) TL4245 Map 5

Chequers

B1368

This civilised 16th-c inn with a smart yet somehow intimate atmosphere, its emphasis largely on dining, stands out as something a little bit special. Downstairs are two warm and cosy comfortably furnished communicating rooms with an open log fire – look out for the priest's hole above the bar. There are some interesting black and white photographs of Fowlmere airfields in both world wars. Upstairs there are beams, timbering and some interesting moulded plasterwork above the fireplace. Attentive but reserved uniformed waiters serve ambitious changing food which may include stilton and walnut pâté (£2.90), marinated herring fillets with sour cream, apple and onion (£3.90), bacon and prawns (£4.80), green thai-style chicken curry (£5.80), grilled venison steak (£8.90) and chocolate and walnut sponge pudding with coffee sauce (£2.80) or English cheeses with walnut bread (£3); maybe nibbles on the bar. Well kept Tetleys and Tolly Original on handpump, freshly squeezed orange juice, a good choice of vintage and late-bottled ports and brandies by the glass, and an excellent choice of very well priced fine wines by the glass. The pleasant garden is particularly well looked after, with white tables under cocktail parasols among the flowers and shrub roses; a light and airy conservatory/function room overlooks it. The current inn sign honours the RAF's No 19 Squadron on one side and the USAF's 339th Fighter Group on the other, whose pilots used the pub. *(Recommended by Neil and Angela Huxter, Susan and Nigel Wilson, Jan and Colin Roe, Derek and Maggie Washington, Amanda Dauncey, J Rudolf, Dr Jim Craig-Gray, Ian Phillips, Steven and Julie Brown, Russell and Margaret Bathie, BHP, PACW, Charles Bardswell, Martin and Pauline Richardson)*

Pubmaster ~ Lease: Norman Rushton ~ Real ale ~ Meals and snacks (till 10) ~ Restaurant ~ (01763) 208369 ~ Children welcome ~ Open 12-2.30, 6-11; closed 25 Dec

GODMANCHESTER (Cambs) TL2470 Map 5

Black Bull

Post St; follow village signposts off A14 (was A604) just E of Huntingdon

There's plenty of character and atmosphere in this heavy-beamed old place by the church, with seats built into the inglenook of the main bar's enormous fireplace, settles forming booths by leaded-light windows, and quite a bit of glinting brassware; a side room up a step is hung with lots of black agricultural and other rustic ironwork. A very wide choice of straightforward but decent food includes sandwiches (from £1.10), soup (£1.45), ploughman's (£3.60), pizza (£4.10), generous cod and chips, steak and ale pie or turkey curry (£5.70), mixed grill (£9.25) and specials such as king prawns in filo pastry (£3.65) and seafood platter (£5.95); puddings from (£1.20); children's menu (£1.50). Well kept Black Bull (made locally for them), Boddingtons, Flowers Original and Whitbreads Castle Eden on handpump; unobtrusive piped pop music; fruit machine. There's a pretty garden behind the car park. *(Recommended by Ian Phillips; more reports please)*

Whitbreads ~ Licensee Colin Dryer ~ Real ale ~ Meals and snacks (till 10pm) ~ Restaurant ~ (01480) 453310 ~ Children welcome till 8.30pm ~ Open 11-2.30(3 Sat); 6-11 ~ Bedrooms: £19/£35

GOREFIELD (Cambs) TF4111 Map 8

Woodmans Cottage (🍴)

Main St; off B1169 W of Wisbech

If you're lucky you may arrive at this cheerfully run, thriving village pub to witness one of their customers' birthday parties with Happy Birthday led by the licensee; if not you'll see plenty of photographs of said events. These celebrations reflect the buoyant enthusiasm of the Aussie licensees and their helpful staff – the food tends to be rich, and their weekend array of about 50 puddings certainly shows commitment. The wide changing choice of main dishes – recent favourites have been chicken kiev and lamb vindaloo (£5.50) – come in really big helpings and are certainly very good value. The spacious modernised bar, with leatherette stools and brocaded banquettes around the tables on its carpet, rambles back around the bar counter. A comfortable side eating area has a growing collection of china plates, as well as 1920s prints on its stripped brick walls, and there's a no-smoking area called 'the Cellar'. Beyond is an attractive pitched-ceiling restaurant so popular that it may be booked some three weeks ahead. At the other end of the pub, a games area has darts, dominoes, pool and CD juke box. Well kept Bass and Greene King IPA on handpump and several Australian wines; bridge school on Monday evenings. There are tables out in a sheltered back terrace, with a few more on a front verandah. *(Recommended by K Kennedy, Jenny and Michael Back, Stuart Earle, R C Vincent, Wayne Brindle, Mark J Hydes, Gordon Theaker, RF and MK Bishop, Ian R Hydes)*

Free house ~ Licensees Lucille and Barry Carter ~ Real ale ~ Meals and snacks (till 10pm; not 25 Dec) ~ Restaurant (closed Sun evening) ~ (01945) 870669 ~ Supervised children welcome away from the bar counter ~ Open 11-2.30, 7-11; closed evenings 25/26 Dec

HINXTON (Cambs) TL4945 Map 5

Red Lion

2 miles from M11 junction 9, 3½ miles from junction 10; just off A1301 S of Great Shelford

They're still collecting bric a brac at this friendly bustling local. This year they've added more stuffed birds and animals, clocks, mirrors and pictures to the friendly mainly open-plan bar which already has some grandfather and grandmother clocks, a barometer, some big prints and quite a lot of smaller rustic pictures on the walls, shelves of china in one corner, and a few beams and timbers hung with horsebrasses. George the Amazon parrot (his repertoire is increasing) perches above the button-back red brocade wall banquette, and there's a stuffed tarantula, egret and guillemot. Well kept Adnams, Bass, Boddingtons, and Greene King IPA on handpump at the central bar counter, also a useful wine list and fresh orange juice. Good sensibly priced and well cooked bar food includes home-made soup (£2.25), ploughman's (£3.75), home-baked ham salad or salmon and broccoli quiche (£4.50), chicken curry and chilli (£4.75), tuna and pasta bake (£4.95), prawn curry (£5.25), stir-fried beef or cold poached salmon (£5.95) and six vegetarian dishes including asparagus quiche (£4.50) and crispy vegetables in black bean sauce and pasta with asparagus and pesto (£4.95); daily specials. Part of the restaurant is no smoking; trivia and unobtrusive piped classical music. Outside the pretty white slightly jettied twin-gabled old building is a neatly kept garden with picnic tables and a paddock with a small pony and goat; there's an unusual heraldic roaring red lion face on the inn-sign. *(Recommended by Ann and Bob Westbrook, John Fahy, Mr and Mrs Tobin, N M Gibbs, Wayne Brindle, Roger Bellingham, Martin and Pauline Richardson, RJH, Jane Kingsbury, Paul Cartledge)*

Free house ~ Licensees James and Lynda Crawford ~ Real ale ~ Meals and snacks (till 10pm; 9.30pm Sun) ~ Restaurant ~ (01799) 530601 ~ Children in eating area of bar and restaurant ~ Open 11-2.30, 6-11

HOLYWELL (Cambs) TL3370 Map 5

Old Ferry Boat

Village and pub both signposted (keep your eyes skinned, it's easy to go wrong!) off A1123 in Needingworth

This big rambling old wisteria-covered thatched building is charmingly set on the site of a monastic ferry house, with lazy tables and cocktail parasols (more on a front terrace) on a manicured rose lawn by the Great Ouse where there's mooring for boats. The six characterful and popular open-plan bar areas (one no smoking) have window seats overlooking the river, very low beams, and timbered and panelled walls; one also has a pretty little carved settle. One of the four open fires has a fish and an eel among rushes moulded on its chimney beam. A stone in the bar marks the ancient grave of the resident ghost Juliette, said to return every year on 17 March. Good bar food from the imaginative menu includes starters like home-made soup (£2.50), chicken bites (£3.25), chicken pâté (£3.50) and garlic prawns (£4.50) and main courses like lunchtime delicious big filled bread sticks (from £2.50) and ploughman's (£4.75), also vegetable and pasta medley (£6.50) fish and chips (£6.75), steak, mushroom and ale pie (£6.95), breast of chicken in tomato, coriander, pepper and olive sauce and the very popular turkey curry pancake topped with melted cheese (£7.50), pork escalope with cider and walnut sauce (£7.75) and lamb cutlets with a peppercorn and french mustard sauce (£8.95); real chips; excellent choice of superb mostly home-made puddings on display (£2.50). Well kept Bass, Charrington IPA, Courage Directors, Nethergate Old Growler and Websters Yorkshire on handpump; friendly, attentive, efficient service even when it gets very busy in summer and at weekends. Fruit machine, trivia and piped music. *(Recommended by Moira and John Cole, Stuart Earle, Jack Morley, David and Glenys Lawson, Joan and Michel Hooper-Immins, Julian Holland, Ted George, Ian Phillips, M and J Back, Basil J S Minson, IE and CA Prosser, Gordon Theaker, Russell and Margaret Bathie, David and Michelle Hedges, Mr and Mrs D T Deas, Paul Cartledge)*

Free house ~ Licensee Richard Jeffrey ~ Real ale ~ Meals and snacks (till 10pm) ~ (01480) 463227 ~ Well behaved children welcome ~ Open 11-3, 6-11 (not Dec 25 eve) ~ Bedrooms: £39.95B/£49.50B

HORNINGSEA (Cambs) TL4962 Map 5

Plough & Fleece ★

Just NE of Cambridge: first slip-road off A45 heading E after A10, then left at T; or take B1047 Fen Ditton road off A1303

There's a wonderfully welcoming homely atmosphere at this friendly and lively village local which is only about ten minutes' drive from the centre of Cambridge. The friendly low black-beamed public bar has comfortably worn high-backed settles and plain seats on the red-tiled floor, a stuffed parrot and a fox by the log fire, and plain wooden tables including a long pine one with an equally long pew to match. Interesting home-cooked bar food includes lunchtime sandwiches (from £1.45), toasties (from £1.75) and ploughman's (£2.90) and starters like devilled crab and smoked haddock in creamy sauce on toast (£3), vegetarian stilton and broccoli flan (£3.25) and grilled oysters wrapped in bacon and served on toast (£5.50); main courses like cottage pie (£3.60), home-cooked ham in cheese sauce with crispy potato topping (£4.85), Cajun fried chicken or salads (£4.90), layers of spinach, tomatoes, onions and roquefort cheese under a puff pastry lid (£4.90), a mixed fish pie flavoured with caerphilly cheese (£5.50), steak and mushroom pie (£6.25), rabbit (£7.25), roast duck with a spicy sauce (£9.50) and beef wellington (£10.50); puddings include treacle tart, lemon cheesecake, chocolate pudding, plum pudding and home-made ginger and brandy ice cream (all £2.30); prices are higher in the evening; prompt, cheerful service. There's a good no-smoking dining room with lots of wood and old bricks and tiles, linked by a terrace to the prettily planted garden. Well kept Greene King IPA and Abbot on handpump, half a dozen good malt whiskies and a couple of vintage ports; dominoes and cribbage. There is easy disabled access. *(Recommended by Liz and Ian Phillips, Mr and Mrs Jones, Stephen Brown, Maysie Thompson, Mr and Mrs S R Maycock, Roy Bromell, Andrew Latchem, Helen Reed, Mrs J Barwell, Wayne Brindle, G W Ayres, Paul Cartledge, J Slaughter, Iain Baillie, P and D Carpenter, Huw and Carolyn Lewis, Mrs L E Baker, Jason Caulkin, Mike Pugh, A T Langton, Dr and Mrs M Bailey, Keith Symons)*

Greene King ~ Tenant Kenneth Grimes ~ Real ale ~ Meals and snacks (not Sun, Mon eve) ~ No-smoking restaurant ~ (01223) 860795 ~ Children over 5 in restaurant only ~ Open 11.30-2.30, 7-11; closed eve 25/26 Dec

HOUGHTON CONQUEST (Beds) TL0441 Map 5

Knife & Cleaver

Between B530 (old A418) and A6, S of Bedford

Bedfordshire Dining Pub of the Year

The emphasis at this finely finished inn is on the very restauranty bar food which is obviously prepared from fresh ingredients. They are serving more fresh and shell fish and use their local smokery for hickory-smoked beef, venison sausages and so forth. The menu which changes every month might include soup of the day (£1.95), French fish soup with rouille, croutons and gruyère or liver pâté (£3), ploughman's (£3.50), a small mixed hors d'oeuvre including shellfish, smoked fish and pâté (£4.50), ciabatta filled with smoked chicken (£4), spaghetti with pancetta, spring onion and shaved parmesan or marinaded herrings in leek and black olive salad (£4.50), fresh crab burger, Toulouse sausages, onion and mushroom tart, chicken and tarragon pie, or meatballs (£4.95), baked focaccia sandwich with whole grilled chicken breast, bacon and tomato (£5.95), and steak baguette (£6.25); home-made puddings like steamed lemon pudding, spicy bread pudding with brandy custard or hazelnut meringue ice cream on the blackboard (£2.25); good cheeseboard which includes many British farmhouse cheeses, cheddar with fruitcake and a lovely Irish blue brie called Abbey (£2.75). You can now choose from a choice of 20 or more good wines by the glass (or 50cl carafe). The welcoming and comfortable bar in this civilised 17th-c brick-built dining pub has a blazing fire in winter, various maps, drawings and old documents on the walls, and a good choice of up to twenty well aged malt whiskies – besides well kept Adnams Extra and Batemans XB on handpump; Stowford Press cider; friendly service and maybe unobtrusive piped classical music. Quite a bit of attention is focused on the restaurant, with its airy conservatory – rugs on the tiled floor, swagged curtains, cane furniture and lots of hanging plants. There are tables out in the neatly kept garden. *(Recommended by Brian and Jill Bond, Joyce and Stephen Stackhouse, Maysie Thompson, Andrew Scarr, Michael Marlow, John C Baker, Philip Russell, Michael Sargent, V Green, R E Rycroft, Peter Burton)*

Free house ~ Licensees David and Pauline Loom ~ Real ale ~ Meals and snacks (not every Sat evening) ~ Restaurant (not Sun evening) ~ (01234) 740387 ~ Children in restaurant only ~ Themed dinners with jazz or classical music some Fri evenings ~ Open 11.30-2.30(2 Sat), 7-10.30(11 Sat); closed Sun evening and 27-30 Dec ~ Bedrooms: £41B/£53B

Pubs in outstandingly attractive surroundings are listed at the back of the book.

KEYSOE (Beds) TL0762 Map 5

Chequers

B660 N of Bedford

The food at this friendly village local is consistently good. As well as the menu there is always a good choice of tasty daily specials on the huge blackboard, with fresh fish on Saturday; sandwiches, interesting home-made soups, tagliatelle with a creamy mushroom and white wine sauce (£4.75), chicken and ham pancake (£6), steak in mustard cream or green peppercorn and brandy sauce (£9.75); Sunday roast (£4.25); puddings like treacle tart, orange cheesecake or fresh fruit pavlova; children's helpings. An unusual stone-pillared fireplace divides the two comfortable beamed and neatly modernised simple rooms – one bar is no smoking. Well kept Hook Norton Best and another beer like Jennings Cumberland that changes every couple of months on handpumps on the stone bar counter; some malts. Video game, dominoes and piped music. The terrace at the back looks over the garden which has a wendy house, play tree, swings and a sand-pit. There is a surcharge for credit cards. *(Recommended by Jenny and Michael Back, S Eldridge, S G Brown, Margaret and Roy Randle)*

Free house ~ Licensee Jeffrey Kearns ~ Real ale ~ Meals and snacks (12-2, 7-9.30) ~ (01234) 708678 ~ Open 12-2.30, 6.30-11; closed Tuesdays

KEYSTON (Cambs) TL0475 Map 5

Pheasant

Village loop road; from A604 SE of Thrapston, right on to B663

Although there have been technical changes in the ownership of this pub, in practice things are continuing very much as before, with the chef/patron still the same, and no sign of relaxation in the high standards we have become used to here. The marvellously imaginative food is still the subject of readers' high praise: it's not cheap but most say it's well worth the money, and along with the absolutely superb wines (including 14 by the glass) this is where the emphasis of this subdued place lies – the owner does assure us that drinkers are as welcome as diners. The regularly changing menu might include haricot bean and truffle soup (£3.50), farmhouse terrine (£3.85), wild boar sausages (£6.25), tagliatelle with sun-dried tomatoes, rosemary and parmesan cheese (£6.95), spinach and ricotta tart with roasted Mediterranean vegetables (£7.50), fried pigeon breasts with red cabbage and thyme (£8.50), chicken with tomato, rosemary, garlic and braised fennel (£8.95), pork tenderloin with sage noodles, spinach and calvados sauce (£9.50), steamed brill with roasted red peppers (£12.95) and char-grilled fillet steak on a tomato confit with haricot beans (£14.50). Puddings might include hot pancakes with coconut ice cream and maple syrup (£3.50), crème caramel with a compote of prunes or jam roly poly (£3.75), lemon citrus tart (£4.50), dark chocolate tart (£5.25) and a selection of unpasteurised British cheeses (£5.50). The same menu is offered throughout this pretty and characterful thatched house – the only difference being that the Red Room has linen napkins, bigger tables and is no smoking. There's a friendly and nicely civilised feel, with low beams, old photographs, leather slung stools and a heavily carved wooden armchair; a high-raftered room that used to be the village smithy has heavy-horse harness and an old horse-drawn harrow. Well kept Adnams Best and three guest beers such as Courage Directors, Morlands Old Speckled Hen and Theakstons XB on handpump; very good friendly service. Some tables under cocktail parasols at the front are laid with tablecloths. No dogs. *(Recommended by Comus Elliott, Margaret and Roy Randle, Peter Burton, Caroline McAleese, Michael Marlow, Gordon Theaker, John Fahy, Basil Minson, Roger and Christine Mash, Dr M V Jones, Martin and Pauline Richardson, John and Tessa Rainsford, Michael Sargent)*

Free house ~ Licensee Roger Jones ~ Meals and snacks (12-2, 6-10) ~ Restaurant ~ (01832) 710241 ~ Children welcome ~ Open 12-3, 6-11

MADINGLEY (Cambs) TL3960 Map 5

Three Horseshoes

Off A1303 W of Cambridge

This well run thatched white pub is part of the same group as the Pheasant at Keysoe above, and very much the same things can be said about the very good imaginative food and the superb wide-ranging wine list (many by the glass). With the emphasis once again on the food and wine dining here errs slightly towards the more formal. The fashionable menu might include green pea soup with prosciutto (£3), crab salad with avocado and pink grapefruit (£4.50), spinach and ricotta ravioli with a lemon, sage and anchovy butter (£5.25) and main courses like couscous tartare with warm sun dried tomatoes and olive polenta (£6.75), pizza with four cheeses or open ravioli of chicken livers (£7), char-grilled chicken breast with parma ham and salsa verde (£8.50), char grilled leg of lamb (£10.50), roast monkfish (£13.75) and puddings like grilled peaches with brandy syrup, vanilla sugar and mascarpone cream (£3), bread and butter pudding (£3.50), praline parfait with passion fruit (£3.75) and sticky toffee pudding with hot butterscotch sauce and rum and raisin ice cream (£4.50) which can be had with a choice of good sweet wines. Adnams, Everards Tiger, Fullers London Pride, Morlands Old Speckled Hen, Timothy Taylor and Wadworths 6X on handpump, lots of malts and freshly squeezed orange juice. The charming traditional bar is comfortably furnished with an open fire. Service is flexible, efficient and attentive. In summer it's nice to sit out on the lawn, surrounded by flowering shrubs, roses and trees.

(Recommended by John Fahy, Julie Peters, Rita Horridge, Wayne Brindle, Maysie Thompson, Paul and Janet Waring, KCH, Jane Kinsbury, Paul Cartledge, B D Jones, Michael Sargent, Martin and Pauline Richardson, Martin Copeman)

Free house ~ Licensees R Stokes and John Hoskins ~ Real ale ~ Meals (11.30-2; 6.30-10) ~ Children welcome ~ Restaurant (not Sun evening) ~ (01954) 210221 ~ Open 11.30-2.30, 6-11

NEWTON (Cambs) TL4349 Map 5

Queens Head ★

2½ miles from M11 junction 11; A10 towards Royston, then left on to B1368

Full of wood smoke from the lovely big log fire and with beer straight from the barrel, this down-to-earth authentic old pub delights readers with its unspoilt charm. The friendly main bar has a low ceiling and crooked beams, bare wooden benches and seats built into the walls and bow windows, a curved high-backed settle on the yellow tiled floor, a loudly ticking clock, and paintings on the cream walls. The little carpeted saloon is broadly similar but cosier. Don't expect anything elaborate to eat: bar food is limited to a good choice of exceptionally good value doorstep sandwiches including banana and smoked salmon and excellent toast and beef dripping (from £1.60), and heartening home-made soup served in mugs or filled baked potatoes (£1.90); in the evening and on Sunday lunchtime they serve tempting plates of cold meat, smoked salmon, cheeses and pâté (from £2.75). Various combinations of Adnams Bitter, Broadside and Extra tapped from the cask, with Old Ale in winter and Tally Ho at Christmas; country wines including elderflower and strawberry, and Crone's cider. Darts in a side room, with shove-ha'penny, table skittles, dominoes, cribbage, fruit machine, and nine men's morris. There are seats in front of the pub, with its vine trellis and unusually tall chimney, or you can sit on the village green.

(Recommended by Frank Gadbois, John Fahy, Karen and Graham Oddey, Susan and Nigel Wilson, Jane Kingsbury, Alan and Eileen Bowker, Ron Gentry, Amanda Dauncey, J Rudolf, David Hedges, Norman Foot, Charles Bardswell, William Pryce, J L Phillips, Peter Douglas, Bob and Maggie Atherton, Mr and Mrs G F Marshall, Stephen and Julie Brown)

Free house ~ Licensee David Short ~ Real ale ~ Snacks (till 10pm) ~ (01223) 870436 ~ Well behaved children in games room ~ Open 11.30(11 Sat)-2.30, 6-11; closed 25 Dec

ODELL (Beds) SP9658 Map 4

Bell

Horsefair Lane; off A6 S of Rushden, via Sharnbrook

By the time we go to press this pretty thatched village pub will be looking spick and span as the friendly chatty landlord here plans to redecorate inside and out. Five warm low-ceilinged linked rooms, some with shiny black beams, loop around the central servery, and have quite a few handsome old oak settles among more neatly modern furniture, a log fire in one big stone fireplace and two coal fires elsewhere. Popular bar food includes sandwiches (from £1.65), ploughman's (from £2.70), omelettes (from £3), breaded plaice fillet, savoury pancakes, home-made vegetable pie or half a roast chicken (£4), home-made lasagne (£4.10), Whitby king prawns (£4.75) and daily specials from the board such as seafood pasta (£4.25), turkey, leek and mushroom pie or steak and kidney pie (£5.25), beef, bacon and cider casserole (£5.95) and pork slices in mustard sauce (£6.25); usual children's dishes (from £1.60). Well kept Greene King IPA, Abbot, Rayments and a seasonal ale on handpump, faint piped music, and good friendly service. The pleasant garden runs back to the Great Ouse, and is full of golden pheasants and cockatiels (and maybe canaries) – as well as a goose called Lucy who's rather partial to lettuce leaves. Further along the road is a very pretty church. No dogs. *(Recommended by John Fahy, Maysie Thompson, Andy and Jill Kassube, Lynda Brightman, Penny and Martin Fletcher, Mr and Mrs Ray, Nick Bentley, Rita Horridge, Mr and Mrs R C Allison)*

Greene King ~ Tenant Derek Scott ~ Real ale ~ Meals and snacks (not Sun evening in winter) ~ (01234) 720254 ~ Children in eating area of bar only ~ Open 11-2.30, 6-11

RISELEY (Beds) TL0362 Map 5

Fox & Hounds

High St; village signposted off A6 and B660 N of Bedford

This is definitely a place for the meat lover, and though very much a pub even describes itself as a steak-house. The long-standing speciality is the cabinet of well hung steaks at one end of the bar counter: you choose which piece of meat you want yours cut from, say how much you want and how you want it cooked, and you're then charged by weight, say £8.80 for 8oz rump, £9.60 for 8oz sirloin, £3 for a steak sandwich. A wide choice of other food includes sandwiches (from £1), home-made soups like stilton and broccoli and leek and potato (£1.95), home-made burger (£3.95), steak and kidney pie or marinaded beef pie (£6.95); good puddings. Plenty of tables spread under the heavy low beams and among timber uprights, with two candlelit side dining rooms. Well kept Charles Wells Eagle with regularly changing guests like Adnams, Felinfoel, Gales, Theakstons and Youngs on handpump, a decent collection of other drinks including a good range of cognacs, unobtrusive piped Glen Miller or light classics, very friendly and helpful service. There are picnic tables in the huge garden. The landlord is great fun – a real personality. *(Recommended by Philip Brindle, Stephen Brown, Dr M V Jones, Bill and Sylvia Trotter, Prof J V Wood, Michael Sargent, George Atkinson)*

Charles Wells ~ Managers Jan and Lynne Zielinski ~ Real ale ~ Meals and snacks (12-1.45, 7-10) ~ Restaurant ~ (01234) 708240 ~ Children welcome ~ Open 11.30-2.30, 6.30-11

STILTON (Cambs) TL1689 Map 5

Bell 🛏 🍷

High Street; village signposted from A1 S of Peterborough

The fine coach-arch in this rather elegant old stone building with its stately curlicued gantry to suspend the pub sign opens on to a sheltered cobbled and flagstoned courtyard, with distances to cities carved on the walls, picnic tables and a well which may date back to Roman times. Two busy but spacious and attractive bars have sturdy upright wooden seats, plush-cushioned button-back banquettes built around the walls and bow windows, big prints of sailing and winter coaching scenes on the partly stripped walls, and a large warm log fire in the fine stone fireplace. Generous helpings of very good bar food (there may be a bit of a wait) include delicious stilton baguettes; vegetable Wellington and stilton sausage (£6.25), chicken kebab (£6.75) and rump steak (£8.50). Well kept Marstons Pedigree, Morlands Old Speckled Hen and Tetleys and a changing guest beer on handpump – they had over 100 last year; large choice of wines by the glass; good friendly service; dominoes, cribbage, backgammon, chess, Mastermind and Scrabble. Chintzy bedrooms make an elegent stay. *(Recommended by John Fahy, George Atkinson, Dr and Mrs G H Lewis, Mrs D E Fryer, Frank W Gadbois, KC, JFM and M West, L M Miall, Alan and Heather Jacques, John Tyzack, Huw and Carolyn Lewis, Mr and Mrs Powell, Roy Smylie, Wayne Brindle, Neil Townend, David and Michelle Hedges, David and Ruth Hollands, Charles and Dorothy Ellsworth, Martin and Pauline Richardson)*

Free house ~ Licensees John and Liam McGivern ~ Real ale ~ Meals and snacks ~ Restaurant ~ (01733) 241066 ~ Children in eating area of bar till 8pm ~ Open 12-2.30(11-3 Sat in summer), 6-11; closed 25/26 Dec evening ~ Bedrooms: £30B/£50B

STRETHAM (Cambs) TL5072 Map 5

Lazy Otter

Cambridge Rd, Elford Closes; off A10 S of Stretham roundabout

During the day the nicest place in this large popular family pub is the no-smoking conservatory which overlooks the Great Ouse – or, if it's a lovely day, at the tables on the neat terrace with the same view. The big garden runs down to the pub's own moorings, and there's a children's play area. Inside where they understand the needs of harassed family travellers it's neat, spacious and comfortable with a relaxed atmosphere, warm fire and friendly helpful staff. Food includes home-made soup (£2.20), big filled baps (from £2.35), filled baked potatoes (from £2.75), burgers (from £3.50), ham and egg or chilli (£4.95), fish and chips, lasagne or vegetarian steak (£5.25), breaded scampi or canelloni filled with ricotta and spinach (£5.95); usual children's menu (£1.50) and puddings (£2.50); Well kept Greene King IPA, Abbot and a seasonal beer such as Sorcerer, Marstons Pedigree and a rotating guest that might be Courage Directors, Greene King Rayments Special or Wadworths 6X, some under light blanket pressure; limited wine list; fruit machine, trivia and piped music. It can get very busy at the weekends. *(Recommended by Stephen and Julie Brown, Liz and Gil Dudley, Wayne Brindle, Stephen and Jean Curtis, K Kennedy, Michael Williamson, R C Vincent, JM and PM, Julian Holland, Nigel and Sara Walker, Clare Dawkins, Gordon Phillips, Ian Phillips, Dr Paul Kitchener, Tom Thomas)*

Free house ~ Licensees Jim Hardy and Stephen Owen ~ Real ale ~ Meals and snacks 12-3; 6-10(12-10 Sat and in summer) ~ Restaurant ~ (01353) 649780 ~ Children welcome ~ Live music Wed night ~ Open 11-11

SUTTON GAULT (Cambs) TL4279 Map 5

Anchor ★ (food award) (wine award)

Village signed off B1381 in Sutton

Cambridgeshire Dining Pub of the Year

The emphasis in this very popular riverside pub is firmly on the superb food, but without detracting from the relaxed old-fashioned atmosphere. The imaginative daily-changing menu (not cheap) might include soup (£3.25), chicken liver, brandy and hazelnut pâté (£4.50), fresh dressed Cromer crab, vegetable and rice filled tomatoes or curried nut loaf with spicy yoghurt (£5.75), whole fresh crab salad, arctic char (similar to trout) or steak and kidney pie (£8.95), supreme of chicken in lemon and tarragon sauce (£9.50), venison (£9.95) and fillet steak dijonnaise (£14.95); puddings include delicious sharp lemon tart, bread and butter pudding with honey and whisky cream, warm bakewell tart and hot sticky toffee pudding (£3.95); half helpings for children. The four heavily timbered gaslit and candlelit cosy rooms have a stylish symplicity with antique settles on the gently sloping floors, along with dining or kitchen chairs and well spaced, stripped and scrubbed deal tables, good lithographs and big prints on the walls, and three log fires; two rooms are now no smoking. Well kept Greene King IPA, Ind Coope Burton and Tolly Original tapped from the cask, very good wine list (including a wine of the week and 10 by the glass), winter mulled wine; freshly squeezed orange juice. No dogs; piped classical music. In summer you can sit outside at the tables or on the bank of the Old Bedford River watching the swans and house martins; the river bank walks are lovely. It is now very much a dining pub – it's best to book, they don't allow short sleeves, and one reader was even warned not to arrive too early for his table as there wasn't really any standing room. *(Recommended by Stephen and Julie Brown, Viv Middlebrook, K Kennedy, Rita Horridge, Stephen and Jean Curtis, Hilary Edwards, Gordon Theaker, Mrs C Archer, John Fahy, Paul and Janet Waring, Julian Holland, Gwen and Peter Andrews, Robin Moore, J S M Sheldon, Wayne Brindle, Trevor Scott, Keith Symons, Professor John and Mrs Patricia White, Michael Sargent, Basil J S Minson, Dr and Mrs M Bailey, Clare Dawkins, Gordon Phillips, V and E A Bolton, Ingrid Abma, Andrew Langbar, Nicholas Law, Paul Cartledge)*

Free house ~ Licensees Robin and Heather Moore ~ Real ale ~ Meals and snacks (till 9.30) ~ (01353) 778537 ~ Well behaved children in no-smoking rooms till 8pm ~ Open 12-2.30, 7(6.30 Sat)-11; closed 25 and 26 Dec ~ Bedrooms: £47.50B/£55B

SWAVESEY (Cambs) TL3668 Map 5

Trinity Foot 🍷

A604, N side; to reach it from the westbound carriageway, take Swavesey, Fen Drayton turnoff

One reader has told us that this very cheery welcoming landlord urged him to try their coffee at four in the afternoon (note their closing times in the rubric below). It's this friendly enthusiasm and the delicious reasonably priced food that make this a really popular place. Fresh fish is delivered daily direct from the East Coast ports and is sold both in the pub and in their fish shop next door (open Tuesday-Saturday 11-2.30, 6-7.30). On the menu there might be smoked fish and fresh herb pâté (£3), herring roes on toast (£3.50), six oysters (£5), grilled butterfish, cod or plaice or tuna kebabs (all £6.75), dressed crab salad (£6.50), grilled fillet of turbot (£9.50), Dover sole (£11), and fresh lobster (£11.50); other dishes include sandwiches (from £1), ploughman's (£3), omelettes (£5.50), grills (from £5.50), and seasonal things like samphire and soft fruits. There are well spaced tables and fresh flowers, a light and airy conservatory, and usually quite a busy atmosphere. Well kept Boddingtons and a guest like Flowers on handpump, lots of wines including New World ones, freshly squeezed orange juice, and coffee that's constantly replenished at no extra charge; cheerful and efficient service. Big enclosed garden of shrubs, trees and lawns; one no-smoking room. *(Recommended by Christine Van der Will, Ian Phillips, Joan Hilditch, J G Cooke, Jane Kingsbury, Michael Sargent, Gordon Theaker, David and Ruth Hollands)*

Whitbreads ~ Tenants H J and B J Mole ~ Real ale ~ Meals and snacks (12-2, 6-9.30) ~ (01954) 230315 ~ Children in eating area of bar ~ Open 11-2.30, 6-11; closed Sun evenings

UFFORD (Cambs) TF0904 Map 5

Olde White Hart

From A15 N of Peterborough, left on to B1443; village signposted at unmarked road on left after about 4 miles

One of the new licensees at this friendly 17th-c village pub has been a regular for over 20 years and has been organising the folk music for the last five, so things are unlikely to change much. The comfortable and welcoming lounge bar is divided in two by an attractive stone chimney, and has wheelback chairs around dark tripod tables and pewter tankards hanging from the beam over the bar counter; Boris the stuffed tarantula is still in residence. The carpeted public bar and the snug both have old-fashioned settles. All bar food is home-made (except the pork and stilton sausages, £5.25, and they're local), and includes doorstep sandwiches (from £1.50), soup (£1.75), creamed garlic mushrooms (£2.50), ploughman's (from £3.25), pork stroganoff (£5.75), steak pie (£4.95), a fresh fish dish like haddock mornay (£5.50) and at least two vegetarian dishes. Well kept Home Bitter, Theakstons Best, XB and Old Peculier, Wadworths 6X and a weekly changing guest on handpump, lots of bottled beers from all over the world, several wines by the glass, and farm ciders. Darts, cribbage, and dominoes, ring-the-bull and captain's mistress. The three acres of gardens have rose arbours, steps and various quiet corners, as well as a sunny terrace with white metal seats and canopy, and a children's play area. It's a good stop for walkers and cyclists; you can camp on the paddock and they intend to allow touring caravans. *(Recommended by Wayne Brindle, Stuart Earle, David and Michelle Hedges, Stephen and Julie Brown, K Kennedy)*

Scottish & Newcastle ~ Tenants Andy Tomblin and Maggie Hurry ~ Real ale ~ Meals and snacks (not Sun evening) ~ Restaurant (not Sun evening) ~ (01780) 740250 ~ Children welcome till 9pm ~ Folk/blues/Cajun/comedy Sun evenings and occasionally midweek ~ Open 11-2.30, 6-11; closed Mon lunchtime and 25 Dec

WANSFORD (Cambs) TL0799 Map 5

Haycock ★ 🍴 🛏 🍷

Village clearly signposted from A1 W of Peterborough

Extremely well trained staff enthusiastically welcome all kinds of people to this well run and civilised golden stone inn. It's now a huge place, but has kept a very personal atmosphere. The fine flagstoned main entry hall has antique hunting prints and a longcase clock. This leads into the lively panelled main bar with dark terracotta walls, a sturdy dado rail above a mulberry dado, and old settles. Through two handsome stone arches is another attractive area, while the comfortable front sitting room has some squared oak panelling by the bar counter, a nice wall clock, and a big log fire. There's an airy stripped brick dining bar by the garden, with sunny modern prints; doors open on to a big terrace with lots of tables. There are two no-smoking areas. Fine bar food includes soup (£2.95), chicken liver pâté (£4.25), sardines fried in garlic butter (£5.85), fresh pasta (from £6.95), spicy pork ribs, fish and chips or mild curried breast of chicken (£7.95), main course antipasto (£8.95), roast salmon (£9.25); home-made puddings like crème brûlée and chocolate truffle cake (from £3.50), and summer terrace barbecues (from £6.95). The outdoor eating area with its big cream Italian umbrellas is very popular. Well kept Adnams, Banks & Taylors Shefford, Bass, Ruddles Best and County, and a guest beer on handpump, a good range of around 11 good house wines by the glass from an exceptional list, and properly mature vintage ports by the glass; freshly squeezed juices. The spacious walled formal garden has boules and fishing as well as cricket (they have their own field). *(Recommended by S G Brown, George Atkinson, Tim and Sue Halstead, John Fahy, Linda Norsworthy, Wayne Brindle, Mrs R Cotgreave, Frank Gadbois, Mrs F M Halle, Martin and Pauline Richardson, Keith and Margaret Kettell, June and Malcolm Farmer, Michael Sargent)*

Free house ~ Licensee Dick Neale and Louise Dunning ~ Real ale ~ Meals and snacks (all day) ~ Restaurant ~ (01780) 782223 ~ Children welcome ~ Occasional jazz Wed evenings; jazz festival week in August ~ Open all day ~ Bedrooms £72B/£98B

If we know a pub has a no-smoking area, we say so.

WOODDITTON (Cambs) TL6659 Map 5

Three Blackbirds

Village signposted off B1063 at Cheveley

This pretty thatched village local is getting more and more popular for its good choice of freshly cooked food which includes soup (£2.10), vegetarian or duck liver pâté (£2.75), dim sum (£2.95), garlic mussels (£3.25), smoked salmon roulade (£3.45), home-cooked ham (£5.50), lasagne and vegetable lasagne (£5.65), vegetable stroganoff (£5.95), beef and Guinness casserole with puff pasty topping (£6.75), venison casserole or lamb oriental (£8.95) and daily specials; good Sunday roasts; the menu is the same in the restaurant. The two comfortably snug and friendly bars have high winged settles or dining chairs around fairly closely spaced neat tables, cigarette cards, Derby-Day photographs, little country prints, and winter fires – the room on the left has the pubbier atmosphere. Well kept Greene King IPA on handpump. Service remains cheerful and efficient even when busy. The attractive front lawn, sheltered by an ivy-covered flint wall, has flowers, roses, and a flowering cherry, with a muted chorus of nearby farm noises; partly no-smoking restaurant; piped music. *(Recommended by Paul and Janet Waring, Wayne Brindle, John Fahy, Martin and Pauline Richardson, Dr and Mrs M Bailey; more reports please)*

Pubmaster ~ Tenant Edward Spooner ~ Real ale ~ Meals and snacks (till 10pm) ~ Restaurant ~ (01638) 730811 ~ Children in eating area of bar and restaurant ~ Open 11.30-2.30, 6.30-11

Lucky Dip

Besides the fully inspected pubs, you might like to try these Lucky Dips recommended to us and described by readers (if you do, please send us reports). Pubs are in Cambs unless we list them as in Beds.

Abbotsley [High Street/St Neots Rd; TL2356], *Eight Bells*: Genuine village pub with good value generous food inc Thurs/Fri fresh fish, well kept Greene King IPA and Abbot *(Howard and Margaret Buchanan)*

Alconbury [Main St, Alconbury Weston; TL1875], *White Hart*: Good straightforward competitively priced food inc home-made chips in characterful pub in charming village; eating areas left and right, back bar with darts, Courage-related ales and an interesting guest beer, very helpful licensees *(Jenny and Michael Back)*

Arlesey, Beds [60 Hitchin Rd; TL1936], *Prince of Wales*: Warmly welcoming local with good home-cooked food from traditional favourites to interesting lamb specialities, well kept Greene King IPA, Abbot and Rayments, darts, dominoes, cribbage and so forth; crowded Fri for live music; well tended spacious garden with jungle gym and memorable bank hol barbecues *(Vic Morrow)*

Arrington [TL3250], *Hardwicke Arms*: Good atmosphere in reopened coaching inn's beamed and panelled lounge, handy for Wimpole Hall; bar food, real ales *(DB, LYM)*

Aspley Guise, Beds [The Square; SP9335], *Bell*: Old dining pub in picturesque village, wide choice of food from simple sandwiches to interesting dishes such as veal with ham and mozzarella or beef fillets with juniper berry sauce and polenta, also reasonable vegetarian choice and good pasta (Italian landlord); welcoming efficient service, Bass and Boddingtons; garden with play area *(Nan Axon)*

☆ **Barrington** [from M11 junction 11 take A10 to Newton, turn right; TL3949], *Royal Oak*: Thatched and heavily beamed and timbered Tudor pub, character rambling bar managed with considerable individuality, pleasant no smoking dining conservatory, tables out overlooking charming green; well kept Greene King IPA and Abbot, prompt friendly staff, food inc wide range of vegetarian dishes generally much enjoyed; maybe piped music, children in one area *(Andrew Latchem, Helen Reed, Trevor P Scott, Joy Heatherley, Gordon Mott, Gill Earle, Andrew Burton, Susan and Nigel Wilson, Paul Cartledge, Nigel Norman, S Brackenbury, Charles Bardswell, RJH, Stephen Brown, Nigel Gibbs, Dr and Mrs M Bailey, LYM)*

☆ **Bartlow** [TL5845], *Three Hills*: Spacious and well established 16th-c family dining pub, neat and tidy, with copper ornaments and olde-worlde pictures, wide choice of bar food inc vegetarian, evening restaurant, Sun lunches, well kept Greene King IPA, decent wines by the glass, very unobtrusive piped music; interesting hill forts nearby *(Paul Cartledge, Ian Phillips, Brian and Jill Bond, Gwen and Peter Andrews, Richard Balls, A M Bateman)*

Bedford, Beds [Goldington Green; TL0751], *Lincolns*: Impressive manor house dating from 1620, original stone fireplaces in bar and two dining rooms, outlook on peaceful cricket green; some concentration on restaurant (food American-based), service brisk and friendly *(Ian Phillips)*

☆ **Bourn** [signed off B1046 and A1198 W of Cambridge; at N end of village; TL3256], *Duke of Wellington*: Well spaced tables in quiet and civilised relaxing bar divided by arches and so forth, good range of generous imaginative food cooked to order (where the locals come to dine out), pleasant attentive staff, well kept Greene King; cl Mon *(Maysie Thompson, Gordon Theaker, Geoff Lee, BB)*

Boxworth [TL3463], *Golden Ball*: Recently refurbished popular dining pub with above-average food *(E A George)*

☆ **Brampton** [Bromholme Lane; signed off A141 Huntingdon Rd opp Hinchingbrooke House; TL2170], *Olde Mill*: Popular Beefeater in beautiful riverside spot, converted mill with working waterwheel and mill race rushing under lounge's glass 'tables', usual good value bar food, upper restaurant, Whitbreads-related real ales, quick pleasant service, tables out by water *(Ian Phillips, Julian Holland)*

Bromham, Beds [Bridge End; nr A428, 2 miles W of Bedford; TL0050], *Swan*: Comfortable beamed village pub with welcoming atmosphere, quick service, open fires, lots of pictures, well kept Greene King IPA and Abbot, decent coffee, popular food inc good value carvery (children allowed here) and salad bar; public bar with darts and fruit machine, pleasant garden *(Michael and Wilma Bishop, John Fahy)*

☆ **Broom**, Beds [23 High St; TL1743], *Cock*: Friendly new licensees and fine atmosphere in attractive and unusual old-fashioned small-roomed pub with well kept Greene King ales tapped from the cask in corridor servery (no bar counter), wide range of food inc good steaks, traditional bar games, real fire; camping in paddock behind *(Michael Marlow, Drs A and A C Jackson, Dr Jim Cowburn, Tim Heywood, Sophie Wilne, Ian Phillips, Robert Bland, LYM)*

Burrough Green [TL6355], *Bull*: Attractive pub with cricketing decor, friendly landlord, well kept ales, separate dining area *(Frank W Gadbois)*

Caddington, Beds [1 Luton Rd; TL0619], *Chequers*: Welcoming and cosy village pub with low-priced real ales, cheap but good home-cooked food, friendly staff; lovely bedrooms *(Jacqueline Walshe, Mrs Patricia Walshe)*; *Cricketers*: Cosy and friendly cheerful local *(Joseph Deveau)*

☆ **Cambridge** [14 Chesterton Rd], *Boathouse*: Nice setting with carpeted extension with verandah overlooking river (wonderful playground on opp bank), unspoilt relaxed atmosphere, L-shaped main room with varnished wood tables and framed prints, eight or so well kept beers such as Brakspears and Boddingtons, good chocie of ciders, decent coffee, generous food, pleasant service; juke box; children welcome, open all day *(P and D Carpenter, Keith and Janet Morris, Tim and Sue Halstead, Kate and Robert Hodkinson, Ian Phillips, Paul Cartledge, LYM)*

☆ **Cambridge** [85 Gwydir St], *Cambridge Blue*: Well kept Nethergate and frequently changed guest beers, good value food (not Sun evening) inc home-made pies and vegetarian dishes, small and simply furnished – one room no smoking; university sports photographs, local paintings, friendly pubby atmosphere, sheltered terrace with children's climbing frame and entertaining model train *(Frank W Gadbois, Susan and Nigel Wilson, P Carpenter, Paul Cartledge, David Brazier, K Kennedy, LYM)*

☆ **Cambridge** [Midsummer Common], *Fort St George*: Picturesque, and very popular for its charming waterside position on Midsummer Common, overlooking ducks, swans, punts and boathouses; extensive but with interesting old-fashioned Tudor core, good bar food and traditional Sun lunches, well kept Greene King real ales, decent wines, games in public bar, intriguing display of historic boating photographs, tables outside *(Alice McLerran, Dr and Mrs P J S Crawshaw, Paul Cartledge, K Kennedy, LYM)*

☆ **Cambridge** [Ferry Path; car park on Chesterton Rd], *Old Spring*: Good individual atmosphere, cosy old-fashioned furnishings and decor, bare boards, gas lighting, lots of old pictures, decent straightforward bar food inc Sun roasts, well kept Greene King real ales, two open fires, back conservatory, summer barbecues; children till 8, has been open all day Sat *(Trevor P Scott, Stephen, Julie and Hayley Brown, Paul Cartledge, LYM)*

☆ **Cambridge** [King St], *Champion of the Thames*: Basic small and cosy pub with friendly welcome, good mix of students and others, wonderfully decorated windows, padded walls and seats, painted anaglypta ceiling, lots of woodwork, no music, well kept Greene King IPA and Abbot; one of the best in the city for atmosphere *(William Pryce, K Kennedy, Andy and Jill Kassube)*

☆ **Cambridge** [Clarendon St], *Clarendon Arms*: Very popular local with well kept Greene King ales, wide choice of good cheap but adventurous bar lunches inc giant crusty sandwiches; open all day; bedrooms clean and comfortable *(Paul Cartledge, I S Thomson, Noel Jackson, Louise Campbell)*

☆ **Cambridge** [Tenison Rd/Wilkin St], *Salisbury Arms*: A dozen or so well kept and well priced real ales and farm ciders in spacious high-ceilinged traditional main bar, good no smoking area, decent basic lunchtime bar food from separate counter inc vegetarian dishes, friendly licensee, games room, TV, maybe jazz Sun lunchtime; can get very busy, open all day Sat *(Paul Cartledge, K Kennedy, Julian Holland, LYM)*

☆ **Cambridge** [Newmarket Rd], *Wrestlers*: Good cheap Thai food the main draw (inc take-aways); good choice of well kept Charles Wells and guest real ales, pool table, student atmosphere and simple furnishings; lively evenings (free live music Thurs-Sat), quieter lunchtime *(Paul Cartledge, Anna Marsh, Dr R M Williamson)*

☆ **Cambridge** [17 Bridge St, opp St Johns Coll], *Mitre*: Recently renovated alehouse-style pub with very friendly attentive service, half a dozen real ales, well priced wines inc some New World ones, attractively priced food from fine sandwiches and hot beef baps up, no smoking area, log-effect fire *(Andy and Jill Kassube, Ian Phillips, David and Gill Carrington)*

Cambridge [19 Bridge St], *Baron of Beef*: Small, friendly and traditional, lots of old photographs, panelling, Greene King ales from uncommonly long counter, buffet food inc good hot beef sandwich *(Paul Cartledge, D K Carter)*; [Bene't St], *Bath*: Recently refurbished scrubbed-floor pub with Whitbreads-related ales, pizzas and other food, sensible prices *(Julian Holland)*; [Newmarket St], *Bird in Hand*: Good changing food from sandwiches up, chilli and curries favoured *(Michael Williamson)*; [Kings St], *Bun Shop*: Atmospheric studenty pub deservedly very popular for food *(Angela Wood)*; [nr war memorial approaching stn], *Flying Pig*: Original small pub very popular with young musicians, piped music from great American blues to customers' occasionally very amateur tapes *(Phil Gilbert)*; [Regent St], *Fountain*: Done out as replica traditional-style pub specialising in real ales – three Theakstons, Youngs Special, Marstons Pedigree and several interesting guest beers from small breweries; limited but good value traditional pie-style food, good mix of ages *(Bob and Sue Ward, Michael Williamson)*; [Barton Rd/Kings Rd], *Hat & Feathers*: Straightforward but currently very popular, with enjoyable atmosphere, well kept Tetleys, good value bar food *(Paul Cartledge, Wayne Brindle)*; [43 Panton St], *Panton Arms*: Straightforward pub well worth knowing for good interesting quickly served food inc exceptionally fresh help-yourself salads *(Anthony Barker, Lawrence Pearse)*; [Barton Rd], *Red Bull*: Old-style bare-boards real ale pub with Whitbreads-related and other beers tapped into jugs from the cask; good sometimes crowdedly studenty atmosphere, juke box, helpful pleasant staff; seating limited, no children *(Trevor P Scott, Wayne Brindle, Stephen and Julie Brown)*; [King St], *St Radegund*: Delightful small pub, very popular with students; good crusty sandwiches, well kept ales such as Fullers London Pride, Hook Norton Best and Nethergate, interesting former-student memorabilia *(Andy and Jill Kassube)*; [Dover St (off East Rd)], *Tram Depot*: Unusual former tram stables with bare bricks, flagstones, old furniture, unconventional layout; reasonably priced bar food (not Sat evening), well kept Everards and wide range of other changing ales, seats out in courtyard; can be crowded with students *(Julian Holland, PC)*

Catworth [High St; B660 between A45 (Kimbolton) and A604; TL0873], *Racehorse*: No news of this rather elegant and formerly highly rated village pub with its log fire and all its bloodstock memorabilia since it closed in late 1994 *(LYM – reports please)*

☆ **Chatteris** [Pickle Fen, B1050 towards St Ives; TL3986], *Crafty Fox*: Wide choice of interesting good value food inc good Sun lunches the mainstay of this unpretentious but distinctive roadside pub with warm welcome and obliging landlord; small bar area with adjacent country-kitchen lounge, big back glass-covered summer-only eating area with fountain, fishpond and mature vines; well kept ales such as Morlands Old Speckled Hen and John Smiths on handpump, piped music *(Julian Holland, Frank W Gadbois, Ian Phillips, LYM)*

Chatteris [South Pk St], *Honest John*: Good atmosphere and well kept real ales inc guest beers in friendly free house *(Alex Nooteboom)*

Chittering [TL4970], *Travellers Rest*: Very friendly and informal, with good food *(Michael Williamson)*

☆ **Clayhithe** [TL5064], *Bridge*: Cosy beamed and timbered bar with good log fire and pretty garden by River Cam; well kept Elgoods and Adnams Bitter and Broadside, pleasant staff, bar food, restaurant; comfortable bedrooms in motel extension *(Wayne Brindle, Martin and Pauline Richardson, LYM)*

Comberton [TL3856], *Three Horseshoes*: Good food, well kept beer *(G Washington)*

☆ **Conington** [Boxworth Rd; signed off A14 (was A604) Cambridge—Huntingdon; TL3266], *White Swan*: Attractive and unpretentious country local with children welcome in several eating areas on right of cheerful traditional bar, games inc bar billiards and juke box on left, good big front garden with play area; good range of popular bar food inc fidgit pie and decent steaks, quick friendly service, well kept Greene King IPA and Abbot tapped from the cask, snuffs; tables outside, play house *(Rich Baldry, Martin and Pauline Richardson, Wayne Brindle, David Campbell, Vicky McLean, BB)*

☆ **Coton** [quite handy for M11, junction 13: 2 miles W of Cambridge off A1303; TL41058], *Plough*: Consistently good well managed Whitbreads food pub with spruce and spacious back bar, more traditional front restaurant, good big garden; good service *(Dono and Carol Leaman, Dr and Mrs M Bailey, P and D Carpenter, LYM)*

☆ **Croydon** [TL3149], *Queen Adelaide*: Sizeable beamed dining bar with standing timbers dividing off separate eating area, comfortable sofas, banquettes and stools, good food inc filled yorkshire puddings and steaks, well kept ales such as Boddingtons and Greene King *(Keith Morris, M A Hendry)*

☆ **Downham** [Main St; sometimes known as Little Downham – the one near Ely; TL5283], *Plough*: Charming little traditional fenland village local with good value home cooking, welcoming service, lots of old photographs and bric-a-brac, Greene King ales under light top pressure, good choice of malt whiskies, tables outside; bustling atmosphere; the friendly well behaved golden retrievers are called Abbot and Indi *(John and Priscilla Gillett)*

☆ **Dry Drayton** [Park St, opp church; signed off A428 (was A45) W of Cambridge; TL3862], *Black Horse*: Unpretentiously straightforward village local with good generous food inc wide vegetarian choice, wide range of beers inc weekly changing guests, friendly prompt service, central fireplace, games area, tables on pretty back terrace and neat lawn; camping/caravanning in meadow behind *(P and D Carpenter, Ian Phillips, Keith and Janet Morris, J Sanderson, Dr and Mrs M Bailey, BB)*

☆ **Dunstable**, Beds [High St; TL0221], *Old Sugarloaf*: Quaint and hospitable former coaching inn with three busy bars, good friendly service, good range of real ales, good local atmosphere; popular bar and restaurant food *(W J Albone, Vanessa Crockett, L K Edlin)*

☆ **Eaton Bray**, Beds [SP9620], *White Horse*: Wide choice of generous well served food and good relaxed atmosphere in rambling old low-beamed dining pub, particularly well run, with timbered dividers, suit of armour in one room, real ales such as Friary Meux Best and Ruddles Best; ranks of tables on back lawn, good walking nearby *(Ian, Kathleen and Helen Corsie, Jenny and Michael Back)*

☆ **Eaton Socon** [Old Great North Rd; village signposted from A1 nr St Neots; TL1658], *White Horse*: Rambling, comfortable and interestingly furnished low-beamed rooms dating from 13th c, relaxing atmosphere, well kept Whitbreads-related and guest ales, friendly service and generally good value fresh food; nice high-backed traditional settles around fine log fire in end room; play area in back garden, children in eating areas; bedrooms *(George Atkinson, LYM)*

☆ **Eaton Socon**, *Crown*: Comfortable little old inn, refurbished but keeping the low beams, open fire and three side areas off bar with separate dining room; good choice of moderately priced food (not Sun) from sandwiches up, wide and interesting choice of perfectly kept real ales served in the northern style, friendly service, nostalgic piped music, restaurant (good steaks); no T-shirts *(S Eldridge, Ian Phillips, John C Baker)*

☆ **Eaton Socon**, *Waggon & Horses*: Popular and busy old open-plan pub with lots of low beams and brasses, Bass and Tetleys-related ales, good value quick generous food inc copious fresh veg, delicious home-made puddings, good Sun lunches; friendly Irish landlord, restaurant *(S Eldridge, George Atkinson, Mrs L E Baker, H Bramwell)*

☆ **Elsworth** [TL3163], *George & Dragon*: Doing well under friendly new licensees, with emphasis on good range of fresh food in attractively furnished and decorated panelled main bar and quieter back dining area, plenty of character and atmosphere, well kept Greene King ales, decent wines, open fire; nice terraces, play area in garden, restaurant; attractive village; closed Sun evening and Mon *(Gordon Theaker, E A George, Martin and Pauline Richardson, Wayne Brindle, LYM)*

Elsworth, *Poacher*: Character free house in beautiful surroundings, friendly landlord, good food, well kept beer *(Maysie Thompson)*

☆ **Ely** [Annesdale; off A10 on outskirts; TL5380], *Cutter*: Lovely riverside setting, with plenty of tables outside and a genuine welcome for children; friendly series of unpretentious bars, decent food, real ales *(Wayne Brindle, John Fahy, J S M Sheldon, JM, PM, LYM)*

☆ **Ely** [Silver St], *Prince Albert*: Good atmosphere in friendly no-nonsense town pub with full range of Greene King ales in peak condition, no juke box or noisy kids, attractive garden below cathedral *(John C Baker, Steve Pickard, Wayne Brindle)*

Ely [2 Lynn Rd], *Lamb*: Pleasing dignified lounge bar with good bar food, handy for cathedral; bedrooms *(W H and E Thomas)*

Felmersham, Beds [Grange Rd; SP9857], *Six Ringers*: Attractive thatched village pub in pleasant Ouse Valley countryside, good value food *(Colin Skevington)*

☆ **Fen Ditton** [High St; TL4860], *Ancient Shepherds*: Generous helpings of good bar food in comfortable and immaculate old-world lounge with settees and no music or fruit machines; friendly helpful staff, restaurant (not Sun) *(Margaret Young, Colin Yardley, Dr and Mrs M Bailey, Trevor P Scott, Paul Cartledge)*

☆ **Fen Ditton** [Green End], *Plough*: Big busy riverside Brewers Fayre pub with promptly served food inc good specials, fresh appetising puddings and children's menu, friendly staff, well kept Whitbreads beers at reasonable prices; nice walk across meadows from town *(Julian Holland, LYM)*

☆ **Fowlmere** [High St; TL4245], *Swan House*: Friendly and comfortable local with enormous log fire, good interesting reasonably priced bar food, good choice of well kept real ales, attentive landlord, piano *(John Fahy)*

Gamlingay [Church St; TL2452], *Cock*: Very old beamed local, friendly and welcoming, with good helpings of simple home-cooked food inc popular Weds OAP bargains *(Anon)*

Glatton [TL1586], *Addison Arms*: Comfortable local atmosphere, good home cooking, reasonably priced drinks *(Andy Cartridge)*

☆ **Grantchester** [TL4354], *Green Man*: Attractively laid out and welcoming, with individual furnishings, lots of beams, good choice of food, Adnams and Tetleys on handpump, extremely pleasant licensees, no music; nice village, a short stroll from lovely riverside meadows; children welcome *(Paul Cartledge, LYM)*

Grantchester, *Red Lion*: Reliable and

spacious food pub with sheltered terrace and good-sized lawn (animals to entertain the many children); well kept beer, helpful staff, restaurant *(Neil and Angela Huxter, LYM)*; [junction Coton rd with Cambridge—Trumpington rd], *Rupert Brooke*: Friendly and cosy renovated beamed pub with Whitbreads-related ales, wide choice of bar food inc vegetarian, discreet piped music *(R I and E B Page, John Fahy)*

☆ **Great Chishill** [TL4239], *Pheasant*: New licensees doing well in unassuming free house with well kept Adnams, Ruddles and Shepherd Neame Spitfire on handpump, good food inc blackboard specials, charming back garden *(Susan and Nigel Wilson, LYM)*

☆ **Guyhirn** [High Rd (off A47); TF3903], *Oliver Twist*: Particularly good choice of reasonably priced food, lots of real ales and dozens of other beers, good atmosphere, big open fire; very popular as lunchtime business meeting place *(G D Lee, E Robinson)*

Hail Weston [just off A45, handy for A1 St Neots bypass; TL1662], *Royal Oak*: Picturesque thatched and beamed pub in quiet and pretty village nr Grafham Water, with cosy log fire, darts, nice big garden with good play area which children can use even if pub's shut; usual bar food, well kept Charles Wells ales with guests such as Adnams Broadside and Morlands Old Speckled Hen, pleasant service, family room *(Andy and Jill Kassube, George Atkinson, Bob and Maggie Atherton)*

☆ **Hardwick** [signed off A428 (was A45) W of Cambridge; TL1968], *Blue Lion*: Friendly local with good food inc quite a lot of fresh fish, well kept beer, very extensive restaurant area, conservatory, Greene King IPA and Abbot; piped music, unobtrusive ginger tom; pretty roadside front garden *(G Washington, Dave Bundock, BB)*

Harlington, Beds [Sundon Rd, off A5120; a mile from M1 junction 12; TL0330], *Carpenters Arms*: Friendly beamed village pub with good value bar food, generous Sun lunch in upstairs restaurant *(Anon)*

☆ **Harston** [48 Royston Rd (A10, nr M11 junction 11); TL4251], *Queens Head*: Consistently generous decent food esp pies (not Sun evening), well kept Greene King IPA and Abbot, quick friendly service, no smoking area; tables outside *(Jim Farmer, Trevor P Scott)*

Henlow, Beds [High St; TL1738], *Engineers Arms*: Welcoming pub with well kept ales inc interesting guest beers rare in the area, quarterly beer festivals, fine open fire, good weekly live folk, blues and rock, traditional games like shut the box, village pictures by local artists *(Vic Morrow)*

☆ **Hexton**, Beds [Pegsdon; B655 a mile E of Hexton; TL1230], *Live & Let Live*: Very snug and traditional, with two rooms opening off tiled and panelled taproom, good cheap food inc vegetarian, Greene King and other real ales kept well, good service, lovely garden below Chilterns *(Jim Farmer, LYM)*

☆ **Heydon** [off A505 W of M11 junction 10; TL4340], *King William IV*: Extraordinary collection of furniture and bric-a-brac, English and continental, in rambling attractively lit partly 16th-c beamed and timbered rooms; tables in garden, paddock with animals; several real ales, bar food, friendly service, central log fire, piped music; bedrooms *(P Carpenter, LYM)*

☆ **Hildersham** [off A604 N of Linton; TL5448], *Pear Tree*: Busy straightforward village local with odd crazy-paved floor, huge woodburner, generous and genuine home cooking inc some unusual dishes and good vegetarian ones as well as usual cheery pub dishes, children's helpings, home-made bread and ice creams; well kept Greene King IPA and Abbot, decent wines, welcoming staff, traditional games, tables in back garden with aviary; children welcome *(Jenny and Michael Back, Keith and Janet Morris, John L Cox, BB)*

Hilton [Potton Rd (B1040); TL2966], *Prince of Wales*: Friendly village local with particularly well kept real ales, decent good value food *(John C Baker)*

☆ **Histon** [High St; TL4363], *Red Lion*: Very jolly new landlord in friendly local with well kept ales such as Benskins Best, Greene King, Marstons Pedigree and Morlands Old Speckled Hen *(Keith Stevens, Wayne Brindle, Paul Cartledge)*

Holme [Station Rd; TL1987], *Admiral Wells*: Recently re-opened after good refurbishment, with well kept ales (up to seven at weekends, esp good Oakham brews), good interesting food such as smoked eel salad and balti dishes *(John C Baker)*

☆ **Huntingdon** [TL2371], *Old Bridge*: Civilised hotel by River Great Ouse, with emphasis on wide choice of good imaginative food inc fine cold table; drinkers just as welcome in charming plush lounge, with excellent choice of good wine by the glass, fine coffee, afternoon teas, good waitress service; monthly jazz nights; attractive gardens with terraces and landing stage; bedrooms excellent, if expensive; in same ownership as Pheasant at Keyston and Three Horseshoes at Madingley (see main entries) *(Julian Holland, E Robinson, John Fahy)*

☆ **Ireland**, Beds [off A600 Shefford—Bedford – OS Sheet 153 map ref 135414; TL1341], *Black Horse*: Welcoming staff and good value food (not Sun evening) in pleasant isolated pub's extensive dining area with brick pillars, beamery and log-effect gas fire; Bass and Stones real ale, good coffee, tables in garden; has been closed Mon *(George Atkinson, Rita Horridge, Richard Holloway, S Eldridge)*

☆ **Kennett** [Bury Rd; TL7066], *Bell*: Delightful old heavy-beamed and timbered inn, neatly and plushly refurbished, with good generous popular food inc some creative dishes, well kept ales such as Greene King, one of the nationals, Nethergate or Shepherd Neame; bedrooms *(Frank W Gadbois, John C Baker, George Atkinson, LYM)*

☆ **Kimbolton** [20 High St; TL0968], *New Sun*:

Good food in pleasant rather bistroish atmosphere, good range of well kept real ales such as Hook Norton *(Prof J V Wood, Stephen Brown)*

☆ **Linslade**, Beds [SP9225], *Globe*: Popular canalside pub with big eating area, extensive range of well presented promptly served food, good choice of beers such as Fullers London Pride, Ridgeway and Wadworths 6X; pleasant walks nearby *(Bill Sykes and others)*

Linton [High St; TL5646], *Crown*: Good food in well run village pub *(Andrew Marshall)*

Littleport [Sandhill Rd; TL5686], *Black Horse*: Friendly new landlady, Hook Norton Old Hookey, Websters, food in bar lounge and restaurant; attractive setting, tables out by river *(Jenny and Michael Back)*; [Station Rd], *George & Dragon*: Friendly new landlord, well kept Badgers, John Smiths and a guest beer, farm cider; open all day *(K Kennedy)*

Luton, Beds [TL0921], *Leaside*: Small Victorian hotel with good choice of particularly good value food in small bar; bedrooms *(V Green)*; [Windmill Rd], *Windmill*: Recently renovated corner pub with Whitbreads ales, good range of cheap standard food inc nice sandwiches, prompt pleasant service *(Ian Phillips)*

March [High St; TL4693], *King William IV*: Welcoming licensees, good range of reasonably priced food, small dining room, Courage beers *(E Robinson)*; [Wisbech Rd], *Men of March*: Warm welcome, good food inc fantastic stilton and cauliflower soup with real French bread, good value wine by the glass *(Moira and John Cole)*

☆ **Marholm** [TF1402], *Fitzwilliam Arms*: Cheerful thatched stone-built inn with attractively refurbished and comfortable rambling three-room bar, good value food, efficient service, well kept Tetleys-related real ales; good big garden *(David and Michelle Hedges)*

Maulden, Beds [TL0538], *White Hart*: Pleasant character thatched low-beamed pub, sympathetically enlarged, with big fireplace dividing bar, lots of tables in separate eating area, good choice of freshly cooked bar food, pleasant efficient service, Whitbreads-related and other beers such as Morlands and Theakstons *(C H and P Stride, Phil and Heidi Cook)*

Milton Bryan, Beds [off B528 S of Woburn; SP9730], *Red Lion*: Welcoming staff and jovial landlord, good range of food and drinks, lovely setting and appearance, happy hour 6-7 *(Steve and Stella Swepston)*

Milton Ernest, Beds [TL0156], *Queens Arms*: Charles Wells pub, rather modernised for some tastes, but well worth knowing as good value B&B stop *(Lady Emma Chanter)*

☆ **Needingworth** [Overcote Lane; pub signposted from A1123; TL3472], *Pike & Eel*: Marvellous peaceful riverside location, with spacious lawns and marina; two separate eating areas, one a carvery, in extensively glass-walled block overlooking water, boats and swans; easy chairs and big open fire in room off separate main plush bar, well kept Adnams, Bass, and Greene King Abbot, friendly and helpful staff, provision for children; clean simple bedrooms, good breakfasts *(Julian Holland, Brian and Jill Bond, LYM)*

Odell, Beds [Little Odell; SP9657], *Mad Dog*: Cosy old beamed and thatched pub with open fire in inglenook, quiet piped music and pleasant garden, handy for Harrold-Odell Country Park; has been very popular for wide choice of good value food and well kept Greene King ales, but long-serving licensees have moved to the Kings Arms in Sandy *(Reports on new regime please)*

☆ **Old Warden**, Beds [TL1343], *Hare & Hounds*: Open fire in beamed character bar, wide choice of generous food, well kept Charles Wells beers, comfortable lounge and dining room – very much geared up for eating; sloping back garden with scramble net and tyre swings; beautiful village, handy for Shuttleworth collection *(Bob Hurling, Rosalind Hodges, Giles Quick, Sue Holland, Dave Webster, Carl Lukens)*

Pampisford [TL4948], *Chequers*: Picturesque pub with lovely window boxes and hanging baskets, pleasant atmosphere despite rather obtrusive games machine, Greene King ales, good standard food *(Keith and Janet Morris)*

Parson Drove [B1166/B1187 W of Wisbech; TF3708], *Swan*: Comfortable and friendly old fenland pub with good choice of good value bar food from sandwiches up inc children's dishes, well kept Elgoods Cambridge and Eldridge Pope Royal Oak on handpump, pictures, brasses, darts and bar billiards in public bar, plusher carpeted lounge, quiet piped music, restaurant; no dogs *(CMW, JJW)*

Peakirk [12 St Pegas Rd; TF1606], *Ruddy Duck*: Very popular traditional village pub, spotless and well cared for, with good range of generous food inc fresh fish and vegetarian; handy for Wildfowl Trust *(P A Wilson)*

☆ **Peterborough** [17 North St; TL1999], *Bogarts*: At least six well kept ales such as Adnams and Bass and good simple food in basic pub handy for the Westgate shopping centre; open all day *(Tony Gayfer, Stuart Earle, Robert Masters)*

☆ **Peterborough** [465 Oundle Rd – off A605 in Woodston], *Botolph Arms*: Attractive ivy-covered flagstone-floored Sam Smiths pub, popular with business people at lunchtime; good facilities for disabled visitors, safe play area *(David and Michelle Hedges)*

Peterborough [Westgate], *Bull*: Rambling atmospheric hotel with numerous bar rooms, nooks and crannies with comfortable arm chairs, low tables and liveried staff; Adnams, decent house wine, limited bar menu inc good sandwiches *(J M Wooll)*; [Thorpewood], *Greenkeeper*: Pleasant modern pub with outside seating and conservatory facing municipal golf course (pub seems to act as club house); cheap, efficiently served menu and Greene King Abbot *(John Wooll)*; [Oundle Rd], *Johnny Byrnes*: Friendly local transformed by new landlord, with well kept Courage-related ales and very quick service in big public bar; games room *(Stuart Earle)*

☆ **Radwell**, Beds [TL0057], *Swan*: Roomy and attractive beamed and thatched pub, two rooms joined by narrow passage, woodburner, lots of prints, unobtrusive piped music, wide choice of good food, Charles Wells Eagle on handpump, decent coffee, hospitable landlord, popular evening restaurant; pleasant garden, small quiet village *(George Atkinson, Maysie Thompson)*

Renhold, Beds [42 Top End; off A428 NE of Bedford; TL0952], *Three Horseshoes*: Friendly and quite lively village local with real fire, fresh flowers and sporting pictures, food inc good value steaks, Sun bar nibbles, well kept Greene King ales, two friendly dogs; satellite TV and fruit machine in public bar, play area in garden; children welcome *(JJW, CMW)*

☆ **Ridgmont**, Beds [handy for M1, junction 13; SP9736], *Rose & Crown*: Consistently good sensible pub food, warm welcome, choice of well kept real ales, good coffee, interesting collection of Rupert Annual covers in well laid out lounge; low-ceilinged traditional public bar with open fire, games inc darts and pool; piped music, stables restaurant (not Mon or Tues evenings); long and attractive suntrap sheltered back garden; children allowed in bar eating area; easy parking, good wheelchair access *(A T Langton, L M Miall, LYM)*

☆ **Sandy**, Beds [Old London Rd; TL1649], *Kings Arms*: Wide choice of well served, plentiful and reasonably priced food, very pleasant atmosphere, competent friendly staff and Greene King ales in two-bar pub with separate restaurant; bedrooms in well built chalets *(Tom Saul)*

☆ *nr* **Sandy** [Deepdale; B1042 towards Potton and Cambridge; TL2049], *Locomotive*: Reliable pub nr RSPB HQ, packed with railway memorabilia; reasonably priced food nicely prepared and presented, friendly staff, well kept Charles Wells Eagle and Bombardier, no smoking area, attractive and sizeable garden with views; piped radio, good service; can be busy weekends; children allowed in eating area *(Dono and Carol Leaman, Ian Phillips, LYM)*

☆ **Sawston** [High St (Cambridge Rd); TL4849], *Greyhound*: Cosy and comfortable L-shaped bar, games room down steps, light and airy high glass-roofed dining room overlooking good big garden, pleasant and obliging staff, good choice of generous prompt food inc vegetarian, open fire, Whitbreads-related real ales, good facilities for children; resident Pyrenean mountain dog *(M and J Back, Martin and Pauline Richardson)*

Sharnbrook, Beds [SP9959], *Swan With Two Nicks*: Well kept Charles Wells beers and guests such as Adnams Broadside and Morlands Old Speckled Hen, adventurous food *(John C Baker, John Fahy)*

☆ **Sharpenhoe**, Beds [Harlington Rd; TL0630], *Lynmore*: Huge helpings of reasonably priced food inc children's dishes in spacious and friendly beamy family lounge and back dining area (good views), well kept ales, good garden for children, big Wendy house; popular with walkers *(the Sandy family)*

☆ **Shefford**, Beds [2 North Bridge St, Clifton Rd; TL1438], *White Hart*: Genuine-feeling old coaching inn, friendly rather than smart, with well kept local Banks & Taylors ales, decent food inc some interesting dishes, friendly landlady, locals and boxer dogs, pleasant lounge, dining room, basic public bar; four bedrooms *(John C Baker, Roz and Bob Hurling, John and Shirley Berrett, Buck and Gillian Shinkman, BB)*

☆ **Shepreth** [12 High St; just off A10 S of Cambridge; TL3947], *Plough*: Changing well kept ales such as Adnams, Boddingtons, Tetleys and Wadworths 6X and popular well presented home-cooked food from sandwiches up in very neatly kept bright and airy local; modern furnishings, bow-tied staff, decent wines, side dining room, piped music; well tended back garden with fairy-lit arbour and pond, summer barbecues and play area *(Trevor Scott, Susan and Nigel Wilson, BB)*

☆ **Silsoe**, Beds [TL0835], *George*: Large pleasant open-plan hotel bar with public end, good bar meals (high chairs provided), restaurant, well kept Greene King IPA and Abbot, big garden with play equipment and pets' corner; organist Sat evening; bedrooms *(Phil and Heidi Cook)*

Souldrop, Beds [off A6 Rushden—Bedford; SP9861], *Bedford Arms*: Clean and spacious, with good choice of good value food in bar with dining section and other areas off; Greene King ales, friendly staff, mainly tiled floor, big stone fireplace, brasses, settles and prints; piped music *(George Atkinson)*

☆ **Southill**, Beds [off B658 SW of Biggleswade; TL1542], *White Horse*: Good atmosphere in well decorated and comfortable lounge, dining room with spotlit well, small public bar with prints, harness and big woodburner; good value food (not Sun evening, and polystyrene plates for outside) inc wide choice of sandwiches and snacks, Whitbreads-related real ales; children in eating areas; delightful big garden with children's rides on diesel-engine miniature train, separate sheltered lawn with bird feeders, garden shop and good play area *(the Sandy family, Joyce and Stephen Stackhouse, LYM)*

St Ives [Merryland; TL3171], *Floods*: Character beamed pub in attractive riverside town, interesting starters, good piping hot main dishes and delicious very sweet puddings *(P and D Carpenter)*; [main st], *Royal Oak*: Warm friendly atmosphere, low beams and open fires, well kept ales, reasonably priced generous food *(Michael J Becker)*

Stow Cum Quy [Newmarket Rd (old A45); TL5260], *Prince Albert*: Genuine cheerful pub notable for at least five lovingly kept changing ales; basic food *(John C Baker, Jamie Henderson)*; [from B1102 follow Anglesey Abbey sign)], *White Swan*: Traditional village pub, casual and cosy; good food at average prices, cooked to order so small delay when busy, inc lots of filled hot baguettes, vegetarian dishes *(C G and B Mason)*

☆ **Stretham** [High St (off A10); TL5374], *Red Lion*: Tastefully done-up village pub with wide choice of good generous food inc some unusual dishes, vegetarian and children's food and Sun lunch, solid pine furniture and old village photographs in lounge, marble-topped tables in pleasant no smoking dining conservatory, five well kept real ales such as Greene King and Nethergate, separate attractive upstairs games room, friendly attentive service; children welcome, picnic-table sets in garden *(CMW, JJW, John C Baker, JM, PM)*

☆ **Studham**, Beds [TL0215], *Red Lion*: Friendly open-plan pub in attractive setting below grassy common, well kept Adnams, Bass, Boddingtons and Ruddles and good generous straightforward food (not Sun); bright and cheerful modernish decor, chatty helpful staff; tables outside, handy for Whipsnade Zoo *(George Atkinson, Mr and Mrs McDougal, LYM)*

Studham [Dunstable Rd], *Bell*: Friendly and welcoming, with good home-made food, four Tetleys-related ales on handpump *(Phil and Heidi Cook)*

☆ **Sutton**, Beds [village signed off B1040 Biggleswade—Potton; TL2247], *John o' Gaunt*: Pretty pink pub nr fine 14th-c packhorse bridge – you have to go through a shallow ford; relaxing cottagey low-beamed lounge bar with easy chairs and low settles around copper-topped tables, newspapers, open fire, simple bar food, well kept Greene King IPA; traditional public bar with hood skittles *(Joyce and Stephen Stackhouse, LYM)*

Sutton [the one in Cambs W of Ely; TL4478], *Chequers*: Good atmosphere in simple but bright and attractive bar with good genuine home cooking inc tempting puddings, well kept Greene King and other ales; forthcoming licensees, hanging baskets of silk flowers for sale *(Chris and Andy Crow, Julian Holland)*

☆ **Swaffham Prior** [B1102 NE of Cambridge; TL5764], *Red Lion*: Welcoming and attractive local in pleasant village, well kept Greene King ales, wide range of food from sandwiches and baked potatoes to steaks, comfortable dining area divided into several separate spaces, quick cheerful service; unusually plush gents' *(J N Child, Alan Kilpatrick)*

☆ **Swavesey** [High St/Market Pl; signed off A14 (ex A604) NW of Cambridge; TL3668], *White Horse*: Welcoming village local with attractive traditional furnishings in public bar, more straightforward spacious lounge and no smoking eating room; good fresh home-cooked food from sandwiches to steaks inc vegetarian dishes and notable curries (not Sun evening or Mon lunch), three Whitbreads-related ales, enterprising wines and spirits, winter Gluhwein, friendly service, children allowed; maybe discreet piped music *(Peter Carpenter, M Thomas, BB)*

Tebworth, Beds [The Lane; SP9926], *Queens Head*: Straightforward well priced food (not Sun) inc perfect chips in light and airy small lounge bar with old plush banquettes, pot plants, open fire; well kept Charles Wells Eagle on handpump and a guest such as Adnams Broadside tapped from the cask; darts, fruit machine and fire in separate bar, friendly welcome, quiet piped music; well spaced picnic tables and swing in raised tree-sheltered garden *(CMW, JJW, Michael and Alison Sandy)*

☆ **The Turves** [W of March; TL3396], *Three Horseshoes*: Real friendly Fenland local, extended with family conservatory, attracting great variety of customers; well kept ales, usually one interesting guest and two nationals, good original food esp fish *(John C Baker, Richard Balls, Stuart Earle)*

☆ **Thorney** [A47/B1040; TF2804], *Rose & Crown*: Wide range of well presented reasonably priced plentiful food, good happy staff, pleasant surroundings; children welcome *(J M and C Day, Eustace A Turner)*

Toddington, Beds [19 Church Sq; handy for M1 junction 12; TL0028], *Sow & Pigs*: Welcoming pub with banquettes, pews and bare boards, amusing pig motifs, well kept Greene King ales, good coffee, wide choice of food (back Victorian-style dining room can be booked for parties), two real fires, friendly landlord; picnic-table sets in small garden *(JJW, CMW)*

☆ **Turvey**, Beds [off A428 NW of Bedford, by church; SP9452], *Three Cranes*: Clean and spacious two-level bar with good range of generous bar food from good sandwiches and ploughman's to big mixed grills, rather formal seating, well kept ales such as Hook Norton Best, Fullers London Pride, decent wines, whiskies and coffee, efficient pleasant staff, unobtrusive piped music; distinctive Victorian portico with jettied upper storey; restaurant, garden with climbing frame; children welcome; bedrooms *(Stephen and Julie Brown, Mary and David Webb, Maysie Thompson, Ian Phillips, Andy and Jill Kassube, BB)*

☆ **Turvey** [Bridge St, at W end of village], *Three Fyshes*: Unfussy and pubby, with lots of character – flagstones, early 17th-c beams, inglenook fires, welcoming staff; good value food from sandwiches and big crusty rolls to substantial hot dishes inc vegetarian, newspapers, traditional games, no music (but maybe TV); beers brewed on the premises, farm ciders; relaxed family atmosphere in garden with access to Great Ouse, summer barbecues, dogs, cats and rabbits; open all day Sat; children and dogs welcome, can get crowded *(Stephen, Julie and Hayley Brown, LYM)*

☆ **Upware** [off A1123 W of Soham; TL5370], *Five Miles from Anywhere, No Hurry*: Friendly service and decent food in aptly named spacious modern free house, fine riverside site *(P and D Carpenter, LYM)*

Waresley [Eltisley Rd; TL2454], *Duncombe Arms*: Friendly well kept pub with wide choice of food in comfortable restaurant, good generous moderately priced bar food inc sandwiches and interesting specials *(Mr and Mrs C A Quick)*

Waterbeach [A10; TL4965], *Slap Up*: Wide choice of good generous food inc carvery and Sun lunch, cold cabinet packed with home-made puddings *(John Whittaker, Andrew Latchem, Helen Reed)*

☆ **Whipsnade**, Beds [B4540 E; TL0117], *Old Hunters Lodge*: Handy for zoo, with children's helpings of some things on the extensive menu – good value uncomplicated food from sandwiches up, esp fish; pleasant snug area on right, plusher modernised main lounge, sofa by roaring fire, good friendly service, well kept Greene King, oil paintings and castle prints, subdued piped music; spacious old-world restaurant *(Brian and Anna Marsden, Nigel Norman, David and Ruth Shillitoe)*

☆ **Whittlesey** [North Side; B1040 towards Thorney; TL2799], *Dog in a Doublet*: Comfortable, clean and quiet riverside pub with bric-a-brac, old prints, well spaced comfortably solid seating; open fire, friendly attentive service, reasonably priced bar food, well kept beer inc Adnams and Greene King, decent wines; handy for Hereward Way walks, restaurant has been open all day Sun *(Stuart Earle)*

☆ **Whittlesford** [off B1379 S of Cambridge; handy for M10 junction 10, via A505; TL4748], *Tickell Arms*: Great atmosphere, ornate heavy furnishings, dim lighting, lovely log fires, attractive flower-filled conservatory, beautiful formal garden, wide range of imaginative bar food, friendly service, well reproduced classical music; closed Mon (exc bank hols); the wines often a better bet than the beers; no credit cards *(Bob and Maggie Atherton, Frank W Gadbois, P I Burton, John Fahy, LYM)*

☆ **Wisbech** [North Brink; TF4609], *Red Lion*: Friendly, comfortable and civilised long front bar in lovely Georgian terrace on River Nene, nr centre and NT Peckover House; very popular lunchtime for good range of good value home-cooked food inc vegetarian and fish, Fri bargain salad bar, well kept local Elgoods beer *(J M Wooll, M J Morgan)*

☆ **Wisbech** [53 North Brink], *Rose*: Cosy, friendly and popular little local in same splendid riverside spot, notable for fascinating choice of changing well kept real ales from small often Northern breweries; good value filled french bread, quick service *(L Priest, PGP, R Martin, Julian Holland)*

Wisbech [West St], *Harlequin*: Pub/restaurant with a difference, friendly licensees, good value food; you can hear the music only in the lavatories *(S Horsley)*

☆ **Woburn**, Beds [SP9433], *Bell*: Pleasant hotel with reliably good food in small dining area and evening restaurant, well kept Greene King Abbot, friendly service, comfortable seating, lots of Spy cartoons, piped music, tables outside; bedrooms *(George Atkinson, Ted Corrin)*

☆ **Woburn** [1 Bedford St], *Black Horse*: Quick obliging service in spacious open-plan food pub with wide choice from sandwiches and baked potatoes to moderately priced steaks cut to order and barbecued in the bar, also children's and vegetarian dishes and special orders; well kept real ales inc Nethergate on handpump; open all day summer Sat and bank hols, summer barbecues in pleasant sheltered garden; children in eating areas *(Ron and Sheila Corbett, Mrs H Ellis, Miss I W Stillman, Andrew Jeeves, Carole Smart, Keith Algar, LYM; more reports on new licensees please)*

Post Office address codings confusingly give the impression that some pubs are in Cambridgeshire, when they're really in the Leicestershire or Midlands groups of counties (which is where we list them).

Cheshire

New entries here this year are the beautifully remodelled Grosvenor Arms at Aldford (excellent wines and a thriving atmosphere), the Bhurtpore at Aston (particularly good beers), the Cheshire Hunt at Pott Shrigley (doing very well under licensees who previously scored a hit at the Stanley Arms up at Bottom of the Oven) and the Swettenham Arms at Swettenham (a popular dining pub); all have good food. Besides new licensees and refurbishment at the Stanley Arms itself, other changes to note here include new licensees for the Spinner & Bergamot at Comberbach, the Fishpool at Delamere, Bells of Peover at Lower Peover and the Bird in Hand in Mobberley; fortunately no drastic developments. It was in this last pub, tied to Sam Smiths, that we found the cheapest beer in the county; the Jolly Thresher at Broomedge (tied to Hydes, another smallish brewer) was also much cheaper than the area average, as was the Rising Sun at Tarporley. This was tied to the regional brewer Robinsons, whose prices were otherwise fairly close to the area norm – that's to say, considerably cheaper than the national average. Another major local presence is Greenalls, who no longer brew but get their beers from Carlsberg-Tetleys; we found beers in their pubs generally fractionally more expensive than the low local average. Food in the area also tends to be good value, with big helpings and quite a bit of individuality. For this we'd particularly pick out the Cholmondeley Arms at Bickley Moss (incomparable, and once again our Cheshire Dining Pub of the Year), the Jolly Thresher at Broomedge, Bells of Peover at Lower Peover, the Sutton Hall Hotel outside Macclesfield, the Swan at Marbury, the Cheshire Hunt at Pott Shrigley, and the Dusty Miller at Wrenbury. In the Lucky Dip section at the end of the chapter, currently notable pubs include the Maypole at Acton Bridge, White Lion at Alvanley, Swan with Two Nicks at Little Bollington, Chetwode Arms at Lower Whitley, Olde Park Gate and Whipping Stocks at Over Peover, Highwayman at Rainow, Legs of Man at Smallwood and the Ferry outside Warrington; we have inspected all these, so can firmly vouch for them. It's worth noting that several of these are Greenalls dining pubs – a growing strength in the area. Finally, note that Chester itself now has a fine choice of interesting pubs.

ALDFORD SJ4159 Map 7

Grosvenor Arms

B5130 S of Chester

There's quite a cosmopolitan feel in this attractively and individually restyled substantial Victorian inn, recently reopened as part of a succesful small family chain. They've cleverly combined traditional decor with a spacious open-plan layout. Buzzing with conversation and quiet piped pop music, the best room is probably the huge panelled library with floor-to-ceiling book shelves on one wall, long wooden floor boards and lots of well spaced substantial tables. Several other quieter rooms are well furnished with good individual pieces including a very comfortable parliamentary type leather settle. Throughout there are plenty of interesting pictures, and the lighting's exemplary. Densely hung with huge low hanging baskets, the terracotta-floored airy conservatory has chunky pale wood garden furniture and opens on to a large elegant suntrap terrace and neat lawn with well spaced picnic sets, young trees and a tractor; the summer barbecues are popular. The good home-made bar food from a bistro-style menu and the blackboard (they could do with a duplicate in such a big pub) includes lunchtime and evening starters like cream of tomato and fresh basil soup (£2.25), thinly sliced chicken breast with stilton salad (£4.75), wild Scotch smoked salmon (£4.95) or ploughman's (£3.95), lunchtime sandwiches (from £2.50) and open sandwiches (from £4.65), macaroni cheese or toad in the hole (£3.95), broccoli and mushroom quiche (£4.95) and rack of ribs (£5.95) and more expensive but generous evening main courses like baked aubergine, potatoes, mushrooms and tomatoes with a yellow pepper and tarragon sauce (£6.45), a pair of fresh trout (£6.95), escalope of turkey with sun-dried tomato and basil sauce (£7.95), braised pheasant (£8.45) and fresh tuna (£8.95). Well kept Boddingtons, Buckleys, Flowers, Moles and Smiles on handpump from the good solid bar counter, a remarkable collection of largely New World wines by the glass, several dozen malt whiskies; two log fires, bar billiards, cribbage, dominoes, chess, Scrabble, Trivial Pursuit. They take some bookings; otherwise best to get there early for a table. *(Recommended by W C M Jones, Paul Craddock, Dr P D Putwain, Mr and Mrs J Williams, Chris Walling, Mr and Mrs W J A Timpson and others)*

Free house ~ Licensees Gary Kidd and Jeremy Brunning ~ Real ale ~ Meals and snacks (till 10pm; not Dec 25) ~ (01244) 620228 ~ Children welcome lunchtime ~ Open 11.30-2.30, 5-11 (Sat 11-11)

ASTON SJ6147 Map 7

Bhurtpore

Off A530 SW of Nantwich; in village follow Wrenbury signpost

It's the interesting well kept beers which stand out here: up to nine changing ones kept in top condition on handpump, most from little-known breweries – on our visit Beartown, Coach House Gunpowder Mild, Hanbys Drawwell, Nethergate IPA, Slaters Premium (from the St George at Eccleshall – see Derbys Lucky Dip), Theakstons Old Peculier, Trough Wild Boar, Woods 15th Aniversary and Worth Old Toss. They have dozens of good bottled beers, too, including Belgian fruit beers, keep a changing farm cider, and try to encourage people to try malt whiskies they've not had before. It can get packed at weekends, but earlyish on a weekday evening or at lunchtime the atmosphere in the carpeted lounge bar is cosy and civilised, and there are some interesting things to look at: rather camped-up Raj memorabilia, good local period photographs, some attractive furniture. Bar food is a strength, including on our visit mushroom and walnut soup, tiger prawns in filo pastry with a lime mayonnaise dip (£3.25), half a dozen curries such as curried kidneys or chicken dansak (£5.25), chicken and ham pancakes or sweet and sour pork (£5.45), loin of lamb (£7.50) and good puddings. Tables in the comfortable public bar are reserved for people not eating; darts, fruit machine, pool, TV; piped country music on our visit (with blues in the restaurant); welcoming service; tables in garden. *(Recommended by Jill and Peter Bickley, Richard Lewis, Sue Holland, Dave Webster)*

Free house ~ Licensee Simon George ~ Real ale ~ Meals and snacks ~ Restaurant ~ (01270) 780917 ~ Open 12-2.30, 6.30-11

The letters and figures after the name of each town are its Ordnance Survey map reference. *How to use the Guide* at the beginning of the book explains how it helps you find a pub, in road atlases or large-scale maps as well as in our own maps.

BARBRIDGE SJ6156 Map 7

Barbridge Inn

Village signposted just off A51 N of Nantwich; OS Sheet 118 map reference 616566

Families are made welcome at this popular canalside pub with a colouring page on the children's menu (crayons from the bar), a play house, climber, swings and slide in the waterside garden, and baby-changing facilities. It's a very friendly and particularly well run place, comfortably modernised and open-plan, and serving a wide choice of good bar food: sandwiches (from £1.75; hot french bread from £2.40), filled baked potatoes (from £1.85), ploughman's (from £3.65), steak and kidney pie (£3.95), gammon and egg (£4.55), spinach and ricotta tortellini (£4.85), seafood crèpes (£4.95), farmhouse grill (£7.35), daily specials such as a 1lb lamb joint marinated in mint sauce (£5.95) or halibut steak with prawns and mushrooms (£6.76), puddings (from £1.85), and roast Sunday lunch (£4.95); the balustraded restaurant area (part of which is no smoking), up steps, overlooks the canal. Well kept Boddingtons and Cains and weekend guest beers on handpump; darts, dominoes, cribbage, fruit machine, video game, and quiet piped music. There's a side conservatory and picnic tables (some under cover) from which you can watch the narrow-boats. Good disabled facilities. *(Recommended by Richard Lewis, Mike and Wendy Proctor, Brian and Anna Marsden, Patrick and Mary McDermott)*

Boddingtons (Whitbreads) ~ Manager W H Eyre ~ Real ale ~ Meals and snacks (all day Sun) ~ (01270) 528443 ~ Children welcome ~ Jazz Thurs evenings ~ Open 11.30-11; 11.30-3, 5.30-11 in winter

BARTHOMLEY SJ7752 Map 7

White Lion ★ £

A mile from M6 junction 16; take Alsager rd and is signposted at roundabout

As we went to press, some changes were afoot at this very attractive black and white timbered pub. The bedrooms (which should be operating again by the time this book is published) were closed while the central heating was overhauled, an outside drinking area at the back of the building was being constructed, and the third bar room was being refitted and a woodburning stove added. But apart from that, it remains very much as it always has been – an unspoilt and friendly place with a good mix of people and no noisy games machines or music. The simply furnished main room has attractively moulded black panelling, heavy oak beams dating back to 1614 (one big enough to house quite a collection of plates), a lovely open fire, Cheshire watercolours and prints on the walls, and latticed windows. Up some steps, a second room has another open fire, more oak panelling, a high-backed winged settle, a paraffin lamp hinged to the wall, and sensibly placed darts, shove-ha'penny, cribbage and dominoes. Very cheap lunchtime bar food includes soup (£1), filled french sticks (£1.30), hot beef sandwiches (£1.50), popular pies like steak and kidney, and cheese and onion oatcake or cornish pasties (£1.30), and particularly good home-made hotpot (£2); on Saturday and Sunday pies and rolls only are available. Very well kept Burtonwood Bitter, Forshaws, Dark Mild and Top Hat on handpump; the cats have their admirers too. It can get very busy at weekends. The early 15th-c red sandstone church of St Bertiline across the road is worth a visit. *(Recommended by David and Shelia, Paul and Gail Betteley, Alastair Campbell, Sue Holland, Dave Webster, Alan and Paula McCully, Barbara Houghton, Nigel Woolliscroft, DAV, D Cox, Dick Brown, John Fazakerley, Barbara Hatfield, Dave Irving, P Bromley, Chris Cook)*

Burtonwood ~ Tenant Terence Cartwright ~ Real ale ~ Lunchtime meals and snacks ~ (01270) 882242 ~ Children welcome except in main bar – must be gone by 9.15pm ~ Spontaneous folk music first Sun lunchtime of month ~ Open 11.30-11; closed Thurs lunchtime ~ Bedrooms: £20S/£35S

We say if we or readers have seen dogs or cats in a pub.

BICKLEY MOSS SJ5549 Map 7

Cholmondeley Arms ★

Cholmondeley; A49 5½ miles N of Whitchurch; the owners would like us to list them under Cholmondeley Village, but as this is rarely located on maps we have mentioned the nearest village which appears more often

Cheshire Dining Pub of the Year

There's no denying that this light and airy converted Victorian schoolhouse puts most emphasis on its excellent food – but they do keep good Boddingtons, Flowers IPA and Original and a weekly changing guest beer such as Weetwood Old Dog on handpump, and were more than happy to welcome several of our readers (wet and bedraggled after a cycle ride) with hot toddies and a seat by the fire. The cross-shaped and high-ceilinged bar has a range of seating from cane and bentwood to pews and carved oak, masses of Victorian pictures (especially portraits and military subjects), patterned paper on the shutters to match the curtains, and a great stag's head over one of the side arches; some of the old school desks are above the bar on a gantry. The daily specials are particularly enjoyable and might include very good stilton or mushroom soup, salmon tartare with a watercress sauce (£3.95), home potted shrimps (£4.25), tasty gruyère and prawn parcels, chicken and coriander curry (£6.95), excellent fishcakes with hollandaise sauce, boiled bacon in parlsey and cider sauce with pease pudding (£7.25), rack of lamb with mint hollandaise (£7.75), quail baked with honey, garlic and soy (£7.95), and puddings such as raspberry trifle, Austrian sherry chocolate cake or lovely bakewell tart; children's dishes. An old blackboard lists ten or so interesting and often uncommon wines by the glass; big (4 cup) pot of cafetiere coffee, teas, and hot chocolate; very friendly, efficient staff. There are seats out on a sizeable lawn, and Cholmondeley Castle and gardens are close by. *(Recommended by Nigel Woolliscroft, R N Hutton, Roger and Christine Mash, Andrew Shore, Paul and Maggie Baker, W C M Jones, Rita and Keith Pollard, Chris Walling, Mike and Wendy Proctor, Basil Minson, D Hanley, Mrs J Oakes, Mrs P Abell, Thorstein Moen, Julie Peters, Barry Hankey, R Ward, Julian Jewitt, Martin Aust, A R and B E Wayer, George Jonas, Sue Holland, Dave Webster, David Shillitoe, Mr and Mrs W J A Timpson, John and Christine Simpson, M G Hart, J and P Maloney, Mr and Mrs J Furber, G E Stait, Gill and Mike Cross, Andrew Stephenson, Maysie Thompson, L W Baal)*

Free house ~ Licensees Guy and Carolyn Ross-Lowe ~ Real ale ~ Meals and snacks (till 10pm) ~ (01829) 720300 ~ Children in eating area of bar till 8pm ~ Open 12-3, 6.30-11 ~ Bedrooms: £36.50S/£50S

BOTTOM OF THE OVEN SJ9872 Map 7

Stanley Arms

From A537 Buxton—Macclesfield heading towards Macclesfield, take first left turn (not signposted) after Cat & Fiddle; OS Sheet 118 map reference 980723

New licensees have taken over this isolated moorland pub and the three cosy rooms have been refurbished – though keeping to traditional styles. Two of the rooms have lots of shiny black lacquered woodwork and plush wall settles and stools around low dimpled copper tables on the new carpet; the third is laid out as a dining-room; open winter fires. Bar food now includes sandwiches, cumberland sausage or cod and chips (£5.50), gammon and egg (£6.35), and daily specials. Well kept Marstons Burton and Pedigree on handpump; dominoes, cribbage and piped music. There are picnic tables on the grass behind. *(Recommended by Jack Morley, F C Johnston, Yolanda Henry, Simon Barber, Wayne Brindle, Richard Lewis; more reports on the new regime please)*

Marstons ~ Tenant Valerie Rowland ~ Real ale ~ Meals and snacks (till 10pm) ~ Restaurant ~ (01260) 252414 ~ Children in restaurant ~ Open 11.30-3(3.30 Sat), 6-11; may close winter Mons if weather very bad

BRERETON GREEN SJ7864 Map 7

Bears Head

1¾ miles from M6, junction 17; fork left from Congleton road almost immediately, then left on to A50; also from junction 18, via Holmes Chapel

Popular with locals who drop in for a drink and a chat, as well as those wanting to eat, the rambling open-plan rooms of this civilised and quietly friendly timber-framed old pub have a relaxed and old-fashioned atmosphere. There are masses of heavy black beams and timbers, some traditional oak panel-back settles and a corner cupboard full of Venetian glass, and in one room, a section of wall (under glass for protection) has had the plaster removed to show the contruction of timber underneath. There are two serving bars, though only one is normally in use. Popular bar food served by neat waiters in brocaded waistcoats consists of home-made soup (£1.75), sandwiches (from £1.95, good steak and onion £5.95), home-made pâté (£3.25), splendid home-made lasagne (£5.55), hot dishes such as gammon and egg, roast chicken with home-made stuffing or grilled fillet of plaice with banana, lemon and butter sauce (from £6.75) and rump steak (£7.95); also daily specials such as very good moules marinières and haddock (from £6.50); very good chips and home-made puddings from the pudding trolley. Bass, Burtonwood Bitter, Courage Directors and a guest beer on handpump, kept in fine deep cellars, a good range of blend and malt whiskies, fine brandies and liqueurs and decent wines (especially Italian); trivia machine, soothing piped music. Outside a pretty side terrace has white cast-iron tables and chairs under cocktail parasols, big black cast-iron lamp clusters and a central fountain; barbecues are held outside on the terrace in the summer. ***(Recommended by John and Pam Smith, Richard Lewis, P Williams, M W Turner, Douglas and Patricia Gott, C H Stride)***

Free house ~ Licensee Roberto Tarquini ~ Real ale ~ Meals and snacks (till 10pm) ~ Restaurant ~ (01477) 535251 ~ Children welcome ~ Trad folk music every other Weds evening ~ Open 12-3, 6-11 ~ Bedrooms: £35B/£52.50B

BROOMEDGE SJ7085 Map 7

Jolly Thresher

A56 E of Lymm

This enjoyable, friendly 16th-c pub is spaciously open-plan with country chairs and tables on stripped boards, prints of some of Lowry's less well known paintings on the papered walls, fresh flowers, two open fires, and swagged curtains. Good value, popular bar food includes lovely soup (£1.25), lunchtime sandwiches (£2; toasties 25p extra), chilli con carne (£3.95), southern fried chicken (£4.95), evening grills like steaks (from £6.25) or Barnsley chop (£7.95), and daily specials such as very good cod and chips and excellent Cajun chicken; well kept Hydes Bitter and Mild on handpump; darts, dominoes and piped music. There are tables out behind, looking over the pub's neat bowling green to the Bridgewater Canal. ***(Recommended by Geoffrey and Brenda Wilson, Richard Lewis, E A Wright, John Broughton, Andy and Jill Kassube, Judith Mayne)***

Hydes ~ Tenant Peter McGrath ~ Real ale ~ Meals and snacks (not Sun evening or Mon) ~ (01925) 752265 ~ Children in eating area of bar ~ Open 11.30-3(4 Sat), 5.30-11

BURLEYDAM SJ6143 Map 7

Combermere Arms 

A525 Whitchurch—Audlem

As well as their main Octoberfest beer festival with around 30 real ales, this friendly 16th-c pub continues to hold various mini beer festivals throughout the year: Bass, Highgate Dark, Worthington Bitter and guest beers on handpump.

The traditionally furnished bar has horsebrasses and tankards on the beams, fox masks on standing timbers, and an unusal circular oak bar. Bar food, with prices unchanged since last year, includes very good soup (£1.30), sandwiches (from £1.40), burgers (from £1.60), ploughman's (from £2.75), fresh cod (£3.95), steak, kidney and mushroom pie in ale (£4.50), home-made lasagne (£4.60), ricotta cheese and spinach cannelloni (£4.65), Turkish lamb (£5.25), steaks (from £7.95), and daily specials; children's menu, Sunday lunch (£5.65). Darts, shove-ha'penny, dominoes, video game, and piped music. There's a children's adventure play complex (50p). *(Recommended by Richard Lewis, Basil Minson, Paul and Maggie Baker, Paul Boot, Martin Aust, Kate and Robert Hodkinson)*

Free house ~ Licensee Neil Murphy ~ Real ale ~ Meals and snacks (12-2.30, 4.30-9.30; all day Sat and Sun) ~ Restaurant (all day Sun) ~ (01948) 871223 ~ Children welcome ~ Open 11-11

COMBERBACH SJ6477 Map 7

Spinner & Bergamot

Village signposted from A553 and A559 NW of Northwich; pub towards Great Budworth

Taking its name from two 18th-c racehorses, this neatly kept pub has new licensees this year. So far, they have changed very little and the front bar still has Toby jugs hanging from the beams, one or two hunting prints on the cream textured walls, red plush button-back built-in wall banquettes, and a warming log fire. The softly lit back dining room has country-kitchen furniture (some of oak), pretty curtains, and a big brick inglenook with a stripped high mantlebeam; brocaded wall seats in the neat red-tiled public bar. Bar food includes home-made soup (£1.85), sandwiches (from £2; toasties or open sandwiches from £3), filled baked potatoes (from £3.20), cottage pie (£3.85), vegetable lasagne (£4.50), and home-made steak and kidney pie or gammon and egg (£5), with evening extras like potted shrimps (£3.50), jumbo scampi in home-made batter (£6.85), and steaks (from £9); daily specials like chicken curry (£6) or fresh grilled halibut with lemon and lime sauce (£7.50), and Sunday roasts. Well kept Greenalls Bitter, Original and Mild on handpump; darts, dominoes, and piped music, and a bowling green outside at the back – bowls can be hired. There are wooden picnic tables on the sloping lawn and lots of flowering tubs and hanging baskets. *(Recommended by Olive and Ray Hebsen, Chris Walling, Simon Barber, Mr and Mrs R Hebson, Roger and Christine Mash, John Broughton, Mr and Mrs C J Frodsham; more reports on the new regime please)*

Greenalls (Allied) ~ Tenants Nigel and Carol Ross ~ Real ale ~ Meals and snacks ~ Restaurant ~ (01606) 891307 ~ Open 11.30-3, 5.30-11; closed evening 25 Dec

COTEBROOK SJ5765 Map 7

Alvanley Arms ⇦

Forest Rd; Junction A49/B5152, N of Tarporley

The bars in this handsome creeper-covered Georgian inn have been refurbished and re-carpeted this year. The main bar has a big open fire, neat high beams, a few hunting and sporting prints, some brasses, and fairly close-set tables (dining-height by the plush wall banquettes around the sides, and lower ones with plush stools in the middle). Well kept Robinsons Mild and Best on handpump from the solid oak bar counter, and several malt whiskies. On the other side of a pleasantly chintzy small hall is a quieter but broadly similar room with more interesting prints and a delft shelf of china; one area is no smoking. Generous helpings of waitress-served food include sandwiches, hotpot (£4.75), steak pie (£4.95), cod and chips with mushy peas (£5.20), duck breast with mango and ginger (£7.25), guinea fowl with a coarse grain mustard sauce (£7.95), and whole lemon sole (£8.25); there may be a wait for food unless you arrive early. The very pleasant garden looks out towards rolling fields and has fairy-lit picnic tables under a small cedar and a pond with geese. They do not take credit cards. *(Recommended by Paul Boot, Simon Barber, Olive and Ray Hebson, Graham Reeve, G B Rimmer, E Riley, Roger and Christine Mash, George Jonas)*

Robinsons ~ Tenants Mr and Mrs J White ~ Real ale ~ Meals and snacks ~ Restaurant ~ (01829) 760200 ~ Children in restaurant ~ Open 11.30-3, 5.30(6 Sat)-11 ~ Bedrooms: £25B/£50B

DELAMERE SJ5669 Map 7

Fishpool

A54/B5152

New licensees had just taken over this attractive and comfortable pub as we went to press, and were hoping to keep things very much the same. The four small room areas (watch out, one of the doors between them is very low) are bright with polished brasses and china, and there's well kept Greenalls Bitter, Mild and Original on handpump. Good bar food includes sandwiches (from £1.75), pies like chicken and ham or beef and mushroom (from £4.50), cumberland sausage in mustard and whisky sauce (£4.75), steaks (from £7.95), specials such as fresh salmon (£5.25), and puddings like apricot crumble (£1.95). The pub is so well placed near the pike-haunted lake and Delamere Forest it can be particularly busy at weekends – best to go early, then. *(Recommended by Mr and Mrs R Bebson, Mrs P Abell, Graham and Lynn Mason, Mr and Mrs Craig, Steve and Karen Jennings, Olive and Ray Hebson, A Craig, Mrs Ann-Marie Colligan)*

Greenalls (Allied) ~ Tenants Richard and Maureen Lamb ~ Real ale ~ Meals and snacks ~ (01606) 883277 ~ Children in eating area of bar until 8pm ~ Open 11-3, 6-11 ~ Bedrooms: £17.50/£35

GREAT BUDWORTH SJ6778 Map 7

George & Dragon

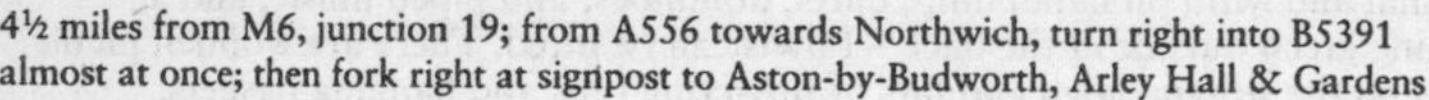

4½ miles from M6, junction 19; from A556 towards Northwich, turn right into B5391 almost at once; then fork right at signpost to Aston-by-Budworth, Arley Hall & Gardens

It's worth walking around the village – one of Cheshire's prettiest – and looking at the church and village stocks before coming to this very friendly 17th-c pub. The rambling panelled lounge has plenty of nooks and alcoves, beams hung with copper jugs, red plush button-back banquettes and older settles, and a fine big mirror with horsebrasses on the wooden pillars of its frame; one area is no smoking at lunchtime. The public bar has plenty of room for traditional pub games such as darts and pool, and there's also dominoes, a fruit machine, video game, trivia and piped music. At busy times families can use the upstairs restaurant, which is no smoking on Sunday lunchtimes. Bar food, with prices unchanged since last year, includes soup (£1.50), sandwiches (from £1.95), dim sum (£2.90), ploughman's (£3.95), salads (from £4.50), vegetarian curry (£4.75), fresh fillet of cod or gammon and egg (£4.95), steaks (from £7.50), daily specials such as liver and onions (£3.95), home-made steak in ale pie (£4.25) or lamb with orange and ginger (£4.75), and puddings (£2); children's menu (£1.95). Well kept Tetleys and two weekly changing guests on handpump, quite a few malt whiskies, and Addlestones cider. The pub is popular with a good cross-section of people – though walkers must leave their muddy boots in the porch. *(Recommended by Richard Lewis, Simon Barber, Graham and Lynn Mason, Tony and Lynne Stark, Peter and Lynn Brueton, S R and A I Ashcroft, Bill and Lydia Ryan, Mrs J M Bell, Simon J Barber, Barbara Hatfield)*

Tetleys (Allied) ~ Lease: Malcolm Curtin ~ Real ale ~ Meals and snacks ~ Upstairs restaurant ~ (01606) 891317 ~ Children in eating area of bar ~ Open 11.30-3, 6-11; all day Sat

HIGHER BURWARDSLEY SJ5256 Map 7

Pheasant

Burwardsley signposted from Tattenhall (which itself is signposted off A41 S of Chester) and from Harthill (reached by turning off A534 Nantwich—Holt at the Copper Mine); follow pub's signpost on up hill from Post Office; OS Sheet 117 map reference 523566

The window with the best view here – overlooking the Cheshire Plain and the Wirral – is in the beamed and timbered bar. The landlord's previous career was as a ship's pilot and some of the decorations are associated with this, such as his Merchant Navy apprenticeship papers, some ship photographs, and a brass ship's barometer – though there's also a parrot, a stuffed pheasant (as well as a picture of one), a set of whimsical little cock-fighting pictures done in real feathers, and big colour engravings of Victorian officials of the North Cheshire Hunt. Over the high stone mantlepiece of the see-through fireplace – said to house the biggest log fire in the county – are some plates, and around the fire is a tall leather-cushioned fender (in front of it Thomas the cat may be sitting). Other seats range from red leatherette or plush wall seats to one or two antique oak settles. Good bar food includes sandwiches and home-made soup, ploughman's, popular fresh fish such as plaice, brill, halibut, john dory and Dover sole (from £6.50), and steaks from their own home-grown Highland cattle (from £9.50); the pleasant conservatory is no smoking in the daytime and is useful for families. Well kept Bass and a guest such as Fullers London Pride or Morlands Old Speckled Hen on handpump, a choice of over 40 malts and quite a few wines; friendly staff. Fruit machine (not in main bar) and piped music. The bedrooms are in an attractively and very comfortably converted sandstone-built barn, and all have views – this year the landlord's flat is to be converted into two further rooms (he is moving to a cottage 100 yards away). Picnic tables on a big side lawn. The pub is well placed for walks along the Peckforton Hills and is half a mile from Tattenhall Fly Fisheries. *(Recommended by F A Eames, Mr and Mrs Craig, Don Kellaway, Angie Coles, Paul Robinshaw, Lynn Sharpless, Bob Eardley, L M Miall, Andrew Stephenson, Barbara Hatfield)*

Free house ~ Licensee David Greenhaugh ~ Real ale ~ Meals and snacks ~ Restaurant ~ Tattenhall (01829) 70434 ~ Children in conservatory till 8pm ~ Horses welcomed, and horse-and-trap rides can be arranged ~ Open 12-3, 6-11 ~ Bedrooms: £40B/£70B

nr LANGLEY SJ9471 Map 7

Hanging Gate

Higher Sutton; follow Langley signpost from A54 beside Fourways Motel, and that road passes the pub; from Macclesfield, heading S from centre on A523 turn left into Byrons Lane at Langley, Wincle signpost; in Sutton (half-mile after going under canal bridge, ie before Langley) fork right at Church House Inn, following Wildboarclough signpost, then two miles later turning sharp right at steep hairpin bend; OS Sheet 118 ref 952696

This cosy old drovers' pub was first licensed nearly 300 years ago but actually built much earlier. The three low-beamed snug little rooms are simply and traditionally furnished and there are big coal fires, a stuffed otter, some attractive old photographs of Cheshire towns, and super views looking out beyond a patchwork of valley pastures to distant moors (and the tall Sutton Common transmitter above them). Down stone steps an airier garden room has much the same view from its picture window. Dominoes, juke box. Reasonably priced bar food includes soup (£2), sandwiches (£2.90), and basket meals (from £4.60), with daily specials such as steak and kidney pie, chicken in tarragon wine, beef roghan josh or drunken bull (all £5.75). Well kept Courage Directors, Ruddles County and John Smiths on handpump, mulled wine in winter; friendly service. Seats outside on a crazy-paved terrace. *(Recommended by Wayne Brindle, Mike and Wendy Proctor, Yolanda Henry, Nigel Woolliscroft, Andy Petersen)*

Free house ~ Licensees John and Lyn Vernon ~ Real ale ~ Meals and snacks (not Thurs) ~ (01260) 252238 ~ Children welcome ~ Open 12-3, 7-11; closed all day Thurs

LANGLEY SJ9471 Map 7

Leathers Smithy

From Macclesfield, heading S from centre on A523 turn left into Byrons Lane at Langley, Wincle signpost; in Langley follow main road forking left at church into Clarke Lane – keep on towards the moors; OS Sheet 118 map reference 952715

Lovely views from this friendly old-fashioned pub look across to the Ridgegate Reservoir, and the steep mass of Teggs Nose (a country park) acts as a backdrop – making it popular with walkers. Inside, the room that readers like best is the lively, partly flagstoned right-hand bar with its bow window seats or wheelback chairs, and roughcast cream walls hung with gin traps, farrier's pincers, a hay basket and other ironwork. On the left, there are more wheelback chairs around cast-iron-framed tables on a turkey carpet, little country pictures and drawings of Cheshire buildings, Wills steam engine cigarette cards and a locomotive name-plate curving over one of the two open fires; faint piped music. The family room is no smoking. Well kept Ind Coope Burton, Jennings Bitter and Snecklifter, Tetleys Bitter and occasional guest beers on handpump, as well as Addlestones cider. Gluhwein in winter from a copper salamander, and a decent collection of spirits, including around 80 malt whiskies and 10 Irish; dominoes. Hearty bar food includes sandwiches (from £1.80), black pudding and mushy pies (£3.60), ploughman's (from £3.90), lasagne (£4.70), vegetarian dishes such as spinach and walnut pancake or cheese and onion quiche (£4.65), good salads (£4.70), home-made steak pie (£4.95), halibut or gammon and egg (£6.20), steaks (from £8.20), and delicious puddings such as butterscotch and walnut fudge cake (£2.70). *(Recommended by Steve Goodchild, Peter Downes, Wayne Brindle, Andrew Stephenson)*

Tetleys (Allied) ~ Tenant Paul Hadfield ~ Real ale ~ Meals and snacks (limited Mon lunchtime, not Mon evening; till 8.30 other evenings, though Fri and Sat till 9.30) ~ (01260) 252313 ~ Children in own room Sat and Sun lunchtime only ~ Occasional pianola music ~ Open 12-3, 7-11

LOWER PEOVER SJ7474 Map 7

Bells of Peover ★

The Cobbles; from B5081 take short cobbled lane signposted to church

Luckily, things seem to have changed very little since the new licensees took over this wisteria-covered pub. It's very neatly kept, and the little tiled bar has side hatches for its serving counter, Toby jugs, and comic Victorian prints, while the original lounge has two small coal fires, antique settles, antique china in the dresser, high-backed windsor armchairs, a spacious window seat, and pictures above the panelling. There's a second similar lounge. Good waitress-served bar food includes soup (£1.85), sandwiches with home-cooked meats (from £2.05; open sandwiches from £3.55), filled baked potatoes (mostly £4.05), home-made quiche (£4.85), attractive salads (from £5.05), home-made pies (£5.45), good daily specials, and several puddings (£2.50). Most people wear a jacket and tie in the restaurant. Well kept Greenalls Best on handpump and several wines. The sheltered crazy-paved terrace in front of the pub faces a lovely black and white timbered church, mainly 14th-c, with fine woodwork inside, and a spacious lawn beyond the old coachyard at the side spreads down through trees and rose pergolas to a little stream. *(Recommended by Roger and Christine Mash, Carl Travis, Mrs P Abell, John Broughton, Kevin and May Bronnsey, Graham and Lynn Mason, John and Pam Smith, Wendy, Liz and Ian Phillips, John Derbyshire, Leith Stuart, P D and J Bickley, Dono and Carol Leaman, S R and A I Ashcroft, George Jonas)*

Greenalls (Allied) ~ Lease: Keith Jones, Peter Slack ~ Real ale ~ Meals and snacks

~ Restaurant (closed Sat lunchtime, Sun evening, Mon) ~ (01565) 722269 ~ Children in restaurant ~ Open 11.30-3, 5.30(6 Sat)-11

MACCLESFIELD SJ9271 Map 7

Sutton Hall Hotel ★

Leaving Macclesfield southwards on A523, turn left into Byrons Lane signposted Langley, Wincle, then just before canal viaduct fork right into Bullocks Lane; OS Sheet 118 map reference 925715

This civilised 16th-c baronial hall is set in lovely grounds with tables on a tree-sheltered lawn – and if staying here, they can arrange clay shooting, golf or local fishing for you. The bar (divided into separate areas by tall black timbers) is furnished mainly with straightforward ladderback chairs around sturdy thick-topped cast-iron-framed tables, though there are a few unusual touches such as an enormous bronze bell for calling time, a brass cigar-lighting gas taper on the bar counter itself, a suit of armour by another big stone fireplace, and a longcase clock; also, some antique squared oak panelling, lightly patterned art nouveau stained glass windows, broad flagstones around the bar counter (carpet elsewhere), and a raised open fire. The menu is not unusual but the food is excellently cooked and presented, and there's friendly waitress service; the range includes home-made soup (£1.55), sandwiches (from £2.10), home-made pâté (£3.40), home-made lasagne (£5), home-made steak and kidney pie or spinach pancakes filled with ratatouille with a sour cream dressing (£5.35), daily specials such as venison sausages, smoked quail or monkfish in batter (from £5.35), and puddings (£2.10). Well kept Bass, Marstons Burton, Stones Best and a guest beer on handpump, 40 malt whiskies, freshly squeezed fruit juice, and decent wines. ***(Recommended by F C Johnston, Kevin and Kay Bronnsey, Nigel Woolliscroft, Mr and Mrs B Hobden, S G Brown, Basil Minson, S R and A I Ashcroft)***

Free house ~ Licensee Robert Bradshaw ~ Real ale ~ Meals and snacks (till 10pm) ~ Restaurant ~ (01260) 253211 ~ Children allowed weekends and bank hol lunchtimes only ~ Open 11-11 ~ Four-poster bedrooms: £68.95B/£85B

MARBURY SJ5645 Map 7

Swan

NNE of Whitchurch; OS Sheet 117 map reference 562457

It's the buoyantly cheerful atmosphere and good mix of customers that readers like at this creeper-covered white pub – run for 25 years by the same licensees. The neatly kept, partly panelled lounge has upholstered easy chairs and other country furniture, a grandfather clock, a copper-canopied fireplace with a good winter fire (masses of greenery in summer), discreet lighting and piped music; part of the room is no smoking. Most of the imaginative food is listed on a board and changes daily: fine soups (£1.50), chicken liver pâté (£2.65), garlic mushrooms (£2.95), Whitby goujons of plaice (£4.85), good spinach and garlic mushroom pancake (£4.75), smoked haddock and prawn cheesebake (£5.45), beef in ale (£5.50), tasty char-grilled lamb chops with orange mint sauce (£5.95), steaks (from £7.50), and puddings like banoffi pie or chocolate and almond torte (£2.50); chips are home-made. Well kept Greenalls Bitter and Original and Tetleys on handpump, forty malt whiskies, and friendly service; darts, dominoes, and piped music. The pub, rebuilt in 1884, is in a quiet and attractive village, a half-mile's country walk from the Llangollen Canal, Bridges 23 and 24. The nearby church is worth a visit. ***(Recommended by Pete Yearsley, Sue and Bob Ward, Bill Sykes, Nigel Woolliscroft, Mr and Mrs R J Phillips, Kate and Robert Hodkinson, Gill and Keith Croxton, Sue Holland, Dave Webster, Barbara Hatfield)***

Greenalls (Allied) ~ Lease: George, Ann and Mark Sumner ~ Real ale ~ Meals and snacks (not Mon lunchtime) ~ Restaurant ~ (01948) 663715 ~ Children welcome ~ Open 12-3, 7-11; closed Mon lunchtime (except bank hols)

MOBBERLEY SJ7879 Map 7

Bird in Hand

B5085 towards Alderley

Bustling and friendly, the cosy low-ceilinged rambling rooms here have warm coal fires and a relaxed, simple atmosphere. There are Toby jugs and other china on a high shelf, comfortably cushioned heavy wooden seats, small pictures on the attractive Victorian wallpaper, and wood panelling in the little snug; the top dining area is no smoking. Under the new licensee, bar food now includes sandwiches, ploughman's, welsh rarebit (£4.25), gammon and egg (£4.95), daily specials such as chilli con carne or tomato and courgette bake (£4.95), and puddings like home-made fruit pie (£1.95); summer afternoon teas, and helpful service. Well kept Sam Smiths OB and Museum on handpump and lots of malt whiskies; darts, dominoes, cribbage, fruit machine, and trivia. It can get crowded, but there are seats outside. ***(Recommended by Chris Westmoreland, Yolanda Henry, R T and J C Moggridge, Richard Lewis, Jill and Peter Bickley)***

Sam Smiths ~ Manager Guy Richardson ~ Real ale ~ Meals and snacks ~ (01565) 873149 ~ Children in eating area of bar ~ Open 11-11

OVERTON SJ5277 Map 7

Ring o' Bells £

Just over 2 miles from M56, junction 12; 2 Bellemonte Road – from A56 in Frodsham take B5152 and turn right (uphill) at Parish Church signpost

The prize-winning hanging baskets in front of this friendly early 17th-c local are quite a sight in summer, and at the back of the building is a secluded garden with tables and chairs, a pond, and lots of trees. Inside, this is very much the sort of place where people tend to talk to each other. There are a couple of little rambling rooms with windows giving a view past the stone church to the Mersey far below; one at the back has some antique settles, brass-and-leather fender seats by the log fire, and old hunting prints on its butter-coloured walls. A beamed room with antique dark oak panelling and stained glass leads through to a darts room (there's also dominoes and cribbage, but no noisy games machines). Good value waitress-served home-made bar food is served at lunchtime only and includes sandwiches and toasties (from £1.35; the steak and onion one is popular, £1.95), stilton, walnut and celery quiche or home-made curry (£3.35), a big breakfast (£3.50), home-made steak, mushroom and ale pie (£3.75), prawn and mushroom filled plaice or salads (£3.95), and puddings (£1.40). Well kept Greenalls Bitter and Original on handpump or tapped from the cask and no less than 80 different malt whiskies served from the old-fashioned hatch-like central servery; cheerful helpful service. The cats are called Blackberry India (who is particularly friendly and is now 15) Lottie, and tabby twins Shula and Tilly. ***(Recommended by G Kelsall and others; more reports please)***

Greenalls (Allied) ~ Tenant Shirley Wroughton-Craig ~ Real ale ~ Lunchtime meals and snacks ~ Children welcome until 8pm (not in bar itself) ~ (01928) 732068 ~ Open 11.30-3, 5.30(6 Sat)-11

PEOVER HEATH SJ7973 Map 7

Dog

Off A50 N of Holmes Chapel at the Whippings Stocks, keep on past Parkgate into Wellbank Lane; OS Sheet 118 map reference 794735; note that this village is called Peover Heath on the OS map and shown under that name on many road maps, but the pub is often listed under Over Peover instead

Some changes here this year include the refurbishment of the bar and dining room and the opening up of a private entrance for residents to get to their rooms; three more bedrooms are planned as well. Around the main bar is an engaging series of small areas with seats ranging from a comfortable easy chair, through wall seats (one built into a snug alcove around an oak table), to the handsome ribbed banquettes in the quiet and spacious no-smoking dining room on the left; logs burn in one old-fashioned black grate and a coal fire opposite it is flanked by two wood-backed built-in fireside seats. Bar food includes home-made soup such as curried apple and parsnip (£2.50), mushrooms in beer batter with garlic dip (£3.85), baked ham and pineapple mornay, haddock and prawn au gratin, roast beef and yorkshire pudding, and rabbit with herbs and mustard (all £6.95), and puddings such as home-made fruit crumble or sticky toffee pudding (£2.50); dishes are 50p more in the evening. Much of the dining area is no smoking. Well kept Flowers IPA, Jennings Mild and Tetleys on handpump, Addlestones cider, lots of malt whiskies, decent wine list, freshly squeezed orange juice and espresso and cappuccino coffee; darts, pool, dominoes, and piped music. There are picnic tables out on the quiet lane, underneath the pub's pretty hanging baskets and an attractive beer garden which is lit in the evenings. *(Recommended by Roger and Christine Mash, Simon Barber, Kevin and Kay Bronnsey, Jill and Peter Bickley, K J Phillips, Mr and Mrs Smith-Richards, Mrs B Lemon, Yolanda Henry, L M Miall, S Ashcroft, Tim Galligan, L Walker, Richard Lewis, Brian Kneale, Helene Thompson, Chris Walling)*

Free house ~ Licensee Frances Cunningham ~ Real ale ~ Meals and snacks ~ Restaurant ~ (01625) 861421 ~ Well behaved children welcome ~ Solo guitar/country music Weds ~ Open 11.30-3, 5.30-11 ~ Bedrooms: £39.50B/£59.50B

PLUMLEY SJ7175 Map 7

Smoker

2½ miles from M6 junction 19: A556 towards Northwich and Chester

Named for a favourite racehorse of the Prince Regent some two hundred years ago, this very popular, well run thatched pub has three well decorated connecting rooms with open fires in impressive period fireplaces; also, comfortable deep sofas, cushioned settles, windsor chairs, and some rush-seat dining chairs, a collection of copper kettles and military prints on dark panelling, and a glass case containing an interesting remnant from the Houses of Parliament salvaged after it was hit by a bomb in World War II. The Edwardian print by Goodwin Kilburne of a hunt meeting outside shows how little the pub's appearance has changed; one area is no smoking. Good home-made bar food includes soup (£1.80), sandwiches (from £1.85), tasty home-made savoury pancakes or pâté (£3.25), macaroni with stilton and port (£3.45), ploughman's (£5.40), fresh plaice or kofta curry (£5.55), home roast ham and pineapple (£6.05), home-made steak and kidney pie or good beef stroganoff (£6.40), steaks (from £8.40), and daily specials; children's dishes (£2.25). Well kept Robinsons Best, Bitter and Hatters Mild on handpump; 30 malt whiskies and a good choice of wines; friendly service. Outside there's a sizeable side lawn with roses and flower beds, and this year the garden has been extended to include a children's play area. *(Recommended by Mrs Pat Crabb, Simon Barber, Andy Cunningham, Gary Roberts, Ann Stubbs, DAV, Mrs B Lemon, Richard Lewis, J and B Gibson, Bronwen and Steve Wrigley, George Jonas, A R and B E Wayer, Nick and Meriel Cox, Dick Brown, M V and J Melling, J E Hilditch, W C M Jones, D Newth, Bill and Lydia Ryan)*

Robinsons ~ Tenants John and Diana Bailey ~ Meals and snacks (11.30-2.30, 6-10) ~ Restaurant (not Sun evening) ~ (01565) 722338 ~ Children in eating area of bar and in restaurant ~ Open 11-3, 5.30-11

We accept no free drinks or payment for inclusion. We take no advertising, and are not sponsored by the brewing industry – or by anyone else. So all reports are independent.

POTT SHRIGLEY SJ9479 Map 7

Cheshire Hunt

At end of B5091 in Bollington, where main road bends left at Turners Arms, fork straight ahead off it into Ingersley Road to follow Rainow signpost, then up hill take left turn signposted Pott Shrigley; OS Sheet 118 map reference 945782

Originally called the Quiet Woman when it was a weekly cattle-auction house, this isolated stone pub got its present name around 1850. There are several small rooms that ramble up and down steps with spindleback and wheelback chairs, solidly built small winged settles, sturdy rustic tables, lovely flower arrangements, beams and black joists, and roaring log fires. Bar food is very good and includes home-made soup (£1.95), sandwiches (from £2), white stilton cheese spiced with nutmeg and peppercorns, breaded, deep fried and set on a fresh apple and cinnamon puree (£3.20), ploughman's or black pudding with Irish soda bread (£3.95), locally made spicy sausages (£4.10), home-made steak and kidney pie (£5.95), chicken in a wine and cream sauce (£6.20), steaks (from £7.95), daily specials, puddings such as home-made cheesecake or apple pie (from £2), and evening extras such as halibut steak with fresh dill and lemon or rack of lamb (£8.95); children's dishes (from £1.95). Well kept Boddingtons, Marstons and guest beers on handpump; no noisy games machines or piped music. Outside, there are seats on three terraces, gardens, and views over pastures. *(Recommended by Alan and Heather Jacques, Jill and Peter Bickley, Andrew Ross)*

Free house ~ Licensee Alan Harvey ~ Real ale ~ Meals and snacks (till 10pm; not Mon lunchtime) ~ Restaurant (open all day Sun) ~ (01625) 573185 ~ Children in eating area of bar and in restaurant ~ Open 12-3, 5.30-11; all day Sun; closed Mon lunchtime

SUTTON SJ9469 Map 7

Ryles Arms 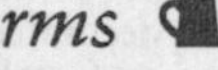

Off A54 Congleton—Buxton, 2¾ miles E of A523 – signposted Sutton 2¾; or coming into Sutton from Macclesfield, fork right after going under aqueduct; OS Sheet 118 map reference 942694

Though people do drop in for a drink, this pleasant slated white stone local is very much a popular dining pub – and owes a lot of its success to the attentive and warmly friendly Irish landlord. The menu and prices are unchanged from last year and include soup (£1.50), sandwiches (from £2), ploughman's (£3.50), tuna and courgette quiche or chicken curry (£5), steak and kidney pie or a good lasagne (£5), gammon and egg or roast beef (£6), and grilled halibut steak (£7.50). The section of the pub by the bar is basically two rooms knocked together, with comfortable seats and french windows leading to a terrace with metal and plastic chairs. On the right is a dining area (no smoking at eating times), with some attractively individual furnishings; the family room is no smoking too. Well kept Coach House Best, Marstons Pedigree, Ruddles Best and County, and John Smiths on handpump, a good choice of whiskies. *(Recommended by Brian and Anna Marsden, Richard Lewis, Peter and Jill Bickley, John Watson; more reports please)*

Free house ~ Licensee Frank Campbell ~ Real ale ~ Meals and snacks (till 10pm) ~ (01260) 252244 ~ Children in family room and in restaurant ~ Open 11.30-3, 7-11; closed 25 Dec

SWETTENHAM SJ8067 Map 7

Swettenham Arms

Village signed off A535 just S of Jodrell Bank or just N of Holmes Chapel – keep following sign; pub behind brick-towered church

Prettily placed in a tucked-away village, this busy but spacious country pub is popular for its wide choice of generous food. The heavily beamed bar has three communicating room areas linked by a sweep of fitted turkey carpet, with some interesting and individual furnishings and a variety of old prints – military, hunting, old ships, reproduction Old Masters and so forth. Wherever you eat, you order food from a separate counter in the end no-smoking dining room (where there's a huge inglenook – the pub has several winter log fires). The range of food is very wide: around 19 starters such as home-made soup (£2.20), whitebait, duck pâté with garlic bread or smoked salmon and prawns (all around £3.95); as many main courses, like marinated lamb, poached salmon, roast beef and yorkshire pudding, and vegetarian dishes (from £7.75); and popular puddings (£2.50). Well kept Boddingtons, Jennings and Tetleys on handpump. You can sit outside at picnic tables on the quiet neat side lawn surrounded by shrubs and trees; the hanging baskets at the front are pretty. The pub's run by the same people as the Dog at Peover Heath. *(Recommended by Chris Walling, Richard Lewis, P H and R Sutcliffe, A Lomas)*

Free house ~ Licensees Frances and James Cunningham ~ Real ale ~ Meals and snacks ~ Restaurant ~ (01477) 571284 ~ Children in eating area of bar ~ Open 11.30-3, 6-11; 11.30-11 Sat

TARPORLEY SJ5563 Map 7

Rising Sun

High St; village signposted off A51 Nantwich—Chester

Very popular locally, this bustling and friendly village pub is pretty in summer with its mass of hanging baskets and flowering tubs. Inside, well chosen tables are surrounded by character seats including creaky 19th-c mahogany and oak settles, and there's also an attractively blacked iron kitchen range (and three open fires), sporting and other old-fashioned prints on the walls, and a big oriental rug in the back room. Good value lunchtime bar food includes sandwiches (from £1.75), filled baked potatoes (from £1.95), home-made cottage pie (£2.95), home-made steak and kidney pie (£4.45), gammon and egg or pork and apple in cider (£5.15), beef in ale (£5.45), and more elaborate dishes in the evening from the restaurant menu; helpful, prompt service. Well kept Robinsons Best and Mild on handpump; fruit machine, maybe unobtrusive piped music. *(Recommended by David and Shelia, Richard Lewis, F J and A Parmenter, Mrs A Abell, Andrew Shore, Paul Boot, Brian Wainwright, A R and B E Sayer)*

Robinsons ~ Tenant Alec Robertson ~ Real ale ~ Meals and snacks (11.30-2, 5.30-9.30) ~ Restaurant ~ (01829) 732423 ~ Open 11.30-3, 5.30-11

WESTON SJ7352 Map 7

White Lion

3½ miles from M6 junction 16; A500 towards Crewe, then village signposted on right

At lunchtime, this pretty black and white timbered old inn fills up quickly with people keen to enjoy the popular food served by smartly dressed staff. The busy low-beamed main room is divided up into smaller areas by very gnarled black oak standing timbers, and has a varied mix of seats from cushioned modern settles to ancient oak ones, plenty of smaller chairs, and a friendly, relaxing atmosphere. In a smaller room on the left are three fine settles, well carved in 18th-c style. Bar food includes home-made soup (£1.50), good sandwiches or batch cakes (from £1.75), chicken liver or smoked salmon pâté (£3), vegetarian quiche or a daily special (£3.95), ploughman's (from £4.50), daily roast (£4.50), poached local Dee salmon (£6.50), steak (£8.25), and big home-made puddings (£1.90). Well kept Bass, Boddingtons, Highgate Dark, and Joules Crown Ale (new to us) on handpump; dominoes, piped music; the restaurant is no smoking – as are some bar areas. Picnic tables shelter on neat grass behind, by the pub's own bowling green. The hotel part is discreetly hidden away at the back. *(Recommended by G S Miller, Richard Lewis, Helen Lowe, Basil Minson, E G Parish, Martin Aust, C H and P Stride, Miss D P Barson)*

Free house ~ Licensee Mrs A J Davies ~ Real ale ~ Meals and snacks (not 25 Dec) ~ Restaurant (not Sun evening) ~ (01270) 500303 ~ Children in eating area of bar and in restaurant ~ Open 11-3, 5-11; closed evening 25 Dec ~ Bedrooms: £47B/£57B

WETTENHALL SJ6261 Map 7

Boot & Slipper

From B5074 on S edge of Winsford, turn into Darnhall School Lane, then right at Wettenhall signpost: keep on for 2 or 3 miles

Set on a small country lane, this attractively refurbished pub has three old shiny dark settles and more straightforward chairs in its beamed main bar, white walls, a big log fire in the deep low fireplace with a fishing rod above it, and a nice chatty and relaxed atmosphere. The modern bar counter also serves the left-hand communicating beamed room with its shiny pale brown tiled floor, cast-iron-framed long table, panelled settle and bar stools; darts, dominoes. An unusual trio of back-lit arched pseudo-fireplaces form one stripped-brick wall and there are two further rooms on the right, as well as a back restaurant with big country pictures. Good bar food includes sandwiches (from £1.30; steak batch £2.50), home-made soup (£1.40), home-made pie of the week (£3.95), salads (from £4), gammon and egg (£5.50), daily specials such as spare ribs (£3.85), peppered cider pork (£4.50) or lamb rogan josh (£4.75), puddings (£1.75), and children's dishes (£2). Well kept Highgate Mild and Marstons Pedigree on handpump, a decent wine list, and quite a few malt whiskies. Outside a few picnic tables sit on the cobbled front terrace by the big car park. *(Recommended by Robert and Ann Lees, Mr and Mrs G R Smith-Richards; more reports please)*

Free house ~ Licensee Rex Challinor ~ Real ale ~ Meals and snacks ~ Restaurant ~ (01270) 528238 ~ Children in eating area of bar ~ Open 11.30-3, 5.30-11 ~ Bedrooms: £26S/£40S

WINCLE SJ9666 Map 7

Ship

Danebridge

This quaint 16th-c pub – one of the oldest in Cheshire – is tucked away in scenic countryside with fine walks all round. The old-fashioned little rooms have a nice atmosphere, very thick stone walls, a coal fire and well kept Boddingtons Bitter and a weekly changing guest beer on handpump; decent wines. Good bar food includes soup (£1.50), filled french bread with chips (lunchtime, from £3), grilled Dane Valley trout (£4.75), gammon and eggs (£5.95), sirloin steak (£7.95), delicious venison casserole, steamed puddings (from £1.95), and children's meals (£1.95); fondue bourguignonne is the house speciality and includes a bottle of house red wine; dominoes, chess, draughts, Monopoly and cards. *(Recommended by Mike and Wendy Proctor, Mr and Mrs J Tyrer, DC, Wayne Brindle, Nigel Woolliscroft, Roger and Christine Mash)*

Free house ~ Licensees Andrew Harmer and Penelope Hinchliffe ~ Real ale ~ Meals and snacks (till 10pm; not winter Mon) ~ (01260) 227217 ~ Well behaved children in family room ~ Open 12-3, 7-11; closed Monday Nov-Mar ~ One bedroom: £25/£40

The opening hours we quote are for weekdays; in England and most of Wales, Sunday hours are 12-3, 7-10.30.

WRENBURY SJ5948 Map 7

Dusty Miller

Village signposted from A530 Nantwich—Whitchurch

The position here is lovely, set by the Llangollen branch of the Shropshire Union Canal and next to a striking counter-weighted drawbridge. Picnic tables are set on a gravel terrace among rose bushes by the water, and they're reached either by the towpath or by a high wooden catwalk above the River Weaver; in summer they hold regular barbecues including whole hog roasts. Inside, there's a friendly welcome and the main area is comfortably modern, with a series of tall glazed arches with russet velvet curtains facing the water, long low hunting prints on the white walls, and tapestried banquettes and wheelback chairs flanking dark brown rustic tables. Further in, there's a quarry-tiled standing-only part by the bar counter, which has well kept Robinsons Best, Frederics and Hartleys XB on handpump; the right-hand side of the lounge bar is no smoking. Dominoes, cribbage, shove-ha'penny, and classical piped music. Imaginative, popular bar food – using local produce where possible – includes sandwiches (lunchtimes), smoked oysters (£3.95), roulade of chicken stuffed with parma ham on a blue cheese sauce or good salmon (£8.50), rack of lamb with honey, rosemary and cider sauce (£8.95), and fresh fish and chips on Tuesday evenings; separate children's menu. *(Recommended by Gordon Theaker, Lynn Sharpless, Bob Eardley, Mark Gillespie, D Deas, John Andrew, Nigel Woolliscroft, Paul Noble, Patrick and Mary McDermott)*

Robinsons ~ Licensee Robert Lloyd-Jones ~ Real ale ~ Meals and snacks ~ Upstairs restaurant (closed Sun evening) ~ (01270) 780537 ~ Children in restaurant ~ Open 12-3, 6-11; all day in high season; closed evening 25 Dec

Lucky Dip

Besides the fully inspected pubs, you might like to try these Lucky Dips recommended to us and described by readers (if you do, please send us reports):

☆ **Acton Bridge** [Hilltop Rd; B5153 off A49 in Weaverham, then right towards Acton Cliff; SJ5975], *Maypole*: Spacious and civilised beamed dining pub, attractive outside with hanging baskets and tubs, good generous varied food in pleasant dining room with lots of brass, copper and china; some antique settles as well as more modern furnishings, two coal fires, friendly service, Greenalls Bitter and Mild on handpump, gentle piped music; seats in well kept garden with orchard behind *(Mrs P Abell, Graham and Lynn Mason, Brian Gregory, LYM)*

Adlington [Wood Lane North – OS Sheet 109 map ref 936818; SJ9180], *Miners Arms*: Improved and extended dining pub, very clean and comfortable, with lots of alcoves and quiet corners, efficient service, good food, usually two guest beers as well as Boddingtons; well suited to families, refurbished play area *(P and M Rudlin, Brian and Anna Marsden)*

Alderley Edge [Brook Lane; SJ8478], *Oakwood*: Well run Whitbreads pub with good range of beers, sensible-sized menu with lots of sandwiches and good reasonably priced piping hot meals, pleasant decor and furnishings *(Mr and Mrs C Roberts)*

Alsager [SJ7956], *Manor House*: Part of hotel complex, pub in old manor house, lots of beams, relaxing atmosphere, good menu, friendly staff, well kept Whitbreads-related beers on handpump; bedrooms *(Richard Lewis)*; [Crewe Rd], *Old Mill*: Particularly well kept Banks's Best, Camerons Strongarm and Marstons Pedigree, good value tasty straightforward food from sandwiches to steaks, friendly efficient staff good with children; big play area with lots of activities, maybe free milk shakes; 12 well equipped bedrooms *(Richard Lewis)*

☆ **Alvanley** [Manley Rd – OS Sheet 117 map ref 496740; SJ4974], *White Lion*: Remarkably wide changing choice of generous food from sandwiches up inc vegetarian and children's dishes in comfortable, civilised and very popular dining pub, friendly service, plush seats in low-ceilinged lounge, games in smaller public bar, Greenalls Mild, Bitter and Original, tables and play area outside with some small farm animals *(Mr and Mrs B Hobden, Myke Crombleholme, Olive and Ray Hebson, Graham and Lynn Mason, Derek and Margaret Underwood, LYM)*

Ashley [3 miles S of Altrincham – OS Sheet 109 map ref 776843; SJ7784], *Greyhound*: Greenalls pub with good generous food, pleasant staff, unlimited well served coffee, Tetleys and a guest ale *(A F C Young)*

☆ **Audlem** [Audlem Wharf – OS Sheet 118 map ref 658436; SJ6543], *Shroppie Fly*: Beautifully placed canal pub, one bar shaped like a barge, good canal photographs, collection of brightly painted bargees' china and bric-a-brac, seats on waterside terrace; usual food, well kept Boddingtons, friendly staff, mainly modern furnishings, children in room off bar and restaurant; open almost all day summer, closed winter lunchtimes *(Nigel Woolliscroft, D Hanley, Julian Jewitt, Tony Hobden, LYM)*

Audlem [A525, Audlem Wharf], *Bridge*: Particularly well kept Marstons and guest ales and good food from sandwiches up in friendly unspoilt pub with coal fire, tiled floor, darts, pool, juke box and games machines; dogs allowed, seats out by canal *(Margaret and Allen Marsden, D Hanley)*

☆ **Beeston** [Bunbury Heath; A49 S of Tarporley; SJ5459], *Beeston Castle*: Good value interesting generous food from huge open sandwiches up inc mouth-watering puddings, in clean, comfortable and well restored pub, welcoming prompt service even when busy, short but well chosen wine list, well kept beers; children until 8 *(Mrs A Bradley, Mrs H Jack, Don Kellaway, Angie Coles, Mr and Mrs D Conroy)*

☆ **Bell o th Hill** [just off A41 N of Whitchurch; SJ5245], *Blue Bell*: Attractive two-roomed heavily beamed country local with decent food, Sun papers, well kept real ales; piped music; nice garden, attractive surroundings *(J Roy Smylie, LYM)*

☆ **Bollington** [Church St; SJ9377], *Church House*: Wide choice of good value quickly served lunchtime food in corner terrace pub, small and busy but warmly welcoming; well kept Tetleys and Theakstons, furnishings inc pews and working sewing-machine treadle tables, separate dining room, friendly prompt staff; piped music *(Bill Sykes, Tim Boddington, C Tan)*

☆ **Bollington** [29 Adlington Rd, heading N off B5091 by railway viaduct], *Vale*: Pleasantly modernised local nr canal walks, comfortable and spotless, with good home-cooked bar food, well kept Thwaites Bitter and Mild and Timothy Taylors Landlord on handpump, very friendly staff, log fire, neat woodside lawn with good play area; closed Mon lunchtime except bank hols, jazz Mon evening *(A F C Young, LYM)*

☆ **Bollington Cross** [SJ9277], *Cock & Pheasant*: Comfortable beamed family lounge bar with log fire, dark wood, old prints, promptly served good value food inc children's dishes in attractive little dining room, conservatory, Boddingtons, plenty of tables in garden, back playground *(C and M M Roberts)*

☆ **Bosley** [Leek Rd (A523); SJ9266], *Harrington Arms*: Cosy roadside pub with wide choice of good generous straightforward home cooking, well kept Robinsons Bitter and Old Stockport on handpump, good decor, friendly landlord, pleasant setting *(Richard Lewis, K H Frostick)*

☆ **Broxton** [Nantwich Rd; A543, nr junction with A41], *Durham Heifer*: Good value food inc interesting specials in welcoming and comfortable beamed dining pub, unobtrusive piped music, good range of drinks; pleasant country views *(Kenneth and Joyce Houghton, Paul Boot)*

☆ **Broxton** [A41/A534 S of Chester; SJ4754], *Egerton Arms*: Consistently good friendly service in spacious black and white pub with well polished old furniture in roomy and attractive dark-panelled bar, stained glass lights above, old plates and prints, discreet piped music, partly no smoking dining area off; wide choice of good food inc lots for children, helpful efficient staff, Burtonwood ales, decent wines; tables under cocktail parasols on balcony terrace with lovely views to River Dee; children very welcome, colouring materials, play area with Wendy house; open all day, bedrooms; *(Jeanne and Tom Barnes, Paul and Maggie Baker, Mr and Mrs R Phillips, D Hanley)*

☆ **Bunbury** [SJ5758], *Dysart Arms*: Old farmhouse converted into cosy and attractive free house with several nooks and crannies, lots of antique furniture, generally old-fashioned atmosphere, Tetleys and Thwaites ales, welcoming landlord, tables in lovely elevated big garden by church *(Mr and Mrs J H Adam, Sue Holland, Dave Webster, Chris Walling)*

☆ **Burtonwood** [Alder Lane; 3 miles from M62 junction 9, signed from A49 towards Newton-le-Willows – OS Sheet 108 map ref 585930; SJ5692], *Fiddle i'th' Bag*: Peaceful waterside spot, friendly, comfortable and spacious, with plenty of alcoves, brassware, pottery and stuffed animals; popular lunchtime for good food, tables outside *(D Grzelka, LYM)*

☆ **Butley Town** [A523 Macclesfield—Stockport; SJ9177], *Ash Tree*: Popular dining pub with wide choice of good bar food, three attractive rooms, good coal fires, well kept Boddingtons/Whitbreads ales, friendly atmosphere *(C A Wilkes, B C Armstrong, LYM)*

☆ **Chester** [1 Russell St, down steps off City Rd], *Old Harkers Arms*: Lofty Victorian canalside building full of bric-a-brac, with four well kept changing ales inc Cains, interesting malt whiskies, decent wines, good choice of varied and unusual food, nicely presented in generous helpings, efficient friendly staff; quiet lunchtime, very lively evening *(Peter Pocklington, D Hanley, David and Judith Woodcock, Richard Lewis, J L Moore)*

☆ **Chester** [Park St, off Albion St)], *Albion*: Lovely welcoming eccentric atmosphere and landlord, masses of WWI memorabilia in three carefully refurbished Victorian rooms, also 40s and 50s things; big helpings of good value home-cooked chip-free lunchtime food inc massive sandwiches and unusual main dishes, Cains and Greenalls beers, quick friendly service; just below city wall *(M A Cameron, Andy and Jill Kassube, Mr and Mrs Craig, Tony and Lynne Stark, Sue Holland, Dave Webster, Brian Kneale, Peter and Jenny Quine, Wayne Brindle, Mike and*

Pam Simpson)

☆ **Chester** [Eastgate Row N], *Boot*: Fine position on The Rows, heavy beams, lots of old woodwork, oak flooring and flagstones, black-leaded kitchen range in lounge beyond food servery, no smoking oak-panelled upper room, good atmosphere, friendly new licensee, cheap well kept Sam Smiths; children allowed *(J and P Maloney, Sue Holland, Dave Webster, M A Cameron, H K Dyson, D R Shillitoe, Andy and Jill Kassube, LYM)*

☆ **Chester** [Lower Bridge St], *Falcon*: Striking building with beams, handsome stripped brickwork, well kept Sam Smiths OB and Museum, decent basic bar food (not Sun), fruit machine, piped music; children allowed lunchtime (not Sat) in airy upstairs room; jazz Sat lunchtime, open all day Sat; can get packed *(M A Cameron, D Hanley, George Atkinson, Richard Lewis, Tony and Lynne Stark, J and P Maloney, H K Dyson, LYM)*

☆ **Chester** [Watergate St], *Old Custom House*: Popular old pub with lots of good pottery and brass in three character rooms, limited choice of very reasonably priced decent food, good range of Marstons ales inc Mild, efficient service, good evening atmosphere, fruit machine in lounge *(Ian Phillips, D Hanley, M A Cameron)*

☆ **Chester** [Upper Northgate St], *Pied Bull*: Attractive and comfortable beamed 16th-c pub, well kept Cains and Greenalls Original, warm welcome, wide choice of generous reasonably priced food even Sun evening, no smoking area; bedrooms *(Dr and Mrs A M Evans, Andrew Shore)*

☆ **Chester** [Tower Wharf, Raymond St; behind Northgate St, nr rly], *Telfords Warehouse*: Interesting pub in former warehouse designed by Thomas Telford, great views over canal basin, well kept ales such as Theakstons and changing guests such as good local Weetwood, good unusual food in pub, cellar wine bar and upper restaurant; blond furniture, nightly live music; children welcome *(Ants Aug, M A Cameron)*

☆ **Chester** [Watergate St], *Watergates*: Wide range of quickly served good food from ploughman's up in lovely medieval crypt – a wine bar, with candlelit tables and good wine choice, but also well kept Cains real ale; can get packed on race days *(Geoff and Angela Jaques, D Hanley, Sue Holland, Dave Webster)*

Chester [94 Lower Bridge St], *Bear & Billet*: Gloriously timbered Jacobean inn reopened after painstaking restoration, nine real ales, 20 well kept wines by the glass, good upstairs restaurant *(Anon; more reports please)*; [Northgate St], *Coach & Horses*: Lots of woodwork, bric a brac and prints, massive range of sandwiches, also baked potatoes, baguettes and fry-ups, two monthly guest ales such as Caledonian IPA and Everards; piped music, fruit machine *(D Hanley)*; [St John St], *Marlborough Arms*: Warm and friendly, doing well under new young landlord, with home-made lunchtime food inc good vegetarian dishes, Whitbreads-related beers *(Paul Weston, George Atkinson)*; [Bridge St], *Olde Vaults*: Panelling and leaded lights, well kept Greenalls, upstairs lounge *(D Hanley)*

Church Lawton [Congleton Rd S (A34) – OS Sheet 118 map ref 828552; SJ8155], *Red Bull*: Large and comfortable, with several rooms inc upstairs lounge and eating area, good choice of bar food, well kept Hartleys XB and Robinsons Bitter and Hatters Mild, friendly landlord; soft piped music *(Richard Lewis)*

☆ **Churton** [Farndon Rd (B5130); SJ4256], *White Horse*: Small village pub with three attractively furnished connecting bars, copper-topped tables, lots of polished bric-a-brac; remarkable range of reasonably priced home-cooked food, quickly and efficiently served, real ales such as Bass and Burtonwood; pool *(G B Rimmer, E Riley)*

Clotton [A51 Chester—Nantwich; SJ5364], *Bulls Head*: Attractively refurbished, with pleasant friendly atmosphere and well presented varied food *(G B Rimmer, C Riley)*

☆ **Congleton** [High St; SJ8663], *Olde Kings Arms*: Superbly timbered former manor house reopened after massive renovation by Marstons, cosy low-beamed separate rooms, open fires, good value real ale, very well priced limited food, well kept Pedigree and Best on handpump *(Richard Lewis, Steve Goodchild)*

Congleton [West St], *Durham Ox*: Comfortable beamed local with plates on walls, cosy seats, Beartown Bitter, John Smiths and Tetley Walkers; pool room, juke box *(Richard Lewis)*

☆ **Crewe** [Nantwich Rd (A534) opp rly stn; SJ7056], *Crewe Arms*: Good value attractive bar meals in comfortable and spacious lounge with Victorian pictures, marble-topped tables, alabaster figurines, curtained alcoves, ornate ceiling; good pubby public bar; Tetleys well kept when it's on, friendly staff, open all day; bedrooms *(E G Parish, Richard Lewis)*

Crewe [58 Nantwich Rd; SJ7053], *British Lion*: Sensitively refurbished and well run, with good atmosphere, Tetleys-related and guest real ales *(Sue Holland, Dave Webster)*[25 Earle St], *Crown*: Original fittings, old-fashioned furnishings and wallpaper; busy main front bar, back games room with pool and juke box, two quietly chatty lounges and drinking corridor; welcoming landlady and locals, well kept Robinsons; handy for Railway Heritage Centre *(Pete Baker)*; [Nantwich Rd], *Earl of Crewe*: Refurbished in back-to-basics style, lots of railway prints and beer memorabilia, panelling, copper cauldrons; cosy atmosphere, good choice of ever-changing real ales kept well, reasonably priced food *(Richard Lewis)*; [Middlewich Rd (A530), Wolstanwood; SJ6755], *Rising Sun*: Big popular pub with well kept Greenalls Original and Best and Stones Best, lots of brass, good food, friendly staff; children's

play area; bedrooms *(Richard Lewis)*
Eaton [the one nr Tarporley; SJ5763], *Red Lion*: Attractive and comfortable, with wide choice of good generous food, good friendly service, separate bar with pool and darts, floodlit bowling green, barbecues and play area; well kept Greenalls and Stones; children welcome *(Richard Lewis)*
Ellesmere Port [Princes Rd; SJ4077], *Princes Arms*: Cosy and welcoming local with down-to-earth customers, decent food, pool *(Michael Hickman)*; [Chester Rd], *Woodland*: Big pub/restaurant with good traditional food, Worthington Best, back bowling green; children welcome in restaurant *(Kevin Smith)*
Faddiley [A534 Wrexham—Nantwich; SJ5753], *Tollemache Arms*: Attractively cottagey thatched and timbered pub which was very popular (and a main entry) under previous tenants who left at the end of 1994 *(LYM)*
Frodsham [Church St; SJ5278], *Rowlands*: Good food, very friendly atmosphere, carefully kept real ales; children welcome *(Roger and Susan Dunn)*
Fullers Moor [A534 – OS Sheet 117 map ref 500542; SJ4954], *Copper Mine*: Comfortable dining pub with interesting copper-mining memorabilia, well kept Bass and Burtonwood Best, children welcome; spacious garden with barbecues and lovely views; handy for Sandstone Trail *(G Hallett, LYM)*
☆ **Gawsworth** [nr Macclesfield; SJ8969], *Harrington Arms*: Farm pub's two small rooms with bare wooden floorboards, fine carved bar counter, well kept Robinsons Best and Best Mild served in big old enamelled jugs *(Dave Irving, LYM)*
Goostrey [111 Main Rd; off A50 and A535], *Crown*: Extended Marstons dining pub keeping lots of beams and pictures, cosy and friendly atmosphere, popular landlord, well kept ale; bedrooms *(Richard Lewis, Mr and Mrs G D Amos, LYM)*; [Station Rd (towards A535)], *Red Lion*: Clean and pleasant modernised open-plan bar and back family restaurant with well kept Boddingtons, Tetleys and a guest such as Shepherd Neame Spitfire on handpump, friendly efficient service, piped music and fruit machines, restaurant, nice garden with play area; children welcome *(Richard Lewis, Robert and Ann Lees, LYM)*
Great Sutton [Capenhurst Lane/New Chester Rd; SJ3876], *Old Wirral Hundred*: Newish Banks's pub with pleasant atmosphere and bargain lunches *(Don Kellaway, Angie Coles)*
☆ **Guilden Sutton** [SJ4568], *Bird in Hand*: Good well presented food in pleasant dining pub, friendly service, well kept beer; children welcome *(Peter E Morris, M A Cameron, John Hillyer)*
Hale [Grove Lane/Wellfield Ln; handy for M56 junction 6; SJ4782], *Well Green*: Big Beefeater with mock Tudor alcoves and indoor water feature; tasty food, attentive obliging service, Whitbreads real ales inc bargain-priced guest, tables on terrace, play area *(JJW, CMW)*
Hartford [Chester Rd (A559 SW of Northwich); SJ6472], *Coachman*: Former coaching inn done up in old-fashioned style with interconnecting rooms off bar, well cooked reasonably priced food, well kept Greenalls, tables out behind *(Mr and Mrs C Roberts, Michael Gittins)*
Hassall Green [SJ7858], *Romping Donkey*: Tetleys-related ales and good value food in small picturesque cottage pub neatly furnished to match appearance, pleasant countryside with canal walks; may not open till 7 *(Tony Hobden, E G Parish, LYM)*
☆ **Hatton** [Warrington Rd (B5356, handy for M56 junction 10); SJ6082], *Hatton Arms*: Cosy 18th-c bar with friendly licensees and locals, open fire, two plainer rooms off; bar lunches inc good value soup and sandwiches, real ales; cobbled pavement outside, local Lewis Carroll connections *(Chris Walling, Andy and Jill Kassube)*
Haughton Moss [Long Lane; off A49 S of Tarporley; SJ5856], *Nags Head*: Good atmosphere, warm and friendly, good food and beer, sensible prices; children welcome *(Philip Leay)*
☆ **Heatley** [Mill Lane; SJ7088], *Railway*: Old original railway pub with four distinct rooms, good cheap bar food inc good barm cakes, superbly kept Boddingtons and guest beers, friendly licensees and Welsh terrier *(Eileen and Alan Gough)*
☆ **Higher Whitley** [1¼ miles from M56 junction 10; A559 towards Northwich; SJ6280], *Birch & Bottle*: Good value food in civilised and attractively decorated pub with well kept Greenalls Mild, Bitter and Original, decent wines, good log fires, attractive conservatory; children allowed if eating *(John Watson, LYM)*
Knutsford [Chelford Rd; SJ7578], *Dun Cow*: Interesting antique and other furnishings and bric-a-brac; doing well under friendly new landlord, with good food, well kept ales and decent wine *(Malcolm Kavanagh)*
☆ **Little Bollington** [the one nr Altrincham, 2 miles from M56 junction 7: A56 towards Lymm, then first right at Stamford Arms into Park Lane – use A556 to get back on to M56 westbound], *Swan with Two Nicks*: Popular and efficiently run beamed village pub full of brass, copper, bric-a-brac and cabaret memorabilia; friendly feel, snug alcoves, antique settles in back room, log fire, wide choice of food esp evening fish, well kept Whitbreads-related real ales, tables outside; attractive hamlet by Dunham Hall deer park *(Bill and Lydia Ryan, Geoffrey and Brenda Wilson, C A Wilkes, LYM)*
Little Leigh [A49, just S of A533; not far from M56 junction 10; SJ6276], *Holly Bush*: As we went to press it seemed possible that this might survive as a largely unspoilt farm-pub of real charm and character, though a history of disputed planning applications still leaves some doubt *(LYM; news please)*
☆ **Lower Peover** [Crown Lane; B5081, off A50;

SJ7474], *Crown*: Good bar food and service and lots of bric-a-brac inc interesting gooseberry championship memorabilia in friendly and attractive L-shaped bar with two rooms off; Boddingtons, dominoes *(Steve Hardy)*

☆ **Lower Whitley** [SJ6179], *Chetwode Arms*: Very popular and relaxing Millers Kitchen dining pub with traditional layout, solid furnishings all clean and polished, warm coal fires, Greenalls Mild and Bitter on handpump, good food and service, children welcome; immaculate bowling green, play area, open all day Sat *(Gary Roberts, Ann Stubbs, Roger and Christine Mash, Brian and Anna Marsden, W C M Jones, Graham and Lynn Mason, LYM)*

☆ **Lymm** [Eagle Brow, nr M6 junction 20; SJ6787], *Spread Eagle*: Character beamed village pub with three well furnished distinct areas inc small snug, cheery atmosphere, well kept Lees on handpump, good home-made bar food, juke box *(Alan Gough)*

☆ *nr* **Macclesfield** [A537 some miles out towards Buxton – OS Sheet 119 map ref 001719; SK0071], *Cat & Fiddle*: Britain's 2nd-highest pub, surrounded by spectacular moorland (though on a trunk road), with magnificent views; spacious, comfortable and clean lounge, roomy flagstoned public bar, Robinsons real ales, decent bar food; busy lunchtime in summer *(Wendy and Ian Phillips, LYM)*

☆ **Mobberley** [opp church; SJ7879], *Church*: Smart but friendly and comfortable, with wide choice of good generous food, great log fire, well kept Greenalls, cheerful service; tables in courtyard, big garden with play area, own bowling green; children welcome *(C and M Roberts, R and A Lees, Bill and Lydia Ryan, Chris Westmoreland)*

☆ **Mobberley** [Town Lane; down hill from sharp bend on B5185 at E edge of 30mph limit], *Roebuck*: Spacious and pleasant open-plan bar with pews, polished boards, panelling and alcoves; well kept Courage-related real ales, good generously served bar food from lunchtime sandwiches up, good friendly service, upstairs restaurant, seats in cobbled courtyard and garden behind, play area; children welcome *(Bill and Lydia Ryan, CR, Chris Westmoreland, LYM)*

Mobberley [Wilsons Mill Lane], *Bulls Head*: Friendly and comfortable low-beamed pub plushly opened up around central open fireplaces, with old pictures, soft lighting, well kept Boddingtons, immaculate bowling green *(Bill and Lydia Ryan, BB)*; [Ashley Rd, towards Altrincham], *Chapel House*: Quiet, friendly and cosy panelled lounge, with particularly well kept Boddingtons, real fire; small games room, courtyard seats *(Bill and Lydia Ryan)*; [Paddock Hill, off B5085 Knutsford—Wilmslow], *Plough & Flail*: Small but comfortable three-roomed pub with big helpings of good food inc fish, quick friendly service, log fire, well kept Boddingtons; restaurant *(Ian Blackwell)*

Mow Cop [Station Rd – OS Sheet 118 map ref 854574; SJ8557], *Cheshire View*: Friendly and simply furnished local with tremendous bird's-eye view of the Cheshire Plain; well kept Marstons Best, Regimental and Pedigree, lots of prints of nearby castle *(Richard Lewis, LYM)*

☆ **Nantwich** [Hospital St – by side passage to central church; SJ6552], *Lamb*: Hotel bar with leather chesterfields and other comfortable seats, well kept Burtonwood Forshaws, decent malt whiskies, good value nicely served generous home-cooked food inc outstanding fish in bar and traditional upstairs dining room, attentive staff; piped music; bedrooms *(W C M Jones, Sue Holland, Dave Webster, BB)*

☆ **Nantwich** [51 Beam St], *Red Cow*: Beautifully rebuilt 15th-c former farmhouse, comfortable and lively, with well kept Robinsons Best, Mild, Old Tom and Hartleys XB *(Sue Holland, Dave Webster, Gordon Theaker, Nick and Alison Dowson)*

Nantwich [High St], *Crown*: Striking Elizabethan inn with rambling comfortably modernised beamed and timbered bar, real ales, bar food, good value attached Italian restaurant, helpful service; comfortable bedrooms *(P D Donoghue, LYM)*; [97 Welsh Row], *Oddfellows Arms*: Cosy and friendly, with well kept Burtonwood, reasonably priced food inc vegetarian, games; very attractive street *(Sue Holland, Dave Webster)*; [High St], *Olde Vaults*: Changing well kept ales such as Exmoor Gold, Marstons Pedigree, Morlands Old Speckled Hen, Tetleys, Shepherd Neame Spitfire, Charles Wells Bombardier, Wychwood Best and Wobbly Bob in tastefully refurbished pub, lots of wood and local prints, some pews, friendly staff; very popular *(Richard Lewis)*; [Hospital St], *Vine*: Handy for lunch, with friendly service, good atmosphere, quiet corners, varied food from hearty sandwiches up, Banks's Bitter and a guest ale *(Sue Holland and Dave Webster)*

Neston [1 Park St; SJ2978], *Brewers Arms*: Traditional pub dating from late 17th-c nr River Dee, good choice of lunchtime food inc sandwiches and vegetarian, five Whitbreads-related ales, good atmosphere *(S A McCann)*

No Mans Heath [A41; SJ5148], *Wheatsheaf*: Low beams, lots of pictures, brasses, wrought iron, comfortable seats, cosy fires, friendly staff, well kept Bass, Ruddles County, Theakstons Best and Worthington Best, usual decent food, relaxing atmosphere; piped music; play area in garden *(Richard Lewis)*

☆ **Ollerton** [A537 – OS Sheet 118 map ref 775769; SJ7877], *Dun Cow*: Pretty country pub, small-roomed and friendly, with attractive and individual furnishings, two fine log fires, well kept Greenalls Cask and Original, drinkable wine, dominoes, shove-ha'penny and darts in small tap room, interesting bar food from sandwiches up inc vegetarian; open all day (inc restaurant in summer), children in snug and restaurant *(Mrs P J Pearce, JHMB, Paul Wreglesworth, Olive and Ray Hebson, LYM)*

☆ **Over Peover** [off A50 S of Knutsford; SJ7674], *Olde Park Gate*: Pleasant quiet atmosphere in several small black-beamed rooms with some attractive furnishings inc fine Macclesfield oak chairs, well kept Sam Smiths, good straightforward bar food from sandwiches up, sensible prices, good friendly service, back public bar where the locals watch Coronation St; family room, tables outside *(Richard Lewis, BB)*

☆ **Over Peover** [Stocks Lane, just off A50], *Whipping Stocks*: Another attractive Sam Smiths pub, with several rooms, good oak panelling and fittings, solid furnishings, well kept ale, popular sensibly priced home-made food, children in eating area, picnic tables in garden with safe play area; can be dominated weekday lunchtime by people from nearby Barclays Bank regional HQ, but relaxing evenings *(Mr and Mrs K H Frostick, DC, LYM)*

☆ **Parkgate** [The Parade; SJ2878], *Red Lion*: Comfortable Victorian pub on attractive waterfront with great view of Welsh hills, food inc good value sandwiches, Tetleys-related ales, 19th-c paintings and beer-mug collection *(FC)*

Parkgate [The Parade], *Boathouse*: Busy but pleasant, with efficient young staff, Greenalls Bitter and Mild and Tetleys, wide choice of usual food, attractive furnishings; conservatory restaurant; trad jazz Tues *(Douglas Copeland, W C M Jones)*; [Boathouse Lane (B5135)], *Parkgate Hotel*: Cosily furnished country house well placed on Dee estuary, stylish pubby bar, warm welcome, tasty lunchtime food, good wines and service; bedrooms *(E G Parish)*

☆ **Plumley** [Plumley Moor Lane; off A556 by the Smoker; SJ7175], *Golden Pheasant*: Spacious series of comfortably modernised rooms inc pool room, well kept Lees Bitter and Mild, decent bar food and good value restaurant, good friendly staff, roomy conservatory overlooking back children's garden, pub gardens and bowling green; children welcome, good well equipped bedrooms *(R H Jones, Richard Lewis, Bill and Lydia Ryan, Simon Barber, LYM)*

Prestbury [SJ9077], *Legh Arms*: Striking long heavy-beamed 16th-c building with gallery, smart atmosphere, tables laid with cloths and cutlery, good choice of good value inventive food, well kept Robinsons *(Steve Goodchild)*

☆ **Rainow** [NE of village on A5002 Whalley Bridge—Macclesfield; SJ9576], *Highwayman*: A favourite for people who like timeless unchanging country pubs: small rooms, low 17th-c beams, good winter fires (electric other times), moorland views, plenty of atmosphere; Thwaites real ales, bar food inc good sandwiches, rather late opening *(Gordon, Dr Roy Partington, Yolanda Henry, Brian and Anna Marsden, LYM)*

Sandbach [10 Market Sq; SJ7661], *Crown*: Very old and picturesque, on cobblestone square with Saxon cross; good food, excellent staff *(Jeffrey Eastburn)*; [Newcastle Rd, 1¼ miles from M6 junction 17], *Old Hall*: Handsome Jacobean hotel with fine panelling and spreading lawns; Ruddles Best in small bar, good restaurant meals, excellent service, agreeable atmosphere; bedrooms comfortable and well equipped *(E G Parish, LYM)*

☆ **Scholar Green** [off A34 N of Kidsgrove; SJ8356], *Rising Sun*: Good country-pub atmosphere, welcoming service, good choice of well kept ales such as Fullers London Pride, Marstons Best and Pedigree, Robinsons, Thwaites and a changing guest, wide choice of generous interesting home-cooked food, family room, pleasantly refurbished restaurant; darts, unobtrusive piped music *(Maeve and Peter Thomson, Dick and Barbara Waterson, Richard Lewis)*

Scholar Green, *Travellers Rest*: Busy, comfortable and cosy, lots of panelling and prints, well kept Banks's, Marstons Best and Regimental, wide choice of good value bar food *(Richard Lewis)*

☆ **Smallwood** [Knutsford Rd (A50 N of Alsager); SJ8160], *Legs of Man*: Comfortable roadside Robinsons pub with carefully matched chairs, banquettes, carpet, curtains and wallpaper, fin de siecle tall white nymphs on columns, lush potted plants, long rather imaginative menu, well kept Best, Fredericks and Best Mild, friendly staff; restaurant, children very welcome; well spaced tables on side lawn with play area *(Richard Lewis, Graham Emmett, Helen Lowe, BB)*

☆ **Smallwood** [Newcastle Rd (A50)], *Bulls Head*: Attractive interestingly decorated dining pub with lots of space and particularly good garden with play area; well kept Burtonwood and Tetleys, decent house wines, imaginative range of well presented generous food inc good puddings, good service; piped pop music, children welcome; quite handy for Biddulph Grange (NT) *(R C Vincent, LYM)*

☆ **Styal** [Altrincham Rd (B5166 nr Ringway Airport); SJ8383], *Ship*: Friendly pub in attractive NT village with good service, wide choice of good food all day, well kept Courage-related ales, children allowed; seats out in front, walks in riverside woods *(Terry Buckland, Dorothee and Dennis Glover)*

Sutton [SJ9273], *Lamb*: Good comfortable low-ceilinged traditional local, Tetleys beer, reasonably priced home cooking inc proper steak and kidney pie, friendly atmosphere and staff *(Tony Young)*; *Olde Kings Head*: Friendly low-ceilinged bar, beautiful stained glass, well kept Boddingtons, Marstons Pedigree and Thwaites, extensive menu; bedrooms *(Richard Lewis)*

Tarporley [High St; SJ5563], *Crown*: Well kept Boddingtons, Tetleys and guest beers, lots of pictures, conservatory, very friendly staff; extensive well priced menu, relaxed atmosphere *(Richard Lewis)*

☆ *nr* **Tiverton** [Wharton's Lock; Bates Mill Lane – OS Sheet 117 map ref 532603; SJ5660], *Shady Oak*: Canalside country pub with plenty of seats and good play area in waterside garden and terrace, fine views of

Beeston Castle, airy lounge, small carpeted conservatory, well kept Courage-related ales, Chef & Brewer food, summer barbecues, moorings *(M A Cameron, LYM)*

Walgherton [London Rd; A51 between Bridgemere Gdn Centre and Stapeley Water Gdns; SJ6949], *Boars Head*: Country-pub atmosphere, good quick food all day from sandwiches up, very friendly staff, reasonably priced Greenalls, large lounge with dining area, bar with games, prints and boars' heads, very big garden with hens in field and play area; bedrooms *(Sue Badel, D Hanley)*

☆ **Walker Barn** [A537 Macclesfield—Buxton; SJ9573], *Setter Dog*: Remote but civilised extended dining pub with windswept moors view, well kept Marstons, good food in small bar and restaurant, good service, roaring fire; handy for Teggs Nose Country Park *(Mike and Wendy Proctor)*

☆ **Warmingham** [Middlewich Rd; SJ7161], *Bears Paw*: Good food inc lots of specials in small bar and restaurant, pool room, children very welcome; good spot by river and ancient church in small hamlet *(Helen Lowe)*

Warrington [Chester Rd, Lower Walton; SJ6085], *Ship*: Well kept Greenalls, good Italian restaurant, reasonably priced bistro; bedrooms very well equipped *(Geoff Charnock)*

☆ *nr* **Warrington** [Fiddlers Ferry; leave A562 in Penketh – park in Station rd off Tannery Lane – OS Sheet 108 map ref 560863], *Ferry*: Picturesquely isolated between Manchester Ship Canal and Mersey, four well kept real ales inc very quickly changing guest beers, over 100 whiskies, good home-cooked food in nice upstairs dining room (not Sun evening), low beams, log fires, provision for children; tables outside with rabbits in hutches, pony paddock, burger trailer *(D Grzelka, John McPartland, Pete Yearsley, LYM)*

Waverton [A41 S of Chester; SJ4663], *Black Dog*: Greenalls dining pub with guest beers such as Arrols 80/- and Theakstons, big tasteful lounge, small garden; occasional jazz evenings, piped music *(D Hanley)*

Wheelock [Mill Lane; A534 Sandbach—Crewe; SJ7559], *Nags Head*: Well furnished bars, good bar food, thriving cottagey atmosphere, brassware, well kept Chesters Bitter and Mild and Boddingtons; secluded walled garden, good canalside and country walks; children welcome, bedrooms *(E G Parish, Richard Lewis)*

Whiteley Green [OS Sheet 118 map ref 924789; SJ9278], *Windmill*: Spacious and attractive garden with summer bar and barbecues, roomy modernised lounge and dining area, good lunchtime bar food, well kept Tetleys-related ales; provision for children; attractive countryside *(C A Wilkes, Brian and Anna Marsden, BB)*

Willaston [Newcastle Rd, Blakelow – OS Sheet 118 map ref 680517; SJ6851], *Horseshoe*: New licensees doing well, reliable standard food, Robinsons Best, Best Mild, Old Stockport and Old Tom, panelled lounge with fire, dining room, public bar; garden with swings *(Sue Holland, Dave Webster)*

Wilmslow [Green Ln; SJ8481], *Blue Lamp*: Banks's conversion of former police station, best described as 'upmarket spit and sawdust'; well kept Bitter, Camerons Strongarm and Marstons Pedigree, usual food from separate counter *(Brian and Anna Marsden)*

Winwick [A49/A573; 1½ miles W of M6 junction 22; SJ6093], *Swan*: Popular lunchtime for generous mainly straightforward food *(G M and J M Smith)*

☆ **Wybunbury** [Main Rd (B5071); SJ6950], *Swan*: Charmingly placed by beautiful churchyard, with seats in garden, well kept beer, reasonably priced genuine home cooking inc interesting dishes, warmly welcoming staff, tasteful furnishings inc some from antiques shop at the back *(Catherine and Andrew Brian, R and A Lees, LYM)*

> Post Office address codings confusingly give the impression that some pubs are in Cheshire, when they're really in Derbyshire (and therefore included in this book under that chapter) or in Greater Manchester (see the Lancashire chapter).

Cleveland *see* Northumbria

Cornwall

This year we've seen a distinct advance in the quality of the food at quite a few Cornish pubs. Places which now stand out for enjoyable meals include the Maltsters Arms at Chapel Amble (fish specialities – it's our choice as Cornish Dining Pub of the Year), the Trengilly Wartha near Constantine (a great all-rounder), the prettily placed Ship at Lerryn, the Roseland at Philleigh (doing very well at the moment), the Ship on the harbour at Porthleven, the Fox & Hounds at Scorrier, the Crown at St Ewe, the well refurbished New Inn on Tresco and (though its primary virtue is its splendid range of real ales) the Old Ale House in Truro; this last pub's developed such a strong and wide appeal that it gains a star award this year. Food's a particular attraction too at three strong new entries this year: the very well run Halzephron on the coast at Gunwalloe south of Helston, the charmingly rambling Crown at Lanlivery and the relaxed and friendly Springer Spaniel at Treburley. The Royal Oak in Lostwithiel also makes the main entries this year; good all round, with a range of ales that's better than usual for Cornwall. Other pubs currently doing particularly well include the atmospheric Cobweb in Boscastle, the Turks Head in Penzance, the Star at St Just in Penwith and the St Kew Inn; and the Pandora near Mylor Bridge and the Eliot Arms at Tregadillett are always well worth a visit. The Turks Head on St Agnes gains a place-to-stay award this year. Other changes include new licensees doing well at the Crows Nest in the hamlet of that name, and at the Punch Bowl & Ladle at Penelewey. Sadly the tenants who last year gained a main entry for the White Hart at St Keverne have left, and the owners of the Carpenters Arms at Metherell are retiring; both are back in the Lucky Dip section, where the strongest current contender for promotion is the Old Inn at Mullion. Other Lucky Dip entries to note particularly include the Napoleon in Boscastle, Coombe Barton at Crackington Haven, Top House at Lizard, New Inn at Manaccan, Royal Oak at Perranwell, Blue Peter among other pubs in Polperro, Lugger at Portloe, Who'd Have Thought It at St Dominick and refurbished Victory in St Mawes. We have inspected virtually all of these, so can vouch firmly for their quality. Drinks prices in the area are rather lower than the national average; in this year's price survey we found that beer in the former Devenish/Cornish Brewery pubs now tied to Greenalls (who no longer brew but get their beers from national brewers) costs about 10% more than in pubs tied to the local St Austell brewery.

BOSCASTLE SX0990 Map 1

Cobweb

B3263, just E of harbour

The room with the most atmosphere here is the lively public bar where both locals and visitors are made welcome by the hard-working and cheerful licensee and his staff. Hundreds of old bottles hang from the heavy beams, there's a cosy log fire, two or three curved high-backed winged settles against the dark stone walls, and a few leatherette dining chairs. Well kept Bass, St Austell Tinners, HSD, and XXXX Mild, and Shepherd Neame Spitfire on handpump, with occasional guest beers, and several malt whiskies. Quickly served, good value bar food includes sandwiches (from £1.40, crab or prawn £3), fine pasties (£1.50), baked potatoes (from £1.50), sausage, egg and chips (£3.25; the chips are good), meaty or vegetarian lasagne (£4.25), steaks (from £6.50), gammon and egg (£7.50), and daily specials; children's dishes (from £1.25). Darts, pool (keen players here), dominoes, video game, and fruit machine; the big communicating family room has an enormous armchair carved out of a tree trunk as well as its more conventional windsor armchairs, and another winter fire. Opening off this a good-sized children's room has a second pool table, and more machines. The pub's position near the tiny harbour can mean crowds in the holiday season. *(Recommended by Alan and Eileen Bowker, Anthony Marriott, M W Turner, R T and J C Moggridge, John Whiting, Jack and Philip Paxton, Brian and Anna Marsden, S Demont, T Barrow, Richard Dolphin)*

Free house ~ Licensees Ivor and Adrian Bright ~ Real ale ~ Meals and snacks (till 10pm) ~ Restaurant (not Sun evening) ~ (01840) 250278 ~ Children in own room and in restaurant ~ Live entertainment Sat evening ~ Open 11-11 – though closed for 2 hours Sat afternoon

CHAPEL AMBLE SW9975 Map 1

Maltsters Arms 🍷

Village signposted from A39 NE of Wadebridge; and from B3314

Cornish Dining Pub of the Year

Although this popular family-run pub places a lot of emphasis on its good food (and has refurbished the no-smoking eating areas), there's a nice pubby atmosphere in the attractively knocked-together rooms (one of which is no smoking): black oak joists in the white ceiling, partly panelled stripped stone walls, heavy wooden tables on the partly carpeted big flagstones, and a large stone fireplace; there's also a side room with windsor chairs and a good upstairs family room. Bar food includes sandwiches, boozy mushrooms (£3.95), bubble and squeak with cold meats or fried egg (£4.25), vegetable rice skillet (£5), sizzle dishes such as chicken with ginger or prawns with chilli (£6), steak in ale pie (£6.50), stir-fried breast of duck with ginger, spring onions and mange tout (£9), with lots of fish specialities such as scallops in wine and cream, local sea trout or lovely whole sea bass baked with herbs, and lovely puddings such as fruit crumbles, bread and butter pudding with brandy and cream, and lemon tart; lots of clotted cream. Well kept Bass, Ruddles County, Sharps Cornish and a beer brewed for the pub by Sharps (who are a new local brewery), and a guest beer on handpump kept under light blanket pressure; around 20 wines by the glass (including a proprietor's choice), several malt whiskies, and several brandies; helpful, friendly staff. Winter darts, cribbage, dominoes, trivia, and piped music. Benches outside in a sheltered sunny corner. *(Recommended by Sue Demont, Tim Barrow, John Woodward, P V Caswell, R and S Bentley, Jack and Philip Paxton, Rita Horridge, Lawrence Bacon, Brian and Anna Marsden, Jennifer Tora, Simon and Natalie Forster, Margaret Mason, David Thompson, Steve and Liz Tilley, Nick Wikeley, S R Chapman, Ted George)*

Free house ~ Licensees David and Marie Gray ~ Real ale ~ Meals and snacks ~ (01208) 812473 ~ Children in restaurant and family room ~ Open 11-2.30, 5.30(6 in winter)-11

CONSTANTINE SW7229 Map 1

Trengilly Wartha 🛏 🍷 ◼

Constantine signposted from Penryn—Gweek rd (former B3291); in village turn right just before Minimarket (towards Gweek); in nearly a mile pub signposted left; at Nancenoy, OS sheet 204, map reference 731282

It's unusual to find a pub that genuinely appeals to most people – but this busy place does just that. The no-smoking conservatory family room is bright and cheery even on a gloomy winter day, the food is very good indeed, there's a splendid choice of real ales, and readers enjoy staying here, too. The low-beamed main bar has a wood-burning stove and modern high-backed settles boxing in polished heavy wooden tables, and the lounge has cushioned wall benches, a log fire and some harness. Up a step from the bar is an eating area with winged settles and tables; darts, pool, bar billiards, cribbage, shove-ha'penny, dominoes, fruit machine, and video and trivia machines. Good, home-made bar food includes soup such as tomato and basil (£2.20; the fish one is delicious £2.40), blue cheese and walnut pâté (£3), ploughman's or leek and cheese soufflé (£4), fresh pizza (£4.20), interesting salads such as candied aubergine with crème fraîche or dressed crab (from £5), cassoulet (£7.50), and lots of fishy daily specials like good mixed fried fish (£3.30), skate wing with caper sauce (£5.80) or salmon steamed in paper with vermouth and fresh herbs (£7.50); children's menu (from £2). Regular festivals are held throughout the year like the Sausage Festival, wine festival, fish one and so forth. They keep an unusually wide choice of drinks for the area, such as well kept Fergusons Dartmoor, St Austell XXXX Mild, Sharps Cornish (a local brewery) on handpump with regularly changing ales from smaller brewers tapped from the cask such as Ash Vine, Berrows, Cotleigh Tawny, Exmoor Gold, Gibbs Mew Bishops Tipple, Otter Bright and so forth. Also, over 40 malt whiskies (including several extinct ones), and a large, interesting wine list (with several by the glass). The pretty landscaped garden has some picnic tables around the vine-covered pergola, an international sized piste for boules, and a lake garden next door to the inn. *(Recommended by Wendy Arnold, Sue Demont, Tim Barrow, P and M Rudlin, R and S Bentley, Anthony Barnes, Andy and Jill Kassube, Mr and Mrs J Woodfield, Jack and Philip Paxton, Canon Michael Bourdeaux, Peter Brimacombe, DJW, Bob and Maggie Atherton, John and Sally Clarke, Charles Lovedale, Mr and Mrs W J A Timpson, S R Chapman, Pat and John Millward, Margaret Kemp)*

Free house ~ Licensees Nigel Logan, Michael Maguire ~ Real ale ~ Meals and snacks ~ Restaurant ~ (01326) 340332 ~ Children welcome ~ Occasional live music ~ Open 11-3 (2.30 winter), 6(6.30 winter)-11 ~ Bedrooms: £36(£42B)/£48(£59B)

CROWS NEST SX2669 Map1

Crows Nest £

Signposted off B3264 N of Liskeard; or pleasant drive from A30 by Siblyback/St Cleer rd from Bolventor, turning left at Common Moor, Siblyback signpost, then forking right to Darite; OS Sheet 201 map reference 263692

On the southern slopes of Bodmin moor, this old-fashioned and friendly 17th-c pub has an interesting table converted from a huge blacksmith's bellows (which still work), an unusually long black wall settle by the big log fire as well as other more orthodox seats and polished tables, and lots of stirrups, bits and spurs hanging from the bowed dark oak beams. On the right, and divided by a balustered partition, is a similar area with old local photographs and maybe flowers on the tablecloths. Under the new licensee, lunchtime bar food includes filled soft rolls (from £1; not Sunday lunchtime), soup (£1.85), ploughman's (£2.75), chips with ham and egg, sausage or chicken (from £2.50), vegetable lasagne (£3.50), and children's dishes (£1.75), with evening grills (from £5.95); Sunday roast lunch (£3.95). Well kept St Austell Tinners and HSD on handpump kept under light blanket pressure; juke box, fruit machine. On the terrace by the quiet lane there are picnic tables. This used to be the pay office/company store where tin and copper miners were paid. No children. *(Recommended by Sue Demont, Tim Barrow, Norma Farris, Mr and Mrs J Woodfield, Jack and Philip Paxton, R L Turnham, R and S Bentley, Jack and Philip Paxton, S Brackenbury, Ted George)*

St Austell ~ Tenant C R Sargeant ~ Real ale ~ Meals and snacks ~ (01579) 345930 ~ Children welcome ~ Open 11-11

FALMOUTH SW8032 Map 1

Quayside

ArwenackSt/Fore St

The simple subterranean-feeling public bar here has a fine range of beers on handpump such as Boddingtons, Courage Directors, Flowers Original, Ruddles County, and Tetleys on handpump with Bass tapped from the cask, and half-a-dozen gravity fed guests like Batemans XXXB, Cotleigh Old Buzzard, Gibbs Mew Bishops Tipple, Otter Ale, Sharps Cornish (a new local brewery), and Shepherd Neame; they hold beer fesitvals during the spring and autumn half-terms; Old Hazy farm cider. There are malt sacks tacked into the counter, lots of beer mats on the panelled walls, book matches on the black ceiling, a big white ensign, a mix of ordinary pub chairs on the bare boards, a log-effect gas fire in the stripped stone fireplace, and a big barrel of free peanuts (which gives an individual touch to the floor covering). Upstairs is the lounge bar (which you enter from the attractively bustling street) with comfortable, new armchairs and sofas at one end, more straightforward tables and chairs at the other, picture windows overlooking the harbour, and huge range of over 219 whiskies (179 are single malts) – the whisky club meets monthly, guests are welcome to tastings. Bar food includes home-made soup (£1.45), doorstep sandwiches (from £2.30), ploughman's (from £3.55), liver and bacon or Chinese vegetables and cashew nuts (£3.50 small, £4.95 regular), pizzas (from £3.95), beef in ale pie (£4.55), puddings (£1.95), and daily specials (lots of fresh fish). There are picnic tables on the tarmac by the Custom House Dock and next to the handsome Georgian harbour-master's office. *(Recommended by Nigel Woolliscroft, P and M Rudlin, Alan and Eileen Bowker, Mark Robinson, Sue Holland, Dave Webster, John Lansdown, John Wooll, David and Michelle Hedges)*

Greenalls ~ Managers David Patterson and Derrick Smith ~ Real ale ~ Meals and snacks (not Sun evening) ~ (01326) 312113 ~ Children welcome ~ Duo Fri and Sat evenings, summer Weds brass band ~ Open 11-11

HELFORD SW7526 Map 1

Shipwrights Arms

Off B3293 SE of Helston, via Mawgan

The draw to this thatched pub is its lovely position above a beautiful wooded creek – best enjoyed in summer when you can sit on the terraces; the top part of the terrace is roofed over with Perspex. Inside there's quite a nautical theme with navigation lamps, models of ships, sea pictures, drawings of lifeboat coxwains and shark fishing photographs – as well as a collection of foreign banknotes behind the bar counter. A dining area has oak settles and tables; winter open fire. Well kept Flowers, Whitbreads Castle Eden and a guest beer on handpump, and bar food such as home-made soup (£2.25), home-made steak and kidney pie (£6.50), steaks (from £7.75), and puddings (£2.95); piped music. It does get crowded at peak times. *(Recommended by Martin and Penny Fletcher, Werner Arend, Adrian and Karen Bulley, A J N Lee, Beverley James, E N Burleton, Nigel Flook, Betsy Brown, Jack and Philip Paxton, Gwen and Peter Andrews, Margaret Kemp, David and Michelle Hedges)*

Greenalls ~ Lease: Charles Herbert ~ Real ale ~ Meals and snacks (not winter Sun or Mon evenings) ~ (01326) 231235 ~ Children in eating area of bar ~ Parking only right outside the village in summer ~ Open 11-2.30, 6-11(10.30 in winter); closed winter Sun evenings

HELFORD PASSAGE SW7627 Map 1

Ferryboat

Signed from B3291

In summer particularly, this pub is popular with families as just ten yards from the terrace is a sandy beach with safe swimming and where you can hire small boats and arrange fishing trips; there's also a ferry across to Helford village (again, summer only), summer barbecues and summer afternoon cream teas. Inside, the big spacious bar has well kept St Austell BB, Tinners, HSD and XXX Mild on handpump, and home-made bar food such as soup, sandwiches (£2.50), steak in ale pie (£4.50), lamb and almond curry or fish pie (£5.25), vegetarian dishes, and a daily fish dish; the restaurant is no smoking. Darts, pool, dominoes, fruit machine, video game, juke box, Sky TV, and quiet piped music. They hold their own regatta on the second Sunday of August. *(Recommended by Werner Arend, Adrian and Karen Bulley, Jim Reid, John Beeken, Anthony Barnes, Mr and Mrs W J A Timpson, Gwen and Peter Andrews, Nigel Woolliscroft, Mr and Mrs C R Little)*

St Austell ~ Manager Steven Brown ~ Real ale ~ Meals and snacks ~ Restaurant ~ (01326) 250625 ~ Children in eating area of bar and in restaurant ~ Live entertainment three times a week in summer ~ Open 11-11; 11-3, 6.30-11 in winter

HELSTON SW6527 Map 1

Blue Anchor £

50 Coinagehall Street

The impression that this old thatched town pub gives is very much that of a basic take-us-as-you-find-us local – though behind that impression (if it's not too busy) you can spot all sorts of signs of age. A series of small, low-ceilinged rooms opens off the central corridor, with simple old-fashioned furniture on the flagstones, interesting old prints, some bared stone walls, and in one room a fine inglenook fireplace. A family room has video game, fruit machines, and darts. They still produce their Medium, Best, 'Spingo' Special (the name comes from the Victorian word for strong beer) and Extra Special ales in what is probably the oldest brewing house in the country. At lunchtimes you can usually go and look round the brewery and the cellar; they also sell farm cider. Bar food includes rolls (£1.10), pasties (£1.50), and some pot meals. Past an old stone bench in the sheltered little terrace area is a skittle alley. The pub is very popular with locals (mainly men). *(Recommended by Mark Walker, Sian Thrasher, Anthony Barnes, Jack and Philip Paxton, Alastair Campbell, Sue Holland, Dave Webster, David and Michelle Hedges)*

Own brew ~ Licensee Kim Corbett ~ Real ale ~ Snacks (12-4) ~ (01326) 562821 ~ Children in family room ~ Live bands Fri evenings ~ Parking sometimes difficult ~ Open 11-11

nr HELSTON SW6522 Map 1

Halzephron

Signposted off A3083, S

In the two years they have been here, the Thomases (both from Cornwall) have turned what was a very run-down pub into a thriving business. They use local suppliers for all their produce and both licensees have a wealth of local knowledge. The pub was built around 500 years ago and was well known as a smugglers' haunt – there still exists a shaft leading to a tunnel which can be reached only from the attic. Good, popular bar food includes sandwiches (from £1.90), home-made soup such as celery and walnut or pea and ham (£2.15; with a cheese roll as well, £4.50), chicken liver or smoked trout pâté (£2.95), grilled goat's cheese on toast (£3.10), ploughman's (from £3.40), daily pasta and vegetarian dishes (£5.30), several platters (from £7.60; crab £8.50), daily specials like pancakes filled with prawns in a tarragon cream sauce, spicy lamb with honey, almonds and spices, lemon sole, scallops in a garlic cream sauce, and char-grilled steaks, and puddings such as tiramisu, cheesecakes or chocolate fudgecake with a butterscotch pecan topping (£2.75). Well kept Furgusons Dartmoor and Sharps Doom Bar on handpump, lots of malt whiskies and liqueurs, and an interesting wine list; darts, dominoes and cribbage. The quietly welcoming pleasant bar has a warm fire in the big hearth, comfortable seating, copper on the walls and mantlepiece, and maybe the three cats (Millie the tortoiseshell, Humphrey the gentle black one, and a lively marmalade one called Mr Chivers); there's also a newly created family room with toys, games and puzzles. Just 300 yards away is Gunwalloe fishing cove, a sandy beach one mile away at Gunwalloe Church Cove, and lots of unspoilt coastal walks with fine views of Mount's Bay. We've not yet had reports on the bedrooms but would expect them to be good. *(Recommended by George and Chris Miller, R P and L E Booth, Sally Andrews, Mick Wood, Bob and Maggie Atherton, P and M Rudlin, Gwen and Peter Andrews, G Atkinson, Paul Weedon, Alan Castle)*

Free house ~ Licensees Harry and Angela Thomas ~ Real ale ~ Meals and snacks (not 25 Dec) ~ Restaurant ~ (01326) 240406 ~ Children in family room and restaurant ~ Open 11.30-3, 6-11; winter evening opening 6.30 ~ Bedrooms: £35B/£50B

LANLIVERY SX0759 Map 1

Crown

Village signposted off A390 Lostwithiel—St Austell

The friendly Cornish licensees in this pretty 12th-c pub are keen to preserve the chatty, relaxed atmosphere – hence no juke box, games machines or pool table. The bar servery is buried at the heart of a rambling series of rooms – the first of which is the small, dimly lit public bar with its heavy beams, slate floor, built-in wall settles and attractive alcove of seats in the dark former chimney; darts. A much lighter room leads off here with beams in the white boarded ceiling, some comfortable, if ancient, burgundy plush sofas in one corner, flowery cushioned black settles, a small cabinet with wood-turning stuff for sale, owl and badger pictures, and a little fireplace with an old-fashioned fire; there's also another tiny similar little room. The slate-floored porch room has lots of succulents and a few cacti, and wood-and-stone seats. Good bar food uses home-grown soft fruit, vegetables and herbs as well as produce from local farmers and fishermen, and includes soup with a home-made roll, sandwiches (from £1.45), pasties (£1.70), ploughman's (from £2.45), home-made curries (from £4.65), vegetarian dishes (from £5.75), several ways of doing scallops, swordfish, trout or lemon sole (from £5.95), home-made steak and kidney pie (£6.15), steaks (from £9.25), four daily specials like lamb chops in a shallot sauce or devilled crab claws, home-made puddings, and a children's menu (from £1.25). Well kept Bass, Sharps (brewed 12 miles away), and Worthington on handpump, and farm cider; dominoes and cards. In the garden are some white cast-iron furniture and picnic tables sheltered by the black-and-white painted building. *(Recommended by Ian Phillips, Jack and Philip Paxton, S Brackenbury, Michael and Joan Johnstone)*

Free house ~ Licensees Ros and Dave Williams ~ Real ale ~ Meals and snacks ~ Restaurant ~ (01208) 872707 ~ Children in restaurant ~ Open 11-3, 6-11 ~ Bedrooms: £23S/£40S

LANNER SW7240 Map 1

Fox & Hounds

Comford; junction A393/B3293; OS sheet 204 map reference 734399

This year, a wildlife pond has been developed in the garden here and a big barbecue area opened up, too. There are pretty hanging baskets and tubs of flowers, and picnic tables on the sheltered and neatly kept back lawn; swings and climber for children. Inside, the rambling bar has black beams and joists, stripped stonework and dark panelling, some comical 1920s prints by Lawson Wood, some high-backed settles and cottagey chairs, and a relaxed atmosphere. One granite fireplace has a woodburning stove, another has a good log fire, and there may be cheerful summer flowers to brighten up the tables. Bar food includes sandwiches, ploughman's, soup (£1.85), cashew nut paella (£4.55), cumberland sausages (£5), vegetarian dishes, seafood mornay (£6.75), steaks (from £9.50), honey roast duck (£10.25), puddings (£2), children's menu (from £1.50), and daily specials. Well kept Bass and St Austell Tinners, HSD and Winter Warmer tapped from the cask; around 14 malt whiskies. Pool, shove-ha'penny, cribbage, dominoes, fruit machine, and piped music. Part of the restaurant is no smoking. *(Recommended by Ian Julian, Alan and Eileen Bowker, Tom Evans, RB, Andy and Jill Kassube, S Brackenbury, Jack and Philip Paxton)*

St Austell ~ Tenants Mike and Sue Swiss ~ Real ale ~ Meals and snacks ~ Restaurant ~ (01209) 820251 ~ Open 11-3, 6-11; 11-11 Sat

LERRYN SX1457 Map 1

Ship

Village signposted from A390 in Lostwithiel

Doing very well at the moment, this neatly kept, hospitable pub is pretty in summer with its flower borders, tubs and hanging baskets, and there are some picnic tables in front of the stone building, with more on a sheltered back lawn which also has a children's play area. Inside, the walls of the bar are hung with photographs of the small seagull-engined craft race, held in December – the winner is the first back to the pub to ring the ship's bell – as well as some old village ones, brasses on beams, and a locally made grandfather clock; part of the lounge bar is no-smoking. A separate room has sensibly placed darts, pool, dominoes, fruit machine, and piped music. Well kept ales might include Bass, Courage Best, Exmoor Gold, Fullers London Pride, Morlands Old Speckled Hen, Otter Ale, and Sharps Cornish on handpump, local farm cider, fruit wines and lots of malt whiskies. Good bar food includes sandwiches, lots of home-made pies like venison, pheasant and cranberry, pumpkin, homity, and steak and oyster pie (all £5.75), and dishes readers have liked such as chicken with orange and honey, good vegetarian choices, spanish pork and olive casserole or home-made chicken kiev, an enjoyable crab salad or local wild salmon, and lovely puddings like wonderful lemon brûlée. You can walk along the bank of the River Lerryn or through the National Trust woodland nearby. There is a self-catering flat for rent. *(Recommended by Gwen and Peter Andrews, S N T Spencer, George Atkinson, Philip Jackson, Patricia Heptinstall, Mr and Mrs J Woodfield, Jack and Philip Paxton, JE, Gerry Hollington, R L Turnham)*

Free house ~ Licensee Howard Packer ~ Real ale ~ Meals and snacks ~ Restaurant ~ (01208) 872374 ~ Well behaved children welcome ~ Open 11.30-3(2.30 in winter), 6-11 ~ Bedrooms: £30

LOSTWITHIEL SX1059 Map 1

Royal Oak

Duke St; pub just visible from A390 in centre

There's an unusually good choice of real ales for the area in this friendly old pub: Bass, Elgoods Greyhound, Fullers London Pride, Marstons Pedigree, Sharps Doom Bar, and Whitbread Original as well as lots of bottled beers from around the world. Popular bar food includes lunchtime sandwiches (from £1.45) and ploughman's (from £2.75), as well as soup (£1.45), salads (from £4.45), vegetarian crêpes (£5.25), steaks (from £7.30), daily specials such as a curry (£4.95), steak and kidney pie (£5.25) or fresh whole plaice (£7.45), puddings (£1.55), and children's dishes (from £1.70). The well kept lounge is spacious and comfortable, with captain's chairs and brown leatherette button-back banquettes on its patterned carpet, a couple of wooden armchairs by the log-effect gas fire, and walls stripped back to the old reddish granite. There's also a delft shelf, with a small dresser in one inner alcove. The flagstoned back public bar has darts, dominoes, cribbage, fruit machine and juke box, and is popular with younger customers. On a raised terrace by the car park are some picnic tables. *(Recommended by Jack and Philip Paxton, G Washington, Peter Williamson, Andy and Jill Kassube, Ron Shelton, Jill Bickerton, Dr John Lunn)*

Free house ~ Licensees Malcolm and Eileen Hine ~ Real ale ~ Meals and snacks ~ Restaurant ~ (01208) 872552 ~ Children in eating area of bar and in restaurant ~ Open 11-11 ~ Bedrooms: £26.50(£29.50B)/£46.50(£51.50B)

LUDGVAN SW5033 Map 1

White Hart

Churchtown; off A30 Penzance—Hayle at Crowlas – OS Sheet 203 map reference 505330

A relaxed atmosphere, lots of locals, and no noisy machines or piped music give this interesting old pub quite a timeless feel. The small and snug beamed rooms have masses of mugs and jugs glinting in cottagey corners, bric-a-brac, pictures and photographs (including some good ones of Exmoor), soft oil-lamp-style lighting, stripped boards with attractive rugs on them, and a fascinating mix of interesting old seats and tables; the two capacious woodburning stoves run radiators too. Good simple bar food (with prices virtually unchanged since last year) includes sandwiches (from £1.10), home-made soup or village-made pasties (£1.60), ploughman's (£2.50; good stilton), sausage and egg (£3), salads (from £3.50), omelettes (£3.75), home-made vegetable or meaty lasagne (£4), steaks (from £7.75), puddings (£1.75), and daily specials such as delicious fresh mackerel (£3), toad in the hole (£3.75), or rabbit casserole (£4.50). Well kept Flowers IPA, Marstons Pedigree and a guest beer tapped from the cask; part of the eating area is reserved for no-smokers. Although the great manority of readers feel this is just how a village pub should be, there has been a smattering of unhappiness in the last year over unwelcoming service – we'd be grateful for reports on this. *(Recommended by J Ingram, K Stevens, Jack and Philip Paxton, R and S Bentley, Richard Wood, Fiona Lewry, J F Doleman, Mr and Mrs D Darby, Anthony Barnes, Mrs B Sugarman, Dr R J Rathbone, Peter Neate, Anthony Barnes)*

Devenish (Greenalls) ~ Tenant Dennis Churchill ~ Real ale ~ Meals and snacks (not Mon evening Oct-May) ~ (01736) 740574 ~ Children in restaurant only ~ Open 11-2.30, 6-11

MITHIAN SW7450 Map 1

Miners Arms

Just off B3285 E of St Agnes

The several cosy little rooms and passages in this 16th-c pub are warmed by winter open fires. The atmospheric small back bar has an irregular beam and plank ceiling, wood block floor and bulging squint walls (one with a fine old wall painting of Elizabeth I), and another small room has a decorative low ceiling, lots of books and quite a few interesting ornaments. Bar food includes sandwiches, ploughman's, crab bake (£3.95), lasagne, beef curry or steak and kidney pie (£5.25), daily specials, and puddings like toffee apple fudge cake (£2.20). The dining room is no smoking; the plump spaniel might be walking around with his 'please don't feed me' notice around his neck. Well kept Bass and Boddingtons on handpump kept under light blanket pressure, and several wines by the glass; friendly service. Dominoes, shove-ha'penny, and piped music. There are seats on the back terrace, with more on the sheltered and cobbled forecourt. *(Recommended by Piotr Chodzko-Zajko, Jerry and Alison Oakes, Jack and Philip Paxton, Bob and Maggie Atherton, Tim and Chris Ford)*

Greenalls ~ Tenant David Charnock ~ Real ale ~ Meals and snacks ~ (01872) 552375 ~ Children welcome ~ Open 12-3, 6-11.30; winter evening opening 7

MORWENSTOW SS2015 Map 1

Bush £

Village signposted off A39 N of Kilkhampton

If unchanging little pubs with few concessions to modern ideas appeal to you, then this ancient place should be just the ticket – the landlord is firmly against piped music, children and dogs. It's one of the oldest pubs in Britain – part of it dates back over 1000 years and a Celtic piscina carved from serpentine stone is still set in one wall. There are ancient built-in settles, flagstones, and a big stone fireplace, and a cosy side area with antique seats, a lovely old elm trestle table, and a wooden propeller from a 1930 De Havilland Gipsy Moth. An upper bar, opened at busy times, is decorated with antique knife-grinding wheels, miners' lamps, casks, funnels, and so forth. Well kept St Austell HSD and Winter Brew (December and January only) both on handpump, and guest beers such as Cotleigh Old Buzzard, Wadworths 6X and Farmers Glory tapped from the cask behind the wood-topped stone bar counter (with pewter tankards lining the beams above it); quite a few malt whiskies and Inches cider. Simple lunchtime bar food includes sandwiches, good home-made soup (£1.50), locally-made pasties (£1.60), ploughman's with a bowl of home-made pickle (£2), home-made stew (£3), crab and coleslaw (£3.50), various daily specials, and puddings like spotted dick or apple pie; no chips. Darts and two friendly cats. Seats outside shelter in the slightly sunken yard. Within a few hundred yards is the famous village church, with a wrecked ship's figurehead as a gravestone for its crew, and Vicarage Cliff, one of the grandest parts of the Cornish coast (with 400-ft precipices) is a ten-minute walk away. *(Recommended by Rita Horridge, Jack and Philip Paxton, S Brackenbury, Alan and Eileen Bowker, Richard Cole, LM, Ian and Nita Cooper, P C Russell, S Demont, T Barrow, David Holloway)*

Free house ~ Licensee J H Gregory ~ Real ale ~ Lunchtime snacks (not Sun) ~ (01288) 331242 ~ Open 12-3, 7-11; closed Mon Oct-Apr, except bank holidays

MOUSEHOLE SW4726 Map 1

Ship

Follow Newlyn coast rd out of Penzance; also signposted off B3315

A traditional fisherman's local right by the harbour in a lovely village, this relaxed place has genuine character in its opened-up main bar: black beams and panelling, built-in wooden wall benches and stools around the low tables, sailors' fancy ropework, granite flagstones, and a cosy open fire. Bar food includes sandwiches (crab £3.50), local mussels (£3.25), local fish dishes, and steaks (from £7.25). On 23 December they bake Starry Gazy pie to celebrate Tom Bawcock's Eve, a tradition that recalls Tom's brave expedition out to sea in a fierce storm 200 years ago. He caught seven types of fish, which were then cooked in a pie with their heads and tails sticking out. Well kept BB, Tinners and HSD on handpump, and several malt whiskies; friendly staff; darts, dominoes, cribbage, and fruit machine. The village does get packed in summer (when parking is virtually impossible) and over the Christmas period when people come to visit the elaborate harbour lights. *(Recommended by Mark Walker, J C Simpson, Gary Nicholls, Peter and Joy Heatherley, Bill Sharpe, Andy and Jill Kassube, Lynn Sharpless, Bob Eardley, DAV, Dr and Mrs A K Clarke, Gwen and Peter Andrews)*

St Austell ~ Tenants Michael and Tracey Maddern ~ Real ale ~ Meals and snacks ~ Restaurant ~ (01736) 731234 ~ Children welcome if kept away from bar ~ Summer parking can be difficult ~ Open 10.30am-11pm ~ Bedrooms: /£40B

nr MYLOR BRIDGE SW8036 Map 1

Pandora ★ ★ 🍷

Restronguet Passage: from A39 in Penryn, take turning signposted Mylor Church, Mylor Bridge, Flushing and go straight through Mylor Bridge following Restronguet Passage signs; or from A39 further N, at or near Perranarworthal, take turning signposted Mylor, Restronguet, then follow Restronguet Weir signs, but turn left down hill at Restronguet Passage sign

The waterside setting for this pretty medieval thatched pub really is lovely – and much appreciated from the picnic tables in front or on the long floating jetty. Quite a few people arrive by boat and there are showers for visiting yachtsmen. Inside is splendidly atmospheric, and the several rambling, interconnecting rooms have low wooden ceilings (mind your head on some of the beams), beautifully polished big flagstones, cosy alcoves with leatherette benches built into the walls, a kitchen range, and a log fire in a high hearth (to protect it against tidal floods); two no-smoking areas. Bar food includes home-made soup (from £1.85), sandwiches (from £2.50), burger (£3.95), pancakes stuffed with mushroom and spinach (£4.50), fish pie (£4.95), crab thermidor (£8.50), daily specials, puddings like home-made treacle tart (£2.30), Sunday roast (from £4.95), and children's dishes (from £1.50). Bass, St Austell Tinners, HSD and BB on handpump from a temperature controlled cellar, several malt whiskies, 20 good wines by the glass, and farm cider; dominoes, winter pool, and winter weekly quiz. It does get very crowded in summer, and parking is difficult at peak times. *(Recommended by Nigel Flook, Betsy Brown, George and Chris Miller, G W Stevenson, C Driver, E N Burleton, Beverley James, Ted George, Jim Reid, Sue Holland, Dave Webster, Bob and Maggie Atherton, Michael Sargent, Andy and Jill Kassube, A J N Lee, D C Pressey, Jerry and Alison Oakes, Pat and John Millward, Gwen and Peter Andrews, Lynn Sharpless, Bob Eardley, Jim and Maggie Cowell, Susan and Nigel Wilson, Penny and Martin Fletcher)*

St Austell ~ Tenant Helen Hough ~ Real ale ~ Meals and snacks (till 10pm in summer) ~ Evening restaurant ~ (01326) 372678 ~ Children in eating area of bar and in restaurant ~ Open 11-11; 12-2.30(3 winter Sat/Sun), 7-11 in winter

PELYNT SX2055 Map 1

Jubilee 🛏

B3359 NW of Looe

This neatly kept and comfortable 16th-c inn, once an old farmhouse, has a relaxed lounge bar with an early 18th-c Derbyshire oak armchair, brown leather and red fabric cushioned wall and window seats, windsor armchairs, magazines stacked under the oak tables, and a good winter log fire in the stone fireplace under the neatly squared oak beams; gleaming brass, fresh flowers, and mementoes of Queen Victoria, such as a tapestry portrait, old prints, and Staffordshire figurines of the Queen and her consort. The flagstoned entry is separated from the bar by an attractively old-fangled glass-paned partition. Good, popular food (with prices unchanged since last year), promptly served by cheery waitresses, includes home-made soup (£2), a good choice of sandwiches (from £1.60), ploughman's (from £2.80), salads (from £4.80), haddock au gratin with prawns (£4.90), local seafood mornay (£5.40), fresh cod (£5.60), gammon and egg (£6.50), sirloin steak (£9.80), and puddings (from £1.80). Well kept Furguson Dartmoor Strong on handpump, several malt whiskies, and quite a few wines. The quite separate public bar has sensibly placed darts, pool, fruit machine, and piped music. A crazy-paved central courtyard has picnic tables with red and white striped umbrellas, pretty tubs of flowers, and barbecues (weather permitting), and there's a well equipped children's play area. *(Recommended by George Atkinson, Ian Phillips, Barbara and Denis Melling, J C Simpson, James Morrell, K and R Beaver, John and Tessa Rainsford, David Burnett, Donna Lowes)*

Free House ~ Licensee Tim Williams ~ Real ale ~ Meals and snacks ~ Restaurant (not Sun evening) ~ (01503) 220312 ~ Children welcome ~ Open 11-3, 6-11 ~ Bedrooms: £35B/£60B

PENELEWEY SW8240 Map 1

Punch Bowl & Ladle

Feock Downs, B3289

A new licensee has taken over this quaint 15th-c pub set near the King Harry ferry and Trelissick Gardens. There are several comfortably furnished, attractive rooms – though the cosy ones in the original part have lots of shipwreck paintings and farm implements around the walls, and an open fire. Well kept Bass, Boddingtons, Flowers Original and guest beers such as Courage Directors or Tetleys on handpump. Bar food such as filled baked potatoes (from £1.95), open sandwiches (from £3.05), salads (from £3.95), chicken in tomato, mushroom and cream (£6.45), beef and stilton casserole (£7.45), at least two fresh fish dishes daily like whole grilled lemon sole (£9.50), daily specials such as chicken and apricot pie or curried vegetables in filo cases (from £5.95), puddings (£2.25), and two Sunday roasts (£4.95); children can have half helpings of adult food or their own menu (from £2.25). Darts, shove-ha'penny, cribbage, dominoes, fruit machine, and piped music. *(Recommended by John Chetwynd-Chatwin, Adrian and Karen Bulley, John Wooll, Jim and Maggie Cowell)*

Greenalls ~ Manager Richard Dearsley ~ Real ales ~ Meals and snacks ~ Restaurant ~ (01872) 862237 ~ Well behaved children welcome ~ Open 11-3, 5.30-11

PENZANCE SW4730 Map 1

Turks Head

At top of main street, by big domed building (Lloyds Bank), turn left down Chapel Street

As good as ever, this friendly pub has a relaxed and chatty main bar interestingly decorated with old flat irons, jugs and so forth hanging from the beams, pottery above the wood-effect panelling, wall seats and tables, and a couple of elbow rests around central pillars. The menu has quite an emphasis on seafood, with crab soup (£1.60), fish pie (£5.25), crab salad (mixed meat £6.70, white meat £7.50), and cold seafood platter (£8.95), as well as sandwiches (from £1.40), filled baked potatoes (from £1.95), ham and egg (£3.25), ratatouille topped with cheese (£4.05), meaty or vegetarian lasagne (£4.35), popular steak and kidney pie (£4.60), good steaks, and puddings. Boddingtons, Flowers Original and Marstons Pedigree on handpump, country wines, and helpful service; juke box, piped music. The sun-trap back garden has big urns of flowers. There has been a Turks Head here for over 700 years – though most of the original building was destroyed by a Spanish raiding party in the 16th-c. *(Recommended by Gary Nicholls, Norma Farris, P and M Rudlin, Bill and Sylvia Trotter, Mark Walker, RB, David Yandle, Neil and Anita Christopher, David Dimock, S Brackenbury)*

Greenalls ~ Tenant William Morris ~ Real ale ~ Meals and snacks (11-2.30, 6-10) ~ Restaurant ~ (01736) 63093 ~ Children in cellar dining room ~ Open 11-3, 5.30-11

PHILLEIGH SW8639 Map 1

Roseland ★

Between A3078 and B3289, just E of King Harry Ferry

There's a good chatty atmosphere in this friendly little 17th c pub – and no noisy games machines or piped music. The low beamed bar has a nice oak settle and antique seats around the sturdy tables on the flagstones, an old wall clock, a good winter fire, and lots of rugby and rowing prints – the landlord's sports. Good, popular home-made bar food using fresh local produce includes pasties (£1.95), home-made soup, sandwiches (from £2.50), home-made chicken liver and sherry pâté (£3.65), ploughman's (from £3.95), filled oven-baked potatoes (from £3.25), beef cobbler (£4.95), fresh local crab salad (£7.25), with evening dishes such as vegetable nut roast (£6.75), local mussels (£6.95), sirloin steak with a red wine sauce (£9.25), and fresh local lobster (24 hours' notice); summer cream teas. Well kept Bass, Greenalls Bitter and Marstons Pedigree on handpump, farm cider from the barrel (summer only), and quite a few malt whiskies; dominoes, cribbage, shove-ha'penny. The pretty paved front courtyard is a lovely place to sit in the lunchtime sunshine beneath the cherry blossom; the birds are unusually tame. The furniture here too is interesting – one table made from a converted well. The quiet lane leads on to the little half-hourly King Harry car ferry across a pretty wooded channel, with Trelissick Gardens on the far side. *(Recommended by R and S Bentley, M E Wellington, Alan and Eileen Bowker, Stephen and Sarah Pleasance, Mr and Mrs P Richardson, R J Walden, Kevin and Tracey Stephens, Michael Sargent, Cdr and Mrs J G Ross, Kevin O Gillies, Jerry and Alison Oakes, Peter and Joy Heatherley, DJW, Lynn Sharpless, Bob Eardley)*

Greenalls (Devenish) ~ Tenant Graham Hill ~ Real ale ~ Meals and snacks ~ Restaurant ~ (01872) 580254 ~ Children welcome ~ Open 11.30-3, 6-11; probably all day July/August

PILLATON SX3664 Map 1

Weary Friar

Best reached from the good Callington—Landrake back road; OS Sheet 201 map reference 365643

In a village hidden away down a maze of Cornish lanes, this pretty 12th-c pub has four characterful and tidy knocked-together rooms (one is no smoking): beam-and-plank ceilings, comfortable seats around sturdy wooden tables, easy chairs by a little coal fire at one end, and a much grander old stone fireplace at the other. Good, popular bar food includes lunchtime sandwiches (£2.50) or ploughman's (from £3.25), as well as soup (£2.50), basket meals or salads (from £4), vegetable or steak in ale pies (£5.50), chicken tikka masala (£6.50), steaks (from £8.50), and puddings (from £2.50). Well kept Bass, Courage Directors, Morlands Old Speckled Hen, and Wadworths 6X on handpump, farm cider, country wines and mulled wine; piped music. There are old-fashioned slatted teak seats outside, in the angle of the L-shaped black-shuttered building and over the quiet lane. *(Recommended by Ted George, James Macrae, Jack and Philip Paxton, R J Walden, J and J O Jones, S Brackenbury, P J Caunt, Bronwen and Steve Wrigley, Ian and Deborah Carrington, Vernon Crockett, Linda and Brian Davis, R L Turnham, M and R Hepburn)*

Free house ~ Licensees Mr and Mrs R Sharman ~ Real ale ~ Meals and snacks (till 10pm) ~ Restaurant (closed Mon) ~ (01579) 50238 ~ Children in eating area of bar ~ Open 11.30-3, 6.30-11 ~ Bedrooms: £35B/£50B

POLKERRIS SX0952 Map 1

Rashleigh

Signposted off A3082 Fowey—St Austell

From the stone terrace here, there are fine views towards the far side of St Austell and Mevagissey Bays and the pub actually borders a lovely isolated beach. Inside, the front part of the bar has comfortably cushioned seats, with local photographs on the brown panelling of a more simply furnished back area; friendly staff and locals, and winter log fire. Good food includes soup (£1.95), sandwiches (from £1.65; open ones from £4.25), ploughman's (from £3.80), pasta and mushroom bake (£4.50), fish or steak pies (£5.50), popular lunchtime cold buffet (from £5.50), daily specials such as fresh cod (£4.95), rabbit and bacon pie (£5.50) and sea trout (£9.75), and puddings (£1.95). Bass, Furgusons Best and Dartmoor, Ind Coope Burton, and St Austell HSD on handpump or tapped from the cask, decent wine list and several malt whiskies; dominoes, cribbage, and trivia. Though parking space next to the pub is limited, there's a large village car park, and there are safe moorings for small yachts in the cove. This whole section of the Cornish coast path is renowned for its striking scenery. *(Recommended by Cdr and Mrs J G Ross, JE, Jack and Philip Paxton, Barbara and Denis Melling, Mrs B Sugarman, Roger Wain-Heapy, A W Lewis, John and Tessa Rainsford, A N Ellis, Mr and Mrs C R Little, Peter and Lynn Brueton)*

Free house ~ Licensees Bernard and Carole Smith ~ Real ale ~ Meals and snacks ~ Restaurant ~ (01726) 813991 ~ Well-behaved children in eating area of bar until 8.30pm ~ Pianist Fri (in summer) and Sat evenings ~ Open 11-3, 6-11; 11.30-2.30, 6.30-11 in winter

POLRUAN SX1251 Map 1

Lugger

Reached from A390 in Lostwithiel; nearby parking expensive and limited, or steep walk down from village-edge car park; passenger/bicycle ferry from Fowey

The two bars in this friendly local have been knocked together and refurbished but still have beams, high-backed wall settles, wheelback chairs, and a slightly nautical theme – big model boats, local boat photographs, and a fish tank. Half the family room is no smoking. Good bar food includes sandwiches, home-made steak and kidney pie (£4.25), smoked haddock pasta (£4.75), seafood curry (£5), and fresh local fish such as whole plaice (£5.50), shark steak (£6.50), and monkfish (£6.95). St Austell BB, Tinners, HSD and XXXX on handpump and Scrumpy Jack cider; darts, pool (winter only), cribbage, fruit machine, and piped music. There are fine views of the little harbour and across to Fowey – and if you arrive by boat, there are steep stone steps leading up to the pub. Good surrounding walks; well behaved dogs allowed. Self-catering cottage available. *(Recommended by Mike Woodhead, George Atkinson, JE, Andy and Jill Kassube, Peter and Audrey Dowsett, Norma Farris, P and J Shapley, David Rule, Peter and Audrey Dowsett)*

St Austell ~ Manager Terry Jones ~ Real ale ~ Meals and snacks ~ Restaurant ~ Children in family room ~ (01726) 870007 ~ Local singer/comedian or middle of road singing duo Thurs and occasional Fri and Sat evenings ~ Open 11-11; 11-3, 6.30-11 in winter

PORT ISAAC SW9980 Map 1

Golden Lion

Fore Street

Looking down on the rocky harbour and lifeboat slip from the windows of this 18th-c pub, you can just imagine the tunnel that used to run from here to a harbourmouth cave in smuggling days. The bar has a fine antique settle among other comfortable seats, decorative ceiling plasterwork, perhaps the pub dog Hollie, and a relaxed, friendly atmosphere – despite the summer crowds. Good home-made food includes sandwiches, ploughman's (from £3.95), fish pie (£5.25), tasty seafood lasagne (£5.45), and fresh seafood platter (£12.75); during the summer, evening meals are served in the bistro. Well kept St Austell Tinners and HSD on handpump and twenty-three malts. Darts, shove-ha'penny, dominoes, cribbage, a fruit machine in the public bar, and piped music. A large cannon sits on the small back terrace. The very steep narrow lanes of this working fishing village are most attractive. *(Recommended by Dave Thompson, Margaret Mason, R T and J C Moggridge, Andy and Jane Beardsley, Lynn Sharpless, Bob Eardley, David and Julie Glover, Graham Tavar, Margaret Mason)*

St Austell ~ Tenants Mike and Nikki Edkins ~ Real ale ~ Meals and snacks ~ Evening summer restaurant ~ (01208) 880336 ~ Children welcome ~ No parking nearby ~ Open 11.30-11; 11.30-3, 6.30-11 winter weekdays

nr PORT ISAAC SX0080 Map 1

Port Gaverne Hotel

Port Gaverne signposted from Port Isaac, and from B3314 E of Pendoggett

In a lovely spot, just back from the sea and close to splendid clifftop walks, this early 17th-c inn has well kept bars with low beams, flagstones as well as carpeting, big log fires, some exposed stone, and an enormous marine chronometer. In spring the lounge is filled with pictures from the local art society's annual exhibition in aid of the Royal National Lifeboat Institution; at other times there are interesting antique local photographs. Bar food includes sandwiches (from £1.60), home-made soup (£2.50), ploughman's (from £2.95), cottage pie (£2.95), salads (from £3.75, half a lobster £8.75), and deep-fried local plaice (£4.95). During the season lunchtime food is served buffet-style in the dining room, as it is on Sunday throughout the year (when food stops at 2 sharp). The rest of the time it's served in the bar or 'Captain's Cabin' – a little room where everything except its antique admiral's hat is shrunk to scale (old oak chest, model sailing ship, even the prints on the white stone walls); the restaurant is no smoking. Well kept Bass, Flowers IPA and Sharps on handpump, a good bin-end wine list with 60 wines, a very good choice of whiskies and other spirits such as ouzo and akvavit, and around 38 liqueurs. Dominoes, cribbage and piped music in the renovated Green Door Bar across the lane, which also has a big diorama of Port Isaac. *(Recommended by Laurence Bacon, Nigel Flook, Betsy Brown, James Macrae; more reports please)*

Free house ~ Licensee Mrs M Ross ~ Real ale ~ Meals and snacks (till 10pm) ~ Restaurant ~ (01208) 880244 ~ Children in eating area of bar and in own area ~ Open 11-11; 11-3, 6-11 in winter; closed early Jan to mid-Feb ~ Bedrooms: £47B/£94B; restored 18th-c self-contained cottages

PORTHALLOW SW7923 Map 1

Five Pilchards

SE of Helston; B3293 to St Keverne, then village signposted

The long-serving landlord has been here now for 30 years. It's a robustly stone-built old place just off the beach with an abundance of salvaged nautical gear, lamps made from puffer fish, and interesting photographs and clippings about local shipwrecks. Well kept Devenish Cornish Original, Greene King Abbot, John Smiths, and Whitbreads Pompey Royal on handpump, and country wines. Lunchtime food includes home-made soup (£1.50), ploughman's (from £3), daily specials (from £2.25), and prawn platter (£6.95); darts in winter, dominoes, and a fruit machine. The attractive cove is largely protected against unsightly development by being owned by its residents. Tides and winds allowing, you can park on the foreshore. Please note that children are not welcome. *(Recommended by A J N Lee, Jack and Philip Paxton, Michael Sargent, Anthony Barnes, E N Burleton, S Brackenbury, DJW, Gwen and Peter Andrews, John and Sally Clarke)*

Free house ~ Licensee David Tripp ~ Real ale ~ Lunchtime snacks ~ (01326) 280256 ~ Open 12-2.30(3 Sat), 6(7.30 in winter)-11; closed Mon from Jan-Whitsun ~ Self-contained flat sleeps 6

PORTHLEVEN SW6225 Map 1

Ship ★

Apart from its marvellous position here with views over the pretty working harbour and out to sea, what readers like so much about this friendly old fishermans' pub is its cheerfully buoyant atmosphere. The knocked-through bar has log fires in big stone fireplaces and some genuine character, and the candlelit dining room shares the same fine view; the family room is a conversion of an old smithy and has logs burning in the huge open fireplace. Well kept Courage Best and Ushers Best and Founders on handpump; dominoes, euchre, fruit machine and piped music. Nicely presented, popular bar food includes sandwiches (from £1.80; fine toasties from £2.45; excellent crusty loaf from £3.50), filled oven-baked potatoes (from £2.30), ploughman's (from £4.50), vegetable curry, steak and kidney pudding or fish pie (£5.25), sweet and sour chicken (£6.95), mussels in garlic butter (£7.95), interesting daily specials like chicken casserole in orange and cointreau, and sirloin steak (£8.75); puddings like home-made apple torte (from £2.25), evening extras such as an excellent big bowl of mushrooms in garlic (£3.95), and children's meals (£1.95). Terraced garden. The harbour is interestingly floodlit at night. *(Recommended by Peter and Audrey Dowsett, Mrs J Jones, Jack and Philip Paxton, Pete and Rosie Flower, John and Vivienne Rice, Beverley James, Bob and Maggie Atherton, Canon Michael Bourdeaux, Mr and Mrs Brackenbury, DAV, John and*

Sally Clarke, Peter and Lynn Brueton, Sue Holland, Dave Webster, Mark Walker, Mr and Mrs C R Little, Martin and Penny Fletcher)

Ushers ~ Tenant Colin Oakden ~ Real ale ~ Meals and snacks ~ (01326) 572841 ~ Children in family room ~ Parking can be difficult in summer ~ Open 11.30-3, 6.30-11; 11.30-2.30, 7-11 in winter

SCORRIER SW7244 Map 1

Fox & Hounds

Village singposted from A30; B3298 Falmouth road

Bar food in this friendly white cottage is popular, so it's worth getting here early for a seat. Served by uniformed waitresses, it might include home-made soup (£1.95), doorstep or open sandwiches (from £2.95), filled baked potatoes (from £2.95), lunchtime ploughman's (from £3.45), omelettes (from £3.95), Lebanese kofta (£4.60), moussaka (£4.70), cumberland sausage or mushrooms in a tomato, basil and sherry sauce with pasta and mozzarella (£4.95), cold prawns in curried mayonnaise (£5.20), fish and broccoli bake (£6.95), sirloin steak (£8.35), daily specials such as parsnip bake (£4.65), liver and bacon or Hawaiian lamb with limes (£4.95), squire's pork (£5.25), and good home-made puddings. Well kept Boddingtons and Flowers Original on handpump. The long bar is divided into sections by a partition wall and low screens and has creaky joists, vertical panelling, stripped stonework, hunting prints, comfortable furnishings, and big log fires, as well as a stuffed fox and fox mask; there's also more seating in a no-smoking front extension, formerly a verandah. The long building – well set back from the road – is prettily decorated outside with hanging baskets and window-boxes, and has new picnic tables under cocktail parasols in front. *(Recommended by Tony Wickett, Gillian Jenkins, S Brackenbury; more reports please)*

Greenalls ~ Tenants David and Linda Halfpenny ~ Real ale ~ Meals and snacks (till 10pm; and see below; not 25 or 26 Dec) ~ (01209) 820205 ~ Well behaved children allowed in eating area of bar, subject to landlord's approval ~ Open 11.30-2.30, 6-11; closed Mon evenings 3 Jan-end Mar/Easter

ST AGNES SW7250 Map 1

Railway

10 Vicarage Rd; from centre follow B3277 signs for Porthtowan and Truro

The older part of this friendly little terraced pub has a remarkable collection of shoes – minute or giant, made of strange skins, fur, leather, wood, mother-of-pearl, or embroidered with gold and silver, from Turkey, Persia, China or Japan and worn by ordinary people or famous men, as well as some splendid brasswork that includes one of the finest original horsebrass collections in the country. As if this wasn't enough to look at, there's also a notable collection of naval memorabilia from model sailing ships and rope fancywork to the texts of Admiralty messages at important historical moments, such as the announcement of the ceasefire at the end of the First World War. Bar food includes home-made soup (£1.95), sandwiches (from £1.95), ploughman's or filled baked potatoes (£3.50), home-made daily specials (£3.95), fresh plaice or lemon sole (£4.65), steak (£7.95), and puddings; children's meals (£2.25). Well kept Boddingtons and Marstons Pedigree on handpump; darts, pool, cribbage, pinball, dominoes, fruit machine and juke box. *(Recommended by Malcolm and Helen Baxter, Jim Reid, Jack and Philip Paxton, S R and A J Ashcroft, R and S Bentley, Andy and Jill Kassube, Paul Cartledge)*

Greenalls ~ Tenant Christopher O'Brien ~ Real ale ~ Meals and snacks (12-2.30, 6-10) ~ (01872) 552310 ~ Children in eating area of bar ~ Quiz night Tues, live music Thurs ~ Open 11-3, 6-11; 11-11 Sat

It is illegal for bar staff to smoke while handling your drink.

ST AGNES (Isles of Scilly) SV8807 Map 1

Turks Head

The Quay

Well worth the boat trip, this marvellously peaceful little slate-roofed white cottage sits just above the sweeping bay, with gorgeous sea views. Across the sleepy lane are a few tables on a patch of lawn above the water, with steps down beside them to the slipway – you can walk down with your drinks and food and sit right on the shore. Inside, there's a growing collection of flags, helmets and banknotes in the simply furnished but cosy and very friendly pine-panelled bar, as well as maritime photographs and model ships; the extension is no smoking. First class bar food includes legendary huge locally made pasties (though they do sell out; £2.90), soup (£1.65), open rolls (from £1.85; crab £3.50), ploughman's (from £3), ham or beef and chips or Cajun vegetable casserole (£4.95), with evening gammon in port wine sauce (£5.25), fresh fish of the day, and sirloin steak (£8.35); children's meals (from £1.75). Ice cream and cakes are sold through the afternoon, and in good weather they do good evening barbecues (£3-7 Tuesday, Thursday and Sunday, July/August only), arranging special boats from St Marys – as most tripper boats leave by 5-ish. Remarkably, they also have real ale which arrives in St Agnes via a beer supplier in St Austell and two boat trips: Furgusons Dartmoor and Strong, Flowers Original and IPA, and Ind Coope Burton, in good condition on handpump, besides decent house wines, a good range of malt whiskies, and hot chocolate with brandy. Darts, dominoes, and cribbage. In spring and autumn hours may be shorter, and winter opening is sporadic, given that only some 70 people live on the island; they do then try to open if people ask, and otherwise tend to open on Saturday night, Sunday lunchtime (bookings only, roast lunch), over Christmas and the New Year, and for a Wednesday quiz night. *(Recommended by Douglas Allen, Pete and Rosie Flower, James Davies, Dorothee and Dennis Glover, Mr and Mrs D Darby, Keith and Janet Morris, P and M Rudlin)*

Free house ~ Licensees John and Pauline Dart ~ Real ale ~ Meals and snacks ~ (01720) 422434 ~ Well behaved children welcome ~ Open 11-11 summer (see text for winter) ~ Bedroom: /£42B

ST BREWARD SX0977 Map 1

Old Inn

Old Town; village signposted off B3266 S of Camelford, also signed off A30 Bolventor—Bodmin

There's a lot of atmosphere in this genuinely friendly small country pub – and a good mix of locals and visitors, too. The two roomed bar has fine broad slate flagstones, banknotes and horsebrasses hanging from the low oak joists that support the ochre upstairs floorboards, and plates on the stripped stonework. The outer room has fewer tables (old ones, of character), an open log fire in big granite fireplace, a piano and sensibly placed darts. The inner room has cushioned wall benches and chairs around its tables, naif paintings on slate by a local artist (for sale cheaply), a good log fire, and a glass panel showing a separate games room with darts, pool table, juke box, video game and fruit machine, where children are allowed; cribbage, dominoes. Popular home-made bar food includes good soup, sandwiches (from £1.50), ploughman's (£3), lovely pasties, fresh plaice (£4.75), a pie of the day (£4.95), vegetarian dishes (from £4.95), two sizes of huge mixed grill (from £6.95), and puddings like good sticky toffee pudding or banoffi pie (£2.20); big helpings. Well kept Bass, John Smiths Best, Ruddles County, and a guest such as Sharps on handpump; the landlord is from the West Highlands and his range of 80 malt whiskies reflects this, only coming from the Highlands and Islands; cheap but decent coffee. Picnic tables outside are protected by low stone walls. There's plenty of open moorland behind, and cattle and sheep wander freely into the village. In front of the building is a very worn carved stone; no-one knows exactly what it is but it may be part of a Saxon cross. *(Recommended by A Preston, John Woodward, A N*

Ellis, Jack and Philip Paxton, Jeff Davies, Jennifer Tora, David Burnett, Donna Lowes, Dave Thompson, Margaret Mason, Ted George)

Free house ~ Licensees Ann and Iain Cameron ~ Real ale ~ Meals and snacks (not 25 Dec) ~ Restaurant ~ (01208) 850711 ~ Children in eating areas and games room ~ Open 12-3, 6-11; winter closing may be 2.30

ST EWE SW9746 Map 1

Crown

Village signposted from B3287; easy to find from Mevagissey

For 39 years, this unspoilt cottage has been run by the same warmly welcoming family. It's a firm favourite of many readers, and the traditional bar has 16th-c flagstones, a very high-backed curved old settle with flowery cushions, long shiny wooden tables, and an ancient weight-driven working spit; the fireside shelves hold plates, and a brass teapot and jug. The eating area with its burgundy coloured carpet, velvet curtains, and matching cushions to go on the old church pews, has been extended this year. Popular food includes good, fresh pasties (95p), sandwiches (from £1.55, local crab in season £3.45, open sandwiches £3.65), tasty soup (£1.65), ploughman's or filled baked potatoes (from £2.95), salads (from £4.50, fresh crab in season £6.95), gammon with egg or pineapple (£7), tasty steaks (from £7.95), grilled lemon sole (£9.45; evenings only), daily specials, and puddings like home-made fruit or very good mincemeat and brandy pies (from £1.65) and their special Green Mountain ice-cream (£3). Well kept St Austell Tinners and HSD on handpump, several malt whiskies and local wine; fruit machine and piped music. Several picnic tables on a raised back lawn. *(Recommended by R and S Bentley, N J Lawless, Mr and Mrs J Woodfield, Michael J Boniface, Dorothee and Dennis Glover, Jack and Philip Paxton, Bob and Maggie Atherton, Colin Harnett, J C Simpson, Peter Cornall, Richard Dolphin, Gwen and Peter Andrews, P and J Shapley)*

St Austell ~ Tenant Norman Jeffery ~ Real ale ~ Meals and snacks ~ Restaurant ~ (01726) 843322 ~ Children in eating area of bar ~ Open 11-3(2.30 winter), 6-11; closed evening 25 Dec ~ Bedrooms: /£34

ST JUST IN PENWITH SW3631 Map 1

Star

Fore Street

Readers who have stayed here have particularly enjoyed the very relaxed, friendly atmosphere in this interesting and unchanging old inn and others, just dropping in for a drink or meal – have found their winter or summer visits just as rewarding. The dimly lit L-shaped bar has tankards hanging over the serving counter, some stripped masonry, appropriately old-fashioned furnishings, a good many mining samples and mementoes, and characterful regulars with dark faces, long curls, beards, and colourful clothes; there's also a separate snug. Good value bar food includes home-made soup (£1.70), pasties (£1.80), ploughman's (£2.90), cheese melties (£3.20), home-made pies with herb potatoes (£4.70), crab averock (£4.90), vegetarian dishes, and all-day breakfast. Well kept St Austell Tinners, HSD and XXXX Mild tapped from the cask, with farm cider in summer, mulled wine in winter, old-fashioned drinks like mead, lovage and brandy or shrub with rum, and decent coffee or hot chocolate with rum and cream; shove-ha'penny, cribbage, dominoes, table skittles, euchre, shut-the-box, chess, Scrabble, fruit machine, trivia and juke box. Attractive back yard with roses, a gunnera, and tables. The bedrooms are simple but comfortably furnished in period style, with notable breakfasts; the pub's not far from the coast path. *(Recommended by Tom Marshall Corser, D Kudelka, Jack and Philip Paxton, P and M Rudlin, Peter and Joy Heatherley, Dave Thompson, Margaret Mason, Bill Sharpe, S Brackenbury, DAV, Andy and Jill Kassube, Mick Hitchman, K R Flack)*

St Austell ~ Tenants Rosie and Peter Angwin ~ Real ale ~ Meals and snacks

(11-3, 6-11 unless very crowded) ~ (01736) 788767 ~ Children in snug with toy box ~ Celtic folk music Mon evenings, guitarist Weds evenings, and impromptu entertainment any time ~ Open 11-11; 11-3, 6-11 mid Nov-end Feb ~ Bedrooms £15/£25(£36B)

ST KEW SX0276 Map 1

St Kew Inn

Village signposted from A39 NE of Wadebridge

A pub since 1779, this is a rather grand-looking stone building with a friendly welcome and a charming and unspoilt atmosphere – no noisy machines or piped music. There are winged high-backed settles and varnished rustic tables on the lovely dark Delabol flagstones, black wrought-iron rings for lamps or hams hanging from the high ceiling, a handsome window seat, pretty fresh flowers, and an open kitchen range under a high mantelpiece decorated with earthenware flagons. Popular food includes sandwiches, home-made soup (£1.75), ploughman's or leeks and bacon in cheese sauce (£3.95), meaty or vegetable lasagne (£4.95), highly praised sirloin steak (£8.95), and evening extras like chicken tikka (£3.25), fish pie (£5.25), king prawns in garlic (£6.95), and hot smoked salmon steak (£7.95); children's menu (from £3.10) and Sunday roast (£4.25). Well kept St Austell Tinners and HSD tapped from wooden casks behind the counter (lots of tankards hang from the beams above it); good service. The big peaceful garden has plenty of space for children to play (and friendly goat called Aneka) and there are picnic tables on the front cobbles. Parking is in what must have been a really imposing stable yard. The church next door is lovely. *(Recommended by Sue Demont, Tim Barrow, R and S Bentley, Rita Horridge, John Whiting, P V Caswell, Jack and Philip Paxton, R T and J C Moggridge, Cdr and Mrs A C Curry, A N Ellis, Lawrence Bacon, Jacquie and Jim Jones, Nick Wikeley, Graham Tayar, Sheilah Openshaw, Paul Adams, Simon and Natalie Forster, A E and P McCully, C J Parsons)*

St Austell ~ Tenants Steve and Joan Anderson ~ Real ale ~ Meals and snacks ~ Restaurant ~ (01208) 841259 ~ Well behaved children in eating area of bar ~ Open 11-2.30, 6-11; closed 25 Dec

ST MAWGAN SW8765 Map 1

Falcon

NE of Newquay, off B3276 or A3059

From the peaceful, pretty garden of this wisteria-covered old stone pub there are good views of the village – as well as plenty of seats, its own wishing well, play equipment for children, and stone tables in a cobbled courtyard. Inside, the big friendly bar has a log fire, small modern settles and large antique coaching prints on the walls, and there's plenty of space for eating the well-presented food, which might include sandwiches (lunchtime only, from £1.55), soup (£1.75; the crab is good £2.15), garlic mushrooms and bacon in white wine and cream (£3.25), home-made steak and kidney pie (£4.95), and steaks (from £8.35), with evening dishes such as fresh cod in a herb batter (£4.50), lamb and cranberry casserole (£4.75), and lemon chicken (£5.25); on summer evenings barbecues are held in the garden. The restaurant is no smoking and there are lots of paintings by two local artists for sale. Well kept St Austell Tinners, HSD and XXXX Mild on handpump; cheery service; darts, dominoes, euchre, trivia, and piped music. A handsome church is nearby. *(Recommended by A Lock, RLW and Dizzy, Norma Farris, Charles E Owens, Catherine C Almond, Piotr Chodzko-Zajko, Jack and Philip Paxton, Ian Phillips, S Brackenbury, D Stokes, Don Kellaway, Angie Coles, Simon and Natalie Forster, Mr and Mrs W J A Timpson, Steve and Liz Tilley, B J Woodford, David Holloway)*

St Austell ~ Tenant Andy Banks ~ Real ale ~ Meals and snacks ~ Restaurant ~ Children in restaurant ~ (01637) 860225 ~ Live jazz or brass bands summer Sun evenings ~ Open 11-3, 6-11 ~ Bedrooms: £15/£34(£42S)

ST TEATH SX0680 Map 1

White Hart

B3267; signposted off A39 SW of Camelford

As well as swords and a cutlass, this friendly village pub is decorated with sailor hat-ribands and ships' pennants from all over the world. A coin collection is embedded in the ceiling over the serving counter in the main bar, which also has a fine Delabole flagstone floor. Between the counter and the coal fire is a snug little high-backed settle. Leading off is a carpeted room, mainly for eating, with modern chairs around neat tables, and brass and copper jugs on its stone mantlepiece; piped music. Generous helpings of simple but popular well presented bar food include sandwiches, filled baked potatoes, home-made pies like steak or chicken and ham (£5.95), popular gammon and steak (£8.95), and Sunday roasts (£4); the restaurant is no smoking. Well kept Ruddles County and Ushers Best on handpump. The games bar has darts, two pool tables, dominoes, fruit machine, video game, and satellite TV with three screens. ***(Recommended by Simon Pyle, David and Julie Glover; more reports please)***

Free house ~ Licensees Barry and Rob Burton ~ Real ale ~ Meals and snacks (till 10pm) ~ Restaurant ~ (01208) 850281 ~ Children welcome ~ Open 11-3, 6-11 ~ Bedrooms: £20/£40

TREBARWITH SX0585 Map 1

Port William

Trebarwith Strand

It's the setting that readers especially like about this converted old harbourmaster's house. From the picnic tables on the terrace there are glorious views over the beach and out to sea. Inside, there's quite a nautical theme with fishing nets and maritime memorabilia decorating the walls, a separate gallery area with work by local artists, and the 'captain's cabin' which has a full-size fishing dinghy mounted on the wall; part of the bar is no smoking. Bar food includes quite a few fish dishes like home-made smoked mackerel pâté (£2.95), pan-fried john dory (£5.95), skate wings in black butter with capers (£6.25), local fresh crab platter (£6.95), good halibut in a mustard, cheese and cream sauce (£7.75) or whole oven-baked brill (£8.50) – as well as home-made soup (£2.25), filled rolls (from £2.25), home-made pasties (£2.50), vegetable curry (£5.25), steak and kidney pie (£5.25), and evening steaks (from £8.95); children's menu (from £1.25). St Austell HSD and Tinners and John Smiths (kept under light blanket pressure) with guests like Courage Directors, Marstons Pedigree, Ruddles County and Ushers on handpump; jugs of sangria and rum punch. Darts, pool, cribbage, fruit machine, video game, trivia and piped music. Dogs welcome and bowl of water provided for them. Mr Hale is hoping to convert the self-catering flats into five bedrooms for 1996. ***(Recommended by Rita Horridge, R T and J C Moggridge, Jeff Davies, S Brackenbury)***

Free house ~ Licensee Peter Hale ~ Real ale ~ Meals and snacks ~ Restaurant ~ (01840) 770230 ~ Children welcome away from main bar area ~ Folk music Fri evening and occasional Sat/mid-week evenings ~ Open 11-11 ~ Bedrooms: see text

TREBURLEY SX3477 Map 1

Springer Spaniel

A388 Callington—Launceston

It's rare to find such a relaxing atmosphere just a step off the main road – this is an object lesson in the welcome travellers should get. The approach extends into their catering, too, as they seem happy to be flexible with the ingredients in their very good, totally home-made food: sandwiches or french bread rolls (from £1.50), freshly-made soup (£2; seafood chowder £2.50), good spiced lentil pâté, terrine of venison with gooseberry and elderflower relish (£3.75), ham and egg (£3.95), cold roast rib of beef with pickles and chips (£4.50), steak and kidney pie (£5.50), grilled lamb cutlets with mint and redcurrant sauce (£6.95), and daily specials like ham and banana mornay (£3.75), breast of goose with onion marmalade, fillet of smoked haddock in a light cheese sauce (£5.95), roast sea bass, and delicious Dover sole, with puddings like lovely fresh lemon tart or chocolate mousse (from £3.25). Well kept Furgusons Dartmoor and St Austell HSD on handpump, New World wines, and farm cider; very friendly service. The bar has a lovely, very high-backed settle by the woodburning stove in the big fireplace, high-backed farmhouse chairs and other seats, and pictures of olde-worlde stage-coach arrivals at inns, and this leads into a room with chintzy-cushioned armchairs and sofa in one corner, a big solid teak table, and games such as bagatelle, backgammon, dominoes, cribbage, and an old-fashioned space game. Up some steps from the main bar is the beamed, attractively furnished restaurant; friendly black cat. They re-named the pub in 1992 after their dog Bertie. ***(Recommended by John and Tessa Rainsford, J Jones, R V L Summers, Jack and Philip Paxton, Jacquie and Jim Jones, Rita Horridge)***

Free house ~ Licensee John Pitchford ~ Real ale ~ Meals and snacks ~ Restaurant ~ (01579) 370424 ~ Children in snug or restaurant ~ Open 11-3, 5.30-11

TREEN SW3824 Map 1

Logan Rock

Just off B3315 – the back rd Penzance—Lands End

After a walk along the wild cliffs – or just to see the nearby Logan Rock (an 80-ton boulder from which the pub takes its name) – you can work up an appetite to enjoy the popular bar food in this friendly and relaxed pub. This might include sandwiches (from £1.50, local crab when available £4.25), good pasties (£1.40), wholesome soup (£1.95), salads (from £4.25, crab £7.25), a popular fish and egg dish they call the Seafarer (£4), lasagne (£4.50), scampi (£5.25), very good charcoal-grilled steaks (from £7.50), and puddings like home-made fruit pie or crumble (£2.10); children's dishes (from £1.40) and afternoon cream teas. They will heat baby foods on request. The low-beamed main bar has a series of old prints telling the story of the rock, high-backed modern oak settles, wall seats, a really warm coal fire, and well kept St Austell Tinners and HSD on handpump. Lots of games such as darts, dominoes, cribbage, fruit machine, video games, winter pool and another fruit machine in the family room across the way; juke box, piped music. Dogs are allowed in if on a lead. There are some tables in a small wall-sheltered garden, looking over fields, with more in the front court. ***(Recommended by Mrs E Howe, Bill Sharpe, George and Chris Miller, Alan and Eileen Bowker, A J N Lee, David Mead, DAV, Dr and Mrs A K Clarke, Anthony Barnes, Alan Castle, Andy and Jill Kassube, Mark Walker)***

St Austell ~ Tenants Peter and Anita George ~ Real ale ~ Meals and snacks (from June-Sept all day, otherwise 12-2, 7-9) ~ Restaurant ~ (01736) 810495 ~ Well behaved children in family room ~ Open 10.30am-11pm; 10.30-3, 5.30-11 in winter

TREGADILLETT SX2984 Map 1

Eliot Arms ★ ★ 🍷

Village signposted off A30 at junction with A395, W end of Launceston bypass

Our most popular Cornish entry, this creeper-covered old house has a charming series of little softly lit rooms with a collection of 72 antique clocks including 7 grandfathers, hundreds of horsebrasses, old prints, old postcards or cigarette cards grouped in frames on the walls, and shelves of books and china. Also, a fine old mix of furniture, from high-backed built-in curved settles, through plush Victorian dining chairs, armed seats, chaise longues and mahogany housekeeper's chairs, to more modern seats, open fires, flowers on most tables, and a lovely ginger cat called

Peewee; inoffensive piped music. The good home-made food comes in very big helpings, and might include soup (£1.95), a dozen ploughman's (from £3.95), cheese and vegetable pasta bake (£4.95), fisherman's crunch (£5.50), home-smoked chicken and ribs with barbecue sauce (£6.95; they have their own smoker and plan to add more smoked dishes), salmon steak in a cream and prawn sauce or whole grilled sole with a lemon and parsley butter (£8.95), and lots of lovely puddings. Well kept Flowers Original, Marstons Pedigree, and a guest beer on handpump, a fine choice of wines, several malt whiskies, and excellent friendly service; darts, shove-ha'penny, table skittles, and fruit machine. A garden beyond the car park has picnic tables, a good climbing frame, swing and playhouse. *(Recommended by Brian and Anna Marsden, R W Brooks, S Lonie, S Tait, Jack and Philip Paxton, Jerry and Alison Oakes, Piotr Chodzko-Zajko, Alan and Eileen Bowker, J and J O Jones, Bob and Maggie Atherton, SC, JC, R and S Bentley, Beverley James, Lynn Sharpless, Bob Eardley, Jeff Davies, S Brackenbury, Nigel Flook, Betsy Brown, Dr and Mrs R Neville, F J Robinson, Mr and Mrs D T Deas, Graham Tayar, Mrs Patricia Nutt, Phil and Anne Smithson, Paul Weedon)*

Free House ~ Licensees John Cook and Lesley Elliott ~ Real ale ~ Meals and snacks (not 25 Dec) ~ (01566) 772051 ~ Children in eating area of bar and two side rooms ~ Open 11-2.30, 6-11; closed 25 Dec ~ Bedrooms: £24/£38

TRESCO (Isles of Scilly) SV8915 Map 1

New Inn

New Grimsby

The light and airy bars here are refurbished using lots of washed-up wood from a ship's cargo – and have a nice pubby atmosphere and picture windows looking out over the swimming pool. Good bar food includes soups that are virtually meals in themselves (£1.90; the fish one is popular), sandwiches (from £1.80; crab £3.65), lunchtime pasta and pizza dishes (from £2.90), filled french bread (from £3.50; local lobster £9), salads with mozzarella, avocado, egg and fresh basil and their own gravadlax or marinated fish (from £3.40), pheasant chasseur (£4.10), local monkfish kebabs (£6.10), and local hake steaks steamed in a champagne and lobster sauce (£8.40), with evening starters (from £1.90) and lots of char-grilled meat and fish (from £5.80). The well regarded no-smoking restaurant also has a separate children's menu. Bass, Boddingtons, Flowers Original, Morlands Old Speckled Hen, and Whitbreads Castle Eden and Pompey Royal on handpump, interesting wines, and a good range of malt whiskies. Pool and juke box (rarely played). There are white plastic tables and chairs in the garden. Many of the people staying here are regular return visitors. *(Recommended by Keith and Janet Morris, Pete and Rosie Flower, Dorothee and Dennis Glover, Neil and Anita Christopher, R J Herd)*

Free house ~ Licensee Graham Shone ~ Real ale ~ Meals and snacks ~ Restaurant ~ (01720) 422844 ~ Children in eating area of bar until 9.30pm ~ Live music twice a month ~ Open 11-11; 11.30-3, 7.30-11 in winter ~ Bedrooms: /£48B

TRESILLIAN SW8646 Map 1

Wheel

A39 Truro—St Austell

General Fairfax used this friendly pub as his headquarters in the closing stages of the Civil War, and it was at Tresillian Bridge that the Royalists finally surrendered to him. The two cosy and traditional original room areas (watch for the low door as you go in) have some timbering and stripped stonework, as well as low ceiling joists, soft lighting, and plush wall seats on the carpet. There are steps from one part to another, though access for the disabled is quite reasonable. Generous helpings of good value bar food include soup (£1.60), large filled rolls (from £2; open sandwiches from £2.95), ploughman's (from £3), vegetarian crumble (£3.85), salads (from £3.70), gammon (£5.75), steaks (from £9.50), home-made daily specials, and puddings (from £2); children's dishes (from £1.45). Well kept Devenish Royal

Wessex and Flowers Original on handpump, coffee and tea; piped music. The neat garden stretches down to a tidal stretch of the River Fal, and has a play area. The distinctive wheel worked into the thatch of the roof makes the pub instantly recognisable. ***(Recommended by R T and J C Moggridge, Jack and Philip Paxton, Piotr Chodzko-Zajko, David Gittins, Mr and Mrs J Woodfield, Deborah and Ian Carrington, P M Lane, Peter Cornall, J I Fraser, Mr and Mrs Barker)***

Greenalls ~ Tenant David Hulson ~ Real ale ~ Meals and snacks (till 10pm Fri and Sat) ~ (01872) 520293 ~ Children in room with no bar ~ Open 11-2.30(3 Sat), 6-11

TRURO SW8244 Map 1

Old Ale House ★ £

7 Quay St/Princes St

It's unusual to find a serious real ale pub (they keep up to 24 real ales here, tapped from the cask) that genuinely appeals to most people but this old-fashioned and warmly friendly back-to-basics place does just that; readers have thoroughly enjoyed their visits. There's some interesting 1920s bric-a-brac, an engagingly old-fashioned diversity of furnishings that would do credit to any small-town auction room, newpapers and magazines to read, and a barrel full of monkey nuts; piped music. Constantly changing, the beers might include Boddingtons, Bass, Cotleigh Old Buzzard and Tawny, Courage Best and Directors, Exmoor Gold, Ale and Beast, Fullers London Pride, Kings Head Golden Goose, Ma Hussons and Kings Ransom, Morlands Old Speckled Hen, Sharps Own, Shepherd Neame Spitfire, Smiles Exhibition, Tetleys, and Wadworths 6X; interesting wines such as damson and birch. The enterprising and varied choice of good food, freshly prepared in a spotless kitchen in full view of the bar, might consist of doorstep sandwiches (from £2.15; delicious hot baked garlic bread with melted cheese from £1.25), filled oven baked potatoes (£2.85), ploughman's (£3.25), hot meals served in a skillet pan like oriental chicken, sizzling beef or liver, bacon and onions (small helpings from £3.25, big helpings from £4.50), lasagne or steak and kidney pie (£3.95), daily specials like crab bake, mussels in white wine or beef and stilton pie, and puddings (from £1.65). Altogether, an excellent departure for Cornwall. No dogs, clean lavatories. ***(Recommended by Jeff Davies, Peter Williamson, Alastair Campbell, Jack and Philip Paxton, Mrs E Howe, P and M Rudlin, Cdr and Mrs A C Curry, Ted George, RLW and Dizzy, M E Wellington, S Brackenbury, Susan and Nigel Wilson, Jeff Davies)***

Greenalls (Devenish) ~ Manager Ray Gascoigne ~ Real ale ~ Meals and snacks (12-2.30, 5-7) ~ (01872) 71122 ~ Impromptu music Mon evening, rock/blues/jazz Thurs evening ~ Open 11-3, 5-11; all day Fri and Sat

Children welcome means the pubs says it lets children inside without any special restriction. If it allows them in, but to restricted areas such as an eating area or family room, we specify this. Places with separate restaurants usually let children use them, hotels usually let them into public areas such as lounges. Some pubs impose an evening time limit – let us know if you find this.

Lucky Dip

Besides the fully inspected pubs, you might like to try these Lucky Dips recommended to us and described by readers (if you do, please send us reports):

☆ **Albaston** [OS Sheet 201 map ref 423704; SX4270], *Queens Head*: Well kept Courage, food inc good pasties, low prices and friendly landlord in big welcoming public bar with changing local industrial memorabilia; handy for Cotehele and Tamar Valley railway *(John and Tessa Rainsford, Jack and Philip Paxton)*

☆ **Altarnun** [just N, OS Sheet 201 map ref 215825; SX2182], *Rising Sun*: Tasty well served simple food in unpretentious but friendly farmers' local with flagstoned bar, six well kept real ales; pretty village *(Tom Evans, A N Ellis, Jack and Philip Paxton)*

☆ **Bodinnick** [across the water from Fowey; SX1352], *Old Ferry*: New owners for beautifully placed inn with character back flagstoned public bar partly cut into rock, lots of boating pictures, bar food, well kept real ales, games room where children allowed; hotel part looking over water, with summer evening restaurant, comfortable roomy bedrooms; lovely walk from Polruan *(R and S Bentley, Jack and Philip Paxton, Gerry Hollington, Lynn Sharpless, Bob Eardley, LYM)*

☆ **Bodmin** [Dunmere (A389 NW); SX0467], *Borough Arms*: Neat, spacious and friendly, with stripped stone, open fire, lots of railway photographs and posters, well kept Bass, Boddingtons and Whitbreads, decent wines, friendly atmosphere, big helpings of good value straightforward food (no sandwiches), unobtrusive piped music, fruit machine; children in side room, picnic tables out among shady apple trees; can get very busy lunchtime in season *(C J Parsons, Peter Williamson, BB)*

Bodmin [5 Higher Bore St], *Masons Arms*: Traditional Cornish pub with steps and low ceilings, well kept Bass, good value bar food *(Andy and Jill Kassube)*

☆ **Bolventor** [signed just off A30 on Bodmin Moor; SX1876], *Jamaica Inn*: Is this a pub or a theme park? But welcoming, with lots of character in clean, comfortable and cosy oak-beamed bar, log fire, parrot, well kept Whitbreads ales, reasonably priced food inc good cream teas; pretty secluded garden with play area, bleak moorland setting *(D K Carter, Bronwen and Steve Wrigley, Gary Nicholls)*

☆ **Boscastle** [upper village, stiff climb from harbour; SX0990], *Napoleon*: Charming 16th-c pub, lots of little low-beamed rooms, interesting Napoleon prints, basic good value food inc vegetarian, well kept Bass and St Austell ales, decent wines, very friendly staff, polished slate floor, big open fire, pool room, children allowed; piped music, maybe folk music; suntrap terrace, second garden too; may close early if quiet *(Jeff Davies, A W Lewis, Jack and Philip Paxton, Brian and Anna Marsden, LYM)*

Boscastle [Harbour], *Wellington*: Long bar with popular food, Whitbreads-related ales, regular live music; comfortable bedrooms *(M Sinclair, BB)*

Bude [Falcon Terrace; SS2005], *Falcon*: Local overlooking canal, lots of quick generous food, well kept St Austell Tinners and HSD, attentive staff; bedrooms *(Dr N Holmes, David Whalley)*

Cadgwith [SW7214], *Cadgwith Cove*: Spacious and comfortable local with seats in pleasant front courtyard overlooking photogenic village's fish sheds and bay; useful for basic food, Whitbreads real ale; separate restaurant with different management *(David and Michelle Hedges, DJW, Sue Holland, Dave Webster, Nigel Woolliscroft)*

☆ **Camborne** [B3303 out towards Helston; SW6440], *Old Shire*: Lots of comfortable chairs and sofas and great coal fire in homely family pub with good value interesting food, friendly helpful staff, good range of beers; garden with summer barbecues, five bedrooms *(Ian Phillips)*

Camborne, *Waggoners Arms*: Cosy intimate local welcoming visitors, Bass, Flowers IPA and Wadworths 6X, simple cheap well prepared food; games machines, piped 60s music *(Alastair Campbell)*

☆ **Camelford** [Main St (A39); SX1083], *Masons Arms*: Friendly newish licensees in unpretentious heavy-beamed stonebuilt pub with St Austell ales, decent value bar food inc children's dishes and good steak and kidney pudding, local photographs, advertising mirrors, houseplants; pool and juke box in one bar; children allowed *(Keith and Janet Morris, Bill and Sylvia Trotter)*

☆ **Cargreen** [off A388 Callington—Saltash; SX4362], *Spaniards Arms*: The star's for its waterside position, with tables on terrace by Tamar – always some river activity, esp at high tide; at least five real ales, small panelled bar, huge fireplace in another smallish room, bar food, big restaurant *(M W Edwards, A N Ellis)*

Cawsand [SX4350], *Old Ship*: Very welcoming, good food *(Simon and Pie Barker)*

Charlestown [SX0351], *Rashleigh Arms*: Good value straightforward food, good range of real ales, quick service, large comfortable lounge, good canalside family room; piped music; big restaurant, seats out by tiny harbour; good value bedrooms *(Jack and Philip Paxton)*

Coverack [SW7818], *Paris*: Friendly old-fashioned Whitbreads pub with lovely views over sea and harbour, well kept Bass, food inc good teas, interesting wooden moulds from Falmouth churchyard; restaurant *(Margaret Cadney, DJW)*

☆ Crackington Haven [SX1396], *Coombe Barton*: Huge place for a tiny village, making the most of the spectacular sea view; friendly service, good bar food inc fresh local fish and vegetarian dishes, home-made puddings, well kept ales inc a new local beer, good coffee, back family room, games room with pool tables; bedrooms *(G T White, P and M Rudlin, Jeff Davies)*

☆ Crafthole [SX3654], *Finnygook*: Clean and comfortable much-modernised lounge bar, decent straightforward food, quick service, Whitbreads-related beers, good coffee, pleasant restaurant, good sea views from residents' lounge; bedrooms good value *(George Atkinson, BB)*

☆ Crantock [SW7960], *Old Albion*: Pleasantly placed thatched village pub with old-fashioned tastefully decorated bar, good range of generously served home-cooked food *(Mark and Nicola Willoughbby, Jack and Philip Paxton, LYM)*

Cremyll [SX4553], *Edgcumbe Arms*: Not at all smart, but super setting by Plymouth ferry, waterside seating, good cheap snacks, Courage Best, quick service, friendly staff *(George Atkinson)*

Cubert [Trebellan; SW7858], *Smugglers Den*: Friendly service, interesting layout and decor, good food *(R W Brooks)*

☆ Duloe [B3254 N of Looe; SX2358], *Olde Plough House*: Welcoming newish licensees doing good interesting reasonably priced food inc grillstones in spacious pub with two log fires, cushioned settles, sewing-machine treadle tables with polished wooden tops; well kept Bass, good wine, locals' area with pool and darts *(Maureen Hobbs, J C Simpson, JE, R Turnham)*

☆ Egloshayle [Wadebridge—Bodmin; SX0172], *Earl of St Vincent*: Good value freshly cooked food, well kept St Austell Tinners and HSD, friendly service, attractive decor inc antique clocks; colourful flowers in summer *(Buffy and Mike Adamson, Mark Billings, Jack and Philip Paxton)*

☆ Falmouth [Maenporth Beach – round Falmouth Bay towards Mawnan; SW8032], *Seahorse*: Smooth smoked-glass cafe/bar in holiday complex, virtually on beach with great estuary view; wide range of good bar food inc fresh fish and some unusual dishes, well kept Ansells and Ruddles County, chilled foreign beers, good friendly service, upstairs restaurant, tables on terrace with boules – busy on barbecue nights; children very welcome *(John Wooll, Adrian Acton)*

☆ Falmouth [The Moor], *Seven Stars*: Unchanging local with wonderfully entertaining vicar-landlord, tatty furnishings, warm welcome, well kept Bass, Flowers Original and St Austell HSD tapped from the cask, minimal food, tables on roadside courtyard *(Robert Weeks, Sue Holland, Dave Webster, John Wooll, Jack and Philip Paxton, BB)*

☆ Falmouth [Custom House Quay], *Chain Locker*: Excellent spot on inner harbour, interesting nautical decor in roomy bare-boards panelled bar, decent straightforward food from side servery, well kept Whitbreads-related ales, fruit machine *(Sue Holland, Dave Webster, LYM)*

Falmouth [Prinslow Lane, Swanvale], *Boslowick*: Good value straightforward food and well kept ale in spacious black and white beamed former manor house; friendly staff, plenty of seats inc plush sofas, log-effect gas fires, family room with games machines; children's play area *(John Wooll)*; [Church St], *Grapes*: Spacious pub with fine harbour view from some seats, plenty of tables, wide range of reasonably priced food esp fish, pleasant staff, Whitbreads-related and other ales *(Gwen and Peter Andrews)*; [Church St], *Kings Head*: Rambling bar with lots of pictures and bric-a-brac, soft settees, easy chairs and firmer dining chairs, well kept Whitbreads-related ales, bar food, winter log fire, piped music *(Alan and Eileen Bowker, LYM)*; [High St], *Star & Garter*: High views over harbour towards Flushing, friendly service, reasonably priced food, Whitbreads-related and interesting guest ales, mixed customers *(Sue Holland, Dave Webster)*

Flushing [SW8033], *Royal Standard*: Trim and traditional unspoilt waterfront local, simple well done food inc good baked potatoes and home-made pasties, real ales such as Bass, Boddingtons, Flowers IPA, Worthington, warm welcome, plenty of genuine characters, pool; unreconstructed outside gents' *(Margaret Cadney, Sue Holland, Dave Webster, Gwen and Peter Andrews)*

☆ Fowey [SX1252], *Ship*: Pubbiest pub here, good value food from sandwiches through local fish to steak, comfortable cloth-banquette main bar with coal fire, pool/darts room, family dining room with big stained-glass window; St Austell Tinners and HSD, relaxed local atmosphere, friendly service; juke box or piped music (may obtrude), dogs allowed; bedrooms old-fashioned, some oak-panelled *(Rita Horridge, Ann and Bob Westbrook, Mike Woodhead, Lindsley Harvard, Margaret Whalley, S Brackenbury, Ted and Jane Brown, BB)*

Fowey [Town Quay], *King of Prussia*: Upstairs bay windows looking over harbour to Polruan, well kept St Austell ales, efficient cheerful service, piped pop music (may obtrude), good value side family food bar, seats outside; bedrooms *(George Atkinson, Mike Woodhead, LYM)*; *Lugger*: Recently redecorated, with unpretentious locals' bar, good inexpensive food in dining area, tables outside; bedrooms *(Ted and Jane Brown, BB)*

Gerrans [SW8735], *Plume of Feathers*: Flowers IPA and Whitbreads BB on handpump, reasonably priced ploughman's and other bar food, padded settles and stools, red carpet, fruit machines; handy for network of NT paths all around *(Frank Cummins)*

☆ **Golant** [off B3269; SX1155], *Fishermans Arms*: Plain but charming waterside local, nice garden, lovely views from terrace and window; warm welcome, good generous straightforward home-made food, well kept Courage-related ales, log fire, interesting pictures, tropical fish *(Nick Wikeley, Jack and Philip Paxton, Andy and Jill Kassube)*

Gorran Haven [SX0141], *Llawnroc*: Friendly village local adjoining hotel overlooking harbour and fishing village; decent bar food, well kept Whitbreads-related ales, well placed tables out in front, barbecues; handy for the Lost Gardens of Heligan; bedrooms *(Norma and Keith Bloomfield, Nick Lawless)*

Grampound [Fore St (A390 St Austell—Truro); SW9348], *Dolphin*: Friendly helpful staff, good value generous food, comfortable chintzy settees and easy chairs *(Colin May)*

Gulval [SW4832], *Coldstreamer*: Good value if not cheap food in unusual high-ceilinged pub, Whitbreads-related ales, friendly staff and cat, cosy restaurant; quiet, pleasant village *(Jo Rees, Jack and Philip Paxton, DAV)*

☆ **Gunnislake** [lower road to Calstock; SX4371], *Rising Sun*: Comfortable 17th-c dining pub with particularly good serious if not cheap food using seasonal produce (helpings not large), interesting curios and antiques, good choice of beers, welcoming licensees, garden with play area; live music Mon *(Richard Weltz, R A Cullingham)*

☆ **Gurnards Head** [B3306 Zennor—St Just; SW4338], *Gurnards Head*: Good choice of food inc nice fish and fresh veg, friendly service, well kept Flowers Original and other ales and decent wine in unspoilt genuine pubby bar, open fires each end; food all day (at least in summer), bedrooms – good base for cliff walks *(Stephen Gibbs, Jeanne Cross, Paul Silvestri, Bill Sharpe)*

Helston [Coinagehall St; SW6527], *Fitzsimmons Arms*: Large bar with several comfortable rooms, well kept Bass, Boddingtons and Flowers, reliable food, separate restaurant area; very popular Fri evening with personnel from nearby naval air base *(Alastair Campbell, Sue Holland, Dave Webster, G Washington)*

☆ **Hessenford** [A387 Looe—Torpoint; SX3057], *Copley Arms*: Comfortable pub with spacious garden and terrace in most attractive riverside position, good range of generous well priced food in bar and restaurant, well kept St Austell ales, big family room, play area; bedrooms *(George Atkinson, Bronwen and Steve Wrigley)*

☆ **Kingsand** [Fore St; towards Cawsand – OS Sheet 201 map ref 434505; SX4350], *Halfway House*: Cosy softly lit low-ceilinged bar around huge central fireplace, smartly simple furnishings, wide choice of food inc well presented fresh local fish, Bass, Charrington and Worthington real ales, decent wines, good staff, unobtrusive piped music, restaurant; comfortable well equipped bedrooms, handy for Mount Edgcumbe and marvellous cliff walks on Rame Head *(Dr K T Nicolson, Mike and Heather Barnes, A Kingstone)*

☆ **Kingsand** [village green], *Rising Sun*: Friendly little old local with massive helpings of good food from sandwiches, pasties and burgers up inc plenty of local fish and incredibly long sausage, good choice of well kept beer and wine, open fire; can get packed *(Derek and Rosemary King, Mike and Heather Barnes, Ann and Bob Westbrook)*

☆ **Lamorna** [off B3315 SW of Penzance; SW4424], *Lamorna Wink*: Simply furnished friendly country local a short walk from pretty cove with good coast walks, decent food served efficiently from hatch inc huge baked potatoes, good pasties and plenty of fish, Whitbreads-related ales; interesting naval memorabilia and pictures *(Shirley Pielou, Alan and Eileen Bowker, Jim Reid, LYM)*

Lands End [SW3425], *Lands End Hotel*: Decent food in big conservatory extension housing bars and pretty bistro-style dining area; obliging staff, tables on terrace; bedrooms priced by view; admission charge – part of extensively developed complex *(Mark Walker, Gary Nicholls)*

Lanreath [off B3359; SX1757], *Punch Bowl*: Unspoilt 17th-c inn of great potential, charmingly traditional flagstoned public bar and comfortable black-panelled lounge, games bar, garden bar, food in bars and restaurant, well kept St Austell ales; bedrooms *(T S Rutter, BB)*

Launceston [SX3384], *White Hart*: Big pub very popular lunchtime for well priced home-made food from good sandwiches up; good choice of beers, nice log fires, dining room *(John and Christine Vittoe)*

☆ **Lizard** [SW7012], *Top House*: Reliably well run pub which with the nearby serpentine shop is the saving grace of this otherwise disappointing village: lots of interesting local sea pictures, fine shipwreck relics and serpentine craftwork in neat bar with generous bar food inc good local fish and seafood specials, interesting vegetarian dishes, well kept Whitbreads-related ales and good choice of other drinks, truly welcoming helpful service, roaring log fire, darts, fruit machine; tables on terrace *(Gwen and Peter Andrews, Peter and Joy Heatherley, John Tyler, Jim Reid, Anthony Barnes, Sue Holland, Dave Webster, W N Brandes, BB)*

☆ **Longrock** [old coast rd Penzance—Marazion; SW5031], *Mexico*: Doing well under welcoming current landlord, with very wide choice of generous good value food, cheerful local atmosphere; former office of Mexico Mine Company, with massive stone walls *(P and M Rudlin, Mark Walker, J M Bowers, Bill Sharpe)*

Looe [SX2553], *Salutation*: Consistently

good simple food inc crab sandwiches and vegetarian dishes, busy with locals and fishermen; fast friendly service, well kept Ushers Best *(Dr and Mrs B D Smith)*
Lostwithiel [North St; SX1059], *Globe*: Traditional pub with great choice of pies (not Mon) *(J Fletcher, Jack and Philip Paxton)*
☆ **Malpas** [off A39 S of Truro; SW8442], *Heron*: Straightforward pub notable for its lovely setting above wooded creek; big helpings of decent quick food inc good home-cooked ham, St Austell Tinners and HSD, log fire, pool, machines, piped music, suntrap slate-paved terrace; children welcome *(S Brackenbury, Michael Sargent, Helen Taylor, R L Turnham)*
☆ **Manaccan** [down hill signed to Gillan and St Keverne; SW7625], *New Inn*: Attractive old pub with tidy and stylish individual furnishings, reasonably priced bar food, well kept Whitbreads-related ales tapped from the cask, lots of atmosphere; big garden with swing, pretty waterside village *(John and Sally Clarke, DJW, Anthony Barnes, Jack and Philip Paxton, LYM)*
Marazion [SW5231], *Station*: Converted station master's house, great views over St Michaels Mount, fresh local fish *(D Kudelka)*
☆ **Mawgan** [St Martin; SW7323], *Old Courthouse*: Prettily placed open-plan split-level pub, very spacious, clean and comfortable, with good choice of food, very well kept Whitbreads-related ales, friendly service, pleasant garden; children welcome *(Nigel Woolliscroft, Adrian and Karen Bulley)*
☆ **Mawnan Smith** [W of Falmouth, off Penryn—Gweek rd – old B3291; SW7728], *Red Lion*: Lots of pictures and bric-a-brac in thatched pub's cosy interconnected beamed rooms inc no smoking room behind restaurant, generous helpings of food from sandwiches to steaks, well kept Bass and other ales, good service; children welcome *(Paul Weedon, Mr and Mrs Hall, Mr and Mrs W J A Timpson, Air Cdr and Mrs A C Curry, Gwen and Peter Andrews, Mrs J Barwell, S R Chapman, LYM)*
☆ **Menheniot** [off A38; SX2862], *White Hart*: Stripped stone, red leatherette button-back seats and lots of brass in friendly relaxing bar with well kept Bass and Boddingtons, wide choice of generous good food (can be taken away); bedrooms well equipped and neatly modernised *(David Burnett, Donna Lowes, Jill Bickerton)*
☆ **Metherell** [Lower Metherell; follow Honicombe sign from St Anns Chapel just W of Gunnislake on A390; SX4069], *Carpenters Arms*: Heavily black-beamed inn with huge polished flagstones and massive stone walls, handy for Cotehele; a long-standing main entry, with cheerful atmosphere, wide choice of good value food from sandwiches up, well kept Bass, Ruddles County, St Austell HSD and a guest beer, good farm ciders and decent wine, but Douglas and Jill Brace who gave it so much character have just retired; children welcome, bedrooms *(LYM; reports on new regime please)*
Mevagissey [off Fore St by post office; SX0145], *Fountain*: Unpretentious friendly local with good simple food, well kept beer, plenty of atmosphere; piano sing-songs some evenings *(Ted George, Jack and Philip Paxton, Paul Cartledge)*; [Polkirt Hill], *Harbour Lights*: Great harbour and bay views, good value straightforward food, well kept Bass, good service; trad jazz Sun lunchtime, tables outside; bedrooms *(Jack and Philip Paxton)*; [Fore St, nr harbour], *Ship*: 16th-c pub with generous food inc good fish and chips, full range of well kept St Austell beers, welcoming licensees; big comfortable room divided into small interesting areas, ships' memorabilia, open fire, friendly cat; fruit machines, piped music; bedrooms *(Ann and Bob Westbrook, Jack and Philip Paxton)*
☆ **Mitchell** [off A30 Bodmin—Redruth; SW8654], *Plume of Feathers*: Rambling comfortable bar with lots of bric-a-brac, generous efficiently served home-made food from sandwiches to hearty grills from open-plan back kitchen, Whitbreads-related ales on handpump, attentive staff, flame-effect gas fire; piped music, darts and winter pool; tables outside, with play area and farm animals; children welcome *(Gwen and Peter Andrews, Bill Sharpe, Jim and Maggie Cowell, P and M Rudlin, LYM)*
☆ **Mullion** [SW6719], *Old Inn*: Lovely thatched pub with dark passages and warren of small rooms, lots of interesting old prints, brasses and nautical items, big inglenook fireplace, good reasonably priced food inc local fish (may be a wait when busy), particularly welcoming service, well kept Whitbreads-related ales, good house wines; piped music; bedrooms, self-catering cottages *(Ian Phillips, S R Chapman, David and Michelle Hedges, Bill and Sylvia Trotter, Gwen and Peter Andrews, George and Chris Miller, Andy and Jill Kassube, C P Scott-Malden, LYM)*
☆ **Newbridge** [A3071 Penzance—St Just – OS Sheet 203 map ref 424316; SW4232], *Fountain*: Beautiful stone house with tables out in garden, well done out with attractive old-fashioned decor inc cheery fire in awesome fireplace, particularly good food inc fresh curried prawns, friendly landlord, well kept real ale inc Mild, great atmosphere *(Tania Woodrow, Patrick Deschenes, Robin and Molly Taylor, Dr D K M Thomas)*
Newtown [the one off B3293, SE of Helston; SW7423], *Prince of Wales*: Small stone pub with welcoming new landlady, interesting food in bar and restaurant inc fish, pretty stone fireplace, Whitbreads ales, pool, darts, maybe piped music; can park caravans behind *(E A George, DJW, Gwen and Peter Andrews)*
Notter [Notter Bridge, just off A38

Saltash—Liskeard; SX3861], *Notter Bridge*: Attractive spot in wooded valley with big picture windows overlooking river, simple decor, wide choice of good value generous food in dining area, well kept beer, games bar, tables on terrace *(Bronwen and Steve Wrigley, Ted George)*

☆ **Padstow** [Lanadwell St; SW9175], *Golden Lion*: Friendly local with pleasant black-beamed front bar, high-raftered back lounge with russet plush banquettes against ancient white stone walls; reasonably priced simple lunches, evening steaks and fresh seafood; well kept Whitbreads and Cornish Original on handpump, piped music, juke box, fruit machines; bedrooms *(M W Turner, P and M Rudlin, Mr and Mrs J Woodfield, BB)*

☆ **Padstow** [Lanadwell St], *London*: Cottagey fishermen's local with good atmosphere, well kept St Austells, sensibly priced food inc good crab sandwiches; bedrooms *(Cdr and Mrs A C Curry, LYM)*

☆ **Padstow** [South Quay], *Old Custom House*: Airy open-plan bar with good unpretentious food inc vegetarian, comfortable chesterfields around open fire, prints of old harbour, big beams and timbers, lots of old trunks and cases; attentive helpful staff, well kept St Austell real ales, restaurant; good spot by harbour, with conservatory; attractive bedrooms *(John and Vivienne Rice, Andy and Jane Beardsley, Ted George, BB)*

☆ **Pendoggett** [SX0279], *Cornish Arms*: Big lively locals' bar with games and piped music, two attractive more sedate front rooms with traditional oak settles on fine slate floor, no smoking coffee room, well kept Bass and Flowers IPA, food in bar and restaurant; provision for children, open all day, terrace with distant sea view; bedrooms *(S Brackenbury, Andrew Low, Jack and Philip Paxton, Graham Tayar, D L Barker, Helen Taylor, LYM)*

Pentewan [just off B3273 St Austell—Mevagissey; SX0147], *Ship*: Friendly local opp harbour, good bar food and reasonably priced Sun lunch, summer lounge bar, open fire in main bar *(S Brackenbury)*

☆ **Penzance** [Barbican; Newlyn rd, opp harbour after swing-bridge; SW4730], *Dolphin*: Welcoming and attractive nautical pub with good harbour views, quick bar food inc good pasties, well kept St Austell ales, great fireplace, big pool room with juke box etc; children in room off main bar; no obvious nearby parking *(Mark Walker, Gary Nicholls, G Washington, LYM)*

Penzance [Chapel St], *Admiral Benbow*: Elaborately nautical decor, friendly staff, decent food, Courage-related ales, children allowed, downstairs restaurant; open all day summer *(Mark Walker, Gary Nicholls, LYM)*; [Quay], *Yacht*: Useful St Austell pub with children's area *(Mark Walker, Gary Nicholls)*

☆ **Perranarworthal** [A39 Truro—Penryn; SW7839], *Norway*: Done up in traditional style with small rooms, lots of rustic bric-a-brac, stuffed birds and fish; big helpings of popular lunchtime bar food, restaurant, Whitbreads-related ales, tables outside *(Jim and Maggie Cowell, LYM)*

Perranporth [SW7554], *Plume of Feathers*: Vegetarians and families welcome, good moderately priced food, friendly service, plenty of seats, beautiful big garden *(Piotr Chodzko-Zajko)*

Perranuthnoe [signed off A394 Penzance—Helston; SW5329], *Victoria*: Comfortable L-shaped bar with coastal and wreck photographs, some stripped stonework, well kept Courage-related ales, bar food, neat coal fire, booth seating in family area, games area; handy for Mounts Bay; bedrooms *(Peter and Joy Heatherley, LYM)*

☆ **Perranwell** [off A393 Redruth—Falmouth and A39 Falmouth—Truro; SW7839], *Royal Oak*: Pleasant unassuming black-beamed village pub, friendly staff and locals, cosy seats, good value bar food inc sandwiches and attractive lunchtime cold table, well kept Whitbreads-related ales and decent wines, good winter fire, provision for children, garden with picnic tables; piped music *(Gwen and Peter Andrews, John Wooll, LYM)*

☆ **Polgooth** [SW9950], *Polgooth*: Much modernised country local with good big family room and (up steep steps) outside play area; popular food, St Austell real ales, pleasant atmosphere *(Jack and Philip Paxton, LYM)*

☆ **Polperro** [The Quay; SX2051], *Blue Peter*: Cosy and unpretentious little low-beamed wood-floored harbourside local with well kept St Austell Tinners and HSD and guest beers, farm cider, log fire, traditional games, piped music, some seats outside; family room, open all day; no food *(Lindsley Harvard, Margaret Whalley, Jack and Philip Paxton, S R and A J Ashcroft, Bryan Hay, George Atkinson, Jerry and Alison Oakes, LYM)*

☆ **Polperro** [Quay], *Three Pilchards*: Low-beamed dim-lit local high over harbour, well kept Ushers, cheap simple food, open fire, neat chatty staff, tables on terrace up 30 steep steps; piped music can be fairly loud, open all day *(George Atkinson, L Harvard, M Whalley, Ted George)*

☆ **Polperro** [top of village nr main car park], *Crumplehorn Mill*: Friendly atmosphere and affordable generous food inc local fish in converted mill, separate dark areas inc upper gallery, beams, stripped stone, flagstones, log fire, comfortable seats, well kept Bass and St Austell HSD and XXXX, farm cider; pool area, piped music (can be fairly loud); good value bedrooms *(L Harvard, M Whalley, J H Bell, George Atkinson, Bryan Hay, BB)*

☆ **Polperro** [bear R approaching harbour], *Noughts & Crosses*: Cheerful riverside bar, soft lighting, comfortable banquettes, beams, stripped stone and panelling; good value food, Ushers ales, pool, fruit machine, good friendly service, upper family room; unobtrusive piped music; pretty street *(George Atkinson, Bronwen and Steve Wrigley)*

Polperro [Fore St], *Ship*: Very welcoming service, well kept Ushers, generous helpings of reasonably priced food, family room, terrace; children welcome *(Anon)*

Port Isaac [SX0080], *Old School*: Good bar food inc home-made soups, spacious terrace overlooking harbour; bedrooms *(Mrs L C Thomson)*

☆ **Portloe** [SW9339], *Lugger*: Well presented bar lunches inc children's dishes, simple easy chairs, two fires, good evening restaurant, decent wines, tables on terrace, pretty setting in attractive village above cove; bedrooms (not all with sea view); restaurant licence – you can't just go for a drink – otherwise clear main entry *(P and J Shapley, Dr R J Rathbone, Stephen Horsley, Mr and Mrs C R Little, S R Chapman, P M Lane, Mr and Mrs W J A Timpson, S Brackenbury, LYM)*

Portmellon Cove [SX0144], *Rising Sun*: Small lower bar and big upper family/games room overlooking sandy cove nr Mevagissey, decent food inc children's and vegetarian, St Austell tapped from the cask, seats outside; bedrooms; has been cl winter *(Jack and Philip Paxton, LYM)*

Portreath [SW6545], *Basset Arms*: Comfortable and welcoming village pub with good food in bar and newish restaurant, well kept beers, unobtrusive piped music; short stroll from beach *(S Howe, Tony Wickett)*

☆ **Portscatho** [SW8735], *Plume of Feathers*: Friendly and comfortable, with good thriving atmosphere, popular good value food in main bar or small eating area, side locals' bar, well kept St Austell Tinners, well reproduced loudish pop music, good staff; pretty fishing village, very popular with summer visitors; dogs allowed *(R and S Bentley, LYM)*

☆ **Poughill** [SS2207], *Preston Gate*: Friendly and busy welcoming local with pews and long mahogany tables on flagstones, log fires, well kept Tetleys-related ales, bar food, darts, some seats outside; children welcome, dogs looked after well *(Richard Cole, Brian Jones, LYM)*

Probus [Fore St; A390; SW8947], *Hawkins Arms*: Friendly local, generous well priced food, well kept St Austell ales; bedrooms *(Andy and Jill Kassube, Jack and Philip Paxton)*

☆ **Quintrel Downs** [East Rd; SW8560], *Two Clomes*: Attractive largely unspoilt former cottage with open fire, apt furnishings, nice mix of customers, well kept ales, reasonably priced food, pleasant landlord; family room *(Tom Evans, Jack and Philip Paxton)*

☆ *nr* **Redruth** [Tolgus Mount; SW6842], *Tricky Dickies*: Isolated former tin-mine smithy, interesting industrial relics, good food, changing well kept beers, partly covered terrace with barbecues; has had live music Tues/Thurs *(P and M Rudlin, Andy and Jill Kassube)*

Roche [SW9860], *Rock*: Roomy originally 14th-c inn with food inc vegetarian in dining and restaurant areas (kitchen open to view), well kept Whitbreads-related ales, pool table in front bar, quiet piped music *(G Washington)*

☆ **Ruan Lanihorne** [off A3078 St Mawes rd; SW8942], *Kings Head*: Good standard home-made food inc good sandwiches in attractive pub overlooking Fal estuary; Tetleys-related real ales, quick friendly service, pleasant atmosphere, china hanging from beams, cigarette cards, no smoking area; suntrap sunken garden and seating area with beautiful view; children welcome; bedrooms *(S Brackenbury, G W Stevenson)*

☆ **Sennen Cove** [SW3526], *Old Success*: 17th-c inn, perhaps best out of season, by clean beach with glorious view along Whitesand Bay; small nautical bar with lots of old photographs, quick generous reasonably priced bar food inc fresh seafood, well kept ales inc Bass, piped music, carvery restaurant; gents' past car park; attractive bedrooms, good breakfasts *(N and J Strathdee, Mrs B Sugarman, Alan Castle, Mr and Mrs D Fellows, Mr and Mrs R Head)*

St Austell [Sandy Hill; SX0152], *Carylon Arms*: Nicely refurbished, with good home-made specials, well kept St Austell ales *(Andy and Jill Kassube)*

☆ **St Dominick** [Saltash; a mile E of A388, S of Callington – OS Sheet 201 map ref 406674; SX3967], *Who'd Have Thought It*: An unlikely favourite – flock wallpaper, tasselled plush seats, Gothick tables, gleaming pottery and copper; reliably good interesting food inc fresh fish (lunch orders may stop 1.30), well kept Bass and Whitbreads-related ales, decent wines, friendly staff, impeccable lavatories, new family sun lounge; quiet countryside nr Cotehele *(S R Chapman, Jacquie and Jim Jones, Mrs C Watkinson, Mr and Mrs J Woodfield, Ted George, John Kirk, LYM)*

☆ **St Issey** [SW9271], *Ring o' Bells*: Neatly modernised cheerful village inn with consistently good food inc children's helpings, well kept Courage, friendly staff, open fire; bedrooms *(N P S Shaw, Mr and Mrs R J Phillips, LYM)*

St Ives [Fore St; SW5441], *Castle*: Comfortable and friendly two-room local, well priced bar food (may be a wait), Whitbreads-related ales, pine panelling, old local photographs, maritime memorabilia, unobtrusive piped music; best out of season *(Shirley Pielou, Bill and Sylvia Trotter)*; [High St], *Queens*: Biggish comfortable dining pub with decent food, family area, friendly atmosphere, pool table; bedrooms *(Bill and Sylvia Trotter)*; [The Wharf], *Sloop*: Extensive artistic connections so the place to go if you're visiting the Tate Gallery; paintings for sale, reliable bar food, reasonable range of real ales *(Sue Holland, Dave Webster)*; [Chapel St], *Three Ferrets*: Small and simple, with good value generous food, pleasant atmosphere, well kept real ale; piped music *(Bill and Sylvia Trotter)*

St Keverne [The Square; SW7921], *Three Tuns*: Cheery local by church with big helpings of cheap straightforward bar food inc good seafood and excellent steaks (landlord was a butcher), well kept Flowers IPA and Original, decent whiskies, woodburner, darts, some nautical decorations, picnic tables out by square; bedrooms *(John and Sally Clarke, Gwen and Peter Andrews, Sue Holland, Dave Webster, Peter and Lynn Brueton)*; [The Square], *White Hart*: Rather more up-market than our other entry here, with handsome bar and bedrooms, and a popular main entry in last edition, but the tenants who did so well (and cooked such excellent fish) were unable to agree terms with Greenalls and left as we went to press, with temporary management taking over *(LYM; reports please)*

St Kew [St Kew Highway (A39 Wadebridge—Bude); SX0375], *Red Lion*: Welcoming local, good value food, well kept beer *(Mr and Mrs Dane, S N T Spencer)*

☆ **St Mabyn** [SX0473], *St Mabyn Inn*: Good interesting food in sympathetically refurbished pub doing well under current regime *(Margaret Mason, David Thompson, Mark Billings, Jack and Philip Paxton)*

☆ **St Mawes** [SW8433], *Victory*: Recently tastefully refurbished, small and cosy, good friendly service, good reasonably priced food, good range of well kept Whitbreads-related ales, interesting sea pictures, children allowed; bedrooms *(Andy Bryant, G W Stevenson, N and J Strathdee, Anthony Barnes, Keith and Janet Morris, LYM)*

☆ **St Mawes**, *Rising Sun*: Pubby front locals' bar, plush hotel bar, attractive conservatory, slate-topped tables on terrace just across lane from harbour wall, lunchtime bar food, evening restaurant and Sun lunches, well kept St Austell BB and HSD on handpump, decent wine list, good service; open all day summer; pretty bedrooms with views *(N and J Strathdee, R and S Bentley, Helen Taylor, LYM)*

☆ **St Merryn** [Church Town (B3276 towards Padstow); SW8874], *Cornish Arms*: Well kept St Austell Tinners and BB and usual bar food inc good steaks in simple but spotless local with fine slate floor and some 12th-c stonework; good games room, picnic tables outside; children over 6 may be allowed in eating area *(Dave Thompson, Margaret Mason, A J N Lee, MJVK, LYM)*

☆ **St Merryn**, *Farmers Arms*: Big busy family dining pub with bright and spacious no smoking dining area, St Austell ales, good value house wine, floodlit well, children's games room with videos and so forth, tables on back terrace; bedrooms *(Don Kellaway, Angie Coles, Andy and Jane Beardsley)*

St Minver [SW9677], *Four Ways*: Straightforwardly friendly, with decent food, well kept Whitbreads-related ales, pretty garden, pleasant surroundings *(Margaret Mason, David Thompson, John Woodward)*

☆ **St Neot** [N of A38 Liskeard—Bodmin; SX1867], *London*: Good imaginative home-made food, well kept real ales, cheerful service, beams and two open fires; attractive village in wooded valley *(Mr and Mrs W J A Timpson)*

St Tudy [off A39 nr Wadebridge; SX0676], *Cornish Arms*: Friendly local with largish front bar, pool room and restaurant, well kept Sharps (new brew from Rock), bar food; children welcome *(Dave Thompson, Margaret Mason)*

☆ **Stratton** [SS2406], *Tree*: Rambling pub with seats in attractive ancient coachyard, very friendly bar rooms, well kept St Austell Tinners, varied well priced bar food, character evening restaurant; bedrooms *(R T and J C Moggridge, LM, Peter and Lynn Brueton, David Holloway, BB)*

☆ **Stratton** [SS2406], *Kings Arms*: Fine old well kept three-room 17th-c free house, six or more regularly changed real ales, varied tempting food; children welcome *(P and M Rudlin, David Holloway)*

Threemilestone [W of by-pass outside village; SW7844], *Oak Tree*: Spacious yet cosy and cheerful bar, Whitbreads-related ales, decent wines, wide changing choice of well presented tasty food, good quick service *(John Wooll)*

Tintagel [Fore St; SX0588], *Cornishman*: Good food from sandwiches up, well kept St Austell ales, flower-filled back terrace *(A J N Lee)*; [Tregatta (B3263 S)], *Min Pin*: This home-brew pub has now closed *(LYM)*

Trebarwith [signed off B3263 and B3314 SE of Tintagel – OS Sheet 200 map ref 058865; SX0585], *Mill House*: Marvellous spot in own steep streamside woods above sea, decent food inc children's dishes in low-key but inviting bar with fine Delabole flagstones, St Austell Tinners and a guest ale, friendly service, restaurant, comfortable bedrooms *(Mark and Nicola Willoughby, John Whiting, LYM)*

Tregrehan Mills [SX0453], *Britannia*: 16th-c inn with food all day running up to tournedos Rossini, restaurant, good choice of real ales; big garden with play area *(Andy and Jill Kassube)*

Trevarrian [B3276 NE of Newquay; SW8566], *Travellers Rest*: Good plentiful food, well kept St Austell beers, good friendly service; can get crowded in summer *(Charles Owens, Catherine Almond)*

☆ **Trevaunance Cove** [The Beach; SW7251], *Driftwood Spars*: Good quickly served fresh food from sandwiches up in former tin-mine store nr beach with huge beams, thick stone walls and log fires, decor highlighting smuggling and lifeboats; reasonable prices, big family room, attractive restaurant, well kept ales, lots of malt whiskies; comfortable bedrooms *(Mark and Nicola Willoughby, Jim Reid, Alan Wheatley)*

Truro [Frances St], *Globe*: Good choice of reliable generous home-made food, well kept Whitbreads-related ales, friendly efficient service, comfortable mix of furnishings inc leather armchairs and sofas, several rooms off central serving area; old panelling and beamery, bottle-glass screens, taxidermy, old prints *(Paul Cartledge, John and Wendy Trentham, P and M Rudlin)*

☆ **Truro** [Kenwyn St], *William IV*: Busy dark-panelled bar with slightly secluded raised areas and lots of bric-a-brac, well kept St Austell beers, decent wine, good value buffet food inc hot dishes in elegantly tiled airy two-level conservatory dining room opening into small flowery garden *(Peter Williamson, John Wooll, Bill Sharpe)*

Truro [Lemon Quay, by central car park], *Market*: Unchanging town local, friendly and simple, with home-made food inc good Cornish pasties, well kept beer *(Mark Walker, Bill and Sylvia Trotter, Anthony Barnes, LYM)*

☆ **Veryan** [SW9139], *New Inn*: Wide choice of good value bar food in neat and homely one-bar local, friendly landlord, well kept St Austell tapped from the cask, quiet seats out behind; bedrooms, lovely village *(Ted George)*

Werrington [outside village; SX3287], *Countryman*: Enormous helpings of food, well kept Bass and St Austell HSD, friendly staff, very popular with locals *(Dr and Mrs N Holmes)*

☆ **Zennor** [SW4538], *Tinners Arms*: Welcoming gently extended country local in lovely windswept setting nr coast path, limited bar food, well kept St Austell Tinners and HSD from casks behind bar, decent coffee, rather spartan feel with lots of granite and stripped pine; friendly cats, no music, tables on attractive new terrace *(Brian and Jill Bond, Peter and Lynn Brueton, Jeanne Cross, Paul Silvestri, Gwen and Peter Andrews, Mike and Heather Barnes, George and Chris Miller, Stephen Horsley, LYM)*

Isles of Scilly

☆ **Bryher** [SV8715], *Hell Bay*: Snug low-ceilinged granite-walled bar with sea views from deep window recesses, pleasant atmosphere, friendly staff, good quickly served cheap bar food (new dining room), attractive gardens with sheltered play area, stroll from beaches; keg beers; well equipped bedrooms *(Keith and Janet Morris, J C Simpson, BB)*

☆ **St Marys – Hugh Town** [The Strand; SV9010], *Atlantic*: Best pub here, big low-beamed L-shaped harbourside bar full of interesting nautical bric-a-brac, wreck salvage and photographs, good cheery atmosphere (esp on live music nights), simple reliable generous bar food inc local fish, well kept St Austell Tinners and HSD, great assortment of customers; piped music (may be obtrusive); family room, no smoking restaurant; good views, esp from small back jetty/terrace; bedrooms in adjacent hotel *(P and M Rudlin, David Mead, Neil and Anita Christopher, BB)*

St Marys – Hugh Town [Silver St (A3110)], *Bishop & Wolf*: Very wide choice of good well presented generous food esp fish, friendly efficient staff, interesting decor with gallery over rd, nets, maritime bric-a-brac, lifeboat photographs, upstairs restaurant, popular summer live music *(Naomi Badcock, Mr and Mrs D Darby, Keith and Janet Morris, Neil and Anita Christopher)*

Tresco [SV8915], *Island*: Upmarket but friendly hotel in beautiful spot, very comfortable bar, excellent reasonably priced food; fine grounds, tables out on terrace by grass (with badminton); right by shore with sweeping sea and island views; bedrooms *(R J Herd, P and M Rudlin, BB)*

Bedroom prices normally include full English breakfast, VAT and any inclusive service charge that we know of. Prices before the '/' are for single rooms, after for two people in double or twin (B includes a private bath, S a private shower). If there is no '/', the prices are only for twin or double rooms (as far as we know there are no singles).

Cumbria

An abundance of friendly and attractive pubs in lovely scenery makes this a fine area for anyone who likes good pubs; many have very good food, too (though it can be pricy), and many are charming places to stay in. New main entries this year, or pubs returning to these pages after an absence, are the Burnmoor at Boot (most attractively placed in a quieter part of the Lakes), the very individual Abbey Bridge Inn up by the ancient priory at Lanercost, the Queens Head at Tirril (doing extremely well under its newish Italian owner), the Mortal Man, a friendly small hotel at Troutbeck, and the Gate at Yanwath; the Queens Head and Gate both have particularly good food. Other pubs currently doing very well here include the Royal Oak at Appleby, the Pheasant at Casterton (gaining our food award this year), the Britannia at Elterwater, the Drunken Duck up above Hawkshead, the Shepherds at Melmerby (a new star award for it), and the Queens Head at Troutbeck (another to gain our star award). Note that quite a few pubs this year have new licensees, with consequent changes. With eight pubs here now qualifying for our food award, and many others doing good fresh home cooking, there's plenty of scope for really enjoyable meals out: from among them, we choose the Queens Head at Tirril as Cumbrian Dining Pub of the Year. Drinks prices are generally at least 10p lower than the national average, with three good local breweries active here – Jennings, Mitchells and Yates (though the cheapest beer we found was at the Blue Bell in Heversham, tied to Sam Smiths of Yorkshire). Main-entry pubs brewing their own are the Sun at Dent (its beers turning up in quite a few other pubs now), Masons Arms on Cartmel Fell and Cavendish Arms in Cartmel, whose very young brewer now does three good real ales. In the Lucky Dip section at the end of the chapter pubs currently standing out include the New Inn at Blencogo, Punch Bowl at Crosthwaite, Dog & Gun in Keswick, Strickland Arms near Levens, Middleton Fells at Middleton, Fat Lamb above Ravenstonedale, Scafell at Rosthwaite, Wasdale Head Inn at Wasdale and Bay Horse at Winton; as we have inspected almost all of these we can confirm their high quality.

ALSTON NY7246 Map 10

Angel

Front Street (A689)

In a quaintly old-fashioned Pennine village and half way up the steep cobbled main street, is this friendly 17th-c stone pub. The black-beamed and timbered L-shaped bar has logs burning in a big stone fireplace, horsebrasses on the beams, brass pans and a coach-horn on the walls, and wheelback chairs and traditional black wall seats around dimpled copper tables. Good value bar food, quickly served, includes sandwiches (from £1.30), soup (£1.35), ploughman's (£2.80), salads (from £3.20), good cumberland sausage (£3.45), mushroom and nut fettucini (£3.95), 12oz gammon and egg (£5.50), 8oz sirloin steak (£7.25), and puddings like sticky toffee or pavlova (£1.65); good Sunday roast, children's meals. Well kept Boddingtons and

Flowers IPA on handpump, and darts, dominoes, and piped music. A sheltered back garden has some picnic tables and umbrellas. ***(Recommended by Jim and Maggie Cowell, H K Dyson, G W Lindley; more reports please)***

Free house ~ Licensees Nicky and Sue Ashcroft ~ Real ale ~ Meals and snacks (not Tues evening) ~ (01434) 381363 ~ Children welcome until 9pm ~ Open 11-5, 7-11 ~ Bedrooms: £14/£28

AMBLESIDE NY3804 Map 10

Golden Rule

Smithy Brow; follow Kirkstone Pass signpost from A591 on N side of town

This is very much an honest Lakeland local, but after a trek over the fells, you can be sure of a friendly welcome from the landlord – even if your boots are a bit muddy. There are lots of local country pictures and a few fox masks decorating the butter-coloured walls, horsebrasses on the black beams, built-in leatherette wall seats, and cast-iron-framed tables. The room on the left has darts, a fruit machine, and dominoes; the one down a few steps on the right is a quieter sitting room. Well kept Hartleys XB and Robinsons Best, Old Stockport, and Hatters Mild on handpump; local pork pies (35p) and filled rolls (£1.25) only; friendly dog. There's a back yard with tables, a small pretty summer garden, and wonderfully colourful window boxes. The golden rule referred to in its name is a brass meausuring yard mounted over the bar counter. ***(Recommended by H K Dyson, Helen Hazzard, David Lewis, Mike and Jo, David Lands, John and Marianne Cooper; more reports please)***

Hartleys (Robinsons) ~ Tenant John Lockley ~ Real ale ~ Limited snacks ~ (01539) 433363 ~ Children welcome ~ Nearby parking virtually out of the question ~ Open 11-11

APPLEBY NY6921 Map 10

Royal Oak ★

Bongate; B6542 on S edge of town

If this very popular old-fashioned coaching inn has a weakness, neither we nor our readers have found it yet. It's a consistently enjoyable place to be – for a drink, a meal or a weekend. Part of the long, low building dates back to the 14th c, and the beamed lounge has old pictures on the timbered walls, some armchairs and a carved settle, and a panelling-and-glass snug enclosing the bar counter; there's a good open fire in the smaller, oak-panelled public bar; dominoes. From an imaginative and most comprehensive menu, the excellent home-made food might include lunchtime sandwiches such as home-cooked ham and beef (from £1.40), superb soup with home-made bread (£1.75), pâté of the day (£2.75), hot green pancakes stuffed with apple and stilton (£2.95), delicious brown Lancashire shrimps (£3.75), cumberland sausage or savoury vegetable crumble (£4.25), fresh fish of the day (£5.95), interesting salads (from £5.95), English gammon and egg or chicken supreme with lemon and tarragon (£6.95), Scottish salmon steak with dill cream sauce (£7.95), pork fillet with mushrooms, madeira and cream (£8.95, evening only), and steaks (from £8.95); adventurous daily specials, children's meals, and puddings (£2). One of the dining rooms is no smoking. They keep a fine range of real ales on handpump: Bongate Special Pale Ale (their own beer made locally) and Theakstons Best, with regular visitors such as Holts, several Maclays ales and Yates Premium, and guest ales mainly from Scotland and Northern England; several malt whiskies, and a carefully chosen wine list with 8 by the glass and quite a few half bottles. In summer the outside is very colourful, with seats on the front terrace among masses of flowers in tubs, troughs and hanging baskets. You can get here on the scenic Leeds/Settle/Carlisle railway (best to check times and any possible delays to avoid missing lunch). ***(Recommended by Mr and Mrs N Evans, Richard Holloway, Anthony Barnes, Karen Eliot, A W Lewis, Malcolm Taylor, Tony Gayfer, Dr Peter Crawshaw, Jack and Heather Coyle, Steve and Julie Cocking, Pat and John Millward, Mike and Ann Beiley, Angela Steele, Jeff***

Davies, S R and A J Ashcroft, Mr and Mrs R Head, Jan and Dave Booth, Simon Watkins, David and Margaret Bloomfield, Lucy James, Dr RKP, David Heath, H K Dyson, Gwen and Peter Andrews, Geoffrey and Brenda Wilson, Jane Kingsbury, Luke Worthington, and others)

Free house ~ Licensees Colin and Hilary Cheyne ~ Real ale ~ Meals and snacks (12-2, 6-9; not 25 Dec) ~ Restaurant ~ (017683) 51463 ~ Well behaved children welcome ~ Open 11-3, 6-11; closed 25 Dec ~ Bedrooms: £27.50/£59.50B

See also entry under nearby BRAMPTON

ARMATHWAITE NY5146 Map 10

Dukes Head

Off A6 a few miles S of Carlisle

A good spot for discovering the attractive Eden Valley, this well kept inn is run by friendly, welcoming licensees. The civilised lounge bar has oak settles and little armchairs among more upright seats, oak and mahogany tables, antique hunting and other prints, and some brass and copper powder-flasks above its coal fire. Good home-cooked bar food includes sandwiches (from £2), ploughman's (£4.95), filled three-egg omelettes (£5.50), courgette, spinach and pasta bake (£6), home-boiled ham (£6.50), sirloin steak (£9), their particular pride roast duck (£9.50), daily specials such as fresh cod in batter (£5.50) or venison in Guinness casserole (£6.40), with children's dishes (£3.60), old-fashioned puddings, and three-course Sunday roast (£8.75); the breakfasts are huge. Well kept Boddingtons and intermittent guest beers on handpump, good wines, nostalgic piped music, and dominoes; separate public bar with darts and pool, two games machines and juke box in back lobby. There are tables out on the lawn behind. The licensees also run the New Crown Inn at Ainstable. *(Recommended by Richard Holloway, A N Ellis, Jean and Douglas Troup, David Heath, Paul and Ursula Roberts)*

Free house ~ Licensee Peter Lynch ~ Real ale ~ Meals and snacks ~ Restaurant ~ (016974) 72226 ~ Children welcome ~ Open 11.30-3, 5.30-11 ~ Bedrooms:£22.50(£27.50B)/£40(£45B)

ASKHAM NY5123 Map 9

Punch Bowl

Village signposted on right from A6 4 miles S of Penrith

Interesting furnishings in the rambling bar of this attractively set busy pub include an antique settle by an open log fire, Chippendale dining chairs and rushwork ladder-back seats around sturdy wooden tables, well cushioned window seats in the white-painted thick stone walls, coins stuck into the cracks of the dark wooden beams (periodically taken out and sent to charity), and local photographs and prints of Askham. The old-fashioned woodburning stove, with its gleaming stainless chimney in the big main fireplace, is largely decorative. Generous helpings of bar food include home-made soup (£2.25), lunchtime sandwiches (£2.50), potted salmon (£2.85), pies like pork and apple or venison with red wine, cranberries and mushrooms (from £5.10), bacon chop in a pineapple curry sauce (£5.40), mushroom and tomato lasagne (£5.95), cumberland tagliatelle (£6), fish pie (£6.20), and steaks (from £9.50); children's dishes (£3). Whitbreads Castle Eden on handpump kept under light blanket pressure and a changing guest beer, and several malt whiskies; cribbage and piped pop music, and in the separate public bar darts, pool, juke box and fruit machine. There are tables out on a flower-filled terrace, and the setting, facing the lower village green, is attractive. *(Recommended by Angus Lyon, James and Patricia Halfyard, G O Cook, J Finney, MJVK, Dr Brian Hamilton, Malcolm Phillips, Ian and Deborah Carrington, S and D Shaw, Kathryn and Brian Heathcote, Lucy James, Dr RLP, H K Dyson, N H and A G Harries)*

Whitbreads ~ Lease: David and Frances Riley ~ Real ale ~ Snacks (lunchtime) and meals ~ (01931) 712443 ~ Children in eating area of bar ~ Open 11.30-3, 6.30(6 Sat)-11; 12-3, 7-11 in winter ~ Bedrooms: £19.50/£39

BASSENTHWAITE NY2332 Map 9

Sun

Village itself, signposted off A591 a few miles NW of Keswick

Though this pleasant inn looks tiny from the outside, the bar rambles around into areas that stretch usefully back on both sides of the servery. There are low 17th-c black oak beams, lots of brasses, built-in wall seats and plush stools around heavy wooden tables, and a good stone fireplace with big logs burning in winter. The landlady is from the Lakes, while her husband is Italian, and the bar food draws on both their backgrounds: minestrone soup (£1.50), squid in batter (£2.50), ploughman's (£3.50), lancashire hotpot (£4), steak and kidney pie, lasagne with garlic bread (£5), pork steaks in mushroom sauce (£6), sirloin steak (£8), and puddings such as syrup sponge or sticky toffee pudding (£2). Well kept Jennings on handpump; dominoes; no dogs. A huddle of white houses looks up to Skiddaw and other high fells, and you can enjoy the view from the tables in the pub's front yard, by a neighbour's blackberry bush. *(Recommended by Richard Holloway, Mrs P Abell, MB, David Heath, Nick Cox, N H White, Brian and Jill Bond, Peter and Lynn Brueton, Michael Wadsworth)*

Jennings ~ Tenants Giuseppe and Josephine Scopelliti ~ Real ale ~ Meals and snacks (12-1.30, 6.30-8.30ish; not Sun evening) ~ (017687) 76439 ~ Children welcome (in side rooms whenever possible) ~ Open 12-2.30, 6-11; may close earlier winter lunchtimes if very quiet; closed Mon lunchtimes Nov-Mar

BASSENTHWAITE LAKE NY1930 Map 9

Pheasant ★ 🛏

Follow Wythop Mill signpost at N end of dual carriageway stretch of A66 by Bassenthwaite Lake

Surprisingly old-fashioned and relaxed, the pubby little bars in this rather smart civilised hotel have Persian rugs on the parquet floor, rush-seat chairs, library seats, and cushioned settles, hunting prints and photographs on the fine ochre walls, and drinks served from a low serving counter. Well kept Bass and Theakstons Best on handpump and quite a few malt whiskies. Good lunchtime bar food includes soup (£1.90), cold roast meat platter or ploughman's (£3.90), potted Silloth shrimps (£4), smoked local trout with cucumber and dill vinaigrette (£4.10), steak and kidney pie (£4.95), smoked venison with black cherries in cumberland sauce (£5.20), grilled cumberland sausage, black pudding, mushrooms and tomato (£5.80), Chinese stir-fried pork fillet (£6.25), and puddings (£2.60); the elegant restaurant is no smoking. If the bars are full, you might want to move to the large and airy beamed lounge at the back, which has easy chairs on its polished parquet floor and a big log fire on cool days; there are also some chintzy sitting rooms with antique furniture (one is no smoking). The hotel is surrounded by very attractive woodlands, with beeches, larches and Douglas firs, and you can walk into them from the garden. This is a very good walking area. *(Recommended by John and Pam Smith, S Fazackerly, C Rowan, John and Christine Lowe, Jack Morley, V and E A Bolton, Jerry and Alison Oakes, Lynn Sharpless, Bob Eardley, Cath and John Howard, WAH, N H White, Nigel Woolliscroft, John Allsopp)*

Free house ~ Licensee W E Barrington Wilson ~ Real ale ~ Lunchtime snacks (no bar food Sun evening) ~ Restaurant ~ (017687) 76234 ~ Children in eating area of bar (not Sun) ~ Open 11-3, 5.30-10.30(11 Sat); 11.30-2.30, 5.30-10.30 in winter; closed 25 Dec ~ Bedrooms: £55B/£68B

Bedroom prices are for high summer. Even then you may get reductions for more than one night, or (outside tourist areas) weekends. Winter special rates are common, and many inns cut bedroom prices if you have a full evening meal.

BEETHAM SD5079 Map 7

Wheatsheaf

Village (and inn) signposted just off A6 S of Milnthorpe

You can't really miss this striking early 17th-c building with its fine black and white timbered cornerpiece – and it's a handy place for the old road to the Lakes. The lounge bar is relaxed and chatty and has lots of exposed beams and joists, attractive built-in wall settles, tapestry-cushioned chairs, a massive antique carved oak armchair, and a cabinet filled with foreign costume dolls. Beyond a little central snug is a tiled-floor bar with darts and dominoes. Good, reasonably priced bar food includes soup (£1.40), sandwiches (from £1.80), home-made hotpot (£3.20), ploughman's (£3.85), home-made pies like cheese or steak and kidney (from £3.30), sausage, liver and bacon (£3.50), steaks (from £6.75), daily specials, and puddings (from £1.60); courteous, friendly staff. If the bar is too crowded, you can eat in the upstairs no-smoking dining room for the same price. Well kept Boddingtons and Thwaites Bitter on handpump, and quite a few malt whiskies. *(Recommended by Prof I H Rorison, Mr and Mrs K H Frostick, R D Knight, Cath and John Howard, Derek and Margaret Underwood, Miss D P Barson; more reports please)*

Free house ~ Licensee Mrs Margaret Shaw ~ Real ale ~ Meals and snacks (11.45-1.45, 6-8.45) ~ Restaurant ~ (015395) 62123 ~ Children welcome till 8.30pm ~ Open 11-3, 6-11; closed evenings 25/26 Dec ~ Bedrooms: £30B/£40B

BOOT NY1801 Map 9

Burnmoor

Village signposted just off the Wrynose/Hardknott Pass road, OS Sheet 89 map reference 175010

In a quieter area than much of Lakeland, this family-run partly 16th-c inn is surrounded by peaceful fells that rise fairly gently at first to Scafell, and by lots of attractive tracks such as the one up along Whillan Beck to Burnmoor Tarn. There are seats outside on the sheltered front lawn, and it's close to Dalegarth Station (the top terminus of the Ravenglass and Eskdale light steam railway). Inside, the beamed and carpeted white-painted bar has an open fire, red leatherette seats and small metal tables. Mrs Foster is Austrian and there are always some speciality dishes on the menu: delicious soup (£1.20), lunchtime ploughman's (£3.40), several flans such as cheese and onion or Austrian smoked ham and cheese (from £3.50), home-cooked cold meats (£4), cumberland game pie (£5.50), Wienerschnitzel (£6.10), sirloin steak (£7.80), and daily specials. They grow a lot of the vegetables themselves, and keep hens and pigs. Well kept Jennings Bitter, Cumberland and Snecklifter on handpump, Austrian wines, and gluhwein in winter; pool and juke box. *(Recommended by John and Heather Bentley, S Fazackerly, C Rowan, John T Ames, J S M Sheldon, Russell and Margaret Bathie, Peter and Lynn Brueton, Helen Hazzard, John and Marianne Cooper)*

Free house ~ Licensees Tony and Heidi Foster ~ Real ale ~ Meals and snacks (12-2, 6-9) ~ Restaurant ~ (019467) 23224 ~ Children welcome till 9pm ~ Open 11-3, 4.45-11 ~ Bedrooms: £23/£48(£52B)

BOWLAND BRIDGE SD4289 Map 9

Hare & Hounds

Village signposted from A5074; OS Sheet 97 map reference 417895

What makes this white-painted pub successful is largely due to Mr Thompson's quick wit and individual attention to customers – he's as deft a publican as he used to be an international footballer. The comfortably modernised bar, divided into smaller areas by stone walls, has oak beams, ladder-back chairs around dark wood tables on the spread of turkey carpet, Liverpool and England team photographs and caps (the landlord used to play for both), reproduction hunting prints, a stuffed pheasant, and open fires. Bar food includes soup (£1.50), sandwiches (from £1.75), pizzas (from £3.95), cumberland sausage (£4.75), coq au vin (£5.95), steaks (from £9.50), daily specials, and 4-course Sunday roast lunch (£8.95); very good, prompt service. Well kept Lakeland Gold from the Cavendish Arms in Cartmel and Tetleys on handpump, and several malt whiskies from a long bar counter with a cushioned red leatherette elbow rest for people using the sensible backrest-type bar stools. Dominoes, video game, and piped music. The climbing roses, window boxes and hanging baskets are pretty in summer, and there are picnic tables in the spacious garden at one side, with more by the road. The pub is set by the bridge itself. *(Recommended by J Finney, H K Dyson, Mark Bradley, Colin and Shirley Brown, Margaret and Arthur Dickinson, S R and A I Ashcroft; more reports please)*

Free house ~ Licensee Peter Thompson ~ Real ale ~ Meals and snacks ~ Restaurant (residents only) ~ (015395) 68333 ~ Children welcome ~ Open 11-3, 5.30-11; winter evening opening 6pm ~ Bedrooms: £33B/£46B(mostly with own bthrm)

BOWNESS ON WINDERMERE SD4097 Map 9

Hole in t' Wall

Lowside

Tucked away in a back street, this bustling and characterful place is much enjoyed by readers. It's Bowness's oldest pub and the friendly licensees welcome regulars and tourists alike. The bar has lots to look at such as giant smith's bellows, and old farm implements and ploughshares, and a room upstairs has handsome plasterwork in its coffered ceiling. On cool days a splendid log fire burns under a vast slate mantlebeam. The tiny flagstoned front courtyard (where there are sheltered seats) has an ancient outside flight of stone steps to the upper floor. Mrs Mitton decides what to cook each day once she gets into her kitchen. There might be sandwiches (from £2.50), vegetarian ratatouille with cheese topping and garlic bread (£4.95), fresh mussels and king prawns in white wine (£5.10), chicken, rump steak and mushrooms in white wine and cream (£5.20), home-made fish pie (£5.25), popular whole roast pheasant with red wine sauce (£6.25), and puddings like lemon meringue pie or fruit cake and cheese (£2). Hartleys XB and Robinsons Frederics, Best, Old Stockport, and Hatters Mild on handpump in excellent condition, home-made lemonade and very good mulled winter wine; darts, pool, fruit machine and jukebox upstairs. If you'd rather catch it on a quiet day, it's better to visit out of season. *(Recommended by Christopher Turner, Richard Lewis, Katie Hornby, Rosemarie Johnson, George Atkinson, Elizabeth and Anthony Watts, John and Marianne Cooper, Alan and Ruth Woodhouse)*

Hartleys (Robinsons) ~ Tenants: Andrew and Audrey Mitton ~ Real ale ~ Meals and snacks (not Sun evening) ~ (015394) 43488 ~ Children in family room off taproom until 9pm ~ Parking nearby can be difficult ~ Open 11-11

BRAITHWAITE NY2324 Map 9

Coledale Inn

Village signposted off A66 W of Keswick; pub then signed left off B5292

Although much of the emphasis here is on the hotel side, those dropping in for a drink or a meal while out walking are just as welcome. The left-hand bar has fine views of Skiddaw and the much closer bracken-covered hills from the window-seats, a winter coal fire, and little 19th-c Lakeland engravings; the green-toned bar on the right, with a bigger bay window, is more of a dining bar. Simple, reliable food includes home-made soup (£1.30), filled baked potatoes (from £2.70), salads (from £4.20), ploughman's (£4.90), cumberland sausage (£5.20), gammon and egg (£5.70), sirloin steak (£8.50), and puddings with custard or cream (£1.85); daily specials, vegetarian meals, and several children's dishes (£1.75). Well kept Jennings Bitter, Theakstons XB, Yates, and Youngers Scotch on handpump or electric pump;

darts, dominoes, trivia and piped music. The dining room is no smoking. The garden has tables and chairs on the slate terrace beyond the sheltered lawn, and a popular play area for children; the pub is perfectly placed at the foot of the Whinlatter Pass – so walkers can start their hike straight from the door. *(Recommended by P and M Rudlin, J Finney, D Hanley, Simon Watkins, Terry and Eileen Stott, Mrs W E Darlaston, JKW, Jon Aldous, Mrs P Abell, V and E A Bolton, Nick Cox, WAH, Dave Davey, Sarah Bertram, Adrian and Gilly Heft)*

Free house ~ Licensees Geoffrey and Michael Mawdsley ~ Real ale ~ Meals and snacks ~ (017687) 78272 ~ Children welcome ~ Open 11-11 ~ Bedrooms: £20S/£50S

BRAMPTON NY6723 Map 10

New Inn

Note: this is the small Brampton near Appleby, not the bigger one up by Carlisle. Off A66 N of Appleby – follow Long Marton 1 signpost then turn right at church; village also signposted off B6542 at N end of Appleby

This year, one of the two cosy little rooms here (the Westmorland Bar) has been refurbished with stripped and polished old pine benches with upholstered cushions, and old pine tables; there's also a good range of local pictures (mainly sheep and wildlife), and a nice little oak table; a stuffed fox is curled on top of the corner TV, and a red squirrel pokes out of a little hole in the dividing wall. The particularly interesting flagstoned dining room has horsebrasses on its low black beams, well spaced tables, and a splendid original black cooking range at one end, separated from the door by an immensely sturdy old oak built-in settle. Good bar food includes lunchtime sandwiches (from £1.20; steak £2.95), ploughman's (£3.50) and pizzas (from £2.75), as well as home-made soup (£1.50), home-made chicken liver pâté with cumberland sauce (£2.50), Morecambe Bay shrimps (£3), steak and kidney pie (£4.70), nut roast (£4.75), spicy stroganoff (£6.95), sirloin steak (£8.30), and puddings like fruit crumble or treacle sponge (£2); 3-course Sunday lunch (£6.50, children £3). Well kept Boddingtons, Theakstons Best, and Youngers Scotch on handpump, and a good choice of whiskies with some eminent malts; friendly service, darts, dominoes and piped music. There are seats on the lawn and a barbecue area. No dogs in bedrooms. In June, the Appleby Horse Fair tends to base itself here. Incidentally another Brampton near Chesterfield has a pub of the same name. *(Recommended by Richard Holloway, Ian Rorison, Christopher Turner, Mark and Caroline Thistlethwaite, Dave Davey)*

Free house ~ Licensees Roger and Anne Cranswick ~ Real ale ~ Meals and snacks ~ Restaurant ~ (017683) 51231 ~ Children in eating area of bar and in restaurant until 9pm ~ Open 11.30-2.30(3 Sat), 6-11; Jan, Feb, Mar opening midday ~ Bedrooms: £18/£36

BUTTERMERE NY1817 Map 9

Bridge Hotel

Readers are very fond of staying here and the views from the bedrooms are marvellous. The inn is set in some of the best steep countryside in the county, and Crummock Water and Buttermere are just a stroll away – it's not surprisingly popular with walkers. The beamed bar is divided into two parts and furnished with settles and brocaded armchairs around copper-topped tables, a panelled bar counter, and some brass ornaments; the flagstoned area is good for walking boots. There's also a friendly and comfortable lounge bar. Good bar food includes home-made soup (£1.90), open sandwiches or ploughman's (£3.60), leek and onion tart (£4.80), Cumbrian hotpot (£5.30), salads (from £5.90), hare, venison and rabbit pie (£6), gammon with egg or poached Borrowdale trout (£6.20), steaks (from £8.70), and puddings (£2.30); Sunday lunch (£5.20); the restaurant is no smoking. In the summer food is served all day, starting with breakfast in the lounge bar between

9-10am and they do afternoon tea and have a high tea menu too. Well kept Black Sheep Best and Special and Theakstons Old Peculier and summer guest beers on handpump, and quite a few malt whiskies; dominoes, cribbage. Outside, a flagstoned terrace has white tables by a rose-covered sheltering stone wall. *(Recommended by Bronwen and Steve Wrigley, Tony Gayfer, Wayne Brindle, Michael Butler, P H Roberts, Dave Lands, J B Neame, Mr and Mrs S Ashcroft, Sarah Geyer, Mick Whelton)*

Free house ~ Licensee Peter McGuire ~ Real ale ~ Meals and snacks ~ Evening restaurant ~ (017687) 70252 ~ Children welcome ~ Open 10.30-11 ~ Bedrooms: £36B/£73B; also, s/c apartments

CARTMEL SD3879 Map 7

Cavendish Arms

Off main sq

The hoped for brewery here has now opened with Nick Murray brewing the very good home brews – Lakeland Gold (which won Best Beer Award at the Wigan Beer Festival), Buttermere Bitter and Cartmel Thoroughbred on handpump; they also keep a couple of guest ales as well, Belgian Trappist bottled beers, and a good choice of malt whiskies. Good bar food includes sandwiches, home-made soup (£2.50), home-made game terrine (pheasant, duck livers and rabbit) with a mango, juniper and poppyseed pickle (£3.95), stir-fried vegetables with tofu and saffron rice (£4.95), steak and mushroom in ale pie (£5.95), lamb cutlets marinated in dark rum and demerara sugar and served with a pine kernel sauce or salmon with lime and ginger butter (£7.95), Aberdeen Angus steaks (from £11.95), and daily specials; helpful, friendly staff and a very nice atmosphere – and although the pub is popular with locals, there's still a warm greeting for visitors. The no-smoking restaurant now has a roasting spit for Sunday lunches. Darts and dominoes. There are tables in front of the pub, with more at the back by the stream, and their flower displays tend to win awards. The landlord will take inexperienced fell walkers on guided treks over the mountains. There are plans to add five more bedrooms. *(Recommended by Jack Morley, George Atkinson, H K Dyson, Malcolm Taylor, Philip Johnson, Wayne Brindle, John Scarisbrick, Mark Holmes, Janis and Neil Hedgecock, Mrs C Thexton, A T Langton, Gill and Maurice McMahon)*

Free house ~ Tom and Nick Murray ~ Real ale ~ Meals and snacks (11.30-2.15, 6-9.30) ~ Restaurant ~ (015395) 36240 ~ Children welcome until 8.30pm ~ Open 11.30-11 ~ Bedrooms: £23B/£46B

CARTMEL FELL SD4288 Map 9

Masons Arms ★

Strawberry Bank, a few miles S of Windermere between A592 and A5074; perhaps the simplest way of finding the pub is to go uphill W from Bowland Bridge (which is signposted off A5074) towards Newby Bridge and keep right then left at the staggered crossroads – it's then on your right, below Gummer's How; OS Sheet 97 ref 413895

Very popular with our readers, this beautifully set place keeps an extraordinary choice of beers. On the five handpumps are two beers brewed on the premises – Amazon (light and hoppy but quite strong) and Big Six or Great Northern – and usually Black Sheep Special, Thwaites White Oak, and a guest. There's also their own damson beer (depending on the fruit crop) and cider using mainly local apples (called Knickerbockerbreaker). A 24-page booklet clearly describes hundreds of imported beers, most stocked and some even imported, which is now in its 15th edition and, considering its scale, is unique. You can be sure of finding some beers here that simply don't exist anywhere else in the country. They also do a brisk trade for instance in Liefmanskriek and Liefmansframbozen (cherry and raspberry beer from Belgium), and have two authentic German beers (Furstenberg Export from the Black Forest and St Georgen Dunkel, a dark lager from Franconia), a genuine Dutch Trappist beer, La Trappe Blonde, on draught (very rarely on draught even in

Holland itself), Bitburger Pils on draught, and a tap for wheat beers. Many of the beers have their own particular-shaped glasses. As well as house wine, the Stevensons keep two white and two red guest wines, often from Australia and Chile. Popular wholesome food (lots of vegetarian choices) includes soup (£2.50), sandwiches (from £3.25), hazelnut and lentil pâté (£4.25), Morecambe Bay potted shrimps (£4.50), ploughman's (£5.50), spicy vegetable burritos or fisherman's pie (£6.50), cumberland sausage and cider casserole or rogan josh (£7.50), home-made puddings like blueberry and apple tart or tiramisu (£2.95), and daily specials such as chicken and smoked cheese bake (£6.25), baked whole trout stuffed with asparagus and prawns (£6.75), and pork fillet in a mustard cream sauce (£7.25). The main bar has low black beams in the bowed ceiling, country chairs and plain wooden tables on polished flagstones, and a grandly Gothick seat with snarling dogs as its arms. A small lounge has oak tables and settles to match its fine Jacobean panelling, and a plain little room beyond the serving counter has pictures and a fire in an open range; the family room has an old-parlourish atmosphere, and there's also an upstairs room which helps at peak times. The setting overlooking the Winster Valley to the woods below Whitbarrow Scar is unrivalled and a good terrace with rustic benches and tables makes the most of the dramatic view. They sell leaflets outlining local walks of varying lengths and difficulty. As it's such a favourite with so many people, don't be surprised if the bar is extremely crowded; it's often much quieter mid-week. *(Recommended by Malcolm Taylor, MJVK, C M Fox, John Scarisbrick, Wayne Brindle, Jenny and Roger Huggins, R J Walden, John and Joan Nash, J H and S A Harrop, James House, LM, Ann Reeder, David Craine, John and Chris Simpson, Tina and David Woods-Taylor, David Heath, Mark Rumsey, H K Dyson, Jack Morley, Mr and Mrs S Ashcroft, Mike and Wendy Proctor, Helen Hazzard, Mick Hitchman, Colin Davies, Sharron Thompson, Philip Dixon, Cath and John Howard, Mark Bradley, Nigel Woolliscroft, TBB, P Barnsley, Ewan and Moira McCall, Paul McPherson, Lynn Sharpless, Bob Eardley, Mr and Mrs Rankine, John and Marianne Cooper, S R and A I Ashcroft, Lucy James, Dr RKP)*

Own brew ~ Licensees Helen and Nigel Stevenson ~ Real ale ~ Meals and snacks (12-2, 6-8.45) ~ (015395) 68486 ~ Children welcome till 9.30pm ~ Open 11.30-11; 11.30-3, 6-11 winter weekdays ~ Four self-catering flats and two self-catering cottages available

CASTERTON SD6279 Map 10

Pheasant

A683 about a mile N of junction with A65, by Kirkby Lonsdale; OS sheet 97, map reference 633796

Going from strength to strength, this civilised white-painted inn has a welcoming and attractive atmosphere. The two comfortably modernised, beamed rooms of the main bar glow with polish and have table lamps and pot plants, padded wheelback chairs, plush wall settles, newspapers and magazines to read, an open log fire in a nicely arched bare stone fireplace with polished brass hood, and souvenir mugs on the mantlepiece; there's a further room across the passage which will have been refurbished by the time this book is published. Well kept Morlands Old Speckled Hen, Theakstons Bitter and XB, and Charles Wells Bombardier on handpump, a small but good wine list from Corney & Barrow, and over 30 malt whiskies. Good, popular bar food includes home-made soup (£2.25), sandwiches (from £2.25), prawn and gruyere pot (£4.50), omelettes (£4.75), locally made black pudding and bacon grill (£4.95), home-made steak and kidney pie (£5.50), courgette and brie lasagne or cold meat platter (£5.95), fresh sardines (£6.25), spicy lamb balti (£6.95), Aberdeen Angus steaks (from £6.50), daily specials such as fresh Irish pike marinated with fresh herbs and lemon juice (£4.25), home-made broccoli and parmesan quiche (£6.25), and cajun-style chicken (£7.25), and puddings (£2.50); hearty breakfasts. The restaurant is no smoking; darts, dominoes, a weekly winter quiz night in aid of the Guide Dogs, and piped music. There are some tables with cocktail parasols outside by the road and the garden has been improved this year. The nearby church (built for the girls' school of Brontë fame here) has some attractive pre-Raphaelite stained glass and paintings. *(Recommended by Malcolm Taylor,*

G C Brown, John Allsopp, Mrs Pat Crabb, Sue Holland, Dave Webster, Michael and Joan Melling, Frank Cummins, Les and Jean Scott, Kim Schofield, W G Burden, Neil Townend, John Allsopp, Dr J A Caldwell)

Free house ~ Licensees Melvin and May Mackie ~ Real ale ~ Meals and snacks ~ Restaurant ~ (015242) 71230 ~ Children welcome ~ Open 11-3, 6-11 ~ Bedrooms: £37B/£64B

CHAPEL STILE NY3205 Map 9

Wainwrights

B5343

In a delightful fellside spot, this white-rendered Lakeland house is surrounded by good walks, and you can enjoy the views from the picnic tables out on the terrace. Inside, there's a relaxed and friendly atmosphere and plenty of room in the characterful slate-floored bar with its old kitchen range and cushioned settles; half the pub is no smoking. Good food includes soup (£1.80), sandwiches (from £1.95), filled baked potatoes (from £2.75), rainbow trout (£6.25), children's dishes (£2.45; free lollipop and children's cocktails, too), and changing daily specials such as a vegetarian dish, chicken with tarragon, white wine and cream, and barnsley chop (from £5.25); good, prompt service. Well kept Theakstons Best, XB and Old Peculier with a summer guest beer like Marstons Pedigree or Morlands Old Speckled Hen on handpump and a decent wine list; dominoes, fruit machine, trivia, and piped music. *(Recommended by Bronwen and Steve Wrigley, Jenny and Roger Huggins, Richared Lewis, H K Dyson, Roger and Christine Mash, Sara Geyer, Mick Whelton, V and E A Bolton, Ewan and Moira McCall, Philip Orbell, John E Crowe)*

Matthew Brown (S & N) ~ Real ale ~ Meals and snacks ~ (015394) 37302 ~ Children welcome ~ Quiz night Weds evening, Folk music every other summer Thurs evening ~ Open 11.30-11; 11.30-3, 6-11 in winter

COCKERMOUTH NY1231 Map 9

Trout

Crown St

If you are a keen fisherman (or would like to become one), then this bustling 17th-c inn is the place for you. They have fishing rights on the River Derwent, and hold fishing weekends for beginners from February to June. The comfortable and friendly bar has low pink plush sofas and captain's chairs around dark polished tables, some patterned plates on the walls, pot plants, and an open fire in the stone fireplace; the coffee lounge (at lunchtime) and the restaurant are no smoking. Well kept Jennings Cumberland, Marstons Pedigree, Theakstons Best and Charles Wells Bombardier on handpump, over 50 malt whiskies, wines of the month, and freshly squeezed orange or grapefruit juices; piped music. Bar food includes home-made soup (£1.40), sandwiches (from £2.35), soup and a sandwich (from £3.60), chicken pâté with cognac and fresh basil (£2.60), ploughman's or mushroom stroganoff (£4.75), gammon and egg (£4.95), home-made steak, kidney and mushroom pie (£5.60), Cantonese prawns (£6.75), 8oz sirloin steak (£8.95), puddings like golden crunchy syrup tart or fresh fruit salad (£2.25), and children's menu (£2.75); prompt, courteous staff. In summer you can eat in the pretty, award-winning gardens, next to the river, and William Wordsworth's birthplace is next door. Dogs welcome. *(Recommended by R J Walden, Prof Ian Rorison, Ian Fraser, David Gittins)*

Free house ~ Licensee Gill Blackah ~ Real ale ~ Meals and snacks ~ Restaurant ~ (01900) 823591 ~ Children welcome ~ Open 10.30-3, 5.30-11 ~ Bedrooms: £57.95B/£74.95B

Pubs brewing their own beers are listed at the back of the book.

DENT SD7187 Map 10

Sun

Village signposted from Sedbergh; and from Barbon, off A683

Just three miles up in the Dale, this pretty pub has set up its own Dent Brewery in a converted barn, and produces their Bitter, Ramsbottom and T'Owd Tup (which they also supply to other pubs all over the country). They also keep Youngers Scotch on handpump. There's a pleasant traditional atmosphere in the bar and fine old oak timbers and beams studded with coins, as well as dark armed chairs, brown leatherette wall benches, lots of local snapshots and old Schweppes advertisements on the walls, and a coal fire; one of the areas is no smoking. Through the arch to the left are banquettes upholstered to match the carpet (as are the curtains). Good value, straightforward bar food includes home-made soup (£1.45), sandwiches (from £1.50), ploughman's (£3.50), home-made pasties (£3.75), home-made steak and kidney pie (£4.25), cumberland sausage (£4.45), gammon and pineapple (£5.25), rump steak (£5.75), puddings (£1.75), and children's helpings (£2.25); pleasant, prompt service; good breakfasts. Darts, pool, dominoes, cribbage, fruit machine, video game, and juke box (in the pool room). There are rustic seats and tables outside. *(Recommended by Peter and Audrey Dowsett, David Varney, JKW, Derek and Margaret Underwood, Richard Houghton, Kim Schofield, H K Dyson, Paul McPherson, Dono and Carol Leaman, Peter and Lynn Brueton, Tina and David Woods-Taylor)*

Own brew ~ Licensee Martin Stafford ~ Real ale ~ Meals and snacks ~ (015396) 25208 ~ Children welcome until 9pm ~ Open 11-11; 11-2.30, 7-11 in winter; closed 25 Dec ~ Bedrooms: /£33

DOCKRAY NY3921 Map 9

Royal

A5091, off A66 W of Penrith

Surrounded by lots of pleasant walks, including one to Aira Force waterfall which is just down the road, this carefully renovated small white inn was once used by William and Dorothy Wordsworth. The unusually spacious, airy and light open-plan bar is comfortably plush with built-in bays of olive-green herringbone button-back banquettes, a spread of flowery pink and blue carpet, and a woodburning stove. For walkers, an area of more traditional seating has stripped settles on flagstones, with darts, cribbage, dominoes, and trivia, and there are unusual leatherette-topped sewing-machine tables throughout. Two dining areas (one no smoking) spread beyond the bar, and good home-cooked food includes soup (£1.75), lunchtime filled rolls (from £2.30), baked potatoes (from £2.50) or choice of lunchtime ploughman's (£4.40), omelettes (£4.95), salads (from £5.50), home-made steak and kidney pie (£5.50), grilled Barnsley chop (£7.25), 8oz sirloin steak (£8.50), and with particularly good dishes of the day such as seafood lasagne, chicken breast stuffed with smoked cheese or braised guinea fowl (£5.75); they use herbs from a good-sized herb garden beyond the car park. Well kept Boddingtons Bitter, Marstons Pedigree, Mitchells Bitter, Theakstons XB, and Whitbreads Castle Eden on handpump, a decent range of malt whiskies, good wines by the glass for this area, and several country wines; helpful friendly staff, unobtrusive piped music. There are picnic tables on a tree-sheltered lawn. *(Recommended by Pat and John Millward, Mark Rumsey, Jack Morley, David Heath, H K Dyson, Roger Berry, Kathryn and Brian Heathcote)*

Free house ~ Licensees James and Sarah Johnson ~ Real ale ~ Meals and snacks ~ Restaurant ~ (017684) 82356 ~ Children in eating area of bar if supervised ~ Open 11-11 ~ Bedrooms:£25B/£50B

The symbol shows pubs which keep their beer unusually well or have a particularly good range.

ELTERWATER NY3305 Map 9

Britannia Inn ★

Off B5343

Even on a mid-winter evening, this unpretentious and friendly little pub is packed with visitors (mainly walkers) – so if you're hoping for a seat, it might be best visited at lunchtime. It's set right in the heart of the Lake District and close to Langdale and the central lakes, with tracks over the fells to Grasmere and Easedale – walking boots are not barred. At the back is a small and traditionally furnished bar, while the front bar has winter coal fires and settles, oak benches, windsor chairs, a big old rocking chair, and a couple of window seats looking across to Elterwater itself through the trees on the far side; there's also a comfortable no-smoking lounge. Well kept Boddingtons Bitter, Jennings Bitter and Mild, and a guest beer on handpump, quite a few malt whiskies, and a well chosen, good value wine list; good service, even when busy. Popular bar food at lunchtime includes home-made soup or filled wholemeal baps (£1.35), ploughman's (£4.05), pizzas (from £4.05), vegetable tikka masala (£5.50), pork chop in cider (£6), steak and kidney pie (£6.30), and evening extras like poached fresh salmon with parsley butter (£8.75) or sirloin steak in red wine (£8.95); daily specials, puddings like home-made sticky toffee pudding (£2.20), and children's dishes (£3.20); super breakfasts. The restaurant is no smoking; darts and dominoes. The front terrace has chairs and slate-topped tables. In summer, people flock to watch Morris and Step and Garland Dancers on the pretty village green opposite. *(Recommended by Jenny and Roger Huggins, Mrs B Lemon, LM, N H and A H Harris, G S Miller, Keith Croxton, Paul Carter, A Preston, Tommy Payne, Dr Diana Terry, S R and A J Ashcroft, John and Maureen Watt, S Fazackerly, C Rowan, Tina and David Woods-Taylor, Fiona Wynn, Terry and Eileen Stott, Jack Morley, H K Dyson, George Atkinson, R J Walden, John and Liz Stevenson, Phil and Heidi Cook, Mr and Mrs Ray, Simon Watkins, Ewan and Moira McCall, Ian and Val Titman, Lorrie and Mick Marchington, Michael and Harriet Robinson, Helen Hazzard, Paul and Sue Merrick, John Atherton)*

Free house ~ David Fry ~ Real ale ~ Meals and snacks ~ Restaurant ~ (015394) 37210 ~ Children welcome ~ Summer parking may be difficult ~ Open 11-11; closed 25 Dec and evening 26 Dec ~ Bedrooms: £26.50/£59S

ESKDALE GREEN NY1400 Map 9

Bower House

½ mile W of village towards Santon Bridge

As there are no noisy machines or piped music, the atmosphere in this old stone-built inn is quietly relaxed and chatty. The lounge bar has a good winter log fire, and cushioned settles and windsor chairs that blend in well with the original beamed and alcoved nucleus around the serving counter; also, a separate lounge with easy chairs and sofas. Popular, good value food includes big helpings of soup (£2), sandwiches (from £2), cumberland sausage or lasagne (£5), salads (from £5), steak and kidney pie (£6), nut roast with fresh tomato sauce (£5.50), sirloin steak (£9.50), and daily specials such as smoked trout pâté (£3), guinea fowl with cranberry sauce (£6.50), and puddings like apple and blackberry crumble or sticky toffee pudding (£2.25 – plus 25p for cream). The restaurant is no smoking. Well kept Courage Directors, Hartleys XB, Theakstons Best and Youngers Scotch on handpump, with guests like Jennings or Robinson, a reasonably priced wine list, and quite a few malt whiskies; friendly staff; dominoes. There's a neatly tended sheltered lawn and garden and on summer Sundays you can watch the cricket on the field alongside the pub. Some of the comfortable bedrooms are in the annexe across the garden. *(Recommended by Wayne Brindle, John Allsopp, J Weeks, Andy and Julie Hawkins, V and E A Bolton, Mr and Mrs Rankine; more reports please)*

Free house ~ Licensee Derek Connor ~ Real ale ~ Meals and snacks (12-2, 6.30-9.30) ~ Restaurant ~ (019467) 23244 ~ Children welcome lunchtime and early evening ~ Open 11-11; closed winter afternoons ~ Bedrooms: £39B/£56B

King George IV

E of village at junction of main rd with rd up to Hard Knott Pass

Both from inside this Georgian-looking pub (it's actually much older), and from the tables in the garden, the Eskdale views are charming. The refurbished bar has traditional wall seats for its handful of tables, giving plenty of space out in the room, there's a comfortable lounge, and a back games room with bar billiards, dominoes, draughts, fruit machine, and piped music; warming winter log fire. A wide choice of generously served good bar food includes home-made soup (£1.60), excellent sandwiches (from £1.70), black pudding in a cider sauce or ploughman's (£4.50), stir-fried vegetables (£5.50), omelettes such as salmon and prawn (£5), steaks (from £8.50), daily specials such as fried liver and onions (£5.20), large juicy tuna steak in herb butter, chicken kiev or evening steaks (from £8.25), with children's dishes (£2.20); quick, welcoming staff. The restaurant is no smoking. Well kept Bass, Marstons Pedigree, Theakstons Best and Old Peculier, and other guests on handpump, and 168 malt whiskies. ***(Recommended by C Driver, Andrew Stephenson, Tina and David Woods-Taylor, Tim Heywood, Sophie Wilne, Peter Watkins, Pam Stanley, Paul and Maggie Baker)***

Free house ~ Licensees Harry and Jacqui Shepherd ~ Real ale ~ Meals and snacks ~ Restaurant ~ (019467) 23262 ~ Children welcome ~ Open 11-11; 11.30-2.30, 6-11 in winter; closed 25 Dec ~ Bedrooms £19.50B/£39B

FAUGH NY5155 Map 9

String of Horses

From A69 in Warwick Bridge, turn off at Heads Nook, Castle Carrock signpost, then follow Faugh signs – if you have to ask the way, it's pronounced Faff

You can be sure of a warm welcome at this attractive 17th-c coaching inn. The open-plan bar is made up of several cosy communicating beamed rooms with log fires in cool weather and some interesting carved furniture including fine old settles and elaborately carved Gothick seats and tables; there are also simpler windsor and other chairs, panelling, brass pots, warming pans, and antique prints. Good bar food consists of sandwiches, home-made soup (£1.75), shrimps in a mild curry mayonnaise (£2.75), cumberland sausage (£4.95), broccoli and cauliflower in spicy tomato and cheese sauce (£4.25), chicken tikka or steak and kidney pudding (£5.50), 8oz sirloin steak (£7.95), daily specials like fish pie (£4.95) or trout hollandaise (£5.75), and puddings such as bread and butter pudding (£2.95). Several malt whiskies and an extensive wine list; darts, pool, dominoes, fruit machine, video game, and piped music. Residents have the use of a Jacuzzi, sauna, solarium and small outdoor heated pool. There are pretty hanging baskets amongst the Dutch blinds and lanterns outside, and lanterns and neat wrought iron among the greenery of the sheltered terrace. ***(Recommended by Jack and Heather Coyle, R E and P Pearce, E V Walder, Tim Heywood, Sophie Wilne, Dr R H M Stewart)***

Free house ~ Licensee Mrs Anne Tasker ~ Meals and snacks ~ Restaurant ~ (01228) 70297 ~ Children welcome ~ Pianist Fri/Sat evening in restaurant ~ Open 11.30-3, 5.30-11 ~ Bedrooms: £58B/£68B

GARRIGILL NY7441 Map 10

George & Dragon

Village signposted off B6277 S of Alston

Looking across a small tree-shaded village green, this stonebuilt ex-posting inn with its massively heavy stone slates is a famous stop for walkers on the Pennine Way, which passes its door. Inside on the right, the bar has very broad polished flagstones, a lovely stone fireplace with a really good log fire, good solid traditional furnishings and a cosy and relaxed atmosphere; there's a separate tartan-carpeted games room with sensibly placed darts, pool and dominoes. The very friendly landlord's wife prepares the good value generous bar food, such as soup (£1.40), sandwiches (from £1.45), filled yorkshire puddings (from £1.75), baked potatoes (from £2.10), cumberland sausage and egg (£3.95), home-made steak pie (£4.25), lentil crumble (£4.50), and sirloin steak (£7.25), with sticky toffee pudding (£1.80), and children's dishes (from £1.75). Well kept McEwans 70/-, Theakstons Best, XB and Old Peculier and changing guest beers on handpump, decent malt whiskies. *(Recommended by Richard Holloway, G W Lindley, David and Margaret Bloomfield; more reports please)*

Free house ~ Licensees Brian and Jean Holmes ~ Real ale ~ Meals and snacks ~ Restaurant ~ (01434) 381293 ~ Children welcome ~ Open 11.30-4, 6.30-11; 12-3, 7-11 in winter ~ Bedrooms:£15/£30, also very cheap small bunkhouse

GRASMERE NY3406 Map 9

Travellers Rest

Just N of Grasmere on A591 Ambleside—Keswick rd; OS sheet 90, map ref 335089

This year, careful refurbishment of this homely and friendly little 16th-c pub has taken place. All of the bedrooms are redecorated and four now have their own bathrooms, and the no-smoking restaurant has been extended and refurbished with beams, church pews and local artefacts; all the settles and chairs have been re-upholstered, too. The comfortable, beamed lounge bar has a relaxed atmosphere, a warming log fire, banquettes and cushioned wooden chairs around varnished wooden tables, local watercolours, suggested walks and coast-to-coast information on the walls, and some horsebrasses by the bar counter; piped classical music. The games room is popular with families: pool, darts, juke box, and piped music. Enjoyable bar food includes home-made soup (£1.95), local trout pâté (£2.95), open sandwiches (from £4.45), ploughman's, chargrilled burger or vegetable brochette (all £4.95), local cumberland sausage and apple sauce (£5.25), steak and kidney pie (£5.75), coq au vin (£5.95), steaks (from £8.85), children's menu (£2.95), daily specials such as good fresh fish, and puddings (£2.65). Well kept Jennings Bitter, Cumberland and Snecklifter on handpump, and at least a dozen malt whiskies. From the picnic tables in the garden you can admire the wonderful views; good nearby walks. *(Recommended by John and Joan Nash, E McCormack, D Hanley, H K Dyson, James House, Mr and Mrs J A Moors, Jack Morley, Simon Watkins, Derek and Margaret Underwood, Paul Boot, Neil Townend, Mr and Mrs G R Smith-Richards, WAH, Tina and David Woods-Taylor, Susan and Alan Buckland, David Lands, Paul and Sue Merrick, Mr and Mrs C Roberts, C A Wilkes, Miss D P Barson)*

Free house ~ Licensees Lynne, Derek and Graham Sweeney ~ Real ale ~ Meals and snacks (12-3, 6-9.30) ~ (015394) 35604 ~ Children in eating area of bar ~ Open 11-11 ~ Bedrooms: £22.95(£29.95)/£45.90(£51.90B)

HAWKSHEAD SD3598 Map 9

Kings Arms

In summer, the place to sit is outside this pretty inn on the terrace overlooking the central square of the lovely Elizabethan village. The cosy and traditional low-ceilinged bar is popular with locals and has comfortable red-cushioned wall and window seats and red plush stools on the turkey carpet, and an open fire. Bar food includes home-made soup (£1.75), local cumberland sausage with spicy apple sauce or mushroom stroganoff (£4.95), ploughman's (from £5.10), battered haddock (£5.30), steak and mushroom pie (£5.50), steaks (from £8.50), and children's menu (£2.75). The restaurant is no smoking. Well kept Greenalls, Tetleys, Theakstons Best and Old Peculier and guest beers on handpump, a good choice of malt whiskies, and maybe summer farm cider. Darts, dominoes, cribbage, fruit machine, and piped pop music. In keeping with the atmosphere of the rest of the place, the bedrooms have coins embedded in the old oak beams. They will organise sea or fresh water fishing trips. The village car park is some way away, but if you're staying at the inn, you'll get a free permit. *(Recommended by John and Chris Simpson, H K Dyson, Richard Lewis, Mr and Mrs R Head, D Cox, John Allsopp, Linda Norsworthy)*

Free house ~ Lease: Rosalie Johnson ~ Real ale ~ Meals and snacks (12-2.30, 6-9.30) ~ Restaurant ~ (015394) 36372 ~ Well behaved children welcome ~ Occasional live folk music/country & western ~ Open 11-11; closed 25 Dec ~ Bedrooms: £28(£33B)/£46(£56B); 2 self-catering cottages close by

Queens Head

This attractive black-and-white timbered pub has heavy bowed black beams in its low-ceilinged open-plan bar, red plush wall seats and plush stools around heavy traditional tables, lots of decorative plates on the panelled walls, and an open fire; a snug little room leads off. Bar food includes lunchtime sandwiches, soup (£2.25), ploughman's (£5), home-made pancakes with nuts and vegetables in a creamy white sauce or steak pie (£6.50), devilled lambs' kidneys (£6.75), kedgeree (£7.50), pork fillet topped with mozzarella cheese and wrapped in bacon (£8.50), seafood dishes, and 9oz sirloin steak (£10.95). The restaurant is no smoking. Well kept Hartleys XB and Robinsons Bitter, Frederics, and Mild on handpump, and quite a few whiskies; dominoes and piped music. Walkers must take their boots off. In summer, the window boxes are pretty. *(Recommended by H K Dyson, Richard Lewis, Simon J Barber, D J and P M Taylor, D Cox, Wayne Brindle; more reports please)*

Hartleys (Robinsons) ~ Tenant Tony Merrick ~ Real ale ~ Meals and snacks (12-2.30, 6.15-9.30) ~ Restaurant ~ (015394) 36271 ~ Children in restaurant if eating and in snug ~ Occasional live jazz ~ Open 11-11 ~ Bedrooms: £35(£45)/£53(£59.50B)

nr HAWKSHEAD NY3501 Map 9

Drunken Duck ★

Barngates; the hamlet is signposted from B5286 Hawkshead—Ambleside, opposite the Outgate Inn; or it may be quicker to take the first right from B5286, after the wooded caravan site; OS Sheet 90 map reference 350013

Immensely popular, this attractive and friendly old pub still manages to make you feel welcome – even at its busiest. There are several cosy and traditionally pubby beamed rooms with tub chairs, cushioned old settles, blond pews, ladderback country chairs, and wheelbacks on the fitted turkey carpet, good winter fires, and maybe the multi-coloured cat and small elderly dog. Around the walls are pictures, cartoons, cards, fox masks, and cases of fishing flies and lures. There have been very few disappointments with the food, which has delighted even some of our most critical vegetarian readers: pâté such as lentil and tomato or walnut and stilton (£2.95), cauliflower and broccoli cheese or fennel, orange and butterbean casserole (£4.95), vegetable and lentil chilli (£5), and spinach and ricotta filo (£5.50); also, filled rolls (£1.95), ploughman's (£3.95), Greek lamb with olives (£5.75), pork and pepper pasta (£5.95), gammon and egg (£6.25), and venison steak in Mexican marinade (£7.95). The dining room is no smoking. Well kept Boddingtons Bitter, Jennings Bitter, Mitchells Lancaster Bomber, Theakstons Old Peculier, Yates Bitter, and a beer brewed for the pub by Yates, called Drunken Duck Bitter on handpump or tapped from the cask, and over 50 malt whiskies. Seats on the front verandah look across to Lake Windermere in the distance; to the side there are quite a few rustic wooden chairs and tables, sheltered by a stone wall with alpine plants along its top, and the pub has fishing in a private tarn behind. *(Recommended by Mr and Mrs Richard Osborne, RLW and Dizzy, C M Fox, John and Christine Lowe, Ian Morley, Richard Lewis, J Finney, John and Chris Simpson, Tina and David Woods-Taylor, John and Maureen Watt, H K Dyson, K H Frostick, George Atkinson, L M Miall, John Scarisbrick, S R and A J Ashcroft, Pat and John Millward, James House, Ann Reeder, David Craine, Bronwen and Steve Wrigley, D Hanley, Mr and Mrs G Arbib, David Wright, Kate and Robert Hodkinson, Mark Bradley, N H White, Mr and Mrs G R Smith-Richards, Jerry and Alison Oakes, V and E A Bolton, C A Wilkes, Frank Cummins, Andrew Scarr, Michael and Rachael Dunlop, Simon and*

Amanda Southwell, M V Fereday, Linda Norsworthy)

Free house ~ Licensee Stephanie Barton ~ Real ale ~ Meals and snacks ~ (015394) 36347 ~ Children in eating area of bar ~ Occasional Morris Dancing ~ Open 11.30-3, 6-11; closed 25 Dec ~ Bedrooms: £50B/£69B

HEVERSHAM SD4983 Map 10

Blue Bell

A6 (now a relatively very quiet road here)

Once a vicarage, this 17th-c country inn has a comfortably civilised bay-windowed lounge bar with warm winter fires, an antique carved settle, cushioned windsor armchairs and upholstered stools on the flowery carpet, pewter platters hanging from the beams, and small antique sporting prints on the partly panelled walls. One big bay-windowed area has been divided off as a children's room, and the long, tiled-floor, quieter public bar has darts and dominoes. Good bar food based on fresh local produce includes sandwiches, home-made soup, lovely Morecambe Bay potted shrimps (£3.95), smoked haddock mornay, local game casserole, vegetarian dishes, steak in ale pie (£5.95), and sizzling sirloin steak platter (£7.95). The restaurant is no smoking. Well kept Sam Smiths OB on handpump, with Museum kept under light blanket pressure, several malt whiskies, a decent wine list, and their own cider; helpful staff. Darts, pool, cribbage, dominoes, fruit machine, and piped music. Crossing over the A6 into the village itself, you come to a picturesque church with a rambling little graveyard; if you walk through this and on to the hills beyond, there's a fine view across to the estuary of the River Kent. The estuary itself is a short walk from the pub down the country road that runs by its side. Pets welcome by arrangement. *(Recommended by Mr and Mrs C Roberts, Wayne Brindle; more reports please)*

Sam Smiths ~ Manager Richard Cowie ~ Real ale ~ Meals and snacks (11-2.30, 6-9.30) ~ Restaurant ~ (015395) 62018 ~ Children welcome ~ Ceilidh 1st/3rd Thurs of month ~ Open 11-3, 6-11; 11-11 Sat ~ Bedrooms: £35B/£64B

INGS SD4599 Map 9

Watermill

Just off A591 E of Windermere

An incredible range of up to 14 real ales is kept on handpump in this warmly friendly family-run inn: Theakstons Best, XB and Old Peculier and Lees Moonraker, and regularly changing guests such as Hexhamshire Devils Water, Hop Back Summer Lightning, Jennings Snecklifter, Kelham Island Pale Rider, Mitchells Lancaster Bomber, Shepherd Neame Spitfire, and Scotts William French and so forth; farm cider and several malt whiskies. There are no fruit machines or juke box and the bars have a chatty atmosphere, a happy mix of chairs, padded benches and solid oak tables, bar counters made from old church wood, open fires, and amusing cartoons by a local artist on the wall; one area is no smoking. The spacious lounge bar, in much the same traditional style as the other rooms, has rocking chairs and a big open fire. Walkers and their dogs (on leads) are welcome. Bar food includes home-made soup (£1.60), lunchtime sandwiches (from £1.95), lunchtime ploughman's (£3.40), local cumberland sausage (£4.25), salads (from £4.80), home-made curry (£5), Whitby scampi (£5.50), local grilled gammon (£5.80), and steak (£9.10); they specialise in real ale casseroles and pies; children's meals (from £2.20). Darts, table skittles and dominoes. The inn is in a lovely spot with the River Gowan bordering the garden and lots of climbing, fell-walking, fishing, boating of all kinds, swimming and pony-trekking within easy reach. Perhaps the attic rooms are due for some attention. *(Recommended by D Hanely, John and Pam Smith, Sue Holland, Dave Webster, J S M Sheldon, Dick Brown, Graham and Lynn Mason, R J Walden, Jeff Davies, Ian Morley, Jenny and Roger Huggins, John Scarisbrick, Jack Morley, Graham and Lynn Mason, Paul Boot, Sharron Thompson, Dick Brown, Mr and Mrs Ashcroft, D Hanley, Wayne Brindle)*

Free House ~ Licensee Alan Coulthwaite ~ Real ale ~ Meals and snacks (not 25 Dec) ~ (01539) 821309 ~ Children in lounge until 9pm ~ Open 12-2.30, 6-11; closed lunchtime 25 Dec ~ Bedrooms: £24S/£40S

KIRKBY LONSDALE SD6278 Map 7

Snooty Fox

Main Street (B6254)

Full of interesting things to look at, the various rooms in this rambling pub are full of stage gladiator costumes, horse-collars and stirrups, mugs hanging from beams, eye-catching coloured engravings, stuffed wildfowl and falcons, mounted badger and fox masks, and guns and a powder-flask. The bar counters are made from English oak, as is some panelling, and there are also country kitchen chairs, pews, one or two high-backed settles and marble-topped sewing-trestle tables on the flagstones, and two coal fires. Good home-made food includes soup (£2), sandwiches (from £2.50), filled baked potatoes (from £2.95), deep-fried gruyere fritter on a peach purée (£3.75), cumberland sausage with onion gravy (£4.95), steak and kidney pudding (£5.75), Sri Lankan chicken curry (£5.95), poached Scottish salmon (£7.25), haunch of venison in claret (£7.95), steaks (from £10.95), and puddings such as sticky toffee pudding with butterscotch sauce or chilled Belgian chocolate mousse with caramel and orange sauce (from £2.95). Well kept Hartleys XB, Theakstons Best, and Timothy Taylors Landlord on handpump, several malt whiskies, and country wines; dominoes, fruit machine and good juke box. There are tables out on a small terrace beside the biggish back cobbled stableyard, with more in a pretty garden; small play area for children. *(Recommended by Peter and Audrey Dowsett, Sue Holland, Dave Webster, Paul McPherson, Neville Kenyon, David Webster, J Weeks, Mr and Mrs C J Frodsham; more reports please)*

Free house ~ Licensee Jack Shone ~ Real ale ~ Meals and snacks (all day) ~ Restaurant ~ (015242) 71308 ~ Children in eating area of bar ~ Open 11-11 ~ Bedrooms: £26B/£46B

Sun 🛏

Market St (B6254)

Locals and visitors of all ages mix quite happily in this atmospheric and friendly little pub. The low beamed, rambling rooms are filled with a collection of some 500 banknotes, maps, and old engravings, and the walls – some of which are stripped to bare stone or have panelled dados – are hung with battleaxes and other interesting antiques, and even a fireplace. Furnishings include window seats and cosy pews and there are good winter fires. Well kept Black Sheep Bitter, Boddingtons, Dent Bitter (from the Sun in Dent) and Youngers No 3 on handpump, and 50 malt whiskies; dominoes, cribbage, trivia, and piped music. A good range of well cooked and presented food includes sandwiches (from £1.95), cumberland sausage (£3.75), feta cheese and spinach strudel (£4.25), beef and Guinness casserole (£4.50), oriental chicken (£5.95), swordfish portuguese (£6.95), steaks (from £6.95), daily specials such as roast rack of lamb or pork stroganoff (£6.95) or grilled halibut steak (£7.25), and puddings like hot chocolate fudgecake or sticky toffee pudding (£2.25); good personal service, and super breakfasts. There's an unusual pillared porch; the steep cobbled alley is also attractive. Some of the bedrooms are in a stone barn with lovely views across the Barbon Fells. *(Recommended by Sue Holland, David Webster, Steve and Julie Cocking, Mr Jackson, B J and J S Derry, Dave McKenzie, David and Ruth Hollands, Kim Schofield, Mike and Wendy Proctor, Michael Marlow)*

Free house ~ Licensee Andrew Wilkinson ~ Real ale ~ Meals and snacks (11-2, 6-10) ~ Restaurant ~ (015242) 71965 ~ Children welcome ~ Open 11-11 ~ Bedrooms: £22(£25B)/£44(£48B)

> It's against the law for bar staff to smoke while handling food or drink.

LANERCOST NY5664 Map 10

Abbey Bridge Inn

Follow brown Lanercost Priory signs from A69 or in Brampton

This unusual inn has to itself a remarkable quiet spot by a strikingly arched medieval bridge, just down the lane from the great 12th-c priory. The pub part is in a side building with high pitched rafters and knobby whited stone walls, formerly a smithy: an attractive combination of very simple furnishings with a relaxed but rather stylish atmosphere and really good food and drink. Using fresh produce, the food at lunchtime includes sandwiches (£1.95), soup (£3), a plate of smoked fish (£3.35), quiche of the day (£4.75), home-made steak or vegetarian pie (£6.50), chicken satay (£7.25), salmon steak (£8.99), and puddings (£2.25); in the evenings it's normally served restaurant-style in a no-smoking gallery up spiral stairs. Well kept and well chosen real ales on handpump change every few days: on our late spring inspection they were Burton Bridge, Fullers Chiswick, Shepherd Neame and Yates; other good drinks, such as the excellent Fentimans ginger beer and quite a few malt whiskies. The understated rustic decor includes charming Ashley Boan prints; large woodburning stove, with a gas heater instead in cool non-winter weather; welcoming service; very faint piped pop music and dominoes. There are a few seats outside. *(Recommended by R E and P Pearce, John Oddey, D and J Tapper, Wayne A Wheeler)*

Free house ~ Licensee Philip Sayers ~ Real ale ~ Meals and snacks ~ Evening restaurant ~ (016977) 2224 ~ Children welcome ~ Open 12-2.30, 7-11; closed 25 Dec ~ Bedrooms £20 (no basin in that one)/£50B

LANGDALE NY2906 Map 9

Old Dungeon Ghyll

B5343

The whole feel of this dramatically set inn is basic but cosy – and once all the fell walkers and climbers crowd in, full of boisterous atmosphere. It's at the heart of the Great Langdale Valley and surrounded by fells including the Langdale Pikes flanking the Dungeon Ghyll Force waterfall – and there are grand views of the Pike of Blisco rising behind Kettle Crag from the window seats cut into the thick stone walls of the bar. Furnishings are very simple and straightforward food includes lunchtime sandwiches (£1.75), filled baked potatoes (£2.75), pizzas (£4.20), cumberland sausage (£4.95), chilli con carne (£5.25), puddings, and children's meals (£2.95); if you are not a resident and want to eat in the restaurant you must book ahead. Well kept Broughton Oatmeal Stout, Jennings Cumberland, Theakstons XB, Old Peculier and Mild, and Yates Bitter on handpump, farm cider, and a fair range of malt whiskies; darts, cribbage and dominoes. It can get really lively on a Saturday night (there's a popular National Trust campsite opposite). *(Recommended by George Atkinson, Dr Diana Terry, David Heath, Wayne Brindle, Bronwen and Steve Wrigley, H K Dyson, Nigel Woolliscroft, Sara Geyer, Mick Whelton, John and Marianne Cooper, Lynn Sharpless, Bob Eardley, Lorrie and Mick Marchington)*

Free house ~ Licensee Neil Walmsley ~ Real ale ~ Meals and snacks (12-2, 6-9) ~ Evening restaurant ~ (015394) 37272 ~ Children welcome ~ Spontaneous live music ~ Open 11-11; closed 24-26 Dec ~ Bedrooms: £25(£30B)/£50(£60B)

LEVENS SD4886 Map 10

Hare & Hounds

Village signposted from A590; since completion of dual carriageway link, best approach is following route signposted for High Vehicles

New licensees have taken over this attractive little village pub and are aiming to keep the cosy atmosphere. The low-beamed, carpeted lounge bar is furnished with a wicker-backed Jacobean-style armchair and antique settle on its sloping floor, as well as old-fashioned brown leatherette dining seats and red-cushioned seats built into the partly panelled walls. There's an interesting display of old fire-engine artefacts. Bar food now includes soup, lunchtime sandwiches (from £1.55; toasties from £1.60), filled baked potatoes (from £3.05), ploughman's (£3.80), salads (from £3.75), cumberland sausage (£4.35), steak and kidney pie (£4.50), chicken curry (£4.75), and sirloin steak (£7.65). At the front is a snug tap room, with darts, cribbage and dominoes; also golden-oldie juke box in the separate pool room, down some steps. Well kept Vaux Samson and Wards Thorne on handpump. The pub is also close to Sizergh Castle. *(Recommended by John Scarisbrick, Peter and Audrey Dowsett, Wayne Brindle, Brian and Anna Marsden, Mike and Wendy Proctor, Paul McPherson; more reports on the new regime, please)*

Vaux ~ Tenants Colin and Sheila Burrow ~ Real ale ~ Meals and snacks ~ Restaurant ~ (015395) 60408 ~ Children welcome ~ Open 11-3, 6-11

LITTLE LANGDALE NY3204 Map 9

Three Shires ☞

From A593 3 miles W of Ambleside take small road signposted The Langdales, Wrynose Pass; then bear left at first fork

The three shires are Cumberland, Westmorland and Lancashire, which used to meet at the top of the nearby Wrynose Pass. There are lovely views over the valley to the partly wooded hills below Tilberthwaite Fells, and seats on the terrace with more on a well kept lawn behind the car park, backed by a small oak wood. Inside, the comfortably extended back bar has antique oak carved settles, country kitchen chairs and stools on its big dark slate flagstones, stripped timbers and a beam-and-joist stripped ceiling, a modern stone fireplace and chimney piece with a couple of recesses for ornaments, and Lakeland photographs lining the walls; an arch leads through to a small, additional area. Bar food includes soup (£1.75), lunchtime sandwiches, ploughman's, home-made pâté (£3.30), home-made steak and kidney pie or mushroom stroganoff (£5.75), liver and onions (£6.25), trout with lemon and herb butter (£6.75), and puddings (£2.50). The restaurant and small public bar are no smoking. Marstons Pedigree, Ruddles County, and Websters Yorkshire on handpump, and quite a few malt whiskies; darts and dominoes. *(Recommended by Richard Lewis, Jack Morley, Tina and David Woods-Taylor, Gillian and Michael Wallace, V and E A Bolton, G C Brown)*

Free house ~ Licensee Ian Stephenson ~ Real ale ~ Meals and snacks (no evening food Dec and Jan) ~ Evening restaurant ~ (015394) 37215 ~ Children welcome until 9pm ~ Open 11-11; 11-3, 8-10.30 in winter; closed 25 Dec ~ Bedrooms: /£68B

LOWESWATER NY1222 Map 9

Kirkstile

From B5289 follow signs to Loweswater Lake; OS Sheet 89, map reference 140210

You can admire the spectacular surrounding peaks and soaring fells from the very attractive covered veranda here – and from the big bow windows in one of the rooms off the bar. The bar itself is low-beamed and carpeted, with comfortably cushioned small settles and pews, partly stripped stone walls, and a big log fire. Decent bar food (with prices unchanged since last year) includes home-made wholemeal filled rolls (from £1.80), good home-made soup (£1.95), filled baked potatoes (from £3.25), home-made pasty (£3.50), ploughman's (£4.15), bean and tomato casserole (£4.50), omelettes (from £4.75), cumberland sausage and egg (£5), sirloin steak (£9.25), daily specials, and puddings; big breakfasts, and helpful, friendly service. Well kept Jennings Bitter and Cumberland on handpump, a fair choice of malt whiskies, and decent wine list; darts, dominoes, cribbage and a slate shove-ha'penny board; a side games room called the Little Barn has pool, fruit

machine, video game and juke box. There are picnic tables on the lawn.
(Recommended by S R and A J Ashcroft, Phil and Karen Wood, John and Christine Lowe, Simon and Chris Turner, Jack Morley, John and Liz Stevenson, Roger and Christine Mash, Ian Rorison, H K Dyson, Nigel Woolliscroft, Dave Lands, Mike and Ann Beiley, John Allsopp, Michael Wadsworth)

Free house ~ Licensees Ken and Shirley Gorley ~ Real ale ~ Meals and snacks (12-2.30, 6-9) ~ Restaurant ~ (01900) 85219 ~ Children welcome ~ Open 11-11 ~ Bedrooms: £32(£42B)/£42(£52B)

MELMERBY NY6237 Map 10

Shepherds ★

About half way along A686 Penrith—Alston

We've decided to give this consistently enjoyable pub a star this year as readers remain delighted with the very good food, hard-working, friendly staff, and well kept beers. As well as their fine range of cheeses – 11 North Country cheeses, 6 other English cheeses, and European Community cheeses of the month – you might find soup like chicken and leek or creamed parsnip (£1.90), ploughman's with home-made roll and lovely pickles (from £3.60), pork and port pâté (£3.40), delicious cumberland sausage hotpot (£5), tagliatelle garniture forestière (£5.40), steak and kidney pie (£5.95), local trout (£6.40), Calcutta beef curry (£6.90), a mountain of excellent spare ribs (£6.20), very tender spiced lamb with yoghurt (£6.80), chicken breast Leoni (£6.90), venison and roquefort crumble (£7.20), and steaks (from £9.60); lots of daily specials such as courgette and pasta bake, lambs' liver lyonnaise or half a roast duckling with a wild mushroom sauce, Sunday roast lunch (£5.40), and delicious puddings such as superb ginger surprise, lemon meringue pie or rich chocolate torrone (£2.25); part of the main eating area is no smoking. Although it's a spacious place, it's best to get there early. Well kept Batemans, Black Sheep Bitter, Boddingtons, Jennings Cumberland and Snecklifter, and Maclays on handpump, as well as 56 malt whiskies, a good wine list, and quite a few bottled continental beers. Lots of pot plants brighten up the bar, which also has cushioned wall seats, sunny window seats, sensible tables and chairs, light-panelling, and an open fire; half the pub is now no smoking. A games bar has darts, pool, dominoes, and fruit machine. Hartside Nursery Garden, a noted alpine and primula plant specialist, is just over the Hartside Pass, and there are fine views across the green to the Pennines.
(Recommended by Richard Holloway, Ann Reeder, David Craine, John and Chris Simpson, E Carter, Laura Darlington, Gianluca Perinetti, Joan and Tony Walker, Michael Butler, Pat and John Millward, Malcolm Taylor, Mrs D M Dunne, T M Dobby, Paul Kitchener, Paul and Janet Waring, Joe and Carol Pattison, Frank Davidson, F J Robinson, Kathryn and Brian Heathcote, Mr and Mrs C Roberts, Dr A and Dr A C Jackson)

Free house ~ Licensees Martin and Christine Baucutt ~ Real ale ~ Meals and snacks (10.30-2.30, 6-9.45) ~ (01768) 881217 ~ Children in eating area of the bar till 8.30pm ~ Open 10.30-3, 6-11; closed 25 Dec ~ Several holiday cottages

NEAR SAWREY SD3796 Map 9

Tower Bank Arms

B5285 towards the Windermere ferry

Beatrix Potter lovers tend to pop into this busy pub after a visit to Hill Top Farm (owned by the National Trust) next door. The low-beamed main bar has high-backed settles on the rough slate floor, local hunting photographs and signed photographs of celebrities on the walls, a grandfather clock, and a good traditional atmosphere; Emma or Maxwell the pub's labradors may be sitting in front of the big cooking range with its fine log fire. Lunchtime bar food includes soup (£1.70), filled rolls (from £2.10), ploughman's (from £3.70), home-made quiche (£4.75), and a home-made pie of the day (£4.90); more substantial evening main meals such as grilled gammon and eggs or Esthwaite trout (£6.75), venison or duckling (£7) and puddings (£2.30). Well kept Theakstons Best, XB and Old Peculier, and Mild, and a weekly changing guest beer on handpump, as well as 28 malt whiskies, Belgian fruit beers and other foreign beers, and wine bottled for the pub; darts, shove-ha'penny, cribbage, dominoes, backgammon and shut-the-box. Seats outside have pleasant views of the wooded Claife Heights. This is a good area for golf, sailing, birdwatching, fishing (they have a licence for two rods a day on selected waters in the area), and walking, but if you want to stay at the pub, you'll have to book well in advance. *(Recommended by Jack Morley, Gwyneth and Salvo Spadaro-Dutturi, G S Miller, S R and A J Ashcroft, H K Dyson, Simon and Amanda Southwell, David Wright, Helen Hazzard, P Barnsley, Tina and David Woods-Taylor, Mike and Jo, Sara Geyer, Mick Whelton, Mrs J Jones)*

Free house ~ Licensee Philip Broadley ~ Real ale ~ Meals and lunchtime snacks (not 25 Dec) ~ Restaurant ~ (015394) 36334 ~ Children welcome at lunchtime; in restaurant in evening ~ 11-3, 5.30(6 in winter)-11; closed evening 25 Dec ~ Bedrooms: £32B/£44B

SEATHWAITE SD2396 Map 9

Newfield

Duddon Valley, nr Ulpha (ie not Seathwaite in Borrowdale)

In a quieter corner of the lakes, this cottagey 16th-c inn has managed to keep a relaxed and genuinely local atmosphere (though at weekends it's popular with walkers and climbers). There's a big round table among others in the slate-floored main bar, a comfortable side room, and a games room with pool, darts, cribbage and dominoes. Good value bar food includes filled french bread (£1.60), proper home-made soup (£1.75), cumberland sausages that are a real challenge (£4.50), home-made steak pie or a vegetarian dish (from £4.50), huge gammon steaks with local farm eggs (£5.95), and good steaks; the restaurant is no smoking. Well kept Theakstons Best, XB and Old Peculier and a guest such as Marstons Pedigree, Morlands Old Speckled Hen or Youngs Special on handpump, a dozen malt whiskies, several Polish vodkas, and good service. Tables out in the nice garden have good hill views. The pub owns and lets the next-door cottages. Well behaved dogs allowed. *(Recommended by Catharine Driver, H K Dyson, Prof I H Rorison, J Jones)*

Free house ~ Licensee Chris Burgess ~ Real ale ~ Meals and snacks ~ Restaurant ~ (01229) 716208 ~ Well behaved children welcome ~ Open 11-3, 6-11; 11-11 Sat ~ S/c flats available

SEDBERGH SD6692 Map 10

Dalesman

Main St

This popular and nicely modernised old pub has lots of stripped stone and beams, cushioned farmhouse chairs and stools around dimpled copper tables, and a raised stone hearth with a log-effect gas fire. Also, tropical fish, a blunderbuss, horsebrasses and spigots, various stuffed animals including a badger and a greater spotted woodpecker, and Vernon Stokes gundog pictures. Through stone arches on the right a no-smoking buttery area serves good value food such as soup (£1.50), filled rolls and toasties (from £2), filled baked potatoes or ploughman's (from £4), steak and kidney pie (£4.95), and daily specials like gammon and egg (£5.95), fresh poached salmon (£6.95), half a roast duckling (£8.95), and a huge mixed grill (£12.50); Sunday lunch (£4.95); friendly, helpful service. Well kept Ind Coope Burton, Tetleys Bitter and Dark Mild, and Theakstons Best on handpump; dominoes, fruit machine, and piped music. There are some picnic tables out in front; small car park. *(Recommended by Lynn Sharpless, Bob Eardley, Dono and Carol Leaman, George Atkinson, Peter and Audrey Dowsett, JKW, Simon and Louise Chappell, Paul McPherson, B Horner)*

Free house ~ Licensees Barry and Irene Garnett ~ Real ale ~ Meals and snacks ~

Restaurant ~ (015396) 21183 ~ Children in eating area of bar ~ Open 11-11; 11-3, 6-11 in winter; closed 25 Dec ~ Bedrooms: £25S/£48B

STAINTON NY4928 Map 10

Kings Arms

1¾ miles from M6 junction 40: village signposted from A66 towards Keswick, though quickest to fork left at A592 roundabout then turn first right

New licensees have taken over this pleasant, modernised old pub, and bar food now includes sandwiches, soup (£1.30), cumberland sausage (£4.05), steak and kidney pie (£4.20), breast of chicken with sage and onion stuffing (£4.25), salads (from £4.30), and gammon with egg (£5.05). The roomy open-plan bar has leatherette wall banquettes, stools and armchairs, wood-effect tables, brasses on the black beams, and prints and paintings of the Lake District on the swirly cream walls. Well kept Boddingtons, Whitbreads Castle Eden, and guest beers on handpump or electric pump. Sensibly placed darts, dominoes, fruit machine, and piped music. There are tables outside on the side terrace and a small lawn. *(Recommended by John and Christine Lowe, Gary Roberts, Ann Stubbs, Richard Holloway, Ursula Thompson, Duncan Redpath, Lorraine Milburn, N H White, Gary Roberts; more reports on the new regime, please)*

Whitbreads ~ Tenants James and Anne Downie ~ Real ale ~ Meals and snacks (not 25 Dec) ~ (01768) 862778 ~ Children in eating area of bar until 9pm ~ Open 11.30-3, 6.30(6 Sat)-11; winter weekday evening opening 7pm

THRELKELD NY3325 Map 9

Salutation

Old main rd, bypassed by A66 W of Penrith

As this friendly and unpretentious little village local is handsomely set below the fells, it's naturally popular with walkers (and the tiled floor is used to muddy boots). The several simply furnished connecting rooms can get quite crowded in summer, but even then there's a good atmosphere and the staff are welcoming. The home-made food is generous and hearty (and prices are unchanged since last year): sandwiches (from £2.15), soup (£2.25), large ploughman's (from £4.35), Hungarian goulash, sweet and sour pork or good steak and mushroom pie (£4.95), jumbo cumberland sausages made in Keswick to the pub's own recipe (not for the faint hearted! £5.85), daily specials like mushroom stroganoff, beef curry madras, or lamb provençale (£4.95), and puddings (from £1.85). Well kept Theakstons Best, XB and Old Peculier and guests like Jennings, Marstons Pedigree, Mitchells Lancaster Bomber and Morlands Old Speckled Hen on handpump. The spacious upstairs children's room has a pool table and juke box (oldies); there are also darts, cribbage, dominoes, video game and trivia. The owners let a couple of holiday cottages in the village. *(Recommended by Dr Pete Crawshaw, Richard Holloway, V and E Bolton, I E and C A Prosser, Nigel Woolliscroft, Paul and Sue Merrick, Nick Cox, David Heath)*

S & N ~ Tenants Ken and Rose Burchill ~ Real ale ~ Meals and snacks (not 25 Dec) ~ (017687) 79614 ~ Children welcome (must be in family room after 9pm) ~ Open 11-3, 5.30-11; 12-2, 6-11 in winter

TIRRIL NY5126 Map 10

Queens Head

3½ miles from M6 junction 40; take A66 towards Brough, A6 towards Shap, then B5320 towards Ullswater

Cumbrian Dining Pub of the Year

Hard-working, friendly new licensees have taken over this popular inn and readers are full of praise for the way things are going. Mr D'Aprile (who is Italian) and his

English wife Lynne used to run a restaurant at Penrith for six years and are putting a lot of effort into the food here – though there's still a good local atmosphere. And readers who have stayed here recently were very pleased with their upgraded bedrooms. The oldest parts of the bar have low bare beams, black panelling, high-backed settles, and a roomy inglenook fireplace (once a cupboard for smoking hams). The floor underneath the carpet is actually raw rock, quarried out for the pub in the early 18th c. Attractively presented, very good food includes good home-made soup (£1.75), home-made chicken liver and brandy pâté (£2.45), stuffed pepper (£3.75), ploughman's (£4.75), quite a few excellent pasta dishes such as paglia e fieno (green and white noodles with smoked salmon, parmesan and cream, fettucine marinara (noodles in tomato sauce with prawns and tuna in white wine) or lasagne (£2.50 starter, £4.95 main course), leek and mushroom croustade (£6.50), steak in ale pie (£6.95), steaks (from £8.25), veal marsala or beef florianna (£10.95), and flambé king prawns or steak Diane (£12.95; not Saturdays); daily fresh fish, roast Sunday lunch (£5.25), and children's dishes (£2.50); friendly, attentive service. Well kept Marstons Pedigree, Morlands Old Speckled Hen, Theakstons Best and Youngers Scotch on handpump; darts, pool, dominoes, and juke box in the back bar. The pub is very close to a number of interesting places, such as Dalemain House at Dacre. *(Recommended by H K Dyson, Neville Kenyon, Johnathan and Ann Tross, G O Cook, Mr and Mrs B Fletcher, Terry and Eileen Stott, Mr and Mrs J Futers, John Barlow)*

Free house ~ Licensees Nunzio and Lynne D'Aprile ~ Real ale ~ Meals and snacks (till 10pm) ~ Restaurant ~ (01768) 863219 ~ Children welcome ~ Open 11-2.30(3 Sat), 6-11 ~ Bedrooms: /£42B

TROUTBECK NY4103 Map 9

Mortal Man

Upper Rd, nr High Green – OS Sheet 90, map ref 411035

Surrounded by marvellous scenery, this popular inn has a warmly welcoming and relaxed atmosphere. The bustling, partly-panelled bar has horse-brasses on its dark beams, a nice medley of seats including a cushioned settle and some farmhouse chairs around copper-topped tables, a big roaring fire, friendly black dog – and no piped music; there's also a small, cosy lounge. Good bar food includes home-made soup (£1.75), smoked salmon pâté or wood pigeon with apple sauce and celery sticks (£2.95), mixed bean casserole, lentil pie or poached salmon with a dill sauce (all £5.75), pork in cider hotpot or beef in ale pie (£6), roast rack of lamb (£7.75), Aberdeen Angus fillet steak (£9.50), and puddings (£2.50). The restaurant, with its big picture windows, is no smoking. Well kept Theakstons Best and Youngers Scotch on handpump; darts and dominoes. *(Recommended by Peter and Audrey Dowsett, A Preston, Gillian and Michael Wallace, Mrs B Lemon, H K Dyson, Mike and Wendy Proctor, Derek and Margaret Underwood, Gill and Mike Cross, I H Rorison, D J and P M Taylor)*

Free house ~ Licensee Christopher Poulsom ~ Real ale ~ Meals and snacks (not Mon evening) ~ Restaurant ~ (015394) 33193 ~ Children in eating area of bar until 9pm ~ Open 12-2.30, 5.30-11 ~ Bedrooms: £35B/£60B

Queens Head ★

A592 N of Windermere

Star quality is beginning to emerge from this bustling 17th-c coaching inn. This last year it has been pleasing more readers than any other pub in the Lake District. The bright bar has cushioned antique settles among more orthodox furniture, a massive Elizabethan four-poster bed as the basis of its serving counter, other fine antique carving, and two roaring log fires in imposing fireplaces. The bar rambles through some half-dozen attractively decorated rooms, including an unusual lower gallery, a comfortable dining area and lots of alcoves and heavy beams. First class, interesting food includes good home-made soup (£1.95), lunchtime filled french bread, fried chicken livers with smoked bacon and shallots in a raspberry vinegar and soya sauce on a warm potato and saffron salad (£3.95), crepes with tarragon and soy with a mild green chilli and smoked tofu filling with gruyère, and served with a fruity salad and new potatoes or super steak, ale and mushroom pie (£5.95), chicken fried in garlic and lemon butter and served with steamed vegetables with a light orange and coriander sauce (£6.95), Scottish salmon with lemon butter and topped with a smoked salmon and herb crumble and served with home-made tagliatelle and an orange beurre blanc (£8.50), fillet of pork with an apple, tarragon and mushroom duxelle in a puff pastry and served with a red wine jus and apple coulis (£9.50), and sirloin steak (£10.50); beautifully presented puddings; helpings are not that big. Well kept Boddingtons, Hartleys XB, Mitchells Lancaster Bomber, Tetleys and guest beers on handpump; helpful, friendly service. Darts, dominoes, and piped music. Plenty of seats outside have a fine view over the Trout valley to Applethwaite moors. *(Recommended by George Atkinson, LM, Jack Morley, Mrs B Lemon, Ernest M Russell, Ian Morley, Gillian and Michael Wallace, D Tapper, Mr and Mrs J Tyrer, Andy and Jill Kassube, A Preston, R W Saunders, Liz and Julian Long, Simon Watkins, RLW and Dizzy, Anne and Brian Birtwistle, Mr and Mrs Jacob, Tina and David Woods-Taylor, Richard Fawcett, Neville Kenyon, Wayne Brindle, J S M Sheldon, H K Dyson, F Jarman, WAH, Lynn Sharpless, Bob Eardley, Sara Geyer, Mick Whelton, Phil and Heidi Cook, Philip Saxon, A Preston, R E and P Pearce)*

Free house ~ Licensees Mark Stewardson and Joanne Sherratt ~ Real ale ~ Meals and snacks ~ Restaurant ~ (015394) 32174 ~ Children welcome ~ Open 11-11; closed 25 Dec ~ Bedrooms: £37.50B/£55B

ULVERSTON SD2978 Map 7

Bay Horse

Canal Foot signposted off A590 and then again by the large factory

Although this rather civilised and very well run inn is mainly popular for its beautifully presented, outstanding food, you will be made just as welcome if you only want a drink and a snack. In the bar the food might include filled home-made baps (£1.45), home-made soup (£1.85), home-made herb and cheese pâté with cranberry and ginger purée (£4.50), pâté or terrine as a main course with salad and baked potato (£6.25), pork and stilton sausages with an apple sauce and a tomato and apricot chutney (£6.75), layers of beef tomato, aubergine, smoked ham and wild mushrooms in a rich sherried egg custard, diced smoked breast of chicken and button mushrooms cooked in a tomato, cream and brandy sauce with a puff pastry topping or flakes of smoked salmon, brandied sultanas and waterchestnuts cooked in a rich cheddar cheese cream sauce, baked with a savoury breadcrumb topping (all £7.50), and home-made puddings (£2.95). There's also the grill with well hung Scotch steaks, and a no-smoking conservatory restaurant (with exceptional views across to Morecambe Bay, and where bookings are essential); the three-course lunch is fine value for £14.50 (separate evening menu). There's a steady flow of real ales on handpump which might include Boddingtons, Fullers London Pride, Marstons Pedigree, and Mitchells Lancaster Bomber, and so forth, a decent choice of spirits, and an impressive and interesting New World wine list; lovely home-made shortbread with the good coffee. The bar has a pubby atmosphere and a huge stone horse's head, as well as attractive wooden armchairs, some pale green plush built-in wall banquettes, glossy hardwood traditional tables, blue plates on a Delft shelf, and black beams and props with lots of horsebrasses. Magazines are dotted about, there's a handsomely marbled green granite fireplace, and decently reproduced piped music; darts, bar billiards, shove-ha'penny, cribbage, and dominoes. Out on the terrace are some picnic tables. They will be holding friendly and informal day cookery demonstrations in their new kitchen. The owners also run a very good restaurant at their Miller Howe hotel on Windermere. *(Recommended by John Derbyshire, Jack Morley, M J Brooks, Anne and Brian Birtwistle, Malcolm Taylor, John and Chris Simpson, Neville Kenyon, Christopher Mobbs, Philip Vernon, Kim Maidment, Ian Morley, A and M Dickinson)*

Free house ~ Licensee Robert Lyons ~ Real ale ~ Lunchtime bar meals and snacks (not Mon) ~ Separate lunchtime and evening restaurant (not Sun or Mon lunchtimes) ~ (01229) 583972 ~ Children in eating area of bar only ~ Open 11-11 ~ Bedrooms: £65B/£130B inc dinner

YANWATH NY5128 Map 9

Gate

2¼ miles from M6 junction 40; A66 towards Brough, then right on A6, right on B5320, then follow village signpost

An engaging combination of really good inventive food with the welcoming environment of an unpretentious village local: our inspection meal consisted of 'black devils' (sliced black pudding in a thin mildly peppery cream sauce – an excellent starter or very light snack at £3.25), tender venison cooked rare with a delicate pink peppercorn sauce (£8.50) and, the most successful dish, a fan of duck breast crisped on the outside but rare and succulent inside with a deftly understated gin and lime pan-reduction sauce (£8.95). Other inventive dishes which readers have praised highly include cumberland sausage and bacon in a mixed bean casserole (£5.25), mushroom pasta in stilton sauce baked with mozzarella (£6.95), and beef fillet with smoked bacon and Rutland cheese (£8.95); also, sandwiches (from £2), home-made soup (£2.25), ploughman's (£4.50), cheese and mushroom crunchy (£5.25), and puddings (£2.50). The simple turkey-carpeted bar, full of chatting regulars, has a log fire in an attractive stone inglenook and one or two nice pieces of furniture and middle-eastern brassware among more orthodox seats; or you can go through to eat in a more staid back two-level no-smoking dining room which is used as a restaurant on Saturday nights. Well kept Theakstons Best and two changing guest beers such as Burton Bridge Bitter and Cropton Two Pints on handpump, good coffee with real cream, obliging service; darts, dominoes, and very unobtrusive piped music; the border collie is called Domino. There are a few picnic tables outside.
(Recommended by Terry and Eileen Stott, David Heath, Gail Swanson)

Free house ~ Licensees Ian and Sue Rhind ~ Real ale ~ Meals and snacks ~ Restaurant ~ (01768) 862386 ~ Children welcome ~ Open 12-3, 6.30(6 Sat)-11; 12-2.30, 7-11 in winter

Lucky Dip

Besides the fully inspected pubs, you might like to try these Lucky Dips recommended to us and described by readers (if you do, please send us reports):

☆ **Alston** [Main St; NY7246], *Turks Head*: Convivial local with limited cheap food, well kept Boddingtons and Theakstons, helpful service, spotless housekeeping; bar counter dividing big front room into two areas, back lounge with cosy fire and small tables; at top of steep cobbled street *(Frank Davidson, Jim and Maggie Cowell, H K Dyson)*

☆ **Ambleside** [Market Sq; NY3804], *Queens*: Neatly comfortable hotel bar, good value food inc vegetarian, generous puddings and good children's menu, prompt friendly service, well kept ales such as Boddingtons, Hook Norton, Jennings, Theakstons XB, separate cellar bar with pool room; well equipped bedrooms *(Simon Watkins, Andy and Penny Scott, H K Dyson, Pat Woodward)*

Ambleside [just above Mkt Sq], *Royal Oak*: Busy beamed and carpeted local with rolls in main bar area and more substantial meals in another section across courtyard; well kept Theakstons XB and Youngers Scotch, friendly staff, outside seats *(George Atkinson, H K Dyson)*

☆ *nr* **Ambleside** [A592 N of Troutbeck; NY4007], *Kirkstone Pass*: Lakeland's highest inn, best out of season, with fine surrounding scenery, snug cheery bar with lots of old photographs and bric-a-brac, good coffee, wide choice of whiskies, well kept Tetleys, friendly staff, parrot and cockatiel, open fire, lively amusements, simple food, maybe piped Classic FM; bedrooms, all with four-posters *(John and Maureen Watt, H K Dyson, John and Joan Nash, LYM)*

Arrad Foot [SD3181], *Armadale*: Attractive dining bar attached to small hotel, wide choice of good food, friendly welcome esp for families; keg beer; bedrooms *(David Heath)*

☆ **Askham** [village crossroads by lower green; NY5123], *Queens Head*: Comfortable two-room beamed lounge, open fire, copper and brass, usual food from sandwiches to steaks, well kept Wards Sheffield Best, children in back bar and dining room, pleasant garden; bedrooms *(Richard Holloway, LYM; more reports on new regime please)*

☆ **Bampton** [NY5118], *St Patricks Well*: Warm friendly local doing well under new landlord, well kept Jennings Bitter and Mild, bar food inc good shepherd's pie and steaks, big open fire, pool room, darts, juke box; a couple of seats outside; bedrooms good value, huge breakfasts *(Mr and Mrs Barker, BB)*

☆ **Barbon** [off A683 Kirkby Lonsdale—Sedbergh; SD6383], *Barbon Inn*: Charmingly set below fells, with sheltered garden, some individual furnishings in small somewhat hotelish rooms off little bar, well kept Theakstons Best and Old Peculier, polite helpful service, decent bar food from sandwiches up inc vegetarian dishes, no smoking restaurant, friendly service; children welcome, old-fashioned bedrooms *(Gill and Mike Cross, Sue Holland, Dave Webster, Mrs M A Kilner, L Grant, Wayne Brindle, Barbara Wensworth, A P Jeffreys, Kim Schofield, H K Dyson, John and Joan Nash, LYM)*

☆ **Bardsea** [SD3074], *Bradylls Arms*: Wide choice of good food from sandwiches to fresh seafood in plushly refurbished old village inn, some stripped stone, lovely Morecambe Bay views from well furnished back conservatory restaurant; Boddingtons and Theakstons real ale, very friendly landlady; garden with play area *(Peter and Lynn Brueton)*

Barrow in Furness [Holbeck Park Av, Roose; SD2069], *Crofters*: Former farmhouse with well kept cheap Thwaites ale, good value home cooking, helpful staff, two bars; music, barbecue park *(M Edwards)*; [General Dr, Isle of Walney], *George*: Good food, friendly staff, two bars – one with good entertainment; nr beach *(Gordon Day)*

☆ **Beckermet** [NY0207], *White Mare*: Good cooking, well furnished connecting rooms, well kept Theakstons, friendly landlord; tables in streamside garden, attractive village *(Irene Shuttleworth)*

☆ **Blencogo** [signed off B5302 Wigton—Silloth; NY1948], *New Inn*: Very good food – real serious cooking – in bright and simply modernised former village local, log fire, Mitchells real ale, decent wines and whiskies, a few big Cumbrian landscapes, pleasant service; but even when not busy unable to feed people arriving just before 8.30 without booking; no food Sat-Mon evenings, maybe faint piped pop music *(Dr and Mrs Young, Helen Gibson, Robert Burn, BB)*

☆ **Bouth** [off A590 nr Haverthwaite; SD3386], *White Hart*: Attractive village pub in good S Lakes walking country, two real fires inc old kitchen range, sloping ceilings and floors, intimate authentic decor, good food under friendly new landlord, real ales, nice gardens; bedrooms *(Gordon Day, Jack Morley)*

Braithwaite [NY2324], *Royal Oak*: Jennings ales, bar meals, pool in back room, piped music *(D Hanley)*

Broughton in Furness [Princes St; SD2187], *Black Cock*: Olde-worlde pub dating from 15th c, good value food, friendly service, cosy fireside, well kept Courage-related ales; open all day Tues; bedrooms *(Michael Taylor)*

☆ **Buttermere** [NY1817], *Fish*: Spacious and smartly refurbished former coaching inn on NT property between Buttermere and Crummock Water, good value bar food from fresh sandwiches to trout, good range of well kept S&N ales; bedrooms *(G O Cook, H and D Payne, BB)*

☆ **Cark in Cartmel** [B5278; follow Holker Hall signs; SD3776], *Engine*: Comfortably refurbished pub with good food from lunchtime sandwiches up, Theakstons Best and XB and Youngers, obliging staff, open fire; restaurant, tables out by little stream; self-contained holiday flats *(Louise and Simon Chappell, M and J Back, BB)*

Carlisle [Botchergate; NY4056], *Caledonian Cask House*: Bare stone and boards, railway memorabilia, bar food, Whitbreads-related ales and guests like Cains, Morlands Old Speckled Hen and Timothy Taylors Landlord; pool, fruit machine *(D Hanley)*

☆ **Cartmel** [The Square; SD3879], *Kings Arms*: Picturesque pub nicely placed at the head of the attractive town square – rambling heavy-beamed bar, mix of furnishings from traditional settles to banquettes, usual bar food and no smoking restaurant all day, well kept Whitbreads-related ales, children welcome, seats outside *(Wayne Brindle, Elizabeth and Anthony Watts, E A George, LYM)*

Cartmel [The Square], *Royal Oak*: Low ceilings, cosy nooks, decent food, well kept Whitbreads-related real ales, polite service; nice big garden *(H K Dyson)*

☆ **Cockermouth** [Main St; NY1231], *Bush*: Well refurbished, open fires, well kept Jennings and guest beers, very friendly bar staff, good lunchtime food *(Ian and Gayle Woodhead, Mike Woodhead, Stephen Crothers)*

☆ **Cockermouth** [Main St], *Huntsman*: Recently well refurbished Jennings pub, good well priced food inc bargain Sun lunch (queues for this), well kept ales, very friendly landlord, quick service even when busy; interesting local photographs, juke box; open all day *(R J Walden, Mike Woodhead)*

☆ **Coniston** [signed from centre; SD3098], *Sun*: Attractively placed below mountains (doubling as rescue post), with interesting Donald Campbell and other Lakeland photographs in traditional back bar, good log fire, bar food, Jennings, Marstons Pedigree and Tetleys from the deep granite cellar; children in eating area and restaurant, darts, dominoes, maybe piped music; open all day; comfortable bedrooms *(G Atkinson, J Finney, G S Miller, MR, RR, LYM)*

☆ **Coniston** [Yewdale Rd], *Black Bull*: Large popular pub with beams, red banquettes and stools, log fires, piped classical music, relaxed atmosphere, filling home-made bar food promptly served, well kept S&N ales, more Donald Campbell photographs; separate bar suiting walkers; restaurant, tables in enclosed courtyard; comfortable good value bedrooms, good breakfasts *(Neil and Anita Christopher, David Heath, Catherine Sawyers, I H Rorison)*

☆ **Cowgill** [nr Dent Stn, on Dent—Garsdale Head rd; SD7587], *Sportsmans*: Fine Dentdale location with good nearby walks; home-made bar food lunchtime and evening, well kept S&N ales, drinkable wine, log fires, plainish bar/lounge with darts in snug at one end and pool room at the other, no piped music; bedrooms overlooking lovely river *(Peter and Audrey Dowsett, E G Parish)*

Crook [B5284 Kendal—Bowness – OS Sheet 97 map ref 471958; SD4795], *Sun*: Quietly straightforward pub with well kept Theakstons and other beers, extensive range of well cooked food, competitively priced wines, welcoming fire *(Leslie and June Lyon, LYM)*

☆ **Crosthwaite** [off A5074 Levens—Windermere; SD4491], *Punch Bowl*: Interestingly rambling many-roomed modernised dining bar with upper galleries, usual food inc bargain steak meals, neat helpful staff, well kept S&N ales, separate games area, some tables outside; children and dogs welcome, restaurant; pleasant roomy bedrooms (readers prefer nos 2 and 3), attractive quiet location *(Roger and Corinne Ball, H K Dyson, Jack Morley, LYM)*

☆ **Deanscales** [A5086 S of Cockermouth; NY0927], *Old Posting House*: Welcoming and comfortable split-level dining pub, good value generous home-made food from sandwiches to steaks, interesting old fittings surviving from posting and coaching days, Lakeland and heavy-horse prints; well kept Jennings Bitter and Cumberland *(M E A Horler, BB)*

Dent [Main St; SD7187], *George & Dragon*: Civilised and peaceful, part pub, part hotel; local Dent beer, good bar meals, bargain Sun lunch, reasonably priced evening restaurant, no piped music; bedrooms comfortable *(Peter and Audrey Dowsett)*

☆ **Durdar** [NY4151], *Black Lion*: Well kept Theakstons Best, very pleasant staff, no smoking room, home-made food in huge helpings, all extremely clean; handy for Carlisle racecourse, not far from M6 junction 42 *(Joe Green)*

☆ **Eskdale** [NY1400], *Brook House*: Wide choice of good generous home-cooked food served cheerfully yet unintrusively in small family-run hotel under new management, with small plush bar, comfortable lounge, open fires, Jennings Cumberland, good views, handy for Ravenglass rly; good bedrooms *(G T and R M Ross)*

☆ **Far Sawrey** [SD3893], *Sawrey*: Simple but comfortable and welcoming stable bar with tables in wooden stalls, harness on rough white walls, big helpings of good simple lunchtime bar food, well kept Black Sheep Bitter and Special and Jennings, pleasant staff; separate hotel bar, evening restaurant; seats on nice lawn, beautiful setting, walkers, children and dogs welcome; bedrooms comfortable and well equipped *(H K Dyson, Jack Morley, Simon Barber, LYM)*

☆ **Glenridding** [back of main car park, top of road; NY3917], *Travellers Rest*: Homely unpretentious bar with big helpings of good simple food for hungry walkers, well kept Whitbreads-related ales, simple newish decor, everyone friendly *(H K Dyson, David Lewis, Russell and Margaret Bathie)*

Grange over Sands [Grange Fell Rd (off B5277); SD4077], *Hardcrag Hall*: Two character 16th-c panelled rooms and dining rooms, friendly service, reasonably priced Thwaites and a weekend guest beer, good choice of reasonably priced bar meals with children's helpings; bedrooms *(John Scarisbrick)*

☆ **Grasmere** [NY3406], *Red Lion*: Ideal spot in lovely village, very friendly staff, tasty bar food in plush lounge bar and cane-chair conservatory, well priced restaurant meals, well kept beers, good range of malt whiskies; good bedrooms *(Andy and Jill Kassube)*

☆ **Grasmere** [main bypass rd], *Swan*: Up-market but relaxed and individual, with friendly service, lively little public bar, quieter old-fashioned lounge popular with older people (this is where children go), oak beams, armchairs, velvet curtains, prints and swords, inglenook log fires; well prepared bar food, keg beer but good malt whiskies, tables in garden, picturesque surroundings, drying room for walkers; easy parking; comfortable bedrooms – a Forte hotel *(Elizabeth and Anthony Watts, H and D Payne, John Atherton, LYM)*

☆ **Grasmere**, *Wordsworth*: Well kept and stylish hotel with cheerful separate Dove & Olive Branch bar for good cheap bar food, log fire and well kept Bass Special; good light lunches in conservatory, nice garden, comfortable bedrooms *(LYM)*

Grasmere, *Tweedies*: Comfortable lounge bar with good standard bar food, well kept Boddingtons and Theakstons on handpump, good service, tartan displays, restaurant *(Simon Watkins, Chris Cook)*

Great Corby [NY4854], *Queens*: Well kept real ales, cosy atmosphere, open fires, friendly licensees *(Raymond A Clarke)*

Great Strickland [NY5623], *Strickland Arms*: Pleasant country pub, good food, Tetleys-related and Jennings real ales, competitive prices *(Stephen Clark)*

☆ **Haverthwaite** [A590 Barrow rd; SD3284], *Dicksons Arms*: Low-beamed bar with woodburning stove, hunting prints, good generous food inc delicious puddings, well kept Jennings, Marstons Pedigree and Moorhouses Pendle Witches Brew, pleasant atmosphere, prompt friendly service; restaurant *(Catherine and Martin Snelling, Margaret and Roy Randle, Roger and Christine Mash)*

Haverthwaite, *Anglers Arms*: Busy local with good value generous food, Theakstons and Youngers No 3 on handpump, overflow upstairs dining room *(R G Bywaters)*

Hawkshead [SD3598], *Red Lion*: Friendly modernised pub with some old-fashioned touches, good log fire, Courage-related ales, usual food, piped music; bedrooms *(Jean and Douglas Troup, H K Dyson, LYM)*

Helton [NY5122], *Helton*: Very welcoming landlord, freshly cooked food inc particularly good cumberland sausage; log fire *(Johnathan and Ann Tross)*

☆ **Hesket Newmarket** [signed from B5299 in Caldbeck; NY3438], *Old Crown*: The friendly and very individual licensees who made this prettily set little inn such a popular main entry for its relaxed atmosphere, unassuming but interesting home cooking and unusual home-brewed beers left in early summer 1995; the new landlord may get the former brewer to go on supplying the beers, but as we went to press was unsure of his other plans – though will not be opening on Mon-Thurs lunchtimes *(LYM; news please)*

☆ **Howtown** [NY4519], *Howtown Hotel*: Stunning setting nr Ullswater, small cosy hotel lounge bar, separate public bar with good lunchtime sandwiches for hungry walkers, restaurant, morning coffee or afternoon tea; welcoming very long-serving owners, well kept Theakstons Best, sound wines by the glass, pleasant garden; bedrooms *(Lucy James, RKP, Ian Rorison)*

☆ **Ireby** [NY2439], *Sun*: Clean and friendly country local with good plentiful food, well kept Jennings, woodburner, beams, brasses and harness, red plush seats and polished tables; no meals Tues lunch; no meals Mon (winter) *(John and Maggie Churcher)*

Ireby, *Paddys Bar*: Friendly pub in small working village below Caldbeck Fells, wide range of beers *(Anon)*

Kendal [SD5293], *Globe*: Civilised but cheerful beamed split-level bar, pleasant decor, good cheap bar food, quick friendly service, separate dining-room upstairs (where children welcome) *(Mr and Mrs C Roberts, Sue Holland, Dave Webster)*; [72 Milnthorp Rd], *Kendal Arms*: Warmly friendly, comfortable and spacious split level bar and conservatory, good attractively presented food, good service, well kept ales *(E G Parish)*

☆ **Keswick** [Lake Rd, off top end Mkt Sq; NY2624], *Dog & Gun*: Lively and unpretentious town local with some high settles, low beams, partly slate floor (rest carpeted or boards), fine Abrahams mountain photographs, log fire; well kept McEwans 80/-, Theakstons Best and Old Peculier and a guest ale, open fires, well presented generous bar food from sandwiches up, friendly efficient staff; piped music; children if eating, no dogs *(Mr and Mrs R J Foreman, P and M Rudlin, Nigel Woolliscroft, D Hanley, Paul and Gail Betteley, Philip Saxon, Jeanne Cross, Paul Silvestri, Mark Bradley, V and E A Bolton, WAH, LYM)*

☆ **Keswick** [St John's St], *George*: Attractive black-panelled side room with good log fire where the poet Southey used to wait for Wordsworth to arrive from Grasmere, also open-plan main bar with old-fashioned settles and modern banquettes under Elizabethan beams; bar food, well kept Theakstons and Yates, smartish restaurant; bedrooms comfortable *(P and M Rudlin, J S M Sheldon, H K Dyson, LYM)*

Keswick [Lake Rd], *Four in Hand*: Cosy, atmospheric back lounge, stage-coach bric-a-brac, wide choice of good reasonably priced food, decent-sized tables in dining room, full Jennings range on handpump, friendly staff; very busy in summer *(Paul and Gail Betteley, Michael Butler)*; [Market Sq], *Keswick Lodge*: Hotel lounge bar with comfortable pubby feel, well kept Jennings and Theakstons, wide choice of reasonably priced bar food, pleasant service; bedrooms *(Ian Fraser and others)*

☆ *nr* **Keswick** [Crosthwaite Rd; by A66, a mile out], *Pheasant*: Small friendly beamed pub with lots of local cartoons, big helpings of limited but good value food, well kept Jennings, particularly friendly prompt service; children if eating; bedrooms *(WAH, Michael Butler, P and M Rudlin, D Hanley)*

☆ *nr* **Keswick** [Newlands Valley – OS Sheet 90 map ref 242217], *Swinside*: Clean and friendly modernised pub in peaceful valley below marvellous crags and fells, well kept Jennings Bitter, Cumberland and Sneck Lifter, decent house wine, open fires, generous bar food, restaurant; tables outside with best view; dogs allowed, open all day Sat and summer, may not open winter lunchtimes; bedrooms *(H K Dyson, Simon Watkins, WAH, Tony Gayfer, V and E A Bolton, LYM)*

Kirkby Lonsdale [SD6278], *Fleece*: Unfashionable local with friendly service, well kept Worthington BB *(Sue Holland, David Webster)*; *Red Dragon*: Quite smart, with Jennings ale, quite a good reasonably priced menu, back restaurant *(PD, AD)*

☆ **Kirkby Stephen** [NY7808], *Kings Arms*: Old-fashioned oak-panelled lounge bar, good home cooking inc good sandwiches, popular lunchtime cold table and dining-room meals, well kept Whitbreads-related beers, friendly helpful owners; darts and dominoes in public bar, tables in walled garden; bedrooms *(Dono and Carol Leaman, LYM)*

Kirkby Stephen [4 Market St], *White Lion*: Uncluttered friendly local, appealing for its lack of frills and heroic domino-players *(Helen McLagan)*

Kirkoswald [NY5641], *Fetherston Arms*: Good value food, pleasant landlord; good reasonably priced bedrooms *(T M Dobby)*

☆ **Langdale** [by car park for Stickle Ghyll; NY2906], *Stickle Barn*: In lovely setting, suiting walkers and mountaineers well, good choice of food inc packed lunches, well kept Courage-related beers, gluhwein and jagertee, fruit machines, maybe loud piped music; big pleasant terrace, open all day in summer; bunkhouse accommodation, live music in loft *(RLW, Dizzy, John and Maureen Watt)*

☆ **Levens** [Sedgwick Rd, by Sizergh Castle gates – OS Sheet 97 map ref 500872; SD5087], *Strickland Arms*: New landlord doing wide choice of generous imaginative well cooked food in 16th-c NT pub, friendly prompt service even when very busy, well kept Marstons Pedigree, Morlands Old Speckled Hen and Theakstons XB, Best and Old Peculier, standard breweryised internal refurbishment but clean and comfortable, with log fire; piped music, pool table, upstairs restaurant, children allowed, good garden; frequent live music Mon/Tues *(R H Rowley, Mr and Mrs C Roberts, Richard Lewis)*

☆ **Lindale** [B5277 N of Grange-over-Sands – OS Sheet 97 map ref 419805; SD4280], *Lindale*: Comfortable spacious bar, good generous reasonably priced food from sandwiches to huge steaks, nice oak-beamed dining area (children welcome here), well kept Whitbreads Castle Eden, good friendly service; bedrooms *(Mr and Mrs C Roberts, Janis and Neil Hedgecock)*

☆ **Lowick Bridge** [just off A5084; SD2986], *Red Lion*: Busy family pub with two spacious, attractive and comfortable areas, well kept Hartleys XB and Robinsons, good choice of generous bar food inc Sun roasts, friendly staff; charming spot *(David Heath, Prof I H Rorison, LM, JCW)*

☆ **Lowick Green** [A5092 SE of village; SD2985], *Farmers Arms*: Charming public bar with heavy beams, huge flagstones, big open fire, cosy corners and pub games (this part may be closed winter), some interesting furniture and pictures in plusher hotel lounge bar across yard, food in bar and restaurant, well kept Theakstons XB and Youngers IPA and No 3, children welcome, open all day; piped music; bedrooms *(LYM; more reports on current regime please)*

Lupton [Cow Brow; A65, nr M6 junction 36; SO5681], *Plough*: Impressive oak beams and stonework, well kept beers, good home-cooked food with summer barbecues, facilities for disabled; beautiful spot *(E G Parish, Jean and Douglas Troup)*

☆ **Middleton** [A683 Kirkby Lonsdale—Sedbergh; SD6288], *Middleton Fells*: Comfortably plush open-plan oak-beamed bar with lots of brasswork (some made by the landlord), three good fires, good choice of popular sensibly priced home-made food, friendly landlord, well kept Boddingtons and Tetleys; games room, juke box, quiz nights; very attractive garden, fine scenery; children welcome *(David Heath, Katie Hornby, Peter and Audrey Dowsett, LYM)*

☆ **Middleton** [A683 Kirkby Lonsdale—Sedbergh; SD6386], *Swan*: Quaint old two-roomed pub, clean, friendly, with lots of individuality; keg beer, but open fire in bar, small but varied choice of good food in second room; particularly good steaks *(David Heath, Mike and Wendy Proctor, LYM)*

☆ **Mungrisdale** [village signed off A66 Penrith—Keswick, a bit over a mile W of A5091 Ullswater rd – OS Sheet 90 map ref 363302; NY3731], *Mill Inn*: Simple pub in lovely valley hamlet, good bar food, Jennings real ale, lots of malt whiskies, plain games room, separate restaurant; children welcome, tables on gravel forecourt and neat lawn sloping to little river; warm pleasant bedrooms (note that there's a quite separate Mill Hotel here) *(V and E A Bolton, LYM)*

Nateby [B6259 Kirkby Stephen—Wensleydale; NY7807], *Black Bull*: Relaxed and friendly country local with roaring log fire, pleasant layout with nice decorations and beams, particularly well kept Theakstons and Youngers beers, good value standard food, good service; bedrooms good value too *(Paul Hindle)*

☆ **Nether Wasdale** [NY1204], *Strands*: Lovely spot below the remote high fells around Wastwater, good range of generous bar food, well kept Hartleys XB and Robinsons, friendly service; bedrooms *(Peter and Lynn Brueton)*

☆ **Newton Reigny** [off B5305 just W of M6 junction 41; NY 4832], *Sun*: Open-plan village inn with plush seats and velvet curtains, stripped stone and wrought iron, central open fire, Courage-related and other ales inc a local guest, popular food from vegetarian dishes to game casseroles and salmon, no smoking restaurant; darts, dominoes and pool off at one end, children away from bar, open all day Sat; piped music, cheap bedrooms *(Richard Holloway, David Bloomfield, LYM; more reports on new regime please)*

Orton [2 miles from M6 junction 38; B6261 towards Penrith; NY6207], *George*: Lovely old inn, very friendly, wonderful peaceful setting, good reasonably priced food and beer; bedrooms comfortable *(Michael and Hazel Lyons)*

☆ **Outgate** [B5286 Ambleside—Hawkshead; SD3699], *Outgate Inn*: Sadly Ian and Katrina Kirsopp who put so much life and individuality into this attractively placed country pub have just left, following a steep rent increase by Robinsons; its three modernised rooms will still be a comfortable refuge, and there will still be their beers, but we don't yet know about food, children, bedrooms, or if there'll still be good jazz on Fri *(LYM; news please)*

☆ **Oxenholme** [½ mile up hill, B6254 towards Old Hutton – OS Sheet 97 map ref 536900; SD5390], *Station*: Tidy, clean and comfortable breweryised country pub, with good generous straightforward food, well kept S&N and Whitbreads-related beers, very friendly staff, log fire, garden; not at station *(Mr and Mrs C Roberts)*

Penrith [NY5130], *George*: Decorous beamed and oak-panelled lounge hall with fine plasterwork, oak settles and easy chairs around good open fire, big bow windows; short choice of reasonably priced lunchtime bar food, well kept Marstons Pedigree, lively back bar, restaurant; comfortable bedrooms *(FD, LYM)*; [Queen St], *Lowther Arms*: Small friendly well run local with wide range of reasonably priced lunchtime food, Theakstons Best and XB, Youngers Scotch and guest ales such as Dent, Marstons Pedigree, Morlands Old Speckled Hen, Timothy Taylors Landlord and Wadworths 6X, real fire; little nearby parking *(Adrian Watson)*

☆ **Penruddock** [NY4327], *Herdwick*: Pleasantly refurbished old pub with consistently good food esp Sun roast, good friendly service, attractive restaurant – worth booking evenings *(Malcolm Taylor and others)*

Pooley Bridge [NY4724], *Sun*: Rather unusual inside, with warm and cosy lounge bar, well kept Jennings ales, good value generously served simple bar food, separate restaurant; tables in garden *(G O Cook)*

☆ **Ravenstonedale** [signed off A685 Kirkby Stephen—M6; NY7204], *Black Swan*: Good food with interesting specials in comfortable and decorous bar with open fire and some stripped stone, well kept Hartleys XB, Robinsons, Theakstons, Worthington, Youngers and a changing guest, lots of country wines, good service, evening restaurant; dogs welcome, tables in pretty tree-sheltered streamside garden over road; comfortable well equipped bedrooms, inc some for disabled *(John Allsopp, SS, Malcolm Phillips, BB)*

Ravenstonedale, *Kings Head*: Friendly two-room beamed bar with log fires, button-back banquettes and dining chairs, good range of generous food, well kept Mitchells, Theakstons XB and Tetleys, separate games room *(R P Knight, LYM)*

☆ *nr* **Ravenstonedale** [Crossbank; A683 Sedbergh—Kirkby Stephen; SD6996], *Fat Lamb*: Remote friendly inn now has well kept Mitchells in brightly modernised bar with pews, log fire in traditional black kitchen range, good local photographs; cheerful service, usual bar food, maybe piped classical music, restaurant, seats out by sheep pastures; facilities for disabled, children really welcome; comfortable bedrooms with own bathrooms *(Malcolm Phillips, Graeme Mew, BB)*

☆ **Rockcliffe** [NY3661], *Crown & Thistle*: Comfortable and clean, well divided so as to be spacious, light and airy yet cosy, wide choice of attractively priced good food in huge helpings, quick friendly service even when busy, well kept Theakstons Bitter and Mild; locally popular games bar *(Mr and Mrs C Roberts, Dorothy and David Young)*

☆ **Rosthwaite** [NY2615], *Scafell*: Extended and refurbished slate-floored walkers' bar, very popular with them for ample good value lunchtime food from sandwiches to steak and salmon, children's helpings of most dishes, full range of Theakstons ales kept well, afternoon teas, log fire, quick friendly service; glassed-in verandah overlooking river, subdued piped music; hotel has cosy sun-lounge bar and dining room; bedrooms not large but good *(I H Rorison, Tony Gayfer, Simon Watkins, H K Dyson, Joe and Carol Pattison, David Heath)*

☆ **Sandside** [B5282 Milnthorpe—Arnside; SD4781], *Ship*: Spacious modernised pub with glorious view of estuary and mountains beyond; friendly staff, decent bar food, well kept S&N real ales, decent wines, summer barbecues, tables out on grass by good children's play area; children allowed in eating area *(John Fazakerley, LYM)*

☆ **Satterthwaite** [SD3492], *Eagles Head*: Small and unpretentious but friendly, with good value generous home-cooked lunchtime food esp soup, sandwiches and home-made pies (also Fri/Sat summer evenings), big log fire, helpful landlord, well kept Thwaites, pool, darts; papers and guidebooks for sale; handy for Grizedale Forest; bedrooms comfortable and clean, shared bathroom; maybe some closures winter esp Mon *(Sue Holland, David Webster, Mrs H H Lord, Margaret and Roy Randle, Sara Geyer, Mick Whelton)*

☆ **Scales** [A66 W of Penrith; NY3427], *White Horse*: Comfortable beamed pub with hunting pictures, cosy corners and good open fires, Jennings real ales, decent food; under new ownership this last year *(Mr and Mrs Jones, Jack Morley, Roger and Christine Mash, LYM; more reports on new regime please)*

☆ **Seatoller** [NY2414], *Yew Tree*: Good low-ceilinged restaurant at foot of Honister Pass in area short of good pubs, well presented imaginative food, efficient friendly staff; you can get just a drink at the bar, but may have to sit out in the garden with it *(Bill Sykes)*

Sedbergh [Finkle St; A683; SD6692], *Red Lion*: Cheerful Jennings local, comfortable and friendly, with good service, fair range of food, well kept ales *(Richard Houghton, BB)*

St Bees [Main St; NX9712], *Queens*: Simple three-room bar, well kept Boddingtons, Theakstons Best and Youngers Scotch, big helpings of good home-made bar food in dining area with big tables; good start or finish for Wainwright's coast-to-coast walk; bedrooms *(M E A Horler, GL)*

☆ **Staveley** [SD4798], *Eagle & Child*: Simple good value home-cooked bar food with fresh veg, well kept Newcastle Exhibition, Tetleys and Theakstons Best, friendly service, bright but comfortable little modern front lounge and more spacious carpeted bar; well kept, with small neat garden; bedrooms inexpensive, good breakfast *(Sue Holland, Dave Webster, Dr and Mrs Baker, David Lands, G Washington, BB)*

Stonethwaite [Borrowdale; NY2613], *Langstrath*: Friendly, neat and clean, with good fresh bar food; delightful village *(H K Dyson, Nigel Woolliscroft)*

☆ **Talkin** [village signed off B6413 S of Brampton; NY5557], *Blacksmiths Arms*: Welcoming and cheerful, good generous quick food in bar or dining room, Sun lunch very popular (booking advisable); well kept Youngers ales on handpump, open fire, local pictures; unobtrusive piped music, fruit machine; five well appointed bedrooms, prettily set village *(Mr and Mrs C Roberts, LM, Graham and Lynn Mason)*

☆ **Thirlspot** [A591 Grasmere—Keswick; NY3217], *Kings Head*: Attractively placed long low beamed bar with wide choice of usual good value home-cooked food, well kept Jennings, Theakstons Best, XB and Mild, Yates and guest such as Marstons Pedigree, inglenook fires, tables in garden, games room with pool, live music Fri; children welcome; good value bedrooms (the hotel part and restaurant are quite separate);

same ownership as Travellers Rest at Grasmere (even same piped music) *(A Rowley, Richard Lewis, Tina and David Woods-Taylor, LYM)*

☆ **Torver** [A593 S of Coniston; SD2894], *Church House*: Decent varied food in small clean tidy low-beamed bar and attractive evening restaurant, pleasant service, splendid hill views, good fire, well kept Whitbreads Castle Eden, big garden; children welcome; open all day at least in summer; bedrooms *(W Mecham, Dr and Mrs P B Baker, SP)*

Torver, *Red Lion*: Good generous food, friendly helpful staff, reasonable prices; children welcome *(Dave)*; *Wilson Arms*: Good beer, log fires, food; no dogs; bedrooms *(Dr Pete Crawshaw)*

☆ **Ulverston** [King St; SD2978], *Rose & Crown*: Good friendly traditional pub atmosphere, good food, well kept Hartleys XB, Robinsons Best Mild and Bitter, quick service even when busy on Sat market day *(Margaret and Roy Randle, Anne and Brian Birtwistle)*

Warwick on Eden [2 miles from M6, junction 43; A69 towards Hexham, then village signposted; NY4657], *Queens Arms*: Unpretentious two-room bar with well kept Tetleys-related ales, some interesting wines, malt whiskies and farm cider, good log fires, straightforward food (not winter Sun evening); tables in side garden with bright play area; open all day Sat; children welcome; bedrooms *(R E and P Pearce, Dave Braisted, LYM)*

☆ **Wasdale Head** [NY1808], *Wasdale Head Inn*: Marvellous fellside setting, spacious panelled main bar with cushioned settles on slate floor and great mountain photographs, adjoining pool room, no smoking snug and children's room; popular if not cheap bar food, well kept Jennings, Theakstons Best and Old Peculier and Yates, decent choice of wines and malt whiskies; the hotel side is good and comfortable; open all day, cl much of winter *(Peter and Lynn Brueton, Dr R H M Stewart, Nigel Woolliscroft, D Baker, Ann Reeder, David Craine, Brian and Anna Marsden, Brian and Jill Bond, Piotr Chodzko-Zajko, H K Dyson, Andrew Stephenson, E A George, David Wright, LYM)*

Windermere [SD4109], *Lamplighter*: Small friendly bar attached to hotel, wide choice of good generous food, well kept Theakstons and Youngers IPA; restaurant *(Liz and Julian Long)*

☆ **Winster** [A5074; SD4293], *Brown Horse*: Large open-plan light and comfortable dining pub with well spaced tables and good log fire; a main entry with food award in the last edition, but the Dohertys responsible for such excellent food left in early 1995; well kept Jennings and Marstons Pedigree, decent wines, children welcome *(LYM; news please)*

☆ **Winton** [just off A685 N of Kirkby Stephen; NY7810], *Bay Horse*: Quiet and friendly, in peaceful moorland hamlet, two unpretentious low-ceilinged rooms with Pennine photographs and local fly-tying, good generous reasonably priced home-cooked food inc fresh veg, well kept Theakstons Best, Jennings Bitter and Cumberland and Youngers Scotch, summer guest beers, pool in games room; may close Tues-Thurs lunchtimes in winter; comfortable modestly priced bedrooms, good breakfasts *(T M Dobby, Alan Dove, LYM)*

Workington [NX9928], *Commercial*: Traditional pub with well kept Jennings, good atmosphere *(Thor-Leif Lundberg)*

Please keep sending us reports. We rely on readers for news of new discoveries, and particularly for news of changes – however slight – at the fully described pubs. No stamp needed: *The Good Pub Guide*, FREEPOST TN1569, Wadhurst, E Sussex TN5 7BR.

Derbyshire and Staffordshire

New main entries this year are the relaxing and individual Waltzing Weasel at Birch Vale (particularly good food and wine, a nice place to stay in), the Olde Nags Head in Castleton (civilised and interesting, another nice place to stay in), the National Trust's Hardwick Inn outside Hardwick Hall (back in these pages after a break) and the cheerful Derby Tup at Whittington Moor on the edge of Chesterfield (mainly for its excellent beers, but good cheap food too). Other pubs currently doing particularly well here include the Moat House in its pretty canalside spot at Acton Trussell, the Druid at Birchover (a very busy dining pub), the unspoilt Olde Gate at Brassington, the Miners Arms at Eyam (emphasis on good home cooking), the welcoming Coach & Horses at Fenny Bentley (a village which now has two microbreweries), the smartly civilised Chequers on Froggatt Edge, the Jervis Arms at Onecote (excellent for families), the Old Crown at Shardlow (good beers, interesting food) and the White Horse at Woolley Moor (a fine all-rounder). We choose as Derbyshire's Dining Pub of the Year the Chequers on Froggatt Edge, and as Staffordshire's Dining Pub of the Year the Olde Dog & Partridge at Tutbury (for its enjoyable carvery). The Lantern Pike at Little Hayfield (we list it under Hayfield) and Packhorse at Little Longstone are both outstanding for the warmth of their welcome; the cheery Yew Tree at Cauldon has an unrivalled collection of curiosities. Food and drinks prices in the area are generally lower than the national average. Much the cheapest beer we found here was at the Brunswick in Derby, for a beer brewed on the premises; the cheapest "branded" drinks we found were at the Yew Tree at Cauldon and Barley Mow at Kirk Ireton, while own brews from the Rising Sun at Shraleybrook and John Thompson near Melbourne were also cheap. In the Lucky Dip section at the end of the chapter, pubs to note particularly include the George & Dragon at Alrewas, Devonshire Arms at Beeley, Navigation at Buxworth, Olde Dolphin and Abbey Inn in Derby, Izaak Walton in Dovedale, St George at Eccleshall, Bluebell at Farnah Green, Cavalier at Grindon, Slaters at Hill Chorlton, Meynell Ingram Arms at Hoar Cross, several entries in Hope, Worston Mill at Little Bridgeford, Royal Oak at Millthorpe, Little Mill at Rowarth, Seven Stars at Sandonbank, both Ticknall entries, George at Tideswell, Wellington in Uttoxeter, George at Waterhouses and Mainwaring Arms at Whitmore; we have inspected the great majority of these and rate them highly.

People named as recommenders after the main entries have told us that the pub should be included. But they have not written the report – we have, after anonymous on-the-spot inspection.

ACTON TRUSSELL (Staffs) SJ9318 Map 7

Moat House

Village signposted from A449 just S of Stafford; the right turn off A449 is only 2 miles (heading N) from M6 jnct 13

This attractive 14th-c timbered building stands in its own six acres of lovely landscaped grounds next to the Staffordshire & Worcestershire canal – there are mooring facilities for narrowboats, and plenty of friendly ducks. The family have a 400-acre farm which supplies some produce for the good bar food, which might include daily specials like mushroom soup (£1.50), roast pork (£4.50), chicken and mushroom pancake with cheese sauce (£4.75), chicken chasseur, venison sausages, leek or stilton bake or steak braised in red wine (£5.25), poached cod fillet in white wine and prawn sauce (£5.50) and entrecote steak. Well kept Banks's Bitter, Marstons Pedigree and about ten guest beers a month on handpump, a good wine list and about ten wines by the glass, and decent range of spirits served in the charming oak-beamed and comfortable bar; pleasant friendly staff. Fruit machine, piped music. *(Recommended by Basil Minson, Dave Braisted, RT and JC Moggridge, Dorothee and Dennis Glover, FJ and A Parmenter, G J Parsons, Peter and Jenny Quine, Graham Reeve, David Heath, John and Christine Simpson)*

Free house ~ Licensees John and Mary Lewis ~ Real ale ~ Meals and snacks (no bar food Sat evening or Sun) ~ Restaurant (not Sun evening) ~ (01785) 712217 ~ Children in restaurant and eating area of bar ~ Open 11-3, 6-11; all day Sat in summer; closed 25/26 Dec

ALSTONEFIELD (Staffs) SK1355 Map 7

George

Village signposted from A515 Ashbourne—Buxton

This beautifully simple 16th-c stone inn is prettily placed by the village green in the middle of a quiet farming hamlet. Locals, campers and hikers gather in the low beamed bar, which has a warm fire, fine collection of old photographs and pictures of the Peak District, and pewter tankards hanging by the copper-topped bar counter. A spacious family room is full of wheelback chairs around tables. Generous helpings of straightforward bar food from a printed menu – you order at the kitchen door – include sandwiches (£1.75), soup (£1.85), ploughman's (from £3.60), meat and potato pie (£4.95), lasagne, chicken, smoked trout or Spanish quiche (£5.20). Well kept Burtonwood Bitter, Forshaws and Top Hat on handpump; dominoes. The big sheltered stableyard behind the pub has a pretty rockery with picnic tables, and there are some stone seats beneath the attractive inn sign at the front; you can arrange with the landlord to camp on the croft. Useful walking country although muddy boots and dogs may not be welcome. *(Recommended by Nigel Woolliscroft, J E Rycroft, Jack and Philip Paxton, Paul and Maggie Baker, John Waller, Harriet and Michael Robinson, Dave Irving, David Atkinson, Jeanne and Tom Barnes, Ian and Emma Potts, Peter Marshall)*

Burtonwood ~ Tenants Richard and Sue Grandjean ~ Real ale ~ Meals and snacks ~ (01335) 310205 ~ Children in one room ~ Open 11-2.30, 6-11

Watts Russell Arms

Hopedale

This 18th-c shuttered stone house is gloriously set outside the village in a deep valley of the Peak District National Park, close to Dovedale and the Manifold. In the cheerful bar the furniture is elegantly comfortable, with brocaded wall banquettes and wheelback chairs and carvers, there's an open fire below a copper hood, a collection of blue and white china jugs hanging from the ceiling, bric-a-brac around the roughcast walls, and an interesting bar counter made from copper-bound oak barrels. Bar food includes soup (£1.75), bacon and tomato baps (£3.10), chilli (£4.50), gammon (£5.95). Well kept Mansfield Traditional, Old Baily and Riding

Mild and a guest like Charles Wells Bombardier or Morlands Old Speckled Hen on handpump, and about ten malts; darts and dominoes. Outside there are picnic tables on the sheltered tiered little terrace, and garden. Popular with walkers and busy at weekends. *(Recommended by Ian Jones, Jack and Phillip Paxton, Paul Robinshaw, Yolanda Henry, David Atkinson, Eric J Locker, Jeanne and Tom Barnes)*

Free house ~ Licensees Frank and Bridgette Lipp ~ Real ale ~ Meals and snacks (not winter Sun evenings) ~ (01335) 310271 ~ Children in eating area of bar (must be over 5) ~ Open 12-3, 7-11

ASHBOURNE (Derbys) SK1846 Map 7

Smiths Tavern

St Johns St; bottom of market place

There's a new licensee at this archetypal old-fashioned town tavern at the foot of the market place. The attractive bar has horsebrasses and tankards hanging from heavy black beams, a delft shelf of antique blue and white china, old cigarette and drinks advertisements, and a black leatherette wall seat facing the bar counter. Steps take you up to a middle room with leatherette seating around barrel tables, a log-effect gas fire and piano, and beyond that a light and airy end dining room has three nice antique settles among more ordinary seats around simple dining tables. Well kept Marstons Best and Pedigree and two guests on handpump. The weekly changing menu includes soup (£1.75), sandwiches (from £1.50), ploughman's (from £3.50), steak and kidney pie (£4.50), lamb cutlets with port, wine and redcurrant (£5.50), entrecote in red wine (£7.25), pepper fillet steak (£8.95), at least two vegetarian dishes like broccoli and hazelnut bake (£4.25) and a daily roast (£4.50). Good friendly service and atmosphere; darts, cribbage, fruit machine and well chosen and reproduced if not quiet piped pop music. *(Recommended by Paul Robinshaw, Anthony Barker, Wayne Brindle, Mr and Mrs D Lawson; more reports please)*

Marstons ~ Tenants John and Elaine Bishop ~ Real ale ~ Meals and snacks (12-2.30, 7-9.30) ~ (01335) 342264 ~ Children in dining room ~ Maybe piano singalongs Fri, Sun ~ Open 11-3, 5-11; all day Thurs, Fri, Sat

ASHFORD IN THE WATER (Derbys) SK1969 Map 7

Ashford Hotel ⇆ 🍷

Church Street; village signposted just off A6 Bakewell—Buxton

Big helpings of very tasty freshly cooked bar food here include sandwiches (from £2) and filled baked potatoes (from £2.50) till 5pm only, and ploughman's (£4.50), steak and mushroom pie (£4.95), lasagne (£5.25), daily roast (£5.95) and trout with almonds (£6.25); usual children's menu (£1.95). The cosy bar in this handsome stone-built hotel has lots of gleaming brass and copper on the stripped brick of the broad stone inglenook fireplace, plush seats and stools around its traditional cast-iron-framed tables on the patterned carpet, and an imposing bar counter. Friendly neatly dressed staff serve well kept Mansfield Best, Old Baily, Riding Best, one of their seasonal beers, and a guest like Charles Wells Bombardier on handpump; decent wines and lots of malt whiskies. Cribbage, dominoes, fruit machine and piped music. There are tables out in the garden. The village is remarkably pretty and the packhorse bridge is lovely; no-smoking lounge and restaurant; highchairs. *(Recommended by Mary Roebuck, Jack and Philip Paxton, M W Turner, Jamie and Ruth Lyons, Ben Grose, Sue Holland, Dave Webster, Alan and Eileen Bowker, Mr and Mrs R F Wright, David and Michelle Hedges, J Weeks, Pat and Tony Young, Ann and Colin Hunt, Brian and Anna Marsden, G J Parsons)*

Free house ~ Licensees John and Sue Dawson ~ Real ale ~ Meals and snacks (midday-9pm) ~ Restaurant ~ Children in eating area of bar and restaurant ~ (01629) 812725 ~ Open 11-11 ~ Bedrooms £50B/£70B

BIRCH VALE (Derbys) SK0286 Map 7

Waltzing Weasel

A6015 E of New Mills

In the last few years this has been transformed into an attractive traditional inn, with a civilised comfortable bar and good natural cooking. The U-shaped bar has comfortably chatty corners, a cheerful fire, a good longcase clock, some handsome oak settles and tables among more usual furniture, houseplants on corner tables, and lots of mainly sporting Victorian prints; there are daily papers on sticks, well kept Marstons Best and Pedigree on handpump, with interesting guest ales such as Churchills or Hartington, a good choice of decent wines and malt whiskies. Though not cheap, the food is a strong point, with current favourites including crayfish tails in garlic mayonnaise (£5), seafood tart (£8.75) and salmon in shrimp sauce (£12.50); on our inspection visit other dishes included celery soup, duck pâté (£3.75), fresh asparagus (£4), a vegetable tart or chicken curry (£6.75), canelloni (£7.50) and – very early in the seaon – roast lamb (£8.75). Puddings and cheeses are excellent. The charming back restaurant has picture-window views of Kinder Scout and the moors, and these are shared by a pretty garden and terrace. Service is obliging and individual. *(Recommended by Jack Morley, Pat and Tony Young, N Duckworth)*

Free house ~ Licensee Mike Atkinson ~ Real ale ~ Meals and snacks ~ Restaurant ~ (01663) 743402 ~ Children in eating area ~ Open 12-3, 6-11 ~ Bedrooms:£45B/£65B

BIRCHOVER (Derbys) SK2462 Map 7

Druid

Village signposted from B5056

There's a vast selection of over 100 dishes on the blackboards lining the long fairly narrow bar at this dining pub. Some favourites, served generously, are soup (£1.70), olive and rosemary bread (£2.60), spare ribs (£3.95), deep-fried Buxton blue cheese (£3.80), New Zealand lip mussels in garlic cream (£4.20), vegetable Wellington (£5.90), steak and kidney pudding (£6.90), poached salmon steak with gooseberry and ginger (£7.90), honey saddle of lamb with red currant and gooseberry (£10.50), and puddings (from £2.50); half-price helpings for children. It's extremely popular so bookings are advisable for evenings and weekends – you probably won't be able to sit down at all if you're not eating. The bustling bar is small and plain, with plush-upholstered wooden wall benches around straightforward tables, and a big coal fire; the Garden Room is reserved for non-smokers. The spacious and airy two-storey dining extension, candlelit at night, is really the heart of the place, with pink plush seats on olive-green carpet, and pepper-grinders and sea salt on all the tables. Well kept Charles Wells Bombardier, Leatherbritches Ashbourne and Belter (from a new small brewer in Fenny Bentley), Mansfield Bitter and one of their seasonal brews, and Morlands Old Speckled Hen on handpump, and a good collection of malt whiskies; good service. A small public bar has dominoes; well reproduced classical music. There are picnic tables in front. *(Recommended by Nigel Woolliscroft, Cathryn and Richard Hicks, John and Christine Lowe, David and Shelia, Neville Kenyon, D Eberlin, Mike and Wendy Proctor, Yolanda Henry, Jamie and Ruth Lyons, Jack and Philip Paxton, Jack Morley, Mr and Mrs Jones, A P Jeffreys, Pauline Crossland, Dave Cawley, Mrs M A Kilner, Roger and Christine Mash, Sue Grossey, Jim Farmer, Mr and Mrs G Turner, Stephen and Julie Brown*

Free house ~ Licensees Brian Bunce and Nigel Telford ~ Real ale ~ Meals and snacks ~ (01629) 650302 ~ Children welcome if eating but must be gone by 8pm ~ Open 12-3, 7-11; closed 25, 26 Dec pm

Real ale to us means beer which has matured naturally in its cask – not pressurised or filtered.

BRASSINGTON (Derbys) SK2354 Map 7

Olde Gate

Village signposted off B5056 and B5035 NE of Ashbourne

The peaceful public bar in this genuinely unspoilt creeper-covered country local is traditionally furnished, with a lovely old kitchen range with lots of gleaming copper pots, pewter mugs hanging from a beam, embossed Doulton stoneware flagons on a side shelf, an ancient wall clock, and rush-seated old chairs and antique settles (one ancient, partly reframed, black oak solid one). Stone-mullioned windows look across lots of garden tables to small silvery-walled pastures. On the left of a small hatch-served lobby, another cosy beamed room has stripped panelled settles, tables with scrubbed tops, and a roaring fire under a huge mantlebeam. Bar food changing day by day includes big open sandwiches, steak and kidney pie (£6.50), balti dishes (£7.50) and popular summer barbecue – Cajun chicken (£7.15) and lamb steaks (£8.95); good puddings; no chips. Well kept Marstons Pedigree and a guest; good selection of malt whiskies; cribbage and dominoes; no children under 10; no-smoking dining room. The Carsington reservoir is five minutes' drive from the pub and is ideal for water sports and so forth. *(Recommended by Mike and Wendy Proctor, Paul Robinshaw, Jack and Philip Paxton, David Atkinson, Neil and Anita Christopher, A P Jeffreys, Chris Raisin, John and Christine Lowe, D Kudelka, Mr and Mrs S Price, David Eberlin, John Beeken, Alan and Judith Gifford, Peter Marshall, Ann and Colin Hunt, J and PM, Norma and Keith Bloomfield, Andy and Jill Kassube)*

Marstons ~ Tenant Paul Burlinson ~ Real ale ~ Meals and snacks (not Mon and Sun eve in winter) ~ (01629) 540448 ~ Children over 10 ~ Open 12-2.30(3 Sat), 6-11; closed Mon lunchtimes in winter

BURTON-ON-TRENT (Staffs) SK2423 Map 7

Burton Bridge Inn £

24 Bridge St (A50)

Simple and unpretentious, this friendly local has beautifully kept own brew beers on handpump – Burton Bridge Bitter, XL, Porter and Festival. At the moment the brewery is at the back in a long old-fashioned yard (you can go round it on Tuesdays if you book in advance), but it's set to move into a newly acquired building further down the yard. It's then very likely that they will extend the pub; country wines; good choice of malt whiskies. The plain walls in the friendly little front bar are hung with notices, awards and brewery memorabilia; even when it's quiet people tend to spill out into the corridor. Basic but good bar snacks such as chip butties (£1), good filled cobs (from £1.45, hot roast pork or beef £1.75), cheese-filled oatcakes (£2.25), and giant filled yorkshire puddings with ratatouille, faggots and mushy peas, a roast of the day or sausages (from £1.85). The panelled upstairs dining room is open at lunchtime only; there's also a skittle alley, with gas lighting and open fires; dominoes. *(Recommended by John Scarisbrook, Alan and Paula McCully, Richard Lewis, Jack and Philip Paxton, Sue Holland, Dave Webster, Barbara Hatfield, Wayne Brindle)*

Own brew ~ Tenant Kevin McDonald ~ Real ale ~ Lunchtime meals and snacks (not Sun) ~ (01283) 536596 ~ Well behaved children in eating area of bar and in upstairs dining room, until 8pm ~ Open 11.30-2.15, 5.30-11; closed bank hol lunchtimes till 7pm

BUTTERTON (Staffs) SK0756 Map 7

Black Lion ★

Village signposted from B5053

Friendly and unspoilt, this 18th-c stone inn has a series of clean and tidy homely rambling rooms. One welcoming bar has a low black beam-and-board ceiling, lots of brassware and china, a fine old red leatherette settle curling around the walls, well polished mahogany tables, and a good log fire. Off to the left are red plush button-back banquettes around sewing-machine tables and Victorian prints, while an inner room has a fine old kitchen range and a loudly squawking parakeet called Sergeant Bilko. Generous helpings of bar food include soup (£1.60), sandwiches (from £1.75), ploughman's and salads (£4.25), steak and kidney pie, lasagne, vegetarian lasagne and stroganoff (£4.75), mixed grill (£8.25) and daily specials such as cumberland sausage bake or cheese and vegetable bake; puddings like spotted dick (£2.25). The four real ales on handpump might include Bass, McEwans 70/-, Morlands Old Speckled Hen, Theakstons Best and Old Peculier or Youngers No 3; several malt whiskies; a cocktail bar is open weekend evenings. Darts, bar billiards, shove-ha'penny, dominoes, cribbage, table football, table skittles, and separate well lit pool room; piped music. Outside picnic tables and rustic seats on a prettily planted terrace look up to the tall and elegant spire of the local church of this pretty conservation village; pleasant views over the Peak National Park. *(Recommended by Nigel Woolliscroft, Paul Robinshaw, M W Turner, Jack and Philip Paxton, Alan and Judith Gifford, S Howe, Dave Irving, Celia Minoughan, Jack Morley, Mayur Shah, Mrs C Blake, Mike and Wendy Proctor, Jed and Virginia Brown, PACW, David and Shelia, Jenny and Roger Bell, Peter Marshall, Paul and Karen Mason, Eric and Jackie Robinson)*

Free house ~ Licensee Ron Smith ~ Real ale ~ Meals and snacks ~ Restaurant (Fri/Sat eve and Sun lunchtime only) ~ (01538) 304232 ~ Children welcome ~ Open 12-3, 7-11; closed Weds lunchtime ~ Bedrooms: £29.38B/£47B

nr BUXTON (Derbys) SK0673 Map 7

Bull i'th' Thorn

Ashbourne Road (A515) six miles S of Buxton, nr Hurdlow; OS Sheet 119 map reference 128665

The fascinating medieval hall at this solid old place has survived since 1472 when the pub was just known as the Bull. The building's great age becomes apparent as soon as you get to the main entrance, where there's a lively old carving of a bull caught in a thornbush, and others depicting an eagle with a freshly caught hare, and some spaniels chasing a rabbit. The hall has panelled window seats in the embrasures of the thick stone walls, handsome panelling, a massive central beam among a forest of smaller ones, and old flagstones stepping gently down to a big open fire. It's furnished with fine long settles, an ornately carved hunting chair, a longcase clock, a powder-horn, and armour that includes 17th-c German helmets, swords, and blunderbusses and so forth. Despite all this, the atmosphere here is that of any straightforward roadside pub; food includes sandwiches, soup (£1.20), steak and kidney pie, scampi or roast beef (£4), sirloin steak (£7), and puddings (£1.50); Sunday roast (£4.50). An adjoining room has darts, pool, dominoes, fruit machine, juke box; piped music; well kept Robinsons Best and sometimes Best Mild on handpump. The simple family room opens on to a terrace and big lawn, with swings, and there are more tables in a sheltered angle in front. There's a holiday flat and adjacent field for caravans and camping. The pub is handy for the High Peak Trail. Coach parties are welcome. *(Recommended by D G Clarke, Roger and Valerie Hill, Jack and Philip Paxton, Mike and Wendy Proctor, Jean Gustavson, Geoffrey and Irene Lindley, Ann and Colin Hunt, Sarah and Steve de Mellow)*

Robinsons ~ Tenant George Haywood ~ Real ale ~ Meals and snacks ~ Restaurant (only used for big parties) ~ (01298) 83348 ~ Children in family room, pool room and restaurant ~ Occasional weekend live groups and karaoke ~ Open 11.30-3, 6.30-11 ~ Two Bedrooms: £16/£32

CASTLETON SK1583 (Derbys) Map 7

Olde Nags Head

Cross St

In the centre of this village famous for its blue john caverns, this small but solid hotel dating from the 17th-c has been attractively fitted out in period style – heavy cut glasses in the elaborately Victorian dining room, charming wallpaper and elegant woodwork in the upstairs lavatories. The civilised and relaxing Turkey-carpeted main bar (no boots) has a faint nostalgic smell of beeswax, and its interesting furnishings include good 18th-c Derbyshire carved oak chairs and settles liberally spread with red plush cushions, cut ruby glass and china in a wall cabinet, small antique tables, and one grander carved one which on our inspection visit had a magnificently arranged bowl of flowers. Lighting is mainly by the lamps for the pictures, and there's a pretty coal fire; faint piped mandolin music on our visit. Friendly uniformed staff serve well kept Bass and Boddingtons from handpump and good coffee, with peanuts on the bar. A good selection of bar food includes sandwiches (from £2.40), soup (£2.60), filled yorkshire pudding (£2.95), soup and half a sandwich (£3.50), prawn fritters (£4.50), grilled mushrooms filled with tuna (£4.95), and main courses like steak and kidney pie (£5.40), usually five vegetarian dishes which might include leek and mushroom crumble (£5.50), fish and chips (£5.60), warm chicken and bacon salad (£6.75) lamb chops (£6.95), salmon and mange tout tagliatelle (£7.75), chicken breast with asparagus (£8.95). Seasonal puddings are from the restaurant trolley; small portions from the menu for children. ***(Recommended by J F M and M West, JM, PM, L Powell, Jack and Philip Paxton)***

Free house ~ Licensee Mrs Carole Walker ~ Real ale ~ Meals and snacks (12-2, 6.30-10.30) ~ Restaurant ~ (01433) 620248 ~ Children in restaurant ~ Open 11-11 ~ Bedrooms:£42.50B/£56B

CAULDON (Staffs) SK0749 Map 7

Yew Tree ★ ★ £

Village signposted from A523 and A52 about 8 miles W of Ashbourne; OS Sheet 119 map reference 075493

A place that creates tremendous debate and diversity of opinion among readers – a great favourite with many, but not all. Tucked unpropitiously between enormous cement works and quarries, this plain roadside local doesn't from the outside suggest any reason for stopping. When we add to this the fact that it does only the most basic snacks, that its seats are somewhat shabby, and that a very good spring-clean wouldn't come amiss (one of its greatest supporters is plagued by a recurring nightmare in which the public health inspectorate shuts it down), you'll wonder why it has any place in this book – let alone our top star rating. It's because shining through all that is the character of its landlord Alan East and above all the unique fascination of the profusion of bizarre mainly Victorian objects that he's crowded into the pub's dimly lit rooms. Perhaps the most impressive are the working Polyphons and Symphonions – 19th-c developments of the musical box, often taller than a person, each with quite a repertoire of tunes and elaborate sound-effects; go with plenty of 2p pieces to work them. But there's also two pairs of Queen Victoria's stockings, ancient guns and pistols, several penny-farthings, an old sit-and-stride boneshaker, a rocking horse, swordfish blades, and even a fine marquetry cabinet crammed with notable early Staffordshire pottery. Soggily sprung sofas mingle with 18th-c settles and a four-person oak church choir seat with carved heads which came from St Mary's church in Stafford; above the bar is an odd iron dog-carrier (don't ask how it works!). As well as all this there's an expanding set of fine tuneful longcase clocks in the gallery just above the entrance, a collection of six pianolas, including a newly acquired electric one, with an excellent repertoire of piano rolls, a working vintage valve radio set, a crank-handle telephone, a sinuous medieval wind instrument made of leather, and a Jacobean four-poster which was once owned by Josiah Wedgwood and still has the original wig hook on the headboard. Remarkably cheap simple snacks like hot pork pies (65p), meat and potato pies, chicken and mushroom or steak pies (70p), hot big filled baps and sandwiches (from 80p), and quiche or smoked mackerel (£2.30). Beers include Bass, Burton Bridge and M & B Mild on handpump or tapped from the cask, and there are some interesting malt whiskies such as overproof Glenfarclas; drinks prices are very low indeed. Darts, shove-ha'penny, table skittles (taken very seriously here), dominoes and cribbage.

Hiding behind a big yew tree, the pub is difficult to spot – unless a veteran bus is parked outside. Dovedale and the Manifold Valley are not far away. *(Recommended by Mike Woodhead, Hilary Dobbie, Jack and Philip Paxton, Graham Bush, Mike and Wendy Proctor, Mrs C Blake, David and Shelia, John and Christine Lowe, Paul Robinshaw, Nigel Woolliscroft, B Adams, Mayur Shah, Sue Holland, Dave Webster, H K Dyson, Roger and Valerie Hill, Tom McEwan, Roger and Jenny Huggins, Ian and Nita Cooper, Wayne Brindle, JM, PM, David and Ruth Hollands, Stephen and Julie Brown, Brian and Anna Marsden, John and Marianne Cooper, Ann and Colin Hunt, Martin Aust, David Ing, Barbara and Norman Wells, Jim and Maggie Cowell, John Scarisbrick)*

Free house ~ Licensee Alan East ~ Real ale ~ Snacks (11-3, 6-9.30 but generally something to eat any time they're open) ~ (01538) 308348 ~ Children in Polyphon room ~ Pianola most nights – played by the landlord ~ Open 10-3, 6-11

CRESSWELL (Staffs) SJ9739 Map 7

Izaak Walton

Village signposted from Draycott in the Moors, on former A50 Stoke—Uttoxeter

The two neatly kept bars in this smart dining pub have little country pictures, dried flowers on walls and beams, pastel flowery curtains, gentle lighting, a little settee in one window and lots of uniform solid country-kitchen chairs and tables in polished pale wood, going nicely with the fawn carpet. Popular bar food includes soup (£2.25), lunchtime baked potatoes (from £1.60), steak and kidney pie or lasagne (£4.95), chicken and broccoli bake (£5.25), poached salmon (£6.95), a choice of about six vegetarian dishes including broccoli and hazelnut bake (£6.50), and daily blackboard specials like lamb and apricot curry (£5.95), game pie or shoulder or rack of lamb with apricot and ginger sauce (£7.95), grilled Dover sole (£8.95) and a fish of the day. All eating areas are now no smoking. Well kept Marstons Pedigree and Best on handpump; piped music; relaxed friendly service. There's a surcharge of 4% on credit cards. *(Recommended by John Scarisbrick, Henry Barclay, David and Shelia, Sue Holland, David Webster, Paul and Maggie Baker, Eric J Locker; more reports please)*

Free house ~ Licensees Anne and Graham Yates ~ Real ale ~ Meals and snacks 12-2; 6(7 winter)-10 ~ Restaurant ~ (01782) 392265 ~ Children in eating area of bar ~ Open 12-2.30, 6(7 winter)-11; all day Sun; closed 25/26 Dec

DERBY SK3435 Map 7

Alexandra  £

Siddals Rd, just up from station

This solid Victorian pub has an attractive 1920s feel to the refurbishments in the lively bar and more comfortable lounge. Each year they serve about 600 different beers – six quickly changing guests alongside well kept Bass, Batemans XB and Mild, Marstons Pedigree and Youngers No 3; rare farm ciders, country wines and around 20 changing malt whiskies. There are good heavy traditional furnishings on dark-stained floorboards, and lovely local railway photographs and shelves of bottles around its walls (they stock a good range of Belgian beers). Popular food includes filled rolls (from £1), a range of ploughman's (£2.55), good chilli con carne or spaghetti bolognese (£2.30), liver and bacon casserole (£2.95), a vegetarian dish and a range of carefully chosen English cheeses (different every week). Quick cheery service; dominoes, a soundless fruit machine and piped music. They may have bedrooms by the time this Guide appears in print. *(Recommended by Richard Lewis, David and Shelia, Chris Raisin, A Summerfield, Jack and Philip Paxton; more reports please)*

Free house ~ Licensee Mark Robins ~ Real ale ~ Meals and snacks (12-2, not Sun) ~ (01332) 293993 ~ Open 11-2.30, 4.30(6 Sat)-11

We say if we know a pub has piped music.

Brunswick £

1 Railway Terrace; close to Derby Midland railway station

They keep a tremendous range, including their own brews, of fourteen, often obscure, very well kept real ales on handpump, and six more tapped from the cask at this very popular traditional old railway pub. There might be Bass, Batemans Mild, Greene King Abbot, Hook Norton Old Hookey, Marstons Pedigree, Theakstons XB and Best, Timothy Taylors Landlord, and Wards Sheffield. Their own brews – you can see the process – include First Brew, Recessionale Second Brew, Railway Porter, Old Accidental and Owd Abusive, and there's a beer festival in early October; draught farm cider. The marvellously friendly high-ceilinged serving bar has heavy, well padded leather seats, whisky-water jugs above the dado, and a dark blue ceiling and upper wall, with squared dark panelling below. The no-smoking room is decorated with little old-fashioned prints and swan's neck lamps, and has a high-backed wall settle and a coal fire; behind a curved glazed partition wall is a quietly chatty family parlour narrowing to the apex of the triangular building. Darts, cribbage, dominoes, fruit machine; good friendly service. Daily changing home-made bar food includes pork pies (75p), filled salad rolls with turkey, beef and ham (£1), home-made soup (£1.25), hot beef, hot turkey or hot traditional sausage beef cobs (£1.50), home-made beef and onion pie (£1.70), cauliflower cheese (£2.50), and beef and mushroom pie in home-brewed porter (£3.50). There are seats in the terrace area behind. *(Recommended by Richard Lewis, Chris Raisin, David and Shelia, Dorothee and Dennis Glover, John Scarisbrick, Jack and Philip Paxton, Andrew Stephenson, Derek and Sylvia Stephenson, Luke Hundleby, D W Gray)*

Free house ~ Licensee Trevor Harris ~ Real ale ~ Lunchtime meals and snacks 11.30-2.30, (rolls only Sun) ~ Restaurant (not open Sun) ~ (01332) 290677 ~ Children in family parlour and restaurant ~ Jazz Thurs evenings ~ Open 11-11

EYAM (Derbys) SK2276 Map 7

Miners Arms

Signposted off A263 Chesterfield—Chapel-en-le-Frith

There's a pleasant restful atmosphere in these three little plush beamed rooms, each with a stone fireplace. The emphasis is very much on the excellent fresh home-made bar food. At lunchtime this includes light and crispy filled baguettes (£1.95), ploughman's with the area's traditional fruitcake (£3.75) and daily changing blackboard specials like carrot and lentil soup (£1.95), good lamb and mint sausages (£3.95), crayfish tail salad (£4.50), beef braised in stout or braised oxtail (£4.95), chicken breast in cream and prawn sauce (£5.25) or cod or plaice mornay (£5.50); puddings like bakewell pudding or trifle (£1.95); good Sunday roast (no bar food then). Well kept Boddingtons on handpump; friendly service. *(Recommended by C T Harrison, Peter and Anne Hollindale, Prof I H Rorison, KC, John and Christine Lowe, Jack and Philip Paxton, Jack Morley, Cathryn and Richard Hicks, W H and E Thomas, M Baxter, M G Hart)*

Free house ~ Licensees Nicholas and Ruth Cook ~ Real ales ~ Lunchtime meals and snacks (not Sun) ~ Evening restaurant open for Sun lunch ~ (01433) 630853 ~ Children welcome ~ Open 12-3, 7-11; closed Sun night and Mon lunchtime and first 2 weeks Jan ~ Bedrooms: £25B/£45B

FENNY BENTLEY (Derbys) SK1750 Map 7

Coach & Horses

A515 N of Ashbourne

This welcoming and quietly friendly 17th-c coaching inn's pleasant little back room has ribbed green built-in wall banquettes and old prints and engravings on its dark green leafy Victorian wallpaper. There are more old prints in the friendly front bar, which has flowery-cushioned wall settles and library chairs around the dark tables on its Turkey carpet, waggonwheels hanging from the black beams, horsebrasses and pewter mugs, and a huge mirror; two cosy log fires; no-smoking area. Popular very good bar food in generous helpings includes soup (£1.40), baps and sandwiches (from £1.10, toasties from £2.50), burger (£1.60), filled baked potatoes (mostly £3.20), salads (from £4.25), beef madras or chilli (£4.95) or breaded plaice, haddock or seafood platter, steak and kidney pie, chicken and mushroom pie, lasagne or vegetarian lasagne and filled yorkshire puddings (£5.25), chicken and broccoli bake and vegetarian mushroom and stilton bake (£5.50); usual children's menu (£2.25). Well kept Bass and Black Bull Bitter and Dovedale (from a small local brewer) on handpump, good coffee, and pleasant service; darts, dominoes and piped music; picnic tables on the back grass by an elder tree, with rustic benches and white tables and chairs under cocktail parasols on the terrace in front of this pretty rendered stone house. Leave muddy boots outside. *(Recommended by Richard Lewis, Brian Horner, Brenda Arthur, Paul Robinshaw, Basil Minson, D Hanley, Jack Morley, Neil and Anita Christopher, Jack and Philip Paxton, David and Shelia, Eric Locker, John Scarisbrick, Geoffrey and Irene Lindley, R H Sawyer, Alan Kilpatrick, Brian and Anna Marsden, Frank Cummins, Ann and Colin Hunt, Wayne Brindle)*

Free house ~ Licensee Edward Anderson ~ Real ale ~ Meals and snacks ~ Restaurant ~ (01335) 350246 ~ Children welcome ~ Open 11.30-2.30, 6-11; closed 25 Dec

nr FOOLOW (Derbys) SK1976 Map 7

Barrel £

Bretton; signposted from Foolow which itself is signposted from A623 just E of junction with B6465 to Bakewell

Perched on an ancient Roman road, this unspoilt inn has views across five counties. Stubs of massive knocked-through stone walls divide the cosy peaceful beamed bar into several areas – the snuggest is at the far end with an open wood fire, a leather-cushioned settle, and a built-in corner wall-bench by an antique oak table. Decorations include local maps and history, an aerial photograph, a rack of clay pipes, poems about the pub and a clock which moves in an anti-clockwise direction; a Delft shelf has lots of old glass and china bottles, and there's a mix of seats including converted wooden barrels. Tasty good value bar food includes sandwiches (from £1.25; double decker 90p extra, toasties from £1.80), filled baked potatoes (£1.95), open wholemeal baps (from £2.60), salads (from £2.60) and chicken, ham and mushroom pie and country pie (£3.30); daily puddings (£1.50); Bass, Boddingtons and Stones on handpump, and a good choice of whiskies. Darts, cribbage, dominoes. There are seats on the breezy front terrace, and the pub is popular with walkers. *(Recommended by Jack Morley, Ian Rorison, Jack and Philip Paxton, Hilary Dobbie, Andy and Jane Bearsdley, Don Kellaway, Angie Coles, Nigel Woolliscroft, John Cadman, Derek and Sylvia Stevenson, I H Rorison, Mrs F M Halle, Sarah and Gary Goldson, Geoffrey and Irene Lindley, M G Hart, Pauline Crossland, Dave Cawley)*

Free house ~ Licensee Derek Smith ~ Real ale ~ Meals and snacks ~ (01433) 630856 ~ Children welcome ~ Folk on Weds evening ~ Open 12-3, 6.30(7 Sat in winter)-11; 12-11 Sat in summer

FROGGATT EDGE (Derbys) SK2477 Map 7

Chequers 🛏

B6054, off A623 N of Bakewell; Ordnance Survey Sheet 119, map reference 247761

Derbyshire Dining Pub of the Year

Although there is some emphasis on dining at this beautifully placed, well run and fairly smart country inn, there is still a pubby atmosphere in the bar, or you can relax in the peaceful back garden. There are antique prints on the white walls which are partly stripped back to big dark stone blocks, library chairs or small high-backed winged settles on the well waxed floorboards, an attractive, richly varnished beam-and-board ceiling, and a big solid-fuel stove; one corner has a nicely carved oak cupboard. Popular and fairly imaginative bar food efficiently served by smartly dressed staff includes soup of the day (£1.25), big sandwiches served with salad and chips (from £3.55), date and walnut strudel (£4.25), rabbit crumble (£4.75), beef cobbler, broccoli and cream cheese quiche or lasagne (£4.85), slices of pork fillet with smoked ham, pineapple and mozzarella (£4.95), lemon and mustard chicken breast (£5.65); puddings like marmalade bread and butter pudding and peach and chocolate cheesecake (from £1.75). Well kept Wards Best on handpump, about 25 malt whiskies and a good wine list. The restaurant is no smoking; piped music. Froggatt Edge itself is just up through the woods behind the inn; no dogs or boots. *(Recommended by Ian Rorison, R N Hutton, John and Joan Calvert, Wayne Brindle, Jack and Philip Paxton, Elizabeth and Anthony Watts, Sue Holland, Dave Webster, Cathryn and Richard Hicks, Leonard Robinson, Pauline Crossland, Dave Cawley, Peter Marshall, Bob Riley, M G Hart, Dr M V Jones, Ann and Colin Hunt, Margaret and Paul Digby, David and Michelle Hedges, Neville Kenyon, Dawn and Phil Garside, Mark Hydes, CW, JW)*

Wards ~ Lease: E and I Bell ~ Real ale ~ Meals and snacks ~ Restaurant ~ (01433) 630231 ~ Children over 14 in restaurant ~ Open 11-3, 5-11 ~ Bedrooms: £39B/£49B

GRINDLEFORD (Derbys) SK2478 Map 7

Maynard Arms

B6521 N of village

There are fine views from this comfortable hotel in the heart of the Peak District. The smart and spacious high-ceilinged main bar has some dark panelling, tapestry wall hangings, comfortable blue-coloured plush seats on the blue patterned carpet, and silver tankards above the bar. Off the hall there's a smaller no smoking green plush bar for restaurant diners. Good bar food includes soup (£1.50), open sandwiches (from £2.95), mushroom stroganoff (£3.95), lamb lasagne, fried lamb's liver, vegetable and mushroom Wellington or steak and stout pie (£4.25), filled yorkshire pudding or anytime breakfast (£4.50) and minted lamb kebabs; daily changing blackboard specials and home-made puddings (£1.75). Well kept Boddingtons and Whitbreads Castle Eden on handpump; piped music; neatly kept garden. New licensees this year. *(Recommended by Mr and Mrs Jones, Mike and Wendy Proctor, Prof I H Rorison, Paul Robinshaw, John Fahy, David and Fiona Easeman, G W H Kerby, Peter Marshall)*

Free house ~ James Lamb and Christina Henry-Lamb ~ Real ale ~ Meals and snacks ~ Restaurant ~ (01433) 630321 ~ Children in restaurant and eating area of bar until 9.30pm ~ Open 11-3, 6-11; 11-11 Sat ~ Bedrooms: £49B/£65B

HARDWICK HALL (Derbys) SK4663 Map 7

Hardwick Inn

2¾ miles from M1 junction 29: at roundabout A6175 towards Clay Cross; after ½ mile turn left signed Stainsby and Hardwick Hall (ignore any further sign for Hardwick Hall); at Stainsby follow rd to left; after 2½ miles staggered rd junction, turn left

This charming 17th-c golden stone house was originally a lodge for the nearby Elizabethan Hall; it's now owned, along with its splendid park, by the National Trust. Now open all day (except Sunday), the several separate rooms have a relaxed old-fashioned atmosphere. The carpeted lounge has varnished wooden tables, comfortably upholstered wall settles, tub chairs and stools, and stone-mullioned latticed windows. One room has an attractive 18th-c carved settle. Popular bar food includes sandwiches (from £1.85), ploughman's (from £3.10), lincolnshire sausage with egg (£3.35), home-made steak and kidney pie (£4.25), a daily vegetarian dish or grilled trout (£4.50), gammon and egg or pineapple (£4.75) and steaks (from £7.25); puddings (£1.85), and children's menu (from £1.95). Well kept Marstons Pedigree,

Morlands Old Speckled Hen, Theakstons XB and Old Peculier and Youngers Scotch on handpump; friendly staff. There are tables outside with a very nice view; it can get crowded. There's a charge for entry to the park, which you can no longer get into from the inn. *(Recommended by Ian Rorison, David Craine, Ann Reeder, A Preston, A and R Cooper, DC, M W Turner, Stephen and Julie Brown, M D Phillips, Ann and Colin Hunt, Andy and Jill Kassube, J F M West, Mayur Shah, Stephen Jones)*

Free house ~ Lease: Peter and Pauline Batty ~ Real ale ~ Meals and snacks 11.30-9.30 (not Sun evening) ~ Carvery restaurant (Tues-Sat, Sun lunchtime) ~ (01246) 850245 ~ Children in restaurant and eating area of bar only ~ Open 11.30-11

HAYFIELD (Derbys) SK0388 Map 7

Lantern Pike

Little Hayfield; A624 towards Glossop

Outstandingly warm and friendly service from the landlady and her team is the hallmark of this villlage local. It's unpretentious but cosy, comfortable, and spick and span, with a warm fire, plush seats, flowers on the tables, lots of brass platters, china and toby jugs; well kept Boddingtons, Flowers IPA, Timothy Taylors Landlord and a guest such as Mitchells Original on handpump, a good selection of malt whiskies. Good well presented home-made bar food includes soup (£1.95), sandwiches from (£2.25), breaded plaice (£4.60), lasagne, chilli and curry (£4.70) and vegetarian dishes like lasagne or leek and mushroom crumble (£4.95); usual children's menu (£2.25) and several dishes on a specials board which might include steak and stout pie (£4.95), chicken balti (£5.50), chicken zingari (£5.95); Sunday roast (£5.25); darts, dominoes, piped nostalgic pop music. Tables on a two-level stonewalled back terrace, served from a window, look over a big-windowed weaver's house to the Lantern Pike itself, and the pub's very well placed for walkers. *(Recommended by Gwen and Peter Andrews, Mike and Penny Sanders, Robert and Ann Lees, Harriet and Michael Robinson, Mike and Wendy Proctor, Mike Woodhead, J E Rycroft, Gordon, Jack Morley, Tony Short, Mr and Mrs J Ireland, A N Ellis)*

Free house ~ Licensee Gerry McDonald ~ Real ale ~ Meals and snacks (12-2.30, 6-9.30; all day weekends and bank holidays) ~ Restaurant open all day Sun ~ (01663) 747590 ~ Children in eating area of bar ~ Open 11-3, 6-11; all day Sat and Sun ~ Bedrooms: £25B/£35B

HOLMESFIELD (Derbys) SK3277 Map 7

Robin Hood

Lydgate; just through Holmesfield on B6054

The oldest part of this friendly rambling moorland inn is around 300 years old. The wide choice of popular food served by smart pleasant staff might include home-made soup (£1.95), sandwiches (from £2.25), filled jacket potatoes (from £2.25), ploughman's (£4.25), lasagne or chilli (£5.25), honey-glazed ham or steak, ale and mushroom pie (£5.95) and puddings like home-made cheesecake or hot chocolate fudge cake (£2.25); there are also quite a few not so cheap daily specials on the blackboard such as chinese-style spare ribs (£1.95), hot roast beef baps (£3.95), grilled lamb cutlets (£6.95) and pork steak in a horseradish sauce or supreme of chicken in stilton sauce (£8.25), and puddings like syrup sponge or bread and butter pudding (£2.35); usual children's menu. It's best to book at weekends. The neat extended lounge area has exposed beams, chintz and paisley curtains, plush button-back wall banquettes around wood-effect tables, partly carpeted flagstone floors, and lovely open fires; piped music. Outside on the cobbled front courtyard there are stone tables, and opposite the pub are a number of footpaths into the Cordwell valley – the views over Chesterfield and Sheffield are fine. *(Recommended by Comus Elliot, A Preston, JP, Sarah and Steve de Mellow, Andrew Stephenson, Mrs Williams, Mr and Mrs W Normington, Mrs F M Halle)*

Free house ~ Licensees Chris and Jackie Hughes ~ Meals and snacks (11.30-2.30, 6-9.30; all day Sun) ~ (0114 289) 0360 ~ Children welcome if eating ~ Open 11.30-3, 6-11

KINGS NEWTON (Derbys) SK3826 Map 7

Hardinge Arms

5 miles from M1 junction 24; follow signs to E Midlands airport; A453, in 3 miles (Isley) turn right signed Melbourne, Wilson; right turn in 2 miles to Kings Newton; pub is on left at end of village

The rambling front bar at this civilised, friendly and well run old place has open fires, beams, a fine panelled and carved bar counter, and blue plush cushioned seats and stools – some in a pleasantly big bow window.There's also a stately and spacious back lounge, and it's popular with the older set and businessmen. The home-made bar food includes sandwiches, salads and various dishes of the day (from £4), and shows what can be done with standbys like steak and kidney pie (£5) and roast beef (£6). Well kept Bass and Ind Coope Burton on handpump, and several malt whiskies; table skittles (Sunday evening only), dominoes; piped music; large car park. *(Recommended by Jack and Philip Paxton, SS, I D Irving, Wayne Brindle; more reports please)*

Free house ~ Licensee Michael Johnson ~ Real ale ~ Meals and snacks (not Mon evenings) ~ (01322) 863808 ~ Children in eating area of bar until 8pm ~ Open 11-2.30, 6-11

KIRK IRETON (Derbys) SK2650 Map 7

Barley Mow

Signposted off B5023 S of Wirksworth

The quietly peaceful pubby atmosphere in the unspoilt little rooms of this handsome Jacobean stone house probably hasn't changed much since it first became an inn some 200 years ago. The timeless small main bar has antique settles on the tiled floor or built into the panelling, a coal fire, old prints, shuttered mullioned windows – and a simple wooden counter behind which reposes a tempting row of casks of real ales, kept well and sold cheaply, such as Adnams, Batemans XXB, Charles Wells Bombardier, Greene King, Hook Norton Best and Old Hookey, Marstons Pedigree, Timothy Taylors Landlord or Wadworths 6X; also Thatcher's farm cider. Another room has cushioned pews built in, oak parquet flooring and a small woodburner, and a third has more pews, tiled floor, beams and joists, and big landscape prints. Filled lunchtime rolls; good value evening meals for residents only. Civilised old-fashioned service, a couple of friendly pugs and a somnolent newfoundland, dominoes and cribbage; one no-smoking room. There's a good-sized garden, as well as a couple of benches out in front; small charming village in good walking country. *(Recommended by A J and M Thomasson, Jack and Philip Paxton, Graham and Lynn Mason, JM, PM, David Eberlin, Michel Hooper-Immins; more reports please)*

Free house ~ Licensee Mary Short ~ Real ale ~ Lunchtime snacks ~ (01335) 370306 ~ Children at lunchtime, not in bar ~ Open 12-2, 7-11 ~ Bedrooms: £25.50B/£37.75B

LITTLE HUCKLOW (Derbys) SK1678 Map 7

Old Bulls Head

Pub signposted from B6049

Well worth a weekend visit (it's now shut for most of the week) this friendly spick and span little village pub has two atmospheric rooms with old oak beams, thickly cushioned built-in settles, interesting collections of locally mined semi-precious stones, antique brass and iron household tools, and a coal fire in a neatly restored stone hearth. One room is served from a hatch, the other over a polished bar counter. Tasty home-made bar food includes sandwiches (from £1.95), filled yorkshire puddings (£3), ploughman's (£3.95), lasagne (£4.95), salmon in asparagus sauce or chicken in leek and stilton sauce (£5), steak and kidney pie (£5.25), poached salmon in a rich asparagus sauce (£5), mixed grill (£7.95) and puddings like rhubarb crumble from a blackboard. Well kept Stones Best from carved handpumps; a good range of well reproduced piped classical music, dominoes. There are tables in the neatly tended garden, which is full of an unusual collection of well restored and attractively painted old farm machinery. *(Recommended by Jack and Phil Paxton, R N Hutton, Basil Minson, DC, Geoffrey and Irene Lindley, Ann and Colin Hunt, Susan Boyle, Eugene Wills, Peter Marshall)*

Free house ~ Licensee Mrs Rita Saxon ~ Real ale ~ Meals and snacks ~ (01298) 871097 ~ Children welcome ~ Cl Mon-Thurs; open Fri-Sun 7-11, also 12-3 Sat and Sun

LITTLE LONGSTONE (Derbys) SK1971 Map 7

Packhorse

Monsal Dale and Ashford Village signposted off A6 NW of Bakewell; follow Monsal Dale signposts, then turn right into Little Longstone at Monsal Head Hotel

The licensee, locals and even the dog offer a marvellously warm welcome at this snug and atmospheric little 16th-c cottage. The two traditional and cosy rooms are simply furnished with country kitchen chairs, cloth-cushioned settles and a more unusual almost batwinged corner chair under the beam-and-plank ceiling. Around the walls are a collection of prettily hung decorative mugs, brass spigots, attractive landscape photographs by Steve Riley, blow-ups of older local photographs and the odd cornet or trumpet. Good, popular bar food includes baps spread with dripping and generously filled with hot well hung beef or with hot pork, apple sauce and stuffing (£2), soup (£2.25) spare ribs (which are a meal in themselves) or stilton garlic mushrooms (£3.25), ploughman's (£4.50), probably three vegetarian dishes like cheese and spinach cannelloni (£4.95), or very tasty, filling steak and kidney pie (£5), lamb steak in stilton sauce (£6.60), steaks or chicken with lemon and coriander (£7.95), and puddings like brandy roulade or steamed puddings (£2.25). Well kept Marstons Best or Pedigree on handpump; darts, dominoes, cribbage. In the steep little garden there's a new terrace, goats and rabbits. *(Recommended by Mike and Wendy Proctor, A J Payne, Nigel Woolliscroft, Paul Robinshaw, Jack Morley, Derek and Sylvia Stephenson, Comus Elliot, Jack and Philip Paxton, David and Shelia, Bronwen and Steve Wrigley, M G Hart, John Fahy, J and PM)*

Marstons ~ Tenants Lynne and Mark Lythgoe ~ Real ale ~ Meals and snacks (12-2, 7-9) ~ Restaurant (Thurs-Sat, bookings only) ~ (01629) 640471 ~ Well behaved children in eating area lunchtime and perhaps early eve ~ Live music Wed nights ~ Open 11-3, 5(6 on Sat)-11; closed 25 Dec evening

nr MELBOURNE (Derbys) SK3825 Map 7

John Thompson

Ingleby; village signposted from A514 at Swarkestone

This large and friendly popular pub takes its name from the enthusiastic landlord who both owns it and brews its highly praised JTS Bitter (you can buy their home-brew kits); Bass is also available on handpump. The big, pleasantly modernised lounge has ceiling joists, some old oak settles, button-back leather seats, sturdy oak tables, antique prints and paintings, and a log-effect gas fire; a couple of smaller cosier rooms open off, with pool, a fruit machine, and a juke box in the children's room, and a no-smoking area in the lounge. As last year, well priced, good but straightforward bar food consists of sandwiches (nothing else on Sundays; the beef is excellent), or a set meal of soup, a cold buffet with very good meats or excellent hot roast beef (£5, not Mondays) and well liked puddings; friendly efficient service. It's in a lovely setting above the River Trent, with lots of tables on the well kept lawns by flowerbeds, and on a partly covered outside terrace with its own serving bar. *(Recommended by Eric Locker, A and R Cooper, J Honnor, J F M West, Jack and Philip Paxton, Wayne Brindle, R J Herd, David and Shelia, Dorothee and Dennis Glover, Cdr Patrick Tailyour, John and Christine Simpson)*

Own brew ~ Licensee John Thompson ~ Real ale ~ Lunchtime meals and snacks (snacks only Sun; cold buffet only, Mon) ~ (01332) 862469 ~ Children in separate room ~ Open 10.30-2.30, 7-11

MONSAL HEAD (Derbys) SK1871 Map 7

Monsal Head Hotel

B6465

The cosy side stable bar once housed the horses which lugged people and their luggage up from the station deep down at the end of the valley viaduct. There's still a bit of a horsey theme, with stripped timber horse-stalls, harness and brassware, as well as flagstones, a big warming woodburning stove in an inglenook, cushioned oak pews around flowery-clothed tables, farm tools, and railway signs and lamps from the local disused station; steps lead up into a crafts gallery. Well kept John Smiths, Marstons Pedigree, Morlands Old Speckled Hen, Ruddles Best and County, and Theakstons Old Peculier on handpump; farm cider; helpful staff; darts. Bar food includes lasagne or ham and mushroom tagliatelle (£4.25), plaice or scampi and a couple of vegetarian dishes like bulgar wheat and walnut casserole (£4.50), home-made leek and mushroom au gratin (£4.75), home-made steak and kidney pie (£5.75), rabbit pie (£8.95), pheasant braised in madeira (£9.50) and mixed grill (£10.50); Sunday roast (£5.95). The back garden has a play area; shove-ha'penny, dominoes. The really dramatic views down the steep Monsal Dale valley to the River Wye are best seen from the front terrace or the upstairs sunlounge of this extended Victorian hotel. Its spacious high-ceilinged front bar is set out like a wine bar, with dining chairs around big tables; it's partitioned off from a no-smoking restaurant area. *(Recommended by Jack and Philip Paxton, Mike and Wendy Proctor, Roger and Valerie Hill, David and Shelia, Phil and Heidi Cook, K Flack, A Preston, Derek and Sylvia Stephenson, John Fahy, Sarah and Gary Goldson, Carolyn Eaton, Mark Watkins, Gwen and Peter Andrews, David and Michelle Hedges)*

Free house ~ Licensee Nicholas Smith ~ Real ale ~ Meals and snacks (12-2.30, 6-9.30) ~ Restaurant ~ (01629) 640250 ~ Children welcome, but not after 7 in Stable bar ~ Open 11-11; closed 25 Dec ~ Bedrooms: £17.50(£20B)/£35(£40B); must be dinner and B&B for two nights at weekends)

ONECOTE (Staffs) SK0555 Map 7

Jervis Arms 

B5053, off A523 Leek—Ashbourne

Doing really well in all respects this bustling 17th-c pub is one of the very few really special family pubs. It's in a lovely moorland setting on the banks of the River Hamps (the licensee does warn that this isn't safe for children) with picnic tables under cocktail parasols on the ashtree-sheltered lawn, a little shrubby rockery, slides and swings, play trees, and a footbridge leading to the car park. Inside, the irregularly shaped main bar has white planks over shiny black beams, window-seats, wheelback chairs, two or three unusually low plush chairs, little hunting prints on the walls, and Toby jugs and decorative plates on the high mantlepiece of its big stone fireplace. A similar but simpler inner room has a fruit machine. There are two family rooms with high chairs. Very well kept Bass, Marstons Pedigree, Ruddles County, Theakstons XB, Old Peculier and Mild, Websters Yorkshire and Worthington on handpump, a fair range of malt whiskies, and Scrumpy Jack cider. Generous helpings of good bar food include soup (£1.20), filled rolls (£1.60), filled baked potatoes (from £3.75), home-made chilli or cottage pie (£3.95), ploughman's (from £4.25), home-cooked ham or roast topside of beef (£4.50), curried nut, fruit and vegetable pie or savoury cheesecake (£4.75), steaks (from £8.25) and puddings including a selection of hot sponges or banana split (£1.95); usual children's meals (from £1.25); very friendly landlord and staff. Darts, dominoes, cribbage, fruit machine, and piped music. A spacious barn behind the pub has been converted to self-catering accommodation; mother and baby room. *(Recommended by Mike and Wendy Proctor, Nigel Woolliscroft, Richard Lewis, Jack and Philip Paxton, John Scarisbrook, Paul Robinshaw, DMT, John Beeken, Susan Boyle, Martin Aust, Myke and Nicky Crombleholme)*

Free house ~ Licensees Robert and Jean Sawdon ~ Real ale ~ Meals and snacks (till 10pm) ~ (01538) 304206 ~ Children welcome, three family rooms ~ Open 12-2.30, 7(6 Sat)-11; all day Sun; closed 25/26 Dec ~ Self-catering barn (with two bedrooms); £125 a week for the whole unit

OVER HADDON (Derbys) SK2066 Map 7

Lathkil

Village and inn signposted from B5055 just SW of Bakewell

Perched on a hillside looking steeply down into Lathkil Dale – one of the quieter dales, with an exceptionaly harmonious spread of pastures and copses – is the little hamlet of Over Haddon, possibly the best situated Derbyshire village. Paths from the village take you straight into this tempting landscape, which has a lot to interest the nature lover. This happily positioned no-nonsense but comfortable place makes the most of the marvellous views, and welcomes walkers (there's a place for muddy boots in the lobby) and at the same time offers some good civilised comforts. The airy room on the right has a warming fire in the attractively carved fireplace, old-fashioned settles with upholstered cushions or plain wooden chairs, black beams, a Delft shelf of blue and white plates on one white wall, original prints and photographs, and big windows. On the left is the spacious and sunny family dining area – partly no smoking – which doubles as a restaurant in the evenings; at lunchtime the bar food is served here from a buffet and includes home-made soup (£1.50), filled cobs (from £1.85), salads (£4.30), beef curry (£4.95), lasagne (£5.10), steak and kidney pie (£5.60), smoked trout (£5.70), and home-made puddings like treacle tart (from £1.95); in the evening a short slightly more expensive menu includes spicy chicken breast with mango chutney (£6.90) and lamb cutlets with red currant jelly (£7.80). Well kept Wards Best, Mild and Thorne Best on handpump; select malt whiskies and new world wine; piped classical music or jazz, shove-ha'penny, dominoes, cribbage. Best to get here early in good weather. *(Recommended by Jack and Philip Paxton, Nigel Woolliscroft, Dorothee and Dennis Glover, Michael and Harriet Robinson, Gwen and Peter Andrews, Prof I H Rorison, Tony Young, Ian Jones, Helen Pickering, Ian Rorison, Mike and Wendy Proctor, L P Thomas, C J Scott, Basil Minson, John Waller, Dr Peter Donahue, Bob Riley, W H and E Thomas, Sue Holland, Dave Webster, Donald Clay, Sarah and Gary Goldson, Andrew Stephenson, Ann and Colin Hunt, John Fahy, Mrs F M Halle, Roger and Christine Mash, Barbara Hatfield, A M McCarthy, Simon Morton, L W Baal)*

Free house ~ Licensee Robert Grigor-Taylor ~ Real ale ~ Lunchtime meals and snacks ~ Evening restaurant (residents only Sun) ~ (01629) 812501 ~ Children in eating area of bar at lunchtime – but must eat a meal ~ Open 11.30-3, 6.30-11 ~ Bedrooms: £32.50S/£60B

SHARDLOW (Derbys) SK4330 Map 7

Hoskins Wharf

3½ miles from M1 junction 24; A6 towards Derby, pub on left

This converted 18th-c warehouse is undergoing further fairly major refurbishments, as Mansfield Brewery turn it into a family dining operation. Keeping our fingers crossed, we've left it in the main entries as its chief charm has always been in the interesting and imposing building and its canal basin surroundings. It is a conversion of a striking tall 18th-c brick-built warehouse, and a branch of the canal actually flows through a sweeping arch in the middle of the bottom bar; to reach the pub you go across a counter-weighted drawbridge. Picture windows overlook the canal basin; there's lots of stripped brickwork, heavy beams and brick flooring. Beers should be from the good Mansfield range – Riding, Traditional and Old Baily. There's plenty of space outside among the weeping willows on a sort of island between the canal branches. *(Reports please)*

Mansfield ~ Real ale ~ Meals and snacks

Old Crown

Cavendish Bridge

This thriving 17th-c coaching inn is well liked for its very good food and interesting range of rather more unusual well kept real ales, so you need to arrive early to be sure of a seat. The menu includes filled rolls or sandwiches (from £1.35), salads (from £4.25), tomato and vegetable tagliatelle (£4.95), seafood platter (£5.95), sirloin steak (£7.75) and puddings (£1.60). Interesting daily specials go in for strong tastes: kidneys, bacon and cumberland sausage provençale or beef and kidney pudding (£5.50), haddock and broccoli puff pie, beef in red wine, stuffed leg of lamb or pork loin rolled with liver, sausage meat, bacon, prunes and stilton (£5.95), sole fillet poached in champagne and cream (£6.25) and chicken breast with ginger, dijon mustard and sherrry (£6.50). They now have planning permission for a restaurant, and will do evening food when it's built. Including guests (nearly always local) they serve well kept Bass, Boddingtons, Felinfoel Double Dragon, Lloyds VIP, Marstons Pedigree, Rudgate Battleaxe, Woodfordes Norfolk Nog, Worth Backside and a beer brewed for them called Wide Eyed and Crownless; nice choice of malt whiskies. The busy friendly beamed bar is full of amazing bric-a-brac including hundreds of jugs and mugs hanging from the beamed ceiling, brewery and railway memorabilia, and lots of pictures. Cribbage and piped music. The garden has a children's play area. *(Recommended by Andrew Stephenson, Alan and Eileen Bowker, Mike Pugh, Andy and Jane Bearsdley, Dr and Mrs J H Hills, Jack and Philip Paxton, Chris Raisin, Wayne Brindle, A and R Cooper, Harry and Irene Fisher)*

Free house ~ Licensees Peter and Gillian Morton-Harrison ~ Real ale ~ Lunchtime meals and snacks ~ (01332) 792392 ~ Children in eating area of bar only ~ Open 11.30-3, 5-11; cl evenings 25/26 Dec

SHRALEYBROOK (Staffs) SJ7850 Map 7

Rising Sun

3 miles from M6 junction 16; from A500 towards Stoke take first right turn signposted Alsager, Audley; in Audley turn right on the road still shown on many maps as A52, but now in fact a B, signposted Balterley, Nantwich; pub then signposted on left (at the T-junction look out for the Watneys Red Barrel)

The lively easy-going atmosphere and an impressive range of beers produced in the brewery behind the pub – usually five appropriately named ones like Dusk, Flare, Rising, Setting, Sunstroke, maybe a stronger brew called Total Eclipse – are the main attractions here; also guest beers from Burton Bridge, Eldridge Pope, Tomintoul and Wadworths. As well as these, there are around 120 malts, 12 cognacs and 100 liqueurs; and foreign beers from Belgium, Germany, Singapore, Spain, and Australia. Food is mostly simple with good pizzas (from £3), cheeseburger (£4), 17 different vegetarian pot meals (£6.50) and beef casserole (£7); friendly service. The well worn, casual bar – at times full of a younger crowd – has shiny black panelling and beams and timbers in the ochre walls, red leatherette seats tucked into the timberwork and cosy alcoves, brasses and some netting, dim lighting, curtains made from beer towels sewn together, and a warm open fire. Dominoes, fruit machine and piped music, possibly an energetic blues club upstairs on Thursday nights. *(Recommended by Sue Holland, Dave Webster, Nigel Woolliscroft, Richard Lewis, Paul and Gail Betteley, Mr and Mrs R J Grout, P Yearsley, David and Shelia, Peter and Lynn Brueton, John Scarisbrook, Derek and Sylvia Stephenson, Mike and Wendy Proctor, John and Joan Nash, Mark and Diane Griast, Dave Braisted, Andrew Stephenson, M S and M Imhoff, Bill and Lydia Ryan)*

Own brew ~ Licensee Mrs Gillian Holland ~ Real ale ~ Meals and snacks (12-2.30, 6.30-10.30) ~ Restaurant ~ (01782) 720600 ~ Children welcome until 9pm unless in restaurant ~ Open 12-3.30, 6.30-11; 12-11 Fri and Sat

TATENHILL (Staffs) SK2021 Map 7

Horseshoe

Off A38 at A5121 Burton exit – then signposted; OS Sheet 128 map reference 203217

Despite this sensitively modernised old pub's popularity, there is plenty of room in its cosy communicating areas. The tile-floored Tap Bar with booth seats and some standing timbers has a family area at the back with a pleasant garden view through picture windows; the square-panelled front part has a flowery carpet, a delft shelf with antique bottles and pictorial plates, and on the left is a smallish self-contained area with a woodburning stove and wheelback chairs around a few tables divided off from the rest by timber and wrought iron. Very quickly served good value bar food includes home-made soup (£1.25), rolls and sandwiches (from £1.70), burgers (from £2.35), ploughman's and vegetarian dishes like nut roast (from £3.75), filled yorkshire pudding, baked potatoes or breaded plaice (£3.95), steak and kidney pie (£4.35), salads (from £4.60), grilled trout (£4.85) and steaks (from £5.95); children's menu (from £2); you must book for the Sunday lunch in the cosy pitched-roof two-level restaurant. Particularly well kept Marstons Pedigree and a guest on handpump, and in winter Owd Roger under light blanket pressure; wines from all ten beaujolais village appellations, direct from the growers; dominoes, cribbage, fruit machine, piped music. The garden has plenty of tables either on the terrace or among small trees, and an enclosed play area on wood chippings with a fort and a huge timber climber; the grill room is no smoking. *(Recommended by Joan and Tony Walker, Peter and Audrey Dowsett, Eric Locker, Dorothee and Dennis Glover, Dave Braisted, Ian and Emma Potts)*

Marstons ~ Tenant Michael Bould ~ Real ale ~ Meals and snacks (all day Sat, not Sun evening) ~ Restaurant (not Sun evening) ~ (01283) 564913 ~ Children in eating area of bar, and in restaurant if over 10 ~ Open 11.30-3, 5.30-11; Sat 11.30-11; closed evening 25 Dec

TUTBURY (Staffs) SK2028 Map 7

Olde Dog & Partridge

A444 N of Burton on Trent

Staffordshire Dining Pub of the Year

The main attraction at this civilised 15th-c dining pub is the excellent carvery restaurant (roast of the day £6.95, prime sirloin of beef with big yorkshire pudding £7.75), so popular that the bar menu is limited to soup (£1.50), sandwiches (from £1.75, open from £2.65) and ploughman's from (£2.75); puddings are from the cold counter in the carvery (from £1.95). Much of the extensive carvery is no smoking and you need to arrive early to be sure of a table; a pianist plays each evening. The stylish bar has two warm Turkey-carpeted rooms, one with red plush banquettes and rather close-set studded leather chairs, sporting pictures, stags' heads and a sizeable tapestry, the other with a plush-cushioned oak settle, an attractive built-in window seat, brocaded stools and a couple of Cecil Aldin hunting prints. Well kept Marstons Pedigree and a guest beer like Morlands Old Speckled Hen or Youngers Special from the small oak bar counter, freshly squeezed orange, and decent wines, some on draught; friendly efficient service. The half timbered frontage is prettily hung with hanging baskets and the neat garden has white cast-iron seats and tables under cocktail parasols, with stone steps between its lawns, bedding plants, roses and trees. The pub is near Tutbury Castle, where Mary Queen of Scots was imprisoned on the orders of Elizabeth I. *(Recommended by Clive Gilbert, Derek and Sylvia Stephenson, I D Irving, Derek and Margaret Underwood, Paul Robinshaw, Peter and Audrey Dowsett, Mrs S Beniston, Ralph and Lorna Lewis, G J Parsons, JM, PM, Wayne Brindle, Mrs S Beniston, David and Shelia, David Wright)*

Free house ~ Licensee Mrs Yvette Martindale ~ Real ale ~ Lunchtime meals and snacks (not Sun) ~ Carvery ~ (01283) 813030 ~ Children welcome ~ Evening and Sunday lunch pianist ~ Open 11-3, 6-11; closed 25/26 Dec ~ Bedrooms: £52.50B/£72.50B

WARDLOW (Derbys) SK1875 Map 7

Three Stags Heads

Wardlow Mires; A623 by junction with B6465

There's a simple unspoilt atmosphere at this friendly little white-painted cottage where walkers, their boots and dogs are welcome; they have four dogs (and some cats) of their own, so the unassuming interior is fairly well worn. The tiny parlour bar has old leathercloth seats, a couple of antique settles with flowery cushions, two high-backed Windsor armchairs and simple oak tables on the flagstones, and a cast-iron kitchen range which is kept alight in winter; one curiosity is the petrified cat in a glass case. Tables in the small, no-smoking dining parlour – where there's an open fire – are bookable. They try to vary the seasonal menu to suit the weather so dishes served on their home-made plates (the barn is a pottery workshop) might include a three-cheese ploughman's (£5), vegetarian dishes like vegetable and apricot casserole or leek and stilton hot pot (from £5), rabbit in mustard and herbs (£6.50), chicken breast in wine with chunky vegetables or rack of lamb (£7); friendly service. Kelham Island Pale Rider and Fat Cat (both brewed by our Sheffield main entry – see Yorks chapter), Springhead Bitter from the little Springhead brewery in Sutton-on-Trent, and Hoskins & Oldfields Old Navigation on handpump, and lots of continental and British bottled beers. Cribbage and dominoes, nine men's morris and chess. The front terrace looks across the main road to the distant hills. The car park is across the road by the petrol station. *(Recommended by Jack Morley, Nigel Woolliscroft, Jack and Philip Paxton, R N Hutton, Comus Elliot, Derek and Sylvia Stephenson, Brian and Anna Marsden, Mike and Wendy Proctor, Peter Lecomber, John Fahy, Bill and Lydia Ryan, Andrew Stephenson)*

Free house ~ Licensees Geoff and Pat Fuller ~ Real ale ~ Meals and snacks (12-3, 7-10) ~ Restaurant ~ (01298) 872268 ~ Children may be allowed until 8.30pm ~ Live folk and Irish music Fri/Sat evening and Sun lunch ~ Open 12-3, 7-11; 12-11 Sat

WARSLOW (Staffs) SK0858 Map 7

Greyhound

B5053 S of Buxton

There's a warm cheery welcome at this plain slated stone building, which takes its name from the Buxton to Uttoxeter coach which used to stop here. The cosy long beamed bar has cushioned oak antique settles (some quite elegant), a log fire, houseplants in the windows, and quietly restrained landscapes on the cream walls. Big helpings of good home-made bar food include filling soup (£1.75), sandwiches (from £1.80), filled baked potatoes (from £3.25), ploughman's (from £4.50), home-made steak, mushroom and ale pie, lasagne or vegetarian curry (£4.95), steak (from £8); puddings (£2), while daily specials might include minted lamb casserole, chicken in leek and cream sauce, chicken and broccoli in creamy peppercorn sauce, seafood mornay or sweet and sour pork (£5.25); traditional Sunday roast (£4.95) and good breakfasts. Well kept Marstons Pedigree and a guest beer such as Burton Bridge

Bitter, Everards Tiger, Jennings Cumberland or Timothy Taylors Landlord on handpump. Pool room, with darts, dominoes, cribbage, and fruit machine; piped classical music at lunchtimes. The simple bedrooms are comfortable and clean. There are picnic tables under ash trees in the side garden, with rustic seats out in front; handy for the Manifold Valley, Alton Towers and Dovedale. The licensees also run the Devonshire Arms in Hartington. *(Recommended by Mike and Wendy Proctor, Paul Robinshaw, Mrs C Blake, Derek and Sylvia Stephenson, R H and V A Rowley, Mr and Mrs H Brierly; more reports please)*

Free house ~ Licensees David and Dale Mullarkey ~ Real ale ~ Meals and snacks ~ (01298) 84249 ~ Children in eating area of bar until 9pm ~ Live 60s/rock and roll music Sat night ~ Open 12-2.30(2 in winter), 7-11; cl Mon lunchtime exc bank holidays, then cl the following Tues lunchtime ~ Bedrooms: £16.50/£33

WETTON (Staffs) SK1055 Map 7

Olde Royal Oak

Off B5053 via Butterton; or off A515 via Hopedale

Set in lovely National Trust walking country, this aged white-painted and shuttered stone village house has a relaxed and timeless atmosphere. The older part of the building has black beams supporting the white ceiling boards (to which a collection of golf clubs has been attached), small dining chairs sitting around rustic tables, a piano surrounded by old sheet music covers, an oak corner cupboard, and a log fire in the stone fireplace; this room extends into a more modern-feeling area with another fire which in turn leads to a carpeted sun lounge looking out on to the small garden. Bar food includes sandwiches (from £1.25), filled baked potatoes (from £1.95), ploughman's (from £3.80 with local cheeses), salads (from £4.35), lasagne (£4.75), local trout (£4.95) and steak (£8.95), puddings like chocolate fudge cake or cheesecake (from £1.95), and children's meals (from £1.95). Well kept Eldridge Pope Royal Oak, Ruddles County and Rutland, Theakstons XB, and a weekly guest beer on handpump, about 18 malt whiskies, and Addlestones cider; darts, dominoes, cribbage, shove-ha'penny and piped music. Places like Wetton Mill and the Manifold Valley are nearby, and behind the pub is a croft suitable for caravans and tents. *(Recommended by Mike and Wendy Proctor, Paul Robinshaw, Jack and Philip Paxton, Paul Perry, Jeanne and Tom Barnes; more reports please)*

Free house ~ Licensee George Burgess ~ Real ale ~ Meals and snacks (not winter Sun evenings) ~ (01335) 310287 ~ Children in family room ~ Open 11.30-3, 6.30-11; 12-2.30, 7.30-11 in winter ~ Bedrooms: /£38S

WHITTINGTON MOOR (Derbys) SK3873 Map 7

Derby Tup £

387 Sheffield Rd; B6057 just S of A61 roundabout

On the outskirts of Chesterfield, this straightforward corner pub keeps a splendid range of real ales on handpump. The regulars are Batemans XB, Exmoor Gold, Kelham Island Fat Cat, Marstons Pedigree, Tetleys, Timothy Taylors Landlord and Theakstons XB and Old Peculier, and there are two quickly changing guest beers – on our inspection visit, Cotleigh Barn Owl and Robinsons Hatters Mild. They also have lots of continental and bottle-conditioned beers, and decent malt whiskies. The unspoiled plain rectangular bar with frosted street windows and old dark brown linoleum has simple furniture arranged around the walls – there's a tremendously long aged red plastic banquette – leaving lots of standing room; two more small unpretentious rooms; fruit machine. Besides sandwiches, the food, changing daily and almost all home-cooked with fresh ingredients, might include mushroom soup (£1.50), spaghetti bolognese or cauliflower cheese (£2.95), chilli con carne or chicken casserole (£3.95) and chicken escalopes in plum sauce or Thai chicken in a delicious creamy peanut sauce (£4.25); efficient, informally friendly landlord, cheerful relaxed atmosphere, darts, cribbage, dominoes, piped rock and blues.

(Recommended by Jack and Philip Paxton, Ian Keenleyside, Andy and Jill Kassube, Peter Marshall, Margaret and Paul Digby)

Free house ~ Licensee David Williams ~ Real ale ~ Meals and snacks (12-2.30, 5 (6 Sat)-7.30; not Sun evening) ~ (01246) 454316 ~ Children in eating area ~ Open 11.30-3, 5(6 Sat)-11

WOOLLEY MOOR (Derbys) SK3661 Map 7

White Horse

Badger Lane, off B6014 Matlock—Clay Cross

The enthusiastic licensees here keep a good balance between the popular food served in the cottagey beamed dining lounge and the original tap room where the cheerful locals gather to organise their two football teams, two boules teams, darts, dominoes and quiz teams – and to enjoy the well kept Bass and Batemans Mild and three guests like Towns Brewery Sunshine or Wards Waggledance on handpump; decent wine. The good value bar food made with local produce is from a choice of about a dozen daily specials which might include kidneys turbigo or moussaka (£4.75), chicken, stilton and cashew nut pie (£4.95), beef cooked with orange and walnuts (£5.25) and fresh salmon and leek tagliatelle (£5.50); also sandwiches (from £2.20), ploughman's (£3.50), steak and kidney pie (£3.95) and game pie (£4); puddings like banana and caramel pie, lemon and ginger crunch and treacle sponge (£2); small no-smoking room at the side of the dining room. There are lovely views across the Amber Valley from the picnic tables in the garden and a very good children's play area with wooden play train, climbing frame and swings for all ages. A booklet describes eight walks from the pub, and the landlord is a keen walker; the pub is handy for Ogden Reservoir. They hold several real ale festivals a year. *(Recommended by Derek and Sylvia Stephenson, John and Christine Lowe, Norma and Keith Bloomfield, Peter and Audrey Dowsett, Geoffrey and Irene Lindley, David and Shelia, Pat and Tony Young, Jack and Philip Paxton, Paul Robinshaw, John Beeken, John Fahy, Ian Jones, Alan and Judith Gifford, Jenny and Brian Seller, R N Hutton, D Kudelka, JJW, CMW, John Honnor, Alan and Judith Gifford)*

Free house ~ Licensees Bill and Jill Taylor ~ Real ale ~ Meals and snacks (11.30-2, 6.30-9; not Sun evening) ~ Restaurant (not Sun evening) ~ (01246) 590319 ~ Children in eating area of lounge bar if eating and in restaurant ~ Open 11.30-2.30(3 Sat), 6.30-11

Lucky Dip

Besides the fully inspected pubs, you might like to try these Lucky Dips recommended to us and described by readers (if you do, please send us reports):

☆ **Abbots Bromley**, Staffs [Mkt Pl; SK0724], *Crown*: Very friendly new licensees doing well, food all fresh inc vegetarian and even home-made chips, well kept Bass and Worthington, spotless much modernised lounge and bright public bar with games; children welcome; good bedrooms *(Dennis D'Vigne, C Whittington, LYM)*

☆ **Abbots Bromley** [High St], *Coach & Horses*: Comfortable and attractive well run Tudor village pub, good helpings of well prepared food in refurbished beamed bar and restaurant, well kept Bass and related beers, friendly staff; good bedrooms *(M A Robinson, D Hanley, H and T Dyal, Tim Bucknall)*

☆ **Abbots Bromley** [Bagot St], *Royal Oak*: Wide choice of good partly Dutch-inspired food in clean, comfortable and attractive dining lounge with efficient polite service (worth booking), well kept Marstons and a guest ale, good wine, interesting restaurant *(Nigel Hopkins, S Howe)*

Alfreton, Der [High St; SK4155], *Olde McDonalds Farm*: Flamboyant farm theme with parachuting chickens, moving sheep heads, funny farm memorabilia in big Edwardian building; pinball, pool, table football and video games in games room, separate eating area, Theakstons Best and XB and Youngers Scotch on handpump, real fires; very busy for Thurs-Sat live entertainment; open all day, facilities for disabled *(Mr and Mrs Russell Allen)*

Alrewas, Staffs [High St; off A38 – OS Sheet 128 map ref 172150; SK1714], *George & Dragon*: Three friendly low-beamed partly knocked together rooms with consistently well kept Marstons, good value generous bar food (not Sun) inc children's dishes, efficient staff, attractive paintings; piped music; pleasant partly covered garden with good play area, children welcome in eating area *(Gordon Smith, Graham Richardson, G P Kernan, G E Stait, Dave Braisted, B M Eldridge, LYM)*

☆ **Alton**, Staffs [SK0742], *Talbot*: Welcoming stone-built pub, small and cosy, with well kept beer, good interesting food, good staff *(Mike and Wendy Proctor)*

Amerton, Staffs [SJ9927], *Plough*: Traditional friendly family-run country pub, good range of ales, good bar menu, large garden with safe well equipped play area; opp farm attraction *(B M Eldridge)*

☆ **Ashbourne**, Der [Ashbourne Green (A515 towards Matlock); SK1846], *Bowling Green*: Well kept Bass, Worthington and two other changing ales, wide choice of good value bar lunches inc vegetarian, friendly atmosphere, straightforward comfort; good bedrooms *(M D Farman, Philip da Silva)*

☆ **Ashbourne**, [Victoria Sq], *Horns*: Attractive olde-worlde 18th-c pub with bay window overlooking steep cobbled street, friendly fast service, good range of food inc home-made pies, well kept Bass, decent coffee *(F A Ward, Tracey Hitchcock, Graham Moore)*

☆ **Ashford in the Water**, Der [SK1969], *Black Bull*: Cosy and homely comfortable lounge with well kept Robinsons ales, nicely presented home-cooked food, quick friendly service; tables out in front *(Brian and Jill Bond, John Waller, Jack and Philip Paxton, Keith Croxton)*

☆ **Ashley**, Staffs [signposted from A53 NE of Market Drayton; SJ7636], *Peel Arms*: Plush and squeaky-clean local with olde-worlde touches such as warming old kitchen range, friendly licensees, well kept Marstons; lovely big garden with swings *(Nigel Woolliscroft, Sue Holland, Dave Webster, Tom and Jeanne Barnes)*

☆ **Ashley**, *Meynell Arms*: Local with good value bar food (not Mon evening) inc popular Sun lunches and take-aways, well kept Bass, M&B Mild and Theakstons, deep sofa, cast-iron stove, timbering, panelling and stripped stone; games in comfortable public bar, children in eating area; vintage tractors in yard *(Tom and Jeanne Barnes, Catherine and Andrew Brian, LYM)*

Audley, Staffs [Nantwich Rd; SJ7951], *Potters Lodge*: Relaxing, with friendly staff, well kept Whitbreads-related ales, wide choice of food inc children's; play area *(Richard Lewis)*

Bakewell, Der [Bridge St; SK2168], *Castle*: Good value food, newspapers to read, smart wine-bar feel but good choice of ales, friendly staff *(Sue Holland, Dave Webster)*; [Market Pl], *Red Lion*: Good food even Sun evening, good choice of ales, no juke box or noisy games, local characters; good value bedrooms *(Ray Loughlin)*

☆ **Bamford**, Der [A6013; SK2083], *Derwent*: Interestingly varied separate rooms off central hall-servery, big pictures and windows, friendly landlord, bar food inc vegetarian, well kept Marstons Best and Pedigree and Stones Best, restaurant, open all day; children welcome, seats in garden; comfortable bedrooms *(Barbara and Norman Wells, Lynn Sharpless, Bob Eardley, Wayne A Wheeler, LYM)*

Bamford, *Yorkshire Bridge*: Much-modernised late 19th-c, warm and cosy, with two gas fires, generous good value food, well kept Whitbreads *(Steve Goodchild)*

Barlow, Der [SK3474], *Peacock*: Smart comfortable lounge and bars, views down valley, well kept Mansfield, well filled rolls, handy for walkers; bedrooms *(Steve Goodchild)*

Barton under Needwood, Staffs [Main St; SK1818], *Middle Bell*: Renovated with beautifully varnished wooden floors, attractive decor and tropical conservatory, Brazilian landlady, food inc chargrills *(B M Eldridge)*

Baslow, Der [Nether Rd; SK2572], *Devonshire Arms*: Small straightforward hotel in pleasant surroundings, usual food inc decent sandwiches, evening restaurant, Marstons Pedigree, Shipstones Mild and Tetleys, quiet piped music, footpath to Chatsworth; bedrooms *(Anthony Barker, Mrs F M Halle)*

☆ **Beeley**, Der [SK2667], *Devonshire Arms*: Black beams, flagstones, stripped stone and plenty of atmosphere, good range of well kept ales inc Black Sheep, Theakstons XB and Old Peculier, queue at nice dining room's counter to order enterprising cheerfully served though not cheap food from sandwiches up, big log fires, no music; attractive rolling scenery nr Chatsworth – can get very busy; children welcome, with upstairs family room and own menu *(Ian and Val Titman, Dr Keith Bloomfield, John and Christine Lowe, D C Alcock, Jack and Philip Paxton, W H and E Thomas, Mike and Wendy Proctor, Dr and Mrs D E Awbery, E D Bailey, BH, LYM)*

Belper, Der [High St – OS Sheet 119 map ref 350485; SK3447], *Grapes*: Friendly horseshoe bar with lounge area, open fires, well kept Marstons Pedigree and guest ales, good choice of reasonably priced lunchtime bar food inc vegetarian; darts, skittles *(Mrs H R Pearce)*

☆ **Biggin**, Der [W of A515; SK1559], *Waterloo*: Wide choice of good value generous mostly home-cooked food inc children's dishes in pleasant bars, welcoming efficient service, Bass; dales views *(Jack and Philip Paxton)*

☆ **Birch Vale**, Der [via Station Rd towards Thornsett off A6015; SK0287], *Sycamore*: Thriving four-roomed dining pub with good reasonably priced food inc children's dishes and rich puddings, well kept ales, friendly helpful service, piped music, fountain in downstairs drinking bar; spacious streamside gardens with good play area, pets' corner and summer bar; restaurant open all day Sun, children welcome, handy for Sett Valley trail; bedrooms comfortable, good breakfast *(S A Moir, LYM)*

Bobbington, Staffs [SO8090], *Red Lion*:

Recently extended traditional pub, good food, pleasant atmosphere, affable staff, Theakstons and two guest beers *(J G and P Greenly)*
Bonsall, Der [SK2858], *Kings Head*: Very welcoming to children, with efficient friendly landlord, good value food inc good vegetarian menu; handy for Limestone Way and other walks *(Mark and Mary Fairman, Jack and Philip Paxton)*
Bottom House, Staffs [A523 SE of Leek; SK0452], *Forge*: Very friendly staff, wide choice of good food and drinks, piped easy listening music *(S Green)*
Boylestone, Der [Harehill; signed off A515, N of A50 junction; SK1735], *Rose & Crown*: Oak-beamed tile-floored traditional country local with enthusiastic singing landlord, well kept beers inc guests *(Jack and Philip Paxton)*
Bradwell, Der [B6049 S of Hope; SK1781], *Valley Lodge*: Comfortable big lounge bar with good guest beers, attentive friendly staff *(David and Michelle Hedges, Jack and Philip Paxton)*
☆ **Brassington**, Der [SK2354], *Miners Arms*: Very welcoming and pubby, with good food, well kept Marstons Pedigree, good-humoured landlord; children welcome, live music some nights; bedrooms *(Dr Roy F Stark, Ian Jones, Jack and Philip Paxton)*
Breaston, Der [Wilsthorpe Rd; SK4634], *Bulls Head*: Concentration on reliably good food inc vegetarian (esp spinach and ricotta canelloni) and good value puddings, swift friendly service, relaxed areas away from dining areas, good atmosphere *(Mrs Ann-Marie Hunt)*
Brewood, Staffs [SJ8808], *Admiral Rodney*: Highly Victorianised, with secluded alcoves, well kept Holt, Plant & Deakins ales, generous good value food, friendly service, games room; can get very busy *(Tony Hobden)*
☆ **Burton on Trent**, Staffs [Shobnall Rd (B5234 towards Abbots Bromley); SK2423], *Albion*: Marstons showpiece pub nr brewery, spacious, comfortable and attractive, with generous good value lunchtime bar food and carvery, well kept Pedigree, good service, family conservatory, roomy separate public bar with games and juke box; big fairy-lit garden with good play area, children's bar, barbecues *(Ian and Emma Potts, LYM)*
Burton on Trent, [Wellington Rd], *Bill Brewer*: Comfortable and welcoming new family pub with outdoor play area, baby-changing room, provision for the disabled; daily-changing home-cooked food (not Sun) inc steak and wine bargain Mon evening, special supper offer early evening, wide range of ales such as Bass, Boddingtons, Marstons Pedigree and Worthington, cheap house wines, freedom from smoke and juke boxes *(B M Eldridge)*; [Black Pool St], *Black Pool*: Comfortably refurbished with attractive antique oak fireplace for coal-effect gas fire in pleasant raised lounge area, polished ash panelling, well kept Batemans Mild, Marstons Bitter and Pedigree, Morlands Old Speckled Hen and Timothy Taylors Landlord, farm cider, lunchtime snacks inc sandwiches and filled cobs; pool, darts and dominoes, new conservatory and garden *(B M Eldridge)*; [Ashby Rd], *Waterloo*: Friendly local with well kept Bass and Marstons, now doing good varied food *(Dave Hayzen-Smith)*
☆ **Buxton**, Der [Bridge St; SK0673], *Railway*: Friendly and popular railway-theme food pub, good atmosphere, varied well cooked food, prompt service *(J C and I F Paterson)*
Buxton [37 High St], *Cheshire Cheese*: Big friendly low-ceilinged open-plan local with dark timber and stained glass, well kept Hardys & Hansons, live music Sun Mon and Weds *(Frog Twissell)*; [North Rd], *Devonshire Arms*: Warm and friendly, good home-cooked food, obliging staff; restaurant *(S F D Kelly)*
☆ **Buxworth**, Der [Silkhill, via B6062 off A6 just NW of Whalley Bridge roundabout – OS Sheet 110 map ref 022821; SK0282], *Navigation*: Busy bright cluttered decor and atmosphere to match in welcoming pub by abandoned canal basin (restoration plans), several low-ceilinged rooms, some canalia and brassware, lacy curtains, cheery staff, real coal and log fires, flagstone floors, good value generous food, four well kept Courage-related and other ales; darts, pool, piped music; tables on sunken flagstoned terrace; open all day; bedrooms *(Pete Yearsley, John Derbyshire, Karl Green, David Ball, Bill Sykes, BB)*
Calver, Der [A623 N of Baslow; SK2474], *Bridge*: Unspoilt but comfortable, with Hardys & Hansons ales, quickly served good value generous usual food, pleasant landlord, nice garden *(Ann and Colin Hunt, Comus Elliot)*
☆ **Castleton**, Der [How Lane; SK1583], *Peak*: Roomy airy bar, dining room with high ceiling and picture window view of Peak hills, wide choice of above-average generous reasonably priced food inc vegetarian, Tetleys and other ales, friendly service *(B and K Hypher, Peter and Anne Hollindale)*
☆ **Castleton** [High St/Castle St], *Castle*: Plush hotel bars with handsome flagstones, beams, stripped stonework, open fires, decent bar food though keg beers; open all day summer, tables outside; good bedrooms *(B M Eldridge, Jack and Philip Paxton, LYM)*
☆ **Castleton**, *George*: Good atmosphere and good value simple food in roomy bars with friendly helpful staff, well kept Bass; tables on wide forecourt; popular with young people – nr YHA; dogs welcome *(JM, PM, Jack and Philip Paxton, R H Sawyer)*
Castleton, *Olde Cheshire Cheese*: Two cheery communicating areas, wide choice of reasonably priced bar food, Wards tapped from the cask, comfortable seats around open fire, piped music, sensibly placed darts; bedrooms *(Tracey Hitchcock, Graham Moore, BB)*
☆ **Cauldon Lowe**, Staffs [Waterhouses; A52 Stoke—Ashbourne; SK0748], *Cross*: Good range of well kept beers and of decent food,

several attractive rooms, charming service, reasonable prices, scenic setting *(Jack and Philip Paxton)*

Chapel en le Frith, Der [SK0680], *Cross Keys*: Pleasant atmosphere and good food (all day Sun) in old pub with smartly decorated restaurant, well kept beers, very friendly service; children welcome *(Lee Goulding, S E Paulley, Jack Morley)*

☆ **Cheddleton,** Staffs [Basford Bridge Lane, off A520; SJ9651], *Boat*: Cheerful local above canal, neat long bar with attractive fireplace in airy new extension, low plank ceilings, fine choice of well kept Marstons and other ales, reliably good cheap waitress-served food, interesting pictures; handy for North Staffs Steam Railway Museum; children welcome, fairy-lit tables outside *(Mike and Wendy Proctor, D G Clarke, Bill Sykes, Jack and Philip Paxton, LYM)*

Chesterfield, Der [residential area; SK3871], *Blue Stoops*: Bar food inc good Sun lunch; bedrooms *(Mrs Pam Deeprose)*

☆ **Chinley,** Der [off A624 towards Hayfield; SK0482], *Lamb*: Profusely decorated three-room stone-built roadside pub with friendly atmosphere, well prepared quick reasonably priced bar food, well kept Bass and other ales; children till 8.30; lots of tables out in front *(Mike and Wendy Proctor, JM, PM, BB)*

☆ **Church Broughton,** Der [OS Sheet 128 map ref 205337; SK2033], *Holly Bush*: Neat and attractive village pub, dining room extended to cope with popularity of good cheap simple home cooking inc Sun lunch; well kept Marstons Pedigree, friendly labradors *(Chris Raisin)*

☆ **Clifton Campville,** Staffs [SK2510], *Green Man*: Low-beamed 15th-c village pub with character public bar, airy modernised lounge, good family atmosphere, well kept Bass, good value bar food; children in family room, garden with swings *(Graham Richardson, LYM)*

☆ **Consall,** Staffs [Consallforge; best approach from Nature Pk, off A522 – OS Sheet 118 map ref 000491; SJ9748], *Black Lion*: Basic unspoilt tavern, popular despite isolation in very old-fashioned canalside settlement, generous cheap individually prepared food (may be delays even for snacks when busy), free-speaking landlady, good coal fire, well kept Marstons Pedigree and Ruddles County on handpump, traditional games, piped music; children welcome; busy weekends, good walking area *(Bill Sykes, Jack and Philip Paxton, LYM)*

☆ **Copmere End,** Staffs [W of Eccleshall; SJ8029], *Star*: Classic simple two-room country local overlooking mere, Bass and guest ale, good interesting home-made food, very friendly service, picnic tables in beautiful back garden full of trees and shrubs; local horticultural society produce for sale Sun lunchtime; children very welcome *(Nigel Woolliscroft)*

Coseley, Staffs [Daisy St; off A4123 B'ham—Wolverhampton; SO9494], *White House*: Interesting constantly changing guest beers such as Blackbeard Deadringer, Burton Bridge Festival and Hardington Moonshine, as well as Holt, Plant & Deakins Bitter and Entire; lots of china cats, piped music, usual food *(Paul and Susan Merrick)*

Cresswell, Staffs [SJ9739], *Hunter*: Pleasant, with interesting paraphernalia *(Anna Brewer)*

☆ **Cutthorpe,** Der [NW of Chesterfield; B6050 well W of village; SK3273], *Gate*: Picture-window views over eastern Peak District from chatty area around bar, neat dining lounge down steps, decent fair-priced food inc bargain lunches popular with older people, well kept ales such as Bass, Boddingtons, Flowers Original and Mansfield Riding, friendly efficient staff, lots of biggish pictures *(Alan and Heather Jacques, S E Paulley, BB)*

Darley Dale, Der [Dale Rd N (A6); SK2663], *Grouse*: Comfortable and welcoming Hardys & Hansons pub with well kept Mild and Bitter, lots of prints, separate games room with pool, slide hockey and juke box, small high-walled back play area; can get a bit smoky; children allowed *(Brian and Anna Marsden)*

☆ **Derby** [Queen St, nr cathedral; SK3435], *Olde Dolphin*: Cosy and civilised 16th-c beamed pub, several rooms inc tiny snug and side room with Offilers Brewery mementoes, wide choice of well kept changing Bass-related and other ales (cut prices Mon evening), good value food, upstairs no smoking dining area (children allowed here), prompt friendly service; newspapers, board games, even a ghost; open all day (inc Sun for food) *(Brian Jones, Norma and Keith Bloomfield, Richard Lewis, Andrew Stephenson, John and Christine Lowe)*

☆ **Derby** [Ley St, Darley Abbey; SK3438], *Abbey Inn*: Interesting for including massive stonework remnants of 11th-c abbey; brick floor, studded oak doors, big stone inglenook, stone spiral stair to upper bar with handsome oak rafters; well kept cheap Sam Smiths, decent lunchtime bar food, children allowed; opp Derwent-side park *(Paul Robinshaw, LYM)*

Derby [13 Exeter Pl], *Exeter Arms*: Friendly staff, good well kept ales, lots of character, *HMS Exeter* memorabilia *(R Lewis)*; [25 King St], *Flowerpot*: Extended real ale pub, friendly staff, lots of old Derby prints *(R Lewis)*; [204 Abbey St], *Olde Spa*: Relaxed old local, well kept Tetleys-related ales, tiled-floor bar, games room, garden with fountain *(Chris Raisin)*; [Exeter Pl], *Royal Standard*: Nicely refurbished; friendly staff, well kept ales *(R Lewis)*; [Irongate], *Vaults*: Cellar below wine bar/cafe with fine choice of largely Whitbreads-related ales *(R Lewis)*

☆ **Dovedale,** Staffs [Thorpe—Ilam rd; Ilam signposted off A52, Thorpe off A515, NW of Ashbourne; SK1452], *Izaak Walton*: Refreshingly informal for sizeable hotel, relaxing low-beamed bar, some distinctive antique oak settles and chairs, good log fire in massive central stone chimney; Ind Coope Burton on handpump, bar food and restaurant, morning coffee and afternoon tea; seats out on lawn by sheep pastures, superb views; bedrooms comfortable *(Mike and Wendy Proctor, Jack and Philip Paxton, D Kudelka, Gwen and Peter Andrews)*

Dronfield, Der [Carr Lane; Dronfield Woodhouse; SK3378], *Miners Arms*: Smartly comfortable, good Tetleys-related beer range, friendly service, delightful garden with play area *(B M Eldridge)*

☆ **Eccleshall**, Staffs [Castle St; SJ8329], *St George*: Keen friendly landlord now brewing his own good Slaters Bitter and Premium, with interesting guest beers; comfortable beamed bar with old prints and open fire, good generous home-cooked food in attractive bistro, good wines; comfortable individually decorated bedrooms *(Richard Lewis, A Shropshall, R Clark)*

Eccleshall, *Royal Oak*: Very old timbered local, friendly staff, lively feel, good value meals *(Richard Lewis)*

Edale, Der [SK1285], *Old Nags Head*: Useful walkers' pub with substantial basic cheap food, open fire, S&N and other ales; children in airy back family room *(Ann and Colin Hunt, Jack and Philip Paxton, LYM)*

Ellastone, Staffs [SK1143], *Duncombe Arms*: Very friendly traditional village pub, good food *(Jenny Sapp, Peter Hudson)*

Elton, Der [SK2261], *Duke of York*: Homely utterly unspoilt old-fashioned local, like stepping back in time; darts in one of three rooms; closed lunchime, open 8-11 *(Ann and Colin Hunt, Jack and Philip Paxton)*

Endon, Staffs [Leek Rd (A53); SJ9253], *Plough*: Busy but cosy, Bass and Worthington Best, friendly staff, good food in self-service Toby carvery *(Richard Lewis)*

☆ *nr* **Endon** [Denford, some way E; SJ9553], *Holly Bush*: Friendly staff, wide range of well kept ale, good value food from sandwiches up; nice rural position on Caldon Canal, very busy in summer *(M F Thomas, Patrick and Mary McDermott, Mike and Wendy Proctor, Mr and Mrs Jones)*

Enville, Staffs [A458 W of Stourbridge; SO8286], *Cat*: Mainly 17th-c, with four bar areas, cheerful fire, very wide choice of ales, good food such as pheasant and apricot pie *(Dave Braisted)*

☆ **Etruria**, Staffs [A53 well away from centre; SJ8647], *Plough*: Small very friendly two-room pub doing well under new licensees, nice atmosphere and decor, coal fire, five Robinsons beers inc Old Tom and Fredericks, wide choice of food esp steaks, will do anything on request from sandwiches up; busy lunchtime and weekends *(Mike and Wendy Proctor, John Scarisbrick)*

Etruria [Festival Park], *China Garden*: Canalside pub with fine choice of Bass-related and other ales, wide choice of cheap food, friendly service, family room, dining room, garden *(Richard Lewis)*

☆ **Farnah Green**, Der [follow Hazelwood signpost off A517 in Blackbrook, W edge of Belper; SK3346], *Bluebell*: Plush smartly run dining pub, good prompt food in relaxing small rooms; sturdy tables out on terrace and in quiet gently sloping spacious side garden, restaurant with inventive cooking, well kept Bass *(Peter Marshall, John Waller, Mike and Jo, BB)*

Fenny Bentley, Der [SK1750], *Bently Brook Lodge*: Attractive old house run for years as country inn with big bar, friendly staff, pleasant atmosphere, decent food, beers from nearby microbrewery, plush restaurant, lovely garden with plenty of tables; handy for Dovedale walks; bedrooms *(John Scarisbrick, B M Eldridge)*

Fernilee, Der [A5002 Whalley Bridge—Buxton; SK0179], *Shady Oak*: Roadside pub in glorious countryside, wide range of well cooked food inc lots of moderately priced specials *(Geoffrey Lindley)*

Findern, Der [25 Main St; SK3030], *Wheel*: Recently refurbished, welcoming staff, well kept Bass and Marstons Pedigree, good value bar food (not Sun eve), Sky TV in separate lounge bar; pleasant garden *(B M Eldridge)*

Flagg, Der [A515 Buxton—Ashbourne; SK1368], *Duke of York*: Good food and service, well kept beer *(Anon)*

☆ **Foolow**, Der [formerly Lazy Landlord; SK1976], *Bulls Head*: Attractive moorland village pub, new owners doing good helpings of interesting though not cheap food in good no smoking restaurant area, also cheaper bar snacks; Wards and Vaux beers and one or two guests, good service *(Adrian and Gilly Heft, Mr and Mrs J A Moors, Mr and Mrs G Archer, LYM)*

☆ **Fradley**, Staffs [Fradley Park signed off A38 Burton—Lichfield, OS Sheet 128 map ref 140140; SK1414], *Swan*: Cheery pub in particularly good canalside spot, food inc good value Sun lunch, well kept Tetleys-related ales inc Mild, traditional public bar and quieter plusher lounge and lower vaulted back bar (where children allowed), lots of malt whiskies, cribbage, dominoes, piped music; waterside tables *(Karen Phillips, Nigel Hopkins, Ian and Emma Potts, Paul Robinshaw, G P Kernan, M Joyner, LYM)*

Gnosall, Staffs [SJ8221], *Navigation*: Overlooking Shrops Union Canal, Wards ales, friendly staff, reasonably priced food in restaurant *(Tony Hobden)*

Great Chatwell, Staffs [SJ7915], *Red Lion*: Friendly village pub, good facilities for children, well kept ales inc many guests, good food (not Mon) inc outstanding chips *(Jean and Douglas Troup, Dave Major)*

☆ **Great Hucklow**, Der [SK1878], *Queen Anne*: Good range of food esp exotic fish, comfortable beamed bar with open fire, two other rooms, one with French windows to small terrace and pleasant garden with lovely views; children welcome, handy for walks *(Roger A Mash, Jack and Philip Paxton, Mike and Wendy Proctor)*

☆ **Grindon**, Staffs [signed off B5033 N of A523; SK0854], *Cavalier*: 16th-c character pub with well kept Wards Best, decent straightforward food, pleasant service; smallish front bar with larger room behind and separate games room, good mix of locals and visitors; pleasant informal garden, attractive countryside *(Dr and Mrs B Baker, Jack and Philip Paxton, Nigel Woolliscroft, Jack Morley, LYM)*

☆ **Hanley**, Staffs [65 Lichfield St; SJ8747], *Coachmakers Arms*: Character unspoilt friendly town pub, three small rooms and drinking corridor, particularly well kept Bass and M&B Mild, skittles *(Nigel Woolliscroft, Sue Holland, Dave Webster)*

Hanley [Lichfield St/Old Hall St], *Albion*: Big busy city pub, quickly served good value basic lunchtime food, no-smoking dining area, interesting photographs *(CW, JW, Sue Holland, Dave Webster)*; *Founder & Firkin*: Recently converted to Firkin formula, simply furnished, lots of wood, old prints, brewery posters etc, brewing own Dogbolter, Poker and Founder; good basic food inc huge filled baps, good atmosphere, juke box *(Richard Lewis)*; [Tontine St], *Tontine Alehouse*: Good generous lunchtime food, well kept Tetleys and Marstons Pedigree *(Dr and Mrs B Baker, N Woolliscroft)*; [centre], *Trinitys*: Former bank, now like an American saloon bar, lots of wood, big back mirror, prints and artefacts, huge choice of good value food, well kept Marstons *(R Lewis)*

☆ **Hartington**, Der [The Square; SK1360], *Devonshire Arms*: Good choice of tasty food at sensible prices, well kept beer, friendly efficient service; bedrooms comfortable *(Mr and Mrs Dolby, Wayne A Wheeler, M P Jefferson, John and Joan Calvert)*

☆ **Hartington**, *Minton House*: Beautifully presented reasonably priced bar food, decent wines, welcoming fire and friendly staff in spick and span hotel – a nice place to stay *(W H and E Thomas, Mrs B H Adams)*

Hartington, *Charles Cotton*: Courage-related ales, good food prepared by French landlady inc superb soups and Staffordshire oakcake with wild mushrooms, basic children's menu; coal fires; bedrooms *(Paul Robinshaw)*

☆ *nr* **Hartington** [Newhaven; A515 a mile N of A5012; SK1561], *Jug & Glass*: Has been attractive low-beamed moorland pub – a popular main entry – with relaxed atmosphere, Bass, Marstons Pedigree and a guest beer, bar food from sandwiches to steaks, a welcome for children, pretty no smoking dining room, tables outside; but as we went to press closed after fire damage, no news yet about reopening *(LYM; reports please)*

Hartshill, Staffs [296 Hartshill Rd (A52); SJ8545], *Jolly Potters*: Well kept Bass and M&B Mild, simple snacks, four little rooms off a drinking corridor *(Nigel Woolliscroft, Sue Holland, Dave Webster)*

Hartshorne, Der [Main St; SK3220], *Admiral Rodney*: Two-bar pub with Bass, Marstons Pedigree and three changing ales, good modestly priced food from filled rolls to steaks, darts, pub games, live music and singalongs; pub cat called Lara; open all day *(Stephen Liverman)*

Hassop, Der [SK2272], *Eyre Arms*: Cosy 17th-c inn with good food in small dining area, courteous friendly landlord *(F J Lascelles Pallin, Geoffrey and Irene Lindley)*

☆ **Hathersage**, Der [A625; SK2381], *George*: Substantial comfortably modernised old inn, good value bar food, calm atmosphere, well kept Boddingtons, decent wine, neat flagstoned back terrace by rose garden; a nice place to stay (the back bedrooms are the quiet ones) *(Margaret and Paul Digby, David Eberlin, LYM)*

☆ **Hathersage** [Leadmill Bridge; A622 (ex B6001) towards Bakewell], *Plough*: Ex-farm with Derwent-side garden, good helpings of good fresh food quickly served even when busy, two dining areas, cheerful staff, well kept ales such as Wadworths 6X, decent wines *(M Baxter, Bill and Beryl Goddard, Geoffrey and Irene Lindley, Ian Rorison)*

☆ **Hathersage** [Church Lane], *Scotsmans Pack*: Big welcoming open-plan local dating from 17th c, good choice of generous nicely presented food, well kept Burtonwood, decent wines; some seats outside; good bedrooms, huge breakfast *(Margaret and Paul Digby, M S Crabtree)*

☆ **Hathersage** [A625], *Hathersage*: Comfortable and friendly, modernised with restraint, good value food in spacious bar and lounge, well kept Courage-related ales, log fires; bedrooms good value *(Dr Paul Kitchener, Mrs F M Halle)*

☆ **Hatton**, Der [Station Rd (A50); by Tutbury rly stn; SK2130], *Castle*: Friendly family-run coaching inn, wide choice of good interesting reaonably priced home-cooked food in bar and restaurant, well kept Bass, Theakstons and Worthington; handy for glassworks, castle and antique shops; bedrooms *(B M Eldridge, G A Clark)*

Haughton, Staffs [Newport Rd (A518); SJ8620], *Shropshire*: Tastefully modernised with exposed roof timbers, very friendly efficient service, wide range of food all week, relaxed atmosphere, pleasant garden *(Paul and Maggie Baker, Cyril Burton)*

☆ **Hayfield**, Der [Market St; SK0387], *Royal*: Well run 18th-c former vicarage, oak panelling, six well kept ales, cheerful atmosphere, good food from young chef with good ideas; pleasantly decorated bedrooms *(Frank Hughes, JM, PM)*

Heage, Der [Old Rd; SK3750], *Black Boy*: Big friendly open-plan pub with real fires, well kept Mansfield Riding and Old Baily, good range of food in restaurant inc wide vegetarian choice, traditional games *(B M Eldridge)*

☆ **Hednesford**, Staffs [Mount St; SJ9913], *West Cannock*: Wide choice of well kept reasonably priced changing beers and good value food in cosy Victorian-style pub, very friendly staff, generous OAP offers Sat and Mon lunchtime; tables outside *(John and Chris Simpson, Steve Owen, Stephen Clough)*

Hednesford [Eskrett St, off Market St], *Mrs O'Rourkes Hen House*: Good fun, hums with life *(David and Shelia)*

☆ **High Offley**, Staffs [towards High Lea –

Bridge 42, Shrops Union Canal; SJ7826], *Anchor*: Unspoilt homely canal pub in same family for over a century, two simple homely rooms, well kept Marstons Pedigree and Owd Rodger and Wadworths 6X tapped in cellar, Weston's farm ciders, sandwiches; children welcome, seats outside, cl Mon-Weds winter; caravan/campsite *(Nigel Woolliscroft)*

☆ **Hill Chorlton**, Staffs [Stone Rd (A51); SJ7939], *Slaters*: Comfortable and attractive beamed bar in farm buildings, good standard bar food from sandwiches up inc vegetarian and Sun roasts, well kept Banks's, Boddingtons and Marstons Pedigree, decent wines, upstairs restaurant, children's room; tables out in attractive garden, animals in barn; bedrooms *(Mayur Shah, Nigel Woolliscroft, Paul and Gail Betteley, Peter and Jenny Quine, Mike and Wendy Proctor, LYM)*

☆ **Hoar Cross**, Staffs [off A515 Yoxall—Sudbury; SK1323], *Meynell Ingram Arms*: Welcoming two-bar traditional country pub, two log fires, good varied reasonably priced food inc popular Sun lunch, well kept Boddingtons and Marstons Pedigree, cheerful staff *(Mrs R Cotgreave, Dorothee and Dennis Glover, M A Robinson, Derek and Margaret Underwood, Jackie Sherrington)*

☆ **Hollington**, Staffs [the one between Alton and Uttoxeter; SK0538], *Raddle*: Extended country pub with good generous bar food inc vegetarian and children's, five well kept ales on handpump, neatly modernised rambling bar, sizeable upstairs family room with own servery, helpful young staff; great views from garden with big play area *(John Scarisbrick, BB)*

☆ **Hope**, Der [Edale Rd; SK1783], *Cheshire Cheese*: 16th-c stonebuilt pub with cosy little up-and-down oak-beamed rooms, interesting good value home cooking, welcoming helpful staff, well kept Stones and Wards, several coal fires; attractive village, children allowed in eating area, walkers welcome; bedrooms *(Sue Demont, Tim Barrow, Jack and Philip Paxton, Sarah and Steve de Mellow, LYM)*

☆ **Hope** [A625 towards Castleton], *Poachers Arms*: Pleasant relaxed atmosphere in modern but traditionally furnished interconnected rooms, friendly staff, wide choice of popular food from sandwiches up, well kept Courage-related ales, children welcome, back conservatory; darts, dominoes, maybe piped music; the two dogs are Barney and Tina; comfortable bedrooms *(B M Eldridge, M G Hart, Jim Farmer, M W Turner, Prof I H Rorison, D Kudelka, John and Christine Lowe, Anthony Barker, LYM)*

Hope [A625 towards Bamford], *Rising Sun*: More hotel than pub, but open all day for good reasonably priced food in extensive lounge and bar areas; children welcome *(Geoffrey and Irene Lindley)*; [1 Castleton Rd], *Woodroffe Arms*: Tastefully redeveloped with several rooms inc conservatory, wide choice of good value food inc children's dishes and Sun lunch, four real ales and Addlestone's cider, real fire, polite service; Sun quiz night, garden with swings; bedrooms *(Geoffrey and Irene Lindley, CMW, JJW)*

☆ **Huddlesford**, Staffs [off A38 2 miles E of Lichfield – OS Sheet 139 map ref 152097; SK1509], *Plough*: Beams, nooks and crannies in pleasant old pub alongside canal and railway, comfortable leather seats, wide choice of good generous food, lower dining area, well kept Ansells, Greenalls Original and Worthington, good range of wines, friendly efficient staff, games area, tables out by water *(M and J Back, Dorothee and Dennis Glover)*

Ilkeston, Der [Station Rd, Ilkeston Junction; formerly the Middleton Hotel; SK4642], *Dewdrop*: Large three-room local by rly in old industrial area, friendly staff, good value bar snacks, Ind Coope Burton, Hook Norton Old Hookey, Kelham Island Pale Rider, Wards Kirby and guests, two coal fires, barbecue; good value bedrooms *(Jack and Phil Paxton, Simon, Julia and Laura Plumbley)*

Ivetsey Bank, Staffs [A5 Telford—Cannock, 5 miles from M6 junction 12; SJ8311], *Bradford Arms*: Well kept Banks's ales, good food esp local steaks, wide vegetarian choice, children's menu, very friendly staff, disabled access; big garden with play area and animals; caravan/campsite *(Paul Lasance)*

Kings Bromley, Staffs [Manor Rd; SK1216], *Royal Oak*: Good choice of well presented generous food inc vegetarian, welcoming staff, immaculate premises *(Mrs J M Wilson)*

☆ **Kinver**, Staffs [A449; SO8483], *Whittington*: Striking black and white timbered Tudor house, genuine Dick Whittington connection, interesting old-fashioned bar, conservatory opening on to fine garden; good value food, well kept Banks's ale, attentive staff, roaring fire *(P and J Grosset, LYM)*

Knighton, Staffs [B5415 Woore—Mkt Drayton; SJ7240], *White Lion*: Large beamed bar with two log fires, smaller side room, dining area, conservatory, well kept Marstons and guests, good food; restaurant (not Mon or Sun evening); large adventure playground *(D Hanley, N Woolliscroft)*

Knockerdown, Der [1½ miles S of Brassington on B5035; SK2352], *Knockerdown Inn*: L-shaped bar and dining room with pictures and bric-a-brac, extensive reasonably priced menu, good value Sun lunch, well kept Banks's Mild and Marstons Pedigree, no piped music, friendly local atmosphere; good views from garden, nr Carsington reservoir; well behaved children may be allowed *(David Eberlin, JJW, CMW)*

☆ **Ladybower Reservoir**, Der [A57 Sheffield—Glossop, at junction with A6013; SK1986], *Ladybower*: Fine views of attractive reservoir from unpretentious open-plan stone pub, clean and spacious; reasonably priced popular food, Tetleys-related ales, red plush seats, discreet piped music; children welcome, stone seats outside, good walks *(P Corris, Prof I H Rorison)*

☆ **Leek**, Staffs [St Edwards St; SJ9856], *Swan*:

Old three-room pub with reasonably priced lunchtime food, no smoking lounge, well kept Bass and guest ales, occasional beer festivals, lots of malt whiskies, choice of coffees; folk club, seats in courtyard *(John Scarisbrick, Mike and Wendy Proctor)*

Leek [Macclesfield Rd], *Dyers Arms*: Vibrantly friendly local with particularly well kept Bass, good value food, good mix of customers, great sporting flavour – landlord footballer Kevin Lewis *(Malcolm Smith)*; [St Edward St], *Wilkes Head*: Three character rooms, swing doors, well kept Whim Magic Mushroom Mild, Hartington and Old Izaak, two guest beers, cut prices Thurs *(John Scarisbrick)*

☆ **Lichfield**, Staffs [Market St; SK1109], *Scales*: Cosy traditional oak-panelled bar with wooden flooring, screens, imitation gas lights, sepia photographs of old Lichfield; meals and snacks, well kept Bass-related and other ales, darts, smart service; suntrap back courtyard *(Luke Hundleby, T G Thomas, LYM)*

☆ **Lichfield** [Tamworth St], *Pig & Truffle*: Good nicely decorated panelled dining pub, reasonable prices, attentive service, well kept ales, good coffee, seats in sunny back yard; piped music; no food Fri-Sun evenings when more a younger person's preserve *(Gary Nicholls, T G Thomas, David and Valerie Hooley, William and Dilys Cliffe)*

Lichfield [Conduit St, opp central mkt], *Earl of Lichfield*: Welcoming Marstons pub, good range of reasonably priced snacks and basic meals, friendly prompt helpful service *(DAV, BB)*; [Bird St], *Kings Head*: Traditional front rooms, good bar food, well kept Marstons Pedigree and Best, conservatory, tables in courtyard *(Gary Nicholls)*

☆ **Little Bridgeford**, Staffs [nr M6 junction 14; turn right off A5013 at Little Bridgeford; SJ8727], *Worston Mill*: Very popular family dining pub, spacious and welcoming, in attractively converted 1814 watermill, wheel and gear still preserved, ducks on millpond and millstream in attractive garden with adventure playground and nature trail (but nr main rly line), conservatory; lots of oak and leather, well kept Marstons Pedigree and other ales, good value wine, wide choice of reasonably priced good food, polite efficient staff, children welcome *(Richard Lewis, Julian Holland, Paul and Gail Betteley, M Joyner, LYM)*

Little Haywood, Staffs [Main Rd; SK0021], *Red Lion*: Close to River Trent; well kept Marstons Pedigree *(Nigel Hopkins)*

☆ **Litton**, Der [off A623; SK1675], *Red Lion*: Pretty village pub/restaurant (you can't just have a drink), above-average food esp game in cosy low-ceilinged partly panelled front rooms or bigger back room with stripped stone and antique prints; huge log fires, good friendly service, well kept Boddingtons, decent wine, quiet piped classical music; dogs allowed; cl weekday lunchtimes, Sun/Mon evenings *(Mr and Mrs David Lee, G W Lindley, JJW, CMW, Mrs D M Everard, LYM)*

Longdon, Staffs [off A51 Rugeley—Staffs; SK0714], *Swan With Two Necks*: Generous home-cooked food inc some good value interesting dishes, friendly helpful staff, well kept ale; lovely village *(Eric J Locker, Nigel Hopkins, Jack and Philip Paxton)*

☆ **Lullington**, Der [SK2513], *Colvile Arms*: 18th-c village pub with basic panelled bar, plush lounge, pleasant atmosphere, friendly staff, piped music, well kept Bass and Marstons Pedigree on handpump, good value snacks, tables on small sheltered back lawn overlooking bowling green; cl weekday lunchtimes *(John Beeken, LYM)*

☆ **Makeney**, Der [Holly Bush Lane; A6 N, cross river Derwent, before Milford turn right, then left; SK3544], *Holly Bush*: Popular old-fashioned pub with good choice of beers brought from cellar in jugs, three roaring open fires; children allowed in conservatory *(Andrew Stephenson, B Adams)*

Mapleton, Der [SK1647], *Okeover Arms*: Small, friendly and comfortable bar, well kept Tetleys-related ales, decent bar food, concerned service, restaurant; good walking country *(S Howe, Anthony Barker)*

Marshlane, Der [B6056 S of Sheffield; SK4079], *Fox & Hounds*: Cosy and friendly, dark beams, pictures, plates and brass, fresh flowers, open fire, separate tap room with darts, well kept Burtonwood Bitter and Forshaws, good coffee, wide choice of good value food, quiet piped music, two friendly dogs; big garden with picnic tables, good play area, goat, good views *(JJW, CMW)*

Matlock, Der [Matlock Bridge; A6 S edge of town; SK2959], *Boat House*: By River Derwent, between rd and cliff of old limestone quarry, friendly unchanging old-fashioned pub with very wide choice of good value food inc lots of well cooked fresh veg, also vegetarian choice; well kept Hardys & Hansons ales, open all day – tea at teatime; interesting walks; bedrooms *(Norma and Keith Bloomfield, Pat and Tony Young)*

Matlock Bath, Der [SK2958], *Temple*: Well established 18th-c hotel with wonderful Derwent valley views, two comfortable bars (one with carvery) and restaurant, good unusual bar menu with Austrian dishes, well kept Jennings and Theakstons; children welcome lunchtime; bedrooms *(Norma and Keith Bloomfield, Mark and Mary Fairman)*

☆ **Melbourne**, Der [SK3825], *White Swan*: Local feel in interestingly restored 15th-c pub with good value imaginative food, friendly service, well kept Marstons Pedigree; can get quite smoky nr bar; pleasant narrow garden; children welcome *(Jack and Philip Paxton, A and R Cooper)*

☆ **Melbourne** [222 Station Rd, towards Kings Newton/Islay Walton], *Railway*: Good old-fashioned chatty local, good value basic well cooked food, attractive dining room, well kept Marstons Pedigree, Timothy Taylors Landlord, Wards and guest beers, tiled and wooden floors, cast-iron gas fireplaces; well behaved children allowed; bedrooms *(Derek and Sylvia Stephenson, Jack and Philip*

Paxton, Wayne Brindle, R and A Cooper)
Melbourne [Ashby Rd (B4587 S)], *Melbourne Arms*: Basic food inc good value sandwiches and fish and chips, well kept Theakstons Best, friendly service; Indian restaurant with impressive menu *(R T and J C Moggridge)*

Mickleover, Der [Station Rd; SK3034], *Great Northern*: The railway has gone but railway prints in pleasant lounge, good value bar food inc big steaks and popular Sun lunches *(Chris Raisin)*

Millers Dale, Der [SK1373], *Anglers Rest*: Good friendly atmosphere, well kept Tetleys and Worthington, great value food – good choice inc vegetarian; cosy lounge with fire and nice old photographs, pool room, very friendly staff; attractive village, good walks *(Rupert Lecomber, Jack and Philip Paxton, Susan Boyle, Eugene Wills)*

☆ **Millthorpe**, Der [Cordwell Lane; SK3276], *Royal Oak*: Stripped stone, oak beams, relaxed welcome for all inc walkers, cosy snug, real fires, inexpensive simple but interesting home-made lunchtime food, well kept Wards on handpump, helpful licensees, no piped music; no children inside, tables out on pleasant terrace; good walks nearby, cl Mon lunchtime exc bank hols *(E W Scott, Norma and Keith Bloomfield, J M Pawson, Chris and Elizabeth Riley, Keith and Sonya Byres, LYM)*

Milton, Der [Main St; just E of Repton; SK3126], *Swan*: Well kept Marstons Pedigree and very friendly service in rather old-fashioned lounge, good range of good value bar food (not Mon, book for Sun lunch), separate bar; garden with play area, attractive village *(B M Eldridge, Sue Holland, David Webster)*

Milwich, Staffs [Smallrice; B5027 towards Stone; SJ9532], *Red Lion*: Bar at end of farmhouse, Bass tapped from the cask, friendly welcome, log fire *(Nigel Woolliscroft, Jack and Philip Paxton)*

☆ **Monyash**, Der [OS Sheet 119 map ref 153665; SK1566], *Bull*: Friendly village pub, good low-priced home-cooked food inc vegetarian, Tetleys-related ales inc Mild, roaring log fire in high-ceilinged bar with pictures and lots of plates, efficient staff, quiet piped music, dining room, pool in small back bar; children and muddy dogs welcome *(Phil and Heidi Cook, Mrs R S Rotbart)*

Moorwood Moor, Der [nr South Wingfield; SK3656], *White Hart*: Good choice of reasonably priced food, spacious and comfortable dining area, tables in garden *(A Preston, Jack and Philip Paxton)*

Muckley Corner, Staffs [A5/A461 (Walsall Rd); SK0806], *Olde Corner House*: Good sensibly priced restaurant-style food, well kept Marstons Pedigree and other ales, friendly atmosphere, pleasant decor; comfortable bedrooms *(M S and M Imhoff, M V Fereday)*

Nether Padley, Der [OS Sheet 119 map ref 258779; SK2577], *Grouse*: Friendly and comfortable back bar welcoming walkers and children, plusher front lounge, good basic food, real ale, nice atmosphere *(A P Jeffreys)*

☆ **Newcastle under Lyme**, Staffs [High St; SJ8445], *Golden Lion*: Good value simple home cooking in comfortably modernised but old-fashioned pub with well kept Bass; handy for open market *(Nigel Woolliscroft, Sue Holland, Dave Webster)*

Newcastle under Lyme [Etruria Rd], *New Victoria*: Theatre bar worth visiting even on non-performance nights, good choice of well kept real ales inc uncommon guest beers, nice atmosphere, bar snacks *(Mike and Wendy Proctor, Nigel Woolliscroft)*; [Bridge St], *Old Brown Jug*: Good home-made lunchtime food, well kept Marstons, live music Thurs *(Nigel Woolliscroft)*

Norbury Junction, Staffs [off A519 Eccleshall—Newport via Norbury; SJ7922], *Junction*: Popular canalside pub, wide range of good reasonably priced home-cooked bar food, good value carvery, well kept beer, friendly efficient service *(Sandra Iles, D Hanley)*

Norton in the Moors, Staffs [SJ8951], *Norton Arms*: Nicely decorated lounge bar, comfortable and homely bar with pool and TV, friendly staff, low-priced bar snacks, Bass on handpump, Highgate Mild and Worthington Best on electric pump *(Richard Lewis)*

Ockbrook, Der [Green Lane; SK4236], *Royal Oak*: Character 18th-c village local, well kept Bass and guests, open fire, quiet atmosphere, good lunches, charming cottage garden *(B M Eldridge)*

Overseal, Staffs [SK2915], *Cricketts*: Bass and guest ales, good value bar food, friendly staff *(Paul Robinshaw)*

☆ **Penkhull**, Staffs [Manor Court St – OS Sheet 118 map ref 868448; SJ8644], *Greyhound*: Relaxed traditional two-room pub in hilltop 'village', particularly good value filling snacks, well kept Marstons Pedigree and Tetleys; children in eating area, picnic tables on back terrace *(David and Shelia, Mike and Wendy Proctor, LYM)*

☆ **Penkridge**, Staffs [Market Pl – handy for M6 junctions 12/13; SJ9214], *Star*: Open-plan but friendly, with good landlord, lots of black beams and button-back red plush, good value generous lunchtime food (extended hours Weds and Sat) with gingham tablecloths in dining area, well kept cheap Banks's and guest ales; piped music; open all day, barbecues *(Graham Reeve, John and Chris Simpson, BB)*

Penkridge [Penkridge Lock], *Boat*: Bustling pub on Staffs & Worcs canal, welcoming landlord, Tetleys-related ales, good value food *(Tony Hobden)*; [A449], *Railway*: Friendly service, cosy atmosphere, separate bar and lounge *(John and Chris Simpson)*

☆ **Pilsley**, Der [off A619 Bakewell—Baslow; SK2471], *Devonshire Arms*: Cosy and welcoming local with limited good value food using fresh Chatsworth ingredients lunchtime and early evening, well kept

Mansfield Riding and Old Baily and other ales on handpump; lovely village handy for Chatsworth Farm and Craft Shops *(DC, G Washington)*

Repton, Der [High St; SK3026], *Bulls Head*: Beams and open fires, ex-stables dining area with original flagstones and boards, wide food choice inc vegetarian and children's, Bass, Ind Coope Burton, Marstons Pedigree and guest beers; families welcome; play area, terrace, garden; attractive village *(B M Eldridge)*

☆ **Ripley,** Der [Buckland Hollow; A610 towards Ambergate, junction B6013 – OS Sheet 119 map ref 380510; SK3851], *Excavator*: Open-plan Marstons Tavern Table with separate dining area and no-smoking area, wide choice of food (all day Sun) inc vegetarian and good children's menu, friendly efficient staff, reasonable prices, particularly well kept Pedigree and other ales *(Mark Bradley, Mike and Penny Sanders)*

Rolleston on Dove, Staffs [Church Rd; SK2427], *Spread Eagle*: Old pub with good range of well kept Bass-related ales, food all day, small restaurant with fresh fish, popular Sunday carvery; attractive village *(B M Eldridge)*

Rough Close, Staffs [SJ9239], *Swynnerton Arms*: Wide choice of reasonably priced bar food, fast polite service *(S Green)*

☆ **Rowarth,** Der [off A626 in Marple Bridge at Mellor sign, sharp left at Rowarth sign, then follow Little Mill sign; OS Sheet 110 map ref 011889 – but need Sheet 109 too; SK0189], *Little Mill*: Beautiful tucked-away setting, unusual features inc working waterwheel, vintage Pullman-carriage bedrooms; wide choice of cheap plentiful bar food all day (may be a wait), big open-plan bar with lots of little settees, armchairs and small tables, Banks's, Hansons, Robinsons Best Mild and Bitter and a guest beer, hospitable landlord, pub games, juke box, busy upstairs restaurant; children welcome, pretty garden dell across stream with excellent play area *(C Findell, Geoffrey and Irene Lindley, Bill and Lydia Ryan, N M Baleham, Mrs J Barwell, TBB, Jack and Philip Paxton, LYM)*

☆ **Rowsley,** Der [A6; SK2566], *Grouse & Claret*: Spacious and comfortable well refurbished Mansfield Landlords Table family dining pub, good reasonably priced food (all day weekends) from carvery counter with appetising salad bar, friendly helpful efficient service, decent wines; good value bedrooms *(Patricia Young, Tim and Lynne Crawford, A Preston, Jack and Philip Paxton, Geoffrey Lindley)*

☆ **Rowsley** [A6], *Peacock*: Decent unpretentious lunchtime bar food (not Sun) in civilised 17th-c small hotel's spacious and comfortable lounge, interestingly old-fashioned inner bar, real ales, friendly efficient staff, attractive riverside gardens, trout fishing; bedrooms good though far from cheap *(Pat Carlen, Jack and Philip Paxton, LYM)*

☆ **Rushton Spencer,** Staffs [Congleton Rd; off A523 Leek—Macclesfield at Ryecroft Gate; SJ9462], *Crown*: Friendly simple local in attractive scenery, with busy front snug, bigger back lounge, games room, S&N ales; food may include interesting Greek dishes *(LYM; reports on current regime please)*

Rushton Spencer [A523], *Royal Oak*: Burtonwood ales, bar food, lots of rally photographs *(D Hanley)*

☆ **Salt,** Staffs [signed S of Stone off A518; SJ9527], *Holly Bush*: Medieval partly thatched timbered pub, modern tasteful back extension, fine inglenook fireplace, well kept ales, generous bar food inc good value lunchtime specials, warm welcome, live music some summer Sats *(David and Shelia, P Bromley, Kate and Harry Taylor)*

☆ **Sandonbank,** Staffs [SJ9428], *Seven Stars*: Popular well decorated dining pub with wide choice of good value generous food from sandwiches up inc vegetarian and weekend carvery, Mon-Weds bargains, obliging service, well kept Burtonwood, several cosy corners, two big open fires, houseplants; two pool tables (winter only), piped music; restaurant, children welcome, seats out behind *(David and Shelia, Paul and Gail Betteley, Catherine and Martin Snelling, LYM)*

☆ **Shardlow,** Der [The Wharf; SK4330], *Malt Shovel*: Friendly 18th-c former maltings attractively set by canal, good changing lunchtime food, well kept Marstons and guest ales; odd-angled walls, good open fire heating two rooms, pleasant service; seats out by water *(A and R Cooper, Jack and Philip Paxton, David and Shelia, Andy and Jane Bearsdley, Bill Sykes, LYM)*

Shebden, Staffs [N of Newport, nr Harpur Adams Ag Coll; SJ7626], *Wharf*: Wide choice of good value simple food, guest beers such as Eldridge Pope Royal Oak and Morlands Old Speckled Hen, bar billiards, games machines; children welcome, big garden and playground, nr canal *(Nigel Woolliscroft)*

Shenstone, Staffs [Main St; SK1004], *Railway*: Airy lounge with leather chesterfields, varied nicely cooked lunchtime food, well kept Marstons ales; barbecue and picnic tables in garden *(Mr and Mrs H S Hill, Gary Nicholls)*

Shenstone Woodend, Staffs [Birmingham Rd nr Lichfield; SK1101], *Highwayman*: Friendly staff, well kept Bass, pleasant Toby carvery restaurant *(Geoffrey and Irene Lindley, Gary Nicholls)*

Shottle, Der [A517 Belper—Ashbourne; SK3149], *Hanging Gate*: Consistently good food inc vegetarian, friendly service; nice spot; children welcome *(Mr and Mrs J Fowden, B B Watling)*

☆ **Smalley,** Der [A608; SK4044], *Bell*: Charming three-room village pub, friendly staff, good helpings of straightforward food, well kept ales such as Batemans XB and XXXB, Marstons Pedigree and Ruddles, good choice of wines, keen landlord; lovely garden *(Jack and Philip Paxton, Mark Bradley)*

☆ **Sparrowpit**, Der [nr Chapel en le Frith; junction of A623 – B6061; SK0980], *Wanted Inn*: Friendly and attractive stonebuilt 16th-c inn, two rooms each with real fire, good value home cooking, well kept Robinsons Bitter and Mild, lots of copper; piped music; picnic tables by car park, beautiful countryside *(D W Gray, Jack and Philip Paxton, Susan Boyle, Eugene Wills, JJW, CMW)*

☆ **Stafford** [turn right at main entrance to station, 100 yards down], *Stafford Arms*: Friendly and comfortable real ale pub with well kept Titanic Best, Premium, Capt Smiths, Lifeboat or Wreckage, Stout and interesting changing small-brewery guests, farm cider, good generous reasonably priced food (all day weekdays), chatty staff, wide range of customers (no under-21s); barbecues and live bands during twice-yearly beer festival; now open all day, can be very busy *(Ken Wright, Richard Lewis, John and Chris Simpson, Sue Holland, Dave Webster)*

☆ **Stafford** [A34/A449 central roundabout, take Access Only rd past service stn], *Malt & Hops*: Rambling comfortable beamed pub with several well kept ales inc Exmoor Gold, big helpings of lunchtime food, low prices, good friendly service, provision for children; evenings esp Thurs-Sat becomes lively young person's place *(Mr and Mrs J C Burton, Richard Lewis, LYM)*

Stafford [Eastgate St], *Forester & Firkin*: Big popular bare-boards Firkin pub with own Dogbolter, Forester and Pecker, lots of framed beer mats and old photographs, good value food; live music nights, very busy weekends *(R Lewis)*; [Eastgate St], *Lord Nelson*: Cosy local with particularly well kept ales such as Boddingtons, Joules, Newcastle Exhibition, Theakstons Best, XB and Old Peculier and Youngers Scotch, farm ciders, friendly staff, good value food *(R Lewis)*; [Mill St], *Nags Head*: Friendly town pub, well kept Bass, Highgate Mild and Worthington Best; loud juke box popular with young people late evening *(G Reeve, R Lewis)*; [Cape Ave], *Oxleathers*: Good atmosphere, friendly staff, Banks's ales, pool, darts, Sky TV; regular live music *(Dale James)*; [Peel Terr, just off B5066 Sandon Rd – formerly Cottage by the Brook], *Tap & Spile*: Constantly changing real ales with good mix of standard and little-known, country wines, friendly staff, tasteful bare boards and bricks with lots of prints; pool, traditional games, live music Weds *(R Lewis)*; [Stone Rd], *Wagon & Horses*: Good local atmosphere, friendly staff *(Thomas Giuliante Jr)*

Stanton, Der [A444; SK2719], *Gate*: Pleasantly refurbished, good value home cooking inc children's dishes, well kept Marstons Pedigree, friendly staff *(Graham Richardson, B M Eldridge)*

☆ **Stanton by Dale**, Der [3 miles from M1 junction 25; SK4638], *Stanhope Arms*: Cosy and attractive rambling pub, friendly staff, well kept Tetleys-related ales, good value generous fresh bar food, upstairs dining room converted from adjoining cottage; unspoilt village *(Dr and Mrs J H Hills, R Johnson)*

Stoke on Trent, Staffs [City Rd, Fenton; SJ8944], *Malt 'n' Hops*: At least four real ales inc one brewed to landlord's own recipe *(David and Shelia)*; [Hill St; SJ8745], *Staff of Life*: Character Potteries local, welcoming even when packed, unchanging layout of three rooms and drinking corridor *(Pete Baker, Sue Holland, Dave Webster)*

☆ **Stone**, Staffs [21 Stafford St (A520); SJ9034], *Star*: Welcoming 18th-c canalside pub with canal photographs and exposed joists in intimate public bar, snug lounge and pleasant family room; well kept Banks's, Camerons and Marstons, good value food inc children's (not Sun evening), open fire, nearby moorings; open all day Apr-Oct *(DC, Tony Hobden, Paul Robinshaw, Colin Buckle, LYM)*

Stramshall, Staffs [SK0735], *Hare & Hounds*: Good food, well kept beer *(G Washington)*

Stretton, Staffs [A5, not far from M6 junction 12; SJ8811], *Bell*: Banks's beer, good food in bar and restaurant, children's area; garden with barbecue *(D Hanley)*

Stretton, Staffs [Craythorne Rd – the one nr Burton on Trent; SK2525], *Craythorne*: Rebuilt pub with good value food, Bass, Marstons Pedigree and Tetleys, pine panelling, good atmosphere; doubles as golf clubhouse *(EAW)*

Sutton cum Duckmanton, Der [A632 Bolsover—Chesterfield; SK4171], *Arkwright Arms*: Biggish friendly roadside pub with good value food, four real ales, comfortable banquettes, darts, fruit machine, juke box; big garden with play area *(JJW, CMW)*

Swindon, Staffs [village centre; SO8690], *Old Bush*: Rambling building with cheap Banks's and bar snacks *(Dave Braisted)*

Swynnerton, Staffs [SJ8535], *Fitzherbert Arms*: New licensees doing good interesting food in traditional country pub, coal fire, good range of beers, friendly atmosphere; bedrooms *(Chris Cronin)*

Taddington, Der [SK1472], *Queens Arms*: Attractively furnished and decorated, welcoming landlord and staff, varied generous nicely presented food inc good children's dishes, Mitchells and Tetleys; quiet village in good walking country *(S and E Howe, Jack and Philip Paxton)*

☆ **Ticknall**, Der [7 High St; SK3423], *Staff of Life*: Very neat, with up to 16 real ales on handpump or tapped from the cask inc ones from distant breweries such as Moorhouses, Pendragon, Shepherd Neame, also wide choice of good popular inexpensive food; good atmosphere, friendly staff, magazines to read, restaurant, good wine list *(Derek and Sylvia Stephenson, Anthony Barker, G Atkinson, Eric Locker, Jack and Philip Paxton, Alan and Heather Jacques, Rona Murdoch)*

☆ **Ticknall** [B5006 towards Ashby de la Zouch], *Chequers*: Small, friendly and full of atmosphere, with vast 16th-c inglenook fireplace (maybe with winter roast chestnuts), bright brass, old prints, well kept Marstons Pedigree and Ruddles, very welcoming landlady, good fresh lunchtime baps and ploughman's (not Sun), seats in sizeable garden *(Alan and Heather Jacques, Jack and Philip Paxton, G Atkinson, Mrs W Bryn Davies, LYM)*

☆ **Tideswell**, Der [SK1575], *George*: Welcoming village inn recently sympathetically refurbished giving more table space for good value generous home cooking, keeping simple traditional decor and furnishings and separate room areas; well kept Hardys & Hansons, friendly landlord, open fire, weekly folk bands; tables in front overlooking pretty village, sheltered back garden; children welcome; good value bedrooms, pleasant walks *(Norma and Keith Bloomfield, Susan Boyle, Eugene Wills, W H and E Thomas, Jack and Philip Paxton, Sarah and Gary Goldson, A F C Young, K Flack, BB)*

Tintwistle, Der [Old Rd; off A628, N side; SK0297], *Bulls Head*: Good food, well kept ales and reasonable prices in low-beamed 16th-c pub, suitable decor *(Tony Owens)*

☆ **Uttoxeter**, Staffs [High St, opp cinema; SK0933], *Wellington*: A few other pubs have either a clergyman landlord or a pet pig but this is the only one we know with both – *Church Times* as well as local papers for customers, wide choice of very good food (copperplate blackboard writing), a dozen Belgian beers among more usual drinks such as well kept Bass, open fire, Classic FM, cosy restaurant; open all day *(Pat Bromley, Ian C Hutchieson)*

Walton, Der [Matlock Rd; B6015 SW of Chesterfield; SK3669], *White Hart*: Two-bar pub with well kept Courage-related ales, play area *(JJW, CMW)*

☆ **Wardlow**, Der [B6465; SK1874], *Bulls Head*: Plushly comfortable country dining pub with decent food, Wards ale, helpful landlord and welcoming staff, provision for children; no dogs or walking boots; simple bedrooms *(Derek and Sylvia Stephenson, Dr and Mrs D E Awbery, Geoffrey and Irene Lindley, Comus Elliot, Brian and Anna Marsden, Jack and Philip Paxton, Roger and Christine Mash, LYM)*

☆ **Waterhouses**, Staffs [SK0850], *George*: Large three-room dining pub, good food similar to Izaak Walton at Cresswell (same management, see main entries) inc children's, Marstons ales, play area; handy for Manifold cycle trail, two bike hire places *(John Scarisbrick)*

☆ **Weston**, Staffs [The Green; off A518 – OS Sheet 127 map ref 978268; SJ9726], *Woolpack*: Well modernised, open-plan but separate areas with cosy corners, reasonably priced good fresh food, small dining room, well kept Marstons and guest ales, smart but pleasant staff, antique furniture inc high-backed settle, polished brass, lovely relaxed well tended gardens by village green *(Peter and Jenny Quine, Bill Sykes)*

Wheaton Aston, Staffs [Canalside, Tavern Br; SJ8412], *Hartley Arms*: Canalside, food, Banks's beers, seats outside *(D Hanley)*

☆ **Whitmore**, Staffs [3 miles from M6 junction 15 – A53 towards Mkt Drayton; SJ8141], *Mainwaring Arms*: Popular old place of great character, rambling interconnected oak-beamed rooms, stone walls, four open fires, antique settles among more modern seats; well kept Bass, Boddingtons, Marstons Pedigree, wide range of foreign bottled beers and ciders, seats outside, children in eating area, no piped music; open all day Fri/Sat, picturesque village *(David Lewis, Catherine and Andrew Brian, D W Gray, Gary Roberts, D P and M E Cartwright, Anthony Birchall, Nigel Woolliscroft, LYM)*

Wingerworth, Der [Derby Rd (A61); SK3767], *Hunloke Arms*: Big Steak pub in imposing early 18th-c stone building, good range of well kept Tetleys-related ales, two raised levels, one furnished with light wood contrasting well with other more traditional one *(B M Eldridge)*

☆ **Winster**, Der [B5056 above village; SK2460], *Miners Standard*: Welcoming local, well kept Marstons Pedigree, Theakstons XB and a guest such as Black Sheep, good value food till 10, big open fires, interesting lead-mining photographs and mineral specimes, well placed darts, restaurant, attractive view from garden; children allowed away from bar *(Barbara Hatfield, Jamie and Ruth Lyons, Jack Morley)*

☆ **Wrinehill**, Staffs [Den Lane; pub signed just off A531 Newcastle—Nantwich; SJ7547], *Crown*: Good range of well kept ales and wide choice of good generous food inc vegetarian in busy but cosy neatly refurbished pub with friendly staff, plush seats, interesting pictures, two open fires, well reproduced pop music; children allowed lunchtime, early evening; cl weekday lunchtimes exc bank hols *(Richard Lewis, LYM)*

Yeaveley, Der [on byroads S of Ashbourne; SK1840], *Horseshoe*: Good food and atmosphere, well kept beer *(G Washington)*

☆ **Youlgreave**, Der [Church St; SK2164], *George*: Handsome stonebuilt local opp church, unpretentious, quick friendly service, good range of reasonably priced home-cooked food, comfortable banquettes, well kept S&N ales; flagstoned walkers' bar, games room, juke box; roadside tables outside *(Harriet and Michael Robinson, JJW, CMW, Sue Holland, Dave Webster, Jack and Philip Paxton)*

☆ **Youlgreave** [High St], *Farmyard*: Low ceilings, flagstones, stone fireplace, old farm tools, character landlord, well kept Mansfield Mild and Riding on handpump, good reasonably priced food, big upstairs restaurant, attractive village; children welcome *(Jack and Philip Paxton)*

☆ **Yoxall**, Staffs [Main St; SK1319], *Crown*: Relaxed atmosphere, good value fresh tasty food, well kept Marstons Pedigree, quick friendly service, cosy refurbished lounge with log-effect gas fire, separate raised dining room; children welcome lunchtime *(B M Eldridge)*

Devon

Some changes to note here include management of the Masons Arms at Branscombe passing to the next generation (lots of wines by the glass, a summer beer festival, new kitchen), friendly new licensees at the Poltimore Arms at Brayford, lots of work on the building and garden of the Coach & Horses at Buckland Brewer (promising reports on its new Portuguese chef), welcoming new people at the Tally Ho in Hatherleigh (good food and wines, as well as keeping the microbrewery going), a new man at the Duke of York at Iddesleigh (high hopes for the pub, which he's known for 40 years), and new licensees at the friendly Millbrook at South Pool (but still in the same family). That otherwise unchanging old favourite the Masons Arms at Knowstone has just about completed its bedroom-refurbishment programme; the Coombe Cellars at Combeinteignhead has been taken over by Whitbreads as a Brewers Fayre (if anything even more of a family place); and the Double Locks on the edge of Exeter has been bought by Smiles, the small Bristol brewer (early reports are good). Pubs currently doing particularly well include the bustling Watermans Arms at Ashprington, the pretty thatched Cott at Dartington, that great all-rounder the Nobody at Doddiscombsleigh, the Dolphin not far from the sea at Kingston, and the beautifully placed Otter at Weston – which gains a star award this year for its great atmosphere (good food, too). Devon is a fine county for eating out in pubs, with a high proportion qualifying for our food award – this year newcomers to this gastronomic elite are the Anchor at Cockwood (seafood cooked in all sorts of ways), the medieval New Inn at Coleford (imaginative use of the best local produce), and the relaxed and friendly Church House at Holne (the specials are the thing there). New Devon main entries are the Red Lion in its peaceful village setting at Broadclyst, the friendly thatched Five Bells at Clyst Hydon (we're betting it'll be very popular indeed), the Manor at Lower Ashton (excellent beers, decent food), the friendly Journeys End prettily placed at Ringmore (another that we're sure will become a readers' favourite), and the delightfully cottagey Northmore Arms at Wonson – well worth tracking down. In the Lucky Dip section at the end of the chapter, current notables (most of them inspected and thoroughly approved by us) include the Bridford Inn, Coppa Dolla at Broadhempston, Artichoke at Christow, Anglers Rest near Drewsteignton, Royal Oak at Dunsford, Red Cow in Honiton, Ley Arms at Kenn, Crabshell at Kingsbridge, Grampus at Lee, New Inn at Moreleigh, Two Mile Oak near Newton Abbot, Ring of Bells at North Bovey, Yard Arm in Plymouth, Stag at Rackenford, the Sandy Park Inn, both Stokenham entries, Floyds Inn at Tuckenhay, both Ugborough entries, the Westleigh Inn and both Widecombe entries; there's a fine choice in both Exeter and Topsham. Drinks prices in the area are typically a shade higher than the national average, with pubs getting their beers from the smaller local breweries generally offering savings of just a few pence a pint. (Note that despite its name Dartmoor is actually produced by the Tetleys-Carlsberg combine.) Quite a few pubs here brew their own beer, and of these we found the Fountain Head at Branscombe, Mildmay Colours at Holbeton and Beer Engine at Newton St Cyres had the most attractive prices – though the cheapest beer of all was a special offer of just over £1 on Websters Green Label at the Normandy Arms at Blackawton.

ABBOTSKERSWELL SX8569 Map 1

Court Farm

Wilton Way; look for the church tower

New licensees have taken over this attractive old farmhouse. The long bar has a mix of seats on the polished crazy flagstones, a woodburning stove in a stripped red granite fireplace, a nice big round table by an angled black oak screen, a turkey rug in one alcove formed by a low granite wall with timbers above, and a long rough-boarded bar counter; a further small room is broadly similar with stripped kitchen tables and more spindleback chairs. On the right of the entrance is the two-roomed public bar with a woodburning stove, and fruit machine, and a simple end room with darts, cribbage and dominoes. Bar food now includes home-made soup (£1.55), doorstep sandwiches (from £1.85), ploughman's (from £2.95), home-cooked ham and egg or mushroom and stilton tagliatelle (£4.25), home-made steak and kidney pie (£5.35), whole grilled fresh local plaice (£5.95), steaks (from £7.95), roast rack of lamb with rich madeira sauce (£8.95), and puddings (£2.25). Well kept Bass, Boddingtons, Flowers IPA and a guest beer on handpump or tapped from the cask. The pretty garden has a wendy house full of bikes and toys to ride for children. ***(Recommended by Joan and Gordon Edwards, Steve Huggins, A E and P McCully, Peter and Jenny Quine, N King)***

Heavitree (who no longer brew) ~ Tenant Robin Huggins ~ Real ale ~ Meals and snacks (till 10pm) ~ (01626) 61866 ~ Children in eating area of bar ~ Occasional live music Fri/Sat ~ Open 11-3, 5-11; 11-11 Sat

ASHBURTON SX7569 Map 1

London Hotel

11 West St

Behind this rather grand but friendly coach house is the brewery where they brew their own beers, served on handpump: Best, Figurehead, Man o' War and Black Velvet Stout. The spacious turkey-carpeted lounge has a central fireplace, little brocaded or red leatherette armchairs and other seats around the copper-topped casks they use as tables, and stripped stone walls; the room spreads back into a softly lit dining area. Bar food includes home-made soup, sandwiches, ploughman's, steak and kidney pie (£4.20), 8oz rump steak £5.80), puddings like home-made apple pie, and daily specials; farm ciders; darts, shove-ha'penny, dominoes, cribbage and piped music. ***(Recommended by Jeanne Cross, Paul Silvestri, Richard Houghton, R J Walden, Cdr Patrick Tailyour, Mr and Mrs McDougal, Nigel and Teresa Brooks)***

Own brew ~ Licensee M Thompson ~ Real ale ~ Meals and snacks ~ Restaurant ~ (01364) 652478 ~ Children welcome ~ Open 11-2.30(3 Sat), 5.30-11 ~ Bedrooms: £27B/£35B

ASHPRINGTON SX8156 Map 1

Durant Arms

Village signposted off A381 S of Totnes; OS Sheet 202 map reference 819571

It's the very good food that visitors and locals like in this friendly and neatly kept gable-ended dining pub. At lunchtime there might be sandwiches (from £1.50), ploughman's (£3), stilton and asparagus flan (£3.50), salmon and broccoli bake

(£3.95), casserole of lamb cutlets (£4.20), big brown pot, good chicken curry with pots of mango chutney, banana and coconut, and crisp poppadum, venison casserole, lamb's liver and bacon or cashew nut paella (all £4.95), with evening dishes such as tomato and basil soup (£1.95), baked avocado and crab (£3.25), baked skate in tarragon butter (£7.15), generous rack of lamb, pork tenderloin with cider and apple sauce (£8.25), monkfish in cream and garlic (£8.50), and roast duckling with orange and brandy sauce (£10.95); very good puddings include lemon meringue pie and crème brûlée; best to book to be sure of a seat. The public bar has been incorporated with the other two bars and has wooden tables and chairs as well as unusual cutaway barrel seats on the red turkey carpet, prints on the wall, and Exmoor, Palmers IPA, and Wadworths 6X on handpump from a temperature controlled cellar, 12 malt whiskies and decent wines; good service. The lower carpeted lounge – where families are allowed – is furnished with settles, tables, chairs, red velvet curtains and a winter fire (there are two others as well); darts, dominoes and piped music. The dog, George II, is a real favourite among customers – particularly children. Tables in the sheltered back garden. *(Recommended by D I Baddeley, David Wallington, B J Harding, T Cobden Pike, Dr P R Davis, P R Ferris, T Aldworth, Mrs Margaret Barker, Gordon)*

Free house ~ Licensees John and Gill Diprose ~ Real ale ~ Meals and snacks ~ (01803) 732240 ~ Children in eating area of bar and in restaurant ~ Open 11.30-2.30, 6-11

Watermans Arms

Bow Bridge, on Tuckenhay road; OS Sheet 202 map reference 812565

Once a smithy and brewhouse, and a prison during the Napoleonic Wars, this riverside pub is flourishing at the moment. The quarry-tiled bar area has a bustling, friendly atmosphere, heavy beams, high-backed settles, built-in wall benches, rustic seats, and candles in bottles, and the comfortable eating area has windsor chairs on its red carpet, more beams, and stripped stone walls; log fires. Good bar food includes home-made soup (£1.95), sandwiches (from £2.25; fresh crab £3.95), ploughman's (£4.95), freshly made pasta carbonara or mushroom stroganoff (£5.95), cold platters (from £6.25), home-made steak and kidney pie or plaice (£6.95), Thai chicken curry (£8.50), roast lamb with rosemary and red wine sauce (£8.95), daily specials, and children's dishes (£2.50); part of the restaurant and the residents' lounge is no smoking. Well kept Bass, Dartmoor, Palmers IPA, and Tetleys on handpump, with a farm cider called Pigsqueal, and Luscombe real apple juice; good, quick service. Dominoes and piped music. There are picnic tables in the flower-filled garden and more by the river where you can watch the ducks (or even swans and kingfishers). More bedrooms have been added this year. *(Recommended by Joy and Paul Rundell, Roger and Susan Dunn, Nigel Spence, Kim Greek, George and Jeanne Barnwell, B H Sharpe, David Wallington, Barry Lynch, Jeanne Cross, Paul Silvestri, Jim and Maggie Cowell, M V and J Melling, T Aldworth, A Plumb, Mrs J Barwell, Alan and Heather Jacques, Paul Boot)*

Free house ~ Licensee Trevelyan Illingworth ~ Real ale ~ Meals and snacks ~ Restaurant ~ (01803) 732214 ~ Children in eating area of bar and in restaurant ~ Open 11-3, 6-11 ~ Bedrooms: £36S/£66S

AXMOUTH SY2591 Map 1

Harbour

B3172 Seaton—Axminster

To be sure of a seat, it's best to get here early as this thatched stone pub is very popular with both locals and visitors. The Harbour Bar has black oak beams and joists, fat pots hanging from pot-irons in the huge inglenook fireplace, brass-bound cask seats, a high-backed oak settle, and an antique wall clock. A central lounge has more cask seats and settles, and over on the left another room is divided from the no-smoking dining room by a two-way log fireplace. At the back, a big flagstoned lobby with sturdy seats leads on to a very spacious and simply furnished family bar. Well kept Devenish Royal Wessex, Flowers IPA and Original, and Whitbreads Castle Eden on handpump; darts and pool. Good bar food includes sandwiches (from £1.50), ploughman's (from £3.25), vegetarian dishes (from £4.75), and fresh fish (from £5); roast Sunday lunch (£4.75), and maybe Sunday cheese and nibbles on the bar; friendly, cheerful service even when busy. They have a lavatory for disabled people, and general access is good. There are tables in the neat flower garden behind. The handsome church has some fine stone gargoyles. ***(Recommended by A Denman, Mrs A M Fishleigh, Basil Minson, Galen Strawson, A Plumb, Brian A Websdale)***

Free house ~ Licensees Dave and Pat Squire ~ Real ale ~ Meals and snacks (not winter Sun evenings) ~ (01297) 20371 ~ Children in family room in summer, in eating area of bar in winter ~ Open 11-2.30, 6-11

BANTHAM SX6643 Map 1

Sloop

Off A379/B3197 NW of Kingsbridge

Just 300 yards over the dunes is a lovely sandy beach with lots of rock pools – and it's one of the best surfing beaches on the south coast – so this 16th-c building does get extremely busy in summer. The black-beamed bar has country chairs around wooden tables, stripped stone walls and flagstones, and easy chairs in a quieter side area with a nautical theme. Bar food includes sandwiches (from £1.75), basket meals (from £2.40), ploughman's (from £3.60), liver and onions (£4.25), vegetable au gratin (£4.95), salads (from £5.45; fresh crab £8.65), steaks (from £8.65), daily specials like hot potted shrimps (£3.25), scallop mornay (£4.85), giant cod or roast pheasant (£7.40), and john dory of whole lemon sole (£7.95); hearty breakfasts. Well kept Bass, Blackawton Bitter, Ushers Best and a guest beer on handpump, Churchward's cider from Paignton, several malt whiskies, and a very good wine list including local ones. Darts, dominoes, cribbage, table skittles, fruit machine, trivia, and piped music. There are some seats at the back. The bedrooms in the pub itself have the most character. ***(Recommended by James Macrae, J and J O Jones, Mrs M Lawrence, B Taylor, Roger and Susan Dunn, Jacquie and Jim Jones, Owen and Margaret Warnock, Anthony Marriott, Peter Lewis, Mr and Mrs C R Little, P and J Shapley, Bill Edwards, Mr and Mrs C R Little, Mrs J Barwell)***

Free house ~ Licensee Neil Girling ~ Real ale ~ Meals and snacks (till 10pm) ~ Restaurant ~ (01548) 560489 ~ Children in eating area of bar and in restaurant ~ Open 11-2.30, 6-11; winter evening opening 6.30 ~ Bedrooms: £27B/£54B; s/c cottages also

BERRYNARBOR SS5646 Map 1

Olde Globe ★

Village signposted from A399 E of Ilfracombe

One reader was happy to find that after a 40-year gap, this characterful old pub was as good as ever. The atmospheric series of dimly lit homely rooms have low ceilings, curved deep-ochre walls (bulging unevenly in places), floors of flagstones or of ancient lime-ash (with silver coins embedded in them) and old high-backed oak settles (some carved) and plush cushioned cask seats around antique tables. Decorations include a profusion of genuinely old pictures, priests (fish-coshes), thatcher's knives, sheep shears, gin traps, pitchforks, antlers, copper warming pans and lots of cutlasses, swords, shields and fine powder flasks. Well kept Courage Directors, John Smiths Bitter, and Ushers Best on handpump, and several country wines; sensibly placed darts, pool, skittle alley, dominoes, cribbage, fruit machine, and piped music. Bar food includes soup (£1.30), sandwiches (from £1.25), pasties (£2.50), ploughman's (£2.60), salads (£3.10), lasagne or good chilli con carne (£3.90), steaks (from £6.95), daily specials (£3.50), puddings (from £1.50), children's dishes (£1.90), and popular main course Sunday lunch (£3.80; 3-course in restaurant £6 – best to book). In high season the restaurant is used as a no-smoking room for bar rather than restaurant meals. There's now a children's activity house in the garden and the crazy-paved front terrace has some old-fashioned garden seats. The village is pretty. Dogs are welcome. *(Recommended by Basil Minson, Dorothy and Leslie Pilson, R J Walden, George and Jeanne Barnwell, Ted George, Graham and Sue Price, Dave and Moyra Burley, John Sanders, Dorothee and Dennis Glover, Jim and Maggie Cowell, S R and A J Ashcroft, Bob Smith)*

Courage ~ Lease: Phil and Lynne Bridle ~ Real ale ~ Meals and snacks (till 10pm) ~ Gaslit restaurant ~ (01271) 882465 ~ Children in family/function room with toys ~ Live entertainment Thurs evenings July/Aug ~ Open 11.30-2.30, 6-11; winter evening opening 7pm

BISHOPS TAWTON SS5630 Map 1

Chichester Arms

Pub signposted off A377 outside Barnstaple

In a pleasantly quiet village, this thatched pub has a rather smart bar with low heavy beams and stout supporting timbers, plush wall banquettes and cushioned wheelback chairs on its patterned carpet, a solid old bar counter, uneven sloping floors, and an open fire. The family room has its own bar: darts, pool, alley skittles, cribbage, dominoes, fruit machine, video game, piped music, and doors out to barbecue area. The restaurant has a no-smoking area. Bar food includes soup (£1.75), sandwiches (from £1.75), filled baked potatoes (from £2.95), meat or vegetable burgers (£2.95), cod in batter (£3.95), tortellini and prawns (£4.95), steaks (from £7.95), and puddings (£2.75). Well kept Bass, Worthingtons, and a guest beer on handpump. There are picnic tables on a flagstoned front terrace, with more in a sheltered back area. *(Recommended by Peter and Audrey Dowsett, R J Walden, Lynn Sharpless, Bob Eardley, E H and R F Warner, P and J Shapley, B M Eldridge)*

Free house ~ Lease: Hugh Johnston ~ Real ale ~ Meals and snacks (till 10pm) ~ Restaurant ~ (01271) 43945 ~ Children in eating area of bar and in restaurant ~ Occasional live entertainment Sun evening ~ Open 11.30-3, 5.30-11; 11.30-11 Sat

BLACKAWTON SX8050 Map 1

Normandy Arms

Signposted off B3207 W of Dartmouth; OS Sheet 202 map reference 807509

There's an interesting display of World War II battle gear in this solid old inn – which still carries some of the bullet scars from when this whole village was commandeered as a training ground to prepare for the Normandy landings. The quaint and cosy main bar has a good log fire and a warmly welcoming atmosphere, as well as bar food such as home-made soup (£1.95), sandwiches (from £1.95, crab £2.95), ploughman's (£3.95), home-made chicken liver pâté (£4.25), home-made steak and kidney pie (£4.95), whole lemon sole (£8.50), pork in cider and cream (£8.75), steaks (from £8.95), and home-made puddings like luscious lemon cake or apple pie (from £2.60). Well kept Bass, Blackawton Bitter, Websters Green Label and a guest beer on handpump. Sensibly placed darts, shove-ha'penny, cribbage and dominoes; well behaved dogs welcome; tables out in the garden, where there's a gaggle of elderly tractors. *(Recommended by Roger and Susan Dunn, Jack and Philip Paxton, George and Jeanne Barnwell, Phil and Anne Smithson, F Tomlin, Paul and Janet Waring, J L Hall, Dennis Heatley, D G King, David Holloway)*

Free house ~ Licensees Jonathan and Mark Gibson ~ Real ale ~ Meals and snacks (not winter Sun evenings) ~ Restaurant ~ (01803) 712316 ~ Children in family room and in restaurant ~ Folk/blues winter Mon evenings ~ Open 11.30-2.30, 6.30-11; 12-2, 6.30-11 in winter ~ Bedrooms: £30B/£48B; not 24-26 Dec

BRANSCOMBE SY1988 Map1

Fountain Head

Upper village, above the robust old church; village signposted off A3052 Sidmouth—Seaton

As well as their own-brewed beers – Branoc, Jolly Geff (named after Mrs Luxton's father, the ex-licensee), and Olde Stoker – this old tiled stone house holds a beer festival on the last weekend in June. They also keep Green Valley farm cider. The room on the left – formerly a smithy – has a log fire in the original raised firebed with its tall central chimney, forge tools and horseshoes on the high oak beams, and cushioned pews and mates' chairs. On the right, an irregularly shaped, more orthodox snug room has a another log fire, white-painted plank ceiling with an unusual carved ceiling-rose, brown-varnished panelled walls, and rugs on its flagstone-and-limeash floor; the children's room is no smoking, and the airedale is called Oscar. Bar food includes cockles or mussels (£1.25), sandwiches (from £1.50; fresh crab when available £2.50), ploughman's (£3.50), home-made steak and kidney pie or home-cooked ham and egg (£4.75), kebabs (£5.95), steaks (from £8.50), daily specials like fried sardines (£3.95) or pasta bake (£4.25), and children's dishes (from £1.95); roast Sunday lunch (November-May), and some winter speciality food nights. Darts, cribbage, dominoes. There are seats out on the front loggia and terrace, and a little stream rustling under the flagstoned path. *(Recommended by Mrs A M Fishleigh, Peter Burton, M Richards, J I Fraser, R J Walden)*

Free house ~ Licensee Mrs Catherine Luxton ~ Real ale ~ Meals and snacks (not 25 Dec) ~ (01297) 680359 ~ Children in own small room; if over 10 can eat in eating area of bar in evening ~ Monthly folk group last Sun lunchtime of month ~ Open 11.30-2.30, 6.30-11; 11.30-2, 7-11 in winter ~ S/c available

Masons Arms

Main St; signed off A3052 Sidmouth—Seaton

Mrs Inglis's son Murray has now taken over the management of this 14th-c inn and has assembled an enthusiastic young team to help him. The kitchen has been re-organised which should cut down on the wait for food, the menu has changed to include more traditional dishes (and vegetarian ones), and they do spit roasts over the open fire in the bar every Thursday – lunchtime leg of lamb, evening rib of beef, a whole pig on the first Friday of each month, and a garlicky French fish speciality called Bourride on Friday lunchtimes. The rambling low-beamed bar has a massive central hearth in front of the roaring log fire, windsor chairs and settles, and a more relaxed atmosphere. The bar food menu was under review as we went to press, but included soup (£1.80), sandwiches (from £1.95; crab £2.90), ploughman's (from £3.50), chicken liver pâté (£3.50), penne with a tomato, oregano and basil sauce (£4.50), deep-fried local fillet of plaice (£5.65), chicken, stilton and walnut strudel (£5.95), steak and kidney pudding (£6.25), peppered rump steak (£6.95), and puddings like raspberry cheesecake (£2.50); summer cream teas (£3). One of the three rooms of the restaurant is no smoking. Well kept Bass, Dartmoor, and Ruddles County and two guest beers such as Morlands Old Speckled Hen or Robinsons on handpump, and they hold a summer beer festival with over 20 real ales and entertainment; ten wines by the glass from a fine list, and Addlestones and Coates ciders. Darts, shove-ha'penny, skittle alley, dominoes, and trivia. Outside, the quiet flower-filled front terrace has tables with little thatched roofs, extending into a side garden. *(Recommended by Guyneth and Salvo Spadaro-Dutturi, Basil Minson, Peter Burton, Mrs A M Fishleigh, WA, Mark and Heather Williamson, J I Fraser, W F C Phillips, M Owton, Mrs J M Corless, B D Jones)*

Free house ~ Licensees Janet Inglis and Murray Inglis ~ Real ale ~ Meals and snacks all day (though reduced in afternoon) ~ Restaurant ~ (01297) 680300 ~ Children in eating area of bar and in restaurant ~ Live entertainment Fri evening in Waterfall Room ~ Open 11-11; 11-3, 6-11 in winter ~ Bedrooms: (some in cottage across road); £22(£37B)/£44(£54B)

BRAYFORD SS6834 Map 1

Poltimore Arms

Yarde Down – three miles from village, towards Simonsbath; OS Sheet 180 map reference 724356

Under friendly new management, this chatty local has a good pubby atmosphere. The main bar has an open fire in the inglenook fireplace, old leather-seated chairs with carved or slatted backs, cushioned wall settles, a little window seat, some interesting tables, and a beam in the slightly sagging cream ceiling with another over the small serving counter; there are photos of hunt meetings and hunting cartoons on the walls. The lounge bar has old guns and wildlife prints by a local artist on the walls, a mix of chairs, and another open fire; darts, pool, shove-ha'penny, juke box, and piped music in the plainly decorated games room. Good bar food now includes sandwiches, home-made soup (£1.75), home-made pâté (£2.25), cannelloni with ricotta cheese and spinach (£3.95), gammon and egg (£5.55), local trout (£5.75), charcoal-grilled salmon fillet in lemon and parsley butter (£6.95), steaks (from £6.95), and puddings like good raspberry pavlova (£2.75). Well kept Cotleigh Tawny and Wadsworth 6X tapped from the cask. In the side garden there are picnic tables. ***(Recommended by Nigel Paine, Jennie Munro, Jim Wingate, Chris Westmoreland, Gethin Lewis, R J Walden, Anthony Barnes, B M Eldridge)***

Free house ~ Licensees Richard and Dawn Austen ~ Real ale ~ Meals and snacks (not 25 Dec) ~ Restaurant ~ (01598) 710381 ~ Children in restaurant ~ Open 11.30-2.30, 6.30-11; closed evening 25 Dec

BRENDON SS7748 Map 1

Rockford

Lynton—Simonsbath rd, off B2332

Completely redecorated inside and out, this homely little inn is surrounded by lovely Exmoor scenery. The original stables and hay loft have been converted into bars and there are lots of old photographs on the walls (which the landlord is happy to describe to you). Bar food includes lunchtime dishes like home-made cottage pie (£2.75), smoked trout (£3.50), or home-made chicken and mushroom pie (£3.95), with evening things such as gammon home-braised in ale with honey glaze (£5.95), and lamb in redcurrant and port or chicken supreme stuffed with prawns (£6.95); well kept Cotleigh Barn Owl, and Courage Best and Directors on handpump, and decent wines. Darts, pool, shove-ha'penny, cribbage, dominoes, and piped music. The pub is set by the East Lyn river with its good salmon, brown trout and sea trout fishing; Watersmeet is closeby, riding can be arranged, and there are lots of fine walks. ***(Recommended by H and D Payne, Mrs C Blake, Dorothee and Dennis Glover, Peter and Audrey Dowsett)***

Free house ~ Licensees D W Sturmer and S J Tasker ~ Real ale ~ Meals and snacks ~ Restaurant ~ (015987) 214 ~ Children welcome in eating area of bar ~ Local folk every 3rd Sat evening of month ~ Open 12-2.30(2 in winter), 7-11; closed weekday lunchtimes 2 weeks Nov and 2 weeks Feb ~ Bedrooms: £18/£36

BROADCLYST SX9897 Map 1

Red Lion ♀

B3121, by church

In a quiet village by some thatched houses and a church with a pinnacled tower, this tiled, ochre-washed old pub has picnic tables on the front cobbles by the wisteria, and more seats in a small enclosed garden across the quiet lane. Inside, the long red-carpeted bar has heavy beams, cushioned window seats, some nice chairs around a mix of oak and other tables, and a collection of carpenters' planes; a flagstoned area has cushioned pews and low tables by the fireplace, and at the end of the L-shaped room are big hunting prints and lots of team photographs. Popular bar food includes home-made soup (£1.60), sandwiches (from £1.80), home-made chicken liver pâté (£2.70), lamb's kidneys in sherry (£3.50), ploughman's (from £3.60), vegetable lasagne (£4.60), steak and kidney pie or pork and apple in cider casserole (£4.80), rump steak (£7.90), daily specials like tandoori chicken (£4.60), Brixham haddock or grilled pork chop (£4.80) or 20oz T-bone steak (£10.95), children's meals (from £2), and puddings (from £2). Well kept Bass, Eldridge Pope Royal Oak, Wadworths 6X, Worthington Best, and a guest like Vaux Waggle Dance on handpump, 8 wines by the glass, and local farm cider; they sell home-produced honey. Darts and a beamed skittle alley. *(Recommended by Patrick Stewart-Blacker, E V M Whiteway, Desmond and Pat Morris, Mrs J M Corless, Canon and Mrs M Bourdeaux, J I Fraser, Denzil Taylor)*

Free house ~ Licensees Stephen and Susan Smith ~ Real ale ~ Meals and snacks (till 10pm) ~ Restaurant (not Sun evening) ~ (01392) 461271 ~ Children in skittle alley and family room ~ Open 11-3, 5.30-11

BROADHEMBURY ST1004 Map 1

Drewe Arms ★

Signposted off A373 Cullompton—Honiton

Although this pretty pub is so popular for its consistently good food (especially the wonderful fresh fish), the friendly licensees continue to try and preserve the unpretentious pubby atmosphere. It's now almost essential to book to be sure of a table, and this year there are no restrictions on eating any of the dishes anywhere in the pub – or in the flower-filled garden: lovely gravadlax, ceviche of scallops, langoustines and garlic mayonnaise or marinated herring with a glass of aquavit (all £4.95), fillet of cod in mustard sauce or salmon and crab cakes (£6.95), fillet of brill with prawns and mushrooms (£7.95), tuna loin with a spicy tomato sauce (£8.95), half a fresh lobster (£10.25), a seafood selection (£17.95) or a three-course meal (£17.95); also, super soups such as chive and potato (£2.45), good open sandwiches (from £4.95), and ploughman's (£4.65). Well kept Otter Bitter, Ale, Bright and Head (from a tiny brewery a few miles from the pub in Luppitt) tapped from the cask, a very good wine list (with good value house wine and six served in two sizes of wine glass), local cider. The bar has neatly carved beams in its high ceiling, and handsome stone-mullioned windows (one with a small carved roundabout horse). On the left, a high-backed stripped settle separates off a little room with three tables, a mix of chairs, flowers on sturdy country tables, plank-panelled walls painted brown below and yellow above with attractive engravings and prints, and a big black-painted fireplace with bric-a-brac on a high mantlepiece. The flagstoned entry has a narrow corridor of a room by the servery with a couple of tables, and the cellar bar has simple pews on the stone floor; dominoes, cribbage and skittle alley. There are picnic tables under cocktail parasols on the lawn that stretches back under the shadow of chestnut trees, towards a church with its singularly melodious hour-bell. The pretty village with its cream-coloured thatched cottages is worth a stroll around. *(Recommended by Martin Walsh, R V Ford, J and J O Jones, D E Kent, John and Fiona Merritt, J W Bridge, Sue Demont, Tim Barrow, D I Baddeley, Jacquie and Jim Jones, Nigel Flook, Betsy Brown, Jeanne Cross, Paul Silvestri, Mark and Michele Aston, John and Sally Clarke, Mr and Mrs J B Merritt, B J Harding, Tim and Chris Ford, Eric and Patricia King, Howard and Margaret Buchanan, Ian Phillips, John and Vivienne Rice, Mr and Mrs J Brown, J I Fraser, John and Tessa Rainsford, M V and J Melling, Jason Caulkin, B and K Hyper, Pat and John Millward)*

Free house ~ Licensees Kerstin and Nigel Burge ~ Real ale ~ Meals and snacks (till 10pm; not Sun evening) ~ Restaurant (not Sun evening) ~ (01404) 841267 ~ Well behaved children in eating area of bar and in restaurant ~ Open 11-3, 6-11

BUCKLAND BREWER SS4220 Map 1

Coach & Horses ★

Village signposted off A388 S of Bideford; OS Sheet 190 map reference 423206

Some changes to this cheerfully run and enjoyable 13th-c pub include its re-thatching and complete redecoration inside and out, and the renovation of the garden following the addition of the new skittle alley last year. The attractively furnished bar has heavy oak beams, comfortable seats including a handsome antique settle, and a woodburning stove in the inglenook; a good log fire also burns in the big stone inglenook of the cosy lounge. A small back room serves as a children's room. Under the new chef, food now includes delicious whitebait, lovely ham and pea soup, good home-made pasties (£2.15), filled baked potatoes (from £2.50), home-baked ham with eggs (£4.50), liver and bacon casserole (£4.75), wonderful local trout or steak and kidney pie (£5.50), chicken chambertin, salmon steak in various sauces or pork medallions in a cream and brandy sauce (all around £6.25), steaks (from £8.75), and puddings like good banoffi pie or treacle tart. Well kept Flowers IPA and Original and a guest beer such as Fullers London Pride on handpump; friendly and efficient service. Pool, darts, dominoes, shove-ha'penny, cribbage, fruit machine, and video game. The two cats are called Amos and Benson. There are tables on a terrace in front, and in the side garden. *(Recommended by A M Stephenson, L Parikian, Jennie Munro, Jim Wingate, Chris Westmoreland, Gethin Lewis, Roger and Susan Dunn, R J Walden, Philip and Joanne Gavins, Rita Horridge, Nigel and Lindsay Chapman, Michael and Joan Johnstone, R J Walden, Mrs Ann Saunders, A E and P McCully, Alan and Julie Wear, Roderic Plinston, Peter J Moore, Chris and Pauline Ford, Nigel and Lindsay Chapman)*

Free house ~ Licensees Kenneth and Oliver Wolfe ~ Real ales ~ Meals and snacks ~ Restaurant ~ (01237) 451395 ~ Well behaved children welcome ~ Occasional Morris dancers ~ Open 11.30-3, 6-11; closed evening 25 Dec ~ Bedrooms: £22B/£36B

BUDLEIGH SALTERTON SY0682 Map 1

Salterton Arms

Chapel Street

This tucked away town pub is very popular for its quickly served, interesting food: sandwiches (from £1.35, steak £3.95), good soup (£1.75), liver and onions (£2.95), steak and kidney pie or chicken chasseur (£4.25), vegetarian dishes such as roquefort and spinach strudel or crunch nut cutlet (£4.75), lunchtime specials like beef goulash or spaghetti bolognese (£4.25), and evening specials such as cod and prawn mornay or crab platter (£6.95), sea bass (£8.50) and steaks (from £7.50); good fresh vegetables, and puddings such as chocolate gunge or banoffi pie (£2); best to book at weekends and for Sunday lunch. The L-shaped bar has dark green plush wall seats and solid chairs around plain pub tables on the new dark red carpet, lots of prints on the walls, and small open fires; a very comfortable upper gallery serves as restaurant. Well kept Courage Best and Directors, John Smiths, and Wadworths 6X on handpump, a good few Irish whiskeys, and neatly uniformed staff; darts, cribbage, dominoes, fruit machine, and piped music. The flowering tubs and hanging baskets are very pretty. *(Recommended by F C Smith, Werner Arend, Marjorie and David Lamb, Mark and Heather Williamson, Mrs J M Corless, Gethin Lewis, George Atkinson, Howard and Margaret Buchanan, B D Jones)*

Free house ~ Licensees Steve and Jennifer Stevens ~ Real ale ~ Meals and snacks (till 10pm) ~ Restaurant ~ (01395) 445048 ~ Children welcome ~ Jazz winter Sun evenings ~ Open 11-3, 5.30-11; 11-11 July and August

BUTTERLEIGH SS9708 Map 1

Butterleigh Inn

Village signposted off A396 in Bickleigh; or in Cullompton take turning by Manor House Hotel – it's the old Tiverton road, with the village eventually signposted off on the left

An unpretentious series of little rooms in this friendly 16th-c village pub are decorated with pictures of birds and dogs, topographical prints and watercolours, a fine embroidery of the Devonshire Regiment's coat-of-arms and plates hanging by one big fireplace. One room has a mix of Edwardian and Victorian dining chairs around country kitchen tables, another has an attractive elm trestle table and sensibly placed darts, and there are prettily upholstered settles around the three tables that just fit into the cosy back snug. Bar food includes filled rolls (lunchtimes, £1.75), home-made soup (£2.25), ploughman's (£3.75), venison sausages with cumberland sauce or chilli pancakes (£4.95), lamb cutlets or Mexican platter (£6.95), rump steak (£9.95), and puddings like treacle tart with clotted cream (£2.25). Well kept Cotleigh Tawny and Barn Owl, and guest beers on handpump, and several malt whiskies; darts, bar billiards, shove-ha'penny, table skittles, cribbage, dominoes, and piped music; jars of snuff on the bar. Outside are tables on a sheltered terrace and neat small lawn, with a log cabin for children. *(Recommended by John Hazel, Rich and Pauline Appleton, Anthony Barnes, Peter and Joy Heatherley, Sally Pidden, George and Jeanne Barnwell, A P Jeffreys, Bill and Beryl Farmer, Mr and Mrs B Hobden, Nigel and Teresa Brooks, Mrs J Horsthuis, Jim and Maggie Cowell, Steve Dark, Alan Carr, Eric and Patricia King)*

Free house ~ Licensees Mike and Penny Wolter ~ Real ale ~ Meals and snacks ~ (01884) 855407 ~ Children welcome lunchtimes only ~ Open 12-2.30(3 Sat), 6-11 ~ Bedrooms: £20/£34

CHAGFORD SX7087 Map 1

Ring o' Bells

Off A348 Moretonhampstead—Whiddon Down

The walled garden behind this big, friendly old pub has been laid to lawn this year and is a real summer suntrap. Inside, the oak-panelled bar has comfortable seats, photographs of the village and local characters on the walls, a log-effect gas fire, and Tabbie the pub cat (now 15 years old); a traditional slate floor should be laid by the time this book is published. Good bar food (the same menu is used in the restaurant) includes sandwiches, home-made soup (£1.95), basket meals (from £3.75), fresh fish and chips (from £4), home-made steak and kidney pie (£4.75), daily specials (from £4.50) such as vegetarian and pasta dishes and fresh fish and shellfish, and home-made puddings (from £1.75); Sunday roasts. Well kept Butcombe Bitter, Exmoor Ale, Wadworths 6X and a monthly guest beer on handpump, Addlestones cider, and decent wines by the glass; darts, shove-ha'penny, cribbage, dominoes, fruit machine, and piped music. Good moorland walks nearby. *(Recommended by Helen McLagan, John and Christine Vittoe, Air Cdr and Mrs A C Curry, Patrick Clancy, A N Ellis)*

Free house ~ Licensee Mrs Judith Pool ~ Real ale ~ Meals and snacks ~ Restaurant ~ (01647) 432466 ~ Children in restaurant ~ Open 11-3(2.30 in winter), 6-11

CHARDSTOCK ST3004 Map 1

George ⟹

Village signposted off A358 S of Chard

Mainly set out for dining, the two-roomed original bar in this neatly thatched 13th-c inn has two good log fires, massive beams, ancient oak partition walls, character furnishings, stone-mullioned windows, and well converted old gas lamps. It's quietly chatty as the piped music is confined to an interestingly laid out two-level back bar. Good food includes sandwiches, kedgeree or spaghetti bolognaise (£4.95), home-made steak and kidney pie or devilled kidneys (£5.25), local trout with lemon butter and almonds (£7.25), chicken en croûte (£8.25), pheasant breasts with a mushroom and madeira sauce (£8.95), and home-made puddings such as sticky toffee pudding with butterscotch sauce or apple fritters with drambuie syrup (£2.75); on Sunday evening the food is more restricted, with soup, home-made pizzas, and salads. Well kept Boddingtons and Flowers Original on handpump; darts, cribbage and alley skittles. There are some tables out in a back loggia by a flint-cobbled courtyard sheltered by the rather attractive modern extensions to the ancient inn, with more in a safely fenced grass area with a climber and swings. The four bedrooms are in a well converted back stable block. The inn has an interesting booklet about its history. Excellent walks nearby. *(Recommended by K S Pike, Margaret and Nigel Dennis, R M Bloomfield, Alan and Judith Gifford, J E Davies, David Eberlin, Gordon; more reports please)*

Free house ~ Licensee John Hall ~ Real ale ~ Meals and snacks ~ Restaurant ~ (01460) 220241 ~ Children in eating area of bar and in top bar ~ Open 11.30-3, 6-11; closed Mon lunchtime ~ Bedrooms: £35B/£42.50B

CHERITON BISHOP SX7793 Map 1

Old Thatch

Village signposted from A30

Enjoyable, generously served food and a friendly welcome are to be found at this busy 16th-c pub – and it's best to get there early to make sure of a seat: sandwiches, home-made soup (£1.55), home-made pâté (£2.40), ploughman's (£2.75), sautéed lamb's kidneys (£2.85), good salads (including an interesting vegetarian one from £4.50), gammon and egg (£4.75), steak and kidney pudding (£4.95), a curry of the day (£5.95), pork tenderloin in a sour cream and mustard sauce (£6.95), 8oz steak (£7.50), daily specials like Armenian lamb, salmon and prawn lasagne or vegetable kebabs with tofu, and puddings such as creole bananas or syllabub (from £2.50). The rambling, beamed bar is separated from the lounge by a large open stone fireplace (lit in the cooler months). Well kept Badger Tanglefoot, Cotleigh Tawny, and Wadworths 6X on handpump, and half-a-dozen wines by the glass or carafe. Dominoes, cribbage, and piped music. We'd be grateful for reports on the bedrooms which we have every reason to believe would be very comfortable. No children. *(Recommended by Jeffrey Aspinall, John and Christine Vittoe, Dorothee and Dennis Glover, John Wooll, P V Caswell, R J Walden, R W Brooks, TOH, Betty Laker, David Burnett, Donna Lowes, Don Kellaway, Angie Coles, John Hazel)*

Free house ~ Licensee Brian Bryon-Edmond ~ Real ale ~ Meals and snacks ~ (01647) 24204 ~ Open 12-3, 6.30-11; 11.30-3, 6-11 Sat; winter weekday opening 7; closed first two weeks Nov ~ Bedrooms: £33B/£45B

CHITTLEHAMHOLT SS6521 Map 1

Exeter Inn ⇦

Village signposted from A377 Barnstaple—Crediton and from B3226 SW of South Molton

This friendly old inn makes a good base for Exmoor National Park with all its outdoor facilities. The bar has an open woodburning stove in the huge stone fireplace, cushioned mate's chairs and stools, settles, and a couple of big cushioned cask armchairs, and an interesting collection of matchboxes, bottles and foreign banknotes. In the side area there are seats set out as booths around the tables under the sloping ceiling. Good bar food served by attentive staff includes home-made soup (£1.65), filled french bread (from £2.10), filled baked potatoes (from £2.25), home-made chicken liver pâté (£2.50), ploughman's (from £3.75), hog pudding (like a haggis, £4.95), vegetarian cheese and nut croquettes or local trout (£5.95), excellent local steaks (£8.95), daily specials, children's meals (from £2.75), and home-made puddings with clotted cream (£2.25); Sunday roast (£4.95). Well kept Dartmoor, Ind Coope Burton, Tetleys and a weekly changing guest beer on handpump or tapped from the cask; freshly squeezed orange juice and farm ciders; darts, dominoes, shove-ha'penny, trivia, and piped music. The dog is called Alice and the cat, Clyde. The terrace has benches and flower baskets. The pub's cricket team play on Sundays. *(Recommended by Derek and Iris Martin, R J Walden, Anthony Barnes)*

Free house ~ Licensees Norman and Margaret Glenister ~ Real ale ~ Meals and snacks (11.30-2, 6-9.30) ~ Restaurant ~ (01769) 540281 ~ Children welcome ~ Open 11.30-2.30(3 Sat), 6-11; closed evenings 25 and 26 Dec ~ Bedrooms: £20S/£40S; s/c available

CHURCHSTOW SX7145 Map 1

Church House

A379 NW of Kingsbridge

The long and cosy characterful bar of this medieval pub has low and heavy black oak beams, cushioned seats cut into the deep window embrasures of the stripped stone walls, an antique curved high-backed settle as well as lots of smaller red-cushioned ones, and a line of stools – each with its own brass coathook – along the long glossy black serving counter; a great stone fireplace has a side bread oven. Bar food, served at the curtained-off end of the bar, includes sandwiches (from £1.75), home-made soup (£2), ploughman's (£2.95), basket meals (from £2.95), fish pie or steak and kidney pie (£4.50), gammon and egg (£7.25), steak (£7.95), home-made fruit pies (£2.10), children's menu (from £1), and popular carvery (£7.95; Wednesday-Saturday evenings and Sunday lunch); the restaurant is no smoking. Well kept Bass and Dartmoor on handpump; cribbage, dominoes, euchre, and fruit machine. Just inside the back entrance there's a conservatory area with a floodlit well in the centre, and there are seats outside. *(Recommended by B Taylor, Owen and Margaret Warnock, Mr and Mrs C Roberts, Alan and Heather Jacques, T Aldworth, Gordon, C and Marjorie Roberts, David Eberlin, Jim and Maggie Cowell)*

Free house ~ Licensees Nick and Vera Nicholson ~ Real ale ~ Meals and snacks (12-1.30, 6.30-9; not 25 or 26 Dec) ~ Restaurant (not Sun evening) ~ (01548) 852237 ~ Children in eating area of bar and in restaurant ~ Open 11-2.30, 6-11

CLYST HYDON ST0301 Map 1

Five Bells

B3176 not far from M5 jctn 28

The cottagey garden in front of this charming and warmly friendly white-painted thatched pub (with reed peacocks on top) is lovely in spring and summer – the owners planted over 10,000 bulbs – and the big window boxes are very pretty, too. Up some steps is a sizeable flat lawn with picnic tables, a waggon filled with flowers, a slide, and pleasant country views. Inside, it's spotlessly kept and very attractive, and the long bar is divided at one end into different seating areas by brick and timber pillars; china jugs hang from big beams that are studded with horsebrasses, many plates line the delft shelves, and there's lots of sparkling copper and brass, and a nice mix of dining chairs around small tables (fresh flowers and candles in bottles), with some comfortable pink plush banquettes on a little raised area. Past the big fireplace is another big (but narrower) room with a pine dresser at one end and similar furnishings. Very good home-made bar food includes sandwiches (from £1.80), soup (£1.95), smoked prawns with garlic mayonnaise (£3.75), platters (from £3.95), courgettes provençale (£4.35), cold rare roast beef with chips and pickles (£5.50), curry (£5.50), daily specials like local asparagus, local venison, broccoli and mushroom pasta, chicken breast with bacon, leek and sherry sauce, smoked fish platter and monkfish with tomato and basil; children's meals (£2.25) and puddings (£2.50). Well kept Cotleigh Tawny, Dartmoor, and Wadworths 6X on handpump; maybe piped music. The golden retrievers are called Willow and Sasha, and the cat, Twinkle. *(Recommended by Timothy Gee, Marian Greenwood, Tony Beaulah, Jacquie and Jim Jones, H Beck, Eric and Patricia King, R M Sparkes, Denzil Taylor)*

Free house ~ Licensees Robin Bean and Charles Hume Smith ~ Real ale ~ Meals and snacks ~ Restaurant ~ (01884) 277288 ~ Well behaved children in eating area of bar ~ Open 11.30-3, 6.30-11

COCKWOOD SX9780 Map 1

Anchor

Off, but visible from, A379 Exeter—Torbay

From the tables on the sheltered verandah here you can look across the road to the bobbing yachts and crabbing boats in the landlocked harbour. And the food has much to do with the sea, too. There are 30 different ways of serving mussels (£5.50 normal size helping, £9.75 for a large one), 14 ways of serving scallops (from £5.25 for a starter, from £10.50 for a main course), and 11 ways of serving oysters (from £5.25 for starter, from £11 for main course); other fresh fish dishes might include fried shark steak or locally caught cod (£5.50), whole grilled plaice (£6.50), local crab platter (£6.95), a shellfish platter (£14.95), and red snapper, bream, grouper and parrot fish. Non-fishy dishes feature as well, such as sandwiches (from £2.25), home-made chicken liver pâté (£3.85), ratatouille (£3.95), home-made cottage pie (£4.50), 8oz rump steak (£8.95), and children's dishes (£1.95). The restaurant is no smoking. The small, low-ceilinged, rambling rooms have black panelling, good-sized tables in various alcoves, and a cheerful winter coal fire in the snug. Well kept Bass, Boddingtons, Eldridge Pope Royal Oak, Flowers IPA, Whitbreads Fuggles, Marstons Pedigree, and two guests on handpump kept under light blanket pressure or tapped from the cask, with rather a good wine list, country wines, 30 malt whiskies, and Inch's cider; dominoes, cribbage, fruit machine, and piped music. Nearby parking may be difficult when the pub is busy – which it usually is. *(Recommended by R W Flux, Jean Cross, Paul Silvestri, Chris Westmoreland, John Beeken, Mrs Pat Crabb, Adrian Alton, Paul and Janet Waring, Ian Phillips, Jim and Maggie Cowell, P M Lane, Jon and Julie Gibson, A E and P McCully, S R and Mrs A J Ashcroft)*

Heavitree (who no longer brew) ~ Tenants T Morran, Miss A L Sanders, Mrs J Wetton ~ Real ale ~ Meals and snacks (till 10pm) ~ Restaurant ~ (01626) 890203 ~ Children in eating area of bar ~ Open 11-11

COLEFORD SS7701 Map 1

New Inn

Just off A377 Crediton—Barnstaple

In an attractive hamlet of thatched cottages, this medieval inn has four interestingly furnished areas that spiral around the central servery: paraffin lamps, antique prints and old guns on the white walls, landscape plates on one of the beams and pewter tankards on another, and ancient and modern settles, spindleback chairs, plush-cushioned stone wall seats, some character tables – a pheasant worked into the grain of one – and carved dressers and chests; the resident parrot is chatty and entertaining. The servery itself has settles forming stalls around tables on the russet carpet, and there's a winter log fire. In the good food they use fresh local produce and dishes might include fresh tomato and bail soup (£2.10), smoked trout and dill mayonnaise (£4.25), king prawns with garlic butter (£4.95), baked stuffed aubergine with tomato and garlic sauce or cheese and garlic agnolotti with wild mushroom sauce (£5.50), wild boar sausages with onion gravy (£5.95), Turkish lamb with herbs and courgettes (£7.50), salmis of guinea fowl with grape and madeira sauce or monkfish marinated in ginger, lime and fennel and grilled (£8.95), john dory with lemon and thyme butter (£9.50), and puddings like pink grapefruit soufflé or dark and light chocolate terrine (£2.50); friendly, helpful staff. Well kept Badger Best, Boddingtons, Otter Ale, and Wadworths 6X on handpump, an extensive wine list, quite a range of malt whiskies, and port; fruit machine (out of the way up by the door), darts, and piped music. Big car park. There are some benches and seats outside by the stream. *(Recommended by Anthony Savage, Howard Clutterbuck, R J Walden, David Watson, Liz and Jake Nelson, Mike Cargill, Graham and Karen Oddey, J L Cox, Steve Williamson, John Hazel, John and Vivienne Rice)*

Free house ~ Licensees Paul and Irene Butt ~ Real ale ~ Meals and snacks (till 10pm) ~ Restaurant ~ (01363) 84242 ~ Children welcome ~ Open 11.30-2.30, 6-11; closed 25 Decand 26 Dec ~ Bedrooms: £32B/£49.50B

Pubs with particularly interesting histories, or in unusually interesting buildings, are listed at the back of the book.

COLYTON SY2493 Map 1

Kingfisher

Dolphin St; village signposted off A35 and A3052 E of Sidmouth, in village follow Axminster, Shute, Taunton signpost

This is very much a homely local with friendly staff and hearty helpings of popular food. There are blue plush cushioned window seats, stools, sturdy elm wing settles and rustic tables, a big open fireplace and walls stripped back to stone. Glasses slotted into the two waggon-wheels hanging above the bar swing in unison when someone in the upstairs family room walks above the beamed ceiling; sensibly placed darts, dominoes, cribbage, fruit machine, video game, and skittle alley. Well kept Badger Best and Tanglefoot, Charles Wells Bombardier, and changing guest ales on handpump. Bar food includes sandwiches (from £1.50, speciality prawn £2.75), filled baked potatoes and ploughman's (from £1.50), plaice, gammon, and a winter daily special (from £3), and home-made cheesecakes and fruit pies (from £1.50). There are tables under cocktail parasols on the terrace, and a lawn with pergola, flower beds and water features. ***(Recommended by Denzil Taylor, Nick Wikeley, Mrs Ann Saunders, Helen Flaherty; more reports please)***

Free house ~ Licensees Graeme and Cherry Sutherland ~ Real ale ~ Meals and snacks (till 10pm) ~ (01297) 552476 ~ Children in family room ~ Open 11-2.30, 6-11

COMBEINTEIGNHEAD SX9071 Map 1

Coombe Cellars

Pub signposted off B3195 Newton Abbot—Shaldon

Now tied to Whitbreads and part of the Brewers Fayre chain – and with new licensees – this waterside pub is very family friendly. Children have an indoor play area, their own menu, baby-changing facilities, highchairs, parties with face painting and games, and an outside play galleon and fenced-in playground in the garden. They hold fun days with magicians, live music, barbecues and beach parties, quiz nights and darts tournaments, and have disabled lavatories and ramped entrances. The estuary setting here is really lovely and at low tide you can watch innumerable wading birds on the mudflats. Pontoons and jetties with tables overlook the water, and there are more tables on big terraces. Lots of water-sports facilities, too – the pub is the base for the South Devon Water Sports Association. There's a pleasure trip service from Teignmouth that takes in this pub. Inside, the long beamed bar has one area with old photographs and pictures of the pub, another with hunting, shooting and fishing items, and yet another with nautical bric-a-brac; comfortable seating, a wood-burning stove, and two log-effect gas fires. Darts, dominoes, fruit machine. Bar food typically now includes sandwiches or baps (from £1.99), vegetable moussaka (£3.99), steak and kidney pudding (£4.20), tagliatelle carbonara (£4.45), gammon and egg (£4.85), fish pie (£4.99), chicken balti (£5.45), steak (£7.85), puddings (£1.99), and children's menu (£3.25). Well kept Boddingtons, Flowers Original and a changing guest such as Wadworths 6X on handpump; several wines by the glass. ***(Recommended by Adrian Zambardino, Debbie Chaplin; more reports on the changes, please)***

Whitbreads ~ Manager Martin Bowers ~ Real ale ~ Meals and snacks (all day) ~ (01626) 872423 ~ Children welcome away from main bar area ~ Open 11-11

CORNWORTHY SX8255 Map 1

Hunters Lodge

Off A381 Totnes—Kingsbridge ½ mile S of Harbertonford, turning left at Washbourne; can also be reached direct from Totnes, on the Ashprington—Dittisham road

As the two rooms of the little low-ceilinged bar in this quietly friendly village inn have only around half-a-dozen red plush wall seats and captain's chairs around heavy elm tables, it can get crowded at holiday times. There's also a small and pretty cottagey dining room with a good log fire in its big 17th-c stone fireplace. Popular bar food includes home-made soup (£1.90), home-cooked honey roast ham (£4.50), grilled sardines (£5.25), home-made steak and kidney pie (£5.45), chicken maryland (£5.95), tandoori halibut (£8.50), guinea fowl or seafood grill (£8.95), and puddings (£2.50); three course Sunday roast (£6.75). Well kept Blackawton Special and Forty-four and Ushers Best on handpump and local Pig Squeal cider; darts, dominoes, shove-ha'penny, children's games, puzzles and colouring place-mats, trivia and piped music; they have four dogs (only let loose after closing time). There are picnic tables on a big lawn stretching up behind the car park, with swings, a climbing frame and summer barbecues, and closer to the pub is a new terrace with flowering tubs and more seats. Several walks start from the pub. *(Recommended by D I Baddeley, B Taylor, Dennis Heatley, David and Tina Woods-Taylor, Gordon, Paul Boot)*

Free house ~ Licensee Robin Thorns ~ Real ale ~ Meals and snacks (till 10pm) ~ Cottagey restaurant ~ (01803) 732204 ~ Children welcome ~ Open 11-3, 6.30-11; closed evening 25 Dec

DALWOOD ST2400 Map 1

Tuckers Arms

Village signposted off A35 Axminster—Honiton

A lovely sight in summer with colourful window boxes, hanging baskets, and tubs, this beautifully kept thatched longhouse has a lovely friendly atmosphere as well as original 800-year-old stripped beams and original flagstones in the bar. Also, a random mixture of dining chairs, window-seats, a pew, a high-backed winged black settle, and oak stripped beams, a woodburning stove, and a log fire in the inglenook fireplace. A side lounge with shiny black woodwork has a couple of cushioned oak armchairs and other comfortable but unpretentious seats, and the back bar has an enormous collection of miniature bottles. Good bar food includes home-made soup (£1.75), potato skins with interesting dips (from £3.25), mushroom stroganoff or tagliatelle with spinach, mushrooms and cream (£7.25), speciality rib-eye steaks (from £7.95), the notably popular 'tiddy' (a big puff pastry with a changing home-made filling from £8.25), rack of lamb with lemon, herbs and garlic or fresh local trout with lemon butter (£10.55), fresh fish like monkfish with ginger, fresh cod baked with a herb and pine nut crust, and king prawns, and puddings (£2.75). Well kept Boddingtons, Flowers Original, Otter Ale, and Wadworths 6X on handpump, and quite a few malt whiskies; table skittles, fruit machine, piped music, and skittle alley. *(Recommended by David Wallington, Mr and Mrs D V Morris, George Atkinson, K S Pike, Pat and Robert Watt, Paul Boot, John and Fiona Merritt, Gordon, R J Walden, Mrs J M Corless, Desmond and Pat Morris)*

Free house ~ Licensees David and Kate Beck ~ Real ale ~ Meals and snacks (till 10pm) ~ Restaurant ~ (01404) 881342 ~ Children in skittle alley and eating area of bar ~ Open 12-3, 6.30-11 ~ Bedrooms: £25S/£40S

DARTINGTON SX7762 Map 1

Cott ★ 🍴 🛏 🍷

In hamlet with the same name, signposted off A385 W of Totnes opposite A384 turn-off

You can be sure of a genuinely friendly welcome from either the Greys or their hard-working staff at this lovely thatched 14th-c inn. And there's a super atmosphere in the communicating rooms of the traditional, heavy-beamed bar with its big open fires, flagstones, and polished brass and horse-harnesses on the white-washed walls; one area is no smoking. Very good food might include sandwiches, steak and kidney pie, fillets of Torbay sole with dill cream and anchovy, spicy gingered pork or sweet pepper and potato pie (all £5.75), braised duck with rhubarb and redcurrant (£6.95), and venison and game sausage casserole (£7.50), with evening dishes such as fillet of lamb with a redcurrant and rosemary sauce (£10.50), roulade of pork tenderloin stuffed with apricots and pine nuts (£11.25), and monkfish tails with garlic butter and fresh local mussels (£11.95); puddings like strawberry roulade, orange and ginger crunch or caramel and banana crumble (£3; clotted cream 50p extra). Part of the restaurant is no smoking. Well kept Bass, Butcombe Bitter and Cotts Wallop (see if you can guess what it really is) on handpump, Inch's cider, 10 interesting wines by the glass, and a good selection of malt whiskies. There's a pub cricket team – they'd welcome enquiries from visiting teams. Harvey the cat still likes to creep into bedroom windows in the middle of the night (despite advancing age), and Minnie and Digger the jack russells are keen to greet visitors. The garden has a new terrace and new seating amidst the attractive tubs of flowers. Good walks through the grounds of nearby Dartington Hall, and it's pleasant touring country – particularly for the popular Dartington craft centre, the Totnes-Buckfastleigh steam railway, and one of the prettiest towns in the West Country, Totnes. *(Recommended by David Holman, Barry A Lynch, Joan and Gordon Edwards, Revd A Nunnerley, Kees van Kempen, H and D Payne, Paul and Janet Waring, George and Jeanne Barnwell, Dr and Mrs Young, Mrs V Coombs, Mr and Mrs D Clements, Nigel Spence, Kim Greek, George Jonas, Simon and Debbie Tomlinson, John and Vivienne Rice, Peter Williamson, Anthony Marriott, Martin Foss, David Wallington, Neil and Anita Christopher, Jim and Maggie Cowell, T A Bryan, David and Tina Woods-Taylor, D G King, M V and J Melling, Mrs S Segrove, A E and P McCully, David Cundy, A Plumb, Patrick Clancy, Peter and Lynn Brueton)*

Free house ~ Licensees David and Susan Grey ~ Real ale ~ Meals and snacks (12-2.15, 6.30-9.30) ~ Restaurant ~ (01803) 863777 ~ Children in restaurant ~ Live entertainment monthly Sun evening ~ Open 11-2.30, 5.30-11; closed evening 25 Dec ~ Bedrooms: £45B/£50B

DARTMOUTH SX8751 Map 1

Cherub

Higher St

This is a lovely 14th-c Grade I listed building and each of the two heavily timbered upper floors juts further out than the one below. Inside, the bar has tapestried seats under creaky heavy beams, red-curtained leaded-light windows, an open stove in the big stone fireplace, and well kept Flowers Original, Morlands Old Speckled Hen, Wadworths 6X and a guest beer on handpump; quite a few malt whiskies. Bar food includes sandwiches, soup (£1.95), filled baked potatoes (from £3.50), ploughman's (from £3.75), smoked haddock in a white wine and cheese sauce (£3.95), chilli con carne or beef in ale stew (£4.95), seafood pasta (£5.95), and poached salmon (£6.75). In summer, the flower baskets are very pretty. *(Recommended by Owen and Margaret Warnock, Mike Woodhead, E Carter, G W Stevenson, Joy and Paul Rundell, Andy and Jill Kassube, Paul and Janet Waring, Gordon, R W A Suddaby, Pat and John Millward, Mr and Mrs A K McCully, Steve Goodchild, John Evans, Wayne Brindle, Joy Heatherley)*

Free house ~ Licensee Steven Hill ~ Real ale ~ Meals and snacks (till 10pm) ~ Restaurant ~ (01803) 832571 ~ Children in restaurant ~ Open 11-11

Royal Castle

11 The Quay

Overlooking the inner harbour, this handsome 17th-c hotel has a bustling atmosphere and quite a lot of character. The left-hand, local bar is decorated with navigation lanterns, glass net-floats and old local ship photographs, and has a mix of furnishings from stripped pine kitchen chairs to some interesting old settles and mahogany tables; one wall is stripped to the original stonework and there's a big log fire. On the right in the more sedate, partly no-smoking carpeted bar, they may do winter spit-roast joints on some lunchtimes; there's also a Tudor fireplace with copper jugs and kettles (beside which are the remains of a spiral staircase), and plush furnishings, including some Jacobean-style chairs. One alcove has swords and heraldic shields on the wall. Well kept Boddingtons, Courage Best, Flowers, and

Ruddles on handpump, quite a few malt whiskies, and local farm cider; welcoming staff. Dominoes, fruit machine, trivia, and piped music. The range of generously served bar food includes lunchtime sandwiches (from £1.45, good crab £2.75) and a choice of ploughman's (from £2.45), as well as home-made soup (£1.65), baked potatoes with hot or cold fillings (from £2.70), cauliflower cheese and bacon (£3.25), home-made steak and kidney pie or smoked haddock and mushroom crumble (£4.50), curry of the day or whole plaice (£4.95), steaks (from £9.95), daily specials like cumberland sausage or half-a-dozen local oysters (£4.50), and puddings (£2.45); curry night on Tuesdays. *(Recommended by T G Thomas, Mr and Mrs A K McCully, Pat and John Millward, George S Jonas, Mr and Mrs R Head, P and J Shapley, A Craig; more reports please)*

Free house ~ Licensee Nigel Way ~ Real ale ~ Meals and snacks (all day) ~ Restaurant ~ (01803) 833033 ~ Children in first-floor library and in eating area of bar ~ Live entertainment in public bar Sun/Tues ~ Open 11-11 ~ Bedrooms: £50B/£80B

DODDISCOMBSLEIGH SX8586 Map 1

Nobody Inn ★ ★

Village signposted off B3193, opposite northernmost Christow turn-off

This is such an enjoyable and well run inn and Mr Borst-Smith – never one to rest on his laurels – continues to make improvements. They keep perhaps the best pub wine cellar in the country – 800 well cellared wines by the bottle and 20 by the glass kept oxidation-free; there's also properly mulled wine and twice-monthly tutored tastings (they also sell wine retail, and the good tasting-notes in their detailed list are worth the £3 it costs – anyway refunded if you buy more than £20-worth); also, a choice of 250 whiskies, Gray's and Inch's farm ciders and well kept Bass, Branscombe Vale Branoc, a beer brewed by Branscombe Vale especially for the pub called Nobodys, and two guest beers on handpump or tapped straight from the cask. The two atmospheric rooms of the lounge bar have handsomely carved antique settles, Windsor and wheelback chairs, and benches, carriage lanterns hanging from the beams (some of which are original), and guns and hunting prints in a snug area by one of the big inglenook fireplaces. Good bar food – they now have their own vegetable garden – includes sandwiches, home-made soup (£1.95), hot wholemeal pitta bread filled with cheese, tomato, onion and herbs (£2.75), coarse home-made duck's liver pâté with port (£3.10), sausages and mash with onion gravy (£3), butter bean casserole (£3.50), mushroom and walnut strudel (£4.10), daily specials like boboti (£4.60), beef and mushroom in ale casserole (£5.20) or spring chicken cooked in an apricot sauce (£5.30), puddings such as warm treacle tart or home-made spiced bread pudding (from £2.20), and a marvellous, constantly changing choice of 40 or 50 west country cheeses (a choice of six £3.50; you can buy them to take away as well). The restaurant is no smoking. There are picnic tables on the terrace, with views of the surrounding wooded hill pastures. The medieval stained glass in the local church is some of the best in the West Country. No children. *(Recommended by Jack and Philip Paxton, George Jonas, Ron Gentry, Nigel Spence, Kim Greek, Lynn Sharpless, Bob Eardley, Charlotte Creasy, Martin Foss, Jane Hosking, Ian Burniston, Chris Westmoreland, David R Babb, Joan and Gordon Edwards, Mike Woodhead, Anthony Marriott, E B Davies, B Taylor, Peter West, Gerry Hollinton, James Nunns, Joan and Gordon Edwards, Mike Cargill, D K Carter, A P Jeffreys, Dennis Dickinson, DAV, R J Walden, John Waller, Steve Huggins, J L Cox, Paul Harrison, S R and A J Ashcroft, Victor Sunderland, S Demont, T Barrow, A Young, D Hayward, Don Kellaway, Angie Coles, John and Vivienne Rice, Mr and Mrs R P Begg)*

Free house ~ Licensee Nicholas Borst-Smith ~ Real ale ~ Meals and snacks (till 10pm) ~ Evening restaurant (not Sun) ~ (01647) 252394 ~ Open 12-2, 6-11; winter evening opening 7; closed evening 25 Dec ~ Bedrooms (some in distinguished 18th-c house 150yds away); £23(£35B)/£33(£59B)

If we know a pub does summer barbecues, we say so.

DREWSTEIGNTON SX7390 Map 1

Drewe Arms

Signposted off A382 NW of Moretonhampstead

Mabel Mudge retired last year aged 99, but as we went to press this old thatched pub was being run by a group of villagers hoping to preserve it very much along her lines: that's to say, a very basic village tavern. There's no serving counter and the well kept real ale (typically Flowers IPA) and draught cider are kept on racks in the tap room at the back. A third room, used occasionally, has a notable herringbone-pattern Elizabethan brick floor. Ham or cheese sandwiches (£1.25); darts, dominoes, cribbage and chess. Castle Drogo nearby (open for visits) looks medieval, though it was actually built earlier this century. *(Recommended by Wendy and Ray Bryn Davies, Jack and Philip Paxton, John Hazel, Gordon, J I Fraser, Lynn Sharpless, Bob Eardley, Barbara and Norman Wells)*

Whitbreads ~ Real ale ~ Lunchtime snacks ~ (01647) 21224 ~ Children welcome ~ Open 11.30-3, 6-11; 11.30-11 Sat

EAST DOWN SS5941 Map 1

Pyne Arms 🍷

Off A39 Barnstaple—Lynton; OS sheet 180, map reference 600415

The low-beamed bar here has lots of nooks and crannies, a very high-backed curved settle by the door (as well as more ordinary pub seating), a wood-burning stove with horse harness and farm tools on the wall above it, horse-racing prints and Guinness and Martell placards on the red walls, and some copper jugs and big barrels; up some steps is a small, no-smoking galleried loft with more tables and chairs. A flagstoned games area has pine-plank wall benches, and pool, darts, shove-ha'penny, cribbage, dominoes, table skittles, fruit machine, and trivia; juke box. Good food from a wide menu includes sandwiches (from £1.55), delicious home-made soup (£1.75), ploughman's (£2.85), home-made pâté (£3.35), home-cooked ham and egg (£4.65), mussels in season prepared in four different ways (£6.25), scampi provençal (£7.25), several veal dishes (£8.35), beef Stroganoff (£9.65), steaks (from £9.65), daily specials such as broccoli au gratin (£4.50), steak and kidney pie (£5.25) or cod provençale (£5.45), and a range of puddings; food service stops promptly at 2pm. Well kept Courage Directors and John Smiths on handpump and five wines by the glass. The boisterous doberman is popular with visitors, though he isn't allowed in the bar. The Black Venus at Challacombe, White Hart at Bratton Fleming, and Station House at Blackmoor Gate are under the same management. Arlington Court is close by. *(Recommended by R J Walden, Andy and Jackie Mallpress, S R and A J Ashcroft, Steve and Carolyn Harvey; more reports please)*

Free house ~ Licensees Jurgen and Elisabeth Kempf ~ Real ale ~ Meals and snacks (till 10pm) ~ (01271) 850207 ~ Children in galleried loft only ~ Open 11-2.30, 6-11; closed 25 Dec

EXETER SX9292 Map 1

Double Locks ★ ☕

Canal Banks, Alphington; from A30 take main Exeter turn-off (A377/396) then next right into Marsh Barton Industrial Estate and follow Refuse Incinerator signs; when road bends round in front of the factory-like incinerator, take narrow dead end track over humpy bridge, cross narrow canal swing bridge and follow track along canal; much quicker than it sounds, and a very worthwhile diversion from the final M5 junction

Although Smiles Brewery have taken over here and installed a couple of managers, early reports are that little has changed in this popular lockside pub. It's a lively place with a good mix of people (though a large percentage are, of course, students) and a fine range of beers on handpump or tapped from the cask: Smiles Bitter, Best and Exhibition with guests like Adnams Broadside, Batemans XXXB, Eldridge Pope Royal Oak, Everards Old Original, Exmoor, Greene King Abbot, and Wadworths 6X; Grays farm cider, several malt whiskies, and organic apple juice. Bar food now includes soup (£1.80), sandwiches (£2), mushrooms on toast (£3.20), filled baked potatoes (from £3.30), ploughman's (£4), feta cheese and spinach pie or ham and eggs (£3.80), ratatouille crêpe (£4.30), breakfast special (£4.75), and home-made puddings like chocolate biscuit cake or sticky toffee pudding (£2.60); summer barbecues. There's quite a nautical theme in the bar – with ship's lamps and model ships – and notably friendly service. Cribbage, trivia, and piped music. There are picnic tables outside and cycle paths along the ship canal. *(Recommended by Mike Gorton, Rita Horridge, Werner Arend, George and Jeanne Barnwell, Andy and Jill Kassube, Jack and Philip Paxton, Jerry and Alison Oakes, Chris Westmoreland, Owen and Margaret Warnock, J M Corless, Paul Weedon, Wayne Brindle, Victor Sunderland, P M Lane, Dr M V Jones, J I Fraser, Pat and John Millward)*

Smiles ~ Managers Tony Stearman and Christopher Edwards ~ Real ale ~ Meals and snacks (all day) ~ (01392) 56947 ~ Children welcome ~ Jazz 1st and 2nd Thurs of month and live entertainment Weds evenings and summer Fri/Sat ~ Open 11-11; closed evening 25 Dec

White Hart ★ 🛏 🍷

66 South St; 4 rather slow miles from M5 junction 30; follow City Centre signs via A379, B3182; straight towards centre if you're coming from A377 Topsham Road

The rambling bar of this well run 14th-c inn is full of atmosphere and interest – it's been a popular meeting place for centuries. Big copper jugs hang from heavy bowed beams in the dark ochre terracotta ceiling, there are windsor armchairs and built-in winged settles with latticed glass tops to their high backs, oak tables on the bare oak floorboards (carpet in the quieter lower area) and a log fire in one great fireplace with long-barrelled rifles above it. In one of the bay windows is a set of fine old brass beer engines, the walls are decorated with pictorial plates, old copper and brass platters (on which the antique lantern lights glisten), and a wall cabinet holds some silver and copper. From the latticed windows, with their stained-glass coats-of-arms, one can look out on the cobbled courtyard – lovely when the wisteria is flowering in May. The Tap Bar, across the yard, with flagstones, candles in bottles and a more wine-barish feel, serves soup, sandwiches, cold meats, steak and oyster pie (£5.50), chicken and chestnut pie (£5.95), char-grilled steaks (from £7.60). There is yet another bar, called Bottlescreu Bill's, even more dimly candlelit, with bare stone walls and sawdust on the floor. It serves much the same food, as well as a respectable range of Davy's wines and pint jugs of vintage port from the wood or tankards of bucks fizz, and in summer does lunchtime barbecue grills in a second, sheltered courtyard. On Sundays both these bars are closed. Bass, Davy's Old Wallop (served in pewter tankards in Bottlescreu Bill's) and John Smiths on handpump or tapped from the cask. Bedrooms are in a separate modern block. *(Recommended by M E Wellington, P and T Ferris, R J Walden, Ron Gentry, F C Johnston, Werner Arend, Wayne Brindle, B A Ferris Harms, John and Vivienne Rice, Barry and Anne, Patrick Clancy, David and Fiona Easeman, Jim and Maggie Cowell, E V M Whiteway, Peter and Audrey Dowsett, J I Fraser)*

Free house ~ Licensee Graham Stone ~ Real ale ~ Meals and snacks (till 10pm) ~ Restaurant ~ (01392) 79897 ~ Children in eating area of bar and in lounges ~ Open 11.30-3, 5-11; 11.30-11 Sat ~ Bedrooms: £54.50B/£78B

EXMINSTER SX9487 Map 1

Turf ★

Follow sign to Swans Nest, signposted from A739 S of village, then continue to end of track, by gates; park, and walk right along canal towpath – nearly a mile

By the last lock of the Exeter Canal before the estuary of the River Exe, this attractively isolated pub has fine views from the bay windows of the pleasantly airy bar out to the mudflats – which are full of gulls and waders at low tide. There are mahogany decking and caulking tables on the polished bare floorboards, church pews, wooden chairs and alcove seats, big bright shorebird prints by John Tennent and pictures and old photographs of the pub and its characters over the years on the walls, and a woodburning stove and antique gas fire. Bar food includes sandwiches (from £2; lots of toasties from £2.55), home-made soup (£2.50), tuna and pasta bake or ploughman's (£4.75), lasagne and garlic bread or beef curry (£5.95), and puddings like apple crumble or sticky toffee pudding (from £2); the dining room is no smoking. Well kept Eldridge Pope Royal Oak, Dartmoor, and Tetleys Bitter on handpump, and a short but thoughtful good value wine list; darts, shove-ha'penny, cribbage, dominoes, trivia, and piped music; friendly, efficient service. The garden has a children's play area; well behaved dogs welcome. To reach the pub you can either walk (which takes about 20 minutes along the ship canal) or take a 40-minute ride from Countess Wear in their own boat, the *Water Mongoose* (bar on board; £3.50 adult, £2.50 child return, charter for up to 56 people £125). They also operate a 12-seater and an 8-seater boat which bring people down the Exe estuary from Topsham quay (15 minute trip, adults £2.50, child £2). For those arriving in their own boat there is a large pontoon as well as several moorings. *(Recommended by Chris Westmoreland, Jeanne Cross, Paul Silvestri, Mike Gorton, J I Fraser, Robin and Peter Etheridge)*

Free house ~ Licensees Clive and Ginny Redfern ~ Real ale ~ Meals and snacks ~ (01392) 833128 ~ Children welcome ~ Open 11-11; closed Nov-March ~ Bedrooms: £25/£50

HARBERTON SX7758 Map 1

Church House

Village signposted from A381 just S of Totnes

It's the daily specials that feature strongly in this ancient village pub, with the standard menu acting as more of a back-up during busy periods. Favourite dishes include deep-fried brie wrapped in bacon with a spicy redcurrant jelly (£3.75), crêpes Florentine au gratin (£5.50), salmon, broccoli and cheesy potato bake (£5.95), steak picado or lamb and fresh spinach balti using freshly ground and roasted spices (£6.95), and puddings like home-made ginger ice cream with clotted cream and brandy snap (£2.75); home-made soup (£1.85), sandwiches (from £1.95), ploughman's (from £3.75), a fry-up (£5.25), grilled whole plaice (£7,75), and steaks (from £7.95). There's some magnificent medieval oak panelling – and the latticed glass on the back wall of the open-plan bar is almost 700 years old and one of the earliest examples of non-ecclesiastical glass in the country (it had been walled off until Victorian times). Furnishings include attractive 17th- and 18th-c pews and settles and there's a large inglenook fireplaces with a wood-burning stove; one half of the room is set out for eating. The no-smoking family room has been refurbished this year. Bass and Courage Best and two weekly-changing guest beers such as Eldridge Pope Royal Oak, Dartmoor, Gibbs Mew Bishops Finger, Marstons Pedigree or Shepherd Neame Spitfire on handpump, and farm cider; darts, dominoes and cards. The pub is in a steep little twisting village, pretty and surrounded by hills. *(Recommended by J H Bell, Jean Cross, Paul Silvestri, Bill Sharpe, Roger Wain-Heapy, T Aldworth, Gordon, David Holloway, Alan and Brenda Holyer, Jim and Maggie Cowell, Marion and R W A Suddaby, Marion and John Hadfield, Steve Huggins)*

Free house ~ Licensees David and Jennifer Wright ~ Real ale ~ Meals and snacks (not 25 Dec) ~ (01803) 863707 ~ Children in family room ~ Occasional Morris men in summer ~ Open 12(11.30 Sat)-2.30(3 Sat), 6-11; closed evenings 25/26 Dec and 1 Jan

HATHERLEIGH SS5404 Map 1

George 🍷

A386 N of Okehampton

Farmers crowd into this friendly inn on Tuesday market day – but visitors are made just as welcome. There's a good atmosphere and particularly helpful, friendly staff in the little front bar in the original part of the building: huge oak beams, stone walls two or three feet thick, an enormous fireplace, and easy chairs, sofas and antique cushioned settles; you can get drinks here throughout market day. The spacious L-shaped main bar was built from the wreck of the inn's old brewhouse and coachmen's loft, and has more beams, a wood-burning stove, and antique settles around sewing-machine treadle tables; a quieter no-smoking extension, with more modern furnishings, leads off this; darts, pool, dominoes, fruit machine and piped music. Well kept Bass, Boddingtons, and Wye Valley on handpump with regularly changing guests, Inch's cider, wines and champagnes by the glass, several malt whiskies, and home-made lemonade and ginger beer in summer. Generous helpings of good, tasty bar food include sandwiches, home-made soup (£2.20), fried halloumi with lime vinaigrette (£2.90), ploughman's (£3.25), spinach and ricotta pie or tagliatelle carbonara (£4.50), delicious mediterranean prawns with garlic mayonnaise (£4.75), steak and kidney pie (£5), Sri Lankan curry (£5.95), a generous mixed grill, steaks (£8.50), and puddings like good treacle tart or super lemon tart (£2.20). In the flood-lit courtyard there are very pretty hanging baskets and window-boxes on the black and white timbering, and rustic wooden seats and tables on its cobblestones; there's also a walled cobbled garden. *(Recommended by Rita Horridge, Moira and John Cole, Jack and Philip Paxton, Derek and Iris Martin, R J Walden, Barry and Anne, Werner Arend, John and Vivienne Rice, Les and Mavis Law, Derek and Margaret Underwood)*

Free house ~ Licensees Veronica Devereux and John Dunbar-Ainley ~ Real ale ~ Meals and snacks (12-2, 6-9.30) ~ Restaurant (closed Sun) ~ (01837) 810454 ~ Children in eating area of bar ~ Open 11-3.30, 6-11; see above ~ Bedrooms: £28.50(£48B)/£49.50(£69.50B)

Tally Ho

Market St (A386)

Cheerful and enthusiastic new licensees have taken over this friendly bustling pub, and although they will obviously stamp their own mark, the own-brewed beers continue, the food is totally home-made and good, and the furnishings remain happily unchanged. The opened-together rooms of the bar have heavy beams, two woodburning stoves (an armchair by one, the other in a very high-mantled smoking-chamber of a hearth), sturdy old oak and elm tables on the partly carpeted wooden floor, decorative plates between the wall timbers, candles in bottles, and shelves of old bottles and pottery; the two cockatiels are called Squeaky and Squashy. Much emphasis is placed on the changing daily specials which might include tagliatelle with meatballs in a cream sauce (£4.95), steak of conger eel in lime and butter sauce (£5.50), roast lamb marinated in Tally Ho! Ale (£5.65), trout (£5.95), Thai green chicken curry (£6.50), and salads such as tiger tail prawns with seaweed or seafood (from £7); also, sandwiches (from £2.35), soup such as cream of tomato and coriander (£2.95), home-made pâté (£3), steaks (from £9.45), and lovely puddings like rhubarb and cinnamon tart or chocolate and banana pie (from £2.10); Wednesday evening is home-made pizza night (from £3.95) and Thursday is grill (or griddle) night (from £5.50). Through a big window in one building of the former back coach yard you can see the spotless copper brewing equipment where they brew deep-coloured quite strongly hopped Potboiler with its sturdily appetising finish, Tarka Tipple, Thurgia, Nutters, and Master Jack's Mild – they will bottle beers for you to take away; also, a decent range of wines, and several malt whiskies. Darts, shove-ha'penny, dominoes, cribbage, trivia, and piped music. There are tables and an aviary in the sheltered garden. *(Recommended by Alan and Eileen Bowker, Richard Houghton, Thomas Neate, Wendy and Ray Bryn Davies, R J Walden, Jack and Philip Paxton; more reports on the new regime, please)*

Own brew ~ Licensees Megan and Jason Tidy ~ Real ale ~ Meals and snacks ~ Evening restaurant (closed Weds/Thurs) ~ (01837) 810306 ~ Well behaved children in eating area of bar and in restaurant ~ Open 11-2.30, 6-11 ~ Bedrooms: £30B/£50B

HAYTOR VALE SX7677 Map 1

Rock ★

Haytor signposted off B3344 just W of Bovey Tracey, on good moorland road to Widecombe

It might be best to book a table if you want to eat in the bar of this rather civilised Dartmoor inn – though there are usually seats in the no-smoking dining room or restaurant. The two communicating, partly panelled bar rooms have easy chairs, oak windsor armchairs and high-backed settles, candlelit, polished antique tables, old-fashioned prints and decorative plates on the walls, and good winter log fires (the main fireplace has a fine Stuart fireback). A wide choice of good bar food includes home-made soup (£1.90), sandwiches (from £2.35), ploughman's (from £4.25), filled baked potatoes (from £3.95), lasagne or 3-egg omelettes using free range eggs (£4.95), steak and kidney pie (£5.55), local rabbit in mustard sauce (£5.65), good aubergine in spicy tomato sauce or curries (£5.95), steaks (from £9.95), and puddings such as apple bread and butter pudding or chocolate terrine (from £2.95); friendly, attentive staff. Well kept Bass, Eldridge Pope Royal Oak and Hardy, and Dartmoor on handpump, and several malt whiskies. In summer, the pretty, well kept large garden opposite the inn is a popular place to sit and there are some tables and chairs on a small terrace next to the pub itself. The village is just inside the National Park, and golf, horse riding and fishing (and walking, of course) are nearby. *(Recommended by G and M Stewart, Mrs J Beale, P H Roberts, John and Vivienne Rice, G W Stevenson, John and Christine Vittoe, Sue Demont, Tim Barrow, Anthony Marriott, Lawrence Bacon, David and Tina Woods-Taylor, Dennis Heatley, David Holloway, Jon and Julie Gibson, Mark and Heather Williamson, T Aldworth, Steve Huggins, W F C Phillips, Patrick Clancy, B A Ferris, P M Lane)*

Free house ~ Licensee Christopher Graves ~ Real ale ~ Snacks (not Sun or Bank Hol) ~ Restaurant ~ (01364) 661305 ~ Children in eating area of bar ~ Open 11-3, 6.30-11; 11-11 Sat ~ Bedrooms: £29.95(£35.95B)/£50(£61.95B)

HOLBETON SX6150 Map 1

Mildmay Colours

Signposted off A379 W of A3121 junction

It's quite a surprise to find this neatly kept, pleasant pub in a quiet village, brewing its own well hopped and fruity beers – Colours Best, SP, 50/1, Old Horse Whip, and Tipster on handpump – you are welcome to look at the brewery. Lots of named tankards hang over the bar counter and there are plenty of bar stools as well as cushioned wall seats and wheelback chairs on the turkey carpet, various horse and racing pictures on the partly stripped stone and partly white walls, and a tile-sided wood-burning stove; an arch leads to a smaller, similarly decorated family area. The separate plain back bar has pool, sensible darts, dominoes, cribbage. Good value, popular bar food includes sandwiches (from £1.80), half pint of garlic prawns (£2.75), home-cooked ham and egg (£3.35), ploughman's or vegetarian nut roast (£3.95), and Mexican dishes such as huevos rancheros or enchiladas (from £4.25), home-made pie of the day (£4.75), steaks (from £7.95), and daily specials such as spiced lentil soup (£2.25), beef balti (£4.95) or skate with capers and black butter (£6.25); children's meals (£2.75), and two course carvery Friday and Saturday evenings and Sunday lunch, £6.95); helpful service. The well kept back garden has picnic tables, a swing and some guinea pigs and rabbits in a big cage, and there's a small front terrace. *(Recommended by B Taylor, Nigel Spence, Kim Greek, Andy and Jill Kassube, D Rowe, Richard Houghton, J C Hathaway, Geoff and Marianne Millin, David Lewis)*

Own brew ~ Licensee Andrew Patrick ~ Real ale ~ Meals and snacks (served throughout opening hours) ~ Upstairs carvery restaurant (closed Mon-Thurs) ~ (01752) 830248 ~ Children in eating area of bar ~ Open 11-3.30, 6-11; occasional all day opening in summer ~ Bedrooms in two cottages opposite: £20B/£40B

HOLNE SX7069 Map 1

Church House

Village signed off B3357 2 or 3 miles W of Ashburton

We've decided to give this well run country inn a Food Award this year – and readers have been full of praise for the imaginative use of fresh local produce, particularly in the daily specials. But this is not just a straightforward dining pub. There's a relaxed and quietly chatty atmosphere where walkers with their well behaved dogs are made just as welcome as those coming to enjoy a meal – no piped music, noisy machines or pool tables. The lower bar has stripped pine panelling and an 18th-c curved elm settle, and is separated from the atmospheric carpeted lounge bar by a 16th-c heavy oak partition; open log fires in both rooms. There are fine moorland views from the pillared porch (where regulars tend to gather). They take great care in preparing their food (even growing some of their own organic vegetables): soup (£1.95), lunchtime sandwiches (from £2.50), home-made pâté (from £2.95), filled baked potatoes (from £3.50), lunchtime ploughman's (from £3.95), 3-egg omelettes (from £3.75), excellent steak and kidney in ale pie (£5.25), local rabbit pie (£5.50), grills (from £5.75), daily specials such as vegetable and pasta bake (£4.95), home-baked ham and parsley sauce or lamb's liver in a sherry cream sauce (£5.75), grilled whole local sole on the bone or pork in ginger and cream (£6.25), baked salmon in lemon and herb butter (£6.75), and puddings like apple charlotte (£2.25). The restaurant is no smoking. Well kept Blackawton Bitter and Shepherds Delight, Eldridge Pope Hardy, Dartmoor, and Wadworths 6X on handpump, Greys farm cider, and decent house wines (several by the glass); darts, dominoes, cribbage, and table skittles in the public bar. The quarter-hour walk from the Newbridge National Trust car park to the pub is rather fine, and there are many other attractive walks nearby, up on to Dartmoor as well as along the wooded Dart valley. Charles Kingsley (of *Water Babies* fame) was born in the village.

(Recommended by Alan Newman, David Mowbray, R J Walden, Nick and Meriel Cox, Dr N Holmes, Jeanne Cross, Paul Silvestri, Mark and Heather Williamson, Anthony Marriott, Mrs J Beale, Ann and David Rose, Simon Evans, T Aldworth, D Goodger, P R Ferris, A Plumb, Simon and Natalie Forster, David Eberlin)

Free house ~ N E and W J Bevan ~ Real ale ~ Meals and snacks ~ Restaurant ~ (01364) 631208 ~ Well behaved children in eating area of bar; over 7 (except residents) in restaurant in evening ~ Occasional local musicians or Morris dancers ~ Open 11.30-3, 6.30-11; winter opening 12 and close 10.30 Sun-Thurs ~ Bedrooms: £22.50(£27.50B)/£39(£50B)

HORNDON SX5280 Map 1

Elephants Nest

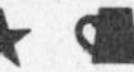

If coming from Okehampton on A386 turn left at Mary Tavy Inn, then left after about ½ mile; pub signposted beside Mary Tavy Inn, then Horndon signposted; on the Ordnance Survey Outdoor Leisure Map it's named as the New Inn

On the spacious, flower-bordered lawn in front of this isolated old pub are some wooden benches and tables that look over the walls to the pastures of Dartmoor's lower slopes. Inside, there are large rugs and flagstones, a beams-and-board ceiling, a good log fire, and cushioned stone seats built into the windows, with captain's chairs around the tables; the name of the pub is written up on the beams in 60 languages. Another room – created from the old beer cellar and with views over the garden and beyond to the moors – acts as a dining or function room or an overspill from the bar on busy nights. Good home-made bar food at lunchtime includes home-made soup (£1.35), home-made pâté (from £3), steak and kidney pie (£4.50), tandoori chicken (£5.20), Aberdeen Angus steaks (from £9.60), daily specials such as Hungarian goulash (£4.50), baked cod with provençale sauce (£5.80), and guinea fowl in orange and Dubonnet sauce (£6); vegetables are £1.20 extra. Well kept Boddingtons Bitter, Palmers IPA, St Austells HSD, and a local and another guest on handpump; farm cider. Sensibly placed darts, cribbage, dominoes, Shut-the-box, and piped music. You can walk from here straight onto the moor or Black Down, though a better start (army exercises permitting) might be to drive past Wapsworthy to the end of the lane, at OS Sheet 191 map reference 546805. They have three dogs, two cats, ducks, chickens, rabbits, and horses; customers' dogs are allowed in on a lead. *(Recommended by Dr and Mrs N Holmes, R J Walden, Andy and Jill Kassube, Andy, Andrew and friends, Nigel Spence, Kim Greek, Phil and Anne Smithson, George and Jeanne Barnwell, Jack and Philip Paxton, Andy and Jackie Mallpress, Paul Boot, Mrs S Segrove)*

Free house ~ Licensee Nick Hamer ~ Real ale ~ Meals and snacks (until 10pm) ~ (01822) 810273 ~ Children in two rooms off bar ~ Folk music 2nd Tues evening of month ~ Open 11.30-2.30, 6.30-11

HORSEBRIDGE SX3975 Map 1

Royal ★

Village signposted off A384 Tavistock—Launceston

This prettily-set pub feels as if it can't have changed much since Turner slept on a settle in front of the fire so that he could slip out early to paint the nearby bridge. Besides the beers brewed on the premises – Horsebridge Best, Right Royal, Tamar and the more powerful Heller – they also keep Bass and Sharps Own on handpump, and country wines. The rooms are simple and old-fashioned and the one on the right room has harness and brasses on the stripped stone walls, vertically panelled cushioned stall seats around neat old tables, and some mate's and wheelback chairs; the one on the left has cushioned casks and benches around three tables on the slate floor, and bar billiards, sensibly placed darts, and dominoes; piped music. There's another small room, called the Drip Tray, for the overflow at busy times. The good variety of freshly cooked bar food at lunchtime includes soup, lots of good ploughman's (from £2.95), and cottage pie or fisherman's pot; also, ricotta cheese and spinach cannelloni, steak and kidney pie, vegetable tikka masala, venison in wine, sherried kidneys, prawn Cantonese, and salads (from £5.50-£6.25), and puddings like treacle pudding or nutty apple and caramel strudel (£2.10); no chips or fried food. The covered area in the garden, presided over by Fred, the resident jackdaw, also has budgies, finches, and so forth, and a big terrace with seats, a rose arbour and hanging baskets. The pub was originally called the Packhorse, and got its present name for services rendered to Charles I (whose seal is carved in the doorstep). No children. *(Recommended by Andy and Jill Kassube, Dr and Mrs N Holmes, Jack and Philip Paxton, James Macrae, Paul and Heather Bettesworth, Richard Houghton, Peter Taylor, John Hazel, Mayur Shah, John and Tessa Rainsford, A N Ellis)*

Own brew ~ Licensees T G and J H Wood ~ Real ale ~ Snacks (lunchtime) and meals (not Sun evening) ~ (01822) 870214 ~ Open 12-2.30, 7-11; closed evening 25 Dec

IDDESLEIGH SS5708 Map 1

Duke of York

B3217 Exbourne—Dolton

A friendly new licensee has taken over this largely 14th-c pub and is determined to preserve its relaxing atmosphere and character – he has known the pub for some 40 years. It's very much the social centre of the village and filled with chatty regulars: rocking chairs by the roaring log fire, cushioned wall benches built into the wall's black-painted wooden dado, stripped tables, and other homely country furnishings. Bar food now includes sandwiches (from £1.50), home-made soup or garlic mushrooms (£1.75), very good local honey-roast sausages with two eggs or ploughman's (£3.95), leek and stilton bake (£4.35), Malay chicken (£4.75), fresh halibut (£5.25), steaks (from £7.95), and puddings like sticky toffee pudding (£2.10); dishes from India, Pakistan and South East Asia on Wednesday evenings. Well kept Adnams Extra, Cotleigh Tawny and perhaps Exmoor Ale tapped from the cask; shove-ha'penny, cribbage, dominoes and sensibly placed darts. Through a small coach arch is a little back garden with some picnic tables under cocktail parasols. Good fishing nearby. *(Recommended by Joan and Gordon Edwards, Paul and Wendy Bachelor, David Wallington, R J Walden, Derek and Iris Martin, Gwen and Peter Andrews)*

Free house ~ Lease: Bill Pringle ~ Real ale ~ Meals and snacks (not Mon evening and see opening hours below) ~ Restaurant ~ (01837) 810253 ~ Children in eating area of bar and in restaurant ~ Open 11.30-3, 6.30-11; closed lunchtimes Mon/Tues/Weds 1 Nov-31 Mar ~ Bedrooms: £20/£40(£44B)

KILMINGTON SY2797 Map 1

Old Inn

A35

Popular locally, this thatched white pub has a characterful, traditionally furnished main bar, comfortable lounge with leather armchairs and sofa around the inglenook fireplace, well kept Bass and Worthington Best on handpump, and darts, dominoes, cribbage, fruit machine, and piped music; skittle alley. Good value food includes sandwiches, basket meals, home-cooked ham and eggs (£3.95), home-made steak, mushroom and Guinness pie (£4.95), and specials like chicken breast filled with spinach and almonds with a garlicky tomato sauce (£8.95) or fresh fish; the little restaurant is no smoking. There are two gardens – a big one by the car park and a more secluded one behind. *(Recommended by David Roberts, John Hazel, N Bushby, W Atkins; more reports please).*

Free house ~ Licensees Carol and Jeff Little ~ Real ale ~ Meals and snacks ~ Restaurant (closed winter Sun/Mon evenings) ~ (01297) 32096 ~ Children in eating area of bar and in restaurant ~ Open 11-2.30, 5.30-11

KINGSKERSWELL SX8767 Map 1

Barn Owl 🛏

Aller Mills; just off A380 Newton Abbot—Torquay – inn-sign on main road opposite RAC post

Carefully run, this 400-year-old ex-farmhouse has three comfortable beamed bars. The large bar has an elaborate ornamental plaster ceiling, antique dark oak panelling, some grand furnishings such as a couple of carved oak settles and old-fashioned dining chairs around the handsome polished tables on its flowery carpet, and a decorative wooden chimney piece; the other rooms have low black oak beams, with polished flagstones and a kitchen range in one, and an inglenook fireplace in the other. Popular bar food includes home-made soup (£2), big sandwiches with interesting side salad (from £2.70, crab £3.75), filled baked potatoes (from £2.95), delicious garlic mushrooms (£3.25), generous ploughman's (from £3.75), quite a few salads (from £5.50; home roast loin of pork £5.95; fine fresh local salmon £7.95), fresh fillet of sole (£5.95), gammon (£6.25), steaks (from £9.95), mixed grill (£10.25), puddings (£2.50), and daily specials like steak and kidney pie (£5.75), salmon, prawn and mushroom pancakes (£5.95), and beef wellington with madeira sauce (£7.95). Well kept Dartmoor, Ind Coope Burton and Wadworths 6X on handpump, 15 malt whiskies, and several wines by the glass. There are picnic tables in a small sheltered garden. *(Recommended by Michael Butler, R W Flux, Peter and Jenny Quine, John A Barker, Steve Goodchild, C and Marjorie Roberts, Peter Pocklington, Tom Evans, John Dowell, Steve Huggins, A E and P McCully, Michael A Butler)*

Free house ~ Licensees Derek and Margaret Warner ~ Real ale ~ Meals and snacks (till 10pm) ~ Restaurant (not Sun) ~ (01803) 872130 ~ Children in restaurant only ~ Open 11.30-2.30, 6-11; winter evening opening 6.30; closed evening 25 Dec, closed 26/27 Dec ~ Bedrooms: £40B/£60B

Pubs close to motorway junctions are listed at the back of the book.

KINGSTEIGNTON SX8773 Map 1

Old Rydon ★

Rydon Rd; from A381/A380 junction follow signs to Kingsteignton (B3103), taking first right turn (Longford Lane), go straight on to the bottom of the hill, then next right turn into Rydon Rd following Council Office signpost; pub is just past the school, OS Sheet 192 map reference 872739

Very popular for its constantly changing and imaginative food, this old pub has a warmly welcoming atmosphere, too. The small, cosy bar has a big winter log fire in a raised fireplace, cask seats and upholstered seats built against the white-painted stone walls, and lots of beer mugs hanging from the heavy beam-and-plank ceiling. There are a few more seats in an upper former cider loft facing the antlers and antelope horns on one high white wall; piped music. Generously served, the bar food might include vegetable, split pea and lovage soup (£1.95), potato pancakes topped with a seafood salad in lemon mayonnaise (£3.25), cauliflower and flat cap mushrooms in a pesto, tomato and cream sauce (£4.40), venison sausages with bubble and squeak in a rich red wine, onion and herb sauce (£4.65), pork and stir-fried vegetable casserole in a rich peanut, coriander, ginger and lemon-grass sauce (£5.65), fisherman's pie with local cod and prawns in a white wine, cream and sorrel sauce (£5.95), and puddings such as amaretto mousse with amaretti biscuits or sticky toffee pudding (£2.50). Well kept Bass, Wadworths 6X, and a changing guest ale on handpump, and helpful service. There's also a prettily planted dining conservatory. Seats in a nice biggish sheltered garden, which also has a swing. ***(Recommended by Barbara Wensworth, Nick Leslie, Alan and Eileen Bowker, D I Baddeley, Kevin Mitchell, Peter and Jenny Quine, Jeanne Cross, Paul Silvestri, Mrs Pat Crabb, Steve Huggins, Thomas Neate, George Atkinson, P and J Shapley, John and Vivienne Rice)***

Free house ~ Licensees Hermann and Miranda Hruby ~ Real ale ~ Meals and snacks ~ Restaurant (closed Sun) ~ (01626) 54626 ~ Children in eating area of bar, but no under 8s after 8pm ~ Open 11-2.30, 6-11; closed 25 Dec

KINGSTON SX6347 Map 1

Dolphin

Off B3392 S of Modbury (can also be reached from A379 W of Modbury)

From this peaceful shuttered 16th-c inn, there are several tracks leading down to the sea. Inside, the several knocked-through beamed rooms have a warmly welcoming atmosphere and rustic tables and cushioned seats and settles around their bared stone walls; one small area is no smoking. Very good home-made bar food includes sandwiches (from £1.50), soup such as onion and coriander or lentil (£1.95), ploughman's (from £3.50), chicken with an apple and calvados sauce or leek and pistachio nut lasagne with garlic bread (£4.95), steak and kidney pie (£5.50), fisherman's pie (£5.95), lamb steak with rosemary and garlic (£6.50), steaks (from £7.95), plaice fillets with an apricot and hazelnut stuffing in a wine, apricot and dill sauce (£8.95), puddings such as chocolate pear pudding or treacle tart (£2.25), and children's meals (from £1.50). Well kept Courage Best and Ushers Founders on handpump. Outside, there are tables and swings. ***(Recommended by R W Brooks, B Taylor, Mr and Mrs C C Mathewman, Roger and Susan Dunn, Norma Farris, B J Harding, David Cundy, Gordon, T Aldworth, Maurice Ingram, Lorraine Flanagan, David Goldstone, Roger Berry)***

Ushers ~ Tenants Neil and Annie Williams ~ Real ale ~ Meals and snacks (till 10pm) ~ (01548) 810314 ~ Children in eating area of bar and in two children's areas ~ Open 11-2.30, 6-11 ~ Bedrooms: £35B/£45B

Looking for a pub with a really special garden, or in lovely countryside, or with an outstanding view, or right by the water? They are listed separately, at the back of the book.

KNOWSTONE SS8223 Map 1

Masons Arms ★ 🛏 🍷

Village signposted off A361 Bampton—South Molton

Marvellously relaxed and full of individual character, this unspoilt 13th-c thatched pub is in a lovely quiet position opposite the village church. It's run in a very personal way by the warmly welcoming licensees and the small untampered main bar always has a good mix of chatty locals and visitors. Ancient bottles of all shapes and sizes hang from the heavy medieval black beams, there are farm tools on the walls, substantial rustic furniture on the stone floor, and a fine open fireplace with a big log fire and side bread oven. A small lower sitting room has pinkish plush chairs around a low table in front of the fire and bar billiards. Bar food can be very good indeed: widely praised home-made soup (£1.75) and pâté (£2.50), ploughman's with proper local cheese and butter in a pot or Greek salad (£3.50), fried plaice (£3.95), home-made pies, varying from day to day, like venison, cheese and leek or rabbit (£4.25), home-made curry (£5.25), good fritto misto (£5.95), and home-made puddings like chocolate torrone or treacle tart (£1.95); specials such as potted pheasant (£2.50), venison casserole with herb dumplings (£4.95) or salmon kedgeree (£5.25); good value Sunday lunch, a popular Thursday curry night, and theme nights about once a month, usually with live music, a special menu and a special drink. The restaurant is no smoking. They often sell home-made marmalades, fruit breads or hot gooseberry chutney over the counter. Well kept Badger Best and Cotleigh Tawny tapped from the cask (and an occasional guest beer), farm cider, a small but well chosen wine list (with around 8 by the glass), and coffee and teas; several snuffs on the counter; darts, shove-ha'penny, bar billiards, dominoes, cribbage, and quiz nights. Maybe weekend evening summer barbecues in the back garden. Charlie the engaging bearded collie likes to join you on a walk at least part of the way; the cats are called Archie and Allie. The refurbishment of the bedrooms is nearly complete. *(Recommended by L Parikian, Jack and Philip Paxton, Dr Peter Donahue, Sue Demont, Tim Barrow, S G N Bennett, Clive Gilbert, N M Baleham, Chris Westmoreland, Jed and Virginia Brown, A E and P McCully, Martin Jones, David Saunders, D B Delany, Robin and Molly Taylor, Patricia Nutt, Jim and Maggie Cowell, Lynn Sharpless, Bob Eardley, John Wootten, Christine Hodgeson, R J Walden)*

Free house ~ Licensees David and Elizabeth Todd ~ Real ale ~ Meals and snacks ~ Restaurant (not Sun evening) ~ (01398) 341231/341582 ~ Children in eating area of bar and in restaurant ~ Occasional live music ~ Open 11-3, 6-11; winter evening opening 7; closed evenings 25/26 Dec ~ Bedrooms: £40/£55B; dogs £1.50

LITTLEHEMPSTON SX8162 Map 1

Tally Ho!

Signposted off A381 NE of Totnes

This is a smashing little pub with a relaxed, friendly and chatty atmosphere – helped by the fact that there are no noisy machines or piped music. The bare stone walls in the cosy low-beamed rooms are covered with growing collections of porcelain, brass, copperware, mounted butterflies, stuffed wildlife, old swords, and shields and hunting horns and so forth; there's also an interesting mix of chairs and settles (many antique and with comfortable cushions), candles on the tables, fresh flowers, panelling, and two ornamental woodburning stoves. Enjoyable and very good, the bar food includes delicious soup (£2.75), sandwiches (from £2.75; lovely crab £3.25), super soused mackerel, mussels in cream and white wine (£2.95), rabbit casserole or steak and kidney pie (£6.50), fresh local plaice (£7.25), Brixham fish pie (£8.50), Aberdeen Angus steaks (from £9.25), fresh roast duckling (£11.50), home-made puddings with clotted cream, and daily specials. Well kept Dartmoor, and Wadworths 6X on handpump from a temperature controlled cellar. The terrace is a mass of flowers in summer. *(Recommended by David Wallington, John A Barker, Peter Burton, Mrs B Lemon, Ian Phillips, Steve Huggins, Alan and Brenda Holyer)*

Free house ~ Licensees Alan and Dale Hitchman ~ Real ale ~ Meals and snacks (till 10pm) ~ (01803) 862316 ~ Children in eating area of bar ~ Open 12-2.30, 6-11; closed 25 Dec

LOWER ASHTON SX8484 Map 1

Manor

Ashton signposted off B3193 N of Chudleigh

The sort of pub that appeals immensely to CAMRA members, this gets quite crowded with chaps enjoying the well kept Wadworths 6X tapped from the cask and Bass, Janners, Theakstons XB and a changing guest ale such as Burton Bridge on handpump, or perhaps the local Green Valley farm cider. This side of things is very much concentrated in the left-hand room, its walls covered in beer mats and brewery advertisements; on the right, two rather more discreet rooms have a wider appeal, bolstered by popular home-made food including sandwiches (from £1.50), soup (£1.60), ploughman's (from £3.50), filled baked potatoes (from £2.60), steak and kidney pie (£4.95) and steaks (from rump £8.50), with a good choice of changing specials (many topped with melted cheese and served with very garlicky garlic bread) such as mixed bean chilli or vegetable and nut curry (£4.50) and beef casserole (£5.25). Service is quick; shove-ha'penny, spoof. The garden outside this creeper-covered house has lots of picnic tables under cocktail parasols (and a fine tall Scots pine); it's a charming valley. No children allowed inside *(Recommended by Marion and John Hadfield, Jeanne Cross, Paul Silvestri, Julian McMahon, Chris Westmoreland)*

Free house ~ Licensees Geoff and Clare Mann ~ Real ale ~ Meals and snacks (12-1.30, 7-9.30; not Mon) ~ Open 12-2.30, 6(7 Sat)-11; cl Mon exc bank holidays

LUSTLEIGH SX7881 Map 1

Cleave

Village signposted off A382 Bovey Tracey—Moretonhampstead

In an attractive village, this warmly friendly old thatched pub has a very pretty sheltered summer garden, full of flowers. Inside, the cosy, low-ceilinged lounge bar has big winter log fires, and attractive antique high-backed settles, pale leatherette bucket chairs, red-cushioned wall seats, and wheelback chairs around the tables on its patterned carpet. The second bar has a large dresser, harmonium, an HMV gramophone, prints, and other similar furnishings; the family room has crayons, books and toys for children. Big helpings of quickly served enjoyable bar food include home-made soup (£1.95), sandwiches (£2.65), pasta with pesto (£3.60), ploughman's (from £3.95), home-made chicken curry (£5.45), home-made steak, kidney and Guinness pie (£5.95), excellent roast pork with apple sauce (£6.25), daily specials such as good lamb chops baked in cider, puddings like lovely apple crumble and clotted cream or gooseberry and almond pie (£2.25), and children's dishes (from £2.95). Well kept Bass, Flowers Original and IPA and a guest like Whitbreads Fuggles on handpump, several malt whiskies, and farm ciders. *(Recommended by G and M Stewart, John and Christine Vittoe, Alan Newman, R J Walden, Mr and Mrs C Roberts, A Lock, Joan and Gordon Edwards, Sue Hobley, John and Vivienne Rice, Werner Arend, David and Tina Woods-Taylor, Patrick Clancy, Steve Huggins, P M Lane)*

Heavitree (who no longer brew) ~ Tenant Alison Perring ~ Real ale ~ Meals and snacks ~ (016477) 223 ~ Open 11-11 (inc Sun); 11-3, 6-11 in winter ~ Children in no-smoking family room ~ Parking may be difficult

LUTTON SX5959 Map 1

Mountain

Off Cornwood—Sparkwell road, though pub not signposted from it

You're sure of a friendly welcome here – from both the licensees and their cats and three dogs. The bar has a high-backed settle by the log fire, some walls stripped back to the bare stone, windsor chairs around old-fashioned polished tables in a larger connecting room, and a fine view over the lower slopes of Dartmoor; the same view is shared by the terrace. Well kept Dartmoor, Wadworths 6X and a guest beer on handpump, several malt whiskies, and farm cider; darts, cribbage, dominoes, and liar dice. Generous helpings of good straightforward bar food include good pasties (£1), sandwiches (from £1.60), soup (£1.70; with a hunk of cheese as well £3), sausage and chips (£2.60), cottage pie (£3.50), ploughman's or ham cooked in cider (£3.80), and chicken kiev. *(Recommended by Roger and Susan Dunn, Mr and Mrs Jones, Andy and Jill Kassube, George and Jeanne Barnwell, J H Bell, J S Poulter)*

Free house ~ Licensees Charles and Margaret Bullock ~ Real ale ~ Meals and snacks (till 10 evening) ~ (01752) 837247 ~ Children in eating area of bar and in own room ~ Open 11-3, 6-11; winter Mon-Weds evening opening 7

LYDFORD SX5184 Map 1

Castle ★

Signposted off A386 Okehampton—Tavistock

As well as a cosy atmosphere and warmly friendly staff, it's the very wide range of food that readers like so much in this charming pink-washed Tudor inn. From a menu that changes sometimes twice a day, there might be soups like cream of celeriac and roasted fennel or tomato and fresh basil (£2.20), Devon Blue, walnut and pork pâté (£3.95), fresh coriander and onion patties with apple mint, roasted cumin and cucumber dip (£5.25), fried black pudding with mustard and parsley sauce and parsnip mash (£5.35), smoked haddock kedgeree fish cakes (£5.45), wild rabbit casserole (£5.55), home-cooked gammon with cider and wholegrain mustard sauce encased in pastry (£5.75), Thai mussel and fresh pineapple curry with saffron and burnt almond rice (£6.35), and puddings like chocolate and raspberry roulade or lemon, wine and brandy mousse (from £2.30); they are also trying organic food and wines, and have an authentic curry night once a month from October to April. Part of the restaurant is no smoking. Well kept Blackawton Devon Gold, Dartmoor, Smiles Best and Wadsworth 6X plus a guest beer on handpump or tapped from the cask, and around 14 wines by the glass, as well as a sparkling wine and bucks fizz. One of the rooms of the twin-roomed bar (where the bar food is served) has low lamp-lit beams, a sizeable open fire, masses of brightly decorated plates, some Hogarth prints, an attractive grandfather clock, and, near the serving-counter, seven Lydford pennies hammered out in the old Saxon mint in the reign of Ethelred the Unready, in the 11th-c; the second room has an interesting collection of antique stallion posters, and both rooms are furnished with country kitchen chairs, high-backed winged settles and old captain's chairs around mahogany tripod tables on big slate flagstones. Unusual stained-glass doors; sensibly placed darts, cribbage, dominoes, and trivia. The terrace in the well kept garden has a pets' corner for residents' children with goats, rabbits, hens and a shetland pony called Wanda. The pub is next to the village's daunting, ruined 12th-c castle and close to a beautiful river gorge (owned by the National Trust; closed Nov-Easter); the village itself was one of the four strong-points developed by Alfred the Great as a defence against the Danes. The planned extension has to wait for an archaeological dig before it can start. *(Recommended by Jacquie and Jim Jones, Andy and Jill Kassube, Anthony Marriott, Mike Gorton, S P Ward, R J Walden, Simon and Debbie Tomlinson, Jack and Philip Paxton, T Cobden Pike, Nigel Flook, Betsy Brown, Howard Clutterbuck, S Lonie, S Tait, J and J O Jones, J R Williams, Frank Cummins, John and Christine Vittoe, Mick Gray, Alan and Brenda Holyer, Richard Davies, Peter and Lynn Brueton, Frank Cummins, P and M Rudlin, Patrick Clancy)*

Free house ~ Licensees Clive and Mo Walker ~ Real ale ~ Meals and snacks ~ Restaurant ~ (01822) 820241/820242 ~ Children in restaurant and snug area; must be over 5 in evening restaurant ~ Open 11.30-3, 6-11; closed evening 25 Dec ~ Bedrooms: £28.75(£38.75B)/£42.50(£52.50B)

LYNMOUTH SS7249 Map 1

Rising Sun ☞

Mars Hill; down by harbour

There are lovely views over the boats in the little harbour and out to sea from this thatched 14th-c inn. The modernised panelled bar has a relaxed chatty atmosphere, as well as cushioned built-in stall-seats on the uneven oak floors, black beams in the crooked ceiling, some stripped stone at the fireplace end, and latticed windows facing the harbour; piped music. Well kept Courage Directors and John Smiths on handpump, and decent lunchtime bar food such as home-made soup (£1.95), filled rolls (from £2.45; crab £3.50), filled baked potatoes (£3.25), ploughman's (£3.95), chilli con carne (£4.25), bacon lardons and crispy croutons on mixed leaves with a walnut dressing (£4.50), and steak, mushroom and Guinness pie (£4.75); the attractive restaurant is no smoking. There's a charming terraced garden behind the inn, cut into the hillside. Shelley reputedly spent his honeymoon with his 16-year-old bride, Harriet, in one of the cottages here. The steep walk up the Lyn valley to Watersmeet (National Trust) and Exmoor is particularly pleasant. ***(Recommended by** John and Christine Vittoe, Gary Gibbon, Mark Berger, Malcolm Fowler, Mr and Mrs M Brown, E B Davies, R J Walden, M D Beardmore, Paul Randall, Dorothee and Dennis Glover, Bill and Beryl Farmer)*

Free house ~ Licensee Hugo Jeune ~ Real ale ~ Lunchtime meals and snacks ~ Restaurant ~ (01598) 53223 ~ Children in restaurant if over 5 ~ Open 11-3, 5.30-11; 11-2.30, 6.30-11 in winter ~ Bedrooms: £39.50B/£79B

MEAVY SX5467 Map 1

Royal Oak

Off B3212 E of Yelverton

In a pretty Dartmoor-edge village, this traditional old pub is run by friendly and helpful licensees. The L-shaped bar has pews from the next door church, red plush banquettes and old agricultural prints and church pictures on the walls, and there's a smaller bar – where the locals like to gather – with a big fireplace and side bread oven, and red-topped barrel seats. Bar food includes sandwiches, soup (the game is very good), ploughman's, home-made chicken curry (£4.75), mussels with cockles, cheese-topped with white wine and garlic sauce or home-made steak and kidney pie (£4.95), puddings like spotted dick or apple pie, and roast Sunday lunch. Well kept Bass, Courage Best, Eldridge Pope Royal Oak, and Otter Bitter on handpump kept under light blanket pressure. Darts, dominoes, and piped music. There are benches and picnic-tables outside the pub by the village green (where the 500-year-old oak tree once had nine men eating inside its trunk). No children. ***(Recommended by** Mr and Mrs J Woodfield, Jeanne Cross, Paul Silvestri, Bill Sharpe, Andy and Jill Kassube, L Powell, R J Walden, Anthony Marriott, A N Ellis, Paul Redgrave, Frank Cummins)*

Free house ~ Licensees Roger and Susan Barber ~ Real ale ~ Meals and snacks (11.30-2.30, 6.30-9.30) ~ (01822) 852944 ~ Open 11.30-3, 6.30-11

MILTONCOMBE SX4865 Map 1

Who'd Have Thought It ★

Village signposted from A386 S of Tavistock

It's a pleasure to visit this attractive 16th-c pub before a visit to Buckland Abbey or the lovely gardens of the Garden House at Buckland Monachorum. The atmospheric, black-panelled bar has a woodburning stove in the big stone fireplace, cushioned barrel seats and high-backed winged settles around solid, polished wooden tables, colourful plates on a big black dresser, and rapiers, sabres and other weapons on its walls; two other rooms (one is no smoking) have seats made from barrels. Generous helpings of popular bar food (with prices unchanged since last year) include sandwiches, home-made soup (£2.25), pâté (£3.25), chicken or vegetable curry (from £3.50), tasty steak and kidney pie (£4.50), rabbit casserole or lamb steak in orange and ginger (£5.25), grilled trout (£6.95), sirloin steak (£8.50), and puddings like cherry and almond strudel or chocolate fudge cake (£2.10); on Sunday lunchtime the food is a bit more restricted but also includes two roasts (£4.25). Well kept Bass, Blackawton Headstrong, Eldridge Pope Royal Oak, Golden Hill Exmoor, and Wadworths 6X on handpump, and Bulmer's and Inch's ciders; efficient staff; dominoes, fruit machine. There are picnic tables on a terrace with hanging baskets by the little stream. No children. *(Recommended by Andy and Jill Kassube, Anthony Marriott, R W Brooks, Ted George, Frank Cummins, R J Walden, Jim and Maggie Cowell, A N Ellis)*

Free house ~ Licensees Keith Yeo and Gary Rager ~ Real ale ~ Meals and snacks ~ (01822) 853313 ~ Folk club Sun evening in lower bar ~ Open 11.30-2.30(3 Sat), 6.30-11

MORETONHAMPSTEAD SX7585 Map 1

White Hart

A382 N of Bovey Tracey

The congenial licensee has now been running this civilised place for 18 years and has been a hotelier in Devon for over 30. The large lounge bar is furnished with oak pews from the parish church, armchairs, plush seats and stools, the hall has a splendidly large-scale 1827 map of Devon by Greenwood, and in the lively public bar there are leatherette seats and settles under a white beam-and-plank ceiling; log fires – and the friendly standard poodles are called Poppy and Rosie. A wide choice of promptly served, popular bar food includes soup (£2.25), sandwiches (from £2.50), lunchtime egg and chips (£3.25), filled baked potatoes (£3.35), ploughman's or vegetable lasagne (£4.50), and steak and kidney or lamb, leek and apricot pie (£5.75), with evening dishes such as a roast of the day (£6.95), chicken in cider, apple and cinnamon in a cream sauce (£8.75) or grilled local trout (£8.95); puddings like treacle tart or bread pudding (£2.50), daily specials, cream teas, and Sunday roast; no children's helpings but an extra plate is available. The restaurant and part of the eating area of the bar are no smoking. Well kept Bass, Boddingtons, and Smiles on handpump, and Luscombe farm cider; darts, cribbage, shove-ha'penny, dominoes, and fruit machine. You can sit on a pew among the flowers in the small back courtyard. Well placed for Dartmoor and good for nearby walks, riding, golf and fishing. *(Recommended by Lynn Sharpless, Bob Eardley, Ernie and Joan Potter, Paul Randall, D Goodger, David Crossley; more reports please)*

Free house ~ Licensee Peter Morgan ~ Real ale ~ Meals and snacks ~ Restaurant and evening grill room ~ (01647) 440406 ~ Children welcome ~ May have to park in the public car park, a short walk away ~ Open 11-11 ~ Bedrooms: £43B/£63B

NEWTON ST CYRES SX8798 Map 1

Beer Engine

Sweetham; from Newton St Cyres on A377 follow St Cyres Station, Thorverton signpost

From the downstairs cellar bar you can see the stainless brewhouse where this friendly old station hotel brews its own beer: Rail Ale, Piston Bitter, and the very strong Sleeper. The spacious main bar has partitioning alcoves, windsor chairs and some button-back banquettes around dark varnished tables on its red carpet. Good, reasonably priced bar food includes speciality sausages like pork and garlic or oriental (£3.75), home-made steak and kidney pie or chicken in barbecue sauce (£4.75), Brixham plaice (£5.25), and rump steak (£6.50); darts, shove-ha'penny, dominoes and cribbage; fruit machine and video game in the downstairs lobby. There's a large sunny garden on several interesting levels with lots of sheltered seating; you can eat out here, too. *(Recommended by John Hazel, Jeanne Cross, Paul Silvestri, Mike Cargill, Peter and Lynn Brueton, Jim and Maggie Cowell)*

Own brew ~ Licensee Peter Hawksley ~ Real ale ~ Meals and snacks (till 10pm) ~ (01392) 851282 ~ Children in eating area of bar ~ Live music Sat evenings and some Sun lunchtimes ~ Open 11.30-2.30, 6-11; 11.30-11 Sat (cellar bar open till midnight Fri/Sat)

NOSS MAYO SX5447 Map 1

Old Ship

Off A379 via B3186, E of Plymouth

At high tide you can reach this 16th-c pub by boat, so it's a popular place with yachtsmen – and there are tables on the terrace overlooking the water. Inside, the two thick-walled bars have a warm, friendly atmosphere and reliably good bar food that includes sandwiches, good pasties, home-made daily specials, really delicious locally caught fish grilled on the bone (from £4), steaks, and nice puddings with clotted cream; 3-course Sunday carvery (£7.50). The restaurant is no smoking. Well kept Bass, Boddingtons, Dartmoor, Wadworths 6X, and a guest like Boddingtons on handpump, and several malt whiskies; swift, helpful service; darts, fruit machine, and piped music. *(Recommended by George Atkinson, A N Ellis, B Taylor, Steve Huggins, Marion and John Hadfield)*

Free house ~ Licensees Norman and Val Doddridge ~ Real ale ~ Meals and snacks (till 10.30pm) ~ Restaurant ~ (01752) 872387 ~ Children welcome ~ Open 11-3, 6-11

PETER TAVY SX5177 Map 1

Peter Tavy

Off A386 nr Mary Tavy, N of Tavistock

New licensees have taken over this 15th-c stone inn and have moved the bar counter to create more space, carried out a lot of restoration work, and exposed original fireplaces and beams. They now offer bedrooms, the garden has been planted with shrubs, and the paddock has been reclaimed. The bar still has a lot of atmosphere, as well as low beams, high-backed settles on the black flagstones by the big stone fireplace (which usually has a good log fire on cold days), smaller settles in stone-mullioned windows, and a snug side dining area; no-smoking area at weekends. Good bar food at lunchtime now includes soup (£1.80), filled baked potatoes (from £1.95), open sandwiches (£2.75) and filled french bread (£3.50), cottage pie (£3.75), ploughman's with local cheeses (£3.95), and steak and kidney pudding (£4.50), with evening dishes such as scallops (£4.95), an Italian dish (£5.75), pork chop in white wine and cider (£7.25), and sirloin steak (£8.45); daily specials such as fresh fish and game, and puddings like fruit crumble or treacle tart (£2.50). Well kept Bass, Courage Directors, Dartmoor, St Austell HSD, Tetleys, and a guest such as Gibbs Mew Bishops Tipple on handpump kept under light blanket pressure or tapped from the cask; over 30 malt whiskies, a fairly priced wine list, and country wines; darts, cribbage, dominoes, and piped music. From the picnic tables in the garden there are peaceful views of the moor rising above nearby pastures. *(Recommended by John Wilson, Werner Arend, Mr and Mrs Jones, Andy, Andrew and friends, Jack and Philip Paxton, Jill Bickerton, Jeanne Cross, Paul Silvestri, Andy and Jill Kassube)*

Free house ~ Licensees Rita Westlake and John Vaughan ~ Real ale ~ Meals and snacks ~ Restaurant ~ (01822) 810348 ~ Children in back room ~ Nearby parking often difficult ~ Open 11.30-2.30, 6.30-11 ~ Bedrooms: £50B

PLYMOUTH SX4755 Map 1

China House ★

Marrowbone Slip, Sutton Harbour, via Sutton Road off Exeter Street (A374)

In a marvellous position overlooking Sutton Harbour, this carefully converted 17th-c waterside pub is Plymouth's oldest warehouse. It's lofty and very spacious but partitioned into smaller booth-like areas, with great beams and flagstone floors, bare slate and stone walls, and lots of nets, kegs and fishing gear; there's even a clinker-built boat. On the left is the main bar with plain wooden seats around dark tables in front of a good log fire – all very chatty, comfortable and relaxed. Under the new managers, food now includes sandwiches (from £2.45), soup (£2.50), filled baked potatoes (from £3.45), a vegetarian dish of the day like mushroom macaroni bake (£4.65), lamb cutlets or fish dishes such as cod in white sauce (£4.95), and puddings (£2.75). The upstairs restaurant is no smoking. Well kept Dartmoor Best and Strong on handpump; fruit machine, trivia and piped music. In front of the pub are some picnic tables, with benches on the verandah. The view from the Barbican across to the pub is lovely. *(Recommended by Anthony Marriott, James Macrae, Mike Woodhead, Peter Williamson, Andy and Jill Kassube, P H Roberts, Nigel Spence, Kim Greek, Jeanne Cross, Paul Silvestri, Brian and Anna Marsden, Shirley Pielou)*

Ansells (Allied) ~ Managers Colin and Ann Head ~ Real ale ~ Meals and snacks ~ Restaurant ~ (01752) 260930 ~ Children welcome ~ Live music Weds-Sun lunchtimes ~ Open 11-11; 11-3, 5-11 in winter

nr POSTBRIDGE SX6780 Map 1

Warren House

B3212 1¾ miles NE of Postbridge

A valuable refuge after a walk on Dartmoor, this remote place has a fire at one end of the bar that is said to have been kept almost continuously alight since 1845; also, simple furnishings such as easy chairs and settles under a beamed ochre ceiling, wild animal pictures on the partly panelled stone walls, and dim lighting (fuelled by the pub's own generator); even in high season there's quite a local atmosphere as the pub is something of a focus for this scattered moorland community. Bar food includes sandwiches, home-made soup (£1.95), filled baked potatoes (from £2.50), good ploughman's (£3.85), a home-made vegetarian dish (£4.10), home-made pies like steak in ale or chicken (from £6), and scampi (£6.30). Well kept Butcombe Bitter, Flowers Original, Gibbs Mew Bishops Tipple, and a guest beer like St Austell HSD and Wadworths 6X on handpump, farm cider and a range of country wines. Darts, pool, cribbage, dominoes, fruit machine, video game, and piped music. This road is worth knowing, as a good little-used route westward through fine scenery. Dogs allowed. *(Recommended by John Hazel, Alan Newman, A N Ellis, Jack and Philip Paxton, Norma Farris, Jeanne Cross, Paul Silvestri, John and Marianne Cooper, R J Walden)*

Free house ~ Licensee Peter Parsons ~ Real ale ~ Meals and snacks (noon-9.30 in summer) ~ (01822) 880208 ~ Children in family room ~ Open 10-11; 11-2.30, 6-11 in winter

POUNDSGATE SX7072 Map 1

Tavistock

Off B3380 at SW end of Ashburton; or from central Dartmoor follow B3357 E, keeping on to bear right past Corndon Tor

In summer, this ancient slated white house has lots of pretty hanging baskets, a lovely back garden with award-winning displays of bedding plants, and picnic tables on the front terrace just above the quiet lane. Inside, there's a friendly village atmosphere and some interesting old features like the narrow-stepped granite spiral staircase, original flagstones, and ancient fireplaces – one with a wood-burning stove, the other with logs. Bar food includes home-made soup (£1.80), bacon and eggs (£2.65), ploughman's (from £3.15), vegetarian crêpes (£3.35), pasta and tuna bake (£4.60), chicken tikka (£5.85), steaks (from £7.95), puddings (from £1.70), and daily specials such as Lyme Bay crab flan (£3.95) or salmon fillet with asparagus and lemon in puff pastry (£4.95). Well kept Courage Best and Ushers Best and Founders from a temperature-controlled cellar, local farm cider, elderflower pressé, and mulled wine and brandied hot chocolate in winter; good welcoming service; darts, cribbage, dominoes, and fruit machine. The family room was once the stable. *(Recommended by Mike Gorton, G and M Stewart, Joan and Gordon Edwards, A N Ellis, Alan Newman, P R Ferris, Dr and Mrs R E S Tanner, Jane Palmer, Les and Mavis Law)*

Ushers ~ Lease: Ken and Janice Comer ~ Real ale ~ Meals and snacks (11.30-2.30, 6-9.30) ~ (01364) 631251 ~ Children in family room ~ Open 11-3, 6-11

RATTERY SX7461 Map 1

Church House

Village signposted from A385 W of Totnes, and A38 S of Buckfastleigh

The original building here probably housed the craftsmen who built the Norman church, and may then have served as a hostel for passing monks. The spiral stone steps behind a little stone doorway on your left as you go in probably date from about 1030 – making this one of the oldest pub buildings in Britain. And there are massive oak beams and standing timbers in the homely open-plan bar, as well as large fireplaces (one with a little cosy nook partitioned off around it), windsor armchairs, comfortable leather bucket seats and window seats, and prints on the plain white walls; the dining room is separated from this room by heavy curtains. Shandy the golden labrador is very amiable and there's a nice black cat with two white paws. Good bar food includes home-made soup, filled rolls, good ploughman's with local cheeses, fresh salmon and prawn mornay (£6.25), country lamb hotpot or spicy red pepper chicken (£6.30), venison casserole (£6.50), roast guinea fowl with blackcurrant and port sauce (£6.60), home-made puddings, and children's dishes. Well kept Dartmoor, St Austell Tinners, and a weekly guest beer on handpump, a range of malt whiskies (up to 40 years old), and decent wines; friendly staff and locals. Outside, there are peaceful views of the partly wooded surrounding hills from picnic tables on a hedged courtyard by the churchyard. *(Recommended by John Evans, R W Brooks, Jack and Philip Paxton, B J Harding, Barry Lynch, Dorothee amd Dennis Glover, Mr and Mrs Jones, Paul and Janet Waring, B Yalor, Joy and Paul Rundell, Anthony Marriott, Neil and Anita Christopher, John and Vivienne Rice, Steve Huggins, D J Elliott, A Plumb, Alan and Brenda Holyer)*

Free house ~ Licensees Brian and Jill Evans ~ Real ale ~ Meals and snacks ~ (01364) 642220 ~ Children in eating area of bar and in dining room ~ Open 11-2.30, 6-11

RINGMORE SX6545 Map 1

Journeys End

Off B3392 at Pickwick Inn, St Anns Chapel, nr Bigbury

In a quiet village, this partly medieval thatched inn was originally used to house the masons working on the nearby church. It's a warmly friendly place with a thatched bar counter in the panelled main bar, bare boards and flagstones, an unusual partly pitched ceiling, soft lighting from a nice mix of lamps, and a blazing log fire. Good bar food includes sandwiches (from £2; hot bacon and mushroom £3), omelettes (£3.50; the Spanish one is recommended), ploughman's (from £3.50), ham and eggs or lentil and split pea moussaka (£4.50), local trout (£5.95), steaks (from £7.95), good daily specials such as cream of wild mushroom soup, home-made pork terrine, oxtail stew, grilled sardines, lemon sole stuffed with asparagus, and tasty chicken with garlic and tarragon, children's meals (£3), and puddings like home-made fruit pies (£2). Well kept Adnams Broadside, Crown Buckley Reverend James, Exmoor Ale, Otter Ale, Shepherd Neame Spitfire, and Charles Wells Bombardier on handpump or tapped from the cask, Stancombe farm cider, and winter mulled wine; fruit machine. The big, attractively planted garden has plenty of seats. The inn is named after the anti-war play written here by R C Sherriff. *(Recommended by Patrick and Lynn Billyeald, David Mowbray, Steve Webb, Marianne Lantree, Lynn Sharpless, Bob Eardley, Tim Brierly, Jeanne Cross, Paul Silvestri, Gordon, M D Hare, David Lewis, David Burnett, Donna Lowes)*

Free house ~ Licensee James Parkin ~ Real ale ~ Meals and snacks ~ Conservatory restaurant ~ (01548) 810205 ~ Children in eating area of bar, in restaurant and in TV room ~ Occasional Folk music Fri evenings ~ Open 11.30-3, 6-11 ~ Bedrooms: £20B/£40B

SHEEPWASH SS4806 Map 1

Half Moon

Off A3072 Holsworthy—Hatherleigh at Highampton

For those who love fishing, this buff-painted, civilised inn is the place to stay as they have 10 miles of private fishing on the River Torridge (salmon, sea trout and brown trout) as well as a rod room, good drying facilities and a small shop stocking the basic things needed to catch fish. There are lots of fishing pictures on the white walls of the neatly kept and friendly carpeted main bar, solid old furniture under the beams, and a big log fire fronted by slate flagstones. Lunchtime bar food is attractively straightforward and good, including sandwiches (£1.50, toasties £2), home-made soup (£1.75), home-made pasties (£2.50), ploughman's (£3.25), home-cooked ham salad (£3.75), and home-made puddings (£2). Well kept Courage Best and Directors, Marstons Pedigree, and an occasional guest like Wadworths 6X on handpump (well kept in a temperature-controlled cellar), a fine choice of malt whiskies, and an extensive wine list; darts, fruit machine, and separate pool room. *(Recommended by John and Vivienne Rice, R J Walden, Heather Martin, Andrew Low, David Gittins, Mr and Mrs J D Marsh)*

Free house ~ Licensees Benjamin Robert Inniss and Charles Inniss ~ Real ale ~ Snacks (lunchtime)~ Evening restaurant ~ (01409) 231376 ~ Children welcome lunchtime only ~ Open 11-2.30, 6-11 ~ Bedrooms: £37.50B/£65.50B

SIDFORD SY1390 Map 1

Blue Ball ★

A3052 just N of Sidmouth

The same family have been running this 14th-c thatched inn since 1912. The low, partly-panelled and neatly kept lounge bar has a bustling, cheerful atmosphere, heavy beams, upholstered wall benches and windsor chairs, lots of bric-a-brac, and a lovely winter log fire in the stone fireplace (there are two other open fires as well); the snug is no smoking. Quickly served bar food includes sandwiches (from £1.60), ploughman's (from £3.25), omelettes or vegetable lasagne (£4.50), salads (from £4.50), chilli con carne (£5), home-made steak and kidney pie (£5.50), and steaks (from £8.75); puddings (£2.25), children's dishes (from £2.25), and good breakfasts. Boddingtons, Devenish Royal Wessex, Flowers IPA, Marstons Pedigree on handpump, kept well in a temperature-controlled cellar. A plainer public bar has darts, cribbage and a fruit machine; piped music. Tables on a terrace look out over a colourful (and award-winning) walled front flower garden, and there are more seats on a bigger back lawn – as well as in a covered area next to the barbecue; safe swing, see saw and play house for children. *(Recommended by Michael Butler, Nick Wikeley, Werner Arend, George and Jeanne Barnwell, Denzil Taylor, Chris Westmoreland, Don and Thelma Beeson, A Denman, Michael Boniface, Martin Pritchard, Nicolas Corker, Malcolm Taylor, Maj D A Daniells, Mrs A M Fishleigh, Dr C E Morgan, Shirley Pielou, D S Beeson, Wayne Brindle, Helen Flaherty, Brian Websdale, Deborah and Ian Carrington, Wally Huggins, Eric and Patricia King, B D Jones, E V N Whiteway, Gordon, J L Alperin)*

Devenish ~ Tenant Roger Newton ~ Real ale ~ Meals and snacks (till 10pm) ~ Well behaved children in eating area of bar ~ (01395) 514062 ~ Open 10.30-2.30, 5.30-11 ~ Bedrooms: £22/£36

Please let us know what you think of a pub's bedrooms. No stamp needed: *The Good Pub Guide*, FREEPOST TN1569, Wadhurst, E Sussex TN5 7BR.

SOURTON SX5390 Map 1

Highwayman ★

A386 SW of Okehampton; a short detour from the A30

You will be quite amazed at the sheer eccentricity of this pub's remarkable design. It doesn't have a lot of the things that people expect from a pub – no real ale and virtually no food – but what it does have is a marvellously well executed fantasy decor that the owners have over the years put great enthusiasm and masses of hard work into. The porch (a pastiche of a nobleman's carriage) leads into a warren of dimly lit stonework and flagstone-floored burrows and alcoves, richly fitted out with red plush seats discreetly cut into the higgledy-piggledy walls, elaborately carved pews, a leather porter's chair, Jacobean-style wicker chairs, and seats in quaintly bulging small-paned bow windows; the ceiling in one part, where there's an array of stuffed animals, gives the impression of being underneath a tree, roots and all. The separate Rita Jones' Locker is a make-believe sailing galleon, full of intricate woodwork and splendid timber baulks, with white antique lace clothed tables in the embrasures that might have held cannons. They only sell keg beer, but specialise in farm cider, and food is confined to a range of meaty and vegetarian pasties (£1); service is warmly welcoming and full of character; old-fashioned penny fruit machine, and 40s piped music. Outside, there's a play area in similar style for children with little black-and-white roundabouts like a Victorian fairground, a fairy-tale pumpkin house and an old-lady-who-lived-in-the-shoe house. You can take children in to look around the pub but they can't stay inside. The period bedrooms are attractive. *(Recommended by Anthony Marriott, Jerry and Alison Oakes, S P Ward, John Hazel, Jack and Philip Paxton, John Davies, Paul Weedon, John and Vivienne Rice, Mr and Mrs A K McCully, Barbara and Norman Wells)*

Free house ~ Licensees Buster and Rita Jones and Sally Thomson ~ Snacks (10-1.45, 6-9.45) ~ (01837) 86243 ~ Open 10-2, 6-10.30; closed 25/26 Dec ~ Bedrooms: £36

SOUTH POOL SX7740 Map 1

Millbrook

Off A379 E of Kingsbridge

The opening hours in this tiny pub (one of the smallest in this book) tend to be adjusted to suit the tide times, as boating visitors like to make the most of the mooring facilities; there are seats on the terrace by the stream with its Aylesbury ducks. Inside, the charming little back bar has handsome windsor chairs, a chintz easy chair, drawings and paintings (and a chart) on its cream walls, clay pipes on the beams, and fresh flowers. Home-made bar food includes home-made soup (£2.25), sandwiches (from £2), ploughman's (from £3.75), cottage pie (£4), chilli con carne (£4.15), fish pie (£5.50), vegetarian dishes, daily specials like moussaka (£4.95), seafood pasta (£6.95) or Scottish sirloin steak (£8.25), and puddings (£2.25). Bass, Ruddles Best, Wadworths 6X and a guest ale on handpump, and Churchwards farm ciders; good, friendly service even when busy. Darts and euchre in the public bar in winter. *(Recommended by Owen and Margaret Warnock, Mike Gorton, David Eberlin, Roger Wain-Heapy, Mrs J Barwell, Bill Edwards)*

Free house ~ Licensees Jed Spedding and Liz Stirland ~ Real ale ~ Meals and snacks ~ (01548) 531581 ~ Children in top bar ~ Open 11-2.30, 5.30-11 – depending on high tide

SOUTH ZEAL SX6593 Map 1

Oxenham Arms ★ 🛏 🍷

Village signposted from A30 at A382 roundabout and B3260 Okehampton turnoff

It's the atmosphere of unhurried calm and history that people like about this friendly inn. It was first licensed in 1477 and has grown up around the remains of a Norman monastery, built here to combat the pagan power of the neolithic standing stone that still forms part of the wall in the family TV room behind the bar (there are actually twenty more feet of stone below the floor). It later became the Dower House of the Burgoynes, whose heiress carried it to the Oxenham family. The beamed and partly panelled front bar has elegant mullioned windows and Stuart fireplaces, and Windsor armchairs around low oak tables and built-in wall seats. The small family room has beams, wheelback chairs around polished tables, decorative plates, and another open fire. Bar food includes soup, sandwiches, good ploughman's, fish and chips, home-made steak, kidney, mushroom and Guinness pie (£4.95), and daily specials such as Greek salad with olives and feta cheese (£3.95), vegetable lasagne (£4.25) or seafood provençal (£4.50). Bass, Dartmoor and Princetown Jail Ale (a local brew and new to us) tapped from the cask, Inch's cider, and an extensive list of wines including good house claret; darts, shove-ha'penny, dominoes, cribbage, and trivia. Note the imposing curved stone steps leading up to the garden (replanted this year) where there's a sloping spread of lawn. *(Recommended by Helen Pickering, James Owen, David Mowbray, John and Christine Vittoe, R W Brooks, Canon Michael Bourdeaux, Jon Pike, Julie Murphy, John and Vivienne Rice, Jack and Philip Paxton, J and J O Jones, R J Walden, Myroulla West, Denzil T Taylor, Peter and Lynn Brueton, Mr and Mrs C R Little, Mike Dickerson, Joan and Gordon Edwards, Mr and Mrs R Copeland, Patrick Clancy, David Holloway, Steve Goodchild, David Gittins, Marion and John Hadfield, DAV, Gordon, Nigel Flook, Betsy Brown)*

Free house ~ Licensee James Henry ~ Real ale ~ Meals and snacks ~ Restaurant ~ (01837) 840244 ~ Children in family room ~ Open 11-2.30, 6-11 ~ Bedrooms: £40B/£50B

STAVERTON SX7964 Map 1

Sea Trout

Village signposted from A384 NW of Totnes

There's always a good mix of locals and visitors in this friendly old village pub. The main bar has low banquettes, soft lighting and an open fire, and the neatly kept rambling beamed lounge bar has cushioned settles and stools, a stag's head above the fireplace, and seatrout and salmon flies and stuffed fish on the walls. There's also a public bar with a pool table, darts, fruit machine, and juke box. Reasonably priced bar food includes home-made soup (£1.85), sandwiches (from £2.50), home-made pâté (£3.25), ploughman's (from £3.75), pork and apple sausages (£3.95), home-cooked ham and egg (£4.75), smoked haddock and prawn crumble or home-made steak and kidney pie (£5.50), local trout (£6.25), salads (from £5.95), and steaks (from £8.50); daily specials, puddings, children's meals (from £2.85), and good Sunday lunch. Well kept Dartmoor on handpump, and efficient, friendly staff. There are seats under parasols in the garden. A station for the Torbay Steam Railway is not far away. *(Recommended by Michael Sargent, Don and Thelma Beeson, J H Bell, Peter and Jenny Quine, Joan and Gordon Edwards, Michael Butler, Rich and Pauline Appleton, Alan and Brenda Holyer, Mr and Mrs A K McCully)*

Free house ~ Licensees Andrew and Pym Mogford ~ Real ale ~ Meals and snacks ~ Restaurant ~ (01803) 762274 ~ Children in eating area of bar ~ Open 11-3, 6-11; closed evenings 25/26 Dec ~ Bedrooms: £39.50B/£50B

STOCKLAND ST2404 Map 1

Kings Arms

Village signposted from A30 Honiton—Chard

It's well worth driving down the narrow lanes to get to this friendly 16th-c pub in order to enjoy the first-class, home-made food. Lunchtime snacks include sandwiches (from £1.50), soup (£2), burgers (from £2), ploughman's or filled pancakes (£3.50), omelettes (from £3.50), steak and kidney pie (£4.50), gammon and egg (£5.50), and children's dishes (from £1.25); from the blackboard there might be Portuguese sardines or garlic mushrooms (£3), pacific prawns in garlic sauce (£4.50), local trout (£6.50), vegetable stir-fry, venison pie or strips of lamb's liver with caramelised onion, tarragon and madeira (£7.50), seafood in filo (£8.50), beef roulade (£9.50), local lemon sole (£11.50), and puddings like morello cherry cheesecake or passion-fruit and ginger soufflé glacé (£3). The dark beamed, elegant dining lounge has solid refectory tables and settles, attractive landscapes, a medieval oak screen (which divides the room into two), and a great stone fireplace across almost the whole width of one end; you can enjoy the same menu in the cosy restaurant with its huge inglenook fireplace and bread oven. Booking is essential; hearty breakfasts. Well kept Badger Best, Exmoor Bitter, Ruddles County, and John Smiths on handpump, over 40 island and west coast malt whiskies (large spirit measures), a good wine list with house wines and special offers by the bottle or glass chalked up on a board, and farm ciders – including Bollhayes cider (methode champenoise). At the back, a flagstoned bar has captain's-style tub chairs and cushioned stools around heavy wooden tables, and leads on to a carpeted darts room with two boards, another room with dark beige plush armchairs and settees (and a fruit machine), and a neat ten-pin skittle alley; table skittles, cribbage, dominoes, video game, and quiet mainly classical piped music. They have tug-of-war training nights on Sunday and Thursday, ladies' league skittles/quiz evening on Monday, men's skittles on Wednesday and Friday, various skittle teams Tuesday and Thursday; the Stockland Fair is held on Whitsun Bank Holiday Monday. There are tables under cocktail parasols on the terrace in front of the white-faced thatched pub and a lawn enclosed by trees and shrubs – summer barbecues on Sunday evenings during school holidays. Well behaved dogs allowed. *(Recommended by Mr and Mrs R J Parish, Mrs J Oakes, Anthony Barnes, Mr and Mrs J B Merritt, Ian Phillips, John and Fiona Merritt, Martin Walsh, Pat and Robert Watt, Margaret and Nigel Dennis, L Roberts, Mr and Mrs D T Deas, R James, Mrs J M Corless, Marion and John Hadfield, Gordon)*

Free house ~ Licensees Heinz Kiefer and Paul Diviani ~ Real ale ~ Snacks (lunchtime) and meals ~ Restaurant ~ (01404) 881361 ~ Well behaved/supervised children in eating area of bar but must be over 12 in restaurant ~ Lyme Bay folk club first Sat in month, varied music every Sun (and bank hol Mon) ~ Open 12-3, 6.30-11; on 25 Dec only open 11-1 ~ Bedrooms: £20B/£30B

STOKE FLEMING SX8648 Map 1

Green Dragon 🍷

Church Rd

Although the landlord might be sailing around the Cape of Good Hope on your visit (the pub is run by Peter Crowther the successful long-distance yachtsman), you can be sure of a friendly welcome. The beamed main part of the bar has two small settles, bay window seats, boat pictures, and maybe Electra or Maia the young Burmese cats, while down on the right is an area with throws and cushions on battered sofas and armchairs, a few books (20p to RNLI), adult board games, a grandfather clock, a wringer, and cuttings about the landlord and maps of his races on the walls. Down some steps is the Mess Deck decorated with lots of ensigns and flags, and there's a playbox of children's games; darts, shove-ha'penny, cribbage, dominoes, trivia, and piped music. Home-made bar food includes soup (£1.70), sandwiches (from £1.80), ploughman's with three cheeses (£3), chicken and mushroom pancakes, fisherman's pie or Italian meatloaf (£4.90), salmon roulade (£5.10), and puddings like chocolate whisky cake or treacle tart (£2.20); they do Sunday breakfasts between 9 and 11am. Well kept Bass, Boddingtons, Eldridge Pope Royal Oak, and Flowers Original on handpump, big glasses of six good house wines from Australia, California, France and Germany, Addlestones cider, and a good range of spirits; you can take the beer away with you. There's a back garden with swings, a climbing frame and picnic tables and a front terrace with some white plastic garden tables and chairs. The tall church tower opposite is interesting. *(Recommended by A Plumb; more reports please)*

Heavitree (who no longer brew) ~ Tenants Peter and Alix Crowther ~ Real ale ~ Meals and snacks (not winter Sun evenings) ~ (01803) 770238 ~ Children welcome ~ Open 11-2.30, 5.30-11

STOKE GABRIEL SX8457 Map 1

Church House ★

Village signposted from A385 just W of junction with A3022, in Collaton St Mary; can also be reached from nearer Totnes; nearby parking not easy

The medieval beam-and-plank ceiling in the lounge bar of this early 14th-c pub is exceptionally attractive, and there's also a huge fireplace still used in winter to cook the stew, a black oak partition wall, window seats cut into the thick butter-colour walls, and decorative plates and vases of flowers on a dresser. The mummified cat in a case, probably about 200 years old, was found during restoration of the roof space in the verger's cottage three doors up the lane – one of a handful found in the West Country and believed to have been a talisman against evil spirits. Home-made bar food includes soup (£1.45), a huge choice of sandwiches and toasties (from £1.65; good cheese and prawn toasties, lovely local river salmon), filled baked potatoes (from £2.35), ploughman's (from £3.25), daily specials like fresh Dart salmon, various platters, and steak and kidney in ale pie, and puddings (from £1.95); well kept Bass, Worthington Best, and a guest ale on handpump, and quite a few malt whiskies. Darts, cribbage, and fruit machine in the little public locals' bar; piped music. There are picnic tables on the little terrace in front of the building. No children. *(Recommended by Peter and Jenny Quine, Mr and Mrs C Roberts, B J Harding, Michael Butler, John and Fiona Merritt, Mr and Mrs A K McCully, Bill and Beryl Farmer, E B Davies, T Aldworth, June and Tony Baldwin)*

Free house ~ Licensee Glyn Patch ~ Real ale ~ Meals and snacks (till 10pm) ~ (01803) 782384 ~ Open 11-3, 6-11; 11-11 Sat

TIPTON ST JOHN SY0991 Map 1

Golden Lion ⇦

Pub signposted off B3176 Sidmouth—Ottery St Mary

The Radfords have been running this busy village pub for 25 years and it's still a popular place with locals and visitors. The bar has an open fire, a comfortable old settee, red leatherette built-in wall banquettes, an attractive gothick carved box settle, a carved dresser, and a longcase clock. Decorations include lots of guns, little kegs, a brass cauldron and other brassware, and bottles and jars along a Delft shelf. Bar food such as soup (£1.50), sandwiches (from £2.40), ploughman's (from £3.45), vegetarian chilli (£3.95), home-made lasagne (£4.55), steak and kidney pie (£4.85), tipsy pork with mushrooms and cream sauce (£7.45), steaks (from £7.95), puddings like gooseberry and apple crumble with clotted cream (from £2), and daily specials like chicken livers with bacon (£3.15), wild rabbit pie (£4.75) or fresh fish. The restaurant and children's area are no smoking. Well kept Bass, Boddingtons, Eldridge Pope Hardy and Whitbreads Castle Eden on handpump, farm cider, fresh local apple juice, a comprehensive wine list, and fruit wines; darts, cribbage, dominoes, and piped music. There are pretty summer hanging baskets, a few picnic tables on the side lawn, a pretty walled area, and a terrace. *(Recommended by Mr and Mrs Turner, Denzil Taylor, George and Jeanne Barnwell, Alan Newman, Mark and Heather Williamson, B D Jones, J I Fraser, Eric and Patricia King, David Holloway, Mrs J M Corless)*

Heavitree (who no longer brew) ~ Tenants Colin and Carolyn Radford ~ Real ale ~ Meals and snacks ~ Small restaurant ~ (01404) 812881 ~ Children in small area next to bar; must be over 7 in evening ~ Open 11-3, 6-11 ~ Two bedrooms: £38.77S

Please let us know of any pubs where the wine is particularly good.

TOPSHAM SX9688 Map 1

Bridge

2¼ miles from M5 junction 30: Topsham signposted from exit roundabout; in Topsham follow signpost (A376) Exmouth on the Elmgrove Road

The unspoilt character of this 16th-c pub remains unchanged – as does the big choice of real ales tapped from the cask in the cosy no-smoking inner sanctum (where only the most regular of regulars sit): Adnams Broadside, Badger Tanglefoot, Barrons Devon Glory, Bass, Branscombe Vale Branoc (see Fountain Head, Branscombe), Eldridge Pope Royal Oak, Gibbs Mew Bishops Tipple, Marstons Owd Rodger, Theakstons Old Peculier, and Wadworths 6X. The little no-smoking parlour, partitioned off from an inner corridor with leaded lights let into the curved high back of one settle, is decorated with a booming grandfather clock, crossed guns, swords, country pictures and rowing cartoons, and mugs hanging from the beams; a bigger room is opened at busy times. Food is confined to pasties (£1), sandwiches (£1.45) and ploughman's (from £3.25). *(Recommended by Jack and Philip Paxton, Andy and Jill Kassube, J I Fraser, Jim and Maggie Cowell, Wayne Brindle, Mark Grist; more reports please)*

Free house ~ Licensee Mrs Phyllis Cheffers ~ Real ale ~ Lunchtime snacks ~ (01392) 873862 ~ Children welcome ~ Open 12-2, 6-10.30(11 Fri/Sat)

Passage

2 miles from M5 junction 30: Topsham signposted from exit roundabout; in Topsham, turn right into Follett Road just before centre, then turn left into Ferry Road

It's the enjoyable fresh fish dishes that draw people to this attractive waterside pub: fresh mussels (in season, £4.95), pollock, grilled monkfish, lemon sole, Dover sole, turbot, cod, halibut, crab and so forth (£5.50-£12); other food includes filled rolls (from £1.50), ploughman's (£3.75), ham and eggs (£3.95), platters (from £3.95; crab, prawn and smoked salmon £5.95), chicken korma or mushroom and nut fettucine (£4.25), steaks (from £7.75), and puddings. Well kept Bass, Boddingtons, Flowers IPA, and Marstons Pedigree on handpump. The traditional bar has leatherette wall pews and bar stools and is decorated with electrified oil lamps hanging from big black oak beams in the ochre ceiling; plank panelling and crazy-paving flagstones in one room; fruit machine and piped music. The front courtyard has benches and tables, and there are more seats down on the quiet shoreside terrace. No children. *(Recommended by Werner Arend, John and Fiona Merritt, George and Jeanne Barnwell, John and Vivienne Rice, B J Harding, Howard and Margaret Buchanan, Eric and Patricia King, A E and P McCully)*

Heavitree (who no longer brew) ~ Licensee David Evans ~ Real ale ~ Meals and snacks ~ Restaurant ~ (01392) 873653 ~ Parking can be a problem ~ Open 11-11

TORBRYAN SX8266 Map 1

Old Church House

Most easily reached from A381 Newton Abbot—Totnes via Ipplepen

This atmospheric inn is built on the site of a very ancient cottage. The bar on the right of the door is particularly attractive, and has benches built into the fine old panelling as well as the cushioned high-backed settle and leather-backed small seats around its big log fire. On the left there are a series of comfortable and discreetly lit lounges, one with a splendid deep Tudor inglenook fireplace with a side bread oven. There's quite a lot of emphasis on the large choice of bar food – which might include sandwiches, home-made soup, whole plaice, beef in ale, chicken breast in a blue cheese sauce or salmon in a white wine sauce (all £4.95), fresh local trout, local pheasant, and daily specials such as liver and bacon or steak and kidney pie. Half-a-dozen well kept real ales such as Brains Dark Mild, Flowers IPA and Original, and maybe two beers named for the pub on handpump or tapped from the cask, up to 20 malt whiskies, and decent wine list. *(Recommended by Joy and Paul Rundell, Sheila and Gordon Haden, Mr and Mrs J Woodfield, Ian Phillips, Patrick Clancy, Gordon, Steve Huggins, P and J Shapley)*

Free house ~ Licensee Eric Pimm ~ Real ale ~ Meals and snacks (till 10pm) ~ Restaurant ~ (01803) 812372 ~ Children welcome away from bar ~ Open 12-3, 6-11 ~ Bedrooms: £35B/£50B

TORCROSS SX8241 Map 1

Start Bay (food award)

A379 S of Dartmouth

They cope well with the customers who flood in to enjoy the fresh fish at this thatched 14th-c pub. The landlord catches some of the fish himself – plaice (£5.30), monkfish (£6.95), scallops (£7.50), and fresh crab or whole lemon sole (£7.95); the lovely cod and haddock comes in three sizes – medium (£3.80), large (£4.90) and jumbo (£6.10 – truly enormous), skate wing in batter (£5.10), crevettes (£5.95), and Dover sole (£9.95). Other food includes sandwiches (from £1.75), ploughman's (from £3), meaty or vegetable lasagne (£4.50), steaks (from £7.95), puddings (£1.75), and children's meals (from £1.60); they warn of delays at peak times (and you will probably have to wait for a table). Well kept Bass and Flowers IPA and Original on handpump, Addlestones and local farm cider, and fresh apple juice. The unassuming main bar has photographs of storms buffeting the pub and country pictures on its cream walls, wheelback chairs around plenty of dark tables or (round a corner) back-to-back settles forming booths, and a winter coal fire; a small chatty drinking area by the counter has a brass ship's clock and barometer; one area is no smoking as is part of the family room. The good winter games room has pool, darts, shove-ha'penny, dominoes, fruit machine, video game, and juke box; there's more booth seating in a family room with sailing boat pictures. Fruit machine in the lobby. On the terrace are some picnic tables looking out over the three-mile pebble beach. The freshwater wildlife lagoon of Slapton Ley is just behind the pub. *(Recommended by Roger Wain-Heapy, B Taylor, Dorothee and Dennis Glover, David Wallington, Alan and Brenda Holyer, C J Pratt, John and Vivienne Rice, Paul and Gail Betteley)*

Heavitree (who no longer brew; Whitbreads tie) ~ Tenant Paul Stubbs ~ Real ale ~ Meals and snacks (11.30-2, 6-10; not evening 25 Dec) ~ (01548) 580553 ~ Children in family room ~ Open 11.30-2.30, 6-11; all day in school holidays; closed evening 25 Dec

TORRINGTON SS4919 Map 1

Black Horse £

High St

Said to have been General Fairfax's headquarters during the civil war, this pretty twin-gabled place is one of the oldest inns in North Devon. It's popular (especially locally) for generously served, good value food: sandwiches (from £1.30; triple deckers £2.55), filled baked potatoes (from £1.70), ploughman's (from £2.90), home-made chicken and mushroom pie (£3.30), roast chicken with gravy (£3.50), home-made steak and kidney pie (£3.65), broccoli and cream cheese bake (£3.75), steaks (from £7.15), daily specials (from £2.70) and roast pork, lamb or beef (£2.90), children's dishes (from £1.75), promptly served Sunday roast lunch, and good vegetables. Well kept Courage Directors, John Smiths, Ushers Best, Wadworths 6X and a regular changing guest beer. The bar on the left has an oak counter, a couple of fat black beams hung with stirrups, a comfortable seat running right along its full-width window, and chunky elm tables; on the right, a lounge has a striking ancient black oak partition wall, a couple of attractive oak seats, muted plush easy chairs and a settee. The restaurant is oak-panelled; darts, shove-ha'penny, cribbage, dominoes, fruit machine, and well reproduced piped music; friendly cat and dogs.

Handy for the RHS Rosemoor garden and Dartington Crystal. *(Recommended by A M Stephenson, Brian and Louisa Routledge, R J Walden, J F Reay, K R Harris, Nigel and Lindsay Chapman, Chris Westmoreland, K H Frostick, Nigel Chapman, David Holloway)*

Ushers ~ Lease: David and Val Sawyer ~ Real ale ~ Meals and snacks (not Sun evening) ~ Restaurant (not Sun evening) ~ (01805) 622121 ~ Children in eating area of bar and in restaurant ~ Open 11-3, 6(6.30 Sat)-11 ~ Bedrooms: £16B/£28B

TOTNES SX8060 Map 1

Kingsbridge Inn

9 Leechwell St; going up the old town's main one-way street, bear left into Leechwell St approaching the top

As we went to press, we heard that the people who have been running this pub for the last few years were leaving, but they expected little change as the ownership will remain the same. The low-beamed rambling bar has an elaborately carved bench in one intimate little alcove, comfortable plush seats and wheelbacks around rustic tables, broad stripped plank panelling, and bare stone or black and white timbering. A small area above the bar (usually reserved by diners) is no smoking. Bar food has been very good and has included sandwiches, soup, welsh rarebit (£2.70), excellent platters (from £4), sweet and sour pork (£5.20), local wild rabbit and prune pie (£6.20), chicken breast with hazelnut cream sauce (£7.20), steaks (from £9.30), and puddings (£2.50). Bass, Courage Best, Dartmoor, Theakstons Old Peculier, and a guest beer on handpump. Nearby ancient Leechwell's worth the walk down and back up the steep hill (reputed to have healing properties). *(Recommended by George and Jeanne Barnwell, Jeanne Cross, Paul Silvestri, Peter and Jenny Quine, David Wallington, George Jonas, Joy and Paul Rundell, Norma Farris, Steve Noakes, Mr and Mrs C Roberts; more reports on the new regime, please)*

Free house ~ Real ale ~ Meals and snacks ~ (01803) 863324 ~ Children in eating area of bar ~ Open 11-2.30, 5.30-11

TRUSHAM SX8582 Map 1

Cridford Inn

Village and pub signposted from B3193 NW of Chudleigh, just N of big ARC works; 1½ very narrow miles

This friendly, atmospheric pub is full of history. During re-thatching, the original Norman roof was discovered, which is possibly the only one in England – and the very early medieval transept window in the bar is said to be the oldest domestic window in Britain and is Grade I listed. The bar has window-seats, pews and chapel chairs around kitchen and pub tables, stout standing timbers, natural stone walls, flagstones, and a big woodburning stove in the stone fireplace. Very good home-made bar food (using only fresh local produce) might include excellent soup like parnsip with ginger or cider and cheese (£2.25), brandy enriched chicken liver pâté with cumberland sauce (£3.50), local cheese platter with chutney, pickles and salad (£4.95), fish and chips (£5.25), lovely smoked salmon (from their own smokehouse) with dill and mustard sauce or steak and kidney pie (£5.75), pork with barbecue sauce (£6.50), Cajun chicken with creole sauce (£7.50), and daily specials such as herrings marinated in madeira (£3.25), spinach and mushroom roulade with spicy tomato sauce or four bean casserole topped with a herb and nut crumble (£5.25), fresh Brixham crab salad (£6.50), and noisettes of lamb in port and redcurrant sauce (£7.50), with puddings such as banoffi pie, lovely brandy snaps filled with seasonal fruit and sorbet or nursery puddings (£3.25). The no-smoking restaurant has a mosaic date stone showing 1081 and the initials of the then Abbot of Buckfastleigh. Well kept Adnams Broadside, Bass, Cotleigh Tawny, and a beer they call Trusham Bitter on handpump, a short but interesting wine list with monthly specials and wines by the glass, local Brimblecombe cider, and country wines. The cats are called

Smudge and Sophie, and the jack russells Patch and Jack; quiet piped music. You can sit on the sun-trap front terrace and they hold summer barbecues with an accordionist. The bedrooms have now been carefully renovated. *(Recommended by Nick and Meriel Cox, Joan and Gordon Edwards, Mike Gorton, Sue Hobley, John and Vivienne Rice, Wendy Arnold, Miss A Battye, John Allsopp, Richard Armstead, Alan and Rose Hogg, R Rawlings, Steve Huggins, Dr Monica Nurnberg, Mrs N Mendelssohn)*

Free house ~ Licensees David and Sally Hesmondhalgh ~ Real ale ~ Meals and snacks (not winter Mon) ~ Evening restaurant (closed Sun and winter Mon) ~ (01626) 853694 ~ Children in top bar but must be gone by 8.30pm ~ Open 12-2.30, 6-11; closed winter Mon and 25 Dec ~ Bedrooms: £37.50B/£55B

WELCOMBE SS2217 Map 1

Old Smithy

Village signposted from A39 S of Harland; pub signposted left at fork; in hamlet of Darracott

This friendly thatched pub is in a lovely rural setting – the lane going past leads eventually to parking down by Welcombe Mouth, which is an attractive rocky cove. The open-plan bar has a chatty, informal atmosphere, log fires at both ends of the room, button-back banquettes and wheelback chairs and little snug windows; the restaurant was once the old forge; piped music. Bar food, popular with the nearby campers and holiday bungalow visitors, is straightforward and includes sandwiches, good pasties, ploughman's (£2.95), scampi (£3.60), and lasagne (£4.95); there's also a no-smoking tea shop. Well kept Boddingtons, Butcombe, Flowers IPA, and Marstons Pedigree on handpump. Darts, fruit machine and piped music. The pretty, terraced, sheltered garden has plenty of seats. *(Recommended by Mr and Mrs Westcombe, R J Walden, Anthony Barnes, Rita Horridge, Jack and Philip Paxton, C P Scott-Malden, Philip and Joanne Gavins, R T and J C Moggridge, James Macrae, Gary Gibbon, Derek and Delia Spindlow, Tim Barrow, Sue Demont, Robin and Molly Taylor)*

Free house ~ Licensees Geoff Marshall and sons ~ Real ale ~ Meals and snacks ~ (01288) 331305 ~ Children welcome until 8.30 ~ Open 11.30-11; 12-3, 7-11 in winter; closed Mon/Tues Nov-Feb ~ Bedrooms: £20/£35

WESTON ST1200 Map 1

Otter ★ 🍴 🍷

Village signposted off A30 at W end of Honiton bypass

Sitting at the picnic tables on the sizeable lawn which runs down to the little River Otter and watching the ducks, is a marvellous way to unwind. There are pretty climbing plants, hanging baskets and flowering tubs, and an animal sanctuary with free-ranging cockerels, hens, rabbits and guinea-pigs. Inside, the very low-beamed main bar has such a good relaxed atmosphere and friendly welcome, that we feel the time has come to award the pub a star. Chamberpots and jugs hang from beams, comfortable chairs sit by the log fire (that stays alight right through from autumn to spring), there's an interesting mix of polished wooden antique tables, wooden chairs, and handsome chapel pews, and candles in bottles; each day a page of the Bible on the lectern that ends one pew is turned, and attractive bric-a-brac includes some formidable arms and armour, horse collar and bits, quite a few pictures, and an old mangle; a veritable library leads off, with quite a few readable books and magazines, as well as board games, darts, shove-ha'penny, cribbage, dominoes, table skittles, a fruit machine, video game, trivia, juke box and piped music; pool and skittle alley, too. Promptly served and very good, the food might include lovely soup like lemon and courgette (£2.30), sandwiches (from £1.85), baked potatoes filled with smoked ham, herb and cheese sauce or creamy stilton and mushroom (from £2.95), potted crab and prawns with Grand Marnier and dill and served in an orange butter (£3.80), peking duck pancake (£4.50), ploughman's (£4.65), super local butcher's sausages (£5.50), steak and kidney pie (£5.75), steaks (£10.15), and changing daily specials like tasty tagliatelle with artichoke, lovely fresh fish dishes, delicious rack of lamb or excellent roast guinea fowl, and pan-fried fresh venison in a peppered sauce. They're good to children: high chairs, a children's menu (£1; suitable baby food, too) with a picture to colour and free lollipop, a box of toys, rocking-horse, and a bike. Well kept Bass, Boddingtons, and Eldridge Pope Hardy on handpump, good inexpensive wines, farm cider, and freshly squeezed orange juice. *(Recommended by Richard Dolphin, R T and J C Moggridge, Rich and Pauline Appleton, F C Johnston, Peter and Audrey Dowsett, Mayur Shah, Mr and Mr D V Morris, S M Gray, Martin Pritchard, Nicolas Corker, Desmond and Pat Morris, Mrs J Blake, E V M Whiteway, T Buckley, L Knight, Gordon)*

Free house ~ Lease: Brian and Susan Wilkinson ~ Real ale ~ Meals and snacks (till 10pm; not 25 Dec) ~ (01404) 42594 ~ Children welcome ~ Piano player Sun and odd times in week ~ Open 11-3, 6-11; only 11-1 on 25 Dec

WONSON SX6790 Map 1

Northmore Arms

Off A388 2 miles from A30, at Murchington, Gidleigh signpost; then at junction where Murchington and Gidleigh are signposted left, keep straight on – eventually, round Throwleigh, Wonson itself is signposted; OS Sheet 191 map reference 674903

Down narrow high-hedged lanes on the north-east edge of Dartmoor, this delightful secluded cottage is a real find – all the more remarkable in this area for being open all day. Its two small connected beamed rooms are modest and informal but very civilised, with wall settles, a few elderly chairs, three tables in one room and just one in the other. There are two open fires, and some attractive photographs on the stripped stone walls. Service is gently welcoming; besides well kept changing ales such as Adnams Broadside, Cotleigh Tawny and Exe Valley Dobs, they have good house wines, and the simple food is good value: sandwiches (from £1.50), steak and kidney pudding (£4), a roast lunch (£4.50), and puddings (£1.75). The small sheltered sloping garden is rustic and very peaceful, with gentle country noises off; excellent walking from the pub (or to it – perhaps from Chagford or Gidleigh Park). This should be a nice place to stay though we've not yet had reports on that. *(Recommended by John Wilson, John Wilkinson, Sean and Wendy McGeeney, T Treagust)*

Free house ~ Licensee M Miles ~ Real ale ~ Meals and snacks ~ (01647) 231428 ~ Well behaved children welcome ~ Open 11-11 ~ Two bedrooms: £15/£25

WOODBURY SALTERTON SY0189 Map 1

Digger's Rest ★

3½ miles from M5 junction 30: A3052 towards Sidmouth, village signposted on right about ½ mile after Clyst St Mary; also signposted from B3179 SE of Exeter

For over 22 years, Mr and Mrs Pratt have run this very welcoming and cosy thatched village pub. It's a popular place with both locals and visitors, and there are heavy black oak beams, comfortable old-fashioned country chairs and settles around polished antique tables, a dark oak Jacobean screen, a grandfather clock, and plates decorating the walls of one alcove; at one end of the bar is a log fire, and at the other is an ornate solid fuel stove. The big skittles alley can be used for families, and there's a games room with darts and dominoes. Well kept Bass, Dartmoor, and Tetleys on ancient handpumps, and local farm ciders; sensibly placed darts and dominoes in the small brick-walled public bar. Good bar food includes home-made soup (£1.55), sandwiches with home-cooked meats (from £2.75; local crab £3.25), ploughman's (£4.25), home-made curry or home-cooked beef with chips (£4.25), salads (from £5.95), steaks (from £8.45), daily specials such as steak and kidney pie (£4.75) or half a roast duck (£8.95), and puddings (£2.25). The terrace garden has views of the countryside. *(Recommended by George and Jeanne Barnwell, Chris Westmoreland, George Atkinson, Mark and Heather Williamson, John and Vivienne Rice, B D Jones, E V M Whiteway, Peter and Lynn Brueton, J E Davies, John Beeken, J I Fraser, Anthony Barnes)*

Free house ~ Licensee Sally Pratt ~ Real ale ~ Meals and snacks (12-1.45, 7-10) ~ (01395) 232375 ~ Children at end of bar or in skittle alley (if not in use) ~ Open 11-2.30, 6.30-11; closed evenings 25/26 Dec

Lucky Dip

Besides the fully inspected pubs, you might like to try these Lucky Dips recommended to us and described by readers (if you do, please send us reports):

☆ **Abbotsham** [the one nr Bideford; SS4226], *Thatched*: Former New Inn reopened after extensive refurbishment integrating old and new well, Bass, Butcombe Bitter, Courage Directors and John Smiths, attractive food, families welcome; tables outside; handy for the Big Sheep *(Chris Westmoreland)*

Abbotskerswell [SX8569], *Butchers Arms*: Tucked-away little old pub, well kept Whitbreads, pleasant nooks and corners *(John A Barker, Steve Huggins, Joan and Gordon Edwards)*

☆ **Appledore** [Irsha St; SS4630], *Royal George*: Friendly local feel in cosy and unspoilt front bar, simple but good fresh food inc local fish and good value Sun roasts in newer eating area with superb estuary views, well kept ales such as Bass, Ind Coope Burton, Morlands Old Speckled Hen, attractive pictures; picnic tables outside, picturesque street sloping to sea *(Chris Westmoreland, Mr and Mrs N Hazzard, Nigel and Lindsay Chapman)*

Appledore [Irsha St], *Beaver*: Well refurbished with raised area overlooking estuary in light uncluttered bar, good food and service, well kept ales such as Bass, Butcombe, Flowers, pool room, views from outdoor tables; children welcome *(A Cull, C Westmoreland)*; [Market St], *Coach & Horses*: Compact cosy three-room pub in picturesque street, fish posters, Courage-related ales *(C Westmoreland)*; [Market St], *Royal*: Simple good value food inc local fish and substantial Sun lunch, well kept Bass and Wadworths 6X, recently improved back family room, benches out on front cobbles; opens for breakfast *(C Westmoreland)*; [quay, by church], *Seagate*: Friendly, good food, Dartmoor ale, fantastic views, children welcome, picnic tables outside; bedrooms pretty *(Mary Reed, Rowly Pitcher, C Westmoreland)*

☆ **Ashburton** [West St; SX7569], *Exeter*: Friendly old-fashioned pub with well kept Courage-related ales, good value food *(John and Tessa Rainsford, Jeanne Cross, Paul Silvestri, Joy and Paul Rundell)*

Ashburton [East St], *Red Lion*: Well run, with good food and well kept beer *(Paul and Heather Bettesworth)*

Avonwick [B3210, off A38; SX7157], *Avon Arms*: Pleasant fairly modern interior, good friendly service, wide range of good food esp pasta, puddings and ice creams (Italian cook), best to book Fri/Sat eve; pleasant riverside garden *(Mr and Mrs J Woodfield)*; [B3210], *Mill*: Good value lunchtime carvery in pretty converted mill with play area in big lakeside garden, friendly service, children's helpings (they have high chairs), Bass on handpump *(John Evans)*

Axminster [Raymonds Hill; A35 nr B3165; SY2998], *Hunters Lodge*: Character 16th-c coaching inn under newish ownership, well kept Bass and Worthington, good value bar and restaurant food inc carvery, big garden with children's play area; well behaved dogs welcome *(John Roberts)*

☆ **Axmouth** [SY2591], *Ship*: Comfortable and civilised, good fresh local fish, well kept Whitbreads-related real ales, good wine and coffee, friendly staff and samoyeds, lots of embroidered folk dolls; attractive garden with sanctuary for convalescent owls *(W C M Jones, A Denman, LYM)*

☆ **Babbacombe** [112 Babbacombe Rd; A379 Torquay—Teignmouth; SX9365], *Masons Arms*: Friendly and atmospheric, three rooms with stripped stone and panelling, good food, well kept Bass and Boddingtons, decent wine, children treated well; very busy evenings *(John Allsopp, N A Morgans)*

Babbacombe [St Marychurch], *Snooty Fox*: Huge rambling pub with nightly live entertainment, Bass, generous usual food *(Michael Butler)*

Barnstaple [SS5533], *Rolle Quay*: Big pub with rather plush lounge, separate bar, skittle alley, good value food, well kept beers inc guests from independent breweries *(Richard Houghton)*

☆ **Beer** [Fore St; ST2389], *Anchor*: Good generous well presented food inc wide choice of superb fresh fish, big helpings, same menu in bar and restaurant; quick friendly service, well kept beer, spacious garden looking over cove, charming village; can get crowded, public car park quite a long walk; bedrooms clean and comfortable *(Basil Minson, Alan A Newman, Mrs B Sugarman, Dennis Dickinson, A W Lewis, Mrs V Rollo, Mr and Mrs Garrett, Don and Thelma Beeson)*

☆ **Beesands** [SX8140], *Cricket*: Attractively basic, in good spot on beach with tables outside; good value food esp crab sandwiches, well kept Whitbreads-related real ales, lots of local history *(Alan and Heather Jacques, Roger Wain-Heapy)*

Belstone [a mile off A30; SX6293], *Tors*: Imposing stone building, good choice of reasonably priced generous food, well kept Butcombe and Otter ales, decent wines; bedrooms, attractive village well placed for N Dartmoor walks *(J L Jones, John and Vivienne Rice)*

☆ **Bickleigh** [SS9406; A396/A3072 N of Exeter], *Fishermans Cot*: Fishing hotel with good well served food inc popular reasonably priced carvery, well kept Bass, good restaurant, tables in garden by River Exe with small weir and ancient bridge; comfortable bedrooms looking over own terrace to river *(Simon and Debbie Tomlinson, E Robinson, Jim and Maggie Cowell, Mr and Mrs R Head, Alan Newman, Mrs J M Corless)*

☆ **Bickleigh**, *Trout*: Thatched pub with comfortable easy chairs in huge bar and dining lounge, sizeable buffet counter with good choice of food from sandwiches up and tempting puddings cabinet, well kept ales such as Cotleigh Tawny, Bass, Boddingtons, Exmoor Gold, nice coffee, efficient enthusiastic young staff; tables on pretty lawn, car park across rd; five well equipped bedrooms, good breakfast *(Mrs G Teall, E Robinson, LYM)*

Bideford [Mkt Sq; SS4526], *Joiners Arms*: Good value food, friendly service, well kept Bass, Dartmoor and a guest such as Fullers, good collection of joiner's tools, dining area *(Richard Houghton, Chris Westmoreland)*; *Kings Arms*: Cheerful and popular pub nr quay, reasonably priced food from good filled rolls up, good Sun lunches, alcovey front bar with Victorian harlequin floor tiles, back raised family area, well kept Whitbreads-related and other ales such as Exmoor Beast; pavement tables *(Nigel and Lindsay Chapman, Rita Horridge, Chris Westmoreland)*

☆ **Bigbury** [St Anns Chapel – B3392 N; SX6647], *Pickwick*: Good choice of bar food, well kept ales such as Bass and Flowers, local farm cider; very friendly rustic-look bar, plainer family extension with pool and other games – children treated well, carvery restaurant; piped music; bedrooms *(David Cundy, LYM)*

☆ **Blackmoor Gate** [SS6443], *Old Station House*: Big dining pub in same local chain as Pyne Arms, East Down (see main entries), with similar food, well kept ales; churchy pews, plush dining chairs, soft red lighting, character no-smoking area with grandfather clock; spacious games area with two well lit pool tables, darts and juke box; big garden with good views; skittle alley; children allowed (but under-5s in small family room only) *(Ian Shorthouse, BB)*

☆ **Blagdon** [Higher Blagdon; pub signed off A385 leaving Paignton; SX8561], *Barton Pines*: Spaciously converted mock-Elizabethan 19th-c mansion, rather town-pub feel in big bar with dining area, good generous food all cooked to order, friendly informative service, provision for families, grand gardens giving views out to sea and over to Dartmoor; caravan site behind *(Mr and Mrs C Roberts, LYM)*

Bolberry [Bolberry Down – OS Sheet 202 map ref 691392; SX6939], *Port Light*: Unlikely building (blocky ex-RAF radar station) alone on dramatic NT clifftop, bright, spacious and popular inside, with decent bar food, well kept Dartmoor, friendly efficient service, restaurant, conservatory, tables in garden with play area; well behaved children allowed; four bedrooms *(Dorothee and Dennis Glover)*

☆ **Brampford Speke** [off A377 N of Exeter; SX9299], *Agricultural*: Good friendly food pub, wide choice of good home cooking inc interesting puddings, attractive prices, well kept Courage, prompt service, gallery restaurant where children allowed; picnic tables on sheltered terrace *(Mrs E McFarland)*

☆ **Brandis Corner** [A3072 Hatherleigh—Holsworthy; SS4103], *Bickford Arms*: Well kept ales inc Bass and Flowers, good service and very wide choice of well presented generous food at reasonable prices esp fresh fish and steaks, in simple 17th-c beamed village local; log fires, games room, restaurant, garden, attractive countryside; bedrooms *(Roderic Plinston, Joan and Gordon Edwards, A B Agombar)*

Branscombe [A3052; SY1988], *Three Horseshoes*: Large rambling roadside pub, Bass and a beer named for the pub, good jazz Fri eve and Sun lunchtimes *(Quentin Williamson)*

☆ **Bridestowe** [old A38; SX5189], *White Hart*: Unpretentious local, partly flagstoned beamed main bar with grandfather clock and games end, some nice old furnishings in lounge, panelled restaurant; good generous food, well kept Palmers, friendly staff, informal streamside back garden, peaceful Dartmoor village; bedrooms *(Chris and Pauline Ford, Dr and Mrs N Holmes, BB)*

☆ **Bridford** [off B3193 Dunsford—Chudleigh; SX8186], *Bridford Inn*: Consistently good food inc popular Sun lunch (worth booking), well kept beers, local cider, dark beams, some well polished antiques, Turkey carpet, big stone fireplace; cl Tues, does not open till 12 and 7 (6.30 Sat); tables on fairylit terrace above quiet village with pretty valley views, well behaved dogs allowed *(Robert and Gladys Flux, Peter Whittle, Claire Harding, Hugh and Peggy Holman, BB)*

☆ **Broadclyst** [Whimple Rd; SX9897], *New Inn*: Good range of reasonably priced food esp fish, well kept Whitbreads-related ales, decent wine, friendly service, in former farmhouse with stripped bricks, boarded ceiling, low doorways, roaring log fires, country and horsey bygones; small restaurant, skittle alley *(A E Brace, E V M Whiteway, E H and R F Warner)*

☆ **Broadhempston** [off A381, signed from centre; SX8066], *Coppa Dolla*: Cheerful buoyant atmosphere and good surprisingly ambitious food in straightforwardly comfortable bar divided by sturdy timber props, well kept ales such as Bass, Dartmoor Best, Palmers and Wadworths 6X, good service, decent wines, log fires, well spaced picnic tables in attractive garden with pleasant views; two apartments *(Harry and Irene Fisher, Peter and Jenny Quine, Joan and Gordon Edwards, BB)*

Broadhempston [The Square], *Monks Retreat*: Black beams, busy decor with lots of copper, brass and china, log fire in huge stone fireplace, very wide choice of straightforward food inc sizzler steaks and midweek bargains, well kept Bass and Teignworthy Reel Ale, very cheerful service; by arch to attractive churchyard, a few picnic tables out in front *(Jeanne Cross, Paul Silvestri, Gordon, BB)*

Buckfastleigh [Totnes Rd; SX7366], *Dartbridge*: Good reasonably priced food, well equipped for families, opp Dart Valley Rly – very popular in summer; ten letting chalets *(Wg Cdr G K A Hollett)*

☆ **Buckland Monachorum** [SX4868], *Drakes Manor*: Well kept Courage-related ales, good friendly service, good value food inc good Sun lunches, beams and oak panelling; public bar with games machines *(G W Stevenson, Mr and Mrs J Woodfield, Bruce Bird)*

☆ **Burgh Island** [SX6443], *Pilchard*: Perhaps has things too easy, given its monopoly, but fun to visit, perched above sea on this tidal island with its great cliff walks; atmospheric smuggly decor, Courage-related ales, basic food (all day summer, lunchtime only winter); piped music, children in downstairs bistro *(Paul McPherson, Nigel Spence, Kim Greek, Tim and Lynne Crawford, Jack and Philip Paxton, Gordon, John and Vivienne Rice, LYM)*

California Cross [SX7052], *California*: Pleasant beamed pub with well kept Dartmoor and Wadworths 6X, good value food, friendly staff, family room, restaurant, garden; very popular *(Dr and Mrs N Holmes)*

Calverleigh [B3221 Tiverton—Rackenford; SS9214], *Rose & Crown*: Attractive, with good value food in decent-sized helpings, pleasant friendly atmosphere *(M Joyner)*

☆ **Chagford** [Mill St; SX7087], *Bullers Arms*: Welcoming local with very wide food range inc vegetarian, reasonable prices, three changing ales, collection of militaria, darts, very friendly licensees; summer barbecues *(John Hazel, John and Christine Vittoe, Joan and Gordon Edwards, Patrick Clancy, LYM)*

Chagford, *Three Crowns*: Distinguished ancient thatched building of great potential though bar furnishings largely modern, popular food, friendly service, Bass and Flowers Original, big fire, stripped-stone public bar with pool and darts; tables on front cobbles and in back garden; good old-fashioned bedrooms *(Ted George, G Washington, John and Christine Vittoe, Gordon, BB)*

☆ **Challacombe** [B3358 Blackmoor Gate—Simonsbath – OS Sheet 180 map ref 695411; SS6941], *Black Venus*: Good range of generous reasonably priced home-cooked food inc delicious puddings, Courage-related ales, good friendly service, low 16th-c beams, pews, decent chairs, stuffed birds, woodburning stove and big open fire, separate games room, attractive large dining area (children over 5 allowed here); in same local chain as Pyne Arms, East Down – see main entries; seats in garden, attractive countryside; bedrooms *(H and D Cox, Neil and Anita Christopher, BB)*

☆ **Chillington** [SX7942], *Chillington Inn*: Friendly village local with old settles, benches and low tables in front bar, good individual chairs in back bar, good bar food often inc local seafood, well kept Bass, Palmers and guests on handpump; restaurant; may be closed winter lunchtimes Mon-Thurs; bedrooms *(P Bass, Alistair Stanier)*

Chip Shop [OS Sheet 201 map ref 436752; SX4375], *Chip Shop*: Friendly local with good value food, welcoming service, well kept Bass, Exmoor and Smiles Best, lots of mirrors, unobtrusive piped music, garden with play house; well placed darts *(Richard Houghton, John Hazel, Jack and Philip Paxton, Andy and Jill Kassube)*

☆ **Christow** [signed off B3193 N of A38; SX8385], *Artichoke*: Pretty thatched local with open-plan rooms stepped down hill, low beams, some black panelling, flagstones, straightforward food inc decent specials, vegetarian, fish and game, big log fire (2nd one in no-smoking end dining room), Whitbreads-related ales; tables on back terrace, pretty hillside village nr Canonteign Waterfalls and Country Park *(Mr and Mrs A K McCully, Mr and Mrs A P Vogt, Joan and Gordon Edwards, M S Crabtree, Mary and William Bankes, BB)*

☆ **Clayhidon** [off A38 via Culmstock, Hemyock; ST1615], *Half Moon*: Simple unfussy decor, all clean and civilised, in welcoming pub with imaginative home-cooked food, well kept Bass and Cotleigh, good house wine; quiet views from picnic tables in garden over road, a couple of well behaved labradors; opens noon *(John and Fiona Merritt, Lady Emma Chanter, BB)*

☆ **Clearbrook** [off A386 Tavistock—Plymouth; SX5265], *Skylark*: Big and busy, with well kept beer, generous good value food, children's room; good Dartmoor views *(Nigel Spence, Kim Greek)*

Clyst St Mary [nr M5 junction 30; SX9790], *Half Moon*: Well kept Bass tapped from the cask in solid friendly old pub next to multi-arch bridge, good value generous food; bedrooms *(Chris Westmoreland, Mike Dickerson)*

Cockington [SX8963], *Drum*: Picturesque thatched and beamed tavern in quaint Torquay-edge village by 500-acre park, spacious and well run, with Tetleys-related ales inc Dartmoor, wide choice of food in bar and two family eating areas, Weds summer barbecues, winter skittle evenings and live music; juke box or piped music; seats on terrace and in attractive back garden *(Michael A Butler, Peter Morgan, Steve Huggins)*

☆ **Cockwood** [SX9780], *Ship*: Comfortable and welcoming 17th-c inn overlooking estuary and harbour, good seafood menu from open crab sandwiches up, Ushers beer, reasonable prices, pleasant quick service, good steep hillside garden 17th-c inn overlooking estuary and harbour with good seafood menu, Ushers beer *(Peter and Jenny Quine, Chris Westmoreland, Ian Phillips)*

☆ **Coffinswell** [SX8968], *Linny*: Very pretty 14th-c thatched country pub with big cheerful beamed bar, fires each end, cosy window seats and alcoves, good value usual food in bar, well kept Bass, Ind Coope Burton and Morlands Old Speckled Hen, open fires, friendly service, children's room, restaurant; picturesque village *(Mr and Mrs A K McCully, Peter and Jenny Quine, T A Bryan, Jim and Maggie Cowell)*

Colaton Raleigh [A376 Newton Poppleford—Budleigh Salterton; SY0787], *Otter*: Warm welcoming pub with family room, good reasonably priced food, lovely big garden *(A Preston)*

Combe Martin [Seaview Hill; SS5847], *Dolphin*: Pleasant spacious local, good reasonably priced food, Worthington, lots of whiskies and liqueurs, friendly licensee, quiet piped music *(John Sanders)*; [Seaside], *Fo'c's'le*: Fantastic beach setting, varied food, friendly attentive service; bedrooms beautifully decorated *(Mary Reed, Rowly Pitcher)*

☆ **Combeinteignhead** [SX9071], *Wild Goose*: Spacious 17th-c beamed pub, lots of hanging jugs and teapots, wide choice of good food from separate servery, good range of changing ales, friendly service, open fire, pool room, darts *(D Cox, George Atkinson)*

☆ **Countisbury** [A39, E of Lynton – OS Sheet 180 map ref 747497; SS7449], *Exmoor Sandpiper*: Rambling heavy-beamed pub with antique furniture, several log fires, usual food from sandwiches to steaks, well kept Flowers Original and Greene King Abbot, restaurant; children in eating area, open all day; comfortable bedrooms *(R V Ford, LYM)*

☆ **Croyde** [B3231 NW of Braunton; SS4439], *Thatch*: Spick-and-span chocolate-boxy decor in popular rambling thatched inn nr surfing beach, generous bar food, well kept Tetleys-related ales, morning coffee, teas, smiling staff, tables outside; restaurant, children in eating area, open all day; piped music; bedrooms *(Mr and Mrs M P Aston, R J Walden, A M Pring, LYM)*

☆ **Croyde** [off B3231 NW of Braunton], *Whiteleaf*: A guest house not a pub, but has won many GPG friends with peaceful comfortable surroundings, truly imaginative fresh food and good wines, and a landlord who certainly knows his pubs (they have been thinking of scaling down the catering side, so check if booking); dogs allowed *(BN)*

Culmstock [S of M5; ST1014], *Culm Valley*: Ancient pub in lovely spot in small village by bridge, friendly licensees and locals, good interesting food in bar and restaurant, ales such as Bass, Bunces Pigswill, Shepherd Neame Bishops Finger, river walk to working wool museum *(Shirley Pielou)*

☆ **Dartmouth** [Smith St; SX8751], *Seven Stars*: Lively beamed and panelled local, quick well priced popular food, ales such as Kilkenny and Wadworths 6X, coal fire; maybe piped pop music, fruit machine; upstairs restaurant, children's room *(T G Thomas, BB)*

Dartmouth [Bayards Cove], *Dartmouth Arms*: Well priced pizzas (can be taken away), marvellous setting *(Steve and Sue Noakes)*; [Victoria Rd], *Seale Arms*: Bar food (not Sun lunch) inc curries and children's, family room with big blackboard and chalks, helpful friendly owners, Courage-related ales, Sunday bar nibbles; nr market; bedrooms *(T G Thomas)*

☆ **Denbury** [The Green; SX8168], *Union*: Spotless well run low-beamed local on edge of old village green, simple food from good sandwiches to steaks inc vegetarian and lots of puddings, Whitbreads-related ales, good coffee; tables in garden by green, quietly pretty sheltered village *(Joan and Gordon Edwards, Bill Sharpe, Jeanne Cross, Paul Silvestri, Steve Huggins, BB)*

☆ **Devonport** [6 Cornwall St; SX4555], *Swan*: Lively riverside local with lots of well kept ales, generous good value snacks, roaring fire, live music most nights with extended opening till midnight *(W Fletcher)*

Devonport [240 James St], *Little Mutton Monster*: Good backstreet pub with good choice of real ales and good value Indian food inc hot chillies *(Andy and Jill Kassube)*

☆ **Dittisham** [The Level; SX8654], *Red Lion*: Welcoming well run local with well kept Bass, open fires, sleeping dogs, good value innovative food in restaurant, friendly licensees, family room; attractive village *(Michael Weaver, B Taylor)*

☆ **Dittisham**, *Ferry Boat*: Big windows make the most of beautiful waterside spot, nr little foot-ferry you call by bell; well kept Courage, bar food inc good pasties *(Jim and Maggie Cowell, Barry A Lynch, Steve Huggins, LYM)*

☆ **Dog Village** [B3185 S – ½ mile off A30 opp airport; SX9896], *Hungry Fox*: Roomy mock-Tudor dining pub, good value home cooking, Whitbreads-related ales, wide range of wines and spirits, good friendly service *(E V M Whiteway)*

☆ **Down Thomas** [SX5050], *Langdon Court*: Increasingly good food in welcoming lounge bar and family room, reasonable prices, good fire, country views, Whitbreads-related ales from ornate servery, picnic tables outside; dogs allowed; interesting country-house hotel with comfortable bedrooms *(Susan Cody, Brian White, Nigel Spence, Kim Greek)*

☆ *nr* **Drewsteignton** [Fingle Bridge, off A38 at Crockernwell via Preston or Drewsteignton; OS Sheet 191 map ref 743899; SX7390], *Anglers Rest*: Idyllic wooded Teign valley spot by 16th-c packhorse bridge, lovely walks; tourist souvenirs and airy cafe feel, but has well kept Cotleigh and Courage ales and reliable food inc children's meals (not Sun); good friendly service, waterside picnic tables *(Jim and Maggie Cowell, Jack and Philip Paxton, T H G Lewis, Jeanne Cross, Paul Silvestri, Alan Newman, John and Christine Vittoe, BB)*

☆ **Dunsford** [just off B3212 NE of

Moretonhampstead – OS Sheet 191 map ref 813891; SX8189], *Royal Oak*: Good unusual reasonably priced food and good friendly service in relaxed village inn's light and airy lounge bar, half a dozen well kept changing ales, local farm ciders, woodburner; steps down to games room, provision for children; quiz nights, piped music may be loud; Fri barbecues in sheltered tiered garden, good value bedrooms in converted barn *(David Burnett, Donna Lowes, John and Christine Vittoe, Carol Whittaker, John Crompton, Jean Cross, Paul Silvestri, LYM)*

East Budleigh [Oak Hill (A376); SY0684], *Rolle Arms*: Good range of local beers, good value standard food, friendly chatty service *(MW, HW, Mr and Mrs D V Morris)*

Ermington [SX6353], *Crooked Spire*: Clean tasteful open-plan dining bar locally popular for generous food inc Sun lunches, friendly efficient service; bedrooms comfortable, with shared bathroom *(Alan and Brenda Holyer, JSE, C Smith)*; *First & Last*: Beautiful setting, lots of ivy and hanging baskets, friendly licensees, simple good cheap food with ample veg, well kept Bass and local beers *(Simon and Debbie Tomlinson, K H Frostick)*

Exbourne [SX6002], *Red Lion*: Doing well under good new landlord, warm atmosphere, well kept Tetleys, Wadworths 6X and a summer guest *(R G Walden)*

☆ **Exeter** [The Quay], *Prospect*: Pleasant setting overlooking waterfront nr Maritime Museum, beams, panelling and settles, old safari pictures and local prints, welcoming feel, wide range of reasonably priced fresh food inc good fish in big dining area up a few steps, well kept Bass and Charrington IPA, helpful staff *(Mr and Mrs David Lee, Wayne Brindle, Tony and Wendy Hobden, June and Tony Baldwin, Jim and Maggie Cowell, John and Vivienne Rice)*

☆ **Exeter** [Martins Lane – just off cathedral close], *Ship*: Pretty 14th-c pub with substantial comfortable furniture in heavy-beamed atmospheric bar, well kept Bass and Boddingtons on handpump, decent generous food, upstairs restaurant *(John and Vivienne Rice, Chris Westmoreland, Barry and Anne, Paul Randall, E V M Whiteway, LYM)*

☆ **Exeter** [The Close; bar of Royal Clarence Hotel], *Well House*: Big windows looking across to cathedral in open-plan bar divided by inner walls and partitions; lots of Victorian prints, well kept changing ales, popular bar lunches inc good salads, good service; Roman well beneath (can be viewed when pub not busy); piped music *(Wayne Brindle, Andy and Jill Kassube, Paul Randall, Graham Reeve, BB)*

☆ **Exeter** [14 Exe St, off Bonhay Rd], *Papermakers*: Pub/wine bar/bistro with charming Continental atmosphere, wide choice of good unusual food, friendly efficient service, Wadworths 6X and guests like Eldridge Pope Hardy and Royal Oak and Greene King Abbot, good wines, reasonable prices *(Prof and Mrs John Webster, Arthur McCartney)*

☆ **Exeter** [Cowick Lane; between A377 and B3212], *Cowick Barton*: Friendly comfortable former 17th-c red sandstone farmhouse, wide choice of good generous food, Bass, Courage Best and Ruddles County on handpump, lots of country wines, good service, log fire, small back restaurant *(Jim and Maggie Cowell, E V M Whiteway)*

Exeter [High St, C&A basement], *Chaucers*: Smart modern pub/bistro/wine bar down lots of steps, candles in bottles, well kept Bass and Tetleys, good range of food, friendly service *(Alan Prine, Graham Reeve, John Atkins, Chris Westmoreland)*; [centre], *Honiton*: Particularly well kept Bass, big helpings of good value tasty food; all clean, friendly pub dog *(Alan Sinclair)*; [St Davids Hill], *Jolly Porter*: Attractive traditional rooms, lively with students and locals, well kept Courage-related and changing guest ales, good cheap plentiful food, snooker room, bric-a-brac and books; jazz Weds *(Jim and Maggie Cowell, Graham Reeve)*; [Bonhay Rd], *Mill on the Exe*: Comfortably done out with old bricks and timbers, good food, St Austell ales, quick friendly service; riverside terrace *(Wayne Brindle, R J Walden, Eric Whiteway, BB)*; [2 Countess Wear Rd], *Tally Ho*: Village-pub feel, interesting spot on River Exe, good value home-cooked food, decent wine *(Arthur McCartney)*; [High St North], *Turks Head*: Friendly busy Beefeater, long two-level book-lined lounge bar, wide choice of bar food, well kept Whitbreads-related ales, upstairs restaurant; where Dickens found the original of Joe, the *Pickwick Papers* fat boy, forever nodding off *(Chris Westmoreland, BB)*

☆ **Exminster** [just off A379; SX9487], *Swans Nest*: Huge choice of reasonably priced honest self-service food from sandwiches up in very popular high-throughput food pub, handy for M5, character furnishings in inviting well arranged rambling dining bar; no-smoking areas, Bass and Dartmoor, attractive carvery, salads and children's dishes, helpful staff; especially good for family groups with children *(D S Beeson, Wg Cdr G K A Hollett, Mr and Mrs C R Little, Mr and Mrs K C B Box, Desmond and Pat Morris, B D Jones, Mrs J M Corless, LYM)*

☆ **Filleigh** [off A361 N Devon link rd; SS6627], *Stags Head*: Good food, generous if not cheap, in friendly and attractive 16th-c thatched pub with lake, neat furnishings, well kept Bass and other beers; bedrooms comfortable and good value, good breakfasts *(Nick and Alison Dowson)*

☆ **Fremington** [B3233 Barnstaple—Instow; SS5132], *New Inn*: Good choice of popular food in bar and restaurant, well kept beer *(Don and Thelma Beeson, R E and P Pearce)*

Frithelstock [just W of Torrington; SS4619], *Clinton Arms*: Remarkable range of food (restaurant has had ostrich and crocodile), Bass tapped from the cask, friendly helpful service; children welcome *(Nigel and Lindsay Chapman, A M Stephenson, R J Walden)*

Frogmore [A379 E of Kingsbridge; SX7742], *Globe*: Wide range of good food in spacious comfortable dining room, good friendly service, children welcome; good bedrooms *(Jennifer Sheridan, R D Bubb)*
Galmpton [Churston Bridge; Dartmouth Rd; SX8956], *Weary Ploughman*: Enterprising licensees, new popular restaurant with freshly cooked food, attentive staff, live music some nights; bedrooms modest but adequate and clean *(Paul and Janet Waring)*
☆ George Nympton [SS7023], *Castle*: Good range of above-average food inc vegetarian, comfortably stylish surroundings; bedrooms comfortable too, fishing rights *(A N E Cox)*
Georgeham [by church; B3231 Croyde—Woolacombe; SS4639], *Kings Arms*: Simple friendly village pub with well kept ales, jazz nights; had a brief moment of glory spring 1995 with outstanding food for a village pub, but this catering arrangement did not last *(L Parikian, S Aldridge)*
☆ Georgeham [Rock Hill; above village – OS Sheet 180 map ref 466399], *Rock*: Cheerful character oak-beamed pub, old red quarry tiles, open fire, pleasant mix of country furniture, lots of bric-a-brac; well kept Courage-related real local farm cider, good bar food; piped music, darts, fruit machine, pool room; tables under cocktail parasols on front terrace, pretty hanging baskets *(B M Eldridge, Jim and Maggie Cowell, BB)*
☆ Hartland Quay [down toll rd; SS2522], *Hartland Quay*: Outstanding cliff scenery, rugged coast walks, genuine atmosphere and good untouched maritime feel with panelling and shipwreck pictures; good value basic home-cooked food, St Austell Tinners, Inch's cider, quick pleasant service, lots of tables outside; reasonably priced bedrooms, hotel has seawater swimming pool *(T Treagust, John Sanders, Jeanne Cross, Paul Silvestri, Nigel and Lindsay Chapman, A M Stephenson, Barry and Anne)*
☆ Hexworthy [village signed off B3357 Tavistock—Ashburton, 3¾ miles E of B3212; SX6572], *Forest*: Solid Dartmoor hotel, comfortable and spacious open-plan bar and back walkers' bar, welcoming staff, good bar food and range of beers; good-sized bedrooms *(J R Williams, Joan and Gordon Edwards, LYM)*
☆ Highampton [A3072 W of Hatherleigh; SS4804], *Golden*: Attractive 16th-c thatched pub with Dartmoor views from garden behind, homely low-beamed alcovey lounge, brasses, watercolours, farm tools, stove in big stone fireplace; good value food, well kept Bass tapped from the cask, pool room; well behaved children allowed *(Chris and Pauline Ford, R J Walden)*
☆ Holcombe Rogus [ST0518], *Prince of Wales*: Spacious and comfortable, no machines or music, friendly atmosphere, good food (not Sun or Tues eves) in elegant dining room with good fire, well kept Cotleigh ales *(Bryan Wheeler)*
☆ Honiton [43 High St; ST1500], *Red Cow*: Busy but welcoming local, nice atmosphere and seating areas, log fires, Courage-related and local ales, decent wines and malt whiskies, good choice of good value food, friendly helpful staff *(K R Harris, Basil Minson, Mrs J Blake, Pat and John Charles)*
Honiton [March Yarcombe, off A303 NE], *Cottage*: Pubby atmosphere, good value home-made food, well priced real ales, skittles, darts, pool; bedrooms *(MAJ, KWJ, Shirley Johnson)*; [Fenny Bridges – A30 4 miles W; SY1198], *Fenny Bridges*: Spacious, with big helpings of good standard food, well kept local beer, quick service; restaurant, tables in garden *(Howard Clutterbuck)*
☆ Horns Cross [A39 Clovelly—Bideford – OS Sheet 190 map ref 385233; SS3823], *Hoops*: Good atmosphere, wide choice of Whitbreads-related ales and of tasty food in attractive thatched dining pub, much modernised inside; friendly if not always speedy service, big inglenook log fires, eating area in central courtyard as well as cosy restaurant and bar, decent wines, provision for children and disabled; comfortable bedrooms *(B Rivers, Jack and Philip Paxton, A B Agombar, LYM)*
Horrabridge [SX5169], *Leaping Salmon*: Friendly atmosphere, good cheap home-made food; beautiful Dartmoor village *(Miss H Goodale)*
☆ Ideford [SX8977], *Royal Oak*: Friendly, dark and cosy thatched village local, lots of Victorian, Edwardian and World War regalia, flags and so forth, well kept Bass, sandwiches, log fire *(Steve Huggins)*
☆ Ilfracombe [Broad St; SS5147], *Royal Britannia*: Sedate but friendly old-fashioned hotel in attractive spot above harbour; low seats, armchairs, copper tables and lots of prints in series of connecting rooms; wide choice of good value bar food inc local fish, well kept Courage-related beers; bedrooms *(B M Eldridge)*
☆ Ilfracombe [Bicclescombe Park Rd (off A361)], *Coach House*: Neat, clean and well run, with good food in pleasant bar, family room and beamed upstairs restaurant *(A J D Hale)*
☆ Instow [Marine Dr; SS4730], *Boathouse*: Good choice of generous good value food, some starters as big as main courses; good service, atmosphere and range of beers, pleasant view over beach, estuary and Appledore *(Mr and Mrs Jacob, R E and P Pearce)*
Instow, *Buccaneer*: New light and airy pub on seafront nr dunes; beers from all over southern half of England, coffee and food *(Chris Westmoreland)*; *Quay*: Just above quay, tables out in front, pleasant open-plan interior, Whitbreads-related ales, friendly service; bar food *(C Westmoreland)*; *Wayfarer*: Popular local with Bass, Whitbreads-related and a guest ale, main room with areas off, some interesting food inc lots of local fish; garden, children welcome *(C Westmoreland)*
☆ Kenn [signed off A380 just S of Exeter; SX9285], *Ley Arms*: Extended rebuilt

thatched pub with polished granite floor and beams in attractive public bar, plush black-panelled lounge with striking fireplace, well kept Bass and Whitbreads-related ales, good wines, popular bar food; piped music, no-smoking family room, games area, sizeable restaurant side *(Gordon, Rich and Pauline Appleton, Graham Reeve, Annette Stewart, Mike Gorton, A E and P McCully, E V M Whiteway, LYM)*

☆ **Kings Nympton** [SS6819], *Grove*: Friendly thatched and beamed family local, well kept Ushers and farm cider, good value food; lots of games, skittle alley, picturesque village *(D B Delany, LYM)*

☆ **Kingsbridge** [quayside, edge of town; SX7344], *Crabshell*: Lovely waterside position, charming when tide in, with big windows and tables outside, wide choice of bar food inc lunchtime shrimp or crab sandwiches and ambitious hot dishes esp local fish; quick friendly staff, well kept Bass and Charrington IPA, decent choice of wines, good farm cider, good fire *(Dorothee and Dennis Glover, Wendy Arnold, Michele and Mike Zinopoulos, Stephen Teakle, D M Shalit, Bill Edwards, BB)*

☆ **Kingsbridge** [Fore St], *Ship & Plough*: Interesting 18th-c pub brewing its own good cheap Blewitts Brains Out, Mild and Trumpet; friendly informative staff, usual food *(S Webb, M Lantree, Richard Houghton)*

Kingsbridge [Mill St], *Hermitage*: Friendly, usual food inc good home-made soup, good coffee, log fire *(Alan Prine)*

☆ **Kingskerswell** [towards N Whilborough – OS Sheet 202 map ref 864665; SX8666], *Bickley Mill*: Rambling converted out-of-the-way mill, comfortable seats, dark wood and brasses, carpet spreading into all the alcoves, popular generous interesting bar food inc vegetarian, well kept ales such as Ansells, Bass, Wadworths 6X, speedy cheerful service; restaurant Weds-Sat evenings; bedrooms *(John Wilson, Mr and Mrs C Roberts)*

☆ **Kingskerswell** [Torquay Rd; SX8767], *Hare & Hounds*: Busy extended food pub with good value carvery and salad bar, good service *(D J Knight, Mrs Jean Knight, Mrs M A Brasher)*

Kingsteignton [Aller Mill; SX8773], *Brown Owl*: Clean and pleasant rooms of character in attractive pub; shame about the piped music *(BAFH)*

Kingswear [Higher St; SX8851], *Ship*: Not particularly stylish, but cosy and welcoming, plenty of locals, generous well priced food served quickly, well kept Bass; one table with Dart views, a couple outside *(Joy Heatherley, Paul and Mitzi Auchterlonie)*

☆ **Knowle** [just off A361 2 miles N of Braunton; SS4938], *Ebrington Arms*: Welcoming and friendly, good value food, well kept Bass and Wadworths 6X, lots of bric-a-brac in comfortable main bar, attractive candlelit dining area; pool room, piped music *(R J Walden, Deborah and Ian Carrington, Steve and Carolyn Harvey, S R and A J Ashcroft, Ian and Nita Cooper, LYM)*

Lamerton [A384 Launceston—Tavistock; SX4476], *Blacksmiths Arms*: Good value generous fresh food, children very welcome *(Paul and Heather Bettesworth)*

☆ **Lee** [SS4846], *Grampus*: Attractive medieval pub short stroll from sea, lots of seats in quiet sheltered garden, wide range of basic but good well presented home-made food, well kept Whitbreads-related ales, decent piped music; two bedrooms; superb coastal walks *(Sue Demont, Tim Barrow, Mr and Mrs Westcombe, LYM)*

Littleham [SS4323], *Clinton Arms*: Cheery family local nr Sandy Bay holiday site, well kept beers and ciders, good range of substantial bar food, play area and animals outside *(Mark Williamson)*

☆ **Loddiswell** [SX7148], *Loddiswell Inn*: Welcoming landlady, well kept Ushers, good choice of freshly cooked generous food inc local ingredients, log fire, thriving local atmosphere *(Alan and Heather Jacques, Dr and Mrs N Holmes)*

☆ **Longdown** [B3212 W of Exeter; SX8690], *Lamb*: Open-plan bar with wide choice of imaginative reasonably priced home-made food in dining area, settees in front alcove, ales such as Dartmoor, Exmoor Gold, Ind Coope Burton *(David Burnett, Donna Lowes, John Stoner)*

☆ **Luton** [Haldon Moor; SX9076], *Elizabethan*: Friendly low-beamed pub with wide range of good value food inc lots of pies and fish, well kept beer *(A P Jeffreys, Julie Bennett)*

☆ **Lympstone** [Exmouth Rd (A376); SX9984], *Nutwell Lodge*: Big modern-looking roadside dining pub, surprisingly attractive inside, with sensibly priced popular food inc good carvery and early lunchtime bargains, well kept Bass and Dartmoor, decent wines, friendly efficient service; children welcome *(B D Jones, John and Vivienne Rice, CW, J I Fraser, Dr P R Davis, LYM)*

Lympstone, *Globe*: Good mix of visitors and locals in relaxed simply furnished two-room pub, popular food esp seafood, quick friendly service, small pleasant restaurant; pretty waterside village *(Shirley Pielou, Chris Westmoreland)*; *Swan*: Recently refurbished under new Irish landlord, welcoming atmosphere, good food, well kept beer *(Richard Armstead)*

Lynmouth [harbour; SS7249], *Rock House*: Small relaxing bar popular with locals, friendly staff, good reasonably priced food, good choice of beer and wine; restaurant, bedrooms, very attractive spot *(John and Christine Vittoe)*

Lynton [Market Pl; SS7249], *Crown*: Welcoming and comfortable lounge bar, decent reasonably priced food, well kept beer and cider, helpful staff; bedrooms *(Dorothee and Dennis Glover, W H and E Thomas)*; [Castle Hill], *Royal Castle*: Wonderful coastal views from terrace, well kept ales inc Butcombe, friendly service, good range of bar food; bedrooms *(Bruce Bird)* *nr* **Lynton** [Martinhoe, towards Heddon's Mouth – OS Sheet 180 map ref 654482; SS6548], *Hunters Inn*: Outstanding setting in lovely wooded NT valley, great walks; good plain food, lots of real ales, good farm cider, cream teas; attractive bedrooms *(Alan and Brenda Holyer, John Matthews)*

☆ **Maidencombe** [Steep Hill; SX9268], *Thatched*: Picturesque extended thatched pub with lovely coastal views, cheap plentiful good food, Tetleys-related ales, quick friendly service, big family room, no-smoking areas, restaurant; attractive garden with small thatched huts (dogs allowed out here but not in pub); children allowed; bedrooms in annexe, small attractive village *(Julie Bennett)*

☆ **Manaton** [SX7581], *Kestor*: Useful Dartmoor-edge inn in splendid spot nr Becky Falls, modern, clean and cheerful; wide range of good value home cooking, well kept changing ales, farm cider, open fire, helpful service; piped music; attractive bedrooms *(Denzil Taylor, G and M Stewart, Mr and Mrs C T Alcock, Mrs Pat Crabb)*

☆ **Marsh** [signed off A303 Ilminster—Honiton; ST2510], *Flintlock*: Welcoming and comfortable 17th-c inn, wide choice of good bar food inc vegetarian, well kept beer and cider, armoury and horsebrasses *(Mrs J M Corless, Howard Clutterbuck)*

Marsh, *Cottage*: Unpretentious genuine country pub, well kept beers, decent wines, good variety of reasonably priced food; bedrooms good, clean and comfortable *(K W Johnson)*

Mary Tavy [A386 Tavistock—Okehampton; SX5079], *Mary Tavy*: Small, unpretentious, welcoming and attractive, Bass, St Austell Tinners and a guest ale, well prepared modest food *(John Wilson, Bruce Bird, Jack and Philip Paxton)*

☆ **Meeth** [A386 Hatherleigh—Torrington; SS5408], *Bull & Dragon*: 16th-c beamed and thatched village pub, Tetleys-related ales with a guest such as Butleigh, decent wines, good value well presented straightforward food using local produce, friendly staff and locals, unobtrusive piped music; children welcome, exemplary lavatories *(A J Blackler, R J Walden, Gill Earle, Andrew Burton, Ron and Sheila Corbett)*

☆ **Merrivale** [B3357; 4 miles E of Tavistock – OS Sheet 191 map ref 459752; SX5475], *Dartmoor*: Welcoming refurbished pub with Dartmoor views, nr bronze-age hut circles, stone rows and pretty river; good value generous basic lunchtime food, well kept ales inc Bass, Courage and one labelled for the pub, water from their 120-ft well, good choice of country wines, open fire, friendly attentive staff, tables outside – very popular summer evenings; good walks *(Mr and Mrs K C B Box, Dr and Mrs N Holmes, Frank Cummins)*

☆ **Molland** [SS8028], *London*: Incredibly unspoilt dim-lit basic Exmoor-edge pub, with Bass and Worthington BB tapped from casks behind bar, good value food inc children's meals in big dining room, log fire, welcoming landlord, upper-crust locals; next to wonderfully untouched church *(Robin and Molly Taylor, Dave Lands, S G N Bennett, T J H Bodys)*

Molland, *Black Cock*: Cotleigh ales, good home-cooked straightforward food, friendly atmosphere, good family room with pool table, heated indoor swimming pool *(Doug and Gill Green, Dave Lands)*

Monkokehampton [SS5805], *Olde Swan*: Small and quiet, well kept beers, friendly locals *(R Pottey)*

Morchard Bishop [signed off A377 Crediton—Barnstaple; SS7707], *London*: Well appointed old coaching inn, good value food in bar or small dining room, attentive service, Boddingtons, Fullers London Pride, Marstons Pedigree and changing guests; lively meeting place for local darts, pool and skittles teams *(Alan and Heather Jacques)*

☆ **Moreleigh** [B3207; off Kingsbridge—Totnes in Stanborough, left in village – OS Sheet 202 map ref 767527; SX7753], *New Inn*: Busy country local with character old furniture, big inglenook, nice pictures, candles in bottles; limited choice of good wholesome home-cooked food served generously, well kept Palmers tapped from the cask; may be closed Sat lunchtime/race days *(Andy and Jill Kassube, David Wallington, Jim and Maggie Cowell, Roger Wain-Heapy, R W A Suddaby, LYM)*

☆ **Mortehoe** [off A361 Ilfracombe—Braunton; SS4545], *Ship Aground*: Open-plan village pub by church with big family room, well kept Whitbreads-related and guest ales, Hancock's cider in summer, decent wine, bar food, log fire; massive rustic furnishings, lots of nautical brassware; pool, skittles and other games, tables outside; piped music may be intrusive, ginger tom; wonderful walking on nearby coast footpath *(S R and A J Ashcroft, Julian Holland, Peter and Audrey Dowsett, Ian and Nita Cooper, Susan and Nigel Wilson, D P and M E Cartwright, Sarah Elliott, Gary Goldson, LYM)*

Mortehoe, *Chichester Arms*: Warm and welcoming, with lots of old village prints, wide choice of reasonably priced usual bar food, Bass and Courage-related ales, helpful service, no piped music *(Peter and Audrey Dowsett, P and J Shapley)*

☆ **Newton Abbot** [East St; SX8671], *Olde Cider Bar*: Fat casks of interesting farm ciders and perries in unusual basic cider house, no-nonsense stools and wall benches, pre-war-style decor; good country wines, snacks inc venison pasties, very low prices; small games room with machines *(Jeanne Cross, Paul Silvestri)*

Newton Abbot, *Jolly Farmer*: Well kept Courage, decent bar food, barn theme, skittle room, juke box *(Steve Huggins, Jeanne Cross, Paul Silvestri)*

☆ *nr* **Newton Abbot** [A381 2 miles S, by turn to Abbotskerswell], *Two Mile Oak*: Atractively quiet and old-fashioned, with good log fire, black panelling, low beams, stripped stone, lots of brasses, candlelit alcoves; wide choice of well prepared reasonably priced bar food, cosy little dining room, well kept Bass, Flowers IPA, Eldridge Pope Royal Oak and guest beers, seats on back terrace, attractive garden *(Joan and Gordon Edwards, Peter and Jenny Quine, LYM)*

☆ **Newton Ferrers** [Riverside Rd East; SX5448], *Dolphin*: Friendly pub in lovely village overlooking yachting harbour, good value food *(David Lewis, David Goldstone)*

☆ **Newton St Cyres** [SX8798], *Crown & Sceptre*: Attractive decor, good imaginative home-made food, friendly staff, Bass and Boddingtons, family area, splendid lawn with trees and stream *(Paul Redgrave, John and Vivienne Rice)*

☆ **Newton Tracey** [5 miles S of Barnstaple on B3232 to Torrington; SS5226], *Hunters*: Friendly old pub with good value bar food, four real ales, log fire, evening restaurant, skittle alley/games room; juke box, fruit machines; tables outside, play area; provision for children *(Mr and Mrs N Hazzard, Nigel and Lindsay Chapman)*

☆ **No Mans Land** [B3131 Tiverton—South Molton; SS8313], *Mount Pleasant*: Traditional country pub with cosy bars, wide range of good inexpensive home-made food from huge sandwiches up, real ales such as Bass and Butcombe, decent wines, friendly service, open fires, ex-forge restaurant; children's room, tables outside *(Mr and Mrs T B Mills, C Roberts)*

☆ **North Bovey** [SX7483], *Ring of Bells*: Bulgy-walled 13th-c thatched inn, well kept Dartmoor, Ind Coope Burton, Marstons Pedigree and Wadworths 6X, farm cider, games etc, good log fire, good value straightforward bar food, restaurant, friendly staff; children welcome; big bedrooms with four-posters; seats outside by lovely tree-covered village green below Dartmoor *(Denzil Taylor, Steve Huggins, J L Hall, George Atkinson, D Cox, LYM)*

North Molton [Sandyway Cross, up towards Withypool; SS7933], *Sportsmans*: Fairly handy for Landacre beauty spot, with well kept Courage-related ales, friendly atmosphere, good food – not cheap, but decent value considering the big helpings *(B M Eldridge)*

☆ **Noss Mayo** [SX5447], *Swan*: Small pub with charming waterside views, good range of bar food inc fresh fish, well kept Courage Best and Directors, old beams, open fire; children welcome, tables outside – peaceful picturesque village *(Shirley Pielou, Margaret and Roy Randle, David Lewis)*

Otterton [SY0885], *Kings Arms*: Comfortably refurbished, with good choice of food, real ale and pleasant service; charming village *(J I Fraser, F J Willy, Mrs J M Corless)*

☆ **Paignton** [27 Esplanade Rd; SX8960], *Inn on the Green*: Big brightly comfortable unpubby bar open all day, useful lunchtime for enormous choice of popular sensibly priced quick food inc two-person bargains, well kept Courage-related ales (and good soft and hot drinks), friendly service; out-of-the-way family room, live music and dancing nightly, restaurant, big terrace looking out over green to sea *(Bruce Bird, Mrs J M Corless, C and M M Roberts, George Atkinson, LYM)*

☆ **Parkham** [SS3821], *Bell*: Spacious and comfortable thatched village pub, good value fresh food, lots of nooks and crannies, log fire, old-fashioned furnishings, choice of real ales *(R J Walden, LYM)*

☆ **Plymouth** [Citadel Rd/Saltram Pl – back of Plymouth Hoe, behind Moat House], *Yard Arm*: In fine spot overlooking the Hoe, attractive woodwork and some interesting nautical bric-a-brac giving character, three levels and intimate snug feel, well kept Courage-related ales and a guest such as Bass, very cheap generous straightforward food inc children's, cheerful service; subdued piped music, children allowed in bottom area, tables outside *(Ian Phillips, Brian Atkin, Brian and Anna Marsden, David Yandle, Mark Walker)*

☆ **Plymouth** [Old George St; Derrys Cross, behind Theatre Royal], *Bank*: Busy three-level pub interestingly converted from former bank, dark wood balustrades, conservatory area upstairs (children allowed here), tables outside; cheerful service, good value food all day, take it on tray – busy at lunchtime for this), well kept Tetleys-related ales; music nights, lively young evening atmosphere *(Andy and Jill Kassube, David Yandle, W Fletcher, Geraldine Berry, Steve Howe)*

Plymouth [Borringdon Terr; Turnchapel signs off A379 Kingsbridge rd; SX4755], *Borringdon Arms*: Well worn local, clean and friendly, with five well kept ales and occasional beer festivals; back conservatory *(B and K Hypher, Andy and Jill Kassube)*; [Commercial Rd, Coxside], *Fareham*: Recently completely refurbished, with well kept St Austells HSD *(Mike Woodhead)*; [21 Breton Side], *Kings Head*: Worth knowing for good range of well kept beers inc their good value Kings Ransom own brew; opens 10am, occasional folk music *(BM, AM, Mike Woodhead, M J Manuel)*; [5 St Andrews St], *Kittys*: Irish theme, real ales, good staff *(Peter Williamson)*; [2 Market Way], *Newmarket*: Very clean though busy, Courage ales, good range of other drinks; good staff *(Peter Williamson)*; [Cumberland Gdns], *Shakespeare*: Friendly family-run pub with well kept ales, good value bar food, reasonably priced bedrooms *(Kirk Taylor)*; [13 Sutton Rd], *Shipwrights Arms*: Simple nicely cooked low-priced food in good Courage local, welcoming fire, kind staff *(C W Jenkins, Mike Woodhead)*; [Grand Parade, West Hoe], *Waterfront*: Pleasant cafe-bar in good spot by Plymouth Sound, big restaurant areas, strict dress code, beers by half-pint or two-pint jug *(Mayur Shah, Nigel Spence, Kim Greek)*

Plympton [Station Rd, central shopping area; SX5356], *Sir Joshua Reynolds*: Good range of well cooked food, comfortable lounge with bookable tables, bar with juke box, pool and darts *(Rich and Pauline Appleton)*

☆ **Princetown** [SX5873], *Plume of Feathers*: Popular unchanging much-extended hikers' pub, good value food inc good pasties, friendly efficient service, well kept Bass and St Austell HSD and Tinners, two log fires, solid slate tables, live music Fri night, Sun lunchtime – can be lively then; children welcome, play area outside; good value bedrooms, also bunkhouse and camping *(David Holloway, Andy and Jill Kassube, John Hazel)*

Princetown, *Prince of Wales*: Friendly no-nonsense local, wide choice of good value straightforward food, Flowers and Wadworths 6X on handpump, large dog and two cats; two huge open fires, granite walls hung with rugs *(John Wilson, Joan and Gordon Edwards, BB)*

Prixford [SS5436], *New Ring o' Bells*: Recently modernised village pub with reasonably priced generous food, friendly service; very handy for Marwood Hill Gardens *(K R Harris, I R Bull)*

☆ **Pusehill** [SS4228], *Pig on the Hill*: Newish family dining pub on farm, pig decorations, plenty of tables in bar, raised gallery and adjacent room through archways; decent food inc children's, well kept Ind Coope Burton, reasonable prices, children's TV room, big adventure playground, boules *(B M Eldridge, Chris Westmoreland)*

☆ **Rackenford** [off A361 NW of Tiverton; SS8518], *Stag*: Good changing fresh and imaginative food and lots of character and atmosphere in interesting 13th-c low-beamed thatched pub with original flagstoned and cobbled entry passage, huge fireplace flanked by ancient settles; friendly service, well kept real ales such as Cotleigh and Exmoor Gold; bedrooms *(Elizabeth Beresford, K Flack, Eric and Patricia King, BB)*

☆ **Rockbeare** [SY0295], *Jack in the Green*: Good value interesting food showing real flair. well kept Bass and Wadworths 6X, good reasonably priced wines, cheerful staff, back restaurant *(John and Vivienne Rice, E V M Whiteway)*

☆ **Salcombe** [off Fore St nr Portlemouth Ferry; SX7338], *Ferry*: Fine spot overlooking water, bottom stripped-stone bar giving on to sheltered flagstoned waterside terrace, top bar opening off street, and between them a good dining bar; well kept Palmers ales *(Alan and Brenda Holyer, B Taylor, Tim and Lynne Crawford, Owen and Margaret Warnock, Richard Hathaway, LYM)*

☆ **Salcombe** [Fore St], *Victoria*: Well placed and attractive, with comfortable lounge, copious good food cooked to order, pleasant eating area, jovial landlord, well kept Bass and Wadworths 6X; segregated children's room, bedrooms *(Tim and Lynne Crawford, Moira and John Cole, A Craig)*

Salcombe [Union St], *Fortescue*: Busy local nr harbour, three bars, terrace, reliable food, well kept Courage Directors; can get busy in summer *(Allan and Philippa Wright, Joy and Paul Rundell)*

☆ **Sampford Courtenay** [B3072 Crediton—Holsworthy; SS6301], *New Inn*: 16th-c thatched pub with well kept Bass and Flowers, good filling food, low-beamed open-plan bar, open fires, nice garden with children's play area and playhouse *(Derek and Iris Martin)*

☆ **Sampford Peverell** [16 Lower Town; a mile from M5 junction 27, village signed from Tiverton turn-off; ST0214], *Globe*: Spacious rather than cosy, with decent generous home cooking, cheerful attentive staff, well kept Whitbreads-related ales, piped music, games in public bar, pool room, skittle alley, tables in front; open all day; children allowed in eating area and family room *(Mrs J M Corless, Ron Shelton, LYM)*

☆ **Sandy Park** [SX7189], *Sandy Park*: Thatched country local with convivial old-fashioned small bar, stripped old tables, built-in high-backed wall seats, big black iron fireplace, real ales such as Cotleigh Tawny, Eldridge Pope Hardy and Wadworths Farmers Glory, decent wines; bar food (not winter Sun/Mon evenings), children in eating area, cosy restaurant; service can slow if busy; simple clean bedrooms *(R J Walden, A R Hards, W Matthews, Joan and Gordon Edwards, Steve Huggins, Bryn Davies, Werner Arend, Lara Kramp-Chopin, LYM)*

Seaton [Marine Cres; SY2490], *Fishermans*: Cheap tasty food all day, good welcome, open fire *(Brian Websdale)*

Shaldon [Fore St; SX9372], *Clifford Arms*: Friendly 18th-c pub in pleasant village, good value home-cooked food inc fresh local fish, well kept Bass and Dartmoor Best, pub games, family room *(B M Eldridge)*; [Ringmore Rd (B3195)], *Shipwrights Arms*: Chatty village local with pleasant river views from back garden, good value basic food, friendly service, Courage Directors *(George Atkinson, LYM)*

☆ **Shiphay** [off A380/A3022, NW edge of Torquay; SX8865], *Devon Dumpling*: Popular for its country style, with good reasonably priced food inc vegetarian, well kept Courage Best, Morlands Old Speckled Hen and Wadworths 6X, cheerful service; plenty of space inc upper barn loft; aquarium, occasional live music, no dogs inside *(Wally Huggins, Mr and Mrs C Roberts)*

☆ **Sidmouth** [Old Fore St; SY1287], *Old Ship*: Shiny black woodwork, ship pictures, wide choice of fair-priced food inc vegetarian, well kept ales such as Boddingtons, Marstons Pedigree, Wadworths 6X; close-set tables but roomier raftered upstairs bar, dogs allowed; just moments from the sea, so can get crowded in summer, but service good and friendly *(Eric and Patricia King, E V M Whiteway, Sarah and Gary Goldson, Jason Caulkin, BB)*

☆ **Sidmouth** [High St], *Tudor Rose*: Well run by friendly long-serving landlord, good value straightforward food in bar and restaurant (where children allowed), well kept Bass, comfortable seats, soft lighting, low ceilings, bric-a-brac from copper kettles to a penny-farthing, quiet piped music *(J I Fraser, M E Wellington, Brian Websdale)*

☆ *nr* **Sidmouth** [Bowd Cross; junction B3176/A3052; SY1089], *Bowd*: Big thatched family roadhouse with attractive garden, bar food, indoor and outdoor play areas *(Gordon, Nick Wikeley, E V M Whiteway, Chris Westmoreland, LYM)*

☆ **Silverton** [14 Exeter Rd; SS9502], *Three Tuns*: Good value food inc fine vegetarian dishes in 17th-c inn's old-fashioned bar or cosy restaurant, well kept Courage Best and Directors, welcoming efficient service; good value bedrooms in new block, handy for Killerton *(Denzil Taylor, Nick Wikeley)*

☆ **Slapton** [SX8244], *Tower*: Atmospheric ancient low-ceilinged flagstoned bar with two open fires, peaceful garden overhung by romantic ivy-covered ruined jackdaw tower; has been a popular main entry, with good food and beer, family room and three simple bedrooms, but closed early 1995; arrangements afoot for reopening under new management as we went to press *(LYM; news please)*

South Brent [Plymouth Rd; SX6960], *Pack Horse*: Relaxed, comfortable and characterful local; good choice of food, good landlord; bedrooms *(H A Dobson)*

South Molton [SS7125], *Bish Mill*: Doing well under dedicated current owners, sparkling clean, with basic home-made bar food inc evening casseroles and steaks, well kept Cotleigh Tawny, restaurant; pretty garden and terrace *(David Wallington)*

☆ **South Tawton** [off A30 at Whiddon Down or Okehampton, then signed from Sticklepath; SX6594], *Seven Stars*: Friendly and unpretentious local, good generous simple food, well kept Bass, Boddingtons and a guest beer, decent wines; pool and other bar games, restaurant (cl Sun and Mon evenings winter); children welcome; bedrooms *(Chris Bartram, LYM)*

South Zeal [SX6593], *Kings Head*: Good bar food *(David Holloway, Jack and Philip Paxton)*

Sparkwell [SX5757], *Treby Arms*: Friendly, warm, very welcoming; good range of beers inc unusual guests, small dining room *(Philo Anne Smithson)*

☆ **Spreyton** [SX6996], *Tom Cobbley*: Friendly village local, generous cheap home-made food, well kept Cotleigh Tawny and occasional guest beers; darts, cards, attractive garden with summer barbecues, dog-loving licensees; comfortable bedrooms sharing bath, big breakfasts *(R J Walden, Jack and Philip Paxton, Giles J Robinson)*

Starcross [SX9781], *Atmospheric Railway*: Named for Brunel's experimental 1830s railway here, basically long pipe enclosing piston connected to train, pumping stations sucking the train along; interesting memorabilia, Whitbreads-related ales *(Alan Newman)*

☆ **Sticklepath** [off A30 at Whiddon Down or Okehampton; SX6494], *Devonshire*: Friendly owners and welcoming locals in 16th-c thatched village inn with good low-priced snacks, bookable Sun lunches and evening meals, friendly and cosy low-beamed slate-floored bar, big log fire, some nice old furniture, comfortable armchairs in room off, St Austell Tinners and HSD, farm cider, magazines to read; open all day Fri/Sat *(Bryn Davies, LYM)*

☆ **Stokeinteignhead** [SX9170], *Church House*: Well restored 13th-c thatched dining pub, good if not cheap food in character bar, dining lounge or restaurant area, delightful spiral staircase, friendly chatty staff, well kept Bass, Flowers IPA and Marstons Pedigree on handpump, farm cider, good coffee; nice back garden with little stream *(Jim and Maggie Cowell, Jeanne Cross, Paul Silvestri, Gordon, John Wilson, George Atkinson, Gethin Lewis)*

☆ **Stokeinteignhead**, *Chasers Arms*: Good value food inc interesting dishes in 16th-c thatched pub/restaurant (you can't go just for a drink); well kept Eldridge Pope Dorset, fine range of house wines, quick friendly service; lovely unspoilt village *(Tom Evans, D I Baddeley, Peter and Jenny Quine, Paul and Janet Waring)*

☆ **Stokenham** [just off A379 Dartmouth—Kingsbridge; SX8042], *Tradesmans Arms*: Tranquil 15th-c thatched cottage with plenty of antique tables neatly set for good simple fresh bar food esp seafood; well kept Adnams and Bass, good malt whiskies, very friendly staff; restaurant, children allowed in left-hand bar, picnic tables outside (nice surroundings), maybe quiet piped classical music; tiny car park, opens noon *(John Allsopp, Paul and Janet Waring, Steve Huggins, Joy and Paul Rundell, Gordon, LYM)*

☆ **Stokenham** [opp church, N of A379 towards Torcross], *Church House*: Rambling open-plan family pub, children's room well stocked with toys etc, attractive garden with play area, fishpond and chipmunks; good food inc fresh fish and other local ingredients, well kept Bass, Eldridge Pope Hardy and Flowers Original, farm cider, decent wines, no-smoking dining room, unobtrusive piped music *(T Aldworth, P and J Shapley, Norma Farris, Roger Wain-Heapy, LYM)*

☆ **Tedburn St Mary** [village signposted from A30 W of Exeter; SX8193], *Kings Arms*: Good choice of sensibly priced food (all day Sun) in attractive old pub, open-plan but comfortable, with big log fire and lots of brass; end games area, well kept real ales, local cider; children in eating area; bedrooms *(E V M Whiteway, J A Kempthorne, LYM)*

Teignmouth [Bitton Park Rd; SX9463], *Golden Lion*: Popular local, two well kept guest beers, pleasant friendly service, traditional public bar with good pool and darts teams *(B M Eldridge)*

Thurlestone [SX6743], *Village Inn*: Good

range of well kept beers and of bar and restaurant meals in nice, if rather up-market, village pub handy for coastal path *(Jeremy Brittain-Long)*

Tiverton [Castle St; SS9512], *Queens Head*: Small friendly local with skittles, darts, euchre, pool and backgammon *(Cliff Salter)*

☆ **Topsham** [Fore St; 2 miles from M5 junction 30; SX9688], *Globe*: Good solid traditional furnishings, log fire and plenty of character in heavy-beamed bow-windowed bar of friendly and relaxed 16th-c inn; low-priced straightforward home-cooked food, well kept Bass, Ushers Best and Worthington BB on handpump, decent reasonably priced wine, civilised locals, snug little bar-dining room, separate restaurant; seats in sheltered courtyard, children in eating area, open all day; good value attractive bedrooms *(Gordon, Mark Walker, E H and R F Warner, B Taylor, Chris Westmoreland)*

☆ **Topsham**, *Lighter*: Spacious and plush, with well kept Badger ales, good friendly staff, decent quickly served bar food, panelled alcoves and tall windows looking out over tidal flats, seats out on old quay; good choice of board games, children in eating area; big good value bedrooms sharing bathroom *(Ian Lock, Gabrielle Coyle, Chris Westmoreland, E V M Whiteway, R J Walden, BB)*

☆ **Topsham** [High St], *Lord Nelson*: Well priced generously served food inc giant open sandwiches, pleasant atmosphere, attentive service *(Alan Newman)*

Topsham [Fore St], *Drakes*: Bass, Boddingtons, Devenish Royal Wessex, a beer named for the pub and guest beers, good choice of wines by the glass, tempting food in upstairs intimate restaurant; good atmosphere *(Adrian Alton)*; [Monmouth Hill], *Steam Packet*: Dark flagstones, scrubbed boards, panelling, stripped masonry, bar food, well kept ales; on boat-builders' quay *(Chris Westmoreland, LYM)*; [68 Fore St], *Salutation*: Done up in Victorian style complete with flagstoned period courtyard; clean and comfortable, friendly staff, well kept beers, good freshly cooked food esp local fish *(K R Harris)*

☆ **Torquay** [Park Lane; SX9264], *Hole in the Wall*: Small two-bar 16th-c local nr harbour, low beams and flagstones, decent food, well kept Courage, friendly licensees, lots of Naval memorabilia, old local photographs, chamber-pots; open all day *(Mr and Mrs C Roberts, Peter and Jenny Quine, Jim and Maggie Cowell)*

Torrington [Old Station House; SS4919], *Puffing Billy*: Popular family pub in former station building, well kept ales, decent wines and food inc good value children's dishes, lots of train memorabilia and pictures, garden interesting for children; handy for Tarka Trail *(Susan and Nigel Wilson, A M Stephenson, P Johns)*

Totnes [SX8060], *Watermans Arms*: Clean and comfortable after recent refurbishment, short choice of good simple food, big fireplace with woodburner, cheerful staff, well kept beer *(Mr and Mrs C Roberts)*

☆ **Tuckenhay** [Bow Creek; out of Totnes, keep on Ashprington rd past Watermans Arms; SX8156], *Floyds Inn (Sometimes)*: Keith Floyd's pub, excellent food in character bar and airy downstairs restaurant, but the prices are too high now to justify a main entry despite its marvellous position by a peaceful wooded creek; Bass, Blackawton, Dartmoor and Exmoor ales, Luscombe farm cider, lots of malt whiskies, decent wines, log fire, juke box, very nice waterside tables with popular barbecues; children in eating area, maybe live music Sun evening *(Mrs J Barwell, A Plumb, Barry A Lynch, Mrs S Segrove, Mrs S Smith, Joy and Paul Rundell, John and Fiona Merritt, Jim and Maggie Cowell, LYM)*

Two Bridges [B3357/B3212; SX6175], *Two Bridges*: Popular old Dartmoor inn, nice log fire in cosy bar, large lounge, usual bar food inc useful buffet lunch from restaurant, afternoon tea; bedrooms *(John and Christine Vittoe, Dr and Mrs N Holmes)*

Tytherleigh [A358 Chard—Axminster; ST3103], *Tytherleigh Arms*: Spacious and comfortable, with good range of usual food inc local fish, Eldridge Pope ales, small restaurant *(M E Wellington, Howard Clutterbuck)*

☆ **Ugborough** [Lutterburn St; off A3121 – signed from A38 W of South Brent; SX6755], *Anchor*: Very wide choice of food inc some splendid unusual dishes, children's food and delicious home-made puddings in restaurant or simple oak-beamed public bar (which still has chatty locals), well kept Bass, Wadworths 6X and guests, decent wines, friendly service, pub games, piped music, tables in garden; bedrooms; attractive village *(Roger Berry, A E Brace, Garth Redgrave, Dr J D Davies, Mr and Mrs Hart, Gordon, LYM)*

☆ **Ugborough**, *Ship*: Well run open-plan dining pub extended from cosy 16th-c flagstoned core, remarkably wide choice of good food inc lots of fresh fish, good fresh veg and farm ice-cream, pleasant efficient waitresses, well kept Bass and Boddingtons; tables outside *(Mr and Mrs C C Mathewman, B Taylor, Dr and Mrs N Holmes, George Atkinson)*

Upottery [ST2007], *Sidmouth Arms*: Attractive pub in pleasant village setting, food inc good Sun lunch; bedrooms *(Gordon, Paul and Heather Bettesworth)*

Walkhampton [SX5369], *Walkhampton*: Fine old Dartmoor-edge village pub, real ales, good food *(Nick Shutt)*

☆ **West Down** [the one up nr Ilfracombe; SS5142], *Crown*: Pleasant village pub with alcovey lounge, good value generous food inc children's and vegetarian, little red plush dining room, family room, discreet back pool/darts room; Flowers Original and other real ales, fine big garden behind with play areas and good shelter *(D P and M E Cartwright)*

Westleigh [½ mile off A39 Bideford—Instow; SS4628], *Westleigh Inn*: Friendly village pub with old pictures in smallish lounge, well kept Ushers, good straightforward home-cooked food esp cottage and fish pies, family atmosphere, gorgeous views down over the Torridge estuary from spacious neatly kept hillside garden, good play area *(Mr and Mrs N Hazzard, Nigel and Lindsay Chapman, Chris Westmoreland, Simon Starr, Mr and Mrs Westcombe, LYM)*

Whimple [off A30 Exeter—Honiton; SY4097], *New Fountain*: Civilised and attractive village local with friendly landlord and good food *(Gordon, LYM)*

☆ **Widecombe** [SX7176], *Olde Inne*: Friendly and cosy, with stripped 14th-c stonework, big log fires in both bars, some concentration on wide choice of good reasonably priced food with prominent restaurant area, Ushers and other beers, friendly service; in pretty moorland village, very popular with tourists though perhaps at its best out of season; room to dance on music nights, good big garden; great walks around *(John Hazel, Julie Peters, Colin Blinkhorn, Michael A Butler, John and Christine Vittoe, Philip and Debbie Haynes, John Hazel, Patrick Clancy, Jack and Philip Paxton, G and M Stewart, LYM)*

☆ **Widecombe** [turning opp Old Inne, down hill past long church house – OS Sheet 191 map ref 720765], *Rugglestone*: New licensees have extended carefully, keeping cosy bar unspoilt with woodburner and dozy dog, splendid value simple home cooking, well kept Bass and Butcombe tapped from the cask, larger room with space for darts etc, no piped music; tables in garden, beautiful quiet streamside setting *(G and M Stewart, John Hazel, Jack and Philip Paxton, P and T Ferris)*

☆ **Winkleigh** [off B3220; SS6308], *Kings Arms*: Beams, flagstones, scrubbed pine tables, woodburner and big separate log fire, good home-cooked food (light snacks Sun evening), Courage-related ales, good efficient service, well reproduced piped music, no-smoking restaurant; small sheltered side courtyard with pool; children over 6 allowed, cottage to let by the week; has been cl Mon *(G Washington, LYM)*

☆ **Winkleigh**, *Winkleigh Inn*: Clean and simple, with well kept real ales, Inch's farm cider, reasonably priced interesting food, lovely garden with view of church tower *(David Burnett, Donna Lowes)*

☆ **Woodbury** [3½ miles from M5 junction 30; A376, then B3179; SY0187], *White Hart*: Consistently good generous food all home-cooked in attractive and comfortable lounge bar or small homely restaurant, good friendly service, well kept Bass and Worthington BB; good locals' bar with many characters, skittle alley with own buffet, peaceful village *(Richard Armstead, George and Jeanne Barnwell, Robert and Gladys Flux)*

Woodbury Salterton [Sidmouth Rd; A3052 Exeter—Sidmouth; SY0189], *White Horse*: Modern spacious pub with consistently good reasonably priced food, well kept ales, comfortably divided dining areas, cheerful service; good children's room and play area; booking essential Sat; bedrooms *(J I Fraser, R W Flux)*

Woolacombe [Ossaborough; unclassified rd signed off B3343 and B3231; SS4543], *Mill*: Welcoming pub with chatty landlord, interesting memorabilia, attractive layout (flagstoned 17th-c former mill); bar food, well kept Courage Directors, good service, large woodburner, pool table; tables in walled courtyard *(A M Pring, J F Reay)*

☆ **Woolfardisworthy** [SS3321], *Farmers Arms*: Small cosy low-ceilinged thatched local, friendly landlord, decent food, spotless housekeeping, well kept Northern guest beers *(David Field, R Pottey)*

Yealmpton [A379 Kingsbridge—Plymouth; SX5751], *Rose & Crown*: Courage pub, pleasant surroundings and service, interesting specialities as well as more usual food *(T Cobden Pike)*

Children welcome means the pubs says it lets children inside without any special restriction. If it allows them in, but to restricted areas such as an eating area or family room, we specify this. Places with separate restaurants usually let children use them, hotels usually let them into public areas such as lounges. Some pubs impose an evening time limit – let us know if you find this.

Dorset

A fine new main entry this year is the Fox at Corscombe, doing very well under friendly licensees with a winning combination of good food and old-fashioned traditional surroundings. The welcoming and relaxed New Inn at Stoke Abbott also makes the main entries this year, after an absence. Other pubs currently doing particularly well include the timeless Spyway at Askerswell (it gains a Beer Award), the bustling Anchor down by the sea near Chideock, the Museum Inn at Farnham (it's our choice as Dorset Dining Pub of the Year), the Scott Arms at Kingston (a new landlord has settled in extremely well), the Marquis of Lorne at Nettlecombe (right back on form after reopening, nothing too much trouble for the current licensees), the prettily placed Thimble at Piddlehinton, and the unchanging Shave Cross Inn at Shave Cross. Several pubs newly gain our Award for well kept beers – the welcoming Three Horseshoes at Burton Bradstock, the New Inn at Cerne Abbas, the relaxed and comfortable Countryman at East Knighton, and the otherwise rather restauranty Pilot Boat in Lyme Regis. Three pubs newly qualifying for our Wine Award are the Red Lion at Cerne Abbas, the recently refurbished New Inn at Church Knowle and the atmospheric and attractively placed Smugglers at Osmington Mills. Prices in the area are on the high side, with beer costing significantly more than the national average; of the local chains, we found pubs tied to Greenalls (who took over the former local brewer Devenish but no longer brew themselves, getting their beers primarily from Whitbreads) and Eldridge Pope tended to have prices even higher than the local average, while Badger and, particularly, Palmers tied pubs tended to be cheaper. There are quite a few pubs to watch – most of these already inspected and approved – in the Lucky Dip section at the end of the chapter: Pickwicks in Beaminster, the Gaggle of Geese at Buckland Newton, Winyards Gap near Chedington, Kings Arms at East Stour, Acorn at Evershot, Avon Causeway at Hurn, Loders Arms at Loders, Crown at Marnhull (very promising new tenants), Bottle at Marshwood, Haven House at Mudeford, Halfway at Norden Heath, Three Elms at North Wootton, Inn in the Park in Poole, Mitre at Sandford Orcas (another particularly promising place) and Springhead at Sutton Poyntz; there's a good choice in Shaftesbury.

ABBOTSBURY SY5785 Map 2

Ilchester Arms

B3157

Readers do like staying at this handsome stone inn, not least because it's ideally placed for exploring Abbotsbury's varied attractions. Most famous amongst these is the ancient Swannery, but just as worthy of attention are the sheltered 20-acre gardens (closed in winter) not far from the remains of the abbey, with unusual tender plants and peacocks. Lanes lead from the back of the pub into the countryside, and you can see the sea from the comfortable back bedrooms. It's a characterful building, with a good cosy atmosphere in the rambling beamed rooms. The bustling main bar has over 1,000 prints on the walls, many depicting swans from the nearby abbey, as well as red plush button-back seats and spindleback chairs around cast-iron-framed and other tables on a turkey carpet, and chesterfield sofas in front of the open log fire. Hunting horns hang from the beams along with stirrups and horsebrasses, there's a stag's head, and some stuffed fish. Well kept Bass, Flowers Orginal, and Wadworths 6X on handpump, with a few malt whiskies; dominoes, cribbage, fruit machine, Sky TV, winter pool, and piped music. Popular bar food includes lunchtime sandwiches (not Sun), soup (£2), Dorset sausage baguette (£2.60), jacket potato with cheese and bacon (£3.95), home-made steak and ale pie (£4.95), roast beef and yorkshire pudding (£5.95), daily specials like stir-fried pork with bean sprouts, seafood such as local lemon sole (£8.95) or red mullet with chive sauce (£9.25), and home-made puddings (all £2.25); children's menu (from £1.95). Big breakfasts are served in the sizeable and attractive no-smoking conservatory restaurant, and there are afternoon teas in the bar. *(Recommended by Philip Orbell, Gordon, A H Denman, Risha Stapleton, Alan Skull, JKW, Basil Minson, George and Jeanne Barnwell, David Brokensha, Bill and Beryl Farmer, Myroulla West, Dr and Mrs J H Hills, Sue Holland, David Webster, Peter Neate, Susan Cody, A Plumb, C J Pratt)*

Greenalls ~ Managers Mike and May Doyle ~ Real ale ~ Meals and snacks ~ Restaurant ~ (01305) 871243 ~ Children in eating area of bar and in restaurant ~ Occasional live entertainment ~ Open 11-11 ~ Bedrooms(not 24-5 Dec): £48.40B

ASKERSWELL SY5292 Map 2

Spyway ★ 🍷 £ 🛏

Village signposted N of A35 Bridport—Dorchester; inn signposted locally; OS Sheet 194 map reference 529933

Blending in perfectly with a part of Dorset where rolling hills, thatched cottages and narrow lanes and bridleways are the norm, this simple country inn has long been a favourite with readers, and at the moment it seems more popular than ever. You can return after a couple of years' absence and feel as though you've only just left, so little changes – the friendly locals may even be sitting in exactly the same spots they occupied when you were last there. The particularly helpful licensee keeps an excellent choice of drinks: Ruddles County, Ushers Best, and Wadworths 6X on handpump, 20 decent wines by the glass, 23 country wines, around 40 whiskies and a big choice of unusual non-alcoholic drinks. The cosy and characterful little rooms have old-fashioned high-backed settles, cushioned wall and window seats, fine decorative china, harness and a milkmaid's yoke, and a longcase clock; there's also a no-smoking dining area decorated with blue and white china, old oak beams and timber uprights. Shove-ha'penny, table skittles, dominoes and cribbage. Promptly served and reasonably priced, the good bar food usually includes a range of generous ploughman's such as hot sausages and tomato pickle or home-cooked ham with pickle (from £3.25), and lots of salads (from £3.95 – the prawn is well-liked), as well as three-egg omelettes (£3.25), sausages and chips (£3.50), haddock or plaice (£3.60), evening extras like gammon and egg (£6.25) or 8oz steak (£8.25), and daily specials like vegetable bake (£3.50) or home-made steak and onion pie (£4.25). Good views from the big back garden, and plenty of pleasant walks along the paths and bridleways nearby. Eggardon Hill, which the pub's steep lane leads up, is one of the highest in the region, with lovely views of the downs and to the coast. No children. *(Recommended by Paul and Sue Sexton, Gordon, Alan Skull, Bill Edwards, JKW, Pete and Rosie Flower, John Beeken, Barry A Lynch, Ron Gentry, K S Pike, Dr and Mrs G H Lewis, George and Jeanne Barnwell, J H Bell, Huw and Carolyn Lewis, Mr and Mrs C R Little, Jim and Maggie Cowell, Paul Harrison, Jason Caulkin, S R Chapman, TOH, Ron Shelton, Chris Warne, Richard Dolphin, Mr and Mrs P B Dowsett, Roger and Sheila Thompson, John Sanders, Wayne Brindle, Pauline Bishop, Ian and Deborah Carrington)*

Free house ~ Licensees Don and Jackie Roderick ~ Real ale ~ Meals and snacks ~ (01308) 485250 ~ Open 10.30-2.30(3 Sat), 6-11

BISHOPS CAUNDLE ST6913 Map 2

White Hart

A3030

The biggish garden is rapidly becoming the centre of attention at this busy grey slate dining pub. Prettily floodlit at night, it's ideal for families, with a play area made up of trampolines, a playhouse with slides, and a sandpit. A covered area has been introduced out here for sitting outside on those summer days when the weather isn't quite so perfect, and as we went to press they told us they were hoping to add a small animal pen with rabbits and guinea pigs. They may have barbecues on summer Friday evenings. The big, irregularly-shaped bar inside has enough space to cater for all tastes and needs, as well as handsomely moulded low beams, ancient panelling, a good variety of seats and tables in decent wood, dark red curtains, and nice lamps. The walls are attractively decorated with brass trays and farming equipment. Good mostly home-made bar food includes sandwiches (£1.95), a wide range of ploughman's such as prawn or local blue vinny (£3.75), salads, vegetarian dishes (£4.95), and daily specials such as beef in Guinness with horseradish dumplings (£5.25), lamb rogan josh or gammon topped with hard-boiled egg and cheese sauce (£5.95); they also do a smaller appetite menu. They grow their own herbs and some of the vegetables. Well kept Badger Best and Tanglefoot on handpump, and they are hoping to stock guest ales; friendly helpful service; darts, alley skittles, fruit machine and piped music. *(Recommended by Brian Chambers, Gary Roberts, Ann Stubbs, Major and Mrs E M Warwick, John Hazel, Keith Widdowson, Marjorie and David Lamb, H D Wharton, J Muchelt, Don and Thelma Beeson, PWV, Guy Consterdine, Mrs C Archer)*

Badger ~ Managers Gordon and Joyce Pitman ~ Real ale ~ Meals and snacks ~ (01963) 23301 ~ Children in family area plus skittle alley ~ Open 11-2.30, 6.30-11 ~ Bedroom: £13/£25

BRIDPORT SY4692 Map 2

George

South St

Boisterous market traders drink to the strains of opera or jazz at this unusual town local, a pub that's a good deal more civilised than you might at first expect. Divided by a coloured-tile hallway, the two sizeable bars are full of old-fashioned charm and lots of genuine character; one is served by a hatch from the main lounge. There are nicely spaced old dining tables and country seats and wheelback chairs, big rugs on tiled floors, a mahogany bar counter, fresh flowers, and a winter log fire, along with an interesting pre-fruit machine ball game. An interesting range of drinks takes in well kept Palmers 200, Bridport, IPA and Tally Ho! on handpump, up to seven brands of calvados, a good wine list (with several available by the half-bottle or glass), local apple juice, and freshly squeezed orange and grapefruit, and there's an espresso coffee machine; friendly service. The wide range of bar food relies heavily on fresh local produce, and might typically include sandwiches (from £1.75), home-made soup (£1.90), home-made pâté (£2.95), ratatouille (£3.50), chicken in cream, mushroom and calvados sauce (£3.75), over a dozen omelettes (£3.95), home-made pies such as ham, chicken and mushroom (£4.75), whole grilled plaice (£4.95) and home-made puddings such as apple tart; you can usually see the licensee at work preparing your meal. Two tables are no smoking. You can only have an evening meal out of season if you make a reservation. *(Recommended by George Atkinson, R C Morgan, Brenda and Rob Fincham, Jeremy Williams, Anne Hyde, Jim and Maggie Cowell; more reports please)*

Palmers ~ Tenant John Mander ~ Real ale ~ Meals and snacks (not Sun lunch or bank holidays – and see note above about evening meals) ~ (01308) 423187 ~ Children in family room ~ Open 10am-11pm (8.30am for coffee every day); closed 25 Dec ~ Bedrooms: £18.50/£37

BURTON BRADSTOCK SY4889 Map 2

Three Horseshoes

Mill St

The cheery welcome is what really stands out about this friendly and well-placed thatched inn; you're always made to feel at home, either by the family in charge (who have been here 17 years now), or from the chatty locals. The pleasant roomy bar has an enjoyable atmosphere, an open fire, comfortable seating, and Palmers 200, Bridport, IPA and Tally Ho! on handpump. Nicely presented promptly served bar food includes burgers (from £2.25), good crab sandwich (£3.20), several ploughman's from (£3.40), steak and kidney pie (£3.85), fish and chips (£4.05), vegetarian pie (£4.50), lasagne (£4.95), grilled gammon (£6.25), crab salad (£7.90), puddings (from £2.15), children's meals (£2.55), and evening extras like beef curry (£5.90), Cantonese prawns (£5.95), and sirloin steak (£10.35). The menu probably has more groan-inducing jokes than have ever before been collected together in one place. The dining room is no smoking, and there's an unusual game called karum, an intriguing mix of shove-ha'penny and snooker. There are tables on the lawn, and Chesil beach and cliff walks are only 400 yards away. The pretty village is worth strolling around. *(Recommended by Basil Minson, Philip Orbell, Alan Skull, Julia Duplock, Ian Phillips, Ron Gentry, JM, PM, Mark and Toni Amor-Segan, Rona Murdoch, Mr and Mrs Red Shimwell, Eric J Locker, Mrs J A Powell)*

Palmers ~ Tenant Bill Attrill ~ Real ale ~ Meals and snacks ~ Partly no-smoking restaurant ~ (01308) 897259 ~ Children in eating area ~ Open 11-2.30, 6(7 winter)-11; closed evening 25 Dec ~ Bedrooms;/£31

CERNE ABBAS ST6601 Map 2

New Inn

14 Long Street

Built as a guest house for the nearby Benedictine abbey, this 15th-c inn has a stone roof estimated to weigh over 200 tons. The comfortable L-shaped lounge bar has oak beams in its high ceiling, seats in the stone-mullioned windows with a fine view down the main street of the attractive stone-built village, and a warm atmosphere. You'll still find the old pump and mounting block in the old coachyard, and behind it there are tables on a big sheltered lawn. They can seem very busy at lunchtime, when bar food includes sandwiches (from £1.80), ploughman's (£3.50), filled baked potatoes (from £3.50), fish and chips (£4.95), a cold carvery (from £5.50), and home-made specials like steak and kidney pie (£5.50) or three-fish grill in sorrel sauce (£7.50); in the evening they usually add soup (£1.90), herb and garlic mushrooms (£2.75), mussels in cider (£3.50), oriental stir-fry (£4.95), Scottish salmon in a herb and garlic sauce (£7.95), skate with black butter and capers (£9), char-grilled steaks (from (£9.50), and puddings such as summer pudding (£3.40). Well kept Eldridge Pope Hardy and Royal Oak on handpump, a good wine list with around 10 by the glass, and several malt whiskies; piped music. A good track leads up on to the hills above the village, where the prehistoric (and rather rude) Cerne Giant is cut into the chalk. *(Recommended by James House, JKW, A Plumb, Jack and Philip Paxton, Geoff Butts, Polly Marsh, Joan and Michel Hooper-Immins, Lynn Sharpless, Bob Eardley, David Holloway, J L Aperin, Andy and Jill Kassube, Major and Mrs E M Warrick, WHBM, Joy and Arthur Hoadley, Major T C Thornton, Paul Boot)*

Eldridge Pope ~ Managers Paul and Vee Parsons ~ Real ale ~ Meals and snacks ~ Restaurant ~ (01300) 341274 ~ Children welcome until 9pm ~ Open 11-3, 6-11 ~ Bedrooms: £25/£30

Most pubs in the *Guide* sell draught cider. We mention it specifically only if they have unusual farm-produced 'scrumpy' or even specialise in it.

Red Lion ♀

Long St

One of the most appealing features of the menu at this neatly kept and friendly pub is that most of the meals are available in a reduced size for those with a smaller appetite. The choice generally includes sandwiches (from £2.10), soup (£1.85), artichoke salad (£2.40), filled baked potatoes (from £3.40), good ploughman's (from £4), omelettes (from £4), asparagus pancake (£4.70), several vegetarian pasta dishes (£4.95), local trout (£6.95), grilled loin of pork (£7.50) and steaks (from £8.95), with puddings such as apricot strudel (£2.20); the prices quoted are for the standard size meals. Some of the vegetables come from local gardeners and allotments. Well kept Wadworths IPA and 6X and two changing guest beers like Bass or Ringwood Fortyniner on handpump, and a decent wine list, with several available by the glass; good cheerful service. Recently refurbished to give a lighter, more cottagey feel, the bar has a handsome wooden counter, wheelback chairs on the green patterned carpet, a good deal of china bits and pieces, and two little areas leading off; darts, skittle alley, piped music. Parts of the building are a lot older than the mid-Victorian frontage suggests, and there's a secluded flower-filled garden. *(Recommended by Paul Carter, James House, Basil J S Minson, Galen Strawson, Lynn Sharpless, Bob Eardley, Jack and Philip Paxton, Arthur and Joy Hoadley, Mike and Heather Barnes, Jane Basso, Sally Edsall, Jason Caulkin, David Holloway, Geoff Butts, Polly Marsh, Rona Murdoch)*

Free house ~ Licensees Brian and Jane Cheeseman ~ Real ale ~ Meals and snacks ~ (01300) 341441 ~ Children in eating areas and bowling alley ~ Open 11.30-3, 6.30-11

Royal Oak

Long Street

Obviously a popular spot for eating at the moment, this cheery Tudor pub can start filling up with lunchtime diners quite quickly, even in winter. The name of the licensees is the only thing that's altered since the last edition, and there certainly hasn't been any change to the friendly feel of the place. Sturdy oak beams line the three flagstoned communicating rooms, the neat courses of stonework decked out with antique china, brasses and farm tools, and lots of shiny black panelling. The open fireplaces are filled with fresh flowers. Well kept Flowers IPA and Original, Morlands Old Speckled Hen and Ringwood Best and Old Thumper on handpump from the uncommonly long bar counter, and half a dozen or so wines by the glass. Well-liked bar food includes sandwiches (from £1.50), winter soup, ploughman's (from £3.75), fried brie with cranberry sauce (£3.95), lasagne (£5), steak and kidney pie or fried lemon sole (£5.25), very good Portland crab salad (£5.50), steaks (from £6.25), gammon and egg (£7.25), changing specials, and puddings such as Jamaican crunch (£2.50). There are seats in the garden. *(Recommended by D Packman, Galen Strawson, James House, Jack and Philip Paxton, Lynn Sharpless, Bob Eardley, Basil Minson, David Holloway, Rona Murdoch, Joy and Arthur Hoadley, G U Briggs, Brig T I G Gray, B B Morgan, Gwyneth and Salvo Spadaro-Dutturi)*

Free house ~ Licensees Brendan and Liz Malone ~ Real ale ~ Meals and snacks ~ Children in eating area of bar ~ (01300) 341797 ~ Open 11-3, 6-11

nr CHIDEOCK SY4292 Map 1

Anchor

Seatown; signposted off A35 from Chideock

What really distinguishes this friendly and welcoming old pub is its splendid position, almost straddling the Dorset Coast Path and nestling beneath the 617 foot Golden Cap pinnacle. Just a few steps from the beach, seats and tables on the spacious front terrace are ideally placed for views, but you'll have to get there early in summer to bag a spot – idyllic seaside coves tend to draw the crowds, and this one is no exception. Several readers really enjoy the cheery holiday bustle in summer, but our own preference is to visit out of season, when the crowds have gone and the cosy little bars seem especially snug and welcoming. The two little rooms have warming winter fires, some sea pictures and interesting local photographs, a few fossils and shells, simple but comfortable seats around neat tables, and low white-planked ceilings; the family room and a further corner of the bar are no smoking, and there are friendly animals (especially the cats). Service is charming and obliging whatever time of year you go. Good bar food includes home-made soup (£2.45), sandwiches (from £1.75, crab £3.45), filled jacket potatoes (from £2.75), ploughman's (£3.75), beef curry (£4.25), home-made steak and kidney pie (£4.95), avocado filled with crabmeat (£5.25), specials such as stuffed peppers (£4.75), pigeon casserole or scallop and mushroom fettucine (£5.75), turkey in hazelnut cream (£6.75), and steak with green peppercorns (£8.45); children's dishes (from £1.95), afternoon clotted cream teas in summer. Well kept Palmers 200, Bridport, IPA and Tally Ho! on handpump, under light top pressure during the winter; freshly squeezed orange juice, and a decent little wine list. Shove-ha'penny, table skittles, cribbage, dominoes, fruit machine (summer only), a carom board, shut-the-box, and piped classical music. There are fridges and toasters in the bedrooms so you can make your own breakfast and eat it looking out over the sea. The licensees now also run the Ferry at Salcombe. *(Recommended by Eric Locker, Richard Dolphin, Christopher Gallop, K S Pike, Jeff Davies, Basil Minson, Jenny and Brian Seller, S Lonie, S Tait, Jeanne Cross, Paul Silvestri, George Atkinson, Mr and Mrs M P Aston, Andy and Jill Kassube, Marjorie and David Lamb, Dr R J Rathbone, D L Barker, Wayne Brindle)*

Palmers ~ Tenants David and Sadie Miles ~ Real ale ~ Meals and snacks (12-9.30 in summer; not winter Sun evenings) ~ (01297) 489215 ~ Well behaved children welcome ~ Folk, blues or jazz most Sat evenings ~ Open 11-11; 11-2.30, 6-11 in winter ~ Bedrooms: £16.50/£33

CHILD OKEFORD ST8313 Map 2

Saxon

Gold Hill; village signposted off A350 Blandford Forum—Shaftesbury and A357 Blandford—Sherborne; from centre follow Gillingham, Manston signpost

One of the most popular features of this friendly old village inn has long been the menagerie in the attractive back garden, the star of which is undoubtedly George, the Vietnamese pot-bellied pig. This year George has appeared on television and in magazines, but rather than becoming an old ham with all the acclaim, he still likes to work for his keep, and we're told he soon shifts late drinkers out of the bar. Other animals include Bass and Barny, the golden retrievers, three cats (William, Henry, and Thomas), contented rabbits in neat hutches, goldfish, an entertainingly wide variety of fowls from khaki campbells to vociferous geese, and a goat, Thea. Inside, the cosy bar is a quietly clubby room with a log fire, and leads through a lethally low-beamed doorway into a rather more spacious side room with a mix of tables including an attractive mahogany one in the centre, plank-panelled dado, and a big woodburning stove in its brick and stone fireplace. Simple, good value and neatly presented food includes lots of sandwiches (from £1.25, prawn £3.50, toasties from £1.50), filled baked potatoes (from £2.10), ploughman's (from £3.35), a daily curry (£3.85), home-cooked ham or shepherd's pie (£3.95), cod in batter (£4.50), home-made steak and kidney pie (£5.50) and 8oz rump steak (£8.95), with several daily specials and puddings such as raspberry and redcurrant pie (£2.50); children's menu (from £1.60). Well kept Bass, Butcombe Bitter and a guest beer on handpump, and a range of fruit wines; shove-ha'penny, cribbage, dominoes, piped music. It's a good place to come after walking on the nearby neolithic Hambledon Hill. Dry dogs are welcome on a lead. Please note, they no longer do bedrooms. *(Recommended by Andy and Jill Kassube, Douglas Adam, Brian Chambers, Marjorie and David Lamb, H D Wharton, John Hazel, Harriet and Michael Robinson, WHBM and others; more reports please)*

Free house ~ Licensees Roger and Hilary Pendleton ~ Real ale ~ Meals and snacks; not Tues evenings, or winter Sun evenings ~ (01258) 860310 ~ Children welcome in top bar ~ Open 11.30-2.30(3 Sat), 7-11

nr CHRISTCHURCH SZ1696 Map 2

Fishermans Haunt £

Winkton: B3347 Ringwood road nearly 3 miles N of Christchurch

Order spring water at this relaxing creeper-covered hotel and it may come from the 17th-c well in one of the series of interconnecting rooms. Each of these areas seems to suit a different mood, and there are a variety of furnishings and eye-catching adornments, from copper, brass and plates to stuffed fish and fishing pictures, and oryx and reindeer heads. At one end of the chain of rooms big windows look out on the neat front garden, and at the other there's a fruit machine and video game; one area is no-smoking. The back garden is a tranquil spot, close to weirs on the River Avon, and with tables among the shrubs, roses and other flowers on the lawn; it looks especially good at night when the building is decked with fairy lights. Good value straightforward bar food includes sandwiches (from £1.50; toasties from £2.10), soup (£1.60), sausages, onion rings and chips (£3.20), chicken nuggets (£3.70) and scampi (£4.50), with specials chalked on a board, a popular cold carvery, and children's meals (£2.75); the prices are unchanged from last year. Well kept Bass, Ringwood Best and Fortyniner, and Wadworths 6X on handpump, cheerful staff; piped music. *(Recommended by P Gillbe, D P and J A Sweeney, Wayne Brindle, J Muckelt; more reports please)*

Free house ~ Licensee James Bochan ~ Real ale ~ Meals and snacks (till 10) ~ Restaurant ~ Children in eating area of bar and in restaurant ~ (01202) 484071 ~ Open 10.30-2.30(3 Sat), 6-11; closed 25 Dec ~ Bedrooms: £32(£36B)/£54(£56B)

CHURCH KNOWLE (Isle of Purbeck) SY9481 Map 2

New Inn ♀

The landlord is very proud of the extensive refurbishments carried out at this comfortable partly-thatched pub over the last year; he reckons most people won't be able to tell anything has changed, though regular visitors may notice the little doorway that was discovered by chance behind one of the walls during the work. An arch connects the two main bar areas, nicely furnished with new farmhouse chairs and dining tables and with a log fire at each end, and by knocking down the wall between the old lounge bar and the restaurant they've been able to create a less formal dining lounge than before; one area is no-smoking. Most people come for the food, the reliable menu featuring dishes such as sandwiches (from £2), tasty home-made soup (£2.20, the Dorset blue vinny is still much enjoyed), good and quite elaborate ploughman's, with a choice of various local cheeses (£4.25), grilled sardines (£4.50), stir-fried prawns (£5), moules marinières, steak and kidney pie or roast of the day (£5.50), mushroom stroganoff (£6.80), game pie (£7), chicken tikka (£7.25), and puddings like lemon brûlée or summer pudding (£2.50), served with clotted cream; children's meals (from £3). You can generally buy locally made cheese to take away. Well kept Devenish Royal Wessex, Flowers Original and a guest such as Boddingtons or Whitbread Castle Eden; they've recently improved the wine list, and their dozen or so wines are all available in two sizes of glass. Good range of coffees and other hot drinks. You can hire the skittle alley for functions. Plenty of tables in the well-sized garden, which has fine views of the Purbeck hills. No dogs. *(Recommended by David Mead, Dr and Mrs J H Hills, Andy Thwaites, Christopher Gallop, Eric Locker, J L Alperin, David Eberlin, Mrs C Watkinson, Jason Caulkin, Charles Bardswell, Dr and Mrs R E S Tanner, Wayne Brindle, Trevor P Scott, Harriet and Michael Robinson, Dr N Holmes, A E and P McCully, G R Sunderland, R H Brown)*

Greenalls (Whitbreads) ~ Tenants Maurice and Rosemary Estop ~ Real ale ~ Meals and snacks ~ Restaurant ~ (01929) 480357 ~ Children in eating area of bar ~ Open 11-3, 6(7 winter)-11; may close winter Mons

If we don't specify bar meal times for a main entry, these are normally 12-2 and 7-9; we do show times if they are markedly different.

CORFE CASTLE (Isle of Purbeck) SY9681 Map 2

Fox

West Street, off A351; from town centre, follow dead-end Car Park sign behind church

The ruins that rise up from behind the very pleasant sun-trap back garden here are some of the most familiar and evocative in the country, and as the pub itself is made from the same stone as the castle, it seems likely that they were both built around the same time. It really is a characterful place, the cosily traditional feel owing a lot to the fact that it's been run by the same family for over 50 years, who despite alterations and additions, have managed to preserve its rather special atmosphere very well. The tiny front bar has small tables and chairs squeezed in, a painting of the castle in its prime among other pictures above the panelling, old-fashioned iron lamps, and hatch service. An ancient well was discovered in the lounge bar during restoration, and it's now on display there under glass and effectively lit from within. There's also a pre-1300 stone fireplace, and another alcove has further ancient stonework and a number of fossils. Promptly served enjoyable bar food includes sandwiches (from £1.95), home-made soup (£1.90), filled baked potatoes (from £3.15), well presented ploughman's (from £3.40), ham, egg and chips (£4.20), home-made steak and kidney pie or plaice (£4.75), daily specials like walnut and lentil bake (£4.75), crab salad (£6.25), sirloin steak au poivre (£8.60), and puddings (from £2.05). Well kept Eldridge Pope Royal Oak, Gibbs Mew Bishops Tipple, Greene King Abbot, Ind Coope Burton, and Wadworths 6X tapped from the cask; good dry white wine. Reached by a pretty flower-hung side entrance, the garden is divided into secluded areas by flower beds and a twisted apple tree, and really comes into its own in summer. The surrounding countryside is worth exploring and there's a local museum opposite. *(Recommended by B and K Hypher, Marjorie and David Lamb, Chris Westmoreland, Andy Thwaites, C A Hall, Alan Skull, D P and J A Sweeney, Nigel Clifton, Jack and Philip Paxton, Geoff Butts, Polly Marsh, Andy and Jill Kassube, David Eberlin, Paul Boot, John Honnor, James Skinner, David Holloway, D G Clarke, Wayne Brindle)*

Free house ~ Licensees Miss A L Brown and G B White ~ Real ale ~ Meals and snacks ~ (01929) 480449 ~ Open 11-3(2.30 winter), 6(6.30 winter)-11; closed 25 Dec

Greyhound

A351

Set directly beneath the battlements of the castle, this old-fashioned place has a notably friendly welcome – even if you arrive just before last orders on a busy summer lunchtime they still seem genuinely pleased to see you. The three small low-ceilinged areas of the main bar have mellowed oak panelling, old photographs of the town on the walls, a collection of old bottles, and flowers on each table; there's also a no-smoking family area. The pub can get crowded in season. Popular bar food includes large filled rolls (from £1.50), home-made winter soup (£2.25), generously filled baked potatoes (from £2.75), ploughman's (£3.25), home-made chilli con carne (£3.50), mushroom and nut fettucini (£3.95), and plenty of seafood such as Mediterranean prawns sautéed in garlic (£6), good fresh crab salad (£8.75), mixed seafood platter (£9.50) or lobster salad with prawns and crab (£12); prompt cheery service. Well kept Boddingtons, Flowers Original, and a guest beer on handpump. Sensibly placed darts, pool (winter), cribbage, dominoes, fruit machine, and juke box. There are benches outside at the front, and more in a small area at the back. Dogs welcome. *(Recommended by D P and J A Sweeney, Chris Westmoreland, Jack and Philip Paxton, John and Joan Nash)*

Whitbreads ~ Lease: A P and P C Southwell ~ Real ale ~ Meals and snacks ~ (01929) 480205 ~ Children in family room ~ Open 11-11; 11-3, 6.30-11 in winter ~ Bedrooms: £20/£40

> If we know a pub has an outdoor play area for children, we mention it.

CORSCOMBE ST5105 Map 2

Fox

On outskirts, towards Halstock

The standing of this cosy thatched pub has shot up in recent months, largely because of the very good thoughtfully prepared food. It's the sort of place where chips, freezers and microwaves are outlawed, and carefully chosen ingredients are supplied by locals and neighbours. The meat for example is specially hung for the pub, the pheasant comes from a nearby estate and a local car mechanic dives for the scallops. What's on the menu each day depends very much on what they feel like cooking that morning: excellent filled baguettes, vegetable soup (£2.75), various ploughman's with home-made chutney, and specials such as local squid with garlic and herbs (£4.50), rabbit casserole (£5.50), tagliatelle carbonara or cod in a crabmeat sauce (£6.25), local crab pancake (£6.50), scallops with shallots and white wine (£9.95), fillet of sea bass with fennel or breast of duck with cranberry (£10.50), and home-made ice creams and puddings (£2.95); they do a good Sunday roast. All meals are freshly prepared (they don't even use a microwave for reheating) so at busy times there may be a delay. Readers like the fact that despite the success of the food this is very much a traditional family-run pub of the old school, just as welcoming if you only want a drink. The room on the right has lots of beautifully polished copper pots, pans and teapots, harness hanging from the beams, small Leech hunting prints and Snaffles prints, Spy cartoons of fox hunting gentlemen, a long scrubbed pine table (a highly polished smaller one is tucked behind the door), an open fire and a newly laid old floor. In the left-hand room there are built-in wall benches, candles in champagne bottles on the cloth-covered or barrel tables, an assortment of chairs, lots of horse prints, antlers on the beams, two glass cabinets with a couple of stuffed owls in each, and an L-shaped wall settle by the stove in the fireplace. Well kept Exmoor, Fullers London Pride, Palmers Bridport and Smiles Best on handpump or tapped from the cask, home-made elderflower cordial, local cider, good wine list; darts, dominoes, bridge, backgammon. Tinker the greyhound and the two labradors Cracker and Bramble love a bit of attention. There's a big table in a covered courtyard with hanging baskets, roses and honeysuckle, and further seats across the quiet village lane, on a lawn by the little stream. This is a nice area for walks.
(Recommended by R Voorspuy, L M Miall, K S Pike, Mrs A Wells, Robert and Jill Maltby, Dr and Mrs J H Hills, Marcus Corah, Alice Valdes-Scott)

Free house ~ Licensee Martyn Lee ~ Real ale ~ Meals and snacks (not 25 Dec) ~ (01935) 891330 ~ Well-behaved children welcome ~ Open 12-2.30, 7-11; 11-11 Sat

CRANBORNE SU0513 Map 2

Fleur-de-Lys

B3078 N of Wimborne Minster

Now practically devoured by encroaching greenery, this lovely old inn is full of reminders of its illustrious heritage. A Gothic arch and a pair of ancient stone pillars are said to have come from the ruins of a nearby monastery, while the walls are lined with historical documents and mementoes of some of the people who have stayed here over the centuries, from Hanging Judge Jeffreys to Rupert Brooke (whose poem about the pub takes pride of place above the fireplace) and Thomas Hardy, who stayed here while writing *Tess of the d'Urbervilles.* The oak-panelled lounge bar is attractively modernised, and there's also a more simply furnished beamed public bar with well kept Badger Best and Tanglefoot on handpump, farm cider, and some good malt whiskies. Very good, popular bar food includes well-liked sandwiches, good soup, variously filled pancakes (£3.95), nutty mushroom layer or steak and kidney pudding (£4.95), halibut with mushrooms in a white wine sauce (£7.95), rack of lamb with rosemary and redcurrant sauce or pork in port and stilton sauce (£8.95), and puddings such as treacle tart or various pavlovas (£2.25). They do a good value Sunday lunch, for which it's best to arrive early. The welcoming landlord has been here 18 years now. Darts, shove-ha'penny, dominoes, cribbage, fruit machine, and piped music. There are swings and a slide on the lawn behind the car park. Bedrooms are comfortable and spacious, and it's an ideal base for exploring the area. *(Recommended by E G Parish, Pat and Robert Watt, H T Flaherty, Henen Pickering, James Owen, D Marsh, Robert and Jill Maltby, Sue Holland, David Webster, C J Pratt, Nigel Clifton, H D Wharton, Alan and Eileen Bowker, John Hazel, Keith Symons, Michael and Harriet Robinson)*

Badger ~ Tenant Charles Hancock ~ Real ale ~ Meals and snacks (not 25 Dec or evening 26 Dec) ~ (01725) 517282 ~ Children in eating area of bar and dining room ~ Open 10.30-2.30, 6-11 ~ Bedrooms: £17.50(£25B)/£38(£42B)

DORCHESTER SY6890 Map 2

Kings Arms

High East St

Always humming with activity, this rather elegant Georgian inn has long played a central role in Dorset history – there are strong links with Nelson, and the handsome first-floor bow window is memorable from Thomas Hardy's *Mayor of Casterbridge.* The spacious and comfortable bar has a civilised yet bustling atmosphere and some interesting old maps and pictures; one historic photograph shows Hardy here with a 1915 film crew. The most popular tables are those around the capacious fireplace, full of eaters enjoying the well-presented bar food: soup (£1.95), well-served sandwiches (from £2.35), ham and mushroom tagliatelli (£4.95), steak and kidney pie or fish and chips (£5.25), salads (from £5.50), chicken stir fry or poached salmon (£6.95), steaks (from £7.65), and several daily specials; they also have evening grills and a coffee shop. Lunchtime service can slow down if they're busy but the neatly dressed staff are consistently friendly and obliging. Well kept Bass, Boddingtons, Courage Directors, Marstons Pedigree, Ruddles County on handpump, Wadworths 6X on handpump, and a range of malt whiskies from the long mahogany bar counter; fruit machine, piped music. *(Recommended by Keith Archer, Ian Phillips, Jack and Philip Paxton, Andy and Jill Kassube, Barbara Hatfield, Peter Neate, Sue Holland, David Webster, Julian Bessa)*

Free house ~ Licensee Richard Lowe ~ Real ale ~ Meals and snacks ~ Restaurants ~ (01305) 265353 ~ Children in eating area of bar and restaurants ~ Live entertaiment Tues and Thurs evening ~ Open 11-3, 6-11; 11-11 Sat ~ Bedrooms: £43.95B/£57.95B

EAST CHALDON SY7983 Map 2

Sailors Return

Village signposted from A352 Wareham—Dorchester; from village green, follow Dorchester, Weymouth signpost; note that the village is also known as Chaldon Herring; Ordnance Survey sheet 194, map reference 790834

Tucked away in a tranquil spot near Lulworth Cove, this long low pub is quite a favourite with some readers, mainly because of its simple friendly atmosphere. It's been sympathetically renovated over the years, but the welcoming bar still keeps much of its original character, and the low-ceilinged stone-floored core now serves as a coffee house. The newer part has open beams showing the roof above, uncompromisingly plain and unfussy furnishings, and old notices for decoration; the dining area has solid old tables in nooks and crannies. A wide range of heartily served bar food takes in sandwiches, soup, filled baked potatoes, burgers, vegetarian meals and popular daily specials such as steak and kidney pie (£4.95) tasty whole gammon hock (£6.25) and local plaice (£6.95); it's worth coming early if you plan to eat, especially on Sunday, when the good value roast is popular. The restaurant is partly no smoking. Well kept Wadworths 6X, Whitbreads Strong Country and a guest beer on handpump, country wines, farm cider, and malt whiskies. Darts, shove-ha'penny, table skittles, dominoes, and piped music. Benches, picnic tables and log seats on the grass in front look down over cow pastures to the village. From nearby West Chaldon a bridleway leads across to join the Dorset Coast Path by the National Trust cliffs above Ringstead Bay. *(Recommended by Marjorie and David Lamb, Jerry and Alison Oakes, E A George, Mr and Mrs B Hobden, Mrs M A Mees, Jason Caulkin, Roger and Jenny Huggins, Charles Bardswell, David Mead, Dr Andrew Brookes, Neil Hardwick, V Regan, D Baker, Frank W Gadbois, John and Joan Nash, Eric J Locker)*

Free house ~ Licensees Bob and Pat Hodson ~ Real ale ~ Meals and snacks ~ Restaurant ~ (01305) 853847 ~ Children in small family room and in restaurant ~ Open 11-2.30, 6.30-11; closed evening 25 Dec

EAST KNIGHTON SY8185 Map 2

Countryman

Just off A352 Dorchester—Wareham; OS Sheet 194 map reference 811857

The atmosphere at this friendly pub is very relaxed and comfortable, but you can tell that plenty of thought and effort is being put into things. The main bar is a long carpeted room with plenty of character, a fire at either end, and a mixture of tables and wheelback chairs with cosier sofas. It opens into several other areas, including a no-smoking family room, a games bar with pool and darts, and a carvery. Quickly served and in big helpings, the wide range of popular bar food might include well filled sandwiches or baguettes (from £1.60), soup (£1.95), omelettes (from £3.10), ploughman's (from £3.85), a good few vegetarian meals like vegetable crumble (from £4.25), salads (from £5.25), prawns or scampi (£5.75), lemon sole (£5.95), daily specials like cod mornay (£4.75) or chicken breast in a creamy pepper sauce (£5), home-made puddings (£2.45) and children's meals (from £2.35); they do a good carvery (£8.95, two courses). Well kept Courage Best and Directors, John Smiths, Morlands Old Speckled Hen, Ringwood Best and Old Thumper, and Wadworths 6X on handpump, Scrumpy Jack cider, good choice of wines, and courteous well trained staff; piped music. Well behaved dogs allowed. There are tables and children's play equipment out in the garden. *(Recommended by Chris Westmoreland, Alan Skull, Jerry and Alsion Oakes, Bruce Bird, Martyn Kearey, Stan Edwards, Marjorie and David Lamb, John and Joan Nash, Steve Webb, Marianne Lantree, Keith Houlgate, Mrs M A Mees)*

Free house ~ Licensees Jeremy and Nina Evans ~ Real ale ~ Meals and snacks ~ Restaurant ~ (01305) 852666 ~ Children welcome ~ Open 11-3, 6-11; closed 25 Dec ~ Bedrooms: £32B/£45B

FARNHAM ST9515 Map 2

Museum

Village signposted off A354 Blandford Forum—Salisbury

Dorset Dining Pub of the Year

If you didn't know better you might easily drive past this unassuming looking old inn, though once you've visited you wouldn't make the same mistake twice. It's a very characterful place, with a particularly friendly landlord who dashes out of the kitchen to make a joke, then rushes back to prepare another meal. The waitress-served food is very much the main draw, with a wide range of regularly changing dishes such as home-made tomato and basil soup (£2.50), sandwiches (from £3.25 with very lavish salad), ploughman's (£3.95), local asparagus (£4.75), vegetable curry (£5.25), mouclade (£5.50 – not unlike moules marinières but easier to eat), venison sausages with red cabbage (£5.75), home-made steak and kidney pie (£5.95), fresh oysters (£6.25), gammon and eggs or pigeon pie (£6.50), salmon and crab fishcakes (£6.95), baked monkfish with Pernod and lime (£9.95), and puddings such as their very popular strawberry pancakes (£3.50). There's a calmly civilised feel to the Coopers Bar, which has green cloth-cushioned seats set into walls and windows, local pictures by Robin Davidson, an inglenook fireplace, and piped classical music. Very well kept Wadworths 6X and changing guests such as Greene King Abbot or Smiles Best on handpump, as well as a large range of decent wines and around twenty-six malt whiskies; darts, pool, trivia machine and juke box. There's a most attractive small brick-walled dining conservatory, leading out to a sheltered terrace with white tables under cocktail parasols, and beyond an arched wall is a garden with swings and a colourful tractor. Good value, simple bedrooms in converted former stables. The rustic village is largely thatch and flint. *(Recommended by Gwen and Peter Andrews, Paul Bachelor, Guy Consterdine, P Gillbe, Phil and Heidi Cook, J H Bell, Robert and Jill Maltby, DC, KC, Bernard and Kathleen Hypher, D and B Carter, K E Wohl, John Hazel, C Fisher)*

Free house ~ Licensee John Barnes ~ Real ale ~ Meals and snacks (service stops at 1.45 lunchtime) ~ Restaurant ~ (01725) 516261 ~ Children in eating areas and restaurant ~ Occasional live entertainment ~ Open 11-3(12 Sat), 6(7 Sat)-11; closed 25 Dec ~ Bedrooms: £35B/£50B

GODMANSTONE SY6697 Map 2

Smiths Arms £

A352 N of Dorchester

We often say that tables at pubs might fill up quickly but perhaps nowhere is that more true than at this 15th-c thatched building – there are only six of them inside. They couldn't add any more even if they wanted to, as this is one of those pubs with a claim to be the smallest in the country, measuring just 39ft lengthways, 14ft across and 12ft high. There are further seats and tables outside on a crazy-paved terrace, or on the grassy mound by the narrow River Cerne. The little bar has some antique waxed and polished small pews hugging the walls (there's also one elegant little high-backed settle), long wooden stools and chunky tables, National Hunt racing pictures and some brass plates on the walls, and an open fire. Well kept Ringwood Best tapped from casks behind the bar; friendly, helpful staff (the landlord is quite a character); piped music. Good home-made food typically includes sandwiches (from £1.35), ploughman's (from £2.90), jumbo sausage (£2.40), quiche (£3.25), chilli con carne (£3.30), a range of salads (from £3.55), home-cooked ham (£4.25), scampi (£4.90), daily specials such as curried prawn lasagne or topside of beef, and puddings. The building was originally a smithy, and Charles II is supposed to have stopped to have his horse shod here. A pleasant walk leads over Cowdon Hill to the River Piddle. Note they don't allow children inside. *(Recommended by John Hazel, Bill Edwards, Jack and Philip Paxton, Ted George, J Muckelt, V G and P A Nutt, David Holloway, John and Joan Nash)*

Free house ~ Licensees John and Linda Foster ~ Real ale ~ Meals and snacks (till 9.45) ~ (01300) 341236 ~ Open 11-3, 6-11; winter evening opening 6.30

KINGSTON (Isle of Purbeck) SY9579 Map 2

Scott Arms

B3069

This creeper-clad stone house is doing exceptionally well at the moment, with every one of the reports we've received over the last year united in high praise for the food, atmosphere, and of course the setting. The views of Corfe Castle and the Purbeck Hills from the well kept garden are quite magnificent, and it's a lovely spot to relax after enjoying one of the area's many good walks. They do get very busy (even in winter), but the rambling warren-like rooms are capable of absorbing more people than you might think. All have old panelling, stripped stone walls, some fine antique prints and a friendly, chatty feel; an attractive room overlooks the garden, and there's a decent extension well-liked by families. The highly regarded bar food includes home-made soup (£2.25), mushrooms in cream and garlic (£2.95), baked avocado with crab and prawn (£3.25), a big proper ploughman's (£3.50), steak and kidney pie (£5.75), quite hot and flavoursome curries and chilli (£5.50), excellent specials such as seasonal crab salad (£6.50), chicken stuffed with spinach and bacon in red wine and strawberry sauce (£7.25) and venison with redcurrant and port sauce, good puddings (there's an unusual oatmeal base on the cheesecake), and children's meals (£2.95); part of the dining room is no smoking. Well kept Boddingtons, Courage Directors, Ringwood Best and Wadworths 6X on handpump; efficient service from pleasant, smiling staff. *(Recommended by David Mead, Chris Westmoreland, E G Parish, John and Joan Nash, P J Caunt, Doreen and Brian Hardham, P Gillbe, Derek Patey, Jack and Philip Paxton, WHBM, B and K Hypher, James House, Alan Skull, Trevor P Scott, Charles Bardswell, John Wheeler, James Skinner)*

Free house ~ Lease: Simon Trevis ~ Real ale ~ Meals and snacks; not 25 Dec ~ (01929) 480270 ~ Children welcome except in bar ~ Acoustic blues every other Weds ~ Open 11-2.30, 6-11

LANGTON HERRING SY6182 Map 2

Elm Tree

Village signposted off B3157

One of the licensees at this slate-roofed cottage used to be a chef at the Dorchester, and in the year or so since arriving here he's worked hard to maintain the pub's reputation for food. Favourite dishes on the menu over the last few months have included sandwiches, artichoke hearts with mushrooms and mozarella (£4.75), good moules marinières (£5.75), and steak and ale pie (£6.95); they also have a brunch menu (£2.95), plenty of fresh fish on the specials board, and a range of interestingly flavoured home-made ice creams. Boddingtons and Greenalls Original on handpump. The main carpeted rooms have beams and walls festooned with copper, brass and bellows, cushioned window seats, red leatherette stools, windsor chairs, and lots of tables; one has some old-fashioned settles and an inglenook. The traditionally furnished extension gives more room for diners. Outside in the pretty flower-filled sunken garden are colourful hanging baskets, flower tubs, and tables; a track leads down to the Dorset Coast Path, which here skirts the eight-mile lagoon enclosed by Chesil Beach. *(Recommended by Basil Minson, P Gillbe, D C Pressey, Howard Clutterbuck and others)*

Greenalls ~ Tenants Roberto D'Agostino, L M Horlock ~ Real ale ~ Meals and snacks (till 10pm) ~ (01305) 871257 ~ Children welcome ~ Open 11-3, 6.30-11

LYME REGIS SY3492 Map 1

Pilot Boat

Bridge Street

Handy for the sea and beaches, this is a very reliable spot for a good meal. The food definitely does seem to be the main attraction, with a wide range of tasty waitress-served dishes: sandwiches (from £1.35, delicious crab £2.95), home-made soup (£1.95; the bouillabaisse is wonderful), good ploughman's (£3.25), excellent crab pâté (£3.50), salads (from £5.25), avocado and sweetcorn bake (£5.50), steak and kidney pie (£5.95), pork and cider casserole (£6.25), several fish dishes such as local trout (£7.50) or whole grilled lemon sole (£9.50), steaks (from £9.50), specials such as plaice fillets stuffed with asparagus (£7.50), and children's dishes (from £1.95, not just burgers and fish fingers). The restaurant is no smoking. Well kept Palmers Bridport, IPA and Tally Ho on handpump, and a decent wine and liqueur list; friendly considerate service. The light, airy and comfortable bar is interestingly decorated with local pictures, Navy and helicopter photographs, lobster-pot lamps, sharks' heads, an interesting collection of local fossils, a model of one of the last sailing ships to use the harbour, and a notable collection of sailors' hat ribands. At the back, there's a long and narrow lounge bar overlooking the little River Lym; darts, dominoes, cribbage. There are seats on a terrace outside. The licensees run another Lyme Regis pub, the Cobb Arms, which has bedrooms. *(Recommended by Bruce Bird, D P and J A Sweeney, Ian Phillips, Nigel Warr, Jill and Antony Townsend, M E Wellington, R C Morgan, TOH, Chris Thomas, C J Pratt, Myroulla West, Joan and Michel Hooper-Immins, Liz and John Soden, Steve Huggins, Stan Edwards, Jason Caulkin, Julian Bressa, A Craig)*

Palmers ~ Tenants Bill and Caroline Wiscombe ~ Real ale ~ Meals and snacks (till 10 in summer) ~ Restaurant ~ (01297) 443157 ~ Children welcome ~ Occasional live entertainment ~ Open 11-3, 6.30-11 (winter 11-2.30, 7-11)

MARNHULL ST7718 Map 2

Blackmore Vale 🍷

Burton Street; quiet side street

The home-made bar food at this welcoming and warmly atmospheric old pub has recently won a couple of awards in the trade press, and it's just as highly regarded by readers. The wide choice of thoughtfully presented dishes includes sandwiches (from £1.40), soup (£1.70), a separate menu of filled baked potatoes (from £1.95), ploughman's (from £3.65), dimsum (£3.75), ham and egg (£4.25), several vegetarian dishes such as nut cutlet en croûte or chestnut patties in red wine sauce (£5.45), steak and kidney pie (£5.45), their speciality Voodoo chicken (£6.95), tipsy crab pie (£7.45), steaks (from £8.45), duck breast with port, cranberry and orange sauce (£8.75), daily specials, and lots of home-made puddings; Friday is fish night, and they generally have three roasts on Sunday. They will bring your food to the garden, where one of the tables is thatched; service can slow down when they're pushed. The comfortably modernised lounge bar is decorated with fourteen guns and rifles, keys, a few horsebrasses and old brass spigots on the beams, and there's a log fire. Well kept Badger Best, Hard Tackle and Tanglefoot on handpump, farm cider and a good wine list. Darts, cribbage, dominoes, shove-ha'penny, fruit machine, piped music, and a skittle alley. Parts of the building date back 400 years, and it started out as a brewhouse and bakehouse for the Strangeways Estate; you can still see the entrance to the old bake oven at the end of the bar, near the fireplace. The pub was used by Thomas Hardy in *Tess of the D'Urbervilles* as the model for Rollivers. ***(Recommended by Richard Dolphin, John Hazel, Keith Stevens, C H and P Stride, Dr and Mrs J H Hills, WHBM, Major T C Thornton)***

Badger ~ Tenants Roger and Marion Hiron ~ Real ale ~ Meals and snacks (till 10pm) ~ (01258) 820701 ~ Children in eating area of bar ~ Open 11.30-2.30, 6.30-11

MILTON ABBAS ST8001 Map 2

Hambro Arms 🛏

Well set in another attractive part of the county, this pretty pub nestles in the heart of a late 18th-c landscaped village, its gently winding lane lined by lawns and cream-coloured thatched cottages. The beamed front lounge bar, reached through a maze of stone corridors, has a bow window seat looking down over the houses, captain's chairs and round tables on the carpet, and in winter an excellent log fire. Well kept Boddingtons and Flowers Original on handpump, good wine list; darts, juke box and fruit machine in the cosy back public bar. Bar food includes sandwiches, soup, ploughman's, fish like halibut or salmon in lobster and prawn sauce, and specials such as pheasant in mushroom and red wine (£6.95) or venison steaks in a rich madeira sauce (£8.95); roast Sunday lunch. The outside terrace has some tables and chairs. No children. ***(Recommended by E G Parish, WHBM, P Gillbe, JN, J Muckelt, Andy Jones, Andy and Jill Kassube, John Honnor, M V and J Melling, Dr and Mrs Nigel Holmes)***

Greenalls ~ Tenants Ken and Brenda Baines ~ Real ale ~ Meals and snacks ~ Milton Abbas (01258) 880233 ~ Open 11-2.30, 6.30-11 ~ Bedrooms: £30B/£50B

Most of the big breweries now work through regional operating companies, with different names. If a pub is tied to one of these regional companies, we put the parent company's name in brackets – in the details at the end of each main entry.

NETTLECOMBE SY5195 Map 2

Marquis of Lorne

Close to Powerstock and can be found by following the routes described under the entry included for that village – see below

This delightful country pub went through something of a sticky patch following the departure of the tenants who had made it such a well-loved main entry, and it even closed for a while, so it's good to see that under the Barretts the place is well and truly back on form. In fact we've had more reports on it over the last year than for any other pub in Dorset, all of them highlighting especially the welcome and attention they've received from the landlord and his wife. One reader was lucky enough to visit when Mr Barrett's brother and friends, all members of a choir, were treating everyone to an impromptu concert. Also coming in for praise is the food, all listed on blackboard menus and typically including dishes like home-made soup (£1.85), sandwiches (from £2.25), ploughman's (£3.45), moules marinières or fresh local asparagus (£3.95), hot spicy crab (£4.25), beef, Guinness and stilton pie (£5.95), pork steak marinated in orange and basil or pasta courgette and stilton bake (£6.25), local plaice with lime butter (£6.95), chicken breast in garlic and herbs (£7.50), grilled trout stuffed with prawns and aspargus (£8.95), mixed grill (£9), and puddings such as treacle tart; the vegetables are excellent. One dining area is no smoking. The bustling main bar has a log fire, mahogany panelling and old prints and photographs around its neatly matching chairs and tables; two dining areas lead off, the smaller of which has another log fire and is no smoking. A wooden-floored snug has darts, cribbage and table skittles. Well kept Palmers Bridport, 200 and Tally Ho! on handpump, and good wine list with usually around eight by the glass; piped music is mainly classical. Outside, the summer hanging baskets are pretty, and the big garden has masses of swings, climbing frames and so forth among the picnic tables under its apple trees. Good breakfasts include a lovely fruit salad. It's quite a drive to get to the pub, but you couldn't hope for a more pleasant journey, through lovely peaceful countryside. *(Recommended by Dr and Mrs J H Hills, P J Hanson, Mrs G Slade, Philip Orbell, Paul and Sue Sexton, M Gibbons, D G Taylor, Philip Herbert, G L and N M S Royal, Avril Hanson, K Guppy, Mr and Mrs M Spring, Gordon, Ms Egan-Strang and others)*

Palmers ~ Tenant Ian Barrett ~ Real ale ~ Meals and snacks ~ (01308) 485236 ~ Children in eating area ~ Open 11-2.30, 6(6.30 winter)-11; closed 25 Dec ~ Bedrooms: £30B/£55B

OSMINGTON MILLS SY7341 Map 2

Smugglers

Village signposted off A353 NE of Weymouth

The Smuggs, as locals like to call this partly thatched stone-built inn, was once the refuge of the King of the smugglers, French Peter. The sea is just a short stroll away down through the pretty combe, and it's easy to see why the pub was considered such a convenient landing place for contraband. It's a well run and spacious place, with shiny black panelling and woodwork dividing the bar into lots of cosy, friendly areas. Soft red lantern-lights give an atmospheric hue to the stormy sea pictures and big wooden blocks and tackle on the walls, and there are logs burning in an open stove. Some seats are tucked into alcoves and window embrasures, with one forming part of an upended boat. Quickly served by friendly staff, the good bar food includes home-made soup (£2), first-rate filled french sticks (from £3.25), ploughman's (£4), filled baked potatoes (from £4.50), artichoke hearts and wild mushrooms in a tomato and basil sauce (£4.75), home-made steak, kidney and mushroom pie (£5.50), a la carte meals such as wild mushroom and nut fettucine (£8) or caribbean chicken (£8.75), and daily specials such as very good monkfish in red wine sauce (£9.50); theme nights like Cajun, French or medieval. Service stays efficient and friendly even when they're busy. Half the restaurant area is no smoking. Well kept Courage Directors, Ind Coope Burton, Morlands Old Speckled Hen, Ringwood Old

Thumper, and Wadworths 6X on handpump, and a fine choice of wines by the glass. Darts, pool and fruit machine are well segregated, dominoes and shut-the-box, and piped music. There are picnic tables out on crazy paving by a little stream, with a thatched summer bar and a good play area over on a steep lawn; barbecues out here in summer. It gets very busy in high season (there's a holiday settlement just up the lane). *(Recommended by Howard and Margaret Buchanan, A Plumb, Keith Pollard, J M T Morris, Mrs B M Fyffe, Charles Bardswell, John and Joan Nash, Peter and Lynn Brueton)*

Free house ~ Licensee Bill Bishop ~ Real ale ~ Meals and snacks ~ Restaurant ~ (01305) 833125 ~ Children in restaurant and family room ~ Occasional jazz, blues and steel bands ~ Open 11-11; 11-2.30, 6.30-11 in winter (closed 25 Dec) ~ Bedrooms: £28B/£55B

PIDDLEHINTON SY7197 Map 2

Thimble

B3143

Buried amongst winding Dorset lanes, this pretty thatched pub is approached by a little footbridge over the River Piddle. It's a pretty spot, with masses of flowers in the garden and attractive floodlighting at night, but while this inevitably means it's something of a crowd-puller, there's never any resulting drop in quality or efficiency. In any case there's plenty of room in the neatly kept and friendly low-beamed bar, where attractive furnishings include an open stone fireplace and a recently discovered deep well. Well-praised and attractively presented bar food includes sandwiches (from £1.60), filled baked potatoes (from £1.75), home-made soup (£2.10), home-made pâté (£2.90), ploughman's (from £3.60), spinach and ricotta cheese cannelloni (£4.65), breaded whole tail scampi (£5.75), steak and oyster pudding (£5.95), gammon and egg (£6.95), steaks (from £9.50), and puddings (£2.50), with weekly specials like chicken stir-fry (£5.20) or beef, venison and strong ale pie (£5.70), and fresh fish such as bream, skate or sea bass (as available); good Sunday roast (£5.35). Well kept Badger Hard Tackle, Eldridge Pope Hardy Country, and Ringwood Best and Old Thumper on handpump, along with farm cider and quite a few malt whiskies; friendly service. *(Recommended by Bronwen and Steve Wrigley, John and Sheila French, Gordon, Christopher Gallop, David Lamb, Julie Peters, Galen Strawson, Jack and Philip Paxton, David Dimock, K E Wohl, R A F Montgomery, G U Briggs, Jason Caulkin)*

Free house ~ Licensees N R White and V J Lanfear ~ Real ale ~ Meals and snacks ~ (01300) 348270 ~ Well-behaved children welcome ~ Open 12-2.30, 7-11

PLUSH ST7102 Map 2

Brace of Pheasants

Village signposted from B3143 N of Dorchester at Piddletrenthide

Charmingly placed in a fold of hills surrounding the Piddle Valley, this long, low 16th-c thatched pub is one of those places where the licensees put genuine enthusiasm and extra care into making their visitors happy. Relaxed but civilised, the beamed bar has good solid tables, some oak window seats as well as the windsor chairs, fresh flowers, a heavy-beamed inglenook at one end with cosy seating inside the old fireplace, and a good log fire at the other. A very wide choice of imaginative but never over-ambitious home-made bar food might include soup (£1.85), crab savoury (£3), ploughman's (from £3.50), asparagus hollandaise or soft herring roes with garlic butter (£3.50), ham , egg and chips (£4.75), venison sausages (£5.25), local plaice (£5.75), pies such as steak and kidney or lamb and rosemary (£6.25), and a la carte dishes such as lemon sole, pork fillet with blue cheese and sherry or rack of lamb with rosemary and redcurrant (£9.75), and steamed salmon and scallops with watercress sauce (£9.95); even the children's menu (from £1.75) is more interesting than the norm. The restaurant and family room are no smoking. Well kept Bass, Flowers Original and Wadworths 6X, and they do country wines;

darts, alley skittles, and dominoes. The friendly labrador is called Bodger. Behind is a decent-sized play garden with swings, an aviary, a rabbit in a cage and a lawn sloping up towards a rookery. Originally a row of cottages that included the village forge, the pub lies alongside Plush Brook, and an attractive bridleway behind goes to the left of the woods and over to Church Hill. *(Recommended by John and Joan Nash, Jerry and Alison Oakes, John Hazel, James House, John and Sheila French, Christopher Gallop, Stan Edwards, K S Pike, H D Wharton, Bronwen and Steve Wrigley, John and Tessa Rainsford)*

Free house ~ Licensees Jane and Geoffrey Knights ~ Real ale ~ Meals and snacks ~ Restaurant ~ (01300) 348357 ~ Children in family room and restaurant ~ Open 11.30(12 in winter)-2.30, 7-11

POWERSTOCK SY5196 Map 2

Three Horseshoes 🍷

Can be reached by taking Askerswell turn off A35 then keeping uphill past the Spyway Inn, and bearing left all the way round Eggardon Hill – a lovely drive, but steep narrow roads; a better road is signposted West Milton off the A3066 Beaminster—Bridport, then take Powerstock road

Fresh fish features very strongly on the menu at this popular dining pub, and they've started running half-day courses demonstrating how to select and cook it; they also do weekend courses where you could end up cooking the meals in the restaurant. If catching the fish is more your angle, the pub is handy for the nearby trout ponds, or you can book a six-hour trip out to sea. Depending on availability, diners might find listed on blackboard fish dishes such as skate wing with capers (£8.95), fillet of brill with onions, wine and cream (£9.50), monkfish tail provençale (£10.50), or char-grilled sea bass (£12.50), while other dishes on the menu (reckoned by readers to be slightly poorer value than in previous years) include filled french sticks or various soups (from £2.50), spinach pancake with cheese sauce (£4.50), moules marinières (£4.95), various pasta dishes (£6.50, with salad and as much bread as you want), good summer kebabs (£7.95), wild rabbit casserole (£8.50), venison in a red wine sauce (£10.50), and puddings like sunken chocolate soufflé or strawberry meringue roulade (from £3). Good breakfasts with home-made marmalade. The restaurant is no smoking. Well kept Palmers Bridport (very nicely priced in summer), 200, IPA and Tally Ho! on handpump, plenty of wines by the glass, and freshly squeezed fruit juice. The comfortable L-shaped bar has country-style chairs around the polished tables, pictures on the stripped panelled walls, and warm fires; you may come across Daisy and Jess, the friendly retrievers, or Charlie the springer spaniel. The garden has swings and a climbing frame, and from the neat lawn rising steeply above the pub, there are lovely uninterrupted views towards the sea. Though they tell us they allow children, a couple of readers with very young children have felt slightly unwelcome. *(Recommended by K S Pike, Susan Mullins, Bill Edwards, PO, Gordon, Mark and Michelle Aston, Barry Lynch, Major and Mrs Warwick, Mrs S A Burrows, F C Johnston, D L Barker, Huw and Carolyn Lewis, Mrs Margaret Barker, J L Alperin, Gethin Lewis, Barbara Hatfield, J Muckelt, C J Pratt, DC, Mr and Mrs J A Wilson, Dr R J Rathbone)*

Palmers ~ Tenant P W Ferguson ~ Real ale ~ Meals and snacks ~ Restaurant ~ (01308) 485328 ~ Open 11-3, 6-11 ~ Bedrooms: £24(£30B)/£40(£50)

SHAVE CROSS SY4198 Map 1

Shave Cross Inn ★

On back lane Bridport—Marshwood, signposted locally; OS Sheet 193, ref 415980

Travelling monks used to lodge at this peaceful partly 14th-c thatched inn on the last stage of their pilgrimage to the shrine of St Wita at Whitchurch. Whilst here many of them picked up the distinctive haircuts that give the pub its name, the best carried out by a landlord apparently known as Atte the Shaver. A visit today doesn't have quite the same fringe benefits, but it's still a notably friendly place well worth tracking down, very popular with readers at the moment. The original timbered bar is a lovely flagstoned room, surprisingly roomy and full of character, with one big table in the middle, a smaller one by the window seat, a row of chintz-cushioned windsor chairs, and an enormous inglenook fireplace with plates hanging from the chimney breast. The larger carpeted side lounge has a dresser at one end set with plates, and modern rustic light-coloured seats making booths around the tables. Popular, promptly served bar food includes fine ploughman's (from £2.75), good sausages (£2.75), steak sandwich (£3.95), mushroom and spinach lasagne (£3.90), salads (from £3.75), vegetable balti (£4.15), kebabs of sweet and sour pork and spicy lamb (£5.95), mixed grill (£7.95), daily specials like tiger prawns in filo pastry (£4.35), chicken, ham and mushroom pie (£4.45), char-grilled shark or swordfish steak (£7.45), puddings such as gooseberry crumble (£1.85), and children's meals (from £1.95). Well kept Badger Best, Bass and Eldridge Pope Royal Oak on handpump, and local cider in summer; cheery ad welcoming staff – one barman is quite skilled at juggling. Darts, alley skittles, dominoes and cribbage. The pretty flower-filled sheltered garden has a thatched wishing-well, a goldfish pool, a children's play area, and a small secluded campsite for touring caravans and campers. *(Recommended by Pete and Rosie Flower, Bill Edwards, Clive Gilbert, M E Wellington, Marjorie and David Lamb, Gordon, G Washington, Alan Skull, Galen Strawson, K S Pike, Ron Gentry, D L Barker, Mrs A R E Bishop, David and Michelle Hedges, David Holloway, Chris Warne, David Eberlin, Chris Tarrant)*

Free house ~ Licensees Bill and Ruth Slade ~ Real ale ~ Meals and snacks (not Mon, except Bank holidays) ~ (01308) 868358 ~ Children in lounge bar ~ Open 12-2.30(3 Sat), 7-11; closed Mon (except bank holidays)

STOKE ABBOTT ST4500 Map 2

New Inn

Village signposted from B3162 and B3163 W of Beaminster

Back as a main entry after several years away, this friendly 17th-c thatched inn is under its current licensees a wonderfully relaxing place to come for a good lunch. The enterprising specials cooked by the landlady are the meals to go for, with favourite dishes this year including their speciality beef pie topped with cheese and onion rather than a crust (£4.25), louisiana chicken (£5) and cashew nut balls in a mushroom sauce (£5.25); they also have a more straightforward menu with sandwiches (from £1.90), ploughman's (from £3), battered fish and the like. The carpeted bar has around 200 horse brasses covering its beams, as well as wheelback chairs and cushioned built-in settles around simple wooden tables, and settles built into snug stripped stone alcoves on either side of the big log fireplace. They found another fireplace with handsome panelling during work on the building. Well kept Palmers Bridport and IPA on handpump; darts, table skittles, piped music. Sheltering behind a golden stone wall which merges into an attractively planted rockery, the well kept garden has a long gnarled silvery log to sit on, wooden benches by the tables, swings, and usually a donkey and some sheep in a paddock. There are nice views from here towards the hills. *(Recommended by Hetty Owen-Smith, Mr and Mrs D Carter, Bill Edwards, Galen Strawson, J L Alperin, John Fisher)*

Palmers ~ Tenants Paul and Donna Bennett ~ Real ale ~ Meals and snacks (not Mon lunchtimes except Bank holidays) ~ (01308) 868333 ~ Children welcome ~ Open 12-2.30, 7-11 ~ Bedrooms: £17.50/35

SYMONDSBURY SY4493 Map 1

Ilchester Arms

Village signposted from A35 just W of Bridport

Even on a Saturday evening you should be able to find a tranquil corner at this attractive old thatched inn, pleasantly tucked away in a peaceful little village. Cosily friendly, the open-plan bar has rustic benches and tables, seats in the mullioned windows, and a high-backed settle built into the bar counter next to the big inglenook fireplace. Another area, also with an open fire, has candle-lit tables and is used mainly for dining in the evening and at weekends; this part of the pub is no smoking. Under their new chef the decent range of bar food includes home-made soup (£2.25), filled rolls or baked potatoes (from £2.50), ploughman's (£3.75), salads (from £3.95), gammon steak or pork dijon (£4.75), vegetarian dishes (from £4.75), lamb cassoulet (£4.95), whole lemon sole (£6.25), and daily blackboard specials such as rabbit in cider (£5.25), veal escalopes in garlic and mushrooms (£6.75), and fillet of plaice stuffed with asparagus (£8.50); children's menu (from £1.75). Well kept Palmers Best, Bridport and 200 on handpump or tapped from the cask, welcoming licensees. Darts, dominoes, cribbage, fruit machine, table and alley skittles, piped music. There are tables outside in a quiet back garden by a stream. The high-hedged lanes which twist deeply through the sandstone behind the village lead to good walks through the wooded low hills above the Marshwood Vale. *(Recommended by Basil Minson, Paul and Sue Sexton, Jenny and Brian Seller, Gordon, Gwyneth and Salvo Spadaro-Dutturi, Dr R J Rathbone, Reg and Carrie Carr, TOH, R M Bloomfield)*

Palmers ~ Tenants Dick and Ann Foad ~ Real ale ~ Meals and snacks (not winter Mon) ~ Restaurant ~ (01308) 422600 ~ Children welcome ~ Open 11-3, 6.30-11; 11.30-2.30, 7-11 winter ~ Bedrooms: £15/30 (family room)

TARRANT MONKTON ST9408 Map 2

Langton Arms

Village signposted from A354, then head for church

Becoming increasingly useful for families especially, this is a very attractive 17th-c thatched inn, prettily placed next to the church in a lovely Dorset village. The good value bar meals are popular, with extensive blackboard menus offering dishes such as Poole Bay crab soup (£2.30), wild boar and venison sausages in red wine gravy or pasta parcels filled with spinach and ricotta cheese (£4.25), sweet and sour prawn fritters, breast of chicken in a cheese and bacon sauce, fillet of salmon in a prawn and white wine sauce, and puddings like coffee and tia maria cheesecake (£1.95); they also have Monday fish and chips (£2.95), Tuesday pizza and pasta (from £3.50), Thursday steaks (from £4.25), and children's meals (2 courses £1.99). The well kept beers change all the time – they've had over 150 brews pass through the handpumps in the last couple of years – but as we went to press they stocked Morlands Old Speckled Hen, Ringwood Fortyniner, Smiles Best and Tisbury Best. Decent wines, some by the glass, helpful staff. The comfortable beamed main bar has settles that form a couple of secluded booths around tables at the carpeted end, window seats, and another table or two at the serving end where the floor's tiled. There's a big inglenook fireplace in the public bar, and an old stable has been converted into a no-smoking restaurant area; darts, pool. The skittle alley doubles as a family room during the day, and there are children's play areas in here and in the garden, where you may also find summer barbecues and a bouncy castle. Tracks lead up to Crichel Down above the village, and Badbury Rings, a hill fort by the B3082 just south of here, is very striking. *(Recommended by Revd A Nunnerley, H T Flaherty, Phil and Heidi Cook, John Hazel, Richard Dolphin, Gary Roberts)*

Free house ~ Licensees Philip Davison, James Cossins, Michael Angel ~ Real ale ~ Meals and snacks (till 10pm) ~ Evening restaurant (not Sun or Mon ~ (01258) 830225 ~ Children in family room ~ Open 11.30-11; 11.30-3, 6-11 winter ~ Bedrooms: £39B/£54B

UPWEY SY6684 Map 2

Old Ship 🍷

Ridgeway; turn left off A354 at bottom of Ridgeway Hill into old Roman Rd

Warmly friendly and cottagey, this pretty little pub has once again been highly recommended for its food over the last year. The generously served meals might typically include home-made soup (£1.95), sandwiches (from £2.25), very good garlic mushrooms (using proper field mushrooms, £3.95), three-egg omelettes (from £3.10), cheese and broccoli quiche or ploughman's (£3.95), ham and egg (£4.75), plaice (£6.25), cold meats with a very good help-yourself salad bar (£6.75), parcel of lamb filled with forcemeat and and rosemary (£7.50), steaks (from £8.95), daily specials like fillet of cod Bretonne (£6.25) or chicken stuffed with pork and herbs in a white wine and mushroom sauce (£7.25), and good puddings; three-course Sunday lunches (£6.95). The several attractive interconnected rooms have a peaceful and welcoming atmosphere, as well as a mix of sturdy chairs, some built-in wooden wall settles, beams, an open fire with horsebrasses along the mantlebeam, fresh flowers on the solid panelled wood bar counter and tables, china plates, copper pans and old clocks on the walls, and a couple of comfortable armchairs. Well kept Boddingtons, Greenalls Original and a weekly changing guest such as Marstons Pedigree on handpump, and a good wine list that always includes a dozen or so by the glass; attentive but unfussy service. There are colourful hanging baskets outside, and picnic tables and umbrellas in the garden. *(Recommended by Ian Phillips, Galen Strawson, John and Val Spouge, O Carroll, Joan and Michel Hooper-Immins, Andy and Jill Kassube, TOH)*

Greenalls ~ Tenant Paul Edmunds ~ Real ale ~ Meals and snacks (not 25 Dec) ~ Restaurant ~ (01305) 812522 ~ Children in eating area ~ Open 11-2.30(3 Sat), 6-11

WEST BEXINGTON SY5387 Map 2

Manor Hotel

Village signposted off B3157 SE of Bridport, opposite the Bull in Swyre

An ancient place first mentioned in the Domesday Book, this smart old hotel is a particularly pleasant place to stay for a few days. You can see the sea from the bedrooms and from the garden, where there are picnic tables on a small lawn with flower-beds lining the low sheltering walls; a much bigger side lawn has a children's play area. Inside, a handsome Jacobean oak-panelled hall leads down to the busy pubby cellar bar, actually on the same level as the south-sloping garden. Small country pictures and good leather-mounted horse brasses decorate the walls, and there are red leatherette stools and low-backed chairs (with one fat seat carved from a beer cask) under the black beams and joists, as well as heavy harness over the log fire. A smart no-smoking Victorian-style conservatory has airy furnishings and lots of plants. Popular bar food includes sandwiches (from £2.05), very good home-made soup (£2.25), ploughman's (£4.25), lobster roulade or devilled crab (£4.65), bangers and mash (£5.95), salads (from £6.05; crab £7.35), brazil nut loaf (£6.75), meat or vegetable lasagne (£6.85), rabbit or steak and kidney pies (£6.95), rack of lamb (£8.95), especially good fish dishes such as lemon sole caprice (£9.95) or monkfish au poivre (£11.45), puddings (£2.95), and children's meals (£3.25); good breakfasts. Well kept Furgusons Dartmoor, Ind Coope Burton and Wadworths 6X on handpump, quite a few malt whiskies and several wines by the glass; alley skittles. Helpful courteous service. *(Recommended by Julia Duplock, Galen Strawson, Basil Minson, Mark and Caroline Thistlethwaite, Mrs J A Powell, Eric and Patricia King, John Coatsworth, Jacqueline White, J Muckelt, KC, W C M Jones, Mr and Mrs M P Aston, J L Alperin, David Brokensha, P J Hanson)*

Free house ~ Licensee Richard Childs ~ Real ale ~ Meals and snacks (till 10pm) ~ Restaurant ~(01308) 897616 ~ Children welcome ~ Open 11-11; closed evening 25 Dec ~ Bedrooms: £47B/£80B

WEST LULWORTH SY8280 Map 2

Castle

B3070

Dorset seems to have more than its fair share of attractive thatched inns and here's another one, in a lovely spot close to Lulworth Cove, with good walks in either direction. The lively public bar has polished flagstones and button-back leatherette seats forming a maze of booths around the tables, and the comfortably furnished lounge, though more modern-feeling, is still cosy, with blue banquettes under the countryside prints on the walls, and pewter tankards hanging from one beam. Decent value bar food includes home-made soup (£1.80), filled rolls (from £1.80), ploughman's (from £3.50), vegetable and cheese bake (£4.50), liver and bacon casserole or steak and kidney pie (£4.90), salmon steak (£6.50), beef stroganoff (£9), seafood stew (£10), steak stuffed with smoked oysters (£12), puddings, and children's meals (from £2.50); very good breakfasts. Very busy in summer, the popular garden has giant chess boards, boules, hopscotch, steeply terraced rose beds, a barbecue area, and good views. Well kept Devenish Wessex, Flowers Original and Marstons Pedigree on handpump, farm cider, several malt whiskies; darts, shove-ha'penny, table skittles, dominoes, cribbage, fruit machine, trivia, backgammon, Scrabble and other board games, piped music. It's best to walk down to the Cove from here as the car park at the bottom is expensive. *(Recommended by Andy Thwaites, Risha Stapleton, B and K Hypher, Annette and Stephen Marsden, Mr and Mrs L Boyle, D J Milner, S Lancaster, Martyn Kearey, W H and E Thomas, Trevor Scott, J L Alperin, Gill Earle, Andrew Burton)*

Greenalls ~ Lease: Graham Halliday ~ Real ale ~ Meals and snacks (11-2, 7-10) ~ Restaurant ~ (01929) 400311 ~ Children in eating area and restaurant ~ Occasional Morris dancing ~ Open 11-2.30, 7-11 ~ Bedrooms: £20(£25B)/£35(£41B)

WORTH MATRAVERS (Isle of Purbeck) SY9777 Map 2

Square & Compass

At fork of both roads signposted to village from B3069

You can leave thirty years or so between visits to this unique little place and still find everything exactly the same. The delightfully unchanging feel has been helped by the fact that it's been run by different generations of the same family for 90 years, with nothing altered in all that time – or at least since decimalisation anyway. Determinedly basic, the old-fashioned main bar has simple wall benches around the elbow-polished old tables on the flagstones, and interesting local pictures under its low ceilings. Well kept Badger Best, Morlands Old Speckled Hen, Ringwood Fortyniner, and Whitbreads Strong Country are tapped from a row of casks behind a couple of hatches in the flagstoned corridor (local fossils back here, and various curios inside the servery), which leads to a more conventional summer bar; Bulmers and Inch's ciders. Bar food is limited to cornish or cheese and onion pasties (80p), served all day; cribbage, shove ha'penny and dominoes. On a clear day the view from the peaceful hilltop setting is hard to beat, looking down over the village rooftops to the sea between the East Man and the West Man (the hills that guard the coastal approach), and on summer evenings the sun setting out beyond Portland Bill. There are benches in front of the pub to admire the view, and free-roaming chickens and other birds may cluck happily around your feet. The pub is at the start of an OS Walkers Britain walk; dogs welcome. *(Recommended by Andy Thwaites, Avril Hanson, Derek Patey, Paul and Sue Sexton, Nigel Clifton, P J Hanson, Chris Westmoreland, D P and J A Sweeney, Jack and Philip Paxton, James Macrae, Gwyneth and Salvo Spadaro-Dutturi, David Warrellow, D G Clarke, David Mead, Geoff Butts, Polly Marsh, Geraint Roberts, A Plumb, R H Brown, Lynn Sharpless, Bob Eardley, Peter Pocklington)*

Free house ~ Licensee Charlie Newman ~ Real ale ~ Snacks ~ (01929) 439229 ~ Children welcome ~ Occasional live music ~ Open 11-3, 6-11; all day summer Sats

Post Office address codings confusingly give the impression that some pubs are in Dorset, when they're really in Somerset (which is where we list them).

Lucky Dip

Besides the fully inspected pubs, you might like to try these Lucky Dips recommended to us and described by readers (if you do, please send us reports):

☆ **Almer** [just off A31; SY9097], *Worlds End*: Big open-plan thatched family dining pub, an efficient operation with very wide food choice, quick service, well kept Badger Best and Tanglefoot; picnic tables out in front and behind, plenty of space with good big well equipped play area *(Mr and Mrs P D Prescott, WHBM, Howard Clutterbuck, BB)*

Ansty [Higher Ansty; ST7603], *Fox*: Unusual inn with good range of food, friendly helpful service, part of bar set aside for non smokers, fantastic collection of Toby jugs and decorative plates, well equipped children's bar, skittle alley, pool table; beautiful countryside *(Keith Widdowson, LYM)*

☆ **Beaminster** [The Square; ST4701], *Pickwicks*: Restaurant with bar rather than pub, but quaint and comfortable, with good atmosphere, interesting real ales, wide choice of good well presented home-cooked food inc good vegetarian dishes; piped opera, friendly landlord; bedrooms *(R MacDonald, Prof and Mrs S Barnett, A J Peile)*

☆ **Beaminster** [The Square], *Greyhound*: Friendly relaxing little 18th-c pub, interesting inside, popular for wide choice of good value food inc interesting vegetarian pâté; well kept Palmers IPA and BB, good friendly service, small family room *(Gordon, C J Pratt)*

Bearwood [Bear Cross, Magna Rd – A341 roundabout; SZ0596], *Bear Cross*: Large, busy pub with wide choice of home-made food inc massive choice of cheap filled baked potatoes; Badger beers *(WHBM)*

Benville Lane [off A356 NW of Dorchester; ST5403], *Talbot Arms*: Small village pub, friendly service, good range of bar food *(Galen Strawson)*

☆ **Bere Regis** [West St; SY8494], *Royal Oak*: Open-plan unpretentious modernised local, thoroughly welcoming, good reasonably priced food, well kept Whitbreads-related ales, woodburner, sensibly placed darts, cribbage, fruit machine; dining room; open all day Fri and Sat; bedrooms *(John and Joan Nash, Peter Cornall, John and Joan Nash, BB)*

Blandford Forum [Market Pl; ST8806], *Greyhound*: Coin and matchbox collections, stripped brick, carved wood, comfortable seats, well kept Badger Best and Tanglefoot and Worthington Dark; bar food, popular restaurant *(John and Joan Nash)*; [77 Salisbury St], *Nelsons*: Welcoming, old beams and sawdust, reasonably priced interesting food in big or small helpings, Sun lunch, newspapers; Boddingtons *(John and Joan Nash)*

Bournemouth [The Square; SZ0991], *Moon on the Square*: Well fitted new Wetherspoons pub, good range of competitively priced beers, awesome helpings of bar food, no-smoking areas, no piped music; good value *(Paul Randall)*

☆ **Bridport** [West Bay; SY4690], *West Bay*: Straightforward pub very popular for good unusual dishes such as bison sausages, lots of fresh local seafood, occasional gourmet evenings; Palmers IPA and Best, tables in garden *(Chris Warne, Jenny and Brian Seller)*

Bridport [West Bay Rd], *Crown*: Good food – interesting real cooking, with deft sauces and herbs from the garden – in unpretentious setting; well kept Palmers beers, welcoming staff, good atmosphere *(Mr and Mrs Tony Allan)*; [East Rd], *Toll House*: Big helpings of good food, charming informal family service; bedrooms (busy road) *(Thorstein Moen)*

Broadmayne [SY7286], *Black Dog*: Comfortably modernised village pub with good range of reasonably priced food inc popular Sun lunch *(David Lamb, BB)*

☆ **Buckhorn Weston** [ST7524], *Stapleton Arms*: Friendly and spacious, wide choice of food inc fresh fish Thurs, steaks Fri, good puddings; pleasant countryside *(Brig T I G Gray, Brian Chambers)*

☆ **Buckland Newton** [ST6904], *Gaggle of Geese*: Pleasant atmosphere in well run comfortably solid pub, attractive decor, friendly dogs and a cat, well kept Bass, Badger Best, Wadworths 6X and a guest beer, decent wines and spirits, good reasonably priced usual bar food, smartish restaurant; spacious pool/snooker and skittle rooms, sizeable grounds *(R J Herd, R G Glover, Maj T C Thornton, John Hazel, BB)*

Burton [just N of Dorchester; SY6891], *Sun*: Recently reopened, very tastefully enlarged, good food, quite busy but service prompt and efficient, friendly manager; huge car park *(John Hazel)*

☆ **Burton Bradstock** [Southover; SY4889], *Dove*: 16th-c thatched inn doing well under current licensees, very pleasant atmosphere, interesting beers, good range of food inc fresh seafood *(Prof and Mrs S Barnett, Ron Shelton)*

Burton Bradstock, *Anchor*: Comfortable, clean and roomy, well kept Courage Best, good choice of good value bar food till 10 *(Galen Strawson)*

Cashmoor [A354 6 miles E of Blandford; ST9713], *Cashmoor*: Well kept Badger family pub in spacious former coaching inn, wishing well in lounge bar, good range of reasonably priced bar food, tables in garden with play area *(Brian Chambers)*

☆ **Charlton Marshall** [A350 Poole—Blandford; ST9003], *Charlton Inn*: Smart and tidy oak-beamed food pub, wide choice of good generous food from sandwiches and lots of baked potatoes up, well kept Badger Best and Tanglefoot, well chosen wine list, quick friendly service, unobtrusive piped music, small garden *(WHBM)*

☆ *nr* **Chedington** [A356 Dorchester—Crewkerne; ST4805], *Winyards Gap*:

Spectacular view from tables in front of tastefully modernised pub with wide choice of traditional food inc lots of home-made puddings, children's and vegetarian dishes, popular Sun lunch; well kept Exmoor Stag, Flowers Original, Wadworths 6X and a guest ale, country wines, no-smoking area, skittle alley, also darts, pool etc; children in dining area, live music Sun evening, self-catering in converted barn; pleasant walks nearby *(E A George, D Marsh, Steve Huggins, Howard Clutterbuck, Marjorie and David Lamb, Ron Shelton, LYM)*

☆ **Chesil** [bear right off A354 into Portland, following Chiswell signs; SY6873], *Cove House*: Modest bare-boards pub in superb spot just above the miles-long Chesil pebble beach, three tables out by sea wall, friendly staff and Whitbreads-related ales; piped music may be obtrusive, and food now not special *(Christopher Gallop, Eric Locker, LYM)*

☆ **Chetnole** [ST6007], *Chetnole Arms*: Lively and welcoming, wide choice of good home cooking, well kept interesting changing ales, local farm ciders, log fires, cheerful staff; nice garden *(Tim Wilde, Dr and Mrs N Holmes)*

☆ **Chideock** [A35 Bridport—Lyme Regis; SY4292], *George*: Thatched 17th-c pub with neat rows of tables in simple front bar, big log fire in dark-beamed plush lounge, wide choice of bar food, well kept Palmers, efficient staff, restaurant, tables in back garden; bedrooms *(Mrs J M Corless, Ron Gentry, Andy Jones, R A F Montgomery, LYM)*

☆ *nr* **Christchurch** [Ringwood Rd, Walkford; just off A35 by Hants border – OS Sheet 195 map ref 222943; SZ2294], *Amberwood Arms*: Eye-catching traditional pub festooned with hanging baskets and flower tubs, imaginative food in bar and comfortable restaurant, friendly staff; some live music, weekly trivia night, picnic tables and play area; open all day *(E G Parish, Cheryl Baker)*

☆ **Colehill** [off A31 E of Wimborne; down hill N of village, right at bottom into Long Lane – OS Sheet 195 map ref 032024; SU0201], *Barley Mow*: Very popular extended thatched 16th-c dining pub, wide range of promptly served food, very reasonable prices, well kept Best and Tanglefoot and a guest such as Charles Wells; attractive beamed and panelled core, good log fires, provision for children, folk music Fri, nice garden with play area *(Alan and Eileen Bowker, John Hazel, Maurice Southon, Peter and Hlia Douglas, LYM)*

☆ **Corfe Castle** [SY9681], *Bankes Arms*: Big busy ex-coaching inn with Whitbreads-related real ales, decent food, long garden with play area, attractive surroundings; children welcome *(R H Brown, Chris Westmoreland, Gwyneth and Salvo Spadaro-Dutturi, B and K Hypher)*

Corfe Mullen [A31 W of Wimborne Minster; SY9798], *Coventry Arms*: Famous Old Trout back to its old name and doing well under new Greenalls regime, Bass, Courage Directors, Morlands Old Speckled Hen, Ringwood Best, and Wadworths 6X tapped from casks, spacious bar; pubbily atmospheric but popular mainly for good straightforward food *(WHBM)*; [Wareham Rd], *Dorset Soldier*: Good food and atmosphere *(Rob Ayres)*

Dorchester [20 High West St; SY6890], *Royal Oak*: Quiet, Eldridge Pope Dorchester, Hardy Country and Royal Oak, good range of straightforward meals in bar or back room; bedrooms *(Marjorie and David Lamb)*; [Weymouth Ave, by Dorchester Sth Stn], *Station Masters House*: Comfortable and roomy railway-theme pub with friendly service, notable for well kept Eldridge Pope ales straight from the handsome adjacent brewery; quick generous sensibly priced food; fruit machines and pool, piped music can be rather loud, open all day Weds-Sat, busy Weds (market opp) *(Barbara Hatfield, Brian Chambers, Stan Edwards)*; [47 High East St], *Tom Browns*: Well run, good home-brewed beer *(JM, PM)*; [40 Allington Ave; A352 towards Wareham], *Trumpet Major*: Bright and fresh, with big family dining conservatory, wide choice of food, good two-course Sun lunch, well kept Eldridge Pope ales, friendly service; play area *(K D Corbett, Joan and Michel Hooper-Immins)*

East End [OS Sheet 195 map ref 996987; SY9898], *Lambs Green*: Much extended, with loudspeaker food announcements etc, but worth knowing for well kept M&B Brew XI and good value tasty well cooked food *(Richard Dolphin)*

☆ **East Stour** [A30, E towards Shaftesbury; ST7922], *Kings Arms*: Spotless and comfortable, with satisfying fresh food inc interesting specials and good puddings, well kept ales inc Bass, friendly family service, local paintings and drawings, model railway locomotive collection, no piped music; restaurant (not Mon) beyond tanks of catfish, public bar with darts and fruit machine; tables outside; children welcome *(Lt Cdr G J Cardew, Canon Kenneth Wills, Mr and Mrs R O Gibson)*

East Stour [The Street], *Fox & Hounds*: Particularly good range of beers, friendly service, interesting bar food *(R H Martyn)*

☆ **Evershot** [off A37 8 miles S of Yeovil; ST5704], *Acorn*: Comfortable stripped-stone bar with wide choice of reliable food from sandwiches to steaks, changing ales such as Palmers and Wadworths 6X, decent wines, fine old fireplaces; games in quiet separate public bar, piped music; children in skittle alley and restaurant; bedrooms comfortable, pretty village in attractive Hardy walking country; no cheques or credit cards under £15 *(Maj and Mrs Warrick, Keith Pollard, LYM)*

Eype [SY4491], *New Inn*: Warm and friendly, well kept Palmers, decent food inc children's; magnificent views *(Stephen Bayley)*

Fiddleford [A357 Sturminster Newton—Blandford Forum; ST8013], *Fiddleford Inn*:

Spacious refurbished pub keeping some nice old touches, good choice of quickly served food in lounge bar, restaurant area and back family area; well kept Courage-related ales, big attractive garden with play area *(Helen Morton, Mr and Mrs R O Gibson, Brian Chambers, LYM)*

☆ **Gillingham** [Peacemarsh; ST8026], *Dolphin*: Good friendly pub with new landlord cooking particularly good value food, wife runs the bar; well kept Badger ales *(R A Cullingham)*

☆ **Gussage All Saints** [signed off B3078 Wimborne—Cranborne; SU0010], *Drovers*: Sturdily furnished country dining pub with peaceful views, generous well presented food, well kept Bass, Marstons Pedigree and Ruddles County on handpump, country wines, friendly service, tables out on terrace, good play area; children in eating area, in summer has been open all day Sat *(Peter Churchill, Phil and Heidi Cook, Sue Holland, Dave Webster, Neil Hardwick, LYM)*

Highcliffe [Walkford Rd; SZ2193], *Walkford*: Good value food in bar and restaurant, wide range of beers and wines, friendly licensees, skittle alley, good play yard with picnic tables; reputed ghost *(Cheryl Baker)*

Hinton St Mary [just off B3092 a mile N of Sturminster; ST7816], *White Horse*: Character local with jovial public bar, comfortable extended lounge, tables in flower garden; reasonably priced bar food (booking advised Sun lunch), cheerful staff; no piped music *(Brian Chambers)*

Holt Heath [SU0604], *Cross Keys*: Energetic and capable new landlady who's done wonders with the garden; Badger Best, plenty of whiskies, good barbecue *(WHBM)*

Horton [B3078 Wimborne—Cranborne; SU0207], *Drusillas*: Picturesque, food inc OAP bargains, cream teas and restaurant; real ales, children welcome, adventure playground *(E G Parish)*

☆ **Hurn** [village signed off A338, then follow Avon, Sopley, Mutchams sign – OS Sheet 195 map ref 136976; SZ1397], *Avon Causeway*: Current management doing well, with good moderately priced food, Wadworths ales and guests such as John Smiths and Ringwood Old Thumper, good choice of wines and spirits, two civilised bars, pleasantly enlarged dining area, welcoming staff; interesting railway decorations, Pullman-coach restaurant by former 1870s station platform, piped music, open all day; bedrooms *(Audrey and Peter Reeves, WHBM, M Joyner, LYM)*

Ibberton [ST7807], *Crown*: Well kept beer, good food, friendly feel *(G Washington)*

Langton Matravers [B3069 nr junction with A351; SY9978], *Ship*: Robust basic local with lively Purbeck Longboard shove-ha'penny, pool, darts, Courage-related ales; children welcome, handy for Putland Farm *(Chris Westmoreland, LYM)*

☆ **Loders** [SY4994], *Loders Arms*: Attractive thatched village pub with small refurbished bar and connecting restaurant, notable for original often elaborate food (not cheap) inc lots of fish; friendly service, unhurried relaxed feel even when busy, well kept Palmers ales, good choice of wines, open fire; bedrooms comfortable and well equipped *(Patrick McGrath, Deborah and Ian Carrington, H G Robertson, Paul and Sue Sexton, John and Sheila French, Mr and Mrs D V Morris)*

☆ **Longham** [A348 Ferndown—Poole; SZ0698], *Angel*: Cosy beamed roadside pub (big car park, can get very busy) well reworked to give children's area away from bar, wide choice of food from sandwiches to steaks inc children's dishes, friendly prompt service, well kept Badger Best and Tanglefoot, unobtrusive piped music; big garden with lots of play facilities *(Peter Churchill, R Wilsono, A Plumb, P Gillbe)*

☆ **Lyme Regis** [25 Marine Parade, The Cobb; SY3492], *Royal Standard*: Buzzing atmosphere in cosy local, open-plan but keeping three separate low-ceilinged areas, with well kept Palmers, good value food inc good cream teas with home-made scones, pool table, suntrap terrace (floodlit at night) leading to beach *(Mr and Mrs J Irving, Neil Williams, Julian Bessa, Jim and Maggie Cowell)*

Lyme Regis [The Cobb], *Cobb Arms*: Spaciously refurbished, interesting local and sea pictures, wide range of bar food, well kept Palmers real ales; next to harbour, beach and coastal walk *(Bruce Bird)*; [Silver St], *Nags Head*: Friendly local, well kept Bass, decent range of reasonably priced food *(Nigel Warr)*

Lytchett Matravers [High St; SY9495], *Chequers*: Low-beamed and cosy, food that's a little bit different, big family room, pleasant good-sized restaurant with central fire and kitchen view, no-smoking conservatory dining area off *(B and K Hypher, Gordon Theaker)*

☆ **Marnhull** [B3092 (Crown Rd nr church); ST7718], *Crown*: Yet another change of tenants in this attractive thatched pub – local people, and early signs are very promising; comfortably refurbished lounge leading to dining area, wide choice of food (not Sun evening) using local produce, inc home-made pies and OAP bargain lunches Tues/Thurs, log fire, well kept Badger ales; charming beamed and flagstoned public bar with another huge fireplace; children in eating area, occasional live music in skittle alley; four comfortable bedrooms *(Brian Chambers, LYM)*

☆ **Marshwood** [B3165 Lyme Regis—Crewkerne; SY3799], *Bottle*: Unspoiled recently rethatched 16th-c country local, inglenook in low-ceilinged newly painted bar, well kept Hook Norton and Wadworths 6X, reasonably priced bar food, small games bar, skittle alley; good spacious garden, pretty walking country *(Marjorie and David Lamb, Ian Phillips, Dr and Mrs J H Hills, Gordon,*

LYM)

Milborne St Andrew [A354 Blandford—Dorchester; SY8097], *Royal Oak*: Friendly two-bar pub with plenty of tables, fair range of food, Badger Best and Tanglefoot *(David Lamb)*

☆ **Morden** [B3075 between A35 and A31 E of Bere Regis; SY9195], *Cock & Bottle*: Extensively refurbished in rustic style, beams and timbering carefully set out of true, comfortably warm and welcoming, good food esp fish and poultry, nice fire, well kept Badger ales; pleasant countryside *(Nigel Flook, Betsy Brown, David Dimock, E G Paris, WHBM)*

Morecombelake [A35 Bridport—Lyme Regis; SY4093], *Ship*: Welcoming atmosphere, good bar food inc generously filled baked potatoes, well kept Palmers *(Paul and Sue Sexton, Gwyneth and Salvo Spadaro-Dutturi)*

☆ **Moreton** [SY8089], *Frampton Arms*: Warmwell Aerodrome theme in public bar, steam railway pictures in lounge bar, friendly landlord, wide choice of good value food, restaurant and conservatory; comfortable bedrooms *(Janet and John Loder, Mrs K E Neville-Rolfe)*

☆ **Mudeford** [beyond huge seaside car park at Mudeford Pier – OS Sheet 195 map ref 182916; SZ1891], *Haven House*: Much-extended, best in winter for old-fashioned feel in quaint old part-flagstoned core and lovely seaside walks (dogs banned from beach May-Sept), very popular summer for position on beach with family cafeteria, tables on sheltered terrace; Whitbreads-related ales, simple bar food, cheerful service *(Mr and Mrs Berner, Rita Horridge, WHBM, B and K Hypher, LYM)*

☆ **Norden Heath** [Furzebrook; A351 Wareham—Corfe Castle; SY9483], *Halfway*: Really interesting authentic Cypriot dishes among more usual home cooking in unpretentious, popular and relaxed thatched main-road pub, well kept Whitbreads-related ales with guests such as Ringwood Best and Twelve Bore; garden with pets' corner *(Mr and Mrs Damien Burke, B and K Hypher, David Lamb, D G Clarke, Chris Westmoreland, Derek Patey)*

☆ **North Wootton** [A3030; ST6514], *Three Elms*: Interesting Matchbox cars and other collections in lively and welcoming pub with wide range of good reasonably priced food esp specials, well kept beers such as Boddingtons, Fullers London Pride and Hook Norton Mild; three bedrooms, good breakfasts; bedrooms *(S G Brown, David Tyzack, Stephen and Julie Brown, Dr A and Dr A C Jackson)*

Piddletrenthide [B3142; SY7099], *Piddle*: Lots of chamber-pots to honour nearby eponymous river's name, good food, spacious garden with picnic tables; a favourite stop for cyclists *(Lee Kreider)*

☆ **Poole** [Pinewood Rd, Branksome Park; off A338 on edge of Poole, towards Branksome Chine – via The Avenue; SZ0590], *Inn in the Park*: Consistently warm welcome in very popular pleasantly redecorated small hotel bar, well kept Bass and Wadworths 6X, good value generous bar food (not Sun evening), attractive dining room (children allowed), log fire, tables on small sunny terrace; comfortable bedrooms, quiet pine-filled residential area above sea *(Mark Hydes, Peter Churchill, J Muckelt, LYM)*

☆ **Poole** [The Quay; SZ0190], *Portsmouth Hoy*: Well done nautical theme, lots of brass, plenty of atmosphere, good choice of reasonably priced food inc generous fish, well kept Eldridge Pope Blackdown Porter, Dorchester, Hardy Country and Royal Oak, smart bar service, nice back dining area, separate no-smoking area; on lively quay *(W H and E Thomas, Paul Barstow, Karyn Taylor, John and Joan Nash, B and K Hypher)*

☆ **Poole** [88 High St], *Old Harry*: Good menu inc lots of fish and seafood in friendly and bustling city local with comfortable seats inc big raised dining area, cheerful service, Bass and Charrington ale *(K R Harris, Basil Minson)*

Poole [Sandbanks Rd, Lilliput], *Beehive*: Not cheap but worth knowing for well kept beers and large no-smoking conservatory-style family eating area; picnic tables *(Audrey and Peter Reeves)*; [Market St], *Guildhall*: Bright family eating pub with good range of seafood *(Nigel Flook, Betsy Brown, LYM)*; [Longfleet Rd/Fernside Rd], *Shah of Persia*: Well refurbished, with no-smoking family area, smart new lavatories, good fresh food, soft piped music, welcoming Welsh licensees and polite staff, well kept Eldridge Pope ales, moderate prices *(Audrey and Peter Reeves and friends)*

☆ **Portesham** [Front St (B3157); SY6086], *Kings Arms*: Large pub with considerable recent extensions, good reasonably priced food inc some unusual dishes, welcoming service, sizeable attractive garden with play area, pond and trout stream *(Stan Edwards, Dave Braisted, B and K Hypher, Mr and Mrs R O Gibson)*

Portland [Top-of-Town; SY6876], *Portland Heights*: Smart hotel with pleasant public bar, reasonably priced food and drinks and fantastic Chesil beach view *(A H Denman)*

☆ **Portland Bill** [SY6870], *Pulpit*: Comfortable food pub in great spot nr Pulpit Rock, short stroll to lighthouse and cliffs; local shellfish as well as usual bar and restaurant food inc vegetarian, well kept Gibbs Mew real ales, friendly efficient staff; piped music *(Eric J Locker, A H Denman, B and K Hypher)*

Preston [A353 Weymouth—Osmington; SY7083], *Bridge*: Cottagey pub with reasonable choice of food and well kept beers; sun-trap garden with swings, etc *(Stan Edwards)*; [A353], *Spice Ship*: Surprisingly big family pub, nautical decor in series of rooms off big central bar, reasonable range of bar food and ales such as Marstons Pedigree, live music popular with nearby caravan-campers *(Stan Edwards)*

☆ **Puncknowle** [Church St; SY5388], *Crown*: Good local atmosphere in 16th-c beamed and thatched flint inn's clean and comfortable open-plan lounge, good choice of reasonably priced home-cooked food esp pies and steak sandwiches, good vegetarian choice, well kept Palmers, decent wines, lots of country wines, very friendly staff; family room, locals' bar; attractive garden, pretty setting opp church; bedrooms *(Neil Hardwick, Paul and Wendy Bachelor, Deborah and Ian Carrington)*

☆ **Sandford Orcas** [off B3148 and B3145 N of Sherborne; ST6220], *Mitre*: Good value attractively presented food (steak and kidney pie praised by many) in tucked-away country local, cosy and comfortable with a good deal of unpretentious character, good service, well kept John Smiths and Wadworths 6X; bedrooms *(D Waters, A G Drake, Stephen Brown, Betty and David Stockwell, LYM)*

☆ **Shaftesbury** [St James St; ST8622], *Two Brewers*: Currently the best pub here, a steep walk down famously photogenic Gold Hill (though you can drive round to it); well divided extensive open-plan turkey-carpeted bar, lots of decorative plates, good choice of reasonably priced popular bar food (children's helpings of any dish) inc good Sun roasts, very friendly service, well kept Courage Best and Directors, Wadworths 6X and guests such as Adnams Best and Batemans XB; picnic tables in garden with pretty views *(Christopher and Sharon Hayle, B and K Hypher, Colin Walls, Alan and Paula McCully, BB)*

☆ **Shaftesbury** [Bleke St], *Ship*: 17th-c local with black panelling, oak woodwork, traditional layout; well kept Badger Best and Tanglefoot, farm cider, bar food with separate eating area, pool and other games in public bar (crowded with young people weekend evenings), tables on terrace, boules *(Barbara Hatfield, Jim and Maggie Cowell, Kevin Booker, Jack and Philip Paxton, Gordon, LYM)*

☆ **Shaftesbury** [The Commons], *Grosvenor*: Charming older-style coaching hotel, warm and comfortable; good genuine fair-priced bar snacks, well kept beers inc Bass, stylish restaurant; ask Reception if you can see the magnificently carved oak 19th-c Chevy Chase sideboard in the first-floor residents' lounge; good bedrooms *(Mrs J A Powell, Alan and Paula McCully)*

☆ **Shaftesbury** [High St], *Mitre*: Cheerfully unpretentious, with quickly served good generous food from sandwiches up inc vegetarian, Blackmore Vale views from back dining room, well kept Eldridge Pope beers, good choice of malt whiskies and wines, daily papers, small suntrap garden; bedrooms *(A E and P McCully, Keith and Janet Morris, Marjorie and David Lamb, B and K Hypher, LYM)*

☆ **Sherborne** [Cooks Lane (nr abbey); ST6316], *Digby Tap*: Thriving unspoilt flagstoned pub with plenty of character, good choice of well kept ales, farm cider, huge helpings of bar food (not Sun), pleasant service, pub games; seats outside *(Ron Shelton, Richard Houghton, Mr and Mrs A P Reeves, Jim Knight, S G Brown, John Hazel, Revd A Nunnerley)*

☆ **Sherborne** [Horsecastles], *Skippers*: Pleasant local bustle, welcoming service, good range of food, well kept Bass and other ales; just outside centre *(John and Joan Nash, John Hazel, Richard Houghton)*

Sherborne [Westbury; off Acreman St opp Cooks Lane], *Britannia*: Friendly local with good value bar food, helpful landlord, well kept beers, pool table and juke box; bedrooms comfortable *(Alistair Harris, Gordon)*; [Swan Passage], *Swan*: Locally popular for well cooked and served food, friendy staff; warmly welcoming atmosphere *(F J Willy, Mr and Mrs Norman Davies)*

Shipton Gorge [off A35/B3157 E of Bridport; SY4991], *New Inn*: Good atmosphere, food inc freshly caught local fish *(Michael Richards)*

Southbourne [Overcliff Dr; about 2 miles W of Hengistbury Head; SZ1591], *Commodore*: Clifftop pub reopened 1995 after refurbishment as Berni inn, comfortable furnishings, separate areas for children and non-smokers, well kept Whitbreads-related beers, lots of naval memorabilia, good well priced food, small terrace *(Mr and Mrs A P Reeves)*

Spetisbury [ST9102], *Drax Arms*: Friendly local, good generous food *(Mrs R Pielou)*

☆ **Studland** [SZ0382], *Bankes Arms*: Wonderful peaceful spot above fine beach, outstanding country, sea and cliff views from huge pleasant garden; friendly and easy-going, substantial simple food, well kept Poole and Whitbreads-related ales, attractive log fire, pool table; children welcome, nr Coast Path; can get trippery in summer, parking can be complicated or expensive if you're not a NT member; bedrooms *(Barbara Hatfield, Nigel Flook, Betsy Brown, Geoff Butts, Polly Marsh, E G Parish, Chris Westmoreland, B and K Hypher)*

Studland [Beach Rd], *Manor House*: Good value food (may have to book – and you can't come just for a drink), quick welcoming service even when busy, comfortable spacious lounge with open fire, conservatory, coast views, attractive garden above beach; attractive bedrooms, handy for walks *(B and K Hypher)*

☆ **Sturminster Newton** [Market Cross (B3092); ST7814], *White Hart*: Welcoming and homely 18th-c thatched inn, warm cosy bar, well kept Badger, reasonably priced bar food, morning coffee, afternoon teas, garden beyond cobbled coach entry; bedrooms comfortable, though road not quiet *(Graham and Lynn Mason)*

☆ **Sutton Poyntz** [off A353 SE of Weymouth; SY7083], *Springhead*: Spacious but cosy, with comfortable furnishings, beams, well kept Eldridge Pope and Marstons Pedigree, decent reasonably priced wines, good choice of tempting food, log fires, welcoming attentive staff, newspapers, bar billiards; lovely spot opp stream in quiet village, good play area in big garden, walks to White Horse Hill and Dorset Coastal Path *(Peter Churchill, Gwyneth and Salvo Spadaro-Dutturi, J H and B V Hartland)*

Swanage [High St; SZ0278], *Black Swan*: Picturesque old pub with garden nr millpond, well kept beers, tasty home-made bar food; maybe piped radio, occasional live music *(Veronica Brown)*; [Ulwell Rd], *Ferryboat*: Quiet refuge with lovely bay view, well kept Tetleys-related ales, food inc speciality pancakes *(Joan and Michel Hooper-Immins, Jack and Philip Paxton)*; [Bell St, Herston – just off 1st turn into town off A351], *Globe*: Pleasant friendly L-shaped local, well kept Whitbreads-related ales *(Chris Westmoreland, D P and J A Sweeney)*; [1 Burlington Rd], *Pines*: Reliably good value popular lunchtime food and well kept beers in big hotel bar; excellent views from garden (a long way from bar); bedrooms comfortable *(John Kirk)*; *Red Lion*: Friendly bar and larger lounge opening on to back terrace with play area, Ringwood and Whitbreads beers; children welcome *(Chris Westmoreland)*; [High St], *Royal Oak*: Pleasant local with good home-cooked food, well kept Wadworths 6X, friendly service *(D P and J A Sweeney)*; [The Square], *Ship*: Reliably well run, good atmosphere, bedrooms *(Jack and Philip Paxton, LYM)*; [High St], *White Horse*: Worth knowing for good value straightforward food inc good spotted dick and custard; friendly welcome, well kept Whitbreads-related ales *(Howard Allen)*

☆ **Sydling St Nicholas** [SY6399], *Greyhound*: Wide choice of good well prepared food with plentiful properly cooked veg, friendly service, well kept Ringwood and Wadworths 6X; tables in small garden, very attractive village *(Galen Strawson)*

☆ **Tarrant Gunville** [ST9212], *Bugle Horn*: Attractive and comfortable country pub, wide choice of good value usual food, welcoming licensees, well kept Ringwood and Wadworths 6X; seats in garden *(John Hazel)*

Tarrant Keynston [ST9304], *True Lovers Knot*: Simple village local with first-class landlord, well kept Badger ales, decent range of food, good atmosphere; children in eating area, big garden *(WHBM, John Hazel)*

☆ **Tolpuddle** [SY7994], *Martyrs*: Genuine home cooking, with good choice and busy restaurant; friendly staff, well kept Badger beers, nice garden with ducks, hens and rabbits *(Joan Nash)*

☆ **Trent** [ST5918], *Rose & Crown*: Traditional relaxed old-fashioned pub, with log fire, flagstone floors, comfortable oak settles, nice pictures, fresh flowers, books, no piped music or machines; wide choice of consistently good quickly served food, decent choice of real ales, dining conservatory; picnic tables behind; children welcome *(LM, Gerry Cox)*

Upwey [B3159, nr junction A354 – OS Sheet 194 map ref 666845; SY6684], *Masons Arms*: Two small rooms, one no smoking, and sizeable garden with play area; a main entry in last edition for excellent atmosphere, individual decor, decent food and well kept Marstons Pedigree, but the tenants left in October 1995 *(LYM; reports on new regime please)*

☆ **Wareham** [South St; SY9287], *Quay*: Light and airy stripped-stone bars, bar food from soup and sandwiches up, comfortable seats, open fire, well kept Whitbreads-related and other ales, friendly staff, children allowed away from main bar; picnic tables out on the quay, parking nearby can be difficult *(David Dimock, B and K Hypher, Chris Westmoreland, John and Joan Nash)*

☆ **Wareham** [41 North St; A351, N end of town], *Kings Arms*: Thriving and very welcomig traditional thatched town local, back serving counter and two bars off flagstoned central corridor, well kept Whitbreads-related ales, reasonably priced bar food (not Fri—Sun evenings), back garden *(R H Brown, Tom Espley, LYM)*

Wareham [14 South St], *Black Bear*: Similar spinal-corridor layout in this bigger 18th-c inn, which has well kept Eldridge Pope Royal Oak and Hardy Country, good choice of bar food, pleasant atmosphere, picnic tables in back yard *(Joan and Michel Hooper-Immins, Bruce Bird, Chris Westmoreland)*

☆ **Waytown** [between B3162 and A3066 N of Bridport; SY4697], *Hare & Hounds*: Wide range of good interesting reasonably priced food inc OAP bargains in friendly attractively refurbished 17th-c pub, good mix of customers, Palmers ales, simple garden with rabbits and chickens *(R E Goldsmith, Dr David Evans)*

☆ **West Bay** [SY4590], *Bridport Arms*: Good range of generous good value food esp locally caught fish in thatched pub on beach nr harbour and cliff walks, friendly staff, well kept Palmers BB, big fireplace in flagstoned back bar, no music; bedrooms *(Dr J R G Beavon, Prof and Mrs S Barnett, Bill Edwards)*

☆ **West Knighton** [off A352 E of Dorchester; SY7387], *New Inn*: Biggish neatly refurbished pub with considerable range of reasonably priced food, small restaurant, quick friendly staff, real ales, country wines, skittle alley, good provision for children; colourful garden, pleasant setting in quiet village with wonderful views *(Stan Edwards, David Lamb)*

☆ **West Stafford** [SY7289], *Wise Man*: Attractive and comfortable 16th-c pub, thatch, beams and toby jugs, with wide choice of good value generous food, friendly staff, well kept Whitbreads-related ales, decent wines and country wines, public bar with darts; nr Hardy's cottage *(R J Walden)*

☆ **West Stour** [ST7822], *Ship*: Carefully cooked food in fresh and attractively furnished pub with big log fire, well kept ales, good range of wines, attentive service, intimate split-level restaurant; garden behind, comfortable bedrooms *(Brig T I G Gray, R A F Montgomery)*

☆ **Weymouth** [Trinity Rd; SY6778], *Old Rooms*: Lovely harbour views over part-pedestrianised street from benches in front of character low-beamed fisherman's pub, well priced straightforward lunchtime food, unpretentious restaurant, friendly staff, well kept Whitbreads-related ales *(Stephen and Anna Oxley, B and K Hypher)*

☆ **Weymouth** [Barrack Rd], *Nothe Tavern*: Roomy well run local with good range of food inc fresh fish, friendly service, well kept Eldridge Pope Royal Oak and Hardy, decent wines; distant harbour glimpses from garden *(Joan and Michel Hooper-Immins, Marjorie and David Lamb, Jonathan Beard, Emma Clarke, C J Pratt)*

Weymouth [Dorchester Rd], *Royal Oak*: Friendly Eldridge Pope pub, lovely exterior decor, warm and comfortable inside with fireside armchairs *(A Plumb)*; [St Nicholas St], *Sailors Return*: Popular local with good helpings of tasty food, quiet piped music *(Veronica M Brown)*

Whitchurch Canonicorum [SY3995], *Five Bells*: Cheerfully unpretentious village local, Palmers ale, basic bar food, helpful staff, children welcome, lovely views; tables out in front, attractive village with fine church, good walking country *(Marjorie and David Lamb, Gwyneth and Salvo Spadaro-Dutturi, Richard Burton)*

☆ **Wimborne Minster** [Victoria Rd, W of town; SZ0199], *Lost Keys*: Chummy, chatty and well run, with good sandwiches, salads and reliable home-cooked hot dishes, well kept Bass and Fullers, Ringwood or Wadworths 6X *(WHBM, Sally Edsall)*

☆ **Wimborne Minster** [Hanham Rd, East Borough], *Dormers*: Partly 17th-c with handsome panelling and ceilings, not a conventional pub but includes spacious pubby bar with well kept Badger Best and Tanglefoot, good food, helpful staff, piped classical music, boxed games; also conservatory-feel coffee shop, restaurant, garden running down to small river *(WHBM)*

☆ **Wimborne St Giles** [SU0212], *Bull*: Imaginative food inc fish fresh daily from Cornwall in comfortable red-carpeted bar with cretonne-cushioned modern settles; Badger ales *(Patrick Freeman, W Mecham, John Hazel)*

Winfrith Newburgh [A352 Wareham—Dorchester; SY8084], *Red Lion*: Wide range of promptly served food inc lighter dishes in comfortable eating place with friendly efficient service, Badger ales; piped music, tables out behind, bedrooms *(Stan Edwards, John and Joan Nash, Mrs M A Mees)*

Winterborne Kingston [SY8697], *Greyhound*: Good value food inc popular carvery, well kept Wadworths 6X, staff friendly even when busy, good atmosphere *(John and Joan Nash)*

☆ **Winterbourne Abbas** [A35 W of Dorchester; SY6190], *Coach & Horses*: Staff deal efficiently even with large coach parties in big roadside pub with extensive lounge bar and long side dining area, cold food counter and hot carvery service, well kept Bass, Eldridge Pope Thomas Hardy and Royal Oak; particularly good well equipped outside play area; bedrooms *(F H Swan, John Sanders, T A Bryan, Stan Edwards, BB)*

Wool [Dorchester Rd; SY8486], *Ship*: Very welcoming, good value quickly served food *(Gerald Bown)*

Durham *see* Northumbria

Essex

This year's crop of new entries confirms that Essex is increasingly a good county for eating out well in pubs: the Bull at Blackmore End and the Green Dragon at Youngs End are both well run dining pubs, with the Bull's food in particular showing a good deal of individuality; the Compasses near Coggeshall has all the attributes of a friendly country pub, but its food is so good that it's close to award standard; and though the chief charm of the Flitch of Bacon at Little Dunmow is its unspoilt welcoming character, its short choice of simple food is most enjoyable. Among existing entries, the food at the Green Man at Gosfield stands out: for the second year running, we choose it as Essex Dining Pub of the Year. Other pubs where food is currently a particular strength include the Swan in its lovely setting at Chappel, the fine old Marlborough Head in Dedham, the very friendly Pheasant at Gestingthorpe (good on vegetarian dishes), the White Hart at Great Yeldham (as the new licensee settles in we feel this may work its way into the top rank), the very well run Bell at Horndon on the Hill, the cheerful Green Man at Little Braxted, the Queens Head at Littlebury (always ringing the changes), and the Eight Bells in Saffron Walden. No less than nine pubs in the county now qualify for our Beer Award, and the same unusually high proportion for our Wine Award. Drinks prices in the county are rather higher than the national average, and have been rising rather faster than elsewhere; we found prices in pubs tied to the regional brewer Greene King around average, but pubs tied to smaller local brewers (Crouch Vale, Ridleys) were cheaper than average. Cheapest of all was the £1-a-pint mid-week special offer at the Queens Head at Littlebury. In the Lucky Dip section at the end of the chapter, pubs to watch particularly at the moment (most inspected and approved by us) include the Wooden Fender at Ardleigh, Shepherd & Dog at Crays Hill, Three Horseshoes at Duton Hill, Cherry Tree at Great Stambridge, Rainbow & Dove at Hastingwood, Cock & Bell at High Easter, Wheatsheaf at High Ongar, Crown at Little Walden, Gardeners Arms in Loughton, Moreton Massey at Moreton, Tower Arms at South Weald and Green Man at Toot Hill.

ARKESDEN TL4834 Map 5

Axe & Compasses ★ 🍷

Village signposted from B1038 – but B1039 from Wendens Ambo, then forking left, is prettier; OS Sheet 154 map reference 482344

There's a fine old-fashioned and relaxed atmosphere in this rambling thatched country pub – and a warm welcome from the friendly licensees, too. A comfortable carpeted saloon bar has a warm coal fire, pastel green-cushioned oak and elm seats, quite a few easy chairs, old wooden tables, lots of brasses on the walls, and a friendly cat called Spikey. The smaller public bar, with cosy built-in settles, has sensibly placed darts and cribbage. Popular meals can be eaten in the bar or the restaurant and might include sandwiches, home-made soup (£2.25), deep-fried mushrooms with garlic mayonnaise (£3.95), mushroom pancake with a creamy cheesy sauce (£6.75), grilled whole lemon sole (£8.75), steaks (from £11.50), and daily specials such as chicken and spinach terrine (£3.95), scallops with mushrooms and onions in white wine and glazed with cheese sauce (£5.25), chicken, leek and bacon crumble (£6.75), and pork loin in a creamy mushroom sauce and glazed with stilton cheese (£7.25); prompt, attentive service. Well kept Greene King IPA and Abbott on handpump under light blanket pressure, a very good wine list, and 21 malt whiskies. There are seats outside on a side terrace with colourful hanging baskets; maybe summer barbecues. The village is very pretty. *(Recommended by Roger Byrne, Tina and David Woods-Taylor, Gwen and Peter Andrews, John Fahy, Mr and Mrs I Walker, E A George, Robin Moore, Martyn Kearey, D K Carter, Penny and Martin Fletcher, Adrian Kelly)*

Greene King ~ Lease: Themis and Diane Christou ~ Real ale ~ Meals and snacks (not winter Sun evening) ~ Restaurant (not winter Sun evening) ~ (01799) 550272 ~ Children in eating area of bar and in restaurant until 8.30 ~ Open 11-2.30, 6-11

BLACKMORE END TL7430 Map 5

Bull 🍷

Signposted via Beazley End from Bocking Church Street, itself signed off A131 just N of Braintree bypass; pub is on Wethersfield side of village

Tucked away down a country lane, this comfortable dining pub has plenty of good snacky things such as sandwiches (home-baked ham £1.95), a well balanced mushroom and thyme or carrot and orange soup (£2.25), interestingly filled baked potatoes (£2.50), ham and eggs (£3.95), slices of potato, onion and mushroom with hazelnuts and sour cream (£3.25), ploughman's (from £3.50), marinated prawns and mushrooms (£3.95) and a warm croissant with Parma ham and brie (£4.25). At the other end of the scale, set lunches (two courses £7.50, three £9.95) are good value, and separate main dishes are cooked with careful attention to ingredients and detail: liver with a rich but not at all cloying redcurrant sauce (£6.95), turkey with an interesting avocado and cider sauce (£8.50), crispy yet succulent duck with a light raspberry sauce (£10.50), very tender new season's lamb cutlets (£10.95). Good vegetables are served separately; potatoes give a choice of good chunky chips, new or dauphinoise; there are lots of home-made puddings such as iced blackcurrant parfait (£3.50); coffee comes with home-made fudge. The flowery-carpeted dining bar has red plush built-in button-back banquettes, low brown-painted beams, lots of menu blackboards, and middle-of-the-road piped music; beyond a massive brick chimney-piece is a family room with lots of agricultural tackle, and at the other end is a prettily cottagey restaurant area. Adnams, Greene King IPA and changing guest ales such as Boddingtons and Mauldons Midsummer Madness and Whiteadder on handpump; decent house wines, and an enterprising list of bin-ends; picnic tables outside. *(Recommended by Gwen and Peter Andrews, Paul and Ursula Randall)*

Free house ~ Licensees Christopher and Mary Bruce ~ Real ale ~ Meals and snacks (12-2, 7-10) ~ Restaurant ~ (01371) 851037 ~ Children if eating ~ Open 12-3, 7-11

CASTLE HEDINGHAM TL7835 Map 5

Bell

B1058 E of Sible Hedingham, towards Sudbury

In summer, a particular highlight of this interesting old coaching inn is the fine big walled garden behind the pub – an acre or so, with grass, trees and shrubs; there are more seats on a small terrace. The beamed and timbered saloon bar has a friendly atmosphere and Jacobean-style seats and windsor chairs around sturdy oak tables, and beyond the standing timbers left from a knocked-through wall, some steps lead up to a little gallery. Behind the traditionally furnished public bar a games room has dominoes and cribbage; piped pop music. One bar is no smoking, and each of the rooms has a good log fire. Promptly served bar food includes soup (£2), ploughman's (£3), mushrooms in garlic butter (£3.50), ham and broccoli bake (£4), liver and bacon casserole, steak and Guinness pie or Thai chicken curry (all £4.50), trout (£6), sirloin steak (£7), and treacle tart (£2); Greene King IPA and Abbot and an occasional guest beer tapped from the cask, and farm cider. The Great Dane is called Lucia. The nearby 12th-c castle keep is worth a visit. *(Recommended by Gwen and Peter Andrews, Anthony Barker, Barbara and Norman Wells, John Fahy; more reports please)*

Grays (Greene King, Ridleys) ~ Tenant Mrs Sandra Ferguson ~ Real ale ~ Meals and snacks (till 10pm; not Mon evening, except bank holidays) ~ (01787) 460350 ~ Well behaved children welcome, except in public bar ~ Jazz last Sun lunchtime of month/first Tues of month, acoustic guitar group Fri evening ~ Open 11.30-3, 6-11; closed evening 25 Dec

CHAPPEL TL8927 Map 5

Swan

Wakes Colne; pub visible just off A604 Colchester—Halstead

The setting for this friendly timbered old pub is marvellous – the River Colne runs through the garden and down to the splendid Victorian viaduct below. And in summer, the sheltered suntrap cobbled courtyard, now partly covered by a canopy, has a rather continental feel with parasols, big tubs overflowing with flowers, and French street signs. Inside, the spacious, rambling and low-beamed bar has standing oak timbers dividing off side areas, banquettes around lots of dark tables, one or two swan pictures and plates on the white and partly panelled walls, and a few attractive tiles above the very big fireplace, filled in summer with lots of plants; one bar is no smoking. Popular and good value bar food includes filled french rolls or sandwiches (from £1.50; the beef are recommended), ploughman's (from £3.25), home-made steak and kidney pie or gammon with pineapple (£4.45), fried cod or rock eel (£4.95), salads (from £4.95), sirloin steak (£8.95), fresh fish dishes, and good puddings. Well kept Greene King Abbot and Rayments on handpump, a good selection of wines by the glass served by notably cheery helpful staff; cribbage, dominoes, and faint piped music. The nearby Railway Centre (a must for train buffs) is just a few minutes' walk away. *(Recommended by Gwen and Peter Andrews, Howard Gatiss, Ian Phillips, David Shillitoe, S R Maycock, John Fahy, Tony and Wendy Hobden, Professor S Barnett, Russell and Margaret Bathie, Barbara and Norman Wells, R A Quantock, Basil J S Minson)*

Free house ~ Licensees Terence Martin and M A Hubbard ~ Real ale ~ Meals and snacks (till 10.15) ~ Restaurant ~ (01787) 222353 ~ Children over 5 in restaurant and eating area of bar ~ Open 11-3, 6-11

CLAVERING TL4731 Map 5

Cricketers

B1038 Newport—Buntingford, Newport end of village

This attractive and comfortably modernised 16th-c dining pub is very popular for its wide choice of interesting home-made bar food: sandwiches, soup (£2.80), terrine of veal and bacon accompanied by an onion and shallot compote (£3.75), tagliatelle with sun-dried tomatoes, broccoli and feta cheese (£3.80), herby pastry tartlet filled with leeks and mussels and baked with mozzarella cheese (£4), steak and kidney pie (£8.25), grilled slices of pork covered in braised celery, walnuts and stilton (£8.75), baked halibut steak on a tomato, chive and leek sauce (£9.25), and duck breast on a sauce of braised lettuce, bacon and peas (£10.80); every Tuesday they hold a fish night (starters from £3, main courses from £5.50), and on Wednesday there's a Pudding Club menu with steak and kidney pudding, roast beef and yorkshire pudding and sweet puddings with custard. The roomy L-shaped bar has lots of beams and standing timbers, pale green plush button-backed banquettes, stools and windsor chairs around shiny wooden tables, gleaming copper pans and horsebrasses, dried flowers in the big fireplace (open fire in colder weather), and fresh flowers; one area is no smoking. Well kept Boddingtons, and Flowers IPA and Original on handpump. The front terrace has picnic tables and umbrellas and colourful flowering shrubs. We'd be grateful to hear from readers who have stayed in the newly opened bedrooms, which look pretty. *(Recommended by Jack Morley, Mr and Mrs I Walker, John Fahy, Maysie Thompson, Adrian M Kelly, Gwen and Peter Andrews, Gordon Theaker, Mrs Gwyneth Holland, Bernard and Marjorie Parkin)*

Free house ~ Licensees Trevor and Sally Oliver ~ Real ale ~ Meals and snacks ~ Restaurant (not Sun evening) ~ (01799) 550442 ~ Children in eating area of bar and in restaurant ~ Open 10.30-3, 6-11

nr COGGESHALL TL8522 Map 5

Compasses

Pattiswick; signposted from A120 about 2 miles W of Coggeshall; OS Sheet 168 map reference 820247

Surrounded by farmland, this secluded, friendly country pub fills up quickly with people keen to enjoy the wide range of very good food. The neatly kept and comfortable bars are spacious and attractive with beams, tiled floors and lots of brass ornaments, and Greene King IPA, Marstons Pedigree and Rayments on handpump. Home-made, the bar food includes soup (£1.50), one-and-a-half rounds of sandwiches (from £2.95), ploughman's (from £3.95), liver and bacon (£5.95), kidneys braised in whisky (£6.95), a choice of eight daily vegetarian dishes (from £6.95), steak, kidney and wild boar pie (£7.95), salmon Italienne (£8.95), lamb shoulder in rosemary and garlic (£10.95), half roast duck in fruit sauce (£11.50), and puddings like passion fruit and caramel bavarois or chocolate, hazelnut and praline torte (£2.50). Darts. Outside there are seats on the lawns. *(Recommended by John Fahy, Quentin Williamson, Hazel Morgan, Pamela Goodwyn, G Neighbour)*

Free house ~ Licensees Chris and Gilbert Heap ~ Real ale ~ Meals and snacks ~ Restaurant ~ (01376) 561322 ~ Children in eating area of bar ~ Open 11-3, 6-11

DEDHAM TM0533 Map 5

Marlborough Head 🛏

Mr and Mrs Wills have been running this nicely old-fashioned inn for over 18 years now – and although it's a very popular place for eating, there's still a good pubby atmosphere. The comfortable central lounge has lots of beams and pictures, a wealth of finely carved woodwork, and a couple of roaring log fires; the beamed and timbered bar is set out for eating with lots of tables (which have a numbered pebble for ordering food) in wooden alcoves around its plum-coloured carpet. An imaginative choice of good bar food might include sandwiches (from £1.95), soup (£1.85), creamy mushroom pot with a warm muffin (£3.85), bacon, mushroom and tomato quiche (£4.45), broad bean and chestnut casserole (£5), braised wild rabbit in mustard sauce (£5.65), cured leg of pork in sweet and sour sauce with exotic fruits (£6), Aga roasted back bacon steak with peaches (£6.45), noisettes of roe deer with pear and cinnamon sauce (£7.50), and very good home-made puddings such as rhubarb crumble, lemon silk crunch or black and white chocolate mousse pâté with milk chocolate sauce (from £2.65); best to get there early to be sure of a table; they also do morning coffee and afternoon teas. Ind Coope Burton and Worthingtons on handpump, kept under light blanket pressure. Seats on the terrace or in the garden at the back (part of which is now the car park). The pub is right in the heart of Constable's old town, directly opposite the artist's school, and the handsome flushwork church tower that features in a number of his paintings. When this became an inn in 1704, it was named for the Duke of Marlborough's victory at Blenheim. *(Recommended by Ian Phillips, Derek and Maggie Washington, John Beeken, Paul Noble, A Preston, Mike Beiley, Joan Hilditch, Andrew Jeeves, Carole Smart, George Atkinson, David and Ruth Hollands)*

Ind Coope (Allied) ~ Lease: Brian and Jackie Wills, Linda Mower ~ Real ale ~ Meals and snacks (all day; not Dec 25) ~ (01206) 323250 ~ Children in eating area of bar and in family room ~ Open 10-11; closed Dec 25 ~ Bedrooms: £32.50S/£50S

FYFIELD TL5606 Map 5

Black Bull

B184, N end of village

It's the wide range of popular, good value food that draws people to this friendly dining pub. There might be stockpot soup (£1.40), sandwiches (from £1.65), filled baked potatoes (from £2.25), ploughman's (£2.50), ratatouille with garlic bread (£2.95), soft roes, chilli con carne or flaked smoked haddock in cheese and wine sauce (all £3.25), spinach and mushroom lasagne (£3.35), chicken roasted with cider, mustard, ginger and spices (£6.25), wing of skate with lemon butter (£7), and kleftiko (shoulder of lamb in herbs and wine, £7.35); the vegetables are nicely cooked. On Thursday evenings a separate fresh fish menu includes sole, plaice and more exotic choices like red snapper. Inside, the series of communicating rooms have low ceilings, big black beams, standing timbers, and cushioned wheelback chairs and modern settles on the muted maroon carpet; warm winter fire. Well kept Courage Directors, Trumans IPA, and Wadworths 6X on handpump under light blanket pressure, darts, dominoes, cribbage, piped music, fruit machine. Under an arbour by the car park is an aviary with budgerigars and cockatiels, and there are picnic tables on a nearby stretch of grass, as well as to the side of the building. *(Recommended by M A and C R Starling, Mayur Shah, Stephen and Jean Curtis, Beryl and Bill Farmer, R C Morgan, Keith Archer, Peter and Joy Heatherley, Gwen and Peter Andrews, C H and P Stride, Mrs Gwyneth Holland, John Fahy, Robert Turnham, Caroline Shearer)*

Free house ~ Licensee Alan Smith ~ Real ale ~ Meals and snacks (12-2 7-9.30) ~ Restaurant ~ (01277) 899225 ~ Children in restaurant ~ Open 11-2.30(3 Sat), 6.30-11

GESTINGTHORPE TL8138 Map 5

Pheasant

Village signposted from B1058; pub at Audley End end

You can be sure of a particularly friendly welcome from the cheerful and outgoing licensees in this simple country pub with its lovely old-fashioned character. The little lounge bar has a big pheasant-print-cushioned bow window seat looking out over the quiet lane to gently rising fields, a raised log fire, and interesting old furnishings: a grandfather clock, arts-and-crafts oak settle, and a pew. The red-walled public bar, with more orthodox pub furniture, has another winter log fire; dominoes, cribbage, shove-ha'penny, and piped music. There's also a family room. Bar food is totally home-made and good value: sandwiches (from £1.50), soup (£1.95), tagliatelle with bacon, tomato, garlic and basil or macaroni cheese (£2.95), shepherd's pie or ploughman's (£3.75), omelettes (from £3.75), good fish pie (£4.50), beany goulash (£5.25), mint-glazed lamb cutlets or aubergine layer bake (£5.95), tiger prawns with spring onion and ginger (£6.95), sirloin steak (£9.75), and puddings such as treacle tart or apricot and almond crumble (from £1.95); no chips or deep-fried meals. Twice a year they hold vegetarian weeks in addition to the normal menu. Well kept Adnams Southwold, Greene King IPA and Abbot, Nethergate Bitter, and a weekly guest beer on handpump, and local cider. The garden has picnic tables looking over the fine views of the countryside, and you can play pétanque out here. *(Recommended by Gwen and Peter Andrews, Pamela Goodwyn, Paul Beckwith, John Fahy, Miss D Morrison, A Kemp, Ian Phillips, Sue Holland, Dave Webster)*

Free house ~ Licensees Adrian and Tricia McGrillen ~ Real ale ~ Meals and snacks (11.30-2.15, 6.30-9.45) ~ (01787) 461196 ~ Well behaved children welcome ~ Occasional live entertainment ~ Open 11-3, 6-11

GOSFIELD TL7829 Map 5

Green Man

3 m N of Braintree

Essex Dining Pub of the Year

As well as particularly good food, you can expect a warm welcome from the cheerfully efficient staff in this busy, well run dining pub. The popular lunchtime cold table has a splendid help-yourself choice of home cooked ham, tongue, beef and turkey (all carved by the landlord), dressed salmon or crab (in season), game pie, salads and homemade pickles (£6.95). Other excellent dishes include soups like game with sherry (£1.90), lovely soft roes on toast with bacon (£3.25), fresh battered cod (£6), delicious liver and bacon or super braised oxtail with dumplings (£6.50), cider-baked hot ham or hot sirloin of beef (£6.85), tender roast shoulder of wild boar (£6.95), really good rare lamb chops in a port and cranberry sauce (£7.25), pheasant in red wine (£7.95), fresh scallops mornay (£8.20), roast duck with gooseberry sauce (£8.50), 20oz T-bone steak (£13.50), and superb puddings like apple charlotte, raspberry pavlova or steamed marmalade pudding (£2.75); the vegetables are fresh and the chips home-made. They have regular themed food evenings with curries and Greek and Italian dishes. The two little bars have a relaxed atmosphere, and the dining room is no smoking. Well kept Greene King IPA and Abbot on handpump, and decent nicely priced wines, many by the glass; darts. *(Recommended by Gwen and Peter Andrews, John Fahy, Tina and David Woods-Taylor, BNF, M Parkin, Paul and Ursula Randall)*

Greene King ~ Lease: John Arnold ~ Real ale ~ Meals and snacks (not Sun evening) ~ Restaurant (not Sun evening) ~ (01787) 472746 ~ Well behaved children in eating area ~ Open 11-3, 6.30-11 (midnight supper licence)

GREAT YELDHAM TL7638 Map 5

White Hart

Poole Street; A604 Halstead—Haverhill

Roger Jones (who was running the civilised Pheasant at Keyston, a popular main entry in Cambridgeshire) has taken over this attractive Tudor house. A lot of refurbishment will take place before the pub is up and running properly: the kitchen is to be completely overhauled, the beer cellar enlarged to allow for them to keep three real ales, a wine cellar opened in a converted extension building, the renovation of the stone and wood floors in the main areas, and complete redecoration throughout; one area will be no smoking. As well as sandwiches and snacks, the food will follow the lines at the Pheasant with dishes such as leek and parma ham risotto, spicy tuna and salmon fishcakes with a peanut and cucumber dressing, wild boar sausages, pork tenderloin with sage noodles, spinach and a calvados sauce, rack of lamb with a redcurrant jus, char-grilled steaks, and puddings such as hot pancakes with coconut ice cream and maple or jam roly poly with custard. Well kept Nethergate Bitter and two guests on handpump, and a fine wine list. The black-and-white building and well-kept garden are very attractive, with seats among a variety of trees and shrubs on the lawns. *(More reports please)*

Free house ~ Licensee Roger Jones ~ Real ale ~ Meals and snacks (till 10pm) ~ Restaurant (not Sun evening) ~ (01787) 237250 ~ Children welcome ~ Open 12-2.30, 6-11

HATFIELD BROAD OAK TL5416 Map 5

Cock 

High St

Real ale drinkers are well looked after in this characterful 15th-c village pub. As well as Adnams Best and Nethergate IPA, there are four changing guest beers such as Fullers London Pride, Jennings Snecklifter, Morlands Old Speckled Hen, and

Shepherd Neame Spitfire on handpump or tapped from the cask – and last year they had over 150 different beers. There's a genuinely old-fashioned atmosphere – helped by the absence of noisy games machines and piped music – as well as beams, wide-planked wooden floors, a no-smoking tap room with open fire (a woodburning stove in another room), and lots of fresh flowers. The walls are decorated with the title sheets of Victorian and Edwardian music hall songs and old advertisements, and there's an untouched Victorian brass railed bar. Popular bar food includes sandwiches, soup such as ham and lentil, brandied chicken liver pâté (£1.95), local smoked trout and salmon parcels or roast summer vegetables with lemon vinaigrette (£2.25), mediterranean lamb with beans or stir-fried chilli and garlic chicken with noodles (£6.50), and roast salmon with fresh tomato and basil coulis (£8.50); good bloody mary and chilli sherry; bar billiards, juke box and darts. *(Recommended by Joy Heatherley, Gwen and Peter Andrews)*

Free house ~ Licensees David Sulway and Pamela Holcroft ~ Real ale ~ Meals and snacks (till 10pm; not Sun evening) ~ Restaurant (not Sun evening) ~ (01279) 718273 ~ Children in eating area of bar ~ Open 12-3, 5.30(6 Sat)-11

HORNDON ON THE HILL TQ6683 Map 3

Bell 🍷

M25 junction 30 into A13, then left into B1007 after 7 miles, village signposted from here

The hard-working licensees are not the sort of people to sit on their laurels (even though this partly medieval pub has been in the family for over 50 years), and continue to win competitions for (again) their wonderful hanging baskets and very good food. The inn is very much a focus for the village – though visitors are made welcome, too. The beamed, open-plan bar has some antique high-backed settles and plush burgundy stools and benches on the flagstones or highly polished oak floorboards, and seats in a bow window at the back with views over the fields. Very good imaginative bar food might include spinach, garlic and potato soup (£2.60), chicken liver pâté with home-made rhubarb chutney (£3.25), smoked haddock fishcakes (£3.60), steak and kidney pie (£4.95), home-made chicken sausages (£5.25), fricasée of monkfish with cucumber and mustard (£10.25), braised shoulder of lamb with tarragon mash (£10.50), calf's liver with shallot gravy (£10.95), fillet of beef with haggis and port wine sauce (£11.50), and puddings like orange sponge pudding with marmalade sauce or white chocolate mousse with bitter coffee sauce (£3.50). They have a changing choice of eight real ales a week on handpump, such as Arundel Gold, Bass, Charrington IPA, Crouch Vale Millennium Gold, and Fullers London Pride, and a huge selection of over 100 well chosen wines from all over the world with 13 by the glass listed on a blackboard with notes on what to drink with your food; you can also buy them off-sales. On the last weekend in June the High Road outside is closed (by Royal Charter) for period-costume festivities and a crafts fair; the pub holds a feast then. We're sure the bedrooms with their Tudor beams would be very nice indeed, but have, as yet, to hear from readers who have stayed here. *(Recommended by M A and C R Starling, Mrs J A Blanks, Nigel Norman, Neville Kenyon, MJVK, Mrs Gwyneth Holland, Gwen and Peter Andrews)*

Free house ~ Licensee John Vereker ~ Real ale ~ Meals and snacks ~ Restaurant ~ (01375) 673154 ~ Children in restaurant ~ Open 11-2.30(3 Sat), 6-11 ~ Bedrooms: /£55B

LAMARSH TL8835 Map 5

Red Lion

From Bures on B1508 Sudbury—Colchester take Station Road, passing station; Lamarsh then signposted

From the tables and small pews (in stalls with red velvet curtain dividers), you can look through the front windows of this friendly old place and enjoy the fine views over the fields and colour-washed houses of the Stour Valley. The bar has a lot of atmosphere, as well as abundant timbering, attractive dried flowers and plants, local scenes on the walls, a roaring log fire, and unobtrusive piped music. Very good changing bar food might include soups such as carrot and orange, huge filled rolls with a very flexible range of fillings (£3.35), stilton and walnut bake or chicken, ham and broccoli pie (£4.95), well-liked salads such as greek-style tuna with feta cheese (£5.25), and home-made puddings such as cherry pie (£2.50). Part of the eating area is no-smoking. Well kept Courage Directors, Greene King IPA, John Smiths, Marstons Pedigree and Wadworths 6X on handpump, a range of malt whiskies, and decent dry white wine by the glass; friendly staff. Pool, darts, cribbage, fruit machine, video game, and trivia. There are swings in the biggish sheltered sloping garden. *(Recommended by Gwen and Peter Andrews, Nigel Norman, Liz, James and Ian Phillips, D Cox, Basil J S Minson)*

Free house ~ Licensees John and Angela O'Sullivan ~ Real ale ~ Meals and snacks (till 10.30) ~ Restaurant ~ (01787) 227918 ~ Children in eating area ~ Very occasional live music ~ Open 11-3, 6-11; 11-11 Sat

LANGHAM TM0233 Map 5

Shepherd & Dog 🍷

Moor Rd/High St; village signposted off A12 N of Colchester

It's worth getting to this warmly friendly local early – especially at lunchtime – to be sure of a seat. But make sure you're really hungry beforehand as helpings are very generous: good sandwiches, celery and dill soup (£1.75), tasty deep-fried brie with cranberry jelly, nice vegetable samosas, stuffed loin of pork with a herby cheese sauce (£4.25), lamb's liver, bacon and black pudding, grilled halibut and anchovy butter (£6.95), monkfish and bacon kebab (£7.25), whole baked mullet (£9.90), and vegetarian dishes; they also hold Greek, Indian, French and American food evenings. Well kept Greene King IPA and Abbot, Nethergate Old Growler and Bitter, and Rayments on handpump, and decent wines. The L-shaped bar, with an interesting collection of continental bottled beers, is kept spick and span, and there's often a sale of books for charity. Tables outside. *(Recommended by Gill and Andy Plumb, John Fahy, M A and C R Starling, Gwen and Peter Andrews, Nigel Clifton, Jeff Davies, Barbara and Norman Wells, D and B Carter, R G Smedley)*

Free house ~ Licensees Paul Barnes and Jane Graham ~ Real ale ~ Meals and snacks (11.30-2.15, 6-9.30) ~ Restaurant ~ (01206) 272711 ~ Children welcome until 9pm ~ Open 11-3, 5.30-11; closed 26 Dec

LEIGH ON SEA TQ8385 Map 3

Crooked Billet

51 High St; from A13 follow signpost to station, then cross bridge over railway towards waterside

New licensees have taken over this small, inviting old place bracingly set right by the sea wall. The homely lounge bar has two big bay windows with good views out to sea, seats built around the walls, a solid fuel stove, and photographs of local cockle smacks on the shiny, yellowing walls; on the left, the bare-floored public bar has a huge log fire and more photographs. Home-made bar food now includes filled baked potatoes (from £2.35), filled french bread (from £2.50), crab platter (£2.75), vegetarian dishes (from £3.50), ploughman's (from £3.75), mussels in mediterranean sauce or chicken curry (£3.95), minced beef and onion pie (£4.25), and steak and kidney pie (£4.95). Well kept Adnams, Benskins, Ind Coope Burton, and Tetleys on handpump, with guest beers such as Marstons Pedigree and Wadworths 6X. Straightforward snacks such as filled rolls (from £1.50), ploughman's (£3), chilli con carne and hot pots (around £3.50). The big terrace has an outside servery used on fine afternoons, and seats from which to watch the shellfish boats in the old-fashioned working harbour; there's a new barbecue area. No children. *(Recommended by Tim Heywood, Sophie Wilne, Nigel Norman, Trevor P Scott, D Cox, A Plumb, Mr and Mrs A N Piper)*

Taylor Walker (Carlsberg Tetleys) ~ Managers Andy and Mairi Heron ~ Real ale ~ Lunchtime meals and snacks (all day bank holidays) ~ (01702) 714854 ~ Live Bluegrass band every other Mon (not high season) ~ Open 11.30-11

LITTLE BRAXTED TL8314 Map 5

Green Man

Kelvedon Road; village signposted off B1389 by NE end of A12 Witham bypass – keep on patiently

This friendly and pretty brick house, tucked away on an isolated lane, is a smashing place for a quiet drink – either in the sheltered garden, or in the traditional little lounge. There's an interesting collection of bric-a-brac, including 200 horse brasses and some harness, mugs hanging from a beam, a lovely copper urn, and an open fire. The tiled public bar leads to a games room with darts, shove-ha'penny, dominoes, cribbage, and fruit machine. Well kept Ridleys IPA, ESX and Spectacular is dispensed from handpumps in the form of 40mm brass cannon shells, and there are several malt whiskies; piped music. Good, home-made bar food includes sandwiches, filled french bread, filled baked potatoes, stuffed mushrooms, a crab and salmon pot, pies such as steak and ale pie or fidget pie (an East Anglian recipe involving onion, apple, bacon and cider), various casseroles (from £4.75), and a popular haggis. There are picnic tables in the sheltered garden behind. No children. *(Recommended by Roxanne Chamberlain, Derek Patey, Alan Budden, John C Baker, George Atkinson, David Cardy, Mrs Gwyneth Holland, Hazel Morgan, Bernard Patrick, Gwen and Peter Andrews, S J Barney, R C Morgan)*

Ridleys ~ Tenants Tony and Andrea Wiley ~ Real ale ~ Meals and snacks ~ (01621) 891659 ~ Open 11.30-3, 6-11; closed evening 25 Dec

LITTLE DUNMOW TL6521 Map 5

Flitch of Bacon

Village signposted off A120 E of Dunmow, then turn right on village loop road

The Walkers reopened this old place two years ago after about a year's disuse, and now run it as a delightfully unspoilt country tavern. It looks across the quiet lane to a broad expanse of green, and has a few picnic tables on the edge; the nearby church of St Mary is well worth a visit. Inside, the small L-shaped bar is simply but attractively furnished, mainly with flowery-cushioned pews, and has prettily arranged flowers on the tables; the ochre walls are timbered. Quietly relaxing at lunchtime during the week, the atmosphere can be vibrantly cheerful in the evenings – especially on one of the Saturdays when they sing through a musical such as *Me and My Girl* around the piano at the back. Home-cooked food is simple but good: generous sandwiches including excellent home-carved ham (£1.75), soup such as spinach (£2.50), cheese and ham ploughman's (£3.25), ham and eggs with a crusty roll (£4), three or four changing hot dishes such as sausage hot-pot (£4.50) or strongly commended steak and kidney pie (£6.50), and a couple of puddings – on our inspection visit, local strawberries (£1.95) and summer pudding (£2.50); good buffet lunch only on Sunday. Well kept Greene King IPA and their seasonal beer and a guest such as Arundel or Woodfordes Wherry on handpump; friendly and thoughtful service; silenced fruit machine. We expect this would be a nice place to stay, but haven't yet had enough reports on this aspect to be sure. *(Recommended by David Oppedisano, Jim Leven, Nikki Moffat)*

Free house ~ Licensees Bernard and Barbara Walker ~ Real ale ~ Meals and snacks ~ (01371) 820323 ~ Children may be allowed in function room if free ~ Open 11-3, 6-11; 11-11 Sat ~ Bedrooms: £25B/£45B

Food details, prices, timing etc refer to bar food – not to a separate restaurant if there is one.

LITTLEBURY TL5139 Map 5

Queens Head

B1383 NW of Saffron Walden; not far from M11 junction 9, but exit northbound only, access southbound only

For those who really enjoy good beers and interesting food, this unpretentious pub is the place to head for. They keep eight real ales such as Bass, Courage Directors, John Smiths and Youngers Scotch with changing guests like Hancocks HB, Marstons Best, Mansfield Riding, and Mauldons Black Adder, have helpful tasting notes, and a bargain £1 a pint for John Smiths on Monday-Thursday. There's an an annual real ale festival with over 70 different beers – and the landlord aims to have 140 different beers every year; also interesting bottled beers, and a decent recently expanded wine list. Good, home-made food changes every day and might include lunchtime sandwiches (from £1.95), soup such as prawn and samphire (£2.20), filled baked potatoes (from £2.50), baked avocado with stilton butter (£2.80), wild boar and apple sausages (£3.10), ploughman's (£4.25), fresh tagliatelle with vegetarian sauces or provençale tarts with garlic pastry (£5.20), gammon with cider and apple (£5.90), pheasant with cranberries (in season, £7.90) and puddings like different treacle tart or banoffi pie (£2.50); they do a two-course weekday lunch (£5), two-course Sunday lunch (£7.95), hold winter themed food evenings, and grow lots of herbs (used in the cooking). The pub is carefully refurbished to make the most of its unassuming appeal – flooring tiles, beams, simple but attractive wooden furniture, old local photographs, bunches of dried flowers and plants, and snug side areas leading off the bar; a part near the restaurant is no-smoking. The atmosphere's vibrant and friendly; darts, shove-ha'penny, cribbage, dominoes and maybe piped music. Tables out in a nicely planted walled garden, and swings, stepping stumps, a climbing frame and slide for children. *(Recommended by Gwen and Peter Andrews, John Fahy, Susan and Nigel Wilson, E D Bailey, H O Dickinson, Peter Saville, Stephen and Jean Curtis, Nigel Clifton, P and D Carpenter, Neil Walden, Ruth Davies, Ian Phillips, Alan and Ruth Woodhouse, John C Baker, Trevor P Scott, Tony Gayfer)*

Free house ~ Licensees Deborah and Jeremy O'Gorman ~ Real ale ~ Meals and lunchtime snacks ~ Restaurant (not Sun evening) ~ (01799) 522251 ~ Children in eating area of bar and in restaurant ~ Open 12-11; limited opening 25/26 Dec ~ Bedrooms: £29.95B/£44.95B

MILL GREEN TL6400 Map 5

Viper

Mill Green Rd; from Fryerning (which is signposted off north-east bound A12 Ingatestone bypass) follow Writtle signposts; OS Sheet 167 map reference 640019

Tables on the neat lawn here look over marvellously cared-for gardens with a mass of colourful summer flowers – and the pub itself is almost hidden by overflowing hanging baskets and window boxes. Inside, it's very much a local and the two little rooms of the lounge have spindleback seats, armed country kitchen chairs, and tapestried wall seats around neat little old tables, and a warming log fire. The parquet-floored taproom (where booted walkers are directed) is more simply furnished with shiny wooden traditional wall seats, and beyond there's another room with country kitchen chairs and sensibly placed darts; shove-ha'penny, dominoes, cribbage and a fruit machine. Three very well kept, monthly changing real ales such as Elgoods, Ridleys and Charles Wells on handpump, served from the oak-panelled counter. Bar snacks include good sandwiches (from £1.70), chilli con carne (£3), and ploughman's (from £3). No children. *(Recommended by Basil Minson, Gwen and Peter Andrews, George Atkinson, D Cox, S J Barney; more reports please)*

Free house ~ Licensee Fred Beard ~ Real ale ~ Lunchtime snacks ~ (01277) 352010 ~ Open 11-2.30(3 Sat), 6-11

Prices of main dishes usually include vegetables or a side salad.

NAVESTOCK TQ5397 Map 5

Plough

Sabines Rd, Navestock Heath (off main rd at Alma Arms)

An enjoyable local atmosphere and an outstanding choice of real ales can be found in this neatly kept country pub. On handpump or tapped from the cask, there may be up to thirteen beers: Brains Dark, Brakspears, Fullers ESB, Cotleigh Harrier and Tawny, Hoskins & Oldfield Supreme, Mauldons White Adder, Otter Bitter, Thwaites Bitter, and Timothy Taylors Landlord; maybe three cask ciders. Several interconnecting rooms have a mix of dark wooden solid chairs with flowery-cushioned seats around polished wooden tables, horsebrasses and dried flowers on the beams, and an open fire. Bar food includes sandwiches, home-made hot dishes (from around £4.50), steaks (from £7.95), weekend barbecues, and a favourite dish called snob's chicken. Darts, cribbage, dominoes and piped music. *(Recommended by Derek Patey, JLP, Joy Heatherley, George Atkinson, D Cox)*

Free house ~ Licensee Ros Willson ~ Real ale ~ Meals and snacks (not Sun evenings) ~ (01277) 372296 ~ Children in eating area of bar ~ Trad jazz monthly, Sun evening ~ Open 11-4, 6-11

NORTH FAMBRIDGE TQ8597 Map 5

Ferryboat £

The Quay; village signposted from B1012 E off S Woodham Ferrers; keep on past railway

This is a lovely unassuming spot, tucked away at the end of the lane down by the River Crouch, with good lonely walks around. It's an attractive 500-year-old weatherboarded pub, simply furnished with traditional wall benches, settles and chairs on its stone floor, nautical memorabilia, old-fashioned lamps, and a few historic boxing-gloves. There's a log fire at one end, and a woodburning stove at the other, and a dining conservatory for families. Good value bar food includes sandwiches (from £1.10), soup (£1.40), ploughman's (from £2.20), deep-fried cod (£2.95), beef and onion pie (£3), ham and egg (£3.50), vegetable chilli (£4), poached halibut (£6), steaks (from £6), venison in port and red wine (£7), puddings (£1.75), and children's meals (£1.50). Well kept Flowers IPA on handpump and guests like Fremlins or Morlands Old Speckled Hen; friendly chatty landlord; shove ha'penny, table skittles, cribbage, dominoes, and piped music. There's a pond with ducks and carp, and seats in the garden. *(Recommended by Derek Patey, Paul Barstow, Karyn Taylor, Gwen and Peter Andrews, Myroulla West, Russell and Margaret Bathie, K and B Moore, George Atkinson)*

Free house ~ Licensee Roy Maltwood ~ Real ale ~ Meals and snacks ~ Restaurant ~ (01621) 740208 ~ Children in family conservatory ~ Open 11-3, 6-11; 12-3, 7-11 in winter

PELDON TL9916 Map 5

Rose

B1025 Colchester—Mersea, at junction with southernmost turn-off to Peldon

The cosy bar in this pink-washed old inn has one or two standing timbers supporting the low ceiling with its dark bowed 17th-c oak beams, creaky close-set tables and some antique mahogany, chintz curtains in the leaded-light windows, and brass and copper on the the mantlepiece of the gothick-arched brick fireplace; the large conservatory is no-smoking. Bar food includes sandwiches, lasagne, steak and kidney pie (£5.70), steaks (from £10.95), and Sunday roast (£6.95). Well kept Boddingtons, Flowers Original, and Tetleys on handpump. The spacious garden is very relaxing with good teak seats and two ponds with geese and ducks. *(Recommended by Hilary Dobbie, Joy Heatherley, Chris Harrison, Barbara and Norman Wells; more reports please)*

Free house ~ Licensees Alan and Ariette Everett ~ Real ale ~ Meals and snacks (until 10pm; not evening 25 Dec) ~ Restaurant (only Fri and Sat evenings) ~ (01206) 735248 ~ Children in conservatory ~ Open 11-3(2.30 in winter), 5.30-11 ~ Bedrooms: £25/£35

PLESHEY TL6614 Map 5

White Horse

Signposted with Howe Street off A130 Dunmow—Chelmsford

As friendly and cheerful as ever, this 15th-c pub has lots of nooks and crannies filled with a fascinating array of jugs, tankards, antlers, miscellaneous brass, prints, books, bottles – and even an old ship's bell. The rooms have a genuinely friendly feel and are furnished with wheelback and other chairs and a mix of dark wooden tables; one fireplace has a woodburning stove, another big brick one has horse-brasses along the mantlebeam, and yet another has an unusual curtain-like fireguard. The snug room by the tiny bar counter has brick and beamed walls, a comfortable sofa, some bar stools and a table with magazines to read, as well as a sonorous clock. Well kept Archers, Batemans, Crouch Vale, Elgoods, Jennings, and Nethergate on handpump, and local cider; fruit machine. Bar food includes good soup (£2), huffers (from £2.50; the bacon and mushroom is lovely), filled baked potatoes or ploughman's (from £3.50), cumberland sausage (£5), lentil bake or steak and kidney pie (£5.50), fresh pasta with a daily sauce (£5.60), and daily specials. Glass cabinets in the big dining room are filled with 1500 miniatures and the room also has sturdy furniture, lots of plants, and an old-fashioned stove in the brick fireplace. Doors from here open on to a terrace with white plastic garden furniture, a grass area with similar seating and a few picnic tables, and a children's play area with slide, swings and a see-saw. The hanging baskets and flowering tubs are very pretty – and the cat is called Tigger. ***(Recommended by Tony Beaulah, Maysie Thompson, J Mayhew, Mike Beiley, Dorothy Pilson, Gwen and Peter Andrews, Professor John White, Patricia White, Paul and Ursula Randall)***

Free house ~ Licensees John and Helen Thorburn ~ Real ale ~ Meals and snacks (till 10pm) ~ Restaurant ~ (01245) 237281 ~ Children welcome ~ Open 11-3, 7-11

RICKLING GREEN TL5029 Map 5

Cricketers Arms 🛏 🍷

Just off B1383 N of Stansted Mountfichet

This is such a happy and friendly family-run inn – and no matter how busy they are, the Proctors really go out of their way to make visitors feel at home. Essex CC play on the village green outside every year, and there are certainly enough cricketing mementoes to make them feel at home. Masses of cricket cigarette cards are displayed on the walls of the softly lit and comfortable saloon bar, the two bays of which are divided by standing timbers; in winter chestnuts are roasted on the log fire. Very good home-made bar food includes tomato and herb soup (£1.95), chicken liver and brandy pâté (£2.95), crab mayonnaise (£3.95), mussels (from £4.95), gammon and egg (£5.75), haddock provençal or vegetable balti (£5.95), chicken in apricots (£6.25), steak and kidney pie (£6.95), prawn and pineapple curry (£7.95), and duck in orange sauce (£9.25). Well kept Flowers IPA and a monthly changing strong Bitter and Mild tapped from the cask, and 24 bottle conditioned beers from all over Britain; 10 wines by the glass. There's a very heavily beamed little stone-floored side family dining area (no-smoking), a separate front bar with pool, darts, cribbage, dominoes, fruit machine and juke box, and a modern back restaurant. A sheltered front courtyard has picnic tables overlooking the cricket green. The bedrooms are in a modern block behind – handy for Stansted Airport, with a courtesy car for guests. ***(Recommended by John Fahy, Gwen and Peter Andrews, Stephen and Jean Curtis, Stephen Brown, Maysie Thompson, K and B Moore, George Atkinson, Hugh and Peggy Colgate, Wayne Brindle)***

Free house ~ Licensees Tim and Jo Proctor ~ Real ale ~ Meals and snacks (till 10) ~ Restaurant ~ (01799) 543210 ~ Children in eating area and family room ~ Open 11-3, 6-11; all day summer Sat/Sun ~ Bedrooms: £40B/£50B

SAFFRON WALDEN TL5438 Map 5

Eight Bells ♀

Bridge Street; B184 towards Cambridge

The very good food continues to draw people to this handsomely timbered black-and-white Tudor inn. As well as lots of daily specials, the menu might include home-made soup (£1.95; the broccoli is good), ploughman's (from £3.45), omelettes (£4.45), dressed Cromer crab with mayonnaise (£4.75), home-made lasagne (£5.75), mushrooms thermidor (£5.95), home-made steak, kidney and mushroom pie (£6.25), skate wing with capers (£7.25), calf's liver with smoked ham, mushroom and cream sauce (£8.50), and steaks (from £10.30); home-made puddings like chocolate and brandy pot or morello cherry cheesecake (£2.50), and children's menu (from £1.85); prompt, attentive and friendly service. Well kept Adnams, Friary Meux, Ind Coope Burton, Tetleys, and a weekly changing guest on handpump, and decent wines by the glass (with a choice of glass size). Partly no-smoking, the restaurant is in a splendidly timbered hall with high rafters, tapestries and flags, and the neatly kept open-plan bar is divided by old timbers, its modern oak settles forming small booths around the tables. There's a family room in the carpeted old kitchen with an open fire. There are seats in the garden. Nearby Audley End makes a good family outing, and the pub is close to some good walks. *(Recommended by Ian Phillips, JKW, John Fahy, Gwen and Peter Andrews, F Tomlin, Dono and Carol Leaman, Judith Mayne, M and B Moore)*

Ind Coope (Allied) ~ Manager David Gregory ~ Real ale ~ Meals and snacks (till 10pm Sat) ~ Restaurant ~ (01799) 522790 ~ Children in restaurant and family room ~ Open 11-3, 6-11

STOCK TQ6998 Map 5

Hoop £ 🍺

B1007; from A12 Chelsmford bypass take Galleywood, Billericay turn-off

A fine range of real ales in this happily unsophisticated village pub includes those from Adnams, Crouch Vale, Exmoor, Hopback, Jennings, Marstons, Nethergate, Wadworths, and Youngs on handpump or tapped from the cask – and over the May Day week, there might be around one hundred to choose from; also, farm ciders, summer country wines, and winter mulled wine. The bustling bar has a friendly and traditional atmosphere, as well as brocaded wall seats around dimpled copper tables on the left, a cluster of brocaded stools on the right, and a coal-effect gas fire in the big brick fireplace. Good value bar food includes home-made soup (£1), sandwiches (from £1.20), filled baked potatoes (from £1.50), omelettes (from £2.50), sausage pie or quiche (from £2.75), ploughman's (from £3), home-cooked ham and egg (£3.25), Lancashire hotpot or steak and kidney pie (£3.50), chicken curry (£4), and daily specials like Irish stew (£3.50), oxtail and dumplings (£4), calf's liver (£4.50), and four fish dishes. Sensibly placed darts (the heavy black beams are studded with hundreds of darts flights), cribbage and dominoes. Lots of picnic tables in the big sheltered back garden, prettily bordered with flowers and where they have occasional summer barbecues and maybe croquet (or boules on the front gravel). The dog is called Misty and the cat Thomas. *(Recommended by Beryl and Bill Farmer, Tina and David Woods-Taylor, Gwen and Peter Andrews, Mike and Pam Simpson)*

Free house ~ Licensee Albert Kitchin ~ Real ale ~ Meals and snacks (throughout opening hours) ~ (01277) 841137 ~ Children in eating area of bar ~ Open 11-11

If you know a pub's ever open all day, please tell us.

TILLINGHAM TL9903 Map 5

Cap & Feathers ★

B1021 N of Southminster

It's the lovely old-fashioned atmosphere that readers like about this characterful old tiled house. Three warmly snug low-beamed and timbered rooms make up the bar, with sturdy wall seats (including a venerable built-in floor-to-ceiling settle), a homely dresser and a formidable woodburning stove, as well as little wheelback chairs with arms and etched-glass brass-mounted lamps; one parquet-floored part has bar billiards (operated by an old shilling, provided at the bar), sensibly placed darts, and table skittles – there's another set in the attractive no-smoking family room, and they have shove-ha'penny, cribbage and dominoes. Daily changing bar food (with prices unchanged since last year) features the distinctively flavoured products of their own smokery, such as smoked fillet of beef (£5.95) or trout (£6.75), as well as their own beef and venison pies, soup (£1.75), lasagne (£4.95), sirloin steak (£10.50), and home-made puddings like apple pie or ice cream. Well kept Crouch Vale Best and two changing guest beers on handpump, farm cider, and country wines; friendly and efficient service. A small side terrace has picnic tables under birch trees. Just down the lane is the village cricket pitch, and the pub fields its own team. *(Recommended by Paul Barstow, Karyn Taylor, George Atkinson, EDB, Gwen and Peter Andrews, A Plumb, Evelyn and Derek Walter, D Cox)*

Crouch Vale ~ Tenant John Moore ~ Real ale ~ Meals and snacks ~ (01621) 779212 ~ Children in no-smoking family room ~ Open 11.30-3, 6-11 ~ Three bedrooms: £20/£30

WENDENS AMBO TL5136 Map 5

Bell

B1039 just W of village

Although this small and friendly village pub is very popular locally, visitors are made to feel welcome, too. It's cottagey inside with spotlessly kept small rooms that ramble engagingly round to the back, with brasses on ancient timbers, wheelback chairs around neat tables, comfortably cushioned seats worked into snug alcoves, and quite a few pictures on the cream walls; good open fires. Good straightforward food includes lunchtime filled home-baked rolls (from £1.65), jalapeno peppers stuffed with cream cheese and chilli sauce (£3.25), ploughman's (£3.50), vegetarian dishes (from £4.95), popular curries (from £5.25), beef in ale pie (£5.95), Cajun chicken or mixed grill (£6.75), and puddings such as spotted dick or treacle tart (£2); popular winter Sunday lunch. Well kept Adnams, Ansells Dark Mild, Eldridge Pope Hardy, and guest beers on handpump; darts, dominoes, Monopoly, and piped music; boules. The very extensive back garden is quite special: an informal layout with a big tree-sheltered lawn, lots of flower borders, unusual plant-holders, plenty of amusements for children (and a goat called Gertie), and a sort of mini nature-trail wandering off through the shrubs). The two dogs are called Kate and Samson. *(Recommended by Gwen and Peter Andrews, Trevor P Scott, Ian Phillips, Neil Barker)*

Free house ~ Licensees Geoff and Bernie Bates ~ Real ale ~ Meals and snacks (not Mon evening) ~ Children in family dining room ~ (01799) 540382 ~ Open 11.30-3(2.30 winter), 6-11

WOODHAM WALTER TL8006 Map 5

Bell

A414 E from Chelmsford; village signposted on left after about 6 miles

This Elizabethan house is most attractive with its striking jettied upper storey. Inside, the neatly kept and friendly lounge bar has old beams and timbers, decorative plates and brass, and is divided into irregularly-shaped alcoves on various levels, with comfortable seats and a log fire. Decent bar food (with prices unchanged since last year) includes a wide choice of well-priced sandwiches (from £1.05), soup (£1.75), real ale pâté (£2.35), plaice or fried egg and sausages (£3.75), steak and kidney pie (£4.95), salmon and broccoli pie (£5.25), prawn curry (£5.50), duck in orange sauce (£7.95) and steaks (from £7.95) – as well as daily specials and vegetarian dishes. There's a prettily decorated dining room in a partly panelled gallery up steps from the main bar. Adnams, Friary Meux, and a weekly guest beer on handpump. *(Recommended by Nigel Norman, Paul Barstow, Karen Taylor, Gwen and Peter Andrews, John Fahy, Quentin Williamson, Paul and Ursula Randall)*

Free house ~ Licensees Alan and Margaret Oldfield ~ Real ale ~ Meals and snacks (not Mon, not winter Sun) ~ (01245) 223437 ~ Children in eating area or separate lounge ~ Open 12-3, 6.30(7 Sat)-11

Cats

Back road to Curling Tye and Maldon, from N end of village

In summer, you can sit in the delightful garden outside this attractively timbered rural pub, and enjoy the views of the peaceful hills. The roof is decorated by prowling stone cats, and the feline theme is continued inside where there are shelves of china cats. The atmosphere is very relaxed, and the rambling low-ceilinged bar is full of interesting nooks and crannies and traditionally decorated, with low black beams and timbering set off well by neat white paintwork; there's a warming open fire. Bar snacks are only served on Thursday, Friday and Saturday lunchtimes; well kept Adnams Southwold and Broadside, Greene King IPA and Abbot and Rayments Special on handpump, and friendly service. The pleasantly chatty landlord would rather we didn't include his pub in the *Guide,* but letting licensees decide for us which pubs not to include would damage our independence almost as much as allowing other landlords to pay for their inclusion, so we have, quite deservedly, included it once more. *(Recommended by John Fahy, Paul and Ursula Randall, Gwen and Peter Andrews; more reports please)*

Free house ~ Real ale ~ Lunchtime snacks (see note above) ~ Open 11-2.30ish, 6.30ish-11; may close if not busy in winter

YOUNGS END TL7319 Map 5

Green Dragon

A131 Braintree—Chelmsford, just N of Essex Showground

This well run dining pub strikes a good balance between its wide range of generous good value food and an attractively pubby atmosphere. The bar part has normal pub furnishings in its two rooms, with a little extra low-ceilinged snug just beside the serving counter; turkey carpet sweeps from the main bar room into the restaurant area, which has an understated barn theme – stripped brick walls, a manger at one end, and low beams supporting the floor of an upper 'hayloft' with steep pitched rafters. At lunchtime (not Sunday) you can have bar food down this end, where the tables are a better size for eating from than in the bar itself. The bar food includes sandwiches (home-cooked ham £1.90), filled baked potatoes (£2.20), ploughman's (from £3.95), chicken and bacon parcels with sage and mushroom sauce (£5.85), and lots of seafood such as dressed crab salad (£6.50), large cod fillet (£6.55) or halibut with saffron and lime vinaigrette (£7.50); vegetables are fresh, puddings good. Well kept Greene King IPA, Abbot and their seasonal beer such as Kings Champion; helpful cheerful service, neat waitresses; unobtrusive piped music (jazz on our inspection visit). The neat back garden has lots of picnic tables under cocktail parasols, a big green play dragon, climbing frame and budgerigar aviary; summer barbecues. *(Recommended by Basil Minson, Mark Walker, John and Val Spouge, Gwen and Peter Andrews)*

Greene King ~ Lease: Bob and Mandy Greybrook ~ Real ale ~ Meals and snacks (till 10 Fri and Sat) ~ Restaurant (evenings, Sun lunch) ~ (01245) 361030 ~ Children in restaurant ~ Open 11.30-3, 6-11

Lucky Dip

Besides the fully inspected pubs, you might like to try these Lucky Dips recommended to us and described by readers (if you do, please send us reports):

Abridge [London Rd (A113); TQ4696], *Maltsters Arms*: Lively up-to-date atmosphere in largely 18th-c beamed pub with two bars, well kept Greene King IPA and Abbot on handpump, open fires *(Robert Lester, Nigel Giddons, John Fahy)*; [Market Pl (A113/B172)], *White Hart*: Pleasantly placed with garden by small river, reasonably priced straightforward lunchtime food in two dining areas off spacious open-plan refurbished bar, Bass and Charrington IPA, RAF fighter-bomber pictures; live jazz Mon-Weds *(M A Starling)*

☆ **Ardleigh** [Harwich Rd; A137 – actually towards Colchester; TM0529], *Wooden Fender*: Welcoming beamed bar, open-plan but traditional, with good home cooking inc Sun lunch, well kept Adnams, Fullers ESB, Greene King IPA and Morlands Old Speckled Hen, friendly character landlord, log fires, restaurant allowing children, a pool in back garden; immaculate lavatories *(Magda and Derek Kelsey, E G Parish, LYM)*

☆ **Bannister Green** [off A131 or A120 SW of Braintree; TL6920], *Three Horseshoes*: Popular and comfortable country local, newish tenants settling in well now, well kept Ridleys, good value food, tables out on broad village green and in garden; children welcome *(Tony Beaulah, LYM)*

Barnston [A130 SE of Dunmow; TL6419], *Bushel & Sack*: Welcoming conversion of former village shop, good reasonably priced food in bar or comfortable restaurant, sitting room in between *(Tony Beaulah)*

☆ **Battlesbridge** [Hawk Hill; TQ7894], *Barge*: Recently refurbished weatherboarded pub by art and craft centre nr Crouch estuary, very popular lunchtime weekends for good value bar meals; well kept Tetleys-related ales and a guest such as Adnams, good service, children's room *(George Atkinson)*

Battlesbridge [Hawk Hill], *Hawk*: Spacious open-plan beamed pub, also handy for craft centre, with Crouch Vale ale, usual food, friendly landlord, chamber-pots and pewter tankards, open fire, fruit machines, maybe local radio; big garden *(George Atkinson)*

Blackmore [The Green; TL6001], *Prince Albert*: Island bar serving five or six knocked-through rooms, wide choice of bar food, well kept Bass, Charrington and Hancocks HB, friendly efficient service, fairly unobtrusive piped music; attractive village with big antique and craft shop *(Joy Heatherley, Gwen and Peter Andrews)*

☆ **Boreham** [Church Rd; TL7509], *Queens Head*: Traditional pub with wide appeal under current licensees, well kept Greene King IPA and Abbot, decent wines, good value lunchtime food inc Weds roast and Sun lunch; snug beamed saloon, more tables down one side of long public bar with darts at end, maybe piped radio; friendly naturally welcoming atmosphere *(Gwen and Peter Andrews)*

Boreham [Colchester Rd], *Six Bells*: Also has reliable food *(George Atkinson)*

Braintree [South St; TL7622], *Wagon & Horses*: Friendly licensees in 19th-c local with good value food inc Sun lunch *(Mr and Mrs S C Graham)*

Brentwood [Magpie Lane, facing Childerditch Common; TQ5993], *Greyhound*: Big popular pub in open countryside, varied food with conservatory dining extension, friendly service *(MJVK)*

Broxted [TL5726], *Prince of Wales*: Friendly L-shaped bar with restaurant and conservatory dining areas, particularly good choice of wines by the glass, Tetleys-related ales with a guest such as Courage Directors, attentive welcoming service, quiet piped music; good garden with play area *(Gwen and Peter Andrews, Mr and Mrs Blake)*

Canfield End [Little Canfield; A120 Bishops Stortford—Dunmow; TL5821], *Lion & Lamb*: Pleasantly refurbished Ridleys pub, clean, quiet and friendly, with good value food in bar and spacious restaurant, willing service; shame about the piped music; back garden with barbecue and play area *(Jez Cunningham, A C Morrison)*

☆ **Chelmsford** [Roxwell Rd, about 2 miles from centre; TL7006], *Horse & Groom*: Attractive mock-Tudor pub with well kept ales, decent wines, good value food inc Sun lunch, good service, big no-smoking dining area, country views from pleasant conservatory, unobtrusive piped music; tables outside *(John and Beryl Kersey, Gwen and Peter Andrews, Paul and Ursula Randall, LYM)*

Chelmsford, *County*: Doing well under new management, good quite pubby atmosphere in hotel bar, well kept Adnams and Greene King IPA, decent wine, good straightforward bar food, pleasant staff; bedrooms *(Gwen and Peter Andrews)*

Chelmsford [Cooksmill Green; A414 5 miles W – OS Sheet 167 map ref 638052; TL6305], *Fox & Goose*: Spaciously extended matey roadside pub with decent quick food *(PR, LYM)*

☆ **Chigwell** [High Rd (A113); TQ4693], *Kings Head*: Striking 17th-c building with strong Dickens connections, lots of memorabilia, some antique furnishings; good value Chef & Brewer bar food, friendly staff, well kept ales, upstairs restaurant; roomy and quiet weekday lunchtimes, can get very crowded weekend evenings; attractive garden *(D Cox, John Fahy, C H and P Stride)*

☆ **Coggeshall** [West St; towards Braintree;

TL8522], *Fleece*: Handsome Tudor pub with thriving local atmosphere, well kept Greene King IPA and Abbot, decent wines, reliable straightforward bar food (not Tues or Sun evenings), cheery service; spacious sheltered garden with play area, next to Paycocke's *(Gwen and Peter Andrews, D P Pascoe, LYM)*

☆ **Coggeshall** [main st], *White Hart*: Lots of low Tudor beams, antique settles among other more usual seats, prints and fishing trophies on cream walls, wide choice of food, Adnams, decent wines and coffee; bedrooms comfortable *(John Fahy, GA, PA)*

☆ **Colchester** [East St; TM0025], *Rose & Crown*: Carefully modernised handsome Tudor inn, timbered and jettied, parts of a former gaol preserved in its rambling beamed bar, good value bar food, real ale; comfortable bedrooms *(Barbara and Norman Wells, LYM)*

☆ **Colchester** [Castle St, off Roman Rd], *Forresters Arms*: Friendly local with well kept Whitbreads-related ales, wide range of food at good prices (even the sandwiches and baked potatoes are imaginative), folk music Tues *(Colin Keane, Dagmar Junghanns)*

Colchester [Lexden Rd; formerly Hospital Arms], *Tap & Spile*: Refurbished quiet attractive interior, partly flagstone, with up to nine changing well kept real ales, small choice of lunchtime food, lots of Essex CC photographs, woodburner; tables in small back courtyard *(Ian Phillips, Stuart Earle, Barbara and Norman Wells)*

☆ **Crays Hill** [London Rd; TQ7192], *Shepherd & Dog*: Spotless bar with low beam-and-plank ceiling, bare boards, soft lighting, good log fire, attractive side conservatory overlooking big nicely lit garden, well kept Tetleys-related ales and a beer brewed for the pub, varied good value straightforward food inc vegetarian and children's, OAP bargains Tues/Thurs, good waitress service; children welcome; fruit machines, quiet piped music, live music Sun pm; good walks *(Paul Barstow, Karyn Taylor, Tony Burke, Mike Beiley)*

Cressing [TL7920], *Three Ashes*: Unpretentious Greene King pub with charming garden, new tenants planning to expand the food side *(News please)*

☆ **Danbury** [Runsell Green; N of A414, just beyond green; TL7905], *Anchor*: Lots of beams, timbering, brickwork and brasses, two log fires, separate games bar, attractive dining conservatory; has had too frequent changes of management for a confident recommendation, but May 1995 latest people doing good generous straightforward food, well kept Adnams and Ridleys *(Paul Barstow, Karyn Taylor, Nigel Norman, LYM)*

☆ **Danbury**, *Griffin*: Quiet and spacious well run Chef & Brewer, 16th-c beams and some older carved woodwork, decent food *(Mrs Gwyneth Holland)*

Debden [High St; TL5533], *Plough*: Friendly welcoming local, newish licensees doing generous good value straightforward food inc Sun roasts, Greene King IPA, Abbot and Rayments, decent house wines; children welcome, fair-sized garden behind *(Sandra Iles)*

☆ **Dedham** [TM0533], *Sun*: Roomy and comfortably refurbished Tudor pub, cosy panelled rooms with log fires in huge brick fireplaces, handsomely carved beams, well kept beer, reasonable wines, good range of generous reasonably priced food, cheerful staff, good piped music; tables on back lawn, car park behind reached through medieval arch, wonderful wrought-iron inn sign; panelled bedrooms with four-posters, good walk to or from Flatford Mill *(Quentin Williamson, John and Wendy Trentham, Mrs Gwyneth Holland, A C Morrison, Ian Phillips)*

Dunmow [just off A120 W; TL6221], *Queen Victoria*: Trim thatched and beamed local, excellent landlord, well kept ales inc Courage Directors, no-smoking area, good straightforward bar food, more interesting restaurant menu *(Robert Bardell, Gwen and Peter Andrews)*

☆ **Duton Hill** [off B184 Dunmow—Thaxted, 3 miles N of Dunmow; TL6026], *Three Horseshoes*: Neatly but gently updated to keep welcoming traditional atmosphere, good choice of reasonably priced food, well kept Flowers Original, Fullers London Pride and Ridleys IPA, friendly licensees, central log fire, interesting social-history memorabilia, fine views from recently tidied garden *(Gwen and Peter Andrews)*

Elmdon [TL4639], *Kings Head*: Attractive rambling local, plush bar with dining area behind, separate spartan games bar, three real ales, decent food, friendly staff, lots of memorabilia, horsebrasses, pictures; attractive back garden with lots of animals and budgerigars *(J C Williams)*

☆ **Feering** [3 Feering Hill; TL8720], *Sun*: Four or five changing perfectly kept ales inc one brewed for the pub by Crouch Vale, good interesting fresh food with Italian tendencies, oak beams and inglenooks, attractive furnishings; very popular *(John C Baker, David Tindal)*

☆ **Fiddlers Hamlet** [Stewards Green Rd, a mile SE of Epping; TL4700], *Merry Fiddlers*: Long low-ceilinged 17th-c country pub profusely decorated with chamber-pots, beer mugs, brasses and plates, Adnams, Morlands Old Speckled Hen and Tetleys on handpump, usual pub food, efficient friendly staff, unobtrusive piped music, occasional live sessions; big garden with play area *(A L Turnbull, Joy Heatherley)*

Finchingfield [TL6832], *Fox*: The splendid pargeting makes this late 18th-c inn one of the best sights in this picture-book village; Greene King ales and a guest such as Morlands Old Speckled Hen, reasonably priced generous food inc bargain OAP lunch, tables in garden *(Gwen and Peter Andrews)*

Fryerning [Mill Green; TL6400], *Cricketers*: Doing well under cheerful newish licensees, popular for wide choice of food inc good puddings – bar full of tables for this; Greene King IPA and Abbot, cricket memorabilia, country views *(Tony Beaulah, John Fahy)*

☆ **Furneux Pelham** [TL4327], *Brewery Tap*: Good food esp fish in friendly refurbished bar with well kept Greene King and Rayments; back garden room and terrace overlooking neat attractive garden *(Geo Rumsey)*

Grays [Duck Rd; TQ6178], *Bull*: Big genuinely old white-painted pub with tiled roof and low beams, big covered dining terrace, attractive garden, good range of bar food, friendly staff *(Ian Phillips)*; [Lodge Lane (A1306 towards Lakeside)], *Treacle Mine*: Big new Americanised pub with several Bass ales and a guest such as Crouch Vale, competitively priced food, two homely eating areas, one no smoking, lots of woodwork, pictures and mining tools, realistic-looking 'mine' in small garden with play area *(Paul Barstow, Karyn Taylor)*

☆ **Great Baddow** [Galleywood Rd; or off B1007 at Galleywood Eagle; TL7204], *Seabrights Barn*: Expensively redeveloped Greene King family pub in rustic raftered barn conversion, lots for children though also a spacious child-free bar, good food (all day Sun), good friendly service, well kept real ales, decent wines, summer barbecues *(Derek Howse, Les Downes, LYM)*

☆ **Great Bromley** [Harwich Rd (B1029 just off A120); TM0826], *Old Black Boy*: 18th-c pub recently reopened after attractive refurbishment, very wide choice of good value food inc lots of fish in bar and restaurant, real ales, decent wines, no-smoking area; big newly done garden *(Alan Budden, Alan J Wilkins)*

Great Chesterford [TL5143], *Crown & Thistle*: Small and busy, good food, well kept beer *(G Washington)*

☆ *nr* **Great Henny** [Henny Street; Sudbury—Lamarsh rd E; TL8738], *Swan*: Tables on lawn by quiet river opp cosy well furnished timbered pub with partly no-smoking conservatory restaurant, decent bar food (not Sun evening), barbecues, well kept Greene King IPA and Abbot; children allowed, maybe piped music *(A Plumb, LYM)*

☆ **Great Horkesley** [Nayland Rd (A134); TL9730], *Rose & Crown*: Lovely old two-floored pub, clean, cosy and welcoming, good varied food, Greene King and other ales, three bars and restaurant *(N Bushby, W Atkins, Quentin Williamson)*

☆ **Great Stambridge** [1 Stambridge Rd; TQ9091], *Cherry Tree*: Spacious but cosy beamed country dining pub with wide choice of well served food from sandwiches up inc good fish and lots of traditional puddings, Courage Directors and Flowers IPA, good wine choice, friendly service, coal-effect gas fire, elegant circular dining conservatory, garden; fairly quiet piped music; very popular, can get crowded *(George Atkinson, Susan and Alan Dominey)*

☆ **Great Waltham** [old A130; TL6913], *Beehive*: Friendly refurbished pub with decent food, well kept Ridleys and Wadworths IPA and 6X, useful malt whiskies, good log fire; tables outside, opp attractive church *(Gwen and Peter Andrews, Mike Barry)*

☆ **Great Warley Street** [TQ5890], *Thatchers Arms*: Pretty Chef and Brewer in attractive village, reliable food, several well kept ales, helpful service *(Norman Foot, Quentin Williamson, John Fahy)*

Hadleigh [London Rd (A13); TQ8087], *Waggon & Horses*: Extensively refurbished as family restaurant rather than pub, reliably good value food *(DP)*

Halstead [Parsonage St; TL8130], *Griffin*: Well kept Greene King IPA, Abbot and Rayments on handpump, reasonably priced food, good company, attractive garden *(Stephen Gard)*

☆ **Hastingwood** [very nr M11 junction 7; follow Ongar sign, then Hastingwood turn; TL4807], *Rainbow & Dove*: Comfortable and very friendly Mway break, low-beamed rooms packed with bric-a-brac, roaring fire, basic food inc good sausages (children allowed in eating area), picnic tables in garden with summer Sun evening barbecues; keg beers, no food Mon/Tues evenings *(Eric and Jackie Robinson, LYM; more reports please)*

☆ **Herongate** [Billericay Rd; A128 Brentwood—Grays; TQ6391], *Green Man*: Doing well under new landlord, with good value food, several clean, bright and welcoming rooms, Adnams and Tetleys-related ales; children allowed in back rooms *(Mrs J Boyt, Graham Bush, George Atkinson)*

Herongate, *Blue Boar*: Busy Chef & Brewer with pleasant nooks and crannies, reliable generous food – you can see into the kitchens *(M A Starling)*; [Dunton Rd – turn off A128 Brentwood—Grays at big sign for Boars Head], *Old Dog*: Friendly and relaxed, with good choice of well kept ales and of lunchtime bar food in long traditional dark-raftered bar, open fire, comfortable back lounge; front terrace and neat sheltered side garden *(D Cox, LYM)*

Heybridge [34 The Street; TL8508], *Heybridge*: Unassuming exterior, but particularly good food *(R D B Todman)*

☆ **High Easter** [TL6214], *Cock & Bell*: Attractive timbered Tudor pub with grand old beams, dining area up steps from lounge, log fire in cheery second bar, generous home-cooked straightforward food, well kept ales such as Batemans, Crouch Vale, Fullers London Pride, Morlands Old

Speckled Hen, friendly service, children welcome; piped radio may obtrude; bedrooms *(Sandra Iles, Roger and Valerie Hill, Gwen and Peter Andrews, LYM)*

☆ **High Ongar** [King St, Nine Ashes – signed Blackmore, Ingatestone off A414 just E; TL5603], *Wheatsheaf*: Comfortable and very welcoming low-beamed country dining pub, some intimate tables in bay-window alcoves, two open fires, fresh flowers, wide choice of home-cooked food (fish and steaks particularly recommended), well kept Whitbreads-related ales and guests such as Crouch Vale, Fullers and Youngs, attentive service, spacious attractive garden with play house *(G Boyes, Walter and Muriel Hagen, MJVK, Dave and Pam Bowell, BB)*

☆ **High Roding** [The Street (B184); TL6017], *Black Lion*: Attractive low-beamed bar dating from 15th century, good food esp authentic Italian dishes, courteous long-serving landlord and cheerful staff, comfortable relaxed surroundings, well kept Ridleys; discreet piped music *(Paul and Ursula Randall, Gwen and Peter Andrews, E J Cutting)*

Little Baddow [North Hill; towards Hatfield Peverel; TL7807], *Rodney*: Attractive low-beamed country local full of nautical brasswork and Nelson memorabilia, well kept Greene King IPA and Rayments and a guest beer, decent food; pool room with unobtrusive piped music, terrace and garden with well equipped play area *(GA, PA)*

Little Bentley [TM1125], *Bricklayers Arms*: Small country local with reliable good value home cooking inc speciality steaks; real ale, welcoming obliging staff *(Jim Kinnear, Pamela Goodwyn, Beryl and Bill Farmer)*

Little Walden [B1052; TL5441], *Crown*: Neat and spacious long low-beamed open-plan bar with fresh flowers and big log fire, good range of generous good food (not Sun evening) esp fish inc several vegetarian dishes, changing ales tapped from the cask such as Adnams, Batemans and Wadworths 6X, welcoming service, unobtrusive piped music; handy for Linton Zoo *(Bill and Lydia Ryan, Gwen and Peter Andrews, Ian Phillips, Peter and Joy Heatherley)*

☆ **Loughton** [103 York Hill, off A121 High Rd; TQ4296], *Gardeners Arms*: Country feel in (and outside) traditional low-ceilinged pub with Adnams and Courage-related ales, two open fires, friendly service, good straightforward lunchtime bar food (not Sun) from sandwiches up with hot dishes all fresh-cooked (so can be delays), children in restaurant *(Joy Heatherley, Gwen and Peter Andrews, John Fahy, LYM)*

Loughton [227 High Rd], *Last Post*: Former post office well converted to Wetherspoon pub, good warming atmosphere, good range of sensibly priced ales, good value food *(Robert Lester, John Fahy)*

☆ **Manningtree** [Manningtree Stn; out towards Lawford; TM1031], *Station Buffet*: Early 1950s feel, long marble-topped bar, three little tables and a handful of unassuming seats; interesting well kept ales such as Adnams, Greene King, Mauldons and Summerskills, good cheap generous simple home-cooked food, friendly service *(John C Baker)*

Manuden [opp church – OS Sheet 167 map ref 491267; TL4926], *Yew Tree*: Open-plan bar with warmly welcoming service, well kept Theakstons Best, short choice of good value lunchtime food, plenty of regulars *(PGP)*

Margaretting [B1002; TL6701], *Spread Eagle*: Simple but spacious, well kept Bass ales, decent cheap food, fine array of daily papers, attentive staff, unobtrusive piped music *(Jenny and Brian Seller, Gwen and Peter Andrews, John Fahy)*

☆ **Margaretting Tye** [TL6800], *White Hart*: Wide choice of good value promptly served food, well kept Adnams and Broadside, Mauldons, Greene King IPA and a guest beer on handpump, friendly staff; piped music; attractive garden by quiet village green, barbecue, good walks *(Mike Beiley, Gwen and Peter Andrews)*

☆ **Mashbury** [towards the Walthams; TL6411], *Fox*: Friendly beamed and flagstoned lounge, old-fashioned long tables, generous homely food, well kept Adnams and Ridleys tapped from the cask, decent wine; dominoes, cribbage, skittles; quiet countryside *(Beryl and Bill Farmer)*

Mill Green [TL6401], *Cricketers Arms*: Genuine country pub in picturesque setting, good food, well kept ales, fine wines *(Clive Rumsey)*

Molehill Green [off A120, E of M11 junction 8; TL5624], *Three Horseshoes*: Attractive thatched pub with low oak beams, settles, big fireplaces, Tetleys-related ales, friendly service, good bar food inc Weds fish night *(John and Shirley Dyson)*

☆ **Moreton** [signed off B184 at Fyfield or opp Chipping Ongar school; TL5307], *Moreton Massey*: Rambling dining pub with attractive array of salvaged rustic beams and timbers, nice mix of tables, a few country nick-nacks, big log fires; doing well under current licensees, with enjoyable food from sandwiches and ploughman's to good range of interesting hot dishes, Adnams, Courage Directors and Morlands Old Speckled Hen, good choice of decent wines by the glass, daily papers, good friendly service; piped music may obtrude a bit; picnic tables under cocktail parasols on side grass *(Gwen and Peter Andrews, Joy Heatherley, M A and C R Starling, BB)*

☆ **Moreton**, *White Hart*: Welcoming local with lovely log fire, nicely quirky layout on different levels with cosy rooms inc two dining rooms off lounge bar, well kept ales such as Adnams, Belchers and Courage, wide choice of home-cooked food inc properly cooked veg; courteous efficient service; bedrooms *(Joy Heatherley, Alan*

and Ruth Woodhouse, E J Cutting)
Mountnessing [TQ6297], *George & Dragon*: Well kept beer, good food *(G Washington)*

☆ **Navestock** [Huntsmanside, off B175; TQ5397], *Alma Arms*: Generous helpings of good value food, good choice of wines, well kept ales such as Adnams, Greene King Abbot and Rayments; low beams, comfortable seats, spacious dining area *(Miss Sandra Iles, H O Dickinson)*

☆ **Norton Heath** [just off A414 Chelmsford—Ongar; TL6004], *White Horse*: Particularly good bar food with a French slant (Tues-Sat lunchtimes) in comfortably modernised long timbered bar, good friendly service, Courage Directors, unobtrusive piped music; bar billiards; restaurant (Tues-Sat evening, Sun lunch); garden with play area; cl Mon *(Richard Siebert)*

☆ **Peldon** [TL9916], *Plough*: Welcoming tiled and white-boarded village local, small and simple; good home-cooked food inc fresh fish, well kept Crouch Vale IPA; pool, quiz and fruit machine *(Chris Harrison, BB)*
Pentlow [Pinkuah Lane; TL8146], *Pinkuah Arms*: Old country pub surrounded by farmland, good traditional food, pool table, darts, open fire; spacious garden with boules and barbecues *(Michael Nardini)*

☆ **Pilgrims Hatch** [Ongar Rd; TQ5895], *Black Horse*: Particularly good home cooking at sensible prices inc fresh veg and huge puddings; friendly service *(K and B Moore)*

☆ **Purleigh** [by church; TL8401], *Bell*: Cosy rambling beamed and timbered pub, nooks and crannies, maybe a big log fire, well kept Adnams and Greene King IPA, good reasonably priced home-made lunchtime food, welcoming landlord; picnic tables on side grass, views over Blackwater estuary *(Gwen and Peter Andrews, LYM)*

☆ **Radwinter** [B1053 E of Saffron Walden – OS Sheet 154 map ref 612376; TL6137], *Plough*: Neatly kept red plush open-plan black-timbered beamed bar with central log fire and separate woodburner; good choice of popular bar food inc vegetarian, well kept Greene King IPA, Nethergate and Charles Wells Bombardier on handpump, decent wine; piped music; very attractive terrace and garden, open countryside; bedrooms *(Gwen and Peter Andrews, Brian and Jill Bond, John and Karen Day, BB)*

☆ **Rayleigh** [39 High St; TQ8190], *Old White Horse*: Attractive pub developed considerably since former world cross country champion Mel Batty took over, good cheap home-cooked food, well kept Charrington IPA, Fullers London Pride, Worthington and guest beers, friendly staff, lots of sporting memorabilia – not just athletics; new back terrace with barbecues; children welcome *(Jenny Sturgess, Mr and Mrs C Wragg, R Walmsley)*

☆ **Rochford** [35 North St (one-way); TQ8790], *Golden Lion*: Pretty white cottage with lots of changing ales, good range of cheap lunchtime snacks inc seven styles of sausage; friendly landlord, wonderful atmosphere, though not smart *(Ian Phillips)*
Roydon [High St (B181); TL4109], *White Hart*: Genuine olde-worlde pub with pleasant atmosphere, friendly staff, good mix of locals and tourists, four well kept real ales, good bar and restaurant food, occasional live music *(K Watts)*
Saffron Walden [10-18 High St; TL5438], *Saffron*: Comfortably modernised former coaching inn, wide choice of waitress-served food in bar and restaurant, tables on terrace *(Dave Bundock)*

☆ **Shalford** [TL7229], *George*: Good value home cooking, lots of exposed brickwork, log fire in enormous fireplace, well kept Greene King IPA and Rayments with a guest such as Adnams Broadside, young smiling staff, lots of children at weekends, no music; tables on terrace *(Gwen and Peter Andrews)*

☆ **South Weald** [Weald Rd (off A1023); TQ5793], *Tower Arms*: Imposing building opp church with several small high-ceilinged rooms, conservatory restaurant (not Sun-Tues evenings), decent Chef & Brewer food, well kept Theakstons Best, Old Peculier and XB and John Smiths, friendly staff; children allowed away from bar; extensive secluded garden with boules (you can hire the balls); picturesque village *(Graham Bush)*
St Osyth [Point Clear Rd; TM1215], *White Hart*: Small family-run pub, very friendly and welcoming, with good food and beer *(Simon Talbot)*
Stebbing [High St; TL6624], *Kings Head*: Beamed 17th-c local, cosy and comfortable, summer barbecues; beautiful village walking trails *(Nikki Moffat)*; [High St], *White Hart*: Lovely lively beamed local, particularly good food *(Nikki Moffat)*

☆ **Stock** [The Square (just off main st); TQ6998], *Bear*: Lovely old building with cosy restaurant, good well cooked and presented food esp fish, Adnams and Tetleys; cat called Rhythm (Blues went missing some time ago) *(Mrs Gwyneth Holland, Keith and Cheryl Roe, M A and C R Starling, A Morgan, Les Downes)*
Stock [Common Rd; just off B1007 Chelmsford—Billericay], *Bakers Arms*: Open-plan beamed pub with smart banquettes, decent food inc vegetarian, attractive restaurant, charming wel kept garden *(Paul Barstow, Karyn Taylor)*

☆ **Stow Maries** [TQ8399], *Prince of Wales*: Well kept Crouch Vale and other changing ales generally from interesting distant small breweries, friendly traditional bare-boards atmosphere, several unspoilt rooms, decent wines and country wines, log fire, small range of good value fresh food inc vegetarian and children's *(Adrian White, Julie King)*

☆ **Sturmer** [The Street; A604 SE of Haverhill; TL6944], *Red Lion*: Warm and welcoming thatched and beamed pub, good choice of generous reasonably priced good food (not Sun evening) esp filling steak and kidney pie; helpful service, convenient layout if you don't like steps; children in dining room and conservatory *(Mrs Carol Canter, W T Aird)*

Thaxted [Mill End; TL6130], *Star*: Cheerful old beamed pub with wide choice of good food even on Sun, well kept Ind Coope Burton, good service *(John Fahy)*

Theydon Bois [Coppice Row (B172); TQ4599], *Queen Victoria*: Well presented quick straightforward food inc good value specials, bright end dining area with interesting nick-nacks, much older front with low ceilings (can get smoky), pleasant bustle; tables on terrace *(Joy Heatherley)*; [Station Rd (off B172)], *Railway Arms*: Small but comfortable refurbished local popular lunchtime with OAPs for cheap food from sandwiches up; prints of old steam engines, well kept Theakstons XB, decent coffee, good friendly service, garden *(Geo Rumsey)*

☆ **Toot Hill** [village signed off A113 S of Ongar and from A414 W of Ongar; TL5102], *Green Man*: Good simply furnished country dining pub with general though not unanimous approval for the food, remarkable choice of wines from a good variety of merchants, inc dozens of champagnes, and ales such as Adnams, Smiles and Love Potion No 9; friendly staff, uncrowded relaxed feel, pretty front terrace, tables in back garden; no children under 10 *(Mick Hitchman, G and T Edwards, Helen Morton, Tony Gayfer, C Slack, A J and M Thomasson, D A Edwards, Warren O'Callaghan, Wayne Brindle, Adrian M Kelly, Mrs M Starling, K and B Moore, Eric and Jackie Robinson, J H Gracey, H O Dickinson, MJVK, LYM)*

☆ *nr* **Waltham Abbey** [very handy for M25 junction 26; A121 towards Waltham Abbey, then follow Epping, Loughton sign from exit roundabout; TL3800], *Volunteer*: Good genuine chow mein and big pancake rolls (unless Chinese landlady away Mar/Apr) and generous more usual food in big open-plan McMullens pub; attractive conservatory, guest beer, some tables on side terrace, pretty hanging baskets; nice spot by Epping Forest, can get very busy weekends *(Dave Braisted, Joy Heatherley, John and Elspheth Howell, BB)*

☆ **White Roding** [TL5613], *Black Horse*: Sprucely well kept Ridleys pub with generous home cooking (not Sun evening; fresh fish Thurs), well kept IPA, welcoming attentive service, bar billiards, very quiet piped music, good atmosphere *(J Kruger, Gwen and Peter Andrews)*

☆ **Wickham Bishops** [TL8412], *Mitre*: Pleasantly refurbished with snug bars and spacious family dining area, reasonably priced food inc some unusual dishes, polite staff, friendly locals, well kept Adnams Extra and Ridleys IPA and ESX, decent wines, good fire *(Gwen and Peter Andrews)*

☆ **Widdington** [High St; signed off B1383 N of Stansted; TL5331], *Fleur de Lys*: Low-beamed and timbered bar with inglenook log fire, seven well kept enterprising real ales, decent wines, straightforward seating, welcoming service, varied food which can hit quite a high; games in back bar, children in restaurant and no-smoking family room, picnic tables on side lawn *(Gwen and Peter Andrews, Caroline Wright, John Fahy, Jack Davey, Audrey and Dennis Nelson, LYM)*

☆ **Wivenhoe** [Black Buoy Hill, off A133; TM0321], *Black Buoy*: Wide choice of ales inc weekly guest in spacious and charming open-plan bar, good food, convivial atmosphere, river views, restaurant *(Mike Harrison)*

Wivenhoe [TM0321], *Rose & Crown*: Friendly riverside pub with well kept ales, good views, jovial licensee, great atmosphere, warm fire, live jazz *(Mike Harrison, Les Downes)*

Woodham Ferrers [Main Rd; TQ7999], *Bell*: Carefully extended attractive beamed lounge/dining area with lots of exposed brickwork, friendly chatty staff, cheap straightforward food, well kept Adnams and Ridleys IPA, good coffee; piped music not too obtrusive, pool, fruit machine; restaurant; nice sheltered garden with well and pond *(Gwen and Peter Andrews, G Washington, George Atkinson)*

Woodham Mortimer [TL8104], *Hurdlemakers Arms*: Quietly placed country local with picnic tables well spaced among trees and shrubs outside, cottagey feel in simply furnished flagstoned lounge with cushioned settles, low ceiling and timbered walls; well kept Greene King IPA and Abbot and Ridleys, good fresh food, darts alley in public bar; summer barbecues, garden children's room with video games *(M J Murphy, Paul Zimmerman, Peter Helsdon, BB)*

Post Office address codings confusingly give the impression that some pubs are in Suffolk, when they're really in Essex (which is where we list them).

Gloucestershire

This chapter is swollen by a number of pubs in those parts of Avon which are to switch to Gloucestershire in the 1996 local gorvernment changes – that is, pubs which would previously have been covered by our Somerset and Avon chapter. It also includes several new main entries: the Green Dragon near Cowley, settling down well under a new landlady; the unpretentious Black Horse at Cranham – good home cooking and excellent beers; the Edgemoor at Edge, more good home cooking and fantastic views; the interesting Old Lodge at Minchinhampton, doing very well under its new management; and the charmingly restored Eliot Arms at South Cerney. Other pubs currently doing particularly well here include the Black Horse at Amberley (good beer, special food offers, fine views), the friendly and busy Catherine Wheel at Bibury, the Bear at Bisley (new licensees settling in extremely well now), the Kings Head at Bledington (our choice as Gloucestershire Dining Pub of the Year), the somewhat hotelish Crown at Blockley, the cheery Bakers Arms in Broad Campden, the New Inn at Coln St Aldwyns (another outstanding place for pub meals), the Wild Duck at Ewen (yet another), the Plough at Ford (good new tenant), the Fox at Great Barrington (getting better all the time), the Olde Inne at Guiting Power (current owners making commendable changes), the Kilkeney Inn at Kilkenny (excellent food), the busy, friendly and characterful White Hart at Littleton upon Severn, the Fox at Lower Oddington (great enthusiasm for wine, food, service and atmosphere), the Bathurst Arms at North Cerney (atmosphere transformed under the new owner), the Anchor at Oldbury-upon-Severn, the Boat at Redbrook (wonderful setting, fine beers, great atmosphere), the friendly and distinctive Daneway at Sapperton, and the charmingly placed Butchers Arms at Sheepscombe. This county is so well endowed with really good pubs that the Lucky Dip section at the end of the chapter is full of fine pubs which are as much worth visiting as many of the main entries. Currently we'd particularly pick out the Gardeners Arms at Alderton, Fox at Broadwell, Eight Bells in Chipping Campden, Tunnel House at Coates, Dog & Muffler near Coleford, the Colesbourne Inn, the Crown at Frampton Mansell, Farmers Arms at Guiting Power, Halfway House at Kineton, Farmers Boy at Longhope, Pickwick at Lower Wick, Catherine Wheel at Marshfield, Masons Arms at Meysey Hampton, White Hart Royal in Moreton in Marsh, Royal Oak in Painswick, Snowshill Arms at Snowshill, both Black Bear and Bell in Tewkesbury, Hare & Hounds at Westonbirt and Old Corner Cupboard in Winchcombe. Pubs tied to the little Donnington brewery, usually simple and unpretentious, are always worth a look; and in our drinks price survey we found them consistently much cheaper than the area's average, which in turn is rather lower than the national average. Apart from them, the cheapest beers we found were in the Ram at Woodchester, the Anchor at Oldbury on Severn and the Bakers Arms in Broad Campden.

ALMONDSBURY ST6084 Map 2

Bowl

1¼ miles from M5, junction 16 (and therefore quite handy for M4, junction 20; from A38 towards Thornbury, turn first left signposted Lower Almondsbury, then first right down Sundays Hill, then at bottom right again into Church Road

It's a mystery why people bother with service stations when they can just as easily eat in places like this popular white cottage, a couple of minutes from the motorway. Brightly decked out in summer with flowering tubs, hanging baskets and window boxes, it's a friendly place, with the staff welcoming and keen to please, and the atmosphere pleasant and relaxed. A long neatly kept beamed bar has blue plush-patterned modern settles and pink cushioned stools and mate's chairs, elm tables, and quite a few horsebrasses; the walls are stripped to bare stone and there's a big winter log fire at one end, with a woodburning stove at the other. Well kept Courage Best and Directors, John Smiths, Wadworths 6X and a weekly changing guest on handpump, some enterprising bottled beers, good value wines, ten malt whiskies, freshly pressed fruit juices, tea or coffee. Good value home-made bar food includes sandwiches (£1.95), soup (£1.95), burgers (from £2.85), filled baguettes (£2.95), ploughman's (£3.95), omelettes (from £4.45), savoury bean hotpot (£4.75), pork and leek sausages (£4.95), chicken balti (£5.65), beef and beer casserole (£6.45), steak and kidney pie (£6.75), daily specials, and puddings (£2.45); they may charge extra to eat from this menu in the attractive little restaurant, part of which is no smoking. Cribbage, dominoes, fruit machine, trivia, piped music. There's a brown spaniel named Charlie, another dog Corrie, and a black and white cat. A back patio area overlooks a field and can be booked for private parties, and there are some picnic tables across the quiet road. *(Recommended by Roy and Sue Morgan, Lindsley Harvard, Margaret Whalley, Mike Woodhead, Howard Clutterbuck, Nigel Clifton, R J Walden, R W Brooks, Keith Pollard, Meg and Colin Hamilton, Brian and Anna Marsden, John and Joan Wyatt, Mr and Mrs R J Phillips, Rona Murdoch, Jennifer Tora, Don Kellaway, Angie Coles, Pat and John Millward, Simom and Amanda Southwell)*

Courage ~ Lease: John Alley ~ Real ale ~ Meals and snacks (till 10) ~ Restaurant ~ (01454) 612757 ~ Children welcome ~ Open 11-3, 5(6 Sat)-11; closed evening 25 Dec ~ Bedrooms: £48.50B/£68.50B (though usually much less at weekends)

AMBERLEY SO8401 Map 4

Black Horse

Village signposted off A46 Stroud—Nailsworth; as you pass village name take first very sharp left turn (before Amberley Inn) then bear steeply right – pub on your left

They have a number of unusual and very good value offers at this bustling and friendly pub; you might find beers for a pound a pint on some evenings for example, and you can order anything from the menu for £3.50 on Monday, or £4 Tuesday-Thursday. There are marvellous views from both the conservatory and dining bar – which has wheelback chairs, green-cushioned window seats, a few prints on the plain cream walls, and a fire in a small stone fireplace; the family bar on the left is no smoking. A fine range of well kept real ales on handpump, such as Archers Best, Eldridge Pope Hardy Country, Furgusons Dartmoor, Smiles Exhibition, Tetleys, Wadworths 6X and Youngs. Bar food includes sandwiches and other straightforward bar meals, as well as popular specials such as Indian baltis, Cajun chicken or bream in creole sauce (£5.95); service is excellent. Darts, pool, alley skittles, cribbage, dominoes. Teak seats and picnic tables on a back terrace (with barbecue) share the same glorious view as the bars, and on the other side of the building, a lawn with pretty flowers and honeysuckle has more picnic tables. The pub is very popular locally. *(Recommended by Lt Col E H F Sawbridge, Dave Irving, Tom McLean, Roger Huggins, Ewan McCall, James and Patricia Halfyard, G C Brown, Paula Williams, S G Brown, Michael Marlow, Tony and Wendy Hobden, Richard and Janice Searle)*

Free house ~ Licensee Patrick O'Flynn ~ Real ale ~ Meals and snacks ~ (01453) 872556 ~ Children welcome ~ Open 12-3, 6-11; 12-11 summer Sats

AMPNEY CRUCIS SP0602 Map 4

Crown of Crucis

A417 E of Cirencester

Several readers have commented on the helpful service here, with one delighted when the landlord nipped upstairs and brought all his luggage back down to the car. Most people come for the reliable good value food: sandwiches (from £1.60), soup (£1.85), vegetable stroganoff pancakes (£3), a lunchtime daily special (£3.45), ploughman's (£3.85), locally made sausages (£3.90), choux buns filled with chicken and mushrooms (£4.95), steak and mushroom pie (£5.40), lamb balti (£5.45), steaks (from £8.95), good home-made puddings (£2), and children's meals (£2.30). It's worth arriving early to be sure of a table; the restaurant is no smoking. The spacious and tastefully modernised bar has a cheery welcoming feel, and some character, and service is efficient and very friendly. Well kept Archers Village, Ruddles County and Theakstons Best on handpump, farm cider, maybe elderflower drinks. In summer, it's most pleasant to sit outside at the many tables on the back grass by a stream with ducks and maybe swans. *(Recommended by Colin Laffan, Pat Crabb, David Holman, Mr and Mrs J Brown, Andrew and Ruth Triggs, E A George, Marjorie and Colin Roberts, Peter Pocklington, Mrs S Smith, Gwen and Peter Andrews, Neil and Anita Christopher, Jan and Dave Booth, The Monday Club, Dave Irving, Roger Huggins, Ewan McCall, Tom McLean)*

Free house ~ Licensee R K Mills ~ Real ale ~ Meals and snacks (till 10) ~ Restaurant ~ Poulton (01285) 851806 ~ Children welcome until 8pm ~ Open 11-11; closed 25 Dec ~ Bedrooms: £31B/£48B

APPERLEY SO8628 Map 4

Farmers Arms

Nr Apperley on B4213, which is off A38 N of Gloucester

You can usually go into the little thatched brewhouse behind this friendly beamed pub and watch them making their own rather tasty Mayhems Oddas Light and Sundowner Heavy. Inside the extended but cosy pub itself it's usually the food that's the centre of attention, so although there's plenty of room at the bar, you'll generally find most people in the comfortable and spacious dining lounge. They have fresh fish delivered daily, which leads to several interesting blackboard specials such as turbot in lime sauce; other popular dishes include open sandwiches (£2.50), soup (£1.75), ploughman's (£3.75), haddock or cod (£4.50-£5.50 depending on how hungry you are), ham and egg (£5.25), a separate menu of vegetarian dishes such as nut wellington or spicy bean burgers (£5.75), beef and ale pie (£5.95) and several steaks (from £7.75), with children's dishes (£3.25 inc sundae) and a wide choice of puddings (£2.50). Service is prompt and very friendly even when they're busy; open fires, piped music. In addition to their own beers they keep Boddingtons and Marstons Pedigree, along with decent wines (including a red and a white wine of the month), and a fair range of malt whiskies. Guns line the beams of the bar, and there are old prints, horseshoes and stuffed pheasants dotted about. The neat garden has picnic tables by a thatched well, with a wendy house and play area. *(Recommended by Neil and Anita Christopher, J Roy Smylie, Mr and Mrs C Roberts, Mrs M Haggie, Kathryn and Brian Heathcote, Dave Irving, Roger Huggins, Ewan McCall, Tom McLean, Derek and Sylvia Stephenson, Mike Pugh)*

Own brew ~ Licensees Geoff and Carole Adams ~ Real ale ~ Meals and snacks (till 10) ~ Restaurant ~ (01452) 780307 ~ Children welcome ~ Occasional live music ~ Open 11-3, 6-11

Waterside pubs are listed at the back of the book.

ASHLEWORTH QUAY SO8125 Map 4

Boat

Ashleworth signposted off A417 N of Gloucester; Quay signed from village

This timeless 15th-c cottage has been run by the same family ever since it was first granted a licence by Charles II. Up a secluded lane right on the banks of the Severn, it's a friendly and uncomplicated place, where the charming landladies really do work hard at preserving the unique character. Spotlessly kept, the front parlour has a great built-in settle by a long scrubbed deal table that faces an old-fashioned open kitchen range with a side bread oven and a couple of elderly fireside chairs; there are rush mats on the scrubbed flagstones, houseplants in the window, fresh garden flowers, and old magazines to read. A back parlour with rugs on its red tiles has plump overstuffed chairs and a sofa, a grandfather clock and dresser, a big dog basket in front of the fire, and shove-ha'penny, dominoes and cards (the front room has darts and a game called Dobbers). A pair of flower-cushioned antique settles face each other in the back room where Arkells BBB and Smiles Best and guests like Oakhill Yeoman and Exmoor Gold are tapped from the cask, along with a full range of Westons farm ciders. They do excellent lunchtime rolls (from £1.20) or ploughman's with home-made chutney (£2.50) during the week, and groups of walkers can book these or afternoon teas. In front, there's a sun-trap crazy-paved courtyard, bright with plant tubs in summer, with a couple of picnic tables under cocktail parasols; more seats and tables under cover at the sides. The medieval tithe barn nearby is striking; some readers prefer to park here and walk to the pub. ***(Recommended by Pete and Rosie Flower, Jack and Philip Paxton, Dr Paul Kitchener, Sara Nicholls, Keith Stephen, Nigel Clifton, Mrs Pat Crabb, Jeff Davies, Michael Launder, Derek and Sylvia Stephenson, Dave Irving, Roger Huggins, Tom McLean, Ewan McCall, Ted George, Richard and Janice Searle, Jed and Virginia Brown, P Neate, K Baxter)***

Free house ~ Licensees Irene Jelf and Jacquie Nicholls ~ Real ale ~ Lunchtime snacks ~ (01452) 700272 ~ Children welcome ~ Open 11-3, 6-11; 11-2.30, 7-11 in winter

AUST ST5789 Map 2

Boars Head

½ mile from M4, junction 21; village signposted from A403

A well-liked and reliable stop on the journey between Wales and England, this small-roomed village pub is unexpectedly rural considering its proximity to the motorway. It generally fills up quite quickly at lunchtimes, but service is always warmly welcoming and efficient. Full of evidence of the landlady's care and attention, the comfortable main bar has well polished country kitchen tables and others made from old casks, old-fashioned high-backed winged settles in stripped pine, some walls stripped back to the dark stone, decorative plates hanging from one stout black beam, big rugs on dark lino, and a log fire in the main fireplace. In another room is a woodburning stove, while a third has dining tables with lace tablecloths, fresh flowers and candles. Popular bar food includes home-made stock-pot soup (£2.20), ploughman's (£3.75), help-yourself salads (from £3), smoked salmon and scrambled eggs (£5.95), daily specials such as home-made steak and kidney or chicken pie, a tasty beef casserole, venison and other game dishes, or winter meals like braised oxtail (from £5.50), whole fresh plaice and Severn salmon (from £7), and good puddings (£2); Sunday lunch (from £5.75), children's helpings. Service can slow down at busy times. Part of the eating area is no smoking. Well kept Courage Best, Flowers Original and a regularly changing guest like Ind Coope Burton on handpump. There's a medieval stone well in the pretty sheltered garden, which has an aviary and rabbits (including Newbury, an enormous lop-eared one), and even a cheery chipmunk. Also a touring caravan site. When the pub was first recorded in the 18th c it stood next to a row of cottages built by the parish for unmarried mothers (even the vicar's daughter was there for a while); a rudimentary version of the CSA tracked down the fathers, who were then fined 17/6. ***(Recommended by Pat*** *and John Smyth, C H and P Stride, David Shillitoe, Pat and Richard Tazewell, J M Mogg, D G Clarke, G K Johns, A D Shore, Margaret Drazin, R Michael Richards, Michael, Alison and Rhiannon Sandy)*

Courage ~ Lease: Mary May ~ Real ale ~ Meals and snacks (till 10; not Sun evening) ~ (01454) 632278 ~ Children in eating area till 9pm ~ Open 11-2.30, 6-11

AWRE SO7108 Map 4

Red Hart

Village signposted off A48 S of Newnham

A bale of straw swings from the pitched rafters of this remote 16th-c pub, a relaxing motion rather in keeping with the overall mood of the place. The red-tiled building is surprisingly tall – with a chimney to match. Attractive and immaculately kept, the L-shaped main part of the bar has a deep glass-covered well, an upholstered wall settle and wheelback chairs; there are plates on a delft shelf at the end, as well as a gun and a stuffed pheasant over the stone fireplace, and big prints on the walls. Cheery staff, and a nice mix of locals and visitors. Well cooked and nicely presented bar food includes sandwiches, home-made soup (£2), home-made chicken liver pâté (£3.50), ploughman's (£3.95), home-baked ham with egg (£4.95), home-made steak and kidney pie (£5.75), popular seafood pancake (£6.75), mixed grill (£6.95), chicken breast in mushroom and cream sauce (£7.95), salmon in a vermouth and prawn sauce (£8.75), and slices of beef with shallots and mushrooms (£10.75). Well kept Wadworths 6X and a changing beer such as Robinsons on handpump, and several malt whiskies; darts, fruit machine and piped music. In front of the building are some picnic tables. *(Recommended by Glenda Jones, Robert Huddleston, A Y Drummond, Paul Boot, Paul Weedon)*

Free house ~ Licensee Patrick Purtill ~ Real ale ~ Meals and snacks (not Sun evenings) ~ Restaurant (not Sun evenings) ~ (01594) 510220 ~ Children welcome ~ Open 11-2.30, 7-11; closed Mon exc bank holiday lunchtimes

BARNSLEY SP0705 Map 4

Village Pub

A433 Cirencester—Burford

A consistently reliable and friendly stone pub near Rosemary Verey's garden, with a good range of bar food that's generally had that little bit of extra thought put into its preparation. A typical lunchtime menu might include interestingly filled bagels or toasted muffins (from £2.50), filled baked potatoes (from £2.50), smoked trout and cream cheese pâté (£3.25), crispy stuffed pepper (£3.35), ploughman's (£3.50), a Quorn dish of the day or steak and kidney pie (£4.95), a good salad or smoked salmon and dill quiche (£5), chicken curry (£5.50), and daily specials. Well kept Butcombe Bitter and Wadworths 6X on handpump, and country wines. The walls of the comfortable low-ceilinged communicating rooms are decorated with gin-traps, scythes and other farm tools, and there are several winter log fires, as well as plush chairs, stools and window settles around the polished tables. The atmosphere is bustling yet unhurried; cribbage, shove ha'penny, and dominoes, piped music. The sheltered back courtyard has plenty of tables, and its own outside servery. *(Recommended by Dave Irving, Roger Huggins, Tom McLean, Ewan McCall, John Bowdler, Andrew and Ruth Triggs, SRP, Maysie Thompson, Paul McPherson, Roger Byrne, K H Frostick, J Weeks)*

Free house ~ Licensee Mrs Susan Wardrop ~ Real ale ~ Meals and snacks ~ Restaurant ~ (01285) 740421 ~ Children welcome ~ Open 11.30-3, 6-11; closed 25 Dec ~ Bedrooms: £29B/£44B

Tipping is not normal for bar meals, and not usually expected.

BIBURY SP1106 Map 4

Catherine Wheel

Arlington; B4425 NE of Cirencester

Like the village around it – reckoned by William Morris to be England's most beautiful – this low-beamed Cotswold stone pub can get very busy with visitors in summer, and the two smaller and quieter back rooms are probably the best place to head for then. The welcoming main bar at the front dates back in part to the 15th century, and has lots of old-fashioned dark wood furniture, a good log fire, gleaming copper pots and pans around the fireplace, and papers to read; it's perhaps at its best on a winter weekday evening. The good choice of well presented and generously served straightforward bar food (very popular with readers at the moment) includes sandwiches (from £2), soup (£2.25), filled baked potatoes or ploughman's (from £3.50), cottage pie (£4.75), meat or vegetable lasagne (£5.50), gammon and egg (£6.25), poached salmon (£6.75), and daily specials; besides special dishes (from £1.50), they'll usually do a small helping of anything else for children, and their Sunday lunch is good. Well kept Archers, Boddingtons, Courage Best, Flowers Original, Tetleys and Whitbreads Best on handpump, and a good few malt whiskies; soft drinks prices have been very fair here. The helpful and friendly service extends to well-behaved dogs, who may be given a Bonio; shove-ha'penny, table skittles, dominoes, cribbage, fruit machine, piped music. There's a good sized and well kept garden behind with picnic tables among fruit trees (and a play area), and some seats out in front. As we said last year, we'd be surprised if this weren't in the running for a stay award, and would be interested to hear what readers think. *(Recommended by Neil and Anita Christopher, Andrew and Ruth Triggs, SRP, Peter and Audrey Dowsett, George Atkinson, Jennie Munro, Jim Wingate, M Joyner, Gordon, R Huggins, D Irving, T McLean, E McCall)*

Free house ~ Licensee Carol Palmer ~ Real ale ~ Meals and snacks (all day) ~ (01285) 740250 ~ Children in family room at front ~ Open 11-11; cl evening 25 Dec ~ Bedrooms: /£50S

BISLEY SO9006 Map 4

Bear

Village signposted off A419 just E of Stroud

Recent reader reports suggest that this elegantly gothic 16th-c inn is better than ever under its current licensees. Popular with enough locals to give it a really rather attractive atmosphere, it's a warmly welcoming and friendly place, with a well-regarded range of home-made food that relies almost completely on fresh local produce. Tasty and good value dishes currently include filled french sticks (from £2.15; melted cheddar and smoked bacon £2.70, 4oz rump steak £3.70), fried potatoes with garlic and herb butter (£3.45) or bacon and sausage (£4), burgers (from £3.70), vegetable pasty filled with fennel, mushrooms and pine kernels in white wine and cream sauce (£4.45), home-made steak and kidney pie (£5.65), daily specials such as mussels with a bacon, garlic and crumb topping (£3.95), pork tenderloin stuffed with garlic, madeira and prunes or monkfish with tomato, garlic and white wine on a bed of pasta (£7.95), whole lemon sole (£8.95), and popular home-made puddings like marmalade sponge (from £1.95). The meandering L-shaped bar has a long shiny black built-in settle and a smaller but even sturdier oak settle by the front entrance, and an enormously wide low stone fireplace (not very high – the ochre ceiling's too low for that); a separate stripped-stone area is used for families. Well kept Bass, Flowers Original, Tetleys, Whitbread Castle Eden and a weekly changing guest on handpump; table skittles, cribbage, dominoes, cards, draughts. A small front colonnade supports the upper floor of the pub, and the sheltered little flagstoned courtyard made by this has a traditional bench; as well as the garden, there's quite a collection of stone mounting-blocks – and quoits. No music or games machines. The steep stone-built village is attractive. *(Recommended by John and Joan Wyatt, R W Brooks, Marjorie and Colin Roberts, Andrew and Ruth Triggs, Martyn Kearey, Roger Huggins, Ewan*

McCall, Tom McLean, Dave Irving, Paul Weedon and others)

Pubmaster ~ Tenants Nick and Vanessa Evans ~ Real ale ~ Meals and snacks (not Sun evening; till 10) ~ (01452) 770265 ~ Children in family room ~ Occasional live music ~ Open 11-3(2.30 winter), 6-11; closed evening 25 and 26 Dec ~ Bedrooms: £16/£36

BLEDINGTON SP2422 Map 4

Kings Head

B4450

Gloucestershire Dining Pub of the Year

It might be cosy, relaxed and attractively set by the village green, but what draws so many people to this pleasantly up-market 15th-c inn is the very good, imaginative food. Don't worry if the range of menus looks a little bewildering at first, you can mix and match dishes from all of them. A typical day's choice might include home-made soup (£1.95), mozzarella and garlic croûton kebab with fresh anchovies (£2.95), sandwiches (£3.25), potato and olive cakes topped with sauté chicken livers and spring onion (£3.25), salad platters (from £3.50), black pudding and poached egg rosti (£4.25), vegetarian bake (£4.50), stuffed rabbit (£4.95), various pasta dishes (£6.25), steak, mushroom and wine pie (£6.95), local trout grilled with white wine, prawns and parsley or veal topped with parma ham and sage cooked with spinach and noodles (£8.95), honey roast duck in brown ale and parsnip sauce or roast quail with chilli raisin sauce (£9.50), whole grilled Dover sole (£11.95), puddings such as lovely fruit pavlova (£2), and children's dishes (from £1.50); they do a good three-course set meal for £9.95. It's worth arriving in plenty of time – they stick very firmly indeed to their afternoon closing time, and food service can stop well before then. In the evening a 10% service charge is added to all meals. The smart but welcoming main bar is full of ancient beams and other atmospheric furnishings, such as high-backed wooden settles, gateleg or pedestal tables, and a warming log fire in the stone inglenook (which has a big black kettle hanging in it); the lounge looks on to the garden. An antique bar counter dispenses well kept Hook Norton Best and Wadworths 6X, as well as two changing guests such as Glenny Hobgoblin, Otter, Shepherd Neame Spitfire or Uley Pigs Ear, local ciders in summer, excellent extensive wine list (with eight by the glass), and 20 or so malt whiskies. They can are get very busy, but service is generally prompt, efficient and friendly. Part of the restaurant area is no-smoking; piped music. The public bar has darts, pool, shove-ha'penny, dominoes, fruit machine, and juke box. The back garden has Aunt Sally and tables that look over to a little stream with lots of ducks that locals often greet by name. *(Recommended by David Holman, Bruce Warren, Gillian and Michael Wallace, Malcolm Taylor, SFAY, Maysie Thompson, D H T Dimock, D G King, D D Collins, Joan and John Calvert, John Waller, Margaret Templeton, Nigel Wilkinson, Peter and Audrey Dowsett, Jerry and Alison Oakes, Mr and Mrs Butler, Stephen Guy, Ted George, Andrew Shore, Neil and Anita Christopher, Graham Reeve, Fred Collier, Gwen and Peter Andrews, Pat and John Millward, M A Watts, Basil Minson, Mr and Mrs Gorton, John and Marianne Cooper, Ann and Bob Westbrook, W C M Jones, T and D Borneo, E J and M W Corrin, Alan Skull, Mrs B Lawton, Alan and Jane Clarke)*

Free house ~ Licensees Michael and Annette Royce ~ Real ale ~ Meals and snacks (till 9.45) ~ Restaurant ~ (01608) 658365 ~ Children in restaurant and garden room extension ~ Occasional jazz ~ Open 11-2.30, 6-11; closed 25 Dec ~ Bedrooms: £40B/£60B

BLOCKLEY SP1634 Map 4

Crown ★

High Street

In the midst of quite an extensive refurbishment programme as we went to press, this smartly civilised Elizabethan inn has long been highly regarded for the fresh fish served in both the hotel-ish restaurant and back bistro. Depending on when you visit, the choice might include sea bream, herring, sprats, whitebait, whiting, salmon, Dover sole, skate, plaice, monkfish, eel, red and grey mullet, trout, shark, lobster, swordfish, and crab; they do a very well-liked seafood fricassée. In the bustling bar, which has a slightly more pubby atmosphere, there may be soup, sandwiches, moules marinières or the enduringly popular cod in beer and chive batter (£5.95), kidneys in mustard sauce (£6.95), and braised oxtail or seafood vol-au-vent (£7.95); they do a good Sunday lunch. Well kept Bass, Butcombe, Crown Buckley Reverend James, Donningtons BB, Hook Norton Best, Tetleys and Wychwood Terrier on handpump, large choice of wines, several malt whiskies; friendly staff. There's an antique settle amongst the more recent furnishings, and leading off from the bar is a snug carpeted lounge with an attractive window seat, windsor chairs around traditional cast-iron-framed tables, and a winter log fire; steps lead up into a little sitting-room with easy chairs, which in turn leads through to another spacious dining room; piped music. The terraced coachyard is surrounded by beautiful trees and shrubs, and there's a hatch to hand drinks down to people sitting out in front, by the lane. If you're staying (it's handy for sights such as Batsford Park Arboretum), breakfasts may include bucks fizz. At weekend lunchtimes parents can leave children in the supervised creche for £4.95, which includes the child's drinks and lunch (though you must book in advance). *(Recommended by Julie Peters, Sara Nicholls, John and Heather Dwane, Martin and Karen Wake, Christopher and Maureen Starling, D G King, P J Caunt, Moira and John Cole, Alain and Rose Foote, Jenny and Michael Back, Neville Kenyon, John Waller, Dr David Clegg, Andy Petersen, George Atkinson, Andrew and Ruth Triggs, Pat and John Millward, D Grzelka, P D and J Bickley, J and S E Garrett, Richard Osborne, Leith Stuart, John and Shirley Dyson, Michael Sullivan, Dorothee and Dennis Glover)*

Free house ~ Licensees John and Betty Champion ~ Real ale ~ Meals (not in bar on Sat) and snacks ~ Restaurant ~ Blockley (01386) 700245 ~ Well behaved children welcome ~ Open 11-3, 5.30-11 ~ Bedrooms: £53B/£78B

BRIMPSFIELD SO9312 Map 4

Golden Heart

Nettleton Bottom; A417 Birdlip—Cirencester

This carefully refurbished and extended country pub has pleasant views down over a valley from the rustic cask-supported tables on its suntrap gravel terrace. The main low-ceilinged bar is divided into three cosily distinct areas with a huge stone inglenook fireplace in one, and traditional built-in settles and other old-fashioned furnishings throughout. A comfortable parlour on the right has another decorative fireplace, and leads into a further room opening on to the terrace. A notable range of well kept beers usually includes a combination of Bass, Fullers London Pride, Hook Norton, Marstons Pedigree, Ruddles Best and Timothy Taylors Landlord on handpump or tapped from the cask; also Scrumpy Jack cider, and a good range of wines by the glass. Very quickly served bar food might include sandwiches, vegetarian pancakes (£5.75), grilled lemon sole, steak and mushroom pudding or hot bacon, chicken and avocado salad (£6.95); there may be a surcharge for using credit cards. They have beer festivals on the spring and August bank holidays, when as well as around 50 beers they have games and hog-roasts. Two areas of the pub are no-smoking. Good walks nearby. *(Recommended by F C Johnston, Thomas Nott, R G Watson, D G King, Mr Chamberlain, Mrs B Lemon, Jack and Philip Paxton, Steve Goodchild, P Neate, Jeff Davies, Martyn Kearey, R M Bloomfield, Dave Irving, Ewan McCall, Roger Huggins, Tom McLean)*

Free house ~ Licensee Catherine Stevens ~ Real ale ~ Meals and snacks (11-2, 6-10) ~ (01242) 870261 ~ Children welcome ~ Occasional live entertainment ~ Open 12-3, 6-11

All *Guide* inspections are anonymous. Anyone claiming to be a *Good Pub Guide* inspector is a fraud, and should be reported to us with name and description.

BROAD CAMPDEN SP1637 Map 4

Bakers Arms ★ £

Village signposted from B4081 in Chipping Campden

Simple, small and genuinely pubby, this cheery ex-granary is the kind of place where locals play dominoes in a corner of the bar, and all the best seats are taken by the cats (the black one is especially hard to shift). The enthusiastic landlady works very hard to keep the unpretentious atmosphere just right; she's planning a big 'tidy-up' over the next few months. There are generally seven real ales on handpump in summer and five in winter, many of which you're unlikely to have ever come across before, with regulars including Donnington BB, Hook Norton, Stanway (a tiny brewery in Stanway House, Winchcombe), and Wickwar Brand Oak; some brews are priced well below the county average. They have beer festivals over the spring and August bank holiday weekends. Good and very reasonably priced food includes ploughman's (£1.95), cottage pie (£2.95), chilli (£3.25), steak and kidney pie (£3.75), and specials such as their very well-liked cheese and ale soup (£1.95), liver and onion casserole or meat loaf (£3.95), tasty beef in beer casserole (£4.25), chicken in white wine sauce (£4.50) and cider and cheese pork chop (£4.75), with a good Sunday roast (£4.25); the children's menu (from £2, with dishes like chicken madras) also suits those with smaller appetites. Very cosy and friendly, the tiny beamed bar has a pleasantly mixed bag of tables and seats around the walls (which are stripped back to bare stone), a log fire under a big black iron canopy at one end with a rocking chair beside it, and another at the other end. The oak bar counter is attractive, and there's a big framed rugwork picture of the pub; darts, cribbage, dominoes. There are white tables under cocktail parasols by flower tubs on a side terrace and in the back garden, some seats under a fairy-lit arbour, and a play area, with Aunt Sally and Tippit. The tranquil village is handy for the Barnfield cider mill. *(Recommended by D G King, Martin Jones, MDN, John Waller, Sara Nicholls, Andrew and Ruth Triggs, H O Dickinson, Simon Small, Christopher and Maureen Starling, Ted George, Jerry and Alison Oakes, Mrs B Lemon, Kathryn and Brian Heathcote, J and S E Garrett, Ann and Bob Westbrook, L Walker, Mrs S Smith, Derek and Sylvia Stephenson, BKA, Roy Smylie, Mrs Pat Crabb, H O Dickinson, Simon and Amanda Southwell, E V Walder, Leith Stuart, Mr and Mrs K H Frostick, Mr and Mrs P B Dowsett, David Heath, Douglas Adam, Basil Minson, Paul Boot)*

Free house ~ Licensee Carolyn Perry ~ Real ale ~ Meals and snacks (till 10 Fri and Sat) ~ (01386) 840515 ~ Children welcome ~ Folk night 3rd Tues of month ~ Open 11.30-11; 11.30-2.30, 6-11 in winter; closed 25 Dec, evening 26 Dec and lunchtime first Sat after Spring Bank Holiday, for local 'Scuttledown Wake'

BROCKHAMPTON SP0322 Map 4

Craven Arms ♀

Village signposted off A436 Andoversford—Naunton – look out for inn sign at head of lane in village; can also be reached from A40 Andoversford—Cheltenham via Whittington and Syreford

Lovely views from this picturesque 17th-c Cotswold inn, well-placed in a smartly attractive hillside village. Inside, there are low beams, thick roughly coursed stone walls and some tiled flooring, and though much of it has been opened out to give a sizeable (and spotlessly kept) eating area off the smaller bar servery, it's been done well to give a feeling of several communicating rooms; the furniture is mainly pine, with some wall settles, tub chairs and a log fire. Well-liked home-made bar food includes soup (£1.95), giant sausage (£2.50), big ploughman's (£3.50), steak sandwich or good beef curry (£4.95), home-made steak and kidney pie (£5.75), broccoli and walnut quiche or gammon and egg (£5.95), cold poached salmon (£8.50), char-grilled sirloin steak (£9.95), and super puddings like sherry trifle or sticky toffee pudding (£2.75), with evening extras such as duck breast in orange and Grand Marnier sauce (£8.95). Well kept Butcombe Bitter, Hook Norton Best, Wadworths 6X and Wickwar BOB on handpump. Service is friendly and efficient, though may be pushed during busy periods. Darts, shove-ha'penny. There are swings in the sizeable garden. *(Recommended by John and Joan Wyatt, Frank Cummins, Neil and Anita Christopher, Dave Irving, Ewan McCall, Roger Huggins, Tom McLean, Mr and Mrs P R Bevins, Mr and Mrs W W Swaitt)*

Free house ~ Licensees Dale and Melanie Campbell ~ Real ale ~ Meals and snacks ~ Restaurant ~ (01242) 820410 ~ Children in eating area and restaurant ~ Open 11-2.30, 6-11; closed 25 Dec

BROCKWEIR SO5401 Map 4

Brockweir

Village signposted just off A466 Chepstow—Monmouth

Close to the Wye in a village where Nelson occasionally entertained Lady Hamilton, this notably friendly 17th-c pub has been pleasantly redecorated in the last couple of years. The bare-stone-walled and beamed main bar has sturdy settles on quarry tiles in the front part, a winter open fire, and brocaded seats and copper-topped tables in a series of carpeted alcoves at the back; pool, cribbage and trivia in the bare-floored and traditionally furnished public bar. Well kept Freeminer Bitter (brewed only four miles away) and Hook Norton Best with a changing guest such as Batemans XXXB on handpump; Bulmers farm cider. Bar food includes sandwiches (from £1.70), soup, tuna bake (£3.20), ploughman's (£3.30), beef in stout (£4.90), scampi (£4.95), and puddings such as pecan pie (£2). Monty, the characterful trailhound, may join you for most of your meal. A covered courtyard at the back opens into a sheltered terrace, and there are picnic tables in a garden behind. As the pub is not too far away from the steep sheep-pastures leading up to Offa's Dyke Path and the Devil's Pulpit, with views over the Wye and Tintern Abbey, it's understandably a popular stop with walkers – though they do have fairly new carpets so appreciate it if muddy boots are removed. Canoeing, horse riding and salmon fishing are available locally. Dogs welcome. *(Recommended by Barry and Anne, Piotr Chodzko-Zajko, Roger and Jenny Huggins, George Atkinson, N C Walker, Bob Riley)*

Free house ~ Licensees George and Elizabeth Jones ~ Real ale ~ Meals and snacks ~ (01291) 689548 ~ Children in family room ~ Open 12-2.30(3 Sat), 6-11 ~ Bedrooms: £25/£36

CHEDWORTH SP0511 Map 4

Seven Tuns

Queen Street, Upper Chedworth; village signposted off A429 NE of Cirencester; then take second signposted right turn and bear left towards church

Friendly and pleasantly remote, this attractively placed Cotswold pub has two bars with completely different characters. On the right, the smarter but cosily atmospheric little lounge has sizeable antique prints, tankards hanging from the beam over the serving bar, comfortable seats, decent tables, a partly boarded ceiling, a good winter log fire in the big stone fireplace, and a relaxed, quiet atmosphere; no muddy boots in here. The basic public bar on the left is more lively, and opens into a games room with darts, pool, pinball, dominoes, fruit machine and video game; there's also a skittle alley (which can be hired). The bar menu has shrunk to allow the chef to concentrate on his daily specials; favourite dishes have included a good steak and ale pie (£4.95), chicken and ham pie (£5.95), and grilled shark steak in garlic (£6.95), as well as game casserole, seafood kebabs, Portuguese sardines, steaks (from £8.85), a good Sunday roast, and children's meals; they may have themed evenings throughout the year (such as the August bank holiday Monday pig roast with live band). Well kept Courage Best and John Smiths on handpump, along with Georges and Old Ambrose, brewed especially for the pub, mulled wine in winter, kir and sangria in summer; obliging service from welcoming, hard-working staff. Across the road is a little walled raised terrace with a stream running through it forming a miniature waterfall. There are plenty of tables both here and under cocktail parasols on a side terrace – perfect for relaxing after a walk through the valley. The famous Roman villa is a pleasant walk away. *(Recommended by Dr A Y Drummond, Andrew and Ruth Triggs, Nick and Meriel Cox, G Washington, Marjorie and Colin Roberts, John and Joan Wyatt, Thomas Nott, Tom McLean, Roger Huggins, Ewan McCall, Dave Irving, Gordon, Audrey and Peter Dowsett, D G King)*

Free house ~ Licensee Brian Eacott ~ Real ale ~ Meals and snacks (not Mon, or 25 Dec) ~ (01285) 720242 ~ Well-behaved children allowed until 9pm, in public bar if eating, otherwise games room ~ Open 12-2.30, 6.30-11; 11.30-3, 6.30-11 Sat; closed Mon lunchtime

CHIPPING CAMPDEN SP1539 Map 4

Kings Arms 🍷

Overlooking the market square, this civilised little 16th-c hotel is more obviously food-orientated than the other places we know in Chipping Campden, but none the worse for that, particularly as the welcome is so genuinely warm and friendly. Not just to grown-ups either, children are given crayons and colouring books, and dogs supplied with bowls of water. The comfortably old-fashioned bar has handsomely carved black beams, a fine stone inglenook fireplace, maybe fresh flowers, and some big bay window seats. Bar food includes lunchtime sandwiches (not Sun), soup (£1.90), chicken livers (£3.50), pasta provençale or a speciality sausage of the day (£4.50), steak and kidney pie or grilled trout with almonds (£4.95), daily specials like chicken kashmir (£4.95) or seafood juliennais (£5.75), puddings such as sherry trifle or lemon and kiwi flummery, and children's meals (£2, including ice cream); best to get there early. Watch out for their special offers, particularly on winter evenings when you may find a three-course meal for £6.50, or a four-course meal in the candlelit restaurant for £12.50 (with a bottle of wine). The very extensive wine list runs to around 72 by the bottle and 10 by the glass. There are seats in the gardens behind, and the hotel is handy for the attractive nearby gardens of Hidcote and Kiftsgate Court. *(Recommended by John Bowdler, Martin and Karen Wake, Mrs J Oakes, Peter Lloyd, Andrew and Ruth Triggs, Ian Rorison, H O Dickinson, Malcolm Davies, Leith Stuart, Derek Allpass, Jill White, Gordon Mott, Peter Lloyd, Kathryn and Brian Heathcote, E G Parish, Prof John and Patricia White, C Turner, Peter Lloyd, JF)*

Free house ~ Licensee Stan Earnshaw ~ Meals and snacks (12-3, 6-9.30) ~ Restaurant ~ (01386) 840256 ~ Children welcome ~ Open 11-11 ~ Bedrooms: £30B/£60B

Noel Arms 🛏 🍷

Some of the antiques and characterful furnishings at this very well run and rather smart old inn look like they could have been here when Charles II is supposed to have been a guest after the Battle of Worcester. The welcoming bar is decorated with casks hanging from its beams, farm tools, horseshoes and gin traps on the bare stone walls, armour, and old oak settles, attractive old tables, seats and newer settles among the windsor chairs; there's a winter coal fire, and a conservatory behind. The small lounge areas are comfortable and traditionally furnished with coach horns, lantern lighting, and some stripped stonework, and the reception area has its quota of pikes, halberds, swords, muskets, and breastplates. Well kept Bass and Hook Norton on handpump, with guest ales such as Brains, Felinfoel Double Dragon, Shepherd Neame Spitfire, Rebellion from the Marlow Brewery, and Uley Old Spot, and a good choice of malt whiskies, brandies, and over 100 wines. Big helpings of good home-made lunchtime bar food such as soup (£2), sandwiches (£2.35), ploughman's (from £3.75), filled baguettes (£3.90), cauliflower and broccoli bake (£3.95), pork, apple and cider casserole (£4.65), chicken and leek pie (£4.85), beef, Guinness and mushroom stew (£5.10), and puddings like toffee, apple and pecan pie (£2.50); friendly efficient service; dominoes, and piped music. There are seats in the old coachyard. *(Recommended by Andrew and Ruth Triggs, DAV, John Waller, C Turner, Col A H N Reade)*

Free house ~ Licensee Neil John ~ Real ale ~ Lunchtime meals and snacks ~ Restaurant ~ Evesham (01386) 840317 ~ Children welcome ~ Jazz summer Sun evenings ~ Open 10.30-3, 6-11; all day Thurs-Sat ~ Bedrooms: £60B/£80B

CLEARWELL SO5708 Map 4

Wyndham Arms 🛏 🍷

B4231, signposted from A466 S of Monmouth towards Lydney

One of the things that really stands out about this neatly kept and civilised country inn is that despite being a hotel it still has a distinctly pubby feel and character. The smart and comfortable beamed bar has red plush seats and velvet curtains, a collection of flat-irons by the log-effect gas fire in its spacious stone fireplace, and two big unusual patchwork pictures on its bared stone walls; cribbage and dominoes. Well kept Flowers Original and Whitbreads West Country PA on handpump, lots of malt whiskies, a very good range of generously served wines by the glass or half bottle – and gherkins, onions and olives on the counter; good service from smartly turned-out staff. Bar food is pricey but excellent quality and worth the extra: home-made soup (£3), sandwiches (from £3.50; open ones from £4), ploughman's (£4.50), home-made pâtés like cheese and fresh herb or chicken liver (£4.55), sausages and egg or smoked haddock with poached egg (£4.95), a daily pasta dish (£5.95), local salmon salad (£6.75), prawn or vegetable curry (£7.50), a vegetarian dish of the day (£7.75), deep-fried lemon sole with home-made tartare sauce (£7.75), liver and bacon (£7.75), steaks (from £10.25), and tasty puddings (£2.50). Breakfasts are very good. Many of the fruits, vegetables and herbs are grown in the garden. Seats out on the neat patios, and a friendly and characterful flat-coated retriever Theo; other dogs welcome. The setting is lovely, and this is an ideal base for exploring the area. *(Recommended by George Atkinson, Dave Irving, M J Morgan, S H Godsell, Dr C E Morgan, Martyn Kearey, M Lithgow, Bob Riley, C W Channon, David and Mary Webb, Tom McEwan, Roger Huggins, Dr and Mrs K Hofheinz, Nick Cox)*

Free house ~ Licensees John, Rosemary and Robert Stanford ~ Real ale ~ Meals and snacks ~ Restaurant ~ (01594) 833666 ~ Children welcome ~ Open 11-11 ~ Bedrooms: £46.50B/£61B

COLD ASTON SP1219 Map 4

Plough

Village signposted from A436 and A429 SW of Stow-on-the-Wold; beware that on some maps the village is called Aston Blank, and the A436 called the B4068

Virginia creepers scramble up the heavy stone walls of this marvellously unspoilt and tiny 17th-c pub. Divided into snug little areas by standing timbers, the bar has a built-in white-painted traditional settle facing the stone fireplace, an old photograph of the pub on the mantlepiece, low black beams, simple old-fashioned seats on the flagstone and lime-ash floor, and a happy mix of customers. Warmly friendly staff serve big helpings of good bar food such as home-baked filled rolls (from £2.50), ploughman's, nicely filled baked potatoes (from £4.25), vegetarian meals like delicious cauliflower cheese (£4.95), home-made pies or chilli (£5.25), barbecued ribs (£5.75), and popular puddings; they don't take credit cards. Do arrive in plenty of time, food service does stop promptly. Well kept Theakstons Best and a guest like Morlands Old Speckled Hen on handpump, mulled wine in winter; darts, cribbage, dominoes, shove-ha'penny, quoits and unobtrusive piped music. The small side terraces have picnic tables under parasols, and there may be Morris dancers out here in summer. No dogs. *(Recommended by Nick and Meriel Cox, Dave Irving, Ewan McCall, Roger Huggins, Tom McLean, Frank Cummins, F J and A Parmenter, Tim Brierly, Gordon, John and Joan Wyatt, Neil and Anita Christopher, George Atkinson)*

Free house ~ Licensee Arthur King ~ Real ale ~ Meals and snacks (till 1.45 lunchtime, 1.30 Sun) ~ (01451) 821459 ~ Children in tiny dining room ~ Open 11-2.30, 6.30-11

COLN ST ALDWYNS SP1405 Map 4

New Inn

On good back road between Bibury and Fairford

They like to boast that, bar only the briefest of hiccups, the purpose and fabric of this popular ivy-covered inn has remained the same throughout the reign of 20 monarchs. In none of that time can it have been quite so civilised as it is today, with a genuinely old-fashioned atmosphere and caring and concerned licensees. The food is outstanding, with a reassuringly short range of regularly changing dishes such as a proper french onion soup (£3.65), soft filled baguettes such as chicken liver parfait with pine nuts (£4.50), smoked haddock gratin with leeks and chives (£4.75), crottin cheese salad with sun-dried tomatoes and crostini (£5.50), ploughman's (£5.95), fishcake with tomato and basil salad (£6.50), liver and bacon with mash and mustard sauce (£7.25), rump steak (£8.50), daily specials, children's meals, and puddings such as custard tart with home-made nutmeg ice cream (£3.80); the carefully prepared vegetables are extra. The two main rooms are most attractively furnished and decorated (you can tell the landlady used to be an interior designer), and divided by a central log fire in a neat stone fireplace with wooden mantlebeam and willow-pattern plates on the chimney breast; also, oriental rugs on the red tiles, low beams, some stripped stonework around the bar servery and hops above it, and a mix of seating from library chairs to stripped pews. Down a slight slope, a further room has a log fire in an old kitchen range at one end, and a stuffed buzzard on the wall. Well kept Hook Norton, Wadworths 6X, Websters and guests on handpump, half a dozen good wines by the glass, and several malt whiskies; very good, friendly service. Cribbage, dominoes, cards, chess and draughts. Lots of seats under umbrellas in the split-level terraced garden; popular sunny weekend barbecues. The peaceful Cotswold village is pretty, and this is good walking country. *(Recommended by A G C Harper, SRP, Neil and Anita Christopher, Bronwen and Steve Wrigley, Dr I H Maine, Colin Laffan, Peter and Audrey Dowsett, Tom McLean, Dave Irving, Ewan McCall, Roger Huggins, Gordon, J and S Askin, Ivor Hockman, Joan Olivier, S J Pearson, George and Heather Tucker, Dr John Evans, Claire and Michael Willoughby, D M St G Saunders, Pat and John Millward, Paula Harrison, Paul McPherson)*

Free house ~ Licensee Brian Evans ~ Real ale ~ Meals and snacks ~ Restaurant ~ (01285) 750651 ~ Children welcome ~ Open 11-2.30, 5.30-11; 11-11 summer Sats ~ Bedrooms: £50B/£75B

nr COWLEY SO9614 Map 4

Green Dragon

Cockleford; pub signposted from A435 about 1½ miles S of junction with A436 – or follow Elkstone turn-off; OS Sheet 163 map reference 969142

Opening time at this attractive stone-fronted pub is signalled by what's becoming quite an unusual tradition, when the landlady serves her six-year old horse Coker a pint of Smiles Best at the front door. He's quite partial to Guinness too, so watch your pint if you're walking past him. The last few years at the Green Dragon have been chequered to say the least, but under the current licensee (who took over just after our last edition was published) things seem to be settling down again nicely. You really get the impression that the pub is her home – she even puts her birthday cards up in the genuinely old-fashioned bar. Full of flowers and candles and free from games or music, this has antique furnishings including an aged dresser, big flagstones in one tiny room and wooden boards in the other, beams, a spacious stone fireplace, and a wood-burning stove; dominoes, cribbage. Well-liked bar food includes a good tomato, mushroom, onion and garlic soup (£1.95), ragout of lamb and apricot or Dragon smokie (£5.95), salmon (£9.25), and sirloin steak in a stilton sauce (£9.95). A good range of beers includes Smiles Best, Exhibition and Mayfly, Fullers ESB, Hook Norton, Shepherd Neame Spitfire, Theakstons Old Peculier and other guests on handpump or tapped from the cask; also farm cider, and a range of malt whiskies. There are terraces outside overlooking Cowley Lake and the River

Churn, and the pub is a good centre for the lovely local walks. Dogs welcome. *(Recommended by John and Joan Wyatt, Dave Irving, Roger Huggins, Tom McLean, Ewan McCall, S C King, Tom Gondris, Frank W Gadbois, Thomas Nott, Malcolm Taylor, G Washington, Mr and Mrs Mullins, Marjorie and Colin Roberts, Paul Boot, Brad, Joni and Kristin Nelson, D Cox, M G Hart, M L and B S Rantzen, Martyn Kearey)*

Smiles ~ Licensee Pia Maria Boast ~ Real ale ~ Meals and snacks (not 25/26 Dec) ~ (01242) 870271 ~ Children in left-hand bar only ~ Jazz/celtic rock every Weds evening ~ Open 11.30-2.30, 6-11; closed evening 25/26 Dec, all day 1 Jan

CRANHAM SO8912 Map 4

Black Horse

Village signposted off A46 and B4070 N of Stroud; up side turning

This unpretentious friendly local, old-fashioned, small and cosy, has good generous home-cooked food, including sandwiches (from £1), soup (£1.65), ploughman's (from £3), and a good changing choice of hot dishes such as cumberland sausage (£3.95), almond nut loaf with pepper sauce (£4.50), fishcakes (£4.95), liver and bacon (£5.25), a half pheasant (£5.50), superb lamb chops (£5.95) and various popular pies from vegetarian (£4.25) to steak and kidney (£6.25); vegetables are fresh, and because this is not out-of-a-packet cooking most things can be had in small helpings for children. Very well kept Boddingtons, Flowers Original, Hook Norton Best, Whitbreads PA and Wickwar Brand Oak on handpump, Stowford Press cider, decent wines. A cosy little lounge has just three or four tables; the main bar is quarry-tiled, with cushioned high-backed wall settles and window seats, and a good log fire; shove-ha'penny, cribbage, dominoes, unobtrusive fruit machine, occasional piped music. Service is very friendly (the licensees are both local), and Truffle the Brittany spaniel is quite a character. Tables in the sizeable garden behind (and in the dining room, where it might be wise to book at weekends) have a good view out over the steep village and wooded valley. *(Recommended by Tom Evans, A Y Drummond, James Skinner, Margaret Drazin, D G Clarke, Nick and Meriel Cox)*

Free house ~ Licensees David and Julie Job ~ Real ale ~ Meals and snacks (not Sun evening) ~ (01452) 812217 ~ Children welcome ~ Occasional folk music or Morris men ~ Open 11.30-2.30, 6.30-11

EBRINGTON SP1840 Map 4

Ebrington Arms

Signposted from B4035 E of Chipping Campden; and from A429 N of Moreton-in-Marsh

The landlord at this unpretentious alehouse has a pottery in the courtyard where he hand throws and fires the crockery used in the restaurant. Very much a local rather than the smarter dining pubs so often found in this part of the world, it nevertheless has a chatty mix of countryfolk and visitors even out of season, and a pleasantly traditional feel that blends in very well with the surroundings. Some fine old low beams, stone walls, flagstoned floors and inglenook fireplaces – the one in the dining room still has the original iron work. The little bar has sturdy traditional furnishings, with seats built into the airy bow window, and a slightly raised woodfloored area. A lower room, also beamed and flagstoned, has stripped country-kitchen furnishings. Decent, simple bar food, generously served, might include sandwiches, filled baguettes (from £3.75), ploughman's, lasagne or ratatouille (£3.95), various types of local sausage (£4.95), gammon and eggs or pies such as chicken, ham and tarragon or a good steak and kidney (£5.45) and steaks (from £8.50). The menu is chalked up on the beams and stretches on for what seems like miles. Well kept Donnington SBA, Hook Norton Best and guests on handpump, Bulmer's farm cider; absolutely no piped music or games machines – just an old-fashioned harmonium. Trophies bear witness to the success of the pub's dominoes team, and you can also play cribbage, darts and shove ha'penny. An arched stone wall shelters a terrace with picnic tables under cocktail parasols. No dogs at least at mealtimes, when even the licensees' friendly Welsh springer is kept out. Handy for Hidcote and Kiftsgate. Some readers feel that more attention might be paid to the housekeeping, though others worry this would alter the unspoilt character of the place. *(Recommended by Ted George, Jerry and Alison Oakes, Barry and Anne, Christopher and Maureen Starling, Martin Jones, P R White, Graham Reeve, P D and J Bickley, D A Edwards, Richard Osborne, David and Helen Wilkins, Leith Stuart, Pam Adsley, E V Walder)*

Free house ~ Licensees Gareth Richards and Andrew Geddes ~ Real ale ~ Meals and snacks (not Sun evening) ~ (01386) 593223 ~ Children in dining room ~ Open 11-2.30, 6-11; closed 25 Dec ~ Bedrooms: £35B

EDGE SO8509 Map 4

Edgemoor

A4173 N of Stroud

The terrace and the big picture windows of this busy food pub share the same hard-to-beat view, looking down over the valley to Painswick, often described as the 'Queen of the Cotswolds'. If you're here at dusk you'll see the lights in the little cluster of houses come on one by one, watched over by the serenely superior church spire towering above them. The highly praised home-made bar food includes sandwiches, unusual starters like kidneys and bacon in cream sauce or deep-fried brie and cranberry, and main courses such as steak pie, fresh fish, vegetarian dishes, and a daily roast; the restaurant may be fully booked for their three-course Sunday lunch, but they have the same menu in the bar. Clean and tidy, the main bar is an orderly place, with West Country cloth upholstery and pale wood furniture on the patterned carpet, and neat bare stone walls. All the dining areas are no-smoking. Butcombe, Smiles, Tetleys and Uley Old Spot on handpump, kept under light top pressure in winter, good wines by the glass, and an interesting range of malt whiskies; piped music. *(Recommended by C Jones, Catherine Hamilton, Christopher and Maureen Starling, Paul Weedon)*

Free house ~ Licensee Chris Bayes ~ Real ale ~ Meals and snacks (not Sun evening ~ Restaurant ~ (01452) 813576 ~ Children in eating area ~ Open 11-3, 6-11; closed Sun evening Oct-Mar

EWEN SU0097 Map 4

Wild Duck ★ 🍴 🍷 🛏

Village signposted from A429 S of Cirencester

Marked out by the odd-looking clock on the outside wall, this lovely 16th-c inn is a most unusual building, in parts more like an old manor house than a typical pub. The high-beamed main bar has a nice mix of comfortable armchairs and other seats, candles on the tables, a fine longcase clock, a talking grey parrot in a cage near the bar, paintings on the coral walls, crimson drapes, magazines to read, and an open winter fire, and another bar has a handsome Elizabethan fireplace and antique furnishings and looks over the garden. The atmosphere is particularly warm and cosy, and the service consistently friendly, but it's the food that people seem to like best, especially the fish, delivered fresh every day from Devon, and including dishes like tuna (£7.95), lemon sole (£8.50), red bream (£8.95), snapper (£9.50), and parrot fish or sea bass (£14.95). Other meals might include soup (£2.50), ploughman's, enjoyable Japanese prawns with cucumber yoghurt or seafood salad with shredded chicken (£4.50), chilli tortillas (£6.50), lamb hash with fried bananas (£7.50), roasted prosciutto ham (£9.95), steaks (from £10.95), and some often really rather inventive daily specials – we've heard especially good things about their peppered strawberries served with cherry tomatoes, or the pork in Pernod served with rice in a pineapple. As well as Duckpond, brewed especially for the pub, well-kept beers might include Fullers London Pride, Theakstons XB and Old Peculier, Wadworths 6X or Youngs Special. Good wines; shove-ha'penny, gentle piped music. The pub does get busy, though there are teak tables and chairs in the sheltered and well-kept garden. On the edge of an attractive village, the pub is handy for Cirencester. *(Recommended by Dave Irving, Roger Huggins, Tom McLean, Ewan McCall, John and Chris Simpson, David Holman, Marjorie and Colin Roberts, John Waller, SRP, Stephen, Julie and Hayley Brown, D G King, N H and A H Harries, Malcolm Taylor, Susan and John Douglas, A C W Boyle, D G King, Dr and Mrs James Stewart, Jan and Dave Booth, Pat and John Millward, F J Robinson, P Neate, Dave Braisted, W C M Jones, John Oddey)*

Free house ~ Licensees Brian and Tina Mussell ~ Real ale ~ Meals and snacks (till 10pm) ~ Restaurant ~ (01285) 770310 ~ Children welcome ~ Open 11-11 ~ Bedrooms: £48B/£65B

FORD SP0829 Map 4

Plough

B4077

Handy for some lovely countryside, this pretty stone pub is doing rather well at the moment, praised by readers for its food, service, and above all the warmly welcoming atmosphere. The gallops for local stables are opposite, and there's quite a racing feel to the place, particularly on the days when the horse owned by a partnership of locals is running at Cheltenham. The beamed and stripped-stone bar has old settles and benches around the big tables on its uneven flagstones, oak tables in a snug alcove, racing prints and photos on the walls, log fires, and a traditional, friendly feel; dominoes, cribbage, shove-ha'penny, fruit machine, piped music, and several board games. Under the new licensee bar food includes good sandwiches, home-made soup (£2.50) and pâtés (£3.45), home-cured ham and egg (£5.50), local trout (£5.75), game casserole, knuckle of lamb or steak and kidney pie (£6.50), and home-made puddings (£2.35). They still have their traditional asparagus feasts every April-June, when the first asparagus spears to be sold at auction in the Vale of Evesham usually end up here. Well kept Donnington BB and SBA served on handpump by obliging staff; also freshly squeezed orange juice, and a range of wines and champagnes. There are benches in front, with rustic tables and chairs on grass by white lilacs and fairy lights, and a play area at the back. This used to be the local court house, and what's now the cellar was the gaol; outside an inviting old sign suggests 'Step in and quaff my nut-brown ale'. Look out for the Llama farm between here and Kineton. *(Recommended by Angus Lyon, D E Kent, Roger Byrne, E V Walder, Sara Nicholls, Andrew and Ruth Triggs, Martin and Karen Wake, George Atkinson, Jack and Philip Paxton, Martin Jones, Gwen and Peter Andrews, Lawrence Pearse, Dave Irving, Roger Huggins, T McLean, Ewan McCall, John and Shirley Dyson, E V Walder, Andy and Jill Kassube, Gordon, Kathryn and Brian Heathcote)*

Donnington ~ Tenant W Skinner ~ Real ale ~ Meals and snacks (not Sun evenings) ~ (01386) 584215 ~ Children welcome ~ Jazz 2nd Tues in month ~ Open 11-11 ~ Bedrooms: £35B/£50B

GREAT BARRINGTON SP2013 Map 4

Fox

Village signposted from A40 Burford—Northleach; pub between Little and Great Barrington

Business is booming at this simple Cotswold inn – trade has increased so much under the enthusiastic current licensees that they've had to add a new car park. Prettily set beside a stone bridge over the Windrush, it's particularly pleasant on sunny days when you can relax on the seats near the landscaped pond in the orchard, or on the riverside terrace; there may be barbecues out here on summer Saturdays. The low-ceilinged little bar has stripped stone walls, two roaring log fires, and rustic wooden chairs, tables and window seats; sensibly placed darts, pool, shove-ha'penny, dominoes, cribbage, fruit machine, and piped music. Well kept Donnington BB and SBA on handpump, and Addlestones cider. The pub dog is called Bruiser (though he's only little). Bar food includes sandwiches (not Sun), mussels (£4.95), salmon fishcakes (£5.95), chicken and mushroom pie (£5.75), beef in ale pie (£6.25), very good steaks supplied by the landlord's father, and giant breakfasts; senior citizens special on Mondays. There's a skittles alley out beyond the sheltered yard, and they have private fishing. *(Recommended by Gordon, Martin Jones, Neil and Anita Christopher, Lawrence Pearse, Dave Irving, Ewan McCall, Roger Huggins, Tom McLean, Martin and Karen Wake, David Holloway, Bronwen and Steve Wrigley, Chris and Annie Clipson)*

Donnington ~ Tenants Paul and Kate Porter ~ Real ale ~ Meals and snacks ~ (01451) 844385 ~ Children welcome ~ Live music monthly ~ Open 11-11; closed evening 25 Dec ~ Bedrooms: £22.50/£40

GREAT RISSINGTON SP1917 Map 4

Lamb

Overlooking the village and its surrounding hills, this partly 17th-c pub has quite a civilised air, but still feels very pubby. On the walls of the cosy two-roomed bar are photographs of the guide dogs the staff and customers have raised money to buy (over 20), as well as a history of the village, plates, pictures, and an interesting collection of old cigarette and tobacco tins. Wheelback and tub chairs with cushioned seats are grouped around polished tables on the light brown carpet, a table and settle are hidden in a nook under the stairs, and there's a log-effect gas fire in the stone fireplace. Bar food includes sandwiches, home-made soup (£2.85), mushrooms stuffed with stilton or deep-fried brie with redcurrant jelly (£3.95), pasta bake (£6.75), local trout with apricot and almond stuffing (£8.75), sirloin steak with a crushed pepper, mushroom and brandy sauce (£10.50), daily specials like home-made sausages or local asparagus (£4.50), and char-grilled liver and bacon (£4.65), and home-made puddings (£2.50); the restaurant is partly no smoking. Morlands Old Speckled Hen and Smiles on handpump, good wine list (with highly praised and well-served wines by the glass), country wines, farm cider, maybe piped classical music. You can sit out in the sheltered hillside garden, or really take advantage of the scenery and walk, via gravel pits now used as a habitat for water birds, to Bourton on the Water. This really is a pleasant place to stay; one of the chintzy bedrooms in the warren of small stairs and doors has a four-poster carved by the landlord, while a newly converted Victorian suite has a period bed and matching dressing table. There's an indoor swimming pool. *(Recommended by George Atkinson, John Waller, Bronwen and Steve Wrigley, Helen Pickering, James Owen, DJW, SRP, R W Brooks, P D and J Bickley, D Walker, Marjorie and David Lamb, D A Edwards, Dr C B Cohen, T and D Archer, Peter and Janet Race, Neil and Anita Christopher, Peter and Rosemary Ellis, Leith Stuart)*

Free house ~ Licensees Richard and Kate Cleverly ~ Real ale ~ Meals and snacks (till 1.45 lunchtime) ~ Restaurant ~ (01451) 820388 ~ Children in eating area of bar and restaurant ~ Open 11.30-2.30, 6.30-11; closed 25/26 Dec ~ Bedrooms: £38B/£52B

GREET SP0230 Map 4

Harvest Home

B4078 just N of Winchcombe

Transformed in the last couple of years by its German chef-patron and his wife, this civilised and relaxed pub majors on its wide choice of good food, such as omelettes (£4.50), king prawns in garlic butter (£5.25), duck and bacon pie (£5.75), salmon baked in flaky pastry with a mushroom and chive sauce (£5.95), steaks from 6oz rump (£6.75), zigeuner schnitzel (fried slices of pork loin with tomato and onion sauce, £7.25) and specials – partly dependent in winter on what the local shooting parties have been able to bag – such as bass in a white wine sauce (£7.35), game pie (£5.75), pheasant (£7.35) or haunch of venison (£7.75). Despite competition from the good steamed puddings, the favourite pudding here is home-baked apple strudel; and this is one of the few places we know serving fresh local brown-cap mushrooms. There are filled baguettes (from £2.50), ploughman's (from £4.25) and children's dishes (from £2.25). The neat, clean bar has a dozen or so well spaced tables, with seats built into the bay windows and other sturdy blue-cushioned seats; there are pretty flower prints and country scenes on the walls, and several dried-flower arrangements. Boddingtons, Morlands Old Speckled Hen, Wadworths 6X and Whitbreads PA on handpump, decent wines, good coffee (spoilt for us by foil-topped milk substitute); darts and fruit machine down at one end (the other, with a good open fire, is no smoking), cribbage, dominoes, unobtrusive piped classical music; helpful and pleasant young staff. There's a big beamed pitched-roof side restaurant (same food, also no smoking). The sizeable garden has a play area and boules, and the narrow-gauge GWR railway passes it. The miniature schnauzers are called Oscar and Boris. *(Recommended by Lorraine Gwynne, Ian and Sheila Richardson, Michael Green, Brian and Genie Smart)*

Whitbreads ~ Lease: Heinz and Lisa Stolzenberg ~ Real ale ~ Meals and snacks ~ Restaurant ~ (01242) 602430 ~ Children in no-smoking areas till 9 ~ Open 10.30-3, 6-11

GRETTON SP0131 Map 4

Royal Oak

Village signposted off what is now officially B4077 (still often mapped and even signed as A438), E of Tewkesbury; keep on through village

An unusual way of arriving here is by steam train, as at weekends, Bank Holidays and two weeks in summer, the Gloucestershire-Warwickshire Railway that runs from Toddington to Winchcombe station stops at the bottom of the garden. The garden itself is very popular in summer, with picnic tables on the flower-filled terrace and under a giant pear tree, a neatly kept big lawn running down past a small hen-run to a play area (with an old tractor and see-saw), and even a bookable tennis court. There's quite a friendly atmosphere in the series of bare-boarded or flagstoned rooms – the pub was once a pair of old stone-built cottages – all softly lit (including candles in bottles on the mix of stripped oak and pine tables), and with dark ochre walls, beams (some hung with tankards, hop bines and chamber-pots), old prints, and a medley of pews and various chairs; the affable setter is called George. The no-smoking dining conservatory has stripped country furnishings, and a broad view over farmland to Alderton and Dumbleton Hills. Well kept John Smiths, Marstons Pedigree, Morlands Old Speckled Hen, Ruddles County, Smiles Best and Wadworths 6X on handpump, around 70 whiskies, and around 40 decent wines. Good value bar food includes main courses like mackerel with yoghurt and french mustard sauce, or celery and stilton pasta bake; darts, shove-ha'penny, fruit machine, piped music. *(Recommended by Jo Rees, Martin Jones, Sara Nicholls, Basil Minson, Brian White, Ewan McCall, Tom McLean, Roger Huggins, Dave Irving, Derek and Sylvia Stephenson)*

Free house ~ Licensees Bob and Kathy Willison ~ Real ale ~ Meals and snacks ~ Restaurant ~ (01242) 602477 ~ Well-behaved children welcome ~ Folk/blues Weds evening ~ Open 11-2.30, 6-11; closed 25/26 Dec

GUITING POWER SP0924 Map 4

Olde Inne

Village signposted off B4068 SW of Stow-on-the-Wold (still called A436 on many maps)

This snug old cottage is doing rather well under the friendly licensees who took over just before our last edition. They've tidied the place up without making any major changes, and their hearty bar food is proving popular, especially the Burmese and Thai specials. The welcoming beamed and gently lit bar has a winter log fire in an unusual pillar-supported stone fireplace, attractive built-in wall and window seats (including one, near the serving counter, that's the height of the bar stools), and small armchairs. The public bar is similarly furnished but also has flagstones and stripped stone masonry, as well as sensibly placed darts, cribbage and dominoes. Bar food includes home-made soup (£2.25), frikadeller (Danish pork rissole, £4.75), steak and kidney pie (£4.95), spicy nut roast (£5.50), half a roast duckling in port wine sauce (£8.50), specials such as Burmese chicken and noodles or felafel with hummus and pitta bread (£5.50), puddings like apple and walnut crumble, and children's meals (£2.95); surcharge for cheque or credit card bills below £10. Well kept Hook Norton and Theakstons Best and guests like Bass, Exmoor Gold and Marstons Pedigree on handpump, several malt whiskies. From the pleasant garden behind are views towards the peaceful sloping fields. Decent walks nearby. Locals know the pub as th'Ollow Bottom thanks to its position in a marked dip in the road. *(Recommended by Mr and Mrs D C Stevens, Maureen Hobbs, Frank Cummins, Margaret Dyke, Philip Orbell, Angus Lyon, Martin Jones, Dave Irving, Roger Huggins, Ewan McCall, Tom McLean, A Y Drummond, John and Shirley Dyson, Gordon, Andy and Jill Kassube)*

Free house ~ Licensees Bill and Julia Tu ~ Real ale ~ Meals and snacks (not 25 Dec) ~ Restaurant ~ (01451) 850392 ~ Children in eating area of bar and restaurant ~ Open 11.30-3(2.30 winter), 6(5.30 Fri)-11

HYDE SO8801 Map 4

Ragged Cot

Burnt Ash; Hyde signposted with Minchinhampton from A419 E of Stroud; or (better road) follow Minchinhampton, Aston Down signposted from A419 at Aston Down airfield; OS Sheet 162 map reference 886012

Nicely set beside a row of chestnut trees in the heart of the Cotswolds, this welcoming cottage with its stone-slab roof is always friendly and chatty. The relaxed and rambling bar has lots of stripped stone and black beams, as well as a traditional dark wood wall settle by the end fire, cushioned wheelback chairs and bar stools, and cushioned window seats; off to the right is a no-smoking restaurant area. A good choice of reasonably priced and well liked home-made bar food includes sandwiches, onion soup (£1.60), pizzas or omelettes (from £3.95), at least five vegetarian meals (from £4.50), fresh fish (from £4.95), steak and kidney pie (£4.95), gammon (£5.95) and steaks (from £8.95). Well kept Bass, Marstons Pedigree, Theakstons Best, Uley Old Spot, and Wadworths 6X on handpump, and several malt whiskies and wines (the landlord used to be in the wine trade); good service; darts, cribbage, fruit machine. There are picnic tables in the garden, and bedrooms in an adjacent converted barn. The garden has an interesting pavilion (now used as a conference or function room). *(Recommended by Dave Irving, Roger Huggins, Tom McLean, Ewan McCall, M J Morgan, Dorothy and Leslie Pilson, Andrew Shore, Neil and Anita Christopher, T Roger Lamble, John and Shirley Dyson, R C Watkins)*

Free house ~ Licensees Mr and Mrs M Case ~ Real ale ~ Meals and snacks ~ Restaurant (closed Sun evening) ~ (01453) 884643 ~ Children in eating area of bar and restaurant ~ Open 11-3, 6-11 ~ Bedrooms: £48B/£60B

KILKENNY SP0018 Map 4

Kilkeney Inn

A436 nr Cheltenham – OS Sheet 163 map reference 007187; if this hamlet is not shown on your map look for Dowdeswell

The emphasis is firmly on food at this comfortable country pub (they call themselves a brasserie now), but it's still the kind of place you can pop into for just a drink. Readers enjoy eating here very much indeed, and no wonder – the meals are excellently prepared and presented, and particularly good quality. The regularly changing menu might include lunchtime filled french sticks (from £2.50) and ploughman's (£3.85), as well as soup (£2.20), tartlet of kidney and mushrooms in red wine (£3.35), gravadlax or avocado, mushroom and cheese bake (£3.50), steak and kidney pie (£5.95), phitivier of mushroom, fennel and wild rice with tomato and coriander sauce (£6.95), pan-fried pork fillet in peach curry sauce (£7.95), rack of lamb with thyme and redcurrant sauce (£8.50), half a roast duck with orange, lime and Cointreau sauce (£10.95), and puddings such as blackcurrant and cassis shortcake or chocolate and amaretto mousse (£2.75); helpful friendly service. Booking is recommended, especially at weekends. The extended and modernised bar, quite bright and airily spacious, has neatly alternated stripped Cotswold stone and white plasterwork, as well as gleaming dark wheelback chairs around the tables, and an open fire. Up at the other end of the same long bar is more of a drinking area, with well kept Hook Norton Best and Ruddles Best on handpump, an excellent range of decent wines and lots of malt whiskies. It opens into a comfortable no-smoking dining conservatory. Attractive Cotswold views, good parking. *(Recommended by Mr and Mrs Mullins, Thomas Nott, Brian White, Christopher Darwent, Sara Nicholls, Mrs B Lemon, S Whittingham, Roger Huggins, Tom McLean, Ewan McCall, Dave Irving, Wyn Churchill, R M Bloomfield, Neil and Anita Christopher, Mrs K E Neville-Rolfe, Andy Petersen, Philip Brown, Mrs Jackson, Frank W Gadbois, Don Kellaway, Angie Coles, Paul Boot)*

Free house ~ Licensees John and Judy Fennell ~ Real ale ~ Meals and lunchtime snacks ~ (01242) 820341 ~ Well behaved children in eating areas ~ Open 11.30-2.30, 6.30-11; closed 25/26 Dec, and Sun evenings Jan-March

KINGSCOTE ST8196 Map 4

Hunters Hall ★ ♀

A4135 Dursley—Tetbury

Somehow even when this civilised, creeper-covered old inn is very busy, the antique furnishings and characterful connecting rooms encourage a timeless and really rather relaxing atmosphere. The series of rooms have fine high Tudor beams, a lovely old box settle, sofas and miscellany of easy chairs by the stone walls and velvet curtains, and sturdy settles and oak tables on the flagstones in the lower-ceilinged public bar. Generally served from a buffet in an airy end room, bar food usually includes dishes like sandwiches (not Sunday lunchtime), soup (£2.20), chicken and pork liver pâté (£2.95), vegetable and cream cheese pancake (£4.95), good home-made steak and kidney pie (small £4.95, large £5.45), cauliflower, mushroom and cheese bake (£5.10), venison, orange and red wine casserole (£6.25), pork loin grilled with smoked bacon and brie (£6.95), home-made puddings (£2.30), and children's meals; there's more space to eat in the no-smoking Gallery upstairs. Well kept Bass, Hook Norton, Marstons Pedigree and Uley Old Spot on handpump, around ten wines by the glass, several malt whiskies and elderberry punch in winter; pleasant and efficient staff. A back room – relatively untouched – is popular with local lads playing pool; darts and juke box. The garden is very much geared towards families, with the highpoint a fortress of thatched whisky-kegs linked by timber catwalks; also a climber and some swings. The licensees also run the Old Lodge at Minchinhampton Common, back as a main entry this year. *(Recommended by Gwen and Peter Andrews, Dave Irving, Roger Huggins, Tom McLean, Ewan McCall, Sara Nicholls, Julie Peters, Brad and Joni Nelson, MM, Nick and Meriel Cox, Dave and Jules Tuckett, MS, Margaret Dyke, Paul McPherson, Peter Neate, Nick Cox, Mrs M Hurst, Michael Marlow)*

Free house ~ Licensee David Barnett-Roberts ~ Real ale ~ Meals and snacks ~ Restaurant ~ (01453) 860393 ~ Children in eating area of bar ~ Open 11-3, 6-11; 11-11 summer Sats ~ Bedrooms: £41B/£62B

nr LECHLADE SU2199 Map 4

Trout

St John's Bridge; 1 mile E of Lechlade on A417

The fishing theme at this bustling old place (first an inn in 1472) extends a lot further than just the name: plenty of stuffed trout and pike and fishing prints on the walls inside, and they still have ancient fishing rights on a two-mile stretch of the river. The big garden runs down to the Thames, and is a good spot to relax after a walk along the footpath; there are seats by the water, or under the venerable walnut tree, as well as boules and Aunt Sally, a summer bar and marquee for families, and fine views over the meadows. A flagstoned part of the atmospheric and low beamed partly panelled main bar offers Courage Best and Directors, John Smiths and a changing guest on handpump; opening off here is a snug area, once the ground-floor cellar, with wooden tables and settles. A third bar leads to the garden. Popular well-presented bar food includes home-made soup (£2.95), home-made pâté (£4.30), ploughman's (from £4.30), locally made sausages (£5.30), macaroni and aubergine bake (£5.75), vegetable curry (£6.25), pizzas (from £6.20), gammon steak (£6.35), salads or seafood crumble (£6.50), rump steak (£9.95), and home-made puddings and daily specials; the dining room is no smoking. Though they do warn of delays at busy times, readers have found these tend to be a little longer than promised, and you may have to wait a while for drinks too. Darts, shove-ha'penny, and video game; the amiable pointer is called Blucher. They have big events the second and last weekends in June (a steam engine and tractor meet on the first one), and a big party on bonfire night. *(Recommended by Peter and Audrey Dowsett, John Wooll, Frank W Gadbois, George Atkinson, Dr Peter Donahue, Sue Cubitt, Gwen and Peter Andrews, Jenny and Brian Seller)*

Courage ~ Lease: Bob and Penny Warren ~ Real ale ~ Meals and snacks (till 10) ~ Restaurant ~ (01367) 252313 ~ Children in eating area of bar and restaurant ~ Trad jazz Tues evenings, modern jazz Sun, pop/rock Fri ~ Open 10-3, 6-11; all day summer Sats

LITTLE WASHBOURNE SO9933 Map 4

Hobnails

B4077 (though often mapped still as the A438) Tewkesbury—Stow-on-the-Wold; 7½ miles E of M5 junction 9

Run by the same family since 1743, this enterprising old place is always friendly and welcoming, however busy it might be. These days their speciality is the enormous choice of large and generously filled baps, ranging from egg and mushroom (£2.25), through liver and onions (£3.50), gammon and pineapple (£3.95) and chicken and mushroom (£4.95) to steak with egg and mushrooms (£6.45); they do a smaller range for children (from 95p). Also on the menu are a choice of soups (£2.20), macaroni cheese (£5.25), a good few vegetarian dishes like lentil curry, a good vegetable casserole topped with a cheese scone or filo pastry parcels with leeks and stilton cheese (£5.40), lasagne (£5.75), curries or lamb casserole (£5.95), and a huge range of around 25 home-made puddings such as treacle and lemon tart, tyrolean chocolate gateau or French fruit flan (£2.75); many of the gateaux are available to take away. The snug and welcoming little front bar has old wall benches by a couple of tables on its quarry-tiled floor, low sway-backed beams hung with pewter tankards, and lots of old prints and horse brasses, and there's a more modern, carpeted back bar with comfortable button-back leatherette banquettes; open fire.One dining room is no-smoking, as is half of a second. Well kept Boddingtons, Flowers Original, Wadworths 6X, and Whitbreads West Country PA on handpump; darts, shove-ha'penny, fruit machine, piped music. A separate skittle alley (with tables) can be hired weekday evenings. Between the two buildings, and beside a small lawn and flower bed, there's a terrace with tables, and children's playground. *(Recommended by Gordon, M Joyner, R J Herd, David Cooke, Neil and Anita Christopher)*

Whitbreads ~ Lease: Stephen Farbrother ~ Real ale ~ Meals and snacks (till 10) ~ Restaurant ~ Alderton (01242) 620237 ~ Children in restaurant ~ Open 11-2.30, 6-11; closed 25/26 Dec

LITTLETON UPON SEVERN ST5990 Map 2

White Hart

3½ miles from M4 junction 21; B4461 towards Thornbury, then village signposted

Several parts of this lovingly restored pantiled pub are still as they were when it was built as a farmhouse in the 1680s, and later extensions have done nothing to harm the old-fashioned feel. There are three atmospheric main rooms, with flagstones in the front, huge tiles at the back, and smaller tiles on the left, along with some fine furnishings that include long cushioned wooden settles, high-backed settles, oak and elm tables, a loveseat in the big low inglenook fireplace, some old pots and pans, and a lovely old White Hart Inn Simonds Ale sign. By the black wooden staircase are some nice little alcove seats, there's a black-panelled big fireplace in the front room, and hops on beams, fresh flowers, and candles in bottles. An excellent no-smoking family room, similarly furnished, has some sentimental engravings, plates on a delft shelf, and a couple of high chairs, and a back snug has pokerwork seats, table football and table skittles; darts, shove ha'penny, cribbage, dominoes, trivia. Good promptly-served bar food includes soup (£1.80), good filled rolls (from £2.80), potato skins with various dips (from £3.45), ploughman's (£3.50), artichokes provençal or cashew nut, apricot and bean casserole (£4.95), turkey, sage and stilton bake (£5.45), fruity chicken curry (£5.65), steak and kidney pie (£5.95), gravadlax (£5.95), seafood and shellfish pie (£6.25), fish specials, puddings (from £1.95), and children's meals £2.50). Well kept Smiles Bitter, Best and Exhibition and Wadworths 6X tapped from the cask, with a guest such as Fullers London Pride, espresso coffee machine. They often get very busy at weekends, but staff are always very pleasant. Picnic table sets sit on the neat front lawn, intersected by interesting cottagey flowerbeds; by the good big back car park are some attractive shrubs and teak furniture on a small brick terrace. Dogs are allowed if on a lead, and there are quite a few walks from the pub itself. *(Recommended by Steve and Carolyn Harvey, Peter and Audrey Dowsett, John and Donna Bush, Pat and John Millward, D G Clarke, C H and P Stride, W Marsh, Carolyn Eaton, Mark Watkins, Dave and Jules Tuckett, Simon and Amanda Southwell)*

Smiles ~ Manager Philip Berryman ~ Real ale ~ Meals and snacks ~ (01454) 412275 ~ Children in restaurant and family room ~ Open 11.30-2.30, 6-11; all day Sat ~ Bedrooms: £29.50B/£39.50B

LOWER ODDINGTON SP2325 Map 4

Fox

Nr Stow-on-the-Wold

This rather elegant place has managed to build its enviable reputation rather quickly, and readers tell us that this year standards seem to have risen still further. The excellent wine list, shipped in conjunction with a highly regarded wine guru, is perhaps what the pub is best known for, but it's also well liked for its warmly friendly service, imaginative food, and relaxed, country house atmosphere. The carefully restored, simply and spotlessly furnished rooms have fresh flowers, flagstones and an open fire, a lovely dining room, and very nice customers; piped classical music. Excellent quality and very well presented, the changing range of food might include watercress soup (£2.25), french bread sandwiches (from £2.95), chicken liver pâté (£2.95), mushrooms in stilton sauce with puff pastry (£3.95), spinach and ricotta cheese cannelloni (£5.50), fettucine with smoked salmon, crème fraîche and dill (£5.95), unusually fresh trout in herb sauce, lamb's liver with bacon, salmon fishcakes or steak, mushroom and Guinness pie (£6.95), sirloin steak (£8.50), puddings such as banana and toffee crumble (£2.50), and daily specials; roast Sunday lunch (£7.95). Well kept Hook Norton Best, Marstons Pedigree and a guest such as Boddingtons or Shepherd Neame Spitfire on handpump, several malt whiskies, sloe gin, elderflower pressé, fresh orange juice, pimms in a jug, and so forth. A good eight-mile walk starts from here. *(Recommended by Martin Jones, M and J Huckstepp, Karen and Graham Oddey, Sara Nicholls, Ian Irving, Frank Cummins, N and J Steadman, Mrs J Oakes, Graham Reeve, Gordon, Stephen Guy, Paul Boot, E J and M W Corrin, Pat and John Millward)*

Free house ~ Licensees Nick and Vicky Elliot ~ Real ale ~ Meals and snacks (till 10pm) ~ (01451) 870555 ~ Children welcome ~ Open 12-3, 6.30-11; closed evening 25/26 Dec

Pubs with attractive or unusually big gardens are listed at the back of the book.

MINCHINHAMPTON SO8600 Map 4

Old Lodge

Minchinhampton Common; from centre of common take Box turn-off then fork right at pub's signpost

Recently reopened under the same owners as the Hunters Hall at Kingscote, this former hunting lodge is superbly placed on the plateau of the National Trust owned Minchinhampton Common. Tables on a neat lawn by an attractive herbaceous border look over grey stone walls to the neatly grazed common and the Iron Age earthworks which surround it. Refurbished with new carpets and substantial pine tables and chairs, the small and snug central bar opens into a pleasant bare-brick-walled room and an airy stripped-stone dining area, both of which are no smoking. Early reports on the bar food are very promising, with the menu including home-made soup (£2.25), ploughman's (£3.95), mussels in white wine and cream sauce or vegetable and pasta bake (£4.75), steak and kidney pie (£5.75), jambalaya (chicken, spicy sausage and prawns in a hot creole sauce, £6.95), puff pastry horn filled with beef and mushrooms or seafood (£7.95), duck breast with honey and apricot sauce (£8.75), Italian ham joint (£9.95), specials such as scampi, prawns and cod in a pernod sauce (£8.95) or fillet steak in a pink peppercorn sauce (£10.95), puddings like treacle and coconut tart (£2.25), and children's meals (£2.40). Marstons Pedigree, Robinsons Best and Thwaites on handpump and electric pump, good range of wines including a wine of the month, and summer drinks like elderflower spritzer. Service is friendly and helpful. No dogs. They share car parking with the adjoining golf club, so lots of cars outside doesn't necessarily mean the pub is full. ***(Recommended by Janet and Paul Boak, Neil and Anita Christopher, D G King)***

Free house ~ Licensees David Barnett-Roberts and Alan Webb ~ Real ale ~ Meals and snacks (till 10) ~ (01453) 832047 ~ Children welcome (last orders from children's menu 7.45) ~ Open 11-3, 6.30(7 winter)-11

NAILSWORTH ST8699 Map 4

Weighbridge ♀

B4014 towards Tetbury

Back in the days when the landlord used to run the bridge from which the pub takes its name, it would cost you 3d for each score of pigs you wanted to take along the turnpike. Readers like the unchanging atmosphere in the relaxed and friendly bar, its three cosily old-fashioned rooms all with antique settles and country chairs, stripped stone walls, and window seats; one even has a bell to ring for prompt service. The black beam-and-plank ceiling of the left-hand room is thickly festooned with black ironware – sheepshears, gintraps, lamps, cauldrons and bellows – while up some steps a raftered loft has candles in bottles on an engaging mix of rustic tables, as well as unexpected decorations such as a wooden butcher's block. Good bar food includes filled rolls (from £1.50), ploughman's (from £3.20), shepherd's pie (£3.80), meaty or vegetarian lasagne (£3.95), a very popular two-in-one pie with cauliflower cheese in one half and steak and mushroom in the other (small £4.60, big £5.80), and puddings like treacle tart or banoffi pie (from £1.95). Well kept Marstons Pedigree, John Smiths, Ushers Founders and Wadworths 6X on handpump, and several wines by the glass (or bottle). Behind is a sheltered garden with swings and picnic tables under cocktail parasols. ***(Recommended by Neil and Anita Christopher, Dave Irving, Ewan McCall, Roger Huggins, Tom McLean, Peter Neate, Kevin and Tracey Stephens, Richard and Janice Searle)***

Free house ~ Licensee Janina Kulesza ~ Real ale ~ Meals and snacks ~ (01453) 832520 ~ Children welcome ~ Open 11-2.30, 7(6.30 Sat)-11; closed 25 Dec

By law pubs must show a price list of their drinks. Let us know if you are inconvenienced by any breach of this law.

NAUNTON SP1123 Map 4

Black Horse

Village signposted from B4068 (shown as A436 on older maps) W of Stow-on-the-Wold

They like to do things their own way at this busy old inn, tucked away in an unspoilt little village. Some readers have found the service a little inflexible, but if you're willing to take the place on its own terms, and don't mind maybe being told where to sit, or what you can and can't do, then a visit here can be really rather memorable. A favourite with the locals, the comfortable bar has simple country-kitchen chairs, built-in oak pews, and polished elm cast-iron-framed tables, black beams and stripped stonework, and a big woodburning stove. Good food includes sandwiches and filled rolls, lunchtime ploughman's, chicken liver pâté, half a pint of smoked prawns (£4), salmon and broccoli fish cakes (£6), barnsley chops or gammon (£7), steaks (from £9), daily specials like ham and mushroom tagliatelle or pork chop valentine, and puddings such as a very well-liked crème brûlée. The Donnington BB and SBA on handpump are nicely priced below the county average, there's a choice of wines by the glass, freshly squeezed fruit juice, and a range of malt whiskies; sensibly placed darts, shove ha'penny, dominoes. Some tables outside. Signs warn that food service stops at 1.15 (it may stop earlier), and however far you've travelled they won't be persuaded to make an exception. *(Recommended by Dr I H Maine, Martin Jones, DP, LP, Gordon, Michael Richards, Andrew and Ruth Triggs, D D Collins, John and Marianne Cooper, D A Edwards, Alex and Beryl Williams, Andy and Jill Kassube, Andrew and Catherine Brian, Mr and Mrs J Brown, Neil and Anita Christopher, D Grzelka)*

Donnington ~ Tenants Adrian and Jennie Bowen-Jones ~ Real ale ~ Meals and snacks (stop at 1.15 lunchtime; not 25 Dec) ~ Restaurant ~ (01451) 850378 ~ Well behaved children over 10 allowed in restaurant~ Open 11-2.30, 6-11; closed evening 25/26 Dec ~ Two Bedrooms: £25/£35

NEWLAND SO5509 Map 4

Ostrich

B4231 Lydney—Monmouth, OS Sheet 162 map reference 555096

Rather civilised but still delightfully informal, this partly 13th-c inn might have current affairs magazines lying around for people to read, candles on the tables, and classical music playing quietly in the background. Well placed in a picturesque village close to the River Wye, it's a particularly attractive building, with creaky floors, uneven walls, and a spacious but cosily traditional low-ceilinged bar. Huge logs burn in the fine big fireplace decorated with a very capacious copper kettle and brass-bound bellows, and comfortable furnishings include cushioned window seats and wall settles, and rod-backed country-kitchen chairs. An excellent choice of eight well kept real ales on handpump might take in interesting brews such as Freeminers Iron Brew, Hardingtons Moonshine, Marstons Pedigree, Ringwood Old Thumper, Ruddles Best, Shepherd Neame Spitfire, Uley Old Spot or Wadworths 6X; also, farm cider, seven or eight wines by the glass, country wines, and over 20 malt whiskies. The often unusual home-made bar food might include good soup (£2), moules marinières (£4), avocado, bacon and mushrooms in a cream sauce or spicy lamb pancake (£4.50), steak and oyster pie (£7.50), and venison medallions in wild mushroom sauce (£10); good vegetables, and they bake all their own bread. Tables out in the small garden, and walkers are welcome if they leave their muddy boots at the door. No children. Readers who've stayed here recently have had vastly differing experiences; don't expect hotel standards or service. *(Recommended by Phil and Heidi Cook, George Atkinson, Steven Coughlan, Mrs B M Innes-Ker, P and M Rudlin, Richard Mattick, Martyn Kearey, Dawn and Phil Garside, Keith J Willoughby, JCT, Sue Demont, Tim Barrow, Mr and Mrs G J Snowball, R G and M P Lumley, Mrs Pat Crabb, Roger Huggins, Dave Irving, Tom McLean, Ewan McCall)*

Free house ~ Licensees Richard and Veronica Dewe ~ Real ale ~ Meals and

snacks (not 25 Dec) ~ (01594) 833260 ~ Open 12-2.30(3 Sat), 6.30-11; closed 25 Dec ~ Bedrooms: £25/£40

NORTH CERNEY SP0208 Map 2

Bathurst Arms 🍷

A435 Cirencester—Cheltenham

Smartened up considerably under its new owner, this handsome old inn seems like a warmly welcoming old friend even on first acquaintance. Civilised without being snooty, the relaxing beamed and panelled bar has a good mix of old tables and nicely faded chairs, old-fashioned window seats, some pewter plates, and a fireplace at each end, one quite huge, and housing an open woodburner. There are country tables in a little carpeted room off the bar, as well as winged high-backed settles forming booths around other tables; all is highly polished and obviously cared for. A good choice of bar food might include sandwiches, home-made pâté (£2.95), warm goat's cheese salad (£3.20), moules marinières (£3.95), various pasta dishes (£4.95), home-made pies, gammon topped with mozarella cheese or salmon fishcakes in prawn and dill sauce (£5.50), panfried monkfish (£7.25), and mixed grill (£7.50). Well kept Arkells BBB, Hook Norton Best, Wadworths 6X and a changing guest on handpump, freshly squeezed fruit juice, good wines; the staff are notably friendly, and there's a very happy feel to the place. They decorate the rooms particularly stylishly at Christmas. The Stables Bar has darts, pool, cribbage, pinball, dominoes, and piped music. The attractive flower-filled front lawn runs down to the River Churn, and there are picnic table sets sheltered by small trees and shrubs, as well as summer barbecues in good weather. *(Recommended by Reece and Mike Gannaway, D M Wilkins, Peter and Audrey Dowsett, TN, Neil and Anita Christopher, D G King, T and D Archer, Dave Irving, Roger Huggins, Tom McLean, Ewan McCall)*

Free house ~ Licensee Mike Costley-White ~ Real ale ~ Meals and snacks ~ Restaurant ~ (01285) 831281 ~ Children welcome ~ Irish/Celtic evenings Tues, occasional live music weekends in Stable bar ~ Open 11-3, 6-11; closed 25 Dec ~ Bedrooms: from £30B/£40B

NORTH NIBLEY ST7496 Map 4

New Inn ★

Waterley Bottom, which is quite well signposted from surrounding lanes; inn signposted from the Bottom itself; one route is from A4135 S of Dursley, via lane with red sign saying Steep Hill, 1 in 5 (just SE of Stinchcombe Golf Course turn-off), turning right when you get to the bottom; another is to follow Waterley Bottom signpost from previous main entry, keeping eyes skinned for small low signpost to inn; OS Sheet 162 map reference 758963; though this is the way we know best, one reader suggests the road is wider if you approach directly from North Nibley

Serving beer here is the Barmaid's Delight; you might be forgiven for thinking such enthusiasm is the result of a particularly successful course in staff training, but in fact Barmaid's Delight is the name of one of this very pubby pub's antique beer engines. Particularly well kept Cotleigh Tawny and WB (a beer brewed specially for the pub), Greene King Abbot, Smiles Best, Theakstons Old Peculier, and changing guests are either dispensed from these or tapped from the cask; the character landlady is quite a real ale expert. Good value home-made bar food includes filled brown baps (from 60p), toasties (from £1.30), ploughman's (from £2.80), egg and bacon quiche (£3.85), steak and onion pie (£3.95), plaice (£4.95), daily specials such as fresh asparagus (in season, £2.75) or tuna and broccoli bake (£3.75), and puddings like bakewell tart (£1.50). The carpeted lounge bar has cushioned windsor chairs and varnished high-backed settles against the partly stripped stone walls, and sensibly placed darts, dominoes, shove-ha'penny, cribbage, and trivia in the simple public bar; piped music. Also Inch's cider and over 50 malt whiskies. It's in a delightful setting in the heart of pleasant walking country; outside is a beautifully kept terrace, with the garden beyond, and then a bowl of quiet pastures, rising to a fringe of woods (worth exploring). At the far end of the garden, is a small orchard with swings, slides and a timber tree-house. To stay here you have to book a long way ahead – and best not to arrive outside opening hours. No children. *(Recommended by D Godden, Jack and Philip Paxton, Thomas Nott, Drs Ben and Caroline Maxwell, Paula Williams, P M Lane, Dave Davey, T M Dobby, Patrick Clancy, D Baker, Dono and Carol Leaman, Jeff Davies)*

Free house ~ Licensee Ruby Sainty ~ Real ale ~ Meals and snacks ~ (01453) 543659 ~ Open 12-2.30, 7-11; closed evening 25 Dec ~ Two bedrooms: £25/£35

OAKRIDGE LYNCH SO9102 Map 4

Butchers Arms

Village signposted off Eastcombe—Bisley road, E of Stroud; or steep lanes via Frampton Mansell, which is signposted off A419 Stroud—Cirencester

Picnic table sets on a stretch of lawn at this well-run pub look down over the valley, and you can really appreciate the village's rather odd remote setting. Not easy to find, it's popular mainly for the good bar food, which might include lunchtime dishes such as sandwiches, ploughman's (from £3.25), cauliflower cheese (£3.50), home-made cottage pie (£3.75), omelettes or brunch (£4.95), beef and stout pie (£5.50), and rib steak (from £6.95), and evening meals like bacon and black pudding with mustard sauce (£3.95), deep-fried baked potato wedges with spicy chicken tikka (£4.95) or haddock and prawns in cheese sauce (£5.50), orange pork stroganoff (£8.95), and lamb cutlets mornay (£9.50); good Sunday roast (£6.95). The prominence given to food hasn't in any way made this less of a drinker's pub – in the evening, food is only served in the Stable Room (just off the main bar area) which keeps the atmosphere warm and lively – and diners can enjoy a drink at the bar before or after their meal. The spacious rambling bar has a few beams in its low ceiling, some walls stripped back to the bare stone, three open fires, and comfortable, traditional furnishings like wheelback chairs around the neat tables on its patterned carpet. Well kept Archers Best, Bass, Goffs Jouster, Hook Norton Old Hookey, Tetleys and Theakstons Best on handpump; darts, dominoes, fruit machine, trivia, and alley skittles. Pretty hanging baskets in summer. Usefully, the pub's car park is up on the level top road, so you don't have to plunge into the tortuous network of village lanes. *(Recommended by Colin W McClerrow, Keith Stevens, Roger and Jenny Huggins, Neil and Anita Christopher, Paul Weedon, Peter and Audrey Dowsett, Dave Irving, Tom McLean, Ewan McCall)*

Free house ~ Licensees Peter and Brian Coupe ~ Real ale ~ Meals and lunchtime snacks ~ Restaurant (Weds-Sat evenings, Sun lunch) ~ (01285) 760371 ~ Children in small ante room only ~ Open 12-3, 6-11

ODDINGTON SP2225 Map 4

Horse & Groom

Upper Oddington; signposted from A436 E of Stow-on-the-Wold

A change of ownership at this friendly Cotswold inn since our last edition, but no change to the warm local atmosphere, or to the lovely garden. Plump trout patrol the little water-garden beyond a rose hedge, and there are picnic tables on the neat lawn below the car park, apple trees, and a fine play area including an enormous log climber and Aunt Sally. The welcoming bar has pale polished flagstones, a big log fire, a handsome antique oak box settle among other more modern seats, some horsebrasses on the dark 16th-c oak beams in the ochre ceiling, and stripped stone walls with some harness and a few brass platters; a quarry-tiled side area has a fine old polished woodburner. From a regularly changing menu, popular and well-presented bar food might include sandwiches (from 2.95), soup (£2.50), taramasalata (£2.75), hot chicken wings or rollmops (£2.90), steak and mushroom pie (£5.50), strir-fried beef or chicken or escalope of pork with mushroom and grain mustard sauce (£6.50), fresh salmon with prawns and mushroom (£6.75), puddings, and children's meals (£3.25); the candlelit dining room is pretty. Three changing real ales on handpump such as well kept Courage Directors, John Smiths, or Marstons Pedigree, decent wines by the glass. The bedrooms are not large, but quaint and comfortable. *(Recommended by Gordon, E A George, Dr D Radley, Moira and John Cole, Bronwen and Steve Wrigley, John and Heather Dwane, Peter and Audrey Dowsett, Ian Irving, John and Shirley Dyson, George Atkinson, Roger Huggins, Dave Irving, Tom McLean, Ewan McCall, Mike and Jill Steer, Fred Collier, Graham Reeve, Paul Boot and others)*

Free house ~ Licensees Graham and Phyllicity Collins ~ Real ale ~ Meals and snacks ~ Restaurant ~ (01451) 830584 ~ Children welcome ~ Open 12-2.30, 6-11; winter evening opening time 7 ~ Bedrooms: £32.50B/£50B

OLD SODBURY ST7581 Map 2

Dog

Badminton Rd

The vast menu at this friendly pub – ideal for a family lunch – has quite an emphasis on fresh fish, with plenty of dishes like plaice, red mullet, shark or tuna, whole fresh sole, Devon scallops or clam fries, and lots of different ways of serving squid (£4.50) and mussels (£4.95). Other dishes include sandwiches (from £1.75), soup (£2.25), ploughman's (£3.95), cottage pie (£4.75), steak and kidney pie or vegetarian moussaka (£4.75), sweet and sour pork (£5.95), curries or Hawaiian chicken creole (£6.25), steaks (from £6.95), puddings (from £1.95), children's meals (from £1.50), and daily specials. It's worth arriving early, they do get busy. The two-level bar and smaller no-smoking room both have areas of original bare stone walls, beams and timbering, low ceilings, wall benches and cushioned chairs, open fires, and a welcoming, cheery atmosphere. Well kept Boddingtons, Flowers Original, Wadworths 6X, and Wickwar Brand Oak on handpump, decent wine list, pimms and sangria by the glass or jug, vintage port, and malt whiskies; helpful, attentive staff. Darts, skittle alley, cribbage, pinball, dominoes, fruit machine, and juke box. Trophy, the border collie, likes playing football with customers. There's a large garden with lots of seating, a summer barbecue area, pets' corner with rabbits, guinea pigs and so forth, climbing frames, swings, slides, football net, see-saws and so forth, and bouncy castle most bank holidays. Lots of good walks nearby. *(Recommended by Basil Minson, Pat and Richard Tazewell, R T and J C Moggridge, Nigel Clifton, Martin and Karen Wake, Paula Williams, Cdr Patrick Tailyour, Simon and Amanda Southwell, Don Kellaway, Angie Coles, Barry and Anne, R C Morgan, N and J Strathdee)*

Whitbreads ~ Lease: John and Joan Harris ~ Real ale ~ Meals and snacks (till 10) ~ (01454) 312006 ~ Children welcome until 9.30 ~ Regular party nights ~ Open 11-11 ~ Bedrooms: £22.50/£35B

OLDBURY-ON-SEVERN ST6292 Map 2

Anchor

Village signposted from B4061

The landlord of this attractively modernised village pub tells us the boules pitch at the bottom of the garden is the biggest in the area. What draws so many people here though is the very good bar food, cooked by the landlord using fresh local produce. The chip-free choice changes daily and might include splendid salads, with many of the ingredients coming from gardens in the village, leek and potato bake or sautéed mushrooms and onion topped with cheese and breadcrumbs (£3.95), salmon in a cream and white wine sauce (£5.50), tenderloin of pork in a cream, brandy and peppercorn sauce (£6.95), fillet of beef en croûte, and well-liked puddings such as apple crumble topped with caramel or sticky toffee pudding (£2.50); prompt and efficient waitress service in no-smoking dining room – best to get there early if you want a seat. Bass tapped from the cask, with Butcombe, Fullers London Pride, Theakstons Best and Old Peculier and Worthingtons Best on handpump, all well priced for the area (the Butcombe was 13p below the county average as we went to press). Also over 75 malts, decent choice of good quality wines, Inch's cider, and freshly squeezed fruit juice; darts, shove-ha'penny, dominoes and cribbage. The comfortably furnished beamed lounge has a curved high-backed settle facing an attractive oval oak gateleg table, winged seats against the wall, easy chairs, cushioned window seats, and a big winter log fire. There are seats in the pretty garden, and St Arilda's church nearby is interesting, on its odd little knoll with wild flowers among the gravestones (the primroses and daffodils in spring are lovely). Lots of paths over the meadows to the sea dyke or warth which overlooks the tidal flats. *(Recommended by Andrew Shore, P H Roberts, M G Hart, Mrs B Lemon, Peter and Audrey Dowsett, Paul Carter, R V Ford, Steve and Carolyn Harvey, Dr and Mrs B D Smith, Adrian M Kelly, John and Pat Smyth, D G Clarke, S Brackenbury, Margaret and Douglas Tucker, C H Stride, Nigel Foster)*

Free house ~ Licensees Michael Dowdeswell, Alex de la Torre ~ Real ale ~ Meals and snacks ~ Restaurant ~ (01454) 413331 ~ Children in dining room ~ Occasional pianist ~ Open 11.30-2.30(3 Sat), 6.30(6 Sat)-11; closed 25 Dec

PARKEND SO6208 Map 4

Woodman

Just off B4234 N of Lydney

Handy for good walks in the Forest of Dean, this relaxing place is spacious and comfortable without being at all plush, with two open fires in the long heavy-beamed and carpeted bar, and wall settles and wheelback chairs around gleaming copper-topped tables. The walls are stripped back to stone in some places, and decorated with monster two-handed saws and some unusual carvings of hounds and badgers. Well-presented bar food includes soup (£1.95), ploughman's (£4), rump steak sandwich or chilli bean and vegetable hotpot (£4.25), steak and mushroom pie or home-cooked ham and egg (£4.75), seafood curry (£5.75), house specialities like good chicken breast in stilton sauce (£5.75), guinea fowl with port and cranberry sauce (£7.25) or giant rack of ribs with barbecue sauce (£8.75), and children's meals (£2.20); they do a three-course Sunday lunch, and the bistro menu is appealing. The service is usually friendly, but can be rather leisurely. Well kept Bass and Boddingtons on handpump, decent wines, and maybe darts, fruit machine, juke box. There are picnic tables out on the front terrace, facing the village green. *(Recommended by Mrs B Sugarman, Neil and Anita Christopher, SRP, MJ, Dave Irving, P G Brown, David and Mary Webb)*

Whitbreads ~ Lease: Pat Buckingham ~ Real ale ~ Meals and snacks (till 10pm) ~ Evening bistro (Thurs-Sat) ~ (01594) 563273 ~ Children in eating area ~ Open 11.30-3.30, 6(7 winter)-11; 11-11 Sat ~ Bedrooms: £25(£30B)

REDBROOK SO5410 Map 4

Boat ◀

Pub's car park is now signed in village on A466 Chepstow—Monmouth; from here 100-yard footbridge crosses Wye (pub actually in Penallt in Wales – but much easier to find this way); OS Sheet 162 map reference 534097

Cross the disused railway bridge from the car park at this wonderfully set pub and you also cross the border into Wales. It's a very pleasant way to approach the place, with the River Wye curving below, and smoke curling up from the chimney of the pub itself. You can sit in the garden (prettily lit at night) with the sound of the water spilling down the waterfall cliffs into the duck pond below. Inside, the cosy bar is cheery and full of character, with lots of pictures of the pub during floods, landscapes, a wall settle, a grey-painted piano, and a woodburning stove on the tiled floor. A fine choice of between eight and ten well kept beers, tapped straight from casks behind the bar counter might include Adnams, Bass, Brains SA, Boddingtons, Butcombe, Exmoor Stag, Hook Norton Best, Shepherd Neame Spitfire, Smiles Best and Exhibition, and Theakstons Best and Old Peculier; good range of country wines. Big helpings of good bar food such as filled baked potatoes (from £1.50), soup (£1.65), ploughman's (£3.40), vegetable curry (£4), leek and roast parsnip stilton bake (£4.15), chilli (£4.20), Mexican chicken lasagne (£4.40), rabbit and sausage pie (£4.45), brie and haddock pie (£4.95), and puddings like strawberry and almond roulade or orange and pear trifle (£1.75). Darts, shove-ha'penny, table skittles, cribbage, dominoes, and trivia, with a quiz night every other winter Monday. They can get busy on sunny days, when it can seem as though the world and his whole family are here. Dogs welcome. *(Recommended by Keith and Audrey Ward, Sue and Mike Lee, Alan and Paula McCully, Jack and Philip Paxton, N Christopher, Piotr Chodzko-Zajko, Mr and Mrs J Brown, Ted George, P and M Rudlin, Dr C E Morgan, Dr R F Fletcher, A J Miller, Robin Cordell, Tony and Lynne Stark, Simon and Amanda Southwell, David Lewis, Roger Huggins, Dave Irving, Tom McLean, Ewan McCall, Alan and Eileen Bowker, R G and M P Lumley, Steve and Liz Tilley, PW, P M Lane, John and Helen Thompson, Gwynne Harper, Paul Boot)*

Free house ~ Licensees Steffan and Dawn Rowlands ~ Real ale ~ Meals and snacks ~ (01600) 712615 ~ Children welcome ~ Folk/rock Tues evening, jazz/blues Thurs ~ Open 11-3, 6-11; 11-11 winter Sats; closed evening 25 Dec

SAPPERTON SO9403 Map 4

Bell

Village signposted from A419 Stroud—Cirencester; OS Sheet 163 map reference 948033

A straightforward and reliable village pub, well run and friendly, and surrounded by good walks. The spacious but warm and cosy carpeted lounge has stripped stone walls and a good log fire; an extension up a couple of steps makes it L-shaped, with sturdy pine tables and country chairs. Well kept Bass, Flowers Original, Wadworths 6X and Whitbreads West Country PA on handpump, and prompt, courteous service. Simple but good value bar food includes sandwiches (from £1.40), soup (£1.75), ploughman's (from £3), good gloucester sausages (£3.25), salads (from £3.25), macaroni cheese (£4.15), half chicken (£4.95), grilled gammon and pineapple (£5.25), and steaks (from £7.40). No credit cards. The large public bar has some old traditional wall settles, and well placed darts, cribbage, dominoes, fruit machine, and trivia; separate skittle alley/function room. There are tables out on a small front lawn. *(Recommended by Ewan McCall, Tom McLean, Dave Irving, Roger Huggins, Jack and Philip Paxton, Thomas Nott, Andrew and Ruth Triggs, Mrs J M White, D G King)*

Free house ~ Licensees Gordon and Violet Wells ~ Real ale ~ Meals and snacks (till 10pm) ~ (01285) 760298 ~ Children in lounge ~ Open 11-2.30, 6.30-11; closed evening 25 Dec

Daneway £

Village signposted from A419 Stroud—Cirencester; from village centre follow Edgeworth, Bisley signpost; OS Sheet 163 map reference 939034

The car park at this bustling and friendly old pub – quite a favourite with some readers – is built over what used to be one of the locks of the neighbouring Thames and Severn Canal; you can still see the corner-stone of the lock gates. Good walks along the canal banks lead off in either direction, and it's particularly worth the short stroll to the entrance of the Sapperton Tunnel, which was used at the end of the 18th-c by the 'leggers', men who lay on top of the canal boats and pushed them through the two-and-a-half mile tunnel with their feet. With a good mix of locals and visitors (it doesn't take many calls before the two begin to overlap), the welcoming bar has a remarkably grand and dominating fireplace, elaborately carved oak from floor to ceiling, and racing and hunting prints on the attractively papered walls. A short range of generously served lunchtime bar food includes good value filled rolls (from 90p, not Sundays), burgers (£2), filled baked potatoes (£2.50), ploughman's (from £2.75), lasagne (£3.75), and beef and Guinness pie (£4.65), with evening extras like gammon steak (£5.50) and rump steak (£7.25), occasional specials, and puddings such as apple pie. Well kept Archers Best, Bass, Wadworths 6X, a well-priced beer brewed for the pub (from a local brewery) and a weekly changing guest on handpump or tapped from the cask, and local farm cider; cheery licenees. Darts, dominoes, shove-ha'penny and ring-the-bull in the public bar, which has a big inglenook fireplace; quoits. The lovely sloping lawn is bright with flower beds and a rose trellis, and lots of old picnic tables look down over the canal and the valley of the little River Frome. There may be a vintage motor cycle club meeting in the car park on some summer Wednesdays. *(Recommended by Roger and Jenny Huggins, Tom McLean, Ewan McCall, Dave Irving, Nick Dowson, Malcolm Taylor, Thomas Nott, F J and A Parmenter, Marjorie and Colin Roberts, Kevin and Tracey Stephens, Peter and Audrey Dowsett, Mike Davies, Andrew and Ruth Triggs, Jack and Philip Paxton, Dave and Jules Tuckett, P and M Rudlin, D A Edwards, Neil and Anita Christopher)*

Free house ~ Licensees J and J Buggins ~ Real ale ~ Meals and snacks ~ (01285) 760297 ~ Children in small no-smoking family room off lounge ~ Open 11-2.30(3 Sat), 6.30-11

SHEEPSCOMBE SO8910 Map 4

Butchers Arms 🍷

Village signposted from B4070 NE of Stroud, and A46 N of Painswick (narrow lanes)

The cricket ground behind this beautifully-placed pub is on such a steep slope that the boundary fielders at one end can scarcely see the bowler. Very much the centre of village activity – with frequent visits from local singing organisations and country dancing clubs – the pub has a good chatty atmosphere free from fruit machines, juke boxes or piped music. The busy bar is decorated with lots of interesting oddments like assorted blow lamps, irons, and plates, and there are seats in big bay windows, log fires, and flowery-cushioned chairs and rustic benches. Well kept Bass, Hook Norton Best, Jennings Cockerhoop, Tetleys and a guest beer on handpump, farm ciders, and a good wine list; darts, cribbage, dominoes, and maybe winter quiz evenings. Good bar food includes soup (£1.50), filled baguettes (from £2.50), ham, cheese and mushroom pancake (£3.50), ploughman's (£3.95), vegetable tikka masala (£4.75), steak and kidney pie (£5.25), mixed grill (£7.75), evening extras like pepperpot beef (£6) or roast duck with grand marnier and citrus fruit sauce (£8.50), specials such as pork cooked in beer with leek and mushrooms (£5.95), or lamb steaks with redcurrant jelly (£6), and puddings like strawberry and redcurrant cheesecake (£2). The restaurant and a small area in the bar are no smoking. There are teak seats below the building, tables on the steep grass behind, and dramatic vistas over the valley. The pub can be quite crowded on summer days and weekends; get here early to bag a table or enjoy the views at their best. *(Recommended by R G Watson, Marjorie and Colin Roberts, Moira and John Cole, Thomas Nott, E J Wilde, Neil and Anita Christopher, Keith Stevens, John and Joan Wyatt, C Smith, David Campbell, Vicki McLean, Simon Warren, Angus Lyon, Mr and Mrs W J Walford, Peter Neate, Paul Weedon, Nick and Meriel Cox, Roger Huggins, Dave Irving, Tom McLean, Ewan McCall, Lawrence Pearse, Gwen and Peter Andrews)*

Free house ~ Licensees Johnny and Hilary Johnston ~ Real ale ~ Meals and snacks (till 10) ~ Restaurant ~ (01452) 812113 ~ Children welcome ~ Open 11-11; 11-2.30, 6.30-11 in winter

SOUTH CERNEY SU0497 Map 4

Eliot Arms

Village signposted off A419 SE of Cirencester; Clarks Hay

In the six years they've had it, the Hicklings have done wonders to this handsome wisteria-draped stone inn. It has an unusual layout: the solidly done little bar servery is where you might expect to find a reception desk, so a bit of a surprise at first (it grows on you), and lots of separate snug places to sit are linked by short passages lined with decorative plates. It's all been done very well, adding up to a good relaxed atmosphere, with some interesting racing-car pictures from Fangio and Moss to Mansell among all the bric-a-brac in the back room – which has a fine log fire. A good choice of decent freshly made bar food includes sandwiches (from £1.50, chip butty £1.75), filled baked potatoes (from £2.50), burgers (from £4.25), chicken and ham or steak and kidney pie (£4.95), gammon and egg (£5.50), scampi thermidor (£6.95), steaks (from sirloin £8.95) and dishes of the day such as tagliatelle niçoise (£4.95), stuffed plaice (£5.25) and beef stroganoff (£5.75); good value children's meals (£2.50), and a popular Wednesday fish night; as well as the cosily attractive little dining room down a step or two, there's a smart separate no-smoking restaurant, and a coffee shop. Well kept Boddingtons, Flowers Original, Wadworths 6X and Whitbreads PA, good range of malt whiskies, German bottled beers, decent teas and coffees, smiling helpful service; shove-ha'penny, and tucked-away silenced fruit machine; skittle alley. There are picnic tables and a swing in the neat back garden. We've not yet had reports on the bedrooms but would expect them to be good. *(Recommended by Roger Huggins, Tom McLean, Dave Irving, Ewan McCall, Dr and Mrs A K Clarke, Nick Dowson*

Free house ~ Licensees Duncan and Linda Hickling ~ Real ale ~ Meals and snacks ~ Restaurants ~ (01285) 860215 ~ Children welcome till 9 ~ Open 10.30am-11pm ~ Bedrooms: £35B/£45B

SOUTHROP SP2003 Map 4

Swan 🍷

Village signposted from A417 and A361, near Lechlade

Still one of the highlights of this rather civilised creeper-covered old pub is the range of excellent and unusually flavoured home-made ice-cream, with delicious concoctions such as apple, ginger and calvados, toffee, hazelnut and Southern Comfort, white chocolate, mint and meringue, or honey and stem ginger, plus sorbets like elderflower and lime, or mango, coconut and Malibu. Other well-liked bar food might consist of stilton and onion soup (£2.80), cottage pie (from £3.25), smoked haddock and prawns in a creamy sauce (£3.50), goat's cheese in puff pastry (£4.85), and buckwheat pancake filled with chicken, bacon and mushrooms (£5.25), with evening extras like tiger prawns in filo pastry, sirloin steak (£9.50) or beef wellington (£9.95). Morlands Original and guest beers such as Archers Golden and Oakhill Bitter on handpump or tapped from the cask, good wine list, and an increasing range of soft drinks; the small restaurant is no smoking. Service is pleasant and friendly. The extended low-ceilinged front lounge has cottagey wall seats and chairs, and winter log fires, while beyond it is a spacious stripped-stone-wall skittle alley, well modernised, with plenty of tables on the carpeted part, and its own bar service at busy times; piped music. There are tables in the sheltered garden behind. The village is pretty, with lovely spring daffodils. *(Recommended by John Bowdler, SRP, Mr and Mrs R J Grout, Mike and Jo, Pat and John Millward, Mrs K E Neville-Rolfe, Mrs S Smith, Dave Braisted, Patrick Freeman)*

Free house ~ Licensees Patrick and Sandra Keen ~ Real ale ~ Meals (not Sun evening) ~ Restaurant (not Sun evening) ~ Southrop (0136 785) 205 ~ Children welcome ~ Open 12-2.30, 7-11

ST BRIAVELS SO5605 Map 4

George 🛏

Locals, walkers and visitors all blend together effortlessly in this lovely old pub, a warmly friendly place oozing with character and history. It has its own ghost, and a Celtic coffin lid dating from 1070, discovered when a fireplace was removed and now mounted next to the bar counter. The three rambling rooms have old-fashioned built-in wall seats, some booth seating, green-cushioned small settles, Toby jugs and antique bottles on black beams over the servery, and a large stone open fireplace. A dining area is no smoking. Well presented and popular home-made bar food includes ploughman's (from £3.95), half a dozen vegetarian meals such as avocado and stilton bake or Italian-style stuffed aubergines, steak and kidney pie or beef curry made with fresh spices (£6.95), char-grilled steaks (from £7.95), seafood provençale (£8.95), and specials such as hock of ham (£5.75) or duck a l'orange (£8.95); the vegetables and potatoes are served in separate dishes. The dining room is no smoking. Well kept Boddingtons, Courage Directors, Marstons Pedigree, and Wadworths 6X on handpump, lots of malt whiskies, good wines, scrumpy jack cider; piped music. Tables on a flagstoned terrace at the back overlook the grassy former moat of a silvery stone 12th-c castle built as a fortification against the Welsh, and later used by King John as a hunting lodge (it's now a Youth Hostel); there are more tables among roses and shrubs, and an outdoor chess board. Lots of walks start nearby, and it's not far to Tintern Abbey. *(Recommended by Howard James, D Godden, Alan and Paula McCully, Mr and Mrs P E Towndrow, Pat and Richard Tazewell, Piotr Chodzko-Zaiko, V G and P A Nutt, Dave and Jules Tuckett, H Anderson, Andrew and Liz Roberts, Andy and Jill Kassube, P J F Westlake, Simon and Amanda Southwell, F C Wilkinson)*

Free house ~ Licensee Bruce Bennett ~ Real ale ~ Meals and snacks ~ Restaurant ~ (01594) 530228 ~ Children in eating area til 9.30 (no crying babies) ~ Open 12-2.30, 6.30-11 ~ Bedrooms: £25B/£40B

STANTON SO0634 Map 4

Mount

Village signposted off B4632 (the old A46) SW of Broadway; Old Snowshill Road – take no through road up hill and bear left

The splendid views are what draw people to this busy pub, and on a clear day you can see beyond the picture-postcard golden stone village below as far as the Welsh mountains. The atmospheric original bar has black beams, cask seats on big flagstones, heavy-horse harness and racing photographs, and a big fireplace. An older spacious extension, with some big picture windows, has comfortable oak wall seats and cigarette cards of Derby and Grand National winners. A no-smoking extension is used in winter as a restaurant and in summer as a more informal eating bar. Well kept Donnington BB and SBA on handpump, and farm cider; friendly staff. Darts, shove ha'penny, dominoes, cribbage, backgammon, chess, and piped music. Straightforward bar food includes sandwiches (from £1.75, tasty toasties £3.50), good ploughman's (£3.95), lasagne (£4.75), steak and kidney pie (£5), and daily specials like hickory smoked chicken; at busy times a PA announces when your meal is ready. You can play boules on the lawn, and there are seats on the terrace. Popular summer Sunday barbecues. *(Recommended by Pam Adsley, Sara Nicholls, Jack and Philip Paxton, Tom Evans, Martin and Karen Wake, Frank Gadbois, George Atkinson, Ted George, Martin Jones, P M Lane, Andrew and Ruth Triggs, E G Parish, Peter and Audrey Dowsett, Michael and Margaret Norris)*

Donnington ~ Tenant Colin Johns ~ Real ale ~ Meals and snacks (not Sun evening) ~ (01386) 584316 ~ Well behaved children welcome ~ Open 11-3, 6-11; 11-11 Sat; closed 25 Dec

STOW-ON-THE-WOLD SP1925 Map 4

Queens Head

The Square

Distinguished by its chatty and friendly atmosphere, this really is a characterful old local, nicely set in a charming village, and easy to spot by its colourful climbing rose and hanging baskets. The most atmospheric part is the traditional flagstoned back bar, with lots of beams and a couple of interesting high-backed settles as well as wheelback chairs, public school football team colours on a back wall, and a big log fire in the stone fireplace. The jovial landlord is quite a racing buff, so there are several horse prints on the walls. The music is piped classical or opera (not in front), and there's shove-ha'penny, a fruit machine, and darts (one of the pub's two dogs can open the doors of the dart board). The busy stripped-stone front lounge is packed with small tables, little windsor armchairs and brocaded wall banquettes. Bar food includes sandwiches, very good soup such as tomato and basil (£1.75), filled baked potatoes, omelettes (from £2.75), popular ploughman's, steak and kidney or lamb and leek pie (£4.95), specials such as asparagus in season (£7.25) and puddings like delicious apricot crumble; they may not do food some winter evenings. Donnington BB and SBA are particularly well kept on handpump; they do mulled wine in winter, and service is quick and helpful. A green bench in front has a pleasant view, and in a back courtyard there are some white tables. *(Recommended by Andrew and Ruth Triggs, Tony and Wendy Hobden, Helen McLagan, John Waller, Pat and Richard Tazewell, Tom Mclean, Ewan McCall, Roger Huggins, Dave Irving, Andy and Jill Kassube, Joan and Michel Hooper-Immins, Mrs B Sugarman, D L Barker, Ralf Zeyssig, J Weeks, Gordon, Richard Lewis)*

Donnington ~ Tenant Timothy Eager ~ Real ale ~ Meals and snacks (not Sun, or Mon evening) ~ (01451) 830563 ~ Children welcome ~ Occasional jazz Sun lunchtimes ~ Open 11-2.30, 6(6.30 Sat)-11

nr STOW-ON-THE-WOLD SP1729 Map 4

Coach & Horses £

Ganborough; A424 2½ miles N of Stow; OS Sheet 163 map reference 172292

The unusual game of bottle-walking has been attracting lots of attention to this friendly little Cotswold pub. The rules are surprisingly hard to explain, but stripped to the basics involve walking then hopping with bottles balanced in the palm of the hand. They hope their annual Wold Championships will become World next year with the inclusion of overseas entrants. The bar area is decorated with good wildlife photographs on the walls and coach horns on its ceiling joists, there's a winter log fire in the central chimney-piece, and leatherette wall benches, stools and windsor chairs on the flagstone floor; steps lead up to a carpeted part with high-backed settles around the tables. This being the nearest pub to the Donnington brewery, the Donnington XXX, BB and SBA on handpump are usually well kept. Tasty bar food includes home-made game soup (£1.95), sandwiches (£2.10), macaroni cheese or cottage pie (£2.50), filled baked potatoes (from £3.25), ploughman's (from £3.50), lasagne or curried chicken (£3.95), home-made steak and kidney pie or grilled Donnington trout (£5.95), mixed grill (£7.50), daily specials such as chicken filled with stilton and port or brie, and puddings (£2); one dining room is no smoking. Decent wines, Addlestone's cider, darts, dominoes, fruit machine and juke box, and a popular skittle alley; some readers feel the piped music can be a little intrusive. The garden has been improved this year, and now has a waterfall and rockery, as well as seats on a terrace and a narrow lawn. The attached field where the three pub dogs play (one an enormous wolfhound) also has a goat and maybe an occasional horse, and is a site for Caravan Club members; slide and swings for children. *(Recommended by Barbara and Dennis Melling, Peter and Audrey Dowsett, Bronwen and Steve Wrigley, A Wallbank, Andy and Jill Kassube, Michael and Margaret Norris, W C M Jones, Philip Brown, E V Walder)*

Donnington ~ Tenant Andy Morris ~ Real ale ~ Meals and snacks ~ (01451) 830208 ~ Children in eating area of bar ~ Occasional live music (usually Sun evening) ~ Open 11-3, 6.30(6 Sat)-11; closed 25 Dec

WOODCHESTER SO8302 Map 4

Ram

South Woodchester, which is signposted off A46 Stroud—Nailsworth

A fine choice of real ales on handpump at this attractive country pub, which at any one time might include Archers Best, Boddingtons, Fullers London Pride and ESB, John Smiths, Morlands Old Speckled Hen, Ruddles Best, and Uley Bitter and Old

Spot. The L-shaped beamed bar has three open fires, some stripped stonework, country-kitchen chairs, several cushioned antique panelled settles around a variety of country tables, and built-in wall and window seats; sensibly placed darts. Bar food might include filled rolls, various ploughman's, several vegetarian meals like aubergine and bean stew (£4.95), steaks (from £6.95), and changing specials such as Thai chicken (£5.45), liver and bacon casserole, sweet and sour pork or ham, turkey and leek pie (£5.95); fresh vegetables and a choice of potatoes. From the picnic table sets on the terrace there are spectacular views down the steep and pretty valley. We've detected a slight lessening of enthusiasm in readers' reports over the last year, so more news would be particularly welcome. *(Recommended by Frank Gadbois, Jack and Philip Paxton, Michael Launder, Roger Huggins, Tom McLean, Ewan McCall, Dave Irving, Paul Boot, Anne Morris, Lawrence Pearse)*

Free house ~ Licensees Michael and Eileen McAsey ~ Real ale ~ Meals and snacks ~ Restaurant (not Sun evening) ~ (01453) 873329 ~ Children welcome ~ Occasional Irish band ~ Open 11-3, 5.30-11; 11-11 Sat

Lucky Dip

Besides the fully inspected pubs, you might like to try these Lucky Dips recommended to us and described by readers (if you do, please send us reports):

☆ **Alderton** [off B4077 Tewkesbury—Stow – OS Sheet 150 map ref 999334; SP0033], *Gardeners Arms*: A favourite with its many regulars for good reasonably priced food in civilised old-fashioned surroundings; interesting restaurant food (evenings not Sun, and weekend lunchtimes; may be booked up), extension keeping bar sensibly separate, with well kept Hook Norton Best, Theakstons Best and XB and Wadworths 6X, lunchtime sandwiches, soup or ham and eggs, log fire, good antique prints, high-backed settles among more usual seats, friendly licensees, tables on sheltered terrace behind the thatched Tudor pub, by well kept garden; children welcome *(D Grzelka, Tricia Kelly, Nick Cox, R J Herd, Mr and Mrs W M Stirling, Norman and Mary Phillips, Neil and Anita Christopher, LYM)*

☆ **Aldsworth** [A433 Burford—Cirencester; SP1510], *Sherborne Arms*: Much-extended modernised dining pub with beams, bric-a-brac and spacious and attractive no-smoking conservatory dining area, good food esp fish, Whitbreads-related ales, log fire, friendly prompt service, lovely garden; fills quickly weekends, lavatory for disabled *(Paul McPherson, Marjorie and David Lamb, Jill Bickerton, E Prince, Mark Bradley)*

Ampney Crucis [turn left at Crown of Crucis and veer left at triangle; SP0602], *Butchers Arms*: Repeated management changes have not helped this pub, but latest team settling in well, with warm friendly atmosphere, well kept Tetleys-related ales with a guest like Marstons Owd Rodger, good value food, log fire *(R Huggins, T McLean, D Irving, E McCall)*

☆ **Ampney St Peter** [A417, ½ mile E of village; SP0801], *Red Lion*: Unspoilt very traditional 17th-c country local, old-fashioned benches facing open fire, informal counterless serving area (well kept Whitbreads PA), welcoming chatty regulars, hatch to corridor; separate room with wall benches around single table, darts, cards and dominoes; cl weekday lunchtimes *(T McLean, R Huggins, E McCall, D Irving, Pete Baker, BB)*

☆ **Andoversford** [signed just off A40; SP0219], *Royal Oak*: Well run, with well kept Bass, Boddingtons and Hook Norton Best, wide choice of good straightforward food, open fire, friendly licensees, chatty local atmosphere, games area with darts, pool and fruit machine; cosy dim-lit dining area with timbered upper gallery *(D Irving, E McCall, R Huggins, T McLean, Philip Brown, BB)*

Andoversford, *Pegglesworth*: Recently converted farmhouse hotel, good food in pleasant bar decorated with sports equipment, well kept Arkells 3B and Morlands Old Speckled Hen, open fires; fabulous views towards the Malvern and Welsh hills, good garden; six comfortable bedrooms *(Dr M E Nicholas)*

☆ **Apperley** [village signed off B4213 S of Tewkesbury, go down lane beside PO opp Sawpit Lane; SO8628], *Coal House*: Airy bar notable for its splendid riverside position, with Bass, Wadworths 6X and a guest ale, red plush seats; front terrace with Severn views, play area *(Derek and Sylvia Stephenson, BB)*

Ashleworth [signed off A417 at Hartpury; SO8125], *Arkle*: Welcoming homely atmosphere, sofas and comfortable seats as well as the usual pub furniture in bar off entrance hall, attractively priced Donnington ales, food inc good farmhouse pie, skittle alley *(T McLean, R Huggins, E McCall, D Irving, David Bloomfield)*; *Queens Arms*: Newish licensees doing good choice of bar food inc some unusual dishes, with lovely fresh veg and two sorts of potato; good range of real ales, friendly cosy bar, attractive restaurant alongside with nice touches like good big mugs of coffee to close *(Keith Stephen)*

Bibury [signed off B4425; SP1106], *Bibury Court*: Beautiful 17th-c hotel with wonderful views, wide range of usual bar snacks and more inventive main dishes such as warm salad of smoked chicken, avocado and toasted cashews; well kept beer, range of wines; bedrooms *(G S and E M Dorey)*

Birdlip [OS Sheet 163 map ref 925144; SO9214], *Royal George*: Spaciously done up with lots of Edwardiana, pictures, variously furnished little room areas; Bass and Boddingtons on handpump, wide range of reasonably priced lunchtime bar food, separate restaurant; bedrooms *(the Monday Club, Neil and Anita Christopher, D G King)*

☆ **Bisley** [SO9006], *Stirrup Cup*: Spacious but bustling local, good choice of enjoyable food inc sandwiches and good value specials, friendly staff *(Robert Huddleston, D Irving, E McCall, R Huggins, T McLean)*

☆ **Blaisdon** [off A48 – OS Sheet 162 map ref 703169; SO7017], *Red Hart*: Well kept changing ales from good small breweries in brightly lit beamed and flagstone-floored village local, good value food (not Sun evening) in unobtrusive dining extension, friendly service, spring beer festival; dogs allowed; tables under cocktail parasols in attractive garden *(John Reed, Ian Phillips, Ted George, Edwin Field, Mr and Mrs D Johnson, JW, HP)*

Blockley [Station Rd; SP1634], *Great Western Arms*: Relaxing comfortable modern-style lounge, simple bar snacks and several specials, well kept Flowers, Hook Norton and Marstons Pedigree, busy public bar on left with games room; attractive village, lovely valley view *(B M Eldridge, Jenny and Michael Back)*

☆ **Bourton on the Hill** [A44 W of Moreton-in-Marsh; SP1732], *Horse & Groom*: Easy chairs, low tables, big log fire and steeplechasing pictures in small but high-ceilinged stripped-stone lounge, bigger more local bar with games; usual bar food, Bass on handpump, decent restaurant (not Sun or Mon evenings), no under-10s; bedrooms good value *(John Le Sage, LYM)*

Bourton on the Water [SP1620], *Old New Inn*: Old hotel next to 1:9 scale model of village built in 1930s by previous landlord, comfortably worn and welcoming, with history *(Gary Nicholls, Dave Irving)*

Brimscombe [off A419 SE of Stroud; SO8602], *Ship*: Named for former shipping canal here (its trans-shipment port, England's biggest in 1700s, now an industrial estate); well laid out to combine roominess with feeling of snugness, varied good value menu, well kept Bass and Boddingtons *(Dave Irving)*

☆ **Broadwell** [off A429 2 miles N of Stow-on-the-Wold; SP2027], *Fox*: Pleasant local opp attractive village's green, with good choice of cheap food made to order inc good fresh veg and delicious puddings, snug eating areas, well kept Donnington, quick friendly service even when busy; bedrooms *(Ted George, Marjorie and David Lamb, Angus Lyon, Sue and Vic North)*

Bussage [SO8804], *Ram*: Good views across valley from terrace, several real ales, good range of food, friendly atmosphere *(Janet and Paul Boak)*

Cam [High St; ST7599], *Berkeley Arms*: Interesting pub with friendly landlord, good beer choice, evening activities *(Julian Jewitt)*

☆ **Camp** [B4070 Birdlip—Stroud, junction with Calf Way; SO9109], *Fostons Ash*: Quietly isolated Cotswold inn with good food inc good value generous Sun roast, fresh veg, well kept Smiles, efficient cheerful service; handy for walks *(John and Joan Wyatt, J Cole)*

Cashes Green [SO8305], *Prince of Wales*: Homely local with well kept decor, straightforward food, Whitbreads-related ales; amiable service, live music Fri *(D G King)*

☆ **Cerney Wick** [SU0796], *Crown*: Roomy modernised lounge bar, neat and clean, opening into comfortable semi-conservatory extension, public bar with pool, darts, fruit machine and log fire, popular straightforward food inc good Sun roasts, well kept Whitbreads-related ales, helpful service; children welcome, good-sized garden with swings, small motel-style bedroom extension *(Neil and Anita Christopher, R Huggins, D Irving, E McCall, T McLean, Mrs P J Peeprose, Neville Kenyon, BB)*

Chalford [Chalford Hill – OS Sheet 163 map ref 895032; SO8903], *Old Neighbourhood*: Well kept Archers Best and local Uley beers, low prices, basic wooden floors and tables, open fire, games machine tucked away in corner; lively atmosphere, very friendly landlord, tables on terrace *(Roger Huggins, Nick Dowson, D Irving, E McCall, T McLean)*

☆ *nr* **Chalford** [France Lynch – OS Sheet 163 map ref 904036], *Kings Head*: Friendly and attractive old country local, well kept beer, wide range of good bar food, no juke box or fruit machine, garden, great views *(Roger Entwistle, Mrs P A Orr)*

☆ **Charlton Kings** [Cirencester Rd; A435; SO9620], *Little Owl*: Clean, friendly and attractive, good range of food in bar and restaurant, Whitbreads-related ales, decent wines, friendly licensees *(Janet and Paul Boak, Mr and Mrs W J B Walford)*

Charlton Kings [London Rd (A40)], *London*: New landlord doing wide range of lunchtime food inc good salads and filled baked potatoes in plush lounge-restaurant, unchanged big public bar, Wadworths 6X and Whitbreads beers; bedrooms *(John and Joan Wyatt)*

Cheltenham [Bath Rd; SO9422], *Bath*: Basic unspoilt 1920s two-bar layout and simple furnishings, friendly landlady, locals' smoke room, well kept Bass and Uley on handpump *(Pete Baker, E McCall, D Irving, R Huggins, T McLean)*; [London Rd; A40 towards Charlton Kings, nr junction A435], *Beaufort Arms*: Thriving local atmosphere, well kept Wadworths ales and a guest such as Badger Tanglefoot, decent food, obliging friendly service *(John and Joan Wyatt, Frank Gadbois)*; [1-3 Montpellier Villas], *Beehive*: Simple bare-boards decor but immaculate, with coal fire, welcoming family atmosphere, wide range of beers and spirits, good house wines, wide choice of food inc imaginative baguette fillings and Sun lunch *(Pam Valentine)*; [Benhall Ave], *National Hunt*:

Modern chalet-style suburban estate pub, spacious and attractive inside, good range of cheap lunchtime bar food, well kept Whitbreads-related and guest ales *(John and Joan Wyatt, B M Eldridge)*; [Grosvenor/High St], *Restoration*: Long dimly lit pub with food servery in raised dining area, opened-out lower area, lots of beams, tons of bric-a-brac, simple wooden furniture, good atmosphere, five or more well kept reasonably priced beers *(Steve Goodchild, Gary Nicholls, Thomas Nott)*

☆ **Chipping Campden** [Church St; SP1539], *Eight Bells*: Heavy-beamed flagstoned 14th-c pub by church, simply and charmingly restored with enormous log fire, fresh flowers, lots of dark wood tables and chairs, cushioned pews, stripped masonry, generous interesting changing food using fresh local ingredients, friendly staff, well kept Tetleys-related and guest beers, decent wines; picnic tables in pleasant courtyard; comfortable bedrooms *(J G Quick, Linda Norsworthy, Martin Jones, Peter and Jenny Quine, MDN, Charles and Lesley Knevitt, Martin and Sarah Constable)*

☆ **Chipping Campden** [High St], *Lygon Arms*: Good welcoming service, lots of horse pictures in carpeted stripped-stone bar, separate eating room and raftered evening restaurant, well kept Donnington SBA, Hook Norton Best, Wadworths 6X and interesting guests such as Ash Vine Challenger or Tomintoul Ceilidh, open fires, good food in back bistro area, restaurant beyond sheltered courtyard with tables; children welcome, open all day exc winter weekdays; decent bedrooms *(Andrew and Ruth Triggs, George Atkinson, Mr and Mrs Thompson, LYM)*

Chipping Campden [Sheep St], *Red Lion*: Simple good value home-cooked food (new upstairs dining room), attractive bar, well priced beer, welcoming staff *(E V Walder, Martin Jones)*

Chipping Sodbury [Bath side of town; ST7282], *Boot*: Friendly and relaxed old pub, little booths *(Dr and Mrs A K Clarke)*; [Market Sq], *Squire*: Friendly landlady, limited good value food inc popular lunchtime doorstep sandwiches *(D G King)*

☆ **Cirencester** [W Market Pl; SP0201], *Slug & Lettuce*: Flagstones, bare boards, lots of woodwork, attractive mix of furnishings inc good big tables, big log fires; well kept Courage ales, good coffee, bar food inc unusual dishes (no chips), friendly helpful staff, children welcome; tables in inner courtyard; piped pop music, very popular with young people evenings *(Marjorie and Colin Roberts, D Irving, R Huggins, T McLean, E McCall, Pat and Richard Tazewell, LYM)*

☆ **Cirencester** [Black Jack St; between church and Corinium Museum], *Golden Cross*: Backstreet Victorian local with longish comfortable bar, sensible tables, simple good value food, three well kept Arkells ales, very friendly service, good beer mug collection; piped music may obtrude; skittle alley, tables in back garden, nr wonderful church *(Marjorie and Colin Roberts, D Irving, R Huggins, T McLean, E McCall, Peter and Audrey Dowsett, Nick and Alison Dowson)*

Cirencester [Dollar St/Gloucester St], *Corinium Court*: Welcoming log fire in cosy smart bar, well kept Hook Norton Old Hookey and Wadworths 6X, decent wine, reasonably priced food, attractive restaurant; entrance through charming courtyard with tables; bedrooms *(Peter and Audrey Dowsett)*; [Stratton], *Drillmans Arms*: Popular old roadside local with reasonable food, good range of beers inc guests ales, lots of weekend bar nibbles *(John Scarisbrick)*; [10-14 Chester St], *Oddfellows Arms*: Cosy backstreet local with good range of well kept strong real ales inc less common ones, changing reasonably priced food, friendly service, live music twice weekly *(Roger Huggins, Nick and Alison Dowson, S G Mullock)*; [Lewis Lane], *Twelve Bells*: Pleasant open-plan backstreet pub, friendly if sometimes rather smoky; coal fire in back room, continental prints, Archers Best, Eldridge Pope Hardy Country and a guest such as Shepherd Neame Bishops Finger, bar food *(Nick and Alison Dowson, Tom McLean)*

Clearwell [SO5708], *Butchers Arms*: Cosy inside with subdued red upholstery, dark woodwork, good open fire; very obliging staff, attractive food inc good cheap fresh filled rolls *(A E and P McCully)*

☆ **Cliffords Mesne** [out of Newent, past Falconry Centre – OS Sheet 162 map ref 699228; SO6922], *Yew Tree*: Good value straightforward food (not Mon) in quiet and comfortable beamed country pub on slopes of May Hill (NT); well kept Courage-related ales and Wadworths 6X; restaurant, children welcome, pool table in separate area, tables out on terrace *(Alan and Jane Clarke, R G and M P Lumley, John and Shirley Dyson)*

☆ **Coates** [follow Tarleton signs from village (right then left), pub up rough track on right after rly bridge, OS Sheet 163 map ref 965005; SO9600], *Tunnel House*: Idyllically placed idiosyncratic beamed country pub by abandoned canal tunnel, mix of aged armchairs, sofa, rustic benches, enamel advertising signs, stuffed mustelids, race tickets, well kept Arches Best, Smiles, Theakstons Best and Wadworths 6X, basic bar food, Sunday barbecues, log fires (not always lit), pub games, big juke box muh appreciated by Royal Agricultural College students; has been a popular main entry, but the very relaxed management style seems to have been slipping into just too casual a mode for some recently; children welcome (good safe play area), camping facilities *(Pat and John Millward, P and M Rudlin, Peter and Janet Race, Mike Davies, Tony and Wendy Hobden, Frank Gadbois, Stephen, Julie and Hayley Brown, Andrew and Ruth Triggs, LYM)*

☆ **Codrington** [handy for M4 junction 18, via B4465; ST7579], *Codrington Arms*: Popular for good value generous well prepared food inc delicious pies and fish and chips;

welcoming service, good range of beers *(KC, Andrew Shore, Meg and Colin Hamilton)*

☆ **Coleford** [Joyford; best approached from Christchurch 5-ways junction B4432/B4428, by church – B4432 towards Broadwell, first left signed Joyford, then lane on right beyond hamlet; OS Sheet 162 map ref 580134; keep your eyes skinned for pub sign hidden in hedge; SO5813], *Dog & Muffler*: Very friendly prettily set country pub with good range of reasonably priced generous bar food in pleasant back conservatory dining room overlooking verandah, log-effect gas fire in olde-worlde bar, old well in foyer, well kept Ruddles County and Sam Smiths on handpump, big games-room extension; sheltered lawn with picnic tables, some under thatched conical roofs, play area, 18th-c cider press by path from car park; bedrooms *(Phil and Heidi Cook, Ted George, Dave Irving, P and M Rudlin, John Hazel)*

☆ **Colesbourne** [A435; SO9913], *Colesbourne Inn*: Comfortable panelled inn taken over autumn 1995 by Bob and Elaine Flaxman, who had previously made the Greyhound at Siddington a very popular main entry – one to watch, with huge log fires in several rooms, hunting prints, settles and oak tables, masses of mugs on beams; Wadworths ales, country wines, bar food which we expect to be good, tables in back garden; comfortable bedrooms *(PD, AD)*

☆ **Duntisbourne Abbots** [A417 N of Cirencester – OS Sheet 163 map ref 978091; SO9709], *Five Mile House*: Unspoiled country tavern, regulars around the single table in little bay-windowed flagstoned bar, tiny snug formed from two huge and ancient high-backed settles; well kept Courage tapped from cask behind perfunctory counter, relaxed atmosphere, home-made pickled eggs (sometimes goose eggs) as well as crisps *(Pete Baker, Jack and Philip Paxton)*

☆ **Dursley** [May Ln, by bus stn; ST7598], *Old Spot*: Simple, friendly pub with great atmosphere, well kept Bass, Uley and two guest beers, friendly landlord, doorstep sandwiches and quick snacks, lots of pig paraphernalia; bar billiards, cribbage, dominoes and boules, no music or machines *(Julian Jewitt)*

☆ **Eastleach Turville** [off A361 S of Burford; SP1905], *Victoria*: Attractive lounge/dining area, pool in separate bar, obliging service, good home cooking, well kept Arkells, nice views; quiet midweek lunchtime, busy evenings esp Sat (when pianist replaces juke box) *(John and Joan Wyatt, Gordon, Paul McPherson)*

☆ **Elkstone** [Beechpike; A417 6 miles N of Cirencester – OS Sheet 163 map ref 966108; SO9610], *Highwayman*: Well kept Arkells real ales, good house wines, fair range of decent standard food, good friendly staff, and considerable character in rambling warren of low beams, stripped stone, alcoves, antique settles among more modern furnishings, log fires; piped music; outside play area, good indoors provision for children *(D Irving, R Huggins, T McLean, E McCall, Thomas Nott, BHP)*

Fairford [Market Pl; SP1501], *Bull*: Friendly beamed hotel, no-smoking areas at mealtimes, interesting menu, helpful staff; Arkells 2B and 3B; bedrooms *(George Atkinson)*

Forest of Dean [B4226 nearly a mile E of junction with B4234; SO6212], *Speech House*: Forte hotel superbly placed in centre of Forest, lovely warm interior with lots of oak panelling, substantial reasonably priced bar food, well kept Bass, afternoon teas, plush restaurant; bedrooms comfortable *(A E and P McCully, Dave Irving, W H and E Thomas)*

Forest of Dean, see: Clearwell, Coleford, Lower Lydbrook, Parkend; and main entries for Clearwell, Newland, Parkend and St Briavels

Foss Cross [A429 N of Cirencester; SP0609], *Hare & Hounds*: Welcoming, with decent food, well kept Bass, Everards Beacon and Tiger and Wadworths 6X, main room with popular fruit machine, couple of small tables and warm fire in second small room; 32-bed motel extension planned *(Roger Huggins, Tom McLean, G Washington)*

Frampton Cotterell [Beesmoor Rd; ST6683], *Golden Lion*: Friendly and popular family dining pub with varied good value generous food (straightforward dishes tipped most strongly), well kept Bass and Ind Coope Burton tapped from the cask *(Dennis Heatley, A D Shore)*

☆ **Frampton Mansell** [off A491 Cirencester—Stroud – OS Sheet 163 map ref 923027; SO9102], *Crown*: Increasingly popular in evenings, well kept ales such as Archers Village, Oakhill Farmers, Wadworths 6X, friendly service, stripped stone lounge bar with dark beam-and-plank ceiling, public bar with darts, food in bar and restaurant; lovely views over village and steep wooded valley; children in eating area, teak seats outside; comfortable bedrooms *(Paul Weedon, D Irving, E McCall, T McLean, R Huggins, LYM)*

Frampton on Severn [The Green; SO7407], *Bell*: Pleasantly gentrified Whitbreads pub by cricket pitch, good range of fairly priced lunchtime food, decent service, Butcombe, Cornish Original and Wadworths 6X *(A Y Drummond)*

☆ **Glasshouse** [by Newent Woods; first right turn off A40 going W from junction with A4136 – OS Sheet 162 map ref 710213; SO7122], *Glasshouse*: Carefully preserved small country tavern with changing well kept real ales tapped from the cask, flagstone floors, log fire in vast fireplace, good value straightforward food, helpful landlady, magnificent British Match poster, darts and quoits, seats on fenced lawn with big weeping willow loved by children; fine nearby woodland walks *(Edwin Field)*

☆ **Gloucester** [Llanthony Rd; off Merchants Rd, S end of Docks], *Waterfront*: Good wide range of ales tapped from the cask in bare-boards black-beamed bar with scrubbed tables, tin helmets, barrels you can chalk on, free peanuts (shells go on the floor), beermat collection; bar billiards, table football, ninepins etc; generous cheap food, eating area up a step with back-to-back cubicle seating; piped music (live some nights), fruit machine, Sky TV; part of docks complex *(Richard Lewis, Ted George, Roger Huggins)*

☆ **Gloucester** [Bristol Rd about 1½ miles S of centre, opp Lloyds Bank], *Linden Tree*: Lively and attractive local with particularly well kept ales – three Wadworths, three interesting guests; good varied straightforward food, back skittle alley *(Joan and Michel Hooper-Immins, Paul Weedon)*

Gloucester [Westgate St/Berkeley St], *Fountain*: Pleasant, comfortable and quiet 17th-c inn handy for cathedral, well kept Whitbreads-related ales, good value straightforward food *(Alan Kilpatrick)*; [Sandhurst Lane], *Globe*: Good value food, esp two-for-the-price-of-one offers *(Tony Lockyer)*; [Westgate St], *New Inn*: Lovely medieval building with courtyard, now a comfortable routine Chef & Brewer with four separate areas, lots of beams and wood, well kept Bass, Boddingtons, John Smiths, Smiles and Worthington BB, two-for-price-of-one meal offers; bedrooms *(Richard Lewis)*; [Westgate St], *Old Crown*: Old-fashioned Victorian pub with well kept Sam Smiths, comfortable upstairs lounge, food inc filling wholemeal baps, friendly staff; handy for Folk Museum *(Marjorie and Colin Roberts)*; [Westgate St], *Tailors House*: Good value quick food, decent real ales; handy for cathedral *(Chris Jackson, Helen Medhurst)*; [81 Southgate St], *Whitesmiths Arms*: Close to docks, unpretentious decor with delightful model boats, cheerful landlord, well kept beers *(Michael Launder)*; [Kimberley Warehouse, Docks], *Willys Steamboat Bar*: Useful Texas-theme bar/bistro, mainly English food, decent wine; helpful friendly staff *(Roy Bromell)*

☆ **Guiting Power** [SP0924], *Farmers Arms*: Friendly licensees doing well in homely and unspoilt partly flagstoned Donnington pub, well kept ales, good value generous home cooking, prompt service, no piped music, walkers welcome – good walks nearby; tables in garden maybe with bank-hols bouncy castle, open all day at least in summer; bedrooms *(Robert Huddleston, Lady Emma Chanter, Dorothy and Leslie Pilson, Mr and Mrs Buckingham, Martin and Karen Wake, John and Joan Wyatt)*

Hanham [Hanham Lock – OS Sheet 172 map ref 647702; ST6470], *Lock & Weir*: Idyllic setting beside River Avon, plain but comfortable inside, range of beers, friendly upbeat service, garden, unobstrusive piped 60s music; children in side rooms *(Andrew Partington)*

Hartpury [Ledbury Rd (A417); SO7924], *Canning Arms*: Charmingly idiosyncratic, with lots of red bows and nick-nacks, horsebrasses on beams, country prints; log fire, Tetleys-related ales, pleasant licensees, decent genuine bar food in eating area; live jazz some nights *(Neil and Anita Christopher, Jo Rees)*

Hawkesbury Upton [ST7786], *Duke of Beaufort*: Friendly landlord, extended uncluttered lounge with dog prints on white walls, TV and darts in quite cosy stripped-brick bar; specialises in cider *(Martin and Karen Wake)*

☆ **Hillesley** [ST7689], *Fleece*: Welcoming attractive local with good traditional furnishings, interesting bar food inc good specials and steaks, no-smoking upper dining bar; well kept Whitbreads-related real ales, decent wines and malt whiskies, friendly landlord; small Cotswolds village surrounded by lovely countryside, nr Cotswold Way; bedrooms *(Robert Huddleston, Pat and Richard Tazewell, M I Ellis, John Hazel, Paul Weedon)*

Kemble [outside village on A433 Cirencester—Tetbury; ST9897], *Thames Head*: Friendly atmosphere, stripped stone, timberwork, cottagey back area with pews and log-effect gas fire in big fireplace, country-look dining-room with another big gas fire, real fire in front area; well kept Arkells Bitter, 2B and 3B on handpump, good value straightforward food, seats outside, children welcome *(D Irving, E McCall, R Huggins, T McLean, LYM)*

☆ **Kineton** [signed from B4068 and B4077 W of Stow-on-the-Wold; SP0926], *Halfway House*: Traditional unpretentious country local in good walking country, well kept cheap Donnington BB and SBA from nearby brewery, simple food inc sensibly priced hot dishes, friendly staff, pub games (and juke box), tables on narrow front terrace and sheltered back lawn, restaurant; children allowed lunchtime, no visiting dogs; simple comfortable bedrooms *(Nick and Meriel Cox, Dr A Y Drummond, Lawrence Pearse, Martin Jones, LYM)*

☆ **Lechlade** [SU2199], *Red Lion*: Traditional village local with wide range of good value food inc good Sun lunches, friendly helpful service, well kept Arkells, restaurant with log fire *(Marjorie and David Lamb, D Irving, R Huggins, T McLean, E McCall)*

Lechlade [The Square], *New Inn*: Good range of well kept ales and wide choice of wholesome reasonably priced food in big busy bar with huge log fire; friendly staff, back restaurant, play area in big garden extending to Thames; bedrooms *(Peter and Audrey Dowsett)*

☆ **Leighterton** [off A46 S of Nailsworth; ST8291], *Royal Oak*: Unpretentious pub with appropriately simple decor and matching extension, four well kept interesting ales, decent straightforward home cooking, friendly landlord, nice garden, quiet village; quite handy for Westonbirt Arboretum *(Margaret Dyke)*

☆ **Little Barrington** [A40 W of Burford; SP2012], *Inn For All Seasons*: Old inn with plenty of character, big log fire, comfortable wing armchairs, magazines; friendly helpful staff, wide choice of generous bar food esp fish, informal restaurant; local beers such as Wychwood Best, piped classical music; tables in garden, bedrooms; may be closed Mon winter *(Martin and Karen Wake)*

Little Witcombe [A417; SO9015], *Twelve Bells*: Routine Beefeater pub, popular and comfortable, with friendly and efficient service, decent food and drink; Travel Inn bedrooms *(TN)*

☆ **Longhope** [Ross Rd (A40); SO6919], *Farmers Boy*: Good wholesome food inc same two-in-one pies as at Weighbridge nr Nailsworth (see main entries) in three big carefully refurbished rooms, one with running water in covered well; stripped stone, farm tools, log fire, relaxed atmosphere, welcoming service, well kept Adnams and Wadworths 6X, no juke boxes or machines; attractive garden *(Mr and Mrs K Box, Neil and Anita Christopher, Mrs B Lemon, Joy Raymond, Mrs Pat Crabb, T Buckley, L Knight)*

☆ **Lower Lydbrook** [Vention Lane; pub signed up single-track rd from B4228 NE of village – OS Sheet 162 map ref 604167; SO5916], *Royal Spring*: Very prettily placed, simple and quiet, with pews and high-backed settles in long beamed lounge looking down valley, wide range of well presented bar food inc good Sun lunch, friendly chatty licensees, log fire, well kept Wadworths; pretty garden built around stream dropping down steep coombe, play area, pets' corner; children very welcome *(Robert Huddleston, Lawrence Pearse, LYM)*

☆ **Lower Swell** [B4068 W of Stow-on-the-Wold; SP1725], *Golden Ball*: Character welcoming local, bright and clean, with Donnington BB and SBA from the pretty brewery just 20 mins' walk away, good range of ciders and perry, bar food, evening restaurant (no food Sun evening); simple bar with log fire, games area behind big chimneystack, garden with occasional barbecues, Aunt Sally and quoits; decent simple bedrooms *(D Grzelka, P J Keen, LYM)*

☆ **Lower Wick** [off A38 Bristol—Gloucester just N of Newport; ST7196], *Pickwick*: Full range of Smiles beers now in bright clean dining pub, very popular (particularly with older people) for generous changing home-cooked food, straightforward but interesting; traditional games inc ancient table skittles, no music, decent wines; rather close-set tables; wonderful countryside and good views despite nearby M5 and rly; children welcome *(A D Shore, Gwen and Peter Andrews, C H and P Stride, John and Pat Smyth, Margaret Dyke)*

Maisemore [SO8121], *Rising Sun*: Generous freshly cooked food inc good Sun lunch, good choice of beers, tables outside with safe play area, skittle alley *(Richard Lewis)*

Mangotsfield [Cossham St; ST6577], *Red Lion*: Two-bar suburban pub, no-smoking dining room (one bar no smoking too), good well priced home-cooked food, efficient service *(K R Harris)*

☆ **Marshfield** [signed off A420 Bristol—Chippenham; ST7773], *Catherine Wheel*: Interesting family-run old pub, attractively renovated, with plates and prints on stripped stone walls, good mix of settles, chairs and stripped tables, impressive fireplace, cottagey back family bar, charming no-smoking Georgian dining room, flower-decked back yard; good food inc Thurs fresh fish, (not Sun), well kept Courage Best and Wadworths IPA and 6X, farm cider, decent wines; golden labrador, darts, dominoes; provision for children *(Susan and John Douglas, Pete and Rosie Flower, Ian Jones, Graham Fogelman, Pat and John Millward, LYM)*

Marshfield [A420], *Crown*: Large busy local with coach entry to yard, big log fire in well furnished beamed lounge, wide choice of competitively priced food esp steaks, well kept Tetleys, Websters and their own Mummers Ale, service very quick even when crowded; children welcome, live music Sat, occasional quiz nights *(Pete and Rosie Flower)*; [A420], *Lord Nelson*: Spacious range of beamed bars with open fires, well kept Bass, Boddington, Worthington BB and a guest beer, wide choice of home-made food (good meat – new landlord was in the trade), bistro restaurant, locals' games bar, enthusiastic licensees; charming small courtyard, bedrooms in cottage annexe *(Pete and Rosie Flower)*

☆ **Meysey Hampton** [off A417 Cirencester—Lechlade; SU1199], *Masons Arms*: Welcoming newish landlord in extensively renovated beamed 17th-c inn with good freshly cooked reasonably priced food, well kept John Smiths and Wadworths 6X, decent wines inc several ports, hospitable atmosphere, good solid furnishings, big inglenook log fire at one end, no-smoking restaurant up a few steps; homely and cosy well equipped bedrooms, good breakfasts *(Paul McPherson, D Irving, E McCall, R Huggins, T McLean, Patricia and Tony Carroll, Matt Richardson, Sarah Orchard, D H and M C Watkinson, BB)*

Mickleton [B4632 (ex A46); SP1543], *Kings Arms*: Comfortable, relaxed and civilised, popular for good value food, with pleasant staff, Whitbreads-related ales, some tables outside; handy for Hidcote and Kiftsgate *(G Washington, BB)*

Minchinhampton [High St; SO8600], *Crown*: Antique settle among other wooden seats, lots of local and sporting prints, separate no-smoking dining room, pleasant service, Whitbreads-related ales and a guest such as Moles Best, good value bar food *(Neil and Anita Christopher)*

Minsterworth [A48 S of Gloucester; SO7716], *Apple Tree*: Friendly and comfortable roadside Whitbreads dining pub based on extended oak-beamed 17th-c farmhouse, decent standard food, open fires, prompt service, unobtrusive piped music, well kept ales; big garden with enclosed play area; open all day – lane beside leads down to the Severn, a good way of avoiding east bank crowds on a Bore weekend *(Thomas Nott)*

☆ **Moreton in Marsh** [High St; SP2032], *White Hart Royal*: Busy and comfortable old-world inn, partly 15th-c, with oak beams, stripped stone, big inglenook fire in lounge area just off main bar, welcoming helpful staff, particularly well kept Bass and Worthington BB, good value straightforward food changing daily in bar and simple but pleasant restaurant, inc good seafood and Sun lunch; a real welcome for children, can get crowded; good value bedrooms *(Derek Allpass, Jill White, Mark Ellis, George Atkinson, Pam Adsley, A E and P McCully, Henry Paulinski, Andrew and Ruth Triggs, N W Neill)*

☆ **Moreton in Marsh** [High St], *Redesdale Arms*: Fine old coaching inn with pictures for sale, prettily lit alcoves and big stone fireplace in comfortable panelled bar on right, well kept Tetleys-related ales with a guest such as Exmoor Stag, good range of tasty food inc vegetarian and large or small helpings, restaurant, darts and fruit machine in flagstoned public bar, TV in back conservatory, friendly helpful staff; tables in big back garden; comfortable well equipped bedrooms *(George Atkinson, Mrs B Sugarman, Fred Collier, Andrew and Ruth Triggs, Annette and Stephen Marsden)*

☆ **Moreton in Marsh** [Market Pl], *Black Bear*: Good value enterprising home-made food, excellent service, warm, comfortable and relaxing lounge, livelier public bar; full range of well kept local Donnington ales, back garden *(Joan and Michel Hooper-Immins, Dr and Mrs M N Edwards, B M Eldridge)*

Moreton in Marsh [High St], *Bell*: Pleasant homely pub with Courage-related ales, good value food all day, efficient service; bar covered with banknotes and beermats, tables (some under cover) in garden *(Andrew and Ruth Triggs)*; [High St], *Inn on the Marsh*: Good reasonably priced restaurant-style food, well kept interesting ales such as Armstrongs, Burton Bradstock, Hook Norton, friendly young staff, comfortable armchairs and settles, dining conservatory; bedrooms *(Annette and Stephen Marsden, Andrew and Ruth Triggs)*

☆ **Nailsworth** [coming from Stroud on A46, left and left again at roundabout; ST8499], *Egypt Mill*: Attractively converted three-floor mill with working waterwheel in one room, static machinery in second area, Ind Coope Burton and Wadworths 6X on handpump, wide choice of good generous bar food inc fresh veg, quick service, good value meals in civilised upstairs restaurant; can get crowded weekends, occasional loud karaoke or jazz evenings; children welcome, no dogs; lovely gardens, good bedrooms *(Dr and Mrs A K Clarke, D Irving, E McCall, R Huggins, T McLean, Mr and Mrs J Brown, Roger Entwistle)*

☆ **Nether Westcote** [SP2120], *New Inn*: Good value home-cooked food, well kept Morrells and good service in warmly welcoming pub, pleasantly unpretentious but cosy and clean; can get busy, piped pop music may be loud; sizeable adjoining campsite, pretty village *(James de la Force, Peter and Audrey Dowsett)*

☆ **North Nibley** [B4060; ST7496], *Black Horse*: Good atmosphere and wide range of generous fresh home-made bar food from ploughman's up in straightforward village local, comfortably old-fashioned, with well kept Whitbreads-related real ales and an interesting guest beer, good log fire, maybe piped music; popular restaurant Tues-Sat evenings, Sun lunchtime, tables in pretty garden; good value cottagey bedrooms, good breakfasts *(Paul Weedon, Pat and Richard Tazewell, Mrs Anne Parmenter, Martin and Karen Wake, T and D Archer, Margaret Dyke, LYM)*

☆ **Northleach** [Cheltenham Rd; SP1114], *Wheatsheaf*: Clean and smartly comfortable, almost more hotel than pub, with pleasantly upmarket atmosphere, quiet piped classical music, very polite friendly staff; good value lunchtime bar food, real ales inc Marstons Pedigree; restaurant, lovely terraced garden; well equipped modern bedrooms *(John Honnor, John and Joan Wyatt)*

☆ **Northleach** [Market Pl], *Red Lion*: Good value generous food from good sandwiches to Sun roasts in straightforward bar with open fire, well kept Courage-related ales, decent coffee, very friendly service; piped music and fruit machines *(Margaret Dyke)*

☆ **Nympsfield** [SO8000], *Rose & Crown*: Friendly village local nr Coaley Peak viewpoint over Severn Valley, handy for Cotswold walks, big helpings of straightforward home-cooked food inc huge ploughman's in recently enlarged and improved eating area, cosy partly stripped-stone lounge with big fireplace, wide choice of ales such as Bass, Boddingtons and Uley Bitter and Old Spot, Australian chardonnay on tap, good quick service even when busy, separate public bar; terrace and garden, good play area; clean and comfortable bedrooms sharing bath and lavatory, big breakfasts *(Margaret Dyke, T M Dobby, Neil and Anita Christopher, Martin and Karen Wake)*

☆ **Painswick** [St Mary's St; SO8609], *Royal Oak*: Busy and attractive old town local with bubbly atmosphere, interesting layout and furnishings inc some attractive old or antique seats, good value honest food (bar nibbles only, Sun) from sandwiches to changing hot dishes inc Thurs fresh fish, well kept Whitbreads-related ales, friendly family service, small sun lounge by suntrap pretty courtyard; children in eating area; can get crowded, nearby parking may be difficult *(D Irving, E McCall, R Huggins, T McLean, E J Wilde, Paul Weedon, G C Hackemer, Michael Marlow, Thomas Nott, Martyn Kearey, LYM)*

Parkend [SO6208], *Fountain*: Friendly and efficient landlord, lots of interesting bric-a-brac, log fires, varied well kept beers; good value usual food *(David and Mary Webb, Mrs C Watkinson)*

Perrotts Brook [A435 Cirencester—

Gloucester; SP0105], *Bear*: Useful roadside pub, Courage-related ales, reasonably priced usual food, friendly landlord, smart interior with good mug collection on beams *(Peter and Audrey Dowsett)*

Pilning [handy for M5 junction 17; ST5585], *Plough*: Recently refurbished, good choice of ales inc Bass and Wadworths 6X, good home cooking, pleasant garden with play equipment *(Steve and Carolyn Harvey)*

☆ **Prestbury** [Mill St; SO9624], *Plough*: Improving range of good very generous food in well preserved thatched village local's cosy and pleasant oak-panelled front lounge, friendly and comfortable; lots of regulars in basic but roomy flagstoned back taproom with grandfather clock and big log fire, well kept Whitbreads-related ales tapped from casks, pleasant back garden *(B M Eldridge, D Irving, E McCall, R Huggins, T McLean)*

Pucklechurch [ST7077], *Rose & Crown*: Pleasant Wadworths pub with sensibly priced well kept ales, decent food promptly served inc Sun roasts and good choice of puddings, seats outside *(DAV, P Neate)*

☆ **Purton** [just upstream from Sharpness village – ie not pub of this name in nearby Berkeley; SO6904], *Berkeley Arms*: Quiet and basic rustic Severnside pub-cum-farm with wonderful estuary view, two character flagstoned rooms with plain high-backed settles, well kept Wadworths 6X, food confined to pickled eggs, crisps, maybe ploughman's; great walks; summer caravanning allowed when there's no risk of flooding *(Paul and Gail Betteley)*

☆ **Quenington** [SP1404], *Keepers Arms*: Cosy and comfortable stripped-stone pub, very friendly, with traditional settles, lots of mugs hanging from low beams, good coal fire, decent food in both bars and restaurant, Whitbreads-related ales, no piped music; bedrooms *(Audrey and Peter Dowsett)*

Randwick [SO8206], *Vine Tree*: Quite spacious hillside village pub, wonderful valley views esp from terrace and garden; well kept Whitbreads-related ales, good choice of food (not Tues), beams, timbering, stripped stone, rush matting, copper-topped tables, plates and Lawson Wood prints on walls, warm welcome; children's play area *(Neil and Anita Christopher, R Huggins, D Irving, T McLean, E McCall)*

Rangeworthy [ST6986], *Rose & Crown*: Friendly two-bar country pub, nautical theme in one room, hunting in the other *(Dr and Mrs A K Clarke)*

Rodborough [SO8404], *Bear*: Flagstoned bar with pleasant window seats, welcoming log fire, good value bar food, well kept Courage; children welcome; comfortable Forte hotel – good base for touring Cotswolds; bedrooms *(Dave Irving, E McCall, R Huggins, T McLean, W H and E Thomas)*

☆ **Shepperdine** [off B4061 N of Thornbury; ST6295], *Windbound*: Well placed on Severn estuary nr Wildfowl Trust Centre, spacious pubby bar with decent straightforward food, well kept beers, attractive pictures, friendly landlord; upstairs room (which has the views) may now be open only for functions; tables on fairylit lawn *(Brian and Jill Bond, John and Donna Bush, LYM)*

Shurdington [A46 just S of Cheltenham; SO8318], *Bell*: Range of beers and well chosen wines at reasonable prices, well served home-cooked food; conservatory looking over playing field; children welcome *(E A George)*

☆ **Siddington** [Ashton Rd; village signed off Cirencester through-traffic system nr industrial estate, and from A419 northbound; SU0399], *Greyhound*: Has been extremely popular main entry, with two log fires and great mix of traditional furnishings and bric-a-brac in sizeable beamed lounge, games in public bar, pleasant garden, good popular bar food and well kept Wadworths and guest beers; but former tenants are now to be found at the Colesbourne Inn (see above), and no news yet on new regime *(LYM; reports please)*

Slad [B4070 Stroud—Birdlip; SO8707], *Woolpack*: Basic village local in splendid setting, lovely valley views, very obliging service, cheap food, well kept Uley Old Spot and Whitbreads-related ales *(Prof I H Rorison, TN, PN, John and Joan Wyatt)*

Slimbridge [Shepherds Patch, by swing bridge across ship canal – OS Sheet 162 map ref 728042; SO7303], *Tudor Arms*: Very handy for Wildfowl Trust and canal, good value home-cooked food in bar and evening restaurant, children's room; bedrooms in small annexe *(Paul Weedon)*

☆ **Snowshill** [SP0934], *Snowshill Arms*: Friendly local feel midweek winter, can be very crowded other times – handy for Snowshill Manor (which closes lunchtime); good popular food, well kept Donnington BB and SBA, efficient service, spruce and airy bar, log fire; charming village views from bow windows and from big back garden; skittle alley, good play area; children welcome if eating, nearby parking may be difficult *(Mr and Mrs P B Dowsett, Nick and Meriel Cox, Patrick Freeman, P and M Rudlin, Richard Lewis, Mrs P J Pearce, D Grzelka, D Hanley, Joan and John Calvert, Pam Adsley, Andrew and Ruth Triggs, LYM)*

☆ **Somerford Keynes** [OS Sheet 163 map ref 018954; SU0195], *Bakers Arms*: Welcoming traditional village local currently doing well, knowledgeable barman may even give tastes of his frequently changing well kept ales, partly stripped-stone lounge bar, food inc good specials; big garden *(Dr and Mrs A K Clarke, D Irving, E McCall, T McLean, R Huggins)*

☆ **Staverton** [Haydon, W of Cheltenham; B4063 – OS Sheet 163 map ref 902248; SO9024], *House in the Tree*: Not in a tree but a pleasantly busy spick-and-span Whitbreads pub with guest ales, good choice of lunchtime food in big dining lounge, more traditional public bar, obliging service; may get crowded at weekends, plenty of tables in garden with pets' corner *(John and Joan*

Wyatt, D Irving, E McCall, R Huggins, T McLean, David and Alison Walker)
Stow-on-the-Wold [The Square; SP1925], *Talbot*: Popular local, less touristy than some here, well kept Wadworths IPA and 6X with a guest such as Everards Tiger, wide choice of good simple food all day, friendly staff; juke box can be intrusive *(Joan and Michel Hooper-Immins, Richard Lewis)*; [The Square], *White Hart*: Decent food in cheery and pleasant old front bar or plush back dining lounge; bedrooms *(Paul McPherson, Mrs P J Pearce, LYM)*
Stroud [Stratford Rd, opp Stratford Park; SO8504], *Old Nelson*: 19th-c Gothick former school converted into pub/restaurant/hotel, decent food in spacious Victorian-style Millers Kitchen family dining areas, solicitous staff, Bass and Tetleys-related ales; pervasive piped music; bedrooms; recommended by a reader who taught here when the school was still kept by Mr Nelson *(John and Joan Wyatt)*
Teddington [Stow Rd, 3½ miles from M5 junction 9; SO9632], *Teddington Hands*: Modernised Whitbreads pub, very welcoming, with Boddingtons, Marstons Pedigree and Shepherds Neame, decent choice of house wines, unusual home-made food esp good fish; handy for Cheltenham Races *(Frank Gadbois, George S Jonas, Norma and Keith Bloomfield)*
☆ **Tetbury** [Gumstool Hill, Mkt Pl; ST8893], *Crown*: Cosy atmosphere, good choice of popular bar food and well kept Hook Norton Best and Whitbreads-related ales in friendly 17th-c town pub with big log fire in long oak-beamed front bar, attractive medley of tables, efficient courteous service, unobtrusive piped music; back family dining conservatory with lots of plants, picnic tables on back terrace; comfortable bedrooms *(Roger Huggins, LM, Karen and Graham Oddey, B and K Hypher, P and J Shapley)*
nr **Tetbury** [Calcot; A4135 W, junction A46; attached to Calcot Hotel; ST8394], *Gumstool*: Smart and busy new cafe-style bar attached to Calcot Hotel, modern tables and seats on flagstones, Bass, varied decent food inc interesting dishes; bedrooms *(D G King)*; [A433 towards Cirencester], *Trouble House*: Pretty 17th-c pub with well kept Wadworths beers, open fire, small quiet lounge, more lively bar with bar billiards and darts in room off, usual food, no music *(Roger Huggins, Karen and Graham Oddey)*
☆ **Tewkesbury** [High St; SO8932], *Black Bear*: Extremely picturesque timbered pub, said to be county's oldest, with rambling heavy-beamed rooms off black-timbered corridors, inviting yet not too crowded, five or six ales such as Shepherd Neame Spitfire and Wychwood Dog and Hobgoblin tapped from the cask, reasonably priced bar food inc good children's menu, very friendly service, riverside lawn *(Sue and Mike Lee, Pat Bromley, Clifford Payton, BB)*
☆ **Tewkesbury** [52 Church St], *Bell*: Interesting hotel bar, plush but not intimidatingly smart, with black oak beams and timbers, some neat William and Mary oak panelling, medieval leaf-and-fruit frescoes, armchairs, settees and tapestries; good choice of decent bar food from sandwiches up inc civilised Sun buffet lunch, comfortable restaurant, well kept Banks's and Wadworths 6X, friendly helpful service, big log fire; garden above Severnside walk, nr abbey; good bedrooms *(Gordon Mott, Andrew and Ruth Triggs, Adrian and Gwynneth Littleton, F M Steiner, BB)*
Tewkesbury [Church St], *Berkeley Arms*: Character medieval timbered inn best seen from narrow passageway outside lounge with jettied windows above, well kept Wadworths Farmers Glory, 6X and IPA, friendly staff, good value food in both bars and back barn dining area with striking ancient rafters; open all day summer, bedrooms *(Joan and Michel Hooper-Immins)*; [out on A38], *Gupshill Manor*: Much restored as Whitbreads pub, with lovely flower garden *(Dave Braisted)*
Thornbury [59 High St; ST6390], *Knot of Rope*: Well appointed reputedly haunted town house, knowledgeable bar staff; unusual for serving real ales by electric pump *(Dr and Mrs A K Clarke)*; [Chapel St], *Wheatsheaf*: Locally popular for good value home cooking with real veg, Sun roast, wide range of real ales *(K R Harris)*
Tockington [ST6186], *Swan*: Spacious stone-built timbered pub, now a free house with wider choice of well kept ales, good range of reasonably priced unusual dishes (service may stop very early Sun), good no-smoking area, friendly staff, tables in garden; quiet village *(E D Bailey, Pat and Richard Tazewell)*
☆ **Tolldown** [under a mile from M4 junction 18 – A46 towards Bath; ST7577], *Crown*: Surprisingly unspoilt off-motorway pub with usual food in heavy-beamed stone bar, no-smoking area, well kept Wadworths, log fire; dominoes, darts and fruit machine, piped music, good garden with play area; children in eating area and restaurant; bedrooms *(Barry and Anne, LYM)*
☆ **Tormarton** [handy for M4 junction 18, signed off A46 N; ST7678], *Portcullis*: Ivy-covered old Cotswold stone inn doing well since reopening under new owners, good atmosphere, ultra-friendly staff, generous interesting food at sensible prices, good range of beers such as Hartington Gold and Otter, log fire (sometimes two), attractive panelled dining room; tables in garden, quiet village; bedrooms *(Meg and Colin Hamilton, Jeff Davies, Pete and Rosie Flower, Barry and Anne)*
Tormarton [also nr M4 junction 18], *Compass*: Very extended off-motorway place with choice of rooms inc cosy local-feeling bar open all day for food, pleasant conservatory, well kept ales inc Smiles, friendly staff, rather pricy restaurant, comfortable bedrooms *(Neville Kenyon, W L G Watkins, Nicholas Roberts, LYM)*
☆ **Twyning** [Twyning Green; SO8936], *Fleet*:

Star is for superb setting, with good river views from big popular welcoming open-plan bar, variety of seating areas inside and out, well kept Whitbreads-related ales, access for the disabled, bar food, boat shop *(DAV, Dr and Mrs A K Clarke)*

☆ **Uley** [The Street; ST7898], *Old Crown*: Welcoming local with long narrow lounge, good value generous food inc children's dishes, well kept Uley and Pigs Ear with a couple of Whitbreads-related ales, darts and fruit machine, pool table in small upstairs room (how did they get it up the spiral stairs?), unobtrusive piped music, attractive garden; bedrooms good value with super breakfast, good base for walks *(Alastair Campbell, Emma Hayes)*

☆ **Wanswell Green** [SO6901], *Salmon*: Good value food, well kept Whitbreads-related real ales, decent wines and cider, two attractive candlelit back dining rooms, busy front bar (esp Fri/Sat night), good friendly staff helpful with children; big front play area; nr Berkeley Castle and Severn walks *(Mr and Mrs J Brown, Andrew Shore, Paul Weedon)*

☆ **Westbury on Severn** [Bell Lane (A48 Gloucester—Chepstow); SO7114], *Red Lion*: Tiled and timbered pub with good interesting generous food, well kept ales inc Hook Norton Best, decent wine, very friendly staff, coal stove; next to churchyard by footpath to Severn, handy for NT gardens *(Philip Lake, Mrs C Watkinson, Mr and Mrs W A Poeton)*

☆ **Westonbirt** [A433 SW of Tetbury – OS Sheet 162 map ref 863904; ST8690], *Hare & Hounds*: Well run old-fashioned hotel bar, comfortable and relaxed, with decent reasonably priced lunches inc salad bar and good cheap rolls, John Smiths, Wadworths IPA and 6X, quick helpful service, pleasant gardens; handy for Arboretum; limited space for families; bedrooms *(Mr and Mrs J Brown, Dr Ian Crichton, D G Clarke, W H and E Thomas)*

☆ **Whitminster** [A38 1½ miles N of M5 junction 13; SO7708], *Old Forge*: Small and unpretentious old beamed pub with welcoming attentive staff, bar food, small restaurant, good choice of beers and wines; children welcome *(D G Clarke, Paul Weedon, P J and S E Robbins)*

☆ **Willersey** [nr Broadway – OS Sheet 150 map ref 106396; SP1039], *Bell*: Tastefully appointed civilised 14th-c golden stone dining pub, comfortable and spotless, with good interesting food, good value though not cheap, from well presented sandwiches up; three Whitbreads-related ales, friendly attentive service; may have to wait for a table unless you book; overlooks delightful village's green and duck pond, tables in garden *(Pam Adsley, Moira and John Cole)*

☆ **Winchcombe** [High St], *Old Corner Cupboard*: Relaxed traditional local at top of attractive village, with hatch-service lobby, small smoke room, lounge with beams, stripped stone, armchairs and good inglenook log fire, attractive small back garden; well kept Hook Norton, Marstons Pedigree and four Whitbreads-related ales, good straightforward bar food from sandwiches up, friendly landlord, board games; bedrooms in self-contained wing *(Neil and Anita Christopher, Peter Mayo, Richard and Janice Searle, DAV, Michael and Derek Slade, Roger Huggins, Tom McLean, R A Baker)*

☆ **Winchcombe** [Abbey Terr], *Plaisterers Arms*: Welcoming 18th-c pub with good generous cheapish food inc vegetarian, children's and good puddings, prompt cheerful service, well kept ales such as Bass, Tetleys, Wadworths and local Goffs Jouster, open fire, plenty of seating inc comfortably worn settles, two bars and dining area, stripped stonework, beams, copper, brass and old tools, lots of steps; play area in attractive garden, long and narrow; comfortable bedrooms *(Mrs M Hamilton, Dr I H Maine, Neil and Anita Christopher, Peter and Janet Race, C and J Roe, DAV, George Atkinson)*

Winchcombe [High St (A46)], *White Harte*: Good all round, agreeable efficient staff, good reasonably priced food; bedrooms spacious with good facilities *(G C Brown)*

Winterbourne Down [Down Rd, Kendleshire; just off A432 Bristol—Yate, towards Winterbourne; ST6679], *Golden Heart*: Large, well furnished and welcoming, with beams, open fires, inglenook, wide choice of reasonably priced food, good friendly service, well kept beer, country view from restaurant; fruit machines; children's room, huge lawns front and back, both with play equipment *(PN)*

☆ **Withington** [signed off A436, A40; from church go S, bearing left – OS Sheet 163 map ref 032153; SP0315], *Mill*: Fine mossy-roofed old stone building with rambling, higgledy-piggledy beamed bar and cosy little side rooms, interesting antique seats, good log fire and lovely streamside gardens (summer barbecues) in peaceful valley; Sam Smiths ales, usual food, gets very busy weekends, piped music may intrude; children allowed, games bar; bedrooms *(D Irving, R Huggins, T McLean, E McCall, Gordon, Helen Pickering, James Owen, George and Chris Miller, Rebecca Mortimer, LYM)*

Woodmancote [Stockwell Lane; SO9727], *Apple Tree*: Popular straightforward food in roomy local with Bass, Wadworths and Whitbreads-related ales; restaurant; garden *(D Walker, Mr and Mrs J Brown)*

Post Office address codings confusingly give the impression that some pubs are in Gloucestershire, when they're really in the Midlands (which is where we list them).

Hampshire

Pubs on top form here these days include the Red Lion at Boldre (very popular dining pub, lots of decent wines by the glass), the Flower Pots at Cheriton (decent food and good atmosphere, brewing its own good beer which can increasingly be found in other Hampshire pubs), the very friendly White Horse at Droxford (gaining two of our awards this year, both as a place to stay and for its beers), the Bush at Ovington (very civilised, lots of character, lovely setting), the Fleur de Lys at Pilley (good food, enterprising licensees), and the Wykeham Arms in Winchester (very good all round, with an outstanding range of wines by the glass – this year it gains its second star). New main entries here are the White Hart at Cadnam (really getting into its stride now, under the Emberleys who made so many friends among readers of the Guide when they were at the New Forest Inn at Emery Down); the Jolly Farmer in Locks Heath (very welcoming and interesting); and the Dever Arms at Micheldever (unusual food, good wines and beers, cheerfully civilised atmosphere). The county's particular strength is in dining pubs – lots to choose from, in both the main entries and the Lucky Dips, with some of Whitbreads' best chain dining pubs being found here now. What's rather more elusive here is the pub with real character: the White Horse above Petersfield stands out for this, and another to hunt down is the Harrow at Steep. The Sun at Bentworth is particularly rare in combining great character and atmosphere with very good food: it's our choice as Hampshire Dining Pub of the Year. In the Lucky Dip section at the end of the chapter, pubs currently showing specially well (most already vetted by us) include the Globe in Alresford, Three Tuns at Bransgore, Tally Ho at Broughton, Castle at Crondall, Horse & Jockey at Curbridge, Chairmakers Arms at Denmead, George at East Meon, Jack Russell at Faccombe, Fox & Hounds at Fair Oak, Jolly Sailor near Fawley, Hen & Chicken at Froyle, Yew Tree at Highclere, Trout at Itchen Abbas, Ship at Langstone, Peat Spade at Longstock, Trusty Servant at Minstead, Ship at Owslebury, Fish in Ringwood, Filly at Setley, White Hart at Sherfield on Loddon, White Lion at Soberton, Fox at Tangley, Fishermans Rest at Titchfield and Hoddington Arms at Upton Grey. Drinks prices are rather higher in Hampshire than the national average: the cheapest pub we found was the Flower Pots at Cheriton, brewing its own beer; pubs tied to Gales tended to be rather cheaper than other tied houses.

ALRESFORD SU5832 Map 2

Horse & Groom

Broad St; town signposted from new A31 bypass

The rambling nooks and crannies give the open-plan bar here a pleasantly secluded feel: neat settles and windsor chairs, black beams and timbered walls partly stripped to brickwork, old local photographs, and shelves of earthenware jugs and bottles. Perhaps the nicest place to sit is at the tables in the three bow windows on the right, looking out over the broad street. Bar food includes sandwiches, baked potatoes (from £3.95), warm salads (£4.25), liver and bacon (£4.75), steak and kidney pie (£5.25), and steaks (from £7.95). Well kept Bass, Boddingtons, Fremlins, Marstons Pedigree and Whitbreads Castle Eden and Strong Country on handpump, kept under light blanket pressure; coal-effect gas fire, unobtrusive piped music. Service can slow down at busy periods. *(Recommended by Caroline Kenyon, Ann and Colin Hunt, Mr and Mrs R J Foreman, Canon Kenneth Wills, KCW, Lynn Sharpless, Bob Eardley, Dawn and Phil Garside, Martin and Karen Wake)*

Whitbreads ~ Lease: Robin and Kate Howard ~ Real ale ~ Meals and snacks ~ (01962) 734809 ~ Children welcome ~ Open 11-11; maybe 11-3, 6-11 in winter

BATTRAMSLEY SZ3099 Map 2

Hobler

A337 a couple of miles S of Brockenhurst; OS Sheet 196 map reference 307990

If you are in tune with the landlord's idosyncratic sense of humour, you'll very much enjoy yourself here. The black-beamed bar – divided by the massive stub of an ancient wall – has a very relaxed feel, and is furnished with pews, little dining chairs and a comfortable bow-window seat. Guns, china, New-Forest saws, the odd big engraving, and a growing collection of customer photographs decorate the walls, some of which are stripped back to timbered brick; the cosy area on the left is black-panelled and full of books. Popular bar food includes home-made soups (£2.50), ploughman's (£3.70), garlic mushrooooms or spaghetti bolognaise (£6.95), barbecued spare ribs (£7.95), grilled trout (£8.95), rack of lamb or Cajun chicken (£9.95), half roasted duck with alcoholic orange sauce (£10.95) and their popular 'Hot Rocks', a hot stone on a plate upon which you cook your own meat. Well kept Bass, Flowers Original, Wadworths 6X and guest beers from small local breweries on handpump, a good range of malt whiskies (over 75) and country wines. In summer a spacious forest-edge lawn has a summer bar, a huge timber climbing fort in the good play area, and picnic tables, as well as a paddock with ponies, pigs, donkeys, a peacock and hens. No children. *(Recommended by Lynn Sharpless, Bob Eardley, D Marsh, C A Hall, Jenny and Brian Seller, Mr and Mrs G P Tobin, Andrew Scarr, Don Kellaway, Angie Coles, Stephen and Anna Oxley)*

Whitbreads ~ Licensee Pip Steven ~ Real ale ~ Meals and snacks (till 10) ~ (01590) 623291 ~ Jazz Tues evening ~ Open 10.30-2.30, 6-11

BEAUWORTH SU5624 Map 2

Milbury's

Turn off A272 Winchester/Petersfield at Beauworth ¾, Bishops Waltham 6 signpost, then continue straight on past village

Surrounded by a Bronze Age cemetery – the Mill Barrow, hence the pub's name – this popular place has fine views from the garden, and good nearby walks. Sturdy beams, stripped masonry, panelling and massive open fireplaces (with good winter log fires) offer reminders of the building's years, and there's a 600-year-old well cut nearly 300 feet into the chalk; the massive treadwheel beside it used to be worked by a donkey. Well kept Courage Directors, Hampshire King Alfred and Pendragon, Shepherd Neame Spitfire, Tetleys and a beer named for the pub on handpump, Addlestones cider, and country wines. Tasty bar food includes home-made soup (£2.25), sandwiches (from £2.65), ploughman's (£2.95), stuffed vegetarian pancake or steak and Guinness pie (£4.95), salmon fillet with garlic and basil (£6.95), steaks (from £8.75), puddings (£2.45), children's dishes (£2.75), and Sunday brunch (from £3.50); service is prompt, efficient and cheerful; best to book at weekends. Skittle alley. *(Recommended by T Roger Lamble, J S M Sheldon, Clive Gilbert, N Matthews, JKW, N*

E Bushby, Miss W E Atkins, M J D Inskip, Canon Kenneth Wills, W J Wonham, Dave Braisted, KCW, Ann and Colin Hunt, Mayur Shah)

Free house ~ Licensees Jan and Lenny Larden ~ Real ale ~ Meals and snacks (till 10) ~ Restaurant ~ (01962) 771248 ~ Children welcome ~ Open 11-2.30(3 Sat), 6-11 ~ Bedrooms: £22.50/£38.50

BENTLEY SU7844 Map 2

Bull

A31 Farnham—Alton, W of village and accessible from both directions at W end of dual carriageway Farnham bypass

Well placed for woodland walks, this little tiled white pub has pretty summer flowering tubs and hanging baskets, and tables on the side terrace, by a fairy-lit Wendy house on stilts. Inside, the low-beamed, traditionally furnished rooms have plenty of interesting local prints, pictures and photographs on the walls, especially in the snug left-hand room, which also has a dimly lit back alcove with a tapestried pew built around a nice mahogany table, and a log-effect gas fire in a big old fireplace. The restaurant area has several comical prewar Bonzo prints. Bar food includes sandwiches (from £2.25), ploughman's (around £4.25), lasagne (£5.50), and home-made steak, kidney and mushroom pie (£6.50), with daily specials like saddle of rabbit or crispy Thai lamb. Courage Best, Fullers London Pride and Wadworths 6X on handpump; darts, fruit machine, piped music. *(Recommended by T Roger Lamble, P J Caunt, D Marsh, Clive Gilbert, James Macrae, Stephen Teakle, John and Vivienne Rice, A D Marsh, Mrs B G Laker, Michael A Butler)*

Courage ~ Lease: Bill Thompson ~ Real ale ~ Meals and snacks (till 10) ~ Restaurant ~ (01420) 22156 ~ Children in eating area of bar and in restaurant ~ Jazz Sun lunchtime ~ Open 11-11

BENTWORTH SU6740 Map 2

Sun

Sun Hill; from the A339 coming from Alton the first turning takes you there direct; or in village follow Shalden 2¼, Alton 4¼ signpost

Hampshire Dining Pub of the Year

There's a fine buoyant atmosphere in this unspoilt cottage and the two tiny communicating rooms are traditional and old-fashioned. Both have open fires in the big fireplaces, a mix of seats like high-backed antique settles with pews and schoolroom chairs, olde-worlde prints and blacksmith's tools, and bare boards and scrubbed deal tables on the left; lots of fresh flowers dotted around and newspapers and interior magazines to read. An arch leads to a brick-floored room with another open fire and hanging baskets. Good, imaginative bar food has earned the pub a food award this year: sandwiches (from £1.90), home-made soup (£2.20), ploughman's (from £3), filled baked potatoes (£3.50), smoked haddock pancakes or particularly good cumberland sausage with onion gravy (£4.50), fresh salmon fishcakes with crab sauce (£5.50), lamb with port and redcurrants (£6), steak and kidney pie or creamy fish bake (£6.50), and puddings like pear or honey and almond tart, individual little sponge puddings or lemon and caramel mousse (£2.50). Well kept Courage Best, Badger Best, Cheriton Pots Ale, Marstons Pedigree, Ringwood Best, Ruddles Best, Wadworths 6X, Worldham Old Dray, and a beer named after the pub (brewed by Hampshire) on handpump; country wines; dominoes. Service is quick and friendly – as are the two dogs, Honey and Ruddles. Several picnic tables under cocktail parasols look over the quiet lane. *(Recommended by Andrew Scarr, Lynn Sharpless, Bob Eardley, Margaret Dyke, A G Drake, Joan and Andrew Life, Dr Ronald Church, Joy and Paul Rundell, Roger Walker, Susan and John Douglas, J S M Sheldon, Guy Consterdine, Julia Stone, Alan and Margot Baker, David Sweeney, G B Longden, Martin and Karen Wake, Brenda and Jim Langley, Phil and Sally Gorton, John and Joan Nash)*

Free house ~ Licensees Richard and Jan Beaumont ~ Real ale ~ Meals and snacks (not Sun evening Nov-Feb) ~ (01420) 562338 ~ Children allowed in garden room, no under 10s after 8pm ~ Occasional Morris dancers (26 Dec and odd Fri nights in summer) ~ Open 12-3, 6-11; closed Sun evening Nov-Mar and 25 Dec

BOLDRE SZ3298 Map 2

Red Lion ★ 🍴 🍷

Village signposted from A337 N of Lymington

Apart from the very good food, what readers like about this pub is that it has remained consistently good over the many years that some of them have known it. The four warmly atmospheric black-beamed rooms are filled with heavy urns, platters, needlework, rural landscapes, and so forth, taking in farm tools, heavy-horse harness, needlework, gin traps and even ferocious-looking man traps along the way; the central room with its profusion of chamber-pots is no smoking. An end room has pews, wheelback chairs and tapestried stools, and a dainty collection of old bottles and glasses in the window by the counter. Good bar food includes home-made soup (£2.50), good sandwiches (from £2.50), quite a few ploughman's or smoked fish pâté (£4.20), unusual and well liked basket meals ranging from sausages to duck with wine-soaked orange slices (from £4.50), slices of smoked duck breast with redcurrant jelly (£4.80), home-made vegetable casserole (£5.50), liver and bacon casserole (£5.90), home-made steak and kidney pie (£6.90), cold home-cooked gammon with two poached eggs (£7.30), daily specials such as rabbit pie or lamb, leek and apricot cobbler (£7.30), or local partridge casseroled in white wine (£8.90), and an interesting range of ice-creams (£2.90). Do get there early, some days tables go within minutes. Well kept Eldridge Pope Dorchester, Hardy Country and Royal Oak on handpump, and up to 20 wines by the glass; prompt and friendly service. In summer, the flowering tubs and hanging baskets are lovely and there's a cart festooned with colour near the car park. No children. *(Recommended by C A Hall, Joan and Michel Hooper-Immins, Mr and Mrs M F Norton, A Y Drummond, D Marsh, R H Rowley, Kim Redling, Tom Gondris, Nigel Flook, Betsy Brown, Jean-Bernard Brisset, Miss E Evans, Gill and Mike Cross, Martin and Pauline Richardson, Martin, Jane, Simon and Laura Bailey, J Watson, Keith and Margaret Kettell, Andrew Scarr, John and Christine Simpson, Jason Caulkin)*

Eldridge Pope ~ Lease: John and Penny Bicknell ~ Real ale ~ Meals and snacks (11-2.15, 6-10.15) ~ Restaurant ~ (01590) 673177 ~ Open 11-3, 6-11

BRAMDEAN SU6128 Map 2

Fox 🍷

A272 Winchester—Petersfield

With the emphasis very much on food, this white 17th-c weather-boarded dining pub does get busy. There's a good relaxing atmosphere in the much modernised and neatly cared for open-plan bar – as well as black beams, tall stools with proper backrests around the L-shaped counter, and comfortably cushioned wall pews and wheelback chairs; the fox motif shows in a big painting over the fireplace, and on much of the decorative china; one area is no smoking. Favourite dishes (with prices virtually unchanged since last year) include sandwiches (from £2.25; good cold meat), good soup (£2.50), ploughman's (£3.95), locally smoked trout (£4.50), king prawns with mayonnaise or mussels and prawns in sherry and garlic butter (£5.50), cauliflower cheese (£6.50), battered cod (£6.95), beef stroganoff (£8.50), and usually lots of fresh fish dishes such as skate, halibut, lobster or salmon steak in lime butter (£10.95). If you're not sure which wine to choose from the extensive wine list, they're quite happy to open a bottle to taste. Well kept Marstons Bitter and Pedigree on handpump; piped music. At the back of the building is a walled-in terraced area, and a spacious lawn spreading among the fruit trees, with a really good play area – trampoline as well as swings and a seesaw. No children inside. *(Recommended by Betty*

Laker, Dave Braisted, Clive Gilbert, J H Bell, T Roger Lamble, Canon Kenneth Wills, Lynn Sharpless, Bob Eardley, Guy Consterdine, W and S Jones, Peter and Audrey Dowsett, Colin Laffan, Ann and Colin Hunt, R K F Hutchings)

Marstons ~ Tenants Jane and Ian Inder ~ Real ale ~ Meals and snacks ~ (01962) 771363 ~ Open 10.30-3, 6-11; closed 25 Dec

BURITON SU7420 Map 2

Five Bells

Village signposted off A3 S of Petersfield

For those aiming to take the ferry from Portsmouth, this unpretentious old country local is very handy. It's attractive and genuinely welcoming, and the low-beamed lounge on the left is dominated by the big log fire, and has period photographs on its partly stripped brick walls, as well as a rather worn turkey carpet on oak parquet; the public side has some ancient stripped masonry, a woodburning stove, and old-fashioned tables. An end alcove with cushioned pews and old fishing prints has board games such as Scrabble (sensibly issued with a referee dictionary). Popular bar food includes lunchtime snacks such as filled french bread (£2.75), and ploughman's or filled baked potatoes (£3.75), as well as soup (£2.50), baked brie and almonds (£3.50), broccoli and stilton bake, barbecue spare ribs or curries (£5.50), lots of salads (from £5.50; dressed crab or half lobster £7.50), steak and kidney pie (£6.95), venison or fresh fish such as crab and sherry bake, whole plaice or smoked haddock (£7.95), steaks (£9.75), and daily specials. Well kept Adnams, Ballards Best, Friary Meux Best, Ind Coope Burton, Ringwood Old Thumper, and Tetleys on handpump; prompt, friendly service. Darts, dominoes, cribbage, and trivia. There are a few tables on sheltered terraces just outside, with many more on an informal lawn stretching back above the pub. They now offer self-catering cottages. *(Recommended by Mike Fitzgerald, Lynn Sharpless, Bob Eardley, Mrs Jane Basso, G R Sharman, JEB, Clive Gilbert, Paul Williams, Ted Burden, Paula Harrison, John and Joy Winterbottom, Barry and Anne, G B Longden, Jack Taylor, Gwen and Peter Andrews, John Carter, Rona Murdoch, J S M Sheldon)*

Free house ~ Licensee John Ligertwood ~ Real ale ~ Meals and snacks (till 10) ~ Restaurant (not Sun evening) ~ (01730) 263584 ~ Children in restaurant and snug ~ Jazz last Mon in month, folk or blues each Weds, Blue Grass first Sun in month ~ Open 11-2.30(3 Sat) 5.30-11

BURSLEDON SU4809 Map 2

Jolly Sailor

2 miles from M27 junction 8; follow B3397 towards Hamble, then A27 towards Salisbury, then just before going under railway bridge turn right towards Bursledon Station; it's best to park round here and walk as the lane up from the station is now closed to cars

Popular with yachtsmen, this charmingly unspoilt pub has tables in the garden under a big yew tree, and even on the wooden jetty – just right for watching all the goings on in the rather pretty yachting harbour. The nautical theme continues inside, with ship pictures, nets and shells in the airy front bar, as well as windsor chairs and settles on its floorboards. The atmospheric beamed and flagstoned back bar, with pews and settles by its huge fireplace, is a fair bit older. Well kept Badger Best and Tanglefoot, Gales HSB, Wadworths 6X, and a beer named for the pub (actually Gribble Bitter) on handpump, and country wines; darts, fruit machine and piped music. Bar food includes soup (£1.95), sandwiches (from £2.50), ploughman's (from £3.95), devilled whitebait (£3.75), sweetcorn fritter with provençale sauce or warm lentil salad (£5.25), steak and mushroom pie (£5.50), and sweet and sour pork (£5.75). The restaurant is no smoking. The path down to the pub (and of course back up again) from the lane is steep. *(Recommended by Jack and Philip Paxton, C A Hall, Ian Phillips, Jenny and Brian Seller, Adrian Zambardino, Debbie Chaplin, R C Hopton, Dawn and Phil Garside, Susan and John Douglas)*

Badger ~ Managers Stephen and Kathryn Housley ~ Real ale ~ Meals and snacks ~ Restaurant ~ (01703) 405557 ~ Children in eating area and restaurant ~ Open 11-2.30, 6-11; 11-11 Sat; closed Dec 25

CADNAM SU2913 Map 2

White Hart

½ mile from M27 junction 1; A336 towards village, pub off village roundabout

The Emberley family who previously ran the New Forest Inn at Emery Down and Fleur de Lys at Pilley as very popular main entries have now concentrated their resources here – a very successful move. They reopened the White Hart in 1994 after an extensive renovation programme that's given a spacious multi-level dining lounge, with good solid furnishings, soft lighting, country prints and appropriate New Forest pictures and mementoes. A wide choice of good attractively presented bar food includes soup (£2.75), ploughman's (£4.25), chicken and spring onion satay or tomato, avocado and mozzarella salad (£4.50), scampi, mushroom stroganoff, leek and spinach strudel with Madeira sauce or curry of the day (£6.75), gigot of lamb with cherry and almond sauce (£8.25) and breast of duck with fresh Victoria plum sauce (£9.25), generous roast beef and yorkshire pudding (£6.95; their roasts come with delicious sauces), with interesting specials and a tempting array of puddings; sauces are delicious. Well kept Flowers Original, King and Barnes Sussex, Morlands Old Speckled Hen and Wadworths 6X on handpump, farm ciders, decent wines listed on a blackboard including about eight good ones by the glass, no games machines; occasional piped music; efficient welcoming service even when it's busy. There are picnic tables under cocktail parasols outside, with a chance of making friends with the resident goat, three horses and five dogs: Victoria, Emma, Prudence, Solo and Freddie. *(Recommended by John Sanders, N E Bushby, Miss W E Atkins, F J Willy, Mark and Heather Williamson)*

Whitbreads ~ Lease: Nick and Sue Emberley ~ Real ale ~ Meals and snacks ~ Restaurant ~ (01703) 812277 ~ Children welcome ~ Open 11-3, 6-11

CHALTON SU7315 Map 2

Red Lion ♀

Village signposted E of A3 Petersfield—Horndean

In a lovely position beneath the village church and overlooking the South Downs, this pretty thatched pub was first licensed in 1503. The heavy-beamed and panelled bar has an ancient inglenook fireplace with a frieze of burnished threepenny bits set into its mantlebeam, and is furnished with high-backed traditional settles and elm tables. Popular bar food includes sandwiches (from £2.20), deep fried brie with redcurrant jelly (£3.25), filled baked potatoes (from £3.25), ploughman's (£3.75) and daily specials such as fruited game casserole (£5.50), guinea fowl in calvados (£6.95), poached salmon with prawns (£7), grilled red sea bream fillet (£7.50), and teriyaki steak (£7.95); families are usually directed to a modern no-smoking restaurant extension. Gales BBB, Best, HSB, Winter Brew, and a guest beer on handpump, several wines by the glass, and over 50 malt whiskies; efficient, friendly service. Fruit machine, piped music, and they run cricket and football teams. Popular with walkers and riders, the pub is fairly close to the extensive Queen Elizabeth Country Park and about half a mile down the lane from a growing Iron Age farm and settlement, and it's only about 20 minutes to the car ferry. *(Recommended by T Roger Lamble, Clive Gilbert, Eileen Akehurst, Penny and Peter Keevil, Theo Schofield, Jack Taylor)*

Gales ~ Managers Mick and Mary McGee ~ Real ale ~ Meals and snacks (not Sun evening) ~ (01705) 592246 ~ Children in restaurant ~ Open 11-3(2.30 in winter), 6-11; closed 25 Dec evening

Soup prices usually include a roll and butter.

CHERITON SU5828 Map 2

Flower Pots

Pub just off B3046 (main village road) towards Beauworth and Winchester; OS Sheet 185 map reference 581282

You can be sure of a warmly friendly welcome from the hard-working licensees in this bustling village local – and very good home-brewed real ales from their micro-brewery, the Cheriton Brewhouse. Very well priced and full of flavour, they offer Cheriton Best, Diggers Gold and Pots Ale. The two little rooms have a really pleasant atmosphere that readers appreciate very much. The quiet and comfortable one on the left has pictures of hounds and ploughmen on its striped wallpaper, bunches of flowers, and a horse and foal and other ornaments on the mantlepiece over a small log fire. Behind the servery there's disused copper filtering equipment, and lots of hanging gin-traps, drag-hooks, scaleyards and other ironwork. Good, popular bar food (with prices unchanged since last year) includes sandwiches (from £1.50, toasted from £1.75), filled jacket potatoes (from £2.50), ploughman's (from £2.75), chilli (£3.50) and beef stew (£3.75); good efficient service. Darts in the neat plain public bar (where there's a covered well), also cribbage, shove-ha'penny and dominoes; the family room has a TV, board games and colouring books. There are old-fashioned seats on the pretty front and back lawns – very useful in fine weather as they can quickly fill up inside. Near the site of one of the final battles of the Civil War, the pub was built in 1840 by the retired head gardener of nearby Avington Park, which explains the unusual name. *(Recommended by Simon Collett-Jones, Canon Kenneth Wills, D A Forsyth, Richard Houghton, Ann and Colin Hunt, Dono and Carol Leaman, Ron Shelton, Jack and Philip Paxton, Martin and Karen Wake, John and Chris Simpson, Nigel Clifton, Drs Ben and Caroline Maxwell, Lynn Sharpless, Bob Eardley, A R and B E Sayer, Phil and Sally Gorton)*

Own Brew ~ Licensees Patricia and Joanna Bartlett ~ Real ale ~ Meals and snacks (till 8.30 Sun evenings, not at all winter Sun evenings) ~ (01962) 771318 ~ Children in family room ~ Open 11.30-2.30, 6-11 ~ Bedrooms: £23B/£42B

CRAWLEY SU4234 Map 2

Fox & Hounds

Village signposted from A272 Winchester—Stockbridge and B3420 Winchester—Andover

This is one of the most striking buildings in a village of fine houses – each timbered upper storey successively juts further out, with lots of pegged structural timbers in the neat brickwork (especially around the latticed windows), and elaborately carved steep gable-ends. The scrupulous workmanship continues inside, with oak parquet, latticed windows, and an elegant black timber arch in the small lounge, and neatly panelled upholstered wall benches around the tables of the beamed main bar. There are fires in both spotlessly maintained rooms – real logs in the lounge, log-effect gas in the other. Good, well presented bar food includes sandwiches, home-made soups (£2.45), mushrooms in garlic butter (£3.75), home-made trout and smoked mackerel pâté (£3.95), mixed bean casserole or spicy cheese and lentil loaf with tangy tomato sauce (£5.95), home-made game and Guinness pie or chicken and asparagus pancake au gratin (£6.50), fresh dressed Poole Bay crab (£6.75), fresh local trout with prawns and mushrooms flamed in brandy (£6.95), and rump steak (£8.95); friendly, careful service. Well kept Gales BBB and Wadworths 6X on handpump. *(Recommended by Phyl and Jack Street, Tim Espley, Roger Byrne, Howard Allen, Philip and Trisha Ferris, Wayne Brindle, J N Tyler, Peter and Susan Maguire, Professor H G Allen, Guy Consterdine, Julia Stone)*

Free house ~ Licensees Doreen and Luis Sanz-Diez ~ Real ale ~ Meals and snacks ~ Restaurant (not Sun evening) ~ (01962) 776285 ~ Children in eating area of bar and in restaurant ~ Open 11.30-2.30(3 Sat), 6.30-11 ~ Bedrooms: £40B/£55B

If we know a pub has a no-smoking area, we say so.

DROXFORD SU6018 Map 2

White Horse

4 miles along A32 from Wickham

Readers really enjoy this rambling 16th-c coaching inn and it's run by a particularly friendly and attentive family. The atmospheric lounge bar is made up of a series of small intimate rooms with attractive furnishings, low beams, bow windows, alcoves and log fires, while the public bar is larger and more straightforward: cribbage, dominoes, pool, shove ha'penny, table football and CD juke box. Well presented, tasty food includes good sandwiches (from £1.60; toasties 25p extra; hot crusty french sticks £2.55), home-made soup (£2), green-lipped mussels (£2.95), ploughman's (from £3.25), Portuguese sardines in garlic butter (£3.95), vegetable curry (£4.95), gammon and egg (£5.35), a brace of locally smoked quail (£5.65), popular steak, mushroom and Guinness pie (£7.95), steaks (from £9.15), and puddings; children's menu (from £1.95). The restaurant is no smoking. Well kept Arundel Gold, Badger Tanglefoot, Butcombe Bitter, Shepherd Neame Spitfire, and Wadworths 6X on handpump, and country wines; prompt professional service. One of the cubicles in the gents' overlooks an illuminated well. There are tables in a secluded flower-filled courtyard comfortably sheltered by the building's back wings. *(Recommended by N Matthews, Clarence Shettlesworth, Barry and Anne, Simon Collett-Jones, Sue Ridout, Mr and Mrs R J Foreman, Lynn Sharpless, Bob Eardley, T W Fleckney, Anne and Colin Hunt, Ian Phillips, John and Joan Nash, Eileen Akehurst, Lt Col E H F Sawbridge, Professor H G Allen, Peter and Audrey Dowsett, Mayur Shah, G B Longden, B S Bowden, I E and C A Prosser, Betty Laker)*

Free house ~ Licensee Sidney Higgins ~ Real ale ~ Meals and snacks (till 9.45) ~ Restaurant ~ (01489) 877490 ~ Children in family room and restaurant ~ Open 11-3, 6-11; closed 25 Dec ~ Bedrooms: £25(£40B)/£35(£50B)

DUMMER SU5846 Map 2

Queen

Half a mile from M3, junction 7; take Dummer slip road

Handy for travellers on the M3, this tiled white cottage is set on a peaceful village lane. It's the popular food that most customers are aiming for: home-made soup (£2.50), a marvellous range of sandwiches (from £2.50), quite a few filled baked potatoes (from £3.95), good cod in their own beer batter (£5.95 medium, £8.95 large), seven types of burger (from £6.50), lasagne (£6.95), steak and kidney pudding (£9.95), Scotch Angus steaks (from £11.95), daily specials, puddings, and roast Sunday lunch (from £6.95); notably cheery and friendly service. The bar is open-plan, but has a pleasantly alcovey feel, with a liberal use of timbered brick and plaster partition walls, as well as beams and joists and an open fire. There are built-in padded seats, cushioned spindleback chairs and stools around the tables on the dark blue patterned carpet, and pictures of queens, old photographs, small steeplechase prints and advertisements. Well kept Courage Best and Directors and Fullers London Pride on handpump; fruit machine in one corner, cribbage, and well reproduced pop music. Picnic tables under cocktail parasols on the terrace and in a neat little sheltered back garden. *(Recommended by Guy Consterdine, Kevin and Tracey Stephens, Gary Roberts, Ann Stubbs, J S M Sheldon, Tina and David Woods-Taylor, KC, Dr and Mrs A K Clarke, Patrick Clancy, Chris Warne, Tony and Wynne Gifford, John Evans)*

Courage ~ Lease: John and Jocelyn Holland ~ Real ale ~ Meals and snacks (till 10) ~ Restaurant ~ (01256) 397367 ~ Children in eating area of bar ~ Open 11-3.30, 5.30-11

If you enjoy your visit to a pub, please tell the publican. They work extraordinarily long hours, and when people show their appreciation it makes it all seem worth while.

IBSLEY SU1509 Map 2

Old Beams

A338 Ringwood—Salisbury

This much extended dining pub is immensely popular for its quickly and efficiently served bar food. From a very wide choice, there might be an appetising cold buffet (from £5.90) as well as sandwiches (from £1.90), curries (£4.70), braised oxtail (£5.60), venison in red wine, pork Normandie or beef bourguignon (all £6.50), char-grilled Scotch steaks (£8.50), and Dover sole (£11.95); they announce when food is ready over an intercom. Well kept Eldridge Pope Royal Oak, Gales HSB, Gibbs Mew Bishops Tipple, Ringwood Best and Old Thumper, Wadworths 6X, and a guest beer on handpump, and country wines. The main room is divided by wooden panelling and a canopied log-effect gas fire, and there are lots of varnished wooden tables and country-kitchen chairs under the appropriately aged oak beams; the conservatory is a great success. Part of the eating area and half the restaurant are no smoking. *(Recommended by P Gilbe, Mr and Mrs B Hobden, P J Caunt, Howard Clutterbuck, Ian Phillips, Jack and Philip Paxton, Wayne Brindle, Stephen and Anna Oxley, Colin Barnett, Ruth Trott, John Watson, RH, Mr and Mrs Hawkins, S Eldridge, D Baker, Basil J S Minson, Dr Gerald W Barnett)*

Free house ~ Licensees R Major and C Newell ~ Real ale ~ Meals and snacks (till 10) ~ Restaurant (not Sun evening) ~ (01425) 473387 ~ Children in eating area, restaurant and family room ~ Open 11-3, 6-11

LANGSTONE SU7105 Map 2

Royal Oak

High Street; last turn left off A3023 (confusingly called A324 on some signs) before Hayling Island bridge

Charmingly placed on the edge of a landlocked natural harbour, this pretty old pub has fine views from the garden (where there's a pets' corner) and from the seats in the bow windows of the bar. At high tide swans come right up to here, much as they must have done in the days when it was a landing point for the 18th-c Langstone Gang, a notorious group of smugglers. The spacious and atmospheric flagstoned bar is simply furnished with windsor chairs around old wooden tables on the wooden parquet and ancient flagstones, and two open fires in winter. Good, straightforward bar food includes filled rolls (from £2.85), mushrooms with wine and cheese sauce (£2.95), garlic prawns (£3.85), ploughman's (from £4.25), lasagne (£5.25), steak and kidney pie (£5.85), and local fish (from £5.95). Well kept Boddingtons, Flowers Original, Gales HSB, and Whitbreads Pompey Royal and Fuggles on handpump; Bulmer's cider; bar billiards, cribbage. *(Recommended by Colin and Ann Hunt, Christopher Perry, Brenda and Jim Langley, Ted Burden, Viv Middlebrook, Richard and Maria Gillespie, David Eberlin, Wayne Brindle, A Craig, J E Hilditch, Ian Phillips)*

Whitbreads ~ Manager Stuart Warren ~ Real ale ~ Meals and snacks (12-9.30) ~ (01705) 483125 ~ Children in eating area of bar and in restaurant ~ Parking at all close may be very difficult ~ Open 11-11; closed evening 25 Dec

LOCKS HEATH SU5006 Map 2

Jolly Farmer

2½ miles from M27 junction 9; A27 towards Bursledon, left into Locks Rd, at end T-junction right into Warsash Rd then left at hire shop into Fleet End Rd; OS Sheet 196 map reference 509062

A happy surprise in this area of largely modern development, this thriving old inn has lots of character and good value well presented food. The small bar on the right and extensive series of softly lit rooms on the left have nice old scrubbed tables, cushioned oak pews and smaller chairs; their ochre walls and beams are hung with a veritable forest of country bric-a-brac, racing prints, Victorian engravings and so on, making for a very cosy feeling that's amplified by the coal-effect gas fires. Though it all feels attractively pubby, everyone's really here to eat. A wide choice of quickly served bar food includes filled baps (from £1.95, steak £4.25), soup (£2.95), ploughman's or seafood sandwiches (from £3.25), spicy crisped vegetables (£4.25), home-baked ham and eggs or steak and kidney pie (£5.45) and specials such as moules marinières (£4.95), whole plaice or mixed meat salad (£5.95), ribeye steak (£6.95) and lobster (£16.95); a three-course Sunday lunch is £9.25. One of the two restaurants is no smoking. Well kept Boddingtons, Flowers Original and Gales HSB on handpump, neat friendly staff, silenced fruit machine. There are tables under cocktail parasols on two sheltered terraces, and as they are very family friendly a good play area with a wendyhouse, trampoline, swings and a seesaw. *(Recommended by Alan Reid, Mrs P McFarlane, Peter and Audrey Dowsett, C H and P Stride, M J Inskip, Colin and Ann Hunt, N Matthews)*

Free house ~ Licensees Martin and Cilla O'Grady ~ Real ale ~ Meals and snacks (11.45-2.30, 6-10.15) ~ Restaurant ~ (01489) 572500 ~ Children welcome ~ Open 10.30-3, 5-11(Thurs, Fri, Sat 10.30-11) ~ Bedrooms: £35S/£45S

LYMINGTON SZ3194 Map 2

Chequers 🍷

¾ mile down Ridgeway Lane; marked as dead end just south of A337 roundabout in Pennington W of Lymington, by White Hart; please note this pub was listed under Pennington in some previous editions

The bar in this pleasantly tucked away yachtsmen's local is simple but stylish, and has polished floorboards and crisp quarry-tiles, a cannon by the fireplace, attractive local landscapes and townscapes above the green dado, and plain chairs and wall pews around wooden or cast-iron-framed tables. A good range of home-made bar food includes lunchtime filled french sticks (from £1.75), soup (£2.50), garlic bread with cheese and prawns or ploughman's (£3.95), and chilli con carne (£4.25), with changing daily specials such as moules marinières, stilton, bacon and walnut salad or ham and leek bake au gratin (£3.50-£4.50), a vegetarian and a pasta dish, fresh fish like haddock mornay, grilled whole plaice, monkfish, halibut or turbot (from £6.50), roast rack of lamb (£7.50), half roast duck with soy sauce and honey (£8.50), steaks (from £8.95), and puddings. Four well kept real ales such as Bass, Flowers Original, Greene King Abbot, Morlands Old Speckled Hen, Whitbreads Strong Country, and Wadworths 6X on handpump, a good value, thoughtful wine list, and quite a few golden rums – mostly from the Caribbean. Very friendly service; well chosen and reproduced piped pop music, cribbage, dominoes and darts. There are picnic tables out in its neat sheltered garden, with teak tables on a terrace below, and more tables in an inner courtyard; there may be barbecues out here in summer. *(Recommended by D Marsh, D Deas, Bernard Phillips, E G Parish, Martin, Jane, Simon and Laura Bailey, W K Struthers; more reports please)*

Whitbreads ~ Lease: Michael and Maggie Jamieson ~ Real ale ~ Meals and snacks (till 10) ~ Restaurant ~ (01590) 673415 ~ Well behaved children welcome away from bar ~ Open 11-3, 6-11; closed 25 Dec

MATTINGLEY SU7357 Map 2

Leather Bottle

3 miles from M3, junction 5; in Hook, turn right-and-left on to B3349 Reading Road (former A32)

This cosy brick and tiled pub is a popular place all year. In summer, there are lots of tubs and baskets of bright flowers, and wisteria, honeysuckle and roses both at the front and in the attractive tree-sheltered garden, and in winter there are roaring log fires in the inglenook fireplaces. The busy beamed main bar is friendly and relaxed, and has brocaded built-in wall seats, little curved low backed wooden chairs, some sabres on the cream wall, a ticking metal clock over one of the fireplaces, and a good local atmosphere. At the back is the characterful cottagey second bar with lots of black beams, an antique clock, country pictures on the walls (some stripped to brick), lantern lighting, sturdy inlaid tables with seats, and a red carpet on bare floorboards. Generous helpings of bar food include sandwiches (from £1.80, toasted ham, mushroom and egg £3.50, steak £4.75), soup (£2.30), ploughman's (from £3.95), good sausages (£5.50), ham off the bone with eggs and chips (£5.80), vegetable balti (£6.20), lasagne (£6.90), salmon, cod and mushroom pie (£7.20), steaks (from £12.50), and puddings like treacle tart or lemon brûlée (from £2.50). Well kept Courage Best and Directors and guest beers such as Badger Tanglefoot, Gales HSB, Hampshire King Alfred's, Worldham Barbarian Bitter, and Wychwood Dogs Bollocks on handpump or tapped from the cask; prompt friendly service; fruit machine. *(Recommended by T Roger Lamble, Thomas Nott, TBB, Clive Gilbert, David Warrellow, Theo Schofield, J N Tyler, D A Edwards, Chris Warne, KC)*

Courage ~ Lease: Richard and Pauline Moore ~ Real ale ~ Meals and snacks (till 10) ~ (01734) 326371 ~ Children welcome ~ Open 11-2.30, 6-11

MICHELDEVER SU5142 Map 2

Dever Arms 🍷

Village signposted off A33 N of Winchester

Since buying it from Whitbreads, the Pennys have transformed this into a very civilised country pub, with interesting food and excellent drinks. The calm and simply decorated bar has beams, chintzy curtains, heavy tables and good solid seats – a nice cushioned panelled oak settle and a couple of long dark pews as well as wheelback chairs; there is a woodburning stove at each end, and a fresh and attractive no-smoking area with lighter-coloured furniture opens off. Apart from a few regular dishes such as soup (£2.25), mushrooms with smoky bacon (£2.95), lunchtime ploughman's (£4.25), vegetarian kebabs with lime sauce and lemon rice (£5.80) and lamb casserole with butter beans (£6.95), most of the generously served food changes from day to day, and might include rigatoni with roasted vegetables or trout and watercress fishcake (£3.95), venison sausages with red cabbage (£4.25), pork, chicken and apricot home-raised pie (£4.95) and gammon served in more adventurous ways than usual (£6.95), with winter game. Well kept Badger Best, Gales HSB, Hop Back Summer Lightning, Maclays Wallace, Pots (from the Flower Pots at Cheriton) and Ringwood Best on handpump; decent interesting wines by the glass and bottle; very good quietly friendly and attentive service; bar billiards and darts up at one end, well chosen and reproduced piped music. There are white cast-iron tables under cocktail parasols on a small sheltered back terrace, and some more widely spaced picnic tables and a play area on the edge of a big cricket green behind. *(Recommended by Mr and Mrs Stewart, Mrs J I Conville, A W Dickinson, Mike Hayes, Joan and John Calvert, George Rodger, Mr and Mrs Hargreaves)*

Free house ~ Licensees Mike and Violet Penny ~ Real ale ~ Meals and snacks (12-2, 7-10; not Sun eve) ~ Restaurant ~ (01962) 774339 ~ Children in family room or eating area of bar ~ Open 11.30-3, 6-11

OVINGTON SU5531 Map 2

Bush ★ 🍷

Village signposted from A31 on Winchester side of Alresford

A firm favourite with many readers, this charming and quietly upmarket little cottage is tucked away down a leafy lane with lots of seats by the River Itchen, and more on a tree-sheltered pergola dining terrace with a good-sized fountain pool. We like it best though on chilly winter weekdays when the atmosphere is undisturbed by lots of people, and the low-ceilinged bar has a warmly cosy feel that immediately makes you feel at home. There's a roaring fire on one side with an antique solid fuel stove opposite, as well as cushioned high-backed settles, elm tables with pews and kitchen chairs, and masses of old pictures in heavy gilt frames on the green walls. Good home-made bar food includes sandwiches (from £1.95), ploughman's (£3.95), avocado and prawn mousseline or marinated herrings (£4.95), spicy vegetable fritter with a sweet and sour sauce or fried chicken (£5.95), grilled local trout or mussels (£6.95), tiger prawns in filo (£7.25), steaks (£9.75), and puddings (£2.50). Service is friendly and prompt, even when it's really busy. Well kept Flowers Original, Gibbs Mew Deacon, Ringwood Fortyniner, Wadworths 6X and Whitbreads Strong Country on handpump; a good choice of wines, country wines, and farm cider. It's handy for the A31, and there are nice walks nearby. *(Recommended by John and Christine Simpson, Mike Fitzgerald, Canon Kenneth Wills, John Fahy, J S M Sheldon, Gwen and Peter Andrews, Martin and Karen Wake, Joan and John Calvert, David Rule, A W Dickinson, Mike Hayes, Clive Gilbert, N Matthews, Derek and Margaret Underwood, James Macrae, Iain McBride, Samantha Hawkins, BKA, Mr and Mrs Craig, David Rule, John Le Sage, Tom Espley, Martin and Pauline Richardson, Roy Smylie, KCW, Jenny and Brian Seller, J L Hall, Mike Davies)*

Free house ~ Licensees Geoff and Sue Draper and Patrick Maguire ~ Real ale ~ Meals and snacks ~ Evening restaurant (not Sun) ~ (01962) 732764 ~ Nearby parking may be difficult ~ Children in eating area of bar ~ Open 11-2.30, 6-11

nr PETERSFIELD SU7423 Map 2

White Horse ★ ★

Priors Dean – but don't follow Priors Dean signposts: simplest route is from Petersfield, leaving centre on A272 towards Winchester, take right turn at roundabout after level crossing, towards Steep, and keep on for four miles or so, up on to the downs, passing another pub on your right (and not turning off into Steep there); at last, at crossroads signposted East Tisted/Privett, turn right towards East Tisted, then almost at once turn right on to second gravel track (the first just goes into a field); there's no inn sign; alternatively, from A32 5 miles S of Alton, take road by bus lay-by signposted Steep, then, after 1¾ miles, turn off as above – though obviously left this time – at East Tisted/Privett crossroads; OS Sheet 197 coming from Petersfield (Sheet 186 is better the other way), map reference 715290

This marvellous old farmhouse is now tied to Gales but they have asked the long-serving landlord (he's been here 22 years) to keep on running it very much as before. It owes a great deal to Jack Eddlestone – indeed, on days when he's not there the place doesn't seem so special. But for many people this is all a traditional country pub should be and the two charming and highly idiosyncratic parlour rooms are full of a relaxing mix of furnishings and bric-a-brac: old pictures, farm tools, drop-leaf tables, oak settles, rugs, stuffed antelope heads, longcase clock, and a fireside rocking-chair to name a few. An excellent and well-priced range of a dozen or so beers on handpump includes the very strong No Name Bitter and Strong, as well as Ballards Best, Gales BBB, Best and HSB, King & Barnes Sussex Bitter and Sussex Mild, Ringwood Fortyniner, Theakstons Old Peculier, and guest beers; country wines, some sparkling, are tapped from small china kegs. Shove-ha'penny, dominoes, cribbage. Bar food generally includes sandwiches, good thick soup (£2.10, winter only, as it's done overnight on the Aga), ploughman's (from £3.10), leek and lentil pie (£3.50), cottage or fisherman's pie (£3.95), and steak and kidney pudding (£4.50). They've usually got local eggs for sale, including organic free range ones, and in season pheasants too. There are of course times (not always predictable, with Sundays – even in winter – often busier than Saturdays) when the place does get packed. Rustic seats (which include chunks of tree-trunk) and a terrace outside; as this is one of the highest spots in the county it can be quite breezy. A nearby field has caravan facilities, and is regularly used for pony club meetings – as well as a landing place for the odd Tiger Moth plane or hot-air balloon. If trying to find it for the first time, keep your eyes skinned – not for nothing is this known as the Pub With No Name. No children. *(Recommended by Kevin and Tracey Stephens, Martin and Penny Fletcher, Christopher Turner, T W Fleckney, F C Johnston, Jack and Philip Paxton, Adrian Zambardino, Debbie Chaplin, David Craine, Ann Reeder, Roger and Valerie Hill, Canon Kenneth Wills, Michael J Boniface, Colin and Ann Hunt, Ian Phillips, E B Davies, John and Christine Simpson, Julie Munday, Martin Robinson, Steve Tasker, Wayne Brindle, David and*

Michelle Hedges, Lynn Sharpless, Bob Eardley, J S M Sheldon, R J Walden, Peter and Lynn Brueton, Jason Caulkin, KCW, James Nunns, Mark and Diane Grist, Owen Upton)

Gales ~ Manager Jack Eddleston ~ Real ale ~ Meals and snacks (not Sun lunchtime) ~ (01420) 588387 ~ Open 11-2.30(3 Sat), 6-11

PILLEY SZ3298 Map 2

Fleur de Lys

Village signposted off A337 Brockenhurst—Lymington

This year, a new marquee with heating and lighting by oil lamps and candles has been installed around the 14th-c wishing well, and there are seats in the garden with its waterfall and dovecote; on Friday and Saturday evenings (weather permitting) they barbecue arournd 10 choices of fresh fish. In the entrance-way is a list of landlords that goes back to 1498 – but there's evidence that an inn of some sort existed here in Norman times, making this the oldest pub in the New Forest. The characterful lounge bar has heavy beams, lots of bric-a-brac and a huge inglenook log fire. Bar food (served all day) includes sandwiches, soup (£2.45), ploughman's (£3.95), venison and wild boar sausages or giant mushrooms filled with stilton and garlic (£4.25), curry (£6.50), nut roast (£6.65), grilled swordfish steak (£7.95), breast of barbary duck in fruits of the forest and grand marnier sauce (£9.75), daily specials such as ham and egg (£5.75), fresh mackerel (£7.25), veal and apricots in brandy (£7.45), and black bream (£9.95), afternoon cream tea (£3.45), and puddings (from £2.65). Well kept Boddingtons, Brakspears, Flowers Original, Marstons Pedigree, Morlands Old Speckled Hen, and Whitbreads Castle Eden on handpump, country wines, and farm ciders. *(Recommended by Dave Braisted, Clive Gilbert, Mr and Mrs Craig, D Marsh, R C Hopton, Mr and Mrs M F Norton, James House, Stephen and Anna Oxley, Lynn Sharpless, Bob Eardley, Andrew Shore, Michael Leigh, Mrs P MacFarlane, Stephen Oxley, Dr M Onton, Julia Stone)*

Whitbreads ~ Lease: Craig Smallwood ~ Real ale ~ Meals and snacks ~ Restaurant ~ (01590) 672158 ~ Children welcome ~ Open 11-11 ~ One bedroom: /£60B

PORTSMOUTH SZ6501 Map 2

Still & West

Bath Square; follow A3 and Isle of Wight Ferry signs to Old Portsmouth water's edge

From the upstairs restaurant or on the terrace, the views of the boats and ships fighting the strong tides in the very narrow mouth of Portsmouth harbour are breathtaking – they seem almost within touching distance. It's a friendly, cheerful place and the habitual haunt of the clergy who attend diocesan meetings at the cathedral. The bar is comfortably decorated in nautical style, ship models, an early brass submarine periscope and so forth, and has very well kept Gales BBB and HSB tapped from the cask, with a guest like Everards Tiger, Morlands Old Speckled Hen or Morrells Varsity, along with some aged whiskies and country wines. Popular bar food includes traditional fish and chips (wrapped in newspaper ready to take away if you want, £2.95), a proper ploughman's (£3.95) and around 10-15 cheeses from around the world. A wider range of meals in the upstairs restaurant features plenty of fresh fish dishes like haddock gratinée (£5.50) or halibut veronique (£7.95). Parking can be quite difficult. The pub is quite near to HMS *Victory*, and can get busy on fine days. *(Recommended by Ann and Colin Hunt, M J D Inskip, Thomas Nott, John Fahy, Canon Kenneth Wills, D Grzelka, Alan Bunt)*

Gales ~ Managers Mick and Lynn Finnerty ~ Real ale ~ Meals and snacks ~ Restaurant ~ (01705) 821567 Children welcome ~ Live music Sun evening ~ Open 11-11

Pubs with outstanding views are listed at the back of the book.

ROCKBOURNE SU1118 Map 2

Rose & Thistle 🍷

Village signposted from B3078 Fordingbridge—Cranborne

In a charming village with the excavated remains of a Roman villa, this attractive thatched 17th-c pub with its smartly civilised atmosphere is mainly popular for its very good bar food. At lunchtime this might include home-made soup (£2.45), ploughman's (from £4.25), locally made sausages (£4.45), tagliatelle carbonara (£5.75), and specials like broccoli and cheese pancake with almond topping (£3.95), liver and bacon with red wine and onion gravy (£5.45), rabbit casserole or steak and kidney pie (£5.95), or fried fillet of lemon sole (£7.95), and evening specials such as lamb steak with an orange and mint sauce (£8.95), monkfish wrapped in bacon and creamy prawn sauce (£9.45) or medallions of beef fillet with a stilton and port sauce (£11.45); lovely puddings; friendly service. Well kept Adnams Broadside, Courage Best, Fullers London Pride, Hopback Summer Lightning, and Wadworths 6X on handpump, with a good range of wines from around the world, some by the glass. The public bar has tables arranged like booths, old engravings, sparkling brass and a good log fire, as well as new furnishings such as lovely polished tables and carved benches; one small area is no smoking; darts, shove ha'penny, and dominoes. There are tables by a thatched dovecot in the neat front garden. *(Recommended by Rob Holt, J O Jonkler, Dave Braisted, Jerry and Alison Oakes, Jason Caulkin, J H L Davis)*

Free house ~ Licensee Tim Norfolk ~ Real ale ~ Meals and snacks ~ Restaurant (not Sun evening) ~ (01725) 518236 ~ Children in eating area of bar and in restaurant (until 9) ~ Open 11-3, 6-11; winter 12-3, 7-10.30

ROTHERWICK SU7156 Map 2

Coach & Horses ☕

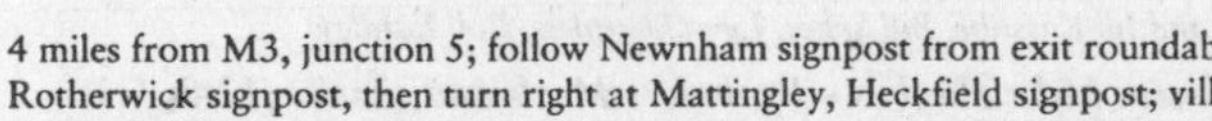

4 miles from M3, junction 5; follow Newnham signpost from exit roundabout, then Rotherwick signpost, then turn right at Mattingley, Heckfield signpost; village also signposted from A32 N of Hook

Friendly new licensees have taken over this creeper-covered 16th-c pub. The two small beamed front rooms each has a stripped brick open fireplace, oak chairs and other interesting furniture, and a fine assortment of attractive pictures; one is tiled, the other flagstoned, and one is no smoking. Good bar food now includes sandwiches, quorn stir-fry or mushroom stroganoff (£5.25), smashing rack of lamb and nice grilled trout, boozy chilli pie (£5.95), chicken piri-piri (£6.25), and whole baby lemon sole (£7.25). Well kept real ales on handpump dispensed at the servery in the parquet-floored inner area include Badger Best, Hard Tackle and Tanglefoot, Gribble Black Adder and Wadworths 6X, and Inch's cider; cribbage, dominoes, backgammon, connect four and a Sunday night quiz. In summer, there are tubs and baskets of flowers, and rustic seats and picnic tables under cocktail parasols. *(Recommended by Gary Roberts, Ann Stubbs, David Wallington, KC, Clive Gilbert, J S M Sheldon, Martin Jones, Chris Warne, Derek and Sylvia Stephenson, D A Edwards, D Cox, Chris and Anne Fluck)*

Badger ~ Managers Sean and Christine McAusland ~ Real ale ~ Meals and snacks (till 10, 9.30 Sun) ~ Restaurant ~ (01256) 762542 ~ Children welcome ~ Open 11-11

SOPLEY SZ1597 Map 2

Woolpack

B3347 N of Christchurch; village signposted off A338 N of Bournemouth

Although quite a number of pubs have live music, few have a pianist every night – much appreciated by readers. It's a friendly place and the rambling low-beamed open-plan bar has a good local atmosphere, red leatherette wall seats and simple wooden chairs around heavy rustic tables, and has both a woodburning stove and a small black kitchen range; there's also a conservatory. Good bar food includes filled rolls, home-made soup (£2.50), venison sausages or good mushroom stroganoff (£4.95), lasagne (£5.25), king prawns in garlic, chilli and coriander (£5.50), Thai chicken curry or gammon and egg (£5.95), seafood pie with muscadet (£6.25), and sirloin steak (£9.95). Well kept Flowers Original and Ringwood Best on handpump; piped music. The garden has seats from which you can watch the ducks dabbling about on the little chalk stream under the weeping willows, by the little bridge. No children. ***(Recommended by J M T Morris, Jerry and Alison Oakes, WHBM, Anna and Steven Oxley, Andy and Jill Kassube)***

Whitbreads ~ Lease: Barbara and Dick Goemaat ~ Real ale ~ Meals and snacks ~ (01425) 672252 ~ Pianist every night ~ Open 11-11

SOUTHSEA SZ6498 Map 2

Wine Vaults £

Albert Rd, opp Kings Theatre

Mr Hughes has now opened his own brewery in this very simple place with Spikes Impaled Ale and Stingor on handpump, as well as guests such as Brewery-on-Sea Spinnaker Bitter, Hampshire King Alfred's, Hop Back Summer Lightning, and Ringwood Old Thumper; they hold beer festivals in May and November with 70 different ales. The bar, usually full of students, has wood-panelled walls, a wooden floor, Wild West saloon-type swing doors, and an easy-going, chatty feel; pool, table football and piped music. Mainly straightforward but very well priced bar food comes in big helpings, from a range that includes sandwiches, soup, and spicy cashew nut casserole (£3.25) and chicken and spinach lasagne (£3.65). The one-eyed black labrador is called Ziggy. No children but dogs are welcome. ***(Recommended by J A Snell, Clive Gilbert, Ann and Colin Hunt, Graham Brooks, Sue Anderson, Phil Copleston, John Beeken, Andy and Jill Kassube, Bill Sykes, Lynn Sharpless, Bob Eardley)***

Own brew ~ Licensee Mike Hughes ~ Real ale ~ Meals and snacks (12-2, 5.30-9.30, 9 weekends) ~ (01705) 864712 ~ Open 11.30-3, 5.30-11; 11.30-11 Fri/Sat

SPARSHOLT SU4331 Map 2

Plough

Village signposted off A272 a little W of Winchester

An innovative new chef is now doing the cooking here and dishes tend to change on a daily basis: home-made soup (£1.95), sandwiches (from £2.60), ploughman's (from £3.10), mushroom and fresh tarragon tagliatelle (£3.95), tuna fish and leek bake (£4.25), Greek spiced meatloaf with olives and a tomato and onion sauce (£4.50), spiced indonesian chicken and vegetable hot pot or wild boar sausages with black pudding and honey and mustard sauce (£4.75), daily specials such as chicken liver and sweet pepper pâté (£2.95), stuffed aubergines with tabbouleh (£6.95), smoked loin of bacon with mustard sauce (£7.25), baked lamb steak and mint crust (£8.25), and Scotch fillet steak with green peppercorn sauce (£11.50); children's dishes (£2.75). Well kept Wadworths IPA and 6X and a guest beer changing fortnightly from countrywide independent breweries on handpump, and a good choice of wines with several by the glass. The extended main bar area has plenty of tables and comfortable seats, and is a pleasant and airy mix of cream paintwork, stripped brick and some panelling; there's a no-smoking area. The side bar has bar billiards, shove-ha'penny, cribbage, and dominoes. There are tables outside, with a climbing frame, and even donkeys and hens. ***(Recommended by Ian Phillips, Howard Allen, D Waters, Lynn Sharpless, Bob Eardley, John and Joy Winterbottom, Alan and Julie Wear)***

Wadworths ~ Tenant Sarah Hinman ~ Real ale ~ Meals and snacks (not Sun evening) ~ (01962) 776353 ~ Well behaved children allowed until 9 ~ Informal music Fri evening ~ Open 11-2.30(3 Sat), 6.30-11; closed evenings 25 Dec/1 Jan

STEEP SU7425 Map 2

Harrow

Take Midhurst exit from Petersfield bypass, at exit roundabout first left towards Midhurst, then first turning on left opposite garage, and left again at Sheet church; follow over motorway bridge to pub

A visit here is like going back 100 years. It's a charmingly old-fashioned family-run place with hops and dried flowers hanging from the beams in the little public bar – as well as a tiled floor, built-in wall benches around scrubbed deal tables, a good log fire in the big inglenook, stripped pine wallboards, and dominoes. Enormous helpings of good simple home cooked bar food include home-made scotch eggs (£1.40), sandwiches (home-cooked ham £2.50), excellent soups overflowing from old-fashioned bowls, huge ploughman's (£3.60), and various quiches, lasagne, cottage pie or cauliflower cheese (£5); puddings include a delicious treacle tart (£2.50). Well kept Boddingtons, Flowers Original and Whitbread Strong Country tapped from casks behind the counter, country wines, Bulmers cider; polite and friendly staff, even when under pressure. The big garden is left free-flowering so that goldfinches can collect thistle seeds from the grass, and there are lots of tables out here. The Petersfield bypass doesn't intrude on this idyll, though you will need to follow the directions above to find it. No children. *(Recommended by Lynn Sharpless, Bob Eardley, P Conrad Russell, Howard Bateman, Jack and Philip Paxton, Christopher Perry, Wendy Arnold, M W Jones, Nick Twining, B S Bowden, Mrs B M Spurr, Prof A N Black, Mark and Diane Grist, Julia Stone; R C Watkins)*

Free house ~ Licensees the McCutcheon family ~ Real ale ~ Meals and snacks ~ (01730) 262685 ~ Open 11-2.30, 6-11

STOCKBRIDGE SU3535 Map 2

Vine

High St (A30)

Handy for Test Valley walks, this bustling old coaching inn is popular for its good food, though without losing a distinctive pubby feel. The open-plan bar is comfortably pleasant, with an interesting combination of woodwork, brickwork and purple papered walls, a delft shelf of china and pewter, and old-gold velvet curtains. Bar food includes sandwiches, soup (£2.50), filled crêpes or seafood pasta (£3.25), ploughman's (£4.25), tasty beef in ale, lamb and apricot pie (£5.25), skate wings (£5.75), curry or gammon and egg (£5.95), steaks (from £6.95), puddings (£2.75), and Sunday roasts (£4.95); best to book, especially at weekends. Boddingtons, Flowers Original, Ringwood Best and a guest ale on handpump. Very good obliging service; piped music. *(Recommended by Wayne Brindle, Mr and Mrs Craig, M J D Inskip, Simon Collett-Jones, Ann and Colin Hunt, J F Burness, Dr and Mrs Nigel Holmes, Mr and Mrs G P Tobin, A R and B E Sayer, John Sanders, D A Edwards)*

Whitbreads ~ Tenant John Green ~ Meals and snacks ~ Restaurant ~ (01264) 810652 ~ Children in restaurant ~ Open 11-2.30(3 Sat), 6-11; maybe all day summer Sats ~ Bedrooms: £22.50/£37.50

TICHBORNE SU5630 Map 2

Tichborne Arms

Village signed off A31 just W of Alresford

After enjoying one of the good nearby walks (the friendly landlord can describe many to you), this attractive thatched pub is a fine place to relax over a drink or a meal. The food is very good and might include sandwiches (from £1.45; toasties from £1.95), home-made soup (£2), liver and bacon nibbles with a home-made dip (£2.25), ploughman's (from £3.30), baked potatoes with a fine range of fillings (from £3.50), daily specials such as rabbit crockpot (£4.50), bolognaise pancakes

(£4.75) or steak, ale and stilton pie (£5.75), and puddings like rhubarb crumble and sticky toffee pudding (£2). The comfortable, square-panelled room on the right has pictures and documents on the walls recalling the bizarre Tichborne Case, when a mystery man from Australia claimed fraudulently to be the heir to this estate, as well as a log fire in an attractive stone fireplace, wheelback chairs and settles (one very long), and latticed windows with flowery curtains. On the left, a larger and livelier room, partly panelled and also carpeted, has sensibly placed darts, cribbage, shove-ha'penny, dominoes and a fruit machine; well kept Boddingtons, Flowers IPA, Wadworths 6X, and Whitbreads Fuggles tapped from the cask, and country wines; excellent friendly service. There are picnic tables outside in the big well kept garden. Dogs are welcome. No children. *(Recommended by Ann and Colin Hunt, Lynn Sharpless, Bob Eardley, Joan and John Calvert, G and M Stewart, JKW, Phil and Sally Gorton, Ron Shelton, Paul Adams, Ewa Sawicka, Martin and Karen Wake, J L Hall, Mayur Shah, Rita and Derrick Barrey, Julia Stone, P J Guy)*

Free house ~ Licensees Chris and Peter Byron ~ Real ale ~ Meals and snacks (12-1.45, 6.30-9.45) ~ (01962) 733760 ~ Open 11.30-2.30, 6-11

UPHAM SU5320 Map 2

Brushmakers Arms

Shoe Lane; village signposted from Winchester—Bishops Waltham downs road, and from B2177 (former A333)

The garden here has been extended to twice its previous size and is well stocked with mature shrubs and trees (it used to be a private garden), and there are picnic tables on a sheltered back terrace among lots of tubs of flowers, with more on the tidy tree-sheltered lawn. Inside, you can be sure of a friendly welcome, and the comfortable L-shaped bar is divided into two by a central brick chimney with a woodburning stove in the raised two-way fireplace; also, comfortably cushioned wall settles and chairs, a variety of tables including some in country-style stripped wood, a few beams in its low ceiling, and quite a collection of ethnic-looking brushes. Well kept Bass, Fullers London Pride, Ringwood Best, and a weekly guest beer on handpump, several malt whiskies, and Gales country wines. Good reasonably priced bar food includes sandwiches, mushroom and sweetcorn stroganoff (£3.95), leeks wrapped in ham with cheese sauce or pasta with chicken and dijon mustard (£4.25), braised beef in mustard sauce (£4.50), sirloin steak with boursin (£8.75); Sunday roasts (£4.95). Sensibly placed darts, dominoes, and cribbage; the friendly dog is called Rosie. There's not much parking nearby. *(Recommended by John and Chris Simpson, John and Joan Nash, N Matthews, Howard Allen, Colin and Ann Hunt, A R and B E Sayer, Lynn Sharpless, Bob Eardley)*

Free house ~ Licensees Sue and Andy Cobb ~ Real ale ~ Meals and snacks ~ (01489) 860231 ~ Children allowed away from bar ~ Open 11-2.30(3 Sat), 6-11

VERNHAM DEAN SU3456 Map 2

George

On the old coach road going NW from Hurstbourne Tarrant; follow Upton signpost from A343; or from A338 5 miles S of Hungerford follow Oxenwood signpost and keep on

Friendly new licensees have taken over this old timbered brick and flint pub. The neatly kept and rambling open-plan bar has beams, a lovely polished elm table, traditional black wall seats built into the panelled dado, some easy chairs, and a log fire in its big inglenook fireplace; the eating area is no smoking. Bar food now includes toasties (£2), corned beef hash (£3.80), bangers and mash (£4), smoked salmon, avocado and egg (£5.50), char-grilled steaks (£8.25), and puddings like treacle tart or sticky toffee pudding (£2.20). Well kept Marstons Best and Pedigree on handpump; darts, shove-ha'penny, dominoes and cribbage. There are seats in the pretty garden behind. *(Recommended by Joy and Paul Rundell, Gordon, Marjorie and David Lamb, Peter and Audrey Dowset, Mark Matthewman, Jack and Philip Paxton, Dr and Mrs A K*

Clarke, Colin and Ann Hunt, Lynn Sharpless, Bob Eardley, Prof A N Black, Brenda and Jim Langley, Alan and Julie Wear, I E and C A Prosser)

Marstons ~ Tenants Candy Lacy-Smith and Derek Pollard ~ Real ale ~ Meals and snacks (not Sun evening) ~ (01264) 737279 ~ Well behaved children in eating area of the bar ~ Open 11.30-2.30(3 Sat), 6-11; closed evening 25 Dec

WELL SU7646 Map 2

Chequers

5 miles W of Farnham; off A287 via Crondall, or A31 via Froyle and Lower Froyle (easier if longer than via Bentley); from A32 S of Odiham, go via Long Sutton; OS Sheet 186 map reference 761467

The snug rooms in this pleasant pub are full of alcoves, low beams, wooden pews and old stools, and GWR carriage lamps, and the panelled walls are hung with lots of 18th-c country-life prints, and old sepia photographs of locals enjoying a drink. Bar food includes bangers and mash (£4.75), chilli con carne or scrambled eggs with smoked salmon (£5.50), home-made game pie (£5.95), and dressed crab (£6.75). Well kept Boddingtons, Flowers Original, and Wadworths 6X on handpump. In the back garden are some chunky picnic tables, and at the front, there's a vine-covered front arbour. *(Recommended by Lynn Sharpless, Bob Eardley, Clive Gilbert, Martin and Karen Wake, James Macrae, John and Christine Simpson, Keith Widdowson, Julia Stone, J A Stein, Susan and John Douglas, Ian Phillips, Dr and Mrs R E S Tanner, A and A Dale)*

Free house ~ Licensee Rupert Fowler ~ Real ale ~ Meals and snacks (till 10) ~ Restaurant (not Sun) ~ (01256) 862605 ~ Children welcome ~ Open 11-3, 5.30-11

nr WHERWELL SU3839 Map 2

Mayfly 🍷

Testcombe; A3057 SE of Andover, between B3420 turn-off and Leckford where road crosses River Test; OS Sheet 185 map reference 382390

Sitting outside at the tables here and watching the trout rise in the River Test is a fine way to spend a warm summer lunchtime. The spacious, beamed and carpeted bar has fishing pictures and bric-a-brac on the cream walls above its dark wood dado, windsor chairs around lots of tables, two woodburning stoves, and bow windows overlooking the water; there's also a conservatory. Popular bar food includes a wide range of cheeses (around three dozen) served with fresh crusty wholemeal bread or home-made quiche (£3.25), (£3.70), smoked trout (£3.95), chicken tandoori (£4), and a selection of cold meats such as rare topside of beef (from £3.60); salads are an extra 70p per spoonful. In the winter they add more hot dishes such as braised oxtail or steak and vegetable pie. It does get very busy and there are queues at busy periods. Well kept Boddingtons, Flowers Original, Morlands Old Speckled Hen and Wadworths 6X on handpump, in winter sensibly kept under light blanket pressure; 12 wines by the glass and country wines; fruit machine and piped music. *(Recommended by Wayne Brindle, Barry A Lynch, P J Caunt, J R Whetton, Anne Parmenter, M J D Inskip, P Gillbe, Martin and Karen Wake, Ian Phillips, Clive Gilbert, L Grant, M Moore, A R and B E Sayer, C H and P Stride, R J Herd, Gill and Mike Cross, Mrs C Archer, Stephen and Jean Curtis, Professor H G Allen)*

Whitbreads ~ Managers Barry and Julie Lane ~ Real ale ~ Meals and snacks (12-9) ~ (01264) 860283 ~ Children welcome ~ Open 11-11

Ideas for a country day out? We list pubs in really attractive scenery at the back of the book – and there are separate lists for waterside pubs, ones with really good garden, and ones with lovely views.

WINCHESTER SU4829 Map 2

Wykeham Arms ★ ★

75 Kingsgate Street (Kingsgate Arch and College Street are now closed to traffic; there is access via Canon Street)

'A gem', 'the best pub I know' and 'simply superb' are just some of the accolades used by readers to describe this marvellous place. Rather smart and stylish, the series of busy rooms radiating from the central bar are furnished with 19th-c oak desks retired from nearby Winchester College (the inkwells imaginatively filled with fresh flowers), a redundant pew from the same source, kitchen chairs and candlelit deal tables and big windows with swagged paisley curtains; all sorts of collections are dotted around. A snug room at the back, known as the Watchmakers, is decorated with a set of Ronald Searle 'Winespeak' prints, a second one is panelled, and all of them have a log fire; several areas are no-smoking. Particularly good food at lunchtime might include good sandwiches, delicious soups like cream of celeriac (£2.25), spinach roulade with smoked ham and tarragon (£3.50), stilton and quince pâté (£3.65), ploughman's (from £3.95), seafood and leek pasta bake (£4.95), and Moroccan lamb meatballs with noodles or pork, sage and apple casserole (£5.25); in the evening they do meals such as beef, Guinness and onion casserole (£8.95), warm courgette and basil terrine (£9.50) or roast rack of Hampshire Down lamb glazed with a port wine jus (£11.25); puddings such as tipsy apricot trifle, lemon and ginger cake or walnut fudge tart (£2.95). Service is welcoming and friendly. There's an excellent seasonally-changing list of wines including over 22 by the glass and by the 250ml and 500ml carafe, several half-bottles, and helpful tasting notes. Also well kept Eldridge Pope Dorchester, Hardy and Royal Oak on handpump, and a number of cognacs and liqueurs. The Alternative Beverage list (an eclectic range of non-alcoholic drinks taking in Horlicks, Ovaltine and Bovril) is working well. There are tables on a covered back terrace, with more on a small but sheltered lawn. The lovely rooms are thoughtfully equipped, and residents have the use of a sauna. No children. *(Recommended by Jenny and Brian Seller, Lynn Sharpless, Bob Eardley, John Whiting, Prof J R Leigh, Linda and Brian Davis, R V Ford, Thomas Nott, Kim Redling, N Matthews, Kevin and Katherine Cripps, N W Neill, Caroline Kenyon, Wayne Brindle, Mike Hayes, Gwen and Peter Andrews, Gill and Mike Cross, Mr and Mrs A Craig, Julia Stone, Wim Kock, Willem-Jan Kock, Hans Chabot, Mayur Shah, K E Wohl, Brenda and Jim Langley, Phil and Sally Gorton, Ted Burden, Paula Harrison, Julia Stone, Mr and Mrs Stewart)*

Eldridge Pope ~ Tenants: Mr and Mrs Graeme Jameson ~ Real ale ~ Meals and snacks ~ Evening restaurant ~ (01962) 853834 ~ If the small car park is full local parking may be difficult – don't be tempted to block up Kingsgate Street itself ~ Open 11-11; closed 25 Dec ~ Bedrooms: £65B/£75B

Lucky Dip

Besides the fully inspected pubs, you might like to try these Lucky Dips recommended to us and described by readers (if you do, please send us reports):

☆ **Alresford** [The Soke, Broad St (extreme lower end); SU5832], *Globe*: Lovely view of 12th-c ponds from new patio doors and attractive garden (with ducks hoping for scraps); Courage-related ales with a guest such as Wadworths 6X, lots of decent wines by the glass, cheapish popular food, friendly staff, big open fire each end, uncluttered decor with quite a lot of local history; piped music, board games; open all day, nearby parking can be difficult *(N Matthews, J Muckelt, Mike Ledwith, R and P F Shelton, KCW, BKA, Martin and Karen Wake, Lynn Sharpless, Bob Eardley)*

Alresford [West St], *Bell*: Georgian coaching inn's relaxing bar recently enlarged to take in former dining room, modest new dining room, decent moderately priced food, well kept Ringwood Best and Old Thumper, good coffee, friendly efficient service, pleasant back courtyard; comfortable bedrooms *(Tony Gayfer, Colin and Ann Hunt, KCW)*

Alton [Church St; SU7139], *Eight Bells*: Very basic but comfortable local with good choice of beers *(Derek Patey)*; [The Butts], *French Horn*: Ushers dining pub with friendly atmosphere, well kept beers; skittle alley *(Richard Houghton)*

☆ **Ampfield** [off A31 Winchester—Romsey; SU4023], *White Horse*: Good value food but also a welcome for drinkers in comfortably done-up extended Whitbreads dining pub with period-effect furniture, log fire, well kept ales, decent wine, very pleasant manageress; good play area, pub backs on to golf course and village cricket green *(KCW, H and D Payne, John and Chris Simpson, Mr and Mrs Craig, Nick Wikeley)*

Arford [SU8336], *Crown*: Tastefully refurbished local with well kept Tetleys-related ales, good freshly prepared food esp big filled baps they call stuffies, also children's and vegetarian *(Charles and Joan Woodhatch, Les Jarman)*

Ashmansworth [SU4157], *Plough*: Two rooms knocked together, slightly austere but civilised and relaxed, with well kept Archers tapped from the cask, friendly landlord *(Gordon)*

Ashurst [A35 Lyndhurst—S'hamptn; SU3310], *Forest*: Holidaymakers' Whitbreads pub, friendly willing staff lift it out of the ordinary; fairly priced food and guest ales *(James Cowell)*

☆ **Avon** [B3347; SZ1498], *New Queen*: Well run attractive dining pub with atmospheric different areas and levels, low pitched ceiling, good range of popular food, friendly service, well kept Badger ales; bedrooms *(WHBM)*

Bank [SU2807], *Royal Oak*: Small atmospheric pub in attractive untouristy village, good choice of food, country wines, shove-ha'penny; chipmunks and goats in garden, stunning scenery; very busy evenings *(Mr and Mrs A J Rapley)*

☆ **Basing** [Bartons Lane (attached to Bartons Mill Restaurant), Old Basing; SU6653], *Millstone*: Simply decorated converted mill in lovely spot by River Loddon, decent good value food, good choice of well kept ales tapped from the cask, good service; big garden *(Brenda and Jim Langley, Jim Reid)*

☆ **Beaulieu** [almost opp Palace House; SU3802], *Montagu Arms*: Civilised and comfortable hotel in attractive surroundings; separate less upmarket Wine Press bar, open all day, has basic lunchtime bar food, well kept Whitbreads-related ales, decent wines, lots of malt whiskies, quick friendly service, picnic tables out on front courtyard, piped pop music; children welcome; comfortable but expensive bedrooms *(Mr and Mrs R J Foreman, E G Parish, Mrs J Styles, LYM)*

☆ **Bighton** [off B3046 in Alresford just N of pond; or off A31 in Bishops Sutton – OS Sheet 185 map ref 615344; SU6134], *Three Horseshoes*: Good simple lunchtime food (maybe just sandwiches in summer) in simple village local with open fire in small lounge, police memorabilia (ex-police landlord), well kept Gales HSB, BBB, winter 5X and Prize Old Ale, lots of country wines, friendly family service; children welcome, geese in garden *(Lyn Sharpless, Bob Eardley, Jack and Philip Paxton, Ian Exton)*

☆ **Bishops Sutton** [former A31 Alresford—Alton; SU6031], *Ship*: Friendly and pleasantly relaxed local, good quickly served bar food *(Colin and Ann Hunt, D Marsh, LYM)*

Bishops Waltham [Church St; SU5517], *Bunch of Grapes*: Character two-room village local, simple and friendly, with bar food, Courage and Ushers ales *(Ann and Colin Hunt, Stephen and Jean Curtis)*

☆ **Bishopstoke** [Fairoak Rd; SU4619], *River*: Warm welcome and well priced home cooking in spacious family pub with interesting things to look at; big safe riverside garden with play area; some live music *(Mrs D Brown, Martyn Yates, John and Chris Simpson, Dr and Mrs A K Clarke)*

Bishopstoke [Church Rd], *Forresters Arms*: Friendly local with well kept ales inc Gibbs Mew Bishops Tipple, lively public bar with darts, cribbage, quieter lounge; attractive garden *(Matthew Roberts)*

Blacknest [SU7941], *Jolly Farmer*: Modern, light and airy dining pub with good value generous quick food inc children's, big open fire one end, family room; tables on sheltered terrace and in garden *(HNJ, PEJ, G B Longden)*

Bordon [SU7935], *Woodlands*: Newly opened spacious pub with well kept Boddingtons, attractive grounds *(Chris Perry)*

☆ **Botley** [The Square; SU5112], *Bugle*: Delightful atmosphere in attractive beamed pub with good generous straightforward food inc fresh fish, Whitbreads-related ales, well trained welcoming young staff, restaurant; tables in flower-filled yard *(Colin and Ann Hunt, John Sanders)*

Botley [Botley Rd, nr stn], *Railway*: Popular good value generous food, fresh veg, quick cheerful service, well priced Marstons with a guest such as Banks's Mild; large comfortable railway-theme bar, extensive restaurant area *(John and Chris Simpson, John Sanders)*

☆ **Braishfield** [Newport Lane; SU3725], *Newport*: Particularly well kept Gales ales in unchanging friendly and unpretentious two-bar village local with simple good value food inc huge sandwiches, country wines, decent coffee, down-to-earth licensees, weekend singsongs; good summer garden with geese, ducks and chickens *(Lynn Sharpless, Bob Eardley, John and Chris Simpson)*

Brambridge [just off B3335 Twyford—Winchester; SU4721], *Dog & Crook*: Modernised open-plan L-shaped bar with Whitbreads-related ales, simple reasonably priced bar food, friendly licensee and dogs; handy for Itchen Way walks *(Ann and Colin Hunt)*

☆ **Bransgore** [Ringwood Rd, off A35 N of Christchurch; SZ1897], *Three Tuns*: Pretty little thatched whitewashed pub with tasteful low-beamed bar, comfortable dining area, quick friendly service, wide range of good food inc vegetarian and imaginative daily specials, Whitbreads-related and other ales, fresh flowers, small restaurant; pleasant back garden with play area and open country views, flower-decked front courtyard; bedrooms *(C C Stamp, Mr and Mrs George Clarke, R S Dancey, D Baker, E G Parish, C A Hall)*

☆ **Bransgore** [Ringwood Rd], *Crown*: Clean and comfortable Brewers Fayre pub with quick friendly service, good value generous food

from sandwiches up inc children's and lots of puddings, Whitbreads-related ales, big garden with good play area *(D Baker, D Marsh)*
Breamore [SU1518], *Bat & Ball*: Bustling pub with decent food *(Joan and John Calvert)*
Brockenhurst [by rly stn; SU2902], *Morant Arms*: Good service in both bars, well kept Eldridge Pope Hardy, no piped music *(Michael Gidding)*; [Lyndhurst Rd], *Snakecatcher*: Long narrow lounge bar with decent food inc children's, well kept Eldridge Pope ales, good choice of wines by the glass, good service, function room doubling as restaurant *(WHBM)*
Brook [B3078 NW of Cadnam; SU2714], *Bell*: More hotel than pub, but friendly and comfortable, with well kept Wadworths 6X, good bar lunches, prompt pleasant service, several spacious rooms leading out into big secluded garden; delightful village *(Derek and Margaret Underwood)*; *Green Dragon*: Big open-plan modernised New Forest pub with good range of quick food in dining area, well kept Whitbreads-related ales, big garden with good enclosed play area *(Jack Taylor, KCW, Dr and Mrs A K Clarke)*
☆ **Broughton** [opp church; signed off A30 Stockbridge—Salisbury; SU3032], *Tally Ho*: Now in same family as Flower Pots, Cheriton (see main entries), sympathetically renovated basic but comfortable local, big plain modern flagstoned bar with darts, hunting-print lounge, well kept beers inc those brewed at the Flower Pots, simple sensibly priced food, welcoming landlord, decent wines in two glass sizes, newly laid-out garden behind *(Lynn Sharpless, Bob Eardley, Howard Allen)*
Bucklers Hard [SU4000], *Master Builders*: Monopoly position in charming carefully preserved waterside village, original core with beams, flagstones and big log fire attractive when not too crowded, Tetleys-related ales, tables in garden; part of a substantial hotel complex, good bedrooms *(W J Wonham)*
Bullington [Bullington Cross; A303/A34; SU4542], *Bullington Cross*: Useful stop with reasonable range of food, very obliging service, comfortable and spacious bar area with Bass and Wiltshire Stonehenge *(Richard Houghton)*
☆ **Burghclere** [Harts Lane, off A34 – OS Sheet 174 map ref 462608; SU4660], *Carpenters Arms*: New licensees in pleasantly furnished small pub with thriving atmosphere, good country views from attractively laid-out dining conservatory, big helpings of reasonably priced bar food, well kept ales, unobtrusive piped music; garden; handy for Sandham Memorial Chapel (NT) *(Bill Capper, D Marsh, Mr and Mrs P Gregory, HNJ, PEJ)*
☆ **Burley** [Bisterne Close, ¾ mile E; SU2003], *White Buck*: Current regime doing well in plushly elegant high-ceilinged pub/restaurant, good choice of reasonably priced food, friendly service, good choice of well kept beers, separate dining room, children's room; dogs allowed, hitching posts, tables on spacious lawn; well equipped bedrooms *(S H Godsell, J M T Morris, D Marsh, WHBM)*
☆ **Bursledon** [Hungerford Bottom], *Fox & Hounds*: Included for handsomely rebuilt ancient Lone Barn behind with cheerful rustic atmosphere, immense refectory table, lantern-lit side stalls, lots of interesting farm equipment, wide choice from food bar, well kept Courage-related real ales, country wines; children allowed only in conservatory connecting it to original pub *(Eamon Green, Jack and Philip Paxton, LYM)*
Cadnam [by M27, junction 1; SU2913], *Sir John Barleycorn*: Pretty thatched pub with beams and dark woodwork, prompt friendly service, good choice of reasonably priced food, Wadworths 6X, good atmosphere *(Keith and Margaret Kettell, W J Wonham, Anthony and Freda Walters)*
☆ **Canterton** [Upper Canterton; off A31 W of Cadnam follow Rufus's Stone signs (no right turn westbound); SU2613], *Sir Walter Tyrell*: Pretty pub by lovely New Forest clearing often with ponies, ideal base for walks; restaurant, wide choice of good value bar food, well kept Courage-related ales, friendly atmosphere, roomy bar and restaurant; big play area, sheltered terrace *(Colin Barnett, Ruth Trott, K Flack)*
Chawton [SU7037], *Greyfriar*: Early 16th-c building with low beams, standing timbers studded with foreign coins, wide range of reasonably priced food, good coffee; opp Jane Austen's house; garden behind *(Joan Olivier)*
Chilworth [A27 Romsey Rd; SU4018], *Clump*: Busy dining pub useful for good value straightforward food, though service may sometimes slow under sheer pressure of numbers; well kept Whitbreads-related ales, conservatory, tables in garden *(John and Chris Simpson, Mr and Mrs A Craig)*
☆ **Crondall** [Croft Lane; SU7948], *Castle*: Welcoming unpretentious village local with good unusual choice of reasonably priced fresh bar food inc finely judged sauces and good Sun lunch; Fullers ales, subdued piped music, jazz evenings, garden, skittle alley, hitching posts for horses *(G S and M P Stewart, J S M Sheldon, Mrs Broadway, Mrs Mitchell)*
Crookham [The Street; SU7852], *Black Horse*: Friendly, good beer, small-village atmosphere *(Kim Redling)*
☆ **Curbridge** [A3051; SU5211], *Horse & Jockey*: Beautiful setting by River Hamble tidal tributary at start of NT woodland trail, well refurbished with separate dining area; well presented good value food, Gales ales, country wines, cheerful licensees, bright helpful staff; lovely garden with trees and fenced play area *(Ruth and Alan Cooper, Ian Phillips, John Sanders, Geoff Holt)*
Curdridge [Curdridge Lane (B3035), just off A334 Wickham—Botley; SU5313], *Cricketers*: Open-plan country pub with banquettes in refurbished lounge area, little-changed public part, welcoming newish

licensee, Marstons ales, above-average food inc good specials, nice dining area; quiet piped music, tables on front lawn *(Ann and Colin Hunt)*

Damerham [on B3078; SU1016], *Compasses*: Friendly and busy recently revamped local, decent food; bedrooms *(Jerry and Alison Oakes)*

☆ **Denmead** [Forest Rd, Worlds End; SU6211], *Chairmakers Arms*: Simple, roomy and comfortable country pub surrounded by paddocks and farmland, welcoming staff, fine range of good value well presented food inc superb sandwiches, new no-smoking dining area, well kept Gales BBB, HSB and XXXL, decent wine, log fires; no music *(Ann and Colin Hunt, John Sanders, C Slack, Eric Heley, LYM)*

Dibden Purlieu [B3054/A326; SU4106], *Heath*: Handy Brewers Fayre with good atmosphere even when busy, family restaurant, lots of children but quiet corners; reasonably priced food, Whitbreads-related ales, swings outside *(E G Parish, Dave Braisted)*

☆ **Downton** [A337; SZ2793], *Royal Oak*: Reliably good home cooking esp pies in neat and quiet partly panelled family pub, half no smoking, with well kept Whitbreads-related ales, decent wines, friendly landlady, unobtrusive piped music; huge well kept garden with good play area *(John Cromar, D Marsh, E G Parish)*

☆ **Droxford** [SU6018], *Hurdles*: Good generous home cooking, pleasant mature staff, well kept ales; not at all pubby *(John Sanders)*

☆ **Dunbridge** [Barley Hill; SU3126], *Mill Arms*: Bright new restaurant area extending into conservatory by garden, bar refurbished but keeps some character, really flavoursome food inc fine pastry for the pies, well prepared veg, home-made bread; real ales such as Hampshire King Alfred *(Howard Allen, Jo Goldsmith)*

☆ **Dundridge** [Dundridge Lane; off B3035 towards Droxford, Swanmore, then right towards Bishops Waltham – OS Sheet 185 map ref 579185; SU5718], *Hampshire Bowman*: Good atmosphere, not too smart, in friendly and cosy downland pub with well kept Archers Golden, King & Barnes Festive and Ringwood Best and Old Thumper tapped from the cask, decent red wine, country wines, good value straightforward food inc vegetarian; children, dogs and walkers welcome, tables on spacious and attractive lawn *(Colin and Ann Hunt, Lynn Sharpless, Bob Eardley, BB)*

☆ **Durley** [Durley Street; just off B2177 Bishops Waltham—Winchester; SU5116], *Robin Hood*: Friendly simple two-bar Marstons pub, log fire, good food inc kangaroo steaks (licensee spent some time in Australia), cheerful waitresses; back terrace and pleasant garden overlooking field *(Ann and Colin Hunt, Malcolm and Wendy Butler)*

Durley [Heathen St – OS Sheet 185 map ref 516160], *Farmers Home*: Wide range of good genuinely home-cooked food inc lots of specials and fine steaks, also vegetarian and children's dishes, well kept Boddingtons, log fire in small bar, big dining area, relaxed atmosphere, efficient obliging staff; big garden with good play area and pets' corner *(Richard Burton, Roger and Corinne Ball)*

☆ **East Boldre** [SU3700], *Turf Cutters Arms*: Roomy and relaxed dim-lit New Forest pub with good original atmosphere, character landlord and very enjoyable food – worth waiting for a table *(Gill and Mike Cross, Andrew Scarr)*

East End [back road Lymington—Beaulieu, parallel to B3054; SZ3697], *East End Arms*: Popular New Forest pub with Ringwood ales, bar food, curious tree trunk in lounge bar *(Michael Andrews)*

☆ **East Meon** [Church St; signed off A272 W of Petersfield, and off A32 in West Meon; SU6822], *George*: Friendly and attractive rambling beamy country pub in lovely setting, cosy areas around central bar counter, scrubbed deal tables and horse tack; well kept Badger Tanglefoot, Ballards, Boddingtons, Flowers and Gales HSB, decent wines, bar and restaurant food, log fire; good outdoor seating arrangements; small but comfortable bedrooms, good breakfast *(R L Martin, Dagmar Junghaans, Colin Keane, Mr Ely, Nic Armitage, Sara Nicholls, J R Smylie, G B Longden, LYM)*

East Meon, *Izaak Walton*: Simple village pub with good fresh food and pleasant welcome; busy weekends *(T W Fleckney)*

☆ **East Tytherley** [SU2929], *Star*: Charming country pub in lovely surroundings, well priced Courage-related, Gales and Ringwoods ales, decent food from sandwiches up, no-smoking lounge bar and restaurant, courteous service, relaxing pubby atmosphere; giant chess and draughts games on forecourt *(Ann and Colin Hunt, D Marsh)*

☆ **Easton** [SU5132], *Chestnut Horse*: Comfortable beamed dining pub in lovely sleepy village, wide choice of good imaginative food, Bass, Charrington IPA, Courage Best, Fullers London Pride, good log fire, smart prints and decorations *(KCW, Lynn Sharpless, Bob Eardley, Brenda and Jim Langley)*

Easton [OS Sheet 185 map ref 511321], *Cricketers*: Good choice of half a dozen real ales such as Eldridge Pope Hardy, Mansfield Old Baily, Ringwood Best and Youngs Special, good straightforward food from ploughman's up, polite landlord and good staff, occasional entertainment such as Morris dancers or country & western *(Ann and Colin Hunt, KCW)*

☆ **Ellisfield** [Fox Green Lane, Upper Common – OS Sheet 186 map ref 632455; SU6345], *Fox*: Comfortable and interesting two-bar village local with well priced food attracting lunchtime trade from Basingstoke, good choice of beers such as Badger Tanglefoot, Hampshire King Alfred, Marstons Pedigree, Theakstons Old Peculier and Wadworths 6X, decent wines and country wines, friendly attentive service; restaurant area, pleasant

garden *(Geoff Kontzle, Tony and Wendy Hobden, J V Dadswell)*
Emery Down [off A35 just W of Lyndhurst; SU2808], *New Forest*: Good position in one of the nicest parts of the Forest, with good walks nearby, tables out on three-level back lawn; attractive softly lit open-plan lounge with log fires, well kept Whitbreads-related real ales, usual food, children allowed; prices on the high side *(D Godden, H T Flaherty, David Shillitoe, Clive Gilbert, LYM)*
Emsworth [High St; SU7406], *Crown*: Small hotel's spacious low-beamed bar with ales such as Courage, Marstons Pedigree, Wadworths 6X, good value bar food inc children's, two cosy coal fires, prompt service; separate eating area; bedrooms *(Ann and Colin Hunt, A J Blackler); Kings Arms*: Friendly local, cosy and traditional, well kept Gales and other ales, decent wines, good home cooking, back restaurant, garden behind *(Peter Couch)*; [35 Queen St], *Lord Raglan*: Welcoming and relaxing little Gales pub with log fire, good range of food esp fish, restaurant; children welcome if eating, garden behind nr water; occasional live music *(Ann and Colin Hunt)*
Eversley [SU7762], *White Hart*: Three different areas suiting darts crowd, smart set and doggie set, good long-serving tenant, straightforward food; open all day *(G V Price)*
☆ **Everton** [3 miles W of Lymington; SZ2994], *Crown*: Good cheap food in relaxing traditional bar with log fire, well kept Bass and Whitbreads-related ales, second lively bar with pool, darts, table football, Sky TV and good juke box, welcoming chatty locals and ex-Navy landlord; picnic tables outside, quite handy for New Forest *(Christopher Francis)*
Ewshot [SU8149], *Windmill*: Well kept Tetleys-related ales, good food, friendly service, enormous garden with putting green and Sunday lunchtime barbecues *(M M Matthews, Chris De Wet)*
☆ **Faccombe** [SU3858], *Jack Russell*: Popular and comfortable country dining pub with attractive conservatory, smart attentive staff, good carefully presented food with separate veg, well kept beer; attractive setting opp village pond; bedrooms spotless and cheerful *(Phyl and Jack Street, HNJ, PEJ, B Adams)*
☆ **Fair Oak** [Winchester Rd (A3051); SU4918], *Fox & Hounds*: Busy, comfortable and attractive open-plan family dining pub with exposed brickwork, beam-and-plank ceilings, soft lighting; wide choice of reasonably priced food (all day weekends) in old-world bar and separate modern family area, friendly service, Courage-related ales, decent wines; piped music; children's play area by car park *(Lynn Sharpless, Bob Eardley, Mr and Mrs A Craig, Colin and Ann Hunt, Joan and John Calvert)*
☆ **Farnborough** [Rectory Rd; nr Farnborough North stn; SU8753], *Prince of Wales*: Good choice of real ales and whiskies in lively and friendly local with three small connecting rooms, good service, lunchtime food; can get very crowded *(KC)*
Farnborough [Cove Rd], *Tradesmans Arms*: Very warm and friendly atmosphere, good fairly priced food *(Julie Taylor)*
☆ **Farringdon** [off A32 S of Alton; Crows Lane, Upper Farringdon; SU7135], *Rose & Crown*: Generous helpings of good value food in welcoming local, clean and bright, with neat back dining room, Marstons and other well kept real ales, decent wines; tables and playthings in well kept back garden *(C H Stride, Rob and Doris Harrison, BB)*
☆ **Fawley** [Ashlett Creek, off A326; SU4703], *Jolly Sailor*: Plushly modernised waterside pub doing well under current friendly regime, promptly served good value food inc Sun carvery and good puddings, Whitbreads-related and guest ales, restaurant, good liner pictures; piped music (live Fri/Sun), children welcome; by dinghy club overlooking busy shipping channel, handy for Rothschild rhododendron gardens at Exbury *(Mr and Mrs P B Dowsett, B W Bailey, Dr M Owton, LYM)*
☆ **Fordingbridge** [14 Bridge St; SU1414], *George*: Good value food inc imaginative dishes, children really welcome in attractive conservatory facing river, tables out on pleasant waterside terrace, friendly atmosphere not unlike a continental bistro *(Mrs Jane Basso)*
☆ **Freefolk** [N of B3400; SU4848], *Watership Down*: Friendly and cosy partly brick-floored bar, lounge and games areas off, real ales such as Archers Best, Brakspears PA and Mild and Hampshire Pendragon, cheap cheerful food with good specials; piped music *(Andy Jones, Peter Churchill)*
☆ **Fritham** [SU2314], *Royal Oak*: Thatched New Forest pub with no concessions to modernity, Ringwood ales tapped from the cask, odd assortment of furniture inc high-backed settles, pots and kettles hanging in wide old chimney; tables in garden with climbing frame, all sorts of passing animals; no food beyond pickled eggs, crisps and occasional barbecues, bring your own sandwiches; children in back room *(Howard Allen, Jack and Philip Paxton, John Beeken, LYM)*
☆ **Frogham** [Abbotswell Rd, off A338/B3078 SE of Fordingbridge; SU1713], *Foresters Arms*: A less basic New Forest pub with Bass, Boddingtons and three well kept changing guest beers, decent wines and country wines, tasty food in small dining room, games room, tables on front verandah; children welcome, open all day Sat, occasional good beer festivals; good walks *(Howard Clutterbuck, Joan and John Calvert, LYM)*
☆ *nr* **Froxfield Green** [back rd Alton—Petersfield; SU7025], *Trooper*: Well kept Bass, Ringwood and guest beers such as Wadworths, interesting good value wines, simple bar food inc good evening steaks, friendly service, candlelight, scrubbed pine tables and bare boards, good views *(Wendy Arnold)*
☆ **Froyle** [Upper Froyle; A31 Alton—Farnham;

SU7542], *Hen & Chicken*: Wide choice of good generous food in cosy 16th-c pub with oak beams and pillars, antique settles, oak tables, huge fireplace among more orthodox furnishings; friendly helpful staff, good range of well kept ales, unobtrusive piped music; tables outside, play area *(Guy Consterdine, Hazel Morgan, Paul and Sue Sexton, LYM)*

Gosport [Stokes Bay Rd, Alverstoke; SZ6099], *Alverbank House*: Nice setting nr sea with Isle of Wight views, more hotel than pub, but comfortable, with several real ales, good choice of bar food, friendly staff, big garden; bedrooms very well appointed *(Peter and Audrey Dowsett)*; [Queens Rd], *Queens*: Popular real ale pub with five well kept beers such as Archers, Black Sheep and Ringwood, basic food, nice atmosphere, family room, good service; parking may be difficult *(B S Bowden, Ann and Colin Hunt, John and Chris Simpson)*

Greywell [from M3 junction 5 take A287 Odiham turning then first right to village; SU7151], *Fox & Goose*: Friendly atmosphere, good bar food; handy for Basingstoke Canal walks *(Margaret Dyke)*

☆ **Hamble** [3 miles from M27 junction 8; SU4806], *Olde Whyte Harte*: Friendly down-to-earth yachtsmen's pub, recently refurbished, with cheap bar food, Gales Best, BBB and HSB, lots of country wines, blazing inglenook log fire, flagstones and low beams; children in eating area, seats outside *(Ian Phillips, John Atherton, LYM)*

Hamble, *Bugle*: Numerous staff in big labyrinthine waterside pub, neat, tidy and comfortable, with standard food, river-view restaurant, Courage-related ales; tables on terrace *(Alan Skull, P M Rudlin, D Marsh, Ruth and Alan Cooper, LYM)*; [High St], *King & Queen*: Lively atmosphere, welcoming staff, well kept beers inc unusual guest beer, huge helpings of good cheap well presented bar food *(Alan Skull)*

☆ **Hambledon** [West St; SU6414], *Vine*: Friendly traditional beamed pub with good range of beers such as Charles Well Bombardier, Fullers London Pride, Gales HSB and BBB, Shepherd Neame Premium, country wines, good simple home cooking (not Tues evening), obliging staff, open fire in lounge, old prints, china, ornaments, farm tools, high-backed settles; shove-ha'penny, darts *(Lynn Sharpless, Bob Eardley)*

Hambledon [Hipley], *Horse & Jockey*: Welcoming staff, well kept Whitbreads-related beers, good reasonably priced food, delightful garden by stream *(John Sanders)*

☆ **Hammer Vale** [Hammer Lane; between A3, A287 and B2131 W of Haslemere; SU8832], *Prince of Wales*: Straightforward open-plan country local with particularly well kept Gales ales inc Dark Mild and winter XXXXX tapped from the cask, friendly staff, good value food *(Mike Fitzgerald, LYM)*

Hartley Wintney [Cricket Green; SU7656], *Cricketers*: Friendly pub handy for serving food on Sun; can be a bit smoky *(Margaret Dyke)*

Havant [East St; SU7106], *Bear*: Big but cosy low-beamed bar, friendly service, good range of ales inc Flowers Original, Ringwood Best and Old Thumper, old prints; coffee lounge and dining room upstairs *(Colin and Ann Hunt)*; [South St], *Old House At Home*: Fine Tudor two-bar pub, enlarged and much modernised, with low beams, two fireplaces in lounge, well kept Gales BBB and HSB, good choice of bar food; piped music (live Sun), back garden *(Colin and Ann Hunt, Tony and Wendy Hobden, LYM)*; [6 Homewell], *Robin Hood*: Cosy old Gales pub with low ceilings in rambling open-plan bar, good mix of customers, beer tapped from the cask, reasonably priced bar meals, open fire; sensible darts *(Colin and Ann Hunt)*

☆ **Hawkley** [Pococks Lane – OS Sheet 186 map ref 746292; SU7429], *Hawkley*: Unpretentious free house with well kept Ringwood Fortyniner and other ales, big helpings of good value bar food, decent choice of wines, no-smoking area, juke box, back restaurant, tables in pleasant garden behind; lovely countryside, lots of walks *(David Martin, Mike Fitzgerald, Ann and Colin Hunt, Jack and Philip Paxton)*

☆ **Heckfield** [B3349 Hook—Reading; SU7260], *New Inn*: Big well run rambling open-plan dining pub with good choice of food, some traditional furniture in original core, two good log fires, well kept ales such as Badger Tanglefoot, Courage Directors, Fullers London Pride, unobtrusive piped music; restaurant (not Sun); bedrooms in comfortable and well equipped extension *(Chris Warne, LYM)*

☆ **Highclere** [Andover Rd; A343 S of village; SU4360], *Yew Tree*: Relaxing comfortably plush dining bar with good value food, good atmosphere, big log fire, friendly efficient service, well kept ales such as Brakspears, Ringwoods Fortyniner, Wadworths 6X, decent wines, some attractive decorations; restaurant; four comfortable bedrooms *(Maureen Hobbs, Guy Consterdine, Gordon, LYM)*

☆ **Hill Head** [Cliff Rd; SU5402], *Osborne View*: Clean and modern clifftop pub with good bar food inc Sun roasts, well kept Badger Best and Tanglefoot, good service and exceptional picture-window Solent views (you need field-glasses to see Osborne House itself); evening restaurant; by bird reserve *(Mr and Mrs A Craig, N Matthews, John Sanders, June and Eric Heley)*

Hinton [A35 4 miles E of Christchurch; SZ2095], *East Close*: Particularly good food (meals not snacks), and well kept ales such as Eldridge Pope, Ringwood or Whitbreads; no-smoking area; bedrooms *(Mark Brock)*

☆ **Hook** [London Rd – about a mile E; SU7254], *Crooked Billet*: Smart and spacious recently refurbished pub with wide choice of good food all day, well kept Courage-related ales, welcoming helpful service, homely open fires, good range of soft drinks, early-evening happy hour, soft piped music; attractive streamside garden with ducks; children welcome *(Anna Marsh, Simon Collett-Jones)*

☆ **Horndean** [London Rd; SU7013], *Ship & Bell*: Big pub/hotel adjoining Gales brewery, full range of their beers kept well, good relaxed local atmosphere in bar with deep well, comfortable snug lounge with steps up to dining room, reasonably priced bar lunches; bedrooms *(Ian Phillips, Penny and Peter Keevil)*

☆ **Horsebridge** [about a mile SW of Kings Somborne – OS Sheet 185 map ref 346303; SU3430], *John o' Gaunt*: Simple unrefurbished village local with well kept Adnams, Palmers IPA and Ringwood Fortyniner, friendly landlord, popular cheap food (not Tues evening), picnic tables outside; by mill on River Test, very popular with walkers weekends, dogs welcome *(Mike Hayes, Peter Churchill, Lynn Sharpless, Bob Eardley, Nick Wikeley, Martyn and Mary Mullins)*

☆ **Houghton** [S of Stockbridge; SU3432], *Boot*: Wide range of tasty well presented food in friendly and well run dining pub, well kept beer, popular restaurant; closed Mon *(DP, A D Marsh, J F Burness)*

Hursley [A31 Winchester—Romsey; SU4225], *Dolphin*: Good relaxed country atmosphere, decent food, hard-working newish licensees, well kept beer *(KCW, Mr and Mrs Craig)*; [in village], *Kings Head*: Smarter open-plan food pub with well kept Bass, Charrington IPA and Wadworths 6X *(KCW)*

Hurstbourne Tarrant [A343; SU3853], *George & Dragon*: Low beams and inglenook, separate rooms and eating area, real ales inc Wadworths 6X, reasonably priced bar food; bedrooms, attractive village *(Colin and Ann Hunt, LYM)*

Hythe [82 Stade St; SU4207], *Hope*: Proper pub with cases of tropical butterflies and spiders, good food inc real scampi, well kept beer *(Alan and Maggie Telford)*

☆ **Itchen Abbas** [4 miles from M3 junction 9; A34 towards Newbury, fork right on A33, first right on B3047; SU5333], *Trout*: Well run smallish pub with discreet partly no-smoking lounge bar, chatty public bar with darts and bar billiards, well kept Marstons Bitter and Pedigree, decent wines, good value changing bar food from sandwiches up inc some interesting main dishes, friendly service, restaurant; pretty side garden with good play area; roomy bedrooms, good breakfast *(Lynn Sharpless, Bob Eardley, KCW, Jenny and Brian Seller, Paul and Fiona Hutt, R H Rowley, Ron Shelton, Dennis H Phillips, W J Wonham, BB)*

☆ **Keyhaven** [SZ3091], *Gun*: 17th-c nautical-theme beamed pub overlooking boatyard, popular at lunchtime particularly with older people for wide choice of generous bar food, well kept Whitbreads-related ales; garden with swings and fishpond; children welcome *(Nick Wikeley, Mr and Mrs A Craig, D Marsh)*

Kings Somborne [SU3631], *Sun*: Cosy cheerful village pub, good value food *(HA)*

☆ **Kings Worthy** [A3090 E of Winchester, just off A33; SU4933], *Cart & Horses*: Useful renovated Marstons Tavern Table family dining pub with softly lit alcoves, lots of well spaced tables, conservatory, reasonably priced home-cooked food, efficient service, tables in pleasant garden with marvellous play houses *(KCW, Nick Wikeley, R T and J C Moggridge, LYM)*

Kingsclere [Swan St; SU5258], *Swan*: 15th-c coaching inn with welcoming local atmosphere, well kept Greene King Abbot and a guest, good food esp burgers, good service *(Sheilah Openshaw)*

☆ **Langstone** [A3023; SU7105], *Ship*: Waterside pub with lovely view from roomy pleasantly decorated bar and upstairs restaurant, good generous food esp fish cooked within sight, obliging service, well kept Gales, country wines, log fire; children's room, seats out on quiet quay *(David Eberlin, Roger Lamble, R K F Hutchings, Wendy Arnold, Penny and Peter Keevil, Jack and Philip Paxton, John and Chris Simpson, Colin and Ann Hunt)*

☆ **Lasham** [SU6742], *Royal Oak*: Comfortable, friendly country pub in attractive spot nr gliding centre, well kept ales such as Courage Best, Eldridge Pope Royal Oak, Marstons Pedigree and Wadworths 6X, good home cooking, log fire; tables outside *(John Castelete, Bruce Bird)*

☆ **Linwood** [signposted from A338 via Moyles Court, and from A31; keep on – OS Sheet 195 map ref 196107; SU1910], *High Corner*: Big rambling pub very popular for its splendid New Forest position, decent straightforward bar food from sandwiches to steaks, quick service even when busy (shame about the Tannoy food announcements), Whitbreads-related ales, restaurant carvery open all day Sun, family room and no-smoking verandah lounge, big neatly kept lawn with sizeable play area; open all day Sat; bedrooms *(Dono and Carol Leaman, LYM)*

☆ **Linwood** [up on heath – OS Sheet 195 map ref 186094], *Red Shoot*: Attractive old furniture and rugs on the floorboards, generous decent food inc good sandwiches, well kept Wadworths IPA, 6X and Morrells Varsity on handpump, friendly staff, nice New Forest setting *(WHBM, Alan Skull)*

Little London [Silchester Rd; SU6359], *Plough*: Cosy unspoilt local with tiled floor, low beams, friendly landlord, well kept Wethereds, Ringwood and guest beers, log fire, attractive garden *(Steve Hyde)*

Littleton [Main Rd; SU4532], *Running Horse*: Small village pub with well kept Gibbs Mew and guest ales, reasonably priced good food; big garden with play area *(P Gillbe)*

☆ **Longparish** [B3048 off A303 just E of Andover; SU4344], *Plough*: Reliably good open-plan pub/restaurant with well served food from sandwiches up, well kept Whitbreads-related ales, good value wine, restaurant allowing children over 4; piped music, can be crowded weekends; attractive garden *(John Evans, G Washington, Keith Symons, LYM)*

☆ **Longstock** [SU3536], *Peat Spade*: Character landlady cooking really good food (can take time) in elegantly rural dining pub, smart, bright and airy, and often fully booked; pot plants and central table with books, adjoining dining room, well kept Ringwood Best and Fortyniner; wines not cheap but unusually wide choice by glass; no dogs – pub dogs in bar; pleasant garden *(Dr and Mrs A K Clarke, Ian Phillips, Martin and Karen Wake, Mike Hayes, BB)*

☆ **Lower Froyle** [SU7544], *Anchor*: Well run, warm and attractive brightly lit pub with wide range good standard food inc sandwiches, cheerful informal service, well kept ales; well in bar, restaurant; piped music; seats outside *(KC, G and M Stewart, John and Vivienne Rice, J S M Sheldon, Lynn Sharpless, Bob Eardley)*

☆ **Lower Wield** [SU6340], *Yew Tree*: Reliably good value welcoming dining pub, well kept beer; closed Mon *(Betty Laker, Mr and Mrs A Craig)*

☆ **Lymington** [Southampton Rd (A337); SZ3295], *Toll House*: Wide choice of reliably good value food (not Sun or Mon evening) inc children's, good friendly atmosphere, well kept Ringwood, Wadworths 6X and several guest beers, pleasant efficient staff, oak beams; good-sized children's room *(D Marsh)*

Lymington [High St], *Angel*: Popular but roomy and peaceful dark-decor modernised bar with largely home-made bar food, three well kept Eldridge Pope ales, tables in attractive inner courtyard; bedrooms *(Joan and Michel Hooper-Immins, D Marsh, LYM)*; [High St], *Champagne Charlies*: Excels in mainly locally caught fish inc outstanding value lobster salad; well kept beer *(D Marsh)*; [Bowling Green, Sway Rd], *Wheel*: Bargain pints, standard reasonably priced food *(C A Hall)*

☆ **Mapledurwell** [off A30 Hook—Basingstoke; SU6851], *Gamekeepers*: Interesting old bar with well kept Eldridge Pope ales, farm cider, good value bar snacks, opening into bigger upmarket restaurant with wide interesting choice of good generous food; good value wines, friendly smart staff; piped music; in lovely thatched village with duckpond *(J S M Sheldon, KC, Simon Collett-Jones, G B Longden)*

Meonstoke [SU6119], *Bucks Head*: Morlands pub with well kept Bass and Old Speckled Hen, country wines, good bar food with fresh veg, garden; lovely village setting, nearby river *(Terry and Eileen Stott, John Sanders)*

☆ **Minstead** [SU2811], *Trusty Servant*: Prettily placed New Forest pub with small bare-boards public bar, unsophisticated back lounge (also small), wide choice of good fresh fish and more usual bar food, well kept changing ales such as Hook Norton Best, Hop Back Summer Lightning, Smiles Best and Wadworths 6X, country wines; sizeable attractive restaurant, airy by day, candlelit by night; comfortable bedrooms *(David Wallington, D Marsh, S Eldridge, Ron Shelton, Malcolm and Wendy Butler, David Sowerbutts, BB)*

☆ **Mortimer West End** [off Aldermaston rd at Silchester sign; SU6363], *Red Lion*: Welcoming country dining pub with lots of beams, stripped masonry and woodwork, good range of Badger and other well kept ales, good log fire; quiet piped music; seats on small flower-filled terrace by quiet road *(KC, LYM)*

New Milton [Ashley Rd; SZ2495], *Ashley*: Good food and service, reasonable prices *(J Boyt)*

☆ **North Gorley** [Ringwood Rd, just off A338; SU1611], *Royal Oak*: Comfortable and welcoming 17th-c thatched pub with beam and plank ceiling, flagstones, panelled dado, generous reasonably priced usual food from sandwiches to steaks inc children's dishes, well kept Whitbreads-related ales, welcoming young staff; children in family room, big well kept garden with swings and climber, idyllic New Forest setting nr pond *(Jerry and Alison Oakes, Lynn Sharpless, Bob Eardley)*

North Waltham [signed off A30 SW of Basingstoke, handy for M3 junction 7; SU5645], *Fox*: Hunting prints and dark furniture in attractive and comfortable bar (with darts and juke box), lounge and restaurant, Ushers Best and Founders, friendly welcoming licensees, wide choice of food inc lots of seasonal game *(Lynn Sharpless, Bob Eardley)*

☆ **North Warnborough** [nr M3 junction 5; SU7351], *Swan*: Friendly canalside village pub with good choice of well priced good food, well kept Courage Best, Marstons Pedigree, Wadworths 6X *(P J Caunt, Margaret Dyke)*

☆ **Oakhanger** [off A325 Farnham—Petersfield; SU7736], *Red Lion*: Lovely old village inn with comfortable lounge, well kept beer, good food esp fresh fish, big log fire, eating area *(Mike Fitzgerald, Mr and Mrs R J Foreman)*

☆ **Odiham** [High St (A287); SU7450], *George*: Old-fashioned inn with short choice of imaginative daily-changing home-cooked food, well kept Courage-related ales, decent wines by the glass, pleasant staff; comfortable little back bar overlooking garden; bedrooms *(F C Johnston, J S M Sheldon, LYM)*

Odiham [Church Sq], *Bell*: Welcoming local in pretty square opp church, well kept Courage-related ales, limited choice of good food, friendly service *(J S M Sheldon)*

Overton [Red Lion Lane; SU5149], *Red Lion*: Village local with changing real ales, open fires, good value food esp Sun roasts, lively public bar with piped music, quieter saloon, garden with good play area; children welcome; live music twice weekly *(Tony Leyland)*

Ower [Salisbury Rd, just off M27 junction 2; SU3216], *Mortimers*: Handy and roomy stop-off with welcoming licensees, catering well for businessmen and families *(Nick Male)*

☆ **Owslebury** [SU5123], *Ship*: Small very popular village local with little-changed character bar, extended family area, decent home cooking, quick friendly service, well kept Marstons; magnificent downland views from two garden areas, children's play area, goat, maybe even bowls practice and cricket net; good walks *(John and Joan Nash, Mark Hydes, Ann and Colin Hunt, M J D Inskip, LYM)*

☆ **Petersfield** [College St; SU7423], *Good Intent*: Locally very popular for wide range of good value home-cooked food (not Mon), real ales such as Bass, Marstons Pedigree and Ringwood Fortyniner, good coffee, efficient friendly service; neat modern feel despite 16th-c beams and timbers, good log fires; cosy restaurant *(Richard and Maria Gillespie, Ron Shelton)*

☆ **Portsmouth** [Bath Sq, Old Town; SU6501], *Spice Island*: Roomy modernised waterside Whitbreads pub with seafaring theme, big windows and outside seats overlooking passing ships, well kept ales, food all day inc vegetarian, family room (one of the few in Portsmouth), bright upstairs restaurant; can be very crowded, as with other pubs here nearby parking may be difficult *(Penny and Peter Keevil, Julie Mundy, Martin Robinson, Colin and Ann Hunt, T Roger Lamble, Thomas Nott)*

☆ **Portsmouth** [High St, Old Town], *Dolphin*: Spacious decorously refurbished old timber-framed pub with ten or more Whitbreads-related and other ales, wide range of food, good log fire, cosy snug; video games; open all day Sat, children welcome in eating area *(Ann and Colin Hunt, KCW, Martyn Hart)*

☆ **Portsmouth** [High St, Old Town], *Sally Port*: Spick-and-span, brightly modernised but still interesting, with reasonably priced good bar food esp fish, well kept Marstons, good friendly staff, upstairs restaurant; comfortable bedrooms *(Shirley Pielou, Ann and Colin Hunt)*

Portsmouth [The Wharf, Camber Dock], *Bridge*: On the wharf, good water views, bar food, upstairs fish bistro, Whitbreads-related ales *(Colin and Ann Hunt, Sue Anderson, Phil Copleston)*; [nr Dockyard], *Lady Hamilton*: Interesting history, wonderful sandwiches *(Mrs Davidson)*; [View Rd, nr continental ferry port], *Rudmore Cellars*: Particularly well kept Tetleys-related ales, interesting pictures *(Ann and Colin Hunt)*

☆ **Ringwood** [The Bridges, West St, just W of town; SU1505], *Fish*: Several cosy places to sit, fishy decorations give endless scope for speculation, well kept ales such as Brakspears and Fullers London Pride, wide choice of good value food, log fire, good obliging service, eating area allowing children, no dogs; tables on riverside lawn, open all day *(Howard Allen, Ian Phillips, S and J Moate, J H L Davis, Wally Huggins, LYM)*

Ringwood [12 Meeting House Lane, behind supermarket], *Inn on the Furlong*: Several rooms, with flagstone floors, stripped brick and oak timbering, conservatory restaurant; full range of Ringwood beers kept well, good value lunchtime bar food; live music some nights, Easter beer festival *(Bruce Bird)*

☆ **Rockford** [OS Sheet 195 map ref 160081; SU1608], *Alice Lisle*: Friendly and pleasant open-plan pub attractively placed on green by New Forest, wide choice of good value food inc good sandwiches and children's helpings in big conservatory-style family eating area, well kept Gales and guest beers, country wines, helpful staff, baby-changing facilities; garden with good play area and pets' corner, ponies wander nearby; handy for Moyles Court *(Mrs Pointon, S Eldridge, Charles Owens, Catherine Almond, BB)*

Romsey [SU3521], *White Horse*: Good bar food, good staff and atmosphere; bedrooms *(David Voice)*

☆ *nr* **Romsey** [Botley Rd; A27 towards N Baddesley – handy for M27 junction 3; SU3621], *Luzborough House*: Extensive Whitbreads family dining pub with interesting series of smaller rooms leading off high-raftered flagstoned main bar, good generous food all day, well kept ales, big log fire, cheerful staff; piped music; children welcome away from bar, tables and play area in spacious walled garden *(Mr and Mrs Craig, Nick Wikeley, N E Bushby, Miss W E Atkins, LYM)*

nr **Romsey** [Greatbridge, A3057 towards Stockbridge; SU3422], *Dukes Head*: Attractively decorated old Whitbreads pub festooned with flowering baskets in summer; wide range of good value food, friendly staff, Strong Country tapped from the cask, inglenook eating places, charming back garden wth old tractor and rabbits *(David Dimock, Ruth and Alan Cooper, D Illing)*; [Woodley, A31 towards Winchester; SU3722], *Hunters*: Whitbreads pub handy for quick all-day food; friendly staff, pleasant atmosphere, well kept ales *(Dennis H Phillips, KCW)*; [bypass, 300 yds from entrance to Broadlands], *Three Tuns*: Deceptively small from the outside, lots of space inside, genuine old beams, open fires, beers such as Bass, Flowers, Ringwood, Wadworths 6X, generous well presented home-made food, good friendly service, afternoon teas, pleasant terrace *(C A Hall)*

☆ **Rotherwick** [High St; SU7156], *Falcon*: Welcoming country local with half a dozen rotating well kept local beers, good reasonably priced food, friendly landlord, open fire; children welcome *(Anna Marsh, Mark Coleman, Stephen Teakle, Jonathan Culver, Andy Guerin)*

Selborne [SU7433], *Queens*: Friendly village pub/hotel with interesting local memorabilia in bar, well kept beer, good value standard food inc children's, open fires; children welcome; bedrooms, very handy for Gilbert White's home *(Michael Jefferson, A J Blackler, Thomas Nott, LYM)*

☆ **Setley** [A337 Brockenhurst—Lymington; SU3000], *Filly*: Relaxing and comfortable, with two contrasting and attractive bars, interesting choice of generous well presented food inc vegetarian, well kept Bass, Ringwood Old Thumper and Wadworths 6X, decent wines, friendly landlord, quick service – very popular with older people (and children) lunchtime; piped music; some tables outside, handy for New Forest walks *(Joan and John Calvert, Lynn Sharpless, Bob Eardley, Derek and Margaret Underwood, C A Hall, D Deas, Dave Braisted, John and Joan Nash, R M Leonard, D Marsh, R Ward, Howard Clutterbuck, Anna and Steven Oxley, LYM)*

☆ **Sherfield on Loddon** [SU6857], *White Hart*: Tidily refurbished and quietly welcoming, with wide choice of generous fresh food prepared to order (so can be a wait if busy), huge inglenook fireplace, friendly efficient service, well kept Courage and guest ales, good choice of wines, interesting coaching-era relics, tables outside; soft piped music; handy for The Vyne *(Simon Collett-Jones, Mr and Mrs T Bryan, Chris Warne, J S M Sheldon, K D and C M Bailey, LYM)*

☆ **Soberton** [signed off A32 S of Droxford; SU6116], *White Lion*: Well run chatty country pub with good value food esp home-made pies, well kept ales inc Burts, scrubbed tables and woodburner in rambling lounge bar, irregularly shaped public bar, quiet views from sheltered garden with play area and sun-trap fairy-lit terrace; children welcome exc public bar *(G B Longden, John Evans, A J Netherton, John and Joy Winterbottom, J S M Sheldon, LYM)*

Southampton [by St Denys Stn; SU4313], *Dolphin*: Recently refurbished in uncluttered bare-boards style, with six changing ales on handpump – mainly Gibbs Mew, Ringwood, Wiltshire; friendly staff, food from hot sandwiches to Sun lunch inc vegetarian, three coal fires, big tables, no-smoking area, some live music *(Richard Mason, Dr M Owton)*; [55 High St, off inner ring rd], *Red Lion*: Interesting for its lofty galleried hall, genuinely medieval, with armour and Tudor panelling; open all day, Courage-related ales *(Mr and Mrs A Craig, LYM)*; [Adelaide Rd, St Denys], *South Western Arms*: Good range of real ales, lots of woodwork with upper gallery; popular with students, easy-going atmosphere *(Dr M Owton, Michael and Derek Slade)*

Southsea [15 Eldon St/Norfolk St; SZ6498], *Eldon Arms*: Half a dozen Eldridge Pope and other changing ales in big comfortable rambling bar with old pictures and advertisements, attractive mirrors, lots of nick-nacks; good range of promptly served food, sensibly placed darts, pool and fruit machine, restaurant *(Ann and Colin Hunt)*; [120 Southsea Terr], *Langtrees*: Whitbreads pub opp Solent-edge green, big well thought-out modern garden, small room areas, open fire, wide range of food, real ales *(Alan J Langlois)*; [The Parade], *Parade*: Big smart L-shaped bar, Whitbreads-related and other ales, reasonably priced simple food, musical instruments and sheet music on walls, interesting fire surround, fancy glass dividers *(Ann and Colin Hunt)*; [Gt Southsea St], *Western*: Cosy free house with plates and old pictures, seven different wines, real ales, decent coffee, interesting lunchtime specials, cheerful atmosphere *(Ann and Colin Hunt, P Neate)*

St Mary Bourne [SU4249], *Bourne Valley*: Clean and friendly, quick service, well kept beers, good choice of ploughman's, good daily specials; bedrooms *(Clive Gilbert)*

☆ **Steep** [Church Rd; Petersfield—Alton, signposted Steep off A325 and A272; SU7425], *Cricketers*: Spacious and airy bare-boards lounge with pews, good solid benches and heavy wooden tables, lots of cricket prints on the panelling, good generous food, well kept Gales ales, decent wines and malt whiskies; restaurant, picnic tables on back lawn with swings and play-house; comfortable good value bedrooms *(JS, B S Bowden, LYM)*

☆ **Stockbridge** [A272/A3057 roundabout, E end; SU3535], *White Hart*: Cheerful and welcoming divided bar, oak pews and other seats, antique prints, shaving-mug collection, reasonably priced bar food, Sun lunches, Bass and Charrington IPA on handpump, country wines, courteous service; children allowed in comfortable beamed restaurant with blazing log fire; bedrooms *(Ann and Colin Hunt, Mr and Mrs R O Gibson, J V Dadswell, Lynn Sharpless, Bob Eardley, Wim Kock, Willem-Jan Kock, Hans Chabot, LYM)*

☆ **Stockbridge** [High St], *Grosvenor*: Good atmosphere and quick cheerfully courteous service in pleasant and comfortable old country-town hotel's two smallish bars and dining room, decent food, Courage Directors and Whitbreads Best, log fire; big attractive garden behind; bedrooms good value *(W and S Jones, Brig D B Rendell, Simon Collett-Jones, BB)*

☆ *nr* **Stockbridge** [Leckford (A30 E); on OS Sheet 185 map ref 405367 as White Hart], *Leckford Hutt*: Comfortable settles, easy chairs and settees, good fire, lots of mugs and tankards, friendly licensees, extraordinarily deep well, good value food inc children's and sandwiches, well kept Marstons Best and Pedigree, good coffee; public bar with table games, quoits, quiet fruit machine and lots of chamber-pots; children in lunchtime family area, friendly dogs allowed later; garden behind *(Charles Bardwell, KCW)*

☆ **Stratfield Saye** [signed off A33 Basingstoke—Reading; SU6861], *New Inn*: Several semi-divided areas inc lounge with log fires, nice prints and plates, cheerful staff, decent bar food inc children's and good puddings, well kept Badger and guest ales, children and dogs welcome; attractive garden with play area, good barbecues, pleasant surroundings *(Klaus and Elizabeth Leist)*

Stroud [A272 Petersfield—Winchester; SU7223], *Seven Stars*: Useful stop with good choice of food from good sandwiches to some exotic dishes served quickly and cheerfully in roomy comfortable open-plan bar, well kept Greene King IPA and Abbot and Wadworths 6X, restaurant; bedrooms very comfortable *(C O Day, Brig J S Green, Gwen and Peter Andrews, Prof A N Black)*

☆ **Stuckton** [village signed S of Fordingbridge, by A338/B3078 junction; SU1613], *Three Lions*: Too restauranty for the main entries, but wide choice of generous, interesting and unusual wholesome food (not Mon) inc good old-fashioned puddings in neat and airy bar; good welcoming service, lots of fresh flowers, well kept Tetleys-related and other ales on handpump, decent wines; closed Sun evening and Mon in winter *(David Cundy, LYM)*

☆ **Swanmore** [Hill Grove – OS Sheet 185 map ref 582161; SU5716], *Hunters*: Spacious and popular dining pub with big family room, wide choice of food inc vegetarian and children's, Courage Directors, good house wine, cheerful attentive staff, lots of carpentry tools; plenty of picnic tables, good big play area; very busy weekends *(Miss D J Hobbs, Mr and Mrs J E C Hobbs, Mr and Mrs A McCall, John Sanders)*

Swanmore, *Rising Sun*: Welcoming pubby atmosphere, good log fires, decent food, well kept beer, comfortable seats *(TBB, Stephen and Jean Curtis)*

☆ **Tangley** [SU3252], *Fox*: Busy little pub with generous good value imaginative food inc excellent puddings, well kept Courage-related and guest ales, good choice of wines, two big log fires, friendly and chatty landlord, prompt helpful service, pleasant restaurant *(Mr and Mrs John Hobbs, John Hazel, Sarah and Graham Rissone)*

☆ **Timsbury** [Michelmersh; A3057 towards Stockbridge; SU3424], *Bear & Ragged Staff*: Very busy Whitbreads country dining pub, airy and comfortable, with wide choice of food all day, several well kept ales, lots of wines by the glass, country wines, tables out in garden, good play area; children in eating area *(Andrew Brookes, A Craig, P J Caunt, S Eldridge, Mr and Mrs Gordon Turner, Joan and Andrew Life, Joan and John Calvert, LYM)*

☆ **Titchfield** [Mill Lane, Segensworth; off A27 at Titchfield Abbey; SU5305], *Fishermans Rest*: Comfortable Whitbreads pub/restaurant in pleasant spot opp Tichfield Abbey, mellow eating area off bar, good choice of well kept ales inc Gales HSB and Wadworths 6X, pleasant atmosphere, friendly service, two log fires, daily papers, fishing memorabilia; tables out behind overlooking river *(Roger and Corinne Ball, M J D Inskip, Terry and Eileen Stott, Sue Anderson, Phil Copleston, N Matthews, Anthony and Freda Walters, John and Chris Simpson, Ann and Colin Hunt, A E Green)*

☆ **Titchfield** [East St, off A27 nr Fareham], *Wheatsheaf*: Popular bar food inc sandwiches and good value Sun roast, friendly landlord, well kept Courage and guest ales such as Bass, Morlands Old Speckled Hen or Theakstons Old Peculier, small restaurant, tables out behind *(David Lewis, John and Chris Simpson, Ann and Colin Hunt)*

Titchfield [High St], *Bugle*: Very popular, efficient and friendly; good restaurant in old barn behind *(N Matthews)*

Totford [B3046 Basingstoke—Alresford; SU5738], *Woolpack*: Friendly pub/restaurant with well kept Gales HSB, Palmers IPA and local Cheriton Pots on handpump, stripped-brick bar, large dining room, good food, open fire; tables outside, lovely setting; bedrooms *(Martyn and Mary Mullins, CH, AH)*

☆ **Totton** [Eling Quay; SU3612], *Anchor*: Nautical photographs, well kept Bass and good value promptly served basic home-cooked food in interestingly placed little creekside local, no frills but friendly; a few tables by quay, handy for NT Tidal Mill *(Ian Phillips, Clive Gilbert)*

☆ **Turgis Green** [A33 Reading—Basingstoke; SU6959], *Jekyll & Hyde*: Enjoyable rambling black-beamed pub with lots of picnic tables in good sheltered garden (some traffic noise), play area and various games; five changing real ales, some interesting furnishings and prints particularly in back room, quick friendly service, wide range of food from sandwiches up, all day inc breakfast; piped music; lavatories for the disabled, children allowed *(Chris Warne, Jim Reid, LYM)*

☆ **Twyford** [SU4724], *Bugle*: Friendly open-plan pub done up in rich post-Victorian style, wide choice of generous reasonably priced good food inc good value Sun lunch, well kept Eldridge Pope ales, decent wines by the glass *(J L Hall, Colin and Ann Hunt)*

Twyford [High St], *Phoenix*: Roomy open-plan Marstons pub with decent food, pleasant restaurant, garden *(Ann and Colin Hunt)*

☆ **Upton** [the one nr Hurstbourne Tarrant; SU3555], *Crown*: Classic comfortable country pub doing well under current licensees, good bar food, well kept beer *(GSS, Nick Bell, BB)*

☆ **Upton Grey** [SU6948], *Hoddington Arms*: Consistently good value interesting food inc excellent puddings in unpretentious two-bar local; well kept Morlands and other ales, Australian wines by glass, friendly service, family room, bar billiards; piped music; garden, attractive village *(G B Longden, Guy Consterdine, Mrs B M Spurr, Jim Reid, Christopher Glasson)*

Wallington [1 Wallington Shore Rd, nr M27 junction 11; SU5806], *Cob & Pen*: Wide choice of good value food, well kept Whitbreads-related ales; large garden *(N Matthews)*; *White Horse*: Well furnished local with pictures of old Fareham, good value lunchtime food popular with executives from nearby industrial estate; well kept Bass tapped from the cask, guest beers *(June and Eric Heley, Terry and Eileen Stott)*

☆ **Warnford** [A32; SU6223], *George & Falcon*: Spacious and comfortable softly lit country pub, popular generous food in bar and restaurant, quick friendly service, piped light classical music, Courage-related ales *(Sue Anderson, Phil Copleston, P Gillbe, Miss D J Hobbs, John Hobbs)*

☆ **West Meon** [High St; SU6424], *Thomas*

Lord: Good atmosphere in attractive cricket-theme village pub, well kept Whitbreads-related ales, good value generous food, friendly new landlord, collection of club ties in lounge; tables in garden *(KCW, Joan and Andrew Life, Colin and Ann Hunt)*

☆ **West Wellow** [nr M27 junction 2; A36 2 miles N of junction with A431; SU2919], *Red Rover*: Warm welcome, wide range of good value food, Whitbreads-related ales, extensive partly no-smoking dining area, friendly staff *(Colin and Ann Hunt, R Pattison)*

West Wellow [Canada Rd; off A36 Romsey—Ower at roundabout, signposted Canada], *Rockingham Arms*: Plush beamed 19th-c pub with good food and drinks, friendly atmosphere and service, open fire; dogs on leads allowed, pool and darts, restaurant; children welcome; garden with play area, small caravan park; on edge of New Forest *(D Marsh, Mr and Mrs Craig)*

☆ **Weyhill** [A342, signed off A303 bypass; SU3146], *Weyhill Fair*: Popular local with well kept Gales HSB, Marstons and Morrells on handpump, weekly guest beers tapped from the cask in the cellar, and wide choice of good value food; spacious solidly furnished lounge with easy chairs around woodburner and old advertisements, smaller family room, no-smoking area; children welcome *(John Watkins, Andy and Jackie Mallpress, Richard Houghton, Bruce Bird, BB)*

☆ **Wherwell** [B3420; SU3941], *White Lion*: Cosy beamed village local with friendly helpful service, good value fresh food esp sandwiches and ploughman's in bar or dining room, Whitbreads-related real ales, log fire, fresh flowers, polished brass, shelves of plates *(Colin Laffan, Ann Cassels-Brown, P J S Mitchell, Mr and Mrs J Woodfield, Dr H C Mackinnon, Stephen Jackman, R A Dean)*

☆ **Whitsbury** [follow Rockbourne sign off A354 SW of Salisbury, turning left just before village; or head W off A338 at S end of Breamore, or in Upper Burgate; SU1219], *Cartwheel*: Smart low-beamed country pub with wide choice of well presented reasonably priced food inc good sandwiches, good range of changing real ales with Aug beer festival, horse-racing decorations, friendly service, neat restaurant; dogs allowed, weekly barbecue in attractive secluded sloping garden with play area; children allowed in restaurant when not in use *(W K Struthers, Jerry and Alison Oakes, Dennis H Phillips)*

☆ **Whitway** [Winchester Rd (old A34); SU4559], *Carnarvon Arms*: Extraordinarily long menu – walls in main bar not big enough to cope with it all; food good and well presented, service helpful, extension of eating area into adjacent barns planned; OAP bargain lunches Tues-Thurs, fish and chips Fri; bedrooms *(HNJ, PEJ)*

☆ **Winchester** [The Square, between High St and cathedral; SU4829], *Eclipse*: Picturesque little partly 14th-c pub with heavy beams, timbers and oak settles, very handy for cathedral; well kept Ringwood Fortyniner and Old Thumper, well done lunchtime bar food inc good value toasties, friendly service, seats outside *(A Craig, Rona Murdoch, Dr and Mrs A K Clarke, A E Green, LYM)*

Winchester [St Cross; SU4727], *Bell*: Well kept Marstons and good atmosphere in unpretentious lounge bar; handy for St Cross Hospital *(Christopher Perry)*; [Southgate St], *Green Man*: Welcoming Marstons local with wide range of food, monthly guest beer *(Etienne Patterson)*; [by Guildhall], *Guildhall*: Decorated in 1930s style, reasonably priced food, Eldridge Pope ales *(Dave Braisted)*; [Morn Hill, Alresford Rd], *Percy Hobbs*: Useful for long food service, with well kept Whitbreads-related ales, pleasant alcoves; pervasive piped music and air conditioning *(KCW)*; [Kingsgate Rd], *Queen*: Quiet, friendly and comfortable two-bar pub in attractive setting nr College (useful car park), with well kept Marstons, good value home cooking *(Mike and Caroline Hayes, John and Chris Simpson)*; [57 Stockbridge Rd (A272 past stn)], *Roebuck*: Cosy sitting-room atmosphere, friendly and welcoming, Marstons and guest ales, good value simple generous food *(Kathy and Peter Nourse)*; [Romsey Rd], *St James*: Small renovated corner pub with scrubbed pine tables, panelling, sepia wallpaper, flagstones, friendly landlord, relaxed atmosphere, full Wadworths range kept well, good value standard bar food inc good range of filled baguettes; small pleasant garden *(Bob Eardley)*; [Stanmore Lane (off Romsey Rd 2 miles out)], *Stanmore*: Friendly efficient staff, reasonably priced food, well kept Eldridge Pope ales; reasonably priced bedrooms *(John and Chris Simpson)*; [Jewry St], *Theatre Royal Bar*: Very small adjunct to theatre, good range of beers *(Christopher Perry)*; [Durngate], *Willow Tree*: Intimate nicely furnished pub in beautiful riverside setting, well presented generous food inc bargain daily special, well kept Marstons beers, friendly service *(Mr and Mrs John Baskwell)*

☆ **Winchfield** [Winchfield Hurst; SU7753], *Barley Mow*: Two-bar local with big new restauranty sunroom, wide choice of good value generous home-cooked food from sandwiches up, friendly staff, well kept Courage-related ales, decent wine, unobtrusive piped music; dogs welcome, nr Basingstoke canal – lots of good walks *(June and Eric Heley, G B Longden, Betty Laker, Liz and Ian Phillips)*

☆ **Woodgreen** [OS Sheet 184 map ref 171176; SU1717], *Horse & Groom*: Busy beamed local, good choice of home-cooked food inc lovely puddings; real ale, log fire, eating area off bar *(Joan and John Calvert, M J Clenshaw)*

Hereford & Worcester

This is a very interesting area for people who like good pubs. It includes quite a number of really unspoilt rustic taverns which have escaped modernisation and refurbishment – a dying breed which has become very rare indeed elsewhere. The Monkey House at Defford is a prime example, and there are several others to be found in the Lucky Dip at the end of the chapter. Moreover, plenty of pubs here which are altogether more civilised than these country alehouses and cider houses have also preserved a great deal of character – the Fleece at Bretforton is perhaps the best example, but there are plenty of others. Pub food has been improving in the area and is now of a generally high standard: the Olde Salutation at Weobley (currently doing very well all round) and the handsome old Feathers in Ledbury both gain our Food Award this year, as does an entirely new main entry, the friendly and civilised Hunters Inn at Longdon. The other new main entry is the Bridge Inn at Michaelchurch Escley – simple good value in a lovely setting. (It's worth noting that these two were the only pubs to qualify, in the batch of 15 potential new entries we inspected here this year.) Other changes to note here include new licensees at the Ancient Camp at Ruckhall (good food still, very interesting wines now) and the Lough Pool at Sellack (friendly and chatty); and the welcoming Sun at Winforton now does bedrooms. Drinks prices in the area are well below the national average: we found the lowest beer prices at the Talbot at Knightwick (a real bargain offer), the Butchers Arms at Woolhope and the Green Man at Fownhope. Pubs currently particularly worth noting in the Lucky Dip section at the end of the chapter include the Penny Farthing at Aston Crews, Riverside at Aymestrey (reopened after a long closure), Green Dragon at Bishops Frome, Cottage of Content at Carey, Old Chequers at Crowle, Old Bull at Inkberrow, King & Castle in Kidderminster, Angel at Kingsland, Talbot in Leominster, Royal George at Lingen, Three Horseshoes at Little Cowarne and nearby Three Crowns at Ullingswick, Fox & Hounds at Lulsley, Cliffe Arms at Mathon, Bell at Pensax, Hope & Anchor in Ross on Wye, Red Lion at Stiffords Bridge, Olde Anchor in Upton upon Severn, Coach & Horses on Weatheroak Hill, Rhydspence at Whitney on Wye and Cardinals Hat in Worcester.

BERROW SO7934 Map 4

Duke of York

A438 Tewkesbury—Ledbury, just E of junction with B4208

This has been a meeting place for centuries – for 15th-c pilgrims making their way from Tewkesbury to Hereford and for local Yorkists in the Wars of the Roses. Today, it's still popular and the two connected rooms of the comfortable bar are full of bustle, as well as beams, nooks and crannies, and a good log fire; there's a small back restaurant (partly no smoking). Bar food includes sandwiches, home-made soup (£1.75), ploughman's (from £2.50), garlic mushrooms (£2.85), cumberland sausage and black pudding with a mild mustard sauce (£3.25), filled yorkshire pudding (from £4.95), home-made steak and kidney pie or broccoli and cream cheese bake (£5.50), mushroom and ham tagliatelle (£5.75), turkey tikka (£6.50), steaks (from £7.25), daily specials, and puddings (£2.20); children's meals (£1.95). Well kept Boddingtons, Fremlins and Ruddles Best on handpump, and farm cider; dominoes, cribbage, and piped music. A spacious garden behind has picnic tables and a slide. The pilgrims' cross in the nearby church is thought to have stood originally in front of the pub. Good walking in the nearby Malvern Hills. *(Recommended by S C King, Anthony and Freda Walters, Graham Reeve)*

Whitbreads ~ Lease: Pam Harber ~ Real ale ~ Meals and snacks ~ Restaurant ~ (01684) 883449 ~ Children welcome until 9 ~ Open 11-3, 6.30-11

BEWDLEY SO7875 Map 4

Little Pack Horse

High Street; no nearby parking – best to park in main car park, cross A4117 Cleobury road, and keep walking on down narrowing High Street; can park 150 yds at bottom of Lax Lane

In a quiet riverside town full of attractive buildings, this characterful pub is tucked away from the summer crowds. It's full of eccentricities and oddities: the walls are covered with various clocks, wood-working tools, Indian clubs, a fireman's helmet, an old car horn, lots of old photographs and advertisements, and even an incendiary bomb; a wall-mounted wooden pig's mask is used in the pub's idiosyncratic game of swinging a weighted string to knock a coin off its ear or snout. There are pews, red leatherette wall settles, a mixed bag of tables on the red-tiled floor, roughly plastered white walls, and low beams. Good, reasonably priced bar food includes home-made soup (£1.75), very substantial sandwiches (weekdays only), filled baked potatoes (£2.95), lasagne or chilli (£3.95), gammon with pineapple or home-baked ham salad (£4.25), the hefty Desperate Dan pie (£4.95), and sirloin steak, with puddings such as jam roly poly with custard (£1.95); friendly service. As well as their own Lumphammer on handpump, they keep Ind Coope Burton and a changing range of guest beers; woodburning stove; fruit machine, video game. No dogs. *(Recommended by Lawrence Bacon, Martin and Karen Wake, Mrs P J Pearce, DMT, Jenny and Brian Seller, Stephen, Julie and Hayley Brown, David and Shelia, Pete Yearsley, P M Lane)*

Carlsberg Tetleys ~ Licensees Peter and Sue D'Amery ~ Real ale ~ Meals and snacks ~ (01299) 403762 ~ Children welcome away from front bar ~ Open 11-3, 6-11 (all day summer Sats)

BIRTSMORTON SO7935 Map 4

Farmers Arms

Off B4208

There's a good old-fashioned rural atmosphere in this attractive black-and-white timbered village pub. On the right a big room rambles away under low dark beams, with some standing timbers, and flowery-panelled cushioned settles as well as spindleback chairs; on the left an even lower-beamed room seems even snugger, and in both the white walls have black timbering. Service is quick and friendly. Popular, good value home-made bar food (with prices unchanged since last yearr) includes filled sandwiches (from £1.10), ploughman's (from £2.20), summer salads (from £2.50), macaroni cheese (£2.60), sausage and chips (£2.95), chicken and vegetable curry (£3.65), steak and kidney pie (£4.75), trout and almonds (£5.50), rump steak (£7.25), and puddings (from £1.40). Well kept Hook Norton Old Hookey and guest beers like Hardington, Hobsons and Woods on handpump; darts in a good tiled area, shove-ha'penny, cribbage, and dominoes. There are seats out on the grass. Plenty of walks nearby, and they have a self-catering cottage. *(Recommended by Neil and Anita Christopher, May Neville-Rolfe, Ted George, Rebecca Mortimer)*

Free house ~ Licensees Jill and Julie Moore ~ Real ale ~ Meals and snacks (11-2, 6-10) ~ (01684) 833308 ~ Children welcome ~ Open 11-2.30(3 Sat), 6-11

BRANSFORD SO7852 Map 4

Bear & Ragged Staff

Powick Rd; off A4103 SW of Worcester

Consistently good food can be found at this stylish dining pub with its proper tablecloths, linen napkins, and fresh flowers: lovely soup, ploughman's (from £5.15), mushroom and watercress pancake with yoghurt dip or lentil and cider roast with garlic spicy tomato sauce (£5.45), faggots and peas (£5.70), beef in red wine (£5.85), grilled sirloin steak (£7.85), daily specials such as fish dishes, creamy chicken in white wine sauce (£5.25), and sirloin strips in green peppercorn and brandy sauce or grilled fillet of salmon with hollandaise (£5.85), and puddings like lemon meringue pie or old-fashioned trifle (from £2.80); vegetables are extra (£2); best to book; on Sunday there are roasts only, they hold a pudding evening every two months (£7.50), a popular singles only dinner party (£10), and cheese and wine evenings every quarter. The interconnecting rooms have a relaxed and cheerful atmosphere (the restaurant is no smoking), an open fire, well kept Boddingtons and Flowers Original on handpump kept under light blanket pressure, and a good range of wines; friendly good-humoured service; darts, cribbage, and piped music. *(Recommended by Christopher and Maureen Starling, W H E Thomas, A Preston, Paul and Elizabeth Anthony, Michael and Margaret Norris, Graham Reeve)*

Free house ~ Licensee John Owen ~ Real ale ~ Meals and snacks (till 10pm) ~ Restaurant ~ (01886) 833399 ~ Well behaved children welcome ~ Piano Fri and Sat evenings ~ Open 12-3, 6-11

BREDON SO9236 Map 4

Fox & Hounds

4½ miles from M5 junction 9; A438 to Northway, left at B4079, then in Bredon follow To church and river signpost on right

This neat thatched place is almost more of a restaurant now, with a wide choice of popular food: home-made soup (£2.25), hot open sandwiches (£3.75), ploughman's (from £3.75), fresh sardines in garlic butter or leeks and ham in cheese sauce (£4.95), chicken curry (£5.25), home-cooked ham and eggs (£5.50), smoked haddock and mushrooms in creamy sauce (£5.75), steaks (from £7.95), and daily specials, vegetarian and children's dishes, and puddings; roast Sunday lunch (£5.95). The comfortable and well-modernised carpeted bar has dressed stone pillars and stripped timbers, a central wood-burning stove, maroon plush and wheelback chairs around attractive mahogany and cast-iron-framed tables and elegant wall lamps. A smaller side bar has assorted wooden kitchen chairs, wheelbacks, and settles, and an open fire at each end. Well kept Boddingtons, Morlands Old Speckled Hen and Wadworths 6X on handpump, also freshly squeezed fruit juice and several malt whiskies. Prompt friendly service; shove-ha'penny. The pub is pretty in summer with its colourful hanging baskets, and some of the picnic tables are under Perspex; there's a thatched wendy house. *(Recommended by W H and E Thomas, D G King, Dave Braisted, James Macrae, G and M Hollis, Ian Jones, E A George, Alan and Jane Clarke, John Kirk, Mr and Mrs A K McCully, Brad and Joni Nelson, George Atkinson, Michael A Butler)*

Whitbreads ~ Lease: Michael Hardwick ~ Real ale ~ Meals and snacks (till 10) ~ Restaurant ~ (01684) 772377 ~ Children welcome ~ Open 10.30-2.30, 6.30-11~ Bedrooms in adjacent private house: £15/£30

BRETFORTON SP0943 Map 4

Fleece ★ ★

B4035 E of Evesham: turn S off this road into village; pub is in centre square by church; there's a sizeable car park at one side of the church

One of the finest old country pubs in Britain, this was a farm owned by one family for nearly 500 years. They first opened it as a pub in 1848 and ran it until 1977 when the last of the line bequeathed it to the National Trust (under the stipulation that no crisps, peanuts and so forth be sold). All the furnishings are original, many of them heirlooms: a great oak dresser holds a priceless 48-piece set of Stuart pewter, there's a fine grandfather clock, ancient kitchen chairs, curved high-backed settles, a rocking chair, and a rack of heavy pointed iron shafts, probably for spit roasting, in one of the huge inglenook fireplaces. There are massive beams and exposed timbers, worn and crazed flagstones (scored with marks to keep out demons), and plenty of oddities such as a great cheese-press and set of cheese moulds, and a rare dough-proving table; a leaflet details the more bizarre items, and there are three warming winter fires. The room with the pewter is no-smoking. Well kept Everards Beacon Bitter, M & B Brew XI and Uley Old Spot and Pigs Ear, country wines and winter mulled wine; the beer festival is held in the second half of July. Bar food includes sandwiches (from £1.30), ploughman's (from £3), sausages (£3.30), lasagne (£3.80), steak and kidney pie (£4.15), locally cured gammon (£4.95), and steak (£6.25). Darts, cribbage, dominoes, shove-ha'penny. In summer, when it gets very busy, they make the most of the extensive orchard, with seats on the goat-cropped grass that spreads around the beautifully restored thatched and timbered barn, among the fruit trees, and at the front by the stone pump-trough. There's also an adventure playground, a display of farm engines, and an aviary. They also hold the village fete and annual asparagus auctions at the end of May. No dogs (they have their own). *(Recommended by Dave Brown, Martin Jones, Lynn Sharpless, Bob Eardley, Phil and Sally Gorton, Richard Holmes, Fran Reynolds, Sara Nicholls, Jack and Philip Paxton, Jerry and Alison Oakes, John and Marianne Cooper, Brad and Joni Nelson, P J Hanson, P D and J Bickley, David Shillitoe, Gordon Mott, Ted George, Arthur Frampton, Leith Stuart, Kathryn and Brian Heathcote, Andy and Jill Kassube, Gordon, D Baker)*

Free house ~ Licensee N J Griffiths ~ Real ale ~ Meals and snacks (not Mon or Sun evenings in Jan and Feb) ~ (01386) 831173 ~ Children welcome ~ Morris men summer weekends ~ Open 11-2.30, 6-11

BRIMFIELD SO5368 Map 4

Roebuck

Village signposted just off A49 Shrewsbury—Leominster

Rather like a restaurant with rooms, this smartly civilised dining pub serves beautifully presented meals – and considering the quality, prices in the bar do seem fair: soup with home-made rolls (£2.70), crab pot with melba toast or black pudding with an apple, spinach and pinekernel pie (£6.25), baked breast of chicken with a light cider and apple sauce (£6.50), steak and kidney pie or baked queen scallops stuffed with mushroom and garlic butter (£7), confit of duck leg on a bed of red cabbage with an orange sauce (£9), lots of tempting puddings like rhubarb and orange terrine with crème fraîche, fresh lemon tart with a fresh fruit coulis or bread and butter pudding with apricot sauce (from £5), and an excellent range of unusual British farmhouse cheeses served with home-made oat cakes and walnut and sultana bread (£6); vegetables are £1.25 extra. The quiet and old-fashioned snug has an impressive inglenook fireplace and another panelled bar has dimpled copper-topped cask tables, decorative plates mounted over dark ply panelling and a small open fire; the popular big-windowed side restaurant is elegant and modern. Caring, pleasant staff serve olives and friandises (good ones) before your bar meal comes. The wine list is enormous and remarkably good, particularly strong on the better burgundy and rhone growers and eleveurs, and New World wines; also Morlands Old Speckled Hen and Woods Parish on handpump, a range of malt whiskies, and local farm cider. Incidentally, there's a family connection with the Walnut Tree at Llandewi Skirrid. *(Recommended by Mike Dickerson, Nigel Woolliscroft, W H and E Thomas, F C Johnston, H and D Payne, J C Green, R M Bloomfield, The Monday Club, Mr and Mrs S Price, Neville Kenyon, Pat and John Millward)*

Free house ~ Licensee Carole Evans ~ Real ale ~ Meals and snacks (not Sun or Mon) ~ Restaurant (closed Sun and Mon) ~ (01584) 711230 ~ Children welcome ~ Open 12-2.30, 7-11; closed Sun, Mon ~ Bedrooms: £45B/£60B

BROADWAY SP0937 Map 4

Crown & Trumpet

Church St, just off High St

This is a lovely golden stone building with a heavy-tiled roof, attractively set close to the church and village green. It's a down-to-earth place, popular locally, with a cheerful and thriving atmosphere, and a cosily unpretentious beamed and timbered bar with dark high-backed settles and a blazing log fire; quiz night on Thursdays, Saturday sing-alongs, and bar billiards, darts, shove-ha'penny, cribbage, dominoes, ring the bull and shut the box at one end, fruit machine and piped music; they also play Evesham quoits here. They keep a guest beer such as local Stanway Bitter alongside Boddingtons, Flowers IPA and Original and Morlands Old Speckled Hen or Wadworths 6X on handpump, all in good condition; winter mulled wine and hot toddies, and Bulmers cider. Good bar food includes sandwiches (£2), ploughman's (from £3.95), steak and kidney pie (£4.75), beef cooked in a local plum sauce (£4.95), rump steak (£7.95), daily specials such as vegetable and bacon bake (£3.95), pork cooked in cider and apples (£4.95), trout topped with stilton and prawns (£6.95); Sunday roast (£4.95), and asparagus menu in season (from £4.45); quick, friendly service; seats out on the front terrace. *(Recommended by D Hanley, DAV, Sheila Keene, Andrew and Ruth Triggs, Pam Adsley, John and Marianne Cooper, Jill and Peter Bickley, Paul Boot, D Hanley, T M Dobby)*

Whitbreads ~ Lease: Andrew Scott ~ Real ale ~ Meals and snacks ~ (01386) 853202 ~ Children welcome ~ Sing-along duo Sat ~ Open 11-2.30, 5-11; 11-11 Sat ~ Bedrooms: /£43B

DEFFORD SO9143 Map 4

Monkey House

Woodmancote; A4104 towards Upton – immediately after passing Oak public house on right, there's a small group of cottages, of which this is the last

One of the few remaining absolutely traditional cider-houses, this pretty black-and-white cottage is set back from the road behind a small garden with one or two fruit trees – you might at first think it just a private house as there's no inn-sign. From a hatch beside the door, very cheap Bulmer's Medium or Special Dry cider is tapped from wooden barrels and poured by jug into pottery mugs. Beer is sold in cans – a concession to modern tastes. They don't do food (except crisps and nuts), but allow you to bring your own. In good weather, you can stand outside with Tess the bull terrier and Tapper the Jack Russell, and hens and cockerels that wander in from an adjacent collection of caravans and sheds; they now have two horses called Murphy and Mandy. Or you can retreat to a small side outbuilding with a couple of plain tables, a settle and an open fire; darts and dominoes. The name came from a drunken customer some years ago who fell into bramble bushes and insisted he was attacked by monkeys. *(Recommended by Derek and Sylvia Stephenson; more reports please)*

Free house ~ Licensee Graham Collins ~ (01386) 750234 ~ Children welcome ~ Open 11-2.30, 6-11; closed Mon evening, all day Tues

DORSTONE SO3141 Map 6

Pandy

Pub signed off B4348 E of Hay-on-Wye

Surrounded by pretty countryside, this enjoyable pub – the oldest in the county – has picnic tables and a play area in the neat side garden. Inside, the friendly licensees will make you very welcome and there's a lovely atmosphere in the neatly kept main room (on the right as you go in): heavy beams in the ochre ceiling, stout timbers, upright chairs on its broad worn flagstones and in its various alcoves, and a vast open fireplace with logs; maybe a couple of slumbering cats. Very good bar food includes sandwiches, home-made soup (£1.95), Welsh lavercakes wrapped in bacon (£3.45), ploughman's (from £4.15), home-cured gravadlax (£5.25), tortellini mornay with spinach and ricotta (£5.35), nut roast (£5.50), seafood crumble (£5.95), lamb and apricot casserole (£6.25), guinea fowl with honey and Welsh whisky (£9.25), daily specials like chicken tikka masala (£5.75), popular red dragon pie (£5.95), fresh fish dishes, and steamed game pudding (£7.95), and puddings such as chocolate mousse with raspberries or bakewell pudding; they hold themed food evenings – medieval, Indian, bangers and mash (10 different sausages) and so forth. Well kept Bass, Smiles Best, Dorothy Goodbody's Golden Summertime Ale (from the Wye Valley Brewery), and guest ales on handpump; lots of malt whiskies and all the Irish ones. A games area with stripped stone walls and a big woodburning stove has darts, cribbage, dominoes, and fruit machine; piped music and quoits; a side extension has been kept more or less in character. The pub was built in 1185 by Richard de Brico to house workers constructing a chapel of atonement for his part in the murder of Thomas à Becket. *(Recommended by Kevin and Tracey Stephens, S C King, Graham and Glenis Watkins, Anthony Barnes, David Morris, Sue Demont, Tim Barrow, M E Wellington, P A Clark, Huw and Carolyn Lewis, K R Wood, Ted George)*

Free house ~ Licensees Chris and Margaret Burtonwood ~ Real ale ~ Meals and snacks (in winter, not Mon lunchtime or all day Tues) ~ (01981) 550273 ~ Children welcome until 9pm ~ Ceilidh band, singers and various bands on bank holidays and on special event evenings ~ Open 12-3, 7-11; in winter closed Mon lunchtime and all day Tues

FOWNHOPE SO5834 Map 4

Green Man

B4224

People like this striking black and white inn so much, that some are prepared to queue in the pouring winter rain until opening time on a Saturday night. Standing timbers create the feel of several separate rooms, and the nicest bar, on the left as you come in from the road, has a big log fire, comfortable armchairs under its high oak beams, long cushioned settles agains the timbered ochre walls (hung with small pictures and brasses), and seats set into tall latticed windows; dominoes and fruit machine. The residents' lounges and the main restaurant are no-smoking. Reasonably priced food includes soup (£1.70), sandwiches (£1.75), ploughman's or deep fried plaice (£3.50), roast local chicken (£3.60), lasagne (£4.50), home-made steak pie or trout with almonds (£5.25), rump steak (£7.40), daily specials such as beef, mushroom and ale casserole or sweet and sour pork (£5.25), puddings (£1.90) and children's meals (£2.90); they do a Sunday carvery in one of the restaurants. Well kept and very attractively priced Courage Directors, Hook Norton Best, Marstons Pedigree, John Smiths, and Sam Smiths OB on handpump, some under light blanket pressure, and Weston's farm ciders; helpful staff. The quiet garden behind has robust benches and seats around slatted tables among the trees and flowerbeds of the big lawn, and there's a play area. The hotel has had quite an interesting history since it first opened in the late 15th c, providing shelter for Colonel Birch and his Roundhead forces the night before they recaptured Hereford in the Civil War, and later used as a Petty Sessions Court; you can stiill see the iron bars to which prisoners were chained, the cell, and the judge's bedroom with a special lock on the door. *(Recommended by John Hazel, N Lawless, John Bowdler, Gordon, Adam Bell, Peter Neate, Paul and Sue Merrick, Ted George, Mr and Mrs B Hobden, Andy and Jill Kassube)*

Free house ~ Licensees Arthur and Margaret Williams ~ Real ale ~ Meals and snacks (till 10) ~ Restaurant ~ (01432) 860243 ~ Children welcome ~ Open 11-3, 6-11 ~ Bedrooms: £31B/£50B

You are now allowed 20 minutes after 'time, please' to finish your drink – half-an-hour if you bought it in conjunction with a meal.

HANLEY CASTLE SO8442 Map 4

Three Kings £

Pub signposted (not prominently) off B4211 opposite Manor House gates, N of Upton upon Severn, follow Church End signpost

This is a genuinely quaint and very unpretentious local where little seems to have changed in the 80-odd years that it has been in the same family. The little tiled-floor taproom on the right is separated off from the entrance corridor by the monumental built-in settle which faces its equally vast inglenook fireplace. A hatch here serves very well kept Butcombe Bitter, Thwaites and usually three guest beers from small independent breweries on handpump, a good range of malt whiskies and farm cider. On the left, another room is decorated with lots of small locomotive pictures, and has darts, dominoes, shove-ha'penny and cribbage. A separate entrance leads to the comfortable timbered lounge with another inglenook fireplace and a neatly blacked kitchen range, little leatherette armchairs and spindleback chairs arounds its tables, and another antique winged and high-backed settle. Straightforward bar food includes soup (75p), sandwiches (from 80p), omelettes (from £1.50), ploughman's (from £1.95), sausage and egg or burgers (£2), and daily specials; there may be some delay. Bow windows in the three main rooms and old-fashioned wood-and-iron seats on the front terrace look across to the great cedar which shades the tiny green. One or two readers feel that poor housekeeping standards here should disqualify this pub from the main entries, though for others this all seems part of the enjoyable feeling of stepping back a few decades in time. ***(Recommended by P and M Rudlin, Derek and Sylvia Stephenson, Dave Thompson, Margaret Mason, John Bowdler, John and Marianne Cooper, DAV, Mike Dickerson, Ian and Nita Cooper, A R Pike, Bill Edwards, W A Wheeler)***

Free house ~ Licensee Mrs Sheila Roberts ~ Real ale ~ Meals and snacks (not Sun evening) ~ (01684) 592686 ~ Children in family room, maybe elsewhere if not busy ~ Singer/guitar Sun evening, sing-along alternate Sat evenings, folk club alternate Thurs evenings ~ Open 11-3, 7-11; closed evening Dec 25 ~ Bedrooms: £27.50B/£45B

KNIGHTWICK SO7355 Map 4

Talbot

Knightsford Bridge; B4197 just off A44 Worcester—Bromyard

The surrounding countryside is quiet and charming and this rambling 14th-c inn is attractively placed by the old bridge over the River Teme. The lounge bar has a variety of interesting seats from small carved or leatherette armchairs to the winged settles by the tall bow windows, heavy beams, entertaining and rather distinguished coaching and sporting prints and paintings on its butter-coloured walls, and a vast stove which squats in the big central stone hearth; there's another log fire, too, though it's not always lit. Well kept (and very cheap for the area) Bass, Hobsons Bitter and Worthingtons on handpump, decent wines by the glass, freshly squeezed orange juice. At its best, the food is very good indeed – if not cheap – and might include sandwiches, soup like tomato and marjoram soup (from £1.95), blue cheese pancake (£4.25), pork, orange and cognac pâté (£4.50), liver and bacon (£6.95), steak and kidney pie (£7.50), asparagus and chicory gratin (£8.50), chicken with lovage (£9.95), venison steak (£10.95), lemon sole (£13.95), and puddings like sticky date and toffee pudding, quince tart or rhubarb and ginger tart (£3.50); helpings are not large. The well furnished back public bar has darts, pool on a raised side area, fruit machine, video game and juke box; dominoes and cribbage. Well behaved dogs welcome. There are some old-fashioned seats outside, in front, with more on a good-sized lawn over the lane by the river (they serve out here too). Some of the bedrooms are above the bar; good breakfasts. ***(Recommended by Jack and Philip Paxton, Gordon, Dave Braisted, Lawrence Bacon, Alan Skull, TLB, P Hunter, R G and M P Lumley, Mr and Mrs Sean Crampton, Rebecca Mortimer, Mr and Mrs Bryn Gardner, Mrs S le Bert-Francis)***

Free house ~ Licensees Annie and Wiz Clift ~ Real ale ~ Meals and snacks ~

Restaurant ~ (01886) 821235 ~ Well behaved children in eating area of bar ~ Folk night alternate Fri, Morris dancers every winter Weds ~ Open 11-11; closed evening 25 Dec ~ Bedrooms: £24.50(£31B)/£42(£56.50B)

LEDBURY SO7138 Map 4

Feathers

High Street, A417

The very atmospheric and rather civilised Fuggles Bar in this elegant and striking mainly 16th-c timbered inn has managed to accommodate both drinkers and diners in marvellous harmony – not easy to do well. Locals tend to gather at one end of the room or at stools by the bar counter and don't feel at all inhibited by those enjoying the imaginative food and fine wines. And if you want to get away from drinkers there are some very snug and cosy tables with nicely upholstered seats with bays around them off to one side. There are beams and timbers, hop bines, some country antiques, 19th-c caricatures and fowl prints on the stripped brick chimney breast (lovely winter fire), and fresh flowers on the tables. Very attractively presented, the good food includes home-made soup (£2.95), penne with red onion, peppers, olives, basil and tomato sauce (£3.95), thai-style prawns in hot garlic sauce (£4.95), good home-made burgers (£5.85), spinach, leek, and two cheese filo with fresh tomato sauce (£7.50), casserole of venison with smoked bacon, red wine and chestnuts (£8.50), fresh salmon with a tomato and basil salsa (£9), stir-fried lamb in coconut, coriander and chilli sauce with egg noodles (£9.25), nice steaks (from £10.50), and puddings like coffee, maple and walnut cheesecake or treacle and pecan nut tart (£3.95); friendly, attentive service. They do good afternoon teas in the more formal quiet lounge by the reception area with comfortable high-sided armchairs and sofas in front of a big log fire. Well kept Bass, Crown Buckley Reverend James, Fullers London Pride, Shepherd Neame Spitfire, and guest beers on handpump, a fine wine list, various malt whiskies, and farm cider. They have their own squash courts. The Prince of Wales whose heraldic feathers give this striking and familiar old building its name was Prince Arthur, who, if he had lived, would have become king in 1509 instead of his brother, Henry VIII. *(Recommended by Ted George, Gordon Theaker, Michael Richards, Michele and Clive Platman, JAH, John Bowdler, David Peakall, TBB, Mike Beiley, R G and M P Lumley, Tony and Wynne Gifford, AT, J Weeks, Derek and Cerys Williams, Alan Skull)*

Free house ~ Licensee David Elliston ~ Real ale ~ Meals and snacks ~ Restaurant (not Sun evening) ~ (01531) 635266 ~ Children in eating area of bar and in hotel lounge area ~ Jazz/rock/live music Thurs evening ~ Open 11-11 ~ Bedrooms: £59.50B/£78.50B

LONGDON SO8336 Map 4

Hunters

B4211 S

If the licensees' former track-record is anything to go by (they ran the Bear & Ragged Staff at Cumnor (Oxon) and the Crown at Hopton Wafers (Shrops), both popular main entries), this friendly and rather civilised pub should do very well indeed. On the right as you go in there are two comfortable armchairs in a bay window, one-person pews and wheelbacks around a mix of tables, plates and dried flowers on a delft shelf, a warm open fire, and photographs of the licensees in racing cars, yachts, and a glider; on the left is a similarly furnished room with flagstones and a big woodburning stove; a small dining room leads off here, and there's a smart heavily beamed restaurant as well. Good, imaginative bar food includes sandwiches (brown, white or crusty from £1.50), ploughman's (£3), home-made soup like cream of tomato and basil (£2.25), fresh seafood pancake (£4.25), steak and kidney pie (£5.95), baked middle cut of fresh cod with lemon and herb butter (£6.25), vegetarian oriental stir-fry (£6.45), steaks (from £8.75), half shoulder of local lamb roasted with honey and rosemary (£8.95), daily specials such as stilton, apple and calvados pâté (£3.45), chicken, ham and sweetcorn potato cakes with parsley sauce (£5.75), smoked bacon, wild mushrooms and cambazola pancakes (£6.95), and flaked salmon and broccoli in a dill cream sauce on pasta spirals (£7.25); puddings, good cheese with biscuits, and children's menu. Well kept Hook Norton Best, Ruddles Best, Stanney Bitter (from the Stanway Brewery in Gloucestershire), and Websters Yorkshire on handpump, and good wine by the glass; regular quiz and theme nights. There's always a lot going on in their six acres of grounds, and the attractive back garden has some picnic tables on the crazy-paved terrace, with more on the big lawn; dogs, rabbits and ponies. *(Recommended by Jo Rees, W L Congreve)*

Free house ~ Licensees Howard and Polly Hill-Lines ~ Real ale ~ Meals and snacks (till 10) ~ Restaurant ~ (01684) 833388 ~ Children welcome ~ Open 11-3, 6-11

LUGWARDINE SO5541 Map 4

Crown & Anchor ♀

Cotts Lane; just off A438 E of Hereford

The several smallish character rooms (one suitable for families) in this attractive old black-and-white timbered inn, are smart and comfortable, with an interesting mix of furnishings, and a friendly and very pleasant atmosphere. A wide choice of food includes interesting dishes such as herring with tomato (£2.75), beef and Beamish pie (£5.50), very popular cod and prawn pie (£6), rabbit with garlic, ginger and soy (£5.75), pork baked with spinach and mozzarella (£6.50), and monkfish pancakes with saffron sauce (£7.50), besides staples such as sandwiches (from £1.25), ploughman's (£3.50), good cold platters (meat £4.50, seafood £5.50) and several vegetarian dishes such as courgette and ricotta lasagne (£5.20); besides usual children's dishes (£2.40), they will do small helpings of some other main courses, and main dishes come with a choice of accompaniments – chips, salad, vegetables, rice, even paella. Well kept Bass, Hook Norton Best, Worthington BB, and weekly guest beers on handpump, decent wines including a clutch of usefully priced bin ends; big log fire. The village has become a dormitory village for Hereford with quite a lot of stylish mainly modern houses. *(Recommended by Kay and Bob Barrow, Lynn Sharpless, Bob Eardley; more reports please)*

Free house ~ Licensees Nick and Julie Squires ~ Real ale ~ Meals and snacks (till 10) ~ (01432) 851303 ~ Children welcome ~ Open 11.30-11

MICHAELCHURCH ESCLEY SO3134 Map 6

Bridge

Off back rd SE of Hay-on-Wye, along Escley Brook valley; or can be reached off B4348 W of Hereford, via Vowchurch, then eventually left at Michaelchurch T-junction, and next left

Tucked away down a steep lane in an attractive valley, this riverside pub is now run by a friendly ex-home economics teacher. In summer, you can sit outside watching the muscovy ducks and brown trout, and they hold special events such as a fund-raising plastic duck race with a pig roast and side shows, and have their own successful raft team; small riverside campsite with hot showers and changing room. Inside, there's a very relaxed local atmosphere in the simple left-hand bar: dark black beams, straightforward pine pews and dining chairs, brocaded bar stools, some paintings of the pub and detailed farm scenes, a TV in one corner, and a very big woodburning stove. The quarry-tiled public bar has sensible darts, two video games, juke box, board games, and a few baby toys. Well kept Bass and Wye Valley Hereford on handpump, several farm ciders, and an unexpectedly good choice of fairly priced wines. Bar food includes home-made soups like pea and ham or cream of cauliflower (£2), fish pâté (£3), vegetarian quiche or omelettes (£4), local sausages with onions and apple sauce (£4.25), fish pie (£5.50), gammon and eggs (£6), rump steak (£8), and puddings such as trifle or cheesecake (£2); Sunday roast lunch needs to be booked two days before; the restaurant is no smoking. *(Recommended by Katheryn Aldersea, Ivan Smith, Patrick Freeman, C J Parsons)*

Free house ~ Licensee Jean Draper ~ Real ale ~ Meals and snacks ~ (not Mon) ~ Restaurant ~ (01981) 510646 ~ Well behaved children welcome until 9.30 ~ Open 12-2.30(3 Sat), 6.30-11; winter evening opening 7; cl Mon lunchtime

MUCH MARCLE SO6633 Map 4

Slip Tavern

Off A449 SW of Ledbury; take Woolhope turning at village stores, then right at pub sign

The landlord of this quiet country pub used to be a nurseryman and the gardens that stretch out behind the building are really lovely and full of interesting plants; the hanging baskets and big urns in front are very pretty, too. There's a well-separated play area, and maybe summer barbecues. Inside is cosy and chatty, with ladder-back and wheelback chairs around the black tables of the immaculately kept lounge bar, angling around the counter to a similar family area. A good point is that the public bar (carpeted too), is divided off only by the bar counter itself – so in the lounge the atmosphere is warmed by the true country voices from over on the other side. Well kept Boddingtons and Hook Norton on handpump, with local farm ciders (the pub is surrounded by Weston's cider-apple orchards), and several wines; pleasant service, muted piped music. As well as good daily specials such as cod cooked in cider or chicken with broccoli in a creamy sauce (£5.25) or prawn and vegetable stir-fry in a Cantonese sauce (£5.75), bar food includes sandwiches, soup (£1.40), ploughman's (£3.50), filled jacket potatoes (£4.15), faggots (£4.75), steak pie (£4.95), vegetable curry (£5.10), and puddings like creamy lemon crunch or chocolate sponge (£2.30). There's more space for eating in the new conservatory (again attractively planted), though it's best to book. *(Recommended by G and M Hollis, Norma Farris, A E and P McCully, Judith and Stephen Gregory, Lynn Sharpless, Bob Eardley, Peter Lloyd, AT, Mr and Mrs J Brown, Mrs Pat Crabb, Mr and Mrs W W Swaitt, Neil and Anita Christopher, Graham Reeve)*

Free house ~ Licensee Gilbert E Jeanes ~ Real ale ~ Meals and snacks ~ Restaurant (not Sun) ~ (01531) 660246 ~ Children welcome ~ Open 11.30-2.30, 6.30-11

OMBERSLEY SO8463 Map 4

Crown & Sandys Arms

Coming into the village from the A433, turn left at the roundabout, into the 'Dead End' road

Civilised and pretty, this Dutch-gabled white inn fills up quickly with people keen to enjoy the good food. The lounge bar has comfortable windsor armchairs, antique settles, a couple of easy chairs and plush built-in wall seats, black beams and some flagstones, old prints, maps and ornamental clocks (which are for sale) on its timbered walls, log fires and maybe daily newspapers; half is no smoking. As well as daily specials which include lots of fresh fish such as monkfish kebabs, red mullet, grilled whole plaice and seafood medley, the menu has sandwiches (from £1.70; toasties from £1.75), filled baked potatoes (from £2.50), ploughman's (from £3.25), home-made soup with filled french bread (£3.50), home-made curry or vegetarian quiche (£4.95), salmon steak with a fish cream sauce (£6.75), puddings (£2.25), and children's meals (from £1.50); best to get here early for a seat. Bass, Hook Norton Best, Hobsons Best, Woods Special, and guest beers on handpump, half-a-dozen wines by the glass, litre or half-litre, and country wines. There are picnic tables in the garden behind the building. No dogs except guide dogs. *(Recommended by Dorothy Pilson, Nick and Meriel Cox, Joan and Michel Hooper-Immins, G S and E M Dorey, John Bowdler, A J Morton, Jeff Davies, Gethin Lewis, C Smith, Martin Jones, John and Joan Humphreys, David Shillitoe, M G Hart, Mr and Mrs J Brown, Alan Skull, E H and R F Warner, Michael and Margaret Norris, George Atkinson, Steve and Jill Taylor, DAV, R M Bloomfield)*

Free house ~ Licensee R E Ransome ~ Real ale ~ Meals and snacks (till 9.45) ~

Restaurant ~ Worcester (01905) 620252 ~ Well behaved children allowed until 7pm ~ Open 11-2.30, 5.30-11; closed 25 Dec and evening 26 Dec ~ Bedrooms: £30S/£40S

Kings Arms

There's always a friendly bustle and a warm welcome at this black-beamed and timbered Tudor pub. The comfortable, informal rooms ramble around various nooks and crannies full of stuffed animals and birds, a collection of rustic bric-a-brac, and four open fires; one room has Charles II's coat of arms moulded into its decorated plaster ceiling – he's reputed to have been here in 1651. Good, popular food includes sandwiches, soup (£2.65), smoked salmon and prawn pâté (£4.95), spicy chicken wings or crunchy nut brie (£5.25), halloumi cheese and courgettes with tomato salsa or Welsh leek sausages (£5.95), char-grilled Cajun chicken breast (£6.95), unsmoked and smoked haddock in a cheese and white wine sauce (£7.50), sea bass or sirloin steak (£9.50), and puddings such as banana and chocolate custard crunch or fresh fruit tartlet with crème anglaise (£3.25). Well kept Bass, Boddingtons and Marstons Pedigree on handpump kept under light blanket pressure, and a decent range of malt whiskies; quick cheerful service, even when busy. A tree-sheltered courtyard has tables under cocktail parasols, and colourful hanging baskets and tubs in summer, and there's a new terrace. *(Recommended by David Tristram, Basil Minson, David Holman, Jack Barnwell)*

Free house ~ Licensees Chris and Judy Blundell ~ Real ale ~ Meals and snacks (till 10, all day Sun) ~ (01905) 620315 ~ Children over 8 in eating area if eating, and must leave by 8.30pm ~ Open 11-2.45, 5.30-11, 12-10.30 Sat; closed 25/26 Dec

PEMBRIDGE SO3958 Map 6

New Inn

Market Square; A44

Beautifully set in the centre of this black-and-white town and overlooking the church – which has an unusual 14th-c detached bell tower beside it – this ancient place has tables on the cobblestones between it and the former wool market. The three simple little rooms of the aged bar are comfortable and atmospheric and have oak peg-latch doors, elderly traditional furnishings including a fine antique curved-back settle on the worn flagstones, and a substantial log fire. Bar food includes sandwiches (from £1.50), ploughman's (£3.25), pitta bread filled with smoked turkey and avocado salad or chicken baked with walnut oil, apricots and prunes (£5), warm seafood salad or lamb cutlets in elderberry wine (£6), and puddings like treacle and lemon tart or hazelnut pavlova (£2.25). Ruddles Best and County and guest beers like Adnams, Marstons Pedigree or Wadworths 6X on handpump, farm cider, and several malt whiskies; darts, cribbage, shove-ha'penny, and dominoes. Lavatories are outside. *(Recommended by Joan and Andrew Life, John Hibberd, Neville Kenyon, Bill Flisher, Sara Nicholls, Steve Goodchild, A E and P McCully, Kevin and Katharine Cripps, M G Hart, P A Clark)*

Free house ~ Licensee Jane Melvin ~ Real ale ~ Meals and snacks ~ Restaurant (not Sun evening) ~ (01544) 388427 ~ Children in eating area of bar until 8.30 ~ Jazz or folk occasional winter evenings ~ Open 11-3, 6-11; 11-2.30, 6.30-11 in winter ~ Bedrooms: £17.50/£35

RUCKHALL SO4539 Map 6

Ancient Camp

Ruckhall signposted off A465 W of Hereford at Belmont Abbey; from Ruckhall pub signed down private drive; can reach it too from Bridge Sollers, W of Hereford on A438 – cross Wye, then after a mile or so take first left, then left again to Eaton Bishop, and left to Ruckhall

New licensees have taken over this tucked-away, stylish inn and have introduced an interesting menu and some good vintage ports, clarets, and pudding wines. The central beamed and flagstoned bar is simply but thoughtfully furnished with comfortably solid green-upholstered settles and library chairs around nice old elm tables. On the left, a green-carpeted room has matching sofas around the walls, kitchen chairs around tripod tables, and a good few sailing pictures. On the right, there are simple dining chairs around stripped kitchen tables on a brown carpet, and stripped stonework; nice log fire. Good bar food now includes sandwiches, smoked salmon terrine or duck breast with onion marmalade (£4.50), home-cured gravadlax (£5), game casserole with herb dumplings (£7), fresh Wye salmon (£7.50), and monkfish with bacon or minted lamb chops (£8). Well kept Hook Norton Best, Whitbreads West Country PA and Woods Parish on handpump, wines drawing on the landlord's private collection of around 600 cases of fine wines. The peaceful rustic views are quite magnificent, and much enjoyed from seats on the terrace among the roses, looking down to the river and beyond. If you're staying try and get the front bedroom which has the same view. *(Recommended by John Bowdler, Joan Olivier, Dr C E Morgan, Mr and Mrs W W Swaitt, R G and M P Lumley, Martin Richards, P A Clark, Mrs S Wright, Peter Yearsley; more reports on the new regime, please)*

Free house ~ Licensees Pauline and Ewart McKie ~ Real ale ~ Meals and snacks (not Sun evening, not Mon) ~ Restaurant (not Mon) ~ (01981) 250449 ~ Children allowed until 7 ~ Live trios and quartets planned ~ Open 12-3, 6.30-11; closed Mon ~ Bedrooms: £48B/£58B

SELLACK SO5627 Map 4

Lough Pool Inn ★ 🍷

Back road Hoarwithy—Ross on Wye; OS Sheet 162 map reference 558268

The friendly new licensees are keen to make customers feel at home in this attractive black and white timbered cottage and circulate as much as possible, chatting to locals and visitors alike. The beamed central room has a log fire at each end, kitchen chairs and cushioned window seats around plain wooden tables, sporting prints and bunches of dried flowers, and a mainly flagstoned floor. Other rooms lead off, with attractive individual furnishings and nice touches like the dresser of patterned plates. Bar food includes soup (£2.10), stilton and port pâté (£2.95), jumbo sausage (£3.60), ploughman's (£3.95), spinach, cheese and mushroom pie or steak and kidney pie (£5.95), moules marinières (£6.50), chicken korma (£6.95), greek-style goat casserole (£8.50), steaks (from £7.95), daily specials such as wild boar casserole, grilled tuna steaks or fresh whole Dover sole, and puddings like chocolate rum pot or orange and carrot cake (from £2.25). ribs in spicy sauce or especially highly praised vegetarian dishes like bean and vegetable goulash or Caribbean fruit curry (£5.75), steak and kidney pie (£5.95), plaice (£6.50), chicken korma (£6.75), steaks, salmon in prawn, mushroom and white wine sauce (£8.45) and the much-loved greek-style goat casserole (£8.50). Well kept Bass, John Smiths and Wye Valley Hereford on handpump, as well as a good range of malt whiskies, local farm ciders and a well-chosen wine list; piped classical music. The neat front lawn has plenty of picnic tables, and the surrounding countryside is lovely and full of walks and bridleways – and provides good fishing, too. *(Recommended by Keith and Audrey Ward, Dr C E Morgan, Gordon, Frank Cummins, Nigel Wilkinson, Graham and Glenis Watkins, P Brown, Alan and Ruth Woodhouse, Roger Byrne, Ted George, Mr and Mrs W W Swaitt; more reports on the new regime, please)*

Free house ~ Licensees Malcolm and Janet Hall ~ Real ale ~ Meals and snacks ~ Restaurant (not Sun evening) ~ (01989) 730236 ~ Well behaved children in restaurant and snug ~ Open 12-3, 6.30-11; closed Dec 25, evening 26 Dec

Please tell us if any Lucky Dips deserve to be upgraded to a main entry and why. No stamp needed: *The Good Pub Guide*, FREEPOST TN1569, Wadhurst, E Sussex TN5 7BR.

ST OWENS CROSS SO5425 Map 4

New Inn

Harewood End

You get such a warm welcome from the licensees in this lovely timbered 16th-c coaching inn that you feel as if you've known them for years. There are lots of nooks and crannies, settles, old pews, beams, timbers, huge inglenook fireplaces in both lounge bar and restaurant, a happy mix of drinkers and diners, and a lively, cheerful atmosphere. Bar food is home-made using only local seasonal produce, and a typical day's choice might include sandwiches (from £2.25), lots of starters (from £2.25), home-made steak and kidney pie (£5.95), popular boozey beef (£6.95), fillet of pork zingara or trout wrapped in bacon (£7.95), and good local steaks (from £10.45); vegetarian dishes, too. Well kept Bass, Hook Norton Old Hookey, Smiles Best, Tetleys, Wadworths 6X, and guest beers on handpump, a good choice of malt whiskies, local ciders, and wines; darts, shove-ha'penny, cribbage, dominoes, and piped music. The eldest of the characterful dobermans is called Baileys, and her two daughters Tia Maria and Ginnie. There are fine views over rolling countryside to the distant Black Mountains, and the hanging baskets are quite a sight. *(Recommended by Martyn Hart, N Lawless, Mrs L K Dix, Alan and Paula McCully, Frank Cummins, Nigel Wilkinson)*

Free house ~ Licensee Nigel Donovan ~ Real ale ~ Meals and snacks (till 10pm Sat) ~ Restaurant ~ (01989) 730274 ~ Children welcome ~ Open 12-2.30(3 Sat), 6-11 ~ Bedrooms: £30B/£50B

WEOBLEY SO4052 Map 6

Olde Salutation

Village signposted from A4112 SW of Leominster; and from A44 NW of Hereford (there's also a good back road direct from Hereford – straight out past S side of racecourse)

Readers have very much enjoyed staying in the pretty bedrooms of this friendly and carefully run Tudor inn – and the food has been so warmly praised that we've given the pub a food award this year. But despite all this, there's a relaxed and traditionally pubby feel and the two areas of the quiet, comfortable lounge – separated by a few steps and standing timbers – have brocaded modern winged settles and smaller seats, a couple of big cut-away cask seats, wildlife decorations, a hop bine over the bar counter, and logs burning in a big stone fireplace; more standing timbers separate it from the neat no-smoking restaurant area, and there's a separate smaller parquet-floored public bar with sensibly placed darts, and a fruit machine; cribbage. Excellent bar food includes soup like carrot and rosemary (£2.20), filled french sticks (from £3.20), ploughman's (from £3.75), stir-fried vegetable pancake with a red pepper sauce (£3.75), smoked salmon roulade with spinach and prawns with a tomato and coriander mayonnaise (£4.10), nice lamb's liver and bacon (£5.65), good home-made lasagne (£5.75), baked cod fillet on a mushroom duxelle with cheese and chive sauce (£6.25), and specials such as pasta and blue cheese bake (£5.50), sweet and sour chicken (£5.75), lovely roast lamb, supreme of pheasant with red wine and mushrooms (£6.50), and puddings like banoffi pie, delicious bread and butter pudding or lemon soufflé (from £3.50); lovely breakfasts. The restaurant is no-smoking. Well kept Boddingtons, Hook Norton Best, and a guest ale on handpump, a good, interesting wine list with lots to explore, and quite a good collection of whiskies; good, helpful service. On a sheltered back terrace are tables and chairs with parasols. *(Recommended by Don Kellaway, Angie Coles, Frank Davidson, Margaret and Nigel Dennis, G and M Hollis, Brian and Barbara Gorton, Gwen and Peter Andrews, Lynn Sharpless, Bob Eardley, Karen Eliot, P Sumner, Thorstein Moen, Mr and Mrs R Sparham, A P Jeffreys, Cath and John Howard, W H and E Thomas, DAV, the Monday Club, A Preston, P A Clark, Simon and Amanda Southwell, R J Walden)*

Free house ~ Licensees Chris and Frances Anthony ~ Real ale ~ Meals and snacks ~ Restaurant (not Sun evening) ~ (01544) 318443 ~ Children in eating area of bar ~ Open 11-3, 7-11; closed Dec 25 ~ Bedrooms: £32.50B/£55B

WINFORTON SO2947 Map 6

Sun

A438 14 miles W of Hereford

A three bedroomed extension has been added to this spotless, friendly little dining pub – which means you can enjoy the imaginative food without having to rush off afterwards. Changing daily, there might be sandwiches, black olive pâté (£2.75), avocado, melon and goat cheese salad (£3.30), Singapore prawn spicy soup (£3.75), Bangkok beef (£5.25), aubergine and vegetable gateaux with wild mushroom sauce (£5.95), rook pie (£7.50), fillet of Welsh lamb with mint and cranberries (£9.50), and puddings such as lemon tart with gooseberry sauce or chocolat au St Emillion (£3.50). There's a really friendly feel to the two beamed areas on either side of the central servery, with an individual assortment of comfortable country-kitchen chairs, high-backed settles and good solid wooden tables, heavy-horse harness, brasses and old farm tools on the mainly stripped stone walls, and two log-burning stoves. Well kept Felinfoel Double Dragon, Hook Norton Best, Jennings Cumberland Bitter, and Woods Parish on handpump, and a dozen or so malt whiskies; sensibly placed darts, cribbage, dominoes, maybe piped music. The neat garden, with some sheltered tables, also has a good timbery play area. *(Recommended by Dr Paul Kitchener, Sally and Bill Hyde, Peter Yearsley, A K Thorlby, Mrs B Sugarman, P A Clark)*

Free house ~ Licensees Brian and Wendy Hibbard ~ Real ale ~ Meals and snacks (not winter Tues) ~ (01544) 327677 ~ Children in eating area of bar ~ Open 11.30-3, 6.30-11; closed Tues evening and all day Tues Nov-June ~ Bedrooms: £29B/£45B

WOOLHOPE SO6136 Map 4

Butchers Arms ★

Signposted from B4224 in Fownhope; carry straight on past Woolhope village

This is such a friendly, relaxed place that it's no wonder so many people enjoy staying here. It's very popular with locals too – always a good sign. The two welcoming bars are often filled with flowers, and one has old-fashioned built-in seats with brocaded cushions, captain's chairs and stools around small tables, very low beams decorated with hops, old photographs of country people on the walls, and a brick fireplace filled with dried flowers. The other, broadly similar though with less beams, has a large built-in settle and another log fire. Good bar food includes lots of lunchtime sandwiches (from £1.95), home-made soup (£2.25), leek and hazelnut terrine wrapped in vine leaves (£3.75), ploughman's with home-made pickles and chutney (from £3.95), stilton, pear and walnut strudel (£4.95), smoked haddock with bacon in a cream and cheese sauce (£5.25), local wild rabbit in cider (£5.50), steak and kidney pie (£6.25), rump steak (£8.95), and puddings like home-made apple pie (from £2.25); very good, hearty breakfasts; the restaurant is no smoking. Well kept Fullers London Pride, Hook Norton Best and Old Hookey, Marstons Pedigree and a guest beer on handpump, local ciders, quite a few malt whiskies, and decent wines. Friendly cat – dogs not welcome. Sliding french windows lead from the bar to a little terrace with teak furniture, a few parasols and cheerful flowering tubs; there's also a tiny willow-lined brook. The countryside around is really lovely – to enjoy some of the best of it, turn left as you come out of the pub and take the tiny left-hand road at the end of the car park; this turns into a track and then into a path; the view from the top of the hill is quite something. *(Recommended by Sally Barker, Lynn Sharpless, Bob Eardley, Norma Farris, John Bowdler, Dr J A T Saul, DMT, Jerry and Alison Oakes, Sarah and Peter Gooderham, Gordon, Denys Gueroult, C L Metz, the Monday Club, Mrs B Sugarman, Paul and Karen Mason, Roy Smylie, Mr and Mrs W W Swaitt, Ian Jones)*

Free house ~ Licensees Patrick Power and Lucinda Matthews ~ Real ale ~ Meals and snacks (till 10 weekends and summer) ~ Restaurant (not Sun evening) ~ (01432) 860281 ~ Well behaved children welcome ~ Open 11.30-3, 6.30(7 Mon-Thurs in winter)-11 ~ Bedrooms: £25/£39

Crown 🍷

In village centre

In the heart of the village, this busy and welcoming old place is popular with locals and visitors. The neatly kept lounge bar is light and airy with dark burgundy plush button-back built-in wall banquettes and stools, a timbered divider strung with hop bines, good wildlife photographs and little country pictures on the cream walls, and open fires. Good bar food includes home-made soup (£1.70), home-made potted stilton with mushrooms (£2.75), home-made bacon and cheese crumpet (£3.25), omelettes (£4.50), vegetarian casserole in yorkshire pudding (£5), fish pie or faggots in onion gravy (£5.25), steak and kidney pie or lamb and cranberry casserole (£5.50), steaks (from £8.50), grilled lemon sole (£10.75), puddings like home-made treacle tart or apricot claffouti (£2.25), and children's menu (from £2.50); the restaurant is no smoking. Well kept Hook Norton Best, Smiles Best, Tetleys and a guest beer on handpump, decent wine list, and farm cider. There are picnic tables under cocktail parasols on the neat front lawn; darts, summer quoits. *(Recommended by Paul and Sue Merrick, Jerry and Alison Oakes, Denys Gueroult, Ardill and Anne Booth, Mrs Pat Crabb, Mr and Mrs W W Swaitt, Derek and Sylvia Stephenson, R G and M P Lumley, Peter Lloyd, Alan Skull, the Monday Club, W F C Phillips, Andy and Jill Kassube)*

Free house ~ Licensees Neil and Sally Gordon ~ Real ale ~ Meals and snacks (till 10) ~ Restaurant ~ (01432) 860460 ~ Well behaved children allowed till 8, though customers with under 10s are asked to check with licensee to avoid there being too many at one time ~ Open 12-2.30, 6.30(6 Sat)-11; winter evening opening 7(6.30 Sat); closed evening 25 Dec

WYRE PIDDLE SO9647 Map 4

Anchor

B4084 NW of Evesham

Formerly boatmen's cottages, this relaxed 17th-c pub is a marvellous place in summer with seats on the spacious lawn that runs down to the River Avon, and views spreading out over the Vale of Evesham as far as the Cotswolds, the Malverns and Bredon Hill; quite a few customers arrive by boat. The big airy back bar shares the same fine view, and there's a friendly and well kept little lounge with a good log fire in its attractively restored inglenook fireplace, comfortably upholstered chairs and settles, and two beams in the shiny ceiling. Very popular bar food includes home-made soup (£2.25), good open baps (from £2.05), ploughman's (£3.50), excellent moules marinières (£4.90), broccoli and brie bake with almonds (£5.60), steak and kidney pie (£5.35), daily specials like Loch Fyne kipper mousse (£2.95), Drambuie haggis or stilton mushrooms in puff pastry (£3.50) navarin of lamb (£6.25), fresh seafood bake (£6.50), and casserole of venison in red wine (£7.75), home-made puddings (from £2), and children's meals (from £3). Friendly, obliging service. Well kept Boddingtons, Flowers IPA and Original, Marstons Pedigree, and Wadworths 6X on handpump and country wines; darts, cribbage, dominoes, fruit machine, and piped music. *(Recommended by G S and E M Dorey, W C M Jones, Lynn Sharpless, Bob Eardley, Jack Barnwell, Michael and Margaret Norris, Peter Pocklington, R J Herd, Simon and Louise Chappell, D R Shillitoe, John and Marianne Cooper, Alan and Jane Clarke, Bronwen and Steve Wrigley, Brad, Joni and Kristin Nelson, Bill Sykes)*

Whitbreads ~ Lease: Michael Senior ~ Real ale ~ Meals and snacks (not Sun evening) ~ River-view lunchtime restaurant (not Sun evening) ~ (01386) 552799 ~ Children in eating area of bar and in restaurant ~ Open 11-2.30(12-3 Sat), 6-11

Post Office address codings confusingly give the impression that some pubs are in Hereford and Worcestershire, when they're really in the Midlands, Shropshire, Gloucestershire or even Wales (which is where we list them).

Lucky Dip

Besides the fully inspected pubs, you might like to try these Lucky Dips recommended to us and described by readers (if you do, please send us reports):

☆ **Abbey Dore** [SO3830], *Neville Arms*: Open-plan local, partly divided by arches, with bays of red plush banquettes in lounge area, real fire, well kept Wye Valley Herefordshire, Supreme and HPA, good coffee, friendly landlord and Devon rex cat, decent bar food; pool, darts, fruit machine (and maybe rather obtrusive TV) in public area; charming Golden Valley countryside *(Derek Allpass, Jill White, Nigel Wilkinson, Mr and Mrs R J Phillips, BB)*

☆ **Aston Crews** [SO6723], *Penny Farthing*: Recently extended partly 15th-c pub, roomy and relaxing, with lots of beams, horse brasses, harness and farm tools, well in bar with skeleton at bottom; interesting good value food, well kept Marstons, decent wines, easy chairs, two restaurant areas, one with pretty valley and Forest of Dean views (shared by tables in charming garden), subdued piped music; bedrooms *(Neil and Anita Christopher, Mrs D Cross, BB)*

☆ **Aymestrey** [A4110; SO4265], *Riverside*: Friendly, well ordered 16th-c half-timbered inn with well kept Bass, Boddingtons, Flowers Original and Marstons Pedigree, decent malt whiskies, generous home-made food (mussels a favourite), relaxed atmosphere (service may not be that quick), friendly licensees, low oak beams, open fires, piped classical music, no games machines; restaurant; attractive terrace gardens by River Lugg; bedrooms *(J M Potter, C R Whitham, Paddy and Marilyn Gibbon, Basil J S Minson)*

Badsey [2 miles east of Evesham on B4035; SP0743], *Round of Gras*: Popular fresh-cooked food, esp asparagus, in straightforward pub with Whitbreads-related ales and log fire *(Kathryn and Brian Heathcote, Dave Braisted, BB)*

☆ **Barnards Green** [junction B4211 to Rhydd Green with B4208 to Malvern Show Ground – OS Sheet 150 map ref 793455; SO7945], *Blue Bell*: Comfortable Marstons dining pub in pleasant setting, wide choice of reasonably priced standard food inc vegetarian, well kept Best and Pedigree, friendly quick service, small no-smoking area, lavatories for the disabled; children allowed till 8, nice garden *(Graham Reeve, LYM)*

Baughton [A4104 Pershore—Upton; SO8741], *Jockey*: Real ales such as Adnams Broadside, Banks's, Woods Parish and Gibbs Mew Bishops Tipple, decent Australian wines, good bar and restaurant food, friendly landlord *(Frank Gadbois)*

Belbroughton [High St (off A491); SO9277], *Queens*: Comfortable local, friendly and clean, good value food, polite staff, well kept beer; quiet village *(Andy Petersen, W L G Watkins, DMT)*

Beoley [SP0669], *Cross & Bowling Green*: Bar, lounge and cottagey dining lounge, Tetleys-related ales *(D Hanley)*

☆ **Bishops Frome** [just off B4214 Bromyard—Ledbury; SO6648], *Green Dragon*: Attractive unspoilt flagstoned pub with plenty of character, good interesting range of well kept beers, fine log fire, reasonably priced simple bar food, games room, seats outside; children welcome, no dogs; open all day Sat *(Gordon, Rebecca Mortimer, Dorothy Pilson, Anthony Byers, LYM)*

Bishops Frome [B4214], *Chase*: Simple village local opp green, wide range of good value generous home-made food, very attentive friendly staff, seats on terrace, children welcome; three comfortable bedrooms *(Jill Easty, Graham Laylee, K D Day)*; *Wheatsheaf*: Very good value own brew beer called Overture, good Chinese/Cantonese evening food (and take away) in lounge area *(Dr and Mrs Baker)*

Bournheath [Dodford Rd; SO9474], *Gate*: Attractive country dining pub with popular food inc lunchtime and early evening bargains, also Cajun specialities and vegetarian, in bar and adjoining restaurant, well kept Boddingtons, Smiles Best and Exhibition and a weekly guest beer; nice garden *(Ian Shorthouse, Chris Wrigley)*

☆ **Bredenbury** [A44 Bromyard—Leominster; SO6056], *Barneby Arms*: Substantial hotel popular for wide range of generous food inc vegetarian and carvery in clean bright busy bar with ceiling joists, horse tack, lots of old woodworking tools; well kept Banks's and Marstons Pedigree, friendly staff; children welcome, big garden, comfortable bedrooms *(Peter Collins, Philip Jackson, Patricia Heptinstall, Graham Bush, John Hazel)*

Bredon [High St; SO9236], *Royal Oak*: Relaxed country pub, open fire, good choice of real ales, pool, darts, friendly staff; skittle alley *(Andrew Aldridge)*

Bretforton [10 Main St; SP0943], *Victoria Arms*: Good choice of home-made specials (not Mon) in clean tidy local with Theakstons Best, XB and Old Peculier *(E Cornish)*

☆ **Broadway** [Collin Lane; follow Willersey sign off A44 NW – marked Gt Collin Farm on OS Sheet 150 map ref 076391; SP0739], *Collin House*: Good bar lunches inc interesting freshly cooked main courses and good traditional puddings in lovely bar of small country hotel, very relaxed and civilised – good log fires, no machines or piped music (but no sandwiches or ploughman's either), very accommodating; nice restaurant not overpriced, good wine list, local beers, proper coffee, pleasant staff; tables outside; comfortable bedrooms *(Lawrence Bacon, Ian Rorison, W C M Jones)*

☆ **Broadway** [Main St (A44)], *Lygon Arms:* Magnificent old inn (run by Savoy group –

far from cheap) with interesting rooms rambling away from attractive oak-panelled bar; sandwiches all day; imaginative bar food in adjoining more intimate Goblets wine bar, with decent wines, wooden tables and pleasant service – does get busy in holiday season; tables in prettily planted courtyard, well kept gardens; children allowed away from bar; bedrooms *(D Hanley, GA, John and Shirley Dyson, LYM)*

Broadway [Main St], *Horse & Hound*: Spacious bay-windowed bar with plenty of woodwork, open fire, china cabinets, dining end with good value food; quick pleasant staff, Whitbreads-related ales with guests such as Hook Norton Old Hookey or Wadworths 6X, Sunday papers *(D Hanley, Neil and Anita Christopher)*

☆ **Brockhampton** [Bringsty Common; off A44 Bromyard—Worcester; SO6955], *Live & Let Live*: Consistently friendly service and well kept beers in basic rustic tavern down rough track over bracken-covered common – only the sign of this black and white half-timbered cottage is visible from the road *(Rebecca Mortimer, Gordon)*

Bromsgrove [78 Birmingham Rd; SO9570], *Hop Pole*: Homely and welcoming, with well kept good value Red Cross OBJ ale, wide range of reasonably priced sandwiches and other snacks *(Dr and Mrs Bill Baker)*

☆ **Bromyard** [Sherford St; SO6554], *Crown & Sceptre*: Wide choice of good generous food inc good veg and children's dishes in simply decorated 17th/18th-c family pub; good dining room, ever-changing guest beers, daily papers, big woodburner in inglenook; popular at weekends; bedrooms *(Douglas and Patricia Gott, Anthony Byers, Rebecca Mortimer)*

Bromyard [Stourport Rd (B4203)], *Holly Tree*: Good value local with cosy lounge, spacious public bar and dining room; Tetleys and Worthington, prompt friendly service, cheap food inc sandwiches *(Neil and Anita Christopher)*

Bromyard Downs [OS Sheet 149 map ref 671559; SO6755], *Royal Oak*: Beautifully placed 18th-c pub with wide views, dining room with huge bay window, John Smiths and Tetleys, pool table in L-shaped bar with interesting woodwork, open fires, friendly staff *(Neil and Anita Christopher)*

☆ **Carey** [signed from good road through Hoarwithy; OS Sheet 149 map ref 564310; SO5631], *Cottage of Content*: Medieval country cottage in lovely peaceful setting, opened up inside but still quite a bit of character, with flagstones, beams, alcoves, stripped pine and other appropriate furnishings; Bass, Hook Norton Best and Old Hookey and Worthington, bar food, traditional games; TV in bar, children welcome, tables outside; bedrooms; generally relaxing and very highly rated, but there has been an undercurrent of 'could do better' concern in some readers' reports *(Dorothy Pilson, R M Bloomfield, Mr and Mrs W W Swaitt, TBB, R G and M P Lumley, Andy and Jill Kassube, Nigel Clifton, Gordon, Jerry and Alison Oakes, Andrew Stephenson, Nigel Wilkinson, Roger and Christine Mash, LYM; more reports please)*

☆ **Castlemorton** [Castlemorton Common; B4208 – OS Sheet 150 map ref 787388; SO7838], *Plume of Feathers*: Lovely little whitewashed country pub doing very well under newish owners, low beams, log fire, warmly welcoming landlady, attractively priced home cooking, Bass, Boddingtons, Hook Norton Best, Morlands Old Speckled Hen and John Smiths, separate darts and dining areas *(Mike Dickerson, A Y Drummond)*

☆ **Chaddesley Corbett** [off A448 Bromsgrove—Kidderminster; SO8973], *Fox*: Recently refurbished to give more space, good cheap home cooking esp bargain lunchtime carvery (get there early for a table), welcoming atmosphere, friendly staff, well kept Theakstons, good service, nice dogs *(W H and E Thomas, David G Pearce, Moira and John Cole)*

Chaddesley Corbett [High St], *Swan*: Good Bathams Mild and Bitter, good snacks such as hot pork sandwiches, jazz Thurs, other live music some weekends *(Dr and Mrs Baker)*

☆ **Claines** [3 miles from M5 junction 6; A449 towards Ombersley, then leave dual carriageway at second exit for Worcester; village signposted from here, and park in Cornmeadow Lane; SO8558], *Mug House*: Ancient basic country tavern in unique churchyard setting by fields below the Malvern Hills, low doorways, heavy oak beams, well kept cheap Banks's Bitter and Mild, minimal choice of basic but generous snacks (not Sun), children allowed in snug away from servery *(John and Phyllis Maloney, LYM)*

Cleeve Prior [Main St (B4085); SP0849], *Kings Arms*: Well run and comfortable, no piped music, good filled french bread and well kept beers *(Wade and Jud Pollard)*

☆ **Clent** [A491 Bromsgrove—Stourbridge; SO9279], *Holly Bush*: Pleasant country pub very popular midweek lunchtime for good range of freshly cooked bar food (may be a wait) esp fish, Holt Plant & Deakins Bitter and Entire *(Jack Barnwell, Dorothee and Dennis Glover)*

Clifton upon Teme [SO7162], *Red Lion*: Civilised and comfortable, rather smart even, with central log fire in big bar, decent food, friendly service; attractive beamed bedrooms, pretty village *(Gordon, Anthony Byers)*

☆ **Clows Top** [A456 Bewdley—Tenbury; SO7171], *Colliers Arms*: Reliable dining pub, roomy and comfortable, with wide choice of food inc vegetarian, no-smoking restaurant, civilised service, log fires, well kept Theakstons Best and XB, unobtrusive piped music; no dogs *(Frank Cummins)*

☆ **Crowle** [SO9256], *Old Chequers*: Smart and busy, with more modern restaurant extension opening off old pubby core of some character, good generous food inc unusual dishes (no sandwiches etc), prompt service, several well kept ales inc Bass *(Graham Reeve, G S and E M Dorey, Mrs Nicola Holden, Miss M Roberts, W H and E Thomas, Martin Lavery, David Jones)*

☆ **Doverdale** [off A449 Kidderminster—Worcester; SO8665], *Ripperidge*: Good food esp fresh fish, separate restaurant, pleasant service and surroundings *(W H and E Thomas)*

☆ **Droitwich** [Copcut Elm (A38 Worcester rd); SO9063], *Trotter Hall*: Part of M A D O'Rourke's 'Little' chain, eccentric mock-up of piggy stately home with appropriate ceiling paintings, waxwork boar musicians, statues and portraits of noble pigs, but also tasty food in the two big basic but comfortable rooms, well kept beers inc Bass and Little Lumphammer; children welcome *(Graham Reeve, David and Shelia, Dave Braisted)*

☆ **Dunhampstead** [just SE of Droitwich; pub towards Sale Green – OS Sheet 150 map ref 919600; SO9160], *Firs*: Civilised and relaxing country local with good home cooking inc some unusual dishes, helpful prompt service, friendly dogs, comfortable conservatory; well kept Bass, popular restaurant, tables in garden – a nice spot in summer, nr canal *(Mr and Mrs R Phillips, Mr and Mrs N C Shaw, LYM)*

☆ **Eardisland** [A44; SO4258], *White Swan*: Interesting old pub in lovely black-and-white village, with armchairs and enormous fire in cosy inner core, two rooms furnished more suitably for eating, pleasant public bar with pool and fruit machine, good back garden with play house: would have been a main entry this year for exceptionally welcoming service (for children too), wide choice of nicely prepared generous food, well kept Marstons ales and attractive bric-a-brac, but Mr Burke the tenant hopes to move to another nearby pub *(BB; reports on new regime please)*

☆ **Elmley Castle** [village signed off A44 and A435, not far from Evesham; SO9841], *Queen Elizabeth*: Ancient tavern in pretty village below Bredon Hill, cheap farm cider and well kept Marstons in attractive old-fashioned tap room, haphazard medley of periods in decoration and furnishings, friendly licensee and locals, maybe piped classical music *(Derek and Sylvia Stephenson, LYM)*

Elmley Castle [Mill Lane], *Old Mill*: Good value lunchtime specials, well kept Whitbreads-related ales, children allowed in eating area; former mill house with lovely secluded garden looking over village cricket pitch to Bredon Hill *(Pam Adsley, LYM)*

Elsdon [SO3254], *Bird in Bush*: Comfortably refurbished pub in remote village overlooking huge green, clean homely lounge, no-smoking area, bar snacks *(Neil Barker)*

Far Forest [A4117 Bewdley—Ludlow, just W of junction with A456; SO7374], *Plough*: Bright and cosy beamed dining area popular lunchtime with older people for nicely cooked food inc vegetarian, pleasant friendly service, well kept Bass, Boddingtons BB, M & B Mild and a guest such as Youngs, woodburner, lots of brass and china; picnic tables on neat lawn, subdued piped pop music; children allowed if eating; good walks *(Frank Cummins, Dave Braisted)*

Fladbury [SO9946], *Anchor*: Unspoilt village local with several areas, friendly service *(Richard Houghton)*

☆ **Flyford Flavell** [½ mile off A422 Worcester—Alcester; SO9754], *Boot*: Unpretentious 18th-c beamed pub with plenty of character, wide range of good generous food (cooked to order so may be a short wait), well kept beer inc Bass, dining conservatory; lovely surroundings *(Geoff and Angela Jaques, M R Smith, Dennis Boddington)*

Fromes Hill [SO6846], *Majors Arms*: Tables in garden with spectacular view (great adventure place for the children if you keep them under control); bar food *(Anthony Byers)*

☆ **Gorcott Hill** [off A435 3 miles S of M42 junction 3; SP0868], *Hollybush*: Quietly placed but lively country pub with wide range of generous home-made bar food inc competitively priced seafood, well kept Bass, good service; busy with office people weekday lunchtime *(Graham Reeve, Ralf Zeyssig)*

Great Witley [SO7666], *Hundred House*: Busy much-modernised coaching inn, friendly staff, well kept Bass, decent food; handy for ruined Witley Court and remarkable church *(Michael Richards)*

☆ **Hadley** [Hadley Heath; A4133 Droitwich—Ombersley; SO8664], *Bowling Green*: Attractively refurbished three-roomed inn with vast range of reasonably priced food inc lots of interesting dishes and good value Sun carvery, also lunchtime sandwiches; well kept Banks's Bitter and Mild, Marstons Pedigree and Hook Norton, good value wines, comfortable bedrooms; has UK's oldest bowling green *(Denys Gueroult, Graham Reeve)*

☆ **Hanbury** [Woodgate; SO9663], *Gate Hangs Well*: Much extended dining pub alone in farmland, open-plan but well divided, with good value attractively presented food inc carvery and fine home-made pies, well kept Bass and Worthington, friendly service; very popular, best to book *(Jean and Richard Phillips)*

Hardwicke [B4348; SO2743], *Royal Oak*: Tastefully renovated, delightful atmosphere, good value food inc good Sun lunch, obliging service; bedrooms comfortable, horses stabled *(Mr and Mrs C Jewers)*

Hereford [69 St Owen St; SO5139], *Barrels*: Well kept Hereford Bitter, HPA, Supreme and Brew 69, also Dorothy Goodbodys and guest beer such as Lloyds VIP, with farm ciders from Bulmer's, Stowford Press and Weston's; open all day *(Richard Lewis)*; [71 St Owen St], *Sun*: City pub caught in a time warp, well kept Bass, Hereford Bitter, Whitbreads PA, guest beers and farm cider

(R Lewis); [St Owen St opp fire stn], *Victory*: Well kept Wye Valley Able Bodied, Powder Monkey and Eight Bells, Whitbreads Glorious Goldings and a guest beer such as Woods Parish, four farm ciders, bar in shape of a ship; bar food, restaurant; formerly the Jolly Roger *(Richard Lewis)*

☆ **Howle Hill** [coming from Ross fork left off B4228 on sharp right bend, first right, then left at crossroads after a mile – OS Sheet 162 map ref 603204; SO6121], *Crown*: Delightful hidden-away pub with good range of well priced tasty food (not Sun evening, Mon; no sandwiches), well kept Whitbreads-related ales, friendly landlord and labradors (no visiting dogs), padded pews; bar skittles, tables in garden; winter opening may be limited *(Colin Laffan, R G and M P Lumley)*

☆ **Inkberrow** [A422 Worcester—Alcester; set well back – OS Sheet 150 map ref 015573; SP0157], *Old Bull*: Friendly newish landlord doing good simple home-made food in photogenic Tudor pub with bulging walls, huge inglenooks, flagstones, oak beams and trusses, and some old-fashioned high-backed settles among more modern furnishings; lots of Archers memorabilia (it's the model for the Ambridge Bull), good range of Whitbreads-related ales, good value coffee; children allowed in eating area, tables outside *(E W Pitts, Peter and Jenny Quine, Anthony Byers, Gordon, Alan and Eileen Bowker, Meg and Colin Hamilton, Anthony R Clemow, LYM)*

☆ **Kempsey** [Green Street – a village, signed off A38 in Kempsey itself; SO8649], *Huntsman*: Bargain eat-as-much-as-you-like lunchtime cold table and short choice of other food (not Sun/Mon evenings) in simply furnished out-of-the-way local with horsey and hunting prints, county cricket memorabilia, well kept Banks's Mild and Bitter on electric pump and Everards Old Original on handpump, friendly great dane called Sam, ditto landlord, daughter and locals; children welcome (though no special food for them, no sandwiches etc) *(Maj T C Thornton, Mike Tucker, Philip Jackson, Patricia Heptinstall, Sue and Mike Lee, Derek and Sylvia Stephenson, Brig J S Green, Nigel Clifton, LYM)*

Kempsey [Bestmans Lane, Kempsey Common], *Farmers Arms*: Good value snacks inc cheap steak bap, M & B Brew XI and John Smiths, collection of full spirits bottles; start for several good circular walks *(Dave Braisted)*; [Main Rd (A38)], *Walter de Cantelupe*: Good value food (not Mon) inc sound local produce and some really adventurous cooking in bar's two small rooms or intimate and relaxing candlelit dining room; great atmosphere, log fire, changing guest beers such as Hobsons Old Henry, Lloyds Derby, Woods Shropshire Lad, wines imported direct from Italy – eight by the glass; no music, friendly labrador, back garden *(Drs Ben and Caroline Maxwell)*

☆ **Kidderminster** [Comberton Hill, in stn; SO8376], *King & Castle*: Welcoming replica of Edwardian refreshment rooms suiting its setting in Severn Valley Rly terminus, steam trains outside, good range of well kept ales changing daily, wide choice of basic good value generous food – even the sandwiches are massive; pleasant if sometimes smoky atmosphere, genuinely friendly service, children welcome; very busy bank hols and railway gala days *(R C Vincent, B M Eldridge, Patrick and Mary McDermott, Henry Brugsch, John C Baker)*

☆ **Kidderminster** [42 Mill Lane; signed off ring rd by A442 to Bridgnorth, fork rt opp General Hosp], *Little Tumbling Sailor*: Decidedly unsmart (lavatories due for upgrading) but has lots of good naval photographs as well as nautical hardware from brass and model ships to saucy figurehead; several rooms around central servery, home-made food from sandwiches up, well kept Holt Plant & Deakins Mild and Entire and Little Lumphammer; piped music (live Mon); well behaved children welcome, small garden with trawler deckhouse and sandpit *(Pete Yearsley, S P Bobeldijk, David and Shelia, Stephen, Julie and Hayley Brown, LYM)*

Kidderminster [centre], *Olde Seven Stars*: Cosy straightforward town house, courteous pleasant service, surprisingly good inventive food *(Jo Rees)*

☆ **Kingsland** [B4360 W of Leominster; SO4561], *Angel*: Timbered former coaching inn with miscellaneous furnishings, some pleasantly faded, in relaxed beamed bar, big stove, fresh flowers, prompt friendly service, good generous often unusual food, well kept Bass, Worthington and Wye Valley Herefordshire, decent sensibly priced wines, maybe loudish piped classical music; attractive restaurant, some tables outside *(Anthony Barnes, BB)*

☆ **Kington** [Church Rd (A44); note this is the Herefs one, handy for Hergest Croft Garden, Hergest Ridge and Offa's Dyke Path, at SO3057], *Swan*: Cosy but airy bar overlooking square, friendly helpful staff, good value food, well kept ales; restaurant; children welcome; bedrooms clean and simple *(Dorothy and Leslie Pilson, James Skinner)*

☆ **Kington** [Victoria Rd], *Olde Tavern*: Wonderful time-warp old place, very idiosyncratic but outstandingly friendly, with small plain often enjoyably crowded parlour, dark brown woodwork, impressive pewter collection, commemorative china; well kept Arkells, chatty landlady; children welcome, though not obviously a family pub *(Dave Irving, Tim Locke)*

Kington [Bridge St], *Queens Head*: Fairly recently reopened, brewing its own good Solstice ales – Golden Torc, Talisman and Capstone; cheap food inc some inventive dishes *(Dave Irving)*

☆ **Ledbury** [New St; SO7138], *Olde Talbot*: 16th-c timbered inn, cheerful and comfortable, with two bars and a restaurant, brass and copper hanging from the beams, well kept beers, wide range of good value food, open fire, tales of a friendly poltergeist; decent bedrooms sharing bath *(Mrs S Wright, LYM)*

Ledbury [A449 SW, junction B4216], *Full Pitcher*: Whitbreads pub done up in the current bit-of-everything 'old' style, open all day for food, with well kept Boddingtons, friendly staff *(A E and P McCully)*; [down passage to church], *Prince of Wales*: Beautifully placed on narrow lane nr market hall, low-beamed front bars, long back room, couple of tables in yard crammed with beautiful flower tubs and hanging baskets; very friendly landlord *(Gordon)*

☆ **Leintwardine** [SO4174], *Sun*: More private house than pub, very unspoilt and welcoming, three tables and benches in red-tiled bar with faded blue wallpaper and roaring fire, lounge with small settee and a couple of chairs is octogenarian landlady's own sitting room, Pitfield PA and Mild real ale drawn from casks in her kitchen *(Roger Huggins, Tom McLean, Dave Irving, Ewan McCall, Jack and Philip Paxton)*

Leintwardine [High St], *Lion*: Well kept Boddingtons and Morlands Old Speckled Hen, good choice of nicely presented good value bar and restaurant food, good service *(Mr and Mrs D Olney)*

☆ **Leominster** [West St; SO4959], *Talbot*: Comfortable and attractive old coaching inn with heavy beams and standing timbers, antique carved settles, log fires with 18th-c oak-panelled chimneybreasts, sporting prints; decent straightforward home-made bar food, well kept Courage-related ales, efficient cheerful service; piped music; bedrooms *(A K Thorlby, P Neate, BHP, BB)*

☆ **Leominster** [South St], *Royal Oak*: Generous cheap home-made food in handsome Georgian-fronted small hotel's bustling locals' bar, friendly service, big log fire, several real ales inc Hook Norton and Woods; can be rather smoky; spotless genuine Edwardian gents'; simple bedrooms *(W F C Phillips, Neil and Anita Christopher, BB)*

Leominster [Broad St], *Grape Vaults*: Friendly little pub with consistently warm welcome, well kept Marstons Pedigree and Best and guests, wide range of good freshly cooked bar meals, no games machines or music *(P Campbell)*

Letton [SO3346], *Swan*: Friendly atmosphere, accommodating service, good reasonably priced food all home made, well kept beers inc local Wye Valley, good games room *(S P Bobeldijk)*

☆ **Lingen** [OS Sheet 149 map ref 367670; SO3767], *Royal George*: Friendly pub combined with PO and shop, Bass, Hook Norton and Morlands Old Speckled Hen, good value bar food, coal fire, plenty of tables in big garden with good hill views, play area, fenced-off water garden; in beautiful country setting nr Kim Davis's alpine nursery and garden *(A K Thorlby, Dorsan Baker, T G Thomas)*

☆ **Little Cowarne** [off A465 S of Bromyard, towards Ullingswick; SO6051], *Three Horseshoes*: Wide choice of good home cooking in quarry-tiled bar and spacious restaurant (lunchtime carvery), well kept Bass and other ales, decent wines, log fire, mix of solid tables and chairs, friendly obliging licensees, disabled access; juke box, pool, darts and fruit machine; lovely country views from terrace and simple pleasant garden; comfortable bedrooms *(Mr and Mrs W W Swaitt, Anthony Byers, J Penford, A E and P McCully)*

☆ **Lulsley** [signed a mile off A44; SO7455], *Fox & Hounds*: Tucked-away dining pub with smallish parquet-floored bar stepping down into neat dining lounge, pretty little restaurant on left, popular food from sandwiches and burgers to duck and cherry sauce, Bass and Worthington BB, decent wines, open fire, colourful enclosed garden with play area; live jazz some Sats *(J Hart, Dave Braisted, Denys Gueroult, JAH, BB)*

☆ **Lyonshall** [SO3355], *Royal George*: Looking up under friendly new owners, clean and inviting, with outstanding floral decorations outside, good food and service, three rooms off central servery, pleasant partly no-smoking dining room; comfortable bedrooms *(A J Major, Vanessa Vassar, Robert Kopun)*

Malvern [SO7845], *Foley Arms*: Good range of food in bar, hotel lounges or on sunny terrace with good views, nice atmosphere in smarter restaurant with good value enterprising menu, Badger Tanglefoot, uniformed staff; bedrooms *(B and K Hypher)*; [74 Wyche Rd], *Wyche*: Clean and comfortable half-timbered pub nr top of Malvern hills, fine view, wide choice of reasonably priced well presented food, quick helpful service; bedrooms *(Philip Jackson, Patricia Heptinstall, P and M Rudlin)*

☆ **Mamble** [just off A456 Bewdley—Tenbury Wells; SO6971], *Sun & Slipper*: Formerly Dog & Duck, reopened 1994 under its original name after refurbishment to a high standard; reasonably priced well cooked food, esp fish, with good choice of veg; bedrooms *(A H Thomas)*

☆ **Mathon** [off A4103 just E of Stiffords Bridge via Cradley; or B4220 N of Ledbury; SO7345], *Cliffe Arms*: Very low heavy beams in three little rooms, flowery-cushioned pews and comfortable kitchen chairs, good relaxed atmosphere, enormous helpings of home-made food, efficient service, well kept Courage-related ales with a guest such as Hobsons Best, back dining room with small band in minstrels' gallery some evenings; streamside garden, lovely setting; children welcome *(Mr and Mrs G Taylor, BB)*

☆ **Monnington on Wye** [A438 Hereford—Hay; SO3744], *Portway*: Pleasantly refurbished roomy 16th-c pub with elegant oak-beamed lounge, good atmosphere, wide range of good imaginative home-cooked bar food inc vegetarian, using local produce; restaurant *(P Hogger, C E Power, Dr Michael Smith)*

Much Dewchurch [SO4831], *Black Swan*: Attractive roomy pub dating back in part to 14th-c, quietly welcoming landlord, real ales such as Bass, Crown Buckleys Rev James and one brewed by them for the pub, Hook Norton Best and Woods Special, decent home cooking *(Gwen and Peter Andrews)*

Newbridge Green [B4211, off A4104 just W of Upton upon Severn; SO8439], *Rose & Crown*: Former Drum & Monkey, reopened late 1994 with Banks's and Marstons ales, attractive food *(Mike Dickerson)*

Newland [A449; SO7948], *Swan*: Good food esp Thai chicken and chicken balti, Wadworths 6X, delightful homely atmosphere *(Philip Jackson, Patricia Heptinstall)*

Ombersley [SO8463], *Cross Keys*: Comfortable atmosphere, good well priced food, good range of ales *(J F Risbey)*

☆ **Pensax** [B4202 Abberley—Clows Top, S of village; SO7269], *Bell*: L-shaped main bar with long cushioned pews on bare boards, solid tables, restrained decor, open fire, dining extension looking over back garden's picnic tables to rolling fields and woods, interesting changing ales, friendly landlord, wide choice of good sensibly priced food, decent coffee; children welcome *(Andy Petersen, Alan Skull, BB)*

☆ **Pershore** [Bridge St; SO9445], *Millers Arms*: Spacious but cosy beamed pub with good value home cooking, friendly atmosphere,well kept Wadworths and guest beers; more of a young people's pub in the evening *(Derek and Sylvia Stephenson)*

☆ **Radford** [Alcester Rd; S of A422 Worcester—Stratford; SP0055], *Wheelbarrow Castle*: Popular beamed pub with new extension, wide choice of good generous reasonably priced food, fish specialities, friendly service, well kept Banks's, Hook Norton and Theakstons *(John and Shirley Dyson, Peter Lloyd)*

Risbury [OS Sheet 149 map ref 560549; SO5554], *Hop Pole*: Basic country tavern in old farm buildings, tiled hallway leads to small bar with tiny serving area, bus seats lined up in pairs and small fireplace; Woods served by jug from barrel in a back room, crisps – no other food; lively welcoming locals *(Graham Bush)*

☆ **Ross on Wye** [Riverside; coming in from A40 W side, 1st left after bridge; SO6024], *Hope & Anchor*: Big-windowed family extension looking out on flower-lined lawns leading down to river, plenty of tables out here (and summer ice-cream bar and barbecues), boating theme in cheery main bar, cosy upstairs parlour bar and Victorian-style dining room, decent food inc good choice for children, well kept Bass and Hancocks HB, farm cider, convivial landlord; open all day, can be crowded weekends, summer boat trips *(Ted George, I H Rorison, the Sandy family, George Atkinson, Lynn Sharpless, Bob Eardley, Christopher Glasson, LYM)*

Ross on Wye [Market Pl], *Crown & Sceptre*: Wide choice of good ale and home-made food; really nice atmosphere *(C Davie)*; [High St], *Rosswyn*: Well kept Courage-related beers, friendly staff and wide choice of reasonably priced bar food in 15th-c inn with curious 17th-c carvings in back bar, open fire; fruit machines round corner, juke box; restaurant, beautiful garden; bedrooms *(DP, LP)*

☆ **Severn Stoke** [A38 S of Worcester; SO8544], *Rose & Crown*: Beautiful 16th-c black and white pub, well modernised keeping low beams, nick-nacks and good fire in character front bar, well kept Courage-related and other real ales, good value generous food inc children's dishes and even on Sun enormous granary rolls, welcoming atmosphere, back room where children allowed; lovely big garden with picnic tables, playhouse and play area *(M A Cameron)*

☆ **Shatterford** [Bridgnorth Rd (A442); SO7981], *Red Lion*: Spotless olde-worlde pub with good atmosphere, good value well cooked food, courteous service, fine views *(W H and E Thomas)*; *Bellmans Cross*: Big pub with Hobsons and Youngs ales, decent straightforward food, sensible prices *(Dave Braisted)*

☆ **Shobdon** [OS Sheet 149 map ref 405625; SO4062], *Bateman Arms*: Comfortable two-bar local with good food, well kept ales, friendly landlord; restaurant; bedrooms *(Ralph and Lorna Lewis)*

Staunton on Wye [SO3645], *New Inn*: Well run 16th-c local, roomy but cosy alcoves, good range of generous home-cooked food inc vegetarian, Courage Directors and Smiles, friendly licensees; boules *(Denis and Kate Dighton, Nigel Foster)*

☆ **Stiffords Bridge** [A4103 W of Gt Malvern; SO7348], *Red Lion*: Roomy and busy main-road country local with good cheery atmosphere, log fire, sensible mix of table sizes, good food from rewarding sandwiches to lots of home-cooked interesting specials, sensible prices, well kept Banks's, Hobsons Best and Marstons Pedigree, local farm cider, pleasant service, tables on trellised terrace; bedrooms *(Steve and Cherri Griffiths, B and K Hypher, Dr David Clegg, LYM)*

☆ **Stockton Cross** [off A49; SO5161], *Stockton Cross*: Wide range of good reasonably priced home-cooked food in beautifully kept squat black and white building, well kept beers, decent wines, welcoming service; attractive garden *(K Baxter, Penny and Ray Perry)*

☆ **Stoke Prior** [Hanbury Rd (B4091); the one nr Bromsgrove, SO9468], *Country Girl*: On the up, with consistently good food and service, big helpings and reasonable prices, good choice of Whitbreads-related ales; handy for walks on Dodderhill Common *(A J Goring, G S and E M Dorey, Dave Braisted)*

☆ **Stoke Works** [Shaw Lane; a mile from M5 Junction 5 – OS Sheet 150 map ref 938656; SO9365], *Bowling Green*: Attractively and comfortably refurbished, with good value food inc children's, well kept Banks's Bitter and Mild, good atmosphere; big garden with beautifully kept bowling green; handy for Worcs & Birmingham Canal *(Graham Reeve)*

Symonds Yat [Symonds Yat W, just off A40; SO5616], *Old Court*: Beautiful old creeper-covered building, very cosy lounge bar with black panelling, open log fire, backwards clock; limited choice of good value bar food, baronial restaurant; open all day Mon-Sat; bedrooms *(A E and P McCully)*

☆ **Tenbury Wells** [Worcester Rd; A456 about 1½ miles E – so inn actually in Shrops; SO6168], *Peacock*: 14th-c inn doing well since recent reopening, several comfortable separate rooms, heavy black beams, views towards River Teme, cheerful log fires, comfortable kitchen chairs and ex-pew settles, well kept Bass, Ind Coope Burton and Tetleys, good food from sandwiches to enterprising well cooked main dishes, good fish and traditional Sun lunches, welcoming landlord, back family room, picnic tables on terrace *(Frank Cummins, LYM)*

☆ **Tenbury Wells** [A4112 S], *Fountain*: Quaint low timbered pub with lots of black beams in open-plan lounge bar, red and gold flock wallpaper, big brass platters, delft shelf of bright china, masses of artificial flowers, coal-effect gas fire, big dining room beyond, side bar with pool; particularly well kept Bass and Courage-related ales, decent wines by the glass, good choice of well home-cooked food inc fine specials, friendly and courteous service, maybe unobtrusive piped music; picnic tables on side lawn with lots of play equipment *(W W Swaitt, Joan and Andrew Life, BB)*

☆ **Tenbury Wells** [Teme St], *Ship*: Snug old town pub with lots of dark wood inc fine Elizabethan beams, little hunting prints and other pictures, well kept changing ales such as Glenny Hobgoblin and Timothy Taylors Landlord, good coffee, good imaginative bar food and Sun lunch in bright dining room with fresh flowers, reasonable prices, friendly landlord and staff, good relaxed atmosphere; piped music may intrude rather; picnic tables in coach yard and on neat sheltered back lawn; comfortable bedrooms *(Graham Reeve, A T Monks, George Atkinson, Michael and Barbara Chance, Roy and Mary Roebuck, BB)*

Tillington [SO4645], *Bell*: Good food in pleasantly done pub with lounge extension, warm welcome, local and other ales, friendly service *(J Penford and others)*

☆ **Trumpet** [A438 Hereford—Ledbury; SO6639], *Verzons*: Late 18th-c former farmhouse, now a cheerful and welcoming small hotel, with good choice of decent food in long comfortable bar-cum-bistro on left, well kept Hook Norton, friendly relaxed staff, restaurant on right; lovely garden with Malvern views; tasteful bedrooms *(Michael Lloyd, J F Risbey)*

☆ **Ullingswick** [Bleak Acre, towards Little Cowarne; SO5949], *Three Crowns*: Charming little low-beamed pub moved gently up market and blossoming under very welcoming and helpful new licensees, good food inc quite a few vegetarian dishes and some exotic dishes (but sandwiches too), real ales, decent wines, open fires, a couple of traditional settles besides more usual seats, plenty of atmosphere; tables in good garden, pretty hanging baskets *(S and S Pines, J and S Holman, Anthony Byers, John Bowdler, Frank Davidson)*

☆ **Uphampton** [SO8364], *Fruiterers Arms*: Small country pub brewing its own Arrowhead, Buckshot and good strong Mild; woodburner, local memorabilia, comfortable armchairs, lunchtime food *(Anon)*

Upper Wyche [Chase Rd off Walwyn Rd; off B4218 Malvern—Colwall, 1st left after hilltop on bend going W; SO7643], *Chase*: Fine views from civilised lounge of genteel rather clubby country pub on Malvern Hills, well kept ales, bar food – may stop well before 2; attractive garden *(Philip Jackson, Patricia Heptinstall, Dr J A T Saul, Anthony and Freda Walters)*

☆ **Upton Bishop** [SO6527], *Moody Cow*: Recently renovated charming country pub with good range of ales inc Courage, Hook Norton and Wye Valley, good generous food inc Sun lunch, helpful service, attractive floorboards; live jazz Thurs *(Mike Dickerson, Dr Paul Kitchener, Malcolm Smith)*

☆ **Upton upon Severn** [High St; SO8540], *Olde Anchor*: Picturesque and rambling but neat and tidy 16th-c pub with helpful service, old-fashioned furnishings, black timbers propping its low beams, lots of copper, brass and pewter, good fire in unusual central fireplace; well kept Courage-related ales, straightforward low-priced food; has been open all day summer, can get crowded evenings then *(D Godden, Ted George, Gordon, J and S Gregory, LYM)*

Upton upon Severn, *Kings Head*: Good riverside setting, extended well furnished lounge bar area, Whitbreads-related ales, separate eating area, food popular at lunchtime *(P and M Rudlin, Martyn Hart)*; [Old St, far end main st], *Little Upton Muggery*: Basic pub tricked out with nearly 4,000 mugs festooning walls and ceiling; generous food, well kept ales *(Bill Sykes, Ted George)*; [Riverside], *Swan*: Relaxed atmosphere and low stripped beams in main riverside bar, well kept Marstons Pedigree, two open fires, boating memorabilia, fruit machine, games machines in anteroom; small smarter bar with sizeable dining room off, good value interesting food; garden with summer barbecues *(Mike Dickerson, Jo Rees, Derek and Sylvia Stephenson, LYM)*

☆ **Upton Warren** [Worcester Rd; SO9367], *Swan*: Good value friendly Greenalls Millers Kitchen dining pub, well kept beers; new bedroom extension *(Dave Braisted)*

☆ **Walterstone** [off A465 at Pandy – OS Sheet 161 map ref 340250; SO3425], *Carpenters Arms*: Cheerful landlady and daughters helping out at weekends in lovely old unspoilt country pub, clean and friendly, with good reasonably priced food, well kept beer, nice kitchen range *(Gordon, Mr and Mrs S Price)*

☆ **Weatheroak Hill** [Icknield St – coming S on

A435 from Wythall roundabout, filter right off dual carriageway a mile S, then in village turn left towards Alvechurch; not far from M42, junction 3; SP0674], *Coach & Horses*: Roomy country pub popular for its wide choice of interesting well kept ales, most from small breweries; plush-seated low-ceilinged two-level lounge bar, tiled-floor public bar, cheap straightforward bar food, modern restaurant, plenty of seats out on lawns and upper terrace; piped music; children allowed in eating area *(Cathy Scott, Richard Baker, Wayne A Wheeler, Mr and Mrs C Roberts, George Atkinson, Lawrence Bacon, LYM)*

☆ **Wellington Heath** [SO7141], *Farmers Arms*: Good friendly service, reliably good food inc good value Sun lunch, well kept Courage Best and Directors, spacious and comfortable; tables on sunny terrace overlooking pretty wooded valley *(Mr and Mrs P Akitt, Anthony and Freda Walters)*

☆ **Whitney on Wye** [pub signed just off A438 about 1½ miles W; SO2747], *Rhydspence*: Good interesting if not cheap food in very picturesque country inn, old-fashioned furnishings, heavy beams and timbers in rambling spick-and-span rooms, pretty dining room, Bass, Hook Norton Best and Robinsons Best, children allowed, tables in attractive garden with fine views over Wye valley, comfortable bedrooms; very few reports in the most recent months, but we suspect this fully deserves a main entry – more reports please *(Ted George, Peter Yearsley, Jane Hosking, Ian Burniston, Colin Laffan, John F Shapley, Phil Putwain, Adrian and Gwynneth Littleton, Frank Cummins, S Demont, T Barrow, LYM)*

Wildmoor [nr M5 junction 4; SO9675], *Wildmoor Oak*: Useful for decent cheap food, M & B ales; collection of foreign number plates *(Dave Braisted)*

☆ **Wolverley** [B4189 N of Kidderminster; SO8279], *Lock*: Cottagey-looking pub with bay window overlooking a lock on the quaint Staffs & Worcs Canal as it negotiates a red sandstone bluff into which the pub is set, some waterside tables, comfortable furnishings, canalia, generous well prepared straightforward food, Banks's and Camerons real ales, good prices and service; lovely spot *(Bill Sykes, P and M Rudlin, Gordon)*

Wolverley, *Live & Let Live*: Good choice of good value food inc midday bargains *(Mr and Mrs M Pearson)*

☆ **Worcester** [31 Friar St], *Cardinals Hat*: The town's oldest pub, busy, cheery and easy-going, with its own-brewed Jolly Roger (see pub of that name, below), Shipwrecked and Flagship, also lots of well kept guest beers – beer mats cover ceiling above bar; comfortable oak-panelled back lounge, open fires, lots of prints, decent cheap home-made food esp soups, good coffee, good service, warming log-effect gas fire, piped music; jug-and-bottle off licence next door, brewery visits can be arranged *(Richard Lewis, Graham Reeve, Frank W Gadbois, David and Shelia, D Hanley)*

☆ **Worcester** [50 Lowesmoor], *Jolly Roger*: Basic down-to-earth stablemate of Cardinals Hat, much enjoyed by those who don't care for airs and graces; good low-priced but strong beers brewed here, interesting guest beers, good generous straightforward cheap food inc speciality sausages, friendly staff, thoroughly unpretentious atmosphere, barrel furniture, stone and wood floors, beams, ship-theme murals, bar shaped like galleon; children welcome; pool, games machine, piped music can be loud, live music Fri and Sat evenings *(Graham Reeve, Sue Anderson, Phil Copleston, Richard Lewis, David Campbell, Vicki McLean)*

☆ **Worcester** [London Rd, about ½ mile from centre], *Little Worcester Sauce Factory*: Fun pub with tiled walls advertising sauces, tiled map of Britain filling ceiling of largest room, lots of stripped pine and sawdust – and lots more sauce; good atmosphere, decent range of hearty good value food, friendly staff, Tetleys-related ales and their own Lumphammer *(Paul Weedon, D Hanley, David and Shelia, Frank W Gadbois, Andrew Jeeves, Carole Smart, JJW, CMW)*

Worcester [Angel Passage, Broad St], *Crown*: Modern busy Greenalls pub, several satellite TVs, generous good straightforward bar food, well kept beer, good photographs of 60s pop stars, very friendly service *(David and Julie Glover, M Borg)*; [Fish St], *Farriers Arms*: Pleasantly furnished lounge, basic public bar, relaxed atmosphere, interesting decorations, decent food, cheerful service; very handy for cathedral *(Ron Leigh, LYM)*; *Severn View*: Open fireplaces, black and white timbering, Home Bitter and Theakstons ales, bar food, good service; piped music; views of river beyond main road *(D Hanley)*

Wychbold [A38; SO9265], *Crown*: A Banks's Milestone dining pub with good value meals, friendly service *(Dave Braisted)*

Wythall [Icknield St; SP0775], *Peacock*: Old-established country pub with good range of real ales, good food from baps to char-grilled steaks, no-smoking area; open all day *(JB)*

☆ **Yarpole** [SO4765], *Bell*: Comfortably smart picturesquely timbered ancient pub extended into former cider mill, lots of brass and bric-a-brac, Hobsons real ales, good straightforward food, skittle alley; tables in sunny garden, very handy for Croft Castle *(Alan Skull, T G Thomas)*

Most pubs in this book sell wine by the glass. We mention wines only if they are a cut above the – generally low – average. Please let us know of any good pubs for wine.

Hertfordshire

There are relatively few free houses in this county, so that a higher than usual proportion of our entries are tied to breweries. This may account for the chopping and changing we tend to find here: this year, the landlord of the Three Horseshoes at Bourne End (a really nice summer pub) has moved to the interesting old Fighting Cocks in St Albans; the cheerful Goat in St Albans has new managers again; the landlord of the Jolly Waggoner at Ardeley (very popular home-cooked food) has also taken on the Bull at Cottered, doing a major refit; and the Sow & Pigs near Wadesmill has a new landlady (readers just as keen as ever). Other changes to note here include four entirely new main entries: the Bushel & Strike at Ashwell (food whenever they're open), the White Horse at Burnham Green (a very popular well run dining pub), the Lytton Arms at Knebworth (an attractive place with excellent beers) and the Plume of Feathers at Tewin (good food in very civilised surroundings). Other places with particularly good food include the Sword in Hand at Westmill (increasingly popular) and the George & Dragon at Watton at Stone, which is again our choice as Hertfordshire Dining Pub of the Year. The Rose & Crown in St Albans has excellent sandwiches. Drinks prices in the area are rather higher than the national average, particularly in pubs tied to the national combines or a non-brewing chain supplied by them such as Greenalls. The Valiant Trooper at Aldbury and (brewing its own) the Fox & Hounds at Barley were outstandingly cheap, and the Garibaldi in St Albans, a Fullers pub, was lower priced than most. In the Lucky Dip at the end of the chapter, pubs we'd particularly pick out include the Greyhound at Aldbury, Farmers Boy at Brickendon, Two Brewers at Chipperfield, Alford Arms at Frithsden, Silver Fox at Hertford Heath, Nags Head at Little Hadham, Green Dragon at London Colney, Coach & Horses at Newgate Street, Cabinet at Reed and Scotsbridge Mill in Rickmansworth; as we have inspected almost all of these we can firmly vouch for them.

ALDBURY SP9612 Map 4

Valiant Trooper

Village signposted from Tring and under a mile E of Tring railway station; Trooper Road (towards Aldbury Common)

Quite an old-fashioned and rustic feel to this characterful and friendly family-run free house, a partly pink-painted and tiled pub near the village pond and stocks. The lively first room, beamed and tiled in red and black, has built-in wall benches, a pew and small dining chairs around the attractive country tables, and a woodburning stove in the inglenook fireplace. In the brown-carpeted middle bar there's some exposed brick work and spindleback chairs and some easily missed signs warning you to 'mind the step'. The far room has nice country kitchen chairs around individually chosen tables, and a brick fireplace; decorations are mostly antique cavalry prints. The simple but very good and well-liked bar food includes a popular range of open sandwiches or filled baked potatoes (from £2.75), ploughman's (£2.75), cottage pie (£4.20), sausage and mash or mixed grill (£4.90), and children's meals (£2.25). The lounge bar is no smoking at lunchtime; pleasant, obliging service. Well kept Bass, Fullers London Pride, Wadworths 6X, Youngs Special and a guest on handpump, along with John Smiths for £1 a pint; during their popular happy hours (12-2 and 5-7), one of the beers and a lager are sold at £1.30 a pint, and spirits are good value too, at £1.50 a double. There are some tables in the small, prettily flowered garden at the back, and the concrete terrace has been reduced and put to grass. Shove-ha'penny, dominoes, cribbage, bridge on Monday nights; dogs welcome – their own big black one is called Alexander. The village itself is fascinating, and handy for some of the very best Chilterns scenery – particularly nice views can be had from around the monument to the Duke of Bridgewater, and the woods close to the pub are very good for walking. *(Recommended by S J Edwards, Nigel and Lindsay Chapman, Peter Saville, John Fahy, Andrew Scarr, Lyn and Bill Capper, Ted George)*

Free house ~ Licensee Dorothy Eileen O'Gorman ~ Real ale ~ Meals and snacks (not Sun or Mon evenings) ~ Restaurant (not Sun evening) ~ Aldbury Common (0144 285) 1203 ~ Children in eating area of bar until 9pm ~ Open 11.30-11

ARDELEY TL3027 Map 5

Jolly Waggoner

Signposted off B1037 NE of Stevenage

Tucked away in a peaceful village, this pretty little pub is well liked by readers for its very good bar food – nothing too fancy or complicated, but carefully prepared by the landlord using fresh produce from local suppliers. Attractively presented dishes include sandwiches (from £1.95), french onion soup (£2.50), locally made sausages (£3.25), ploughman's (from £3.95), excellent salads (from £4.25), home-made burgers (£4.50), vegetable and pasta bake or their very popular Arnold Bennett ommelette filled with smoked haddock and cheese (£5.50), salmon fillet (£9.95), calf's liver (£10.95), and delicious puddings; booking is essential for their Sunday lunch, and there's a £1 surcharge for credit cards. Sensitively refurbished by the brewery, the comfortable bar has lots of open woodwork and a relaxed and civilised atmosphere, while the restaurant (extended into the cottage next door) is decorated with modern prints. Friendly, flexible service. Well kept Greene King IPA and Abbot tapped from the cask, good range of wines; darts, cribbage, dominoes, fruit machine and piped music. The garden is looking very pretty at the moment; there may be boules out here on Monday evening. The landlord also runs a main entry pub at Cottered. *(Recommended by Bob and Maggie Atherton, Anthony Barnes, Wayne Brindle, Cyril S Brown, Charles Bardswell, David Surridge, Andrew Scarr, Martyn Kearey, Prof John and Mrs Patricia White)*

Greene King ~ Tenant Darren Perkins ~ Real ale ~ Meals and snacks (not Mon) ~ Restaurant (not Sun evening) ~ (01438) 861350 ~ Well behaved children welcome (must stay seated); no babies ~ Open 12-2.30(3 Sat), 6.30-11; closed Mon lunchtime

ASHWELL TL2639 Map 5

Bushel & Strike

Off A507 just E of A1(M) junction 10, N of Baldock, via Newnham; also signposted off A1 southbound; and off A505 Baldock—Royston; car park down Swan Lane off main street

The front part of this cheerful open-plan pub is devoted to eating, with a food display cabinet in front of a big stripped dresser on the left. The wide popular choice includes sandwiches (from £1.80), filled baked potatoes (£3), steak and kidney pie or six bean medley (£5.95), sizzler-stone dishes such as beef teriyaki or Cajun chicken (£6.95), rack of lamb (£7.95) and calf's liver with bacon, mushroom and Madeira (£8.95); good Sunday buffet lunch. Their approach to dining hours is flexible: and you can order food whenever they are open. Neatly laid tables have careful flower arrangements, and there are attractive hunting and coaching prints and local colour photographs – this is a pretty village, with some ancient timbered houses. The back part has some interesting seats including several cut from casks, and a coal-effect gas fire; beyond is a well furnished restaurant extension with the same menu and old farm tools as decoration. Well kept Adnams Broadside, Charles Wells Bombardier, Eagle and Fargo and a guest such as Badger Best or Theakstons XB on handpump or sometimes under light blanket pressure, very friendly staff. There are tables out on a small terrace and more spacious lawn, under a big apple tree and flowering cherry; no-smoking restaurant and buffet area. *(Recommended by N S Holmes, H Bramwell, Susan and Nigel Wilson)*

Charles Wells ~ Tenant Michael Mills-Roberts ~ Real ale ~ Meals and snacks (all licensing hours exc Sun eve) ~ Restaurant ~ (0146 274) 2394 ~ Children welcome ~ Open 11-3, 6-11(11.30-3, 5.30-11 Fri; 11-11 Sat)

AYOT ST LAWRENCE TL1916 Map 5

Brocket Arms ★

B651 N of St Albans for about 6 miles; village signposted on right after Wheathampstead and Marshall's Heath golf course; or B653 NE of Luton, then right on to B651

This white-painted and tiled 14th-c brick pub is a delightfully traditional place, simple and unspoilt, and reeking with atmosphere and genuine character. While the appeal of some similar old pubs has been adversely affected by shifting the emphasis towards dining, no such concessions have occurred here, and readers like it all the more for that. Well off the beaten track in lovely countryside and down some very narrow lanes, it has two bustling low-ceilinged rooms, with orange lanterns hanging from the sturdy oak beams. There's a big inglenook fireplace (often too hot to sit in), a big coal fire in the back room (which can be a bit cold in winter if the fire isn't lit), a fishtank in the dining room fireplace, magazines to read, and a long built-in wall settle in one parquet-floored room. Pictures by a local artist are for sale; darts, dominoes, shove ha'penny, piped music. A good range of beers on handpump includes Greene King Abbot and IPA, Theakstons Best and Wadworths 6X with two weekly changing guests such as Gibbs Mew Bishops Tipple or Eldridge Pope Royal Oak; Rosies farm cider and Stowpress keg cider. The short new bar menu includes stilton and onion soup or filled french sticks (£2.50), filled baked potatoes, a good salad buffet, chicken and potato or pork and turkey pies (£5), king prawns in a crispy garlic and herb coating (£6), daily specials, and puddings (£2); they do ploughman's (from £4) all day. Afternoon teas weekends and bank holidays. It can get very crowded at weekends when the service might suffer a little; it may also be a little smoky then. The extensive sun-trap walled garden has a summer bar and a children's play area. The pub is haunted by the ghost of a Catholic priest who was tried and hanged here during the Reformation. Just over the road are the romantic remains of a medieval church, when it was the monastic quarters for the nearby romantically ruined Norman church. Nearby is the house of George Bernard Shaw, also reputedly haunted, not by Shaw, but his friend T E Lawrence. *(Recommended by M W Turner, Nigel Norman, Peter and Joy Heatherley, Nick and Alison Dowson, Phil and Heidi Cook, Nigel Hopkins, Tom McLean, Roger Huggins, Howard James, Martin and Pauline Richardson, Andy Thwaites, JMB, J A Boucher, J and P Maloney, Wayne Brindle*

Free house ~ Lease: Toby Wingfield Digby ~ Real ale ~ Meals and snacks ~ Partly no-smoking restaurant (not Sun or Mon evening) ~ (01438) 820250 ~ Children in restaurant ~ Open 11-11; 11-3, 6-11 Sat ~ Bedrooms: £40/from £55B

BARLEY TL3938 Map 5

Fox & Hounds

Nr Junction of B1368 and B1039, SE of Royston

A favourite with James I when he was hunting from Royston, this attractive 15th-c local is currently well regarded for its excellent range of well kept beers and wide choice of good bar food. As well as their own very well priced Nathaniel's Special and the somewhat stronger Flame Thrower, the range of beers on handpump includes Boddingtons and Whitbread Castle Eden, and six changing guests from around the country; lots more during their real ale festivals. Also farm ciders, a good range of wines by the bottle or glass and several malt whiskies. The blackboard menu generally covers an entire wall, and features carefully prepared dishes such as soup (£1.75), chestnut and wine pâté (£3.25), spare ribs (£3.45), pies such as steak and kidney or venison and onion (from £5.55), rabbit and mustard casserole (£5.95), lots of vegetarian dishes such as cashew nut paella or avocado and corn bake (£5.95), salmon dill and potato bake (£6.95), trout stuffed with prawns and asparagus (£7.95), half a roast duck with mango (£8.25), and children's meals (from £1.75). There's a well-furnished series of low-ceilinged and alcovey rambling rooms, with substantial log fires on both sides of a massive central chimney. The dining area with its odd-shaped nooks and crannies was originally the kitchen and cellar; half of it is now no smoking. Friendly staff, locals and cat, and a fine range of games, from darts (two league darts teams), bar billiards and dominoes (two schools), to shove-ha'penny, cribbage, fruit machine and skittles; also a league cricket team, and pétanque. They have disabled lavatories and ramp access to dining room at the back. ***(Recommended by Frank Gadbois, Charles Bardswell, M E Wellington, David Craine, Ann Reeder, Susan and Nigel Wilson, Dave Braisted, Joy Heatherley, David and Valerie Hooley, Karen Phillips, Ben Grose, K and B Moore, R L Turnham, Stephen and June Curtis)***

Own brew ~ Licensee Rita Nicholson ~ Real ale ~ Meals and snacks ~ Restaurant ~ (01763) 848459 ~ Well-behaved children welcome until 9pm ~ Open 12-2.30, 6-11 (all day summer Sats)

BOURNE END TL0206 Map 5

Three Horseshoes

Winkwell; narrow lane just off A41 Berkhamsted—Hemel Hempstead

In summer the setting of this pretty little black-and-white pub is hard to beat, right beside a canal and looking down to an unusual swing bridge. Tables on the terrace and more tables out among tubs of flowers by the water are well placed for views of the nearby narrowboat basin. A good deal older than most canal pubs (it's said to date back to the 16th c). There are three cosy and homely rooms with low beamed ceilings, an aga, and three roomy inglenook fireplaces, one still with its side bread oven. Furnishings are comfortable and traditional, and there are gleaming horsebrasses and harness around the softly-lit walls. A recent extension directly overlooks the canal through the bay windows. A good range of real ales on handpump might include Benskins Best, Eldridge Pope Royal Oak, Ind Coope Burton, Marstons Pedigree, Tetleys and a weekly changing guest; friendly and relaxed staff. As well as sandwiches, bar food might include hot dishes such as fisherman's pie (£5.25), sheep shank (£6.95), and 16oz fresh trout (£7.95). It can sometimes be difficult to find a seat inside – though that tends to be in fine weather, when the outside tables come into play anyway. ***(Recommended by M W Turner, Mr and Mrs Hillman, Nigel and Lindsay Chapman, John Fahy, David Shillitoe, David Wright, BKA, Ted George, Mr and Mrs M P Aston)***

Ind Coope (Allied) ~ Manager David Mehsen ~ Real ale ~ Meals and snacks (not Sun evening) ~ (01442) 862585 ~ Children welcome ~ Open 11-11

BURNHAM GREEN TL2516 Map 5

White Horse

Off B1000 N of Welwyn, just E of railway bridge by Welwyn Station

Facing a broad green, this thriving and very civilised dining pub fills quickly at lunchtime, especially with older people with an eye for value: food then includes sandwiches (from £1.40), local sausages (£2.75), ploughman's (£2.85), filled baked potatoes (from £3.40), vegetable lasagne (£3.90), omelettes (from £3.90), gammon (£6.25) and steaks (from £8.25 for 8oz sirloin), with dishes of the day such as skate with black butter, hake with lemon butter sauce (£4.75) or dressed Cromer crab (£5.75), and several home-made puddings (£1.95). In the evening prices are a shade higher, with several more elaborate dishes such as stuffed guineafowl (£9.50), but no sandwiches etc. The nicest part – get there early for a chance of a seat – is the original black-beamed bit by the bar, with solid traditional furnishings, hunting prints, corner china cupboards and log-effect gas fire in two small communicating areas. There are many more tables in a two-floor extension with pitched rafters in its upper gallery, no smoking downstairs. A back brick terrace by a fountain has neat teak garden furniture, with picnic tables on grass by a pond beyond, and a gentle country view. Well kept Adnams, Bass, Fullers London Pride, Ind Coope Burton, Tetleys and Theakstons Best and Old Peculier on handpump, quick friendly service by neatly uniformed staff. *(Recommended by Phil and Heidi Cook, Martyn Kearey, Neil O'Callaghan, Stephen and Jean Curtis)*

Free house ~ Licensees Richard Blackett and Nicky Hill ~ Real ale ~ Meals and snacks ~ Restaurant ~ (01438) 798416 ~ Children in restaurant ~ Open 11-3, 6-11

COTTERED TL3129 Map 5

Bull

A507 W of Buntingford

The landlord of the Jolly Waggoner at Ardeley now also looks after this attractive pub, and as we went to press they were beginning a major refit. Attractively set among trees and greenery, it's already had a fair bit of brewery attention over the last couple of years, with a new conservatory, and extensions to the restaurant. The latest plans involved adding a grill house which by now should be serving fresh meats, fish and salad. The low-beamed front lounge is roomy and comfortable, with lots of horsebrasses, a formidable collection of cream jugs hanging from the beams and around the walls, and a good fire; unobtrusive piped music. A second bar has darts, dominoes, cribbage, fruit machine, and a video game. Well kept Greene King IPA and Abbot on handpump, decent wines, quick pleasant service. The well reworked sizeable garden has boules and a play area. *(Recommended by Charles Bardswell, Bob and Maggie Atherton, Phil and Heidi Cook; more reports please)*

Greene King ~ Lease: Darren Perkins ~ Real ale ~ Meals and snacks ~ Restaurant ~ (01763) 281243 ~ Children welcome ~ Open 12-3, 6-11; cl evening 25/26 Dec

ESSENDON TL2708 Map 5

Salisbury Crest

West End; off B158 Hertford—Potters Bar

The pleasant country views from the back terrace and garden here seem especially attractive at dusk, though there are seats and tables to enjoy them during the day as well. It's very much a proper pub, chatty and friendly, with beams, brasses, coach horns, and a warming open fire in the big copper-hooded fireplace. A smallish bar on the right has green plush cushions on traditional vertical-panelling wall seats. Good value straightforward bar food might include sandwiches, soup (£2.25), good fresh mussels or ploughman's (£3.75), chilli con carne, lamb cutlets in tomato and garlic or chicken with smoked sausage in garlic and mushroom sauce (all £5.95), and home-made puddings such as pecan pie (£2.95). Well kept Ansells and Greene King IPA and Abbot, a good range of spirits, and decent house wines. The cosy and stylish two-room restaurant has a cheerful and relaxed atmosphere too, despite its smartness. *(Recommended by Neil O'Callaghan, Gordon Pitt; more reports please)*

Free house ~ Licensee Ray Curson ~ Real ale ~ Meals and snacks ~ Restaurant ~ (01707) 876314 ~ Children in restaurant ~ Open 11-2.30(3.30 Sat), 5.30-11

Pubs staying open all afternoon are listed at the back of the book.

FLAUNDEN TL0100 Map 5

Bricklayers Arms

Village signposted from A41; Hogpits Bottom – from village centre follow Boxmoor, Bovingdon road and turn right at Belsize, Watford signpost

Coated in Virginia creeper, this low cottagey tiled pub is a peaceful, inviting spot, especially in summer when the tables in the lovely old-fashioned garden are surrounded by foxgloves against sheltering hawthorn and ivy hedges. The emphasis is very much on the good value bar food, with generously served dishes such as soup (£1.95), sandwiches (from £2.85), filled baked potatoes (from £3.15), ploughman's (from £3.95), local sausages (£5.45), chicken curry or fish pie (£5.95), vegetable stir fry (£6.95), bricklayer's feast – ribs, chicken wings and potato skins coated with barbecue sauce and garlic dip (£6.45), beef in ale pie (£6.95), steaks (from £11.75), fish, daily specials, and puddings (£3.45); there's an excellent à la carte menu too. The warmly decorated friendly and busy low-beamed bar has dark brown painted traditional wooden wall seats, open winter fires, and stubs of knocked-through oak-timbered walls that give a snug feeling to the three original rooms. There's a back dining room, and there may be nibbles on the bar; darts, cribbage. A good range of well kept (though not cheap) beers on handpump takes in Adnams, Chiltern Beechwood, Marstons Pedigree, Shepherd Neame Spitfire and two guests, and there's a good range of wines; prompt professional service from welcoming staff. It gets packed at the weekends, so arrive early for a table. Just up the Belsize road there's a path on the left, through woods, to more Forestry Commission woods around Hollow Hedge. *(Recommended by Heather Couper, Nigel and Lindsay Chapman, J Slaughter, Rhoda and Jeff Collins, David Goldstone, Gwyneth Holland, Iain Baillie, Simon Collett-Jones, Peter Watkins, Pam Stanley, Nigel Chapman, Bill Capper)*

Free house ~ Licensee R C Mitchell ~ Real ale ~ Meals and snacks (no sandwiches Sun) ~ Restaurant ~ (01442) 833322 ~ Children in eating area and restaurant ~ Open 11-2.30(3 Sat), 6-11

GREAT OFFLEY TL1427 Map 5

Green Man ♀

Village signposted off A505 Luton—Hitchin

Very much a food pub these days, this big, busy place benefits from an impressive sweeping view from the spacious and elegant conservatory, looking down across the picturesque garden, pond and waterfall, and beyond to the flatter land below stretching for miles to the east. The flagstoned terrace around three sides of the conservatory has plenty of chairs and tables and a profusion of flowers in hanging baskets and tubs, while inside the bars have low moulded beams, lots of antique farm-tool illustrations, wheelback and spindleback chairs around simple country pine scrubbed tables, some stripped brick, an open fire and a woodburning stove. An airier right-hand room has countryside prints, a cabinet of trophies, cushioned built-in wall seats, and another big woodburner with a row of brass spigots decorating the chimneypiece. Generously served lunchtime meals such as soup (£1.25), sandwiches and large filled rolls (from £2.25), filled baked potatoes, ploughman's (from £2.95), hot salt beef sandwich (£3.50), broccoli cream cheese bake or pies such as steak and kidney or chicken, ham and leek (£4.95), good lunchtime help-yourself salads (from £6), gammon (£6.25), and puddings like apple pie (from £2); they do a daily carvery (£6). Boddingtons, Courage Directors, John Smiths, Marstons Pedigree, Ruddles County and Websters on handpump, and a decent choice of wines by the glass; friendly cat, piped music, fruit machine. Attention to detail extends to the lavatories, where gentlemen will find a shoeshine kit and nailbrush, and ladies tissues, brushes and a settee. Children are encouraged to play in the front garden, where there are swings and a slide, rather than the back. *(Recommended by Howard James, Susan and Nigel Wilson, Nigel Norman, Ian Phillips, Mrs C Watkinson, Sue Grossey, K and B Moore, Michael and Alison Sandy, Bob and Maggie Atherton, Andrew Jeeves, Carole Smart, Nic Armitage)*

Free house ~ Licensee Raymond H Scarbrow ~ Real ale ~ Meals and snacks (cold food all day; no food Sun afternoon) ~ Restaurant (open all day Sun) ~ (01462) 768256 ~ Children welcome ~ Open 10.30am-11pm

KNEBWORTH TL2320 Map 5

Lytton Arms

Park Lane, Old Knebworth, 3 miles from A1(M) junction 7; A602 towards Stevenage, 2nd roundabout right on B191 towards Knebworth, then right into Old Knebworth Lane; at village T-junction, right towards Codicote

Facing a park-like green, this handsome Victorian pub's heart is its collection of 13 handpumps, serving well kept Bass, Fullers London Pride, Nethergate, Theakstons Best, Woodfordes Wherry, and quickly changing guest beers: on our inspection visit close to VE Day these included Adnams May Day, Banks & Taylors Victory Gold, Brewery on Sea Dive Bomber, Elgoods Cambridge, McMullens Oatmeal and Morlands Hope & Glory – at which point we surrendered gracefully. In his seven years here Mr Nye has served over 1,300 different real ales, and he keeps Staropramen beer from Prague on draught, and almost 100 bottled beers including plenty of Trappist and lambic ones. There are country wines, four dozen malt whiskies, Weston's Old Rosie farm cider, and hot chocolate and herb teas as well as coffee; in the winter, hot gluhwein served by the log fire, with chestnuts roasting. Several solidly furnished big-windowed carpeted rooms, some panelled and each with a slightly different decor (railway memorabilia here, old Knebworth estate photographs there), ramble around the big central servery, ending in a newish no-smoking conservatory with orderly pale tables on its shiny brown tiles; the dining area is also no smoking. Bar food includes sandwiches (from £1.65), soup (£1.85), filled baked potatoes (from £2.90), ploughman's (£3.80), ham and egg (£4.20), popular O'Hagan sausages (£4.30), home-made steak and mushroom pie (£5.30) and a fine mixed grill (£7.40), with children's dishes (from £2.10); there may be a delay at busy times. There are picnic tables on the front grass, and the safely fenced back garden has a play area; summer barbecues. Dominoes, shove-ha'penny, maybe piped music; hard-working landlord, friendly efficient service; Rimau the three-legged cat has now got used to being called Tripod. *(Recommended by P Neate, Sir John Stokes, Steve Watkins, Adrian Entecott)*

Free house ~ Licensee Stephen Nye ~ Real ale ~ Meals and snacks ~ (01438) 812312 ~ Children in conservatory ~ Open 11-3, 5-11; all day Fri/Sat

RUSHDEN TL3031 Map 5

Moon & Stars

Village signposted from A507 Baldock—Buntingford, about 1 mile W of Cottered

A pleasantly unassuming village local, with welcoming regulars and staff, and quite an intimate atmosphere in the unspoilt and cottagey little bar. There's a vast inglenook fireplace beneath the heavy-beamed low ceiling, and leading off is a table-filled no-smoking lounge bar. Straightforward but well-liked and good value bar food might include sandwiches, soup (£2.95), stilton and ale pâté (£3.25), ploughman's, ham and egg, good fresh fish and chips on Thursday evening, steak and kidney pie (£5.50), chicken with apricots and brandy (£7.25), and steaks (from £8.95); they're particularly proud of the home-made puddings (£2.25). Also Sunday roasts, and cream teas on summer Sunday afternoons. Well kept Greene King IPA and Abbot on handpump, and a short, decent wine list. Very friendly service; darts, dominoes, shove-ha'penny, cribbage, fruit machine, pétanque, piped music. The two dogs are called Fred and Lucy. There are good views from the tables on the rolling lawns that extend up the hillside and benches at the front. This is another of those pubs where not all the spirits are drinkable – the ghost here has apparently been known to turn off the gas in the cellar. *(Recommended by Bob and Maggie Atherton, Tony and Wendy Hobden, John Whitehead, D A Edwards, Robert Turnham, Martyn Kearey, David and Ruth Hollands, Diane Foster, Martin Danzebrink, Paul Kitchener, R A Buckler)*

Greene King ~ Tenants Robbie and Gill Davidson ~ Real ale ~ Meals and snacks (not Mon, or evening Sun) ~ (01763) 88330 ~ Children over 5 in eating area lunchtime only ~ Open 12-2.30, 6(6.30 Sat)-11; closed Mon lunchtime ~ Bedroom: £27.50B/£35B

ST ALBANS TL1507 Map 5

Fighting Cocks

Off George Street, through abbey gateway (you can drive down, though signs suggest you can't)

Readers visiting this enchanting spot for the first time have told us they'd expected it to be quite touristy because of the building's age and history, and been pleased to discover that this is not the case – it's a proper pub, with a good friendly feel. When it first opened as an alehouse about 400 years ago it was called the Round House because of its rather odd shape. It later became known as the Fisherman before it took its present name – a reference to the modernised Stuart cock-fighting pit that is still evident as a sunken area (now with nice seating) below the much-modernised bar. Some sort of building is said to have been here since the foundation of the Abbey in 793 and the years before it became an inn are filled with periods as a battlemented gatehouse, a mill and a boathouse. Though it's changed a good deal since then, heavy low beams still give a trace of its heritage, and a good log fire in the inglenook fireplace, a stuffed cock in a cabinet, some pleasant window alcoves, and other nooks and corners add to the atmosphere. Well kept changing beers such as Ind Coope Burton, Marstons Pedigree, Tetleys, Timothy Taylors Landlord and Wadworths 6X on handpump; cask conditioned cider. Sensibly limited bar food includes popular filled wholemeal baps (from £2.35), excellent ploughman's (from £3.40), vegetarian dishes (from £3.50), steak and kidney or fighting cock's pie (£4.25), and daily specials. Seats in the attractive garden look down to the river with its ducks. *(Recommended by Mark Matthewman, Ted George, David Goldstone, Brian Marsden, K E Wohl, Mr and Mrs P Aston, Professor John White, George Atkinson, P A Hubble)*

Ind Coope (Allied) ~ Manager Cilla Palmer ~ Real ale ~ Meals and snacks ~ (01727) 865830 ~ Children welcome ~ Open 11-11

Garibaldi

61 Albert Street; off Holywell Hill below White Hart Hotel – some parking at end of street

Bigger than the rather unprepossessing facade suggests, this bustling town pub manages to attract a real mix of age groups, and though quite a favourite with the younger set, it's rated rather highly by older readers too. There's a good friendly atmosphere in the refurbished Victorian style bar, which angles round the central island servery. Up some steps is a little tiled-floor snug, while a separate food counter on a lower level opens out into a neat and cosy little no-smoking conservatory. Victorian and Edwardian theatrical prints decorate the walls. Bar food includes sandwiches, curried apple soup (£1.75), butternut squash risotto (£3.50), popular enchiladas (£3.75), normandy-style pork (£3.80), and steak and ale pie (£4.50). Nicely priced and well kept Fullers Chiswick, London Pride, ESB and Hock on handpump; cribbage, dominoes, fruit machine, decent piped pop music. The pub has its own cricket team. A side yard has a few picnic tables. *(Recommended by BKA, Jan and Colin Roe, Brian Marsden, Martin Kay, Andrea Fowler, J A Boucher and others)*

Fullers ~ Manager Anna-Maria Quick ~ Real ale ~ Meals and snacks (not Sun evening) ~ Restaurant (closed Sun evening) ~ (01727) 855046 ~ Children in conservatory until 9 ~ Live blues music at least once a month ~ Open 11-11; closed evening 25 Dec

There are report forms at the back of the book.

Goat

Sopwell Lane; a No Entry beside Strutt and Parker estate agents on Holywell Hill, the main southwards exit from town – by car, take the next lane down and go round the block

This historic inn can trace its landlords as far back as at least 1686, and since our last edition there's been another name to add to the list. In the 18th c it had the most extensive stables of any pub in the county, and though the attractive building has changed enormously since those days, the several areas rambling around the central bar are full of character, as well as a profusion of eye-catching decorations – stuffed birds, chamber pots, books, prints and so forth; there's an open fire in winter. It's a popular place, especially with students, so there's usually a cheery boisterous atmosphere, even more so during their well-received live jazz. Boddingtons, Greene King Abbot and IPA, Marstons Pedigree, Wadworths 6X and a changing guest on handpump; good range of malt whiskies. Home-made bar food includes dishes like filled baked potatoes (from £2.25), big roast beef baguette (£2.95), scampi, and home-made pies (from £4.50); Sunday lunch (£4.95). Fruit machine, trivia and piped music. There are tables on the neat lawn-and-gravel smallish back garden, and maybe barbecues out here in summer. ***(Recommended by Susan and Nigel Wilson, Brian Marsden and others; more reports please)***

Devenish ~ Managers Colin and Dee Rowberry ~ Real ale ~ Meals and snacks (not evenings Fri, Sat or Sun) ~ (01727) 833934 ~ Children in eating area ~ Jazz Sun lunchtime ~ Nearby parking may be difficult ~ Open 11.30-2.30(3 Sat), 5.30(6 Sat)-11; closed evening 25 Dec

Rose & Crown

St Michaels Street; from town centre follow George Street down past the Abbey towards the Roman town

The friendly landlord at this relaxed and rather civilised pub is American, and his speciality American style gourmet sandwiches are reckoned by some readers to be the best sandwiches they've ever had in a pub. They range from cheese, apple and lettuce (£2.45) to more elaborate concoctions such as ham, salted peanuts, red leicester and tomato (£2.60), pastrami, apple and aspargus (£3.20), or liver pâté, bacon, swiss cheese, lettuce and french mustard (£3.70); all are attractively served with home-made potato salad and sweet pickled cucumber. A short choice of other dishes includes standard sandwiches (from £1.35), chilli con carne (£3.75), various pasta dishes (from £4.35), and moussaka (£4.95). The beamed public bars are firmly traditional (no games machines or music), and have unevenly timbered walls, old-fashioned wall benches, a pile of coffee-table magazines, chintzy curtains and cushions and black cauldrons in a deep fireplace; big fire in winter. Well kept Adnams, Greenalls Original, Tetleys, Wadworths 6X and a weekly changing guest on handpump; farm ciders, a dozen or so malt whiskies, winter hot punch and tea or coffee; efficient service. Darts (placed sensibly to one side), dominoes, cribbage. Lots of tables and benches along the side and at the back of the pub with shrubs and roses, flower beds and hanging baskets. ***(Recommended by Nigel Hopkins, Mark Hydes, Russell and Margaret Bathie, Brian Marsden and others)***

Greenalls (Allied) ~ Tenant Neil Dekker ~ Real ale ~ Lunchtime meals and snacks (not Sun) ~ (01727) 51903 ~ Children in lounge area lunchtime only ~ Irish and Scottish folk Thurs eve, acoustic club Sun ~ Open 11.30-3, 5.30(6 Sat)-11

TEWIN TL2714 Map 5

Plume of Feathers 🍷

Village signposted off B1000 NE of Welwyn Garden City; Upper Green Road, N end of village, OS Sheet 166 map reference 273153

Bought by the Mitchells of the Bricklayers Arms at Flaunden, this has now been transformed into a roomy but cosy dining pub, civilised and quiet, with very well spaced tables in several different low-ceilinged communicating areas. The nicest is up some steps at one side: a big oriental rug, easy chairs and sofas, a low table, oak-panelled bookcases covering most of one wall – very snug and clubby. Decor is generally very low key, with just a few carefully chosen prints on the cream walls. Behind the bar is a pretty pink-tablecloth restaurant, and there are well spaced picnic tables in a pleasant back garden overlooking a golf course, with some more tables out in front. Good interesting bar food, all home-made from fresh ingredients, includes soup (£2.90), filled potato skins (from £4.25), beetroot, asparagus and cashew salad (£4.95), pork and leek sausages (£5.25), tagliatelle (£5.50), steak and kidney pudding (£6.50), salmon fishcakes (£6.95) and Thai seafood curry (£7.50), with a few changing specials such as fillet of brill (£5.95) or well flavoured duck fillets with pepper, carrot and leek strips on a sizzler stone (£6.50); they'll do a bowl of olives (£1.25), and sandwiches including large mixed platters. Well kept Adnams, and changing beers such as Bass, Boddingtons, Hancocks HB, Marstons Pedigree and Morlands Old Speckled Hen; decent wines by the glass, including vintage and late-bottled ports. *(Recommended by Neil O'Callaghan)*

Free house ~ Licensees David Berry and Liz Mitchell ~ Real ale ~ Meals and snacks ~ Restaurant ~ (01438) 717265 ~ Children in restaurant ~ Open 11-2.30(3 Sat), 6-11

WADESMILL TL3517 Map 5

Sow & Pigs

Thundridge (the village where it's actually situated – but not marked on many road maps, which is why we list it under nearby Wadesmill); A10 just S of Wadesmill, towards Ware

Warmly welcoming under the new landlady, this cheerful village pub has a great deal of charm and character. The natural focus is the plank-panelled central serving bar, which has a small ship's wheel and binnacle, a rustic table supported by two barrels in the bay of the cosy window seat, and, as the name of the pub suggests, quite a porcine theme. There are lots of little piggies in a glass cabinet and amusing pictures in this vein on the wall. More spacious rooms lead off on both sides – the dining room on the right has dark beams and massive rustic tables, while the area on the left has a timber part divider, and a couple of steps half way along, helping to break it up. Very good generously served bar food includes sandwiches (from £1.50), soup (£1.75), ploughman's (from £3.25) and mixed grills (£7.50), various daily specials like beef in Guinness, liver and bacon, hock of ham with honey glaze and salad, or pigeon pie (from £4.95), and their speciality yorkshire fish and chips – haddock in an unusual batter (£5.25). Well kept Adnams, Greenalls Original, Shipstones and Wadworths 6X on handpump, along with a weekly changing guest. There are picnic tables under cocktail parasols, with their own service hatch, on a smallish fairylit grass area behind by the car park, sheltered by tall oaks and chestnut trees. Access directly onto the A10 can be difficult. *(Recommended by Joy Heatherley, John Fahy, Martyn Kearey, Sue Grossey, R C Vincent, K and B Moore, S M Wallace)*

Greenalls ~ Tenant Meriel Riches ~ Real ale ~ Meals and snacks ~ Restaurant ~ (01920) 463281 ~ Children welcome ~ Open 11-3, 5.30-11; all day Sat

WATTON AT STONE TL3019 Map 5

George & Dragon ★ 🍴 🍷

Village signposted off A602 about 5 miles S of Stevenage, on B1001; High St

Hertfordshire Dining Pub of the Year

It's mainly the excellent bar food that draws so many people to this popular old place, though it stands out too for its pleasantly sophisticated atmosphere. A typical day's menu might include sandwiches (from £1.10), home-made soup (£1.60), ploughman's (£3.25), filleted smoked eel with strips of bacon (£4.50), cornets of smoked salmon filled with avocado mousse (£4.95), flemish-style beef carbonnade (£6.75), lamb's liver in a cream, brandy and black pepper sauce (£6.85), salmon baked in whiskey and lemon juice (£7.75), medallions of venison in a port wine and juniper berry sauce or half a fresh lobster (£11.50), daily specials, and highly regarded puddings. The very good separate restaurant is partly no-smoking. Proper napkins, antiques and daily newspapers add to the smart feel of the place; it's best if you at least wear shirts with sleeves. They do get busy (you may have problems finding a table unless you arrive early), but service always remains friendly and briskly efficient. Well kept Greene King Abbot and IPA on handpump, under light blanket pressure; several malt whiskies and good house wines by half-pint or pint carafes, and a selected house claret. The carpeted main bar has country kitchen armchairs around attractive old tables, dark blue cloth-upholstered seats in its bay windows, an interesting mix of antique and modern prints on the partly timbered ochre walls, and a big inglenook fireplace. A quieter room off, with spindleback chairs and wall settles cushioned to match the green floral curtains, has a hunting print and old photographs of the village above its panelled dado. Fruit machine, summer quiz nights, and boules in the pretty extended shrub-screened garden. The pub is handy for Benington Lordship Gardens. *(Recommended by G L Tong, Nigel Norman, Maysie Thompson, Howard James, Peter Saville, M E Wellington, Joy Heatherley, Mrs C Archer, Bob and Maggie Atherton, Neil O'Callaghan, Hazel Morgan, Bernard Patrick, Patricia White and Prof John White, Huw and Carolyn Lewis, J A Boucher)*

Greene King ~ Lease: Kevin Dinnin ~ Real ale ~ Meals and snacks (till 10; not Sun evening) ~ Restaurant (not Sun evening) ~ (01920) 830285 ~ Children in small family room and restaurant ~ Occasional live entertainment ~ Open 11-2.30, 6-11(11-11 Sat); closed evening Dec 25

WESTMILL TL3626 Map 5

Sword in Hand

Village signposted W of A10, about 1 mile S of Buntingford

Perhaps the prettiest building in a particularly beautiful village, this colour-washed local is well liked for its friendly feel and tasty home-made food. Now all on blackboards, the popular changing menu might include dishes such as soup (£2.50), garlic and herb prawns (£3.50), warm avocado and smoky bacon salad (£3.95), ham, egg and chips (£4.50), lamb balti (£5.50), steak and kidney pudding (£5.95), pigeon breast with port and mustard sauce (£6.50), chicken breast with garlic mushrooms and mozzarella cheese (£7.50), and char-grilled sirloin steak with stilton and madeira sauce (£9.50). Booking is advisable in the restaurant. Well kept Greene King IPA and Abbot and a guest on handpump, changing range of wines. Traditional and comfortable, the beamed bar has photographs and prints on the cream and brown timbered walls, elaborate furnishings, cushioned seats on the turkey carpet, good log fires, a relaxed and happy atmosphere, and maybe Scruffy, the playful little dog. They were planning to extend the dining area as we went to press. There are seats on a terrace surrounded by climbing roses and clematis, and more in the partly crazy-paved side garden running down to the fields, where a play area has a log cabin, slide, and an old tractor to climb on. The sword in hand comes from the crest of Thomas Greg, a local landowner, for whom the pub's first landlord (also the village blacksmith) made the tools used on his Caribbean sugar plantations; cribbage, shove-ha'penny and piped music; nice walks nearby. The landlord sometimes organises classic car shows. *(Recommended by Dr Paul Kitchener, John Fahy, Maysie Thompson, Quentin Williamson, Huw and Carolyn Lewis, Martin Kearey, Martin and Jane Bailey)*

Free house ~ Licensees David and Heather Hopperton ~ Real ale ~ Meals and snacks ~ Restaurant ~ (01763) 271356 ~ Well behaved children welcome ~ Open 12-3, 6(6.30 winter)-11; closed evening 25 Dec ~ Bedrooms: /£39.50B

Post Office address codings confusingly give the impression that some pubs are in Hertfordshire, when they're really in Bedfordshire or Cambridgeshire (which is where we list them).

Lucky Dip

Besides the fully inspected pubs, you might like to try these Lucky Dips recommended to us and described by readers (if you do, please send us reports):

☆ **Aldbury** [SP9612], *Greyhound*: Simple old Georgian-faced inn by village duckpond below Chilterns beechwoods, handy for walks and popular with locals for good bar food; cosy snug eating areas with separate drinks and food serveries in passage between them, efficient welcoming service, well kept Tring Brewery beer; children welcome; a hospitable place to stay *(Ted George, Mr and Mrs W R R Bruce, David Evans, LYM)*

☆ **Amwell** [village signposted SW from Wheathampstead; TL1613], *Elephant & Castle*: Secluded and spacious floodlit grass garden behind low-beamed ancient pub with inglenook fireplace, panelling, stripped brickwork, 200-ft well shaft in bar; bar food (not Sun), well kept Benskins, Ind Coope Burton and guest beers on handpump; restaurant; children in eating area *(Nigel Norman, Helen Morton, Mr and Mrs N Hazzard, J and P Maloney, LYM)*

☆ **Ashwell** [High St; TL2639], *Three Tuns*: Flower-decked 18th-c inn with lots of pictures, stuffed pheasants and antiques in opulently Victorian lounge, good range of very quickly served food, Greene King IPA and Abbot, good coffee, friendly staff; more modern public bar with pool; bedrooms *(George Atkinson, Susan and Nigel Wilson)*

Ashwell [nr stn, just off A505], *Jester*: Good range of beers inc Boddingtons, Morlands Old Speckled Hen and Wadworths 6X, reasonably priced food, pleasant garden behind; bedrooms *(Susan and Nigel Wilson)*; [69 High St], *Rose & Crown*: Comfortable refurbished open-plan local, beams and log fire, freshly cooked food inc vegetarian in bar and restaurant (children allowed), Greene King Abbot, IPA and Rayments, pleasant service, darts and machines at plainer public end; tables in big pretty country garden *(Phil and Heidi Cook)*

☆ **Ayot Green** [off B197 S of Welwyn, nr A1(M) – OS Sheet 166 map ref 222139; TL2213], *Waggoners*: Friendly, good well presented bar food, three cosy well kept areas, lots of mugs hanging from low ceiling, separate eating area, good range of real ales, good service and atmosphere even on a lively Sat night, quiet suntrap back garden with play area, wooded walks nearby *(Fiona and Paul Hutt, Hazel R Morgan)*

Baldock [Whitehorse St; TL2434], *Rose & Crown*: Former coaching inn with well kept Greene King IPA and Abbot, good atmosphere, decent food *(K Glanville)*

Batford [Lower Luton Rd; B653, S of B652 junction; TL1415], *Gibraltar Castle*: Large Fullers pub smartly done in old-fashioned style, low beams, sparkling glass and brassware, cosy window alcoves, interesting militaria; well kept beers, food (not Sun – bar nibbles then), friendly staff and locals, some tables on front roadside terrace *(Michael Sandy, Dr and Mrs A K Clarke)*

☆ **Benington** [just past PO, towards Stevenage; TL3023], *Bell*: Generous food, efficient service, well kept beer in lovely old pub with unusual stag-hunt mural over big fireplace; secluded village *(Charles Bardswell, M E Wellington)*

☆ **Berkhamsted** [Gravel Path; SP9807], *Boat*: Lively atmosphere, lovely canalside setting, well kept Fullers Chiswick, London Pride and ESB, decent wines, lunchtime food (not Sun); fruit machine and piped music; children in eating area lunchtime *(Alan Stourton, Nigel and Lindsay Chapman, Comus Elliott, LYM)*

Bishops Stortford [a mile N; TL4821], *Red White & Blue*: Small and unostentatious, with good range of ales, tasty daily specials, fine service *(Jack Davey)*

Boxmoor [St Johns Rd; TL0306], *Three Blackbirds*: Half a dozen good quickly reasonably priced main dishes in roomy well appointed pub with no-smoking area *(J A Gardner)*

☆ **Brickendon** [1 Brickendon Lane; S of Hertford – OS Sheet 166 map ref 323081; TL3208], *Farmers Boy*: Roomy refurbished village pub in attractive spot, wide choice of good value food from sandwiches up, dining area, Greene King ales, friendly service, seats in back garden and over road *(Chris Mawson, A C Morrison, Martyn Kearey, K C Phillips)*

Brookmans Park [Bradmore Green; TL2504], *Brookmans Park*: Spacious and comfortable interwar pub in quiet local shopping area, food area with screens between tables, Whitbreads-related ales, straightforward food, pleasant chatty staff *(Keith and Janet Morris)*

Bushey [25 Park Rd, off A411; TQ1395], *Swan*: Old-fashioned largely unspoilt one-room backstreet pub, welcoming and homely; well kept Tetleys-related ales, darts, cribbage and dominoes *(Pete Baker, LYM)*

Chandlers Cross [TQ0698], *Clarendon Arms*: Friendly traditional country pub with well kept Marstons Bitter and Pedigree, Ruddles County and a guest beer, attractive verandah, lots of tables and cocktail umbrellas; handy for woodland walks, bar lunches (not Sun) *(Richard Houghton, Jonathan and Helen Palmer)*

☆ **Chipperfield** [The Common; TL0401], *Two Brewers*: Forte country hotel with surprisingly relaxed and pubby dark-beamed main bar, cushioned antique settles, well kept Bass, Greene King IPA and Abbot, Marstons Pedigree and a guest beer; popular lunchtime bar food in bow-windowed lounge with comfortable sofas and easy chairs, good restaurant; overlooks pretty tree-flanked cricket green; children allowed in lounge and restaurant, open all day Sat; comfortable bedrooms *(J S M Sheldon, John Misselbrook,*

Richard Houghton, Peter Watkins, Pam Stanley, Neil O'Callaghan, Janet Pickles, LYM)

Chipperfield [The Street], *Royal Oak*: Friendly relaxed atmosphere and well kept beer in two small neatly kept bars, log fire, soft piped music, no juke box; good bar food at reasonable prices *(Bob West)*

☆ Chorleywood [The Swillet; from M25 junction 17 follow Heronsgate signpost; TQ0295], *Stag*: Open-plan dining pub, but still a welcoming place for a drink, with well kept Tetleys-related ales, good atmosphere, no piped music or fruit machines; popular if not cheap food (not Sun evening) from sandwiches up inc imaginative dishes and lovely puddings, tables on back lawn, children's play area; busy weekends *(SMG, N M Baleham, Helena Reid, Peter Saville, Richard Houghton)*

Chorleywood [Long Lane, Heronsgate; off junction 17], *Land of Liberty, Peace and Plenty*: Friendly take-us-as-you-find-us local with well kept Courage-related beers, interesting guest ales from far afield, half-a-dozen Belgian beers on tap; limited range of freshly made bar food; TV may be loud *(Stan Edwards)*; [Rickmansworth Rd; A404 just off M25 junction 18], *White Horse*: Relaxing but quickly served bar lunches from sandwiches up in old two-bar pub with extended refurbished lounge, Greene King IPA, Abbot and Rayments, unobtrusive piped music; livelier evenings *(Jim Reid)*

☆ *nr* Datchworth [Bramfield Rd, Bulls Grn; TL2717], *Horns*: Relaxed and pretty 15th-c country pub, beams and inglenook log fire, rugs on brick floor, china and pictures; good sensibly priced straightforward food, well kept Whitbreads-related ales, good cider and coffee, welcoming staff, small snug; seats among roses on crazy paving overlooking green *(George Atkinson, LYM)*

Elstree [Watling St; TQ1795], *Cat & Fiddle*: Attractive unspoilt country pub with good food and wide range of well kept ales; not cheap *(Leslie Fryer)*; [Medburn; A5183 towards Radlett], *Waggon & Horses*: Well kept Adnams, Greenalls Original and a guest like Caledonian 80/- or Exmoor Gold, chatty welcoming landlady, bar food, exposed oak beams, gleaming brassware, blue and white china, fresh flowers, open fire; attractive garden with good views *(N M Baleham)*

☆ Flamstead [High St; TL0714], *Three Blackbirds*: Cosy low-beamed pub, partly Tudor, with chatty landlady, two real fires, old dark wood and brickwork, pictures, brass and copper; quick service, well kept Courage-related ales, Greene King and Marstons Pedigree, good value food; friendly bull terrier, pool, darts and fruit machine in games area; piped local radio; good walks nearby; children welcome *(JJW, CMW)*

☆ Flaunden [TL0100], *Green Dragon*: Attractive and comfortable Chilterns pub with several changing well kept ales, partly panelled extended lounge with small back restaurant area, darts and shove-ha'penny in traditional 17th-c small tap bar; reasonably priced straightforward food, friendly service, fruit machine; very popular Sun lunchtime; charming well kept garden with summer-house and aviaries *(Simon Collett-Jones, LYM)*

☆ Frithsden [from Berkhamsted take unmarked rd towards Potten End, pass Potten End turning on right then take next left towards Ashridge College; TL0110], *Alford Arms*: Secluded Whitbreads country local brewing its own ales, pleasant old-world atmosphere, good plain bar food from filled rolls up (step down to nicely furnished eating area), quick friendly service, open all day Sat; darts, bar billiards, fruit machine; in attractive countryside, picnic tables out in front *(Bill Capper, Ted George, Maurice Southon, Nigel and Lindsay Chapman, LYM)*

Goffs Oak [Andrews Lane; TL3103], *Prince of Wales*: Friendly country local with good food, big garden *(Mike Cahill)*

☆ Graveley [TL2327], *Waggon & Horses*: Former coaching inn with comfortable beamed and timbered lounge, big open fire, good choice of straightforward food popular lunchtime with Stevenage businesspeople, Whitbreads-related ales; locals' snug by door where Brin the pub's terrier can be found; big terrace by village duckpond, summer lunchtime barbecues *(Charles Bardswell)*

Great Offley [towards Kings Walden; TL1427], *Red Lion*: Good food, reasonable choice of Whitbreads-related and other ales, log fire in small, simple and cosy low-ceilinged central bar, friendly welcome, restaurant; piped music; bedrooms *(Ian Phillips)*

☆ Halls Green [NW of Stevenage; TL2728], *Rising Sun*: Charming 18th-c beamed country pub with big open fire in small lounge, darts area behind fireplace, dining conservatory, decent food inc doorstep sandwiches and popular Sun lunch, well kept McMullens Country, AK Mild and a guest beer on handpump; huge garden with big children's play area, terrace and barbecue *(Norman and Gill Fox, Phil and Heidi Cook)*

☆ Harpenden [Kinsbourne Green; 2¼ miles from M1 junction 10; A1081 towards town, on edge; TL1015], *Fox*: Pews, antique panelling, two log fires, lots of bric-a-brac and masses of prints in big but cosy and relaxing lounge bar, good value food, smaller public bar; friendly efficient staff, Tetleys-related and several other well kept ales with March real ale festival, good coffee; children welcome, play area in big garden *(Phil and Heidi Cook, BB)*

Harpenden [Cravells Rd], *Carpenters Arms*: Friendly landlord and staff, good home cooking, well kept beers and neat terrace garden *(R A Buckler)*; [High St/Station Rd], *Harpenden Arms*: Old-fashioned pub divided by original chimneybreasts, with comfortable lounge, pinball machine in public part, light and airy restaurant end with some Thai dishes (not weekend evenings); well kept Fullers ales *(Michael Sandy, Martin Kay, Andrea Fowler)*; [East Common; TL1314],

Three Horseshoes: Pleasant country pub with tables out by quiet common, good bar food, changing Whitbreads-related ales; can get crowded weekend lunchtimes but tables can be reserved; children welcome *(Andrew Jeeves, Carole Smart, LYM)*

☆ **Hatfield** [Park St, Old Hatfield; TL2308], *Eight Bells*: Quaint and attractive old beamed pub, pleasantly restored, well kept Tetleys-related and a guest ale, decent reasonably priced bar food, couple of tables in back yard, piped music; open all day, occasional live music; best at quiet times, crowded Fri/Sat nights *(Nick and Alison Dowson, Christopher Turner)*

Hemel Hempstead [A41; TL0506], *Swan*: Small pub with good range of beers, little dining room with good food cooked and served by owner, darts and snooker *(Mr Horwood)*

☆ **Hertford** [The Folly; TL3213], *Old Barge*: Nicely placed canalside pub, long and low, good service even when hectic, friendly helpful young staff, lots of barge pictures etc, Tetleys-related ales kept well, decent food inc good ploughman's and vegetarian; fruit and games machines *(George Atkinson, P Corris, LYM)*

☆ **Hertford** [Fore St], *Salisbury Arms*: Relaxing hotel lounge, well kept McMullens inc AK Mild, cheerful service, decent food (not Sun evening); splendid Jacobean staircase to bedrooms *(P Corris)*

☆ **Hertford** [33 Castle St], *White Horse*: Small intimate no-frills free house, very pubby, with open fire between the two bars, interesting furniture in upstairs no-smoking lounge, good range of real ales inc ones brewed on premises, wide range of fruit wines, friendly service; popular with younger people *(Richard Houghton, Neil O'Callaghan)*

☆ **Hertford Heath** [B1197, signed off A414 S edge of Hertford; TL3510], *Silver Fox*: Bustling and friendly well kept rather suburban-feeling local, very popular lunchtime (busy most nights too) for sensibly priced food from sandwiches up inc good range of puddings, quick service, particularly well kept Adnams, Tetleys and Theakstons Best and Old Peculier; busy most evenings too; relaxing sheltered back terrace with fountain *(Martyn Kearey, G L Tong, A C Morrison, Stephen and Jean Curtis, Audrey and Dennis Nelson, Neil O'Callaghan, Rita Horridge, BB)*

Hertingfordbury [TL3112], *White Horse*: Tastefully refurbished Forte hotel, good food in bar with comfortable settees, separate restaurant; children welcome; bedrooms *(Fiona and Paul Hutt)*

☆ **Hinxworth** [Main St, just off A1(M); TL2340], *Three Horseshoes*: Thatched, beamed and timbered dining pub popular for changing choice of good food (not Sun evening, Mon) inc children's and Sun roast; big brick inglenook, small dining extension, well kept Greene King IPA and Abbot, friendly licensees, no juke box or piped music; big garden with swings, climbing frames and maybe friendly wandering pig *(Neil O'Callaghan, G L Tong, Joyce and Stephen Stackhouse)*

Hitchin [Bancroft; TL1929], *Assizes*: Old beamed pub with spit-and-sawdust feel, mix of young and old, good changing range of well kept sensibly priced real ales, beer festivals spotlighting particular regions, good lunchtime food (not Sun), upstairs restaurant Thurs-Sat *(John)*

Hoddesdon [Dobbs Weir – OS Sheet 166 map ref 385083; TL3808], *Fish & Eels*: Spacious pub prettily placed opp weir on River Lea, huge sandwiches, garden with play area; handy for Rye House, nature reserve behind, long river walks *(Mrs P Pearce)*

Hunton Bridge [Bridge Rd, just off A41 N of Watford; TL0800], *Kings Head*: Good value varied food, well kept beer, good service; garden excellent for children *(N M Baleham)*

Kings Langley [60 High St; TL0702], *Rose & Crown*: Popular and welcoming, with good warm fires, attractive pictures and lamps, Tetleys-related and guest ales; plenty of character despite games machines; frequent live music *(N M Baleham)*

Kinsbourne Green [A1086; TL1015], *Fox*: Busy but welcoming, nine real ales on handpump with up to 50 at March and May beer festivals, well priced bar food inc several vegetarian specials *(Phil and Heidi Cook)*

☆ **Langley** [off B656 S of Hitchin, on edge of Knebworth Park; TL2122], *Farmers Boy*: Friendly low-beamed and timbered local under new management, huge inglenook fire one end, woodburner at the other, small public bar behind; lots of brasses, old photographs and prints, well kept Greene King IPA and Abbot, wide-ranging bar food from toasties up; garden behind *(Phil and Heidi Cook)*

☆ **Little Berkamstead** [1 Church Rd; TL2908], *Five Horseshoes*: 17th-c beams and stripped brickwork, two log fires, well kept Greene King and Tetleys-related ales, decent wines, wide range of good generous bar food inc sandwiches and vegetarian, quick responsive service; good restaurant; garden with picnic tables, busy in summer *(A C Morrison, Martyn Kearey)*

☆ **Little Hadham** [The Ford, just off A120 W of Bishops Stortford; TL4322], *Nags Head*: Good freshly cooked changing food inc lots of fresh fish in 16th-c country dining pub's cosy and relaxed heavily black-beamed interconnecting rooms, clean and comfortable; well kept Greene King IPA, Abbot, Rayments and a seasonal beer tapped from the cask, decent wines, freshly squeezed orange juice, efficient friendly staff, old local photographs, guns, copper pans; restaurant; children welcome *(Gwen and Peter Andrews, Martyn Kearey, J D Patrick, George Atkinson, Ben Grose, LYM)*

☆ **Little Wymondley** [by Stevenage/Hitchin bypass, nr Hitchin; TL2127], *Plume of Feathers*: Good food and friendly obliging service in comfortably refurbished pub; alsatian called Leah *(Charles Bardswell)*

☆ **London Colney** [Waterside; just off main st by bridge at S end; TL1704], *Green Dragon*: An attractive find, friendly and immaculate, with good value generous food (not Sun), lots of beams and brasses, soft lighting, well kept Tetleys-related and guest ales, decent wine; prettily set riverside tables *(Mrs C Archer, LYM)*

☆ **Much Hadham** [B1004 – OS Sheet 167 map ref 428197; TL4219], *Bull*: Attractive old pub with good choice of well presented food, well kept Tetleys-related ales, unspoilt inglenook public bar, nicely worn-in comfortable banquettes in roomy dining lounge, smaller back family dining room; children welcome, unusually big garden *(PACW, R A Buckler, Martyn Kearey, PH, JH, Dr Ronald Church, LYM)*

☆ **Much Hadham** [Hertford Rd, about ¼ mile outside], *Jolly Waggoners*: Family country pub with friendly animals in huge garden, good home-cooked food inc children's dishes and choice puddings, pleasant efficient service, Greene King ales, good range of malt whiskies, nice window seats; handy for Hopleys nursery *(Martyn Kearey, Joy Heatherley)*

☆ **Newgate Street** [a mile N of Cuffley; TL3005], *Coach & Horses*: Heavy beams and flagstones in civilised country pub by church, wide choice of bar food inc vegetarian, well kept Tetleys-related and guest ales, efficient friendly service, two open fires, built-in black wall pews, lots of brasses; picnic tables in sheltered garden, good walks nearby *(Norman Foot, J Giles Quick, Nigel Norman, LYM)*

Northaw [B157; TL2802], *Two Brewers*: Friendly bar staff, wide range of beers and cider, cheap tasty food *(Neil O'Callaghan)*

☆ **Nuthampstead** [TL4034], *Woodman*: Out-of-the-way thatched and weatherboarded free house with welcoming locals, good range of well kept real ales, tasty reasonably priced food, inglenook log fire, pleasant garden *(David Surridge, Leslie Fryer)*

☆ **Potters Crouch** [leaving St Albans on Watford rd via Chiswell Green, turn right after M10 – OS Sheet 166 map ref 116052; TL1105], *Holly Bush*: Particularly well kept Fullers Chiswick, London Pride and ESB, good generous simple food, efficient service, decent wines, spacious feel with good-sized tables, lots of pictures, plates, brasses and antlers, old-fashioned lighting; busy weekends; good big garden with picnic tables *(A C Morrison, N M Baleham, S J Edwards, Roy and Mary Roebuck, MK, AF)*

☆ **Puckeridge** [TL3823], *White Hart*: No news yet of new licensees in cosy rambling dining pub with welcoming fire, lots of wooden armchairs as well as button-back banquettes, McMullens ales, good tables outside; has been open all day Sat *(LYM; reports on new regime please)*

Redbourn [A5183 about 2½ miles from M1 junction 9; TL1012], *Chequers*: Useful and friendly flagstone-floored Chef & Brewer with dark wood fittings, screened dining area, usual food, well kept Courage Directors, good coffee; family room *(George Atkinson)*

☆ **Reed** [High St; TL3636], *Cabinet*: Friendly and relaxed tiled and weatherboarded house, a pub for centuries, with helpful welcoming service, log fire in little rustic parlourish public bar, pleasant lounge, five well kept ales, good generous food, helpful staff, tables in big garden with pond and flowers *(Joyce and Stephen Stackhouse, Ann Griffiths, Simon Watkins, LYM)*

☆ **Rickmansworth** [Scots Hill Rd; off Park Rd (A412) towards Watford; TQ0594], *Scotsbridge Mill*: Well kept Whitbreads-related ales, pleasant willing staff, good food in bar and Beefeater restaurant, stunning setting – rambling and comfortable former water mill with River Chess running through, well spaced waterside tables outside *(the Shinkmans)*

☆ **Sandridge** [High St; TL1610], *Rose & Crown*: Clean and comfortable dining pub with wide range of generous changing straightforward food inc five rich soups and lots of main courses, good service, several Whitbreads-related and other ales *(J A Boucher, Andrew Scarr, Helena Reid)*

Sarratt [The Green; TQ0499], *Cricketers*: Lovely village setting handy for Chess Valley walks, well kept Courage Best and Directors, good choice of tasty food, welcoming service; dining area, tables outside *(Douglas Bail, David Craine, Ann Reeder)*

Sawbridgeworth [Cambridge Rd; TL4814], *Gate*: At least seven quickly changing real ales, all in peak condition *(Richard Taylor)*; [Hand Lane], *Hand & Crown*: Wide choice of good value generous food, fresh veg *(Geo Rumsey)*

☆ **St Albans** [Holywell Hill; TL1507], *White Hart*: Comfortable and civilised if a bit formal, two small bar areas opening into larger one with tables; antique panelling, handsome fireplaces and furnishings, courteous helpful service, some bar food bargains esp Weds lunchtime businessman's special, food all day Sat; restaurant, Tetleys-related and guest ales; bedrooms *(Michael, Alison and Rhiannon Sandy, Brian Marsden, LYM)*

St Albans [2 Keyfield Terr, off London Rd], *Beehive*: Done up in spit-and-sawdust style, with period photographs, Whitbreads-related ales, bar food (not Fri/Sat, but summer evening barbecues Fri-Sun); piped music may be loud (live Thurs), quiz night Tues; good atmosphere, popular with young people *(Nick Dowson)*; [Fishpool St], *Black Lion*: Well kept Bass, Charringtons IPA and Fullers London Pride in relaxing hotel lounge with discreet piped music; good Italian restaurant; bedrooms *(Brian Marsden, Nigel Hopkins)*; [Hatfield Rd], *Crown*: All-day food in beamed pub with Courage Best, Greene King IPA, Marstons Pedigree and Wadworths 6X; quiz night Mon and Thurs, juke box; popular with students *(Anon)*; [36 Fishpool St], *Lower Red Lion*: Friendly and popular, with changing often interesting real ales, live music Weds, two lounges, log fire, red plush seats; tables in pleasant back garden; bedrooms *(David Goldstone, P A Hubble)*; [London Rd], *Milehouse*: Imposing and comfortable, fine old beams, panelling, huge fireplace, pleasant seats and polished tables, wide choice of nicely presented food, attentive staff; juke box, TV *(GB)*; [Victoria St], *Philanthropist & Firkin*: New pub in former library, making good use of the space – very pleasant at quieter times, can get packed and smoky some evenings; Tetleys and its own Dogbolter, Bookworm and Verulamium ales, Weds comedy night upstairs, occasional live music *(Nick and Alison Dowson)*; [St Michaels], *Six Bells*: Friendly and well kept low-beamed food pub on site of an old Roman bath house, well kept Allied and a guest real ale, big helpings of good value freshly cooked food *(David Goldstone, Brian Marsden, LYM)*; [28 George St], *Tudor*: Whitbreads-related ales, pleasant decor, quiz night Weds, upstairs restaurant *(Nick Dowson)*; [High St], *Vintry*: Big new pub in former Barclays Bank building, very simple, light and spacious; good bar service, Bass, Greene King and Morlands Old Speckled Hen; very busy Fri/Sat evenings *(Anon)*; [4 Keyfield Terr, round corner from Garibaldi], *White Hart Tap*: Small but friendly, with well kept Tetleys and Worthington BB, good value lunchtime food, tables outside; open all day, live band Tues *(Anon)*; [Upper Dagnall St], *White Swan*: Older customers than some pubs here, with well kept Boddingtons, Marstons Pedigree and Wadworths 6X *(Anon)*

☆ *nr* **St Albans** [Tyttenhanger Green, off A414 E – OS Sheet 166 map ref 182059], *Plough*: Spacious and friendly, with polite prompt service, lovely longcase clock, good log fire, at least seven real ales kept well, good straight-forward bar food (no Sun lunch); bar billiards, walls festooned with old beer bottles and nick-nacks, friendly young staff, big garden with play area *(Huw and Carolyn Lewis)*

Stevenage [164 High St; TL2324], *Chequers*: Refurbished open-plan high-ceilinged Greene King pub with good value standard lunchtime bar food, busy weekdays; pool, juke box *(G L Tong)*

Therfield [off A505 Baldock—Royston; TL3336], *Fox & Duck*: Village pub refurbished by good new landlord, four ales on handpump, good value food, good children's garden with climbing frames, swings and tree house *(Susan and Nigel Wilson)*

☆ **Thorley Street** [A1184 Sawbridgeworth—Bishops Stortford; TL4718], *Coach & Horses*: Really good family atmosphere, well kept changing Tetleys-related and guest ales, courteous service, generous good value quickly served bar food, Readers Union books, decent wine; children very welcome; good garden with play area *(Mr and Mrs C Holmes)*

Tring [Tring Hill; SP9211], *Crows Nest*: Beefeater with good range of decent food, well kept Whitbreads-related ales, massive garden with good play area, though oddly no service out here *(R C Vincent)*; [Bulbourne; B488 towards Dunstable, next to BWB works; SP9313], *Grand Junction Arms*: Characterful canalside pub under new management, big redesigned open-plan bar with raised side eating area, canal photographs and memorabilia, play area in big garden overlooking canal (barbecues and Sat evening live music out here); Adnams, Greenalls and Wadworths 6X, interesting good value food *(Phil and Heidi Cook)*; [King St], *Kings Arms*: Good changing range of well kept beers inc the local Ridgeway, attractively priced generous tasty food, individual decor with emerald green ceiling, panelling, enamel signs, no-smoking area *(Mike Pugh)*

Walkern [B1036; TL2826], *Yew Tree*: Good unpretentious atmosphere in ancient pub, wide choice of genuine well cooked food, boxer dog called Bruce *(Charles Bardswell)*

☆ **Water End** [B197 N of Potters Bar – OS Sheet 166 map ref 229042; TL2204], *Old Maypole*: Low ceilings, big inglenook fire, lots of brasses, miniatures and bric-a-brac; good value basic food, well kept Greene King IPA and Abbot, friendly service, family room; outside tables *(Chris Mawson)*

Watford [17 Estcourt Rd; TQ1196], *Golden Lion*: Interesting range of guest beers (and customers), plenty of atmosphere, decent food *(Dave Middleburgh)*; [Leavesden High Rd], *Hare*: Two-bar pub with good value food, well kept Bass and Fullers London Pride, facilities for children and disabled people *(David Appleby)*

Watton at Stone [13 High St (A602); TL3019], *Bull*: Nice atmosphere in picturesque old country pub refurbished since 1992 fire, Tetleys-related ales, good well priced food with Chinese accent; beams, massive inglenook, public bar with darts and unobtrusive juke box; restaurant, big back garden *(Martyn Kearey)*

Wheathampstead [Gustard Wood; off B651 1½ miles N, towards Shaws Corner; TL1716], *Cross Keys*: Impressively friendly staff in attractively placed country pub in rolling wooded countryside, comfortable pleasantly slightly dated feel, Tetleys-related and guest ale *(Paul A Kitchener, LYM)*; [Gustard Wood; OS Sheet 166 map ref 172164], *Tin Pot*: Not much from outside but a pleasure inside, new owners really offer personal touch; dogs welcome; bedrooms excellent, good breakfast *(Sue Elliott)*

☆ **Whitwell** [B651; TL1820], *Eagle & Child*: Good choice of reasonably priced food and well kept Whitbreads-related ales in snug, comfortable and relaxed pub with a good deal of intrinsic character and interesting bric-a-brac; welcoming licensees, cats, good play area in back garden *(Bill Capper, LYM)*

☆ **Whitwell** [67 High St (B651)], *Maidens Head*: First-class landlord and friendly staff in clean McMullens local with good value food esp gammon, well kept ales tapped from the cask, good coffee, interesting key-ring collection, seats in safe children's garden *(Sir John Stokes)*

Humberside *see* Yorkshire

Isle of Wight

The Seaview Hotel in Seaview has such good specials that this year we choose it as Isle of Wight Dining Pub of the Year; it's currently doing very well indeed, all round. Another pub with particularly good specials is the welcoming Red Lion at Freshwater, and authentic Italian cooking stands out at the very individually run Bonchurch Inn in Bonchurch. Other places we'd firmly recommend for an enjoyable meal out include the friendly Crown at Shorwell (much more room there now, too) and the well run Wheatsheaf in Yarmouth. The Wight Mouse part of the Clarendon Hotel at Chale stands out as the best family pub on the island, though there's plenty for adults to enjoy there too. Drinks prices on the island are rather higher than the national average; we found the Seaview Hotel much the cheapest place for beer. Local beers to look out for include Goddards from Ryde, and Burts (now that Hartridges the Hampshire-based drinks firm have revived the name of the island's former Newport brewery, with plans for a small chain of tied pubs). In the Lucky Dip at the end of the chapter, pubs we'd currently note particularly are the Eight Bells in Carisbrooke, Travellers Joy at Northwood, Chequers at Rookley, New Inn at Shalfleet and Sloop at Wootton Bridge.

ARRETON SZ5486 Map 2

White Lion £

A3056 Newport—Sandown

Shortly before we went to press new licensees took over at this cream-painted village pub, still one of the most popular on the island, and one of the few that has managed to keep much of its original character. Cosy and relaxing, the roomily comfortable beamed lounge bar has guns, shining brass and horse-harness on the partly panelled walls, and cushioned windsor chairs on the brown carpet. The smaller, plainer public bar has dominoes, cribbage, shove ha'penny, table skittles and winter darts. Very good value bar food includes sandwiches (from £1.80), soup (£1.95), ploughman's (from £2.50), filled baked potatoes (from £2.75), steak and kidney pie or broccoli and mushroom quiche (£3.25), smoked haddock pasta (£3.75), chicken korma (£4.75), lemon sole bonne femme (£6.50) and home made specials. Well kept Bass, Whitbreads Strong Country, Wadworths 6X and a changing guest tapped from casks behind the bar, with an interesting cask-levelling device. There's a family Cabin Bar (full of old farm tools) in the pleasing garden, and you can also sit out in front by the tubs of flowers – you may need to as it does get very busy. The village church is 12th-c and houses the Isle of Wight Brass Rubbing Centre; there's a craft village nearby. *(Recommended by D H and M C Watkinson, Jack Barnwell, Simon Collett-Jones, David P Sweeney, Martyn and Mary Mullins; reports on the new regime please)*

Whitbreads ~ Lease: Mark and Rucky Griffith ~ Real ale ~ Meals and snacks (not Mon evening) ~ (01983) 528479 ~ Children in eating area ~ Open 11-3, 7-11

Prices of main dishes usually include vegetables or a side salad.

BONCHURCH SZ5778 Map 2

Bonchurch Inn

Bonchurch Shute; from A3055 E of Ventnor turn down to Old Bonchurch opposite Leconfield Hotel

It's the mixture of good, well priced Italian and English cooking and the rather different atmosphere that attracts readers to this old stone inn. The licensees come from Italy, so really know how to cook their native dishes, as well as how to greet their customers with gusto – you might be welcomed by an exuberant succession of enthusiastic handshakes. They're very flexible with what's on the menu, and may do special requests, particularly if you're vegetarian. A typical day's bar menu includes sandwiches (from £2), minestrone soup (£1.80), pizza or ploughman's (£3), spaghetti bolognese (£4), canelloni with spinach, seafood risotto, or fettuccine carbonara (£4.25), duckling with orange sauce (£6), and puddings such as zabaglione (£3); children's helpings. There's a small cosy dining room, but on sunny days it's rather nicer to sit at one of the tables in the flower-filled cobbled courtyard, which even without the pub's Italian connections seems very continental. It's enclosed by buildings worked into the steep rock slope. Inside, the high-ceilinged and friendly public bar – at its best when busy – is partly cut into the steep rocks of the Shute, and conjures up an image of salvaged shipwrecks with its floor of narrow-planked ship's decking, and seats of the sort that old-fashioned steamers used to have; there's also a smaller saloon. Courage Best and Directors tapped from the cask, Italian wines by the glass, a few bottled French wines, and coffee; darts, bar billiards, shove-ha'penny, table tennis, dominoes and cribbage. ***(Recommended by Michael and Harriet Robinson, Martyn and Mary Mullins, Lynn Sharpless, Bob Eardley; more reports please)***

Free house ~ Licensees Ulisse and Aline Besozzi ~ Real ale ~ Meals and snacks (11.30-2.15, 6-10.30) ~ Restaurant ~ (01983) 852611 ~ Children in family room ~ Open 11-3, 6.30-11; closed Dec 25 ~ Bedrooms; £17/£34

CHALE SZ4877 Map 2

Clarendon / Wight Mouse ★ 🍷

In village, on B3399, but now has access road directly off A3055

This bustling, well-organised place is perhaps the complete family pub, but still remains a favourite with grown-up readers as well. Children are not just tolerated but enthusiastically welcomed, and a great deal of thought has been put into keeping them amused. There are play areas inside and out, pony rides on Sid and Arthur, the well-liked Shetland pony, a pets' corner, and maybe even Punch and Judy shows in the spacious sheltered back garden. More restful souls can soak up the lovely views out towards the Needles and Tennyson Downs. Inside it's an extended, rambling, atmospheric place, the original core hung thickly with musical instruments, and with guns, pistols and so forth hanging over an open log fire. One end opens through sliding doors into a pool room with dark old pews, large antique tables, video game and juke box, while at the other is an extension with more musical instruments, lots of china mice around a corner fireplace, decorative plates and other bric-a-brac, and even part of a rowing eight hanging from its high pitched ceiling. The turkey-carpeted family room extends beyond a two-way coal-effect gas fire, with quite close-set pews around its tables, hunting prints, and more decorative plates. A very good range of drinks includes well kept Boddingtons, Fuggles Imperial, Marstons Pedigree, Morlands Old Speckled Hen and Wadworths 6X on handpump, an outstanding choice of around 365 whiskies, nearly 50 wines, and some uncommon brandies, madeiras and country wines. Popular, generously served bar food includes sandwiches (from £1.80, fresh crab £3.40, toasties 25p extra), home-made soup (£1.80), ploughman's (from £3.10), a few vegetarian dishes like a daily pasta bake (£3.90), salads or burgers (from £3.90), ham and eggs (£4.10), Wiener schnitzel (£4.60), a daily curry, Mexican hot chilli con carne in taco shells (£5.40), fisherman's platter or gravadlax (£7.30), giant mixed grill (£7.60), steaks (from £8.80), daily specials, and children's meals (from £1.50); puddings include ice cream made at a farm nearby (which is open to visitors). Despite serving hundreds of meals every day, service is always efficient and smiling. Darts at one end, dominoes, fruit machine, pinball, pool. Live music every evening is never too loud for conversation. They run a mini-bus service for four or more people (£3 a person). *(Recommended by Joan and Michel Hooper-Immins, T Roger Lamble, Mike Starke, Phil and Heidi Cook, R F and M K Bishop, Paul and A Sweetman, John Farmer, Nigel Gibbs, Chris and Kim Elias, J M Campbell, Mr and Mrs D E Powell, John and Christine Simpson, Paul Cartledge, Andrew Stephenson, Sue Anderson, Phil Copleston)*

Free house ~ Licensees John and Jean Bradshaw ~ Real ale ~ Meals and snacks (noon-10pm) ~ Restaurant ~ (01983) 730431 ~ Children in eating areas and three family rooms ~ Live music every night ~ Open 11am-midnight ~ Bedrooms: £25(£28B)/£50(£56B)

nr COWES (EAST) SZ5092 Map 2

Folly

Folly Lane – which is signposted off A3021 just S of Whippingham

Yachtsmen have long used this shipshape old pub as a place to moor their boats and take a shower, and thanks to the installation of a proper weather station, they can now pick up weather forecasts and warnings too. Very prettily set on the river bank of the estuary, the pub has big windows offering a birds-eye view of the boats on the water, and in summer seats on a waterside terrace. The maritime connections go back a long way, as the original building was based around a beached sea-going barge; the roof still includes part of the deck. The nautically themed opened-out bar has a wind speed indicator, barometer and a chronometer around the old timbered walls, as well as venerable wooden chairs and refectory-type tables, shelves of old books and plates, railway bric-a-brac and farm tools, old pictures, and brass lights; it can get busy. Bar food includes generously filled sandwiches (from £2.25), soup (£1.85), potato skins (£2.75), ploughman's (£3.95), home-made chilli or steak and kidney pie (£4.65), a help-yourself casserole, steak (£8.85), daily specials, fresh fish, and children's meals (£2.25); Sunday roast (£5.25). In winter they do a three-course meal for £4.75, and have theme nights with special menus on Fridays. Well kept Boddingtons, Flowers Original, Morlands Old Speckled Hen, Wadworths 6X and Whitbreads Strong Country on handpump under light blanket pressure, several rums such as West Indian Amber, and Gales country wines; bar billiards, shove ha'penny, table skittles, dominoes, fruit machine, trivia, and sometimes fairly loud piped music. There's a bouncy castle in the landscaped garden in summer, and it's not far to Osborne House. If you're coming by land, watch out for the sleeping policemen along the lane. *(Recommended by Dr and Mrs A K Clarke, Peter and Audrey Dowsett, Andy Cunningham, A E R Albert, Martyn and Mary Mullins, Derek and Margaret Underwood, John Watson, Bill and Beryl Farmo, Martin, Jane, Simon and Laura Bailey, Chris and Kim Elias, R F and M K Bishop)*

Whitbreads ~ Managers John and Christine Pettley ~ Real ale ~ Meals and snacks (all day, from 9am for breakfast) ~ (01983) 297171 ~ Children in eating area and restaurant ~ Keyboard player Thurs, Sat, and summer Sun evenings ~ Open 11-11 (9 for breakfast)

FRESHWATER SZ3487 Map 2

Red Lion

Church Place; from A3055 at E end of village by Freshwater Garage mini-roundabout follow Yarmouth signpost and brown sign to Hill Farm Riding Stables, then take first real right turn signed to Parish Church

For a couple of months each year this charming place is pretty much self sufficient in fresh vegetables, and the apples, plums, peas, herbs and even nettles grown in the garden all find their way onto the menu. Lots of thought and enthusiasm is put into the carefully prepared food, and as well as a standard menu with sandwiches (from £1.65), filled baked potatoes (from £3.50), ploughman's (from £2.95), vegetable lasagne (£4.25), and ham, egg and chips (£4.95), they have a big blackboard of daily specials such as stinging nettle soup (£2.20), chicken liver pâté (£3.25), devilled crab pots (£4.50), meatloaf with home-made chutney (£5.50), chicken breast in lemon and pepper sauce, beef in ginger or steak and kidney pie (£5.75), pork medallions with cider, apples and cognac or whole lemon sole (£7.50), rack of lamb with elderberry and port (£7.95), local lobster salad (£11.95), and good puddings such as sherry and mincemeat crumble, or their popular home-made ice creams like banana and lemon or brandy alexander (£2.20); Sunday lunch (£5.75). In a picturesque setting beside the church, the pub is very much at the heart of the local community, and the cheery landlord and locals encourage a notably friendly and welcoming feel. The atmospheric bar is smartly traditional, with open fires, comfortable low grey sofas and sturdy country-kitchen style furnishings on mainly flagstoned floors with bare boards at one end, and a good mix of pictures and china platters on the walls; it can get a little smoky at busy times. Well kept Boddingtons, Flowers Original, Goddards Best (brewed on the island) and Morlands Old Speckled Hen on handpump, as well as White Monk cider (cask-conditioned on the island for three years in an oak barrel to a Carthusian monks' recipe); fruit machine, darts, shove-ha'penny, dominoes, bardo, jenga and shut the box. The piped music is mainly classical. There are picnic tables on a sheltered back lawn edged by neat flower beds. Good walks for nature lovers nearby, especially around the River Yar. *(Recommended by Simon Collett-Jones, Jeanne Cross, Paul Silvestri, Mrs C Watkinson, R F and M K Bishop, Cathryn and Richard Hicks, Michael and Harriet Robinson, Alison Bond, Bill Edwards, Robert and Gladys Flux, M and A Cook, Barry Hall, John Watson, Nigel Gibbs)*

Whitbreads ~ Lease: Michael Mence ~ Real ale ~ Meals and snacks (not winter Sun evening) ~ (01983) 754925 ~ Well behaved supervised children welcome ~ Open 11.30-3(11-4 Sat), 5.30(6Sat)-11

NITON SZ5076 Map 2

Buddle

From A3055 in extreme S of island, take road to St Catherine's lighthouse

Nicely off the tourist track, this friendly old house is one of the island's oldest pubs, though it operated without a licence until 1850. For many years it was the haunt of notorious local smugglers, and though it no longer has the same reputation for drinking and carousing, the pub still retains something of the atmosphere of those long gone days. The modernised characterful bar – which can get busy – still has its heavy black beams and big flagstones, a broad stone fireplace with a massive black oak mantlebeam, and old-fashioned captain's chairs around solid wooden tables; pewter mugs and so forth hang on the walls. A couple of areas are no-smoking. They generally have up to nine real ales available, the changing range perhaps including Adnams, Bass, Boddingtons, Burts, Flowers Original, Greene King Abbot and Morlands Old Speckled Hen on handpump or tapped from the cask; also a range of wines by the bottle or the glass and local wines and ciders. Service is consistently pleasant and welcoming. Unsurprising but reliable and generously served bar food includes sandwiches in winter, soup (£1.95), garlic mushrooms (£2.75), vegetable samosas (£2.95), chilli con carne (£4.25), breaded plaice (£4.35), mushroom and kidney bean stroganoff (£4.45), steak (from £8.75), puddings (from £1.95), and children's meals (from £1.75); good chips. Along one side of the lawn, and helping to shelter it, is what they call the Smugglers' Barn, which doubles as a family dining area and function room. Shove ha'penny, cribbage, dominoes, fruit machine, trivia, and juke box. The cat is called Marmaduke and there are friendly dogs. You can look out over the cliffs from the well cared for garden, with its tables spread over the sloping lawn and stone terraces; at night you may be able to see the beam of the nearby lighthouse sweeping round the sea far below. Good walks nearby. *(Recommended by HNJ, PEJ, T Roger Lamble, Peter and Audrey Dowsett, Phil and Heidi Cook)*

Whitbreads ~ Lease: John and Pat Bourne ~ Meals and snacks (11.30-3, 6-9.45) ~ Niton (0983) 730243 ~ Children welcome away from bar ~ Regular live music in summer ~ Open 11-11 (winter Mon-Thurs 11-3, 6-11)

SEAVIEW SZ6291 Map 2

Seaview Hotel

High Street; off B3330 Ryde—Bembridge

Isle of Wight Dining Pub of the Year

The terrace of this pleasantly restrained little hotel does indeed look out over the sea, and further, across to the south coast. Inside it's a lot more pubby than you might expect, especially in the cosily old-fashioned back bar, which has lots of nautical nick-nacks such as oars, a ship's wheel, porthole cover, and block and tackle around its dimly lit ochre walls, a log fire, and traditional pub furnishings on the bare boards; it can be busy with young locals. The airier bay-windowed bar at the front is more relaxed and civilised, and has a splendid array of naval and merchant ship photographs, as well as Spy nautical cartoons for *Vanity Fair,* and original receipts from Cunard's shipyard payments for the *Queen Mary* and the *Queen Elizabeth;* it has a line of close-set tables down each side on the turkey carpet, and a pleasantly chatty relaxed atmosphere. The freshly made bar food is very popular with readers, with particularly praised dishes including sandwiches (from £1.95; tasty prawn and fresh local crab when available), soup (£2.20), ploughman's or crispy chicken wings (£3.65), roasted pepper and bacon salad with black olives and sun dried tomatoes (£4.95), seafood quiche with mussels, prawns, cream, fresh herbs and cheese (£5.95), entrecote steak (£9.95), whole or half lobster salads (from £10.95), and puddings like treacle sponge (£2.75); herbs come from the garden, and they do a good Sunday roast. Excellent, courteous service. The restaurant is no-smoking. Flowers IPA and local Goddards on handpump (the former very well priced for the area), decent wine list, local apple juice, and a choice of malt whiskies; darts, cribbage and dominoes and piped music. There are tables on the front terrace and sun porch, and more in a sheltered inner courtyard. *(Recommended by D H and M C Watkinson, Shirley Pielou, Jack Barnwell, Simon Collett-Jones, Andrew Stephenson, DJW, Mr and Mrs D E Powell, John Watson)*

Free house ~ Licensees Nicholas and Nicola Hayward ~ Real ale ~ Meals and snacks ~ Restaurant (not Sun evening, except bank holidays) ~ (01983) 612711 ~ Children in eating area of bar ~ Open 10.30-3, 6-11 ~ Bedrooms: £40B/£60B

SHANKLIN SZ5881 Map 2

Fishermans Cottage

Bottom of Shanklin Chine

Picturesquely tucked into the cliffs, this unpretentious thatched cottage enjoys one of the nicest and most unusual settings of any pub we know. It's only a few minutes' walk to Shanklin's Esplanade, but seems a lot more remote, especially if you're sitting at one of the tables on the terrace looking towards the beach and sea, with the sound of the surf in the background. It's best to go during the day, as the terrace does lose the sun in the evening. Inside, the clean low-beamed and flagstoned rooms are still cosy after a recent refurbishment, with photographs, paintings and engravings on the stripped stone walls. Decent bar food includes sandwiches (from £1.70), sausage and chips (£2.70), ploughman's (from £2.90), salads (from £3.70, crab and prawn £5.90) scampi (£4.90), and a pint of prawns (£5.80). Courage Directors on handpump, coffee all day, and a range of local country wines; polite and friendly bar staff. Fruit machine, piped music; wheelchair access. It's a lovely walk to here along the zigzagged path down the steep and sinuous Chine, the beautiful gorge that was the area's original tourist attraction (there may be a charge for this route in summer), though do remember before starting out in winter that the pub is closed out of season. *(Recommended by Mr and Mrs P C Clark, John and Christine Simpson, Reg Nelson, Sarah Bullard; more reports please)*

Free house ~ Licensees Mrs A P P Springman and Mrs E Barsdell ~ Meals and snacks (11-3, 6-9, not Sun) ~ (01983) 863882 ~ Children welcome ~ Live entertainment two evenings a week ~ Open 11-11; cl Nov-Mar

SHORWELL SZ4582 Map 2

Crown

B3323 SW of Newport; OS Sheet 196 map reference 456829

Recently refurbished and doubled in size, this civilised pub remains a real local, in spite of the holidaymakers. Friendly, chatty, and slightly off the beaten track, it has an enchanting garden, with picnic tables and white garden chairs and tables looking over a little stream that broadens out into a wider trout-filled pool with prettily planted banks. The front entry to the pub is over a footbridge and through a little garden with a pump. Still characterful, the warm and cosy beamed two-room lounge bar has blue and white china in a carved dresser, old country prints on the stripped stone walls, other individual furnishings, a cabinet of model vintage cars, and a winter log fire with a fancy tilework surround; one area is no-smoking. Black pews form bays around tables in a stripped-stone room off to the left, with another log fire; the stone window ledges are full of houseplants. Consistently popular bar food includes sandwiches, fisherman's pie (£4.95), chicken breast in apricot and brandy sauce or salmon escalope with fennel and pernod (£6.50). Well kept Badger Tanglefoot, Boddingtons, Flowers Original and Wadworths 6X on handpump, local apple juice, cider and country wines. Efficient service from cheery staff and landlord; darts, fruit machine, trivia, boules, faint piped music. *(Recommended by Simon Collett-Jones, Mrs C Watkinson, HNJ, PEJ, D H and M C Watkinson, DJW, Phil and Heidi Cook, Nigel Gibbs, Martyn and Mary Mullins, Andrew Stephenson)*

Whitbreads ~ Tenant Mike Grace ~ Real ale ~ Meals and snacks (till 10pm; not 25 Dec) ~ (01983) 740293 ~ Children welcome ~ Open 10.30-11; 10.30-3, 6-11 in winter

VENTNOR SZ5677 Map 2

Spyglass

Esplanade, SW end; road down very steep and twisty, and parking can be difficult

The landlord has filled this splendidly placed pub with a genuinely interesting jumble of memorabilia that just keeps growing and growing. Wrecked rudders, ships' wheels, old local advertisements, stuffed seagulls, an Admiral Benbow barometer and an old brass telescope are just some of the things dotted around the snug separate areas of the mostly quarry-tiled bar. Furnishings include pews around traditional pub tables, with a carpeted no-smoking room at one end and a family area (with piped pop music) at the other. A spacious sunny terrace is perched on top of the sea wall with views along the bay. Bar food includes sandwiches (from £1.85), filled baked potatoes (£2.75), ploughman's (£3.35), salads (from £4.25), chilli con carne or several vegetarian meals like vegetable kiev (£4.50), home-made cottage pie (£4.65), seafood lasagne (£5.25), crab (£6.50), a whole fresh local lobster (£11.75), and daily specials like ham and leek bake or beef beaujolais (£5.95). Well kept Badger Best and Tanglefoot on handpump, with changing guest beers tapped from the cask; on special occasions such as a lifeboat support week there may be half a dozen or more. Also White Monk cask-conditioned cider. Fruit machine, video game, piped music, and a boat rocker for children. They have no objection to dogs or muddy boots. *(Recommended by D P and J A Sweeney, P Neate, Sue Anderson, Phil Copleston, Reg Nelson, June and Malcolm Farmer; more reports please)*

Free house ~ Licensees Neil, Stephanie and Rosie Gibbs ~ Real ale ~ Meals and snacks; afternoon tea in summer ~ (01983) 855338 ~ Children in family room ~ Live traditional Irish or jazz every night ~ Open 10.30-11; 11-3, 7-11 in winter ~ Bedrooms: /£35B

Places with gardens or terraces usually let children sit there – we note in the text the very very few exceptions that don't.

YARMOUTH SZ3589 Map 2

Wheatsheaf

Bridge Rd

Readers particularly like the consistency of this unstuffy place, something that comes across not just in the very good bar food, but in the service, atmosphere, and welcome, all of which can be happily relied on. Generously served and reasonably priced meals might include soup (£1.50), sandwiches (from £2), filled baked potatoes (from £2.20), crusty rolls (£2.30), particularly good value ploughman's (from £2.75), burgers (from £3.20), smoked trout fillet (£3.25), four giant garlic mussels (£3.45), salads (from £3.50), home-cooked gammon (£4.50), trout with stilton sauce or almonds (£5.25), steaks (from £7), puddings (from £1.90), and good blackboard daily specials like Japanese king prawns (£3.25), fresh black bream with grape and wine sauce (£5.45), game pie (£5.95), dressed crab platter (£8.95) and the impressive lobster platter with prawns, garlic mussels and smoked trout (£10.95); they're happy to modify dishes to suit tastes. Don't be put off by the slightly unprepossessing street frontage – inside it's comfortable and spacious, with four eating areas including a light and airy conservatory. Service is very quick and friendly. Four well kept beers such as Boddingtons, Flowers Original, Goddards or Morlands Old Speckled Hen on handpump; fruit machine, pool (winter only) and juke box (in public bar). The pub is particularly handy for the ferry. *(Recommended by HNJ, PEJ, Dr and Mrs A K Clarke, Clive Gilbert, Martyn and Mary Mullins)*

Whitbreads ~ Lease: Anthony David and Mrs Suzanne Keen ~ Real ale ~ Meals and snacks (11-2.30, 6-9.30) ~ (01983) 760456 ~ Children in harbour lounge and conservatory ~ Open 11-3, 6-11

Lucky Dip

Besides the fully inspected pubs, you might like to try these Lucky Dips recommended to us and described by readers (if you do, please send us reports):

☆ **Bembridge** [Station Rd; SZ6487], *Row Barge*: Open-plan, with unpretentious nautical decor (nr harbour), well kept Whitbreads-related and other ales, farm cider, good pizzas and other food, friendly landlord; bedrooms *(Martyn and Mary Mullins, June and Malcolm Farmer, David White)*

Brading [56-57 High St; A3055 Sandown—Ryde; SZ6086], *Bugle*: Big helpings of good straightforward food inc children's in three roomy areas, pretty floral wallpaper, quicky friendly service, well kept Flowers IPA, Goddards Special, Wadworths 6X; piped music; restaurant, supervised children's room with lots of games and videos, garden *(Mr and Mrs J Beere)*

☆ **Carisbrooke** [High St; SZ4888], *Eight Bells*: Spotless refurbished dining pub well set at foot of castle, bigger than it looks inside, with Whitbreads-related and other beers such as the well priced local Goddards, good value very generous fresh straightforward food, friendly staff; charming garden behind running down to swan-filled lake, also play area *(HNJ, PEJ, Martyn and Mary Mullins, Mr and Mrs M Farmer)*

☆ **Carisbrooke** [Park Cross; Calbourne Rd, B3401 1½ miles W; SZ4687], *Blacksmiths Arms*: Quiet well kept hillside family pub, panoramic views from dining room and terraced back garden, friendly helpful staff, Badger, Hampshire Pendragon and Ruddles ales, good value bar food; children welcome *(John Beeken, D H and M C Watkinson, Michael Andrews)*

Cowes [25 High St; SZ4896], *Pier View*: Quiet split-level pub with wooden floors, good service and well kept beer *(Dr and Mrs A K Clarke)*; [Watchhouse Lane], *Union*: Small Gales pub with good atmosphere, Adnams as guest beer, bar food, cosy side room; bedrooms *(Michael Andrews)*

Culver Down [seaward end nr Yarborough Monument; SZ6385], *Culver Haven*: Isolated clifftop pub with superb Channel views, modern, clean and very friendly, with good straightforward home cooking inc fresh veg, fair prices, quick service, Burts and Eldridge Pope on handpump, choice of five different fresh coffees; big restaurant; piped music; children and pets welcome, small terrace *(Mr and Mrs D S Enock)*

Downend [A3056, at crossroads; SZ5387], *Hare & Hounds*: Rethatched, refurbished and extended, lots of beams and stripped brickwork, two bars, dining area with friendly waitress service, decent straightforward food, Goddards Special and Whitbreads-related ales, good views from terrace, nice spot by Robin Hill Country Park which has good play area *(June and Malcolm Farmer, Simon Collett-*

Jones, Jack Barnwell, BB)
Fishbourne [Fishbourne Rd; from Portsmouth car ferry turn left into no through road; SZ5592], *Fishbourne Inn*: Delightful inn with warm, friendly staff, good food inc crab sandwiches and exotic ice cream *(D H and M C Watkinson)*
Freshwater Bay [SZ3386], *Albion*: Big modern popular bar overlooking bay, neat quick service, generous salads and hot dishes, well kept beer; terrace; bedrooms comfortable *(Peter and Audrey Dowsett)*
Godshill [Eden Dale; SZ5282], *Taverners*: Comfortable pub doing well under experienced new owners, good food, well kept Courage-related ales, evening restaurant, tables in courtyard; no car park – public one 200 yds away *(Jack Barnwell)*
Gurnard [Princes Esplanade; SZ4795], *Woodvale*: Big main bar with picture windows overlooking Solent, glass-panelled ceilings, decent range of standard food inc bargain steaks, obliging staff, smaller bar and billiards room *(HNJ, PEJ)*
Havenstreet [off A3054 Newport—Ryde; SZ5690], *White Hart*: Ancient building with two clean, comfortable and really pubby bars with well kept ales, varied generous food esp pies with fresh veg and splendid salads, reasonable prices; interesting beer-bottle collection *(David Sweeney, F D Wharton, Rozelle Say)*
☆ **Hulverstone** [B3399 – OS Sheet 196 map reference 398840; SZ3984], *Sun*: A pub to look at, with thatch, charming flower-filled garden, even village stocks; friendly informal newish licensees, well kept Gales BB and HSB tapped from the cask, food inc good home-made steak and kidney pie; piped music; sea views *(Anne Parmenter, Adrian Stopforth)*
☆ **Limerstone** [B3399 towards Brighstone; SZ4382], *Countryman*: Large brightly lit high-ceilinged open-plan bars and restaurant area, mock dark beams, white paintwork, horse/farming equipment and pictures, lots of tables with candles and flower decorations, usual bar food from filled rolls to steaks, prompt polite service, Badger Best and Tanglefoot, Charles Wells Eagle and Ind Coope Burton on handpump; moderate piped music; front garden with sea view *(Michael Andrews, HNJ, PEJ, D P and J A Sweeney, Phil and Heidi Cook)*
☆ **Newchurch** [OS Sheet 196 map reference 562855; SZ5685], *Pointer*: Genuine village local, friendly and unpretentious, with good generous straightforward home cooking, well kept Gales BBB and HSB, good range of country wines; brightly lit plush lounge, flame-effect fires, old photographs, L-shaped games bar on right, spotty dogs, pleasant back garden with floodlit boules area *(David Sweeney, HNJ, PEJ, LYM)*
☆ **Newport** [St Thomas Sq; SZ4988], *Wheatsheaf*: Inn dating back to 17th century, in attractive old part by parish church; recently comfortably upgraded but keeping good atmosphere, with friendly helpful staff, good generous reasonably priced food; children welcome, comfortable bedrooms *(HNJ, PEJ, Eric Phillips)*
Newport [High St], *Cask & Crispin*: Recently reopened, with full range of Burts beers – first pub in what Hartridges the new parent company hope will be a chain on the island and in Hants; good bar food, pleasant atmosphere, no piped music *(Martyn and Mary Mullins)*
☆ **Niton** [off A3055; SZ5076], *White Lion*: Straightforward food done well in clean, roomy and comfortable pub with good no-smoking section, children's dishes and Sun lunches, welcoming landlord, well kept Greene King Abbot, good atmosphere; children welcome, nice setting *(David Sweeney, Anne Parmenter, Adrian Stopforth)*
☆ **Northwood** [85 Pallance Rd; off B3325 S of Cowes; SZ4983], *Travellers Joy*: Not the smartest pub, but this busy local is a boon to serious real ale drinkers on the island, with ten or so kept well, inc several rare visitors; good range of generous reasonably priced simple bar food, friendly staff, old island prints; fruit machine, subdued piped music; family room, garden behind with swings and lots of rabbits; open all day Fri/Sat and summer *(Nigel Gibbs, Michael Andrews)*
☆ **Rookley** [Niton Rd; pub signed off A3020; SZ5183], *Chequers*: A straightforward menu, but good cooking using fresh ingredients, with plenty of veg served separately, at most attractive prices; clean and spacious plush refurbished lounge bar looking over road to rolling downland, friendly service, well kept Courage-related ales, small log fire, partly flagstoned games area on left; Lego in family room, mother-and-baby unit, picnic tables out on grass, realistic play house in safely fenced play area *(Jack Barnwell, Anne Parmenter, Martyn and Mary Mullins, HNJ, PEJ, BB)*
Sandown [12 Fitzroy St; SZ5984], *Castle*: Interesting free house with six real ales, lunchtime food inc home-made sausages, civilised atmosphere lunchtimes, live music evenings *(Joan and Michel Hooper-Immins)*; [High St], *Kings Bar*: Cafe-bar with good service, fine sea views, lunchtime food, Terry O'Neill photographs, Sky TV; popular with young people, piped music may be loud *(Terry King)*
Seaview [Esplanade; B3340, just off B3330 Ryde—Brading; SZ6291], *Old Fort*: Spacious, light and airy, more cafe-bar than pub, with commanding sea views, good choice of beers, prompt efficient service, wide choice of generous usual food inc cold buffet *(HNJ, PEJ, Jack Barnwell)*
☆ **Shalfleet** [A3054 Newport—Yarmouth; SZ4189], *New Inn*: More restaurant than pub, majoring on generous seafood, but good atmosphere with roaring log fire in traditional panelled and flagstoned bar, stripped stone dining lounge with big stripped pine tables, restaurant, no-smoking

family area; well kept Gales HSB and island beers on handpump, decent wines, country wines and coffee, service cheerful even when crowded, children in eating area, open all day summer *(Robert and Gladys Flux, Michael Andrews, P Neate, Anne Parmenter, Alison Bond, Dr and Mrs A K Clarke, DJW, D H and M C Watkinson, LYM)*

Shanklin [Chine Hill; SZ5881], *Chine*: Reopened after extensive tasteful refurbishment – beams and flagstones, separate bright family conservatory; wide choice of good food (not Sun evening, Tues or Sat) inc good value specials; lovely wooded setting with good sea views *(L R Stubbington)*; [High St Old Town; A3055 towards Ventnor], *Crab*: Picturesque thatched pub with pleasant tables outside; modernised bar with Whitbreads-related ales, rows of tables in dining area, quickly served family food; open all day *(Reg Nelson, David Sweeney, LYM)*; [Esplanade], *Longshoreman*: Comfortable low-beamed seafront pub with good Sandown Bay views, old Island photographs *(David Sweeney, Reg Nelson)*

Shide [SZ5088], *Barley Mow*: Unpretentious light and airy open-plan pub, chatty and friendly, with genial hard-working landlord, wide choice of generous home-cooked fresh food at low prices, very subdued piped music, Whitbreads *(HNJ, PEJ)*

Totland [Alum Bay Old Rd; SZ3286], *Highdown*: Brightened up and doing well under new owners, with fresh well cooked food inc some unusual dishes and good sauces, smart little new dining room, good pleasant service; piped music; picnic tables out in raised paddock area; bedrooms *(HNJ, PEJ)*

☆ **Whitwell** [High St; SZ5277], *White Horse*: Wide range of food inc vegetarian, and full Gales beers range, in well furnished big interconnected beamed bars; cheerful quick service, horse brasses, log fire, muted piped music *(Martyn and Mary Mullins)*

Whitwell [OS Sheet 196 map reference 521779], *Sun*: Good food, well kept beer; clean and friendly *(Anne Parmenter)*

☆ **Wootton Bridge** [A3054 Ryde—Newport; SZ5492], *Sloop*: Reliable Whitbreads Brewers Fayre pub, very popular, with good value generous food, lots of tables in huge spacious split-level bar, smart upmarket decor, friendly quick service, subdued piped music; nice setting, fine views over yacht moorings *(HNJ, PEJ, Barry Hall)*

☆ **Wroxall** [Clarence Rd (B3327); SZ5579], *Star*: Welcoming two-bar local, plush and tidy, with good choice of reasonably priced straightforward food, big open fire in cosy tiled public bar, well kept cheap Burts ales *(Jason Reynolds, HNJ, PEJ)*

☆ **Yarmouth** [St James' Sq; SZ3589], *Bugle*: Peaceful lounge, lively bar with counter like galleon stern, dark panelling, food from well filled sandwiches to grills inc children's dishes, well kept Whitbreads-related ales; piped music can be rather loud; restaurant, children's room with pool and video game, sizeable garden, summer barbecues; good big airy bedrooms – make sure you get one that's not over the bar *(Dr and Mrs A K Clarke, Chris and Kim Elias, LYM)*

☆ **Yarmouth** [Quay St], *George*: Sizeable hotel with Solent views from austerely panelled nautical bar, relaxing atmosphere, good bar food esp seafood, popular restaurant, courteous staff, well kept Burts, decent wine; big garden running down to shore with outside summer bar, barbecue area and lovely view; bedrooms comfortable *(Dr and Mrs A K Clarke, K Flack, Ian Pickard)*

Yarmouth [Quay St], *Kings Head*: Cosy pub opp car ferry, well kept ales, good food inc well prepared local fish, plush seats, friendly staff, open fires, unobtrusive piped music; can get crowded; bedrooms *(Dr and Mrs A K Clarke)*

Kent

A good clutch of new main entries here consists of the Albion in Faversham, a new place with very good food in simple but civilised surroundings; the picturesque Red Lion at Hernhill; the Hare at Langton Green, a fine interestingly redesigned dining pub; the firmly unspoilt Shipwrights Arms at Oare (reopened after a closure under enterprising new licensees); and the Fox & Hounds on Toys Hill, an unchanging country tavern in beautiful countryside. Other pubs currently doing specially well here include the very welcoming and thoroughly Kentish Flying Horse at Boughton Aluph, the Dove among the orchards at Dargate (newish licensees doing a grand job), the George at Newnham (becoming a real favourite for meals out – we choose it as Kent Dining Pub of the Year), the well run Bottle House just outside Penshurst and the Spotted Dog with its lovely view over Penshurst Place (both have above-average food), the Ringlestone Inn (oozing character, good lunchtime buffet), Sankeys in Tunbridge Wells (excellent fish and seafood) and the Pepper Box at Ulcombe (developing really well, with good thoughtfully presented food). There are some strong contenders, most already inspected by us, in the Lucky Dip section at the end of the chapter; we'd pick out the White Horse at Boughton Street, Canterbury Tales in Canterbury, Ship at Conyer Quay (but the landlord who's made it such an interesting main entry is planning to leave – grab it while you can), Kentish Rifleman at Dunks Green, Elephant in Faversham, Harrow at Ightham Common, Rock near Penshurst, Coopers Arms in Rochester, Clarendon in Sandgate, Bull at Sissinghust, Chequers at Smarden, Tiger at Stowting, Harrow at Warren Street, Pearsons in Whitstable (chiefly for its fish restaurant), Bull at Wrotham and Walnut Tree at Yalding. The Hooden Horse pubs are good value, appealingly young at heart. Beer prices in the area are generally on the high side; the cheapest drinks we found were in the Red Lion at Hernhill. We found that in pubs tied to the local brewer Shepherd Neame prices tended to be lower than the area average.

---

nr BIDDENDEN TQ8538 Map 3

Three Chimneys

A262, a mile W of village

One reader cheerfully drove 72 miles to get to this civilised and atmospheric old country pub. Nestling into the ground with its tiny windows and entrance, the lovely building has been here so long it has a slightly organic appearance. At the back the lusciously growing garden with nut trees at the end (probably the habitat of the very boisterous grey squirrels) has densely planted curving borders with flowering shrubs and shrub roses, that seem to permeate the garden room. The rambling series of small, very traditional rooms are huddled under low oak beams with simple wooden furniture and old settles on flagstone and coir matting, some harness and sporting prints on the exposed brick walls, and good winter log fires. The simple public bar has darts, shove-ha'penny, dominoes and cribbage. For many people the main draw is the very good food, sensibly limited to around four starters and main courses each day, though selected from quite a wide-ranging repertoire; favourite dishes include cock a leekie soup (£2.80), potted stilton in port and walnuts (£3.25), egg and anchovy mousse (£3.50), curried scallops and prawns (£3.95), courgette and mushroom quiche (£4.95), mixed bean casserole (£5.50), pork with date and apricot stuffing (£5.95), chicken and leek pie (£6.40), duck and pheasant casserole (£6.80), beef with chestnuts and celery (£6.85), and puddings such as pumpkin and mincemeat pie (£2.70) or glazed pear tart (£2.90), served with fresh Jersey cream. You can book tables in the garden room. A good range of well kept real ales tapped from the cask: Adnams Best, Brakspears, Harveys Best (and Old in winter), Marstons Pedigree, Morlands Old Speckled Hen and Wadworths 6X, along with a very dry Biddenden local cider, and a carefully chosen wine list with a range of half bottles (as well as local wine) and about twenty malt whiskies. Sissinghurst gardens are just down the road. *(Recommended by Richard and Ruth Neville, D B Stanley, E Carter, Martin Hickes, R G and J N Plumb, Tony and Wendy Hobden, John Fahy, K Burvill, Richard Fawcett, R Misson, Hilary Dobbie, J H Bell, Mike and Joyce Bryant, Mr and Mrs Hillman, Paul Adams, Simon Morton, N M Gibbs, Gordon, K Flack, Tim Galligan, M A and C R Starling, George Moore, Colin Laffan, L G Milligan, N H and A H Harries)*

Free house ~ Licensees C F W Sayers and G A Sheepwash ~ Real ale ~ Meals and snacks (till 10pm) ~ Biddenden (01580) 291472 ~ Children in garden room ~ Occasional live entertainment ~ Open 11-2.30, 6-11; closed 25/26 Dec

BOUGH BEECH TQ4846 Map 3

Wheatsheaf

B2027, S of reservoir

Flower beds and fruit trees fill the sheltered side and back gardens of this lovely pub, thought by locals to have started off as a hunting lodge belonging to Henry V. Inside the variety of heads and horns on the walls and above the massive stone fireplaces certainly indicate that someone has been hunting during its long history, though the sword from Fiji, crocodiles, stuffed birds, squirrels and even an armadillo suggest a wider ranging field than that provided by the chase around Tudor Hever. The atmosphere is congenial and welcoming, as are the staff and the old-school landlord. The neat central bar has unusually high ceilings with lofty oak timbers and divided from this by standing timbers – formerly an outside wall to the original building – is the snug. Other similarly aged features include a piece of 1607 graffito, 'Foxy Galumpy', thought to have been a whimsical local squire; also cigarette cards, swordfish spears and the only manatee in the south of England. The public bar has an attractive old settle carved with wheatsheaves, shove-ha'penny, dominoes, cribbage, and sensibly placed darts and other board games. The good heartily served bar food has quite an emphasis on home-cooked pies (from £4.95), along with curries and chillis made with fresh ground spices (from £4.95), and a variety of fish dishes, pasta, salads, and local game in season; watch out for the lead shot. Service can slow down at busy times. Well kept Boddingtons, Fremlins, Flowers Original, Morlands Old Speckled Hen and a couple of changing guests on handpump or tapped from the cask, decent wines, vintage ports, Scrumpy Jack cider, and a variety of malts; piped music. The friendly cat might jump on your lap as soon as you find a seat. There's a rustic cottage and boat in the garden for children to play on. *(Recommended by Reece and Mike Gannaway, Dr Michael Smith, Colin Laffan, Simon Pyle, George Atkinson, D A Edwards, Ian Phillips)*

Whitbreads ~ Lease: Elizabeth and Peter Currie ~ Real ale ~ Meals and snacks (12-2.30, 6-10) ~ (01732) 700254 ~ Children in eating area of bar ~ Folk music Weds evening ~ Open 11-3, 6-11(11-11 Sat)

BOUGHTON ALUPH TR0247 Map 3

Flying Horse

Boughton Lees; just off A251 N of Ashford

Built to catch the hungry pilgrim traffic on its way to Canterbury, this marvellously Kentish 15th-c pub is particularly well liked by readers for its notably friendly welcome. It's an especially nice place to come in summer, when you can sit outside and watch cricket on the broad village green. A few clues to the building's age still remain, mainly in the shiny old black panelling and the arched windows (though they are a later Gothic addition). Two ancient spring water wells were uncovered during restoration work, and these are now illuminated and covered at ground level with walk-over glass. The open-plan bar has lots of standing room so never seems too crowded, as well as comfortable upholstered modern wall benches, fresh flowers on many tables, hop bines around the serving area, horse brasses, and stone animals on either side of the blazing log fire. From the back room, big doors open out onto the spacious rose filled garden, where there are seats and tables. Good bar food such as sandwiches, mussels (£3.50), home-made steak and kidney pie (£4.95), Indonesian nasi goreng (£5.25), several fish dishes (from £5.25), lamb cutlets (£5.50), roast pheasant in season (£5.95), and peppered steaks (£7.50); maybe barbecues in summer, good breakfasts. Well kept Courage Best, John Smiths, Marstons Pedigree, Morlands Old Speckled Hen, Wadworths 6X and a weekly changing guest on handpump; decent wine list, and a range of malts. Shove-ha'penny, cribbage, dominoes, fruit machine and sometimes noticeable piped music. *(Recommended by Werner Arend, George Jonas, Reece and Mike Gannaway, John Hardie, S G Brown, James House, Dave Braisted)*

Courage ~ Lease: Howard and Christine Smith ~ Real ale ~ Meals and snacks ~ Restaurant (not Sun evening) ~ (01233) 620914 ~ Children in restaurant and well room ~ Occasional live music ~ Open 11-3, 6-11 (11-11 Sat) ~ Bedrooms: £20/£35

BOYDEN GATE TR2265 Map 3

Gate Inn ★

Off A299 Herne Bay—Ramsgate – follow Chislet, Upstreet signpost opposite Roman Gallery; Chislet also signposted off A28 Canterbury—Margate at Upstreet – after turning right into Chislet main street keep right on to Boyden; the pub gives its address as Marshside, though Boyden Gate seems more usual on maps

The cheery licensee has just celebrated his twentieth year at this charming and unpretentious old place. Readers who've known it all that time say nothing has changed in the intervening period – it's still a fine example of an unspoilt and traditional village pub, quite a focus for local activities ('MCC' here stands for Marshside Cricket Club), but welcoming and friendly to visitors. Distinctly pubby, the bar has pews with flowery cushions around tables of considerable character, hop bines hanging from the beam, a good winter log fire (which serves both quarry-tiled rooms), and attractively etched windows; there are photographs on the walls – some ancient sepia ones, others new. Unfussy but tasty, the well prepared good value bar food includes enterprising sandwiches with lots of pickles (from £1.25, black pudding £1.35), filled baked potatoes (from £1.90), home-made burgers (from £1.65), garlic mushrooms (£1.90), a range of ploughman's (£3.60), home-made vegetable flan (£3.75), sliced pepper or home-cooked ham spicy hotpots (£4.10), mixed grill (£4.50), and puddings; they use organically grown local produce where possible, and you can generally buy local honey and free-range eggs. The eating area is no smoking at lunchtime. Well kept Shepherd Neame Bitter, Spitfire, and Bishops Finger tapped from the cask, with country wines, local apple juice, and coffee; they take care to give individual service. Sensibly placed darts, as well as shove-ha'penny, bar billiards, dominoes, and cribbage. They can get very busy at weekends. On a fine evening, it's marvellously relaxing to sit at the picnic tables on the sheltered side lawn listening to the contented quacking of what seems like a million happy ducks and geese (they sell duck food inside – 5p a bag). There may be Morris dancers in summer. *(Recommended by David R Shillitoe, David Hodgkins, Chris Westmoreland, Tommy Payne, Gwen and Peter Andrews, W Walters, Jacquie and Jon Payne, Martin and Pauline Richardson, Louise Weeks, Mr and Mrs Joseph Williams, Stephen Brown)*

Shepherd Neame ~ Tenant Christopher Smith ~ Real ale ~ Meals and snacks ~ (01227) 860498 ~ Children in eating area of bar and in family room ~ Pianist Sun evening, jazz Tues, folk Friday ~ Open 11-2.30(3 Sat), 6-11

BROOKLAND TQ9926 Map 3

Woolpack

Just out of village; off A259

It's surprising we don't get more reports about this crooked white early 15th-c cottage, huddling low against the flat landscape. Once the Beacon Keeper's house, it has all the smuggling connections you'd expect, and plenty of old-fashioned character and atmosphere. Its tremendous age is immediately apparent in the ancient entrance lobby with uneven brick floor and black painted pine panelled walls. On the right the simple but homely softly lit main bar has basic cushioned plank seats in a massive inglenook fireplace, and a painted wood effect bar counter hung with plenty of water jugs. Some of the ships' timbers in the low-beamed ceiling may date from the 12th c. On the new quarry tiled floor is a long elm table with shove ha'penny carved into one end, other old and new wall benches (a lazy cat sleeps on one) and chairs at mixed tables around the walls, and characterful photos of the locals (and perhaps their award winning sheep). To the left of the lobby a sparsely furnished tiny room leads to an open-plan games room with central chimney stack, modern bar counter, and young locals playing darts or pool; cribbage, dominoes, fruit machine, piped music. Well kept Shepherd Neame Best, Bishops Finger and Spitfire on handpump. Straightforward but well priced and generously served bar food includes sandwiches (from £1.40, home-cooked ham £1.80, crab or prawn £2.30), soup (£2.25), shepherd's pie (£2.75), filled baked potatoes (from £3.25), ham, egg and chips or ploughman's (£3.50), a pint of prawns (£3.95), lasagne or chilli (£3.95), trout (£5.95) and mixed grill or sirloin steak (£7.25). Tables outside look down the garden to a stream, where the pub has fishing rights. *(Recommended by Simon Morton; more reports please)*

Shepherd Neame ~ Tenants John and Pat Palmer ~ Real ale ~ Meals and snacks ~ (01797) 344321 ~ Children in family bar until 9pm ~ Open 11-3, 6-11

CHIDDINGSTONE TQ4944 Map 3

Castle 🍷

Village signposted from B2027 Tonbridge—Edenbridge

An integral part of the wonderfully picturesque cluster of unspoilt Tudor houses that makes up Chiddingstone, this rambling old inn probably dates back to the 15th c, and could have been where Anne Boleyn found shelter when she was stranded in a terrible blizzard on her way to nearby Hever. The handsome, carefully modernised beamed bar has an attractive mullioned window seat in one small alcove, latticed windows, well made settles forming booths around the tables, and cushioned sturdy wall benches; it might get busy with visitors in summer so it's worth arriving early for a table. Well kept Harveys Sussex, Larkins Traditional (brewed in the village) and a changing beer like Shepherd Neame Best on handpump; also a good range of malt whiskies, coffee, liqueur coffees, and tea, and an excellent choice of over 150 wines (the quality is reflected in the prices, though the house wines should suit all pockets). Darts, shove-ha'penny, dominoes and cribbage. Bar food includes home-made soup (£2.55), open sandwiches (from £3.45), home-made pâté (£3.65), filled baked potatoes (from £4.05), a daily pasta dish (£4.80), ploughman's (£4.90), very hot chilli con carne (£5.15), half a dozen giant snails (£5.30), salads (from £6.95) and a changing two or three course meal (from £9.95), with starters like moules marinières or marinaded prawns, and main courses like salmon in caper and parsley sauce or pigeon casseroled in real ale; puddings such as cointreau ice cream, chocolate torte or home-made cheesecake (£2.45). The landlord has been here for more than thirty years. The pretty back garden has a small pool and fountain set in a rockery and tables on a brick terrace and neat lawn. There are more tables at the front opposite the church, and the countryside around here is lovely. Recent reports suggest service can be a little erratic. *(Recommended by J S M Sheldon, Jenny and Brian Seller, E D Bailey, Steve Goodchild, C H and P Stride, Paul McKeerer, L G Milligan, David and Michelle Hedges, Andy Petersen, Ian Phillips, Penny and Martin Fletcher, David Wright, Thomas Nott)*

Free house ~ Licensee Nigel Lucas ~ Real ale ~ Meals and snacks (until 15 minutes before closing time) ~ Restaurant ~ (01892) 870247 ~ Children in saloon bar and restaurant ~ Open 11-3, 6-11; all day Sat

DARGATE TR0761 Map 3

Dove

Village signposted from A299

Surrounded by strawberry fields and orchards, this old-fashioned honeysuckle-clad brick house is a very pretty, peaceful spot, well-liked by readers. The sheltered garden is particularly attractive, with roses, lilacs, paeonies and many other flowers, picnic tables under pear trees, a dovecot with white doves, a rockery and pool, and a swing. The carefully refurbished rambling rooms are now bare-boarded once again (the current licensees took away the carpets), and as well as a good winter log fire have photographs of the pub and its licensees throughout the century; piped music. Well kept Shepherd Neame Bitter and Spitfire, and an unusual strong local cider. In addition to the sandwiches (from £2.50), and ploughman's, the good value daily changing menu might include promptly-served dishes like seafood pancake (£5.65), home-made steak and kidney pie (£4.95), and gammon in port wine (£5.50). A bridlepath leads up from the pub (along the charmingly-named Plumpudding Lane) into Blean Wood. *(Recommended by Ian Irving, Ian Phillips, David Rule, Mrs M Henderson, S G Brown, Mr and Mrs J Back, D K Carter, Simon Small)*

Shepherd Neame ~ Tenants Paul and Alison Anderson ~ Real ale ~ Meals and snacks ~ (01227) 751360 ~ Well behaved children welcome ~ Open 11-3, 6-11 (closed evening 25 Dec)

FAVERSHAM TR0161 Map 3

Albion

Follow road through town and in centre turn left into Keyland Road; just before Shepherd Neame Brewery walkway over road turn right over bridge, bear right, first right into public car park

Patrick Coevoet, the French chef and licensee here, is known to us for his previous work at two other main entries in this Guide. The soundly imaginative home-cooked blackboard menu is a sensible length and might include ploughman's (from £3.20), warm salad of chicken liver and wild mushrooms with raspberry vinegar dressing (£3.95), tagliatelle with hazelnuts and bacon or spinach, mushroom and stilton pancakes (£5.95), local dressed crab (£7.25), escalope of salmon in spinach, prawn and cream sauce (£8.20), fried calf's liver with sherry and cream (£9.25), fresh fish from the Whitstable market, and popular puddings like mango sorbet with vanilla ice cream, fresh fruit and a fruit coulis, mango tarte tatin, plum pudding or steamed date and apple pudding (£2.50). There's a pleasant chatty atmosphere in the light and airy open-plan room, where locals gather at the central bar; it has simple but solid mixed old pine furniture on wood and sisal flooring. The pale pea green walls have some nautical paraphernalia and old pine mirrors. Big picture windows and french doors open out on to willow trees along the bank of Faversham Creek (arrive early and walk for about an hour along the path that follows the river) with boats and some new and old industrial buildings. The picnic tables out on the walkway make this a delightful place to spend a summer evening. As the Shepherd Neame Brewery is just across the river the Bishops Finger, Master Brew and Spitfire on handpump are just as perfectly kept as you'd expect. *(Recommended by Mrs M Henderson; more reports please)*

Shepherd Neame ~ Tenants Patrick Coevoet and Josephine Bridges ~ Real ale ~ Meals and snacks (12-2, 7-9.30; Fri, Sat 7-10; not Mon and Sun evenings) ~ (01795) 591411 ~ Children away from bar area ~ 11-3, 6.30(Fri and Sat 6)-11

GROOMBRIDGE TQ5337 Map 3

Crown 🍷

B2110

The blackboards at this quaint and carefully preserved Elizabethan inn aren't all used to display the menu – one is usually reserved for a vocabulary-building word of the day. The tile-hung house is prettily set at the end of a horseshoe shaped row of comely cottages, surrounding a lovely steep green with views to the village below. Once the haunt of smugglers en-route between London and Rye, the series of snug, atmospheric rooms is decorated with various antique bottles – many accompanied by an anecdote the landlord is only too happy to share. It's a relaxed and chatty place, with a cheery bustle around the long copper-topped serving bar, and logs quietly burning in the big brick inglenook; lots of old teapots and pewter tankards on the walls. The end room, normally for eaters, has fairly close-spaced tables with a variety of good solid chairs, a log-effect gas fire in a big fireplace, and an arch through to the food ordering area. The walls, mostly rough yellowing plaster with some squared panelling and some timbering, are decorated with small topographical, game and sporting prints, and a circular large-scale map with the pub at its centre; some of the beams have horsebrasses. A pretty little parlour serves as an overflow for eaters, and is bookable too. The range of tasty bar food usually consists of dishes like home-made soup (£1.60), garlic mushrooms (£3), vegetarian tortellini in tomato, garlic and pepper sauce (£3.50), home-baked honey roast ham (£4.80), and chicken provençale or lamb steak in red wine with mushrooms (£5); nicely cooked vegetables, Sunday roast. Service is flexible, and it's the kind of place where cream comes in a jug. Well kept Courage Directors, Harveys IPA and Ruddles County on handpump, good value house wines (by the glass as well), and local Biddenden cider; shove-ha'penny, cribbage and backgammon. There are picnic tables on the sunny front brick terrace or on the green. Across the road is a public footpath beside the small chapel which leads, across a field, to moated Groombridge Place (the gardens of which are now open to the public) and fields beyond. *(Recommended by W J Wonham, Hilary Dobbie, Keith and Audrey Ward, Stella Knight, Colin Laffan, P Neate, Jason Caulkin, Chris and Anne Fluck, Mavis and John Wright, Lawrence Pearse, Richard Waller, K Flack, Joy and Arthur Hoadley)*

Free house ~ Licensees Bill and Vivienne Rhodes ~ Real ale ~ Meals and snacks (not Sun evening) ~ Evening restaurant (not Sun) ~ (01892) 864742 ~ Children in eating area and restaurant ~ Occasional Morris dancers in summer, mummers in winter ~ Open 11-2.30(3 Sat), 6-11; 11-11 summer Sats ~ Bedrooms: £22/£38

nr HADLOW TQ6352 Map 3

Artichoke

Hamptons; from Hadlow—Plaxtol road take second right (signposted West Peckham), the pub has a new sign on the grass verge; OS Sheet 188, ref 627524

This isolated little cottage is one of those pubs that somehow manages to suit every season. On a sunny summer day you can sit under the awning on the fairy-lit front terrace, or on the wooden seat built around the lime tree, and gaze across the surrounding countryside. And in winter the two atmospheric little rooms are warmed by a woodburning stove and an inglenook fireplace filled with tree trunk sized logs. The very busy bars are filled with fairly closely spaced cushioned high-backed wooden settles, wooden farmhouse-kitchen chairs, upholstered wrought-iron stools matching unusual wrought-iron, glass-topped tables on the turkey carpet, and beams in the low ceilings; lots of gleaming brass, some country pictures (mainly hunting scenes), antique umbrellas, old storm lamps, and a fox mask. Home-made bar food includes vegetable soup (£2.25), crispy prawn brochettes or ploughman's (£3.95), pies such as steak and kidney or chicken and mushroom (£5.95), mixed grill (£6.95), specials such as salmon and prawn gratin or chicken, pepper and courgette bake (£5.95), steaks (from £9.25), and puddings (£2.50). Fullers London Pride, Greene King Abbot, and Youngs Special on handpump, with a good range of spirits. *(Recommended by Nigel Wikeley, L M Miall, Rev M R Kemp, David and Fiona Easeman, G B Longden, J Muckelt, Mrs J M Aston, K Flack)*

Free house ~ Licensees Terence and Barbara Simmonds ~` Real ale ~ Meals ~ Restaurant (not Sun eve) ~ (01732) 810763 ~ Children in eating area of bar ~ Open 11.30-2.30, 6.30-11; closed winter Sun evenings

HERNHILL TR0660 Map 3

Red Lion

Off A299 at Highstreet roundabout via Dargate; or off A2 via Boughton Street and Staplestreet; follow Hernhill church signs

It's particularly pleasant to sit outside this very pretty Tudor inn which is ideally set next to the church and village green, bright with daffodils in spring. The long narrow densely beamed and flagstoned interior with new pine tables throughout is often crowded with people gathering for the popular food served in big helpings (order from one side of the bar): soup (£1.75), chicken liver pâté (£2.95), moules marinières (£3.25 or £5), courgette and nut burgers (£3.50), scampi (£4.25), vegetable lasagne (£4.50), seafood carbonara (£5.25), salmon fillet with cucumber and dill sauce (£6.95), chicken breast with stilton and mushroom sauce (£7.95) and breast of duck with redcurrant and damson sauce (£8.95). There is a restaurant upstairs. Good range of well kept real ales including Boddingtons, Fullers London Pride, Morlands Old Speckled Hen and Shepherd Neame Master Brew; log fires in winter; very good play area in garden; boules; piped pop music which can be quite loud; darts. *(Recommended by Peter and Pat Frogley, Chris Westmoreland)*

Free house ~ Nicola and Michael White ~ Real ale ~ Meals and snacks (till 10) ~ Restaurant (not Sun eve) ~ (01227) 751207 ~ Children welcome away from bar ~ Open 11-3, 6-11 ~ Bedrooms: £30/£40

LAMBERHURST TQ6635 Map 3

Brown Trout ♀

B2169, just off A21 S of village nearly opposite entrance to Scotney Castle

The densely hung vermillion hanging baskets stand out starkly against the white-painted facade of this busy pub; even in winter the show is marvellous with baskets and tubs of pansies. Fresh fish from Billingsgate is still the distinguishing feature, with meals such as soft roes on toast (£3.90), half a dozen oysters (£3.95), Mediterranean prawns in garlic butter (£4.95), 10oz fresh fillet of plaice (£4.95), wing of skate (£6.95), dressed crab with prawns (£7.50), and whole lobster (£13.95); also non-fishy dishes like soup (£1.95), lasagne (£4.95), pork chops (£6.25) and steaks (from £8.95), with a good value two-course steak meal (including a bottle of wine) at £13.95 for two. Service is generally welcoming and friendly, though does slow down at busy periods. You may have to book ahead, particularly on Saturday evenings. The small bar has a big central counter surrounded by russet hessian walls with small country prints, glowing copper and brass hanging thickly from the beams, and eight or nine tables – most people tend to eat in the biggish extension dining room which has many closely set tables and a fish tank. Changing beers such as Harveys or Larkins on handpump, a large choice of wines and freshly squeezed fruit juices; side fruit machine, faint piped music. Picnic tables under cocktail parasols on the sloping front grass to the road and a large, safe garden behind with swings, slides and trampolines; there may be barbecues out here on summer Sundays. The licensee also runs the Rainbow Trout in Rotherfield, and the Tickled Trout at West Farleigh. *(Recommended by Peter and Pat Frogley, Margaret and*

Nigel Dennis, Mr and Mrs P Brocklebank, B J Harding, Martin Jones, Maysie Thompson, Ian Phillips, K Flack)

Whitbreads ~ Lease: Joseph Stringer ~ Real ale ~ Meals and snacks (till 10) ~ Restaurant ~ (01892) 890312 ~ Children welcome ~ Open 10.30(11 in winter)-3.30, 6-11; closed evening 25 Dec

LANGTON GREEN TQ5538 Map 3

Hare 🍷

A264 W of Tunbridge Wells

Already very popular, this civilised and individual dining pub only takes bookings in one room, so even at their busiest times you should be able to get a table without booking (maybe a short wait). The fairly extensive and imaginative menu is changed twice a day and listed on a large blackboard. Generous helpings of well presented food prepared from fresh ingredients might include mushrooms in tomato and garlic topped with melted cheese (£3.95), fried potato wedges topped with smoked bacon, mushroom and sauce cheese (£4.25), fried lamb's kidneys lightly chillied (£4.95), seafood cocktail with prawns, smoked salmon, crab meat and smoked mackerel (£6.95), grilled lemon sole or chicken breast on tagliatelle with wild mushroom sauce (£8.95), half roast garlic crumbed shoulder of lamb with redcurrant sauce (£9.95), platter of roast beef, ham, chicken liver terrine, stilton, cheddar cheese, smoked mackerel and prawns for two (£17.95), a very popular seafood platter for two (£29.95) and delightfully presented puddings on huge plates like bread and butter pudding, banoffee pie on a fruit coulis and spotted dick and custard (£2.95). Once you've ordered at the bar, you're served by attentive young waitresses. The knocked-through ground floor of this spacious turn of the century inn is light and airy, with good-sized rooms, high ceilings and lots of big windows. The interior is enthusiastically decorated in spirit with its age, with dark-painted dados below light walls and dark ceilings, oak furniture and turkey carpets on stained wooden floors, and largely period romantic pastels and bric-a-brac (including a huge collection of chamber-pots). There's a civilised and conversational atmosphere in the big room at the back which is probably the one to head for. Old books and pictures crowd its walls, as well as two big mahogany mirror-backed display cabinets. It has lots of large tables (one big enough for at least 12) on a light brown carpet; french windows open on to a terrace with picnic tables, looking out on to a tree-ringed green (you don't see the main road). Well kept Greene King Abbot and Rayments; decent wines; about 35 malt whiskies; piped pop music in front bar area. *(Recommended by Mrs D McFarlane, Jonathan Nettleton, Julia Lawrence, E V J Rushton, Mr and Mrs Bishop, Mr and Mrs Hancock)*

Greene King ~ Tenant Brian Whiting ~ Real ale ~ Meals and snacks ~ (01892) 862419 ~ Children welcome away from bar ~ Open 11.30-2.30; 6-11

NEWNHAM TQ9557 Map 3

George ★ 🍷

44 The Street; village signposted from A2 just W of Ospringe, outside Faversham

Kent Dining Pub of the Year

Several readers tell us this distinctive 16th-c village pub is rapidly becoming one of their favourites. The Dickensian atmosphere and above-average bar food are the main reasons cited, but the place is obviously very well cared for, with tremendous attention to detail evident in the neat furnishings and decor, and the beautiful flower arrangements. The very good bar food might include dishes such as sandwiches (from £1.20), delicious soup (£2), pheasant eggs Florentine (£3.25), courgettes bolognese or moules marinières (£3.75), cheese topped cottage pie (£3.80), a good variety of ploughman's and salads (from £4.25, avocado and prawns £6), pasta of the day or chilli con carne (£4.60), vegetarian parcel (£5.30), steak and kidney pie or pudding (£5.95 or £6.25), game pie (£6.30), fillets of sole Dieppoise (£8.30), lemon and ginger poussin on a bed of caramelised onions (£8.40), memorable rack of lamb (cooked pink £8.50), pot roast half shoulder of lamb glazed with mint jelly (£10.75), fillet steak with port and cream sauce (£11.95), and puddings (not Sunday) such as chocolate roulade or an old-fashioned suet pudding (£2.50); they use local fruit and vegetables as much as possible. Service does stop bang on 1.30pm on a Sunday, so get there well before then if you plan to eat. No credit cards. The spreading series of atmospheric rooms have prettily upholstered mahogany settles, dining chairs and leather carving chairs around candlelit tables, table lamps and gas-type ceiling chandeliers, rugs on the waxed floorboards, early 19th-c prints (Dominica negroes, Oxford academics, politicians), a cabinet of fine rummers and other glassware, and a collection of British butterflies and moths; hop bines hang from the beams and there are open fires. Well kept Shepherd Neame Bitter, Best, Bishops Finger and Spitfire on handpump, four wines by the glass and more by the bottle, and unobtrusive, better-than-usual piped music; shove-ha'penny, cribbage, dominoes, fruit machine. There are picnic tables in a spacious sheltered garden with a fine spreading cobnut tree, below the slopes of the sheep pastures. Dogs allowed (drinking bowl in lobby). Good walks nearby. *(Recommended by Wayne Brindle, Tina and David Woods-Taylor, Chris Westmoreland, Mrs M Henderson, Derek Patey, P M Lane, Stephen and Julie Brown, Ben Regan)*

Shepherd Neame ~ Tenant Simon Barnes ~ Real ale ~ Meals and snacks (till 10pm, till 1.30 sharp Sun; not Sun evening, not Mon) ~ (01795) 890237 ~ Children welcome ~ Open 10-3, 6-11; they close at 2 Sun lunchtimes

OARE TR0163 Map 3

Shipwrights Arms

Ham Road, Hollow Shore; from A2 just W of Faversham, follow Oare—Luddenham signpost; fork right at Oare—Harty Ferry signpost, drive straight through Oare (don't turn off to Harty Ferry), then left into Ham Street on the outskirts of Faversham, following pub signpost

It's quite an adventure getting to this splendidly unspoilt 17th-c tavern, back as a main entry after several years away. Situated in the middle of marshland, 3ft below sea level, it's reached by a daunting and determinedly bumpy track that you might at first think leads absolutely nowhere; readers whose cars have delicate suspension can well understand why so many customers seem to arrive by boat. Low-roofed, dark and cosy, the three relaxed little bars are as traditional and rustic as any fans of this type of pub could wish for. Separated by standing timbers and wood part-partitions or narrow door arches, they're filled with a medley of seats from tapestry cushioned stools and chairs through some big windsor armchairs to black wood-panelled built-in settles forming little booths. Lighting is by generator (and water is pumped from a well), and there are hops and pewter tankards hanging over the bar counter, copper kettles, boating pictures, flags or boating pennants on the ceilings, several brick fireplaces, and a wood-burning stove. Simple bar food such as burgers (from £1.80), good pizzas (from £2.50), steak and kidney pie (£4.15), and seafood platter (£4.20); part of the eating area is no smoking. Well kept beers such as Flowers IPA and Original, Goachers Mild and Light, and Shepherd Neame Bitter and Spitfire tapped from casks behind the counter, and a strong local farm cider; darts, cribbage, dominoes, backgammon, piped music. Very friendly service. The small front and back gardens outside the white weather-boarded and tiled building lead up a bank to the path above the creek where lots of boats are moored. *(Recommended by Werner Arend, Mrs M Henderson, Chris Westmoreland)*

Free house ~ Lease: Simon Claxton ~ Real ale ~ Meals and snacks ~ (01795) 590088 ~ Children in eating area ~ Open 11-3, 7-11; 11-11 Sat

PENSHURST TQ5243 Map 3

Bottle House

Coldharbour Lane, Smarts Hill; leaving Penshurst SW on B2188 turn right at Smarts Hill signpost, then bear right towards Chiddingstone and Cowden

Standing alone in quiet countryside, this friendly family-run 15th-c free house is still a very popular choice with readers for food; the only complaint we've had about the meals in the last year is that it's too difficult to choose what to have. The very wide range includes filled jacket potatoes and ploughman's (from £4.25), cheese, vegetable and onion pie or breaded lemon sole (£5.95), chicken madras, steak and kidney pudding or avocado and brie salad (£6.95), king prawns in oriental pastry (£7.95), lamb steak in a green peppercorn sauce (£8.95), and specials such as smoked haddock stuffed with salmon mousse in filo pastry (£7.50) or fillet of beef stuffed with boursin cheese and wrapped in bacon (£11.95); good puddings and Sunday lunch. It soon fills up, but even when busy service remains efficient and notably welcoming. The relaxed low-beamed front bar has an exposed brick floor, smoothed with age, extending to behind the polished copper topped bar counter, and an atmosphere that seems comfortable as soon as you walk in. Big windows look out to a patio area with climbing plants and hanging baskets around picnic tables under cocktail parasols, and beyond to the quiet fields and oak trees. Down a step, the unpretentious main red-carpeted bar has massive behopped supporting beams, two large stone pillars with a small brick fireplace inbetween with a copper hood and stuffed turtle to one side, and old paintings and photographs on mainly plastered walls. To the far right, an isolated extension forms a small pine panelled snug hung with part of an extensive collection of china pot lids; the rest are in the low ceilinged, well appointed dining room. Scattered throughout the pub is the licensee's collection of old sewing machines. Well kept Harveys, Ind Coope Burton, and Larkins from nearby Chiddingstone on handpump (they've won awards for their cellar), cider from Chiddingstone too, and local wine; unobtrusive piped music. Dogs welcome (they may offer them biscuits). The affable licensees run another Kent main entry, the George & Dragon at Speldhurst. *(Recommended by James House, Margaret and Nigel Dennis, Keith and Audrey Ward, Ian Jones, Jon Carpenter, P J Guy, Mary Defer, G T White, R and S Bentley, P Neate, Colin Laffan, T O Haunch, Mark and Nicola Willoughbby)*

Free house ~ Licensees Gordon and Val Meer ~ Real ale ~ Meals and snacks (till 10) ~ Restaurant (not Sun evening) ~ (01892) 870306 ~ Children welcome ~ Open 11-2.30, 6-11

Spotted Dog 🍷

Smarts Hill; going S from village centre on B2188, fork right up hill at telephone box: in just under ½ mile the pub is on your left

Twenty miles of countryside stretch before you from the terrace of this popular pub, with the lush upper Medway valley curling round below towards medieval Penshurst. A quaint tiled house perched on the side of a hill, it's still the unusually good bar food that readers seem to like the most. Covering up to five blackboards, the range of meals might change twice a day, with particularly well received dishes over the last year including avocado, mozzarella and basil plait (£5.45), quarter leg of lamb (£7.45), venison, wild mushroom and madeira pie (£7.95), and whole grilled Dover sole (£13.95); they also do sandwiches, soup, and ploughman's, and lots of fresh fish like tuna, red snapper or parrot fish, vegetarian meals such as aubergines stuffed with chilli, vegetables and cheese or wild mushroom and cashew nut stroganoff, and puddings like cherry strudel or treacle tart. You go down a few steps to enter the neatly kept and heavily beamed and timbered bar, which has some antique settles as well as wheelback chairs on its rugs and tiles, a fine brick inglenook fireplace, and attractive moulded panelling in one alcove. It's quite small, so there may be an overflow into the restaurant at busy times; staff stay smiling amidst the cheery bustle. Well kept Adnams, Eldridge Pope Royal Oak, King & Barnes Sussex, and Wadworths 6X on handpump, along with Old Spotty – a Best Bitter brewed specially for the pub by Courage. The wine list is good (lots from the New World, even some from Penshurst); unobtrusive piped music. Lots of room for children to play outside. *(Recommended by Hilary Dobbie, Nigel Wikeley, Roger and Valerie Hill, Mark Steavenson, Peter Harrison, M E A Horler, J H Bell, Steve Goodchild, Keith and Audrey Ward, P Neate, Paul McKeerer, J Muckelt, Simon Morton, David Wright, Colin Laffan)*

Free house ~ Licensee Andy Tucker ~ Real ale ~ Meals and snacks ~ Restaurant ~ (01892) 870253 ~ Children in eating area of bar ~ Open 11.30-2.30, 6-11; closed 25 Dec

PLUCKLEY TQ9243 Map 3

Dering Arms

Near station, which is signposted from B2077 in village

Quite astonishing when seen for the first time, this atmospheric old pub has a uniquely handsome castle-like exterior, with cleanly cut Dutch gables topping the massive grey stone blocked walls above heavy studded oak doors. The unusual arched mullioned 'Dering' windows took the family name when a member of the clan escaped from the Roundheads by climbing through one, and subsequently decreed that all houses built on the estate should have similar fenestration – you can still see lots locally. The strikingly high ceilinged echoing bar still has something of a baronial feel – it's not hard to imagine huge dogs lounging on the wood and stone floors in front of the great log fireplace. Decorations are stylishly simple, with a variety of good solid wooden furniture – the smaller bar is similar; dominoes, shove ha'penny. Very popular bar food includes sandwiches (from £1.40), ploughman's (£3.50), all-day breakfast (£3.95), a daily pie or pasta dish (£5.95) and very well presented blackboard specials such as potted crab or mussels in cider and cream sauce (£3.95), good monkfish with bacon and orange sauce, fillet of red bream, braised oxtail, or rabbit in mustard and ale (£9.65), and fillet of halibut meunière (£10.65); puddings like sherry trifle or caramel rice pudding (£2.50). The restaurant menu is very good (probably worth booking), and they do a cafetiere of coffee with home-made almond shortbread (£1.20). Every six weeks they have gourmet evenings, elaborate black-tie affairs with seven courses. Well kept real ales on handpump include Goachers Maidstone Light, Real Mild, Gold Star (summer), Porter (winter) and Dering ale, a beer they brew specially for the pub; good extensive wine list, home-made lemonade, local cider. There's a vintage car rally once a month, and in summer garden parties with barbecues and music from jazz to classical string quartets. *(Recommended by E Carter, Dave Braisted, Hilary Dobbie, J Fane, Miss M Byrne, Viv Middlebrook, Nigel Gibbs, Nicola Thomas, Paul Dickinson)*

Free house ~ Licensee James Buss ~ Real ale ~ Meals and snacks (till 10pm; not Sun evening) ~ Restaurant (not Sun evening) ~ (01233) 840371 ~ Children in eating area and restaurant ~ Occasional jazz or string quartet in summer ~ Open 11-3, 6-11; closed 26/27 Dec ~ Bedrooms: £28/£36

RINGLESTONE TQ8755 Map 3

Ringlestone ★

M20 Junction 8 to Lenham/Leeds Castle; join B2163 heading N towards Sittingbourne via Hollingbourne; at water tower above Hollingbourne turn right towards Doddington (signposted), and straight ahead at next crossroads; OS Sheet 178 map reference 879558

Characterful is the best word to describe this timeless 16th-c inn, and it's a word that just as easily describes several of the former licensees, not least the mother and daughter who, dressed in full evening dress, would carefully vet each approaching customer, often using a shotgun to send packing those they didn't like the look of. These days the food is one of the main draws, especially the help-yourself hot and cold lunchtime buffet – well worth the queues for meals like herrings in madeira or mussels provençale (£3.95), macaroni with tuna and clams (£3.75), and cidered chicken casserole or peppered beef goulash (£4.50). Evening meals might include a thick vegetable and meat soup with sherry (£2.95), smoked mackerel salad (£4.35), leek and spinach pasties (£4.50), coconut and banana curry (£5.85), a good range of unusual pies such as ham, leek and parsnip wine or chicken and bacon in cowslip wine (£7.35), fresh trout (£8.35), and puddings such as chocolate, plum and elderberry trifle or brandy bread pudding (£2.95); many of these dishes turn up more cheaply as part of the lunchtime buffet. Changing well kept real ales tapped from casks behind the bar or on handpump and chalked up on a board might include brews such as Felinfoel Double Dragon, Harveys Best, Shepherd Neame Bishops Finger and Spitfire, Tetleys, Theakstons Best and Old Peculier, and Whitbreads Best; also 24 country wines (including sparkling ones), and fresh fruit cordials. The central room has farmhouse chairs, cushioned wall settles, and tables with candle lanterns on its worn brick floor, and old-fashioned brass and glass lamps on the exposed brick and flint walls; there's a wood-burning stove and small bread oven in an inglenook fireplace. An arch from here through a wall – rather like the outside of a house, windows and all – opens into a long, quieter room with cushioned wall benches, tiny farmhouse chairs, three old carved settles (one rather fine and dated 1620), similar tables, and etchings of country folk on its walls (bare brick too). Regulars tend to sit at the wood-panelled bar counter, or liven up a little wood-floored side room. Hard-working, friendly staff. There are picnic tables on the two acres of beautifully landscaped lawns, with shrubs, trees and rockeries, and a water garden with four pretty ponds linked by cascading waterfalls, a delightful fountain, and troughs of pretty flowers along the pub walls. Well behaved dogs welcome.

(Recommended by Wayne Brindle, R G and J N Plumb, Martin Hickes, Tina and David Woods-Taylor, E D Bailey, Gwen and Peter Andrews, E Carter, Beverley James, Dr G M Regan, Nicola Thomas, Paul Dickinson, E D Bailey, A B Dromey, Stephen Brown, D A Edwards)

Free house ~ Licensees Michael Millington-Buck and Michelle K Stanley ~ Real ale ~ Meals and snacks ~ Restaurant (not Sun eve) ~ (01622) 859900 ~ Children welcome ~ Open 11.30-3, 6-11; closed 25 Dec

SELLING TR0456 Map 3

White Lion 🍷

3½ miles from M2 junction 7; village signposted from exit roundabout; village also signposted off A251 S of Faversham

Nudging excellence in every department, this pleasantly tucked-away 300 year-old coaching inn is a mass of colour in summer with its riotous hanging baskets. Warmly atmospheric and welcoming, the comfortable bar is decorated with moss and dried flowers, and has two huge brick fireplaces (with a spit over the right-hand one) with fires in winter, pews on stripped floorboards, and an unusual semi-circular bar counter; maybe quiet piped music. Good, generously served bar food includes sandwiches (from £1.25), home-made soup (£2.25), garlic and herb pâté or smoked salmon mousse (£2.95), ploughman's (from £3.50), salads (from £4.75), several vegetarian meals like mushrooms in a spicy provençal sauce with cheese (£5.75), steaks (from £7.50), specials such as traditional beef pudding or steak and kidney pie (£4.95), curries including chicken and coconut (£5.95), and a range of home-made puddings; smaller helpings for younger and older customers. Monday is curry night, and they do Sunday roasts. Well kept Shepherd Neame Mild, Best and Spitfire on handpump, extensive wine list (with some by the glass), and a range of malt whiskies. The welcoming landlord is a trumpet-player, and may even play on jazz nights. There are rustic picnic tables in the attractive garden behind.

(Recommended by Ian Irving, E G Prish, Nigel Foster, Stephen Brown, Evelyn and Derek Walter, D K Carter)

Shepherd Neame ~ Tenant Anthony Richards ~ Real ale ~ Meals and snacks ~ Restaurant (not Sun evening) ~ (01227) 752211 ~ Children welcome (in family room) ~ Live music second and last Tues of month ~ Open 11-3, 6.30-11; closed 25 Dec

nr SMARDEN TQ8842 Map 3

Bell ★ 🍷 🍺

From Smarden follow lane between church and The Chequers, then turn left at T-junction; or from A274 take unsignposted turn E a mile N of B2077 to Smarden

This pretty peg-tiled old local doubled as a pub and a blacksmith's forge from 1630 to earlier this century. It's very pleasant sitting in the garden amongst the mature fruit trees and shrubs, looking up at the attractive rose-covered building with its massive chimneys – though on sunny weekends you're hardly likely to have the place to yourself; small sandpit out here for children. Inside, the snug little low beamed back rooms still have something of the flavour of past times, as well as bare brick or rough ochre plastered walls, brick or flagstone floors, pews and the like around simple tables (candlelit at night), and inglenook fireplaces; one room is no smoking. The larger airy white painted and green matchboarded bar has a beamed ceiling and quarry tiled floor, a woodburning stove in the big fireplace, and a games area with darts, pool, cribbage, dominoes, fruit machine and juke box at one end. Straightforward bar food includes home-made soup (£1.75), sandwiches or toasties (from £2.20, rump steak £3.45), home-made pâté (£2.45), pizzas (from £2.95), ploughman's (from £3.50), shepherd's pie (£3.60), salads (from £4.75), plaice (£5.25), steaks (from £8.25), and puddings like home-made chocolate crunch cake (£1.95); usual children's and vegetarian meals. You might have to wait for meals at busy times. Well kept Flowers Original, Fremlins, Fullers London Pride, Goachers Maidstone, Harveys Best, Marstons Pedigree and Shepherd Neame Best on handpump, eight wines by the glass, and local Biddenden cider. There's a gathering of vintage and classic cars on the second Sunday of each month. *(Recommended by Jack and Philip Paxton, Gordon Milligan, E N Burleton, Mr and Mrs P Brocklebank, Hilary Dobbie, Ian and Emma Potts, Colin Laffan, Simon Small, Elizabeth and Klaus Leist, Mrs C Dasey, Viv Middlebrook, D Cox, Gordon)*

Free house ~ Licensee Ian Turner ~ Real ale ~ Meals and snacks (till 10pm, 10.30 Fri and Sat) ~ (01233) 770283 ~ Children in large bar only ~ Open 11.30-2.30(3 Sat), 6-11; closed 25 Dec ~ Bedrooms: £20/£32

SOLE STREET TQ6567 Map 3

Compasses

Back lane between Godmersham (A28) and Petham (B2068); OS Sheet 189 map reference 095493

A real treat once you've tracked it down, this well preserved and pleasantly remote 15th-c brick tavern is becoming quite a favourite with families. The hard-working licensees have put a lot of effort into upgrading the big garden over the last year or so, and around its tables and fruit trees you'll now find three well stocked aviaries, goats and sheep, a couple of wooden play houses and a steel climbing frame; on fine summer lunchtimes the landlady might bring out her cockatoo, B Bob. It's very atmospheric inside, particularly in the little room at the back with its narrow wooden wall benches around the big kitchen table on the polished flagstone floor, a carefully restored massive brick bread oven, and enamelled advertisement placards on the walls. The front bar is a long, narrow room with beams in the shiny ochre ceiling, simple antique tables on its polished bare boards, rows of salvaged theatre seats along some walls, and a log fire in winter; bar billiards, piped music. The piano isn't just for decoration – they invite any customer who wants to play to have a go. Very good, popular bar food includes soup (£1.95), filled rolls freshly baked on the premises (from £1.80), large filled french sticks (from £2.95), dimsum (£3.65), ploughman's (from £3.75), filled baked potatoes (from £4.50), lentil crumble or battered cod (£5.20), cheese and potato pie (£5.50), well liked puff-pastry pies such as steak and kidney or chicken and sweetcorn (£5.95), chicken tikka (£6.25), stir-fried Cantonese prawns and vegetables or puff pastry parcel with cheese and prawns (£6.95), peppered steak (£10.95), and lots of elaborate ice cream sundaes (from £2.95). Well kept Boddingtons, Fullers London Pride and ESB, Whitbreads Castle Eden and a guest on handpump, Biddenden local cider and fruit wines. Service is very friendly, and readers tell us the cheery landlord has a good sense of humour. The area is good for walking, and cobwebbed with footpaths. *(Recommended by L M Miall, D B Stanley, Wim Cock, David Bloomfield, Peter Hitchcock, Ron and Sheila Corbett, Paul Adams)*

Free house ~ Licensees John and Sheila Bennett ~ Real ale ~ Meals and snacks (till 10 Fri) ~ (01227) 700300 ~ Children in Garden room ~ Open 12-3, 6.30-11 all year

SPELDHURST TQ5541 Map 3

George & Dragon 🍷

Village signposted from A264 W of Tunbridge Wells

Based around a 13th-c manorial hall, this marvellously distinguished half timbered building is one of the oldest pubs in the south of England. As with so many ancient places there have been a few changes, with the addition of heavy oak beams during modernisation – although to be fair this was in 1589. Some of the flagstones are bigger than any we've ever seen, and it's said that Kentish archers returning from their victory at Agincourt rested on them in 1415. The spacious open-plan bar, part-panelled and part plastered, has as its centrepiece a huge sandstone fireplace with a vast iron fireback that's over three hundred years old; seating is on high backed wooden benches at several old wood topped cast iron tables. To the left is a carpeted bar with a comfortable sofa and padded banquettes, exposed beams, rough plaster, a grandfather clock that marks the half hour and a small fireplace. Well kept Fullers London Pride, Harveys Best and Youngs Special on handpump, with lots of malt whiskies and a large wine cellar of around 140 bins; fruit machine, piped music. Efficiently served bar food includes home-made soup (£2.95), spicy chicken wings with chilli dip (£3.50), deep fried brie with apple and calvados sauce (£3.95), ploughman's or filled baked potatoes (from £4.25), chilli (£4.95), meat or vegetable lasagne (£5.95), steak, kidney and Guinness pie (£6.95), dressed crab, Cajun chicken or hot or cold poached Scotch salmon (£7.95), and lamb steak with green pepper sauce or rack of hickory smoked ribs (£8.95). The first-floor restaurant under the original massive roof timbers is striking. There are white tables and chairs on the neat little lawn, ringed with flowers, in front of the building. It can get busy at weekends, especially at night. The licensees also run the Bottle House at Penshurst. *(Recommended by Alan and Eileen Bowker, J S M Sheldon, M A and C R Starling, Winifrede D Morrison, Paula Williams, Keith and Audrey Ward, Hilary Dobbie, Peter Neate, Gwen and Peter Andrews, Colin Laffan, Thomas Nott)*

Free house ~ Licensees Gordon and Val Meer ~ Real ale ~ Meals and snacks (till 10pm; not Sun evening) ~ Restaurant (not Sun evening) ~ (01892) 863125 ~ Children welcome ~ Monthly jazz supper ~ Open 11-11

TOYS HILL TQ4751 Map 3

Fox & Hounds

Off A25 in Brasted, via Brasted Chart and The Chart

The fairly firm but very kind Mrs Pelling doesn't allow mobile phones in her pub, and there are little notices by the open fires that say 'no unofficial stoking'. There are no frills, fruit machines, juke boxes or background music at this marvellously traditional, down-to-earth and slightly eccentric remote country local. When your eyes have adjusted to the dim light you can sit comfortably on one of the homely and well worn old sofas or armchairs which are scattered with cushions and throws, and read the latest *Country Life, Hello* or *Private Eye*. Some of the aged local photographs, letters and pictures on the nicotine-stained walls don't look as if they've moved since they were put up in the 1960s, and it's unlikely that much, including the decor, has changed since then. Bar food is at an absolute minimum with filled rolls (from £1.30) and lunchtime ploughman's (from £3.45). Well kept Greene King IPA and Abbot on handpump; occasional sing-songs around the piano. The garden is particulary lovely with picnic tables on a good area of flat lawn surrounded by mature shrubs. As you approach this peaceful retreat from the pretty village (one of the highest in the county) you will catch glimpses through the trees of one of the most magnificent views in Kent. There are good walks nearby, and it's handy for Chartwell and for Emmetts garden. *(Recommended by John and Elspeth Howell, Jenny and Brian Seller)*

Greene King ~ Tenant Mrs Pelling ~ Real ale ~ Snacks ~ (01732) 750328 ~ Children away from bar, lunchtime only ~ 11.30-2.30(3 Sat), 6-11; closed 25 Dec

TUNBRIDGE WELLS TQ5839 Map 3

Sankeys

39 Mount Ephraim (A26 just N of junction with A267)

Still reckoned by many to be the best place to come for fish in the whole of the south east, this splendid seafood restaurant has a delightfully pubby downstairs cellar bar, complete with gas-lighting and York-stoned floor. Lively and relaxed, it's decorated with old mirrors, prints, enamel advertising signs, antique beer engines and other bric-a-brac (most of which has been salvaged from local pub closures) and french windows lead to a sun-trap walled garden with white tables and chairs under cocktail parasols. The four rooms upstairs have Spy prints on the walls, plush dining chairs and old pews; the two back rooms are no smoking. The excellent restaurant menu is also available in the bar, and might include dishes like potted shrimps (£4.50), stuffed clams or local oysters in a shallot dressing (£5), lemon sole meunière or seafood paella (£9), bouillabaisse (£10), roast monkfish with garlic (£13), grilled halibut or gilt headed bream (£13.50), bass steamed with spring onions, soy and ginger (£15.50), plateau de fruit de mer (£16), and lobster (from £19); the bar menu features filled baguettes (£3), home-made pâté or a daily pasta dish (£4), fish soup or home-made lamb and chilli sausages (£4.50), vegetarian meals (£5.50), cous cous or chicken breast filled with crab meat (£6.50), duck cassoulet (£7.50), and rack of lamb (£10). Some combination of Harveys, King and Barnes or Shepherd Neame ales from an antique beer engine, though most people seem to be taking advantage of the superb wine list; they also have quite a choice of unusual teas, running to Black Dragon Oolong and Japanese Sencha. You need to get there early in the evening for a table in the bar. *(Recommended by Roger and Valerie Hill, Hilary Dobbie, G L Tong, J A Snell)*

Free house ~ Licensee Guy Sankey ~ Real ale ~ Meals and snacks (12-3, 7-10) ~ No-smoking restaurant (not Sun) ~ (01892) 511422 ~ Children welcome ~ Live music Sun evenings ~ Open 12-11; 12-3, 6-11 Sat; closed 25 Dec

ULCOMBE TQ8550 Map 3

Pepper Box

Fairbourne Heath (signposted from A20 in Harrietsham; or follow Ulcombe signpost from A20, then turn left at crossroads (with sign to pub)

Until faily recently this relaxed and cosy old inn was also the village shop, bakery and butcher, and for a while it was used as a clearing house for smuggled spices. It's very nicely placed on high ground above the weald, looking out over a great plateau of rolling arable farmland. For many people the main attraction is the very good bar food, with thoughtfully prepared dishes such as home-made soup (£1.95), chicken satay (£3.50), haddock mousse with prawns, wrapped in smoked salmon (£3.60), a daily curry (£5.20), asparagus pancakes (£5.50), steak and kidney pudding (£5.90), stir-fried beef in black bean sauce (£6.50), sole bonne femme (£7), and specials such as braised chicken in a cream and lime sauce (£6), calf's liver and bacon (£6.50), or roast rack of lamb (£6.80); they also do lunchtime sandwiches, good puddings, and a Sunday roast. The friendly, homely bar has standing timbers, low beams hung with hops, copper kettles and pans on window sills, some very low-seated windsor chairs, wing armchairs, and a sofa and two armchairs by the splendid inglenook log fire. A side area is more functionally furnished for eating, and there's a very snug little dining room that's ideal for dinner-parties. Very well kept Shepherd Neame Bitter, Bishops Finger and Spitfire on handpump or tapped from the cask, and fruit wines and malt whiskies; efficient, courteous service. If you're in the garden, with its small pond, swing and tables among trees, shrubs and flower beds, you may catch a glimpse of the deer that sometimes come up, but if not you're quite likely to meet Jones the tabby tom, the other two cats, or Boots the plump collie. The name of the pub refers to the pepperbox pistol – an early type of revolver with numerous barrels. *(Recommended by R Suddaby, Tony Gayfer, Werner and Karla Arend, Evelyn and Derek Walter, Chris and Pauline Ford, M A and C R Starling; more reports please)*

Shepherd Neame ~ Tenants Geoff and Sarah Pemble ~ Real ale ~ Meals and snacks (not Sun evening) ~ Restaurant (not Sun evening) ~ (01622) 842558 ~ Children in restaurant ~ Live music Sun evening ~ Open 11-3, 6.30-11

Lucky Dip

Besides the fully inspected pubs, you might like to try these Lucky Dips recommended to us and described by readers (if you do, please send us reports):

☆ **Addington** [just off M20, junction 4; TQ6559], *Angel*: 14th-c inn in classic village green setting, plenty of well spaced tables, usual food inc generous ploughman's, quick friendly service, reasonable prices; Courage-related ales *(L M Miall, Mark Percy)*

Ash [the one nr Sandwich; TQ5R2858], *Dover Arms*: Friendly local with good choice of reasonably priced food, pleasant decor inc plate collection, separate public bar with pool, darts, juke box etc; children welcome if eating *(Ross Mackenzie)*

☆ **Ashford** [Silverhill Rd, Willesborough; TR0241], *Hooden Horse on the Hill*: Done up cheerfully in unpretentious style, well kept ales inc Goachers and five guests, good food inc Mexican specialities, friendly courteous staff *(John Baker)*

Ashurst [A264 by rly stn; TQ5038], *Bald Faced Stag*: Welcoming pub with well kept Harveys, some emphasis on food, good choice inc good value Sun lunch, daily papers; pleasant garden with play area, country walks nearby *(E G Parish, G Futcher)*

☆ **Aylesford** [handy for M2 junction 3 or M20 junction 6, via A229; 19 High St; TQ7359], *Little Gem*: Tudor pub, very cosy and quaint, with tiny front door, lots of atmosphere, interesting upper gallery; good range of interesting real ales, bar lunches (can be a wait) and evening snacks, flame-effect gas fire; children welcome, piped radio *(Bob Happ, Sheldon Barwick, LYM)*

Badlesmere [Ashford—Faversham; TR0054], *Red Lion*: Character Shepherd Neame pub, beams and panelling, slightly raised front area; garden behind *(Chris Westmoreland)*

☆ **Barham** [Elham Valley Rd (B2065); TR2050], *Dolls House*: Attractive old-fashioned pub in beautiful Elham Valley, good value food inc many vegetarian dishes, good beer range inc Morlands Old Speckled Hen, prompt friendly service, dolls and doll pictures *(Louise Weekes)*

☆ **Barham** [The Street], *Duke of Cumberland*: Pleasant open-plan local with good value generous straightforward lunchtime food, Whitbreads-related ales, bedrooms, caravan site *(L M Miall)*

Beltring [A228/B2160; TQ6747], *Brookers Oast*: Smart former oast house, bar food, Fremlins and Flowers ales; next to Whitbreads Hop Farm *(Quentin Williamson)*

Benenden [TQ8033], *Bull*: Imaginative bar and restaurant food, huge range of ciders, Harveys and Hook Norton ales *(Comus Elliott)*; [The Street (B2086)], *King William IV*: Low-ceilinged village local with country furnshings, Shepherd Neame ales, reasonably priced food, good log fire; games in public bar, small garden *(Comus Elliott, LYM)*

Benover [B2162; TQ7048], *Woolpack*: Pretty tile-hung pub with well kept ales, good bar food inc vegetarian in panelled and beamed lounge, games in public bar, summer barbecues on big lawn; attractive walks nearby *(David Appleton, LYM)*

☆ **Biddenden** [High St; TQ8538], *Red Lion*: Plush but friendly old inn in lovely village, good straightforward food, well kept Whitbreads-related ales *(Andy and Jackie Mallpress, Gordon)*

Bilsington [TR0334], *White Horse*: Good traditional English food like game stew and dumplings, good range of puddings, well kept beers, big new restaurant area with Sun spit-roasts; no loud music *(D B Stanley)*

Birchington [Station Rd; TR3069], *Seaview*: Handy place to stay, simple but clean, with pleasant helpful people, big breakfast fry-up *(Mary and Peter Clark)*

Birling [nr M20 junction 4; TQ6860], *Nevill Bull*: Emphasis on good nicely presented food; friendly service and atmosphere; well kept Whitbreads-related ales *(Comus Elliott)*

☆ **Bodsham** [Bodsham Green; TR1045], *Timber Batts*: Attractive and busy, with very wide range of tasty food, good service, unspoilt country setting *(Mrs J A Trotter, Comus Elliott)*

☆ **Boughton Street** [¾ mile from M2 junction 7, off A2; TR0559], *White Horse*: Carefully restored dark-beamed bars and timbered dining room, decent food all day inc early breakfast, good attentive service, well kept Shepherd Neame inc Porter on handpump, good tea and coffee; tables in garden, children allowed; bedrooms comfortable and well equipped – back ones quiet *(Miss M Byrne, Mrs M Henderson, LYM)*

Boxley [TQ7759], *Kings Arms*: Friendly village pub, nice building, good choice of ales and of sensibly priced straightforward food inc good sandwiches, good garden for children; pleasant walks around *(E D Bailey, Dr T E Hothersall)*

☆ **Brabourne** [Canterbury Rd, E Brabourne; TR1041], *Five Bells*: Pleasant and comfortable atmosphere, helpful staff, good food modestly priced, well kept Courage-related ales, log fire; tables in garden *(Douglas and Margaret Chesterman)*

☆ **Brasted** [A25, 3 miles from M25 junction 5; TQ4654], *White Hart*: Spacious relaxing lounge and extension sun lounge, interesting Battle of Britain bar with signatures and mementoes of Biggin Hill fighter pilots, well kept Bass and Charrington IPA; children welcome, big neatly kept garden; food in bar and restaurant, can get very busy weekends; bedrooms *(M E A Horler, Rob and Doris Harrison, Sandra Iles, Gordon Smith, C O Day, LYM)*

☆ **Brasted** [A25], *Bull*: Friendly local with well kept Shepherd Neame ales, intimate dining lounge, separate public bar with darts and maybe skittles; tables in garden *(Paul McKeerer, B B Morgan)*

☆ **Bridge** [53 High St, off A2; TR1854], *White Horse*: Good fresh food and very pleasant service in smartly comfortable good value dining pub with cosy interconnected rooms inc civilised restaurant, several real ales, good choice of wines; attractive village *(J F Webley, R F and M K Bishop, Mrs Hilarie Taylor)*

Broadoak [TR1661], *Golden Lion*: Pleasant airy two-bar village pub with Shepherd Neame ales, bar food, restaurant; picnic tables on lawn with play area, dovecote, pet sheep *(Chris Westmoreland)*; *Royal Oak*: Smallish Whitbreads pub with open fire, farm tools, tables outside with play area *(Chris Westmoreland)*

Burham [Burham Common, just W of Blue Bell Hill; not far from M2 junction 3 – OS Sheet 178 map ref 733628; TQ7362], *Robin Hood*: Three small bars, good-sized garden with picnic tables, aviaries, barbecue/shop; pleasant, cosy place deep in the woods and Downs *(A W Lewis)*

☆ **Canterbury** [12 The Friars; just off main St Peters St pedestrian area], *Canterbury Tales*: Small friendly pub, relaxing and civilised, with good range of changing local and distant ales maybe inc Belgian cherry beer, decent bar food, smart helpful staff, clean and airy lounge – popular lunchtime with local businesspeople; opp Marlow Theatre *(David Dimock, John A Barker, Robert Gomme, Malcolm Wight, Mark Thompson, Julian Holland)*

Canterbury [Upper Bridge St], *Flying Horse*: Well kept beers, good helpings of tasty food, friendly efficient service *(W Bailey, Julian Holland)*; [St Stephens], *Olde Beverlie*: Spacious, clean and warm with cheerful comfortable atmosphere, interesting beams and wattle ceiling, attractive red stone floor, Toby jugs, pleasing fireplace; Whitbreads-related ales, lunchtime food, neat well planted walled garden *(Chris Westmoreland)*; [Watling St, opp St Margaret St], *Three Tuns*: Real ales such as John Smiths and Theakstons, friendly people, pleasant atmosphere; bedrooms *(John A Barker)*

Capel Le Ferne [A20 towards Folkestone; TR2439], *Valiant Sailor*: Friendly and clean, with good range of beers and popular generous food *(Walter and Muriel Hagen)*

Challock [Halfway Crossing; TR0050], *Half Way House*: Good value food, pleasant atmosphere *(Daren Keates)*

Chatham [Dock Rd; TQ7567], *Command House*: Superb location by the water, just below the churchyard of what is now the Medway Heritage Centre, with Victorian fort above; limited food *(Ian Phillips)*

Chiddingstone Causeway [B2027; TQ5146], *Little Brown Jug*: Spaciously and comfortably done out in olde-brick-and-beam style, good choice of ales inc local Larkins and of wines, friendly welcome, wide range of promptly served food, restaurant; attractive garden with play area; bedrooms *(Angela and Alan Dale, MD, ND, Colin Laffan)*

☆ **Chilham** [off A28/A252; TR0753], *White Horse*: On prettiest village square in Kent, with a couple of tables out on the corner; comfortably modernised beamed bar, food from sandwiches up (has been available all day in summer exc Tues evening, maybe lunchtimes only winter), Whitbreads-related ales, good winter log fire, quiet piped music, restaurant *(James House, W J E Kock, W J Kock, LYM)*

☆ **Chillenden** [TR2653], *Griffins Head*: Reliable food and good service in attractive beamed, timbered and flagstoned 14th-c pub with three comfortable rooms, big log fire; pleasant small garden surrounded by wild roses *(Phil Godwin, L M Miall, M Veldhuyzen)*

☆ **Cliffe** [TQ7376], *Black Bull*: Good genuine Malaysian bar food in friendly cosy village pub with good choice of well kept ales, weekday evening basement restaurant, darts/pool room, quiet juke box, no machines, very welcoming to children *(James Curran, Margaret Hung)*

☆ **Cobham** [B2009, handy for M2 junction 1; TQ6768], *Leather Bottle*: Beautifully laid-out extensive colourful garden with fishpond and play area, masses of interesting Dickens memorabilia, ancient beams and timbers (but extensive modernisation); usual bar food and real ales; quiet, pretty village; bedrooms *(Ian and Nita Cooper, E D Bailey, George Atkinson, Thomas Nott, LYM)*

☆ **Conyer Quay** [from A2 Sittingbourne—Faversham take Deerton St turn, then at T-junction left towards Teynham, then follow Conyer signs; TQ9664], *Ship*: Sadly Mr Heard, the ebullient landlord who has made this so lively, has decided to retire and as we went to press was putting it on the market; if he's still there you can rely on an unsurpassed range of wines, spirits and beers, and lots of fun; but in any event the pub's well worth a visit for its creekside position and attractively old-fashioned small-roomed layout *(Mrs M Henderson, Malcolm Wight, Gwen and Peter Andrews, S May, Ian and Emma Potts, E D Bailey, Andrew Jeeves, Carole Smart, Ian Philips, John Watson, Chris Westmoreland, LYM)*

Coopers Corner [B2042 Sevenoaks—Edenbridge; TQ4849], *Frog & Bucket*: Not smart, but youthful and lively, with barbecue, pub food, real ale inc one brewed for the pub, live bands, happy mix of locals and bikers *(K Flack)*

☆ **Cowden** [Holtye Common; A264 S of village – actually just over border in Sussex; TQ4539], *White Horse*: Wide choice of good generous attractively priced food esp fish, also vegetarian dishes, in bar and spacious dining room, carp swimming under glass panels in its floor; warm friendly atmosphere, barbecues *(Jill Reeves, R D Knight)*

☆ **Cowden** [Cowden Pound; junction B2026 with Markbeech rd; TQ4642], *Queens Arms*: Unspoilt two-room country pub like something from the 1930s, with splendid landlady, well kept Whitbreads, darts; strangers quickly feel like regulars *(Pete Baker)*

Cowden [High St], *Fountain*: Good local atmosphere, a welcome for strangers, traditional pub games, well kept Whitbreads-related ales, reasonable prices *(Patrick Jennings)*

☆ **Cranbrook** [High St; TQ7735], *Hooden Horse*: Good lively atmosphere, friendly courteous staff, good range of beers, fine choice of food inc delicious Mexican meals *(Hilary Dobbie)*

Darenth [Darenth Rd; TQ5671], *Chequers*: Popular food esp good value home-cooked Sun lunch in warm and friendly traditional local, can book tables in pleasant room behind bar *(Comus Elliott, Mr and Mrs Hillman)*

Deal [Beach St; TR3752], *Kings Head*: Seafront pub with fine views, good value food *(Jim Clugston)*

Dungeness [by old lighthouse; TR0916], *Britannia*: Friendly, good value food inc fresh local fish *(Vic and Rene Coue)*

Dunkirk [TR0759], *Red Lion*: Smart beamed multi-level pub with Whitbreads-related ales, dining room, well kept garden with goldfish pool which is also visible from inside; room for caravans *(Chris Westmoreland)*

☆ **Dunks Green** [Silver Hill; TQ6152], *Kentish Rifleman*: Early 16th-c, with good choice of bar food, friendly licensees, Larkins and Whitbreads-related ales, decent wine, prompt efficient service even when busy, no machines; dogs welcome; plenty of seats in unusually well designed garden behind *(L M Miall, Robert Huddleston, John and Elspeth Howell)*

☆ **Eastling** [The Street; off A251 S of M2 junction 6, via Painters Forstal; TQ9656], *Carpenters Arms*: Pretty and cottagey oak-beamed pub with big fireplaces front and back, welcoming Irish licensees, decent food (not Sun evening), well kept Shepherd Neame, some seats outside; children allowed in restaurant; small but well equipped bedrooms in separate building, huge breakfast *(A N Ellis, Mrs M Henderson, Paula Harrison, Mary and Peter Clark, LYM)*

☆ **Edenbridge** [74 High St; TQ4446], *Old Crown*: Fairly recently reopened Tudor pub with good well priced food inc bargain suppers, four real ales; one of the last pubs to have kept its 'gallows' inn-sign stretching right across the road *(John A Archer, LYM)*

☆ **Elham** [St Marys Rd; TR1743], *Kings Arms*: Good interesting reasonably priced food, reliably good service, attractive lounge bar, good open fire, steps down to big dining area; pool table in public bar; charming village *(L M Miall, Alan and Maggie Telford)*

Elham [High St], *Rose & Crown*: Attractive old building, friendly landlord, good food and beer; bedrooms *(Robert Bray)*

Etchinghill [TR1639], *New Inn*: Friendly neatly kept pub with good food, good service, well kept beers *(W M Holden)*

☆ **Eynsford** [TQ5365], *Malt Shovel*: Spacious dining pub handy for castles and Roman villa, wide range of generous bar food inc lots of seafood (lobster tank), Whitbreads-related ales, friendly staff, nice atmosphere *(G Futcher, Colin Laffan, Nigel Gibbs, D W Welton, Martyn Hart)*

Eynsford [Riverside], *Plough*: Friendly local with good value food from snacks to full meals, well kept beer, good atmosphere *(David C Thompson)*

Eythorne [TR2849], *Crown*: Small pub with particularly good restaurant, friendly service *(Martin Hickes)*

Farningham [High St; TQ5466], *Chequers*: Old open-plan village local with full range of Fullers ales and Morlands Old Speckled Hen, home-made bar food, friendly welcome; can be a bit smoky *(Michael Wadsworth)*

☆ **Faversham** [31 the Mall, handy for M2 junction 6; TR0161], *Elephant*: Very picturesque flower-decked terrace town local with good range of food inc imaginative vegetarian dishes, good choice of changing ales, prompt welcoming service, simple but attractive furnishings on stripped boards; summer barbecues *(Mrs K E Neville-Rolfe, Mrs M Henderson, Louise Weekes, Jack and Philip Paxton, C J Parsons, BB)*

Folkestone [nr harbour; TR2336], *Carpenters*: Pleasant staff, super fish *(Marian Greenwood)*; [42 North St], *Lifeboat*: Good atmosphere, well kept Bass, Fullers London Pride and Wadworths 6X ales, reasonably priced bar food inc good value sandwiches *(Alan and Eileen Bowker)*; [Ferries Mead], *Master Brewer*: Modern estate pub with well prepared home-cooked food, good beer and coffee, very warm welcome *(Ian Phillips)*

Fordcombe [TQ5240], *Chafford Arms*: Pretty pub, recently tastefully extended by long-serving licensees, with charming garden, Whitbreads-related ales, local cider, interesting food esp fish *(D D Collins)*

☆ **Fordwich** [off A28 in Sturry; TR1759], *Fordwich Arms*: Generous helpings of decent plain cooking inc fresh veg in civilised and handsome pub with open fire in attractive fireplace, Whitbreads-related ales, discreet piped music; spacious garden by River Stour *(Russell and Margaret Bathie, G S and E M Dorey, LYM)*

☆ **Four Elms** [B2027/B269 E of Edenbridge; TQ4648], *Four Elms*: Busy dining pub, welcoming and comfortable, impressive choice of reliably good generous food, well kept Courage Directors and Harveys, decent wine, good service, two big open fires, some interesting decorations inc huge boar's head; children allowed, tables outside; juke box, fruit machine; handy for Chartwell *(Colin Laffan, Margaret and Nigel Dennis, Alan Kilpatrick, David and Michelle Hedges, Rhoda and Jeff Collins, BB)*

Goathurst Common [Whitley Row, just N – OS Sheet 188 map ref 499529; TQ4952], *Chimneys*: Spacious and pleasing reproduction decor, Whitbreads-related ales, quickly served well presented straightforward food, flame-effect gas fire *(Jenny and Brian Seller)*

☆ **Goudhurst** [TQ7238], *Star & Eagle*: Striking medieval inn with settles and Jacobean-style seats in heavily beamed open-plan bar, good bar food, well kept Whitbreads-related ales, decent wine, good service; lovely views esp from tables out behind; children welcome, bedrooms comfortable *(Ralph A Raimi, Derek Howse)*

☆ *nr* **Goudhurst** [A262 W], *Green Cross*: Good value genuine home cooking, real ales inc some unusual ones, enjoyable if not exactly pubby atmosphere, open fires and friendly staff; beamed dining room for residents; bedrooms light and airy, good value *(A Preston)*

Grain [High St; TQ8876], *Hogarth*: Well preserved old pub with good atmosphere, wide choice of beers, food in bar and restaurant; useful for its Isle of Grain location *(Paul Welsh)*

☆ **Great Chart** [Chart Rd; TQ9842], *Hooden Horse*: Almost entirely Mexican menu, six changing well kept ales and local farm cider in quarry-tiled two-roomed pub, beams a forest of hop bines; cheap and cheerful furnishings, good lively atmosphere, friendly staff, piped blues *(Jim Penson, Hilary Dobbie, BB)*

☆ **Hadlow** [Ashes Lane (off A26 Tonbridge Rd); TQ6349], *Rose Revived*: Friendly and attractive 16th-c pub with well kept beers inc Harveys and King & Barnes, good bar food inc well filled fresh sandwiches *(D and B Carter, E D Bailey)*

Hartlip [Lower Hartlip Rd; TQ8464], *Rose & Crown*: Popular country pub with friendly service, Ruddles Best and County, atmospheric candlelit Victorian-style conservatory restaurant *(R Owen)*

☆ **Hawkhurst** [Pipsden – A268 towards Rye; TQ7730], *Oak & Ivy*: Comfortable and attractive old panelled inn with well kept Whitbreads-related ales, friendly staff, generous good value home cooking in no-smoking dining end, roaring log fires; attractive restaurant, popular Sun roasts *(Sue and Mike Todd)*

☆ **Heaverham** [Watery Lane – OS Sheet 188 map ref 572587; TQ5658], *Chequers*: Good choice of good food and friendly service in attractive two-bar country pub with well kept range of beers; lots of birds both caged and free in big garden *(LM, E D Bailey)*

Hernhill [Staplestreet; TR0660], *Three Horseshoes*: Smallish attractively unpretentious Shepherd Neame pub with good value simple food, interesting earthenware bottle collection *(Chris Westmoreland)*

☆ **Hever** [TQ4744], *Henry VIII*: Very handy for Hever Castle, with fine panelling and beams, inglenook fireplace, lots of Henry VIII decorations; friendly and comfortable feel, well kept local and other beers, decent wines, good service, bar food; children truly welcome, maybe piped radio; pondside lawn *(CR, RR, LYM)*

☆ **Hodsoll Street** [TQ6263], *Green Man*: Pretty pub on village green, lots of hanging baskets, big garden with play area, aviary and pet's corner; quiet inside, with good food (not Sun/Mon pm), well kept beer, cheerful staff, log fires, no music *(Sandra Powell, E D Bailey)*

☆ **Hollingbourne** [Eyhorne St; B2163, off A20; TQ8454], *Dirty Habit*: Dim-lit old pub with lots of different old kitchen and dining tables and chairs, nicely wonky floors, interesting food, well kept ales, decent house wines, flame-effect gas fire in big fireplace, games area, unobtrusive juke box; on Pilgrims Way, handy for Leeds Castle *(Peter and Joy Heatherley)*

Hollingbourne [Eyhorne St – OS Sheet 188 map ref 833547], *Windmill*: Interesting, comfortable and welcoming, with various different levels and nooks around central servery, quick food, well kept Whitbreads-related ales, sunny garden with children's play area *(Mrs P J Pearce)*

Horsmonden [TQ7040], *Gun & Spitroast*: Pleasant old-fashioned pub on village green, good range of Tetleys-related beers, wide choice of good value food inc frequent spit-roasts, good smart service *(Comus Elliott, R D Knight)*

Ickham [just off A257 W of Canterbury; TR2257], *Duke William*: Friendly comfortable front bar, more formal seating behind with restaurant and conservatory, very wide choice of good food, well kept beers such as Adnams, Fullers, Shepherd Neame and Youngs; smart garden *(Chris Westmoreland, Stephen and Julie Brown)*

☆ **Ide Hill** [off B2042 SW of Sevenoaks; TQ4851], *Cock*: Pretty village-green local, neatly modernised, with well kept Greene King, straightforward bar food (not Sun evening, only sandwiches Sun lunchtime), fine log fire, bar billiards, piped music, some seats out in front; handy for Chartwell and nearby walks – so gets busy, with nearby parking sometimes out of the question *(Colin Laffan, Dr Michael Smith, David Dimock, LYM)*

☆ **Iden Green** [B2086; TQ8032], *Royal Oak*: Doing very well under new licensees, with really good home-cooked food, good atmosphere and service *(Peter and Liz Moore)*

Iden Green [signed off B2086], *Woodcock*: 17th-c country pub with good traditional English food in comfortable and friendly rural setting *(Mr Cornock)*; [A262 E of Goudhurst], *Peacock*: Charming traditional low-beamed lounge with flagstones and massive fireplace, well kept Whitbreads-related ales, simple food inc good ploughman's, friendly staff, plain public bar with music and games, good big garden; packed with young people Sat night *(Comus Elliott)*

☆ **Ightham Common** [Common Rd; TQ5755], *Harrow*: Particularly good fresh food in cosy and unpretentious country local with sparse wooden furniture, roaring log fire, papers to read, pool, darts, board games and jigsaws, well kept Greene King IPA and Abbot, friendly staff; restaurant evenings and Sun; bedrooms *(Ingrid Abma, Andrew Langbar, Russell Isaac, David Wright, John and Elspeth Howell)*

☆ **Ivy Hatch** [off A227 N of Tunbridge; TQ5854], *Plough*: Fastidious French cooking, good wines, attractive candlelit surroundings, delightful conservatory and garden; has been a highly rated main entry, but since 1994 or so, though still well worth knowing, has tilted too firmly into restaurant mode (especially regarding service and prices) to stay in the main listings *(Simon Small, Mrs P D McFarlane, Tony Gayfer, LYM)*

nr **Ivy Hatch** [Stone Street, which is also signed off A25 E of Sevenoaks; TQ5754], *Snail*: Former Rose & Crown, and still has its splendid rambling garden, but has declared its intention of getting away from a pub image, and though still friendly with decent food and beers early reports suggest that it's succeeding *(LYM)*

Kemsing [Cotmans Ash; TQ5558], *Rising Sun*: Attractive old country pub, several guest beers, interesting range of generous bar food, garden with aviary *(John and Elspeth Howell)*

Knockholt [TQ4658], *Harrow*: Well kept beer *(G Washington)*

☆ *nr* **Lamberhurst** [Hook Green (B2169 towards T Wells); TQ6535], *Elephants Head*: Ancient rambling country pub with wide choice of food inc vegetarian, well kept Harveys, heavy beams, some timbering, brick or oak flooring, log fire and woodburner, plush-cushioned pews etc; darts and fruit machine in small side area, picnic tables on back terrace and grass with play area (peaceful view), and by front green; nr Bayham Abbey and Owl House, very popular with families weekends *(C R and M A Starling, BHP, LYM)*

Lamberhurst [B2100; TQ6735], *Horse & Groom*: Welcoming village local with good variety of well priced well presented generous food, well kept Shepherd Neame, darts, massive tie collection; bedrooms *(Lesley Neville)*

Lenham [The Square; TQ8952], *Dog & Boar*: Friendly inn with decent choice of food, Shepherd Neame ales; good value bedrooms, pretty village *(W C A Simmons)*

☆ **Littlebourne** [4 High St; TR2057], *King William IV*: Good freshly prepared food, friendly service, good range of well kept ales, interesting wines inc New World ones; bedrooms *(Desmond and Gillian Bellew, Mr and Mrs Blake, S D Samuels)*

Littlebourne [62 The Hill (A257)], *Evenhill House*: Locally popular for good food, decent wines, well kept beers *(Paul Buckland)*

Maidstone [Earl St; TQ7656], *Earls*: Recently reopened by Courage, plush and polished – a well done example of the style *(Comus Elliott)*; [Earl St], *Hogs Head*: Whitbreads pub done up with bare floors and scrubbed pine tables, six or seven real ales, good well priced lunches *(Comus Elliott)*; [Tonbridge Rd], *Walnut Tree*: Lively Courage local with well kept Best and Directors and Wadworths 6X, live R & B Mon, jazz Sun lunchtime, comedy night *(Gerry Heath)*

nr **Maidstone** [Weavering Street Village; TQ7855], *Fox & Goose*: Unchanging civilised local priced to keep out the riff-raff, well kept Courage Best, John Smiths, Morlands Old Speckled Hen and Wadworths 6X, public bar with darts but no pool or juke box, limited food *(Comus Elliott)*

Marden [Staplehurst Rd; TQ7444], *Stilebridge*: Enjoyable local with well kept real ale, good food *(Mike Darling)*; *Unicorn*: Comfortable local with wide choice of reasonably priced food, nice restaurant area, welcoming staff *(R A Quantock)*

Marshside [TR2265], *Hog & Donkey*: Idiosyncratic pub with Whitbreads-related ales, small room with tables, chairs, sofas and bright cushions strewn around; car park may be full of cars even if pub empty – landlord collects them *(Chris Westmoreland)*

☆ **Meopham** [Meopham Green; A227 Gravesend—Wrotham; TQ6466], *Cricketers*: Neatly kept 17th-c pub with seats out overlooking green, more in back garden, cricket memorabilia, Tetleys-related ales, usual food, friendly service, tasteful modern restaurant extension; piped music *(Gwen and Peter Andrews)*

☆ **Mersham** [OS Sheet 179 map ref 049341; TR0539], *Farriers Arms*: Smart and attractive three-room local based on early 17th-c forge, good value straightforward food, well kept Tetleys-related ales, good friendly service; exceptionally well kept pleasant gardens behind; bedrooms *(Duncan Redpath)*

Milstead [TQ9058], *Red Lion*: Small friendly country pub, landlord cooks well *(Chris and David Mathews)*

☆ **Nettlestead** [Nettlestead Green; B2015 Pembury—Maidstone; TQ6852], *Hop Pole*: Wide range of decent food and well kept ales such as Adnams Extra and Fullers London Pride in attractively extended pub with central fire, friendly service, fresh flowers, decent wine; among orchards *(Mr and Mrs A P Reeves, John and Elspeth Howell)*

☆ **Oad Street** [nr M2 junction 5; TQ8662], *Plough & Harrow*: Nice old village pub opp craft centre, friendly landlord, well kept Shepherd Neame and half a dozen changing ales, good value home cooking, one small bar, another much larger, light and airy at the back; children welcome; picnic tables in secluded back garden *(Chris Westmoreland)*

☆ **Offham** [TQ6557], *Kings Arms*: Warm welcome, well kept Courage Best, good range of bar food, log fire, lots of old tools; piped music; attractive village *(K Flack)*

Offham [Church Rd], *Red Lion*: Welcoming staff, log fire, good food, Theakstons real ale, reasonable prices; monthly live music *(W C A Simmons)*

☆ **Otford** [High St; TQ5359], *Crown*: Pretty pub with character beamed bar, opp pond in delightful village with pleasant walks; friendly staff, good sandwiches and some really imaginative home cooking, well kept Tetleys-related ales, decent house wines; occasional jazz evenings, lovely garden behind *(Russell and Margaret Bathie, Mrs S J Findlay, Jan and Colin Roe, Thomas Nott)*

☆ **Otford** [66 High St], *Horns*: Cosy 15th-c beamed pub with big inglenook log fire, attentive friendly service, good food, well kept ales inc Harveys and King & Barnes *(E D Bailey)*

☆ **Otford** [High St], *Bull*: Pleasant place for decent bar food inc sandwiches, well kept Courage-related ales, helpful service; good family room, attractive garden *(Thomas Nott)*

Painters Forstal [village signposted off A2 at Ospringe; TQ9958], *Alma*: Friendly two-bar weatherboarded village pub with well kept Shepherd Neame, picnic tables on lawn *(Chris Westmoreland)*

Pembury [High St; TQ6240], *Black Horse*: Small pleasantly modernised low-beamed local with well kept ales inc Harveys and one brewed locally for the pub, friendly staff, log fire, decent quick food, tidy little restaurant/carvery; children's garden neat and well kept *(Thomas Nott, Gary Wood)*

☆ **Penshurst** [centre; TQ5243], *Leicester Arms*: Neatly kept hotel bar in charming village by Penshurst Place, extended eating area, quiet corners, wide choice of good bar food, well kept real ale, prompt friendly service even when rather crowded; children welcome, decent bedrooms *(Cedric and Ruth Reavley, P Neate, Tim and Pam Moorey)*

☆ *nr* **Penshurst** [Hoath Corner – OS Sheet 188 map ref 497431], *Rock*: Charmingly old-fashioned untouristy atmosphere in tiny beamed rooms, wonky brick floors, good value sandwiches and generous home cooking, well kept local Larkins and other ales, inglenook, ring the bull; children and dogs welcome; tables outside, beautiful countryside nearby *(J A Snell, Keith Widdowson, R and S Bentley, Dr D R Pulsford, BB)*

☆ **Pluckley** [TQ9245], *Black Horse*: Cosy, comfortable and attractive, with vast inglenook, various nooks and crannies, generous choice of decent food, big restaurant area popular for business lunches; friendly staff and black cat, well kept Whitbreads-related ales, interesting board games; children allowed if eating; pleasant orchard garden, good walks *(Michael Butler, E D Bailey, Martin Hickes, Mr and Mrs P Brocklebank)*

☆ **Pluckley** [Munday Bois], *Rose & Crown*: Welcoming little pub with nicely furnished dining room, good varied food, interesting wines, well kept ales, reasonable prices, good service; friendly dog *(Barbara and Alec Jones, R Misson)*

Ramsgate [Paragon (seafront); TR3865], *Churchills*: Spacious pub done up with old building materials and farm tools, views of port and yacht marina, Ringwood Old Thumper, Theakstons Old Peculier and half a dozen changing guest ales, good value food, back restaurant; children welcome, Weds jazz downstairs, Sun folk and blues *(Ian Parsons, Colin Hammond)*

☆ **Rochester** [10 St Margarets St; TQ7467], *Coopers Arms*: Quaint and interesting ancient local, good bustling atmosphere with fine mix of customers, friendly licensees, comfortable seating, good value bar lunches, well kept Courage-related ales;

can be a bit smoky; handy for castle and cathedral *(Elizabeth and Klaus Leist, A W Lewis, W J E Kock, W J Kock, Mrs M Henderson, Steve Goodchild)*

☆ **Rolvenden Layne** [TQ8530], *Another Hooden Horse*: Beams, hops and candlelight, popular good value home-made food inc Mexican, good range of beers, local ciders and wine, good friendly staff; no music or machines *(Paul Adams, Ewa Sawicka, Peter and Vivian Symes)*

Ruckinge [B2067 E of Ham Street; TR0233], *Blue Anchor*: Well kept and friendly, with Whitbreads-related ales, good value home-cooked food, tastefully furnished conservatory; garden with pretty pond *(Rob and Doris Harrison, D B Stanley)*

☆ **Sandgate** [Brewers Lane – main rd towards Hythe, then 100 yds or so after it emerges on to sea front park opp telephone box on R (beware high tides) and walk up steep cobbled track beside it; TR2035], *Clarendon*: Good food inc delicious clams and treacle puddings in fine low-beamed backstreet local just above sea, simple comfortable furniture, friendly licensees, consistently well kept Shepherd Neame esp Spitfire with a guest such as Eldridge Pope, marvellous Kent CC cricket memorabilia, splendid dog *(Terry Buckland, Ian Phillips, L M Miall)*

Sandgate [High St], *Ship*: Busy pub with eight changing well kept ales, cheap cheerful home-made bar food, good service, character landlord, seafaring theme, genuinely old furnishings; seats outside *(A B Dromey, Alan and Maggie Telford)*

Sandwich [Cattlemarket/Mote Sole; TR3358], *Red Cow*: Carefully refurbished old pub with welcoming staff, Boddingtons, King & Barnes Sussex, Morlands Old Speckled Hen, Wadworths 6X and Scarlet Lady on handpump, two old fireplaces, old prints and photographs, garden bar, hanging baskets *(Alan and Eileen Bowker)*

☆ **Sarre** [TR2565], *Crown*: Carefully restored pub making much of its long history as the Cherry Brandy House, good range of reasonably priced home-cooked food, well kept Shepherd Neame; comfortable bedrooms *(Wim Kock)*

☆ **Sevenoaks** [London Rd, nr stn; 2½ miles from M25 junction 5;TQ5355], *Halfway House*: Quiet and friendly partly 16th-c local with beams and brasses, well kept Greene King IPA, Abbot and Rayments, wide range of reasonably priced home-made food inc good fresh veg, good service, obliging landlord *(Pam and Tim Moorey, Ian Phillips)*

Sevenoaks [centre], *Hogs Head*: Lively and popular traditional local, good range of ales, decent food, pool table etc *(Stacey Goldsmith)*; [A225 just S], *Royal Oak Tap*: Good range of well kept Whitbreads-related and other ales, original bar snacks such as good hot salt beef sandwiches, two real fires, big conservatory; quite independent of neighbouring Royal Oak Hotel *(Ian Phillips, B J Harding)*

☆ *nr* **Sevenoaks** [Godden Green, off B2019 just E; TQ5555], *Bucks Head*: Picturesque old village-green local in pretty spot by duckpond, surrounded by cherry blossom in spring; particularly well kept Courage-related and guest beers, friendly atmosphere, decent bar food, cosy furnishings; children really welcome; in attractive walking country nr Knole *(Cedric and Ruth Reavley, Tony Gayfer, David Wright)*

Shipbourne [Stumble Hill; TQ5952], *Chaser*: Hotel in lovely spot by village church and green, a comfortable place to stay; cheerful public bar, ambitious bar food in bistro-like end part with candles and stripped pine, friendly service, well kept beers, decent wines, hard-working landlady, high-vaulted restaurant, tables outside *(Christopher Dent, E G Parish, Steve Goodchild)*

☆ **Shoreham** [TQ5161], *Kings Arms*: Pretty and popular, with good food inc good value ploughman's, Ruddles beer, interesting coaching-theme decorations inc waxwork ostler, free Sun bar nibbles, tables outside; quaint unspoilt village on River Darent, good walks *(Jenny and Brian Seller)*; [High St], *Royal Oak*: Simple old-fashioned local, well kept beer, good value traditional home-cooked food, summer barbecues *(S Atkinson)*

☆ **Sissinghurst** [TQ7937], *Bull*: Good food esp (not weekday lunchtimes or Mon eve) authentic pastas and pizzas in roomy welcoming pub with some armchairs, shelves of books and china, big pleasant dark-beamed restaurant area, quick willing service, Whitbreads-related ales, quiet piped music, fruit machine; neat quiet garden *(Joy Heatherley, Joan and Gordon Griffes, R G and J N Plumb, Comus Elliott, Mr and Mrs F G Browning)*

☆ **Smarden** [TQ8842], *Chequers*: Cosy and relaxed beamed local with plenty of character, log fire, comfortable seats, good varied rather special food inc vegetarian dishes and fresh veg, well kept Courage ales, decent wines, big cat, no music or machines; pleasant tables outside; bedrooms simple (and some within earshot of bar) but good value, with huge breakfast *(Gordon, Marian Greenwood)*

☆ **Snargate** [Romney Marsh; B2080 Appledore—Brenzett – OS Sheet 189 map ref 990285; TQ9828], *Red Lion*: Old-fashioned unspoilt 19th-c pub with well kept Adnams and Batemans tapped from the cask *(Phil and Sally Gorton, Pete Blakemore)*

☆ **Southfleet** [off A2 via A227 S towards Southfleet; or from B262 turn left at Ship in Southfleet then sharp right into Red St – pub about half-mile on right; TQ6171], *Black Lion*: Character two-room local, with good generous bar food from ploughman's up, well kept Adnams, Greene

King Abbot and Courage-related beers, cheerful staff, handsome no-smoking restaurant; children in eating area; good barbecue in big shrub-sheltered garden *(Ian and Nita Cooper, Michael and Jenny Back, Darren Ford, LYM)*

☆ **St Margarets at Cliffe** [High St; TR3644], *Cliffe Tavern Hotel*: Attractive clapboard-and-brick inn opp church with friendly newish licensees, two cats and a singing dog, good log fire, well kept Greene King and Shepherd Neame ales, simple bar and larger open-plan lounge, secluded back walled garden, good if not cheap food in dining room; has been open all day Sat, allowing well behaved children; bedrooms, inc some in cottages across yard *(Sue and Bob Soar, LYM)*

☆ **St Margarets Bay** [on shore below Nat Trust cliffs; TR3844], *Coastguard*: Tremendous views (to France on a clear day) from modernised seaside pub, open all day in summer; well kept sensibly priced real ales, good range of food esp vegetarian; children welcome; lots of tables out below NT cliff, summer Sun afternoon teas out here *(J Ryeland, R Misson, Mark Thompson, J Watson, LYM)*

☆ **St Mary in the Marsh** [TR0628], *Star*: Relaxed remote pub run by friendly family, well kept Shepherd Neame inc Mild tapped from the cask; bedrooms attractive, with views of Romney Marsh *(A Preston)*

☆ **Stalisfield Green** [off A252 in Charing; TQ9553], *Plough*: Good choice of well presented home-cooked food inc good fish, friendly service, big but tasteful side extension, tables in big garden, attractive setting and good view *(Evelyn and Derek Walter)*

Staplehurst [Chart Hill Rd – OS Sheet 188 map ref 785472; TQ7847], *Lord Raglan*: Landlord cooks well, charming landlady, in 17th-c beamed pub with three open fires, good coffee, no piped music; picnic tables outside *(R D Knight)*

Stockbury [Stockbury Green; TQ8361], *Harrow*: Good food on big platters inc enormous starters, well kept Shepherd Neame ales with a guest beer, good choice of wines, friendly landlord, log fire and woodburner *(R Owen)*

Stone Street [by-road Seal—Plaxtol – OS Sheet 188 map ref 573546; TQ5754], *Padwell Arms*: Small and friendly, with good choice of reasonably priced generous specials, friendly staff; real ales *(H W and R Owen)*

☆ **Stowting** [off B2068 N of M20 junction 11; TR1242], *Tiger*: Charming country pub of considerable individuality, with attractive unpretentious furniture, candles on tables, faded rugs on bare boards, bar food from sandwiches to steaks, well kept Adnams, Boddingtons, Everards Tiger, Ind Coope Burton, Tetleys, Wadworths 6X and guest beers, Biddenden farm cider, good log fire, tables outside with occasional barbecues; well behaved children allowed, good jazz Mon *(A B Dromey, Christopher M McNulty, Comus Elliott, Ian Phillips, Dave Braisted, LYM)*

Street End [B2068 S of Canterbury; TR1453], *Granville*: Solid and friendly, with well kept beers, wide choice of decent bar food, autographed cricket bats *(W J E Kock, W J Kock)*

☆ **Tenterden** [High St; TQ8833], *Woolpack*: Striking 15th-c inn with several oak-beamed rooms inc family dining room, inglenook log fires, pleasant atmosphere, good generous home-cooked food, friendly service, well kept Whitbreads-related and other ales, decent coffee; open all day; comfortable bedrooms *(J Watson)*

Tonbridge [High St; TQ5946], *Chequers*: Good value food, well kept beer, friendly efficient staff, Tudor beams, tables outside; comfortable bedrooms *(Steve Hall)*; [125 High St], *Rose & Crown*: Nice old Forte hotel with pleasant atmosphere, welcoming staff, good food; bedrooms *(Stella Knight)*

☆ **Tunbridge Wells** [Tea Garden Lane, Rusthall; TQ5639], *Beacon*: Comfortable sofas, stripped wood, good really friendly atmosphere and imaginative food from filled french bread to Sun lunch, interesting wines; live music or theatre downstairs weekends; lovely views from terrace *(Peter Neate, Hilary Dobbie, BB)*

Tunbridge Wells [Spa Hotel, Mt Ephraim], *Equestrian Bar*: Stylish and comfortable bar with unusual equestrian floor-tile painting and steeplechasing pictures, good polite helpful service, fine choice of bar food inc excellent bangers and mash, well kept real ales; hotel lounge takes overflow; bedrooms *(E G Parish, LYM)*; [Chapel Pl/Castle Sq], *Grapevine*: Useful stop nr Pantiles, wide range of bar food, friendly service *(Mrs H Dobbie)*; [The Common], *Mount Edgcumbe*: Hotel's newly refurbished bar, simple decor with lots of bricks, hops and wood, good views over the common, good choice of food with unusual variations like jellied eel ploughman's, obliging service; bedrooms *(Hilary Dobbie, LYM)*; [Lower Green Rd, Rusthall], *Red Lion*: Charming quiet village pub, old oak beams, two open fires; friendly landlord, wide range of food inc Sun lunch *(E V J Rushton)*

☆ *nr* **Tunbridge Wells** [High Rocks; out just over the Sussex border; TQ5638], *High Rocks*: Good jazz nights in extensively refurbished pub with good value food, hard-working staff, big restaurant; open all day, children welcome; beautiful garden, attractive views *(Simon Small)*

Upchurch [TQ8467], *Crown*: Welcoming Courage village pub with big log fire, home-made dishes of the day *(Ian Phillips)*

Waltham [TR1048], *Lord Nelson*: Imaginative sandwiches, pleasant atmosphere, Goachers, Greene King and Harveys beers, lots of good pictures, good garden *(Comus Elliott)*

☆ **Warren Street** [just off A20 at top of North Downs – OS Sheet 189 map ref 926529;

TQ9253], *Harrow*: Quiet and comfortable dining pub neatly extended around 16th-c low-beamed core, consistently good friendly service, generous food, above average if not cheap, well kept Shepherd Neame and a guest beer on handpump, flowers and candles, big woodburner, faint piped music; restaurant (not Sun evening) with attractive conservatory extension; good bedrooms, on Pilgrims Way *(J A Snell, Comus Elliott, Colin McKerrow, Mary and Peter Clark, BB)*

☆ **West Farleigh** [B2010 off A26 Tonbridge—Maidstone; TQ7152], *Tickled Trout*: Good food esp fish in pleasant bar and attractive dining room, well kept Whitbreads-related ales, fast friendly service; Medway views (esp from garden), path down to river with good walks *(E D Bailey, LYM)*

West Malling [High St; TQ6857], *Bear*: Good home cooking, immaculate housekeeping, well kept beer, friendly efficient service; plenty of room *(J W Joseph, Mark Walker)*; [High St], *Joiners Arms*: Friendly two-bar local with big open fire in saloon, bar lunches (not Sun), Shepherd Neame ale; open all day Sat *(Mark Walker)*

☆ **West Peckham** [TQ6452], *Swan*: Wide range of good food inc some original recipes, Harveys on handpump; wonderful country setting, popular on summer weekends *(K Flack, C O Day)*

Westbere [TR1862], *Yew Tree*: Cosy warm free house with very friendly landlord, good reasonably priced food *(Chris and Dave Mathews)*

Westerham [Market Sq; TQ4454], *George & Dragon*: Welcoming Chef & Brewer with good pubby atmosphere, lots of memorabilia from General Wolfe's 1758 visit onwards, good service, decent traditional Sun lunches, Courage-related ales *(Dave Braisted)*

☆ **Whitstable** [Sea Wall; TR1166], *Pearsons*: What makes this special is the good fresh fish and seafood in the cheerful little upstairs seaview restaurant – sadly this is not at the moment available in the bar, which has more usual pub food, a nautical decor, well kept Whitbreads-related ales, decent wines, and a huge lobster tank in its lower flagstoned part; piped music, very friendly staff, children welcome in eating areas *(Mr and Mrs Barnes, E D Bailey, Mrs M Henderson, L M Miall, Thomas Nott, James Macrae, Ted George, John Watson, LYM)*

Wickhambreaux [TR2158], *Rose*: Three smallish panelled rooms with log fire in big fireplace, good fish-oriented food, Whitbreads-related ales; on village green *(Chris Westmoreland)*

☆ **Wingham** [Canterbury Rd; TR2457], *Dog*: Medieval beams, lots of character, good range of Whitbreads-related ales, good food, welcoming staff; comfortable bedrooms *(P G Hicks, M A Watkins)*

Wormshill [The Street; TQ8757], *Blacksmiths Arms*: Lovely recently renovated isolated low-beamed country cottage, open fire, friendly staff, well kept Shepherd Neame ales and guests, good varied food (not Tues evening) inc vegetarian and doorstep sandwiches; beautiful garden with country views *(R Owen)*

☆ **Worth** [The Street; TR3356], *St Crispin*: Thriving friendly and relaxed refurbished pub with eight well kept ales inc four changing guests, wide range of good value fresh food in bar and restaurant, charming garden; comfortable bedrooms, lovely village position not far from beach *(Russell and Margaret Bathie, A B Dromey)*

☆ **Wrotham** [signed 1¾ miles from M20, junction 2; TQ6159], *Bull*: Welcoming helpful service in attractive 14th-c inn with good food, log fires, well kept Whitbreads-related ales, decent wines; children welcome, separate restaurant; comfortable bedrooms, huge breakfasts, attractive village *(P Walker, Pierre Haddad, LYM)*

☆ **Wye** [signed off A28 NE of Ashford; TR0546], *Tickled Trout*: Good summer family pub with lots of tables and occasional barbecues on pleasant riverside lawn, spacious conservatory/restaurant; rustic-style bar with usual bar food, Whitbreads-related ales; children welcome *(LM, LYM)*

☆ **Yalding** [Yalding Hill; TQ7050], *Walnut Tree*: Attractive beamed bar on several levels with inglenook and interesting pictures, welcoming staff, good bar food inc some interesting dishes, wide restaurant choice, Fremlins, Harveys and Wadworths 6X; bedrooms *(John and Elspeth Howell, C R and M A Starling, Jenny and Brian Seller, Mr and Mrs P Brocklebank)*

Lancashire (including Greater Manchester and Merseyside)

With plenty of bargains in both food and drinks, this area's pubs stand out as offering exceptional value for money. Character is often a very strong point here too, and it's an area we always look forward to inspecting because of the genuine friendliness we find in virtually all the pubs here – whether or not they make the main-entry grade. In fact this year we have found two excellent newcomers: the Eagle & Child at Bispham Green (good all round, with most attractive antique decor), and the Black Horse at Croston (smartened up a lot since we last saw it, with excellent real ales); the Assheton Arms in the charming village of Downham is also back among the main entries after a break, as is the charming Station Buffet in Stalybridge. Other pubs currently doing specially well here include the Black Dog at Belmont (very cheap beer, attractively priced food), the hillside Moorcock at Blacko (good dining pub), the friendly Old Rosins near Darwen, the Taps in Lytham (a relaxed real ale pub), the Royal Oak in Manchester (terrific for cheese), the Inn at Whitewell (which despite going rather upmarket is giving more enjoyment to more readers than any other pub in the area) and the cosy New Inn at Yealand Conyers, where the food under its current painstaking licensees stands out so clearly that we choose it as Lancashire Dining Pub of the Year. In the Lucky Dip section at the end of the chapter, pubs showing specially well these days (most already inspected by us) include the Coach & Horses at Bolton by Bowland, Crown & Thistle in Darwen, Globe in Dukinfield, Strawbury Duck at Entwistle, Farmers Arms at Heskin Green, Egerton Arms near Heywood, Ship at Lathom, Robin Hood at Mawdesley, Kettledrum at Mereclough, Hark to Bounty at Slaidburn and Freemasons Arms at Wiswell. As we've said, this is an area of low pub prices, with the regional brewers Robinsons and Thwaites holding prices well below the national average, and plenty of good local brewers such as Burtonwood, Holts, Hydes, Lees, Mitchells and Sam Smiths to look out for too; Hydes prices still hover around the £1 mark.

---

nr BALDERSTONE (Lancs) SD6332 Map 7

Myerscough Hotel

Whalley Rd, Salmesbury; A59 Preston—Skipton, over 3 miles from M6 junction 31

This bustling 18th-c pub is always friendly and welcoming. At lunchtime it's a popular food stop, usually busy with families, businessmen or workers from the British Aerospace plant across the road. In the evening the softly lit beamed bar has a pleasant relaxed and cottagey feel with less emphasis on food and more on the pub side. There are well made and comfortable oak settles around dimpled copper or heavy cast-iron-framed tables, as well as nice pen and ink drawings of local scenes, a painting of the month by a local artist, and lots of brass and copper. The serving counter has a nice padded elbow rest, and dispenses well kept Robinsons Best and Mild and occasionally Hartleys XB on handpump, and several malt whiskies; darts, shove-ha'penny, dominoes, and fruit machine. Good bar food includes home roast beef and yorkshire pudding, braised steak, mushrooms and onions and chicken or beef curry (£4.50) and puddings. There are picnic tables, bantams and their chicks, and rabbits in the garden; very handy for the M6. *(Recommended by John and Pam Smith, Russell and Margaret Bathie; more reports please)*

Robinsons ~ Tenant John Pedder ~ Real ale ~ Meals and snacks (12-2, 6.30-8.30) ~ (01254) 812222 ~ Well behaved children in front room at mealtimes ~ Weds quiz night ~ Open 11.30-3, 5.30-11 ~ Bedrooms: /£55S

BELMONT (Lancs) SD6716 Map 7

Black Dog

A675

This cosy and unpretentious characterful little 18th-c farmhouse is a real favourite with readers, not least because of the very good value food and drinks. We like the way they've kept it pubby by not taking bookings, but it does tend to fill up quickly so get there early for a table. The original cheery and traditional small rooms are packed with antiques and bric-a-brac, from railwaymen's lamps, bedpans and chamber-pots to landscape paintings, as well as service bells for the sturdy built-in curved seats, rush-seated mahogany chairs, and coal fires. The atmosphere is perhaps best on a winter evening, especially if you're tucked away in one of the various snug alcoves, one of which used to house the village court. The landlord may be happily whistling along to the piped classical music; twice a year they have a small orchestral concert, and on New Year's Day at lunchtime a Viennese concert. The well kept Holts Bitter is still very good value, only £1.01 a pint as we went to press. Very popular, good value and highly praised bar food includes home-made soup (£1.20; they do a winter broth with dumplings, £1.50), sandwiches (from £1.30; steak barm cake £1.70), ploughman's (from £3), steak and kidney pie, scampi, gammon or lamb cutlets (£3.80), steaks (from £5.80), well liked salads with various fruits like grape, banana and strawberry and a landlord's summer salad (English and continental meats for the 'big salad eater') and daily specials like pork in stilton and celery sauce, grilled pork chops in cream and madeira sauce, braised steak in red wine or pepperoni, pasta and chilli bake. There may be some delays to food service at busy times. An airy extension lounge with a picture window has more modern furnishings; morning coffee, darts, pool, shove-ha'penny, dominoes, cribbage, and fruit machine. From two long benches on the sheltered sunny side of the pub there are delightful views of the moors above the nearby trees and houses; there's a track from the village up Winter Hill and (from the lane to Rivington) on to Anglezarke Moor, and paths from the dam of the nearby Belmont Reservoir. *(Recommended by S R and A J Ashcroft, Andrew Hazeldine, Gordon Tong, John and Pam Smith, Graham and Lynn Mason, Howard Bateman, Kevin Potts, Bill and Lydia Ryan, Patrick Clancy, JJW, CMW, Comus Elliott, Andy and Julie Hawkins, Richard Davies)*

Holts ~ Tenant James Pilkington ~ Real ale ~ Meals and snacks (not Mon or Tues evenings except for residents) ~ (01204) 811218 ~ Children welcome away from bar ~ Open 12-4, 7-11 ~ Bedrooms: £29B/£38B

BILSBORROW (Lancs) SD5139 Map 7

Owd Nells

Guy's Thatched Hamlet, St Michaels Road; at S end of village (which is on A6 N of Preston) take Myerscough College turn

Part of a thriving little complex called 'Guy's Thatched Hamlet' which has transformed a previously neglected stretch of canal – purpose-built and artificial to be sure, but still a great place for a family day out. There's an expanding hotel with indoor pool and gym, and various craft and tea shops. The three or four spacious communicating rooms of the pub have an easy-going rustic feel, with their mix of brocaded button-back banquettes, stable-stall seating, library chairs and other seats, high pitched rafters at either end, and lower beams (and flagstones) by the bar counter in the middle; a couple of areas are no smoking. Children are made especially welcome; there may be free lollipops and bags of bread for feeding the ducks. Colourful seats out on the terrace, part of which is covered by a thatched roof; a small walled-in play area has a timber castle, and you can play cricket or boules. There may be Morris dancers out here on summer weekends. Good helpings of American-style bar meals such as soup (£1.20), cheese and pickles (£2.70), hot roast beef sandwich (£3.50), steak sandwich (£4), ploughman's (£4.10), curried chicken (£4.35), half a BBQ chicken (£4.50), steak and kidney pudding (£4.60), also afternoon sandwiches (from £2.50) and scones (£1.40) and tasty evening finger snacks like fingers of breaded mozzarella with a chilli dip (£1.85), deep-fried sticks of celery (£2), deep-fried strips of chicken breast (£2.45) and goujons of fresh fish with a dip (£2.95); children's menu (£2.25). Waitress service is prompt and professional even under pressure – it often gets busy, especially in school holidays. Well kept Whitbreads Castle Eden and an interesting choice of weekly changing guests like Cains, Dents, Flowers Original, Mitchells, Moorhouses Pendle Witches Brew and Robinsons Best on handpump, several wines including a bargain house champagne, tea and coffee; darts, video game, fruit machine, Connect-Four, and unobtrusive piped pop music. ***(Recommended by Rosemarie Johnson, Carl Travis, Sarah and Gary Goldson, Graham Bush, Bronwen and Steve Wrigley, D Grzelka, Gill and Keith Croxton, Brian and Jill Bond, Jim and Maggie Cowell, Fred Collier, John Atherton, Alan Reid)***

Free house ~ Licensee Roy Wilkinson ~ Real ale ~ Meals and snacks (all day) ~ Next-door restaurant (all day inc Sun) ~ (01995) 640010/640020 ~ Children welcome ~ Various live entertainments ~ Open 10.30-11; cl 25 Dec ~ Bedrooms: £37B/£42B

BISPHAM GREEN (Lancs) SD4914 Map 7

Eagle & Child

Maltkiln Lane (Parbold—Croston rd, off B5246)

Since buying this striking three-storey dark brick pub from Whitbreads in 1992 the owner Martin Ainscough has largely rebuilt it, in an attractively understated old-fashioned style. Though the civilised bar is largely open-plan, it's well divided by stubs of walls. There are fine old stone fireplaces, oriental rugs and some coir matting on flagstones, old hunting prints and engravings, and a mix of individual furnishings including small oak chairs around tables in corners, and several handsomely carved antique oak settles – the finest apparently made partly from a 16th-c wedding bed-head. House plants stand on a big oak coffer. A particularly good range of well kept beers on handpump consists of Boddingtons, Coach House Gunpowder Dark Mild, Theakstons Best and Thwaites, with three or four changing guest ales which on our inspection visit were Hanby Scorpio Porter, Timothy Taylors Landlord and Worth Alesman; Symond's farm cider, decent wines, a good collection of malt whiskies, friendly and interested service; maybe piped pop radio. This year they have won planning permission to install their own microbrewery in the handsome side barn. Food benefits from the fact that the Ainscoughs farm much of the land around Parbold, so there may be well hung meat from their herd of pedigree Galloways, and vegetables and herbs are mostly local. On our visit, good sound food included sandwiches, mushroom and mixed peppeı soup (£1.35), smoked chicken and pasta salad (£2.10), smoked salmon and prawn mousse (£3.10), beef baguette with soup or cheese (£3.50), braised oxtail (£4.70), steak and ale pie (£4.75), liver and bacon (£4.95), lemon sole poached with grapes and champagne (£5.25), and gammon (£6.10). A change of chef was imminent as we went to prèss, with menus expected to become even more individual (we'd very much like reports on this aspect). There is a neat if not entirely orthodox bowling green behind, and the pub garden has just been restored. Harry the dog is not the most sober individual (especially if there are hot-air balloons around). *(Recommended by Keith Croxton, Maurice and Gill McMahon, Tim Kent)*

Free house ~ Manager Monica Evans~ Real ale ~ Meals and snacks (12-2, 6-9) ~ (01257) 462297 ~ Children in eating area ~ Quiz night Tues ~ Open 12-3, 5.30-11

BLACKO (Lancs) SD8541 Map 7

Moorcock

A682; N of village towards Gisburn

In a superb position high on the moors, this isolated old stone inn has breath-taking views from the big picture windows in the spaciously comfortable bar, which has a lofty ceiling and cream walls hung with brass ornaments. There's a slight leaning towards dining, and one of the main draws is certainly the well presented bar meals which are all home-made by the landlady and might include moussaka (£3.95), sweet and sour chicken or pork (£4.50), tuna steaks or swordfish in dill (about £4.95), Mediterranean mixed fish with garlic, chicken breast with brandy cream and mushroom sauce (£5.50), salmon and asparagus mornay (£5.95) and rump steak brushed with garlic (£6.95). They do a number of lamb dishes including rack of lamb, with the meat coming from their own flock. Most dishes are served with garlicky cream potatoes; puddings from the blackboard include a brandy snap basket with elderflower ice cream and strawberries, meringue nest with forest fruits and cream, crème brûlée, toffee nut tart, or lemon and ginger cheesecake (all £2.50). Well kept Thwaites Bitter on handpump; efficient and cheery service. The attractively landscaped back garden is very busy at weekends, though quieter during the week; there's usually a goat, a couple of lambs, game cocks, and lots of white doves. The pub used to be a farmhouse and the landlord maintains the tradition, often out with his sheep around the Blacko Tower a mile or so across the moors. His collie puppies go to other working farms as far afield as Ireland, Canada and America. *(Recommended by Mr and Mrs R Hebson, Bronwen and Steve Wrigley, J A Swanson, Roger and Christine Mash, K C Forman, Laura Darlington, Gianluca Perinetti, Wayne A Wheeler, Gwen and Peter Andrews, Paul McPherson)*

Thwaites ~ Tenant Elizabeth Holt ~ Meals and snacks (till 10) ~ (01282) 614186 ~ Children welcome ~ Open 12-2.30, 6-12; cl 25 Dec

BLACKSTONE EDGE (Gtr Manchester) SD9716 Map 7

White House

A58 Ripponden—Littleborough, just W of B6138

In the 1700s the young men of Littleborough would gather here having guarded the mail coach across these bleak and moody moors. The highwaymen have gone but the panoramic views stretching for miles into the distance remain and the Pennine Way crosses the road just outside. Even in summer it somehow manages to seem windswept up here. The busy, welcoming and cheery main bar has a turkey carpet in front of a blazing coal fire and a large-scale map of the area. The snug Pennine Room opens off here, with brightly coloured antimacassars on its small soft settees, and there's a new extension. A spacious room on the left has a big horseshoe window looking over the moors, as well as comfortable seating. Good helpings of homely bar food include vegetable soup (£1.20), sandwiches (from £2), cumberland sausage with egg (£3.25), steak and kidney pie, roast chicken breast or vegetarian quiche (£3.75), chilli, beef curry or lasagne (£4), also, daily specials and home-made apple pie (£1.20); children's meals (£1.50). Good friendly service. Two well kept beers on handpump such as Moorhouses Pendle Witches Brew, Theakstons Best and Timothy Taylors Landlord, farm cider, and malt whiskies; trivia, fruit machine. It's a popular stop for walkers, whose muddy boots can be left in the long, enclosed porch. *(Recommended by Geoffrey and Irene Lindley, Ron and Sheila Corbett, Laura Darlington, Gianluca Perinetti, Ian and Emma Potts, Paul Wreglesworth)*

Free house ~ Licensee Neville Marney ~ Real ale ~ Meals and snacks (11.30-2; 7-10) ~ Restaurant ~ (01706) 378456 ~ Children welcome ~ Open 11.30-3, 7(6 Sat)-11

BRINDLE (Lancs) SD6024 Map 7

Cavendish Arms

3 miles from M6 junction 29; A6 towards Whittle-le-Woods then left on B5256

Several cosy little rooms, each with quite a distinct character, ramble around a central servery at this snugly civilised old pub. Some of the woodwork partitions have fascinating stained glass scenes with lively depictions of medieval warriors and minstrels. Many of them commemorate the bloody battle of Brundenburg, a nasty skirmish between the Vikings and Anglo-Saxons on the Ribble estuary. If it's quiet the friendly licensees are very happy to chat about the pub's history, and there are lots of pictorial plates and Devonshire heraldic devices in plaster on the walls; comfortable seats, discreet flowery curtains. Well kept Burtonwood Best on handpump, and a good choice of malt whiskies; darts and dominoes. Simple bar food includes soup (£1.50), home-made beef or chicken pie (£4), seafood platter (£4.75), home-made lasagne or crispy battered cod (£5), grilled salmon (£5.25) and roast beef and yorkshire pudding (£5.50), daily specials, and puddings (from £1.50). There are white metal and plastic tables and chairs on a terrace by a rockery with a small water cascade, with another table on a small lawn behind. It's nicely set in a tranquil little village, and there's a handsome stone church across the road. *(Recommended by Cyril Higgs, John and Pam Smith, K C Forman, Paul Boot, Mr and Mrs J H Adam, Peter and Lynn Brueton, G McKaig, Helen Hazzard)*

Burtonwood ~ Tenant Peter Bowling ~ Real ale ~ Meals and snacks (12-2, 5.30-9; not Sun evening) ~ Restaurant (not Sun evening) ~ (01254) 852912 ~ Children welcome till 9pm ~ Open 11-3, 5.30-11; cl Dec 25

CHIPPING (Lancs) SD6243 Map 7

Dog & Partridge 🍷

Hesketh Lane; crossroads Chipping—Longridge with Inglewhite—Clitheroe, OS Sheet 103 map reference 619413

Parts of this comfortable and relaxed inn date back to 1515, though it's been much modernised since, extra eating space now spreading over into a nearby stable. Good home-cooked bar food usually includes dishes like sandwiches (from £2), soup (£1.80), ploughman's (£4.25), three vegetarian dishes like leek and mushroom crumble (£5), steak and kidney pie (£6), roast duckling or seasonal game dishes (£7) and sirloin steak (£7.50); the home-made chips are particularly well liked and they do various fish and game specials. The main lounge, quite snug and with rather a genteel feel, is comfortably furnished with small armchairs around fairly close-set low wood-effect tables on a blue patterned carpet, brown-painted beams, a good winter log fire, and multi-coloured lanterns; service is friendly and helpful. Tetleys, Tetleys Mild and a guest on handpump, over 60 wines, and a good range of malt whiskies; piped music; jacket and tie are preferred in the restaurant. *(Recommended by Dr T E Hothersall, Peter Churchill; more reports please)*

Free house ~ Licensee Peter Barr ~ Real ale ~ Meals and snacks (12-1.45, 7-9.45, not Sat evening; 3-9.30 Sun) ~ Restaurant (inc Sun lunch) ~ (01995) 61201 ~ Children welcome ~ Open 12-3, 7-11

> Cribbage is a card game using a block of wood with holes for matchsticks or special pins to score with; regulars in cribbage pubs are usually happy to teach strangers how to play.

CROSTON (Lancs) SD4818 Map 7

Black Horse £

Westhead Road; A581 Chorley—Southport

Completely refurbished in the last few months, this now has a quietly comfortable Victorianised appeal, with carpets, attractive wallpaper, solid upholstered wall settles and cast-iron-framed pub tables, a fireplace tiled in the Victorian manner and reproduction prints of that period (also a couple of nice 1950s street-scene prints by M Grimshaw), and a remarkable back dining room very heavily furnished in reproduction Victorian. The main appeal is in the good changing range of well priced beers; the owners also have the leases of two high-throughput Preston real ale pubs (Fox & Grapes and Market Tavern – see Lucky Dip), so bulk buying gives them a real edge over many other free houses. Theakstons Best, XB and Mild are on regularly, and they have another five rotating among a batch of at least 16 which is changed weekly; on our inspection visit these were Cartmel Buttermere, Coach House Gunpowder Mild, Newcastle Brown, Worth Best and Youngers No. 3; also bargain spirits doubles. Simple reliable bar food includes sandwiches (from £1.35), filled baked potatoes (£1.75), a cheap dish of the day such as steak pie and chunky home-cut chips (£2), several OAP bargains (£2.25 inc coffee), chilli con carne (£2.75), breaded haddock or cheese and onion quiche (£2.95) and gammon and egg or chicken kiev (£3.25), with children's dishes (£1.50); darts, pool, cribbage, dominoes, fruit machine, juke box, maybe TV. There are picnic tables outside, and a good solid safely railed-off play area; the pub has its own crown bowls green, and now also a boules pitch (boules available from the bar). ***(Recommended by John Fazakerley, C A Hall)***

Free house ~ Licensees John and Anne Welsh ~ Real ale ~ Meals and snacks (12-2.30, 5-8) ~ Restaurant ~ (01772) 600338 ~ Children in restaurant ~ Open 11-11

nr DARWEN (Lancs) SD6922 Map 7

Old Rosins

Pickup Bank, Hoddlesden; from B6232 Haslingden—Belthorn, turn off towards Edgeworth opposite the Grey Mare – pub then signposted off to the right; OS Sheet 103 map reference 722227

It's always a surprise to find a popular place in such a remote spot, but then this attractively set hotel does have particularly friendly staff, a good pubby atmosphere and lovely views over the moors and down into the wooded valley. The open-plan bar is comfortably furnished with red plush built-in button-back banquettes, and stools and small wooden chairs around dark cast-iron-framed tables. Lots of mugs, whisky-water jugs and so forth hang from the high joists, while the walls are decorated with small prints, plates and old farm tools; there's also a good log fire. Parts of the bar and restaurant are no smoking. Well kept Boddingtons, Flowers Original, Marstons Pedigree and Theakstons Old Peculier on handpump or tapped from the cask, plenty of malt whiskies and coffee; maybe piped music. The generously served good value bar food, usually served all day, includes good home-made soup (£1.30), sandwiches (from £1.85; open sandwiches from £3) and ploughman's (£3.25), pork satay (£2.50), vegetable spring rolls (£3.50), salads (£3.60), home-made pizzas (from £3.75), freshly battered plaice (£3.95), delicious beef in Old Peculier or chicken tikka (£4.25), and sirloin steak (£7.25); puddings (£1.75), and children's meals. There are picnic tables on a spacious crazy-paved terrace. Readers have enjoyed their murder weekends and other themed evenings. ***(Recommended by Gary and Sarah Goldson, G L Tong, Bronwen and Steve Wrigley, Graham and Lynn Mason, Laura Darlington, Gianluca Perinetti, Brian Horner, Brenda Arthur, RJH, Tim Galligan, David Eberlin)***

Free house ~ Licensee Bryan Hankinson ~ Real ale ~ Meals and snacks (12-10.30) ~ Restaurant ~ (01254) 771264 ~ Children welcome ~ Open 12-11 ~ Bedrooms: £39.50B/£49.50B

DOWNHAM (Lancs) SD7844 Map 7

Assheton Arms

From A59 NE of Clitheroe turn off into Chatburn (signposted); in Chatburn follow Downham signpost; OS Sheet 103 map reference 785443

Fish is something of a speciality at this intimate and well preserved old place, which is charmingly set in a stonebuilt village spreading along a duck-inhabited stream. The best choice is at the weekend (arrive early as it fills up quickly) when they'll usually have delicious potted Morecambe Bay shrimps (£3.95), smoked salmon, gravadlax or roast smoked salmon (£4.95), good grilled plaice (£6.50), monkfish with mixed peppercorns and brandy (£8.50), scallops (£8.95), smoked fish platter (£9.95), sea bass (£10.95) and possibly oysters, crab and lobster. There's also a wide range of reasonably priced and generously served bar food, such as tasty home-made ham and vegetable soup (£1.95), sandwiches (not Saturday evening or Sunday lunchtime; from £2.75), stilton pâté (£3.25), cauliflower and mushroom provençale (£4.95), home-made steak and kidney pie (£5.25), venison and bacon casserole (£6.95) and steaks (from £8.95), puddings including a good toffee gateau and French lemon tart (£2.25), and children's dishes (£2.75); the chips are excellent. The rambling, beamed and red-carpeted bar has olive plush-cushioned winged settles around attractive grainy oak tables, some cushioned window seats, and two grenadier busts on the mantlepiece over a massive stone fireplace that helps to divide the separate areas. Well kept Boddingtons, Flowers Original and Whitbreads Castle Eden under light blanket pressure; decent wines by the glass or bottle; piped music; picnic tables outside look across to the church. *(Recommended by M Joyner, Mr and Mrs J Tyrer, Bronwen and Steve Wrigley, John Fazakerley, K C Forman, Gwen and Peter Andrews, Julie and Andrew Hawkins, Peter Walker, Wayne Brindle)*

Whitbreads ~ Tenants David and Wendy Busby ~ Real ale ~ Meals and snacks (till 10pm) ~ (01200) 441227 ~ Children welcome ~ Open 12-3, 7-11

GARSTANG (Lancs) SD4845 Map 7

Th'Owd Tithebarn ★

Signposted off Church Street; turn left off one-way system at Farmers Arms

Inside this beautifully set creeper-covered canalside barn it's a bit like an old-fashioned farmhouse kitchen parlour. There's an old kitchen range, prints of agricultural equipment on the walls, masses of antique farm tools, stuffed animals and birds, and pews and glossy tables spaced out on the flagstones under the high rafters. Waitresses in period costume with mob-caps complete the vintage flavour, and upstairs you'll find the Lancaster Canal Museum and Information Centre. Sitting on the big stone terrace is particularly pleasant, with plenty of ducks and boats wending their way along the water. Straightforward bar food includes home-made vegetable soup (£2.25), ploughman's (£3.55), burger (£4.20), steak pie (£4.55), vegetarian quiche or roast pork (£4.75), roast beef and yorkshire pudding (£5.25) and sirloin steak (£7.50); puddings (from £1.65), ice creams (from £1.75), and a good choice of meals for children (from £1.75). Well kept Mitchells Original and Lancaster Bomber on handpump; lots of country wines, and a fine antique bar billiards machine. It can get busy. *(Recommended by Peter and Audrey Dowsett, Cyril Higgs, Dorothee and Dennis Glover, Rosemarie Johnson, Winifrede D Morrison, MJVK, Mike and Wendy Proctor, Lynn Sharpless, Bob Eardley, Andy and Julie Hawkins)*

Mitchells ~ Managers Kerry and Eunice Matthews ~ Real ale ~ Meals and snacks (till 10pm; 9.30 Sun) ~ Restaurant ~ (01995 604486) ~ Children welcome ~ Open 11-3, 7(6 Sat)-11; cl Mon (exc lunchtime bank holiday Mons)

GOOSNARGH (Lancs) SD5537 Map 7

Bushells Arms 🍴 🍷

4 miles from M6 junction 32; A6 towards Garstang, turn right at Broughton traffic lights (the

first ones you come to), then left at Goosnargh Village signpost (it's pretty insignificant – the turn's more or less opposite Whittingham Post Office)

Tremendous care and attention is given to the food here. The constantly changing specials menu is largely determined by the availability of good fresh ingredients, often local, and has a Mediterranean tendency, so lots of olive oil, beans, garlic and olives. They make a number of unusual soups like lovage or Dutch pea with ham and garlic sausage, also lamb's liver with onions and thyme in a sherry cream sauce and bean casserole, cod steaks with garlic, lemon, tomato and olives or Turkish mixed vegetable casserole (£5.50), chicken fillet in a creamy mustard and fresh dill sauce (£6) and fresh fish daily. The usual menu includes soups (£1.30), spring rolls, samosas or falafels (£2), tandoori chicken wings (£2.50), chilli or cheese and broccoli flan (£4.50), steak and kidney pie (£5), stifatho (a Greek beef stew), or chicken fillet filled with smoked bacon, asparagus, grated cheese in hollandaise sauce and wrapped in puff pastry (£6), and a traditional local set menu with black pudding, a pastie, cheeses and a shortbread flavoured with caraway seeds and known as Goosnargh cake. Crisp and fresh vegetables include tasty potatoes, done with garlic, cream, peppers and parmesan; delicious puddings like apricot and rhubarb crumble, gooseberry pie with hyssop, pecan pie or chocolate soufflé (all £2); also children's dishes (£1.75) There may be delays at peak periods (mainly evenings and weekends), but service is friendly, and they're still happily serving lunches not long before closing time. The spacious, modernised bar has lots of snug bays, each holding not more than two or three tables and often faced with big chunks of sandstone (plastic plants and spotlit bare boughs heighten the rockery effect); also soft red plush button-back banquettes, with flagstones by the bar; fruit machine. Two areas are no smoking. The well chosen and constantly developing range of wines is excellent, with some New World ones and several half bottles, as well as changing wines of the month; the list gives useful notes to help you choose. Also well kept Boddingtons and Tetleys on handpump, and several malt whiskies. Tables in a little back garden, and hanging baskets at the front. The signal for opening the doors at lunchtime is the tolling of the church clock, and haunted Chingle Hall is not far away. *(Recommended by Barry Lynch, Sarah and Gary Goldson, E J and M W Corrin, J and P Maloney, Tom Ross, Dave Braisted, Andy and Julie Hawkins, Fred Collier, Mike and Jo, Sue Holland, Dave Webster, D Grzelka, Michael A Butler, Mr and Mrs M A Cook, John Watson, Paul Boot)*

Whitbreads ~ Tenants David and Glynis Best ~ Meals and snacks (till 10pm) ~ (01772) 865235 ~ Very well behaved children in eating area of bar until 9pm ~ Open 12-3, 6-11; cl 25 Dec and occasional Mondays

Horns 🍷

Pub signed from village, about 2 miles towards Chipping below Beacon Fell

This nicely set former coaching inn is much older than the building's brightly mock-Tudor facade (over 200 years old, in fact) suggests. The polished but snug rooms haven't changed much since they were built, and all have log fires in winter. Dotted around are a number of colourful flower displays – a good indication of the care and effort the friendly licensees put into running the place. Beyond the lobby, the pleasant front bar opens into attractively decorated middle rooms with antique and other period furnishings, and there's a thriving, enjoyable atmosphere. Tasty bar food includes wholesome soups (£1.75), beautifully presented sandwiches (from £2), plaice, roast pheasant or steak and kidney pie (£4.95), gammon and egg (£5.50), a daily roast and fresh fish of the day like halibut or scallops, and evening steaks, all nicely served with freshly cooked, piping hot chips; home-made puddings like sherry trifle or an excellent sticky toffee pudding (£3.50). A very good range of up to ten or so wines by the glass, an extensive wine list, a fine choice of malt whiskies, but keg Tetleys; cheerful and helpful young staff, piped music. *(Recommended by S R and J R Ashcroft, Andy and Julie Hawkins, John Atherton, J A Boucher)*

Free house ~ Licensees Elizabeth Jones and Mark Woods ~ Meals and snacks (not Sat evening or Sun lunch) ~ Restaurant ~ (01772) 865230 ~ Children welcome if dining ~ Open 11.30-3, 6.30-11; cl Mon lunchtime ~ Bedrooms: £40B/£65B

LIVERPOOL SJ4395 Map 7

Philharmonic ★ £

36 Hope Street; corner of Hardman Street

There's a delightful contrast between the wonderful opulence of the exquisitely decorated rooms and the cheery bustle and chat of the friendly staff and visitors at this marvellously elegant late Victorian gin palace. At the heart of its splendid fittings is a mosaic-faced serving counter, from which heavily carved and polished mahogany partitions radiate under the intricate plasterwork high ceiling. The echoing main hall is decorated with stained glass including contemporary portraits of Boer War heroes such as Baden-Powell and Lord Roberts, rich panelling, a huge mosaic floor, and copper panels of musicians in an alcove above the fireplace. More stained glass in one of the little lounges declares Music is the universal language of mankind and backs this up with illustrations of musical instruments; there are two plushly comfortable sitting rooms. Lavatory devotees may be interested to know that the famous gents' are original 1890s Rouge Royale by Twyfords: all red marble and glinting mosaics, these alone earn the pub its star, in the view of many readers. Well kept Ind Coope Burton, Jennings, Tetleys Bitter and Imperial and Walkers Bitter and Best on handpump, some malt whiskies and cask cider; fruit machine, trivia and juke box. Good value home-made bar food includes soup (99p), filled baguettes (£1.95, hot £2.15), and various well-priced dishes like lasagne, steak and kidney pie, haddock or chilli con carne (all £3.95), gammon (£4.60), rump streak (£6.45) and mixed grill (£7.65). On Sunday there is a three-course Sunday lunch (£4.95). *(Recommended by Alice McLerran, B Adams, John O'Donnell, Andrew Stephenson, M W Turner, Jonathan Mann, Abagail Regan, Geraint Roberts, G T White, Mr and Mrs S Ashcroft)*

Walkers (Carlsberg Tetleys) ~ Manager Phil Ross ~ Real ale ~ Meals and snacks (not Sun eve) ~ Restaurant ~ (0151) 709 1163 ~ Children in restaurant only ~ Weds quiz night ~ Open 11.30-11

LYTHAM (Lancs) SD3627 Map 7

Taps £

A584 S of Blackpool; Henry Street – in centre, one street in from West Beach

This is a stop for the serious drinker – the bar stools have seat belts, and the enthusiastic landlord is forever hunting out new beers. Each time he changes a barrel it's to a different beer; he tells us he's had over 1,000 to date. As they change so often, we can't tell you exactly what to expect, but to give you an idea of the width of the range on a typical day this last summer he had Everards Chesters Mild, Flowers Original, Marstons Pedigree, Colonel Peppers Lemon Ale, Timothy Taylors Golden Best and Wadworths IPA; Boddingtons is more or less a regular fixture. There's a really good friendly and unassuming atmosphere in the Victorian-style bare-boarded bar, which has plenty of stained glass decoration in the windows with depictions of fish and gulls reflecting the pub's proximity to the beach, also captain's chairs in bays around the sides, open fires, and a coal-effect gas fire between two built-in bookcases at one end. As well as a TV for special sporting events there's a bit of a rugby theme, with old photographs and portraits of rugby stars on the walls; piped music, shove-ha'penny, fruit machine and juke box. Once again at the same good value prices as last year, simple lunchtime bar food includes soup (85p), filled baked potatoes (from 90p), sandwiches (from £1.40, toasties from £1.70), and cold platters (from £2.95), with hot home-made daily specials like cottage pie, steak and ale pie, chicken curry and lasagne (£3.25); the ham and beef is home-cooked. There are no meals on Sunday, but instead they have free platters of food laid out, with tasty morsels like black pudding, chicken wings or minted lamb. *(Recommended by Carl Travis, Simon Barber, Sue Holland, Dave Webster, Rosemarie Johnson, Graham Bush, R W Saunders, Alan and Eileen Bowker, Kevin Potts, Fred Collier, Andy and Julie Hawkins)*

Whitbreads ~ Manager Ian Rigg ~ Real ale ~ Lunchtime meals and snacks (free snacks only on Sun) ~ (01253) 736226 ~ Children in eating area during meal times ~ Open 11-11

MANCHESTER SJ8498 Map 7

Dukes 92 £

Castle Street, below the bottom end of Deansgate

This lively place is under the same ownership as the well established Mark Addy (see below) and has a similar excellent choice of splendid value cheeses and pâtés, served in huge helpings with granary bread (£3). They also serve a soup in winter, filled baked potatoes (from £2.50) and various salads. You'll find it right in the heart of old industrial Manchester in an area of vigorous redevelopment by the site of the original Roman fort; don't be disheartened by the hulking old warehouses, smoky railway viaduct and disused canals you pass to get there. The spacious building has been stylishly converted from old canal-horse stables, with black wrought-iron work contrasting boldly with whitewashed bare plaster walls, a handsome marble-topped bar, and an elegant spiral staircase to an upper room and balcony. Up here are some modern director's chairs, but down in the main room the fine mix of furnishings is mainly rather Edwardian in mood, with one particularly massive table, and chaises-longues and other comfortable seats. Well kept Boddingtons, Marstons Pedigree and a changing guest on handpump; they also serve a Belgian wheat beer called Hoegarden on handpump, and quite a few Belgian fruit beers; decent wines and a large selection of malts, friendly staff; piped music. There are some tables out by the canal basin which opens into the bottom lock of the Rochdale Canal. Events in the forecourt may include jazz and children's theatre, and there's lots of theatre in the new function room. *(Recommended by Liz, Wendy and Ian Phillips, Carl Travis, Dr M Bridge, Rupert Lecomber, P M Mason, Brian Wainwright, Margaret and Allen Marsden)*

Free house ~ Licensee Thomas Joyce ~ Real ale ~ Snacks ~ (0161) 839 8646 ~ Children welcome away from bar till 7pm ~ Theatre in the function room ~ Open 11.30-11

Lass o' Gowrie £

36 Charles Street; off Oxford Street at BBC

This simple and characterful place has a lively charm of its own, especially if you don't mind the crowd of good-natured university students or possibly having to drink your own-brew pint on the pavement outside in true city-centre pub style. It's only this busy on Friday and Saturday nights during term times, but it's always fairly popular. The simple appearance of the long bar with its gas lighting and bare floorboards is one of the distinctive things about the place, but it's the malt-extract beers that people like best. Named for their original gravity (strength), LOG35 is quite lightly flavoured and slips down very easily, while LOG42 is a little meatier. Seats around a sort of glass cage give a view of the brewing process in the micro-brewery downstairs in the cellar. There's also well kept Whitbreads Castle Eden and Classic ales as they are released on handpump, and Biddenden farm cider; it might take some while to get served at busy periods. Hop sacks drape the ceiling, and the bar has big windows in its richly tiled arched brown facade, as well as mainly stripped walls. Good value bar food, unchanged since last year, includes sandwiches (from £1.25) and big filled baps (from £1.45), vegetable lasagne or moussaka (£3), cottage pie (£3.20) and chicken curry (£3.30); efficient cheery service. The volume of the piped pop music really depends on the youth of the customers at the time; fruit machine, trivia. *(Recommended by Bill and Lydia Ryan, Andy and Julie Hawkins, Terry Buckland, Paul Jones, Neil H Barker, Bill Ryan)*

Own brew (Whitbreads) ~ Manager Joe Fylan ~ Real ale ~ Lunchtime meals and snacks ~ (0161) 273 6932 ~ Children over 2 in small side room and raised area until 6pm ~ Open 11.30-11; cl 25 Dec

Marble Arch £

73 Rochdale Rd (A664), Ancoats; corner of Gould St, just E of Victoria Station

This striking late Victorian drinking house has an incredible range of 12 well kept beers on handpump. The choice changes regularly but typically takes in brews like Fullers London Pride, Goachers, Hydes Anvil, Marstons Pedigree and Owd Roger, Mitchells Best, Oak Wobbly Bob, Titanic Captain Smith and Lifeboat, and Youngs Special. They also keep a good choice of bottled beers (including Belgian Trappist beers) and a selection of country wines. Bar food, served in the lounge extension at the back, includes huge filled barm cakes, beef burgers, filled baked potatoes, chips and curry sauce or sandwiches (from £1.20), lasagne or chilli (£2.25). The decor is Victorian in style with extensive marble and tiling (particularly the frieze advertising various spirits, and the chimney breast above the carved wooden mantlepiece), a sloping mosaic floor, rag-rolled walls, magnificently restored lightly barrel-vaulted high ceiling, and walls partly stripped back to the glazed brick. Bar billiards, dominoes, cribbage, pinball, fruit machine, jukebox and lively background music. On the third Wednesday of the month the Laurel and Hardy Preservation Society, the Sons of the Desert, meet here and show old films. *(Recommended by Paul Carter, Andrew Hazeldine, Bill and Lydia Ryan, Simon J Barber)*

Free house ~ Managers John and Janet Oshea ~ Real ale ~ Meal and snacks 12-9 (not Sun) ~ (0161) 832 5914 ~ Children in eating area of bar ~ R & B, jazz or folk Fri and Sat evenings ~ Open 12-11(7-10.30 Sun) closed Bank Hol lunchtimes, and all day 25 and 26 Dec

Mark Addy ♀ £

Stanley Street, Salford, Manchester 3; look out not for a pub but for what looks like a smoked glass modernist subway entrance

If the man in the moon ever came to Manchester this is where you'd find him, because at any one time they have a choice of up to 50 different cheeses from all over Britain and Europe. Served with granary bread (£3), it comes in such huge chunks you probably won't be able to finish your helping – a doggy-bag is thoughtfully provided; there's also a range of pâtés including a vegetarian one (£3), and maybe winter soup. Well converted from waiting rooms for boat passengers, it has quite a civilised and trendy atmosphere, especially in the flower-filled waterside courtyard from where you can watch the home-bred ducks. Inside, the series of barrel-vaulted red sandstone bays is furnished with russet or dove plush seats and upholstered stalls, wide glassed-in brick arches, cast-iron pillars, and a flagstone floor. Well kept Boddingtons, Marstons Pedigree and fortnightly changing guests like Timothy Taylors Landlord on handpump, quite a few wines; piped music. They get very busy, so it is worth getting there early, and they prefer smart dress. It's named after a 19th-c man who rescued (at different times) over 50 people from drowning in the River Irwell outside. *(Recommended by JJW, CMW, Paul Carter, Carl Travis, M A Cameron, John O'Donnell, Dr M Bridge, Caroline Wright, Dawn and Phil Garside)*

Free house ~ Licensee Sara Louise Ratcliffe ~ Real ale ~ Snacks (11.30-8, Sun 12-3) ~ (0161) 832 4080 ~ Children welcome away from bar till 8pm ~ Open 11.30-11

Royal Oak (🍴) £

729 Wilmslow Road, Didsbury

One wonders why it is that Manchester has so many really superb cheese pubs – in our view, this is the pick of them. Over the last 30-odd years, Mr Gosling has been enthusiastically tracking down cheeses from all over the place, and you'd be hard pushed to think of one he doesn't keep. It's unusual to be served with less than a pound of even the rarer ones, with a substantial chunk of bread, salad and extras such as beetroot and pickled onions (£3 for a choice of two cheeses, take-away bags provided); there are also pâtés and winter soup. Particularly well kept Batemans Mild, Marstons Bitter and Pedigree and guests on handpump, and some sherries and ports from the wood; efficient, friendly service. The exterior is fairly ordinary; although the interior was very badly damaged by fire not long ago and a wonderful collection of theatre memorabilia lost, the busy bar has been restored much to its original state, with antique theatre bills and so forth again gradually filling it. There are some seats outside. *(Recommended by Roger and Christine Mash, Simon Barber, Mark*

Hydes, Ian Phillips, Brian and Anna Marsden, John O'Donnell, Yolanda Henry, P Yearsley, Stephen and Julie Brown, Bill and Lydia Ryan, Martin Richards)

Marstons ~ Tenant Arthur Gosling ~ Real ale ~ Lunchtime snacks (not weekends or bank holidays) ~ (0161) 445 3152 ~ Open 11-11; cl evening 25 Dec

Sinclairs Oyster Bar £

Shambles Square, Manchester 3; in Arndale Centre between Deansgate and Corporation Street, opposite Exchange Street

You'll probably be as surprised as we were to find this timeless 18th-c pub incongruously set in the middle of the Arndale shopping centre. The delightfully old-fashioned interior is split up into lots of snugs and (partly no smoking) dining areas, the interesting rooms have low ceilings, squared oak panelling, and traditional furnishings such as small-backed stools that run along a tall old-fashioned marble-topped eating bar. The larger room upstairs has low old-fashioned wall settles, a scrolly old leather settee, pictures of old Manchester, and good lunchtime bar food such as sandwiches (from £1.10), ploughman's (£2.50), chilli, quiches or various vegetarian dishes (£3.20), steak pie or vegetarian or chicken kievs (£3.60), lamb in mint and pepper sauce (£3.80), beef and oyster pie (£3.90); prices are unchanged from last year. Friendly welcoming service from neatly uniformed barmaids. Very well kept and well priced Sam Smiths OB and Museum on handpump, chess, dominoes, cribbage, draughts, fruit machine, and piped music. There are picnic tables outside in the pedestrians-only square. *(Recommended by John O'Donnell, Keith Stevens, John and Pam Smith, Bill and Lydia Ryan; more reports please)*

Sam Smiths ~ Manager Darren Coles ~ Real ale ~ Lunchtime meals and snacks (12-5) ~ (0161) 834 0430 ~ Children in eating area till 6pm ~ Nearby parking difficult ~ Open 11-11

MARPLE (Gtr Manchester) SJ9588 Map 7

Romper

Ridge End; from A626 Stockport Road in Marple, coming in from Manchester side, look out for Church Lane on your right (third turning after railway bridge and just after a garage); once in Church Lane, follow The Ridge signposts; OS Sheet 109 map reference 965966

There's a fairly smart atmosphere at this beautifully positioned country dining pub, alone on the steep side of the Goyt valley – there are good views from a fairly large raised terrace area. Reliable home-made food in big helpings such as lunchtime open sandwiches (not Sunday) with freshly sliced turkey, ham and beef, ploughman's (£4.95), cumberland sausage (£5.50), six vegetarian dishes (from £5.75), steak, kidney, ale and mushroom pie or gammon (£5.95), sirloin steak (£8.95), mixed grill or T-bone steak (£11.95); Sunday roast (£5.50); home-made fruit pies (£1.95). The four knocked-through oak-beamed rooms have soft blue corduroy seats and some antique settles around the many tables; there's soft lighting and gentle piped music. Well kept Boddingtons, Marstons Pedigree, Theakstons Old Peculier, Timothy Taylors Landlord and Wadworth 6X on handpump, with about 30 malt whiskies and a decent wine list; efficient service from friendly staff. There's a pretty walk down towards the Peak Forest Canal from a car park attractively set in hilly common, 100 yards along the Marple road. *(Recommended by Roger and Christine Mash, Bill Sykes, Gordon, Andrew and Ruth Triggs, Peter Childs, Ian and Emma Potts)*

Free house ~ Licensees Geoff and Patty Barnett ~ Real ale ~ Meals and snacks (till 10 Fri, Sat; 12-9.15 Sun) ~ (0161) 427 1354 ~ Children in eating area, no under-7s after 7pm ~ Open 12-2.30(3 Fri, Sat), 6-11; 12-10.30 in winter

People don't usually tip bar staff (different in a really smart hotel, say). If you want to thank them – for dealing with a really large party say, or special friendliness – offer them a drink.

MELLOR (Gtr Manchester) SJ9888 Map 7

Devonshire Arms

Longhurst Lane; follow Mellor signpost off A626 Marple—Glossop and keep on up hill; note that this is Mellor near Stockport, NOT the other one on the north side of Manchester

This friendly and unpretentious place is particularly popular for its good lunchtime food, all of which is carefully home-made and usually includes quite a few curries and spicy dishes: pea and ham and carrot and mint soup (£1.60), potted shrimps or hummus (£3.25), mussel chowder (£3.45), steamed fresh mussels (£4), courgettes provençale or ploughman's (£4.25), smoked sausage, egg curry or tortellini (£4.95), seafood pasta, bean curry or spiced chick pea curry (£5.25), diced chicken and peppers in a spicy sherry sauce (£5.25), tarragon salmon, braised oxtail or beef in Guinness (£5.50), and only a couple of puddings including popular crêpes with orange and Grand Marnier (£3.25). The Harrisons take obvious pride in their pub and do their best to make sure strangers feel at home. The cheerful little front bar has a couple of old leather-seated settles among other seats, lots of old local and family photographs, and a sizeable Victorian fireplace with a deep-chiming clock above it. A couple of small back rooms, attractively papered and with something of a period flavour, both have their own Victorian fireplaces – the one on the right including an unusual lion couchant in place of a mantlepiece. Robinsons Best and Mild on electric pump, a decent collection of spirits including about 50 malt whiskies, several New World wines, and good coffee (which comes with a little pot of fresh cream); cribbage, shove-ha'penny and dominoes; possibly background radio. There are picnic tables out in front, and behind, where an attractively planted terrace leads back to a small tree-sheltered lawn. Walkers are welcome if they take their boots off. *(Recommended by Roger and Valerie Hill, Roger and Christine Mash, John Derbyshire; more reports please)*

Robinsons ~ Tenant Brian Harrison ~ Real ale ~ Meals and snacks every lunchtime and Mon evening ~ (0161) 427 2563 ~ Well behaved children in eating area ~ Trad jazz Thurs evenings ~ Open 11.30-3.30, 5.30-11

NEWTON (Lancs) SD6950 Map 7

Parkers Arms

B6478 7 miles N of Clitheroe

In the middle of a cluster of neat stone cottages, this spacious and pretty black and white pub is delightfully set in a bowl of tree-sheltered pastures between Waddington Fell and Beatrix Fell, with the River Hodder below. Well spaced picnic tables on the big lawn look down towards the river, and beyond to the hills. The very well liked and generously served bar food might include soup (£1.60), very generous sandwiches (from £1.95), barbecue ribs (£2.95), steak and kidney pie (£4.95), and a big choice of daily blackboard specials like trout stuffed with crab and basil, venison steak, roast beef or prawn and salmon pancakes (£4.95); excellent service. Some of the joists in the very friendly and welcoming bar are from the same oak used to repair the Blitz-damaged Houses of Parliament. Plenty of stuffed animals and paintings on the walls in here, as well as red plush button-back banquettes, a mix of new chairs and tables and open fire. Beyond an arch is a similar area with sensibly placed darts, pool, dominoes, fruit machine, video game and discreet piped music. Boddingtons, Flowers IPA, Black Sheep Bitter and a guest like Tetleys on handpump. They have a friendly black labrador (who has been known to bring customers a stick to throw) and jack russell. *(Recommended by Wayne Brindle, Sarah and Gary Goldson, S R and A J Ashcroft, Arthur and Margaret Dickinson, K C and B Forman, Fred Collier, John Broughton, Bob Riley, Kevin Potts, J M Halle)*

Whitbreads ~ Tenant Nicholas Hardman ~ Real ale ~ Meals and snacks ~ Restaurant ~ (01200) 446236 ~ Children welcome ~ Open 11-3, 6-11; all day summer Sundays; cl 25 Dec ~ Bedrooms: £20/£35

RABY (Merseyside) SJ3180 Map 7

Wheatsheaf

The Green, Rabymere Road; off A540 S of Heswall

This half-timbered, thatched and white-washed country cottage (known locally as the Thatch) is a really authentic and traditional local in almost every way. The little rooms are simply furnished and characterful, with an old wall clock and homely black kitchen shelves in the central bar, and a nice snug formed by antique settles built in around its fine old fireplace. A second, more spacious room has upholstered wall seats around the tables, small hunting prints on the cream walls and a smaller coal fire. As well as sandwiches there's a huge range of toasted sandwiches, often extending to unusual kinds such as black pudding, and there may be hot dishes like steak and kidney pie, gammon, scampi and plaice. Beers on handpump might include Cains Traditional, Courage Directors, Ind Coope Burton, Tetleys, Theakstons Best, XB and Old Peculier, Thwaites and Youngers Scotch, and there's also a good choice of malt whiskies. The old-fashioned feel extends to the service and opening hours, and under 18s are strictly excluded. *(Recommended by Phil Putwain, S R and A J Ashcroft, Fred Collier, Tony and Lynne Stark, Basil Minson, Mr and Mrs C Roberts, Brian Kneale, Don Dellaway, Angie Coles; more reports please, particularly about prices and food and beer details – year after year the landlord refuses to give us any information)*

Free house ~ Licensee Ian Cranston ~ Real ale ~ Lunchtime meals and snacks (not Sun) ~ Open 11.30-3, 5.30-10.30

RIBCHESTER (Lancs) SD6435 Map 7

White Bull

Church Street; turn off B6245 at sharp corner by Black Bull

Although this stately stone pub was built in 1707, the Tuscan pillars of the entrance porch have been in the area for nearly 2,000 years. Behind the pub are the remains of a Roman bath house, and there's a small Roman museum close by. It's a popular stop for lunchtime food and can get busy, so it's worth getting there early for a table. Good value bar meals include soup (£1.30), open sandwiches (from £1.70), stuffed mushrooms or crispy prawns (£2.45), steak and kidney pie (£4.15), ploughman's, lasagne or chilli (£4.25), lamb chops (£4.95) and various steaks with a choice of toppings (from £6), and changing specials such as swordfish with garlic and prawns and braised shoulder of lamb; children's menu. Service is caring and attentive, even during busy periods, and children are made particularly welcome. The spacious and attractively refurbished main bar has comfortable old settles, and is decorated with Victorian advertisements and various prints, as well as a stuffed fox in two halves that looks as if it's jumping through the wall; most areas are set out for eating during the day, and you can also eat out in the garden behind. Well kept Boddingtons, Flowers IPA, Theakstons Best and a monthly changing guest like Greene King Abbot on handpump, occasionally kept under light blanket pressure, good range of malt whiskies, a blackboard list of several wines by the glass or bottle; darts, dominoes, fruit machine, piped music. Just up the road is an excellent Museum of Childhood. *(Recommended by Paul McPherson, Phil and Dilys Unsworth, W Bailey; more reports please)*

Whitbreads ~ Lease: Marilyn and Bob Brooks ~ Real ale ~ Meals and snacks (not Mon evening; 12-9 Sun and bank holidays) ~ (01254) 878303 ~ Children welcome ~ Occasional jazz or folk night ~ Open 11.30-3, 6.30-11; all day Sun and bank holidays

STALYBRIDGE (Gtr Manchester) SJ9698 Map 7

Stalybridge Station Buffet £

Any disheartened commuter will enjoy this unique and much-loved if rather basic Victorian-style bar, which is a delightful and unpretentious reminder of the days when the railways were still part of the Empire's glory – it's a must for fans of unusual bars. As it's full of railway memorabilia, including barge and railway pictures set into the marble-topped red bar counter, and more railway pictures and some old station signs on the high walls, train buffs will be fascinated too. In keeping with the modern British Rail story it's long been under threat of closure, but a dedicated campaign has kept it going in the face of all odds, and with Tameside Council now supporting it things are looking relatively hopeful. Instead of the usual station food they serve very good value traditional cafe snacks including delicious black-eyed peas (60p), hot or cold pies with black peas (from 60p), sandwiches (80p), and tea made freshly by the pot which you can enjoy as you're watched over by the image of Queen Victoria etched in the glass of a great mirror above the fire. Very well kept Grays Best (new to us) and three guest beers on handpump in summer and on tap in winter; various Belgian bottled beers and occasional farm ciders; trivia. *(Recommended by Mike Smith, Andrew Hazeldine, Wayne Brindle, Rupert Lecomber; more reports please)*

Free house ~ Licensee Ken Redfern ~ Real ale ~ Snacks ~ Children welcome ~ Folk singers Sat evening ~ Open 5-11; Fri and Sat 12-3, 7-11

TOCKHOLES (Lancs) SD6623 Map 7

Rock 🍷

Village signposted from A666 S of Blackburn; OS Sheet 103 map reference 663233

There's a delightful northern friendliness and flexibility at this really homely and welcoming moorland inn. Combine this with the tremendous amount of dedicated hard work put in by the Gallaghers (when we spoke to Dominic he told us he'd been up since 6am at the fish market and preparing their home-cooked pies) and the result is a wonderfully relaxing place to visit. You won't find the 30 or so constanty varying wines on a written list, but as it's the landlord's hobby he'll be delighted to chat about them, and as he enjoys finishing a good bottle himself you can try virtually any by the glass; well kept Thwaites Bitter, Mild and Scallywag on handpump, a variety of unusual malt whiskies including some Indian ones, and some unusual liqueurs. The very tasty home-made bar food in big reasonably priced helpings includes a soup of the day like carrot, herb and onion (£1.75), sandwiches (from £1.55), ploughman's (£2.25), cheese and onion pie (£3.85), home-made steak pie (£3.95), roasts, gammon or chicken baked in wine (£4.65), sirloin steak (£7.95), and changing specials like calamari in a crunchy crispy batter (£2.80), New Zealand mussels in white wine (£3.25), snails in garlic (£3.55), beef in ale or pork baked in cider, tarragon and herbs (£5.50). Do talk to the landlord if there's nothing on the menu you fancy or you're a vegetarian, as long as they're not too busy and they've got the ingredients they'll sort something special out; lots of puddings (from £1.75); occasional flambé evenings; booking advisable at weekends. The two-room beamed bar is cosy, with wall banquettes, moiré curtains, brass ornaments around the neat fireplace, old sporting prints on the cream-coloured walls and plates on a delft shelf, some really old. On the left by the bar counter (which has unusually comfortable swivel bar stools) there's some dark brown panelling. Unobtrusive piped music, fruit machine. There are tables out on a small terrace. On a clear day from the back dining area you may be able to see not only rolling well wooded pastures, but the coast some 20 miles away – look out for Blackpool Tower and about three times a year even the Isle of Man. *(Recommended by Laura Darlington, Gianluca Perinetti, G L Tong, S and J Cumming/Johnson, Gordon Tong, John Fazakerley, Jim and Maggie Cowell; more reports please)*

Thwaites ~ Tenants Dominic and Maureen Gallagher ~ Real ale ~ Meals and snacks (not Mon lunchtime, exc bank holidays; all day Sun) ~ (01254) 702733 ~ Children welcome until 8.45pm ~ Open 12-2, 7-12; Sun 12-11; cl Mon lunchtime

UPPERMILL (Gtr Manchester) SD9905 Map 7

Cross Keys £

Runninghill Gate; from A670 in Uppermill turn into New Street, by a zebra crossing close to the chapel; this is the most practical-looking of the lanes towards the high moors and leads directly into Runninghill Gate, but is still steep and more than a mile long

This friendly and chatty low-beamed moorland pub is very much at the heart of the local community, and at lunchtimes especially you start to feel quite at home with the local atmosphere, particularly if you're sitting on one of the comfortable old settles. Among various clubs and teams that gather here (including the Gun Club, which meets for clay pigeon shooting every other Sunday at 10 am) you can watch the Saddleworth Clog and Garland Dancers practising their clog dancing on the old flag floor in the kitchen every Monday night. One room has an original cooking range, another, overlooking the lonely moorland Saddleworth church, has local prints and drawings for sale. Good value simple bar food includes soup (£1), sandwiches (from £1.20, toasted from £1.30), lasagne or sausage, chips and peas (£2.85), steak and kidney pie, ploughman's or plaice (£3.50), scampi or turkey nuggets (£3.75), and puddings like apricot crumble (from £1.30); children's menu (£1.85). Well kept Lees Bitter and Mild on handpump, lots of malt whiskies; darts, dominoes, cribbage and fruit machine. There's a side terrace and a stylish flagstoned back terrace with bright flowers sheltered by a dry stone wall; there's a new adventure playground out here. The setting is lovely, and tracks from behind the pub lead straight up towards Broadstone Hill and Dick Hill. *(Recommended by Jack and Philip Paxton, Chris Westmoreland, Andrew and Ruth Triggs, G J Parsons, Bronwen and Steve Wrigley)*

Lees ~ Tenant Philip Kay ~ Real ale ~ Meals and snacks (11.30-8, Sun 12-3) ~ (01457) 874626 ~ Children in two side rooms till 8pm ~ Clog dancing Mon evenings, folk Weds evenings ~ Open 11-11

WHARLES (Lancs) SD4435 Map 7

Eagle & Child

Church Road; from B5269 W of Broughton turn left into Higham Side Road at HMS Inskip sign; OS Sheet 102 map reference 448356

Little changes from year to year at this quiet and friendly thatched country ale house. It's well worth visiting because scattered through the very neatly kept rooms is the landlord's marvellous collection of lovely antique furnishings including some fine ancient oak seats, the most interesting of which can be seen in the L-shaped bar, where a beamed area round the corner past the counter has a whole cluster of them. One of the highlights is a magnificent, elaborately carved Jacobean settle which originally came from Aston Hall in Birmingham, carrying the motto *exaltavit humiles*. There's also a carved oak chimneypiece, and a couple of fine longcase clocks, one from Chester, and another with a nicely painted face and an almost silent movement from Manchester. The plain cream walls are hung with modern advertising mirrors and some older mirrors, and there are a few exotic knives, carpentry tools and so forth on the plastered structural beams; even when it's not particularly cold, there should be a good fire burning in the intricate cast-iron stove. Well kept Boddingtons and three regularly changing guests such as Cains Traditional, Wadworths 6X or Wards on handpump; darts in a sensible side area, friendly cat. One or two picnic tables outside. Do please note it's closed on weekday lunchtimes, and there is no food. *(Recommended by Graham Bush, John Atherton, Mr and Mrs G Goldson; more reports please)*

Free house ~ Licensees Brian and Angela Tatham ~ Real ale ~ No food ~ (01772) 690312 ~ Open 7-11 (and 12-3 Sat; usual Sun hours)

WHITEWELL (Lancs) SD6546 Map 7

Inn at Whitewell ★ ★ 🛏 🍷

Most easily reached by B6246 from Whalley; road through Dunsop Bridge from B6478 is also good

This tremendously popular place is beautifully set deep in the Forest of Bowland and surrounded by well wooded rolling hills set off against higher moors. It has such a civilised atmosphere and such individual furnishings that at times it has the air of a hospitable country house. The inn also houses a wine merchant (hence the unusually wide range of around 180 wines available – the claret is recommended), an art gallery, and a shop selling cashmere, shoes and so forth, and owns several miles of trout, salmon and sea trout fishing on the Hodder; with notice they'll arrange shooting. A real bonus is that although it gets very busy, it's very spacious inside and out, so usually stays peaceful and relaxing. The old-fashioned bar has antique settles, oak gateleg tables, sonorous clocks, old cricketing and sporting prints, log fires (the lounge has a very attractive stone fireplace), and heavy curtains on sturdy wooden rails; one area has a selection of newspapers, local maps and guide books. The public bar has darts, pool, shove-ha'penny and dominoes, with a 1920s game-of-skill slot machine; there's a piano for anyone who wants to play. Down a corridor with strange objects like a stuffed fox disappearing into the wall is the pleasant sun-trap garden, with wonderful views across the Hodder and down to the valley. Popular lunchtime bar food includes soup (£2), big sandwiches (from £3), cumberland sausage, salads or ploughman's (from £5), steak and kidney pie (£5.60), fisherman's pie (£5.80), weekend oysters, steaks (£9.50), home-made puddings like chocolate roulade (£2) and British hand-made cheese (from £2.50); there's an à la carte menu and slightly different evening dishes, and they serve coffee and cream teas all day. Well kept Boddingtons and Marstons Pedigree on handpump. Some of the spacious and beautifully refurbished bedrooms even have their own CD players; the gents', incidentally, now have cricketing prints – more decorous than many readers will remember. *(Recommended by Nick and Meriel Cox, Nigel Woolliscroft, Graham Bush, Laura Darlington, Gianluca Perinetti, R C Foster, Howard Bateman, Helen Pickering, Robert and Ann Lees, Phil and Karen Wood, Wayne Brindle, Jim and Maggie Cowell, J Royce, Geoff and Sue Abbott, S R and A I Ashcroft, Neville Kenyon, Andy and Julie Hawkins, J Roy Smylie, Nic Armitage, Paul McPherson, L P Thomas, Bob and Janet Lee, John and Phyllis Maloney, Barry and Lindsey Blackburn, Jonathan Mann, Abagail Regan)*

Free house ~ Licensee Richard Bowman ~ Real ale ~ Meals and snacks (not Sat evening if a big function is on) ~ Restaurant (not Sun lunchtime) ~ (01200) 448222 ~ Children welcome ~ Open 11-2, 6-11 ~ Bedrooms: from £49B/£65B

YEALAND CONYERS (Lancs) SD5074 Map 7

New Inn

3 miles from M6 junction 35; village signposted off A6 N

Lancashire Dining Pub of the Year

This simple early 17th-c ivy-covered stone pub is getting really popular for its novel and imaginative blackboard specials, which reflect the slightly theatrical approach to flavours that one might expect from a chef trained by John Tovey, of the famous Miller Howe up in the Lakes. They could include chicken liver parfait with a traditional ale bread (£4.25), gravadlax of salmon with mustard and honey mayonnaise and caviar tartlets (£4.95 or £6.50), baked tripe (£5.25), quails stuffed with chicken and pistachio mousse on date chutney with a rich port gravy (£6.50) or poached chicken breast stuffed with banana on home-made rhubarb chutney with cream Pernod sauce (£7.50). Readers make particular mention of the really imaginative salads which come with most dishes. Puddings like apple crème brûlée, bilberry jelly topped with vanilla custard, rich creamy macaroni pudding and sticky toffee pudding (from £2.95) are no less creative. For the not so adventurous the short menu is more straightforward: filled baps (from £2.25), filled baked potatoes (from £2.75), bobotie, cumberland sausage, quiche of the day or potato bake (£4.95). There is a good friendly and professional reception, though understandably with a clear emphasis on dining, in this atmospheric and charming old place. On the left is a simply furnished little beamed bar with a log fire in the big stone fireplace, and on the right are two communicating cottagey dining rooms with black furniture to match the shiny beams, an attractive kitchen range and another winter fire. The restaurant is no smoking. Well kept Robinsons Best, Frederics, Hartleys XB, Hatters Mild and Old Tom on handpump, a good choice of about twenty malt whiskies, home-made lemonade. Dominoes, cribbage, piped music. A sheltered lawn at the side has picnic tables among roses and flowering shrubs. *(Recommended by A N Ellis,*

Nick and Meriel Cox, George Atkinson, P A Legon, Bronwen and Steve Wrigley, Mrs P J Carroll, R J Walden, David and Gill Carrington, Eric Locker, Rev J E Cooper, Mike Tucker, Martin, Jane, Simon and Laura Bailey, Paul McPherson, Olive Carroll, P Barnsley, Colin and Shirley Brown, David Bloomfield, Michael A Butler, Prof I H Rorison, Brian Kneale, Wayne Brindle, Derek and Margaret Underwood)

Hartleys (Robinsons) ~ Tenants Ian and Annette Dutton ~ Real ale ~ Meals and snacks (all day till 9.30) ~ Restaurant ~ (01524) 732938 ~ Children in eating area of bar and restaurant ~ Open 11-11(winter 11-3, 5.30-11)

Lucky Dip

Besides the fully inspected pubs, you might like to try these Lucky Dips recommended to us and described by readers (if you do, please send us reports):

Adlington [5A Market St (A6); SD5912], *White Bear*: Basic town local with well kept S & N ales, cheap food, pool table in back bar; can be smoky; safely enclosed back terrace with lots of play equipment *(Richard Davies, BB)*

☆ **Altrincham** Gtr Man [Navigation Rd, Broadheath; junction with Manchester Rd (A56); SJ7689], *Old Packet House*: Pleasantly restored local with attractive Victorianised decor, shiny black woodwork, good solid furnishings, turkey carpet, well kept Boddingtons, Websters and Wilsons, open fires, good bar food inc lots of sandwiches and well presented salads, some fresh-cooked hot dishes, nice plush back dining room, prompt friendly service; fruit machines, juke box; under same ownership as Dog at Peover Heath (see Cheshire main entries); small sheltered back terrace, well equipped bedrooms *(Ian Phillips, Brian Jones, BB)*

Altrincham [Stamford St], *Malt Shovels*: Friendly local with good Sun quiz night, good pin ball machine, decent food *(Cormac McCaughey)*

Ashton in Makerfield Gtr Man [Edge Green Rd; SJ5799], *Harrow*: New managers putting effort into good choice of well presented food, well kept real ale; good children's play area *(F E Hughes)*

☆ **Ashton under Lyne** [Mossley Rd (A670); SJ9399], *Hartshead*: Panoramic views over Manchester from Brewers Fayre family dining pub with baby changing, children's lavatories, own menu, marvellous outdoor play area, Lego etc inside; generous standard food, can get very busy summer weekends and bank hols, open all day *(Ian and Emma Potts, J Mayhew)*

☆ **Ashton under Lyne** [152 Old St], *Witchwood*: Lively pub with bands virtually every night (worth the admission), well kept ales such as Boddingtons, Courage Directors and John Smiths, lunchtime snacks (not Sun), low prices *(Graham Reeve)*

Atherton Gtr Man [Lovers Lane; SD6703], *Masons Arms*: Local with good value popular food (not Mon) inc home-made specials, well kept Tetleys, friendly family service *(Annette and Stephen Marsden)*

☆ **Barnston** Mer [Barnston Rd (A551); SJ2883], *Fox & Hounds*: Good value quickly served straightforward food from ploughman's up inc very popular Sun lunch, Courage-related and guest ales, plates, prints, brasses, fox masks and brushes, even decorative clothes rack over kitchen range, in partly flagstoned long lounge bar; pretty summer courtyard and garden with outside bar; by farm and lovely wooded dell *(Paul Boot, Mr and Mrs C Roberts, A Craig)*

☆ **Bashall Eaves** [SD6943], *Red Pump*: Welcoming tucked-away country pub with good imaginative home cooking inc good value Sun lunch, Whitbreads-related ales, two log fires, restaurant, two bedrooms, own fishing on River Hodder *(A and M Dickinson, Paul McPherson)*

Billington [SD7235], *Judge Walmsley*: Victorian pub in fine setting, outstanding evening food from two Thai cooks *(D J Poole)*

☆ **Birkenhead** Mer [Claughton Firs, Oxton; SJ3289], *Shrewsbury Arms*: Particularly well kept Cains and Whitbreads-related real ales in friendly and bustling pub, spacious lounge recently refurbished with extension in character, good bar food, hard-working landlord; tables on terrace *(Tony and Lynne Stark)*

Birkenhead, *Commodore*: Wide choice of well kept S & N and other rarer ales in friendly bare-boards backstreet local with pool, live music nights and good basic food *(Richard Lewis)*; [128 Conway St], *Crown*: Multi-roomed town centre alehouse with a dozen interesting real ales, Weston's farm cider, good basic food, low prices *(R Lewis)*

☆ **Blackpool** [204 Talbot Rd; opp Blackpool North stn; SD3035], *Ramsden Arms*: Attractive decor with masses of bric-a-brac and pictures, friendly helpful staff, well kept Boddingtons, Jennings and Tetleys with guests such as Cains and Robinsons, over 40 whiskies, cheap food, CD juke box, games; good value bedrooms *(Bill and Beryl Farmer, Bill and Lydia Ryan, Andrew Hazeldine)*

Blackpool [Talbot Sq], *Counting House*: Converted bank with good value standard food, well kept Whitbreads-related ales, well equipped upstairs sea-view family room, cheerful service *(R C Vincent)*; *Dunes*: Particularly well kept Boddingtons, good cheap home-made food; delightful hanging baskets and window boxes; bedrooms *(Kevin Potts)*; [Preston Old Rd, Marton], *Mere Park*: Newly refurbished with very friendly atmosphere, good value food inc bargain Sun lunch, helfpul licensees, children welcome *(Carol Thomas)*; [Queens Prom], *Uncle Toms Cabin*: Good food, friendly staff, tables outside, nightly entertainment in season *(Existing reporter)*

Blackrod [38 Little Scotland; SD6110], *Gallaghers*: Consistently well kept ales, good food in bar and restaurant *(Mr Ormrod)*

☆ **Bolton** Gtr Man [606 Halliwell Rd; SD7108], *Ainsworth Arms*: Unpretentious and friendly, with particularly well kept Tetleys-related and guest beers, basic good value food, quick service, pub games, old-fashioned smoke room; busy evenings, helpful attitude to wheelchairs *(Bill and Lydia Ryan, Andrew Hazeldine)*

☆ **Bolton** [36 Pool St], *Howcroft*: Good value lunches and well kept Tetleys-related ales in well preserved friendly old local with lots of small screened-off rooms, Addlestone's cider, plenty of games inc pinball, darts, bar billiards; bowling green, occasional live music *(Bill and Lydia Ryan, Andrew Hazeldine)*

☆ **Bolton** [52 Junction Rd, Deane; SD6808], *Kings Head*: Attractive local with central servery for flagstoned bar and two lounges, well kept Walkers Bitter, Mild, Best and Winter Warmer, massive stove, good reasonably priced lunchtime food, pleasant atmosphere; seats out overlooking church or back bowling green *(Andrew Hazeldine)*

Bolton [Eagle St, off Bradshawgate], *Anchor*: Cosy and friendly, particularly well kept Bass-related ales, good ship watercolours *(Andrew Hazeldine)*; *Queens Moat House*: Limited but good snacks for no more than the price of a normal pub lunch (though beers pricy), restaurant interestingly converted from old church; good bedrooms *(Gordon Tong)*; [127 Crook St], *Sweet Green*: Friendly local with four small rooms off central bar, green decor, well kept Tetleys-related and guest ales, basic lunchtime food; darts, pool, seats outside *(Andrew Hazeldine, Bill and Lydia Ryan)*

☆ **Bolton by Bowland** [SD7849], *Coach & Horses*: Quietly welcoming comfortable pub with pleasantly untouristy traditional decor in lovely streamside village with interesting church; good fresh well presented food to suit the season, well kept Whitbreads-related beers, coal fires, restaurant (where children may be allowed); get there early weekends for a table *(J A Boucher, Jim and Maggie Cowell, Roger Berry, Paul McPherson, GTW)*

☆ **Brierfield** [Burnley Rd (A682), just off M65 junction 12; SD8436], *Waggon & Horses*: Comfortable and beautifully restored and fitted-out late Victorian small-roomed local, lots of interest, well kept Thwaites Bitter, Craftsman and Mild on handpump, good malt whiskies, warm fires; bar food (not evenings Sun-Weds), children allowed away from servery, open all day Fri/Sat *(J E Hilditch, LYM)*

Bromborough Mer [Pool Lane; SJ3582], *Village Pub*: Part of big hotel and leisure complex, open all day with simple lunchtime bar food inc sandwiches, Sun carvery, guest beers; can get busy, entertainment most nights inc live bands *(Graham and Lynn Mason)*

Bromley Cross Gtr Man [Chapeltown Rd (B6391); SD7213], *King William IV*: Friendly three-room country local with cosy settee in small area down steps by window, popular and good value new mainly Italian restaurant *(Bronwen and Steve Wrigley)*

☆ *nr* **Broughton** [not far from M6 junction 32 via A6 N; left into Station Lane about a mile after Broughton traffic lights; SD4937], *Plough at Eaves*: Two homely low-beamed carpeted bars, well kept Thwaites Bitter and Craftsman, lots of malt whiskies, usual food inc children's helpings, darts, pool and other games, piped music, well equipped play area outside; cl Mon/Tues *(Sarah and Gary Goldson, JM, PM, LYM)*

Burscough [SD4310], *Ship*: By canal locks, good choice of well kept guest beers, friendly atmosphere, well cooked lunchtime food *(Mr and Mrs J Tyrer)*

☆ *nr* **Bury** [Nangreaves; off A56/A666 N under a mile E of M66 junction 1, down cobbled track; SD8115], *Lord Raglan*: Notable for its lonely moorside location, with great views; lots of bric-a-brac in traditional front bar, big open fire in back room, plainer blond-panelled dining room (where children allowed); well kept S&N real ales, interesting foreign bottled beers, hearty bar food *(Laura Darlington, Gianluca Perinetti, LYM)*

Cheadle Hulme Gtr Man [by rly stn; SJ8787], *Cheadle Hulme Hotel*: Fairly modern Holts pub with well kept cheap beer, big open elevated lounge area, restaurant *(Chris Westmoreland)*

☆ **Chorley** [Friday St, behind stn; SD5817], *Malt 'n' Hops*: Friendly and comfortable pub done out in traditional old tavern style, wide range of well kept changing ales from small northern brewers, bar food *(Mary Moore)*

☆ **Churchtown** Mer [off A565 from Preston, taking B5244 at Southport; SD3618], *Hesketh Arms*: Smart and spacious Victorian-style dining pub with good value fresh food from chip butties to roast beef inc children's helpings; Tetleys Bitter and Mild on handpump from central servery, open fires, lively atmosphere, Weds jazz; attractive partly thatched village nr Botanic Gardens *(BB)*

☆ **Churchtown**, the different Lancs one [nr church, off A586 Garstang—St Michaels-on-Wyre; SD4843], *Punchbowl*: Good choice of good food in attractive mock-Tudor beamed pub/restaurant with panelling, stained glass, lots of stuffed animals; friendly staff, well kept Tetleys and Dark Mild, good fires; lavatory for disabled people; another lovely village *(J A Boucher)*

Conder Green [Cockerham Rd (A588); not far from M6 junction 33; SD4556], *Stork*: Attractive 17th-c pub with good views from outside seats; several cosy panelled rooms, Whitbreads-related ales, good coffee, good home cooking inc vegetarian in bar or separate dining room ; bedrooms, handy for Glasson Dock *(Dennis D'Vigne)*

☆ **Cowan Bridge** [Burrow-by-Burrow; A65 towards Kirkby Lonsdale; SD6277], *Whoop Hall*: Spacious, spruce and comfortable open-plan bar with interesting quick food all day from 8am from popular buttery, well kept Boddingtons and Theakstons Best and XB, decent wines, pleasant restaurant; tables outside with play area; children allowed in eating area; well appointed bedrooms *(Frank Cummins, Sue Holland, David Webster, LYM)*

☆ **Croston** [Out Lane (off A581) – OS Sheet 108 map ref 486187; SD4818], *Lord Nelson*: Welcoming and relaxed old-fashioned local with well kept Whitbreads-related ales, decent straightforward food, no juke box or machines (TV in side family room), Nelson theme inc the Trafalgar message in flags on a mast outside *(John Smith, Andy and Julie Hawkins, F A Noble)*

Croston [Town Rd], *Grapes*: Good value home cooking in dining room off bar (booking advisable weekends), friendly staff, well kept beers *(D Grzelka, Janet Lee, Robert Lester)*

☆ **Darwen** [Roman Rd, Grimehills; SD6922], *Crown & Thistle*: Small and cosy two-room country dining pub with good if not cheap food (all tables set for diners, must book Fri/Sat), fresh flowers, moorland views, well kept Thwaites Bitter and Mild *(Neville Kenyon, Bronwen and Steve Wrigley)*

Delph Gtr Man [SE0009], *Old Bell*: Good food in comfortable bar and restaurant, friendly efficient service, real ale *(A McEwen)*

☆ **Diggle** Gtr Man [Diglea Hamlet, Sam Rd; village signed off A670 just N of Dobcross; SE0008], *Diggle Hotel*: Modernised three-room hillside pub popular lunchtime and early evening for food from sandwiches to duck, steaks and generous Sun roasts, inc children's dishes; well kept Boddingtons and Timothy Taylors Golden Best and Landlord, decent wines, good choice of malt whiskies, good coffee, friendly service, soft piped music, rustic fairy-lit tables among the trees, quiet spot just below the moors; opens noon *(Bill Sykes, K C and B Forman, BB)*

Dobcross Gtr Man [SD9906], *Swan*: Beamed pub below the moors, well kept Bass, good reasonably priced food; children welcome *(Anon)*

☆ **Dukinfield** Gtr Man [Globe Sq; SJ9497], *Globe*: Welcoming family-run pub with generous and genuine home cooking inc good value Sun lunch, well kept John Smiths and Tetleys, good comfortable atmosphere, games room; children welcome, open all day weekdays, bedrooms clean and comfortable, attractive surroundings nr Lower Peak Forest Canal; only a shortage of recent reports keeps it out of the main entries this year *(Graham Reeve, Mike Pugh, Ian and Emma Potts, LYM)*

☆ **Eccles** Gtr Man [33 Regent St (A57 – handy for M602 junction 2); SJ7798], *Lamb*: Untouched Edwardian Holts local with splendid etched windows, fine woodwork and furnishings; cheap well kept beer, full-size snooker table *(Bill and Lydia Ryan, Andrew Hazeldine)*

Eccles [133 Liverpool Rd, Patricroft, a mile from M63 junction 2], *White Lion*: Another classic Edwardian Holts local with drinking corridor, games in lively vaults bar, separate smoke room (with weekend sing-songs) and quiet lounge *(Pete Baker)*

Eccleston [Towngate; B5250, off A581 Chorley—Southport; SD5117], *Farmers Arms*: Big but friendly low-beamed pub/restaurant with good traditional food (not that cheap) all day, well kept largely Whitbreads-related ales, black cottagey furniture, red plush wall seats, rough plaster covered with plates, pastoral prints, clocks and brasses; darts; parking can be a problem when busy; bedrooms *(John Fazakerley)*

Egerton Gtr Man [Belmont Rd; SD7114], *Wright Arms*: Beamed coaching inn in very attractive scenery below Rivington Pike, warmly furnished and friendly, with good value bar food, restaurant, good range of beers, popular garden *(B M Eldridge)*

☆ **Entwistle** [Overshores Rd; village signed off Blackburn Rd N of Edgworth – OS Sheet 109 map ref 726177; SD7217], *Strawbury Duck*: Cosy dim-lit beamed and flagstoned country pub by isolated station – trains from Blackburn and Bolton; well kept Boddingtons, Marstons Pedigree and Timothy Taylors Best and Landlord with a weekly guest beer, popular bar food (all day Sat and Sun) inc Indian and children's dishes; games room, restaurant, good unobtrusive piped music (live Thurs), tables outside; children till 8.30; cl Mon lunchtime; comfortable bedrooms, good Pennine walks *(Bronwen and Steve Wrigley, Mr and Mrs Ashcroft, Chris Pierce, Bill and Lydia Ryan, Simon and Chris Turner, Andy and Jill Kassube, LYM)*

Fence [Wheatley Lane rd, just off A6068; SD8237], *Fence Gate*: Good-natured cosy local with well kept beers inc guests, bright pleasant young staff, good fresh food inc brasserie; bedrooms *(I Tattersall)*; [Pendle Forest], *Forest*: Refurbished pub with interesting reasonably priced food using excellent sometimes unusual fresh ingredients *(F J Robinson)*

Fleetwood [The Esplanade, nr tram terminus; SD3247], *North Euston*: Architecturally interesting Victorian hotel with decent food and real ales; bedrooms *(Sue Holland, Dave Webster)*

Formby Mer [Massams Lane; SD2808], *Freshfield*: Enjoyably refurbished in 'spit & sawdust' style, very popular esp weekends; good choice of well kept beers, good value food esp sausages *(G P Fogelman)*

☆ **Freckleton** [off A584 opp The Plough; towards Naze Lane Ind Est, then right into Bunker St; SD4228], *Ship*: Genuinely old, big windows looking out over the watermeadows from roomy nautical-theme main bar, good value bar food (not Mon evening) from sandwiches to bargain big steaks, Boddingtons on handpump, airy upstairs carvery and buffet, tables outside; children provided for *(J A Boucher, Jim and Maggie Cowell, LYM)*

Freckleton, *Coach & Horses*: Pleasantly refurbished lively local with Whitbreads-related ales, darts in separate bar *(Graham Bush)*

☆ **Galgate** [A6 S of Lancaster, handy for M6 junction 33; SD4755], *Plough*: Particularly well kept Boddingtons and several guest beers, good reasonably priced food inc super sandwiches, friendly efficient young licensees; open all day *(Dr H Huddart)*

☆ **Garstang** [northbound section of one-way system; SD4845], *Wheatsheaf*: Small and cosy neatly kept low-beamed pub with gleaming copper and brass, good range of well priced freshly cooked food inc notable specials (esp fish), good service, decent malt whiskies *(J Roy Smylie, BB)*

Gatley Gtr Man [SU8488], *Horse & Farrier*: Comfortable old coaching inn with attached restaurant, Hydes ale, reasonably priced food *(Chris Westmoreland)*

Glasson [nr Glasson Dock; SD4456], *Stork*: Welcoming and popular, with well kept beer, hard-working licensees, neat restaurant; clean bedrooms *(Richard Fawcett)*

Great Harwood [Railway Rd; SD7332], *Royal*: Good choice of changing well kept ales, many continental bottled beers, good range of food esp mixed grill; comfortable well equipped bedrooms *(Louis Cropper)*

Grindleton [off A69 via Chatburn; SD7545], *Duke of York*: Busy village pub with good if not cheap home-cooked food *(Simon Woodhouse)*

Halebarns Gtr Man [SJ7986], *Bulls Head*: Lively local with good food, wide choice of well kept beers, attractive garden with bowling green; entertainment some nights *(Ursula Tucker)*

Halton [Church Brow; SD5065], *White Lion*: Good atmosphere, well kept Mitchells beer; good quiz night Weds *(P A Legon)*

☆ **Haslingden** [Hud Rake; SD7823], *Griffin*: Opened 1994, brewing its own cheap Bitter, Mild, Stout, Porter, Sunshine, and the occasional Special, in the cellar; basic but clean and quiet, no juke box or games machines; take-home jugs available *(Carl Travis, Markus Buckley, Rosemarie Johnson)*

Hawkshaw Gtr Man [91 Ramsbottom Rd; SD7615], *Red Lion*: Recently attractively renovated, good food in bar and restaurant, well kept Thwaites, Timothy Taylors and Charles Wells beers; comfortable bedrooms, by River Irwell *(Andy and Jill Kassube)*

Haydock Mer [Liverpool Rd nr racecourse; SJ5797], *Angle*: Very good value food, esp T-bone steak *(J Mealea)*

☆ **Heaton with Oxcliffe** [shd be signed Overton off B5273 Lancaster—Heysham; SD4460], *Golden Ball*: Isolated by River Lune, road sometimes cut off at high tide; three cosy little low-beamed traditional rooms with hatch service and antique settles; very friendly staff, well kept Mitchells, reasonably priced food, warm fires, evening restaurant; seats outside; children welcome; open all day Sat in summer *(S R and A J Ashcroft, LYM)*

☆ **Heskin Green** [Wood Lane; B5250, N of M6 junction 27; SD5214], *Farmers Arms*: Cheerful sparkling clean country pub, spacious but cosy, with wide choice of well kept Whitbreads-related and good guest ales, heavy black beams, brasses and china, good value home cooking in two-level dining area, very friendly staff; picnic tables outside, good play area, pets' corner, peacocks and doves; open 12-11 *(Comus Elliott, Ray and Liz Monk, BB)*

Heswall Mer [45 Gayton Rd, lower village; SJ2782], *Victoria*: Two comfortable bars with Victorian decorations, overlooking River Dee and Welsh hills; good choice of food, very pleasant young staff, nice garden behind; bedrooms *(E G Parish)*

☆ *nr* **Heywood** Gtr Man [off narrow Ashworth Rd; pub signed off B6222 on Bury side of N Heywood; SD8513], *Egerton Arms*: Good interestingly prepared food from sandwiches up, imaginative vegetables and vegetarian dishes, lovely puddings, in isolated hillside pub with great views esp from terrace; good service, comfortable sofas and easy chairs in plush lounge by smart restaurant, simpler bar with old farm tools and coal fire even in summer, big-windowed small extension; keg beer, huge car park *(Graham Reeve, Laura Darlington, Gianluca Perinetti, Ian and Amanda Wharmby, BB)*

Hindley Gtr Man [Ladies Lane, by stn; SD6104], *Edington Arms*: Friendly and busy local with six well kept ales inc Holts,

Moorhouses Premier, and Savages Head brewed for the pub; back pool table *(Andrew Hazeldine)*; *Wiganer*: Convivial pub with Rugby League photographs and memorabilia everywhere; cheap Whitbreads-related ales and snacks *(Andrew Hazeldine)*

☆ **Holden** [the one up by Bolton by Bowland – OS Sheet 103 map ref 777494; SD7749], *Copy Nook*: Well renovated, with pleasant efficient staff (family connection with Horns at Goosnargh – see main entries), wide choice of good food, well kept beer *(Michael and Joan Melling)*

Hornby [SD5869], *Royal Oak*: Long low-beamed bar with well kept Thwaites, food inc good filled rolls, friendly service; darts, TV and games machine at one end, juke box, piped music *(Mr and Mrs M St-Amour)*

Hoylake Mer [Stanley Rd; SJ2289], *Green Lodge*: Famous old hotel associated with nearby Royal Liverpool golf links and many previous championships; well kept Burtonwood, good value food; bedrooms *(Maurice and Gill McMahon)*

Hurst Green [OS Sheet 103 map ref 685379; SD6838], *Shireburn Arms*: Quiet comfortable 17th-c hotel in idyllic setting with panoramic Ribble valley views, good reasonably priced food, Thwaites and other ales; separate tea room, occasional pianist ; bedrooms *(Jim and Maggie Cowell)*

Inglewhite [3 miles from A6 – turn off nr Owd Nells, Bilsborrow; SD5440], *Green Man*: Enthusiastic newish licensees doing good food; Greenalls kept particularly well *(Jim and Maggie Cowell)*

☆ **Irby Mer** [Irby Mill Hill, off Greasby rd; SJ2684], *Irby Mill*: Well kept Boddingtons, Cains Bitter and Dark Mild, Jennings, Tetleys, Theakstons Best and two guests such as Burts Nipper and Maclays, good house wines and decent lunchtime food (not Sun) in four low-beamed largely flagstoned rooms, straightforward pub furniture, coal-effect gas fire, relaxed local atmosphere, a few tables outside *(Tony and Lynne Stark, Maurice and Gill McMahon, E G Parish, Andrew Pollard, Paul Boot, BB)*

☆ **Lancaster** [Canal Side; parking in Aldcliffe Rd behind Royal Lancaster Infirmary, off A6 – cross canal by pub's footbridge], *Water Witch*: Cheerful canalside pub attractively converted from 18th-c barge-horse stabling, well kept real ales, flagstones, stripped stone, rafters and pitch-pine panelling; games room, juke box/piped music – louder as the night wears on; bar food, upstairs restaurant, seats outside; children allowed in eating areas, open all day Sat *(Brian Kneale, P Lawson, LYM)*

Lancaster [centre], *Jolly Sailor*: Popular nautical-theme pub with lots of woodwork, well kept Mitchells Best, Lancaster Bomber and Christmas Cracker, bar food *(Richard Lewis)*; [by M6 junction 34], *Lancaster Posthouse*: Hotel not pub, but roomy comfortable bar overlooking indoor swimming pool has well kept Courage Directors; friendly service, reliable restaurant ; comfortable bedrooms *(N H and B Ellis, BB)*

☆ **Lathom** [Wheat Lane, off A5209; Parbold Rd after Ring o' Bells heading into Burscough; SD4512], *Ship*: Big and busy well run pub tucked below canal embankment, several separate rooms with decor varying from interestingly cluttered canal memorabilia through naval pictures and crests to hunting prints, lots of copper and brass, cheap popular lunchtime food served promptly, friendly staff, ten well kept changing real ales, often interesting; games room *(S R and A J Ashcroft, D Grzelka, Gary and Sarah Goldson, John Fazakerley, Mike Schaffel, James Cowell, Philip and Carol Seddon, BB)*

Little Lever Gtr Man [SD7507], *Jolly Carter*: Clean tidy pub with modern decor, friendly helpful staff, good value food, well kept Boddingtons *(S G Brown)*

☆ **Liverpool** [Grafton St], *Cains Brewery Tap*: Splendid Victorian architecture, wooden floors, plush snug, lots of old prints, wonderful bar, flame-effect gas fire, newspapers; cosy relaxing atmosphere, friendly staff, good well priced food, and above all well kept attractively priced Cains ales with interesting guest beers and a popular brewery tour ending here with buffet and singing *(Richard Lewis, Stephen and Jean Curtis, Chris Walling, Andrew Stephenson)*

☆ **Liverpool** [Albert Dock Complex], *Pump House*: Relaxing multi-level conversion of dock building, good Mersey views, lots of polished dark wood, bare bricks, mezzanine and upper gallery with exposed roof trusses; marble counter with bulbous beer engines and brass rail supported by elephants' heads, tall chimney; wide choice of generous cheeses, some hot food, friendly efficient service; waterside tables, boat trips in season; keg beers, busy weekend evenings *(Geraint Roberts, John Fazakerley)*

☆ **Liverpool** [A5036 continuation S; promenade drive by former Garden Festival site], *Britannia*: Fantastic view across wide expanse of Mersey; welcoming efficient staff, good reasonably priced food *(Eric Locker, Brian Kneale)*

Liverpool Mer [Exchange St E], *Andersons*: Comfortable pub/wine bar, popular with business people for good cheap food like corned beef hash, Cains Dark Mild and Bitter, Marstons Pedigree *(R Lewis)*; [17 Cases St], *Globe*: Well kept Bass, Cains Bitter and Dark Mild, Higsons Bitter and Mild in local with tiny sloping-floor back lounge, friendly licensees, lots of prints of old Liverpool; lunchtime filled baps *(R Lewis)*; [23 Cumberland St], *Poste House*: Small comfortable backstreet local with room upstairs, well kept beers, lunchtime meals, friendly licensees *(R Lewis)*; [Roscoe

St], *Roscoe Head*: Small friendly pub, quiet and civilised, with outstandingly well kept Tetleys and maybe Jennings, immaculate tie collection *(Steve and Karen Jennings, Andrew Stephenson)*; [Dale St], *Ship & Mitre*: Friendly local with very wide changing choice of well kept unusual beers, good value food, friendly staff, pool *(R Lewis)*; [86 Wood St], *Swan*: Good range of well kept ales in backstreet bare-boards pub with rock juke box, Mon live music, good value home-cooked lunches, friendly staff *(R Lewis)*; [24 Rainford Gdns], *White Star*: Traditional basic local with well kept Bass-related and other beers such as Cains and Shepherd Neame, lots of woodwork and prints, friendly service *(Rich Sharp, R Lewis, H Novack)*

Longridge [SD6039], *Corporation Arms*: Friendly local with good value food inc Sun lunch, well kept Boddingtons, decent wine *(Paul Reeves, Wilfrid Murphy)*

Lowton Gtr Man [Golborne Rd; just off A580; SJ6196], *Hare & Hounds*: Attractive white-painted pub with rustic feel, oak beams, brass and earthenware, well kept Tetleys, friendly atmosphere, good range of food *(B M Eldridge)*

☆ **Lowton** Gtr Man [443 Newton Rd (A572 1½ miles S of A580; SJ6297], *Travellers Rest*: Friendly and relaxed, with good range of tasty food in bar and restaurant, friendly staff, small cosy rooms off main area, Greenalls ales, clocks, tapestry of pub; tables outside *(Olive and Ray Hebson, D Grzelka)*

Lydgate Gtr Man [51 Stockport Rd; SD9603], *White Hart*: Recently tastefully and extensively refurbished, with some concentration on good if not cheap food in separate area, log fires in most rooms, Boddingtons, Coach House Innkeepers, John Smiths Magnet, Lees and Websters on handpump; pretty village *(A J E Sykes)*

Lytham [Church Rd; SD3627], *County*: Well kept Boddingtons in spaciously refurbished pub ; good value bedrooms *(Graham Bush)*

☆ **Manchester** [127 Gt Bridgewater St, Oxford St side], *Peveril of the Peak*: Three traditional rooms around central servery, busy lunchtime but welcoming and homely evenings, with well kept Courage-related ales, cheap basic lunchtime food (not Sun), good service; lots of mahogany and stained glass, sturdy furnishings, interesting pictures, pub games inc table football; lovely external tilework, seats outside; children welcome, cl weekend lunchtimes *(Terry Buckland, Andrew Hazeldine, Bill and Lydia Ryan, Paul Carter, LYM)*

☆ **Manchester** [50 Great Bridgewater St; corner of Lower Mosley St], *Britons Protection*: Chatty, genuine and well run, with fine tilework and solid woodwork in rather plush front bar, attractive softly lit inner lounge with coal-effect gas fire, battle murals in passage leading to it; well kept though not cheap Ind Coope Burton, Jennings and Tetleys, good bar lunches, quiet and relaxed evenings; handy for GMEX centre *(Bill and Lydia Ryan, Paul Carter, Terry Buckland, BB)*

☆ **Manchester** Gtr Man [Honey St; off Red Bank, nr Victoria Stn], *Queens Arms*: Small welcoming pub with well kept Batemans XXXB, Mitchells Best, Timothy Taylors Landlord and Best, Theakstons Old Peculier and six changing guest beers, simple but often unusual lunchtime and evening bar food, coal fire, bar billiards, good juke box, bottle collection; open all day weekdays; unexpected views of Manchester across the Irk Valley and its railway lines from pleasant garden with new play area, worth penetrating the surrounding viaducts, scrapyards and industrial premises *(Brian Wainwright, S G Brown, D W Gray, Mark Stevens, Bill and Lydia Ryan, Andrew Hazeldine)*

☆ **Manchester** [4a Helmshaw Walk; nr Upper Brook St (A34), off Kincardine Rd/Whitekirk Cl], *Kings Arms*: Good cheap own-brewed West-Coast-style Yakima Grande Pale Ale, Ginger Beer (the real thing, packs a punch), and Old Soporific (stupefyingly strong); good value unusual lunchtime food, friendly staff, sparse furnishings, good-natured no-frills atmosphere; an improbable find, given the area *(Bill and Lydia Ryan, Andrew Hazeldine)*

☆ **Manchester** [6 Angel St; off Rochdale Rd], *Beer House*: Lively basic local with ten or so well kept changing ales (extra in summer), also farm ciders, Leifmanns Kriek and good range of bottled foreign beers; eclectic juke box, robust cheap bar snacks. lots of old local prints *(Richard Lewis, Bill and Lydia Ryan, Richard Wood, Fiona Lewry, Brian Wainwright)*

Manchester [Berry Brow, Clayton Bridge], *Bay Horse*: Friendly and relaxing, beams and lots of brass, good home-cooked food, Tetleys, summer barbecues; pleasant garden *(B M Eldridge)*; [66 Oldham St], *Castle*: Unspoilt traditional bar with Robinsons Mild, Bitter, Best and Old Tom from fine bank of handpumps, blues Thurs *(Andrew Hazeldine, Bill and Lydia Ryan)*; [86 Portland St], *Circus*: Two tiny rooms with very well kept Tetleys from cramped corridor bar; cl afternoons, and often looks closed other times (you have to knock) *(Bill and Lydia Ryan, Andrew Hazeldine)*; [71 Old Bury Rd, Whitefield, nr Besses o' the Barn Stn], *Coach & Horses*: Multi-room coaching inn built around 1830, little changed, very popular and friendly, with well kept Holts, table service, darts, cards *(Pete Baker)*; [Windsor Crescent (A6), opp Salford Univ], *Crescent*: Lively three-room studenty pub with fine changing choice of beers, good juke box *(Bill and Lydia Ryan, Andrew Hazeldine, Rupert Lecomber)*; [95 Cheetham Hill Rd (A665)], *Derby Brewery Arms*: Huge showpiece Holts pub with well kept cheap beer from the nearby brewery, good value lunchtime food hatch *(Brian Wainwright, S G Brown)*; [Wilmslow Rd, Fallowfield], *Friendship*: Reasonably priced food inc wide vegetarian choice in 1930s pub refurbished in modern style; piped music may be rather loud *(Ian Phillips)*; [High St, opp Arndale Centre], *Hogshead*: About 20 changing beers, many Whitbreads-related, food inc lots of speciality sausages; open all day *(John O'Donnell)*; [2 Portsmouth St, off Dover St nr Univ Student Union], *Jabez Clegg*: Lively long and lofty studenty bar with Whitbreads-related ales, raised area with 3-floor spiral stair leading nowhere, part like Bavarian beer keller with long tables; open all day, lunchtime food *(John O'Donnell)*; [47 Ducie St], *Jolly Angler*: Unpretentious backstreet local, small and friendly, with well kept Hydes, pool and darts, informal folk singing Mon, open all day Fri/Sat *(Pete Baker, Andrew Hazeldine, Bill and Lydia Ryan, Brian Wainwright, BB)*; [Bloom St, Salford], *Kings Arms*: Victorian pub with good choice of well kept real ales *(Andrew Hazeldine)*; [Wilmslow Rd, Didsbury], *Old Cock*: A dozen or more changing ales in big bare-boards pub with large wooden benches, bare boards, mix of locals and students; cheapish food, good fruit machine, tables outside, open all day Sun *(Graham Gowland, Martin Bennett)*; [Portland St], *Old Monkey*: Superb new central Holts pub, good comfortable design, cheap good beer *(S G Brown)*; [310 Deansgate], *Pig & Porcupine*: Split-level purpose-built pub with good friendly character, open all day (cl Su evening); wheelchair access *(Andrew Hazeldine)*; [Wilmslow Rd, Withington], *Red Lion*: Long low cottage-style Marstons pub opening into big two-level complex of plush seating with conservatory, friendly staff, popular good value food (not Sun evening), well kept Pedigree, Banks's Mild and a guest such as Bull Mastiff Ebony; bowling green *(Bill and Lydia Ryan, Matthew Callaghan, Ian Phillips)*; [15-17 Windmill St], *Royal Central*: Well kept Boddingtons, lots of brass and dark wood, food inc good specials; restaurant overlooks GMEX *(R V McKenna)*; [Sackville St], *Swinging Sporran*: Good beer, reasonable prices, good atmosphere *(Paul King)*; [37 Swan St], *Walkers*: Small and rather new, with well kept ales such as Batemans XB, Fullers London Pride, Marstons Pedigree and a couple of guests, lunchtime and evening food *(Andrew Hazeldine)*; [122 Gt Ancoats St], *White House*: Friendly local with big lounge and vault with pool table, well kept cheap ales alternating between Holts, Cains and others *(Andrew Hazeldine, Bill and Lydia Ryan)*; [43 Liverpool Rd, Castlefield], *White Lion*: Busy but friendly and comfortable, with good inexpensive food in nicely decorated dining area, four Whitbreads-related and guest ales, seats outside overlooking site of Roman fort; very handy for GMEX *(Paul and Karen Mason, Andrew Hazeldine)*; [139 Barlow Moor Rd, Didsbury], *Woodstock*: Impressive, roomy and welcoming conversion of old house hidden from road by trees, Bass (maybe drinks table service), good generous food inc vegetarian *(John O'Donnell)*

☆ **Mawdesley** [Bluestone Lane; follow Eccleston sign from village which is signed off B5246 Parbold—Rufford; SD5016], *Robin Hood*: Busy, neat and comfortable open-plan refurbished pub with button-back wall banquettes, reproduction Victorian prints, decorative plates, stained-glass seat dividers, some stripped stone; good value generous straightforward home cooking with fresh veg and cheap children's helpings, small pretty upstairs restaurant (often booked well ahead), friendly atmosphere and good service, well kept Whitbreads-related and guest ales, decent wines, children's room; piped nostalgic pop music, fruit machine; picnic tables on neat side terrace, good fenced play area *(Fred Collier, John Fazakerley, Jim and Maggie Cowell, Keith Croxton, BB)*

☆ **Mereclough** [302 Red Lees Rd; off A646 Burnley—Halifax – OS Sheet 103 map ref 873305; SD8730], *Kettledrum*: Friendly and cosy country local currently doing well, with wide choice of good value genuine home cooking, five well kept Courage and Theakstons ales, good service, fine views, extraordinary collections esp gruesome knives, partly no-smoking gaslit upstairs dining room; children allowed away from main bar till 9, seats outside *(Wayne Brindle, LYM)*

Morecambe [19 Bare Lane, Bare; SD4665], *Dog & Partridge*: Ten real ales inc Boddingtons and Timothy Taylors, freshly cooked bar food; new licensees have kept traditional interior *(Dr and Mrs Baker)*

Mossley Gtr Man [Manchester Rd (A635 N); SD9802], *Roaches Lock*: Canalside pub with Whitbreads-related beers, eating area, friendly efficient service, benches overlooking towpath *(Chris Westmoreland)*

☆ **Mottram** Gtr Man [off A57 M'ter—Barnsley; at central traffic lights turn opp B6174 into Broadbottom Rd; SJ9995], *Waggon*: Generous reliable food served very promptly all day in comfortable open-plan local, sensible prices, well kept Robinsons Best and Best Mild on electric pump, friendly waitresses, big central fire, good wheelchair access; picnic tables and good play area outside *(Michael and Janet Hepworth, BB)*

Much Hoole [Liverpool Old Rd (A59 SW of Preston); SD4723], *Rose & Crown*: Huge squarish pitched-roof family dining room with very popular good value home-cooked food (not Sun) esp fish, locals' bar with banquettes and piped pop music (may be loud, TV may be on too), games area with pool; Greenalls and Tetleys on handpump; children not unwelcome *(Jim*

and Maggie Cowell, Janet Lee)
New Brighton Mer [Magazine Lane; SJ2994], *Magazine*: Friendly bar with small rooms leading off, nr prom *(Don Kellaway, Angie Coles)*
New Hey Gtr Man [113 Huddersfield Rd; SD9311], *Bird in the Hand*: Quiet friendly local with particularly well kept Sam Smiths OB, real fire in lounge, games in smoke room *(Bill and Lydia Ryan, Andrew Hazeldine)*
Newburgh [A5209 Standish—Ormskirk; SD4710], *Red Lion*: Previously popular dining pub taken under management by Burtonwood, given the usual treatment with flame-effect gas replacing coal fires etc, and a standardised menu, but still useful for food all day; piped music, cheerful service, bedrooms *(LYM)*
Oakenclough [NE of Garstang; SD5347], *Moorcock*: Good views, lots of olde-worlde charm, beams and exposed stonework, open fires, good food, live entertainment Sat evenings *(Simon Woodhouse)*
Ogden Gtr Man [Lanebottom; E of New Hey; SD9512], *Bulls Head*: Good generous food esp chips, well kept beer and quick friendly staff *(Mr and Mrs Wharmby)*
Oldham Gtr Man [161 St John St, Lees; SD9504], *Grapes*: 19th-c stone pub, two warm beamed rooms, friendly service, Tetleys-related ales; open all day *(Thomas Williams, Louise North)*; [Den Lane, Springhead], *Peels Arms*: Two homely beamed rooms, well kept Whitbreads-related ales, reasonably priced bar lunches *(Thomas Williams)*
Ormskirk [County Rd; SD4108], *Hayfield*: Relaxing refurbished pub with Courage-related ales, good range of well priced main courses, good friendly service *(Dr and Mrs Griffin)*
Oswaldtwistle [Haslingden Old Rd; A677/B6231; SD7327], *Britannia*: Attractive traditional core with log-burning ranges, reasonably priced bar food with some emphasis on fresh fish, friendly atmosphere, Thwaites Bitter and Mild; sun-trap back terrace and play area; food all day Sun, children in family restaurant *(John Fazakerley, LYM)*
☆ **Parbold** [Alder Lane (A5209); SD4911], *Stocks*: Relaxed local atmosphere in two rooms off island bar extending into roomy beamed dining area with separate servery doing good value home-cooked food (not Sun evening) inc vegetarian and sizzlers; well kept Tetleys Bitter and Dark Mild and a guest such as Archers, busy evenings *(Rona Murdoch, Comus Elliott, Andrew Hazeldine, BB)*
☆ **Pendleton** [SD7539], *Swan With Two Necks*: Welcoming olde-worlde village pub below Pendle Hill, good value interesting well presented food with lots of fresh veg, well kept ale *(Mrs Lyn Jones, LYM)*
Pleasington [Pleasington Lane; SD6426], *Railway*: Good variety of wholesome plain food, friendly landlord; can get a bit smoky *(S and J Cumming-Johnson)*
Poulton Le Fylde [Ball St; SD3439], *Thatched House*: Busy thatched pub with well kept Whitbreads-related and guest ales *(Rosemarie Johnson)*
Preesall [192 Park Lane; towards Knott End; SD3647], *Black Bull*: Tetleys pub with friendly landlord, good guest beer, wide range of generous good value food; well liked by older people *(Kevin Potts)*
Preston [166 Friargate; SD5330], *Black Horse*: Thriving friendly old-fashioned pub with full Robinsons ale range and Hartleys XB, lunchtime food, side rooms, upstairs 1920s-style bar, unusual curved and tiled main bar, panelling, stained glass and mosaic floor; pictures of old town, lots of artefacts, good juke box *(Richard Lewis, Graham Bush)*; [17 Fox St], *Exchange*: Lunchtime food, Theakstons and Youngers ales (cheap Thurs); pool, juke box *(R Lewis)*; [15 Fox St], *Fox & Grapes*: Busy traditional pub with bare boards, basic fittings, old Preston pictures, lunchtime food, well kept Theakstons and Youngers – huge throughput of No 3 *(R Lewis)*; [30 Avenham St], *Gastons*: Multi-level two-bar pub with its own Arkwright Mild, Bitter, Clog Dancer, Torchlight, Pierpoints and a guest like Jennings Snecklifter all well kept; pool, darts, fruit machine, TV; decent wines and bar food *(R Lewis)*; [33 Market St], *Market*: Next to Preston's Victorian covered market, ornately decorated cabinet, comfortable seating, friendly staff, lunchtime food, back pool table and good juke box; well kept Matthew Browns and Theakstons *(R Lewis)*; [35 Friargate (by Ringway)], *Old Black Bull*: Recently converted into basic alehouse with good mix of customers inc lots of students, lots of well kept changing beers, good value food; unmodified prewar green-tiled frontage with original stained glass *(Graham Bush, R Lewis)*; [24 Lancaster Rd, by Guildhall], *Stanley Arms*: Gin palace interior with fine mirrors, bare boards, four areas, different levels; friendly staff, popular lunchtime food, 16 handpumps with well kept changing ales from small breweries, German and Belgian beers, Bulmer's cider; pool room, TV, can be packed evenings, weekend bouncers *(R Lewis, Graham Bush)*; [rly stn], *Station Bar*: One of the few serving real ale – Bass and Thwaites Daniels Hammer; can be smoky, with machines and music *(R Lewis)*
Rawtenstall [Newchurch Rd; SD8123], *Red Lion*: Open fire, well kept Wilsons, good bar food; small restaurant *(Brian Richardson)*
☆ **Riley Green** [A675/A6061; SD6225], *Royal Oak*: Cosy low-beamed three-room pub nr canal, decent reliable food, Thwaites Bitter and Mild, friendly efficient service; ancient stripped stone, open fires, seats from high-backed settles to red plush armchairs, turkey carpet, soft lighting, interesting model steam engines; can be packed

weekends *(John Fazakerley, Bronwen and Steve Wrigley, BB)*
Rimington [SD8045], *Black Bull*: Free house with Theakstons bitter, good innovative bar snacks, restaurant *(W J Proctor)*
Ringley [right off A667 at sign for Kidds Garden Centre; SD7605], *Horseshoe*: Good for a quiet drink, with good value lunchtime food; three areas off main bar, interesting local pictures, pleasant back garden ; well behaved children lunchtime *(Bronwen and Steve Wrigley)*
☆ **Rochdale** Gtr Man [Cheesden, Ashworth Moor; A680 towards Edenfield; SD8316], *Owd Betts*: Isolated but cosy moorland pub with great views, three low-beamed areas, oak settles, brasses, open fires, stripped stone; well kept Greenalls Bitter and Mild, food inc good sandwiches, efficient friendly service *(J E Rycroft, K H Frostick, BB)*
Rochdale Gtr Man [Toad Lane; SD8913], *Baum*: Lots of old advertisements, conservatory, seats in garden, reasonably priced food, well kept Boddingtons, John Smiths and Ruddles, TV and piped music; handy for Rochdale Pioneers Museum *(JJW, CMW, Steven Williams)*; [470 Bury Rd; A6222/A6452 continuation], *Cemetery*: Wide choice of well kept real ales and bottled beers in old-fashioned pub high above rd, good bare-boards parlour, two comfortable little Victorian-style lounges, tiled facade with etched windows *(Grant Redfern)*
Roughlee [nr Nelson; SD8440], *Bay Horse*: Old village pub in beautiful valley with pleasant restaurant, good value meals inc fine puddings *(A and M Dickinson)*
Sale Gtr Man [Rifle Rd, nr M63 junction 8; SJ8092], *Jacksons Boat*: Fishing memorabilia, Tetleys-related ales, food from separate servery (limited Sun), real country feel despite being handy for Mway; walks in Mersey Valley Country Park *(P Yearsley)*
☆ **Simonstone** [Trapp Lane, off School Lane – Simonstone—Sabden trans-Pendle rd, OS Sheet 103 map ref 776356; SD7735], *Higher Trapp*: Attractive refurbished bar with good views, well kept beer; bedrooms *(Wayne Brindle)*
☆ **Slaidburn** [B6478 N of Clitheroe; SD7152], *Hark to Bounty*: Charming Forest of Bowland village, relaxed country atmosphere, friendly new licensees doing well; decor a pleasant mix of old and new, open fire, brasses, lots of tables with new chef doing good value interesting food, S&N ales, good value wines; a nice place to stay, good walks *(Richard R Dolphin, Bronwen and Steve Wrigley, LYM)*
Southport Mer [Union St; SD3316], *Guest House*: Traditional unspoilt town pub with well kept Whitbreads-related ales, Cains Mild and two guest beers, limited food, no music *(Julian Desser)*
St Helens Mer [Cooper St; SJ4996], *Turks Head*: Full range of Cains beers kept well, also Holts; friendly atmosphere *(James Featherstone)*
Stalybridge Gtr Man [Mottram Rd; SJ9698], *Hare & Hounds*: Converted to a traditional rather upmarket town chop house, Lees on handpump *(Neville Kenyon)*
☆ **Standish** [very handy for M6 junction 27/28], *Beeches*: Comfortable modern seats and decent food in roomy steakhouse-style dining pub, partly flagstoned; decent food, Walkers real ale, good value wines, friendly efficient service; bedrooms *(D Grzelka)*
☆ **Standish** Gtr Man [Platt Lane, Worthington – OS Sheet 108 map ref 575114; SD5711], *Crown*: Civilised oasis, chesterfields, armchairs, fresh flowers and open fire in comfortable panelled bar, well kept ales such as Bass, Bass Mild and Boddingtons, airy dining extension with wide range of good reasonably priced food, pleasant conservatory; children allowed away from bar *(D Grzelka, Ardill and Anne Booth, Paul Boot, LYM)*
Standish, *Forresters Arms*: Greenalls local with good value food esp specials and home-made pies in big dining area, Greenalls Original *(Annette and Stephen Marsden)*
☆ **Stockport** Gtr Man [552 Didsbury Rd (off A5145), Heaton Mersey; SJ8691], *Griffin*: Thriving unspoilt local with cheap well kept Holts Bitter and Mild in four unpretentiously Victorian rooms off central servery with largely original curved-glass gantry, basic furnishings, no piped music; lunchtime food in dining extension, seats outside *(N P Greensitt, BB)*
☆ **Stockport** [14 Middle Hillgate; SJ8991], *Red Bull*: Beamed and flagstoned local, very friendly and well run, with very well kept Robinsons Best and Best Mild from nearby brewery, good value bar lunches (not Sun), substantial settles and seats, open fires, lots of pictures and brassware, traditional island servery; quiet at lunchtime, can get crowded evening *(Bill and Lydia Ryan, LYM)*
☆ **Stockport** [12 Little Underbank; steps from St Petersgate], *Queens Head*: Long narrow late Victorian pub with separate snug and back dining area; good bustling atmosphere, reasonable bar food, well kept Sam Smiths on handpump, rare brass cordials fountain, daily papers, old posters and adverts; some live jazz, otherwise piped; famous narrow gents' *(Bill and Lydia Ryan, S Demont, T Barrow)*
Stockport [Market Pl], *Bakers Vaults*: Good value generous home-made food such as Thai chicken curry or Cajun chicken *(Louise Woolliscroft)*; [82 Heaton Moor Rd], *Plough*: Cheap pleasant food and well kept Tetleys-related beers in big open-plan pub with numerous dark little corners, idiosyncratic landlady *(Lee Goulding)*
☆ **Summerseat** Gtr Man [½ mile from M66 junction 1 northbound, off A56 N via Bass Lane then Cliffe Avenue, then bear right], *Waterside*: Striking conversion of tall

19th-c cotton-mill building, flagstones, tiles, restored machinery, attractive setting with tables outside; good range of well kept ales, decent wine, authentic Thai food (landlord's wife from Thailand); service can sometimes slow down; very popular with young people evenings, piped pop music may be loud *(Gordon Tong, Peter Crawshaw, LYM)*

☆ **Tarleton** [70 Church Rd; off A59/A565 Preston—Southport; SD4420], *Cock & Bottle*: Popular village dining pub with wide choice inc interesting starters, lots of game and fish; Thwaites Best Bitter and Mild, friendly service, separate public bar *(John and Jane Horn, Jim and Maggie Cowell, K R and I Hall)*

☆ **Thornton Hough** Mer [Church Rd (B5136); SJ3081], *Seven Stars*: Decorous two-room dining with easy chairs and sofa as well as banquettes and wheelback chairs, Whitbreads-related ales with guests such as Cains, tables outside; bedrooms *(John Allsopp, Mr and Mrs C Roberts, Don Kellaway, Angie Coles, LYM)*

Tunstall [A683 S of Kirkby Lonsdale; SD6173], *Lunesdale Arms*: Friendly and attractive village pub, food entirely fresh, well kept beers, good wine; pretty village, Bronte church *(Mr and Mrs Sayers)*

☆ **Waddington** [SD7243], *Lower Buck*: Traditional friendly and busy local with Theakstons and other well kept ales, popular food, hatch-service lobby, front bar with built-in dresser, plain back room, pool room; pretty village *(J A Boucher, Wayne Brindle, BB)*

Waddington [SD7146], *Waddington Arms*: Two airy rooms with woodburners, well kept Morlands Old Speckled Hen, Theakstons Mild and Bitter and a beer brewed for the pub, Waddingtons Bitter, imaginative well prepared food (not Mon) using fresh local produce, well chosen piped music, no-smoking area; children welcome; bedrooms *(Arthur and Margaret Dickinson)*

Westhead [Wigan Rd; SD4307], *Prince Albert*: Lots of character, smallish rooms, open fires, real ales, good value food; comfortable newly converted bedrooms *(Philip and Carol Seddon)*

☆ **Westhoughton** Gtr Man [490 Wigan Rd; SD6505], *Hartcommon*: Basic three-roomed traditional local with well kept Theakstons Best and a guest such as Marstons Pedigree, pub games, friendly landlord *(Andrew Hazeldine, Bill and Lydia Ryan)*

Westhoughton [2 Market St (A58)], *White Lion*: Traditional small-roomed hatch-service pub with well kept Holts *(Bill and Lydia Ryan, Andrew Hazeldine)*

White Stake [Wham Lane; not far from M6 junction 29; SD5126], *Farmers Arms*: Popular mainstream dining pub with eight changing Whitbreads-portfolio guest beers *(Jim and Maggie Cowell, Fred Collier)*

Wigan Gtr Man [69 Poolstock Lane; SD5805], *Beer Engine*: Up to a dozen or so changing ales, live music – several bands at annual beer festival; other events inc Laurel & Hardy festival *(Kerry Docherty)*; [New Market St], *Tudor House*: Basic but cosy, with unusual changing guest beers, good range of food all day, coal fires, popular with students esp evenings and weekends; live rock most Weds, Irish Thurs; tables outside; bedrooms *(Peter Bird)*

☆ **Wiswell** [just NE of Whalley; SD7437], *Freemasons Arms*: Cosy and pubby, with wide choice of good value well presented interesting food (must book restaurant Sat evening), friendly efficient service, good range of beers, lots of malt whiskies; lovely village below Pendle Hill; cl Mon/Tues evening *(A and M Dickinson, Dr and Mrs D E Awbery)*

☆ **Woodford** Gtr Man [550 Chester Rd; A5149 SW of BAe entrance; SJ8882], *Davenport Arms*: Unspoilt traditional country pub, simple but comfortable, with small rooms, coal fires, friendly staff, well kept Robinsons Best and Best Mild, good reasonably priced home cooking lunchtime (toasted sandwiches evening), good games room, no-smoking room; tables on front terrace and in attractive garden *(Pat and Tony Young, P and M Rudlin)*

Woodley Gtr Man [Hyde Rd; A560 Stockport—Hyde; SJ9392], *Lowes Arms*: Well kept Robinsons on electric pump, carefully cooked food at sensible prices, friendly atmosphere, unobtrusive piped music *(Wes Perry)*

☆ **Wrea Green** [Station Rd; SD3931], *Grapes*: Busy but roomy open-plan local with well cooked imaginative food in pleasant clean dining area, well kept Boddingtons, Marstons Pedigree and Theakstons, open fire, efficient courteous staff; tables out overlooking village green, picturesque neighbouring church *(Cyril Higgs, Graham Bush)*

Wrightington Bar [Mossy Lea Rd; B5250, nr M6 junction 27; SD5313], *Tudor*: Good reasonably priced food in bar and separate restaurant, friendly atmosphere, old-world charm with beams and open fires *(John Winstanley)*

Post Office address codings confusingly give the impression that some pubs are in Lancashire when they're really in Yorkshire (which is where we list them).

Leicestershire, Lincolnshire and Nottinghamshire

Pubs doing specially well in these counties at the moment include the Blue Ball at Braunston (very good food, nice atmosphere), the Martins Arms at Colston Bassett (smart and upmarket, with very good imaginative food), the White Horse at Empingham (very popular food, by Rutland Water), the very foody Old Barn at Glooston (closed lunchtimes nowadays), the friendly Bewicke Arms at Hallaton, the old-fashioned Cap & Stocking at Kegworth (Bass from a jug), the friendly Nelson & Railway near its parent brewery in Kimberley, the Wig & Mitre in Lincoln (good food all day from 8am), the civilised Nevill Arms at Medbourne (a very nice place to stay at), the Red Lion at Newton (another civilised place, very good cold buffet), the Peacock at Redmile (a lovely place for a meal out – we choose it as Leicestershire Dining Pub of the Year), and the grand old George in Stamford (much loved over the years). Two of this year's new main entries here are very strong indeed on good beer – the handsomely resurrected Victoria in Beeston, and the Brewers Arms in Snaith, an attractively converted mill which brews its own. Two – the Chequers at Gedney Dyke and the Bakers Arms at Thorpe Langton – have really memorable food. In Nottinghamshire, drinks prices are well below the national average; they are close to average in Leicestershire and Lincolnshire. We found pubs tied to the local breweries Batemans and Hardys & Hansons tended to be particularly cheap. In the Lucky Dip section at the end of the chapter, pubs showing specially well these days include the Welby Arms at Allington, Tally Ho at Aswarby, Reindeer at East Bridgford, Five Bells at Edenham, Finch Hatton Arms at Ewerby, Black Horse at Grimston, Old White Hart at Lyddington, Muskham Ferry at North Muskham, King William at Scaftworth, Vine at Skegness, Old Brewery at Somerby, Bramley Apple in Southwell, White Hart at Tetford, Finches Arms at Upper Hambleton, Cross Keys at Upton, Black Horse at Walcote and Noel Arms at Whitwell; we have inspected the great majority of these and can firmly vouch for their appeal. There is a better choice of pubs in Nottingham than in either Lincoln or Leicester.

As Humberside is being abolished and divided between North Yorkshire and Lincolnshire in summer 1996, we have included pubs south of the Humber (covered by a Humberside chapter in previous editions) here instead this year.

BEESTON (Notts) SK5338 Map 7

Victoria

Dovecote Lane, backing on to railway station

This roomy pub – carefully converted from what was an almost derelict railway hotel – has now been taken over by Tynemill, the small group run by Chris Holmes who was a leading light in the Campaign for Real Ale in its early days. The friendly manager here used to run the Lincolnshire Poacher in Nottingham, another of these pubs, and his brother works in the kitchen here. Anyone who has enjoyed the thoroughly traditional feel of the Poacher will certainly like this. It's quite long and narrow, the three downstairs rooms keeping their original layout and windows, with the woodwork and floorboards stripped to show the grain, an unfussy decor, good chatty atmosphere and simple solid traditional furnishings. The area on the left has now been reworked for sensibly priced food service – including lots of filled rolls (from £1), winter steak and kidney pie (£4.95), chicken with tarragon, cream and white wine or fresh tuna steak (£5.50), steaks (from £7.95), and breast of barbary duck with Cointreau and orange sauce (£8.95); a higher than usual proportion is vegetarian, such as spicy stuffed aubergines or cauliflower and broccoli bake with spinach and ricotta (£3.95), and goat's cheese wrapped in vine leaves and served with tabbouleh or stilton and walnut tart (£4.25). Puddings like apple crumble, caramel tart or jam roly poly (£1.50), and Sunday roast lunch (£4.95); the eating area is no smoking. The main focus is on the well kept changing real ales on handpump – ten or more, from independent breweries, with four regulars such as Batemans XB, Courage Directors, Marstons Pedigree, and Sam Smiths OB, and guests that change maybe twice a day like Bathams Bitter, Enville Ale, Hop Back Mild, Malton Pale Ale, Woodfordes Wherry, and Yates Bitter. Also, Biddenden and Lanes ciders, 100 malt whiskies and 20 others, and several wines by the glass; dominoes, cribbage and occasional piped music. There are picnic tables in a pleasant area outside, looking over on to the station platform – the trains pass within feet. *(Recommended by Jack and Philip Paxton, David and Shelia, Jane Hosking, Ian Burniston, Andrew Abbott, Andy and Jane Beardsley, Gary Siddall)*

Free house ~ Licensee Neil Kelso ~ Real ale ~ Meals and snacks (12-2.30, 5-8) ~ (0115) 925 4049 ~ Children in eating area till 8 ~ Jazz every 2nd Sunday, folk once a week ~ Open 11-3, 5-11 Mon-Thurs; 11-11 Fri/Sat

BRAUNSTON (Leics) SK8306 Map 4

Blue Ball

Village signposted off A606 in Oakham

Although much emphasis is obviously placed on the very good food here, what readers also like is the relaxed and informal atmosphere. It's said to be Rutland's oldest pub and the main area preserves its original form of separate rooms, while the furnishings and decorations – not too fussy – are individual and interesting. Well presented, the food might include home-made pâté of the day (£2.95), moules marinières, a choice of cheeses with salad and a walnut oil dressing or stilton soufflé (£3.50), spicy fish cakes (£3.95), tagliatelle with tomato, garlic and basil sauce (£4), spare ribs (£4.95), spaghetti with ginger and vegetables (£5), and puddings such as summer pudding with a raspberry coulis, sloe gin and redcurrant bavarois with a vanilla sauce or profiteroles (£2.50); children's menu (£4.50); very good service, even when busy. Well kept Bass, Greene King Abbot, Marstons Bitter and Pedigree, Tetleys, and Timothy Taylors Landlord on handpump, and up to 8 wines by the glass (including one sparkling). Dominoes, shove-ha'penny (not much used), and piped music; one room is no smoking. The licensees also own the Peacock at Redmile in the same county. *(Recommended by Jim Farmer, S G Brown, D Goodger, Julie Peters, David and Shelia, Joan and Michel Hooper-Immins, Brian and Jill Bond, Stephen Brown, Brian Atkin)*

Free house ~ Licensees Colin and Celia Crawford ~ Real ale ~ Meals and snacks (12-2, 6.30-10) ~ Restaurant (closed Sun evening and all day Mon) ~ (01572) 722135 ~ Children welcome ~ Open 12-3, 6-11

Old Plough ⚲

Village signposted off A606 in Oakham

This is a very attractive place – both inside and out – and although there's now quite an emphasis on the good food, the atmosphere is still nice and pubby and they hold lots of social and sporting events for locals. A good choice of attractively served meals includes home-made soup (£1.85), really big filled rolls (from £2.75), filled baked potatoes (from £2.95), king scallops with a japanese, ginger and honey glaze (£4.50), vegetable or steak and kidney pies or fresh Whitby scampi (£6.95), game pie (£7.25), lemon chicken fillets (£7.50), salmon and ricotta cannelloni (£7.95), steaks (from £9.95), and puddings like brandy snap and Baileys cheesecake, fresh fruit salad or mulled wine pudding (from £2.25); very good service. The traditional bars have upholstered seats around cast-iron-framed tables under the heavy and irregular back beams, and plenty of brass ornaments on the mantlepiece. At the back is a stylish modern no-smoking conservatory dining room. The lounge bar has well kept Oakham Jeffrey Hudson, Ruddles Best, and John Smiths on handpump, a good, interesting well noted wine list, and Scrumpy Jack cider. The carpeted public bar has darts in winter; maybe piped music. Picnic tables shelter among fruit trees, and there's a boules pitch. The inn-sign is attractive. *(Recommended by M and J Back, George Atkinson, Paul Cartledge, Jim Farmer, L Walker, David and Gillian Phillips, J D Cloud)*

Free house ~ Licensees Andrew and Amanda Reid ~ Real ale ~ Meals and snacks (till 10) ~ Restaurant ~ (01572) 722714 ~ Children welcome ~ Open 11-3, 6-11; closed 25 Dec

BURROUGH ON THE HILL (Leics) SK7510 Map 4

Stag & Hounds

Village signposted from B6047 in Twyford, 6 miles S of Melton Mowbray

New licensees have taken over this little village pub, and are placing a lot of emphasis on their freshly cooked, home-made food using home-grown herbs – no freezer packs or microwaves. From a changing menu there might be garlic mushrooms with hot stilton sauce or mozzarella, beef tomatoes and basil (£2.95), moules marinières (£3.50), chicken with mustard, tarragon, grapes and white wine or fresh salmon in cucumber and basil (£6.95), steaks (from £7.50), baked halibut in fresh tomato and tarragon sauce (£7.95), monkfish on a bed of roasted mediterranean vegetables (£10.50), and home-made puddings (from £2.95). Well kept Courage Directors, Marstons Pedigree, Morlands Old Speckled Hen, and a beer they call Burrough Hill Dry Hopped brewed only for them on handpump. The bar has traditionally pubby furnishings and good open fires; piped music. There are seats in the garden, with a children's play area. *(Recommended by David and Glenys Lawson, David and Shelia, J D Cloud, Stephen Brown; more reports on the new regime, please)*

Free house ~ Licensees Craig and Barbara Pinnick ~ Real ale ~ Meals and snacks (not Mon) ~ (01664) 454375 ~ Children welcome ~ Open 12-3, 6-11; closed Mon lunchtime

COLEBY (Lincs) SK9760 Map 8

Bell 🛏

Far Lane; village signposted off A607 S of Lincoln, turn right and right into Far Lane at church

Built in 1759, this welcoming and reliable dining pub has added three new en-suite double rooms this year. It's a cosy place, and the three communicating carpeted rooms each has a roaring winter log fire, low black joists, pale brown plank-panelling, a variety of small prints, and 60 number plates from around the world. Generously served and nicely presented food includes soup (from £1.50), doorstep sandwiches (from £1.95), garlic mushrooms in tomato and basil sauce (£2.50), burger or sausages (£2.95), cauliflower and broccoli au gratin (£4.75), beef, mushroom and Guinness pie (£5.95), beef napoli (slices of beef wrapped around a minced pork and cheese stuffing in a tomato and basil sauce £7.25), and chicken en croute with smoked salmon and prawns (£7.95); Wednesday night is fish night with fresh fish delivered daily from Grimsby. Well kept Bass, Flowers Original, and Tetleys on handpump, and several malt whiskies; friendly service. There's a quite separate pool room, darts, dominoes, juke box, and satellite TV. Several picnic tables outside, and walks along the Viking Way. *(Recommended by Caroline Kenyon, M and J Back, Ian Phillips, Roger Bellingham, Mr and Mrs J Brown, Lawrence Pearse)*

Pubmaster ~ Tenants Robert Pickles and Sara Roe ~ Real ale ~ Meals and snacks (till 10) ~ Restaurant ~ (01522) 810240 ~ Children welcome ~ Live bands Fri evenings ~ Open 11.30-3, 6-11 ~ Bedrooms: /£35B

COLSTON BASSETT (Notts) SK7033 Map 7

Martins Arms

Signposted off A46 E of Nottingham

Some changes to this civilised and rather smart place include the landscaping of the one acre garden, the completion of the new lavatories, and the opening up of a bedroom with private sitting room – they will be adding two more rooms shortly. But it's the food that readers like most with much emphasis on the fresh, daily-delivered produce, and home-made chutneys, vinegars, and petit fours. In the bar, this might include sandwiches and rolls (from £2.75; walnut and brie with slices of smoked chicken £3.95, and pan-fried chilli beef in warm pitta bread £4.95), Welsh rarebit or potato cake filled with stilton or cheddar (£4.95), creamed smoked haddock topped with a poached egg and finished with a mornay sauce, a fine ploughman's with Melton Mowbray pork pie with local ham, stilton or cheddar, slices of apple, and pickles, home-made gnocchi with fresh tomato and basil sauce or chicken sausages with a leek salad, fish hot pot with a fennel sauce topped with puff pastry or sauté of duck and rabbit with figs and thyme, with bacon, stout and dumplings (£8.95), sirloin steak (£11.95), and lovely puddings such as sweet crêpes filled with a lemon mincemeat with a warm brandy cream sauce, mascarpone and yoghurt terrine with a caramel sauce or sticky toffee pudding (£3.50). They have occasional gourmet or wine tasting evenings; smart uniformed staff. Well kept Adnams, Bass, Batemans XB and XXXB, Greene King Abbot, Hook Norton Best, Mitchells Lancaster Bomber, Morlands Old Speckled Hen, and Timothy Taylors Landlord on handpump, a good range of malt whiskies and cognacs, an interesting wine list, an open fire, and a proper snug. Furnishings are a comfortable lived-in mix. No music, just the murmur of conversation; cards and croquet, and they can arrange riding and ballooning. The well laid out restaurant is decorous and smart, with well spaced tables. The pub is run by the same people as the Crown at Old Dalby, also a main entry in this chapter. No children. *(Recommended by Jack and Philip Paxton, David and Shelia, Malcolm Taylor, Brian Atkin, Brian White, David Raine, Andy and Jane Beardsley, Roy Bromell, R K Wright)*

Free house ~ Licensees Lynne Strafford Bryan and Salvatore Inguanta ~ Real ale ~ Meals and snacks (till 10; not Sun or Mon evenings) ~ Restaurant (not Sun evening) ~ (01949) 81361 ~ Open 12-3(2.30 if very quiet), 6-11

DONINGTON ON BAIN (Lincs) TF2382 Map 8

Black Horse

Between A153 and A157, SW of Louth

Walkers are fond of this busy village pub as it's on the Viking Way (muddy boots must be left in the hall), and there are views across the rolling Wolds; picnic tables in the back garden. Inside, much emphasis is placed on the popular bar food, served in relaxed, cheerful surroundings: soup (£1.95), filled baked potatoes (from £1.95), ploughman's (£2.95), omelettes (from £4.25), macaroni cheese or cottage pie (£4.50), steak pie or vegetable nut bake (£4.75), trout and almonds (£5.25), steaks (from £5.95), a huge mixed grill (£10.25), children's dishes (£1.50) and specials such as rack of ribs with barbecue sauce (£5.95), chicken a la king (£6.95), and breast of duck in an orange sauce (£7.50). Well kept Adnams, Courage Directors, John Smiths, Ruddles Best and Shepherd Neame Spitfire on handpump; friendly service. A softly lit little inner room has some unusual big murals of carousing Vikings, while the snug back bar, with cushioned seats by the log fire in the reconstructed brick inglenook, has very low black beams, and antlers around the wall lanterns. There's more room in the main bar area, popular with locals, and with some heavy-horse prints and harness, a very twisty heavy low beam under its ceiling joists, and a big woodburning stove; the public bar (another log fire) has a games room off, with darts, pool, dominoes, video game and juke box; maybe unobtrusive piped music. No dogs. *(Recommended by PGP, Nigel and Lindsay Chapman, Caroline Kenyon, Julie Peters, Derek and Sylvia Stephenson, Stephen Brown, Paul S McPherson, Anthony Barnes)*

Free house ~ Licensees Tony and Janine Pacey ~ Real ale ~ Meals and snacks (till 10) ~ (01507) 343640 ~ Children in eating area of bar and in games room; not late in evening ~ Open 11.30-3, 7-11; closed Mon lunchtime Jan-Apr ~ Bedrooms: £25S/£40S

DRAKEHOLES (Notts) SK7090 Map 7

Griff Inn

Village signposted from A631 in Everton, between Bawtry and Gainsborough

Seats in the neatly kept landscaped gardens here are quite a draw in summer, and you can look down over the canal basin and the flat valley of the River Idle. The former Chesterfield Canal passes under the road through a long tunnel and is now restored and navigable; a map in the lounge shows the route. The civilised and carefully colour-matched main lounge bar has small plush seats around its tables, and little landscape prints on silky-papered walls; one bar is no smoking. Bar food includes sandwiches, salads (from £3.75), carvery (from £3.95), steak pie or gammon and egg (£4.75), seafood platter (£5.95), and daily specials (from £4.95). As well as the no-smoking restaurant, there's a more airy brasserie-style summer restaurant and a cosy cocktail bar. Boddingtons, Flowers, and Whitbreads Castle Eden on handpump; friendly service; trivia and piped music. *(Recommended by R and C E Nightingale, Mrs M J Aston, June and Tony Baldwin, Simon Collett-Jones, Paul Cartledge)*

Free house ~ Licensees Michael and Barbara Edmanson ~ Real ale ~ Meals and snacks (till 10) ~ Restaurant ~ (01777) 817206 ~ Children welcome ~ Open 11.30-3, 5.30(7 Sat)-11 ~ Bedrooms: £35B/£50B

DYKE (Lincs) TF1022 Map 8

Wishing Well

21 Main Street; village signposted off A15 N of Bourne

A surprise among much more modern houses, this friendly village inn has a good solid reputation for good value, tasty food. Well-served dishes include sandwiches (from £1.80), cheddar ploughman's (£3.50), lincolnshire sausages (£4.25), a selection of home-made pies (from £4.50), vegetarian fuellitine, prawn salad or lemon sole (£4.95) and daily specials; popular Sunday lunch (£8.50) for which booking is essential, huge puddings, children's dishes. At the dining end of the long, rambling front bar there is indeed a wishing well, as well as lots of heavy beams, dark stone, brasswork, candlelight and a cavern of an open fireplace. The carpeted lounge area has green plush button-back low settles and wheelback chairs around individual wooden tables. Well kept Greene King Abbot and Tetleys on handpump, with guest beers such as Batemans Strawberry Fields, Bunces Old Smokey and Eldridge Pope Cricketers. The quite separate public bar, smaller and plainer, has sensibly placed darts, pool, shove-ha'penny, dominoes, fruit machine and juke box. There's a play area by the garden. *(Recommended by Jenny and Michael Back, F J and A Parmenter, Mark and Caroline Thistlethwaite, Mark Hydes, Edward Storey, M J Morgan)*

Free house ~ Licensee Barrie Creaser ~ Real ale ~ Meals and snacks ~ Restaurant (closed Sun evening) ~ (01778) 422970 ~ Children welcome ~ Open 11-3, 6-11 ~ Bedrooms: £19.50S/£39S

EMPINGHAM (Leics) SK9408 Map 4

White Horse

Main Street; A606 Stamford—Oakham

There's always a cheerful bustle in this consistently popular old inn, and the licensees work very hard to make sure they are offering what people want. This year they have completely refurbished all the bedrooms (some are in a delightfully converted stable block). The open-plan lounge bar has a big log fire below an unusual free-standing chimney-funnel, lots of fresh flowers, and a very relaxed and comfortable atmosphere; one eating area is no-smoking. Well presented, good bar food includes home-made soup (£1.95), chicken liver or stilton and leek pâtés (£2.95), chicken, ham and mushroom pie (£5.50), ploughman's (£5.85), moules marinières or vegetable enchilada (£5.95), chicken breast filled with cheese and wrapped with bacon (£6.25), steaks, and puddings like sherry trifle or bread and butter pudding (£2.95); they also offer morning coffee and afternoon tea. Helpings are big, and vegetables are served separately in a little dish. Well kept Courage Directors, John Smiths, Ruddles County, Wadworths 6X, and a guest beer on handpump, kept under light blanket pressure; fruit machine and piped music. Outside are some rustic tables among urns of flowers, and the pub is on the edge of Europe's largest man-made lake, with good water-sports facilities. *(Recommended by Gordon Theaker, A and M Dickinson, AMM, CP, Peter Brimacombe, Alan and Heather Jacques, A M McCarthy, H Bramwell, Rita Horridge, V and E A Bolton, Philip da Silva)*

Courage ~ Lease: Roger Bourne ~ Real ale ~ Meals and snacks (till 10) ~ Restaurant ~ (01780) 460221 ~ Well behaved children in eating area of bar and in Orange Room ~ Open 11-11 ~ Bedrooms: £32(£42B)/£45(£55B)

EXTON (Leics) SK9211 Map 8

Fox & Hounds

Signposed off A606 Stamford—Oakham

Just two miles from Rutland Water, this strikingly tall stone building is handy for walkers on the Viking Way, and there are seats among large rose beds on the well kept back lawn, overlooking paddocks. Inside, the high-ceilinged lounge bar has some dark red plush easy chairs as well as wheelback seats around lots of dark tables, hunting and military prints on the walls, brass and copper ornaments, and a winter log fire in a large stone fireplace. Bar food includes soup (£2.40), ploughman's (from £3.50), liver and bacon (£5.50), lasagne or home-made steak and kidney pie (£6.25), and local trout (£7.75), with evening extras like scampi (£5.95) or rump steak (£9.50). Well kept Sam Smiths OB and guests like Fullers London Pride and Tetleys on handpump; piped music. The lively and quite separate public bar has darts, pool, cribbage, dominoes, juke box, fruit machine, and video game. Service can slow down if coach parties are in. *(Recommended by Stephen Brown, Tony Gayfer, Michael Betton, Jim Farmer, WHBM, H Bramwell, L Walker; more reports please)*

Free house ~ Licensee David Hillier ~ Real ale ~ Meals and snacks ~ Restaurant (not Sun evening) ~ (01572) 812403 ~ Children in eating area of bar ~ Open 11-3, 6-11 ~ Bedrooms: £22/£36

GEDNEY DYKE (Lincs) TF4125 Map 8

Chequers

Village signposted off A17 Holbeach—Kings Lynn

A few feet below sea level, this warmly welcoming small Fenland village pub appropriately serves lots of really fresh fish and seafood, changing day by day depending on what's available, such as grilled plaice, lemon sole, skate wing, Cromer crabs and Brancaster scallops. There's a wide choice of other good freshly cooked attractively presented food, too, including sandwiches, ploughman's or slices of smoked chicken on strips of vegetables, coated with a peanut, chilli and sesame dressing (£3.50), smoked salmon and prawn roulade (£4.95), steak and mushroom pudding (£5.50), Mediterranean vegetable and polenta pudding with fresh tomato coulis or mushroom and sweetcorn timbale with star anise sauce (£5.95), Cajun spiced pork steak on noodles with a yoghurt and herb dip (£6.50), and chicken breast filled with mozzarella cheese and roasted with bacon or a South African dish with spiced minced lamb with apricots and almonds in an almond sauce (£6.95); also speciality ice-creams, and enjoyable old-fashioned puddings such as bread and butter with whisky sauce; roast Sunday lunch. Everything's kept spotless, with an open fire in the bar, a small rather old-fashioned no-smoking restaurant area at one end, and an elegantly done new dining conservatory at the other, overlooking a garden with picnic tables. Well kept Adnams Bitter and Mild, Bass, Batemans XXXB, Greene King Abbot, and Morlands Old Speckled Hen on handpump, four or five decent wines by the glass, elderflower pressé, good coffee with real cream, friendly licensees, polite attentive service. ***(Recommended by G P Kernan, Viv Middlebrook, R and L Scrimshaw, Mark and Caroline Thistlethwaite, Peter Hann, F J and A Parmenter, John Honnor)***

Free house ~ Licensee Judith Marshall ~ Real ale ~ Meals and snacks (12-1.45, 7-9) ~ Restaurant ~ (01406) 362666 ~ Children welcome ~ Open 12-2, 7-11; closed 25/26 Dec

GLOOSTON (Leics) SP7595 Map 4

Old Barn ★

From B6047 in Tur Langton follow Hallaton signpost, then fork left following Glooston signpost

Over the last winter, this 16th-c pub was altered to offer two no-smoking bars instead of the restaurant with its attendant bar; tables can be reserved here. The unchanged lower beamed main bar has stripped kitchen tables and country chairs, pewter plates, Players cricketer cigarette cards, and an open fire. The same blackboard menu is now offered throughout the pub: sautéed avocado, mushrooms and peppers on granary toast or marinated fresh salmon (£3.95), hot roast beef sandwich (£4.75), pork fillet rossini (£8.95), supreme of chicken with prawns and pernod (£9.25), roast duck breast with a gooseberry and walnut glaze (£9.95), and medallions of beef fillet in black bean sauce (£12.25). Due to their busy evenings and remote situation, the pub is closed on weekday lunchtimes; on Saturday lunchtime they only serve snacks – good Sunday lunch (3 courses £9.50). Four well kept real ales on handpump rotated from a wide choice of beers like Adnams Broadside, Bass, Batemans XB, Fullers London Pride, Greene King Abbot and IPA, Hook Norton Old Hookey, Morlands Old Speckled Hen, Nene Valley Rawhide, Theakstons Best, and Wadworths 6X; decent wines (several by the glass). There are a few old-fashioned teak seats in front, with picnic tables by roses under the trees behind. The french-style shower-and-wash cabinets please readers, but might perhaps suit best those with at least a modest degree of mobility. Well behaved dogs welcome. ***(Recommended by F Davy, David Atkinson, H Paulinski, Margaret and Roy Randle, Eric Locker, Frank Cummins, Jim Farmer, A J Morton, Stephen, Julie and Hayley Brown, Joan and Michel Hooper-Immins, Gwen and Peter Andrews)***

Free house ~ Licensees Charles Edmondson-Jones and Stewart Sturge ~ Real ale ~ Meals and snacks (not weekday lunchtimes or Sun evening) ~ Restaurant (not Sun evening) ~ (01858) 545215 ~ Well behaved children welcome ~ Open 7-11 during the week; 12-2.30, 7-11 Sat; closed Sun evening ~ Bedrooms: £37.50B/£49.50B

We say if we or readers have seen dogs or cats in a pub.

GRANTHAM (Lincs) SK9135 Map 7

Beehive £

Castlegate; from main street turn down Finkin Street opposite St Peter's Place

This simple no-frills pub's real claim to fame is its remarkable sign – a hive full of living bees, mounted in a lime tree. Happily they're kept 25 feet up. It's been here since at least 1830, and probably the eighteenth century, making this one of the oldest populations of bees in the world. Bar food includes a good value basic ploughman's with cheddar or stilton (from £2.40), sandwiches or filled jacket potatoes, home-made chilli con carne (£2.50), gammon (£2.95), changing daily specials (from £2.50) and home-made puddings (from £1.55); cheerful service. The bar itself is comfortably straightforward, with Boddingtons, Woodfordes Wherry and two guest beers on handpump; fruit machine, trivia, video game, good juke box and satellite TV. The back bar is no smoking at lunchtime. *(Recommended by Derek and Sylvia Stephenson, Bernard and Marjorie Parkin, Brian White, RB, Ian Phillips)*

Free house ~ Licensee S J Parkes ~ Real ale ~ Lunchtime meals and snacks (not Sun) ~ (01476) 67794 ~ Children welcome ~ Open 11.30-11; 11.30-5, 7-11 Sat; closed 25 Dec

HALLATON (Leics) SP7896 Map 4

Bewicke Arms ★

On good fast back road across open rolling countryside between Uppingham and Kibworth; village signposted from B6047 in Tur Langton and from B664 SW of Uppingham

From the front of this old thatched inn you can watch the various activities on the village green, especially entertaining on Easter Monday when there's a 'bottle-kicking' race (they actually use miniature barrels), or in the summer when there may be Morris dancing. Picnic tables on a crazy-paved terrace behind the whitewashed building look over the ex-stableyard car park to the hills behind. Inside, there's a friendly welcome for locals and visitors alike, and the unpretentious beamed main bar has two small oddly shaped rooms with farming implements and deer heads on the walls, pokerwork seats, old-fashioned settles (including some with high backs and wings), wall benches, and stripped oak tables, and four copper kettles gleaming over one of the log fires; the bottom room is no-smoking during the week. Big helpings of well-liked bar food include basics like sandwiches, ploughman's, and grills, with daily specials such as egg and prawn mayonnaise (£3.95), deep-fried brie with cranberry dip (£4.45), meaty or vegetarian lasagne (£5.85), fresh local trout with dill and lemon butter (£6.80), chicken boursin (£7.60), chicken breast with bacon and mushrooms in a port, cream and fresh rosemary sauce (£8.20), and puddings such as treacle sponge and custard (£2.50); get there early for a seat (though they take bookings on Saturday evening). Service is charming and flexible. Well kept Marstons Pedigree, Ruddles Best and County and Websters Yorkshire on handpump; darts, fruit machine in the side corridor, and piped music. No dogs. They have a big self-catering apartment to rent. *(Recommended by Wayne Brindle, Jack and Philip Paxton, D Goodger, Eric Locker, Jim Farrmer, Margaret and Roy Randle, Rona Murdoch, Mr and Mrs J Back, P G Plumridge, David and Shelia)*

Free house ~ Licensee Neil Spiers ~ Real ale ~ Meals and snacks ~ Restaurant ~ (01858) 555217 ~ Well behaved children welcome ~ Open 12-2.30, 7-11

HECKINGTON (Lincs) TF1444 Map 8

Nags Head

High Street; village signposted from A17 Sleaford—Boston

Comfortable and rather cosy, the left-hand part of the snug two-roomed bar in this 17th-c village pub has a coal fire below the shiny black wooden chimney-piece in what must once have been a great inglenook, curving into the corner and taking up the whole of one end of the small room – it now houses three tables, one of them of beaten brass. On the right there are red plush button-back built-in wall banquettes, small spindleback chairs, and an attractive bronze statuette-lamp on the mantlepiece of its coal fire; also, a lively watercolour of a horse-race finish (the horses racing straight towards you), and a modern sporting print of a problematic gun dog. From an ever-changing menu, bar food might include soup (£1.95), sandwiches (from £1.95), garlic mushrooms (£2.95), pears, stilton and spinach grilled on toast (£3.50), smoked salmon quiche (£4.25), homity pie (£4.50), steak and kidney pie (£4.95), beef olive with mushroom and red wine sauce (£5.50), fresh salmon with cream, lemon and chive sauce (£5.74), and puddings like fruit crème brûlée or sticky toffee pudding (£2.50); Sunday roast. Well kept Wards Sheffield Best and Kirby Strong on handpump; cheery, efficient service; pool, shove-ha'penny, trivia, and juke box. The garden behind has picnic tables, and it's not far to an unusual eight-sailed windmill. *(Recommended by P R Morley, Howard James, DC, Anthony Barnes, Brian Horner, Brenda Arthur, Owen Davies, Susan and John Priestley, F J and A Parmenter)*

Wards ~ Lease: Bruce and Gina Pickworth ~ Real ale ~ Meals and snacks ~ (01529) 460218 ~ Well behaved children welcome ~ Open 11-3, 5-11 ~ Bedrooms: £22/£32

HOSE (Leics) SK7329 Map 7

Rose & Crown

Bolton Lane

There are usually eight real ales on handpump at a time in this welcoming, atmospheric pub – often including brews you won't often find in this area, from smaller breweries in the west country or in the north; forthcoming beers are posted up on the walls. Over the past year these have included Ashvine Tanker and Hop and Glory, Badger Best, Eldridge Pope Hardy, Felinfoel Double Dragon, Fullers London Pride, Gibbs Mew Bishops Tipple, Hardingtons Best and Old Lucifer, Harviestoun Manor, Moorhouse Pendle Witches Brew, Oakhill Yeoman and Wickwar Brand Oak, Shepherd Neame Spitfire, and Wye Valley to name just a few. They also stock several malt whiskies. The more-or-less open-plan bar has red plush furnishings, and pool, darts, cribbage, dominoes, a fruit machine, trivia and juke box. The restaurant and part of the lounge bar are no smoking. Bar food includes filled rolls (from £1.25), home-made soup (£1.55), garlic mushrooms (£1.80), ploughman's (from £3.75), steaks (from £6.55), gammon and egg or trout and almonds (£6.75), salads (from £6.75), daily specials such as deep-fried camembert (£1.95), fillet of pork au poivre (£7.95), and fresh salmon with a brandy and lobster sauce (£8.50), and puddings (£1.95). There are tables on a fairy-lit sheltered terrace behind the building and a fenced family area at the rear of the car park. Campers and caravanners are welcome. *(Recommended by Chris Raisin, Joan and Michel Hooper-Immins, D C Roberts, June and Malcolm Farmer, Jack and Philip Paxton, Andrew Stephenson, J D Cloud, Stephen Brown, R M Taylor)*

Free house ~ Licensees Carl and Carmel Routh ~ Real ale ~ Meals and snacks (till 10, 9 Sun) ~ Restaurant ~ (01949) 60424 ~ Children in eating area of bar ~ Open 12-2.30, 7-11; closed 25 Dec

KEGWORTH (Leics) SK4826 Map 7

Cap & Stocking ★ £

Under a mile from M1 junction 24: follow A6 towards Loughborough; in village, turn left at chemists' down one-way Dragwall opposite High Street, then left and left again, into Borough Street

Each of the two determinedly simple front rooms in this friendly little pub has a coal fire, and on the right there's lots of etched glass, big cases of stuffed birds and locally caught fish, fabric-covered wall benches and heavy cast-iron-framed tables, and a cast-iron range; the back room has french windows to the garden. There's a genuinely old fashioned flavour which extends to Bass being served the traditional way in a jug direct from the cask, and they also keep Hancocks HB, M & B Mild, and Ruddles County on handpump, with a guest such as Badger Tanglefoot, Courage Directors, Mansfield Old Baily, Shepherd Neame Bishops Finger or Vaux Waggle Dance. Good value bar food includes filled rolls (from 80p; hot ones from £1), soup (£1.25), ploughman's (from £3.20), pizzas (from £3.40), chilli con carne or vegetable curry (£3.50), Hungarian goulash (£4.25), beef stroganoff (£4.95), daily specials such as apricot pork, Sri Lankan chicken or Szechuan meatballs (from £3.95), and puddings like hot treacle sponge (£1). Dominoes, cribbage, trivia, Monday evening quiz, and floodlit boules in the pleasant garden. *(Recommended by R and A Cooper, AMM, CP, Jane Hosking, Ian Burniston, Peter and Jenny Quine, D R E Berlin, Jim Farmer, Dr and Mrs J H Hills, Karen Eliot, Jack and Philip Paxton, G C Hackemer, Mike and Kathleen York, David Eberlin, A J Morton, Dave Braisted, R N Hutton, Stephen Brown, John and Carol Holden, Norma and Keith Bloomfield, Paul Wreglesworth, Wayne Brindle, Mrs Elizabeth Howe, Derek and Sylvia Stephenson, Mayur Shah)*

Bass ~ Lease: Graham and Mary Walsh ~ Real ale ~ Meals and snacks ~ (01509) 674814 ~ Children welcome ~ Open 11.30-3, 6(6.30 in winter)-11

KIMBERLEY (Notts) SK5044 Map 7

Nelson & Railway £

2 miles from M1 junction 26; Kimberley signposted from exit roundabout, pub in Sation Rd, on right from centre

Not surprisingly, the Hardys & Hansons Bitter, Classic and Mild ales here are particularly well kept – the brewery is directly opposite; several malt whiskies. It's a friendly place and the beamed bar and lounge have an attractive mix of period Edwardian-looking furniture, and are interestingly decorated with brewery prints and railway signs; it can get busy. Good value food includes sandwiches (from £1.10; hot rolls from £1.45), soup (£1.20), burgers (from £1.65), filled baked potatoes (from £1.95), cottage pie (£2.50), tomato and vegetable tagliatelle (£3.95), chicken curry (£4.50), gammon and egg (£4.95), sirloin steak (£5.95), puddings (£1.65), and children's meals (£1.50); good housekeeping, efficient service; darts, alley skittles, dominoes, cribbage, fruit machine, chess, Scrabble and juke box. There are tables and swings out in a good-sized cottagey garden. The unusual name comes from the days when the pub was just yards away from two competing railway stations. *(Recommended by M W Turner, Jane Hosking, Ian Burniston, M Carey, A Groocock, Alan and Eileen Bowker, Gary Roberts, Ann Stubbs, Jack and Phillip Paxton, Wayne Brindle, TBB, G P Kernan, CW, JW, Derek and Sylvia Stephenson, Barbara Wensworth, Mark Bradley, Ian and Nita Cooper, Professor Ron Leigh)*

Hardys & Hansons ~ Tenants Harry and Pat Burton ~ Real ale ~ Meals and snacks (12-2.30, 5.30-9) ~ (0115) 9382177 ~ Children in eating area of bar ~ Open 11-3, 5-11 Mon-Weds, all day Thurs-Sat ~ Bedrooms: £18/£31

KNIPTON (Leics) SK8231 Map 7

Red House

Village signposted off A607 Grantham—Melton Mowbray

You may be welcomed in the hall of this fine, Georgian ex-hunting lodge by friendly dogs and cats – a bit like a private house. The roomy turkey-carpeted bar, divided by a central hearth with a woodburning stove, has sturdy old-fashioned furnishings, hunting pictures, a delft shelf of sporting or game bird decorative plates, and a relaxed, friendly atmosphere. A neatly furnished no-smoking conservatory opens off the airy no-smoking restaurant, and a good choice of rewarding bar food might include black pudding fritters or linguine napolitan (£2.95), ploughman's (£3.95), aubergine and tomato lasagne or lattice tart of oyster mushrooms, peppers and crème fraîche (£5.25), cassoulet of rabbit and pigeon, chicken breast in honey and lemon sauce or roast lamb on ratatouille (£5.45), and home-made puddings such as deep sour cherry tart with a fruity glaze or poached pears (£2.45). Well kept Marstons Pedigree, Tetleys and a guest beer changing weekly such as Jennings Cumberland or Morlands Old Speckled Hen on handpump and electric pump, a good choice of wines including 120 bin-ends, 20 malt whiskies, and quite a few brandies and ports; service is friendly and obliging. The public bar area has darts, cribbage, and fruit machine; there may be unobtrusive piped music. *(Recommended by Derek and Sylvia Stephenson, Jack and Philip Paxton, David and Shelia, A and R Cooper, R A Hobbs, Elizabeth and Anthony Watts, R M Taylor)*

Free house ~ Lease: Robin Newport ~ Real ale ~ Meals and snacks ~ Restaurant ~ (01476) 870352 ~ Children welcome till 9 ~ Occasional trad jazz or folk ~ Open 11-3(4 Sat), 6-11 ~ Bedrooms:£21.50(£32.50B)/£32(£46.50B)

LAXTON (Notts) SK7267 Map 7

Dovecote

Signposted off A6075 E of Ollerton

Friendly and welcoming, this redbrick house is next to three huge medieval open fields, and this is one of the few parts of the country still to be farmed using this historic method. Every year in the third week of June the grass is auctioned for haymaking, and anyone who lives in the parish is entitled to a bid – as well as to a drink. A former stable block behind the pub has a visitor centre explaining it all. A window in the central room by the bar still looks out over the village to the church tower, and there are brocaded button-back built-in corner seats, stools and chairs, and a coal-effect gas fire; it opens through a small bay which was the original entry into another similar room. Around the other side a simpler room with some entertaining Lawson Wood 1930s tourist cartoons leads through to a pool room with darts, juke box, fruit machine, cribbage and dominoes. Bar food includes sandwiches (from £1.50), home-made soup (£1.70), home-made steak and kidney pie or lasagne (£4.20), mushroom stroganoff (£4.25), lemon chicken (£4.60), paella (£4.70), seafood au gratin (£4.90), steaks (from £6.50), and children's meals (£2); pleasant service. Well kept Mansfield Riding and a couple of guest beers on handpump or electric pump; helpful service. There are white tables and chairs on a small front terrace by a sloping garden with a disused white dovecote, and a children's play area. *(Recommended by Geoffrey and Irene Lindley, R F Wright, David and Shelia)*

Free house ~ Licensees Stephen and Betty Shepherd ~ Real ale ~ Meals and snacks ~ (01777) 871586 ~ Children welcome ~ Open 11.30-3.30, 6.30-11

LINCOLN SK9872 Map 8

Wig & Mitre ★ (food) (wine)

29 Steep Hill; just below cathedral

On the steeply picturesque alley that runs down from the cathedral towards the centre, this very civilised and welcoming old town pub still has some of its original 14th-c features, such as exposed oak rafters and part of the medieval wattle-and-daub by the stairs. Downstairs, the cheerful, simpler bar has pews and other straightforward furniture on its tiles, and a couple of window tables on either side of the entrance; the upstairs dining room has settees, elegant small settles, Victorian armchairs, shelves of old books, and an open fire. It's decorated with antique prints and more modern caricatures of lawyers and clerics, with plenty of smart magazines and newspapers lying about – the kind of place you'd feel comfortable in on your own. What makes this pub really special is the incredible range of food that they serve from lots of different menus, some changing twice a day and served non-stop from 8 o'clock in the morning to around midnight. They're happy to let you mix and match items from the various lists, and however rushed or busy they are service always stays cordial and efficient. The several menus vary in style and price but a rough selection of dishes might include sandwiches (from £2.95), good soup (£3.25), good farmhouse cheeses with biscuits or fresh bread (£3.50), a proper breakfast (£5), warm salad of smoked chicken with crispy bacon and quail eggs (£5.50), baked cheese soufflé with cream and ham (£5.75), chicken, mushroom and tarragon pie (£6), sauté of lamb's sweetbreads with mushrooms in a tarragon mustard cream (£6.95), mixed tagliatelle with asparagus, spinach and sun-dried tomatoes in a creamy blue cheese sauce (£8), roast saddle of rabbit with bacon, mushrooms, herbs and white wine sauce (£10.95), collops of monkfish with pink peppercorn dressing (£12.50), and puddings such as chocolate and brandy terrine with coffee sauce or tiramisu cheesecake (£2.95). There's an excellent and extensive, if somewhat pricy, selection of over 95 wines, many of them available by the glass, with an emphasis on South African, Australian, Chilean or other regional wines. Sam Smiths OB and Museum on handpump, lots of liqueurs and spirits, freshly squeezed orange juice and good coffee. *(Recommended by Ian Phillips, Leigh and Gillian Mellor, Susan and Alan Dominey, H K Dyson, Joan and Michel Hooper-Immins, E J Wilde, David and Shelia, Caroline Kenyon, Dr and Mrs A K Clarke, A M McCarthy, Graham and Karen Oddey, Michael Sargent, P Neate, Rita Horridge, Mrs A Loxley, M Baxter, B R Shiner)*

Sam Smiths ~ Tenants Michael Hope and Paul Vidic ~ Real ale ~ Meals and snacks (8am-11pm) ~ Restaurant ~ (01522) 535190 ~ Children welcome ~ Open 8am-11pm, including Sun; closed 25 Dec

LOUGHBOROUGH (Leics) SK5319 Map 7

Swan in the Rushes £

The Rushes (A6)

'A rattling good old-fashioned pub' is how one reader describes this chatty place – and many agree with him. The overall character is lively down-to-earth informality with a friendly welcome and good food. But the main draw is the fine collection of beers – interesting German, Belgian and other bottled beers, and on handpump well kept Archers Golden, Boddingtons, Marstons Pedigree, and Springhead Roaring Meg, and four regularly changing guests; two ciders, a good range of malt whiskies, and country wines. There are several neatly kept separate room areas, each with its own style – though the most comfortable seats are in the left-hand bay-windowed bar (which has an open fire) and in the snug back dining room. It can get very crowded, but service is good. Very reasonably priced, the home-made bar food includes filled rolls, a variety of ploughman's (from £2.95), tagliatelle bolognaise or chilli con carne (£2.95), broccoli and cauliflower mornay filled pancakes (£3.40), bobotie, beef in ale or chicken in apple wine (£3.95), 8oz rump steak (£4.50), and puddings like apple strudel (£1.30). Shove-ha'penny, cribbage, dominoes, juke box, and backgammon. The simple bedrooms are clean and cosy, and breakfasts excellent. *(Recommended by Joan and Michel Hooper-Immins, Bruce Bird, David and Shelia, S G Brown, Jack and Philip Paxton, Jim Farmer)*

Free house ~ Licensee Andrew Hambleton ~ Real ale ~ Meals and snacks (12-2, 6-8.30; not Sat/Sun evenings) ~ Children in dining room ~ Blues or R&B Sat evening, occasional folk Fri evening ~ Open 11-2.30, 5-11; 11-11 Fri/Sat ~ Bedrooms: £20(£25B)/£30(£35B)

LYDDINGTON (Leics) SP8797 Map 4

Marquess of Exeter

Village signposted off A6003 N of Corby

After a painstaking refurbishment using original techniques and raw materials (there was a terrible fire last year), this warmly welcoming and handsome stone hotel is now up and running again. It's well liked for its friendly atmosphere, and they do good bar food such as sandwiches (£1.50), soup (£1.75), broccoli and tomato bake (£4.75), liver and sausage casserole or home-made lasagne (£4.95), a pie of the day or honey-roast rack of lamb with a peach coulis (£5.95), gammon and egg (£7.10), sirloin steak (£7.95), and home-made puddings (£1.85). Good service from neatly welcoming staff. Well kept Ruddles Best and County on handpump. The pub is named after the Burghley family, who have long owned this charming village. *(Recommended by Jim Farmer, John Dennett; more reports please)*

Free house ~ Licensee L S Evitt ~ Real ale ~ Meals and snacks ~ Restaurant (not Sun evening) ~ (01572) 822477 ~ Children in restaurant ~ Open 11.30-3, 6-11 ~ Bedrooms: £40B/£55B

MEDBOURNE (Leics) SP7993 Map 4

Nevill Arms

B664 Market Harborough—Uppingham

Very much enjoyed by readers at the moment, this bustling and handsome old mullion-windowed pub is attractively placed by a little footbridge over the River Welland where there are ducks (this is becoming a popular spot for plastic yellow duck races for charity). The appealing main bar has an especially cheerful atmosphere, as well as two winter log fires, chairs and small wall settles around its tables, a lofty, dark-joisted ceiling and maybe a couple of dogs or a cat. A spacious back room by the former coachyard has pews around more tables (much needed at busy times), and there's a conservatory with newspapers – but in summer most people prefer eating at the tables outside on the grass by the dovecote. Well kept Adnams, Ruddles Best and County and two fortnightly changing guests on handpump, and country wines. Good value bar food includes home-made soup (£1.95), sandwiches (from £1.55, open sandwiches £3.25), egg and prawn mayonnaise or ploughman's (£3.25), interesting cheese platters, filled baked potatoes (£3.45), chilli con carne (£4.75), daily specials, puddings, and children's meals (£1.95). Darts, shove-ha'penny, table skittles, cribbage, dominoes, with hopp-la, shut-the-box, and Captain's Mistress on request. Readers particularly enjoy staying here, and the licensees have bought a neighbouring cottage in order to extend their bedrooms. *(Recommended by A J Morton, Margaret and Roy Randle, M J Morgan, Joan and Michael Hooper-Immins, Philip Orbell, Eric Locker, Frank Cummins, R K Wright, P G Plumridge, Douglas and Patricia Gott, Mr and Mrs Ray, WHBM, Ian and Sue Mackenzie)*

Free house ~ Licensees E F Hall and Partners ~ Real ale ~ Meals and snacks (till 9.45) ~ (01858) 565288 ~ Children welcome ~ Open 12-2.30, 6-11 ~ Bedrooms: £40B/£50B

NEWTON (Lincs) TF0436 Map 8

Red Lion ★

Village signposted from A52 E of Grantham; at village road turn right towards Haceby and Braceby; pub itself also discreetly signed off A52 closer to Grantham

With prices unchanged for two years, the food in this civilised old place is as good as ever. What readers still like best is the range of excellent imaginatively displayed salads. You choose as much as you like, with six different types of fish such as fresh salmon, nine cold meats, and pies; a small helping is £6.95, normal £7.95, and large £8.95, with children's helpings £3.50. The home-made soups are also very good (£1.90), and there's a choice of hot dishes in the winter months including one or two local specialities such as stuffed chine of pork or spicy lincolnshire sausages; they also do rich puddings, a Sunday carvery, and sandwiches on request. The licensee used to be a butcher, and it does show – the meat and fish could hardly taste better. The welcoming and very neatly-kept communicating rooms have old-fashioned oak and elm seats and cream-rendered or bare stone walls covered with farm tools, malters' wooden shovels, a stuffed fox, stag's head and green woodpecker, pictures made from pressed flowers, a dresser full of china, and hunting and coaching prints. Very well kept Bass and Batemans XXXB on handpump; fresh flowers, friendly service, unobtrusive but well reproduced piped music, a fruit machine, and nice dogs. During the day and at weekends two squash courts run by the pub can be used by non-members. The neat, well sheltered back garden has some seats on the grass and on a terrace, and a good play area. The countryside nearby is ideal for walking, and acccording to local tradition this village is the highest point between Grantham and the Urals. *(Recommended by Gordon Thornton, Michael and Susan Morgan, F J and A Parmenter, Howard and Margaret Buchanan, E J Wilde, Alan and Eileen Bowker, June and Malcolm Farmer, Malcolm Phillips, Brian and Jill Bond, RB, Chris Walling, Roy Briggs, Barbara Taylor)*

Free house ~ Licensee Graham Watkin ~ Real ale ~ Meals and snacks (till 10) ~ (01529) 497256 ~ Children welcome ~ Open 11.30-3, 6-11; closed 25 Dec

NORMANTON ON TRENT (Notts) SK7969 Map 7

Square & Compass

Signposted off B1164 S of Tuxford

The bar in this cosy village pub has fresh flowers and an attractive grandfather clock, and is divided by an enormous woodburning stove in a central brick fireplace. There are several more or less separate snug areas, alcoves and bays, mainly with green plush furnishings, farming photographs, a flowery red carpet, red curtains and roughcast shiny cream walls; piped music. Good value bar food includes soup (£1.10), sandwiches (from £1.10), burgers (from £1.40), home-made pâté (£2.25), double sausage and egg (lunchtime, £2.45), steak and kidney pie (from £3.95), mushroom and nut fettucine or curry (£4.25), chicken kiev (£4.50), sirloin steak (£7.25), puddings (from £1.60), and children's meals (from £1.60); Sunday roast. Well kept Adnams, Bass, Everards, Stones and Theakstons Best on handpump. The public side has pool, table skittles, cribbage, dominoes, juke box. Outside, there are seats and a children's play area with wendy house, swings, and Mother Hubbard boot house. *(Recommended by Derek and Sylvia Stephenson, L R Jackson, Mike and Maggie Betton, Mrs M Littler, John Honnor, Jean-Bernard Brisset, Eamon Green, Wayne Brindle)*

Free house ~ Licensee Janet Lancaster ~ Real ale ~ Meals and snacks (till 9.45) ~ Restaurant (not Sun evening) ~ (01636) 821439 ~ Children welcome ~ Open 12-3, 6-11, 12-11 Sat ~ Family bedroom: £26S

NOTTINGHAM SK5640 Map 7

Fellows Morton & Clayton £

54 Canal Street (part of inner ring road)

From a big window in the quarry tiled glassed-in area at the back of this carefully converted canal building, you can see the little brewery that makes the very good own-brew real ales: Samuel Fellows and Matthew Claytons; both are well kept on handpump and very reasonably priced. They also keep Boddingtons, Flowers IPA, Timothy Taylord Landlord, Wadworths 6X and Whitbreads Castle Eden. It's a softly lit place with a good pubby atmosphere, screens of wood and stained glass, dark blue plush seats built into its alcoves, wooden tables, some seats up two or three steps in a side gallery, and bric-a-brac on the shelf just below the glossy dark green high ceiling; a sympathetic extension provides extra seating. Satisfying bar food includes filled rolls (from 80p), home-made soup (£1.25), ploughman's (from £2.40), burgers (from £2.50), cauliflower cheese (£2.95), home-made steak and kidney pie (£3.25), home-made lasagne (£3.60), freshly battered haddock (£3.95), tandoori chicken (£4.25), and rump steak (£5.95); prompt, friendly service. Well reproduced nostalgic pop music, trivia, fruit machine and maybe newspapers on a rack. There's a terrace with seats and tables. In the evening (when, as we say, they don't do food) it seems to aim more at young people. The canal museum is nearby, and Nottingham station is just a short walk away. *(Recommended by M Jovner, Richard Lewis, Andy and Jane Beardsley, Howard James, Jack and Philip Paxton, Norma and Keith Bloomfield, Jane Hosking, Ian Burniston, BKA, David and Shelia)*

Own brew (Whitbreads) ~ Lease: Les Howard ~ Real ale ~ Lunchtime meals and snacks (11.30-6.30) ~ Restaurant (not Sun evening) ~ (0115) 9506795 ~ Children in restaurant ~ Open 11-11; cl 25 Dec

Lincolnshire Poacher

Mansfield Rd; up hill from Victoria Centre

Every day, this cheery town pub offers twelve or eighteen different dishes on its menu, cooked mainly by the landlord or his brother. Good value and interesting, the choice might include hazelnut pâté or baked stuffed aubergines (£3.75), broccoli and roquefort quiche or home-made faggots (£3.95), liver and chorizo casserole (£4.25), steak and kidney pie (£4.75), baked ham with parsley sauce or Somerset pork casserole (£4.50), roast breast of chicken Sicilian (£4.95), and puddings; no chips, and efficient, pleasant service. They have a splendid arrangement with Batemans under which the pub can serve Bass, Marstons Pedigree and four guest ales alongside perfectly kept Batemans XB, XXXB, Salem Porter, Valiant, and Victory Ale on handpump; also good ciders, and over 70 malt whiskies and 10 Irish ones. The big wood-floored front bar has wall settles and plain wooden tables, and is decorated with breweriana; it opens on to a plain but lively room on the left, from where a corridor takes you down to the chatty panelled back snug. It's very popular with young people in the evenings and can get smoky, though less so in the conservatory overlooking tables on the terrace behind. *(Recommended by Jack and Philip Paxton, Jane Hosking, Ian Burniston, Andy and Jane Beardsley, Richard Lewis, G P Fogelman, Mr and Mrs B F Condon, David and Shelia, Geoffrey and Irene Lindley, Dr Keith Bloomfield)*

Batemans ~ Lease: Neil Kelso and Laurence McDowall ~ Real ale ~ Meals and snacks (12-3, 5-8; not evenings Sat or Sun) ~ (0115) 9411584 ~ Children in conservatory ~ Occasional live entertainment ~ Open 11-3, 5-11; 11-11 Fri/Sat

Olde Trip to Jerusalem ★

Brewhouse Yard; from inner ring road follow The North, A6005 Long Eaton signpost until you are in Castle Boulevard then almost at once turn right into Castle Road; pub is up on the left

Although this unusual pub is mainly 17th c, its cavern may have served as cellarage for an early medieval brewhouse which stood here. The upstairs bar is unique: cut into the sandstone rock below the castle, its panelled walls soar narrowly into the dark cavernous heights above. Unfortunately, this part is often closed at lunchtime. The friendly downstairs bar is also mainly carved from the rock, with leatherette-cushioned settles built into the dark panelling, barrel tables on tiles or flagstones, and more low-ceilinged rock alcoves. Well kept real ales include Hardys & Hansons Kimberley Classic, Best, and Mild, and Marstons Pedigree on handpump. Home-made bar food includes cobs and sandwiches (from £1.25), filled baked potatoes (from £2.20), giant yorkshire puddings with lots of fillings (£3.95), and daily specials such as steak and kidney pie or a vegetarian dish (up to £4.95); cribbage, dominoes, chess, fruit machine, ring-the-bull; seats outside. The pub may close for refurbishment November/December 1995. No children. *(Recommended by Jack and Philip Paxton, Richard Lewis, Jane Hosking, Ian Burniston, Andy and Jane Beardsley, Howard James, Mark and Diane Grist, Richard Houghton, David and Shelia, Paul and Ursula Randall)*

Hardys & Hansons ~ Manager Patrick Dare ~ Real ale ~ Lunchtime meals and snacks ~ (0115) 9473171 ~ Open 11-11

Sir John Borlase Warren £

1 Ilkeston Rd; Canning Circus (A52 towards Derby – pub faces you as you come up the hill from city centre)

Friendly new managers have taken over this traditional local, attractively placed opposite Georgian almshouses. It takes its name from the distinguished naval commander who in 1798 defeated an attempted French invasion of Ireland off Kilkenna, and there are plenty of prints commemorating his career on the walls of the half-dozen communicating rooms. Other pictures range from early humorous advertisements and Victorian sentimental engravings to a big chromolithograph of Queen Victoria's Diamond Jubilee procession, as well as etched mirrors, engraved glass, comfortable parlourish seating, swirly Victorian acanthus-leaf wallpaper, and dark brown Anaglypta dado. Well kept Greenalls Original, Shipstones Bitter and Tetleys on handpump. Bar food, from a counter in the downstairs room, includes filled rolls (from £1.25), filled baked potatoes (£2.25), chilli con carne or nut and mushroom fettucine (£3.25), and steak in ale pie (£3.30). The eating area is no smoking at lunchtime. At the back a garden has tables sheltering under an old tree, and there may be barbecues out here in summer. *(Recommended by Jack and Philip Paxton, Andy and Jane Beardsley, Jane Hosking, Ian Burniston, David and Shelia, Brian White)*

Greenalls ~ Managers Ian and Alison Occleshaw ~ Real ale ~ Lunchtime meals and snacks ~ (0115) 9474247 ~ Children welcome (not Fri/Sat evenings) ~ Open 11.30-3, 5-11; 12-3, 6.30-11 Sat

OLD DALBY (Leics) SK6723 Map 7

Crown ★

By school in village centre turn into Longcliff Hill then left into Debdale Hill

This rather smart creeper-covered ex-farmhouse has a new, much travelled head chef this year who the licensees say adds lots of style to their menu. They grow their own herbs and still make their own bread, vinegars and ice creams – no microwaves or chips: soup (£2.95), sandwiches and rolls (from £2.95), vegetarian potato cake filled with stilton or cheddar (£4.95), chicken liver terrine with an apple compote (£5.95), a hash with chicken, potatoes, onions, tomatoes, olives, poached egg and toast points (£6.95), a fine ploughman's (£7.50), spicy crab cakes with a cocktail sauce (£7.95), home-made steak and rabbit pie (£8.95), sautéed calf's livers with apples and brandy (£9.50), rack of lamb with tomato and leeks in a mint au jus (£10.95), Scottish sirloin steak (£12.95), puddings like chocolate orange soufflé cake or winter fruits warmed in mulled wine, served with home-baked shortbread (£3.50), and interesting cheeses (£4.50). Well kept Adnams Broadside, Black Sheep, Brakspears, Greene King Abbot, Hook Norton Best, Marstons Pedigree, Morlands Old Speckled Hen, Shepherd Neame Spitfire, Timothy Taylors Landlord, Wadworths 6X and Woodfordes Wherry and Baldric on handpump, an interesting wine list, quite a few malt whiskies and several brandies and Italian liqueurs served by staff wearing black-and-white uniforms and bow ties. Despite the emphasis on food, the pub still keeps much of its original layout and feel, and the three or four little rooms have black beams, one or two antique oak settles, William Morris style armchairs and easy chairs, hunting and other rustic prints, fresh flowers, and open fires; the snug and newly refurbished large dining room are no smoking. One room has darts and cards. There are plenty of tables on a terrace, with a big, sheltered lawn (where you can play boules) sloping down among roses and fruit trees. The licensees run another main entry, the Martins Arms at Colston Bassett. *(Recommended by A and R Cooper, Anthony Barker, Brian White, Nigel Flook, Betsy Brown, Jane Hosking, Ian Burniston, Jack and Philip Paxton, Paul and Sue Merrick, D K Carter, Stephen Brown, David and Helen Wilkins, V and E A Bolton, Sue and Brian Wharton, Ted George)*

Free house ~ Licensees Lynne Strafford Bryan and Salvatore Inguanta ~ Meals and snacks (till 10) ~ Restaurant (not Sun evening) ~ (01664) 823134 ~ Children allowed in games room and dining rooms (away from bar and Tap Room) ~ Open 12-3(2.30 if quiet), 6-11

OLD SOMERBY (Lincs) SK9633 Map 8

Fox & Hounds

B1176 E of Grantham

The several little rooms here have a friendly atmosphere – as well as some copper-topped tables, comfortable seating upholstered in a hunting-print fabric, and pictures on the same theme. One room is no smoking. Good bar food includes home-made soup (£1.60), sandwiches or spectacular jumbo rolls (from £1.90; ham, banana and grilled cheese £2.40, steak £4), home-made pâté (£3), ploughman's (£3.45), home-made lasagne (£4.60), freshly-battered Grimsby haddock, plaice or halibut (from

£5.35), steaks (from £8.85), vegetarian dishes and daily specials, puddings (£2.10), and Sunday lunch (£5); quite a few fresh fish dishes in the restaurant. Well kept Marstons Pedigree, Ruddles County and John Smiths on handpump. There's a large garden with plenty of tables and chairs, and a big car park. *(Recommended by Stephen Brown, Derek and Sylvia Stephenson; more reports please)*

Free house ~ Licensees Tony and Karen Cawthorn ~ Real ale ~ Meals and snacks (not Mon) ~ Restaurant (not Sun evening) ~ (01476) 64121 ~ Children in eating area of bar until 8 ~ Open 11.30-2.30, 7-11.30; closed Mon (except bank holidays)

REDMILE (Leics) SK7935 Map 7

Peacock

Off A52 W of Grantham at Belvoir Castle, Harlby, Melton signpost, then right at crossroads signposted Redmile

Leicestershire Dining Pub of the Year

'Quite the best pub meal I've had for years' says one well travelled reader – and many would agree with him. But it's not just the food that comes in for such warm praise – the staff are particularly friendly and helpful and the happy mix of locals and visitors creates an enjoyably bustling atmosphere. They aim for a French flavour with dishes and tell us that prices are unchanged since last year: very good lunchtime filled french sticks, delicious celery soup (£1.90), baked avocado and stilton (£3.50), tagliatelle with a sauce of smoked bacon, onion, mushroom, tomato and basil (£4.75), poached eggs with mushrooms and bacon in red wine sauce, king prawns provençale (£5.15), chicken Dijon or delicious red mullet baked with tomato and basil, sirloin steak or marvellous pan-fried slices of duck with a blackcurrant sauce (both £8.50), and lots of perfect puddings such as caramelised apple tart or poached meringue and banana flambé; vegetables are very good, while service is prompt and efficient. There's also a pretty little no-smoking restaurant, with a three course set menu for £12.95. It can get busy at lunchtimes and they recommend booking. The range of well kept beers on handpump includes Bass, Greene King Abbot, Marstons Pedigree, Tetleys, and Timothy Taylors Landlord, and a guest beer, and they have an interesting wine list including fairly priced bottles and some by the glass; occasional special events such as cookery demonstrations or wine tastings. Despite the emphasis on eating, the spotless beamed rooms have an easy-going pubby feel, as well as pews, stripped country tables and chairs, the odd sofa and easy chair, some stripped golden stone, old prints, chintzy curtains for the small windows, and a variety of wall and table lamps; the snug and the conservatory are no smoking. Open fires, darts, cribbage, dominoes, maybe unobtrusive piped music, and tables outside. The pub is in an extremely pleasant tranquil setting near Belvoir Castle. *(Recommended by Viv Middlebrook, David and Shelia, DC, Jack and Philip Paxton, June and Malcolm Farmer, Chris Raisin and friends, Andy and Jane Beardsley, David and Helen Wilkins, David Atkinson, Michael Lyne, Roxanne Chamberlain, Nigel Hopkins, T Whitford, Mike and Jo, Mark and Mary Fairman, Sue and Brian Wharton, Wendy Arnold, Dr Sheila Smith, Derek and Sylvia Stephenson)*

Free house ~ Licensees Celia and Colin Craword ~ Real ale ~ Meals and snacks (12-3, 6.30-10) ~ Restaurant ~ (01949) 842554 ~ Children welcome ~ Open 11-11

RETFORD (Notts) SK6980 Map 7

Market

West Carr Road, Ordsall; follow Retford Leisure Centre sign off A620 W, then after West Carr Road Industrial Estate sign on your right take first left turning up track which – if you look closely – is signed for the pub; or, on foot, from Retford Rly Stn follow footpath under S of frontage, turn R at end

It's worth tracking this friendly pub down – don't be put off by the unexceptional-looking exterior or its surprising location amongst the factories of a light industrial estate. They keep a marvellous range of up to 14 well kept beers with helpful notes detailing each brew: Bass, Boddingtons, Marstons Pedigree, Morlands Old Speckled

Hen, Shepherd Neame Spitfire, Theakstons Best and XB, Thwaites White Oak, Youngers No 3 and guest beers on handpump. Very good value and tasty home cooked bar food includes sandwiches, hot beef roll (£1.65), burgers (from £3.10), home-made pie (£4.25), steak (£5.95), and their popular fresh Scarborough haddock weighing over one pound (£8.50); cheery and obliging service. The cosy bar has green plush wall banquettes and dimpled copper or dark wood tables, and pantiles over the bar servery, with an open fire at one end and a little blue plush snug at the other. A spacious conservatory dining room opens off this, and in turn gives on to a small terrace with white tables; dominoes, cribbage and piped music. *(Recommended by CMW, JJW, Alan and Eileen Bowker, Peter Marshall, John C Baker; more reports please)*

Free house ~ Licensee Raymond Brunt ~ Real ale ~ Meals and snacks (till 10) ~ Restaurant ~ (01777) 703278 ~ Children in eating area of bar ~ Jazz 3rd Sun of month (lunchtime) ~ Open 11-4(3 in winter), 6-11; 11-11 Sat

SIBSON (Leics) SK3500 Map 4

Cock

A444 N of Nuneaton

This thatched and timbered country pub dates back to the 13th c, with proof of its age in the unusually low doorways, ancient wall timbers, heavy black beams, and genuine latticed windows. An atmospheric room on the right has comfortable seats around cast-iron tables, and more seats built in to what was once an immense fireplace, which they like to say provided sanctuary for Dick Turpin when his pursuers got too close. His horse, apparently, would hide out in the cellars. The room on the left has country kitchen chairs around wooden tables, and what was the bar billiards room is now a no-smoking dining area. Generous helpings of good value bar food include home-made soup (£1.50), good sandwiches (from £1.50), home-made pâté (£2), steak and kidney pie or beef curry (£4.95), honey roast ham and egg (£5.50), steaks (from £7.50), daily specials such as leek and mushroom stroganoff (£5.50), and sizzling Texas beef, lamb's liver provençale or stuffed lamb's hearts (all £5.95), children's menu (£2.50), and home-made puddings (£2); they have regular gourmet evenings. It can seem cramped at times but that just adds to the cosy atmosphere. Well kept Bass and M & B Brew XI on handpump; excellent service; bar billiards, fruit machine and piped music. A little garden and courtyard area has tables and a barbecue. The restaurant (in a former stable block) is popular, the summer hanging baskets are attractive, and they have a caravan field (certified with the Caravan Club). *(Recommended by Thomas Nott, Paul and Janet Waring, Mike and Wendy Proctor, Jack and Philip Paxton, Stephen Brown, Julie Peters, Dennis and Dorothee Glover, John Cadman, Graham and Karen Oddey)*

Bass ~ Lease: Graham and Stephanie Lindsay ~ Real ale ~ Meals and snacks (not Sun lunchtime) ~ Restaurant (not Sun evening) ~ (01827) 880357 ~ Children in eating area of bar ~ Open 11.30-2.30(3 summer Sat), 6.30(6 Sat)-11

SNAITH (Lincs) SE6422 Map 7

Brewers Arms

10 Pontefract Rd

Filling something of a gap in our North Lincolnshire pub map, this is an attractive conversion of a former mill, very clean and newly refurbished, with old local photographs, exposed ceiling joists and a neat brick and timber bar counter – which for most people will be the main focus of attention. The reason is that this is the home of a fine set of beers gaining growing favour in pubs selling them elsewhere – Old Mill Bitter, Mild, Bullion and Nellie Dean on electric pump. Unusually, they also do their own lager. You can arrange to see around the brewery (in a quite separate building). The bar food is good too, with soup (£1.20), fine sandwiches, prawn cocktail (£2.35), vegetable curry or broccoli potato bake (£3.95), lasagne (£4.25), battered cod or haddock fillet (£4.50), breaded scampi or gammon steak

(£4.75), and daily specials (from £3.95). There are also good value home-cooked restaurant meals, with green plush chairs and turkey carpet in a fresh and airy conservatory-style dining area (no-smoking) with a pine plank ceiling and lots of plants. Beware of joining the skeleton at the bottom of the old well. Fruit machine, piped music. *(Recommended by Thomas Nott, C A Hall)*

Own brew ~ Manager John McCue ~ Real ale ~ Meals and snacks ~ (01405) 862404 ~ Children welcome in eating area of bar ~ Open 11-3, 6-11 ~ Bedrooms:£40B/£52B

STAMFORD (Lincs) TF0207 Map 8

George ★ ★

71 High St, St Martins; B1081 leaving town southwards

Even when this lovely old coaching inn was just a fuelling stop on the Great North Road (as one reader remembers it first) there was a marvellous atmosphere. Of course, today it's much more sophisticated but remains a very special place to many people, because despite its elegance there's always a warmly pubby flavour and relaxed feel, and you will be made as welcome coming for a drink as you would coming to stay for a week. The current building dates from 1597 when it was built for Lord Burghley, but there are still parts of a much older Norman pilgrims' hospice, and a crypt under the cocktail bar that may be 1000 years old. In the 18th and 19th c it was a bustling coaching inn, with 20 trips a day each way from London and York, and two of the front rooms are still named after these destinations. They have a medley of seats ranging from sturdy bar settles through leather, cane and antique wicker to soft settees and easy chairs, while the refurbished central lounge has sturdy timbers, broad flagstones, heavy beams, and massive stonework. The nicest place for lunch (if it's not a warm sunny day) is the indoor Garden Lounge, with well spaced white cast-iron furniture on herringbone glazed bricks around a central tropical grove, and a splendidly tempting help-yourself buffet (from £9.90). Other bar food includes soup (£3.40), chicken liver pâté with an orange and redcurrant sauce (£4.95), toasted club or Danish open sandwiches (from £6.55), pasta dishes like fettucini with fresh and smoked salmon in cream sauce or pasta parcels filled with ricotta cheese and spinach tossed in mushrooms and cream (£7.25), gruyere cheese fritters with a quince jelly, local sausages or lovely burgers (£7.95), fresh haddock and chips (£8.45), home-made steak and kidney pudding (£9.45), char-grilled steaks (from £11.50), and puddings (£3.60); they do a range of cheaper sandwiches and ploughman's in the York bar. Adnams and Ruddles Best on handpump, but the best drinks are the Italian wines, many of which are good value and sold by the glass; also freshly squeezed orange juice, filter, espresso or cappuccino coffee. Welcoming staff. The cobbled courtyard at the back is lovely in summer, with comfortable chairs and tables among attractive plant tubs and colourful hanging baskets; waiter drinks service. Besides the courtyard, there's a neatly maintained walled garden, with a sunken lawn where croquet is often played. *(Recommended by Chris Raisin and friends, Ian Phillips, Jack and Philip Paxton, Gordon Thornton, Lynn Sharpless, Bob Eardley, David and Shelia, Caroline Kenyon, Bernard and Marjorie Parkin, Stuart Earle, Graham and Karen Oddey, Mr and Mrs T F Marshall, Michael Sargent, Thomas Nott, WHBM)*

Free house ~ Licensees Ivo Vannocci and Chris Pitman ~ Real ale ~ Meals and snacks (12-11) ~ Two restaurants ~ (01780) 55171 ~ Children welcome ~ Open 11-11 ~ Bedrooms: £72B/£105B

STRETTON (Leics) SK9416 Map 7

Ram Jam

Great North Rd (A1)

Although this very civilised place looks like a traditional coaching inn from the outside, once inside it's rather like a continental coffee house or smart wine bar with an efficient little all-day partly no smoking snacks bar serving food and drinks from breakfast-time on. Meals are consistently good and imaginatively presented, and might include soup (£2.50) grilled aubergine topped with a peanut and sesame oil dressing (£2.95), filled granary baps (£3.95), hash brown potatoes topped with two poached eggs and grilled bacon (£4.25), tagliatelle with parmesan, lemon zest and roasted garlic (£4.95), grilled sausages with onion marmalade (£5.95), roast cod topped with a chickpea crust and bacon snips (£6.25), sirloin steak (£9.95); friendly, efficient service, even under pressure. The comfortably airy modern lounge bar has Mexican hand-made tiles, sofas around turkey carpets, old breadboards and modern china on the cream walls, and neat contemporary seats; it opens out at the rear to a leisurely no-smoking restaurant. Good wines, freshly squeezed orange juice, fresh-ground coffee and so forth. There are teak seats on the terrace at the back looking up to the orchard behind (some traffic noise here, of course, though the bedrooms are surprisingly quiet); big car park. *(Recommended by Chris Westmoreland, Mark Hydes, Chris Raisin, Karen and Graham Oddey, Geoffrey and Irene Lindley, Michael Sargent, Simon Collett-Jones)*

Free house ~ Licensee Tim Hart ~ Meals and snacks (7am-10pm) ~ Restaurant ~ (01780) 410361 ~ Children welcome ~ Open 11-11 (snack bar open earlier for breakfast); closed Dec 25 ~ Bedrooms: £46.35B/£60.80B

THORPE LANGTON (Leics) SP7492 Map 4

Bakers Arms 🍴

Village signposted off B6047 N of Market Harborough

This corner of Leicestershire seems to breed really good pubs with an enviable facility. This particular thatched pub tucked away in a small village has been refurbished and extended as a spacious dining pub, and has become very popular indeed in the evenings for its combination of good food and really welcoming warmth. Furnishing is simple, with straightforward seating and stripped pine tables: some draw a parallel with the Peacock at Redmile. Certainly, what counts most is the quality of the cooking, with fresh ingredients and good presentation. A wide changing choice both of starters and of main dishes – all on blackboards – might include home-made soup (£2.50), home-made chicken liver pâté with melba toast (£3.25), tandoori chicken with mint yoghurt (£3.50), sweet and sour vegetables or avocado and tomato bake (£6.25), chicken breast with garlic mushrooms wrapped in bacon with a thyme sauce (£8.45), fillet of sea bream with caper sauce (£8.95), monkfish with fresh herbs panfried in butter (£9.50), grilled Dover sole or fillet steak with a horseradish crust and brandy sauce (£12.95), and puddings such as fruit crumbles, sticky toffee pudding or profiteroles (£2.75); you will need to book up some time ahead. Well kept Ind Coope Burton and Tetleys on handpump, and an extensive wine list with 5 by the glass; good friendly service, and no games or piped music. There are picnic tables in the garden. *(Recommended by J D Cloud, D J Etheridge, Brian Atkin, Mike and Margaret Banks)*

Free house ~ Manageress Kate Hubbard ~ Real ale ~ Meals and snacks (see opening times) ~ Restaurant ~ (01858) 545201 ~ Children in snug till 8pm ~ Pianist Fri evenings ~ Open Tues-Fri 6.30-11; 12-2.30, 6.30-11 Sat; cl weekday lunchtimes, Sun evening, all day Mon

UPTON (Notts) SK7354 Map 7

French Horn

A612

This bustling pub is well regarded locally for eating, and at lunchtimes you may find most tables set out ready for meals. From a changing menu, there might be sandwiches (from £1.25), soup (£1.45), mushrooms stuffed with stilton in a port and redcurrant sauce (£2.85), steak pie (£4.50), and very good specials like sweet and sour rack of ribs (£4.95), kebabs in chilli sauce (£5.25), grilled sea bream with prawns (£5.65), guinea fowl in a black cherry sauce or poached salmon in a cream and dill sauce (£6.95), and lots of puddings like coffee meringue or white chocolate profiterole gateau (£2.25). Usefully they also do a range of sandwiches and hot snacks all afternoon. The neat and comfortable open-plan bar (refurbished this year) has a nicely relaxed feel, as well as cushioned captain's chairs, wall banquettes around glossy tables, and watercolours by local artists on the walls. Well kept Vaux Double Maxim and Waggle Dance and Wards Bitter and Thorn on handpump, and several wines by the glass; staff are friendly and efficient. The big sloping back paddock, with picnic tables, looks over farmland. *(Recommended by David Caudwell, Alan and Eileen Bowker, Sarah and Peter Gooderham, Jack and Philip Paxton, Phyl and Jack Street, Ian and Val Titman, David and Shelia)*

Wards ~ Licensee Joyce Carter ~ Real ale ~ Meals and snacks ~ Restaurant ~ (01636) 812394 ~ Children welcome ~ Open 11-11

WELLOW (Notts) SK6766 Map 7

Olde Red Lion

Eakring Road; pub visible from A616 E of Ollerton

The original deeds for this 16th-c pub set out what really was just a peppercorn rent, one peppercorn per year to be precise; you can still see the deeds on the wall of one of the bars. Some things have changed since then, but very much a fixed feature over most of the period has been the village's May Day celebrations, and windows in the low-beamed front room look out on their centrepiece, a tremendously tall brightly spiral-painted maypole. There's a comfortably furnished series of rooms and photographs tracing the building's development on the partly panelled walls. The food has a great local reputation for value – a combination of low prices and big helpings – so it's best to get here early if you want to eat: good sandwiches (from £1.50), crispy vegetable parcels (£3.50), home-made steak and kidney pie (£4.25), lasagne (£4.95), halibut steak (£5.95), steaks (from £6.95), mixed grill (£9.95), daily specials and children's menu (£1.95); best to book for Sunday lunch; the dining area is no smoking. Well kept Courage Directors, Morlands Old Speckled Hen, Ruddles Best and County, John Smiths Magnet and guest beers on handpump; quick service; dominoes, table skittles. An L-shaped strip of grass above the car park has picnic tables under cocktail parasols, and a set of swings. *(Recommended by Derek and Sylvia Stephenson, Ants Aug, Gordon Tong, M Joyner, David and Shelia, L Grant)*

Free house ~ Licensee Richard Henshaw ~ Real ale ~ Meals and snacks (till 10) ~ Restaurant ~ (01623) 861000 ~ Children in eating area and restaurant ~ Occasional folk evenings and summer Morris dancers ~ Open 11.30-3, 5.30-11, all day summer Sats; closed Dec 25

WOODHOUSE EAVES (Leics) SK5214 Map 7

Pear Tree

Church Hill; main street, off B591 W of Quorndon

Don't be put off by the rather modern exterior – this is a busy, well run pub with a friendly landlord. It's the upper flagstoned food area which is special, with pews forming booths around the walls, flagstone floor, and a pitched roof giving a pleasantly airy and open feel at lunchtime; at night, despite low lighting, the atmosphere is pleasantly lively. The end food servery looks straight through into the kitchen, which does generous helpings of good food such as sandwiches (from £1.85), soup (£2), mushrooms and bacon in garlic butter (£3.95), ploughman's (£4.25), burgers (£5.25), grilled nut cutlets (£5.75), spit-roast chicken (£6.25), sirloin steak (£9.50), and puddings (£2.25). There's a log fire in an attractive Victorian fireplace, and decent wines. The lower part of the pub is a straightforward comfortable turkey-carpeted local, with well kept Ind Coope Burton, Marstons Pedigree and Tetleys on handpump and an open fire. Outside there are a few picnic tables under cocktail parasols, with a summer bar by an arbour of climbing plants;

good nearby walks. *(Recommended by J Honnor, Stephen, Julie and Hayley Brown, Jack and Philip Paxton, A and R Cooper, George Atkinson, Andrew Stephenson)*

Ansells ~ Lease: Richard Dimblebee ~ Real ale ~ Meals and snacks (till 10) ~ (01509) 890243 ~ Children welcome ~ Open 11-3, 6-11

Lucky Dip

Besides the fully inspected pubs, you might like to try these Lucky Dips recommended to us and described by readers (if you do, please send us reports):

☆ **Acresford**, Leics [A444 Burton—Nuneaton; SK3113], *Cricketts*: Attractive and well run, with good home-cooked food inc vegetarian, well kept Bass, Marstons Pedigree and regional ales, good range of other drinks, friendly service; attractive garden and setting *(Graham Richardson, Ian Phillips, B M Eldridge)*

☆ **Alford**, Lincs [29 West St (A1004); TF4576], *White Horse*: Neat and comfortable, with dark green plush and dimpled copper, well kept Bass, Batemans XB and Worthington Best, good range of Polish vodkas, good value fresh-cooked food in bar and restaurant, good service; bedrooms *(Gordon Theaker, George and Sheila Edwards, LYM)*

☆ **Allington**, Lincs [The Green – 2 miles N of A52 Nottingham—Grantham; SK8540], *Welby Arms*: Attractively and interestingly decorated local, clean and congenial, with good range of reasonably priced home-cooked food inc fresh fish and vegetarian, no-smoking section in eating area, particularly well kept Bass, John Smiths, Timothy Taylors Landlord and guests such as Woods Wonderful; good staff, friendly landlord and standard poodles *(John C Baker, Derek and Sylvia Stephenson, Tony Gayfer, Stuart and Alison Exley)*

Ashby de la Zouch, Leics [Market St; SK3516], *Queens Head*: Cosy beamed pub handy for shoppers and business people; good range of well priced food, Marstons Pedigree, friendly staff *(George Atkinson)*

☆ **Ashby Folville**, Leics [SK7011], *Carington Arms*: Half a dozen well kept Everards, Adnams and other interesting guest ales and jovial obliging landlord in attractively placed spacious and comfortable Tudor-style country pub, solid rural home cooking inc good chips; children welcome, nice garden, maybe calves or horses in back paddock *(Jim Farmer, O K Smyth)*

Ashby Parva, Leics [off A426 N of Lutterworth; not far from M1 junction 20; SP5288], *Holly Bush*: Roomy but cosily and comfortably divided, with good value generous food, restaurant area, efficient service, well kept beers inc guests; barbecues in garden *(George Atkinson, Ted George)*

☆ **Aswarby**, Lincs [A15 Folkingham—Sleaford; TF0639], *Tally Ho*: Small but imposing stone-built oak-beamed country inn, neat civilised traditional furnishings, big log fire and woodburning stove, friendly service, well kept Adnams, Batemans XB and a guest beer on handpump, good food with veg cooked to perfection, smart interesting restaurant with piped classical music; tables and timber play fort on grass behind, by sheep meadow; bedrooms comfortable and well equipped, in neatly converted block behind; nearby church worth a visit *(Sqn Ldr and Mrs P A Bouch, F J and A Parmenter, Chris Walling, June and Malcolm Farmer, LJBH, John and Zoe Chamberlain, BB)*

☆ **Barholm**, Lincs [TF0810], *Five Horseshoes*: Old-fashioned relaxed village local, clean and cosy, with well kept Adnams, Batemans and interesting guest beers; old farm tools, stuffed birds, tables in garden, paddocks behind *(David and Michelle Hedges, LYM)*

Barnoldby le Beck, Lincs [SW of Grimsby; TA2303], *Ship*: Nautical-theme country pub with good sensibly priced food in bar and comfortable dining room, attentive staff, wide range of drinks, pleasant setting *(Gordon B Thornton)*

☆ **Barnsdale**, Leics [just off A606 Oakham—Stamford; SK9008], *Barnsdale Lodge*: Well appointed and pleasant country inn, former farmhouse, with lots of interesting old artefacts, attractive character furnishings, good range of good food inc cream teas, Morlands Old Speckled Hen, Ruddles and Tetleys, friendly staff; bedrooms comfortable *(Gordon Theaker, Alan and Heather Jacques)*

☆ **Barrow upon Soar**, Leics [Mill Lane, off South St (B5328); SK5717], *Navigation*: Extended split-level pub based on former barge-horse stabling, attractive and comfortable, with lovely canal view from small back terrace with moorings; good value straightforward bar food, interesting bar top made from old pennies, central open fire, friendly landlord; well kept Courage Directors, Marstons Pedigree and Shipstones, skittle alley, piped music *(Dr K Bloomfield, Stephen Brown)*

Barrow upon Soar [OS Sheet 129 map ref 573173], *Soar Bridge*: Interesting spot nr busy canal lock, friendly service and atmosphere, flowers in panelled lounge, good value home-cooked food inc several vegetarian dishes (prompt stop to food service), Everards and Adnams; unobtrusive piped music *(Jim Farmer)*

☆ **Bathley**, Notts [SK7759], *Crown*: Should be well worth knowing, as taken over by the Paczesnys who made the Muskham

Ferry at North Muskham a popular main entry *(Reports please)*

Belchford, Lincs [E of A153 Horncastle—Louth; TF2975], *Blue Bell*: Three well kept interesting guest beers, simple food inc delicious home-made pies, nicely refurbished bar *(Caroline Kenyon)*

Belmesthorpe, Leics [Shepherds Walk; TF0410], *Bluebell*: Quaint and friendly olde-worlde village pub with good fire, well kept Marstons Pedigree and Ruddles County, good value lunchtime bar food (not Sun) *(Jack Pettit)*

Belton, Leics [off A512/A453 between junctions 23 and 24, M1; SK4420], *Queens*: Former coaching inn with well kept Bass, two pleasant bars, restaurant, pleasant staff; cheap food very popular with older people at lunchtime; bedrooms *(Beryl and Terry Bryan)*

Billesdon, Leics [Church St; SK7202], *Queens Head*: Beamed and partly thatched village pub with good food in bar and upstairs restaurant, friendly atmosphere, local beer *(J R M Black)*

Billingborough, Lincs [High St; TF1134], *Fortescue Arms*: Cosy traditional atmosphere, beams, open fires, country bygones, Ansells, Bass, Ind Coope Burton, Kilkenny and a guest ale, good value food, dining room, cheerful service (can slow when busy at weekends); tables under apple trees in big garden *(Dave and Margaret Bush)*

Blackfordby, Leics [Main St; SK3217], *Black Lion*: Newly refurbished, with good range of well kept ales inc Bass, Courage and Tetleys, bar food (not Weds) *(B M Eldridge)*

☆ **Blyth**, Notts [SK6287], *White Swan*: Well kept Whitbreads-related ales esp Castle Eden, good food from sandwiches up inc good fresh fish, in cosy neatly kept pub with big open fires, friendly landlord; may be piped music; good A1 break, by duck pond *(Paul Cartledge, Ian Finney, E J Cutting)*

☆ **Boston**, Lincs [Wormgate; TF3244], *Goodbarns Yard*: Tasteful modern pub and restaurant with well kept Courage and guest beers, good bar food inc some interesting spicy snacks *(Frank W Gadbois, A W Dickinson, Bill Isaac)*

Boston [Horncastle Rd (B1183)], *Kings Arms*: Fine spot by canal opp tall working windmill, airy front bar, plush little back bar, well kept Batemans Mild, XB and XXXB, friendly efficient landlady, usual bar food; bedrooms modern and comfortable with cheery furnishings *(Frank W Gadbois, BB)*; [Spilsby Rd (A16)], *Mill*: Clean roadside pub with restaurant feel, usual bar food with bargain three-course meals, friendly efficient service, Batemans, quiet piped music; seats out in front *(K D Day)*

Bourne, Lincs [Mkt Pl; TF0920], *Angel*: Well kept Youngers IPA, tasty bar food, attractive saloon bar, friendly service; bedrooms *(Frank W Gadbois)*

Bramcote, Notts [Derby Rd; junction A6007/B5010; SK5037], *Sherwin Arms*: Large prewar roadhouse with comfortable banquettes, wide choice of good value food (not Sun evening), well kept Shipstones, picnic tables outside; piped music can be loud *(JJW, CMW)*

☆ **Brandy Wharf**, Lincs [B1205 SE of Scunthorpe; TF0197], *Hankerin*: Odd and interesting, esp for cider enthusiasts like the landlord (over 60 varieties here), decor inc all sorts of cider items from posters to drinking pots, odd foot poking through ceiling of dim-lit lounge; lovely open fire, good value generous plain food inc wonderful real chips, summer cider shop; riverside setting with good moorings, slipways; cl Christmas, New Year, Mon winter lunchtimes *(Jane Kingsbury)*

☆ **Breedon on the Hill**, Leics [A453 Ashby—Castle Donington; SK4022], *Holly Bush*: Comfortably plush, with low black beams, lots of brass, sporting plates etc, well kept Marstons Pedigree and Tetleys, bar food (stops early lunchtime; not Sun), restaurant (can be fully booked Sat, cl Sun), no-smoking area, friendly efficient staff; piped music (live Mon); some tables outside, nice bedrooms; interesting village with Anglo-Saxon carvings in hilltop church above huge limestone face *(Nan Axon, Gordon Theaker, Rona Murdoch, Norma and Keith Bloomfield, A and R Cooper, BB)*

Bruntingthorpe, Leics [Cross St; SP6089], *Joiners Arms*: Good food inc Sun lunch in beamed dining area, Hoskins ales, lots of china and brasses, friendly staff; cl weekday lunchtimes; handy for aviation museum *(George Atkinson, A R Hipkins)*

Bunny, Notts [Nottingham—Loughborough; SK5728], *Rancliffe Arms*: Good food and atmosphere, well kept beers, sensible prices, friendly staff *(Ruth and Alan Cooper)*

Burton upon Stather, Lincs [N of Scunthorpe; SE8717], *Sheffield Arms*: Good choice of well kept ales and of generous food in attractively furnished old-fashioned stone pub, old photographs *(JLP)*

Carlton on Trent, Notts [Ossington Rd; signed just off A1 N of Newark; SK7964], *Great Northern*: Large comfortable pub next to railway line, lots of railway memorabilia, family room and big play area; Mansfield Riding, Springfield and guest ales, decent food, good housekeeping *(Jack and Philip Paxton, Chris Westmoreland)*

Castle Donington [90 Bondgate (B6504); SK4427], *Cross Keys*: Friendly and snug low-ceilinged pub, good food popular lunchtime with airport office staff, well kept beers *(Dr & Mrs A K Clarke, R and A Cooper)*; [A453, S end], *Nags Head*: Beamed dining pub with good food, well kept beer, decent wine, friendly service *(Stephen Newell, Dr and Mrs A K Clarke)*

☆ *nr* **Castle Donington** [Kings Mills], *Priest House*: Good food and atmosphere in rambling beamed dining bar of watermill turned hotel, with medieval tower; friendly helpful staff, real ales inc one brewed for the pub, children really welcome; 50 acres of wooded grounds by River Trent, fishing, canoeing; bedrooms excellent *(Ruth and Alan Cooper, Dr and Mrs A K Clarke, Michael and Margaret Norris, LYM)*

☆ **Catthorpe**, Leics [just off A5 S of Gibbet Island; SP5578], *Cherry Tree*: Good value food in attractive well run country local, friendly, cosy, clean and warm, with pleasant atmosphere, dark panelling, lots of plates and pictures, coal-effect fire, attentive service, particularly well kept Bass and Hook Norton Best; piped radio; cl Mon/Tues lunchtimes *(Ted George, B Adams, Cdr Patrick Tailyour)*

Caunton, Notts [off A616 Newark—Ollerton; SK7460], *Plough*: Well prepared tasty food in dining area off L-shaped bar, pleasant staff, friendly attentive landlady *(Phyl and Jack Street)*

Caythorpe, Lincs [SK9348], *Red Lion*: Good service, varied menu, changing range of beers; obviously care about quality *(Peter Burton)*

Church Langton, Leics [B6047 about 3 miles N of Mkt Harborough; just off A6; SP7293], *Langton Arms*: Popular and welcoming country pub, smartly extended, with wide choice of good value interesting food inc vegetarian and weekly OAP lunches, helpful friendly staff, candlelit dining area, well kept Marstons Pedigree and other ales *(Jim Farmer, Gerald Roxbury)*

Claybrooke Magna, Leics [SP4988], *Woodcutter*: Pleasant unassuming free house with well kept Bass, carpeted lounge with restaurant and public bar areas, decent well priced food, pleasant friendly landlord, maybe piped radio *(George Atkinson)*

Claypole, Lincs [SK8449], *Five Bells*: Cheery bustle in spotless village pub with well kept Batemans and Wards, simple wholesome food at reasonable prices inc real chip butties, good friendly service, games; well equipped play area *(John C Baker, P White)*; [Main St], *Woolpack*: Full range of Marstons beers and a guest like Morlands Old Speckled Hen or Timothy Taylors Landlord, all kept well, freshly made simple but interesting food, great community atmosphere in quite unspoiled local *(John C Baker)*

☆ **Cleethorpes**, Lincs [Kingsway; TA3008], *Willys*: Modern bistro-style pub brewing its own good beers, also well kept guest beers and good value straightforward lunchtime food; quiet jukebox, Humber estuary views; annual beer festival *(Andy and Jill Kassube)*

Cleethorpes [Kingsway], *Kings Royal*: Good choice of real ales in well run pub, now inc locally brewed Leaking Boot *(Garry Fox)*

Clifton, Notts [Farnborough Rd; SK5534], *Winning Post*: Friendly local with pool and darts in games bar, refurbished lounge, family room, smoke room with dominoes; open all day Friday and Saturday; quiz night Tues, live weekend entertainment, bank hol extravaganzas; lavatories for the disabled *(Mr and Mrs R J Allen)*

Clipstone, Notts [Old Clipstone; B6030 Mansfield—Ollerton – OS Sheet 120 map ref 606647; SK6064], *Dog & Duck*: Friendly and comfortably plush three-room pub with amazing teapot collection, good value basic home cooking, family dining room, well kept Home ales and Theakstons XB *(Norma and Keith Bloomfield, M and J Back)*

Coleby, Lincs [Hill Rise; SK9760], *Tempest Arms*: Roomy, friendly and comfortable, with well kept Batemans XB and Courage-related ales, food Thurs-Sat, friendly staff and spaniel, wonderful view from pretty garden; on Viking Way *(Ian Phillips)*

Coleorton, Leics [SK4017], *Angel*: Modernised old inn with attractive oak beams, coal fires and somewhat wonky floor; friendly, with well kept Marstons *(Dr and Mrs A K Clarke)*

☆ **Coningsby**, Lincs [Boston Rd (B1192); ½ mile NW of village – OS Sheet 122 map ref 242588; TF2458], *Leagate*: Dark old heavy-beamed fenland local with three linked areas, ageing medley of furnishings inc great high-backed settles around the biggest of the three log fires; prompt attractively priced straightforward food, several Courage-related and other ales; piped jazz or pop music, fruit machine; rustic garden with play area; children if eating *(Caroline Kenyon, Maxine Larkin, Robin Etheridge, K D Day, Mark Hydes, LYM)*

Countesthorpe, Leics [SP5895], *Axe & Hand*: Convivial village local with Tetleys-related ales, friendly staff; not a dining pub *(C Elliott)*

☆ **Cowbit**, Lincs [Barrier Bank; A1073 S of Spalding; TF2618], *Olde Dun Cow*: Wide choice of good value bar food, ales such as Batemans XXXB, Boddingtons, Morlands Old Speckled Hen, Theakstons Best and XB, friendly waitress service in pleasant black and white split-level bar with old oak beams, antique notices, restaurant one end, games area at the other; bedrooms *(M and J Back)*

☆ **Cropston**, Leics [15 Station Rd (B5328); SK5510], *Bradgate Arms*: Much modernised extended village pub with traditional snug, well kept Banks's Bitter and Mild and guest beers, wide choice of standard Milestone Tavern food from separate servery for sunken no-smoking family dining area, friendly service; skittle alley, fruit machines, piped music, can get crowded; biggish garden with play area, handy for Bradgate Park *(JJW, CMW, Graham Norman, A and R Cooper, Jim Farmer, LYM)*

Croxton Kerrial, Leics [1 School Lane; A607 SW of Grantham; SK8329], *Peacock*: 17th-c pub with five real ales, good varied choice of reasonably cheap food (inc takeaways), long bar with real fire partitioned off at one end, some nick-nacks, quiet piped music – the sort of place where even out-of-practice strangers are tempted to play pool; children and dogs welcome, picnic tables in garden *(JJW, CMW, David and Shelia)*

Cuckney, Notts [High Croft; SK5671], *Greendale Oak:* Good range of reasonably priced bar food, swift service even when very busy midweek lunchtime, roomy but cosy L-shaped bar, good coffee, evening restaurant; bedrooms *(Peter and Audrey Dowsett, Geoffrey and Irene Lindley)*

Dunton Bassett, Leics [The Mount; off A426/B581 S of Leicester; SP5490], *Crown & Thistle*: Chatty and welcoming newish licensees, good value food inc children's, eating area, skittles/darts area; piped pop music; garden and terrace with play area *(JJW, CMW)*

☆ **East Bridgford**, Notts [Kneeton Rd, off A6075; can also be reached from A46; SK6943], *Reindeer*: Comfortable and spotless, with several eating areas, good generous food inc interesting dishes, cooked to order (so may be a wait), quick friendly service, changing real ales such as Charles Wells Bombardier, open fire; need to book at weekends; attractive village *(Derek and Sylvia Stephenson, Andy and Jill Kassube, Mrs K E Nicholson)*

East Langton, Leics [signed off B6047; the Langtons also signed off A6 N of Mkt Harborough; SP7292], *Bell*: Decent food in pleasant bar with stripped stone walls, log fire, glossy beams *(George Atkinson, LYM)*

Eastwood, Notts [Newthorpe; SK4846], *Foresters Arms*: Charming lounge packed on weekend piano nights, bar with darts and dominoes, Hardys & Hansons ales; skittles, small play area, barbecues *(Jack and Philip Paxton)*; [Newthorpe Common; SK4745], *Lord Raglan*: Friendly local with homely attractive lounge, big comfortable bar, good value food inc a good vegetarian choice, pool table, darts and skittles areas, quiz night Weds; spacious garden, not far from D H Lawrence trail *(Mike Barrett)*

☆ **Edenham**, Lincs [A151; TF0621], *Five Bells*: Wide choice of generous usual bar food in neat busy modernised dining lounge, well kept Marstons Pedigree and Tetleys, two log fires, piped music, lots of foreign banknotes, soft lighting; back restaurant/function room, tables in garden with good play area; children welcome *(M and J Back, Mrs J A Blanks, LYM)*

Edwinstowe, Notts [High St; SK6266], *Black Swan*: Decent straightforward food, well kept beer, cheerful service; handy for Sherwood Forest walks *(M Joyner)*

☆ **Elkesley**, Notts [just off A1 S of Blyth; SK6975], *Robin Hood*: Big helpings of good food inc imaginative dishes in well furnished lounge/dining room, games machines and pool in public bar; well kept Whitbreads-related ales, picnic tables and play area in garden by A1 *(Christopher Turner, Gordon Smith, JJW, CMW)*

☆ **Elston**, Notts [A46 SW of Newark; SK7548], *Coeur de Lion*: Good bar food, well kept Bass and obliging neat staff in extraordinary building with pinnacles, domes, lancet windows, steep roofs, tall chimneys, elevated terraces; decorous panelled bar with soft russet plush seats, country prints and engravings, two candlelit dining rooms, one upstairs with soaring pitched and raftered ceiling *(David and Ruth Hollands, BB)*

Enderby, Leics [26 High St; SP5399], *Chatsworth*: Good choice of good food inc unusual dishes, good choice of real ales; gets very busy, can book *(Paul and Melonie Fox)*

☆ **Epperstone**, Notts [SK6548], *Cross Keys*: Friendly old small two-bar village pub, locally popular for good value hearty home-cooked food esp pies; well kept Hardys & Hansons beers, cheerful service; pleasant countryside *(Andy and Jill Kassube, Norma and Keith Bloomfield, Moira and John Cole)*

Epworth, Lincs [High St; SE7804], *Loco*: Well kept beers, good food in restaurant or bar, lots of railway memorabilia *(Andrew Maufe)*; [The Square], *Red Lion*: Several separate beamed areas, roaring fire, Tetleys and Youngs, good food, friendly efficient waitress service *(Ian and Freda Millar)*

☆ **Ewerby**, Lincs [TF1247], *Finch Hatton Arms:* Substantial plushly furnished well decorated mock-Tudor pub with good atmosphere, efficient friendly staff, well kept Stones Best and Wards Sheffield Best on handpump, coal fire, decent bar food, smart restaurant, comfortable back locals' bar; bedrooms *(P R Morley, BB)*

Fishtoft, Lincs [A52 Boston—Wainfleet; TF3642], *Ball House*: Looks more a house than a pub, good generous fresh food using local produce, lots of fresh veg, vegetarian dishes, Batemans and other beers *(Miss J Sanderson)*

Frampton, Lincs [signposted off A16 S of Boston; TF3239], *Moores Arms*: Friendly character pub with well kept Bass, good food, popular lunchtime with Boston businessmen; perhaps the prettiest Fenland village *(V and E A Bolton, Peter Burton)*

☆ **Frisby on the Wreake**, Leics [Main St; SK6917], *Bell*: Friendly roomy pine-beamed local with brass, oil paintings and real fire, family room in back extension, good choice of well kept real ales, fair range of wines, decent coffee, decent straightforward lunchtime food, different evening choice – good value and quality; smaller back family room; piped music, smart dress required; tables outside *(CMW, JJW, Joan and Michel Hooper-Immins)*

Gaddesby, Leics [SK6813], *Cheney Arms*: Two-room pub refurbished under newish landlord, big comfortable lounge with open fire and Dambusters mementoes, bare-boards bar with racehorse prints, Everards Beacon and Tiger, good bar food running up to roast wild boar; well kept back garden; bedrooms *(Stephen Brown)*

Gainsborough, Lincs [Lord St; SK8189],

White Hart: Helpful friendly staff, Courage-related ales, big helpings of good value food *(Ann Griffiths)*

☆ **Gedney**, Lincs [Chapelgate, just off A17 W of Long Sutton; TF4024], *Old Black Lion*: Good warmly welcoming service, wide choice of good value quickly served food inc fresh veg, Whitbreads-related ales, good house wines *(John Wooll, Ray Tunnicliff, Mrs R Finlay)*

☆ **Glaston**, Leics [A47 Leicester—Peterboro, E of Uppingham; SK8900], *Monckton Arms*: Attractive stone inn quite handy for Rutland Water, with three neat and friendly little rooms in bar, picnic tables on sheltered terrace by sizeable modern extension, comfortable bedrooms; a popular main entry in last edition, with well kept Bass, Marstons Pedigree and Tetleys and a wide choice of good value fresh-cooked bar food, but licensees left as we went to press, with no news of replacements *(LYM; reports please)*

☆ **Grantham**, Lincs [High St; SK9135], *Angel & Royal*: Remarkable worn medieval carved stone facade, ancient oriel window seat in upstairs plush bar on left, massive inglenook in friendly high-beamed main bar opp (has had spit-roasts), well kept Bass and occasional guest beers, bar food; bedrooms in comfortable modern Forte hotel block extending behind *(George Brisco, LYM)*

Grantham [Vine St], *Blue Pig*: Another of the few buildings here to survive the great fire of 1660, beams, character, well kept beer, welcoming service, simple bar food, three rooms – one with machines *(RB, Ian Phillips)*

☆ **Great Casterton**, Lincs [village signed off A1; TF0009], *Crown*: Neat stripped-stone bar with high booth seating, inglenook log fire, friendly atmosphere, good range of well kept ales, good value home-cooked bar food; simpler back bar, old-fashioned seats in pretty little garden opp attractive church *(DC, Christopher Turner, BB)*

Greatford, Lincs [TF0811], *Hare & Hounds*: The Podmores who made this unpretentious local a popular main entry with their enterprising food are now to be found at the Ship at Surfleet Seas End *(LYM)*

☆ **Greetham**, Leics [B668 Stretton—Cottesmore; SK9214], *Wheatsheaf*: Consistently good value generous food served till 11 inc lots of char-grills and Fri bargain steak suppers in welcoming unpretentious L-shaped communicating rooms, well kept Tetleys and Whitbreads on handpump, attentive staff, coal fire, soft piped music; pool and other games in end room, restaurant, tables on side grass; live music Sat *(Jenny and Michael Back, Jim Farmer, BB)*

☆ **Grimston**, Leics [off A6006 W of Melton Mowbray; SK6821], *Black Horse*: Comfortable, suave and sparkling clean, with good imaginatively presented straightforward bar food – all freshly cooked, so takes time; remarkable collection of cricket memorabilia (landlord happy to talk about it), well kept Marstons Pedigree, open fire, discreet piped music; no food Sun, cl Sun evening and Mon exc bank hols; attractive village with stocks and 13th-c church *(Colin McKerrow, David and Shelia, J H Gracey, Patrick Clancy, LYM)*

☆ **Gunthorpe**, Notts [Trentside; SK6844], *Tom Browns*: Converted riverside school house with good really unusual interesting food in bar and restaurant, Theakstons and two guest beers, overnight moorings *(Andy and Jill Kassube)*

Halam, Notts [SK6754], *Waggon & Horses*: Attractive old building housing popular mainstream good value dining pub *(Paul Gretton, J Finney)*

☆ **Hallaton**, Leics [North End; SP7896], *Fox*: Warm and friendly local with good value bar food inc five vegetarian dishes such as wonderful vegetarian yorkshire pudding, good Sun carvery; well kept Marstons Pedigree and Tetleys, Spanish landlord; children welcome; tables out by village duckpond *(Carole Cox, Rona Murdoch)*

Halstead, Leics [SK7405], *Salisbury Arms*: Village pub with lovely country views from restaurant conservatory, good varied food, good choice of beers inc local brew *(P and J Farrow)*

☆ **Halton Holegate**, Lincs [B1195 E of Spilsby; TF4165], *Bell*: Pretty village local, simple but comfortable and welcoming, with wide choice of decent home-made food inc outstanding fish and chips, vegetarian dishes and Sun lunches, well kept Bass, Batemans and Mansfield Old Baily, aircraft pictures, pub games, maybe piped music; children in eating area and restaurant *(D W Gray, Derek and Sylvia Stephenson, LYM)*

Heath End, Leics [SK3621], *Saracens Head*: Basic two-room farm pub by Staunton Harold Reservoir visitor centre; Bass tapped from the cask, warm coal fires, very cheap sandwiches *(Jack and Phil Paxton)*

Horncastle, Lincs [West St; TF2669], *Fighting Cocks*: Unpretentious oak-beamed local with quick cheerful service, wide range of good value food inc gigantic garnished yorkshire puddings, Batemans, Courage Directors, Marstons Pedigree and M & B Brew XI, open fire each end *(A W Dickinson, Chris Mawson)*; *Kings Head*: Thatched pub with well kept Batemans, good home-made food, unexpected decor in lavatories – as in a private house *(Frank W Gadbois)*

☆ **Hough on the Hill**, Lincs [SK9246], *Brownlow Arms*: Wide range of good value well cooked and presented food (not weekday lunchtimes) in attractive 17th-c pub's relaxing lounge, sofas and comfortable chairs, well kept Marstons Pedigree and changing guest beers, decent wines, friendly efficient service; pubby separate bar, good restaurant; good value pretty bedrooms, good breakfasts, peaceful picturesque village *(Norman and Gill Fox, R A Hobbs, RB, V and E A Bolton)*

☆ **Illston on the Hill,** Leics [off B6047 Mkt Harborough—Melton; SP7099], *Fox & Goose*: Welcoming and idiosyncratic pub full of interesting decorations, well kept Everards Mild, Beacon, Old Original and Tiger, good coal fires, friendly licensees; no food *(J D Cloud, Jim Farmer, BB)*

☆ **Kegworth,** Leics [towards West Leake – OS Sheet 129 map ref 501268; SK5026], *Station*: Attractively refurbished, with stripped brickwork and open fires, two rooms off small bar area, new upstairs dining room, well kept Bass and Worthington, well served good food; tables on big back lawn; bedrooms *(David Eberlin, A and R Cooper, Jack and Philip Paxton)*

Kegworth, *Red Lion*: Unpretentious pub with well kept beer and good home cooking *(David and Shelia)*

Kibworth Beauchamp, Leics [Leicester Rd; SP6893], *Coach & Horses*: Popualr food in welcoming pub with well kept Bass, log fires *(Eric Locker)*

☆ **Kibworth Harcourt,** Leics [Main St (just off A6); SP6894], *Three Horseshoes*: Unassuming quiet village pub with well kept Bass and Marstons Best and Pedigree, decent straightforward generous food (not Sun evening), friendly service, comfortable plush seating, side eating areas; piped music, children welcome; tables on attractive back terrace *(Eric Locker, Brian Atkin, PC, Gwen and Peter Andrews, LYM)*

☆ **Kilby Bridge,** Leics [A50 S of Leicester; SP6097], *Navigation*: Fine canalside position with waterside garden, several areas, some small and cosy, off central bar, big dining area, generous usual food, warm welcome, well kept Tetleys-related ales and Marstons Pedigree on handpump, good coffee; huge fish in tank in lounge, piped music, fruit machines, busy bookable restaurant; children welcome, no dogs *(George Atkinson, P G Topp, Jim Farmer, J Haywood)*

Kimberley, Notts [Nottingham Rd; SK5044], *Stag*: Cosy old pub with small lounge, busy bar, low oak beams, table skittles, Tetleys-related ales, play garden at back *(Jack and Philip Paxton)*

Kirby Muxloe, Leics [Main St; SK5104], *Royal Oak*: Pleasant pub with good value early-bird lunch and wide range of good if not cheap filled french sticks, full Everards range and one or two guest beers; piped music *(Derek and Sylvia Stephenson, Gerald Roxbury)*

Kirkby on Bain, Lincs [TF2462], *Ebrington Arms*: Very welcoming, pleasant meals, genial landlord, good range of guest beers *(Arthur and Susan Brough)*

☆ **Knossington,** Leics [off A606 W of Oakham; SK8008], *Fox & Hounds*: Unspoilt small village pub with coal fire in cosy comfortable lounge, pool room for younger customers, friendly licensees, well kept Courage-related ales, huge choice of malt whiskies, reasonably priced food inc unusual dishes, summer barbecues in big garden *(Dave and Pat Heath, Jack and Philip Paxton, Anthony Barnes, J D Cloud)*

☆ **Lambley,** Notts [Church St; SK6245], *Woodlark*: Well preserved and interestingly laid out, careful extension into next house giving extra lounge/dining area, good value lunches and more ambitious evening meals, cheerful welcome, well kept S & N ales, wide range of pub games inc pool room, table skittles and skittle alley; children in annexe *(Alan and Eileen Bowker, BB)*

Langham, Leics [Bridge St; SK8411], *Noel Arms*: Comfortable and attractively furnished low-ceilinged lounge, smart covered terrace, well kept beers inc Ruddles from nearby brewery, usual bar food *(Jim Farmer, LYM)*

☆ **Langworth,** Lincs [A158 Lincoln—Wragby; TF0676], *New Station*: Pleasant pub (station long gone, railway still there) with roomy conservatory, well kept Courage-related ales, reasonably priced wine, generous food esp super fresh fish and chips, Sunday carvery *(Michael Clark, John C Baker)*

☆ **Leicester** [9 Welford Pl; corner Newarke St/Welford Rd], *Welford Place*: Spacious semicircular Victorian bar overlooking busy streets, an air of gravitas – quiet, comfortable, almost clubby; Ruddles Best and County, good choice of decent wines and other drinks, friendly and obliging service; good changing bar food, palatial stone stairs to tasteful restaurant; under same management as main-entry Wig & Mitre in Lincoln *(O K Smyth, Susan and Nigel Siesage, Julie Peters)*

☆ **Leicester** [Silver St/Carts Lane], *Globe*: Clubbily local old-fashioned three-room pub with lots of woodwork, gas lighting, coal-effect gas fire, peaceful upstairs dining room with good value simple lunchtime food; well kept Everards and guest beers such as Enville and Morlands Old Speckled Hen; juke box *(Brian and Anna Marsden, Joan and Michel Hooper-Immins, Paul Cartledge, BB)*

☆ **Leicester** [Charles St], *Rainbow & Dove*: Big open-plan bare-boards bar nr station with well kept Banks's Mild and Bitter, Hansons Mild, Camerons Strongarm and four guest ales, farm cider, good service, plain well cooked food weekday lunchtimes; students evening, professionals too lunchtime, live music Sun evening, regular beer festivals *(Joan and Michel Hooper-Immins, Paul Cartledge, J D Cloud)*

☆ **Leicester** [131 Beaumanor Rd; off Abbey Lane (A5131), rt fork S from A6 at Red Hill Circle], *Tom Hoskins*: Tap for Hoskins small brewery – group brewhouse tours can be arranged; flagstones, floorboards, panelling, varnished pews, brewery memorabilia; well kept cheap Hoskins and guest ales, limited but good value lunchtime food (not Sun), traditional games and fruit machine; can get smoky *(A G Roby, LYM)*

Leicester [156 Belgrave Gate], *Bowlturners Arms*: Friendly local with well kept Tetleys-related ales (Shipstones), skittle alley *(Richard Houghton)*; [Pocklingtons Walk], *Lamplighters*: Interesting modern pub with neon above bar, stained-glass round ceiling, ceiling fans, bric-a-brac piled on shelves; well kept Mansfield beers inc Riding, good well priced lunchtime food inc children's, good atmosphere; piped music *(Brian and Anna Marsden, Joan and Michel Hooper-Immins, R and A Cooper)*; [139 London Rd], *Marquis of Wellington*: Lively Edwardian pub with swift professional service, good filled lunchtime rolls and simple changing hot dishes inc evening pot meals, well kept Adnams, Everards and guest beers, interesting bric-a-brac; popular with professional people lunchtime, more studenty evening; colourful back courtyard with murals and attractive plants *(JCW, Paul Cartledge, Joan and Michel Hooper-Immins, J Weeks)*; [Welford Rd (A50), Victoria Park], *New Road*: Comfortably plush, with several Tetleys-related ales, beams and ochre walls; subdued piped music *(Brian and Anna Marsden)*; [Highcross St], *Red Lion*: Nicely decorated central pub, particularly well kept Burtonwood beers; soft piped music *(G W Mason)*; [Butt Close Lane, nr bus stn], *Salmon*: Cosy and welcoming Banks's pub nr Shires shopping centre, reasonably priced well kept beer, single drinking area round a semicicular bar *(Brian and Anna Marsden)*; [King St], *Vin Quatre*: Good atmosphere, popular with young professionals, reasonable prices *(Marc Tournier)*; [centre], *Wellington*: Big island bar, comfortable seats in bays around tables, small no-smoking area, decent wine, limited nourishing cheap snacks quickly served by friendly staff *(John Wooll)*

☆ **Lincoln** [Bunkers Hill], *Lincolnshire Poacher*: Careful renovation by Mansfield, roomy and comfortable bar area with old chairs and books, Lincolnshire memorabilia inc interesting prints, big dining part with no-smoking areas, good range of food inc local dishes, Riding and Old Baily real ale, attentive considerate service; play areas inside and (with video surveillance) outside; open all day Sun *(Mike and Maggie Betton, Gordon Thornton)*

☆ **Lincoln** [Steep Hill], *Browns Pie Shop*: Wide choice of good food inc popular chunky pies; restaurant licence only, but does have Everards Tiger and Ruddles Best as well as decent wines, comfortable seats, friendly staff, pleasant traditional atmosphere *(ILP, Gordon Thornton)*

Lincoln [25 Lindum Rd (Wragby rd)], *Adam & Eve*: Civilised pub, one of the oldest here, opp gate to cathedral close; well kept John Smiths and Theakstons, bar food; boules, tree-shaded play area *(Ian Phillips, HKD)*; [Doddington Rd (B1190, outskirts)], *Swanholme*: Comfortable and friendly new pub delightfully placed by lake, Bass and Worthington in pleasant bar, big dining area with facilities for children and children's helpings *(Gordon Thornton)*; [Burton Lane End, off A57 Saxilby rd SW], *Woodcocks*: Well done modern family pub with outside playground, supervised indoor play area, plenty of high chairs in dining areas, children's menus; good varied decor, Marstons beers, reasonably priced food, friendly staff, pleasant spot nr canal walk *(David and Ruth Hollands, Gordon Thornton)*

Littlethorpe, Leics [Station Rd; not far from M1 junction 21; off B4114; SP5496], *Plough*: Friendly 16th-c thatched pub, local pictures and china in lounge, smoke room with darts, copper tabletops and kettles, decent food inc good cheeseburgers, dining room, Everards ales and a guest such as Shepherd Neame Bishops Finger, piped local radio, bedlington terriers wandering around; children welcome, picnic tables outside *(JJW, CMW, George Atkinson)*

Long Bennington, Lincs [SK8344], *Reindeer*: Busy welcoming local with good choice of home-cooked food in bar and more formal dining lounge, good wines, friendly efficient service *(Donald and Margaret Wood, Robert Jordan)*; [Main St], *Royal Oak*: Another popular and comfortable local, well kept Marstons Pedigree, good home cooking, decent wines, welcoming service, games room, skittle alley, back garden; sociable children well catered for *(Stewart Boyd, Roy W Sowden, D G Stentiford)*

Long Sutton, Lincs [Main St; off bypass A17 Kings Lynn—Holbeach; TF4222], *Crown & Woolpack*: Good generous low-priced home cooking (sandwiches only, Mon-Weds) in thriving unpretentious local with panelled back dining room, good Sun lunch (must book), Bass, Worthington BB and one or two guest beers such as Black Sheep or Kilkenny, roaring fire; dominoes, piped music (may be rather loud) *(Michael and Jenny Back)*

☆ **Loughborough**, Leics [The Rushes (A6); SK5319], *Black Lion*: Wide range of Hoskins and other beers, stripped pine and pews, bare boards and sawdust in front bar area, cosier back lounge; very helpful bar service, good value simple food, peaceful at lunchtime but noisy evenings; handy for canal basin *(A and R Cooper, Dr and Mrs A M Evans, Joan and Michel Hooper-Immins)*

Loughborough [Wards End], *Blacksmiths Arms*: Well kept ales inc Hoskins Mild and Bitter, Marstons Pedigree, Newcastle Exhibition and Theakstons Old Peculier and XB; good range of modestly priced food esp pies *(Tim and Ann Newell, Alan and Kristina Thorley)*; *Great Central*: Attractively refurbished, popular lunchtime for good value food, friendly atmosphere; bedrooms *(A and R Cooper)*; [Churchgate], *Three Nuns*: Recently refurbished, good range of beers and country wines; good well priced food the main lunchtime draw, evening popular with students *(A and R*

Cooper)

☆ **Louth**, Lincs [Cordeaux Corner, Brackenborough – off bypass; TF3289], *Brackenborough Arms*: Two welcoming bars with well kept Marstons and Stones, wide choice of bottled beers, food inc good generous home-cooked pies and fresh Grimsby fish and chips; good bedrooms in new wing *(W P J Elderkin, Stephen, Julie and Hayley Brown)*

Louth [Cornmarket], *Masons Arms*: Beautifully restored. with friendly landlord, several well kept ales, good vegetarian food, good dining room (former masonic lodge meeting room); bedrooms *(Frank W Gadbois)*

Lowdham, Notts [1 Southwell Rd; SK6646], *Magna Charta*: Hardys & Hansons pub with good range of food, plenty of tables, pleasant bar area *(Mike and Maggie Betton)*

☆ **Lutterworth**, Leics [34 Rugby Rd (A426 S); very handy for M1 junction 20; SP5484], *Fox*: Friendly and clean, with comfortable dining chairs in lounge, decent food inc good vegetarian special, well kept Whitbreads-related ales, good coffee, very friendly and accommodating landlord, open fires; video game but no piped music; tables in garden *(Frank Davidson, George Atkinson, Frank Cummins)*

Lutterworth [Market St], *Greyhound*: Attractive 18th-c coaching inn, friendly service, Tetleys-related ale, good well presented bar food from sandwiches up; restaurant; bedrooms *(R T Moggridge)*

☆ **Lyddington**, Leics [SP8797], *Old White Hart*: Traditional village inn with two small atmospheric flagstoned bars, enterprising good value food (not Sun evening) with fresh veg, well kept Greene King Abbot, decent wines, friendly service, restaurant; safe and pretty summer garden *(Stephen, Julie and Hayley Brown, Wayne Brindle, Rev J E Cooper, Roy Collings, W Elderkin)*

Mansfield, Notts [39 Leeming St; SK5561], *Tap & Spile*: Two-roomed town pub nr market, several well kept real ales, annual beer festival, lunchtime and evening food; games in back room, children in no-smoking snug *(Jack and Philip Paxton)*

☆ **Manton**, Leics [St Marys Rd; SK8704], *Horse & Jockey*: Unspoilt character pub with big coal fire, warmly welcoming landlord, good range of promptly served food, well kept Mansfield Riding and Old Baily; can get busy even in winter; comfortable bedrooms, not far from Rutland Water *(Jack and Philip Paxton)*

☆ **Maplebeck**, Notts [signed from A616/A617; SK7160], *Beehive*: Snug little unspoiled beamed country tavern, traditional furnishings, open fire, free antique juke box, Mansfield ale, tables on small terrace with grassy bank running down to small stream – very peaceful *(Eamon Green, LYM)*

☆ **Mapperley**, Notts [Plains Rd (B684); SK6043], *Travellers Rest*: Friendly and popular, open all day, with half a dozen well kept S & N ales and a guest beer, wide choice of good value food all day (not after 2 Sun/Mon) inc vegetarian and children's, good ordering system, popular lunchtime no-smoking area, back family building with adjacent play area *(Alan and Eileen Bowker, Bruce Bird)*

Mareham le Fen, Lincs [A115; TF2861], *Royal Oak*: Interesting partly thatched 14th-c building with pleasant interior, well kept Batemans XB and a guest such as John Smiths, friendly atmosphere, limited good value food *(Joan and Michel Hooper-Immins, M J Morgan)*

☆ **Market Bosworth**, Leics [The Square; SK4003], *Black Horse*: Village local popular for wide choice of reasonably priced food, keen attentive service and well kept Marstons Pedigree and Tetleys; restaurant; bedrooms, attractive village *(the Monday Club, Jim Farmer, Graham Richardson, David Atkinson)*

☆ **Market Bosworth** [Mkt Pl], *Softleys*: Wine bar/restaurant (you more or less have to eat, but it does have well kept Hook Norton Best and Wadworths 6X) in fine old building with oak beams, brassware, hanging mugs, grand fireplace; good individually prepared food inc sandwiches and changing hot dishes, some interesting; very friendly service, decent wine, spotless housekeeping, attractive upstairs dining room; closed Mon; bedrooms *(P J Caunt, Roy Bromell, George Atkinson, Dorothee and Dennis Glover)*

Market Bosworth [Rectory Lane], *Inn on the Park*: Good value reliable food in dining pub with smart bar, polite welcoming staff, well kept Bass; beautiful spacious grounds *(C J Pratt, K Walton)*

☆ **Market Deeping**, Lincs [Market Pl; TF1310], *Bull*: Low-ceilinged alcoves, little corridors, interesting heavy-beamed medieval Dugout Bar; well kept Everards Tiger and Old Original and guest beers, good value bar food (not Sun or Mon evening), attractive eating area, no piped music lunchtime, helpful friendly service, restaurant; seats in pretty coachyard; children in eating areas; open all day Fri, Sat *(Norma and Keith Bloomfield, LYM)*

☆ **Market Harborough**, Leics [High St; SP7388], *Three Swans*: Comfortable and handsome coaching inn with fine range of bar food inc good lunchtime ploughman's and toasties in plush and peaceful front lounge bar, fine conservatory or attractive suntrap courtyard, decent wines, good coffee, very friendly and helpful staff; Courage-related ales, upstairs restaurant; bedrooms *(Joan and Michel Hooper-Immins, Stephen Brown, Jim Farmer)*

Market Overton, Leics [High St, nr church; SK8816], *Black Bull*: Attractive pub with artificial pool and waterfall by entrance, thriving lounge bar with Ruddles, Theakstons and Youngs, wide choice of good bar meals, restaurant; get there early Sun and in summer *(Eddie and Iris Brixton)*

☆ **Markfield**, Leics [A50 just under a mile from M1 junction 22; SK4810], *Field Head*: Huge beamed lounge/dining area around central bar, pictures, antiquey bits and pieces, uncounted nooks and corners; good reasonably priced generous food in bar and restaurant, friendly attentive staff, Hoskins and other ales, decent house wine; bedrooms, huge breakfasts *(George Atkinson, the Monday Club, O K Smyth)*

☆ **Marston**, Lincs [2 miles E of A1 just N of Grantham; SK8943], *Thorold Arms*: Pleasantly refurbished, with good food and atmosphere, friendly service, well kept ales *(Peter Burton, Jeanne and Tom Barnes)*

Minting, Lincs [The Green; off A158 Lincoln—Horncastle; TF1873], *Sebastopol*: Comfortable and attractive country pub, cosy and low-beamed, with good restaurant food (must book at busy times), homely sofas in carpeted public bar, fish tank built into wall; cl Mon *(Mike and Maggie Betton)*

☆ **Morton**, Notts [SK7251], *Full Moon*: Rambling 16th-c local, comfortably enlarged but not spoilt, very popular even midweek for good fairly priced food inc fish, vegetarian and Indian specialities and lots of puddings; well kept Theakstons and guest beers, prompt welcoming service; children welcome, delightfully out-of-the-way hamlet *(Ian and Val Titman, Geoffrey and Irene Lindley)*

☆ **Mountsorrel**, Leics [Loughborough Rd, off A6; SK5714], *Swan*: Particularly good unusual home cooking with a very deft touch in two unshowy whitewashed bars with log fires and red banquettes, well kept Batemans and Theakstons, wide choice of good wines by the glass, unusual non-alcoholic drinks, very pleasant but uneffusive welcome; walled back garden leading down to canalised River Soar; bedrooms; *(Anthony Barnes, A and R Cooper)*

☆ **Navenby**, Lincs [High St; car park behind is off East Rd; SK9858], *Kings Head*: Small village pub with decent food inc good varied puddings in pleasant no-smoking area off bar, interesting nick-nacks, books, quick friendly service, well kept Bass, no piped music *(P Neate, Peter Burton, Roger and Linda Nicklin)*

☆ **Newark**, Notts [London Rd, nr Beaumond Cross; SK8054], *Mail Coach*: Generous reasonably priced lunchtime food (not Sun), well kept Tetleys-related ales and changing guest beers in comfortable interestingly decorated communicating areas, friendly service, decent wines, open fires, traditional games, sheltered back courtyard; open all day, live blues Sat *(Lorna and Bill Tyson, Graham Gowland, Paul Gretton)*

☆ **Newark** [Northgate], *Malt Shovel*: Welcoming and comfortably refurbished old-fashioned local with good doorstep sandwiches and lunchtime hot dishes inc fresh veg, well kept Timothy Taylors Landlord, Wards Sheffield Best and guest beers, choice of teas, very friendly staff *(Lorna and Bill Tyson)*

☆ **Newton Burgoland**, Leics [Main St; off B586 W of Ibstock; SK3708], *Belper Arms*: Friendly and interesting pub said to date from 13th century, good reasonably priced food in roomy lounge and low-beamed areas off, lots of bric-a-brac, well kept Marstons, restaurant; big garden with play area *(Julie Peters)*

Normanton on Soar, Notts [Main St – OS Sheet 129 map ref 518230; SK5123], *Plough*: Popular two-bar mock-Tudor village local in beautiful setting by River Soar, nice atmosphere and decorations, well kept Marstons Pedigree and Tetleys, attentive friendly staff; children's playground *(A and R Cooper, Chris Raisin)*

☆ **North Muskham**, Notts [Ferry Lane; village signed just off A1 N of Newark; SK7958], *Muskham Ferry*: Warmly welcoming pub in splendid location on River Trent, tastefully redecorated, with wider range of food, well kept Courage-related ales and changing guest beers, attentive staff, relaxing views, children very welcome; waterside garden *(David and Shelia, Bill Flisher, Adam and Joan Bunting, Mary Moore, J Finney, Celia Minoughan, D and B Carter, Arthur and Margaret Dickinson, Malcolm Phillips, D Grzelka, LYM)*

☆ **Norton Disney**, Lincs [Main St; off A46 Newark—Lincoln; SK8859], *St Vincent Arms*: Attractive village pub with well kept Batemans Mild and XXXB, Marstons Pedigree, three interesting guest beers, open fire, good value plain food from sandwiches up, pleasant landlord; tables and big amusing adventure playground out behind *(Derek and Sylvia Stevenson, Sarah and Peter Gooderham)*

☆ **Nottingham** [18 Angel Row; off Market Sq], *Bell*: Quaint low-beamed 15th-c pub with Bass, Eldridge Pope Royal Oak, Jennings Bitter, Marstons Pedigree and Theakstons Old Peculier and a guest like Mansfield Old Baily kept well in extraordinarily deep sandstone cellar, three bustling timbered and panelled bars (very crowded and maybe smoky late evening), nice window seats in calmer raftered upstairs room used as lunchtime family restaurant – good value simple well presented lunchtime food; good value wines, quick friendly service; trad jazz Sun lunchtime (rolls only then), Mon and Tues evenings; open all day weekdays *(Joan and Michel Hooper-Immins, Norman Smith, Norma and Keith Bloomfield, Chris Raisin, Eamon Green, LYM)*

Nottingham [117 Hartley Rd, Radford; SK5540], *Boulevard*: Busy, friendly town pub, very cheap Youngers Scotch, games bar with pool, darts and snooker, lots going on in the evenings, entertainment, pub games etc *(Russell Allen)*; [2 Canal St], *Canal*: New pub with Batemans, Deakins Stag, Everards Beacon, Mansfield Old Baily, Bitter, Riding and Mild and guest beers, good friendly staff, meals, November beer festival *(Richard Lewis)*; [Mansfield Rd], *Filly & Firkin*: Nice straightforward interior, its own brews Dogbolter, Filly, Rocks and two guest beers, this chain's usual good value food *(R Lewis)*; [Mansfield Rd], *Golden Fleece*: Good choice of Tetleys-related ales *(R Lewis)*; [Balloon Wood, Wollaton; SK5139], *Gondola*: Friendly pleasantly refurbished local, welcoming lounge, public bar with pool, darts and dominoes, good value food, Home Mild and Bitter, quiz night Thurs, live entertainment Thurs-Sun; pleasant rural setting, open all day *(Mr and Mrs R J Allen)*; [Mansfield Rd, Carrington; SK5642], *Grosvenor*: Big busy open-plan pub with real fire, interesting continental beers inc fruit beers, good choice of about eight guest beers, good value food inc Sun roast; lavatories for the disabled *(Mr and Mrs R J Allen)*; [273 Castle Bvd, Lenton; SK5438], *Grove*: Busy studenty pub, recently opened upstairs real ale bar with particularly well kept Theakstons XB, good food inc big pies and yorkshire puddings, interesting bottled beers and brewery memorabilia, pleasant staff, quiz nights Tues, TV upstairs for football and rugby *(Russell and Carolynne Allen, Anna Brewer)*; [North Sherwood St], *Hole in the Wall*: Friendly landlord, shiny wooden floor, bar food, fine choice of beer such as Deakins Stag, Mansfield Riding, Bitter, Old Baily and Mild, Timothy Taylors Landlord and two guest beers *(R Lewis)*; [91 Front St, Arnold; SK5845], *Horse & Jockey*: Warm and friendly traditional town pub, good range of beers with weekly changing guest, continental bottled beers and Belgian fruit beers, open fires, food inc good pies all day *(Mr and Mrs R J Allen)*; [Trent Bridge], *Larwood & Voce*: On the edge of the cricket ground, reasonably priced bar food, well kept Theakstons *(Andy and Jill Kassube)*; [Wellington Circus], *Limelight*: Lively bar and restaurant attached to Playhouse theatre, nine constantly changing well kept ales, occasional modern jazz *(R Lewis, David and Shelia, Derek and Sylvia Stevenson)*; [Clumber St], *Lion*: Friendly efficient service, Theakstons ales, reasonably priced meals; separate dining room *(SB)*; [Wilford St (A453 at canal bridge)], *Navigation*: Basic bar food, real ales such as Banks's Bitter, Mild and Time Warp, weekly guests like Camerons Strongarm; popular with students *(R Lewis)*; [Nuthall Rd, Cinderhill; SK5343], *Red Lion*: Busy and friendly, popular with students lunchtime, locals evening; big open-plan bar with pool and darts in games area, comfortable raised area, Theakstons, well priced lunchtime food (not Sun); children welcome, summer barbecues, live music Mon; open all day *(Mr and Mrs R J Allen)*; [Alfreton Rd], *Red Lion.*: Good range of beers, good reasonably priced food with Tues supper bargain, Sun breakfast with papers *(David and Shelia)*; [Maid Marion Way], *Salutation*: Ancient back part with beams, flagstones and cosy corners, plusher modern front, cheap cheerful food, up to a dozen changing ales inc interesting ones, sensible prices and good atmosphere *(David and Shelia, Keith Stevens, George Atkinson, Graham Bush, BB)*; [Mansfield Rd, Arnold – opp Burnt Stump Park, nr Papplewick pumping stn; SK5845], *Seven Mile*: Usual Beefeater food, five well kept Whitbreads-related ales, tasteful decor, no-smoking area, friendly service, piped music, old photographs, plants etc *(JJW, CMW)*; [132 Park Lane, Bosford], *Standard of England*: Open-plan local with pool, pinball, darts, dominoes etc, Sky TV, good range of drinks inc very cheap Youngers Scotch, lots of bank hol activities *(R J Allen)*; [Sheriffs Way, Queensbridge Rd], *Tom Hoskins*: Good choice of beers such as Batemans Mild, Cains Mild, Hoskins Beaumanor, Old Nigel and Penns *(R Lewis)*; [off Market Sq], *Yates Wine Lodge*: Lively and traditional, good range of drinks esp wines *(Chris Raisin)*

Nuthall, Notts [Nottingham Rd (B600, away from city), off A610 nr M1 junction 26; SK5144], *Three Ponds*: Tastefully refurbished Hardys & Hansons roadhouse with garden and play area, well kept Kimberley Classic on handpump, good value food with cheaper meals for OAPs, good coffee; piped music may obtrude *(JJW, CMW)*

Oakham, Leics [2 Northgate; SK8508], *Wheatsheaf*: Friendly two-room 17th-c pub nr church, Adnams and Everards Beacon and Tiger, open fire, usual food *(George Atkinson)*

Peatling Magna, Leics [SP5992], *Cock*: Thriving village local with two rooms, cosy log fire, good value generous food, friendly staff, lots of events *(C Elliott, Louise Wordsworth)*

Peatling Parva, Leics [SP5889], *Shires*: Comfortable seats, Ruddles beers, big garden, good range of food, friendly service, piped music not too obtrusive *(George Atkinson)*

☆ **Pleasley**, Notts [handy for M1 junction 29; A617 Mansfield—Chesterfield; SK5064], *Old Plough*: Comfortably and attractively extended, wide range of good value food from sandwiches to well priced steaks, well kept Ind Coope Burton, Tetleys, Mansfield Old Baily and guests such as Thwaites Craftsman *(Andy and Jill Kassube, Derek and Sylvia Stephenson)*

Plumtree, Notts [just off A606 S of Nottingham; SK6132], *Griffin*: Civilised and tastefully refurbished, good generous food in airy conservatory, well kept Hardys & Hansons *(Mrs J Barwell, Chris Raisin, Ruth and Alan Cooper)*

Radcliffe on Trent, Notts [SK6439], *Round Oak*: Real ale and generous wholesome food at reasonable prices; character not its strongest point *(David and Shelia)*

☆ **Ranby**, Notts [just off A1 by A620 Worksop—E Retford; SK6580], *Chequers*: Nice building in superb canalside spot, delightful waterside terrace, some mooring, weekend boat trips; well kept beer, cheerful service, attractive and comfortable inside, dining room with farm tools and bric-a-brac; children welcome, open all day, reasonably priced food noon-10 *(David Campbell, Vicki McLean, Mr and Mrs Buckley)*

☆ **Ravenshead**, Notts [177 Main Rd (B6020); SK5956], *Little John*: Well organised modern pub with comfortable airy lounge, good value bar food, games in smaller public bar, aquarium between bars, well kept Mansfield, restaurant; weekend barbecues, no dogs *(JJW, CMW, LYM)*

☆ **Redmile**, Leics [off A52 Grantham—Nottingham; SK8036], *Olde Windmill*: Welcoming and comfortable lounge and dining room, well kept Everards and other ales, good range of generous good value bar food; less crowded than our main entry here; tables on terrace and in garden *(Elizabeth and Anthony Watts, Dr and Mrs J H Hills)*

☆ **Rothwell**, Lincs [Caistor Rd (A46); TF1599], *Nickerson Arms*: Convivial and attractive open-plan bar, good imaginative if not cheap food with some emphasis on fish, wide choice of well kept ales such as Batemans, Tetleys, Timothy Taylors Landlord, friendly and relaxed atmosphere; children welcome, tables outside *(Nigel and Lindsay Chapman)*

Ryhall, Leics [TF0310], *Old Green Dragon*: Interesting old pub doing well under current regime, Bass, Greene King and Tetleys ales, well priced food *(K H Frostick)*

☆ **Saddington**, Leics [S of Leicester between A50 and A6 – OS Sheet 141 map ref 658918; SP6591], *Queens Head*: Welcoming and popular, with enterprising landlord, good food inc good Sun lunch in recently refurbished dining room with lovely view, OAP bargain lunches, well kept Adnams, Everards Beacon and Tiger and Ruddles *(Cdr Patrick Tailyour, Elizabeth and Anthony Watts)*

☆ **Scaftworth**, Notts [A631 Bawtry—Everton; SK6692], *King William*: Pleasant country pub reopened under welcoming new tenants, three rooms with old high-back settles and plain tables and chairs, pictures, new carpets; well kept Whitbreads-related ales, decent home cooking, darts and pool, friendly little dog; big garden, play area *(JJW, CMW, David Alcock, LYM)*

Scalford, Leics [SK7624], *Plough*: Neat newly decorated free house doing well under newish landlady, well kept Greene King Abbot, notable food *(Sara Nathan)*

☆ **Scotter**, Lincs [The Green; SE8801], *White Swan*: Charming spot by village green on duck-populated river bank, wide choice of good sensibly priced bar food inc children's helpings, real ales, separate dining room menu; 12 luxury bedrooms *(Gordon Thornton)*

Selston, Notts [Church Ln, nr M1 junction 27; SK4553], *Horse & Jockey*: Very traditional, with up to ten real ales tapped from the cask, bank hol beer festivals, outside lavatories, small play area; open all day Mon and Sat *(Jack and Phil Paxton)*

Shawell, Leics [not far from M6 junction 1; village signed off A5/A427 roundabout – turn right in village; SP5480], *White Swan*: Creeper-covered dining pub which has been popular for good food in roomy dining room, well kept ales and friendly service *(News of current regime please)*

☆ **Shearsby**, Leics [A50 Leicester—Northampton; SP6290], *Chandlers Arms*: Good food inc Indian, vegetarian and even vegan in small welcoming stonebuilt pub with well kept Marstons Pedigree and other ales such as Adnams and Greene King, relaxing atmosphere, Dutch landlady, well chosen piped music; attractive back terrace garden, picturesque village; children allowed in one room for lunch, no motorcyclists *(George Atkinson, Jim Farmer)*

☆ **Sheepy Magna**, Leics [Main St (B4116); SK3201], *Black Horse*: Neatly kept village pub with good value generous food from filled rolls up, friendly licensees, well kept Ansells Mild and Marstons Pedigree on handpump, games in lively public bar, family area, tables on pleasantly arranged back terrace *(M and J Back, LYM)*

Shepshed, Leics [Iveshead Rd, handy for M1 junction 23; SK4719], *Jolly Farmers*: Character beamed pub, nicely carpeted, plates on wall, friendly staff, well kept beer, efficiently served well priced good food inc evening steak special and bargain Sat lunch *(R and A Cooper)*; [Betton St], *Pied Bull*: Cosy thatched pub with beams, fireplaces etc, friendly staff, good reasonably priced food esp filled baked potatoes, beers such as Batemans Champion and Dark Mild, Marstons Pedigree and Monks Habit *(R and A Cooper)*; [Ashby Rd], *White Horse*: Popular local and businessmen's main road house, nice atmosphere, good value generous home-made food, lawns behind *(A and R Cooper)*

☆ **Sibson**, Leics [A444 N; SK3500], *Millers*: Large hotel around converted bakery and watermill, mill wheel and stream nr entrance, even a small fountain in flagstoned corridor to low-beamed lounge bar with Courage-related ales and good range of good value popular food, one table made from old millstone; afternoon teas, handy for Twycross Zoo and Bosworth Field; bedrooms good *(Christopher Bearfoot)*

☆ **Sileby**, Leics [Swan St; SK6015], *White Swan*: Small unspoilt sidestreet pub with comfortable and welcoming dining lounge, interesting good value generous home-cooked food (not Sun eve or Mon) inc vegetarian and superb puddings, home-baked bread, well kept Marstons Pedigree, entertaining boxer dogs, small tasteful restaurant; children's playroom in converted back bowling alley with closed-circuit TV *(Ruth and Alan Cooper, P and J Farrow, Jim Farmer)*

☆ **Skegness**, Lincs [Vine Rd, Seacroft (off Drummond Rd); TF5660], *Vine*: Dating mainly from late 18th c, comfortable well run bar overlooking drive and own bowling green, imposing antique seats and grandfather clock in turkey-carpeted hall, juke box in inner oak-panelled room; three well kept Batemans real ales, good reasonably priced bar food, restaurant, tables on big back sheltered lawn with swings; bedrooms, peaceful suburban setting *(Peter Burton, A and R Cooper, Derek and Sylvia Stephenson, Norma and Keith Bloomfield, LYM)*

Skellingthorpe, Lincs [SK9272], *Stones Arms*: Friendly local with good reasonably priced food, well kept ale, superb welcoming service *(Marcus Underwood)*

Skillington, Lincs [SK8925], *Cross Swords*: Small and pleasant, with good hospitable service; food not that cheap but good *(Gene Hawkins)*

Smeeton Westerby, Leics [SP6792], *Kings Head*: Well kept Bass, good food inc bargain lunches *(G W Mason)*

☆ **Somerby**, Leics [High St; SK7710], *Old Brewery*: Roomy modernised pub, on the market as we go to press but meantime business as usual – interesting cheap Parish ales brewed in pub yard (popular group brewery tours inc supper and unlimited drink), hearty cheap home-cooked food inc formidable mega grill, roaring open fires, cheery relaxed atmosphere, thriving bar, cosy lounge; shame about the piped music; children very welcome, tables in garden, boules and play area *(Joan and Michel Hooper-Immins, Richard Houghton, A and R Cooper, Jack and Philip Paxton, J D Cloud, Rona Murdoch, BB)*

☆ **Southwell**, Notts [Church St (A612); SK6953], *Bramley Apple*: Friendly pub with generous good value food inc fresh fish, well kept Batemans XB, Marstons Pedigree and a guest beer, attractively worked Bramley apple theme, eating area screened off by stained glass *(Andy and Jill Kassube, Mrs J Barwell, BB)*

Southwell, *Saracens Head*: Cosy beamed and panelled character bar with good value lunches and well kept Courage-related ales, in interesting old Forte hotel (where Charles I spent his last free night); good service, children in eating area or restaurant; bedrooms comfortable *(Andy and Jill Kassube, LYM)*

☆ **Spalding**, Lincs [Herring Lane/Double St; TF2618], *Lincolnshire Poacher*: Good choice of S & N and other constantly changing ales, polished tiles in bar, other rooms off inc dining area, good home-made food, friendly service, open fires, old enamel advertising signs everywhere; seats on green overlooking river, but traffic a bit intrusive *(J Honnor, George and Sheila Edwards, Ian Phillips)*

Spalding [Broad St], *Punch Bowl*: Good food and atmosphere, seats outside *(David Mason)*; [Pinchbeck Rd], *Royal Mailcart*: Reasonably priced generous food in lounge with dining area, Bass and Courage-related ales, friendly helpful staff, bar and games room on left, smart Regency-style back restaurant (must book Sun lunch) *(Michael and Jenny Back)*

☆ **Stamford**, Lincs [High St, St Martins (B1081 S); TF0207], *Bull & Swan*: Solidly traditional, with three low-beamed connecting rooms, gleaming copper and brass, log-effect gas fires, tables out in former back coachyard; has had good generous standard food, well kept Bass and Tetleys, friendly service; children welcome, bedrooms *(LYM; reports on current regime please)*

Stamford [All Saints Pl], *Crown*: Obliging staff, good value food and well kept Ruddles County in large rambling stonebuilt pub's panelled bar and no-smoking dining room; bedrooms *(K D Day, G B Longden)*; [5 Cheyne Lane], *Hole in the Wall*: Cosy and busy – may have to wait for a table; good food, well kept beers *(Cdr Patrick Tailyour)*; [19 Maiden Lane], *Kings Head*: Small homely pub with friendly staff, well kept Flowers and Tetleys, decent food *(Tim and Ann Newell)*; [Broad St], *Lord Burghley*: Old pub with new licensees, good atmosphere and service, well kept Bass, Fullers London Pride, Ruddles County and Timothy Taylors Landlord, farm cider, food (not Sun evening) inc good steak and kidney pie and steamed puddings; pleasant small walled garden *(Joan and Michel Hooper-Immins, P Tetley)*

Stathern, Leics [Church St; SK7731], *Red Lion*: Beams, flagstones, open fire, well kept Whitbreads-related ales, warm homely atmosphere; can get very busy *(Chris Raisin, G Doyle)*

Staunton in the Vale, Notts [SK8043], *Staunton Arms*: Friendly and welcoming, well kept Marstons Pedigree, good value food *(Nigel Hopkins, Peter Burton)*

Stoke Golding, Leics [SP3997], *George & Dragon*: Comfortable local, wide range of good value food, hard-working licensees, Ansells, Marstons and Tetleys *(Sue and Mike Todd)*

☆ **Stretton**, Leics [signed off A1; SK9416], *Jackson Stops*: Informal homely thatched pub in quiet village tucked away just off A1, well kept Ruddles Best and County, decent wines, good food, open fires, pleasant atmosphere; local for three-nation fighter squadron at RAF Cottesmore with lots of relevant memorabilia *(RB, Ian Phillips, LYM)*

☆ **Surfleet Seas End**, Lincs [off A16 N of Spalding; TF2728], *Ship*: Now run by the Podmores whose good natural cooking previously won a main entry for the Hare & Hounds at Greatford *(Michael and Susan Morgan)*

Susworth, Lincs [Main St; SE8302], *Jenny Wren*: Overlooking River Trent, lots of panelling, oak beams and brasses, various nooks and crannies, good rather upmarket food inc lots of seafood, Brains, Shepherd Neame Bishops Finger and John Smiths, real fire; polite service, some picnic tables outside *(Michael Swallow, JJW, CMW)*

☆ **Sutton Cheney**, Leics [Main St – off A447 3 miles S of Mkt Bosworth; SK4100], *Royal Arms*: Lots of tables in friendly dining pub's three smallish low-ceilinged rooms, each different; good local atmosphere, wide choice of good value food with good fresh veg, two open fires, well kept Marstons and changing guest beers; upstairs restaurant, family conservatory with wishing well, lots of picnic tables in big garden with good children's play area; handy for Bosworth Field and Mallory Park, can get busy *(Jim Farmer, Mike and Wendy Proctor, Roy Bromell, Julie Peters)*

☆ **Sutton in the Elms**, Leics [Coventry Rd; B4114, just S of B581 – quite handy for M69 junction 2, and M1 – OS Sheet 140 map ref 509937; SP5194], *Mill on the Soar*: Thriving atmosphere in roomy converted watermill – stripped brickwork, some rugs and carpet on the flagstones, brown beams and joists festooned with china and copper, conservatory area, river views from upstairs restaurant, quickly served good value bar food, Everards and guest ales; children welcome; good value bedrooms in separate comfortably modern block *(T M Dobby, LYM)*

Swineshead Bridge, Lincs [A17 Swineshead—E Heckington; TF2142], *Barge*: Useful lunch stop, relaxing uncrowded front room, some attractive old curios, good value food, pool table in public bar, quiet garden with swing; children given puzzle and picture to colour *(Bronwen and Steve Wrigley)*

Swinhope, Lincs [off B1203 NE of Mkt Rasen; TF2196], *Clickem*: Good choice of beers, decent range of unusual bar food *(Nigel and Lindsay Chapman)*

☆ **Swithland**, Leics [SE end of village; between A6 and B5330, between Loughborough and Leicester; SK5413], *Griffin*: Very much a local, with Everards and other well kept beers, reasonable choice of food, pleasant decor, attractive prices; gardens by stream with horses, nice setting *(A and R Cooper, Andrew Stephenson, Tony and Joan Walker, LYM)*

Tattershall Thorpe, Lincs [B1192 Coningsby—Woodhall Spa; TF2259], *Blue Bell*: Attractive pub with big lavatera bushes all round, food inc good Sun roast, small dining room, attentive service even when busy, Adnams Broadside, Marstons Pedigree, Morlands Old Speckled Hen and Tetleys, Sun bar nibbles; piped pop music; tables in garden *(JJW, CMW)*

Tealby, Lincs [11 Kingsway, off B1203; TF1590], *Kings Head*: Warm welcome, oak beams, good choice of food inc speciality local sausages; picture-postcard village *(Gordon Thornton)*

☆ **Tetford**, Lincs [OS Sheet 122 map ref 333748; TF3374], *White Hart*: Early 16th-c pub doing well under current regime, with good atmosphere, well kept Mansfield ales, wide choice of interesting food inc some bargains and good options for children; old-fashioned settles, slabby elm tables and red tiled floor in pleasant quiet inglenook bar, no-smoking snug, basic games room; seats and swings on sheltered back lawn, simple bedrooms *(Mike and Maggie Betton, MJH, Nigel and Lindsay Chapman, LYM)*

Thornton, Leics [Main St; S of M1, junction 22; SK4607], *Bricklayers Arms*: Traditional old village local with several cosy rooms, real fire and old photographs in beamed bar, Everards Tiger, Beacon and Mild and Morlands Old Speckled Hen, basic good value menu; piped radio *(JJW, CMW)*

Thorpe on the Hill, Lincs [SK9065], *Railway*: Unspoilt country local with Hamilton Ellis LMS prints of pre-1923 railway scenes, friendly landlord, well kept Mansfield ales *(John C Baker)*

☆ **Thurgarton**, Notts [Southwell Rd; A612; SK6949], *Red Lion*: Wide choice of good generous bar food, particularly well kept Mansfield ales, lovely fire, restaurant; pleasant surroundings and garden, children welcome *(Elizabeth and Anthony Watts, M J Radford)*

☆ **Timberland**, Lincs [Station Rd; TF1258], *Penny Farthing*: Pleasant and spacious stripped-stone beamed lounge locally popular for good generous lunchtime bar food and evening dining room (not Mon exc residents), Tetleys and Youngers Scotch, decent house wine, unobtrusive piped music, local paintings for sale; bedrooms *(W P J Elderkin)*

Tinwell, Leics [Crown Lane; TF0006], *Crown*: Cosy and convivial village local, wide choice of good food *(Peter Francon-Smith)*

Tur Langton, Leics [off B6047; follow Kibworth signpost from village centre; SP7194], *Crown*: Well kept Bass and Marstons Pedigree, attractive furnishings from antique curved settle to chintzy easy chairs, restaurant; tables on pleasantly planted terraces and in sheltered back courtyard; cl weekday lunchtimes *(Paul Cartledge, LYM)*

Twyford, Leics [10 Main St; off B6047 E of Leicester; SK7210], *Saddle*: Comfortable L-shaped bar under new management, well kept Mansfield Old Baily and Riding, open fire, reasonably priced food, games end; charming little beamed dining area *(JJW, CMW, Stephen, Julie and Hayley Brown)*

Ullesthorpe, Leics [Main St; SP5087], *Chequers*: Enterprising go-ahead pub with very wide choice of reasonably priced food in bar and restaurant, attentive service, beams and flagstones *(Miss D P Barson, Cdr Patrick Tailyour)*

☆ **Upper Hambleton**, Leics [village signposted from A606 on E edge of Oakham; SK9007], *Finches Arms*: Outstanding views of Rutland Water from tables on back gravel terrace and picture-window restaurant extension, good choice of food inc interesting dishes and good veg, built-in button-back leatherette banquettes and open fire in knocked-through front bar, well kept Bass and other ales on handpump; friendly staff *(Eric Locker, M J Morgan, David and Michelle Hedges, Mr and Mrs Peakman, GW, BW, Wayne Brindle, BB)*

☆ **Uppingham**, Leics [High Street W; SP8699], *White Hart*: Wide choice of good value simple tasty food using local produce, inglenook fire in panelled front lounge, quite a warren of passages and rooms, two well kept Courage-related ales with a guest such as Morlands Speckled Hen, reasonably priced wines, good service, back restaurant; bedrooms *(O K Smyth, George Atkinson, Eric Locker, R H Jones)*

☆ **Upton**, Notts [Main St (A612); SK7354], *Cross Keys*: Splendid atmosphere in rambling heavy-beamed bar with good welcoming service, lots of alcoves, central log fire, masses to look at from sporting cartoons and local watercolours to decorative plates and metalwork, interesting medley of furnishings; well kept Batemans XXXB, Boddingtons, Brakspears, Marstons Pedigree and guest beers, decent wines; friendly dog, unobtrusive piped music, folk evenings; children in back extension with carved pews or dovecote restaurant *(Duncan Small, Lorna and Bill Tyson, A C Morrison, John Fahy, W D Crane, Derek and Sylvia Stephenson, K H Frostick, D R E Berlin, David and Shelia, Brian and Jill Bond, LYM)*

☆ **Walcote**, Leics [1½ miles from M1 junction 20, A427 towards Market Harboro; SP5683], *Black Horse*: Authentic Thai food (not Mon or Tues lunchtime) cooked by the landlady, in good value big helpings, well kept ales such as Hook Norton Best and Old Hookey, Timothy Taylors Landlord, Judges Old Growler, interesting bottled beers and country wines, no-smoking restaurant; glossy varnish on the bar tables wouldn't come amiss *(Cathy Scott, Richard Baker, Dr and Mrs D E Awbery, Graham Reeve, David and Shelia, H Paulinski, Jim Farmer, Frank Cummins, LYM)*

Walkeringham, Notts [High St; SK7792], *Three Horseshoes*: Popular place in remote village nr River Trent, pretty flowers and hanging baskets, simple old-fashioned decor, wide choice of good food with good sauces, fresh lightly cooked veg; well kept beer inc a guest *(M and J Godfrey)*

☆ **Watnall Chaworth**, Notts [3 miles from M1 junction 26: A610 towards Nottingham, left on to B600, then keep right; SK5046], *Queens Head*: Tastefully extended old pub with wide range of good value food, Home Bitter and Mild, Theakstons XB and Old Peculier, efficient friendly service; snug bar and dining area, beams and stripped pine, coal fires; fruit machine, piped music; picnic tables in spacious garden with big play area; open all day Fri/Sat *(Jack and Philip Paxton, JJW, CMW, Mike and Penny Sanders)*

Welby, Lincs [SK9738], *Rose & Crown*: Interesting food, Shepherd Neame Spitfire *(June and Malcolm Farmer)*

☆ **Welham**, Leics [SP7692], *Old Red Lion*: Popular for good value food inc bargain lunchtime pies and steaks, Marstons Pedigree and guests on handpump, good service, several wines; lovely fire *(S A Moir, Norman Smith)*

West Deeping, Lincs [Main St; TF1109], *Red Lion*: Attractive bar, long and low, with plenty of tables, roaring coal fires each end, old stonework and beams, real ales such as Bass, Ansells and Ind Coope Burton, wide choice of bar food from sandwiches up inc vegetarian, prompt welcoming service; games room *(M and J Back)*

Westwoodside, Lincs [off B1396 W of Haxey – OS Sheet 112 map ref 726988; SK7599], *Park Drain*: Good value traditional food, friendly staff, well kept beers; building is unusual, built for coal mine that was never sunk, interesting decor, bright paintwork outside, colonial-style portico *(Andrew Maufe)*

☆ **Whitwell**, Leics [A606 Stamford—Oakham; SK9208], *Noel Arms*: Wide choice of above-average generous waitress-served home-cooked food (till 10) inc delicious puddings, in spacious plush and decorous dining lounge, cheerful local atmosphere in original unpretentious little front rooms, Ansells and Ruddles Best and County, friendly efficient staff, afternoon teas (not Mon), suntrap tables outside, occasional barbecues; piped music, can get busy; handy for Rutland Water, children welcome; bedrooms *(Prof John and Patricia White, Dr M V Jones, Miss P A Wilson, LYM)*

☆ **Whitwick**, Leics [B587 towards Copt Oak; quite handy for M1 junction 22; SK4514], *Bulls Head*: Welcoming L-shaped plush beamed bar with splendid views over Charnwood Forest – highest pub in Leics; well kept Tetleys-related ales, quickly served home-cooked food (lunchtime, not Sun) using good ingredients; friendly staff, back games room with piped music, big garden with menagerie of farm animals; children very welcome away from bar *(E G Wright, J D Cloud, A and R Cooper, George Atkinson, Jenny and Michael Back)*

Willingham, Lincs [Gainsborough Rd; SK8784], *Fox & Hounds*: Jolly, efficient licensees, well kept beer and good value tasty food in busy and welcoming country local *(Juliette Phillips)*

Wing, Leics [3 Top St, signed off A6003 S of Oakham; SK8903], *Cuckoo*: Lovely thatched house, open-plan bar split into two, friendly staff and locals, Bass, Marstons Pedigree and guest beers; pretty village with interesting medieval turf maze *(Jack and Philip Paxton)*; [Top St], *Kings Arms*: Attractively restored early 17th-c inn with stripped stonework, big fireplaces, comfortable well equipped bedrooms in modern annexe; has been closed, but as we went to press was scheduled for reopening *(LYM; news please)*

☆ **Woodhall Spa**, Lincs [Kirkstead; Tattersall Rd (B1192 Woodhall Spa—Coningsby); TF1963], *Abbey Lodge*: Attractively and discreetly decorated food pub, warm, cosy and popular, with some antique furnishings, prompt welcoming service, wide range of good value bar food inc fine omelettes and Sun lunches, well kept real ale, RAF memorabilia *(Dr J Lunn, Bill and Sheila McLardy)*

☆ **Woodhouse Eaves** [Brand Hill; beyond Main St, off B591 S of Loughborough – OS Sheet 129 map ref 533148], *Wheatsheaf*: Plush open-plan country pub, welcoming service, good if pricy home-cooked food inc vegetarian, several well kept ales, decent wines, log fires; floodlit tables outside *(Jack and Philip Paxton, A and R Cooper, Norma and Keith Bloomfield, Andrew Stephenson, P J Caunt, LYM)*

Woodhouse Eaves, *Bulls Head*: Good home-cooked food, pleasant decor with books, beams and bric-a-brac, relaxed atmosphere, good young staff *(Mr and Mrs A Cooper, Roy Briggs, Barbara Taylor)*

☆ **Woolsthorpe**, Lincs [the one nr Belvoir, signed off A52 Grantham—Nottingham; SK8435], *Rutland Arms*: Comfortable and relaxed country pub with good value nicely presented food esp fish, well kept Whitbreads-related ales, welcoming if not always swift service, lounge with some high-backed settles, hunting prints and brasses, family extension with old furniture, open fire, video juke box, bric-a-brac, separate dining room; two pool tables in annexe; play equipment on big lawn, quiet spot nr restored canal *(Elizabeth and Anthony Watts, Norma and Keith Bloomfield, Chris de Wet)*

Woolsthorpe, *Chequers*: Promising village pub refurbished and reopened by French chef/patron, well kept real ale, good if not cheap food *(David and Shelia, BB)*

Worksop, Notts [off Mansfield Rd; SK5879], *Manor Lodge*: Old-fashioned no-frills pub in former 16th-c manor house, interesting choice of strong ales, good value food most nights and weekends, no machines or juke box, popular Fri live music *(Bob Ward)*

☆ **Wymeswold**, Leics [A6006; SK6023], *Hammer & Pincers*: Extensively refurbished in exposed-beam style, clean, bright and spacious, with pine furniture in four or five rooms on several levels, good value generous food, well kept Bass, Ruddles County, Marstons Pedigree, Theakstons Best and XB and guest beers, friendly service; tables on terrace, neat garden *(Ruth and Alan Cooper, Stephen Brown, John and Zoe Chamberlain, David and Shelia, Jim Farmer)*

Wymeswold [45 Far St], *Three Crowns*: Good welcoming atmosphere, good value food, nicely furnished with character, couple of dogs *(A and R Cooper)*

☆ **Wymondham**, Leics [Edmonthorpe Rd; off B676 E of Melton Mowbray; SK8518], *Hunters Arms*: French chef/patron doing interesting dishes as well as more usual food in cosy and friendly two-bar pub with restaurant, well kept ales such as Bass, Batemans, Greene King IPA and Abbot; very popular weekends *(Norma and Keith Bloomfield, V and E A Bolton)*

Wysall, Notts [off A60 at Costock, or A6006 at Wymeswold; SK6027], *Plough*: Friendly, lively and attractive, well kept Bass and guest ales, nice mix of furnishings, soft lighting, log fire, french doors to terrace and good garden; no cooked lunches Sun *(A and R Cooper, Chris Raisin and friends, Dr and Mrs J H Hills)*

Post Office address codings confusingly give the impression that some pubs are in Leicestershire, when they're really in Cambridgeshire (which is where we list them).

Lincolnshire *see* Leicestershire

see Leicestershire

Midlands (Northamptonshire, Warwickshire and West Midlands)

New entries here include the Butchers Arms at Farnborough, reopened by friendly and hardworking new licensees; the George at Lower Brailes, an old Cotswold inn with particularly good home cooking; the friendly well run Star at Sulgrave, with lots of interesting things to look at; and two Spanish-run places, the White Swan at Harringworth (a peaceful old inn, with good food), and the Bell at Monks Kirby (the tapas are what to go for here, and the wines are very good). Other pubs currently doing well here include the Bell at Alderminster (imaginative food, friendly atmosphere – our choice as Midlands Dining Pub of the Year), the Olde Coach House at Ashby St Ledgers (very good all round – a star award this year), the Falcon at Fotheringhay (anoher fine all-rounder, with emphasis on food), the Fox & Hounds at Great Wolford (newish owners settling in extremely well now – and reopening the bedrooms), the Howard Arms at Ilmington (interesting country cooking – gains a Food Award this year), the Fleur de Lys at Lowsonford (new manager with a fine track record), the busy Slug & Lettuce in Stratford (the food's now approaching Award quality), and the very friendly Bulls Head at Wootton Wawen (a sensibly short choice of good food). The Bulls Head at Clipston deserves a special mention for its remarkable range of whiskies – well over 400 now. If you've not seen it before, the Crooked House in Himley is well worth a visit for its extraordinary lopsidedness (it's a good pub, too). The Vine next to its brewery in Brierley Hill is a fine example of a traditional Black Country town local; the Case is Altered at Five Ways could hardly be bettered as an unchanging country tavern. For lovers of zany eccentricity the Little Dry Dock in Netherton and Pie Factory in Tipton have a lot to offer. In the Lucky Dip section at the end of the chapter, pubs to note specially include the revived Bartons Arms in Birmingham, Navigation at Cosgrove, William IV in Coventry (Coventry pubs seem generally more interesting than those in Birmingham), Great Western at Deppers Bridge, Eastcote Arms at Eastcote, Castle on Edge Hill, Marston Inn at Marston St Lawrence, Sondes Arms at Rockingham, Black Swan and Garrick in Stratford, Three Conies at Thorpe Mandeville, Plough at Warmington, Heart of England at Weedon, Bell at Welford on Avon, Royal Oak at Whatcote, Three Horseshoes at Wixford and Great Western in Wolverhampton. Drinks prices in the area as a whole are around the national average – but in the West Midlands they are generally much lower than average, with cheap regional and local brewers such as Banks's and Bathams. Away from this cheap heartland, the best prices we found were in the Case is Altered at Five Ways and Fox & Hounds at Great Wolford; good value local breweries to look out for are Donnington and Hook Norton.

ALDERMINSTER (War) SP2348 Map 4

Bell

A3400 Oxford—Stratford

Midlands Dining Pub of the Year

A new conservatory and terrace have been added to this rather civilised place so you can enjoy the very good, imaginative food overlooking the garden and open countryside. And although the emphasis is based very much on the waitress-served food, readers also like the friendly service and bustling atmosphere. Using fresh produce (no fried food at all), the range of meals changes every day but might include dishes such as soups like carrot and orange (£2.50), waterchestnuts with bacon in a sweet and sour sauce (£3.25), sausages in mustard and honey (£3.95), chicken liver with port and hazelnuts (£4.25), monkfish in lime and ginger (£5.25), spinach and nut pancakes or fresh pasta with pesto sauce (£6.50), fresh fishcakes with watercress sauce (£6.75), good crispy-topped lamb in cider (£7.75), pork chop in creamy mushroom and rosemary sauce (£7.95), steak, kidney and oyster pie or pheasant and venison and pigeon pie (£8.95), mixed seafood casserole (£9.25), and good puddings like tipsy sherry trifle or chocolate, brandy and almond torte (£2.95); also, two-course lunch (weekdays; £5.95), and popular theme evenings like French or Indian. The communicating areas of the spacious bar have a panelled oak settle and plenty of stripped slatback chairs around wooden tables on the flagstones and wooden floors, little vases of flowers, small landscape prints and swan's-neck brass-and-globe lamps on the cream walls, and a solid fuel stove in a stripped brick inglenook; dominoes. Most of the restaurant is no smoking. Fullers London Pride and Whitbreads Fuggles on handpump, a good range of wines (from Berry Bros & Rudd) by the glass, and freshly squeezed juice; obliging, friendly service. The pub is just four miles from Stratford. *(Recommended by Maysie Thompson, Kay Neville-Rolfe, Christine van der Will, Moira and John Cole, Martin Jones, Pam Adsley, Nigel Wilkinson, Mrs J Oakes, David Shillitoe, Peter Lloyd, Roy Bromell, Stephen Richards, David and Ruth Hollands, Mrs R Bennett, A Cowell, Peter Neate, the Monday Club)*

Free house ~ Licensees Keith and Vanessa Brewer ~ Real ale ~ Meals and snacks ~ (01789) 450414 ~ Children welcome ~ Singers/Caribbean evenings and special events ~ Open 12-2.30, 7-11; closed evenings 24 Dec-1 Jan

ASHBY ST LEDGERS (Northants) SP5768 Map 4

Olde Coach House ★

4 miles from M1, junction 18; A5 S to Kilsby, then A361 S towards Daventry; village is signposted left. Alternatively 8 miles from M1 junction 16, then A45 W to Weedon, A5 N to sign for village.

It would be very difficult to find fault with this thriving ivy-covered inn – readers seem pleased with very friendly and efficient service, well kept beers and nice wine, good food, and neat bedrooms. The several comfortable, rambling little rooms have high-backed winged settles on polished black and red tiles, old kitchen tables, harness on a few standing timbers, hunting pictures (often of the Pytchley, which sometimes meets outside), Thelwell prints, and a big winter log fire. A front room has darts, pool, video game and piped music. Popular waitress-served bar food includes home-made soup (£1.95), filled rolls (from £1.95), field mushrooms filled with a stilton mousse (£3.50), meat or vegetable pies (from £5.25), home-made lasagne, balti or brie and broccoli in a flaky pastry case (all £5.95), rainbow trout baked with mushrooms, bacon and prawns (£8.50), steaks (from £9.50), local venison steak (£10.25), and puddings (£2.50); children's menu (from £1.95), and good Sunday lunch menu (main courses from £5.75). The dining room is no smoking. Well kept Everards Old Original, Flowers Original, Hook Norton Old Hookey, Jennings Cumberland, and a beer named for the pub on handpump, with lots more during their spring beer festivals; 12 wines by the glass, and fresh orange juice. Service is always smiling. There are seats among fruit trees and under a fairy-lit arbour (maybe summer barbecues), and a marvellous activity centre for children; disabled entrance and baby-changing facilities, too. The pub is well placed in an attractive village full of thatched stone houses, and the nearby manor house was owned by one of the gunpowder plotters. *(Recommended by Peter and Jenny Quine, Mayur Shah, Martin Wright, KC, David Alcock, Simon Collett-Jones, Sally Pidden, Gordon Theaker, Nigel Flook, Betsy Brown, Andrew and Ruth Triggs, S Marsden, Hilary Dobbie, Derek and Sylvia Stephenson, Graham and Lynne Mason, Cathy Scott, Richard Baker, John and Elliott Gwynne, Miss D P Barson, Julie Peters, G P Kernan)*

Free house ~ Licensees Brian and Philippa McCabe ~ Real ale ~ Meals and snacks ~ (01788) 890349 ~ Children welcome ~ Open 12-2.30, 6-11; 12-11 Sat ~ Bedrooms: £42B/£50B

BADBY (Northants) SP5559 Map 4

Windmill

Village signposted off A361 Daventry—Banbury

Efficiently run by courteous licensees, this thatched coaching inn is a good mixture of old fashioned charm and tasteful modernisation. There's a good friendly feel in the thriving bars, both of which have beams, flagstones and lace, cricketing pictures and appropriately simple country furnishings in good solid wood; there's an enormous inglenook fireplace in one area and a cosy and comfortable lounge. By the time this book is published the planned new bar in the restaurant and new lounge area will be up and running. Promptly served, good food includes home-made soup (£1.75), sandwiches (from £1.75), stilton mushrooms or pork liver, bacon and brandy pâté (£3.25), filled baked potatoes (from £3.25), ploughman's (£3.95), pasta with vegetables and a cheese sauce or lasagne (£5.25), chicken and ham pie (£6.50), char-grilled Cajun chicken (£7.25), steaks (from £8.95), daily specials such as chilli peppers filled with cream cheese (£3.95) or liver and bacon (£5.95), puddings such as lime cheesecake (£2.50), and children's menu (£2.50). Well kept Bass, Boddingtons, Flowers Original, Wadworths 6X and occasionally, Morlands Old Speckled Hen on handpump. Dominoes, video game, piped music. There are tables outside, with a children's play area beyond the car park. *(Recommended by Mayur Shah, Nick Wikeley, Bob and Maggie Atherton, N H and A H Harris, Mrs P Wilson, Simon Collett-Jones, Sheila and Terry Wells, George Atkinson, Paul Burdett, Christopher and Sharon Hayle, Stephen, Julie and Hayley Brown, Gunnar Arholt and family, Michael Marlow, John Fahy)*

Free house ~ Licensees John Freestone and Carol Sutton ~ Real ale ~ Meals and snacks ~ Restaurant (Fri, Sat and Sun lunchtime) ~ (01327) 702363 ~ Children in eating area of bar and in restaurant ~ Jazz last Fri in month, light dance jazz 2nd Sat ~ Open 11.30-3, 5.30-11; all day summer Sats ~ Bedrooms: £39.50B/£49B

BRIERLEY HILL (W Midlands) SO9187 Map 4

Vine £

Delph Rd; B4172 between A461 and A4100, near A4100

Full of local character, this lively place is warmly welcoming and keeps very well priced beer – as it should, being right next to the brewery: Bitter and Mild (dark, unusually full-flavoured with a touch of hops, and outstanding value) on handpump, with Delph Strong in winter. The front bar has wall benches and simple leatherette-topped oak stools, a snug on the left has solidly built red plush seats, and the back bar has brass chandeliers and more seats. Good, fresh lunchtime snacks include old-fashioned sandwiches (£1), faggots and peas (£1.70) and marvellous-value salads (from £1.70). Darts, cribbage, dominoes, fruit machine, video game and trivia. It can get crowded. The pub is known in the Black Country as the Bull & Bladder, from the good stained glass bull's heads and very approximate bunches of grapes in the front bow windows. *(Recommended by Stephen Brown, W L G Watkins, Anthony Marriott, Graham Reeve, Dr Bill Baker)*

Bathams ~ Manager Melvyn Wood ~ Real ale ~ Lunchtime snacks (not Sun) ~ (01384) 78293 ~ Children in own room ~ Blues Sun evening ~ Open 12-11

CLIPSTON (Northants) SP7181 Map 4

Bulls Head

B4036 S of Market Harborough

The black beams in this friendly slate-roofed local glisten with countless coins, carrying on an odd tradition started by US airmen based nearby in World War II – they used to wedge the money waiting for their next drink in cracks and crannies of the ancient woodwork. The bar is cosily divided into three snug areas leading down from the servery, with comfortable seats, sturdy small settles and stools upholstered in red plush, a grandmother clock, some harness and tools, and a log fire. Well kept Bass, Batemans, Boddingtons, Flowers Original, Fullers Chiswick, Greene King IPA, Marstons Pedigree, and Shepherd Neame Bishops Finger on handpump, and an incredible choice of malt whiskies – they had 430 varieties at the last count. The long back games bar, lively in the evenings, has darts, pool, table skittles, dominoes, fruit machine, video game, juke box, and piped music. Good bar food includes sandwiches and other light snacks, and daily specials such as cumberland sausage (£3.95), Drunken Bull pie (£4.95), Dijon chicken or local trout poached in white wine (£5.95), and T-bone steak topped with stilton (£9.95). Outside, a terrace has a few white tables under cocktail parasols – maybe summer barbecues. *(Recommended by Mike and Margaret Banks, Jack Morley, John FHY, Eric Locker, B Adams, Caroline Kenyon, L Walker, J Cox, Stephen, Julie and Hayley Brown, Wayne Brindle, Mr and Mrs K H Frostick)*

Free house ~ Licensees Colin and Jenny Smith ~ Real ale ~ Meals and snacks (not evening Sun or Mon) ~ (01858) 525268 ~ Children welcome ~ Occasional live entertainment ~ Open 11.30-2.30, 6.30-11; closed Mon lunchtime and 25 Dec ~ Bedrooms: £29.50B/£35.50B

COVENTRY (W Midlands) SP3379 Map 4

Old Windmill £

Spon Street

A new licensee has taken over this attractive and unpretentious timber-framed 15th-c pub with its rambling series of tiny cosy old rooms. One is little more than the stub of a corridor, another has carved oak seats on flagstones and a woodburner in a fine ancient inglenook fireplace, and another has carpet and more conventionally comfortable seats. There are exposed beams in the uneven ceilings, and a back room preserves some of the equipment which used to be used for brewing here. Nowadays the beers are well kept Courage Directors, Ruddles Best and County, Wadworths 6X, Websters Yorkshire, and a guest beer on handpump; Bulmers cider; cribbage, dominoes, fruit machine, juke box and piped music. At lunchtime you order food at the kitchen door, and that's where it's handed to you: filled batches (from £1.50), steak in ale or pasty with chips (£2.50), vegetable pasty (£2.55), and rainbow trout or haddock (£2.75). The pub is popular with students, extremely busy on Friday and Saturday evenings. Handy for the Belgrave Theatre. *(Recommended by Hazel Morgan, Ann Griffiths, Graham Reeve, John and Marianne Cooper)*

Courage ~ Lease: Barrie Webster ~ Real ale ~ Lunchtime meals and snacks ~ (01203) 252183 ~ Children welcome ~ Open 11-11; closed 25 Dec

CRICK (Northants) SP5872 Map 4

Red Lion

A mile from M1 junction 18; A428

Handy for the M1, this comfortable old thatched pub has a pleasant low-ceilinged bar with stripped stonework, a notably relaxed chatty air, and two roaring log fires (filled in summer with big, bright copper dishes and brassware); it's quietest and snuggest in the inner part of the bar. Lunchtime snacks include sandwiches and ploughman's, with steak and kidney pie or roast of the day (£3.75), and chicken kiev, gammon, stuffed plaice, roast duck, trout and different steaks (between £5 and £8.50), available in the evening; only sandwiches and ploughman's Sunday lunchtimes. Well kept Hook Norton Best, Courage Directors, Marstons Pedigree, and Websters Yorkshire on handpump. No noisy games machines or piped music. In summer, you can eat on a Perspex-roofed sheltered terrace in the old coach yard, with lots of pretty hanging baskets. There are a few picnic tables under cocktail parasols on grass by the car park. *(Recommended by TBB, G S Miller, George Atkinson, Roger and Christine Mash, K H Frostick, Mayur Shah, Gwyneth Holland, Cathy Scott, Richard Baker, Barbara and Norman Wells, Mrs J Barwell)*

Free house ~ Lease: Tom and Mary Marks ~ Real ale ~ Meals and snacks (not Sun evenings) ~ (01788) 822342 ~ Children in snug lunchtime only ~ Open 11.30-2.30, 6.30-11

EAST HADDON (Northants) SP6668 Map 4

Red Lion

High St; village signposted off A428 (turn right in village) and off A50 N of Northampton

Whether you are dropping into this civilised golden stone hotel for a drink, a snack or restaurant meal, you will be made just as welcome. It's a popular old place, with most people coming for the high quality daily changing bar food: sandwiches or soups (£2.95), ploughman's or home-made pâté (£5.95), home-made salmon fishcake with tomato and basil sauce, stuffed aubergines with feta cheese in tomato sauce or sausage casserole (£6.95), braised oxtail hotpot with dumplings (£7.95), fresh dressed crab or beef in red wine (£8.95), and puddings like bakewell tart or banana and apple upside-down cake (£3.25); they do a three-course set Sunday lunch – worth booking. The neat lounge bar has oak panelled settles, library chairs, soft modern dining chairs, and a mix of oak, mahogany and cast-iron-framed tables; also, white-painted panelling, recessed china cabinets, old prints and pewter, and little kegs, brass pots, swords and so forth hung sparingly on a couple of beams. The small public bar has sturdy old-fashioned red leather seats. The pretty separate restaurant is good, as are the breakfasts. Very well kept Charles Wells Eagle and Bombardier, Morlands Old Speckled Hen, and Youngs Special on handpump, and decent wines; attentive, friendly service; piped music. The walled side garden is very attractive, with lilac, fruit trees, roses and neat little flower beds; it leads back to the bigger lawn, where there are well spaced picnic tables. There are more tables under cocktail parasols on a small side terrace, and a big copper beech shades the gravel car park. *(Recommended by Maysie Thompson, George Atkinson, Heather Couper, Mayur Shah, R H Jones, Mark and Toni Amor-Segan, Mrs Gwyneth Holland, Howard and Margaret Buchanan, Mrs B Sugarman, Ian Fordham, G L Tong, D Jackson)*

Charles Wells ~ Tenants Mr and Mrs Ian Kennedy ~ Real ale ~ Meals and snacks (not Sun evening) ~ Restaurant (not Sun evening) ~ (01604) 770223 ~ Children in eating area of bar and in restaurant lunchtimes; must be over 12 in evenings ~ Open 11-2.30, 6-11; closed 25 Dec ~ Bedrooms: £42B/£59B

Though we don't usually mention it in the text, most pubs will now make coffee – always worth asking. And many – particularly in the North – will do tea.

ETTINGTON (War) SP2749 Map 4

Chequers £

A422 Banbury—Stratford

The outside of this traditional village local has been decorated this year and lots of flower tubs and window boxes added. There are tables and chairs out on the neat back lawn and on an awninged terrace, with more hanging baskets; an Aunt Sally pitch has been added. Inside, the refurbished lounge has attractive sporting prints on the wall, and is set out for eating. The front bar is more straightforward, with sensibly placed darts, shove-ha'penny, dominoes, cribbage, fruit machine and piped music. Quickly served good bar food includes sandwiches (popular bacon, mushrooms and tomato in french bread £2), daily specials like turkey and ham pie, pork and apple casserole or braised liver and onions (£3.50), rabbit casserole or pigeon pie, and nice home-made puddings like rhubarb crumble or banoffi pie (£2.25); on Tuesday and Thursday lunchtimes, they offer a special two-course lunch for OAPs (£3.95). Changing beers such as Bass, Hook Norton Best and Brew XI on handpump; pool room, and a spacious conservatory with garden tables and chairs. *(Recommended by F J and A Parmenter, Ted George, Dennis H Phillips)*

Free house ~ Licensee Mike Deacon ~ Real ale ~ Meals and snacks (not Mon evenings) ~ (01789) 740387 ~ Children over 5 in dining area if eating ~ Open 11-3, 5.30-11

FARNBOROUGH (War) SP4349 Map 4

Butchers Arms

Off A423 N of Banbury

The Robinsons have worked hard at renovating this creeper-covered pub and readers are very pleased with the result. The main lounge bar has lots of pine furniture and fittings, flagstone floors and some carpet, maybe piped classic FM, and well kept Bass, Boddingtons and Marstons Pedigree with weekly guests like Batemans, Hartleys, Oakhill Best, Morlands Old Speckled Hen, Robinsons, Wadworths 6X or Charles Wells Bombardier; decent wine list, too. There's a dining extension with big timbers, and a front public bar. Bar food includes sandwiches (from £1.85), soup (£2.35), filled french sticks or toasted bread filled with ham and cheese and topped with a fried egg (£2.85), home-made pâté (£3.85), lots of ploughman's (£4.30), omelettes, steak and kidney pie or lamb curry (£4.85), mushroom stroganoff (£6.85), children's dishes (£1.85), and puddings like banoffi pie, treacle tart or fruit crumble (£2.85); friendly staff. Darts, dominoes, fruit machine, and piped music. The pub, with its matching stable block opposite, is set well back from the village road, and there's a safely fenced-in front lawn, with seats on another flower-edged lawn which slopes up behind. *(Recommended by George Atkinson, Richard Houghton, Jill and Peter Bickley)*

Free house ~ Licensee Kathryn Robinson ~ Real ale ~ Meals and snacks (till 10) ~ Restaurant ~ (01295) 690615 ~ Children welcome ~ Live music Fri evenings ~ Open 12-3(4 Sat), 7-11

FIVE WAYS (War) SP2270 Map 4

Case is Altered

Follow Rowington signposts at junction roundabout off A4177/A4141 N of Warwick

The bar in this tiled white-painted brick cottage has been licensed to sell beer for over three centuries. It's a marvellously unchanging place with no food, no children or dogs, and no noisy games machines or piped music – but you can be sure of a delightfully warm welcome from the landlady, cheery staff and regulars. The small, unspoilt simple main bar is decorated with a fine old poster showing the Lucas Blackwell & Arkwright brewery (now flats) and a clock with its hours spelling out

2

The Good Pub Guide

The Good Pub Guide
FREEPOST TN1569
WADHURST
E. SUSSEX
TN5 7BR

Please use this card to tell us which pubs *you* think should or should not be included in the next edition of *The Good Pub Guide*. Just fill it in and return it to us – no stamp or envelope needed. And don't forget you can also use the report forms at the end of the *Guide*.

ALISDAIR AIRD

YOUR NAME AND ADDRESS (BLOCK CAPITALS PLEASE)

☐ *Please tick this box if you would like extra report forms*

REPORT ON *(pub's name)*

Pub's address

☐ **YES MAIN ENTRY** ☐ **YES *Lucky Dip*** ☐ **NO don't include**

Please tick one of these boxes to show your verdict, and give reasons and descriptive comments, prices etc

☐ Deserves FOOD award ☐ Deserves PLACE-TO-STAY award

REPORT ON *(pub's name)*

Pub's address

☐ **YES MAIN ENTRY** ☐ **YES *Lucky Dip*** ☐ **NO don't include**

Please tick one of these boxes to show your verdict, and give reasons and descriptive comments, prices etc

☐ Deserves FOOD award ☐ Deserves PLACE-TO-STAY award

Thornleys Ale, another defunct brewery; there are just a few sturdy and old-fashioned tables, with a couple of leather-covered sturdy settles facing each other over the spotless tiles. From this room you reach the homely lounge (usually open only weekend evenings and Sunday lunchtime) through a door lit up on either side. A door at the back of the building leads into a modest little room, usually empty on weekday lunchtimes, with a rug on its tiled floor and a bar billiards table protected by an ancient leather cover (it takes pre-decimal sixpences). Well kept Ansells Mild and Traditional, Flowers Original, and very well priced Sam Smiths OB served by rare beer engine pumps mounted on the casks that are stilled behind the counter. Behind a wrought-iron gate is a little brick-paved courtyard with a stone table under a chestnut tree. *(Recommended by P J Hanson, Wayne Brindle, B Adams, Ted George, Pete Baker, J Dwane, Michael and Derek Slade, the Monday Club)*

Free house ~ Licensee Gwen Jones ~ Real ale ~ (01926) 484206 ~ Open 11.30-2.30, 6-11 (closed evening 25 Dec)

FOTHERINGHAY (Northants) TL0593 Map 5

Falcon ★

Village signposted off A605 on Peterborough side of Oundle

In a village full of history, this stylish old place is most enjoyable. Readers are full of praise for the particularly good service, the relaxed and friendly atmosphere, and very satisfying food. The comfortable lounge has cushioned slatback armchairs and bucket chairs, antique engravings on its cream walls, winter log fires in stone fireplaces at each end, lovely dried flower arrangements, and a hum of quiet conversation; the landlord prefers to keep the simpler public bar for the locals. There's also a conservatory which is popular for Sunday lunch. Good bar food includes leek and potato or french onion soup (£2.90), chicken or duck pâté (£3), a really excellent proper ploughman's (£3.50), herrings in a curry sauce (£3.60), quail's eggs with smoked salmon (£4.60), vegetarian lasagne, steak and kidney pie or West African baboti (£4.90), barbecued spare ribs (£5.10), fresh grilled plaice fillets with asparagus (£7), roast duckling with apple and rosemary stuffing (£7.20), braised venison in a port and orange sauce (£8.20), and steaks (from £8.80); in summer you can eat on the terrace. Well kept Adnams Bitter and Broadside, Elgoods Cambridge, Everards Beacon Bitter, Nethergate IPA, and Ruddles County on handpump, and wines of the month; darts, shove-ha'penny, cribbage and dominoes. Behind is a well liked neat garden with seats under the chestnut tree. The vast church behind is worth a visit, Richard III was born in the village, and the site of Fotheringhay Castle is nearby (where Mary Queen of Scots was executed in 1587). *(Recommended by Maysie Thompson, Bernard and Marjorie Parkin, Comus Elliott, David Tew, Tom Evans, M J Morgan, E D Bailey, Arthur and Margaret Dickinson, Dr Paul Kitchener, Roy Bromell, Thomas Nott, David and Mary Webb, Alain and Rose Foote)*

Free house ~ Licensee Alan Stewart ~ Real ale ~ Meals and snacks (not Mon, not 25-30 Dec) ~ Restaurant ~ (01832) 226254 ~ Children welcome ~ Open 10-3, 6-11

GREAT WOLFORD (War) SP2434 Map 4

Fox & Hounds

Village signposted on right on A3400 3 miles S of Shipston on Stour

Doing very well indeed at the moment, this unspoilt and characterful 16th-c stone pub is the sort of friendly place where both the licensees and locals make visitors feel at home. The old-fashioned open-plan bar is rather cosy, with low beams and flagstones, a pair of high-backed old settles and other comfortable seats around a nice collection of candlelit old tables, well cushioned wall benches and a window seat, old hunting prints on the walls, and a roaring log fire in the inglenook fireplace with its fine old bread oven. A small tap room serves eight weekly changing beers like Boddingtons, Eldridge Pope Hardy, Hook Norton Best, M & B Brew XI, Marstons Pedigree, Morlands Old Speckled Hen, Shepherd Neame Spitfire, Smiles

Best, Thwaites Bitter, and Wychwood Dogs Bollocks on handpump, and over 120 malt whiskies. Good, interesting bar food includes home-made soup (£1.95), sandwiches (from £2.50), ploughman's (£3.95), daily specials such as fresh grilled sardines, chicken and broccoli gratin, beef and prune ragout or fresh local salmon (£2.95-£7.95), steaks (from £6.50), and puddings (£2.75). On the terrace outside is a well. Please note, they now do bedrooms. *(Recommended by Henry Paulinski, George Atkinson, Charlotte Creasy, John Bowdler, Michael Heald, Brian White, Martin Jones, H O Dickinson, Gordon, Michael Sargent)*

Free house ~ Licensees Graham and Anne Seddon ~ Real ale ~ Meals and snacks ~ (01608) 674220 ~ Children in eating area of bar ~ Open 12-3, 6-11 ~ Bedrooms: /£30S

HARRINGWORTH (Northants) SP9298 Map 4

White Swan

Seaton Road; village SE of Uppingham, signposted from A6003, A47 and A43

In a pretty village with a famous 82-arch railway viaduct as backdrop, this stonebuilt Tudor inn still shows signs of its coaching days, in the blocked-in traces of its carriage-entry arch. Good food in very large helpings is prepared by its Spanish chef/patron and includes soup (£2.50), ploughman's (from £4.25), lasagne (£5.25), chicken borito (£5.75), tagliatelle carbonara (£5.95), chicken grilled with stilton (£6.75) and sirloin steak (£8.25). The recently refurbished central bar area has good solid tables, a woodburning stove, and old village photographs (in which many of the present buildings are clearly recognisable). There are comfortable settles in the roomy and welcoming lounge/eating area, which is decorated with a collection of carpenter's planes and other tools; a quieter dining room has a number of old rolling pins on the walls. Well kept Greene King IPA and Abbot and a guest beer such as Marstons Pedigree or Theakstons XB; spotless housekeeping, friendly staff happy to chat about local beauty-spots; tables outside on a little terrace. *(Recommended by Mr and Mrs J F Batstone, Joan and Michel Hooper-Immins, Alan and Heather Jacques, Bernard and Marjorie Parkin, Mary and David Webb*

Free house ~ Christine Sykes and Miguel Morena ~ Real ale ~ Meals and snacks (12-2, 7-10; till 9 Sun) ~ Restaurant ~ (01572) 747543 ~ Open 11.30-2.30, 6.30-11~ Bedrooms:£37.50B/£40(£50B)

HIMLEY (W Midlands – though see below) SO8889 Map 4

Crooked House ★

Pub signposted from B4176 Gornalwood—Himley, OS Sheet 139 map reference 896908; readers have got so used to thinking of the pub as being near Kingswinford in the Midlands (though Himley is actually in Staffs) that we still include it in this chapter – the pub itself is virtually smack on the county boundary

As a result of mining, this pub is literally staggering. Getting the doors open is an uphill struggle, and on one table a bottle on its side actually rolls 'upwards' against the apparent direction of the slope. For a 10p donation you can get a big ball-bearing from the bar to roll 'uphill' along a wainscot. At the back is a large, level and more modern extension with local antiques. Well kept and extremely well priced Banks's Bitter and Mild, and Marstons Pedigree on handpump; dominoes, fruit machine and piped music. Good value bar food includes sandwiches (not Sunday), a smokie (£2.95), scampi (£3.50), and home-made steak and kidney pie (£3.65). The conservatory is no smoking at lunchtimes and there's a spacious outside terrace. *(Recommended by S G Brown, Gordon, Andrew Jeeves, Carole Smart, Graham Reeve, John Hazel, the Monday Club; more reports please)*

Banks's ~ Manager Gary Ensor ~ Real ale ~ Meals and snacks (lunchtimes and Sat evenings) ~ (01384) 238583 ~ Children in food area at lunchtime only, no under 3s ~ Open 11-11; 11.30-2.30, 6.30-11 in winter

ILMINGTON (War) SP2143 Map 4

Howard Arms 🍴 🍷

Village signposted with Wimpstone off A34 S of Stratford

Since Mr Thompson has personally taken over the running of this smart and very neatly kept golden-stone pub – as opposed to employing managers – things seem to be getting better and better. And although much emphasis is placed on the very good food, there's still a good pubby feel and quite a few drinkers in the heavy-beamed bar; this has rugs on polished flagstones, comfortable seats, highly polished brass, and open fires (one is in a big inglenook, screened from the door by an old-fashioned built-in settle). A snug area off from here is no-smoking. From an interesting menu, there might be all-time favourites like crispy cod (£5.50), steak and kidney pie (£5.75), rabbit and black pudding pie (£6), gammon and egg or oxtail stew and dumplings (£6.25), and boiled bacon with parsley sauce, with puddings such as plum and brandy crumble or bread and butter pudding (£2.75); also, sandwiches and ploughman's (lunchtime), broccoli and stilton soup (£2), crispy calamari with herb dip (£3.50), tagliatelle verde with a ragout of wild mushrooms (£5.75), king prawn balti (£6.50), crisp duck with an orange sauce (£8.50), and steaks (from £8.95); particularly good 3-course Sunday lunch (£11.50). Well kept Boddingtons, Everards Tiger, and Marstons Pedigree on handpump, decent wines, and excellent freshly pressed apple juice; friendly, polite service, and nice labrador; shove-ha'penny and Aunt Sally on Thursday evenings. The garden in summer is lovely and the sheltered lawn has fruit trees, a colourful herbaceous border and well spaced picnic tables, with more tables on a neat gravel terrace behind. It's nicely set beside the village green, and there are lovely walks on the nearby hills (as well as strolls around the village outskirts). *(Recommended by Dr I H Maine, John Bowdler, Nigel Hopkins, Moira and John Cole, Martin Jones, M J Radford, Pam Adsley, Mrs J Oakes, P J Hanson, E V Walder, Mrs Nicola Holden, Ann and Bob Westerook, Kathryn and Brian Heathcote, John and Marianne Cooper, Andrew Shore, Peter Lloyd, Margaret and Allan Marsden, Colin Mason)*

Free house ~ Licensee Alan Thompson ~ Real ale ~ Meals and snacks (not winter Sun evenings) ~ Restaurant (not winter Sun evenings) ~ (01608) 682226 ~ Well-behaved children welcome ~ Open 11-2.30, 6-11; closed evening 25 Dec ~ Bedrooms: £30B/£50B

KENILWORTH (War) SP2871 Map 4

Virgins & Castle

High St; opposite A429 Coventry Rd at junction with A452

This nice old-fashioned town pub has several separate rooms opening off the inner flagstones-and-beams servery, and there's a couple of simply furnished small snugs (one with flagstones and the other with rugs on its bare boards) flanking the entrance corridor; down a couple of steps, a large room has heavy beams, a big rug on ancient red tiles, and matching seat and stool covers. Also, a carpeted lounge with more beams, some little booths, hatch service, and a good warm coal fire, and a new upstairs room with juke box, bar billiards, pool table, pin table and football table, fruit machine and big TV. Bar food includes good value sandwiches (from £1.20), ploughman's (£2.95), and daily specials like steak and kidney pie or beef stew (£4); traditional Sunday roast. Well kept Bass, Davenports, Greenalls Original, and guest beers on handpump. Seats outside in a sheltered garden. *(Recommended by Dave Thompson, Margaret Mason, John Allsopp, Dr M V Jones, Michael and Derek Slade, George Atkinson, Steve and Karen Jennings)*

Davenports (Greenalls) ~ Manager A P Roberts ~ Real ale ~ Meals and snacks ~ Restaurant ~ (01926) 53737 ~ Children in restaurant ~ Traditional jazz summer Suns, folk muusic Tues ~ Open 11-11

Pubs in outstandingly attractive surroundings are listed at the back of the book.

LANGLEY (W Midlands) SO9788 Map 4

Brewery ★ £

1½ miles from M5, junction 2; from A4034 to W Bromwich and Oldbury take first right turn signposted Junction 2 Ind Estate then bear left past Albright & Wilson into Station Rd

From tractor seats in a back corridor you can see through a big picture window into the brewhouse here – a charmingly think-small subsidiary of Allied Breweries, the Ind Coope empire, where they produce their Entire – full-flavoured, quite strong and much loved by beer-drinkers. The simple Tap Bar serves this and the ordinary Holt, Plant and Deakins Bitter, brewed up in Warrington, and has lots of plates and Staffordshire pottery, and a coal-effect gas fire. The Parlour on the left has plates and old engravings on the walls, a corner china cabinet, brass swan's neck wall lamps, a coal fire in a tiled Victorian fireplace with china on the overmantle, and dining chairs or sturdy built-in settles around four good solid tables. A red-tiled kitchen, divided off by shelves of Staffordshire pottery and old books, is similarly furnished, with the addition of lots of copper pans around its big black range; darts, cribbage, dominoes, quiz night every other Tuesday, and piped big band and classical music. Straightforward bar food (written up rather waggishly on a blackboard) includes very good value doorstep sandwiches with hot roast beef, roast ham and cheese, roast pork and stuffing, even black pudding and onion (£1.60), and a home-made dish of the day such as steak and kidney pie, macaroni cheese, chicken curry or Cornish pasties (£1.95); friendly service. It's hard to believe that this pub was only built in 1984. *(Recommended by S G Brown, David and Shelia, Christopher Darwent, Mike and Wendy Proctor, B Adams, John and Christine Simpson, Brian and Anna Marsden, Ian and James Phillips)*

Holt, Plant & Deakins (Allied) ~ Manager Tony Stanton ~ Real ale ~ Lunchtime meals and snacks (not Sun) ~ (0121) 544 6467 ~ Children in eating area lunchtimes and early evenings ~ Open 11-2.30, 6(7 Sat)-11

LAPWORTH (War) SP1670 Map 4

Navigation

Old Warwick Rd (B4439 Warwick—Hockley Heath)

In summer and at weekends, this busy local is very popular with canal-users. There are seats on a back terrace or on the sheltered flower-edged lawn running down to the water, maybe barbecues, Morris dancers or even travelling theatre companies out here then, and outside hatch service; it's all prettily lit at night. Inside, the flagstoned bar is decorated with brightly painted canal ware and cases of stuffed fish, and has high-backed winged settles, seats built around its window bay and a coal fire in its high-mantled inglenook. A second quieter room has tables on its board-and-carpet floor – and a dresser with dominoes, shut-the-box, and board games. Straightforward bar food includes lunchtime sandwiches (from £1.75), quiches, curries or steak and kidney pie (£5.25), steak (from £6.95), and puddings (£1.85); service can slow down when busy – as it often is on sunny days – but stays friendly and obliging. Well kept Bass, M&B Brew XI, and a guest beer on handpump, and summer cider; fruit machine. *(Recommended by David Shillitoe, Wayne Brindle, Dave Thompson, Margaret Mason, George Atkinson, Gary Roberts, Ann Stubbs, D Alcock, Stephen Brown, Roger and Jenny Huggins, Richard Lewis, Brian Jones, Graham Reeve, Mark Grist, Dennis H Phillips, Derek and Sylvia Stephenson)*

M&B (Bass) ~ Lease: Andrew Kimber ~ Real ale ~ Meals and snacks ~ (01564) 783337 ~ Children in eating area until 9 ~ Occasional Morris dancing, folk music ~ Open 11-2.30, 5.30-11; 11-11 Sat

LITTLE COMPTON (War) SP2630 Map 4

Red Lion

Off A44 Moreton-in-Marsh—Chipping Norton

There's a pleasant, friendly atmosphere in this simple but civilised low-beamed stone inn, and the comfortable lounge has snug alcoves and a couple of little tables by the log fire. A dining area leading off has good generously served home cooked food such as home-made soup (£1.95), large filled granary rolls (from £2.25), ploughman's (from £3.55), celery, apple and prawn salad (£3.75), home-cooked ham and egg (£4.85), lasagne or bean and vegetable chilli (£5.50), home-made steak and kidney pie (£5.95), good marinated swordfish steak (£7.25), lots of steaks (from £8.60; 32oz £25.50), roast duck with black cherry, peach and orange curaçao sauce (£8.95), and king prawns in garlic butter (£12.25). Booking is recommended on Saturday evenings especially. The plainer public bar has another log fire, and darts, pool, cribbage, fruit machine, juke box and Aunt Sally. Well kept Donnington BB and SBA on handpump and an extensive wine list; good service; piped music. The bedrooms are good value. No dogs – even in garden (where there's a children's play area with climbing frame). It's a handy base for touring the Cotswolds. *(Recommended by Pam Adsley, Martin Jones, Mr and Mrs P Smith, H O Dickinson, Marion and John Hadfield, Chris Warne, Mrs A Binns, Gordon)*

Donnington ~ Tenant David Smith ~ Real ale ~ Meals and snacks ~ Restaurant ~ (01608) 674397 ~ Children in eating area of bar ~ Occasional folk music ~ Open 11-2.30, 6-11 ~ Bedrooms: £24/£36 (no under 8s)

LOWER BRAILES (War) SP2630 Map 4

George

B4035 Shipston on Stour—Banbury

Our simple inspection meal here was excellent: a beautifully dressed Parma ham salad (£4.95), and an exemplary steak sandwich (£4.50). Other thoughtfully prepared and presented dishes served in good helpings include starters like soup (£2), pâté (£2.95), prawn cocktail (£3.75), smoked salmon (£4.95) and main courses like rabbit stew and salmon en croûte, lasagne or chilli con carne (£5.95), steak and kidney pie (£6), plaice (£6.95), citrus chicken breast (£7.25), duck breast with orange sauce (£9.75) and grilled dover sole (£11.75); good home-made puddings like bread and butter pudding, pecan pie or steamed chocolate (all £2.85). The big and airy bar on the right has substantial windows on two sides, with several good-sized stripped pine tables on its light lino-tiled floor, and a woodburner in the inglenook. The back bar has an oriental rug on a brown carpet, and polished tables around dark panelled walls with built-in brocade seats. The same food's served in an attractive flagstoned country-style restaurant. Service is relaxed, but with a steady old-fashioned attentiveness. Well kept Hook Norton Best, Old Hookey and Mild on handpump, lots of malt whiskies; darts, dominoes, shove ha'penny, cribbage, piped music. At the back is a large, attractive shrub-surrounded garden with picnic-sets on an end terrace. *(Recommended by Jane Dobby, G Washington, James Sargeant, H D Spottiswoode)*

Hook Norton ~ Tenants Jane and Peter Brown ~ Real ale ~ Meals and snacks ~ Restaurant ~ (01608) 685223 ~ Children in restaurant and lounge ~ Open 11.30-3, 6-11 ~ Bedrooms: £38B/£48B

LOWSONFORD (War) SP1868 Map 4

Fleur de Lys

Village signposted off B4439 Hockley Heath—Warwick; can be reached too from B4095 via Preston Bagot

Under a friendly and efficient new licensee this year (he has run several of our main entry pubs in the past), this canalside pub is rather smart and civilised. The spreading bar has lots of low black beams in the butter-coloured ceiling, brocade-cushioned mate's, wheelback and dining chairs around the well spaced tables, and rugs on the flagstones and antique tiles; it's at its most parlourish on the left, with a sofa and some bookshelves, and down steps on the right is a log fire and a couple of long settles. Bar food can now be eaten anywhere (rather than restricted to certain areas) and might include stilton mushrooms (£2.55), sandwiches (with a bowl of soup as well, £3.85), ploughman's (from £3.95), fish and chips (£4.75), vegetable crumble or steak and kidney pudding (£4.95), salads like hot chicken and bacon (from £5.75), pork steak with apple and dijonnaise sauce (£5.95), sirloin steak (£8.45), and puddings (from £1.95); there may be delays when busy. Well kept Boddingtons, Flowers Original, Wadworths 6X and a guest beer on handpump, and decent wines including good New World ones (lots by the glass); several open fires, newspapers and magazines, fruit machine, and unobtrusive piped classical music. In summer, the picnic tables down on the grass among tall weeping willows by the Stratford-upon-Avon Canal are a most pleasant place to sit and watch the ducks and moored barges; there's a well equipped play area too. *(Recommended by James Macrae, Roy Bromell, P J Hanson, Wayne Brindle, KC, Michael Begley, Mayur Shah, G B Longden, John Fahy, Nigel Flook, Betsy Brown, Don Kellaway, Angie Coles, Dorothy and Leslie Pilson, David Heath, P J F Westlake, Mr and Mrs R J Phillips, Dorothee and Dennis Glover, Brian and Anna Marsden, Wendy Arnold, Graham Reeve)*

Whitbreads ~ Manager David Tye ~ Real ale ~ Meals and snacks ~ (01564) 782431 ~ Children in eating area of bar ~ Open 11-11

MONKS KIRBY (War) SP4683 Map 4

Bell

Just off A427 W of Pailton; Bell Lane

The very traditional appearance of this timbered and flagstoned old pub is rather deceptive, because with its chatty Spanish landlord the warmly comfortable and informal atmosphere is distinctly southern European. The landlord's little girl wanders cheerfully round the rambling rooms with a friendly big alsatian, while locals gather happily round the bar. What makes this place really special is that as well as the more usual bar food there's a surprisingly comprehensive Spanish menu: you can make a splendid meal from the good range of garlic-drenched tapas dishes served in little frying pans, such as grilled sardines, prawns in white wine, garlic and chilli, Spanish salami cooked in garlic and white wine, squid fried in butter or cooked modizo-style, king prawns in garlic and chilli, and scallops cooked with white wine, tomato, lemon juice and breadcrumbs (from £2.75). Main courses include a vegetable paella (£6.25), grilled loin of pork with garlic, white wine, lemon and parsley (£8.25), paella (£9.50), honey-roasted saddle of lamb with red wine sauce (£9.95), steak flamed with port and topped with pâté (£11.75), and plenty of fish such as salmon in creamy seafood sauce (£8.75), fish in a white wine and caper sauce (£9.95), mixed sea grill (£11.75) and lobster thermidor (£15.75). Well kept Boddingtons, Flowers Original and Whitbreads Fuggles Imperial on handpump. There's a very good wine list, ports for sale by the bottle and a healthy range of brandies and malt whiskies. In keeping with the general style, the informal back terrace has rough-and-ready rustic woodwork and a pretty little view across a stream to a buttercup meadow. Fairly loud piped music. *(Recommended by John and Marianne Cooper, the Monday Club)*

Free house ~ Licensees Paco and Belinda Maures ~ Real ale ~ Meals and snacks ~ (01788) 832352 ~ Children welcome ~ 12-2, 7-11 (cl Mon lunchtime)

NASSINGTON (Northants) TL0696 Map 5

Black Horse

Consistently good food from an elaborate menu continues to draw people to this civilised 17th-c pub. With the emphasis firmly on fresh local produce, there might be soup (£2.65), home-made pâté (£2.95), prawns and scallops in a creamy cheese sauce (£3.45), spanish-style tortilla (£4.25), steak sandwich (£5.25), seafood pancake (£5.95), lots of vegetarian dishes such as mushroom and edam pie or vegetable and cream cheese crumble (both £6.75), pork sautéed with walnuts and apples served with a marsala wine sauce or strips of turkey in an almond, hazelnut, peanut and coriander sauce (£9.35), rich game casserole marinated in herbs and wine (£9.45), breast of duck with a sauce of black cherries, brandy and raisins (£9.95), puddings (£2.85) and children's meals (£2.45); they hold imaginative monthly themed food evenings, too (best to book well in advance). A splendid big stone fireplace in the lounge bar is thought to have come from Fotheringhay Castle (which had been destroyed some time earlier) when the pub was built. There are easy chairs and small settees, a beamed ceiling, and a pleasant, relaxed atmosphere; piped music. The bar servery, with panelling from Rufford Abbey, links the two comfortable rooms of the restaurant. Bass, John Smiths, Tetleys and a guest beer on handpump, a very good varied wine list, with several half bottles, and a good few malt whiskies; service is efficient and friendly. You can sit out on the very well-tended attractive sheltered lawn, with plenty of flowers and plants. *(Recommended by Wayne Brindle, Roger Bellingham, Mary and David Webb, Mrs J M Day, Andy Thwaites)*

Free house ~ Licensees Roland Cooke and Jonathan Reid ~ Real ale ~ Meals and snacks (till 9.45) ~ Restaurant ~ (01780) 782324 ~ Children welcome ~ Monthly theme nights with music ~ Open 12-3, 7-11

NETHERTON (W Midlands) SO9387 Map 4

Little Dry Dock

Windmill End, Bumble Hole; you really need an A-Z street map to find it or OS Sheet 139, map reference 953881

Full of character and atmosphere, this tiny, eccentric place has an entire narrow-boat squeezed into the right-hand bar and used as the servery (its engine is in the room on the left). There's also a huge model boat in one front transom-style window, winches and barge rudders flanking the door, marine windows, and lots of brightly coloured bargees' water pots, lanterns, jugs and lifebuoys; fruit machine, trivia, and piped music. They have their own Little Lumphammer ale as well as Holt, Plant & Deakins Entire and Ind Coope Burton, and fruit wines; friendly service. Bar food includes sandwiches, soup (£1.75), black pudding thermidor (£2.10), faggots and peas (£4.45), home-made lasagne (£4.65), gammon and egg (£5.20), steak and kidney in Guinness pie (£5.25), rump steak (£6.25), and puddings (from £1.75). There are pleasant towpath walks nearby. *(Recommended by Anthony Marriott, Howard West, Pat and John Millward, Mike and Wendy Proctor, Andrew Jeeves, Carole Smart, Basil J S Minson, Pete Yearsley, Patrick and Mary McDermott, James and Ian Phillips, Ron Fletcher, Stephen, Julie and Hayley Brown)*

Carlsberg Tetley ~ Tenant Frank Pearson ~ Real ale ~ Meals and snacks (12-2.30, 6-10) ~ (01384) 235369 ~ Children welcome ~ Irish folk music Mon evenings ~ Open 11-3, 6-11

NEWBOLD ON STOUR (War) SP2446 Map 4

White Hart

A34 Shipston on Stour—Stratford

The airy, beamed main bar in this friendly pub – partly divided by stub walls and the chimney – has modern high-backed winged settles, seats set into big bay windows, a fair amount of brass, and a gun hanging over the log fire in one big stone fireplace. A wide range of good, reasonably priced food includes home-made soup (£1.95), home-made chicken liver pâté or garlic mushrooms in cream and white wine (£3.50), home-baked ham and eggs or grilled fresh local trout with almonds (£5.85), chicken breast poached in cider with rosemary and fresh cream (£6.95), steaks (from £6.95), and daily specials like lamb's kidneys with sherry and cream (£5.85) or curried prawns with fresh pineapple (£6.75); best to book weekend evenings and Sunday lunch. The roomy back public bar has pool, dominoes, fruit machine, trivia and juke box; Bass and Worthingtons Best on handpump. There are some picnic tables under cocktail parasols in front of the pub, with its well tended hanging baskets. *(Recommended by Derek Allpass, Jill White, C Fisher, Marion and John Hadfield; more reports please)*

M & B (Bass) ~ Lease: Mr and Mrs J C Cruttwell ~ Real ale ~ Meals and snacks (not Sun evening) ~ Restaurant (not Sun evening) ~ (01789) 450205 ~ Children welcome ~ Open 11-2.30(3 Sat), 6-11

OUNDLE (Northants) TL0487 Map 5

Mill

Barnwell Rd out of town; or follow Barnwell Country Park signs off A605 bypass

Next to Barnwell Country Park, this imposing old mill building, dating back to the early 16th-c, has picnic tables under cocktail parasols among willow trees by the pond, with more on side grass and some white cast-iron tables on a flagstoned terrace. It's popular with diners who like the wide choice of well-served meals including sandwiches (not Sunday), home-made soup (£2.95), garlic mushrooms (£3.75), ploughman's (from £3.75), burgers (from £4.55), local sausages and egg (£4.95), lots of pizzas (from £4), quite a few Mexican dishes like tortilla pancakes filled with spiced chicken and deep-fried (chimichanges, £7.55), nacho chips with chilli con carne or vegetable chilli with black olives and sour cream (muchos nachos, £7.95), and sizzling platters with meat or vegetables and sour cream and tortilla pancakes (from £9.95). Stairs outside take you up to the most popular part, the Trattoria, which has stalls around tables with more banquettes in bays, stripped masonry and beams, and a millstone feature; its small windows look down over the lower millpond and the River Nene. A rather dimly lit ground floor bar has red leatherette button-back built-in wall banquettes against its stripped-stone walls; on the way in a big glass floor panel shows the stream race below the building. Two-thirds of the bar is no smoking. Courage Best and Directors on handpump; top-floor restaurant (more beams, and the corn hoist); bar billiards. *(Recommended by Frank Cummins, Mr and Mrs G Hart, Peter Watkins, Pam Stanley; more reports please)*

Free house ~ Licensees Noel and Linda Tulley ~ Real ale ~ Meals and snacks (till 10pm) ~ Restaurant (not Sun evening) ~ (01832) 272621 ~ Well behaved children in eating area ~ Open 12-3, 6.30-11

Ship £

West St

The genuinely welcoming landlord and his sons give this well-worn and unpretentious local a buoyantly cheerful atmosphere that readers like very much. The heavily beamed lounge bar is made up of three rooms that lead off the central corridor on the left: up by the street there's a mix of leather and other seats including a very flowery piano stool (and its piano), with sturdy tables and a log fire in a stone inglenook, and down one end a panelled snug has button-back leather seats built in around it. This is no-smoking – if you light up you have to donate £1 to the RNLI. Well kept Bass, Marstons Pedigree, Nethergate IPA, and Tetleys on handpump. Bar food includes sandwiches (from £1.30), home-made soup (£1.60), filled baked potatoes (from £1.70), ploughman's or sausages and beans (£2.50), home-made smoked salmon pâté (£2.75), home-cooked ham and egg (£3), fried cod (£3.20), home-made steak and kidney pie or vegetable lasagne (£4.50), steaks (from £7.50), and lunchtime daily specials such as pork chop in cider and apple, mince with mashed potatoes or Barnsley double lamb chops (£2.50-£3), and puddings. Sunday lunchtimes they just do a roast and pies. Smiling, efficient service. Dominoes, maybe free Sunday nuts and crisps on the bar. The tiled-floor public side has pinball, fruit machine, video game, and juke box. A series of small sheltered terraces strung out behind has wooden tables and chairs, lit at night. Several of the bedrooms are in a new extension. *(Recommended by George Atkinson, Bernard and Marjorie Parkin, Norma and Keith Bloomfield, Tom Evans)*

Free house ~ Licensee Frank Langridge ~ Real ale ~ Meals and snacks (till 10) ~ (01832) 273918 ~ Children welcome ~ Occasional live music ~ Open 11-3, 6-11; 11-11 Sat ~ Bedrooms: £20(£27.50B)/£35(£45B)

PRIORS MARSTON (War) SP4857 Map 4

Falcon

Hellidon Rd; village signposted off A425 Daventry Rd in Southam; and from A361 S of Daventry

Civilised and friendly, this handsome old pub has a neatly kept main bar that rambles around into an L beyond the log fire in the big high-mantled stone fireplace, with well padded high-backed winged settles on its cheerfully patterned carpet; a couple of big framed mirrors alongside the country pictures give a feeling of extra space, and there's a no-smoking area. Generous helpings of popular bar food include soup, sandwiches, tequila chicken, fettucini or monkfish (£8.95), lemon sole (£9.50), steaks using prime Scottish beef, and puddings; daily specials and regular theme nights. Well kept ABC Best, Everards Beacon and Old Original, Ind Coope Burton, and Marstons Pedigree on handpump. *(Recommended by Mrs J Oakes, P J Caunt, Jill and Peter Bickley, Stephen, Julie and Hayley Brown, John and Marianne Cooper, Clive Watkins, John Fahy; up-to-date reports please)*

Free house ~ Licensees Stephen and Jane Richards ~ Real ale ~ Meals and snacks (till 10) ~ (01327) 260562 ~ Well behaved children allowed until 9 ~ Open 12-3, 7-11 ~ Bedrooms: £25S/£35S

Holly Bush

From village centre follow Shuckburgh signpost, but still in village take first right turn by telephone box, not signposted

This year, the friendly licensee has opened up bedrooms in this characterful golden stone building – once the village bakehouse. The small beamed rambling rooms have old-fashioned pub seats and stripped stone walls, and there may be up to three winter open fires. Good bar food includes sandwiches (£2.25), ploughman's or home-made burger (£4.25), filled baked potatoes (£3.25), cumberland sausage and egg (£3.50), three-egg omelette (£4.25), home-made meaty or vegetarian lasagne or nice chicken tikka masala (£4.95), beef and Guinness pie (£5.95), salmon steak with herb butter (£6.95), steaks (from £8.95), and puddings (£2.50); children's menu (£2.50), Sunday roast (£5.25), and occasional pig roasts. Well kept Bass, Hook Norton Best, Marstons Pedigree, Theakstons Old Peculier, and Wadworths 6X on handpump; darts, pool, fruit machine, trivia, juke box, and piped music. *(Recommended by Michael Jeanes, George Atkinson, Stephen, Julie and Hayley Brown, Jill and Peter Bickley, Clive Watkins)*

Free house ~ Licensee Mark Hayward ~ Real ale ~ Meals and snacks ~ Restaurant ~ (01327) 260934 ~ Children welcome ~ Open 12-3, 5.30(6 Sat)-11 ~ Bedrooms: £30B/£40B

SAMBOURNE (War) SP0561 Map 4

Green Dragon

A435 N of Alcester, then left fork onto A448 just before Studley; village signposted on left soon after

This friendly village green pub is a pretty place in summer with its climbing roses around the shuttered and timbered facade, and picnic tables and teak seats among flowering cherries on a side courtyard, by the car park. Inside, the modernised beamed communicating rooms have a good cheery atmosphere as well as little armed seats and more upright ones, some small settles, and open fires; piped music. Good bar food includes nice sandwiches, home-made soup (£2.25), home-made pâté (£2.50), omelettes (from £3.95), sausage and mash, home-made steak and kidney pie and very good curry (all £4.95), vegetable tagliatelle with a saffron cream sauce (£5.50), steaks (from £9.25), puddings (£2.25), and children's menu (from £2.50); an à la carte section has more adventurous dishes such as pan-fried tuna steak teriaki (£8.95), prawns and scallops in filo pastry (£9.95), and beef en croûte with a lemon stuffing in a madeira sauce (£11.75). Well kept Bass, Hobsons, and M & B Brew XI on handpump; cheerful, attentive service. *(Recommended by K Neville-Rolfe, Ian Phillips, Jerry and Alison Oakes; more reports please)*

M & B (Bass) ~ Lease: Phil and Pat Burke ~ Real ale ~ Meals and snacks (till 10; not Sun) ~ Restaurant (not Sun) ~ (01527) 892465 ~ Children in eating area of bar and in restaurant ~ Open 11-3, 6-11

SHUSTOKE (War) SP2290 Map 4

Griffin

5 miles from M6, junction 4; A446 towards Tamworth, then right on to B4114 and go straight through Coleshill; pub is at Furnace End, a mile E of village

Real ale buffs crowd into this friendly and unpretentious village local to enjoy the beers brewed from their micro-brewery (Church End Vicar's Ruin, Pew's Porter, Cuthbert's, and summer N Reg), as well as guests such as Blackmore's Dead on Arrival, Burton Bridge Summer Ale, and Steam Packet Bargee, all from a servery under a very low, thick beam; farm ciders also. The low-beamed, L-shaped bar has an old-fashioned settle and cushioned cafe seats (some quite closely packed), sturdily elm-topped sewing trestles, lots of old jugs on the beams, beer mats on the ceiling, and log fires in both stone fireplaces (one's a big inglenook); the conservatory is popular with families. Lunchtime bar food includes sandwiches (from £1.20), steak and ale pie (£4), cod or haddock (£5), and 12oz sirloin steak (£5.50); they may sell local fresh eggs. There are old-fashioned seats and tables on the back grass, a children's play area, and a large terrace with plants in raised beds. *(Recommended by Graham Richardson, Mrs J Oakes, Kate and Robert Hodkinson, Stephen Brown, Mrs Gwyneth Holland, J Dwane, the Monday Club, Andrew Jeeves, Carole Smart, CW, JW, Richard Lewis, Graham Reeve)*

Own brew ~ Licensees Michael Pugh and Sydney Wedge ~ Real ale ~ Lunchtime meals and snacks (not Sun) ~ (01675) 481205 ~ Children in conservatory ~ Open 12-2.30, 7-11; closed evenings 25/26 Dec

STRATFORD UPON AVON (War) SP2055 Map 4

Slug & Lettuce

38 Guild Street, corner of Union Street

Perhaps best in the early evening or on weekday lunchtimes – before the crowds set in – this is a cheerfully friendly place serving very good food (it's very handy if you're going on to the theatre). You can see some of the meals being prepared at one end of the long L-shaped bar counter, with dishes like home-made leek, potato and sweetcorn soup (£2.45), home-made smoked trout pâté or creamy garlic mushrooms (£4.45), black pudding topped with bacon, egg, tomato and melted cheese, pork and chive sausages in a creamy Dijonnaise sauce, vegetarian puff pastry parcel or baked chicken in a mushroom and mild mustard sauce (all £5.75), sautéed lamb's liver with bacon in a port and onion gravy (£9.75) and excellent grilled breast of duckling in a plum and cassis sauce (£10.95); helpful staff. The bar has pine kitchen tables and chairs on rugs and flagstones, a few period prints on stripped squared panelling, a newspaper rack, and a solid fuel fire; cribbage and piped music. Well kept beers such as Ansells, Ind Coope Burton, Tetleys, and a guest beer on handpump, and decent wine. There's a small flagstoned back terrace, floodlit at night, with lots of flower boxes and sturdy teak tables under cocktail parasols, with more up steps. As the evening goes on the pub becomes a favourite with younger customers. *(Recommended by Ted George, David and Shelia, Dr and Mrs A K Clarke, Lawrence Pearse, Maury Harris, Clifford Payton, Sara Nicholls, Dr I H Maine, Peter Neate, K Baxter, Cdr Patrick Tailyour)*

Ansells (Allied) ~ Manager Neil Miller ~ Real ale ~ Meals and snacks (5.30-9; all day Thurs-Sat) ~ (01789) 299700 ~ Children in eating area of bar ~ Open 11-3, 5.30-11; all day Thurs-Sat

SUDBOROUGH (Northants) SP9682 Map 4

Vane Arms

High St; A6116 Corby—Thrapston

Mr Tookey is a real beer enthusiast and more than happy to talk you through his marvellous range of real ales – they vary so much that it's almost like a continuous beer festival. There's usually nine well kept and often rare brews on at a time, such as Adnams Broadside, Churchills Pride, Eldridge Pope Royal Oak, Elgoods GSB, Oakham Old Tosspot and JHB, Theakstons Old Peculier, Thwaites Craftsman, and Woodfordes Victory. If you're not sure which to have, they do a sample tray for about five pounds, with around a third of a pint of each; they also keep a couple of Belgian fruit beers, farm cider and lots of country wines. The welcoming and comfortable main bar has some stripped stonework, and good inglenook fireplaces with open fires in winter (and perhaps Nelson the dog in front of one of them); one area is no smoking. There's a small public bar with darts, pool, table skittles, fruit machine, video game, and piped music. A wide range of freshly cooked food includes sandwiches, home-made soup (£1.95), mushrooms in stilton sauce (£2.95), good steak and kidney pie (£5.50), breast of chicken with stilton wrapped in bacon and encased in puff pastry (£7), venison steak (£7.50), steaks (from £9), a weekly changing fresh fish dish, lots of popular Mexican dishes featuring dishes like spicy chicken wings (£2.95), tacos (£5.95) and fajitas (£7.95); helpful, friendly service. *(Recommended by S G Brown, Eric Locker, Wayne Brindle, Julian Holland, Joan and Michel Hooper-Immins, David and Michelle Hedges, Derek and Sylvia Stephenson, D H and M G Buchanan, Stephen, Julie and Hayley Brown)*

Free house ~ Licensees Tom and Anne Tookey ~ Real ale ~ Meals and snacks (not Sun or Mon evenings) ~ Restaurant (not Sun evening) ~ (01832) 733223 ~ Children welcome ~ Open 11.30-3, 5.30(6 Sat)-11; closed Mon lunchtime Bedrooms: £30B/£45B

SULGRAVE (Northants) SP5545 Map 4

Star

E of Banbury, signposted off B4525; Manor Road

On the road to George Washington's ancestral home, this hospitable small creeper-covered stonebuilt inn has a neat bar divided by a timbered and leaded-light screen. The part by the big inglenook fireplace (with a paper skeleton on its side bench) has polished flagstones, the other part a red carpet, and furnishings are mainly small pews, cushioned window seats and wall benches, kitchen chairs and cast-iron-framed tables. Lots of things to look at include front pages of newspapers from notable days (Kennedy's assassination, say), collections of this and that, and some rather jokey stuffed animals. The staff are welcoming and friendly, as are one or two very regular locals. Seasonal dishes from the changing blackboard might include starters like soup or chicken liver pâté (£2.50), guacamole and tortilla or hummus and pitta (£2.95), filo-wrapped tiger prawns or prawn and smoked egg mayonnaise (£3.95), and main courses like lasagne or a really huge steak and kidney pie (£4.95), chicken rogan josh, smoked cheese, leek and potato pie or courgette, feta and basil quiche (£5.95), smoked breast of chicken (£6.25), salmon steak or cold smoked trout (£6.95), leg of lamb steak or grilled swordfish (£7.95), turkey, pork and cranberry pie (£8.95) and 12oz rump steak (£9.50); they do good double-decker sandwiches (from £1.95) and ploughman's (£3.75). Well kept Hook Norton Best, Old Hookey and a monthly changing guest ale like Fullers London Pride on handpump. no-smoking back restaurant; piped music. There are some tables outside. We've not yet had reports on the bedrooms, but would expect this to be a nice place to stay. *(Recommended by George Atkinson, Keith Archer, Leith Stuart)*

Hook Norton ~ Tenant Andrew Willerton ~ Real ale ~ Meals and snacks ~ Restaurant ~ (01295) 760389 ~ Open 11-2.30, 6-11 (closed 25 Dec) ~ Bedrooms: £25B/£40B

THORNBY (Northants) SP6775 Map 4

Red Lion

Welford Road; A50 Northampton—Leicester

Pleasantly unchanging, this stylish cream-painted slated brick roadside pub is a friendly place. The bar has logs burning in an open stove, pewter tankards hanging from a beam, decorative plates densely covering the walls, and china jugs and steins on a shelf and hanging over the bar. Carefully chosen furnishings include individual old-fashioned lamps, a lovingly polished big golden table that sits between a couple of pews in one of the bay windows, and deep leather armchairs and sofa in one of two smallish areas opening off; it does help if you like dogs – they have three friendly ones; shove-ha'penny, cribbage, dominoes, shut-the-box, chess, bagatelle, and piped music. Good home-made bar food includes sandwiches, home-made soup (£2.25), lasagne (£5.50), home-made steak in ale pie or well-liked curry (£5.95), steaks (£8.95), lunchtime meaty or vegetarian burgers (£2.95) or filled yorkshire pudding (£3.95), daily specials such as fresh mushrooms in cream and garlic (£2.95) or prawn and cauliflower gratinée (£5.95), fresh fish and vegetarian dishes, and quite a few evening extras; children's helpings. Well kept Hook Norton Best, Marstons Pedigree, Robinsons Best, Timothy Taylors Landlord, Wadworths 6X and a guest beer on handpump. There are some seats outside. *(Recommended by Cdr Patrick Tailyour, M J Morgan, Wayne Brindle, L M Miall, George Atkinson, Frank Cummins, Mr and Mrs Hillman)*

Free house ~ Licensee Caroline Baker ~ Real ale ~ Meals and snacks ~ Small restaurant ~ (01604) 740238 ~ Well behaved children welcome ~ Open 12-2.30, 6.30(5 Fri)-11; 11.30-11 Sat

TIPTON (W Midlands) SO9592 Map 4

M A D O'Rourkes Pie Factory

Hurst Lane, Dudley Rd towards Wednesbury (junction A457/A4037) – look for the Irish flag

This friendly, if rather eccentric pub, is a pastiche of a 1940s pork butcher's, with all sorts of meat-processing equipment from the relatively straightforward butcher's blocks to the bewilderingly esoteric (part of the fun is trying to guess what it's all for), not to mention strings of model hams, sausages and so forth hanging from the ceiling. Labels for pigs' heads mounted on the walls tell you about the dogs and abbots that are alleged to go into their recipes. In fact the food's good solid value and might include black pudding thermidor (£2.25), a roast of the day (£4.25), faggots and peas (£4.50), shepherd's pie or leek and stilton bake (£4.75), the gargantuan Desperate Dan cow pie complete with pastry horns (£5.25), and sweet puddings such as spotted dick and jam rolypoly (from £1.95); children's dishes (£2.50). The atmosphere is buoyant, and service is cheerful. They have their own variable but generally good Lumphammer ale, and Ansells Mild, Holt Plant & Deakins Mild and Entire and a guest beer; fruit machine, trivia, and piped music. Though it's roomy, with more space upstairs, it can get very busy (packed on Friday and Saturday evenings), especially if there's a party from a Black Country coach tour wandering around in a state of tickled shock. *(Recommended by S G Brown, Mike and Wendy Proctor, Ian Phillips, Mr and Mrs D T Deas, Stephen and Julie Brown, David and Shelia)*

Carslberg Tetley ~ Managers Chris and Sharon Wood ~ Real ale ~ Meals and snacks (till 10) ~ (0121) 557 1402 ~ Children welcome ~ Irish singer Mon evening, duo Weds evening ~ Open 11-3, 6-11

TWYWELL (Northants) SP9478 Map 4

Old Friar

Village signposted from A14 about 2 miles W of Thrapston

The attractively furnished bar in this busy pub has wooden carvings of friars on the beams and brick fireplaces, and there are plain wooden tables, tub chairs and settles.

It's a very foody place, with most of the tables set for eating: sandwiches and snacks (from £1.50), home-made soup (£1.90), stilton mushrooms (£2.75), vegetable stroganoff (£5.75), lasagne (£5.50), steak and kidney pie or cold meats from the carvery (£5.95), a hot carvery (£6.95), and steaks (from £7.95); children's menu. Part of the dining area is no smoking. Well kept Ansells Best, Shepherd Neame Spitfire, Tetleys, and Theakstons XB on handpump served from the brick bar counter; hard-working helpful staff; darts, pool, shove-ha'penny, cribbage, dominoes, fruit machine and piped music. No dogs. The garden has tables and a children's play area, with a bouncy castle on Sundays. ***(Recommended by R C Vincent, Stephen Brown; more reports please)***

Carlsberg Tetleys ~ Tenant Yvonne Joan Crisp ~ Real ale ~ Meals and snacks (till 9.45) ~ Restaurant ~ (01832) 732625 ~ Children in eating area of bar and in restaurant ~ Open 11-2.30(5.30 Thurs), 6-11; 11-11 Sat

WEST BROMWICH (W Midlands) SP0091 Map 4

Manor House

2 miles from M6, junction 9; from A461 towards Wednesbury take first left into Woden Rd East; at T-junction, left into Crankhall Lane; at eventual roundabout, right into Hall Green Rd. Alternatively, 5 miles from junction 7.

Built for the Deveraux and de Marnham families in the 1300s, though a manor house was recorded on this site two centuries earlier, this small manor house is a remarkable place: you enter through the ancient gatehouse, across the moat, and inside, the main room is actually a great flagstoned hall, where massive oak trusses support the soaring pitched roof (the central one, eliminating any need for supporting pillars, is probably unique). This is now mainly an eating area (no smoking), and around the walls are a few lifesize medieval effigies, with as a centrepoint a rather unusual knight in armour, every 40 minutes or so turning round on his horse – which even neighs. A fine old sliding door opens on to stairs leading up to a series of smaller and cosier timbered upper rooms, including a medieval Solar bar, which again have lovely oak trusses supporting their pitched ceiling beams. There are blue carpets and plenty of tables, and comfortably cushioned seats and stools around small tables, with the occasional settle; a snug Parlour Bar is tucked in beneath the Solar. The emphasis is pretty much on eating, and they do now call themselves a restaurant, but it is all rather jolly, and families are made especially welcome. Their meals are styled as feasts (and helpings are huge), with mostly char-grilled dishes like chicken or steak or a pound of cod with plenty of chips (£3.95), though they also do a well-liked steak and kidney pie and good value Sunday lunch; they put sparklers in their home-made ice cream for children. Well kept Banks's Bitter and Mild on electric pump, and Scrumpy Jack cider; fruit machines, piped music. Efficient, courteous staff. A broad stretch of grass leads away behind the moat, towards the modern houses of this quiet suburb; a car park is sensitively tucked away behind some modern ancillary buildings. ***(Recommended by Andrew Stephenson, Mike Woodhead, M W Turner, Gary Nicholls, M Joyner, Stephen, Julie and Hayley Brown, Steve and Liz Tulley)***

Banks's ~ Managers Les and Rose Millard ~ Real ale ~ Meals and snacks (12-2.30, 6-9.30) ~ Restaurant ~ (0121) 588 2035 ~ Children welcome ~ Medieval banquets Fri, quiz night Sun ~ Open 11.30-3, 5.30-11

WITHYBROOK (War) SP4384 Map 4

Pheasant ♀

4 miles from M6, junction 2; follow Ansty, Shilton signpost; bear right in Shilton towards Wolvey then take first right signposted Withybrook – or, longer but wider, second right into B4112 to Withybrook

This pleasant old village pub is cosy in winter with its good open fires, and the spacious lounge has a serving counter flanked by well polished rocky flagstones, lots of plush-cushioned wheelback chairs and dark tables on the patterned carpet, a few farm tools on its cream walls, and a friendly, relaxed atmosphere. Popular bar food includes home-made soup (£1.25), sandwiches (£1.50), lentil and mushroom au gratin (£4.75), ploughman's (£4.95), omelettes (from £4.95), home-made steak and kidney pie or braised liver and onions (£5.50), fish pie (£6.25), braised pheasant(£7.25), steaks (from £7.50), fresh fish of the day, and puddings such as fruit crumble (£2). Well kept Courage Directors and John Smiths on handpump kept under light blanket pressure, and a good range of wines, many available by the half-bottle or glass; fruit machine in the lobby, and piped music (sometimes quite loud). There are tables under lantern lights on a brookside terrace, and the bank opposite is prettily planted with flowers and shrubs. Parking can be difficult at busy times.

(Recommended by Geoff Lee, JJW, CMW, David and Shelia, Mayur Shah, Roy Bromell, Cdr Patrick Tailyour, Cath and John Howard, G L Tong, Stephen, Julie and Hayley Brown, Ian and Nita Cooper, Paul and Sue Merrick, Cathy Scott, Richard Baker)

Free house ~ Licensees Derek Guy, Alan and Rene Bean ~ Real ale ~ Meals and snacks (till 10) ~ (01455) 220480 ~ Children welcome ~ Open 11-3, 6.30-11; closed 25/26 Dec

WOOTTON WAWEN (War) SP1563 Map 4

Bulls Head

Stratford Road; A34 N of Stratford

A charming black and white timbered building dating back several hundred years. Inside, it's warmly welcoming and heavily beamed with quite an emphasis on the good food. The attractive low-ceiling L-shaped lounge has massive timber uprights, decorations and furnishings that go well with the building, and rugs setting off the good flagstones; there's also a rather austere taproom with pews and a sawdusted floor, and a handsome restaurant. There are fresh flowers, and service by the notably friendly young staff is quick. Generous helpings of good often unusual food from a sensibly short menu include home-made soup (£2.50), mixed mushrooms in a creamy dill sauce in puff pastry (£4.50), soft herring roes on toast (£4.95), smoked salmon ravioli in a creamy white wine sauce (£5.25), pork and chive sausages or seafood tartlet (£5.50), broccoli and blue brie pancakes (£6.75), char-grilled chicken breast with chilli butter (£7.95), brown braised beef with fresh herb dumplings (£8.50), calf's liver and bacon or char-grilled sirloin steak (£10.50), and puddings such as rich toffee and banana crumble (more like a tartlet) or chewy raspberry pavlova (£2.85). Well kept Fullers London Pride, Greene King Abbot, Marstons Pedigree, Morlands Old Speckled Hen, and Wadworths 6X on handpump, and several wines by the glass. There are tables out in the garden, with some in a vigorous young vine arbour. It's handy for walks by the Stratford Canal.

(Recommended by Roy Bromell, Mike Begley, Dorothee and Dennis Glover, George Atkinson, Susan and John Douglas, Leith Stuart, Pat and Roger Fereday, the Monday Club, Joyce and Stephen Stackhouse, John Clements, Dr Vanessa Potter)

Free house ~ Licensee John Willmott ~ Real ale ~ Meals and snacks (12-2.30, 6-10) ~ Restaurant ~ (01564) 792511 ~ Children welcome ~ Open 12-3, 6-11; closed 25 Dec

Post Office address codings confusingly give the impression that some pubs are in the Midlands, when they're really in the Derbyshire, Leicestershire or Shropshire areas that we list them under.

Lucky Dip

Besides the fully inspected pubs, you might like to try these Lucky Dips recommended to us and described by readers (if you do, please send us reports):

☆ **Abthorpe**, N'hants [Silver St; signed from A43 at 1st roundabout S of A5; SP6446], *New Inn*: Partly thatched take-us-as-you-find-us country local in quiet village, rambling dim-lit bars, beams, stripped stone, inglenook fireplace, attractively priced home cooking (not Sun/Mon), well kept Hook Norton Best and Old Hookey and a guest such as Fullers London Pride, good choice of malt whiskies, friendly service, lots of old family photographs etc; big garden with goldfish pool and aviary *(George Atkinson, BB)*

☆ **Alcester**, War [Kings Coughton (A435 towards Studley); SP0859], *Moat House*: Clean, comfortable and very well run, with welcoming service, good choice of good generous food and of well kept ales *(A H Thomas, Jack Barnwell)*

Alcester [Stratford Rd], *Cross Keys*: Down to earth, with good food at very low prices *(A H Thomas)*; [34 High St], *Three Tuns*: Unspoilt. Flagstone floors, low ceilings and armchairs, own-brew beer and other ales, pleasant service, cheery customers *(Graham Reeve, Richard Houghton)*

Allesley, W Mid [73 Birmingham Rd; SP2981], *Rainbow*: Basic busy local in lopsided ancient building, a pub from the early 1950s, popular for cheap lunchtime food; own-brew beer and Courage Best and Directors, can be crowded with young people at night *(Richard Houghton, Geoff Lee)*

☆ **Alveston**, War [end of village, off B4086 Stratford—Wellesbourne; SP2356], *Ferry*: Long open-plan dining pub with comfortable brocaded seating, low-key decor and log fire, in nice spot with path along River Avon; has been a very popular main entry for good food and atmosphere and well kept real ales and wines, but the Russons who made it so good left in summer 1995 *(LYM; reports on new regime please)*

☆ **Amblecote**, W Mid [Collis St; SO8985], *Robin Hood*: Cosy and informal open-plan local, good changing range of particularly well kept ales inc Bathams, the unique honeyed Enville and a Mild, farm ciders, good value food in dining area, friendly staff, children allowed till 8.30 if eating; comfortable bedrooms *(Richard Houghton, Chris Wrigley, Graham Reeve, Steve Spinks, Ian Jones)*

Ansley, War [Birmingham Rd; SP2991], *Lord Nelson*: Friendly local with particularly good service, good food *(Louis Fearnhead)*

Ansty, War [B4065 NE of Coventry; SP3983], *Rose & Castle*: Nr canal, some canal-theme decorations, low beams, decent food; Bass and Walkers Winter Warmer *(Dave Braisted)*

☆ **Apethorpe**, N'hants [Kings Cliffe Rd; TL0295], *Kings Head*: Stonebuilt pub in attractive conservation village, cosy bar with pool, comfortable lounge with real fire, good value bar food (not Mon), arch to big dining area with separate menu (inc Mon), real ales such as Fullers London Pride, Marstons Pedigree, polite service; children welcome, picnic tables in small enclosed garden *(JJW, CMW, Julian Holland)*

☆ **Ardens Grafton**, War [towards Wixford – OS Sheet 150 map ref 114538; SP1153], *Golden Cross*: Pleasant L-shaped room with lots of antique dolls in cabinets, also teddy bears, toy rabbits etc, photographic magazines (local society meets here), Shakespearean murals; generous helpings of good bar food, restaurant with antique doll collection, well kept ales inc interesting guest beers, very welcoming efficient service, unobtrusive piped music, fruit machine; seats outside, nice views *(George Atkinson, John and Marianne Cooper)*

Ashorne, War [SP3057], *Cottage*: Friendly small local with food area at one end, good generous food; may cl weekday lunchtimes *(Fiona and Paul Hutt)*

☆ **Ashton**, N'hants [the one NE of Oundle, signed from A427/A605 island; TL0588], *Chequered Shipper*: Well kept Adnams, Marstons Pedigree and two other real ales in attractive pub on green of thatched Tudor-style village, peacocks outside, unusual inn sign using different coloured nails; friendly staff, open fire, fish tanks, stuffed birds, butterflies and so forth; can get crowded; children welcome, on Nene Way *(Stephen, Julie and Hayley Brown)*

Ashton, N'hants [Stoke Rd; the other one, off A508 S of M1 junction 15; SP7850], *Old Crown*: 18th-c family-oriented modernised local, all clean and neat, with roomy lounge/dining area (children allowed), big bar, darts and pool at back, beams, muskets, pictures and dolls of Henry VIII and wives, substantial meals with no shortage of chips, well kept Charles Wells Eagle, Bombardier and Boddingtons, piped music; big garden behind *(George Atkinson, Brian and Anna Marsden)*

☆ **Aston Cantlow**, War [SP1359], *Kings Head*: Pretty village pub not far from Mary Arden's house in Wilmcote, lots of timbers and low beams, flagstones, inglenook, cheery log fire, well used old furniture inc settles, grandfather clock; good prompt straightforward food (not Sun or Mon evenings) from sandwiches to steaks, well kept Whitbreads-related ales, friendly landlord and cat *(John and Marianne Cooper, Jerry and Alison Oakes, Mr and Mrs C Roberts, LYM)*

☆ **Aynho**, N'hants [SP5133], *Cartwright Arms*: Neatly modernised 16th-c former posting inn, friendly staff and customers, good home-made lunchtime bar food, Bass, Hook Norton Best and Morlands Old Speckled Hen, reasonably priced restaurant, a few tables in pretty corner of former coachyard; bedrooms comfortable and attractive *(Dave Braisted, Maxine Coleman, BB)*

☆ **Aynho** [Wharf Base, B4031 W], *Great Western Arms*: Interesting unpretentious pub with good cheap bar food in roomy informal dining areas, log fire, well kept Hook Norton Bitter and Mild, GWR memorabilia; bar billiards, video game, children's room; big garden by Oxford Canal, with moorings *(George Atkinson, Frank Gadbois)*

Balsall Common, W Mid [Balsall St; SP2377], *Saracens Head*: Recently Victorianised large Maltster dining pub with good straightforward bar food in roomy series of interconnecting rooms, some 16th-c beams and flagstones, well kept Tetleys-related ales, friendly service; muted piped music, video games *(the Monday Club, Dave Braisted, Roy Bromell)*

Barford, War [Wellesbourne Rd; A429 S of Warwick; SP2760], *Granville Arms*: Comfortable, with good range of fairly priced bar food, quick friendly service, beams, oak chairs and tables; children welcome *(K D Day)*

Barnacle, War [signed off B4029 in Shilton, nr M6 junction 2; SP3884], *Red Lion*: Quiet straightforward two-room pub with good range of substantial good value food (not Sun lunchtime), well kept Bass and M & B ales, pleasant staff; seats out in covered front area *(John and Marianne Cooper, Ted George, Geoff Lee)*

Barnwell, N'hants [TL0484], *Montagu Arms*: Delightfully old-fashioned village pub with four well kept ales inc Hook Norton Old Hookey, bar food, nice atmosphere, friendly staff; garden has potential *(Frank W Gadbois, David Hedges)*

Barston, W Mid [Barston Ln; from M42 junction 5, A4141 towards Warwick, first left, then signed; SP2078], *Bulls Head*: Attractive partly Tudor village local, oak-beamed bar with log fires and Buddy Holly memorabilia, comfortable lounge with pictures and plates, dining room, friendly relaxed service, good value basic food, well kept Bass, M & B Brew XI and Tetleys, secluded garden, hay barn behind *(Richard Waller, CMW, JJW, L Harvard, K Warren, M Whalley, Pete Baker)*; [Barston Lane], *Malt Shovel*: Friendly old-fashioned local with well kept Bass, decent food, no gaming machines, great landlady, pleasant garden *(Ian Corner)*

Berkswell, W Mid [Spencer Lane; signed from A452; SP2479], *Bear*: Rambling timbered Chef & Brewer dining pub in attractive setting, with tables on pleasant tree-sheltered back lawn, Crimean War cannon in front; village church worth a visit *(George Atkinson, LYM)*

☆ **Birmingham** [144 High St, Aston (A34) – easily reached from M6 junction 6], *Bartons Arms*: Magnificent specimen of Edwardian pub architecture, with inventive series of richly decorated rooms from the palatial to the snug; has recently been taken in hand and cleaned up by landlord who previously won good reputation at the Olde Dolphin in Derby; well kept M & B ales, limited food, plans to instal microbrewery – should be a winner soon *(Graham Reeve, Frances Fox, Richard Green, LYM)*

☆ **Birmingham** [Cambridge St], *Prince of Wales*: Fine traditional local in lovely old building, welcoming long-serving Irish landlord, genuine hatch-served snug, two quiet and comfortable back parlours one of them frozen in 1900, ochre walls, bare floors, lively friendly atmosphere, excellent service, particularly well kept Ansells Bitter and Mild and Ind Coope Burton; wide choice of good food, piped Irish music, can get packed *(Cdr P Tailyour, Jack Barnwell)*

☆ **Birmingham** [36 Winson St, Winson Green], *Bellefield*: Unspoilt friendly sidestreet local with Georgian smoking room, beautiful Victorian tiles, notable bar ceiling; Everards Mild, Tiger and Old Bill and guest beers, interesting bottled beers and occasional beer festivals; good value rather unusual bar food, pub games, music, terrace for children *(J W Busby, Richard Lewis)*

Birmingham [Stephenson St; in Midland Hotel, off New St], *Atkinson Bar*: Busy male-oriented atmosphere in dark old-style place, lots of books and pictures, good interesting range of ales tapped from the cask and kept under light blanket pressure, some served only by the pint mug; very handy for New Street stn and city centre *(George Atkinson, Brian Jones, Graham Reeve)*; [Corporation St/Staniforth St], *Ben Jonson*: Well kept Banks's and Tetleys, generous helpings of popular good value lunchtime food inc Sun *(A J Freestone)*; [22 Gt Hampton St, Hockley], *Church Tavern*: Comfortable and friendly, well known for huge helpings of good value food; well kept Tetleys-related ales inc Holt Plant & Deakins Entire *(Wayne A Wheeler, David Tyzack)*; [Wellington Rd/Birchfield St], *Crown & Cushion*: Lively local with courteous staff, cheap usual food inc some local additions, Ansells ale *(Peter Weir)*; [Bristol Rd, Bournbrook], *Gun Barrels*: Large lounge with bar food, live and piped music and videos, grill room, bar with pool, video games and fruit machines; lavatories for disabled; children welcome *(D Hanley)*; [176 Hagley Rd, Edgbaston], *Hagley Duck*: Masses of bric-a-brac in front bar, wide choice iof real ales behind, farm cider; smart dress required *(Graham Reeve, Gary Nicholls)*; [Palisades], *Newt & Cucumber*: Good range of beers inc Bass, Highgate Dark, Theakstons Best, Worthingtons Best and two constantly changing guests, cut prices 5-7.30, well priced food *(R Lewis)*; [176 Edmund St], *Old Contemptibles*: Spacious and comfortable Edwardian pub with lofty ceiling and lots of woodwork, popular with office workers for good value food lunchtime and early evening (not Sat eve or Sun); well kept Bass, M & B Brew XI, Highgate Dark Mild and changing guest beers such as Exmoor Stag and Hook

Norton Old Hookey, occasional beer festivals, friendly staff; piped music, pinball *(Wayne A Wheeler, Richard Lewis, D Hanley, LYM)*; [Cambridge St], *Prince of Wales*: Ansells and Marstons Pedigree, bar meals, good atmosphere; piped music *(D Hanley)*; [Pershore Rd, Selly Park], *Selly Park*: Large beamed lounge and bar with alcoves, china plates, pictures, lunchtime bar food, Bass and Ruddles, fruit machine *(D Hanley)*; [Bristol Rd, Selly Oak], *Varsity*: Massive split-level lounge, partly wood-floored, with eight TV screens above bar, crystal ceiling balls, Ansells, Ind Coope Burton and Ruddles, piped music; University haunt *(D Hanley)*; [Ruston St], *Vine*: Good backstreet atmosphere, well kept Ansells *(Dave Braisted)*; [Grosvenor St W], *White Swan*: Ansells pub with roomy lounge, good value bar food, good atmosphere; TV, piped music *(D Hanley)*

Bishops Itchington, War [Fisher Rd; 2 miles from M40 junction 12; SP3857], *Malt & Shovel*: Handy stop for reasonable range of cheap food inc bargain Sun lunch, quick service; cosy and friendly pub, with small dining room, interesting things to look at; tiny bar and lounge do get packed at lunchtime *(Tony and Wynne Gifford, Ian Phillips)*

☆ **Blakesley**, N'hants [High St (Woodend rd); SP6250], *Bartholomew Arms*: Genuine country pub, lots of bric-a-brac in two cosy beamed bars, short choice of good bar food inc vegetarian and good value rolls, friendly staff, well kept Marstons Pedigree, pleasant enclosed back garden with summerhouse; children welcome in one bar *(Christopher and Sharon Hayle, Martin and Penny Fletcher, Ted Corrin)*

Blisworth, N'hants [High St; not far from M1 junction 15A; SP7253], *Royal Oak*: 17th-c beamed pub, long and narrowish, with open fire, hospitable landlord, Courage-related ales, well served food inc tasty sandwiches all day inc Sun; Nr Grand Union canal with Courage-related beers and reasonable food at fair prices (all day inc Sun), coffee and tea; pool table, piped music; garden, nr Grand Union canal *(George Atkinson, N and J Strathdee)*

Bloxwich, W Mid [Broad Lane; SK0002], *Sir Robert Peel*: Good value traditional food, well kept Bass and Stones, good staff *(Paul Beswick)*

Boughton, N'hants [Church St; off A508 N of Northampton; SP7566], *Whyte-Melville*: Pleasant, recently renovated, with wide range of food, Morlands Old Speckled Hen, log fire, Victorian pictures, mainly board floor, friendly attentive service, piped music; spacious, but can get very busy lunchtime *(George Atkinson)*

☆ **Braunston**, N'hants [Little Braunston; outside village, just N of canal tunnel; SP5466], *Admiral Nelson*: Popular former 1730 farmhouse in lovely setting by lock and hump bridge, with pleasant waterside garden and towpath walks; well kept Batemans and Courage-related real ales, good value quick bar food inc children's, restaurant *(George Atkinson, Geoffrey Pegram, John and Elizabeth Guywnne)*

Bretford, War [A428 Coventry—Rugby; SP4377], *Queens Head*: Roomy refurbished dining pub, very popular lunchtime with business people and OAPs, wide choice of good value food inc vegetarian, children's and good sandwiches, Marstons Pedigree and Ruddles, chatty staff; garden with big play area *(the Monday Club, George Atkinson)*

Brierley Hill, W Mid [Dudley Rd; SO9187], *Blue Brick*: Good choice of well kept ales, great landlord, huge chip butties *(Roger Abrahams)*

☆ **Brinklow**, War [Fosse Way; A427, fairly handy for M6 junction 2; SP4379], *Raven*: 15th-c beams and open fire in dark-panelled lounge, more basic bar with alcoves and plants, collection of mugs and frog curios, good range of usual food inc vegetarian, well kept Marstons, good friendly service; piped local radio; tables on lawn with various pets; said to be haunted *(CW, JW)*

Brixworth, N'hants [Northampton Rd; SP7470], *George*: Modern, warm and friendly pub behind facade of reputed 14th-c coaching inn, two big beamed rooms with lots of pictures, central fire, reasonably priced food; Charles Wells ales and a guest like Youngs Winter Warmer; piped music; noted Saxon church in village *(George Atkinson, Norma and Keith Bloomfield)*

Broom, War [High St; SP0853], *Broom Tavern*: Attractive brick and timber-framed pub, comfortable and relaxing, popular for food *(Gordon)*

Bubbenhall, War [Lower End; off A445 S of Coventry; SP3672], *Malt Shovel*: Building attractive inside and out, small bar and larger L-shaped lounge rather geared to food, beams, brass and copper, comfortable banquettes, quiet piped music, real flowers on the tables, play area with basketball net, wide range of reasonably priced lunchtime and evening food, Ansells, Bass, Tetleys and Marstons Pedigree on handpump *(JJW, CMW)*

☆ **Bugbrooke**, N'hants [14 Church St; SP6757], *Five Bells*: Cheerful little old-fashioned pub in attractive village, low ceilings, good reasonably priced food esp steaks in dining areas (one no smoking), Courage-related ales, efficient service, games room; children truly welcome *(Keith Croxton, Matthew Adams, Mr and Mrs S Forster)*

Bulwick, N'hants [Main St; just off A43 Kettering—Duddington; SP9694], *Queens Head*: Interesting old local in beautiful village setting opp church, changing ales from small breweries, wide choice of good value food – must book for Sun roast *(David Ellis, K H Frostick)*

Burton Green, War [SW of Coventry; SP2675], *Peeping Tom*: Consistently good value food from French chef/patron, good wines *(Anon)*

Burton Latimer, N'hants [Bakehouse Lane; SP9075], *Olde Victoria*: Good well priced, prompt friendly service, good range of beers; spotless *(Mr and Mrs J Taylor)*

☆ **Castle Ashby**, N'hants [SP8659], *Falcon*: 16th-c beams, open fire, good food in bar and restaurant; bedrooms beautifully decorated, good breakfast; preserved village on Marquess of Northampton's estate *(Andy and Jill Kassube)*

Church Lawford, War [Green Lane; formerly White Lion – OS Sheet 140 map ref 450765; SP4476], *Old Smithy*: Spacious thatched and beamed free house, recently renovated, with dark woodwork in L-shaped lounge on various levels, good range of food from separate servery, Ansells Mild, Marstons Pedigree and local Judges Old Gavel Bender, good service, games room *(George Atkinson)*

☆ **Churchover**, War [handy for M6 junction 1, off A426; SP5180], *Haywaggon*: Carefully modernised old pub with good range of reasonably priced food in two snug eating areas, friendly atmosphere, Courage Best and Directors; on edge of quiet village, beautiful views over Swift valley *(Alain and Rose Foote, BB)*

☆ **Claverdon**, War [B4095; SP1964], *Red Lion*: Pleasant village pub with home-cooked food, friendly quick service and well kept Whitbreads-related real ales; clean and spacious back saloon (where children allowed), small plush front L-shaped lounge, log fire, sheltered terrace, garden and play area with country views; may not open until after noon some days *(Roy Bromell, Margaret Cadney, BB)*

☆ **Collingtree**, N'hants [High St; 1¼ miles from M1 junction 15; SP7555], *Wooden Walls of Old England*: Thatched pub with stripped stonework, low black beams, model galleon and some other nautical memorabilia, well kept Deakins Royal Stag and Mansfield Riding, friendly staff, well priced standard food; table skittles and fruit machine in one bar; lots of picnic tables, swings and tuck shop in back garden *(Mark and Toni Amor-Segan, Jeffrey Brown, PGP, George Atkinson, BB)*

Collyweston, N'hants [Main St; A43 4 miles SW of Stamford; SK9902], *Cavalier*: 19th-c pub extended into older cottages, very friendly staff and cat, lounge with glass walkway over cellars and steps, central fire, Batemans XB, Ruddles, interesting menu, pool table, piped music, separate restaurant; garden; bedrooms *(George Atkinson)*

☆ **Cosgrove**, N'hants [Thrupp Wharf, towards Castlethorpe; SP7942], *Navigation*: Lovely canalside setting, good range of well kept beers, usual pub food, helpful obliging staff, building itself of some character; children welcome *(C Driver, Duncan Small, Karen and Graham Oddey, BB)*

☆ **Coventry**, W Mid [1059 Foleshill Rd, handy for M6 junction 3; SP3379], *William IV*: Extensive range of notable totally authentic Indian food, remarkably good value, and well kept M & B beers in well run prewar estate pub *(John Allsopp, Dave Thompson, Margaret Mason)*

☆ **Coventry** [Hill St, by S end of Leigh Mills car park], *Gatehouse*: The couple who made the Town Wall here really popular and distinctive in the late 1980s and early 1990s are now serving particularly well kept ales (starting with Bass and Brew XI) and good home-cooked food from giant doorstep sandwiches up in this newly opened pub, formerly gatehouse to the Leigh Mills worsted factory *(Brian Randall)*

Coventry [1 The Butts], *Fowl & Firkin*: Typical friendly Firkin atmosphere, good beers brewed here *(Richard Houghton)*; [Lockhurst Lane, just off Foleshill Rd towards M6 junction 3], *Stag & Pheasant*: Cheerful free house, good food from vegetarian to carvery with almost instant service; music loud without being objectionable *(Geoff Lee)*; [Bond St, behind Coventry Theatre], *Town Wall*: Compact unspoilt Victorian pub, with engraved windows, open fire in small T-shaped lounge, simple bar with TV for big sports events, tiny clubby snug and flower-filled back yard; well kept Bass and M & B Brew XI, good value home-cooked food inc generous doorstep sandwiches *(Brian Randall)*

Cranford St John, N'hants [42a High St; 3 m E of Kettering just off A14; SP9277], *Red Lion*: Generous varied reasonably priced food inc bargain OAP lunches in attractive two-bar stone pub, Flowers Original and Tetleys, decent house wine, good service; pleasant garden, quiet village *(David and Mary Webb, Meg and Colin Hamilton)*

☆ **Deppers Bridge**, War [4 miles N of M40 junction 12; B4451; SP4059], *Great Western*: Roomy and airy family pub, non-stop model train clattering round overhead, interesting train photographs, generous helpings of promptly served food inc lots of children's specials, Ansells and Holt Plant & Deakins Entire from new-fangled dispensers, decent wines, good service; play area, tables on terrace *(Margaret Cadney, Ted George, George Atkinson)*

☆ **Dorridge**, W Mid [Four Ashes Rd; SP1775], *Drum & Monkey*: Comfortable, spacious and efficient Greenalls Millers Kitchen dining pub, wide choice of reliable good value food, well kept Tetleys-related ales, no-smoking dining area; big garden with play area *(Michael and Margaret Norris, JB)*

☆ **Dorridge** [Grange Rd (A4023)], *Railway*: Small largely unspoiled local, well kept Bass and M & B Brew XI, friendly family service, limited choice of good value food (10p extra for thick-sliced sandwiches), no music or machines; small garden *(Brian Jones, Dave Braisted, Martin Richards)*

☆ **Duddington**, N'hants [A43 just S of A47; SK9800], *Royal Oak*: Attractive stone inn, very courteously and efficiently run, spotless and comfortable, with plush banquettes, gleaming brass inc wartime shell cases, lots of pictures, open fire; wide choice of popular food, Ruddles County, Portuguese wines strong on the list; nice garden and terrace; bedrooms *(Frank Davidson, George*

Atkinson, Bernard and Marjorie Parkin)

☆ **Easenhall**, War [SP4679], *Golden Lion*: 16th-c inn with tasteful and comfortable lounge, beams and dark panelling, comfortable seating, big helpings of good value food inc good Sun carvery, efficient welcoming service even when busy, Boddingtons, Flowers Original and Theakstons Best, log fire; spacious attractive garden with terrace, barbecue, pet donkey; well equipped bedrooms *(Mark and Toni Amor-Segan, George Atkinson)*

☆ **Eastcote**, N'hants [Gayton Rd; village signed off A5 3 miles N of Towcester; SP6753], *Eastcote Arms*: Attractive unspoilt traditional layout, well kept Hook Norton Best and Jennings, very friendly new licensees, limited range of lunchtime food inc cheap toasties, log fire, small new restaurant, pretty garden *(George Atkinson, K H Frostick, LYM)*

Easton on the Hill, N'hants [TF0104], *Oak*: Pleasant and friendly, good simple home-cooked food, Marstons Pedigree *(Tony Gayfer)*

☆ **Eathorpe**, War [car park off Fosse Way; SP3868], *Plough*: Big helpings of good food inc some bargain meals in long neat and clean split-level lounge/dining area with matching walls, carpets and table linen, huge fish in tank by bar, good friendly chatty service; good cappuccino with mints *(George Atkinson)*

Ecton, N'hants [High St; SP8263], *Three Horseshoes*: 18th-c stone pub with two-level bar, well kept ale, enjoyable atmosphere; said that Benjamin Franklin's grandfather had a smithy in the yard *(Bill Gottschalk)*

☆ **Edge Hill**, War [SP3747], *Castle*: Interesting and well refurbished renovated 18th-c battlemented folly with good value proper pub food, well kept Hook Norton Best and Old Hookey and a guest ale, Stowford Press cider, friendly efficient service, drawbridge to turreted lavatories; children welcome; fabulous views through trees from garden perched over steep slope of Edge Hill *(N and J Strathdee, Richard Lewis, Margaret Dyke, LYM)*

☆ **Ettington**, War [Banbury Rd (A422 towards Stratford); SP2749], *Houndshill*: Neat dining pub with good value food in pleasant surroundings, very popular with families and OAPs; S & N ales, stripped stone and beams, good service, tables in big pleasant garden, good views from front; good well equipped bedrooms *(George Atkinson, Mr and Mrs R Head)*

Evenley, N'hants [The Green; SP5834], *Red Lion*: Small friendly local with strong cricket connections, opp attractive village green; some flagstones, Banks's and Marstons Pedigree, decent choice of wines, reasonably priced food inc good sandwiches and Sun lunch *(B A Ford, George Atkinson, Calum and Susan Maclean)*

Gaydon, War [Church St, very handy for M40 junction 12; SP3654], *Malt Shovel*: Mix of locals and visitors, Whitbreads-related ales, food inc home-made pies and nicely filled rolls *(Mick Gray)*

Gayton, N'hants [SP7054], *Queen Victoria*: Refurbished village pub, very popular weekends, with some emphasis on wide range of food from modern servery area, hunting prints in comfortable back lounge, well kept real ales inc Hook Norton, pleasant staff, darts and hood skittles in lively front public bar, piped music, pool room *(Mr and Mrs S Forster, LYM)*

Geddington, N'hants [Bridge St; just off A43 Kettering—Corby; SP8983], *Star*: Good food at reasonable prices, well kept beers, attractive bar, restaurant, tables outside – pleasant setting not far from picturesque packhorse bridge, handy for Broughton House *(K H Frostick, WHBM)*

Great Billing, N'hants [SP8162], *Elwes Arms*: 16th-c friendly traditional village pub, food from good hot roast beef sandwiches to tempting Sun lunch *(Mrs S Wilkinson)*

☆ **Great Brington**, N'hants [SP6664], *Fox & Hounds*: Comfortable low-beamed local with half a dozen changing well kept ales, good reasonably priced food, very friendly staff, two log fires, flagstones and bare boards, stone walls, newspapers to read, games room with table skittles, juke box or eclectic piped music, quaint outside gents'; garden with food service and play area, charming village nr Althorp House; children welcome *(Guy Turner)*

Great Everdon, N'hants [SP5857], *Plough*: Spotless, with attentive young tenants, coal fires, particularly well kept Banks's Mild and Bitter, wide choice of low-priced appetising food, dining room; spacious garden *(Guy Turner)*

☆ **Great Oxendon**, N'hants [SP7383], *George*: Stylish and civilised, with consistently good restaurant and bar food inc some imaginative dishes, obliging attentive service, pleasant no-smoking conservatory *(Mr and Mrs P Wilkinson, Cdr Patrick Tailyour)*

☆ **Hampton in Arden**, W Mid [1½ miles from M42 junction 6 via village slip rd from exit roundabout; SP2081], *White Lion*: Unpretentious inn, genuinely old without stressing its age; unfussy beamed lounge, real fire, nautical decor inc navigation lights, friendly staff, quick good value bar food (not Sun) from sandwiches to steaks inc children's dishes, well kept Bass, M & B Brew XI and John Smiths, decent wine, public bar with cribbage and dominoes, back dining room; children allowed; attractive village, handy for NEC *(Thomas Nott, Martin Wright, John Fahy, Keith Pollard, Neville Kenyon, L Harvard, K Warren, M Whalley, Malcom Fowlie and Jenny Williams, Roy Bromell, LYM)*

☆ **Hampton Lucy**, War [E of Stratford; SP2557], *Boars Head*: Convivial old beamed local, traditional decor, log fire, brasses, well kept ales inc Ind Coope, prompt friendly service, straightforward well priced food; small garden, pretty village nr Charlcote House *(P J Hanson)*

Harborne, W Mid [High St; SP0284], *Green Man*: M & B ales with guests like Morlands Old Speckled Hen, bar food, big lounge and bar, big TV, darts, pool, juke box, fruit machine *(D Hanley)*

Harbury, War [Mill St; just off B4451/B4452 S of A425 Leamington Spa—Southam; SP3759], *Shakespeare*: Popular and reliable dining pub with linked beamed rooms, stripped stonework, inglenook log fire, well kept Whitbreads-related ales, good hospitable service, horsebrasses, garden room, separate pool room; children allowed in one area; tables in back garden with aviaries *(George Atkinson, M and J Back)*

☆ **Harpole**, N'hants [High St; nr M1 junction 16; SP6860], *Bull*: Comfortable old-fashioned village pub with cosy lounge and eating area, consistently good value generous food, well kept Courage-related ales, quick friendly service, log fire in big inglenook, basic bar and games room, small terrace; no dogs *(Keith Croxton, Dr M V Jones, K H Frostick)*

☆ **Harrington**, N'hants [High St; off A508 S of Mkt Harborough; SP7779], *Tollemache Arms*: Civilised beamed Tudor pub in isolated stonebuilt village, Charles Wells ales, very friendly staff, good home-cooked fresh food inc unusual dishes and good soup, open fires, small back garden; children welcome; clean and attractive bedrooms *(K H Frostick, George Atkinson)*

☆ **Hawkesbury**, W Mid [close to M6 junction 3, exit past Moat House northwards on Longford Rd (B4113), 1st right into Black Horse Rd, cross canal and into Sutton Stop; SP3684], *Greyhound*: Good interesting pies and other generous food with delicious proper chips, good puddings with custard, lots of nick-nacks from ties to toby jugs, well kept Bass and Banks's Mild, coal-fired stove, unusual tiny snug; booking essential for the Pie Parlour – lots of canalia and quite private olde-worlde atmosphere; tables and safe play area in delightful garden by junction of Coventry and N Oxford Canals; children welcome *(D W Gray, Graham Reeve, the Monday Club, Geoff Lee)*

☆ **Hellidon**, N'hants [off A425 W of Daventry; SP5158], *Red Lion*: Clean, cosy and comfortable lounge and bars in beautiful setting overlooking village green, tables outside, pleasant walks nearby; good value well served food in bar and restaurant, well kept real ales inc Bass, welcoming landlord, woodburner, games room; bedrooms *(Mr and Mrs K H Frostick, Hilary Aslett, George Atkinson)*

Higham Ferrers, N'hants [College St (A6); SP9668], *Green Dragon*: Good choice of ales inc local Nene Valley Rawhide, low-priced food inc steaks bought by weight, friendly service, really big garden with dovecote in walls *(George Atkinson, Stephen, Julie and Hayley Brown)*

☆ **Hillmorton**, War [Crick Rd; outskirts, where A428, railway and canal intersect; SP5274], *Old Royal Oak*: Refurbished and extended Marstons Tavern Table with vast family dining area, carpeted lounge, flagstoned bar, good value food, real ales; good play areas inside and out, nappy-changing facilities, lavatories for the disabled; piped music; open all dat Sat, tables out on canalside terrace *(Alain and Rose Foote, George Atkinson)*

Himley, W Mid [Stourbridge Rd; SO8791], *Dudley Arms*: Generous good value food, quick, cheerful and helpful staff, well spaced comfortable furniture; Wolverhampton & Dudley ales *(G M and J M Smith)*

☆ **Hinton in the Hedges**, N'hants [off A43 W of Brackley; SP5536], *Crewe Arms*: Busy 17th-c pub with two roomy old-fashioned alcovey bars and modern extension, good choice of reasonably priced good food from sandwiches up, well kept beers such as Boddingtons, Hook Norton Best, Marstons Pedigree and Morlands Old Speckled Hen, good coffee, friendly family atmosphere, good service, games room, some picnic tables outside *(Dr and Mrs James Stewart, Mark and Diane Grist)*

☆ **Hockley Heath**, W Mid [Stratford Rd (A34 Birmingham—Henley-in-Arden); SP1573], *Wharf*: Friendly modernised Chef & Brewer, quick good value generous straightforward food inc Sun roasts, Courage-related ales, plenty of seats; darts, TV, games machines, piped pop music; children welcome; attractive garden with adventure playground by Stratford Canal, interesting towpath walks *(Dennis Phillips, JJW, CMW)*

☆ **Holcot**, N'hants [Main St; SP7969], *White Swan*: Attractive partly thatched two-bar village inn with Bass, Boddingtons, Morlands Old Speckled Hen, Tetleys and a Cumbrian beer brewed for the pub, good reasonably priced food (not Sun-Weds evening) inc good value Sun lunch, friendly helpful staff, games room with skittles, pool and darts; children welcome; bedrooms *(JJW, CMW, M and J Back, Eric J Locker, Meg and Colin Hamilton)*

☆ **Kenilworth**, War [High St; SP2871], *Clarendon House*: Comfortable traditional hotel, welcoming and civilised, with partly panelled bar, antique maps, prints, copper, china and armour, well kept Flowers IPA and Original and Hook Norton Best and Old Hookey, decent wines, good value simple bar food, interesting restaurant specials, pleasant helpful staff; bedrooms good value *(Tony and Joan Walker, Martyn E Lea, George Atkinson)*

☆ **Kenilworth** [Castle Hill], *Clarendon Arms*: Busy dining pub with good value food in several rooms off long partly flagstoned bar and in largish upstairs dining room; reductions for children and over-55s, efficient staff, Courage-related ales; opp castle *(Thomas Nott, Geoff Lee, Colin Mason)*

Kenilworth [Castle Green], *Queen & Castle*: Busy Beefeater opp castle, quick well cooked food, friendly staff, well kept Whitbreads-related ales, quaint corners, beams and pictures; piped pop music, games machines; extensive lawns, good play area *(Geoff Lee, George Atkinson, Bill Sykes)*; [68 Warwick Rd], *Tut 'n' Shive*: For the young at heart, crooked mirrors, holes in ceiling, old doors hanging crazily, slogans painted on walls and roof, wheelbarrow in roof joist, odds and ends of seats inc a sitz-bath – and half a dozen or more interesting well kept ales; friendly staff, some food, piped music (may be rather loud) *(George Atkinson, Basil Minson)*

Kettering, N'hants [1 Sheep St, Market Pl; SP8778], *Cherry Tree*: Good reasonably priced home-cooked food all day (not after 6 Tues, afternoon break Sun), good welcome, gas fire, well kept Charles Wells, no piped music *(Cdr Patrick Tailyour)*; *Prince of Wales*: Welcoming local with well kept Bass and Tetleys, weekly live music, Irish landlord – St Patricks Day has to be seen to be believed *(Steve Barber)*

Kingswinford, W Mid [55 High St; SO8888], *Old Courthouse*: Eight real ales inc Bass, Bass Special, Bathams, John Smiths and Youngs Winter Warmer, good range of food in conservatory bistro; bedrooms *(DAV)*

☆ **Lamport**, N'hants [Harborough Rd (A508); SP7574], *Lamport Swan*: Imposing stone building with good views, wide range of good value standard food in busy bar and cosy restaurant, well kept Courage Directors, good friendly service; children welcome *(Paul Amos, Mr and Mrs B Verlander, Cathy Scott, Richard Baker, Mr and Mrs G Hughes, Mr and Mrs S Forster, Mrs E Laughton)*

☆ **Leamington Spa** [Campion Terr; SP3165], *Somerville Arms*: Neat and cosy character local with tiny unspoilt Victorian back lounge, several well kept Tetleys-related ales, friendly staff, some memorabilia; no food *(Steve and Liz Tilley, Stephen and Jean Curtis)*

Leek Wootton, War [Warwick Rd; SP2868], *Anchor*: Busy and welcoming, with lounge and smaller bar, good choice of tasty food (not Sun), friendly efficient service, particularly well kept Bass; welcoming to walkers, popular with older people, picnic tables in pleasant garden behind *(George Atkinson, the Monday Club, Geoff Lee, Kate and Harry Taylor)*

☆ **Lighthorne**, War [a mile SW of B4100 N of Banbury; SP3355], *Antelope*: 17th-c stonebuilt dining pub, two comfortable and clean bars (one old, one new) with Cromwellian theme, wide choice of good reasonably priced food inc old-fashioned puddings, separate dining area; well kept Flowers IPA and Wadworths 6X, pleasant service; piped music; little waterfall in banked garden, attractive village *(Mr and Mrs R C Allison, Jill and Peter Bickley, George Atkinson)*

☆ **Lilbourne**, N'hants [Rugby Rd; 4 miles from M1 junction 18; A5 N, then 1st right; SP5677], *Bell*: Neat and comfortable modern lounge bar with good value simple bar food, super service even when busy; seats outside, children welcome *(Ted George, LYM)*

Little Brington, N'hants [4½ miles from M1 junction 16, first right off A45 to Daventry; also signed from A428; SP6663], *Saracens Head*: New tenants and new character, lots of pictures, books and odds and ends (though not as much as before), Fullers London Pride, Wadworths 6X and Whitbreads Pompey Royal, bar food from cheap filled rolls up, log fire, spacious extended lounge with alcoves and red telephone box, restaurant, games bar; piped music; tables in neat back garden, handy for Althorp House and Holdenby House *(George Atkinson, LYM)*

☆ **Little Harrowden**, N'hants [Main St; SP8771], *Lamb*: Good interesting reasonably priced home-cooked food (not Sun evening) in spotlessly refurbished 17th-c pub, three-level lounge with log fire, brasses on beams, intimate dining area, well kept Charles Wells and two guest ales, decent coffee, friendly attentive staff, quiet piped music; public bar, games room with hood skittles; children welcome; garden, delightful village *(N E Johnson, M E Lane, John C Baker, George Atkinson)*

☆ **Long Itchington**, War [Church Rd; SP4165], *Harvester*: Efficiently served good value straightforward food in neat and tidy pub with three well kept Hook Norton and a guest ale, small relaxed restaurant, friendly staff *(George Atkinson, Ted George)*

☆ **Long Itchington** [off A423], *Two Boats*: Another neat pub, with lively canal views from alcove window seats, generous reasonably priced food, well kept ales such as Bass, Boddingtons, Hook Norton, Whitbreads West Country PA, pleasant 60s piped music, live music Fri/Sat; open all day *(Bill Sykes)*

Long Lawford, War [1 Coventry Rd (A428); SP4776], *Sheaf & Sickle*: Four or five well kept beers, good value fresh simple bar food in small cosy lounge and biggish bar with darts and dominoes, small restaurant, friendly staff; garden, open all day Sat *(Alain and Rose Foote, JJW, CMW)*

☆ **Lower Quinton**, War [off A46 Stratford—Broadway; SP1847], *College Arms*: Wide range of generous fresh food inc good Sun roasts, well kept Whitbreads-related ales, welcoming efficient service, spacious open-plan lounge with stripped stone and heavy beams, unusual highly polished tables inc one in former fireplace, leather seats, partly carpeted parquet floor; games in public bar; on green of pretty village *(Martin Jones)*

☆ **Lowick**, N'hants [off A6116; SP9780], *Snooty Fox*: Spacious two-room open-plan beamed lounge with stripped stonework, old-fashioned prints, big log fire, Courage-related and guest ales, good value bar food esp fish (service can slow), decent wines, fresh coffee, top-hat fox behind bar; piped music; popular restaurant with central open fireplace; some live music; nearby church worth a visit *(Darren Ford, Roy Bromell, Penny and Martin Fletcher, Wayne Brindle, LYM)*

☆ **Marston St Lawrence**, N'hants [off A422 Banbury—Brackley; SP5342], *Marston Inn*: Little oak-beamed village pub, looks like a farmhouse from outside, with books on windowsill, lots of interesting bric-a-brac, friendly landlord and cat attached to its usual chair – gives a feeling of visiting friends; food inc generous sandwiches, children's and vegetarian dishes, more elaborate evening choice (not Sun or Mon evening); open fire, good dining room, well kept Hook Norton; big garden, traditional games inc Aunt Sally *(Mrs J Oakes, LYM)*

☆ **Marston Trussell**, N'hants [SP6985], *Sun*: More hotel than pub, with comfortable bedrooms, but well worth knowing for delicious home-made food, decent house wines, helpful staff *(Mrs Davidge, Anthony Barnes, Cdr Patrick Tailyour)*

Mears Ashby, N'hants [Wilby Rd; SP8466], *Griffins Head*: Quiet country pub with bucolic views, congenial licensees, attractive pictures, well kept ales *(Bill Gottschalk)*

Meriden, W Mid [Main Rd; SP2482], *Bulls Head*: Very wide choice of good value generous bar food in large, busy pub dating from 15th century, agreeable atmosphere, efficient staff; well kept Adnams Broadside and Bass, ancient staircase to restaurant *(Margaret and Howard Buchanan, Noel Lawrence)*

☆ **Middleton**, War [OS Sheet 139 map ref 175984; SP1798], *Green Man*: Busy extended beamed family dining pub with good standard food, M & B beers *(D Hanley)*

Netherton, W Mid [Baptist End Rd; SO9387], *White Swan*: Tastefully decorated old-fashioned lounge, generous cheap bar food, Bass ales *(Dave Braisted)*

Newbold on Avon, War [SP4777], *Barley Mow*: Busy local with good value promptly served straightforward food inc children's dishes and Sun lunch, horseracing pictures, conservatory eating, well kept beer, friendly service; big spacious garden with play area *(Alain and Rose Foote, MS, Cathy Scott, Richard Baker)*

Newton Bromswold, N'hants [Church Lane; E of Rushden; SP9965], *Swan*: Homely and friendly village local with largish mock-Tudor lounge, well kept Greene King IPA and Abbot, fairly priced food (not Mon evening), real fire, games room with darts and skittles; piped music, books for charity sale; big garden *(JJW, CMW, Michael Marlow)*

Newton Regis, War [SK2707], *Queens Head*: Clean and spacious, with friendly staff, Adnams and Highgate Mild beers, good value standard well presented food; small sun-trap garden *(George Atkinson)*

☆ **Northampton** [Wellingborough Rd; SP 7560], *Abington Park*: Large Victorian town pub brewing its own good beers, several bars, lunchtime bar food, friendly helpful staff, restaurant, family room; piped pop music, games machines; picnic tables outside, handy for cricket ground *(Cathy Scott, Richard Baker)*

Northampton [Old Kingsthorpe; SP7464], *Queen Adelaide*: Surprisingly good food, well kept ales, interesting warplane photographs *(Philip Orbell)*; [London Rd (B526)], *Queen Eleanor*: Well kept Courage-related and Theakstons ales, play areas inside and out, open all day Sat/Sun *(JJW, CMW)*

Norton, N'hants [off A5 N of Weedon; SP6063], *White Horse*: Old village pub doing well under obliging current landlord, well kept Charles Wells ales and a guest such as Hook Norton Old Hookey, good coffee, good food in beamed lounge with dining annexe, public bar with pool and skittles; piped music *(George Atkinson, Peter Phillips)*

☆ **Offchurch**, War [off A425 Radford Semele; SP3565], *Stags Head*: Pleasant low-beamed thatched dining pub with wide choice of good value generous food inc good vegetarian dishes, friendly service, well kept Bass, unobtrusive piped music; tables in good-sized garden with play area *(Nigel and Sue Foster, the Monday Club)*

☆ **Old**, N'hants [Walgrave Rd; N of Northampton between A43 and A508; SP7873], *White Horse*: Very welcoming log fire, cheery atmosphere, well kept Banks's and Marstons Pedigree, decent wines, wide choice of good value food inc some interesting snacks; ample seating *(Eric J Locker, K H Frostick)*

☆ **Old Hill**, W Mid [Waterfall Lane; off Station Rd, between A4099 Gorstyhill Rd and A459 Halesowen Rd; SO9685], *Wharf*: Popular chatty drinking pub with eight or so well kept largely S & N real ales, cheap food (not Sun) inc children's dishes, pool, juke box, pinball and other games, family area, tables in canalside garden with play area; occasional live music *(Dave Braisted, LYM)*

☆ **Old Hill** [132 Waterfall Lane], *Waterfall*: Genuine down-to-earth local with well kept Bathams, Everards and Hook Norton and three or four interesting guest beers, farm cider, popular plain food from good filled rolls to Sun lunch, tankards and jugs hanging from boarded ceiling; piped music *(Graham Reeve, Dave Braisted)*

☆ **Oldbury**, W Mid [Church St, nr Savacentre; SO9888], *Waggon & Horses*: Impressive Edwardian tiles and copper ceiling in busy town pub with well kept changing ales such as Adnams Best, Boddingtons, Everards Beacon, Best, Mild and Old Original, Holdens XB, Hook Norton Old Hookey, Marstons Pedigree, Morlands Old Speckled Hen and Shepherd Neame Bishops Finger, wide choice of food inc balti dishes in bar and upstairs restaurant, friendly staff, simple furnishings, Black Country memorabilia *(Andy Petersen, Richard Lewis)*

☆ **Orlingbury**, N'hants [signed off A43 Northampton—Kettering, A509 Wellingborough—Kettering; SP8572], *Queens Arms*: Beautifully clean and well looked after, with six well kept ales such as Fullers London Pride and Oak Wobbly Bob, welcoming staff, food inc super sandwiches and ham and egg, cheap coffee, occasional live music; play area *(George Atkinson, Stephen Brown)*

☆ **Oundle**, N'hants [52 Benefield Rd; TL0388], *Black Horse*: Generous popular home-made food inc excellent puddings, wide evening choice and good Sun lunch, in bright clean bar with comfortable dining room, changing ales such as Bass, Batemans Victory and XXXB, Mitchells Lancaster Bomber and John Smiths, roaring fire, helpful friendly staff, games room with piped music; 10ft model black horse outside *(Jenny and Michael Back, David and Mary Webb)*

☆ **Pailton**, War [B4027 Coventry—Lutterworth; SP4781], *White Lion*: Biggish nicely furnished 18th-c pub/restaurant popular for wide range of quickly served decent food inc two-sitting Sun lunch and children's dishes, good range of wines, well kept beers; play area in garden; cl Mon; bedrooms *(George Atkinson, Geoff Lee)*

Pailton [B4027 Lutterworth—Coventry], *Fox*: Well kept M & B Brew XI, Theakstons XB and Worthington Best, farm cider, good value food inc vegetarian and children's; tables and big jungle gym outside; bedrooms *(George Brink, Geoff Lee)*

☆ **Princethorpe**, War [High Town; junction A423/B4453; SP4070], *Three Horseshoes*: Friendly old coaching inn with lots of brass, beams, plates, pictures, comfortable settles and chairs; Judges Barristers, Marstons Pedigree, Ruddles County and John Smiths, country wines, good value freshly prepared food inc children's, vegetarian and Sun lunch, good service, no-smoking eating area, open fire; pleasant big garden with play equipment *(Richard Waller, George Atkinson, JJW, CMW)*

☆ **Priors Hardwick**, War [SP4756], *Butchers Arms*: Medieval oak beams, flagstones, panelling and antiques in friendly upmarket Portuguese-run pub/restaurant (not Sat lunch or Sun evening); log fire and keg beer in small welcoming inglenook bar, country garden *(Jill and Peter Bickley, T M Dobby, D Marsh)*

☆ **Pytchley**, N'hants [SP8574], *Overstone Arms*: Good changing choice of food inc some exotic specials in long countrified dining room packed every evening, often with big parties; runs like well oiled machine, landlord keeping eye on everything; well kept Courage-related beers with a guest such as Batemans; tables in garden, attractive countryside *(Howard and Margaret Buchanan, Peter Titmuss)*

Radford Semele, War [A425 2 miles E of Leamington Spa; SP3464], *White Lion*: Smartly refurbished big Millers Kitchen, good value food, Tetleys-related ales; garden *(George Atkinson, Steve and Liz Tilley)*

☆ **Ratley**, War [OS Sheet 151 map ref 384473; SP3847], *Rose & Crown*: Handsome old beamed local of golden stone, recently reopened by friendly family with three lively roan cocker spaniels; woodburning stove in flagstoned area on right, big log fireplace in carpeted area on left; cosy atmosphere, Badger Tanglefoot and Charles Wells Eagle and Bombardier, good home-cooked food inc superb puddings; tables in small garden, nr lovely church in small sleepy village *(George Atkinson)*

Raunds, N'hants [16 Grove St; SP9972], *Globe*: Popular local with well kept beers, competitively priced food, darts and pool in games room, lots of activities; tables in garden *(Mr and Mrs John Hackett, Mr and Mrs D Phillips)*

Ravensthorpe, N'hants [Church Lane; SP6670], *Chequers*: Wide range of bar food, interesting well kept beers inc Jennings Cumberland, Sam Smiths OB and Thwaites, lots of bric-a-brac in L-shaped bar, friendly locals, efficient service *(Bruce Bird)*

Roade, N'hants [1 High St; just off A508 S of M1 junction 15; SP7551], *Cock*: Solid lunchtime bar food, Marstons Pedigree, Theakstons and guest beers such as Buchanans Best, plates, horse brasses, living flame gas fire; piped music; children in lounge bar *(Penny and Martin Fletcher, KM, JM)*

☆ **Rockingham**, N'hants [SP8691], *Sondes Arms*: Nicely set civilised beamed pub with welcoming service, quiet piped music, good if not cheap home-made food inc some really unusual dishes and lower-priced smaller meals, well kept Charles Wells Eagle and Bombardier and Youngs Special, restaurant; super views *(Alain and Rose Foote, Frank Cummins, D W Gray, Bernard and Marjorie Parkin)*

☆ **Rowington**, War [Old Warwick Rd (B4439); SP2069], *Cockhorse*: Homely cottage-style Edwardian pub in pleasant rural setting, simple tasty pub food inc nice big hand-cut chips, friendly attentive staff, small bar with inglenook and fruit machine, second room with tables; picnic tables and flower tubs in front, pets' corner behind; dogs allowed *(Susan and John Douglas)*

Ryton on Dunsmore, War [High St; SP3874], *Blacksmiths Arms*: Friendly village local, good bar food, Bass and M & B *(D Marsh)*

☆ **Sedgley**, W Mid [Bilston St (A463); SO9193], *Beacon*: Unspoilt local brewing its own good well priced Sarah Hughes Surprise Bitter and Dark Ruby Mild in restored tower brewery, two or three other well kept ales from tiny circular serving area with hatches to several Victorian rooms, family room and conservatory; seats on terrace *(John Scarisbrick)*

☆ **Shipston on Stour**, War [Church St; SP2540], *Horseshoe*: Pretty timbered inn with open-plan largely modern bar, lots of maroon plush, generous straightforward bar food with good chips, big fireplace with copper pans above, chintzy restaurant; Courage-related ales with a guest such as Butcombe, decent coffee, darts, no piped music; small flower-decked back terrace; bedrooms pretty, bright and clean *(Diane Percivall, Pam Adsley, BB)*

☆ **Shipston on Stour** [Station Rd (off A3400)], *Black Horse*: Ancient thatched and beamed pub with good value bar food, well kept Home, Ruddles, Theakstons XB, Websters and a guest beer, properly pubby atmosphere, friendly staff and locals, log fire, small restaurant, back garden with terrace and barbecue, newfoundland dog and a couple of cats *(Margaret Dyke, Dr and Mrs J H Hills, Chris and Anne Fluck)*

☆ **Shipston on Stour** [High St], *White Bear*: Massive settles, good range of beers and cheerful atmosphere in traditional front bar, simple comfortable back lounge, interesting good value generous food, tables in small back yard and benches on street; bedrooms *(Michele and Clive Platman, A Cowell, LYM)*

Shrewley, War [off B4439 Hockley Heath—Warwick; SP2167], *Durham Ox*: Small friendly country pub, wide choice of good reasonably priced food, real ales, spacious garden *(Roy Bromell, Dave Braisted, LYM)*

Shustoke, War [B4114 Nuneaton—Coleshill; SP2290], *Plough*: Rambling local done up in olde-worlde style with brass galore, cheap food, Bass and M & B beers *(Dave Braisted)*

Shuttington, War [SK2505], *Wolferstan Arms*: Good recently refurbished family pub with imaginative reasonably priced menu, long-serving staff, wide views from restaurant; garden and play area *(Graham Richardson)*

☆ **Sibbertoft**, N'hants [SP6782], *Red Lion*: Small, civilised and welcoming pub with huge range of good generous food inc vegetarian, well kept Bass and Tetleys, decent wines, good service, piano, magazines, lovely big tables, comfortable seats *(Jim Farmer)*

☆ **Slipton**, N'hants [Slipton Ln; SP9479], *Samuel Pepys*: 16th-c two-bar pub nicely refurbished with old beams, exposed stonework, open fire, watercolours and decorative plates; wide choice of food inc interesting dishes and OAP bargain lunch, prompt friendly service, five well kept ales, decent wines, good coffee, conservatory; good views from garden with play area; children allowed in restaurant *(Jeremy Wallington, David and Mary Webb, CMW, JJW, D Howitt)*

Smethwick, W Mid [100 High St; SP0288], *Blue Gates*: Good service, attractive new refurbishment, huge upstairs room with stage and bar *(Ajaib Singh Diu)*

Snitterfield, War [Smiths Lane/School Rd; off A46 N of Stratford; SP2159], *Fox Hunter*: Comfortable L-shaped bar/lounge, wide range of food, M & B Brew XI and Ruddles County, hunting pictures; piped music, fruit machine, children allowed; tables outside *(JJW, CMW)*

Solihull, W Mid [Hillfield Rd; SP1479], *Hillfield Hall*: Reliable Toby grill with good friendly service, restaurant overlooking garden *(Michael and Margaret Norris)*

☆ **Southam**, War [A423, towards Coventry; SP4161], *Old Mint*: 14th-c pub open all day Sat, considerable potential in two character heavy-beamed rooms, well kept Bass, Hook Norton Best, Marstons Pedigree, Timothy Taylors Landlord, Wadworths 6X and guest ales, country wines, winter hot punch, open fire; darts, fruit machine, piped music *(Steve and Liz Tilley, Geoff Lee, Nigel Foster, John and Marianne Cooper, John Fahy, David Shillitoe, LYM)*

Stoke Albany, N'hants [1 Harborough Rd; SP8088], *White Horse*: Decent food inc generous starters and wide vegetarian choice, Bass, welcoming young licensees *(Eric Locker)*

☆ **Stoke Bruerne**, N'hants [3½ miles from M1 junction 15 – A508 towards Stony Stratford then signed on right; SP7450], *Boat*: Ideal canal location by beautifully restored lock opp British Waterways Museum and shop; little character flagstoned bar by canal, more ordinary back lounge without the views (children allowed in this bit), tables by towpath; well kept Marstons Best and Pedigree, Sam Smiths OB and Theakstons XB; no-smoking restaurant (not Mon lunchtime) and all-day tearooms, pub open all day summer Sats *(Piotr Chodzko-Zajko, Rita Horridge, Mrs J Barwell, D Deas, Ian Phillips, LYM)*

☆ **Stoke Doyle**, N'hants [S of Oundle; TL0286], *Shuckborough Arms*: Good choice of food, esp vegetarian, in peaceful welcoming L-shaped panelled bar or dining room; well kept ales inc guests, log fires, comfortable chesterfields, helpful landlord, no music or fruit machines, games room with hood skittles; picnic tables in garden with play area; bedrooms good, with own bathrooms *(N S Smith, Erica Head, CW, JW)*

Stonebridge, War [Coventry Rd, Stonebridge roundabout; just off M42 junction 6; SP2183], *Malt Shovel*: Big spacious Toby restaurant handy for NEC, good value standard food, decent service, comfortable seats *((Mayur Shah))*

☆ **Stonnall**, W Mid [Main St, off A452; SK0703], *Old Swann*: Wide choice of good food inc fine sandwiches (booking advised for Sun lunch), friendly and efficient service, particularly well kept Bass and a guest such as Youngs *(Dorothee and Dennis Glover, Jack Barnwell)*

Stourbridge, W Mid [Brook Rd; nr stn; SO8984], *Seven Stars*: Extensive imaginative generous food inc all-day cold snacks in large Victorian pub with impressive wooden carved bar, decorative ceramic tiles, well kept beers inc Bathams and Theakstons; very busy, friendly atmosphere *(Dr and Mrs Baker)*

☆ **Stratford upon Avon**, War [Southern Way; SP0255], *Black Swan*: Great atmosphere, mildly sophisticated, in neat 16th-c pub nr Memorial Theatre – still attracts actors, lots of signed RSC photographs; plainly served bar food at moderate prices, Whitbreads-related ales, friendly service (can be slow to warm up – and not all take kindly to the 'no bikers' notice), open fire, children allowed in small dining area; attractive terrace looking over the riverside public gardens – which tend to act as summer overflow; known as the Dirty Duck *(Susan and John Douglas, James Hanson, Ralph Hunter, Gary Nicholls, Greg Grimsley, Buck and Gillian Shinkman, LYM)*

☆ **Stratford upon Avon** [High St, nr Town Hall], *Garrick*: Another rather theatrical pub – but younger, more alternative, with lots of character, engaging sawdust-floor and stripped-stone decor, cosy front bar, busier back one, central open fire, well kept Whitbreads-related real ales, sensibly priced bar food inc good puddings (popular with office workers lunchtime), friendly service, thoughtfully chosen piped music; children allowed in dining room when food being served; fine tilting timbered building *(George Atkinson, Ted George, B Carter, D Hanley, Gary Nicholls, Andy and Gill Plumb, Dr and Mrs A K Clarke, LYM)*

☆ **Stratford upon Avon** [Chapel St], *Shakespeare*: Smart hotel based on handsome lavishly modernised Tudor merchants' houses, comfortable lounge with plush settees and armchairs, huge log fire, tables in sheltered courtyard; also comfortable Froth & Elbow bar with settles, armchairs and limited but attractive and reasonably priced hot and cold buffet served promptly, but not always open and may not always have real ale; bedrooms comfortable and well equipped, though not cheap *(George Atkinson, John and Christine Vittoe, J M Wooll, LYM)*

Stratford upon Avon, *Arden*: Hotel bar useful for Memorial Theatre, Courage Best and Directors, Flowers Original, good baguettes, tasty bread and butter pudding; very popular, get there early; bedrooms *(Christopher and Maureen Starling)*; [Rother St/Greenhill St], *Old Thatch*: Friendly local, decent wine, well kept beer *(John and Christine Vittoe)*; [Ely St], *Queens Head*: Decent food inc Sun lunch, M & B and guest beers *(D Hanley)*; [Warwick Rd, opp Midland Red bus depot], *Red Lion*: Large friendly Brewers Fayre pub by canal, reasonably priced standard food, good range of real ales, modern pub games; children welcome, play area *(Alain and Rose Foote, Dr and Mrs A K Clarke)*; [Rother St], *White Swan*: Forte hotel's comfortable old-fashioned beamed bar with 16th-c wall painting of Tobias and the Angel, leather armchairs, antique settles, fine oak panelling, lunchtime bar snacks, quick friendly service; children in eating area; bedrooms *(John and Christine Vittoe, George Atkinson, G S and A Jaques, LYM)*; [Church St], *Windmill*: Cosy old pub beyond the attractive church, wide choice of reasonably priced bar food inc vegetarian, Whitbreads-related ales; welcoming even when busy *(Richard Lewis, John and Christine Vittoe, Geoffrey and Irene Lindley)*

Stretton on Dunsmore, War [off A45 and A423; SP4172], *Shoulder of Mutton*: Friendly village local with snug Victorian panelled public bar, particularly well kept M & B Mild and Brew XI on handpump, cards and dominoes, pictures of old Coventry, spotless furniture; spacious 1950s lounge with two darts boards; cl Mon-Thurs lunchtime, erratic opening Sat lunchtime *(Ted George, Pete Baker)*

☆ **Studley**, War [Icknield St Dr; left turn off A435, going N from B4093 roundabout; SP0763], *Old Washford Mill*: Attractive ivy-covered converted watermill, different levels, quiet alcoves, three different restaurants in varying styles, provision for children, real ales tapped from the cask (some brewed on the premises), country wines, internal millstream and interesting old mill machinery; pretty waterside gardens with good play area, ducks and black swan *(Patricia Tovey, LYM)*

Studley [Alcester Rd (A435)], *Little Lark*: Reasonable choice of good modestly priced food, well kept real ale, printing-equipment theme, friendly bustling atmosphere *(Tom Gondris, David and Shelia)*

☆ **Sutton Bassett**, N'hants [SP7790], *Queens Head*: Peaceful village pub with good if not cheap food using herbs from own garden, changing well kept ales such as Tetleys, Marston Moor Cromwell Bitter and Brewers Droop and Smiles Exhibition, welcoming Irish landlord, upstairs restaurant; some seats out beyond car park *(Joan and Michel Hooper-Immins, Stephen and Julie Brown)*

Sutton Coldfield, W Mid [Chester Rd (A452) New Oscott; SP0994], *Tailors*: Good reasonably priced food inc game, good choice of beers, wine-bar atmosphere evenings; open all day *(Lynn Fellows)*

Tanworth in Arden, War [SP1170], *Bell*: Roomy lounge with well kept Whitbreads-related ales, bar food inc good dish of the day, outlook on peaceful village green and lovely 14th-c church; children in eating area and restaurant *(Dave Braisted, LYM)*

☆ **Temple Grafton**, War [a mile E, towards Binton; off A422 W of Stratford; SP1255], *Blue Boar*: Attractive food-oriented early 17th-c pub with beams, several log fires, darts in flagstoned side room, tables on terrace; has been a popular main entry for its unusual combination of freshly cooked really good food at low prices, well kept Donnington BBA, Flowers Original, Hook Norton Best and Wadworths 6X, decent wines and friendly pubby atmosphere, with a welcome for children, but the licensee left in early summer 1995 *(LYM; reports on new regime please)*

☆ **Thorpe Mandeville**, N'hants [former B4525; SP5344], *Three Conies*: Attractive creeper-clad pub with brasses, low beams, some stripped stone, gin trap over inglenook fireplace, horse-racing photographs and conversation, furnishings to suit the old building; decent bar food, well kept Hook Norton and Old Hookey on handpump, good choice of wines and spirits, friendly efficient service, games room, restaurant; children welcome, lots of seats in big garden *(Janet and Bill Cliverd, Leith Stuart, George Atkinson, David and Marguerite Morgan, Graham and Karen Oddey, Geoffrey Pegram, Joan and Ian Wilson, L Walker, LYM)*

☆ **Thorpe Waterville**, N'hants [A605 Thrapston—Oundle; TL0281], *Fox*: Friendly old pub with wide range of enjoyable food inc huge steaks, reasonable prices, coal fire, Charles Wells ales, log-effect fire, quiet piped music, weekend restaurant, welcoming prompt service; children allowed, no dogs, small garden with play area *(David and Michelle Hedges, Mrs Meg Hamilton)*

☆ **Titchmarsh**, N'hants [village signed from A604 and A605, just E of Thrapston; TL0279], *Wheatsheaf*: Popular evening dining pub, good local atmosphere, good home-made bar food, Hook Norton and Marstons Pedigree, lots of exposed stonework, golfing memorabilia, pool room, restaurant, cat and dogs, piped music; children allowed in eating areas; cl Mon evening, weekday lunchtimes *(George Atkinson, LYM)*

☆ **Towcester**, N'hants [Watling St; SP6948], *Saracens Head*: Attractive coaching inn, panelled bar with carpets on pine boards, other old features, interesting *Pickwick Papers* connections, Victorian dining room, short but good range of food, Charles Wells Eagle and Bombardier, neat staff; well equipped bedrooms *(Ian Phillips, George Atkinson, Brig J S Green, Karen and Graham Oddey, LYM)*

Towcester [104 Watling St], *Brave Old Oak*: Expensively restored, with nice furnishings, lovely panelling, decent food, Banks's ales on electric pump, family room; not sure about the heraldic shields, decorative lighting, fruit machine and piped music; bedrooms *(George Atkinson, K H Frostick)*; [Watling St; A5 S, opp racecourse], *Folly*: Thatched pub with decent cheap food, well kept Charles Wells ales, friendly staff, garden with play area *(Helen Jeanes, Christopher and Sharon Hayle)*

☆ **Ufton**, War [White Hart Lane; just off A425 Daventry—Leamington, towards Bascote; SP3761], *White Hart*: Friendly old hilltop pub with fine views from garden – perhaps its strongest feature (though Tannoy food announcements out here); big lounge/dining area, wide range of usual food, well kept Greenalls and Wadworths 6X, friendly service; boules *(George Atkinson, Steve and Liz Tilley, Rona Murdoch)*

Upper Boddington, N'hants [SP4753], *Plough*: Limited choice of good food, fine landlord, lovely Dolls Parlour *(B Adams)*

Upper Gornal, W Mid [Kent St; SO9291], *Britannia*: Authentic Black Country atmosphere, especially in back room originally laid out for table drinks service *(Peter Green)*

Wakerley, N'hants [Main St; SP9599], *Exeter Arms*: Good range of ales such as Adnams Broadside or Marstons Pedigree, good basic home-made food (not Mon), well trained staff in former hunting lodge nr Wakerley Woods, good views and walks over Welland Valley, two connecting rooms with woodburner, local photographs, friendly black labrador; piped music, fruit machine, occasional live music *(CMW, JJW, Richard Clarke)*

Walsall, W Mid [Blue Lane W/Shaw St; SP0198], *Hammakers Arms*: Clean and welcoming lounge, well kept Banks's beers, good value food inc choice of Sun roasts *(John Winterbottom)*

☆ **Warmington**, War [High St; signed off B4100, handy detour between M40 junctions 11 and 12; SP4147], *Plough*: Early 17th-c, with good log fire in cosy and homely low-beamed bar with winged high-backed settle, well kept Hook Norton Best, Marstons Pedigree and guest beer, simple generous bar food (not Sun evening) inc good sandwiches, cheery service; children in eating area *(John Atherton, N and J Strathdee, TBB, J E Rycroft, Alan and Jane Clarke, Bob and Maggie Atherton, Steve and Karen Jennings, Martin and Karen Wake, LYM; more reports please)*

Warmington, N'hants [Peterborough Rd; just off A605 NE of Oundle; TL0791], *Red Lion*: Pleasant attentive landlord, dark beams, pictures and china in lounge, bar with TV, dining lounge with some no-smoking tables; well kept Bass, Highgate Dark Mild and Worthington Best, good value food (not Sun evening); garden with play area and barbecue *(JJW, CMW, John Dyer)*

☆ **Warwick** [11 Church St], *Zetland Arms*: Pleasant no-frills town pub with limited choice of cheap bar food (not weekend evenings), well kept Tetleys-related ales, friendly quick service, functional lounge bar; sheltered garden surprisingly good – secluded, interestingly planted, lovingly kept; children may be allowed; bedrooms, sharing bathroom *(D Hanley, Brad and Joni Nelson, Michael and Derek Slade, LYM)*

Warwick [Crompton St, nr racecourse], *Old Fourpenny Shop*: Friendly M & B pub with well kept guests like Adnams or Butterknowle, bar meals *(D Hanley)*; [11 Market Pl], *Tilted Wig*: Imaginative range of Tetleys-related and other ales, good range of wines, wide choice of good value food (not Sun evening), good friendly service, part stone floors, good views over square, rather a winebar feel; live jazz and folk Sun evening, open all day Fri/Sat and summer *(Richard Lewis, D Hanley, Joan and Tony Walker)*; [West St, towards racecourse and Stratford], *Wheatsheaf*: Well laid out, with well kept Tetleys-related and guest ales, wide range of bar meals; pool, fruit machine, bric-a-brac, two friendly cats, good atmosphere; bedrooms *(D Hanley)*

☆ **Weedon**, N'hants [3 miles from M1 junction 16; A45 towards Daventry; SP6259], *Heart of England*: Big 18th-c pub with panelled eating area, busy attractively refurbished lounge bar with small areas and pool table off, particularly well kept changing ales such as Hook Norton Best, Mansfield Riding and Old Baily, Theakstons Best and XB, good freshly cooked food inc some unusual dishes (may be a wait), restaurant with new conservatory, good friendly easy-going service; piped music, children welcome; big garden leading down to Grand Union Canal, good value pine-furnished bedrooms *(Peter Phillips, JJW, CMW, Robin Tillbrook, Peter J Kearns)*

☆ **Weedon** [junction A5/A45], *Globe*: Usefully placed attractive country hotel with comfortable atmosphere, freshly prepared bar food inc vegetarian and take-aways, small helpings for children or OAPs, Marstons Bitter and Pedigree, Websters Yorkshire and a guest such as Clarks Burglar Bill, friendly service, log fire, restaurant, picnic tables outside; bedrooms *(JJW, CMW, Sue and Mike Todd)*

Weedon [Stowe Hill (A5 S)], *Narrow Boat*: Warm and welcoming well worn-in main bar, good range of bar food in high-raftered ex-kitchen family dining room, summer barbecues, well kept Charles Wells ales with a guest such as Adnams; good generous Cantonese restaurant, spacious and airy, with canal and country views (booking advised Sat); very busy in summer, spacious terrace, big garden by canal; bedrooms in motel extension *(David Tonkin, Bill Sykes, LYM)*

☆ **Welford**, N'hants [SP6480], *Shoulder of Mutton*: Sensibly priced straightforward food (not Thurs) inc children's dishes in friendly and well kept 17th-c inn's arch-linked open-plan bar, Batemans XB and Ruddles Best, good coffee, piped music; skittle room, good back garden with play area, lovely village nr canal marina *(Gordon Theaker)*

☆ **Welford on Avon**, War [High St (Binton Rd); SP1452], *Bell*: Dim-lit dark-timbered low-beamed lounge, flagstoned public bar with darts, pool and so forth, open fires, good friendly staff, well kept Whitbreads-related ales, generous straightforward food inc good value Sun lunch, dining conservatory (children allowed here); piped music; tables in pretty garden and back courtyard; attractive riverside village *(Bob and Maggie Atherton, Peter Williams, Jenny and Michael Back, Martin Lavery, Marjorie and David Lamb, Thomas Nott, LYM)*

Welton, N'hants [off A361/B4036 N of Daventry; SP5866], *White Horse*: Pleasant bars, very friendly landlord, good value food, real ales *(Anon)*

West Bromwich, W Mid [Hill Top (A41 W); SP0091], *Dovecot*: Newish local with M & B beers and cheap good food in big dining area; they do keep doves *(Mr and Mrs T Bryan)*

☆ **Whatcote**, War [SP2944], *Royal Oak*: Dating from 12th century, quaint low-ceilinged small room, huge inglenook, Civil War connections, lots to look at, animal skins on wall; wide choice of decent straightforward bar food (not usually quick unless you ask specially), friendly service, real ales such as Marstons Pedigree, picnic tables outside; children in eating area *(Ann and Bob Westbrook, Mrs J Oakes, L Walker, LYM)*

Whitacre Heath, War [Station Rd; off B4114 at Blyth End E of Coleshill; SP2192], *Swan*: Pleasant pub with interesting agricultural decorations *(Dave Braisted)*

Willenhall, W Mid [Wolverhampton St; SO9698], *Brewers Droop*: Interesting changing well kept ales, good value simple lunches, evening meals Fri/Sat; folk music upstairs Thurs *(Graham Reeve, John Winterbottom)*

☆ **Willey**, War [just off A5, N of A427 junction; SP4984], *Old Watling*: Polished flagstones, stripped masonry and plenty of cosy corners, good neatly kept furnishings, open fire, quick friendly service, generous good value enterprising bar food, well kept Adnams, Banks's and Courage-related beers *(Geoff Lee, Ted George)*

☆ **Wilmcote**, War [The Green; 3 miles NW of Stratford, just off new A46 bypass; SP1657], *Swan House*: Genteel country hotel with glass-topped well in 18th-c beamed lounge, welcoming efficient service, good home-made food inc sizzle steaks in bar and restaurant, well kept Bass, Hook Norton Best and Theakston XB; comfortable bedrooms, front terrace overlooking Mary Arden's cottage, tables in back garden *(Joan and Michel Hooper-Immins)*

☆ **Wixford**, War [SP0954], *Three Horseshoes*: Roomy pub with consistently good generous food inc interesting specials and good range of puddings, charming landlord and staff, well kept Flowers IPA *(Peter Lloyd, John Close, W H and E Thomas, Moira and John Cole)*

☆ **Wolverhampton**, W Mid [Sun St, behind old low-level stn; SO9198], *Great Western*: Classic three-bar backstreet pub with well kept Bathams and Holdens, very promptly served good value plain food inc huge cheap filled cobs, lots of railway memorabilia, friendly staff, tables in yard with good barbecues and extension marquee; parking limited lunchtime *(Mr and Mrs H S Hill, Richard Lewis, Graham Reeve, John Winterbottom, DAV, J Dwane)*

Wolverhampton [Princess St], *Feline & Firkin*: Friendly traditional-style pub with fine choice of well kept ales, decent food *(Jared Warner)*; *Mermaid*: Above-average food lunchtime and early evening, lively meeting-place later *(R D Hopkins)*

nr **Wolverhampton** [Penn Wood Lane, Penn Common (actually just over Staffs border); SO9094], *Barley Mow*: Tiny 17th-c country pub with good home-made food using meat from local butcher; friendly welcome, real ales and cider, reasonable prices; children's play area *(Mrs L M Peach)*

Woodnewton, N'hants [TL0394], *White Swan*: Friendly country local with well kept ales such as Fullers London Pride, Morlands Old Speckled Hen, Shepherd Neame Spitfire, good value food inc Sun lunch *(Derek Thomas)*

☆ **Yelvertoft**, N'hants [49 High St; SP5975], *Knightley Arms*: Comfortably refurbished, simple clean lounge divided by log fire, plates, brasses and pictures, solid wooden furnishings, small neat dining area, good home-cooked food inc children's, Bass, Marstons Pedigree and Websters Yorkshire, good coffee, hood skittles; garden, occasional barbecues *(George Atkinson, Alan Chantler)*

Norfolk

More and more pubs here are now giving customers the benefit of one of the area's great assets – good fresh fish and seafood. For food generally, the welcoming and individual Saracens Head near Erpingham still stands out as having exceptionally good imaginative cooking; two other pubs currently doing very well for meals out are the Hoste Arms in Burnham Market and (with particularly good specials) the Hare Arms at Stow Bardolph. It's the Hoste Arms that we choose as this year's Norfolk Dining Pub of the Year: much more room than the Saracens Head, and at the moment generating a great deal of enthusiasm among readers. Other pubs here that have recently been filling our postbag with warm reports are the rather restauranty Ratcatchers at Cawston, the Rose & Crown at Snettisham (new licensees settling in very well), and the lively Three Horseshoes at Warham. Three enjoyable new Norfolk entries are the lively White Horse in Blakeney, the very relaxed George & Dragon at Cley next the Sea (ideally placed for bird-watchers), and the friendly Crown in Mundford (good unusual food). In the Lucky Dip section at the end of the chapter, pubs worth watching particularly these days include the Three Swallows at Cley next the Sea, Crown at Gayton, Earle Arms at Heydon, Swan at Hilborough, Angel at Larling, Sculthorpe Mill at Sculthorpe, Ship at South Walsham, Ferry House at Surlingham and Sutton Staithe at Sutton Staithe. Norwich has a good choice of enjoyable pubs. Drinks prices are rather higher than the national average, and have been rising rather more than elsewhere; the two cheapest places we found were the Ostrich at Castle Acre and Crown at Colkirk, both tied to the regional brewer Greene King. The local Woodfordes beers are always worth looking out for as good value.

ALDBOROUGH TG1834 Map 8

Black Boys

Signposted off A140 S of Roughton

On summer Sunday afternoons the cricket team use this friendly little pub as their pavilion during matches on the adjacent broad village green. New licensees have taken over since our last edition, and though they're keen to maintain the village local feel, there's still quite an emphasis on bar food. Generously served dishes might include sandwiches (from £1.50), soup (£1.95), filled baked potatoes (from £2.80), ploughman's (£2.95), ham egg and chips (£3.75), carrot and cheese bake (£3.95), steak and kidney pie or barbecue spare ribs (£4.50), pork chops in a mild mustard sauce (£4.75), steaks (from £7.25), and specials such as chicken stir fry (£4.50) or boiled ham in mustard and apricot sauce (£4.75); children's helpings. The neatly-kept and comfortable bar has pleasantly low-key furnishings such as brocaded chairs, green leatherette button-back wall banquettes and cast-iron-framed tables, as well as old local photographs, a log fire and lots of fresh flowers; darts, dominoes, fruit machine, piped music. Well kept Ansells, Flowers Original and Tetleys on handpump, decent wines. There are tables outside in the little courtyard and colourful flowering tubs and hanging baskets. *(Recommended by Geoff Lee, Paul Craddoug, Dr and Mrs M Bailey, Mrs E Stratton, Sheila and Brian Wilson, R C Vincent, A E Barwick, Rita Horridge, Frank Davidson)*

Pubmaster ~ Tenant Mrs Jeanette Coleman ~ Real ale ~ Meals and snacks (not evening 25 Dec) ~ Restaurant ~ (01263) 768086 ~ Children welcome ~ Open 11-3, 6-11; all day Sat, and maybe summer

BLAKENEY TG0243 Map 8

Kings Arms

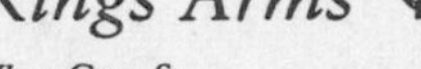

West Gate St

Mr and Mrs Davies have been running this cheery local for 20 years now, and many of their staff have been with them all that time too. Perhaps that accounts for the consistency of the place, which draws people back time and time again whenever they're in the area. Relaxed and welcoming, the three simply furnished, knocked-together rooms have some interesting photographs of the licencees' theatrical careers, other pictures including work by local artists, and what's said to be the smallest cartoon gallery in England in a former telephone kiosk; two areas are no smoking. Tasty bar food includes soup (£2), popular sandwiches (from £1.20), filled baked potatoes (from £3.20), ploughman's (from £3.90), vegetable lasagne (£4.50), fresh local fish like mussels (winter only), crab (summer only), haddock or cod (£5), or grilled trout (£6.50, evenings only), evening salads (from £6.50), steaks (£9.50), puddings such as home-made crumble (from £2.50), and good children's meals (£2.75) – the fish fingers may be home-made; daily specials include seasonal local produce such as fresh asparagus. Very well kept (though not that cheap) Marstons Pedigree, Ruddles County, Websters, Woodfordes Wherry or Nog and a guest like Shepherd Neame Spitfire on handpump, freshly squeezed orange juice; cribbage, dominoes, fruit machine. The large garden has lots of tables and chairs and a separate, equipped children's area, there are baby-changing facilities, too. The date 1760 is picked out in black tiles on the red roof. As it's just a short stroll to the harbour, this pretty white cottage can get crowded at peak times, especially in summer. They can supply information on boat trips out to the seals and birds of Blakeney Point. Dogs welcome. *(Recommended by Stephen, Julie and Hayley Brown, Rita Horridge, Mike and Heather Barnes, Mr and Mrs Jones, K H Frostick, Thomas Nott, David and Michelle Hedges, L Walker, Bill Edwards, Peter and Pat Frogley, Sue Demont, Tim Barrow, Charles Bardswell, Riley and Jean Coles)*

Free house ~ Licensees Howard and Marjorie Davies ~ Real ale ~ Meals and snacks (all day weekends and school holidays) ~ (01263) 740341 ~ Children welcome ~ Open 11-11 ~ Self-catering flatlets available upstairs

White Horse

4 High Street

In a good spot close to the harbour, this small hotel's bar arrangements were reworked a few years ago to give one long bar which has now been attractively refurbished, making it more relaxed and comfortable but keeping a lively and pleasantly pubby atmosphere; besides cribbage and dominoes, there's a good collection of other games such as Connect-4, well kept Adnams, Boddingtons, and Flowers Original, and a good choice of reasonably priced wines, especially from the New World. It does get very busy in the holiday season, but even then there's a good leavening of local people, and brisk service by pleasant young staff rarely slows. There's wheelchair access, though a step across the middle of the bar. Good value well presented bar food includes sandwiches (from £1.25), soup (£1.95; the cockle chowder is good, £3), salads (from £4.50), steak and kidney pie or lasagne (£4.95), daily specials like vegetarian stuffed marrow (£4.95) and Oriental pork or tagliatelle with mushrooms, bacon and pesto sauce (£5.50), local fresh fish dishes, and home-made puddings like treacle tart or bread and butter pudding (£2.25). There's an elegant white-painted restaurant, and tables out in a suntrap courtyard. *(Recommended by Charles Bardswell, Mike and Heather Barnes, Alan and Mary Reid, Susan and John Priestley, Jonathan and Helen Palmer, Mick Hitchman, Frank Davidson, Andy Whitaker, Peter and Pat Frogley)*

Free house ~ Licensee Daniel Rees ~ Real ale ~ Meals and snacks ~ Restaurant (Tues-Sat evening only) ~ (01263) 740574 ~ Children in restaurant and two other rooms ~ Open 11-3, 6-11 ~ bedrooms: £30B/£60B

BLICKLING TG1728 Map 8

Buckinghamshire Arms

Off B1354 N of Aylsham

Like the hall it guards the gates of, this busy Jacobean inn is owned by the National Trust. The small front snug is simply furnished with fabric cushioned banquettes, and has pictures and memorabilia of bare knuckle fighters (especially Jem Mace the Norfolk-born world champion), while the bigger lounge has neatly built-in pews, stripped deal tables, and landscapes and cockfighting prints. A plain family room is no smoking. Tasty bar food includes home-made soup (£1.95), sandwiches, a good, proper ploughman's (£4.50), game, pork and port wine pie or vegetable curry risotto (£4.75), baked smoked gammon (£5.25), spiced crab au gratin (£5.75), steak and mushroom crumble in Adnams ale (£6.75), and home-made puddings (£2.30). Well kept Adnams Best and Broadside, Burton Bridge Bitter and Festival, Sam Smiths OB and Woodfordes Wherry on handpump, and good range of wines and malt whiskies. Recent reports suggest service can be a little disorganised. There are picnic tables under cocktail parasols on the lawn, and they may serve food from an out-building here in summer. Blickling Hall is open from April to mid-October only, and closed Mondays and Thursdays, though you can walk through the park at any time. *(Recommended by Jerry and Alison Oakes, Tim and Sue Halstead, Wayne Brindle, John Wooll, June and Malcolm Farmer, Peter Plumridge, Paul Cartledge, Sue Demont, Tim Barrow, Thomas Nott)*

Free house ~ Licensees Danny and Wendy Keen ~ Real ale ~ Meals and snacks ~ Evening restaurant (not Sun or Mon) ~ (01263) 732133 ~ Children in restaurant ~ Open 11-3, 6-11 ~ Pianist in restaurant most winter Fri evenings ~ Three double bedrooms: £45S/£60S

BURNHAM MARKET TF8342 Map 8

Hoste Arms 🛏 🍷

The Green (B1155)

Norfolk Dining Pub of the Year

With its art gallery, sophisticated food, and well-thought-out music programme, this handsome 17th-c hotel is a long way from your average village local, but for those who like their pubs smart and civilised it's becoming hard to beat. Boldly redecorated this year, the convivial bars have massive log fires and a very relaxed, unstuffy feel; the panelled bar on the right has a series of watercolours showing local scenes of what you might see on various walks from the hotel, and there's a bow-windowed bar on the left. The excellent bar food is served in the front lounge, music room and conservatory, with a range of dishes such as soup (£2.75), pâté (£3.50), half-a-dozen local oysters (£4.75), pasta with tomato and mushroom sauce (£5.75), splendid honey glazed ham hock (£6), salmon and crab fish cake with a coconut and curry sauce (£6.25), Chinese seaweed and mushroom ball stir-fry (£6.50), chicken, leek and smoked bacon pie (£7), char-grilled poussin with a soft pepper and chilli salsa (£7.25), monkfish and king prawn brochette (£8.25), daily specials, and puddings (£2.95); a two-course evening meal in the restaurant is £15.75. One of the restaurants is no smoking; the owner may play the grand piano. Well kept Woodfordes Wherry, Ruddles County and a changing guest like Shepherd Neame Spitfire on handpump, good wine list (with lots by the glass or half bottle), decent choice of malt whiskies, and freshly squeezed orange juice; nice sitting room, and professional service by friendly staff. Morning coffee and afternoon tea in the conservatory. At the back is a pleasant walled garden with tables on a terrace. It can be busy at weekends. *(Recommended by Amanda Dauncey, J Rudolf, Stuart Earle, Stephen, Julie and Hayley Brown, Frank Gadbois, John Wooll, M J Morgan, Charles Bardswell, Wayne*

Brindle, David Culley, Brian Atkin, Iain Baillie, Peter and Pat Frogley, Mrs F M Halle, Mrs R Cotgreave, Alan Reid)

Free house ~ Licensees Pauline Osler, Paul Whittome ~ Real ale ~ Meals and snacks (till 10pm summer; set lunch only 25 Dec) ~ Restaurant ~ (01328) 738777 ~ Children welcome ~ Jazz Mon and Fri evenings ~ Open 11-11 ~ Bedrooms: £48/£66B

BURNHAM THORPE TF8541 Map 8

Lord Nelson

Village signposted from B1155 and B1355, near Burnham Market

Nelson knew this characterful old pub as the Plough, and held a party here before leaving the village to take command of his 64-gun ship the *Agamemnon* in 1793. There have been a few changes in the couple of years since the current friendly and enthusiastic licensees took over (a new kitchen and other sensitive upgradings), but nothing to spoil the place's unique atmosphere or appeal. Pictures and memorabilia of the Admiral line the walls, and there's no bar counter – just a small room with well waxed antique settles on the worn red flooring tiles, and smoke ovens in the original fireplace. A no-smoking eating room has flagstones, an open fire, and more pictures of the celebrated sailor. Straightforward bar food includes home-made soup (£1.80), sandwiches (from £1.70), sausage and egg (£3.10), English breakfast (£3.50), ploughman's (£3.80), salads (from £3.75), omelettes (from £3.80), a home-made pie of the day (£4.75), good vegetarian dishes, daily specials, and children's meals (from £2.50); briskly attentive waitress service. Well kept Greene King Abbot and IPA and Woodfordes Nelson's Revenge tapped from the cask in a back stillroom, and there's an unusual rum concoction called Nelson's Blood; shove-ha'penny, dominoes, draughts, chess, and piped music. Inside lavatories are planned, and they're keen to make the pub popular with families – a highchair is available, and there's a play area outside. *(Recommended by Bob Arnett, Judy Wayman, Peter and Pat Frogley, Stephen, Julie and Hayley Brown, Wayne Brindle, Alan Reid, Huw and Carolyn Lewis, Charles Bardswell, Bill Edwards, P G Plumridge)*

Greene King ~ Lease: Lucy Stafford ~ Real ale ~ Meals and snacks ~ (01328) 738241 ~ Children in separate family room ~ Live music once a month ~ Open 11-3, 6-11

CASTLE ACRE TF8115 Map 8

Ostrich £

Stocks Green; village signposted from A1065 N of Swaffham; OS Sheet 144 map reference 815153

Cheerful and unfussy, this reliable old place is the only pub on the ancient Peddars Way. Well placed on the tree-lined green, it was largely rebuilt in the 18th c, but still has some signs of its older origins, with exposed 16th-c masonry and beams and trusses in the high ceiling. The L-shaped, low-ceilinged front bar has a huge old fireplace with a swinging potyard below its low mantlebeam (which may be used in winter for cooking soups and hams), straightforward furnishings, and big photographs of the local sights on the walls; it may get a little smoky at busy times. Good value bar food includes sandwiches (from £1.20), pizzas (from £1.70), several ploughman's (from £2.50), plaice (£2.95), and grills (from £5), with specials like Cajun chicken; children's meals (from £1). The full range of Greene King beers is well kept on handpump; dominoes, cribbage, fruit machine, and piped music. Picnic tables in the sheltered garden, where they're developing a herb garden for use in the kitchen. There's a Cluniac monastery in the village, as well as the remains of a Norman castle. *(Recommended by Peter and Pat Frogley, Graham and Sandra Poll, Charles Bardswell, J R Williams, Dr and Mrs M Bailey, Sue Anderson, Phil Copleston, Wayne Brindle, R C Vincent, Michael Sargent, D Goodger, John and Elizabeth Gwynne)*

Greene King ~ Tenant Ray Wakelen ~ Real ale ~ Meals and snacks (till 10.30pm; not 25/26 Dec) ~ (01760) 755398 ~ Children in family room ~ Jazz every 2nd and 3rd Weds of month, Folk last Weds of month ~ Open 12-2.30, 7-11 ~ Bedrooms: £15S/£30S

CAWSTON TG1323 Map 8

Ratcatchers 🍷

Eastgate, 1 mile S of village; heading N from Norwich on B1149 turn left towards Haveringland at crossroads ½ mile before the B1145 turn to Cawston itself

This busy place offers some of the best food in the area, though as it increasingly sees itself as a restaurant you may not feel so comfortable coming for just a drink. All the meals are freshly prepared, with real effort put into their preparation – they bake their own bread, make their own herb oils, chutney, purées and stocks, and pickle their own samphire. There may be a 30-40 minute wait as everything is cooked to order, but it is worth it: the meals have won several national awards. The menu typically includes soups (£2.15), sandwiches (from £2.25), traditional Norfolk pork cheese (£2.95), smoked fillet of mackerel (£3.95), local butcher's sausages with home-made garlic bread (£4.55), ploughman's (£4.95), salads (from £5.45), over a dozen vegetarian dishes such as herb pancakes (£5.95), potato and onion thermidor (£6.45), or Indonesian stir-fry (£6.75), several pies like game or a good steak and kidney (£6.35), tagliatelli carbonara (£6.85), chicken breast flamed in brandy with black peppercorns (£8.95), steaks (from £9.95), big mixed grills (from £12.65; they need 24 hours' notice), excellent fresh fish from Billingsgate, daily specials like guinea fowl in a grape and white wine glaze (£7.95), smoked pike mousse with Scottish salmon steak in a chardonnay sauce (£8.35), or escalope of veal panfried with tiger prawns, mushrooms and vodka (£9.85), puddings including white belgian chocolate cheesecake (£4.65), and children's meals (£3.95); British cheese menu. It's pretty much essential to book most evenings, as they get very busy – service may slow down then. No credit cards. Three well kept real ales on handpump such as Adnams Extra, Bass and Hancocks HB, country wines, several malt whiskies; open fires, piped music. As well as the L-shaped beamed bar with its interesting solid wood tables and dining chairs bought at local auctions, there's a quieter and cosier no-smoking, candlelit dining room on the right. Bedrooms are planned for this spring. *(Recommended by Mrs B Lemon, H O Dickinson, Tom Thomas, P F Devitt, Peter and Pat Frogley, Tony Kemp, Rachel Weston, Wayne Brindle, Patrick Clancy, Mrs M E Parry-Jones, K D Day, Mr and Mrs J F Baskerville, John and Christine Simpson, Dr G W Barnett, Paul Cartledge)*

Free house ~ Licensees Eugene and Jill Charlier ~ Real ale ~ Meals and snacks (till 10pm) ~ Restaurant (not Sun evening) ~ (01603) 871430 ~ Children in eating area and restaurant ~ Open 11.45-2.30, 6-11; closed 25/26 Dec

CLEY NEXT THE SEA TG0443 Map 8

George & Dragon 🛏

Holt Road; off A149 W of Sheringham

This handsome Edwardian inn overlooks Cley Marshes and St George's Scrape – magic names for bird-watchers, as the salt-marsh sanctuary is rich in sightings of rarities, which are meticulously recorded in the sighting diary that has pride of place on a special lectern; the inn also has its own hide. There's a cosy bar much used by friendly locals, and a larger more comfortable lounge and dining area where most of the walkers, cyclists and bird-watchers seem to congregate – and where a plaque records the foundation of the Norfolk Naturalists' Trust in 1926. Lots of St George artefacts include a lively stained-glass window. Among the wide choice of carefully prepared bar food strong in local recipes, dishes which have recently been finding special favour with readers include cider-pickled herrings (£3.25), large crab salad (£5.50), fresh scampi (£5.50), steak and kidney pie (£5.50), lemon sole filled with crabmeat (£6.95), their speciality pan haggerty which is a Cumbrian dish of layered baked potatoes, cheese and onion served with bacon, sausage and tomatoes (£5.50) and two or three winter Sunday roasts (£5.50); smoked fish is treated imaginatively, and helpings are generous. Well kept Greene King IPA, Abbot and a Greene King seasonal ale on handpump, attentive polite staff. Across the rather busy road but well screened from it is an attractive and peaceful sizeable garden, with a boules pitch; the exit from the small car park can be a little unnerving. *(Recommended by S G MacSwiney, Mike and Heather Barnes, Noel Jackson, Louise Campbell, John Beeken, Peter and Pat Frogley, Eric Locker, R C Hopton)*

Free house ~ Rodney Sewell ~ Real ale ~ Meals and snacks ~ (01263) 740652 ~ Open 11-2.30, 6.30-11 ~ Bedrooms:£30/£40(£50B)

COLKIRK TF9126 Map 8

Crown 🍷

Village signposted off B1146 S of Fakenham; and off A1065

The buzz of cheerful conversation flows through this unpretentious and friendly red-brick building, and though you'll find a good few people eating, it's still very much a proper traditional village pub. Comfortable and welcoming, the public bar and small lounge both have open fires, solid straightforward country furniture, rugs and flooring tiles, and sympathetic lighting; the no-smoking dining room leading off is pleasantly informal. Good promptly served bar food includes lunchtime sandwiches (from £2) and ploughman's (£3.50), soup (£1.85), pâté (£2.95), herring fillets in a cream, madeira and caper sauce (£3.10), salads (from £4.50), goujons of haddock with a yoghurt dip or cheese-topped vegetable bake (£4.75), chicken in a wine and tarragon sauce (£5.95), steaks with a cream and peppercorn sauce (from £6.25), and daily specials such as devilled kidneys (£5.10), fruity pork curry (£5.25), or fresh crab salad (£5.50); they're starting to do more fresh fish. Well kept Greene King IPA, Abbot and Rayments on handpump, several malt whiskies, and a good range of wines – they'll happily open any bottle of wine you want from their list of several dozen, even for just a glass; friendly staff, helpful landlord. Darts, shove ha'penny, table skittles, cribbage, dominoes, fruit machine. What was the bowling green is now a garden extension to the sun-trap patio, with picnic table sets. *(Recommended by Rita and Keith Pollard, E M Goodman-Smith, Michael Sargent, Sue Anderson, Phil Copleston)*

Greene King ~ Tenant P Whitmore ~ Real ale ~ Meals and snacks (service stops at 1.30 on Sunday); not 25/26 Dec ~ (01328) 862172 ~ Children welcome until 9pm ~ Open 11-2.30, 6-11

DERSINGHAM TF6830 Map 8

Feathers

Manor Road; B1440 towards Sandringham

Readers enjoy sitting in the neatly landscaped garden of this handsome Jacobean inn, where there's a play area with swings, slide and a sand-pit. A small terrace overlooking here leads into the relaxed and characterful main bar, comfortably furnished with soft plush seats, wall settles, carved wooden chairs, and dark panelling and carving. One of the fireplaces, flanked by two brass warming pans, is still dominated by the Prince of Wales' feathers, as the pub was a favourite with the future Edward VII when he was visiting nearby Sandringham. Another bar is similarly furnished. The Adnams and Bass on handpump are joined by a weekly changing guest such as Uley Pigs Ear or Woodfordes Wherry, with maybe a couple more in summer. Generously served bar food includes sandwiches (from £1.25), soup (£1.50), ploughman's (£3.50), chicken and ham pie (£3.95), daily specials such as steak and beer pie or pork in cider sauce (£4.45), leek and stilton bake (£4.95), puddings (from £1.60), and children's meals (£1.60). Darts, pool, bar billiards, fruit machine, trivia, piped music. They can get busy in summer. *(Recommended by Geoffrey and Brenda Wilson, Wayne Brindle, Mark and Caroline Thistlethwaite, K H Frostick, Graham and Sandra Poll, John Wooll, Mrs F M Halle, John Mr and Mrs Ray, Eric Locker, Charles Bardswell, Rita Horridge, R C Vincent)*

Bass ~ Lease: Tony and Maxine Martin ~ Real ale ~ Meals and snacks (till 10pm) ~ Restaurant (not Sun evening) ~ (01485) 540207 ~ Children welcome ~ Open 11-2.30, 5.30-11; closed evening Dec 25 ~ Bedrooms: £25/£40

ERPINGHAM TG1631 Map 8

Saracens Head

Address is Wolterton – not shown on many maps; Erpingham signed off A140 N of Aylsham, keep on through Calthorpe, then where road bends right take the straight-ahead turn-off signposted Wolterton

The landlord of this remote and civilised redbrick inn clearly enjoys putting the meals together, and his enthusiasm has this year once again prompted a good few letters of unstinting praise. While it's the excellent food that readers like best, they also appreciate the warm welcome, and the fact that success in the kitchen hasn't encouraged the place to abandon its pubby roots. The regularly changing menu might include duck and orange soup (£2.50), goose and apple pâté (£3.50), splendid Morston mussels in cider and cream or delicious deep-fried brie and apricot sauce (£3.95), braised pigeon in a fruity sauce (£5.95), grilled fillet of large local trout (£7.25), stir-fry white fish with orange and ginger (£6.75), vine leaves stuffed with goat's cheese and tomato sauce (£6.95), wok-sizzled medallions of wild venison with rosemary and sherry (£8.25), and puddings like sticky brown bread and butter pudding or lemon tart (£2.50); two-course lunches (£4.50), two-course Sunday supper (£5.50), and three-course monthly feasts (£11.50); booking is almost essential. The two-room bar is simple and stylish, with high ceilings and tall windows giving a feeling of space, though it's not large, and around the terracotta walls are a mix of seats from built-in leather wall settles to wicker fireside chairs, solid-colour carpets and curtains, log fires and flowers on the mantlepieces. It looks out on a charming old-fashioned gravel stableyard with picnic tables; they plan to add a bar for light snacks out here. There's a pretty little four-table parlour on the right – cheerful nursery colours, and another big log fire. Very well kept Adnams and a guest beer such as Felinfoel Double Dragon, Morland Old Speckled Hen, or Morrells Varsity on handpump; decent malt whiskies. The wine list is developing rather interestingly, with some shipped direct from a French chateau; friendly service. There isn't a designated no-smoking area, but ashtrays have to be requested. ***(Recommended by John and Moira Cole, Rita Horridge, Anthony Barnes, Stephen, Julie and Hayley Brown, Paul Craddoug, Richard Dolphin, Mr and Mrs Duncan, John and Tessa Rainsford, Peter and Pat Frogley, John and Christine Simpson, BHP, Mrs D Morton, Sue Demont, Tim Barrow, Dr and Mrs M Bailey, Charles Bardswell, Thomas Nott, Nick and Carolyn Carter)***

Free house ~ Licensee Robert Dawson-Smith ~ Real ale ~ Meals and snacks ~ (01263) 768909 ~ Well behaved children welcome ~ Occasional jazz nights ~ Open 11-3, 6-11; closed 25 Dec ~ Bedrooms: £35B/£50B

HOLKHAM TF8943 Map 8

Victoria

A149 on Burnham Overy Staithe—Wells-next-the-Sea rd; near Holkham Hall

Tables on the front corner terrace of this well-run brick-and-flint inn look across the neat flower-fringed front lawn to the rich coastal pastures beyond the road. Handy for both Holkham Hall and the sandy shores and nature reserves, the pub has several homely communicating rooms, simply furnished with leatherette wall banquettes, stools and dining chairs, plants and paintings, and in one room some easy chairs; a separate comfortable lounge has seats in bay windows. Well kept Ansells, Greene King IPA and Tetleys on handpump. Bar food includes sandwiches, ploughman's (from £3.50), steak and kidney pie or fresh crab salad (£4.95), Holkham fish pie (£5.25), fresh fish like sole, cod, halibut or plaice (from £5.95), and steaks (from £8.95); dominoes, cribbage, piped music. There are more tables behind in the former tiled stableyard. ***(Recommended by Anthony Barnes, Mike and Heather Barnes, Charles Bardswell, Mr and Mrs R O Gibson, Peter and Pat Frogley, S G MacSwiney)***

Free house ~ Lease: Peter Hoskins ~ Real ale ~ Meals and snacks ~ Restaurant (not Sun evening) ~ (01328) 710469 ~ Children in restaurant ~ Open 11-3, 6-11; all day Sat ~ Bedrooms: £25B/50B

HUNWORTH TG0635 Map 8

Hunny Bell

Village signposted off B roads S of Holt

Easily identified by its unusual sign, this reliable pub overlooks the village green. The cosy L-shaped bar has windsor chairs around dark wooden tables, comfortable settees (some of which are grouped around the log fire) and Norfolk watercolours and pictures for sale hanging above the panelling dado; one room is no smoking. Well kept Adnams Best, Greene King Abbot and Woodfordes Wherry on handpump, quite a few malt whiskies, and decent wines. Bar food includes sandwiches (from £1.75), soup (£2), home-made pâté (£2.50), ploughman's (£3), local sausages (£3.75), salads (from £4.25), home-made steak and kidney pie or home-cooked ham and egg (£4.50), vegetable lasagne (£4.75), daily specials, evening steaks (from £8.50), puddings (from £2), and children's meals (£2.50). Darts, dominoes, cribbage and piped music. The garden is an especially pleasant place to sit on a nice day, when there's bar service to the tables on the lawn; children's play area and maybe weekend barbecues. Sally King's father runs the Kings Head at Letheringsett. *(Recommended by Charles Bardswell, John and Elizabeth Guynne, Peter and Pat Frogley, Wayne Brindle)*

Free house ~ Licensees Sally and Thomas King ~ Real ale ~ Meals and snacks (12-2, 6-9) ~ Restaurant ~ (01263) 712300 ~ Children in eating areas and separate room during food hours ~ Occasional live music ~ Open 11-3, 5.30-11

KINGS LYNN TF6220 Map 8

Tudor Rose

St Nicholas St (just off Tuesday Market Place – main square)

The snug little front bar of this half-timbered former nunnery is probably the most atmospheric place for a drink in the town centre, with the friendly staff and chatty customers generating a very relaxed and cosy feel. Delightfully old-fashioned, it has high beams, reproduction squared panelling, a big wrought-iron wheelrim chandelier, and newspapers to read. The quite separate back bar is more spacious, and has sturdy wall benches, video games, trivia, fruit machine and juke box. Good value bar food includes soup (£1.60), sandwiches or tasty home-made hoagies (from £1.50), stilton and leek bake (£2.75), ploughman's (£3.75), home-made chilli (£3.95), Greek salad (£4.95), home-cooked ham and egg (£3.50), steak and kidney pie (£5.50), sirloin steak (£7.50), and puddings like delicious treacle tart. Well kept Bass, Boddingtons, Woodfordes Wherry and a guest beer on handpump, a fine choice of whiskies, and decent wines. The upstairs raftered restaurant is no smoking. There are seats in the garden. Bedrooms are simple and modern but comfortable, and some have a pretty view of St Nicholas's Chapel. *(Recommended by R C Vincent, Ron Leigh, John Wooll, Anna Marsh, Rita Horridge)*

Free house ~ Licensees John and Andrea Bull ~ Real ale ~ Meals and snacks ~ Restaurant ~ (01553) 762824 ~ Children in eating area of bar and in restaurant ~ Maybe summer live music every two weeks ~ Open 11-11 ~ Bedrooms: £38.50B/£50B

LETHERINGSETT TG0538 Map 8

Kings Head

A148 just W of Holt

The unusually shrill voice you might hear on the way into this consistently friendly country pub belongs to the talking parrot who stands guard over the entrance hall. The walls of the bar are decorated with various interesting prints, pictures and other items, including a signed poem by John Betjeman, and you may come across two decorative cats (the white one is called Harrold). There's also a small plush lounge, and a separate games room with darts, pool, shove ha'penny, dominoes, cribbage, fruit machines, and piped music. Reasonably priced bar food includes sandwiches (from £2, toasties £2.75), filled baked potatoes (£3), ploughman's (£3.25), salads (from £4.50, local crab in season £4.75), home-cooked ham or home-made steak and kidney pie (£4.75), vegetable tikka masala (£5), and evening steaks (from £8.50); children's meals (£2.75), and a good Sunday lunch (£4.95). Well kept Adnams, Bass, Greene King IPA and Abbot and Shepherd Neame Spitfire on handpump, a dozen malt whiskies, and good service. The spacious lawn has plenty of tables, and is quite attractive on a sunny day. Not far from an interesting water mill, the pub is in a very pleasant setting opposite a church with an unusual round tower. Dogs allowed. *(Recommended by John Wooll, Bill Edwards, Rita Horridge, R C Vincent)*

Free house ~ Lease: Thomas King ~ Real ale ~ Meals and snacks ~ Restaurant (not Sun evening) ~ (01263) 712691 ~ Children in eating area at meal times ~ Middle-of-the-road live music Mon ~ Open 11-11

MUNDFORD TL8093 Map 5

Crown

Crown Street; village signposted off A1065 Thetford—Swaffham

On the quiet village square, this attractive 17th-c former posting inn has a huge open fireplace in a flint wall in its cosy beamed lounge bar, which has captain's chairs around highly polished tables, interesting local advertisements and other memorabilia, and a very relaxed and welcoming atmosphere. A spiral iron staircase with *Vanity Fair* cartoons beside it leads up to the club room (a useful overflow if the pub is unusually busy) as well as the recently redone garden and terrace – and brings the food down from the upstairs kitchen. The varying, good, modestly priced choice might include superb soups such as smoked chicken and almond (£1.75), good sandwiches (from £1.50), burgers (from £2), hot butterfly prawns (£3.25), a warm pigeon breast and bacon salad with toasted pine nuts and a raspberry dressing (£3.75), gravadlax (£3.95), mushroom pancake with proper chips and a salad (£4.50), steak and kidney pie (£5.50), stir-fried vegetables with sherry and oyster sauce and crisped aubergine slices (£8.95), braised brill, salmon and scallops (£10.95) and a formidable mixed grill (£11.95). Puddings (from £2.20) are quite something, and the cheeses (£2.95) excellent. The attractive restaurant is also upstairs. There are more heavy beams in the separate red-tiled locals' bar on the left, which has cast-iron-framed tables, another smaller brick fireplace with a copper hood, sensibly placed darts, dominoes, fruit machine, a juke box and a screened-off pool table. Well kept John Smiths, Sam Smiths OB, Websters Yorkshire, Woodfordes Wherry and (from the new local Iceni Brewery) Boadicia and daunting Deidree of the Sorrows; good choice of malt whiskies, decent house wines (including a barsac by the glass); cheerful service. *(Recommended by P Devitt, Charles Bardswell, Francine Dupre, Jane and Mike Blanckenhagen, Sue Demont, Tim Barrow, Andy Mottram, C E Power, Frank Cummins, Frank Davidson)*

Free house ~ Licensee Barry Walker~ Real ale ~ Meals and snacks ~ Restaurant ~ (01842) 878233 ~ Children welcome ~ Open 11-11 ~ Bedrooms:£29.50B/£45B

NORTH CREAKE TF8538 Map 8

Jolly Farmers

B1355 N of Fakenham

The landlord at this welcoming village pub can't stand the sight of gnomes, so you'll usually find about 40 of them stealthily imported by customers to torment him; one cheeky little chap they used as a doorstop last summer seemed in desperate need of a new belt. The two cheerful and homely small bars have a relaxed, chatty atmosphere (there's no piped music), a winter open fire, displays of dried flowers in summer, and a good mix of locals and visitors. Good quality home-made bar food includes lunchtime filled rolls (from £1.75), home-made pâté (£2.75), ploughman's (£3.75), steak, kidney and ale pie (£5.15), chicken breast with wine, parsley, tomato, onions and garlic (£6.75), pork in cider and cream (£6.95), sirloin steak (£9.25), several well-prepared fresh fish dishes (some supplied direct from the fishermen at Wells), and usually a couple of Thai specials; they have a Thai buffet on Wednesday evenings. Well kept Bass, Greene King Abbot and IPA and Ind Coope Burton on handpump or tapped from the cask, decent wines; service is friendly, attentive and efficient. Bar billiards, cribbage, dominoes, and fruit machine; tables in sheltered garden. The flintstone village is charming. *(Recommended by Mr and Mrs K Tidy, Rita and Keith Pollard, John Wooll, John Beeken, Charles Bardswell)*

Pubmaster (Allied) ~ Tenant Peter Whitney ~ Real ale ~ Meals and snacks (not Mon lunch, or winter Mon evenings ~ Restaurant ~ (01328) 738185 ~ Children in eating area of bar ~ Open 11.30-2.30(3 Sat), 6.30-11

NORWICH TG2308 Map 5

Adam & Eve

Bishopgate; follow Palace Street from Tombland N of the Cathedral

The striking Dutch gables here were added in the 14th and 15th c, but the pub itself is much older, thought to date back to at least 1249, when it was a brewhouse for the workmen building the cathedral; their pay consisted of bread and beer, a simple but practical minimum wage. Prettily decked out in summer with award-winning tubs and hanging baskets, this is a cosy, characterful place, perhaps at its best at lunchtimes when lawyers, clerks and defendants from the neighbouring law courts fill the old-fashioned little rooms with a good cheery bustle. The traditionally furnished bars are said to be haunted by a number of ghosts (including Lord Sheffield, hacked to death close by in a 16th-c peasant rebellion), though more substantial features include antique high-backed settles, one handsomely carved, cushioned benches built into partly panelled walls, and tiled or parquet floors; the snug room is no smoking. Well-liked generously served bar food includes sandwiches, granary baps or filled french bread (from £1.65, excellent prawn £2.50), cheese and ale soup with a pastry top (£2.80), ploughman's (from £3.20), salads (from £3.65), shepherd's pie (£3.80), vegetable pie (£3.85), pork casseroled in cider and rosemary (£4.10), game pie (£4.20), puddings like home-made spicy bread and butter pudding (from £1.90), and daily specials such as steak and kidney pie, chicken breasts with almond and apricot, or tiger prawns wrapped in filo pastry (£4.55); very good Sunday roasts (£4.55), with five vegetables. Well kept Adnams, John Smiths, Morlands Old Speckled Hen, Ruddles County, and Wadworths 6X on handpump or tapped from the cask, a wide range of malt whiskies, quite a few decent wines by the glass or bottle, and Addlestones cider; there's a fine range of pewter tankards above the serving counter. An outside terrace has seats. *(Recommended by Sarah and Gary Goldson, Neil O'Callaghan, John T Ames, Anthony Barnes, John and Christine Lowe, John Wooll, Nick and Alison Dowson, R C Morgan, Andrew and Catherine Brian, Ian Phillips, Pat Carlen, Michael Badcock, Thomas Nott)*

Courage ~ Lease: Colin Burgess ~ Real ale ~ Meals and snacks (12-7) ~ (01603) 667423 ~ Children in eating area of bar ~ Open 11-11

REEDHAM TG4101 Map 5

Ferry

B1140 Beccles—Acle; the ferry here holds only two cars but goes back and forth continuously till 10pm, taking only a minute or so to cross – fare £2 per car, 25p pedestrians

It's been a busy year at this splendidly-placed Broads pub – they've refurbished the bar, replaced the roof, extended the kitchens and added a new restaurant area, all signs of its growing popularity. The ideal approach is by boat, either on the interesting working chain ferry or on a holiday hire boat; there are very good moorings (and showers for boaters). Plenty of well spaced tables on the terrace look out over the River Yare and all its traffic, whether that be colourful yachts, graceful swans or even the occasional wherry. The highly praised and generously served bar food might include sandwiches (from £1.40), game soup (£2.30), poached egg Florentine (£2.50), ploughman's (£3.95), stuffed vine leaves in red pepper sauce or lamb's kidneys (£5.25), home-made curry (£5.50), half a local pheasant (£5.85), prawns poached in a white wine, tomato, herb and cream sauce (£5.95), grilled lamb noisettes (£7.95), steaks (from £9.95), fresh fish from Lowestoft, and children's meals (from £2); excellent vegetables. The restaurant is no smoking. Well kept Adnams Best and Broadside, Woodforde's Wherry, and a guest like Charles Wells Eagle on handpump, quite a few malt whiskies, country wines, and good cheerful staff. Cool and relaxing even on the hottest day, the secluded back bar has antique rifles, copper and brass, and a fine log fire, while in the long front bar comfortable banquettes line the big picture windows, and there are robust rustic tables carved from slabs of tree-trunk; cribbage, dominoes, fruit machine, video game and piped music. They're well geared up for families, with arrangements for baby food, and changing facilities. The woodturners shop next door is worth a look. *(Recommended by David Nicholls, D Goodger, Geoffrey and Brenda Wilson, David and Julie Glover, Bronwen and Steve Wrigley, Sarah and Gary Goldson, Mrs M A Kilner, Tina and David Woods-Taylor, Mrs D Morton, Dennis and Margaret Kilner)*

Free house ~ Licensee David Archer ~ Real ale ~ Meals and snacks (till 10) ~ Restaurant ~ (01493) 700429 ~ Children welcome ~ Open 11-3, 6.30-11; 11-2.30, 7-11 in winter

RINGSTEAD TF7040 Map 8

Gin Trap

Village signposted off A149 near Hunstanton; OS Sheet 132 map reference 707403

A handsome spreading chestnut tree shelters the car park of this attractive white-painted pub. Copper kettles, carpenters' tools, cartwheels, and bottles hang from the beams in the lower part of the well-kept and friendly bar, there are toasting forks above an open fire (which has dried flowers in summer), a couple of man-traps ingeniously converted to electric candle-effect wall lights, and captain's chairs and cast-iron-framed tables on the green-and-white patterned motif carpet. A small no-smoking dining room has quite a few chamber pots suspended from the ceiling, and high-backed pine settles; you can book a table in here. Well kept Adnams, Bass, Greene King Abbot, Woodfordes Nog and a beer brewed by Woodfordes for the pub on handpump; freshly squeezed orange juice; efficient happy staff. Decent bar food includes lunchtime sandwiches (£1.75), ploughman's (from £3), nut cutlet (£3.95), home-made steak and kidney pie or lasagne (£5), steaks (from £8.25), daily specials, mainly home-made puddings (£2.40), and children's meals (from £1.75); there may be nibbles on the bar counter on Sunday lunchtimes. The walled back garden has seats on the grass or small paved area and pretty flowering tubs. The pub is close to the Peddar's Way; hikers and walkers are welcome, but not their muddy boots. There's an art gallery next door, and boules in the back car park. *(Recommended by John Wooll, M J Morgan, J F Doleman, R C Vincent, Graham and Sandra Poll, Amanda Dauncey, J Rudolf, David Eberlin, John Beeken, Peter and Pat Frogley, L Walker, Charles Bardswell, Dave Braisted)*

Free house ~ Brian and Margaret Harmes ~ Real ale ~ Meals and snacks (not winter Sun evenings) ~ (01485) 525264 ~ Well-behaved children welcome in dining room and eating area until 9pm ~ Occasional piano player ~ Open 11.30-2.30, 6.30(7 winter)-11; closed 25 Dec

SCOLE TM1579 Map 5

Scole Inn ★

A140 just N of A143

Over the centuries this stately old coaching inn has provided shelter for people such as Charles II and Nelson, as well as less celebrated figures who had to make do with the famous round bed that could sleep up to 30 at a time. With its magnificently rounded Dutch gables, it's a fascinating building with a real sense of history –

though you have to use your imagination to visualise the notorious local highwayman John Belcher riding his horse up the huge oak staircase to shelter from the law. There are several magnificent fireplaces (even one in the ladies' lavatory), and the high-beamed lounge bar has a 17th-c iron-studded oak door, antique settles, and leather-cushioned seats and benches around oak refectory tables on its turkey carpets. The bare-boarded public bar has stripped high-backed settles and kitchen chairs around oak tables. Bar food includes sandwiches (from £1.55), pitta bread filled with chicken satay or sausage and bacon (£3.25), stir-fry (£5.75), and steak and kidney pie (£5.95). Well kept Adnams Best and Broadside, and a changing guest on handpump; cribbage, dominoes, and piped music. The completion of the local bypass this spring should reduce the traffic noise a couple of readers have noticed.
(Recommended by Gwen and Peter Andrews, Wayne Brindle, R C Morgan, V and E A Bolton, Rita Horridge, Derek and Sylvia Stephenson, Eric and Jackie Robinson, Ian Phillips)

Free house ~ Licensee Norman Jones ~ Real ale ~ Meals and snacks (till 10pm) ~ Restaurant ~ (01379) 740481 ~ Children welcome ~ Open 11-11 ~ Bedrooms: £52B/£66B

SNETTISHAM TF6834 Map 8

Rose & Crown ★ 🍷

Village signposted from A149 bypass S of Heacham; pub in Old Church Rd just S of centre

The colourful garden of this pretty white cottage is particularly attractive, with picnic tables among the flowering shrubs, and two spectacular willow trees. The new licensees have extended and improved the adjoining adventure playground, and added cages of guinea pigs and parakeets to entertain children. They plan a few changes inside as well, though nothing to alter the particularly welcoming and traditional feel of the four bustling bars. The cosy locals' bar at the back has perhaps the nicest atmosphere, along with tapestried seats around cast-iron-framed tables, and a big log fire. At the front is an old-fashioned beamed bar with lots of carpentry and farm tools, cushioned black settles on the red tiled floor, and a great pile of logs by the fire in the vast fireplace (which has a gleaming black japanned side oven). There's also an airy carpeted room with plush seats around tables with matching tablecloths, and pictures for sale on the wall, and an extensive family room, which they hope to improve over the next few months; two areas are no smoking. Tasty bar food might include soup (£1.95), ploughman's (£3.75), open sandwiches (£3.50), leek, stilton and potato bake (£4.75), tagliatelli carbonara (£4.95), vegetable curry (£5.25), beef and Guinness pie (£6.50), steaks (from £8.50), daily specials such as pork in yoghurt or lemon sole filled with seafood and crab, and children's meals. They now have five real ales on handpump, Adnams Bitter and Broadside, Bass, and two changing guests, and their 20 or so wines are all available by the glass; also freshly squeezed orange juice, and afternoon teas. Friendly, helpful service.
(Recommended by John Wooll, M J Morgan, Chris and Richard Potts, JKW, Roger Byrne, Wayne Brindle, David Eberlin, Charles Bardswell, Stephen and Jean Curtis, D Grzelka, Neil and Ruth Walden, Margaret and Roy Randle, Andrew and Catherine Brian, Mrs J Barwell)

Free house ~ Licensees Anthony Goodrich and Annette Smith ~ Real ale ~ Meals and snacks ~ Restaurant (not Sun evening) ~ (01485) 541382 ~ Children in restaurant and garden room ~ Twice-monthly jazz in winter ~ Open 11-11; 11-3, 5-11 winter weekdays ~ Bedrooms: £35B/£50B

STIFFKEY TF9743 Map 8

Red Lion

A149 Wells—Blakeney

A popular pub in an unspoilt village, across the road from a stream with ducks and swans. The oldest parts of the happy, chatty bar have a few beams, aged flooring tiles or bare floorboards, open fires, a mix of pews, small settles, built-in wooden wall seats and a couple of stripped high-backed settles, a nice old long deal table among quite a few others, and oil-type or lantern wall lamps. Big helpings of good, well presented bar food such as sandwiches, soup (£2.20), soft herring roes (£3.35), chicken liver parfait (£3.75), steak and kidney pie (£4.95), salads (£5.25), a daily pasta dish (£6.50), steaks (from £8.15), excellent fresh fish specials, and children's meals (from £1.95). Well kept Greene King Abbot, Woodfordes Wherry and a couple of guest beers on handpump or tapped from the cask; friendly and efficient staff. A games room, detached from the main building, has darts, cribbage and dominoes. The back restaurant leads into a conservatory, and there are wooden seats and tables out on a back gravel terrace, and on grass further up beyond. Some pleasant walks nearby. *(Recommended by John Beeken, J Honnor, Derek and Sylvia Stephenson, Paul Craddock, Jenny and Michael Back, Rita Horridge, Sarah King, Partrick Forbest, Charles Bardswell, Peter and Pat Frogley, BHP, Walter Reid, Roy Bromell)*

Free house ~ Manager Jo Wishart ~ Real ale ~ Meals and snacks ~ (01328) 830552 ~ Children in eating area ~ Live blues Fri evenings ~ Open 11-3(2.30 in winter), 6(7 winter)-11

STOW BARDOLPH TF6205 Map 5

Hare Arms 🍷

Just off A10 N of Downham Market

Chicken and peacocks wander around outside this bustling country pub, which is rapidly becoming quite a favourite with some readers. Very welcoming and congenial, the comfortable old bar, decorated with old advertising signs and fresh flowers, has plenty of tables around its central servery, and a good log fire; two ginger cats and a sort of tabby wander round socialising. It opens into a spacious heated and well planted no-smoking conservatory, and that in turn opens into a pretty garden with picnic tables under cocktail parasols. Very well presented and tasty bar food includes sandwiches, good home-made pâté, mussel chowder (£2.75), vegetarian pancakes (£5.25), and a wide range of changing hot dishes such as fresh skate in caper butter, lamb and apricot pie, sea bream and yellow pepper sauce, chicken breast wrapped in oak-smoked bacon in an asparagus sauce, or beef olives in red wine gravy (all £5.75); fresh fish and local game are particular specialities. Friendly, efficient service. Well kept Greene King IPA, Abbot, and Rayments on handpump, good range of wines and malt whiskies, and maybe cockles and whelks on the bar counter; fruit machine. The friendly licensees will soon have been here for 20 years. *(Recommended by John Wooll, M J Morgan, Stephen, Julie and Hayley Brown, Mark Hydes, Tom Thomas, Wayne Brindle, Gordon Tong, Caroline McAleese, Richard Dolphin, Charles Bardswell, Basil J S Minson, Alan Reid, Rita Horridge, John and Sally Clarke, S G MacSwiney, V and E A Bolton, Thomas Nott, Brian and Jill Bond)*

Greene King ~ Tenants Trish and David McManus ~ Real ale ~ Meals and snacks (till 10pm) ~ Restaurant (not Sun evening) ~ (01366) 382229 ~ Children in conservatory ~ Open 11-2.30, 6-11; closed 25/26 Dec

SWANTON MORLEY TG0117 Map 8

Darbys 🍺

B1147 NE of Dereham

The farming background of the owners of this cosy beamed country pub shows in the agricultural equipment and gin traps around the bar, and in the tractor seats which line the long, attractive serving counter. It's a cheery place, with friendly locals and good food, but stands out especially for its excellent range of perfectly kept real ales: Adnams Bitter and Broadside, Woodfordes Wherry and Mardlers Mild, and four unusual changing guests from all around the country. There are fresh flowers on the pine tables, and a good log fire (with the original bread oven alongside). Generous helpings of enjoyable bar food like shellfish chowder with coconut (£2.50), filled baguettes (from £2.95), garlic and stilton mushrooms or ploughman's (£3.75), blue cheese and vegetable pasta bake (£4.85), venison and turkey pie

(£6.25), steamed chicken breast with a cockle, prawn, cashew and whisky sauce (£6.50), steak and kidney pudding (£7.50), and puddings such as chocolate, fruit and nut slice or lemon crunch flan (£2.25); the dining room is no smoking. The staff stay friendly and helpful even when they're busy, and there are two dogs, a labrador and a border collie; darts, dominoes, cribbage, piped music, children's room with toy box, and challenging play area out in the garden. The bedrooms are in carefully converted farm buildings, and there's plenty to do if you're staying – the family also own the adjoining 720-acre estate, and can arrange clay pigeon shooting, golf, fishing, nature trails, and craft instruction. *(Recommended by Jenny and Michael Back, Graham and Sandra Poll, Ruben Brage, J Cox, R C Vincent)*

Free house ~ Licensee John Carrick ~ Real ale ~ Meals and snacks (till 9.45) ~ Restaurant (not Sun evening) ~ (01362) 637647 ~ Children welcome ~ Open 11-2.30, 6-11; 11-11 Sat; closed evening 25 Dec ~ Bedrooms: £18(£20B)/£36(£40B)

THOMPSON TL9196 Map 5

Chequers

Griston Road; village signposted off A1075 Thetford—Watton; OS Sheet 144 map reference 923969

An American reader was particularly pleased to find this attractive 14th-c thatched pub in the Guide – she lived here in her early childhood, and seeing the entry brought back lots of memories. Nicely placed off the beaten track in good walking country, it has benches, flower tubs and wall baskets outside, and a large garden with picnic tables and a children's play area. Inside, the three main rooms have crooked oak wall timbers completely covered with original brass and copper artefacts, farming tools, Victorian corkscrews and boot-scrapers and so forth, plenty of exposed beams, genuinely old wheelback and spindleback chairs, and uncommonly low doors and ceilings (one is only five feet high so do watch your head). At one end there's an antique-filled dining bar with a high gabled ceiling and an inglenook fireplace; the small snug is a family room. Bar food – not really the pub's main draw – includes sandwiches (from £1.75), soup (£1.95), filled baked potatoes (from £2.75), home-made mackerel pâté (£2.75), big ploughman's (from £3.50), vegetable chilli (£3.75), home-made steak and kidney pie (£4.25), a daily special, and a big mixed grill (£7.50). Well kept Adnams, Ind Coope Burton, Tetleys, Woodfordes Wherry, and two guests on handpump, local farm cider; dominoes, cribbage. *(Recommended by Mr and Mrs Jones, Wayne Brindle, G E Rich, L Walker, Margaret Drazin, Mrs D Morton, Mick Hitchman, Frank Cummins, M and J Back, Derek and Sylvia Stephenson, V and E A Bolton)*

Free house ~ Licensees Bob and Wendy Rourke ~ Real ale ~ Meals and snacks (till 10pm) ~ (01953) 483360 ~ Children welcome ~ Open 11-3, 6-11

THORNHAM TF7343 Map 8

Lifeboat

Turn off A149 by Kings Head, then take first left turn

This old favourite seems to have been going through a rocky patch recently, but we're optimistic that the worst is over. It's perhaps at its best in winter, when the rooms are moodily lit with antique paraffin lamps, and five warming fires keep out the chill from the remote coastal sea flats. The chatty main bar has low settles, window seats, pews, and carved oak tables on the rugs on the tiled floor, great oak beams hung with traps and yokes, shelves of china, and masses of guns, swords, black metal mattocks, reed-slashers and other antique farm tools. Under the new licensee bar food includes sandwiches (from £2.25), home-made soup (£2.50), pork and chicken liver pâté (£3.75), ploughman's (£4.75), 6oz burger (£6.75), half chicken with barbecue sauce (£7.50), 10oz rib-eye steak (£9.95), daily specials such as fresh fish, and children's meals (£2.95). Adnams, Greene King IPA and Abbot, and Woodfordes Wherry on handpump, and local farm cider. Up some steps from the simple conservatory is a terrace with picnic tables, a climbing frame, and a slide. *(Recommended by M E A Horler,*

Jane Kinsbury, John Wooll, Eric Locker, R Clarke, David Culley, M J Morgan, Alastair Campbell, Alan Reid, Sarah King, Patrick Forbest, Charles Bardswell, Les and Jean Scott, Col A H N Reade, Ingrid Abma, Andrew Langbar, Dave and Carole Jones, Peter and Pat Frogley, Dave Braisted, Mr and Mrs Graham, Mrs J Barwell; more reports please)

Free house ~ Licensee Stephen Carter ~ Real ale ~ Meals and snacks (till 10pm) ~ Restaurant ~ (01485) 512236 ~ Children welcome ~ Open 11-11 ~ Bedrooms: £40B/£65B

TITCHWELL TF7543 Map 8

Manor Hotel

A149 E of Hunstanton

Readers do enjoy visiting this comfortable hotel, very handy for the nearby RSPB reserve, and looking out over the coastal flats to the sea. The tranquil lounge has chintzy sofas, magazines, an open fire, and a good naturalists' record of the wildlife in the reserve, while a small bar opening off this has attractive patterned beige wallpaper, grey plush wall banquettes, small round tables, Impressionist prints, and another open fire. Over on the right is a room rather like a farmhouse kitchen with pine furniture, a welsh dresser with unusual mustards and pickles on it, and a collection of baskets and bric-a-brac. There's also a pretty no-smoking restaurant with french windows that open on to a sizeable and sheltered neatly kept lawn with sturdy white garden seats. A sensibly short range of good bar food, served in the pine room, might include sandwiches, soup (£2.95), very good oysters from the creek (85p each, or in winter poached with white wine, garlic and cream £5.95), carrot and nut roast (£6.95), home-made steak and kidney pie or prawn curry (£7.95), fillet of seabass with hollandaise sauce (£8.95), specials such as crab salad (£4.95) or lobster thermidor (£17.95), and children's meals (£3.95). Greene King IPA and Abbot on handpump; particularly helpful and pleasant licensees and staff. Lots of good walks and footpaths nearby. *(Recommended by M J Morgan, Mr and Mrs R O Gibson, Miles and Deborah Protter, Charles Bardswell, Les and Jean Scott, John and Sally Clarke)*

Free house ~ Licensees Ian and Margaret Snaith ~ Real ale ~ Meals and snacks ~ Restaurant (not Sun evening) ~ (01485) 210221 ~ Children welcome ~ Open 12-3, 6-11 ~ Bedrooms: £39B/£78B

TIVETSHALL ST MARY TM1686 Map 5

Old Ram

Ipswich Rd; A140 15 miles S of Norwich

Well run and consistently reliable, this carefully refurbished 17th-c inn is a popular place to come for a good meal. Service is flexible and unflustered, and the food well cooked and very generously served. The wide choice of dishes includes filled rolls (from £2.25), ploughman's (£4.95), burgers (from £5.25), salads (from £6.50), home-made steak and kidney pie or aubergine and mushroom bake (£6.50), big cod fillet in home-made batter (£7.50), gammon (£8.50), daily specials such as pork ribs (£8.50), skate in caper butter sauce (£8.95), or duck in an orange and cointreau sauce (£10.95), steaks (from £10.95), and formidable puddings (from £2.75). Well kept Adnams, Ruddles County, Websters and Woodfordes Ram on handpump, decent house wines, several malt whiskies, and freshly squeezed orange juice; unobtrusive fruit machine and piped music. The spacious main room, ringed by cosier side areas, has standing-timber dividers, stripped beams and brick floors, a longcase clock, antique craftsmen's tools on the ceiling, and a huge log fire in the brick hearth; other rooms ramble off and there are pretty lamps and fresh flowers. An attractive, no-smoking dining room with an open woodburning stove and big sentimental engravings leads to another comfortable dining room and gallery, with Victorian copper and brassware. Seats on the sheltered, flower-filled terrace and lawn behind. No dogs. Well-liked by families, this is very much a dining pub – there aren't many tables or stools for drinkers. *(Recommended by Frank Davidson, Hazel Morgan, B Horner, Evelyn and Derek Walter, V and E A Bolton, Jan and Peter Shopland, John C Baker)*

Free house ~ Licensee John Trafford ~ Real ale ~ Meals and snacks (from 7.30 for breakfast – non-residents welcome – till 10pm); not 25/26 Dec ~ (01379) 676794 ~ Children in eating area of bar but under 7s must leave by 8pm ~ Open 11-11; closed 25/26 Dec ~ Bedrooms: £43B/£61B

UPPER SHERINGHAM TG1441 Map 8

Red Lion

B1157; village signposted off A148 Cromer—Holt, and the A149 just W of Sheringham

Doing well under its current licensees, this little flint cottage is delightfully simple, but very relaxing and comfortable, and since they took on their new chef reports on the food have been unanimously enthusiastic. They use home-grown herbs and fruit, fish is local, and the rabbits and pheasant are caught in the woodland behind the pub. Typical dishes might include Morston moules marinières (£2.95), spicy baked fresh cromer crab (£5.25), chicken breast with honey and mushrooms (£5.65), lamb's kidneys in wholegrain mustard sauce (£5.75), and puddings like treacle tart or apple crumble (£1.95); they do a good Sunday roast (£5.75), as well as three-course Wednesday evening feasts, and monthly fish nights. Well kept Adnams Best, Greene King Abbot and Woodfordes Victory on handpump, with over 60 malt whiskies and a wide range of wines; prompt, pleasant service. The two quiet small bars have stripped high-backed settles and country-kitchen chairs on the red tiles or bare boards, plain off-white walls and ceiling, a big woodburning stove, newspapers to read, and maybe several cats; dominoes and cribbage. The no-smoking snug is ideal for families. *(Recommended by Miles and Deborah Protter, John Wooll, Tom Thomas, Rita Horridge, Wayne Brindle, Geoff Lee, Peter and Pat Frogley, John and Tessa Rainsford, K D Day, Sue Demont, Tim Barrow, Lorna and Bill Tyson, Mrs R Cotgreave, J S M Sheldon)*

Free house ~ Licensee Jason Baxter ~ Real ale ~ Meals and snacks ~ (01263) 825408 ~ Well-behaved children welcome ~ Open 11.30-3(2.30 winter), 6(7 winter)-11; closed Sun evenings Dec-Mar ~ Bedrooms: £18/£36

WARHAM TF9441 Map 8

Three Horseshoes

Warham All Saints; village signposted from A149 Wells-next-the-Sea—Blakeney, and from B1105 S of Wells

Genuinely unspoilt and old-fashioned, this cheery local is partricularly popular with readers at the moment, well liked especially for its lovely pubby atmosphere and tasty home-made food. The three friendly gas-lit rooms have a sturdy red leatherette settle built around the yellowing beige walls, stripped deal or mahogany tables (one marked for shove-ha'penny), an antique American Mills one-arm bandit still in working order (it takes the new 5p pieces), a big longcase clock with a clear piping strike, a Norfolk twister on the ceiling (you give it a twist and according to where it ends up you pay for the next round), and a log fire. The generously served bar food might include sandwiches (from £1.80), home-made soup such as smoked haddock and fennel (£2), soused local herrings (from £2.50), potted smoked fish or ploughman's with home-made pickle (£2.80), local mushrooms in cheese sauce (from £3.50), fisherman's pie (£4.90), tasty rabbit pie (£5.25), children's dishes (from £2), and puddings like spotted dick (the sponge is deliciously light) or apple and blackberry pie (£2.20); good vegetables. Decent house wines and home-made lemonade as well as notably well kept Greene King IPA and Abbot on handpump, and Woodfordes Nelson's Revenge and Wherry tapped from the cask. Shove-ha'penny, dominoes, and fruit machine, and one of the outbuildings houses a wind-up gramophone museum – opened on request. There are rustic tables out on the side grass. The lavatories are currently outside, though they plan to add inside ones this year. *(Recommended by Alan and Mary Reid, Wayne Brindle, John Hobbs, Mr and Mrs Jones, Mrs P Brown, John Beeken, Sheila and Brian Wilson, Laura Ballantyne, Eric J Locker, Sarah King, Patrick Forbest, G E Stait)*

Free house ~ Licensee Iain Salmon ~ Real ale ~ Meals and snacks (not Dec 25/26) ~ No-smoking restaurant ~ (01328) 710547 ~ Children in eating area of bar ~ Occasional pianola Sat evenings ~ Open 11-3, 6-11 ~ Bedrooms: £20/£40(£44B)

WINTERTON-ON-SEA TG4919 Map 8

Fishermans Return

From B1159 turn into village at church on bend, then turn right into the lane

People who've stayed at this traditional brick and flint pub tell us the cosy and friendly atmosphere leads to much more breakfast table chat than usual. Warmly welcoming and characterful, the white-painted, panelled lounge bar has a good, relaxed feel and neat brass-studded red leatherette seats and a winter log fire, while the panelled public bar has low ceilings and a glossily varnished nautical air. Popular home-made bar food includes toasted sandwiches (from £1.20), filled baked potatoes (from £2.25), cottage pie (£3.25), ploughman's (£3.50), meat, vegetable or even prawn burgers (from £4), omelettes (from £4.50), steaks (from £9.50), daily specials such as mixed bean hotpot (£4), smoked haddock mornay (£5.25), or boozy beef pie (£5.75), puddings like home-made cheesecake (£2), and children's dishes (£2.50); good breakfasts. Well kept Adnams, Bass, Elgood Cambridge, John Smiths and a guest on handpump, various wines including their own label, and around 30 malt whiskies; darts, dominoes, cribbage, pool, fruit machine and piped music. Excellent service. Seats in the quiet lane have nice views, as do the sheltered garden and terrace, which opens out from the back bar. The characterful bedrooms, up the steep curving stairs, have low doors and uneven floors. *(Recommended by David Lingard, Peter and Pat Frogley, Hazel Morgan, Andrew and Catherine Brian, Michael Badcock, G E Stait, Paul Harrison, J Soden, E Hobday, D Newton, S Place, Sue and Dominic Dunlop)*

Free house ~ Licensees John and Kate Findlay ~ Real ale ~ Meals and snacks ~ (01493) 393305 ~ Well behaved children in small dining room in winter, in garden room in summer ~ Open 11-2.30, 6(7 winter)-11; 11-11 summer Sats ~ Bedrooms: £30/£45

WOODBASTWICK TG3315 Map 8

Fur & Feather

Village signposted from Horning off A1062; or off B1140

A careful conversion of thatched cottage buildings, this increasingly busy place only opened in 1992, but you'd imagine it had always been a pub, so carefully has the work been done. Comfortable and roomy, and olde-worlde without being overdone, its main draw for many is the full range of well kept ales from Woodforde's brewery next door. These interesting brews crop up individually elsewhere (sometimes as other Norfolk pubs' unnamed house brews), but are very rarely found all together: Broadsman, Wherry, Mardlers Mild, Baldric, perhaps Phoenix or XXX, Nog (a strong dark ale, good for keeping out the winter cold), very strong Headcracker, Pride, and the relatively new Nelson's Revenge and Porter. The bar food sounds ordinary, but is all made with fresh ingredients (even the burgers), and is generously served: sandwiches (from £1.95), a truly giant sausage, filled large yorkshire pudding, meatloaf, ribs, home-made lasagne or beef in ale pie (£5.50), and puddings. The restaurant, and part of the bar, is no smoking. The staff stay friendly and very efficient even when busy; piped music. There are tables out in the garden, with jazz and barbecue evenings in summer. We know very few good pubs in this part of the county, so the continued development of this one – in a picturesque estate village – is very good news indeed. *(Recommended by R C Vincent, Wayne Brindle, John and Shirley Dyson, Brian Horner, Brenda Arthur, Susan Kerner, John C Baker, Jonathan and Gillian Shread, Mr and Mrs B Heath, Adrian Pearce, Bryan Hay)*

Woodfordes ~ Tenants John Marjoram and J Skelton ~ Real ale ~ Meals and snacks ~ Restaurant (Tues-Sat evenings) ~ (01603) 720003 ~ Children in restaurant ~ Open 11-3(12-2.30 winter), 6-11; closed evening 25 Dec

Lucky Dip

Besides the fully inspected pubs, you might like to try these Lucky Dips recommended to us and described by readers (if you do, please send us reports):

Barford [Watton Rd; B1108 7 miles W of Norwich; TG1107], *Cock*: Good value straightforward food, welcoming helpful licensees *(John Wooll)*

☆ **Bawburgh** [TG1508], *Kings Head*: Wide choice of good bar food from baked potatoes to lobster, some unusual dishes; big helpings, good range of real ales, friendly service; lively place with lots of tables and small restaurant *(Dr G W Barnett, Brian and Jean Hepworth, Sue Anderson, Phil Copleston)*

☆ **Binham** [B1388 SW of Blakeney; TF9839], *Chequers*: Very old and unspoilt (outside lavatories), friendly atmosphere, well cooked good value promptly served food inc imaginative dishes (Sun lunch very popular), ales inc Adnams and Woodfordes Wherry and Headcracker, fireplaces each end – one huge; commanding position in pretty village *(Charles Bardswell, Derek and Sylvia Stephenson, Alastair Campbell, Mike and Heather Barnes)*

☆ **Brancaster Staithe** [A149; TF7743], *Jolly Sailors*: Good freshly cooked specials in simple but rather upmarket old-fashioned pub with well kept Greene King, decent wines, distinct sense of style; provision for children, log fire, attractive dining room, sheltered tables in nice garden with enclosed play area *(Charles Bardswell, M J Morgan, LYM)*

☆ **Brandon Creek** [A10 Ely—Downham Market; TL6091], *Ship*: Good summer pub, in lovely spot on junction of the creek with the Great Ouse, tables out by the moorings; spacious bar with massive stone masonry in sunken area that used to be a forge, open fire one end, woodburner the other, friendly staff, ales inc Hook Norton, usual bar food *(Chris and Andy Crow, LYM)*

☆ **Bressingham** [A1066 Thetford—Diss; TM0781], *Garden House*: Thatch, beams and timbering, particularly well kept ales such as Adnams, Butcombe and Woodfordes Wherry, good food inc vegetarian, popular restaurant; opp steam museum, handy for Bressingham Garden; tables in garden *(John C Baker)*

Brisley [TF9521], *Bell*: Good spot on edge of village common, olde-worlde long beamed bar, Whitbreads-related ales, good service, wide choice of popular food inc fresh veg, evening fish restaurant; tables out on green; children welcome; bedrooms *(John Wooll, Brenda Crossley)*

☆ **Briston** [B1354, Aylsham end of village; TG0532], *John H Stracey*: Long-standing landlord, friendly service and wide choice of good value food in clean and well run country dining pub, fresh fish Tues, other speciality evenings, well kept Tetleys and a seasonal winter warmer, comfortable seats, log fire, dog and cat; popular restaurant; good value bedrooms with good breakfasts – nice for people who like being part of family *(John Beeken, R C Vincent, G E Rich)*

☆ **Caistor St Edmunds** [Caistor Lane; TG2303], *Caistor Hall*: Unusual bar with 18th-c shop-front counter, comfortable lounge and library, bar food from good sandwiches up, decent wine; lovely grounds, nr Roman camp; good well furnished bedrooms *(Ian Phillips)*

California [Beach Rd; TG5114], *California Tavern*: Newish modern seafront pub (replacing a victim of sea erosion); very neat and clean, with added beams, games and pool room on left, eating area on right continuing round the back (children allowed here), usual food inc good filled french stick; Boddingtons Mild and Bitter, open all day at least in summer *(Jenny and Michael Back, TN)*

☆ **Cantley** [TG3805], *Cock*: Wide choice of good value food in friendly pub with Woodfordes Wherry and guest beers, conservatory, garden; dogs and children welcome *(Mrs M A Kilner)*

☆ **Carleton St Peter** [N of village; up track off lane Claxton—Langley Green, by River Yare – OS Sheet 134 map ref 350044; TG3402], *Beauchamp Arms*: Big homely Edwardian pub with moorings on Yare, good food, real ales inc Adnams and Woodfordes, armchairs, pool table, restaurant *(Mrs M A Kilner, David and Kate Smith)*

☆ **Castle Rising** [TF6624], *Black Horse*: Comfortable tastefully refurbished Beefeater family dining pub in pleasant village setting, good value food, Whitbreads-related and guest ales, friendly service; children welcome, no dogs, tables out under cocktail parasols *(R C Vincent, Graham and Sandra Poll, Charles Bardswell, M J Morgan, John Wooll, Jane Kingsbury)*

☆ **Cley next the Sea** [The Green, nr church; TG0443], *Three Swallows*: Very friendly staff, banquettes around long high leathered tables, second simpler bar, decent generous home cooking, well kept Greene King IPA, good wines; on attractive village green, barbecues in attractive garden with croquet, aviary and lovely view of church; bedrooms simple but clean and comfortable, handy for the salt marshes *(Geoff Lee, Mike and Heather Barnes, Mrs M A Mees, S G MacSwiney)*

Cockley Cley [TF7904], *Twenty Churchwardens*: Attractive bar food, well kept Adnams, courteous landlord, pleasant waitresses; beams, darts alcove; plenty of worthwhile places to visit nearby *(Frank Cummins, Graham and Sandra Poll)*

☆ **Coltishall** [Church St (B1354); TG2719], *Red Lion*: Modernised family pub, away from water but pleasant setting; decent straightforward generous food inc good puddings, Whitbreads-related ales and Weasel brewed for them by Woodfordes, very friendly staff, several attractive split-level rooms, restaurant; tables out under cocktail parasols, good play area; bedrooms *(S Kerner, David Craine, Ann Reeder, M Berry, Bob and Sue Ward, R C Vincent, John and Shirley Dyson)*

Coltishall [The Common], *Rising Sun*: Big Chef & Brewer on pretty bend of River Bure, very useful for boaters, with moorings; Courage-related ales, food from sandwiches up, waterside and other outside tables, family room, friendly service even when busy; piped music *(David and Julie Glover, Bronwen and Steve Wrigley, LYM)*

☆ **Colton** [TG1009], *Ugly Bug*: Good atmosphere in friendly and attractive family-run lakeside barn conversion, separate dining area with good choice of consistently good value straightforward food inc vegetarian, well kept ales inc Adnams Old, sensible choice of wines, good atmosphere and service; children in conservatory, big garden, fishing; two comfortable bedrooms *(Frank Davidson, R C Vincent)*

☆ **Cromer** [Promenade; TG2142], *Bath House*: Welcoming seafront inn with lots of dark wood, well kept Greene King Abbot and guest beer, standard bar food inc good lunchtime sandwiches, dining room; plenty of tables out on prom; bedrooms *(G D Lee)*

☆ **Denver Sluice** [TF6101], *Jenyns Arms*: Pleasant modernised pub with waterside lawns and terrace overlooking boats, ducks and swans; friendly staff, good generous food inc vegetarian, lots of antiques; handy for Welney wildfowl reserve *(David and Mary Webb, Charles Bardswell, M Scarratt)*

☆ **Dereham** [Swaffham Rd; TF9913], *George*: Good cheap home-cooked bar lunches, good carvery, Courage-related and other ales, carefully attentive landlord; bedrooms good *(Frank Davidson, G Washington, Mary Moore)*

Dereham [High St], *Bull*: Reasonably priced food, affable service *(Frank Davidson, John and Shirley Dyson)*

Dersingham [nr church; TF6830], *Gamekeepers Lodge*: Comfortably refurbished old building, reasonable choice of well cooked and presented generous food, pleasant dining room (children welcome here); tables outside *(John Wooll, Graham and Sandra Poll)*

Ditchingham [Norwich Rd; TM3391], *Duke of York*: Good helpings of well presented home-cooked food inc seafood specials, friendly welcome *(Tom Thomas)*

☆ **Docking** [High St; TF7637], *Pilgrims Reach*: Good generous straightforward food, friendly staff, Adnams Bitter and Broadside, small bar (can be busy), quiet restaurant; tables on attractive sheltered back terrace, children's room *(John Wooll, M J Morgan, Mrs M A Mees)*

Downham Market [TF6103], *Crown*: 17th-c coaching inn with welcoming newish owners, well kept Batemans Best and Crown Buckley Reverend James, restaurant with good reasonably priced food, friendly alsatian; comfortable bedrooms, big breakfasts *(Ben Grose)*

East Barsham [B1105 3 miles N of Fakenham; TF9133], *White Horse*: Pleasantly refurbished and extended, long main bar with big log fire, attractive dining area, well kept ales such as Woodfordes Headcracker, reasonably priced food in bar and restaurant; piped music, darts; children welcome; bedrooms *(Alastair Campbell, M J Morgan)*

☆ **East Harling** [High St (B1111); TL9986], *Nags Head*: Plush seats in three neat bars and no-smoking tiled-floor dining room (children allowed here), wide range of good food inc Sun lunch, prompt friendly service, John Smiths and Whitbreads; juke box; big garden with boules and aviary; not far from Snetterton *(Jenny and Michael Back, Anthony Barnes)*

East Rudham [TF8228], *Cat & Fiddle*: Good welcome, usual food done well with evening griddle specialities, special offer steaks Fri evening, bargain weekday three-course lunches *(Geoff Lee)*

☆ **East Ruston** [Oak St; back rd Horning—Happisburgh, N of Stalham; TG3427], *Butchers Arms*: Big helpings of well presented food in well run comfortable village pub with good range of well kept ales, lots of golf talk, restaurant, attractive garden, pretty hanging baskets *(Tony Kemp, Rachel Weston)*

East Winch [A47; TF6916], *Carpenters Arms*: Friendly atmosphere and staff, Greene King IPA and Abbot and a guest beer, good food inc special offers; well managed restaurant *(Graham and Sandra Poll)*

Erpingham [OS Sheet 133 map ref 191319; TG1931], *Spread Eagle*: Full range of Woodfordes distinctive ales kept well, cheerful friendly staff, usual ploughman's and salads, pool table, neat garden *(D W Gray)*

Fakenham [Bridge St; TF9229], *Wensum Lodge*: Relaxing attractive bar with good reasonably priced food, good service; comfortable bedrooms *(Mr and Mrs Simpson)*

☆ **Gayton** [TF7219], *Crown*: Consistently good food (not Mon evening or Sun) esp help-yourself buffet – roasts winter, impressive salads and cold meats summer, appetising puddings; attractive flower-decked pub, simple yet stylish inside, with some unusual old features, well kept Greene King beers, friendly efficient service, comfortable seats, games room; tables in sheltered garden *(G E Rich, Gordon Thornton, Sheila and Brian Wilson, M J Morgan, June and Malcolm Farmer, Graham and Sandra Poll, LYM)*

Gooderstone [The Street; TF7601], *Swan*: Good choice of beers inc guests; big garden *(Graham and Sandra Poll)*

☆ **Great Bircham** [Main Rd; TF7632], *Kings Head*: Good food inc delicious fish stew and Italian dishes in spacious Edwardian country inn, relaxed and comfortable, with good open fire, friendly welcome, Bass and Charrington IPA, fine Italian wines; bedrooms, attractive village *(Charles Bardswell, John Wooll)*

☆ **Great Cressingham**; [Water End; just off A1064 Swaffham—Brandon; OS Sheet 144 map ref 849016; TF8401], *Windmill*: Roomy family pub with three beamed bars, cosy nooks and crannies, huge log fireplace, lots of farm tools, conservatory, games room; good value standard food, quick service, well kept Adnams, Batemans, Bass, Sam Smiths and guest beers; well kept big garden, dogs allowed *(Charles Bardswell, G Washington, Anthony Barnes)*

Great Yarmouth [Havelock Rd; TG5207], *Red Herring*: Cosy warmly welcoming backstreet pub, nice decor, at least six well kept changing ales such as Adnams and Woodfordes Mild, good value food inc wide choice of good local sausages *(Chris and Pam Dearmun, K Kennedy)*

☆ **Hainford** [TG2218], *Chequers*: Friendly thatched cottage in charming setting, wide range of well prepared food, real ales such as Adnams, Hook Norton Old Hookey and Morlands Old Speckled Hen, big airy bar area and rooms off, pleasant staff, well laid-out gardens with play area; children welcome *(Ian Phillips)*

☆ **Happisburgh** [by church; TG3830], *Hill House*: Long comfortable bar with plenty of character, fire each end, well kept Adnams, Marstons Pedigree, Tetleys and Woodfordes Wherry, wide choice of good generous food inc original dishes, welcoming service, restaurant (children allowed here); tables outside front and back (can get breezy if the wind comes in off the sea); bedrooms, pleasant setting *(Charles Bardswell, Roy Bromell, Alastair Campbell)*

Harpley [off A148 Fakenham—Kings Lynn; TF7825], *Rose & Crown*: Interesting reasonably priced food inc unusual vegetarian dishes in small comfortable lounge, decent wine, friendly hard-working landlord; high chairs provided; quietly attractive village *(John Wooll)*

☆ **Hempstead** [signed from A148 in Holt, pub towards Baconsthorpe; TG1137], *Hare & Hounds*: Unspoilt and laid-back country pub with tiled floor, big woodburner, mix of old-fashioned furnishings and lots of pine, well kept ales such as Bass, Adnams, Greene King Abbot, M & B Mild, Stones and Woodfordes Wherry, modest food choice; a couple of geese patrolling the informal garden, with a pond, rockery and play area *(Mrs R Cotgreave, Geoff Lee, Peter and Pat Frogley, G Washington, PC, LYM)*

☆ **Heydon** [village signposted from B1149; TG1127], *Earle Arms*: Tucked away in remote-seeming estate village, flagstones, bare boards, country furnishings; new licensees doing interesting French bistro-style food using local produce, lots of fresh fish and vegetarian dishes *(Mrs P Holman, LYM)*

☆ **Hilborough** [A1065; TF8100], *Swan*: Welcoming early 18th-c pub with good simple home cooking done to order (so may be a wait), well kept ales such as Bass, Fullers ESB, Greene King IPA and Abbot, Woodfordes Norfolk Nog and interesting guest beers, plenty of old-fashioned pub and board games, friendly landlord, small back restaurant; picnic tables on pleasant sheltered lawn *(Frank Cummins, Charles Bardswell, Jane and Mike Blanckenhagen, Graham and Sandra Poll, BB)*

Hillington [TF7225], *Ffolkes Arms*: Large and comfortable, with wide range of beers, popular Sun carvery, good choice of bar food, garden behind; reasonably priced bedrooms in former barn *(Graham and Sandra Poll, M J Morgan)*

☆ **Holme next the Sea** [Kirkgate St; TF7043], *White Horse*: Generous food – good straightforward value for money; welcoming pub popular with locals and visitors, big garden *(John and Sally Clarke, John Wooll, Charles Bardswell)*

☆ **Holt** [White Lion St; TG0738], *White Lion*: Georgian pub with good simple freshly cooked food in welcoming small bar and restaurant, three well kept ales, big garden; bedrooms *(June and Malcolm Farmer)*

Holt [Bull St], *Kings Head*: Good home cooking, specials for children and OAPs, Theakstons, cheerful atmosphere, small restaurant *(John Wooll)*

Horning [Lower St; TG3417], *Swan*: Big popular Brewers Fayre dining pub on River Bure, open all day, wide range of reasonably priced food, good service, cream teas, seats out by water; bedrooms *(A Denman)*

☆ **Horsey** [just visible down lane 'To The Sea' from B1159 in S bends; TG4522], *Nelsons Head*: Isolated but very welcoming, kept carefully simple, with good range of bar food inc vegetarian and Austrian dishes, ales such as Adnams, Flowers and Woodfordes Wherry, unobtrusive piped classical music, family room, local paintings, some nautical touches, darts, fruit machine; restaurant, small but attractive garden; quiet spot nr coast, handy for Horsey Mill and Mere *(Nigel and Sara Walker, BB)*

Hoveton [TG3018], *Black Horse*: Small, cosy and quiet, separate dining area, polished tables and chairs, horse pictures, prompt friendly service, wide range of generous food *(A H Denman)*

Hunstanton [St Edmunds Terr; TF6842], *Marine Bar*: Very welcoming staff, good range of beers, wide range of reasonably priced food served all day inc enormous ploughman's; holiday flat *(M Tack)*

Ingham [B1151 E of Stalham; TG3826], *Swan*: This attractive thatched inn has been reported closed *(News please)*

Itteringham [TG1430], *Walpole Arms*: Delightfully old-fashioned village pub on River Bure, lively atmosphere, decent food and beer *(John and Elizabeth Gwynne, Anthony Barnes)*

Kings Lynn [Gayton Rd, Gaywood; TF6320], *Wildfowler*: Comfortable and relaxed even when busy, popular food, well kept Tetleys-related beers, friendly staff *(John Wooll)*

☆ **Larling** [Norwich Rd (A11); TL9889], *Angel*: 16th-c local transformed by friendly new owners, pretty dining room with good well cooked food from ploughman's to steaks, unspoiled bar with open fire, well kept Adnams, Greene King IPA and a beer called Biffys Best; open all day *(A M Pring, John C Baker, Frank W Gadbois)*

Little Plumstead [TG3112], *Brick Kilns*: Very good choice of vegetarian, vegan and ordinary food in good helpings; Courage-related ales *(S Anderson)*

Loddon [just off A146 Norwich—Lowestoft;

TM3698], *Swan*: Cosy and pleasant 17th-c coaching inn in attractive village, long bar with lounge at one end and upstairs bar with pool table and video games, good range of well cooked food, seats in yard outside *(Bronwen and Steve Wrigley)*

Longham [TF9415], *White Horse*: Very well kept beer in friendly traditional village pub with wide choice of good value home-cooked food; pleasant garden *(M E Farbrother)*

☆ **Middleton** [Fair Green; off A47 Kings Lynn—Norwich; TF6616], *Gate*: Hard-working landlord doing well in unpretentious creeper-covered village local, well kept Bass, good straightforward bar food, cosy beamed bar with horsebrasses, lots of bric-a-brac, pews, cushioned settle and milk churns, open fire; games bar with pool and machines, pretty side garden with good value barbecues *(R C Vincent, Graham and Sandra Poll)*

Middleton [A47], *Crown*: Roomy pub with good atmosphere, guest ales *(Graham and Sandra Poll)*

☆ **Neatishead** [Irstead Rd; TG3420], *Barton Angler*: Good reasonably priced straightforward food, well kept Greene King ales, comfortable and homely bar, friendly staff, well furnished no-smoking restaurant, lovely quiet gardens; good bedrooms, two with four-posters – a nice place to stay *(Myra and Keith Massey, Michael and Lorna Helyar)*

Neatishead, *White Horse*: Multi-roomed pub with keen family in charge, well kept ales, popular food; piped music may be obtrusive *(Bob and Sue Ward)*

☆ **North Elmham** [B1110 N of E Dereham; junction with B1145; TF9820], *Kings Head*: Welcoming old-fashioned inn, neat and tidy, with good well presented food from sandwiches up served quickly in log-fire lounge or lovely small dining room; public bars, Courage-related ales and Greene King IPA; nr interesting ruins; bedrooms *(John and Elizabeth Gwynne, Gordon Mott)*

North Walsham [Mkt Sq; TG2730], *Kings Arms*: Small town hotel with plush back lounge (children allowed), small carvery off, lively front bar with pool room, Courage-related ales, decent wine, cheap food; bedrooms *(John Wooll)*

North Wootton [TF6424], *House on the Green*: Roomy lounge, affable landlord, decent wine, wide range of food cooked to order inc good vegetarian dishes; good-sized garden *(John Wooll)*

☆ **Norwich** [10 Dereham Rd], *Reindeer*: No-frills bare-boards smoky-ceilinged pub worth knowing for its own-brewed beer and well kept guests (you can see the brewery), dining area with reasonable range of generous food inc perfectly cooked fresh veg, relaxed atmosphere, friendly staff, occasional folk bands; not crowded outside University terms *(Richard Houghton, Jill Palios, P Corris, Sue Anderson, Phil Copleston)*

☆ **Norwich** [Wensum St; S side of Fye Bridge], *Ribs of Beef*: Warm and welcoming, with wide choice of Woodfordes and other ales, farm cider; comfortable main room upstairs, attractive smaller downstairs room with river view and some local river paintings, lunchtime food from filled baps up; can be studenty evenings, but without deafening music *(Thomas Nott, Ian Phillips, Mrs M A Kilner)*

☆ **Norwich** [King St], *Ferryboat*: Pleasant riverside Greene King pub with a good deal of character, traditional beamed old-fashioned front part, steps down through spacious raftered and flagstoned back dining area to riverside garden with play area and barbecue *(Thomas Nott, Mrs M A Kilner, LYM)*

Norwich [Riverside Rd, opp Bishops Bridge], *Bridge House*: 17th-c Whitbreads pub opp Bishops Bridge, well kept ales inc Flowers, big helpings of good plain food presented nicely at very low prices, inc bargain steaks and good salads; service very prompt, helpful and friendly *(Sarah and Gary Goldson)*; [61 St Augustines St], *Catherine Wheel*: Tucked-away oak-beamed pub with good house wine, modest bar menu, good value upstairs restaurant *(John and Wendy Trentham)*; [2 Timber Hill], *Gardeners Arms*: Warm and welcoming, with different small themed areas inc convincing kitchen, more room in former yard which now has glass roof; real ales inc Murderer – recalling pub's former name *(Ian Phillips)*; [Orford Pl, off SE end of Haymarket], *Lamb*: Open-plan, standard food with nursery puddings, Courage-related ales, satellite TVs *(Thomas Nott, Jan and Colin Roe)*; [Trafford Rd], *Trafford Arms*: Friendly local with good value food, real ale inc Milds and many guest beers *(Allen Morrison)*; [Dove St], *Vine*: Tiny, not smart, with wider range of food and drink than you'd expect from the size, frequent live folk music, some seats out in pedestrian street *(Thomas Nott, Peter Smee)*; [Oak St], *White Lion*: Friendly traditional Tap & Spile local with lots of bare wood, good choice of ales, simple cheap bar food inc OAP midweek bargains; quiet lunchtime, lively evening, darts and bar billiards in smaller bar *(S Demont, T Barrow, June and Perry Dann)*

☆ **Old Hunstanton** [part of Le Strange Arms Hotel, Golf Course Rd; TF6842], *Ancient Mariner*: Attractively furnished old bar, comfortable and interesting, with lots of dark wood, bare bricks and flagstones, several little areas inc upstairs gallery, good value usual food, up to half a dozen well kept ales inc Adnams and Broadside, Bass and Charrington IPA, decent wines, open fire, papers and magazines, friendly staff; bedrooms *(Les and Jean Scott, John Wooll, D E Cattell)*

Oxborough [TF7401], *Bedingfeld Arms*: Peaceful setting opp NT Oxburgh Hall, decent food inc roasts on Sun and bank hols, good choice of beer inc Boddingtons and Butcombe Bitter, friendly staff; tables and swings outside; bedrooms *(R C Vincent)*

Potter Heigham [A1062 Wroxham Rd; TG4119], *Falgate*: Charming refurbished pub with Tetleys-related and guest beers, good food in restaurant, friendly service; fruit machine, piped music; aviaries out behind; bedrooms *(David and Julie Glover)*

Pulham Market [TM1986], *Crown*: Food inc

good popular Sun lunch in restaurant (must book) *(Brenda Crossley)*
Ranworth [signed off B1140 Norwich—Acle; TG3514], *Maltsters*: Fine position across quiet lane from Ranworth Broad, rather nautical decor, decent food, friendly prompt service, Courage-related ales; superb nature trail nearby *(Hazel Morgan, LYM)*
☆ **Rollesby** [A149; TQ4416], *Horse & Groom*: Straightforward renovated pub worth knowing for good value generous home-made food esp seafood; clean and comfortable, with well kept Boddingtons, good friendly service; fish and steak restaurant, decent wines; well equipped bedrooms in new wing *(Mr and Mrs M Bailey, D Middleton, Susan Kerner)*
Salthouse [A149 Blakeney—Sheringham; TG0743], *Dun Cow*: Warmly welcoming straightforward old country pub by salt marshes, popular with ramblers and bird-watchers; decent bar food, Flowers Original and Tolly, tables outside *(Geoff Lee, Peter and Pat Frogley)*
☆ **Sculthorpe** [off S side of A148 2 miles W of Fakenham; TF8930], *Sculthorpe Mill*: Sympathetically converted mill popular in summer for its spacious waterside garden; beamed bar, lots of nooks and crannies, open fire, well presented bar food inc good home-made puddings, well kept beers such as Brakspears and Greene King IPA, friendly service, restaurant *(John Wooll, H Jones, M J Morgan, Alastair Campbell, Anthony Barnes, R C Vincent, Mrs J Barwell)*
☆ **Sedgeford** [B1454, off A149 Kings Lynn—Hunstanton; TF7136], *King William IV*: Happy casual atmosphere, good value bar food inc Sun roast with good veg, fast friendly service, well kept Bass and Worthington, restaurant; children allowed in lounge if eating, live music Tues *(John Wooll, Graham and Sandra Poll)*
Sheringham [seafront; TG1543], *Crown*: Good choice of beers and good generous home-cooked food inc vegetarian in two big bars with friendly efficient service, pool table, sea views also from attractive terrace; children welcome, open all day summer, handy for coast walks *(Mrs Jackie Deale, M Tack)*; [High St], *Lobster*: Almost on seafront, old Singer treadle tables in nice lounge, food inc crab, lobster and fish specials; public bar's juke box can sometimes be heard in lounge *(A M Pring)*; [seafront], *Two Lifeboats*: Lovely sea view from comfortable lounge, big helpings of enjoyable usual bar food inc fresh fish (no-smoking dining area), well kept Greene King ales, friendly service; shame about the piped music; bedrooms *(Peter and Pat Frogley, Michael Badcock, Geoff Lee)*
Skeyton [TG2425], *Goat*: Reported closed *(News please)*
Smallburgh [A149; TG3225], *Crown*: Small thatched village inn, beams and big log fires, good simple home-made food in bar and restaurant, well kept Greene King, Tolly and guest ales, welcoming service, attractive garden; bedrooms *(Dr M V Jones, Roger and Pam McIntee)*
☆ **South Creake** [B1355 Burnham Mkt—Fakenham; TF8535], *Ostrich*: Pleasantly homely with pine tables in long bar, good range of food cooked to order (so can be delays) using fresh ingredients, well kept Adnams, Greene King IPA and Woodfordes, friendly staff *(Charles Bardswell)*
South Lopham [The Street (A1066); TM0481], *White Horse*: Restored by new licensees, with original fireplace and oak beams; good home-cooked food inc Sun lunch, Adnams, Greene King IPA and Marstons Pedigree *(Anon)*
☆ **South Walsham** [TG3713], *Ship*: Small friendly village local with traditional brick and beamed bars, well kept Adnams Bitter, Woodfordes Wherry and (new to us) Chalk Hill Bitter, good generous specials inc vegetarian and lovely puddings, gourmet nights (not Sun), good service, welcoming NZ landlord; pool table; tables on front elevated terrace and more in back garden; children's room, play area with friendly goats *(John Beeken, Eric J Locker, John and Shirley Dyson, Susan Kerner, Bronwen and Steve Wrigley)*
☆ **South Wootton** [Nursery Lane; TF6422], *Swan*: Good value home-made food in small old-fashioned two-bar pub overlooking village green, duckpond and bowling green; conservatory dining area, well kept Courage-related ales and Greene King IPA, small enclosed garden with slide and swing *(John Wooll)*
St Olaves [TM4599], *Decoy*: Good food with fresh veg and decent choice of puddings, pleasant landlord, no pretensions *(Mrs D Stutters)*
☆ **Stanhoe** [Main St (B1155); TF8036], *Crown*: Roomy and comfortable open-plan pub with good affable landlord, deservedly popular home cooking with good specials such as jugged hare, Elgoods beer, decent wine and coffee; well behaved children allowed *(John Wooll, E J Taylor, Mrs S R Waite)*
Stoke Holy Cross [TG2301], *Wildebeest Arms*: New licensee doing good French bistro-style food; good wines, espresso coffee *(Roz Waller, Richard Goodenough)*
Strumpshaw [TG3508], *Shoulder of Mutton*: Genuine unimproved village local, a good escape from the yuppies *(Mr Walker)*
☆ **Surlingham** [from village head N; pub on bumpy track into which both village roads fork; TG3206], *Ferry House*: Lively and enjoyable riverside pub (though no view from the bar), comfortably modernised, friendly and unpretentious, by rowing-boat ferry over Yare; sensibly priced standard bar food inc vegetarian and Sun roasts, Courage-related ales, central woodburner, traditional pub games, restaurant; children welcome, with own menu; winter evening opening may be restricted, very busy with boats and visitors in summer – free mooring; handy for RSPB reserve *(John Beeken, Sarah and Gary Goldson, Ian Phillips, LYM)*
☆ **Sutton Staithe** [village signposted from A149 S of Stalham; TG3823], *Sutton Staithe*:

Attractive pub in a particularly unspoilt part of the Broads; cosy alcoves, built-in seats, flagstones, oak beams, an antique settle among more modern furnishings, well kept Adnams and other ales tapped from the cask, usual food inc children's, good puddings and all-day filled long rolls, helpful staff, restaurant; children welcome, flower-filled courtyard; good nearby moorings, bedrooms *(Roy Bromell, Bronwen and Steve Wrigley, LYM)*

Swaffham [1 Station St; TF8109], *George*: Comfortable and friendly small-town hotel, good value food, Greene King IPA and Abbot; children welcome; bedrooms *(John Wooll)*

Tasburgh [A140; TM1996], *Countryman*: Welcoming main-road pub with decent reasonably priced usual food, willing service, well kept Adnams and two other ales, decent wine *(Frank Davidson, Anthony Barnes, John and Wendy Trentham)*

☆ **Thetford** [White Hart St], *Thomas Paine*: Consistently good value bar food and reliable service in friendly and roomy hotel bar, well kept Adnams and Tolly Original, decent wines, open fire; children welcome; bedrooms *(Sheila and Brian Wilson, LYM)*

☆ **Thornham** [Church St; TF7343], *Kings Head*: Pretty old pub with lots of hanging baskets, tables out on front gravel, low-beamed bars with banquettes in well lit bays, welcoming new landlord, usual food, Greene King IPA and Abbot, Marstons Pedigree and Tetleys, open fire, no-smoking area; dogs allowed; three homely and comfortable bedrooms *(Mr ands Mrs K Tidy)*

☆ **Thursford** [TF9833], *Crawfish*: Good home-made food and well kept Flowers Original in cosy relaxed bar and simple side restaurant, fresh flowers, open fire, a few curios, helpful waitresses, decent wine; unobtrusive piped music, occasional live music *(Alastair Campbell, K H Frostick, John Wooll, J and Z Chamberlain)*

Thurton [TG3300], *George & Dragon*: Modest open-plan pub, helpful service, modestly priced food *(John and Wendy Trentham)*

☆ **Titchwell** [A149; TF7543], *Three Horseshoes*: Good range of generous bar food and well kept Adnams and Woodfordes Wherry in refurbished bar with rough walls, exposed wood, beams and struts, log fires; friendly staff, family room, restaurant; play area in garden overlooking RSPB reserve; peaceful and comfortable bedrooms pleasantly furnished in antique pine, handy for beach *(R B Berry, John Beeken, Mrs M A Mees, Dr P Mummery)*

Titchwell [Main St], *Briarfields*: Hotel not pub, but most attractive, with very good value meals in comfortable surroundings, good beer and wine in back bar, terrace overlooking salt marshes, suntrap courtyard with pond; bedrooms *(John Wooll)*

Walcott [B1159, nr church S of village; TG3532], *Lighthouse*: Exceptionally friendly, busy inn with helpful landlord and good food inc interesting vegetarian dishes; children in dining room and function room *(Roy Bromell)*

☆ **Walsingham** [Common Place/Shire Hall Plain; TF9236], *Bull*: Particularly good friendly atmosphere and interesting simply furnished interior, with well kept Ind Coope Burton and Tolly Original, decent food, tables out in the busy village square; much used by pilgrims – collects clerical visiting cards *(Walter Reid, J and Z Chamberlain, Alastair Campbell)*

☆ **Wells next the Sea** [The Buttlands; TF9143], *Crown*: Bustling heavy-beamed Tudor bar and quieter back rooms behind three-storey Georgian facade, well kept Adnams, interesting pictures inc Nelson memorabilia, good log fire, Marstons Pedigree and Tetleys, bar food inc sandwiches and children's dishes, popular restaurant, children allowed in small back conservatory; piped music; charming setting *(Sue Demont, Tim Barrow, M J Morgan, Gordon Pitt, John Wooll, Charles Bardswell, Peter and Pat Frogley, Wayne Brindle, LYM)*

Wereham [off A134; TF6801], *George & Dragon*: Cosy and friendly beamed pub, Hancocks HB; nice surroundings *(Graham and Sandra Poll)*

☆ **West Beckham** [Bodham Rd; TG1339], *Wheatsheaf*: Good choice of well kept Greene King and other ales and good reasonably priced food in friendly comfortable beamed pub with cottagey doors and banquettes, feature log fire; children's room, garden; bedrooms clean, comfortable and cheap, with good breakfasts *(Geoff Lee, Dr and Mrs M Bailey, John and Tessa Rainsford)*

☆ **West Walton** [School Rd; N of Wisbech; TF4713], *King of Hearts*: Comfortably upgraded dining pub with wide choice of good genuine food in smartly furnished bar and restaurant, full range of Elgoods and a guest; holds key for lovely next-door church *(Sheila and Brian Wilson)*

Weston Longville [signed off A1067 Norwich—Bawdswell in Morton – OS Sheet 133 map ref 114158; TG1115], *Parson Woodforde*: Clean and spacious beamed pub, with willing service, usual bar food, well kept ales such as Adnams, Bass and Woodfordes Wherry *(Frank Davidson, Anthony Barnes)*

Weybourne [A149 W of Sheringham; TG1042], *Ship*: Big bar, dining area and restaurant with short choice of good straightforward food in huge helpings; good coffee *(Roy Bromell)*

☆ **Wiveton** [TG0342], *Bell*: Now reopened, with comfortable and attractive gently lit bar, newspapers and magazines, good value simple home cooking, well kept Woodfordes Wherry, welcoming young landlord, pine tables in big glass extension, pleasant garden beyond; charming spot by green and church; dogs welcome *(John Wooll, Frank Davidson)*

☆ **Wreningham** [TM1598], *Bird in Hand*: Polite service in tastefully refurbished dining pub with good varied reasonably priced food inc unusual vegetarian dishes; well kept Whitbreads-related and Woodfordes ales, cosy Victorian-style panelled dining area, local bygones and Lotus car photographs; good friendly service *(Ian Taylor, R C Morgan, Sue Anderson, Phil Copleston, Anthony Barnes, Andy Whitaker)*

Northamptonshire *see* Midlands

Northumbria (including Durham, Northumberland, Cleveland and Tyne & Wear)

Good value both for generous food (with an increasing amount of really fresh fish) and for drink, this area has some fine individual pubs, often in attractive surroundings. Pubs doing specially well here at the moment include the Percy Arms at Chatton (a comfortable place to stay, with 12 miles of fishing), the welcoming Dipton Mill Inn at Diptonmill, the civilised Queens Head at Great Whittington (a new main entry, good interesting food), the Milecastle up on the moors near Haltwhistle, the Cook & Barker Arms at Newton on the Moor (an excellent all-rounder), the Chain Locker in North Shields (good fish), the rather smart Rose & Crown at Romaldkirk, the interesting and very friendly Olde Ship at Seahouses, and the prettily located Pheasant at Stannersburn, up near Kielder Water. Of these, the Rose & Crown currently has most to offer for an enjoyable meal out: we choose it as Northumbria Dining Pub of the Year. Quite a few pubs in the Lucky Dip section at the end of the chapter stand out as worthy of special note: the Saddle in Alnmouth, Lord Crewe Arms at Bamburgh, Shepherd & Shepherdess in Beamish, Rob Roy in Berwick, Black Bull at Corbridge, Three Tuns at Eggleston, Duke of York at Fir Tree, General Havelock at Haydon Bridge, High Force Hotel at High Force, Cross Keys at Thropton, Hadrian at Wall and Beresford Arms at Whalton; as we have inspected most of these, we can vouch for their appeal. Newcastle has plenty of choice, including a growing number of interesting warehouse conversions. As we've said, drinks prices in the area are well below the national average: we found the Chain Locker in North Shields and Cooperage in Newcastle, both selling local beers, specially cheap.

BLANCHLAND (Northumberland) NY9750 Map 10

Lord Crewe Arms

This magnificent partly Norman building in a pretty moorland village near the Derwent Reservoir was originally attached to the guest house of a monastery – part of the cloister still stands in the neatly terraced gardens. The cosy and simply furnished barrel-vaulted crypt bar has plush bar stools, built-in wall benches, ancient flagstones and stone and brick walls that are eight feet thick in some places; Vaux Samson on handpump; darts. Upstairs, the quietly welcoming Derwent Room has low beams, old settles, and sepia photographs on its walls, and the Hilyard Room has a massive 13th-c fireplace where the Jacobite Tom Forster (part of the family who had owned the building before it was sold to the formidable Lord Crewe, Bishop of Durham) is said to have hidden after escaping from prison in London, on his way to exile in France. His loyal sister still haunts the place, asking guests to deliver a message to her long dead brother. Simple bar food includes soup (£1.80), filled white rolls (mostly £2.80), pasta shells with tomatoes, mushrooms, butter beans and cheese (£4), ploughman's (£4.50), fish cakes (£4.75), wild boar and pheasant pie (£5.50), and puddings (£2.40). The evening bar menu is a bit shorter with slightly more expensive dishes like prawn cocktail (£3.25), pork and beef sausages (£6.50), breaded chicken breast (£8) and baked salmon (£8.25). Staff will happily arrange variations of the main menu for children. On Sunday the menu may be limited to soup and a cold buffet with Sunday lunch served in the restaurant; afternoon teas with home-made cakes. There's a pleasant enclosed garden. *(Recommended by Gordon, Karen and Graham Oddey, GSB, John Fazakerley, R J Walden, Peter Race)*

Free house ~ Licensees A S Todd, Peter Gingell, Ian Press ~ Real ale ~ Meals and snacks ~ Restaurant ~ (01434) 675251 ~ Children welcome ~ Open 11-3, 6-11.30 ~ Bedrooms: £65B/£98B

CARTERWAY HEADS (Northumberland) NZ0552 Map 10

Manor House

A68 just N of B6278, near Derwent Reservoir

The good sensibly balanced menu is one of the main draws at this simple slate-roofed stone house. Changing daily and generously served, the choice might typically include soup such as tomato and mint (£1.95), cumberland sausage (£3.85), creamy pasta with chilli and peppers or mushroom gratin (£5.35), honey roast ham (£6), dill herrings with crème fraîche (£6.50), babotie (£6.95), grilled chicken breast with red onion confit (£7.30), baked salmon with coriander (£7.50) and grilled turbot with oyster mushrooms and cream (£9.50), and puddings like sticky toffee pudding or lemon mousse (£2.85) or their own ice creams (£2.10). The very good table d'hôte menu is available throughout the building and might include brill mousseline with tomato and coriander, wild salmon en papillote with lime butter, and honey and mixed spice wafers with raspberries, (£16.50 including coffee); no-smoking restaurant; attentive service in a fairly relaxed atmosphere. There's a changing range of very well kept beers such as Big Lamb, Black Sheep, Butterknowle and Wadworths IPA on handpump, a farm cider, fresh apple juice, up to 20 malt whiskies, and decent wines. The comfortable refurbished lounge bar has picture windows with fine southerly views over moorland pastures, and a wood-burning stove. The beamed locals' bar is furnished with pine tables, chairs and stools, old oak pews, and a mahogany bar. Darts, dominoes and piped music. Rustic tables out on a small side terrace and lawn. *(Recommended by Roger Bellingham, GSB, M Borthwick, M J Morgan, Karen and Graham Oddey, Anne Cherry, A L Carr, Margaret and Nigel Dennis, Dr I H Maine, R Heaven, John Fazakerley, R J Walden, John Oddey, Kay and Mark Denison, Paul Boot)*

Free house ~ Licensee Anthony Pelly ~ Real ale ~ Meals and snacks ~ Restaurant ~ (01207) 255268 ~ Children in eating area of bar ~ Open 11-3, 6-11; closed 25,26 Dec ~ Bedrooms: £22/£38.50

CHATTON (Northumberland) NU0628 Map 10

Percy Arms

B6348 E of Wooller

As well as being very popular for good reasonably priced bar food, this partly creeper-covered friendly stone local has 12 miles of private fishing for residents where you may find salmon, sea trout or stocked rainbow trout. Bar meals include soup (£1.85), home-made pâté (£2.95), home cooked ham salad or tuna pasta salad (£4.65), breaded scampi, vegetable tikka masala or chicken curry (£5.25), fresh trout (£7.55), fillet of salmon (£8.75) and roast half duckling (£8.95); children's dishes (£2.75), and puddings like home-made trifle (from £1.95) or cheesecake (£2.45); all meat is locally butchered and dishes are served with fresh vegetables; good breakfasts. The attractively lit comfortable bar is clean and spacious with wooden wall seats upholstered in pale brocade. The carpeted lounge area has recently been redecorated in bottle green with striped green and gold bench seating, there's an armchair or two among other seats in a family area through a stone-faced arch, and round on the other side a similarly furnished tiled-floor section leads through to a stripped-stone eating area. Well kept Theakstons XB on handpump and a fine selection of about two dozen malt whiskies; open fire, unobtrusive piped music; public bar with darts, pool, dominoes, fruit machine, video game and juke box. There are picnic tables on its small front lawn above the village road, and a holiday cottage is available; large comfortable bedrooms. No dogs in public areas. *(Recommended by Gordon, James Macrae, June and Tony Baldwin, Leigh and Gillian Mellor, A N Ellis, Dr and Mrs J H Hills, Jack and Heather Coyle, BB, Neil Townend, Thomas Nott, Les and Jean Scott, Mr and Mrs C Brown, John Allsopp, Chris and Anne Fluck, Jeanne and Tom Barnes)*

Free house ~ Licensees Pam and Kenny Topham ~ Real ale ~ Meals and snacks (12-1.30, 6.30- 9.30) ~ Restaurant ~ (01668) 215244 ~ Children welcome ~ Open 11-3, 6-11 ~ Bedrooms: £20B/£40B

CORBRIDGE (Northumberland) NY9964 Map 10

Wheatsheaf ⇦

Watling St (former A69, just N of centre)

One of the main draws at this pleasant old house is the good range of well prepared and generously served bar food – there's a large conservatory dining area. The popular lunchtime bar menu includes sandwiches (£1.35), mince pie or cumberland sausage (£3.75), half roast chicken or fried cod (£3.95) and cold roast pork, salads or beef goulash (£4.25); puddings on display (£1.85); children's menu (from £2.50) and a daily blackboard special. Dishes are marginally more expensive in the evening with a few additions like grilled trio of lamb (£6.95) and chicken ragout (£6.75). The lounge bar on the left has comfortable ribbed wall banquettes and cushioned chairs, pink patterned wallpaper above a darker toning dado and below a delft shelf packed with china, some old-fashioned pictures, and roughened burnt orange paintwork between the beams. It opens through a chubby balustrade into a dining area with lots of little china bells on a delft shelf. Well kept Darleys Thorne and Vaux Waggledance on handpump, and a good choice of wines and malt whiskies; prompt friendly service. Darts, dominoes, trivia and piped music; some picnic tables out on the side grass. Out in the stable yard are a couple of strange stones, thought to be of Roman origin, and said to represent the gods Janus and Ceres; 5% charge for credit cards. *(Recommended by Ian Phillips, Gordon, Julie Peters, A Craig, John Oddey, Margaret and David Bloomfield, R M Macnaughton, Graham and Karen Oddey, Paul Boot, Graham and Lynn Mason, Margaret and David Bloomfield)*

Vaux ~ Lease: Gordon Young ~ Real ale ~ Meals and snacks (12-9.30) ~ Restaurant ~ (01434) 632020 ~ Children welcome ~ Singer Sat evenings, once monthly ~ Open 11-11 ~ Bedrooms: £37.50B/£49.50B

COTHERSTONE (Durham) NZ0119 Map 10

Fox & Hounds ⇦

B6277 – incidentally a good quiet route to Scotland, through interesting scenery

Prettily placed overlooking a picturesque village green this white-painted old country dining pub has new licensees since the last edition of this Guide but we're sure it will continue as a quiet and charming place to stay. The cosy beamed bar has various alcoves and recesses, with comfortable furnishings such as thickly cushioned wall seats, local photographs and country pictures on the walls, and a winter open fire. The food served in the L-shaped lounge bar includes sandwiches (£1.50), soup (£1.95), spicy whitebait (£3.45), king prawns in garlic (£4.95), ploughman's (£4.45), chicken curry, steak sandwich or giant filled yorkshire pudding (£4.95), salads or vegetable provençal (£5.95), mixed grill or deep fried haddock (£6.95), grilled lamb cutlets (£7.95), seafood platter (£12.95); puddings (£2.25), local cheeses (£2.95); efficient and courteous service; one restaurant is no smoking. Well kept Hambleton Best, White Boar (from the same supplier as Hambleton) and John Smiths Bitter on handpump, a fair choice of malt whiskies. The pub and is handy for various walks and attractions. No pets. *(Recommended by Eric and Jackie Robinson, V Green, B D Atkin, Peter and Lynn Brueton, Mrs J R Thomas, Susan and Rick Auty; more reports please)*

Free house ~ Licensees Michael and May Carlisle~ Real ale ~ Meals and snacks (12-3, 7-9.30) ~ Restaurant ~ (01833) 650241 ~ Children welcome ~ Open 11-11 (winter 11-3, 6.30-11) ~ Bedrooms: £37.50B/£50B – children must be over 9 to stay here

CRASTER (Northumberland) NU2620 Map 10

Jolly Fisherman £

Off B1339 NE of Alnwick

Perched high in a lovely fishing town (the splendid clifftop walk to Dunstanburgh Castle is close by) this unpretentious local has really fabulous views from its little garden or big picture windows over the harbour to the sea. As well as being popular with workers from the kippering shed opposite and from the harbour the relaxed and atmospheric original bar (particularly the snug by the entrance) really welcomes strangers into the relaxed and friendly swing of things. Simple but popular snacks include toasties or home-made stottie pizzas (£1.30), excellent local crab and salmon sandwiches (£1.60, smoked salmon £2.60) and prawns in mayonnaise (£1.60). Well kept Wards Thornes Best and Vaux Lorimers Best Scotch on handpump; darts, shove-ha'penny, dominoes, cribbage, juke box, fruit machine and trivia. *(Recommended by Dr I H Maine, D Stokes, Caroline Wright, Christopher Turner, J H and S A Harrop, Karen and Graham Oddey, M Carey, A Groocock, Gordon, Julie Munday, Martin Robinson, Verity Kemp, Richard Mills, Stephen Brown, Mrs M A Kilner, David Pither, Jonathan Mann, Abigail Regan, June and Tony Baldwin, P D and J Bickley, Thomas Nott, Mr and Mrs C Brown, D Devine)*

Vaux ~ Lease: W P Silk ~ Real ale ~ Snacks (available during opening hours) ~ (01665) 576461 ~ Children welcome ~ Open 11-11 (winter 11-3; 6-11)

DIPTONMILL (Northumberland) NY9361 Map 10

Dipton Mill

Off B6306 S of Hexham at Slaley, Blanchland and Dye House, Whitley Chapel signposts and HGV route sign

There's a wonderfully cheerful and relaxing atmosphere in the homely rooms of this very popular little local, and a warm welcome from the friendly landlord. Well kept Theakstons Best, as well as Hexhamshire Bitter, Devils Water, Shire and Whapweasel from a local brewery about two and half miles from the pub are served in the snug little bar which has dark ply panelling, red furnishings and open fires; quite a few malt whiskies; darts, bar billiards, shove ha'penny and dominoes. Good value, reliable lunchtime bar food efficiently served includes soup (£1.40), nicely presented sandwiches (from £1.40, the thick rare beef, £1.75, are recommended), ploughman's (£2.75), salads (from £3.25), smoked salmon or cheese and onion flan (£3.50), steak and kidney pie or mince and dumplings (£3.80) and chicken breast in sherry sauce or bacon chop in cider sauce (£4.10) served with good fresh vegetables; puddings like lime cheesecake or syrup sponge (£1.40); home-made cakes and coffee (£1.40); no evening food. The garden is a particularly nice place to unwind, perhaps on the sunken crazy-paved terrace by the restored mill stream, or by the pretty plantings and aviaries. There may be barbecues here on summer weekends. It's in a very peaceful wooded valley and there are easy-walking footpaths nearby. *(Recommended by A L Carr, Mike Pugh, Karen and Graham Oddey, Duncan Small, John Oddey, Dr R H M Stewart, Stephen Brown, Edward Watson)*

Free house ~ Licensee Geoff Brooker ~ Real ale ~ Lunchtime meals and snacks ~ (01434) 606577 ~ Children in games room ~ Open 12-2.30, 6-11; closed 25 Dec

GREAT WHITTINGTON (Northumberland) NZ0171 Map 10

Queens Head

Village signposted off A68 and B6018 just N of Corbridge

In an attractive and very neatly kept stonebuilt village just north of Hadrian's Wall, this early 18th-c pub has always had a warm and friendly atmosphere, but under its present licensees has been developing a much wider appeal. Behind its simple stone exterior, two comfortable beamed rooms with a step between have been refurbished in a gently rustic style, with log fires, a mural over the fireplace near the bar counter, some handsome carved oak settles among other more modern furnishings, old prints and a collection of keys. One of the biggest changes has been the introduction of a wider choice of good changing relatively upmarket home-made bar food listed on a blackboard: sandwiches (from £1.75), ploughman's (£4.50), salads, goujons of fresh haddock, and vegetarian dishes like mushroom stroganoff or nut, corn and cheese casserole (£4.95), beef and ale pie, wild boar and duck pie or breast of chicken with leek and stilton sauce (£5.95), sole mornay (£6.50), sirloin steak (£9.75); good puddings like lemon roulade, summer pudding, sticky toffee pudding and a fruit pie (£2.95). Well kept Queens Head which is brewed for them by the local Hadrian Brewery, Hambleton Bitter and two others which are usually Boddingtons or Courage Directors; decent choice of malt whiskies, friendly attentive service, unobtrusive piped music; there's a no-smoking area in the newish and attractive back restaurant. There are six picnic tables on the small front lawn. ***(Recommended by GSB, Dr R H M Stewart, JJW, CMJ, J D K Hyams, Philip and Helen Heppell, John Oddey)***

Free house ~ Ian Scott ~ Real ale ~ Meals and snacks ~ (01434) 672267 ~ Children in eating area ~ Restaurant ~ Open 12-3, 6-11 (closed 25 Dec evening)

nr HALTWHISTLE (Northumberland) NY7164 Map 10

Milecastle

Military Rd; B6318 NE – OS Sheet 86 map reference 715660

This cosily refurbished remote moorland 17th-c pub effectively combines really good generously served food with warm and genuine hospitality and a peaceful chatty atmosphere (no machines or piped music here). With quite an emphasis on game the imaginative menu includes splendid home-made sausages, particularly venison (£4.75) and cumberland (£5.95), sausage swirls – sausage meat in flaky pastry like a Swiss roll), and interesting pies (around £5.95) such as beef and venison, wild boar and duckling, turkey, ham and chestnut, pheasant and claret, or coulibiac pie – salmon with rice, mushroom and parsley. There are half a dozen or so good dishes of the day. The local meat is well hung and the fresh local vegetables good, as are soups (£1.75) such as spiced tomato, and puddings such as chocolate and orange cake or treacle tart (£2). Sandwiches (from £2.35) and ploughman's (from £3.95) tend to be dressed up with a great deal of salad. Well kept changing real ales such as Black Sheep, Jennings and Tetleys on handpump; a very decent collection of malt whiskies and a good wine list. The snug small rooms of the beamed bar, decorated mainly with brasses, horsey and local landscape prints and attractive dried flowers, do get very busy in season (or when two dozen local farmers arrive in force); there's a lunchtime overflow into the small comfortable restaurant. Good friendly chatty service; a splendid coal fire, with a welcome for walkers (but no rucksacks allowed); some white plastic seats and tables outside in a sheltered walled garden with a dovecote. ***(Recommended by A and D B, V Green, Pat and Robert Watt, John Honnor, Roger Berry, R T and J C Moggridge, Dr A M Rankin, Julia Stone)***

Free house ~ Licensees Ralph and Margaret Payne ~ Real ale ~ Meals and snacks ~ Restaurant (not Sun eve) ~ (01434) 320682 ~ Children over 5 ~ Open 12-2.30, 6.30-11

HEDLEY ON THE HILL (Northumberland) NZ0859 Map 10

Feathers

Village signposted from New Ridley, which is signposted from B6309 N of Consett; OS Sheet 88 map reference 078592

Inside this quaint village local the three well kept turkey-carpeted traditional bars have beams, woodburning stoves, stripped stonework, solid brown leatherette settles, country pictures, and a particulary relaxed and welcoming atmosphere. Well kept Boddingtons and Jennings Cumberland, and a continuously changing local favourite guest ale, possibly Hexhamshire Big Lamp, Butterknowle or Hadrian, are served on handpump; around 30 malt whiskies; dominoes, bar billiards and alley skittles. The well balanced continually changing choice of very good value popular food is restricted to weekends only as the landlady does not want to turn the pub into an eating house: soups such as tomato and mint (£1.75), tuna pasta bake or ploughman's (£3.50), fennel and courgette au gratin (£3.65), summer vegetable tart (£3.85), creamy chicken with spring onions, mushrooms and spinach (£4.75), babotie (£4.95), salmon steak or greek beef casserole with tomatoes, oregano and wine (£5.25), and puddings like rhubarb fudge crumble, chocolate roulade with strawberry sauce and sticky toffee pudding (£1.95); children's meals. Every Easter Monday, this friendly and traditional little stone local holds a barrel race – which ends a weekend mini beer festival with around 20 real ales to choose from. *(Recommended by John Fazakerley, JJW, CMW, Kay and Mark Denison, R and G Underwood, Susan and Rick Auty; more reports please)*

Free house ~ Licensees Marina and Colin Atkinson ~ Real ale ~ Weekend meals and snacks ~ (01661) 843607 ~ Children in family room ~ Irish/Northumbrian folk night (bring your own instruments) 2nd Tues of each month ~ Open 6-11; 12-3, 6-11 Sat

MATFEN (Northumberland) NZ0372 Map 10

Black Bull

Village signposted off B6318 NE of Corbridge

The hard work they put into the gardens of this charming old creeper-covered long stone inn paid off marvellously last year as they won a couple of "In Bloom" awards for their pretty hanging baskets, shrubs and bedding plants – there are plenty of seats outside on the terrace. The spacious turkey-carpeted main bar which is popular with visitors at lunchtime and locals in the evening has windsor chairs, copper-topped tables, and steeplechasing pictures, and there's a side room with red plush button-back built-in wall banquettes, and attractive 1940s photographs. Good, fresh, well presented bar food includes soup of the day (£1.50), duck liver pâté with cumberland sauce (£3.75), fillet of haddock or filled yorkshire pudding (£4.75), honey glazed breast of chicken with toasted almonds (£4.85), scampi, chicken and leek pie or steak and kidney pie (£4.95), home-made cooked ham (£5.25), oak smoked trout fillets (£5.50), roast beef (£5.75) game pie (£7.25), and smoked salmon (£7.50), and puddings (£2.95); good, fresh vegetables. They will do sandwiches, and in addition you can order from the seasonally varying, and very good, restaurant menu; part of the restaurant is no smoking. Well kept Black Bull, Morlands Old Speckled Hen, Theakstons Best, and guests in summer on handpump, a good choice of over 20 malt whiskies, log fires, sensibly placed darts, dominoes, fruit machine, and juke box. No dogs. *(Recommended by Jack and Heather Coyle, Margaret and Nigel Dennis, J P Burke, T M Dobby, R and G Underwood, BB, R Deeming, John Allsopp, John Oddey, Mrs A Gray, J Derek Robb)*

Free house ~ Licensees Colin and Michele Scott ~ Real ale ~ Meals and snacks ~ Restaurant ~ (01661) 886330 ~ Children in eating area of bar ~ Open 11-11; (winter 11-3; 6-11) ~ Bedrooms: £32.50B/£55B

Pubs brewing their own beers are listed at the back of the book.

NEW YORK (Tyne & Wear) NZ3370 Map 10

Shiremoor House Farm ★

Middle Engine Lane/Norham Road; from A1 going N from Tyne Tunnel, right into A1058 then next left signposted New York, then left at end of speed limit (pub signed); or at W end of New York A191 bypass turn S into Norham Road, then first right (pub signed)

The company that transformed the derelict farm buildings here won an award for their sensitive and understated work. Gentle lighting in several well divided spacious areas cleverly picks up the surface modelling of the pale stone and beam ends. There's a delightful mix of interesting and extremely comfortable furniture, a big kelim on the broad flagstones and warmly colourful farmhouse paintwork on the bar counter and several other tables, as well as conical rafters of the former gin-gan, a few farm tools, and good rustic pictures such as mid-West prints, big crisp black-and-white photographs of country people and modern Greek bull sketches. Bar food includes venison sausage or diced pork in coarse-grain mustard sauce (£3.75), breast of chicken with prawn and garlic sauce, blanquette of lamb or coronation chicken salad (£3.95), prawn salad (£4.95) and rack of lamb or rump steak with pepper sauce (£5.95). The granary extension is good for families with high chairs, and bottle or baby food warmed on request. Well kept Black Sheep Special, Stones Best and Theakston's Best on handpump, decent wines by the glass, polite and efficient young staff. No music or games machines; Monday evening quiz. A separate bar serves the equally attractive rather smart restaurant. It can get crowded at weekday lunchtimes. There are picnic tables on neat grass at the edge of the flagstoned farm courtyard, by tubs and a manger filled with flowers; no-smoking area. *(Recommended by Karen and Graham Oddey, E V Walder, Roger Bellingham, Barbara and Norman Wells, John Oddey, Chris and Anne Fluck, Trevor Scott, Neil Townend, John Coatsworth, Jacqueline White)*

Sir John Fitzgerald Ltd ~ Licensees M W Garrett and C W Kerridge ~ Real ale ~ Meals and snacks (all day Sun) ~ Restaurant ~ (0191) 257 6302 ~ Children in eating area of bar and in restaurant ~ Open 11-11

NEWCASTLE UPON TYNE (Tyne & Wear) NZ2266 Map 10

Bridge Hotel £

Castle Square (in local A-Z street atlas index as Castle Garth); right in centre, just off Nicholas St (A6215) at start of High Level Bridge; only a few parking meters nearby, but evening parking easy

The atmosphere at this well preserved bustling and chatty Victorian bar varies according to the time of day. As it's next door to the Crown court lawyers rub shoulders with businessmen and shoppers at lunchtime, while in the evening it's popular with a lively younger set. The imposing, neatly kept old-fashioned lounge has high ceilings, a bar counter equipped with unusual pull-down slatted snob screens, decorative mirrors, brown leather banquettes and elegant small chairs on its rust carpet, and a massive mahogany carved fireplace. In the public bar, which has some cheerful stained glass, there's a good (sometimes loud) jukebox, pool, pinball, dominoes, a video game, and fruit machine. Well kept Courage Best, Theakstons Best and XB and a weekly changing guest beer on handpump; simple bar snacks include toasted sandwiches (90p) and wholemeal stottie cakes with meat and salad (£1.10); friendly service. Tables on the flagstoned back terrace are by the remains of the city wall that look down over the Tyne and its bridges. *(Recommended by Karen and Graham Oddey, GSB, Julian Holland, Stephen and Julie Brown)*

Sir John Fitzgerald Ltd ~ Licensee Walter Richurby and Andrew Gubbie ~ Real ale ~ Lunchtime sandwiches ~ (0191) 232 7780 ~ No children ~ Folk and blues club Mon, other live music Thurs and occasional Fri ~ Open 11-3, 5-11; 11-11 Sat

The knife-and-fork rosette distinguishes pubs where the food is of exceptional quality.

Cooperage £

32 The Close, Quayside; immediately below and just to the W of the High Level Bridge; parking across road limited lunchtime, easy evening

This waterfront Tudor house which is one of Newcastle's oldest buildings was actually once a cooperage but today it's the beer rather than the casks that makes it worthy of attention. They're so busy with locals, businessmen and students that they'll generally get through about 15 a week with a usual choice of seven real ales on handpump including regulars such as Ind Coope Burton, Marstons Owd Rodger and Tetleys, three guests such as Ansells Mild, Benskins, Flowers Original, Friary Meux, Fullers ESB, Marstons Pedigree, or Timothy Taylors Landlord and one of three ales from their own Hadrian brewery – Gladiator, Centurion and Emperor; also handpulled Addlestones and Bulmers ciders. The small bustling bar has huge Tudor oak beams and exposed stonework, and there's extra seating in the lounge area by the pool room; fruit and trivia machines and a juke box. Very good value lunchtime bar food from a changing a menu and quickly changing blackboard is served with fresh seasonal vegetables and home grown herbs; ham and vegetable broth and yellow split pea soup (£1.10), grilled North Shields kipper fillets (£2.20) and other fresh fish from the quay, hot roast pork and stuffing in a stottie bun (£2.75), a vegetarian dish like mushrooms, leek and cauliflower cheesebake (£3), steak, mushroom and ale pie (£3.75), cod fillet bake with a light lager (£3.95) and a daily special like minced beef and ale pie and a pint of beer (£3), and home-made puddings like brandy bread and butter pudding or hot apple and lemon sponge (£1.20); Sunday lunch (£4.95). The pub, near the waterfront, is close to the Sunday outdoor market. *(Recommended by Richard Lewis, S G Brown, Noel Jackson, Louise Campbell, Julian Holland, John Oddey)*

Free house ~ Licensee Michael Westwell ~ Real ale ~ Meals and snacks (11-7) ~ Restaurant (not Sun evening) ~ Newcastle (0191) 232 8286 ~ Children in eating area of bar and in restaurant lunchtime only ~ Open 11-11

Crown Posada £

31 The Side; off Dean Street, between and below the two high central bridges (A6125 and A6127)

The marvellous facade of this bustling city centre pub with its pre-Raphaelite stained-glass windows and imposing golden crown could easily be that of a grand old bank or post office. Inside there's lots of architectural charm such as an elaborate coffered ceiling in cream and dusky pink, and delightful oddities including a line of gilt mirrors each with a tulip lamp on a curly brass mount which match the great ceiling candelabra, stained glass in the counter screens, and Victorian flowered wallpaper above the brown dado (with its fat heating pipes along the bottom – a popular footrest when the east wind brings the rain off the North Sea). It's a very long and narrow room, making quite a bottleneck by the serving counter, and beyond that, a long soft green built-in leather wall seat is flanked by narrow tables. Well kept Bass, Boddingtons, Butterknowle Conciliation, Jennings and Theakstons Best on handpump and tap; lunchtime sandwiches and toasties (£1); friendly barmen, chatty customers; fruit machine. On some weekday evenings you can find it quiet, with regulars reading the papers put out in the front snug, but by Friday it should be quite packed. Note that they don't allow children. *(Recommended by Richard Lewis, S G Brown, Mrs M A Kilner, Thomas Nott, Noel Jackson, Louise Campbell)*

Sir John Fitzgerald Ltd ~ Manager Malcolm McPherson ~ Real ale ~ Lunchtime snacks ~ (0191) 232 1269 ~ Open 11-11

NEWTON ON THE MOOR (Northumberland) NU1605 Map 10

Cook & Barker Arms

Village signposted from A1 Alnwick—Felton

One reader still remembers when the popular restaurant was a blacksmith's shop – which dates in parts back to the 1700s – and the entire inn was limited to what is now the bar area. The extra space is really needed these days because this place is really popular for very good, imaginative bar food: hot sandwiches from (£3.25), vegetarian dishes like Tunisian bean salad or filled croissants (£3.95), spaghetti vongole (£4.80), a daily pie like steak and kidney or chicken, ham and mushroom, grilled lamb's liver and bacon, terrine of sole and wild salmon or baked avocado with Northumbrian goat's cheese (all £4.95); puddings like sticky toffee pudding, bread and butter pudding or baked rice condé (from £2); well kept Courage Directors and Theakstons Best on handpump and two guests which might include Charles Wells Bombardier or Youngers No 3; about 30 good malt whiskies, and decent wines; hardworking, really friendly licensees and good prompt service – even when busy. The unfussy, long beamed and gently atmospheric bar has a coal fire at one end with a coal-effect gas fire at the other, stripped, partly panelled walls, brocade-seated settles around oak-topped tables, framed banknotes and paintings by local artists on the walls, brasses, and a highly polished oak servery. What was the old storeroom now has tables, chairs and an old settle, and darts – it's popular with locals – and the games room has scrubbed pine furniture, french windows leading onto the terrace, and darts, dominoes, fruit machine and juke box. *(Recommended by GSB, E J Wilde, Ian Phillips, Laura Darlington, Gianluca Perinetti, Adam and Joan Bunting, Julie Peters, John Allsopp, Dr I H Maine, Mr and Mrs J A Stewart, Jack and Heather Coyle, Tim and Sue Halstead, Roger Bellingham, Julia Stone, Mike Eeckelaers, B B Pearce, Reg and Carrie Carr, Gerald and Su Mason, G A Pearce, Jack Morley, June and Tony Baldwin, Les and Jean Scott)*

Free house ~ Licensees Lynn and Phil Farmer ~ Real ale ~ Meals and snacks ~ Evening restaurant ~ Shilbottle (01665) 575234 ~ Children in eating area of bar ~ Open 11-3, 6-11 ~ Bedrooms: £30B/£60B

NORTH SHIELDS (Tyne & Wear) NZ3468 Map 10

Chain Locker £

New Quay

Dwarfed by the surviving 1816 wharfside commercial buildings – now largely flats – you'll find this simple and welcoming late Victorian two-storey brick pub close to the pedestrian ferry landing area. There's quite a nautical theme, with seafaring pictures and navigational charts and maps on the walls (some giving a detailed account of the Falklands campaign), also stools and wooden wall benches around small tables (the one on your left as you go in, built over a radiator, is prized in winter), an open fire and local literature and arts information. Four impeccably kept real ales on handpump (two are weekly changing guests) such as Ind Coope Burton, Tetleys, Timothy Taylors Landlord and Hadrian Chainlocker; malt whiskies, farm ciders. Dominoes, fruit machine and piped music. Extremely good, reasonably priced bar food includes lunchtime sandwiches and a good amount of excellent local fresh fish such as garlic mussels (£2.50), smoked fish pie (£3.35) or salmon (£4.75) and oysters if you order them in advance, also steak pie (£3.65). They may have free biscuits and cheese on a Sunday, when they sometimes organise boat trips. *(Recommended by John Prescott, John Oddey, Karen and Graham Oddey, J A Stewart, Mrs M A Kilner, Jonathan Mann, Abigail Regan; more reports please)*

Free house ~ Licensee Wilfred Kelly ~ Real ale ~ Meals and snacks (12-2.30, 6-9.30; not Sun evening) ~ Restaurant (not Sun evening) ~ (0191) 258 0147 ~ Children welcome ~ Folk music Fri evening ~ Open 11-4, 6-11; 11-11 Sat

Wooden Doll

103 Hudson Street; from Tyne Tunnel, follow A187 into town centre; keep straight ahead (when the A187 turns off left) until, approaching the sea, you can see the pub in Hudson Street on your right

Quite a few people stop at this unpretentious place just to see the densely hung collection of well over a hundred paintings by local artists. Or if you'd rather look at the real thing there's a fascinating seagull's-eye view from the covered glassed-in verandah down on to the bustling boats and warehouses of the Shields Fish Quay, with the derricks and gantries beyond. Past them is the sweep of the outer harbour with its long piers, headlands, and low Black Middens rocks. The simple and unassuming wooden floored bar and lounge have a couple of chesterfields, red plush seats and Formica-topped cast-iron tables, and a coal-effect gas fire. A fine range of well kept real ales on handpump might include Ind Coope Burton, Tetleys and Timothy Taylors Landlord; friendly service. The new licensee had only been here two days as we went to press and the menu hadn't yet been finalised but will probably be Tetley's own Farmhouse Platter standard menu and a specials board with lots of fresh fish specials from the Quay; much of the eating area is no smoking. Dominoes, fruit machine, and piped music. *(Recommended by J A Stewart, JJW, CMW, Leonard Dixon, Graham and Karen Oddey, John Oddey, Mrs M A Kilner)*

Carlsberg Tetleys ~ Manager Neil Goodenough ~ Real ale ~ Meals and snacks (not Sun evenings) ~ (0191) 257 3747 ~ Children till 8pm ~ Live music Sat evening ~ Open 11-3, 6-11.30(Sat 11-11.30)

PIERCEBRIDGE (Durham) NZ2116 Map 10

George

B6275 over bridge just S of village

In a magnificent riverside setting by the River Tees the gardens of this old coaching inn have several pleasant eating areas surrounded by colourful flowerbeds; you may see herons and even kingfishers. This is also said to be where the clock stopped short, never to go again, when the old man died, and the venerable timepiece still stands silently in the hallway. The three characterful bars have no less than five open fires in one room or another and solid wood furniture, and it's well worth a visit to the Ballroom Bar – just that, a bar inside a fully-fitted ballroom (open only for special functions or during barbecues); piped music. A wide choice of popular bar food includes sandwiches (£1.95), quite a few starters like good soup, smoked mackerel fillet or pâté (all £2.25), vegetarian dishes such as fruit, vegetable and nut curry or vegetable medley in hollandaise (all £4.85), huge salads or cod in mushroom sauce (£4.85), steak and kidney pie (£4.95), cream of seafood vol au vent (£5.95), pork in oyster sauce (£6.50), stilton and chicken parcel (£8.25) and poached salmon in hollandaise (£9.45), good steaks (from £9.50); puddings such as blackcurrant meringue nest or brandy snaps and apricot (£2.25), four course breakfasts (£5.95), afternoon tea, and Sunday lunch; attentive service. John Smiths, Ruddles County and Theakstons Best on handpump, malt whiskies, and decent wines; they often close the bars in the afternoon, but continue to serve beers in the tea room; piped music. The bedrooms are in the converted stables. Attractively positioned on the alternative, scenic route between Scotch Corner and Edinburgh, the inn is handy for various Roman remains. A fort once stood just over the bridge and there are some interesting excavations on display. *(Recommended by Andrew and Ruth Triggs, Paul and Janet Waring, John Fazakerley, Mrs Cook, Brian Webster, G and B Hartley, Verity Kemp, Richard Mills, R T and J C Moggridge, J M Turner, Mr and Mrs N Bogg, R J Walden, J S Poulter, George Morrison)*

Free house ~ Licensee John Wain ~ Real ale ~ Meals and snacks (12-2, 6-10) ~ Restaurant ~ (01325) 374576 ~ Children in eating area of bar and in Farmhouse restaurant; children over 10 in Riverside restaurant ~ Open 11-11 ~ Bedrooms: £48B/£58B

RENNINGTON (Northumberland) NU2119 Map 10

Masons Arms

Stamford Cott; B1340 NE of Alnwick

Off the beaten track and close to the sea this friendly and well-run old coaching inn has an attractive beamed lounge bar with wheelback and mate's chairs around solid wooden tables on the patterned carpet, plush bar stools, lots of brass, pictures and photographs on the walls, and a relaxed atmosphere; the dining rooms have pine panelling and wrought-iron wall lights. Boddingtons, Marstons Pedigree and Ruddles Best on handpump; and piped music. Popular bar food includes lunchtime only sandwiches, home-made soup (£1.90), home-made chicken liver and brandy pâté (£3.75), fried haddock (£4.95), three bean casserole or cream cheese vegetable bake (£5.45), game casserole (£5.95), gammon steak or chicken coated with orange and lemon sauce (£6.25), steaks (from £9.55), a choice of daily specials; puddings like chocolate gateaux or sherry trifle cheesecake (£2.25), and children's meals. There are sturdy rustic tables on the little front terrace, surrounded by lavender. The bedrooms are in recently converted stables. *(Recommended by Christopher Turner, June and Tony Baldwin, Mrs P Abell, Les and Jean Scott, Mark Bradley, Mrs M Armstrong, Duncan Redpath, Lorraine Milburn, P D and J Bickley)*

Free house ~ Licensees Frank and Dee Sloan ~ Real ale ~ Meals and snacks ~ Restaurant ~ (01665) 577275 ~ Children in restaurant up to 8pm; no infants in evening ~ Open 12-2, 6.30-11 ~ Bedrooms: £33B/£43B

ROMALDKIRK (Durham) NY9922 Map 10

Rose & Crown

Just off B6277

Northumbria Dining Pub of the Year

This fairly smart old hotel is popular as a peaceful and well run place to stay and for its good stylish food. Fresh fish is delivered twice a week, they use fresh pasta and dress their salads with toasted sunflowers. Blackboard specials are particularly interesting and might include moules marinières baked with cream and Cotherstone cheese (£3.95), baked fillet of whiting with oyster mushrooms and chives (£6.95), lamb's kidneys with grain mustard sauce (£5.95) and woodpigeon with juniper and onion confit or char-grilled rump of venison with madeira sauce (£8.95) or pan fried strips of beef fillet with green peppercorns. The popular lunchtime bar menu includes home-made soup (£2.65), filled brown baps (from £2.65), rich chicken liver pâté (£3.50), pasta with Cotherstone cheese in fresh tomato sauce (£3.95), sausages, black pudding and onion confit (£4.25), ploughman's with their own pickled onions and chutney (£4.95), sautéed chicken livers, bacon and walnuts with fresh pasta (£5.50), steak and kidney pie with mushrooms and ale (£7.50). In the evening there are additional dishes like pork fillet in sherry and cream sauce with fresh pasta (£7.95) or char-grilled chicken breast with garlic butter (£8.50); puddings like hot sticky toffee pudding, hot apple and Calvados tart, lime meringue pie and rum and chocolate pot. The beamed traditional bar has old-fashioned seats facing the log fire, a Jacobean oak settle, cream walls decorated with lots of gin traps, some old farm tools and black and white pictures of Romaldkirk at the turn of the century, as well as a grandfather clock, and lots of brass and copper. The smart Crown Room, where bar food is served, has more brass and copper, original coloured etchings of hunting scenes, and farm implements; the hall is hung with wine maps and other interesting prints; no-smoking oak-panelled restaurant. Theakstons Best and Old Peculier on handpump and about eight wines by the glass; good service. In the summer, the tables outside look out over the village green, still with its original stocks and water pump. The village is close to the superb Bowes Museum and the High Force waterfall, and has an interesting old church. *(Recommended by Maysie Thompson, Jack and Heather Coyle, H B Parker, Paul and Janet Waring, Christopher Beadle, R J Walden, John Cadman, Catheryn and Richard Hicks, John Fazakerley, John Honnor, Mavis and Hon Wright, Peter Race, Noel Jackson, Louise Campbell, Leonard Dixon)*

Free house ~ Licensees Christopher and Alison Davy ~ Real ale ~ Meals and snacks (12-1.30, 7-9) ~ Restaurant (not Sun evening) ~ (01833) 650213 ~ Children welcome ~ Open 11-3, 5.30-11; closed 25/26 Dec ~ Bedrooms: £54B/£75B

Planning a day in the country? We list pubs in really attractive scenery at the back of the book.

SEAHOUSES (Northumberland) NU2232 Map 10

Olde Ship ★

B1340 coast road

While you sit surrounded by a treasure-trove of nautical memorabilia in the marvellously atmospheric bar you can look through the one clear window (the other windows have stained-glass sea pictures), across the harbour to the Farne Islands and watch the Lonstones lighthouse shine across the fading evening sky and listen to the small talk of the local fishing fraternity. Everywhere you look in the small and friendly rooms there are shiny brass fittings, sea pictures and model ships, including a fine one of the North Sunderland lifeboat and a model of Seahouses' lifeboat *The Grace Darling*, as well as ship's instruments and equipment and a knotted anchor made by local fishermen; all the items are genuine. Even the floor of the saloon bar is scrubbed ship's decking and if it weren't for the real fire you could almost be forgiven for thinking you really were on a boat. There is another low-beamed snug bar, and an improved family area at the back. Popular bar food includes sandwiches (£1.75), crab or vegetable soup (from £1.50), steak and kidney pie, beef olives, fisherman's pie, Dorset jugged steak and lamb hot pot (all £4.50); puddings such as ginger trifle, chocolate sponge and custard or raspberry pie (£2); a different evening menu includes crunchy cod bake, lasagne and chicken breasts and broccoli with mayonnaise, curry and cheese (all £5.50). This year they've increased their real ales to seven including Black Bull, Charles Wells Bombardier, Longstone Bitter (a tasty ale from a micro-brewery just along the road at Belford), Marstons Pedigree, Morlands Old Speckled Hen, McEwans 80/-, Theakstons Best and XB and Youngers No 3, some kept under light blanket pressure; they also serve several malt whiskies, a hot toddy and mulled wine in winter, and some uncommon bottled beers; dominoes, trivia, and piped music. Pews surround barrel tables in the back courtyard, and a battlemented side terrace with a sun lounge looks out on the harbour. An anemometer is connected to the top of the chimney. You can book boat trips to the Farne Islands Bird Sanctuary at the harbour, and there are bracing coastal walks, particularly to Bamburgh, Grace Darling's birthplace. *(Recommended by Christopher Turner, Paul and Janet Waring, James Macrae, Julie Peters, Laura Darlington, Gianluca Perinetti, Gordon, Leigh and Gillian Mellor, June and Tony Baldwin, Trevor and Christine Millum, A Craig, Stephen and Julie Brown, Michael A Butler, D Devine, Duncan Redpath, Lorraine Milburn, Penny and Peter Keevil, Julie Munday, Martin Robinson, Thomas Nott)*

Free house ~ Licensees Alan and Jean Glen ~ Real ale ~ Meals and snacks ~ Restaurant ~ (01665) 720200 ~ Children in restaurant and Locker room ~ Open 11-3, 6-11 ~ Bedrooms: £34B/£68B

STANNERSBURN (Northumberland) NY7286 Map 10

Pheasant

Kielder Water road signposted off B6320 in Bellingham

Originally a farm in the early 17th-c this friendly and pleasantly unpretentious stone inn is beautifully located in a very peaceful valley just below Kielder Water. There are picnic tables out in the streamside garden, a pony-paddock behind, and quiet forests all around. The red-carpeted largely stripped-stone lounge is traditional, comfortable and attractive, and the separate public bar, similar but simpler, opens into a games room with darts, pool and dominoes; in the evenings there's a happy mix of locals and visitors. There is a no-smoking carpeted country dining room; besides sandwiches, very good home-cooked bar food with fresh vegetables includes lasagne, vegetarian lasagne, vegetable pasta bake, steak and kidney pie and oven crisp haddock (all £5.25) and smoked salmon salad (£6.50). Prices are a bit higher in the evening; good Sunday lunch. Well kept Ind Coope Burton, Tetleys and occasional guests on handpump, a very good collection of malt whiskies, decent wines, good welcoming service. Breakfasts are good. *(Recommended by J D K Hyams, D and J Tapper, Paul and Janet Waring, John Allsopp, Mrs M A Kilner, Ian and Sue Stratford)*

Free house ~ Licensees Walter and Irene Kershaw ~ Real ale ~ Meals and snacks ~ Restaurant ~ (01434) 240382 ~ Children in eating area till 9pm ~ Open 11-3, 5.30-11 (winter 12-2, 7-11; closed Mon in Jan and Feb) ~ Bedrooms:£30B/£52B

WARENFORD (Northumberland) NU1429 Map 10

Warenford Lodge

Just off A1 Alnwick—Belford, on village loop road

One of the main draws here is the attractively presented, good and often imaginative home-made bar food which tends towards foreign country cooking and might include home-made soup or baked egg Florentine (£1.95), lentil, hazelnut and mushroom pâté (£2.75), braised kidney with couscous (£3.90), Turkish aubergine salad or tagliatelle with wild mushroom and walnut sauce (£4.50), Andalucian casserole (£5.50), crispy haddock (£5.70), a substantial and very good fish soup or monkfish in tamarind sauce (£7.90) and stincotto, Italian shank of pork roasted with wine and herbs (£10.90), and puddings like fresh fruit salad with Kirsch, steamed chocolate pudding or toffee and banana ice cream (£2.50); decent selection of wines and malt whiskies; good choice of teas. From the outside it looks like an ordinary small stone house – there's no pub sign – so beware of driving straight past. Although quite old the bar looks modern with cushioned wooden seats around pine tables, some stripped stone walls, and a warm fire in the big stone fireplace; steps lead up to an extension which has comfortable easy chairs and settees around low tables, and a big woodburning stove. *(Recommended by Christopher Turner, Laura Darlington, Gianluca Perinetti, Trevor and Christine Millum, Jill and Peter Bickley, Penny and Peter Keevil, Les and Jean Scott, Thomas Nott, G A Peace)*

Free house ~ Licensee Raymond Matthewman ~ Meals and snacks (not Mon, not lunchtimes except weekends when lunchtime service stops 1.30) ~ Evening restaurant ~ (01668) 213453 ~ Children in restaurant ~ Open 7-11 (closed weekday lunchtimes and Mon except bank holidays), plus 12-2 Sat and Sun

Lucky Dip

Besides the fully inspected pubs, you might like to try these Lucky Dips recommended to us and described by readers (if you do, please send us reports):

☆ **Allendale**, N'land [NY8456], *Golden Lion*: Friendly old pub with Flowers and Websters Yorkshire, country wines, wide choice of good value food (not Mon) inc vegetarian, partly no-smoking dining area with more room upstairs, two real fires, pictures, old bottles, willow-pattern plates; games area with pool and darts, piped music; children welcome; bedrooms *(JJW, CMW)*

Allendale [B6295], *Hotspur*: Good value food and three real ales in roomy and friendly pub with unusual bow windows and carvings, piped music, pool etc; children welcome; bedrooms *(JJW, CMW)*; [Market Pl, B6295], *Kings Head*: Six changing S & N and interesting guest ales, newspapers, big log fire, cheerful service, reasonably priced bar food inc children's, children welcome; Fri evening rock, folk or blues; darts, dominoes, chess and outdoor quoits; comfortable bedrooms *(CW, JW, GSB, Edward Watson)*

☆ **Allenheads**, N'land [just off B6295; NY8545], *Allenheads*: Entertaining landlord, antiques and bric-a-brac from floor to ceiling (esp in pool room), huge helpings of good straightforward cheap food, well kept Tetleys-related ales, decent coffee, real fire, friendly alsatian; dining room; tables outside, with more machinery; bedrooms *(David and Margaret Bloomfield, JJW, CMW)*

☆ **Alnmouth**, N'land [N'land St; NU2511], *Saddle*: Wide choice of well cooked keen-priced food inc fresh fish, good puddings and memorable first-class cheeseboard in clean and friendly old pub rambling through several rooms, unpretentious and homely; well kept S & N and local ales, decent wines, helpful staff, paintings for sale; comfortable bedrooms, good breakfast *(Penny and Peter Keevil, Meg and Colin Hamilton, Mrs P Abell, D T Deas)*

Alnmouth, *Schooner*: Georgian coaching inn with one busy bar, another quieter with red plush seats, interesting local and nautical pictures, bar food, changing real ale, conservatory, candlelit Italian restaurant *(Teresa and Nigel Brooks)*

Alnwick, N'land [Fenkle St; NU1913], *Market Tavern*: No-frills pub with good value generous food, friendly efficient service, warm atmosphere *(Chris and Anne Fluck, Duncan Redpath, Lorraine Milburn)*

☆ **Anick**, N'land [signed NE of A69/A695 Hexham junction; NY9665], *Rat*: Quaint little pub, friendly and nicely refurbished, with good home-cooked food from hot counter inc good fresh veg, Sun roasts and puddings, well kept Courage-related ales and Scrumpy Jack cider, lovely north Tyne views, good service, friendly cat; children welcome, lovely garden with well planted boots *(Penny and Peter Keevil, Joan and Stephen Sloan, V Green)*

☆ **Bamburgh**, N'land [NU1835], *Lord Crewe Arms*: Small hotel with interesting bric-a-brac and good log fire in comfortable and relaxing back lounge bar, more straightforward side bar (children, can get noisy, service may not be swift), usual bar food, restaurant, tables outside; main draw for tourists is great position by green below magnificent coastal castle; dogs allowed; bedrooms comfortable, good breakfasts esp kippers *(D Stokes, D T Deas, Dorothy and David Young, Thomas Nott, Gordon, Julia Stone, Catheryn and Richard Hicks, LYM)*

☆ **Barnard Castle**, Dur [Market Pl; NZ0617], *Golden Lion*: Generous good value home-cooked lunchtime food inc children's helpings in two roomy and comfortable unpretentious bars, well kept Bass and Youngers Scotch, warm welcome, children's room; decent bedrooms *(Penny and Peter Keevil, Brian Kneale, John Fazakerley, BB)*

Barnard Castle, *Old Well*: Friendly landlady, good atmosphere, big helpings of food from sandwiches up inc baked potatoes filled to request, extremely good chips *(M Borthwick)*

☆ **Barrasford**, N'land [NY9274], *Barrasford Arms*: Friendly country local with blazing fires in compact bar, good value generous straightforward home cooking; keg beer and can be smoky; dining room, residents' lounge, children's room; lovely sandstone building with wonderful views, good value bedrooms handy for Hadrian's Wall (but early-morning quarry traffic passes) *(C Smith, Laura Darlington, Gianluca Perinetti)*

☆ **Beamish**, Dur [NZ2254], *Shepherd & Shepherdess*: Very useful for its position nr outstanding open-air heritage museum; good range of quick fairly priced straightforward food, standard layout with tables around walls, but comfortable, with good service, well kept Vaux Samson and Wards Sheffield Best, coal fires; can get crowded, piped music; children welcome, tables and play area with fibreglass monsters out among trees; has been open all day *(R A Hobbs, Mrs M A Kilner, Mr and Mrs C Brown, Trevor Scott, Derek and Sylvia Stephenson, LYM)*

Beamish [far side of Beamish Open Air Museum – entry fee], *Sun*: Turn-of-the-c reconstruction, part of the museum; very basic real period feel, with well kept McEwans 80/-, Theakstons Best and Youngers No 3, filled rolls; it does get packed *(Lesley Sones, LYM)*

☆ **Belford**, N'land [Market Pl; village signed off A1 S of Berwick; NU1134], *Blue Bell*: Good service and welcoming atmosphere in family stable bar (the Belford Tavern) with plentiful bar food inc children's and cut-price OAPs' helpings, keg beer, darts, pool and piped music; separate more upmarket hotel lounge, pleasantly old-fashioned restaurant; children in eating areas, comfortable bedrooms *(Thomas Nott, Christopher Turner, Arthur and Liz Burt, LYM)*

☆ **Bellingham**, N'land [NY8483], *Cheviot*: Good-natured village local reopened by welcoming and hard-working new young licensees, inviting open fire, plentiful well prepared bar food, interesting upstairs dining room with kitchen range; reasonably priced bedrooms, good breakfast *(Gordon, Wayne A Wheeler, J D K Hyams)*

Bellingham, *Rose & Crown*: Good basic village pub with well kept beer, simple food, low prices; very friendly *(J D K Hyams)*

☆ **Berwick upon Tweed**, N'land [Dock View Rd, Spittal (Tweedmouth); NT9952], *Rob Roy*: Outstanding local fish a speciality in quiet and cosy seaview pub, fishing-theme traditional bar with roaring fire and polished wood floor, friendly landlord; keg beers but good fresh coffee; bedrooms *(Jim and Maggie Cowell, Christopher Turner, Thomas Nott)*

☆ *nr* **Berwick upon Tweed** [West Allerdean; 5 miles S – B6354 towards Duddo, Etal – OS Sheet 75 map ref 965465], *Plough*: Cheerful homely country local out by farm, chapel and sheep fields, woodburner in traditional lounge, bar done out with lots of standard rustic memorabilia, good value straightforward food in pine-furnished back dining room, back games bar; Tetleys-related beers, Burmese cats, pleasant garden with splendid Cheviot views and play area *(Jean and Douglas Troup, Les and Jean Scott, Thomas Nott, Roger Berry)*

Bishop Middleham, Dur [NZ3332], *Dun Cow*: Original good value food cooked by newish landlord's Thai wife; keg beers *(Mike and Sue Walton)*

nr **Bowes**, Dur [A66 about 4 miles W – OS Sheet 91 map ref 927124; NY9212], *Bowes Moor*: A snow-line refuge from the bleak westbound dual carriageway, breakfast for passing reps, bar food, restaurant, welcoming licensees; good value house wine *(Frank Davidson)*

Butterknowle, Dur [Wham, off B6282; NZ1126], *Malt Shovel*: Isolated extended stonebuilt country pub, drawings, prints and horse tack in long bar, well kept local Butterknowle ales and Boddingtons, good value bar food 5-11 and Sat lunchtime, Sun lunch, good coffee, attentive service, open fire; fruit machines, piped music; children very welcome *(Duncan Small, JJW, CMW)*

☆ **Catton**, N'land [B6295 N of Allendale; NY8358], *Crown*: Friendly and cosy traditional pub with good value home-cooked food till 10 inc children's and lots of sandwiches, roaring log fire, Butterknowle and Theakstons, good teas and coffee, jovial landlord, pool, darts, juke box, piped music; small garden; well behaved children and dogs welcome *(JJW, CMW)*

☆ **Coatham Mundeville**, Dur [Brafferton Lane;

off A68, ¼ mile from A1(M); NZ2920], *Foresters Arms*: Good food, generous and sensibly priced, well kept Black Sheep, John Smiths Magnet and Theakstons Best, pleasant helpful staff *(R J Walden, Norman Beer)*

☆ **Coatham Mundeville** [part of Hallgarth Hotel; from A1(M) turn towards Brafferton off A167 Darlington rd on hill], *Stables*: Pleasantly converted roomy and lofty stone outbuildings with no-smoking eating area, four well kept S & N ales, side family conservatory, decent food inc Sun lunch; bedrooms *(R J Walden)*

☆ **Corbridge**, N'land [Middle St; NY9964], *Black Bull*: Roomy and friendly low-ceilinged pub with wide range of well kept Whitbreads-related and guest ales, country wines, good house wines, good generous food, traditional settles on stone floor, mix of comfortable chairs, roaring fire, nice friendly atmosphere; open all day *(Noel Jackson, Louise Campbell, Ian Phillips, Graham and Lynn Mason, J D K Hyams, Jane, Stuart and Caroline)*

Corbridge [Newcastle Rd], *Angel*: Small hotel with very welcoming neat staff and above-average bar food inc big mixed grill in plushly comfortable lounge; locals' back bar, restaurant, S & N beers; bedrooms *(P D Smart, LYM)*; [Station Rd], *Dyvels*: Unassuming but pleasant, with well kept Bass and unusual guest beers, tables outside; good value bedrooms *(Paul Boot)*

☆ **Cornforth**, Dur [Metal Bridge; off B6291 N; NZ3134], *Wild Boar*: Comfortable and welcoming, with bric-a-brac in main bar, overhead model railway in big friendly family room, good value generous fresh bar food, upstairs bistro, Bass and interesting guest ales, prompt obliging service; garden with big play area and rides on miniature railway; BR intercity trains run by *(CW, JW, M P Wood)*

Darlington, Dur [nr Market Sq; NZ2915], *Pennyweight*: Welcoming mock-Victorian Vaux city bar, good range of guest beers inc Big Lamp Prince Bishop, other local brews and Tetleys *(Martin Hickes)*

Durham [Saddler St], *Brewer & Firkin*: Closest pub to the castle and cathedral, decent food, six well kept ales, interesting memorabilia *(Jim Brunt)*; [84 New Elvet], *City*: Wide range of decent food in spacious series of knocked-through much refurbished rooms (dates from 17th century), comfortable banquettes, bric-a-brac, well kept Tetleys and Imperial; bedrooms *(John Fazakerley, Jim Brunt, Ian Phillips)*; [next to court building], *Court*: Good choice of Bass-related ales and of reasonably priced generous food inc fine chips all day (not Sun); pleasant surroundings, good service *(Eddie Mackenzie, Jim Brunt)*; [A167 S of Nevilles Cross], *Duke of Wellington*: Busy but spacious Victorian-style local popular for wide range of decent food inc vegetarian and home-cooked; well kept Bass, Worthington and a guest such as Adnams, attentive service; children welcome *(John Allsopp, Pat Woodward, John Fazakerley)*; [Old Elvet], *Dun Cow*: Decidednly unsmart but engaging traditional town pub in pretty black-and-white timbered cottage, cosy front bar, cheap snacks, well kept Whitbreads Castle Eden; children welcome *(Gordon, LYM)*; [New Elvet], *Half Moon*: Well kept Bass and Worthington, old-school bar service, some basic snacks even on Sun; comfortable lower bar, bare-boarded top one, can be a little smoky *(Mrs M Kilner, John Fazakerley)*; [Market Sq], *Market*: Refurbished in traditional style, two levels, S & N ales with a guest such as Jennings Cumberland and various Belgian ales, good value pies *(Mark Fawcitt, Dr Terry Murphy)*; [¼ mile E of junction A1(M)/A690], *Ramside Hall*: Large hotel and function suite, but useful for carvery and wide choice of reasonably priced self-service food; good sandwiches *(Pat Woodward)*; [Sadler St, between Market Sq and cathedral], *Shakespeare*: Busy unpretentious front bar, charming panelled front snug, back room with simple cheap bar snacks and signed actor photographs, lots of malt whiskies, S & N ales, efficient new landlady; children welcome, open all day – convenient for castle, cathedral and river *(Ian Phillips, LYM)*

Ebchester, Dur [B6309 outside; NZ1055], *Derwent Walk*: Attractive and welcoming, doing well under present licensees, with five well kept ales, comfortable dark settles and chairs, good home-cooked food; superb views *(John Oddey)*

☆ **Egglescliffe**, Clvd [NZ4214], *Pot & Glass*: Three warmly welcoming panelled rooms with some slabby tree-trunk tabletops, stools and settles, well kept Bass, friendly staff, good value food; darts, no music; tables on terrace, lovely setting behind church *(C A Hall)*

☆ **Eggleston**, Dur [off B6278 N of Barnard Castle; NY9924], *Three Tuns*: New local licensees in attractive pub set charmingly by broad sloping Teesdale village green, log fire and some interesting furniture in locals' relaxing traditional beamed bar, generous straightforward food (not Sun evening) in big-windowed back room, Whitbreads Castle Eden and an occasional guest beer; tables on terrace and in garden; children welcome *(Clive Gilbert, LYM)*

☆ **Eglingham**, N'land [B6346 Alnwick—Wooler; NU1019], *Tankerville Arms*: Busy village dining pub, some stripped stonework, coal fire each end, well kept Stones and Theakstons XB, decent choice of wines and malt whiskies, children welcome, restaurant; tables in garden *(John Oddey, LYM)*

Ellingham, N'land [signed off A1 N of Alnwick – OS Sheet 75 map ref 167257; NU1726], *Pack Horse*: Friendly well run dining pub in quiet village, small bar and separate dining room (may have to wait for a table), efficient service, good choice of generous food; Theakstons on handpump *(A Preston, Philip and Helen Heppell)*

Elwick, Clvd [¼ mile off A19 W of Hartlepool; NZ4532], *McOrville*: Warm and cosy, friendly service, good basic food *(Mrs P Heslop, JHBS)*

☆ **Etal**, N'land [off B6354 SW of Berwick;

NT9339], *Black Bull*: Pretty thatched pub in attractive village nr steam railway by ruins of Etal Castle, nice walks; modernised lounge with well kept Lorimers Scotch, Tetleys and Wards Sheffield Best, usual food; can get a bit crowded *(GSB, Roger Berry, F A Noble, LYM)*

☆ **Fir Tree**, Dur [A68 West Auckland—Tow Law; NZ1434], *Duke of York*: Wide choice of reliable food in comfortable roadside pub with dining room off cosy wing-chair bar; Bass, Stones and Worthington, good value house wines, cheerful competent staff, racing prints; children welcome, tables outside; now does bedrooms *(Caroline Shearer, Anthony Bradbury, Mrs K I Burvill, P J Keen, BB)*

☆ **Framwellgate Moor**, Dur [Front St; NZ2745], *Tap & Spile*: Good range of well kept beers, decent food at low prices; child-friendly, one room with board games, another with pool and fruit machine *(Mark Havers)*

Gateshead, T & W [Leam Lane (A194); NZ2662], *Lakeside*: Big pub with Courage Directors, John Smiths and Stones ales, bar food inc fresh pizzas and pastas; popular with young people evenings – seven video juke boxes *(Trevor Crawford)*; [Eighton Banks; quite handy for A1(M); NZ2758], *Ship*: Popular and comfortable open-plan pub with bar food (not Sun lunchtime – nibbles instead), great views, well kept Vaux Samson on handpump, good garden for children *(M Borthwick)*

☆ **Greta Bridge**, Dur [hotel signed off A66 W of Scotch Corner; NZ0813], *Morritt Arms*: Interesting and prettily placed old hotel with unusual Pickwickian mural in sturdily traditional civilised bar, attractive garden with play area, restaurant; has been a popular main entry with good reasonably priced bar food, friendly service and well kept Butterknowle Conciliation, but the Mulley brothers who ran it for so long have now sold it; comfortable bedrooms *(SS, LYM; more reports on new regime please)*

Guisborough, Clvd [NZ6016], *Tap & Spile*: Well established favourite decorated in simple style with warm, friendly atmosphere, reasonably priced food till 7, changing beers *(Andy and Jill Kassube)*

☆ **Haltwhistle**, N'land [Rowfoot, Featherstone Pk – OS Sheet 86 map ref 683607; NY6860], *Wallace Arms*: Pleasant rambling former farmhouse reopened by friendly new landlord, wife does lunchtime soup and sandwiches (barn restaurant should also be open by now), well kept local Hexhamshire Devils Water and Whap Weasel, some malt whiskies, thick stone walls, beams, open fires; tables outside with play area, lovely fell views, bedrooms *(Leonard Dixon)*

Haswell, Dur [Front St; NZ3843], *Grey Horse*: Clean and hospitable, good food in Victorian lounge *(Tom Kenmire)*

☆ **Haydon Bridge**, N'land [NY8464], *General Havelock*: Civilised and individually decorated dining pub with limited choice of lunchtime bar food (not Sun), also atmospheric Tyne-view stripped stone restaurant (evenings exc Sun, and Sun lunch) with good interesting if rather pricy full meals; well kept Tetleys, good wines by the glass, efficient friendly service, children and dogs allowed; cl Mon/Tues, also early Jan and Sept, also week after Easter *(AB, DB, Mr and Mrs C Brown, Caroline Wright, B B Pearce, LYM)*

☆ **Hexham**, N'land [Priestpopple; E end of main st, on left entering from Newcastle; NY9464], *County*: Reliably good straightforward lunches from particularly good sandwiches up in cosy hotel lounge, good friendly waitresses, proper coffee; bedrooms *(Dr R H M Stewart)*

☆ **High Force**, Dur [B6277 about 4 miles NW of Middleton; NY8728], *High Force*: Good service and good choice of food in bar of beautifully placed high-moors hotel, named for England's highest waterfall nearby and doubling as mountain rescue post; good range of malt whiskies, children allowed; attractively upgraded bedrooms *(DC, LYM)*

☆ **Holy Island**, N'land [NU1343], *Lindisfarne*: Small red plush bar and simple dining room with well prepared usual food from local crab sandwiches up, keg beer but remarkable number of malt whiskies, pleasant friendly staff, morning coffee, teas and high teas; unobtrusive piped music, children welcome, well kept garden; bedrooms good value *(Julia Stone, Leigh and Gillian Mellor, A Craig, Christopher Turner, John Hazel, Dorothy and David Young)*

Holy Island, *Northumberland Arms*: Small welcoming local, open fire, limited food, friendly cockatoo called Cocky (a sucker for toast crusts); bedrooms *(John Hazel, Mrs M A Kilner, MAB)*

Holystone, N'land [NT9503], *Salmon*: Comfortably furnished Coquet Valley local, good value simple food, Vaux Samson, open fire, lively pool room; in attractive countryside close to venerable Lady's Well, good nearby walks *(JJW, CMW, LYM)*

Horsley, N'land [B6528; just off A69 Newcastle—Hexham; NZ0966], *Lion & Lamb*: Stripped stone, comfortable settles and other seats, stove and log-effect gas fire in attractive lounge, larger dining area, family room; good value well presented food, Whitbreads Castle Eden and Marstons Pedigree, friendly welcome *(JJW, CMW, John Oddey)*

Kielder, N'land [NY6393], *Anglers Arms*: Big pub with good range of food served quickly, handy for Kielder Water and castle *(J D K Hyams)*

Knarsdale, N'land [A689 Alston—Brampton, just N of Slaggyford; NY6854], *Kirkstyle*: Friendly London landlord, well kept Boddingtons, big helpings of bar food lunchtime and evening *(Leonard Dixon)*

Lamesley, T & W [minor rd S of Gateshead A1 western bypass; NZ2558], *Ravensworth Arms*: Large S & N stonebuilt good value dining pub, two well kept Theakstons ales, games machines, pervasive piped music; play area and picnic tables outside; open all day, children welcome *(JJW, CMW, M Borthwick)*

☆ **Lanchester**, Dur [NZ1647], *Queens Head*: Good generous often interesting food, well kept Vaux beers, decent wines and friendly and attentive Swedish landlady in comfortable high-ceilinged village pub *(Anon)*

Langley Park, Dur [NZ2245], *Centurion*: Promising new management, with good atmosphere and good food, Vaux Samson *(Janet Lee)*

Lesbury, N'land [NU2412], *Coach*: Nicely furnished clean and comfortable small bar with sectioned-off lounge area, pool room and restaurant, food from bar snacks to Fri steak suppers and Sun lunch, Hexhamshire Devils Water and Shepherd Neame Bishops Finger *(Teresa and Nigel Brooks)*

Longframlington, N'land [NU1301], *Granby*: Comfortably modernised two-room bar very popular for very wide choice of generous food from sandwiches to steaks, good collection of malt whiskies, decent wines, restaurant; bedrooms in main building good, with big breakfasts *(Laura Darlington, Gianluca Perinetti, Roger A Bellingham, LYM)*

☆ **Longhorsley**, N'land [Linden Hall Hotel, a mile N of village; NZ1597], *Linden Pub*: Sprucely converted ex-granary pub behind country house conference hotel in extensive grounds; briskly served limited but generous bar food, a couple of well kept Whitbreads-related ales, gallery restaurant, quite a few old enamel advertising signs; children welcome, bedrooms in main hotel *(Dave Irving, Mike Pugh, GSB, Thomas Nott, A Craig, LYM)*

☆ **Lowick**, N'land [2 Main St (B6353), off A1 S of Berwick; NU0139], *Black Bull*: Comfortable and attractive main bar and small back bar in pleasant country pub, popular dining room with good choice of food inc vegetarian, McEwans ale, friendly attentive staff; on edge of small pretty village *(Les and Jean Scott, Christopher Turner)*

Marske by the Sea, Clvd [Coast Rd; NZ6423], *Ship*: Big three-bar mock-Tudor local with nautical theme, usual food, well kept Theakstons *(Mr Kerslake)*

☆ **Middleton in Teesdale**, Dur [Mkt Pl; NY9526], *Teesdale*: Lounge bar with very attentive service, good value if not cheap food, well kept Tetleys, log fire; comfortable bedrooms *(SS, Jack and Heather Coyle)*

Middleton St George, Clvd [A67 a mile W; NZ3412], *Old Farmhouse*: Big old farmhouse, fully refurbished two years ago in vernacular style with flagstones and wooden furnishings; wide range of generous food, good range of beers, friendly licensees, family dining area, big play area in garden *(Allan and Philippa Wright)*

Morpeth, N'land [Manchester St; NZ2086], *Tap & Spile*: Two cosy rooms, easy-going and friendly, with seven well kept ales, farm cider, nice food made by good landlady, fair prices, folk music Sun afternoons, dominoes, cards, darts etc, fruit machine; children welcome, open all day *(K Kennedy, JJW, CMW)*

☆ **Newcastle upon Tyne** [33 Shields Rd, Byker], *Tap & Spile*: Excellent choice of interesting well kept ales in well run traditional pub with games in front bar, quieter solidly furnished back room, lunchtime sandwiches; only an absence of recent reports keeps it out of the main entries *(LYM)*

☆ **Newcastle upon Tyne** [High Bridge], *Duke of Wellington*: Small and comfortable, with well kept ales such as Marstons Pedigree, Tetleys and Timothy Taylors, good range of bar food, low prices; lots of 19th-c prints and documents, many connected with Wellington; open all day, next to market so gets very busy *(Mrs M A Kilner)*

Newcastle upon Tyne [High Bridge], *Bacchus*: Well kept Stones, Tetleys, Theakstons XB, Youngers IPA and a guest beer, good value food (not Sun), some lovely old mirrors in the bar; surprisingly big inside, but cosy and comfortable when not too busy *(Eric Larkham, John O'Donnell)*; [Broad Chare], *Baltic Tavern*: Well kept Whitbreads-related ales in spacious and comfortably converted riverside warehouse, lots of stripped brick and flagstones or bare boards (as well as plusher carpeted parts) in warren of separate areas, good value bar food *(David Jackson, LYM)*; [Chillingham Rd], *Chillingham Arms*: Beautifully furnished and fitted, fine woodwork, five well kept ales and a couple of guest beers, occasional mini beer festivals, good cheap lunchtime food inc Sun *(Eric Larkham)*; [St Peters Basin], *Fog on the Tyne*: Overlooking marina, modern but nicely decorated, with maritime pictures; four or five well kept ales, welcoming helpful staff, changing choice of bar food inc some impressive dishes and al dente veg; piped music *(John, Karen and Graham Oddey)*; [44 The Side, Quayside], *Off Shore*: Good value lunchtime food esp carvery in interestingly converted nautical-feel warehouse, well kept Courage Directors and other ales, friendly atmosphere; younger crowd evenings *(John, Karen and Graham Oddey)*; [Quayside, by New Law Courts], *Waterline*: Stylish conversion of ground floor of old bonded warehouse; lots of oak beams and pillars, nooks and crannies, maritime bric-a-brac, oak tables and chairs; welcoming staff, well kept mainly S & N ales, food inc good cheap steaks *(John Oddey)*

Newton, Clvd [A173; NZ5713], *Kings Head*: Neat and airy modernised dining pub, pleasant surroundings nr Roseberry Topping, good value food inc excellent range of sandwiches and Sun lunch, friendly attentive service, wide choice of beer, good coffee; tables out on terrace *(D P Wilcox, Jack and Heather Coyle, G K and D M Holden)*

☆ **Newton by the Sea**, N'land [The Square, Low Newton; NU2426], *Ship*: Straightforward local quaintly tucked into top corner of courtyard of old cottages facing beach and sea, keg beers, coffee, tea and ices, pool table; children welcome, tables out on green; bedrooms *(R and G Underwood, Gordon)*

Newton by the Sea [High Newton; NU2325], *Joiners Arms*: Village local with friendly bustling landlady trotting back and forth with huge platefuls of delicious fish and chips *(Gordon)*

North Bitchburn, Dur [NZ1733], *Red Lion*: Good food, well kept beer *(Jim Brunt)*

Otterburn, N'land [NY8992], *Tower*: Good bar meals, real ale, log fire and morning coffee or afternoon tea in bar and plush lounge of sprawling 1830s Gothick castellated hotel built around original 13th-c peel tower; bedrooms comfortable and good value *(Neil Barker, LYM)*; *Percy Arms*: Useful haven with generous often imaginative bar food, friendly waitresses, splendid roaring fire, Theakstons XB and Youngers Scotch; small front lounge; back bar with juke box popular with young locals and soldiers, can be smoky; comfortable bedrooms *(H Bramwell, Leigh and Gillian Mellor, J Roy Smylie)*

Ovington, N'land [signed off A69 Corbridge—Newcastle; NZ0764], *Highlander*: Good value bar food, three S & N ales, restaurant, games room with pool and darts; quiet piped music, garden with play area; open all day summer; bedrooms *(JJW, CMW, Jack and Heather Coyle)*

Ponteland, N'land [Main St; NZ1773], *Seven Stars*: Huge range of S & N and other ales inc Courage Directors and Marstons Pedigree, lots of bottled beers, pleasant old-fashioned refurbishment, efficient friendly service, good value food *(John, Karen and Graham Oddey)*

Redcar, Clvd [High St; NZ6125], *Lobster*: Traditional pub with elegantly updated lounge, good basic sandwiches with home-baked bread, well kept Sam Smiths ales *(Stephen Kerslake)*

Riding Mill, N'land [NZ0262], *Wellington*: Large S & N chain dining pub with Theakstons ales, piped music, disabled access and promising new licensees; children welcome, play area and picnic tables outside *(JJW, CMJ)*

☆ **Romaldkirk**, Dur [NY9922], *Kirk*: Cosy and friendly little two-room pub, well worn but clean, with wide choice of interesting good value food (not Tues), well kept Black Sheep, Butterknowle and Whitbreads-related beers, good coffee, 18th-c stonework, good log fire, darts, piped popular classics; picnic tables outside in attractive moorland village; doubles as PO *(JJW, CMW, John Fazakerley)*

Running Waters, Dur [A181 E of Durham; NZ3240], *Three Horseshoes*: Friendly dining pub with good reasonably priced home-cooked food in pleasant enviroment, views over Durham; attractive bedrooms *(John Allsopp, Meg and Colin Hamilton)*

☆ **Saltburn by the Sea**, Clvd [A174 towards Whitby; NZ6722], *Ship*: Beautiful setting among beached fishing boats, sea views from tasteful nautical-style black-beamed bars and big plainer summer dining lounge; good range of bar food, Tetleys on handpump, quick friendly service, good evening restaurant (not Sun), children's room and menu, seats outside; busy at holiday times *(Ken Smith, LYM)*

☆ **Seaton Sluice**, Dur [A193 N of Whitley Bay; NZ3477], *Waterford Arms*: Wide choice of very generously served freshly cooked fish and seafood (all day summer Suns, not winter Sun evenings) besides other food in roomy recently refurbished seaside pub with partly no-smoking restaurant, well kept Wards Bitter and Thorne, Vaux Samson and Waggledance, children allowed; piped music; newly redone bedrooms *(Wendy Arnold, Mrs M A Kilner, JJW, CMW, LYM)*

☆ **Sedgefield**, Dur [Front St; NZ3629], *Dun Cow*: Large attractive village inn with wide choice of good value interesting bar food in two bars and restaurant, welcoming service, S & N and guest ales, good range of whiskies; children welcome; bedrooms sharing bathrooms *(Geoff Hughes)*

Sedgefield [Front St], *Black Lion*: 17th-c coaching inn with original cobbled courtyard and outbuildings, dark beams, old open range, lots of bric-a-brac – cosy and friendly; good value meals, well kept Tetleys *(B M Eldridge)*

☆ **Shincliffe**, Dur [A177 S of Durham, three buses an hour from the door; NZ2941], *Seven Stars*: Cosy village inn, small but quietly smart, traditionally furnished in one half, with remarkable fireplace in the other; good choice of substantial food from bar snacks to restaurant meals, friendly Hungarian landlord and chatty locals, well kept Wards and Vaux Samson, some seats outside; attractive village; cheap well equipped spotless bedrooms, good breakfasts (they don't let children stay) *(Comus Elliott, Derek and Sylvia Stephenson)*

Slaley, N'land [B6306 S of Hexham; NY9858], *Travellers Rest*: Friendly early 18th-c pub of great architectural interest, good value standard food lunchtime and Fri/Sat evening, lots of brass and books, two real fires, friendly dog, games area, keg beers; garden with picnic tables and swing, lovely countryside *(J D K Hyams)*

☆ **South Shields**, T & W [South Foreshore; beach rd towards Marsden; NZ3766], *Marsden Rattler*: Real ale and basic food served in pleasant friendly seafront bar area or in two railway carriages with original seats, windows and curtains; conservatory, all-day tea, coffee and cakes, evening restaurant *(GSB)*

South Shields [100 Greens Pl], *Beacon*: Overlooking river mouth, with well kept Vaux Samson, friendly atmosphere, central bar, stove in back room, good value food; darts, fruit machine, piped music *(JJW, CMW)*; [Ocean Rd], *Kirkpatricks*: Large dining pub (former marine college) opp library/museum, comfortable and tastefully converted with well kept Whitbreads-related ales, extensive lunchtime food, newspapers; piped pop music, fruit machines *(JJW, CMW)*; [51 Coronation St, Mill Dam], *Steamboat*: Interesting nautical bric-a-brac, friendly landlord, five real ales, sandwiches; usually open all day, nr river and market

place *(JJW, CMW)*
St Johns Chapel, Dur [Market Pl; A689 Alston—Stanhope; NY8838], *Golden Lion*: Comfortable and relaxed open-plan village pub pleasantly decorated with stuffed animals and birds, horse brasses, cigarette cards, ornaments etc; outgoing landlord, Butterknowle and Jennings ales, good value simple food inc Sun lunch and home-grown veg; pool, juke box, fruit machine; open all day, tea, coffee; bedrooms *(JJW, CMJ, Graham Bush)*
☆ **Stannington**, N'land [just off A1; NZ2279], *Ridley Arms*: Good straightforward food at reasonable prices in spacious open-plan main bar, pleasant and cosy in rustic style, efficient helpful staff, quiet lounge, restaurant; well kept Whitbreads Castle Eden *(GSB, Mrs M A Kilner, LYM)*
Stockton on Tees, Clvd [Knowles St; NZ4218], *Sun*: Well kept beer at attractive prices, friendly staff *(Sean)*
Sunderland, T & W [Green Terr; NZ4057], *Fitzgeralds*: Busy city pub with two bars, one rather trendy (nr University), and very popular food – get there early to avoid a sell-out Fri/Sat night or Sun lunch *(Heath Jackson)*
☆ **Thropton**, N'land [NU0302], *Cross Keys*: Friendly small three-roomed village local, decent pub food, Bass and Hancocks HB, open fires in cosy beamed main lounge, darts, satellite TV; attractive terraced garden looking over village to the Cheviots, tame cockerel, hens, pig and guinea-pig called Henri; open all day at least in summer *(JJW, CMW, Leigh and Gillian Mellor, LYM)*
Toft Hill, Dur [A68 N of W Auckland; NZ1528], *Sportsman*: Welcoming landlady, well kept Theakstons, food inc good value thick broth with chunky veg, good coffee *(R M Macnaughton)*
☆ **Tynemouth**, T & W [Tynemouth Rd (A193); ½ mile W of Tynemouth Metro stn; NZ3468], *Tynemouth Lodge*: Particularly well kept ales and farm ciders, cheap lunchtime filled rolls and coal fire in genuine-feeling friendly and quiet little Victorian-style pub *(LYM)*
Ulgham, N'land [NZ2392], *Forge*: Comfortable and airy lounge opening on to terrace and sheltered neat lawn with play area, cheery high-ceilinged public bar (former village smithy), well kept S & N ales, welcoming efficient service, good straightforward food in attractive dining room *(John Oddey, LYM)*
☆ **Wall**, N'land [NY9269], *Hadrian*: Solidly cushioned two-room bar with good bar food inc some interesting dishes, well kept Vaux ESB and Samson, reconstructions of Romano-British life, friendly new owners, polite staff; Victorian dining room; children welcome; bedrooms – back ones quieter, with good views *(Mr and Mrs D W Moss, John Oddey, Dr S W Tham, LYM)*
☆ **Warden**, N'land [½ mile N of A69; NY9267], *Boatside*: Pleasant friendly dining pub, good range of good food, good service *(Catheryn and Richard Hicks)*
☆ **Warkworth**, N'land [6 Castle Terr; NU2506], *Sun*: 17th-c hotel below castle in attractive village not far from sea, friendly helpful staff, homely atmosphere, well kept S & N ales, wide choice of reasonably priced good food inc local fish; children welcome, bedrooms with good views *(Leigh and Gillian Mellor)*
Warkworth [23 Castle St], *Hermitage*: Clean, friendly and well run typical small-town pub, generous well served food from sandwiches up, well kept Courage-related beers, cheerful obliging staff, small plush upstairs restaurant *(Mrs J Boyt, BB)*; [3 Dial Pl], *Masons Arms*: Warm and cosy thriving local, good friendly service, big helpings of good value food, well kept S & N beers *(Jim and Maggie Cowell, John Watson)*; [Castle St], *Warkworth House*: Cosy bar tastefully refurbished with comfortable sofas, helpful friendly staff, good choice of spirits, well kept Bass and Stones; decent bar meals *(Teresa and Nigel Brooks)*
☆ **West Woodburn**, N'land [NY8987], *Bay Horse*: Welcoming service in simple open-plan bar with red plush banquettes and other seats, open fire, well kept Theakstons XB, usual bar food inc vegetarian and children's, games room; children welcome, airy dining room, a couple of picnic tables in riverside garden; only roasts, Sun lunch; cl Mon/Tues lunchtime in winter; clean and comfortable modernised bedrooms *(Dr and Mrs P J S Crawshaw, Russell Grimshaw, Kerry Purcell, Roger Berry, LYM)*
☆ **Whalton**, N'land [NZ1382], *Beresford Arms*: Very good genuine home cooking at reasonable prices in pleasant civilised bar or dining room, friendly staff, well kept Vaux Lorimers Scotch and Wards; attractive village *(R and G Underwood, C A Hall, Jill and Peter Bickley)*
White le Head, Dur [N of Stanley on B6311; NZ1754], *Highlander*: Friendly 19th-c pub with copper-topped tables, banquettes, pictures and gas fire in lounge, small homely dining room, good value food, attentive obliging service, Batemans and Vaux Samson; persian cat, quiet piped music (live Thurs), pool in bar *(JJW, CMW)*
Whittonstall, N'land [NZ0857], *Anchor*: Attractive village pub doing well after major refurbishment by new owner – welcoming and comfortable, three well kept ales, increasingly varied choice of good food inc very popular Sun lunch *(John Oddey)*
Wolsingham, Dur [Market Pl; NZ0737], *Black Bull*: Well kept Vaux Samson and Double Maxim, small choice of nicely presented generous standard food, lounge on right, public bar with games room on left *(M and J Back, David Bloomfield)*
nr **Wooler**, N'land [B6351 N; NT9928], *Tankerville Arms*: Good service, good range of tasty meals; bedrooms *(Arthur and Liz Burt)*
Wylam, N'land [Station Rd; NZ1265], *Boathouse*: Has been friendly and popular, with good range of well kept ales and decent food *(Reports on new regime please)*

Nottinghamshire *see* Leicestershire

see Leicestershire

Oxfordshire

This county is brimming with good pubs – attractive and individual buildings, often in fine surroundings, run with flair, and often with really good food. Those doing outstandingly well at the moment, with very enthusiastic reports from many readers, include the fine old Lamb in Burford, the idiosyncratic Turkish-run Plough at Clifton Hampden, the cheerful thatched Plough at Finstock, the consistently friendly old Crown at Nuffield, the beamed and flagstoned Bell at Shenington, and the civilised little Red Lion at Steeple Aston. Though a good few established main entries have Food Awards, including the Bear & Ragged Staff at Cumnor, blossoming under its new landlord, we are taking the unusual step of naming an entirely new main entry here as our Oxfordshire Dining Pub of the Year – the charming Boars Head at Ardington. Other interesting new entries here this year are the heavy-beamed old Boot at Barnard Gate, the welcoming Five Bells at Broadwell, the pretty thatched Half Moon at Cuxham, the very friendly Royal Oak at Ramsden and the delightfully redesigned old Three Horseshoes in Witney; all include food as one of their strengths, though in most it's character that predominates. As we've said, this county does stand out for its proliferation of really good pubs. This means that the general quality of the Lucky Dip section at the end of the chapter is unusually high; for example, though we have chosen as our Oxford main entry a pub which has a distinctive appeal for visitors, the Dip includes several others which are very well worth going to. Burford too has good alternative choices. Elsewhere, we'd particularly pick out the Horse & Groom at Caulcott, Tite at Chadlington, Trout at Godstow (at least for its surroundings), Anchor among close rivals in Henley, Dog & Duck at Highmoor, Crown at Pishill, Chequers at Weston on the Green and Kings Head at Wootton. Drinks prices in the county are rather higher than the national average, with the main local brewer, Brakspears, tending to be relatively pricy; pubs tied to Hook Norton, however, stood out as much cheaper than most in the area, and two free houses, the Romany at Bampton and the Trout at Tadpole Bridge, were also relatively very cheap, getting their beers from national combines but holding the price down well.

ADDERBURY SP4635 Map 4

Red Lion 🛏 🍷

A423 S of Banbury; not far from M40 junction 11

It can be hard to drag yourself away from the deep sofas at this carefully refurbished and comfortably civilised old stone inn. It's been offering the same restful atmosphere for quite some time now – on one of the terracotta walls is a list of all the landlords since 1690, along with various quotations and pithy sayings. The right-hand bar has high stripped beams, prints, comfortable chairs, and a lovely big inglenook; the left-hand bar is more for eating, with cosy floral tablecloths, and leads through to the comfortable and prettily decorated residents' lounge. An attractive back dining room and part of the lounge are no smoking. Lots of people are here for the very good food, which might include soup (£1.95), filled baguettes (from £2.50), garlic mushrooms or stilton and port pâté (£3.50), ploughman's (£5.25), various pasta dishes or leek and potato bake (£5.95), lamb stew (£6.95), a pie of the day (£7.95), beef bourguignon (£9.95), chicken stuffed with mushrooms and lobster sauce (£10.95), and good puddings; three-course Sunday lunch (£10.95). Well kept Hook Norton Best, Ruddles County, Websters, and Wadworths 6X on handpump, and 14 wines by the glass; very friendly, efficient service. Tables out on the well kept garden terrace.

(Recommended by John Waller, TBB, David and Shelia, D C T and E A Frewer, John and Christine Lowe, Laurence Keane, Chris Cook, P D and J Bickley, Gordon, Roger Huggins, Dave Irving, Tom McLean, Ewan McCall, Neil and Susan Spoonley, Graham Reeve, The Monday Club, Dr and Mrs D E Awbery)

Free house ~ Licensees Michael and Andrea Mortimer ~ Real ale ~ Meals and snacks (till 10pm) ~ Restaurant ~ (01295) 810269 ~ Children welcome ~ Open 11-11 ~ Bedrooms: £45B/£55B

ARDINGTON SU4388 Map 2

Boars Head

Village signposted off A417 Didcot—Wantage, 2 miles E of Wantage

Oxfordshire Dining Pub of the Year

In the last couple of years this former village local has been transformed into a civilised and upmarket dining pub, increasingly booked out for exceptionally good value interesting food, so much so that an extension is planned. It has three well cared-for interconnecting rooms, with low beams and timbers, fresh flowers, old pictures and photographs and a pleasant light-coloured wood block floor. One room's primarily for eating, with pine settles and well spaced big pine tables, the others have smaller country tables and chairs – still with room for drinkers. Good house wines pass muster even with readers used to the very best in clarets; well kept Fullers London Pride, Morlands and occasional guests; friendly licensees. The regularly changing blackboard menu might include smoked chicken with mango and jalapenos (£4.95), Mexicorn sweetcorn pie with Thai curry and apple sauce (£7.95), john dorey (£9.75) and roast duck with elderberry and raspberry vinegar (£9.95), and imaginative puddings like meringue and sorbet layers or coconut mousse with roast bananas (all £3.80). In a peaceful and attractive village, the pub is part of the Ardington estate; good walks nearby.

(Recommended by R C Watkins, A T Langton, JE, Jed and Virginia Brown, Richard Willmott, Col A H N Reade, M Popham, T R and B C Jenkins, J W Rayson)

Free house ~ Tenants Duncan and Liz Basterfield ~ Real ale ~ Meals and snacks (not Sun, Mon evening) ~ Restaurant ~ (01235) 833254 ~ Well behaved children in eating area ~ Open 11.30-2.30, 6-11; cl 25, 26 Dec

BAMPTON SP3013 Map 4

Romany £

Bridge St; off A4095 SW of Witney

A former grocer's shop (you can still see the hooks for ham projecting through the ceiling), this unassuming 17th-c local offers exceptional value for money – as we went to press the cheapest beer was a good 26p cheaper than the county average, and though the bar food holds few surprises you'd be hard pushed to find a decent meal for less, especially in this area. Even the bedrooms cost half of what you might expect to pay elsewhere. The comfortable bars have plush cushioned windsor chairs and stools around wooden tables, plates and prints on the partly stripped stone walls, and a winter open fire. Well kept Archers Village, Hook Norton Best, Morlands Original and two changing guest beers, handpumped from the Saxon cellars below the bar; cribbage, dominoes, fruit machine, trivia, and piped music. The menu includes sandwiches (from 95p; toasties from £1.20), home-made soup (£1.25), home-made pâté (£1.55), filled baked potatoes (from £1.85), ploughman's (£2.10), sausage, egg, beans and chips (£2.20), salads (from £2.65), lamb's liver and onions or home-made lasagne (£2.70), home-made pies like steak and kidney or chicken and mushroom (£2.90), a good few vegetarian dishes like tomato, celery and cashew nut risotto or vegetable chilli (£2.95), braised pork chop (£3.65), and steaks (from £4.35 for 6oz sirloin); best to book for their popular Sunday lunch. Friendly, hard-working licensees. The restaurant is no smoking. The big garden has picnic tables, Aunt Sally, and a children's play area with tree house, see-saw, and mushroom slide and house. *(Recommended by Marjorie and David Lamb, Meg and Colin Hamilton, CMW, JJW, Sue Anderson, Phil Copleston, Mrs L Lailey)*

Free house ~ Licensees Bob and Ursula Booth ~ Real ale ~ Meals and snacks (11-2.30, 6-9.30) ~ Restaurant ~ (01993) 850237 ~ Well behaved children welcome ~ Open 11-11 ~ Bedrooms: £21B/£30B

BARNARD GATE SP4010 Map 4

Boot

Village signposted off A40 E of Witney

Decidedly a dining pub, this heavy-beamed old place has very friendly and natural service which keeps the atmosphere pleasantly informal, though admittedly unpubby. A wide choice of well cooked food in generous helpings includes sandwiches (from £2), ploughman's (£3.75), grilled king prawns (£4.25), a lunchtime special which includes coffee like kidneys with bacon and bearnaise sauce (£5.95), two or three vegetarian dishes like two mushrooms filled with spinach and pine nuts, and provençal vegetables with a cheese sauce (£7.95), an authenic Thai curry (£8.95), Aberdeen Angus sirloin (10oz £12.95) and lots of fresh fish. The decor is pleasant and civilised in a gently rustic way, with good solid country tables and chairs on bare boards, and stout standing timbers and stub walls with latticed glass breaking up the main area; there's a huge log fire, and a good no-smoking area. Decent wines, well kept Hook Norton Best and two guests like Boddingtons, Flowers Original, Fullers London Pride or Wychwood Best, espresso coffee. There are tables out in front of the stone-tiled stone pub, which despite being so handy for the A40 is out of earshot. *(Recommended by Dr H Y Chan, Tony and Sarah Thomas, Michael Sargent, T H G Lewis, Lindsay Gregory, Adam Hodge)*

Free house ~ George Dailey ~ Real ale ~ Meals and snacks (12-2, 6-10) ~ Restaurant ~ (01865) 881231 ~ Children welcome ~ Open 11-3, 6-11; cl 25 Dec)

BARFORD ST MICHAEL SP4332 Map 4

George

Lower Street, at N end of village: coming from Bloxham, take first right turn

So obviously the centre of the local community that at times it feels almost like the village hall, this is a very attractive 17th-c golden stone pub, with a thatched roof and mullioned windows. The three rambling modernised rooms have cushioned rustic seats and captain's chairs around the dark wood tables, open fires, and a growing collection of company and regimental ties hanging from the beams, most donated by customers over the last few years. Over the fireplace there's a big painting of the Battle of Agincourt, using many of the locals as the soldiers. Promptly served bar food includes sandwiches and good value hot dishes like chilli con carne (£3.40), steak and kidney or chicken, gammon and leek pie (£3.95), and chicken tikka (£4.50). Well kept Adnams, Badger Tanglefoot, Wadworths 6X and guest beers on handpump, lots of country wines. The plump and friendly staffordshire bull terrier is called Jay-Jay; darts, pool, shove-ha'penny, pinball, cribbage, dominoes, fruit machine, video game, trivia and piped music. The pleasant garden has picnic tables, an adventure playground, and views over fields. Just up the road is a caravan/camp site with trout fishing. *(Recommended by David and Shelia, John Bowdler, Wayne Brindle, Marjorie and David Lamb; more reports please)*

Free house ~ Licensees Spencer and Theresa Richards ~ Real ale ~ Meals and snacks (not evenings Sun and Mon) ~ Restaurant (not Sun evening) ~ (01869) 338226 ~ Children in games room ~ Folk/blues Mon evenings ~ Open 12-2.30, 6-11; 12-11 Sat

BECKLEY SP5611 Map 4

Abingdon Arms

Village signposted off B4027

The imaginative food here is still the main draw, but the garden is rather pleasant too, with the small formal flower-edged lawn just behind dropping quietly and spaciously away into the shadows of groves of fruit trees, willows and other shrubs and trees. There's a gently floodlit terrace, along with well spaced tables, a summer-house, and a little fountain. The good, sensibly short menu changes with the seasons; in summer you may find dishes such as Greek salad with taramasalata and feta cheese (£5.50), pasta with tuna, red peppers, stuffed olives and pine nuts (£5.95), whole avocado with prawns and chilli mayonnaise (£6.85), or fresh crab with ginger dressing (£7.45), while in winter they do things like a proper bouillabaisse, baked aubergine stuffed with lentils and apricot, chicken and mushroom curry, and smoked chicken with an apple, yoghurt and nutmeg sauce (all £5.95). Puddings include home-made truffled ice cream or apple and almond tart (£2.35). Every other Friday from October-Easter they do excellent three or four-course themed menus, with dishes from France, Italy or the Holy Land; booking is essential for these. No credit cards. Well kept Hook Norton and Wadworths 6X on handpump, a good range of wines, and quite a few malt whiskies. The comfortably modernised simple lounge has neat flower displays on the tables and cloth-cushioned seats built around the wall, and a smaller public bar on the right has a couple of antique carved settles (one for just one person), and bar billiards; dominoes, shove-ha'penny. No children. Recent reports suggest they can have trouble with the service. *(Recommended by K Chenneour, Alan Skull, A M Rankin, John Waller, Adam and Elizabeth Duff, Michael Sargent, L Walker, Terry and Eileen Stott, Walter Reid, Dave Braisted, T G Brierly, TBB, A T Langton)*

Free house ~ Licensee Hugh Greatbatch ~ Real ale ~ Meals and snacks (not Sun evening) ~ (01865) 351311 ~ Open 11.30-2.30, 6.30-11; Sunday opening 8; closed evening 25 Dec

BINFIELD HEATH SU7478 Map 2

Bottle & Glass ★

Village signposted off A4155 at Shiplake; from village centre turn into Common Lane – pub at end, on Harpsden Road (Henley—Reading back road)

One reader well remembers his first visit to this idyllic-looking thatched and black and white timbered 15th-c pub in 1959, and on a recent return trip was delighted to see nothing has changed since. The neatly kept, low-beamed bar still has scrubbed, ancient tables, a bench built into black squared panelling, spindleback chairs, attractive flagstones, and a roaring log fire in the big fireplace. The smaller, relaxed side room, similarly decorated, has a window with diamond-scratched family records of earlier landlords; shove ha'penny, dominoes. Written up on blackboards, the range of promptly served bar food typically includes lunchtime sandwiches, cumberland sausages with egg or mussels grilled in garlic and herb butter (£4.50), chicken livers with bacon, garlic and cream (£4.95), oxtail casserole (£5.95), fresh salmon fillet (£6.95), and medallions of fillet steak in a peppered sauce (£9.95); friendly staff. Brakspears Bitter, and seasonal Old or Special on handpump, and quite a few malt whiskies. The lovely big garden has old-fashioned wooden seats and tables under little thatched roofs (and an open-sided shed like a rustic pavilion). No children or dogs. *(Recommended by Ted and Jane Brown, P J Caunt, Gordon, Simon Collett-Jones, Clifford Payton, TBB)*

Brakspears ~ Tenants Mike and Anne Robinson ~ Real ale ~ Meals and snacks (lunchtime service stops 1.45); not Sun evening ~ (01491) 575755 ~ Open 11-3, 6-11

Bedroom prices normally include full English breakfast, VAT and any inclusive service charge that we know of.

BIX SU7285 Map 2

Fox

On A4130 Henley—Wallingford

Distinguished by its general atmosphere of relaxing calm, this friendly creeper-clad brick house is well off the main tourist routes, so while it does get busier at weekend lunchtimes, during the week it's an ideal place to come for that get-away-from-it-all drink. Cosy and quietly welcoming, the L-shaped panelled lounge bar has beams, armchairs and settles making the most of the big log fires, and gleaming brasses. There's another log fire and some settles in the connecting wood-floored farmers' bar, with darts, dominoes and a fruit machine. Quickly served, good value bar food includes sandwiches (from £1.65), pasties (£1.95), popular soup (£2.25), ploughman's (from £3.35), ratatouille (£3.55), lasagne or steak and kidney pie (£4.75), beef and venison burgers (£4.95), daily specials like steak and mushroom casserole or winter game (£5.25), puddings (£1.95), and a Sunday roast (£5.50). Well kept Brakspears Bitter and seasonal Old or Special on handpump, picnic tables in the good-sized garden behind. The friendly dog is called Henry, and there's a much-used hitching rail for horses outside. No children. You can book a horse and cart to bring you here at weekends; see the entry at Hailey for details. *(Recommended by Gordon, TBB, Bill Ingham, Marjorie and David Lamb, D D Collins, David Wright, P J Caunt, David Warrellow, N and J Strathdee, Frank Cummins)*

Brakspears ~ Tenants Richard and Sue Willson ~ Real ale ~ Meals and snacks (not Mon evening) ~ (01491) 574134 ~ Open 11-3, 7-11; closed 25 Dec

BLEWBURY SU5385 Map 2

Red Lion

Chapel Lane, off Nottingham Fee; narrow turning northwards from A417

In winter you can roast chestnuts over the big open fire at this welcoming 18th-c Downland pub. Genuinely atmospheric and friendly, the engaging beamed bar has upholstered wall benches and armed seats on its scrubbed quarry tiles, cupboards and miniature cabinets filled with ornaments, foreign banknotes on the beams, and a steadily ticking station clock; a no-smoking bar is popular with families. A nicely concise choice of good freshly prepared bar food at lunchtime includes toasties such as chicken liver pâté or avocado and smoked cheese (£3.50), smoked mackerel and orange salad (£4), ploughman's (£4.10), liver and bacon in a port wine sauce (£5), and pan-fried plaice (£5.50), with evening dishes such as pork tenderloin in calvados (£7.50) and lemon sole (£8); puddings like treacle tart (£2.30). Well kept Boddingtons and Brakspears Bitter on handpump, decent wines, and a good range of non-alcoholic drinks; dominoes, cards, backgammon. The extended garden has a terrace with quite a few seats and tables. *(Recommended by M W Turner, R C Watkins, Marjorie and David Lamb, Geraint Roberts, Susie Northfield, A T Langton)*

Brakspears ~ Licensee Roger Smith ~ Real ale ~ Meals and snacks ~ Restaurant ~ (01235) 850403 ~ Children welcome in part of bar and restaurant till 9pm ~ Open 11-2.30, 6-11; all day Sat; closed evening 25 Dec

BLOXHAM SP4235 Map 4

Elephant & Castle

Humber Street; off A361, fairly handy for M40 junction 11

Regulars at this warmly welcoming Cotswold stone local have been playing on the same hardy shove ha'penny board for over a century now; it's the sort of place where things don't change much as a rule, and that's one of the reasons why readers like it. The relaxed and elegantly simple public bar has a striking 17th-century stone fireplace and a strip wood floor, and the comfortable lounge, divided into two by a very thick wall, has a good winter log fire in its massive fireplace too; sensibly placed darts, dominoes, cribbage, fruit machine, and trivia. Good value straightforward bar food includes soup (90p), decent sandwiches (from £1.50, the ham is recommended), ploughman's (from £1.75), steak and kidney pie, lasagne, or haddock (£3.50), and rump steak (£6.50). Well kept and extremely well priced Hook Norton Best (11p less than the county average as we went to press), Old Hookey, summer Haymaker, and monthly guest beers from small independent brewers; thirty or so malt whiskies. The flower-filled yard has Aunt Sally in summer and there are barbecues on Saturday evenings and Sunday lunchtimes. *(Recommended by TBB, Stephen Brown, Gordon, Tom Evans, David Campbell, Vicki McLean)*

Hook Norton ~ Tenant Chas Finch ~ Real ale ~ Lunchtime meals and snacks (not Sun) ~ Restaurant (not Sun) ~ (01295) 720383 ~ Children in eating area of.bar ~ Open 10-3, 6(5 Sat)-11

BRIGHTWELL BALDWIN SU6595 Map 4

Lord Nelson

Brightwell signposted off B480 at Oxford end of Cuxham or B4009 Benson—Watlington

Still the best place in this neck of the woods for a relaxed but civilised meal, this nice old place was named after the celebrated seaman during his own lifetime, though they had to rechristen it a little when the Admiral was presented with a peerage. There's still quite a naval theme in the bar on the left, where the plain white walls are decorated with pictures and prints of the sea and ships, there are some ship design plans, and a naval sword hangs over the big brick fireplace in the wall (which divides off a further room). Most tables are laid out for eating, especially at weekends, and may be reserved. Some of the most popular dishes on the changing menu currently include mixed leaves with avocado, parmesan cheese, bacon and croutons (£4.25), Thai-style chicken curry (£7.50), sauté of lamb's liver and bacon (£7.95), smoked haddock in a mild curry sauce or duck and orange pie (£8.25), and salmon fishcakes in a chive butter sauce (£8.75); they do some rather unusual soups, and a good two or three course Sunday lunch (from £11.50). Service is friendly and helpful; one of the barmaids has been here for over 20 years. John Smiths and Ruddles County on handpump, a good wine list, and a decent choice of French country wines. Furnishings are comfortably modernised, with wheelback chairs (some armed), country kitchen and dining chairs around the tables on its turkey carpet, candles in coloured glasses, orange lanterns on the walls, and pretty, fresh flowers; piped music. There's a verandah at the front, and tables on a back terrace by the attractive garden or under its big weeping willow, beside the colourful herbaceous border. The village church is worth a look. *(Recommended by Sue Demont, Tim Barrow, Nigel Wikeley, Susan and Alan Dominey, Gordon, Joan Olivier, C Moncreiffe, Michael Sargent, Margaret Dyke)*

Free house ~ Licensees Peter Neal, Richard Britcliffe ~ Real ale ~ Meals and snacks (till 10) ~ Restaurant (not Sun evening) ~ (01491) 612497 ~ Well-behaved children in restaurant ~ Open 12-3, 6.30-11; closed Sun evening, and all day 26 Dec

BROADWELL SP2503 Map 4

Five Bells

Village signposted off A361 N of Lechlade, and off B4020 S of Carterton

Hit by a fire in 1992, this small 16th-c former coaching inn spent some time closed and boarded up, but has emerged as a friendly and attractive country pub. The neatly kept low-beamed lounge has a sizeable dining area off to the right (very busy on Sunday lunchtimes), and another separate dining room which overlooks the spacious, well kept and attractive garden – where they have Aunt Sally, and grow some of the vegetables they use in the kitchen. There is a pleasant mix of flagstones and carpeting; wheelchair access. Consistently good straightforward food freshly cooked to order changes from day to day, and typically might include open sandwiches (from £1.50), home-made soup (£1.95), ploughman's (£3.25), vegetable pasta bake (£4.50), steak and kidney pudding or salmon and prawn gratin (£4.95), stilton chicken (£5.50), steaks (from £8.50), and puddings like fruit crumbles or pavlovas (£2.25). Flowers IPA, Hook Norton Best and Wadworths 6X, good house wine, big log fires, and friendly attentive service. The public bar has games machines; piped music. *(Recommended by Joan Olivier, Mr and Mrs R J Foreman, K Neville-Rolfe, Marjorie and David Lamb, Calum and Susan Maclean)*

Free house ~ Licensees Trevor and Ann Cooper ~ Real ale ~ Meals and snacks (not Mon) ~ Restaurant (not Mon) ~ (01367) 860076 ~ Children in lower dining room ~ Open 11.30-2.30, 6.30-11; closed Mon, evening 25 Dec, 26 Dec ~ Chalet bedrooms: /£35B

BURCOT SU5695 Map 4

Chequers

A415 Dorchester—Abingdon

This pretty black-and-white thatched pub has its own decent little art gallery, refurbished this year after an unfortunate contretemps with a council cleaning lorry. The smartly comfortable beamed lounge seems more spacious than you might have expected from outside; it has an open fire, and a very relaxed and friendly atmosphere. Well kept Archers Village, Ruddles County, and Ushers Best on handpump, with some good whiskies and unusual spirits and liqueurs. Relying very much on fresh local produce, the home-made bar food might include sandwiches, soup (£1.99), bacon and stilton rolls with cranberry sauce (£3.25), ploughman's (£3.99), tomato and aubergine crumble (£4.99), venison and apricot pie (£5.45), steak and kidney pudding (£5.60), baked trout with almonds (£7.25), and a Sunday roast (£5.25); they bake their own bread. There are tables among roses and fruit trees on the neatly kept roadside lawn, and the front is colourfully decked out with flowers in summer. Good access for wheelchairs. *(Recommended by Nigel Norman, Gordon, Hazel Astley, Geraint Roberts, Ian Phillips)*

Free house ~ Lease: Mary and Michael Weeks ~ Real ale ~ Meals and snacks (not Sun evening) ~ Restaurant ~ (01865) 407771 ~ Children in eating area of bar and in gallery (until 9pm) ~ Grand piano Fri and Sat evenings; brass band concerts ~ Open 11-2.30, 6-11

BURFORD SP2512 Map 4

Angel 🍷

14 Witney St, just off main street; village signposted off A40 W of Oxford

Dating back in part to the 14th c, this pleasant old inn is still a popular choice for its very good, and often rather unusual food. The monthly changing menus might include dishes like lunchtime sandwiches (they may not do these when busy at weekends), chicken liver and brandy pâté (£3.95), baked mussels (£4.95), tagliatelli with pesto and sun-dried tomatoes (£5.25), venison, mushroom and red wine pie (£6.95), smoked haddock and prawn au gratin (£7.95), char-grilled lamb steak with minted crème fraîche and a warm bean mash (£8.95), pan-fried chicken breast on a bed of spinach with bacon and gruyère cheese (£9.50), daily specials such as fresh fish delivered twice a week from Cornwall – dressed crab, scallops, red snapper, lemon sole and so forth and good puddings like home-made ice cream or pecan fudge tart (£2.95). The long beamed and panelled bar has antique furnishings and attractive old tables on its weathered flagstones, cushioned wall settles, wheelback chairs and an open fire; it leads out onto a terrace with a pretty walled garden beyond. Steps lead up from the main bar to a no-smoking dining room, and there's another charmingly cosy eating area beyond, with a huge log fire and stripped stone walls. It all looks rather atmospheric when candlelit at night. Well kept Brakspears Bitter, Flowers IPA, Marstons Pedigree, and Shepherd Neame Spitfire on handpump, good wines by the glass, and friendly and considerate service; dominoes and cribbage. We'd have thought this place might deserve our stay award, so would be interested to hear what readers think. *(Recommended by J R Tunnadine, M Joyner, D C T and E A Frewer, Karen and Graham Oddey, Nigel Woolliscroft, Jane Hosking, Ian Burniston, Michael Sargent, Paul McPherson, Stephen Brown, Mark Bradley, Marion and John Hadfield, Viv Middlebrook, David Holloway)*

Free house ~ Licensee Mrs Jean Thaxter ~ Real ale ~ Meals and snacks 12-2, 7-9.30 ~ Restaurant ~ (01993) 822438 ~ Children in eating area of bar ~ Open 11.30-3, 6.30-11; Jan/Feb closed Sun evening and Mon ~ Bedrooms: £35B/£45B

Lamb ★ ★

Sheep Street; A40 W of Oxford

Readers who like this civilised 500-year-old Cotswold inn do tend to fall for it rather heavily – 'heaven on earth' is how one described it recently. What appeals most is the combination of old-fashioned elegance and character with an easy-going, friendly local feel, so that although there's quite an emphasis on the stylish, carefully prepared food, it's very much somewhere that people wander in for a drink and a chat. The spacious beamed main lounge has distinguished old seats including a chintzy high winged settle, ancient cushioned wooden armchairs, and seats built into its stone-mullioned windows, bunches of flowers on polished oak and elm tables, oriental rugs on the wide flagstones and polished oak floorboards, and a winter log fire under its fine mantlepiece. Also, attractive pictures, shelves of plates and other antique decorations, a grandfather clock, and a writing desk. The public bar has high-backed settles and old chairs on flagstones in front of its fire. Good bar lunches might include filled baguettes (from £2.50), home-made soups like cream of parsnip and coriander (£2.95), ploughman's or chicken liver pâté (£4.25), courgette and shellfish au gratin (£5.75), warm asparagus and cashew nut salad (£5.95), pork, celery and apricot casserole (£6.25), beef bourguignon or steak and kidney pie (£6.95), and puddings like lime and stem ginger cheesecake or warm chocolate and pecan nut pie; in the evening they do meals like fillet of sea bass with a prawn and rosemary purse (£14.95) or duck with caramelised pears in brandy sauce (£15.75), or a three-course dinner (£21). Note they don't do bar meals Sunday lunchtimes, though there may be free dips then; the restaurant is no smoking. Well kept Wadworths IPA, 6X and winter Old Timer are dispensed from an antique handpump beer engine in a glassed-in cubicle. A pretty terrace leads down to small neatly-kept lawns surrounded by flowers, flowering shrubs and small trees, and the garden itself can be really sunny, enclosed as it is by the warm stone of the surrounding buildings. The bedrooms are old-fashioned and chintzy. *(Recommended by Ian Carpenter, Jane Hosking, Ian Burniston, David R Shillitoe, Dr Ian Crichton, C Driver, Nigel Wilkinson, John Evans, Leith Stuart, Mr and Mrs Hillman, Nigel Woolliscroft, E B Davies, John Bowdler, Karen and Graham Oddey, Adam and Elizabeth Duff, Lynn Sharpless, Bob Eardley, M V and J Melling, David Holloway, David Mair, Dr H Y Chan, A Cowell, Stephen Brown, Jean-Bernard Brisset, Paul McPherson, Gordon Theaker, Gordon, Michael Marlow, Mrs J M Bell, John and Marianne Cooper, J Weeks, Mike and Jo, Mark Bradley, Brian Jones)*

Free house ~ Licensee Richard de Wolf ~ Real ale ~ Lunchtime bar meals and snacks ~ Evening restaurant ~ (01993) 823155 ~ Children welcome ~ Open 11-2.30, 6-11; closed 25/26 Dec ~ Bedrooms: £35(£57.50B)/£85B

nr CHINNOR SU7698 Map 4

Sir Charles Napier

Spriggs Alley; from B4009 follow Bledlow Ridge sign from Chinnor; then, up beech wood hill, fork right (signposted Radnage and Sprigg Alley) then on right; OS Sheet 165 ref 763983

Here's an appealingly individual hybrid – the delicious bar food couldn't be further from what you'd normally class as pub grub, but then nor is this decidedly civilised place quite a restaurant. The comfortable simply furnished rooms are rather traditional (even homely), and at quiet moments during the week you'll generally feel quite welcome coming for just a drink, particularly in the cosy little front bar. At other times you may find the whole place is virtually dedicated to the stylish back restaurant, and there's little point coming at weekends unless you want to eat. The style and quality of the meals really is first class, though as the price of a starter is similar to what you might pay elsewhere for a main course, it's definitely somewhere to come for a treat. A typical day's bar menu might include pear and watercress soup (£3), poached mussels with shallots, dill and cream (£5), crostini of pigeon and mushrooms with truffle oil (£5.50), pan-fried baby Cornish squid with lemon (£6.50), roast scallops with sorrel and bacon (£7.50), mushroom crêpe (£8.50), braised guinea fowl with caramelised orange (£10.50), baked john dory with fennel and cardamom (£11.50), fillet of beef with juniper berries and red wine (£12), and puddings (£5). Sunday lunch is distinctly fashionable – in summer it's served in the crazy-paved back courtyard with rustic tables by an arbour of vines, honeysuckle and wisteria (lit at night by candles in terracotta lamps). An excellent range of drinks takes in well kept Wadworths IPA and 6X tapped from the cask, champagne on draught, an enormous list of exceptionally well chosen wines by the bottle (and a good few half-bottles), freshly squeezed orange and pink grapefruit juice, Russian vodkas and 30 malt whiskies. Piped music is well reproduced by the huge loudspeakers, there's a good winter log fire, a smartly relaxed feel and friendly staff. The back restaurant is decorated with sculpture by Michael Cooper. The croquet lawn and paddocks by the beech woods drop steeply away to the Chilterns, and there's a boules court out here too. *(Recommended by N M Baleham, B W and S J, Heather Couper, Gordon, Tina and David Woods-Taylor)*

Free house ~ Licensee Julie Griffiths ~ Real ale ~ Bar meals (not Sat evening or Sun) ~ Restaurant (not Sun evening) ~ (01494) 483011 ~ Children welcome lunchtimes; in evenings if over 8 ~ Open 12-2.30, 6.30-11; closed Sun evening and all day Mon

CHRISTMAS COMMON SU7193 Map 4

Fox & Hounds

Hill Rd from B4009 in Watlington; or village signposted from B480 at junction with B481

Mobile phones are strictly banned from this tiny unspoilt cottage – they wouldn't quite fit with the timeless feel of the place. In lovely Chilterns countryside, it's a favourite spot for local walkers to end up in, especially during the bluebell season. Always welcoming and friendly, the cosy beamed bar on the left is plainly furnished with three tables and wooden wall benches or bow-window seats, a little carpet down on the red-and-black flooring tiles, two sturdy logs to sit on in the big inglenook – which has a fire burning even in summer – and a framed Ordnance Survey walker's map on one cream wall. The room on the right is popular with locals and pretty much for drinking only, though you may also see the three cats and a friendly alsatian. Lunchtime food such as winter soup, sandwiches (from £1.50), ploughman's (£2.50; summer only) and sausage, egg and chips (£3.50); sandwiches only on Sundays and Mondays. Well kept Brakspears Bitter, Special and winter Old tapped from the cask in a back still room, good coffee; darts, shove-ha'penny, dominoes, cribbage. There are old-fashioned garden seats and sitting-logs by the roses and buddleia on the front grass beyond a small gravel drive, with picnic tables beside the house. The outside lavatories are in keeping with the pub's basic atmosphere. *(Recommended by Margaret Dyke, Jack and Philip Paxton, Pete Baker, R C Morgan, M W Turner, Jamie and Sarah Allan, Gordon)*

Brakspears ~ Tenant Kevin Moran ~ Real ale ~ Lunchtime snacks (service stops 1.45) ~ (01491) 612599 ~ Children allowed in games room until 9pm ~ Open 12-2.30, 6-11

CHURCH ENSTONE SP3724 Map 4

Crown 🛏

From A34 take B4030 turn-off at Enstone

The River Glyme flows past this creeper-covered Cotswold stone inn, a popular stop with diners come to explore the surrounding area. The comfortable beamed bar has brown plush button-back wall banquettes and windsor chairs on the brown patterned carpet, open fires, and prints on the bare stone walls; the dining area extends into the pleasant conservatory, which leads out into a little back garden. Reliable bar food includes sandwiches, good soup (£1.95), ploughman's, steak, kidney and mushroom pie or beef and Guinness casserole (£4.95), chicken kiev (£5.95), lemon sole (£6.25), steaks (from £7.95), vegetarian specials, and good home-made puddings; good traditional breakfast. No credit cards. Well kept Boddingtons, Flowers Original and Marstons Pedigree on handpump from the horseshoe bar, and a range of malt whiskies; service is attentive and friendly. The restaurant and part of the upper bar are no smoking. There are some white metal tables and chairs in front. *(Recommended by David Logan, Mr and Mrs Hillman, George Atkinson, John Bowdler, Jenny and Michael Back, C A Hall, Wayne Brindle, Lynn Sharpless, Bob Eardley, H O Dickinson)*

Free house ~ Licensees Peter Gannon and Jean Rowe ~ Real ale ~ Meals and snacks (not 25 Dec) ~ Restaurant ~ (01608) 677262 ~ Children in restaurant ~ Open 12-3, 7-11; closed evening 25 Dec ~ Bedrooms: £30B/£38(£42B)

CLANFIELD SP2802 Map 4

Clanfield Tavern 🍷

A4095 5 miles S of Witney

It's the excellent daily changing bar food that lifts this pretty village inn firmly out of the ordinary. As well as sandwiches (from £1.75), soup (£1.95) and ploughman's (£3.75), there might be imaginative dishes like smoked brie-filled mushrooms with barbecue sauce (£5.75), breast of chicken with tarragon, tomatoes, cream and white wine (£6.50), smoked haddock goujons (£6.95), escalope of pork dijonaise (£7.45), grilled monkfish with a light fennel sauce (£7.45), lamb cutlets in red wine and rosemary sauce (£7.75), trout fillets with king prawn and leek sauce, and lovely puddings such as fresh lemon and ginger cheesecake (£2.50); the excellent vegetables are served separately, and they do a good Sunday lunch. Service is pleasant and welcoming. Several flagstoned, heavy-beamed and stone-walled small rooms (one partly no smoking) lead off the busy main bar, furnished with settles and various chairs and seats cut from casks, as well as brass platters, hunting prints, and a handsome open stone fireplace crowned with a 17th-c plasterwork panel. Boddingtons, Hook Norton Best and Flowers IPA on handpump, and quite a few bin end wines; dominoes, shut-the-box, shove-ha'penny, cribbage and piped music. It's pretty in summer, with tiny windows peeping from the heavy stone-slabbed roof and tables on a flower-bordered small lawn that look across to the village green and pond. *(Recommended by Peter and Audrey Dowsett, Mr and Mrs G Turner, Sheila Keene, Joan and Ian Wilson, John Waller)*

Free house ~ Licensee Keith Gill ~ Real ale ~ Meals and snacks (11.30-2, 6-10) ~ Cottagey restaurant ~ (01367) 810223 ~ Children welcome ~ Open 11.30-2.30, 6-11 ~ Bedrooms: £40/£50B

CLIFTON SP4831 Map 4

Duke of Cumberlands Head 🛏 🍷

B4031 Deddington—Aynho

There's quite an emphasis on food at this thatched old village pub, though drinkers still feel welcome, especially in the spacious and simply but stylishly refurbished lounge with its lovely log fireplace. Though the licensee changed just before our last edition, the chef remains the same, and bar food includes dishes like sandwiches, soup (£2.25), garlic mushrooms (£3.25), ploughman's (£3.75), fresh asparagus (£4), local sausages (£4.95), Hungarian goulash or steak and stout pie (£5.75), grilled plaice (£6.75), puddings like cherry and almond tart (£3), and a Sunday roast; on summer Sunday evenings (they're closed then in winter) the only food is from a buffet. The restaurant is no smoking until 10pm. Well kept Adnams Southwold, Boddingtons, Hook Norton, King Alfred and Wadworths 6X on handpump, good wines by the glass, and 25 or so malt whiskies. There are tables out in the garden, and the canal is a short walk away. Bedrooms are in a new but sympathetic extension – you drive under it to park. *(Recommended by R T and J C Moggridge, Karen and Graham Oddey, Jim Reid, E A George, Mick Gray, Eric Locker, V G and P A Nutt, S Demont, T Barrow, G E Stait, Simon Stern, J Dawe, Gordon Theaker, N J Clifton, E A George, R G and M P Lumley, Gordon, David and Mary Webb)*

Free house ~ Licensee Nick Huntington ~ Real ale ~ Meals and snacks (not Sun evening) ~ Restaurant (not Sun or Mon evenings) ~ (01869) 338534 ~ Children in eating area until 9pm ~ Open 12-3, 6.30-11; closed winter Sun evenings ~ Bedrooms: £25S/£45S

CLIFTON HAMPDEN SU5495 Map 4

Plough

On A415 at junction with Long Wittenham turn-off

There were quite a few raised eyebrows a couple of years back when Mr Bektas decided to make this popular old pub completely no smoking, but he clearly knew what he was doing – trade has doubled since. Readers rate it very highly indeed, not least because of the friendly landlord's unusually accommodating attitude. Usually wearing tails or an evening suit, he's quite happy to serve any meal at any time (even if that means a full breakfast at five o'clock in the afternoon), will perhaps drive you home if you've indulged too much, and even offers his wife and daughter as babysitters while parents enjoy a quiet meal in the restaurant. It is very much a place people come to for a meal, with a range of tasty dishes such as home-made soup (£2.45), sandwiches (from £2.75), good oak smoked fish platter (£4.25), pasta with chicken, vegetables, and hazelnuts or with sun-dried tomatoes, parmesan, prawns and basil (£3.85; main course £5.25), steak in beer pie (£5.95), lovely chicken stir-fry (£6.25), sautéed lamb's liver and bacon (£8.50), salmon with pommary mustard and white wine sauce (£10.25), and puddings (£2.50); a three-course meal is £16.50. The cream to go with the several kinds of coffee comes in a pewter cup, and the sugar in a silver-plated bowl. The opened-up bar area has beams and panelling, black and red floor tiles, antique furniture, attractive pictures, and a friendly, relaxed atmosphere; it's said to be haunted by a benign presence that neatly upturns empty glasses. Well kept Courage Best, Ruddles County, and Websters Yorkshire on handpump, plenty of good wines, and a dozen malt whiskies. Some tables and seats outside. They now have an extra couple of bedrooms, with the fruit bowls a nice extra touch. *(Recommended by Peter Churchill, John Wooll, Heather Couper, John Waller, Mrs K J Putman, V Beynon, M Willcox, Margaret Dyke, Mrs J M Campbell, Jack and Philip Paxton, Wayne Brindle, Bob Rendle, Miss J F Reay, Stephen Brown, Eamon Green, Susie Northfield, D R Stevenson, Ian Phillips, David Wright, T A Bryan, Paul McPherson)*

Courage ~ Lease: Yuksel Bektas ~ Real ale ~ Meals and snacks (served all day) ~ Restaurant ~ (01865) 407811 ~ Children welcome ~ Open 11-11 ~ Bedrooms (one with four-poster): £39.50B/£55B

CROPREDY SP4646 Map 4

Red Lion

Off A423 4 miles N of Banbury

A friendly pub in a lovely setting, this thatched 15th-c pub is the kind of place where the locals might advise you as to what to choose from the menu. A short walk from a pretty lock and the Oxford Canal, it stands opposite a handsome old church with a raised churchyard, some of the graves in which are reminders of the Civil War battle that took place nearby. The simply furnished and old-fashioned bar still has high-backed settles under its ancient low beams, seats in one of the inglenooks, quite a lot of brass, plates and pictures on the walls, and winter open fires; the two rooms on the right are more for eating. Popular home-made bar food includes sandwiches (from £1.50), soup (£2.25), ploughman's (from £3.60), jumbo pork sausage (£3.25), steak and kidney pie or vegetarian tortellini bake (£4.75), chicken taco salad (£4.95), daily specials, evening steaks and Mexican fajitas, and puddings; children's menu (from £1.95), and Sunday roasts. There may be a wait at busy times. Well kept Courage Directors, John Smiths, and Ruddles Best on handpump; darts, pool, cribbage, fruit machine, trivia, and piped music. Welcoming American landlady. Seats in the small back garden. *(Recommended by D C T Frewer, Karen and Graham Oddey, Paul Robinshaw, A G Drake, Norma and Keith Bloomfield, Dr D K M Thomas)*

Courage ~ Lease: John Dando ~ Real ale ~ Meals and snacks ~ (01295) 750224 ~ Children in restaurant ~ Parking may be difficult in summer ~ Open 11.30-3, 6-11; 12-3. 6.30-11 winter

CUDDESDON SP5903 Map 4

Bat & Ball

S of Wheatley

Every inch of wall-space here is covered with cricketing memorabilia programmes, photographs, porcelain models in well-lit cases, score books, cigarette cards, pads, gloves and hats, and signed bats, bales and balls. The collection grows all the time, and this year the Cricket Memorabilia Society held a meeting and auction in the comfortable and immaculately kept L-shaped bar. Always friendly and welcoming, the pub has low ceilings, beams, a partly flagstoned floor, and a cheery, straightforward atmosphere. Very well liked bar food includes doorstop sandwiches (£2, lunchtime only), soup (£2.50), meat or spicy bean burgers (£4), vegetarian pasta or pancakes (£4.75), Cajun chicken or tiger prawns in wine and garlic (£5.75), rack of ribs with barbecue sauce (£6.50), lamb filled with smoked cheese, spinach, and sun-dried tomatoes (£7.50), 10oz sirloin steak (£9.75), and puddings (£2.50); Sunday roasts. Well kept Flowers Original, Marstons Pedigree and Whitbread Castle Eden on handpump, along with another beer brewed for them by Flowers; shove-ha'penny, dominoes, and piped music. A very pleasant terrace at the back has seats, Aunt Sally, and good views over the Oxfordshire plain; they plan a new extension out here to replace the current conservatory. *(Recommended by David Campbell, Vicki McLean, Peter and Audrey Dowsett, Walter Reid, LM, Derek and Sylvia Stephenson, Marjorie and David Lamb, Richard Atkinson)*

Free house ~ Licensee David Sykes ~ Real ale ~ Meals and snacks ~ (01865) 874379 ~ Children in eating area ~ Open 12-2.30, 6-11 ~ Bedrooms: £35S/£40S

CUMNOR SP4603 Map 4

Bear & Ragged Staff (food award symbol)

19 Appleton Road; village signposted from A420: follow one-way system into village, bear left into High St then left again into Appleton Road signposted Eaton, Appleton

The former licensees of the Fish at Sutton Courtenay have moved to this smart old place, and brought with them the same style of imaginative food that encouraged us to write so highly of that pub in our last edition. Characterised by dim lights, candle-lit tables, and roaring log fires, the comfortably rambling, softly lit bar has a relaxed but decidely civilised atmosphere, as well as easy chairs, sofas and more orthodox cushioned seats and wall banquettes; one part has polished black flagstones, another a turkey carpet. Written up on blackboards, the bar food may not be cheap, but it is very good, and makes unusual use of fresh ingredients: soup (£2.50), sandwiches such as sun dried tomato and goat's cheese (£4.95) or steak and onion (£5.95), mushroom and chive risotto (£5.25), spaghetti carbonara (£5.95), smoked haddock and poached eggs (£6.25), brochette of lamb's kidneys and mustard (£6.75), fresh fish and chips (£7.50), spatchcocked chicken and sweetcorn fritters or gambas pil pil (£8.95), and daily specials. Bass and Morrells Bitter and Varsity on handpump, plus a wide range of decent wines; piped music. Service is pleasant and obliging and there's a wooden high chair for children. The building is named for the three-foot model of a Warwick heraldic bear which guards the large open fire. *(Recommended by Roger Byrne, Heather Couper, Jim Reid, Joan Olivier, Frank Cummins, Nigel Norman, D C T Frewer, J V Dadswell, Sue Demont, Tim Barrow, Peter and Audrey Dowsett, Lynn Sharpless, Bob Eardley)*

Morrells ~ Tenants Bruce and Kay Buchan ~ Real ale ~ Meals and snacks (till 10) ~ Restaurant ~ (01865) 862329 ~ Children in eating area of bar and restaurant ~ Open 11-11

CUXHAM SU4588 Map 4

Half Moon

4 miles from M40, junction 6; B480

A nicely refurbished thatched and rather cottagey village pub, back as a main entry again thanks mainly to the good range of food carefully prepared by the hard-working licensees. Immaculately kept, the friendly and comfortable low-beamed bars have country-style furnishings, an inglenook fireplace with winter log fires or summer flower displays, and a few clues to one of the landlord's interests – vintage motorcycles. The good range of bar food might include lunchtime sandwiches, ploughman's (from £3.25), breaded brie salad (£5.75), pies such as beef, ale and mushroom or chicken and tarragon, spinach and nut pancakes, gammon or stir-fried Cantonese prawns (all £5.95), and children's meals; prompt, cheery service. Well kept Brakspears PA, SB and winter Old on handpump; darts, shove ha'penny, table skittles, cribbage, dominoes. There are seats sheltered by an oak tree on the back lawn, as well as a climbing frame and maybe summer barbecues. Dogs welcome. Across the road a stream runs through this quiet village. *(Recommended by Marjorie and David Lamb, Mr and Mrs Gregory, Gordon, Michael Sargeant, Graham Reeve, Calum and Susan McLean)*

Brakspears ~ Tenant Simon Daniels ~ Real ale ~ Meals and snacks (not Sun evening) ~ (01491) 614110 ~ Children in separate room ~ Open 12-2.30(3 Sat), 6-11

DEDDINGTON SP4631 Map 4

Kings Arms

Horsefair, off A423 Banbury—Oxford

A pleasant place to linger, this charming 16th-c coaching inn always has a happy, bustling atmosphere, and cheerful, smiling service. The nook-and-crannied bar, full of cheery locals, has black beams and timbering, white-painted stone walls, and one stone-mullioned window in the front has a good sunny window seat. The carpeted lounge has attractive settles and other country furnishings, and a side bar has bar billiards, shove-ha'penny, table skittles, cribbage, dominoes, trivia and satellite TV; Tuesday evening quiz. There's a good fire in the old stone hearth, and well chosen piped music from 1930s big bands to Handel or Vivaldi. Well presented bar food includes lunchtime sandwiches (not Sun), ham, egg and chips (£3.95), liver, bacon and onions (£4.50), steak in ale pie (£4.85), pork steak with black pudding and stilton sauce (£5.50), various baltis (especially on their Friday balti night), and halibut with herb butter (£6.95); they serve pizzas through to 10.30pm (from £3.95). Well kept Adnams, Tetleys, Wadworths 6X, and two monthly changing guests on handpump, plus a range of malt whiskies and eight wines by the glass. They plan to add bedrooms by the summer. *(Recommended by Gwen and Peter Andrews, David and Shelia, Meg and Colin Hamilton, M Joyner, Dr Stern, Miss Dawe, Frank Gadbois, Eric Locker)*

Free house ~ Licensees Susan and Nigel Oddey ~ Real ale ~ Meals and snacks ~ Restaurant ~ (01869) 38364 ~ Children in eating area ~ Jazz first Thurs of month ~ Open 11.30-3, 6-11; all day Sat

DORCHESTER SU5794 Map 4

George

High St; village signposted just off A4074 Maidenhead—Oxford

The very good food at this lovely old coaching inn has been drawing high praise recently, especially the unusual home-made breads served with the bar meals, with flavours such as curry and apricot, ratatouille, malted fruit, leek and bacon, and even chocolate. Accompanying these are well presented and imaginative dishes such as open sandwiches, three cheeses deep-fried in choux pastry with port mayonnaise (£3.95), stilton and smoked bacon in a light mustard sauce baked on field mushrooms and topped with a herb crust (£4.50), free-range omelette (£5.20), pasta with sun-dried tomatoes, anchovies and olives (£6.75), a daily casserole or grilled chicken breast with panfried pineapple slices and brandy sauce (£6.75), oyster mushroom and spinach strudel (£7), fresh fish (£7.75), and puddings like pear and caramel pavlova, or milk, white and plain chocolate mousses on a mint anglaise (£3.50); roast Sunday lunch. The civilised beamed bar is comfortably old-fashioned with an open fire in the big fireplace, cushioned settles and leather chairs. Well kept Brakspears Bitter, and guests like Greene King IPA or Tetleys on handpump, good wine by the glass from a quite exceptional wine list of over 130 bin-ends, and a range of malt whiskies. Pleasant and welcoming service. The inn was originally built as a brewhouse for the Norman abbey that still stands opposite. *(Recommended by Jack and Philip Paxton, John Wooll, Professor John White and Patricia White, George Atkinson, P L Warwick, Susie Northfield, John Waller, TBB, Adam and Elizabeth Duff)*

Free house ~ Licensee Brian Griffin ~ Real ale ~ Meals and snacks ~ Restaurant ~ (01865) 340404 ~ Children in restaurant ~ Open 11-3, 6-11 ~ Bedrooms: £55B/£70B

EAST HENDRED SU4588 Map 2

Wheatsheaf 🍷

Chapel Square; village signposted from A417

A warmly welcoming place that manages to cater to all tastes whilst still remaining firmly at the heart of the village, this is a most attractive 16th-c black and white timbered pub just below the Downs. There are high-backed settles and stools around tables on quarry tiles by a log-burning stove, some wall panelling, cork wall tiles, and a tiny parquet-floored triangular platform by the bar; low, stripped deal settles form booths around tables in a carpeted area up some broad steps. Promptly served, rather good bar food might include sandwiches, filled baked potatoes (from £2.95), curry or chicken tikka (£4.75), good home-made steak and kidney pie (£4.95), and daily specials like vegetable moussaka, local trout or medallions of lamb in a rich port and mint sauce (£6.95), half roast duck in orange and brandy sauce (£7.50), and fillet steak stuffed with stilton in port wine sauce (£11.50), and puddings; three-course Sunday lunch (£7.95). The dining room is no smoking. Well kept Morlands Original, Old Speckled Hen and Tanners Jack on handpump, a few malt whiskies, and wines by the glass; darts, dominoes, piped music, and maybe Bonnie, the golden labrador. The garden behind is colourful with roses and other flowers beneath conifers and silver birch; out here too is a budgerigar aviary, Aunt Sally, a play area for children with swings and so forth, and barbecues on summer Sunday evenings. The nearby church is interesting – its Tudor clock has elaborate chimes but no hands. *(Recommended by H O Dickinson, A T Langton, Susan and Alan Dominey, M W Turner, Geraint Roberts, Tom McLean, A E and P McCully, Marjorie and David Lamb)*

Morlands ~ Tenants John and Maureen Donohue ~ Real ale ~ Meals and snacks (till 10pm) ~ Restaurant ~ (01235) 833229 ~ Children welcome ~ Open 11-3, 6-11

EXLADE STREET SU6582 Map 2

Highwayman 🛏 🍷 ☕

Signposted just off A4074 Reading—Wallingford

One of the things that stands out about this comfortably cosy rambling inn is the notably friendly atmosphere – a couple of readers feel it's among the most welcoming pubs they've ever been in, and all the staff are cheerful and smiling.

Mostly 17th-c (though some parts go back another 300 years or so), the two beamed rooms of the bar have quite an unusual layout, with an interesting variety of seats around old tables and even recessed into a central sunken inglenook; an airy conservatory dining room has more seats, and it is a place where most of the space is given over to people eating. Not that cheap, but generally worth the extra, bar food might include sandwiches, soup (£2.95), garlic mushrooms with bacon and white wine (£4.95), lasagne (£6.50), steak, Guinness and mushroom pie or seafood pancake (£6.95), steaks (from £9.50), and weekly changing specials such as game consomme (£5.75), devilled kidneys (£5.95), saddle of rabbit in cider and cream (£12.95) or grilled Dover sole (£13.95). Well kept Brakspears, Fullers London Pride, Gibbs Mew Bishops Tipple, and changing guests like Hook Norton Old Hookey and Shepherd Neame Spitfire on handpump, freshly squeezed orange juice, decent wines, winter mulled wine, Pimms in summer; piped music in restaurant. The attractive garden has tables with fine views. The friendly mongrel is called Willie and the black and white spaniel, Saigon. The pub can be very busy at weekends. ***(Recommended by Sheila Keene, Jack and Philip Paxton, Mayur Shah, Brian and Anna Marsden, SD, JD, Mike Beiley, Chris Warne, Marjorie and David Lamb)***

Free house ~ Licensees Carole and Roger Shippey ~ Real ale ~ Meals and snacks (12-2.30, 6-10.30) ~ Restaurant ~ (01491) 682020 ~ Children in restaurant ~ Open 11-3, 6-11 ~ Bedrooms: £45S/£55S

FARINGDON SU2895 Map 4

Bell

Market Place; A420 SW of Oxford, then right into A417 – the village is now by-passed

Slightly refurbished under its new licensees, the old-fashioned bar of this bustling 16th-c inn has a timeless atmosphere that on market day reminds some readers of the kind of pubs Dickens and Hardy liked to write about. The wide gates at the front entrance are a reminder of the period when it was a favourite stop on the stagecoach route, and an ancient glazed screen through which customers would have watched the coaches trundling through the alley to the back coach yard is now the hallway. The bar has comfortable red leather settles, a restored old mural, Cecil Aldin hunting prints, and, notably, a 17th-century carved oak chimney-piece over the splendid inglenook fireplace. Well kept Badger Tanglefoot, Wadworths IPA and 6X and a changing guest like Adnams Broadside on handpump (kept under light blanket pressure), several malt whiskies; piped music. Bar food includes sandwiches (from £1.85), filled baked potatoes (from £2.80), tagliatelli carbonara (£3.95), ham, egg and chips (£4.50), mushroom stroganoff (£4.95), steak and kidney pie (£5.25), chicken kiev (£5.95), daily specials and puddings. The cobbled and paved yard, sheltered by the back wings of the pub, has wooden seats and tables among tubs of flowers. ***(Recommended by John Wooll, Tom McLean, Roger Huggins, Barry and Anne, Gordon, Peter and Audrey Dowsett; more reports on the new regime please)***

Wadworths ~ Tenant Darren Rawlings ~ Real ale ~ Meals and snacks (11am-10pm) ~ Restaurant ~ (01367) 240534 ~ Children welcome ~ Live entertainment winter Sat evening ~ Open 9.30-11; closed 25 Dec ~ Bedrooms: £45B/£55B

FERNHAM SU2992 Map 4

Woodman

A420 SW of Oxford, then left into B4508 after about 11 miles; village a further 6 miles on

Snugly cosy and rustic, the heavily beamed rooms in this atmospheric 17th-c country pub have an amazing assortment of old objects like clay pipes ready-filled for smoking, milkmaids' yokes, leather tack, coach horns, an old screw press, some original oil paintings and good black and white photographs of horses. Comfortable seating includes cushioned benches, pews, and windsor chairs, and the candle-lit tables are simply made from old casks. Over the bar there's a collection of over a hundred hats, and in winter you can mull your own wine or beer over the big log fire;

another bar area is in the former barn. Changing bar food might include liver and bacon casserole, spicy sausages, home-made cottage or steak and kidney pies (all £4.50), curries (from £5.40), Chinese prawns (£5.50), and puddings like chunky apple flan or treacle sponge (£2). OAPs who visit regularly get a substantial discount; fruit machine, piped music, friendly dog and two entertaining cats. Well kept Bass, Fullers London Pride, Marstons Pedigree, Morlands Old Speckled Hen, and Theakstons Old Peculier are tapped from casks behind the bar, though at £2 for the cheapest pint they're rather expensive; we think it's these high prices that explain why recent reports on this individual place have been rather less enthusiastic than usual. *(Recommended by Roger and Valerie Hill, Bill Bailey, Peter and Audrey Dowsett and others)*

Free house ~ Licensee John Lane ~ Real ale ~ Meals and snacks (not Mon) ~ (01367) 820643 ~ Children in eating area of bar ~ Open 11-3, 6.30-11; closed Mon lunchtime

FINSTOCK SP3616 Map 4

Plough

The Bottom; just off B4022 N of Witney

Two brothers took over this neatly refurbished thatched old pub just as our last edition was published, and as they are both dog lovers, they've decorated the walls with various doggy-related paraphernalia, including rosettes from canine chums they've exhibited at Crufts. Their own lhasa apso is called Jumbo, and other dogs are welcome in the garden (on a lead) and public bar; they'll usually be offered water or food. Clean, comfortable and relaxed, the long, rambling bar is nicely split up by partitions and alcoves, with an armchair by the open log-burning stove in the massive stone inglenook, tiles up at the end by the servery (elsewhere is carpeted), and a cosy feel under its low oak beams. Bar food includes sandwiches, and specials such as apricot stuffed chicken legs in brandy sauce (£5.95), pork loin strips with grain mustard sauce (£6.45), beef wellington with madeira gravy (£7.95), and fresh fish from Cornwall; booking is recommended on Saturday evenings. A comfortable low-beamed stripped-stone no-smoking dining room is on the right. Well kept Adnams Broadside, Boddingtons, Hook Norton Best and Old Hookey, and a weekly changing guest on handpump, farm cider and fruit cocktails in summer, mulled wine in winter, and a decent choice of wines and malt whiskies; maybe unobtrusive piped music. Service is friendly, swift, and efficient. A separate games area has darts, bar billiards, cribbage, dominoes, and a fruit machine. There are tables (and Aunt Sally) in the good, sizeable garden. Dogs and their owners should find this good walking country. *(Recommended by G W A Pearce, DMT, Peter and Audrey Dowsett, Amanda Clement, Andrew Campbell, John Waller, D Bryan, S Demont, T Barrow, David Heath)*

Free house ~ Licensee K J Ewers ~ Real ale ~ Meals and snacks ~ Restaurant ~ (01993) 868333 ~ Children in eating area of bar ~ Open 12-3, 6-11; 12-11 Sat ~ One bedroom: £32B/£45B

FYFIELD SU4298 Map 4

White Hart

In village, off A420 8 miles SW of Oxford

Still feeling very much a village inn despite the passing trade, the humble-looking exterior houses an impressive medieval building, with soaring eaves, huge stone-flanked window embrasures, and an attractive carpeted upper gallery making up the main room – a grand hall rather than a traditional bar. A low-ceilinged side bar has an inglenook fireplace with a huge black urn hanging over the grate, and a framed history of the pub on the wall. The priests' room and barrel-vaulted cellar are dining areas; three areas are no smoking. Well kept real ales might include Boddingtons, Greene King Abbot, Hook Norton Best, Theakstons Old Peculier and Wadworths 6X on handpump or tapped from the cask; a range of country wines, Weston's cider. Bar food includes lunchtime sandwiches, soup (£2.25), home-made pâté (£2.95), vegetable curry or cheese pie (£5.25), home-made steak and kidney pie (£5.75), local trout (£6.25), chicken tarragon (£7.50), steaks (from £8.50), and daily specials such as venison casserole (£8.50); pleasantly welcoming service. Shove-ha'penny, dominoes, darts, cribbage, trivia, and piped music. A heavy wooden door leads out to the rambling, sheltered and flowery back lawn, which has a children's playground. *(Recommended by D C T and E A Frewer, Dave Irving, Tom McLean, Ewan McCall, Roger Huggins, Nigel Norman, NN, Audrey and Peter Dowsett, M Lithgow, Gordon, Jon Carpenter)*

Free house ~ Licensee John Howard ~ Real ale ~ Meals and snacks (till 10pm) ~ Restaurant ~ (01865) 390585 ~ Children allowed in several rooms ~ Open 11-3, 6-11; closed 25/26 Dec

GREAT TEW SP3929 Map 4

Falkland Arms ★ ★

Off B4022 about 5 miles E of Chipping Norton

For many people this is still the classic country pub, and though you'll never be able to appreciate its charms on your own, the hordes of visitors that flock here in season do nothing to spoil an atmosphere that's as unique as it is timeless. Inside, the splendid partly panelled bar has a wonderful inglenook fireplace, high-backed settles and a diversity of stools around plain stripped tables on flagstones and bare boards, one, two and three handled mugs hanging from the beam-and-board ceiling, dim converted oil lamps, and shutters for the stone-mullioned latticed windows. At the bar counter, decorated with antique Doulton jugs, mugs and tobacco jars, you can buy clay pipes filled ready to smoke, some 50 different snuffs, tankards, a model of the pub, and handkerchiefs; the snug (used as a breakfast room in the mornings) is no smoking. As well as the regular Badger Tanglefoot, Donnington BB, Hook Norton Best and Wadworths 6X, they always have five well kept guest beers, along with 30 or so country wines, 60 malt whiskies, a couple of farm ciders, and hot punch in winter; darts, shove-ha'penny, dominoes, cribbage, and table skittles. Straightforward lunchtime food usually includes sandwiches, sausage and pickle (£4.80), and beef and pâté pie or gingered lamb casserole (£5). There are tables outside in front of the pub, with picnic tables under umbrellas in the garden behind – where there's a dovecot. Weekday lunchtimes are generally the least crowded times to visit. You have to go out into the lane then back in again to use the old-fashioned lavatories. Staying here is delightful (two of the rooms have four-posters), though if you're planning to come at a weekend you may have to book up to three months in advance; it's rare to find a place like this with bedrooms but no evening food. The sense of unimproved charm you get from the pub is evident throughout the whole of the enchanting golden-stone thatched village – or at least it is when the many visitors don't clog up the streets with cars; there's a specially built car park 60 yards or so away from the pub to try to keep the place as unspoilt as possible. The licensees also run the Reindeer in Banbury, which has been very attractively restored. *(Recommended by Alan Skull, Mrs J M Campbell, P and M Rudlin, Dr Peter Donahue, C Moncreiffe, David Campbell, Vicki McLean, D C T Frewer, S G Brown, Lynn Sharpless, Bob Eardley, A G Drake, John Bowdler, Jack and Philip Paxton, Mark Williams, P J Pearce, Nigel Wikeley, Karen and Graham Oddey, Meg and Colin Hamilton, Graham and Lynn Mason, Leith Stuart, Christopher and Sharon Hayle, Ewan McCall, Dave Irving, Roger Huggins, Tom McLean, Gordon, N and J Strathdee, John Waller, Jim and Maggie Cowell, WHBM, John and Christine Simpson, J Wedel, Roy Smylie, John and Shirley Dyson, Michael Marlow, The Monday Club, Paul Boot, S Demont, T Barrow, Wayne Brindle, Frank Gadbois, Ted George)*

Free house ~ Licensees John and Hazel Milligan ~ Real ale ~ Lunchtime meals and snacks (not Sun and Mon, except bank holidays) ~ (01608) 683653 ~ Children in eating area of bar at lunchtime ~ Folk music Sun evening ~ Open 11.30-2.30, 6-11; closed Mon lunchtime except bank holidays ~ Bedrooms: £30(£35S)/£45(£50S)

It is illegal for bar staff to smoke while handling your drink.

HAILEY SU6485 Map 2

King William IV ★ £

Note – this is the hamlet of Hailey, near Ipsden (not the larger Hailey over in west Oxon); signposted with Ipsden from A4074 S of Wallingford; can also be reached from A423; OS Sheet 175 map reference 641859

On a summer evening you can sit among the smartly-painted old farm equipment on the lawn behind this charmingly old-fashioned pub and look across to peaceful, rolling pastures. Inside, the relaxed beamed bar has some good sturdy furniture on the tiles in front of the big winter log fire, and so many well restored farm implements that it could almost be a museum; the timbered bare brick walls are covered with root cutters, forks, ratchets, shovels, crooks, grabbers, man-traps, wicker sieves, full-size carts, ploughs, and a pitching prong, all with details of their age, use and maker – there's even a couple of dried bladders. Two broadly similar carpeted areas open off. Well kept Brakspears PA, SB, and Old tapped from casks behind the bar, and farm ciders; Simple food consists of filled rolls such as ham, cheese and pickle, or corned beef (from 70p – the only evening food), and lunchtime pasties (95p), pies, and ploughman's (£3). They've happily got another Shire horse – Duke – who's already a favourite with customers (and with their children). The perfect way to arrive is by Ian Smith's horse and wagon service; he arranges rides from Nettlebed to the pub where you then have a ploughman's or supper and gently return through the woods and via Stoke Row back to Nettlebed (01491-641324 to book). *(Recommended by Jack and Philip Paxton, Adrian Pearce, Roderic Plinston; more reports please)*

Brakspears ~ Tenant Brian Penney ~ Real ale ~ Snacks ~ (01491) 680675 ~ Children in eating area at lunchtime ~ Open 11-2.30, 6-11

nr HOOK NORTON SP3533 Map 4

Gate Hangs High 🍷

Banbury Rd; a mile N of village towards Sibford, at Banbury—Rollright crossroads

This welcoming and rather isolated country pub has long been a handy find for travellers in the area, as indicated by the sign outside:

The gate hangs high, and hinders none,
Refresh and pay, and travel on.

Well-run by friendly licensees, it has quite an emphasis on dining, with good promptly served bar food typically including dishes such as soup (£1.95), ploughman's (£3.25), cauliflower, sweetcorn and cheese crumble (£5.50), rare roast beef salad (£5.95), steak and kidney pie (£6.50), loin of pork with sweet and sour sauce (£7.25), honey baked ham with local asparagus and cheese sauce (£7.50), and fresh salmon in lemon butter (£8.25). The bar has joists in the long, low ceiling, a brick bar counter, stools and assorted chairs on the carpet, and a gleaming copper hood over the hearth in the inglenook fireplace. Well kept Hook Norton Best and Old Hookey on handpump, a good wine list, and a range of malt whiskies; dominoes. The broad lawn, under holly and apple trees, has swings for children to play on – though one reader feels the once-fine view has been a little spoilt by the tents and caravans at the end. Five miles south-west are the Bronze Age Rollright Stones – said to be a king and his army who were turned to stone by a witch. *(Recommended by Mr and Mrs Box, Marjorie and David Lamb, B E Tarver, John Bowdler, P and M Rudlin, John and Shirley Dyson, Graham and Karen Oddey, M Pearlman)*

Hook Norton ~ Tenant Stuart Rust ~ Real ale ~ Meals and snacks (not Sun evening) ~ Restaurant (not Sun evening) ~ (01608) 737387 ~ Children in eating area of bar and in restaurant ~ Open 11.30-3, 6.30-11

HOOK NORTON SP3533 Map 4

Pear Tree 

Village signposted off A361 SW of Banbury

The Hook Norton brewery is barely 100 yards down the lane from this attractive pub, so you can rely on them serving perfectly kept Hook Norton Best and Old Hookey, along with the seasonal Haymaker or Twelve Days. Still essentially an honest unspoiled village local, its appeal has been somewhat broadened over the last few years, and on early weekday evenings especially (when it's less busy), you'll find this a very pleasant place to visit. The refurbished and knocked together bar area has country-kitchen furniture, including long tables as if for communal eating, a well-stocked magazine rack, open fires blazing away merrily, and a friendly and relaxed atmosphere; maybe locals drifting in with their dogs. Sensible piped music (Handel on Palm Sunday), shove ha'penny, cribbage, dominoes, trivia. Good value food includes generous sandwiches (from £1.70), filled baked potatoes (from £1.85), soups such as cauliflower, cheddar and mustard (£1.95), ploughman's (from £3.35), cottage pie, vegetable curry or lasagne (£3.95), beef in ale casserole (£4.90), daily specials such as pheasant in gin (£5.25) or grilled trout (£5.95), and puddings like pear and strawberry crumble (£1.60); meals are served rather simply to enable them to be eaten standing up – they don't want the emphasis of the place to shift away from drinking. Welcoming landlord, good service. The sizeable garden is attractive, with a play area, chickens and rabbits, Aunt Sally, and popular Sunday barbecues. The pub tends to get crowded on summer weekends. *(Recommended by George Atkinson, David Campbell, Vicki McLean, Robert Gomme, Tom Evans, Sue Holland, Dave Webster)*

Hook Norton ~ Tenants Steve and Wendy Tindsley ~ Real ale ~ Meals and snacks (not evenings Sun/Tues) ~ (01608) 737482 ~ Children welcome till 9pm ~ Occasional live entertainment ~ Open 12-2.30(3 Sat), 6-11 ~ Bedroom: £20S/£35S

KELMSCOT SU2499 Map 4

Plough

NW of Faringdon, off A417 or A4095

Not far from the Thames and the former summer home of William Morris, this rather pretty inn is the kind of place where the locals like to chat, and the licensee is happy to offer advice on local walks. Nicely refurbished, there's an attractively traditional small bar, homely and warmly welcoming, with ancient flagstones and stripped stone walls, and a larger cheerfully carpeted back room, decked out in a way that probably wouldn't have displeased Morris himself, but without any unnecessary gloss; interesting prints on its uncluttered walls. A wide choice of home-cooked food includes sandwiches (from £1.55, toasted from £1.75), soup (£2), ploughman's (from £3.50), ham, egg and chips (£3.95), pork in cider (£5.25), steak and kidney pie (£5.95), fresh local trout (£6.75), buckwheat pancakes filled with spicy vegetables (£6.95), cajun-style red snapper (£7.25), puddings like home-made orange and cointreau cheesecake, children's meals (from £1.50), and Sunday roasts (£4). Well kept Morlands Original and a guest such as Bass or Mansfield Old Baily on handpump, a good range of malt whiskies, attentive service; darts, shove-ha'penny, cribbage, dominoes, fruit machine, trivia, occasional piped music. The attractive garden has unusual flowers, tables and Aunt Sally, and there are Thames moorings a few minutes' walk away. *(Recommended by Mrs P J Pearce, Peter and Audrey Dowsett, David Campbell, Vicki McLean, David and Jane Warren, P and J Shapley, Martin and Karen Wake, Roger Huggins, Tom McLean, Dave Irving, Ewan McCall, D C Humphreys)*

Free house ~ Licensees Trevor and Anne Pardoe ~ Real ale ~ Meals and snacks ~ Restaurant ~ (01367) 253543 ~ Children welcome ~ Singer or duo Sat evening ~ Open 11-11 ~ Bedrooms: £35B/£45B

LEWKNOR SU7198 Map 4

Olde Leathern Bottle

Under a mile from M40 junction 6; just off B4009 towards Watlington

The kind of place where the landlord may strike up a conversation with you if you're on your own, this warmly friendly, bustling pub is popular with a good mix of people. The two rooms of the bar have heavy beams in the low ceilings, open fires, rustic furnishings and an understated decor of old beer taps and the like; the no-smoking family room is separated only by standing timbers, so you don't feel cut off from the rest of the pub. The dogs are called Penny (the doberman) and Charlie (the west highland white). Popular and generously served home-made bar food includes sandwiches (lunchtime only, from £1.95), good soup, ploughman's (from £3.75), filled baked potatoes (from £4.10), a late breakfast (from £4.25), various curries (from £4.50, the chicken is recommended), steak and kidney pie (£4.95), gammon and egg (£5.95), steaks (from £7.95), daily specials like chicken pasta bake (£4.25) or fresh whole lemon sole (£8.95), and home-made puddings (£2); quick, obliging service. Well kept Brakspears Bitter, SB and winter Old on handpump, plus Boddingtons in summer; dominoes and piped music. There are tables on the sizeable lawn alongside the car park; this is a very pretty village. *(Recommended by Dave Braisted, Roger Huggins, Martin and Jane Bailey, TBB, M W Turner, Graham Reeve, Gordon, Michael Sargent, Marjorie and David Lamb, C G and B Mason, D A Edwards, Dorothee and Dennis Glover, Lynn and Bill Capper, K H Frostick)*

Brakpears ~ Tenants Mike and Lesley Fletcher ~ Real ale ~ Meals and snacks (till 10pm Fri/Sat) ~ (01844) 351482 ~ Children in family room and lounge bar ~ Open 11-2.30(3 Sat), 6-11

LITTLE MILTON SP6100 Map 4

Lamb

3 miles from M40, junction 7; A329 towards Wallingford

The long thatched roof hangs low over the honey-coloured walls of this inviting 17th-c stone pub, prettily set in rolling farmland. The old-fashioned and simple beamed bar has little windows in the stripped stone walls that are so near the ground you have to stoop to look out, lots of tables with wheelback chairs, soft lighting, and plenty of happy people eating and drinking. Well kept Bass, Benskins, and Ind Coope Burton on handpump, friendly service. Favourite meals over the last year have included tasty green-lipped mussels in garlic, beef and Guinness casserole or tiger prawns with chilli dip (£6.95), and roast half shoulder of lamb with port and redcurrant sauce (£8.95), and the varied menu also includes sandwiches and children's meals. In summer the quiet garden is lovely: hanging baskets, tubs of flowers, roses, a herbaceous border, fruit trees, and swings. It can get quite crowded at lunchtimes. *(Recommended by Dave Braisted, Tim and Ann Newell, Keith Stevens, Gordon, Dave Irving, Ewan McCall, Roger Huggins, Tom McLean, A T Langton, TBB)*

Ind Coope ~ Tenant David Bowell ~ Real ale ~ Meals and snacks (till 10pm) ~ (01844) 279527 ~ Children in eating area of bar ~ Open 11-2.30, 6.30-11; closed evening 25 Dec

MAIDENSGROVE SU7288 Map 2

Five Horseshoes

W of village, which is signposted from B480 and B481; OS Sheet 175, map reference 711890

The sheltered garden behind this busy little brick house has been redeveloped over the last year, and now has a rockery, some interesting water features, and fine views down over the Chiltern beechwoods; they have an outside bar and maybe barbecues out here in summer. It's the excellent, imaginative food that most people come for, with a varied range of bar meals such as soup (£2.50), welsh rarebit or ploughman's (£3.95), baked potatoes filled with things like prawns in tomato and brandy mayonnaise (from £5.75), smoked salmon pâté (£4.95), pancakes with spicy Thai vegetables or smoked chicken and mushroom (£5.95), steak and kidney pie (£6.80), several stir-fried meals (from £6.95), seafood sausage (£7.95), a proper cassoulet with haricot beans and goose (£8.25), stincotto (£9.05), and crab thermidor (£9.50); the landlord collects fresh fish from the markets twice a week. Well kept Brakspears

Bitter, Special and winter Old on handpump, and a dozen wines by the glass; darts. The rambling bar is furnished with mostly modern wheelback chairs around shiny dark wooden tables – though there are some attractive older seats and a big baluster-leg table, as well as a good log fire in winter; the low ceiling in the main area is covered in bank notes from all over the world, mainly donated by customers. There's a separate bar for walkers where boots are welcome, and a dining conservatory (booking is pretty much essential in here at weekends). *(Recommended by Susan and Alan Dominey, Heather Couper, Andy Thwaites, S and P Hayes, Gordon, Jean Gustavson, Michael Sargent, Brad Wilson, Chris Warne, Ian Phillips, Dr Gerald Barnett, Mark Hydes, David Warrellow, K Harvey)*

Brakspears ~ Tenant Graham Cromack ~ Real ale ~ Meals and snacks ~ Conservatory restaurant ~ (01491) 641282 ~ Children in restaurant and separate family room ~ Open 11.30-2.30, 6-11; closed 25/26 Dec

MOULSFORD SU5983 Map 2

Beetle & Wedge

Ferry Lane; off A329, 1½ miles N of Streatley

Even our elastic definition of pub is stretched by this smart riverside hotel, so this may well be the last year we include it as a main entry. You can still pop in for just a drink, but it does seem to be getting increasingly formal – for example, readers who had previously eaten with their dog by the water were told on a recent visit that they no longer served riverside meals and that dogs were not allowed. Having said all that, the food is excellent, and if you can afford to treat yourself, a meal here is hard to beat. The most pubby part is the Boathouse bar/restaurant by the river, where there's a nice mix of old chairs around polished wooden tables, oak saddle-beams, a tiled floor, flint and brick walls, and quite a chatty atmosphere. The excellent menu in here might include fish soup (£5.50), moules marinières (£5.75), ploughman's with interesting cheeses (£7.25), tagliatelli with pesto, tomato and pinenuts (£7.50), artichoke heart filled with wild mushrooms or spicy sautéed cuttlefish with bean sprouts and spring onion (£7.80), rib-eye steak (£10.75), wing of skate with tomato, fennel and capers (£12.75), roast monkfish tail with baby onions and sun-dried tomatoes (£13.50), and puddings such as deep fried bananas and coconut with apricot sauce or apple and blackcurrant crumble (£5.95); you'll probably need to book at weekends. Well kept (though expensive) Adnams Best, Badger Tanglefoot, and Wadworths 6X on handpump, an extensive wine list, and freshly squeezed orange juice. Service is exemplary. The waterside lawn, flanked by roses, has robustly old-fashioned garden furniture. Rowing boats are available nearby. *(Recommended by Nigel Wilkinson, Jamie and Ruth Lyons, N M Baleham, M W Turner, Dave Carter, Pippa Bobbett)*

Free house ~ Licensees Richard and Kate Smith ~ Real ale ~ Meals and snacks (till 10pm) ~ Restaurant (not Sun evening, or Mon) ~ (01491) 651381 ~ Well-behaved children welcome ~ Open 11.30-2.30, 6-11; closed 25 Dec ~ Bedrooms: £80B/£95B

MURCOTT SP5815 Map 4

Nut Tree

Off B4027 NE of Oxford, via Islip and Charlton-on-Otmoor

The friendly landlord of this civilised low-thatched old house is a master butcher, so you can count on very good steaks and other meats if – as most people tend to do – you're coming to eat. It's in a lovely spot, especially pretty in summer, when there are colourful hanging baskets, ducks on a pretty front pond, trim lawns, and usually plenty of animals such as donkeys, peacocks and rabbits. In the garden you'll also find Aunt Sally, and an unusual collection of ten gargoyles, each loosely modelled on one of the local characters, and carved into a magnificently grotesque form from a different wood. Nine of them hang in the walnut tree and one from a pillar overlooking the well. Inside, the welcoming beamed lounge is decorated in stylish shades of red, and has fresh flowers on its tables (set for food), and a winter log fire; there's also a small back conservatory-style extension. The good bar food includes sandwiches (from £2.50), locally-made sausages (£3.50), veal, ham and egg pie, quite a few fresh fish dishes (from £5.50), steak and kidney pie (£6.50), daily specials, and various chicken and vegetarian meals. Hook Norton and Morrells Oxford on handpump, along with changing guests such as Whichwood Wychert or Wadworths 6X; a fair number of malt whiskies, and a decent range of wines. Darts, shove-ha'penny, cribbage and dominoes, all on Sunday only. The pub is handy for walks through the boggy Otmoor wilderness, and from the M40 (junction 9). *(Recommended by Brian White, Sue Demont, Tim Barrow, Roger Byrne, Richard Dolphin, T M Dobby, Nigel Flook, Betsy Brown, Gordon, Michael Sargent, Alan and Margot Baker, N and J Strathdee, John Waller, TBB)*

Free house ~ Licensee Gordon Evans ~ Real ale ~ Meals and snacks (not Sun) ~ Restaurant (not Sun) ~ (01865) 331253 ~ Children in restaurant ~ Open 11-3, 6.30-11

NUFFIELD SU6687 Map 2

Crown 🍷

A423/B481

Very friendly and popular, this attractive little partly 17th-c brick-and-flint pub seems to have that extra little bit of imagination put into everything, from the decor to the very good food. At the moment their changing range of five or six uncommon cheeses stands out as particularly unusual, with blends such as gubbeen (an Irish vegetarian cheese) or leicester whirl offered with biscuits, or a ploughman's (£3.50). The menu also includes sandwiches, soup (£2.75), baked mussels in a garlic cream sauce (£3.95), tasty wild boar and red wine sausages (£5.25), vegetarian risotto (£5.50), steak, kidney and beer pie or bacon chop with honey and topped with mustard and parsley butter (£5.95), pizza with prawns, cockles, squid and mussels (£6.50), stir-fried beef and noodles (£7.95), grilled scampi with monkfish (£8.50), daily specials, and lots of puddings; everything is home-made, and service is prompt and friendly. Well kept Brakspears Bitter, Special and OBJ on handpump, a good range of decent wines, and cappuccino and espresso coffee. The heavily beamed lounge has country furniture, roaring log fire in a fine inglenook fireplace, a relaxed atmosphere, and shelves of golf balls (there's an adjacent golf course); cribbage, dominoes. The public bar has another big log fire, and there's a third family room, and a friendly cat. Tables out in front, or under cocktail parasols in the partly terraced back garden. Very handy for Nuffield Place, the home of the late Lord Nuffield of Morris cars fame, the pub is right on the Ridgeway Long Distance Path, and they can put you in touch with local people who do B&B. *(Recommended by Mrs H Astley, Professor J R Leigh, Heather Couper, Gordon, R N Carter, Joan Olivier, Dick Brown, R D Knight)*

Brakspears ~ Tenants Ann and Gerry Bean ~ Real ale ~ Meals and snacks (till 9.45, 9.30 Sun) ~ (01491) 641335 ~ Children in small room off bar, lunchtimes only ~ Open 11-2.30(3 Sat), 6-11; closed 25/26 Dec, and evening 1 Jan

OXFORD SP5106 Map 4

Turf Tavern

Bath Place; via St Helen's Passage, between Holywell Street and New College Lane

The narrow alleyways that shield this little pub from the rest of the world aren't shown on that many maps, but even though it might seem a million miles and a hundred years away from the bustle of the city, it's generally the Oxford pub that the majority of visitors head to first. This is probably because it's the most obviously pretty one, especially in summer, when tables in the three attractive walled-in flagstoned or gravelled courtyards around the old-fashioned building become as precious as any of the books in the Bodleian. Inside, the two little rooms have a snug feel, dark beams, and low ceilings, and are still much as Hardy described it when Jude the Obscure discovered that Arabella the barmaid was the wife who'd left him years before; there's also a bar in one of the courtyards. A changing range of real ales might include any combination of Archers Village, Boddingtons, Flowers Original, Fullers London Pride, Greene King Abbot, Marstons Pedigree, Mr Morlands Old Speckled Hen or Wadworths 6X, on handpump or tapped from the bar; they have occasional beer festivals. Also country wines, farm ciders, and a good mulled wine in winter. Straightforward bar food (served rather inconveniently from an outside servery) includes lots of filled baps, hot or cold, like bacon, egg and tomato or chicken tikka mayonnaise, and hot dishes like vegetarian lasagne, traditional roasts, or steak and mushroom pie (all around £4.85). In winter the braziers in the courtyard are very atmospheric to huddle around. ***(Recommended by Wayne Brindle, David and Shelia, John Wooll, David Campbell, Vicki McLean, Dave Irving, Roger Huggins, Tom McLean, Ewan McCall, Mr and Mrs R J Foreman, Nigel Wooliscroft, Walter Reid, Julian Bessa, Sue Demont, Tim Barrow, Mrs Pat Crabb, Gordon, Neil and Elaine Piper, N and J Strathdee, Martin Jones, Eamon Green, Tim and Ann Newell, Jim and Maggie Cowell)***

Whitbreads ~ Manager Trevor Walter ~ Real ale ~ Meals and snacks (all day May-Sept) ~ (01865) 243235 ~ Children in back bar only ~ No nearby parking ~ Open 11-11

RAMSDEN SP3515 Map 4

Royal Oak 🛏

Village signposted off B4022 Witney—Charlbury

This unpretentious village pub has the sort of friendly and cosy atmosphere that makes most people wish they could stay longer – and in cool weather the cheery log fire certainly helps. It also has a wide range of good generous sensibly priced food cooked by the landlord, including interesting specials such as creole chicken with herbed, spiced rice (£7.25), guinea fowl with a fresh peach and armagnac sauce (£7.95) or monkfish with tomato and Pernod sauce (£9.50), as well as regular dishes such as fresh salmon and crab fishcakes with lobster sauce (£7.25), stilton, leek and mushroom pie (£7.75), half shoulder of English lamb with a sage and cider sauce (£9.25), and seafood paella (£9.50); home-made puddings like pancake pie with banana, currants and cream, treacle and almond tart or lemon meringue pie (£2.75), and good Sunday lunches. The traditional bar is simply furnished and decorated but comfortable, without the clutter of nick-nacks that sometimes passes for atmosphere – it has the real thing instead; no noisy games or piped music. Well kept Archers, Banks's, Hook Norton Best and guest beers on handpump, decent wines, very obliging service; evening dining room. Dogs allowed. The cosy bedrooms are in separate cottages. ***(Recommended by John Waller, Rosemary Harris, F M Bunbury)***

Free house ~ Licensee Jon Oldham ~ Real ale ~ Meals and snacks till 10pm) ~ Restaurant ~ (01993) 868213 ~ Children welcome ~ Open 11.30-2.30, 6.30-11 ~ Bedrooms: £27.50B/£40B

ROKE SU6293 Map 2

Home Sweet Home ★

Village signposted off B4009 Benson—Watlington

The low-walled garden at the front of this rather smart thatched and tiled old house looks out on to the quiet hamlet, and is ideal for an excellent lunch on a sunny day; there are lots of flowers around the tables out by the well. Inside, the two smallish, bare-boarded and stone-walled rooms of the bar have a good country atmosphere, as well as heavy stripped beams, leather armed chairs, a few horsey or game pictures such as a nice Thorburn print of snipe, and big log fires – one with a great high-backed settle facing it across a hefty slab of a rustic table. On the right, a carpeted room with low settees and armchairs, and an attractive corner glass cupboard, leads through to the restaurant. Very good bar food includes sandwiches, a splendid steak and kidney pudding (£6.50), fresh salmon fishcakes with parsley sauce (£6.95), calf's liver with crispy bacon or chicken roulade (£7.95), and puddings like treacle sponge (£2.25); readers particularly like the vegetables. Well kept Brakspears Bitter and Eldridge Pope Royal Oak on handpump, and a good choice of malt whiskies. ***(Recommended by Mrs M Lawrence, Nicholas Stuart Holmes, John Waller, N Cooke, David Wright, Eamon Green)***

Free house ~ Licensees Jill Madle, Peter and Irene Mountford ~ Real ale ~ Meals and snacks (till 10pm) ~ Restaurant ~ (01491) 838249 ~ Well behaved children welcome ~ Open 11-3, 5.30-11

SHENINGTON SP3742 Map 4

Bell 🍷

Village signposted from A422 W of Banbury

Nicely set and well run by a notably friendly landlady, this 17th-c golden stone cottage is rather popular with readers at the moment, mainly for its warm welcome and good home-cooked food. The heavy-beamed and carpeted lounge has old maps and documents on the cream wall, brown cloth-cushioned wall seats and window seats, and vases of flowers on the tables; the wall in the flagstoned area on the left is stripped to stone and decorated with heavy-horse harness, and the right side opens into a neat little pine-panelled room (popular with locals) with decorated plates on its walls; darts, cribbage, dominoes, coal fire. Favourite dishes on the menu over the last few months have included sandwiches, well-flavoured soups like parsnip, steak and kidney pie or almond, celery and cashew nut bake (£5.75), salmon in cucumber sauce (£7.50), duck in black cherries (£8.95), and puddings such as a good sticky toffee pudding. They also do the lunches for the local junior school. Well kept Boddingtons and Hook Norton Best on handpump, and a good choice of wines from Berry Bros; good, cheery service. There's a tortoiseshell cat called Willow and a west highland terrier, Lucy. The tables at the front look across to the green. ***(Recommended by John Bowdler, David Lewis, Maysie Thompson, Jon Carpenter, S C King, George Jonas, Jill and Peter Bickley, Piotr Chodzko-Zajko, Joan Olivier, Mr and Mrs W W Swaitt, Mr and Mrs C Moncreiffe, Alex Nicholls, Adele Faiers, G Diamond, R T and J C Moggridge)***

Free house ~ Licensee Mrs J J Dixon ~ Real ale ~ Meals and snacks (till 10) ~ (01295) 670274 ~ Children in eating area of bar ~ Open 12-3, 6.30(6 Sat)-11 ~ Bedrooms: £15(£18B)/£30

SHIPTON-UNDER-WYCHWOOD SP2717 Map 4

Lamb ★ 🍴 🍷 🛏

Just off A361 to Burford

Civilised and stylish, this old sandstone pub certainly has quite an emphasis on food, but there's plenty of room for drinkers too. They now have their popular cold buffet all year round, and other well liked choices from the bar menu include sandwiches (from £2.50), home-made soup, Loch Fyne gravadlax or pan-fried scallops (£5.50), baked ham with cider sauce (£7.50), crispy roast duck (£10.50), lots of fresh fish such as Dover sole, crab (£10.50) or lobster (£12.95), and puddings like lemon and ginger cheesecake (£2.95); vegetables are well presented, salads well dressed, and breakfasts very good indeed. The beamed bar has quite a relaxed feel, as well as a fine oak-panelled settle, a nice mix of solid old farmhouse-style and captain's chairs on the wood-block floor, polished tables, cushioned bar stools, solid oak bar counter, pictures on old partly bared stone walls, and newspapers on rods to read. The restaurant (where some readers felt they had to be on their best behaviour) is no smoking. Well kept Hook Norton Best and Wadworths 6X on handpump, several malt whiskies, carefully chosen wines and champagne by the glass. In summer, you can sit at tables among the roses at the back. No children. ***(Recommended by Stephen***

Brown, A M Rankin, Ewan McCall, Dave Irving, Roger Huggins, Tom McLean, S Demont, T Barrow, Martin Jones, the Monday Club, Michael Sargent, Mark and Toni Amor-Segan, Mrs J M Bell, Dr Stern, Miss Dawe, Adam and Elizabeth Duff, Mark Bradley, T R and B C Jenkins, George and Chris Miller)

Free house ~ Licensees Mr and Mrs L Valenta ~ Real ale ~ Meals and snacks (till 10) ~ Restaurant (not Sun evening) ~ (01993) 830465 ~ Children in eating area and restaurant ~ Open 11-3, 6-11; closed Mon ~ Bedrooms:£58B/£65B

Shaven Crown

Perhaps the glory of this striking heavily stone-roofed inn is the medieval courtyard garden behind, little changed since the days when it was used as an exercise yard by monks. A tranquil place on a sunny day, it has old-fashioned seats set on the stone cobbles and crazy paving, with a view of the lily pool and roses. The inside of the building is rather impressive too, with a magnificent double-collar braced hall roof, lofty beams and a sweeping double stairway down the stone wall. A fine beamed bar has a relief of the 1146 Battle of Evesham, as well as seats forming little stalls around the tables and upholstered benches built into the walls. Good bar food – with prices unchanged from last year – includes soup (£2.15), ploughman's (from £2.95), smoked haddock mousse or mushroom and walnut pancake (£3.95), a mild curried meat loaf, home-baked ham or salmon, cod and dill fishcakes (£5.25), steak, kidney and mushroom pie (£5.75), sirloin steak (£8.95), daily specials, and puddings like treacle tart, lemon soufflé or home-made ice creams (from £1.40); the restaurant is no smoking. Well kept Hook Norton Best and two guests such as Greene King Abbot and Morlands Old Speckled Hen on handpump, well-chosen wine list with a dozen or so half-bottles and a wine of the week, and very good, friendly service. The pub has its own bowling green. This was originally a hospice for the monastery of Bruern in the 14th century, and parts of it are said to have been used as a hunting lodge by Elizabeth I; the residents' lounge, the medieval hall, is lovely. *(Recommended by Marjorie and David Lamb, Tom McLean, Ewan McCall, Roger Huggins, Dave Irving, Moira and John Cole, Frank Cummins, S May, David Campbell, Vicki McLean, John Drew, Dr C I Haines, Peter and Iris Jones, T R and B C Jenkins, Peter and Anne Hollindale, Susan and John Douglas, R G Barton, Heather Thomas, Peter and Rosemary Ellis)*

Free house ~ Licensees Trevor and Mary Brookes ~ Real ale ~ Meals and snacks (not Dec 25) ~ Restaurant ~ (01993) 830330 ~ Children welcome – but no under 5s in restaurant in evening ~ Open 12-2.30, 7-11 ~ Bedrooms: £33B/£66B

SOUTH LEIGH SP3908 Map 4

Mason Arms

3m S of A40 Witney-Eynsham

Considering how handy this delightful thatched country pub is to the A40, it's astonishing how much of a rustic idyll it can seem; one reader remembers being held up on the single-track lane that runs down to it by a fat sow waddling along as if she had all the time in the world. It's a nice place to stay: there are continental breakfasts in the fridge in the room and you may be woken by the comforting sound of bleating sheep in the adjacent little field. Peacocks and chickens potter around the sweeping lawns behind, and there are picnic tables in a small grove by some quite bizarrely-shaped trees and little bushes. Inside, the flagstoned lounge is separated into two halves by a wrought-iron divider, and has lots of polished copper and brass, built-in cushioned settles curving around the corners, a panelled bar counter, an open fire with stone hearth at one end, and a log-effect gas fire at the other; a couple of readers have found the piped music obtrusive. Good home-made bar food includes sandwiches (from £1.95), soup (£1.95), liver pâté (£2.75), ploughman's (£3.75), spicy chicken and smoked ham pancake or a vegetarian dish of the day (£5.25), liver and smoked bacon casserole (£6.75), home-made steak and kidney pie (£6.95), trout in a pink wine sauce (£7.25), and specials such as pheasant in red wine; Sunday roasts. Well kept Sow-lye (brewed for them) and Theakstons Best on handpump, a good range of cognacs and malt whiskies, and lots of wines. Dylan Thomas used to pop in here while writing *Under Milk Wood* at the nearby Manor House. *(Recommended by Joan Olivier, J C S Weeks, Ian Rorison, Sue Demont, Tim Barrow, Nigel Norman, LP, DP, the Monday Club, Mr and Mrs J Brown, Dr P Mummery)*

Free house ~ Licensee Geoff Waters ~ Real ale ~ Meals and snacks (not Sun evening or Mon) ~ Restaurant (not Sun evening or Mon) ~ (01993) 702485 ~ Children welcome ~ Open 11-2.30, 6.30-11; closed Mon ~ Bedrooms: £34.50B/£48.50B

SOUTH STOKE SU5983 Map 2

Perch & Pike ♀

Off B4009 2 miles N of Goring

Those who knew this attractive flint pub before it reopened under the Robinsons a couple of years back will be surprised to learn that it's very much a place for eating now, with rather imaginative and notably well-presented meals. You're still quite welcome to come for a drink, but it really would be a shame not to sample Mrs Robinson's cooking, and enjoy what really is quite a civilised eating experience: diners have linen table napkins in old napkins rings, and bone-handled cutlery gleaned from antique markets. The menu changes every couple of weeks, but as well as sandwiches you might find dishes such as Thai fish cakes with cucumber dip (£4.50), grand marnier and chicken liver pâté or char-grilled squid with coriander and mint chutney (£4.95), pork and cider sausages with olive oil mash and beer and caramelised onion gravy (£7.50), artichoke hearts, roast peppers and gruyère cheese baked in puff pastry and served with watercress sauce (£8.95), chicken fillet with pesto (£9.95), and puddings such as banana cheesecake (£3.75); everything is home-made. With a good pubby feel after a careful refurbishment, the relaxing bar has quite a light and spacious feel, as well as open fires, comfortable seats, and a nice assortment of tables. Well kept Brakspears Bitter and Special on handpump from an old oak bar, and around 15 good wines by the glass. The window boxes are pretty, and there are seats out on the large flower-bordered lawn. The Thames is just a field away. *(Recommended by J M M Hill, Colonel A H N Reade, Nicholas Holmes, Mr and Mrs P G Wright, Joan Olivier, Pippa Bobbett, Dick Brown, Gordon)*

Brakspears ~ Tenants Michael and Jill Robinson ~ Real ale ~ Meals and snacks (not Sun evening) ~ Restaurant ~ (01491) 872415 ~ Children in room next to bar ~ Open 12-2.30, 6-11; closed 25 Dec

STANTON ST JOHN SP5709 Map 4

Star

Pub signposted off B4027; village is signposted off A40 heading E of Oxford (heading W, the road's signposted Forest Hill, Islip instead); bear right at church in village centre

Interestingly arranged over two levels, this bustling old pub has quite a chatty feel to its little low-beamed rooms. One has ancient brick flooring tiles and the other quite close-set tables, while up a flight of stairs (but on a level with the car park) is a busy and well refurbished extension with rugs on flagstones, pairs of bookshelves on each side of an attractive inglenook fireplace, old-fashioned dining chairs, an interesting mix of dark oak and elm tables, shelves of good pewter, terracotta-coloured walls with a portrait in oils, and a stuffed ermine. Well kept Badger Tanglefoot, Wadworths IPA, Farmers Glory, 6X and winter Old Timer on handpump, country wines and hot toddies. Behind the bars is a display of brewery ties, beer bottles and so forth; shove-ha'penny, dominoes, cribbage, and often noticeable piped music. The family room is no smoking. The wide range of promptly served bar food might include sandwiches, asparagus in season, chicken tikka or beef curry (£4.95), pies such as pork and cider or turbot and mushroom, corned beef hash or smoked haddock and bacon au gratin (all £5.25), vegetarian meals like bulgur wheat and walnut pie, and puddings (served with clotted cream) such as banana and ginger cheesecake. The walled garden has picnic tables among the rockeries, and swings and a sandpit. There are annual classic car rallies, and it gets busy then. *(Recommended by Nigel Norman, Gordon, A M Rankin, Martin, Jane and Laura Bailey, Calum and Susan McLean, A M Stephenson, Marjorie and David Lamb, Kate and Robert Hodkinson, Jon Carpenter, Mark Whitmore, S Demont, T Barrow, Joan Olivier, T G Brierly, Michael and Janet Hepworth, Robert Gomme, Walter Reid, Terry and Eileen Stott*

Wadworths ~ Tenants Nigel and Suzanne Tucker ~ Real ale ~ Meals and snacks (till 10pm) ~ (01865) 351277 ~ Children in eating areas and family room ~ Folk music first Sun of month ~ 11-2.30(3 Sat), 6.30-11; closed 25/26 Dec

STEEPLE ASTON SP4725 Map 4

Red Lion ♀

Off A4260 12 miles N of Oxford

By anyone's standards this is a lovely little pub, but it's made extra special by the exceptionally friendly and welcoming landlord. Here now for 21 years, he tells a good tale, and seems to go out of his way to make everyone feel at home. He is also very keen on his wines – the cellar contains over 100 different vintages. The comfortable partly panelled bar has beams, an antique settle and other good furnishings, and under the window a collection of interesting language and philosophy books that crossword fans find compelling. Good, popular lunchtime bar food might include tasty stockpot soup (£1.85), sandwiches (from £1.85), excellent ploughman's with nicely ripe stilton (£3.60), home-made pâté (£3.60), summer meals like smoked salmon platter (£5) or summer salads such as crab (£6), and various winter hot-pots and casseroles (from £4); the evening restaurant is more elaborate. Well kept (and reasonably priced) Badger Tanglefoot, Hook Norton Best and Wadworths 6X on handpump, and a choice of sixty or so malt whiskies. The sun-trap front terrace with its lovely flowers is a marvellous place to relax in summer. *(Recommended by D C T and E A Frewer, Alan Skull, Gordon, Nigel Norman, B Pullee, Dr Ann Wintle, Roger Huggins, Dave Irving, Tom McLean, Ewan McCall, P A Reynolds, Lynn Sharpless, Bob Eardley, Margaret Dyke, A W Dickinson, Michael Sargent, Dorothee and Dennis Glover)*

Free house ~ Licensee Colin Mead ~ Real ale ~ Lunchtime bar meals and snacks (not Sun) ~ Evening Restaurant (closed Sun and Mon and two weeks late Sept-early Oct) ~ (01869) 340225 ~ Children in restaurant ~ Open 11-3, 6-11

STEVENTON SU4691 Map 4

North Star

The Causeway; central westward turn off main road through village, which is signposted from A34

Named after an 1837 steam engine (which accounts for some of the pictures around the walls), this is a marvellously unspoilt and simple pub, where you could be forgiven for thinking it's still some time around the early 1920s. A low half-hidden door leads through a porch into the main bar, where a high-backed settle faces a row of seats around a couple of elm tables; decorations include a polished brass track gauge, and interesting local horsebrasses. There's no bar counter – the Morlands Mild, Bitter and Best are tapped from gleaming casks and surrounded by lots of neatly stacked bottles, bars of chocolate, crisps and so forth; recent reports suggest the beer quality can vary. Cheap ploughman's, and friendly, chatty licensees. There's also a simply furnished dining room, and a small parlourish lounge with an open fire; cribbage. The garden is entered from the road through a small yew tree arch, and grass at the side has some old-fashioned benches. Unfortunately the licensees wouldn't answer any of our questions this year, so we'd be particularly grateful for up-to-date news and prices. *(Recommended by Pete Baker, Jack and Philip Paxton, Gordon, Nic Armitage; more reports please)*

Morlands ~ Tenant Mr R Cox ~ Real ale ~ Meals and snacks (weekday lunchtimes only) ~ (01235) 831309 ~ Open 10.30-2.30, 6.45-11

SWINBROOK SP2811 Map 4

Swan

Back road 1 mile N of A40, 2 miles E of Burford

Covered in wisteria, this quietly traditional 400-year-old place is another genuinely old-fashioned country pub, not far from the River Windrush and its bridge. The tiny interior is cosy, peaceful, and dimly-lit, with simple antique furnishings and a wood-burning stove in the flagstoned tap room and the back bar; darts, shove-ha'penny, dominoes and cribbage. Popular lunchtime bar food might include sandwiches, fish pie or venison in ale (£5.50), and rabbit cooked with wine, tomatoes and herbs (£5.60), with more imaginative seasonally changing evening dishes such as roast poussin stuffed with stilton, spinach and chopped ham in cream and Madeira sauce, lots of game and fresh fish; it might be a good idea to book in the evening. Morlands Original and Wadworths 6X on handpump, and farm ciders; there's an old english sheepdog. There are old-fashioned benches outside by the fuchsia hedge. No dogs or children and no muddy boots in the carpeted dining room. *(Recommended by Roger and Jenny Huggins, A M Rankin, Dave Irving, Ewan McCall, Tom McLean, Richard Marjoram, Jerry and Alison Oakes, Tony Walker, John Waller)*

Free house ~ Licensee H J Collins ~ Real ale ~ Meals and lunchtime snacks (12-1.30, 6.30-8.45; not Sun evening) ~ Restaurant (not Sun or Mon) ~ (01993) 822165 ~ Open 11.30-2.30, 6-11; closed evening 25 Dec

TADPOLE BRIDGE SP3300 Map 4

Trout

Back road Bampton—Buckland, 4 miles NE of Faringdon

At Easter folk singers gather at this warmly friendly 18th-c Thames-side pub and fill the air with unaccompanied singing or old-fashioned instruments. Summer is definitely the time to come, when the garden really makes the most of its enviable setting; with small fruit trees, pretty hanging baskets, and flower troughs, it's a very pleasant spot to while away a couple of hours. You can fish on a two-mile stretch of the river (the pub sells day tickets), and there are moorings for boaters. A wide choice of good, promptly served bar food includes very well priced sandwiches (from 90p; toasties from £1.30), ploughman's (from £3.50), beef and basil lasagne or cauliflower and broccoli bake (£4.25), home-cooked ham and egg (£4.50), sirloin steak (£8.10), specials such as rabbit stew (£4.25), chicken curry (£4.75) or steak and kidney pie (£4.85), and puddings like spotted dick (£1.60); the dining room is no smoking. Archers Village, Gibbs Mew Bishops Tipple and Trout (brewed specially for them), and Morlands Original on handpump; efficient, cheery service. The small L-shaped bar has flagstones, attractive pot plants on the window sills and mantlepiece, and a good pubby atmosphere; darts, dominoes, piped music and Aunt Sally. A marquee at the back provides extra seating for busy days, and they offer overnight moorings and space for caravans and camping. Sadly the welcoming landlord passed away not long after our last edition, but the rest of the family continue to run it in just the same congenial way. *(Recommended by Georgina Cole, Marjorie and David Lamb, Joan Olivier, Roger and Jenny Huggins, Derek and Sylvia Stephenson, George Atkinson, Dr M I Crichton)*

Free house ~ Licensee Mrs Maureen Bowl ~ Real ale ~ Meals and snacks ~ (01367) 870382 ~ Children in dining room and marquee only ~ Singer or duo most Fri evenings ~ Open 11.30-11 (11.30-2.30, 5.30-11 winter weekdays)

Children – if the details at the end of an entry don't mention them, you should assume that the pub does not allow them inside.

TOOT BALDON SP5600 Map 4

Crown

Village signed from A423 at Nuneham Courtenay, and B480

The landlady's very good cooking is still one of the main draws to this bustling and friendly country pub. The simple beamed bar has a log fire, solid furnishings on the tiled floor, and a pleasant atmosphere. The good, homely and generously served bar food might include sandwiches and ploughman's, as well as changing specials like beef carbonnade or steak, kidney and oyster pie (£5.95), baked trout with lemon and fresh herbs, barnsley chop with yoghurt and mint, or chicken supreme with cream, wine and herbs (£6.95), and various grills (from £8.95); it may be best to book, especially at weekends. Well kept Morlands Original on handpump, along with interesting guests such as Adnams Broadside, Charles Wells Bombardier, or Wychwood Best; shove-ha'penny, darts. Hard-working but warmly welcoming licensees, and a friendly cream labrador, Ben. Aunt Sally, summer barbecues, and tables on the terrace. *(Recommended by Marjorie and David Lamb, A T Langton, T R and B C Jenkins, Margaret and Roy Randle, Margaret Dyke, Canon and Mrs M A Bourdeaux, R C Watkins)*

Free house ~ Licensees Liz and Neil Kennedy ~ Real ale ~ Meals and snacks (not evenings Sun/Mon) ~ Restaurant ~ (01865) 343240 ~ Children welcome ~ Open 11-3, 6.30-11

WATLINGTON SU6894 Map 4

Chequers

2¼ miles from M40, junction 6; Take B4009 towards Watlington, and on outskirts of village turn right into residential rd Love Lane which leads to pub

Readers love the cosy and peaceful atmosphere of this cheerful old place, but are especially happy in the notably pretty garden – quite refreshing after the bustle of the main street – with picnic tables under apple and pear trees, and sweet peas, roses, geraniums, begonias, and rabbits. The rambling bar has a low panelled oak settle and character chairs such as a big spiral-legged carving chair around a few good antique oak tables, red-and-black shiny tiles in one corner with rugs and red carpeting elsewhere, and a low oak beamed ceiling darkened to a deep ochre by the candles which they still use; steps on the right lead down to an area with more tables. A vine-covered conservatory looks out over the garden. A good range of popular bar food takes in sandwiches, ploughman's, soup (£2), deep-fried camembert (£3.80), king prawns in filo pastry (£4), lentil and aubergine moussaka (£5), summer salads, cauliflower cheese and crispy bacon (£5.50), steak and kidney pie (£6.50), gammon steak (£7.50), salmon supreme (£8.50), steaks (from £9.50), specials like honey-glazed king prawn and monkfish kebab (£8.20), chicken with apricot and ginger sauce (£8.50), or calf's liver with bacon (£9.50), and puddings such as pecan and maple tart (£3); vegetables are extra (which can make some meals a little expensive). Well kept Brakspears Bitter and Special on handpump, friendly staff. The cheese shop in Watlington itself is recommended. *(Recommended by TBB, Gwen and Peter Andrews, Gordon, Bill Ingham, I E and C A Prosser, Michael Sargent, Tony and Wynne Gifford)*

Brakspears ~ Tenants John and Anna Valentine ~ Real ale ~ Meals and lunchtime snacks ~ Restaurant ~ (01491) 612874 ~ Children in conservatory ~ Open 11.30-2.30, 6-11

WITNEY SP3510 Map 4

Three Horseshoes 🍷

78 Corn Street

This 17th-c Cotswold stone pub has a charming beamed and flagstoned bar, with a thriving welcoming atmosphere, two log fires, a longcase clock, willow-pattern plates on a welsh dresser, an attractive oriental rug, and a good mix of solid old tables with country-kitchen chairs and long benches. Particularly good traditional food runs from simple lunch snacks such as filled french bread (£2.95), baked potatoes (£3.45), and cold platters, shepherd's pie and sausage and beans (all £3.50), to specials such as leek bake with almonds and cheese topping or roast chicken (£4.95) and fresh bass or lamb balti (£6.50), and evening dishes such as fresh mushrooms with blue cheese and cream (£3.40), smoked chicken with hazelnuts, avocado and raspberry vinegar (£4.15), giant spanish omelette (£4.95), pasta with spicy sausage, sun-dried tomatoes and pine nuts or popular yorkshire pudding filled with roast beef (£5.25), pancakes filled with broccoli, bacon and Swiss cheese (£6.95), poached salmon with a lemon and chive butter sauce (£7.95), a good Sunday lunch, and bargain steaks on Thursday evening; they have just started driving to Portsmouth to get their fresh fish. Well kept Morlands and a guest ale such as Charles Wells Bombardier, good house wines, attentive service; smaller candlelit dining room and back snug leading off. Dominoes, cribbage, Scrabble, backgammon, and chess. There are teak seats out in front of the stonebuilt inn, well hung with flower baskets. *(Recommended by Mrs J Burton, John Waller, Brian Heywood)*

Free house ~ Licensees Ben and Libby Salter ~ Real ale ~ Meals and snacks ~ Restaurant ~ (01993) 703086 ~ Children in family room till 7.30pm ~ Open 11.30-2.30, 6.30-11; closed 26 Dec

WOODSTOCK SP4416 Map 4

Feathers

Market St

Just as nearby Blenheim isn't a typical family home, this rather sophisticated Cotswold stone hotel is a long way from your average local, but if you haven't had enough grandeur after visiting the Duke of Marlborough's domicile, then it's the ideal place to head to for refreshment. You're quite welcome to come for just a drink, that is if you can afford to pay £2.35 for a pint of Wadworths 6X without batting an eyelid. The food is also priced a little higher than in a conventional pub, but the quality is first-class; the short but thoughtful and imaginative menu might include pea and ham soup (£3.25), quail's eggs with saffron mayonnaise (£3.50), warm goat's cheese with chorizo and watercress (£4.25), filo pastry leaves filled with flat mushrooms and spinach and nutmeg (£6.25), confit of duck with braised red cabbage (£7.75), halibut and tuna kebab with Mediterranean vegetables (£8.95), and puddings like warmed chocolate and pecan tartlet (£4.75). Vegetables are extra. The pubbiest part is the old-fashioned garden bar at the back with a small bar in one corner, oils and watercolours on its walls, stuffed fish and birds (a marvellous live parrot, too), a central open fire, and a relaxed, tranquil atmosphere; it opens on to a splendid sunny courtyard with attractive tables and chairs among geraniums and trees. A good choice of malt whiskies, freshly squeezed orange juice, and home-made lemonade; efficient, courteous service. Get there early for a table; no dogs. *(Recommended by Walter Reid, Nigel Wikeley, George Atkinson, Tim Barrow, Sue Demont, Marion and John Hadfield)*

Free house ~ Licensee Tom Lewis ~ Real ale ~ Bar meals (not Sat/Sun evenings) ~ Restaurant (not Sun evening) ~ (01993) 812291 ~ Children in eating area ~ Open 11-3, 6-11 ~ Bedrooms: £78B/£99B

WYTHAM SP4708 Map 4

White Hart

Village signposted from A34 ring road W of Oxford

Summer evenings are a particularly good time to come to this picturesque creeper-covered pub, when there might be barbecues in the lovely walled rose garden. Under new management once again, it's a nicely traditional place, with high-backed black settles built almost the whole way round the cream walls of the partly panelled, flagstoned bar, wheelback chairs, a shelf of blue and white plates, and a fine relief of a heart on the iron fireback; they can get busy at lunchtimes. Well kept ABC Best, Ind Coope Burton, Tetleys, and a guest beer on handpump, and a good choice of malt whiskies. Bar food from the food servery includes filled baked potatoes (from £1.55), help-yourself salads (from around £2.85), fish like plaice, trout or halibut (from £5.50), steaks (from £7), mixed grill (£9.20), daily specials like steak and kidney pie, pasta dishes or chilli (£5.25), and puddings (£2.25). The pub's name is said to have come from a badge granted to the troops of Richard II after the Battle of Radcot Bridge in 1390. *(Recommended by Sheila Keene, P H Roberts, Joan Olivier, Roger Byrne, A M Rankin, John Sanders, Prof A N Black, Julian Bessa, Peter and Anne Hollindale, Terry and Eileen Stott, Walter Reid, the Monday Club)*

Ind Coope (Allied) ~ Managers Don and Louise Tran~ Real ale ~ Meals and snacks ~ (01865) 244372 ~ Children in several rooms ~ Open 11-11; winter 11-2.30, 5.30-11

Lucky Dip

Besides the fully inspected pubs, you might like to try these Lucky Dips recommended to us and described by readers (if you do, please send us reports):

☆ **Abingdon** [St Helens Wharf; SU4997], *Old Anchor*: Lovely riverside position, flagstoned back bar with shoulder-height serving hatch, little front bar looking across Thames, roomy lounge, panelled dining room overlooking neat almshouse gardens; well kept Morlands on handpump, good atmosphere, usual food inc children's, friendly service *(Alan Kilpatrick, Mr and Mrs G D Amos, Geraint Evans)*

Adderbury [Tanners Lane, off Bloxham rd towards W end of village; SP4635], *White Hart*: Old-fashioned seats, pictures, log fire and heavy beams in small friendly tucked-away pub with good bar snacks and well kept Whitbreads-related ales; garden *(George Atkinson, LYM)*

☆ **Alvescot** [B4020 Carterton—Clanfield – OS Sheet 163 map ref 273045; SP2604], *Plough*: Welcoming village pub with wide range of good standard food inc vegetarian and good value Sun lunch (must book), lounge with end dining area, attentive staff, old maps, quiet piped music, well kept Wadworths and guest such as Adnams, decent wines, good coffee, log fire; separate public bar *(Marjorie and David Lamb)*

☆ **Ardley** [B430 (old A43) just SW of M40 junction 10; SP5427], *Fox & Hounds*: Wide range of good food, welcoming courteous staff, charming furnishings more like home than pub, two attractive inglenooks, Banks's ales *(Mr and Mrs J Taylor, W L G Watkins, Dave Braisted)*

Ashbury [SU2685], *Rose & Crown*: Comfortable recent renovation, good range of usual food inc good puddings, friendly staff, sensible prices; bedrooms – ideal for Ridgeway walkers *(Nick Cox, Meg and Colin Hamilton, Anne Cargill)*

☆ **Asthall** [off A40 at W end of Witney bypass, then 1st left; SP2811], *Maytime*: Very wide choice of well served food very popular with older people midweek, small back locals' bar, slightly raised plush dining lounge neatly set with tables, more airy conservatory restaurant (children allowed), Morrells and Wadworths 6X, prompt service; in tiny hamlet, nice views of Asthall Manor and watermeadows from garden, big car park; good bedrooms around striking courtyard *(A M Rankin, T G Brierly, BB)*

Balscott [signed off A422 W of Banbury; SP3841], *Butchers Arms*: Chatty and welcoming village local, one room divided into public end with darts, cards and dominoes, and lounge end; well kept Hook Norton *(Pete Baker)*

☆ **Banbury** [47 Parsons St, off Market Pl; SP4540], *Reindeer*: Well restored 17th-c building, beams, panelling, handsome log fires, well kept Hook Norton Best, country wines, good coffee, snuffs, clay pipes, good generous food; shame about the piped music *(George Atkinson, BB)*

Banbury [Parsons Lane], *Wine Vaults*: Bare boards, basic fittings, dark-partitioned areas off, Morrells Varsity and Graduate, extensive range of bottled beers, good cheap down-to-earth food *(George Atkinson, Ted George)*

Bessels Leigh [A420; SP4501], *Greyhound*: Refurbished and extended as useful big family dining pub, well kept beers and varied food, children's room with lots of toys, play area outside; piped music may obtrude *(Peter and Audrey Dowsett, Brig J S Green)*

Bletchingdon [Station Rd; B4027 N of Oxford; SP5017], *Blacks Head*: Pleasant local overlooking village green, long-serving licensees, good value usual food, well kept Ansells or Flowers IPA, darts, cards and dominoes in public bar, pool room, garden with Aunt Sally; at its best Thurs eve – informal singalong *(Pete Baker)*

☆ **Blewbury** [London Rd; SU5385], *Blewbury Inn*: Friendly and comfortably mellowed character downland village pub with hotch-potch of old furniture and attractive log fire in cosy beamed bar, unusually good food in small dining room inc fine evening set menu; bedrooms *(Lorraine Webster, Gordon)*

Bloxham [High St, off A361; SP4235],

Joiners Arms: Homely and bustling local with friendly chatty staff, five S & N ales, good coffee, decent wine, two fires and lots of brasses; piped music, fruit machines *(George Atkinson, Gordon, BB)*

Boars Hill [between A34 and B4017; SP4802], *Fox*: Attractive and relaxed timbered pub in pretty countryside with rambling rooms on different levels, huge log fireplaces, reasonably priced bar food, friendly service, real ales such as Tetleys and Wadworths 6X, no piped music; restaurant; big garden with play area *(Susan and Alan Dominey)*

☆ **Bodicote** [Goose Lane/High St, off A4260 S of Banbury; SP4537], *Plough*: Old, quaint and dark, friendly rather forthright landlord, well brewed beers inc Porter from own brewery attached, three other well kept ales, country wines, wide choice of well cooked straightforward food, good service; old beams, pictures and brasses, dining area *(George Atkinson, CMW, JJW)*

☆ **Buckland** [SU3497], *Lamb*: Plushly refurbished and extended 18th-c stone building in tiny village, clean, with good value changing real food (not Mon) inc some memorable and imaginative dishes; smart helpful service, real ale, decent wines *(A T Langton, Mr and Mrs M Miles, J C Cetti)*

☆ **Bucknell** [handy for M40 junction 10; SP5525], *Trigger Pond*: Quaint and welcoming village pub with big helpings of good popular reasonably priced food, well kept changing ales such as Hook Norton Best, Glenny Wychwood and a Wadworths seasonal brew, friendly service, pleasant garden *(L M Miall, Marjorie and David Lamb)*

☆ **Burford** [High St (A361); SP2512], *Bull*: Comfortable sofas in interestingly restored long narrow beamed and panelled hotel bar, Courage-related ales and a guest such as Wadworths 6X, woodburner, good choice of wines by the glass, wide choice of bar food, friendly attentive service, restaurant; piped music; children welcome, open all day; good value comfortable bedrooms *(A D Crafter, Mrs P J Pearce, Gordon, Mark Bradley, LYM)*

☆ **Burford** [High St], *Mermaid*: Long narrow beamed and flagstoned bar with row of softly lit tables, panelling and stripped stonework, no-smoking conservatory, jettied upper floor, popular generous food all day, well kept Morlands Original, Old Masters and Old Speckled Hen, open fire; pianist Fri/Sat evenings; no facilities for small children *(Gordon, Stephen G Brown, Mrs L Lailey, Jane Hosking, Ian Burniston, David Holloway, John and Shirley Dyson, Mark Bradley, D Hanley, LYM)*

☆ **Burford** [A40], *Inn for All Seasons*: Smartly kept and welcoming, with low beams, old prints, stripped stone and flagstones, good food inc fish fresh from Brixham, real ales inc Wadworths 6X, decent wine, friendly staff; good bedrooms *(Peter and Audrey Dowsett, Philip Jackson, Patricia Heptinstall)*

Burford [Witney St], *Royal Oak*: Stripped stone, generous popular food inc imaginative variety of good value home-made quiches, well kept Wadworths ales, bar billiards, friendly staff *(Mark Bradley, Jim Reid)*

Cassington [SP4510], *Red Lion*: Welcoming low-ceilinged mid-terrace local with well kept Marstons, old-fashioned settles, old prints *(R Huggins, D Irving, T McLean, E McCall, Gordon)*

☆ **Caulcott** [Lower Heyford Rd (B4030); SP5024], *Horse & Groom*: Part-thatched creeper-covered 16th-c pub doing well under friendly new licensees, smartened up without losing its cosy and homely feel; L-shaped bar with dining end, good straightforward home cooking, good log fire in stone fireplace, beams, brasses, Charles Wells Bombardier and Hook Norton Old Hookey; garden with picnic tables under cocktail parasols *(D C T and E A Frewer, Joan Olivier, Gordon)*

☆ **Chadlington** [Mill End; off A361 S of Chipping Norton, and B4437 W of Charlbury; SP3222], *Tite*: Comfortable and welcoming rambling local with settles, wooden chairs, prints, good value often original food, well kept ales such as Badger Best, Palmers Tally Ho and Wadworths IPA, decent wines, congenial landlord, rack of guidebooks; children welcome; lovely views, suntrap garden and terrace, pretty Cotswold village, good walks nearby *(G E de Vries, Jon Carpenter, John Waller, D C T and E A Frewer, M M Matthews)*

☆ **Chalgrove** [High St; SU6396], *Red Lion*: Friendly and pleasantly restored old village pub, good value generous straightforward home-cooked food, well kept Brakspears, Hook Norton and other ales inc interesting guests such as Greene King Sorcerer and Ridleys, log fire and woodburner, beams, partly tiled floor, small restaurant, sizeable garden with Sun lunchtime barbecues; owned by local church trust for over 350 years; lavatory for disabled (but car park some way off); children welcome *(Joan Olivier, Marjorie and David Lamb, Graham Reeve)*

☆ **Charlbury** [SP3519], *Bell*: Small and attractive civilised bar, warm and friendly, with flagstones, stripped stonework, huge open fire, short choice of good interesting bar lunches (not Sun) from sandwiches up, well kept Hook Norton and Wadworths real ales, wide choice of malt whiskies, decent if pricy restaurant; children in eating area; comfortable bedrooms, good breakfasts *(Gordon, Michael Sargent, LYM)*

Charlbury [Sheep St], *Farmers*: Friendly and cosy 17th-c local, lounge split into several areas, oak beams, inglenook fireplace and original Victorian stove, traditional pub games, Ansells on electric pump, good value food in low-key side eating area or neat back restaurant *(George Atkinson, Jon Carpenter)*

Charney Bassett [SU3794], *Chequers*: Popular and comfortable two-room village-green pub with some emphasis on decent freshly prepared food (not Mon) inc range of curries; drinkers welcome too, with well kept

Fullers London Pride, Morlands and Theakstons XB, some singalongs (landlady plays spirited piano), pool; piped music may be rather loud; children welcome *(Pete Baker, Peter and Audrey Dowsett)*

☆ **Checkendon** [OS Sheet 175 map ref 666841; SU6684], *Black Horse*: Gloriously old-fashioned Brakspears country pub tucked into woodland well away from main village, friendly, unpretentious and kept by the same family for many decades; three interconnecting rooms, open fire, unfashionable armchairs, well kept ale tapped from the cask in a back room (ladies' beyond that), pickled eggs, sandwiches, darts; antiquated gents'; fine walking country *(Pete Baker, Phil and Sally Gorton, Tom McLean, Roger Huggins, Jack and Philip Paxton)*

☆ **Chipping Norton** [High St; SP3127], *Blue Boar*: Wide range of well priced food, homely rambling beamed bar divided by arches and pillars, big papier-mâché mannikins in back eating area with long flagstoned conservatory; three Courage-related ales and Theakstons XB, good cider, quick friendly service even if busy, Sun bar nibbles *(John and Shirley Dyson)*

Chipping Norton [Goddards Lane], *Chequers*: Three nicely old-fashioned rooms, well kept Fullers, impressive French-run new evening restaurant; tables in courtyard *(David Campbell, Vicki McLean, Martin Kay, Andrea Fowler)*; [High St], *Fox*: Comfortable and friendly, with well kept Hook Norton ales, rambling lounge, open fire, upstairs restaurant (can be used for lunchtime bar food), friendly service; children welcome; well equipped good value bedrooms *(Andy and Jill Kassube, LYM)*

Chislehampton [B480 Oxford—Watlington, opp B4015 to Abingdon; SU5998], *Coach & Horses*: Small comfortable 16th-c pub, homely but civilised bar and lounge with well kept ales inc Flowers and Hook Norton, big log fire, cheerful licensees; good choice of well prepared food inc good puddings in dining area with polished oak tables, padded chairs and wall banquettes; well kept terraced gardens overlooking fields next to River Thame; well appointed bedrooms in back courtyard *(Mr and Mrs J Brown, Gordon, JCW)*

Cholsey [98 Papist Way; SU5886], *Morning Star*: Spotless, with warm and friendly staff and decor, flower arrangments, wide choice of good reasonably priced food *(J D Wilson)*

☆ **Clifton Hampden** [towards Long Wittenham, S of A415; SU5495], *Barley Mow*: Chef & Brewer a short stroll from the Thames, famous from *Three Men in a Boat;* commercialised, but still has character, with very low beams, oak-panelled family room; usual food, Courage-related real ales, piped music, restaurant, tables in well tended garden; bedrooms *(Jack and Philip Paxton, Eamon Green, Geraint Roberts, Joan Olivier, LYM)*

☆ **Coleshill** [OS Sheet 174 map ref 236937; SU2393], *Radnor Arms*: Cosy atmospheric bar dominated by huge forge chimney, two coal-effect gas fires, lots of smith's tools; Flowers tapped from the cask, good choice of reasonably priced food cooked to order inc tasty home-made pies and fresh veg, friendly quick service, garden behind; piped music; charming village, lots of good walks *(Peter and Audrey Dowsett, Tim Brierly, D Lawson)*

Cottisford [Juniper Hill; N of village, off A43 opp radio masts just S of B4031; SP5832], *Fox*: Quiet little village free house, Hook Norton beers; no food *(Calum and Susan Maclean)*

☆ **Crawley** [OS Sheet 164 map ref 341120; SP3412], *Lamb*: Good lunchtime bar food and wider choice of interesting evening dishes, all home-cooked using good ingredients, in 17th-c stone-built village pub on several levels; well kept Wychwood Shires and Wadworths 6X, decent wines, friendly hard-working licensees, small family area, restaurant; lots of tables in pleasant garden *(Joan Olivier, Marjorie and David Lamb, John Waller, Andrew and Rachel Fogg)*

☆ **Crays Pond** [B471 nr junction with B4526, about 3 miles E of Goring; SU6380], *White Lion*: Clean and welcoming low-ceilinged pub with open fire, attractive conservatory, well kept Courage-related real ales, good inventive if not cheap food (not Tues evening), big garden with play area *(G B Longden, Susan and Alan Dominey)*

Crowell [B4009, 2 miles from M40 junction 6; SU7499], *Shepherds Crook*: Traditional pub attractively refurbished with stripped brick, timber and flagstones, good cheap filling home-made food in carpeted raftered dining area, decent wines, very friendly landlord, exemplary lavatories; views from tables out on green *(Nigel Henbest, Heather Couper, Gordon)*

Crowmarsh Gifford [72 The Street (A4130); SU6189], *Queens Head*: Nice old pub, a bit like a sensitively converted barn, with good attractively priced food, well kept Boddingtons, friendly atmosphere; children in dining area, tables in garden *(Chris and Linda Elston)*

Culham [A415 Abingdon—Dorchester; SU5095], *Waggon & Horses*: Useful for spacious grassy outdoor seating area with play equipment, bouncy castle and barbecues; reasonably priced standard food, Morrells ales, good value wine, log fires *(John Wooll)*

Cumnor [Abingdon Rd; SP4603], *Vine*: Very wide choice of food in carpeted back dining area with wheelback chairs; well kept ales, picnic tables in attractive back garden; service may slow a bit when busy *(Joan Olivier, Nick Wedd)*

Deddington [Oxford Rd (A4260); SP4631], *Holcombe*: Good food and well kept beer in pleasant, comfortable and welcoming 17th-c low-beamed stripped-stone hotel bar; sheltered terrace and lawn, restaurant, comfortable bedrooms *(H D Spottiswoode)*

☆ **Denchworth** [SU3791], *Fox*: Picturesque old

thatched pub, welcoming and relaxing, with two good log fires in low-ceilinged comfortable connecting areas, good range of reasonably priced food inc good puddings, Morlands Old Speckled Hen and Revival Mild, helpful landlord, unobtrusive piped music, beamed restaurant; peaceful garden *(Marjorie and David Lamb, Peter and Audrey Dowsett, Gordon)*

☆ **Dorchester** [High St; SU5794], *Fleur de Lys*: Small comfortable 16th-c village pub opp abbey, very appealing to foreign visitors, with wide choice of good value home cooking, all fresh (not Mon; no sandwiches), Bass, Flowers IPA and Morlands, friendly service; unobtrusive piped music *(Tim and Ann Newell, Tim and Carol Gorringe, P J Keen, R C Watkins, Dorothy and Leslie Pilson)*

Dorchester, *White Hart:* Big beamed bar with attached restaurant, good range of beers ; bedrooms *(David and Alison Walker, Jack and Philip Paxton)*

☆ **Drayton** [A422 W of Banbury; SP4241], *Roebuck*: Freshly prepared imaginative food in bar and evening restaurant and genuinely welcoming staff in comfortable and cosy creeper-covered pub with well kept ales inc Boddingtons, Fullers London Pride and Hook Norton Best, solid fuel stove *(F M Bunbury, Edward and Anne Good, George Atkinson)*

☆ **Duns Tew** [SP4528], *White Horse*: 16th-c beamed pub in pretty village, rugs on flagstones, oak panelling, stripped masonry, enormous inglenook, settles, sofas and homely stripped tables, big pretty dining extension, several well kept ales, good open fires; comfortable bedrooms in former stables; the landlord who turned this former local into more of a hotel/restaurant has now left and we've no news of his successor *(Reports please)*

East Challow [SU3788], *Leather Bottle*: Recently re-opened after burning down in 1990, now more of a restaurant; good choice of meals *(Marjorie and David Lamb)*

☆ **East Hendred** [Orchard Lane; SU4588], *Plough*: Enjoyable straightforward bar food in beamed village pub's attractive and airy main bar, Morlands ales, quick friendly service, farm tools; attractive garden with good play area *(Geraint Roberts, BB)*

Eaton [SP4403], *Eight Bells*: Low-beamed Tudor Morlands pub with two bars, dining room, tables outside; decent bar food inc vegetarian *(Joan Olivier)*

Enslow [Enslow Bridge; off A4095 about 1½ miles SW of Kirtlington; SP4818], *Rock of Gibraltar*: Good value Beefeater, tall building with modern eating extension overlooking canal, beams, stripped stone, bright narrowboat paintwork, hospitable landlady, ample good food inc very individual puddings, Courage-related ales *(Mrs P J Peeprose)*

Epwell [off B4035; SP3540], *Chandlers Arms*: Chatty 16th-c local in attractive out-of-the-way village, friendly landlord, well kept Hook Norton ales, limited choice of good food; quiet little garden *(George Atkinson)*

☆ **Ewelme** [off B4009 about 5 miles SW of M40 junction 6; SU6491], *Shepherds Hut*: Well run, with good value food, well kept Morlands Bitter and Old Masters, welcoming staff, pot plants, darts and fruit machine; piped pop music; children welcome; tables and swing in garden *(Nick Holmes, JJW, CMJ)*

Eynsham [Newlands St; SP4309], *Newlands*: Cosy flagstoned bar with choice of generous good value food, friendly staff, decent wine, inglenook log fire, stripped early 18th-c pine panelling; very busy and bustling weekends, piped music *(D C T and E A Frewer)*; [B4044 towards Swinford Bridge], *Talbot*: Oldish beamed building with good range of fresh food inc OAP bargains, friendly staff, long bar popular with staff from modern factory next door; pleasant walk along Thames towpath; piped music may be loud *(T G Brierly, MB)*

☆ **Faringdon** [Market Pl], *Crown*: Unpretentious old inn with flagstones and panelling – good atmosphere when they light the log fires; reasonably priced well presented food in bar or buttery, good value Sun lunch, friendly staff, well kept Hook Norton and Morlands, no piped music; children welcome; good bedrooms, lovely summer courtyard *(Gordon, Peter and Audrey Dowsett)*

☆ **Fifield** [Stow Rd (A424); SP2318], *Merrymouth*: Isolated rambling old pub with relaxed atmosphere, flagstones, lots of stripped stone, bay windows, farm tools on low beams, open fires, Donnington and perhaps other ales, unobtrusive piped music, food in bar and restaurant; tables on terrace and in back garden; children allowed one end; bedrooms *(Marjorie and David Lamb, Gordon, Mr and Mrs John W Jones, Joan Olivier, LYM)*

Filkins [A361 Burford—Lechlade; SP2304], *Lamb*: Decent generous food (limited Sun) and well kept Morlands Original, Old Masters and Old Speckled Hen in two-bar stonebuilt local, part Elizabethan, warm, friendly and comfortable; big garden, pleasant new bedrooms; cl Mon *(K H Frostick)*

☆ **Fulbrook** [SP2513], *Masons Arms*: Welcoming and chatty village pub with limited range of good value home cooking inc good puddings, nice open fire, well kept beer, good service, bar billiards, locals with dogs *(John and Marianne Cooper, Tim Brierly)*

☆ **Godstow** [SP4809], *Trout*: It's the marvellous position that makes this creeper-covered medieval pub special (and a big tourist draw), with a lovely terrace by a stream clear enough to watch the plump perch, and peacocks in the grounds – one of the nicest summer spots in England; much extended and commercialised, with large snack room, children's area, garden bar and restaurant –

we're not recommending it for food; Bass and Charrington ale, mulled wine in winter *(Jim and Maggie Cowell, Lynn Sharpless, Bob Eardley, Paul Stanfield, Ann and Bob Westbrook, T A Bryan, Adrian Zambardino, Debbie Chaplin, Julie Munday, Martin Robinson, Prof A N Black, Gordon, Julian Bessa, Tim and Ann Newell, LYM)*

Goring [SU6080], *Catherine Wheel*: Genuine enjoyable local in pretty Thames village, good value food in bar and restaurant, friendly licensee, good log fire *(Tony Merrill, Jack and Philip Paxton, John and Pam Smith)*; [Manor Rd], *John Barleycorn*: Friendly traditional village local with prints in cosy beamed lounge bar and good choice of well priced food in adjoining eating area, well kept Brakspears, pool in public bar, pleasant atmosphere, helpful service; bedrooms clean and simple *(Dick Brown, Georgina Cole)*

☆ **Goring Heath** [off A4074 NW of Reading – OS Sheet 175 map ref 664788; SU6679], *King Charles Head*: Charming small-roomed rambling country pub of great potential with lovely big garden and idyllic woodland setting, good walks nearby; good value home-cooked food, well kept beers, relaxed atmosphere, friendly staff; furnishings and decor more modern than you'd expect from cottagey appearance *(Tim Brierly, LYM)*

Great Milton [The Green; a mile from M40 junction 7; SP6202], *Bull*: Well kept pub with cordial welcome, Morrells Bitter and Varsity, nicely presented above-average simple pub food inc good value generous ploughman's, two bars, picnic tables on back lawn with play area *(Frank Cummins)*; *Bell*: This small friendly pub, previously popular for interesting home cooking and real ales, may be converted to a private house following the landlord's death in 1994 *(News please)*

☆ **Grove** [Station Rd (A338); by former Wantage Road stn; SU4191], *Volunteer*: Comfortably modernised local with exceptional friendly service, down-to-earth family feel, nine real ales inc two guests, wide choice of good reasonably priced food inc authentic Bangladeshi, Indian and Pakistani dishes *(HNJ, PEJ, Rachel Hunter)*

Grove, *Bell*: Relatively new well laid out local with good atmosphere, reasonably priced beer, Sun quiz matches, trivia machine, pool *(Dylan Prentiss)*

Hailey [B4022 a mile N of Witney; SP3512], *Lamb & Flag*: Extremely friendly welcome, well served food inc some home-cooked things, no fancy prices, well kept Morlands, friendly dog called Scrap *(B H H Pullen)*

☆ **Henley** [Friday St; SU7882], *Anchor*: Now the town's cosiest and most relaxing pub, though so much a local that one-off visitors can sometimes feel a bit out of place; cottagey and attractive, almost right on the Thames, with nice mix of homely country furniture and bric-a-brac in softly lit parlourish beamed front bar (one armchair for Cognac the friendly boxer), huge helpings of reasonably priced food, well kept Brakspears, friendly and obliging landlady; darts, bar billiards, piano and TV in room on right, caged birds in eating area, back dining room, elegant cat; charming back terrace with rabbit hutch; here and there piles of the sort of stuff you might find dumped around a loosely run family home; children welcome *(Gordon, Brian and Anna Marsden)*

☆ **Henley** [5 Market Pl], *Three Tuns*: Heavy beams and panelling, two rooms opened together around old-fashioned central servery with well kept Brakspears, straightforward generous home-cooked food all day, floodlit back terrace and separate games bar with pinball, juke box and fruit machine; no children *(Gordon, Andy Thwaites, Graham and Karen Oddey, TBB, Brian and Anna Marsden, David Warrellow, LYM)*

☆ **Henley** [West St], *Row Barge*: Friendly simple local, its cosy low-beamed bar dropping down the hill in steps, good value home cooking, well kept Brakspears, darts, big back garden; lively young weekend crowd *(Brian and Anna Marsden, Andy Thwaites, Gordon, Derek and Sylvia Stephenson)*

Henley [Hart St, by the bridge], *Angel*: Prime spot by river, attractive unspoilt interior, nice waterside terrace (plastic glasses for this), Brakspears beer, very popular restaurant *(Gordon, Robert Weeks)*; [Riverside], *Little White Hart*: Large comfortable civilised hotel bar with lots of regatta pictures and bric-a-brac inc three suspended racing skiffs, lots of spoons (shortened oars); gas lighting, friendly landlord; bedrooms *(Gordon, David Warrellow)*; [Bell St], *Old Bell*: Well kept Brakspears in homely and attractive heavily beamed bar with wall-length window filled with pot plants, back dining room *(Gordon, James Koger)*; [Greys Hill], *Saracens Head*: Traditional pub with good range of well kept beers, welcoming atmosphere *(Mark Maynard)*

☆ **Highmoor** [B481 N of Reading, off A423 Henley—Oxford; SU6984], *Dog & Duck*: Cosy and cottagey low-beamed country pub with chintzy curtains, floral cushions, lots of pictures – not at all twee; relaxing and comfortable bar on left, dining room on right, log fire in each, smaller dining room behind, good food, friendly service, well kept Brakspears Bitter, Old and Special; tables in garden *(Gordon, Andy Petersen)*

Hook Norton [SP3533], *Sun*: Particularly good food from sandwiches to exotic dishes, and well kept Hook Norton ales from the nearby brewery, in expensively refurbished combination of two formerly separate pubs; restaurant, comfortable bedrooms *(Philip and Debbie Haynes, Helen Hazzard, Tom Evans)*

Islip [B4027; SP5214], *Red Lion*: Wide choice of well presented generous quick food in three cosy if not especially pubby eating areas inc main tankard-decorated dining room and conservatory, Tetleys-related ales, decent wine; lavatories for the disabled, good garden with barbecue and play area (no children allowed in) *(D C T and E A Frewer)*

☆ **Kidmore End** [Chalkhouse Green Rd, signed from Sonning Common; SU6979], *New Inn*: Pretty black and white country dining pub, well run, with good mainly home-cooked food, well kept Brakspears PA, SB and Old, decent wines, modern furnishings in beamed main room, efficient service, maybe piped music; small children's side room, tables in attractive large sheltered garden with pond and boules piste; can be busy weekends *(Clifford Payton, Mike and Heather Barnes, Brian and Anna Marsden)*

☆ **Kingston Lisle** [SU3287], *Blowing Stone*: Neat roomy traditional-style public bar, small relaxing refurbished lounge bar, big dining conservatory; wide choice of decent food from generous sandwiches up, decent wine, good range of changing ales such as Fullers London Pride, Marstons Pedigree, Morlands Old Speckled Hen, Wadworths 6X, friendly efficient service; attractive village, handy for Ridgeway walks; pretty garden; bedrooms clean and pretty if small *(Elizabeth Chalmers, Peter and Audrey Dowsett, R T and J C Moggridge)*

☆ **Long Wittenham** [SU5493], *Machine Man*: Good choice of genuine food freshly made to order, full range of Eldridge Pope beers kept well with one or two good guest beers, decent wines; traditional welcoming unfussy local atmosphere, darts; bedrooms *(Marjorie and David Lamb, John C Baker)*

☆ **Long Wittenham**, *Plough*: Good choice of reasonably priced prompt bar food in low-beamed lounge, rustic furniture, lots of brass, games in public bar, inglenook log fires, welcoming landlord, Ushers ales, pool and children's room; Thames moorings at bottom of long spacious garden; bedrooms *(Marjorie and David Lamb, Eamon Green)*

Long Wittenham, *Vine*: Cosy beamed village local with comfortable two-level bar, unusual pewter, pictures and bric-a-brac, bar food, friendly landlord, well kept Morlands ales, Aunt Sally *(Gordon)*

☆ **Longworth** [SU3899], *Blue Boar*: Cosy country local with plenty of character, two good log fires and unusual decor (skis on beams etc); usual food, well kept Bass and Morrells Best, piped music, friendly quick service *(Audrey and Peter Dowsett, P A Shewry)*

☆ **Lower Assendon** [B480; SU7484], *Golden Ball*: Friendly renovated pub with good food, well kept Brakspears, log fire *(David Warrellow, Mr and Mrs S Price)*

☆ **Lower Heyford** [21 Market Sq; SP4824], *Bell*: Charming and very welcoming beamed pub in sleepy village, good value simple home-cooked food from home-made sausages in a cob up, good range of beers inc Greene King Abbot, stylishly presented coffee; charming building *(Meg and Colin Hamilton)*

☆ **Marsh Baldon** [the Baldons signed off A423 N of Dorchester; SU5699], *Seven Stars*: Good interesting rather restauranty generous food (no sandwiches; only barbecues some Sat lunchtimes) in large open room; decent wines, good coffee; on attractive village green *(A T Langton, Marjorie and David Lamb)*

☆ **Marston** [Mill Lane, Old Marston – OS Sheet 164 map ref 520090; SP5208], *Victoria Arms*: Quiet spot by River Cherwell, attractive waterside grounds inc spacious terrace, good play area, punt moorings; full Wadworths range and guest beers, generous good value food (not Sun evening in winter) from chunky sandwiches up, lots of tables in main room and smaller ones off, real fires; piped music, children and dogs allowed; lavatory for disabled; beware vicious sleeping policemen *(Joan Olivier, George Atkinson, BB)*

Middleton Stoney [A43/B4030; SP5323], *Jersey Arms*: Small 19th-c stonebuilt hotel, low and rambling, with cosy traditional oak-beamed bar, comfortable adjoining panelled lounge, good bar food, Theakstons ales, good coffee, friendly helpful staff; garden; bedrooms comfortable *(D C T and E A Frewer, Nigel Foster, George Atkinson)*

Milton [the one nr Didcot; SU4892], *Admiral Benbow*: Small friendly pub doing well under new regime, well kept Morrells ales, reasonably priced bar food, garden *(A T Langton)*

Milton [off Bloxham Rd – the one nr Adderbury; SP4535], *Black Boy*: Lively old-world oak-beamed bar in former coaching inn, well kept beers; candlelit restaurant using local produce with creole and other exotic dishes, very popular Thurs-Sat nights *(L H King)*

☆ **Milton under Wychwood** [High St; SP2618], *Quart Pot*: Good atmosphere in spotless pub with good choice of French-influenced good value home-cooked food, delicious puddings, Fri steak night, Adnams and Morlands Old Speckled Hen, friendly licensees; garden, attractive Cotswold village *(Mrs J Burton, Sue and Bob Ward)*

Minster Lovell [just N of B4047 – OS Sheet 164 map ref 314112; SP3111], *Old Swan*: Interesting and attractive old inn with upmarket country-house atmosphere, roaring log fire, deep armchairs, rugs on flagstones, tables in lovely garden, good restaurant; does do expensive sandwiches as well as light lunches, but not really a place to drop into for a casual drink now; bedrooms *(Christopher Gallop, Dr and Mrs A K Clarke, LYM)*

☆ **Nettlebed** [A423; SU6986], *White Hart*: Civilised rambling two-level beamed bar, handsome old-fashioned furnishings inc fine grandfather clock, discreet atmosphere, good log fires, well kept Brakspears, spacious restaurant; not cheap; children welcome; modernised bedrooms *(Jack and Philip Paxton, Gordon, LYM)*

Nettlebed [Watlington Rd], *Sun*: Attractive welcoming pub with well kept Brakspears, lots of jugs hanging from old beams, good choice of food, dining room; sheltered attractive garden with climbing frame, swing and barbecue *(David Craine, Ann Reeder)*

☆ **Newbridge** [A415 7 miles S of Witney; SP4001], *Maybush*: Low-beamed Thamesside local, unpretentious and warmly welcoming, tables set for good range of decent bar food (no sandwiches) at sensible prices, well kept Morlands, clothes presses and other bric-a-brac; moorings, pretty and neatly kept waterside terrace *(Michael Sargent, D H T Dimock, A T Langton, Mayur Shah, LYM)*

☆ **Newbridge**, *Rose Revived*: Big pub well worth knowing for its lovely big lawn by the upper Thames, across the road from our other entry here, prettily lit at night (good overnight mooring free); inside knocked through as Morlands Artists Fayre eatery – promptly served usual food all day inc Sun carvery, Morlands real ales, piped music, fruit machines; children welcome, comfortable bedrooms with good breakfasts *(L M Miall, Peter and Audrey Dowsett, B H H Pullen, Gordon, Neil and Angela Huxter, LYM)*

☆ **Noke** [signed off B4027 NE of Oxford; SP5413], *Plough*: Cheerful country pub on the edge of Otmoor, wide range of low-priced unpretentious food in big helpings, quick friendly service, well kept Morlands, no dogs; tables in pretty garden, busy on a sunny day *(Marjorie and David Lamb, Joan Olivier, D C T and E A Frewer, LYM)*

North Hinksey [off A34 southbound just S of A420 interchange; SP4805], *Fishes*: Comfortable old-fashioned open lounge, good original food inc fresh veg and imaginative vegetarian dishes, OAP bargains Mon-Thurs, children's dishes, well kept Morrells, friendly attentive staff, pleasant sun room; soft piped music; big streamside garden with play area and two Aunt Sally pitches, path across fields towards Oxford, along causeway originally built by John Ruskin to give students experience of healthy outdoor labour *(Jon Carpenter, Joan Olivier)*

☆ **North Leigh** [New Yatt Rd – OS Sheet 164 map ref 384132; SP3813], *Woodman*: Roomy and welcoming stonebuilt village pub with good choice of reasonably priced freshly prepared food, real ales such as Glenny Witney and Wychwood, Hook Norton Best and Wadworths 6X, Easter and bank hol beer festivals, decent wines, proper coffee, good service; daily papers, big garden; bedrooms comfortable *(Marjorie and David Lamb, Joan Olivier)*

☆ **North Newington** [High St, just W of Banbury; SP4139], *Roebuck*: Attractively refurbished dining pub with wide range of good value interesting home-made food from good filled rolls up, quiet bistro atmosphere, individual furnishings, well kept ales inc Morlands and unusual guests, good wines and country wines, open fires, lovely briards, friendly service, piped classical music; children very welcome, good garden with play area and animals *(George Atkinson, John Bowdler and others)*

North Newington [High St], *Blinking Owl*: Friendly stone village inn, lots of owl pictures, good food, Black Sheep and Stones, nice fire, hospitable attentive staff; two bedrooms *(George Atkinson)*

Northmoor [B4449 SE of Stanton Harcourt; SP4202], *Red Lion*: Small stonebuilt village inn of medieval origins, heavily beamed bar and small dining room off, welcoming open fire, wide range of home-cooked bar food inc fine chips, pleasant helpful licensees *(D C T and E A Frewer)*

☆ **Oxford** [Holywell St], *Kings Arms*: Big front bar, half a dozen cosy and comfortably worn-in side and back rooms each with a different character and customers, vibrant atmosphere, well kept Youngs and guest such as Morlands Original and Wadworths 6X, good choice of wines, no-smoking coffee room, decent bar food, papers provided, tables on pavement; very busy and popular with students, but civilised – no music or games, no attempt to hurry you *(Walter Reid, Jim and Maggie Cowell, M Joyner, Elizabeth and Klaus Leist, D Irving, E McCall, R Huggins, T McLean, Wayne Brindle, Gordon, BB)*

☆ **Oxford** [Binsey Lane; narrow lane on right leaving city on A420, just before Self Operated Storage], *Perch*: Lovely thatched pub in pleasant setting with big garden off riverside meadow; big, busy and not cheap, but low ceilings, flagstones, stripped stone, high-backed settles as well as more modern seats, log fires; bar food, no-smoking eating area (children allowed), Tetleys-related ales and Wadworths 6X, decent wine, friendly helpful staff, unobtrusive piped music; particularly good play area, summer marquee and barbecues, landing stage, attractive waterside walks; no dogs (the pub dog's called Mr Chips) *(Joan Olivier, D C T Frewer, Julian Bessa, Eamon Green, Ann and Bob Westbrook, Jim and Maggie Cowell, Margaret Dyke, LYM)*

☆ **Oxford** [Alfred St], *Bear*: Lots of atmosphere in four friendly little low-ceilinged and partly panelled rooms, often packed; massive collection of vintage ties, simple food most days inc sandwiches (kitchen may be closed Weds), good range of well kept Tetleys-related and other ales from centenarian handpumps on rare pewter bar counter, no games machines, tables outside; open all day summer *(Walter Reid, Julian Bessa, W Fletcher, Robert Gomme, Gordon, Terry and Eileen Stott, Eamon Green, Tim and Ann Newell, LYM)*

☆ **Oxford** [St Giles], *Eagle & Child*: Busy rather touristy pub (tiny mid-bars full of actors' and Tolkien/C S Lewis memorabilia), but students too; nice panelled front snugs, tasteful modern back extension with no-smoking conservatory, rather pricy well kept Tetleys-related ales and Wadworths 6X, reasonable range of snacky food, piped classical music, newspapers *(E McCall, D Irving, R Huggins, T McLean, D C T Frewer, Tim and Ann Newell, Nigel Woolliscroft, Billy Whiteshoes Johnson,*

Julian Bessa, Gordon, David and Shelia, Terry and Eileen Stott, John Waller, BB)

☆ Oxford [Broad St], *White Horse*: Small and busy, sandwiched between bits of Blackwells bookshop; mellow oak, ochre ceiling, beautiful view of the Clarendon building and Sheldonian, well kept Tetleys-related and Wadworths ales, friendly licensees *(Julian Bessa, Walter Reid, Gordon, Adrian Zambardino, Debbie Chaplin, D Irving, E McCall, R Huggins, T McLean, Tim and Ann Newell, BB)*

☆ Oxford [North Parade Ave], *Rose & Crown*: Friendly and unspoilt old local with character landlord, popular well priced bar lunches inc middle eastern specialities and Sun roasts, Tetleys-related ales, decent wine; ref books for crossword buffs, no piped music or machines, piano available for good players, jazz Tues; traditional small rooms, pleasant back yard with motorised awning and big gas heaters – children not allowed here or inside unless with friends of landlord *(Gordon, N Hardyman, E McCall, D Irving, R Huggins, T McLean, John Waller, Julian Bessa, S Demont, T Barrow, BB)*

Oxford [Chester St], *Chester Arms*: Friendly local with well kept ale, good food, low prices, easy-going mix of all sorts *(Marc Harrison)*; [Iffley Rd], *Fir Tree*: Really good mix in proper local – relief from young-dominated central pubs; tempting pizzas *(David and Shelia)*; [39 Plantation Rd – 1st left after Horse & Jockey going N up Woodstock Rd], *Gardeners Arms*: Relaxed local and University atmosphere in large, comfortable open-plan pub, good value filling home-made food inc vegetarian in back room where children allowed, well kept Morrells, real cider, tables outside *(Jon Carpenter, LYM)*; [George St], *Grapes*: Still has some of its original features, quieter than most central Oxford pubs *(Walter Reid)*; [Iffley Lock – towpath from Donnington Bridge Rd, between Abingdon Rd and Iffley Rd], *Isis*: Included for beautiful location – beer used to come by punt; early 19th-c former farmhouse with play equipment in large attractive garden, right on river; Morrells beers, lots of rowing mementoes, log fire *(Jim and Maggie Cowell, Jon Carpenter)*; [Banbury Rd, Summertown], *Kings Arms*: Tastefully extended with alcoves added for eating and drinking, very good value simple food from baked potatoes to steaks inc fine salads, friendly staff; children welcome if well behaved, busy lunchtime *(David Campbell, Vicki McLean)*; [St Giles/Banbury Rd], *Lamb & Flag*: Well kept ales, good food when it's available, very friendly service, can be packed with students; back rooms with exposed stonework and panelled ceilings have more atmosphere, and look out over quiet lane *(Walter Reid, Joseph Biernat, N Hardyman)*; [14 Gloucester St, by central car park], *Oxford Brewhouse*: Very mixed furnishings and bric-a-brac on several rambling floors, dark but lively, with stripped brickwork and woodwork, lots of well kept real ales at a price, loud piped music, food (not Sat or Sun evenings) from well laid out servery, seats in small courtyard, monthly live music; children in upper levels *(S Demont, T Barrow, Eamon Green, Geraint Roberts, LYM)*; *Plough*: Unusual range of good value food, Morrells ales, Norwegian landlord *(Geoff and Angela Jaques)*; [Iffley], *Prince of Wales*: Pleasantly refurbished, with good mix of customers, relaxed feel, well kept Wadworths, regular beer festivals; seats outside *(Jon Carpenter)*; [67 Cranham St, Jericho], *Radcliffe Arms*: Good value generous food inc lots of pizzas; popular with younger crowd *(J M and K Potter)*; [Beaumont St], *Randolph Hotel*: Comfortable and welcoming, clubby decor, good place for a quiet cocktail; Osbert Lancaster paintings of the Zuleika Dobson story; bedrooms *(Walter Reid, BB)*; [Woodstock Rd], *Royal Oak*: Lots of little rooms, celebrity pictures in front bar, separate food bar, games area with darts, pool etc *(E McCall, D Irving, R Huggins, T McLean, Gordon)*; [Friars Entry, St Michael St], *Three Goats Heads*: Two good-sized friendly and attractive bars, relaxed downstairs, more formal up; well kept cheap Sam Smiths, good choice of quick generous food, dark wood and booths *(K Regan, Sue Demont, Tim Barrow, A Y Drummond, M Joyner)*; [129 High St], *Wheatsheaf*: Well kept Marstons Pedigree, Morrells Bitter, Varsity and Graduate and a guest beer tapped from the cask, simple snacky food; bare boards, simple wooden seats *(Dr Peter Donahue)*

☆ Pishill [B480 Nettlebed—Watlington; SU7389], *Crown*: Ancient country pub with attractively presented good home-cooked bar food (not Sun or Mon evenings) from sandwiches to steaks, three blazing log fires, black beams, standing timbers, well kept Brakspears, Flowers Original and a guest beer, picnic tables on attractive side lawn, nice surroundings; bedrooms in separate cottage; children allowed Sun lunchtime in restaurant *(Jack and Philip Paxton, P A and M J White, Eamon Green, S J Tasker, David Warrellow, S and P Hayes, Michael Sargent, Helen Hazzard, LYM)*

☆ Pyrton [SU6896], *Plough*: Cosy 17th-c thatched pub with decent generous freshly cooked food inc vegetarian and interesting specials, Weds pasta night, well kept Adnams, Brakspears and Fullers ESB, prompt friendly service, spotless old-fashioned stripped-stone beamed main bar with big woodburner, evening dining area; cl Mon evening, picnic tables outside *(Marjorie and David Lamb, P J Keen, Margaret Dyke, Bill Capper)*

☆ Radcot [Radcot Bridge; A4095 2½ miles N of Faringdon; SU2899], *Swan*: Sheltered and attractive Thames-side garden, with boat trips from pub's camping-ground opp (lift to bring wheelchairs aboard); well kept Morlands, log fire, straightforward food inc good value sandwiches and afternoon teas, piped pop music (may be loud), pub games, lots of stuffed fish; children in eating area; bedrooms clean and good value, with good breakfast *(S Demont, T Barrow, LYM)*

Rotherfield Greys [SU7282], *Maltsters Arms*: Pretty and pleasantly modernised pub by church, Brakspears PA, SB and Old reasonably priced for area, wide choice of food inc children's menu, back garden with picnic tables; handy for Greys Court (NT), good walks *(Mr and Mrs N Hazzard, Brian and Anna Marsden)*

Rotherfield Peppard [Gallowstree Rd; SU7181], *Greyhound*: Homely, pretty and cottagey country pub with some concentration on good home-made food; friendly landlord, good choice of beers, attractive garden with boules piste *(Gordon, Maysie Thompson)*

Russells Water, *Beehive*: This old-world pub, popular in previous editions, is now a private house *(LYM)*

Salford Hill [junction A44/A436; SP2628], *Cross Hands*: Pleasant stonebuilt beamed country pub open all day Sat and summer Fri, with usual food inc nice sandwiches and good value ploughman's, Bass, Hook Norton Best, Morrells Graduate, Wadworths 6X and Worthington, friendly people; games room, camping area behind *(Jenny and Michael Back, LYM)*

Sandford on Thames [Henley Rd, off A423 S of Oxford; SP5301], *Fox*: Friendly local spruced up by new young landlord, simple unspoilt public bar with darts, cards and dominoes, smaller lounge, coal fire, well kept Morrells Mild and Bitter *(Pete Baker)*

☆ **Satwell** [just off B481, 2 miles S of Nettlebed; follow Shepherds Green signpost; SU7083], *Lamb*: Cosy and attractive 16th-c low-beamed cottage, very small (so can get cramped), with tiled floors, friendly licensees, huge log fireplace, well kept Brakspears, traditional games, bar food from sandwiches up inc good ploughman's, tables outside *(John Carter, Gordon, LYM)*

☆ **Shilton** [SP2608], *Rose & Crown*: Mellow 17th-c low-beamed stonebuilt village local with good choice of well prepared home-cooked food at reasonable prices, friendly staff, well kept Morlands Bitter, Old Masters and Old Speckled Hen on handpump, woodburner, soft piped music, darts in beamed and tiled public bar, tables in sizeable garden; pretty village *(Marjorie and David Lamb, Calum and Susan Maclean, Joan Olivier)*

Shiplake [SU7678], *Plowden Arms*: Neatly opened up friendly local, with good range of food made by landlord's daughter, well kept Boddingtons and Brakspears, children's room; handy for Thames walk *(TBB, Gordon, P J Caunt)*

☆ **Sibford Gower** [SP3537], *Wykham Arms*: Low-beamed thatched 17th-c pub with good food (not Mon), well kept Hook Norton Best and Old Hookey, Mansfield Old Baily, Morlands Old Speckled Hen and Wadworths 6X, lots of country wines, big garden with play area and country views, good walks; only a curious absence of reports keeps it out of the main entries this year *(LYM)*

Sibford Gower [Burdrop], *Bishop Blaize*: Friendly efficient service, good value food, Hook Norton Best, John Smiths and Theakstons Best and XB; very old building, nicely kept, with children's corner in big garden, good views *(P and M Rudlin)*

Sonning Common [B481; SU7080], *Bird in Hand*: Small cosy areas with lots of pictures and old advertisements, popular food, real locals, well kept Courage-related ales, lovely back garden with pretty country views *(Gordon)*; [Blounts Court Rd; just off B481 Reading—Nettlebed, NE of centre], *Butchers Arms*: Well designed A E Hobbs between-wars pub with well kept Brakspears Mild, PA and SB, big family room, decent food inc good Sun lunch, pleasant garden adjoining woodland with picnic tables, excellent play area with weekend children's entertainment; bedrooms *(Brian and Anna Marsden, Gordon, LYM)*

☆ **Souldern** [SP5131], *Fox*: Charming beamed stone pub, well kept Hook Norton and other real ales, good interesting though not speedy bar food from ploughman's up, friendly German landlady, nice village location; comfortable bedrooms, good breakfasts *(T A Bryan, N and J Strathdee)*

☆ **South Moreton** [SU5588], *Crown*: Above-average home-made food inc some interesting dishes in tastefully opened-out family country pub with friendly character landlord, particularly well kept Wadworths and guest ales tapped from the cask, friendly service; children allowed, discount scheme for OAPs, theme and entertainment nights *(Susie Northfield, Ailsa Wiggans, R C Watkins)*

☆ **Sparsholt** [SU3487], *Star*: Small choice of good home-cooked food in friendly and relaxed old racing-country local, comfortable furnishings, log fire, attractive pictures, welcoming landlord, attentive staff, Fullers London Pride, Morlands Original, Worthington BB, daily papers, subdued piped music, back garden; pretty village *(Jed and Virginia Brown)*

Standlake [High St; SP3902], *Bell*: Unusual plush restaurant/bar area and separate lounge bar, good well presented food inc interesting dishes, well kept Morlands *(Alison Smith, S Holder)*

☆ **Steventon** [SU4691], *Cherry Tree*: Spacious and relaxing interconnecting rooms, dark green walls, two or three old settles among more modern furnishings, unobtrusive piped music, film-star pictures, stuffed woodpecker and squirrel, nice bay window; Charles Wells Eagle, Morlands and Wadworths 6X, popular quick straightforward food, open fire *(Gordon, Roger Huggins, Tom McLean)*

☆ **Stoke Lyne** [off B4100; SP5628], *Peyton Arms*: Unspoilt tiny snug, bigger public bar with good range of traditional games (no juke box or machines), pleasant garden with Aunt Sally, particularly welcoming landlord and customers, well kept Hook Norton tapped from the cask; no food *(Peter Baker, Jack and Philip Paxton)*

☆ **Stoke Row** [Newlands Lane, off B491 N of Reading – OS Sheet 175 map ref 684844; SU6884], *Crooked Billet*: Opened-up country pub/restaurant with wide choice of good interesting home-cooked meals, well kept Brakspears ales tapped from the cask, racks of decent wines, good log fires; no longer a place for just a drink; big garden, by Chilterns beech woods *(Jack and Philip Paxton, Clifford Payton, LYM)*

☆ **Stoke Row** [Kingwood Common, a mile S, signed Peppard and Reading – OS Sheet 175 map ref 692825], *Grouse & Claret*: Very much a dining pub, pleasant traditional interior with cosy nooks, friendly helpful service, well run restaurant area with good changing food, good choice of wines; piped music *(Simon Collett-Jones, the Monday Club)*

Stoke Row [SU6784], *Cherry Tree*: Two local bar rooms, one room like someone's drawing room, another with pool; friendly licensees and locals, Brakspears tapped from the cask in back stillage room *(Gordon, Jack and Philip Paxton)*; [Witheridge Hill], *Rising Sun*: Friendly Brakspears pub distinguished by the lovely crisp rolls served with almost everything; outstanding ploughman's *(Dick Brown)*

☆ **Stoke Talmage** [signed off A40 at Tetsworth; SU6799], *Red Lion*: Unspoilt country tavern, basic, friendly and welcoming, with cards and dominoes in parlour-like lounge, well kept Butcombe and Morlands, great character landlord; pleasant garden *(Pete Baker, Jack and Philip Paxton, Matthew Jones, D Irving, E McCall, R Huggins, T McLean)*

Stratton Audley [off A421 NE of Bicester; SP6026], *Red Lion*: Welcoming village pub with stripped stone and beams, suitably old varnished wooden furniture, basic low-priced menu, Badger Best, Ruddles and Wadworths 6X, cordial service; small garden, pretty village *(D C T Frewer, Robin Cordell)*

☆ **Sutton Courtenay** [SU5093], *George & Dragon*: Attractive and interesting 16th-c pub with good choice of fair-priced home-made food from sandwiches upwards inc popular Sun lunch, well kept Morlands, good range of decent wines; relaxed atmosphere, candlelit restaurant; no dogs (even in garden), friendly cat called Orwell (his namesake is buried in the graveyard overlooked by picnic tables on the back terrace) *(Marjorie and David Lamb)*

☆ **Sutton Courtenay** [Appleford Rd (B4016)], *Fish*: Bruce Buchan who made this dining pub an extremely popular main entry for his inventive cooking can now be found at the Bear & Ragged Staff in Cumnor – see main entries; attractive layout, Morlands ales, decent wines, no-smoking back dining area *(LYM; reports on new regime please)*

Sutton Courtenay, *Swan*: Smiling service, pleasant atmosphere, well kept beers, decent fresh food *(Tim Brierly, A T Langton)*

Swalcliffe [Bakers Lane; just off B4035; SP3737], *Stags Head*: Village local with reasonably priced food, well kept Hook Norton, good friendly service, huge collection of jugs hanging from ceiling, no music; sizeable garden with play area *(Tony Walker)*

☆ **Sydenham** [SP7201], *Crown*: Welcoming rambling low-ceilinged bar with a little lamp in each small window, unusual choice of good interesting food, Morrells ales, good choice of wines by the glass, friendly cats, relaxed homely atmosphere, dominoes and darts; picturesque village, views of lovely church *(Heather Couper, Nigel Herbert, Jack and Philip Paxton, Gordon, Marjorie and David Lamb)*

☆ **Tackley** [SP4720], *Gardiners Arms*: Comfortable and welcoming lounge bar with well presented good value bar food inc good vegetarian choice and bar food as well as full meals even on Sun, attentive friendly staff, coal-effect gas fire, well kept Morrells ales; entirely separate public bar with darts and piped pop music, bookable bowling alley, picnic tables on grass by car park; handy for Rousham House *(Margaret Dyke, T G Brierly)*

Tetsworth [handy for M40 junctions 6 and 7; SP6801], *Lion on the Green*: Very welcoming and unpretentious, with wide choice of good value generous food inc good Sun lunch, real fire, no dogs; big new antiques centre nearby – which was formerly the Swan Inn *(Margaret Dyke, Mrs A Wiggans)*

☆ **Thame** [Cornmarket; SP7005], *Abingdon Arms*: Good generous bar food inc home-made fresh pasta and speciality doorstep sandwiches, attentive friendly service, well kept Bass, Brakspears, Fullers London Pride, good well identified choice of bottled beers, small no-smoking front lounge and no-smoking bar, bright and basic main bar with bare boards and oriental rugs, three real fires; piped music; tables in garden with swings *(N and J Strathdee, C Aquilino)*

Thame, *Bird Cage*: Quaint black and white beamed and timbered pub, bare boards, some carpet, loads of old nick-nacks, open fires, cigarette cards, homely chairs; short reasonably priced bar lunch menu, well kept Courage-related ales, good bar food, piped music, friendly staff *(Ted George, LYM)*; [High St], *Black Horse*: Traditional old inn with attractive panelled and chintzy back lounge, simple dining area, sunny covered basic back area, good range of standard food, well kept Bass, good coffee, friendly atmosphere; open for breakfast; bedrooms *(George Atkinson, John Waller)*; [High St], *Rising Sun*: Flagstones and bare boards in three linked rooms, well kept Hook Norton and Morlands ales, good food inc huge rolls and notable burgers, real fire *(N and J Strathdee)*

☆ **Thrupp** [off A4260 just N of Kidlington; SP4815], *Boat*: Relaxing and friendly little

16th-c stone-built local in lovely canalside surroundings, quick good value home-cooked food, well kept Morrells, no piped music; restaurant, waterside garden *(Sue Demont, Tim Barrow, Geoff Lee, H D Spottiswoode, M Joyner)*

☆ **Towersey** [down drive nr Chinnor Rd/Manor Rd crossroads; SP7304], *Three Horseshoes*: Unpretentious flagstoned country pub with good value food inc nicely presented fresh veg, old-fashioned furnishings in two low-beamed bars, good log fire, well kept Bass and Tetleys-related ales, small restaurant; piped music, darts; biggish garden with fruit trees and play area; children allowed lunchtime *(Tina and David Woods-Taylor, John Waller, Bill Capper, LYM)*

Uffington [SU3089], *Fox & Hounds*: Friendly old local with wide choice of fairly priced straightforward food, lots of horse-related bric-a-brac, bottles and horse prints, good log fire, decent wine, Morrells beer; garden with play area; charming village, interesting weekend museum; handy for White Horse Hill *(Tim Brierly, Audrey and Peter Dowsett)*

Upper Heyford [SP4926], *Barley Mow*: Worth knowing for well kept ales *(M Joyner)*

Wallingford [St Leonards Ln; SU6089], *Little House Around the Corner by the Brook*: Welcoming and comfortable smallish tasteful bar with pews, good well presented home-made food inc imaginative children's dishes, changing real ales, raised dining area with antique furniture, fresh flowers, candles; piped music; next to church in beautiful spot by brook *(A P Seymour, Dominic and Sue Dunlop)*

☆ **Wantage** [Mill St; past square and Bell, down hill then bend to left; SU4087], *Lamb*: Low beams and timbers, choice of attractively and comfortably furnished seating areas, well kept Morlands, good choice of generous reasonably priced fresh bar food, friendly staff, good play area *(Marjorie and David Lamb, Geraint Roberts, LYM)*

Wantage [Market Pl], *Bear*: Comfortable chairs and settees in big bustling bar, Morlands ales, wide choice of food, friendly and attentive staff, newspapers, no-smoking area; piped music; restaurant, bedrooms *(George Atkinson, BB)*

☆ **Warborough** [Thame Rd (off A329 4 miles N of Wallingford); SU5993], *Cricketers Arms*: Particularly welcoming neat local with attractive decor, good range of freshly prepared reasonably priced usual food (not Sun/Mon evenings), well kept Morlands, proper bar and dining area, good smart service, friendly jack russell, tables and boules piste outside *(Marjorie and David Lamb, Frank Cummins)*

Warborough [The Green South; just E of A329], *Six Bells*: Generous fair value home-made food in low-ceilinged thatched pub with country furnishings, big fireplace, separate dining area, Brakspears ales; tables in back orchard, cricket green in front, boules; children in eating area *(Marjorie and David Lamb, LYM)*

Wendlebury [a mile from M40 junction 9; signed from A41 Bicester—Oxford; SP5619], *Red Lion*: Pleasant pub garden with grotesque wooden statues and food for the rabbits (25p a bag); Badger and Worthington ales, usual food inc good cheap sausages with egg *(Dave Braisted)*

☆ **West Hanney** [SU4092], *Plough*: Pretty thatched pub with attractive timbered upper storey, original timbers and uneven low ceilings, homely panelled lounge with open fire in stone fireplace, unusual plates, brasses and exotic butterflies, very friendly landlord, good value simple tasty food inc good fresh ploughman's, quiches and omelettes, Tetleys-related ales, interesting whiskies, darts in public bar; back garden with aviaries; children welcome *(HNJ, PEJ, Gordon, Rachel Hunter, R C Watkins)*

☆ **West Hendred** [Reading Rd; off A417 – OS Sheet 174 map ref 447891; SU4488], *Hare*: Civilised local, homely and welcoming, very popular for generous good value food served till late evening; decent wine, Morlands ale, two bars – one eating, one drinking *(A T Langton, R C Watkins, M W Turner, Peter and Audrey Dowsett)*

☆ **Westcott Barton** [Enstone Rd (B4030); SP4325], *Fox*: Spacious yet cosy characterful stonebuilt village pub with friendly Italian landlord, good value food inc good Italian dishes as well as traditional English ones and Sun roast, intimate restaurant (not Sun evening), seven well kept real ales, good wines, plans for brewing own beer; lovely view from garden across sheep meadow to church *(Frank W Gadbois, David Campbell, Vicki McLean)*

☆ **Weston on the Green** [A43, a mile from M40 junction 9; SP5318], *Chequers*: Busy thatched pub, clean and friendly, with profusion of old jars, brasses, stuffed fox and ferrets etc in long comfortable raftered bar, view of Thai cook producing good value food inc ethnic dishes, well kept Fullers, farm cider, pleasant staff; tables under cocktail parasols in attractive garden with animals *(Mrs Susan Gibson, Chris and Chris Ellis, Frank W Gadbois, Martin Kay, Andrea Fowler, D C T and E A Frewer)*

☆ **Weston on the Green**, *Ben Jonson*: Thatched pub with wide choice of good value generous food, some very spicy, well kept Bass and Greene King, good house wine, daily papers, enthusiastic young landlord, comfortable dark wood settles in welcoming beamed lounge bar, snug with roaring winter fire, discreet pool room; usually open all day; children very welcome; big sheltered garden with occasional barbecues *(D C T and E A Frewer, David Campbell, Vicki McLean)*

Wheatley [Church Rd; SP5905], *Sun*: Small and friendly, with limited tasty bar food, well kept reasonably priced Flowers and Ind Coope Burton; pleasant garden *(D N Roberts)*

☆ **Whitchurch** [SU6377], *Greyhound*: Pretty cottage with neat relaxed low-beamed L-shaped bar, bric-a-brac inc signed miniature cricket bats, good value food, well kept Tetleys-related ales and Wadworths 6X, polite service, no music or machines; dogs on leads allowed, pleasant garden; nr Thames toll bridge in attractive village, good walks *(Gordon, Dr Andrew Brookes, Mark and Diane Grist)*

Whitchurch Hill [SU6378], *Sun*: Friendly village pub with good varied generous food inc vegetarian, sensible prices, amiable licensees, big garden with animals *(Miss N Price)*

Witney [Market Sq; SP3510], *Eagle Vaults*: Popular comfortable pub with good hot buffet, Bass and Worthington BB, several adjoining lounges, family room, back garden; open all day Thurs market day *(Peter and Audrey Dowsett)*; [Market Sq], *Marlborough*: Relaxed and comfortable recently refurbished bar and lounge, Courage-related ales, good house wine; piped classical music *(Peter and Audrey Dowsett)*

Wolvercote [First Turn; SP5009], *Plough*: On edge of Oxford, tables outside looking over rough meadow to canal, recently enlarged and completely refurbished – armchairs and Victorian-style carpeted bays in main lounge, flagstoned dining room opening off, traditional snug, good-sized public bar with pool and games machines; wide choice of popular food, three well kept Morrells ales, decent wines; piped local radio *(Michael Sargent, N Hardyman)*

☆ **Woodstock** [Park St; SP4416], *Bear*: Handsome old inn with pleasant bar on right, cosy alcoves, tasteful medley of well worn wooden antique armchairs, chintz cushions, paintings, sporting trophies, log fire, Bass and Morrells Bitter, good fresh sandwiches and bar lunches, good service; not cheap; restaurant; good bedrooms – Forte *(Gordon, G C Hackemer)*

☆ **Woodstock** [A44 N], *Black Prince*: Traditional timbered and stripped-stone pub with old-fashioned furnishings, armour, swords, big fireplace, dining room with good simple bar food inc Mexican dishes and pizzas till late, well kept Hook Norton and Theakstons Old Peculier; occasional live music or nostalgic DJ; children allowed; tables out on grass by small river *(David and Alison Walker, David Campbell, Vicki McLean, M Joyner)*

Woodstock [A44 2 miles N], *Duke of Marlborough*: Tiny bar serving attractively furnished restaurant with dark oak and chintz, wide choice of food inc unusual dishes, Tetleys-related ales, friendly staff *(Eddie and Iris Brixton)*; [12 Oxford St], *Punch Bowl*: Pleasant and spacious old beamed inn, attentive helpful staff *(George Atkinson)*; [22 Market St], *Star*: Good food from good sandwiches to hot dishes, quick courteous service even o a busy Sunday *(Dr T Grant)*

☆ **Woolstone** [SU2987], *White Horse*: Attractive and welcoming partly thatched 16th-c pub in secluded downland valley village, good varied quickly served unpretentious food (not cheap) inc several vegetarian dishes, Arkells BBB and Wadworths 6X poured with a creamy head, decent wines, efficient service, two big open fires in spacious beamed and part-panelled room, children allowed in eating area; sheltered garden; lovely spot, handy for White Horse; four charming good value bedrooms *(Paul Randall, JEB, M R Roper-Caldbeck, Colin McKerrow, Rona Murdoch, Peter and Audrey Dowsett)*

☆ **Wootton** [Chapel Hill, off B4027 N of Woodstock], *Kings Head*: Well run dining pub with old oak settles and chintzy sofas in beamed and stripped-stone 17th-c bar, neat spacious restaurant, good interesting food esp fish, well kept Courage Directors, Hook Norton Best and Wadworths 6X, decent wines, fresh orange juice; well behaved children in eating area, maybe piped music; four bedrooms *(John Bowdler, Sue Demont, Tim Barrow, LYM)*

☆ **Wootton** [Glympton Rd (B4027) N of Woodstock], *Killingworth Castle*: 17th-c inn with good atmosphere, big helpings of good sensibly priced home-cooked food using fresh produce inc delicious puddings, chatty Canadian licensees, pleasant garden; bedrooms cosy and comfortable *(Caroline Beloe, Dick Little, Margaret Dyke, Andrew Bill)*

☆ **Wroxton** [Church St; off A422 at hotel – pub at back of village; SP4142], *North Arms*: Good value wholesome bar food in pretty thatched stone pub's simple but comfortable modernised lounge, well kept Morrells, cheerful service, log fire, lots of beer mugs; character restaurant (not Mon); darts, dominoes, fruit machine, weekly summer folk music; attractive quiet garden, lovely village *(N and J Strathdee, LYM)*

Yarnton [Woodstock Rd (A44); SP4712], *Grapes*: Useful Big Steak pub with extensive menu, attractive stone walls, beams and gas-effect fire in big bar and dining areas, well kept Adnams and Tetleys, garden tables *(Iris and Eddie Brixton)*

The Post Office makes it virtually impossible for people to come to grips with British geography, by using a system of post towns which are often across the county boundary from the places they serve. So the postal address of a pub often puts it in the wrong county. We use the correct county – the one the pub is actually in. Lots of pubs which the Post Office alleges are in Oxfordshire are actually in Berkshire, Buckinghamshire, Gloucestershire or the Midlands.

Shropshire

There's particularly good food to be had at the very restauranty but atmospheric Feathers at Brockton (a new entry – straight in with a Food Award), the attractive little Stables at Hope, the Unicorn in Ludlow (now clearly the town's most enjoyable pub), the Talbot in Much Wenlock (though the licensees have changed the chef's the same), the stylish Hundred House at Norton, and the very chatty Wenlock Edge Inn. It's the Unicorn in Ludlow which gains our award as Shropshire Dining Pub of the Year: for a really relaxed meal out we'd suggest its restaurant, though the lively bar is most enjoyable. It also gains a Place to Stay Award this year. Other pubs currently doing particularly well here include the welcoming old Royal Oak at Cardington, the very traditional Red Lion at Llanfair Waterdine, the Horse Shoe at Llanyblodwel (an exciting find for many readers, but we've not yet had reports on the new people who moved in this summer), and the Longville Arms at Longville (rather plain in appearance, but a very happy atmosphere). In the Lucky Dip section at the end of the chapter, pubs making their mark over the last few months include the Railwaymans Arms in Bridgnorth, Crown at Claverley, Sun and White Horse in Clun, Plume of Feathers at Harley, Bear at Hodnet, Meadow and Olde Robin Hood in Ironbridge, Green Dragon at Little Stretton, Crown at Munslow and Stiperstones at Stiperstones. There are several attractive places in Ludlow, and Shrewsbury has a very wide choice, especially for real ale enthusiasts. Drinks prices in the county are rather lower than the national average; the cheapest pubs we found were the Plough at Wistanstow and Three Tuns in Bishops Castle, both brewing their own, and the Lion of Morfe at Upper Farmcote, pricing its Banks's ales most attractively. Besides Woods (next door to the Wistanstow pub), among interesting local ales to be found in the area readers have recently been particularly enjoying Hobsons from Cleobury Mortimer, Hanby (reviving Wem's brewing tradition) and (actually from Staffordshire) the unusual slightly honeyed Enville Ale.

BISHOPS CASTLE SO3289 Map 6

Three Tuns

Salop Street

Inside this quirky beamed pub there's a no-frills welcoming air. There's a good family run feel with lots of rustic appeal in the vinyl floored bar with low backed settles that form three niches on one side with padded settles against the walls and comfortable chairs around heavy walnut tables. On the other side is a long wall settle and three big kitchen tables. Their popular own brew beers – XXX Bitter, Mild, an old-fashioned dark somewhat stoutish ale called Steamer and winter Old Scrooge – are produced in the many-storied Victorian brewhouse across the yard. Each stage of the brewing process descends from floor to floor within the unique tower layout (it's a Grade 1 listed building) and if the landlord isn't too busy he will happily give you a tour on request. Good value home-made bar food includes soup (£1.50), burgers (from £3), ploughman's (from £3.50), chilli con carne or cottage pie

(£4.70), fisherman's pie, scampi or lemon sole (£4.95) and steaks (from £9), quite a few vegetarian dishes like bean and mushroom stroganoff, mushroom and cashew nut pilaf or bean and mushroom stroganoff (from £4.50) and lots of Indian dishes like onion bhajees or vegetable samosas (£2.50), chicken tikka, beef madras or mixed vegetable curry (£5), and steaks (from £9); puddings like treacle tart or carrot cake (from £1.75). Hall's and Weston's ciders, some very reasonably priced bottles of wine; malt whiskies; dominoes and quoits. There's a small garden and terrace. ***(Recommended by Mike and Penny Sanders, Richard Lewis, Amanda Dauncey, Nigel Woolliscroft; more reports please)***

Own brew ~ Licensee Dominic Wood ~ Real ale ~ Meals and snacks ~ Restaurant ~ (01588) 638797 ~ Well behaved children welcome ~ Open 11.30-3, 6.30-11 (closed 25 Dec)

BRIDGES SO3996 Map 6

Horseshoe £

Near Ratlinghope, below the W flank of the Long Mynd

This attractive old pub is delightfully placed by the little River Onny. It's an interesting building (especially the windows), and the single large bar, tidily comfortable and bright, has a good log fire, and local paintings for sale. There is a small dining room off, and promptly served decent home-made food prepared from local produce in season includes toasted sandwiches (from £1.95), Shropshire blue ploughman's (£2.50), vegetable lasagne (£2.65) and chilli con carne (£2.95). The changing choice of well kept real ales is altogether better than you could expect out here, such as Adnams Extra and Southwold, Shepherd Neame Spitfire and two regularly changing guests. Weston's farm cider; friendly service; darts and dominoes, and the landlord's a real individual. There are tables outside, and the pub's very handy for walks on the Long Mynd itself and on Stiperstones – despite its isolation, it can get very busy in summer. ***(Recommended by Nigel Woolliscroft, Jenny and Brian Seller)***

Free House ~ John Muller ~ Real ale ~ Lunchtime meals and snacks ~ (01588) 650260 ~ Children in lounge area ~ Open 12-2.30(3 Sat), 6-11(closed lunchtimes Mon to Thurs in winter)

BROCKTON SO5894 Map 4

Feathers (symbol)

B4378

This stylish restauranty pub has changed tremendously since it last appeared in the Guide over ten years ago. Its charmingly atmospheric beamed rooms have been fashionably updated with stencilling on terracotta or yellow colour wash walls throughout. The constantly changing seasonal blackboard menu might include Greek salad (£3.45), pâté or stuffed mushrooms (£3.75), garlic king prawns (starter £5.75), toasted vegetable and mozarella tartlets or brie parcels wrapped in filo (£5.45), stir fried strips of chicken, steak, peppers and onions served on a sizzle plate (£8.95), lemon sole (£9.75), half a duck or peppered steak (£11.95) and an excellent Sunday lunch. The landlord tells us that they will cook anything on request as long as they have the ingredients in the kitchen. Puddings might include cherries poached in brandy, rum baked bananas or bread and butter pudding (£2.75). Well kept Banks and Marstons Pedigree. One room is no smoking and they have a policy not to sell cigarettes; waitress service throughout; piped music. ***(Recommended by P Fisk, Anthony Marriott, J Evans, Wayne Brindle; more reports please)***

Free house ~ Licensee Mr Hayward ~ Real ale ~ Meals and snacks (6.30-9.30) ~ (01746) 785202 ~ Children welcome ~ Open 6.30-11(also 12-3 Sat and Sun; cl Mon) ~ Bedrooms

If we know a pub has an outdoor play area for children, we mention it.

CARDINGTON SO5095 Map 4

Royal Oak £

Village signposted off B4371 Church Stretton—Much Wenlock, pub behind church; also reached via narrow lanes from A49

There are lovely views over hilly fields from the tables in the rose filled front courtyard of this pretty and welcoming wisteria covered white stone inn. The friendly rambling bar has low beams, old standing timbers of a knocked-through wall, hops draped along the bar gantry, a vast inglenook fireplace with a roaring winter log fire, cauldron, black kettle and pewter jugs, and gold plush, red leatherette and tapestry seats solidly capped in elm. Home-made lunchtime bar food includes macaroni cheese (£2.50), cauliflower cheese (£2.70), cottage pie or good fidget pie (£3.50), lasagne or vegetarian lasagne (£4.15) and fish and chips (£5), and puddings like excellent treacle sponge and custard. Well kept Bass on handpump under light blanket pressure and two other beers, usually Boddingtons, Hook Norton Old Hookey, Wadworths 6X or Worthingtons. There's dominoes and cribbage in the main bar and a no-smoking area. Walkers are welcome and a mile or so away – from the track past Willstone (ask for directions at the pub) – you can walk up Caer Caradoc Hill which looks over scenic countryside; there may be two boxer dogs. *(Recommended by Paul Carter, Nigel Woolliscroft, Dave Braisted, Joan and Andrew Life, Andy and Gill Plumb, D Hanley, Paul Boot, Wayne Brindle, The Monday Club, A G Roby)*

Free house ~ Licensee John Seymour ~ Real ale ~ Meals and snacks (12-2; not Mon) ~ Children welcome lunchtime ~ (01694) 771266 ~ Open 12-2.30, 7-11; closed Mon except bank holidays

HOPE SJ3401 Map 6

Stables ★

Drury Lane, Hopesgate; pub signposted off A488 S of Minsterley, at the Bentlawnt ¾, Leigh 1¾ signpost – then take first right turn; or closer to Minsterley, turn off at Ploxgreen – but a mile and a half of single-track road

As it would be a real shame to miss the chance of a meal at this charming little cream-washed stone cottage it's worth taking careful note of their food serving times which are fairly limited. Promptly served lunchtime food changes every day, but typically includes soup (£2), chicken liver pâté (£2.90), local sausage (£4.50), cheese, tomato and aubergine bake (£5.50), stilton and mushroom pancakes (£5.60), diced pork with honey and mustard or creamy salmon and broccoli pancake (£5.75), lamb curry (£5.80), beef and Guinness casserole (£6.50), lamb's liver and bacon or oven baked cod fillets with cream and cheese (£7.50), country rabbit pie (£7.85), roast rack of lamb with mint and onion sauce (£8.25); puddings (£2.50). There are only four tables in the cottagey no-smoking dining room so booking is worth while. The warmly hospitable black-beamed L-shaped bar has comfortably cushioned or well polished wooden seats around attractive oak and other tables, hunting prints of varying ages and degrees of solemnity, well chosen china, and a log fire in the imposing stone fireplace; in a back room (with copper-topped cask tables) are some big prints of butterflies and herbs. Well kept Benskins, Tetleys and Woods Special on handpump, with Addlestones cider in summer, decent wines and spirits, and half-a-dozen malt whiskies; darts, shove-ha'penny, trivia, cribbage, dominoes; several cats (Winge is the characterful ginger tom) and Corrie and Kelly the gruffly friendly mother-and-daughter cream-coloured labradors. There's a lovely view from the front tables, over unspoilt rolling pastures to the Long Mountain; behind, you look over the Hope Valley to the Stiperstones. *(Recommended by Martyn G Hart, Wayne Brindle, Helen Pickering, James Owen, Basil Minson, Anthony Marriott, Nigel Wooliscroft, Roger and Christine Mash, DC, W C M Jones, A G Roby, WAH, the Monday Club)*

Free house ~ Licensees Denis and Debbie Harding ~ Real ale ~ Meals and snacks (12-1.30, 7-8.30 not Sun-Tues evening) ~ Restaurant (Thurs-Sat evenings)~

(01743) 891344 ~ Open 11.30-2.30(12-2 in winter), 7-11; cl Mon, a week in Feb and a week in early summer

LLANFAIR WATERDINE SO2476 Map 6

Red Lion

Village signposted from B4355 approaching eastwards; turn left after crossing bridge

At the back of this atmospheric old place tables look over the River Teme, the border of England and Wales, and there are more seats among the roses in the quiet lane at the front. The very traditional heavily beamed rambling lounge bar has cosy alcoves, easy chairs, some long, low settles and little polished wooden seats on its turkey carpet, and a woodburner. Perhaps even nicer is the small black-beamed taproom, with plain wooden chairs on its flagstoned floor, and table skittles, dominoes, cribbage, shove-ha'penny, and sensibly placed darts; quoits. Good home-made food includes sandwiches (from £1.50), home-made soup (£1.65), ploughman's (from £3.10), and blackboard specials like chilli, pasta, steak and kidney pie, beef in garlic or salmon (from £3.75 to £9.20). Well kept Marstons Pedigree, Tetleys and a guest on handpump kept under light blanket pressure; good selection of whiskey and draft ciders; friendly service. No walking boots inside; piped music. The area is renowned for beautiful walks (a good stretch of Offa's Dyke is nearby) and designated as an area of outstanding natural beauty. Small but comfortable rooms, very good large breakfasts. *(Recommended by Helen Pickering, James Owen, Mike and Penny Sanders, Gwen and Peter Andrews, Basil Minson, N C Walker, R J Walden)*

Free house ~ Licensee Mick Richards ~ Real ale ~ Meals and snacks (12-1.30, 7-9, not Sun evening) ~ (01547) 528214 ~ Open 12-2, 7-11; closed Tues lunchtime ~ Bedrooms: £17.50(£25B)/£35(£45B)

LLANYBLODWEL SJ2423 Map 6

Horse Shoe

Village and pub signposted from B4396

A delightful stretch of the River Tanat rushes around boulders under a little red stone bridge beside this lovely early 15th-c inn. You can sit at the tables outside and watch children splash in the water, or there's a mile of fly-fishing for trout, grayling or late salmon (free for residents, day tickets otherwise). The simple low beamed front bar with an old black range in the inglenook fireplace has traditional black built-in settles alongside more modern chairs around oak tables on a reclaimed maple floor and lots of brass and china. In the rambling rooms leading off you'll find darts, shove-ha'penny, dominoes, cribbage, a fruit machine, and piped music. The dining room is oak panelled. New licensees arrived here on the day we went to press and the menu hadn't yet been fixed, but as the landlady is from an Italian family there are bound to be a few Italian dishes on the specials board. The landlord has ordered a new beer dispensing system and will keep Marstons Best and Pedigree and a mild. *(Recommended by Basil Minson, Keith Glossop, Mrs P J Carroll, R N Hutton, Paul McPherson, Graham and Lynn Mason; more reports please)*

Free House ~ Licensees Dennis and Jessica Plant ~ Real ale ~ Meals and snacks (11.30-2, 7-10; not Sun, Mon evening) ~ Restaurant ~ (01691) 828969 ~ Children welcome in eating area ~ Open 11.30-3, 6.30-11 ~ Bedrooms: £30/£35S

LONGVILLE SO5494 Map 4

Longville Arms

B4371 Church Stretton—Much Wenlock

There's a particularly good welcome for families at this popular and happy big-windowed inn, and it's set in a rather beautiful part of the country that's accessible to lots of local attractions. Of the two spacious bars the left one is simpler with sturdy elm or cast-iron-framed tables, leatherette banquettes and a woodburning stove at each end. The right-hand lounge has dark plush wall banquettes and cushioned chairs, with some nice old tables. There's a wide range of good-value homely bar food, including soup (£1.50), deep fried camembert with home-made chutney (£3.50), fresh grilled trout with almonds (£5.25), scampi (£5.95), Cajun chicken breast (£6.30), sirloin steak (from £7.90), as well as specials of the day; usual children's meals (from £2) and excellent puddings (from £1.80). Well kept Bass, Marstons Pedigree and Worthington BB on handpump and a guest in summer; selection of wines from the new world and Irish whiskies; darts and piped music. There are picnic tables under cocktail parasols in a neat terraced side garden, with a good play area. Besides the good value bedrooms, there's a good self-contained flat in an adjacent converted barn; superb breakfasts. *(Recommended by Ron Leigh, Andy and Gill Plumb, Anne and Sverre Hagen, P and M Kehely, Nigel Wolliscroft, Adrian and Karen Bulley, Mrs B Garmston, Dr and Mrs T O Hughes, Desmond and Rhona Crilly, the Whalley family, the Staughton family)*

Free house ~ Licensee Patrick Egan ~ Real ale ~ Meals and snacks (not Tues) ~ Restaurant ~ (01694) 771206 ~ Children welcome ~ Open 12-3, 7-11; closed Tues lunchtime ~ No smoking bedrooms: £20S/£35S

LUDLOW SO5175 Map 6

Unicorn

Lower Corve St, off Shrewsbury Rd

Shropshire Dining Pub of the Year

There's a delightfully relaxed and warmly welcoming atmosphere at this beautiful old family run 17th-c inn, which is built in a row of black-and-white houses along the banks of the River Corve. Friendly locals – including lots of well behaved stable lads and jockeys – gather in the single large beamed and partly panelled bar which has a huge log fire in a big stone fireplace. There's a timbered, candlelit restaurant (where they prefer you not to smoke). Consistently well prepared, not over elaborate but extremely good, fresh bar food (you can also choose from the restaurant menu) is written up on a blackboard and might include sandwiches (from £1.75), home-made vegetable soup (£2.50), filled baked potatoes (from £2.50), prawns in garlic or mushrooms in stilton sauce (£3.50), home-made liver pâté (£3.25), ploughman's (£3.75), mushroom and broccoli bake, bacon or mushroom and cauliflower bake or home-cooked ham salad (£4.25), breaded plaice (£4.75), grilled trout (£6.25), salmon with cucumber and lemon sauce or steaks (from £7.50), pork with brandy and rosemary (£7.75), Cumberland duck (£10.50) and a good choice of around ten home-made puddings (with lots of traditional English ones) (all £2.50); there's a fairly interesting selection of vegetarian and even vegan dishes like Moroccan orange salad (£2.75) or asparagus pancake (£5.25) or nut roast (£5.50); attentive, cheerful and willing service. Well kept Bass and Worthington BB on handpump. Beyond the car park is a terrace with tables sheltering pleasantly among willow trees by the modest river. Warm and comfortable timbered bedrooms are a good size; good breakfasts. *(Recommended by J Honnor, Robert Boote, Basil Minson, Barry Lynch, Gillian Jenkins, Mrs C J Richards, Pat and John Millward, Rona Murdoch, Nan Axon, Sally Barker, Bob and Maggie Atherton, J Weeks, Mrs E Smith, M Joyner, Mike and Wendy Proctor, Richard and Maria Gillespie, Nigel Woolliscroft)*

Free house ~ Licensees Alan and Elisabeth Ditchburn ~ Real ale ~ Meals and snacks ~ Restaurant ~ (01584) 873555 ~ Well behaved children welcome ~ Open 12-3, 6-11 ~ Bedrooms: £20B/£40B

MUCH WENLOCK SJ6200 Map 4

George & Dragon

High St

The eccentric landlord at this bustling, friendly and unpretentious town local has put together a delightful collection of pub paraphernalia. Hanging from the beams is possibly the biggest pub collection of water jugs – about a thousand – in England. The cosy atmospheric rooms are lined with old brewery and cigarette advertisements, bottle labels and beer trays and some George-and-the-Dragon pictures. There are a few antique settles as well as conventional furnishings, and a couple of attractive Victorian fireplaces (with coal-effect gas fires) and an old till on the bar. At the back, the quieter snug old-fashioned rooms have black beams and timbering, little decorative plaster panels, tiled floors, a stained-glass smoke room sign, a big George-and-the-Dragon mural as well as lots of smaller pictures (painted by local artists), and a little stove in a fat fireplace. Very good freshly prepared bar food (some dishes may be slightly more expensive in the evening) includes stilton and walnut pâté or prawns in lime and ginger (£3.25), Thai chicken or spinach pancakes (£4.75), rabbit in mustard and cider sauce (£4.85), home-baked ham with parsley sauce or beef cobbler (£4.95), steak and kidney pie (£6.50) and roast breast of duck with spiced apricot sauce (£8); home-made puddings like hot sticky toffee pudding, meringues with fudge sauce or home-made ginger ice cream (£2.25). Well kept Hook Norton Best Bitter and three guest beers like Charles Wells Bombardier, Hobsons Best and a Wye Valley Dorothy Goodbody seasonal ale on handpump; music, often jazz from a vintage wireless. It can get busy and smoky. *(Recommended by Anthony Marriott, Mike and Wendy Proctor, Tom Rodabaugh, Nigel Woolliscroft, Richard Lewis, Mike and Penny Sanders, R M Bloomfield, A E and P McCully, David and Ruth Hollands, J Weeks, Mrs E Smith, M Joyner, Richard and Maria Gillespie)*

Free house ~ Licensee Eve Nolan ~ Real ale ~ Lunchtime meals and snacks (not Sun evening) ~ Evening restaurant (not Sun evening) ~ (01952) 727312 ~ Well behaved children, must be over seven in the evening ~ Open 11-2.30, 6-11; cl 25 Dec evening

Talbot

High Street

Just up the road from our other entry in the town this civilised 14th-c building which was originally part of Wenlock Abbey has quite a different appeal. There are several neatly kept areas with lovely flowers, comfortable green plush button-back wall banquettes around highly polished tables, low ceilings, two big log fires (one in an inglenook). The walls are decorated with prints of fish and brewery paraphernalia. Tim Lathe has now retired but as the new licensee is staying with the same staff, chef and type of menu we expect the very good food to remain as popular as ever. At lunchtime the attractively presented range includes soup (£2.50), filled baked potatoes (from £2.95), ploughman's (from £2.75), Greek salad (£3.50), lentil crumble (£5.50), omelettes (from £5.75), mince filled pancake with cheese (£5.75) and poached salmon (£6.50) and daily specials like sweet and sour pork (£5.25) and oxtail casserole (£7.95). The evening menu might include breast of chicken with orange and ginger or with yoghurt, cucumber and mint (£6.25), mushroom and stilton gratin, lamb's liver fried with juniper and red wine or sautéed lamb's kidneys with sherry and cream (£6.95) and lamb chops (£7.75); puddings like fruit crumble or bread and butter pudding (£2.25); Sunday roast lunch (£9.45); no-smoking restaurant. Well kept changing ales might include Courage Directors, John Smiths and Morlands Old Speckled Hen on handpump; good value wines. Through the coach entry, there are white seats and tables in an attractive sheltered yard. *(Recommended by Basil Minson, Mrs J Ingram, M Joyner, Janet and Peter Race, Richard Lewis, Roger and Valerie Hill, Anthony Marriott, Colin Laffan, WAH, Neil Tungate, C S Bickley, D Deas, Roy and Mary Roebuck, Cyril Burton, P M Lane, Mike and Wendy Proctor, Martin Aust)*

Free house ~ Licensee Sean Brennan ~ Real ale ~ Meals and snacks (not 25 Dec) ~ Restaurant ~ (01952) 727077 ~ Well behaved children allowed (no pushchairs) ~ Open 10-3, 6-11 ~ Bedrooms: £45B/£90B

Please let us know of any pubs where the wine is particularly good.

NORTON SJ7200 Map 4

Hundred House

A442 Telford—Bridgnorth

The beautifully appointed rooms of this old hotel are filled with interesting, even elegant, furnishings. The carefully refurbished bar is divided into several spick and span separate areas, with old quarry tiles at either end and modern hexagonal ones in the main central part, which has high beams strung with hop-bunches and cooking pots. Steps lead up past a little balustrade to a partly panelled eating area where stripped brickwork looks older than that elsewhere. Handsome fireplaces have log fires or working Coalbrookdale ranges (one has a great Jacobean arch with fine old black cooking pots), and around sewing-machine tables are a variety of interesting chairs and settles with some long colourful patchwork leather cushions. Good bar food includes soup of the day (£2.50), ploughman's (£3.95), sausage and mash (£4.95), lasagne or vegetarian savoury pancake (£6.50), steak and kidney, lamb cutlets, chicken chasseur or fisherman's pie (£6.95) and sirloin steak (£9.95); children's menu (£3.75). If the restaurant is very busy on a Saturday night, they may well stop doing bar meals. Well kept Flowers Original and HP&D Entire on handpump, with Heritage Bitter (light and refreshing, not too bitter) brewed for them by a small brewery; over 50 wines; lots of malt whiskies. Dominoes, cribbage and piped music; no dogs. Seats out in a neatly kept and prettily arranged garden which has an enchanting herb garden to supply the kitchen; interested visitors can also tour the licensees' own garden. *(Recommended by Heather Couper, Roger Byrne, Basil Minson, Malcom Fowlie, Jenny Williams, Paul Cartledge, the Monday Club, Nigel Hopkins, Mr and Mrs P F Meadows, D Jones, George Atkinson, J Weeks, M Handley)*

Free house ~ Licensees Henry, Sylvia and David Phillips ~ Real ale ~ Meals and snacks (12-2.30, 7-10) ~ Restaurant ~ (01952) 730353 ~ Children welcome ~ Open 10-3, 6-11 ~ Bedrooms: £59B/£69B

PULVERBATCH SJ4202 Map 6

White Horse

From A49 at N end of Dorrington follow Pulverbatch/Church Pulverbatch signposts, and turn left at eventual T-junction (which is sometimes signposted Church Pulverbatch); OS Sheet 126 map reference 424023

Plenty of regulars crowd into the atmospheric bar of this cosy and character-filled pub, but there's a very warm welcome to strangers too. The several rambling areas have black beams and heavy timbering, as well as unusual fabric-covered high-backed settles and brocaded banquettes on its turkey carpet, sturdy elm or cast-iron-framed tables, and an open coalburning range with gleaming copper kettles. A collection of antique insurance plaques, big brass sets of scales, willow-pattern plates, and pewter mugs hang over the serving counter, and there's even a good Thorburn print of a grouse among the other country pictures. Big helpings of decent bar food, such as cullen skink (heavily creamed smoked fish soup) or sandwiches (from £1.50), burgers (from £2.75), omelettes (from £3.25), filled baked potatoes (from £1.95), sausage and egg (£3.50), crumbed fish of the day (£4.25), chicken and mushroom pancake (£4.75), lamb curry (£5.50), chicken chasseur (£5.75) and beef stroganoff (£8.75); children's menu (from £1.35); puddings like pecan and treacle pie or cheesecake (£1.85) and ice creams (£1.25). Well kept Boddingtons, Flowers Original and Wadworths 6X on handpump, several decent wines by the glass, and a huge selection of over 100 malt whiskies. Darts, juke box, friendly efficient service. The quarry-tiled front loggia with its sturdy old green leatherette seat is a nice touch. The entrance is around the back of the pub. *(Recommended by G Washington, Basil Minson, A P Jeffreys, Mary and Peter Rea, Mrs P Langridge, Joy Heatherley, Janet Bord, Paul S McPherson)*

Whitbreads ~ Lease: James MacGregor ~ Real ale ~ Meals and snacks (till 10pm) ~ (01743) 718247 ~ Children welcome ~ Open 11.30-3, 7-11

UPPER FARMCOTE SO7792 Map 4

Lion of Morfe £

Follow Claverley 2½ signpost off A458 Bridgnorth—Stourbridge

The interesting and traditional public bar with wood-backed wall seats on red tiles and a game trophy over the coal fire is quite a contrast to the more modern conservatory and comfortable lounge at this country pub. The smart brown-carpeted lounge bar has pink plush button-back built-in wall banquettes in curving bays, and a good log fire; it opens into the no-smoking conservatory, which has cushioned cane chairs around glass tables on the red-tiled floor. The carpeted pool room has a big black kitchen range, darts, dominoes and fruit machine. At lunchtime it's popular with an older set who gather for the promptly served and extremely good value bar food which includes filled baked potatoes (from £1.75), steak and kidney pie or cottage pie (£2.95) and lasagne, braised steak or pork in cider (£3.15); daily specials; friendly service. Well kept and priced Banks's Bitter and Mild and Bass on electric pump or handpump. The pleasant garden has picnic tables under cocktail parasols on a terrace, and a lawn spreading out into an orchard with a floodlit boules piste. *(Recommended by Heather Couper, Basil Minson, Barbara and Denis Melling, DMT, the Monday Club, Pete Yearsley, Frank Cummins, DAV)*

Free house ~ Licensees Bill and Dinah Evans ~ Real ale ~ Meals and snacks (not Fri, Sat, Sun) ~ (01746) 710678 ~ Children in eating area of bar and conservatory ~ Folk club first Sat of the month, jazz night second Thurs of the month ~ Open 11.30-3.30(4 Sat)(Mon 12-2), 7-11

WENLOCK EDGE SO5796 Map 4

Wenlock Edge Inn ★

Hilltop; B4371 Much Wenlock—Church Stretton, OS Sheet 137 map reference 570962

As ever this smashing pub continues to be one of the most welcoming and chatty places in the Guide. The really rather special atmosphere is down to the way the family cheerfully draws their guests into the run of things and generates a flow of interesting conversation. The cosy talkative feel is perhaps at its best on the second Monday in the month – story telling night, when the right hand bar is packed with locals telling tales, some true and others a bit more dubious. In the right hand bar is a big woodburning stove in an inglenook, as well as a shelf of high plates, and it leads into a little dining room. The room on the left has pews that came from a Methodist chapel in Liverpool, a fine oak bar counter, and an open fire. The good fresh home-made bar food tends towards British food and might include honey baked ham or steak and mushroom pie (£5.40), applejack chicken (£6.50) and sirloin steak (£8.60); no chips; puddings like tipsy banana, treacle tart or lemon pudding (from £2.25); excellent breakfasts (try the sausage). Well kept local Hobsons Best and Town Crier Robinsons and Websters Best on handpump, interesting whiskies, decent wines by both glass and bottle, and no music – unless you count the deep-throated chimes of Big Bertha the fusee clock. Water comes from their own 190 foot well. There are some tables on a front terrace and the side grass. The building is in a fine position just by the Ippikins Rock viewpoint and there are lots of walks through the National Trust land that runs along the Edge. *(Recommended by DMT, Richard Lewis, Gwen and Peter Andrews, Nigel Woolliscroft, Brian and Margaret Beedham, Barbara and Denis Melling, Nigel Clifton, Mike and Penny Sanders, Paul Carter, Jeff Davies, Gwen and Peter Andrews, G and M Hollis, Mike and Wendy Proctor, Brian and Margaret Beedham, Anthony Marriott, Phil and Carol Byng, Andrew Stephenson, Martyn Hart, Andrew Shore, Audrey Scaife, David Holman, F Jarman, M Joyner, Andy and Gill Plumb, Basil Minson, David Eberlin, Mrs D Jones, Maureen and Keith Gimson, M Cox, Gordon Mott, Susan Holmes, R M Bloomfield, Paul McPherson, Roberta O'Neill, R J Walden, H O Dickinson, Martin Aust, M G Hart, Mr and Mrs D Tapper, Wayne Brindle, Lynn Sharpless, Bob Eardley, Bob and Maggie Atherton, Roy Smylie, Dick Brown, A G Roby)*

Free house ~ Licensee Stephen Waring ~ Real ale ~ Meals and snacks (not Mon

except Bank holidays) ~ Restaurant ~ (0174 636) 403 ~ Children in restaurant (not under 10 if after 8pm Sat) ~ Open 11.30-2.30, 6.30-11; closed Mon lunchtime except Bank holidays; cl 25 Dec ~ Bedrooms: £40S/£55S

WHITCHURCH SJ5345 Map 7

Willey Moor Lock

Pub signposted off A49 just under two miles N of Whitchurch

There's a lovely view of the Llangollen canal and its colourful narrowboats from this pretty lock keeper's cottage with white tables under cocktail parasols on a terrace. To get here you cross a little footbridge over the canal and its rushing sidestream. Inside, several neatly decorated carpeted rooms have low ceilings, a large teapot collection, a decorative longcase clock, brick-based brocaded wall seats, stools and small chairs around dimpled copper and other tables, and two winter log fires. Popular bar food includes cheese and onion pie or minced beef and onion pie (£3.50), chicken curry (£4), breaded plaice (£4.50), home-made steak and kidney pie (£4.85) and about seven vegetarian dishes like chilli, lasagne or burgers (from £3.50); puddings like jam roly poly or chocolate fudge cake (£1.80); usual children's menu (from £2). Food stops one hour before closing, subject to seasonal variations. Well kept Theakstons and two guests like Butterknowle Conciliation, Hanby Drawwell and Treacleminer or Wadworths 6X on handpump; large selection of malt whiskies; fruit machine, piped music, and several dogs and cats. There's a children's play area with swings and slides. *(Recommended by Basil Minson, D Hanley, Sue and Bob Ward, J and P Maloney, Mr and Mrs R J Phillips, Nigel Woolliscroft, Mrs R Gregory, Mr and Mrs Jones, Kate and Robert Hodkinson, Colin Davies, Martin Aust)*

Free house ~ Licensee Mrs Elsie Gilkes ~ Real ale ~ Meals and snacks ~ Restaurant ~ (01948) 663274 ~ Children welcome away from bar area ~ Open 12-2.30(2 in winter), 6-11; cl 25 Dec

WISTANSTOW SO4385 Map 6

Plough 🍷

Village signposted off A49 and A489 N of Craven Arms

This surprisingly modern, high raftered and brightly lit own brew pub has been taken into the direct management of Wood Brewery who produce Woods Parish, Shropshire Lad, Special, the strong Wonderful and some seasonal brews in the older building next door. The pub also serves a couple of guests, two farm ciders, about 16 wines by the glass, and there's a fine display cabinet of bottled beers. Popular home made bar food includes mushrooms filled with stilton and leeks (£3.95), steak, kidney and ale pie (£4.95), chicken breast stuffed with walnut, orange and Shropshire blue or salmon and lime in coriander (£6.95), halibut with white wine (£7.80). The games area has darts, pool, fruit machine, video game and juke box; maybe piped music. Outside there are some tables under cocktail parasols. *(Recommended by J C Green, Martyn Hart, Wayne Brindle, John and Joan Wyatt, Basil Minson, A E and P McCully, A G Roby, L S Pay, K Baxter, M G Hart)*

Own brew ~ Licensees Colin James and Edward Wood ~ Real ale ~ Meals and snacks ~ (01588) 673251 ~ Children in eating area of bar lunchtime only ~ Open 12-3, 7-11(cl Mon lunchtime)

Real ale to us means beer which has matured naturally in its cask – not pressurised or filtered. We name all real ales stocked. We usually name ales preserved under a light blanket of carbon dioxide too, though purists – pointing out that this stops the natural yeasts developing – would disagree (most people, including us, can't tell the difference!).

Lucky Dip

Besides the fully inspected pubs, you might like to try these Lucky Dips recommended to us and described by readers (if you do, please send us reports):

☆ **All Stretton** [SO4695], *Yew Tree*: Comfortable beamed bars, handy for Long Mynd, with good bar food, well kept Bass and Worthington BB, quick helpful service, quiet piped music, restaurant; children welcome *(A G Roby)*

Ash [Ash Magna; SJ5739], *White Lion*: Genuine village local with good atmosphere enhanced by newish character landlord, friendly bar service, old-fashioned feel, good choice of real ales, blazing fires *(Sue Holland, Dave Webster, Sue and Bob Ward)*

Astley [A53 Shrewsbury—Shawbury; SJ5319], *Dog in the Lane*: Tetleys-related ales, reasonably priced good straightforward food, beamed lounge with good brass, copper and china decor; tables outside *(M Joyner, D Hanley)*

Boningale [A464 NW of W'hampton; SJ8102], *Horns*: Three friendly bars with real ales such as St Austell HSD as well as more local Enville and Hook Norton, wholesome nicely presented food inc magnificent brunch, panelled dining room *(Dave Braisted, J Evans)*

☆ **Bridgnorth** [Stn; A458 towards Stourbridge; SO7293], *Railwaymans Arms*: 1940s-style station bar in Severn Valley steam railway terminus, lots of atmosphere esp on summer days; four or five well kept changing Black Country and other interesting ales, simple summer snacks, coal fire, railway memorabilia inc lots of signs, superb mirror over fireplace, seats out on platform; children welcome; car-parking fee refundable against train ticket or what you spend here *(Nigel Woolliscroft, Graham Reeve, Pete Yearsley, B M Eldridge, LYM)*

☆ **Bridgnorth** [Northgate], *Bear*: Friendly and relaxed town pub with good fresh lunchtime food (not Sun), gourmet nights Thurs and special occasions, Bathams, Ruddles and many changing guest ales, good choice of bottled beers, decent wines; tables in sheltered enclosed garden *(K W Grimshaw)*

Bridgnorth, *Golden Lion*: Pleasantly decorated friendly pub with good ploughman's and baked potatoes; no chips *(Alain and Rose Foote)*; [Whitburn St], *Kings Head*: Old timbered pub with pretty unusually patterned windows, good value food from cheap sandwiches and baked potatoes up *(Pete Yearsley, Mrs P J Pearce)*; [Old Ludlow Rd (B4364, a mile out)], *Punch Bowl*: Unpretentious beamed and panelled 17th-c country pub, good generous food inc fresh veg and good carvery, Marstons Pedigree, superb views; piped music *(Pete Yearsley, Jeanne Cross, Paul Silvestri, Wayne Brindle)*

☆ **Burwarton** [B4364 Bridgnorth—Ludlow; SO6285], *Boyne Arms*: Pleasant and friendly country pub with generous reasonably priced home-made food, changing well kept ales such as Bass, Ind Coope Burton and Woods; tables in garden, bedrooms *(J C Joynson, C S Bickley)*

Church Stretton [Affcot; SO4593], *White House*: Good food from interesting menu, Austrian chef, beautiful surroundings *(Paul and Jayne Ruiz)*

☆ **Claverley** [High St; off A454 Wolverhampton—Bridgnorth; SO7993], *Crown*: Very picturesque pub in lovely village. Interesting old-fashioned heavy-beamed bar, really friendly service, good competitively priced home-made food (not Sun-Weds evenings) cooked just as you ask, well kept Banks's, open fires, splendid family garden; dogs allowed, long Sat opening; children allowed in eating area *(Wayne Brindle, LYM)*

Claverley, *Plough*: Busy and welcoming, good simple bar food, good range of Tetleys-related ales; separate bistro *(Pete Yearsley, the Monday Club)*

nr **Claverley** [Upper Ludstone (B4176, just S of A454); SO8095], *Woodman*: Small and clean house, with generous good food at good prices, real ales; garden *(C S Bickley)*

☆ **Cleobury Mortimer** [Church St; SO6775], *Kings Arms*: 16th-c inn with pleasant atmosphere, well kept Hook Norton, Timothy Taylors Landlord and Wye Valley, varied reasonably priced food inc vegetarian and good sandwiches; comfortable bedrooms *(P and M Rudlin, Dennis Boddington)*

☆ **Clun** [High St; SO3081], *Sun*: Tudor timbers and beams, some sturdy antique furnishings, enormous open fire in flagstoned public bar, well kept ales inc Banks's Bitter and Mild, Marstons Pedigree and Woods Special, quiet atmosphere, friendly landlord; children allowed in eating area, tables on sheltered back terrace; bedrooms, lovely village *(Janet Pickles, Colin Laffan, Wayne Brindle, John Evans, Catherine Haynes, Steve Wheldon, LYM)*

☆ **Clun** [Market Sq], *White Horse*: Cosy, welcoming and neatly kept beamed L-shaped bar with inglenook and woodburner, well kept Bass, Woods and Worthington, farm cider, decent bar food inc vegetarian and good puddings, friendly efficient service; children welcome, tables in back garden; bedrooms *(Catherine Haynes, Steve Wheldon, P Tetley, Margaret Horner, Michael Hinkley)*

Coalbrookdale [Wellington Rd; SJ6704], *Coalbrookdale*: Seven changing well kept real ales, good often imaginative food, friendly staff, good mix of people *(Mrs L M Peach)*

☆ **Coalport** [Salthouse Rd, Jackfield; nr Mawes Craft Centre, over footbridge by china museum – OS Sheet 127 map ref 693025; SJ6902], *Boat*: Cosy waterside pub in delightful part of Severn Gorge, basic with some character, coal fire in lovely range, food inc cheap roast meat baps and good value Sun lunch, well kept Banks's Bitter and Mild, welcoming service, darts; summer barbecues on tree-shaded lawn *(Basil Minson, BB)*

Coalport, *Shakespeare*: Simple friendly cream-washed pub by pretty Severn gorge park, also handy for china museum, with good value generous lunches, Tetleys-related ales *(Eddie and Iris Brixton, BB)*

Corfton [B4368 Much Wenlock—Craven Arms; SO4985], *Sun*: Good value simple home-cooked food inc children's and bargain Sun lunch, well kept Whitbreads-related ales, pleasant lounge bar, lively and cheery locals' bar; tables on terrace and in good-sized garden with good play area; piped music *(Mr and Mrs D E P Hughes, BB)*

☆ **Ellesmere** [Scotland St; SJ4035], *Black Lion*: Attractively refurbished with bare boards, ornaments, prints, high-backed settles etc, very pleasant staff, well kept Banks's Mild and Marstons Pedigree *(Rita and Keith Pollard, D Hanley)*

Ellesmere [Birch Rd], *White Hart*: Attractive little black and white pub, perhaps the oldest in Shrops, with well kept Marstons, friendly landlord; not far from canal *(A D Marsh, D Hanley)*

Gledrid [SJ2937], *Poachers Pocket*: Newly refurbished eating house, well kept beers, big helpings of good value food, garden overlooking Llangollen Canal; several rooms, one no smoking *(Bill Sykes)*

Goldstone [Goldstone Wharf; off A529 S of Mkt Drayton, at Hinstock; SJ7128], *Wharf*: Very pleasant gardens by Shropshire Union canal, hot food, cold buffet, well kept beer; children welcome *(Nigel Woolliscroft)*

Grinshill [off A49; SJ5323], *Elephant & Castle*: Early Georgian inn with Bass, bar meals inc good value Sun lunch, juke box, restaurant; tables outside, pleasant walks; bedrooms *(D Hanley)*

Hadnall [A49 6 miles N of Shrewsbury; SJ5220], *Saracens Head*: Snug, with interesting old photographs, marvellous pork and apple sausages in good sauce, Burtonwood ales *(Dave Braisted)*

☆ **Hampton Loade** [SO7586], *Lion*: Fine old stripped-stone inn with good unusual food, friendly efficient service, lots of country wines, good day-ticket fishing on River Severn; very busy in summer or when Severn Valley Rly has weekend steam spectaculars, quiet otherwise; tucked away at end of road that's not much more than a track for the last ¼ mile *(George Atkinson)*

☆ **Harley** [A458 NW of Much Wenlock; SJ5901], *Plume of Feathers*: Friendly and comfortable beamed pub with big open fire, reasonably priced food inc interesting specials, well kept Courage-related and guest ales, cheerful efficient service, darts, piped music (Sun evening live); spacious dining room, tables outside; bedrooms with own baths *(Graham Reeve, B and K Hypher, David Hanley, Wayne Brindle)*

Harmer Hill [SJ4822], *Bridgewater Arms*: Brewers Fayre pub with big dining area, good standard food; play area *(D Hanley)*

Heathton [OS Sheet 138 map ref 813925; SO8192], *Old Gate*: Wide choice of good bar food, charming rooms on different levels, well kept Tetleys-related ales, good choice of wines, big garden *(Nick Whear)*

Hengoed [Higher Hengoed (Oswestry—Weston Rhyn rd off B4579; don't follow Hengoed sign off A5); SJ2933], *Last*: Beamed dining area, red plush lounge, games room with two pool tables, darts, fruit machine; exceptionally friendly landlord, usual food, well kept Bass, Boddingtons, Daleside Old, Eldridge Pope Hardy Country, Fullers ESB, Sam Powells Old Sam; used to have a dog who could tell one pint from another – we found the two present ones can't *(Brian and Anna Marsden)*

☆ **Hinstock** [Wood Lane, just off A41 9 miles N of Newport; SJ6926], *Falcon*: Friendly atmosphere, well kept ales inc Bass, decent wines and malt whiskies, popular good value food in bar and restaurant inc cheap Sun lunch, good pleasant service, no music; welcoming licensees now spreading their energies over Elephant & Castle at Grinshill too *(Basil Minson, RW, SW)*

☆ **Hodnet** [SJ6128], *Bear*: Welcoming 16th-c pub with good range of reasonably priced food inc imaginative dishes, well kept Courage-related ales, friendly obliging service; sofas and easy chairs in foyer, sizeable refurbished bar wearing in nicely now and popular with locals, restaurant with small no-smoking area and corner alcove with glass-tile floor over unusual sunken garden in former bear pit; six good value comfortable bedrooms, opp Hodnet Hall gardens *(John and Joan Holton, G Washington, Mrs S Kellaway, Mr and Mrs Swainbank, R M Bloomfield, D D Moores, J Mealea, Mervyn Wilkinson, Paul Carter, P D Donoghue)*

☆ **Hopton Wafers** [A4117; SO6476], *Crown*: Attractive creeper-covered inn, cosy warmly decorated beamed bar with big inglenook fire and woodburner, lots of miscellaneous tables and chairs, good choice of bar food, well kept Whitbreads-related ales, good house wines, restaurant with no-smoking area, tables on terraces and in streamside garden, provision for children, pretty timbered bedrooms; has been a general favourite, perhaps needs to tighten up some details now *(A E and P McCully, Rita Horridge, George Atkinson, E A C and S J C Sutton, KC, Basil Minson, the Monday Club, C Smith, John Hibberd, LYM)*

☆ **Ironbridge** [Buildwas Rd; SJ6704], *Meadow*: Popular and welcoming Severnside dining pub, newish but done in old-fashioned style with cigarette cards, tasteful prints and brasses, wide choice of good value generous freshly prepared food in lounge and downstairs restaurant (must book Sun lunch), well kept Banks's and Courage-related ales, decent wines, friendly efficient service; pretty waterside garden only slightly marred by partly tree-screened power station on opposite bank *(John Fazakerley, Iris and Eddie Brixton, D Hanley, Basil Minson, Susan Christie)*

☆ **Ironbridge** [Waterloo St], *Olde Robin Hood*: Friendly pub in attractive riverside setting by bridge, doing well under pleasant new landlord; five comfortable connecting rooms with various alcoves, lots of gleaming brass and old clocks; well kept Bass-related beers and guests such as Charles Wells Bombardier, Morlands Old Speckled Hen and Shepherd Neame Bishops Finger, good atmosphere, good value standard food inc sandwiches; seats out in front, handy for museums complex; good value bedrooms *(D Hanley, John Cox, George Atkinson, Alan and Paula McCully)*

☆ **Ironbridge** [Blists Hill Open Air Museum – follow brown museum sign from M54 exit 4, or A442], *New Inn*: Rebuilt Victorian pub in this good heritage museum's recreated working Victorian community (shares its opening hours); friendly staff in period dress, well kept Banks's ales, pewter measure of mother's ruin for 2½d (money from nearby bank), good pasties, gas lighting, traditional games, upstairs tearoom; back yard with hens, pigeon coop, maybe children in costume playing hopscotch and skipping; children welcome *(George Atkinson, WAH, A E and P McCully, LYM)*

Ironbridge [off Madeley rd], *Horse & Jockey*: Good food esp steak and kidney pie, also vegetarian; Bass and Morlands *(Mike and Wendy Proctor, Dave Braisted)*; [Wharfage], *White Hart*: Particularly good value comfortable bedrooms *(N Silverstone)*

Ketley [Holyhead Rd (old A5); M54 junction 6, pass Tesco to roundabout signed Ketley; SJ6810], *Pudding*: In the mould of other 'Little' pubs, but with added suet; popular at lunchtime for pleasant food (free puddings for visibly pregant women), well kept Tetleys-related ales and Lumphammer *(Patrick and Mary McDermott, David and Shelia, P Yearsley)*

☆ **Knockin** [Main St; NW of Shrewsbury; SJ3422], *Bradford Arms*: Popular and busy, with good fresh food, well kept beer and friendly service in relaxing not overdecorated bar *(Robert W Buckle, Alex Mazaraki)*

Knowbury [SO5775], *Penny Black*: Good food inc interesting more elaborate evening dishes, lunchtime Sun carvery, curry/pasta nights, barbecues etc; well kept Morlands Old Speckled Hen and Theakstons XB *(Mike and Alison Cargill)*

☆ **Leebotwood** [A49 Church Stretton—Shrewsbury; SO4898], *Pound*: Attractive and comfortable beamed and thatched roadside, generous good value food, friendly staff, restaurant *(D Hanley)*

☆ **Linley** [pub signed off B4373 N of Bridgnorth; SO6998], *Pheasant*: Unspoilt country local in lovely spot, good honest food (not Sun if busy), attractive prices, interesting choice of real ales; individual landlord *(Wayne Brindle, LYM)*

☆ **Little Stretton** [Ludlow Rd; village well signposted off A49; SO4392], *Green Dragon*: Welcoming and quietly popular civilised dining pub, reasonably priced straightforward food, pleasant service, well kept Tetleys, Wadworths 6X, Woods and a guest such as Whitbreads Scarlet Lady, decent wines and malt whiskies, children in eating area and restaurant; tables in prettily planted garden, handy for Cardingmill Valley (NT) and Long Mynd *(Joan and Andrew Life, DC, Mike and Penny Sanders, DAV, Nigel Woolliscroft, Nick and Meriel Cox, Mr and Mrs Jones, LYM)*

☆ **Little Stretton** [Ludlow Rd], *Ragleth*: Comfortably worn-in bay-windowed lounge, huge inglenook in brick-and-tile-floored public bar, reasonably priced home-made standard food from sandwiches to steaks, friendly landlord, quick service, well kept Ansells Mild and Best, Marstons Pedigree, Woods Parish and guest beers, tables on lawn by tulip tree; children welcome, restaurant *(Nigel Woolliscroft, Andy and Gill Plumb, LYM)*

Longden [Longden Common; SJ4406], *Red Lion*: Well kept Burtonwood and occasional guest beers, snug with pool table, dominoes and cribbage, good value generous food inc children's, lots of space outside for families with weekend fun days *(Amanda Dauncey)*

Longdon upon Tern [SJ6215], *Tayluer Arms*: Big Millers Kitchen with good value bar food, Tetleys-related ales, children's area, piped music, jungle barn outside *(D Hanley)*

Loppington [B4397; SJ4729], *Dickin Arms*: Cosy two-bar pub with heavy beams, open fire, Bass, Wadworths and Youngers beers, good food inc good value Sun lunch, dining room *(D Hanley)*

☆ **Ludlow** [Church St, behind Buttercross; SO5174], *Church*: Comfortable banquettes, attractive prints and paintings, good value straightforward bar food (ploughman's or roast lunch only, Sun), well kept Courage-related and summer guest ales, prompt friendly service, no-smoking restaurant, quiet piped music; children allowed, open all day; comfortable bedrooms *(D Hanley, A E and P McCully, A G Roby, DKP, Rita Horridge, Mr and Mrs R J Phillips, LYM)*

☆ **Ludlow** [Bull Ring/Corve St], *Feathers*: Hotel famous for glorious timbered facade, striking inside with Jacobean panelling and carving, period furnishings; you may be diverted to a humbler but tastefully refurbished side bar for the good sandwiches and other decent bar food, or a casual drink – well kept Flowers Original and Wadworths 6X; efficient pleasant service, restaurant, good parking; comfortable bedrooms, not cheap *(D Hanley, Gwen and Peter Andrews, Lawrence Pearse, LYM)*

☆ **Ludlow** [Broadgate/Lower Bridge St – bottom of Broad St], *Wheatsheaf*: Wide range of good value food inc interesting dishes and cheap Mon/Tues steak nights in nicely furnished traditional 17th-c pub spectacularly built into medieval town gate;

well kept Bass, M & B and Ruddles County, choice of farm ciders, friendly owners, restaurant; attractive beamed bedrooms, warm and comfortable *(E W Lewcock, Mrs J Burgess)*

Madeley [Coalport Rd; SJ6904], *All Nations*: Spartan but friendly one-bar pub which has been brewing its own distinctive well priced pale ale for many decades, in the same family since the 1930s; good value lunchtime sandwiches, handy for Blists Hill *(Pete Baker)*; [Cuckoo Oak Roundabout], *Cuckoo Oak*: Reasonably priced food, Banks's ale *(Dave Braisted)*

☆ **Munslow** [B4368 Much Wenlock—Craven Arms; SO5287], *Crown*: Very wide and imaginative choice of generous good value home-made food with al dente veg in traditional old country local, mix of furnishings in warm and friendly beamed lounge with flagstones, stripped stone, good open fire and friendly dog; small snug, games room; its own reasonably priced beer and others kept well; children welcome, open all day summer *(Wayne Brindle, Mrs Jupp, Judy and Jerry Hooper)*

Neenton [B4364 Bridgnorth—Ludlow; SO6488], *Pheasant*: Charming welcoming village pub, well kept real ale, good reasonably priced food, open fires in panelled lounge; restaurant *(R J Seaward)*

☆ **Nesscliffe** [A5 Shrewsbury—Oswestry; SJ3819], *Old Three Pigeons*: Very popular for very friendly staff, Whitbreads-related ales, coffee all day, log fires, restaurant; Russian tank and lots of other used military hardware outside, also plenty of seats; opp Kynaston Cave, good cliff walks *(Lawrence Bacon, David Warrellow, Martin and Penny Fletcher, D Hanley, K H Frostick)*

☆ **Newcastle** [B4368 Clun—Newtown; SO2582], *Crown*: Cheerful and friendly, with good value usual bar food in quite spacious lounge bar with log fire and piped music, lively locals' bar with darts, pool and so forth in games room, well kept Bass and Worthington BB, decent wines, friendly great dane called Bruno; tables outside; charming well equipped bedrooms, attractive walks *(J C Green, DC, Nigel Woolliscroft, LYM)*

☆ **Newport** [Chetwynd End (A41 N); SJ7519], *Bridge*: Good service, tasty reasonably priced simple home-cooked food and well kept Bass in small, cosy and friendly 17th-c black and white local with small separate restaurant; reasonably priced bedrooms *(A D Marsh)*

☆ **Northwood** [SJ4634], *Horse & Jockey*: Friendly low-beamed pub with good range of decent reasonably priced food, well kept beer, good friendly service, lots of horse and jockey memorabilia; play area *(Myke and Nicky Crombleholme)*

Oswestry [Willow St; SJ2929], *Butchers Arms*: Beams, nooks and crannies, real ales inc guest, exotic bottled beers, good cheap food; young end with pool table etc *(Paddy Moindrot)*

Picklescott [SO4399], *Bottle & Glass*: Out-of-the-way country pub, pleasant bar with open fire, good range of food, well kept Flowers, friendly service; bedrooms *(D E P and I D Hughes, J R Smylie)*

☆ **Pipe Gate** [A51 Nantwich—Stone; SJ7441], *Chetwode Arms*: Friendly comfortably refurbished family pub with wide choice of good food in bar and attractively priced carvery restaurant, no-smoking area, pleasant efficient staff, Tetleys-related and interesting guest beers, open fire; play area *(D Hanley)*

Queens Head [A5 SE of Oswestry, towards Nesscliffe; SJ3427], *Queens Head*: Friendly staff, good food, good choice of ales inc guest beers; nice canal and country walks *(Pete McMahon)*

Rodington [SJ5914], *Bulls Head*: Village pub with well kept Burtonwood beers, reasonably priced generous meals inc traditional puddings *(M Joyner, D Hanley)*

☆ **Ryton** [SJ7603], *Fox*: Smart country pub, very friendly and relaxed, with comfortable lounge bar and dining area, extensive range of good food, lots of interesting pictures, friendly landlord; stunning views of surrounding hills *(Amanda Dauncey, R M Bloomfield)*

☆ **Shifnal** [High St; SJ7508], *White Hart*: Comfortable and good value olde-worlde half-timbered pub in pretty village, good range of interesting changing well kept ales, good promptly served standard food inc fresh veg, very welcoming staff *(W L G Watkins, Alan and Paula McCully)*

☆ **Shrewsbury** [Abbey Foregate], *M A D O'Rourkes Dun Cow Pie Shop*: Zany but homely decor, good range of good value food, friendly staff, welcoming atmosphere, lots of jugs hanging from ceiling, well kept Tetleys-related ales and Lumphammer; attractive timber-framed building *(D Hanley, Patrick and Mary McDermott, Dave Braisted, Michael Begley, David and Shelia, BB)*

☆ **Shrewsbury** [New St/Quarry Park; leaving centre via Welsh Bridge/A488 turn into Port Hill Rd], *Boat House*: Comfortably modernised pub in lovely position opp park by Severn, river views from long lounge bar, tables out on sheltered terrace and rose lawn; popular esp with younger people for ales such as Cains Formidable, Fullers London Pride, Jennings Cumberland, Morlands Old Speckled Hen, Theakstons XB, Timothy Taylors Landlord, Wadworths 6X, Whitbreads Castle Eden and a seasonal beer, good choice of food (some all day), friendly staff, children welcome, summer barbecues *(Alan Castle, D Hanley, John Hibberd, LYM)*

Shrewsbury, *Black Bull in Paradise*: Recently renamed and reopened, Tetleys and Theakstons, pictures, prints and bric-a-brac in connecting bar and lounge with end dance floor; piped music, fruit machines *(D Hanley)*; [16 Castle Gates], *Castle Vaults*: Friendly if worn old timbered local with eight changing mainly unusual ales such as Burton Bridge, Hanby Treacleminer, Hobsons and Ross Hartcliffe, good choice of wines and other drinks, good landlord; generous helpings of good food in adjoining Mexican restaurant, little roof garden with spiral staircase up towards castle; bedrooms good *(K Harvey, Richard Lewis, Ian Phillips)*; [Swan Hill/Cross Hill, nr old Square], *Coach & Horses*: Pine-panelled snug, pleasant bar and restaurant with carvery, well kept Bass and guest beers such as Marstons Pedigree and Timothy Taylors Landlord, good home-made food, attentive service; pretty flower boxes outside *(R M Bloomfield, D Hanley)*; [Dogpole], *Cromwells*: Pub with wine bar and restaurant, beers inc Ruddles and guests like Woods Special and Whistle Belly Vengeance (from Plymouth), good value food, speciality sandwiches, piped music *(D Hanley)*; [48 St Michaels St (A49 ½ mile N of stn)], *Dolphin*: Five different well kept ales changing each week; can be smoky, but cosy and interesting, with gas lighting, no music or machines *(K Harvey, Lloyd Bradley)*; [Mardol], *Kings Head*: Pleasant low-beamed timbered pub with well kept Bass, Highgate Mild, M & B Brew XI, Morlands Speckled Hen and Vaux Sampson, lunchtime food, interesting medieval painting uncovered on old chimney breast; open all day *(Richard Lewis, Alan and Paula McCully)*; [Wyle Cop], *Lion*: Grand largely 18th-c Forte inn with cosy oak-panelled bar and sedate series of high-ceilinged rooms opening off, obliging staff, Bass under light carbon dioxide blanket, reasonably priced bar food and bargain Sun lunches; children welcome; bedrooms comfortable *(R C Vincent, LYM)*; [Church St], *Loggerheads*: Guest beers such as Hardys & Hansons and Youngs Winter Warmer in four rooms, one filled entirely by single scrubbed wooden table; bar food, good lively atmosphere *(D Hanley)*; [Welshpool Rd, The Mount – just off Frankwell Island], *Old Bucks Head*: Quiet pub with Bass-related beers, food *(D Hanley)*; [Milk St, nr St Julians Craft Centre], *Old Post Office*: Big split-level pub with plenty of bric-a-brac and brass, bar food, Marstons ales; piped music *(D Hanley)*; [Mardol], *Pig & Truffle*: Spacious feel, with interesting woodwork, lots of pig pictures, spacious atmosphere, well kept Tetleys-related ales, good value interesting food, welcoming staff *(DAV, D Deas)*; [Smithfield Rd], *Proud Salopian*: Welcoming local with well kept changing ales such as Bass, Boddingtons, Burtonwood Mild, Cains, Hartleys XB, Morlands Old Speckled Hen and a Whitbreads seasonal beer; lunchtime food, darts, pool; open all day *(Richard Lewis)*; [Fish St], *Three Fishes*: Extensively refurbished heavy-beamed pub with massive choice of real ales such as Adnams Broadside, Bass, Brains SA, Boddingtons Mild, Burts Vectis Venom, Courage Directors, Eldridge Pope Thomas Hardy, Everards Tiger, Fullers London Pride and ESB, Jennings Sneck Lifter, Mansfield Old Baily, Ruddles County, Rymans Reserve, Theakstons XB, Whitbreads Trophy and Glorious Goldings, Woods Parish; bar food inc Sun lunch, juke box, open all day; now no smoking *(D Hanley, Neil Calver, Alain and Rose Foote)*; [Welshpool Rd (A458) outside city], *Welsh Harp*: Large lounge, dining area and restaurant, some cricket memorabilia, old advertisements in balcony, good quick food, Bass; pool, darts, bowling green *(D Hanley)*; [Wenlock Rd (car park London Rd)], *White Horse*: Newly renovated Big Steak pub, usual food inc daily specials, real ales such as Tetleys and Harveys, pleasant friendly staff *(Ian Phillips)*

☆ **Stiperstones** [village signed off A488 S of Minsterley – OS Sheet 126 map ref 364005; SO3697], *Stiperstones*: A good find, open all day, with good value simple food inc vegetarian all day too; welcoming little modernised lounge bar with comfortable leatherette wall banquettes, lots of brassware on ply-panelled walls, well kept Woods Parish, pleasant service, darts in plainer public bar, maybe unobtrusive piped music; restaurant, tables outside, good walking nearby *(Colin Laffan, BB)*

Telford [Long Lane (A442); SJ6710], *Bucks Head*: Hotel bar with well kept Tetleys-related ales, good quick food inc children's and good value Sun lunch, family eating area and restaurant; piped music; bedrooms *(D Hanley)*

Tibberton [SJ6820], *Sutherland Arms*: Village local with pool in lively young left-hand bar, more sedate lounge on right, newly extended restaurant at back; food inc imaginative dishes and various steaks *(Adrian Zambardino, Debbie Chaplin)*

☆ **Tilley** [just S of Wem; SJ5128], *Raven*: Well kept dining pub, bright, clean and attractive, with very good service and food, separate restaurant *(Richard J Holloway)*

☆ **Tong** [A41 towards Newport, just beyond village; SJ7907], *Bell*: Reliable reasonably priced food inc children's and good value Sun lunch in friendly and efficient Milestone Tavern dining pub, well kept Banks's and Marstons Pedigree, olde-worlde stripped brickwork, big family room, dining room, unobtrusive piped music, no dogs; pleasant back conservatory, big garden, attractive countryside nr Weston Park *(Mr and Mrs D T Deas, Michael and Margaret Norris, R M Bloomfield, Jean and Douglas Troup, M Joyner, the Monday Club)*

Trench [Trench Rd; SJ6913], *Duke of York*: Greenalls pub with big split-level lounge, big bar with pinball, pool, darts and piped music; bar food inc Sun lunches *(D Hanley)*

Uckington [B5061; old A5 E of Atcham; SJ5810], *Horseshoes*: Decent big Brewers Fayre pub with Whitbreads-related ales, children's eating area and play area *(D Hanley, M Joyner)*

Upper Ludstone [A454/B4176; SO8095], *Royal Oak*: Interesting collection of caps behind the bar, food inc fine cold pork pie; Banks's beer *(Dave Braisted)*

☆ **Upton Magna** [Pelham Rd; SJ5512], *Corbet Arms*: Good value cheap food and well kept

Banks's ales in big L-shaped lounge bar with armchairs by log fire; darts and juke box in smaller public bar, friendly staff; handy for Attingham Park (NT), busy at weekends *(J and P Maloney, Paul Carter)*

Wentnor [SO3893], *Crown*: 16th-c dining pub (all tables may be reserved) with popular home-made food, well kept Boddingtons, Morlands Old Speckled Hen and Woods Shropshire Lad, good range of malt whiskies, big log fire, very friendly spaniel; tables outside; four good bedrooms, fine views, caravan and camp site *(Mike and Penny Sanders)*

Weston Heath [SJ7713], *Plough*: Purple decor, sensibly priced food, Ansells *(Dave Braisted)*

☆ Whitchurch [St Marys St; SJ5341], *Old Town Hall Vaults*: Good value promptly served home-cooked lunchtime food in attractive and civilised 18th-c pub, well kept Marstons Bitter and Pedigree, cheerful service; piped light classics – birthplace of Sir Edward German *(Roger Reeves, M Joyner, Sue Holland, David Webster)*

Whittington [A495 Ellesmere rd; just off A5; SJ3331], *Olde Boot*: Good value generous food and charming staff in comfortable pub attractively placed by 13th-c castle; bedrooms *(W L G Watkins)*

☆ Woofferton [A49 Shrewsbury—Leominster; SO5269], *Salwey Arms*: Well kept Bass and Tetleys, good food in bars and restaurant, welcoming efficient service *(Phil and Carol Byng, David Holman)*

☆ Woore [London Rd (A51); SJ7342], *Falcon*: Huge choice of impressively presented generous fresh food in plain roadside building with good friendly service even when busy, well kept Marstons, interesting prints; dining room more comfortable for eating than bars; nr Bridgemere garden centre *(Paul and Gail Betteley, D Hanley, Mr and Mrs D T Deas)*

Yockleton [SJ4010], *Yockleton Arms*: Consistently good food at competitive prices, good friendly service, well kept Boddingtons, small but well chosen wine list *(Dr S J Shepherd, J B Oakley)*

***Please* keep sending us reports. We rely on readers for news of new discoveries, and particularly for news of changes – however slight – at the fully described pubs. No stamp needed: *The Good Pub Guide*, FREEPOST TN1569, Wadhurst, E Sussex TN5 7BR.**

Somerset and Avon

The local government reorganisation planned for summer 1996 affects this chapter more than most. The county of Avon, which in previous editions we have included in the Somerset chapter, is to be largely reabsorbed into Somerset – more or less as things were before the last reorganisation 20 years ago. So most pubs in what used to be Avon will now be in Somerset, and will continue to be found in this chapter. However, that part of Avon roughly north of Bath and Bristol is to be absorbed into Gloucestershire; all the main entries and Lucky Dip pubs in that area – quite a number – will now be found in the Gloucestershire chapter instead. Despite these 'defections', this chapter still includes a mass of really good pubs, the numbers swollen this year by some particularly interesting new main entries: the civilised Horse & Groom at East Woodlands (really well presented good food), the cottagey and relaxed Kingsdon Inn at Kingsdon (good food here too), the very friendly and unusual old Talbot in the charming village of Mells, and the Full Moon at Rudge – brought gently upmarket while keeping considerable character. Other pubs currently doing specially well here include the cheerful old Globe at Appley (good interesting food), the Ashcott Inn at Ashcott (decent food in pleasant surroundings), the warmly friendly Malt Shovel at Bradley Green, the charming Strode Arms at Cranmore (an excellent dining pub), the New Inn at Dowlish Wake (seems better and better each year – gains a star award this year), the friendly Hood Arms at Kilve, the Royal Oak at Luxborough (one of the West Country's real pub gems), the consistently very enjoyable Notley Arms at Monksilver, and the Rose & Crown at Stoke St Gregory (not haute cuisine, but such very popular honest food that this year it gains a Food Award, and is our choice as Somerset Dining Pub of the Year). The comfortable and atmospheric back bar of the Luttrell Arms in Dunster (new manageress) has been an enjoyable surprise for many readers, considering this is a Forte hotel rather than a pub; at the other end of the scale, the wonderfully unchanging Tuckers Grave at Faulkland and the idiosyncratic and almost equally unspoilt Rose & Crown at Huish Episcopi score very highly for individuality. Congratulations to the charming Royal Oak at Winsford, up and running again after meticulous restoration following a bad fire and almost worse water damage. In the Lucky Dip section at the end of the chapter, pubs showing strongly in recent months include the Lamb in Axbridge, Crown at Bathford, Red Cow at Brent Knoll, Fitzhead Inn at Fitzhead, Hope & Anchor at Midford, Ship in Porlock, Greyhound at Staple Fitzpaine, Masons Arms in Taunton, both West Pennard entries and Rest & Be Thankful at Wheddon Cross. As we have inspected most of these we can give them a clear thumbs-up. There's a massive choice in Bristol, though not so many really outstanding pubs in Bath as such a fine city deserves. Drinks prices in the area are below the national average, especially in pubs getting their beers from the region's smaller breweries. The cheapest places we found were the Fox & Badger at Wellow (a locally supplied free house) and the White Hart at Trudoxhill (brewing its own good beers). Quite a few rewarding local beers to look out for include Butcombe, Cotleigh, Exmoor, Oakhill and – an increasing presence – Smiles.

APPLEY ST0621 Map 1

Globe

Hamlet signposted from the network of back roads between A 361 and A38, W of B3187 and W of Milverton and Wellington; OS sheet 181 map ref 072215

This is the kind of friendly old place where the licensees remember you from your last visit. It's full of cheerful character, and although the food is very good indeed, the locals like to come here for a drink and a chat and discuss the cricket and skittles teams. A stone-flagged entry corridor leads to a serving hatch from where Cotleigh Tawny and Barn Owl are served on handpump, and they have farmhouse cider made in a neighbouring village. The simple beamed front room is relaxed and chatty, with benches and a built-in settle, bare wood tables on the brick floor, and pictures of magpies. What used to be a pool room at the back is now used mainly for eating, while a further room has easy chairs and other more traditional ones; darts, shove-ha'penny, and alley skittles. Good generously served bar food might include filled rolls (from £1.15), good home-made soup (£2.25), mushrooms in cream, garlic and horseradish (£3.25), ploughman's (from £3.95), a light cold egg pancake filled with prawns, celery and pineapple in marie rose sauce (£4.75), home-made steak and kidney pie in stout or spinach and pasta with mushrooms, sweetcorn, walnuts and cream topped with melted stilton (£5.95), fresh salmon with chive, white wine and cream sauce (£7.95), steaks (from £7.95), breast of local chicken stuffed with pine nuts, bacon, raisins and apricots and served with a madeira sauce (£8.95), and puddings like home-made treacle tart or hot banana pancake (from £2.75); children's dishes (£3.25), and popular Sunday roast (£5.25). The restaurant is no-smoking. Seats, climbing frame and swings outside in the garden; the path opposite leads eventually to the River Tone. ***(Recommended by R V Ford, S G N Bennett, Mr and Mrs T J Rigby, G S and E M Dorey, John Hazel, H and D Cox, John A Baker, Pete and Rosie Flower, Patrick Freeman, S G N Bennett)***

Free house ~ Licensees A W and E J Burt, R and J Morris ~ Real ale ~ Meals and snacks (till 10) ~ Restaurant (not Sun evening) ~ (01823) 672327 ~ Children in eating area of bar ~ Open 11-3, 6.30-11; closed Mon lunchtime, except bank holidays

ASHCOTT ST4337 Map 1

Ashcott Inn

A39 about 6 miles W of Glastonbury

Popular at lunchtime, this attractively refurbished and pleasantly atmospheric old pub has stripped stone walls and beams in the bar, as well as good oak and elm tables, some interesting old-fashioned seats among more conventional ones, and a log-effect gas fire in its sturdy chimney. Bar food includes home-made soup (£1.75), sandwiches (from £1.95), home-made chicken liver pâté (£2.95), ploughman's (£3.95), oriental stir-fry (£4.75), cider-baked ham with two eggs (£4.95), salads (from £4.95 with a choice of dressing), beef in ale pie (£5.50), 6oz rump steak (£5.95), grilled plaice (£6.95), puddings like home-made fruit pie (£2.25), and good, thoughtful children's meals (£2.75). Well kept Butcombe Bitter, Flowers Original and a regularly changing guest on handpump; friendly service; darts, cribbage, dominoes, shove-ha'penny, fruit machine, alley skittles and piped music. Seats on the terrace, and a pretty walled garden which the no-smoking restaurant overlooks. ***(Recommended by Judith and Stephen Gregory, Neville Kenyon, Margaret Dyke, H Beck, R W Brooks, Dorothy and Leslie Pilson, Mr and Mrs Jones, Ralf Zeyssig, Bill and Beryl Farmer, Mark and Diana Bradshaw, E H and R F Warner, H F Cox, Brig J S Green)***

Heavitree (who no longer brew) ~ Managers Tony and Bernice Massey ~ Real ale ~ Meals and snacks ~ Restaurant (not Sun evening) ~ (01458) 210282 ~ Well behaved children in eating area of bar and in restaurant ~ Open 11-11; 11-3, 5.30-11 in winter

nr ASHILL ST3217 Map 1

Square & Compass

Windmill Hill; turn left off A358 when see Stewley Cross Garage on a side road

From the upholstered window seats in this nicely remote pub you look over the rolling pastures around Neroche Forest; there's other comfortable seating in the cosy little bar (with extra room for eating), and an open fire in winter. Good hearty bar food includes sandwiches, home-made soup, filled baked potatoes, ploughman's, mixed salami platter (£4.50), sweet and sour quorn (£4.95), tagliatelle with a mozzarella and sun-dried tomato sauce (£5.75), lamb and aubergine harrissa (£5.95), and swordfish steak with balsamic dressing (£7.50); good daily specials, children's menu, and Sunday roast. They have occasional themed food and music evenings, such as Italian, Irish or Spanish, and a well liked fish and chip evening on Thursday. Well kept Bass, Boddingtons, Exmoor Bitter, Flowers Original, and Whitbreads Fuggles on handpump; darts, shove ha'penny, cribbage, dominoes and piped music. Outside on the grass are picnic tables and a good children's play area with badminton and volleyball. There's a touring caravan site. *(Recommended by Mr and Mrs Westcombe, M E Wellington, Howard Clutterbuck, John A Barker, Helen Taylor, Ian, Janet and Joanne James, Linda and Brian Davis)*

Free house ~ Simon and Ginny Reeves ~ Real ale ~ Meals and snacks ~ (01823) 480467 ~ Children welcome ~ Occasional Fri evening music ~ Open 11.30-2.30, 6.30-11

BATH ST7565 Map 2

Old Green Tree

12 Green St

You can be sure of a warm welcome in this smart but unpretentious town pub, and the three oak-panelled little rooms are cosy and chatty with a thriving, genuinely old-fashioned atmosphere. The main bar can get quite busy (thanks to its size), but service always remains efficient, attentive and friendly; there's a comfortable lounge on the left as you go in, its walls decorated with wartime aircraft pictures, and the back bar is no-smoking. The big skylight lightens things up attractively. Good home-made bar food includes soup (£3), good ploughman's or large rolls (from £3.30), spaghetti with cheese, wine and herbs or tomato and parmesan (£4.50), home-made chicken liver and mushroom pâté with lots of garlic and brandy or super bangers and mash with a sauce of apple, cream, cider and whole grain mustard (£4.80), rare beef or seafood platters (£6), and daily specials; helpings are usually quite generous. There are usually five well kept beers on handpump at a time, with some emphasis on ales from local breweries such as Bridgwater, Cottage, Hardington Best, Uley, and Wickwar Brand Oak, and there's an eclectic choice of other drinks that includes some uncommon wines; they do a good Pimms in summer, fine bloody marys and hot punches in winter; no games or piped music. The gents', though good, are down steep steps. *(Recommended by Roger Wain-Heapy, Simon and Pie Barker, A Reimer, J Drew, K Neville-Rolfe, Dr and Mrs A K Clarke, Simon and Amanda Southwell, A Plumb, Bob Riley, Peter Churchill, Roger Huggins, Dave Irving, Ewan McCall, Tom McLean)*

Free house ~ Nick Luke ~ Real ale ~ Lunchtime meals and snacks (not Sun) ~ Children in eating area of bar if over 10 ~ Open 11-11; closed Sun lunchtime

> If we don't specify bar meal times for a main entry, these are normally 12-2 and 7-9; we do show times if they are markedly different.

BLAGDON ST5059 Map 2

New Inn

Church Street, off A368

From the picnic tables at the back of this neat and old-fashioned pub there are lovely views looking down over fields to wood-fringed Blagdon Lake, and to the low hills beyond. Inside, the two warm and individualistic rooms are spotless and full of character, and have some comfortable antique settles – one with its armrests carved as dogs – as well as little russet plush armchairs, mate's chairs and so forth. The ancient beams are decorated with gleaming horsebrasses and some tankards, big logs burn in both stone inglenook fireplaces, and decorations include advertisements for Slades now-defunct ales from Chippenham. There's a dog and a plump cat (no dogs allowed in the garden). Enjoyable lunchtime bar food includes home-made soup (£2), sandwiches (£2.25; weekday toasties £2.40), ploughman's (from £3.80), sausages (£3.60), filled baked potatoes (from £3.60), home-made steak and kidney pie (£4.40), seafood platter (£5.10), cold meat platters (from £5.95), daily specials, puddings (£2.50), children's meals (£2.75), and evening grills (from £6.75). Well kept Butcombe and Wadworths IPA and 6X on handpump; darts, shove-ha'penny, table skittles, dominoes, trivia, and piped music. The pub can get busy at weekends. No children. ***(Recommended by R W Brooks, Gwen and Peter Andrews Don Kellaway, Angie Coles, P H Roberts, Brig J S Green, Roger Huggins)***

Wadworths ~ Licensee M K Loveless ~ Real ale ~ Meals and snacks (till 9.45, 10.15 Fri and Sat) ~ (01761) 462475 ~ Open 11-2.30, 7-11; closed evenings 25/26 Dec

BRADLEY GREEN ST2538 Map 1

Malt Shovel

Pub signposted from A39 W of Bridgwater, near Cannington; though Bradley Green is shown on road maps, if you're booking the postal address is Blackmoor Lane, Cannington, BRIDGWATER, Somerset TA5 2NE; note that there is another different Malt Shovel on this main road, three miles nearer Bridgwater

Nicely tucked away in a remote hamlet, this warmly friendly family-run inn has rebuilt and enlarged the skittle alley this year. The homely no-frills main bar has various boating photographs, window seats, some functional modern elm country chairs and little cushioned casks, sturdy modern winged high-backed settles around wooden tables, and a black kettle standing on a giant fossil by the woodburning stove. There's also a tiny snug with white walls and black beams, a solid oak bar counter with a natural stone front, and red tiled floor. Tasty, straightforward food includes lunchtime sandwiches (from £1.40, crusty rolls £1.80) and ploughman's (from £3.10), as well as particularly good soup, pasta and spinach mornay (£3.55), smoked haddock cheesy bake (£3.85), filled baked potatoes (from £4.10), steak and kidney pie (£4.35), salads (from £4.40), gammon and egg (£4.70), fisherman's pie (£5.75), steaks (from £8.25), daily specials, and puddings; children's meals (from £1.95), and good breakfasts. Well kept Butcombe, John Smiths and guest on handpump, decent wines, and farm cider; piped radio and short mat bowls. The family room opens on to the garden, where there are picnic tables and a fishpond. The bedrooms fit in with the comfortable simplicity of the place. West of the pub, Blackmore Farm is a striking medieval building. ***(Recommended by Anthony Barnes, Paul Randall, Bruce Bird, Andy Thwaites, G W A Pearce, Maysie Thompson, Steve Dark, the Shinkmans, Joan Coleman, Dr Bill Baker, John A Barker, Douglas Allen)***

Free house ~ Licensees Robert and Frances Beverley ~ Real ale ~ Meals (not winter Sun evening) and lunchtime snacks ~ Restaurant (not winter Sun evenings) ~ (01278) 653432 ~ Children in family room and in restaurant ~ Open 11.30-2.30(3 Sat), 6.30(7 winter)-11 ~ Bedrooms: £21.50(£30B)/£30(£38B)

It's against the law for bar staff to smoke while handling food or drink.

BRISTOL ST5872 Map 2

Highbury Vaults £

St Michaels Hill, Cotham; main road out to Cotham from inner ring dual carriageway

The new licensee in this classic atmospheric cornerhouse has every intention of keeping the traditional atmosphere unchanged, with no noisy games or piped music. There's a cosy and crowded front bar with the corridor beside it leading through to a long series of little rooms with wooden floors, green and cream paintwork, old-fashioned furniture and prints, including lots of period Royal Family engravings and lithographs in the front room. It's one of the handful of pubs tied to the local Smiles brewery, so has all their beers well kept on handpump at attractive prices, as well as two monthy guests such as Badger Tanglefoot, Gales HSB, Reverend James, and Charles Wells Bombardier. Very cheap bar food includes filled rolls (60p), vegetable curry (£2.50), chilli con carne or broccoli and two-cheese bake (£2.60),pork and apple in cider (£2.70), and beef and walnut casserole (£2.80). Darts, dominoes and cribbage. It's very popular with students in term time, and can get busy at weekends. They keep a crossword dictionary for quieter moments. A nice terrace garden has tables built into a partly covered flowery arbour – not large, but a pleasant surprise for the locality; maybe summer barbecues. In early Georgian times it was a lock-up where condemned men ate their last meal, and some of the bars can still be seen on the windows. *(Recommended by C Smith, Dr and Mrs A K Clarke, Paul Carter, Gwen and Peter Andrews, Pat and John Millward, William Pryce, Paul Cartledge, Simon and Amanda Southwell)*

Smiles ~ Manager Bradd Francis ~ Real ale ~ Meals and snacks (12-2, 5.30-8.30; not Sat/Sun evenings) ~ (0117) 973 3203 ~ Open 12-11; closed 25/26 Dec

CATCOTT ST3939 Map 1

King William

Village signposted off A39 Street—Bridgwater

Handy for the M5, this neatly kept cottagey pub has a spacious bar with traditional furnishings such as kitchen and other assorted chairs, brown-painted built-in and other settles, window seats, stone floors with a rug or two, and Victorian fashion plates and other old prints. One of the big stone fireplaces has had its side bread oven turned into a stone grotto with kitsch figurines. Decent bar food includes sandwiches (from £1.50), home-made soup (£1.80), ploughman's (from £2.90), home-made steak and kidney pie, shepherd's pie or vegetable lasagne (£4.45), curry of the day (£4.60), smoked haddock in cider sauce (£4.65), pork chop glazed with apricots and honey (£5.50), trout with almonds (£6.75), steaks (from £7.95), lemon sole (£8.95), specials and puddings (from £1.85); friendly service, pleasant landlord. Eldridge Pope Dorchester, Royal Oak, and Hardy, and Palmers BB on handpump, with farm cider and a good range of malt whiskies; darts, fruit machine, and dominoes. A large extension at the back includes a skittle-alley and a glass-topped well. *(Recommended by Adrian M Kelly, John A Barker, Ted George, Jonathan and Amanda Checkley)*

Free house ~ Licensee Michael O'Riordan ~ Real ale ~ Meals and snacks (till 10) ~ (01278) 722374 ~ Children in eating area of bar ~ Open 11.30-3, 6-11

CHURCHILL ST4560 Map 1

Crown

Skinners Lane; in village, turn off A368 at Nelson Arms

Full of unspoilt charm and friendliness, this rural cottage is not for those who like their comforts more on the modern side – as they may feel a little out of place. The only noise is likely to be the low chatter of other customers (or maybe the piano), and the only game you're likely to come across is dominoes. Many people come just for the beer, as there's a constantly changing range of well kept ones such as Bass, Butcombe, Eldridge Pope Hardy, Greene King Abbot, Morlands Old Speckled Hen and Palmers IPA all tapped from casks at the back, along with a nice light but well hopped bitter brewed for the pub by Cotleigh; also a range of country wines, and local Axbridge wine. The small and local stone-floored and cross-beamed room on the right has a wooden window seat, an unusually sturdy settle, and built-in wall benches; the left-hand room has a slate floor, and some steps past the big log fire in a big stone fireplace lead to more sitting space. Generously served bar food includes a good home-made soup (in winter, £2), rare beef sandwich (£2.50), a good ploughman's, various casseroles (from £3.50-£5.50), and chilli con carne (£3.95). They can be busy at weekends, especially in summer. There are garden tables on the front and a smallish but pretty back lawn with hill views; the Mendip Morris Men come in summer. Good walks nearby. *(Recommended by Derek and Sylvia Stephenson, Pete Yearsley, M W Turner, Mr and Mrs J Brown, Roger Wain-Heapy, A C Stone, P H Roberts, Sally Pidden, Simon and Amanda Southwell, David Holloway, Dr and Mrs B D Smith, Peter Lecomber, William Price, Pat and John Millward)*

Free house ~ Licensee Tim Rogers ~ Real ale ~ Lunchtime meals and snacks ~ (01934) 852995 ~ Children in eating area of bar ~ Open 11.30-3.30, 5.30-11

CLAPTON IN GORDANO ST4773 Map 2

Black Horse

4 miles from M5 junction 19; A369 towards Portishead, then B3124 towards Clevedon; in N Weston opp school turn left signposted Clapton, then in village take second right, maybe signed Clevedon, Clapton Wick

This is an excellent stop from the M5, and the little flagstoned front garden is exceptionally pretty in summer with a mass of flowers in tubs, hanging baskets and flowerbeds; there are some old rustic tables and benches, with more to one side of the car park and in the secluded children's play area with its sturdy wooden climber, slide, rope ladder and rope swing. Paths from here lead up Naish Hill or along to Cadbury Camp. Inside this 14th-c pub, the partly flagstoned and partly red-tiled main room has a relaxed, friendly atmosphere, pleasant window seats, winged settles and built-in wall benches around narrow, dark wooden tables, amusing cartoons and photographs of the pub, and a big log fire with stirrups and bits on the mantlebeam. A window in an inner snug is still barred from the days when this room was the petty-sessions gaol; high-backed settles – one a marvellous carved and canopied creature, another with an art nouveau copper insert reading East, West, Hame's Best – lots of mugs hanging from its black beams, and plenty of little prints and photographs. There's also a simply furnished children's room, just off the bar, with high-backed corner settles and a gas fire; darts, dominoes, cribbage, fruit machine, and piped music. Good quickly-served bar food includes filled rolls and french sticks (from £1.75), ploughman's (from £3), and various changing hot dishes like sausage, bacon and mushroom casserole or garlic and coriander chicken (from £3.75). Well kept Courage Best, Marstons Pedigree, and Wadworths 6X on handpump or tapped from the cask; farm cider. *(Recommended by Alan and Heather Jacques, Jack and Philip Paxton, WHBM, P A Neate, Heather and Howard Parry, Jerry and Alison Oakes)*

Courage ~ Tenants Nicholas Evans and Alfonso Garcia ~ Real ale ~ Lunchtime meals and snacks (not Sun) ~ (01275) 842105 ~ Children in family room ~ Live music Mon evenings ~ Open 11-3, 6-11; 11-11 Fri/Sat

COMBE HAY ST7354 Map 2

Wheatsheaf

Village signposted from A367 or B3110 S of Bath

Perched on the side of a steep wooded valley, this busy country pub has three dovecotes built into the walls, tables on the spacious sloping lawn looking down to the church and ancient manor stables, and good nearby walks. The pleasantly old-fashioned rooms have low ceilings, brown-painted settles, pews and rustic tables, a very high-backed winged settle facing one big log fire, old sporting and other prints, and earthenware jugs on the ledges of the little shuttered windows. Popular bar food includes home-made soup (£2.50), ploughman's (from £3.90), game terrine (£3.95), garlic mushrooms or quiche (£4.50), hot baked ham (£5), pheasant or venison (£7.50), sea bass (£8.95), daily specials like chicken livers (£4.75) or rack of lamb (£8.75), and puddings (£2.75). Well kept Courage Best and a guest like Wadworths 6X tapped from the cask; friendly staff (and dog). *(Recommended by Howard Clutterbuck, Ron Gentry, Roger Wain-Heapy, Kevin and Tracey Stephens, Steve and Carolyn Harvey, Dr and Mrs A K Clarke, Michael and Janet Hepworth, R M Bloomfield, Paul Weedon, John Hazel)*

Free house ~ Licensee M G Taylor ~ Real ale ~ Meals and snacks ~ Restaurant ~ (01225) 833504 ~ Children in eating area of bar and in restaurant ~ Open 11-2.30, 6.30-11

COMPTON MARTIN ST5457 Map 2

Ring o' Bells

A368 Bath—Weston

Perhaps at its best when the summer crowds have gone, the snugly traditional front part of this country pub has a wonderfully cosy feel, rugs on the flagstones, and inglenook seats right by the log fire. In summer, you may prefer to go up the step to a cool and spacious carpeted back part, with largely stripped stone walls and pine tables. Good value food remains the same as last year: sandwiches (from £1.25), soup (£1.65), ploughman's (from £3.15), lasagne or mushroom, broccoli and almond tagliatelli (£3.95), grilled ham and eggs (£4.20), generous mixed grill, beef in beer (£4.95), daily specials such as lamb and apricot casserole or skate wings (£4.95), and children's meals (or helpings). Well kept Bass, Butcombe, John Smiths, Wadworths 6X and guest on handpump, farm cider, and country wines; friendly helpful service, maybe quiet piped classical music. The public bar has darts, shove-ha'penny, dominoes and cribbage, and a spacious, no-smoking family room has table skittles, trivia, and bar billiards just outside; a rocking-horse, toys, and baby-changing facilities. There's a decent-sized garden with fruit trees, sturdy tables, and a good play area, and it's not far from Blagdon Lake and Chew Valley Lake. No dogs. *(Recommended by Roger and Jenny Huggins, Tom Evans, E H and R F Warner, Jack and Philip Paxton, R L W and Dizzy, Gwyneth and Salvo Spadaro-Dutturi, A R and B E Sayer)*

Free house ~ Licensee Roger Owen ~ Real ale ~ Meals and snacks (till 10 Fri/Sat) ~ Children in eating area of bar and in no-smoking family room ~ (01761) 221284 ~ Open 11.30-3, 6-11

CRANMORE ST6643 Map 2

Strode Arms ★ Ⓨ 🍷

West Cranmore; signposted with pub off A361 Frome—Shepton Mallet

Pretty views through the stone-mullioned windows in this early 15th-c former farmhouse look down to the village duckpond. But it's the food that people really like here – we've decided to give it a Food Award this year: filled french bread (from £2), soup (£2.20), very good egg mayonnaise with prawns, capers, smoked trout, anchovy and asparagus tips (£3.75), lovely scallops and bacon (£4.85), excellent home-made steak and kidney with bubble and squeak pie or ham and eggs (£4.95), salmon fishcakes (£7), roast rack of lamb roasted with rosemary (£8.25), daily specials such as Greek meatballs with spicy tomato sauce (£5.75), cider-baked ham (£5.95), vegetarian strudel (£6.25), and puddings like spicy pear ginger bread or oven-baked rice pudding with caramel and almonds (from £2.20); Sunday roasts; friendly service. The smartly relaxed bar has charming country furnishings, a grandfather clock on the flagstones, fresh flowers and pot plants, remarkable old locomotive engineering drawings and big black-and-white steamtrain murals in a central lobby, good bird prints, newspapers to read, and lovely log fires in handsome fireplaces. Well kept Flowers IPA, Marstons Pedigree and Wadworths 6X on handpump, an interesting choice of decent wines by the glass and lots more by the bottle, farm cider, and quite a few liqueurs and ports. There's a front terrace with some benches and a back garden. On the first Tuesday of each month, there's a vintage car meeting, and the pub is handy for the East Somerset Light Railway. *(Recommended by Roger Wain-Heapy, Kevin and Tracey Stephens, Mrs C Blake, John Wooll, Tom Evans, Ted George, A D Sherman, R V Ford, M G Hart, Donald Godden, John Hazel, A Nunnerley, John and Tessa Rainsford, Pat and Robert Watt, Stephen Brown, D B Dockray, David Wright, R J Walden, David and Ann Pert, David Holloway, P M Lane)*

Free house ~ Licensees Rodney and Dora Phelps ~ Real ale ~ Meals and snacks (till 10 Fri/Sat) ~ Cottagey restaurant ~ (01749) 880450 ~ Children in restaurant ~ Open 11.30-2.30, 6.30-11; closed Sun evening Oct-Feb

CROSCOMBE ST5844 Map 2

Bull Terrier

A371 Wells—Shepton Mallet

New licensees have taken over this handsome building, one of the county's oldest inns. The neat lounge ('Inglenook') bar has cushioned wooden wall seats and wheelback chairs around neat glossy tables, pictures on its white walls, attractively moulded original beams, a log-effect gas fire in a big stone fireplace with a fine iron fireback, and a red carpet on its flagstone floor. A communicating ('Snug') room has more tables with another log-effect gas fire, and there's a third in the parquet-floored 'Common Bar', by the local noticeboard; also, a family room. Bar food includes sandwiches (from £1.40), soup (£1.95), ploughman's (from £2.75), pancakes stuffed with spinach and peanuts (£4.95), lasagne (£5.25), home-made steak and kidney pie (£5.35), trout with almonds (£6.75), steaks (from £9.95), home-made specials, and puddings such as apple strudel or butterscotch and walnut fudge cake. Well kept Butcombe, Greene King Abbot, Hook Norton Old Hookey, and Smiles Best, Theakstons XB, and Wadworths 6X on handpump; dominoes, chess, draughts, shove ha'penny and cribbage. At the back is an attractive walled garden. There's a two-mile footpath to Bishop's Palace moat in Wells. *(Recommended by James Macrae, Colin and Ann Hunt, R L W and Dizzy, Roger Wain-Heapy, A D Sherman, Tom Evans, Brig J S Green, Kevin and Tracey Stephens, Stephen Boot, Revd A Nunnerley; more reports on the new regime, please)*

Free house ~ Licensees Barry and Ruth Vidler ~ Real ale ~ Meals and snacks (not winter Sun evenings or all day Mon 1 Oct-1 Apr) ~ (01749) 343658 ~ Children in no-smoking family room ~ Open 12-2.30, 7-11; closed on Mondays from 1 Oct to 1 Apr ~ Bedrooms: £30B/£48B

DOULTING ST6443 Map 2

Poachers Pocket

Follow Chelynch signpost off A361 in village, E of Shepton Mallet

It's worth getting to this warmly welcoming and friendly 17th-c pub early to enjoy the popular, generously served meals. The modernised bar has some black beams, a crackling log fire in the end stripped-stone wall, one or two settles, small wheelback or captain's chairs, gundog pictures on the white walls, and flagstones by the bar counter (though it's mainly carpeted). Generous helpings of food include soup (£1.70), sandwiches and rolls (from £1.50), ploughman's (from £2.90), home-made quiche or cauliflower cheese (£4.10), tasty home-made steak and kidney pie (£4.25), home-cooked ham and egg or lasagne (£4.50), poacher's pie (pheasant, rabbit and venison, £6.10), fresh trout (£6.50), steaks (from £8.50), and puddings (from £1.80). Well kept Butcombe Bitter, Oakhill, Wadworths 6X and a guest on handpump, and local farm cider; darts, shove-ha'penny, cribbage, dominoes. There's a garden at the back, with pleasant views of the surrounding countryside. They don't do bedrooms, but are happy to help with the good farmhouse B & B next door. *(Recommended by A D Sherman, Kevin and Tracey Stephens, Dr and Mrs J Hampton, Bob Smith, W F C Phillips, R J Walden)*

Free house ~ Licensees Ken and Stephanie Turner ~ Real ale ~ Meals and snacks (till 10) ~ (01749) 880220 ~ Children in eating area of bar ~ Open 11.30-3, 6-11

DOWLISH WAKE ST3713 Map 1

New Inn ★ 🍴

Village signposted from Kingstone – which is signposted from old A303 on E side of Ilminster, and from A3037 just S of Ilminster; keep on past church – pub at far end of village

Over the ten years that the licensees have run this spotlessly kept village pub, readers have been consistently happy with the friendly welcome and reliably good food – indeed, for some, it's their favourite Somerset pub. Good value and efficiently served meals typically include sandwiches (from £1.45), ploughman's (from £2.75), Bellew sausage or omelettes (from £2.95), stuffed mushrooms £2.95), ham and egg (£3.75), vegetarian dishes like pasta (£3.25) or nut roast (£3.70), stir-fried liver (4.25), chicken tikka masala (£4.35) and a daily special such as steak and kidney pudding, with evening à la carte dishes like butterfly prawns (£3.25), Swiss specialities such as raclette (cheese and baked potatoes, £5.25) or a steak fondue (£7.95), duck mandarin (£9.75), paella (£9.95), beef fillet stuffed with stilton in mushroom and wine sauce (£10.25), and a choice of puddings like excellent lemon brûlée or coconut sorbet; no credit cards. The bar's dark beams are liberally strung with hop bines, and there's a stone inglenook fireplace with a woodburning stove, and old-fashioned furnishings that include a mixture of chairs, high-backed settles, and attractive sturdy tables. Well kept Butcombe, Theakstons Old Peculier and Wadworths 6X on handpump; a decent choice of whiskies, and Perry's cider. This comes from just down the road, and the thatched 16th-c stone cider mill is well worth a visit for its collection of wooden bygones and its liberal free tastings (you can buy the half-dozen different ciders in old-fashioned earthenware flagons as well as more modern containers; it's closed on Sunday afternoons). In a separate area they have darts, shove-ha'penny, dominoes, cribbage, table skittles as well as alley skittles and a fruit machine; maybe piped music. In front of the stone pub there's a rustic bench, tubs of flowers and a sprawl of clematis; the pleasant back garden has flower beds and a children's climbing frame, and dogs are allowed here. *(Recommended by Galen Strawson, Mr and Mrs D V Morris, Margaret and Nigel Dennis, Nigel Wilkinson, Douglas Allen, Howard Clutterbuck, Beverley James, C P Scott-Malden, Mrs J Ashdown, Major and Mrs Warrick, Revd A Nunnerley, Guy Consterdine, John and Fiona Merritt, Pauline Bishop, TOH, Janet Pickles, Desmond and Pat Morris, David and Michelle Hedges)*

Free house ~ Licensees Therese Boosey and David Smith ~ Real ale ~ Meals and snacks (till 10; not Sun evening Nov-Mar) ~ (01460) 52413 ~ Children in no-smoking family room ~ Open 11-3, 6-11

DUNSTER SS9943 Map 1

Luttrell Arms 🛏

A396

A new licensee has taken over this rather civilised and imposing old place – much in keeping with the character of the old town and castle. The comfortable back bar is the place to head for, with a relaxed and pleasant atmosphere, high beams hung with bottles, clogs and horseshoes, a stag's head and rifles on the walls above old settles and more modern furniture, and friendly, attentive staff. Ancient black timber uprights glazed with fine hand-floated glass, full of ripples and irregularities, separate the room from a small galleried and flagstoned courtyard. Promptly served bar snacks include home-made soup (£1.95), ploughman's (from £2.95), filled french sticks (from £3.25), macaroni cheese or all day breakfast (£4.50), steak and kidney pie (£5.75), daily specials and puddings (£2.25); imaginative evening meals, and Sunday lunch. Well kept Bass and Courage Directors on handpump; dominoes. In the gardens there are cannon emplacements dug out by Blake in the Civil War when – with Praise God Barebones and his pikemen – he was besieging the Castle for six months. The town, on the edge of Exmoor National Park, is pretty. *(Recommended by Mr and Mrs Hillman, David R Shillitoe, Peter and Joy Heatherley, H and D Payne, Neville Kenyon, G W Stevenson, B M Eldridge, Basil J S Minson, Michael and Harriet Robinson, John and Christine Vittoe, Jim and Maggie Cowell, Joan Olivier)*

Free house (Forte) ~ Manageress Margaret Coffey ~ Real ale ~ Meals and snacks ~ Restaurant ~ (01643) 821555 ~ Children in eating area of bar ~ Open 10.30-11 ~ Bedrooms: £75B/£95B

EAST LYNG ST3328 Map 1

Rose & Crown

A361 about 4 miles W of Othery

Warmly friendly and relaxed, this is a lovely place for a drink and a chat beside the winter log fire in its modernised old stone fireplace. The traditional open-plan lounge bar has beams, a corner cabinet of glass, china and silver, a court cabinet, a bow window seat by an oak drop-leaf table, copies of *Country Life*, and a relaxed, unchanging atmosphere. Generous helpings of decent, straightforward food include sandwiches (from £1.40), soup (£1.85), ploughman's (from £3), home-cooked ham and egg (£3.65), omelettes (from £4.10), Mexican bean pot or savoury vegetable crumble (£4.95), salads (from £4.95), trout (£5.60), steaks (from £9.15), mixed grill (£9.95), duckling in orange sauce (£10.75), daily specials, and puddings such as home-made sherry trifle (£2.45); pleasant waitress service. Well kept Butcombe and Eldridge Pope Royal Oak and Hardy on handpump; skittle alley and unobtrusive piped light music. The back garden (largely hedged off from the car park) is prettily planted and there are picnic tables. *(Recommended by A and J Tierney-Jones, Pete Yearsley, Richard Dolphin, Colin and Ann Hunt, Shirley Pielou, Stephen Brown, Brig J S Green, John and Tessa Rainsford)*

Free house ~ Licensee P J Thyer ~ Real ale ~ Meals and snacks (till 10) ~ Restaurant ~ (01823) 698235 ~ Children in restaurant ~ Open 11-2.30, 6.30-11; Bedrooms: £25B/£40B

EAST WOODLANDS ST7944 Map 2

Horse & Groom

Signed off Frome bypass off A361/B3092 junction

On the edge of the Longleat estate, this is a small and civilised pub serving particularly good food – though there's also a fine choice of real ales in the small pleasant bar on the left with its stripped pine pews and settles on dark flagstones: Adnams Best, Batemans XB, Butcombe Bitter, Fullers London Pride, Hook Norton, Shepherd Neame, and Wadworths 6X tapped from the cask. Good wines by the glass. The small comfortable lounge has an easy chair and settee around a coffee table, two small solid dining tables with chairs, a big stone hearth with a small raised grate, and a relaxed atmosphere (no piped music); there's also a big no-smoking dining conservatory. Very well presented food included filled home-made french bread (from £1.60), ploughman's (from £2.95), prawn and sweetcorn chowder (£3.50), lovely liver, bacon and onion (£4.75), broccoli and mushroom mornay or pasta carbonara (£4.80), smoked haddock topped with mozzarella (£5.50), and delicious cod with mussels and prawns (£6); five or six interesting vegetables are served separately on a side plate; helpful service. Shove-ha'penny, cribbage and dominoes. You can sit in the nice front garden at some picnic tables by five severely pollarded limes and there are attractive flower troughs and mini wheelbarrows filled with flowers; more seats behind the conservatory. The village is very quiet. *(Recommended by Pat and Robert Watt, Paul and Janette Adams)*

Free house ~ Licensee Timothy Gould ~ Real ale ~ Meals and snacks (not Sun evening, not Mon) ~ Restaurant (not Sun evening) ~ (01373) 462802 ~ Children in small lounge bar ~ Open 11.30-2.30(3 Sat), 6.30-11

EASTON IN GORDANO ST5276 Map 2

Rudgleigh

Martcombe Rd; 1 mile J19 M5; Easton in Gordano sign; stay on A369 – don't take village turnoff

Even when really busy, the atmosphere here remains happy and cheerful, and the staff are efficient and friendly. It's the food that people come for (usefully served all day) and there are masses of specials such as fresh faggots in onion gravy (£4.50), lamb's liver, bacon and onions or cold meat platter with chips and pickles (£4.75), three roasts and a home-made nut one or baked ham and cauliflower cheese (£4.95), whole grilled fresh plaice (£5.50), and peppered rump steak (£6.95), with home-made puddings such as apple crumble, Turkish delight gateau or jam roly poly (£2); half-helpings and half-price for children (or their own good menu from £1.85); also, filled rolls (from £1.55), home-made soup (£1.95), ploughman's (from £3.10), vegetable lasagne (£4.60), ham and egg (£4.75), home-made steak and kidney pie (£4.75), and steaks (from £6.50). Well kept Courage Best, Marstons Pedigree and Smiles Best on handpump. The main bar is divided into two smallish rooms, with the area on the right beyond a dividing wall set for food and decorated with jugs on beams, a delft shelf, and blue and white plates on cream walls; the lounge area has lots of toby jugs hanging from the beams, and brocaded wall benches and some red plush stools round shiny tables on the red flowery carpet. On the left of the entrance is another room with more jugs on beams that leads through to a big family dining room; fruit machine and piped music. The back garden has quite a few orderly picnic tables, a big timber climber and swings, and a post-and-rail fence onto the cricket pitch; there are more picnic tables by the busy road. *(Recommended by Tom Evans, Donald Godden, J and F Gowes, Vivienne and Brian Joyner, Nigel Gibbs)*

Courage ~ Lease: Michael and Joyce Upton ~ Real ale ~ Meals and snacks (11am-10pm – not all day Sun) ~ Restaurant ~ 01275 372363 ~ Children in family room ~ Open 11-11

EXEBRIDGE SS9224 Map 1

Anchor ⇦

B3222 S of Dulverton

Set in a peaceful spot beside the handsome three-arched bridge over the Exe, this inn is mentioned in R D Blackmore's *Lorna Doone*. There are well-spaced tables in the sheltered garden that look down over the river and the trout or salmon swimming gently upstream through its shallow waters. The pub has fishing rights and they can organise a number of other local sports. Inside, the main front bar has individually chosen tables and seats such as a big winged settle and a nice old library chair among more orthodox furnishings, some carpet on its floor tiles, Cecil Aldin hunting prints and Exmoor pictures above the stripped wooden dado, some hunting trophies, and a warm woodburning stove; piped music. Bar food includes good sandwiches (from £1.40), home-made soup (£1.95), filled baked potatoes (from £2.25), local pasty (£3.25), sausage, egg and chips (£3.50), omelettes (from £3.75), ploughman's (from £3.95), curry (£4.25), steak and kidney pie (£4.50), moussaka or lasagne (£5.50), broccoli and cream cheese bake (£5.95), local trout (from £6.50), 8oz rump steak (£8.95) and quite a wide choice of children's dishes (£2.35). There's a back games bar with darts, pool, shove-ha'penny, cribbage, dominoes, and trivia and two fruit machines divided by a flexiwall from a lounge bar with button-back leather chesterfields, modern oak tables and chairs, and french windows to the garden, which has a play area. Well kept John Smiths, Ruddles County, Ushers Best, and Websters Yorkshire (called 'Doone' here); alley skittles. *(Recommended by David R Shillitoe, John Evans, Clive Gilbert, Mr and Mrs Hillman, Elizabeth and Anthony Watts, Jed and Virginia Brown, John Hazel)*

Free house ~ Licensees John and Judy Phripp ~ Real ale ~ Meals and snacks (till 10) ~ Restaurant ~ (01398) 323433 ~ Children in eating area of bar ~ Open 11-3, 6-11 ~ Bedrooms: £35B/£60B

FAULKLAND ST7354 Map 2

Tuckers Grave £

A366 E of village

For many years, this wonderfully atmospheric little place has claimed the title of the smallest pub in the Guide. It's a warmly friendly, basic and homely cider house, and a flagstoned entry opens into a teeny unspoilt room with casks of well kept Bass and Butcombe Bitter on tap and Cheddar Valley cider in an alcove on the left. Two old cream-painted high-backed settles face each other across a single table on the right, and a side room has shove-ha'penny. There's a skittle alley and tables and chairs on the back lawn, as well as winter fires and maybe newspapers to read. Food is limited to sandwiches (75p) and ploughman's at lunchtime. *(Recommended by Roger Huggins, Tom McLean, Dave Irving, Ewan McCall, Pete Baker, Kevin and Tracey Stephens, Arthur and Annette Frampton, Jack and Philip Paxton, Pete Baker, J S Poulter, John and Phyllis Maloney, Pat and John Millward)*

Free house ~ Licensees Ivan and Glenda Swift ~ Real ale ~ Lunchtime snacks (not Sun) ~ (01373) 834230 ~ Children welcome ~ Open 11.30-3, 6-11

FRESHFORD ST7859 Map 2

Inn at Freshford

Village signed off B3108

Part of this pub's attraction is its quiet countryside position by an old stone bridge over the River Frome; you can sit at the many seats and enjoy the views over the valley from the pretty flower-filled gardens. The comfortably modernised and interestingly decorated bar has a relaxed atmosphere and well kept Bass, Ruddles County, and Ushers Summer Madness on handpump, and a decent wine list; part of the bar is no smoking; open fire, piped music. A huge daily changing choice includes good meals like sandwiches, home-made soup, around 40 main courses such as salmon in tarragon sauce (£6.50), oak-smoked chicken in Dijon sauce or pan-fried loin of pork (£6.95) and mini leg of lamb (£7.95), fillet steak, a dozen or so vegetarian dishes and lots of puddings; best to book. Good walks along the riverbank that leads to the Kennet & Avon canal. *(Recommended by Andrew Partington, Roger Wain-Heapy, Chris Downward, GSB, A D Sherman, Ron Gentry, R L W and Dizzy, Kevin and Tracey Stephens, Andrew Shore, Brig T I G Gray, Simon and Amanda Southwell, Peter Neate, Dennis and Joan Rouse, Brian Barefoot, Dave and Jules Tuckett and others)*

Courage ~ Lease: Stephen Turner ~ Real ale ~ Meals and snacks (till 10) ~ Restaurant (not Sun evening) ~ (01225) 722250 ~ Children welcome ~ Open 11-3, 6-11

HASELBURY PLUCKNETT ST4710 Map 1

Haselbury Inn

A3066 E of Crewkerne

The good food and atmosphere here are very much those of a dining pub rather than somewhere to drop in for a casual drink – though they keepa good range of well kept real ales tapped from the cask: Butcombe, Charles Wells Bombardier, Morlands Old Speckled Hen, Liquid Assets (Eldridge Pope) Potters Pride, Smiles Best, Teignworthy Reel Ale and Spring Tide, and Wadworths 6X; also, draft German lagers, a good choice of wines, and country wines. Bar food usually includes soup (£1.50), ploughman's (£3.50), filled baked potatoes or pizzas (from £4), lamb's kidney and bacon tagliatelli or seafood platter (£5.50), lemon sole (£8), charcoal-grilled steaks (from £9), quite a few daily specials, and puddings like apple strudel or treacle tart (from £2); the restaurant is no smoking – best to book at weekends; piped music. Plants and fresh or dried flowers in the windows, chintz armchairs and sofas around the fire and television set, and in one half candlelit wooden tables with unusually heavy red-cushioned cask seats. There are picnic tables in the garden. *(Recommended by B E Tarver, S G Brown, Rich and Pauline Appleton, Nigel Wilkinson, Guy Consterdine; more reports please)*

Free house ~ Licensee James Pooley ~ Real ale ~ Meals and snacks all day ~ Restaurant ~ (01460) 72488 ~ Children welcome ~ Open 12-3, 7-11; closed Mon

HINTON ST GEORGE ST4212 Map 1

Poulett Arms 🍷

Village signposted off A30 W of Crewkerne; and off Merriott road (declassified – former A356, off B3165) N of Crewkerne; take care – there is another pub of the same name a mile or so away, at a roundabout on the former A30

Friendly and cheerful new licensees have taken over this popular dining pub – and early reports from readers are very favourable. The larger dining room has plush chairs and a couple of high-backed settles, big black beams, stripped masonry, an imposing stone fireplace, a few pistols and brasses, and two cosy smaller rooms opening off – one with a big disused inglenook fireplace. Good bar food includes sandwiches or filled french bread (from £1.50), home-made soup (£2.50), ploughman's (from £3.75), omelettes (from £4.25), ham and egg (£4.50), meaty or vegetable lasagne (from £4.50), daily specials such as home-made steak and kidney pie (£5.50), fish of the day (from £6.95), poached salmon with lobster sauce (£7.45), and guinea fowl with cumberland sauce (£8.95), and children's dishes. Well kept Bass, Cotleigh Tawny, John Smiths, and changing guest beers on handpump, and a compact but carefully chosen wine list; cribbage, dominoes, maybe unobtrusive piped music. There's also a skittle alley with darts, and a friendly jack russell called Murphy. The prettily planted back garden at this bustling pub has some white tables under cocktail parasols, near a real rarity – a massive pelota wall. *(Recommended by JKW, Revd A Nunnerly, Mr and Mrs D V Morris, E M Clague, Jill Bickerton, Margaret and Nigel Dennis, Nigel Wilkinson, A Wood, Guy Consterdine, J Weeks, A E and P McCully)*

Free house ~ Licensees Sandy and Marian Lavelle ~ Real ale ~ Meals and snacks ~ Restaurant ~ (01460) 73149 ~ Children in eating area of bar ~ Open 11-3, 6.30-11

HUISH EPISCOPI ST4326 Map 1

Rose & Crown £

A372 E of Langport

Apart from a bit of sprucing up, this wonderfully unspoilt old cider house remains happily unchanged. It's been in the same family for over 120 years now and is known locally as Eli's, after the present landlady's father, who held the licence for 55 years (having taken over from his father-in-law – who also ran the place for 55 years). The atmosphere and character are determinedly unpretentious and warmly friendly, and there's no bar as such – to get a drink, you just walk into the central flagstoned still room and choose from the casks of well kept Bass, Boddingtons, and changing guests, or the wide choice of Somerset farm ciders (and local cider brandy) and country wines which stand on ranks of shelves all around (prices are very low); this servery is the only thoroughfare between the casual little front parlours with their unusual pointed-arch windows and genuinely friendly locals. Food is simple and cheap: generously filled sandwiches (from £1.30, toasted £1.60), soup (£1.50), beans on toast (£1.60), ploughman's (from £2.80) and vegetarian spinach and ricotta parcels (£3.25); good helpful service. Shove-ha'penny, chess, dominoes and cribbage, and a much more orthodox big back extension family room has darts, pool, trivia, juke box and a pin ball machine; skittle alley. There are tables in a garden outside, and a second enclosed garden with a children's play area. George the dog will welcome a bitch but can't abide other dogs. A beer festival is held in the adjoining field every September, and on some summer weekends you might find the pub's cricket team playing out here; good nearby walks. *(Recommended by Mrs C*

Blake, Mr and Mrs J Woodfield, Gwyneth and Salvo Spadaro-Dutturi, John Hazel, Pete Baker, Rich and Pauline Appleton, S G Brown, John Hazel, Bill Sharpe, R J Walden, John and Phyllis Maloney, John Sanders)

Free house ~ Licensee Eileen Pittard ~ Real ale ~ Snacks (any time during opening hours) ~ (01458) 250494 ~ Children welcome ~ Open 11.30-2.30, 5.30-11; all day Fri/Sat

KELSTON ST7067 Map 2

Old Crown

Bitton Road; A431 W of Bath

Carefully restored and genuinely preserved, the four small rooms in this atmospheric old place have beams strung with hops, interesting carved settles and cask tables on polished flagstones (all appealingly lit in the evenings by candlelight), logs burning in an ancient open range (there's another smaller, open range and a Victorian open fireplace – both with coal-effect gas fires), and lovely tableau photographs. Well kept Bass, Butcombe, Smiles Best, and Wadworths 6X and winter Old Timer on handpump; shove-ha'penny and dominoes. Lunchtime bar food includes home-made soup (£1.85), ploughman's (from £3.65), cottage pie (£4.70), ham and leek pie (£4.90), a daily vegetarian dish, beef and Guinness casserole (£5.90), steaks (from £8.95) and puddings like fruit crumble or sticky toffee pudding (£2.80); helpful service. Picnic tables under apple trees in the neat, sheltered back garden look out towards distant hills; you'd hardly believe you were just four miles from Bath's city centre. The car park is over quite a fast road. No children. *(Recommended by Gwen and Peter Andrews, James House, Jon Lyons, J S Rutter, Simon and Amanda Southwell, Dave and Jules Tuckett, Fiona Dick, A Plumb)*

Free house ~ Licensee Michael Steele ~ Real ale ~ Lunchtime meals and snacks (not Sun) ~ Restaurant (not Sun) ~ (01225) 423032 ~ Open 11.30-3, 5-11

KILVE ST1442 Map 1

Hood Arms

A39 E of Williton

The good food in this friendly and welcoming village inn is so popular that it's advisable to book a table beforehand. The menu might typically include sandwiches (from £1.20), home-made soup (£2.25), home-made pâté (£2.25), good ploughman's (£3.40), substantial salads (from £3.75), hot daily specials such as steak and kidney pie, aubergine bake, haddock and cauliflower cheese or salmon pie, and home-made puddings like very good treacle tart (£2.50); attentive service. It gets quite restauranty in the evenings. The straightforwardly comfortable and carpeted main bar has a woodburning stove in the stone fireplace (decorated with shining horsebrasses on their original leathers) and leads through to a little cosy lounge with red plush button-back seats. The restaurant is no-smoking. Well kept Boddingtons and Flowers Original on handpump; cribbage, alley skittles and gentle piped music. A sheltered back terrace, by a garden with a prettily planted old wall behind, has white metal and plastic seats and tables. Please note – they close at 2pm on Sunday lunchtimes. The back bedrooms are the quietest. *(Recommended by Don and Thelma Beeson, Barry and Anne, David and Mary Webb, R V Ford, Pat and Richard Tazewell, G W Stevenson, Jim and Maggie Cowell, Mr and Mrs M A Steane, R and G Underwood, David and Mary Webb, John Hazel)*

Free house ~ Licensees Robbie Rutt and Neville White ~ Real ale ~ Meals and snacks (till 10) ~ Restaurant (Weds-Sat evenings) ~ (01278) 741210 ~ Open 11-2.30, 6-11 ~ Bedrooms: £37B/£62B

KINGSDON ST5126 Map 2

Kingsdon Inn

Off A303 at Podimore Island

This pretty little thatched cottage looks rather like a private house from outside – you even walk up a path through the garden to a neat green painted door with a brass knocker. Inside, it's friendly and relaxed, and on the right are a few low sagging beams, some very nice old stripped pine tables with attractive cushioned farmhouse chairs, more seats in what was a small inglenook fireplace, and an open woodburning stove with colourful dried and artificial fruits and flowers on the overmantle; down three steps through balustrading to a light, airy room with peach-coloured cushions on stripped pine built-in wall seats, curtains matching the scatter cushions, more stripped pine tables, and a big leaf and flower arrangement in the stone fireplace (open fire in winter). Another similarly decorated room has more tables and another fireplace. Very good food, served by efficient, helpful staff, includes at lunchtime, celery and stilton soup (£1.90), soused herring fillets with dill sauce (£3.40), filled french bread (£3.90), cheese and asparagus quiche (£3.90), baked haddock and prawn mornay (£4.60), braised oxtail in Guinness (£5.20), baked cod with herbs and lime butter (£5.60), and puddings such as raspberry and almond tart or rhubarb and orange crumble (from £1.90); evening dishes like mushrooms and bacon in garlic cream (£3.60), grilled goat's cheese salad with walnut dressing (£3.90), wild local rabbit in Dijon mustard sauce (£8.90), local pigeon breasts in port wine sauce (£9.20), roast rack of lamb with rosemary (£9.80), and baked sea bream fillet with tomato and herbs (£10.20). Well kept Boddingtons, Fullers London Pride, Hook Norton Best, Oakhill Best, Shepherd Neame Spitfire, and Smiles Best on handpump; shove-ha'penny, cribbage and darts, and they have rugby, cricket and golf teams; quiet piped music. Picnic tables and umbrellas on the grass. *(Recommended by Gethin Lewis, Galen Strawson, John Hazel, Pat and Robert Watt, Mr and Mrs J G Davies, Dr B Moyse)*

Free house ~ Licensee Duncan Gordon ~ Real ale ~ Meals and snacks (not Sun evening) ~ (01935) 840543 ~ Children in eating area of bar; must be over 5 in evenings ~ Open 11-3, 6-11

KNAPP ST3025 Map 1

Rising Sun 🍷

Lower Knapp – OS Sheet 182 map reference 304257; off A38/A358/A378 E of Taunton

If you like fresh fish and seafood, then this lovely 15th-c Somerset longhouse is the place to head for and there are plenty of blackboards listing the enormous range they have available each day. There might typically be starters like crab fish cakes or bouillabaise (£3.85) and countless imaginative main courses such as black bream marinated in lemon and rosemary (£9.60), poached skate or bass grilled with ginger, brown sugar and soy sauce (£11), scallops poached in vermouth, red mullet niçoise or salmon in asparagus sauce (all £11.55), monkfish provençale (£11.80), brill with a prawn and mushroom filling (£12), john dory poached in a garlic, prawn, fennel and mussel sauce (£13.45), and red snapper in tangy wine, rum and herb sauce (£14.25); they also do good plain bar food like open sandwiches (from £3.40), Welsh rarebit (£2.75), ploughman's (£3.50), ham and egg (£4.50), and a well-liked Sunday lunch. The big single room has well moulded beams, woodwork, and some stonework in its massive rather tilting walls, two inglenook log fires, and a relaxed atmosphere. Well kept Bass, Boddingtons and Exmoor on handpump; decent wine list. The staff (and dogs – Pepi the poodle and Pompey, who weighs in at nine stone) are very welcoming; background classical music. Part of the restaurant is no smoking. There are fine country views from the sun-trap terrace. *(Recommended by Colin W McKerrow, Pete Yearsley, Nigel Paine, Major and Mrs Warrick, E H and R F Warner, Anthony Clemow, Michael Boniface, S Brackenbury, Marion and John Hadfield, Stephen Brown, P Neate, John A Barker)*

Free house ~ Licensee Tony Atkinson ~ Real ale ~ Meals and snacks ~ Restaurant ~ (01823) 490436 ~ Children in restaurant ~ Open 11.30-2.30, 6.30-11 ~ Bedrooms: £25/£36

Prices of main dishes usually include vegetables or a side salad.

LANGLEY MARSH ST0729 Map 1

Three Horseshoes ★

Village signposted off B3227 from Wiveliscombe

This is a good honest pub, neatly kept and simple, and tucked away in the Somerset hills. They keep a fair choice of real ales tapped from the cask such as Furgusons Dartmoor, Palmers IPA, Ringwood Best, Wadworths 6X, and various guests, and Perry's farm cider. The menu changes constantly (though they tell us prices have not) and might include filled rolls, home-made soup, a choice of salads or filled baked potatoes, chilli con carne or liver and onion casserole (£3.95), butter bean and brandy stew or courgette and mushroom bake (£4.50), lamb in Pernod or fish pie (all £4.95), fillet steak (£10.50), fondues (£15 for two people), and puddings such as mincemeat, apple and brandy pancakes or creamy cheese cake (all £1.85); no chips or fried food, and a lot of the vegetables come from the garden. The dining area is no smoking. The back bar has low modern settles and polished wooden tables, dark red wallpaper, planes hanging from the ceiling, banknotes papering the wall behind the bar counter, a piano, and a local stone fireplace; the lively front room has sensibly placed darts, shove-ha'penny, table skittles, dominoes, cribbage and bar billiards; separate skittle alley; piped music. It is small, so they can get crowded. The pub's elderly alsatian is called Guinness and their new puppy is called Ruddles. You can sit on rustic seats on the verandah or in the sloping back garden, with a children's climbing frame and a view of farmland. In fine weather there are usually vintage cars outside. ***(Recommended by K H Frostick, George Jonas, Anthony Barnes, GSD, EMD, Debbie Jones, John Hazel, Pete and Rosie Flower, H F Cox, Alan Carr)***

Free house ~ Licensee John Hopkins ~ Real ale ~ Meals and snacks ~ (01984) 623763 ~ Well behaved children allowed away from bar ~ Occasional spontaneous 'fiddle/squeeze box' sessions with local Morris Dancing musicians ~ Open 12-2.30(3 Sat), 7-11

LITTON ST5954 Map 2

Kings Arms

B3144; off A39 Bath—Wells

Partly 15th-c, this tiled white building is reached down a flight of steps from the car park. There's a big entrance hall with polished flagstones, and the bars lead off to the left with low heavy beams and more flagstones; a nice bit on the right beyond the huge fireplace has a big old-fashioned settle and a mix of other settles and wheelback chairs; a full suit of armour stands in one alcove and the rooms are divided up into areas by standing timbers. It does get busy at weekends but the friendly staff manage to cope cheerfully. Tasty bar food includes sandwiches (from £2.35), garlic mushrooms (£3.15), onion bhajis (£3.45), lots of platters (from £3.50), ham and egg (£4.35), ploughman's (from £4.35), battered cod (£4.65), chicken and broccoli bake (£6.95), chicken tikka (£7.25), and king prawns in garlic butter (£9.50). Well kept Bass, Courage Best, and Wadworths 6X on handpump. The tiered, neatly kept gardens have picnic tables, excellent heavy wooden play equipment including a commando climbing net, and slides and baby swings; the River Chew runs through the bottom of the garden. ***(Recommended by Wendy and Paul Bachelor, E H and R F Warner, JCW, P H Roberts, Don Kellaway, Angie Coles)***

Free house ~ Licensee Neil Sinclair ~ Real ale ~ Meals and snacks (till 10) ~ (01761) 241301 ~ Children in big family room ~ Open 11-2.30, 6-11

LUXBOROUGH SS9837 Map 1

Royal Oak ★

Kingsbridge; S of Dunster on minor rds into Brendon Hills – OS Sheet 181 map reference 983378

Even when the pub's full of cheerful, chatty locals, the licensees go out of their way to make sure that visitors feel just as welcome – and it's this warm friendliness that readers like so much about this unspoilt and characterful pub. The three chatty and warmly atmospheric rooms have flagstones in the front public bar, beams and inglenooks, a real medley of furniture, and good log fires. Well kept real ales such as Batemans XXXB, Cotleigh Tawny, Exmoor Gold, Flowers IPA, and Wychwood Hobgoblin tapped from the cask, and two farm ciders. Popular bar food includes home-made soup (£1.95), huge sandwiches (from £2.25), filled baked potatoes (from £2.95), home-made port and stilton pâté (£3.95), good ploughman's (from £3.95), lamb curry (£4.85), vegetable and stilton pie (£4.95), salads (from £4.95), beef and Beamish pie (£5.25), daily specials such as turkey and tarragon pie (£5.95), fresh scallops in a mustard and dill sauce (£7.25), fillet of venison in cumberland sauce (£9.85), puddings (£2.25), and children's meals (£2.65); there's a wider choice in the evening (booking is recommended). Pool, dominoes, winter darts – no machines or music. Tables outside. The comfortable bedrooms fit in with the simple style of the place, and breakfasts are good. *(Recommended by Sue Demont, Tim Barrow, Dave Thompson, Margaret Mason, Mrs K N Fowler, Sue and Bob Ward, G W Stevenson, Mrs C Blake, Jack and Philip Paxton, John Hazel, R V Ford, Mr and Mrs P E Towndrow, John Humphreys, Anthony Barnes, R T and J C Moggridge, Paul Randall, Angela Basso, Jean Gustavson, J Wedel, Jed and Virginia Brown, Peter and Audrey Dowsett, R Ward, John A Barker, Kevin and Katharine Cripps, James Nunns, Colin Keane, Dagmar Junghanns, Basil J S Minson, Jan and Dave Booth, DC, Graham Pettener, H O Dickinson, Joan Coleman, Clem Stephens)*

Free house ~ Licensees Robin and Helen Stamp ~ Real ale ~ Meals and snacks (till 10) ~ Restaurant ~ (01984) 640319 ~ Children in eating area of bar ~ Folk music Fri ~ Open 11-2.30, 6-11; Dec-Mar evening opening 7 ~ Bedrooms: £20/£30

MELLS ST7249 Map 2

Talbot

W of Frome; off A362 W of Buckland Dinham, or A361 via Nunney and Whatley

In an interestingly preserved feudal village with a lovely church, this unspoilt 15th-c coaching inn is a friendly place with a warm welcome for locals and visitors. Off the informally planted cobbled courtyard, where there are cane chairs around tables, is an attractive room with fresh flowers and candles in bottles on the mix of tables, stripped pews, mate's and wheelback chairs, and sporting and riding pictures on the walls, which are partly stripped above a broad panelled dado, and partly rough terracotta-coloured. A small corridor leads to a nice little room with an open fire; piped music. Good food from a varied menu includes home-made soup (£1.95), home-made pork and chicken liver pâté or creamy garlic mushrooms on toast (£3.50), ploughman's (£3.95), ratatouille flan (£4.25), lasagne or duck and cherry pie (£4.50), tagliatelle with smoked salmon and prawns in a cream sauce (£5.25), steak and kidney pie or stuffed pancakes with a savoury beansprout filling topped with cheese (£6.50), grilled whole lemon sole with herb butter (£7.50), steaks (from £8.95), daily specials such as casserole of wild boar with port, pheasant braised with bacon and red wine or fillet of salmon wrapped in pastry with ginger butter (from £7.50). Well kept Bass, Butcombe and a guest such as Wadworths 6X on handpump, and good wines; well chosen staff. The two-roomed public bar has an appealing room nearest the road with big stripped shutters, a high dark green ceiling, a mix of chairs and a tall box settle, candles in bottles on the stubby pine tables, a rough wooden floor; the locals' room has sports trophies, darts and simple furnishings; skittle alley. They hold an Irish music weekend during the second week of September and a Daffodil Weekend with 350 members of the English Civil War Society over the Easter weekend. The village was purchased by the Hornby family of the 'Little Jack Horner' nursery rhyme and the direct descendants still live in the manor house next door. *(Recommended by Mike and Sue Moss, John and Pat Smyth, Michael Richards, Mr and Mrs Adams, Davie Leonard, Jed and Virginia Brown)*

Free house ~ Lease: Roger Elliott ~ Real ale ~ Meals and snacks ~ Restaurant ~ (01373) 812254 ~ Children welcome ~ Open 12-3, 6-11 ~ Bedrooms: £25B/£39B

MONKSILVER ST0737 Map 1

Notley Arms ★ (food award symbol)

B3188

Sometimes only ten minutes after opening, all the tables in this pub have been snapped up by people keen to enjoy the consistently good food. The characterful beamed and L-shaped bar is relaxed and friendly, with fresh flowers, small settles and kitchen chairs around the plain country wooden and candle lit tables, original paintings on the black-timbered white walls, a couple of woodburning stoves and a pair of cats. Bar food changes daily but might include home-made soup (£1.95), sandwiches (from £2.25), very good ploughman's (from £2.75), filled baked potatoes (from £2.85), pasta with bacon, cheese and cream (£3.95), tomato and mozzarella tart or wild mushroom strudel (£4.50), seafood lasagne (£4.75), creamy mild lamb curry (£5.25), popular Chinese red roast pork (£5.75), beef and Beamish pie or chicken breast with apple and tarragon stuffing (£6.25), trout (£7.50), and puddings like fresh fruit crumbles, summer strawberry cheesecake or home-made ice creams (from £2.25). Well kept Courage Best, Exmoor Ale, Morlands Old Speckled Hen, Ushers Best, and Wadworths 6X on handpump; dominoes and trivia, and alley skittles. Families are well looked after, with colouring books and toys in the bright little family room. There are more toys outside in the immaculate garden, running down to a swift clear stream. *(Recommended by Peter and Joy Heatherley, Howard Clutterbuck, Paul and Susan Merrick, Jim Reid, Dorothy Pilson, Mrs K N Fowler, R V Ford, John and Christine Vittoe, Mrs C Blake, G S and E M Dorey, Mr and Mrs Westcombe, Mr and Mrs Hillman, W H and E Thomas, Mrs C Watkinson, A Plumb, Dr R J Rathbone, M D Beardmore, Joan Olivier, John and Christine Vittoe, Kevin and Katharine Cripps, Jerry and Alison Oakes, Debbie Jones)*

Courage ~ Tenants Alistair and Sarah Cade ~ Real ale ~ Meals and snacks (not 25 Dec or 1st 2 weeks in Feb) ~ (01984) 656217 ~ Children in eating area of bar ~ Open 11.30-2.30, 6.30-11; closed 25 Dec

MONTACUTE ST4916 Map 2

Kings Arms

A3088 W of Yeovil

New licensees have taken over this civilised golden stone inn and have opened up new lounge and restaurant areas, added more bedrooms and new lavatories, and introduced a new chef. The emphasis leans strongly towards the popular food, with dishes such as home-made soup (£1.95), sandwiches (from £2.50), Mediterranean prawns with garlic and lemon (£4.25), vegetable and nut pancake (£4.50), steak, mushroom and Guinness pie (£5.25), chicken supreme (£5.50), sirloin steak (£9.75), daily specials such as local mussels, squid in batter, ham hock and mushy peas, brill in a creamy crab sauce or trout stuffed with almonds and banana, and puddings like apple and cinnamon raisin pie (£2.25); Sunday roast lunch. Well kept Bass and Boddingtons and a local guest beer on handpump (one under light blanket pressure), and quite a few New World wines. Part of the walls at the front of the lounge bar are stripped back to the handsome masonry, and comfortable furnishings include grey-gold plush seats, soft armchairs, chintz sofas, and a high curved settle. The restaurants are no smoking. The pretty village includes the stately Elizabethan mansion of the same name, and behind the hotel the wooded St Michael's Hill is owned by the National Trust. *(Recommended by F J Willy, Wendy Arnold, Nick and Meriel Cox, Michael Boniface, Guy Consterdine, Ron and Anne Fowler, P J Caunt, David and Fiona Easeman, Major and Mrs E M Warrick, J L Alperin)*

Free house ~ Licensees Jonathan and Karen Arthur ~ Real ale ~ Meals and snacks ~ Restaurant ~ (01935) 822513 ~ Children in eating area and restaurant ~ Open 11.30-2.30, 6-11 ~ Bedrooms: £49B/69B

If you know a pub's ever open all day, please tell us.

NORTON ST PHILIP ST7755 Map 2

George ★

A366

Originally built to house merchants buying wool and cloth from the rich sheep-farming Hinton Priory at the great August cloth market, this remarkable old building has been a pub for nearly 600 years. There's a fine half-timbered and galleried back courtyard, an external Norman stone stair-turret, massive stone walls and high mullioned windows. Furnishings are simple: square-panelled wooden settles, plain old tables, wide bare floorboards, and lofty beams hung with hops. A long, stout table serves well kept Bass, and Wadworths IPA, 6X and seasonal beers on handpump. A panelled lounge is furnished with antique settles and tables; it's all perhaps more atmospheric in winter when the fires are lit. Bar food (with prices unchanged since last year) includes soup (£2.25), cheese and leek pancakes (£3.25), filled baguettes or baked potatoes (£3.75), ploughman's (£3.95), meat or fish platters (from £5.50), tortellini and blue cheese bake with broccoli, trout baked with bananas and almonds (£6.75), gammon (£6.95), daily specials, and puddings like treacle tart (£2.75); Sunday roast (£6.95). Darts, pool and dominoes. The Duke of Monmouth stayed here before the Battle of Sedgemoor, and after their defeat his men were imprisoned in what's now the Dungeon cellar bar. When a sympathetic customer held the courtyard gate open for them as they were led out to their execution, he was bundled along with them and executed too. They hope to have bedrooms by mid 1996. *(Recommended by Jack and Philip Paxton, James House, Arthur and Annette Frampton, Howard Clutterbuck, Tom McLean, Roger Huggins, Ewan McCall, Dave Irving, BHP, Wim Kock, Willem-Jan Kock, Hans Chabot, Pat and John Millward, Viv Middlebrook, John and Phyllis Maloney, Jerry and Alison Oakes)*

Wadworths ~ Tenants Andrew and Juliette Grubb ~ Real ale ~ Meals and snacks (till 10 Sat; not evening Dec 25 and 26) ~ Lunchtime restaurant ~ (01373) 834224 ~ Children welcome ~ Open 11-3, 5.30(5 Sat)-11 ~ Bedrooms planned

OVER STRATTON ST4315 Map 1

Royal Oak

From A303 Yeovil—Taunton road, take Ilminster turning at South Petherton roundabout; pass Esso garage and take first left to village

A good break from the busy A303, this popular dining pub has cosily extended dark-flagstoned bars with a mixture of pews, settles or dining chairs, scrubbed deal farmhouse kitchen tables, and a stuffed pheasant. The beams have been prettily stencilled with an oakleaf and acorn pattern, the walls are stripped to bare stonework or attractively ragrolled red, and log fires burn, sometimes even in summer. Under the new manager, food now includes home-made soup (£2.25), creamy garlic mushrooms (£3.75), lamb's kidneys with pasta in a port and cream sauce (£3.95), ploughman's or interestingly filled baked potatoes (£4.25), home-made burgers with spicy barbecue sauce (small helping £4.25, hearty helping £5.95), beef curry or home-made lasagne (small helping £4.50, hearty helping £5.95), seafood tagliatelle (small helping £4.75, hearty helping £6.25), salads (from £5.95), steaks (from £8.45), daily specials such as crab Mexicana (£3.75), moules marinières (£4.75), and pork and apricot medallions (£9.95), children's dishes (from £2.75), and puddings like poached fresh pear with hot butterscotch sauce (from £2.50). The restaurant is no smoking. Well kept Badger Best and Tanglefoot, and Wadworths 6X on handpump, and several malt whiskies. On a floodlit reconstituted-stone terrace sheltered by the back wings of the building are quite a few picnic tables, with more on a further sheltered gravel terrace with a barbecue; a play area for toddlers has swings, slides, climbing frame and a sandpit, and for older children, there's a mini assault course and three trampolines. *(Recommended by Gethin Lewis, M E Wellington, Major and Mrs E M Warrick, S G Brown, Guy Consterdine, Andrew and Helen Latchem, Helen Taylor, John and Vivienne Rice, Dr R J Rathbone)*

Badger ~ Manager Brian Elderfield ~ Real ale ~ Meals and snacks (11.30-2.15, 6.30-10) ~ Restaurant ~ (01460) 240906 ~ Children in restaurant ~ Open 11-3, 6-11

RUDGE ST8251 Map 2

Full Moon

Off A36 Bath—Warminster

Much bigger inside than you'd guess from outside, this attractive rustic pub was bought by the Giffords as a run-down, erratically open cider house. In a way, they were lucky because it meant that the inn was totally unspoilt and they have tried to keep the old character while building up a considerable reputation for well kept real ales and generous helpings of good food. The two rooms on the right have low white ceilings with a few black beams, a woodburning stove in a big stone fireplace with riding boots on the mantlebeam, a built-in settle by the bar, big shutters by the red velvet-cushioned window seats, and wheelbacks and slatback chairs around mainly cast-iron framed tables. Other rooms are similarly furnished except the smallish flagstoned dining room with stripped pine tables and high traditional settles; there's also a small plush restaurant and a big back carpeted extension alongside the skittle alley. The whole feel is gently upmarket. Generous helpings of lunchtime bar food include soup (£1.95), pâté (£3.25), ploughman's (from £3.45), omelettes (from £4.25), curry with coconut and mango (£4.65), home-cooked ham with two eggs or nut and broccoli bake (£4.95), breast of chicken with garlic and lemon butter (£5.25), and sirloin steak (£7.95), with evening dishes such as black pudding with apple purée (£3.95), seafood tagliatelle (£4.25), tart hongroise (shallots, mushrooms, and tomatoes topped with melted cheese, £7.25), fresh local trout oven baked with capers and herb butter (£8.95), and roast rack of English lamb with a calvados and peach sauce (£10.45); children's dishes (£2.25). Well kept Bass, Butcombe and Wadworths 6X on handpump, and Thatcher's cider. ***(Recommended by A D Sherman, Dan Mather, Brian and Judith Young)***

Free house ~ Licensee Patrick Gifford ~ Real ale ~ Meals and snacks (not Sun evening) ~ Restaurant (not Sun evening) ~ (01373) 830936 ~ Children welcome ~ Open 12-3, 6-11; winter evening opening 7; closed Mon lunchtime 1 Oct-Easter ~ Bedrooms: £30B/£45B

SOUTH STOKE ST7461 Map 2

Pack Horse £

Village signposted opposite the Cross Keys off B3110, leaving Bath southwards – just before end of speed limit

The Williams family continue to offer a cheery welcome to locals, office workers at lunchtime, and walkers at weekends. The entrance alleyway that runs through the middle is still a public right of way to the church, and used to be the route along which the dead were carried to the cemetery. It stops along the way at a central space by the serving bar with its well kept Courage Best, and Ushers Best and Founders on handpump. The ancient main room has a good local atmosphere, a heavy black beam-and-plank ceiling, antique oak settles (two well carved), leatherette dining chairs and cushioned captain's chairs on the quarry-tiled floor, a log fire in the handsome stone inglenook, some Royalty pictures, a chiming wall-clock, and rough black shutters for the stone-mullioned windows (put up in World War I); the cupboard in the fireplace used to be where they kept drunks until they sobered up. There's another room down to the left (with less atmosphere). Remarkably good value home-made bar food includes filled rolls, good pasties or sausage plait (80p), ploughman's, a Wednesday special of roast lunch and pudding (£2.50), daily specials (£1.60-£2), and two course Sunday lunch (£3); friendly staff. Rather fine shove-ha'penny slates are set into two of the tables, and there are darts, dominoes, and fruit machine. The spacious back garden, with swings, looks out over the stolid old church and the wooded valley. *(Recommended by Brian Pearson, Peter Neate, Roger Huggins, Dave Irving, Ewan McCall, Tom McLean, Ron Gentry, Roger Wain-Heapy)*

Ushers (Courage) ~ Tenant Colin Williams ~ Real ale ~ Snacks ~ (01225) 832060 ~ Children in eating area of bar ~ Open 11-4, 6-11; all day Sat

STANTON WICK ST6162 Map 2

Carpenters Arms

Village signposted off A368, just W of junction with A37 S of Bristol

The Coopers Parlour on the right in this low tiled-roof inn has one or two beams, red-cushioned wall pews around heavy tables, fresh flowers, and swagged-back curtains and houseplants in the windows; on the angle between here and the bar area there's a fat woodburning stove in an opened-through corner fireplace. The bar has a pubby atmosphere, a big log fire, wood-backed built-in wall seats and some red fabric-cushioned stools, and stripped stone walls. Diners are encouraged to step down into a snug inner room (lightened by mirrors in arched 'windows'), or to go round to the sturdy tables angling off on the right; most of these tables get booked at weekends. Tasty bar food includes home-made soup (£1.95), filled french sticks (from £2.50), ploughman's (£3.55), mushrooms and bacon sautéed with sherry, cream and onions (£3.95), chilli con carne (£4.75), good lamb's liver and bacon (£6.50), fillet of lemon sole meuniere (£7.25), roast rack of English lamb with redcurrant and apple jelly (£7.95), steaks (from £9.25), and home-made puddings (from £2.75); good breakfasts. Well kept Bass, Butcombe, Wadworths 6X, and Worthington Best and Toby on handpump, and a decent wine list; cribbage, fruit machine, TV, boules, and piped music. There are picnic tables on the front terrace. *(Recommended by DJW, Tom Evans, P H Roberts, John and Priscilla Gillett, Brian Atkin, Charles and Dorothy Ellsworth, L G Holmes, Peter Churchill, George Jonas, Dave and Jules Tuckett, Simon and Amanda Southwell, P M Lane, A R and B E Sayer, M G Hart)*

Free house ~ Licensee Nigel Pushman ~ Real ale ~ Meals and snacks (till 10) ~ Restaurant (not Sun evening) ~ (01761) 490202 ~ Children welcome (though no facilities for them) ~ Open 11-11 ~ Bedrooms: £45.50B/£59.50B

STOGUMBER ST0937 Map 1

White Horse

From A358 Taunton—Williton, village signposted on left at Crowcombe

This pleasant pub is set opposite the red stone church in a quiet conservation village. The long room is neatly kept and has old-fashioned built-in settles, other settles and cushioned captain's chairs around the heavy rustic tables on the patterned carpet, and an open coal fire in cool weather; piped classical music. Good, reasonably priced food includes sandwiches (from £1.10), home-made vegetable soup (£1.50), salmon mousse (£2.40), ploughman's, ham and egg or omelettes (£3.10), vegetable pasty (£3.70), seafood lasagne (£3.90), liver and bacon casserole (£4.40), steak and kidney pudding (£5.80), steaks (from £8.80), and puddings like walnut tart or apple crumble (from £1.30); best to book for Sunday lunch, and breakfasts are good; prompt service. Well kept Cotleigh Tawny and Exmoor on handpump, and farm cider in summer. A side room has sensibly placed darts and a fruit machine; shove-ha'penny, dominoes, cribbage, and video game – as well as a separate skittle alley. The garden is quiet except for rooks and sheep in the surrounding low hills. *(Recommended by Bruce Bird, Jim Reid, Paul and Susan Merrick, Roger Wain-Heapy, Alan Carr, Joan Coleman, Pat and Robert Watt, J R Williams, David and Fiona Easeman, Colin Keane, Dagmar Junghanns, John Hazel)*

Free house ~ Licensee Peter Williamson ~ Real ale ~ Meals and snacks (11-2, 6-10) ~ (01984) 656277 ~ Children in dining room ~ Open 11-2.30, 6-11 ~ Bedrooms: £25B/£35B

STOKE ST GREGORY ST3527 Map 1

Rose & Crown

Woodhill; follow North Curry signpost off A378 by junction with A358 – keep on to Stoke, bearing right in centre and right again past church

Somerset Dining Pub of the Year

Many people tell us they enjoy this warmly friendly 17th-c cottage so much that they return again and again – and are always delighted. This year, the cheerfully enthusiastic Browning family are adding jacuzzi bathrooms to the bedrooms in the inn, and are opening a cottage annexe with more bedrooms, a residents' lounge, and a pets' corner for children. The neatly kept and rather jolly bar is decorated in a cosy and pleasantly romanticised stable theme: dark wooden loose-box partitions for some of the interestingly angled nooks and alcoves, lots of brasses and bits on the low beams and joists, stripped stonework, and appropriate pictures including a highland pony carrying a stag; the evening pianist is proving popular. Many of the wildlife paintings on the walls are the work of the landlady, and there's an 18th-c glass-covered well in one corner. Mrs Browning's two sons are responsible for the cooking (they bake their own bread and produce their own marmalade), and use fresh local ingredients – the eggs come from their own chickens. This year, we are giving the pub a Food Award which we feel reflects the top quality of their honest dishes (which come in very generous helpings): sandwiches in their own granary bread (from £1.25), soup (£1.50), ravioli and garlic bread (£4.35), omelettes (£4), scrumpy chicken, grilled liver and bacon, grilled skate wings, cold seafood platter or gammon and pineapple (all £4.95), mushroom, tomato and bean bake or nut roast chasseur (£5.75), steaks (from £7.50), Scotch salmon (£9.50), and puddings (£2.25); very good value OAP's lunch, excellent breakfasts, three-course evening menu (£11.50; lots of choice), and a good three-course Sunday lunch (£7.25). Service is prompt and obliging. One small dining area is no smoking. Well kept Eldridge Pope Hardy and Royal Oak, and Exmoor on handpump; large selection of Taunton ciders, decent wines; unobtrusive piped classical music, shove-ha'penny, and dominoes. Under cocktail parasols by an apple tree on the sheltered front terrace are some picnic tables; summer barbecues. In summer residents have use of a heated swimming pool. The pub is in an interesting Somerset Levels village with willow beds still supplying the two basket works. ***(Recommended by A and J Tierney-Jones, Mr and Mrs G Abbott, R V Ford, Marion Greenwood, Stella Knight, J Taylor, Brian and Anna Marsden, P H Roberts, Mr and Mrs J Brown, Angela and Gordon Abbott, John and June Hayward, A Preston, E H and R F Warner, Lindsey Harvard, Margaret Whalley, Tina Bird, Mrs E M Downard, Mrs T Froud, John le Sage, John A Barker, Paul Collins, Anna Lindars, Peter D Keane, John and Fiona Merritt, Stephen Brown)***

Free house ~ Licensees Ron and Irene Browning ~ Real ale ~ Meals and snacks (till 10) ~ Restaurant ~ (01823) 490296/490184 ~ Children welcome ~ Open 11-3, 6.30-11 ~ Bedrooms: £22.50/£36

STOKE ST MARY ST2622 Map 1

Half Moon

2¾ miles from M5 junction 25; A358 towards Ilminster, then first right, then right at T-junction and follow the signs. Westbound turn left at sign ¾ mile after the traffic lights

Each of the five neat open-plan main areas in this much-modernised village pub is furnished and decorated with a good deal of character and individuality, and there's quite a roomy and relaxed feel. There's quite an emphasis on the food, served by efficient and friendly uniformed staff: sandwiches (from £1.50), soup (£1.65), ploughman's (from £3.50), filled baked potatoes (from £3.95), breadcrumbed chicken (£4.95), steak in ale pie (£5.25), broccoli and cream cheese bake (£5.50), orange and mint lamb steak (£6.95), pork casserole with apples and cider or seafood pasta (£7.95), steaks (from £7.95), puddings (from £2.45), and children's dishes (from £3.95); two dining areas are no smoking. Well kept Boddingtons, Theakstons Best, and Wadworths 6X on handpump. Picnic tables on a well kept lawn and more tables on a small gravel terrace. *(Recommended by J E N Young, CR, Dr C E Morgan, S E Brown, Shirley Pielou, Ian and Deborah Carrington, Prof A N Black, Richard R Dolphin)*

Whitbreads ~ Lease: Pat and Jan Howard ~ Real ale ~ Meals and snacks (till 10) ~ Two restaurants ~ (01823) 442271 ~ Children in eating area of bar ~ Open 11-2.30, 6-11

TRISCOMBE ST1535 Map 1

Blue Ball

Village (and pub) signposted off A358 Taunton—Minehead

From the picnic tables on the narrow terraced lawns built into the steep and peaceful slope here, there are fine views of the Brendon hills; good nearby walks. Inside this friendly thatched and rather cottagey little pub is a neat brown-beamed bar with sporting prints on the white walls, piped light classical music, and barely more than half a dozen tables – one tucked under the mantlebeam of what used to be a monumental brick and stone fireplace; the no-smoking conservatory does relieve the seasonal pressure on space. Well kept Butcombe, Cotleigh Barn Owl, Otter Ale, and St Austell HSD on handpump, and farm cider; dominoes, cribbage, skittle alley, piped music. They have a cocker spaniel, Chadwick, and other dogs are welcome on a lead. Quickly served bar food might include sandwiches, soup (£2.25), venison pâté (£2.65), ploughman's (£3.50), filled giant pancakes (£3.95), pork sausages or broccoli and cream cheese quiche (£3.95), spinach and nut lasagne (£5.25), lamb goulash (£5.50), local duck in orange sauce (£5.85), steaks (from £6.95), and puddings like treacle tart or apple pie (£1.95). The lavatories are in an unusual separate thatched building, and there's a bedroom suite (separate from the pub). *(Recommended by Anthony Barnes, Mrs K N Fowler, Colin Keane, Dagmar Junghanns, Debbie Jones, A Plumb, Jed and Virginia Brown, Dr R J Rathbone; more reports please)*

Free house ~ Licensee Nanette Little ~ Real ale ~ Meals and snacks (not Sun evening) ~ (01984) 618242 ~ Children in eating area and conservatory ~ Open 11-2.30, 7-11; winter lunchtime opening 12; closed Sun evening Oct-end May ~ Bedroom: /£35B

TRUDOXHILL ST7443 Map2

White Hart

Village signposted off A361 Frome—Wells

Friendly new licensees have taken over this creeper covered pub but continue to brew their own real ales from the busy little Ash Vine Brewery (which they'll show you if they're not too pushed): well-flavoured light Ash Vine Bitter and delicate Trudoxhill, through the smooth Challenger and Black Bess Porter to the stronger mid-brown Tanker and rich winter Hop & Glory. As well as these there may be guest beers; country wines. The long, attractively carpeted, stripped-stone bar, really two room areas, has beams supporting broad stripped ceiling boards and a thriving, relaxed atmosphere. It's mostly table seating, with a couple of easy chairs by the big log fire on the right (there's a second at the other end), and some seats in the red velvet curtained windows; piped music. A very wide choice of food now includes home-made soup (£1.80), filled french bread (from £2.40), quite a few burgers (from £2.50), omelettes (from £4.20), devilled kidneys (£4.50), cottage pie (£4.80), vegetable casserole or ham and two eggs (£4.90), home-made steak and kidney pie or beef curry (£5.30), seafood quiche (£5.50), tuna steak (£6.80), mixed grill (£10.90), good steaks, children's menu (from £1.90), and puddings like treacle tart or apple pie (from £2.20); they plan themed food evenings. There are picnic tables on a flower-filled sheltered side lawn. *(Recommended by Derek and Sylvia Stephenson, Dennis Heatley, Peter Woods, Andrew and Ruth Triggs, Colin and Sarah Pugh, George Atkinson, Steve Goodchild, Brig J S Green, Mike and Sue Moss, Tony and Joan Walker; more reports on the new regime, please)*

Own brew ~ Licensees Peter Stockdale and Sally Tuffnell ~ Real ale ~ Meals and snacks (till 10) ~ Restaurant ~ (01373) 836324 ~ Children in eating area of bar ~ Open 12-3(4 Sat), 7(6.30 Sat)-11

WAMBROOK ST2907 Map 1

Cotley

Village signposted off A30 W of Chard; don't follow the small signs to Cotley itself

It's well worth negotiating the miles of high-hedged country lanes to reach this warmly friendly country pub. It has a smart but unpretentious local atmosphere and the simple flagstoned entrance bar opens on one side into a small plush bar, with beyond that a two-room dining area, one of which is no smoking; various open fires. An extension is often used for painting sessions, and the results (complete with price-tags in case you see something you like) can be seen around the walls of the various rooms. Good, pleasing bar food includes home-made soup (£1.75), sandwiches (from £2.20), sausage and chips (£2.75), filled baked potatoes (from £3.25), creamed mushrooms with tarragon (£3.50), ploughman's (from £3.65), omelettes (from £4.95), vegetable minty pie (£5.75), devilled kidneys with port and cream or ham and egg (£5.95), fresh baked plaice (£6.50), chicken with stilton sauce (£6.95), steaks (from £9.25), fresh water prawns in a sweet and sour sauce (£9.50), and puddings (from £1.95); service is friendly and obliging. The restaurant is no smoking. Well kept Flowers Original and Wadworths 6X on handpump, and a good choice of wines; pool, skittle alley, and piped music. Out in the garden below are some picnic tables, with a play area and goldfish pool. Quiet on weekday lunchtimes, it can be very busy at weekends. Lots of lovely walks all around. ***(Recommended by Gwyneth and Salvo Spadaro-Dutturi, Mr and Mrs D V Morris, M E Wellington, Margaret and Nigel Dennis, R T and J C Moggridge, Clem Stephens, David Eberlin, Doug and Doris Nash, Major D A Daniels, Mr and Mrs Bird)***

Free house ~ Licensee D R Livingstone ~ Real ale ~ Meals and snacks (till 10) ~ Restaurant ~ (01460) 62348 ~ Children welcome ~ Open 11-3, 7-11 ~ Bedrooms: £20B/£30B

WELLOW ST7458 Map 2

Fox & Badger

Village signposted on left on A367 SW of Bath

A good mix of locals and office people from Bath come to this simple, flagstoned place with its friendly country atmosphere. The attractively furnished flagstone-floored bar has seats built into snug alcoves, small winged settles with cushions to match the curtains, flowers on the tables, a handsome fireplace and a pleasantly chiming clock, three log fires in winter. Exmoor Ale is sold at the extraordinary price of just £1.10 a pint, and they also have well kept Boddingtons, Butcombe Bitter, and Wadworths 6X on handpump, and Thatchers farm cider. The cosy carpeted public bar has darts, shove-ha'penny, table skittles, dominoes, cribbage, trivia, fruit machine and piped music, there's also a conservatory, and a skittle alley. Reasonably priced wholesome bar food includes sandwiches (£1.50), home-made soup (£2), ploughman's (from £3.30), nut paella, home-made spinach, mushroom and tomato lasagne, home-made steak pie or honey-baked ham and egg (all £4.95), grilled local trout (£5.95), steaks (from £6.95), daily specials, and puddings (£1.99); a good Sunday roast; there may be summer barbecues in the courtyard. ***(Recommended by Jenny and Michael Back, Meg and Colin Hamilton, S G N Bennett, Bob Riley, Betty and Ken Cantle, Mr and Mrs K Box, Roger Huggins, Dave and Jules Tuckett, MH, A Plumb)***

Phoenix Inns ~ Tenant Ray Houston ~ Real ale ~ Meals and snacks ~ Restaurant ~ (01225) 832293 ~ Children in eating area of bar and in skittle alley (under 10s must be gone by 9) ~ Open 11-3, 6-11; 11-11 Thurs/Fri

Pubs close to motorway junctions are listed at the back of the book.

WEST HARPTREE ST5556 Map 2

Blue Bowl

Off A368 Bath—Weston

Under a new licensee, this extended stonebuilt country dining pub has an engaging series of separate rooms, with wheelback chairs around lots of tables, some traditional built-in wall seats, and a delft shelf of decorative china. Another room around the corner on the left has big windows, another delft shelf, landscape pictures, a stripped panelling dado, and pews or sturdy light pine chairs around the tables. Bar food now includes sandwiches (from £1.40; doorsteps £2.45), ploughman's (from £2.50), home-made spaghetti bolognaise (£3.75), home-baked ham and egg (£3.80), steak in ale pie (£4.50), plaice with prawns and mushrooms (£5.95), steaks, and puddings (£1.95). Well kept Butcombe Bitter, Courage Best, and Wadworths 6X on handpump. Tables out on the back terrace look out over meadows, and there are picnic tables on quite a spacious stretch of safely fenced lawn. *(Recommended by Don Kellaway, Angie Coles, Martyn G Hart, L Mercer, Peter Churchill; more reports on the new regime, please)*

Courage ~ Lease: John Sales ~ Real ale ~ Meals and snacks ~ (01761) 221269 ~ Well behaved children allowed ~ Open 12-2.30, 6-11 ~ Bedrooms:£25/£25

WEST HUNTSPILL ST3044 Map 1

Crossways

2¾ miles from M5 junction 23 (A38 towards Highbridge); 4 miles from M5 junction 22 (A38 beyond Highbridge)

A popular lunchtime break from the motorway, this is a spacious 17th-c dining pub. The main part of the bar has dining-room chairs, a mixture of settles, seats built into one converted brick fireplace and good winter log fires in the others. At one end there's more of a dining-room, prettily decorated with old farm machinery engravings, Albert and Chic cartoons (chiefly about restaurants), and 1920ish hunting prints – on Friday and Saturday evenings this area becomes a no-smoking bistro. The other end has an area with big winged settles making booths, and there's a family room with bamboo-back seats around neat tables. Bar food includes generous sandwiches (from £1.60), home-made soup (£2), garlic mushrooms (£3), ploughman's (£3.20), steak and kidney pie (£4.80), gammon and egg (£6), steaks (from £8.50), daily specials such as seafood soup, cashew nut moussaka, curried prawn quiche, and spiced lamb and apricot pie, and puddings such as sherry trifle (£2.20); children's meals (£1.80). Well kept Butcombe Bitter, Flowers IPA and Original, Eldridge Pope Royal Oak, Exmoor Stag and Gold, Oakhill Best, and Smiles Best on handpump, with a changing and often unusual guest; a good choice of malt whiskies, freshly squeezed orange juice and Rich's farm cider. Darts, cribbage, dominoes, shove ha'penny, fruit machine, video game and skittle alley. There are picnic tables among fruit trees in quite a big garden. If you're staying, the back rooms are quieter. *(Recommended by Richard Dolphin, Alan and Eileen Bowker, Gareth and Kay Jones, P H Roberts, B J Harding, JCW, E D Bailey, Patrick Clancy, Bill and Beryl Farmer, Tom Evans, K R Waters, Dorothee and Dennis Glover, Graham and Karen Oddey)*

Free house ~ Licensee Michael Ronca ~ Real ale ~ Meals and snacks (till 10) ~ Restaurant (Fri/Sat evenings and Sun lunch only) ~ (01278) 783756 ~ Children welcome except in main bar ~ Jazz monthly Sun lunchtime ~ Open 12-3, 5.30(6 Sat)-11; closed Dec 25 ~ Bedrooms: £24B/£34B

WINSFORD SS9034 Map 1

Royal Oak

In Exmoor National Park, village signposted from A396 about 10 miles S of Dunster

After a bad fire and terrible water damage, this lovely thatched inn had to be closed for six months. As we went to press, they were nearing the end of the massive rebuilding programme – which has had to be painstakingly done as the pub is 12th/13th-c and a listed building. Mr Steven says the work has been so meticulous that most people would not really notice the difference, and they should be up and running by the time this book is published. From the cushioned big bay-window seat in the cosy lounge bar you look across the road towards the village green and foot and packhorse bridges over the River Winn; horse brasses and pewter tankards hang from the beam above the attractively panelled bar counter, there are windsor armed chairs and cushioned seats on the new carpet, and a splendid iron fireback in the big stone hearth (with a log fire in winter). Another similarly old-fashioned bar has been extended back into what was a store room, creating more eating space. A new menu was being drawn up when we spoke to Mr Steven and they aim to introduce pubby dishes such as steak and kidney pudding, home-made chicken pie, old-fashioned casseroles, and fish dishes (from around £5); also, home-made soup (£2), sandwiches (from £2), ploughman's (£3.95), good pasties, and so forth; evening steaks. Well kept Flowers IPA and Original on handpump with a guest beer tapped from the cask, and an excellent range of other drinks, particularly liqueurs and brandies; friendly staff. The bedrooms (where most of the fire damage occurred) have been totally upgraded, and they do a useful guide to Exmoor National Park identifying places to visit. Good nearby walks – up Winsford Hill for magnificent views, or over to Exford. *(Recommended by Sir John Stokes, T H G Lewis, John and Christine Vittoe, Peter and Audrey Dowsett, Neil and Anita Christopher; more reports please)*

Free house ~ Licensee Charles Steven ~ Real ale ~ Meals and snacks ~ Restaurant (not Sun evening) ~ (01643) 851455 ~ Children in eating area of bar ~ Open 11-2.30, 6-11 ~ Bedrooms: £67.50B/£90B

WITHYPOOL SS8435 Map 1

Royal Oak 🛏 🍷

Village signposted off B3233

The bedrooms and restaurant have been redecorated here this year – which will make this tucked away Exmoor inn an even nicer place to stay. The smartly cosy beamed lounge bar, popular with locals, has a stag's head and several fox masks on its walls, comfortable button-back brown seats and slat-backed chairs, and a log fire in a raised stone fireplace; another quite spacious bar is similarly decorated. Good bar food includes home-made soup (£1.85), sandwiches (from £1.95), snails grilled with garlic butter and parsley (£3.25), ploughman's (from £3.65), filled baked potatoes (from £3.75), home-cooked ham and chips (£5.25), two big venison and bacon sausages with two free range eggs (£6), good steaks (from £6.50), half crispy duck (£10.25), daily specials (fresh fish and game), and puddings. Well kept Flowers IPA and Whitbreads Castle Eden on handpump, farm cider, decent wine by the bottle, half litre, and litre, and a fair number of malt whiskies, cognacs and armagnacs; helpful, friendly staff. It can get very busy (especially on Sunday lunchtimes), and is popular with the local hunting and shooting types; cribbage and dominoes. There are wooden benches on the terrace, and just up the road, some grand views from Winsford Hill, with tracks leading up among the ponies into the heather past Withypool Hill. The River Barle runs through the village itself, with pretty bridleways following it through a wooded combe further upstream. For guests, they can arrange salmon and trout fishing, riding (stabling also), clay pigeon shooting, rough shooting, hunting, sea fishing from a boat and trips to see wild red deer. This is another pub with a *Lorna Doone* connection; R D Blackmore stayed here while writing the book. *(Recommended by R I Hartley, Barry and Anne, James House, H and D Payne, Mr and Mrs Box, S H Godsell, R J Walden, Jim and Maggie Cowell, Clem Stephens, Michael and Harriet Robinson)*

Free house ~ Licensee Michael Bradley ~ Real ale ~ Meals and snacks ~ Restaurant ~ (01643) 831506 ~ Children in restaurant only (if over 8) ~ Open 11-2.30(3 Sat), 6-11; closed 25/26 Dec ~ Bedrooms: £32(£46B)/£56(£68B)

Lucky Dip

Besides the fully inspected pubs, you might like to try these Lucky Dips recommended to us and described by readers (if you do, please send us reports):

Abbots Leigh [Pill Rd; A369, between M5 junction 19 and Bristol; ST5473], *George*: Friendly main-road dining pub with huge choice of attractively presented food, real ales inc Marstons Pedigree, quick service; no children *(Alan and Heather Jacques, D Godden, J Weeks, LYM)*

Allerford [the one W of Taunton; ST1825], *Victory*: Up to ten well kept ales in friendly and popular extended pub, good value straightforward food in bar and restaurant, quiz machine; skittle alley *(John and Fiona Merritt, Rich and Pauline Appleton)*

☆ **Ashcott** [High St; ST4337], *Ring o' Bells*: Wide choice of food inc vegetarian, well kept Bass and Worthington BB, decent wines and helpful service in comfortable and genuine three-room village local; skittle alley, fruit machines, restaurant with soft piped music *(John A Barker, Douglas Allen, John Hazel)*

☆ **Ashcott**, *Pipers*: Comfortable and roomy, with raj fans, good range of food in eating area, Courage-related ales, prompt welcoming service, log fire, pleasant roadside garden *(Howard and Lynda Dix, Brig J S Green)*

☆ **Axbridge** [The Square; quite handy for M5; ST4255], *Lamb*: Interesting rambling old pub in attractive square, with good generous food, welcoming service, well kept ales such as Butcombe and Wadworths 6X, farm cider, log fire, pub games, skittle alley, pretty little garden; children in eating area; old-world spacious bedrooms, huge breakfast *(Peter Cornall, Martyn Hart, Brig J S Green, Colin and Ann Hunt, Mr and Mrs A K McCully, Stephen Horsley, LYM)*

☆ **Backwell** [Farleigh Rd; A370 W of Bristol; ST4968], *George*: Former coaching inn doing well under new licensees, well priced bar food, wide choice in restaurant inc delicious puddings and Sun lunch, well kept Ushers, good choice of wines; children welcome *(Alan and Paula McCully, John Walmsley)*

☆ **Barrington** [ST3818], *Royal Oak*: Welcoming old stone pub in pretty village, handy for Barrington Court, with small cosy lounge, chatty public bar and skittle alley; has been popular for unusual range of quickly changing real ales and of innovative bar food *(Richard R Dolphin, Dave Williams; reports on new regime please)*

☆ **Barrow Gurney** [Barrow St (B3130, linking A370/A38 SW of Bristol; ST5367], *Princes Motto*: Very welcoming unpretentious local with well kept Bass and other ales such as Boddingtons, Butcombe and Smiles Best; snug traditional tap room, long room up behind, cheap wholesome lunchtime snacks *(Mr and Mrs A K McCully, David Eberlin, Tim and Chris Ford, LYM)*

Barrow Gurney [Bridgwater Rd (A38)], *Fox & Goose*: Old farmhouse pub newly refurbished with restaurant extension, emphasis on good generous home-cooked food; Courage-related ales *(Robert and Gladys Flux)*

☆ **Batcombe** [off A359 Bruton—Frome; ST6838], *Batcombe*: Low-beamed 14th-c inn behind church in pretty village, wide choice of good attractively presented home-made food inc vegetarian, well kept Flowers Original, Marstons Pedigree and Oakhill, attentive service, big log fire and woodburning stoves, copper and brass, games room, comfortable minstrel's gallery; children really welcome, busy with families weekends (playroom, children's videos Sun), tables in walled garden with new play area; two bedrooms with own bathrooms *(R H Martyn, Mark Burne)*

☆ **Bath** [Mill Lane, Bathampton (off A36 towards Warminster or A4 towards Chippenham)], *George I*: Attractive creeper-covered canalside pub, wide choice of good food inc fish and vegetarian, good log fires, well kept Bass and Courage Directors, busy weekends but service still quick and friendly; dining room by towpath, no-smoking family room, tables on quiet safe spacious back terrace with garden bar (traffic noise at front); can get crowded, esp weekends *(B and K Hypher, Dr and Mrs A K Clarke, Martin W Elliott)*

☆ **Bath** [23 The Vineyards; the Paragon, junction with Guinea Lane], *Star*: Several small dimly lit interconnecting rooms separated by glass and panelling, basic old-fashioned furnishings, particularly well kept Bass, Butcombe and Wadworths 6X in jugs from the cask, friendly enthusiastic landlord, low prices *(Pete Baker, BB)*

Bath [Walcot St], *Bell*: A musicians' pub, with well kept Butcombe, Wadworths 6X and guest beers, superb value filled rolls, friendly efficient service; frequent free music *(Bill Bailey, Dr and Mrs A K Clarke)*; [Abbey Green], *Crystal Palace*: Biggish modernised bar, sheltered courtyard and heated conservatory, with straightforward food (not Sun evening) inc lunchtime snacks, Eldridge Pope Dorchester, Hardys, Royal Oak and Blackdown Porter, log fire; fruit machines, video game, pinball, piped music *(Marjorie and David Lamb, Dr and Mrs A K Clarke, LYM; more reports on present newish regime please)*; [1 Lansdown Rd], *Farm House*: Pleasant setting on hill overlooking Bath, good choice of food and beer, jazz some evenings *(Anon)*; [Avon Buildings], *Golden Fleece*: Unpromising outside, but good food and impressive array of real ales like Courage Best, Marstons, Wadworths 6X and a recherché guest beer *(Roger Wain-Heapy)*; [Westgate Rd], *Mulligans*: Small simple Irish bar, good lunchtime snacks, traditional music, impressive choice of whiskeys, pleasant staff *(Dr and Mrs A K Clarke)*;

[Daniel St], *Pulteney Arms*: Good atmosphere, popular with Rugby players, well kept Ushers, worthy chip baps, good choice of juke box music *(Stephen O'Connor)*; *Sam Weller*: Well kept Bass and Wadworths 6X, good food cooked to order inc all-day breakfast, friendly young staff, lively mixed clientele *(Meg and Colin Hamilton)*; [42 Broad St], *Saracens Head*: Useful for decent food, cheaper than in many pubs here, inc generous Sat cold table; well kept Courage, quick service *(Meg and Colin Hamilton, Caroline Wright, Dr and Mrs A K Clarke)*

☆ **Bathford** [2 Bathford Hill, signed off A363; ST7966], *Crown*: Spacious and attractively laid out, with relaxed cafe-bar atmosphere, four or five distinct but linked areas inc no-smoking garden room, interesting decorations, good log fire; very wide choice of tasty home-cooked food from filled rolls up inc vegetarian (maybe a wait), well kept Bass, Marstons Pedigree and Ushers Best, decent wines, box of books for children, papers and guidebooks for adults; tables on terrace, nice garden; cl Mon lunchtime exc bank hols *(Meg and Colin Hamilton, GSB, Dr Andrew Brookes, A Curry, Dr and Mrs A K Clarke, RLW, Dizzy, Bob Riley, Catherine Hamilton, D Eberlin, Pat and John Millward, P R Phelps, Adam and Elizabeth Duff, Joy Heatherley, LYM)*

☆ **Bayford** [ST7229], *Unicorn*: Very welcoming beamed and flagstoned pub with big helpings of good value food, well kept Butcombe, Fullers London Pride and guest ales; four good simple bedrooms with own bathrooms, great breakfast *(John Honnor)*

Beckington [Bath Rd/Warminster Rd; ST8051], *Woolpack*: Calm old well refurbished inn with good food, good reasonably priced wines, warm welcome; no-smoking area, nice quiet lounge, good village bar; comfortable bedrooms, delightfully furnished *(Mr and Mrs Paul Adams, Ian Jagoe)*

Berrow [N of Burnham on Sea; ST2952], *Berrow*: Unpretentious friendly local with skittle alley and small dining room, extensive menu inc vegetarian and bargain steaks, good value generous helpings *(Bill and Sylvia Trotter)*

☆ **Biddisham** [off A38 Bristol—Bridgwater, not far from M5 junction 22; ST3853], *New Moon*: Large attractive family eating area in open-plan beamed pub with genuine well presented good value straightforward food, good friendly service; enclosed verandah, picnic tables in small garden *(Mr and Mrs D J Nash, Mark Undrill)*

☆ **Bishops Lydeard** [A358 towards Taunton; ST1828], *Kingfishers Catch*: Run as restaurant despite pub licence, but reliable for good choice of consistently good value food from lunchtime ploughman's and other snacks to steaks; neat, cottagey and relaxing, with welcoming quick service *(Shirley Pielou, BB)*

Bishops Wood [off B3170 S of Taunton; ST2512], *Candlelight*: New management doing well in roomy yet cosy pub with extensive and unusual menu from sandwiches up, fresh veg, pleasant new dining room *(Shirley Pielou)*

Blagdon [Bath Rd; A368; ST5059], *Live & Let Live*: Cosy partly panelled back bar with log fire and sporting prints, generous bar food maybe inc trout caught by landlord, good Sun lunch, well kept Ushers Founders, sensibly placed darts, pool and other pub games, restaurant; handy for fishing on Blagdon Lake; bedrooms *(Frank and Daphne Hodgson, LYM)*

☆ **Brendon Hills** [junction B3190/Elsworthy—Winsford; ST0434], *Raleghs Cross*: Isolated roadside inn nearly 1,200 ft high, views to Wales on clear days, good walking country; huge comfortably modernised bar with rows of banquettes, plenty of tables outside with play area, wide choice of popular generous food (some tables no smoking), carvery Fri/Sat evening and Weds, well kept Exmoor and Flowers Original; children in retaurant and family room; open all day summer; bedrooms *(John Hazel, Janet Pickles, Peter Watkins, Pam Stanley, R W Brooks, Mr and Mrs Hillman, M Joyner, Jill Bickerton, LYM)*

☆ **Brent Knoll** [2 miles from M5 junction 22; right on to A38, then first left; ST3350], *Red Cow*: Sensibly short choice of good well priced food inc proper veg and beautifully served Sun lunch in warmly welcoming spotless dining lounge where children allowed, with well spaced tables, quick pleasant staff, well kept Whitbreads-related ales, skittle alley, pleasant sheltered gardens *(Adrian and Gwynneth Littleton, Andrew Shore, Philip Brown, Elizabeth and Anthony Watts, BB)*

☆ **Bristol** [Upper Maudlin St/Colston St], *Brewery Tap*: Civilised and tasteful haven from city bustle, tap for Smiles brewery with their beers kept well, also interesting Continental bottled ones; small but clean and attractive, with good atmosphere even when packed; filled rolls, real fire; drinks 11-8, cl Sun *(R Marleyn, Simon and Amanda Southwell)*

☆ **Bristol** [St Thomas Lane, off Redcliff St/Victoria St], *Fleece & Firkin*: Lively atmosphere in lofty dim-lit 18th-c wool hall stripped back to stone and flagstones, basic furniture, well kept Smiles, lunchtime food (not Sun) inc gigantic filled baps, pleasant staff, live music Weds-Sat, children weekends *(RLW, Dizzy, LYM)*

☆ **Bristol** [Sion Pl, off Portland St], *Coronation Tap*: Friendly little bustling old-fashioned low-ceilinged tavern famous for its fat casks of interesting farm ciders, also Courage Best and Directors; simple lunchtime food, busy with students weekend evenings *(Gordon Mott, Don Kellaway, Angie Coles, LYM)*

Bristol [Bedminster; ST5670], *Albert*: Well kept Smiles, popular jazz evenings *(Don Kellaway, Angie Coles)*; [off Boyce's Ave, Clifton; ST5773], *Albion*: Friendly and unpretentiously old-fashioned pub with unusual flagstoned courtyard off cobbled alley, well kept Courage ales, simple snacks *(LYM)*; [The Triangle], *Aunties*: Small city pub with good atmosphere, newish licensee with good track record *(Barry and Anne)*; [Bell Hill, Stapleton; ST6176], *Bell*: Roomy red brick pub with welcoming licensees, well kept beers, good home-made meals, spotless dark woodwork *(A E and P McCully, Dr and Mrs A K Clarke)*; [14 Berkley Sq], *Berkley Square*: Smart wine-bar style pub with exciting decor inc a crazy Eiffel Tower; well kept Smiles *(Dr and Mrs A K Clarke)*; [Stokes Croft (A38)], *Brewhouse*: Old pub reopened with own brewery producing several good ales; friendly helpful service, pleasant atmosphere, help-yourself barrel of shell-on peanuts *(Richard Houghton)*; [20 Pembroke Rd, Clifton], *Channings Hotel*: Friendly local upstairs, with welcoming staff, good choice of changing guest beers and well kept Bass, Flowers, Smiles and Tetleys; downstairs completely different, student pub with music, pool, games machines; bedrooms *(D J Atkinson)*; [Regent St, Clifton], *Clifton*: Well done new conversion in traditional style, good food in back bar, well kept beers on electric pump, friendly staff, snugs in front bar with sports TV, all clean and comfortable; bar billiards, board games, no piped music; will be great when it's developed a more lived-in feel *(D J Atkinson, Caroline Grant)*; [Queens Rd], *Colonel Jaspers*: Large cellar bar with sawdust on floors, anything from own-brand real ale to a pipe of port *(Dr and Mrs A K Clarke)*; [Baltic Wharf, Cumberland Rd], *Cottage*: Converted customs house in dockland redevelopment, Boddingtons, Flowers IPA and Ruddles County on handpump, reasonably priced well cooked lunchtime food, efficient friendly staff, plenty of space; piped music; open all day, fine views of Bath landmarks from terrace *(Gwen and Peter Andrews, J Morrell, Bob Riley)*; [Lewington Rd, Fishponds; ST6376], *Fishponds*: Friendly refurbished local doing well under new landlord, two well kept real ales, reasonably priced bar food, keen darts players; open all day Sat *(Roy Kempton)*; [The Triangle, Clifton], *Hobgoblin*: Nice surroundings and good lunchtime atmosphere; crowded with young people evening *(Don Kellaway, Angie Coles)*; [Jacobs Wells Rd, Clifton], *Hope & Anchor*: Brews its own Lucifer ales, also well kept guest such as Badger Tnaglefoot, Marstons Pedigree, Timothy Taylors Landlord, good varied home-made food, summer evening barbecues in picturesque garden inc unusual sausages; occasional live music; popular with university students *(Mike Lucas)*; [centre], *Horn & Trumpet*: Well kept Boddingtons, Marstons Pedigree and Wadworths 6X; very busy Fri/Sat nights *(Anon)*; [Whiteladies Rd], *Kings Arms*: Particularly worth knowing for Sunday roasts *(Arabella Sanders)*; [32 Park St], *Le Chateau*: Grand mix of real-ale pub, wine bar, bistro, conservatory, Victorian memorial; best at weekends, esp Sun with bar nibbles and free papers *(Dr and Mrs A K Clarke, RLW, Dizzy)*; [off King St/Welsh Back], *Llandoger Trow*: By docks, making the most of its picturesque past; draught sherries, eclectic array of liqueur coffees, some concentration on food *(Gillian Washington)*; [off Corn St], *Market*: Panelled bar with old casks, good atmosphere, Smiles and Whitbreads, reasonably priced lunches inc soup, sandwiches and pies *(Nick and Meriel Cox)*; [127 St Georges Rd, Hotwells; ST5772], *Myrtle Tree*: Tiny, so small it has no cellar and barrels of well kept Bass are kept at the end of the bar *(Dr and Mrs A K Clarke)*; [17-18 King St], *Naval Volunteer*: Well done re-creation of traditional city pub, long bar buzzing with conversation, nice dark wood decor, when Admiral Benbow bar open (formerly next-door pub) has a good range of ales inc Bass and Smiles *(John and Phyllis Maloney, Richard Houghton)*; [45 King St], *Old Duke*: The Duke of the sign is Ellington – inside festooned with jazz posters and one or two instruments, side stage has good bands every night, and at Sun lunchtime; decent value simple food, well kept Courage Best and Directors, packed evenings *(Paul Carter, BB)*; [Gloucester Rd], *Prince of Wales*: Warm and friendly, plush seats, well kept Courage beers and Butcombe, simple lunchtime snacks, pleasant staff *(Gwen and Peter Andrews)*; [The Mall, Clifton], *Royal Oak*: Friendly efficient staff, great atmosphere *(Don Kellaway, Angie Coles)*; [St Michaels Hill], *Scotchman & his Pack*: Thoughtful range of good value well presented food in straightforward pub, lively with students and staff from nearby hospitals *(Barry and Anne)*; [15 Upper Maudlin St], *Sea Horse*: Recently taken over by nearby Smiles brewery, sympathetically refurbished *(Dr and Mrs A K Clarke)*; [Victoria St], *Shakespeare*: Elegantly refurbished partly panelled 17th-c pub with well kept Bass, Courage Best and Directors and Wadworths 6X, friendly quick service, open fire, good atmosphere, quiet back lounge *(Ian Phillips)*; [Lower Redland Rd], *Shakespeare*: Edwardian suburban local with quick friendly service, pleasant inexpensive bar food, well kept Bass and Wadworths 6X; no piped music *(A D Halls)*; [Lower Park Row], *Ship*: Low-ceilinged long narrow bar with nautical memorabilia, dimly lit back balcony, spiral stairs down to lower area with pool table, small lounge, several well kept ales such as Smiles and Wadworths 6X, reasonably priced food; small sunny terrace, well reproduced piped music esp evening *(Simon and Amanda Southwell)*; [off Whiteladies Rd, next to Clifton Down rly stn], *Steam Tavern*: Friendly Australian-run local in cosy former station house, wide choice of changing well kept ales, Australian theme – everything upside-down, strine phrases on walls *(Tony Reid)*; [St Michaels Hill, Cotham], *White Bear*: Friendly, with lots of comfortable seating, well kept Courage Directors and Wadworths 6X, no music; popular with students *(D J Atkinson)*

☆ **Broomfield** [1½ miles out on Bishops Lydeard—Bridgwater rd; ST2033], *Travellers Rest*: Attractive two-room pub with three separate sitting areas in largest room; attentive staff, Whitbreads-related ales, wide choice of pleasantly served food inc good soups and pies, log fires; tables outside, well placed for Quantocks *(John A Barker, Shirley Pielou)*

☆ **Bruton** [High St; ST6834], *Castle*: Good solid food value and changing choice of well kept ales in friendly and unpretentious town local, small darkish bars, striking mural of part of town in skittle alley, tables in sheltered back garden; children in eating area and skittle alley *(Canon Kenneth Wills, LYM)*

☆ **Castle Cary** [ST6332], *George*: Welcoming and tranquil old thatched coaching inn, quiet and civilised, with no-smoking lounge, very cosy small front bar with big inglenook, interesting choice of good reasonably priced fresh bar food, attractive dining room (cl Sun), smiling attentive staff, well kept Bass and Butcombe, decent wines inc local ones, good atmosphere; 16 comfortable and spacious bedrooms *(Steve Goodchild, Derek and Sylvia Stephenson, Gwen and Peter Andrews)*

☆ **Catcott** [ST3939], *Crown*: Comfortable and atmospheric old local, good food inc imaginative dishes, friendly service, well kept beer *(T J H Bodys, MJVK)*

☆ **Charlton Musgrove** [B3081, 5 miles SE of Bruton; ST7229], *Smithy*: Neatly refurbished 18th-c pub, sparkling clean, with stripped stone, heavy beams, log fires, home-cooked food inc Sun lunch, Butcombe, Fullers London Pride and Wadworths 6X, good welcoming service; arch to small restaurant overlooking garden, skittle alley and pool table *(E J Wilde, WHBM)*

☆ **Chilcompton** [Broadway; ST6452], *Somerset Wagon*: Four well kept ales and wide range of consistently good food, very popular with businessmen weekdays, in cosy, friendly and atmospheric pub with lots of settles, log fire, books, stuffed animals and militaria *(Susan Bourton, R F Wilson)*

☆ **Chilthorne Domer** [ST5219], *Carpenters Arms*: Comfortable and very welcoming, with good sensibly priced home-cooked traditional food inc lots of puddings, well kept Boddingtons, Marstons Pedigree and Wadworths 6X, friendly efficient service, open fire, fresh flowers; pleasant countryside *(Matthew Phillips, Lt Col James Kay, Alan and June Lucas)*

Churchill [Bristol Rd (A38); ST4560], *Churchill Inn*: Spacious and comfortable family pub, good prompt service, six well kept ales, usual bar food inc children's and Sun lunch; fruit machines, Sky TV *(Mr and Mrs Peter Woods, P H Roberts)*

☆ **Clevedon** [Elton Rd; ST4071], *Little Harp*: On the prom, spacious and popular, terrace and conservatory looking towards Exmoor and the Welsh hills, good helpings of food inc vegetarian and substantial sandwiches, well kept Bass *(Mr and Mrs A K McCully, Tom Evans, JCW)*

☆ **Clevedon** [15 The Beach], *Moon & Sixpence*: Substantial seafront Victorian family dining pub with good choice of generous food, efficient friendly service, balconied mezzanine floor with good sea views to Brecon Beacons, well kept Bass and Smiles tapped from the cask *(A Preston, Alan and Paula McCully)*

☆ **Combe Florey** [off A358 Taunton—Williton, just N of main village turn-off; ST1531], *Farmers Arms*: Neatly rebuilt picturesque thatched and beamed pub with popular food, plenty of tables outside, good log fire, well kept Bass *(Howard Clutterbuck, BB)*

Combe St Nicholas [2½ miles N of Chard; ST3011], *Green Dragon*: Unpretentious local, with good reasonably priced food (ex-butcher landlord – always a good sign), welcoming service, well kept Bass, decent wines, open fire; well behaved children allowed; bedrooms *(Howard Clutterbuck)*

Combwich [ST2542], *Anchor*: Good comfortable pubby atmosphere, fine open fire in lounge, hens scratching in yard; food inc good sandwiches *(M M A Clark)*

Compton Dando [Court Hill; ST6464], *Compton*: Two-bar stonebuilt village local in lovely setting; traditional games *(Dr and Mrs A K Clarke)*

☆ **Congresbury** [St Pauls Causeway; ST4363], *Old Inn*: Tucked-away local, friendly and peaceful, with well kept Bass, Marstons Pedigree, Smiles and Wadworths 6X, decent cheap food, open fire, ancient stove, hundred of matchboxes on low beams *(P M Lane, Mr and Mrs A K McCully, Ron Shelton)*

Congresbury [Brinsea Rd (B3133)], *Plough*: Old flagstoned pub with three distinctive seating areas off main bar, two open fires, old prints, farm tools and sporting memorabilia; basic lunchtime food, well kept ales inc Bass, Crown Buckley Reverend James, Shepherd Neame Spitfire and Wadworths 6X, enthusiastic darts team, table skittles, shove ha'penny and cards, welcoming jack russell called Pepper; small garden with boules, aviary and occasional barbecues *(Alan and Paula McCully)*; [Wrington Rd], *White Hart & Inwood*: In new hands and modernised with conservatory extension, good interesting varied food, fair range of beers *(Dr and Mrs B D Smith)*

Corfe [ST2319], *White Hart*: Good attractively presented food esp huge filled baps and daily specials, efficient pleasant service, attractive layout, guest beers such as Whitbreads Pompey Royal *(Shirley Pielou)*

☆ **Corton Denham** [OS Sheet 183 map ref 634225; ST6322], *Queens Arms*: Attractive and well kept old stonebuilt village inn, comfortable smallish main bar with woodburner, fresh flowers and brasses, Welsh landlord takes great pride in changing guest beers – four a week such as Exmoor, Holdens, Old Stone and Trough; good fresh reasonably priced food; nr Cadbury Castle, bedrooms with good views *(Ian and Val Titman, John and Joan Nash)*

Cossington [Middle Rd; ST3540], *Red Tile*: Welcoming, with Butcombe, Exmoor and John Smiths, fine choice of ports, good food inc daily fresh Brixham fish and speciality steaks, well kept garden with big adventure play area *(Steve Olive)*

Culbone Hill [A39 W of Porlock; opp toll rd from Porlock Weir; SS8247], *Culbone Stables*: Spruced-up unpubby open-plan place with neat light wood tables and chairs, worth knowing for moderately priced sandwiches and bar food, well kept Bass ales and one brewed for them, good farm cider; bedrooms, Exmoor views *(PR)*

☆ **Dinnington** [ST4012], *Rose & Crown*: Good atmosphere in attractive unspoilt country pub with good value home cooking esp seafood, good range of real ales *(Michael Duck, David and Fiona Easeman)*

☆ **Ditcheat** [village signed off A37 and A371 S of Shepton Mallet; ST6236], *Manor House*: Pretty village pub, unusual arched doorways connecting big flagstoned public bar to comfortably relaxed lounge and close-tabled eating area, friendly welcome, very wide choice of good attractively priced food inc unusual puddings, well kept Butcombe and Youngers, open fires, skittle alley, tables on back grass *(Gwen and Peter Andrews, Derek and Iris Martin, P and J Rush, BB)*

☆ **Dulverton** [High St; SS9127], *Lion*: Good food and helpful service in old-fashioned country-town hotel with well kept Exmoor and Ushers on handpump, decent wine and coffee; pleasant setting *(Gwen and Peter Andrews, J C Simpson)*

☆ **East Coker** [ST5412], *Helyar Arms*: Tastefully extended village pub in attractive setting, good reasonably priced food esp fish, super service, good range of ales, oak beams, nice decor *(Wg Cdr J W Lovell)*

☆ **Edington Burtle** [Catcott Rd; ST3943], *Olde Burtle*: Good reasonably priced food inc fresh fish in bar and restaurant, lovely log fire, well kept beer, attractive and friendly local atmosphere *(Gethin Lewis, P H Roberts)*

Edington Burtle, *Tom Mogg*: Modernised country pub with emphasis on food inc generous Sun lunch, well kept Butcombe and John Smiths, terrace and garden *(Nigel and Helen Aplin)*

☆ **Exford** [The Green; SS8538], *Crown*: Traditional old local with pine furniture, log fire and attractive streamside garden, now under same management as Royal Oak at Withypool (see main entries), with welcoming service, well kept beer, decent wines, wide range of reasonably priced imaginative food *(Debbie Leam, Mrs C Watkinson, Ron Shelton)*

Failand [B3128 Bristol—Portishead; ST5271], *Failand*: Simply furnished typical country pub, good usual bar food *(Mrs C Watkinson)*

☆ **Farleigh Hungerford** [A366 Trowbridge—Norton St Philip; ST8057], *Hungerford Arms*: Attractive smartly furnished pub with good views, decent food in main bar, more airy room off, and popular lower-level restaurant, well kept Courage-related ales, friendly service *(Ted George)*

☆ **Fitzhead** [ST1128], *Fitzhead*: Cosy and popular village pub with good unusual specials esp fish and game as well as good more straightforward dishes, well kept Cotleigh Tawny and guest ales, good choice of wines, friendly atmosphere, enthusiastic young licensees, furniture made by landlord; piped music mostly Irish, very busy weekends *(A Kersey-Brown, Mrs Joyce Brotherton, Dave Williams)*

☆ **Glastonbury** [Northload St; ST5039], *Who'd A Thought It*: Good often original food esp fish, well kept ales such as Bass, Eldridge Pope Blackdown Porter and Thomas Hardy and Palmers, decent wines, coal fires, friendly service, enthusiastic landlord, very supportive regulars, stripped brickwork, flagstones and polished pine, exuberant collection of bric-a-brac and memorabilia, entertaining decorations in lavatories, no-smoking restaurant; bedrooms cosy and comfortable, good breakfasts *(P M Lane, Annette and Stephen Marsden, Dr and Mrs J D Abell, Andrew and Helen Latchem, Martin Copeman)*

☆ **Glastonbury** [High St], *George & Pilgrims*: 15th-c inn with magnificent carved stone frontage, good front bar with relaxed atmosphere, heavy tables, handsome stone fireplace and traceried stained-glass bay window; rest of pub, and food and service, more ordinary; well kept Bass and Wadworths 6X, children in buffet and pleasant upstairs restaurant, occasional live music; good clean bedrooms *(Colin and Ann Hunt, Gwen and Peter Andrews, John and Phyllis Maloney, LYM)*

Glastonbury [27 Benedict St], *Mitre*: Good value food inc fresh fish, home-made pies and big puddings, good range of well kept beer inc John Smiths; gets very busy *(Annette and Stephen Marsden)*; [4 Chilkwell St (A361, SE of centre)], *Riflemans Arms*: Chatty popular local with real ales such as Flowers IPA, Eldridge Pope Royal Oak and Palmers, farm cider, good games room, play area and sunny terrace *(Dr Wolf Thandoy, BB)*

☆ **Hallatrow** [ST6357], *Old Station*: Formidable collection of bric-a-brac from 1936 newspapers to beeping car coming through wall, model train running around ceiling, wide changing choice of food, well kept Bass and other ales, lovely staff; garden behind *(D G Clarke, Mike Pugh, Alan and Paula McCully, John and Wendy Trentham)*

Halse [off B3227 Taunton—Bampton; ST1427], *New Inn*: Enjoyable generous food, good range of beers, obliging attentive service; bedrooms clean and homely, with good breakfasts *(Julian and Louise Thomas)*

☆ **Hardway** [rd to Alfreds Tower, off B3081 Bruton—Wincanton at Redlynch; pub named on OS Sheet 183 map ref 721342; ST7234],

Bull: Neat and attractive country dining pub, very popular locally esp with older people weekday lunchtimes, warm comfortable bar, character dining rooms, log fire, well kept Butcombe and Wadworths 6X, farm cider; piped music; tables in nice garden over road, handy for Stourhead Garden *(H and D Cox, Pat and Robert Watt, Pat and John Smyth, Michael Porter, W and S Jones, John and Joan Nash)*

☆ **Haselbury Plucknett** [off N side of A30 about 1½ miles from Crewkerne; ST4711], *Old Mill*: Great atmosphere, good food inc interesting dishes in bar and charming dining room; duck pond and tables outside *(Brian and Peggy Pinfold, Chris and Joan Woodward)*

☆ **Hatch Beauchamp** [old village rd, not bypass; ST3220], *Hatch*: Wide choice of good honest food, very welcoming licensees, lots of copper and brass in carpeted lounge bar with attractive bow-window seats, well kept Butcombe and Teignworthy Reel Ale, farm ciders; games room across yard; good value immaculate bedrooms *(Richard Dolphin, S G Pielou, BB)*

Henstridge [A30 Shaftesbury—Sherborne, junction with A357; ST7119], *Virginia Ash*: Big popular rambling pub, wide choice of food in large restaurant, particularly good puddings and ices, family area, no-smoking area, very accommodating service; morning coffee, tables outside with play area *(Basil J S Minson, Stephen Brown)*

Hillfarance [ST1624], *Anchor*: Peaceful and pretty country local with lots of flower tubs outside, good straightforward food inc children's in attractively redecorated bar and two good eating areas, good value evening carvery, family room with Wendy house, speedy friendly service, well kept beers, garden with play area; bedrooms, caravan site, holiday apartments *(Shirley Pielou, Rich and Pauline Appleton)*

Hinton Blewett [village signed off A37 in Clutton; ST5957], *Ring o' Bells*: Charming low-beamed stone-built country local with good value home cooking (not Sun evening), well kept Wadworths Devizes and 6X on handpump, log fire, pleasant view from tables in sheltered front yard; children welcome *(Robert Huddleston, LYM)*

Hinton Charterhouse [off A36 S of Bath; ST7758], *Rose & Crown*: Friendly and attractive panelled bar with well kept Bass, Butcombe and Smiles tapped from casks, decent food in bar and restaurant; loud live folk music some evenings *(David and Barbara Davies, M G Hart)*

Holford [A39; ST1541], *Plough*: Busy village local with popular food inc good value Sun roasts and lots of steaks, well kept Boddingtons; handy for wonderful Quantocks walks *(David Wright, John Hazel, G W A Pearce)*

☆ **Holton** [ST6827], *Old Inn*: Friendly 16th-c inn with beams, ancient flagstones, log fire, lots of atmosphere; interesting cheap snacks and other food in bar and restaurant (popular weekdays with businessmen and older people), good service, real ales and ciders, tables on terrace *(Gethin Lewis, Maj and Mrs E M Warrick)*

☆ **Horsington** [village signposted off A357 S of Wincanton; ST7023], *Half Moon*: Good atmosphere in knocked-through bars with beams and stripped stone, oak floors, inglenook log fires; well presented home-made food, well kept Adnams, Wadworths IPA and 6X and a guest beer, decent wines, good service, dogs and cats; restaurant Thurs-Sat evening, big back garden with play area; good value bedrooms in chalets *(Geraldine Berry, LYM)*

Howley [ST2609], *Howley Tavern*: Spacious bar with wide choice of imaginative bar food inc vegetarian, Bass, Flowers Original and changing guest beers, decent wines, attractive old-world restaurant; bedrooms *(MAJ, Shirley Johnson)*

☆ **Ilchester** [The Square; ST5222], *Ivelchester*: Friendly inn with outstanding food in bar and restaurant inc sensational puddings; bedrooms extremely comfortable; bedrooms *(David Surridge)*

☆ **Keinton Mandeville** [off A37; ST5430], *Quarry*: Comfortably refurbished pub popular for generous reasonably priced straightforward food inc local seafood, welcoming service, well kept ales, cosy restaurant, skittle room, attractive garden *(Ted George, Adam and Joan Bunting, Nick Cox, John Hazel, Derek and Iris Martin, P and J Rush)*

☆ **Keynsham** [Bitton Rd; ST6568], *Lock Keeper*: Straightforward bar in lovely spot by Avon with lock, marina and weir, good food inc good shellfish open sandwich and steak sandwich, well kept Bass, impressive children's room in sort of cavern down steep stairway with murals; big riverside garden with boules *(Tom Evans)*

Kingsbury Episcopi [ST4321], *Wyndham Arms*: New owner preserving unspoilt style of flagstoned country pub with roaring open fires, good value food, well kept Bass *(S G Brown)*

Lansdown [N towards Dyrham; ST7269], *Blathwayt Arms*: Large comfortable Whitbreads pub with well kept Boddingtons, good top-up policy, good value generous food; open all day *(Dave Irving, Dr and Mrs A K Clarke)*

☆ **Leigh upon Mendip** [ST6847], *Bell*: Comfortable 16th-c beamed village local with wide range of good value home-cooked bar food, good choice of well kept real ales, roaring log fire, efficient service, pleasant restaurant; skittle alley *(J and R S Glover, Fiona Dick)*

Long Ashton [172 Long Ashton Rd; ST5570], *Angel*: Nice pub with log fire in main bar, children's rooms, small courtyard *(Don Kellaway, Angie Coles)*

☆ **Long Sutton** [A372 E of Langport; ST4625], *Devonshire Arms*: Friendly, unpretentious and homely, with good wide-ranging menu inc unusual dishes and lots of fish, two or three well kept real ales, restaurant; bedrooms spacious and clean, with good breakfasts; bedrooms *(Stephen Brown, Janet and Harvey Tooth)*

☆ **Long Sutton**, *Lime Kiln*: Very wide choice of good generous attractively presented food and friendly service in uncluttered pub with three well kept real ales, log fire, restaurant; good modern bedrooms *(Mrs S Knight)*

Lower Langford [ST4660], *Langford*: Roomy and attractive family dining pub with good tasty food, decent wines, great children's room with lots of toys, accommodating staff; pleasant terrace *(Chris and Joan Woodward, Belinda Seaton)*

Mark [ST3747], *White Horse*: Spacious and attractively old-world pub dating from 17th century, with wide choice of home-cooked food, well kept Flowers and guest beers, good friendly service, some decent malt whiskies; good garden with playground *(John Abbott, Philip Brown)*

Marston Magna [ST5922], *Marston*: Helpful cheerful licensees, good service, recently improved interior, old beams, lovely main restaurant, good reasonably priced food, good house wine *(Wg Cdr J W Lovell)*

☆ **Midford** [ST7560], *Hope & Anchor*: Homely and clean, with welcoming service, particularly good interesting food in bar and restaurant end, well kept Butcombe, good Spanish wines, welcoming service; tables outside, video security in car park *(N C Walker, Mr and Mrs Paul Adams, Bill Bailey)*

☆ **Milborne Port** [A30 E of Sherborne; ST6718], *Queens Head*: Beamed lounge with very good choice of generous good value home-cooked food, good range of well kept ales and farm ciders, friendly service, games in public bar, skittle alley, quiet restaurant; tables in sheltered courtyard and garden with play area; children welcome (except in bars); three cosy good value bedrooms *(Mr and Mrs K Box, LYM)*

Milborne Port [High St], *Kings Head*: Good atmosphere in refurbished village pub, snug, bar and dining areas, Eldridge Pope beers, good snacks and meals inc good value children's helpings; good choice of wines *(John Sanders)*

☆ **Milton Clevedon** [High St (B3081); ST6637], *Ilchester Arms*: Homely and comfortable early 17th-c beamed and stripped-brick pub with friendly landlord, rustic bric-a-brac, wide choice of reasonably priced food, well kept Palmers and Wadworths 6X, piano, smaller restaurant bar; lovely hill views from garden and conservatory; no food Sun, cl Mon lunchtime *(John Hazel)*

☆ **Misterton** [Middle St; ST4508], *White Swan*: Beautifully kept, comfortable and friendly, with charmingly served good food cooked by landlady, first-class range of beers, framed tapestries, collection of old wireless sets; attractive new garden behind, skittle alley *(MK, Mrs C H Drew, G C V Clifton, Douglas Allen)*

Monkton Combe [ST7762], *Wheelwrights Arms*: Small country inn with attractively laid-out bar, wheelwright and railway memorabilia, wide choice of reasonably priced wholesome food, well kept ales such as Adnams, Butcombe and Wadworths 6X, big open fire, tiny darts room at end, fruit machine, quiet piped music; well equipped small bedrooms in separate block *(Mike and Kathleen York, LYM)*

☆ **Montacute** [ST4916], *Phelips Arms*: Roomy and airy pub with varied good freshly cooked fair-priced food inc sandwiches, friendly efficient service, well kept beers; HQ of Yeovil branch of Monster Raving Loony Party; tables in garden, delightful village, handy for Montacute House *(Maj and Mrs E M Warrick, Donald Godden, A Preston, S G Brown, Wendy Arnold)*

Moorlinch [signed off A39; ST3939], *Ring of Bells*: Welcoming new landlord and friendly atmosphere, good hearty food, four well kept real ales; attractive lounge with open fires *(A E and P McCully, A and J Tierney-Jones)*

☆ **Nether Stowey** [Keenthorne – A39 E of village; not to be confused with Apple Tree Cottage; ST1939], *Cottage*: Warm and cheerful local with generous good value simple food, Butcombe and Flowers Original, friendly service, comfortable music-free dining lounge with woodburner, aquarium, interesting pictures; games room with two pool tables, juke box and machines (children allowed here); skittle alley, tables on terrace *(John Hazel, LYM)*

☆ **North Brewham** [ST7236], *Old Red Lion*: Stone-floored low-beamed former farmhouse with good food, pleasant atmosphere, well kept Butcombe, Fullers and Greene King ales, friendly and efficient service; handy for King Alfred's monument which is nearby; good if rather pricey food, pleasant atmosphere, and friendly; *(Derek and Sylvia Stephenson, John Hazel)*

North Curry [Queens Sq; ST3225], *Bird in Hand*: Attractive beamed and timbered local with well kept ales, public bar, lounge bar and restaurant; has recently emerged, under a new landlord, from a short phase as 'The Old Coaching Inn' *(Richard Dolphin)*

☆ **North Perrott** [ST4709], *Manor Arms*: Attractively modernised 16th-c pub on pretty village green, inglenook, beams and mellow stripped stone, good value imaginative freshly made food from sandwiches up in bar and cosy restaurant, well kept Boddingtons and Smiles, decent wines, cheerful atmosphere, very welcoming landlord, pleasant garden with adventure play area; two good value comfortable bedrooms in coach house *(G C V Clifton, Ian and Rosemary Wood, Canon Kenneth Wills, Desmond and Pat Morris, Maureen Hobbs, J Dobson)*

Norton sub Hamdon [ST4615], *Lord Nelson*: Good food, friendly customers and staff; pretty village *(Mrs G E Fisher)*

Nunney [11 Church St; signed off A361 Shepton Mallet—Frome; ST7345], *George*: Rambling much modernised open-plan bar with stripped stone walls, log fire, four well kept changing ales such as Exmoor and Wadworths 6X, food inc giant steaks in bar and restaurant, afternoon teas, piped music; rare 'gallows' sign spanning road, in quaint village with stream and ruined castle; bedrooms *(Mike and Sue Moss, BB)*

☆ **Panborough** [B3139 Wedmore—Wells; ST4745], *Panborough Inn*: Friendly and spacious 17th-c village inn with wide interesting range of generous food inc vegetarian and splendid puddings; several clean, comfortable and attractive rooms, inglenook, beams, brass and copper, pleasant attentive service, real ales, unobtrusive piped music; skittle alley, small restaurant, tables in front terraced garden; bedrooms comfortable *(Peter Cornall, Dono and Carol Leaman, K R Harris)*

☆ **Pitminster** [OS Sheet 193 map ref 219191; ST2118], *Queens Arms*: Unspoilt village pub with rather basic bar area, new management eager to please, seven real ales, imaginative wines, good bar food from fine crab sandwiches up, wonderful fish restaurant in pleasant dining room; bedrooms now have own bathrooms *(Lady Emma Chanter, Shirley Pielou)*

☆ **Pitney** [ST4428], *Halfway House*: Friendly and simply furnished old-fashioned pub concentrating on some nine well kept real ales such as Cotleigh Tawny and Oakhill; three log fires, food inc speciality curries *(Arthur and Anne Frampton, Andy Jones)*

☆ **Polsham** [A39 N of Glastonbury; ST5142], *Camelot*: Well run roomy 18th-c dining pub with wide choice of promptly served good food in bar, restaurant and conservatory looking over fields; Palmers and a local beer brewed for the pub, big children's area, terrace; bedrooms *(Brig J S Green, R V Ford, Mr and Mrs K Box)*

☆ **Porlock** [High St (A39); SS8846], *Ship*: Picturesque thatched huge-chimneyed partly 13th-c pub, traditional low-beamed front bar with flagstones, inglenooks each end, hunting prints, plush back lounge, well kept Bass, Cotleigh Old Buzzard, Courage Best and a local guest beer, good country wines, bar food, pub games and pool table, garden; children welcome in eating area; bedrooms; has been a very highly rated main entry and still gives much pleasure, but needs to pull its socks up a bit before we can recommend it universally again *(John Hazel, John and Marianne Cooper, Jan and Dave Booth, W A Wheeler, A Plumb, Dorothee and Dennis Glover, Joan Coleman, Jim and Maggie Cowell, Gwen and Peter Andrews, Christopher and Sharon Hayle, Georgina Cole, Risha Stapleton, Jack and Philip Paxton, Dave Thompson, Margaret Mason, George and Jeanne Barnwell, Don and Thelma Beeson, Mr and Mrs Westcombe, LYM)*

☆ **Porlock Weir** [separate from but run in tandem with neighbouring Anchor Hotel; SS8547], *Ship*: Prettily restored old inn included for its wonderful setting by peaceful harbour, with tables in terraced rose garden and good walks; usual bar food, Courage-related and Exmoor ales and good welcoming service in straightforward family Mariners Bar; roaring fire, attractive bedrooms; not to be confused with the above nearby pub of the same name *(James Nunns, Risha Stapleton, David Wright, Paul Randall, Elizabeth and Anthony Watts, LYM)*

Portbury [½ mile from A369 (off M5 junction 19); ST5075], *Priory*: Pleasant main bar, well kept Bass, bar food inc decent baked potatoes (may take a time) *(TE)*

Portishead [Nore Rd; ST4777], *Hole-In-One*: Originally a golf club house and includes former windmill tower; lovely setting overlooking Severn estuary, great value winter meals offers *(A Kilpatrick)*; [High St], *Poacher*: Locally popular for wide range of good value fresh food inc real veg; Butcombe and Courage ales *(K R Harris)*

☆ **Priddy** [off B3135; ST5450], *New Inn*: Convivial low-beamed pub, modernised but still traditional, doing well under new licensees, with good log fire, spacious conservatory, good value food inc interesting dishes, well kept Bass, Eldridge Pope Hardy and Wadworths 6X, good local cider and house wines, good welcoming service, skittle alley; motorcyclists made welcome; bedrooms comfortable and homely, on quiet village green *(Arthur and Anne Frampton, Paul Nicholson, WHBM, David Logan, Jim and Maggie Cowell)*

☆ **Priddy** [from Wells on A39 pass hill with TV mast on left, then next left – OS Sheet 183 map ref 549502], *Hunters Lodge*: Very unassuming walkers' and potholers' inn taken over by local small Oakhill Brewery, well kept ales tapped from casks behind the bar, welcoming atmosphere, simple good food inc bread and local cheese and OAP bargain lunches, log fire, flagstones; tables in garden *(R H Martyn, Barry and Anne, LYM)*

☆ **Priddy** [off B3135], *Queen Victoria*: Relaxed old-fashioned country pub with flagstones and good open fires, interesting bric-a-brac, friendly staff; well kept Butcombe and other ales tapped from the cask, organic beers, farm ciders and perries, reasonably priced standard food; motorcyclists made welcome; good garden for children over road *(John and Phyllis Maloney, Peter and Wendy Begley)*

Radstock [Walnut Buildings; ST6954], *Tyning*: Long bar in old building, lots of pub games *(Dr and Mrs A K Clarke)*

Rickford [ST4859], *Plume of Feathers*: Log fire, friendly staff, bar food *(Don Kellaway, Angie Coles)*

☆ **Ridgehill** [Crown Hill – pub signed from village; ST5262], *Crown*: Interesting old pub, authentically old-fashioned, with attractive restaurant, skittle alley, lovely views from terrace *(Mary Reed, Rowly Pitcher, Dr and Mrs A K Clarke, G Hart)*

☆ **Rowberrow** [about ½ mile from A38 at Churchill; ST4558], *Swan*: Good bar food from fine sandwiches up and quick courteous service in olde-worlde pub with comic hunting prints and grandfather clock, well kept Bass and Wadworths 6X; good walking country *(Mr and Mrs A K McCully, Gethin Lewis)*

Ruishton [Ilminster Rd (A358); just off M5 junction 25; ST2626], *Blackbrook*: Busy Country Carvery dining pub with wide choice of generous decent food inc children's in open-plan beamed bar, several roomy wooden-screened areas inc carvery and family area, quick helpful service, Courage-related ales; good-sized garden with play area *(Gill and Keith Croxton, Prof A N Black)*

Shepton Mallet [63 Charlton Rd; ST6445], *Thatched Cottage*: Comfortable, with varied bar food; bedrooms with own baths *(Pat Woodward)*

Shoscombe [off A366, A367 or A362 E of Radstock; ST7156], *Apple Tree*: Good atmosphere in basic bar, carpeted lounge with dividing wooden screen, real ales inc Otter and Oakhill; piped music may be loud *(T McLean, R Huggins, E McCall, D Irving)*

Somerton [Church Sq; ST4828], *White Hart*: Attractive 18th-c stonebuilt inn with good food at most attractive prices – good value; friendly service *(P B Arbib)*

Sparkford [A303; ST6026], *Sparkford*: Former Bass pub now run as popular free house by new young licensees, good varied buffet, well kept beers *(Canon Kenneth Wills)*

☆ **Staple Fitzpaine** [ST2618], *Greyhound*: Relaxing sophisticated atmosphere under charming and ebullient newish landlord in interesting rambling country pub with antique layout, flagstones and inglenooks; friendly service, well kept Whitbreads and interesting local real ales such as Juwards, good food *(Tina Bird, Richard Dolphin, Margaret and Nigel Dennis, LYM)*

Stoke sub Hamdon [ST4717], *Fleur de Lis*: Popular and friendly old village local with good well priced food, well kept beers and local ciders, friendly landlady; bedrooms *(Lisa Girling, Steven Robins)*

Tatworth [A358 S of Chard; ST3206], *Olde Poppe*: Very old, with good inexpensive bar snacks, restaurant menu, well kept beers, unusual reasonably priced wines *(MAJ, KWJ, Shirley Johnson)*

☆ **Taunton** [Magdalene St], *Masons Arms*: Fine friendly town pub, often very busy, with good range of well kept ales inc Exmoor, good reasonably priced food from efficient food counter, comfortably basic furnishings, no music or pool tables; good bedrooms *(Bill and Beryl Farmer, Howard Clutterbuck, John Barker, Hugh Donnelly)*

☆ **Thurloxton** [ST2730], *Maypole*: Several different welcoming and attractive areas, very wide choice of generous food from filled baps up, chatty landlord, quick friendly service, Whitbreads-related ales, biggish no-smoking area, soft piped music, skittle alley; peaceful village *(Shirley Pielou, Pete Yearsley, Thomas Neate)*

Trull [Church Rd; ST2122], *Winchester Arms*: Welcoming lively local, good lunchtime food inc fresh veg, good value suppers in small dining room, new licensees settling in well *(Shirley Pielou)*

☆ **Upton Noble** [ST7139], *Lamb*: Small comfortable stripped-stone village local with lovely views and big garden; has been very popular for adventurous food, good service and well kept beer, but as we went to press there was talk of its closing *(News please)*

☆ **Watchet** [Swain St; ST0743], *West Somerset*: Unpretentious, attractive and welcoming, with good cheap food, well kept Cotleigh Tawny and Courage-related ales, nice courtyard with rockery; bedrooms with own bathrooms *(Bob Smith)*

☆ **Waterrow** [A361 Wiveliscombe—Bampton; ST0425], *Rock*: Well run, clean and attractive, charming setting in small valley village; well kept ales inc Cotleigh Tawny and Exmoor Gold, wide choice of home-made food, attractive prices, log fire in smallish friendly bar exposing the rock it's built on, couple of steps up to lunchtime dining room doubling as evening restaurant; good well equipped bedrooms *(Jill Bickerton, Patrick Freeman, Pete and Rosie Flower)*

Wedmore [ST4347], *New Inn*: Good generous food inc speciality ham, vegetarian and children's dishes in cosy and welcoming olde-worlde pub, real ales inc Butcombe and guests, good wines by the glass, jovial landlord and landlady; *(Adrian Acton, Pam and Gerald Roxbury)*

☆ **Wells** [High St, nr St Cuthberts; ST5545], *City Arms*: Good choice of good value food inc unusual dishes in big L-shaped bar and upstairs restaurant of attractively converted largely early 18th-c building – some parts even older (said to have been a Tudor jail); Butcombe and Smiles ales, decent wines, friendly prompt service *(M G Hart, Howard Clutterbuck, John and Phyllis Maloney)*

☆ **Wells** [St Thomas St], *Fountain*: Good vaue generous imaginative food in pleasantly pubby downstairs bar with roaring log fire and popular upstairs restaurant – worth booking weekends, good Sun lunch; friendly quick staff, well kept Courage-related ales, farm cider, good choice of wines, piped music; right by cathedral; children welcome *(John and Phyllis Maloney, Dominic Barrington, Martyn G Hart)*

Wells [42 Southover], *Full Moon*: Basic quiet pub away from the busy High St, small but good value menu, small snug with tables for meals, no-smoking dining room, four real ales, log fires, unobtrusive piped music; tables in big garden; live music Tues *(Brig J S Green)*

☆ **West Bagborough** [ST1633], *Rising Sun*: Welcoming local in tiny village below Quantocks, family service, short choice of fresh generous home-cooked food, well kept Exmoor and Oakhill Farmers, unobtrusive piped music, darts, table skittles, big log fires; bedrooms comfortable, with own bathrooms *(John A Barker, Anthony Barnes, Dr B and*

Mrs P B Baker)
West Camel [ST5724], *Walnut*: Smartly upmarket pub with several real ales, good service and imaginative range of food; very popular Sun (no sandwiches, ploughman's etc then); bedrooms *(A Kilpatrick, Mr and Mrs Copeland)*

☆ **West Pennard** [A361 Glastonbury—Shepton Mallet; ST5438], *Apple Tree*: Well renovated, with flagstones, exposed brickwork, beams, good woodburner, comfortable seats, thatch above main bar, second bar and two eating areas; wide choice of impressive food (landlady watches cooking standards so closely that there may be a wait), well kept Bass, Cotleigh Golden Eagle and Worthington BB, good coffee, pleasant staff; can get crowded lunchtime; tables on terrace *(June and Tony Baldwin, Richard Dolphin)*

☆ **West Pennard** [A361 E of Glastonbury], *Lion*: Short choice of rewarding subtly flavoured food in three neat dining areas opening off small flagstoned and black-beamed core with log fire in big stone inglenook, second log fire in stripped-stone family area, well kept local real ales, welcoming staff; bedrooms comfortable and well equipped, in neatly converted side barn *(W F C Phillips, Canon Kenneth Wills, Mike and Sue Moss, BB)*

Weston in Gordano [B3124 Portishead—Clevedon; ST4474], *White Hart*: Good straightforward food, welcoming helpful service, friendly atmosphere *(MJVK)*

Weston Super Mare [ST3261], *Britannia*: Quiet and friendly pub well off the crowded high street, good bar snacks inc cheap sandwiches *(Brig J S Green)*; [seafront, N end], *Claremont Vaults*: Most windows face towards the sea, with wonderful views down the beach or across the bay, helped by floor being raised about a foot; good choice of cheap lunchtime bar food, three or four well priced real ales, plush furnishings, friendly service *(A C Stone, Ian Phillips)*

Westport [B3168 Ilminster—Curry Rivel; ST3819], *Old Barn Owl*: Peaceful and attractive stripped stone bar, long and narrow, with three small dining areas and separate children's area; wide choice of good food inc fresh veg and unusual dishes, well kept Boddingtons and Wadworths 6X; no piped music; bedrooms *(Shirley Pielou)*

☆ **Wheddon Cross** [A396/B3224, S of Minehead; SS9238], *Rest & Be Thankful*: Good range of home-cooked food from children's dishes to salmon en croute and helpful attentive staff in quietly welcoming comfortably modern two-room bar with buffet bar and restaurant, well kept Courage-related ales, hot drinks, log fire, aquarium and piped music; communicating games area, skittle alley, public lavatory for the disabled; bedrooms *(Clem Stephens, Patrick and Patricia Derwent, LYM)*

☆ **Widcombe** [Culmhead – OS Sheet 193 map ref 222160; ST2216], *Holman Clavel*: Simple but comfortable and charming rustic pub named after its massive holly chimney-beam, good cheap home-cooked bar food, welcoming hard-working landlord, well kept Cotleigh and Flowers Original, nice atmosphere; dogs welcome, handy for Blackdown Hills *(Richard R Dolphin, BB)*

Williton [Long St; ST0740], *Royal Huntsman*: Good range of food, clean and comfortable *(K R Harris)*

Witham Friary [signposted from A361 – OS Sheet 183 map ref 745409; ST7441], *Seymour Arms*: Unchanging unspoilt local, two characterful rooms, hatch servery, warm welcome for visitors, well kept Ushers tapped from the cask, local farm cider; darts, cards, dominoes – no juke box or machines; pleasant garden *(Pete Baker)*

Woolavington [ST3441], *Prince of Wales*: Well kept beer, decent food, good friendly atmosphere, fruit machine, juke box, skittle alley; Thurs pig racing *(Nigel Holman)*

☆ **Woolverton** [A36 N of village; ST7954], *Red Lion*: Roomy beamed pub, panelling, flagstones and rugs on parquet, well kept Bass and Wadworths 6X, very wide choice of wines by the glass, winter mulled wine, straightforward food inc popular filled baked potatoes; open all day *(Dave and Jules Tuckett, LYM)*

Wrantage [A378 E of M5 junction 25; ST3022], *Canal*: Small welcoming three-roomed pub with well kept Cotleigh Tawny and others, farm cider, log fires, usual food nicely and quickly served in bar and dining room; darts, skittle alley, garden with play area *(Pete Yearsley)*

Yarlington [ST6529], *Stags Head*: Friendly and obliging landlord, good bar food, well kept beer, nice garden *(A Speakman)*

Bedroom prices normally include full English breakfast, VAT and any inclusive service charge that we know of. Prices before the '/' are for single rooms, after for two people in double or twin (B includes a private bath, S a private shower). If there is no '/', the prices are only for twin or double rooms (as far as we know there are no singles). If there is no B or S, as far as we know no rooms have private facilities.

Staffordshire *see* Derbyshire

see Derbyshire

Suffolk

This county's many good pubs, often in fine old buildings, include several really civilised dining pubs, leavened with a healthy mix of unspoilt thoroughly pubby places. Pubs which have been generating particular enthusiasm among readers in the last few months include the chatty Queens Head at Blyford (good generous food), the rather hotely Bell at Clare (new landlord doing very well), the Ship at Dunwich (very popular and busy, but the staff cope excellently), the well run and welcoming Beehive at Horringer (quite adventurous popular food), the interesting old Swan at Hoxne (good specials), the friendly and properly pubby Plough just outside Hundon (good genuine food), the civilised old Red Lion at Icklingham (gaining a Food Award this year), the Angel in Lavenham (a fine all-rounder, outstandingly popular), the unpretentious Brewers Arms in Rattlesden (really good cosmopolitan food cooked by the landlord), the Crown in Southwold (doing wonderfully well all round), the civilised Angel at Stoke by Nayland (a most alluring dining pub), and the warmly friendly Gardeners Arms at Tostock. In a very close-run race between the Red Lion at Icklingham, the Crown in Southwold, the Angel at Stoke by Nayland and the Brewers Arms at Rattlesden, it's the Brewers Arms which we choose as Suffolk Dining Pub of the Year. The Plough & Sail at Snape (a new main entry this year) looks like becoming a winner with its new catering, and the new licensees at the Trowel & Hammer at Cotton are going down well – already gaining our Wine Award, and looking towards a Food Award. The Crown at Hartest is another newcomer, an interesting old place in delightful surroundings, with good food. New licensees at the Kings Head at Laxfield look like serving its charmingly old-fashioned character well. The Golden Key at Snape, a fine all-rounder, now has bedrooms; we expect they'll be in line for a Place to Stay Award, and it's not far off a Food Award now, too. In the Lucky Dip section at the end of the chapter, pubs to note particularly (most inspected by us, and therefore firmly vouched for) include yet another Snape pub, the Crown, and also the White Horse at Badingham, Queens Head at Bramfield, Oyster at Butley, Peacock at Chelsworth, Kings Arms at Haughley, White Horse at Risby, Star at Wenhaston and Crown at Westleton. Drinks prices here are roughly in line with the national average, and vary less from pub to pub than in most areas. There's little to choose on price grounds between Adnams and Greene King, the dominant suppliers here, though there are few finer pleasures for lovers of real ale than sampling Adnams on its home ground in Southwold's many excellent pubs; the Crown there, one of East Anglia's very top pubs, had some of the cheapest beer we found in the whole county.

Post Office address codings confusingly give the impression that some pubs are in Suffolk when they're really in Norfolk or Cambridgeshire (which is where we list them).

ALDEBURGH TM4656 Map 5

Cross Keys

Crabbe Street

In summer, this attractive old pub is at its most popular – thanks to its position. A courtyard at the back opens directly on to the promenade and shingle beach, and there are wooden seats and tables out here to take in the view; the hanging baskets are colourful. Inside, the two communicating rooms are divided by a sturdy central chimney with wood-burning stoves on either side, and they keep Adnams Bitter, Broadside, Mild and winter Old on handpump. Bar food includes open sandwiches (from £2.80), ploughman's (£4.25), vegetarian meals such as spinach and mushroom lasagne, fisherman's pie, chicken curry or steak, kidney and ale pie (£5.50-£5.75), scallops au gratin (£5.40), and seafood platter (£11.50); dominoes, cribbage and fruit machine. It can get a little smoky at times. *(Recommended by Stuart Earle, Colin McKerrow, Basil J S Minson, R G Smedley, Anna Marsh, Neil Powell, Gwen and Peter Andrews, BKA; more reports please)*

Adnams ~ Tenant G Prior ~ Real ale ~ Meals and snacks (not winter Sun evenings) ~ (01728) 452637 ~ Children in eating area ~ Open 11-3, 6-11; 11-11 July/Aug

BILDESTON TL9949 Map 5

Crown 🍷

104 High St (B1115 SW of Stowmarket)

Behind this handsome timbered 15th-c inn is an attractive two-acre garden with picnic tables sheltering among shrubs and trees. Inside, you can be sure of a friendly welcome from the Hendersons in the comfortable beamed bars with dark wood tables, its armchairs and wall banquettes upholstered to match the floral curtains, latticed windows, an inglenook fireplace (and a smaller more modern one with dried flowers), and old fashioned prints and facsimiles of old documents on the cream walls. Good food includes home-made soup (£1.95), sandwiches (from £1.95; three-tier ones from £3.95), filled baked potatoes (from £2.50), warm filo tart filled with avocado and scrambled egg (£3.75), game terrine (£3.95), omelettes (£4.95), fresh tagliatelle with ham, mushrooms and cheese in white wine and cream sauce (£5.25), and daily specials such as cod fillet in beer batter (£4.95), steak and kidney pie (£5.95), pork steak with celery and stilton sauce (£6.95), and sautéed guinea fowl with leeks and crispy bacon (£7.95); part of the restaurant is no smoking. Well kept Adnams, Bass, Nethergate and a guest like Mansfield Old Baily or Shepherd Neame Spitfire on handpump, several malt whiskies, James white cider and a thoughtful wine list. Darts, bar billiards, shove-ha'penny, table skittles, cribbage, dominoes, fruit machine, and piped music. We have every reason to think the charming bedrooms here would be very comfortable, and would be grateful for reports. *(Recommended by Gwen and Peter Andrews, Ian Phillips)*

Free house ~ Licensees Mr and Mrs E Henderson ~ Real ale ~ Meals and snacks ~ Restaurant ~ (01449) 740510 ~ Children in eating area of bar ~ Open 11-11; closed evening 25 Dec ~ Bedrooms: £20(£35B)/£35(£55B)

BLYFORD TM4277 Map 5

Queens Head

B1123

Although it's the popular food that people like most about this thatched old village pub, there's a warm, friendly and cosy atmosphere, too. The attractively furnished, unfussy low-beamed bar has some antique settles, pine and oak benches built into its cream walls, heavy wooden tables and stools, and a huge fireplace filled with antique lamps and other interesting implements. They still use water from the original well.

Good, popular food includes lunchtime sandwiches, home-made quiche or ploughman's, moussaka and vegetarian pasta, with evening dishes like home-made game soup (£2.50), pâté (£2.95), spinach and tomato cannelloni (£5.25), fresh large Lowestoft cod in batter (£6.25), steak and kidney pie (£6.65), whole roast pheasant with burgundy sauce (£7.45), large baked greek-style lamb (£8.95), half a roast duck in a mango and peach sauce (£9.35), and sirloin steak (£10.50); the restaurant is no smoking. Well kept Adnams Bitter, Mild, and Broadside, and a guest ale on handpump. There are seats on the grass outside, and a good play area for children. The small village church is opposite, and another church a mile south at Wenhaston has a fascinating 15th-c wall-painting. *(Recommended by Gwen and Peter Andrews, June and Perry Dann, Wayne Brindle, Dave Carter, Joan Hilditch, Andy and Jill Plumb, Mrs P J Pearce, Thomas Nott, D and B Carter, Mr and Mrs D J Carmichael)*

Adnams ~ Tenant Tony Matthews ~ Real ale ~ Meals and snacks ~ Restaurant ~ (01502) 478404 ~ Children in eating area of bar ~ Open 11-3, 6.30-11 ~ Bedrooms: /£40B

BRANDESTON TM2460 Map 5

Queens Head

Towards Earl Soham

A real centre for village life, this well run country pub has a big rolling garden – delightful in summer – with plenty of tables on the neatly kept grass among large flower beds; also, a play tree, climbing frame, and slide. Inside, it's simply decorated with some panelling, brown leather banquettes and old pews in the open-plan bar, divided into separate bays by the stubs of surviving walls; shove-ha'penny, cribbage, dominoes, and faint piped music. Good value bar food includes sandwiches (from £1.50; hoagies from £2), home-made soup (£1.80), home-made chilli (£3.95), ploughman's (from £3.95), home-baked gammon and egg or home-made nut and mushroom pancake (£4), home-made sausage and onion pie or lasagne (£4.50), evening extras like smoked oysters au gratin (£3.50), fillet of pork in apple and cider sauce (£6.95) and poached salmon steak (£7.50), and puddings (£2.20). Well kept Adnams Bitter on handpump with Broadside, and Mild kept under light blanket pressure; helpful staff. The inn has a caravan and camping club site at the back. You can visit the nearby cider farm. *(Recommended by Dr and Mrs M Bailey; more reports please)*

Adnams ~ Tenant Tony Smith ~ Real ale ~ Meals and snacks (not Sun evenings) ~ (01728) 685307 ~ Children in family room ~ Jazz 3rd Mon in month ~ Open 11.30-2.30, 6-11 ~ Bedrooms: £17/£34

nr CHELMONDISTON TM2037 Map 5

Butt & Oyster

Pin Mill – signposted from B1456 SE of Ipswich

From the plenty of seats outside this simple old bargeman's pub, there are fine views over the River Orwell and the wooded slopes beyond and you can watch the boats going up and down. The same views can also be had from the bay window inside, where there's quite a nautical theme to match the surroundings. The half-panelled little smoke room is pleasantly worn and unfussy, with model sailing ships around the walls and high-backed and other old-fashioned settles on the tiled floor; spare a glance for the most unusual carving of a man with a woman over the mantlepiece. Good bar food includes sandwiches (from £1.20; not on Saturday or Sunday lunchtimes), ploughman's (from £2.65), home-made pies and quiches (from £4), popular self-service salads and weekend lunchtime buffet (from £4.50), home-made daily specials like steak and kidney pie, chicken casserole, seafood pots or mushroom stroganoff (all around £4.50), and a selection of puddings (all £2). Cobbolds IPA, Tolly Bitter, Original, Shooter and Mild, and a guest beer such as Bass on handpump; winter darts, shove-ha'penny, dominoes and shut-the-box. A good time to visit the pub would be when the annual Thames Barge race is held (end June/beginning July). No dogs. *(Recommended by Jack and Philip Paxton, Pamela Goodwyn, Stuart Earle, David Peakall, Graham Reeve, Basil J S Minson, J L Phillips)*

Pubmaster ~ Tenants Dick and Brenda Mainwaring ~ Real ale ~ Meals and snacks (till 10pm in summer; not 25 Dec) ~ (01473) 780764 ~ Children welcome except in main bar ~ Open 11-11; 12-10.30 Sun; 11-3, 7-11 in winter; closed evening 25 Dec

CLARE TL7645 Map 5

Bell ♀

Market place

The new licensee in this attractive timbered hotel has changed what was the conservatory into more of an eating Garden Room which opens onto the terrace and down to a little lawn. The rambling lounge bar has splendidly carved black beams and old panelling and woodwork around the open fire, comfortable armchairs on the green carpet and village notices on the hessian walls, giving it a nicely relaxed local feel. There are two other rooms – one with masses of prints (mainly to do with canals) – on its walls. Good food includes ploughman's (from £3.95), cod and prawn bake, steak and kidney pie, fish and chips, pasta carbonara or leek, lentil and broccoli hotpot (all £4.50), lamb cutlets or rump steak (£9), daily specials (£2.50-£9), puddings (from £2.50), and children's dishes (£2). The restaurant is no smoking. Well kept Nethergate Bitter and IPA and a guest beer on handpump, and good wines; darts, pool, fruit machine. Several other striking buildings in the village include the remains of the priory and the castle (which stands on prehistoric earthworks). *(Recommended by W Aird, Gwen and Peter Andrews, J C S Weeks, Tom Thomas, Heather Martin, W H and E Thomas, Walter and Susan Rinaldi-Butcher, Dr and Mrs M Bailey)*

Free house ~ Licensee Giovanni Testagrossa ~ Real ale ~ Meals and snacks ~ Restaurant ~ (01787) 277741 ~ Children welcome ~ Open 11-11 ~ Bedrooms: £45B/£39.95(£55B)

COTTON TM0766 Map 5

Trowel & Hammer ♀

Mill Rd; take B1113 N of Stowmarket, then turn right into Blacksmiths Lane just N of Bacton

One of the new owners here – Julie Huff – used to be part-owner at another of our main entries, the Royal Oak, Yattendon in Berkshire which is a very civilised dining pub; so we have high hopes for this partly thatched and partly tiled white pub. Much emphasis will be placed on the food and they are keeping the same chef, so many popular Greek dishes will remain: taramasalata, lamb kebabs (£4.25), moussaka, and a popular kleftiko cooked with plenty of oregano (£5.95), as well as sandwiches (from £1.20), gazpacho (£1.95), ploughman's (from £3.25), steak and kidney in ale pie (£4.90), fresh fish such as cod meuniere (£5.25), and puddings like chocolate and walnut ganache, summer pudding or lemon cheesecake (£2.75); Friday night is popular paella night (£6.25). Well kept Adnams, Boddingtons, and Greene King IPA and Abbot on handpump, and an interesting wine list; pool, fruit machine, and piped music. The spreading lounge has wheelback and one or two older chairs and settles around a variety of tables, lots of dark beamery and timber baulks, a big log fire, and at the back an ornate woodburning stove; some decorative changes are planned. Work is also planned on the already pretty back garden with its neat climbers on trellises, picnic tables and fine swimming pool. *(Recommended by Gwen and Peter Andrews, John C Baker, Brian Jones, Dave Braisted; more reports on the new regime, please)*

Free house ~ Licensees Julie Huff and Simon Piers-Hall ~ Real ale ~ Meals and snacks (11.30-2, 6.30-10) ~ Restaurant ~ (01449) 781234 ~ Children in eating area of bar ~ Open 11.30-3, 5.30-11; 11.30-11 Sat

DENNINGTON TM2867 Map 5

Queens Head

A1120

Set in gardens alongside the church, this Tudor pub is one of Suffolk's most attractive pub buildings. For centuries – until quite recently – it was owned by a church charity, and inside, you feel it may easily once have been a chapel: the arched rafters of the steeply roofed part on the right certainly give that impression. The main L-shaped room has carefully stripped wall timbers and beams – the great bressumer beam over the fireplace is handsomely carved – some carpet and some traditional flooring tiles, brick bar counters, and solid traditional furnishings. There are sandwiches (from £1.40) and a choice of ploughman's (from £3.65), as well as soup (£1.95), cottage pie (£2.95), tiger prawns in filo pastry and garlic dip (£3.25), cheesy pork pot, kidneys in cream and mustard sauce or lamb and courgette bake (all £3.95), mushroom stroganoff (£4.25), very good fisherman's pie (£4.35), steak and kidney pie (£5.50), steaks (from £8.95), and puddings like apricot sponge pudding with a butterscotch, pistachio and apricot sauce, orange mousse or coffee and whisky trifle (£2.50); vegetables and chips are extra (from £1); they serve breakfast, too, from 9am. Well kept Adnams Bitter and Broadside and a guest such as Wadworths Farmers Glory on handpump; piped music. The side lawn, attractively planted with flowers, is sheltered by some noble lime trees, and has picnic tables; this backs onto Dennington Park where there are swings and so forth for children. *(Recommended by Wayne Brindle, Tony and Wendy Hobden, Donald Rice, C H and P Stride)*

Free house ~ Licensees Ray and Myra Bumstead ~ Real ale ~ Meals and snacks ~ Restaurant ~ (01728) 638241 ~ Children in family area ~ Open 11.30-2.30, 5.30(6 Sat)-11

DUNWICH TM4770 Map 5

Ship ★

In what is left of a charming village (coastal erosion has put most of it under the sea), this delightful old pub remains a firm favourite with readers. At peak times it does get very crowded but the staff remain in command of the situation and are helpful and friendly. The traditionally furnished bar has benches, pews, captain's chairs and candle-lit wooden tables on the tiled floor, a wood-burning stove (cheerfully left open in cold weather) and lots of old fishing nets and paintings on the walls. Good lunchtime food includes home-made soup (£1.50), cottage pie (£3.25), ploughman's (from £3.50), macaroni cheese (£3.50), and chicken and mushroom pie or wonderfully fresh fish and chips (£4.50), with evening dishes like black pudding fried with apple or creamy mushrooms (£3.75), salads (from £6.75), fresh fish crumble (£7.50), rump steak (£7.75), fresh fish of the day (from £7.75), and puddings (£2.75). Well kept Adnams Bitter, Broadside (in summer) and winter Old, and Greene King Abbot on handpump at the handsomely panelled bar counter. The public bar area has dominoes, cribbage, fruit machine, video game, and piped music. There's a conservatory and attractive, sunny back terrace, and a well kept garden with an enormous fig tree. In summer a couple of theatre companies put on productions out here, and there may be Morris dancers. The pub is handy for the RSPB reserve at Minsmere. *(Recommended by G and T Edwards, Nigel Wikeley, Nigel Woolliscroft, Dr Peter Crawshaw, MJVK, Jenny and Brian Seller, Nick and Mary Baker, John Beeken, Andy and Jill Plumb, June and Perry Dann, Helen Crookston, Mrs M A Mees, Mr and Mrs R P Begg, Brenda and Jim Langley, Mary and David Webb, M J V Kemp, Basil Minson, Mr and Mrs G M Edwards, Rita Horridge, Jan and Peter Shropland, Neil Powell, Brian Viner, David Warrellow, Rob and Doris Harrison, Dr and Mrs M Bailey, George Atkinson, Katie and Steve Newby)*

Free house ~ Licensees Stephen and Ann Marshlain ~ Real ale ~ Meals and snacks ~ Evening restaurant ~ (01728) 648219 ~ Children welcome away from main bar ~ Open 11-3(3.30 Sat), 6(6.30 in winter)-11; closed evening 25 Dec ~ Bedrooms: £22/£44(£54S)

EARL SOHAM TM2363 Map 5

Victoria

A1120 Stowmarket—Yoxford

This unpretentious pub has been redecorated this year, and the relaxed bar has kitchen chairs and pews, plank-topped trestle sewing-machine tables and other simple country tables with candles, tiled or board floors, stripped panelling, an interesting range of pictures of Queen Victoria and her reign, and open fires. It's popular for its interesting range of beers brewed on the premises, and you can visit the microbrewery that produces the Victoria Bitter, a mild called Gannet, and a stronger ale called Albert, and take some home with you. Bar food includes sandwiches (from £1.50), soup, ploughman's, burgers (£2.25), chilli (£3.50), pizzas (£3.75), vegetable lasagne (£4.25), and pork with apple and cider or beef curry (£4.50). Darts, shove ha'penny, cribbage, dominoes, cards and backgammon; seats out in front and on a raised back lawn. The pub is close to a wild fritillary meadow at Framlingham and a working windmill at Saxtead. *(Recommended by Stuart Earle, John C Baker, V and E A Bolton, Derek and Sylvia Stephenson, Dr and Mrs P J Crawshaw, Wayne Brindle, Dr and Mrs M Bailey; more reports please)*

Own brew ~ Licensees Clare and John Bjornson ~ Real ale ~ Meals and snacks ~ (01728) 685758 ~ Impromptu folk music Tues and Fri evenings ~ Open 11.30-2.30, 5.30-11

ERWARTON TM2134 Map 5

Queens Head

Village signposted off B1456 Ipswich—Shotley Gate; pub beyond the attractive church and the manor with its unusual gate (like an upturned salt-cellar)

Just as popular in winter as in summer, this warmly welcoming and friendly pub is well liked for its enjoyable food. The comfortably furnished bar has a relaxed, homely feel, bowed 16th-c black oak beams in the shiny low yellowing ceiling, and a cosy coal fire. The same menu is served in both the bar and more modern restaurant and includes sandwiches, good soups like carrot, apple and celery or broccoli and ginger (£1.90), ploughman's (£3.50), home-made lasagne or moussaka, curry, spicy cod with Cajun dip or mushroom and nut fettucine (all £4.95), deep-fried seafood basket (£5.75), big gammon steak with egg (£6.30), daily specials like chicken breast in peach and almond sauce or strips of lamb's liver in madeira sauce (£4.95), fresh fish and seasonal game, and puddings such as strawberry, redcurrant and yoghurt cheesecake or apple bakewell (£1.95). Well kept Adnams Bitter and winter Tally Ho and Old, Greene King IPA, and Morlands Old Speckled Hen on handpump; a decent wine list with several half bottles, and a wide choice of malt whiskies; friendly service. Darts, bar billiards, shove-ha'penny, cribbage, dominoes, and piped music. The gents' have a fascinating collection of navigational maps. The terrace has fine views over fields to ships on the Stour and the distant Parkeston Quay. Nearby Erwarton Hall with its peculiar gatehouse is an interesting place to visit. *(Recommended by Paul and Juliet Beckwith, A Albert, Peter Woolls, M A and C R Starling, Graham Reeve)*

Free house ~ Licensees Mr B K Buckle and Mrs Julia Crisp ~ Real ale ~ Meals and snacks ~ Restaurant ~ (01473) 787550 ~ Children in restaurant ~ Open 11-3, 6.30-11; 11-2.30, 7-11 in winter; closed Dec 25

FRAMSDEN TM1959 Map 5

Dobermann

The Street; pub signposted off B1077 just S of its junction with A1120 Stowmarket—Earl Soham

You can be sure of a particularly warm welcome in this charmingly restored old thatched pub – for visitors as well as regulars. The two spotless and friendly bar areas have very low, pale stripped beams, a big comfy sofa, a couple of chintz wing armchairs, and a mix of other chairs, plush-seated stools and winged settles around polished rustic tables; there's a wonderful twin-facing fireplace, photographs of show rosettes won by the owner's dogs on the white walls, and a friendly tabby, Tinker. A good choice of well kept beers on handpump includes Adnams Bitter and Broadside and three constantly changing guests like Bass, Marstons Pedigree, and Morrells Varsity; efficient service, piped music. Good bar food includes sandwiches (from £1.45), home-made soup or deep fried squid (£2.95), home-made chicken liver pâté or brown shrimps (£3.45), huge ploughman's (from £4.95), spicy nut loaf with tomato sauce (£5.25), mixed grill or home-made curry (£6.95), home-made steak and mushroom pie (£7.25), fish au gratin (salmon, prawns, cod and smoked haddock, £7.95), seasonal game pie (£9.95), steaks (from £9.95), and puddings (from £2.25). They play boules outside, where there are picnic tables by trees and a fairy-lit trellis, and lots of pretty hanging baskets and colourful window boxes. They host the Framsden pram race every year at the end of June. No children. *(Recommended by Gwen and Peter Andrews, June and Perry Dann, Wayne Brindle, G E Rich, Sheila and Terry Wells)*

Free house ~ Licensee Susan Frankland ~ Real ale ~ Meals and snacks (11.30-2, 7-9.45) ~ (01473) 890461 ~ Open 11.30-2.30, 7-11 ~ Bedroom: £20B/£30B

GREAT GLEMHAM TM3361 Map 5

Crown

Between A12 Wickham Mkt—Saxmundham, B1119 Saxmundham—Framlingham

The hard working licensees deserve all the praise that comes their way. Readers very much like staying here (the breakfasts are good), and it's a very nice place to enjoy a meal or a quiet drink, too. The open-plan lounge has two enormous fireplaces with logs blazing in winter, beams, one or two big casks, brass ornaments or musical instruments, wooden pews and captain's chairs around stripped and waxed kitchen tables, and a chatty atmosphere. Local photographs and paintings decorate the white walls, and there are plenty of fresh flowers and pot plants, with more in a side eating room. Well kept Bass and Adnams Bitter, Broadside and winter Old from old brass handpumps; good choice of malt whiskies and decent wines. Now listed on blackboard, the good promptly served bar food includes filled rolls (from £1.60), ploughman's (from £3), slices of locally smoked chicken breast with cumberland sauce (£3.25), grilled Thai chicken breast (£5.95), smoked haddock baked in cream or tenderloin of pork with white wine and mushroom sauce (£6.25), salmon fishcakes with lemon butter or lamb cutlets with rosemary and redcurrant sauce (£6.50), and puddings such as very popular cape brandy pudding or chocolate truffle torte flavoured with rum (£2.50). The restaurant is no smoking. Shove-ha'penny, dominoes, cribbage, chess, Solitaire. There's a neat, flower-fringed lawn, raised above the corner of the quiet village lane by a retaining wall; seats and tables under cocktail parasols out here. *(Recommended by Colin Pettit, John Fahy, K H Frostick, Derek and Sylvia Stephenson, G W H Kerby, Gwen and Peter Andrews, Basil J S Minson, Jeff Davies, W J Wonham, Rob and Doris Harrison, Wayne Brindle)*

Free house ~ Licensee Roger Mason ~ Real ale ~ Meals and snacks (not Mon) ~ Restaurant ~ (01728) 663693 ~ Children in eating area of bar and in restaurant ~ Open 12-2.30(3 Sat), 7-11 ~ Bedrooms: £20S/£38B

HARTEST TL8352 Map 5

Crown

B1066 S of Bury St Edmunds

Attractive and relaxed, this welcoming pink-washed pub at the sunny end of the village green concentrates on good reliable reasonably priced food. It's the sort of place that's ideal if you don't like steps – no dark corners, a roomy layout, yet plenty of interest. By the impressive brick fireplace with its big log fire are some intriguing old farm tools, the spotless bar has some pleasant village prints and horse brasses, and there are some unusual tree-carving paintings. Besides two dining areas there's a family conservatory. The well prepared and presented home-made food includes good sandwiches (from £1.50), notable changing soups such as cream of cauliflower, chunky fish soup or duck and vegetable (£1.75), a massive ploughman's (£3), a vegetarian dish of the day such as home-made vegetable and pasta bake (£4.80), lovely fresh fish such as fresh dressed crab, fried brill, whiting done with Abbot ale and salmon in chive and lemon sauce (£5-£7; they also do a take-away fish and chips £3), winter steak and kidney pie (£5.50), chicken in a white wine and mushroom sauce (£6), Scotch 10oz sirloin steak (£9), and puddings such as double chocolate flan or sherry trifle (£2.25); they do a Monday night four-course meal (from £6.50). Well kept Greene King ales, decent house wines, quick consistently pleasant service, a happy chatty atmosphere, maybe quiet piped music. The pretty garden has picnic tables among shrubs and trees, and there are more tables under cocktail parasols on a sunny terrace. *(Recommended by Gwen and Peter Andrews, P Devitt, Pamela Goodwyn, W T Aird)*

Free house ~ Licensees Paul and Karen Beer ~ Real ale ~ Meals and snacks ~ Restaurant ~ (01284) 830250 ~ Children welcome ~ Open 11-3, 6-11; closed 25/26 Dec

HORRINGER TL8261 Map 5

Beehive

A143

This is a welcoming and well run place with a relaxed atmosphere and quite an emphasis on quickly served adventurous food. A typical choice of dishes might include nibbles such as olive and tomato bread, a dish of olives or savoury dip with corn chips (from £1.35), soup (£2.50), mushrooms in a cream, garlic and tarragon sauce (£3.50), home-made taramasalata (£3.95), ploughman's (£4.75), steak sandwich (£4.95), omelette filled with prawns and creamy lobster sauce (£5.95), platter of cold roast beef with horseradish cream or pasta and mushrooms in light cream and lemon sauce (£6.50), poached smoked haddock topped with egg and rich cheese sauce (£6.95), stir-fry chicken (£7.95), daily specials like lamb's sweetbreads in apple and tarragon cream sauce (£7.95) or fish platter (£8.95), and around eight home-made puddings (£2.75). The little rambling rooms have been redecorated this year: flagstones and coir, stripped panelling or brickwork, some very low beams in some of the furthest and snuggest alcoves, carefully chosen dining and country kitchen chairs with tartan cushions, one or two wall settles around solid tables, picture-lights over lots of 19th-century prints, and a woodburning stove. Their dog Muffin is very good at making friends, though other dogs aren't really welcome. The gents' has a frieze depicting villagers fleeing from stinging bees. Well kept Greene King IPA and Abbot on handpump and decent changing wines with half-a-dozen by the glass. A most attractively planted back terrace has picnic tables, with more seats on a raised lawn. *(Recommended by Rita Horridge, BNF, M Parkin, Pamela Goodwyn, JKW, Howard and Margaret Buchanan, Jane Kinsbury, John C Baker, Stuart Earle, W T Aird, G Washington, Susan May, Sue and Dominic Dunlop, Dr and Mrs M Bailey, F M and A F Walters, Thomas Nott, Keith Wilson, N M Williamson, Wayne Brindle, Simon Morton, Lawrence Bacon, Martin and Pauline Richardson, Richard Balls)*

Greene King ~ Tenants Gary and Dianne Kingshott ~ Real ale ~ Meals and snacks ~ (01284) 735260 ~ Children welcome ~ Open 11.30-2.30, 7-11

HOXNE TM1777 Map 5

Swan

Off B1118; village signposted off A140 S of Diss

Even on a busy day, this carefully restored late 15th-c house is relaxed and peaceful

– and it's popular with visitors and locals of all ages. The front bar has two solid oak counters, heavy oak floors, and a deep-set inglenook fireplace, with an armchair on either side and a long bench in front of it; you can still see the ancient timber and mortar of the walls. A fire in the back bar divides the bar area and snug, and the dining room has an original wooden fireplace. Well presented good bar food includes daily specials such as leek and watercress soup (£2.25), spinach and garlic terrine (£2.75), aubergine slices baked with tomato and mozzarella or pepper and tomato tart with goat's cheese (£3.95), nut and herb loaf (£3.95), pork satay with peanut sauce (£4.95), cod and prawn gratinée (£5.95), and king prawn tails provençale (£6.95); also, ploughman's (from £2.95), a choice of omelettes (£3.25), tasty pancakes filled with mushrooms and cheese (£4.25), gammon (£4.50), plate of salamis with black olives (£4.75), and steaks (from £8.50); fresh vegetables £2.50. If you're sitting outside and waiting for your food order, keep your eye on the roof; rather than use a Tannoy, they briefly sound a school bell and then prop scoreboard type numbers up there when your meal is ready. Service remains quick even at busy times. Well kept Adnams Bitter and winter Old and Tally Ho and Greene King Abbot on handpump or tapped from the cask, and decent wines; pool, shove-ha'penny, dominoes, cribbage, and juke box. The extensive lawn behind is used for croquet, and is a very tranquil place to sit in summer on the hand-made elm furniture, sheltered by a willow and other trees and its shrub-covered wall. Nearby is the site of King Edmund the Martyr's execution; the tree to which he was tied for it is now reputed to form part of a screen in the neighbouring church. *(Recommended by P H Roberts, Gwen and Peter Andrews, Wayne Brindle, Dr Ronald Church, Pamela Goodwyn, Mr and Mrs D J Carmichael, J Honnor, V and E A Bolton)*

Free house ~ Licensees Tony and Frances Thornton-Jones ~ Real ale ~ Meals and snacks (not Sat evening or all day Sun) ~ Restaurant (Sat evening and Sunday lunch) ~ (01379) 668275 ~ Children in eating area of bar ~ Open 12-2.30(3 Sat), 5.30-11; closed 25 Dec

HUNDON TL7348 Map 5

Plough

Brockley Green; on Kedington road, up hill from village

In summer, the gardens behind this extended and modernised pub are a relaxing place to enjoy a drink. There's a terrace with a pergola and ornamental pool, croquet, boules, and fine views over miles of East Anglian countryside; the pub's two friendly retrievers may be out here, too. The neat carpeted bar still has a double row of worn old oak timbers to mark what must once have been the corridor between its two rooms; there are also low side settles with Liberty-print cushions, spindleback chairs, and sturdy low tables on the patterned carpet, lots of horse brasses on the beams, and striking gladiatorial designs for Covent Garden by Leslie Hurry, who lived nearby. The meals are very good, with an emphasis on fresh local produce; the daily changing bar menu might include lunchtime sandwiches (from £1.95), filled french bread (from £2.50), home-made soup (£2.75), ploughman's (from £3.75), gammon and egg (£5.50), pasta shells with parma ham (£5.95), steak and Guinness pie (£6.50), daily specials like tomato and ricotta cheese tortellini (£4.95), seafood bake or fresh sardines (£5.95), scampi tails and prawns in saffron sauce (£6.25), whole plaice stuffed with crab (£6.95), and winter pheasant and rabbit dishes. Well kept Greene King IPA, Mauldons, and a weekly guest beer on handpump, and freshly squeezed orange juice; piped music. Parts of the bar and restaurant are no-smoking. It's also a certified location for the Caravan Club, with a sheltered site to the rear for tourers. The pub has been run by the same friendly family for three generations. *(Recommended by Mr and Mrs Albert, Stephen Boot, W T Aird, Aubrey Bourne, Frank W Gadbois, JLP, Pamela Goodwyn)*

Free house ~ Licensees David and Marion Rowlinson ~ Real ale ~ Meals and snacks ~ Restaurant ~ (01440) 786789 ~ Children welcome ~ Open 11-3, 5-11 ~ Bedrooms: £39.50B/£55B

ICKLINGHAM TL7772 Map 5

Red Lion

A1101, Mildenhall—Bury St Edmunds

Although this civilised and rather smart thatched and whitewashed pub is mainly popular for its very good food, there is a reasonable area in front of the bar and log fire where drinkers are welcome. The smartly refurbished bar has heavy beams, a nice mixture of wooden chairs, candlelit tables, fresh flowers, antlers over the inglenook fireplace, old fishing rods and various stuffed animals, piped classical music, and newspapers; they sell clay pipes and tobacco. Served by pleasant staff, the food might include soup (£2.10), sandwiches (from £2.10), good cheese platter (£3.95), whole prawns in garlic butter (£4.95), excellent sausages in onion gravy (£4.45), shepherd's pie (£5.95), a vegetarian dish of the day (£6.25), English lamb chops with fresh mint sauce (£7.95), plenty of super fresh fish from Lowestoft such as local Larkwood trout or fresh sardines in garlic butter (£7.45), delicious fresh lemon sole (£9.65), fillet of red fish with paprika butter (£9.95), whole grilled sea bass with red pepper sauce (£13.95), daily specials, game in season, and lovely puddings such as hot chocolate nut pudding, sticky treacle tart or chocolate roulade (£3.05). Well kept Greene King IPA and Abbot, and Rayments on handpump, lots of country wines and elderflower and citrus pressé. Picnic tables on a raised back terrace face the fields – including an acre of the pub's running down to the River Lark, with Cavenham Heath nature reserve beyond. In front (the pub is well set back from the road) old-fashioned white seats overlook the car park and a flower lawn. It's close to West Stow Country Park and the Anglo-Saxon Village. *(Recommended by Michael Marlow, Mrs Heather Martin, Tony Gayfer, Jan and Colin Roe, Rita Horridge, J F M and M West, R C Vincent, K H Frostick, Ian Phillips, Dr Ronald Church, S Brackenbury, John and Elspeth Howell, Thomas Nott, Dr and Mrs M Bailey, R H Brown)*

Greene King ~ Lease: Jonathan Gates ~ Real ale ~ Meals and snacks (till 10) ~ Restaurant ~ (01638) 717802 ~ Children welcome ~ Open 12-3, 6-11

IPSWICH TM1744 Map 5

Brewery Tap

Cliff Rd

This year, Tolly Cobbold are celebrating 250 years of brewing in Ipswich. Below the brewery nestles this attractive pink-washed house which is the ground floor of what was the Cobbold family home in the 18th c. There are fully guided brewery tours every day at midday from May-September and at the same time on Saturday and Sunday during October-April; other tours by arrangement. Inside, several very welcoming smallish room areas cluster around the main bar, with decently spaced solid small tables, some armchairs, rugs on polished boards. Some brickwork's been stripped back, and elsewhere some original lathework exposed. There are pictures of the docks and other local scenes, though the best picture is the real-life one framed by the heavy curtains around the big windows – the boats you can often see passing outside. One room is no smoking. The atmosphere is civilised, and the good range of food includes giant filled baps (from £2.25), filled baked potatoes (from £2.50), beef and tomato pasta or lasagne (£4.95), steak and kidney pie (£5.50) and vegetarian dishes from a daily specials board like pineapple paella (£4.95) and home-made puddings (£2.15). Well kept Tolly Mild, Bitter, Original, Tolly-Shooter and Old Strong in winter, and Cobbolds IPA all on handpump, and the full range of Tolly bottled beers; piped music. A games area has darts, bar billiards, shove-ha'penny, cribbage, dominoes, and fruit machine. The back room looks into the brewery's steam-engine room, and a door from the pub leads straight into the brewery. *(Recommended by Neil Calver, C H and P Stride, Ian Phillips)*

Tolly ~ Manageress Jill Willmott ~ Real ale ~ Meals and snacks (not Sun or Mon evenings) ~ (01473) 281508 ~ Children in eating area of bar ~ Jazz last Sun of month ~ Parking restrictions daytime ~ Open 11-11

IXWORTH TL9370 Map 5

Pykkerel

Village signposted just off A143 Bury St Edmunds—Diss

Several neatly kept small rooms lead off the central servery in this popular dining pub, and all have moulded Elizabethan oak beams, attractive brickwork, and big fireplaces, as well as antique tables and chairs and Persian rugs on the gleaming floors; there's a similarly furnished dining area, and a small back sun lounge facing a sway-backed Elizabethan timbered barn across the old coach yard. The emphasis is firmly on the good bar food: sandwiches, soup (£2.10), good cheese platter (£3.95), sausages in onion gravy (£4.45), shepherd's pie (£5.95), vegetarian dishes (from £5.95), steak in ale pie (£6.95), pork chops with whole grain mustard (£7.25), rump steak (£8.95), plenty of very good fresh fish such as local rainbow trout (£7.45), fillet of codling (£8.95), lemon sole or whole grilled plaice (£9.65), and puddings. Well kept Greene King IPA and Abbot on handpump, and pleasantly brisk service. On a goodish stretch of grass under a giant sycamore are some picnic tables. *(Recommended by Julian and Liz Long, Peter and Joy Heatherley, Michael Marlow, Andrew Scarr, Wayne Brindle, J F M West, Tony Gayfer, Charles Bardswell, John C Baker, Richard Balls, BHP, F C Johnston, Dr and Mrs M Bailey, Andrew McKeand, F M and A F Walters)*

Greene King ~ Lease: Ian Hubbert and A Kydd ~ Real ale ~ Meals and snacks (till 10) ~ Restaurant ~ (01359) 230398 ~ Children welcome ~Open 12-2.30, 6-11

LAVENHAM TL9149 Map 5

Angel ★

Market Pl

This carefully-renovated Tudor inn appeals to nearly everybody – and we certainly have more favourable reports about it than for any other pub in the county. There is a strong emphasis on the particularly good food but readers have stressed that those wanting just a quick drink are made more than welcome by the helpful, friendly staff, and the atmosphere is very civilised and relaxed. Changing frequently, the carefully cooked food may include courgette and lentil soup (£2.50), home-made pork pie and chutney (£3.95), lunchtime ploughman's (£4.25), smoked prawns with lemon mayonnaise (£4..50 – they do all their own smoking), steak and ale pie (£5.95), courgette, tomato and mushroom gratin (£6.75), calf's liver with orange and sage or skate wine with sweet pepper and basil sauce (£8.25), lamb chops marinated with garlic and rosemary (£8.95), saddle of venison with grapes and brandy (£10.25), and puddings such as strawberry tart, chocolate fudge cake or steamed orange and apricot pudding (£2.95); Sunday lunch roast rib of beef and yorkshire pudding or roast leg of lamb (£6.25). One of the eating areas is no-smoking. The green-carpeted main bar on the right feels very up-to-date, with piped light classics, lots of shelves of readable books, and blonde furniture including heavy kitchen tables and chairs; one table shaped like a piano-top occupies a bay window, with a nice polished wooden seat running around it to look out on the little market square of this pretty village, and its Guildhall (NT). The open-plan area loops around the servery to a more softly lit dark-beamed part on the left, with some sofas and mate's chairs around darker tables. There's a big log fire in the inglenook, under a heavy mantlebeam and the 16th-c pargeted ceiling. Well kept Adnams, Mauldons White Adder, Nethergate Bitter, Shepherd Neame Spitfire, and Websters Yorkshire on handpump, quite a few malt whiskies, decent wines by the glass and a good choice by the bottle; the back area is a family room. They have a good range of board games, and hold a chess night on Tuesdays, a bridge night Thursdays and a quiz on Sundays; darts, dominoes, cribbage, trivia, and piped music. The big ginger cat is called Dilly, the one without a tail is Stumpy, and they now have Guinness, too. There are picnic tables out in front, and white tables under cocktail parasols in a sizeable sheltered back garden; it's worth asking if they've time to show you the interesting Tudor cellar. *(Recommended by Paul and Ursula Randall, Dominic and Sue*

Dunlop, Jack and Philip Paxton, Bernard and Ann Payne, R G and J N Plumb, P H Roberts, C H and P Stride, John Evans, Gwen and Peter Andrews, Mirr R M Tudor, John C Baker, Frank Gadbois, Nigel Flook, Betsy Brown, Dr I H Maine, Pamela Goodwyn, Tom Thomas, Joan Hilditch, JKW, Alain and Rose Foote, Rosemary Harris, Andy Thwaites, Derek and Margaret Underwood, Paula Shillaw, Keven Whitcombe, Tina and David Woods Taylor, Joy Heatherley, R and S Bentley, Eric and Jackie Robinson, Mr and Mrs R Leeds, Keith Symons, Gina and Billy Olphert, D A Edwards, Anne Campbell, J H Seddon, David and Ruth Hollands, Dougie Paterson, Hugh Stewart, G E Rich)

Free house ~ Licensees Roy and Anne Whitworth, John Barry ~ Real ale ~ Meals and snacks ~ Restaurant ~ (01787) 247388 ~ Children welcome ~ Classical piano Fri evenings and some lunchtimes ~ Open 11-11; closed 25/26 Dec ~ Bedrooms: £37.50B/£50B

Swan ★

A very striking timbered Elizabethan building, this rather smart hotel has an atmospheric little tiled-floor bar buried in its heart with leather chairs and memorabilia of the days when this was the local for the US 48th Bomber Group in the Second World War (many Americans still come to re-visit old haunts); the set of handbells used to be employed by the local church bellringers for practice. From here it's an easy overflow into the drift of armchairs and settees that spreads engagingly through a network of beamed and timbered alcoves and more open areas. Well kept Greene King IPA, Marstons Pedigree and Morlands Old Speckled Hen on handpump. Overlooking the well kept and sheltered courtyard garden is an airy Garden Bar, where at lunchtime a buffet counter serves soup (£2.50), sandwiches (from £3.50; £4.50 for smoked salmon), British cheeses and biscuits (£4.50), honey-baked ham and roast turkey salad (£5.95), a vegetarian dish, a daily hot dish of the day (£8.95), and home-made puddings (£2.95); also, morning coffee and afternoon tea. There is also a lavishly timbered no-smoking restaurant with a minstrel's gallery. Amongst the other fine buildings in this once-prosperous wool town is the Tudor Guildhall, which has a small folk museum. *(Recommended by Mrs Heather Martin, A and M Dickinson, Nigel Flook, Betsy Brown; more reports please)*

Free house (Forte) ~ Licensee M R Grange ~ Real ale ~ Lunchtime meals and snacks ~ Restaurant ~ (01787) 247477 ~ Children welcome ~ Pianist every night ~ Open 11-3, 6-11 ~ Bedrooms: £80B/£130B

LAXFIELD TM2972 Map 5

Kings Head

Behind church, off road toward Banyards Green

The old-fashioned front room in this thatched Tudor pub has a high-backed built-in settle on the tiled floor and an open fire, and a couple of other rooms have pews, old seats, scrubbed deal tables, and some interesting wall prints; the atmosphere is local and welcoming. Under the new licensees, bar food includes sandwiches (from £1.50), soup (£1.90), grilled sardines (£3.75), ploughman's (£3.85), cheese flan (£3.95), rabbit pie, liver and bacon or steak and kidney pie (£4.95), and steak (£8); no piped music or machines, just a very nice traditional feel. Well kept Adnams Bitter, Broadside, Extra and winter Old and Tally Ho, and Greene King IPA on handpump, and farm cider; darts, shove ha'penny, cribbage. Going out past the casks in the back serving room, you find benches and a trestle table in a small yard. From the yard, a honeysuckle arch leads into a sheltered little garden and the pub's own well kept and secluded bowling, badminton and croquet green. *(Recommended by MJVK, Jack and Philip Paxton, Nick and Alison Dowson, David Alchin, Elizabeth and Klaus Leist, Derek and Sylvia Stephenson, David Ball; more reports on the new regime please)*

Free house ~ Managers Adrian and Sylvia Read ~ Real ale ~ Meals and snacks ~ Restaurant ~ (01986) 798395 ~ Children in restaurant ~ Occasional folk nights ~ Open 11-3, 6-11

LEVINGTON TM2339 Map 5

Ship

Gun Hill; village signposted from A45, then follow Stratton Hall sign

This year, a new no-smoking dining room/bar area has been added to this charming traditional inn, using beams taken from an old barn, flagstones, and lots of nautical bric-a-brac. The other rooms also have quite a nautical theme, too, as the pub is popular with users of the local marina: lots of ship prints and photos of sailing barges, beams and benches built into the walls, and in the middle room a marine compass set under the serving counter, which also has a fishing net slung over it. There are also a number of comfortably upholstered small settles, some of them grouped round tables as booths, and a big black round stove; there's a second no-smoking area. High quality home-made bar food includes a good ploughman's, stilton and walnut quiche (£5.25), king prawns in garlic butter (£5.50), braised steak with leek and stilton sauce, chicken with asparagus sauce, lamb with ginger and apricots and avocado and sweetcorn bake (all £5.95), and puddings such as black cherry flan or bread and butter pudding (£2.50). Service is friendly and professional. Well kept Flowers Original, Greene King IPA, Ind Coope Burton, Tetleys, and Tolly Cobbolds IPA on handpump or tapped from the cask, and country wines; cribbage, dominoes. If you look carefully enough, there's a distant sea view from the benches in front. In summer, the hanging baskets are magnificent. No dogs or children. ***(Recommended by Rita Horridge, Keith Archer, Stuart Earle, Pamela Goodwyn, C H and P Stride, J L Phillips)***

Pubmaster ~ Tenants William and Shirley Waite ~ Real ale ~ Meals and snacks (not Sun/Mon/Tues evenings) ~ (01473) 659573 ~ Folk music first Tues of month ~ Open 11.30-3, 6-11

LONG MELFORD TL8645 Map 5

Bull

A134

An inn since 1580, this fine timbered building was originally a medieval manorial great hall. The calm front lounge – divided by the remains of an oak partition wall – has big mullioned and leaded windows, lots of oak timbering, a huge brick fireplace with log fire, a longcase clock from Stradbrook, a rack of daily papers, and various antique furnishings. Supporting the beautifully carved high main beam is a woodwose – the wild man of the woods that figures in Suffolk folk-tales. A more spacious back bar has armed brown leatherette or plush dining seats around antique oak tables, dark heavy beams, and sporting prints on the cream timbered walls; cribbage, dominoes, piped music. The Mylde lounge and the restaurant are no smoking. Bar food remains unchanged since last year and includes sandwiches (from £1.25), soup (£1.95), traditional ploughman's (£3.50), a daily special pie, roast of the day (£5.50) and seafood platter (£5.95); it can be busy at lunchtimes. Well kept Courage Directors, Greene King IPA, and Nethergate Old Growler on handpump, various malt whiskies, and helpful staff. There are tables in the paved central courtyard. Nearby, the Elizabethan Melford Hall and moated Tudor Kentwell Hall are both fine buildings, in attractive grounds. ***(Recommended by Ian Phillips, John Evans, A and M Dickinson, F M and A F Walters)***

Free house (Forte) ~ Manager Peter Watt ~ Meals and snacks (limited menu Sun; not 25 Dec) ~ Restaurant (not Sun evening) ~ (01787) 378494 ~ Children welcome ~ Live entertainment Fri/Sat and Sun lunch ~ Open 11.30-3, 6-11; closed 25 Dec ~ Bedrooms: £75B/£95B

ORFORD TM4250 Map 5

Jolly Sailor

This aptly named and unspoilt smugglers' inn was built mainly from wrecked ships' timbers in the 17th c. There are several cosily traditional rooms served from counters and hatches in an old-fashioned central cubicle, and an uncommon spiral staircase in the corner of the flagstoned main bar – which also has 13 brass door knockers and other brassware, local photographs, and a good solid fuel stove; a small room is popular with the dominoes and shove-ha'penny players, and has draughts, chess and cribbage too. The full range of Adnams ales (including the seasonal ones) is well kept on handpump, and both locals and staff are friendly. Good value home-made bar food includes chilli con carne (£3.60), local fish and chips (£3.75), and omelettes, steak pie, sweet and sour pork, home-cooked ham and egg and roast leg of lamb (all £3.95). The dining room is no smoking. Tables and chairs in the big garden. The setting is very pleasant, by a busy little quay on the River Ore, opposite Orford Ness and close to marshy Havergate Island, where avocets breed. *(Recommended by Frank Cummins, Keble Paterson, June and Perry Dann, Ian Phillips, Neil Powell, Basil Minson)*

Adnams ~ Tenant Philip M Attwood ~ Real ale ~ Meals and snacks (not Tues/Thurs evenings 1 Oct-Easter; not 25/26 Dec) ~ (01394) 450243 ~ Children in dining room if eating ~ Open 11.30-2.30, 7-11 ~ Bedrooms: /£32

RATTLESDEN TL9758 Map 5

Brewers Arms

Signposted on minor roads W of Stowmarket, off B1115 via Buxhall or off A45 via Woolpit

Suffolk Dining Pub of the Year

There's a fine range of surprisingly cosmopolitan dishes cooked by the landlord in this welcoming 16th-c pub. As well as filled rolls the choice might typically include soup like tomato, carrot and coriander (£1.85), hummus and pitta bread (£2.85), fresh asparagus mousse with cucumber sauce (£2.95), venison and pistacchio nut terrine with cumberland sauce or prawns in a cheese fondue sauce (£3.25), and a dozen or so interesting daily changing main courses like spaghetti with mushrooms, coriander and stilton sauce (£4.85), spinach and ricotta cheese pancakes (£5.20), lamb and aubergine lasagne or chicken, tomato and pinenut risotto (£5.50), lamb kofta meatballs (£6.25), delicious rabbit basque (£6.45), beef and Guinness pie or chicken stuffed with leeks and stilton in a sherry sauce (£7.25), with puddings such as apple and banana cinnamon filo pie with rum and fudge sauce (£2.85). Very welcoming and friendly service, and well kept Greene King Abbot and IPA on handpump, and decent wines including some from a local vineyard. The small but lively public bar on the right has shove-ha'penny, cribbage and trivia, and on the left, the pleasantly simple beamed lounge bar has horsebrasses, and individually chosen pictures and bric-a-brac on the walls. It winds back through standing timbers to the main eating area, which is partly flint-walled and has a magnificent old bread oven. French windows open on to a garden edged with bourbon roses, with a boules pitch. *(Recommended by MDN, Stuart Earle, P Devitt, J F M West, Dr Ronald Church, Pamela Goodwyn, Gwen and Peter Andrews, P J Guy, Andrew McKeand, Basil Minson, Donald and Margaret Wood, Caroline Shearer, Ian and Nita Cooper, Mr and Mrs R Leeds)*

Greene King ~ Tenant Ron Cole ~ Real ale ~ Meals and snacks (not Mon, Sun evening or all last week Jun/1st week Jul) ~ (01449) 736377 ~ Well behaved children welcome ~ Jazz every Thurs evening ~ Open 12-2.30(3 Sat), 7-11; closed Mon, closed Sun evening

REDE TL8055 Map 5

Plough

Village signposted off A143 Bury St Edmunds—Haverhill

A couple of our well seasoned readers are more than happy to do an 80-mile round trip several times a year to enjoy the imaginative food here. Typically, there might be turkey in a cream sauce with garlic and cheese topping (£5.50), lamb with artichokes and fennel, hot, spicy chicken, smoked pork chop in orange and melon sauce or vegetable cobbler (all £5.95), wild boar and venison pie (£6.50), stuffed quail in soya sauce (£7.50), fresh fish and game in season, steaks (from £9.50), and puddings such as excellent lemon crush pie, lovely strawberry and raspberry mousses, or in winter the popular Wenceslas tart, a combination of mince, almonds and raisins (£2.50). They also do ploughman's and salads (particularly good beef or Cromer crab), and the little evening restaurant does things like moules au gratin, poached salmon, and steaks, as well as a three course Sunday lunch. Service friendly and helpful; decent wines. The simple and traditional cosy bar has copper measures and pewter tankards hanging from low black beams, decorative plates on a delft shelf and surrounding the solid fuel stove in its brick fireplace, and red plush button-back built-in wall banquettes; fruit machine, unobtrusive piped music. In front of the building are some picnic tables, with more in a sheltered cottage garden behind, where there's a little dovecote. *(Recommended by Gwen and Peter Andrews, Tony and Wendy Hobden, Captain S Hood, J L Phillips, Wayne Brindle, Dr and Mrs M Bailey, J W Cockerton)*

Greene King ~ Lease: Brian and Joyce Desborough ~ Meals and snacks (not Sun evenings) ~ Evening restaurant (not Sun evening) ~ (01284) 789208 ~ Well behaved children in eating area of bar and restaurant ~ Open 11.30-3, 7-11

SNAPE TM3959 Map 5

Golden Key ★

Priory Lane

Bedrooms have been opened in this quietly elegant and rather civilised inn this year, new kitchens installed, the dining room extended a bit, and a terrace constructed at the back near the small sheltered and flower-filled garden; there are plenty of white tables and chairs from which you can enjoy the view. Food is doing very well at the moment and might include good soups such as mixed bean or cauliflower and stilton (£2.95), filled rolls made to order (from £1.50), home-made pâté like chicken liver and cognac or kipper (£2.95), good sausage, egg and onion pie or lovely smoked haddock quiche (£5.50), steak and mushroom or prawn and broccoli pie (both £6.95), honey roast ham (£6.95), grilled lamb chops (£7.95), plenty of fresh fish such as local crab, lemon sole, Dover sole, sea trout, bass and fresh lobster (from £8.95), steaks (from £8.95), and very good home-made puddings like hot lemon cake or chocolate brandy cake (from £2.95). The full range of Adnams beers on handpump (including the seasonal ones), and several malt whiskies. The low-beamed stylish lounge has a winter open fire, an old-fashioned settle curving around a couple of venerable stripped tables and a tiled floor, and at the other end there are stripped modern settles around heavy Habitat-style wooden tables on a turkey carpet, and a solid fuel stove in the big fireplace. The cream walls are hung with pencil sketches of customers, a Henry Wilkinson spaniel and so forth. A brick-floored side room has sofas and more tables. They tend to get busy at weekends. *(Recommended by June and Perry Dann, John Fahy, Pat Woodward, Christine Herxheimer, Derek Patey, Phil and Heidi Cook, J L Phillips, Wayne Brindle, R D Knight, Simon Cottrell, Derek and Sylvia Stephenson, Basil Minson, M A and C R Starling)*

Adnams ~ Tenants Max and Susie Kissick-Jones ~ Real ale ~ Meals and snacks ~ Snape (01728) 688510 ~ Children in eating area ~ Open 11-3, 6-11 ~ Bedrooms: £30B/£50B

Plough & Sail 🍷

Snape Maltings Riverside Centre

David Grimwood was one of the first to introduce the 'simple sophisticated' style of country furnishings and decor which, coupled with interesting natural cooking, has now entered the mainstream of the best type of dining pub. He ran the White Horse at Easton and the Old Chequers at Friston (both in Suffolk) which were very popular main entries under his leadership, and is now in charge of the cooking here as well as at the River Bar Restaurant and Granary Tea Rooms – also part of the Snape Maltings Riverside Centre (which stretches out behind the pub and includes the famous concert hall, art gallery, craft shop, a house and garden shop, and so forth). The buff-coloured pub is a long narrow building with the bar facing you as you walk through the door; beyond this on the right is a raised airy eating room with attractive pine furniture and – to one side – a settle in front of the open fire; beyond this is the busy little restaurant. To the left of the bar and down some steps is a quarry-tiled room with dark traditional furniture. The atmosphere is relaxed and friendly. Wonderfully fresh food includes snacks such as sandwiches (from £1.95; open ones from £3.75), a choice of three home-made soups (from £2.95), home-made pâté such as dark mushroom and cream cheese or smoked mackerel and horseradish (£3.75), and a proper ploughman's (from £3.50), as well as changing dishes like terrine of smoked salmon and trout (£3.50), salad of local smoked prawns with a yoghurt and mint dressing or warm salad of chicken livers with honey and sesame (£3.75), cold salt beef with pickled walnuts, home-made sausage pie with pickles or Cromer crab salad (£5.95), herb-crusted chicken with garlic and roquefort (£6.25), grilled wing of skate with cashews (£6.50), and baked bass with local samphire (£7.95); puddings such as strawberry shortbread, upside-down ginger pudding or tayberry and apple crumble tart (£3.25). Well kept Adnams Best and Broadside and Greene King IPA and Abbot on handpump, and a fine wine list with a few by the glass; darts. No children. The big enclosed back terrace has lots of picnic tables and a giant chess set (popular with children who are not allowed inside). *(More reports please)*

Free house ~ Licensee G D Gooderham ~ Real ale ~ Meals and snacks ~ (01728) 688413 ~ Open 11-3, 5.30-11

SOUTHWOLD TM5076 Map 5

Crown ★

High Street

People are quite prepared to sit outside this smart old hotel for some time waiting for the doors to open – just to be sure of getting a seat. But it's not just the marvellous food and drink that people like so much, it's the fact that this is a most enjoyable place to stay (and the breakfast is interesting) and the staff are helpful and friendly, even when under pressure. The elegant main bar has a relaxed atmosphere, large beams, pretty, fresh flowers on the mix of kitchen pine tables, a stripped curved high-backed settle and other dark varnished settles, kitchen chairs and some bar stools, newspapers to read, and a carefully restored and rather fine carved wooden fireplace; the small no-smoking restaurant with its white cloths and pale cane chairs leads off. The smaller back oak-panelled locals' bar has more of a traditional pubby atmosphere, red leatherette wall benches and a red carpet. There's a particularly carefully chosen wine list, with a monthly changing choice of 20 interesting varieties by the glass or bottle kept perfectly on a cruover machine. Adnams brewery is nearby, and the Crown is understandably their flagship: they have the full range of Adnams wines by the bottle (well over 288, which you can get from the cash and carry by the mixed dozen round the corner), and perfectly kept Adnams Bitter, Broadside, Mild, and winter Old on handpump; also a good choice of malt whiskies, tea, coffee and herbal infusions. The very good, creative bar food changes every day, but might typically include aubergine and garlic soup with red pepper cream (£1.95), warm salad of chicken livers with assorted mushrooms, croutons and crispy bacon (£3.95), walnut crumb tart with leek, walnut and red pesto cream or mussels with tomato and garlic (£6), grilled pigeon breast on baby spinach with goat's cheese dressing or local venison sausages with parsley mash (£7.25), baked fillet of local cod with a chilli and lemon crust and tomato and chilli salsa or fresh Thai crabcake with fresh coriander and coconut dressing (£7.50), gingered Scotch salmon with fresh tomato butter or Moroccan chicken with fruit and nut couscous (£7.65), and puddings such as hot cherry and apple crumble tart with crème fraîche or baked chocolate cheesecake with a thin chocolate sauce (£2.95); most of the main courses can also be enjoyed as starters. The no-smoking restaurant does a good three-course lunch for £15.50. Shove-ha'penny, dominoes and cribbage. There are some tables in a sunny sheltered corner outside. *(Recommended by Pat Woodward, M J Morgan, D S Cottrell, John and Sheila French, Gwen and Peter Andrews, G M K Donkin, John and Moira Cole, Mr and Mrs D S Price, Pat and Roger Fereday, Gill and Andy Plumb, Dave Carter, Tom Thomas, JKW, Dr Ronald Church, Rita Horridge, James Macrae, Nigel Woolliscroft, Mrs F M Halle, C Fisher, V and E A Bolton, Hazel Morgan, Bernard Patrick, Thomas Nott, Keith*

Symons, Martin Richards, Rosemary Harris, Dr and Mrs P Crawshaw, Evelyn and Derek Walter, Anna Marsh, Anthony and Freda Walters)

Adnams ~ Manager Anne Simpson ~ Real ale ~ Meals and snacks (12.15-1.45, 7.15-9.45; not 25-26 Dec, 1 Jan) ~ Restaurant ~ (01502) 722275 ~ Children in eating area ~ Open 10.30-3, 6-11; closed first week Jan ~ Bedrooms: £38B/£58B

STOKE BY NAYLAND TL9836 Map 5

Angel

B1068 Sudbury—East Bergholt; also signposted via Nayland off A134 Colchester—Sudbury

Although this civilised old place is first and foremost a dining pub, drinkers are made welcome, too, and the staff are friendly and efficient. Attractively presented and delicious, the home-made food includes soup (£2.45), fishcakes with remoulade sauce or mushroom and pistachio pâté (£3.95), deep fried cambazola with cranberry sauce (£4.50), vegetarian filo parcels served with fresh tomato coulis (£5.75), steak and kidney pudding or roast loin of pork with crackling, apple mousse and red cabbage (£5.95), supreme of chicken filled with brie and rolled in crushed hazelnuts or roast ballotine of duckling with cassis sauce (£7.95), honey glazed roast rack of lamb (£8.95), brochette of scallops wrapped in bacon (£9.50) and lovely puddings like dark chocolate ganache gateau (£3); vegetables are very good; it's worth arriving early or booking in advance. The comfortable main bar area has handsome Elizabethan beams, some stripped brickwork and timbers, a mixture of furnishings including wing armchairs, mahogany dining chairs, and pale library chairs, local watercolours and older prints, attractive table lamps, and a huge log fire; the atmosphere is relaxed, even when the pub is busy (which it usually is). Round the corner is a little tiled-floor stand-and-chat bar – with well kept Adnams, Greene King IPA and Abbot and Nethergate Bitter on handpump; extensive wine list and good coffee. One room has a low sofa and wing armchairs around its woodburning stove, and Victorian paintings on the dark green walls. There are cast-iron seats and tables on a sheltered terrace. No children. *(Recommended by Gwen and Peter Andrews, MN, DN, Pamela Goodwyn, JKW, Eric and Jackie Robinson, R W Hillyard, John Evans, Quentin Williamson, Nicholas Holmes, C H Stride, Mrs T Froud, Mr and Mrs G M Edwards, Sue Demont, Tim Barrow, Hazel Morgan, Bernard Patrick, Ian Phillips, M A and C R Starling)*

Free house ~ Licensee Peter Smith ~ Real ale ~ Meals and snacks ~ Restaurant ~ (01206) 263245 ~ Open 11-2.30, 6-11; closed 25/26 Dec ~ Bedrooms: £44B/£57.50B

THORNHAM MAGNA TM1070 Map 5

Four Horseshoes

Off A140 S of Diss; follow Finningham 3¼ signpost, by White Horse pub

New licensees have taken over this popular, handsome thatched pub and the pub is now not open all day. The extensive and rambling bar is well divided into alcoves and distinct areas, and there are very low and heavy black beams, some tall windsor chairs as well as the golden plush banquettes and stools on its spread of fitted turkey carpet, country pictures and farm tools on the black-timbered white walls, and logs burning in big fireplaces; the area with the inside well is no smoking. A wide choice of good food, quickly served by uniformed waitresses might include sandwiches, ploughman's, vegetarian dishes (£5.95), chicken and apricot pie with walnuts and mushrooms (£6.50), and various daily fish, offal and game dishes (£7.95-£9.95); the restaurant is no smoking. Well kept Adnams, Courage Best and Directors, and John Smiths on handpump, some malt whiskies and country wines, and piped music. In summer, you can sit at the picnic tables beside the flower beds on a sheltered lawn. Thornham Walks nearby consists of nearly 12 miles of permissive footpaths on the beautiful and privately owned Thornham Estate and there is a half mile hard-surfaced path through the parkland, woodland and farmland which is suitable for wheelchairs and pushchairs as well as those with walking difficulties. The thatched church at Thornham Parva is famous for its ancient wall paintings. *(Recommended by*

Keith Archer, Richard Balls, Davie Craine, Ann Reeder, Andrew McKeand, A G Drake, Clare and Gordon Phillips, John C Baker, Basil Minson, John Honnor)

Free house ~ Licensees Peter and Pam Morris ~ Real ale ~ Meals and snacks ~ Restaurant ~ (01379) 678777 ~ Children in eating area of bar ~ Open 12-3, 6.45(6.30 Sat)-11 ~ Bedrooms: £35B/£50B

TOSTOCK TL9563 Map 5

Gardeners Arms 

Village signposted from A45 and A1088

Readers really enjoy this delightfully unspoilt pub – for the really warm welcome from the licensees (and the locals) and for the very good food. The smart lounge bar has a bustling villagey atmosphere, low heavy black beams, and lots of carving chairs around the black tables. Good value, the food includes sandwiches (from £1.40; toasties £2.50), tasty soup (£1.75), ploughman's with home-made granary rolls (from £3), home-made vegetarian pizza (£4), home-made quiche (£4.25), sausage, egg, chips and beans (£4.25), gammon steak (£4.95), very popular daily specials such as Thai beef curry with stir-fried vegetables on noodles (£5.75) and an increasing number of fish dishes, and puddings (£2.25). Very well kept Greene King Abbot and IPA on handpump. The lively tiled-floor public bar has darts, pool, shove-ha'penny, dominoes, cribbage, juke box, and fruit machine. The picnic table sets among the roses and other flowers on the sheltered lawn are a lovely place to sit and watch the local team playing steel quoits on the pitch. *(Recommended by Richard Fawcett, Ian Phillips, Phillip Fox, Neville Kenyon, Joan Hilditch, Wayne Brindle, Jenny and Michael Back, A H Thomas, Donald and Margaret Wood, Charles Bardswell)*

Greene King ~ Tenant Reg Ransome ~ Meals and snacks (not Mon or Tues evenings or Sun lunchtime) ~ Restaurant (not Sun lunchtime) ~ (01359) 270460 ~ Children in eating area of bar ~ Open 11.30(11 Sat)-2.30, 7-11

WALBERSWICK TM4974 Map 5

Bell

Just off B1387

For those who like unpretentious and unchanging pubs, this ancient place is just the ticket – but the relaxed style of service and housekeeping does not appeal to everyone. The characterful, rambling bar has the flooring bricks and oak beams that it had 600 years ago when the sleepy little village was a flourishing port, curved high-backed settles on the well worn flagstones, tankards hanging from oars above the bar counter, and a woodburning stove in the big fireplace; to one side is a more conventionally comfortable area decorated with local photographs; maybe Fingle, the friendly Irish wolfhound. Bar food includes soup, sandwiches (from £1.50), ploughman's (from £3), good local fish with chips (£4.50), and a good choice of summer help-yourself salads (from £4.50, the fresh Cromer crab is good); in winter they do a wide range of hot dishes such as shepherd's pie or steak and kidney pie (from £4.50); children's helpings. The restaurant is no smoking. Well kept Adnams Bitter, Broadside and Extra on handpump and several malt whiskies; darts, shove-ha'penny, cribbage, dominoes, trivia, and fruit machine. It can get busy (and noisy) in summer, and service then can be rather haphazard. Most of the bedrooms look over the sea or the river. This is a nice spot close to the beach, with a well-placed hedge sheltering the seats and tables on the sizeable flower-filled lawn from the worst of the sea winds. To really make the most of the setting, it's worth taking the little ferry from Southwold, and then enjoying the short walk along to the pub. *(Recommended by Gill and Andy Plumb, Derek Patey, MJVK, Neil Powell, Evelyn and Derek Walter, Mrs F M Halle, BKA, D and B Carter, M J V Kemp, Derek and Sylvia Stephenson)*

Adnams ~ Tenant F A Stansall ~ Real ale ~ Lunchtime meals and snacks ~ Evening restaurant ~ (01502) 723109 ~ Children welcome away from saloon bar ~ Folk music first Sun of month ~ Open 11-11 ~ Bedrooms: £35/£50(£60B)

Lucky Dip

Besides the fully inspected pubs, you might like to try these Lucky Dips recommended to us and described by readers (if you do, please send us reports):

Aldeburgh [The Parade; TM4656], *Brudenell*: Clubbily furnished rather old fashioned large hotel right on the beach (sandbags by the doors), included for the magnificent sea views from the bar; good service, comfortable bedrooms *(George Atkinson, O K Smyth)*; [Market Pl, opp Moot Hall], *Mill*: Friendly nautical atmosphere, local fishermen in bar – good food cooked to order includes local fish; good service, well kept beer, sensible prices, separate cosy no-smoking dining room *(N S Smith, M Catterick and friends)*; [222 High St], *White Hart*: Friendly and individual refurbished Victorian local, well kept Adnams, remarkable range of spirits, good comfortable bedrooms *(Anna Marsh, Neil Powell)*; [Seafront], *White Lion*: Well kept Adnams, good value food, pleasant cheerful service *(Rita Horridge)*

☆ **Aldringham** [B1122/B1353 S of Leiston; TM4461], *Parrot & Punchbowl*: Neatly kept beamed pub with good food from downstairs servery, dining-room meals Fri/weekend (must book then), lots of decent wines, well kept Whitbreads-related ales; piped music, children welcome; sheltered garden with a couple of swings, nice craft centre opp *(Mrs P M Goodwyn, BB)*

☆ **Badingham** [TM3068], *White Horse*: Old-fashioned pub with attractive stripped brickwork and beams, longcase clock by huge open range with woodburner, wholesome reasonably priced straightforward bar food inc vegetarian and children's, well kept Adnams, relaxing atmosphere, well reproduced piped music in public bar; neat bowling green, nice rambling garden *(A H Thomas, John Beeken, Gwen and Peter Andrews, LYM)*

☆ **Bardwell** [The Green; TL9473], *Six Bells*: Comfortably modernised beamed pub dating back to 16th century, wide choice of good food inc fresh fish, well kept Adnams and Wadworths 6X, extensive wine list, log fires, good atmosphere; restaurant, games evening Sun, folk music weekly, children and dogs welcome; garden with play area and Wendy house; attractive pine-furnished bedrooms *(Mrs P M Goodwyn, M J Morgan, Charles Bardswell, Richard Balls)*

Barnham [Barnham Rd; TL8779], *Grafton Arms*: Quiet country pub with good choice of food, well kept beers *(William Buxton)*

☆ **Barton Mills** [A11, by Five Ways roundabout; TL7173], *Bull*: Rambling pleasantly dated bar with big fireplaces, well kept Adnams, Bass, Worthington BB and a guest beer, decent wines, good local atmosphere, reasonably priced standard bar food served noon-10 (not Sun) and good summer salad bar, separate grill room, piped music; children allowed in eating area; bedrooms *(Thomas Nott, Roy Bromell, Ian Phillips, BB)*

Beyton [TL9362], *Bear*: Unrefurbished village local with particularly well kept Courage-related and guest beers, sandwiches and rolls, very friendly cheerful owners *(John C Baker)*

☆ **Blythburgh** [A12; TM4575], *White Hart*: Beautifully placed open-plan family dining pub opp magnificent church; good reasonably priced food inc cold buffet, fine ancient beams, woodwork and staircase, big open fires, well kept Adnams Bitter, Old and Broadside, decent wines, quick conscientious service; children in eating area and restaurant, open all day Fri/Sat; spacious lawns looking down on tidal marshes *(N S Smith, Hazel R Morgan, G M K Donkin, LYM)*

☆ **Boxford** [Broad St; TL9640], *Fleece*: Unpretentious partly 15th-c pub with cosy panelled bar on right, airy lounge bar with wonderful medieval fireplace, armchairs and some distinctive old seats among more conventional furnishings; good home cooking, well kept Tolly, welcoming landlord, good live jazz Fri *(John Prescott, LYM)*

☆ **Bramfield** [A144; TM4073], *Queens Head*: Friendly pleasantly refurbished high-beamed lounge bar, particularly good service, good fresh food, big log fire, well kept Adnams Bitter, Old and Broadside, piped music; darts in public bar; restaurant *(F J and P A Apicella, Dr Ronald Church, Pamela Goodwyn, June and Perry Dann)*

Bucklesham [TM2442], *Shannon*: Much extended old village pub now embraced by Ipswich suburbs; well kept Tolly, vast sandwiches *(David Bloomfield)*

Bungay [Broad St; TM3491], *Green Dragon*: Town local brewing its own good beers, food inc very good filled baked potatoes and good value specials, liberal attitude towards children; piped music may be loud, very popular with young people – side room quieter *(Keith and Janet Morris, G Washington)*

☆ **Bury St Edmunds** [7 Out Northgate St, Station Hill; TL8564], *Linden Tree*: Wide choice of generous cheap food in busy attractively renovated family dining pub with friendly quick service, well kept Greene King IPA and Rayments, wines in two glass sizes, nice atmosphere, popular conservatory restaurant, good well kept garden *(Richard Balls, Sheryl Bailey, Frank Davidson, Rick and Carol Mercado, Stuart Earle, J F M West)*

☆ **Bury St Edmunds** [Crown St – park in back yard off Bridewell Lane], *Dog & Partridge*: Good atmosphere in rambling town pub with bar, snug and several lounge areas – old, very old and new linked together; well kept Greene King from nearby brewery, fair choice of food, friendly efficient service;

games room, restaurant area; more a young people's pub evenings *(J F M West, PGP)*

☆ **Bury St Edmunds** [Whiting St], *Masons Arms*: Good range of reasonably priced food, well kept Greene King IPA and prompt friendly service in busy but comfortable and relaxing dining lounge with lots of oak timbering; more of a local evenings *(K D Day, Nigel Woolliscroft, PGP)*

Bury St Edmunds [Angel Hill], *Angel*: Thriving country-town hotel with good value straightforward food in bar, Regency dining room and cellar grill room, excellent friendly service, Adnams; bedrooms comfortable *(Mrs R C F Martin)*; [Guildhall St], *Black Boy*: Big open-plan pub with side game and sitting areas, Greene King beers, welcoming landlord, reasonably priced food and drink *(PGP)*; [The Traverse], *Cupola House*: Started as a wine bar but now seems to be operating as pub, with good value bar food *(Tom Gondris)*; [Traverse, Abbeygate St], *Nutshell*: Perhaps the country's smallest pub inside (though it's said 102 people once squeezed in); friendly and cosy, with particularly well kept Greene King IPA and Abbot, lots of odd bric-a-brac; attractive corner facade; cl Sun and Holy Days *(Cdr Patrick Tailyour, Michael Marlow)*; [39 Churchgate St], *Queens Head*: Good choice of interesting real ales, cheap food, very quick service; much modernised, busy with professionals at lunchtime and young people Fri/Sat evening; may be open all day *(Richard Balls, F M and A F Walters)*

☆ **Butley** [B1084; TM3651], *Oyster*: Good varied fresh food inc seafood, spicy sizzler dishes and children's menu in small-roomed pub, modernised but pleasant, with informal furniture, well kept Adnams, very friendly landlord, open fires; pleasant outside area with rabbits, doves and budgerigars; folk nights *(Pat and Robert Watt, P J and S E Robbins, Catherine Boardman, Norman Smith, Dr and Mrs P J S Crawshaw, Pamela Goodwyn)*

Buxhall [Mill Green; village signed off B1115 W of Stowmarket, then L at Rattlesden sign; TM0057], *Crown*: Tucked-away country pub with snug little bar and side room, fair choice of bar food, Adnams Broadside and Greene King IPA, open fires, games in separate public bar, restaurant; children allowed if eating, pleasant garden *(Stuart Earle, BB)*

☆ **Cavendish** [High St (A1092); TL8046], *Bull*: Attractive 16th-c beamed pub with wide range of good value food, pleasant atmosphere, good service, well kept Adname, nice fireplaces; bar, dining area, garden with barbecue; fruit machines, darts and pool, no piped music; children welcome, bedrooms *(JJW, CMW, Dr and Mrs N Holmes)*

☆ **Chelsworth** [The Street; near Bury St Edmunds; TL9848], *Peacock*: Lots of Tudor brickwork and exposed beams in attractive old pub, some emphasis on dining now, with wide choice of food inc unusual dishes and good fresh veg, comfortable tables and good service, several well kept changing ales, decent coffee, nice small garden; open all day Sat; bedrooms – the two at the back are quieter; pretty village *(Tom Gondris, Dr I H Maine, J L Phillips, P Devitt, Wayne Brindle, George Atkinson, LYM)*

Clare [High St; TL7645], *Swan*: Straightforward village pub doing well under current licensees – she cooks quite splendidly *(W T Aird, BB)*

Cockfield [Stows Hill; A1141 Lavenham Rd; TL9054], *Three Horseshoes*: Cosy and friendly village pub with Greene King ales, in attractive building; has had good food from superb doorstep sandwiches to delicious puddings, but licensee moved to Cambridge in summer 1995 *(Tony Hepworth, Frank W Gadbois, Mrs Gill Janzen; reports on new regime please)*

Cratfield [TM3175], *Cratfield Poacher*: Well kept Adnams and Greene King IPA and Abbot, stuffed animals, bottle collection, character landlord *(Nick and Alison Dowson)*

Cretingham [TM2260], *Bell*: Comfortable pub mixing striking 15th-c beams, timbers and big fireplace with more modern renovations and furnishings, Adnams and changing guest beers, bar food inc vegetarian and children's; no-smoking lounge and restaurant with Sun lunch (service may slow if busy); traditional games in public bar, family room, may open all day in summer; seats out in rose garden and on front grass *(V and E A Bolton, June and Perry Dann, LYM)*

Darsham [just off A12; TM4169], *Fox*: Friendly service, good reasonably priced food inc fresh veg and home-made puddings; restaurant *(June and Perry Dann)*

☆ **East Bergholt** [Burnt Oak, towards Flatford Mill; TM0734], *Kings Head*: Well kept attractive beamed lounge with comfortable sofas, interesting decorations, quick welcoming service, usual bar food, well kept Tolly, decent coffee, piped classical music (juke box in plain public bar); lots of room in pretty garden, flower-decked haywain, baskets and tubs of flowers in front *(Pamela Goodwyn)*

☆ **Eastbridge** [TM4566], *Eels Foot*: Good atmosphere and friendly folk in what has been a simple unspoiled local with well kept Adnams, generous cheap basic home-made bar food inc vegetarian (no winter evening meals), crisp varnish, red leatherette, bright carpet or lino, lively informal Thurs music nights; tables on quiet front terrace, children in eating area; pretty village, handy for Minsmere bird reserve and heathland walks; landlord left summer 1995, no reports yet on successor *(June and Perry Dann, Derek and Maggie Washington, LYM; news please)*

☆ **Easton** [N of Wickham Mkt, Earl Soham rd; TM2858], *White Horse*: Unspoilt country pub, two neatly kept rooms with open fires, Tolly ales, food in bar and restaurant – has been very good, but the friendly landlord of last year's main entry has now left; children

in eating area, garden with good play area *(John Fahy, BS, JS, LYM; reports please)*
Elmswell [Station Rd, just off A45 nr Woolpit; TL9964], *Fox*: Particularly good imaginative vegetarian food, esp spinach strudel *(C Gilbert)*
Felixstowe Ferry [TM3337], *Ferry Boat*: Well kept ales tapped from the cask in unpretentious 17th-c pub tucked away between golf links and dunes nr harbour and Martello tower, simple bar food, pleasant staff, interesting photographs of turn-of-the-c long-frock local bathing belles *(Rita Horridge, LYM)*
Felsham [TL9457], *Six Bells*: Greene King ales in open-plan rural local with wide choice of food inc wonderful pies, real shortcrust pastry, fresh veg *(Stuart Earle)*
Finningham [TM0669], *White Horse*: Decent food, pleasant atmosphere; handy for walkers *(Pamela Goodwyn)*
☆ **Framlingham** [Market Hill; TM2863], *Crown*: Old-fashioned heavy-beamed public bar opening into hall and comfortable character lounge with armchairs by log fire, decent bar food, Adnams on handpump, help-yourself morning coffee, restaurant; comfortable period bedrooms – traditional small Forte inn *(Ian Phillips, LYM)*
☆ **Friston** [B1121; just off A1094 Aldeburgh—Snape, 4.5 m NE of Aldeburgh; TM4160], *Old Chequers*: Stylish dining pub with simple country pine furnishings, airy decor, well stocked bar; has been a very popular main entry, with excellent service, a good choice of interesting good value food inc a carefully prepared lunchtime buffet, and well kept Adnams, guest beers and wines, but the Grimwoods who made it so successful have moved to the Plough & Sail at Snape – see main entries *(LYM; reports on new regime please)*
Great Barton [Thurston Rd; minor rd from Bury, parallel to A143; TL8967], *Flying Fortress*: Former farmhouse HQ of USAF support group, on edge of Rougham ex-airfield – the original for the film *Twelve O'Clock High*; long bar backing on to big comfortable modern lounge area, Whitbreads-related ales and three good well kept guest beers, wide range of food cooked here inc good Newmarket sausages, friendly staff, take-away wines *(John C Baker, Frank Gadbois)*
☆ **Great Wenham** [The Row, Capel St Mary Rd; TM0738], *Queens Head*: Creative Indian food (not Mon evening) among other dishes in friendly and comfortable traditional country pub with four well kept interesting changing ales, good value wines; families welcome in cosy snug *(Richard Balls, John C Baker)*
Great Wratting [TL6848], *Red Lion*: Adnams pub in lovely setting, huge garden behind with two goats, three dovecotes and a goldfish pond; bedrooms *(Frank W Gadbois)*
Grundisburgh [TM2250], *Dog*: Pleasant atmosphere, good food inc bargain OAP lunches Mon; doing well under current newish management *(Pamela Goodwyn)*
Halesworth [High St; TM3877], *White Hart*: Good food inc fresh veg and good home-made puddings *(June and Perry Dann)*
☆ **Haughley** [centre; TM0262], *Kings Arms*: Clean and peaceful beamed dining lounge with lots of shiny dark tables, smaller lounge and busy public bar with games; cheerful prompt service, wide choice of fair-priced bar food (curries, pies, fish and steaks all praised), log fire, well kept Greene King IPA, Abbot and Rayments, piped music; tables and play house on back lawn *(Ian and Nita Cooper, Joan and Michel Hooper-Immins, Basil Minson, BB)*
☆ **Haughley** [Station Rd – towards Old Newton by level crossing], *Railway*: New licensees doing good value food inc some adventurous dishes in unpretentious but individual traditional country local with well kept Greene King IPA, Mild, Abbot and guest beers such as Burton Bridge and Fremlins, log fire; children in neat back room *(John Baker, BB)*
Hitcham [The Street; B1115 Sudbury—Stowmarket; TL9851], *White Horse*: Good food in bar and restaurant of friendly local with obliging service, well kept Greene King Abbot *(Stuart Earle)*
☆ **Holbrook** [Ipswich Rd; TM1636], *Compasses*: Good value food inc interesting dishes in bar and restaurant, welcoming staff, log fire, well kept ales inc Flowers and Tolly, garden with play area *(A Albert)*
☆ **Horringer** [TL8261], *Six Bells*: Has burst into life since renovation and extension, energetic and ebullient landlord copes well with greatly increased business, as does wife in kitchen; comfortable and uncluttered, with good range of reasonably priced food, well kept Greene King, bright back conservatory opening on to garden ideal for small children on a nice day *(W T Aird, Mrs Heather Martin, Andrew McKeand)*
☆ **Huntingfield** [TM3374], *Huntingfield Arms*: Neat pub overlooking green, light wood tables and chairs, pleasant combination of beams and stripped brickwork, good range of attractively presented bar food inc good fresh fish, well kept Adnams, friendly service, restaurant, games area with pool beyond woodburner *(Gwen and Peter Andrews)*
☆ **Icklingham** [62 The Street; TL7772], *Plough*: Good range of home-made food, well kept Adnams, Greene King IPA and a couple of guests such as Ansells and Boddingtons, friendly atmosphere, lots of cricketing memorabilia and books, subdued piped music; big garden with play area *(George B Spenceley, Frank W Gadbois)*
Ipswich [Dogs Head St, nr Buttermarket; TM1744], *Plough*: Busy but welcoming anti-lager town local with ten well kept real ales, big scrubbed refectory tables, plain floorboards, light and airy, bar billiards *(Keith Stevens, Tina Hammond)*
☆ **Kersey** [signed off A1141 N of Hadleigh; TL9944], *Bell*: Quaint flower-decked Tudor building in picturesque village, low-beamed

public side with tiled floor and log fire divided from red plush lounge by brick and timber screen, well kept Courage-related ales with a guest such as Adnams, decent house wines, rather pricy bar food, restaurant, sheltered back terrace with fairy-lit side canopy; children allowed, small caravan site *(W H and E Thomas, Tony and Wendy Hobden, V and E A Bolton, Tina and David Woods-Taylor, Frank Cummins, C H and P Stride, Basil J S Minson, J N Child, LYM)*

☆ **Layham** [Upper St, Upper Layham; TM0240], *Marquis of Cornwallis*: Beamed 16th-c pub with plush lounge bar, nicely prepared straightforward food inc good ploughman's, fresh veg and home-made meringues, popular lunchtime with businessmen and retired locals, well kept beers such as Marstons Pedigree; good valley views, picnic tables in extensive riverside garden, open all day Sat in summer; bedrooms handy for Harwich ferries *(Mrs P M Goodwyn, O K Smyth, R G and J N Plumb)*

☆ **Lidgate** [TL7257], *Star*: Relaxed and homely old beamed pub with huge log fire (used for winter Sun spit-roasts), interesting regular food cooked to order (so may be a wait) inc good fresh ingredients and often a Spanish emphasis; well kept Greene King IPA and Abbot under light CO2 blanket, decent wines by the glass, fresh coffee, good welcoming service, no music; doubles as PO, lovely garden; children welcome *(Gwen and Peter Andrews, Dr and Mrs M Bailey, Wayne Brindle)*

☆ **Lindsey** [Rose Green; TL9744], *White Rose*: Half-timbered pub out in the country, recently beautifully restored and reopened by welcoming new owners as restauranty dining pub; lovely log fire; good value food inc good variety of veg and imaginative puddings, well kept local and national beers *(T Gondris, John and Brenda Gibbs, R G and J N Plumb)*

Little Bealings [Sandy Lane; TM2347], *Admirals Head*: Good choice of food in restaurant and bar, well kept ales such as Adnams, Bass, Fullers Chiswick and Greene King; warmly welcoming atmosphere *(Frank W Gadbois, G Reeve)*

Little Glemham [A12; TM3458], *Lion*: Good welcoming service, well kept Adnams, wide choice of good value food inc fresh veg, real puddings, weekday OAP bargain lunches; superb aviary behind *(June and Perry Dann)*

☆ **Long Melford** [Hall St; TL8645], *Cock & Bell*: Attractive pink-washed pub doing well under friendly new management, busy and cheerful, with five real ales and a weekly guest, good fresh food cooked to order; one to watch; bedrooms *(Dave Bundock, Mrs T A Uthwaitt, Frank W Gadbois)*

Long Melford, *Black Lion*: Very much a hotel/restaurant now, but it does have bar food – really distinguished, too; good wines *(F C Johnston)*; *Crown*: Recently reopened after renovation, with attractive interior fireplaces and dining room, friendly staff and owners, good value food, well kept Bass, Greene King, Hancocks HB and Joules on handpump; bedrooms *(Frank W Gadbois, BB)*; [Hall St], *George & Dragon*: Well refurbished, with roaring log fires, good food in bar or separate dining room, no-smoking area; Greene King real ales, decent wines, good individual service, bar billiards; regular live jazz or blues (can be noisy weekends), sheltered garden and courtyard; open all day exc Sun; five comfortable bedrooms *(John and Wendy Trentham)*; [main rd, N end of village], *Hare*: Popular pub with good choice of reasonably priced mainly home-made food inc some unusual dishes, good choice of ales, friendly service, log fire in small back bar, larger front bar, dining area, upstairs dining room; attractive garden *(Brian and Louisa Routledge, H O Dickinson, David Dimock)*

☆ **Martlesham** [off A12 Woodbridge—Ipswich; TM2547], *Black Tiles*: Good spacious family pub with pleasantly decorated bistro-style garden-room restaurant, big woodburner in characterful old bar, wide choice of good inexpensive generous quick home-made food, quick service from smart attentive staff, well kept Adnams Bitter and Broadside and a guest beer, tables in garden; has been open all day *(Graham Reeve, C H and P Stride, Mrs Jacqueline Deale, George Atkinson, LYM)*

Martlesham [Martlesham Heath], *Douglas Bader*: Under new management; good choice of filled baguettes and other food inc good fish and generous puddings; friendly staff, tables outside *(J M Deale)*

☆ **Melton** [Wilford Bridge; TM2851], *Wilford Bridge*: Light and roomy country pub with good value food inc local fish in bar and restaurant, steak nights Mon/Tues, takeaways, friendly service; nearby river walks *(Hazel R Morgan, Mary and David Webb, Andrew Day)*

☆ **Mendham** [TM2782], *Sir Alfred Munnings*: Good cheerful atmosphere in big comfortable open-plan bar with good value neatly served bar food, well kept Adnams and other real ales, unobtrusive piped music, restaurant; children welcome, bedrooms, swimming pool for residents *(Pamela Goodwyn, LYM)*

Mildenhall [Main St; TL7174], *Bell*: Well kept Courage Best and Directors in old inn's spacious beamed bar, open fires, friendly service, good value generous food; darts, juke box; comfortable bedrooms *(Clare Dawkins, Gordon Phillips, Frank W Gadbois)*; [134 High St], *White Hart*: Attractively renovated old hotel with decent reasonably priced food in back bar and restaurant inc good carvery, three Tetleys-related real ales; bedrooms *(Frank Gadbois)*

☆ **Monks Eleigh** [The Street; B1115 Sudbury—Stowmarket; TL9647], *Swan*: Clean and comfortably modernised lounge bar with good range of home-cooked bar food, three real ales, open fire, welcoming efficient service, pleasant dining extension; bedrooms *(H R Bevan, MN, DN)*

Newbourne [TM2643], *Fox*: Very popular lunchtime for straightforward home cooking using fresh local produce and home-grown herbs, cosy drinking area around fire, separate family room; pretty hanging baskets, lots of tables out in front *(Pamela Goodwyn, C H and P Stride)*

☆ **Newmarket** [High St; TL6463], *Rutland Arms*: Good reasonably priced bar food and very quick service in elegant yet relaxed two-room Georgian bar, well kept Adnams, tucked-away fruit machine, restaurant; handy for National Museum of Horseracing; bedrooms good value – the ones overlooking the lovely cobbled yard are very quiet *(W H and E Thomas, R C Vincent)*

Newmarket, *Bedford Lodge*: Fine hotel bar with good bar food; bedrooms *(W T Aird)*; *New Wellington*: Good genuine pub with busy bar, tables in saloon, good Irish landlord *(W T Aird)*

Newton [A134 4 miles E Sudbury; TL9140], *Saracens Head*: Comfortable lounge with small log fire, reasonably priced food cooked by landlord, Adnams, Flowers and Tolly; pool in recently redecorated bar; overlooks village pond and green, ducks and geese among the picnic tables *(Ian Phillips)*

☆ **Norton** [Ixworth Rd (A1088); TL9565], *Dog*: Good value food in nice old pink-washed local with pretty hanging baskets, functional eating areas, relatively unspoilt lounge bar, Greene King ales *(Charles Bardswell)*

☆ **Orford** [Front St; TM4250], *Kings Head*: Pleasant old inn, welcoming new licensees (wth friendly dog), decent food from sandwiches up with an emphasis on fresh fish in bar and restaurant, Adnams ales, decent wines; creakily quaint uneven-floored bedrooms *(David Dimock, John Evans, LYM)*

☆ **Pakenham** [signed off A1088 and A143 S of Norwich; TL9267], *Fox*: Friendly village local with good mix of ages, well kept Greene King IPA, Abbot and Rayments, cheerful quick service, wide choice of decent food; beamed lounge with attractive Skegness advertising posters and so forth (can get smoky), flame-effect gas stove, games room, small neat dining room; tables in streamside garden with ducks, fieldful of motley animals behind; children welcome *(Charles Bardswell, Phill Unti)*

☆ **Ramsholt** [off B1083 – OS Sheet 169 map ref 307415; TM3141], *Ramsholt Arms*: Extended former ferryman's cottage alone among pinewoods by Deben estuary, lovely walks along bank, big garden and sunny terrace; two recently refurbished bars, one with fine river view and maybe winter log fire; usual bar food promptly and pleasantly served, real ale; children very welcome *(Lorna and Bill Tyson, Janette Mace, Keith Archer, Mrs P J Pearce, Mrs Hilarie Taylor, LYM)*

☆ **Rattlesden** [High St; TL9758], *Five Bells*: Very friendly traditional village pub, well worn in, with perfectly kept Adnams, Charles Wells Eagle and Bombardier, Wadworths 6X and a guest beer; famous for its big dog Beamish, who really does drink his namesake stout *(John C Baker, Charles Bardswell)*

Redgrave [TM0477], *Cross Keys*: Friendly village local with comfortable lounge bar, well kept Adnams, popular Sun quiz night; can be rather smoky *(David Craine, Ann Reeder, Pamela Goodwyn)*

Reydon [Wangford Rd; TM4978], *Cricketers*: Good choice of good food served piping hot by friendly staff, Adnams beers and wines, light and airy bar, tables in garden; bedrooms *(D and B Carter, J E N Young)*

☆ **Risby** [a mile off A45; TL7966], *White Horse*: Doing well under current management, with well kept Courage and guest beers, decent generous food inc some adventurous dishes, attractive and interesting decor and furnishings, log fire, beams, brickwork and panelling *(John Baker, Pat Crabb, LYM)*

☆ **Rumburgh** [TM3481], *Buck*: Pretty country local, clean, tidy and rambling, with cheap good food, lots of character, well kept ales such as Adnams Extra, friendly atmosphere, cards, juke box, fruit machine and pool table in end room; quiet back lawn *(Nick and Alison Dowson)*

Saxtead Green [B1119; TM2665], *Old Mill House*: Nicely placed opp working windmill, with sizeable garden and pretty back terrace; newly refurbished in 'country fayre' style, with popular food in bar and restaurant, pleasant service *(Wayne Brindle, June and Perry Dann, LYM)*

Shottisham [TM3144], *Sorrel Horse*: Good food, homely surroundings, Tolly ales, log fire, garden *(Dr Peter Crawshaw)*

☆ **Snape** [B1069; TM3959], *Crown*: Attractive and relaxed low-ceilinged cottagey L-shaped bar with lots of pictures, tall seating on old hop tubs, amiable dog contemplating big fire in atmospheric front part supposed to be model for the Boar in Britten's *Peter Grimes*; smaller dining room with log-effect gas fire; big helpings of good distinctive if not cheap food, often with Mediterranean leanings, inc good seafood and puddings, Adnams Bitter, Broadside and Old on handpump, civilised service; tables in sizeable garden with pond; bedrooms well equipped *(C R Whitham, Pamela Goodwyn, Phil and Heidi Cook, A E R Archer, A H Thomas, Neil Powell, LYM)*

South Cove [B1127 Southwold—Wrentham; TM4981], *Five Bells*: Very varied good food inc home-made puddings *(G M K Donkin)*

☆ **Southwold** [7 East Green; TM5076], *Sole Bay*: Homely little Victorian local opp brewery (and the lighthouse sharing its name), moments from the sea; genuine and friendly, sparkling clean, with particularly good value simple lunchtime food (not Sun) esp local smoked sprats, well kept Adnams, chatty landlord, friendly locals and dog (other dogs allowed), tables on side terrace and with the budgies in yard *(V and E A Bolton, M J Morgan, Thomas Nott, Mr and Mrs J Woodfield, Rob and Doris Harrison,*

Stuart Earle, Gill and Andy Plumb, Wayne Brindle, MJVK, Keith and Janet Morris, BB)

☆ **Southwold** [Market Pl], *Swan*: A more traditional hotel than the Crown, with good choice of very tasty fresh interesting bar food (not cheap) in quiet comfortable back bar, chintzy and airy front lounge, good polite service, well kept Adnams and Broadside on handpump and the full range of their bottled beers, decent wines and malt whiskies; ambitious restaurant; good bedrooms inc garden rooms where (by arrangement) dogs can stay too *(Gwen and Peter Andrews, A H Thomas, Peter Woolls, V and E A Bolton, Pam and Tim Moorey, Rob and Doris Harrison, LYM)*

☆ **Southwold** [42 East St], *Lord Nelson*: Bustling cheerful little local nr seafront, low ceilings, panelling and tiled floor, with random old furniture and lamps in nice nooks and crannies, well kept Adnams Mild, Bitter, Broadside and Old on handpump, good basic lunchtime food, staff very pleasant even when busy, sheltered back garden; open all day, children welcome *(John McGee, Stuart Earle, Neil Powell, MJVK, Nigel Woolliscroft, Derek Patey, BB)*

☆ **Southwold** [Blackshore Quay; from A1095, right at Kings Head – pass golf course and water tower], *Harbour*: Very popular basic local by the black waterside net-sheds, tiny low-beamed front bar, upper back bar with lots of nautical bric-a-brac even ship-to-shore telephone and wind speed indicator; simple but imaginative food (not Sun evening, just fish and chips in newspaper Fri evening/Sat lunch), well kept Adnams Bitter and Broadside, coal fires, solid old furnishings, friendly staff, darts, table skittles, tables outside with play area, ducks and animals – can be a bit untidy out here *(V and E A Bolton, MJVK, Susan Kerner, Rob and Doris Harrison, LYM)*

☆ **Southwold** [High St], *Kings Head*: Perhaps the most conventional of the Adnams pubs here, well run and spacious, with lots of maroon and pink plush, very wide choice of promptly served good interesting food esp fish with good fresh veg, well kept Adnams, decent house wines, friendly staff; comfortable family/games room with well lit pool table; decent bedrooms in house across road *(Brenda and Jim Langley, Derek and Maggie Washington, MJVK, BB)*

☆ **Southwold** [South Green], *Red Lion*: Quiet but very receptive local, tidy, comfortable and relatively quiet, with big windows looking over green to sea, ship pictures, brassware and copper, elm-slab barrel tables, pale panelling; well kept Adnams Bitter, Broadside and Mild, good range of good value basic food (seafood recommended), family room and summer buffet room, tables outside; right by the Adnams retail shop; bedrooms small but comfortable *(Thomas Nott, MJVK, David Craine, Ann Reeder, Jeff Davies, BB)*

☆ **Sproughton** [Old Hadleigh Rd – from A45 Claydon interchange go through village then left down unmarked dead end; TM1244], *Beagle*: Plushly comfortable 1920s timber-framed pub, beamery and inglenooks, decent food popular lunchtime with Ipswich businessmen, Whitbreads-related ales and maybe a guest such as Adnams, good service, back conservatory *(Ian Philips)*

Stoke by Nayland [TL9836], *Crown*: Spacious, quiet and comfortably modernised rooms, decent straightforward food served piping hot (but smoking allowed in eating area), Tolly on handpump, restaurant; good with children; bedrooms *(AJ, JJ, LYM)*

☆ **Stradishall** [A143; TL7452], *Cherry Tree*: Two small traditional beamed bars, good reasonably priced straightforward bar food inc vegetarian, pleasant atmosphere, open fires, Greene King beers under light pressure; friendly ducks and pond in huge rustic garden (dogs allowed here); outside gents' *(Gwen and Peter Andrews, BB)*

Stradishall, *Royal Oak*: Two-bar country pub with good cheap bar food served till 10, well kept Nethergate and Mauldons, welcoming landlord *(Dave Bundock)*

☆ **Sudbury** [Acton Sq; TL8741], *Waggon & Horses*: Comfortable welcoming local with interesting decor, great atmosphere, character landlord, good plain food even Sun afternoon, well kept Greene King ales, bar billiards *(Frank Gadbois)*

Sudbury, *Angel*: Busy town pub between church and theatre, with good value food inc popular bargains for two, Greene King ales *(Tony and Wendy Hobden)*

☆ **Sutton** [TM3046], *Plough*: Cosy little bar with button-back banquettes, spacious side restaurant and well equipped games room, bar food from sandwiches up inc some good home-made dishes and local fish, well kept Flowers IPA and Original and Tolly Bitter and Mild, children welcome, tables in garden *(Michael and Maggie Betton, LYM)*

Sweffling [TM3463], *White Horse*: Decent lunches, pleasant atmosphere; handy for walkers *(Pamela Goodwyn)*

☆ **Thorndon** [off A140 or B1077, S of Eye; TM1469], *Black Horse*: Friendly and individual country pub with good well presented food from sandwiches to unusual main dishes inc good puddings and restaurant Sun lunch; beams, timbers, stripped brick, ancient floor tiles, several well kept ales, tables on spacious lawn with country views; well behaved children in eating areas *(Pamela Goodwyn, LYM)*

Thorpe Morieux [TL9453], *Bull*: Village local reopened under new owners, deceptively big inside with predominantly public bar and small games room, Adnams, guest beer and Addlestones cider on handpump, wide-ranging menu inc good steaks, friendly jovial landlord *(Stuart Earle)*

Thurston [TL9365], *Victoria*: Wide choice of reasonably priced food inc good vegetarian choice, separate eating area, well kept Greene King ales, welcoming atmosphere, efficient service *(Richard Balls, Pamela Goodwyn)*

☆ **Trimley St Martin** [TM2736], *Hand in*

Hand: Popular and welcoming extended local, reliably good generous pub food inc vegetarian, fish and bargain special, quick friendly service, good atmosphere, new restaurant *(Mrs J M Deale)*

☆ **Ufford** [Lower St; TM2953], *White Lion*: Good reasonably priced home-cooked food and well kept Tolly in basic, clean, small and friendly pub; open central fireplace *(Dr and Mrs M Bailey)*

☆ **Wangford** [High St; TM4679], *Angel*: 17th-c inn, recently well refurbished, with decent food, good friendly service, informal atmosphere; comfortable bedrooms, ideal for restful holiday break *(DT, Dr and Mrs N Holmes)*

☆ **Wenhaston** [TM4276], *Star*: Quiet and unassuming well run country pub with good reasonably priced home cooking (not Sat or maybe Mon – landlady's day off), well kept Adnams and freshly squeezed orange juice, pleasant views; helpful service, sun-trap lounge, games in public bar, tables on sizeable lawn *(Rob and Doris Harrison, Pamela Goodwyn, Derek Patey, Gwen and Peter Andrews, LYM)*

Wenhaston [Main St], *Compasses*: Well kept beer, good food inc Sun lunch, friendly licensees; tables on lawn; good value bedrooms, wholesome English breakfast *(Mr and Mrs K W Burr)*

West Row [NE of Mildenhall; TL6775], *Judes Ferry*: Newish licensees doing good food in well renovated pub with well kept Adnams Broadside and two guests such as Greene King IPA and Sam Smiths, lots of local photographs, garden by River Lark *(Frank W Gadbois)*

☆ **Westleton** [B1125 Blythburgh—Leiston; TM4469], *Crown*: Upmarket extended country inn with interesting comfortable bar, no-smoking dining conservatory, restaurant, pretty garden with aviary and floodlit terrace, beautiful setting, good walks nearby, 19 quiet comfortable bedrooms; several well kept ales, good wines, malt whiskies and farm cider, log fire, home-made food that can be excellent in bar and evening restaurant (children allowed); treading the narrow tightrope between pub and restaurant/hotel and as the many recommenders show for the most part doing it deftly, but some feel the balance taking price into account isn't quite right *(V and E A Bolton, Dr and Mrs M Bailey, H R Bevan, BKA, Rosemary Harris, Mr and Mrs R P Begg, Gwen and Peter Andrews, Richard Balls, Basil Minson, D and B Carter, M J Morgan, BP, AP, Pamela Goodwyn, Liz and Gil Dudley, MJVK, LYM)*

☆ **Westleton**, *White Horse*: Warm friendly pub in same beautiful village, good value range of generous food inc children's, well kept Adnams, garden with climbing frame *(M G and S M Keegan, Gill and Andy Plumb, H R Bevan, A H Thomas)*

Wickhambrook [Meeting Green; TL7554], *Greyhound*: Well kept real ale (tea and coffee too), genuine welcome for all inc children, motorcyclists, dogs, weekly live music, bank hol barbecues with bouncy castle *(Peter Sprot)*

☆ **Woodbridge** [73 Cumberland Rd; opp Notcutts Nursery, off A12; TM2749], *Cherry Tree*: Agreeable freshly made generous straightforward food inc vegetarian doorstep sandwiches, Flowers Original, Tetleys and Tolly, friendly staff, open fire, stuffed fox, motley collection of books, 60s piped music, fruit machines; no dogs, garden with swings etc *(JCW, Mrs Jackie Deale, George Atkinson)*

☆ **Woodbridge** [Seckford St], *Seckford Arms*: Interesting pub with Mexican accent in decor and good food, well kept Adnams and often unusual guest beers, extrovert landlord, children welcome in garden lounge; open all day *(George Atkinson, Jack and Philip Paxton)*

Woodbridge [centre], *Bull*: 16th-c inn with good value food, well kept Adnams, accommodating landlord, friendly service; small but comfortable bedrooms, good kipper breakfasts *(Mark Yovish)*; [signed off A12 bypass, N of town], *Seckford Hall*: Tudor hotel with dark but friendly bar, genuinely pubby atmosphere, immaculately kept Adnams, decent wines, good value food; garden with lake, leisure centre and swimming pool; bedrooms *(Gwen and Peter Andrews)*; [New St], *Tap & Spile*: Six real ales, old beams, skittles, decent wines *(Stuart Earle)*

Wortham [Bury Rd; TM0877], *Dolphin*: Pleasant pub with good balance between welcoming local atmosphere and varied range of imaginative food; Adnams *(David Craine, Ann Reeder)*

Yoxford [TM3968], *Kings Head*: Good food, well kept beer *(G Washington)*

Stars after the name of a pub show exceptional quality. One star means most people (after reading the report to see just why the star has been won) would think a special trip worth while. Two stars mean that the pub is really outstanding – many that for their particular qualities cannot be bettered.

Surrey

Pubs currently doing well here include the Drummond Arms at Albury (some enjoyable summer Sunday spitroasts, and gains a Place to Stay Award this year), the traditional old Dolphin at Betchworth, the civilised Donkey at Charleshill, the relaxed and prettily set White Horse at Hascombe, the pretty little Plough at Leigh, the King William IV on its steep hillside at Mickleham (gains a Food Award this year), the unspoilt good value Scarlett Arms at Walliswood (very popular lunchtime for good value country food), and the civilised Onslow Arms at West Clandon. Outshining all of these for its delicious creative food is the cheerfully old-fashioned Woolpack at Elstead: it's our choice as Surrey Dining Pub of the Year. Two new main entries which we can also recommend for enjoyable meals out are the Fox & Hounds at Englefield Green on the edge of Windsor Park, and the well run George in Oxted. Lucky Dip pubs attracting special attention in recent months have been the Abinger Hatch at Abinger, Sun at Dunsfold, Queens Head at East Clandon, Plough at Effingham, Woodcock at Felbridge (for character), Parrot at Forest Green, Cock at Headley, Punch Bowl near Ockley, both Outwood entries, Ship in Ripley, Brickmakers Arms at Tandridge, Three Horseshoes at Thursley, Bulls Head at West Clandon, Brickmakers Arms and other Windlesham pubs, and Wotton Hatch at Wotton; we have inspected most of these, so can recommend them directly. Drinks prices in the county are very high – even the cheapest pubs we found, the Donkey at Charleshill (tied to Morlands), the White Lion in Warlingham (Bass) and the Dolphin at Betchworth (Youngs), though much cheaper than the local average, would look expensive if transported say to the West Midlands or the North.

ALBURY TQ0547 Map 3

Drummond Arms ⇐

Off A248 SE of Guildford

The streamside garden overhung with branches and leaves at this well run pub is particularly lovely with ducks and pheasant wandering among the tables. There's a friendly, civilised atmosphere in the wood panelled bar with soft seats and alcoves and in the pleasant conservatory which overlooks the garden. Big helpings of tasty bar food include sandwiches (from £1.50, toasties from £1.75), soup (£1.95), sausages (£2.95), ploughman's (from £3.50), filled baked potatoes (from £3.95), salads (from £4.95), gammon and pineapple (£6.95), and sirloin steak (£9.95), with about 15 good daily specials such as soft roes in garlic (£3.95), home-cured salmon or traditional home-made pies (from £4.95) and stilton filled pheasant breast wrapped in ham (£8.95). On Sunday lunchtimes in summer they spit roast a large pig outside on the new covered terrace where they sometimes have popular themed food evenings. Well kept Courage Best and Directors, King & Barnes Festive, Broadwood, Youngs and a guest on handpump; friendly service which can be a little slow when it gets busy. The village is rewarding to stroll through. *(Recommended by Mayur Shah, Anthony Byers, Andy and Jill Plumb, John Pettit, Sue and Bob Ward, Mr and Mrs D Simons, Ian Phillips, Mrs Hilarie Taylor)*

Free house ~ Licensee David Wolf ~ Real ale ~ Meals and snacks (till 10pm Fri/Sat) ~ Restaurant (not Sun evening) ~ (01483) 202039 ~ Children over 5 welcome in restaurant ~ Open 11-2.30(3 Sat), 6-11 ~ Bedrooms: £38B/£50B

ALBURY HEATH TQ0646 Map 3

William IV

Little London; off A25 Guildford—Dorking to Albury, first left to Albury Heath; go over railway and take first left to Peaslake, then right towards Farley Green; OS Sheet 187 map reference 065468

The three warmly friendly little rooms at this traditional family-run pub (which can get very busy) each has a different atmosphere. The main stone-floored bar has a big chunky elm table with a long pew and a couple of stools, beams in the low ochre ceiling, an enormous basket of dried flowers in the big brick fireplace (with a hearty log fire in winter), and an ancient baboon dressed in a jacket and hat in one corner. A tiny room leading off one end has an L-shaped elbow rest with a couple of stools in front of it, a table and settle and darts. Up a few steps at the other end of the main bar is a simple dining room with gingham-clothed tables, two glass cases with stuffed owls and a piano. On the first Saturday evening of the month they hold a seafood evening. The fish is bought fresh that day from Billingsgate by the licensee and depending on the market might include green-lipped mussels (£4), whitebait or Mediterranean prawns (£4.50), Dover sole (£10), lobster (£14). On the third Saturday in the month they do a whole spit-roasted lamb, pig or venison. The rest of the time the small but selective menu includes home-made dishes like sandwiches (from £1.80), generous ploughman's (from £3.60), cottage pie (£4.20), home-cooked ham, egg and chips or beef and Guinness pie (£4.50) and game pie or mutton casserole (£5.20) and puddings like treacle tart, banoffi pie or tiramisu (all £2.50); Sunday roast lunch (£5.60). Changing real ales might include well kept Boddingtons, Courage Best, Greene King Abbot, Whitbreads Castle Eden and local Hogs Back; shove-ha'penny and cards. The little garden in front has some picnic tables under umbrellas, and old cast-iron garden furniture. It's in the heart of the country and surrounded by lovely walks. *(Recommended by Jenny and Brian Seller, Nigel Flook, Betsy Brown, Helen Morton, Mr and Mrs B Matthews, Andy and Jill Plumb, Anthony Byers, A J N Lee, D and J Tapper, Mr and Mrs Williams, Susan and John Douglas, Mr and Mrs C Moncreiffe, Tim Galligan, Graham Pettener, J N Tyler, Don Mather, Tim Galligan, Mr and Mrs D E Powell, Martin Jones)*

Free house ~ Licensees Mike and Helen Davids ~ Real ale ~ Meals and snacks (12-2.30, 7-10) ~ Restaurant ~ (01483) 202685 ~ Children welcome ~ Open 11-3, 5.30-11 (cl 25 Dec)

BETCHWORTH TQ2049 Map 3

Dolphin

The Street; 2½ miles W of Reigate on A25 turn left into Buckland, then take the second left

There's an unaffected and friendly pubby atmosphere at this cosy little village local with unspoilt nostalgic touches like three coal fires and a well chiming longcase clock. The homely front room is furnished with kitchen chairs and plain tables on the 400-year-old scrubbed flagstones, and the carpeted back saloon bar is black-panelled with robust old-fashioned elm or oak tables. A wide range of consistently good, generous bar food includes soup (£1.75), ploughman's (from £3.25), filled baked potato (from £3.45), sausage and egg (£3.15), vegetable lasagne or lasagne (£4.65), calamari or scampi (£4.80) and gammon steak (£5.55); daily specials; puddings like spotted dick or apple pie (£1.95). Very well priced Youngs Bitter and Special, and Porter in summer and Winter Warmer in winter, on handpump, and a cruover machine guarantees that most wines can be served by the glass; very friendly and efficient service; darts, dominoes, cribbage, fruit machine and shove-ha'penny. There are some seats in the small laurel-shaded front courtyard and picnic tables on a lawn by the car park, opposite the church and on the back garden terrace. Get there early, as it doesn't take long for it to get busy, sometimes with a lively younger crowd. No children. *(Recommended by J S M Sheldon, Jack Taylor, John Pettit, David Peakall, DWAJ, G R Sharman, Jenny and Brian Seller, Alison Ball, David Norris, P Gillbe, Jamie and Ruth Lyons, Mayur Shah, M D Hare, A Plumb, Mrs R Maxwell, Dick Brown, Don Mather, Douglas Jeffery, Ian Phillips)*

Youngs ~ Managers: George and Rose Campbell ~ Real ale ~ Meals and snacks (12-2.30, 7-10) ~ (01737) 842288 ~ Open 11-3, 5.30-11; cl 25 Dec evening)

BLACKBROOK TQ1846 Map 3

Plough 🍷

On byroad E of A24, parallel to it, between Dorking and Newdigate, just N of the turn E to Leigh

There's some emphasis on the impressive and imaginative daily specials at this light and airy cream and terracotta decorated pub: stilton, chestnut and onion soup (£2.45), deep fried mozarella with tomato, onion and basil salsa (£3.45), goat's cheese salad with warm ragout of mushroom, onion and sultanas (£3.75), creamy vegetable and cheese pie (£4.95), ragout of honeyed lamb with spiced fruits (£5.95), poached salmon with prawn and cucumber sauce (£8.75) and venison with cumberland sauce (£8.95) and lovely puddings like champagne sorbet in chocolate cup, spiced cranberry and apple pie and hot carrot pudding (£2.45). The regular menu is more standard and includes filled baked potatoes (from £2.95), ploughman's (£3.75), ratatouille niçoise (£4.95), lasagne (£5.25), prawn curry (£5.45) and sirloin steak (£9.45). Well kept King & Barnes Sussex, Broadwood, Festive, Old Ale in winter and seasonal beers on handpump, freshly squeezed orange juice, 14 good wines by the glass, including a wine of the month, vintage port by the glass, and about 20 country wines. There are fresh flowers cut from the garden on the tables and sills of the large linen curtained windows in the no-smoking saloon bar. Down some steps, the public bar has brass-topped treadle tables, a formidable collection of ties as well as old saws on the ceiling, and bottles and flat irons; pleasant, friendly staff; piped music. Tess the blind black labrador puts in an appearance after 10pm. At the back is a sizeable secluded cottage garden with a good few tables and children can play in the prettily painted Swiss playhouse furnished with tiny tables and chairs. In summer the white frontage is decked with bright hanging baskets and window boxes. The countryside around here is a particularly good area for colourful spring and summer walks through the oak woods. *(Recommended by John Pettit, Cathryn and Richard Hicks, Derek and Maggie Washington, Winifrede D Morrison, Neville Kenyon, Jamie and Ruth Lyons, Tina and David Woods-Taylor, A Plumb, D J Penny, Gwen and Peter Andrews, David Ing, Sue Demont, Tim Barrow, J S M Sheldon)*

King & Barnes ~ Tenants: Chris and Robin Squire ~ Real ale ~ Meals and snacks (not Mon evening) ~ (01306) 886603 ~ Children over 14 in bar ~ Open 11-2.30(3 Sat), 6-11; cl 25, 26 Dec and 1 Jan

CHARLESHILL SU8944 Map 2

Donkey

Near Tilford, on B3001 Milford—Farnham; as soon as you see pub sign, turn left

There's a gentle, civilised atmosphere at this charming old-fashioned 18th-c cottage, and during the week it's a popular lunchtime stop for the ladies of the county. Lots of polished stirrups, lamps and watering cans decorate the walls of the brightly cheerful saloon, furnished with prettily cushioned built-in wall benches and wheelback chairs, while the lounge has a lovely old high-backed settle and a couple of unusual three-legged chairs, as well as highly polished horsebrasses, a longcase clock, some powder pouches, swords on the walls and beams. The reasonably priced home-made bar food in helpings suitable for people with smaller appetites includes sandwiches and toasted sandwiches (from £2), filled baked potatoes (from £2.30) and four home-made daily specials like curries, lasagne and pies (all £4.95). A no-smoking conservatory with blond wheelback chairs and stripped tables, fairy lights and some plants, has sliding doors into the garden. Well kept Morlands IPA, Old Speckled Hen and Charles Wells Bombardier on handpump kept under light blanket pressure; Gales country wines; may sometimes be quiet piped music, shove-ha'penny, dominoes and cribbage. The garden is very attractive, with bright flowerbeds, white garden furniture, a tiny pond, an aviary with cockatiels and a big fairy-lit fir tree. Children's play area has been smartened up since last year. *(Recommended by Winifrede D Morrison, J S M Sheldon, Mr and Mrs T A Bryan, DAV, Ian Phillips, Keith Widdowson, Mr and Mrs D E Powell, R B Crail, G B Longden, Ron and Sheila Corbett, Bill Capper)*

Morlands ~ Lease: Peter and Shirley Britcher ~ Real ale ~ Meals and snacks (not Sun evening) ~ (01252) 702124 ~ Children in conservatory ~ Open 11-2.30, 6-11; cl 25, 26 Dec evening

COBHAM TQ1060 Map 3

Cricketers

Downside Common; 3¾ miles from M25 junction 10; A3 towards Cobham, 1st right on to A245, right at Downside signpost into Downside Bridge Rd, follow road into its right fork – away from Cobham Park – at second turn after bridge, then take next left turn into the pub's own lane

Larger than the superb characterful frontage suggests, the splendidly ancient spacious open plan interior has crooked standing timbers – creating comfortably atmospheric spaces – supporting heavy oak beams so low they have crash-pads on them. In places you can see the wide oak ceiling boards and ancient plastering lathes. Simple furnishings, horse brasses and big brass platters on the walls, and a good winter log fire. About 14 daily changing specials might include cauliflower and broccoli cheese (£3.55), toad in the hole (£3.75), moules marinières (£4.50), Cajun chicken, pork Tuscany and lamb provençale (£5.25), beef stroganoff (£5.95), lemon sole (£6.25) and duck a l'orange (£6.95). There's also a list of about 22 different salads every day. Well kept Ruddles Best and County, and Websters Yorkshire on handpump. Get there early for a table, especially on a Sunday when it's very popular. It's charmingly set with lots of tables overlooking the broad village green, and at the back is a delightfully neat garden with standard roses, dahlias, bedding plants, urns and hanging baskets. Dogs welcome. *(Recommended by John Pettit, S G Brown, Jamie and Ruth Lyons, G W and I L Edwards, Andy Cunningham, Christopher Gallop, Giles Quick, Adrian Zambardino, Debbie Chaplin, Piotr Chodzko-Zajko, Dave Irving, George Atkinson, John and Joan Calvert, Martin and Karen Wake, Guy Consterdine, Stephen G Brown, Clem Stephens, R C Vincent, Ray Cuckow, H G M Osbourne, Mayur Shah, A Plumb)*

Courage ~ Lease: Wendy Luxford ~ Real ale ~ Meals and snacks (till 10pm) ~ Restaurant (not Sun evening) ~ (01932) 862105 ~ Children in Stable Bar ~ Open 11-2.30, 6-11

COLDHARBOUR TQ1543 Map 3

Plough

Village signposted in the network of small roads around Abinger and Leith Hill, off A24 and A29

Just one of the main draws at this remote pretty black-shuttered white house is their excellent range of ten very well kept real ales which might include Adnams Broadside, Badger Best and Tanglefoot, Batemans XB, Fullers London Pride, Ringwood Old Thumper, Shepherd Neame Spitfire and Wadworths 6X on handpump. They also have a short but interesting wine list, country wines and Biddenden farm cider. Something of a characterful alternative for this county, it's busy with a less conventional, younger and perhaps gentrified crowd who are at home in the well worn, interior and easy going, open minded atmosphere. The two bars have stripped light beams and timbering in the warm-coloured dark ochre walls, with quite unusual little chairs around the tables in the snug red-carpeted room on the left, and little decorative plates on the walls and a big open fire in the one on the right – which leads through to the restaurant. Decent home-made bar food includes vegetarian chilli (£4.95), stuffed aubergine with cheddar sauce (£5.75), chicken, leek and stilton pie (£5.95), steak, onion and ale pie (£6.50), grilled fish kebabs marinaded in olive oil, coriander and garlic (£6.95) and puddings like banoffee pie or apple and marzipan tart (£2.25). The games bar on the left has darts, pool, cribbage, shove-ha'penny, dominoes, and there is piped music. Outside there are picnic tables by the tubs of flowers in front and in the terraced garden with fish pond and waterlilies; its good walking country – walkers are welcome and dogs are allowed if on a lead but not in the restaurant (which has a no-smoking area). ***(Recommended by Jenny and Brian Seller, Sue Demont, Tim Barrow, S G N Bennett, Tom and Rosemary Hall, Dick Brown, John Davies, Jon Carpenter, A Plumb)***

Free house ~ Licensees Richard and Anna Abrehart ~ Real ale ~ Meals and snacks ~ Restaurant ~ (01306) 711793 ~ Children in eating area of bar and family room ~Open 11.30-3, 6.30-11; 11.30-11 Sat if busy ~ Bedrooms: £25(£30B)/£40(£50B)

COMPTON SU9546 Map 2

Harrow

B3000

The food at this cheerful dining pub has become so popular that they've turned the lounge area into a restaurant. Their excellent hot or cold seafood platter (£11.50) is particularly well liked. Blackboard menus are scattered around the pub, and with prices tending towards the top end of the range might include ploughman's (£4.75), moules marinières (£7), plaice in beer batter or salmon and broccoli bake (£7.50), steak and Guinness pie (£8) and sirloin streak (£9.75); you will probably need to book on Friday and Saturday evenings. Well kept Burton, Harveys Sussex Best and Tetleys IPA on handpump. The brightly lit main bar has interesting racing pictures below the ancient ceiling – mostly portraits of horses, jockey caricatures and signed race-finish photographs. Opening off here are more little beamed rooms with latched rustic doors, and nice touches such as brass horse-head coat hooks, photographs of the area, and a bas relief in wood of the pub sign; piped music. You can sit outside in summer, round by the car park but looking out to gentle slopes of pasture. In the pretty village the art nouveau Watts Chapel and Gallery are interesting, and the church itself is attractive; Loseley House is nearby too. ***(Recommended by John and Vivienne Rice, Jonathan Nettleton, Mr and Mrs G Turner, DC, Adrian Zambardino, Debbie Chaplin, Derek and Margaret Underwood, Thomas Nott, MS, Dawn and Phil Garside, Guy Consterdine, Tim Galligan, A and A Dale, James Nunns)***

Carlsberg Tetleys ~ Lease: Roger and Susan Seaman ~ Real ale ~ Meals and snacks (12-3, 6-10; breakfast 7.30-12) ~ (01483) 810379 ~ Children welcome ~ Open 11-3, 5.30(6 Sat)-11 ~ Bedrooms: /£35B

Withies

Withies Lane; pub signposted from B3000

The tiny and genuinely pubby low beamed bar at this magnificent 16th-c family run free house has a massive inglenook fireplace which is lit with a roaring log fire even on summer evenings, some attractive panels of 17th-c carving between the windows, and settles (one rather splendidly art nouveau). As there is quite an emphasis on the smart and much pricier restaurant the bar menu is short and straightforward and includes soup (£2.50), sandwiches (from £3), Withies or smoked salmon pâté or ploughman's (£3.25), cumberland sausages (£3.90), filled baked potatoes (from £4) and seafood platter (£6.50). Well kept ales on handpump are Bass, King & Barnes Sussex and Friary Meux. The delightfully immaculate garden overhung with weeping willows has tables under an arbour of creeper-hung trellises, more on a crazy-paved terrace and yet more under old apple trees; the neat lawn in front of the steeply tiled white house is bordered by masses of flowers. *Recommended by MW, HW, Helen Morton, Mayur Shah, Winifrede D Morrison, Guy Consterdine, Jenny and Brian Seller, DC; more reports please)*

Free house ~ Licensees Brian and Hugh Thomas ~ Real ale ~ Meals and snacks (12-2.30, 7-10) ~ Restaurant (not Sun evening)~ (01483) 421158 ~ Children welcome ~ Open 11-3, 6-11; closed 25, 26 Dec evening

EFFINGHAM TQ1253 Map 3

Sir Douglas Haig

The Street; off A246 W of Leatherhead

This busy free house is a popular and reliable place for a good value lunch. Straightforward home-cooked bar food in generous helpings served with a choice of up to five fresh vegetables includes good filled baguettes, daily specials (from £3.75), steak and kidney pie (£4.75), a steak menu (from £5.95); Sunday roast (from £4.75). The roomy building was almost completely rebuilt a few years ago. At one end of the long room there's an eating area with an open fire, small settles, banquettes and kitchen chairs, and at the other end, another open fire, a wood-stained floor, stools, an armchair, and shelves of books. Well kept Boddingtons, Fullers London Pride, Gales HSB, Wadworths 6X and a montly guest on handpump; quick, friendly service. There's a back lawn and terraced area with seats and tables; fruit machine, video game, juke box, and a TV in the corner of the lounge. *(Recommended by Andy and Jill Plumb, John Pettit, Anthony Byers, Brian and Jenny Seller, Jamie and Ruth Lyons, A M Pickup, Mr and Mrs Evans; more reports please)*

Free house ~ Licensee Laurie Smart ~ Real ale ~ Meals and snacks ~ (01372) 456886 ~ Children over 14 only ~ Open 11-3; 5.30-11(11-11 Sat) ~ Bedrooms: £45B/£55B

ELSTEAD SU9143 Map 2

Woolpack

The Green; B3001 Milford—Farnham

Surrey Dining Pub of the Year

Even though this cheerful and warmly welcoming place is busy most of the time there's always a lovely relaxed and informal atmosphere. The main draw is the deliciously creative food that's chalked up daily on a big board near the food servery. Quite often the chef devises new recipes to use carefully purchased fresh ingredients which are then served in good value gigantic helpings, and might include ploughman's (from £3.75), mussels in herb and garlic butter (£3.95), hot breaded blue cheese with cranberry and port or almond breaded chicken strips with cranberry and orange sauce (£4.25), a good selection of vegetarian dishes such as mushroom stroganoff (£4.50), chicken tikka, Thai fish cakes with peanut, chilli and cucumber sauce, or chicken and ham, cod and prawn and steak and kidney pies (£6.95), pork steak in apricot Schnapps and thyme (£8.25), turkey escalopes in vermouth, mushroom and tarragon sauce (£8.75) and pigeon breast in blackberry wine and cream sauce or goose breast with gooseberry, sherry and sage sauce (£8.95), all served with tastily prepared fresh vegetables such as beetroot in creamy sauce, leeks with crunchy topping and cheesy potatoes; every day there's a fresh selection of glorious home-made puddings in big helpings like crème brûlée, choux ring filled with cream, bananas and raspberries, filled pavlovas, rum truffle cake and date and toffee cake (all £2.90); good attentive service. There's a fair amount of wool industry memorabilia, such as the weaving shuttles and cones of wool that hang above the high-backed settles in the long airy main bar, which also has window seats and spindleback chairs around plain wooden tables. There are fireplaces at each end. The large dog basket tucked into a corner is the home of Taffy, a golden retriever. Leading off here is a big room decorated with lots of country prints, a weaving loom, scales, and brass measuring jugs; the fireplace with its wooden pillars, lace frill is unusual. In the family room there are nursery-rhyme murals and lots of dried flowers hanging from the ceiling, and a door that leads to the garden with picnic tables and a children's play area. Well kept Burton ale, Greene King IPA and Tetleys tapped from the cask; quite a few wines by the glass and bottle. Dominoes, cribbage, backgammon, fruit machine. *(Recommended by Alan Skull, Paul Carter, G and M Stewart, Rhoda and Jeff Collins, Clive Gilbert, Mr and Mrs R O Gibson, Bob and Maggie Atherton, Ian Phillips, Mike Fitzgerald, J S M Sheldon, DAV, Mr and Mrs G Turner, Mrs Ailsa Wiggans, G C Hackemer, Guy Consterdine, Anna Marsh, I E and C A Prosser, Lynn Sharpless, Bob Eardley, Tim Galligan, Martin and Karen Wake, Phil and Sally Gorton, Martin Jones, Angela and Alan Dale, Ray Cuckow, Stephen and Julie Brown)*

Friary Meux (Carlsberg Tetleys) ~ Lease: J A Macready and S A Askew ~ Real ale ~ Meals and snacks (till 9.45) ~ Restaurant ~ (01252) 703106 ~ Children in restaurant and family room ~ Open 11-2.30, 6-11; closed eve 25 and all day 26 Dec

ENGLEFIELD GREEN SU9970 Map 2

Fox & Hounds

Bishopsgate Road; off A328 N of Egham

On the edge of Windsor Park and a very short stroll from the main gate to the Savile Garden, this smart 17th-c pub backs on to a riding stables, so there's quite a coming and going of riders if you're sitting out at the picnic tables on the neat and pretty front lawn. Inside is civilised in a well mellowed countrified way, popular without being overcrowded, with good sturdy wooden tables and chairs, prints in sets of four, some stuffed animals and fading red gingham curtains. The bar has good sandwiches (from £1.70), soup (£3.25), baguettes (Saturday and Sunday, from £2) with a great range of fillings and good salad garnishes, and pâté (£5.25). There's a tantalising variety of well presented food in the attractive back dining room, candlelit at night, with a blackboard menu brought to your table and more choice on further wall boards: anything from lots of starters (from £3.25) to home-made steak and kidney pudding (£9.50) to fresh fish dishes like fresh tuna in a lime and tarragon butter (£11.50), wild salmon (£12.75), whole sea bass with garlic basil oil (£14.50), and rack of English lamb, calf's liver with bacon and onion or half a roast duckling with orange sauce (all £12.50); also set Sunday lunch; separately served vegetables are fresh and not overcooked. Prompt friendly service, well kept Courage Best and Directors, John Smiths and a guest such as Greene King IPA on handpump, decent wines. There are more tables on a back terrace. *(Recommended by Caroline Raphael, Simon Collett-Jones, John and Joan Calvert, Julian Bessa, Mayur Shah, Ian Phillips, Donald J Arndt)*

Courage ~ Licensees John Mee and Bobby King ~ Real ale ~ Meals and snacks ~ Restaurant ~ (01784) 433098 ~ Well behaved children welcome ~ Jazz Mon evening ~ Open 11-3, 6-11; closed evening 25 Dec

HASCOMBE TQ0039 Map 3

White Horse

B2130 S of Godalming

There's a relaxed and comfortable atmosphere in the simple character-filled rooms of this rose-draped inn which is tucked away in a pretty village among lovely rolling wooded country lanes on the Greensand Way. Outside there are plenty of tables, some on a little terrace by the front porch and lots spread out at the back on an attractive spacious lawn with roses. It's especially popular for generous helpings of interesting and varied bar food from the blackboard including huge sandwiches, home-made soup (£2.25), home-made pies (£4.50), home-made steak burgers or swordfish steaks (£6.95), whole seabass and charcoal grill specialities; all home-made puddings like bread and butter pudding and sticky toffee pudding (from £3); best to get there early for a table at lunchtime, especially at weekends; quick cheerful service. The cosy atmospheric inner beamed area has a wood-burning stove and quiet small-windowed alcoves that look out onto the garden, and there's a conservatory with blue check tablecloths and light bentwood chairs. Well kept Badger Best, King and Barnes Sussex and Wadworths 6X on handpump; quite a few wines. Darts, shove-ha'penny, dominoes, fruit machine and piped music. The National Trust's Winkworth Arboretum, with its walks among beautiful trees and shrubs, is nearby. *(Recommended by Alan Skull, Mr and Mrs Damien Burke, Chris and Inky Hoare, Keith and Audrey Ward, Brian and Jenny Seller, Nicola Thomas and Paul Dickinson, Liz and Ian Phillips, Mrs Hilarie Taylor, DAV, Michael Sargent)*

Ind Coope ~ Lease: Susan Barnett ~ Real ale ~ Meals and snacks (12-2.20, 7-10) ~ Restaurant (not Sun evening) ~ (01483 208258) ~ Children welcome ~ Open 11-3, 5.30(6 Sat)-11

LALEHAM TQ0568 Map 3

Three Horseshoes

Junction 1 of M3, then W on A308; village signposted on left on B376

This busy 13th-century stone-flagged tavern is at its best on warm summer days when the facade is almost hidden by wisteria, hanging baskets and cartwheels. It does pull the crowds – just as it did when the likes of Lily Langtry, Gilbert and his partner Sullivan, Marie Lloyd and Edward VII when he was Prince of Wales, all customers, boosted its popularity. It's been comfortably modernised, and the dusky open-plan bar has plush burgundy seats on the red carpet, lots of big copper pots and pans hanging from beams, interesting cock-fighting prints on the red walls, and blacksmith's tools hanging over the main fireplace. One small alcove has high-backed settles, and there's a no-smoking conservatory. Under the new licensees popular bar food in big helpings includes an excellent choice of sandwiches or baguettes (from £1.65), ploughman's (from £3.95), huge filled baked potatoes (from £4.95), salads (from £6.25), seafood platter (£8.45), warm cheese salad (£6.75) and daily blackboard specials like duck breast with orange sauce, plaice fillet with prawns and mushrooms, steak and kidney pie, half roast shoulder of lamb, poached salmon with herb butter and a vegetarian lasagne or nut roast and steaks (from £5), and puddings like sherry trifle, chocolate fudge cake or hot waffles and maple syrup (from £2.50). Well kept Fullers London Pride, Gales HSB, Ruddles Best and County, Websters Yorkshire and a guest on handpump with a happy hour between five and seven weekday evenings; decent wines, efficient service and piped music. There are plenty of tables in the rather distinctive creeper-filled garden, and just a short walk away is a grassy stretch of the Thames popular with picnickers and sunbathers. *(Recommended by Stephen Brown, Ian Phillips, Ron and Sheila Corbett, M Carey, A Groocock, Simon Collett-Jones, Wayne Brindle, Clem Stephens, Margaret and Nigel Dennis, Jeff and Rhoda Collins, TBB, D Tapper)*

Courage ~ Lease: A Shore and A Murray ~ Real ale ~ Meals and snacks (12-2.30, 5-9.30) ~ Restaurant (cl Sun evening)~ (01784) 452617 ~ Children in conservatory ~ Open 11-11 (cl 25 Dec)

LEIGH TQ2246 Map 3

Plough

3 miles S of A25 Dorking—Reigate, signposted from Betchworth (which itself is signposted off the main road); also signposted from South Park area of Reigate; on village green

You'll find this pretty tiled and weatherboarded cottage with its welcoming family-run atmosphere in an attractive setting overlooking the village green. On the right is a very low beamed cosy white walled and timbered dining lounge and on the left, the more local pubby bar has a good bow-window seat and an extensive listing of games from which customers can choose to play darts, shove-ha'penny, dominoes, table skittles, cribbage, trivia, the fruit machine, the video game, Jenca, chess or Scrabble; piped music. Popular bar food includes sandwiches (from £1.75), soup (£1.95), pâté

(£2.50), garlic mussels or ploughman's (from £3.95), filled baked potatoes (from £3.25), ham, egg and chips (£4.50), lasagne (£4.75) and sirloin steak (£9.50), and tasty daily specials including good seafood, and puddings like hot chocolate fudge cake, apple pie and blackberry and apple pancake rolls (from £1.95). Booking is recommended especially at weekends when it can get a bit cramped. Well kept King & Barnes Bitter, Broadwood, Festive and Wealdman and seasonal ales on handpump. There are picnic tables under cocktail parasols in a pretty side garden bordered by a white picket fence. No credit cards; parking nearby is limited; handy for Gatwick airport. *(Recommended by Anthony Byers, Jerry Bemis, Mayur Shah, Keith and Audrey Ward, Wayne Brindle, Martin Jones, Richard Oxenham, Nicola Thomas, Paul Dickinson; more reports please)*

King & Barnes ~ Tenant Sarah Broomfield ~ Real ale ~ Meals and snacks (till 10) ~ Restaurant ~ Children in restaurant ~ (01306) 611348 ~ Open 11-2.30 (3 Sat), 5-11

MICKLEHAM TQ1753 Map 3

King William IV

Byttom Hill; short but narrow steep track up hill just off A24 Leatherhead—Dorking by partly green-painted restaurant, just N of main B2289 village turnoff; OS Sheet 187 map reference 173538

Rather unusually placed, this relaxed and unpretentious 18th-c inn is cut into the hillside – so there's quite a climb – with panoramic views down the hill from the snug plank-panelled front bar. The more spacious back bar is quite brightly lit with kitchen-type chairs around its cast-iron-framed tables. There are decent log fires, fresh flowers on all the tables and a serviceable grandfather clock. It's popular for a wide range of fairly imaginative blackboard specials – vegetarian food is a bit of a speciality – which might include attractively presented spinach and aubergine lasagne (£4.95), lamb hot pot or sausages like pork and leek, lamb and apricot or mustard and honey (£5.25), Thai vegetable curry or baked brie in filo pastry (£5.50), Cajun chicken salad (£5.75), spinach and nut bake (£5.95), steak and kidney pie or seafood pie (£6.50), cold poached salmon salad with strawberry and avocado salad or lamb chops with redcurrant and tarragon (£6.95), poached salmon with tomato and herb dressing (£7.25), seafood casserole (£7.50), sirloin steak with wild mushroom sauce (£9.25), and puddings like hot choclocate fudge cake, caramel apple tart and treacle tart (£2.50). Well kept Adnams, Badger Best, Boddingtons, Hogs Back, Ringwood Fortyniner and a guest on handpump; quick and friendly service; good coffee. Dominoes; piped radio can be noticeable. The lovely terraced garden is neatly filled with sweet peas, climbing roses and honeysuckle and plenty of tables (some in an open-sided wooden shelter). A path leads straight up through woods where it's nice to walk after lunch. *(Recommended by David Shillitoe, Tom and Rosemary Hall, Adrian Zambardino, Debbie Chaplin, LM, Ron Gentry, Eddie Edwards, F Jarman, R A Buckler, Derek and Maggie Washington, Mayur Shah, Andy and Jill Plumb, A G Drake, N H and A H Harries, Nic Armitage, Mr and Mrs Gordon Turner, Mark and Diane Grist, Thomas Neate, Ian Phillips, Rhoda and Jeff Collins, Susan and Alan Buckland, G R Sutherland)*

Free house ~ Licensees C D and J E Grist ~ Real ale ~ Meals and snacks (till 9.45, not Mon evening) ~ Restaurant ~ (01372) 372590 ~ Children in eating area of small bar and restaurant, over 14 in main bar ~ Occasional folk/country groups in summer ~ Open 11-3, 6-11; closed 25 Dec

OXTED TQ3951 Map 3

George

High St, Old Oxted; off A25 not far from M25 junction 6

Even when it's busy this very well run pub stays relaxed and welcoming, with the thriving chatty and contented feel that you seem to get only in places which have done away with games machines and piped music. Furnishings are neat, tidy and comfortable, with attractive prints on the walls and a pleasant restaurant area. A wide choice of consistently good food, well presented in generous helpings, includes sandwiches (from £2; sausage and onion £2.75), deep-fried brie with cranberry sauce (£4.25), burgers or vegetarian dishes (from £4.95), cheese platter (£5.95), steak and kidney pie (£6.25), well hung steaks cut to the size you want (from £8.95), fresh seafood such as oysters, halibut, salmon, Dover sole and giant prawns, daily specials such as Oriental lamb, fish and chips, roast lamb or spare ribs (from £5.50), and puddings (from £2.95). Well kept Adnams Bitter, Bass, Boddingtons, Fullers London Pride, Harveys Sussex, and Wadworths 6X on handpump, decent house wines, efficient friendly service; tables outside. *(Recommended by David and Michelle Hedges, G R Sharman, Maureen and Keith Gimson, Hugh and Peggy Colgate, Mr and Mrs J Irving, Susan and Alan Buckland, Cathryn and Richard Hicks, J S M Sheldon)*

Free house ~ Licensees John and Helen Hawkins ~ Real ale ~ Meals and snacks (12-9.30; till 10 Sat) ~ Restaurant ~ (01883) 713453 ~ Children in restaurant if over 8 ~ Open 11-11

PIRBRIGHT SU9455 Map 2

Royal Oak

Aldershot Rd; A324S of village

They have seven well kept rotating real ales – many are Whitbread related – at this neatly kept Tudor cottage, which might include Adnams, Batemans, Boddingtons, Charles Wells Fargo, Flowers Original, Fuggles IPA, Greene King IPA, Marstons Pedigree, Youngs Special or Timothy Taylors Landlord; about fifteen wines by the glass and bottle; several malt whiskies. There's a rambling series of snug side alcoves with heavy beams and timbers, ancient stripped brickwork, and gleaming brasses set around the big low-beamed fireplace which roars in the winter. It's neatly furnished with wheelback chairs, tapestried wall seats and little dark church-like pews set around neat tables, decorated with fresh flowers in summer. Bar food includes filled baked potatoes and large filled baps (from £2.50), steak and ale pie (£5.25), pork in cream sauce with apples (£5.50), chicken breast with ginger and mango (£5.95), ribs and steaks (£7.95). In summer the award winning huge front garden is a mass of colour and pretty in the evening with fairy lights although it can be a bit noisy with passing traffic; the large garden at the back has become very popular. Interesting walks are accessible from the large car park, where walkers may leave cars if permission is gained from the licensee. *(Recommended by H West, Thomas Nott, Guy Consterdine, Paul Carter, Martin and Karen Wake, Ian Phillips, KC, Mike Davies, Susan and John Douglas; more reports please)*

Whitbreads ~ Manager John Lay ~ Real ale ~ Meals and snacks ~ Restaurant ~ (01483) 232466 ~ Children in restaurant ~ Open 11-11 (including Sunday)

PYRFORD LOCK TQ0458 Map 3

Anchor

Lock Lane; 3 miles from M25 Junction 10; south on A3, then slip road signposted Ockham, Ripley and Send, past RHS Wisley Gardens to second bridge

It's the splendid location of this busy modern pub that makes it a main entry. From picnic table sets on the big open terrace there's a fine view of the canal narrowboats as they leave the dock and edge under the steeply hump-backed road bridge and through the locks of the River Wey Navigation. The view is almost as good from the conservatory and the partly carpeted and partly brick-floored bar with big picture windows and comfortable furnishings. Upstairs is full of narrow-boat memorabilia. Good bar food includes home-made specials (from £4.75), ploughman's (£3.75), steak and kidney pie (£4.45), large salad selection (from £4.50), scampi (£5.45), gammon steak (£5.15); daily vegetarian special (from £4.15), all served with chips and peas, children's menu (from £2) and puddings (£1.75); friendly, efficient staff but you may have to queue to place your order which will then be called on a

Tannoy; Courage Best and Directors and Theakstons Best and XB on handpump; fruit machine, video games, piped music, pinball and juke box sometimes even outside. Always busy on a sunny day, partly owing to the pub's proximity to the Royal Horticultural Society's Wisley Gardens. *(Recommended by DWAJ, Peter and Joy Heatherley, Ron Gentry, V Green, A J and G Jackson, David Shillitoe, Mr and Mrs D Simons, P Gillbe, John Pettit, Douglas Jeffery, Stephen Barney; more reports please)*

S & N ~ Managers Paula and Steven Lucie ~ Real ale ~ Meals and snacks ~ (01932) 342507 ~ Children under 14 till 9pm ~ Open 11-11 (winter 11-3, 6.30-11)

SHAMLEY GREEN TQ0343 Map 3

Red Lion

B2128 S of Guildford

The very pleasant interior of this fairly smart dining pub is cosy with a red glossed ceiling, rows of books on high shelves and on the cream walls old photographs of cricket played on the opposite village green. The good mix of furniture includes a handsome panel-back armed settle, red-brocaded high-backed modern settles forming booths around tables, some kitchen chairs and a couple of antique clocks. Most tables are laid for meals with a fairly big choice from the menu and blackboard which might include sandwiches (from £2.95), soups such as ham and lentil, mushroom with croûtons (£3.25), ploughman's (from £3.65), grilled stuffed mushrooms (£5.85), moules farcie or home-baked ham, egg and chips (£6.45), ham and melon salad (£6.75), dijon peppered chicken (£8.75), seafood salad or lamb medallions (£9.25), giant prawns (£10.75), lamb cutlets (£11.45) and lemon sole veronique (£12.95); vegetarian dishes like spinach and mushroom crêpes or mushroom tagliatelle (£6.45); usually they do a Sunday lunch, although not necessarily in summer (£7.95); children can have small portions of some dishes; home-made puddings (all £3.25) like lemon meringue pie and fresh strawberry roulade. Well kept Abbot ale, Flowers Original, Friary Meux and Tetleys, and a good selection of wines. Handmade wooden tables outside. *(Recommended by Guy Consterdine, Ian Phillips, R Sinclair-Taylor, Michael and Carol Meek, Steve Goodchild, Tim Galligan)*

Free house ~ Licensee: Ben Heath ~ Real ale ~ Meals and snacks (11-3, 6-10) ~ Restaurant ~ (01483) 892202 ~ Children welcome ~ Open 11-11 ~ Bedrooms: £35B/£40B

WALLISWOOD TQ1138 Map 3

Scarlett Arms ★

Village signposted from Ewhurst—Rowhook back road; or follow Oakwoodhill signpost from A29 S of Ockley, then follow Walliswood signpost into Walliswood Green Road

As this straightforward little country inn is a particularly popular lunchtime stop for notably good value homely cooking you need to arrive early for a table. Served in hearty portions (mostly with chips and peas) favourite dishes include steak and kidney pie, rabbit pie, chicken with mushroom and white wine sauce, ham and cheesy leek bake, lasagne, moussaka or Lancashire hot pot (£4.50), pheasant casserole (£5.50) and Thursday and Sunday lunchtime roast (£4.75). The red-tiled white building was once a pair of labourers' cottages and the original small-roomed layout has been carefully preserved. The three neatly kept communicating rooms have low black oak beams, deeply polished flagstones, simple but perfectly comfortable benches, high bar stools with backrests, trestle tables, country prints, photographs of locals and two roaring log fires all winter. Well kept King & Barnes Sussex, Broadwood, Festive and Wealdman and a guest ale on handpump. Darts, bar billiards, cribbage, shove-ha'penny, table skittles, dominoes and a fruit machine in a small room at the end. There are old-fashioned seats and tables with umbrellas in the pretty well tended garden. *(Recommended by DWAJ, Margaret and Nigel Dennis, N H and A H Harries, G W and I L Edwards, Peter Lewis, P Gillbe, J S M Sheldon, Keith and Audrey Ward, Anthony Byers, Martin Richards, Andy and Jackie Mallpress, Graham Pettener, Mrs J M Aston, LM))*

King & Barnes ~ Tenant Mrs Pat Haslam ~ Real ale ~ Meals and snacks ~ (01306) 627243 ~Children over 14 ~ Open 11-2.30, 5.30-11

WARLINGHAM TQ3658 Map 3

White Lion

B269

Well worth a small detour if you're heading in or out of London, the marvellously aged warren of dark-panelled rooms in this delightfully unspoilt early Tudor coaching inn are full of nooks and crannies, an impressive old inglenook fireplace, low beams, and even tales of secret passages and ghosts. There's also plenty of deeply aged plasterwork, wood-block floors and high-backed settles, while a side room decorated with amusing early 19th-c cartoons has darts, a trivia machine and a fruit machine. Served in the bigger, brighter room at the end of the building the good value bar food includes sandwiches (£1.60), huge filled cottage loaves (£2.50), beef curry, chilli, cottage pie or steak and kidney pie (£3.95), roast (£4.25) and steaks (£4.95); good service. Bass, Charringtons IPA and Fullers London Pride and two constantly rotating guests like Youngs or M&B Brew XII on handpump; piped music in the eating area; no smoking during lunchtime meal serving hours there. The well kept back lawn, with its rockery, is surrounded by a herbaceous border; there may be outside service here in summer. *(Recommended by Jenny and Brian Seller, Helen Taylor, Graham Pettener, E G Parish, Wayne Brindle, B B Morgan; more reports please)*

Charringtons (Bass) ~ Manager Julie Evans ~ Real ale ~ Meals and snacks (not Sun eve) ~ (01883) 624106 ~ Children in eating area of bar till 8pm ~ Open 11-11

WEST CLANDON TQ0452 Map 3

Onslow Arms

The Street (A247)

The spacious rambling rooms at this handsome early 17th-c country inn have heavy beams, nooks and crannies, polished brass and copper, leaded windows, carved settles on the flagstones or thick carpets and log fires in inglenook fireplaces (one has an unusual roasting spit). There's a quietly comfortable atmosphere with fresh flowers, soft lighting, and courteous, friendly and professional service. A fine choice of around eight changing real ales well kept on handpump might include a Badger Ale, Bass, Boddingtons, Courage Best and Directors, Fullers London Pride, King & Barnes, a Ringwood ale or Youngs Special; a very good German keg lager. Beautifully prepared home-made bar food from the blackboard is served with fresh vegetables and includes sandwiches, coquille St Jacques (£3.85), tagliatelle niçoise (£4.50), chicken and mushroom pie (£5.25), steak, kidney and oyster pie (£5.85), cold meats carved from joints and help yourself salads and a popular carvery, and puddings; many, many more elaborate dishes in the stylish candlelit (partly no-smoking) restaurant. The village is pretty and in summer, the award-winning hanging baskets, flower filled tubs, shrubs and flower-laden cart outside on the flagged courtyard are a marvellous sight. *(Recommended by Gillian and Michael Wallace, J S M Sheldon, TBB, John and Shirley Dyson, Paul Carter, June and Malcolm Farmer, Thomas Nott, Susan and John Douglas, John and Heather Dwane, Dr and Mrs A K Clarke, A E and P McCully, Ian Phillips, R B Crail)*

Free house ~ Licensee Alan Peck ~ Real ale ~ Meals and snacks (till 10pm); not Sun evening ~ Restaurant ~ (01483) 222447 ~ Children in eating area of bar and in restaurant ~ Open 11-2.30, 5.30-11

Post Office address codings confusingly give the impression that some pubs are in Surrey when they're really in Hampshire or London (which is where we list them). And there's further confusion from the way the Post Office still talks about Middlesex – which disappeared in 1974 local government reorganisation.

Lucky Dip

Besides the fully inspected pubs, you might like to try these Lucky Dips recommended to us and described by readers (if you do, please send us reports):

☆ **Abinger Common** [Abinger signed off A25 W of Dorking – then right to Abinger Hammer; TQ1145], *Abinger Hatch*: Lovely country setting nr pretty church and duck pond in clearing of rolling woods, welcoming old-fashioned character bar with heavy beams, flagstones, basic furnishings, log fires, half a dozen well kept ales, inc interesting guest beers, country wines, wide choice of usual bar food, piped music, restaurant; provision for children; may have Sun afternoon teas, open all day bank hols and for village fair – around second weekend June *(Jenny and Brian Seller, Nigel Harris, Susan and John Douglas, Ron Gentry, Winifrede D Morrison, LYM)*

Addlestone [Row Town; TQ0464], *Cricketers*: Wide range of good well prepared food, pleasant garden with bouncy castle tucked away from general view *(Ian Phillips)*

Alfold [TQ0334], *Alfold Barn*: Enterprising new management in magnificently raftered dining pub – have had doorstep salesmen offering discount meals for deposit up front *(Steve Goodchild)*

Badshot Lea [SU8648], *Crown*: Homely and very friendly little no-frills local, big helpings of simple good value fresh food, Fullers ales, efficient service *(Ray Cuckow, Ian Phillips)*

☆ **Banstead** [High St, off A217; TQ2559], *Woolpack*: Spotless Chef & Brewer always busy for consistently good value food from sandwiches up inc children's dishes, good friendly service, well kept Courage-related ales, cosily decorated lounge, good no-smoking area; occasional free jazz, open all day *(DWAJ, John Pettit, P C Strange)*

☆ **Beare Green** [A24 Dorking—Horsham; TQ1842], *Dukes Head*: Good atmosphere and generous straightforward food in attractive roadside pub with good service, open fires, Tetleys-related real ales; pleasant garden *(G Washington, LYM)*

☆ **Bletchingley** [2 High St, 2½ miles from M25 junction 6, via A22 then A25 towards Redhill; TQ3250], *Plough*: Generous helpings of good reasonably priced food in spacious bar or (same price) restaurant of extended pub with well kept ales such as King & Barnes, Tetleys and Wadworths 6X; friendly efficient staff, tables in big garden *(David Voice, David and Michelle Hedges, Chrystabel Austin, Doreen and Brian Hardham)*

Bletchingley [11 High St], *Whyte Harte*: Low-beamed open-plan bars with old prints, big inglenook log fire, plush settles, rugs and parquet, fruit machine, well kept Tetleys-related ales, usual food; seats outside, has been open all day Sat; children in dining room; bedrooms clean and comfortable *(Alan Castle, Jenny and Brian Seller, Craig Mayer, LYM)*; [Little Common Lane, off A25 on Redhill side of village], *William IV*: Quaint old country pub, prettily tile-hung and weatherboarded, with comfortable little back dining room, well kept Bass and Worthington BB, good atmosphere, efficient friendly service; seats in nice garden with summer barbecues Sat evening and Sun lunchtime *(David Hedges, Julian Charman, LYM)*

Blindley Heath [A22; T645], *Farmhouse Table*: Attractive pub with good roadside parking, intimate village bar, rambling areas split into cosy smaller ones; good carvery restaurant Tues-Sun, good polite service; children welcome *(E G Parish)*

Brockham [Brockham Green; TQ1949], *Royal Oak*: Refurbished pub esp friendly to children – and dogs – good garden with play area, good if not cheap food, Tetleys-related ales, beautiful location on green *(Chris and Chris Ellis)*

☆ **Byfleet** [104 High Rd; TQ0661], *Plough*: Medley of furnishings in friendly and lively pub with good value straightforward bar food, well kept Courage and guest ales, lots of farm tools, brass and copper, log fire, dominoes; prices low for Surrey; picnic tables in big pleasant garden *(B and K Hypher, Hugh Wood, Andy Davies)*

Caterham [235 Stanstead Rd, Whitehill; TQ3354], *Harrow*: Good value food inc Sun, well kept Tetleys-related ales, jolly and helpful staff *(Brian and Jenny Seller)*; [High St], *Olde King & Queen*: Delightfully renovated Fullers local with welcoming manager, well kept beers, good value wholesome food (not Sun) *(D and J Tapper)*

☆ **Charlton** [142 Charlton Rd, off B376 Laleham—Shepperton; TQ0869], *Harrow*: Comfortable and friendly carefully modernised thatched 17th-c pub, short choice of generous interesting no-frills food (tables can be booked), particularly good service even when crowded, well kept Morlands, plenty of seats *(Ian and Wendy Phillips, S H Collett-Jones, W L G Watkins)*

Chelsham [Vanguard Way, over the common – OS Sheet 187 map ref 372590; TQ3659], *Bull*: Traditional village-green country pub with good fair-priced home-cooked food Tues-Sat and Sun lunch, table service, welcoming new licensees; tables outside *(E G Parish, M D Hare)*

☆ **Chertsey** [London St (B375); TQ0466], *Crown*: Typical relaxed Youngs pub with attractively renovated Victorian-style bar, well kept ales, back food area, restaurant, good service, conservatory, tables in courtyard and garden with pond; children welcome; smart 30-bedroom annexe *(Richard Houghton, Comus Elliott)*

☆ **Chertsey** [Ruxbury Rd, St Anns Hill (nr Lyne); TQ0267], *Golden Grove*: Busy local with lots of stripped wood, cheap straightforward home-made food from sandwiches up (not Sat-Mon evenings) in pine-tabled eating area, well kept Tetleys-related and Gales ales; piped music, fruit and games machines; big garden with friendly dogs and goat, play area, wooded pond – nice spot by woods *(Ian Phillips, Clem Stephens, Rhoda and Jeff Collins, T A Bryan)*

☆ **Chiddingfold** [A283; SU9635], *Crown*: Picturesque old inn in attractive surroundings, afternoon teas in hotel side with ancient panelling, fine carving, massive beams and tapestried restaurant; simpler side family bar with real ales such as Badger Tanglefoot and Charles Wells, decent food using fresh herbs etc, tables out on verandah; children allowed in some areas; has been open all day, very crowded 5 Nov (fireworks out on green); bedrooms *(Paula Harrison, Margaret and Nigel Dennis, Angela and Alan Dale, JE, LYM)*

☆ **Chilworth** [Dorking Rd; TQ0247], *Percy Arms*: Roomy nicely refurbished well lit bar, good choice of food, lunchtime bargains (not Sun), well kept Greene King ales and good service; pretty views of vale of Chilworth from garden behind, pleasant walks *(John and Heather Dwane)*

Chilworth [Blackheath; off A248 across the level crossing, SE of Guildford], *Villagers*: Attractive pub with lots of rooms, nooks and corners, old pews, interesting home-cooked food from superb sandwiches up, well kept Morlands Speckled Hen, decent wines and port, very friendly and eager-to-please young staff; pretty village, pleasant walks *(TOH, Mr and Mrs B Matthews)*

☆ **Chipstead** [3 miles from M25, junction 8; A217 towards Banstead, right at second roundabout; TQ2757], *Well House*: Cottagey and comfortable partly 14th-c pub with lots of atmosphere, good simple lunchtime food (not Sun) from sandwiches up, very welcoming efficient staff, log fires in all three rooms, well kept Bass and guest beers, good pot of tea; dogs allowed; attractive garden with well reputed to be mentioned in Doomsday Book, delightful setting *(Elizabeth and Klaus Leist, David Peakall, Ian Phillips, Maureen and Keith Gimson, Beverley James, LYM)*

☆ **Chipstead** [B2032, Chipstead Valley – OS Sheet 176 map ref 273575; TQ2757], *Ramblers Rest*: Sensitively refurbished pub in collection of partly 14th-c buildings which used to be Dean Farm restaurant, extensive range of different seating areas with different atmospheres, panelling and low ceilings, plenty of antiques and polished furniture; well kept Whitbreads-related ales, reasonably priced straightforward food inc generous ploughman's, welcoming service, hot-water jugs for baby-milk bottles; big pleasant garden behind, decent walks nearby; let down by the pervasive piped music; open all day inc Sun *(Helen Morton, Jenny and Brian Seller, TOH, Eddie Edwards)*

Chobham [High St; 4 miles from M3 junc 3; SU9761], *Sun*: Well kept low-beamed lounge bar in quiet timbered Courage pub, a reliable refuge *(Martin Richards, LYM)*

☆ **Cobham** [Plough Lane; TQ0960], *Plough*: Cheerful easy-going atmosphere in pretty black-shuttered local with comfortably modernised low-beamed lounge bar, well kept Courage ales, helpful staff, pine-panelled snug with darts, lunchtime food; piped pop music may be rather loud some evenings; seats outside *(John Pettit, Ian Phillips, LYM)*

Cobham [Old Lane], *Black Swan*: Lively country local with lots of brass blowlamps, reasonably priced food in bar and restaurant, 14 real ales, very friendly staff, piped music of the Kate Bush era, frequent discos; big garden with plenty of seats, seesaw, swings, climbing frame and slide *(G W and I L Edwards)*; [Tilt Rd, off Stoke Rd], *Running Mare*: Attractive old local overlooking green, very busy Sun lunchtime and lively Thurs evening, good food, barbecue, great Canadian barkeeps *(S A Mackenzie, Betty Winge)*; [A245 Pains Hill/Byfleet Rd, by Sainsburys], *Snail*: Former Little White Lion, now a brasserie, but real care is taken with the beer and the young staff are efficient and friendly, the cottagey communicating rooms are attractive and comfortable and the food is good; handy for Painshill Park *(Anthony Byers, Mrs J A Blanks)*

☆ **Dorking** [81 South St; TQ1649], *Cricketers*: Bustling little Fullers pub, very neat and tidy, with solidly comfortable furniture, cricketing pictures on stripped brick walls, limited choice of no-nonsense food (not Fri, Sat evening or Sun lunch), well kept Chiswick, London Pride and ESB, low prices, pleasant back terrace with barbecues; open all day *(D J Penny, Jeff and Rhoda Collins, John Pettit, MS, Dr H Huddart, LYM)*

Dorking [Horsham Rd], *Bush*: Simple no-frills pub with well kept Boddingtons and Fullers, good value lunches, friendly unobtrusive service *(Dr H Huddart)*; [45 West St], *Kings Arms*: Low half-timbered pub in antiques area, part-panelled lounge divided from bar by timbers, back dining area, nice lived-in old furniture, warm relaxed atmosphere, good choice of home-cooked food, friendly service, six real ales inc King & Barnes; open all day *(Ian Phillips, Gary T Callaghan, James Richardson)*

Dormansland [B2028 NE; TQ4042], *Plough*: Warm traditional atmosphere in old building in quiet village, many original features, real ales inc well kept Flowers Original, good value carefully prepared generous food inc traditional puddings, young helpful staff; busy weekday lunchtime *(E G Parish)*; [High St], *Royal Oak*: Pretty pub with wide choice of good value home cooking inc unusual dishes, friendly service, darts, character dogs, well kept garden; children welcome *(Lee Crozier, R and S Bentley)*

☆ **Dunsfold** [TQ0036], *Sun*: Consistently good reasonably priced food inc interesting dishes in elegantly symmetrical 18th-c beamed pub on attractive green, friendly old-fashioned atmosphere, scrubbed pine furniture, helpful staff, well kept Tetleys-related ales, log fires; separate cottage dining room; children welcome *(D Sykes-Thompson, Rhoda and Jeff Collins, LYM)*

☆ **East Clandon** [TQ0651], *Queens Head*: Traditionally refurbished timbered pub, currently very well run, with small connecting rooms, big inglenook log fire, fine old elm bar counter, bookcases, pictures, copperware, relaxed atmosphere; decent bar food (not cheap), well kept ales, no lunchtime piped music; some tables outside *(John Evans, E G Parish, R B Crail, A Monte, G B Longden, A E and P McCully, LYM)*

East Horsley [TQ0952], *Barley Mow*: Pleasant old-fashioned pub with extremely long-serving licensee, Greene King and Tetleys-related ales, fair choice of reasonably priced food, nice restaurant *(R B Crail)*

☆ **Effingham** [Orestan Lane; TQ1253], *Plough*: Good value honest home cooking (veg and potatoes may be extra) inc enjoyable Sun lunch in civilised local with two coal-effect gas fires, beamery, panelling, old plates and brassware in long lounge, no-smoking extension, well kept Youngs, efficient staff ; popular with older people – no dogs, children or sleeveless T-shirts inside, lots of tables in big informal garden with play area and out in front; convenient for Polesdon Lacey *(John Pettit, John Ashley, A M Pickup, Mr and Mrs R J Foreman, Christopher Gallop, Mr and Mrs David Cure, Sue and Mike Todd)*

☆ **Egham** [34 Middle Hill, just off A30 towards Englefield Green; TQ0171], *Beehive*: Small, very friendly and often busy, with half a dozen well kept Gales and other ales inc one brewed for the pub by Gales, quickly but individually prepared food, polite service, nice garden *(Ian Phillips, Richard Houghton)*

Egham [38 High St], *Crown*: Crowded local with good food and wide choice of beers inc full Theakstons range and Tennents, Ushers and Youngs; spartan furnishings *(Ian Phillips)*; [1 North St], *Foresters Arms*: Welcoming local with reliably well kept Courage-related beers and decent food *(Joy Cooper)*

Ellens Green [TQ1035], *Wheatsheaf*: Consistently well kept King & Barnes, decent food, good service, busy local atmosphere *(Keith and Audrey Ward)*

Elstead [Farnham Rd; SU9143], *Golden Fleece*: Straightforward building but tall plants add a slightly exotic air and it has good reasonably priced authentic Thai food; busy, with good atmosphere *(Dr N Kennea, Martin and Karen Wake)*

Englefield Green [Wick Lane, Bishopsgate; SU9970], *Sun*: Lived-in pub with well kept Courage-related ales and Youngs Special, decent wines, good choice of food from sandwiches up, reasonable prices, daily papers; biscuit and water for dogs, handy for Savile Garden and Windsor Park *(Ian Phillips, Julian Bessa)*

Epsom [TQ2160], *Barley Mow*: Friendly Fullers local, useful food *(Robin Cordell)*; [Downs Rd, Epsom Downs], *Derby Arms*: Popular and reliable refurbished Toby dining pub with reasonably priced food in bar and added restaurant, inc carvery; friendly helpful service, open all day Sun *(Mr and Mrs A H Denman)*; *Tattenham Corner*: Big Beefeater pub-restaurant next to racecourse, prompt friendly service, good range of standard bar snacks, changing Whitbreads-related and other ales, play area and barbecue in garden *(R C Vincent, E G Parish)*

Ewell [High St; TQ2262], *Green Man*: Big between-wars pub with reasonably priced lunchtime food, sizeable back dining area, well kept beers; piped music, fruit machines, darts; handy for riverside walks *(John Pettit)*; [1 London Rd], *Spring*: Spacious Bass pub with friendly new management, sporting pictures, Fullers London Pride and Worthington BB, good value restaurant, pianist some Sunday lunch times (happy hour then); fruit machine, pool *(G W and I L Edwards)*

Ewhurst [The Street; TQ0940], *Bulls Head*: Extensively refurbished village local, good range of meals, superb garden opp village green *(Steve Goodchild)*; [Pitch Hill; a mile N of village on Shere rd], *Windmill*: Spacious series of hillside lawns give lovely views, as does conservatory restaurant; smart modern bar behind, good interesting food (snacks not cheap), well kept ale such as Wadworths 6X; lovely walking country *(Jenny and Brian Seller, Gwen and Peter Andrews, Alex and Beryl Williams, LYM)*

Fairmile Common [A307 Esher—Cobham; TQ1161], *Fairmile*: Redeveloped as comfortable and spotless Greenalls Millers Kitchen family dining pub with well cooked, served and priced food inc , Tetleys, Courage Best and Greenalls Traditional on handpump, smaller helpings for children or OAPs, good staff, Courage and Tetleys-related ales, spacious gardens; bedrooms *(Anthony Byers, R B Crail)*

☆ **Farleigh** [Farleigh Common; bus route 403 from Croydon; TQ3659], *Harrow*: Former barn with stripped-flint brickwork, rustic decoration inc farm tools and other bric-a-brac, even an owl high in the rafters; good lunchtime food from sandwiches up (not Sun), raised no-smoking area, well kept Bass, cheerful staff; separate locals' bar, tables on big lawn with pasture behind; popular with younger people evening *(Graham Pettener)*

☆ **Farncombe** [signed from Catteshall industrial estate on outskirts of Godalming beyond Sainsburys; SU9844], *Ram*: Huge choice of ciders, cider cocktails and country wines in attractive 16th-c timbered white pub in charming setting, three separate bars with coal-effect fires in old brick hearths, parquet floors, heavy beams, lots of fabric-covered pews, interesting choice of food lunchtime and evening inc good ploughman's, very friendly staff, Fullers London Pride; spacious streamside shaded garden with big carved wooden ram, lots of swings, slides and climbing frames, pretty flowered terrace and barbecue; occasional Morris men, mummers etc *(Giles Quick, Gill Cory, Linda Adams)*

☆ **Felbridge** [Woodcock Hill – A22 N; TQ3639], *Woodcock*: Busy little flagstoned bar opening on to richly furnished room a bit like a film props department, spiral stairs up to another opulent room, candlelit and almost boudoirish, nice small Victorian dining room off; also big seafood restaurant; well kept Harveys, Ringwood Old Thumper, Charles Wells Bombardier, piped music (can be loud and late), relaxed atmosphere – service can be very leisurely; children in eating area, open all day, some tables outside; bedrooms *(John and Janet Wigley, L M Miall, Rita Horridge, Adrian Zambardino, Debbie Chaplin, Alan Skull, Dr Paul Kitchener, LYM)*

Felbridge [London Rd (A22)], *Star*: Spacious pleasantly furnished pub, good for families, with suntrap no-smoking conservatory, willing helpful service, good choice of beers on handpump, good food *(E G Parish)*

☆ **Fickleshole** [Featherbed Lane; off A2022 Purley Rd just S of A212 roundabout; TQ3860], *White Bear*: Rambling interestingly furnished partly 15th-c family country pub with lots of small rooms, well kept ales such as Felinfoel and Fullers, bar food, fruit machine, video game, piped music; children welcome, jazz Weds, open all day Sat; play area in sizeable garden *(Jenny and Brian Seller, J S M Sheldon, LYM)*

☆ **Forest Green** [nr B2126/B2127 junction; TQ1240], *Parrot*: Quaint rambling country pub, pleasant and comfortable, with pervasive parrot motif, well kept Courage ales, good often interesting food (many tables reserved, giving it something of a restaurant feel in the evening), good cheerful service even when crowded; children welcome, open all day; plenty of space outside by cricket pitch, good walks nearby *(P Gillbe, A H Denman, Winifrede D Morrison, Ian Phillips, LYM)*

Frensham [SU8341], *Holly Bush*: Good value food in good-sized helpings, big and bright interior *(Paula Williams)*

☆ **Friday Street** [TQ1245], *Stephen Langton*: Welcoming country local in charming spot, behind cottages in secluded valley below Leith Hill (good walks), good if not cheap usual food with real chips (no sandwiches), good log fire, attractive prints, Charrington IPA and Youngs, popular restaurant, tables in front courtyard; bar lavatories down steps outside *(Dick Brown, Peter Lewis, Jenny and Brian Seller, J S M Sheldon)*

☆ **Godalming** [Ockford Rd, junction Portsmouth Rd (A3100) and Shackstead Lane; SU9743], *Inn on the Lake*: Cosy and comfortable family bar with well presented reasonably priced bar food inc vegetarian, well kept Whitbreads-related and guest real ales, decent wines, log fire and friendly staff; elegant restaurant with indoor fishpond and grand piano, good choice of wines; tables out in lovely garden overlooking lake, summer barbecues; rather steep car park; bedrooms *(Ian Phillips)*

Godalming [Mill Lane, High St S end], *Red Lion*: Lively pub formed from several old properties inc mayor's lodging and courthouse (cellar was gaol); interesting range of real ales, good coffees inc cappuccino, public and lounge bars, good friendly service; open all day weekdays *(George Atkinson)*; [Church St], *Star*: Friendly 16th-c local in cobbled pedestrian street, lively atmosphere, good range of beer, good food inc ingeniously filled baguettes; tables under trees in yard behind *(Paul Stephens)*

☆ **Godstone** [128 High St; under a mile from M25 junction 6, via B2236; TQ3551], *Bell*: Recent extensive refurbishments in 14th-c pub, comfortable beamed bar with lots of old prints, pictures and artefacts, smaller snug, bigger alcovey restaurant with good interesting food inc Malaysian and other exotic meals; Tetleys-related ales, unusual new Victorian-style conservatory, garden; lavatories with disabled access and nappy-changing; bedrooms *(E G Parish, D and A Walters, LYM)*

Godstone [A25 towards Bletchingley], *Hare & Hounds*: Good food pub with wide choice, nice atmosphere *(Gordon Smith, D Deas)*

☆ **Gomshall** [Station Rd (A25); TQ0847], *Compasses*: Attractive and well run, with well kept Gibbs Mew Bishops Tipple and Wiltshire, good well presented food (not cheap but good value), quick service, lots of tables; pleasant garden over duck stream with abundant weeping willows; walkers welcome *(B and B Matthews, G R Sharman)*

Grayswood [A286 NE of Haslemere; SU9234], *Wheatsheaf*: Modernised with conference rooms etc, almost more like a golf club than a pub, but good interesting food, well presented and generous if not cheap, in bar and restaurant with neo-classical frescoes, reasonably priced wines; bedrooms *(Paula Williams)*

Great Bookham [Church Rd; TQ1354], *Old Windsor Castle*: Warm and friendly local, good food popular for business lunches, big back garden with play area *(Stephan Freeman)*

Guildford [Madrid Rd; SU9949], *Astolat*: Modern pub with Bass and other changing well kept ales, pleasant garden with romantic nooks *(Gerry O'Connor)*; [Rydes Hill, Aldershot Rd], *Cricketers*: Friendly local with well kept Courage-related and guest ales, wide range of decent food *(Alan Hudson)*; [Woodbridge Rd], *Forger & Firkin*: Brews its own good Dogbolter and other ales, also strong home-brewed cider and guest ales; weekend live music *(Chris O'Prey)*; [Millbrook; across car park from Yvonne Arnaud Theatre, beyond boat yard], *Jolly Farmer*: Attractive spot overlooking the Wey Navigation, nice atmosphere, friendly young staff, decent food, good range of beers *(G C Hackemer, D J and P M Taylor)*; [46 Chertsey St], *Spread Eagle*: Busy and cheerful town local with well kept Courage-related and interesting changing guest beers, good value simple lunchtime food *(Phil and Sally Gorton, Anthony Byers, Anna Marsh)*

☆ **Headley** [Church Lane, village signed off B2033 SE of Leatherhead; TQ2054], *Cock*: Congenial much-modernised Tudor village local, light and airy, with pews forming table booths, usual bar food (not Sun evening), children allowed in restaurant, well kept Tetleys-related and guest ales, efficient service; games end, piped music may get louder as the night wears on; dogs welcome, tables outside – attractive setting, good walks *(Jenny and Brian Seller, TOH, Ron Gentry, Ian Morley, Julian Bessa, John Pettit, A Plumb, Roger and Valerie Hill, TBB, David Peakall, Ben Grose, LYM)*

☆ **Hersham** [6 Queens Rd; TQ1164], *Bricklayers Arms*: Friendly atmosphere in well kept and clean pub, bigger than it looks, with wide choice of good value genuinely home-cooked bar food from servery at back of lounge, good wines, separate bar with pool; small secluded garden; comfortable bedrooms *(Ian and Liz Phillips, Michael Sage)*

Holmbury St Mary [TQ1144], *Kings Head*: Friendly and cosy, in popular walking country, with food worth waiting for, well kept Ringwood Best and Fortyniner, local farm cider; informal sloping back garden *(Jenny and Brian Seller, Tom and Rosemary Hall)*

Horley [Church Rd; quite handy for M23 junction 9, off Horley turn from A23; TQ2842], *Olde Six Bells*: Interesting as a building – part of heavy-beamed open-plan bar was probably a medieval chapel, and you can still detect the traces; otherwise best viewed as a local, with Bass and Charrington IPA, upstairs raftered dining room, conservatory, open all day weekdays *(J S M Sheldon, LYM)*

Horsell [Horsell Birch; SU9859], *Cricketers*: Fine setting, spacious well kept gardens with barbecues, wide choice of reasonably priced popular food inc Sun lunch, range of beers, friendly atmosphere *(Mr and Mrs D Lockwood, Mr and Mrs G Evans)*; [123 High St], *Red Lion*: Good helpings of cheap food in welcoming well renovated pub with pleasant terrace, picture-filled converted barn where children allowed; good walks nearby *(Ian Phillips, A J Blackler)*

Horsell Common [Chertsey Rd; The Anthonys; A320 Woking—Ottershaw; SU9959], *Bleak House*: Warm and friendly, with decent food, comfortable seats, real ales, picnic tables and barbecues on back lawn; good walks to the sandpits which inspired H G Wells's *War of the Worlds (Ian Phillips)*

☆ **Hurtmore** [just off A3 nr Godalming by Hurtmore/Shackleford turn-off; SU9545], *Squirrels*: Roomy, comfortable, fresh and airy, with upmarket feel, sofas, country-kitchen furniture, partly no-smoking restaurant and conservatory, children's playroom, books for adults and children, decent bar food and restaurant inc sizzle-stone cooking, good friendly service, well kept Courage-related ales, facilities for disabled people; pleasantly converted bedrooms *(Gwen and Peter Andrews, R B Crail, Mrs J A Blanks, LYM)*

☆ **Irons Bottom** [Sidlow Bridge; off A217 – OS Sheet 187 map ref 250460; TQ2546], *Three Horseshoes*: Isolated but popular local, rather sophisticated feel, with new landlord doing well – he's a careful cook using good ingredients, and the menu reflects his time abroad; five or six excellently kept real ales such as Fullers London Pride, Glenny Wychwood or local Hogs Back Tea, quiz night Tues, summer barbecues *(Roger Byrne, Jim Bunting, Don Mather, Jenny and Brian Seller)*

☆ **Kenley** [Old Lodge Lane; left (coming from London) off A23 by Reedham Stn, then keep on; TQ3259], *Wattenden Arms*: Popular dark-panelled traditional country local nr glider aerodrome, well kept Bass and Charrington IPA, lunchtime bar food, prompt service, crisp-loving cat, patriotic and WWII memorabilia, seats on small side lawn; actually just inside London, but by long tradition we list it under Surrey *(B B Morgan, Jenny and Brian Seller, LYM)*

☆ **Kingswood** [Waterhouse Lane; TQ2455], *Kingswood Arms*: Spacious and busy pub, with good value straightforward food, cheerful quick service, Courage-related ales, airy conservatory dining extension; spacious rolling garden with play area *(Chris Jackson, Helen Medhurst)*

Knaphill [Anchor Hill; SU9658], *Royal Oak*: Friendly character local, Courage-related ales; small restaurant area *(Ian Phillips)*

☆ **Leatherhead** [Chessington Rd; A243 nr M25 junction 9; TQ1656], *Star*: Long-serving landlord keeps up fine friendly atmosphere, good choice of generous food inc good specials, nice waitress service, log fire, well kept King & Barnes and Courage-related ales *(J S M Sheldon, Ian Phillips)*

Leatherhead [57 High St], *Dukes Head*: Busy and friendly, with good range of bar food from separate servery, beams, timbers and open fire, good coffee, small front bar with pool and games machine; piped music; handy for good riverside walks *(John Pettit)*

☆ **Leigh** [S of A25 Dorking—Reigate; TQ2246], *Seven Stars*: Pretty country local with friendly landlord, bar food (emphasis on meals rather than snacks) all week, Tetleys-related ales, inglenook fireplace, horse-racing pictures, darts alley in public bar; flower-filled garden, maybe summer Sun barbecues; no children *(Derek and Maggie Washington, LYM)*

Limpsfield [outside village; TQ4148], *Grasshopper*: Tastefully extended and refurbished partly Tudor beamed pub with reasonably priced bar food, Charrington real ale, friendly staff, comfortable chairs, unobtrusive piped music *(Gwen and Peter Andrews)*

Lingfield [Church Rd; from centre towards racecourse, then left after 100 yds; TQ3843],

Star: Spacious recently renovated village pub with hops on beams, flagstones, two open fires, candlelit tables, well kept Whitbreads-related and guest beers, strong cider, wide choice of wines, Mexican as well as traditional food; children welcome, well kept garden *(Steve and Lesley Coppin)*

☆ **Lower Kingswood** [Buckland Rd; just off A217; TQ2453], *Mint Arms*: Family-run, with good value food all day inc Sun, friendly service, wide choice of ales such as Courage Best, Fullers London Pride, Gales HSB, King & Barnes, Theakstons Old Peculier, Wadworths 6X and Youngs, lots of brasses and copper, pool and darts in games area, big garden with play area *(DWAJ, Mr and Mrs G W Edwards)*

Lyne [Lyne Lane; TQ0166], *Royal Marine*: Small, friendly and cosy, neat as a new pin, unpretentious but well presented home-cooked food; Boddingtons, Flowers and Wadworths 6X *(Ian Phillips)*

☆ **Martyrs Green** [Old Lane, handy for M25 junction 10 – off A3 S-bound, but return N of junction; TQ0957], *Black Swan*: Extensively enlarged, with simple furnishings, fine range of a dozen or more well kept real ales, good service, log fire, generous bar food; can get crowded with young people evenings, piped pop music may be loud then; open through afternoon (happy hour from 3), tables in woodside garden with play area; attractive setting, handy for RHS Wisley Garden *(John Pettit, Andy Cunningham)*

☆ **Merstham** [Nutfield Rd; off A23 in Merstham, or follow Nutfield Ch, Merstham 2 signpost off A25 E of Redhill; TQ3051], *Inn on the Pond*: Individually furnished rambling country local with good choice of bar food (roast only, Sun), half a dozen well kept interesting ales, decent coffee, good service, piped radio; family conservatory, sheltered back terrace, views over scrubland (and small pond and nearby cricket ground) to N Downs *(Mrs G M E Farwell, BB)*

☆ **Mickleham** [Old London Rd; TQ1753], *Running Horses*: Popular refurbished 16th-c beamed village pub attractively placed nr Box Hill, interesting choice of food, well kept Tetleys-related real ales, two open fires, pleasant and comfortable newish dining extension/conservatory; nice view from pretty courtyard garden *(J S M Sheldon, Ian Phillips, John Pettit, G W and I L Edwards)*

☆ **Mogador** [from M25 up A217 past 2nd roundabout, signed off; TQ2452], *Sportsman*: Interesting and welcoming low-ceilinged local with almost a cult following, quietly placed on Walton Heath, popular with walkers and riders; well kept Pilgrims Progress and Wadworths 6X, good if not cheap food inc Sun lunch (bookable tables), friendly service, darts, bar billiards; dogs welcome if not wet or muddy; tables out on common, on back lawn, and some under cover *(Jenny and Brian Seller, W A Evershed, Owen Upton)*

Newdigate [TQ2042], *Six Bells*: Popular local with good choice of usual food *(J and M Ratcliff, Mrs C Watkinson)*; [Parkgate Rd], *Surrey Oaks*: Interesting layout, rustic lantern-lit booth seating off flagstoned beamed core with big log fire, friendly atmosphere; good big garden with rockery and water feature; usual bar food, Sun carvery, Tetleys-related ales, games area; children welcome *(Anthony Byers, Roger and Jenny Huggins, K D and C M Bailey, LYM)*

☆ **Norwood Hill** [Leigh—Charlwood back rd; TQ2343], *Fox Revived*: Attractive cottagey old-fashioned furnishings in spacious bare-boards country pub, good value food inc some interesting dishes in big double dining conservatory, Tetleys-related ales, pleasant atmosphere, spreading garden *(Jason Caulkin, LYM)*

Oatlands [Anderson Rd; TQ0965], *Prince of Wales*: Attractive and cosy, with lively friendly atmosphere, well kept real ales, two coal fires; restaurant *(Mike Davies)*

☆ **Ockham** [Ockham Lane – towards Cobham; TQ0756], *Hautboy*: Spectacular red stone Gothick building, now a small hotel, but with pubby feel and good food in character upstairs brasserie bar, darkly panelled and high-raftered, with oil paintings and minstrels gallery; friendly service, table on cricket-view terrace and in secluded orchard garden; chintzy bedrooms *(Susan and John Douglas, BB)*

Ockley [TQ1439], *Old School House*: Good value generous food esp fresh fish in bar and restaurant, friendly service, good wines, wonderful log fire *(Mrs R Maxwell, J S M Sheldon)*

☆ *nr* **Ockley** [Oakwoodhill – signed off A29 S; TQ1337], *Punch Bowl*: Friendly, welcoming and cosy country pub with huge inglenook log fire, polished flagstones, lots of beams, well kept Badger Best and Tanglefoot and Wadworths 6X, wide choice of decent bar food, lots of traditional games, juke box (can be loud); children allowed in dining area, tables outside with flower tubs and maybe weekend barbecues; has been open all day *(Dave Braisted, Ted Burden, Winifrede D Morrison, J S M Sheldon, Mr and Mrs D Carter, LYM)*

☆ **Ottershaw** [222 Brox Rd; TQ0263], *Castle*: Comfortable and friendly, with plethora of farm tools etc, stripped brick and beamery, decent food (popular for business lunches), well kept changing Tetleys-related and other real ales, open fire, no-smoking dining area; garden with tables in pleasant creeper-hung arbour *(Andy Giles, Martin Richards, Ian Phillips)*

☆ **Outwood** [off A23 S of Redhill; TQ3245], *Bell*: Friendly and attractive 17th-c country dining pub recently extended and refurbished for the late 1990s, olde-worlde main bar, wide choice of food which can be eaten here or in sparser restaurant area, indoor barbecues, summer cream teas, good choice of well kept ales, log fires, children welcome, has been open all day; pretty garden with country views *(E G Parish, Mrs K I Burvill, Margaret Dyke, LYM)*

☆ **Outwood** [from village head out towards Coopers Hill and Prince of Wales Rd], *Dog & Duck*: Welcoming rambling beamed country cottage, open all day, with good mix of furnishings, huge log fires, half a dozen well kept Badger and guest ales, popular food all day, lots of board games etc; children in restaurant, tables outside *(RH, Andy and Jill Kassube, B N J Tye, G S B G Dudley, David Hedges, LYM)*

Oxshott [Leatherhead Rd (A244); TQ1460], *Bear*: Youngs pub with well kept beer, conservatory dining room, friendly courteous staff, usual pub food with fresh veg, occasional summer barbecues in small garden *(Richard Payne, PR)*

☆ **Oxted** [High St, Old Oxted; TQ3951], *Crown*: Good choice of well kept ales and wide choice of good value food in Elizabethan pub with Victorian-panelled upper dining bar, busier and livelier downstairs bar, friendly efficient staff; children welcome weekends *(John Ingham)*

Peaslake [TQ0845], *Hurtwood*: Former Forte small prewar country hotel in fine surroundings, doing well since recent independence, with good individually prepared bar food (worth the wait) and well kept local Hogs Back ale in friendly village bar; popular restaurant, comfortable bedrooms *(Stephan Freeman, E N Burleton, BB)*

Puttenham [Seale Lane; SU9347], *Good Intent*: Lots of atmosphere, good range of attractively presented reasonably priced food, constantly changing range of real ales, Inch's farm cider, roaring log fire, very friendly *(Ian Phillips)*

Puttenham [Hook Lane; just off A31 Farnham—Guildford; SU9347], *Jolly Farmer*: Well presented standard Harvester bar food in good helpings, help-yourself salad bar, welcoming efficient young staff, several comfortable rooms with an overall Victorian feel, well kept Courage Best and Directors, children welcome; picnic tables outside *(G C Hackemer, LYM)*

Ranmore Common [3 miles S of Effingham; TQ1451], *Ranmore Arms*: Very welcoming relaxed service, big log fire, well kept Courage-related ales, bar food, unusual building as if once cafe or bungalow but olde-worlde inside; lots of tables outside, with barbecues – the play houses have seen better days *(Ron Gentry)*

☆ **Redhill** [St Johns; TQ2650], *Plough*: Small welcoming old-fashioned pub with interesting bric-a-brac, open fires, well kept Tetleys-related ales, reasonably priced food inc vegetarian, friendly efficient staff *(Andy and Jill Kassube)*

Reigate [Doversgreen Rd, Doversgreen (A217 S); TQ2647], *Beehive*: Very hospitable, good food, pleasant staff *(W L G Watkins)*

☆ **Reigate Heath** [3 miles from M25 junction 8, off Dorking-bound A25 via Flanchford Rd and Bonnys Rd; TQ2349], *Skimmington Castle*: Quaint country pub up bumpy track, with character bar and cosy rooms off (one no smoking), Flowers IPA and Greene King IPA and Abbot, usual bar food (only snacks Sun lunch, not Sun evening); dogs allowed, tables outside with pretty views, good walks *(J S M Sheldon, David Peakall, LYM; more reports on new regime please)*

☆ **Ripley** [High St; TQ0556], *Ship*: Wide choice of reasonably priced well prepared mainly home-made lunchtime bar food from sandwiches up in welcoming 16th-c local with low beams, flagstones, cosy nooks, log fire in vast inglenook; well kept Courage-related beers, very friendly efficient service, small raised games area with bar billiards, window-seats and stools rather than chairs; small high-walled terrace *(Stephen Barney, Bill Capper, Ian Phillips, Michael Launder)*

Ripley [High St], *Anchor*: Old-fashioned low-ceilinged connecting rooms in Tudor inn with usual bar food, games in public bar, well kept Tetleys-related ales, tables in coachyard *(Steve Mott, R B Crail, BB)*; [High St], *Half Moon*: Pleasant open-plan local refurbished in current rather bare style, with well kept Adnams, Fullers and guest ale such as Brakspears or Wadworths 6X from central servery, bar snacks, interesting quiet piped music *(Mike Davies, Gilly S-G)*; [Newark Lane (B367 Pyrford rd], *Seven Stars*: Friendly young people's local with generous food inc special Fri/Sat suppers *(Simon Fisher, Beccy Harvey)*

Rowledge [Cherry Tree Rd; SU8243], *Cherry Tree*: Well kept Courage Best and Directors, good food, interesting landlady, traditional country-pub atmosphere, garden with play area *(Sian Thrasher)*

Send [Cartbridge; TQ0155], *New Inn*: Nice spot by canal with appropriate memorabilia, good value generous food, Tetleys-related and other ales, cheerful staff; piped music *(Ian Phillips, G W and I L Edwards)*

☆ **Sendmarsh** [Marsh Rd; TQ0454], *Saddlers Arms*: Friendly and atmospheric partly beamed local with well kept Tetleys-related ales, good reasonably priced food inc vegetarian and Sun lunch, lots of brasses inc warming pans and ladles, some toby jugs, back room hung with whisky-water jugs; notable Christmas decorations, tables outside *(G W Edwards, Ian Phillips)*

Shackleford [Pepperharrow Lane; SU9345], *Cyder House*: Wide range of well kept ales inc Piston Broke and Old Shackle brewed here, farm ciders, good food inc children's, very friendly obliging staff, firm pine furniture, piped pop music, picnic tables on back lawn; nice village setting *(Lesley Sones, D J Underwood)*

Shalford [Broadford Rd; TQ0047], *Parrot*: Big canalside pub with very clean bars, ample helpings of tasty good value bar food, separate pleasant conservatory grill restaurant, several well kept real ales, friendly efficient staff; attractive garden *(Mrs H M T Carpenter, Steve Goodchild, Ian Phillips)*

☆ **Shepperton** [Church Sq (off B375); TQ0867], *Kings Head*: Immaculate old pub in quiet and attractive square, inglenook fireplace, neat panelling, oak beams, highly polished floors and furnishings, various discreet little rooms, big conservatory extension; good value unpretentious bar food, well kept Courage-related and other ales, attentive service, sheltered back terrace; children welcome, open all day Sat *(Ian Phillips, John and Christine Simpson, Ron Corbett, LYM)*

☆ **Shepperton** [Russell Rd], *Red Lion*: Attractive old wisteria-covered pub in nice spot across rd from Thames, plenty of tables on terrace among fine displays of shrubs and flowers, more on lawn over road (traffic noise) with lovely river views and well run moorings; quick bar food, well kept Courage-related ales with a guest such as Fullers London Pride, restaurant, very friendly staff *(David Sweeney, Nigel Flook, Betsy Brown)*

☆ **Shepperton** [152 Laleham Rd], *Bull*: Small unassuming local with good simple food at sensible prices inc bookable Sun lunch (food area themed as teddy bears' picnic), well kept Courage, Tetleys and Morlands Old Speckled Hen, friendly helpful staff, tables outside; live music some nights; bedrooms with own bathrooms *(David Sweeney, Ian Phillips, Ron Corbett)*

Shepperton [Watersplash Rd, off B376 to Laleham], *Barley Mow*: Consistently good, with nice atmosphere, pubby decor, decent food (not Sun evening), well kept beer; bedrooms *(Ron and Sheila Corbett)*; [Shepperton Lock, Ferry Lane], *Thames Court*: Busy 1930s pub with striking upper gallery overlooking Thames and moorings; quiet nooks and corners in low-lit lower panelled bar, roomy mezzanine, well kept Bass and Flowers IPA, bar food, children in eating area; popular with older people lunchtime, pleasant service, attractive Thamesside garden *(B and K Hypher)*; [Church Sq], *Warren Lodge*: Comfortable hotel bar with big picture window overlooking pretty Thamesside garden, good value evening restaurant; bedrooms *(Ian Phillips)*

☆ **Shere** [village signed off A25 3 miles E of Guildford; TQ0747], *White Horse*: Striking half-timbered medieval pub in beautiful village, uneven floors, massive beams, oak wall seats, two log fires, one in a huge inglenook, Tudor stonework – very ancient and atmospheric and a delight to look around; also functions as a Chef & Brewer dining pub which has not seemed on top form in the last year or so; tables outside, children in eating area *(John Pettit, Sarah and Jamie Allan, G R Sharman, Maurice Southon, LYM)*

Shere [Shere Lane], *Prince of Wales*: Quick obliging service, decent food, well kept Youngs, tropical fish, nice garden; children allowed *(John Pettit)*

☆ **South Godstone** [Tilburstow Hill Rd; TQ3648], *Fox & Hounds*: Welcoming low-beamed pub, cosy and comfortable, with well kept Greene King, good generous reasonably priced food, old prints, some high-backed settles, relaxing garden *(Graham Pettener)*

☆ **Staines** [124 Church St; TQ0471], *Bells*: Cosy and welcoming, with well kept Courage-related ales, wide choice of popular simple food, friendly staff, traditional furnishings and central fireplace, darts, cribbage, fruit machine, quiet juke box; plenty of seats in big garden *(Ian Phillips, Simon Collett-Jones)*

☆ **Staines** [The Hythe; S bank, over Staines Bridge], *Swan*: Splendid Thamesside setting, well kept Fullers ales, friendly helpful staff, tables on pleasant riverside verandah, conservatory, good value food in bar and restaurant; moorings; bedrooms comfortable *(George Atkinson, M P Naworynsky, Martin Kay, Andrea Fowler, LYM)*

Staines [Moor Lane], *Swan on the Moor*: Welcoming pub on green, seeming deep in country, with well kept ales such as Adnams, Boddingtons, Camerons and Wadworths 6X, good range of decent bar food, good garden with lots of picnic tables and big aviary *(Ian Phillips)*; [1 Penton Rd], *Wheatsheaf & Pigeon*: 1920s Courage pub with good food in largish bar/lounge and small dining area, esp fresh fish – evenings may be booked weeks ahead; known locally as the Wee & Pee *(Ian Phillips)*

Sunbury [Thames St, Lower Sunbury; TQ1068], *Flower Pot*: Quiet and pleasant, with attentive cheerful young staff, good home-made food esp apple and cherry pie; separate dining area *(Rhoda and Jeff Collins)*; [64 Thames St], *Magpie*: Pleasantly refurbished, with good views from street-level upper bar, riverside gardens, Gibbs Mew beers, reasonably priced food; bedrooms *(Ian Phillips)*

☆ **Sutton** [Raikes Hollow; B2126 – this is the Sutton near Holmbury St Mary; TQ1046], *Volunteer*: Attractive good-sized terraced garden in lovely quiet setting, low-beamed traditional bar with bric-a-brac and military paintings, Tetleys and Courage-related ales, decent wines inc port, quickly served food *(Winifrede D Morrison, David Hedges, R B Crail)*

Tadworth [Box Hill Rd; TQ2256], *Hand in Hand*: Roomy extended pub, handy for Box Hill, with well kept Courage, good simple bar food inc Sun lunch, friendly service *(John Pettit)*

☆ **Tandridge** [off A25 W of Oxted; TQ3750], *Barley Mow*: Refurbished under welcoming new management, roomy but quite cosy bar, log fires, attentive service, modest range of bar food, restaurant with strong Italian leanings; no music or games machines, big garden; interesting church nearby, good walks to Oxted or Godstone *(M D Hare, W J Wonham)*

☆ **Tandridge** [Tandridge Lane, off A25 W of Oxted], *Brickmakers Arms*: Good atmosphere in popular and pretty country dining pub, dating to 15th century but much extended and modernised, with good range of freshly made food inc some German dishes and lots of fish (no cold snacks Sun), well kept Whitbreads-related ales, decent wines inc local ones, restaurant with good log fires, prompt friendly service *(D and K Pinks, Gordon Smith, J R Tunnadine, Mark and Nicola Willoughby, Margaret and Nigel Dennis, Tamzie and Duncan Hollands)*

Tatsfield [Westmore Green; TQ4156], *Old Ship*: Bass, Charrington IPA and Worthington, lots of interesting pictures and bric-a-brac, good value varied food inc Sun lunch in restaurant with log fire, friendly helpful staff *(G W and I L Edwards)*

Thames Ditton [Weston Green Rd; TQ1567], *Harrow*: Doing well under new managment, decent food, prompt efficient service, well kept beer, unobtrusive piped music *(W L G Watkins)*

Thorpe [Sandhills Ln; Thorpe Green; TQ0268], *Rose & Crown*: Particularly good outdoor children's area with play things and pets' corner; Courage and Theakstons ales, friendly efficient staff, wide range of decent food *(Christopher Gallop)*

☆ **Thursley** [just off A3 SW of Godalming; SU9039], *Three Horseshoes*: Recently refurbished cosy and polished country pub, not cheap but good, with two good log fires, well kept Gales HSB and BBB, country wines, well presented food, prompt friendly service, tables in attractive back garden with barbecues; restaurant; has been open all day Sat *(Jenny and Brian Seller, Brenda Laing, Charles Hobbis, Ian Phillips, LYM)*

☆ **Tilford** [SU8743], *Barley Mow*: The star's for the setting between river and geese-cropped cricket green nr ancient oak, with waterside garden; decent mainly home-made food (helpings not that big), good service, well kept Courage ales, good open fire in big inglenook, comfortable traditional seats around scrubbed tables, interesting prints; small back eating area, weekend afternoon teas; darts, table skittles *(Mr and Mrs Williams, Martin and Karen Wake, Tim Galligan, Joy and Paul Rundell, G C Hackemer, G and M Stewart, Jenny and Brian Seller)*

Upper Halliford [TQ0968], *Goat*: Good buffet starters, pleasant efficient service and surroundings *(Ron and Sheila Corbett)*

Virginia Water [Callow Hill; TQ0067], *Rose & Olive Branch*: Comfortable Morlands pub with guest beer such as Theakstons, good range of genuinely home-cooked food, friendly helpful service *(Ian Phillips, G B Longden)*

☆ **Walton on Thames** [50 Manor Rd, off A3050; TQ1066], *Swan*: Three-bar riverside Youngs pub with lots of interconnecting rooms, huge neatly kept garden leading down to Thames, attractive restaurant, good moderately priced generous food, well kept ales, friendly service; moorings, riverside walks *(Ian Phillips, R B Crail, Mayur Shah, John and Christine Simpson)*

Walton on Thames [Riverside, off Manor Rd], *Anglers Tavern*: Unassuming ordinary pub tucked away on the Thames towpath, first-floor river-view restaurant, some peaceful tables out by the boats; boat hire next door *(Ian Phillips, Mayur Shah)*; [Church St], *Regent*: Very cheap beers and average-priced food in new Wetherspoons pub on site of former cinema, a bit barn-like *(R B Crail)*; [Sunbury Lane], *Weir*: Wide range of good food, elderly all-wood decor, lots of pictures, big terrace with picnic tables and superb view over river and weir; lovely towpath walks *(Romey Heaton)*

☆ **Walton on the Hill** [Chequers Lane (fairly handy for M25 junction 8); TQ2255], *Chequers*: Pleasant mock-Tudor Youngs pub with several rooms rambling around central servery, well kept ales, good value quick lunchtime bar food, restaurant (children allowed here), friendly service, terrace and neat sheltered garden with good summer barbecues; evenings busy with younger people; trad jazz Thurs *(Ian Phillips, Adrian Zambardino, Debbie Chaplin, LYM)*

☆ **Walton on the Hill** [Deans Lane], *Blue Ball*: Facing common nr duck pond, cosily refurbished, well run and much enjoyed by enthusiastic regulars (some of whom have followed the tenants here from their previous pub the Fox & Grapes in London SW19); wide choice of decent well priced food, good atmosphere, smart staff, five Courage-related and other ales, decent New World wines, big garden with barbecue; restaurant open all day Sun *(Sir Simon Tilden and others)*

☆ **Walton on the Hill** [Walton St], *Fox & Hounds*: Decent food esp puddings in chatty bar and pleasant adjoining restaurant (must book), well kept Bass, Fullers London Pride and two other ales, brisk service, nice surroundings *(Ian Phillips, Andy and Gill Plumb, LYM)*

☆ **Warlingham** [Limpsfield Rd, Worms Heath; TQ3857], *Botley Hill Farmhouse*: Converted farmhouse, more restaurant than pub, but good generous reasonably priced bar food too, and well kept (but rather pricy) ales such as Boddingtons, Flowers, Greene King, Pilgrims and Shepherd Neame Spitfire; friendly efficient service, children welcome, with attractions for them; cream teas, wonderful North Downs views, good walking country; very busy weekends, with live music *(D and J Tapper, Gareth Woodward-Jones, Duncan Forsyth, Mrs H M Cook)*

West Byfleet [behind stn; TQ0460], *Claremont*: Roomy, with cheap simple food, good young atmosphere, two pool tables, fruit machines and video games *(Rob Andrews)*

☆ **West Clandon** [The Street; TQ0452], *Bulls Head*: Friendly and comfortably modernised 16th-c country local, very popular esp with older people lunchtime for good value enjoyable food (same food evenings, can be quiet then), raised inglenook dining area, bookable Sun lunch, good waitress service, Courage Best, Marstons Pedigree and Wadworths 6X, decent wine, welcoming long-serving landlord, small lantern-lit bar with open fire and some stripped brick, old local prints, games room with darts and pool; lots of tables and good play area in garden, convenient for Clandon Park, good walking country *(D P and J A Sweeney, DWAJ, John Pettit, Ian Phillips, G W and I L Edwards, R B Crail)*

☆ **West Horsley** [The Street; TQ0753], *Barley Mow*: Attractive traditional village local, flagstones, beams, extraordinary collection of pig ornaments, well kept ales inc Greene King, decent wines and spirits, good value lunchtime food, small restaurant *(John and Heather Dwane, Anthony Byers)*

West Horsley [The Street], *King William IV*: Comfortable and relaxing, very low beams but plenty of space, well kept Courage Directors and Best and Harveys, log fire, welcoming staff; usual food inc children's *(John Pettit, P J Keen)*

☆ **Westcott** [A25; TQ1448], *Crown*: Friendly busy local with attentive staff, interesting decor, generous fresh food, good coffee, small back games room; lovely cottage garden *(S J Penford, T A Bryan)*

Westcott [A25], *Prince of Wales*: Cheerful fairly modern local, sensible choice of well prepared good value bar food *(Brian and Jenny Seller, John Pettit)*

☆ **Weybridge** [Cross Rd/Anderson Rd, off Oatlands Dr; TQ0764], *Prince of Wales*: Attractively restored and friendly, with relaxed country-local feel, good choice of reasonably priced bar food, well kept ales such as Adnams, Boddingtons, Fullers London Pride, Tetleys and Wadworths 6X, ten wines by the glass, coal-effect gas fires, imaginative restaurant menu *(R B Crail, Ian Evans, James Nunns)*

Weybridge [Thames St], *Farnell Arms*: Reliably good value well cooked food inc generous roasts, well kept Badger Best, Tanglefoot and Hard Tackle *(R B Crail)*; [Princes Rd], *Jolly Farmer*: Warm and cosy, with interesting reasonably priced food, well kept and priced Fullers London Pride; lovely garden with terrace and barbecue, nr cricket ground *(Maurice Southon)*; [Thames St], *Old Crown*: Friendly old-fashioned three-bar waterside pub, Courage-related and other ales, decent range of food *(Ian Phillips, Comus Elliott)*; *Volunteer*: Pleasant and unassuming, fresh flowers and prints, tables inc nice big bay-window one, gentle piped classical music; fresh unusual food, events such as beaujolais nouveau breakfast *(Sue Grossey)*

☆ **Windlesham** [Chertsey Rd], *Brickmakers Arms*: Popular well run dining pub with good interesting food esp fish, cheerful busy bar, well kept Courage and other ales, wide choice of wines, very friendly service, daily papers; well behaved children allowed in restaurant, attractive garden with boules and barbecues, lovely hanging baskets *(Guy Consterdine, Bob Atkinson, Ian Phillips, Joy and Paul Rundell)*

☆ **Windlesham** [A30/B3020 junction; SU9264], *Windmill*: Eleven interesting well kept real ales changing weekly, two or three beer festivals a year with massive choice and live music; one long bar, separate side room, busy welcoming atmosphere, youngish customers; friendly landlord, good range of country wines, decent food, unobtrusive piped music; some seats outside *(Richard Houghton, Dr M Owton, Dr C P Dell, Mike Davies, Joy and Paul Rundell)*

Windlesham [Church Rd], *Half Moon*: Big lively friendly local, very wide range of well kept ales inc Fullers London Pride, Wadworths 6X and guests like Adnams Best, Batemans XXXB, Smiles Exhibition and Theakstons, good value straightforward food inc good Sun family lunch, cheerful quick service, modern furnishings, log fires, piped music, silenced fruit machine, interesting WWII pictures; huge beautifully kept garden popular with families *(R B Crail, Dr M Owton, MD, Mrs C Blake, Mike Davies)*

☆ **Witley** [Petworth Rd (A283); SU9439], *White Hart*: Largely Tudor, with beams, good oak furniture, inglenook fireplace where George Eliot drank; good range of well kept ales, very wide choice of good value food, friendly staff; seats outside, play area *(Charles Hobbis, G Washington)*

Wood Street [White Hart Lane; SU9550], *White Hart*: Country local dating from 16th century, good choice of well kept real ales inc five changing guests, big bar area set out for diners *(Richard Houghton, Tim Lake, Robert May)*

Worcester Park [Cheam Common; TQ2266], *Old Crown*: Good value generous varied food in comfortable pub pleasantly done out in beamed farmhouse style, Courage-related ales, friendly staff, restaurant; garden *(G W and I L Edwards, John Sanders)*

Worplesdon [Fox Corner; SU9854], *Fox*: Doing well under current friendly owners, rural atmosphere, occasional guest ale, bar food inc good ploughman's and any sandwich of your choice; big garden with swings *(Lucienne Suter, Steve Merson)*; [A322 Guildford—Bagshot], *White Lion*: Square red brick roadhouse, airy and pleasant, with standard food, Courage and Hook Norton beers *(Thomas Nott)*

☆ **Wotton** [A25 Dorking—Guildford; TQ1247], *Wotton Hatch*: Traditional little low-ceilinged tiled-floor front bar with open fire, central locals' bar with games, interesting well cooked food, well kept Fullers, friendly staff, decent wines, family restaurant and conservatory; garden with play area and impressive views *(Gwen and Peter Andrews, Winifrede D Morrison, LYM)*

Wrecclesham [Sandrock Hill Rd; SU8245], *Sandrock*: Good range of well kept ales mostly from smaller breweries in simply converted local, real fire, no piped music, friendly staff, games room and garden *(G C Hackemer, Lucienne Suter, Steve Merson)*

Sussex

Sussex is full of fine pubs, with a good deal of character – just as well, as this is where our editorial offices are now housed. Among the best at the moment are the rustic little Rose Cottage at Alciston, the unspoilt Blue Ship near Billingshurst, the smart foody George & Dragon at Burpham, the cheap and cheerful Six Bells at Chiddingly (new family extension), the very welcoming Old House At Home at Chidham, the White Harte in Cuckfield (good lunchtime value), the Elsted Inn at Elsted (great country cooking), the civilised Griffin at Fletching (a favourite for food), the Halfway Bridge at Lodsworth (doing very well all round, but especially for food), the Crabtree at Lower Beeding (another most enjoyable dining pub) and the tucked-away Bull at Ticehurst. Of these, the Elsted Inn, the Griffin, the Halfway Bridge and the Crabtree are tops for really enjoyable meals out, and to them we'd add a fine new main entry, the Horseguards at Tillington; from this shortlist we choose as Sussex Dining Pub of the Year the Elsted Inn at Elsted. Other interesting new main entries here this year are the Blacksmiths Arms at Donnington, the Royal Oak at East Lavant (a lovely find), and the idiosyncratic Snowdrop in Lewes. In the Lucky Dip section at the end of the chapter pubs we'd particularly pick out (most inspected and approved by us) include the Black Horse at Amberley, Cricketers at Berwick, Anchor Bleu at Bosham, George & Dragon near Coolham, Lamb in Eastbourne, Anglesey Arms at Halnaker, Sussex Brewery in Hermitage, Black Jug in Horsham, George & Dragon at Houghton, Hare & Hounds at Stoughton, White Horse at Sutton, Lamb at West Wittering and New Inn at Winchelsea. There's a good interesting choice in Brighton. Drinks in the county cost more than the national average. In our price survey we found that pubs supplied by the Sussex firms of Harveys and King & Barnes tended to be cheaper than those supplied by the national breweries. The two cheapest places we found were the Bull at Ticehurst (a free house stocking beers from local breweries including a fine new one called Rother Valley) and the thriving Italian-run Golden Galleon near Seaford (brewing its own).

ALCISTON TQ5005 Map 3

Rose Cottage (food award)

Village signposted off A27 Polegate—Lewes

One of a minority of pubs to be in the same family for more than one generation is this rustic little wisteria-covered cottage. Perhaps this explains why the once-common Sussex custom of long-rope skipping on Good Friday lunchtime to make the crops grow faster lives on here. It's not surprising that the genuinely old-fashioned charm of this warmly traditional place makes it a real favourite with locals and some readers. Small and cosy it soon fills up, so get there early for one of the half-dozen tables with their cushioned pews in the relaxed and friendly well used bar – under quite a forest of harness, traps, a thatcher's blade and lots of other black ironware, with more bric-a-brac on the shelves above the dark pine dado or in the etched glass windows. In the mornings you may also find Jasper, the talking parrot.

Most people come for the very good promptly served food, which includes wholesome soup of the day, a proper ploughman's (£3.50), sausages and chips (£3.75), honey roast ham (£5.50), scampi (£6.25) and 10oz rump steak (£8.95) and daily blackboard specials such as a fresh fish of the day, cheesy topped garlic mussels (£3.65 or £6.95), rabbit and bacon pie, turkey or chicken and ham pie (£4.95), beef and ale pie (£5.50), char-grilled leg of lamb steak with cream of tarragon sauce or wild rabbit in cream and mustard sauce (£6.25) or local venison braised in port and Guinness (£7.95). There's a lunchtime overflow into the no-smoking restaurant area; service is welcoming and efficient, though it may stop promptly. Well kept Harveys and a guest like Morlands Old Speckled Hen on handpump; Merrydown cider and five decent wines by the glass, bottle or half litre including a wine of the month; log fires, maybe piped classical music. There are some seats under cover outside, and a small paddock in the garden has geese, ducks and a chicken. House martins and swallows return year after year to nests above the porch, seemingly unperturbed by the people going in and out beneath them. *(Recommended by Tony Hobden, Colin Laffan, R and S Bentley, Dave Braisted, Norma Farris, Ian Phillips, E N Burleton, E G Parish, Alan Skull, R D Knight, T A Bryan, James Nunns, R J Walden, Adrian and Gilly Heft, Ben Grose)*

Free house ~ Licensee Ian Lewis ~ Real ale ~ Meals and snacks (till 10, 9.30 Sun) ~ Evening restaurant (not Sun) ~ (01323) 870377 ~ Children in eating area and restaurant ~ Open 11.30-2.30, 6.30-11; closed 25, 26 Dec

ALFRISTON TQ5103 Map 3

Star

One of the main reasons for visiting this fairly smart old Forte hotel is the wonderfully atmospheric front part of the building which was built in the 15th c by Battle Abbey as a guest house for pilgrims. The facade is particularly worth a look, as it's studded with curious medieval carvings, mainly religious. The striking red lion on the corner – known as Old Bill – is more recent, and was probably the figurehead from a wrecked Dutch ship. Amongst the antiquities in the bustling heavy-beamed bar is a wooden pillar that was once a sanctuary post; holding it gave the full protection of the Church, and in 1516 one man rode a stolen horse from Lydd in Kent to take advantage of the offer – and so avoid the death penalty. Elegant furnishings include a heavy Stuart refectory table with a big bowl of flowers, antique windsor armchairs worn to a fine polish and a handsome longcase clock; the fireplace is Tudor. The simple bar menu includes home-made soup (£1.95), sandwiches from (£2), filled baked potato (from £2.95), ploughman's (from £4.25), salads (from £3.50) and blackboard specials. There's also a no-smoking lounge. Bass on handpump, a good range of wines by the glass and malt whiskies; service is excellent, with nothing too much trouble. The comfortable bedrooms are in an up-to-date part at the back. Board games are available, and if you're staying they can arrange a wide range of activities. *(Recommended by E G Parish, P Gillbe, J E Hilditch)*

Free house (Forte) ~ Manager Richard Hobden ~ Real ale ~ Meals and snacks (snacks only Sun) ~ Restaurant ~ (01323) 870495 ~ Children in eating area ~ Open 11-3, 6-11 ~ Bedrooms: £83.25B/£106B

ASHURST TQ1716 Map 3

Fountain 

B2135 N of Steyning

Behind the Georgian facade of this delightfully unspoilt old place is a charmingly rustic 16th-c country pub, quite foody at times, but with a strong local following that makes sure it never loses its relaxed traditional feel. The tap room on the right is the one to head for, with its scrubbed old flagstones, a couple of high-backed wooden cottage armchairs by the log fire in its brick inglenook, two antique polished trestle tables and usually six well kept real ales on handpump or tap. The range typically might include Adnams Broadside and Extra, Courage Best and Directors, Fullers London Pride, John Smiths, Youngs Special. A bigger carpeted room with its orginal beams and woodburning stove is where most of the popular homecooked bar food is served: fresh cod or quiche (£5.55), vegetables in light pastry (£6.45), steak and kidney pie or suet and bacon pudding (£6.95) and poached salmon in light pastry (£8.45); Sunday roasts (£6.95). Service is cheery and efficient, but can slow down at busy periods; booking is advisable in the evenings. A gravel terrace has picnic tables by an attractive duckpond, and there are swings and a see-saw (and regular barbecues) in the pretty enclosed garden with fruit trees and roses. They have a cheery black labrador; shove-ha'penny. They've recently extended the restaurant, and an adjoining barn has been converted into a function room with skittle alley. *(Recommended by Romey Heaton, Margaret and Nigel Dennis, Winifrede D Morrison, Tony and Wendy Hobden, Mrs S M Lee, Jenny and Brian Seller, Dave Irving, David Holloway, Alison Burt, Pippa Bobbett, John Beeken, R and S Bentley)*

Free house ~ Licensee Maurice Caine ~ Real ale ~ Meals and snacks ~ Restaurant (not Sun evening) ~ (01403) 710219 ~ Children in restaurant till 8pm ~ Open 11-2.30, 6-11; closed evenings 25, 26 Dec

nr BILLINGSHURST TQ0925 Map 3

Blue Ship

The Haven; hamlet signposted off A29 just N of junction with A264, then follow signpost left towards Garlands and Okehurst

Genuinely simple, this charmingly quiet and unpretentious little pub is tucked away down a remote country lane. In winter the friendly bar is a cosy haven with a blazing fire, and in summer you can relax at the tree-shaded side tables or by the tangle of honeysuckle around the front door. The completely unspoilt beamed and brick-floored front bar has a hatch service and an inglenook fireplace, and a corridor leads to a couple of similar little rooms; there may be a couple of playful cats. Straightforward bar food includes dishes like sandwiches (from £1.70), ham and vegetable soup (£2.35), ploughman's (from £3.30), macaroni cheese (£3.95), cottage pie (£4.15), lasagne (£4.95), steak and kidney pie or scampi (£5.50), and puddings like fruit crumble, treacle tart or gateaux (all £2.30); good helpings and service. Well kept King & Barnes Broadwood, Sussex and winter Old tapped from the cask. A games room has darts, bar billiards, shove-ha'penny, cribbage and dominoes. It can get crowded with a pleasant mix of the educated middle aged, country locals and pleasant young people, particularly at weekends. There's a large beer garden with a play area. They have a gun club and run their own shoot. *(Recommended by Peter Lewis, Tony and Wendy Hobden, John Fahy, J S M Sheldon, Peter Lewis, A M Pickup, Bruce Bird; more reports please)*

King & Barnes ~ Tenant J R Davie ~ Real ale ~ Meals and snacks (not evenings Sun or Mon) ~ (01403) 822709 ~ Children in two rooms without bar ~ Open 11-3, 6-11 (closed 25 Dec evening)

BLACKBOYS TQ5220 Map 3

Blackboys

B2192, S edge of village

The string of old-fashioned and unpretentious little rooms at this partly black-weatherboarded 14th-c inn have dark oak beams, bare boards or parquet, lots of bric-a-brac, antique prints and a good inglenook log fire. There's rather a good atmosphere in the spacious bar on the left where you'll find a novel version of ring-the-bull – ring-the-stag's-nose which one of the friendly locals will happily explain, darts, shove-ha'penny, dominoes, table skittles, cribbage, space game, and a juke box. A big range of good waitress-served home-made food includes rack of spare ribs (£4.95), seafood pancake or tagliatelle arabbicata (£5.50), steak and kidney pie (£5.95) and baked crab mornay with garlic prawns (£7.95). Well kept Harveys

Armada, BB, Pale Ale and seasonal brews on handpump and cask conditioned cider. There's masses of space outside, with rustic tables in the back orchard, some seats overlooking the pretty front pond, a play area with an exciting wooden castle and quite a few animals, and a barn with a big well equipped playroom. *(Recommended by B R Shiner, Colin Laffan, Alan Skull; more reports please)*

Harveys ~ Tenant Patrick Russell ~ Real ale ~ Meals and snacks (12-2.30, 6.30-10) ~ Restaurant ~ (01825) 890283 ~ Children in restaurant ~ Open 11-3, 6-11; closed evening 25 Dec

BRIGHTON TQ3105 Map 3

Cricketers

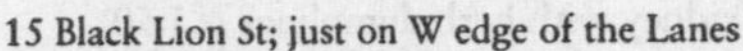

15 Black Lion St; just on W edge of the Lanes

Not far from the seafront you'll find this cheery bustling town pub. The two down-to-earth, friendly and smallish pubby rooms are really atmospheric with Victorian furnishings and lots of bric-a-brac like old record sleeves, musical instruments, hot-water bottles, lots of engraved glass and red plush, and copper and brass, and even a stuffed bear. As the chef is a vegetarian you are likely to find quite a few interesting meat-free daily specials like red bean and aubergine moussaka (around £4.50); other specials like pork and stilton pie (£4.50). The printed menu includes sandwiches (from £1.55), ploughman's (from £2.60), filled baked potatoes (from £2.75), giant yorkshire pudding (£3.75), steak and kidney pie (£4.25), fresh grilled plaice (£4.65), and home-made puddings (from £1.75). Well kept Courage Directors, Morlands Old Speckled Hen and Youngs Special tapped from the cask; efficient service. The pub is popular with students and young people in the evenings, but at lunchtimes the customers are a little more mixed, and the atmosphere and music nicely old-fashioned. The side courtyard is now covered and forms part of the eating area. When built in the 16th c it was called the Laste and Fishcart and used by the London fishbuyers from the nearby market. It got its new name when James Ireland had a cricket field nearby (now houses). *(Recommended by Margaret and Roy Randle, Gill Earle, Andrew Burton, R J Walden, Dr Keith Clements, Sheila Keene, Mrs C A Blake, Sir Simon Tilden, John and Mavis Wright, Barbara and Norman Wells, JM, PM, Chris and Anne Fluck, Simon Collett-Jones, Russell and Margaret Bathie)*

Courage ~ Lease: Jan Jackson and Steve Hannington ~ Real ale ~ Meals and snacks (all day Weds-Sat, not Sun or Mon evening) ~ Restaurant (not Sun or Mon evening) ~ (01273) 329472 ~ Children in restaurant ~ Brazilian and Latin American Sun evening ~ Open 11-11

BROWNBREAD STREET TQ6715 Map 3

Ash Tree

Village signposted off the old coach road between the Swan E of Dallington on B2096 Battle—Heathfield and the B2204 W of Battle, nr Ashburnham

In a delightfully isolated hamlet tucked away down narrow country lanes nestles this warmly welcoming 400-year-old pub. The cosy beamed bars – candlelit at night – have three inglenook fireplaces, stripped brickwork, nice old settles and chairs. Very good bar food includes sandwiches (from £1.50), soup (£1.95), crab mousse (£3.95), beef curry or steak and kidney pie (£4.95), chicken, ham and mushroom pie (£5.45), diced beef with walnuts, pork and vegetables, lamb with rosemary, tomatoes and wine or chicken breast with calvados (£5.50), seasonal game dishes (from £5.50), seafood parcel (£6.95), and puddings like boozy coffee pudding, apricot mousse and date and walnut flan (£2.50). Well kept Fullers London Pride, Harveys Best, Morlands Old Speckled Hen and a guest on handpump. Darts, pool, shove-ha'penny, cribbage, dominoes, fruit machine, video game and a discreet juke box in the simple games room on the left; classical piped music. There's a pretty garden with picnic tables; new licensees this year. *(Recommended by D L Barker, Mr and Mrs R D Knight, Robert Huddleston, Tim and Pam Moorey; more reports please)*

Free house ~ Licensees Malcolm and Jennifer Baker ~ Real ale ~ Meals and snacks (not Mon) ~ Restaurant ~ (01424) 892104 ~ Children in eating area and restaurant ~ Open 12-3, 7-11; closed Mon

BURPHAM TQ0308 Map 3

George & Dragon

Warningcamp turn off A27 a mile E of Arundel, then keep on up

It's worth booking as this smart and comfortable pub gets very busy with people gathering for the very popular good bar food which might include sandwiches (from £2.40, club sandwiches £4.25), soup (£2.60), ploughman's (£3.50), filled baked potatoes (from £3.60), chicken breast filled with garlic (£6.95) and daily specials like avocado with Selsey crab (£4.95), steak and kidney with herb dumplings (£5.50), duck and black cherry pie (£6.50) and skate wing and capers (£8.25), and a delicious selection of home-made puddings like white chocolate mousse, summer pudding or sticky toffee pudding (all £2.70). The immaculately kept spacious and civilised open plan bar has good strong wooden furnishings and an interesting range of constantly changing beers such as Arundel Best, Ash Vine, Cotleigh Courage Directors, Hop Back and Timothy Taylors Landlord, on handpump or electric pump; lots of Irish whiskies. It's charmingly set in a remote hill village of thatch and flint, and there are splendid views down to nearby Arundel Castle and the river. The nearby partly Norman church has some unusual decoration. No dogs. *(Recommended by Colin Laffan, T J Moorey, Derek and Sylvia Stephenson, Mrs Romey Heaton, TOH, John Fahy, M A Gordon Smith, Tina and David Woods-Taylor, R W Tapsfield, N Bushby, W Atkins, Derek and Maggie Washington, David Holloway, Alison Burt, R T and J C Moggridge, Peter Lewis, Jenny and Brian Seller, Mr and Mrs A H Denman, G Washington, Tim and Pam Moorey, Tony and Wendy Hobden)*

Belchers Pubs ~ Tenants James Rose and Kate Holle ~ Real ale ~ Meals and snacks (till 9.45; not Sun evening in winter) ~ Restaurant (not Sun evening) ~ Arundel (01903) 883131 ~ Occasional live music ~ Open 11-2.30, 6-11; closed Sun evenings 1 Nov until Easter

BURWASH TQ6724 Map 3

Bell

A265 E of Heathfield

There's a nice genuinely pubby atmosphere in the friendly L-shaped bar on the right which has an armchair by its big log fire (two fires if it's cold), all sorts of ironwork, bells and barometers on its ochre Anaglypta ceiling and dark terracotta walls, and well polished built-in pews around tables. The room on the left is broadly similar, but quieter (and greener); darts, shove-ha'penny, table skittles, cribbage, dominoes, trivia and piped music. Well kept Batemans XB, Federation Buchanan's Best, Gales HSB and Harveys on handpump, and some new world wines. Under the chirpy new manager bar food includes sandwiches (from £2.50), ploughman's (from £2.95), a couple of vegetarian meals like a huge salad (£3.50) or vegetable lasagne, hot dishes such as home-made steak and kidney pie, chilli or curry (around £4.50), fresh fish with crab and lobster in season, and puddings like home-made apple pie and cheesecake. The bedrooms (oak beams, sloping floors) are fairly basic and the road can be noisy at night. The pub is mentioned in Kipling's *Puck of Pook's Hill*, and is handy for Batemans, the lovely Jacobean ironmaster's house the writer made his home. Seats in front of this flower-covered mainly 17th-c local look across the road to the pretty village's church. Car park at the back. *(Recommended by Fiona Dick, A and J Hoadley, Norma Farris, D A Edwards, R D Knight, J E Hilditch)*

Free House ~ Lease: Colin and Gillian Barrett and Sarah Jennings ~ Real ale ~ Meals and snacks (not Sun evening) ~ Restaurant (not Sun evening) ~ (01435) 882304 ~ Children welcome till 9.30 ~ Open 11-3.30, 5.30-11 ~ Bedrooms: £25B/£35B

BYWORTH SU9820 Map 2

Black Horse

Signposted from A283

There's a particularly attractive garden at this old pub, and the top tables on a steep series of grassy terraces, sheltered by banks of flowering shrubs, look across a drowsy valley to swelling woodland. A small stream runs along under an old willow by the more spacious lawn at the bottom. There's a relaxed and informal atmosphere in the simple bar with basic scrubbed wooden tables, pews and bare floorboards. The log fires may not always be lit in winter when there may be a paraffin heater or two. Bar meals include large baguettes (£3.65), soup (£2.75), filled baked potatoes (£3.95), ploughman's (£3.95), and daily specials such as spaghetti bolognaise (£5.25), fisherman's pie (£6.50), john dory with prawn and caper sauce (£7.25), chicken with lemon and black pepper (£8.50) and halibut with fennel and celery (£8.75); children's meals (£3.50). It can be busy at weekends, especially in summer, so it's worth booking then. Well kept changing beers like Ballards Best, Fullers London Pride, Gales HSB and Youngs Ordinary on handpump, good wines; efficient service; darts, shove ha'penny, cribbage. *(Recommended by Mrs M Rice, Tom and Rosemary Hall, Dr M V Jones, Karen and Graham Oddey, Viv Middlebrook, W K Struthers, John and Mavis Wright, Tony Hobden, Alan and Eileen Bowker, Philip and Trisha Ferris; more reports please)*

Free house ~ Paul Wheeler-Kingshott and Jenny Reynolds ~ Real ale ~ Meals and snacks (11.30-1.45, (till 2 at weekends), 6-9.45) ~ Restaurant ~ Petworth (01798) 342424 ~ Children in restaurant ~ Open 11-3, 6-11

CHIDDINGLY TQ5414 Map 3

Six Bells ★ £

Village signed off A22 Uckfield—Hailsham

It's quite a surprise to find such a cosmopolitan atmosphere in this beautifully remote part of the countryside. It's all down to the charismatic character of the quick-witted landlord Paul, who although born just up the road joined the navy and travelled the world in his early teens. If it's not busy he'll come over and chat to you just out of a natural welcoming curiosity and he'll certainly remember your face the next time you visit. The lovely old beamed rooms are full of characterful solid old wood furniture with some pews and antique seats, lots of fusty old artefacts and interesting bric-a-brac, and plenty of old pictures and posters including bits of local history and log fires. The recent sensitive extension provides some much needed family space; darts, dominoes and cribbage. A wonderful alliance of characterful locals and visitors of all types and ages from artists and musicians through chicken farmers and the very well heeled to friendly bikers gather in this really leisurely environment. One big draw is the tasty straightforward and extremely good value home-made bar food such as French onion soup (90p), a delicious selection of grilled french breads (from £1.10, the famous 'Paul's special' is well worth a try), meat or vegetarian lasagne (£1.85), steak and kidney pie (£2.40), filled jacket potatoes (from £2.70), ploughman's (from £3), cheesy vegetable bake or vegetable korma (£3.10), chilli con carne, chicken curry or spicy prawns Mexicano (£3.60), spare ribs in barbecue sauce (£3.75). Vegetables charged separately are 60p; generous puddings like raspberry pavlova or treacle tart (£2). In the evening at weekends there is some emphasis on the carefully segregated live music in the bareboarded bottom barn-like bar when it really does get very spirited and is probably not the time for a quiet meal, but if you enjoy the atmosphere of a London jazz venue then it's worth going for the good music Sunday lunchtime. Well kept Courage Best and Directors and Harveys on handpump or tap. Outside at the back, there are some tables beyond a big raised goldfish pond, and a boules pitch; the church opposite has an interesting Jeffrey monument. Nicely set where the Weald Way crosses the Vanguard Way, it's a pleasant area for walks. There are vintage and Kit car meetings outside the pub once a month. *(Recommended by K and E Leist, John and Mavis Wright, Ian Phillips, D L*

Barker, Michael Sargent, P J Caunt, Nicola Thomas, Paul Dickinson, Rob and Doris Harrison, Desmond Barker, Alan Skull, J E Hilditch)

Free house ~ Licensee Paul Newman ~ Real ale ~ Meals and snacks (11-2.30, 6-10) ~ (01825) 872227 ~ Children in family room ~ Jazz, blues and other live music in the barn Tues, Fri, Sat and Sun evenings, Jazz Sun lunch ~ Open 10.30-3, 6-11(12 Tue, Fri and Sat)

CHIDHAM SU7903 Map 2

Old House At Home

Cot Lane; turn off A259 (old A27) at the Barleycorn pub

This quiet and cosy out-of-the-way old place forms part of a peaceful cluster of farm buildings. An extensive range of very good food, in big helpings, includes sandwiches (from £1.50), filled baked potatoes (from £3), ploughman's (from £3.25), mussels in a cream and wine sauce (£3.75), salads (from £4.25), fisherman's pie (£4.95), steak and kidney pie (£5.25), grilled trout with almonds (£6.75), steaks (from £8), crab stuffed breast of chicken with white wine, cream and prawn sauce (£8.75), and a good selection of vegetarian dishes like chilli (£4.95) and mushroom and asparagus pie (£5.50); children's meals (£2.50). Booking is recommended for summer evenings. Even if lots of the customers appear to be eating the very genuinely friendly staff still have plenty of time for people coming for just a drink: well kept real ales such as Badger Best, Ringwood Best and Old Thumper, Old House (Burts Nipper), and a guest beer on handpump, as well as a good selection of country wines and several malt whiskies. The homely and welcoming timbered and low-beamed bar has Windsor chairs around the tables, long seats against the walls, a welcoming log fire and a large friendly German Shepherd. It's quite handy for good walks by Chichester harbour, and in summer has a couple of picnic tables on its terrace, with many more in the garden behind. *(Recommended by Ann and Colin Hunt, David Eberlin, Derek and Margaret Underwood, Kevin and Katherine Cripps, Lesley McEwen, Lawrence Pearse, Nigel Clifton, T M Fenning, Peter Lewis, Mr and Mrs R O Gibson, Keith Stevens, Rita Horridge, R T and J C Moggridge)*

Free house ~ Licensees Andy Simpson and Terry Brewer ~ Real ale ~ Meals and snacks (till 10) ~ Restaurant ~ (01243) 572477 ~ Children welcome ~ Open 11.30(12 Sat)-2.30(3 Sat), 6-11; closed evening 25 Dec

COWBEECH TQ6114 Map 3

Merrie Harriers

Village signposted from A271

Once a farmhouse, this white clapboarded village pub still has something of the cheery atmosphere of an old-fashioned farm parlour in the friendly public bar where you're still welcome to drop in for just a drink. The food is still well liked too, with the wide lunchtime menu including sandwiches (from £1.80), home-made soup (£2.25), filled cottage rolls, ploughman's (from £3.25), vegetarian quiche (£4.75), salads, steak and kidney pie (£6.50), various fresh local fish like grilled lemon sole (£9.95) and puddings like apple pie or summer pudding; in the evening they have dishes such as a mixed grill or steaks (from £8.95), and they do a good Sunday roast. Well kept Flowers IPA and Harveys Best on handpump, good choice of wines; friendly, professional service. The beamed and panelled public bar has a traditional high-backed settle by the brick inglenook as well as other tables and chairs, and darts; rustic seats in the terraced garden. *(Recommended by Robert Gomme, Christoper Turner, J H Bell, Colin Laffan; more reports please)*

Free house ~ Licensees J H and C P Conroy ~ Real ale ~ Meals and snacks ~ Restaurant ~ (01323) 833108 ~ Children in restaurant ~ Open 11-3, 6-11

We say if we know a pub has piped music.

CUCKFIELD TQ3025 Map 3

White Harte £

South Street; off A272 W of Haywards Heath

There is a rather appealing traditional feel at this pretty partly medieval tile-hung pub, with its beams, polished floorboards, some parquet and ancient brick flooring tiles, standing timbers, and small windows looking out on to the road. Furnishings in the public bar are sturdy and comfortable with a roaring log fire in the inglenook, and sensibly placed darts. The more comfortable partly carpeted lounge has a few local photographs, comfortable padded seats on a slightly raised area, some fairly modern light oak tables and copper-topped tables and a brick bar counter. The straightforward lunchtime food is very good value and popular so you need to get there early for a table: ploughman's (from £3), and salads, scampi and chips but most people tend to go for the five or so home-cooked bargain specials (£3.50) such as fisherman's, chicken and mushroom, turkey or steak and kidney pies, stuffed marrow and stilton and celery quiche – there is always one vegetarian option. The specials tend to go by about 1.30, so it pays to be there early. Well kept King & Barnes Bitter and Broadwood on handpump, popular landlord (who say's he's not as cheery as he used to be but we don't believe him) and pleasant friendly service; fruit machine, shove-ha'penny. The village is very pretty. *(Recommended by DWAJ, David Holloway, Terry Buckland, Mrs R D Knight)*

King & Barnes ~ Tenant Ted Murphy ~ Real ale ~ Lunchtime meals and snacks (not Sun) ~ (01444) 413454 ~ Well behaved children welcome in eating area of bar at lunchtime ~ Open 11-3, 6-11

DITCHLING TQ3215 Map 3

Bull

2 High St; B2112, junction with B2116

There's still masses of historical atmosphere at this beamed 14th-c building which continued to serve as the local courthouse even after it became a coaching inn. The peacefully relaxed main bar – undisturbed by music or machines – is attractively furnished with carpet strips on the bare boards, old oak chests and settles, striking elm and mahogany tables, a longcase clock, old prints and photographs above the wooden dado and an inglenook fireplace. Along with some other refurbishments and general smartening up the new licensees have turned the little snug into a comfortable family room. Good bar food includes tiger prawns in filo pastry (£3.80), home-cooked gammon or seafood platter (£5.50), a pint of garlic prawns (£6.25), steaks (from £9.50), and puddings like apple pie or bakewell pudding (£2.25), and a daily changing specials board which might include gammon, leek and tomato bake (£4.90), vegetarian dishes (from £4.70), quiches (£5.20), fresh fish (from £5.50) and steak and kidney pie or chicken and asparagus pie (£6.20). Well kept Boddingtons, Flowers Original, King & Barnes Sussex, Morlands Old Speckled Hen and Whitbreads on handpump; good selection of malt whiskies. The restaurant is no-smoking. Picnic tables in the good-sized pretty Downland garden which is gently lit at night look up towards Ditchling Beacon, and there are more tables on a suntrap back terrace; a reader tells us there is fairly good wheelchair access. The charming old village is a popular base for the South Downs Way and other walks. *(Recommended by Sheila Keene, Dr Keith Clements, David Holloway, Guy Consterdine, Frank Cummins, Peter Churchill, John Beeken, Colin Laffan, JM and PM, R J Walden, D A Edwards, Mavis and John Wright)*

Whitbreads ~ Lease: John and Jannette Blake ~ Real ale ~ Meals and snacks ~ Restaurant ~ (01273) 843147 ~ Children welcome in family snug and restaurant ~ Open 11-3, 6-11(11-11 Sat); closed evening Dec 25 ~ Bedrooms: £35.50B/£47.50B

Tipping is not normal for bar meals, and not usually expected.

DONNINGTON SU8502 Map 2

Blacksmiths Arms

South off A27 on to A286 signed Selsey, almost immediate left on to B2201

It's the really friendly welcome and relaxed atmosphere that make this homely little white roadside cottage a new main entry this year. The landlord – who'll possibly be standing at the bar discussing the day's races with the locals – will turn to shake your hand when you arrive and introduce the barmaid. The small down-to-earth rooms are completely crammed with bric-a-brac: the low ceilings densely hung with hundreds and hundreds of little jugs, walls crowded with Victorian prints and a grandfather clock, and an interesting old cigarette vending machine on the sill of one of the pretty little windows. The furniture on a patterned carpet is all solid and comfortable, including several 1950s sofas. Well kept real ales are usually Arundel Ostler, Bass, Badger Best, Fullers London Pride, Morlands Old Speckled Hen, Ringwood Best and Wadworths 6X on handpump. Bar food includes sandwiches (£1.60), ploughman's (£3.95), lasagne (£6.95), steak and kidney pie (£7.25), Selsey crab salad (£8.95), 10oz sirloin steak (£9.95), and children's dishes like baby whale fishcakes and pizzas (from £2); fruit machine and piped pop music. Set next to the road, it seems a shame that they haven't kept the garden as spic and span as inside, but children will find it hard to tear themselves away from the well fenced play area where the grass is virtually obscured by more ride-on-toys (some of them have seen better days) than this editor has ever seen, there's also a plastic tree house and swings. ***(Recommended by Ann and Colin Hunt, John and Tessa Rainsford, Bruce Bird, N E Bushby, Miss W E Atkins, Keith Stevens)***

Free house ~ Licensees Fergus and Gill Gibney ~ Real ale ~ Meals and snacks (till 10, not Sun evening or 25 Dec) ~ Restaurant (not winter Sun evening) ~ (01243) 783999 ~ Children welcome ~ Open 11-2.30, 6-11

EARTHAM SU9409 Map 2

George

Signposted off A285 Chichester—Petworth; also from Fontwell off A27 and Slindon off A29

There's a really friendly and personal welcome at this cheery bustling pub which is prettily set in a lovely part of the county. You need to arrive early to be sure of a table as they don't take table bookings and it is very popular for good well presented bar food which might include filled baked potatoes (from £2.95), farmhouse cottage rolls (from £3.35), duck and pigeon pie (£5.50), venison escalope (£8.25), fresh salmon (£8.45) and quite a few vegetarian dishes. Well kept Gales Best, BBB and HSB, Ringwood Fortyniner and Old Thumper and a guest which changes every three weeks on handpump; quick service by very helpful, courteous staff. The cosy lounge is pleasantly comfortable without being fussily overdecorated, and there's a pubbier public bar; both have a relaxed atmosphere despite being busy. Darts, shove-ha'penny, cribbage, fruit machine and piped music. no-smoking area in the restaurant. ***(Recommended by R T and J C Moggridge, John and Joy Winterbottom, Mr and Mrs Hawkins, Paul Robinshaw; more reports please)***

George Gale ~ Manager Andrew Harvey ~ Real ale ~ Meals and snacks ~ Restaurant ~ (01243) 814340 ~ Children welcome in eating area of bar and restaurant ~ Open 11-11 (winter 11-3, 6-11)

EAST LAVANT SU8608 Map 2

Royal Oak

Signed off A286 N of Chichester

Just a stones throw out of Chichester the atmosphere at this pretty little white house perched steeply above the narrow lane is gloriously peaceful. The very relaxed and spacious open plan bar with modest wood furniture is refreshingly cool in summer and wonderfully cosy with two open fires and a woodburner in winter. It's simply and cleanly decorated, relying on the good natural structure and substance of the building. Thick black skirting provides a pleasingly clean line between the almost bare cream and exposed brick walls and the turkey rugs on the mellow wood, brick and tiled floor. Two charming little sash windows at the front hung with simple dark green cotton curtains look straight on to two picnic tables in a profusion of mature shrubs and flowers crammed into a tiny little terraced front garden. Rambling around the back and side are more captivating little terraced bricked or grassed areas with some metal furniture, picnic-sets, a pergola, and tubs and baskets spilling with flowers and roses. Particularly good bar food includes lobster bisque (£3.95), filled baked potatoes or king prawns in filo pastry (£4.50), smoked salmon pâté (£4.95), mixed cheese salad platter (£5.75), peppers stuffed with ricotta and pine kernels with tomato sauce (£7.50), steak and Guinness pie or halibut supreme with chive and lemon sauce (£8.50), chicken breast with a tarragon and mushroom sauce or chicken marinated in fresh mint and rosemary and char-grilled (£9.50), seafood and avocado salad (£10.95). There is no children's menu but they will happily bring along a small plate. Well kept Gales BBB on tap and HSB and a guest chosen by the brewery like Adnams Extra on handpump are served from the brick bar. Very friendly service and landlord. Car park is across the road. *(Recommended by J H L Davies, J A Snell, Mike Forder, A J Blackler, Viv Middlebrook, Dr and Mrs A K Clarke, Phil and Sally Gorton, Jonathan Phillips)*

Gales ~ Tenant Stephen Spiers ~ Real ale ~ Meals and snacks ~ (01243) 527434 ~ Open 11-2.30(3 Sat), 6-11; closed 25 and 26 Dec

EASTDEAN TV5597 Map 3

Tiger 🍷

Pub (with village centre) signposted – not vividly – from A259 Eastbourne—Seaford

Usefully positioned on the South Downs Way, this low-beamed old-fashioned local is a lovely spot to stop at lunchtime and relax on the seats outside and take in the splendid setting. It's on the edge of a secluded, sloping green lined with low cottages, most of them – like the pub itself – bright with flowering climbers, roses and other flowers. The lane leads on down to a fine stretch of coast culminating in Beachy Head. It seems more idyllic than ever since the closure of the roads around the green, so not surprisingly it does get busy, especially in summer, when the green becomes a sort of overflow. The smallish rooms have low beams hung with pewter and china, traditional furnishings including polished rustic tables and distinctive antique settles, old prints and so forth. The only music you're likely to hear will be from the visiting Morris dancers. Regularly changing beers might include well kept Adnams Broadside, Boddingtons, Flowers Original and Harveys Best on handpump; decent choice of wines by the glass and several interesting vintage bin-ends. Under the new licensees varying bar food, in good helpings, includes a short but good choice of home-made dishes listed on a blackboard such as avocado with stilton mayonnaise or local sausage ploughman's (£3.95), fresh fish and chips (£4.95), tagliatelle carbonara (£5.25) and game stew with herb dumplings or fishcakes with dill mayonnaise (£5.95). Efficient service from helpful staff. *(Recommended by John Fahy, Colin Laffan, Keith Stevens, Brian Jones, RLW and Dizzy, Peter Churchill, Graham Pettener, Ben Grose, Alec and Marie Lewery)*

Free house ~ Licensees Jonathan Steel and Nicholas Denyer ~ Real ale ~ Meals and snacks (not Sun evening) ~ (01323) 423209 ~ Children welcome in upstairs room ~ Open 11-2.30, 6(winter 6.30)-11

ELSTED SU8119 Map 2

Elsted Inn ★ 🍴

Elsted Marsh; from Midhurst left off A272 Petersfield Rd at Lower Elsted sign; from Petersfield left off B2146 Nursted Rd at South Harting, keep on past Elsted itself

Sussex Dining Pub of the Year

As well as winning our award for Best Natural Cooking in last year's edition the licensees here recently contributed as users of mainly local fresh ingredients to Radio 4's Food Programme 'Food Miles Debate'. There is no doubt that their policy of using gloriously fresh local produce like local game, green Jersey cream, fine asparagus and soft fruit from a local farm, bread made locally at the National Trust Bakery at Slindon, free range eggs and English field-raised veal shines through in the splendid home-cooked food they serve in generous portions. From an imaginative changing selection dishes might include some old favourites like handcut sandwiches (from £2), ploughman's (from (£4.50), filled baked potatoes (from £4.75), spinach and walnut roulade (£6), Irish stew, braised oxtail or Sussex bacon pudding (£6.50), home-cooked ham salad, beef in beer pie or rabbit in mustard sauce (£7), game pie, steak and kidney pudding or chicken breast in cream and capers (£7.50), fresh crab salad (£8.25) and duck breast in honey and ginger or crab salad (£8.50), and puddings like blackcurrant cheesepots, treacle tart or dark chocolate mousse (from £2.75), and gorgeous home-made ice creams (from £2); they do children's helpings, and during the week they do a set two-course lunch (£6.50), quite often have themed evenings or even competitions like the best cake baked by a man! There's a separate cottagey candlelit dining room and they do take credit cards. As well as Fullers London Pride and a guest on handpump they keep all six locally brewed Ballards beers. Before Ballards moved some of the beers were brewed here by the landlord, and they still celebrate L'Ale Nouveau Night when a beer cask is rolled down the road to the pub from the brewery. The two friendly and cosy bars have simple country furniture on wooden floors, local photographs on the cream walls, an open fire in the Victorian fireplace, and two big friendly dogs; darts, dominoes, shove-ha'penny, cribbage, backgammon. Children are made very welcome and although dogs are welcome as well one area of the lovely sizeable enclosed garden with tables and boules is kept dog free. *(Recommended by Dr Keats, Lynn Sharpless, Bob Eardley, A, J and G, Bruce Bird, Roger Berry, J F Reay, Chris and Anne Fluck, Viv Middlebrook, Alan Skull, Tony and Susan McDonald, G Bint, Tony and Wendy Hobden, John and Joy Winterbottom, Peter Lewis, Ian Jones, Howard West)*

Free house ~ Licensees Tweazle Jones and Barry Horton ~ Real ale ~ Meals and snacks (12-3, 7-9.30) ~ Restaurant ~ (01730) 813662 ~ Children in eating area and restaurant ~ Folk music first Sun evening of the month ~ Open 11-3, 5.30(6 Sat)-11; closed evening 25 Dec ~ Bedrooms: £17.50/£30

Three Horseshoes ★

Village signposted from B2141 Chichester—Petersfield; also reached easily from A272 about 2 miles W of Midhurst, turning left heading W

Set at the end of a hamlet, the snug little rooms at this cosily old-fashioned 16th-c pub are full of rustic charm, with enormous log fires, antique furnishings, ancient beams and flooring, attractive prints and photographs, and night-time candlelight. Good regularly changing home-made food includes soups (£2.95), generous ploughman's with a good choice of cheeses (£4.50), avocado with stilton and a mushroom sauce topped with bacon (£4.95), chicken and bacon casserole with celery and fennel, rabbit and pigeon casserole (£6.95), steak, kidney and ale pie (£7.50), Scotch sirloin steak with spring onions, shallots and a red wine sauce and puddings like delicious treacle tart (you can take it away) or raspbery and hazelnut meringue (£2.95). Well kept changing ales racked on a stillage behind the bar counter might include Ballards Best and Golden Bine, Cheriton Pots and Diggers Gold, Fullers London Pride and Hook Norton Best to name a few – they tend to concentrate on brews from smaller breweries; farmhouse ciders and summer Pimms. Service is friendly and obliging, and the staff stay smiling even when busy; darts, dominoes and cribbage. The prettily-planted and recently tidied garden with its free-roaming Bantams has wonderful views over the South Downs. *(Recommended by Gill and Mike Cross, T Roger Lamble, A J Blackler, K G Mather, Angela and Alan Dale, John Evans, R K Knight, Nigel Wikeley, Wendy Arnold, S Demont, T Barrow, Clive Gilbert, John Sanders, Lynn Sharpless, Bob Eardley, A G Drake)*

Free house ~ Licensee Andrew Beavis ~ Real ale ~ Meals and snacks (not winter Sun evenings) ~ Restaurant ~ (01730) 825746 ~ Well behaved children in eating area and restaurant ~ Open 11-2.30(3 Sat), 6-11; closed Sun night from October to Easter

FIRLE TQ4607 Map 3

Ram

Signposted off A27 Lewes—Polegate

The bustling bars of this simple family-run village pub are still mainly unspoilt, with comfortable seating, soft lighting, log fires in winter, and a nice, convivial feel; the snug is no smoking. Well kept Harveys Best, Otter Bitter, Mansfield Old Bailey and Worthington on handpump, and decent wines (including three produced locally). Cooked by the landlord's son, the daily changing choice of good bar food might include local sausages with oven baked, mixed mashed potato, red cabbage, onion and cheese (£5.15), homity pie or broccoli or mushroom tart (£5.85), seafood pie (£5.95) and steak and mushroom pudding or chicken and mushroom pie (£8.15). Darts, shove-ha'penny, dominoes, cribbage and toad in the hole. The gents' has a chalk board for graffiti, and there are tables in a spacious walled garden behind. Nearby Firle Place is worth visiting for its collections and furnishings, and the pub is handy for a particularly fine stretch of the South Downs, and for Glyndebourne. *(Recommended by D L Barker, SRP, D A Edwards, F M Steiner, JM, PM, John Beeken, Margaret and Nigel Dennis, Adrian and Gilly Heft, Mavis and John Wright, Dick Brown, LM, D S Cottrell)*

Free house ~ Licensees Michael and Keith Wooller and Margaret Sharp ~ Real ale ~ Meals and lunchtime snacks ~ (01273) 858222 ~ Children in non-serving bars till 9pm ~ Folk 2nd Mon and 1st, 2nd 4th Wed in month, and piano Sat lunchtimes ~ Open 11.30-3, 7-11; closed evening Dec 25 ~ Bedrooms: £50(£60S)

FLETCHING TQ4223 Map 3

Griffin ★

Village signposted off A272 W of Uckfield

This old country inn in a pretty spot just on the edge of Sheffield Park is one of those genuinely civilised and enthusiastic places that just naturally keeps on getting everything exactly right. The imaginative daily changing seasonal menu is especially good and might include dishes like chilled carrot and mint soup (£3.25), salad of roasted red onions and parmesan (£3.95), chicken and wild mushroom terrine (£4.25), and main courses like foccaccio filled with salami, mozzarella and tomato (£4.50), chilli (£5.95), feta, sundried tomato and baby sweetcorn salad (£6.25), spicy spare ribs (£6.50), steak and Guinness pie or rabbit pie (£6.95), and puddings like sticky toffee pudding, crushed soft fruit and meringue or ice cream like brown bread and armagnac (£3.25). It's worth going on a Thursday when they have their fish night and the menu could include hot prawn curry (£6.95), grilled brill with butter and Pernod sauce (£7.95), chicken and monk fish kebab with chilli, lemon grass and coriander (£8.95) or a salad of char-grilled tuna with tartare sauce (£10.95). Every Sunday in spring and summer if the weather is fine there's a barbecue with maybe a spitroast pig or lamb. Well kept Badger Tanglefoot, Fullers London Pride, Harveys Best and a changing guest on handpump, a very good wine list including some English ones and several New World, and various cognacs and malt whiskies; pleasant friendly service. The beamed front bar has a cosy and relaxed 1930s feel – straightforward furniture, squared oak panelling, some china on a delft shelf, a big corner fireplace, and a small bare-boarded serving area off to one side. The landlord may be playing the piano. A separate public bar has darts, pool, pinball, fruit machine, video game, juke box and chess and backgammon. Picnic tables under cocktail parasols on the back grass have lovely rolling Sussex views; there are more tables on a sheltered gravel terrace which is used for dining on warm evenings, and volleyball can be played on the Sheffield lawn. Three of the four attractively individual bedrooms have four-posters. They can be terribly busy at weekends in summer, and, probably because they're so pushed, the generally high standards of food can wobble a little then. *(Recommended by R J Walden, R and S Bentley, John Beeken, Alan Skull, Julie Peters, Colin Blinkhorn, John and Tessa Rainsford, Jill Bickerton, Alan and Eileen Bowker, Margaret and Nigel Dennis, David R Shillitoe, Cathryn and Richard Hicks, Tony and Wendy Hobden, SRP, E D Bailey, Richard Bowden, Christopher P Glasson, D A Edwards, Tim Barrow, Sue Demont, Joan and John Calvert, Jamie and Ruth Lyons, Mr and Mrs A Dale, Winifrede D Morrison, Nicola Thomas, Paul Dickinson, John and Mavis Wright, J S M Sheldon, Colin Laffan, Mr and Mrs Heron)*

Free house ~ Licensees James and Nigel Pullan and John Gatti ~ Real ale ~ Meals and snacks (till 10 Fri, Sat) ~ Restaurant (not Sun evening) ~ (01825) 722890 ~ Children welcome ~ Piano Fri/Sat evenings, Sun lunchtime ~ Open 12-3, 6-11; 11.30-11 Sat, closed 25 Dec ~ Bedrooms: /£55B

FULKING TQ2411 Map 3

Shepherd & Dog

From A281 Brighton—Henfield on N slope of downs turn off at Poynings signpost and continue past Poynings

This charmingly atmospheric little pub used to sell illicit liquor to thirsty shepherds on their way to Findon sheep fair and the partly panelled cosy bar still has shepherds' crooks and harness on the walls, as well as antique or stoutly rustic furnishings around the log fire, with maybe fresh flowers on the tables. Popular well prepared bar food in decent helpings from a changing choice might include sandwiches (from £3, smoked salmon £4.95), moules marinières (£4.50), a wide choice of ploughman's (from £4.25), a vegetarian dish like vegetable pancakes or lasagne (£5.25), beef and Guinness pie (£6.50), big summer salads (£5.95), lemon sole (£6.50), trout (£6.95), a fresh whole wing of skate with whole grain mustard and capers (£7.50), tender sirloin steak (£9.50), and delicious home-made puddings such as chocolate torte or banoffi pie (all £2.75). Try and get there early, especially if you want a prime spot by the bow windows; service can slow down at the busiest times (summer weekends, maybe). Well kept Courage Directors, Harveys BB, and Websters Yorkshire on handpump, plus a couple of changing guests, often from smaller breweries. The series of pretty planted grassy terraces, some fairy-lit, with a little stream running down to the big stone trough, and an upper play lawn sheltered by trees, have views across to the sweeping downs, and a path leads straight up to the South Downs Way. *(Recommended by Mrs M Rice, John and Mavis Wright, R Suddaby, Ian Jones, T Roger Lamble, David Eberlin, Dr Keith Clements, J Dobson, Frank Cummins, Christopher P Glasson, Mark Percy, David Holloway, Simon Small, R D Knight)*

Free house ~ Licensees Anthony and Jessica Bradley Hull ~ Meals and snacks ~ (01273) 857382 ~ Open 10-3(winter 2.30), 6-11; Sat 11-11; closed 25 Dec

GUN HILL TQ5614 Map 3

Gun 🛏

From A22 NW of Hailsham (after junction with A269) turn N at Little Chef

The Wealden Way runs through the lovely country garden of this big country inn which is prettily decked with clematis, honeysuckle and hanging baskets. They don't mind muddy boots, and indeed that sort of customer-comes-first thinking is very much the keynote of the place; plenty more flowers, and fairy-lit trees, in the big well hedged garden, which also has a big play area and some seating in a recently refurbished barn. Inside the busy, well-run and notably friendly warren of rooms there are alcoves under the oak beams, and although most of the furnishings are aimed at diners, there are some more individual pieces, with brasses, copper, pewter, prints and paintings on the panelled walls. In one corner is an Aga, still used for cooking in the winter, and there are several open fires, one in a fine inglenook; a couple of areas are no-smoking. Some oak floorboards from the original 15th-c building which was badly damaged long ago by fire were discovered by chance a couple of years ago when they took up the carpets. Well kept Harveys, Flowers Original and Larkins and a guest like Brakspear or Marstons on handpump, a good choice of wines by the glass, farm ciders, country wines and freshly squeezed fruit juice; cheery young service, with a good mix of ages among the many customers (they don't mind small children). Tasty good value food includes soup (£2.50), onion pie or pasta with a tomato sauce and ricotta and chedder sauce (£5.60), marinaded breast of chicken, poached and served on a bed of spinach with a cheese and wine sauce (£5.80), whole black bream stuffed with prawns, cucumber and herb (£6.80) and lots of fresh fish from Newhaven such as haddock, plaice or lobster and crab when available. They mark the healthiest dishes on the menu, and use wholesome, low-fat ingredients wherever possible. There may be a slight delay at busy periods. Cream teas in the afternoon. *(Recommended by Mr and Mrs Albert, Eddie Edwards, John Beeken, Roger Bellingham, Ian Phillips, Alec and Marie Lewery, Colin Laffan, W A Putland, James House, S G N Bennett, Dick Brown)*

Free house ~ Licensees R J and M J Brockway ~ Real ale ~ Meals and snacks (12-10; winter 12-2, 6-10) ~ (01825) 872361 ~ Children in eating area of bar ~ Open 11-11 inc Sun (11-3 6-11 winter); closed 25 and 26 Dec ~ Bedrooms: £26(£30B)/£32(£36B)

HARTFIELD TQ4735 Map 3

Anchor

Church Street

A delightful mix of all types of customers mingle comfortably at this welcoming old local on the edge of Ashdown Forest. Old advertisements and little country pictures decorate the walls above the brown-painted dado, and there are houseplants in the brown-curtained small-paned windows of the cheerful heavy-beamed bar, with a woodburner, which rambles informally around the central servery. There's a good choice of beers, with very well kept Boddingtons, Flowers Original, Fremlins, Harveys best, Marstons Pedigee and Wadworths 6X on handpump, in addition to guest ales such as Adnams Broadside, Larkins Porter, Palmers Tally Ho and Theakstons Old Peculier. The front verandah soon gets busy on a warm summer evening, when the usual relaxed and contented atmosphere is even more evident than usual. Good bar food includes sandwiches (from £1.30), soup (£2), filled baked potatoes (from £2.50), ploughman's (from £3), pâté (£3.25), sausage and chips, vegetable curry or cheese and spinach pancake (£3.50), cod niçoise (£4.25), spicy seafood pancake or tagliatelle with crab and spinach in a cheese sauce (£4.75), steak sandwich (£5), beef kebab with cumberland sauce (£8), puddings (from £1.50), and children's menu (£2.50); quick friendly service. Darts in a separate lower room; shove ha'penny, cribbage, dominoes, and piped music. It's only been a pub since the last century, but dates back much further, with spells as a farmhouse and women's workhouse. There's a play area in the popular garden and dogs are welcome. *(Recommended by Colin Laffan, D A Edwards, David Peakall, Nigel Wikeley, the Shinkmans; more reports please)*

Free house ~ Licensee Ken Thompson ~ Real ale ~ Meals and snacks (till 10) ~ Restaurant (not Sun evening) ~ (01892) 770424 ~ Children welcome ~ Open 11-11; closed evening 25 Dec ~ Bedrooms: £25S/£35S

nr HEATHFIELD TQ5920 Map 3

Star

Old Heathfield – head East out of Heathfield itself on A265, then fork right on to B2096; turn right at signpost to Heathfield Church then keep bearing right; pub on left immediately after church

This very ancient place – prettily placed and well out of Heathfield itself – has been an inn ever since it was built in 1328 so its massive irregular stonework would have seen pilgrims resting from their way along this high ridge across the Weald to Canterbury. There is a wonderfully historic atmosphere in the L-shaped beamed bar which has rustic furniture, some panelling, murals depicting a connection with the founding of Jamestown in America, as well as window seats and tables by a huge inglenook fireplace which is particularly cosy in cold weather. The really good bar food includes dishes like a dozen anchovy fillets with minced onion and crusty bread (£4.65), mussels in saffron, white wine, garlic and cream (£4.95), smoked fish platter, smoked duck breast or half a shoulder of lamb (£7.95) and lobster tails (£10.95). The restaurant is partly no smoking. Well kept Harveys Best, King and Barnes Sussex and two guests on handpump; darts, shove ha'penny, cribbage, dominoes and piped music. Turner painted the lovely view of rolling oak-lined sheep pastures that you get from the imaginatively planted sloping garden, and it really is impressive. There's a hedged-off children's play area and a floating population of rabbits, cats and birds – maybe even an owl and a couple of peacocks. The neighbouring church is also rather interesting, with its handsome Early English tower. *(Recommended by Colin Laffan, John Collard, Jason Caulkin, Hilary Dobbie, R K Knight, Roger Price, Mr and Mrs J Stern, Jill Bickerton)*

Free house ~ Real ale ~ Lease: Mike and Sue Chappell ~ Meals and snacks (not Sun evening) ~ Restaurant ~ (01435) 863570 ~ Children welcome ~ Jazz some Sundays ~Open 11.30-3, 5.30-11

KINGSTON NEAR LEWES TQ3908 Map 3

Juggs

The Street; Kingston signed off A27 by roundabout W of Lewes, and off Lewes—Newhaven road; look out for the pub's sign – may be hidden by hawthorn in summer

This 15th-c tile-hung cottage, covered with roses in summer, was named for the fish-carriers who passed through between Newhaven and Lewes, and there's still a lovely old fashioned country feel. Inside the medley of furnishings and decorations in the rambling beamed bar is one of the most interesting we know of in the area, with particularly good prints, pictures and postcards on the walls. Bar food includes good open sandwiches (from £2.75), taramasalata or ploughman's (£2.95), local sausages (£2.95), pitta bread with grilled ham, tomato, mushrooms and cheese or chicken tikka (from £4.25), an interesting vegetarian dish (£4.50), very good huge steak and kidney pudding (£7.50), daily specials such as caramelised onion and parmesan cream quiche, mushroom roast with tomato sauce, three cheese potato bake or chicken curry, and good puddings like bread and butter pudding or red berry brûlée (£2.50); children's meals (£2). The restaurant and another small area are no smoking. An unusual and rather effective electronic bleeper system lets you know when meals are ready, and it's worth getting there early, they do get busy. Particularly well kept Harveys Sussex, King & Barnes Broadwood and a guest on handpump, with a wider choice than usual of non-alcoholic drinks and a wine of the month; helpful, welcoming service; log fires, dominoes, shove-ha'penny. There are a good many close-set rustic teak tables on the sunny brick terrace; a neatly hedged inner yard has more tables under cocktail parasols, and there are two or three out on grass by a timber climber and commando net. *(Recommended by David Holloway, Bruce Bird, Martin Jones, Dr Keith Clements, Frank Cummins, R J Walden, Barbara and Norman Wells, LM, Alec and Marie Lewery, Alan Skull, Andrew Partington, Julian Holland)*

Free house ~ Licensees Andrew and Peta Browne ~ Real ale ~ Meals and snacks (not Sun lunchtime) ~ Restaurant (not Sun lunchtime) ~ (01273) 472523 ~ Well behaved children away from bar servery area ~ Open 11-3, 6-10.45(Sat 11); closed Dec 25, 26, evening Jan 1

KIRDFORD TQ0126 Map 3

Half Moon

Opposite church; off A272 Petworth—Billingshurst

Fresh fish – and a very good range of it – is the outstanding feature at this 17th-c family run inn. Carefully chosen by the licensees who have links with Billingsgate going back 130 years they may include such rarities as tile fish, porgy, parrot fish, soft shell crabs, Morton Bay bugs, scabbard fish, razor shells, mahi mahi, and baramundi (all from around £10, though higher for some of the more unusual dishes). Do remember though that fresh fish is seasonal, so there may be times when the range isn't as big as you might hope. They also do more familiar fish like sword fish, bass, lobster, tiger prawns and snapper, as well as dishes like sandwiches (from £1.90), home-made soup (£2.50), ploughman's (£4.20), good salads, home-made lasagne or steak and kidney pie (£5.50). Well kept Arundel Best, Boddingtons, Flowers Original, Fullers London Pride and Youngs Special, some under light blanket pressure; local wine, ciders and apple juice. Service is friendly and welcoming, but can slow down when they get busy. The simple partly flagstoned bars are kept ship-shape and very clean; darts, pool, cribbage, dominoes; piped music. The restaurant is partly no-smoking. There's a big garden with swings, a large boules area and a barbecue area at the back, and more tables in front facing the pretty village's church. *(Recommended by J S M Sheldon, Winifrede D Morrison, C H and P Stride, John and Mavis Wright, R B Crail, Joan G Powell, Michael J Boniface, Guy Consterdine, LM, Ron Gentry, R D Knight, Martin Richards, Rosemary and Maxine, Clem Stephens, M A Gordon Smith)*

Whitbreads ~ Lease: Anne Moran ~ Real ale ~ Meals and snacks ~ Restaurant ~ (01403) 820223 ~ Children welcome till 9pm ~ Occasional live music ~ Open 11-3, 7-11

LICKFOLD SU9226 Map 2

Lickfold Inn

This elegantly restored Tudor inn has a wonderfully characterful garden that spreads over a good few interestingly planted levels, each with a couple of private little seating areas. There may be barbecues out here in summer. In winter big log fires in the enormous brick bar fireplace create a lovely cosy atmosphere and cast subtly flickering shadows on the antique furnishings. In summer the fires are replaced by more tables, but at any time you'll still find the smart Georgian settles, heavy Tudor oak beams, handsomely moulded panelling, and ancient herringbone brickwork under rugs. Chalked up on a blackboard, the changing home-made bar food might include lunchtime sandwiches (from £1.75), ploughman's, sausage or ham, egg and chips or filled baked potatoes (£3.95) and lunchtime and evening lasagne or liver, bacon and onion (£5.95), winter oxtail stew, steak and kidney pie, chicken tikka or strips of beef in chilli sauce (£6.25), and puddings such as home-made ginger pear dumplings, treacle tart or local ice creams (£2.50); good Sunday roast lunches. Well kept Fullers ESB and London Pride and four to six guests such as Adnams Best, Badger Best and Tanglefoot, Ballards Best, Harveys Best or Hop Back Summer Lightning ; good coffee. Note they don't allow children. *(Recommended by G C Hackemer, Mrs M Rice, R W Flux, Guy Consterdine, David Holloway, Alison Burt, Keith and Audrey Ward, J S M Sheldon, Susan Handley, Howard West, Alec and Marie Lewery, Ian Phillips, J F Reay)*

Free house ~ Licensees Ron and Kath Chambers ~ Real ale ~ Meals and snacks (not Sun or Mon evenings) ~ (01798) 861285 ~ Open 11-2.30(3 Sat), 6-11; closed Mon evenings, 25 Dec ~ Bedrooms: £25B/£50B

LEWES TQ4110 Map 3

Snowdrop

South Street; off Cliffe High Street, opp S end of Malling Street just S of A26 roundabout

Dwarfed below a great chalk cliff, this straightforward brick building is named for something much grimmer than you'd imagine – the Christmas Eve avalanche of 1836, when hundreds of tons of snow falling from the cliff demolished several houses on this spot, burying nine people alive. You can see a dramatic painting of the event in Anne of Cleves House (Southover High Street). As something of an alternative main entry for the GPG, the interior is a decided oddity, its decor like the Steptoes' living room crossed with a ship's cabin, with a glorious profusion of cast iron tables, bric-a-brac and outlandish paraphernalia that no doubt owes much to the next-door antique shop. Unfolding the rather dreamlike maritime theme, downstairs there are three ships' figureheads dotted around, walls covered with rough sawn woodplank and upstairs a huge star chart painted on a dark blue ceiling, and a sunset sea mural with waves in relief. There's a very laid-back atmosphere, quiet at lunchtime but a young people's preserve, and lively to match, in the evenings, when the juke box can be loud. They serve no red meat and the light hearted menu includes sandwiches (from £1.50), moules Brit, burritos or large home-made pizzas (from £4.25, seafood £6), Sunday roast free range chicken, a fresh fish like trout or smoked salmon salad (£4.50), garlic prawns (£5), and lots of vegan and vegetarian dishes like burgers (£2.50), lasagne, stuffed marrow or brown rice with stir fried vegetables (£3.50), vegan pasta (£4), and good value puddings like Jamaican banana, chocolate fudge cake or summer fool (£1.25-£2); small portions for children. Five (occasionally up to seven) well kept real ales such as Brewery on Sea Avalanche, Gales HSB, Harveys Hop Back Summer Lightning and Raindance (a wheat beer), Shepherd Neame Spitfire on handpump, good coffee, friendly licensees; pool, chess, cards and a giant chess board in the car park. There are a few tables in the garden. ***(Recommended by Caroline Driver, P Simms; more reports please)***

Free house ~ Licensees Tim and Sue May ~ Real ale ~ Meals and snacks 12-3(2.30 Sun), 6(7 Sun)-9 ~ (01273) 471018 ~ Children under supervision ~ Live jazz Mon evening and probably live music Fri and Sat night ~ Open 11-11 (closed 25 Dec)

LODSWORTH SU9223 Map 2

Halfway Bridge ★

A272 Midhurst—Petworth

This bright and roomy smartly civilised family-run pub is really doing very well at the moment. There is tremendous attention to detail in all aspects of its running which makes for a delightfully pleasing visit. Along with the impressive welcome and friendly atmosphere, service is generally faultless, with good personal touches. The inventive and impeccably home-cooked food comes in a sensibly stylish range that might include moules marinières (£3.95), fish soup with rouille and croûtons (£4.50), feta cheese and garlic olives or venison sausages with bubble and squeak (£4.95), lamb's liver and bacon, chicken with spinach, mushrooms and apricots or steak sandwich (£5.95), kidneys in Dijon and fromage frais (£6.25), parma ham and parmesan salad (£6.50), grilled lamb chops (£6.95), skate in black butter and capers (£8.50), poached salmon with Dijon and tarragon sauce (£8.95), grilled sirloin with tomato and basil sauce (£9.50), and fresh local game in season. Home-made puddings like walnut treacle tart or gooseberry and cinnamon crumble (£3), and various Sunday roasts; it gets busy at weekends so booking is advisable. The three or four comfortable rooms loop around the central servery. Attractive fabrics have been used for the wood-railed curtains and pew cushions, alongside good oak chairs and an individual mix of tables (many of them set for dining). Down some steps the charming country dining room with stripped boards has a dresser and longcase clock. Log fires include one in a well polished kitchen range (this area is no smoking). On the walls are paintings by a local artist. A good range of well kept beers includes well kept Cheriton Pots Ale, Flowers Original and Gales HSB, a guest like Adnams or Fullers London Pride, and a dark beer in winter like Harveys Old on handpump; farmhouse cider and a select but very good range of wines, with several by the glass and a few bin-ends. Dominoes, shove ha'penny, cribbage, backgammon, scrabble, shut the box and mah jong. At the back there are attractive new blue wood tables and chairs on a terrace with a pergola. ***(Recommended by Angela and Alan Dale, J O Jonkler, J S M Sheldon, Dave Braisted, M A Gordon Smith, Clive Gilbert, Mrs J A Banks, Paul Williams, Larry Hansen, Peter Lewis, W K Struthers, G C Hackemer, Sue Demont, Tim Barrow, Dr Keith Clements, Simon Small, Kevin and Katherine Cripps, Guy Consterdine)***

Free house ~ Licensees Sheila, Edric, Simon and James Hawkins ~ Real ale ~ Meals and snacks (till 10) ~ Restaurant ~ (01798) 861281 ~ Children over 10 in restaurant ~ Open 11-3, 6-11; closed winter Sun evenings

LOWER BEEDING TQ2227 Map 3

Crabtree

A281 S of village, towards Cowfold

One reader tells us it's difficult to explore anywhere else with this marvellous place nearby and it's easy to understand why. Standards haven't dropped at all since this was Sussex Dining Pub of the Year last year, and although the choice of daily changing very imaginative food isn't huge it indicates fresh and careful home-preparation. As well as sandwiches (from £1.95) and ploughman's (from £3.50), both using their homemade bread, specials might include spicy fish soup with coconut milk, lemon grass and fresh herbs (£4.50), salad of pigeon breast with orange, bacon and walnut vinaigrette (£4.75), mushroom, baby corn and asparagus risotto or pancake with stir fried vegetables and fresh coriander (£6.10), rabbit with capers and olives (£7.50), spicy chicken in a mushroom, peanut and chilli sauce with fresh coriander (£7.75) and grilled fillet of Scotch salmon with cumin, fennel and pesto topping (£8.10), and puddings like apple and cinnamon pie, banana cheesecake or rhubarb and apple crumble (from £3). The cosy beamed bars have an air of civilised simplicity, and there's plenty of character in the back no-smoking restaurant. Well kept King and Barnes Sussex, Festive and Mild on handpump (cheaper in the public bar), and King and Barnes seasonal brews, and good wines; prompt, friendly service. Darts and bar billiards. A pleasant back garden has seats, and there may be barbecues and live music out here on summer evenings. The pub is very handy for Leonardslee Gardens, which are closed in winter. *(Recommended by Martin and Catherine Horner, Mrs J A Blanks, R and S Bentley, Guy Consterdine, David Holloway, Cathryn and Richard Hicks, TOH, R J Walden, Mrs M Rice, Christoper Glasson, GB, CH, John and Mavis Wright, Debbie Leam, Terry Buckland)*

King & Barnes ~ Tenants Jeremy Ashpool and Nick Wege ~ Real ale ~ Lunchtime meals and snacks ~ Restaurant (not Sun evening) ~ (01403) 891257 ~ Children welcome ~ Occasional live entertainment Sun evenings ~ Open 11-3, 5.30-11

LURGASHALL SU9327 Map 2

Noahs Ark

Village signposted from A283 N of Petworth; OS Sheet 186 reference 936272

This welcoming old pub spectacularly decked with flower baskets in summer has been an inn since it was built in 1537 when it was given its present name with reference to the narrow causeway over the formerly marshy ground at its front. Now the tables on the grass in front look onto the pretty village green. Good bar food which can also be chosen from the restaurant menu includes sandwiches (from £2.50, toasties such as bacon and mushroom £3.50), ploughman's (from £3.50), tuna and pasta bake or tomato and vegetable tagliatelle (£5.25), steak and kidney pudding (£5.75), lamb cutlets (£6.75), calf's liver and bacon (£7.75), chicken breast with leek and stilton sauce (£9.25), poached salmon with asparagus sauce (£9.45) and fillet steak with mushroom and tomato (£12.75). In summer there are flowers in the two neatly furnished bars which in winter are replaced by warm log fires (one in a capacious inglenook). Well kept Greene King Abbot, IPA and Rayments on handpump; friendly service. Darts, shove-ha'penny, table skittles, dominoes, and cribbage. Possibly the loos could do with some attention. *(Recommended by John and Mavis Wright, J S M Sheldon, G B Longden, R D Knight, M Judd, Mrs M Rice, Chris Duncan, S G N Bennett, David Holloway, Roger Price, Mrs B M Spurr, J A Snell, Ian Phillips, G C Hackemer)*

Greene King ~ Tenant Kathleen G Swannell ~ Real ale ~ Meals and snacks (not

Sun evening) ~ Restaurant (not Sun) ~ (01428) 707346 ~ Children welcome ~ Occasional bands, theatre or concerts in garden marquee on summer evenings ~ Open 11.30(12 winter)-2.30, 6(6.30 winter)-11

MAYFIELD TQ5827 Map 3

Middle House

High St; village signposted off A267 S of Tunbridge Wells

This marvellously historical black-and-white timbered inn was built in 1575 and very unusually for a pub is Grade I listed. The place to head for on a winter evening before your meal is the comfortable russet chesterfields cosily grouped in the tranquil lounge area, gently lit by the flickering log fire in a fine ornately carved fireplace (disputedly by Grinling Gibbons). The largely original and uncluttered but comfortable chatty L-shaped beamed main bar is dominated by a massive fireplace surrounded by menu boards at one end, and as this is still very much a friendly village local a TV at the other end. It's worth glancing into the little restaurant which has marvellous old panelling and into a little room that was once a chapel. The wide choice of regularly changing bar food in not cheap but reliably big helpings includes ploughman's (£3.50), open sandwiches (from £4.25), pies like steak and kidney pie, venison and mushroom or chicken and leek (£6.50), pineapple, almonds, sultanas and rice with a curry sauce in a pineapple shell and grilled with a cheese and yoghurt topping (£7.25), pasta with salmon and prawns or grilled trout (£7.95), rack of lamb with honey and ginger (£9.50), black bream fillets sautéed in Chinese black bean and spring onion sauce or poached salmon filled with prawns and avocado and wrapped in filo with rose wine and pink peppercorn sauce (£9.95), and puddings like fruit crumbles, brûlée or banoffi pie (£2.95); there's some handsome panelling in the restaurant. Well kept Greene King Abbot, Harveys Best, Wadworths 6X, and a guest like Fullers ESB or Morlands Old Speckled Hen on handpump; darts, shove-ha'penny, fruit machine, trivia, and piped music. Afternoon tea is served in the fairly formal terraced back garden which has picnic tables, white plastic sets with cocktail parasols, nice views, and a slide and a log house for children; bedrooms are attractive and comfortable. ***(Recommended by Mike and Heather Watson, Jeremy Collins, Colin Laffan; more reports please)***

Free house ~ Licensee Monica Blundell ~ Real ale ~ Meals and snacks ~ Restaurant (not Sun evening) ~ (01435) 872146 ~ Children welcome ~ Open 11-11; ~ Bedrooms: £35(£45B)/£45(£55B)

Rose & Crown

Fletching Street; off A267 at NE end of village

In summer this pretty little weather-boarded 16th-c inn with little windows peeping out from behind the colourful baskets and tubs and rustic tables on the front stoop is delightfully appealing. Several bars wander round the tiny central servery, though it's the two cosy little front rooms – often packed with locals – that are the most atmospheric with low beams, benches built in to the partly panelled walls, an attractive bow window seat, low ceiling boards with coins embedded in the glossy ochre paint, and a big inglenook fireplace which gets the place really roasting in winter. Very popular bar food includes fresh salmon terrine or parma ham salad (£3.50), chilli prawns (£4.25), cottage pie (£3.95), chilli (£4.50), lamb and apricot pie or slices of aubergine with tomato, herbs and mozzarella (£5.95), fisherman's pie (£6.25), cumberland sausage (£6.50), steak and kidney pudding or spinach and vegetable cannelloni (£6.95), filled yorkshire pudding or chicken and spinach curry (£7.95), roast rack of lamb (£8.25), lamb fillets with redcurrant and rosemary (£8.75) and strips of steak with hot chilli and coconut sauce (£8.95). Well kept Bass, Boddingtons, Greene King Abbot, Flowers IPA and Harveys Best on handpump, many new world wines, a sizeable bin end list, and a range of malt whiskies; darts, bar billiards, shove-ha'penny, dominoes and cribbage, piped music at lunchtime. The bedrooms are very pretty and comfortable although there may be a little noise from the restaurant below. *(Recommended by Pam and Tim Moorey, John and Mavis Wright, Edward Bace, Margaret and Nigel Dennis, Brenda and Ralph Barber, Norma Farris, Sue Demont, Tim Barrow, P J Sykes, Pauline Bishop, Mrs S Gooch, Penny and Martin Fletcher)*

Free house ~ Licensee Sean McCorry ~ Real ale ~ Meals and snacks (till 10) ~ Restaurant ~ (01435) 872200 ~ Children in eating area of bar ~ Open 11-11, (winter 11-3, 5.30-11, all day Sat) ~ Bedrooms: £44.95B/£61.90B

MIDHURST SU8821 Map 2

Spread Eagle

South St

Most of this smart and very atmospheric old hotel dates back to the 17th-c but parts of the original building of 1430 still remain and it was described by Hilaire Belloc in *The Four Men* as 'the oldest and most revered of all the prime inns of this world'. Most impressive is the spacious massively beamed and timbered lounge, with its dramatic fireplace, imposing leaded-light windows looking out on the most attractive part of this old town, and handsome yet quite unpretentious old armchairs and settees spread among the rugs on the broad-boarded creaking oak floor. There's apparently a secret room six feet up one chimney. The atmosphere is one of restful luxury, but despite the opulence it's a friendly, welcoming place. A concise lunchtime bar menu consists of vegetable soup (£4.25), tomato, bacon and cheese tart or chicken liver parfait with a toasted brioche (£5.25), a daily special (£5.25), smoked haddock topped with welsh rarebit (£5.50), and puddings (£2.50); the well-regarded, partly no-smoking recently refurbished restaurant has a wider choice. They do good cream teas at weekends. The lounge opens onto a secluded courtyard. Fullers London Pride on handpump, not cheap but well kept; shove-ha'penny, cribbage, dominoes, trivia, maybe piped music. *(Recommended by Mrs M Rice, Paul Carter, JS, Ian Phillips, Graham and Karen Oddey, Martin Jones, Paula Harrison; more reports please)*

Free house ~ Licensees Pontus and Miranda Carminger ~ Real ale ~ Lunchtime meals and snacks (not Sun) ~ Restaurant ~ (01730) 816911 ~ Well behaved children welcome ~ Open 11-2.30, 6-11 ~ Bedrooms: £69B/£85B

NORMANS BAY TQ6805 Map 3

Star

Signposted off A259 just E of Pevensey; and from Cooden, off B2182 coast road W out of Bexhill

This friendly old smugglers' pub is a consistently reliable place for a meal or a drink – though you might find it difficult to decide what to have. There are rarely less than 10 well kept real ales on handpump, with beers like Charles Wells Bombardier, Harveys Best, Hop Back Summer Lightning, Marstons Owd Roger and a variety of other frequently changing brews from nearby or further afield. They also do lots of continental bottled beers, good country wines (the local apple is recommended), and a wider range of lagers and ciders than you'll usually come across. There is a selection of around 100 different dishes on the menu, some served in very big helpings – they hand out doggy bags and warn on the menu with a little elephant picture of the things that might defeat even a smuggler-sized appetite: half-dozen or so vegetarian dishes such as hot Boston beans, harvest pie, nut roast or pastas (from £4.75), a choice of fresh local fish (from £4.50 – the fishermen's huts are just down the road), a dozen or more starters like soup (£1.75), and ploughman's (from £3.95), ham and eggs (£4.50), scampi or half a roast chicken with a jumbo sausage (£6.50), pork chops (£6.75), half shoulder of lamb (£7.50), a good selection of steaks (from £8.75), and a few blackboard specials like lemon sole (£6.95) and beef wellington (£10.95); masses of puddings (from £2.50) – people especially like their large waffles (£4.25); children's dishes (£2.25). The atmosphere is notably welcoming and relaxed, especially in the spaciously modernised bar with comfortably cushioned seats spreading over the carpet of a brick-pillared partly timbered dining lounge; piped music, games in the children's room. Friendly staff cope admirably even when busy. It's particularly popular in summer, when you can relax in the hawthorn-sheltered treeside garden with a play area and there are more tables on a small front terrace; there may be barbecues in summer. Paths inland quickly take you away from the caravan sites into marshy nature reserve. *(Recommended by Colin Laffan, Alec and Marie Lewery, E G Parish, R J Walden)*

Free house ~ Licensee Francis Maynard ~ Real ale ~ Meals and snacks (till 10) ~ (01323) 762648 ~ Children in own room ~ Jazz Tues evening and other live music Sun lunchtime ~ Open 11-3.30, 6-11, maybe all day in summer

NUTHURST TQ1926 Map 3

Black Horse

Village signposted from A281 SE of Horsham

The cosy relaxed main bar of this old-fashioned welcoming black-beamed country pub has big Horsham flagstones in front of the inglenook fireplace. At one end it opens out into other carpeted areas including the dining room. There are interesting pictures on the walls, and magazines to read; cribbage, dominoes, piped music. A good range of well kept beers on handpump includes Adnams, Eldridge Pope Hardy Country and Royal Oak, Greene King Abbot, King & Barnes Sussex, Tetleys and Wadworths 6X, Gales country wines and a fair wine list. Promptly served bar food such as soup (£2.50), doorstep sandwiches or sausage, chips and beans (£2.95), ploughman's (from £3.75), filled baked potatoes (from £3.95), chilli or breaded plaice (£5.25), a pie of the day (£5.75), cannelloni romagna (£5.95), and changing specials like chicken panang or prawns piri piri; children's menu (£1.75). The restaurant is no smoking. Service is friendly and efficient but a service charge of 10% will be added for parties of five or more. They're just as welcoming if you turn up wet and muddy after sampling one of the area's lovely woodland walks. *(Recommended by LM, R J Walden, Clive Gilbert, Wayne Brindle, G Washington, Mr and Mrs Hunns, R and S Bentley, R T and J C Moggridge, Mavis and John Wright)*

Free house ~ Licensees Trevor and Karen Jones ~ Real ale ~ Meals and snacks (11.45-2.30, 6-9.45) ~ Restaurant (not Sun evening) ~ (01403) 891272 ~ Children in restaurant ~ Open 11-3, 6-11

OVING SU9005 Map 2

Gribble ■

Between A27 and A259 just E of Chichester, then should be signposted just off village road; OS Sheet 197 map reference 900050

This delightfully pretty rose covered red brick and thatched cottage was the private home of Rose Gribble for 90 years until she died about a decade ago and a local farmer decided the village needed a pub. The friendly bar – which could have been a pub for centuries – is full of heavy beams and timbering with old country-kitchen furnishings and pews, and the very lovely garden has chunky wood furniture among the apple trees and a covered seating area. The tasty range of beers brewed in the pub's own microbrewery includes the enduring favourites Gribble Ale, Reg's Tipple, Black Adder II, Pluckling Pheasant, Pigs Ear and Wobbler; they also have Badger Best on handpump, with lots of country wines and farm cider. Home-cooked bar food seems to be improving and includes open sandwiches (from £2.50), burgers (from £3.75), ploughman's (from £3.95), ham and eggs, Oriental vegetables or ratatouille au gratin (£4.75), steak and mushroom pie (£5.25), fisherman's pie (£5.45), Mexican chicken with kidney beans, sweetcorn in a tomato and chilli sauce, chicken and ham cooked in cider and cheese sauce (£5.95), battered seafood platter (£6.45), sirloin steak (£9.45); they do smaller helpings of most meals, as well as children's dishes (£2.45); puddings on the blackboard. On the left, a family room with a toy box and pews provides perhaps the biggest no-smoking area we've so far found in a Sussex pub, and also has shove-ha'penny, dominoes, cribbage, a fruit machine and a separate skittle alley. *(Recommended by Colin Laffan, Jonathan Phillips, John Sanders, R T and J C Moggridge, Clive Gilbert, Ted Burden, Lynn Sharpless, Bob Eardley, N E Bushby, Winifrede Morrison, Paul Carter, R J Walden, Eamon Green)*

Own brew (Badger) ~ Managers Ron and Anne May ~ Real ale ~ Meals and snacks ~ (01243) 786893 ~ Children in family room ~ Open 11-2.30, 6-11, all day Sat

nr PUNNETTS TOWN TQ6220 Map 3

Three Cups 

B2096 towards Battle

Burning in the big fireplace under a black mantlebeam dated 1696 are logs that one could just as easily describe as tree trunks. The peaceful and friendly long low-beamed bar of this unspoilt traditional local also has attractive panelling, and comfortable seats, including some in big bay windows overlooking a small green. A back family room leads out to a small covered terrace, with seats in the garden beyond – where you'll find chickens and bantams and a good safe play area. Good value unassuming food includes sandwiches, filled baked potatoes (from £2.75), prize-winning local giant sausages (£3.25), home-made steak or chicken pie (£4.50), half a roast chicken (£6.75) and steaks (from £7.50); part of the eating area is no smoking. Four well kept changing beers such as Arkells and Harveys Best and two guests on handpump. Darts, table skittles, shove-ha'penny, dominoes, cribbage and quiet piped music. There's space for five touring caravans outside. There are good walks from here, on either side of this high ridge of the Weald. *(Recommended by John Le Sage, R D Knight, F A Noble, James Nunns)*

Beards ~ Tenants Leonard and Irenie Smith ~ Real ale ~ Meals and snacks ~ (01435) 830252 ~ Children in restaurant and family room ~ Open 11-3, 6.30-11

ROWHOOK TQ1234 Map 3

Chequers

Village signposted from A29 NW of Horsham

This pleasantly rustic and genuinely characterful old-fashioned place remains unspoilt by the kind of modernisations that seem to blight so many of its type (in spite of yet another new licensee). The snugly unpretentious beamed and flagstoned front bar has black beams in its white ceiling, upholstered benches and stools around the tables on its flagstone floor, and an inglenook fireplace; up a step or two, there's a carpeted lounge with a very low ceiling. Changing blackboard bar food includes filled cottage loaves (£2.95), steak and ale pie, lasagne and braised liver and onions (£5.95), courgette and mushroom bake (£6.25), saddle of lamb stuffed with leeks, almonds and herbs (£9.25), grilled halibut with tartlets of crab and prawn with chive butter (£10.25) and wild boar steak with raspberries and blackberries (£10.75). Well kept Flowers Original, Fullers London Pride and King and Barnes Sussex under light blanket pressure, and a good range of wines with several by the glass; friendly service, piped music. Shove-ha'penny, dominoes and cribbage. A sunny little front terrace borders the quiet lane, and there are a good few tables in the peaceful and prettily planted side garden, with more on another crazy-paved terrace; good children's play area with swings, see-saw, wendy house, slide and climbing frame; boules. *(Recommended by Stella Knight, J S M Sheldon, Clive Gilbert, Martin Richards, Chris and Chris Ellis, Angela and Alan Dale, Alan Whiting, George Atkinson, C R and M A Starling, David Rule)*

Whitbreads ~ Tenant Sarah Luff ~ Real ale ~ Meals and snacks ~ Restaurant ~ (01403) 790480 ~ Children in restaurant ~ Open 11-3, 6-11

Pubs with outstanding views are listed at the back of the book.

RYE TQ9220 Map 3

Mermaid

Mermaid St

In one of the loveliest old Sussex towns this beautiful ancient smugglers' inn, with its black and white timbered facade and distinctive sign hanging over the steeply cobbled street, dates back mainly to the fifteenth and sixteenth centuries and has changed little since those days. In a little back bar a picture of the scene 70 years ago shows the furnishings have scarcely altered since. All that seems to have changed in the past couple of hundred years or so is the addition of electricity and a relaxing of the atmosphere: it used to be a favourite with gangs of notorious smugglers, who kept their loaded pistols by the side of their tankards while drinking. The ghost of a serving maid who lost her heart to one of those smugglers is said to return just before midnight. Fine panelling, antique woodwork and rare frescoes fill the civilised rooms, and there are some unusual intricately carved antique seats, one in the form of a goat, as well as an enormous fireplace. The cellars that hold the well kept Bass, McEwans and Morlands Old Speckled Hen served on handpump date back seven centuries; good wine list, ports and sherries. Readers have enjoyed the restaurant, where there's a salad buffet (about £7), and simple dishes such as soup, sandwiches and ploughman's may also be requested; it's the kind of place where they'll ask you which colour bread you'd prefer and how you'd like the meat in your hot beef sandwich. Hearty breakfasts. There are seats on a small back terrace, and in summer there may be local brass band concerts in the car park; piped music. *(Recommended by Mr and Mrs H and E Hanning, Mrs M Rice, PN, Thomas Nott, Linda and Brian Davis; more reports please)*

Free house ~ Licensee Robert Pinwill ~ Real ale ~ Restaurant ~ Rye (01797) 223065 ~ Children in eating area of bar ~ Open 11-11 ~ Bedrooms: £49.50(£63.80B)/£96.80(£118.80B)

nr SEAFORD TV4899 Map 3

Golden Galleon

Exceat Bridge; A259 Seaford—Eastbourne, near Cuckmere

Although this really popular inn has probably one of the smallest microbreweries in the country the licensee's rather literary brother – do ask about some of the beers' names – does manage to produce a very good range of up to twelve really popular own brew beers; at any time they have about six well kept on handpump which could include Cuckmere Haven Best, Guv'nor, Golden Peace, Gentleman's Gold and an old fashioned cask conditioned stout, Saxon King. These are served alongside a range of about six other beers from smaller brewers and might include Harveys Armada, Greene King Abbot or IPA, Shepherd Neame Bishops Finger or Spitfire and many others on handpump or tapped from the cask; there's also freshly squeezed orange juice, a decent selection of malts, continental brandies and Italian liqueurs and cappuccino or espresso coffee. Having said that it's really the excellent food that draws most people here, and as the very chatty sincere landlord is Italian you can expect lots of properly prepared Italian dishes in plentiful helpings: soup (£2.45), diced chicken with lettuce and home-made garlic mayonnaise (£3.35), ploughman's (from £3.50), a good help-yourself salad counter (from £3.75), garlic bread grilled with mozzarella and covered with parma ham or Italian seafood salad (£3.95), filled baked potatoes (from £4.50), breaded chicken (£5.50), fried or steamed fish of the day (£5.75), swordfish steak (£9.25) and large pork joint cooked on the bone with wine and herbs (£9.95), and specials like lasagne, spaghetti carbonara, chicken in tomato and ginger sauce, popular deep fried cod in garlic and dill batter or pork tenderloin; half-helpings of most things for children; various theme nights; no credit cards. Inside around two-thirds of the turkey-carpeted bar and dining area with its neat rows of tables is no smoking. The high trussed and pitched rafters give this quite an airy feel and there's a nice little side area with an open fire. They recently added a conservatory and hope to start further extensions in the spring; piped music.

At most times of the year there's a cheerily bustling feel that some find more reminiscent of an Italian trattoria than a typical pub, and it does get very busy at the weekends and during holiday periods. There are good views from tables in the sloping garden towards the Cuckmere estuary and the Seven Sisters Country Park which is just over the nearby Cuckmere River. You can walk along it to the sea or there are walks inland to Friston Forest and the Downs. *(Recommended by John Beeken, H D Spottiswoode, Alan Skull, John Fahy, Martin and Karen Wake, P J Guy, Brian Jones, R and S Bentley, Dr Keith Clements, Richard Houghton)*

Own brew ~ Licensee Stefano Diella ~ Real ale ~ Meals and snacks (12-2, 6-9) ~ (01323) 892247 ~ Children in conservatory ~ Open 11-2.30(3 Sat), 6-11

STOPHAM TQ0218 Map 3

White Hart 🍷

Off A283 between village turn-off and Pulborough

One of the highlights at this peaceful place is the fabulous fresh fish restaurant menu which you can also choose from in the bar: seafood salad (£3.25), sole and salmon roulade (£4.95), medallions of monkfish pan-fried in garlic and herbs (£5.50), smoked eel fillets (£5.95), baked salmon with broccoli and cheese or plaice fillets filled with salmon mousse in a champagne sauce (£9.95), pan fried fillets of tuna in a tangy lemon sauce, maritime mixed grill or shark steak in a peppercorn sauce (£10.50). The equally popular bar food includes good homemade sandwiches (from £1.35, soup (£1.90), ploughman's (from £3.20), spicy sausage made to their own recipe (£3.50), kedgeree or devilled kidneys (£3.95), meat or vegetable lasagne or spinach ravioli (£4.20), steak and mushroom pie (£4.50), fish pie (£4.75), and children's meals (£1.90). The three relaxing, cosy and comfortable beamed rooms are quite a draw in their own right with well kept Boddingtons, Flowers Original and Morlands Old Speckled Hen on handpump, about 25 bottled beers from around the world, and decent wines including several New World by the glass, half-bottle and bottle; darts, shove-ha'penny, cribbage, dominoes, fruit machine, and piped jazz or big band music. The beamed candlelit restaurant and usually one bar are no smoking. Tables on the lawn across the road make the most of this attractive spot and the graceful seven-arched medieval bridge which was constructed in 1309. There are tree-lined grass walks down by the meeting of the Arun and Rother rivers, and a play area is across here too. *(Recommended by DC, John Beeken, Tony and Wendy Hobden, John and Mavis Wright, David Holloway, T Roger Lamble, John and Tessa Rainsford, R T and C E Moggridge, John Fahy, J S M Sheldon, A C Morrison, A H Denham, Mrs M Rice)*

Whitbreads ~ Lease: John Palmer and Linda Collier ~ Real ale ~ Meals and snacks (not Sun evenings Oct-May) ~ Restaurant ~ (01798) 873321 ~ Children welcome ~ Live entertainment in garden bank holiday Mons ~ Open 11-3, 6.30(7 winter Mon-Thurs)-11

nr TICEHURST TQ6830 Map 3

Bull 🍺

Three Legged Cross; coming into Ticehurst from N on B2099, just before Ticehurst village sign, turn left beside corner house called Tollgate (Maynards Pick Your Own may be signposted here)

The garden at this delightfully relaxed and peaceful old pub tucked away down little lanes is a must on a lovely summer evening with tables beside an ornamental fish pond looking back at the building, covered in climbing roses and clematis. It's based around a 14th-c Wealden hall, and the original core with its huge log fire in winter is where the editors of this Guide head on the rare occasions they make it out of the office. A series of small flagstoned, brick-floored or oak parquet rooms run together, with heavy oak tables and seats of some character; a dubious round pool table, darts, dominoes and cribbage. Not surprisingly it's a popular place, with the friendly very low beamed rooms soon filling up. The food in more than adequate helpings is very well liked and to give but a few examples includes soup (£1.75), home-cooked filled baguettes (£2.50), steak and mushroom pie or lamb's liver with Madeira (£5.25), 12oz rump steak (£5.50) and shoulder of lamb for two (£13.95), and home-made puddings like apple strudel, summer pudding or bread and butter pudding. They do more elaborate meals in the restaurant extension. Service is friendly and efficient. Well kept Bull Best (Worthington beer that's named for them), Fullers London Pride, Harveys Best, Morlands Old Speckled Hen, locally brewed Rother Valley Level Best and a changing guest. Although they don't have a fancy children's play area they are very children friendly and usually have a bouncy castle at weekends, there's also plenty of room on the pub's own "soccby" pitch; a couple of boules pitches; maybe an outside bar and barbecue. It's handy for visiting the lovely gardens of Pashley Manor. *(Recommended by K and E Leist, Richard Fawcett, Colin Laffan, Tom McLean, Roger Huggins, Mr and Mrs J Liversidge, Mr and Mrs Jones, R Suddaby, Mrs C A Blake, Ian Phillips, Sue Demont, Tim Barrow, Penny and Peter Keevil, J H Bell, Andy Thwaites)*

Free house ~ Licensee Josie Wilson-Moir ~ Real ale ~ Meals and snacks (not Sun or Mon evenings) ~ Restaurant ~ (01580) 200586 ~ Children welcome ~ Open 11-3, 6.30-11

TILLINGTON SU9621 Map 2

Horseguards

Village signposted from A272 Midhurst—Petworth

The new licensees have turned this neat, friendly pub into much more of a dining place now, with a menu that changes twice daily. At lunchtime there may be home-made soup (£2.20), home-made terrines like avocado and chicken or monkfish and turbot and a salad of mixed seafood (all £3.50), and whole grilled plaice or cod with almonds in nut brown butter (£4.50), with more elaborate evening dishes such as chicken breast or duck with sauces (£6.50 and £8.20 respectively), rack of lamb (£7.45), and lots of fish like big grilled lemon sole, Dover sole or fillets of salmon and scallops in filo pastry with a sauce (from around £6); home-made puddings (£2.20), and Sunday roast beef (£4.95). Badger Best, Wadworths 6X and a beer brewed for the pub on handpump. From the seat in the big black-panelled bow window of the beamed front bar pub, there's a lovely view beyond the village to the Rother Valley; darts, piped music. There's a terrace outside, and more tables and chairs in a garden behind. The church opposite is 800 years old. *(Recommended by D J Cooke, Mrs Lili Lomas, Norman Foot, Frank Cummins, Keith Walton)*

Free house ~ Licensees Rex and Janet Colman ~ Real ale ~ Meals and snacks ~ Open 11-3, 6-11; closed 25 Dec

WEST ASHLING SU8107 Map 2

Richmond Arms

Mill Lane; from B2146 in village follow Hambrook signpost

You can get quite a shock when you see the astonishing range of well kept real ales at this unpretentious and notably friendly out-of-the-way village pub. There are usually ten of them on at a time, from all over the country, with a typical selection including Boddingtons, Brakspears, Greene King Abbot, Marstons Pedigree, Morlands Old Speckled Hen, Timothy Taylors Landlord, Youngs Special and a couple of more unusual brews you might not often find in this part of the world; also farm ciders, country wines, Belgian fruit beers and continental bottled beers. The furnishings fit in well – the main room's dominated by the central servery, and has a 1930s feel, with its long wall benches, library chairs, black tables and open fire (maybe with a couple of black cats in front of it). Readers like the good choice of well-priced no-nonsense food such as sandwiches (croque monsieur £3), excellent ploughman's, filled baked potatoes, home-made spinach and mushroom lasagne, vegetarian cannelloni, chilli con carne or curry (£4.20), game pie (£5.60) and salmon en croûte (£6.80). Service is consistently obliging and flexible, even when the pub is busy, as it often is, especially at weekends. Bar billiards, shove-ha'penny, dominoes, cribbage, and trivia and fruit machines in the games room; the skittle alley doubles as a function and family room. There's a pergola, and some picnic tables by the car park. *(Recommended by Deek and Sylvia Stephenson, John Beeken, Ann and Colin Hunt, Phil and Sally Gorton, Alan Kilpatrick, Barbara Hatfield)*

Free house ~ Licensees Bob and Christine Garbutt ~ Real ale ~ Meals and snacks (12-3, 6.30-10) ~ (01243) 575730 ~ Children welcome ~ Tues quiz night ~ Open 11-3, 5.30-11, all day Sat in summer; closed evening Dec 26

WINEHAM TQ2320 Map 3

Royal Oak 

Village signposted from A272 and B2116

The sort of charming and unchanging pub where the invention of snazzy tills, fruit machines and even beer pumps has gone by unnoticed. It's a nicely old-fashioned place, with the emphasis on drinking rather than eating, and can also pride itself on being one of the prettiest pubs in the county. The layout and style are commendably traditional, with very low beams above the serving counter, decorated with ancient corkscrews, horseshoes, racing plates, tools and a coach horn, along with basic old-fashioned furniture and logs burning in an enormous inglenook. It must have looked very like this when the current landlord first came here nearly 50 years ago. Well kept beers tapped from the cask in a still room on the way to a little snug include Boddingtons, Harveys BB, Wadworths 6X and Whitbreads Pompey Royal; darts, shove-ha'penny, dominoes, cribbage. A limited range of bar snacks such as fresh-cut or toasted sandwiches (from £1.25, roast beef £1.75 or smoked salmon £2.25) and home-made soup in winter (£1.50); good courteous service. The neat front lawn has wooden tables by a well. On a clear day male readers may be able to catch a glimpse of Chanctonbury Ring from the window in the gents'. The pub looks especially inviting at night. *(Recommended by Alec and Marie Lewery, Alan Skull, Mayur Shah, Comus Elliott, D E Clough, Terry Buckland)*

Whitbreads ~ Tenant Tim Peacock ~ Real ale ~ Snacks (available throughout opening hours) ~ (01444) 881252 ~ Children in family room ~ Open 11-2.30, 5.30(6 Sat)-11; closed evening 25 Dec

WITHYHAM TQ4935 Map 3

Dorset Arms

B2110

The interior of this 16th-c inn is much older than its Georgian facade suggests. It's set well back from the road and has white tables on a brick terrace raised well above the small green. There's a short flight of outside steps up to the L-shaped bar, which at the end of the climb has sturdy tables and simple country seats on the wide oak floorboards, a good log fire in the stone Tudor fireplace, and a splendidly welcoming atmosphere. It's got quite a good reputation for mostly home-made food, prepared as much as possible from local ingredients. The menu includes sandwiches (from £1.70), soup (£2.10), ploughman's (from £3.60), filled baked potatoes (£3.65), fresh vegetables baked in cream and white wine sauce topped with cheese and parsley (£6.65), fried strips of breast of chicken with garlic and white wine (£7.45), breaded lemon sole (£7.95), pork tenderloin fried with onions and garlic with a spicy tomato sauce (£9.20), strips of veal pan fried with mushrooms, madeira and cream (£9.75) and half a brandy and orange glazed roast duckling with nut stuffing (£10.35); blackboard specials like smoked salmon and dill flan (£3.95), lamb and apricot pie (£4.25) and steak and wild mushroom pie (£4.50). Well kept Harveys BB and IPA, with their Porter in March and Tom Paine throughout July all on handpump, a reasonable wine list including some local ones; friendly, efficient service. Darts, dominoes, shove ha'penny, cribbage, fruit machine and piped music. The countryside around here is nice and the nearby church has a memorial to Vita Sackville-West. *(Recommended by Margaret and Nigel Dennis, R A Dean, Colin Laffan, P Gillbe, J S M Sheldon, Richard Waller)*

Harveys ~ Tenants John and Sue Pryor ~ Real ale ~ Meals and snacks (not Mon evening) ~ Restaurant (not Sun evening) ~ (01892) 770278 ~ Children in restaurant and lounge area ~ Open 11.30(11 Sat)-3, 5.30(6 Sat)-11

Lucky Dip

Besides the fully inspected pubs, you might like to try these Lucky Dips recommended to us and described by readers (if you do, please send us reports):

☆ **Alfriston** E Sus [TQ5103], *Market Cross:* Olde-world atmospheric low-beamed white-panelled bar with smuggling mementoes, good value bar food from sandwiches to steaks (snacks only, Sun lunch), well kept Courage Best and Directors, good choice of wines by the glass, friendly staff, tables in garden; children allowed in eating area and conservatory; can get crowded *(Mark Percy, Keith Stevens, LYM)*

Alfriston [High St], *George*: 14th-c timbered inn, roomy heavy-beamed bar with huge fireplace, extensive menu inc lots of fish, efficient service, well kept King & Barnes, intimate candlelit dining area; comfortable attractive bedrooms, good breakfasts *(John Beeken, E G Parish)*

☆ **Amberley** W Sus [off B2139; TQ0111], *Black Horse*: Attractive flagstoned village pub, up a flight of steps, its beams festooned with sheep and cow bells; wide choice of good simple home-cooked bar food from ploughman's to steaks, fine real chips, well kept Bass, Flowers and Worthington BB, farm cider, lovely open fires, friendly atmosphere, nice garden; children in eating area and restaurant, occasional folk music, two big dogs, sleepy cat *(Mr and Mrs Michael Boxford, Guy Consterdine, John Beeken, Mavis and John Wright, Mrs M Rice, LYM)*

☆ **Amberley** [Houghton Bridge, B2139], *Bridge*: Attractive, busy open-plan dining pub with pretty riverside terrace garden, good range of fresh food inc local fish, well kept Flowers Original, country wines, pleasant service, interesting pictures, unobtrusive piped music; provision for children; bedrooms *(R T and J C Moggridge, A E and P McCully, Peter Lewis, N E Bushby, Mrs D Bromley-Martin, Russell and Margaret Bathie)*

☆ **Amberley** [Rackham Rd], *Sportsman*: Off the beaten track, three small rooms, conservatory and garden, lovely views, genuine home-cooked food from sandwiches up inc good vegetarian, decent wines and country wines, well kept ales, friendly welcome *(Mrs M Rice, Julie Peters, Colin Blinkhorn, LM, Robert W Buckle)*

☆ **Angmering** W Sus [TQ0704], *Spotted Cow*: Harveys, King & Barnes and other ales, good value straightforward food very popular weekdays with older people, cheerful attentive service, picnic tables in roomy garden with good separate play area; dogs allowed, at start of lovely walk to Highdown hill fort *(Ian Phillips)*

☆ **Ardingly** W Sus [B2028 2 miles N; TQ3429], *Gardeners Arms*: Cheerful olde-worlde dining pub with good choice of home-made food inc fresh fish and good value specials, welcoming and attractive if not exactly pubby bar with big log fire in inglenook, cheerful staff, well kept King & Barnes, Theakstons and Courage-related real ales, morning coffee and tea, maybe soft piped music, no children; well spaced tables out among small trees, handy for Borde Hill and Wakehurst Place *(Mrs R D Knight, John Pettit, John and Judith Wells, Mr and Mrs Jones)*

☆ **Ardingly** [Street Lane], *Ardingly Inn*: Comfortable pub with wide choice of good generous straightforward food with good veg, OAP discounts, pleasant staff, decent wines; bedrooms reasonably priced *(Don and Thelma Beeson, F M Furlonger, Margaret and Nigel Dennis)*

☆ **Arlington** E Sus [Caneheath, off A22 or A27; TQ5407], *Old Oak*: 17th-c, with big cosy L-shaped beamed bar, dining room, popular reasonably priced food (not Mon; Tues is bangers and mash night), well kept Badger, Harveys and usually a guest beer tapped from the cask, pleasant staff, log fires, peaceful garden; children allowed, handy for Bluebell Walk *(J H Bell, R and S Bentley, Alan Skull, A Albert)*

☆ **Arlington**, *Yew Tree*: Welcoming neatly modernised two-bar village local, reliable generous home cooking, well kept Fullers London Pride and Harveys with a guest such as Morlands Old Speckled Hen, log fires, efficient service, subdued piped music, darts; restaurant, good big garden and play area by paddock with farm animals *(Tony Albert, John Beeken, Peter Churchill, Jason Caulkin, BB)*

☆ **Arundel** W Sus [High St; TQ0107], *Swan*: Comfortably refurbished L-shaped lounge and restaurant, good choice of bar food inc vegetarian, full range of good Arundel beers with a guest such as Fullers London Pride, all well kept; good bedrooms *(Bruce Bird, Mrs M Rice, Derek and Sylvia Stephenson, LYM)*

Arundel [Mill Rd, eventually], *Black Rabbit*: Lovely spot, tables by river and on verandah with colourful hanging baskets and window boxes looking across to water meadows and castle, long picture-window bar; well kept

Badger Best and Tanglefoot, bar food till 3, open all day summer; piped music may be loud; children in eating areas, well converted 'play boat' *(John Beeken, Romey Heaton, Dr Keith Clements, T Roger Lamble, LYM)*; [School Hill, by cathedral], *St Marys Gate*: Quiet comfortable open-plan bar with alcoves, lots of horse-racing caricatures, generous good value home-cooked bar food, Badger Best and Tanglefoot and guest beer, good service, restaurant; unobtrusive piped music; bedrooms quiet and good value *(Bruce Bird, Mrs M Rice)*

Balls Cross W Sus [signposted off A283 N of Petworth; SU9826], *Stag*: Small flagstoned 15th-c pub with inglenook, reasonably priced food, seats outside *(Mrs M Rice, Bruce Bird)*

Barcombe E Sus [N of Lewes; TQ4114], *Anchor*: Charming gardens and boating on very peaceful river outside remote inn with small clubby bar and restaurant; bedrooms *(Matthew de la Haye, BB)*; [Barcombe Mills], *Anglers Rest*: Tasty imaginative meals, good range of ales such as Adnams Broadside, Anchor Golden, Hop Back Summer Lightning and Brewery on Sea; may be piped music; big sheltered garden, verandah, children's play house; good walks *(John Beeken)*

☆ **Barnham** W Sus [OS Sheet 197 map ref 961043; SU9604], *Murrell Arms*: Genuine old pub with lots of pictures, old maps etc, Gales tapped from the cask, good simple cheap food esp cheese or bacon doorsteps; games inc ring-the-bull *(Tony and Wendy Hobden)*

☆ **Battle** E Sus [25 High St; TQ7416], *George*: Upmarket part pine-panelled bar/bistro, clean and well run, with well kept Harveys, friendly staff, good teas; no music, open all day; bedrooms *(P J Caunt)*

☆ **Berwick** E Sus [Lower Rd, S of A27; TQ5105], *Cricketers:* Heavily beamed country pub, well placed for walkers and very busy weekends, with beautiful olde-worlde garden, well kept Harveys Bitter and Porter tapped from the cask, good value simple home-made food, log fires, friendly service *(Adrian and Gilly Heft, John and Mavis Wright, D L Barker, Paul and Heather Bettesworth, Susie Northfield, Andrew Partington, Tom and Rosemary Hall, Peter Chrismas)*

Bexhill E Sus [Little Common Rd, Little Common; A259 towards Polegate; TQ7107], *Denbigh*: Attractive and friendly small bar and dining area, good choice of real ales, good well priced food, pleasant staff; good friendly pub *(Christopher Turnier)*

Billingshurst W Sus [High St; A29; TQ0925], *Olde Six Bells*: Picturesque partly 14th-c flagstoned and timbered pub with well kept King & Barnes, good bar food, inglenook fireplace, pretty roadside garden *(Dave Lands, LYM)*

☆ **Binstead** W Sus [Binstead Lane; about 2 miles W of Arundel, turn S off A27 towards Binstead – OS Sheet 197 map ref 980064; SU9806], *Black Horse*: 17th-c, with ochre walls and open fire in big bar, good range of real ales, darts and pool one end, welcoming young licensee, good choice of food in bar and reasonably priced restaurant; idyllic garden with country views; bedrooms *(Tony and Wendy Hobden, Bruce Bird, Mrs M Rice)*

Birling Gap E Sus [TV5596], *Birling Gap*: Hotel's nicely decorated separate bar just above seashore, old thatching and carpentry tools, pleasant atmosphere, usual bar food; bedrooms *(Peter and Lynn Brueton, E G Parish)*

Blackham E Sus [A264 towards E Grinstead; TQ4838], *Sussex Oak*: Friendly new licensees, well kept beers, good reasonably priced food *(June and Perry Dann)*

Boarshead E Sus [Eridge Rd, off A26 bypass; TQ5332], *Boars Head:* Unspoilt old and cosy place by pleasant farmyard, big log fire, flagstones, simple good reasonably priced food; piped music turned down if asked *(R D Knight, BB)*

Bognor Regis W Sus [56 London Rd; SZ9399], *Alex*: Friendly, warm, cosy and clean, good value generous food inc hot pork in home-baked bread (Sat) and Sun lunch, Courage-related and King & Barnes ales, huge mug and jug collection *(J Wisden, Jan and Colin Roe, Roger Byrne)*

Bolney W Sus [TQ2623], *Bolney Stage*: Timbered dining pub with wide range of food inc huge mixed grill, reasonable prices, prompt friendly service, popular with locals; handy for Sheffield Park and Bluebell Railway *(A H Denman)*; [The Street], *Eight Bells*: Good attractively presented food, attentive courteous staff, clean and comfortable bars, real ales *(S W Whytehead)*

☆ **Bosham** W Sus [High St; SU8003], *Anchor Bleu*: Lovely sea and boat views from low-beamed waterside pub, in attractive village; well kept Courage-related beers, log-effect gas fire, decent fresh if pricy buffet (some dishes sell out early), seats outside; very popular with tourists, service can take a while in summer *(Mrs M Rice, Peter and Audrey Dowsett, David Dimmock, Colin and Ann Hunt, Eamon Green, Jill Franklin, LYM)*

☆ **Brighton** [100 Goldstone Villas, next to Hove Rly Stn; TQ2805], *Hedgehog & Hogshead*: Bare floorboards, scrubbed tables, church pews, big windows, relaxed atmosphere; brews its own Brighton Breezy and strong Hogbolter, maybe Hedgehog or Hogswill – you can see the brewery; also two guest beers, farm cider, good plentiful food, live music Fri, piped music may be loud other evenings; good service, very popular with young people Sat evening *(Richard Houghton, Nigel Turley, Tony and Wendy Hobden, David Holloway)*

☆ **Brighton** [13 Marlborough Pl], *King & Queen*: Medieval-style lofty main hall, generous good value food, pleasant cheerful service, well kept beer, pool table, flagstoned courtyard; good free jazz most evenings (when parking tends to be difficult) and Sun lunchtime *(P Corris, LYM)*

Brighton E Sus [Portland Rd, Hove], *Aldrington*: Colourful customers, well kept beer, three pool tables *(Stephen Constable)*; [New Rd, off North St, by Theatre Royal], *Colonnade*: Vibrant theatrical atmosphere, velvet, mirrors and interesting theatre posters and photographs from 20s to 80s; lots of character, good friendly service, some snacks, tiny front terrace Despite being extremely busy much of the day and evening, there is always good service and a friendly atmosphere *(Dr Keith Clements)*; [Surrey St], *Evening Star*: Brews two beers itself, with impressive range of well kept guest beers inc ones rare here; bare boards, simple furnishings, friendly service; no food Sun *(Richard Houghton, David Holloway, Bruce Bird)*; [The Lanes], *Font & Firkin*: Clever refurbishment of what appears to have been a church, with mezzanine floor; pleasant service, own brew beers, bar food and good value Sun roasts *(Richard Houghton)*; [105 Southover St, Kemp Town], *Greys*: Strongly recommended for consistently good food inc adventurous original recipes in civilised surroundings *(Tony Pickup)*; [33 Upper St James's St, Kemp Town], *Hand in Hand*: Busy local brewing its own beers, also Badger Best and Tanglefoot, food such as sandwiches, pies and pizzas weekday lunchtimes, Sun roast potatoes; good service *(Richard Houghton, Andy Cameron)*; [by Metropole Hotel], *Hole in the Wall*: Friendly and enjoyable local *(Jim Merrett)*; [Market St, Lanes], *Pump House*: Friendly, lively and relaxed, light and airy but cosy, with very mixed age groups, good choice of wines *(John Wooll, Dr and Mrs A K Clarke)*; [Regency Sq], *Regency*: Renovated by new licensees, now ornate and fun; well stocked bar, quickly served fresh sandwiches and other food *(Christopher Glasson)*; [Castle Sq], *Royal Pavilion Tavern*: Huge pub with lots of separate well refurbished areas, Bass ale, all sorts of food inc speciality fresh-carved roast in baguettes with yorkshire pudding and stuffing, efficient service *(Ian and Colin Roe, LYM)*; [Hove St, Hove], *Ship*: Pleasant relaxed atmosphere, friendly service; bedrooms *(Dr Keith Clements)*; [East St], *Sussex*: Busy and well run, open all day, with tables out in the square *(Dr Keith Clements)*

☆ **Broad Oak** E Sus [A28/B2089 – the one N of Brede; TQ8220], *Rainbow Trout*: Amazing variety of well cooked food served by pleasant waitresses in attractive bustling old bar and big adjacent restaurant extension; gets very crowded but plenty of room for drinkers, with wide range of beers, wines and spirits *(J H Bell, Leslie W Clark)*

☆ **Burwash** E Sus [TQ6724], *Rose & Crown*: Timbered and beamed local tucked away down lane in pretty village, wide choice of ales such as Bass, Charrington IPA and Shepherd Neame, decent wines, good log fire, friendly service, generous bar food, restaurant; tables on quiet lawn; bedrooms *(Joy and Arthur Hoadley, BB)*

Burwash Weald E Sus [A265 2 miles W of Burwash; TQ6624], *Wheel*: Decent food all day in well kept open-plan pub with big log fire, well kept Harveys and other ales, some tables outside; doing well under current friendly licensees *(BB)*

Chailey E Sus [Lewes rd; TQ3919], *Five Bells*: Enjoyable and well kept, with wide changing choice of food all day, big log fire, well stocked bar, good service *(A H Denman)*

Chalvington E Sus [village signed from A27 and A22, then follow Golden Cross rd; TQ5209], *Yew Tree*: Isolated country pub, low beams, stripped bricks and flagstones, inglenook fireplace, straightforward bar food, well kept Harveys and Fremlins; attractive little walled terrace, extensive grounds inc own cricket pitch *(John and Mavis Wright, BB)*

☆ **Charlton** W Sus [off A286 Chichester—Midhurst; SU8812], *Fox*: Cosy old rooms with low beams, no-smoking family extension and restaurant, attractive sheltered garden with Downs views, decent bar food, Ballards Best, Gales HSB and several S & N ales, bedrooms *(PC, Clive Gilbert, LYM; more reports on new regime please)*

Chichester W Sus [3 Broyle Rd; SU8605], *Bell*: Good range of beers, interesting wines, good food inc super puddings, attentive service *(Pauline and Robbie Robertson)*; [North St], *George & Dragon*: Lively theatrical atmosphere and clientele, good soup and pasta, big helpings *(David Betts)*; [3 St Pancras], *Nags Head*: Large oak-panelled pub with shelves of old books, emphasis on food but lively atmosphere for casual drinker *(Dr and Mrs A K Clarke)*; [South St], *White Horse*: Part Tudor, part Georgian, single cosy long bar with settles and ochre walls, end food counter, darts, bar billiards and fruit machine nr main entrance; can be crowded with younger drinkers and foreign students on summer weekends *(Mrs M Rice)*

☆ **Chilgrove** W Sus [just off B2141 Petersfield—Chichester; SU8214], *White Horse*: More smart restaurant than pub, in idyllic downland setting with small flower-filled terrace and big pretty garden, lovely spot on a sunny day; good food in bar too, remarkable list of outstanding wines, welcoming landlord; lunches cheaper than evening *(Mrs M Rice, Dr Brian Hamilton, Mrs D Bromley-Martin)*

☆ *nr* **Chilgrove** [Hooksway; off B2141 Petersfield—Chichester, signed Hooksway down steep track; SU8116], *Royal Oak*: Smartly simple country tavern in very peaceful spot, beams, brick floors, country-kitchen furnishings, huge log fires; home-made standard food inc vegetarian, several well kept ales, games, attractive seats outside; provision for children, has been cl winter Mons *(Peter Taylor, Keith Stevens, Mrs M Rice, Eamon Green, LYM)*

Cocking W Sus [SU8717], *Blue Bell*: Doing well under keen young licensees, good range of ales such as Boddingtons and Gillespies, tempting choice of pleasantly served food inc good ample filled baked potatoes and

ploughman's *(Tom and Rosemary Hall)*
Cocking Causeway W Sus [just S of Midhurst; SU8819], *Greyhound*: Very pleasant service, Courage-related ales, good genuinely home-made food inc interesting specials; pewter pots, woodworking tools etc *(J F Sanders)*
Colgate W Sus [TQ2332], *Dragon*: Atmospheric and cosy, friendly staff, good local beers, big garden *(Wayne Brindle)*
☆ **Compton** W Sus [SU7714], *Coach & Horses*: Friendly and spotless, with well kept Fullers ESB, King & Barnes and Gales HSB and Mild, traditional walkers' bar, plusher beamed lounge, good range of food in bars and restaurant; Flemish landlady *(Colin and Ann Hunt, Roger Lamble)*
☆ *nr* **Coolham** W Sus [Dragons Green; TQ1423], *George & Dragon*: Charming small and ancient pub doing well under current young licensees, decent straightforward pub food inc exceptional handcut chips, well kept King & Barnes Festive and Broadsword, big inglenook, unusually low beams, pub games; children in eating areas; well spaced tables out in big orchard garden *(Colin Laffan, Gordon, Mrs M Rice, LYM)*
Copsale W Sus [signed off A24; TQ1725], *Bridge*: Welcoming modern pub handy for walks, basic food, King & Barnes beers, jazz Sun lunchtimes, garden with play area, busy weekends *(Mrs M Rice, J E C Hobbs)*
☆ **Cousleywood** E Sus [TQ6533], *Old Vine*: Attractive dining pub with lots of old timbers and beams, wide range of generously served decent food (jazz suppers Mon), good house wine, well kept ales; rustic pretty restaurant on right, rather more pubby area by bar, a few tables out behind *(Colin Laffan, BB)*
Cowfold W Sus [Horsham Rd; TQ2122], *Coach House*: Recently tastefully refurbished and well run, with good food *(Ron Gentry)*
Crawley W Sus [Broadwalk; TQ2636], *Hogs Head*: A lunchtime-only recommendation, with good range of ales inc Marstons Pedigree, inexpensive basic food inc filled baps *(Ian Phillips)*; [High St], *Old Punch Bowl*: New Greene King pub which has done time as a bank, Abbot, Black Baron and Charrington IPA, food in good-sized helpings *(Alec and Marie Lewery)*; [Balcombe Rd (B2036)], *Parsons Pig*: Very lively, mostly 25+ age group, plenty of atmosphere, decent food *(Neil McMath)*
☆ **Crowborough** E Sus [Boarshead St, just off A26 towards Eridge; TQ5130], *Boars Head*: Peaceful and welcoming, low 16th-c beams, well kept beer, simple well cooked food, log fire *(Mrs R D Knight, Andrew Hamilton, Peter Coward)*
☆ **Danehill** E Sus [School Lane, Chelwood Common; off A275; TQ4128], *Coach & Horses*: Good home-cooked food inc vegetarian, well kept Harveys, Greene King and guest beers, hard-working licensees, good atmosphere, pews in bar, decent house wine; ex-stables dining extension *(Ron Gentry)*
☆ **Dell Quay** W Sus [SU8302], *Crown & Anchor*: Modernised 15th-c pub on site of Roman quay, yacht-harbour views from garden and comfortable bow-windowed lounge bar, panelled public bar with unspoilt fireplace, Courage-related ales, Marstons Pedigree and Wadworths 6X; good choice of popular food esp fish in bar and restaurant *(Eamon Green, Ann and Colin Hunt, BB)*
☆ **Dial Post** W Sus [B2244, off A24; TQ1519], *Crown*: Comfortable, with upmarket food in bar and restaurant, Courage-related and more local beers, log fires, no-smoking bar area *(Mrs M Rice)*
☆ **Ditchling** E Sus [West St; TQ3215], *White Horse*: Popular local, very busy weekends, with well kept Harveys and changing guest beers, unpretentious food from sandwiches up, quick service, log fire, bar billiards, shove ha'penny etc, unobtrusive piped jazz, live alternate Thurs/Fri *(John Laws, Ian and Colin Roe, JM, PM)*
☆ **Duncton** W Sus [set back from A285 N; SU9617], *Cricketers Arms*: Lively and friendly, with jovial and extremely helpful landlord, quickly served good original home-cooked food and good value filled rolls; well kept Shepherd Neame Spitfire, lots of cricket memorabilia; some seats outside *(Dr L Kopelowitz, Leslie Payne, Jan and Colin Roe)*
Durrington W Sus [Salvington Rd; TQ1104], *Lamb*: Food inc good value Sun lunch (no food Sun evening), recently refurbished saloon, darts and bar billiards in locals' public bar, welcoming service, play equipment in side garden *(Mrs M Rice)*
☆ **Easebourne** W Sus [SU8922], *Olde White Horse*: Cosy local with decent promptly served bar food inc good fish, friendly welcome, Greene King IPA and Abbot, small log fire, traditional games in tap room, tables on back lawn and in courtyard *(I D and W McCaw, Angela and Alan Dale, M A Gordon Smith, Mr and Mrs R O Gibson, G C Hackemer, LYM)*
☆ **East Ashling** W Sus [SU8207], *Horse & Groom*: Recently extended and refurbished, good popular food, pleasant new landlord and young staff; one to watch *(Roger Lamble, Colin and Ann Hunt, Keith Stevens)*
East Chiltington E Sus [Chapel Lane, 2 miles N of B2116; TQ3715], *Jolly Sportsman*: Simple bar, pool room and small dining room, well kept King & Barnes, John Smiths and Wadworths 6X, well presented bar food, rustic furniture and play area in lovely garden next to small nursery run by landlord's father-in-law; South Downs views, nice spot, good walks *(John Beeken)*
☆ **Eastbourne** E Sus [The Goffs, Old Town; TV6199], *Lamb*: Two main heavily beamed traditional bars off pretty Tudor pub's central servery, spotless antique furnishings, good inglenook log fire, well kept Harveys Best, Armada and Old, friendly polite service, well organised food bar, upstairs dining room (Sun lunch), no music or machines; dogs seem welcome, children allowed in very modernised side room; by ornate church

away from seafront; popular with students evenings *(E B Davies, Carol A Riddick, Dave Braisted, Kenneth Mason, Adrian and Gilly Heft, D L Barker, Pam Adsley)*

☆ **Eastbourne** [Holywell Rd, Meads; just off front below approach from Beachy Head], *Pilot*: Lively, comfortable and friendly, prompt food inc good crab salad in season, pleasant landlady, well kept real ales, good ship photographs; garden *(Carol A Riddick, Keith Stevens, Mrs L M Tansley)*

Eastbourne [14 South St], *Dolphin*: Well refurbished intimate pub, coal fires, well kept Bass, Fullers London Pride and Harveys, wide choice of good well priced bar food from sandwiches to Sun lunch, good mix of old tables in restaurant with grand piano; piped music, crowded Saturday afternoon *(W and P J Elderkin and friends, B R Shiner)*; [Terminus Rd], *Terminus*: Not smart, but welcoming (to children too), with well kept Harveys, lunchtime food, busy old-fashioned bar *(W and P J Elderkin and friends, Barbara and Norman Wells)*

☆ **Fairwarp** E Sus [just off B2026, near Uckfield; TQ4626], *Foresters Arms*: Popular, homely and welcoming, recently smartened up outside, with good home cooking inc some unusual dishes and fresh veg, well kept King & Barnes ales, efficient Polish staff, friendly fat dogs, huge fishtank in public bar, pretty village setting nr Weald Way and Vanguard Way footpaths *(Colin Laffan, Alan Skull)*

☆ **Fernhurst** W Sus [The Green, off A286 beyond church; SU9028], *Red Lion*: Heavy-beamed old pub tucked quietly away by green nr church, good reasonably priced food inc interesting specials, attractive layout and furnishings, friendly quick service, several well kept real ales, no-smoking area, good relaxed atmosphere; children welcome, pretty garden *(P Gillbe, G C Hackemer, Jenny and Brian Seller, BB)*

☆ **Findon** [off A24 N of Worthing; TQ1208], *Gun*: Unchanging civilised low-beamed village pub with good generous food inc fresh veg, friendly service, well kept Whitbreads-related ales; attractive sheltered lawn, pretty village in horse-training country below Cissbury Ring; busy weekends *(Mrs M Rice, J C Brittain-Long, LYM)*

☆ **Findon** W Sus [High St], *Village House*: Good food from home-made soup to fish and local game in welcoming converted 16th-c coach house, oak tables, lots of racing silks and pictures, big open fire, wide range of alternating beers, good cheerful service, restaurant popular for Sun lunch, small attractive walled garden; bedrooms *(Mr and Mrs D E Powell)*

Fishbourne W Sus [99 Fishbourne Rd; A27 Chichester—Emsworth; SU8404], *Bulls Head*: Welcoming landlord, particularly well kept ales – all Gales ales and guests such as Fullers London Pride and Youngs Special; good choice of bar food (not Sun evening), log fires, no-smoking area, children's area, skittle alley, boules pitch, restaurant *(Bruce Bird, J A Snell, Keith Stevens)*

☆ **Fittleworth** W Sus [Lower St (B2138); TQ0118], *Swan*: Prettily placed 15th-c pub with big inglenook log fire in friendly and comfortable lounge, good bar food with unusual specials and good Sun lunch in attractive panelled side room with landscapes by Constable's deservedly less-known brother George, courteous helpful staff, piped music; games inc pool in public bar, well spaced tables on big sheltered back lawn, good walks nearby; open all day Thurs-Sat, children in eating area; good value well equipped bedrooms *(Helen and Stuart Dawson, Winifrede D Morrison, Ian Phillips, Mrs M Rice, LYM)*

Frant E Sus [A267 S of Tunbridge Wells; TQ5835], *Abergavenny Arms*: Cosy pub, some emphasis on restaurant side, but now also has six well kept ales such as Bass, Burts, Hogsback and Rother Valley Level Best tapped from the cask, from unusual climate-controlled glass-fronted chamber; log fire, bar billiards *(D L Barker)*; [village rd], *George*: Beamed pub with five real ales inc Morlands Old Speckled Hen, good food in bar and restaurant, friendly staff, log fire, garden with barbecues *(M Buckingham, J S M Sheldon)*

☆ **Funtington** W Sus [SU7908], *Fox & Hounds*: Welcoming old beamed pub extensively refurbished by newish owners, imaginative choice of well cooked fresh food, comfortable and attractive dining extension, Courage-related ales, farm cider, real ginger beer, huge log fire, reasonably priced wines, good coffee, no music, good waiter service *(Penny and Peter Keevil, Viv Middlebrook)*

☆ **Glynde** E Sus [TQ4509], *Trevor Arms*: Well kept Harveys, good range of food, small dining room, pleasant staff, sizeable garden – very busy at weekends; nice spot, good walks (no muddy boots allowed) *(Adrian and Gilly Heft, L M Miall)*

Graffham W Sus [SU9217], *Foresters Arms*: Warmly welcoming peaceful pub, good reasonably priced food, pleasant traditional atmosphere, no music *(R D Knight)*

☆ **Graffham** W Sus [SU9217], *White Horse*: Pleasant family pub with good South Downs views from conservatory, small dining room, terrace and big garden; good well served food, great newish landlord, very friendly staff, a welcome for walkers *(Miss D J Hobbs, Sylvia and Lionel Kopelowitz)*

Hadlow Down E Sus [A272 W of Heathfield; TQ5324], *New Inn*: Looks a bit derelict, with junked machinery outside, but an interesting experience – back to the 1950s, with snacks on shelves behind the bar, Harveys beers inc Mild on handpump, pool room, very friendly family with plenty of stories to tell; houses the post office *(Tom McLean, Roger Huggins, Jason Caulkin)*

☆ **Halnaker** W Sus [A285 Chichester-Petworth; SU9008], *Anglesey Arms*: Genuine food of the type that can be quickly cooked to order, and occasional interesting Spanish specialities, in bright friendly bar with traditional games, well kept King & Barnes and Tetleys-related ales, good wines (again inc direct Spanish imports), smart simplicity in candlelit stripped-pine-and-flagstones dining room (where children allowed), tables in garden *(J H L Davis, Roger Lamble, Ron Shelton, J and P Maloney, Betty Weaver, LYM)*

☆ **Hammerpot** W Sus [A27 4 miles W of Worthing; TQ0605], *Woodmans Arms*: Welcoming low-beamed 16th-c pub with interesting prints, horsey bric-a-brac, well kept Gales and King & Barnes, generous varied food inc giant yorkshire puddings; seats in pleasant garden *(Tony and Wendy Hobden, Bruce Bird, David Holloway)*

☆ **Hartfield** E Sus [Gallipot St; B2110 towards Forest Row; TQ4735], *Gallipot*: Good atmosphere in comfortable L-shaped bar with a couple of well kept ales such as Fullers London Pride, obliging licensees, wide range of good genuine home cooking, no music, log fire, restaurant, dogs allowed if announced; on edge of attractively set village, good walks nearby *(Colin Laffan, R and S Bentley, Neil and Jenny Spink)*

☆ **Hartfield** [A264], *Haywaggon*: Spacious and welcoming beamed pub, very popular with OAPs lunchtime for good reliable low-priced simple bar food in attractive dining room (doubles as evening restaurant), well kept real ale, quick service *(Colin Laffan, Margaret and Nigel Dennis)*

☆ **Hastings** E Sus [14 High St, Old Town; TQ8109], *First In Last Out*: Good reasonably priced beers brewed here, farm cider, friendly landlord, chatty atmosphere, attractive booths formed by pews, no games or juke box; interesting simple lunchtime food, free Sun cockles, central log fire *(Rob and Doris Harrison, Chris Fluck, Friedolf Joetten, Christopher Turner)*

Hastings [E Beach St], *London Trader*: Old town pub well refurbished, plenty of character and atmosphere *(Steve Cooper)*; [Old Town], *Pump House*: Fine old building with low beams and so forth, well kept Shepherd Neame *(Chris Fluck)*

Henfield W Sus [A281; TQ2116], *White Hart*: 16th-c village pub with tools hanging from low beams, horse brasses, paintings, prints and photographs, log fire, Flowers Original and other ales, large popular dining area with good straightforward food and good friendly service, tables on terrace and in garden *(G W and I L Edwards, Brian and Jenny Seller)*

☆ **Hermitage** W Sus [36 Main Rd (A259); SU7505], *Sussex Brewery*: Cosy atmosphere and good log fires in simple small friendly town pub with bare bricks, sawdust on boards and flagstones; well kept Archers Golden, Badger Best, Tanglefoot and Hard Tackle, Charles Wells Bombardier, Wadworths 6X and an ale brewed for them, good value simple food from sandwiches up inc masses of speciality sausages, two neat restaurants, one up a few steps is cosy with shiny wood floors, no machines or piped music, small courtyard; can get very busy, open all day Sat *(Ann and Colin Hunt, Rob and Doris Harrison, P K Broomhead, BB)*

Herstmonceux E Sus [Gardner St; TQ6312], *Brewers Arms*: Unspoilt 16th-c local with particularly good choice of well kept ales, decent food, welcoming licensees; boules *(Peter Thompson)*

☆ **Holtye** E Sus [A264 East Grinstead—Tunbridge Wells; TQ4539], *White Horse*: Unpretentiously refurbished old village pub with friendly and helpful young staff, well kept ales inc Brakspears, generous bar food and popular carvery restaurant with illuminated aquarium set into floor; good facilities for the disabled; bedrooms *(the Shinkmans, Mrs R D Knight)*

☆ **Hooe** E Sus [A259 E of Pevensey; TQ6809], *Lamb*: Prettily placed dining pub, extensively refurbished with lots of stripped brick and flintwork, one snug area around huge log fire and lots of other seats, very wide choice of generous popular food from well filled sandwiches up, well kept Harveys, quick friendly service *(A H Denham, Mr and Mrs Jones, G Washington)*

☆ **Horsham** W Sus [31 North St; TQ1730], *Black Jug*: Good country atmosphere in attractively refurbished panelled pub/restaurant, good choice of often imaginative food esp pies and puddings, well kept John Smiths and Marstons Pedigree, good changing house wines, friendly staff *(Ken Hollywood, Simon Hurst, Don and Thelma Anderson, Peter Walters, Susan Lee)*

☆ **Houghton** W Sus [B2139; TQ0111], *George & Dragon*: Fine old timbered pub with civilised rambling heavy-beamed bar, nice comfortable mix of furnishings inc some antiques, pleasing usual food, Courage Directors, John Smiths, a beer brewed locally for the pub and a guest ale, charming garden with pretty views; children (and maybe dogs) welcome *(John Fahy, Margaret and Nigel Dennis, Clive Gilbert, A E and P McCully, Dr D K M Thomas, Dr M V Jones, Pippa Bobbett, J H Bell, David Holloway, LYM)*

Hunston W Sus [B2145 Chichester—Sidlesham; SU8501], *Spotted Cow*: Very handy for towpath walkers, quite small but attractive and welcoming, big garden with outside tables, good lunchtime snacks inc super sandwiches, bigger evening meals *(Shirley Pielou)*

☆ **Icklesham** E Sus [TQ8816], *Queens Head*: Friendly open-plan three-level beamed family pub with generous varied appetising food inc vegetarian, around a dozen changing real ales, Biddenden cider, decent wines, lots of nooks, crannies and different levels inc no-smoking area, big log fire; garden has fine views *(Amanda Hodges, Bruce Bird, D B Stanley, G S and E M Dorey, Ernest M Russell)*

Icklesham, *Oast House*: Friendly 17th-c pub, good range of popular straightforward food, well kept Adnams and Youngs, free Sun seafood nibbles, silk flower arrangements (for sale); attractive garden *(Mick and Mel Smith, J Baker)*

Isfield E Sus [1 m off A26; TQ4417], *Laughing Fish*: Simply modernised village local with well kept Harveys Best, PA and

Old, good honest home-cooked bar food, tables in small garden with enclosed play area; children welcome, right by Lavender Line *(John Beeken, BB)*

Kingsfold W Sus [A24; TQ1636], *Cromwells*: Generous good value food, Whitbreads-related ales, quick friendly service; evenings has rather a night-club atmosphere, with soft lighting, loud piped music *(Dave Irving)*

Kingsfold W Sus [Dorking Rd; A24 Dorking—Horsham, nr A29 junction; TQ1636], *Dog & Duck*: Comfortable old country pub, well kept King & Barnes and other ales, good value nicely presented food (not after 2 lunchtime) inc popular lunches and Weds curry nights *(Alan Whiting, Dave Irving, DWAJ)*

☆ **Lambs Green** W Sus [TQ2136], *Lamb*: Quaint old beamed pub well refurbished to give more space, friendly helpful staff, well kept beers such as Wadworths 6X and Youngs, good varied changing food, good value considering helping size, restaurant; nice log fire *(Doreen and Brian Hardham, Steve Goodchild, BB)*

☆ **Lewes** E Sus [Castle Ditch Lane/Mount Pl; TQ4110], *Lewes Arms*: Welcoming old-fashioned traditional local below castle mound, cosy front lounge and two larger rooms (one with pool), well kept Harveys and other ales, limited range of basic bar food, daily papers *(Phil and Sally Gorton, Alan Skull, John Beeken)*

☆ **Lewes** [22 Malling St], *Dorset Arms*: Good bar food esp fresh fish Fri lunchtime in popular, civilised and friendly 17th-c pub with well kept Harveys, well equipped family room, restaurant, outside terraces; comfortable bedrooms *(Alan Skull, Andrew Partington)*

Lewes [Offham Rd], *Chalk Pit*: Fine choice of beers, good range of reasonably priced food, very friendly staff *(Alan Skull)*; [main st], *White Hart*: Nice old building with side coach entrance, good value bar food, good service, Harveys beers; restaurant *(Colin Laffan)*

☆ **Lindfield** W Sus [98 High St (B2028); TQ3425], *Bent Arms*: Good bar food inc spit-roasted beef (lunchtime Mon, Tues, Fri, Sat) turned by model steam-engine, other interesting bric-a-brac, antique and art deco furnishings and stained glass; good bar food, good choice of well kept ales, friendly waitresses; attractive garden, children in restaurant and eating area; bedrooms *(Don Mather, LYM)*

☆ **Litlington** E Sus [The Street; between A27 Lewes—Polegate and A259 E of Seaford; TQ5201], *Plough & Harrow*: Cosy beamed front bar in attractively extended flint local, friendly efficient licensees, six well kept changing real ales, decent wines by the glass; consistently good home cooking, dining area done up as railway dining car (children allowed here); back lawn with children's bar, aviary and pretty views; live music Fri *(A Plumb, Neil H Barker, Colin Laffan, LYM)*

☆ **Littlehampton** W Sus [Wharf Rd; westwards towards Chichester, opp rly stn; TQ0202], *Arun View*: Comfortable and attractive 18th-c inn right on harbour with river directly below windows, Whitbreads-related ales, wide choice of reasonably priced decent bar food, restaurant (wise to book), flower-filled terrace; summer barbecues evenings and weekends; bedrooms *(Mrs M Rice, Ruth and Alan Cooper)*

Littlehampton [Western Rd], *Marine*: Good atmosphere in relaxed and chatty local *(Derek Wilkins)*

☆ **Lodsworth** W Sus [SU9223], *Hollist Arms*: Relaxed atmosphere in two small cosy bars and big cheerful dining room, varied food, well kept Ballards ales, darts, shove ha'penny etc *(Mrs M Rice, H West, Anne Watson)*

Lower Dicker E Sus [TQ5511], *Potters*: Small bright and friendly local, Bass and changing guest beers, well presented food *(Robert and Gladys Flux)*

Loxwood W Sus [B2133; TQ0431], *Onslow Arms*: Spacious and pleasant, by Wey & Arun Canal under restoration, with good bar food, well kept full King & Barnes range; picnic tables in garden *(Mike Davies)*

Maplehurst E Sus [TQ1924], *White Horse*: At least six well kept ales such as Cains, Harveys and King & Barnes, decent food, beams, pub cat *(Paul Comerford)*

☆ **Midhurst** W Sus [North St; SU8821], *Angel*: Smart partly 16th-c coaching inn with brasserie-like concentration on good reasonably priced food esp puddings, charming bar cosy and welcoming despite plain tables and hard seats, good service, well kept beer; comfortable bedrooms *(Mrs M Rice, Roger Lamble, N Matthews, Mr and Mrs Michael Boxford)*

☆ **Midhurst** [opp Spread Eagle], *Bricklayers Arms*: Good reasonably priced home-cooked food inc good value Sun roast, well kept Greene King IPA and Abbot, two cosy bars, sturdy old oak furniture, 17th-c beams, old photographs and bric-a-brac *(R A Dean, G W and I L Edwards)*

Midhurst [Petersfield Rd (A272 just W)], *Half Moon*: Useful Big Steak pub with well kept Tetleys-related ales, good value meals, quick friendly waitresses *(Colin Laffan, G Washington)*; [Red Lion St], *Swan*: Good value fresh food all day from 8.30 breakfast, well kept Harveys PA and Best, lots of black beams, plain public bar, small upper lounge, small back restaurant; bedrooms *(Joan and Michel Hooper-Immins)*; [Wool Lane/Rumbolds Hill (A272)], *Wheatsheaf*: Attractive unpretentious low-beamed half-timbered 16th-c pub with good value generous food, very friendly staff, King & Barnes and other beers *(Brian Hutton, Mrs M Rice)*

☆ **Milton Street** E Sus [off A27 Polegate—Lewes, ¼ mile E of Alfriston roundabout; TQ5304], *Sussex Ox*: Attractive family country pub beautifully placed below downs, big lawn and marvellous play area; good atmosphere inside, well kept ales such as

Harveys Best, popular food, pleasantly simple country furniture, brick floor, woodburner, one lively and one quieter family room; lots of good walks, busy weekends *(Jonathan Fry, Andrew Partington, LYM)*

☆ **Netherfield** E Sus [Netherfield Hill, just off B2096 Heathfield—Battle; TQ7118], *Netherfield Arms*: Friendly low-ceilinged country pub with good choice of well kept ales and wines, wide choice of good bar food, inglenook log fire, no-smoking area, restaurant, no music; lovely garden *(John and Vi Collins)*

☆ **Newhaven** E Sus [West Quay; follow West Beach signs from A259 westbound; TQ4502], *Hope*: Big-windowed pub overlooking busy harbour entrance, upstairs conservatory room and breezy balcony tables with even better view towards Seaford Head, well kept Flowers, Harveys and Wadworths 6X, reasonably priced simple food inc seafood specialities, friendly service, darts and pool in airy public bar, waterside terrace *(Keith Mills, LYM)*

Newick E Sus [Allington Rd (A272 W); TQ4121], *Bricklayers Arms*: Good choice of reasonably priced restaurant food (Sun lunch very popular), well kept Harveys, interesting pictures and cigarette cards; tables on terrace and lawn with particularly good play area, goats and duck pond *(G W and I L Edwards)*; [A272, by green], *Bull*: Roomy and attractive, lots of beams and character, good relaxing atmosphere, reasonable choice of moderately priced food in sizeable eating area, good service, well kept mainly Courage-related ales *(Colin Laffan, Alan Kilpatrick, Alec and Marie Lewery)*; [Church Rd], *Royal Oak*: Friendly licensees, decent food (plans to extend restaurant), Flowers Original and Harveys *(G W and I L Edwards)*

Newpound Common W Sus [TQ0627], *Bat & Ball*: Country pub with open fires, good reasonably priced food, well kept King & Barnes ales; big garden, campsite *(Dave Lands)*

☆ **Northchapel** W Sus [A285 Guildford—Petworth; SU9529], *Half Moon*: Beams, open fire, home-made food, local beer, lots of old country tools; garden with tame goose, big red tractor, even old buses; live music last Mon of month *(Sue Anderson, Phil Copleston, Ian Phillips)*

Nyetimber W Sus [255 Pagham Rd; SZ8998], *Inglenook*: Charming atmosphere, good food, attractive garden behind; comfortable bedrooms *(Gillian and Michael Wallace)*; [Pagham Rd], *Lamb*: Warm, welcoming pub with good value food in bar and restaurant (must book Sat), good range of beers, Portuguese chef/patron *(M Judd)*

Offham E Sus [A275 N of Lewes; TQ4012], *Blacksmiths Arms*: Comfortable and peaceful, decent home-cooked food, well kept Harveys Best and Shepherd Neame, good service, log fire in big stone fireplace *(R D and S R Knight)*

☆ **Pagham** W Sus [Nyetimber Lane; SZ8897], *Lion*: Cosy 15th-c pub with two bars, wooden seating, uneven flooring, low beams, good value imaginatively prepared food, well kept Ringwood beers and good malt whiskies, cheerful service, small restaurant, big terrace; very popular in summer *(Mrs M Rice, Mark Parsons, Jan and Colin Roe, David and Rebecca Killick)*

☆ **Pett** E Sus [TQ8714], *Two Sawyers*: Friendly pub with character main bar, small public bar, back snug, small oak-beamed back restaurant where children allowed; well kept ales inc two from new neighbouring Olde Forge microbrewery, log fires, welcoming staff, good if not cheap food; big garden with swings and boules pitch; bedrooms *(D B Stanley, Richard Houghton)*

☆ **Petworth** W Sus [Coultershaw Bridge, just off A285 1½ miles towards Chichester; SU9719], *Badger & Honeyjar*: Victorian pub in idyllic riverside setting, cottagey feel, attentive staff, good choice of music and of beers, eclectic choice of tempting food; tables outside *(R Wilson)*

☆ **Petworth** [A283 towards Pulborough], *Welldiggers*: Stylishly simple low-ceilinged dining pub with good value restaurantish meals; plenty of tables on attractive lawns and terraces, lovely views *(Mrs M Rice, LYM)*

Petworth [Angel St], *Angel*: Olde-worlde hotel with Bass, Badger Tanglefoot and Worthington, cheerful landlord, chatty locals, good weekend carvery; bedrooms *(Shelagh and Denis Dutton)*

☆ **Playden** E Sus [A268/B2082; TQ9121], *Peace & Plenty*: Small welcoming homely pub with roaring log fire in hop-hung lounge bar, well kept Greene King Abbot and Rayments, comfortable armchairs, wooden benches; good value tasty food in softly lit dining room with portraits, tables outside *(Mr and Mrs C J Sanders, John T Ames, Mark Percy)*

☆ **Plumpton** E Sus [Ditchling Rd (B2116); TQ3613], *Half Moon*: Picturesque and cosy, with varied reasonably priced food (not Sun evening) inc all sorts of quiches, well kept King & Barnes, John Smiths and Wadworths 6X, prompt friendly service, log fire; evening restaurant, rustic seats in big garden with Downs view, play area inc tractors *(Tony and Wendy Hobden, John Beeken, Mrs R D Knight, Alec and Marie Lewery)*

Poundgate E Sus [A26 Crowborough—Uckfield – OS Sheet 199 map ref 493289; TQ4928], *Crow & Gate*: Keen young landlord, wide choice of decent food inc OAP bargain lunches and well kept Bass, Harveys Best and Worthington BB; pleasant beamed bar with big copper-hooded fireplace, restaurant *(Colin Laffan)*

☆ **Poynings** W Sus [TQ2612], *Royal Oak*: Varied popular bar food inc vegetarian and good fish, well kept Courage-related ales and a guest such as Harveys, cosy but plenty of room, good staff, attractive side garden – very popular in summer, parking on narrow rd can sometimes attract parking tickets *(David Holloway, Alison Burt, Winifrede D Morrison, Alec and Marie Lewery, Mrs M Rice)*

Rake W Sus [Portsmouth Rd (A3 S of Liphook); SU8027], *Sun*: Comfortable and well run dining pub with wide choice of generous home cooked food, quick friendly service, log fires, Bass, Gales BBB and HSB *(Gentian Walls, G C Hackemer)*

☆ **Ringmer** E Sus [off A26 just N of village turn-off; TQ4412], *Cock*: Heavily beamed country pub with welcoming newish landlord, good inglenook log fire, piped music, no-smoking lounge, restaurant, well kept Gales HSB, Harveys Best, Morlands Old Speckled Hen and Ruddles, huge range of bar food, piped music, seats out on good terrace and in attractive fairy-lit garden; children allowed in overflow eating area *(John Beeken, Tony and Wendy Hobden, John and Mavis Wright, LYM)*

☆ *nr* **Ringmer** [outside village; A26 Lewes—Uckfield, S of Isfield turnoff], *Stewards Enquiry*: Good varied food inc good vegetarian and reasonably priced Sun roasts in tastefully refurbished olde-worlde beamed pub; good service, well kept Harveys, children welcome; some outside tables, play area *(Alan Skull, Alec Lewery, Tony and Wendy Hobden)*

☆ **Ripe** E Sus [signed off A22 Uckfield—Hailsham, or off A27 Lewes—Polegate via Chalvington; TQ5010], *Lamb*: Interestingly furnished snug little rooms around central servery, attractive antique prints and pictures, nostalgic song-sheet covers, Victorian pin-ups in gents'; generous home-made food inc children's and Sun roast, well kept Courage-related ales and a guest such as Harveys, several open fires, friendly service; pub games ancient and modern, pleasant sheltered back garden with play area and barbecues *(Adrian and Gilly Heft, Tony and Wendy Hobden, Anthony Barnes, LYM)*

Robertsbridge E Sus [High St; off A21 to Hastings; TQ7323], *Seven Stars*: New Scottish landlord, welcoming staff, 11 real ales on handpump, new restaurant *(Nigel Paine)*

Rogate W Sus [SU8023], *Wyndham Arms*: Welcoming village local with well kept Ballards, King & Barnes and Ringwood ales, well cooked bar food *(J O Jonkler)*

Rotherfield E Sus [TQ5529], *Rainbow Trout*: Dining pub under same management as Brown Trout at Lamberhurst (see Kent main entries), similar food concentrating on fresh fish, Whitbreads-related and other ales; under local pressure have put up sign behind with old Kings Arms name *(Colin Laffan)*

Rottingdean E Sus [TQ3702], *Plough*: Comfortable pondside local with good value food inc huge home-made pies, well kept beers, extensive wine list, quick friendly service, upstairs restaurant, small back terrace; live jazz Sun *(Linda and Brian Davis)*

☆ **Rusper** W Sus [High St; village signed from A24 and A264 N and NE of Horsham; TQ2037], *Plough*: Padded very low beams, panelling and big inglenook, good value straightforward food, good range of real ales, lovely log fire, bar billiards and darts in raftered room upstairs; fountain in back garden, pretty front terrace, occasional live music; children welcome *(Dr and Mrs A K Clarke, Andy and Jackie Mallpress, DWAJ, G W and I L Edwards, LYM)*

Rustington W Sus [TQ0502], *Lamb*: Good food, well kept beer *(G Washington)*; *Windmill*: Quick service, good bar snacks, friendly staff; garden with play equipment *(Romey Heaton)*

☆ **Rye** E Sus [Gun Gdn, off A259; TG9220], *Ypres Castle*: Pronounced WWI-style, as Wipers, simple and friendly, in fine setting up towards the tower, with great view, big lawn; wide choice of good home cooking esp fish using good ingredients, well kept changing ales such as Hook Norton, Morrells and a Mild, old yachting magazines, local event posters, piped music; open all day in season *(A Preston, John T Ames, Jay Voss, Bruce Bird)*

☆ **Rye**, *Hope & Anchor*: Good value food esp fresh fish; friendly and pleasant *(Rob and Doris Harrison, Russell and Margaret Bathie)*

Rye Harbour E Sus [TQ9220], *Inkerman Arms*: Friendly unpretentious pub nr nature reserve, good food inc fresh fish and old-fashioned puddings, well kept Greene King ales; boules *(H R Taylor, Marian Greenwood)*

☆ **Salehurst** E Sus [½ mile off A21 T Wells—Battle – OS Sheet 199 map ref 748242; TQ7424], *Salehurst Halt*: L-shaped bar in station building by dismantled line, good plain wooden furnishings, friendly staff, good log fire, old prints and photographs, well kept Harveys and Wadworths IPA and 6X, decent wines, limited but varied choice of imaginative generous food, pleasant garden, pretty village with 14th-c church; bedrooms *(Mr and Mrs A Park)*

☆ *nr* **Scaynes Hill** E Sus [Freshfield Lock; off A272 by petrol station at top of village, via Church Lane signpost; TQ3623], *Sloop*: Tucked-away country pub with sofas and armchairs, games room off basic public bar, lots of tables out in neat garden by derelict Ouse Canal; generous bar food inc children's, well kept Harveys Best and guest beers, lots of country wines; piped music, relaxed service; children in eating area, handy for Bluebell steam railway, not far from Sheffield Park *(Stella Knight, Ron and Sheila Corbett, Tony Walker, Keith and Audrey Ward, John and Mavis Wright, Tony and Wendy Hobden, R J Walden, Simon Pyle, LYM)*

Sedlescombe E Sus [TQ7718], *Queens Head*: Welcoming and comfortable village-green local, big inglenook log fire, Doulton toby-jugs, hunting prints, limited good value bar food, Flowers, decent coffee; restaurant, attractive garden *(E G Parish, Rob and Doris Harrison)*

Selmeston E Sus [A27; TQ5006], *Barley Mow*: Long rambling bar with open fire, hunting prints, chamber-pots, Bass, Flowers Original and Harveys beers, wide choice of good food, attentive helpful staff, no-smoking children's area, restaurant; tables outside *(Michael and Jenny Back, Norma Farris)*

☆ **Selsfield** W Sus [Ardingly Rd; B2028 N of Haywards Heath, nr West Hoathly; TQ3434], *White Hart*: Heavy low 14th-c beams and timbers, big log fire, wide choice of bar food inc some original dishes, well kept Gales, King & Barnes and Tetleys, good service; tastefully converted barn restaurant, picnic tables on side lawn above steep wooded combe, walks nearby; children welcome, handy for Wakehurst Place *(Joan and John Calvert, Dave Carter, David Holloway, LYM)*

Shipley W Sus [towards Coolham; TQ1422], *Countryman*: Early 19th-c, with inglenook log fire, darts and billiards in welcoming flagstoned locals' public bar, open fire in cosy carpeted saloon, restaurant extension with wide choice up to grills and steaks, also bar food; play equipment in pretty garden *(Mrs M Rice)*

☆ **Shoreham by Sea** W Sus [Upper Shoreham Rd, Old Shoreham; TQ2105], *Red Lion*: Interesting if dim-lit old low-beamed pub with generous well cooked bar food inc popular Sun lunch, no-smoking dining room, well kept Courage-related ales with a guest such as Wadworths 6X from end bar, occasional beer festivals, decent wines, log fire in unusual fireplace, pretty sheltered garden; river walks, good South Downs views *(R T and J C Moggridge, Mrs M Rice, Jim and Maggie Cowell, M Carey, A Groocock, Ian Phillips)*

☆ **Shortbridge** E Sus [Piltdown – OS Sheet 198 map ref 450215; TQ4521], *Peacock*: Good tasty food in attractive 16th-c beamed and timbered pub with real ales such as Boddingtons, Morlands Old Speckled Hen and Websters Yorkshire, big inglenook, Turkey rugs on oak parquet, soft lighting, dining area; sizeable garden with playhouse *(Caroline Alcock, P J Keen, Lesley Sones, BB)*

☆ **Sidlesham** W Sus [Mill Lane, off B2145 S of Chichester; SZ8598], *Crab & Lobster*: Individual old country local with log fire in attractive traditional bar, plusher side lounge, charming back garden looking over to the coastal bird-reserve and silted Pagham Harbour; limited choice of good bar food (not Sun evening) sometimes inc fresh seafood, well kept Arundel Stronghold and Gales Best and BBB, country wines, traditional games *(John Beeken, John and Tessa Rainsford, Lynn Sharpless, Bob Eardley, Mrs M Rice, Ann and Colin Hunt, LYM)*

Slaugham W Sus [OS Sheet 198 map ref 257281; TQ2528], *Chequers*: Small bar, grill and restaurant, well kept King & Barnes Sussex and Festive, good food inc cheaper lunchtime bar snacks, emphasis on seafood; enormous wine list; tables on front terrace, opp church among pretty cottages by bridleway to Handcross; bedrooms *(LM, James House)*

☆ **Slindon** W Sus [Slindon Common; A29 towards Bognor; SU9708], *Spur*: Smallish attractive 17th-c pub, interesting reasonably priced food, fresh veg in separate dish, enormous open fire, well kept Courage-related beers; separate games room with darts and pool, children welcome, sizeable restaurant, pleasant garden *(TOH, Doreen and Brian Hardham)*

Slinfold W Sus [The Street; TQ1131], *Kings Head*: Good country food, Whitbreads-related ales, polite attentive staff, tables in big garden; bedrooms *(Jason Caulkin)*

☆ **South Harting** W Sus [B2146; SU7819], *White Hart*: Attractive unspoilt pub with good generous home cooking, lots of polished wood, hundreds of keys, big log fire in cosy snug, cheerful service, well kept Tetleys-related ales, decent coffee, restaurant, separate public bar; well behaved dogs allowed, children in games room; good garden behind for them too, with spectacular Downs views *(Mrs M Rice, Colin and Ann Hunt, Alison and Mike Stevens, Dr Brian Hamilton)*

☆ **South Harting**, *Ship*: Good value food in informal unspoilt local with Palmers and Eldridge Pope beers, upobtrusive piped classical music, dominoes; nice setting in pretty village *(Jenny and Brian Seller, Colin and Ann Hunt, John Evans)*

Southwick W Sus [The Green; TQ2405], *Cricketers*: Three long comfortable bars, separate dining area with sturdy Tudor furniture, nicely furnished family room, food inc children's and cream teas; good cheerful service, live entertainment Weds *(Paulina Blowes)*

Staplefield W Sus [TQ2728], *Jolly Sportsman*: Good atmosphere, log fire, good genuine home cooking (so may be a wait), nice garden *(Ron Gentry)*; [Warninglid Rd], *Victory*: Charming whitewashed pub opp village cricket green, dovecote in roof, picnic tables outside with play area; Gales and King & Barnes beer, wide choice of food, welcoming licensees *(R J Walden, Steve Moore)*

☆ **Stedham** W Sus [School Lane (off A272) – OS Sheet 197 map ref 856223; SU8522], *Hamilton Arms*: Proper English pub run by friendly Thai family, good reasonably priced Thai food in bar and restaurant; pretty hanging baskets, seats out by quiet lane, good walks nearby *(KC , John Pearce)*

☆ **Steyning** W Sus [41 High St; TQ1711], *Chequer*: Character largely Tudor pub with labyrinth of bars and seating areas, friendly staff, good range of well kept Whitbreads-related beers, wide choice of generous food from good snacks up, friendly efficient service *(David Dimock, R T and J C Moggridge)*

☆ **Steyning** [130 High St], *Star*: Flagstoned front bar, carpeted back one furnished in pine, rural memorabilia, no-smoking room, cheerful licensees, well kept Whitbreads-related and guest ales, wide choice of good home cooking (can sometimes be a wait); piped music, regular live music; nice gardens, one with climbing frame and rabbits *(Mike Elkerton, Ian Carter, Tony and Wendy Hobden, Susan Lee)*

☆ **Stoughton** W Sus [signed off B2146 Petersfield—Emsworth; SU8011], *Hare & Hounds*: Much modernised pub below downs with reliably good home-cooked food in airy pine-clad bar, big open fires, half a dozen changing well kept ales such as Adnams Broadside and Gibbs Mew Bishops Tipple, friendly staff, restaurant, back darts room, tables on pretty terrace; nr Saxon church, good walks nearby; children in eating area and restaurant *(Colin and Ann Hunt, Chris McGivern, Miss A G Drake, Keith Stevens, LYM)*

☆ **Sutton** W Sus [nr Bignor Roman villa; SU9715], *White Horse*: Unspoilt ivy-clad traditional pub, simple and clean, island servery separating bare-boards bar from dining area, good choice of good value well presented generous food using local materials inc game and fish, flowers on tables, well kept Batemans, Courage, Youngs and guest beers, log fire, friendly staff; tables in garden, pretty downs-foot village; good value bedrooms, comfortable and well equipped *(LM, Tim Galligan, Sarah Quick, G Washington, Peter Lewis, Mr and Mrs P G Wright)*

Tangmere W Sus [SU9006], *Bader Arms*: Modern, with lots of aircraft and WW2 RAF pictures, inc Douglas Bader himself; Badger best and Tanglefoot, wide choice of well presented promptly served good food inc OAP bargains *(DAV)*

Turners Hill W Sus [East St; TQ3435], *Crown*: Spacious increasingly restaurant-oriented dining pub (though sandwiches still available, and two well kept Tetleys-related ales), different levels (one with pitched rafters), log fire, pleasant decor with pictures etc, decent wines, soft piped music, tables outside, pleasant valley views from back garden; children welcome; two bedrooms *(E G Parish, John Pettit, BB)*; [Lion Lane], *Red Lion*: Simple plain cheap food using good fresh ingredients, friendly staff *(Jason Caulkin)*

☆ **Upper Dicker** E Sus [TQ5510], *Plough*: Wide choice of good generous bar food, Courage-related and King & Barnes real ales, log fire and quick friendly service in homely three-room pub, busy evenings; children's swings in big garden *(Tony Albert)*

☆ **Wadhurst** E Sus [Mayfield Lane (B2100 W); TQ6131], *Best Beech*: Well run dining pub, pleasant bar on left with wall seats, quiet but individual decor and coal fire, eating area on right, usual food well cooked from sandwiches to juicy steaks, well kept Harveys and other ales, decent wines; good value bedrooms *(J H Bell, Jill Bickerton, BB)*

Wadhurst [St James Sq (B2099)], *Greyhound*: Pretty village pub strongly supported by local regulars, wide choice of usual bar food and set Sun lunch in neat restaurant or pleasant beamed bar with big inglenook fireplace, real ales such as Bass, Fullers, Harveys, Ruddles County and Tetleys, no piped music; tables in well kept back garden; bedrooms planned *(R Hale, BB)*

☆ **Walderton** W Sus [Stoughton rd, just off B2146 Chichester—Petersfield; SU7810], *Barley Mow*: Pretty village pub with warm and cosy flagstoned bar, comfortable and attractive lounge, two log fires, huge helpings of good bar food inc notable ploughman's and Sun lunch, well kept Gales ales and country wines, cheerful staff, popular skittle alley; children welcome, fine garden *(Viv Middlebrook)*

☆ **Waldron** E Sus [High St; Blackboys—Horam side rd; TQ5419], *Star*: Lively village local with big inglenook log fire in panelled bar, restaurant off, fair range of standard pub food with some interesting specials, Bass, Charrington IPA, Harveys and Charles Wells Bombardier, no music, friendly service *(Tony Albert, P Saville, Tony Watson, Roger Price)*

☆ **Warbleton** E Sus [TQ6018], *Warbil in Tun*: Extended dining pub with good freshly cooked food esp meat, fresh veg, wide choice of puddings, beams and red plush, good friendly service, big log fire, well kept Flowers IPA and Harveys, good coffee, relaxed civilised atmosphere, hard-working licensees; tables on roadside green *(J H Bell, R D and S R Knight, Alan Skull)*

☆ **Warnham** W Sus [Friday St; TQ1533], *Greets*: 15th-c pub with beams, uneven flagstones and inglenook log fire, lots of cosy corners, well kept Whitbreads-related ales, decent wines, wide choice of good home cooking (not Sun evening) inc fine Sun lunch, friendly service; convivial locals' side bar *(B Perrotton, Jim Povey, Howard Gregory, G W and I L Edwards, Jason Caulkin, Margaret and Nigel Dennis)*

☆ **Washington** W Sus [just off A24 Horsham—Worthing; TQ1212], *Franklands Arms*: Well kept, roomy and welcoming, with wide choice of good food esp pies and seafood mornay, several well kept ales, decent house wines, prompt service; big bar, smaller dining area, games area with pool and darts; tables in neat garden, quiet spot yet busy weekends *(Mrs M Rice, Guy Consterdine, Alec and Marie Lewery, Mrs J A Blanks, Jenny and Brian Seller, Cathryn and Richard Hicks)*

☆ **West Chiltington** W Sus [Church St; TQ0918], *Elephant & Castle*: Friendly pub behind ancient church, good range of reasonably priced food freshly cooked by South African landlord, good chips, well kept King & Barnes ales, no music; good garden *(Shelagh and Denis Dutton, Barbara and Alec Jones)*

☆ **West Chiltington** [Smock Alley, just S], *Five Bells*: Consistently good reasonably priced fresh food, full range of King & Barnes beers kept well and other ales from small breweries, good service, pleasant atmosphere *(M Morgan, H R Taylor)*

West Dean W Sus [A286 Midhurst—Chichester; SU8512], *Selsey Arms*: Warm and friendly, log fire, lots of horse racing pictures and memorabilia, big dining area, reasonably priced good food *(Rita and Derrick Barrey)*

☆ **West Hoathly** W Sus [signed off A22 and B2028 S of E Grinstead; TQ3632], *Cat*: Sadly Gonzalo Burillo the tenant of this charming ancient tiled pub (a main entry since the Guide's earliest days) died shortly before we went to press, and his widow has decided to leave, so we can't tell how things will turn out for it; it's delightfully placed in a pretty hilltop village, with fine views and lots of character, and has had good food, well kept Boddingtons, Harveys BB and Wadworths 6X; children allowed *(LYM; news please)*

West Marden W Sus [B2146 2 miles S of Uppark; SU7713], *Victoria Arms*: Good value home-made food inc interesting dishes and good sandwiches in pleasant rustic surroundings, well kept Gibbs Mew, decent house wines, quick service, restaurant *(G and M Stewart)*

☆ **West Wittering** W Sus [Chichester Rd; B2179/A286 towards Birdham; SU7900], *Lamb*: Immaculate 18th-c country pub, several rooms neatly knocked through with tidy new furnishings, rugs on tiles, well kept ales such as Bunces Benchmark, Cheriton Pots, Ind Coope Burton, Harveys Old, Ringwood Fortyniner, decent wines, interesting reasonably priced food, log fire, welcoming efficient service; tables out in front by road and in small sheltered back garden, with outside salad bar on fine days; busy in summer *(Colin and Ann Hunt, Ted Burden, Caron Gilbert, Mrs D Bromley-Martin, Tim and Sue Halstead, BB)*

Westbourne W Sus [Silverlock Pl; SU7507], *Cricketers*: Simple open-plan village local with Gales ales, friendly licensees, darts one end, piped 60s music (not too loud), occasional live music; garden with chipmunks and canaries *(Ann and Colin Hunt)*; [North St], *Good Intent*: Friendly two-bar local with well kept Tetleys and a guest ale, real fires, darts, juke box, monthly live music *(Ann and Colin Hunt)*

☆ **Wilmington** E Sus [just off A27; TQ5404], *Giants Rest*: Doing well under current friendly landlord, with imaginative sensibly priced home-made food, ales such as Adnams, Fullers and Harveys, simple attractive furnishings in small chatty rooms; picnic tables outside; bedrooms *(Alan Skull, E G Parish)*

☆ **Winchelsea** E Sus [German St; TQ9017], *New Inn*: Variety of solid comfortable furnishings in well decorated bustling rambling rooms, some emphasis on wide choice of food inc good fresh fish (sandwiches too), well kept changing ales such as Badger Tanglefoot, Harveys PA, Smiles and Wadworths 6X, decent wines and malt whiskies, friendly waitress service; separate public bar with darts, children in eating area, pretty bedrooms (some sharing bathrooms), delightful setting *(Colin Laffan, J R Whetton, David and Fiona Easeman, Angeline Chan, Jack Taylor, Maysie Thompson, D A Edwards, Gerry Z Pearson, Dr T E Hothersall, LYM)*

☆ **Wisborough Green** W Sus [TQ0526], *Three Crowns*: Good reasonably priced food inc big ploughman's and popular Sun lunch served very quickly in friendly refurbished stripped-brick-and-beams pub, clean and polished; well kept ales such as Greene King Abbot, efficient and obliging young staff, sizeable garden *(Colin Laffan, Howard West, John and Elspeth Howell, David Dimock)*

Worth W Sus [TQ3036], *Cowdray Arms*: Large popular country pub, good choice of well prepared lunchtime meals, real ales with occasional festivals, good friendly service; garden with play area *(Dave Irving, John Pettit)*

☆ **Worthing** W Sus [High St, W Tarring; TQ1303], *Vine*: Good friendly unpretentious local, small, cosy and comfortable and welcoming, with good choice of well kept ales inc distant rarities (and yearly beer festival), good daily special and other food, attractive garden *(Ian Phillips, Dave Irving, Mrs M Rice)*

Worthing [Portland Rd, just N of Marks & Spencer], *Hare & Hounds*: Friendly and busy recently extended pub with good range of reasonably priced bar food; no car park but three multi-storeys nearby *(Brian Hutton, Tony and Wendy Hobden)*; *Hogshead*: Decent food, good choice of real ales *(Robert Heaven)*; [Salvington Rd, Lower Salvington; TQ1205], *John Seldon*: Refurbished Victorian pub, friendly young staff, wide choice of lunchtime food, spacious quiet saloon, smaller public bar with darts and quiz teams popular with younger people, tables in big courtyard and on side terrace; occasional Morris dancers *(Mrs M Rice, Tony and Wendy Hobden)*; [Richmond Rd], *Wheatsheaf*: Popular and comfortable open-plan pub with well kept ales, good reasonably priced food, welcoming atmosphere *(Tony and Wendy Hobden, Mike Appleton)*

Yapton W Sus [Maypole Lane; signed off B2132 Arundel rd – OS Sheet 197 map ref 977042; SU9703], *Maypole*: Friendly staff, customers and cats, two log fires in music-free lounge, generous helpings of reasonably priced home-cooked food (not Sun or Tues evenings), well kept Ringwood Best, Youngers IPA, a Mild and four interesting guest ales, beer festivals Easter and August bank hol *(Bruce Bird, Tony and Wendy Hobden)*

Tyne & Wear *see* Northumbria

Tyne & Wear *see* Northumbria

Warwickshire *see* Midlands

West Midlands *see* Midlands

Wiltshire

Doing especially well here these days are the Red Lion at Axford (good food with emphasis on fish), the Cross Guns near Bradford-on-Avon (a very successful dining pub), the Three Crowns at Brinkworth (another very popular dining pub), the White Hart at Ford (standing out as one of the nicest pubs in Britain – one of the very few to gain all our Awards), the Bell at Ramsbury (outstandingly successful current licensees, well in the running for a Food Award now), the Barge at Seend (making the most of its canalside location) and the mainly no-smoking restauranty Lamb at Semington. The new Spanish landlord for the Harrow at Little Bedwyn is very promising. All these in their way are enjoyable places for a meal out, and to them we'd add the the Talbot at Berwick St John, the Quarrymans Arms at Box, the Red Lion in Lacock, the Wheatsheaf at Lower Woodford (a successful refurbishment), the Silver Plough at Pitton, the Old Mill in Salisbury, the Rattlebone at Sherston, and two new main entries, the Raven at Poulshot and the George & Dragon at Rowde. Particularly as so many readers have enjoyed its refreshingly smoke-free atmosphere, it's the Lamb at Semington which we choose as Wiltshire Dining Pub of the Year. In the Lucky Dip section at the end of the chapter, we'd like to call special attention to the Crown at Alvediston, Greyhound at Bromham, Fox & Goose at Coombe Bissett, Bell at Great Cheverell, Angel at Heytesbury, Carpenters Arms at Sherston, Spread Eagle at Stourton, Red Lion at West Dean and Seven Stars just outside Woodborough; as we have so far been able to inspect only a few of these promising places ourselves, we'd be very grateful for further reports on them. Salisbury has a good choice of pubs – and indeed of interesting breweries, from the little Hop Back to the long-established Gibbs Mew. Wadworths is probably the county's most favoured well known brewery, though Arkells has its admirers. Smaller names to look out for are Archers, Bunces, Foxley, Moles, Oakhill (actually from Somerset) and Wiltshire. Perhaps because of the relative strength of smaller breweries here, drinks prices are just a shade below the national average and have held steadier here recently than almost anywhere else. The cheapest pubs we found were the George and the Red Lion, both in Lacock, both tied to Wadworths, and both actually cheaper than last year, and the Vine Tree at Norton and the Rattlebone at Sherston, both free houses getting their beer from a small local brewer.

AXFORD SU2370 Map 2

Red Lion

Turn-off in Marlborough A345/346 signposted Mildenhall and Ramsbury; Axford is between them

Regular visitors to this pretty flint-and-brick pub say it improves on each visit. The emphasis is very much on the food, but drinkers are made just as welcome as those coming for a meal – and you're quite likely to be greeted as a local on your first visit. Still with the accent on fish, and beginning to concentrate more on the blackboard specials, the range of food might include sandwiches, courgette and tomato soup, lovely smoked salmon roulade, good potted stilton in port, smoked prawns (£3.75), smoked trout (£4.50), lovely sardines or plaice (£7.25), river trout, mullet (£7.95), crayfish (£8.50), lamb fillet (£9.50), lemon sole (£9.95), steaks (from £10.25), local game such as pheasant or partridge (£10.50), Dover sole (£12.50), and fresh lobster (£15.50); salads and vegetables are very fresh and crisp, no chips, but excellent sauté potatoes. There are comfortable cask seats and other solid chairs on the spotless parquet floor of the bustling beamed and pine-panelled bar, with picture windows for the fine valley view; the restaurant is no-smoking. Well kept Foxley Dog Booter (brewed about a mile away), Greene King Abbot, Hook Norton Best, Shepherd Neame Spitfire and Wadworths 6X on handpump, and decent wines including local and New World ones; darts, shove-ha'penny, cribbage, dominoes, fruit machine, and unobtrusive piped music; pleasant quick service. The sheltered garden has picnic tables under cocktail parasols, swings, and lovely views. *(Recommended by Michael and Hazel Lyons, Kevin and Kay Bronnsey, Alan and Paula McCully, Pat and Robert Wyatt, Mr and Mrs Smith, S C King, Colin Laffan, Derek and Sylvia Stephenson, Peter and Audrey Dowsett, R T and J C Moggridge, H Anderson, Nigel Clifton, JE)*

Free house ~ Licensees Mel and Daphne Evans ~ Real ale ~ Meals and snacks (till 10) ~ Restaurant ~ (01672) 520271 ~ Children welcome ~ Open 11-3, 6(6.30 winter)-11 ~ Bedrooms: £30B/£45B

BARFORD ST MARTIN SU0531 Map 2

Barford

Junction A30/B3089

The popularity of this neatly kept old place has been steadily increasing in the two or three years since the current licensees arrived. Their Friday evening Israeli barbecues (all year round, from 7pm) are especially well liked, and other reliable food includes soup (£1.95), filled baked potatoes or big sandwiches (£2.50), ploughman's (from £4.25), falafel with hummus (£4.50), ham and two eggs (£4.75), broccoli and mushroom casserole or cottage pie (£4.95), steak and kidney pie (£6.50), steaks (from £8.95), children's dishes (£2.95), and puddings (£2.25); friendly service. The front bar has dark squared oak panelling, cushioned wall benches, dark seats and tables, and a big log fire in winter; it's generally busier in the evenings than at lunchtime. Well kept Badger Best and Charles Wells Eagle on handpump, and quite a few country wines; darts and piped music. Part of the restaurant is no smoking. They've added a new garden at the back, and there are tables on a terrace outside. The upgraded bedrooms may well deserve our stay award, so we'd be particularly interested to hear from readers who've stayed here. *(Recommended by Dr and Mrs A K Clarke, John and Christine Vittoe, Gordon, Dr and Mrs N Holmes)*

Badger ~ Tenant Ido Davids ~ Real ale ~ Meals and snacks (11.30-3, 7-10) ~ Restaurant ~ (01722) 742242 ~ Children welcome ~ Open 11.30-11; 11.30-3, 7-11 winter ~ Summer folk duets and Morris dancers ~ Bedrooms: £28B/£40B

BERWICK ST JOHN ST9323 Map 2

Talbot

Village signposted from A30 E of Shaftesbury

In a pleasant and peaceful village, full of thatched old houses, this well-run and friendly Ebbe Valley pub is a popular place for eating, especially in the evening, when the tables are candle lit. The single long, heavy beamed bar is simply furnished, with cushioned solid wall and window seats, spindleback chairs, a comfortable kitchen armchair at one end, and a high-backed built-in settle at the other, heavy black beams and cross-beams (nicely shaped with bevelled corners), and a huge inglenook fireplace with a good iron fireback and bread ovens. Adnams Best and Broadside, Bass, and Wadworths 6X on handpump, decent wines. Carefully prepared bar food includes delicious home-made chicken and mushroom soup (£2.95), excellent ploughman's, pasta with a stilton and walnut sauce (£4.95), good curries, steak and kidney pie (£6.95), fresh skate, steaks, and lovely home-made puddings like treacle tart or bread and butter pudding (£3.25); note there is no food on Sunday lunchtimes. Cribbage, dominoes, piped music. Some tables on the back lawn, with swings for children. *(Recommended by G and M Stewart, Gordon, Howard Allen, H D Wharton, S G N Bennett, John Hazel, Tina and David Woods-Taylor)*

Free house ~ Licensees Roy and Wendy Rigby ~ Real ale ~ Meals and snacks (not Sun) ~ Restaurant ~ (01747) 828222 ~ Children in eating area of bar; no under 7s in evening ~ Open 11.30-2.30, 7(6.30 Sat)-11; closed Sun evening

BOX ST8268 Map 2

Quarrymans Arms

Box Hill; off A4 just W of Rudloe

One reader visiting this isolated place feared her allergy to garlic would prevent her from having the meal she particularly fancied, but the chef was happy to replace all the garlic in the dish with rosemary. Other readers have found the service equally helpful and friendly, but what they praise most highly is the quality of the food. A typical day's menu might include sandwiches, tasty home-made soup (£2.25), stilton and asparagus pancake (£3.25), mussels and prawns baked in white wine and garlic (£3.50), wheat and walnut casserole (£5.25), steamed sea bass with garlic and chive sauce (£6.95), pork dijonnaise or pan-fried red snapper fillets with an orange and lemon butter sauce (£7.95), steaks (from £8.25), daily specials, and puddings such as chocolate terrine with a raspberry coulis (£3.50); good vegetables. Well kept Bass, Butcombe, Wadworths 6X, and guests like Wickwar Brand Oak on handpump, good wines, 40 malt whiskies, and ten or so vintage cognacs. Darts, shove-ha'penny, cribbage, dominoes, fruit machine, trivia, boules, cricket, and piped music. Despite the popularity of the food the much-modernised bar is still the kind of place you can come to for just a drink. Interesting quarry photographs and memorabilia cover the walls, and there are dramatic views over the valley; the snug is no-smoking. Picnic-table sets outside. The pub is ideally situated for cavers, potholers and walkers, and runs interesting guided trips down the local Bath stone mine. *(Recommended by Meg and Colin Hamilton, Gwen and Peter Andrews, S A Moir, Roger and Jenny Huggins, Pat and John Millward, Peter and Lynn Brueton, Paul Weedon)*

Free house ~ Licensees John and Ginny Arundel ~ Real ale ~ Meals and snacks (12-3, 6-10.30) ~ Restaurant ~ (01225) 743569 ~ Children welcome away from bar ~ Open 11-11; 11-4, 6-11 Mon/Tues ~ Bedrooms: £25/£30

nr BRADFORD-ON-AVON ST8060 Map 2

Cross Guns

Avoncliff; pub is across footbridge from Avoncliff Station (road signposted Turleigh turning left off A363 heading uphill N from river in Bradford centre, and keep bearing left), and can also be reached down very steep and eventually unmade road signposted Avoncliff – keep straight on rather than turning left into village centre – from Westwood (which is signposted from B3109 and from A366, W of Trowbridge); OS Sheet 173 map reference 805600

Very well liked by readers at the moment, this idyllically set country pub is definitely a place to come to for a meal, and one that's extraordinarily good value considering the quality. Generously served dishes might include sandwiches (from £1.30), home-made pâté (£2), very good stilton or cheddar ploughman's (from £3.20), home-made steak and kidney pie (£4.75), various fish dishes, steaks (from £5.20; 32oz £11), lemon sole (£5.95), trout (£4.10), and duck in orange sauce (£5.95) with delicious puddings (from £1.50). Well kept Courage Best and Directors, John Smiths, Ushers

Best and a guest beer on handpump; good service. There's a nice old-fashioned feel to the bar, with its core of low 17th-c, rush-seated chairs around plain sturdy oak tables (most of which are set for diners, and many of them reserved), stone walls, and a large ancient fireplace with a smoking chamber behind it; piped music. There may be a system of Tannoy announcements for meal orders from outside tables. From the pretty terraced gardens, floodlit at night, there are splendid views down to the wide river Avon, taking in the maze of bridges, aqueducts (the Kennet & Avon Canal) and tracks that wind through this quite narrow gorge. Walkers are very welcome, but not their muddy boots. The pub gets very busy, especially at weekends and summer lunchtimes, so if you want to eat it's probably best to book. *(Recommended by Tony and Wendy Hobden, Meg and Colin Hamilton, Andrew Shore, Richard Dolphin, Andrew Partington, Mrs E M Astley Weston, Dr Diana Terry, A D Sherman, Ron Gentry, Roger Wain-Heapy, John and Christine Simpson, Peter Neate, Dr and Mrs R E S Tanner, Mrs S H Godsell, Paul Weedon)*

Free house ~ Licensees Dave and Gwen Sawyer ~ Real ale ~ Meals and snacks (till 9.45) ~ (01225) 862335 ~ Children in eating area ~ Open 11-3, 6.30-11 (closed 25 and evening 26 Dec)

BRINKWORTH SU0184 Map 2

Three Crowns

The Street; B4042 Wootton Bassett—Malmesbury

When the barman here asks your name as he takes your food order, he may well remember it for the rest of your visit. The bar food really is very good indeed – a little pricier than you might pay elsewhere, but with a corresponding leap in quality and flavours; several readers reckon it's amongst the best food they've ever had in a pub or restaurant. Changing daily and relying on fresh local produce, the choice might include very good crusty filled rolls, home-made pies like steak and kidney or beef and venison (£8.25), crispy sautéed vegetables on a bed of leeks topped with puff pastry (£8.50), parcels of apple, stilton, sultanas and spices (£8.95), an elaborate chicken tandoori pie with bananas and spring onion (£9.95), half a locally smoked chicken with sherry, shallot and cream sauce or fillet of brill with shallots and Vermouth (£11.95), duck supreme in brandy and peppercorn sauce, accompanied by a roast quail stuffed with sausagemeat (£12.45), and home-made puddings (£3.50); best to arrive early in the evening as they don't take bookings. The bustling little rambling bar has a very good pubby feel in all its little enclaves, big landscape prints and other pictures on the walls, some horse-brasses on the dark beams, a dresser with a collection of old bottles, log fires, tables of stripped deal (and a couple made from gigantic forge bellows), with green-cushioned big pews and blond chairs, and a no-smoking conservatory extension; sensibly placed darts, shove-ha'penny, dominoes, cribbage, chess, trivia, fruit machine, piped music. Well kept Archers Village, Bass, Boddingtons, Marstons Pedigree, and Wadworths 6X on handpump (maybe kept under light blanket pressure), and an expanding wine list; prompt efficient service. The garden stretches around the side and back, with well spaced tables, and looks over a side lane to the village church, and out over rolling prosperous farmland. *(Recommended by Ian Phillips, Andrew Shore, D G Clarke, Dr Diana Terry, M G Hart, Pat Crabb, E Carter, Nabil Tarazi, Roger Huggins, Dave Irving, Tom McLean, Ewan McCall, R M Bloomfield, Basil Minson, TBB, Sarah Rissone, J P Gale, Mrs S Smith, Mrs J M Bell, Jane Byrski, Michael Hunt)*

Whitbreads ~ Lease: Anthony Windle ~ Real ale ~ Meals and snacks ~ (01666) 510366 ~ Children in eating area of bar until 9pm ~ Open 10-2.30(3 Sat), 6-11; closed 25 Dec

CHICKSGROVE ST9629 Map 2

Compasses

From A30 5½ miles W of B3089 junction, take lane on N side signposted Sutton Mandeville,

Sutton Row, then first left fork (small signs point the way to the pub, but at the pub itself, in Lower Chicksgrove, there may be no inn sign – look out for the car park); OS Sheet 184 map reference 974294

Well placed in a delightful hamlet, this lovely thatched house has new licensees again, though it will take more than that to affect an atmosphere that's taken so many centuries to develop. The characterful bar has old bottles and jugs hanging from the beams above the roughly timbered bar counter, farm tools, traps and brasses on the partly stripped stone walls, and high-backed wooden settles forming snug booths around tables on the mainly flagstone floor. It's very peaceful and pleasant sitting in the garden or the flagstoned farm courtyard. All home-made, the changing bar food includes dishes such as soup, sandwiches, deep-fried brie with herb crust (£2.95), steak and Guinness pie or pork in cider (£5.95), and puddings like lemon flan; friendly service. Adnams, Bass, Tisbury Best, Wadworths 6X, and a guest beer on handpump; darts, shove-ha'penny, table skittles, and shut-the-box. Lots to do nearby. *(Recommended by Eddie Edwards, D B McAlpin, Lawrence Bacon, Mr and Mrs R H Martyn, James Nason, Simon Harris, John E Rumney, Geoffrey Culmer, G M Betteridge, S K Robinson, Gordon, Jerry and Alison Oakes; more reports on the new regime please)*

Free house ~ Licensees Tony Lethbridge, Sarah Dunham ~ Real ale ~ Meals and snacks ~ (01722) 714318 ~ Children welcome ~ Open 11-3. 6.30-11; closed Mon, except bank holidays when closed following Tues ~ Bedrooms: £25B/£40B

CORSHAM ST8670 Map 2

Two Pigs

A4, Pickwick

Pubs that concentrate just on beer rather than food or families are becoming all too rare these days, so this old-fashioned and characterful place is a splendidly quirky example of what's fast becoming a dying breed. They don't serve any food whatsoever, and under 21s aren't allowed – instead the emphasis is firmly on drinking, with well kept Pigswill (from local Bunces Brewery), and four changing guest beers like Foxleys Barking Mad, Hop Back Summer Lightning, Uley Pigs Ear and so forth, mostly from smaller independent breweries; also a range of country wines. The very narrow long bar has stone floors, wood-clad walls and long dark wood tables and benches; a profuse and zany decor includes enamel advertising signs, pig-theme ornaments, and old radios, a bicycle and a canoe. The atmosphere is lively and chatty (no games machines and only blues piped music), the landlord entertaining, and the staff friendly, and there's a good mix of customers, too. A covered yard outside is called the Sty. You have to time your visit carefully – the pub is closed every lunchtime, except on Sunday. *(Recommended by Dr and Mrs A K Clarke; more reports please)*

Free house ~ Licensees Dickie and Ann Doyle ~ Real ale ~ (01249) 712515 ~ Live blues Mon evenings ~ Open 7-11, plus 12-2.30 Sun

DEVIZES SU0061 Map 2

Bear

Market Place

All manner of notable characters have visited this rambling 17th-c coaching inn over the years, from well-known literary figures to heads of state. George III stayed here on his way to Longleat, though the address of welcome that local big-wigs had prepared for the stopover was a little spoilt when the borough Recorder due to deliver it became overwhelmed by the occasion and suddenly lost his voice. Chatty and busy, the pleasantly old-fashioned main bar has big winter log fires, fresh flowers, black winger wall settles, muted red button-back cloth-upholstered bucket armchairs around oak tripod tables, and old prints on the walls. The traditionally styled Lawrence room (named after Thomas Lawrence the portrait painter, whose father once ran the inn), separated from the main bar by some steps and an old-fashioned glazed screen, has dark oak-panelled walls, a parquet floor, shining copper pans on the mantlepiece above the big open fireplace, and plates around the walls; part of this room is no-smoking. Straightforward bar food includes sandwiches (from £1.75), home-made soup (£1.95), filled baked potatoes, three-egg omelettes or ploughman's (from £2.95), ham, egg and chips (£3.25), 8oz sirloin steak (£7.50), and home-made puddings (£1.95); there's a wider range of meals in the Lawrence room with dishes such as steak and kidney pudding or hot-pot with herb dumplings (£3.95) – you can have these in the bar too. Well kept Wadworths IPA and 6X and a guest beer are served on handpump from an old-fashioned bar counter with shiny black woodwork and small panes of glass, along with freshly squeezed juices, decent wines, and a good choice of malt whiskies; especially friendly and helpful service. Wadworths beers are brewed in the town, and from the brewery you can get them in splendid old-fashioned half-gallon earthenware jars. *(Recommended by A D Sherman, John Hazel, Tom McLean, Ewan McCall, Roger Huggins, Dave irving, John and Christine Vittoe, Gwen and Peter Andrews, David Holloway, Colin and Ann Hunt, Dr M I Crichton, Wim Kock, Willem-Jan Kock, Hans Chabot, Jane Starkey, Ian and Nita Cooper, Gordon Mott)*

Wadworths ~ Tenant W K Dickenson ~ Real ale ~ Meals and snacks (till 10 Fri-Sun) ~ Restaurant (not Sun evening) ~ (01380) 722444 ~ Children in eating area of bar ~ Open 10am-11pm; 10-3, 6-11 Mon-Weds in winter; closed 25/26 Dec ~ Bedrooms: £45B/£70B

EBBESBOURNE WAKE ST9824 Map 2

Horseshoe

On A354 S of Salisbury, right at signpost at Coombe Bissett; village is around 8 miles further on

The pretty little garden at this lovely pub has seats that look out over the steep sleepy valley of the River Ebble, and a paddock at the bottom with four goats, and a Vietnamese pot-bellied pig. Particularly welcoming to visitors and locals alike, it really is a characterful place, and a good few readers can't resist being drawn back again and again. The beautifully kept bar has fresh garden flowers on the tables, lanterns, farm tools and other bric-a-brac crowded along its beams, and an open fire. Simple but well-cooked home-made bar food might include sandwiches (£2.75), fresh trout pâté (£4.95), locally made faggots or lasagne (£5.95), fresh battered cod or home-made pies like fine venison, steak and kidney, fish or chicken and mushroom (all £6.25), specials such as liver and bacon or watercress and mushroom lasagne (£5.95), and excellent home-made puddings; good breakfasts and three course Sunday lunch (£8.95). Well kept Adnams Broadside, Ringwood Best, Wadworths 6X and a couple of tapped from the row of casks behind the bar, farm cider, country wines, and several malt whiskies. Booking is advisable for the small no-smoking restaurant, especially at weekends when they can fill up quite quickly. The barn opposite is used as a games room with darts, pool and a fruit machine. *(Recommended by Jerry and Alison Oakes, Tom and Rosemary Hall, Dr Diana Terry, G W Stevenson, Michael and Hazel Lyons, Jason Caulkin, Dennis Heatley, Ted Burden, John and Joan Nash, Gordon, R and Mrs P F Shelton)*

Free house ~ Licensees Anthony and Patricia Bath ~ Real ale ~ Meals and snacks (not Mon evening) ~ Restaurant ~ (01722) 780474 ~ Children in eating area of bar at discretion of licensees ~ Open 11.30-3, 6.30-11; closed evening 25 Dec ~ Bedrooms: £25B/£40B

FORD ST8374 Map 2

White Hart ★

A420 Chippenham—Bristol; follow Colerne sign at E side of village to find pub

Last year this enduring favourite was our Pub of the Year, and readers still rate it as one of the best in the country. The combination of exceptionally good food, the atmospheric bar, friendly licensees, and range of well kept beers is one that's hard to beat; service is always attentive and cheerful – even when they're really busy – and despite the number of people eating it's very much a place for those wanting just a drink. After all this the setting is something of a bonus, even though on a sunny day there's nothing more pleasant than sitting out on the terrace by the stone bridge and trout stream. The weekly-changing menu might include sandwiches, soups such as leek and potato or chicken and vegetable (from £1.50), ploughman's (from £3.95), Cornish mussels in a white wine cream sauce (£4.25), a couple of well-priced specials such as warm guinea fowl salad (£4.75) or chicken and avocado stir-fry (£4.95), and more elaborate meals like vegetarian ravioli with a fricassé of wild mushrooms (£7.95), grilled whole lemon sole or excellent pork tenderloin with root vegetables, shallots, and a madeira cream sauce (£8.50), supreme of salmon with saffron tagliatelli and black olive purée (£9.95), roast baby poussin with caramelised apples and grapes, flamed with calvados (£10.95), and fillet of beef on a crispy garlic crouton topped with onion marmalade and avocado salsa (£12.50); the good puddings are generously served. There are heavy black beams supporting the white-painted boards of the ceiling, tub armchairs around polished wooden tables, small pictures and a few advertising mirrors on the walls, and a big log-burning stove in the ancient fireplace (inscribed 1553). The beers include well kept Badger Tanglefoot, Bass, Boddingtons, Flowers IPA, Marstons Pedigree, Smiles Best and Exhibition, and Theakstons Old Peculier on handpump; farm ciders, a dozen malt whiskies, and fine wines; piped music. It's a lovely place to stay and there's a secluded swimming pool for residents. *(Recommended by Kevin and Kay Bronnsey, Peter and Joy Heatherley, Andrew Shore, Brian Pearson, TBB, Roger and Susan Dunn, Dr and Mrs A K Clarke, Jeff Davies, M W Turner, Mayur Shah, D G King, Alan and Paula McCully, Pat and Jon Millward, Paul Boot, Mrs Anne Parmenter, Simon and Amanda Southwell, Dr C E Morgan, Jane and Steve Owen, R C Morgan, Barbara Hatfield, Mrs M Lawrence, A R and B E Sayer, Paul Weedon, Susan and John Douglas, P Neate, Dave Irving)*

Free house ~ Licensees Chris and Jenny Phillips ~ Real ale ~ Meals and snacks (till 10) ~ Restaurant ~ (01249) 782213 ~ Children in eating area and restaurant ~ Open 11-3, 5-11 ~ Bedrooms: £43B/£59B

HINDON ST9132 Map 2

Lamb

B3089 Wilton—Mere

Dating back in part to the 13th-c, this civilised solidly built old inn has a roomy long bar, split into several areas, with the two lower sections perhaps the nicest. There's a long polished table with wall benches and chairs, and a big inglenook fireplace, and at one end a window seat with a big waxed circular table, spindleback chairs with tapestried cushions, a high-backed settle, brass jugs on the mantlepiece above the small fireplace, and a big kitchen clock; up some steps, a third, bigger area has lots of tables and chairs. Bar food includes sandwiches, local mussels with cream and garlic (£4.50), venison and pigeon casserole or steak and kidney pie (£5.25), grilled leg of lamb (£5.75), dressed local crab or grilled skate wings with caper butter (£6.25), and a roast Sunday lunch; the restaurant is no smoking. They usually do cream teas throughout the afternoon. Batemans Valiant, Boddingtons, Eldridge Pope Hardy, Exmoor Gold, Fullers London Pride, local Tisbury Thomas Beckett, and Wadworths 6X on handpump, and a range of whiskies including all the malts from the Isle of Islay. Service can slow down when they get busy, though remains helpful and friendly. There are picnic tables across the road (which is a good alternative to the main routes west). No dogs. Readers have found the lavatories rather basic. *(Recommended by D H and B R Tew, Anthony Barnes, Paul Randall, John Evans, John and Christine Vittoe, Ian Phillips, Mrs J A Blanks, Gordon, Peter and Audrey Dowsett, F C Johnston, A R Hands, W Matthews, John and Joan Nash, David Surridge, M Owton, Joan and Ian Wilson, Joy Heatherley, F C Johnston, Patrick Clancy, S G Brown, Robert Tattersall, Colin Laffan)*

Free house ~ Licensee John Croft ~ Real ale ~ Meals and snacks (till 10pm) ~ Restaurant ~ (01747) 820573 ~ Children welcome ~ Open 11-11 ~ Bedrooms: £38B/£55B

KILMINGTON ST7736 Map 2

Red Lion

Pub on B3092 Mere—Frome, 2½ miles S of Maiden Bradley; 3 miles from A303 Mere turn-off

To the delight of several readers, this unpretentious and friendly 400-year-old place is very much a pub first rather than somewhere concentrating on diners. The busy bar is very cosy and comfortable, with an interesting display of locally-made walking sticks, a curved high-backed settle and red leatherette wall and window seats on the flagstones, photographs on the beams, and a couple of big fireplaces (one with a fine old iron fireback) with log fires in winter. A newer no-smoking eating area has a large window and is decorated with brasses, a large leather horse collar, and hanging plates. Good value simple bar food includes home-made soup (£1.50), filled baked potatoes (from £2.40), toasted sandwiches (from £2.50), ploughman's (from £3.25), steak and kidney or lamb and apricot pie (£3.65), meat or vegetable lasagne (£4.50), specials such as very good home-cooked ham (£3.50), and evening extras like grilled gammon steak (£3.95). Butcombe and Marstons Pedigree on handpump (maybe under light blanket pressure), along with a guest like Hop Back Summer Lightning or Tisbury Best; also farm cider and elderflower pressé. Sensibly placed darts, dominoes, shove-ha'penny and cribbage. Picnic table sets in the big garden, and maybe Kim, the labrador. It's very popular with walkers, and a gate leads on to the lane which leads to White Sheet Hill where there is riding, hang gliding and radio-controlled gliders. Stourhead Gardens are only a mile away. *(Recommended by R H Martyn, J H Bell, Mrs R Humphrey, Brig T I G Gray, Guy Consterdine, Anthony Barnes, Mayur Shah, John Honnor, Dr J W Macleod, Colin and Jan Roe)*

Free house ~ Licensee Chris Gibbs ~ Real ale ~ Meals and snacks (not evenings Mon-Thurs and Sun, or 25 Dec) ~ (01985) 844263 ~ Children in eating area of bar till 9pm ~ Open 11-3, 6.30-11 ~ Bedrooms: £15/£30

LACOCK ST9168 Map 2

George

One of the talking points at this atmospheric old place has long been the three-foot treadwheel set into the outer breast of the magnificent central fireplace. This used to turn a spit for roasting, and was worked by a specially bred dog called, with great imagination, a Turnspit. Dating back to 1361, the pub is one of the oldest buildings in this much-loved National Trust village, and has been run for the last ten years by the same courteous and friendly licensee. Often very busy indeed, the bar has a low beamed ceiling, upright timbers in the place of knocked-through walls making cosy corners, armchairs and windsor chairs, seats in the stone-mullioned windows and flagstones just by the bar. The well kept Wadworths IPA, 6X, and Farmers Glory on handpump are very reasonably priced, and there's a decent choice of wines by the bottle. Bar food includes sandwiches, home-made soup (£1.95), vegetable tikka triangles (£2.95), lasagne or moules bonne femme (£5.50), beef teriyaki (£5.95), local rainbow trout or chicken stuffed with stilton in a leek sauce (£6.95), specials like pork and leek sausages (£5.50) or broccoli and cream cheese bake (£5.75), steaks (from £7.75), children's meals (£2.75), and puddings like spotted dick or apple and blackberry pie (£2.50). Darts, shove-ha'penny, cribbage, dominoes and piped music. There are picnic tables with umbrellas in the back garden, as well as a play area with swings, and a bench in front that looks over the main street. It's a nice area for walking. The bedrooms are up at the landlord's farmhouse, and free transport to and from the pub is provided. *(Recommended by TBB, Peter Neate, Andrew and Ruth Triggs, Colin and Ann Hunt, Stephen G Brown, P J Howell, Joan and Michel Hooper-Immins, Mrs B M Spurr, Tom McLean, Roger Huggins, Dave Irving, Ewan McCall, Joy Heatherley)*

Wadworths ~ Tenants John and Judy Glass ~ Real ale ~ Meals and snacks (till 10pm) ~ Restaurant ~ (01249) 730263 ~ Children welcome ~ Open 10-3, 5-11, all day summer Sats ~ Bedrooms – see above: £25B/£35B

Red Lion

High Street; village signposted off A350 S of Chippenham

Plain from the outside but spacious and welcoming once in, this tall brick Georgian inn is generally the only pub in Lacock open all day. Recently refurbished and reupholstered, the long bar is divided into separate areas by cart shafts, yokes and other old farm implements, and the old-fashioned furniture includes a mix of tables and comfortable chairs, turkey rugs on the partly flagstoned floor, and a fine old log fire at one end. Plates, paintings, and tools cover the walls, and there are stuffed birds, animals and branding irons hanging from the ceiling. A wide range of good home-made bar food includes filled rolls and baguettes (from £2.50), ham and egg (£3.50), filled baked potatoes (from £3.50), ploughman's (from £4.25), vegetarian dishes (£4.60), speciality sausages like Thai or leek and ginger (£4.95), vegetarian meals (£5.50), daily specials like spicy lamb and apricot casseroles or pies such as steak and kidney or popular beef and stilton (£5.95), plenty of fresh fish like halibut, trout or sea bass (from £6.95), puddings like sticky toffee pudding (£2.50), and children's helpings or meals (from £1.95). Throughout the afternoon they serve light snacks and afternoon tea; the restaurant is no smoking. Well kept Wadworths IPA and 6X and a guest beer like Lancaster Bomber on handpump; fruit machine, video game, piped music. The pub is close to Lacock Abbey and the Fox Talbot Museum. *(Recommended by Tony and Wendy Hobden, Nikki Moffat, Marjorie and David Lamb, TBB, Andrew and Ruth Triggs, John and Wendy Trentham, Joy Heatherley, Mrs S Spevack, Alan and Heather Jacques, June and Tony Baldwin, Fiona Dick, Janet Pickles)*

Wadworths ~ Managers Roger and Cheryl Ling ~ Real ale ~ Meals and snacks (12-3, 7-10) ~ Restaurant ~ (01249) 730456 ~ Children in eating area ~ Open 11-11; 11-3.30, 6-11 in winter ~ Bedrooms: £35B/£50B

nr LACOCK ST9367 Map 2

Rising Sun

Bowden Hill, Bewley Common; on back road Lacock—Sandy Lane

New licensees again at this bustling pub, which is blessed with one of the most splendid views we know. Seats on the two-level terrace look out right over the Avon valley, some 25 miles or so away; it's a particularly attractive sight around sunset. Inside, the three little rooms have been knocked together to form one simply furnished and characterful area, with a mix of old chairs and basic kitchen tables on stone floors, stuffed animals and birds, country pictures, and open fires. Well kept Moles IPA, Bitter, 97 and Landlords Choice, and a weekly guest beer on handpump; friendly service. Bar food includes sandwiches, celery and stilton soup (£1.95), home-made chicken liver pâté (£2.25), avocado and prawn salad (£4.20), pies such as game, steak and kidney or chicken and mushroom (£4.95), and a Sunday roast (£4.95). Darts, dominoes, shove-ha'penny, and cribbage. *(Recommended by Kevin and Kay Bronnsey, Ron Gentry, John Hazel, F J and A Parmenter, Derek and Sylvia Stephenson, TBB, Tom McLean, Roger Huggins, Dave Irving, Ewan McCall, Chris and Anne Fluck, John Willard, Alan and Heather Jacques, Joy Heatherley, P and J Shapley, Stephen Brown)*

Free house ~ Licensees Tony and Julie Page ~ Real ale ~ Meals and snacks ~ (01249) 730363 ~ Children in eating area of bar ~ Singer Weds evening ~ Open 11-3, 6-11

LITTLE BEDWYN SU2966 Map 2

Harrow ♀

Village signposted off A4 W of Hungerford

This welcoming village pub is owned by the locals, which might account for the very friendly feel you notice as soon as you go in. There's been a change of management since our last edition, and the Spanish roots of the helpful new landlord may come through in some of the cooking – especially the popular and properly prepared paella which they do every Sunday lunchtime (£6). Other well presented meals might include sweet potato and parsnip soup (£2), spicy bean stew (£2.95), mussels in tomato, garlic and white wine (£3.95), gravadlax or sweetbreads with bacon, garlic and mushrooms (£4.25), smoked chicken and avocado salad (£5.25), and Tuscan rabbit or oxtail in a rich wine sauce (£8.95); the restaurant is no smoking. Free from music or games machines, the three rooms have quite a relaxed and chatty feel, as well as a massive ship's wheel on the left, a mixture of country chairs and simple wooden tables on the well waxed boards (one table in the bow window), a bright mural of scenes from the village, and a big woodburning stove; the two inner rooms have a fine brass model of a bull and locally done watercolours and photographs for sale. Well kept Hook Norton Best and two monthly changing guests on handpump, and lots of changing New World wines by the glass. There are seats out in the small, pretty garden, and the pub's a couple of hundred yards from the Kennet & Avon Canal. *(Recommended by Iain McBride, Samantha Hawkins, J E Ellis, Pat Crabb, Anthony Byers, J A and E M Castle, J M M Hill, M E A Horler, Kevin and Kay Bronnsey, N C Walker, P M Lane, TBB, JE, George Atkinson, Alan Kilpatrick)*

Free house ~ Licensees Luis and Angela Lopez ~ Real ale ~ Meals and snacks (not Mon) ~ Restaurant ~ (01672) 870871 ~ Children welcome ~ Open 11-3, 5.30(6 Sat)-11; closed Mon lunchtime and 1 Jan ~ Bedrooms: £22B/£37B

LOWER CHUTE SU3153 Map 2

Hatchet

The Chutes well signposted via Appleshaw off A342, 2½ miles W of Andover

One of the county's most attractive pubs, this thatched 16th-c place has a splendid 17th-c fireback in the huge fireplace, with a big winter log fire in front. The beams seem especially low, and look down over a mix of captain's chairs and cushioned wheelbacks set neatly around oak tables. Good bar food includes sandwiches, home-made soup (£2.25), ploughman's (from £2.95), good moules marinières (£3.95), salads (from £3.95), cottage pie (£4.25), steak and Guinness pie (£5.25), tiger prawns in filo pastry (£6.25), and puddings. Well kept Adnams, Greene King Abbot, Marstons Pedigree, Wadworths 6X and a changing guest on handpump, and a range of country wines. Darts, shove-ha'penny, dominoes, cribbage, and piped music. There are seats out on a terrace by the front car park, or on the side grass, as well as a children's sandpit. *(Recommended by Gordon, Kevin and Kay Bronnsey, Brenda and Jim Langley, Mrs K Johnson, I E and C A Prosser)*

Free house ~ Licensee Jeremy McKay ~ Real ale ~ Meals and snacks ~ Restaurant ~ (01264) 730229 ~ Children in separate restaurant ~ Open 11.30-3, 6-11 ~ Self-contained flat available, prices on request

LOWER WOODFORD SU1235 Map 2

Wheatsheaf

Leaving Salisbury northwards on A360, The Woodfords signposted first right after end of speed limit; then bear left

The refurbishments mentioned in last year's Guide are now complete, and already prompting praise in our postbag. There are more tables for eating, full disabled facilities, baby-changing areas, and new kitchens and lavatories, all sympathetically done so as not to alter the welcoming and rather cosy feel of the place. From a wide menu, the good, popular bar food includes home-made soups like lentil and carrot (£1.65), spinach terrine (£2.95), ploughman's (£3.35), filled baked potatoes or open sandwiches (from £3.45), home-made chicken curry (£4.65), prawn korma (£4.85), potato, leek and cheese bake (£4.95), home-made steak and kidney pie (£5.95), stuffed plaice (£6.05), gammon and egg (£6.35), steaks (from £8.95), puddings (from £2.45), and children's dishes (from £1.65); part of the dining room is no smoking. Well kept Badger Best, Hard Tackle and Tanglefoot on handpump, promptly served by helpful, friendly staff; dominoes and cribbage. The big walled garden has picnic tables, a climber and swings, and is surrounded by tall trees; barbecues out here in summer. *(Recommended by S Jones, Clive Gilbert, Nigel Wikeley, L M Miall, Jerry and Alison Oakes, Don and Thelma Beeson, Ralf Zeyssig, Patricia Nutt, Joy Heatherley, W and S Jones, Mayur Shah, J E N Young)*

Badger ~ Tenants Peter and Jennifer Charlton ~ Real ale ~ Meals and snacks (till 10pm) ~ (01722) 782203 ~ Children in eating area of bar ~ Open 11-2.30, 6.30(6 Sat)-11(10.30 winter Mon-Thurs); closed 25 Dec

MALMESBURY ST9287 Map 2

Suffolk Arms

Tetbury Hill; B4014 towards Tetbury, on edge of town

Now back under brewery management, this enjoyable creeper-covered old stone house is still a favourite stop with quite a few readers. The softly lit, knocked-through bar has comfortable seats such as a chintz-cushioned antique settle, sofa and easy chairs, captain's chairs, and low windsor armchairs, and copper saucepans and warming pans on the stripped stone walls; a stone pillar supports the beams, leaving a big square room around the stairs which climb up apparently unsupported. There's also a lounge, and flowers may decorate the tables. Bar food includes unusual sandwiches (from £2.85), filled baked potatoes (from £3.50), steak and kidney pie (£5.35), 10oz gammon steak (£5.70), half chicken (£6.50), noisettes of lamb (£6.95), darne of salmon (£7.35), and steaks. Well kept Wadworths IPA and 6X and a changing guest on handpump. The neat lawns outside have some seats. Wadworths were planning a refurbishment just as we went to press. *(Recommended by Roger Byrne, Pauline Bishop, Roger and Valerie Hill, Peter Neate, Brian Pearson, Peter and Audrey Dowsett, Michael Sargant, Graham and Karen Oddey, TBB)*

Wadworths ~ Manager Michael Lakin ~ Real ale ~ Meals and snacks ~ (01666) 824323 ~ Children welcome ~ Open 11-2.30, 6-11

NORTON ST8884 Map 2

Vine Tree

4 miles from M4 junction 17; A429 towards Malmesbury, then left at Hullavington, Sherston signpost, then follow Norton signposts; in village turn right at Foxley signpost, which takes you into Honey Lane

An attractive building in an equally pretty setting, this converted 18th-c mill house enjoys a blossoming reputation for its rather good food. Bar snacks include ploughman's (from £2.65), basket meals (from £2.90), filled baked potatoes (from £3.70), home-made beefburger or nutburger (£4.60), and home-made lasagne (£5.25), and the fuller menu features things like home-made soup (£2.60), a warm quiche of duck and fennel on a tangerine coulis (£2.90), fennel, vermouth and potato hotpot (£4.25), braised red snapper with tomato and dill sauce (£8.75), chicken breast filled with cream cheese, garlic and tomato with an oyster mushroom sauce (£8.95), steaks (from £9.40), honey-roast duckling breast with an apricot and coconut cream sauce (£9.75), puddings like toffee apple and pecan pie (from £2.25), and children's meals (£2.05); best to book, especially at weekends, and there's a 5% discount if you pay with cash. The three smallish rooms open together with plates, small sporting prints, carvings, hop bines, a mock-up mounted pig's mask (used for a game that involves knocking coins off its nose and ears), lots of stripped pine, candles in bottles on the tables (the lighting's very gentle), and some old settles. Well kept Wadworths 6X and a beer named for the pub on handpump, along with a couple of guests like Archers Golden or Foxley Best. There are picnic tables under cocktail parasols in a vine-trellised garden with young trees and tubs of flowers, and a well fenced separate play area with a fine thatched fortress and so forth; they have stables at the back. *(Recommended by Colin and Alma Gent, Peter Neate, N K Kimber, Gwen and Peter Andrews, Vivien Lewis, Dave Irving, Roger Huggins, Tom McLean, Ewan McCall)*

Free house ~ Licensee Ken Camerier ~ Real ale ~ Meals and snacks (till 10pm) ~ Restaurant ~ (01666) 837654 ~ Children in eating area of bar and in restaurant ~ Open 12-2.30, 6.30-11; closed Tues

PITTON SU2131 Map 2

Silver Plough ★ 🍴 🍷

Village signposted from A30 E of Salisbury

While most people come to this civilised dining pub for the food (and some for the wines), one reader was highly impressed on his visit by the woodwork, noting that the quality of the tables, seats and timbers is all rather high. A farmhouse until the Second World War, it now has jugs, glass rolling pins and other assorted curios hanging from the beamed ceilings in the main bar, paintings and prints on the walls, and oak settles; piped music. There's a skittle alley next to the snug bar. The emphasis is very much on the food though, with regularly changing menus typically including tasty dishes such as soup (£2.60), particularly good marinated dill herrings (£3.75), green-lippd mussels in a wine, cream and herb sauce (£3.95), ploughman's (£3.95, maybe with unusual cheeses), home-made fish cakes with coriander and fresh chilli dip (£4.25), salmon in Cajun spices with lime butter (£7.95), char-grilled lamb with pear and rosemary sauce (£8.95), barbary duck with deep fried spring greens (£9.25), and sirloin steak with caramelised onions and peppercorn sauce (£10.95); three-course Sunday lunch (£10.95). Well kept Courage Directors, Eldridge Pope Hardy, John Smiths and Wadworths 6X on handpump, a fine wine list including 10 by the glass and some well-priced and carefully chosen bottles, a good range of country wines, and a worthy choice of spirits. While service is generally friendly and efficient, a couple of readers have found it slightly disinterested at times. There are picnic tables and other tables under cocktail parasols on a quiet lawn, with an old pear tree. *(Recommended by Mayur Shah, Gwen and Peter Andrews, Jerry and Alison Oakes, Dr and Mrs N Holmes, E and C A Prosser, Tim Galligan, Joy Heatherley, Nic Armitage, Dawn and Phil Garside, Martin and Karen Wake, W and S Jones, Lynn Sharpless, Bob Eardley, Jean-Bernard Brisset, Brian and Jill Bond)*

Free house ~ Licensee Michael Beckett ~ Real ale ~ Meals and snacks ~ Restaurant (not Sun evening) ~ (01722) 72266 ~ Children in eating area ~ Open 11-3, 6-11

POTTERNE ST9958 Map 2

George & Dragon

A360 beside Worton turn-off

Convivial is the word for this 15th-c thatched house, originally built for the Bishop of Salisbury – it's the kind of place where you instantly feel at home. Furnishings include old bench seating and country-style tables, banknotes from around the world, and water jugs, and there's a pleasant traditional atmosphere. You can still see the fireplace and old beamed ceiling of the original hall. Good reasonably priced bar food includes sandwiches (from £1.35), soup (£1.65), baked potatoes (from £2.95), ploughman's (from £3.50), various omelettes (from £3.50), chilli con carne (£3.95), chicken curry or various crêpes such as chicken and ham or spinach and stilton (£4.25), ham and egg (£4.50), rainbow trout with prawns and mushrooms (£5.50), steaks (from £5.75), and puddings (from £2.15); three-course Sunday lunch (£7.25). The dining room is no smoking. Well kept Wadworths IPA and 6X and a guest beer on handpump. A separate room has pool, darts, shove-ha'penny, dominoes, and a fruit machine, and through a hatch beyond here is a unique indoor .22 shooting gallery (available for use by visiting groups with notice to arrange marshals and insurance); there's a full skittle alley in the old stables. At the back of the pub is a small museum of hand-held agricultural implements. There's a pleasant garden and a sun-trap yard with a grapevine. *(Recommended by Tom McLean, Ewan McCall, Roger Huggins, Dave Irving, Jan and Colin Roe, Mrs Anne Parmenter, John and Joan*

Nash, Mr and Mrs C R Saxby, Dr and Mrs C S Cox, David Logan, Derek and Trish Stockley, David Holloway, G Hart, Mr and Mrs N Hazzard)

Wadworths ~ Tenants Richard and Paula Miles ~ Real ale ~ Meals and snacks (not Mon, except bank hol lunchtime) ~ (01380) 722139 ~ Children in eating area of bar ~ Open 12-2.30(3 Sat), 7-11 (closed Mon lunch except bank holidays) ~ Bedrooms: £19.50/£35

POULSHOT ST9559 Map 2

Raven

Village signposted off A361 Devizes—Seend

We'd heard nothing of this tucked-away pub for some six years, until a report from our reader Mr Laffan (often a bell-wether, when it comes to exploring promising new pub pastures) suggested that it has now become well worth finding. And so it proved when – spurred on by other reports culminating in a hot recommendation from the doughty Andrewses we tried it for ourselves. Neat enough from the outside, especially in contrast to the long rather shaggy nearby village green, it's spick and span inside, the two cosy and intimate rooms of the black-beamed bar well refurbished with sturdy tables and chairs and comfortable banquettes; there's an attractive no-smoking dining room. The landlord keeps personal charge of the kitchen, and his slightly unusual touch gives a distinctive edge to the cooking and presentation of even quite regular dishes. Worthwhile starters and snacks have included good minestrone and other soups (£2.10), ploughman's (from £2.65), interesting salads such as shrimp, avocado and apple (£3.65), and deft fresh pasta dishes (£5.45); reasonably priced main courses include burgundy beef or seafood crumble (£6.20), grilled lamb steaks with red wine and cranberry sauce (£7.05), and poached fresh salmon with parsley sauce (£7.20), with a choice of good fresh vegetables. Given its value, the food's becoming very popular with older people at lunchtime. Particularly well kept Wadworths IPA, 6X and a seasonal ale tapped straight from the cask; neat welcoming staff, and a thriving chatty atmosphere; outside gents'. *(Recommended by Colin Laffan, Gwen and Peter Andrews, Meg and Colin Hamilton, Tony and Wendy Hobden, Tony Beaulah, G Washington)*

Wadworths ~ Tenants Susan and Philip Henshaw ~ Real ale ~ Meals and snacks (not 25 or 26 Dec) ~ Restaurant ~ (01380) 828271 ~ Children in restaurant ~ Open 11-2.30, 6.30-11; closed evening 25 Dec

RAMSBURY SU2771 Map 2

Bell

Village signposted off B4192 (still shown as A419 on many maps) NW of Hungerford, or from A4 W of Hungerford

This comfortably civilised pub is proving particularly popular at the moment, partly for its friendly feel and chatty atmosphere, but mainly for its rather better than average food. Well presented and cheerfully served, meals might include lunchtime sandwiches (from £1.75) and ploughman's (£3.95), soup (£2.30), king prawns wrapped in filo pastry with a sweet and sour dip (£4.25), a trio of locally-made sausages with bubble and squeak (£4.95), mushroom and cashew nut stroganoff (£5.95), fillet of hake with a creamy mussel and basil sauce (£6.95), home-made beef and ale pie (£7.50), steaks (from £7.95), specials such as red mullet on roasted peppers with balsamic vinegar (£7.95) or medallions of pork layered with brie and topped with provençale sauce (£8.45), children's meals (from £1.95), home-made puddings like treacle tart or apricot crumble, and a very good Sunday lunch. Tables can be reserved in the restaurant, though the same meals can be had in the bar; one section is no smoking. Victorian stained glass panels in one of the two sunny bay windows look out onto the quiet village street, and a big chimney breast with open fires divides up the smartly relaxed and chatty bar areas, nicely furnished with polished tables and fresh flowers. Well kept Eldridge Pope Royal Oak, Hook Norton

Best, Wadworths 6X and IPA and a guest on handpump, decent wines, and 20 malt whiskies; evening piped music. There are picnic tables on the raised lawn. Roads lead from this quiet village into the downland on all sides. *(Recommended by Alan and Paula McCully, Roger Wain-Heapy, Gordon, J M M Hill, Kevin and Kay Bronnsey, R C Morgan, Mr and Mrs Jenkinson, Annabel and Chris, Dr M Ian Crichton, W K Struthers, Evelyn and Derek Walter, Susie Northfield, Peter and Audrey Dowsett)*

Free house ~ Licensee Graham Dawes ~ Real ale ~ Meals and snacks ~ Restaurant ~ (01672) 520230 ~ Children welcome except in bar ~ Open 12-3, 6-11

ROWDE ST9762 Map 2

George & Dragon

A342 Devizes—Chippenham

Exceptionally good food draws people so strongly to this interesting old pub that especially on Saturday evening or at Sunday lunchtime you're most unlikely to get a table without booking. Though its emphasis is primarily on food, it's kept admirably to its pub roots; the bar has some interesting furnishings, plenty of dark wood, and a log fire (with a fine collection of brass keys by it), the bare-floored dining room has quite plain and pubby-feeling tables and chairs, and the Wadworths Henrys, IPA and 6X on handpump are kept well. The food really is quite special, making several readers doubt whether they've had anything else quite so good from a pub in recent years. Ingredients are fresh and well chosen, cooking is light and deft, unusual tastes perk up familiar dishes (mint, honey and strawberry transforming a melon starter, for example), and Cornish fish fresh daily is a special highlight, with subtle sauces or just a light hollandaise. The choice includes scallops, skate, monkfish, john dory, turbot, and lobster (from £10); also, salmon fishcakes or cheese soufflé (starter £4.50, main course £8), steak and kidney pie or lamb cooked in yoghurt and coriander (£9), steaks (from £10), and loin of pork with prune and armagnac or breast of duck with a honey and rhubarb compote (£11). You must try to leave room for a pudding (£4): coconut cream with mango and pineapple, say, or meringue with a chocolate, mocha and coffee-bean sauce, rhubarb and Cointreau crumble or plum and armagnac tart, with a jug of help-yourself cream. Several dishes come in two sizes, and the set lunch (two courses £8.50, three £10) is good value. The atmosphere is leisurely and relaxed, and service is friendly, welcoming and efficient. Skittle alley. *(Recommended by Gwen and Peter Andrews, F J and A Parmenter, John Hazel, G P Kernan, Mr and Mrs T F Marshall, I E and C A Prosser, Pat and John Millward, Mr and Mrs Peter Woods)*

Wadworths ~ Licensees Tim and Helen Withers ~ Real ale ~ Meals and snacks (till 10; not Sun or Mon) ~ Restaurant ~ (01380) 723053 ~ Children welcome ~ Open 12-3, 7-11

SALISBURY SU1429 Map 2

Haunch of Venison ★

1 Minster Street, opposite Market Cross

It's the quite splendid building that stands out at this venerable old pub, built some 650 years ago as the church house for St Thomas's, just behind. There are massive beams in the ochre ceiling, stout red cushioned oak benches built into its timbered walls, genuinely old pictures, a black and white tiled floor, and an open fire; a tiny snug opens off the entrance lobby. A quiet and cosy upper panelled room has a small paned window looking down onto the main bar, antique leather-seat settles, a nice carved oak chair nearly three centuries old, and a splendid fireplace that dates back to the building's early years; behind glass in a small wall slit is the smoke-preserved mummified hand of an unfortunate 18th-c card player. Well kept Courage Best and Directors on handpump from a unique pewter bar counter, with a rare set of antique taps for gravity-fed spirits and liqueurs; over 150 malt whiskies, decent wines (including a wine of the week), and a range of brandies. Bar food, served in the lower half of the restaurant, includes sandwiches (from £2.25), ploughman's (from £3.95), vegetarian pasta (£4.50), and always a salad or pie with venison, while the restaurant menu features things like pasta with pinenuts and sun-dried tomatoes (£6.95) or fish stew (£9.95). The pub can get a little smoky. *(Recommended by Jerry and Alison Oakes, Lynn Sharpless, Bob Eardley, Andrew and Ruth Triggs, JM, PM, Kevin and Kay Bronnsey, Gordon, Dr Diana Terry, T A Bryan, Jenny and Brian Seller, Colin and Jan Roe, Wim Kock, Willem-Jan Kock, Hans Chabot, J L Alperin, PWV, Wayne Brindle, Peter Neate, Susan and John Douglas)*

Courage ~ Tenants Antony and Victoria Leroy ~ Real ale ~ Meals and snacks (not Sun evening) ~ Restaurant ~ (01722) 322024 ~ Well behaved children in eating areas ~ Nearby parking may be difficult ~ Open 11-11 (closed Dec 25)

Old Mill 🍷

Town Path, W Harnham

The classic cathedral view from this perfectly placed little hotel may be familiar from Constable's paintings, and the church is a lovely ten-minute stroll across the meadow. The present building dates back to 1550 when it was Wiltshire's first papermaking mill, and in summer you can sit out by the mill pool; stay the night and the only noises in the early hours will be rushing water and quacking ducks. The two smallish square beamed bars are simply furnished with small polished wooden tables and comfortable settles and chairs, there's a collection of over 500 china and other ducks, and a friendly relaxed atmosphere. A fine choice of fresh fish and shellfish comes direct from local boats at Poole and from the west coast of Scotland – see daily specials for crab salad, langoustines, sea bass, salmon and so forth: moules marinières (£4.95), spicy Cajun fish (£5.70), seafood special (a sort of fish stew, £6.20), and salmon koulibiac (£7). Also, sandwiches (from £1.90), vegetable soup (£2.25), ploughman's (£3.85), very good mixed bean and pepper chilli (£5.50), steak and kidney pie (£5.70), and venison casserole (£5.95); well kept Boddingtons, Flowers Original, Hop Back GFB and Summer Lighning and a guest on handpump, and decent malt whiskies and wines; piped music. On summer evenings the garden is nicely floodlit. *(Recommended by JM, PM, Peter and Audrey Dowsett, John and Christine Vittoe, W K Struthers, Tim and Felicity Dyer)*

Free house ~ Licensees Roy and Lois Thwaites ~ Real ale ~ Meals and snacks (11-2.30, 6-10.30pm) ~ Restaurant (not Sun evening) ~ (01722) 327517 ~ Children in eating area of bar ~ Open 11-2.30, 6-11 ~ Bedrooms: £40B/£60B

SEEND ST9361 Map 2

Barge

Seend Cleeve; signposted off A361 Devizes—Trowbridge, between Seend village and signpost to Seend Head

The look and style of this splendidly restored canalside pub may have changed quite a lot over the last few years (it's not the tiny place it was when we first knew it), but there certainly hasn't been any change to its popularity – indeed these days it seems to be more popular than ever. The picnic tables among former streetlamps in the neat waterside gardens are the perfect place for idly watching the barges and other boats on the Kennet and Avon Canal, and there are moorings by the humpy bridge. Inside, there's a strong barge theme in the friendly and relaxed bar, perhaps at its best in the intricately painted Victorian flowers which cover the ceilings and run in a waist-high band above the deep green lower walls. A distinctive mix of attractive seats includes milkchurns and the occasional small oak settle among the rugs on the parquet floor, while the walls have big sentimental engravings. The watery theme continues with a well stocked aquarium, and there's also a pretty Victorian fireplace, big bunches of dried flowers, and red velvet curtains for the big windows. Generously served food such as soup (£1.50), open sandwiches (from £2.75), home-made pâté (£3.25), ploughman's and filled baked potatoes (£3.25), lasagne or butter bean roast (£5.25), steak and mushroom in ale pie (£5.75), chicken in a tomato, pesto and almond sauce on a bed of tagliatelli (£5.95), hickory-smoked ribs (£6.25), 8oz sirloin steak (£8.95), children's dishes (£1.95), and puddings (from £2.50); the restaurant extension is no smoking. Well kept Badger Tanglefoot, Wadworths IPA and 6X, and a guest beer on handpump; mulled wine in winter. Good service; trivia. They do get busy – you may find queues to get in the car park. *(Recommended by R C Watkins, Tony and Wendy Hobden, Colin Laffan, F J and A Parmenter, R H Rowley, Ron Gentry, Peter Neate, Jerry and Alison Oakes, John Hazel, Mrs C Archer, Gwen and Peter Andrews, C H and P Stride, Pat and Robert Watt, I E and C A Prosser, John and Tessa Rainsford)*

Wadworths ~ Tenant Christopher Moorley Long ~ Real ale ~ Meals and snacks (till 10pm Fri/Sat) ~ Restaurant ~ (01380) 828230 ~ Well behaved children welcome ~ Open 11-2.30, 6-11

SEMINGTON ST9461 Map 2

Lamb

99 The Strand; A361 a mile E of junction with A350, towards Devizes

Wiltshire Dining Pub of the Year

A good few readers can hardly praise this civilised eatery enough, with all the letters we've had about it this year highlighting one particular feature – maybe the way the landlord opened the door to welcome a couple he'd seen approaching, the proper fish knives with the fish, the delicious chewy fruit and nut pudding, or most of all the provision made for non-smokers. Smoking is banned throughout the entire pub on Saturday evenings, and at other times there are generally only five tables set aside for smokers. It's very much somewhere to come and enjoy the very good food rather than a casual drink, especially on Saturday evenings or Sunday lunchtimes when you might find the latter impossible; booking is recommended for meals then. From a changing menu, the food might include sandwiches, home-made soup (£2.50), herrings in a dill sauce (£2.95), bobotie (£5.50), chunks of chicken, celery and mushrooms in a cheese sauce (£6.75), braised steak with sherry and mushrooms (£6.95), breast of barbary duck with marsala (£7.50), guinea fowl with orange sauce (£7.95), medallions of beef in a wine sauce (£9.25), fresh fish from Cornwall like lemon sole, monkfish or plaice, and excellent home-made puddings such as white chocolate flan or chocolate and cherry roulade (£2.95); vegetables are good – you might find nuts mixed with the carrots. A series of corridors and attractively decorated separate rooms radiates from the serving counter, with antique settles, a woodburning stove, and a log fire. Well kept Eldridge Pope Hardy and Dorchester on handpump, and good, reasonably priced wines. Excellent service from very friendly, helpful staff; maybe piped classical music. There is a pleasant walled garden with tables, and outside service when the weather is fine. *(Recommended by Peter Neate, Andrew Shore, A D Sherman, Mr and Mrs E H Warner, James and Patricia Halfyard, Pat and John Millward, S H Godsell, Gwen and Peter Andrews, Mrs B Davidson, R C Watkins, Mrs L Powell, G W A Pearce, Don Mather, P C Wilding, Elizabeth Donnelly, Mr and Mrs H Roberts, Mr and Mrs Lionel Stone, Wendy Bateman, David Leonard)*

Free House ~ Licensee Andrew Flaherty ~ Real ale ~ Meals and snacks ~ Restaurant (not Sun evening) ~ (01380) 870263 ~ Children welcome ~ Open 12-2.45, 6.30(6 Sat)-10.30(11 Sat); closed Sun evenings in winter

SEMLEY ST8926 Map 2

Benett Arms

Turn off A350 N of Shaftesbury at Semley Ind Estate signpost, then turn right at Semley signpost

An attractive and characterful building just across the green from the church, this little village inn is a friendly and welcoming place – the kind of pub where they're happy to rustle up some sandwiches if you arrive too late for lunch. The two cosy rooms are separated by a flight of five carpeted steps, and have one or two settles and pews, a deep leather sofa and chairs, hunting prints, carriage lamps for lighting, a pendulum wall clock, and ornaments on the mantlepiece over the log fire. Down by the thatched-roof bar servery, the walls are stripped stone; upstairs, there's a dark panelling dado. Attractively presented bar food includes sandwiches (from £1.50), home-made soup (£2.35), ploughman's (£3.65), omelettes or fresh trout (£4.95), good leek and cheese bake or home-made steak and kidney pie (£4.95), gammon with pineapple (£5.95), 8oz rump steak (£8.95), fresh fish and game specials, and puddings like lemon and ginger crunch or chocolate mousse with rum (£2.95); big breakfasts. Well kept Gibbs Mew Bishops Tipple, Deacon and Salisbury Best on handpump, kept under light blanket pressure, farm cider, four chilled vodkas, 18 malt whiskies, lots of liqueurs, and a thoughtfully chosen wine list, including a good few by the glass; dominoes, cribbage. There are seats outside. Well behaved dogs welcome. ***(Recommended by F C Johnston, Mrs S A Mackenzie, Gordon, Mr and Mrs Smith, Nigel Clifton, Stephen Brown, Tim Barrow, Sue Demont, Paul A Kitchener)***

Gibbs Mew ~ Tenant Joe Duthie ~ Real ale ~ Meals and snacks (till 10pm) ~ Restaurant (not Sun evening) ~ (01747) 830221 ~ Children in eating area of bar and in restaurant ~ Open 11-2.30, 6-11; closed 25/26 Dec ~ Bedrooms: £29B/£44B

SHERSTON ST8585 Map 2

Rattlebone

Church St; B4040 Malmesbury—Chipping Sodbury

Well liked for its very good bar food, this busy 16th-c pub takes its name from local hero John Rattlebone, who fought bravely to help Edmund Ironside defeat Canute in the Battle of Sherston in 1016. He received a mortal wound during the fracas, but covered it with a tile until the battle was won, so stemming the flow of blood, before dying on this spot. There are several rambling rooms and nooks and crannies with low beams, pink walls, pews and settles, country kitchen chairs around a mix of tables, big dried flower arrangements, and lots of little cuttings and printed anecdotes; the atmosphere is pleasant and relaxed; piped classical music. The public bar has a hexagonal pool table, darts, table skittles, fruit machine, cribbage, dominoes and juke box; alley skittles and four boules pitches. The wide choice of good food includes lunchtime filled rolls (from £2.25) and ploughman's (£3.50), home-made soup (£2.25), grilled goat's cheese with nut dressing (£3.95), vegetable crepes (£5.75), mushroom and chestnut stroganoff or steak and kidney pie (£6.25), generous prawn salad (£6.50), escalope of turkey with smoked cheese, apple and cream (£8.50), pork tenderloin with stilton and cream sauce topped with cashew nuts (£8.75), steaks (from £8.75), and puddings like fruit crumble (£2.50); good fresh vegetables. Part of the restaurant is no smoking. Well kept Bass, Smiles Best, Wadworths 6X, a beer named for the pub, and a regularly changing guest on handpump, 50 malt whiskies, 20 rums, fruit wines, Westons cider, decent wines, and quick service. The smallish garden is very pretty with flower beds, a gravel terrace, boules, and picnic tables under umbrellas. The old core of the village is very pretty. ***(Recommended by Michael Richards, D G Clarke, Barry Gibbs, Simon and Amanda Southwell, Paul Weedon, Mrs Pat Crabb, N Cole, Dave and Jules Tuckett, Mr and Mrs R D King)***

Free house ~ Licensees David and Ian Rees ~ Real ale ~ Meals and snacks (till 10pm; not 25 Dec) ~ Restaurant ~ (01666) 840871 ~ Children in eating area of bar and in restaurant ~ Open 11.30-3, 5.30-11; 11.30-11pm Sat

WOOTTON RIVERS SU1963 Map 2

Royal Oak 🍷

Village signposted from A346 Marlborough—Salisbury and B3087 E of Pewsey

Popular mainly for its very extensive range of home-made bar food, this pretty 16th-c thatched pub is just a short stroll from the Kennet & Avon Canal. The choice of meals includes lunchtime sandwiches (£1.75), soup (£1.90), basket meals (from

£2.50), ploughman's (from £3.75), lots of salads (from £3.50; avocado and prawn £5.50), pickled herrings in dill with sour cream, apple and walnut (£4.50), ratatouille with toasted brie topping (£6), local trout (£6.25), steak and Guinness pie (£6.50), lamb with spices, apricot and almonds (£7.90), lemon sauce (£7.50), gammon and egg or chicken with Cajun spices (£8), fresh lemon sole (£9), steaks (from £10), and puddings such as sticky treacle and almond tart or sherry trifle (£2.75); three-course Sunday lunch (£9.95). Booking is recommended in the evenings, when some customers may be quite smartly dressed. The friendly L-shaped dining lounge has slat-back chairs, armchairs and some rustic settles around good tripod tables, a low ceiling with partly stripped beams, partly glossy white planks, and a woodburning stove. The timbered bar is comfortably furnished, and has a small area with darts, pool, bar billiards, cribbage, chess, Monopoly, fruit machine, trivia and juke box. Well kept Boddingtons, Wadworths 6X and a monthly changing guest on handpump or tapped from the cask, interesting whiskies, and a good wine list (running up to some very distinguished vintage ones). They do seem to be more interested in diners than drinkers, and service can slow down at busy times. There are tables under cocktail parasols in the back gravelled yard. The thatched and timbered village is worth exploring, particularly the 13th-c church. The family also run the True Heart at Bishopstone, and the Pheasant at Shefford Woodlands. ***(Recommended by Margaret Dyke, Guy Consterdine, Annabel and Chris, M Carey, A Groocock, R J Herd, David Wright, A R and B E Wayer, Gwen and Peter Andrews, P M Lane, Jim and Maggie Cowell, Wim Kock, Willem-Han Kock, Hans Chabot, Mark and Toni Amor-Segan, Joy Heatherley, Brian Bannatyne-Scott, H Anderson, Mark and Diane Grist, Mrs C Watkinson, Ann and Colin Hart, JE, John and Sherry Moate)***

Free house ~ Licensees John and Rosa Jones ~ Real ale ~ Meals and snacks ~ Restaurant ~ (01672) 810322 ~ Children welcome ~ Open 11-3, 6(7 winter)-11, all day Sat; closed 25 Dec and evening 26 Dec ~ Bedrooms (in adjoining house): £25(£27.50B)/£35(£35B)

WYLYE SU0037 Map 2

Bell

Just off A303/A36 junction

Very handy for Stonehenge, this cosy country pub is nicely set in a peaceful village next to the church. The neatly kept and black-beamed front bar has one of the inn's three winter log fires, and sturdy rustic furnishings that go well with the stripped stonework and neat timbered herringbone brickwork. The friendly alsatian can leap from behind the bar counter into the public bar without any running start. A side eating area has plenty of tables, as well as straightforward food such as soup (£2.50), ploughman's, local ham with free range eggs (£5.35), marinated chicken breasts (£6.95), a big mixed grill (£8.95), daily specials, children's dishes, and a Sunday roast (£5.85); some readers have enjoyed their meal very much, though recent reports have been a little mixed. Badger Best, Wadworths 6X and a guest beer on handpump, and a good range of country wines. The back area – partly no-smoking – has dominoes and fruit machine. There are seats outside, some on a pleasant walled terrace. ***(Recommended by Peter Woods, Clive Gilbert, Stephen Brown, A Lilley, N Virgo, Mr and Mrs R O Gibson, Ian Phillips, A J N Lee, W K Struthers, Tony and Joan Walker, Fiona Dick, E J Robinson, R J Walden, T A Bryan)***

Free house ~ Licensees Steve and Ann Locke ~ Real ale ~ Meals and snacks (till 10 Fri/Sat) ~ (01985) 248338 ~ Children welcome till 9pm ~ Open 11.30-2.30, 6-11 ~ Bedrooms: £25B/£39.50B

> If a service charge is mentioned prominently on a menu or accommodation terms, you must pay it if service was satisfactory. If service is really bad you are legally entitled to refuse to pay some or all of the service charge as compensation for not getting the service you might reasonably have expected.

Lucky Dip

Besides the fully inspected pubs, you might like to try these Lucky Dips recommended to us and described by readers (if you do, please send us reports):

☆ **Aldbourne** [SU2675], *Crown*: Spacious well kept village pub with friendly quick service, pleasant atmosphere, good value straightforward food, well kept Courage-related ales, huge log fire, interesting bric-a-brac, quiet piped music; tables under cocktail parasols in neat courtyard *(Ann and Colin Hart, Colin Laffan, P Neate)*

☆ **Aldbourne** [The Green (off B4192)], *Blue Boar*: Well kept Archers Village, Wadworths IPA and 6X and wide choice of food from home-made soup and generous sandwiches up in spaciously refurbished Tudor pub; picnic tables outside, beautiful village-green setting *(R T and J C Moggridge)*

☆ **Alderbury** [Chute End, off A36; SU1827], *Green Dragon*: Lovely olde-worlde Tudor pub in delightful village setting, good bar snack and restaurant menus served by hatted and aproned chef, warm welcome, Badger ales, small public bar and comfortably modernised lounge; garden with big play area and weekly barbecues *(John Beeken, S J Penford, LYM)*

☆ **Alvediston** [ST9723], *Crown*: Welcoming thatched low-beamed country inn carefully extended behind without spoiling the comfortable and attractive rather upmarket main bar, generous helpings of unusual food, well kept Courage, Ringwood and Wadworths, good prices, friendly efficient service, pretty garden, peaceful location; good bedrooms *(Jerry and Alison Oakes, WHBM, Pat and Robert Watt, Susan May, G M Betteridge, S K Robinson, Gordon, W Marsh, LYM)*

Amesbury [SU1541], *New Inn*: Good considerate welcome to dogs and old people etc, well kept beers, wide range of food *(Brian White)*

☆ **Ansty** [ST9526], *Maypole*: Good food in relaxed attractive surroundings, well kept Butcombe, Fullers London Pride and Wadworths 6X, decent wines, log fire, warm welcome, chintzy bedrooms; still open in 1995 and a strong recommendation while it remains so, but owners have been considering turning it into a private house *(Dr and Mrs N Holmes, Jerry and Alison Oakes, J M T Morris, Jason Caulkin, H D Wharton, Tina and David Woods-Taylor, LYM)*

Ashton Keynes [SU0494], *White Hart*: Smart village local with good reasonably priced food, well kept Flowers, good log fire, friendly efficient service; piped music; delightful village *(Audrey and Peter Dowsett, P A C Neate)*

☆ **Avebury** [A361; SU0969], *Red Lion*: Much-modernised thatched pub in the heart of the stone circles; pleasant original core, friendly staff, usual food from unpubby restaurant extension, well kept Whitbreads-related ales *(Anne Cargill, Ralph Lee, Wim Kock, Willem-Jan Kock, Hans Chabot, John and Christine Vittoe, LYM)*

Badbury [off A345 S of Swindon; SU1980], *Bakers Arms*: Quiet, clean and comfortable village local with central fire, Arkells Bitter and BBB, decent simple food (not Mon), piped music, darts and games machine; children welcome, garden *(CW, JW, Peter and Aubrey Dowsett)*

☆ **Beckhampton** [A4 Marlborough—Calne – OS Sheet 173 map ref 090689; SU0868], *Waggon & Horses*: Friendly stone-and-thatch pub handy for Avebury and open all day, full range of Wadworths ales and a guest beer kept well, good coffee, old-fashioned unassuming atmosphere (though the new green paint's hardly an improvement), understated Dickens connections, wide choice of good value bar food, teas, family room (and children's helpings on request), pub games and machines, CD juke box, pleasant garden with good play area; parking over road, no dogs; bedrooms *(D G Clarke, Gwen and Peter Andrews, G Washington, George Atkinson, Dick and Peggy Stacy, Marjorie and David Lamb, Mr and Mrs A L Budden, Kevin and Kay Bronnsey, Brig J S Green, LYM)*

☆ **Biddestone** [The Green; ST8773], *White Horse*: Busy local, traditional and relaxing, small cosy carpeted rooms, good cheap food, well kept Courage ales, welcoming landlord, shove-ha'penny, darts and table skittles; overlooks duckpond (where Kermit and friends splashed down in *The Great Muppet Caper*) in picturesque village, tables in good garden with swings and pen of birds and rabbits; bedrooms *(the Shinkmans, Bill and Peggy Gluntz, Roger Huggins, Tom McLean, Dr and Mrs A K Clarke)*

☆ **Bishops Cannings** [SU0364], *Crown*: Welcoming local next to handsome old church in pretty village, good range of food in huge helpings, Wadworths beers, friendly efficient staff; walk to Kennet & Avon Canal *(Georgina Cole, Chris De Wet, Marjorie and David Lamb, John and Chris Simpson)*

Bishopstone [SU2483], *White Hart*: Good evening food, well kept Gibbs Mew, good friendly service *(HNJ, PEJ, Dr and Mrs N Holmes)*

☆ **Box** [A4, Bath side; ST8268], *Northey Arms*: Relaxed and welcoming open-plan pub with deep red walls, homely decor and lovely view; marvellously varied mix of traditional and exotic home cooking, well kept real ales, decent wines, good service, restaurant, children welcome; nice garden *(Graham and Pauline Loveday, MH, CH)*

☆ **Bradford on Avon** [Silver St; ST8261], *Bunch of Grapes*: Unusual and atmospheric, on two levels in picturesque steep street, with good choice of generous food, well kept Smiles and other ales, good service *(Mrs Joan Harris)*

Bradford on Avon [Masons Hill], *Dandy Lion*: Enjoyably diverse food and good wine list in upstairs restaurant, busy old-world downstairs pub part popular with young people, nice atmosphere and friendly staff *(Paul Weedon, Richard Dolphin)*; [Trowbridge Rd], *Gongoozler*: Modern pub/restaurant nr marina, good view of canal boats *(Dr and Mrs A K Clarke)*

☆ **Broad Chalke** [SU0325], *Queens Head*: Wide range of good home-cooked food inc unusual dishes at reasonable prices, welcoming service, well kept beer, decent wines and country wines, good coffee, attractive furnishings, no music; wheelchair access from back car park, tables in pretty courtyard; comfortable well equipped bedrooms *(John and Christine Vittoe, Buffy and Mike Adamson)*

☆ **Broad Hinton** [High St; off A4361 about 5 miles S of Swindon; SU1076], *Crown*: Unpretentious welcoming local, pleasant and roomy open-plan bar, well kept Arkells BB, BBB, Kingsdown and Mild, straightforward home-cooked food from sandwiches up, good friendly service, unobtrusive piped music; attractive restaurant, unusual gilded inn sign, spacious garden; bedrooms *(June and Tony Baldwin, Nick and Meriel Cox, LYM)*

Brokerswood [ST8352], *Kicking Donkey*: Lovely rural setting, delightful lawn, welcoming service, several bars and various nooks, log fires, good food *(Robert W Brooks)*

☆ **Bromham** [ST9665], *Greyhound*: Good food esp fish and puddings in two thriving attractively lit bars with lots of enjoyable bric-a-brac, blazing log fires, even a well; interesting real ales, decent wines, small intimate restaurant; skittle alley, pool and darts; big garden *(James Fletcher, Mr and Mrs Parmenter, John Hazel, Ray Watson)*

☆ **Burcombe** [SU0730], *Ship*: Doing well under new management, clean and comfortable, with wide range of good reasonably priced food, country wines *(S Jones, Julie Ashton, A D Shore)*

☆ **Burton** [B4039 Chippenham—Chipping Sodbury; ST8179], *Plume of Feathers*: Cosy old beamed pub with good well presented generous food, decent wines inc many Australian, well kept Bass, Smiles and Tetleys, relaxing atmosphere, log fire; bedrooms *(James Fletcher)*

☆ **Castle Combe** [signed off B4039 Chippenham—Chipping Sodbury; ST8477], *Castle Inn*: Old-world country inn in famously picturesque village, clean and attractive, lounge overlooking village street, separate locals' bar, new conservatory, tables on terrace; open fires, good home-made food inc all-day snacks, efficient service, Courage-related ales, coffee and cream teas; children welcome, bedrooms *(Andrew and Ruth Triggs, D G King)*

☆ **Castle Combe** *White Hart*: Pretty stone-built pub, attractive inside, with beams, flagstones and big log fire, Wadworths Henrys, Farmers Glory and 6X and a guest such as Adnams, friendly staff, talking mynah, decent food, family room, games room and tables in sheltered courtyard *(Andrew and Ruth Triggs, LYM)*

☆ **Charlton** [B4040 toward Cricklade; ST9588], *Horse & Groom*: New licensees concentrating on good well presented home-cooked food in recently completely refurbished civilised and relaxing pub with good log fire, well kept Archers and Wadworths, farm cider, decent wines; restaurant (good value Sun lunch), tables outside; has been cl Mon *(P A C Neate, Gary Gibbon, Mike Davies, LYM)*

☆ **Chilmark** [B3089 Salisbury—Hindon; ST9632], *Black Dog*: Well kept Adnams and Brakspears and good value bar food in comfortably modernised 15th-c local with armchairs and *Country Life* by the log fire in the lounge, fossil ammonites in the stone of another bar, games in third bar; decent coffee *(Colin and Ann Hunt, LYM)*

Chirton [A342; SU0757], *Wiltshire Yeoman*: Newish young couple doing good food and beer at very low prices *(John Hazel)*

Cholderton [A338 Tidworth—Salisbury; SU2242], *Crown*: Cosy and welcoming thatched inn, plentiful bar snacks, Gibbs Mew real ale, bar billiards in small tap room *(Michael Butler)*

☆ **Christian Malford** [B4069 Lyneham—Chippenham, 3½ miles from M4 junction 17; ST9678], *Mermaid*: Long bar pleasantly divided into areas, good popular food inc some interesting dishes, well kept Bass, Courage Best, Wadworths 6X and Worthington BB, decent whiskies and wines, some attractive pictures, bar billiards, darts, fruit machine, piped music (live Thurs), tables in garden; bedrooms *(Patrick Godfrey, Tracy Madgwick, BB)*

Coate [Marlborough Rd, nr Swindon; SU1783], *Spotted Cow*: Spacious and recently renovated, walls full of Victorian pictures, good low-priced food, generous decent wine *(Richard Mattick)*

Collingbourne Ducis [SU2453], *Last Straw*: Attractive and cottagey thatched pub with good value well presented food in separate dining room and comfortable bar area, real ales, pleasant service, good open fire *(Anthony and Freda Walters, M Joyner, D G Clarke)*; *Shears*: Popular racing-country local with good food in bar and restaurant, well kept beers; low-cost bedrooms *(Hamish Mathews)*

Collingbourne Kingston [SU2355], *Cleaver*: Friendly service, local atmosphere, well kept Wadworths 6X, basic generous food *(R T and J C Moggridge)*

☆ **Coombe Bissett** [Blandford Rd (A354); SU1026], *Fox & Goose*: Good reasonably priced food (interesting vegetarian, fine puddings) and Wadworths 6X and other ales in thriving spacious open-plan pub by delightful village green; good service, rustic refectory-style tables, coal fires, old prints, hanging chamber-pots; piped music (classical at lunchtime), children catered for, evening restaurant; picnic tables on terrace and in garden with play area, good access for wheelchairs *(W J Wonham, John and Elizabeth Chaplin, E A George, Sue and Mike Todd, John Hazel, Gordon, Stan Edwards, Ian Phillips)*

Corsley [A362 Warminster—Frome; ST8246], *White Hart*: Pleasantly furnished, with good food, well kept low-priced Oakhill ales, friendly landlord; handy for Longleat *(Don Mather, Andrew and Ruth Triggs)*

Corsley Heath [A362 Frome—Warminster; ST8245], *Royal Oak*: Generous helpings of reasonably priced food, very friendly service, Wadworths Henrys, Farmers Glory and 6X, two small bars, back children's room, big garden, restaurant; handy for Longleat *(Andrew and Ruth Triggs)*

Corston [A429, N of M4 junction 17; ST9284], *Radnor Arms*: Friendly newish mangement, good food, well kept beer *(G Washington)*

☆ **Corton** [off A36 Warminster—Wilton; ST9340], *Dove*: Attractive country pub reopened under new ownership, well refurbished inc new hardwood floors, good straightforward food, well kept Oakhill real ale *(Patrick Freeman, LYM)*

Crockerton [just off A350 Warminster—Blandford – OS Sheet 183 map ref 862422; ST8642], *Bath Arms*: Welcoming new licensees, good lunchtime food, no fruit machines or juke box *(Ernest Lamb)*

Crudwell [A429 N of Malmesbury; ST9592], *Plough*: Quiet lounge with open fire, bar with darts and juke box, pool room, dining area with comfortable well padded seats and more in elevated part; well kept ales such as Bass, Boddingtons, local Foxley, Morlands Old Specked Hen and Wadworths 6X *(Roger and Jenny Huggins, D Irving, T McLean, E McCall)*

Derry Hill [ST9570], *Lansdowne Arms*: Friendly and efficient refurbished Wadworths pub, well kept ales, good imaginative food, open fire, restaurant, garden with good play area; handy for Bowood *(Chris and Anne Fluck, John Hazel)*

☆ **Devizes** [Long St; SU0061], *Elm Tree*: Wide choice of good food and well kept Wadworths IPA and 6X in cosy and cheerfully welcoming heavy-beamed local, decent house wines, no-smoking area; piped music; restaurant, bedrooms *(John and Tessa Rainsford, John Hazel, John and Chris Simpson, Joy Heatherley)*

☆ **Devizes** [Monday Mkt St], *White Bear*: Friendly and cosy relaxing 15th-c beamed pub with antiques and lots of atmosphere, well kept Wadworths IPA and 6X, good range of good value food, welcoming prompt service, entertaining landlord; good big bedrooms *(David Holloway, Joy Heatherley, Ian and Ruth Prior)*

Devizes [New Park St], *Castle*: Tastefully refurbished, with well kept Wadworths IPA, 6X and Henrys, good straightforward food with fresh veg; open all day, bedrooms *(John and Chris Simpson, David Holloway)*

☆ **Donhead St Andrew** [off A30 E of Shaftesbury, just E of Ludwell; ST9124], *Forester*: Small old country pub with inglenook fireplace, very friendly staff, good choice of well kept beers, reasonably priced food inc good sandwiches; interesting locals, live music weekends *(Dr and Mrs A K Clarke, John Hazel)*

☆ **East Knoyle** [The Green; ST8830], *Fox & Hounds*: In attractive spot with beautiful view, pleasant layout, big fire, six well kept real ales, good varied choice of well cooked food *(M V Ward, Mrs D E Fryer)*

Enford [off A345; SU1351], *Swan*: Unspoilt village local with Bunces Old Smokey and Hop Back Special; decent well made food, free tasty bar nibbles *(Howard and Margaret Buchanan)*

☆ **Farleigh Wick** [A363 Bath—Bradford; ST8064], *Fox & Hounds*: Clean and welcoming low-beamed rambling bar, highly polished old oak tables and chairs, gently rural decorations; good fresh food, attractive garden; can get packed weekends *(Meg and Colin Hamilton, A D Sherman)*

☆ **Fonthill Gifford** [2 miles from A303; ST9232], *Beckford Arms*: Friendly old stonebuilt pub with huge log fire in attractive relaxing lounge bar, wide range of moderately priced bar food, well kept Ruddles Best, local country wines, nice conservatory; in lovely countryside; bedrooms *(Pat and Robert Watt, John Dawson, Steve Goodchild, G Fisher)*

Foxham [NE of Chippenham; ST9777], *Foxham*: Small, friendly and cosy, extensive views from front, broad food choice inc vegetarian and Indonesian/Malay curries; piped music *(Peter and Wendy Begley)*

☆ **Great Cheverell** [off B3098 Westbury—Mkt Lavington; ST9754], *Bell*: Spaciously extended, very popular for hearty good value food on big plates with lots of trimmings; comfortable chairs and settles, cosy little alcoves, well kept Courage-related ales and Wadworths 6X, upstairs dining room, friendly attentive service *(Colin Laffan, A D Sherman, Gwen and Peter Andrews, JE)*

Great Hinton [3½ miles E of Trowbridge; ST9059], *Linnet*: Pleasantly refurbished village local with good value home-made food from sandwiches up, well kept Wadworths IPA and 6X, keen young licensees, separate dining room, picnic tables outside, pretty village *(G Washington, John Hazel)*

Great Wishford [SU0735], *Royal Oak*: Very wide choice of food in pleasant old pub in pretty village, well kept Courage-related and other ales, big family dining area, log fires; pretty village *(J C Brittain-Long, Paul Weedon, Dr Diana Terry, LYM)*

☆ **Hannington** [SU1793], *Jolly Tar*: Wide choice of good value honest food, well kept Arkells BB, BBB and Kingsdown, welcoming landlord, big log fire in lounge bar, ships' crests on beams, stripped stone and flock wallpaper; games bar, skittle alley, upstairs grill room; piped music; good robust play area in big garden, tables out in front too; pretty village *(Mr and Mrs P B Dowsett, D M Futcher, BB)*

Heddington [ST9966], *Ivy*: Simple thatched village local with good inglenook fireplace in low-beamed bar, timbered walls, well kept Wadworths tapped from the cask, bar food, children's room; seats outside the picturesque house *(John Hazel, Roger Huggins, LYM)*

☆ **Heytesbury** [High St; ST9242], *Angel*: Well kept and attractively refurbished 16th-c inn, charming dining room opening on to secluded garden behind, wide choice of consistently good interesting food, home-baked bread and cakes for sale, Ash Vine, Marstons Pedigree and Border and Ringwood (the lovely dog's called Marston, too), friendly helpful service; popular with army personnel and can sometimes be a bit noisy, though not off-putting; bedrooms comfortable and attractive *(BHP, DP, P and P Fullerton, Nigel Clifton, Peter Brimacombe, John A Baker, David Surridge)*

☆ **Highworth** [Market Pl; SU2092], *Saracens Head*: Comfortable and relaxed rambling bar, several distinct interesting areas around great central chimney block, friendly service, wide choice of good value straightforward bar food (limited Sun) inc vegetarian and children's, well kept Arkells BB and BBB, no piped music, tables in sheltered courtyard; open all day weekdays, children in eating area; comfortable bedrooms *(Peter and Audrey Dowsett, LYM)*

Highworth [St Michaels Ave], *Goldfinger*: Small neat estate pub, well kept Morrells *(Dr and Mrs A K Clarke)*; [High St], *Wine Cellar*: Archers and a guest beer, good range of wines and whiskies, friendly atmosphere, interesting cellar environment; good prices, opens 7, cl Mon-Thurs lunchtimes *(Denis Thurley)*

☆ **Hindon** [High St; ST9132], *Grosvenor Arms*: Welcoming pleasant bar, decent food inc interesting dishes, well kept beers, good house wines, notable Irish coffee *(Geoffrey Culmer, John Evans, Clifford Payton)*

☆ **Horningsham** [by S entrance to Longleat House; ST8141], *Bath Arms*: Smartly civilised old inn, modernised without being spoilt; good interesting food in bar and restaurant, courteous staff, well kept Bass, Eldridge Pope Thomas Hardy and Wadworths 6X, lots of liqueurs and good malt whiskies, aircraft pictures, various dogs; extra charge for credit cards; attractive gardens, dogs allowed on lead here; bedrooms well equipped, clean and comfortable, pretty village *(Bill Bailey, Fiona Dick)*

☆ **Kington Langley** [handy for M4 junction 17; Days Lane; ST9277], *Hit or Miss*: Huge helpings of good food from interestingly filled baguettes to enterprising and unusual main dishes, clean bar with big no-smoking area, darts in room off, restaurant with good log fire; well kept Courage ales and another such as Exmoor or Moles; cl Mon, attractive village *(Meg and Colin Hamilton, P J Caunt)*

☆ **Landford** [Hamptworth; village signed down B3079 off A36, then right towards Redlynch; SU2519], *Cuckoo*: Unpretentious thatched cottage with well kept real ales such as Adnams Broadside, Badger Best and Tanglefoot, Bunces Best, Wadworths IPA and 6X, cheap filled rolls, pies and pasties, impromptu folk music Fri and maybe Sat and Sun; children in small room off bar; tables outside, big play area and bantams *(K Flack, LYM)*

Liddington [a mile from M4 junction 15, just off A419; SU2081], *Village Inn*: Wide choice of good quick lunchtime bar food in split-level bar with Arkells ales, log fire, no piped music; bedrooms simple but clean *(Peter and Audrey Dowsett)*

Limpley Stoke [Woods Hill, off A36 S of Bath; ST7861], *Hop Pole*: Relaxing stone-built pub with dark panelling, old pictures, big log fire, no-smoking lounge; bar food inc children's (not Sun evening), Courage ales and good choice of genuine guest beers, a good few malt whiskies; summer weekend barbecues in big garden *(Andrew Partington, LYM)*

☆ **Lockeridge** [signed off A4 Marlborough—Calne just W of Fyfield; SU1467], *Who'd A Thought It*: Very welcoming Scots landlord, good choice of good value food, well kept Wadworths IPA and 6X and a guest beer such as Charles Wells Eagle, plush seats in lounge with eating area, separate public bar, log fire; family room, delightful back garden with play area; interesting village *(Marjorie and David Lamb, JEB, Brig Green)*

☆ **Luckington** [High St; ST8383], *Old Royal Ship*: Go-ahead young landlady keeping traditional friendly country-local style alongside good range of innovative food; well kept real ales, farm cider, decent wines (two glass sizes), darts, garden with play area; bedrooms *(M J Morgan, Jerry and Jan Fowler)*

Ludwell [A30; ST9122], *Grove Arms*: Lovely interior, good varied food, restaurant *(Sally and Bill Hyde)*

Malmesbury [Abbey Row; ST9287], *Old Bell*: Lovely old traditional hotel looking across churchyard to Norman abbey, good service, decent food, log fires, Ushers Best and Wadworths 6X, attractively old-fashioned garden providing well for children; bedrooms *(Rosie and Peter Angwin, Bill Bailey, LYM)*; [High St], *Smoking Dog*: Cosy if sometimes smoky beamed and stripped stone local with changing well kept ales such as Archers, Courage Best, Greene King Abbot, Smiles Best and Wadworths 6X, farm ciders, log fires; decent bistro, small garden; bedrooms *(D Irving, R Huggins, T McLean, E McCall, D M Futcher, Steve Hayward, Michael Richards, Larry Alen)*

Manton [High St; SU1668], *Oddfellows Arms*: Fairly small local, well kept Wadworths, country wines, good straightforward food, big garden *(Paul Randall, KB, Nick and David Clifton)*; [High

St], *Up The Garden Path*: Very friendly largish beamed bar with good food (only the finest steak for their steak and kidney pie), no-smoking restaurant *(Mrs C Watkinson, HNJ, PEJ, Mr and Mrs A L Budden)*

☆ **Marlborough** [1 High St; SU1869], *Bear*: Large Victorian inn with impressive central log fire, well kept Arkells Bitter, 3B, Kingsdown and Yeomanry, good often interesting home-cooked food in old-fashioned side bar, small front lunchtime tapas bar (evening restaurant), medieval-style banqueting hall for special occasions, skittle alley; bedrooms inc good value family room *(Mr and Mrs C Holmes, Annabel and Chris, D Irving, E McCall, R Huggins, Tom McLean)*

☆ **Marlborough** [High St], *Sun*: Heavy 16th-c beams, parquet floor and shiny black panelling, plainer lounge on left (children allowed here), well kept Bass and Hook Norton Best, good coffee, decent food esp fresh fish, log fire, friendly staff; seats in small courtyard; piped music, live some nights; friendly staff; bedrooms simple but comfortable and reasonably priced *(George Atkinson, David Griffiths, Kim Ryan Skuse, Gordon, LYM)*

☆ **Marston Meysey** [SU1297], *Spotted Cow & Calf*: Pretty Cotswold stone pub, good value generous bar food, well kept Flowers IPA, Wadworths 6X and two guest beers, welcoming landlord, raised stone fireplace, candlelit restaurant (evening, also Sun lunch); fruit machine and piped music may be rather intrusive; spacious garden with lots of play equipment, picturesque village *(Jan and Dave Booth)*

Mere [Castle St; ST8132], *Old Ship*: 16th-c building with log fires, good value food esp in interesting timber-walled restaurant, cosy hotel bar, spacious separate more pubby bar across coach entry divided into cosy areas by standing timbers, bar games and piped music; children allowed in eating area; good value bedrooms *(S Crockett, Mr and Mrs P Bradley, LYM)*

Minety [SU0290], *White Horse*: Good value generous home cooking in cosy and comfortably refurbished bars or restaurant, four real ales, welcoming service; pleasant lakeside setting *(Mrs C Wise, M Tuohy, Mrs P Green)*

☆ **Netherhampton** [SU1029], *Victoria & Albert*: Cosy and friendly low-beamed pub with antique furniture on polished flagstones, well kept Courage-related ales, good choice of wines, good carefully cooked food, maybe unobtrusive piped music, fruit machine in side room; nice long garden behind with own serving hatch *(Jerry and Alison Oakes, Dr Diana Terry)*

☆ **Nettleton** [ST8178], *Nettleton Arms*: Very wide choice of good generous bar food in renovated 16th-c pub with quiet no-smoking restaurant, interesting minstrels' gallery; good range of reasonably priced well kept beers, welcoming licensees, cosy corners in bar; occasional live music; bedrooms *(Paul Weedon, Neville Kilford)*

☆ **Newton Toney** [off A338 Swindon—Salisbury; SU2140], *Malet Arms*: Very popular (esp with Army officers) for good imaginative food in bar and restaurant; good local atmosphere *(Jerry and Alison Oakes, Dr and Mrs N Holmes)*

Nomansland [SU2517], *Lamb*: Lovely New Forest setting on Hants border, wide choice of good value bar food with decent vegetarian choice, lots of puddings, Ringwood bitter, friendly donkeys, attractive old-fashioned building *(Richard Burton)*

☆ **North Newnton** [A345 Upavon—Pewsey; SU1257], *Woodbridge*: Open all day for eclectic world-wide food inc imaginative vegetarian dishes, also afternoon teas; well kept Wadworths 6X, good wines and coffee, friendly service, log fire, newspapers and magazines; big garden with boules, fishing available; bedrooms, small camping/caravan site *(George Atkinson, Peter Brimacombe, Howard and Margaret Buchanan, Joseph Steindl)*

Nunton [SU1526], *Radnor Arms*: Friendly helpful staff, cheerfully busy bar and staider restaurant, good food inc enormous crab salad, very friendly dog, attractive garden popular with children *(Martin and Karen Wake)*

☆ **Odstock** [SU1526], *Yew Tree*: Fine old thatched country dining pub, bewildering choice of good wholesome food esp fresh fish and game, good range of real ales, nice unpretentious atmosphere *(J V Dadswell, Prof J M White, BB)*

☆ **Ogbourne St Andrew** [SU1872], *Wheatsheaf*: Good bar food, friendly landlord, very pleasant atmosphere; tables in garden behind *(Dr and Mrs Nigel Holmes, Mr and Mrs K H Frostick)*

Ogbourne St George [A345 Marlboro—Swindon; SU1974], *Old Crown*: Very well managed, well kept beer, good imaginative food, warm welcome *(Michael Gidding)*

Ramsbury [Crowood Lane/Whittonditch Rd; SU2771], *Crown & Anchor*: Friendly relaxed beamed village pub with good reasonably priced imaginative food, well kept Bass, Tetleys and usually a guest beer, lots of malt whiskies, pool in public bar; children welcome, garden *(Mr and Mrs P Smith)*

Redlynch [N of B3080; SU2021], *Kings Head*: Comfortable cottagey 16th-c pub reopened after refurbishment by new owners, concentration on good home-cooked food from lunchtime sandwiches to hot dishes with fresh veg *(MJS)*

Rowde [ST9762], *Cross Keys*: Newish licensees, very competitive prices, food quickly and attractively produced *(John Hazel)*

☆ **Salisbury** [New St], *New Inn*: No smoking throughout; heavy beams and timbering, recent refurbishment with quiet cosy nooks and crannies in small eating area off main bar, good range of food, friendly staff, well kept Badger beers; pleasant garden, handy for cathedral *(Dr Diana Terry, Wayne*

Brindle, Brian Bannatyne-Scott, John and Christine Vittoe, BB)

☆ **Salisbury** [Milford St], *Red Lion*: Mix of old-fashioned seats and modern banquettes in two-roomed nicely local-feeling panelled bar opening into other spacious and interesting areas, medieval restaurant, well kept Bass, Ushers, Wadworths 6X and a strong guest beer, lunchtime bar food, loggia courtyard seats; children in eating areas; bedrooms comfortable *(Jerry and Alison Oakes, JM, PM, LYM)*

☆ **Salisbury** [Castle St], *Avon Brewery*: Old-fashioned city bar, long, narrow, busy and friendly, with dark mahogany, frosted and engraved curved windows, friezes and attractive pictures, two open fires; competitively priced food (not Sun evening), well kept Eldridge Pope ales, decent wines, maybe classical piped music; long sheltered garden running down to river; open all day *(Mr and Mrs A P Reeves, Ron Shelton, Wayne Brindle, LYM)*

Salisbury [Winchester St], *Coach & Horses*: Nice old place with fresh pleasant decor, comprehensive imaginative menu, home-baked bread, attentive but unobtrusive service, well kept beer *(Rosemary Bayliss)*; [Wilton Rd, opp main Police stn], *Hogs Head*: Good value, clean and comfortable, very cheerful staff, good atmosphere, big menu *(Sylvia Jones)*; [Wilton Rd], *Horse & Groom*: Single big bar catering for younger set; good beers *(Dr and Mrs A K Clarke)*; [St John St], *Kings Arms*: Creaky old Tudor inn, darkly panelled and heavily beamed, with friendly staff, comfortable furnishings, good choice of wines and real ale, food in bar and restaurant; well furnished bedrooms *(Wayne Brindle, John and Christine Vittoe, LYM)*; [Woodside Rd, Bemerton Heath; SU1230], *Moon*: Very smart friendly estate pub on outskirts, well kept Gibbs Mew *(Dr and Mrs A K Clarke)*; [Wilton Rd], *Wilton*: Recently refurbished, not too chintzy, very friendly and still a genuine local *(Dr and Mrs A K Clarke)*

Seend [A361; ST9461], *Bell*: Unpretentious country pub, prompt friendly service, well kept Wadworths, small choice of good food (not Mon evening), small cosy lounge *(Gwen and Peter Andrews, John Hazel, Mr and Mrs N A Spink)*; [Seend Cleeve], *Brewery*: Genuine local, very obliging landlord, no music, bar billiards, low prices; no food Tues evening, open all day Sat *(John Hazel)*

Shalbourne [just of A338 S of Hungerford; SU3163], *Plough*: Old low-beamed local on green, well refurbished under chatty newish licensees, cosy and nicely furnished lounge doubling as good evening restaurant, no piped music; tables, play area and barbecues outside *(HNJ, PEJ)*

☆ **Sherston** [B4040 Malmesbury—Chipping Sodbury; ST8585], *Carpenters Arms*: Cosy beamed village pub with extraordinarily wide choice of food inc lots of fresh fish, well kept Whitbreads-related ales tapped from the cask, newly varnished tables on floors now carpeted, open fires, friendly efficient staff, dining area; tables in pleasant garden *(G Hart, Peter Cornall, Margaret and Douglas Tucker, Dave Irving, Roger Huggins, Tom McLean)*

South Marston [SU1987], *Carpenters Arms*: Good value food in pub recently much-extended in successful olde-worlde farmhouse style, well kept Arkells and Marstons, friendly staff, good helpings of well priced wholesome food *(Alan and Paula McCully, Dave Irving, Jeff Davies)*

Staverton [B3105 Trowbridge—Bradford-on-Avon; ST8560], *Old Bear*: Wide choice of good food in stone pub's long bar divided into sections, big fireplace, friendly helpful staff; booking recommended Sun lunchtime *(Meg and Colin Hamilton)*

☆ **Stibb Green** [SU2262], *Three Horseshoes*: Friendly and spotless old-world pub with inglenook log fire in small beamed front bar, second smaller bar, wide range of good food, well kept Wadworths ales, country wines, farm cider, lively landlord *(Gordon, Kevin and Kay Bronnsey, H Anderson)*

☆ **Stourton** [Church Lawn; follow Stourhead signpost off B3092, N of junction with A303 just W of Mere; ST7734], *Spread Eagle*: NT pub in lovely setting at head of Stourhead lake (though views from pub itself not special), currently well managed, with pleasant cool and spacious back dining room popular mainly with older people; standard food till 3, and evening, Ash Vine, Bass and Wadworths 6X, friendly waitress service, open fire in parlour bar, tables in back courtyard; bedrooms *(Wendy Arnold, Janet Pickles, Fiona Dick, Nick and Meriel Cox, John A Barker, G Washington, Christopher Gallop, S Jones, WHBM, LYM)*

Stratton St Margaret [SU1787], *Rat Trap*: Pleasant and comfortable, wide choice of reasonably priced food popular lunchtime with office staff, Arkells 3B *(Peter and Audrey Dowsett)*

Swindon [Prospect Hill; SU1485], *Beehive*: Well hidden lively local popular with college students and older people with a faintly bohemian streak, particularly well kept Morrells, simple lunchtime food, Irish folk nights; don't expect plush seats *(Tom McEwan)*

Teffont Magna [ST9832], *Black Horse*: Simple stonebuilt pub in attractive village, friendly landlord, wide range of food, Boddingtons and Wadworths 6X, children's play area in pleasant garden *(John Hazel, Keith Widdowson, LYM)*

☆ **Upton Lovell** [ST9440], *Prince Leopold*: Civilised dining pub concentrating on its nicely decorated restaurant – imaginative food, candlelight even at lunchtime, decent good value wines, cheerful staff; lovely riverside garden maybe with taco bar, comfortable quiet bedrooms *(Mr and Mrs Paul Adams, Patrick Freeman)*

☆ **Wanborough** [2 miles from M4 junction 15; Callas Hill, former B4507 towards Lower Wanborough and Bishopstone; SU2083], *Black Horse*: Popular down-to-earth pub with lovely downland views, limited good generous cheap food from doorstep sandwiches up (snacks only, Sun lunchtime), well kept low-priced Arkells 2B and 3B, in winter Kingsdown tapped from the cask, welcoming landlord (and Bill and Ben the golden retrievers), beams, tiled floor, antique clock; lounge doubling as homely Mon-Sat lunchtime dining room; piped music; informal garden with play area; children very welcome *(Peter and Audrey Dowsett, Alan and Paula McCully)*

☆ **Wanborough** [Foxhill; from A419 through Wanborough turn right, 1½ miles towards Baydon], *Shepherds Rest*: Friendly atmosphere in remote pub up on the Ridgeway, very busy in summer and recently extended into plusher dining area; good value well presented food, well kept Flowers IPA and Original and Marstons Pedigree, welcoming service, lots of tables in low-beamed lounge with hunting prints and brasses, attractive redone garden with play area; children and walkers welcome, camping *(Mrs Barker, I E and C A Prosser)*

☆ **West Dean** [SU2527], *Red Lion*: Very relaxed well kept country pub in lovely peaceful surroundings, with tables out by tree-sheltered village green running down to pretty stream-fed duckpond, play area; simple lounge with easy chairs and open fires, games inc bar billiards in small plain back bar; well kept Cheriton Pots, Hop Back Summer Lightning and (new to us) Balkesbury Bitter, good value interesting food inc tempting puddings and Sun lunch, no-smoking raised dining area, unhurried service; bedrooms spacious, light and fresh *(Ann and Colin Hunt, Lynn Sharpless, Bob Eardley, T A Bryan, LYM)*

☆ **Wilcot** [SU1360], *Golden Swan*: Very pretty old steeply thatched pub by Kennet & Avon Canal, unpretentiously welcoming, lots of china hanging from beams of two small rooms, well kept Wadworths IPA and 6X and in winter Old Timer, friendly retrievers and prize-winning cat; reasonably priced bar food, dining room; rustic tables on pretty front lawn, field with camping, occasional folk and barbecue weekends, children welcome; good value bedrooms, big and airy *(WHBM, Meg and Colin Hamilton, H Anderson, LYM)*

Wilton [Market Pl; SU0931], *Wiltons*: Smart little place with accent on food and nice friendly atmosphere; no-smoking area; discos some nights *(Dr and Mrs A K Clarke)*

☆ **Wingfield** [ST8256], *Poplars*: Clean and friendly country local with decent food inc splendid snacks, well kept Wadworths, quick pleasant service, no juke box or machines, own cricket pitch *(Fiona Dick, Geoff Summers, BB)*

☆ **Winterbourne Monkton** [A361 Avebury—Wroughton; SU0972], *New Inn*: Small friendly village local with basic traditional bar, well kept Adnams, Wadworths 6X and a guest such as Hook Norton Old Hookey, decent cider, reasonably priced bar food, darts, fruit machine, subdued piped music; restaurant; comfortable bedrooms in converted barn, good breakfast *(Rona Murdoch)*

☆ **Woodborough** [Bottlesford, towards Pewsey – OS Sheet 173 map ref 112592; SU1159], *Seven Stars*: Charming friendly thatched country pub with roaring log fires, attractive panelling, well kept Badger Tanglefoot, Wadworths 6X and guest beer, good value excellently prepared food cooked by French chef/patron, regular supplies direct from France, good wine list, two restaurant areas; pretty garden, in 7 acres *(Mr and Mrs S Larkin, Colin Murray-Hill, Peter Brimacombe, Neville Burrell, Nick and David Clifton)*

Wootton Bassett [High St; SU0682], *Hogs Head*: Friendly refurbished town pub, bare boards, good range of real ales, lots of video and other games *(Dr and Mrs A K Clarke)*

Wroughton [High St; SU1480], *Carters Rest*: Full range of Archers ales kept well, several guest beers, welcoming licensees, decent food *(Callum Mills)*

Yorkshire

Our Yorkshire chapter, always very large, is swollen further this year by the addition of those east Yorkshire pubs which would formerly have been included in Humberside, but which now join North Yorkshire as part of the 1996 local government reorganisation. Yorkshire's pubs stand out for character; for the warmth of their welcome; and for value generally low prices, and when it comes to food service a generosity which can overwhelm southerners. For enjoyable meals out, pubs currently doing particularly well here include the very imaginative Crab & Lobster at Asenby (one of England's best dining pubs), the Three Hares at Bilbrough (very foody, but unusually friendly too), the Malt Shovel at Brearton (good new licensees who formerly ran a small Scottish hotel which featured strongly in our companion Good Weekend Guide), the Abbey Inn in its lovely setting at Byland Abbey, the Durham Ox at Crayke (great atmosphere), the Blue Lion at East Witton (another pub that ranks high on the national scale), the rather restauranty Kaye Arms on Grange Moor, the thriving and bustling Angel at Hetton, the very civilised George & Dragon at Kirkbymoorside (gaining a Food Award this year), the warmly friendly Horseshoe up at Levisham, the Gold Cup at Low Catton (doing well after a refurbishment), the quietly upmarket Black Bull at Moulton, the Nags Head at Pickhill (though the licensee brothers have been here for 25 years it still seems to be improving – another place to gain our Food Award this year), the Milburn Arms at Rosedale Abbey (very imaginative, now approaching a Food Award), the warmly welcoming Sawley Arms at Sawley, the charming little Fox & Hounds at Starbotton, the relaxed Old Hall at Threshfield, the Wombwell Arms at Wass (a nice place to stay, too); and three interesting new main entries, the White Hart at Pool, the Three Acres at Shelley (expensive, but the food's quite exceptional) and the Bay Horse at Terrington. From among all of these, it's the Angel at Hetton which we choose as Yorkshire Dining Pub of the Year. As we've said, prices generally in the area are low. Typically, a pint of beer costs 20p less than the British average, and in the last year prices have stayed steadier here than almost everywhere else – it's clear from our price survey that Yorkshire's very independent-minded free houses are driving particularly hard bargains with their suppliers. Pubs tied to Sam Smiths were among the cheapest, and we found good prices also in those tied to Clarks or Timothy Taylors. We were able to buy a pint of beer for under £1 still at the Horse Shoe at Egton Bridge, and for little more at the St Vincent Arms at Sutton upon Derwent and the Greyhound at Saxton. With over 250 pubs now qualifying for the Lucky Dip section at the end of the chapter, we shortlist here a few that are currently showing really well (most of them inspected and approved by us): in North Yorkshire, the Falcon at Arncliffe, Rose & Crown at Bainbridge, Birch Hall at Beck Hole, Royal Oak at Dacre Banks, Cross Keys at East Marton, Black Horse in Grassington, Wainstones at Great Broughton, Bridge at Grinton, Queens Head at Kettlesing, Forresters Arms at Kilburn, Red Lion at Langthwaite, Lister Arms at Malham, Olde Punch

Bowl at Marton cum Grafton, Black Swan in Middleham, Freemasons Arms at Nosterfield, Black Bull at Reeth, White Horse at Rosedale Abbey, Pipe & Glass at South Dalton, White Dog at Sutton Howgrave, Tan Hill Inn on Tan Hill, Wensleydale Heifer at West Witton and Countryman at Winksley; and in South and West Yorkshire, the Swan at Aberford, Griffin at Barkisland, Cow & Calf at Grenoside, Sands House outside Huddersfield, Windmill at Linton, Robin Hood at Pecket Well and Ring o' Bells in Thornton. There's no shortage of good pubs in Leeds and York.

ALDBOROUGH (N Yorks) SE4166 Map 7

Ship

Village signposted from B6265 just S of Boroughbridge, close to A1

As this neatly kept old pub is opposite the ancient church and near the Roman town with its museum and Roman pavements, it is popular with visitors for morning coffee. The heavily beamed bar has some old-fashioned seats around heavy cast-iron tables, sentimental engravings on the walls, and a coal fire in the stone inglenook fireplace. Popular bar food includes home-made soup (£1.60), well filled sandwiches (from £1.95), garlic mushrooms (£2.75), ploughman's or giant yorkshire pudding with roast beef (£4.50), home-made steak and kidney pie, lasagne or home-made chicken curry (£4.95), battered cod (£5.75), steaks (from £7.25), weekly specials, vegetarian dishes, and Sunday roast lunch (£7.50). Well kept John Smiths, Tetleys, and Theakstons Old Peculier on handpump, and quite a few malt whiskies. There are seats on the front terrace or on the spacious lawn behind. *(Recommended by Neil and Angela Huxter, Martin Hickes, T M Dobby, R A Hobbs, J L Cox, Beryl and Bill Farmer)*

Free house ~ Licensee Duncan Finch ~ Real ale ~ Meals and snacks (not Sun evening) ~ Restaurant (not Sun evening) ~ (01423) 322749 ~ Children in eating area of bar ~ Open 11-2.30(3 Sat), 5.30-11 ~ Bedrooms: £29S/£40S

ALLERTHORPE (N Yorks) SE7847 Map 7

Plough

Off A1079 nr Pocklington

One reader arrived at this idyllic little pub shortly after the evening opening time and found he was the only customer; fifteen minutes later it was absolutely packed. The friendly village feel and welcome are quite a draw, but also standing out are the splendid daily specials cooked by the landlord: generously served meals such as venison in red wine sauce, poached fresh salmon with a prawn sauce, rack of lamb in honey, mint and redcurrant sauce, braised dishes like English lamb's liver and onions, steak and onions, or lamb's kidneys. More standard dishes include soup (£1.65), very good sandwiches (£1.95), ploughman's (£3.65), home-made pâté (£3.65), lasagne (£4.95), scampi (£5.30), steaks (from £8.95), children's meals, and puddings (£2.20); vegetarian dishes available on request. Best to arrive early for the Sunday roast lunch (£4.95). The cheery two-room lounge bar has snug alcoves (including one big bay window), hunting prints, some wartime RAF and RCAF photographs (squadrons of both were stationed here), and open fires; the games – pool, dominoes, shove-ha'penny, cribbage, fruit and video machine and juke box – are in an extension. Well kept reasonably priced Theakstons XB and Old Peculier and Tetleys on handpump. The garden is a pleasant spot to relax, and it's not far to the attractive lily-pond gardens and stuffed sporting trophies of Burnby Hall. *(Recommended by Ian Phillips, John and Sheila French, Roger Bellingham, Lee Goulding)*

Free house ~ Licensees David and Janet Booth ~ Real ale ~ Meals and snacks ~ Restaurant ~ (01759) 302349 ~ Children in eating area, games room and restaurant ~ Open 12-3, 7-11

APPLETREEWICK (N Yorks) SE0560 Map 7

Craven Arms

Village signposted off B6160 Burnsall—Bolton Abbey

This stone-built country pub is a warmly atmospheric place with roaring fires (one in an ancient iron range) in its small cosy rooms, attractive settles and carved chairs among more usual seats, and beams that are covered with banknotes, harness, copper kettles and so forth; the landlord is quite a character. Generous bar food includes home-made soup (£1.60), sandwiches (from £1.65), garlic mushrooms (£2.65), ploughman's (£3.75), cumberland sausage and onion sauce or home-made steak and kidney pie (£4.40), tuna bake (£4.70), vegetable bake (£4.80), ham and egg (£5.40), steaks (from £8.20), and daily specials such as vegetable cannelloni (£4.80), game dishes (around £5), and fish; quick table service in the charming small dining room. Well kept Boddingtons, Tetleys, Theakstons Best, Old Peculier, and XB, Youngers, and a summer guest beer on handpump, 24 malt whiskies, and decent, keenly priced wines; darts, shove-ha'penny, cribbage, dominoes – no music. Picnic tables in front of the pub look south over the green Wharfedale valley to a pine-topped ridge – and in summer, the pub is popular with walkers; there are more seats in the back garden. *(Recommended by Prof S Barnett, Gwen and Peter Andrews, J E Rycroft, K H Frostick, D Goodger, A Wilson, Mark Bradley, Paul Cartledge, Paul and Gail Betteley, C Roberts, L Walker, M E A Horler, Nicola Thomas, Paul Dickinson)*

Free house ~ Licensees Jim and Linda Nicholson ~ Real ale ~ Meals and snacks (not 25 Dec) ~ (01756) 720270 ~ Children welcome ~ Open 11.30-3, 6.30-11

ASENBY (N Yorks) SE3975 Map 7

Crab & Lobster ★

Village signposted off A168 – handy for A1

So popular is the imaginative food in this thatched dining pub, that people tend to queue up before the doors open. And although this does mean that it's always busy, the atmosphere is instantly relaxing and there's a warm, friendly buzz of conversation. The menu is chalked over all the dark beams and joists in the characterful rambling L-shaped bar: soups such as fish soup and rouille, crab and lobster bisque or bean and vegetable (£2.95), tartlet of smoked haddock, spinach and hollandaise (£3.95), crab and potato cake, crisp bacon and buttered cabbage or crispy Chinese stir-fry and ginger minted butter (£4.50), spinach and ricotta lasagne with nutmeg cream (£4.75), shellfish ravioli, basil and lemon grass (£5.50), spaghetti of spiced meatballs with tomato chutney (£7.95), braised shank of lamb with gratin potatoes (£9.25), red mullet with mediterranean vegetables or boned saddle of rabbit with oven dried tomatoes and mustard (£9.50), calf's liver with smoked bacon and horseradish rosti (£11.50), salt seared beef fillet on caesar's salad (£12.95), and puddings like warm chocolate tart with vanilla glace, chocolate and Grand Marnier trufflecake or iced honeycomb nougatine with sugared apples (£3.95); presentation is excellent. They do excellent sandwiches and Sunday roast beef, and there are usually nibbles on the bar counter. Theakstons Best, Timothy Taylors Landlord, and Youngers Scotch and No 3 on handpump, good wines by the glass, with interesting bottles. Cosily cluttered, the bar has an interesting jumble of seats from antique high-backed and other settles through settees and wing armchairs heaped with cushions to tall and rather theatrical corner seats and even a very superannuated dentist's chair; the tables are almost as much of a mix, and the walls and available surfaces are quite a jungle of bric-a-brac, with standard and table lamps keeping even the lighting pleasantly informal; well reproduced piped music. There are rustic seats on a side lawn, and out on a front terrace by tubs of flowers; maybe summer barbecues Friday and Saturday evenings and Sunday lunchtime, running to tiger prawns, lobster and suckling pig. A permanent marquee is attached to the restaurant. *(Recommended by Robert and Ann Lees, Tim and Sue Halstead, John and Chris Simpson, Martin Hickes, S Head, Robin and Lucy Harrington, W C M Jones, David Surridge, Tony Gayfer, P D and J Bickley, Geoffrey and Brenda Wilson, Prof J V Wood, Brian Bannatyne-Scott, C J Hartley, Andrew and*

Ruth Triggs, M J Marriage, David Wright, Dr Philip Jackson, Katie and Steve Newby, John Knighton)

Free house ~ Licensees David and Jackie Barnard ~ Real ale ~ Meals and snacks (not Sun evening) ~ Restaurant (not Sun evening) ~ (01845) 577286 ~ Children in eating area of bar ~ Jazz/blues evenings ~ Open 11.30-3, 6.30-11; closed Sun evening

ASKRIGG (N Yorks) SD9591 Map 10

Kings Arms

Village signposted from A684 Leyburn—Sedbergh in Bainbridge

There are three atmospheric, old-fashioned bars in this Georgian manor house. The very high-ceilinged central room has an attractive medley of furnishings that includes a fine sturdy old oak settle, nineteenth-century fashion plates, a stag's head, hunting prints, and a huge stone fireplace; a curving wall with a high window shows people bustling up and down the stairs and there's a kitchen hatch in the panelling. The small low-beamed and oak panelled front bar has period furnishings, some side snugs, and a lovely green marble fireplace. A simply furnished flagstoned back bar has yet another fire, and a fruit machine, and juke box. Darts, shove-ha'penny, dominoes, and cribbage. Bar food (with prices unchanged since last year) includes lunchtime sandwiches (from £1.85; filled french bread and open sandwiches from £3.25), soup (£2.25), stir-fried vegetables (£4), coq au vin or salmon with parsley sauce (£5.25), steak and kidney pie (£5.55), gammon and eggs (£5.95), grilled lamb cutlets, children's dishes (from £1.95), daily specials, and home-made puddings like sticky toffee pudding with butterscotch sauce (£2.50); the restaurants are no smoking. Well kept Dent Bitter, Theakstons XB, and Youngers Scotch and No 3 on handpump, quite a few malt whiskies, and a very good wine list (including interesting champagnes); pleasant, helpful staff. The two-level courtyard has lots of tables and chairs. *(Recommended by Mark and Caroline Thislethwaite, Eddie Edwards, Roger and Corinne Ball, JKW, John Fazakerley, Sara Nicholls, J Royce, Annette Moore, Chris Pearson, Viv Middlebrook, Martin and Pauline Richardson, Andrew and Ruth Triggs, Mark Bradley, D Goodger, Margaret Mason, David Thompson, Paul Cartledge, M J Morgan)*

Free house ~ Licensees Raymond and Elizabeth Hopwood ~ Real ale ~ Meals and snacks ~ Restaurant (not Sun evening) ~ (01969) 650258 ~ Children in eating area of bar and in restaurant ~ Regular live entertainment ~ Open 11-3(5 Sat), 6.30-11 ~ Bedrooms: £55B/£85B

BEVERLEY (N Yorks) TA0340 Map 8

White Horse ('Nellies')

Hengate, close to the imposing Church of St Mary's; runs off North Bar

Some of the locals at this rather special old place might still recall its determinedly traditional former landlady Nellie Collinson (she's still remembered in the pub name), who didn't even have a bar counter and was one of the very last to enforce a men-only rule. To call it unspoilt barely does the pub justice, as little can have changed since the days in the 18th-c when John Wesley preached in the back yard; even then the building was over 350 years old. Readers love this place for the basic but very atmospheric little rooms, huddled together around the central bar, with antique cartoons and sentimental engravings on the nicotine-stained walls, brown leatherette seats (with high-backed settles in one little snug), basic wooden chairs and benches, a gaslit pulley-controlled chandelier, bare floorboards, a deeply reverberating chiming clock, and open fires – one with an attractively tiled old fireplace. Well kept and very cheap Sam Smiths OB and Museum on handpump. There's a daily changing menu with very cheap, simple, quickly served food which might include sandwiches (£1.30), filled baked potatoes (£1.95), a vegetarian dish like vegetable lasagne, and steak and kidney pie (£3.75); Sunday roast (£3.75). A games room has darts, dominoes, trivia and two pool tables – these and the no-smoking room behind the bar are the only modern touches. Those whose tastes are for comfortable modern pubs may find it a little spartan, anyone else will quickly feel at home. *(Recommended by Pete Baker, JJW, CMW, Andy and Jill Kassube, A Craig, David and Ruth Hollands, Annette Moore, Chris Pearson, John Honnor)*

Sam Smiths ~ Lease: John Southern ~ Real ale ~ Lunchtime meals and snacks (not Mon) ~ (01482) 861973 ~ Children welcome except in bar ~ Folk music Mon, Jazz Weds nights ~ Open 11-11 (cl 25 Dec)

BILBROUGH (N Yorks) SE5346 Map 7

Three Hares

Off A64 York—Tadcaster

Although it's the food that readers like so much in this smartly refurbished dining pub, the charming licensees and their staff are genuinely welcoming and friendly. They tell us they are committed towards using fresh local produce cooked in a modern, forward-thinking way and dishes include specials such as calf's liver on a bed of fresh spinach with a shallot and red wine sauce or breast of guinea fowl roasted onto a sherry and honey sauce and topped with a julienne of deep-fried vegetables (£6.95), fillet of Whitby cod topped with Farndale goat's cheese crust, grilled onto a fresh tomato coulis (£7.25), and tuna steak marinaded in citrus and lime and grilled with herb butter or whole Brixham lemon sole with lime butter (£7.95); also, lunchtime sandwiches (not Sunday), home-made soup, chicken and pistachio pâté with warm olive bread or tartlets of Wensleydale cheese and watercress with a red onion salad (£2.95), potted duck confit with marrow chutney and sun-dried tomato bread (£3.95), field mushrooms stuffed with tofu and cashew nuts baked under a herb crust and served with a herb dressing (£5.75), local rabbit pie (£5.95), pasta with frazzled prosciutto ham, roasted peppers and a shallot and garlic dressing (£6.50), goujons of fresh sole in a crisp batter with a dill and lemon mayonnaise (£6.95), stir-fried chicken and king prawns in a black bean sauce (£7.25), and sirloin steak (£9.75), with puddings such as rich terrine of dark chocolate and praline, baked ginger and syrup pudding and home-made ice creams (£2.75). They sell the recipes over the counter for charity. Well kept John Smiths and Timothy Taylors Landlord and changing guests like Black Sheep Bitter and Special, Fullers London Pride, Marstons Pedigree, Theakstons XB, and Wadworths 6X on handpump, and a good, interesting wine list (Mr Whitehead's wholesale wine business is thriving). The old village smithy now forms part of the no-smoking restaurant and the old forge and implement hooks are still visible, and the prettily papered walls of the traditional bar are hung with pictures of the village (taken in 1904 and showing that little has changed since then), and polished copper and brass; dominoes and piped music. The churchyard close to the pub is where Sir Thomas Fairfax, famous for his part in the Civil War, lies buried. *(Recommended by Viv Middlebrook, Lawrence Bacon, Tim and Sue Halstead, Bill and Beryl Farmer, Nick Wikeley, Caroline and Gerard McAleese)*

Free house ~ Lease: Peter and Sheila Whitehead ~ Real ale ~ Meals and snacks (not Mon) ~ Restaurant (not Sun evening or Mon) ~ (01937) 832128 ~ Well behaved children in eating area of bar and in restaurant but must be gone by 8pm ~ Open 12-2.30, 7(6.30 Fri/Sat)-11; closed Mon (except bank holidays), and evenings 26 Dec and 1 Jan

BINGLEY (W Yorks) SE1039 Map 7

Brown Cow

Ireland Bridge; B6429, just W of junction with A650

Just below the old stone bridge over the River Aire, this genuinely unpretentious pub has a friendly open-plan main bar, divided into smaller and snugger areas: comfortable easy chairs and captain's chairs around black tables on the carpet, a high shelf of toby jugs under the dark ceiling, and lots of pictures and some brass on the partly panelled walls. Bar food includes home-made soup (£1.75), sandwiches (from £1.95; double-deckers from £2.25), filled yorkshire puddings (from £2.25), home-made pâté (£2.95), ploughman's (£3.50), home-made lasagne or broccoli and leek bake (£4.95), steaks (from £5.95), house specials such as home-made steak and kidney pie, ham shank and mushy peas or poached haddock with prawns (all £4.95), daily specials, and puddings; the restaurant is no smoking. Well kept Timothy Taylors Bitter, Best, Ram Tam (in winter) and Landlord on handpump; piped music. Below a steep bluebell wood is a sheltered corner terrace behind with tables and chairs – some of them sturdy pews. There are several antique shops in the town. *(Recommended by Nigel Hey, S E Paulley, Graham Peel, Katie and Steve Newby, WAH, Roger Huggins, Tom McLean, Annette Moore, Chris Pearson, Bill and Lydia Ryan, Michael Wadsworth, P A and M J White)*

Timothy Taylors ~ Tenants Simon and Madeleine Dibb ~ Real ale ~ Meals and snacks ~ Restaurant (not Sun evening) ~ (01274) 569482 ~ Children welcome ~ Trad jazz Mon evening ~ Open 11.30-3, 5.30-11

BLAKEY RIDGE (N Yorks) SE6799 Map 10

Lion

From A171 Guisborough—Whitby follow Castleton, Hutton le Hole signposts; from A170 Kirkby Moorside—Pickering follow Keldholm, Hutton le Hole, Castleton signposts; OS Sheet 100 map reference 679996

On the highest point of the North Yorkshire Moors National Park (1325 ft up and with spectacular views), this 16th-c inn is thought to have been founded by the Order of Crouched Friars to lighten up their poverty; it was then used in the mid 18th-c by local farmers who sold surplus corn to horse breeders and stable owners. The cosy and characterful beamed and rambling bars have open fires, a few big high-backed rustic settles around cast-iron-framed tables, lots of small dining chairs on the turkey carpet, a nice leather settee, stripped stone walls hung with some old engravings and photographs of the pub under snow (it can easily get cut off in winter); the atmosphere is bustling and friendly. Big helpings of bar food include soup (£1.95), lunchtime sandwiches (£2.25) and ploughman's (£4.45), home-cooked ham and egg, home-made steak and mushroom pie, vegetarian chilli, Whitby cod in batter or lasagne (all £5.45), butterbean and vegetable curry (£6.25), steaks (from £8.95), and puddings like chocolate sponge with custard or profiteroles (£2.25); Sunday roasts, children's dishes (£3.25), and good breakfasts; quick service even when busy – which it usually is. Well kept Bass, Tetleys, Theakstons Best, Old Peculier, XB and Mild, and Youngers No 3 on handpump; dominoes, fruit machine and piped music. *(Recommended by M Borthwick, R M Macnaughton, Bronwen and Steve Wrigley, Andy and Jill Kassube, John and Christine Simpson, Ian Boag, Fred Collier, Tina and David Woods-Taylor, Andrew and Ruth Triggs, Rupert Lecomber)*

Free house ~ Licensee Barry Crossland ~ Real ale ~ Meals and snacks (11.30-10) ~ Restaurant (all day Sun) ~ (01751) 417320 ~ Children welcome ~ Open 10.30am-11pm ~ Bedrooms: £15.50(£25.50B)/£43(£51B)

BRANDESBURTON (N Yorks) TA1247 Map 8

Dacre Arms

Village signposted from A165 N of Beverley and Hornsea turn-offs

An inn has stood here since the 16th-c, and for some time it was one of the most important posting stations in the East Riding. Travellers weren't the only people to enjoy some kind of hospitality – a snug area on the right once housed the local Court of Justices, while a long-since vanished secret room provided a hiding place for fugitive Jacobites. Still a welcoming spot today, the rambling rough-plastered modernised bar is vividly furnished with plenty of tables, and has a roomily comfortable feel. Well liked and generously served bar food includes sandwiches, soup (£1.50), filled yorkshire puddings (from £3.95), meat or vegetable lasagne

(£4.75), smoked salmon tagliatelle (£5.50), southern fried chicken (£5.35), strips of fillet steak, cooked with Drambuie and cream on a bed of rice (£5.75), seafood thermidor or smoked haddock and prawn bake (£6.50), steaks (from £7.80), puddings (from £2), and children's meals (from £2.50); readers have praised the home-made chips. Well kept Boddingtons, Tetleys, Theakstons Old Peculier and guests on handpump, lots of malt whiskies, and freshly ground coffee; darts, dominoes, fruit machine, video game, and piped music. The landlord traditionally holds the post of Treasurer for the Franklin Dead Brief, a society formed in 1844 to pool money to help those who can't afford funerals; their Annual General Meeting is held here the first Wednesday in February. *(Recommended by KC, R Suddaby, Anthony Barnes; more reports please)*

Free house ~ Lease: Martin Rowe ~ Real ale ~ Meals and snacks (12-2, 6.30-10.30; not 25 Dec, no sandwiches Sun) ~ Restaurant ~ (01964) 542392 ~ Children in eating area of bar and restaurant ~ Open 11-2.30(3 Sat), 6.30(5 Sat)-11

BREARTON (N Yorks) SE3261 Map 7

Malt Shovel 🍴 🍷

Village signposted off A61 N of Harrogate

Friendly, professional new licensees (who previously ran a highly thought of hotel in Scotland) have taken over here. They are aiming to maintain the appeal and character of this unspoilt village free house but are gradually introducing their own style of totally home-made food with great success. Several heavily-beamed rooms radiate from the attractive linenfold oak bar counter with plush-cushioned seats and a mix of tables, an ancient oak partition wall, both real and gas fires, and lively hunting prints. From a changing menu, the very good food might include sandwiches, ploughman's, wonderful mussels with home-baked bread, leek and wensleydale quiche or cumberland sausage with onion and Guinness gravy (all £3.95), nut roast with pesto cream sauce (£4.75), steak, kidney and mushroom pie or honeybaked ham with grain mustard and honey sauce (£4.95), lamb shanks braised in wine with garlic and mint (£5.20), delicious large fillet of fresh haddock in batter (£5.50), seafood pie (£5.75), fresh sea bream with caper butter (£6.70), steaks (from £6.95), and puddings like apple and rhubarb crumble, excellent chocolate fudge cake or baked banana cheesecake with toffee sauce and cream (£2). They now keep five real ales on handpump: Black Sheep Bitter, Daleside Bitter, Old Mill Traditional, Theakstons Best and local guests, a good choice of malt whiskies, and decent wines; darts, shove-ha'penny, cribbage, and dominoes. There are tables behind, on the terrace and the grass. *(Recommended by Viv Middlebrook, Geoffrey and Brenda Wilson, Dorothy and David Young, Janet and Peter Race, S Thompson, Christine and Christopher Challis, Bob and Maggie Atherton, Andrew and Ruth Triggs, R A Whitehead, Tim and Sue Halstead, Catherine and Andrew Brian, Mayur Shah, G Dobson, Paul Boot, Mark Bradley, S Brackenbury, Ann and Bob Westerook)*

Free house ~ Licensees Leslie and Charlotte Mitchell ~ Real ale ~ Meals and snacks (not Sun evening, not Mon) ~ (01423) 862929 ~ Children in eating area of bar ~ Open 12-2.30, 6.45-11; closed Mon

BUCKDEN (N Yorks) SD9278 Map 7

Buck 🍷

B6160

In a glorious setting in upper Wharfedale with fine moorland views, this busy inn is surrounded by lots of footpaths and lanes. Inside, the modernised and extended open-plan bar has upholstered built-in wall banquettes and square stools around shiny dark brown tables on its carpet – though there are still flagstones in the snug original area by the serving counter – local pictures, hunting prints, willow-pattern plates on a delft shelf, and the mounted head of a roebuck on the bare stone wall above the log fire. Efficiently served by helpful uniformed staff, bar food includes home-made soup with home-made roll (£2.45), home-made duck liver pâté (£3.95), mixed hors d'oeuvres (£4.50), swordfish steak or supreme of chicken with mushrooms, shallots, mustard and brandy cream (£7.95), local breast of pheasant (£8.75), steamed Scottish salmon fillet with light lobster and prawn sauce (£8.95), pork fillet on pesto-flavoured noodles (£9.45), and puddings like sticky toffee pudding or caramelised orange and Cointreau tart (from £2.95); the restaurant is no smoking. Well kept Black Sheep Bitter and Special, Theakstons Best, Old Peculier and XB, and a guest beer on handpump; good choice of malt whiskies and decent wines. Darts, dominoes, crirbbage, and piped music. *(Recommended by Anthony Marriott, Anne and Brian Birtwistle, J C Simpson, TBB, Prof S Barnett, Mike and Ruth Dooley, Jack and Heather Coyle, C Roberts, A Barker, E J and M W Corrin, Lee Goulding, P D and J Bickley, Ray and Liz Monk, Catherine and Richard Hicks, Annette Moore, Chris Pearson)*

Free house ~ Licensee Nigel Hayton ~ Real ale ~ Meals and snacks ~ Evening restaurant ~ (01756) 760228 ~ Children in eating area of bar ~ Open 11-11 ~ Bedrooms: £34B/£68B

BURNSALL (N Yorks) SE0361 Map 7

Red Lion

B6160 S of Grassington, on Ilkley road; OS Sheet 98, map reference 033613

This is a nice place to stay as most of the bedrooms have views of the River Wharfe and village green. There are tables on the front cobbles that enjoy the view towards Burnsall Fell, with more seats on a big back terrace; fishing permits for 7 miles of river are sold here. The bustling main bar has sturdy seats built in to the attractively panelled walls (decorated with pictures of the local fell races), windsor armchairs, oak benches, rugs on the floor, and steps up past a solid fuel stove to a back area with sensibly placed darts (dominoes players are active up here, too). The carpeted, no-smoking front lounge bar, served from the same copper-topped counter through an old-fashioned small-paned glass partition, has a log fire. Good bar food includes home-made soup (£2.50), lunchtime sandwiches (£2.95), Cumbrian air-dried ham cured in molasses and served with their own chutney (£3.95), gruyere, broccoli and asparagus tart (£5.75), ploughman's or lamb's liver and bacon (£5.95), steak and kidney pie (£6.25), gammon with free range eggs (£6.95), sirloin steak (£8.95), daily specials such as hake, monkfish, lemon sole, crab, and seasonal game (pheasant, mallard, pigeon and partridge), and puddings such as sticky toffee pudding with caramel sauce or sherry trifle; the restaurant is no smoking. Well kept Tetleys Bitter, Theakstons Best and guest beers on handpump, malt whiskies, and a good wine list with several by the glass. *(Recommended by D Goodger, C H and P Stride, Gwen and Peter Andrews, JCW, Mark Bradley, Mary Moore, G Dobson, Wayne Brindle, Bill and Lydia Ryan, Simon Watkins; more reports please)*

Free house ~ Licensee Elizabeth Grayshon ~ Real ale ~ Meals and snacks (12-2.30, 6-9.30) ~ Restaurant ~ (01756) 720204 ~ Children welcome ~ Open 11.30-4, 5-11 ~ Bedrooms: £39B/£65B

BYLAND ABBEY (N Yorks) SE5579 Map 7

Abbey Inn

The Abbey has a brown tourist-attraction signpost off the A170 Thirsk—Helmsley

As popular as ever for particularly good food, this attractive pub is in a lovely setting opposite the Abbey ruins. The rambling, characterful rooms have some discreet stripping back of plaster to show the ex-abbey masonry, big fireplaces, oak and stripped deal tables, settees, carved oak seats, and Jacobean-style dining chairs on the polished boards and flagstones, bunches of flowers among the candles, various stuffed birds, cooking implements, little etchings, willow-pattern plates, and china cabinets. In a big back room an uptilted cart shelters a pair of gnomelike waxwork yokels, and there are lots of rustic bygones; piped music. Served by neat and friendly waitresses bar food might include lunchtime sandwiches, home-made chicken liver pâté, fried sardines with a green herb and mustard sauce or broccoli and blue cheese tartlet with a spinach and dill sauce (all £3.80), apricot and nut roast (£6.75), turkey, apricot and redcurrant roulade or fillet of pork stuffed with black pudding on an onion sauce (£8), breast of pheasant stuffed with chicken and sage mousse on a Drambuie sauce (£8.25), sea bass with ginger and garlic butter or venison steak with plum sauce (£9.50), and puddings like lemon ginger crunch cheesecake, chocolate roulade or rhubarb crumble (£2.75); good vegetables. Well kept Black Sheep Bitter and Theakstons Best on handpump, and an interesting wine list. No dogs. There's lots of room outside in the garden. *(Recommended by Steve and Julie Cocking, Simon Chappell, Louise Chappell, R F Grieve, Anthony Barnes, Tim and Sue Halstead, Martin Hickes, R N Hutton, Andy and Jane Beardsley, G Dobson, SS, Andrew and Ruth Triggs, The Mair Family, David Rogers, Pat Crabb, H Bramwell, Ann and Frank Bowman, Paul and Ursula Randall, Beryl and Bill Farmer, Pat and Robert Watt, Mr and Mrs R M Macnaughton, John Lawrence, John and Christine Simpson, B B Pearce)*

Free house ~ Licensees Peter and Gerd Handley ~ Real ale ~ Meals and snacks (not Sun evening, not Mon) ~ (01347) 868204 ~ Children welcome ~ Open 11-2.30, 6.30-11; closed Sun evening and all day Mon

CARLTON (N Yorks) SE0684 Map 10

Foresters Arms

Off A684 W of Leyburn, just past Wensley; or take Coverdale hill road from Kettlewell, off B6160

Mr Higginbotham is now running this comfortable ex-coaching inn on his own. It's set in a pretty village in the heart of the Yorkshire Dales National Park, and the emphasis is firmly placed on the imaginative food. There's a good atmosphere, open log fires, low beamed ceilings, and well kept John Smiths, Theakstons Best, Websters Yorkshire, and a guest beer on handpump. Bar food now includes soup or parfait of chicken livers (£2.25), grilled fresh sardines (£3.50), baked crab and asparagus gateau (£3.75), whole grilled plaice (£8.25), mushroom ragout with pasta (£8.50), fricassée of smoked chicken with tagliatelle (£8.75), grilled leg of lamb with lentil cassoulet (£9.25), fillet of beef with sun dried tomato and pesto (£10.50), and puddings like apple and cinammon tart with vanilla sauce, hot mango soufflé or terrine of bitter chocolate (from £2.50); good wines and well liked fruit purée drinks. Part of the restaurant is no smoking; darts, dominoes, shove-ha'penny, and piped music. There are some picnic tables among tubs of flowers. As we went to press, there were a couple of readers unhappy with the welcome and value for money – we obviously hope this was a temporary lapse. *(Recommended by JKW, Ian Morley, Caroline Kenyon, Viv Middlebrook, E J Wilde, J Royce, J Durrant, E J Wilde; more reports please)*

Free house ~ Licensee Barrie Higginbotham ~ Real ale ~ Meals and snacks (not Sun evening, not Mon) ~ Restaurant (not Sun evening, not Mon) ~ (01969) 640272 ~ Children in eating area of bar ~ Open 12-3, 6.30-11 ~ Bedrooms: £30S/£55S

CARTHORPE (N Yorks) SE3184 Map 10

Fox & Hounds ★

Village signposted from A1 N of Ripon, via B6285

As we went to press, the licensee told us that they would shortly be refurbishing the cosy L-shaped bar in this pretty little extended village house. At the moment, the bar has quite a few mistily evocative Victorian photographs of Whitby, a couple of nice seats by the larger of its two log fires, plush button-back built-in wall banquettes and chairs, plates on stripped beams, and some limed panelling; some readers have found the piped music rather obtrusive this year. An attractive high-raftered restaurant leads off with lots of neatly black-painted farm and smithy tools. The menu is the same in the bar and no-smoking restaurant (best to book for the restaurant – they don't take bookings in the bar) and might include roasted tomato or broccoli and apple soups (£2.25), terrine of duckling with home-made apple chutney (£3.95), seafood hors d'oeuvres (£4.95), baby chicken cooked in Theakstons beer (£7.45), good rolled lemon sole fillets filled with fresh salmon and prawns in white wine sauce (£7.95), rack of English lamb (£8.95), fillet steak stuffed with mushrooms and garlic (£10.45), daily specials such as curried vegetable pancake (£3.95), prawn and queen scallop au gratin (£4.95), steak and kidney pie (£6.25), Whitby sea trout with ginger and spring onions (£7.95), and lobster (from £12.50); puddings such as apple and cinnamon flan, tipsy trifle or lemon sponge with tangy lemon sauce (from £2.75); decent wines with bin-ends listed on a blackboard. *(Recommended by Mrs D Cross, Adrian Jackson, Cynthia Waller, W A and S Rinaldi-Butcher, Brian Kneale, Mrs E A Galewski, Malcolm Pettit, Mr and Mrs David J Hart, D Cummings, Leonard Dixon, Janet and Peter Race, Frank Davidson)*

Free house ~ Licensee Howard Fitzgerald ~ Meals and snacks (not Mon) ~ Restaurant (not Mon) ~ (01845) 567433 ~ Children welcome but no small ones after 8pm ~ Open 12-2.30, 7-11; closed Mon and first week of the year from Jan 1

COXWOLD (N Yorks) SE5377 Map 7

Fauconberg Arms ★ 🛏 🍷

In an interesting and pretty village, this civilised old stone pub is much enjoyed by readers. The two cosy and spotless knocked-together rooms of the lounge bar have fresh flowers and gleaming brass, cushioned antique oak settles and other fine furniture, and a marvellous winter log fire in an unusual arched stone fireplace; there's also an old-fashioned back locals' bar for those wanting an informal drink and a chat. One menu serves both the bar and restaurant and Mrs Jaques's love of food shines through: lunchtime dishes such as home-made soup (£1.95), sandwiches (from £2.45), chicken liver and ham terrine with home-made fruit chutney and tomato and apple salad (£3.25), fresh salmon mousse with a cucumber mayonnaise (£3.65), stuffed aubergine with red lentils, cumin and apricots (£5.25), steak and kidney pie (£5.75), pan-fried lamb with a mint and apple gravy (£6.75), and sirloin steak (£8.95), with evening meals like hot buttered shrimps (£3.75), breast of chicken Barbados style (£5.75), pink trout fillets (£6.25), home-made tomato and garlic pasta envelopes (£10.25), and breast of pheasant with caramelised shallots, apricots, almonds and madeira (£10.75). Puddings like white chocolate mousse, apple creme caramel or fresh fruit crumble (£2.95). Well kept John Smiths, Tetleys Bitter, Theakstons Best, and Youngers on handpump, and an extensive wine list with blackboard bin ends available by the glass. Darts, dominoes, fruit machine, juke box and piped music. The inn is named after Lord Fauconberg, who married Oliver Cromwell's daughter Mary. *(Recommended by Martin, Chris and Andy Crow, Bronwen and Steve Wrigley, Michele and Clive Platman, Bob and Maggie Atherton, John and Sheila French, Andy and Jane Beardsley, Andrew and Ruth Triggs, Joan Lawrence, H Bramwell, Pat Crabb, Paul Wreglesworth, Paul Cartledge, Brian Kneale, Simon Collett-Jones, Janet Pickles, Gill Earle, Andrew Burton)*

Free house ~ Lease: Robin and Nicky Jaques ~ Meals and snacks (not Mon evening in winter) ~ Restaurant (not winter Sun evening) ~ (01347) 868214 ~ Children welcome ~ Open 11-3, 6.30(6 Sat)-11; winter evening opening 7pm ~ Bedrooms: £24/£40

CRACOE (N Yorks) SD9760 Map 7

Devonshire Arms

B6265 Skipton—Grassington

In the middle of a small Dales village, this honest, neatly kept pub is run by friendly and chatty licensees. The bar has low shiny black beams supporting creaky white planks, polished flooring tiles with rugs here and there, gleaming copper pans round the stone fireplace, and little stable-type partitions to divide the solidly comfortable furnishings into cosier areas: built-in wall settles and pews with brocaded seats and scatter cushions around sturdy rustic or oak tripod tables. Above the dark panelled dado are old prints, engravings and photographs, with a big circular large-scale Ordnance Survey map showing the inn as its centre. Enjoyable bar food includes home-made soup (£1.65), sandwiches (from £1.75), filled yorkshire puddings (from £4.25), steak and kidney pudding or chicken, ham and leek pies (£5.25), daily specials like shepherd's pie, chilli con carne, pasta dishes, breast of duck or monkfish, and home-made puddings such as cheesecakes or sticky toffee pudding (£2.50), and evening poached Scotch salmon (£5.50), and steaks (from £8.20); sliding doors lead to a snug restaurant where bar meals can be eaten during the week. Well kept Tetleys and Theakstons Best, XB, and Old Peculier (summer only) on handpump, and malt whiskies; a trivia machine is tucked discreetly away by the entrance; darts, dominoes, shove-ha'penny, table skittles, and piped music. There are picnic tables on a terrace flanked by well kept herbaceous borders, with more seating on the lawn; and a small dog called Juno may watch you coming and going from his position on the roof (his large airedale friend Jasper does not follow him up there, luckily). *(Recommended by Gwen and Peter Andrews, Wayne Brindle, Paul J Bispham, E A George, T M Dobby, E G Parish, Ann and Bob Westerook, Richard Waller, TBB, Geoff and Angela Jaques; more reports please)*

Free house ~ Licensees John and Jill Holden ~ Real ale ~ Meals and snacks ~ Restaurant ~ (01756) 730237 ~ Children welcome ~ Open 11.30-3, 6.30(6 Sat)-11; closed evening 25 Dec ~ Bedrooms: £25B/£40B

CRAY (N Yorks) SD9379 Map 7

White Lion ★

B6160, Upper Wharfedale N of Kettlewell

The countryside surrounding this warmly friendly former drovers' hostelry is superb and the pub is the highest in Wharfedale (1,100 ft up by Buckden Pike). You can sit at the picnic tables above the very quiet, steep lane, or on the great flat limestone slabs in the shallow stream which tumbles down opposite. Inside, the simply furnished bar has a relaxed, traditional atmosphere, a lovely open fire, seats around tables on the flagstone floor, shelves of china, iron tools and so forth, and a high dark beam-and-plank ceiling; there's also a no smoking family snug. Good honest bar food includes tasty soup (£1.95), sandwiches (from £2.75), filled yorkshire puddings (from £2.75), cumberland sausage (£4.95), vegetable or meaty lasagne (£5.25), evening dishes such as home-made chicken liver pâté (£2.75), gammon and egg (£6.75), and steaks (from £10.25), daily specials, and puddings (£2.10); good breakfasts. Well kept Moorhouses Premier and Pendle Witches Brew, and Tetleys Bitter on handpump; dominoes. *(Recommended by E J and M W Corrin, Eddie Edwards, Anthony Marriott, Keith J Smith, Lynn Sharpless, Bob Eardley, Caroline Kenyon, D Goodger, Nicola Thomas, Paul Dickinson, Joanne Newton, David Wright, Neville Kenyon, Mr and Mrs K H Frostick, Andrew McKeand)*

Free house ~ Licensees Frank and Barbara Hardy ~ Real ale ~ Meals and snacks ~ (01756) 760262 ~ Children in two rooms ~ Limited parking ~ Open 11-11; 11-2.30, 6.30-11 winter weekdays ~ Bedrooms: £30S/£45S

CRAYKE (N Yorks) SE5670 Map 7

Durham Ox

Off B1363 at Brandsby, towards Easingwold

A smashing pub with a really good atmosphere – and popular with both locals and visitors alike. The old-fashioned lounge bar has venerable tables and antique seats and settles on the flagstones, pictures and old local photographs on the dark green walls, a high shelf of plates and interestingly satirical carvings in its panelling (which are Victorian copies of medievel pew ends), polished copper and brass, and an enormous inglenook fireplace with winter log fires (flowers in summer). Some of the panelling here divides off a bustling public area which has a good lively atmosphere and more traditional furnishings. There is a framed illustrated written acount of the local history dating back to the 12th c, and a large framed print of the original famous Durham ox which weighed 171 stones. Darts and fruit machine. Consistently good bar food includes sandwiches (from £2), ploughman's (£3.95), mushroom stroganoff (£4.25), large fresh grilled haddock (£5.50), lasagne, fish pot, steak and kidney pie or curry (all under £5.50), 12oz sirloin steak (£8.95), and puddings (£2.25). Well kept Banks's, Camerons Bitter and Crown, and Marstons Pedigree on handpump. The tale is that this is the hill which the Grand Old Duke of York marched his men up; the view from the hill opposite is wonderful. ***(Recommended by Roger Bellingham, P Sumner, Tim and Sue Halstead, Ian Morley, Andrew and Ruth Triggs)***

Free house ~ Licensee Ian Chadwick ~ Real ale ~ Meals and snacks (not Sun evening) ~ Restaurant ~ (01347) 821506 ~ Children welcome ~ Open 12-3, 7-11 ~ Bedrooms: £25/£35

CROPTON (N Yorks) SE7588 Map 10

New Inn

Village signposted off A170 W of Pickering

This spotlessly kept and comfortably modernised village inn is home of the Cropton Brewery and their own robustly flavoured beers include Two Pints, King Billy, Special Strong and Scoresby Stout (brewery trips are encouraged), with guests like Boddingtons and Tetleys Bitter on handpump; several malt whiskies. The airy lounge bar has Victorian church panels, terracotta and dark blue plush seats, lots of brass, a small open fire, and a collection of teddies (made in the village) wearing Cropton Brewery t-shirts. The no-smoking family conservatory downstairs has farmhouse-style chairs around wooden tables. Substantial helpings of good bar food include lunchtime sandwiches (not Sunday), home-made soup and pâté, venison sausages in rich gravy (£4.95), nut roast with barbecue sauce or salmon fishcakes (£5.50), chicken burgundy or steak and kidney pie (£5.75), chicken tikka (£6.50), their speciality shoulder of lamb with rosemary and thyme (£7.25), and steaks (from £8.50; 24oz rump £14.50); friendly staff. The elegant small no-smoking restaurant is furnished with genuine Victorian and early Edwardian furniture. Pleasant service; darts, dominoes, fruit machine, video game, pool room, and juke box. There's a neat terrace and garden with pond. Comfortable, good value bedrooms. ***(Recommended by Andy and Jill Kassube, David and Rebecca Killick, Mike Pugh, D and J Johnson, Keith and Margaret Kettell, Joy Heatherley, Paul Wreglesworth, Martin Jones, Paul Cartledge, Paul Noble, Roger and Christine Mash)***

Own brew ~ Licensee Michael Lee ~ Real ale ~ Meals and snacks ~ Restaurant ~ (01751) 417330 ~ Children in conservatory, restaurant, and pool room ~ Open 11-3, 6-11; 11-11 Sat; 12-2.30, 7-11 in winter ~ Bedrooms: £35B/£53B

EAST WITTON (N Yorks) SE1586 Map 10

Blue Lion

A6108 Leyburn—Ripon

On several occasions, readers arriving when they considered it too late for food have been delighted to find that the friendly and helpful staff have been happy to cater for them. And for many people, this stylish and characterful pub is one of their favourites. The big squarish bar has high-backed antique settles and old windsor chairs and round tables on the turkey rugs and flagstones, ham-hooks in the high ceiling decorated with dried wheat, teazles and so forth, a delft shelf filled with appropriate bric-a-brac, a couple of prints of the Battle of Omdurman, hunting prints, sporting caricatures and other pictures on the walls, a log fire, and daily papers; the friendly black labrador is called Ben. Particularly good, very popular bar food might include sandwiches, excellent french-style cheese platter, warm onion or lovely crab and parmesan tarts (£3.95), confit of duckling on a potato and black pudding gallette served with a pine kernel and red wine vinaigrette salad (£4.50), scorched king scallops with a sun dried tomato butter on a tossed salad (£5.50), roast rabbit leg stuffed with herb butter and served with braised cabbage and grain mustard sauce (£8.50), poached fillet of smoked haddock with raclette cheese and asparagus on a fresh mussel broth (£9.25), roast fillet of salmon with caramelised onions and tomato with a ginger butter sauce (£9.40), sautéed strips of beef with a tarragon cream, paprika and brandy sauce served with creamed gnocci (£9.95), and char-grilled venison steak with wild mushrooms and madeira sauce (£11.50); lovely puddings and good breakfasts. Well kept Boddingtons, Theakstons Best, and Timothy Taylors Landlord on handpump, and decent wines. Picnic tables on the gravel outside look beyond the stone houses on the far side of the village green to Witton Fell, and there's a big pretty back garden. *(Recommended by Mr and Mrs Carrera, J Royce, Martin Chapman, John and Chris Simpson, Gwen and Peter Andrews, S Head, Michael and Susan Morgan, Paul J Cornerford, C Wilson, Jack and Philip Paxton, David and Ruth Hollands, Jean Gustavson, Ian S Morley, Robert and Ann Lees, Martin Hickes, Dr I H Maine, Jack and Heather Coyle, J E Rycroft, Jack Hill, Rob Noble, Andrew Shore, Annette Moore, Chris Pearson, Mayur Shah, Walter and Susan Rinaldi-Butcher, Michael Butler, Bill Edwards, Frank Davidson, P D and J Bickley, Jim Farmer, M J Morgan)*

Free house ~ Lease: Paul Klein ~ Real ale ~ Meals and snacks ~ Restaurant (closed Sun evening) ~ (01969) 624273 ~ Children welcome ~ Open 11-11 ~ Bedrooms: £39B/£70B

EGTON BRIDGE (N Yorks) NZ8105 Map 10

Horse Shoe

Village signposted from A171 W of Whitby; via Grosmont from A169 S of Whitby

Charmingly placed in an Esk-side hamlet, this peaceful place has some comfortable seats on a quiet terrace and lawn beside a little stream with ducks and geese; a footbridge leads to the tree-sheltered residents' lawn which runs down to the river. Inside, the bar has high-backed built-in winged settles, wall seats and spindleback chairs around the modern oak tables, a big stuffed trout (caught near here in 1913), a fine old print of a storm off Ramsgate and other pictures on the walls, and a warm log fire. Good bar food served by very friendly staff includes home-made soup (£2), lunchtime sandwiches (from £2.10), stilton mushrooms (£2.95), home-made steak and kidney pie, vegetarian fettucine or cold ham and egg (all £5.95), good bacon chops with peach sauce (£6.50), vegetarian fettucine, and steaks, with daily specials, good fresh vegetables and nice breakfasts. Well kept Tetleys Bitter, Theakstons Best, Old Peculier and XB on handpump, and a weekly guest beer; darts, dominoes, cards, and piped music. Perhaps the best way to reach this beautifully placed pub is to park by the Roman Catholic church, walk through the village and cross the River Esk by stepping stones. Not to be confused with a similarly named pub up at Egton. *(Recommended by Michael Butler, Phil and Heidi Cook, Nick Lloyd, Enid and Henry Stephens, Dr and Mrs Frank Rackow, Carol and Dennis Clayson, Margaret Mason, David Thompson, Andrew and Ruth Triggs, Mayur Shah, B B Pearce, D L Parkhurst, Bronwen and Steve Wrigley)*

Free house ~ Licensees David and Judith Mullins ~ Real ale ~ Meals and snacks (not 25 Dec) ~ Restaurant ~ (01947) 85245 ~ Children are allowed in a back area only ~ Open 11-3.30, 6.30-11; closed evening 25 Dec ~ Bedrooms: £26(£30B)/£38(£46B)

ELSLACK (N Yorks) SD9249 Map 7

Tempest Arms

Just off A56 Earby—Skipton; visible from main road, and warning signs ¼ mile before

It's the food that people like here – and apart from the fish specials listed on a board and their new lunchtime smorgasbord, there might be home-made soup (£1.75), sandwiches (from £2.75, 6oz steak £4.75), rillettes of pork pâté with an orange and onion chutney (£2.75), filo pastry parcels filled with smoked haddock and spring onion laid on a fresh chive cream sauce (£3), salad nicoise (£3.75), a platter of pâté, cheese and pickles (£3.95), vegetarian dishes (£4.75), home-made steak, kidney and mushroom pie in Guinness (£5.95), steamed breast of cornfed chicken with a lemon and tarragon sauce (£6.50), loin of pork with a cider and apple cream sauce (£6.75), and sirloin steak (£8.50); children's dishes (£3.25). The series of quietly decorated areas have small chintz armchairs, chintzy cushions on the comfortable built-in wall seats, brocaded stools, and lots of tables, quite a bit of stripped stonework, some decorated plates and brassware, and a log fire in the dividing fireplace. Well kept Tetleys Bitter, Thwaites Bitter and Craftsman, and Theakstons on handpump, good house wines by the glass or bottle, and malt whiskies; darts, dominoes, and piped music. Tables outside are largely screened from the road by a raised bank. *(Recommended by Mike and Maggie Betton, Gary Roberts, Ann Stubbs, Gwen and Peter Andrews, G C Hackerner, John Allsopp, J Royce, Prof S Barnett, Eric and Jackie Robinson, Karen Eliot, D H and M G Buchanan, John and Joan Nash, Julie Peters, Hugh and Peggy Colgate, Stephen and Brenda Head, Paul McPherson, Mary Moore, Susan and Rick Auty)*

Free house ~ Licensee Francis Boulongne ~ Real ale ~ Meals and snacks (11.30-2.15, 6.30-10) ~ Restaurant ~ (01282) 842450 ~ Children welcome ~ Open 11.30-3, 6.30-11; 11.30-11 summer Sat; closed evening 25 Dec ~ Bedrooms: £46B/£52B

FLAMBOROUGH (N Yorks) TA2270 Map 8

Seabirds 🍷

Junction of B1255 and B1229

Doing rather well at the moment, this straightforward village pub near the cliffs of Flamborough Head has quite a shipping theme in its cheerful public bar. Leading off here the comfortable lounge has a whole case of stuffed seabirds along one wall, as well as pictures and paintings of the local landscape, a mirror glazed with grape vines, and a wood-burning stove; there's a good mix of holidaymakers and locals. The fresh fish daily specials are still the meals to go for, though the other dishes are well liked too, with a range that includes sandwiches, soup (£1.60), prawns in garlic butter (£3.70), yorkshire pudding filled with three cumberland sausages (£3.95), home-made steak and mushroom pie (£4.70), haddock mornay (£5.60), and evening extras like broccoli and cream cheese bake (£4.95), salmon in a tarragon, chervil and butter sauce (£6.95), or pork with onions in a white wine and paprika sauce (£7.95). Well kept John Smiths and a weekly changing guest on handpump, good reasonably priced wine list, a wide range of whiskies and liqueurs, and hot mulled wine in winter. Friendly, hardworking staff; piped music. There's a family room in the garden. *(Recommended by Chris Westmoreland, Andy and Jane Beardsley, Ian Rorison, Roger A Bellingham, David Eberlin, R N Hutton, E J Wilde, DC, Mark Bradley, Roger and Christine Mash, Martin and Pauline Richardson, Joy Heatherley, Lawrence Bacon, Jean Stott, Eric J Locker, Ann and Bob Westbrook)*

Free house ~ Licensee Jean Riding ~ Real ale ~ Meals and snacks (not evening Sun or Mon in winter) ~ Restaurant (not Sun evening in winter) ~ (01262) 850242 ~ Children in eating area of bar and restaurant ~ Open 11-3, 7(6.30 Sat)-11

GOATHLAND (N Yorks) NZ8301 Map 10

Mallyan Spout

Opposite church; off A169

As well as warm winter log fires, the three spacious lounges in this ivy-clad stone hotel have fine views of the garden, Moors and Esk Valley. The traditional bar has a relaxed atmosphere, well kept Malton PA on handpump, and popular food such as sandwiches, good home-made soup (£2.25), home-made pâté (£4.75), ploughman's with home-made chutney and pickle (from £4.75), deep-fried goujons of Whitby plaice (£5.50), pot-roast knuckle of lamb with flageolets (£5.95), casserole of oxtail with butterbeans in red wine sauce (£6.50), grilled whole lemon sole (£8.50), king prawns in herb and garlic butter (£9.95), 12oz sirloin steak (£11.50), and puddings (from £2.75); you can buy their home-made jams, sauces and chutneys to take home. 20 malt whiskies and good wines. One room is no smoking; dominoes. The Mallyan Spout waterfall is close by. Quite a lot of the filming for the *Heartbeat* TV series is done in the village and the cast stay here. *(Recommended by Phil and Heidi Cook, Andy and Jill Kassube, Frank Cummins, Susan and Walter Rinaldi-Butcher, Jim and Maggie Cowell, Lawrence Bacon, Jean Scott, Andrew and Ruth Triggs, Geoff and Angela Jaques, Frank Davidson, David and Julie Glover)*

Free house ~ Licensee Judith Heslop ~ Real ale ~ Meals and snacks ~ Restaurant ~ (01947) 896206 ~ Children in eating area of bar; must be over 6 in evening ~ Open 11-11 (may close earlier if weather is bad) ~ Bedrooms: £45B/£70

GOOSE EYE (W Yorks) SE0340 Map 7

Turkey

High back road Haworth—Sutton-in-Craven, and signposted from back roads W of Keighley; OS Sheet 104 map ref 028406

Reached down high-walled lanes at the bottom of a steep valley, this pleasant pub is popular for its generously served food: sandwiches such as hot roast beef (£2.50), cheese and onion quiche (£4.40), fillet of breaded haddock (£4.60), good steaks (from £6.90; 32oz rump £13), daily specials like filled yorkshire puddings (£3.80), and puddings (from £1.90); Tuesday night is curry night (under £5). Well kept (and much liked) Gooseye Bitter and Pommies Revenge (brewed by a local man), Ind Coope Burton, and Tetleys on handpump. The various cosy and snug alcoves have brocaded upholstery and walls covered with pictures of surrounding areas, and the dining areas are no smoking; piped music. A separate games area has darts, dominoes, cribbage, fruit machine, trivia, and juke box. *(Recommended by Mike and Ruth Dooley, Jenny and Brian Seller, Jamie and Ruth Lyons, Lorna and Antti Koskela, WAH, Jan and Dave Booth, Tony Hall)*

Free house ~ Licensees Harry and Monica Brisland ~ Real ale ~ Meals and snacks (not Mon) ~ Restaurant ~ (01535) 681339 ~ Children welcome until 8.30 ~ Open 12-3, 5.30-11; 12-5, 7-11 Sat; closed Mon evening

GRANGE MOOR (W Yorks) SE2215 Map 7

Kaye Arms 🍴 🍷

A642 Huddersfield—Wakefield

This civilised and busy dining pub is very much somewhere to come for a special occasion and people tend to dress accordingly. The good, imaginative, totally home-made food changes regularly but might include sandwiches (rare beef £1.90), home-made soup (£1.95), jellied terrine of chicken and ham with home-made piccallili (£3.25), king prawns and langoustine in a lime mayonnaise (£4.50), mature cheddar cheese soufflé with waldorf salad and provençal vegetable gratin (£5.95), fresh salmon fishcake with parsley sauce or char-grilled venison sausages on braised red cabbage and apple (£5.10), good bressola, hand-breaded Whitby scampi (£5.95), beef in Guinness and orange with horseradish dumplings and winter vegetables (£7.95), baked fillet of cod with mushroom duxelle, breast of chicken in filo pastry with wild mushroom sauce (£8.60), and good steaks (from £10.75); lovely home-made bread, fine vegetables, and puddings (from £2.80). A thoughtful wine list with exceptional value house wines, 10 by the generous glass and wines of the month, and decent malt whiskies. The U-shaped dining lounge has black mate's chairs and black tables, panelled dado, quict pastel-coloured wallpaper with decorative plates, a high shelf of hundreds of malt whisky bottles, and a brick fireplace; almost imperceptible piped music. The Yorkshire Mining Museum is just down the road. *(Recommended by Andrew and Ruth Triggs, Michael Butler, Geoffrey and Brenda Wilson, Neil Townend, A Preston, Russell Hobbs, Mark Bradley, Stephen and Brenda Head)*

Free house ~ Licensee Stuart Coldwell ~ Meals and snacks (till 10pm) ~ (01924) 848385 ~ Children allowed at lunchtimes only ~ Open 11.30-3, 7(6.30 Sat)-11; closed Mon lunchtime

HARDEN (W Yorks) SE0838 Map 7

Malt Shovel

Follow Wilsden signpost from B6429

Refurbished this year, the three spotlessly clean rooms in this handsome dark stone building (one is no smoking at lunchtime) have blue plush seats built into the walls, kettles, brass funnels and the like hanging from the black beams, horsebrasses on leather harness, and stone-mullioned windows; one has oak-panelling, a beamed ceiling, and an open fire. Good value bar food includes soup (£1.10), hot beef sandwiches (£3), giant yorkshire pudding with beef (£3.25), home-made steak pie (£4.25), fresh haddock (£4.50), and daily specials. Well kept Tetleys on handpump, and efficient service; dominoes and piped music. The pub is in a lovely spot by a bridge over Harden Beck, and the big garden is open to the public. *(Recommended by Nigel Hey, James Macrae, M J Brooks, WAH)*

Carlsberg Tetleys ~ Managers Keith and Lynne Bolton ~ Real ale ~ Lunchtime meals and snacks (not Sun) ~ (01535) 272357 ~ Children in eating area of bar until 8pm ~ Open 11.45-3, 5.30-11; 12-11 Sat

HAROME (N Yorks) SE6582 Map 10

Star

2 miles south of A170, near Helmsley

The bar in this friendly thatched pub has a dark bowed beam-and-plank ceiling, a copper kettle on the well polished tiled kitchen range (with a ship in a bottle on its mantlepiece), and 'mousey Thompson' furniture; there's a coffee loft up in the thatch, popular with families at lunchtime. Good home-made food includes sandwiches, hot black pudding with whisky (£2.95), welsh rarebit with stilton and chutney (£3.95), medallions of fresh salmon with chives, cucumber and cream (£4.95), breast of chicken with white wine, mushrooms, cream and brandy or seafood crepe (£7.95), rack of lamb with orange and Grand Marnier cream sauce (£8.95), and mincemeat and brandy tart (£2.50). Well kept Tetleys, Theakstons Best and Old Peculier and Timothy Taylors Landlord on handpump. Darts, dominoes, cribbage, Scrabble, and piped music. On a sheltered front flagstoned terrace there are some seats and tables, with more in the garden behind which has an old-fashioned swing seat, a trampoline, fruit trees, and a big ash. *(Recommended by Willie Bell, Geoffrey and Brenda Wilson, Jack and Philip Paxton, R F Grieve, Joy Heatherley, Andrew and Ruth Triggs, Mrs E H Hughes, Paul S McPherson, S Demont, T Barrow)*

Free house ~ Licensee Terry Rowe ~ Real ale ~ Meals and snacks (not Mon, not Tues lunchtime or Sun-Weds evenings) ~ Evening restaurant (they do Sun lunch, closed Sun evening) ~ (01439) 770397 ~ Children welcome ~ Open 12-3, 6.30-11; winter evening open 7pm; closed Mon, closed Tues lunchtime

nr HARROGATE (N Yorks) SE2852 Map 7

Squinting Cat

Whinney Lane, B6162 W of Harrogate; turn at traffic lights down Pannel Ash Rd; at roundabout near sports centre, bear right along Whinney Lane; pub on left after about ¾ mile; OS Sheet 104 map reference 287525

A new licensee has taken over this ex-farmhouse – popular with a good mix of people. The original rambling bar rooms have dark oak panelling, beam and plank ceilings, some copper warming pans and horsebrasses, and a stained-glass cat worked into a latticed bow window. The barn-like beamed extension has York stone walls (re-fashioned from an old railway bridge) hung with pictures, pine chairs and tables in one part with re-covered armchairs in another, old grain sacks, barrels, and bottles, and nautical wooden pulley systems radiating out from a minstrel's gallery complete with boat. Bar food includes home-made soup (£1.75), sandwiches (from £2.25), home-made pâté (£2.50), cold platters (from £3.95), steak and kidney pie or lasagne (£4.95), steaks (from £5.25), and half-a-dozen changing daily specials (from £6.25). Well kept Tetleys Bitter and guest beers that change every two weeks on handpump; piped music, dominoes and fruit machine. There are tables outside. The North of England Horticultural Society's fine gardens on the curlew moors at Harlow Car are just over the B6162. *(Recommended by Geoffrey and Brenda Wilson, M J Marriage, Mayur Shah, Paul Cartledge, R M Sparkes, WD, David Watson)*

Tetleys (Allied) ~ Manager Tony Dempsey ~ Real ale ~ Meals and snacks ~ Restaurant ~ (01423) 565650 ~ Open 12-11

HATFIELD WOODHOUSE (S Yorks) SE6808 Map 7

Green Tree

1 mile from M18 junction 5: on A18/A614 towards Bawtry

Now that the no-smoking restaurant has been refurbished, the courteous licensees are aiming to start on the comfortably modernised series of connecting open-plan rooms and alcoves – work should be finished by the time this book is published. Bar food (with prices virtually unchanged since last year) includes soups such as broccoli, mushroom, red pepper and courgette (£1.50), very good sandwiches, ploughman's (£2.95), lots of fresh fish delivered three times a week from Grimsby such as halibut, haddock, cod, lobster, crab and salmon (from £3.95), steak and kidney pie or a roast of the day (£4.20), vegetarian rogan josh or vegetable and tofu casserole (£4.50), and puddings like sticky toffee and date pudding or treacle sponge; menus for children and OAPs. Well kept Thorne Bitter, Timothy Taylors Landlord and Vaux Bitter and Waggle Dance on handpump; prompt service; fruit machine and piped music. *(Recommended by A N Ellis, E J Wilde, John Cadnam, JJW, CMW, Joan and Andrew Life, Paul Cartledge, Brian Horner, Brenda Arthur)*

Wards (Vaux) ~ Managers Peter and Avril Wagstaff ~ Real ale ~ Meals and snacks (till 10) ~ Evening restaurant (not Sun, but they do Sun lunch) ~ (01302) 840305 ~ Children welcome ~ Open 11-3, 5-11 ~ Bedrooms: £25S/£35S

HEATH (W Yorks) SE3519 Map 7

Kings Arms

Village signposted from A655 Wakefield—Normanton – or, more directly, turn off opposite Horse & Groom

As we went to press, new licensees had just taken over this old-fashioned pub. It's in a fine setting – which is a surprise being so close to Wakefield – with picnic tables on a side lawn, and a nice walled flower-filled garden; more seats along the front of the building facing the village green. Inside, the dark-panelled original bar has plain elm stools and oak settles built into the walls and a fire burning in the old black range (with a long row of smoothing irons on the mantlepiece). A more comfortable extension has carefully preserved the original style, down to good wood-pegged oak panelling (two embossed with royal arms), and a high shelf of plates; there are also two other small flagstoned rooms, and the conservatory opens onto the garden. Bar food now includes soup (£1.40), sandwiches (from £1.65), ploughman's (£3.25), fish and chips, filled yorkshire pudding, steak pie or lasagne (from £3.95), steaks (from £7), and puddings (from £1.95). As well as cheap Clarks Bitter and Festival, they also serve guests like Tetleys Bitter and Timothy Taylors Landlord on handpump. *(Recommended by MKP, JLP, Michael Butler, S Thompson, D M Parsloe, MJVK, Mark Bradley, J L Phillips, Gerry McGarry, Ian and Nita Cooper, Graham Reeves) larks ~ Managers Karen and John Battle ~ Real ale ~ Meals and snacks ~ Gas-lit restaurant (open all day Sun until 8) ~ (01924) 377527 ~ Children welcome ~ Open 11.30-3, 5.30-11*

HECKMONDWIKE (W Yorks) SE2223 Map 7

Old Hall

New North Road; B6117 between A62 and A638; OS Sheet 104, map reference 214244

This was once the home of the Nonconformist scientist Joseph Priestley – and it's the 15th-c building itself that readers like. There are lots of old beams and timbers, latticed mullioned windows with worn stone surrounds, brick or stripped old stone walls hung with pictures of Richard III, Henry VII, Catherine Parr and Priestley, and comfortable furnishings. Snug low-ceilinged alcoves lead off the central part with its high ornate plaster ceiling, and an upper gallery room, under the pitched roof, looks down on the main area through timbering 'windows'. Under the new licensee, decent, straightforward waitress-served bar food includes sandwiches (not Sunday), pie of the day (£3.95), chicken kiev (£4.25), gammon and egg (£4.75), and mixed grill (£6.50). Well kept (and cheap) Sam Smiths OB on handpump; darts, fruit machine, and piped music. *(Recommended by Laura Darlington, Gianluca Perinetti, Michael Butler, Monica Shelley, Paul Cartledge, Andrew and Ruth Triggs, Tony Hall, Mark Bradley, Mrs Gwyneth Holland)*

Sam Smiths ~ Manager Keith Dunkley ~ Real ale ~ Meals and snacks ~ (01924) 404774 ~ Children welcome ~ Open 11.30-2.30, 6-11

HELMSLEY (N Yorks) SE6184 Map 10

Feathers 🍷

Market Square

On market day (Friday) the atmospheric older part in this handsome three-storey inn is full of locals and visitors: heavy medieval beams and dark panelling, a big log fire in the stone inglenook fireplace, unusual cast-iron-framed tables topped by weighty slabs of oak and walnut, and a venerable wall carving of a dragonfaced bird in a grape vine. The main inn has its own comfortable lounge bar. Well prepared bar food includes sandwiches, soup (£1.95), good ploughman's, salmon pâté (£3), sausage and egg (£3.50), home-made lasagne or broccoli quiche (£4.95), home-made steak pie (£6.25), deep-fried battered prawns in sweet and sour sauce (£6.50), gammon and egg (£6.75), steaks (from £10.50), and daily specials. Well kept Morlands Old Speckled Hen, John Smiths, Theakstons Best and Old Peculier, and weekly guest ales on handpump, and a large choice of wines chalked on a blackboard; friendly service, darts, dominoes, and piped music. There's an attractive back garden with seats and tables. Rievaulx Abbey (well worth an hour's visit) is close by. *(Recommended by Dr Jim Craig-Gray, Andrew and Ruth Triggs, Joan and Andrew Life, J E Ryecroft, G C Brown, John and Christine Simpson, Peter Race)*

Free house ~ Licensees Lance and Andrew Feather ~ Real ale ~ Meals and snacks ~ Restaurant (not Sun evening) ~ (01439) 770275 ~ Children welcome ~ Open 10.30-11; closed 25 Dec ~ Bedrooms: £25(£35B)/£50(£60B)

HETTON (N Yorks) SD9558 Map 7

Angel ★ 🍴 🍷

Just off B6265 Skipton—Grassington

Yorkshire Dining Pub of the Year

People come from miles around to enjoy the marvellous food in this very well run, friendly dining pub – and to be sure of a table, it's essential to arrive almost as the doors open. Served by hard-working uniformed staff, there might be home-made soup (£2.60; lovely rustic fish soup with aioli £3.25), queen scallops baked with garlic and gruyere (£4.20), seafood baked in filo pastry served on lobster sauce (£4.25), an open sandwich of smoked salmon, cream cheese, smoked bacon and home-made chutney (£4.95), tagliatelle with smoked salmon and broccoli (£5.95), roasted cod fillet with herb crumb topping and leek and mushroom sauce (£6.75), ploughman's (£6.90), chicken breast stuffed with prawns and smoked bacon with lemon sauce (£8.25), seafood hors d'oeuvre (£8.35), winter braised oxtail (£8.50), confit of duck with braised Normandy red cabbage and orange and thyme sauce (£8.90), good calf's liver and bacon with bubble and squeak (£10.50), summer seafood platter (£15.95), daily specials and fish dishes, and puddings like crème brûlée, sticky toffee pudding or rich chocolate marquise with orange compote (from £3.50). Well kept Black Sheep Bitter and Special, and Boddingtons on handpump, over 300 wines (24 by the glass) and quite a few malt whiskies. The four timbered and panelled rambling rooms have lots of cosy alcoves, comfortable country-kitchen chairs or button-back green plush seats, Ronald Searle wine snob cartoons and older engravings and photographs, log fires, a solid fuel stove, and in the main bar, a Victorian farmhouse range in the big stone fireplace; the snug is no smoking. Sturdy wooden benches and tables are built on to the cobbles outside. *(Recommended by Mr and Mrs J Tyrer, Wayne Brindle, Lynn Sharpless, Bob Eardley, Bernard and Marjorie Parkin, Simon Barber, Darren and Clare Jones, Geoffrey and Brenda Wilson, MJVK, Dr and Mrs M Locker, Dr and Sue Griffin, Neville Kenyon, Robert and Ann Lees, Janet and Peter Race, Gwen and Peter Andrews, Tony Hall, Nicola Thomas, Paul Dickinson, Annette Moore, Chris Pearson, Paul Boot, Mike and Jo, Brian and Jill Bond, C Hedderman, John and Joan Nash, E A George, Stephen and Brenda Head, Mark Bradley, Karen Eliot, Paul and Gail Betteley)*

Free house ~ Licensee Denis Watkins ~ Real ale ~ Meals and snacks (till 10) ~ Restaurant (closed Sun evening) ~ (01756) 730263 ~ Well behaved children in eating area of bar ~ Open 12-2.30, 6-10.30; closed 3rd week Jan

HUBBERHOLME (N Yorks) SD9178 Map 7

George

Village signposted from Buckden; about 1 mile NW

This remote and unspoilt old Upper Wharfedale building was J B Priestley's favourite pub. The two small and well kept flagstoned bar-rooms have heavy beams supporting the dark ceiling-boards, walls stripped back to bare stone and hung with antique plates, seats (with covers to match the curtains) around shiny copper topped tables, and an open stove in the big fireplace. Good bar food includes sandwiches, home-made soup (£1.90), home-made pâté (£2.50), cumberland sausage (£4.95), meaty or vegetarian lasagne (£5.50), steak and kidney pie (£5.65), vegetable stir fry (£5.95), chicken breast stuffed with boursin cheese and white wine sauce (£7.45), fillet of salmon with parsley sauce (£8.95), steaks (from £8.95), and puddings (£2.20). Very well kept Theakstons Best and Youngers Scotch and No 3 on handpump, and around 20 malt whiskies. Darts, dominoes, cribbage, and a game they call 'pot the pudding'. There are seats and tables overlooking the moors and River Wharfe – where they have fishing rights. *(Recommended by Lynn Sharpless, Bob Eardley, JKW, John Le Sage, Prof and Mrs S Barnett, Eddie Edwards, Caroline Kenyon, Jack and Philip Paxton, Anthony Marriott, K H Frostick, J L Phillips, John and Joan Nash, M J Morgan, Bill and Lydia Ryan, Lee Goulding)*

Free house ~ Licensees Jerry Lanchbury and Fiona Shelton ~ Real ale ~ Meals and snacks ~ Restaurant ~ (01756) 760223 ~ Children in eating area of bar ~ Open 11.30-3, 6(6.30 winter)-11; 11.30-11 Sat ~ Bedrooms: £25/£35(£45B)

HULL (N Yorks) TA0927 Map 8

Minerva 

From A63 Castle Street/Garrison Road, turn into Queen Street towards piers at central traffic lights; some metered parking here; pub is in pedestrianised Nelson Street, at far end

Following a recent refurbishment of the microbrewery at this picturesque Georgian pub, they hope to start brewing extra beers for local special events, and maybe a winter warmer, in addition to the current Pilots Pride. The town has long been renowned for its beer, and the expression eating Hull Cheese was coined as a euphemism for having a bit to drink. The pub is in the heart of the attractively restored waterfront and bustling marina, so is a great spot from which to watch the harbour goings-on; you might prefer to do this from inside, as the views of the Humber Bridge are unusually good, and the tables on the pavement outside can be a little breezy. Repainted just before we went to press, the several thoughtfully refurbished rooms ramble all the way round a central servery, and are filled with comfortable seats, interesting photographs and pictures of old Hull (with two attractive wash drawings by Roger Davis) and a big chart of the Humber. A tiny snug has room for just three people, and a back room (which looks out to the marina basin, and has darts) houses a profusion of varnished woodwork. As well as their own beer and Tetleys, they have three well kept guests on handpump. Good sized helpings of straightforward bar food such as hot or cold filled baguettes (from £1.95), soup (99p), burgers (from £1.90), filled baked potatoes (from £1.65), ploughman's (£3.25), salads (from £3.25), fried haddock, steak and kidney pie or lasagne (£3.95), and mixed grill (£7.65), with at least five daily specials, three of which are vegetarian; on Sundays they serve a roast and specials only. The lounge is no-smoking when food is being served. Piped music from the fine reproduction Wurlitzer juke box (the real 'works', with the records, are actually in a completely different place); dominoes, fruit machine, video game. Quiz night every Tuesday. *(Recommended by Chris Westmoreland, J S M Sheldon, Miranda Hutchinson; more reports please)*

Own brew (Tetleys) ~ Managers Eamon and Kathy Scott ~ Real ale ~ Meals and snacks (not evening Sat or Sun) ~ (01482) 326909 ~ Children in eating area of bar ~ Open 11-11; closed 25 Dec

Olde White Harte ★ £

Off 25 Silver Street, a continuation of Whitefriargate; pub is up narrow passage beside the jewellers' Barnby and Rust, and should not be confused with the much more modern White Hart nearby

You can almost feel the history in this beautifully preserved ancient tavern, tucked away in a cosy courtyard amongst narrow alleyways. Perhaps one of the nicest things about it is that despite its heritage, this is very much a busy working pub, with at lunchtimes especially a friendly bustle and popularity that's firmly up to the minute. For a more intimate atmosphere come on a quiet weekday evening, when you can gently absorb the fascinating interior. In the downstairs bar attractive stained glass windows look out above the bow window-seat, carved heavy beams support black ceiling boards, and two brocaded Jacobean-style chairs sit in the big brick inglenook with its frieze of Delft tiles. The curved copper-topped counter serves well kept Youngers IPA and No 3, Smiles Exhibition, Theakstons Old Peculier and XB and a guest, as well as 14 malt whiskies. Otherwise very similar, the second bar has a turkey carpet; dominoes, shove ha'penny, table skittles, cribbage, fruit machine, trivia. Resting on the zigzagging old stairs which go straight up to the dining area is a fine long case clock. Very reasonably priced simple, traditional bar food includes sandwiches, made to order salads, and hot dishes such as corned beef and onion pie (£2.25), steak pie (£2.75) and lasagne (£2.95); they also do Sunday lunch. Service is friendly and obliging. Seats in the courtyard outside. It was in the heavily panelled room up the oak staircase that in 1642 the town's governor Sir John Hotham made the fateful decision to lock the nearby gate against Charles I, depriving him of Hull's arsenal; it didn't do him much good, as in the Civil War that followed, Hotham, like the king, was executed by the parliamentarians. *(Recommended by N Haslewood, I Pocsk, Chris Westmoreland, David and Shelia, Ray Hebsen, Stephen E Millard, J S M Sheldon, Martyn and Mary Mullins)*

Youngers (S & N) ~ Managers Brian and Jenny Cottingham ~ Real ale ~ Lunchtime meals and snacks ~ Lunchtime restaurant ~ (01482) 326363 ~ Children in restaurant ~ Quiz nights Mon ~ No nearby parking ~ Open 11-11

KIRBY HILL (N Yorks) NZ1406 Map 10

Shoulder of Mutton

Signposted from Ravensworth road about 3½ miles N of Richmond; or from A66 Scotch Corner—Brough turn off into Ravensworth, bear left through village, and take signposted right turn nearly a mile further on

You can be sure of a friendly welcome from the licensees in this peaceful, ivy-fronted ex-farmhouse. There's a stone archway between the lounge and public bar, green plush wall settles around simple dark tables, local turn-of-the-century photographs of Richmond, and open stone fireplaces. Good bar food includes lunchtime sandwiches (not Sun; the cold roast beef is marvellous), lots of vegetarian dishes (from £4.50), steak and kidney pie (£4.50), good haddock (£5.25), steaks (from £7.95), and daily specials (£4.50); children's dishes. Well kept Black Sheep Bitter, Ruddles County, John Smiths, and Websters Yorkshire on handpump, and quite a few malt whiskies; darts, dominoes, cribbage, and piped music. The yard behind has picnic tables and fine views, and the tree-shaded church opposite has an unusually tuneful bell. *(Recommended by Mr and Mrs A G Pollard, SS, Andrew McKeand)*

Free house ~ Licensees Mick and Anne Burns ~ Real ale ~ Meals and snacks (not Mon lunchtime) ~ Restaurant ~ (01748) 822772 ~ Children in eating area of bar until 9 ~ Sing-a-long Mon evenings ~ Open 12-3, 7-11; closed Mon lunchtime ~ Bedrooms: £25B/£39B

KIRKBYMOORSIDE (N Yorks) SE6987 Map 10

George & Dragon

Market place

The warmly friendly licensees treat the bar in this particularly civilised 17th-c coaching inn as their front room, and all visitors as their guests to be welcomed on entering – and thanked when they leave. There are fresh flowers and daily newspapers, the panelling has been stripped back to its original pitch pine, brass-studded solid dark red leatherette chairs are set around polished wooden tables, horse-brasses are hung along the beams, and there are lots of photographs, prints, shields and memorabilia connected with cricket and rugby on the walls (they have sporting celebrity dinners each quarter), and a blazing log fire; no games machines, pool or juke boxes, and the piped music is either classical or jazz, and not obtrusive. The very good bar food is English and natural, using only fresh produce: lunchtime sandwiches in home-baked buns, home-made soup (at least one is vegetarian, £1.95), smoked duck and apricot terrine (£3.25), black pudding with apple and onion (£3.75), venison sausages with braised onions (£4.50), spinach and cheese roulade (£5.25), steak and kidney pie (£6.25), rabbit casserole with green ginger wine (£6.50), seafood hot pot in fennel flavoured sauce or Sunday lunch roast rib of beef and yorkshire pudding (£6.90), pigeon pie (£7.50), pork fillet in fruit sauce, 10oz sirloin steak (£9.95), and puddings like sherry trifle, wildberry cheesecake and chocolate fruit and nut slice (£2.60); the game and fish is local, breakfasts are delicious, and they offer children's helpings. The attractive no-smoking restaurant was the old brewhouse until the early part of this century. Well kept Black Sheep, John Smiths Bitter, Timothy Taylors Landlord and Theakstons XB on handpump, a fine wine list including up to 10 by the glass, and over 30 malt whiskies; backgammon. There are seats under umbrellas in the back courtyard and a surprisingly peaceful walled garden for residents to use. The bedrooms are in a converted cornmill and old vicarage at the back of the pub. Wednesday is Market Day. *(Recommended by Dr Jim Craig-Gray, Caroline Jarrett, Roger Bellingham, F M Bunbury, K A Barker, John and Joan Calvert, Anne and John Barnes)*

Free house ~ Licensees Stephen and Frances Colling ~ Real ale ~ Meals and snacks ~ Restaurant ~ (0751) 433334 ~ Well behaved children welcome ~ Open 10-3, 6-11 ~ Bedrooms: £44B/£68B

KIRKHAM (N Yorks) SE7466 Map 7

Stone Trough

Kirkham Abbey

A new licensee has taken over this attractively situated inn and readers are enjoying coming here very much. The several beamed, cosy and interesting rooms have warm log fires, a friendly atmosphere, and well kept Bass, Boddingtons, Fullers London Pride, Jennings Cumberland, Marstons Pedigree, Tetleys, Theakstons, and Timothy Taylors Landlord and so forth on handpump. Good bar food includes home-made soup (£2.50), home-made pâté or sausage, egg and chips (£3.50), moussaka or home-baked ham and eggs (£5.75), ploughman's, vegetable bake or home-made seafood pie (£5.95), daily specials like honey-roast knuckle of lamb with white onion sauce or lemon sole stuffed with prawns and grapes (£9.75), steaks (from £10.95), and puddings (£2.95). The no-smoking farmhouse restaurant has a fire in an old-fashioned kitchen range. Darts, pool, bar billiards, shove-ha'penny, table skittles, cribbage, dominoes, fruit machine, video game, trivia, and piped music. There's a good outside seating area with lovely valley views; fine nearby walks. *(Recommended by Christopher Turner, Prof S Barnett, C A Hall, Roger Bellingham, Thomas Nott, F J and A Parmenter)*

Free house ~ Licensee Holly Dane ~ Real ale ~ Meals and snacks (not winter Mon lunchtime) ~ Restaurant ~ (01653) 618713 ~ Well behaved children welcome ~ Open 12-2.30(3 Sat), 6(5.30 Sat)-11; winter evening opening one hour later; closed winter Mon lunchtime

KNARESBOROUGH (N Yorks) SE3557 Map 7

Blind Jacks ◼

Market Place

There are no noisy games machines or piped music in this listed Georgian building – just a chatty atmosphere and half-a-dozen real ales on handpump: Ind Coope Burton and Tetleys Bitter and four daily-changing guests such as Goose Eye Bitter, Hambleton Thoroughbred, Moorhouses Black Cat Mild, and Timothy Taylors Landlord. Also, country wines, foreign bottled beers and farm cider. The two downstairs rooms – stripped brick on the left and dark panelling on the right – have bare floor boards, pews (the one on the right as you go in has a radiator built in behind, which is lovely on a cold day), cast-iron long tables, brewery posters mainly from the south (Adnams, Harveys, Hook Norton, Shepherd Neame), lots of framed beermats, and nice old-fashioned net half-curtains; upstairs restaurant. Under the new licensees, good bar food includes sandwiches (from £1.40), home-made soup (£1.50), mackerel pâté (£1.95), home-made burgers (from £2.50), filled baked potatoes (£2.75), and cheese and tomato quiche or chilli (£3.95), with evening dishes like button mushrooms with bacon and onions (£2.50), lamb and apricot hotpot (£4.75), seafood casserole (£5.25), gammon and eggs (£5.95), and sirloin steak (£7.50); dominoes. Civilised children by arrangement only. *(Recommended by Prof S Barnett, Tim and Ann Newell, Drs A and A C Jackson, CW, JW)*

Free house ~ Licensees A N J Warnes and Ian Fozard ~ Real ale ~ Meals and snacks (not Sun evening or Mon lunchtime) ~ Restaurant (not Sun evening) ~ (01423) 869148 ~ Open 11.30-11; 11.30-3, 6-11 Mon/Tues

LASTINGHAM (N Yorks) SE7391 Map 10

Blacksmiths Arms ◼

Off A170 W of Pickering at Wrelton, forking off Rosedale rd N of Cropton; or via Appleton or via Hutton-le-Hole

New licensees have taken over this little village pub and reports as we went to press are that extensive building works are afoot. What won't change is the lovely surrounding countryside and the tracks through Cropton Forest. The comfortable, oak beamed bar has a good winter fire, an attractive cooking range with swinging pot-yards, some sparkling brass, and cushioned windsor chairs and traditional built-in wooden wall seats. Well kept Church Bitter and Curate's Downfall, John Smiths and Websters Yorkshire on handpump. Bar food includes sandwiches (from £1.35), soup (£1.50), steak and mushroom pie (£4.45), and steak (£8.95); they do a breakfast service for campers and caravanners in the area. A traditionally furnished, no-smoking dining area opens off the main bar, and serves Sunday roasts and evening meals; a decent range of malt whiskies. There is a pool and games room as well as darts, dominoes, cribbage, fruit machine, and video game. The ancient nearby church has a Norman crypt. *(Recommended by G Neighbour, Duncan Redpath, Lorraine Milburn, Bob and Maggie Atherton; more reports on the new regime, please)*

Free house ~ Licensees Mike and Janet Frank ~ Real ale ~ Meals and snacks ~ Restaurant ~ (01751) 417247 ~ Well behaved children welcome ~ Open 11-3, 6.30-11; 11-11 Sat ~ Bedrooms: £16.50/£33

LEDSHAM (W Yorks) SE4529 Map 7

Chequers

Claypit Lane; a mile W of A1, some 4 miles N of junction M62

This neatly kept village pub has remained consistently enjoyable over the years – and no matter how busy things are, the landlord and staff are as welcoming as ever. The old-fashioned little central panelled-in servery has several small, individually decorated rooms leading off, with low beams, lots of cosy alcoves, a number of Toby jugs, log fires; well kept John Smiths, Theakstons Best, Youngers Scotch and Number 3 on handpump. Good, straightforward bar food includes home-made soup (£1.95), sandwiches (from £2.75), ploughman's (£4.25), scrambled eggs and smoked salmon (£4.85), lasagne (£4.95), pasta bake (£5.45), generous grilled gammon and two eggs (£6.75), steaks (from £7.25), around four popular daily specials such as kidneys with bacon in a red wine sauce (£4.35), chicken in a white wine, mushroom and cream sauce (£5.25), haddock mornay (£5.45), and steak and mushroom pie (£5.85), and puddings (£2.25); there may be a loaf of crusty bread with bowls of dripping and sliced onion on the bar to help yourself to. A sheltered two-level terrace behind the house has tables among roses and is popular with families. *(Recommended by M D Phillips, Tim and Sue Halstead, K H Frostick, Roger Bellingham, Roy Bromell, John and Sheila French, Caroline Wright, Mark J Hydes, Mark Bradley, F M Bunbury, John C Baker, Paul Cartledge, Mayur Shah)*

Free house ~ Licensee Chris Wraith ~ Real ale ~ Meals and snacks (not Sun) ~ Restaurant (not Sun) ~ (01977) 683135 ~ Children in separate room ~ Open 11-3, 5.30-11; 11-11 Sat; closed Sun

LEEDS (W Yorks) SE3033 Map 7

Whitelocks ★ £

Turks Head Yard; alley off Briggate, opposite Debenhams and Littlewoods; park in shoppers' car park and walk

It's best to try and visit this marvellously preserved and atmospheric pub early so you can appreciate the unchanging Victorian decor. The long and narrow old-fashioned bar has polychrome tiles on the bar counter, stained-glass windows and grand advertising mirrors, and red button-back plush banquettes and heavy copper-topped cast-iron tables squeezed down one side. Good, reasonably priced lunchtime bar food includes bubble and squeak, sausages and home-made Scotch eggs (all 75p), sandwiches (£1.25) or yorkshire puddings (£1.10), home-made quiche (£1.20), very good meat and potato pie (£2), and jam roly poly or fruit pie (95p); when it gets busy you may have to wait for your order, though the staff are very cheerful and pleasant. Well kept McEwans 80/-, Theakstons Bitter, Youngers IPA, Scotch and No 3 on handpump; quiz evenings every Tuesday in top bar. At the end of the long narrow yard another bar has been done up in Dickensian style. *(Recommended by G P Kernan, Amanda Dauncey, Chris Westmoreland, Basil Minson, Martin Hickes, J Royce, Paul Cartledge, Annette Moor, Chris Pearson, Tony and Wendy Hobden, Mark Bradley, Tony Hall, Reg Nelson)*

Youngers (S & N) ~ Manager Julie Cliff ~ Real ale ~ Meals and snacks (11-8; not Sun evening) ~ Restaurant (not Sun evening) ~ (0113) 245 3950 ~ Children in top bar at lunchtime and in restaurant ~ Open 11-11

LEVISHAM (N Yorks) SE8391 Map 10

Horseshoe

Pub and village signposted from A169 N of Pickering

Set at the top of a lovely, unspoilt village, this bustling family pub has picnic tables on the attractive village green – popular on warm days. Inside, there's a particularly welcoming atmosphere, and the well kept, recently decorated bars have brocaded seats, a log fire in the stone fireplace, and bar billiards, dominoes and piped music. Good bar food includes home-made soup (£1.95), sandwiches (from £2.60; the steak one is delicious £4.50), egg mayonnaise using free range eggs (£2.90), a good ploughman's (£4.45), fresh Whitby haddock (£5.25), prawn thermidor (£5.30), steak and kidney pie or beef curry (£5.50), gammon and egg (£5.90), Cajun chicken (£6.50), steaks (from £9.95), daily specials, vegetarian dishes, children's menu (£2.95), and puddings (£2.25); the restaurant is no smoking. Well kept Malton Double Chance (summer only), Tetleys Bitter, and Theakstons Best, XB and Old Peculier on handpump, and 40 malt whiskies. Three to five times a day in spring and autumn, and seven times in summer, two steam trains of the North Yorks Moors Railway stop at this village. *(Recommended by C A Hall, Chloe Gartery, David Surridge, M Borthwick, Bob and Maggie Atherton, Andrew and Ruth Triggs, Anne and Sverre Hagen, John Allsopp, Mark Whitmore, Simon Collett-Jones)*

Free house ~ Licensees Brian and Helen Robshaw ~ Real ale ~ Meals and snacks (not 25 Dec) ~ Restaurant ~ (01751) 460240 ~ Children welcome till 9.30pm ~ Open 10.30-3, 6.30-11; 11.30-2.30, 7-11 in winter; closed evening 25 Dec ~ Bedrooms: £22/£44(£46B)

LEYBURN (N Yorks) SE1191 Map 10

Sandpiper

Market Place – bottom end

Both visitors and locals alike are assured of a friendly welcome in this neatly kept little 17th-c stone cottage. There's a cheerful bustling atmosphere, and the bar has a couple of black beams in the low ceiling, a stuffed pheasant in a stripped-stone alcove, antlers, and just seven tables, even including the back room up three steps – where you'll find attractive Dales photographs, Toby-jugs on a delft shelf, and a collection of curious teapots. Down by the nice linenfold panelled bar counter there are stuffed sandpipers, more photographs and a woodburning stove in the stone fireplace. There's also a neat dining area on the left; dominoes and piped music. Carefully cooked good bar food includes home-made soup like spicy chicken and tomato (£1.75), sandwiches (from £1.75), home-made pork and liver pâté (£3.25), ploughman's (£3.95), lasagne (£4.75), salads (£4.75), puddings (£2.25), evening dishes like chicken stuffed with spinach and served with stilton sauce or pork tenderloin with orange sauce (£7.25), steaks (£9.95), and daily specials such as deep-fried mushrooms in beer batter (£3.25), cumberland sausage (£3.75), and fresh seafood or steak and kidney pies, beef curry or liver and bacon (all £4.75). Well kept John Smiths, Theakstons Best and Old Peculier, Websters Yorkshire, and a weekly guest like Dent Ramsbottom Strong Ale, Jennings Cumberland or Shepherd Neame Spitfire on handpump, around 100 malt whiskies, and bin-end wines. The friendly English pointer is called Sadie – no other dogs allowed. There are lovely hanging baskets, white cast-iron tables among the honeysuckle, climbing roses, cotoneaster and so forth on the front terrace, with more tables in the back garden. *(Recommended by Michael and Susan Morgan, John and Chris Simpson, J H and S A Harrop, Dono and Carol Leaman, J E Rycroft, F and S Barnes, G S and A Jaques, M J Morgan, Andrew and Ruth Triggs, Jerry and Alison Oakes, M E A Horler, Noel Jackson, Louise Campbell)*

Free house ~ Licensees Peter and Beryl Swan ~ Real ale ~ Meals and snacks ~ Evening restaurant ~ (01969) 622206 ~ Well behaved children welcome until 8pm ~ Open 11-2.30(3 Fri/Sat), 6.30-11 ~ Bedrooms: /£40B

LINTHWAITE (W Yorks) SE1014 Map 7

Sair

Hoyle Ing, off A62; 3½ miles after Huddersfield look out for two water storage tanks (painted with a shepherd scene) on your right – the street is on your left, burrowing very steeply up between works buildings; OS Sheet 110 map reference 101143

If Mr Crabtree is not too busy, he is glad to show visitors the brewhouse in this unspoilt rough-and-ready place: pleasant and well balanced Linfit Bitter, Mild and Special, Old Eli, Leadboiler, Autumn Gold, and the redoubtable Enochs Hammer; there's even stout (English Guineas) – and a porter (Janet St). Thatchers farm cider and a few malt whiskies. The quaint cluster of rooms is furnished with pews or smaller chairs, bottle collections, beermats tacked to beams, rough flagstones in some parts and carpet in others, and several big stone fireplaces; The no-smoking room is being refurbished. The room on the right has darts, shove-ha'penny, cribbage, dominoes, and juke box; piano players welcome. There's a striking view down the Colne Valley – through which the Huddersfield Narrow Canal winds its way; in the 3½ miles from Linthwaite to the highest and longest tunnel in Britain are 25 working locks and some lovely countryside. No food. *(Recommended by Jack and Philip Paxton, Bill and Lydia Ryan, H K Dyson, Reg Nelson, AT, RT; more reports please)*

Own brew ~ Licensee Ron Crabtree ~ Real ale ~ (01484) 842370 ~ Children in three rooms away from the bar ~ Folk music 1st Tues of month ~ Open 7-11 only on weekdays; 12-3, 7-11 Sat, Sun and Bank holidays (not Good Fri)

LINTON IN CRAVEN (N Yorks) SD9962 Map 7

Fountaine

On B6265 Skipton—Grassington, forking right

The setting for this welcoming pub is very pretty and there are seats outside looking over the village green to the narrow stream that runs through this delightful hamlet; you can eat out here on fine days. The little rooms are furnished with stools, benches and other seats, and lots of original water colours and prints, several with sporting themes. Good, popular bar food includes home-made soup (£2), sandwiches (from £3), garlic mushrooms with cream (£3.50), broccoli, cheddar and potato bake (£4.95), good steak and kidney pie (£5.45), Whitby scampi (£5.50), breast of chicken in a lemon, prawn and white wine sauce (£6.25), sirloin steak (£8.75), daily specials such as yorkshire pudding filled with steak and onions in ale, liver and bacon (£4.95) and fresh battered Whitby haddock (£5.95) and puddings (£2); children's dishes (£3.50). Well kept Black Sheep Bitter and Special and Theakstons XB and Old Peculier on handpump; decent malt whiskies. Darts, dominoes, cribbage, and ring the bull. The Linton Room is no smoking. The pub is named after the local lad who made his pile in the Great Plague – contracting in London to bury the bodies. *(Recommended by Prof and Mrs S Barnett, Roger and Christine Mash, Wayne Brindle, Helen McLagan, J R Whetton, Mike and Ruth Dooley, Gwen and Peter Andrews, Caroline Kenyon, Tony Hall, Geoffrey and Brenda Wilson, Wendy Arnold, C H Stride, C Roberts, R E and M Baggs, Wayne Brindle, Sylvia Dutton)*

Free house ~ Licensee Francis Mackwood ~ Real ale ~ Meals and snacks (not Sun or Mon evenings) ~ (01756) 752210 ~ Children welcome away from main bar area ~ Open 12-2.30(3 Sat), 7-11

LITTON (N Yorks) SD9074 Map 7

Queens Arms

From B6160 N of Grassington, after Kilnsey take second left fork; can also be reached off B6479 at Stainforth N of Settle, via Halton Gill

The attractive two-level garden here has stunning views over the fells and there are fine surrounding walks – a track behind the inn leads over Ackerley Moor to Buckden and the quiet lane through the valley leads on to Pen-y-ghent. Inside, the main bar on the right has a good coal fire, stripped rough stone walls, a brown beam-and-plank ceiling, stools around cast-iron-framed tables on the stone and concrete floor, a seat built into the stone-mullioned window, signed cricket bats, and a large collection of cigarette lighters. On the left, the red-carpeted room has another coal fire and more of a family atmosphere with varnished pine for its built-in wall seats, and for the ceiling and walls themselves. Popular bar food includes soup and sandwiches, filled baked potatoes, ploughman's, vegetarian dishes (£3.65-£6.95), good lasagne, home-made pies like rabbit or steak and kidney (£4.95), gammon and egg (£5.25), and steaks (£9.50). Well kept Youngers Scotch on handpump; darts, dominoes, shove-ha'penny, and cribbage. *(Recommended by David Varney, Philip and Elizabeth Hawkins, Gwen and Peter Andrews, John and Joan Nash, Mark and Toni Amor-Segan, Stephen Barney, TBB, John Cadman)*

Free house ~ Licensees Tanya and Neil Thompson ~ Real ale ~ Meals and snacks ~ (01756) 770208 ~ Children in eating area of bar ~ Open 12(11.30 Sat)-3, 7(6.30 Sat)-11 ~ Bedrooms: £21.50/£32(£39B)

LOW CATTON (N Yorks) SE7053 Map 7

Gold Cup

Village signposted with High Catton off A166 in Stamford Bridge or A1079 at Kexby Bridge

Firmly on the up at the moment, this friendly and comfortable white-rendered house has been nicely spruced-up over the last year or so. Popular with the cheery locals, the three communicating rooms of the lounge have a very relaxed atmosphere, with open fires at each end, plush wall seats and stools around good solid tables, flowery curtains, some decorative plates and brasswork on the walls. You can rely on a warmly unfussy welcome and good home-cooked food, from a range that might include soup (£1.50), lunchtime sandwiches (from £1.65), crusty rolls (from £2.70), and ploughman's (£3.25), steak and mushroom pie (£4.40), fisherman's pie (£4.95), and more elaborate evening dishes like trout wrapped in bacon and stuffed with spinach and hazelnuts, or lamb in cumberland sauce; the recently extended restaurant has candlelit dinners on Thursday and Friday, and pleasant views of the surrounding fields. Well kept John Smiths and Tetleys on handpump, good coffee, decent wines. The back games bar is comfortable, with a well lit pool table, darts, dominoes, fruit machine, video game, and well reproduced music. There may be fat geese in the back paddock. *(Recommended by H Bramwell, Roger Bellingham, Rita and Keith Pollard, Ian Phillips)*

Free house ~ Licensees Ray and Pat Hales ~ Real ale ~ Meals and snacks (all day weekends) ~ Restaurant ~ (01759) 371354 ~ Children in eating area ~ Open 12-3, 7-11, all day Sat; closed Mon lunch (exc bank holidays)

MASHAM (N Yorks) SE2381 Map 10

Kings Head ⛟

Market Square

The broad partly tree-shaded market square in this lovely village is just opposite, and the handsome inn's hanging baskets and window boxes are most attractive; there are picnic tables under cocktail parasols in a partly fairy-lit coachyard. Inside, the two opened-up rooms of the neatly kept and spacious lounge bar – one carpeted, one with a wooden floor – have green plush seats around wooden tables, a big War Department issue clock over the imposing slate and marble fireplace, and a high shelf of Staffordshire and other figurines. From an extensive menu, there might be soup and lunchtime sandwiches (not Sun), ploughman's, steak and kidney pie, cod, gammon and egg or scampi (from £4.95), mixed grill (£6.50), steaks (from £7.95), and daily specials; friendly, helpful service. Well kept Theakstons Best, XB and Old Peculier and occasional guests on handpump; fruit machine, dominoes, piped music. Wednesday is market day. *(Recommended by Caroline Jarrett, Clive Gilbert, Brian Horner, Brenda Arthur, Brian Kneale, M J Morgan, Fred Collier, F and S Barnes, Andrew and Marian Ruston, G Dobson, Paul and Ursula Randall, Murray Dykes)*

Scottish & Newcastle ~ Manager Paul Mounter ~ Real ale ~ Meals and snacks ~ Restaurant ~ (01765) 689295 ~ Well behaved children welcome until 9.30 ~ Open 11-11 ~ Bedrooms: £39B/£58B

White Bear ★

Signposted off A6108 opposite turn into town centre

As Theakstons old stone headquarters buildings are part of this pub and the brewery is on the other side of town, the Theakstons Best, XB, Old Peculier, and Mild on handpump here are very well kept; tours can be arranged at the Theakstons Brewery Visitor centre (01765 89057, extension 4317, Weds-Sun); morning visits are best. The traditionally furnished public bar is packed with bric-a-brac such as copper brewing implements, harness, pottery, foreign banknotes, Fairport Convention and Jethro Tull memorabilia, and stuffed animals – including a huge polar bear behind the bar. A much bigger, more comfortable lounge has a turkey carpet. Bar food includes sandwiches, home-made soup (£1.50), ploughman's, curries, beef in Old Peculier or steak and kidney pie (£4.75), and daily specials. Shove-ha'penny, dominoes, cribbage, fruit machine and CD juke box. In summer there are seats out in the yard. *(Recommended by Margaret Mason, David Thompson, Andrew and Ruth Triggs, David and Julie Glover, Jan and Dave Booth, Andrew and Marian Ruston, Jim Farmer, Richard Houghton)*

Scottish & Newcastle ~ Tenant Mrs Lesley Cutts ~ Real ale ~ Meals and snacks (not Sat or Sun evenings) ~ (01765) 689319 ~ Children in lounge bar ~ Live music Sat evenings ~ Open 11-11; closed evening 25 Dec ~ Two bedrooms: /£35

MELTHAM (W Yorks) SE0910 Map 7

Will's o' Nat's 🍷

Blackmoorfoot Road; off B6107

Quite alone in a fine spot up on the moors, this well run pub is popular with readers for its wide choice of good value food. There might be soup (£1.10), sandwiches (from £1.40), deep-fried black pudding with apple fritters (£2.95), ploughman's (from £3.25), deep-fried fresh haddock or wild boar sausage with onion sauce (£3.50), leek and cream cheese pie or chicken curry (£3.85), steak and kidney pie (£3.95), baked fresh cod in mushroom sauce (£4.30), chicken and broccoli lasagne (£4.60), gammon and eggs (£4.65), steaks (from £7.45), children's dishes (from £1.85), and several puddings (from £1.90) such as lime and lemon crunch pie or treacle sponge; cheeses are traditionally made and are farmhouse or from a small dairy (£2.40). Well kept Oak Mill Bitter and Tetleys Bitter and Mild on handpump, a good little wine list, and a large collection of malt whiskies. By the bar there are heavy wooden wall seats cushioned comfortably in pale green corduroy around heavy old cast-iron-framed tables, and the cream walls have lots of interesting old local photographs and a large attractive pen and wash drawing of many local landmarks, with the pub as its centrepiece. A slightly raised, partly no-smoking dining extension at one end, with plenty of well spaced tables, has the best of the views. Dominoes, fruit machine and piped music (not obtrusive). The pub is situated on both the Colne Valley and Kirklees circular walks and close to Blackmoorfoot reservoir (birdwatching). The name of the pub means 'belonging to or run by William, son of Nathaniel'. *(Recommended by M Borthwick, Laura Darlington, Gianluca Perinetti, John and Elizabeth Cox, H K Dyson, Andrew and Ruth Triggs, Stephen and Brenda Head, Neil Townend, J L Phillips)*

Carlsberg Tetleys ~ Lease: Kim Schofield ~ Real ale ~ Meals and snacks (till 10pm) ~ Restaurant ~ (01484) 850078 ~ Children welcome until 9pm ~ Open 11.30-3(3.30 Sat), 6(6.30 Sat)-11

MOULTON (N Yorks) NZ2404 Map 10

Black Bull

Just E of A1, 1 mile S of Scotch Corner

The high standards are being maintained in this decidedly civilised place. The bar has a huge winter log fire, fresh flowers, an antique panelled oak settle and an old elm housekeeper's chair, built-in red-cushioned black settles and pews around the cast iron tables (one has a heavily beaten copper top), silver-plate Turkish coffee pots and so forth over the red velvet curtained windows, and copper cooking utensils hanging from black beams. A nice side dark-panelled seafood bar has some high seats at the marble-topped counter. Excellent bar snacks include lovely smoked salmon: sandwiches (£3.25), pâté (£4.50), and smoked salmon plate (£5.25); they also do a very good home-made soup served in lovely little tureens (£2), black pudding and pork sausage with caramelised apple (£4.25), Welsh rarebit and bacon (£4.50), spinach and cream cheese lasagne (£4.75), memorable seafood pancakes or hot tomato tart with anchovies and black olives (£5.25), and puddings (2); you must search out someone to take your order – the bar staff just do drinks. In the evening, you can also eat in the polished brick-tiled conservatory with bentwood cane chairs or in the Brighton Belle dining car – though they also do a three-course Sunday lunch. Good wine, and a fine choice of sherries. Service can seem a little unbending to first-time visitors, but most people quickly come to appreciate the dry humour and old-fashioned standards. There are some seats under trees in the central court. *(Recommended by SS, Beryl and Bill Farmer, Jack and Heather Coyle, R J Walden, Mike Farrell, G M Joyce, Ralph A Raimi, Roger A Bellingham)*

Free house ~ Licensees Mrs A Pagendam and Miss S Pagendam ~ Lunchtime bar meals and snacks (not Sun) ~ Restaurant (not Sun evening) ~ (01325) 377289 ~ Children over 7 in restaurant ~ Open 12-2.30, 6-10.30(11 Sat); closed Sun evening

MUKER (N Yorks) SD9198 Map 10

Farmers Arms

B6270 W of Reeth

A good mix of locals, walkers and tourists enjoys this lovely little unpretentious Dales pub. It's in a remote spot with fine surrounding walks and there are interesting drives up over Buttertubs Pass or to the north, to Tan Hill and beyond. Inside, the cosy bar has a warm open fire and is simply furnished with stools and settles around copper-topped tables. Promptly served, value-for-money food includes soup (£1.50), lunchtime filled baps and toasties or vegetable or meaty burgers (£1.85), filled baked potatoes (£2.50), omelettes (£4), chicken curry, steak pie or lasagne (£4.25), vegetarian meals (£4.50), gammon and egg (£5.10), sirloin steak (£7.95), children's dishes (from £2.35) and puddings (£2). Well kept Butterknowle Bitter, Theakstons Best, XB and Old Peculier, and Youngers Scotch on handpump; darts and dominoes. *(Recommended by Viv Middlebrook, Richard Hathaway, JKW, Eddie Edwards, Lesley Sones, Peter and Lynn Brueton, Mrs B Garmston, Margaret Mason, David Thompson, Andrew and Ruth Triggs, Barbara and Dick Waterson, Peter Churchill, Martin and Pauline Richardson, M J Morgan, Bill Edwards)*

Free house ~ Licensees Chris and Marjorie Bellwood ~ Real ale ~ Meals and snacks ~ (01748) 886297 ~ Children in eating area of bar ~ Open 11-3, 6.30-11; 11-11 Sat; winter evening opening 7

NEWTON ON OUSE (N Yorks) SE5160 Map 7

Dawnay Arms

Village signposted off A19 N of York

At the bottom of the neatly kept lawn behind this friendly black-shuttered, 18th-c inn are moorings on the River Ouse – you can fish here, too (and walk along the river banks); picnic tables and other tables on the terrace, and a children's play-house and see-saw. Inside, on the right of the entrance is a comfortable, spacious room with a good deal of beamery and timbering and green plush wall settles and brown plush chairs around wooden or dimpled copper tables. To the left is another airy room with red plush button-back wall banquettes built into bays and a good log fire in the stone fireplace; lots of brass and copper, coins, and an old cash register. Popular bar food includes sandwiches, filled yorkshire puddings (£3.95), a roast of the day (£4.95), steak in ale pie (£5.95), fresh poached salmon (£6.95), chicken wrapped in bacon in filo pastry or plaice calypso (£7.95), gigot of lamb with a cream, mint and onion sauce (£8.50), honey-roast duckling (£8.95), and sirloin steak with a bacon, cream and red wine sauce (£9.95); huge breakfasts. Well kept Boddingtons, Marstons Pedigree, John Smiths, Tetleys, and Theakstons Best, XB and Old Peculier on handpump, decent house wines, and several malt whiskies; darts, pool, fruit machine, and unobtrusive piped music. Benningbrough Hall (National Trust) is five minutes' walk away. *(Recommended by J C Brittain-Long, Mrs J Shedlow, Keith Pollard, Mary and Alan Garner, E Carter, M D Phillips, H Bramwell, Mayur Shah, Rhoda and Jeff Collins, John Knighton, Murray Dykes, H K Dyson, R M Macnaughton)*

Free house ~ Licensees John and Angela Turner ~ Real ale ~ Meals and snacks ~ Restaurant ~ (01347) 848345 ~ Children welcome ~ Pianist Saturday evenings ~ Open 11.30-3, 6.30-11; 11.30-11 Sat ~ Bedrooms: £20/£40

NUNNINGTON (N Yorks) SE6779 Map 7

Royal Oak

Church Street; at back of village, which is signposted from A170 and B1257

Attentive staff serve the generous helpings of well presented food in this attractive little dining pub. And although all the dishes are good, it's the home-made daily specials that receive the most praise: steak and kidney casserole with herb dumpling, breast of chicken in orange and tarragon or fisherman's pot (£7.50), and roast duckling with orange sauce (£8.95); also, home-made soup, sandwiches, very good ploughman's, gammon and egg, and steaks; good Sunday lunch. Well kept Ind Coope Burton, Tetleys and Theakstons Old Peculier on handpump; friendly, efficient service. The high black beams of the bar are strung with earthenware flagons, copper jugs and lots of antique keys, one of the walls is stripped back to the bare stone to display a fine collection of antique farm tools, and there are open fires; the carefully chosen furniture includes kitchen and country dining chairs or a long pew around the sturdy tables on the turkey carpet, and a lectern in one corner. Near the car park there are a couple of tables on a little terrace with a good view. Handy for a visit to Nunnington Hall (National Trust). *(Recommended by Tim and Sue Halstead, Patrick Renouf, John and Christine Simpson, Roger A Bellingham, Brian Kneale, Andy Thwaites)*

Free house ~ Licensee Anthony Simpson ~ Real ale ~ Meals and snacks (not Mon) ~ (01439) 748271 ~ Children over 8 only ~ Open 12-2.30, 6.30-11; closed Mon

Real ale may be served from handpumps, electric pumps (not just the on-off switches used for keg beer) or – common in Scotland – tall taps called founts (pronounced 'fonts') where a separate pump pushes the beer up under air pressure. The landlord can adjust the force of the flow – a tight spigot gives the good creamy head that Yorkshire lads like.

nr OTLEY (W Yorks) SE2047 Map 7

Spite

Newall-with-Clifton, off B6451; towards Blubberhouses about a mile N from Otley, and in fact just inside N Yorks

Although the name above the door here will be different, Mr Gill is the brother-in-law of the previous landlord and has also been the chef. It's a popular place with locals with a cheerfully straightforward atmosphere, beamed ceilings, plain white walls hung with some wildfowl prints and a collection of walking sticks, traditional pub furniture, and a good log fire. Bar food includes soup (£1.70), sandwiches (from £1.85), ploughman's (£4.20), home-made steak pie (£4.30), roast pork, lamb or beef (from £4.50), daily specials like meat and potato pie (£4.30), sugar roast ham (£4.50), and duckling (£5.95), and puddings (£1.80). Well kept John Smiths Bitter, Theakstons Best, and Websters Yorkshire on handpump; dominoes and unobtrusive piped music. The neat, well-lit little rose garden has white tables and chairs. *(Recommended by Gwen and Peter Andrews, J E Rycroft, Mike and Ruth Dooley, Ben Grose, Mark Bradley, Dave Davey, M and J Back)*

Courage ~ Lease: Philip Gill ~ Real ale ~ Meals and snacks (not Sun or Mon evenings) ~ Restaurant ~ (01943) 463063 ~ Children in eating area of bar until 9 ~ Open 11.30-3, 6(5.30 Fri)-11; 11.30-11 Sat

PENISTONE (S Yorks) SE2402 Map 7

Cubley Hall

Mortimer Road; outskirts, towards Stocksbridge

Originally a grand Edwardian villa, this interesting place has a spreading bar with panelling, an elaborately plastered ceiling, and lots of plush chairs, stools and button-back built-in wall banquettes on the mosaic tiling or turkey carpet. Leading off this spacious main area are two snug rooms and a side family sun lounge which gives a nice view beyond the neat tree-sheltered formal gardens to pastures in the distance; there's a second children's room, too. One room is no smoking. Efficiently served by neat waitresses, bar food includes sandwiches, soup, omelettes, home-made tagliatelle (£3.95), generous salads, various pies (£4.95), jumbo cod and chips (£5.95), and steaks. Well kept Boddingtons, Flowers, Tetleys Bitter, Marstons Pedigree, and a regular guest beer on handpump, quite a few malt whiskies and other spirits, and a fair choice of wines; dominoes, fruit machine, and piped music. Out on the terrace are some tables and the attractive garden has a good children's play house and adventure playground. *(Recommended by Martin Aust, George Atkinson, Geoffrey and Brenda Wilson, J F M West, Stephen and Brenda Head)*

Free house ~ Licensee John Wigfield ~ Real ale ~ Meals and snacks (not 25 Dec) ~ Restaurant (all day on Sunday) ~ (01226) 766086 ~ Children in two family rooms ~ Open 11-3, 6-11

PICKHILL (N Yorks) SE3584 Map 10

Nags Head

Village signposted off A1 N of Ripon, and off B6267 in Ainderby Quernhow

The friendly Boynton brothers have now been running this busy dining pub for 25 years. And it's still the generous helpings of popular food using fresh produce that attract most people. Praise this year has been consistently high and we feel they have earned their Food Award: sandwiches (from £2; hot roast sirloin of beef £3.75), soup (£2.25), home-made kipper pâté (£3.50), crispy mussels with shrimp sauce (£3.75), grilled skate wings with tarragon and nut brown butter (£4.25), cottage pie (£4.95), half roast chicken with bacon (£5.25), home-made fishcakes with seafood sauce (£6.50), and evening dishes such as noisette of pork with herb and mustard crust (£7.95), grilled whole lemon sole or oven-roasted duck breast with a lime and ginger sauce (£9.95), and rare fillet of venison with bramble and port sauce (£12.95); puddings such as steamed lemon and rhubarb sponge with lemon sauce or Irish coffee chocolate cake and cheese cake cream (£2.95); good breakfasts; the restaurant is no smoking. Well kept Hambleton Bitter (the brewery is a couple of miles away), John Smiths, Theakstons Best, XB and Old Peculier, and an occasional guest beer on handpump; a good choice of malt whiskies and good value wines (several by the glass); the friendly service does slow down under pressure. The busy tap room on the left has masses of ties hanging as a frieze from a rail around the red ceiling, and the beams are hung with jugs, coach horns, ale-yards and so forth; the smarter lounge bar with deep green plush banquettes and a carpet to match has pictures for sale on its neat cream walls. Another comfortable beamed room (mainly for restaurant users) has red plush button-back built-in wall banquettes around dark tables. One table's inset with a chessboard, and they also have cribbage, darts, dominoes, shove ha'penny, and faint piped music. *(Recommended by Hilary Edwards, John Allsopp, John and Chris Simpson, Andrew and Ruth Triggs, Mr and Mrs D S Price, V Green, Jack Morley, David Surridge, June and Tony Baldwin, Paul Cartledge, Martin Jones, Noel Jackson, Louise Campbell, Beryl and Bill Farmer)*

Free house ~ Licensees Raymond and Edward Boynton ~ Real ale ~ Meals and snacks (till 10pm) ~ Restaurant (closed Sun evening) ~ (01845) 567391 ~ Well behaved children in eating area of bar and in restaurant ~ Open 11-11 ~ Bedrooms: £34B/£48B

POOL (W Yorks) SE2445 Map 7

White Hart

Just off A658 S of Harrogate, A659 E of Otley

Rebuilt internally just a few years ago, this popular and welcoming family dining pub now seems as if it's been this way for centuries – four rooms, with a quiet and comfortable atmosphere, restrained country decor with a pleasant medley of assorted old farmhouse furniture, a mix of stone flooring and carpet. The emphasis is on generous fresh food cooked to order, with two of the rooms no smoking. There are outstanding sandwiches (from £1.95), main dishes such as filled yorkshire pudding (£4.25), liver, bacon and onion (£4.50), steak and kidney or chicken, ham and mushroom pies (£4.75), fish and chips (£4.95), huge salads (from £4.95), broccoli and brie parcel with sherry, cream and tomato sauce (£5.25), steaks (from £6.55), hunter's chicken (£6.95), big mixed grill (£7.25), and daily specials like grilled chicken breast with creamy mushroom sauce (£5.95). Good fresh vegetables are cooked to perfection, and there's a choice of chips, new or baked potatoes. The last Tuesday of the month has a popular fish evening. Good friendly service, well kept Stones, Timothy Taylors Landlord, Worthington and a guest beer like Everards Tiger on handpump, a well priced wine list, and log fire in main bar; fruit machine and piped jazz or classical music. There are tables outside, with a play area well away from the road. This part of lower Wharfedale is a pleasant walking area, and despite the emphasis on dining, walkers don't feel at all out of place here. *(Recommended by Gerald and Su Mason, Lynne Gittins, Ben Grose)*

Bass ~ Manager David McHattie~ Real ale ~ Meals and snacks (all day) ~ (0113) 284 3011 ~ Children in no-smoking rooms ~ Open 11-11; 12-10.30 Sun

RAMSGILL (N Yorks) SE1271 Map 7

Yorke Arms

Take Nidderdale rd off B6265 in Pateley Bridge; or exhilarating but narrow moorland drive off A6108 at N edge of Masham, via Fearby and Lofthouse

Nearby Gouthwaite Reservoir takes its name from the Yorke family's mansion (now under the water) and this small country hotel was the shooting lodge. The carefully refurbished bars have open log fires, two or three heavy carved Jacobean oak chairs, a big oak dresser laden with polished pewter and other antiques. Bar food includes sandwiches, home-made soup (£1.95), sautéed mushrooms with bacon, garlic and cream or black pudding thermidor (£3.95), grilled fillet of fresh plaice with parsley butter or battered cod (£5.95), lasagne (£6.25), chicken in white wine and mushroom sauce (£6.95), and salmon with a lemon and chive cream sauce (£7.95). They prefer smart dress in the no-smoking restaurant in the evening. The inn's public rooms are open throughout the day for tea and coffee, and shorts are served in cut glass. You can walk up the magnificent if strenuous moorland road to Masham, or perhaps on the right-of-way track that leads along the hill behind the reservoir, also a bird sanctuary. *(Recommended by Andrew and Ruth Triggs, Robert and Ann Lees, Grodon Theaker, J Peters, Andrew and Marian Ruston)*

Free house ~ Licensees Mr and Mrs MacDougall ~ Lunchtime bar meals and snacks ~ Restaurant ~ (01423) 755243 ~ Children welcome ~ Open 11-11; closed evening 25 Dec to non-residents ~ Bedrooms: £40B/£60B

REDMIRE (N Yorks) SE0591 Map 10

Kings Arms

Wensley—Askrigg back road: a good alternative to the A684 through Wensleydale

Relaxed and unassuming, this friendly village local is tucked away in an attractive small village. The simply furnished bar is neatly kept and has a long soft leatherette wall seat and other upholstered wall settles, red leatherette cafe chairs or dark oak ones, round cast-iron tables, a fine oak armchair (its back carved like a mop of hair), and a wood-burning stove. Popular bar food includes good soup, sandwiches, omelettes (£4.95), meaty or good vegetarian lasagne (£5.45), good steak and kidney pie (£5.95), grilled local trout (£6.95), chicken with garlic or stilton (£7.65), half a roast duck (£9.95), steaks (from £10.95), and daily specials like steak and mushroom pie (£5.95) or local wild boar in Black Sheep Bitter (£6.95); Sunday roast lunch (£4.95, best to book), and there may be cheese and crackers on the bar; the restaurant is no smoking. Well kept Black Sheep, Black Bull and Lightfoot, Cropton Two Pints, John Smiths, Theakstons Black Bull and Lightfoot, and Village Brewer White Boar Bitter (a local micro-brewery) on handpump, 56 malt whiskies, and decent wines. The Staffordshire bull terrier is called Kim. Darts, pool, dominoes, and cribbage; quoits. There are tables and chairs in the pretty garden, which has a superb view across Wensleydale; fishing nearby. Handy for Castle Bolton where Mary Queen of Scots was imprisoned. *(Recommended by JKW, J H and S A Harrop, Ray and Liz Monk, Lesley Sones, Richard Hathaway, P D and J Bickley, Paul S McPherson, Geoff and Angela Jaques, Jim Farmer, Ray and Liz Monk, Michael Butler, Andrew and Ruth Triggs, John Honnor, M J Morgan)*

Free house ~ Licensee Roger Stevens ~ Real ale ~ Meals and snacks ~ Restaurant ~ (01969) 622316 ~ Children in eating area of bar and in restaurant until 9 ~ Open 11-3, 6-11 ~ Two bedrooms: £18/£34

RIPPONDEN (W Yorks) SE0419 Map 7

Old Bridge

Priest Lane; from A58, best approach is Elland Road (opposite Golden Lion), park opposite the church in pub's car park and walk back over ancient hump-backed bridge

On the opposite side of the medieval pack horse bridge over the little River Ryburn from the church (and from this pub's popular restaurant), stands this friendly place – run for 32 years by the same licensee. The three communicating rooms are each on a slightly different level and have a relaxed atmosphere, oak settles built into the window recesses of the thick stone walls, antique oak tables, rush-seated chairs, a few well-chosen pictures, and a big wood-burning stove. Bar food (with prices unchanged since last year) includes a popular weekday lunchtime cold meat buffet which always has a joint of rare beef, as well as spiced ham, quiche, Scotch eggs and so on (£7.50, with a bowl of soup and coffee). In the evenings, and at lunchtime on Saturdays (when it's busy) dishes change quite often, but might include smoked trout pâté (£3.50), beef and lamb meatballs with spicy tomato sauce (£3.75), sauté of beef with walnuts, orange and ginger, fresh mild smoked haddock pancakes or chicken and broccoli lasagne (all £4.25), and puddings like sticky toffee pudding (£1.75); they will cut fresh sandwiches (from £1.80). Well kept Black Sheep Special, Ryburn Best, Timothy Taylors Best and Golden Mild, and a weekly guest beer on handpump, several malt whiskies, and interesting wines, many by the glass. *(Recommended by Monica Shelley, James Macrae, Laura Darlington, Gianluca Perinetti, Roger and Christine Mash, Ann and Bob Westerook, Mark Bradley, Stephen and Brenda Head, Geoffrey and Brenda Wilson, Neville Kenyon)*

Free house ~ Licensee Ian Beaumont, Manager Timothy Walker ~ Real ale ~ Meals and snacks (till 10) ~ Restaurant (not Sun) ~ (01422) 822595 ~ Children lunchtimes only and must be over 12 in restaurant ~ Open 11.30-3.30, 5.30-11; 12-11 Sat

ROBIN HOODS BAY (N Yorks) NZ9505 Map 10

Laurel

Village signposted off A171 S of Whitby

At the heart of one of the prettiest and most unspoilt fishing villages on the North East coast stands this cosy white pub. The friendly beamed main bar bustles with locals and visitors, and is decorated with old local photographs, Victorian prints and brasses, and lager bottles from all over the world; there's an open fire. Bar food consists of lunchtime sandwiches (from £1.20) and winter soup. Well kept Marstons Pedigree, Ruddles Best, John Smiths, and Theakstons Old Peculier on handpump; darts, shove-ha'penny, table skittles, dominoes, cribbage, video game. In summer, the hanging baskets and window boxes are lovely. *(Recommended by Jack and Philip Paxton, Mike and Wendy Proctor, Andrew Hazeldine, Mayur Shah)*

Free house ~ Lease: David Angood ~ Real ale ~ Lunchtime snacks ~ (01947) 880400 ~ Children in family room ~ Open 12-11 ~ Well equipped cottage to rent next to pub

ROSEDALE ABBEY (N Yorks) SE7395 Map 10

Milburn Arms

The easiest road to the village is through Cropton from Wrelton, off the A170 W of Pickering

On a warm summer day, the picnic tables on the terrace and in the garden here are a pleasant place to enjoy a pint of Bass, Stones, Theakstons Best, XB and Old Peculier, and a fortnightly guest well kept on handpump; the steep surrounding moorland is very fine. Inside, the L-shaped and beamed main bar is traditionally furnished and neatly kept, and has 30 malt whiskies, and seven good house wines by the glass. Good, interesting bar food includes sandwiches (from £1.95), home-made soup (£2.25), home-made potted duck liver with home-made chutney (£3.95), home-cured beef with piccalilli or black pudding with apples, onions and garlic (£4.50), breast of chicken wrapped in bacon in a tarragon and mushroom sauce or home-made steak and kidney pie (£5.95), baked cod with fresh crab crust and lemon hollandaise (£6.50), tagliatelle with fresh wild mushrooms and pesto sauce (£6.95), Aberdeen Angus sirloin steak (£9.25), daily specials like beef bourguignon with olive oil mash (£6.50), skewer of salmon, monkfish and king prawns (£6.95), and roast sea bass with bean sprouts and ginger (£9.50), and puddings such as home-made apple pie, steamed lemon and ginger pudding or treacle tart (£2.50); super breakfasts. The restaurant is no smoking. *(Recommended by Frank Cummins, David Surridge, Duncan Redpath, Lorraine Milburn, Martin Hickes, Bronwen and Steve Wrigley, David Ing, Mike and Maggie Betton, Julie Peters, G S and A Jaques, Joyce and Stephen Stackhouse, Roger and Christine Mash, Joy Heatherley)*

Free house ~ Licensee Terry Bentley ~ Real ale ~ Meals and snacks ~ Restaurant ~ (01751) 417312 ~ Well behaved children in eating area of bar till 8.30 ~ Open 11.30-3, 6.30-11 ~ Bedrooms: £44.50B/£74B

SAWLEY (N Yorks) SE2568 Map 7

Sawley Arms 🍷

Village signposted off B6265 W of Ripon

One of the main things readers have liked here this year is the warmth of the welcome and kind service – Mrs Hawes has been running this rather smart pub for 27 years now. A series of small turkey-carpeted, newly refurbished rooms has log fires and comfortable furniture ranging from small softly cushioned armed dining chairs and comfortable settees, to the wing armchairs down a couple of steps in a side snug; there may be daily papers and magazines to read, and a panelled area is no smoking. Good bar food includes lunchtime sandwiches, home-made soups (£2.30), salmon mousse or stilton, port and celery pâté (£3.95), steak pie, plaice mornay, chicken in mushroom sauce or steak pie (£5.75), and quite a few puddings such as lovely bread and butter pudding (£3.50); decent house wines and quiet piped music. The pub is handy for Fountains Abbey (the most extensive of the great monastic remains – floodlit on late summer Friday and Saturday evenings, with a live choir on the Saturday). The lovely gardens, flowering baskets and tubs do win awards (Britain in Bloom winner, twice) and a new summer house is planned. ***(Recommended by Mrs P J Pearce, F J Robinson, Gwen and Peter Andrews, Neville Kenyon, Dorothy and David Young, Maysie Thompson, Roger and Christine Mash, John and Joan Nash, A M McCarthy, Peter Race)***

Free house ~ Licensee Mrs June Hawes ~ Meals and snacks (not Sun or Mon evenings) ~ Restaurant ~ (01765) 620642 ~ Children in restaurant if over 9 ~ Open 11.30-3, 6.30-11; closed Mon evenings except bank holidays

SAXTON (N Yorks) SE4736 Map 7

Greyhound

Village signposted off B1217 Garforth—Tadcaster; so close to A1 and A162 N of Pontefract

Next to the church – where Lord Dacre who fell at the Battle of Towton in 1461 is buried upright on his horse – is this convivial village local which remains happily unchanged. The unspoilt, cosy and chatty taproom on the left has a coal fire burning in the Victorian fireplace in the corner, a cushioned window seat by the mouth of the corridor as well as other simple seats, and ochre Anaglypta walls and a dark panelled dado; an etched glass window looks into the snug with its sturdy mahogany wall settle curving round one corner, other traditional furniture, fancy shades on the brass lamps, and browning Victorian wallpaper. Down at the end of the corridor is another highly traditional room, with darts, shove-ha'penny, and dominoes. Well kept (and very cheap) Sam Smiths OB tapped from casks behind the counter; during the week, they will make sandwiches on request – at the weekends they are on offer. In summer the pub is very pretty with a climbing rose, passion flower, and bedding plants, and a couple of picnic tables in the side courtyard. This is also the community Post Office (Monday, Tuesday and Thursday 8.45am to 10.45am). Lotherton Hall Museum is nearby. ***(Recommended by Chris Westmoreland, Thomas Nott)***

Sam Smiths ~ Manager Colin McCarthy ~ Real ale ~ Sandwiches (lunchtime) ~ (01937) 557202 ~ Children in tap room ~ Open 12-3, 5.30-11; 11-11 Sat

SETTLE (N Yorks) SD8264 Map 7

Royal Oak 🛏

Market Place; town signposted from A65 Skipton—Kendal

Although the licensees in this large stone inn remain the same, they are installing a manager to help them. A good mix of customers creates a bustling, friendly atmosphere in the almost open-plan bar – though enough walls have been kept to divide it into decent-sized separate areas. There are plenty of tables, dark squared oak or matching oak-look panelling, and a couple of elegantly carved arches with more carving above the fireplaces. Lights vary from elaborate curly brass candelabra through attractive table lamps and standard lamps with old-fashioned shades to unexpectedly modernist wall cubes. Bar food includes home-made soup (£1.95), sandwiches (closed, Danish or warm french bread from £2.45, Jamaican with prawn, pineapple, banana and coleslaw £4.40), rich game terrine with plum sauce (£3.40), filled yorkshire puddings (£4), savoury vegetable pancakes (£4.50), ploughman's (£4.90), battered haddock (£5.80), steak and Guinness pie (£6), gammon and egg (£6.40), sirloin steak (£9.50), children's dishes (£3), and puddings (from £2.35). Well kept Boddingtons Bitter, Flowers IPA and Original, Whitbreads Castle Eden, and maybe guest beers on handpump, and decent wines; courteous service. Readers say the Settle & Carlisle railway (only 5 minutes away) is worth a trip, and the Tuesday market here is very good. Some road noise (absurdly heavy quarry lorries cut through the attractive small town – they should certainly be kept out). *(Recommended by Lynn Sharpless, Bob Eardley, Mr and Mrs R Behson, JKW, Karen Eliot, Brian Horner, Brenda Arthur, Dave and Carole Jones, Mary Moore, Catheryn and Richard Hicks, Mark Bradley)*

Whitbreads ~ Tenants Brian and Sheila Longrigg ~ Real ale ~ Meals and snacks (noon-10pm) ~ Restaurant ~ (01729) 822561/823102 ~ Children welcome until 8.30 ~ Singer/pianist/guitar Fri evenings ~ Open 11-11 ~ Bedrooms: £31.50B/£52.25B

SHEFFIELD (S Yorks) SK3687 Map 7

Fat Cat £

23 Alma St

Much enjoyed by readers, the cheap own-brewed beer here – Kelham Island Bitter – is named after the nearby Industrial Museum; they also serve well kept Marstons Pedigree, Timothy Taylors Landlord, and Theakstons Old Peculier, and six interesting guest beers on handpump (usually including another beer from Kelham Island), and keep foreign bottled beers (particularly Belgian ones), country wines, and farm cider. Cheap bar food (with prices unchanged since last year) includes sandwiches, soup, and main dishes like pork and pepper casserole, pasta with nutty Cheshire sauce, salmon and potato pie (all £2.50), puddings such as creamy nectarine and chocolate crunch (80p); Sunday lunch; cribbage, dominoes and Monday evening quiz night 10pm. The two small downstairs rooms have coal fires and simple wooden tables and burgundy-coloured seats around the walls, with a few advertising mirrors and an enamelled placard for Richdales Sheffield Kings Ale; the one on the left is no-smoking. Steep steps take you up to another similarly simple room (which may be booked for functions) with some attractive prints of old Sheffield; there are picnic tables in a fairylit back courtyard. *(Recommended by David and Shelia, Jack and Philip Paxton, R N Hutton, R Holmes, F Reynolds, Terry Barlow, Paul Cartledge)*

Own brew ~ Licensee Stephen Fearn ~ Real ale ~ Lunchtime meals and snacks ~ (01742) 728195 ~ Children allowed upstairs if not booked, until 8pm ~ Open 12-3, 5.30-11; closed 25/26 Dec

SHELLEY (W Yorks) SE2112 Map 7

Three Acres

Roydhouse; B6116, off A629 SE of Huddersfield

This 18th-c former coaching inn is more hotel and restaurant than pub, with style and prices to match, but over the years it's given readers a good many really enjoyable meals out. Moreover, its roomy and pleasantly civilised traditional lounge bar, with old prints and so forth, has well kept changing ales such as Holt, Plant and Deakin Deakin's Downfall, Mansfield Bitter, Riding and Old Baily, Timothy Taylors Landlord, and Charles Wells Bombardier on handpump, and a good choice of malt whiskies. Bar food includes yorkshire pudding with onion gravy (£2.75), a wide range of thoughtfully prepared sandwiches such as home-made cumberland sausage with fried onions and mild mustard mayonnaise, poached salmon with cucumber and watercress or ox tongue, tomato and piccalilli (from £2.75), and changing dishes such as home-made soup (£2.95), moules marinières (£4.95), deep-fried brie with cherry tomato compote, salad and walnut dressing (£4.95), breast of smoked chicken and grapes with lemon mayonnaise, crispy lardons and salad (£6.50), steak hache with caramelised onions, salmon fishcakes with hollandaise sauce, a freshly carved roast of the day or a fine steak and kidney pie (£6.95), and king prawns piri-piri (£7.95). Many readers however opt for the set-price three-course restaurant lunch (£12.95), which might include monkfish with bacon, mille feuilles with salmon and scallops, sautéed kidneys with duck and onion confit, warm goat cheese salad or warm venison sausage salad, and main dishes such as liver and onions, pheasant, quails, or sea trout with scallops. The choice of wines, admittedly not cheap, is so exceptional that one wine-merchant reader could not recall coming across anything to match it in other comparably smart pubs. Service is good and friendly even when busy, and the relaxing atmosphere may be helped along by a pianist playing light music. There are fine views across to Emley Moor, occasionally livened up by the local hunt passing. Breakfasts are excellent. *(Recommended by Stephen and Brenda Head, Michael Butler, Neil Townend, Keith and Margaret Kettell, John Allsopp, David R Shillitoe)*

Free house ~ Licensees Neil Truelove, Brian Orme ~ Real ale ~ Meals and snacks (12-2, 7.30-9) ~ Restaurant ~ (01484) 602606 ~ Children welcome ~ Open 12-3, 6-11; closed Sat lunchtime ~ Bedrooms:£47.50B/£57.50

SICKLINGHALL (N Yorks) SE3648 Map 7

Scotts Arms

Leaving Wetherby W on A661, fork left signposted Sicklinghall

The friendly main bar here is divided up by stubs of the old dividing walls which give it a less open-plan feel. Seats are built into cosy little alcoves cut into the main walls, there's a curious sort of double-decker fireplace with its upper hearth intricately carved, and a big inglenook fireplace. Bar food includes sandwiches, soup (£1.55), burgers (from £2.65), vegetable lasagne (£3.95), steak and mushroom pie or fish and chips (£4.25), gammon and pineapple (£5), and puddings (£1.95). Well kept Theakstons Best, XB and Old Peculier, and a guest such as Morlands Old Speckled Hen on handpump; darts, dominoes, pinball, fruit machine, video game, CD juke box and unobtrusive piped music, and down steps a separate room has pool. In summer, the hanging baskets, flowering tubs and neat garden here are a riot of colour; there are seats and tables, a children's play area with slide, climbing frame and wooden animals, and summer barbecues. *(Recommended by Mrs P J Pearce, David Varney, David Watson, Roy Bromell, Dr A and Dr A C Jackson, Paul Cartledge, Pat Crabb, Margaret Mason, David Thompson, Mark Bradley)*

S & N ~ Manager Carl Lang ~ Real ale ~ Meals and snacks (not 25 Dec) ~ Restaurant (not Sun evening) ~ (01937) 582100 ~ Children in eating area of bar ~ Live band Sun evenings ~ Open 12-3, 6-11; 12-11 Sat

SKIDBY (N Yorks) TA0133 Map 8

Half Moon

Main Street; off A164

New licensees have taken over here since our last edition, and though they plan to make a few changes to the menu, they intend keeping the emphasis on what's always been the highlight – the unique loaf-sized but feather-light filled yorkshire puddings. Fingers crossed that they've inherited the closely guarded secret ingredient that has made these so popular in all the years we've known the place. The wide range generally runs from traditional onion gravy (£2.60, or £3 with vegetarian gravy), through chilli and curry (£4.55) to roast beef (£4.90); other efficiently served dishes might include soup (£1.60), burgers (from £2.55) and steak and kidney pie with suet pastry (£4). Brightly decorated and rather homely, the old-fashioned partly panelled front tap-room has long cushioned wall benches, old elm tables, a little high shelf of foreign beer bottles and miniatures, a tiled floor, and a fire. The more spacious communicating back rooms have an airier feel, as well as an unusually big clock; darts, bar billiards, shove ha'penny, dominoes, cribbage, fruit machine, piped music. Part of the eating area is no-smoking until 8.30pm. John Smiths and Marstons Pedigree on handpump, with a wide range of malt whiskies and an Irish gin. The landscaped garden area beside the car park has a children's play area with a suspended net maze, and in summer a bar with sweets, ice cream and fizzy drinks. A black and white windmill is nearby. *(Recommended by M J Morgan, Stephen Brown, Andy and Jane Beardsley, David and Shelia, Andy and Jill Kassube, Jane Kingsbury, Joy Heatherley, J S M Sheldon, J L Phillips, John Hazel; reports on the new regime please)*

John Smiths (Courage) ~ Lease: Betty Stephanie Bielby and Ruth Auchterlounie ~ Meals and snacks (noon till 10) ~ (01482) 843403 ~ Children in eating area of bar; no under 14s after 8.30 ~ Live music Tues, rock'n'roll first Fri of month ~ Open 11-11; cl evening Dec 25

SOWERBY BRIDGE (W Yorks) SE0623 Map 7

Moorings 

Off Bolton Brow (A58) opposite Java Restaurant

On a warm day you can sit at the tables on the terrace outside this attractively converted ex-canal warehouse and enjoy looking over the basin where the Rochdale and Calder & Hebble Canals meet. Inside, the spacious beamed bar has big windows and stone walls and is decorated with grain sacks and old pulley wheels and so forth; there's a separate eating area. The lounge bar is pleasantly furnished with wooden stools, tile-top tables and fabric-covered seats built against the stripped stone walls (which are decorated with old waterways maps and modern canal pictures), and the big windows and very high ceiling give a relaxed and airy atmosphere. A lobby leads to a no-smoking family room alongside, similarly furnished; cribbage, fruit machine and piped music. Good, reasonably priced bar food includes home-made soup (from £1.50), filled granary cobs (from £2.75), home-made chicken liver pâté (£2.95), filled baked potatoes (from £2.95), vegetable bake (£4.50), home-made pie of the day or gammon (£5.95), steaks (from £8.95), daily specials, puddings (£1.95), children's dishes (£1.95), and Sunday roast (£4.50). Well kept Moorhouses Bitter, Theakstons Best and XB, Youngers Scotch and a regularly changing guest beer on handpump, lots of bottled Belgian beers, and quite a few malt whiskies. *(Recommended by Laura Darlington, Gianluca Perinetti, Andrew and Ruth Triggs, R E and P Pearce, Mike and Ruth Dooley, Mark Bradley, E J and M W Corrin, Paul Boot, J L Phillips, Patrick Clancy, Roxanne Chamberlain)*

Free house ~ Lease: Miss Christine Krasocki ~ Real ale ~ Meals and snacks (till 10 Fri/Sat; not Sun evening) ~ Restaurant (not Sun evening) ~ (01422) 833940 ~ Children in no-smoking family room ~ Open 11.30-3, 5.30(6.15 Mon)-11; Sat 11-11

STARBOTTON (N Yorks) SD9574 Map 7

Fox & Hounds 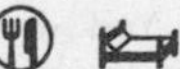

B6160 Upper Wharfedale rd N of Kettlewell; OS Sheet 98, map reference 953749

Outside this prettily placed little Upper Wharfedale inn there are seats in a sheltered corner that enjoy the view over the hills. But it's the good, interesting food that most people come here for: home-made soups such as courgette and broccoli or chicken and vegetable (£1.85), good devilled mushrooms (£2.50), stilton and walnut pâté (£2.95), almond risotto with peanut sauce or mixed bean casserole (£4.75), steak and mushroom pie (£5.75), chicken and leek crumble (£5.95), good Moroccan-style lamb (£6.95), and puddings like honey and brandy cheesecake, fudgy nut and raisin pie or sticky toffee pudding (£2.20); at lunchtime they also offer filled french bread, ploughman's, and filled yorkshire puddings, with evening chicken and fish dishes (from £7.25), and daily specials; the dining area is no smoking. The bar has traditional solid furniture on the flagstones, a collection of plates on the walls, whisky jugs hanging from the high beams supporting ceiling boards, a big stone fireplace (with an enormous fire in winter), and a warmly welcoming atmosphere. Well kept Black Sheep, Theakstons Best and guests like Marstons Pedigree and Moorhouses Premier on handpump, and around 36 malt whiskies. Dominoes, cribbage, chess, draughts, and well reproduced, unobtrusitve piped music. *(Recommended by Wayne Wheeler, John and Chris Simpson, A D Shore, Neil and Angela Hunter, TBB, John and Judith Wells, Paula Shillaw, Keven Whitcombe, Andrew McKeand)*

Free house ~ Licensees James and Hilary McFadyen ~ Real ale ~ Meals and snacks (see below) ~ (01756) 760269 ~ Children welcome ~ Open 11.30-3, 6.30-11; closed Mon Nov-Mar; closed Jan-mid-Feb ~ Bedrooms: £30S/£50S

SUTTON UPON DERWENT (N Yorks) SE7047 Map 7

St Vincent Arms

B1228 SE of York

While this cosy old family-run pub has established quite a reputation as a place to eat, it's also ideal for drinkers, with an excellent range of usually nine well kept beers on handpump. Exceptionally well priced (the cheapest brew is around 20p less than what we found to be the county average), the choice usually consists of Boddingtons, John Smiths, Mansfield Riding and Timothy Taylors Landlord, and regulary changing ales like Adnams Extra, Charles Wells Bombardier, Fullers London Pride, Rudgate Viking, or Shepherd Neame Spitfire; also a range of malt whiskies, and very reasonably priced spirits. Good friendly service. The landlord's son is a chef, and the excellently presented bar food is all home-made; generously served dishes might include sandwiches (from £1.55), steak and kidney pie or lasagne (£5.50), steaks (from £9), and changing specials such as fresh fish, sausage and mash (£3), pork stroganoff (£7), a daily stir-fry (£7.50) and duck breast in orange (£8.50). Booking might be a good idea, especially at weekends. One restaurant area is no smoking. The parlour-like, panelled front bar has traditional high-backed settles, a cushioned bow-window seat, windsor chairs and a coal fire; another lounge and separate dining room open off. No games or music. An attractive garden has tables and seats, and there are pleasant walks along the nearby River Derwent. The pub is named after the Admiral who was granted the village and lands by the nation as thanks for his successful commands – and for coping with Nelson's infatuation with Lady Hamilton. *(Recommended by Jeff Seaman, Roger A Bellingham, Ann and Colin Hunt, C A Hall, Dr P R Davis, Geraldine Liddell)*

Free house ~ Licensee Phil Hopwood ~ Real ale ~ Meals and snacks ~ Restaurant ~ (01904) 608349 ~ Children welcome (must be well behaved in restaurant) ~ Open 11.30-3, 6-11; closed eve Dec 25

TERRINGTON (N Yorks) SE6571 Map 7

Bay Horse

W of Malton; off B1257 at Hovingham (towards York, eventually signposted left) or Slingsby (towards Castle Howard, then right); can also be reached off A64 via Castle Howard, or via Welburn and Ganthorpe

In an unspoilt village on one of the rolling old coach roads that make the most of the Howardian Hill views, this charming country pub has a peaceful and timeless atmosphere. The cosy lounge bar has a roaring log fire, country prints, china on delft shelves and magazines to read, and a traditional public bar has darts and an enthusiastic dominoes school. There's a dining area handsomely furnished in oak, and a back family conservatory with farm tools. Good generously served food includes sandwiches (from £1.65), ploughman's (£4.95), starters such as Wensleydale fritters with chives, celery and walnuts (£2.65), warm buttered crab with toast (£3), and terrine of wild boar and chestnuts (£3.50), with main courses like steak and kidney pie (£5.25), fish pie with Scarborough Woof, bacon and prawns (£5.95), chicken with sausage, sweetcorn and herbs topped with asparagus sauce (£6.50), vegetarian dishes like hazelnut and vegetable loaf or quorn, leek and red wine bake (£5.25), and puddings like blueberry and lemon cream meringue or syrup and walnut tart (£2.25); children's menu (from £1.25). Welcoming and cheerful licensees, excellent friendly service, well kept John Smiths, Youngers IPA, and Theakstons best, Old Peculier and XB on handpump. There are tables out in a small but attractively planted garden. *(Recommended by Mr and Mrs R P Begg, Ann and Colin Hunt; more reports please)*

Free house ~ Licensees Robert and Jill Snowdon ~ Real ale ~ Meals and snacks (not Sun evening, not Tues) ~ (01653) 648416 ~ Children in conservatory ~ Open 12-3, 6.30-11; closed 25 Dec

THORNTON WATLASS (N Yorks) SE2486 Map 10

Buck

Village signposted off B6268 Bedale—Masham

After nine years here (with the same two cooks), the friendly licensees are happy to report that things are much as before – though they have added two new bedrooms this year. The pleasantly traditional right-hand bar has a relaxed atmosphere, handsomely upholstered old-fashioned wall settles on the carpet, a fine mahogany bar counter, a high shelf packed with ancient bottles, several mounted fox masks and brushes (the Bedale hunt meets in the village), and a brick fireplace. Good, popular food at lunchtime might include filled french bread (on Sundays, stuffed with hot roast pork £2.25 or roast beef £2.50), soups such as cheese and ale or carrot and apple (£1.95), a good rarebit with Wensleydale cheese and local ale on toast with crispy bacon (£3.25), locally smoked kipper and scrambled egg (£3.95), lovely mussels in basil and cream sauce (£3.95 starter, £4.95 main course), favourites such as lasagne or Whitby cod and chips (£5.70), beef braised in real ale (£6.50), breast of duck in a honey and soy sauce (£8.95), pork fillet in creamed mushrooms (£7.25), and fresh salmon fillet in a cucumber and dill sauce; good vegetables. The restaurant is no smoking; summer weekend barbecues. Well kept Black Sheep, John Smiths, Theakstons Best, and a guest beer on handpump, and around 40 malt whiskies. The beamed and panelled dining room is hung with large prints of old Thornton Watlass cricket teams. A bigger plainer bar has darts, pool, and dominoes. The low stone building – with its lovely hanging baskets – looks past a grand row of sycamores to the village cricket green (they have a team), and has two quoits pitches in the garden (with league matches on summer Wednesday evenings, practice Sunday morning and Tuesday evening). Trout fishing on the Ure, and an equipped children's play area. Their walking holidays remain popular. *(Recommended by Viv Middlebrook, J R Whetton, Allen Sharp, Philip and Elizabeth Hawkins, M J Morgan, E R Shlackman, Frank Davidson, Geoff and Angela Jaques, Tina and David Woods-Taylor, G Roberts, RB)*

Free house ~ Licensees Michael and Margaret Fox ~ Real ale ~ Meals and snacks (not 25 Dec) ~ Restaurant ~ (01677) 422461 ~ Well behaved children welcome ~ Organ singalong Sat evening, 60s/70s, country & western Sun evening ~ Open 11-2.30, 6-11; 11-11 Sat; closed evening 25 Dec ~ Bedrooms: £30S/£40(£48S)

THRESHFIELD (N Yorks) SD9763 Map 7

Old Hall

B6265, just on the Skipton side of its junction with B6160 near Grassington

This is the sort of place that people like to linger in – and there's a happy mix of locals and visitors creating a good, lively atmosphere. The three communicating rooms have simple, cushioned pews built into the white walls, a high beam-and-plank ceiling hung with pots, unfussy decorations such as old Cadburys advertisements and decorative plates on a high delft shelf, and a tall well blacked kitchen range. Using fresh, seasonal ingredients, the good bar food (with prices unchanged since last year) might include a crispy pancake stuffed with ricotta cheese, leeks and mushrooms (£2.95), chicory wrapped in Bavarian smoked ham with gruyere cheese (£3.45), grilled haloumi cheese topped with a lime and caper dressing or a vegetarian antipasta of artichokes, forest mushrooms, roasted peppers and Italian onion (£3.50), late breakfast (the home-made sausages are lovely), warm salad of duck with an orange citrus dressing (£3.75), gado gado – stir fried cabbage, chillis and peppers in a satay sauce – or nasi goreng (£5.95), pan-fried Scarborough woof with garlic, mushrooms and smoked bacon (£6.25), chicken breast marinaded in grapefruit and honey (£6.75), fillet of fresh haddock with a tomato and garlic sauce (£7.95), guinea fowl cooked in a coriander and cumin sauce or lovely individual lamb joint with redcurrant and mint sauce (£8.95), and puddings like passion fruit torte, stilton and pear pie or bread and butter pudding (£2.25); get there early to bag a table. Well kept Theakstons Best, Timothy Taylors Bitter and Landlord and Youngers Scotch on handpump, with guest beers in summer and quite a few malt whiskies. Darts, dominoes, and maybe piped pop music. A neat side garden, partly gravelled, with young shrubs and a big sycamore has some tables and an aviary with cockatiels and zebra finches. This is, of course, a fine base for Dales walking; there's a 15th-century cottage behind the inn for hire. *(Recommended by Gwen and Peter Andrews, JKW, Bob and Maggie Atherton, Wayne Brindle, Graham Bush, M Joyner, Paul J Bispham, A D Shore, Dr and Mrs P J S Crawshaw, Prof S Barnett, Mary Moore, Brian Kneale, Stephen and Brenda Head, M E A Horler, Jim Paul, Andrew Shore, Neville Kenyon, Nicola Thomas, Paul Dickinson, Tony Hall)*

Free house ~ Licensees Ian and Amanda Taylor ~ Real ale ~ Meals and snacks (not Sun evening, not Mon) ~ Restaurant (not winter Sun evenings) ~ (01756) 752441 ~ Children welcome ~ Open 11.30-3, 6-11 (closed Mon evening) ~ Bedrooms: £25/£35

WAKEFIELD (W Yorks) SE3321 Map 7

Tap & Spile

77 Westgate End

The new licensees have carried on the fine range of real ales kept in this traditional gas-lit pub. As well as their regulars like Tap & Spile Premium (brewed for them by Ushers) and Charles Wells Eagle, there are guests like Hadrian Gladiator Bitter, Hardington Special Pale, Hambleton Thoroughbred, Marston Moor Cromwell Bitter, and Steam Packet Chatterley on handpump. There's a fine chatty and relaxed atmosphere in the main bar with its flagstones, leatherette cushioned built-in wooden wall seats with high backs, snob-screens, Victorian-style flowery wallpaper, honey-coloured vertical-planked dado, and brewery mirrors; several little rooms leading off the corridor; attractive Victorian fireplaces with tiled surrounds. Cheap bar food now includes sandwiches (£1.30; with salad and crisps £1.80), filled yorkshire puddings (from £1.30), and daily specials like steak in ale pie, Mediterranean chicken or pork chops in mustard sauce (£3). No children. *(Recommended by Michael Butler, Wayne Brindle, Ian and Nita Cooper, Gerry McGarry, Mark Bradley, Dave and Carole Jones)*

Free house ~ Licensees Ann and Jim Haigh~ Real ale ~ Lunchtime meals and snacks (12-2) ~ (01924) 375887 ~ Open 12-11

WASS (N Yorks) SE5679 Map 7

Wombwell Arms

Back road W of Ampleforth; or follow brown tourist-attraction sign for Byland Abbey off A170 Thirsk—Helmsley

Although it's the interesting food that people like most here, there's warm praise from readers for the friendly welcome, good wines, and very nice atmosphere. The little central bar is cosy and tasteful and the three low-beamed dining areas are comfortable and inviting and incorporate a former 18th-c granary. Using fresh often local ingredients, lunchtime food might include sandwiches (from £1.95), lovely ploughman's with home-made pickles (£3.95), hot salad of chicken livers (£4.25), smoked salmon and scrambled eggs (£4.95), and specials like venison sausages in red cabbage (£5.15), cashew nut curry or tagliatelle with a cream, bacon and pepper sauce (£5.50), chicken provencale (£5.95), and minted lamb with rosemary (£6.75); evening dishes such as chicken in red wine, shallot and bacon sauce (£7.35), baked fillet of sea bass or breast of guinea fowl (£8.25), and sirloin steak with a three mustard sauce (£10.95), with puddings like bread and butter pudding, treacle tart or sticky toffee pudding (£2.95); lots of good crisp vegetables and vegetarian options. Well kept Black Sheep, Timothy Taylors Landlord, and a guest such as Everards Old Original or Wadworths Old Timer on handpump, and decent malt whiskies; dominoes, Scrabble, Trivial Pursuits. *(Recommended by Andy and Jane Beardsley, John and Chris Simpson, Bob and Maggie Atherton, John and Pippa Stock, SRP, David Surridge, W Rinaldi-Butcher, Paul McPherson, W C M Jones, H Bramwell, Pat Crabb, John and Carol Holden, Wendy Arnold, G W H Kerby)*

Free house ~ Licensees Alan and Lynda Evans ~ Real ale ~ Meals and snacks ~ (01347) 868280 ~ Children in eating area of bar (no under-5s evening) ~ Open 12-2.30, 7-11; closed Sun evening and all day Mon in winter, closed Mon lunchtime in summer, and 10 days in Jan ~ Bedrooms: £24.50B/£49B

WATH-IN-NIDDERDALE (N Yorks) SE1467 Map 7

Sportsmans Arms

Nidderdale rd off B6265 in Pateley Bridge; village and pub signposted over hump bridge on right after a couple of miles

Most people come to this delightful 17th-c inn to enjoy the marvellous food – though there is a bar where locals do drop in for just a drink. A choice of fresh fish might include moules marinières, fresh dressed crab, Scarborough woof sautéed in butter with prawns, almonds and capers, scallops tossed in garlic butter and glazed with mozzarella or fresh monkfish in a grape and mushroom sauce, delicious plaice veronique, and Whitby turbot on a bed of spinach and sorrel with a wine, grape and mousseline sauce (all from £6.95-£7.50); also, good home-made soup (£2.75), ploughman's with locally-made cheeses (£4.60), prawns in wholemeal bread with a tomato flavoured mayonnaise (£5.90), breast of local chicken sautéed and served with garlic butter or marvellous loin of pork with a mustard and mushroom sauce (£6.90), and puddings like crème brûlée or chocolate roulade (£3) and a tremendous range of 18 cheeses (many local). Excellent 3-course restaurant Sunday lunch (£13.50). There's a very sensible and extensive wine list with an emphasis on the New World, good choice of malt whiskies, several Russian vodkas, and attentive service; open fire, dominoes. Benches and tables outside. *(Recommended by Gwen and Peter Andrews, Bob and Maggie Atherton, Andrew and Marian Ruston, Geoffrey and Brenda Wilson, Nicola Thomas, Paul Dickinson, C H Stride, Peter Race, K and R Beaver, Andrew Shore, Stephen and Brenda Head; more reports please)*

Free house ~ Licensee Ray Carter ~ Meals and snacks ~ Evening restaurant (not Sun evening; they do Sun lunches) ~ (01423) 711306 ~ Children welcome until 9pm ~ Open 12-3, 6.30-11; closed 25 Dec ~ Bedrooms: £35(£38S)/£55(£58S)

WIDDOP (W Yorks) SD9333 Map 7

Pack Horse

The Ridge; from A646 on W side of Hebden Bridge, turn off at Heptonstall signpost (as it's a sharp turn, coming out of Hebden Bridge road signs direct you around a turning circle), then follow Slack and Widdop signposts; can also be reached from Nelson and Colne, on high, pretty road; OS Sheet 103, map ref 952317

This year, three bedrooms have been opened up in this busy moorland pub – which will no doubt prove popular with walkers. The bar has window seats cut into the partly panelled stripped stone walls that take in the moorland view, sturdy furnishings, and warm winter fires. Generous helpings of good bar food (with prices unchanged since last year) include sandwiches (from £1.30, double-deckers from £2.40, open sandwiches on french bread from £3), burgers (from £2.50), cottage hotpot (£2.95), ploughman's (£3.50), home-made steak and kidney pie (£4.50), steaks (from £6.25), and specials such as grilled halibut or sea bass and rack of lamb (£8.95); vegetarian dishes and puddings. Well kept Black Sheep, Theakstons XB, Thwaites Bitter and Craftsman, and Youngers IPA on handpump; around 100 single malt whiskies, and some Irish ones as well. There are seats outside. *(Recommended by Laura Darlington, Gianluca Perinetti, Patrick Renouf, Cynthia Waller)*

Free house ~ Licensee Andrew Hollinrake ~ Real ale ~ Meals and snacks (till 10pm; not winter Mon evenings or winter weekdays) ~ (01422) 842803 ~ Children welcome until 8pm ~ Open 12-3, 7-11; closed weekday lunchtimes and Mon Oct-Easter ~ Bedrooms: £28B/£40B

WIGGLESWORTH (N Yorks) SD8157 Map 7

Plough

B6478

This is a pleasant place to stay and there are various little rooms surrounding the bar area – some spartan yet cosy, others smart and plush, including the no-smoking panelled dining room and snug; there's also a conservatory restaurant with fine panoramic views of the Dales and Ingleborough. Popular bar food includes daily specials like rabbit pie, stir-fry vegetable pancake with neapolitan sauce or salmon with a smoked salmon mousse and hollandaise sauce, as well as an american-style menu with pit barbecue dishes (meat is cooked slowly over aromatic woods like hickory, mesquite and oak): oak-smoked eggs with home-made mayonnaise (£1.95), filled savoury pancakes (from £3.95), sandwiches like hot beef or Cajun chicken (from £4.25), hickory chicken (£4.95), salads (from £4.95), halibut steak smoked in mesquite (£6.50), a huge shoulder of lamb (£7.25), smoked steak (£9.45), puddings like pecan pie or cheesecake (£2.50), and children's dishes (from £2.50). Well kept Boddingtons and Tetleys on handpump and a decent wine list; good, friendly service; darts. The garden is attractive. *(Recommended by Steve and Julie Cocking, JKW, Anthony Barnes, Joan and Tony Walker, John Allsopp, K H Frostick)*

Free house ~ Licensee Brian Goodall ~ Real ale ~ Meals and snacks ~ Restaurant ~ (01729) 840243 ~ Children in eating area of bar and in restaurant ~ Open 11.30-2.30, 7-11 ~ Bedrooms: £32.50B/£55B

WIGHILL (N Yorks) SE4746 Map 7

White Swan ★

Village signposted from Tadcaster; also easily reached from A1 Wetherby bypass – take Thorpe Arch Trading Estate turnoff, then follow Wighill signposts; OS Sheet 105 map reference 476468

As well as the tiny characterful front bar – popular with locals – this homely and unspoilt village pub also has a bar opposite with lots of racing prints, a small lobby that's also a favoured place for locals to gather, and a back bar with a mix of old chairs and tables, and quite a few decorative plates, and old theatrical memorabilia and sporting prints on the wall; a dining room leads off this; open fires in most rooms. Bar snacks include sandwiches (from £1.50 to jumbo ones at £3.30), pies such as steak, game, fish and chicken (from £4.20), and puddings (£2.50); on Sunday they do a roast lunch only (three courses £8.50), and they do a three course evening meal in the restaurant Thursday-Saturday evenings (£14.50). Well kept Boddingtons, Marstons Pedigree, Stones, and Tetleys Bitter on handpump; piped music. There's a terrace overlooking the garden where there are lots of seats. *(Recommended by Dave Braisted, Tim and Sue Halstead, Chris Westmoreland, B D Atkin, Paul Cartledge, Mark Bradley)*

Free house ~ Licensee Mrs Rita Arundale ~ Real ale ~ Meals and snacks (not Sun or Mon evenings) ~ Restaurant ~ (01937) 832217 ~ Children in restaurant or family room ~ Open 12-3, 6-11

WORMALD GREEN (N Yorks) SE3065 Map 7

Cragg Lodge

A61 Ripon—Harrogate, about half way

Probably the widest choice of malt whiskies in the world is housed in this comfortably modernised dining pub. There are nearly 1,000 of them, including two dozen Macallans going back to 1937. They have 16 price bands, between £1.15 and £6.50, depending on rarity – with a 17th 'by negotiation' for their unique 1919 Campbelltown. Also, well kept Tetleys Bitter and Theakstons Best, XB and Old Peculier on handpump, several distinguished brandies, and mature vintage port by the glass. The big open-plan bar is laid out for eating and has Mouseman furniture as well as little upholstered chairs around dark rustic tables, horse brasses and pewter tankards hanging from side beams, a dark joist-and-plank ceiling, and a coal fire. Bar food at lunchtime includes soup (£1.30), sandwiches (from £1.35), ploughman's (£2.80), home-made steak and kidney pie (£3.50), vegetarian nut cutlets or lasagne (£3.90), gammon and egg (£4.50), steaks (from £7.50), and a daily roast; in the evenings, there's a larger, more elaborate menu, with more emphasis on fish such as halibut Bretonne (£6), fish pie (£6.50), and salmon and plaice in a white wine and grape sauce (£6.80). The restaurant is no smoking. Shove-ha'penny, cribbage, dominoes and piped music. There are picnic tables under cocktail parasols on the side terrace, with more in a sizeable garden and pretty hanging baskets in summer. The pub is popular with older people. *(Recommended by Mary Moore, David Surridge, Kevin Potts, Paul Cartledge; more reports please)*

Free house ~ Licensee Garfield Parvin ~ Real ale ~ Meals and snacks ~ Restaurant (not Sun evening) ~ (01765) 677214 ~ Children in eating area of bar ~ Open 11.30-2.30, 6-11 ~ Bedrooms: £30B/£45B

YORK (N Yorks) SE5951 Map 7

Black Swan

Peaseholme Green; inner ring road, E side of centre; the inn has a good car park

Deservedly popular, this interesting pub is an enjoyable and surprisingly unspoilt place. The busy black-beamed back bar has wooden settles along the walls, some cushioned stools, and a throne-like cushioned seat in the vast brick inglenook, where there's a coal fire in a grate with a spit and some copper cooking utensils. The cosy panelled front bar, with its little serving hatch, is similarly furnished but smaller and more restful. The crooked-floored hall that runs along the side of both bars has a fine period staircase (leading up to a room fully panelled in oak, with an antique tiled fireplace). Under the new licensee, good bar food includes sandwiches (£1.95), filled french sticks (£3.25), generously filled giant yorkshire puddings, 6oz gammon steak, home-made steak pie or vegetable curry (all £3.95), and ploughman's, home-made lasagne or ham and mushroom tagliatelle (£4.50). The dining area is no-smoking. Well kept Bass, Stones, Timothy Taylors Landlord and Worthingtons on handpump. If the car park is full, it's worth knowing that there's a big public one next door. The timbered and jettied facade here and original lead-latticed windows in the twin gables are very fine indeed. *(Recommended by Chris Westmoreland, Jamie and Ruth Lyons, Ann and Colin Hunt)*

Bass ~ Manager Pat O'Connell ~ Real ale ~ Meals and snacks (11.30-2.30, 5-8 Mon-Thurs; no food weekend evenings) ~ (01904) 625236 ~ Children in separate room ~ Folk Thurs evening ~ Open 11-11 ~ Bedrooms: £25B/£50B

Pubs staying open all afternoon are listed at the back of the book.

Olde Starre

Stonegate; pedestrians-only street in centre, far from car parks

As this is in one of Yorks's prettiest streets, visitors tend to pop in here while shopping – it is the city's oldest licensed pub (1644). The main bar has original panelling, green plush wall seats, a large servery running the length of the room, and a large leaded window with red plush curtains at the far end. Several other little rooms lead off the porch-like square hall – one with its own food servery, one with panelling and some prints, and a third with cream wallpaper and dado; the tap room is no smoking. Well kept Ruddles County, John Smiths Best, and Theakstons Best and XB on handpump, and decent whiskies; piped music, fruit machine and CD juke box. Bar food includes sandwiches (£2.50), vegetarian burger (£3.50), ploughman's, steak and kidney pie or lamb's liver, onion and sausage (£3.95), half roast chicken (£4.35), and puddings (£1.95); Sunday roast lunch (£4.50); helpful staff. Parts of the building date back to 900 and the cellar was used as a hospital in the Civil War. *(Recommended by John Fazakerley, Mark Walker, Andrew and Ruth Triggs, M Borthwick, Ann and Colin Hunt, Jamie and Ruth Lyons, J R Whetton, Paul Cartledge)*

S & N ~ Managers Bill and Susan Embleton ~ Real ale ~ Meals and snacks (11.30-3, 5.30-8) ~ (01904) 623063 ~ Children in three areas away from bar until 8pm ~ Open 11-11

Spread Eagle

98 Walmgate

Mansfield Brewery have now taken over this narrow, popular pub, and as well as Mansfield Riding, Bitter and Old Baily on handpump, they have guests such as Theakstons XB, Timothy Taylors Landlord, and Youngers No 3; country wines and malt whiskies. The main bar is a dark vault and two smaller, cosier rooms lead off – lots of old enamel advertisements and prints on the walls, and a friendly atmosphere. A wide choice of bar food might include sandwiches (from £1.85), various pasta dishes with different sauces (from £3.50), vegetarian dishes (£5), and cashew chicken (£6.35). Fruit machine, trivia, juke box, and piped music. *(Recommended by Gary Nicholls, Ants Aug; more reports please)*

Mansfield Brewery ~ Manager Adrian Wilkinson ~ Real ale ~ Meals and snacks (noon-10pm Mon-Sat) ~ Restaurant ~ (01904) 635868 ~ Children welcome ~ Live Blues Sun lunchtime ~ Open 11-11

Tap & Spile £

Monkgate

As ever, it's the fine choice of around ten well kept real ales that draws people to this traditionally furnished pub: Tap & Spile Premium and Bitter, Old Mill Bitter and Theakstons Old Peculier, and seven constantly changing guests on handpump; five ciders, country wines, and some malt whiskies. The big split-level bar has bare boards, green leatherette wall settles right around a big bay window, with a smaller upper area with frosted glass and panelling; darts, shove-ha'penny, cribbage, dominoes, fruit machine, video game, and piped music. Simple cheap bar food includes sandwiches (from £1.35), filled baked potatoes (from £1.35), filled giant yorkshire puddings (from £2.95), and daily specials including vegetarian dishes (from £2.95); popular Sunday roast lunch (£3.95). There are a few picnic tables outside. This is part of the small chain of pubs with this name. *(Recommended by Drs A and A C Jackson, Christ Westmoreland, Jamie and Ruth Lyons, Brian Wainwright, Mr and Mrs Lawson, Andrew Stephenson)*

Pubmaster ~ Managers Ian Kilpatrick and Vicky Office ~ Real ale ~ Meals and snacks (noon-2.30; 12-7 Sat) ~ (01904) 656158 ~ Children in separate area till 8.30 ~ Live Blues Sun; quiz Weds evening ~ Open 11.30-11 ~ Bedrooms: £34/£34

Lucky Dip

Besides the fully inspected pubs, you might like to try these Lucky Dips recommended to us and described by readers (if you do, please send us reports):

☆ **Aberford** W Yor [Old North Rd; best to use A642 exit off A1; SE4337], *Swan*: Thriving attractively refurbished dining pub, lots of black timber, prints, pistols and cutlasses, cosy layout, staggering choice of good value generous food, Sun carvery, separate ticket system for each course, well kept Whitbreads-related ales, generous glasses of wine, polite uniformed staff, more upmarket upstairs restaurant; comfortable bedrooms *(Andy and Jill Kassube, Mark Bradley, Roy Bromell, Michael Butler, L Sovago)*

Aberford [Old North Rd], *Arabian Horse*: Friendly and relaxed beamed local, lunchtime food, S & N real ales, open fires; open all day Sat *(Mark Bradley, Michael Butler)*

Acaster Malbis N Yor [(and Wheelhouse Restaurant); SE5945], *Ship*: Pleasant riverside inn, very busy in summer (caravan sites nearby), tempting food, well kept Timothy Taylors Landlord, friendly service, attractive garden with play area; bedrooms clean and comfortable *(John C Baker, Chris Westmoreland)*

Ainthorpe N Yor [NZ7008], *Fox & Hounds*: Good fresh food inc much vegetarian, open fires, Theakstons and guest ales; friendly *(M Borthwick)*

☆ **Aldbrough St John** N Yor [off A1 signed to Piercebridge, then signed off to left; NZ2011], *Stanwick Arms*: Lovely country pub with happy staff, good food with Barbados influence in bar, bistro and restaurant, Black Sheep and John Smiths Magnet, all clean and tidy; seats outside; children welcome, bedrooms *(J A Rae, Nichola Watson)*

Ampleforth N Yor [Main St; SE5878], *White Swan*: Extensive modern lounge/dining bar in small attractive village, wide choice of generous food inc popular Sun lunch, front country bar with several real ales inc a guest beer, lots of malt whiskies, darts and a couple of fruit machines; decent wines, good friendly service; back terrace *(H Bramwell, Pat Crabb, Simon Collett-Jones)*

☆ **Appleton Roebuck** N Yor [SE5542], *Shoulder of Mutton*: Cheerful and attractive pub/steak bar overlooking village green, wide choice of good value food, Sam Smiths OB and Museum, quick service; can be crowded with caravanners summer; bedrooms *(Neil O'Callaghan, Michele and Clive Platman)*

Appleton Wiske N Yor [NZ3905], *Short Horn*: Modern pub handy for wide range of generous usual bar food, well kept Bass; separate Sky TV room, occasional discos *(Tim Heywwod, Sophie Wilne)*

☆ **Appletreewick** N Yor [SE0560], *New Inn*: Welcoming stonebuilt pub with good value simple food inc good sandwiches, well kept beers, interesting photographs, pub games; in fine spot, lovely views, garden; bedrooms *(Gwen and Peter Andrews, Bernard and Marjorie Parkin, LYM)*

☆ **Arncliffe** N Yor [off B6160; SD9473], *Falcon*: Classic old-fashioned haven for walkers, matchless setting on moorland village green, absolutely no frills, Youngers tapped from cask to stoneware jugs in central hatch-style servery, generous plain lunchtime bar snacks, open fire in small bar with elderly furnishings and humorous sporting prints, airy back sunroom (children allowed here lunchtime) looking on to garden; run by same family for generations – they take time to get to know; cl winter Thurs evenings; bedrooms (not all year), good breakfasts and evening meals – real value *(Mark Undrill, Neil and Angela Huxter, Brian Wainwright, Sally Johnson, Bill and Lydia Ryan, Mark Bradley, TBB, LYM)*

☆ **Askwith** W Yor [3 miles E of Ilkley; SD1648], *Black Horse*: Biggish family pub in lovely spot, good views from terrace, good choice of well cooked food (best to book Sun lunch), well kept ales inc Theakstons Best and XB, pleasant helpful staff, open fire *(Mark Bradley, Prof S Barnett)*

Aston S Yor [Main St, opp Aston Hall; SK4685], *Yellow Lion*: Good local atmosphere, well kept Whitbreads related ales; handy for M1 junction 31 *(Dave Reese)*

☆ **Austwick** N Yor [just off A65 Settle—Kirkby Lonsdale; SD7668], *Game Cock*: Prettily placed below the Three Peaks, pleasant atmosphere in simple old-fashioned beamed back bar, sensibly priced food (not Mon evening), well kept Thwaites, good fire, children allowed in no-smoking restaurant, seats outside with good play area; bedrooms *(Derek and Margaret Underwood, JKW, LYM)*

☆ **Aysgarth** N Yor [SE0088], *George & Dragon*: Cosy and friendly bar with lots of bric-a-brac, portraits of locals by landlord, also spacious polished hotel lounge with antique china, grandfather clock; ample helpings of good value usual food inc some vegetarian and Sun roasts, five well kept ales inc Hambleton, good friendly service, a welcome for dogs, separate pool area; bedrooms *(Richard Houghton, Michael Butler)*

☆ **Bainbridge** N Yor [A684 Leyburn—Sedbergh; SD9390], *Rose & Crown*: Ancient inn overlooking moorland village green, charming old-fashioned beamed and panelled front bar with big log fire, locals' bar with pool, juke box etc, John Smiths Magnet and Websters Yorkshire, bar food from sandwiches up, restaurant; children welcome, open all day, comfortable bedrooms *(Geoff and Angela Jaques, Mark Bradley, JKW, Frank Cummins, Michael Butler, M J Morgan, LYM)*

☆ **Bardsey** W Yor [A58; SE3643], *Bingley Arms*: Ancient pub with decor to match, very wide range of good value bar food (stops 8) in spacious lounge divided into separate areas inc no smoking, Tetleys Bitter and Mild and Timothy Taylors Landlord, pleasant speedy service, smaller public bar, picturesque upstairs brasserie, charming quiet terrace with interesting barbecues inc vegetarian; bedrooms comfortable *(Annette Moore, Chris Pearson, David Craine, Ann Reeder, Mark Bradley, Paul Cartledge)*

☆ **Barkisland** W Yor [Stainland Rd; SE0520], *Griffin*: Welcoming and tastefully refurbished cottagey rooms inc cosy oak-beamed parlour, open fires, lots of woodwork, good value food, well kept Bass, Ryburn Best and Worthington BB and maybe a potent cheap ale brewed here, restaurant *(S Bradley, Ann and Bob Westbrook, H K Dyson, Anselm Bassano, LYM)*

Barkston N Yor [A162 Tadcaster—Sherburn; SE4936], *Ash Tree*: Thriving, intimate and comfortable, full Theakstons range, decent food; small garden *(Chris Westmoreland)*

☆ **Barnsley** S Yor [Cundy Cross; Grange Lane (A633); SE3706], *Mill of the Black Monks*: Former watermill said to date from 12th century, lovely old stonework in split-level bar and restaurant, five S & N real ales, candlelight, saucy ghost; shame about the piped pop music, live music most nights; big garden with picnic tables, mature trees, swings, pens of ducks and small animals, maybe bouncy castle *(CW, JW, Richard Holmes, Fran Reynolds, Mark Bradley)*

Bawtry S Yor [SK6593], *Granby*: Straightforward pub, useful for the area *(LM)*; [Gainsborough Rd], *Ship*: Reasonably priced bar food inc bargain-for-two *(E Robinson)*

☆ **Beck Hole** N Yor [OS Sheet 94 map ref 823022; NZ8202], *Birch Hall*: Unique unchanging pub-cum-village shop in lovely spot by bridge over river in beautiful steep-valley village, nr Thomason Fosse waterfall, steam railway; hot and cold drinks, Black Sheep, Theakstons Best and XB, sandwiches with home-baked bread, hot pies and other refreshments served through hatch, two rooms, welcoming landlord; ancient outside mural, benches out in front, steep steps up to charming little side garden with nice view *(Mayur Shah, Michael Williamson, Elizabeth and Anthony Watts, Chris Westmoreland, Martyn and Mary Mullins, Andy and Jill Kassube, Jack and Philip Paxton)*

Bedale N Yor [Market Pl; SE2688], *Olde Black Swan*: Nice old bustling beamed pub with well kept Theakstons, good value food inc hearty sandwiches, proper coffee *(Dr and Mrs A K Clarke, Robert W Buckle)*

Beighton S Yor [Eckington Rd; SK4483], *Belfry*: Welcoming local with well kept Stones and Tetleys, big sofas by open fire, good value restaurant; popular Sun disco *(Karen Wait)*

Bempton N Yor [B1229; TA1972], *White Horse*: Pleasant pub with wholesome bar meals *(Dave Braisted)*

☆ **Beverley** N Yor [TA0340], *Beverley Arms*: Spacious traditional oak-panelled bar in comfortable and well run Forte hotel with well kept ales, choice of several decent places to eat inc interesting former coachyard (now enclosed) with formidable bank of the ranges that were used for cooking; good bedrooms, some with Minster view *(Andy and Jill Kassube, Roger Bellingham, LYM)*

Beverley [Wednesday Mkt], *Queens Head*: Cosy, with well kept Wards and Darley Thorne and guests such as Adnams Extra, cheap meals evenings too *(Q Williamson)*

Bishop Thornton N Yor [SE2664], *Drovers Arms*: Spacious beamed bar with open fire, friendly staff, good food and decent choice of drinks *(Stephen R Holman, S Barclay)*

Bishopthorpe N Yor [SE5947], *Ebor*: Very popular and lively local nr main entrance to Archbishop of York's Palace (hence name), beautiful hanging baskets and big well planted garden; lounge opening into dining area, good standard food esp steaks, friendly quick service, Sam Smiths; children welcome *(Shirley Pielou, Thomas Nott)*

☆ **Bolton Percy** N Yor [SE5341], *Crown*: Basic unpretentious country local, well kept Sam Smiths, generous simple food (not Mon or Tues), low prices, friendly dogs, tables on sizeable terrace with ageing pens of ornamental pheasants, quiet setting nr interesting 15th-c church and medieval gatehouse; children welcome *(Nick Wikeley, Paul Cartledge)*

☆ **Boroughbridge** N Yor [St James Sq; SE3967], *Black Bull*: Lovely old pub in attractive village, well kept John Smiths, decent coffee, good range of bar food, friendly service; cosy rooms leading off bar, restaurant, new bedrooms wing *(Ann and Colin Hunt, Mr MacGwire)*

Bradford W Yor [Preston St (off B6145); SE1633], *Fighting Cock*: Busy bare-floor basic alehouse with good choice such as Black Sheep, Exmoor Gold, Sam Smiths, Timothy Taylors, Theakstons, also farm ciders, foreign bottled beers, snacks, coal fires *(Susan and Nigel Wilson, Reg Nelson)*; [Westgate], *New Beehive*: Gaslit and candlelit Edwardian inn popular with musicians, artists, bohemians and students, lots of rooms inc good pool room, huge range of beers, nice back courtyard; live music below; bedrooms *(J Royce)*; [Kirkgate/Ivegate], *Rams Revenge*: Well kept Clarks, Theakstons and guest beers in unpretentious pub with old pews, wooden floor, upper gallery, fine old Bradford prints; lunchtime bar food, folk music, relaxed atmosphere; clock from former town gatehouse on this site in back room *(Bill and Lydia Ryan)*; [Grattan Rd/Barry St], *Castle*: Plain town local owned by group of small independent brewers, distinguished by its good collection of cheap well kept unusual real ales such as Goose Eye Bitter and Wharfedale, Griffin Lions, Merry Marker, Riding Bitter and Mild, Ryburn, Timothy Taylors Golden Pale; basic cheap food, well reproduced piped music (maybe some live) *(BB)*

Bramham W Yor [Claypit Lane; just off A1 2 miles N of A64; SE4243], *Chequers*: Reliably

good food *(K H Frostick)*; [Town Hill], *Swan*: Unspoilt local with engaging landlady, super mix of customers, well kept Vaux Bitter and Samson *(Les Brown)*
Bramhope W Yor [SE2543], *Fox & Hounds*: Popular civilised two-roomed pub with well kept Tetleys Mild and Bitter, lunchtime food, open fire; children welcome, has been open all day *(Mark Bradley, Annette Moore, Chris Pearson)*
Breighton N Yor [SE7134], *Olde Poachers*: Front courtyard gives coaching-inn impression but inside seems more medieval and gothic; comfortable main bar with sofas and easy chairs, big eating area like medieval banqueting hall, good choice of bar food *(Ian Morley)*
Bridlington N Yor [184 Kingsgate; A165, just outside; TA1867], *Broadacres*: Good value clean and spacious Country Carvery, Courage-related ales, play area outside *(SB)*
☆ **Brighouse** W Yor [Brookfoot; A6025 towards Elland; SE1524], *Red Rooster*: Real ales such as Old Mill, Marstons Pedigree, Moorhouses Pendle Witches Brew, Timothy Taylors Landlord and several guests in homely smallish pub divided into areas which feel like separate rooms inc one with books to read or buy; brewery memorabilia, knowledgeable landlord, open fire *(Mark Bradley, Jack and Philip Paxton)*
Brompton on Swale N Yor [B6271; off A1 S of Scotch Corner; SE2299], *Crown*: Good range of food popular with locals, moderate prices *(Mr and Mrs I B White)*
Brotherton N Yor [off A1 at Ferrybridge; SE4826], *Fox*: Good honest welcoming local, cheap plentiful home-cooked bar food *(R and C Underwood)*
☆ **Burnt Yates** N Yor [B6165, 6 miles N of Harrogate; SE2561], *Bay Horse*: Friendly 18th-c dining pub with log fires, low beams, brasses; wide range of bar food, pleasant restaurant, traditional atmosphere; shame about the TV; bedrooms in motel extension *(Roy Bromell, SB, Peter Marren)*
☆ **Burton Leonard** N Yor [off A61 Ripon—Harrogate; SE3364], *Hare & Hounds*: Good generous food inc fresh veg and good chips in cheerful spotless beamed bar and spacious restaurant, well kept Black Sheep, John Smiths and Tetleys, decent wines, friendly service, paintings, copper and brass on walls, big fairy-lit beech branch over ceiling, cosy coffee lounge, no games or jukebox *(Paul J Bispham, Dorothy and David Young, Peter Race, Prof and Mrs S Barnett, Kathryn and Brian Heathcote)*
Burton Salmon N Yor [just off A162 N of Ferrybridge; SE4927], *Plough*: Well kept ales such as Shepherd Neame Bishops Finger, intimate yet spacious bar opening on to nice walled garden, side restaurant *(Chris Westmoreland)*
☆ **Cadeby** S Yor [off A1(M) via A630, then Sprotbrough turn; SE5100], *Cadeby Inn*: Biggish, with open fire and lots of house plants in back lounge, quieter front sitting room, no-smoking snug, separate games area; usual bar food, well kept Courage Directors, John Smiths and Magnet, Sam Smiths OB and Tetleys, over 200 malt whiskies, seats out in front; children in eating area, open all day Sat *(John and Elspeth Howell, F J Robinson, Paul Cartledge, Mark Bradley, Roy Bromell, David Ing, LYM)*
Carlton N Yor [SW of Stokesley; NZ5004], *Blackwell Ox*: Picturesque village location, good bar food and separate Thai menu, Bass, Bull and two other ales on handpump, atmospheric bars (one with cigarette cards), open fires ; bedrooms, handy for coast-to-coast and Cleveland Way walkers *(David Varney)*
Carperby N Yor [a mile NW of Aysgarth; SE0189], *Wheatsheaf*: Friendly local in quiet village, good atmosphere, well kept Theakstons, bar food inc good sandwiches and ploughman's, separate well furnished rooms, restaurant for residents; bedrooms *(Michael Butler, Annette Moore, Chris Pearson)*
☆ **Cawood** N Yor [SE5737], *Ferry*: Very old and cosy, with smallish comfortable rooms, massive inglenook, stripped brickwork, well kept Adnams, Mansfield Riding and a good range of other ales, good reasonably priced food cooked to order, friendly informal service, tables out on grass by river with swing bridge and flagstone terrace above *(Chris Westmoreland, D R Clarke)*
Chapel Haddlesey N Yor [quite handy for M62 junction 34; off A19 towards Selby; SE5826], *Jug*: Homely little two-roomed village pub, once a blacksmiths' and said to be haunted, copper-topped round tables, comfortable banquettes and stools, jugs hanging from beams, wide choice of cheap food, Mansfield Bitter and Riding, John Smiths, Timothy Taylors Landlord and Packet Porter, garden and play area *(JJW, CMW)*
☆ **Chapel le Dale** N Yor [B5655 Ingleton—Hawes, 3 miles N of Ingleton; SD7477], *Old Hill*: Basic stripped-stone flagstone-floor bar with potholing pictures and Settle railway memorabilia, roaring log fire in cosy back parlour, well kept Dent and Theakstons Bitter, XB and Old Peculier, generous simple home-made food in separate room inc good beef sandwiches and pies, plenty of vegetarian; juke box; children welcome; bedrooms basic but good, with good breakfast – wonderful isolated spot *(Jenni Mitchell-Gibbs, Nigel Woolliscroft, LYM)*
☆ **Clapham** N Yor [off A65 N of Settle; SD7569], *New Inn*: Riverside pub with small comfortable panelled lounge, friendly service, Dent, John Smiths, Tetleys and Youngers No 3, public bar with games room, popular bar food, smart restaurant; bedrooms comfortable and reasonably priced, all with own bathroom; handy for walks *(T M Dobby, J H and S A Harrop, M and J Back)*
☆ **Clifton** W Yor [Westgate; off Brighouse rd from M62 junction 25; SE1623], *Black Horse*: Comfortably smart village local popular for good generous food in restaurant;

cosy oak-beamed bars, well kept Whitbreads-related beers; bedrooms comfortable *(Mark Bradley, Andrew and Ruth Triggs, RJH, Michael Butler)*

☆ **Cloughton** N Yor [N of village; TA0096], *Hayburn Wyke*: Good reasonably priced food inc good value Sun carvery in attractive old rose-covered pub nr NT Hayburn Wyke and Cleveland Way coastal path, lots of tables outside, red-cushioned settles in beamed L-shaped bar, restaurant and eating area beyond; well kept John Smiths, Theakstons Best and Youngers, friendly efficient staff, well behaved children and babies welcome; bedrooms *(Andrew and Ruth Triggs, M Borthwick)*

☆ **Cloughton Newlands** N Yor [A171; TA0196], *Bryherstones*: Outstanding welcome, several interconnecting rooms, well kept Youngers, over 50 whiskies, big helpings of well prepared food inc fresh fish and veg, lots of miniatures in cases; one room has two pool tables, quieter room upstairs; children welcome, delightful surroundings *(Mike and Wendy Proctor, T M Dobby, Keith and Margaret Kettell, David and Julie Glover)*

Cottingham N Yor [West Green; TA0633], *Blue Bell*: Pleasantly placed, with good dining area, attentive service, some concentration on steaks *(R Suddaby)*

☆ **Dacre Banks** N Yor [SE1962], *Royal Oak*: Good food inc some interesting recipes and good veg in cosy and comfortable open-plan village pub with beautiful valley views, two lounge areas with interesting old photographs, open fire in front part, restaurant, well kept Black Sheep, John Smiths and Tetleys, friendly young owners, unusual piped music; tables outside, boules; bedrooms *(Prof S Barnett, Geoffrey and Brenda Wilson, Andrew and Marian Ruston, Mrs B M Fyffe, J A Penny)*

Dalton N Yor [between A19 and A168, S of Thirsk; SE4377], *Jolly Farmers of Olden Times*: Good value for bed, breakfast and evening meal, very cheerful owners; just two bedrooms *(Ernest Lee)*

Danby N Yor [NZ7109], *Duke of Wellington*: Roomy and popular, with wide choice of good value well cooked food inc vegetarian, welcoming service, good coffee ; bedrooms very well appointed *(Bruce and Maddy Webster, Bob Ellis)*

Dewsbury W Yor [Chidswell Lane, Shaw Cross; SE2523], *Huntsman*: Converted cottages alongside urban-fringe farm, pleasant decor and atmosphere, lots of brasses and bric-a-brac, Stones, Worthington BB and maybe other ales; no food evening or Sun/Mon lunchtime, busy evenings *(Michael Butler)*; [Station], *West Riding Refreshment Rooms*: Unusual new station buffet, with six real ales changing every few days, many from local breweries such as Blackmoor, food all healthy as licensee is a nutritionist *(Laura Anderson)*

Dore S Yor [A625 SW of Sheffield; SK3081], *Dore Moor*: Just out of city on edge of Peak Park, well restored by helpful new owners, lots of stripped pine, good value ample food, good range of beers inc Stones and guests *(Alan and Heather Jacques)*

Driffield N Yor [Market Pl; TA0258], *Bell*: Elegant and popular 18th-c inn with delightful old-fashioned restaurant, long comfortable red plush bar, former Corn Exchange used as stripped-brick eating area with lots of leafy-looking hanging baskets, good bar food and splendid imaginative salad bar; comfortable bedrooms *(Gordon Thornton, Roger Bellingham)*

☆ **Dunford Bridge** S Yor [Windle Edge Lane; off A628 Barnsley—M'ter OS Sheet 110 map ref 158023; SE1502], *Stanhope Arms*: Cheerful and nicely placed family pub below the moors around Winscar Reservoir, friendly attentive service, good value straightforward food from sandwiches to big Sun lunch, OAP lunches (not Sat-Mon), afternoon teas summer Suns, well kept Timothy Taylor Landlord, Mansfield Riding and Bitter and (new to us) White Rabbit Spring Ale, pool room (with fruit machine); piped music can be a bit loud; sizeable garden with camping ground, occasional live music *(JJW, CMW, BB)*

☆ **East Keswick** N Yor [Main St; SE3644], *Duke of Wellington*: Tasty generous home-cooked straightforward food (not Mon) inc good veg and traditional puddings, big ornate Victorian dining room, convivial bar with big open fire (loud juke box and lots of local youth Sat night), friendly staff *(David Varney)*

☆ **East Layton** N Yor [A66 not far from Scotch Corner; NZ1609], *Fox Hall*: Wide choice of bar food and good friendly service in panelled bar with cosy booths, sporting prints, more open back part with big south-facing window, well kept Theakstons Best (more ales in summer), good range of malt whiskies and wines; games room, juke box, piped music; tables on back terrace; evening restaurant, Sun lunches; children and well behaved dogs welcome; bedrooms comfortable, good breakfasts *(Andrew and Ruth Triggs, LYM)*

☆ **East Marton** N Yor [Marton Bridge; A59 Gisburn—Skipton; SD9051], *Cross Keys*: Welcoming old-fashioned pub attractively set back behind small green nr Leeds & Liverpool Canal, log fire, interesting decor and furnishings, good range of food at tempting prices, wide choice of well kept ales inc Ruddles, Theakstons and John Smiths, decent wines, friendly helpful staff, children's area (where the food counter is), evening restaurant; tables outside *(Kevin Potts, Bronwen and Steve Wrigley, M E A Horler, Jack Hill, Dr and Mrs D E Awbery, LYM)*

East Morton W Yor [SE1042], *Busfield Arms*: Attractive country cottage with ivy around door, impressively run as food pub, with wide choice, well kept Bass, Stones and Worthington, good range of wines, warmly friendly atmosphere *(B M Eldridge, D Stokes)*

☆ **East Witton** N Yor [over ½ mile on road to Middleham; SE1586], *Cover Bridge*: Idiosyncratic and informal old riverside country local with two simple little rooms,

Black Sheep, John Smiths and Theakstons Best, country wines, simple bar food, pub dogs; children welcome, sizeable rough garden, open all day; bedrooms *(M J Morgan, Bill Edwards, Andrew and Ruth Triggs, LYM)*

Eccup W Yor [off A660 N of Leeds; SE2842], *New Inn*: Popular isolated Tetleys pub with big lounge and family room, good range of bar meals and sandwiches, friendly efficient service; children's play area; well placed for good walks, on Dales Way and nr Harewood Park *(D Stokes, Tim and Sue Halstead)*

Egton N Yor [NZ8106], *Horseshoe*: Traditional low-beamed moorland village pub with good value basic food such as pizzas and yorkshire puddings, good choice of starters, well kept Tetleys and Theakstons Bitter and Old Peculier, warm welcome, open fire; may be closed some winter lunchtimes; not to be confused with the Horse Shoe down at Egton Bridge *(Bronwen and Steve Wrigley, Andy and Jill Kassube, M Borthwick)*

☆ **Egton Bridge** N Yor [signed off A171 W of Whitby; NZ8005], *Postgate*: Moorland village local with relaxed and informal atmosphere, decent bar food, Camerons Lion and Strongarm, Flowers IPA, Ind Coope Burton and Tetleys, traditional games in public bar, tables on sunny flagstoned terrace; can get a bit smoky; open all day, good value bedrooms *(Joy Heatherley, John Honnor, F M Bunbury, LYM)*

Elland W Yor [Park Rd, quite handy for M62 junction 24; SE1121], *Barge & Barrel*: Friendly old-fashioned pub with huge helpings of cheap food, wide changing range of good beers, family room (with air hockey), piped radio; seats by industrial canal *(Lee Goulding, Mike Woodhead)*; [Park Rd], *Colliers Arms*: Warmly friendly, Sam Smiths beers, good range of home-made bar food, back conservatory and seats by canal *(B M Eldridge)*

Ellerby N Yor [just off A174 Whitby rd; NZ8015], *Ellerby Inn*: Pleasant country inn in small village with nice moorland strolls nearby, good range of bar food (or choice from fancier restaurant menu), John Smiths and Tetleys ales and good choice of malt whiskies, lovely secluded back garden surrounded by flowery rockeries; bedrooms *(Bronwen and Steve Wrigley, Michael Butler)*

☆ **Embsay** N Yor [Elm Tree Sq; SE0053], *Elm Tree*: Civilised well refurbished open-plan beamed village pub with good bar food inc good-sized children's helpings, good service, old-fashioned prints, log-effect gas fire; well kept changing ales such as Bateman XB, Cains Bitter, Fullers London Pride, Scarlet Lady, Pennine Golden and Wadworths 6X, games area, juke box; busy weekends esp evenings; comfortable bedrooms *(Mr and Mrs I B White)*

☆ **Escrick** N Yor [E of A19 York—Selby – OS Sheet 105 map ref 643425; SE6343], *Black Bull*: Warm cosy atmosphere, well spaced tables in bar, good imaginative if not cheap food in good-sized dining area, decent wines, welcoming landlord; very popular weekends ; bedrooms *(Ian S Morley, Roger Bellingham, John T Ames)*

☆ **Etton** N Yor [3½ miles N of Beverley, off B1248; SE9843], *Light Dragoon*: Recently refurbished roomy country local with wide range of decent bar food, well kept Youngers Scotch and IPA, inglenook fireplace, pleasant service, garden with play area *(Roger Bellingham, Andy and Jill Kassube, E J Wilde, BB)*

Faceby N Yor [NZ4903], *Sutton Arms*: Emphasis on dining – good food, well kept beer, 30s and 50s bric-a-brac *(J A Rae)*

Fairburn N Yor [just off A1; SE4727], *Bay Horse*: Very comfortable, with good generous cheap food, pleasant staff, decent beers *(Douglas and Margaret Chesterman)*

☆ **Farndale East** N Yor [Church Houses; next to Farndale Nature Reserve; SE6697], *Feversham Arms*: Friendly walkers' pub in lovely daffodil valley, two unspoilt smallish rooms with flagstone floors and real fires, well kept Tetleys, very good value home-cooked food, open fire, pleasant restaurant, high standard of service; very popular weekends; nice small garden, good bedrooms, big breakfasts *(Lee Goulding, Chris Westmoreland, Geoff and Angela Jaques, Elizabeth and Anthony Watts, Ian Boag)*

Felixkirk N Yor [SE4785], *Carpenters Arms*: Comfortable 17th c free house in picturesque small village, big helpings of decent food, real ale, smart restaurant with own menu inc popular Sun lunch (should book), pleasant service *(F J and A Parmenter)*

Ferrybridge W Yor [off A1 on B6136 Castleford Rd; SE4824], *Golden Lion*: Good value pub by Aire/Calder Navigation, impressive views of motorway above and old road bridge in background; well kept Tetleys, fine buffet lunch *(Comus Elliott)*

☆ **Finghall** N Yor [Akebar Park; off A684 E of Leyburn; SE1890], *Friars Head*: Good imaginative fresh food in attractively converted barn, Black Sheep, John Smiths and Theakstons, good coffee, pleasant service, log fire, attractive stonework and beams, cosy nooks, large conservatory; looks over bowling green and pay-as-you-play golf, adjacent caravan site *(Dono and Carol Leaman, J H and S A Harrop, Michael and Susan Morgan)*

Flamborough N Yor [Dog & Duck Sq; junction B1255/B1229; TA2270], *Royal Dog & Duck*: Friendly local with two homely comfortable beamed rooms, well kept Bass, usual food esp local fish ; bedrooms *(Martin and Pauline Richardson, Chris Westmoreland)*

Foggathorpe N Yor [A163 E of Selby; SE7537], *Black Swan*: Popular local refurbished under pleasant new management, well kept John Smiths and Black Sheep, generous simple fresh bar food inc thick hand-cut chips *(P J Keen)*

Fylingdales N Yor [A171 S of Whitby; SE9399], *Flask*: Good variety of well priced fresh food in pleasant moorland pub, recently extensively refurbished; children's room play area, attractive bedrooms *(Mr and Mrs M St-Amour)*

☆ **Galphay** N Yor [off B6265 Ripon—Pateley Bridge; SE2573], *Galphay Inn*: Good food inc speciality roasts and very hospitable prompt service in cosy dining pub, one side pine-panelled with matching solid tables and settles, adjoining larger more open area with pictures; S & N beers on handpump, decent house wine, log fire; cl Mon evening and weekday lunchtimes *(Peter Churchill, David Hagen)*

☆ **Gargrave** N Yor [Church St/Marton Rd; SD9354], *Masons Arms*: Friendly well run local on Pennine Way, between river and church, well kept Whitbreads-related real ales, generous quick bar food inc vegetarian, copper-canopied log-effect gas fire dividing two open-plan areas; bowling green behind; children if well behaved *(Wayne Brindle, Dave Braisted)*

Gargrave, [A65 W of village], *Anchor*: Big Brewers Fayre family pub worth knowing for all-day food service (from 7.30 b'fast) and superb play area, with canalside tables; welcoming competent service, Whitbreads-related real ales, good wheelchair access; piped music; economically run bedrooms in modern wing *(Elizabeth and Anthony Watts, George Atkinson, RB)*

Giggleswick N Yor [Brackenbar Ln; A65 Settle bypass; SD8164], *Old Station*: Handy stop on Settle bypass, generous straightforward home-made food in L-shaped bar with brasses, railway prints and dining end, no-smoking restaurant, friendly staff, well kept John Smiths and Tetleys Mild and Bitter; bedrooms *(J L Phillips, John Allsopp)*

Gillamoor N Yor [SE6890], *Royal Oak*: Good bar food, clean, comfortable and roomy beamed and panelled bars, well kept beer; handy for Barnsdale Moor *(F M Bunbury)*

Goathland N Yor [NZ8301], *Goathland*: Welcoming big bar, smaller plush lounge, well kept Camerons Bitter and Strongarm, wide choice of bar food inc local scampi, stripped-stone restaurant; seats out in front, doubles as pub in *Heartbeat*; comfortable bedrooms *(Andrew Hazeldine, Andy and Jill Kassube)*

Goldsborough N Yor [handy for A1; SE3856], *Bay Horse*: Very well prepared food, good garden, quiet village ; bedrooms *(Geoff and Angela Jaques)*

☆ **Grassington** N Yor [Garrs Lane; SE0064], *Black Horse*: Comfortable open-plan modern bar, very busy in summer, with well kept Black Sheep Bitter and Special, Tetleys and Theakstons Best and Old Peculier, open fires, generous straightforward home-cooked bar food inc children's and fine ploughman's, cheerful service, darts in back room, sheltered terrace, small attractive restaurant; bedrooms comfortable, well equipped and good value *(Paul J Bispham, Prof and Mrs S Barnett, NT, PD, Bill Sharpe, Mrs E Howe, Gill Cambridge, BB)*

☆ **Grassington** [The Square], *Devonshire*: Busy and comfortable hotel, good window seats overlooking sloping village square, interesting pictures and ornaments, open fires, good range of well presented food in big well furnished dining room, good family room, friendly efficient service, McEwans 80/- and full range of Theakstons ales, tables in back garden; well appointed good value bedrooms, good breakfasts *(Gwen and Peter Andrews, Roy Smylie, Andrew and Marian Ruston, Jean and Douglas Troup, LYM)*

☆ **Great Ayton** N Yor [High Green; off A173 – follow village signs; NZ5611], *Royal Oak*: Wide range of generous good food, well kept Theakstons ales, helpful service, friendly unpretentious bar with open fire in huge inglenook, beam-and-plank ceiling, bulgy old partly panelled stone walls, traditional furnishings inc antique settles, long dining lounge (children allowed); pleasant views of elegant village green from bay windows; bedrooms *(G S and A Jaques, John Fazakerley, LYM)*

Great Ayton [Low Green], *Buck*: Pleasant pub across road from local riverside beauty spot, changing well kept Whitbreads-related ales, June beer festival, popular food inc vegetarian; a few tables outside *(Duncan Redpath, Lorraine Milburn)*

☆ **Great Broughton** N Yor [High St; NZ5405], *Wainstones*: Good value varied food and well kept Tetleys in pleasantly unpretentious hotel bar, friendly efficient staff, good restaurant, children welcome; bedrooms *(B B Watling, G Neighbour)*

Great Broughton, *Black Horse*: Exceptionally friendly welcome, decent food, ales such as Tetleys Imperial; handy for Cleveland Way and coast-to-coast path; bedrooms cheap and simple (improvements scheduled) *(David Varney)*

Great Ouseburn N Yor [SE4562], *Crown*: Interesting decor, good range of beers, wide choice of food inc imaginative dishes *(Tim and Sue Halstead)*

☆ **Grenoside** S Yor [Skew Hill Lane; 3 miles from M1 junction 35 – OS Sheet 110 map ref 328935; SK3293], *Cow & Calf*: Peaceful contrast to M1, worth the effort of finding this neatly converted farmhouse, three friendly connected rooms, one no smoking, high-backed settles, brass and copper hanging from beams, plates and pictures, good value hearty home-cooked bar food (not Sun evening; till 8.15) inc children's, well kept Sam Smiths OB and Museum on electric pump, tea and coffee; piped music; family room in block across walled former farmyard with picnic tables; splendid views over Sheffield, open all day Sat *(CMW, JJW, G Washington, KCH, LYM)*

Grewelthorpe N Yor [SE2376], *Crown*: Well kept beer inc Theakstons, good straightforward food, whistling landlord *(Colin McKerrow)*

☆ **Grinton** N Yor [B6270 W of Richmond; SE0598], *Bridge*: Unpretentious riverside inn in lovely spot opp charming church, two bars, very friendly service, well kept Black Sheep

Special, John Smiths Magnet and Theakstons, decent wines, good range of good value food inc good steaks; attractive tables outside, front and back; bedrooms with own bathrooms; open all day *(Paul and Janet Waring, Patrick and Lynn Billyeald, Richard Houghton, E G Parish, Andrew and Ruth Triggs, Rhona and Peter Fear)*

☆ **Halifax** W Yor [Paris Gates, Boys Lane – OS Sheet 104 map ref 097241; SE0924], *Shears*: Hidden down steep cobbled lanes among tall mill buildings, dark unspoilt interior, warm welcome, well kept Marstons Pedigree, Timothy Taylors Landlord and unusual guest beers; very popular lunchtime for good cheap food from hot-filled sandwiches to home-made pies, curries, casseroles etc; sporting prints, local sports photographs, collection of pump clips and foreign bottles; seats out above the Hebble Brook *(Madeleine Cheung, Mike Woodhead, Lee Goulding, Annette Moore, Chris Pearson)*

Halifax [Bull Green], *Lewins*: Old pub refurbished in olde-worlde style, Bass, Stones, Robinsons and guests on handpump, good food, wooden floors, settles and high-back chairs *(Mike Woodhead)*; [New Rd, nr stn], *Pump Room*: No-frills pub very popular for its dozen or so well kept changing ales; clean and friendly *(Ian and Mike Woodhead, Gayle Butterfield, Carl Travis)*; [Sun Fold, South Parade], *Three Pigeons*: Good range of well kept real ales such as Black Sheep, Boddingtons, Tetleys and Timothy Taylors Landlord, guests such as Jennings *(Mike Woodhead)*

☆ **Hampsthwaite** N Yor [Main St; about 5 miles W of Harrogate; SE2659], *Joiners Arms*: Good food esp well presented good value Sun lunch, well kept Courage-related ales, decent wines, smallish bar, well spaced dining room tables, good atmosphere and friendly staff; nice village setting *(Geoffrey and Brenda Wilson, Andrew and Marian Ruston, F J Robinson)*

Harewood W Yor [diagonally opp Harewood House; SE3245], *Harewood Arms*: Busy former coaching inn opp Harewood House, three attractive, comfortable and spacious lounge bars, wide choice of good food, friendly prompt service, well kept ales inc Sam Smiths OB, decent wines, coffee and afternoon tea *(Janet Pickles, B M Eldridge)*

☆ **Harrogate** N Yor [31 Tower St; SE3155], *Tap & Spile*: Basic but very friendly bare-boards stripped-stone pub, three clean and pleasant rooms, up to ten changing well kept and well described ales, helpful staff, cheap basic lunchtime bar food, daily papers; open all day Sat, packed on live band nights *(Mark Bradley, Lorena Catarina Soto, Andrew and Marian Ruston)*

☆ **Harrogate**, [Crimple Lane; A59/B6161 towards Skipton], *Travellers Rest*: Two-room country pub in pleasant valley setting, real fires in both rooms; shining woodwork, oak beams, friendly service; good freshly prepared cheap food inc fish, well kept Tetleys and Theakstons Best *(C A Hall, Andrew and Ruth Triggs)*

Harrogate [Montpellier Gdns], *Drum & Monkey*: Not a pub but well worth knowing for downstairs fish bar, eat at bar or pub-style tables, good wines; busy, noisy and friendly *(Neville Kenyon)*; [off Crag Lane by Harlow Carr Gardens], *Harrogate Arms*: Wide choice of good food, helpful staff, real ales, quiet setting with tables outside and play area *(Dono and Carol Leaman)*; [off E Parade], *Regency*: Comfortable town pub with well kept Bass and Tetleys, ad lib coffee, good service, good value generous home-cooked food all day *(Ian Boag)*

☆ **Hartoft End** N Yor [Pickering—Rosedale Abbey rd; SE7593], *Blacksmiths Arms*: Attractive, immaculate and civilised 16th-c wayside inn by moors, originally a farmhouse and gradually extended, lots of original stonework, brasses, cosy nooks and crannies, relaxing atmosphere, good bar food inc excellent fish and fresh veg, attractive new restaurant with cane furnishings ; bedrooms *(Bronwen and Steve Wrigley, Enid and Henry Stephens)*

Hawes N Yor [High St; SD8789], *Crown*: Traditional local with good range of well priced quickly served bar food, well kept Theakstons Best, XB and Old Peculier, friendly service, coal fire each end; walkers welcome, children allowed away from bar; seats out on cobbled front forecourt *(R A Hobbs, Paul and Gail Betteley, Peter and Lynn Brueton)*; [High St], *White Hart*: Friendly, warm and cosy, busy around bar, quieter on left, wide choice of reasonably priced food in bar and restaurant, welcoming service; bedrooms good value *(Richard Houghton, G W Lindley)*

☆ **Hawnby** N Yor [SE5489], *Hawnby*: Good choice of well cooked generous food in spotless inn, lovely location in village surrounded by picturesque countryside, a magnet for walkers; Vaux beers, good unhurried service, owl theme; tables in garden with country views; neat bedrooms *(David and Margaret Bloomfield, Andrew and Ruth Triggs)*

☆ **Haworth** W Yor [Main St; SE0337], *Fleece*: Small partly panelled rooms, not too touristy, with flagstones, some carpeting, plants in pots and hanging baskets, well kept Timothy Taylors ales on handpump, coal fires in stone fireplaces, tasty reasonably priced food most lunchtimes, friendly staff; maybe piped disco/pop music *(Andrew Baren)*

Haworth [Main St], *Black Bull*: Was Branwell B's main drinking place, now a rather touristy Whitbreads pub, open all day, with good value food noon-8.30, six real ales, quiet piped music and games machines; some no-smoking tables, children welcome ; bedrooms *(JJW, CMW)*; [West Lane], *Old White Lion*: Very good value food and well kept Courage-related ales inc the new Wilsons BB, good popular restaurant (booked up Sat); warm and comfortable, very handy for museum; decent bedrooms, though not large *(R MacDonald, Jenny and Brian Seller, Paul McPherson, Nigel Hey)*

Hebden Bridge W Yor [Pecket Well; A6033 out towards Keighley; SD9928], *Robin Hood*: Well kept Tetleys and Theakstons, good value food, four clean and attractive rooms with toby jugs and nice views, cheerful welcoming landlord; bedrooms *(H K Dyson, M E A Horler)*

☆ **Helmsley** N Yor [Market Pl; SE6184], *Crown*: Warm and friendly beamed front bar opening into bigger unpretentious central dining bar, wide choice of good value food and enjoyable teas, good service, range of well kept beers, roaring fires, tables in sheltered garden behind with conservatory area; bedrooms pleasant *(H Bramwell, BB)*

☆ **Helmsley** [Market Pl], *Black Swan*: Smart and attractive Forte hotel, not a pub, but pleasant beamed and panelled bar with carved oak settles and windsor armchairs, cosy and comfortable lounges with a good deal of character, attentive staff, charming sheltered garden; good place to stay – expensive, but comfortable and individual *(Owen and Margaret Warnock, BB)*

Helmsley [Market Pl], *Royal Oak*: Friendly inn with good food inc roasts and filled Yorkshire puddings, well kept Camerons; bedrooms good *(Andy and Jill Kassube)*

☆ **Helperby** N Yor [SE4470], *Farmers*: Friendly unspoilt local with pine country furniture, good value food, small restaurant, Theakstons Best, XB and Old Peculier, comfortable games room with fruit machine and darts, tables in garden; bedrooms *(Andrew and Ruth Triggs)*

Helperby [Main St], *Golden Lion*: Particularly good choice of ales from smaller brewers, good simple bar food, cosy atmosphere, friendly staff *(Charlie Brook)*

Hemingfield S Yor [Beech House Rd, off A633 SE of Barnsley; SE3901], *Lundhill*: Early 19th-c, now considerably enlarged, with several areas off bar, dark beams, lots of brass, very friendly atmosphere, four real ales, weekend bar food, upstairs no-smoking restaurant, picnic tables outside *(JJW, CMW)*

☆ **Hepworth** W Yor [38 Towngate, off A616 SE of Holmfirth – OS Sheet 110 map ref 163069; SE1606], *Butchers Arms*: Friendly L-shaped bar, jovial landlord, partly panelled stone walls, open fire, Boddingtons, Tetleys and Timothy Taylors Landlord, bar food, evening restaurant; pool and darts at one end; open all day Fri/Sat *(JJW, CMW)*

High Bentham N Yor [Main St; SD6769], *Coach House*: Low beams, alcoves, nooks and crannies, oak tables, fresh flowers; clean and welcoming, with imaginative food inc good fish choice and fine chips, Robinsons ales; lovely white linen restaurant *(John and Bridget Dean)*

☆ **Holme** W Yor [SE1006], *Fleece*: Cosy pleasant rooms, lots of lifeboat memorabilia, well kept Tetleys, Theakstons and Youngers, good coffee, popular fresh pub food inc special offers, very welcoming landlord, efficient staff, real fire, pool/darts room, quiet piped music; attractive village setting below Holme Moss TV mast, great walks *(Bill Sykes, J E Rycroft, Chloe Gartery, Gwen and Peter Andrews)*

Holme on Spalding Moor N Yor [SE8038], *Red Lion*: Well run, clean and comfortable, with good bar food and seafood restaurant, friendly staff, eclectic range of wines, sunny terrace with koi carp; bedrooms *(H Bramwell)*

☆ **Holmfirth** W Yor [Victoria Sq – OS Sheet 110 map ref 143082; aka Rose & Crown; SD1408], *Nook*: Character local, tiled floor, low beams and basic furnishings, friendly atmosphere, Timothy Taylors and other well kept ales; fruit machine, video game; streamside seats outside *(Rupert Lecomber, Jack and Philip Paxton)*

☆ **Holywell Green** W Yor [handy for M62 junction 24; SE0820], *Rock*: Comfortably refurbished in Victorian style, with cosy bar areas, conservatory, well kept Black Sheep, Theakstons and Youngers, open fire, decent bar food, massive choice of good restaurant food; well decorated bedrooms *(James Cowell, Andy and Jill Kassube)*

☆ **Honley** W Yor [SE1312], *Jacobs Well*: Good value bar food with some imaginative dishes, good range of well kept beers inc Tetleys and Thwaites, decent whiskies and wines; friendly atmosphere, pleasant surroundings *(J L Phillips, Stephen and Brenda Head)*

Hopperton N Yor [A59 Harrogate—York; SE4256], *Masons Arms*: Good food esp steaks, very leisurely atmosphere, well kept Bass; evenings only *(Les Brown)*

Horsforth W Yor [Long Row; SE2438], *Queens Arms*: Old character pub, warm and friendly atmosphere, well kept Bass, Stones and Worthington, good value bar food (not weekends), picnic tables outside *(B M Eldridge)*

Hotham N Yor [Main St; quite handy for M62 junction 38; SE8934], *Hotham Arms*: Friendly and busy, with comfortable banquettes, smallish back dining area partly no smoking, good value food (not Mon/Tues evenings), good-natured attentive service, Black Sheep, Boddingtons Mild and Tetleys, TV and fruit machine, games room *(JJW, CMW)*

☆ **Hovingham** N Yor [SE6775], *Worsley Arms*: Good value well prepared food, interesting choice esp vegetarian, in friendly and welcoming back bar comfortably furnished for eating, well kept John Smiths, Malton Double Chance and Theakstons Mild, good coffee, kind staff, lots of Yorkshire cricketer photographs esp from 1930s and 40s; nice tables out by stream; pleasant bedrooms *(F J and P Parmenter, R M Macnaughton, BB)*

☆ **Huddersfield** W Yor [Crosland Moor; SE1115], *Sands House*: Very popular dining pub with wide choice of good value tempting unusual food inc thoughtful children's dishes and classic puddings, oblong bar full of contemptorary clocks and watches, lots of woodwork, well kept Boddingtons, cheerful welcoming staff; downstairs dining room, children welcome *(H K Dyson, Andrew and Ruth Triggs, Malcolm J Steward)*

☆ **Huddersfield** [Chapel Hill, just outside ring rd – OS Sheet 110 map ref 143162], *Rat & Ratchet*: Now brewing its own Experimental Ale, besides wide range of well kept ales inc Marstons Pedigree, Smiles, Timothy Taylors Landlord and Best and lots of changing guest beers; bare boards in bar and adjoining room, two more comfortable rooms up steps, basic well cooked cheap bar food inc Weds curry night *(David Whitehead, Tony and Wendy Hobden)*

Huddersfield [A640 towards Denshaw], *Buckstones*: Smart recent open-plan refurbishment, Bass and Timothy Taylors Landlord; glorious view over Marsden Moor from seats outside *(Chris Westmoreland)*; [market area], *Dog & Gun*: Comfortably plush friendly local with well kept Bass, Stones Best and Worthington Best; pool *(Richard Lewis)*; [Colne Bridge – B6118 just off A62 NE], *Royal & Ancient*: Spacious, comfortable and popular, with log fires, good interesting bar food, Bass and Whitbreads ales, restaurant *(M A Butler, A Preston)*

☆ **Hull** N Yor [Land of Green Ginger, Old Town; TA0927], *George*: Handsomely preserved traditional long Victorian bar, open all day; lots of oak, mahogany and copper, good choice of cheap, generous and tasty lunchtime food inc good fish, well kept Bass and Stones, good service, piped music; can get very busy – get there early; handy for the fine Docks Museum; children allowed in plush upstairs dining room *(J S M Sheldon, Andy and Jill Kassube, Chris Westmoreland)*

Hull [Clive Sullivan Way], *Alexandra*: Cheerful local, plentiful cheap food *(Bob Lilley)*; [Greenwood Ave/Beverley Rd (A1079)], *Humber Pilot*: Newish, comfortable and friendly, reasonably priced basic food, well kept Mansfield Riding and Bitter, piped music, TV, lots of games machines – mainly a young person's pub *(JJW, CMW)*; [nr New Theatre], *New Clarence*: Sensibly refurbished, partitioned to give a degree of cosiness; dark panelling, stone floors, Tetleys-related and other ales *(Chris Westmoreland)*; [193 Collingham Rd], *Newland Park*: Modernised 1930s hotel, good standard pub food inc lunchtime carvery at reasonable prices, decent beers, good service, pleasant atmosphere *(Roger Bellingham)*; [150 High St – quiet Old Town lane S of centre], *Olde Black Boy*: Little black-panelled low-ceilinged front smoke room, lofty 18th-c back vaults bar (with juke box strong on golden oldies, fruit machine, TV); well kept Tetleys-related and other ales, bar food, friendly staff, interesting history *(Chris Westmoreland, BB)*; [Posterngate], *Schnapps Bar*: Wide range of continental mainly German beers, mainly bottled, with eight from big Bavarian or Austrian-style pot founts; broad mix of ages, coffee too *(Chris Westmoreland)*; [Alfred Gelder St (close to Guildhall)], *White Hart*: Mansfield pub with heavy tiled bar, high ceiling, ornate wood and glasswork *(Chris Westmoreland)*

Hunton N Yor [SE1992], *Countrymans*: Warmly welcoming village inn, beautiful old beams, panelling, teapot collection and brasses, comfortable seats, no-smoking dining room, Courage Directors, John Smiths and Theakstons Best, good usual lunchtime bar food (cl Mon-Thurs lunchtime at least in winter), pool room; seven well equipped bedrooms *(Michael and Susan Morgan)*

☆ **Hutton le Hole** N Yor [SE7090], *Crown*: Friendly local with good service and food, well kept Tetleys, lots of whisky-water jugs, busy friendly atmosphere; children welcome; small pretty village with wandering sheep *(I McCaskey, Chris and Andy Crow)*

☆ **Ingbirchworth** S Yor [Welthorne Lane; off A629 Shepley—Penistone; SE2205], *Fountain*: Neat and spacious red plush turkey-carpeted lounge, cosy front bar, comfortable family room, open fires; generous bar food inc exotic salads and superb puddings, well kept Tetleys, well reproduced pop music, friendly service, tables in sizeable garden overlooking reservoir *(Peter and Carolyn Clark, BB)*

Ingleton N Yor [SD6973], *Three Horse Shoes*: Friendly, good for walkers; good value bar snacks *(Dave Braisted)*

☆ **Jackson Bridge** W Yor [Sheffield Rd; off A635 Holmfirth—New Mill – OS Sheet 110 map ref 165076; SE1607], *Red Lion*: Well kept Tetleys and guests such as Bass, Black Sheep, Fullers London Pride and Theakstons Best, Old Peculier and XB, decent wines, good food from basic bar meals to more extravagant reasonably priced dishes, three friendly cosy rooms with dark wooden tables and chairs, red wall seats, plates and *Last of the Summer Wine* pictures, open fire, frequent jazz nights *(Jenny Wilson)*

☆ **Jackson Bridge** W Yor [Scholes Rd, signed off A616], *White Horse*: Low-ceilinged small-roomed pub with blue plush wall seats and dining chairs, simple home-cooked early lunches, well kept Bass and Stones, coffee from 9am, friendly landlord, more *Last of the Summer Wine* pictures, pool room looking out on charming waterfall and ducks behind *(JJW, CMW)*

Keighley W Yor [SE0641], *Black Bull*: Attractive inn with decent food, by 16th-c church *(Andrew Adams)*

☆ **Kettlesing**, N Yor [signed off A59 W of Harrogate; SE2256], *Queens Head*: Dining pub doing well under friendly new management, nicely presented good food in wide price range, popular weekday lunchtimes with older people, lots of quite close-set tables, well kept Theakstons Best and XB, Youngers Scotch, good house wines, quick service, unobtrusive piped music, attractive and interesting decorations *(F J Robinson, BB)*

☆ **Kettlewell** N Yor [SD9772], *Racehorses*: Comfortable and civilised, recently refitted, with good value well prepared food, Black Sheep, John Smiths and Theakstons, good choice of wines, log fires, attentive service; well placed for Wharfedale walks; bedrooms good, with own bathrooms *(Bill and Lydia*

Ryan, A Barker, Geoff and Angela Jaques, Peter Churchill, BB)

Kettlewell, *Bluebell*: Roomy simply furnished knocked-through local with snug areas and flagstones, well kept Black Sheep and S & N ales, reasonably priced straightforward food; pool room, piped music, children's room, tables on good-sized back terrace; bedrooms *(Peter Churchill, A Barker, BB)*; *Kings Head*: Lively old character local away from centre, well kept Black Sheep and other ales, good value food; pool room, bedrooms *(John Cadman, Bill and Lydia Ryan, A Barker, BB)*

☆ **Kilburn** N Yor [SE5179], *Forresters Arms*: Next to 'mouseman' Thompson furniture workshops (visitor centre opp), largely furnished by them; big log fire, varied well presented food, well kept Black Sheep and Theakstons Best, games and piped music; restaurant, well behaved children allowed, open all day; suntrap seats out in front, pleasant village; bedrooms clean, cheerful and bright *(Andrew and Ruth Triggs, Martin Hickes, Jim Farmer, Dono and Carol Leaman, Ian Boag, Mrs R Humphrey, LYM)*

☆ **Kilnsey** N Yor [Kilnsey Crag; SD9767], *Tennant Arms*: Pleasant staff, decent bar food, well kept Tetleys and Theakstons Best and Old Peculier, open fires, interesting decorations; piped music; views of spectacular overhanging crag from restaurant; comfortable bedrooms all with private bathrooms, good walks *(D Stokes, Neville Kenyon)*

Kirkby Overblow N Yor [SE3249], *Shoulder of Mutton*: Attractive layout, interesting decor, two log fires, well kept Tetleys, bar food, tables in lovely garden with play area by meadows; new licensees no longer doing bedrooms *(BB)*

Kirkbymoorside N Yor [Market Pl; SE6987], *Kings Head*: Cosy and unpretentious, doing well under friendly newish licensees, flagstoned walkers' bar (boots allowed), lounge opening into sheltered courtyard and garden, well priced food all home-made inc crunchy fresh veg, well kept beer; bedrooms *(Helen Orchison, BB)*

Kirkheaton W Yor [known as the Kirkstele; SE1818], *Beaumont Arms*: Pleasant and hospitable, relaxed and efficient, well kept beers, comfortably furnished *(A Preston)*

Knaresborough N Yor [High Bridge, Harrogate Rd; SE3557], *Yorkshire Lass*: Big pub-restaurant in fine riverside position, close to Mother Shipton's Cave with picturesque views from terrace; lively decoration, more than welcoming Scottish landlord, good generous food, comfortable dining room, well kept Courage-related ales, daily papers; live jazz/blues some nights; bedrooms well equipped and good value *(Martin Hickes)*

Langsett S Yor [A616 nr Penistone; SE2100], *Waggon & Horses*: Spotless comfortable pub on moors main road, welcoming helpful staff, blazing log fire, good plain home cooking inc popular Sun lunch, well kept Bass and Stones *(Cynthia Waller, Michael Butler)*

☆ **Langthwaite** N Yor [just off Reeth—Brough rd; NZ0003], *Red Lion*: Unspoilt, individual and relaxing, in charming dales village, with local books and maps, basic cheap nourishing lunchtime food, Black Sheep, Theakstons XB and Youngers Scotch, country wines, tea and coffee; well behaved children allowed lunchtime in very low-ceilinged (and sometimes smoky) side snug, quietly friendly service; good walks all around, inc organised circular ones from the pub *(Ray and Liz Monk, Peter Churchill, J H and S A Harrop, Andrew and Ruth Triggs, Geoff and Angela Jaques, LYM)*

☆ **Lealholm** N Yor [NZ7608], *Board*: Two-bar pub with good range of food inc big filled yorkshire puddings and good puddings, Camerons, big log fire favoured by Billy the monster pub cat; riverside garden, nice spot *(Mike and Maggie Betton)*

☆ **Leeds** W Yor [Gt George St], *Victoria*: Well preserved ornate Victorian pub with grand etched mirrors, impressive globe lamps extending from the ornately solid bar, smaller rooms off; well kept Tetleys inc Mild, friendly smart bar staff, reasonably priced food from end serving hatch *(Reg Nelson, Chris Westmoreland)*

☆ **Leeds** [37 Waterloo Rd, Hunslet; SE3131], *Garden Gate*: Archetypal ornate but much more down-to-earth Victorian pub with various rooms off central drinking corridor, well worth a look for its now near-unique style and intricate glass and woodwork; Tetleys Bitter and Mild foaming with freshness, farm cider, no food; open all day, can be boisterous evenings *(Annette Moore, Chris Pearson, Chris Westmoreland, Paul Cartledge, LYM)*

☆ **Leeds** [Hunslet Rd], *Adelphi*: Well restored handsome Edwardian tiling, woodwork and glass, several rooms, impressive stairway; particularly well kept Tetleys (virtually the brewery tap), good cheap lunchtime bar food, live jazz Sat *(Reg Nelson)*

☆ **Leeds** [86 Armley Rd, by Arkwright St], *Albion*: Very jolly, as if it's always party-time; three well restored interesting rooms, well kept Boddingtons and Tetleys from superb brass handpumps, good service, good value filling snacks, separate pool room; the original for the 00-gauge model railway pub *(David Campbell, Vicki McLean)*

☆ **Leeds** [Headrow, Kirkgate, by indoor mkt], *Duck & Drake*: No-frills big pub with a dozen or more well kept reasonably priced real ales inc obscure local brews, bustling friendly atmosphere, simple substantial food, open fire; loud live music Sun, Tues and Thurs nights, quieter back room *(Mark Bradley, Chris Westmoreland)*

☆ **Leeds** [North St (A61)], *Eagle*: Well kept reasonably priced Timothy Taylors and several guest beers usually from distant smaller breweries in 18th-c pub with choice of basic or plush bars, sensible food, helpful staff; pleasant for lunch, good bands in back bar weekends; bedrooms *(PGP, LYM)*

☆ **Leeds** [9 Burley Rd, junction with Rutland St], *Fox & Newt*: Interesting choice of mainly

Whitbreads-related ales as well as several brewed in the cellar here, good value limited standard lunchtime food, cheery neo-Victorian decor, well reproduced piped music; open all day, children welcome, dogs allowed evening *(Thomas Nott, Roger A Bellingham, LYM)*

Leeds [Meanwood], *Beer Exchange*: Comfortably renovated, with eight well kept real ales inc many from smaller breweries, no-smoking area, good food *(Andy and Jill Kassube)*; [Great George St], *George*: Good central well preserved Tetleys drinking pub, cheap, welcoming and lively, at its best during the week *(PGP, Reg Nelson)*; [off Wetherby rd, nr Sheepscar interchange], *New Roscoe*: Replacing a pub submerged by Sheepscar interchange, airy and busy, regular live music (esp Sun lunch), often Irish *(Chris Westmoreland)*; [The Calls], *Shears Yard*: Newish wine bar/restaurant, tables in yard, plenty of room inside, good choice of reasonably priced wines; good fresh food inc tapas-style mini dishes *(Kathryn and Brian Heathcote)*; [The Calls], *Sparrows Wharf*: Vaulted converted warehouse basement, informal, spacious and comfortable, Bass beers and Timothy Taylors Landlord, food lunchtime and evening, some seats on timber balcony over river *(Chris Westmoreland)*; [alley off Boar Lane parallel to Duncan St], *Whip*: Welcoming and lively, two or three alcoves in narrow front bar, back room, good choice of Tetleys-related ales *(Chris Westmoreland)*; [New Briggate], *Wrens*: Relaxing Tetleys pub with theatre posters and lots of summer plants, good snacks, no-smoking room *(Chris Westmoreland, Paul Cartledge)*

☆ **Leyburn** N Yor [Market Pl; SE1191], *Golden Lion*: Relaxing bay-windowed two-room bar, quite light and airy, with log-effect gas fire in eating area, good value generous straightforward bar food, evening restaurant; good beer brewed to their own recipe in Harrogate as well as Theakstons, decent coffee, friendly service, tables out in front; open all day, dogs allowed; bedrooms good value *(M J Morgan, BB)*

☆ **Linton** W Yor [Main St; SE3947], *Windmill*: Polished country atmosphere in small rooms with pewter tankards for the locals, antique settles, oak beams, longcase clock; generous helpings of good food (not Mon or Sun evening, very busy Sun lunchtime), well kept Theakstons Best and XB and Youngers Scotch, friendly staff, affluent feel; tables in pleasant garden, car park through coaching entrance *(C M F Harrison, Geoffrey and Brenda Wilson, Mark Bradley, LYM)*

Little Weighton N Yor [SE9833], *Black Horse*: Wide choice of generous home-cooked food, quick pleasant service, very reasonable prices *(E J Wilde)*

Lothersdale N Yor [Dale End; SD9646], *Hare & Hounds*: Comfortable and welcoming village pub on Pennine Way; John Smiths and Tetleys, good prompt lunchtime food at competitive prices; quiet midweek, busy with families weekend *(G W Lindley, A Preston)*

Low Marishes N Yor [SE8277], *School House*: Smart country family pub, good generous food inc fresh veg, well kept real ales *(Andy and Jill Kassube)*

☆ **Low Row** N Yor [B6270 Reeth—Muker; SD9897], *Punch Bowl*: Friendly youth-hostelish family bar, open all day in summer, with well kept Theakstons Best, XB and Old Peculier and guests, Easter beer festival, rows of malt whiskies, wide choice of good value food, log fire, games room; fine Swaledale views; popular tea room 10-5.30 with home-made cakes, small shop, bicycle and cave lamp hire, folk music Fri; good basic bedrooms, also bunkhouse, big breakfast *(Mark Bradley, John Unsworth)*

☆ **Malham** N Yor [SD8963], *Lister Arms*: Friendly and relaxed open-plan lounge, busy weekends, with good interesting bar food inc Mexican, well kept changing ales inc Black Sheep, Moorhouses Pendle Witches Brew and Wadworths 6X, even Liefmans Kriek and Franboyen in summer, lots of malt whiskies, roaring fire, helpful staff, restaurant famous for steaks, games area with pool; seats outside the substantial stone inn overlooking green, more in back garden – nice spot by river, ideal for walkers; bedrooms *(Dr J A Spencer, Paul McPherson, Prof and Mrs S Barnett, Mary Moore, Neil Calver, R E and M Baggs, D Goodger, J A Swanson)*

☆ **Malham**, *Buck*: Big village pub now doing well under welcoming newish local couple, good varied food prepared to order, well kept Black Sheep and Theakstons, log fires, comfortable lounge and big hikers' bar, separate candlelit dining room; decent well equipped bedrooms, many good walks from the door *(Geoffrey Stait, Pat Westbury, Neil Calver)*

Malton N Yor [Weston; SE7972], *Blacksmiths Arms*: Good local with warm country atmosphere, John Smiths and Tetleys *(Christopher Turner)*; [Market Pl], *Kings Head*: Ivy-covered pub, comfortable inside, with wide choice of good bar food, at least five well kept beers *(Andy and Jill Kassube)*; [Yolkersgate], *Mount*: Interesting local with lots of pictures etc, good choice of good value food, John Smiths, Tetleys and guest beers *(Christopher Turner)*; [Old Malton], *Royal Oak*: Friendly helpful service, good guest beers, good generous quickly served standard food inc Whitby seafood platter; tables in garden, children welcome *(K J Hillier, Dr Philip Jackson)*

☆ **Market Weighton** N Yor [SE8742], *Londesborough Arms*: Recently completely refurbished, two old-fashioned real ale bars with brass footrail along counter, John Smiths and Tetleys, interesting ambitious bar and restaurant food, decent wine, good civilised atmosphere, friendly staff; comfortable well equipped bedrooms *(Tony Gayfer, LYM)*

☆ **Marton cum Grafton** N Yor [signed off A1 3 miles N of A59; SE4263], *Olde Punch Bowl*: New chef doing good interesting very elegantly presented food in attractive old pub with comfortable and roomy heavy-beamed open-plan bar, open fires, brasses, framed old advertisements and photographs; Tetleys and Youngers Scotch and No 3, decent wines, no piped music, welcoming service, restaurant; children welcome, good play area and picnic tables in garden *(Viv Middlebrook, LYM)*

☆ **Masham** N Yor [Silver St, linking A6168 with Market Sq; SE2381], *Bay Horse*: Good range of good value straightforward bar food, friendly staff, Black Sheep and Theakstons ales – both produced in this village; children allowed *(Andrew and Marian Ruston, Richard Houghton)*

Methley W Yor [Main St; SE3926], *New Bay Horse*: Refurbished pub with ex-rugby footballer landlord, well kept Tetleys, enormous helpings of reasonably priced bar food (not Sun or Mon evenings), big children's room, big well furnished garden and play area *(A Dyson)*

☆ **Middleham** N Yor [SE1288], *Black Swan*: Very welcoming cheerfully civilised local atmosphere in immaculate heavy-beamed stripped stone bar with sturdy furniture inc high-backed settles built in by big stone fireplace, good attentive service, wide choice of reasonably priced filling and tasty bar food, well kept John Smiths, Theakstons Best, XB and Old Peculier, racing memorabilia; maybe piped pop music; separate dining room, tables on cobbles outside and in sheltered back garden; charming village in good walking country; bedrooms comfortable, clean and spacious, with own bathrooms *(D Grzelka, Neil and Angela Huxter, Michael Butler, Carol and Dennis Clayson, Philip da Silva, John and Chris Simpson, Jim Paul, Gordon Theaker, LYM)*

Middleham, *Black Bull*: Attractively refurbished by hard-working new young couple, good food inc fine nachos, well kept beer, good service; bedrooms *(Carol and Dennis Clayson)*

☆ *nr* **Midgley** W Yor [signed from Hebden Br, with evening/Sun bus to pub; coming from Halifax on A646 turn right just before Hebden Bridge town centre on to A6033 towards Keighley, take first right up steep Birchcliffe Rd and keep on to the top – OS Sheet 104 map ref 007272; SE0027], *Mount Skip*: Spectacular views of Pennines and mill-town valleys, welcoming staff, well kept Tetleys and Timothy Taylors Bitter, Landlord and Golden Best, good log fire, lots of prints and old photographs, china and brasses, generous cheap food inc two sizes for children; games area, unobtrusive piped music, restaurant, benches outside – right by Calderdale Way footpath; children allowed (not late); cl Mon lunchtime Oct-Easter, Tues lunchtime Jan-Easter *(Bruce Bird, Mark Bradley, LYM)*

☆ **Midhopestones** S Yor [off A616; SK2399], *Midhopestones Arms*: Character 17th-c pub, flagstones, stripped stone and pine, three small rooms, woodburner, pictures, assorted chairs, tables and settles; eight well kept ales inc Courage-related ones, Barnsley, Timothy Taylors Landlord and Wards, friendly staff, log fires, good value home cooking (not Sun evening) esp Sun lunch, breakfasts too; restaurant, seats outside; children welcome *(John B Dickinson, David and Lynn Lambley, CMW, JJW)*

Morton on Swale N Yor [SE3292], *Swaledale Arms*: Welcoming atmosphere, well kept Theakstons Best, good food (but not too foody), comfortable (not too luxurious), nice staff *(Comus Elliott)*

New Mill W Yor [Penistone Rd (A635); SE1808], *Crossroads*: Attractive roadside pub with Mansfield Riding and Old Baily, proper coffee, good value bar food inc children's Tues-Sun, friendly service, open fire and small aquarium in bar, kitchen range and darts in smaller tiled-floor room leading off, adjoining raftered partly no-smoking dining barn; nice garden with country views; cl Mon *(Andrew and Ruth Triggs, JJW, CMW)*

North Rigton N Yor [SE2748], *Square & Compass*: Comfortably modernised, good choice of reasonably priced good meals, restaurant *(James Marshall)*

North Stainley N Yor [SE2977], *Staveley Arms*: Old country pub with decent generous bar food, popular carvery Thurs-Sat evening and Sun lunch, rustic bric-a-brac ; bedrooms comfortable and well priced *(Andy and Jill Kassube)*

Northallerton N Yor [High St; SE3794], *Golden Lion*: Good atmosphere and well kept Hambleton in Forte ex-coaching inn's pleasant bar, good inexpensive food in attractive eating area, good coffee; bedrooms *(Roger Bellingham)*

☆ **Nosterfield** N Yor [B6267 Masham—Thirsk; SE2881], *Freemasons Arms*: Warm and friendly civilised open-plan bar and dining area, two log fires, beams and flagstones, Empire bric-a-brac, well kept Black Sheep and Theakstons, decent wines, sensible choice of good interesting food (not Mon evening), smiling service; tables outside, very pleasant surroundings; children welcome *(Martin and Tracy Land, David and Judith Hart, Andrew and Kathleen Bacon, H J Sharp, Mrs B J Head)*

Nun Monkton N Yor [off A59 York—Harrogate; SE5058], *Alice Hawthorn*: Modernised down-to-earth beamed village local with lots of brass etc, big brick inglenook fireplace, Tetleys and other ales, freshly prepared basic food, keen darts players; on broad village green with pond and lovely avenue to church and Rivers Nidd and Ouse *(Viv Middlebrook, T A Bryan, Tim and Sue Halstead, BB)*

☆ **Oakworth** W Yor [Harehills Lane, Oldfield; 2 miles towards Colne; SE0038], *Grouse*: Comfortable, interesting and spotless old pub packed with bric-a-brac, gleaming copper, lots of prints and china, attractively individual furnishings; particularly good lunchtime soup, filling sandwiches and cold dishes (not Mon), charming evening restaurant, well kept Timothy Taylors, good range of spirits, entertaining landlord, good service, good

Pennine views *(WAH, A and M Dickinson)*

☆ **Osmotherley** N Yor [The Green; SE4499], *Golden Lion*: Friendly family service, wide range of good bar food inc good puddings, well kept John Smiths Magnet, decent coffee, tables out overlooking village green; 44-mile Lyke Wake Walk starts here; may be closed Mon lunchtime *(Geoff and Angela Jaques)*

☆ **Osmotherley**, *Three Tuns*: Concentration on wide choice of interesting fresh food worth the wait in roomy and comfortable back dining room, small simple front bar, well kept Theakstons Best, XB and Old Peculier, smart friendly service, attractive coal fire; tables out in pleasant garden with lovely views; children welcome; comfortable bedrooms, good walks nearby *(Roger Berry, Martin Hickes, Geoff and Angela Jaques, John and Chris Simpson, Thomas Nott, R F Grieve, RB, Andrew and Ruth Triggs, J N Child, Dr Terry Murphy, M D Phillips)*

Ossett W Yor [Dewsbury Rd; SE2820], *Red Lion*: Good if not cheap food *(Martin Aust)*; [Manor Rd], *Victoria*: Wide-ranging reasonably priced food inc Sun carvery, changing beers such as Greene King Abbot, Marstons and Tetleys; cl Mon-Thurs lunchtime *(Michael Butler)*

☆ **Oswaldkirk** N Yor [signed off B1363/B1257 S of Helmsley; SE6279], *Malt Shovel*: Former small 17th-c manor house, heavy beams and flagstones, fine staircase, simple traditional furnishings, huge log fires, two cosy bars (one may be crowded with well heeled locals), family room, interestingly decorated dining room; well kept Sam Smiths OB and Museum, good fresh simple well presented food (maybe not Mon/Tues, and may sometimes stop before 2), interesting garden; children may be allowed *(M and J Back, Dr J Johnson, LYM)*

Otley W Yor [Boroughgate; SE2045], *Bay Horse*: Very old local with low beams and well kept ales; can be rather cramped *(Ben Grose)*; [Bondgate], *Rose & Crown*: Comfortable stonebuilt pub with friendly staff, wide range of mainly Whitbreads-related ales, good menu (not Fri/Sat evenings); can be busy lunchtime *(Lynne Gittins, Ben Grose)*

☆ **Oxenhope** W Yor [A6033 Keighley—Hebden Bridge; SE0335], *Waggon & Horses*: Welcoming stripped-stone moorside pub with good views, good range of generous food till late evening, Tetleys and Theakstons, open fires, pleasant simple decor, cheerful service, separate dining room; children welcome *(WAH, LYM)*

Oxenhope [off B6141 towards Denholme], *Dog & Gun*: Well kept Timothy Taylors Landlord and Best in roomy bar with olde-worlde decor, open fire each end, usual bar food, bistro-style restaurant, nice views *(WAH)*

☆ *nr* **Pateley Bridge** N Yor [Fellbeck; B6265, 3 miles E; SE2066], *Half Moon*: Good setting handy for Brimham Rocks, open all day, with spaciously airy modernised decor, well kept Timothy Taylors Landlord and Theakstons, generous good quick bar food, welcoming staff; piped music, fruit machines; children welcome, bedrooms in chalets *(Roger Berry, WAH, LYM)*

nr **Pateley Bridge** [Nidderdale rd N – OS Sheet 99 map ref 148665; SE1466], *Water Mill*: Well converted mill in pleasant setting, one of England's largest working waterwheels; cavernous bar with well kept Marstons Old Peculier, Theakstons XB and Youngers Scotch, good value food, open all day; picnic tables in big garden with good play area; bedrooms *(Lawrence Pearse)*

☆ **Pecket Well** W Yor [A6033 N of Hebden Bridge; SD9929], *Robin Hood*: Warmly welcoming jovial landlord, two rooms with lots of sporting prints, attractive stone fireplace in separate pool room, banquettes in stripped-stone vaulted-ceiling dining area, careful home cooking inc good veg, well kept Tetleys and Theakstons Best and Old Peculier, decent wines, friendly dog called Kiwi *(Gwen and Peter Andrews, Cynthia Waller, Mrs E Howe)*

☆ **Pickering** N Yor [18 Birdgate; SE7984], *Black Swan*: Attractive hotel keeping pubby atmosphere in smart plush bar, good service, good value tasty food, well kept Black Smith and Courage-related beers; well furnished restaurant; bedrooms *(Ann and Colin Hunt, Andy and Jill Kassube, Andrew Hazeldine, Q Williamson)*

Pickering [Market Pl], *Bay Horse*: Welcoming heavy-beamed plush bar with old-fashioned prints and horsey bric-a-brac, big fire, well kept John Smiths, generous good value food, bigger back public bar, upstairs restaurant *(Ann and Colin Hunt, BB)*; [Market Pl], *White Swan*: Two small bars, good traditional well priced bar food inc vegetarian, well kept Camerons and Theakstons, pleasant staff, busy but comfortable family room, good restaurant with interesting wines; bedrooms comfortable, good breakfast *(Andy and Jill Kassube, John T Ames, Willie Bell)*

☆ **Pocklington** N Yor [5 Market Pl; SE8049], *Feathers*: Roomy open-plan lounge with banquettes (busy Tues market day), usual bar food, well kept Theakstons Best and Youngers Scotch, helpful landlady; children welcome, timbered restaurant, no-smoking conservatory, quiz and jazz nights, comfortable motel-style bedrooms *(Julie Peters, LYM)*

Pool [A658 towards Harrogate; SE2445], *Hunters*: Up to eight well kept ales, balcony for warm weather, open fires for cold *(Chris Westmoreland)*; [A659 towards Arthington], *Wharfedale Arms*: Pleasant lively food pub with separate restaurant, quick service masterminded by vocal Italian landlord, good value bar food, Tetleys *(D Stokes)*

☆ **Potto** N Yor [Cooper Lane; NZ4704], *Dog & Gun*: Roomy tucked-away pub with open fire in plush L-shaped bar with alcove seating, charming lounge with interesting decor, wide choice of bar food inc delicious puddings, friendly family service, attractive evening restaurant; bedrooms spacious and tidy, big breakfast *(JV)*

☆ **Pudsey** W Yor [SE2233], *Beulah*: Comfortable and friendly old-fashioned pub with superb views, reasonably priced bar snacks, good interesting food cooked to order in small restaurant, well kept Tetleys, friendly efficient service *(R B and H Rand)*

Pudsey [Town St, Farsley; SE2135], *Old Hall*: Good food and atmosphere *(John Spear)*

Queensbury W Yor [Mountain; A644 Brighouse—Denholme; SE1030], *Mad Ma Jones's*: Well kept changing ales such as Black Sheep, Morlands Old Speckled Hen and Theakstons, bright cheerful landlord who knows about beer, old kitchen-style bar, imitation hams, old linen press and memorabilia, enjoyable low-priced food esp cow pie *(Jenny and Brian Seller, Janice and Peter Rush)*

Ravensworth N Yor [off A66; NZ1408], *Bay Horse*: Attractive stone-built split-level beamed local, clean and smart, with good varied food inc vegetarian and children's, Theakstons ales; children welcome, picnic tables facing village green *(Mike and Sue Walton, JJW, CMJ)*

☆ **Reeth** N Yor [just off B6270; SE0499], *Black Bull*: Friendly local with traditional dark beamed and flagstoned L-shaped bar, separate lounge, well kept Tetleys and Theakstons, reasonably priced usual bar food, open fires – can be smoky; children welcome, pool and other games; at bottom of fine broad sloping green; comfortable bedrooms, good breakfast *(Margaret Mason, David Thompson, Chris and Andy Crow, Michael Butler, Gwen and Peter Andrews, LYM)*

☆ **Reeth** [Market Pl (B6270)], *Kings Arms*: Popular dining pub by green, with oak beams, pine pews around walls, log fire in big 18th-c stone inglenook, warm plum carpet, quieter room behind; good reasonably priced food, friendly service, well kept Theakstons, John Smiths and Tetleys; children very welcome; bedrooms *(Gwen and Peter Andrews)*

Richmond N Yor [Finkle St; NZ1801], *Black Lion*: Well kept ales, friendly service, lots of cosy separate rooms inc no-smoking lounge, good atmosphere, dark traditional decor, bar food; bedrooms reasonably priced *(Ben Grose)*

☆ **Ripley** N Yor [off A61 Harrogate—Ripon; SE2861], *Boars Head*: Beautiful old hotel with long flagstoned bar, neat and well run, with tables in series of stalls, good value bar food, well kept Archers, Theakstons Best and XB and other guest beers, smart friendly service, plenty of tables in charming garden; good restaurant; comfortable if not cheap bedrooms *(Andrew and Ruth Triggs, Tim and Sue Halstead, David Surridge, Colin and Ann Hunt, David and Ruth Hollands)*

☆ **Ripon** N Yor [Bridge Lane, off Bondgate Green (itself off B6265); or cross bridge nr cathedral and turn left along path; SE3171], *Water Rat*: Good value generous food inc wide vegetarian choice, well kept Vaux and interesting guest ales, good service; pleasantly bustling, unassuming but well furnished, prettily set by footbridge over River Skell with ducks and weir, charming view of cathedral from riverside terrace; friendly service *(GSB, Dr and Mrs D Awbery, A Craig, Colin and Ann Hunt)*

Ripon [Allhallow Gate, off Mkt Sq], *Golden Lion*: Small and cosy, well kept Theakstons, wide choice of good well priced food in bar and small back restaurant, friendly staff *(Roger Berry, Ants Aug)*

☆ **Robin Hoods Bay** N Yor [King St, Bay Town; NZ9505], *Olde Dolphin*: Roomy 18th-c inn stepped up above sea front in attractive little town; unpretentious furnishings, friendly service, convivial atmosphere, well kept cheap Courage, good open fire, bar food inc local seafood, popular back games room; dogs welcome in bar if well behaved, piped music, Fri folk club; can get crowded weekends, long walk back up to village car park; bedrooms basic but very cheap *(Mike and Wendy Proctor)*

Robin Hoods Bay [The Dock, Bay Town], *Bay*: Fine sea views from cosy picture-window bar, well kept Courage-related ales, log fires, generous home-made food with separate dining area; maybe piped music, well behaved children may be allowed in room up steps; tables outside; bedrooms *(Mike and Wendy Proctor, Chris and Andy Crow, Andrew Hazeldine)*

Roecliffe N Yor [SE3766], *Crown*: Extended without losing atmosphere, good food and service *(Janet and Peter Race)*

☆ **Rosedale Abbey** N Yor [300 yds up Rosedale Chimney; SE7395], *White Horse*: Cosy and comfortable farm-based country inn with local feel in interestingly decorated bar, lots of character, well kept Tetleys and Theakstons, quite a few wines and good choice of malt whiskies, good generous reasonably priced home-made bar food esp range of pies, restaurant, lovely views from terrace (and from bedrooms); children allowed if eating, open all day Sat; bedrooms – a nice place to stay *(Ron Monk, Ian S Morley, Paul Cartledge, Bronwen and Steve Wrigley, J L Phillips, LYM)*

☆ **Runswick Bay** N Yor [NZ8217], *Royal*: Super setting, lovely views over fishing village and sea from welcoming big-windowed plain front lounge with interesting marine fishtank, limited choice of good value food inc huge helpings of fresh local fish, cosy bustling atmosphere, well kept John Smiths, nautical back bar, terrace; bedrooms *(Mike and Wendy Proctor, Michael Butler, LYM)*

Runswick Bay N Yor [NZ8217], *Runswick Bay*: Decent straightforward food cooked to order *(Michael Williamson)*

☆ **Saxton** N Yor [B1217 Towton—Garforth about a mile outside; SE4736], *Crooked Billet*: Tidy and well run extended pub doing a huge trade in very reasonably priced food esp giant sandwiches, pies and enormous yorkshire puddings – get there early for a seat; friendly comfortable atmosphere, well kept John Smiths, efficient service *(Thomas Nott,*

John Broughton, F and Dorothy Twentyman, Janet Pickles, Chris Westmoreland)

☆ **Saxton** [Headwell Lane], *Plough*: Smart dining pub, small bar with blackboard over blazing coke fire, good choice of food (not Sun evening) inc interesting specials, good veg and beautifully presented puddings in adjacent dining room, well kept Theakstons, decent house wine, good coffee; cl Mon *(Roy Bromell, BKA)*

Scammonden Reservoir W Yor [A672; SE0215], *Brown Cow*: Friendly landlord, good rotating guest beers such as Maidens Water, Marstons Pedigree, Morlands Old Speckled Hen and Tetleys Imperial, cheap bar food inc children's, in old-fashioned pub with long bar; breathtaking scenery, overlooking M62, moors and Scammonden dam *(H K Dyson)*

☆ **Scarborough** N Yor [Vernon Rd; TA0489], *Hole in the Wall*: Great atmosphere and well kept Malton Double Chance, Theakstons BB, XB and Old Peculier and good changing guest beers in friendly three-roomed local with one long central bar, country wines, no piped music or machines; cheap basic lunchtime food *(Andrew Hazeldine, Dave Braisted)*

Scarborough [Falsgrave], *Tap & Spile*: Wide choice of beers inc cheap Big Lamp and changing guests in busy friendly old-style bare-boards pub with open fires, no juke box, food; open all day *(Glenn Morris)*

☆ **Scawton** N Yor [SE5584], *Hare*: Low and pretty, much modernised, with a couple of cosy settees, simple wall settles, little wheelback armchairs, air force memorabilia; friendly service, well kept Home, Theakstons Best and Old Peculier, decent straightforward food, two friendly dogs, eating area, pool room; tables in big back garden with caged geese, nice inn-signs; children welcome, handy for Rievaulx *(Andrew and Ruth Triggs, BB)*

☆ **Scorton** N Yor [B1263 Richmond—Yarm, just outside village – off A1 just N of Catterick; NZ2500], *St Cuthberts*: Friendly local atmosphere, welcoming efficient service, good value well presented imaginative fresh food inc good generous Sun lunches and vast choice of puddings, well kept Theakstons; restaurant *(Paul and Ursula Randall, Mr Ramsden, Mr and Mrs C J Davey, Keith Davey, Sarah Thomas)*

☆ **Seamer** N Yor [Main St; TA0284], *Copper Horse*: Generous good food in friendly no-smoking dining areas off main bar, beams, brasses, bare stone, part wood-floored and part carpeted, with gold plush bar stools and wooden chairs around cast-iron-framed tables; pleasant helpful service, Youngers, restaurant; cl Mon in winter; pretty village *(Ian S Morley)*

Settle N Yor [SD8264], *Golden Lion*: Bright red plush in cheerful high-beamed bar with enormous fireplace, bar, well kept Thwaites, games in lively public bar, horses still stabled in coachyard *(Dave and Carole Jones, LYM)*

Sheffield [Crookes; SK3287], *Ball*: Around eight well kept real ales, quiz nights *(M Porter)*; [66 Victoria St, off Glossop Rd], *Bath*: Local with good atmosphere, well kept ales inc guests, big main bar, small lounge with fire, good landlady *(H A Dobson)*; [Henry St], *Cask & Cutler*: Small pub beside new tramway, five well kept changing ales from small breweries, food inc unusual sausages, lots of posters, friendly landlord, sensibly placed pool table, no juke box; annual beer festival *(Jack and Philip Paxton, Simon, Julia and Laura Plumbley)*; [Broad Lane], *Fagans*: Warm and welcoming, with friendly staff, well kept Tetleys, wide range of malt whiskies, no juke box, live music Fri *(Andrew Hilton, Jack and Philip Paxton)*; [Division St, corner of Westfield Terr], *Frog & Parrot*: Largely bare-boarded with lofty ceiling, huge windows, comfortable banquettes up a few steps, lively studenty cafe-bar atmosphere in evenings, interesting beers brewed on the premises – one fearsomely strong *(Paul Cartledge, LYM)*; [Crookes], *Noahs Ark*: Good choice of beers and of generous good cheap food *(M Porter)*; [3 Crookes Rd, Crookes], *Old Grindstone*: Busy Victorian pub with good cheap food inc good Sun roast, Timothy Taylors Landlord, Vaux Waggle Dance and Wards, teapot collection, obliging service, friendly black cat, games room with pool etc, no piped music, jazz Mon *(CMW, JJW, M Porter)*; [255 Ecclesall Rd], *Pomona*: Large comfortably modernised suburban pub with wide choice of good value food 11-9 (not Sun), Theakstons XB and Youngers Scotch and No 3, conservatory, snooker room, games machines *(JJW, CMW)*; [Tofts Lane, just off Rivelin Valley Rd], *Rivelin*: Popular pub with reasonably priced food, Bass and Tetleys on handpump, pelmets with plates and horse brasses, ideal for walkers *(Andrew and Ruth Triggs)*; [Millhouses Lane], *Robin Hood*: Open-plan Big Steak pub split into cosy areas, each attractively decorated, well kept Tetleys-related beers, conservatory and outside eating area *(B M Eldridge)*; [86 Brown St], *Rutland Arms*: Jolly place handy for the station and the Crucible; good wine and beer, plentiful good value food *(Jenny Garrett)*; [610 Redmires Rd], *Three Merry Lads*: Big Steak pub with uninterrupted views, good range of Tetleys-related beers, friendly staff, pleasant garden with play area *(B M Eldridge)*

☆ **Shepley** W Yor [Station Rd, Stocksmoor; Thunderbridge and Stocksmoor signed off A629 N; SE1810], *Clothiers Arms*: Good atmosphere in softly lit rooms inc games room, conservatory extension, polite helpful staff and friendly landlord; bar food (not Sun or Mon evenings), downstairs carvery, Tetleys and Theakstons, tables out on balconies; quiet countryside *(M A Butler)*

☆ **Shepley** [Penistone Rd – OS Sheet 110 map ref 197088], *Sovereign*: Very popular welcoming open-plan L-shaped dining lounge with low beamery, red carpets and upholstery, yucca plants, restaurant leading off, generous unpretentious good value fresh food, Bass and Worthington BB, moderately priced wines, good atmosphere, attentive

service; garden, provision for children *(M A Butler)*
Sheriff Hutton N Yor [The Square; SE6566], *Highwayman*: Cosy old coaching inn overlooking castle; log fires, snug bars, oak beams in lounge and dining room, decent range of beers, big garden; 12th-c church *(B M Eldridge)*
Shipton N Yor [SE5559], *Dawnay Arms*: Well kept beer, good food *(G Washington)*
Shiptonthorpe N Yor [A1079 Mkt Weighton—York; SE8543], *Crown*: Increasingly popular for good food inc Sun lunch, good service, well kept beer *(Roger Bellingham)*
☆ **Sinnington** N Yor [SE7586], *Fox & Hounds*: Good generous home-cooked food inc interestig veg and good value Sun lunch, two clean and welcoming bar areas, dining area, impressive service even when busy, nice paintings and old artefacts, cosy fires, well kept Bass and Camerons, separate pool room; attractive village with pretty stream and lots of grass; cosy well equipped bedrooms *(Mr Rymer, Mrs Boothman, Miss Halse, Elizabeth and Anthony Watts, Enid and Henry Stephens, Rita and Keith Pollard)*
☆ **Skerne** N Yor [Wansford Rd; TA0455], *Eagle*: Quaint and unspoilt village local with two simple rooms either side of hall, coal fire, well kept Camerons from rare Victorian cash-register beer engine in kitchen-style servery, chatty locals, friendly landlord brings drinks to your table; no food, open 7-11 Mon-Fri, 12-2 weekends *(Jack and Philip Paxton, Pete Baker)*
☆ **Skipton** N Yor [Canal St; from Water St (A65) turn into Coach St, then left after canal bridge; SD9852], *Royal Shepherd*: Busy old-fashioned local in pretty spot by canal, good low-priced basic food served quickly, well kept Whitbreads-related ales, decent wine, friendly service, unusual sensibly priced whiskies, open fires and photographs of Yorks CCC in its golden days in big bar, snug and dining room, tables outside, games and juke box *(Leonard Dixon, Ray and Liz Monk, Prof and Mrs S Barnett)*
Skipton [Swadford St], *Cock & Bottle*: Old-fashioned local with well kept real ales, simple good food, welcoming licensees, darts, fruit machines, Sun evening live music; small play area out behind *(Cath Scaife)*
☆ **Slaithwaite** W Yor [B6107 Meltham—Marsden; SE0813], *White Horse*: Friendly and attractively set moorland inn with good quick unusual home-cooked food, Tetleys and Timothy Taylors Landlord, small bar with log fire, comfortable lounge on right, attractive restaurant area on left, tables out on front flagstones; children welcome; two bedrooms sharing bath, huge breakfast *(Andrew and Ruth Triggs, Louise Knowles, Sarah Harvey)*
Slaithwaite [Cop Hill], *Rose & Crown*: Marvellous Colne Valley and moor views, recently refurbished (even a bit posh for the area), with well kept Tetleys *(H K Dyson)*; [B6107 Meltham—Marsden], *White House*: Imposing inn high on the south side of the Colne Valley; Tetleys, Theakstons and Youngers Scotch, long dining area on left of small central bar, public bar to left; restaurant, piano, efficient friendly staff *(Andrew and Ruth Triggs)*
☆ **Snape** N Yor [SE2784], *Castle Arms*: Enterprising food in comfortable and homely pub with cosy inglenooks, open fires, friendly licensees, well kept ale, decent wines, attractive small dining area; pleasant village *(Paul Wreglesworth)*
Sneaton N Yor [Beacon Way; NZ8908], *Wilson Arms*: Wider choice of food under very friendly new tenants, well kept Theakstons Best, good open fires, newly decorated dining room *(M Borthwick, Andrew Hazeldine)*
☆ **South Dalton** N Yor [OS Sheet 106 map ref 964454; SE9645], *Pipe & Glass*: Friendly new licensee in quiet dining pub prettily set by Dalton Park, well kept Theakstons Best, Morlands Old Speckled Hen and Youngers IPA, good choice of food inc vegetarian and good chips, some high-backed settles, old prints, log fires, beams and bow windows, conservatory, restaurant, children welcome, tables in garden with play area *(Keith and Rita Pollard, Eric J Locker, Karen and Graham Oddey, J S M Sheldon, M and J Back, LYM)*
☆ **Sowerby** W Yor [Steep Lane; SE0423], *Travellers Rest*: Several cosy little rooms, open fire, wide choice of good generous reasonably priced food, friendly service; fine country setting, good view over Halifax and Calderdale Valley from garden (lovely at night) *(L G Milligan, Ian and Amanda Wharmby)*
Spennithorne N Yor [SE1489], *Old Horn*: Small cosy low-beamed 17th-c inn, renovated but not spoilt, with games area, separate dining area, well kept Marstons Pedigree, John Smiths and Theakstons Best, simple choice of good home-cooked food inc good veg, decent wine, warm welcome, friendly locals, unobtrusive piped music; two bedrooms with own bathrooms *(Michael and Susan Morgan, Mike and Penny Sanders, D Grzelka)*
Spofforth N Yor [A661 Harrogate—Wetherby – OS Sheet 104 map ref 366507; SE3650], *Railway*: Sam Smiths pub with ordinary bar, simple unfussy lounge, garden and play area, straightforward inexpensive food *(Thomas Nott)*
☆ **Sprotbrough** S Yor [Lower Sprotbrough; 2¾ miles from M18 junction 2; SE5302], *Boat*: Three roomy and interestingly furnished areas in busy ex-farmhouse by River Don, big stone fireplaces, latticed windows, dark brown beams, bar food inc good ploughman's and wide choice of hot dishes (no sandwiches), well kept Courage-related beers, farm cider, helpful staff; piped music, fruit machine, no dogs; big sheltered prettily lit courtyard, river walks; restaurant (Tues-Sat evening, Sun lunch); open all day summer Sats *(Peter Marshall, LYM)*

☆ **Stainforth** N Yor [B6479 Settle—Horton-in-Ribblesdale; SD8267], *Craven Heifer*: Friendly dales village pub, small, cosy and clean, with well kept Thwaites, log fire, reasonably priced bar food inc well filled sandwiches; bedrooms simple but comfortable, fine breakfast *(M E A Horler, A N Ellis)*

Staithes N Yor [NZ7818], *Cod & Lobster*: Superb waterside setting in unspoilt fishing village under sandstone cliff, well kept beers inc Camerons Best and Strongarm, lovely views from seats outside; quite a steep walk up to top car park *(Andrew Hazeldine, LYM)*; *Royal George*: Small and friendly, nr harbour, with locals' bar on right, three plusher interconnected rooms, straightforward food, Burton Bridge, Camerons Bitter and Strongarm, children welcome; piped music, darts *(Phil and Heidi Cook)*

Stanbury W Yor [SE0037], *Old Silent*: Clean and up-to-date moorland village pub with conservatory, separate games room, juke box; well kept Theakstons, straightforward food, open fire, welcoming service, friendly restaurant; bedrooms *(WAH, Mark and Rachel Hirst, LYM)*

☆ **Staveley** N Yor [signed off A6055 Knaresborough—Boroughbridge; SE3663], *Royal Oak*: Prettily laid out beamed and tiled-floor pub locally popular for unusual home-cooked food in bar and restaurant, Tetleys-related ales, welcoming service, broad bow window; tables on front lawn *(Dorothy and David Young, LYM)*

☆ **Stokesley** N Yor [1 West End; NZ5209], *White Swan*: Simple country pub with regularly changing interesting ales, pizzas, no music *(G S and A Jaques, E J Cutting)*

☆ **Stutton** N Yor [SE4841], *Hare & Hounds*: Wide choice of good food at sensible prices (inc good Sun lunch) in cosy and unspoilt low-ceilinged stone-built pub unusually done out in 1960s style; good welcoming service, well kept and priced Sam Smiths OB, decent wine, restaurant; children allowed if eating; lovely long sloping garden with toys for children *(Paul Cartledge, Chris Westmoreland, Peter and Lois Haywood, Tim and Sue Halstead)*

☆ **Sutton** S Yor [follow Askern, Campsall sign off A1 S of Barnsdale Bar, then signed from Campsall; SE5512], *Anne Arms*: Creeper-covered stone house open all day, small cottagey rooms crammed with decorative china, family conservatory, John Smiths Magnet; the tenants who made it popular for hearty good value home-cooked meals left in summer 1995, taking at least part of the china collection *(LYM; news please)*

☆ **Sutton Howgrave** N Yor [signed off B6267 just W of A1; SE3279], *White Dog*: This charming immaculate cottage has been a popular main entry for many years, with really good food (open only at lunchtime), good wines and friendly service; catch it while you can, as at the end of 1995 Basil and Pat Bagnall are converting it to a private house for their retirement – with our best wishes *(LYM)*

☆ **Sutton on the Forest** N Yor [B1363 N of York; SE5965], *Rose & Crown*: Two-roomed dining pub with friendly newish licensees, good cooking and fresh ingredients, Theakstons ales, decent wines *(Andrew Argyle, W Rinaldi-Butcher)*

☆ **Sutton under Whitestonecliffe** N Yor [A170 E of Thirsk; SE4983], *Whitestonecliffe*: Beamed roadside pub with wide range of good value traditional generous bar meals (can be eaten in small restaurant) inc fresh fish and good puddings, open fire in relaxing and comfortable front lounge, back pool/family room with juke box and fruit machine, pleasant tap room with traditional games; John Smiths, Tetleys and Theakstons Best, decent wines, good friendly service; children welcome; back bedroom wing *(Andrew and Ruth Triggs, Martin Hickes)*

☆ **Tadcaster** N Yor [1 Bridge St; SE4843], *Angel & White Horse*: Tap for Sam Smiths brewery, cheap well kept OB and Museum, friendly staff, big helpings of good simple lunchtime food (not Sat) from separate counter; longish bar with alcoves at one end, fine oak panelling and solid furnishings but piped pop music; restaurant (children allowed there); the dappled grey dray horses are kept across the coachyard, and brewery tours can be arranged – tel (01937) 832225; open all day Sat *(Brian Kneale, Chris Westmoreland, Susan and Nigel Wilson, Paul Cartledge, LYM)*

☆ **Tan Hill** N Yor [Arkengarthdale (Reeth—Brough) rd, at junction with Keld/W Stonesdale rd; NY8906], *Tan Hill Inn*: Simple furnishings, flagstones and big open fires in Britain's highest pub, on the Pennine Way, nearly five miles from the nearest neighbour; well kept Theakstons Best, XB and Old Peculier (in winter the cellar does chill down – for warmth you might prefer coffee or whisky with hot water), good choice of hearty food from sandwiches up, some good old photographs, games room, occasional singalong accordion sessions, quite a heady atmosphere; children welcome, open all day at least in summer; bedrooms, inc some in newish extension; often snowbound, with no mains electricity (juke box powered by generator) *(Jim Farmer, Lesley Sones, Richard Houghton, Barry A Lynch, M J Morgan, Bronwen and Steve Wrigley, D Tolson, LYM)*

Tankersley S Yor [Church Lane; SK3399], *Tankersley Manor*: More hotel than pub, restored 17th-c manor house with extensions, comfortable, with good food; bedrooms *(Andrew and Ruth Triggs)*

☆ **Thirsk** N Yor [Market Pl; SE4382], *Golden Fleece*: Comfortable two-room bar with good reasonably priced food from sandwiches up, well kept Whitbreads-related ales, pleasant service, view across square from bay windows; restaurant, bedrooms *(Dono and Carol Leaman, Andrew and Ruth Triggs, Barbara and Norman Wells)*

Thoralby N Yor [SE0086], *George*: Small lively Dales village local with generous sensibly priced food, Black Sheep, John Smiths and Websters, darts, dominoes; good clean cheap bedrooms *(Ray and Liz Monk, Richard Hathaway)*

☆ **Thornton** W Yor [Hill Top Rd; SE0933], *Ring o' Bells*: Wide choice of well presented good home cooking inc fresh fish, meat and poultry specialities, classy restaurant; Courage-related ales, very welcoming service *(Stephen and Brenda Head, Mrs Pam Deeprose, Geoffrey and Brenda Wilson, F J Willy, Nick Haslewood, A D Shore)*

☆ **Thornton in Lonsdale** N Yor [just NW of Ingleton; SD6976], *Marton Arms*: Quiet country pub with antique pine furniture, 15 well kept real ales, farm cider, lots of malt whiskies, good bar food inc good pizzas, enormous gammon and daily specials, efficient friendly service even when busy; children welcome, attractive Dales setting; bedrooms *(Paul J Bispham, Andy and Jill Kassube, John Hazel, Mr and Mrs J Connor, Richard Houghton)*

Thornton le Clay N Yor [SE6865], *White Swan*: Enthusiastic regulars giving strong support to friendly old-fashioned dining pub with popular food inc vegetarian, well kept ales such as Black Sheep and Youngers Scotch, decent wines, log fires, tables on terrace; good view from impeccable ladies' *(Eileen Walker and others)*

Thruscross N Yor [off A59 Harrogate—Skipton, or B6255 Grassington—Pateley Br; SE1558], *Stone House*: Moorland pub with beams, flagstones, stripped stone, dark panelling and warm fires; generous bar food, well kept ales, traditional games, sheltered tables outside; children welcome *(Prof and Mrs S Barnett, LYM)*

☆ **Thurlstone** S Yor [OS Sheet 110 map ref 230034; SE2303], *Huntsman*: Well run old stone-built pub with good range of well kept ales inc Flowers and Marstons, welcoming atmosphere, lunchtime bar food, coal fire *(Michael Butler)*

Tickhill S Yor [Sunderland St; A631 Bawtry rd; SK5993], *Scarbrough Arms*: Cheerful pub with lots of brass and barrel tables, decent food, cheerful staff, well kept Ruddles County; swings out behind *(Simon and Louise Chappell)*

☆ **Todmorden** W Yor [550 Burnley Rd, Knotts; A646 – OS Sheet 103 map ref 916257; SD9125], *Staff of Life*: Attractive partly flagstoned pub with stone-vaulted bar, home-cooked food inc vegetarian, Jennings ales and ones brewed locally by Robinwood *(Annette Moore, Chris Pearson, LYM)*

Towton N Yor [A162 Tadcaster—Ferrybridge; SE4839], *Rockingham Arms*: Bright and friendly extended pub popular for good food esp fish and chips, horsey theme in comfortable front room, welcoming efficient service, well kept Vaux Bitter and Samson, good coffee, revolving back pool table *(John Broughton, Roy Bromell, Chris Westmoreland)*

☆ **Ulley** S Yor [Turnshaw Rd; 2 miles from M1 junction 31 – off B6067 in Aston; SK4687], *Royal Oak*: Friendly and cosy stone-built pub in lovely countryside by church, very popular for good range of good value bar food, attractive and intimate inexpensive restaurant (must book); well kept cheap Sam Smiths OB, stable-theme beamed lounge with rooms off, helpful service, quiet piped music, good children's room, big garden; can get packed on warm summer evenings, esp Sat *(Gordon Theaker, GSB, Paul Robinshaw, WAH)*

Upper Poppleton N Yor [A59 York—Harrogate; SE5554], *Red Lion*: Reasonably priced food inc good vegetarian in dark and cosy olde-worlde bars and dining areas, quiet and welcoming – popular with older people and businessmen; pleasant garden; bedrooms *(Mr and Mrs I B White)*

Wakefield W Yor [Westgate; SE3321], *Henry Boons*: Well kept Clarks (from next-door brewery) and Timothy Taylors, very cheap food, pleasant traditional bare-boards furnishings – good for lunch *(Andy and Maureen Pickering)*

Walkington N Yor [35 East End; B1230 Beverley—South Cave; SE9937], *Barrel*: Local by village duckpond refurbished in comfortable old-world style, welcoming service, well kept Boddingtons, Marstons Pedigree, Stones, Websters and Whitbreads, good cheap unfussy food cooked to order *(Thomas Nott, JJW, CMW, C A Hall)*; [B1230], *Dog & Duck*: Popular dining pub with good bar food in long lounge or small restaurant; well kept Mansfield and Riding ales, decent wine, pleasant atmosphere, good service *(Roger Bellingham)*; [B1230], *Ferguson Fawsitt Arms*: Mock-Tudor bars in 1950s style, with good choice of properly cooked good value food and good puddings from airy no-smoking flagstone-floored self-service food bar, very popular lunchtime with older people; friendly cheerful service, decent wine; tables out on terrace, games bar with pool table *(Roger Bellingham, John Bestley, LYM)*

Walsden W Yor [A6033 S of Todmorden; SD9322], *Bird i' th' Hand*: Small roadside pub with wide choice of good home-cooked food; always busy, usually queue outside for strict 7pm opening *(M J Halliday)*

Warley W Yor [SE0525], *Maypole*: Good value generous food, well kept Marstons Pedigree *(Howard Bateman)*

☆ **Warthill** N Yor [village signed off A64 York—Malton and A166 York—Great Driffield; SE6755], *Agar Arms*: Popular steak pub, other food too inc lunchtime sandwiches and children's; softly lit and nicely decorated welcoming L-shaped bar and extension, open fires, well kept Sam Smiths on electric pump, decent house wine, pleasant staff; pretty spot opp duckpond *(D Baker, BB)*

☆ **Welburn** N Yor [SE7268], *Crown & Cushion*: Tidy stonebuilt village pub with two connecting rooms, good value home cooking inc good Sun lunch, well kept Camerons Bitter and Strongarm and Tetleys, decent wine, welcoming staff, games in public bar, restaurant; piped music; attractive small back garden with terrace; children in eating areas, has been closed Mon lunchtime in winter *(F J and P Parmenter, Geoffrey and Brenda Wilson, LYM)*

Wentbridge W Yor [Great North Rd (off A1); SE4817], *Blue Bell*: Several communicating rooms, beams, stripped stone, bric-a-brac and solid wooden tables, chairs and settles; wide choice of quick generous food inc Sun evening, friendly efficient service, well kept Tetleys, Theakstons Best and Timothy Taylors Landlord; family room, good view from garden *(John Watson, G Washington, Mark Bradley, CW, JW, John Coatsworth, Jacqueline White)*

☆ **Wentworth** S Yor [3 miles from M1 junction 36, village signed off A6135, pub on B6090; can also be reached from junction 35 via Thorpe; SK3898], *George & Dragon*: Friendly rambling split-level bar, home-cooked food, good choice of guest ales, assorted old-fashioned furnishings, ornate stove in lounge, back small games room, restaurant, benches in front courtyard *(Mark Bradley, Cathy Scott, Richard Baker, Peter Marshall, LYM)*

☆ **Wentworth** [village centre], *Rockingham Arms*: Good choice of reasonably priced food (not Sun evening) inc inventive specials in friendly pub with wooden chairs and settles, hunting pictures, open fires, stripped stone, rooms off inc a dining room and family room, cheerful service, several well kept S & N real ales; piped music; tables in attractive garden with own well kept bowling green; has been open all day; bedrooms *(Mark Bradley, G P Kernan, LYM)*

West Burton N Yor [on green, off B6160 Bishopdale—Wharfedale; SE0186], *Fox & Hounds*: Welcoming unpretentious local in idyllic Dales village around long green; simple generous inexpensive fresh food inc children's, Black Sheep and Theakstons ales, residents' dining room, children welcome; nearby caravan park; good modern bedrooms *(Michael Butler, Richard Hathaway, Frank Hughes, Dr Philip Jackson, Patricia Heptinstall)*

☆ **West Witton** N Yor [A684 W of Leyburn; SE0688], *Wensleydale Heifer*: Clean and comfortable low-ceilinged front lounge with small interconnecting areas, big attractive bistro, separate restaurant too, generous carefully prepared food inc interesting dishes and seafood, good log fire, attractive prints, pleasant decor and civilised atmosphere; good service even when busy, small bar with well kept Theakstons; comfortable bedrooms in main building and nearby houses *(D Grzelka, Keith Croxton, Michael and Susan Morgan)*

Wheldrake N Yor [SE6845], *Wenlock Arms*: Good value food in modernised village pub, efficient service, John Smiths and Marstons Pedigree, darts in big main bar, restaurant; live music Sat *(Ann and Colin Hunt)*

Whiston S Yor [Turner Lane, nr M1 junction 33; SK4590], *Golden Ball*: Extended old food-oriented pub, well kept Tetleys and other ales, one no-smoking eating area, relaxed atmosphere; TV, piped music, no food Sun evening *(JJW, CMW, Paul Cartledge)*

☆ **Whitby** N Yor [Church St; nr 199 Steps, East Side; NZ9011], *Duke of York*: Comfortable beamed pub down by harbour entrance, lovely views from lounge, friendly and lively atmosphere, good value bar food inc local cod and good vegetarian range, well kept Courage-related ales; open all day summer *(Ken Smith, Andy and Jane Beardsley, Andrew Hazeldine, M Borthwick, Andy and Jill Kassube)*

Whitby [Bagdale], *Bagdale Hall*: Hotel in handsome and carefully restored medieval former manor, well kept Tetleys, good choice of spirits, piped classical music, fine restaurant with some light meals, welcoming owners; six comfortable bedrooms, of character, huge breakfast *(Peter and Anne Hollindale, D L Parkhurst)*; [41 Church St], *Black Horse*: Tastefully refurbished to reflect its age (gas lights, stained glass); well kept Tetleys and Marstons Pedigree, well priced snacks and lunchtime meals; seafaring memorabilia *(Andrew Hazeldine, Jack and Philip Paxton)*; [Bridge St, just over bridge to E/Old Whitby], *Dolphin*: Pleasant atmosphere, wide range of bar food, well kept Camerons and Theakstons *(Andy and Jill Kassube)*; [Flowergate], *Little Angel*: Friendly spotless local with well kept John Smiths and Tetleys, boating theme, good value generous lunchtime food, service friendly and quick even if busy, children allowed if well behaved *(Andrew Hazeldine)*; [New Quay Rd], *Tap & Spile*: Well decorated, no-smoking area, good bar food inc local cod, up to eight well kept ales, country wines *(Andy and Jill Kassube)*

Whitwood W Yor [SE3723], *New Wheatsheaf*: Spacious comfortable bar with Tetleys, wide choice of straightforward food with help-yourself veg, games area *(Neil and Anita Christopher)*

Wilberfoss N Yor [off A1079 E of York; SE7351], *Oddfellows Arms*: Friendly staff, good generous food inc vegetarian in tasteful beamed dining extension, good Sun carvery, Bass and Stones, good house wine, interesting pictures, delft shelf *(K J Hillier, H Bramwell)*

☆ **Winksley** N Yor [off B6265 Ripon—Pateley Bridge; SE2571], *Countryman*: Attractive heavily beamed stone-walled downstairs bar, bar food inc notable bookmaker's lunch and good puddings, Theakstons and Websters, decent whiskies, coffee and tea, helpful staff, simple upstairs family/games room, tables on fairy-lit front terrace and out behind, restaurant; handy for Fountains Abbey and Studley Royal; has been cl Mon lunchtime (all day Mon in winter) *(Dr Philip Jackson, Patricia Heptinstall, LYM)*

Woodkirk W Yor [Leeds Rd; SE2725], *Black Bull*: Very smooth Sam Smiths, friendly people, well priced good food *(Laura Anderson)*

Worsborough S Yor [A61 opp country park and watermill; SE3503], *Red Lion*: Friendly pub, open all day, two bars and raised eating area, good value Sun lunch, books and pictures; children welcome; quiet piped music, pool, fruit machine; garden with play area *(JJW, CMW)*

Wortley S Yor [Halifax Rd; A629 N of Sheffield; SK3099], *Wortley Arms*: Stonebuilt coaching inn with big lounge (no-smoking area), tap room and dining room, brewing its own Earls Ale, also Reindeer, Stones and Youngers; piped pop music, open all day *(JJW, CMW)*

Wragby W Yor [A638 nr Nostell Priory; SE4117], *Spread Eagle*: Four homely low-beamed rooms with well kept Bass and Sam Smiths, well presented generous food, evening restaurant; tap room with photographs of regulars as youngsters *(D Isling, M A Butler)*

☆ **York** [High Petergate], *Hole in the Wall*: Good atmosphere in rambling open-plan pub handy for Minster, beams, stripped brickwork, turkey carpeting, plush seats, well kept Mansfield beers, good coffee, cheap simple food noon-8 inc generous Sun lunch, friendly efficient service, juke box, piped music not too loud; open all day *(Roger A Bellingham, Chris Westmoreland, C H Stride, John Fazakerley, D J and P M Taylor, LYM)*

☆ **York** [18 Goodramgate], *Royal Oak*: Cosy black-beamed 16th-c pub with big helpings of good value imaginative bar food (limited Sun evening) served 11.30-7.30, quick friendly service, well kept Camerons, Ind Coope Burton and Tetleys, wines and country wines, good coffee; prints, swords and old guns, no-smoking family room; can get crowded *(Chris Westmoreland, C H Stride, JJW, CMW, BB)*

☆ **York** [26 High Petergate], *York Arms*: Snug little basic panelled bar, big refurbished no-smoking lounge, second cosier partly panelled lounge full of old bric-a-brac, prints, brown-cushioned wall settles, dimpled copper tables and an open fire; quick friendly service, well kept Sam Smiths OB and Museum, good value simple food lunchtime and early evening, no music; handy for Minster, open all day *(Paul Cartledge, Michele and Clive Platman, Keith and Cheryl Roe, BB)*

☆ **York**, [7 Stonegate], *Punch Bowl*: Attractive local with small rooms, helpful service, good lunchtime food, up to six well kept ales; good value bedrooms *(Mark Walker, Graham and Lynn Mason, Andy and Jill Kassube, Chris Westmoreland)*

York [9 St Martins Lane, Micklegate], *Ackhorne*: Former Acorn, traditional bare-boards look, well kept Black Sheep, a beer brewed for the pub by Hadrian, and changing ales from independent local breweries, basic food such as chip butties *(Steve Phillips)*; [55 Blossom St], *Bay Horse*: Basic but pleasant rambling pub, lots of nooks and alcoves, nice back room with button-back leather seats, original old cash register; food inc good value seafood platter *(Martin Hickes, BB)*; [53 Fossgate], *Blue Bell*: Two small friendly panelled rooms, coal fires, several well kept Vaux ales, fresh lunchtime sandwiches and pickled eggs *(Chris Westmoreland, Pete Baker)*; [29 Bootham], *Bootham Tavern*: Popular untouristy drinkers' pub with four well kept Tetleys ales, cosy lounge, friendly landlord *(Richard Lewis)*; [Church St], *Golden Lion*: Big open-plan modern pub with stripped brick walls, fair range of good food at lunchtimes (quieter than other places), quick attentive service, well kept Courage-related ales *(Mark Walker)*; [23 Market St], *Hansom Cab*: Dark panelling, wall seats, wing chairs, side alcoves, good value quick food counter, willing service *(Michele and Clive Platman)*; N Yor [9 Lendal], *Judges Lodging*: Low-arched cellar bar, lots of little rooms, good food here and in restaurant, well kept Theakstons; comfortable bedrooms *(Richard Horan)*; [Kings Staithe just below Ouse Bridge], *Kings Arms*: Fine riverside position with picnic tables out on cobbled waterside terrace; bowed black beams and flagstones inside, straightforward furnishings and bar food from sandwiches up, CD juke box can be loud; open all day *(Geoff and Angela Jaques, LYM)*; [Lendal], *Lendal Cellars*: Broad-vaulted medieval cellars carefully spotlit to show up the stripped masonry, hand-crafted furniture and cask seats on stone floor, interconnected rooms and alcoves, well kept Whitbreads and a guest ale *(Chris Westmoreland, BB)*; [Tanners Moat/Wellington Row], *Maltings*: Good range of guest beers from small breweries, decent well priced pub food with vast helpings of chips, chip butties, welcoming service, interesting salvaged fittings like suburban front door for ladies', plenty of atmosphere; handy for Rail Museum *(G P Wood, Mark Walker, Mick Popka, A Summerfield, J Royce)*; [by Monk Bar], *Monkbar Cloisters*: Part of fairly new small hotel, smart but welcoming decor, Tetleys-related ales, good restaurant ; bedrooms *(Chris Westmoreland)*; [Goodramgate], *Old White Swan*: Characterful rambling Victorian and Georgian bars, delightful covered courtyard, bar food; doing well under new licensees, popular with younger people at night *(Martin Hickes)*; [North St, opp Viking Hotel], *Tap & Spile*: Three smallish rooms, good reasonably priced changing local beers, good simple wholesome food; relaxed and friendly *(Chris Westmoreland)*; [Merchantgate, between Fossgate and Piccadilly], *Red Lion*: Low-beamed rambling rooms with some stripped Tudor brickwork, relaxed old-fashioned furnishings, well kept Courage-related ales, bar snacks and summer meals, tables outside, good juke box or piped music *(Chris Westmoreland, LYM)*; [Goodramgate], *Snickleway*: Snug little old-world pub, lots of antiques, copper and brass, coal fires, good simple wholesome lunchtime snacks (not Sun), unobtrusive piped music, prompt service, well kept John Smiths *(Mark Walker, Shuni Davies)*; [Museum St], *Thomas's*: Plush cheerful Victorian-style pub, assorted sports bric-a-brac, good value straightforward food *(Michele and Clive Platman)*

London
Scotland
Wales
Channel Islands

London

Pubs currently doing particularly well here include the Chandos, the Lamb, the Olde Cheshire Cheese, the Olde Mitre, the Princess Louise (all Central), the Olde White Bear, the Spaniards (both North), the George, the Ship (both South), the Churchill Arms and the Kings Arms (both West). We have included a number of new main entries this year: the distinguished Victorian Albert and the altogether cosier little Seven Stars (both Central), the atmospheric if rather touristy Anchor and the White Cross, a delightful riverside pub with a remarkable range of wines by the glass (both South), and in West London the Eel Pie (back in these pages after an absence, for its good beers) and the Ladbroke Arms (notably good food, for London). For the second year running, the Eagle in Farringdon Road (EC1) romps home as London Dining Pub of the Year. Though in other London pubs food tends to be pretty functional rather than a major draw, it does tend to be relatively cheap. Drinks prices by contrast are very high in Central London, particularly in pubs tied to or supplied by the big national brewers, who still control a high proportion of London's pubs. We found these had used their local monopoly to put up their prices by nearly 10p a pint over the year, whereas pubs getting their beers from elsewhere had scarcely changed their prices at all. The local chain of Wetherspoons pubs such as Hamilton Hall make a point of keeping their drinks prices down; we also found the Olde White Bear in Hampstead (North London) very cheap indeed. Pubs supplied by the local Fullers brewery tend to be cheaper than average, as do many Youngs pubs.

CENTRAL LONDON

Covering W1, W2, WC1, WC2, SW1, SW3, EC1, EC2, EC3 and EC4 postal districts

Parking throughout this area is metered throughout the day, and generally in short supply then; we mention difficulty only if evening parking is a problem too. Throughout the chapter we list the nearest Underground or BR stations to each pub; where two are listed it means the walk is the same from either

Albert (Westminster) Map 13

52 Victoria Street, SW1; ⊖ St James's Park

Dwarfed by the faceless cliffs of dark modern glass around it, this Victorian showpiece still towers above them in architectural merit. It's one of the great sights of this part of London, handsome, colourful and harmonious. Inside, the ground floor is a huge open-plan bar, with good solid comfortable furniture, gleaming mahogany, original gas lamps, and by day a fresh and airy feel however busy it gets, thanks to great expanses of heavily cut and etched windows along three sides. Despite the space, on weekday lunchtimes it's packed with civil servants, sprinkled often enough with a few familiar faces from the House of Commons (the Division Bell sounds here). Service from the big island counter is swift and friendly (particularly obliging to overseas visitors), with well kept Courage Directors, John Smiths, Ruddles Best, Theakstons Best and XB, Wadworths 6X and Websters Yorkshire on handpump. The separate food servery is good value, with sandwiches (from £1.30), ploughman's (£3), salads (from £3.50) and five home-cooked hot dishes such as cottage pie, steak pie, quiche or lasagne (all £4.25). The upstairs restaurant does an eat-as-much-as-you-like carvery, better than average (all day inc Sunday, £13.95). Piped music is never obtrusive, and noticeable only at quiet times. *(Recommended by Robert C Ward Jr, Mary Sikorski, John Ames, Mark Walker, Richard Waller)*

Scottish & Newcastle ~ Managers Roger and Gill Wood ~ Real ale ~ Meals and snacks (11-10.30) ~ Restaurant ~ (0171) 222 5577 ~ Open 11-11; cl 25-26 Dec

Argyll Arms (Oxford Circus) Map 13

18 Argyll St W1 ⊖ Oxford Circus, opp tube side exit

Pick your tube exit carefully when surfacing at Oxford Circus and you may be greeted with the handsome frontage of this bustling place, liberally festooned with plants and flowers, rather than the swarms of stressed-out shoppers that more typically characterise the area. It's a delightful surprise to find the pub so traditional given its position, with the three cubicle rooms at the front the most atmospheric and unusual. All oddly angular, they're made by wooden partitions with distinctive frosted and engraved glass, with hops trailing above. A long mirrored corridor leads to the spacious back room, with the food counter in one corner; this area is no-smoking at lunchtime. Chalked up on a blackboard (which may also have topical cartoons), the choice of meals includes good and unusual sandwiches like generously filled stilton and grape (£2.35) or smoked salmon and cream cheese (£3.25), ploughman's (£4.25) and main courses such as salads, a pie of the day such as steak and kidney (£4.85), and roast beef (£5.85). Adnams, Greene King IPA, Marstons Pedigree, Tetleys and a couple of often unusual guests like Blackwytch or Tomintoul Stag on handpump, maybe under light blanket pressure, and Addlestone's cider; welcoming, efficient staff; two fruit machines, piped pop music. The quieter upstairs bar, which overlooks the busy pedestrianised street (and the Palladium theatre if you can see through the foliage outside the window), is divided into several snugs with comfortable plush easy chairs; swan's neck lamps, and lots of small theatrical prints along the top of the walls. The gents' has a copy of the day's *Financial Times* on the wall, and there's a popular penned area outside with elbow-height tables. The pub can get busy. *(Recommended by Per Ness, Christopher Gallop, John Fazakerley, Ian Phillips, Gordon, Brian and Anna Marsden)*

Nicholsons (Allied; run as free house) ~ Managers Mike and Sue Tayara ~ Real ale ~ Meals and snacks (11-9; not Sun) ~ 0171-734 6117 ~ Children welcome ~ Open 11-11; closed Sun, Jan 1

Black Friar (City) Map 13

174 Queen Victoria Street, EC4; ⊖ Blackfriars

An inner back room of this well-known pub has some of the best fine Edwardian bronze and marble art-nouveau decor to be found anywhere – big bas-relief friezes of jolly monks set into richly coloured Florentine marble walls, an opulent marble-pillared inglenook fireplace, a low vaulted mosaic ceiling, gleaming mirrors, seats built into rich golden marble recesses, and tongue-in-cheek verbal embellishments such as Silence is Golden and Finery is Foolish. The whole place is much bigger inside than seems possible from the delightfully odd exterior, and that's quite a good thing – they do get very busy, particularly after work; lots of people spill out onto the wide forecourt in front, near the approach to Blackfriars Bridge. See if you can spot the opium smoking-hints modelled into the fireplace of the front room. Lunchtime bar food includes filled rolls (£2.50), baked potatoes or ploughman's (£2.95), and salads; service is obliging and helpful. Well kept Adnams, Brakspears, Tetleys, Wadworths 6X and an Allied beer named for Nicholsons on handpump; fruit machine. If you're coming by Tube, choose your exit carefully – it's all too easy to emerge from the network of passageways and find yourself on the other side of the street or marooned on a traffic island. *(Recommended by Chris Westmoreland, Karen and Graham Oddey, Gordon, A Plumb, David and Michelle Hedges, Andy Thwaites)*

Nicholsons (Allied) ~ Manager Mr Becker ~ Real ale ~ Lunchtime meals (11.30-2.30) ~ 0171- 236 5650 ~ Open 11.30-10(11 Thurs/Fri); closed weekends and bank hols

Chandos (Covent Garden) Map 13

29 St Martins Lane, WC2; ⊖ Leicester Square

While at times it can seem all of London is meeting in the bare-boarded downstairs area of this impressive pub, it's the upstairs Opera Room that those in the know head for. Quieter and more atmospheric (as well as surprisingly spacious), it's rather like a cross between a typical pub and a chattily civilised salon, with secluded alcoves, low wooden tables and panelling, and comfortable leather sofas. Opera memorabilia is dotted around the walls, and the small orange, red and yellow leaded panes of glass in the windows give the place a slightly theatrical hue – as well as rather effectively distancing the bustle outside. Food is served up here, at lunchtime including dishes like sandwiches, soup, cottage pie, steak and stilton stew, chicken and almond casserole or steak and kidney pie (all £4), chicken in white wine (£4.50), and jumbo battered cod (£4.75), with Sunday roasts, and evening extras such as rump steak (£7.50). Well kept and Sam Smiths OB and Museum on handpump (maybe under light blanket pressure in summer), at distinctly un-London prices; darts, pinball, fruit machines, video game, trivia and piped music. The pub can get very busy in the early evening (especially downstairs) but the atmosphere is always cheery and relaxed, and the service friendly and helpful. On the roof facing the National Portrait Gallery they have an automaton of a cooper at work (10-2, 4-9). Lots of attractions and theatres are within easy walking distance of here, with the Coliseum (home of the English National Opera) just around the corner. If that's where you're headed don't be tempted to dawdle – our research officer was enjoying the pub so much he almost lost track of the time, and even though he arrived at the theatre only a minute late had to stand up for the whole of the first half (which naturally was more than twice as long as the second). *(Recommended by Gill and Andy Plumb, Neil and Anita Christopher, Susan and Nigel Wilson, Chris Westmoreland, Mike Davies, Andy Thwaites, Wayne Brindle, John Fazakerley)*

Sam Smiths ~ Manager Neil Park ~ Real ale ~ Meals and snacks (11.30-3.45, 5.30-9.30) ~ 0171-836 1405 ~ Children in eating area of Opera room till 6pm (7 Sun-Weds) ~ Open 11-11; closed Dec 25

Cittie of Yorke (Holborn) Map 13

22 High Holborn, WC1; find it by looking out for its big black and gold clock; ⊖ Chancery Lane

Rather like a huge baronial hall, the main back room of this busy old place is quite amazing when seen for the first time, the extraordinarily extended bar counter (the longest in Britain) stretching off into the distance, vast thousand-gallon wine vats resting above the gantry, and big bulbous lights hanging from the astonishingly high raftered roof. It does get packed at lunchtime and in the early evening, particularly with lawyers and judges, but most people tend to congregate in the middle, so you should still be able to bag one of the intimate, old-fashioned and ornately carved cubicles that run along both sides. The unique triangular Waterloo fireplace, with grates on all three sides and a figure of Peace among laurels, used to stand in the Grays Inn Common Room until barristers stopped dining there. A smaller, comfortable wood-panelled room has lots of little prints of York and attractive brass lights, while the ceiling of the entrance hall has medieval-style painted panels and plaster York roses. There's a lunchtime food counter in the main hall with more in the downstairs cellar bar: filled baps, ploughman's (£3.95), salads (£4.50), and several daily changing hot dishes such as beef in red wine and mushroom pie, spicy chicken lasagne, paella, lamb in redcurrant sauce or seafood bake (all £3.95). Well-priced Sam Smiths OB and Museum on handpump; darts, pinball, dominoes, fruit machine, trivia and piped music. There's been a pub on the site since 1430, though the current building owes more to the 1695 coffee house which stood here behind a garden; it was reconstructed in Victorian times using 17th-c materials and parts. *(Recommended by GSB, Gordon; more reports please)*

Sam Smiths ~ Manager Stuart Browning ~ Real ale ~ Meals and snacks (12-2.30, 5.30-10) ~ 0171-242 7670 ~ Children in eating area ~ Open 11.30-11 weekdays; closed Sun

Dog & Duck (Soho) Map 13

Frith Street, W1; ⊖ Tottenham Court Rd/Leicester Square

This delightful little corner house is right in the heart of fashionable Soho, and in good weather especially there tend to be plenty of people spilling onto the bustling street outside. On the floor by the door is a mosaic of a dog, tongue out in hot pursuit of a duck, and the same theme is embossed on some of the shiny tiles that frame the heavy old advertising mirrors. The little bar counter is rather unusual, and serves well kept Marstons Pedigree, Timothy Taylors Landlord, Tetleys, an Allied beer brewed for Nicholsons, and a guest on handpump; doorstep sandwiches (from £1.70). The main bar really is tiny, and it's mostly standing room only, with some high stools by the ledge along the back wall, though there are seats in a roomier area at one end, and in an upstairs bar overlooking the street. No machines or piped music – though if you fancy a few tunes Ronnie Scott's Jazz Club is near by. *(Recommended by Chris Westmoreland, Gordon, Mark Walker, Gill Earle, Andrew Burton)*

Nicholsons (Allied) ~ Manageress Mrs Gene Bell ~ Real ale ~ Snacks (not weekends) ~ 0171-437 4447 ~ Open 12-11; closed Sat and Sun lunchtimes, opening 6 Sat evening

Eagle (City) Map 13

Farringdon Rd; opposite Bowling Green Lane car park; ⊖ Farringdon/Old Street

London Dining Pub of the Year

It's unusual to find a London pub where the food is the centre of attention, and even rarer to come across one with meals as good as these. Highly distinctive and made with the finest quality produce, the choice changes at least once every day, and there's quite an emphasis on Mediterranean dishes (particularly Spanish and Italian). On a typical day you could sample Andalucian chickpea and mussel soup (£3.50), Greek or lebanese-style feta salads (£6), fettucini with barlotti beans and pancetta or pappardelle with chicken livers and sage (£6.50), Italian sausages with sweet roast onions and rocket (£7), Tuscan pork loin roast with garlic, fennel and parsley (£7.50), fabada (a Spanish stew with butter beans, chorizo, pork, ham and black pudding, £8), seafood and rabbit paella (Friday lunchtimes only, £8), sea bass with fennel, tomato, olives and basil (£9.50), and Spanish or Italian cheeses (£4.50); they may run out of some dishes fairly early. The open kitchen forms part of the bar, and furnishings in the single room are simple but stylish – school chairs, circular tables and a couple of sofas on bare boards, modern paintings on the walls (there's an art gallery upstairs, with direct access from the bar). The atmosphere is lively and chatty and although there's quite a mix of customers, it is popular with media folk (*The Guardian* is based just up the road); it's best to get here before 12.30 if you want a seat at lunchtime. Well kept Charles Wells Bombardier and Eagle and Ruddles County on handpump, decent wines including a dozen by the glass, good coffee, and properly made cocktails; piped music. In the evenings it's more traditionally pubby, though again seats and tables are fiercely coveted then. *(Recommended by Andrew Stephenson, Chris Westmoreland, Ian Phillips, Nicola Thomas, Paul Dickinson, Sarah King, Patrick Forbes)*

Free house ~ Licensees Michael Belben and David Eyre ~ Real ale ~ Meals (12-2.30, 6.30-10.30) ~ 0171-837 1353 ~ Children welcome ~ Open 12-11; closed Sat, 2-3 weeks at Christmas, bank holidays

Tipping is not normal for bar meals, and not usually expected.

Front Page (Chelsea) Map 12

35 Old Church Street, SW3; ⊖ Sloane Square, but some distance away

One of the especially nice things about this smartly stylish place is that although it can get busy in the evening (on Fridays in particular), it fills up rather slowly, so that if you arrive around six o'clock you may have the place almost to yourself. Even at its busiest it's never too crowded, the civilised atmosphere is chatty but rarely loud, and there's a good mix of people around the heavy wooden tables or pews and benches. Huge windows with heavy navy curtains and big ceiling fans give the place a light and airy feel, and one cosy area has an open fire; lighting is virtually confined to brass picture-lights above small Edwardian monochrome pictures, and there are newspapers to read (if they see you're waiting for someone they quite often bring these across to you). Big blackboards at either end list the nicely presented bistro-style food: smoked chicken and ham salad (£5.25), duck liver and bacon salad with raspberry vinaigrette (£5.50), crabcakes with beetroot salad (£5.70), venison stir-fry or grilled fillet of plaice with prawn butter sauce (£6.25), cheese fondue (for two, £8.50), and puddings like baked bananas (£3). Well kept Boddingtons, Ruddles County and Websters Yorkshire on handpump; decent wines; quick, pleasant, smiling service. Major sporting events may be shown on a big TV screen. Outside, there are big copper gaslamps hanging above pretty hanging baskets. The same people run the Sporting Page not too far away (see dips), and a couple of other pubs, including the Chequers at Well (see Hampshire main entries). *(Recommended by Dr and Mrs A K Clarke, James Macrae; more reports please)*

Courage ~ Lease: Rupert Fowler, Philip Osborne ~ Real ale ~ Meals (12-2.30, 7-10) ~ Children welcome ~ 0171-352 0648 ~ Open 11-3, 5.30-11; closed two days at Christmas

Glassblower (Piccadilly Circus) Map 13

42 Glasshouse Street, W1; ⊖ Piccadilly Circus

Undergoing a complete refurbishment as we went to press (they were closed for two months in the summer of 1995), this vibrant pub is a useful retreat from the shops of Regent Street. An enormous gently-flickering copper and glass gaslight hangs from the centre of the ceiling in the main bar, with more gaslight-style brackets around the walls. There are also lots of untreated rough wooden beams with metal wheel-hoops hanging on them, plain wooden settles and stools, and sawdust on gnarled floorboards; lots of beer towels, framed sets of beer mats and bottle tops. The pub's position means it's well liked by visitors to London at lunchtime, and in the evenings it can get very busy (and smoky) – you might find it quieter in the lounge bar upstairs, and you're certainly more likely to find a table there. A wide range of real ales on handpump includes Courage Best and Directors, John Smiths, Theakstons Best, Old Peculier and XB and a changing guest; also a good few malt whiskies and Scrumpy Jack cider. Food such as filled baguettes (from £2.85), popular fish and chips (£4.95) and home-made daily specials (£4.85); table service upstairs. Fruit machine, video game, trivia, and juke box. There are hanging flower-baskets outside. *(Recommended by Chris Westmoreland, John Fazakerley, Gordon, David Craine, Ann Reeder, Neil and Anita Christopher, Mark Walker, Wayne Brindle, Richard Waller)*

S & N ~ Manager Mervyn Wood ~ Real ale ~ Meals and snacks (11.30-9 Mon-Thurs, 11-5.30 Fri and Sat; not Sun evening) ~ 0171-734 8547 ~ Children in upstairs bar only ~ Open 11-11; closed 25 Dec

Grenadier (Belgravia) Map 13

Wilton Row, SW1; the turning off Wilton Crescent looks prohibitive, but the barrier and watchman are there to keep out cars; walk straight past – the pub is just around the corner; ⊖ Knightsbridge

Nestling in a smartly peaceful mews behind Knightsbridge, this snugly characterful place is proud of its connections with the Duke of Wellington, whose officers used it as a mess for a while; there's a grand painting of the Duke presiding over a military banquet after Waterloo, along with smart prints of Guardsmen through the ages. Standing outside in summer is lovely, watching the sky slowly darken behind the pub's patriotically painted red, white and blue frontage, and forgetting for a while that you're anywhere near the centre of London; if you get there first you may be lucky enough to bag the bench. There aren't many seats in the cramped front bar either, but you should be able to plonk yourself on one of the stools or wooden benches, as despite the charms of this engaging little pub it rarely gets crowded. Friendly, helpful staff serve well kept Courage Best, Theakstons Best, Morlands Old Speckled Hen and Youngs Special on handpump from the rare pewter-topped bar counter – or they can shake you a most special Bloody Mary. Reasonably priced bar food served straight from the kitchen includes soup (£2.95), ploughman's (£3.95), and hot dishes like sausage and beans (£4.25) or scampi (£5.25); they're usually quite happy to serve snacks like a bowl of chips. The tiny back restaurant is a little pricey, but just right for a cosy dinner with someone special. It's reckoned to be the most haunted pub in London, famous for its well-documented poltergeist. ***(Recommended by James Macrae, Liz and Benton Jennings, Gordon; more reports please)***

S & N ~ Manager Paul Gibb ~ Real ale ~ Meals and snacks (12-2.30, 6-10) ~ Intimate candlelit restaurant ~ 0171-235 3074 ~ Children in restaurant ~ Open 12-11; closed evening 24 Dec and all day 25/26 Dec and 1 Jan

Hamilton Hall (Bishopsgate) Map 13

Liverpool Street Station, EC2; ⊖ Liverpool St

You can always spot a Wetherspoons pub – you'll come away from the bar convinced they've undercharged you for your drinks, until the next round when you find the prices really are that low. Now the chain has conquered virtually all parts of London they're slowly but surely expanding around the rest of the country too, and this busy place is pretty much their flagship. It was once the ballroom of the Great Eastern Hotel, and still has much of the original stunning Victorian baroque decor. Plaster nudes and fruit writhe around the ceiling and fireplace, and there are fine mouldings, chandeliers, and mirrors; the upper level was added during the exemplary conversion, and a good-sized section is no-smoking. Comfortable small armchairs and stools are grouped into sensible-sized areas, and filled by a good mix of customers; it can get very crowded indeed early in the evening, when tables will be at a premium. As at other pubs in the chain, reliable bar food, brought to your table, includes filled granary baps or ciabatta rolls (from £1.85), soup (£1.95), filled baked potatoes (from £2.55), burgers (from £3.25), fish and chips (£3.45), sausage hotpot (£4.25), pies like chicken and broccoli or steak and kidney (£4.45), tuna and spinach mornay or chicken with cashew nuts (£4.95), daily specials and puddings like chocolate cream pie (£1.95); Sunday roast (£4.95). Well kept Courage Directors, Greene King Abbot and IPA, Theakstons Best and XB, and Youngers Scotch on handpump, all at very good prices – the Youngers Scotch is often just 99p a pint; fruit machine, trivia. Friendly, efficient staff. There are plenty more Wetherspoons houses dotted around the Lucky Dips – most share the same standards of food, beer and service. ***(Recommended by Christopher Gallop, Eddie Edwards, Neil Barker, John Fahy, Sue Demont, Tim Barrow, Derek Patey, Comus Elliott and others)***

Free house ~ Licensee Dave Chapman ~ Real ale ~ Meals and snacks (11-10pm) ~ 0171-247 3579 ~ Open 11-11; closed 25/26 Dec, 1 Jan

Lamb ★ (Bloomsbury) Map 13

94 Lamb's Conduit Street, WC1; ⊖ Holborn

Victorian London lives on at this unspoilt, atmospheric place, little changed since the last century and easily one of our more popular entries in the capital. It's famous for its cut-glass swivelling 'snob-screens' all the way around the U-shaped bar counter, but sepia photographs of 1890s actresses on the ochre panelled walls and traditional cast-iron-framed tables with neat brass rails around the rim very much add to the overall effect. Decimal currency doesn't quite fit in, and when you come out you almost expect the streets to be dark and foggy and illuminated by gas lamps.

Sandwiches (£1.15, not Sunday), ploughman's (£3.50), and quite a few salads are available all day, and, until 2.30, they do hot dishes such as home-made pies or steak and kidney pudding (£3.95), and daily specials like curry or vegetable lasagne; Sunday carvery in restaurant (£4.95). Consistently well kept Youngs Bitter and Special on handpump, with Warmer in winter; prompt service, chatty landlord, and a good mix of customers. There are slatted wooden seats in a little courtyard beyond the quiet room which is down a couple of steps at the back; dominoes, cribbage, backgammon. No machines or music. A small room at the back on the right is no smoking. It can get very crowded, especially in the evenings. *(Recommended by Gordon, Chris Westmoreland, B J Harding, Margaret Whalley, Lindsley Harvard, Nicola Thomas, Paul Dickinson, Timothy Gee)*

Youngs ~ Manager Richard Whyte ~ Real ale ~ Meals and snacks (11.30-10) ~ 0171-405 0713 ~ Children in eating area of bar ~ Open 11-11; closed evening 25 Dec

Lamb & Flag (Covent Garden) Map 13

33 Rose Street, WC2; off Garrick Street; ⊖ Leicester Square

Still very much as it was when Dickens described the Middle Temple lawyers who frequented it when he was working in nearby Catherine Street, this historic old pub is a well liked place for Londoners to meet after work, and you'll almost always find plenty of people standing in the little alleyways outside, even in winter. It was out here on a December evening in 1679 that Dryden was nearly killed by a hired gang of thugs; despite several advertisements in newspapers he never found out for sure who was behind the dastardly deed, though the most likely culprit was Charles II's mistress the Duchess of Portsmouth, who suspected him of writing scurrilous verses about her. It's a lot safer these days (though watch out for the darts in the tiny plain front bar), but they still celebrate Dryden Night each year. Very well kept Courage Best and Directors, John Smiths, Morlands Old Speckled Hen and Wadworths 6X on handpump, and a good few malt whiskies. The busy low-ceilinged back bar has high-backed black settles and an open fire, and in Regency days was known as the Bucket of Blood from the bare-knuckle prize-fights held here. It fills up quite quickly, though you might be able to find a seat in the upstairs Dryden Room, which has a choice of several well kept cheeses and pâtés, served with hot bread or French bread, as well as doorstep sandwiches (£3), roast beef baps (Mon-Fri, £3.45), ploughman's (£3.50), and hot dishes like shepherd's pie or bangers and mash (£3.95). The pub is very handy for Covent Garden. *(Recommended by Chris Westmoreland, Susan and Nigel Wilson, C Smith, Bob and Maggie Atherton, Gordon, SRH, Margaret Whalley, Lindsley Harvard, Howard and Margaret Buchanan, Caroline Wright)*

Courage ~ Lease: Terry Archer and Adrian Zimmerman ~ Real ale ~ Lunchtime meals (till 2.30) and snacks (12-5); not Sun ~ (0171) 497 9504 ~ Live jazz Sunday evening ~ Open 11-11; closed 25-6 Dec and 1 Jan

Museum Tavern (Bloomsbury) Map 13

Museum Street, WC1; ⊖ Holborn or Tottenham Court Rd

It may be the presence of the British Museum just over the road that accounts for the civilised and even rather bookish feel you might find in quiet moments (late afternoon, say) at this old-fashioned little Bloomsbury pub. Karl Marx is fondly supposed to have had the odd glass here, and it's tempting to think that the chap scribbling notes or earnestly studying a weighty tome at the next table is working on a similarly seminal set of ideas. The single room is simply furnished and decorated, with high-backed benches around traditional cast-iron pub tables, and old advertising mirrors between the wooden pillars behind the bar. A good range of well kept (though even for this area not cheap) beers includes well kept Courage Best and Directors, John Smiths, Theakstons Best, Old Peculier and XB and a couple of guests like Morlands Old Speckled Hen or Wadworths 6X on handpump; they also have several wines by the glass, and a choice of malt whiskies. Available all day from a servery at the end of the room, bar food might include salads (£3.80), ploughman's

(£3.95), vegetarian meals like vegetable curry (£4.25), and hot dishes such as steak and ale or cottage pies (£4.95). Fruit machine. Tables may be hard to come by at lunchtime, when it's very popular with tourists and visitors to the Museum, but unlike most other pubs in the area, it generally stays pleasantly uncrowded in the evenings. There are a couple of tables outside under the gas lamps and 'Egyptian' inn sign. *(Recommended by Gordon, Chris Westmoreland, Ian Phillips, Andy Thwaites, Martin and Pauline Richardson)*

S & N ~ Managers John and Carmel Keating ~ Real ale ~ Meals and snacks (11-10) ~ 0171-242 8987 ~ Children in eating area of bar till 5pm ~ Open 11-11, 12-10.30 Sun; closed evening 25 Dec

Nags Head (Belgravia) Map 13

53 Kinnerton St, SW1; ⊖ Knightsbridge

Hidden away in an attractive and peaceful little mews, this snug little gem really doesn't seem like a London pub at all. Cosy and homely (it's one of those pubs that claims to be the capital's smallest), it feels almost rural, and you could be forgiven for thinking you'd been transported to an old-fashioned pub somewhere in a sleepy country village, right down to the friendly locals chatting around the unusual sunken bar counter. It's rarely busy, even at weekends, and the atmosphere is always relaxed and welcoming; it's the kind of place where they greet you when you come in and say goodbye as you leave – not exactly the norm in this neck of the woods. Warmly traditional, the small, panelled and low-ceilinged front area has a wood-effect gas fire in an old cooking range (seats by here are generally snapped up pretty quickly), and a narrow passage leads down steps to an even smaller back bar with stools and a mix of comfortable seats. There's a 1930s What-the-butler-saw machine and a one-armed bandit that takes old pennies, as well as rather unusual piped music, generally jazz, folk or show tunes. The well kept Adnams and Tetleys are pulled on attractive 19th c china, pewter and brass handpumps. Decent food includes sandwiches (from £2.50), filled baked potatoes (£2.95), ploughman's (£3.65), real ale sausage, mash and beans (£3.75), salads (from £3.85), chilli con carne or steak and mushroom pie (£3.95) and specials like roast pork or cod mornay (£4.50); there's a £1 service charge added to all dishes in the evenings. There's a solitary bench outside. *(Recommended by Susan Douglas, Gordon; more reports please)*

Free house ~ Licensees Kevin and Peter Moran ~ Real ale ~ Meals and snacks (11-9) ~ 0171-235 1135 ~ Children in eating area of bar ~ Open 11-11

Old Coffee House (Soho) Map 13

49 Beak Street, W1; ⊖ Oxford Circus

The downstairs bar of this friendly little cornerhouse is a busy jumble of stuffed pike and foxes, great brass bowls and buckets, ancient musical instruments (brass and string sections both well represented), a good collection of Great War recruiting posters, golden discs, death-of-Nelson prints, theatre and cinema handbills, old banknotes and so forth – even a nude in one corner (this is Soho, after all). Upstairs, the food room has as many prints and pictures as a Victorian study. It's a useful place to know about for a decent well-priced lunch, and can be surprisingly peaceful too. The choice of meals is rather wider than you'll find in most other pubs in the area, with a range including sandwiches, filled baked potatoes (from £2.20), burgers (from £2.95), various platters (from £3.75), lots of hot dishes like chicken, ham and leek pie, macaroni cheese, chilli, lasagne, tuna and pasta bake, or winter stews and casseroles (all £3.95), and puddings (£1.70); on Sundays and in the evenings they only do toasted sandwiches. Well kept Courage Best and Directors and Marstons Pedigree on handpump; helpful, attentive service. *(Recommended by Gordon, G Atkinson; more reports please)*

Courage ~ Lease: Barry Hawkins ~ Real ale ~ Lunchtime meals and snacks (12-3; evenings and Sun toasted sandwiches only) ~ (0171) 437 2197 ~ Children in upstairs food room 12-3pm ~ Open 11-11

Olde Cheshire Cheese (City) Map 13

Wine Office Court; off 145 Fleet Street, EC4; ⊖ Blackfriars

One of London's most famous old pubs, this bustling 17th-c former chop house has cellar vaults dating back to before the Great Fire. Over the years Congreve, Pope, Voltaire, Thackeray, Dickens, Conan Doyle, Yeats and perhaps Dr Johnson have visited its unpretentious little rooms, and some of them probably came across the famous parrot that for over 40 years entertained princes, ambassadors, and other distinguished guests. When she died in 1926 the news was broadcast on the BBC and obituary notices appeared in 200 newspapers all over the world; she's still around today, now stuffed and silent. Up and down stairs, the various bars and rooms have bare wooden benches built in to the walls, sawdust on bare boards, and on the ground floor high beams, crackly old black varnish, Victorian paintings on the dark brown walls, and a big open fire in winter; darts, bar billiards, fruit machine and piped music. Surprisingly untouristy, it's been extended in a similar style towards Fleet St. Snacks include sandwiches and filled rolls, and in the downstairs bar ploughman's (£3.50) or hot dishes such as chicken casserole with cheese scones, lamb tikka, vegetarian quiche, and beef and ale pie (all £3.95). Well kept (and, as usual for this brewery, well priced) Sam Smiths Old Brewery and Museum on handpump, friendly service. *(Recommended by R T and J C Moggridge, Karen and Graham Oddey, Jamie and Ruth Lyons, John Ames, Chris Westmoreland, Gordon, John Fazakerley)*

Sam Smiths ~ Licensees Gordon Garrity ~ Meals and snacks (all day; not Sun evening) ~ Restaurant (not Sun evening) ~ 0171-353 6170 ~ Children welcome ~ Open 11-11; closed Sun evening and bank holidays

Olde Mitre £ (City) Map 13

Ely Place, EC1; there's also an entrance beside 8 Hatton Garden; ⊖ Chancery Lane

Readers very much enjoy tracking down this interesting little pub, tucked away rather incongruously on the edge of the City. The carefully rebuilt tavern with its quaint facade carries the name of an earlier inn built here in 1547 to serve the people working in the nearby palace of the Bishops of Ely. The dark panelled small rooms have antique settles and – particularly in the back room, where there are more seats – old local pictures and so forth. An upstairs room, mainly used for functions, may double as an overflow at peak periods; on weekdays, the pub is good-naturedly packed between 12.30 and 2.15, with an interesting mix of customers. Popular bar snacks include really good value sandwiches such as ham, salmon and cucumber or egg mayonnaise (£1, including toasted), as well as filled rolls (from 70p), sausages (80p), and pork pies or scotch eggs. Well kept Friary Meux, Ind Coope Burton and Tetleys on handpump; notably friendly, chatty staff; darts. There are some seats with pot plants and jasmine in the narrow yard between the pub and St Ethelreda's church. The iron gates that guard Ely Place are a reminder of the days when the law in this distrit was administered by the Bishops of Ely; even today it's still technically part of Cambridgeshire. *(Recommended by Ian Phillips, A W Dickinson, Tim Heywood, Sophie Wilne, John Fazakerley, Christopher Gallop, Chris Westmoreland, Helen Hazzard, Gordon)*

Taylor-Walker (Allied) ~ Manager Don O'Sullivan ~ Real ale ~ Snacks (all day) ~ 0171-405 4751 ~ Open 11-11; closed weekends and bank holidays

Orange Brewery (Pimlico) Map 13

37 Pimlico Road, SW1; ⊖ Sloane Square

A recent refurbishment of this lively and friendly pub has seen the two original bars knocked into one, with what was the Pie and Ale Shop now transformed into a viewing area looking down into the pub's own little brewery. Every week they produce over 500 gallons of their popular ales – SW1, a stronger SW2, Pimlico Light and Pimlico Porter, and Victoria lager; they may also have a couple of guest beers on handpump. A new range of bar food is built around the beers too, with dishes such as sausages with beer and onion gravy (£2.95) or beef and beer pie (£4.25) flavoured with their SW2; they also do sandwiches, salads and ploughman's. Above the simple wooden chairs, tables and panelling, are various examples of vintage brewing equipment and related bric-a-brac, and there's a nicely tiled fireplace; fruit machine, piped music. You can book tours of the brewery. Seats outside face a little concreted-over green beyond the quite busy street. *(Recommended by James Macrae, Christopher Trueblood, James House, A W Dickinson, Andy Thwaites, Ian Phillips, Richard Waller)*

Own brew (though tied to S & N) ~ Manager Billy Glass ~ Real ale ~ Meals and snacks (12-10; limited choice Sun) ~ 0171-730 5984 ~ Children in eating area of bar ~ Open 11-11; winter 12-3, 7-10.30

Princess Louise (Holborn) Map 13

208 High Holborn, WC1; ⊖ Holborn

This deservedly popular old-fashioned gin-palace is for many visitors the quintessential London pub, and it certainly has plenty in common with the city it represents so well; big, bustling, and full of a richly diverse assortment of people, it's grandly elegant but bang-up-to-date, with calmer corners away from the crowds, and, despite all that seems familiar, enough that's individual to mark it out as unusual. The long main bar serves a fine range of regularly changing real ales, well kept on handpump, such as Adnams Best, Bass, Brakspears PA, Batemans XB, Courage Best, Gales HSB, Theakstons Best, Wadworths 6X and maybe a couple of more unusual guests; also several wines by the glass – including champagne. Neat, quick staff. They do good sandwiches (from £1.75) just about all day. The elaborate decor includes etched and gilt mirrors, brightly coloured and fruity-shaped tiles, and slender Portland stone columns soaring towards the lofty and deeply moulded crimson and gold plaster ceiling. The green plush seats and banquettes are comfortable, and the gents' are the subject of a separate preservation order. The quieter upstairs bar has excellent authentic Thai meals (quite a draw in themselves) – though these are now served weekday lunchtimes only. *(Recommended by Sue Demont, Tim Barrow, Ian Phillips, Andy Thwaites, Gordon, Chris Westmoreland, David Wright, Howard and Margaret Buchanan, Stephen R Holman, Margaret Whalley, Lindsley Harvard)*

Free house ~ Licensee Joseph Sheridan ~ Real ale ~ Snacks and weekday lunchtime meals ~ 0171-405 8816 ~ Open 11-11; 12-3, 6-11 Sat; closed 25/26 Dec

Red Lion (Mayfair) Map 13

Waverton Street, W1; ⊖ Green Park

The special Bloody Marys at this relaxed and civilised Mayfair pub can certainly make quite an impression – one reader is still recovering from the rather potent Medium Spicy concoction, and can't imagine how anyone could manage the Very Spicy option. Very relaxed and civilised, the main L-shaped bar has small winged settles on the partly carpeted scrubbed floorboards, London prints below the high shelf of china on its dark-panelled walls, and something of the atmosphere of a smart country pub. A very good range of well kept beers includes Courage Directors, Greene King IPA, Morlands Old Speckled Hen, Robinsons Best, Theakstons Best and XB and Wadworths 6X on handpump. Reliably good food, served in the back bar, includes sandwiches (from £2.20), and main courses like their very well liked cumberland sausage, duck and venison pie or stuffed cabbage leaves (all £4.75), and chargrilled burger with stilton cheese (£5.50); they home-cook all their meats. Unusually for the area, food is served morning and evening seven days a week. It can get crowded at lunchtime. The gents' has a copy of the day's *Financial Times* at eye level. *(Recommended by Bob and Maggie Atherton, Adrian Zambardino, Debbie Chaplin, Gordon, Mark Walker)*

S & N ~ Manager Raymond Dodgson ~ Real ale ~ Meals and snacks ~ Restaurant ~ 0171-499 1307 ~ Children in eating area of bar and in restaurant ~ Open 11-11; 11-3, 6-11 Sat

Seven Stars (City) Map 13

53 Carey St, WC2; ⊖ Holborn (just as handy from Temple or Chancery Lane, but the walk through Lincoln's Inn Fields can be rather pleasant)

Facing the back of the Law Courts, this tranquil pub is a uniquely timeless little gem. We're not using the word little lightly – on our last visit it was hard to tell whether the customers (barristers and legal folk on the whole) were standing in the peaceful street outside because it was sunny, or because there's so little space inside. The door, underneath a profusion of hanging baskets, is helpfully marked General Counter, as though you couldn't see that the simple counter is pretty much all there is in the tiny old-fashioned bar beyond. Lots of caricatures of barristers and other legal-themed prints on the walls, and quite a collection of toby jugs, some in a display case, the rest mixed up with the drinks behind the bar. Courage Best and Directors on handpump, and good value bar snacks such as sandwiches (from £1.10), filled baguettes (from £1.30), sausages (80p), pork pies (£1.35) and maybe a couple of hot dishes like beef in red wine (£2.80); you'll probably have to eat standing up – the solitary table and stools are on the left as you go in. A cosy room on the right appears bigger than it is because of its similar lack of furnishings; there's a flame-effect fire, and shelves round the walls for drinks or leaning against. The friendly landlord (often on his own behind the bar) is quite likely to start up a conversation as soon as he sees you approaching. Stairs up to the lavatories are very steep – a sign warns you climb them at your own risk. *(Recommended by Chris Westmoreland, Gordon, W T Aird)*

Courage ~ Lease: John Corley ~ Real ale ~ Snacks ~ 0171-242 8521 ~ Open 11-10 weekdays only, may close earlier if not busy; closed weekends except Sat of Lord Mayor's Show

Star (Belgravia) Map 13

Belgrave Mews West – behind the German Embassy, off Belgrave Sq; ⊖ Knightsbridge

The feel of this warmly traditional place is very un-London, and though it can get busy at lunchtime and on some evenings, there's a pleasantly quiet and relaxed local feel outside peak times. One reader feels it's the sort of pub you might see in an old black and white film. Service is very obliging and helpful; they're quite happy being flexible with the menu or providing something slightly different if they can. The small entry room, which also has the food servery, has stools by the counter and tall windows; an arch leads to a side room with swagged curtains, lots of dark mahogany, stripped mahogany chairs and tables, heavy upholstered settles, globe lighting and raj fans. The back room has button-back built-in wall seats, and there's a cosy room upstairs. Good value bar food includes sandwiches (£1.30), salads, hot lunchtime specials like fish and chips, steak pie or corn beef hash (around £3.50), and evening dishes like barbecue chicken (£4.90) and steaks (£6.30); they do sandwiches on Saturdays, but otherwise there's no food at weekends. Very well kept and priced Fullers Chiswick, ESB and London Pride served by friendly staff. Outside in the attractive mews are pretty flowering tubs and hanging baskets. *(Recommended by LM, B J Harding, Gordon, Ian Phillips, John Fazakerley, Richard Waller)*

Fullers ~ Managers Bruce and Kathleen Taylor ~ Real ale ~ Meals and snacks (not Sat or Sun) ~ 0171-235 3019 ~ Children allowed if eating ~ Open 11.30-3, 5(6.30 Sat)-11, 11.30-11 Fridays and every day for two weeks before Christmas; closed Dec 25/26

Sun (Bloomsbury) Map 13

63 Lamb's Conduit St, WC1; ⊖ Holborn/Chancery Lane

Scottish and Newcastle have added this pleasantly spartan bare-boards pub to their empire since our last edition, but there haven't been any changes – the landlord is still the same, and the emphasis remains firmly on the astonishing selection of real ales. There are always between 10 and 16 different brews on handpump, easily the widest choice in London (and probably a good deal further, too), rotated from an even wider range in the cellar. A typical turnout might take in Adnams Broadside, Badger Best and Tanglefoot, Bass, Brakspears, Courage Best and Directors, Ruddles Best and County, Theakstons Best, XB and Old Peculier, and Wadworths 6X and Farmers Glory. The wall is taken up with an alphabetical listing of all the beers they have stocked, with details of their strengths. Furnishings are simple and basic, with a few tables around the U-shaped bar counter, and a couple of picnic-table sets in the street outside. Straightforward bar food includes toasted sandwiches (from £1.40), filled baguettes (from £2), burgers (from £2.30), ploughman's (£3.50), and hot dishes like curry, lasagne or a pie (around £3.50); several malt whiskies, darts, fruit machine, video game, trivia, piped music, TV. After work the pub might be packed with smart-suited City folk or medical staff from the several hospitals nearby. They sometimes organise tours of the cellar. *(Recommended by Peter Nakaji, Chris Westmoreland, Tina Hammond, Margaret Whalley, Lindsley Harvard)*

S & N ~ Licensee Gary Brown ~ Real ale ~ Meals and snacks (12-2.30, 6-10) ~ 0171-405 8278 ~ Children in eating area of bar ~ Open 11-11

Westminster Arms (Westminster) Map 13

Storey's Gate, SW1; ⊖ Westminster

Handily placed near Westminster Abbey and Parliament Square, this traditional local has a lot in common with any other place where nearby workers come for a drink at the end of the day – except that most of these people, one way or another, work in government. For many the main draw is the fine range of real ales on handpump, typically including Adnams, Bass, Brakspears PA, Theakstons Best, Wadworths 6X, Westminster Best brewed for them by Charringtons, and often unusual weekly changing guests; they also do decent wines. Furnishings in the busy main bar are simple and old-fashioned, with proper tables on the wooden floors and a good deal of panelling; there's not a lot of room, and they do get very busy, so come early for a seat. Pleasant, courteous service. Most of the food is served in the downstairs bar, quite different in character with some of the tables in cosy booths: various salads and ploughman's, Mexican pasta (£4.50), lasagne, shepherd's pie or steak and kidney pie (£5), and fish and chips or scampi. Piped music in this area, and in the upstairs restaurant, but not generally in the main bar; fruit machine. There are a couple of tables and seats by the street outside. *(Recommended by Mark Walker, Sue Demont, Tim Barrow, Dr J R G Beavon, John Fazakakerley, Richard Waller)*

Free house ~ Licensees Gerry and Marie Dolan ~ Real ale ~ Meals and snacks (11-10; not Sunday evening) ~ Restaurant (not Sun) ~ 0171-222 8520 ~ Children in eating area and upstairs restaurant ~ Open 11-11; closed Dec 25-6

NORTH LONDON

Parking is not a special problem in this area unless we say so.

Compton Arms (Canonbury) Map 12

4 Compton Avenue, off Canonbury Lane, N1; ⊖ Highbury & Islington

Quite a peaceful haven this, hidden away up a mews, free from games machines or music, and with a delightfully relaxing little crazy paved back terrace, with benches and cask tables among flowers under a big sycamore tree. Well run by friendly staff, the low-ceilinged rooms are simply furnished with wooden settles and assorted stools and chairs, with local pictures on the walls. Well kept Greene King Abbot, IPA and Rayments on handpump, and good value bar food such as sandwiches, burgers (£2.50), salads (from £2.75), hot dishes like chicken kiev or gammon and egg (from around £3), and a Sunday roast (£3.50). It's a shame we don't get more reports about this very pleasant (if tiny) local. *(Recommended by Sue Demont, Tim Barrow; more reports please)*

Greene King ~ Managers W and P Porter ~ Real ale ~ Meals and snacks (11-10) ~ 0171-359 6883 ~ Children welcome ~ Open 11-10

Holly Bush (Hampstead) Map 12

Holly Mount, NW3; ⊖ Hampstead

The walk up the little hill from the tube station to this cheery place is delightful, along some of Hampstead's most villagey streets and past several of its more enviable properties. London seems so far away you'd hardly think you were so close to Hampstead High Street. The atmospheric front bar has real Edwardian gas lamps, a dark and sagging ceiling, brown and cream panelled walls (decorated with old advertisements and a few hanging plates), open fires, and cosy bays formed by partly glazed partitions. Slightly more intimate, the back room, named after the painter George Romney, has an embossed red ceiling, panelled and etched glass alcoves, and ochre-painted brick walls covered with small prints and plates. During the week bar food includes toasted sandwiches (from £1.40), ploughman's (£2.95), and pasta, chilli or shepherd's pie (around £3.25), with maybe home-made scouse at weekends (the cheery licensees are from Liverpool), a daily vegetarian dish, and traditional Sunday roasts (£4.75). Benskins, Ind Coope Burton, Tetleys and a frequently changing guest on handpump; darts, shove-ha'penny, cribbage, dominoes, fruit machine, and video game. Good friendly service. ***(Recommended by Don Kellaway, Angie Coles, Gordon, Wayne Brindle, Margaret Whalley, Lindsley Harvard)***

Taylor-Walker (Allied) ~ Manager Peter Dures ~ Real ale ~ Meals and snacks (12.30-3, 5.30-11) ~ 0171-435 2892 ~ Children in coffee bar ~ Twice weekly live music jazz Sun night, 60s guitarist weds ~ Nearby parking sometimes quite a squeeze ~ Open 11-3(4 Sat), 5.30(6 Sat)-11; closed evening 25 Dec

Olde White Bear (Hampstead) Map 12

Well Road, NW3; ⊖ Hampstead

Several readers consider this villagey neo-Victorian place to be the best London pub they've ever visited. Friendly and traditional, it's well liked for its relaxing and almost clubby feel, amidst which all sorts of Londoners feel comfortable, from the young chap in the corner doing the crossword, to the old gentleman reading his magazine with a monocle. The dimly-lit main room has lots of Victorian prints and cartoons on the walls, as well as wooden stools, cushioned captain's chairs, a couple of big tasselled armed chairs, a flowery sofa, handsome fireplace and an ornate Edwardian sideboard. A similarly-lit small central room has Lloyd Loom furniture, dried flower arrangements and signed photographs of actors and playwrights. In the brighter end room there are elaborate cushioned machine tapestried pews, and dark brown paisley curtains. Good bar food includes soup, sandwiches or filled baked potatoes (from £1.90), ploughman's (£3.50), fish and chips (from £3.50), hot dishes like cottage pie or steak and kidney pie (£4.25), and the very popular Greek platter – a huge salad with olives, dips, pitta bread and feta cheese (£4.50). Very well priced, the range of beers on handpump includes Adnams, Ind Coope Burton, Greene King Abbot, Tetleys, Wadworths 6X and Youngs Bitter; they also have a dozen or so malt whiskies, and maybe winter mulled wine. Darts, shove ha'penny, cribbage, dominoes, fruit machine, piped music. Note they don't allow children inside, and parking may be a problem – it's mostly residents' permits only nearby. ***(Recommended by Tom McLean, Roger Huggins, Walter Reid, Wayne Brindle, Gordon, Don Kellaway, Angie Coles)***

Taylor Walker (Allied) ~ Lease: Peter and Margaret Reynolds ~ Real ale ~ Meals and snacks ~ 0171-435 3758 ~ Open 11-11

Spaniards Inn (Hampstead) Map 12

Spaniards Lane, NW3; ⊖ Hampstead, but some distance away

Named after the Spanish ambassador to the court of James I (who is said to have lived here), this charming former toll-house is a very atmospheric and comfortable place, authentically old-fashioned, with open fires, genuinely antique winged settles, candle-shaped lamps in pink shades, and snug little alcoves in the low-ceilinged oak-panelled rooms of the attractive main bar. A very nice sheltered garden has slatted wooden tables and chairs on a crazy-paved terrace which opens on to a flagstoned walk around a small lawn, with roses, a side arbour of wisteria and clematis, and an aviary. Well kept Bass, Fullers London Pride, Hancocks BB and a guest like Adnams Extra on handpump; friendly service, piped music. Daily changing bar food includes stilton ploughman's (£3.75), home-made quiche or vegetable lasagne (£4.95), ratatouille (£4.25), vegetable lasagne (£4.75), and beef and Guinness pie (£5.75); the food bar is no-smoking at lunchtime. A quieter upstairs bar may be open at busy times. It's very handy for Kenwood, and indeed during the 1780 Gordon Riots the landlord helped save the house from possible disaster, cunningly giving so much free drink to the mob on its way to burn it down that by the time the Horse Guards arrived the rioters were lying drunk and incapable on the floor. The pub and a similar little whitewashed outbuilding opposite are responsible for the slight bottlenecks you sometimes come across driving round here; they jut out into the road rather like King Canute holding back the tide of traffic, and cars all have to slow down to squeeze past. Dogs welcome. *(Recommended by Nigel Flook, Betsy Brown, Gordon, Roger Huggins, Tom McLean, Mr and Mrs Garrett, N and M Foster, S J Elliott, E G Parish)*

Charringtons (Bass) ~ Manager D E Roper ~ Real ale ~ Meals and snacks (12-9.30) ~ 0181-455 3276 ~ Children in eating area of bar and in upstairs bar ~ Open 11-11

Waterside (King's Cross) Map 13

82 York Way, N1; ⊖ King's Cross

King's Cross is hardly what you'd call London's most appealing area for visitors, but that makes discovering this friendly little oasis all the more rewarding. Readers very much enjoy sitting on the unexpectedly calm outside terrace overlooking the Battlebridge Basin, and on sunny days you might find a barbecue out here. The building really isn't very old but it's done out in firmly traditional style, with stripped brickwork, latticed windows, genuinely old stripped timbers in white plaster, lots of dimly lit alcoves (one is no-smoking), spinning wheels, milkmaid's yokes, and horse brasses and so on, with plenty of rustic tables and wooden benches. Some of the woodwork was salvaged from a disused mill. Adnams, Boddingtons, Flowers IPA, Marstons Pedigree and a guest on handpump, as well as wines on draught; bar billiards, pinball, fruit machine, video game, trivia and sometimes loudish juke box. As we went to press they were just about to introduce a Berni menu, but the rest of the pub should stay unchanged. No dogs inside. *(Recommended by Chris Westmoreland, S R and A J Ashcroft, James Macrae, N C Walker, Nigel Flook, Betsy Brown, A W Dickinson, CW, JW, Ian Phillips, Don Kellaway, Angie Coles, Dr and Mrs A K Clarke)*

Whitbreads ~ Managers Liz Hickey and Colin Smith ~ Real ale ~ Meals and snacks (12-2.30, 5-8.30) ~ (0171) 837 7118 ~ Open 11-11; closed 25/26 Dec and 1 Jan

SOUTH LONDON

Parking is bad on weekday lunchtimes at the inner city pubs here (SE1), but is usually OK everywhere in the evenings – you may again have a bit of a walk if a good band is on at the Bulls Head in Barnes, or at the Windmill on Clapham Common if it's a fine evening

Alma ♀ (Wandsworth) Map 12

499 York Road; ⇌ Wandsworth Town

Travelling by rail into Waterloo you can see this bustling pub rising above the neighbouring rooftops as you rattle through Wandsworth Town. Stylish, civilised and just that little bit different, it has an authentic French cafe-bar feel, and a real air of chattily relaxed bonhomie. Even when it's very full with smart young people – which it often is in the evenings – service is careful and efficient; one reader visiting late the night before Christmas Eve was impressed with the way the staff were coping amongst the discarded paper hats and cracker debris. There's a mix of chairs around cast-iron-framed tables, lots of ochre and terracotta paintwork, gilded mosaics of the Battle of the Alma, an ornate mahogany chimney-piece and fireplace, bevelled mirrors in a pillared mahogany room divider, and pinball and a fruit machine. The popular but less pubby dining room has a fine turn-of-the-century frieze of swirly nymphs; there's waitress service in here, and you can book a particular table. Youngs Bitter, Porter, Special and Winter Warmer on handpump from the island bar counter, decent house wines (with several by the glass), freshly squeezed orange juice, good coffee, tea or hot chocolate, newspapers out for customers. Unusual and tasty, the good value bar food includes sandwiches (£1.40), soup (£2.50), croque monsieur (£2.45), mussels with garlic, parsley, cream and Scrumpy Jack cider (£3.20), filo parcels stuffed with tofu, spring onion, baby corn and mushrooms (£3.90), vegetable cous-cous or toasted muffins with ham and poached egg (£4.50), chicken breast with a creamy ginger, coriander and cashew nut sauce, or leg of lamb with fresh chillis and curry with spinach and mushrooms (£6), daily fresh fish, and steak (£9.25). If you're after a quiet drink don't come when there's a rugby match on the television. Charge up their 'smart-card' with cash and you can pay with a discount either here or at the management's other two pubs, the Ship at Wandsworth (see below) and the Coopers Arms, SW3. *(Recommended by P Gillbe, Ian Phillips, Susan and John Douglas; more reports please)*

Youngs ~ Tenant Charles Gotto ~ Real ale ~ Meals and snacks (12-11; not Sun evening) ~ Restaurant (not Sun evening) ~ 0181-870 2537 ~ Children welcome ~ Open 11-11; closed 25 Dec

Anchor (South Bank) Map 13

34 Park St, Bankside, SE1; Southwark Bridge end; ⊖ London Bridge

A maze of little rooms and passageways, this atmospheric riverside pub has an unbeatable view of the Thames and the City from its busy front terrace. It dates back to about 1750, when it was built to replace an earlier tavern, possibly the one that Pepys came to during the Great Fire of 1666. 'All over the Thames with one's face in the wind, you were almost burned with a shower of fire drops,' he wrote. 'When we could endure no more upon the water, we to a little ale-house on the Bankside and there staid till it was dark almost, and saw the fire grow.' The rambling series of rooms have creaky boards and beams, black-panelling, and old-fashioned high-backed settles as well as sturdy leatherette chairs. Even when it's invaded by tourists (it can seem a little commmercial at times) it's usually possible to retreat to one of the smaller rooms. Adnams Southwold, Courage Best and Directors, John Smiths, Marstons Pedigree, Morlands Old Speckled Hen and Ruddles County on handpump; darts, bar billiards, three fruit machines, video game, trivia, fairly loud juke box, and piped music. Standard bar food includes sandwiches (from £2.95), winter soup, ploughman's (£2.95), and hot dishes like beef and ale pie or vegetable lasagne (£4.50); they do a Sunday roast in the restaurant. The pub can get smoky, and service can slow down at busy periods. There's an increasing number of satisfying places to visit nearby; the Clink round the corner is particularly worth a look. *(Recommended by Paul Randall, Jim Honohan, Don Kellaway, Angie Coles, David and Michelle Hedges, Dr and Mrs A K Clarke)*

Greenalls ~ Licensee Danny Phillips ~ Real ale ~ Meals and snacks (11.30-3, 5-9) ~ Restaurant ~ 0171-407 1577 ~ Children allowed away from bar ~ Open 11-11, 12-10.30 Sun; closed 25/26 Dec, 1 Jan

Bulls Head 🍷 (Barnes) Map 12

373 Lonsdale Road, SW13; ⇌ Barnes Bridge

Top-class modern jazz groups perform at this imposing riverside pub every night, and they're quite a draw. You can hear the music quite clearly from the lounge bar (and on peaceful Sunday lunchtimes from the villagey little street as you approach), but for the full effect and genuine jazz club atmosphere it is worth paying the admission to the well equipped music room. Back in the bustling bar alcoves open off the main area around the island servery, which has Youngs Bitter and Special on handpump, around a hundred or so malt whiskies, and decent wines. Around the walls are large photos of the various jazz musicians and bands who have played here; darts, dominoes, cribbage, Scrabble, chess, cards, fruit machine and video game in the public bar. All the food is home-made, including the bread, pasta, sausages and ice cream, and they do things like soup (£1.50), sandwiches (from £1.80, hot roast meat £2), pasta or home-baked pie (£3.50), and a popular carvery of home-roasted joints (£3.50); service is efficient and very friendly. Bands play 8.30-11 every night plus 12-2pm Sundays, and depending on who's playing prices generally range from £3.50 to £6. *(Recommended by Bob and Maggie Atheron, Susan and John Douglas; more reports please)*

Youngs ~ Tenant Dan Fleming ~ Real ale ~ Meals and snacks ~ Evening restaurant (not Sun evening, though they do Sun lunch) ~ 0181-876 5241 ~ Children welcome ~ Jazz every night and Sun lunchtime ~ Nearby parking may be difficult ~ Open 11-11

Crown & Greyhound (Dulwich) Map 12

73 Dulwich Village, SE21 ⇌ North Dulwich

Just right for summer, this imposing place is blessed with a very pleasant big two-level back terrace, with a good many picnic-table sets under a chestnut tree; you'll generally find a salad bar and ice cream stall out here on sunny days. Inside is grand and astonishingly spacious – it gets very busy in the evenings but there's enough room to absorb everyone without any difficulty. The most ornate room is on the right, with its elaborate ochre ceiling plasterwork, fancy former gas lamps, Hogarth prints, fine carved and panelled settles and so forth. It opens into the former billiards room, where kitchen tables on a stripped board floor are set for the good bar food. Changing every day (the friendly landlady likes to try out new recipes and ideas), the choice might include enormous doorstep sandwiches and toasties (from £2.10), evening filled baked potatoes (from £2), ploughman's (£3.25), vegetarian dishes such as mushroom and spinach strudel, and a range of specials like pork and cheese filo parcels, chicken, leck and stilton crumble, good lamb fennel casserole, or steak and mushroom pie (all around £4.75); popular Sunday carvery (£5.95) – get there early, they don't take bookings. A central snug leads on the other side to the saloon – brown ragged walls, upholstered and panelled settles, a coal-effect gas fire in the tiled period fireplace, and Victorian prints. Well kept Ind Coope Burton, Tetleys, Youngs Bitter and unusual monthly changing guests like Arrols 80/- on handpump; fruit machines, video game, and piped music. There's a no-smoking family area on the right. The pub is handy for walks through the park. *(Recommended by Sue Demont, Tim Barrow, Andy Thwaites, Christopher Gallop, David Wright, E G Parish, Lee Goulding)*

Taylor Walker (Allied) ~ Managers Bernard and Sandra Maguire ~ Real ale ~ Meals and snacks (12-2.30, 5.30-9; not Sun evening) ~ Restaurant (not evenings Sun) ~ 0181-693 2466 ~ Children in restaurant and no-smoking family room ~ Open 11-11

Cutty Sark (Greenwich) Map 12

Ballast Quay, off Lassell St, SE10; ⇌ Maze Hill, from London Bridge, or from the river front walk past the Yacht in Crane St and Trinity Hospital

Since our last edition a new licensee has taken over this attractive late 16th-c white-painted house. Particularly striking as you approach is the big upper bow window jettied out over the pavement, which, from inside, offers good views across to the Isle of Dogs. Full of atmosphere and conjuring up images of the kind of London we imagine Dickens once knew, the bar has flagstones, rough brick walls, wooden settles, barrel tables, open fires, low lighting and narrow openings to tiny side snugs – all very cosy, and, says one reader, just as it was in the 50s. Various pithy sayings are chalked up on the old slates. A roomy eating area has food such as sandwiches, soup (£1.95), topside of beef served hot in a home-made baguette (£4.25), vegetable stroganoff (£4.95), grilled honey and lemon chicken or half rack of ribs with home-made barbecue sauce (£5.45), and steak and onion braised in Guinness (£5.95). Well kept Bass, Worthington Best and a fortnightly changing guest on handpump, several malt whiskies, and a new wine list with a dozen or so by the glass. An elaborate central staircase leads up to an upstairs area; fruit machine, trivia, juke box. There are waterside tables on a terrace across the narrow cobbled lane. The pub can be very busy with young people on Friday and Saturday evenings. *(Recommended by Robert Gomme, Jenny and Brian Seller; more reports please)*

Free house ~ Licensee Terry McCormack ~ Real ale ~ Meals and snacks ~ 0181-858 3146 ~ Children welcome ~ Live music Tues/Thurs/Fri evening ~ Open 11-11

Fox & Grapes (Wimbledon) Map 12

Camp Rd, SW19; ⊖ Wimbledon

Another change of licensees at this well-set pub, ideally placed on the edge of Wimbledon Common. It's especially pleasant on summer evenings when the doors are open and you can sit out on the grass. The neatly comfortable main bar has no surprises – traditional pub furniture, a bit of beamery, log-effect fire and so forth, with a good chatty atmosphere at lunchtimes. There's a step or two down to a rather cosier area. A wide choice of home-made bar food includes sandwiches, soup (£2.75), deep fried brie and camembert en croûte (£3.95), ploughman's (£4.25), spinach and stilton pancake (£4.95), a roast of the day (£5.60), steak and kidney pie (£5.75), poached salmon (£6.75), sirloin steak (£8.95) and changing daily specials. Well kept Courage Best and Directors, Marstons Pedigree, and Wadworths 6X on handpump; farm cider, mulled wine in winter, piped music. *(Recommended by Per Ness, A J N Lee, Colin Pearson, D and B Thomas, John and Shirley Dyson; reports on the new regime please)*

Courage ~ Lease: John O'Connor ~ Real ale ~ Meals and snacks (12-10) ~ 0181-946 5599 ~ Children welcome ~ Open 11-11

George ★ (Southwark) Map 13

Off 77 Borough High Street, SE1; ⊖ Borough or London Bridge

This splendid looking 17th-c coaching inn is such a London landmark that it's easy to forget it's still a proper working pub, and a good one too. It was noted as one of London's 'fair Inns for the receipt of travellers' in 1598, and rebuilt on its original plan after the great Southwark fire in 1676. For a while it was owned by Guys Hospital next door, and then by the Great Northern Railway Company, under whose stewardship it was 'mercilessly reduced' as E V Lucas put it, when the other wings of the building were demolished. Now preserved by the National Trust, the remaining wing is a unique survival, the tiers of open galleries looking down over a cobbled courtyard with plenty of picnic tables, and maybe in summer Morris men or performing players from the nearby Globe Theatre. It's just as unspoilt inside, the row of simple ground-floor rooms and bars all containing square-latticed windows, black beams, bare floorboards, some panelling, plain oak or elm tables and old-fashioned built-in settles, along with a 1797 'Act of Parliament' clock, dimpled glass lantern-lamps and so forth. The snuggest refuge is the simple room nearest the street, where there's an ancient beer engine that looks like a cash register. They use this during their regular beer festivals (the third week of each month), when they might have up to 14 unusual real ales available; the ordinary range includes Boddingtons, Flowers Original, Fullers London Pride, Whitbread Castle Eden and a changing guest on handpump. Also farm cider, and mulled wine in winter; darts, bar billiards, table skittles and trivia. A short choice of bar food might include triple-decker sandwiches (from £1.50), soup (£2), cumberland sausage (£2.75), ploughman's (£3), and home-made pies like steak and mushroom (£3.75); pleasant service. A splendid central staircase goes up to a series of dining rooms and to a gaslit balcony. Unless you know where you're going (or you're in one of the many tourist groups that flock here during the day in summer) you may well miss it, as apart from the great gates there's little to indicate that such a gem still exists behind the less auspicious looking buildings on the busy high street. *(Recommended by James Macrae, A W Dickinson,*

Gordon, Mark Walker, Buck, Calire and Paul Shinkman, Don Kellaway, Angie Coles, Sue Demont, Tim Barrow, Walter Reid)

Whitbreads ~ Manager John Hall ~ Real ale ~ Lunchtime meals and snacks ~ Restaurant (not Sun; often used for groups only – check first) ~ 0171-407 2056 ~ Children in eating area of bar and in restaurant ~ Nearby daytime parking difficult ~ Globe Players, Morris dancers and Medieval Combat Society during summer ~ Open 11-11; closed 25/26 Dec, 1 Jan

Hole in the Wall (Waterloo) Map 13

Mepham Street, SE1; ⊖ Waterloo

The loud rumbling you may hear as you sip your pint at this no-frills drinkers' pub is nothing to be alarmed about, nor should you worry if the walls start to shake – it's just another train passing overhead. The deep red brick ceiling is in fact part of a railway arch, and the main bar is virtually underneath Waterloo Station. A wide range of regularly changing well kept beers on handpump includes Adnams, Bass, Boddingtons, Everards Tiger, Greene King IPA, King and Barnes Sussex, Ruddles County, Theakstons Best, Websters Yorkshire and Youngs Ordinary and Special; they also stock various malt and Irish whiskies. The furnishings are very basic, and a good range of amusements includes a loudish juke box, pinball, two fruit machines, trivia and a couple of video games. Basic bar food includes sandwiches, home-made pies (£2.95), chilli con carne, home-cooked meats, and salads. A smaller front bar is rather smarter. *(Recommended by Tony Dickinson, Owen Walker)*

Free house ~ Licensee Ulick Burke ~ Real ale ~ Meals and snacks all day ~ Weekday daytime parking difficult ~ 0171-928 6196 ~ Open 11-11; 11-4, 7-11 Sat; closed Dec 25

Horniman (Southwark) Map 13

Hays Galleria, Battlebridge Lane; ⊖ London Bridge

The spacious and gleaming bar at this elaborate and rather smart-looking pub is rather like a cross between a French bistro and a Victorian local – and something else besides. There's a set of clocks made for tea merchant Frederick Horniman's office showing the time in various places around the world, and the area by the sweeping bar counter is a few steps down from the door, with squared black, red and white flooring tiles and lots of polished wood. Steps lead up from here to various comfortable carpeted areas, with the tables well spread so as to allow for a feeling of spacious relaxation at quiet times but give room for people standing in groups when it's busy; part of the upstairs area is no-smoking. Bar food includes filling triple-decker sandwiches (from £3.15), ploughman's, and daily changing hot dishes like steak and mushroom pie or a couple of vegetarian meals; they do a four-course carvery (£12.75). Well kept Adnams, Brakspears, Ind Coope Burton, Tetleys, Timothy Taylor Landlord, Wadworths 6X, and maybe a changing guest on handpump. A tea bar serves tea, coffee, chocolate and other hot drinks, and Danish pastries and so forth; a hundred-foot frieze shows the travels of the tea. Pinball, fruit machine, trivia, unobtrusive piped music. Wonderful views of the Thames, *HMS Belfast* and Tower Bridge from the picnic-table sets outside. The pub is at the end of the visually exciting Hays Galleria development, several storeys high, with a soaring glass curved roof, and supported by elegant thin cast-iron columns; various shops and boutiques open off. *(Recommended by D Cox, David and Michelle Hedges, Ian Phillips, Andy Thwaites; more reports please)*

Nicholsons (Allied) ~ Managers Bette Bryant and Dennis Hayes ~ Real ale ~ Meals and snacks (12-3.30) ~ Carvery restaurant (not Sun evening) ~ 0171-407 3611 ~ Children welcome till 8pm ~ Occasional live entertainment ~ Open 10am-11pm (till 4 Sat, 3 Sun); closed evenings 24/31 Dec and all day 25/26 Dec

Pubs brewing their own beers are listed at the back of the book.

Market Porter (Southwark) Map 13

9 Stoney Street, SE1; ⊖ London Bridge

This friendly place is where the market workers and porters traditionally came for a drink at the start or the end of the day. Busy and atmospheric, it's particularly well liked today for its range of well kept beers, one of the most interesting and varied in London. As well as the Market Bitter and Special brewed for them, the choice of eight ales on handpump might include a combination of Bishops Traditional, Harveys Best, Otter Bright, Spinnaker Buzz, Timothy Taylor Landlord, Wadworths 6X and Youngs Bitter. The main part of the long U-shaped bar has rough wooden ceiling beams with beer barrels balanced on them, a heavy wooden bar counter with a beamed gantry, cushioned bar stools, an open fire with stuffed animals in glass cabinets on the mantlepiece, several mounted stags' heads, and 20s-style wall lamps. A decent choice of promptly served bar food includes sandwiches or filled rolls (from £1.95), deep fried jalapeno peppers stuffed with cream cheese (£2.75), ploughman's (£3.25), all-day breakfast (£3.85), pasta with smoked haddock, prawns and mushrooms (£4.95), chicken tikka (£5.95), steaks (from £7.95), and changing daily specials; Sunday lunch. Obliging service; darts, shove ha'penny, cribbage, dominoes, fruit machine, video game, pinball, and piped music. A small partly panelled room has leaded glass windows and a couple of tables. Part of the restaurant is no smoking. The company that own the pub have similar establishments in Reigate and nearby Stamford St. *(Recommended by Don Kellaway, Angie Coles, Michael Boland, Sue Demont, Tim Barrow, David and Michelle Hedges)*

Free house ~ Licensee Steve Turner ~ Real ale ~ Lunchtime meals and snacks (not Sat) ~ Restaurant (not Sun evening) ~ 0171-407 2495 ~ Children in restaurant, anywhere at weekends ~ Open 11-11 (11-3, 7-11 Sat)

Phoenix & Firkin ★ (Denmark Hill) Map 12

5 Windsor Walk, SE5; ⇌ Denmark Hill

Lively, loud, and crowded in the evenings, this vibrant place is a real favourite with some readers. It's an interesting conversion of a palatial Victorian railway hall, but the atmosphere, rather than the architecture, is what draws so many people in. A model railway train runs back and forth behind the food bar, and there are paintings of steam trains, old-fashioned station name signs, a huge double-faced station clock (originally from Llandudno Junction in Wales), solid wooden furniture on the stripped wooden floor, old seaside posters, Bovril advertisements, and plants. At one end there's a similarly-furnished gallery, reached by a spiral staircase, and at the other arches lead into a food room; fruit machine, trivia, pinball. Their own Phoenix, Rail and Dogbolter on handpump, and maybe one or two guest beers. The piped music may be loud, especially in the evenings when the pub is popular with young people (it can be a little smoky then too); you can enjoy a quieter drink at lunchtimes. Straightforward food includes big filled baps (from £2.10), a good cold buffet with pork pies, salads, quiche and so forth, and a couple of daily hot dishes like steak and kidney pie or beef curry (£3.80). There are a couple of long benches outside, and the steps which follow the slope of the road are a popular place to sit. *(Recommended by Dr and Mrs A K Clarke, Andy Thwaites, Dr M Owton, Sarah King, Patrick Forbes)*

Own Brew ~ Manager Andrew Lowson ~ Real ale ~ Meals and snacks (12-8.30) ~ 0171-701 8282 ~ Children in eating area of bar till 5pm ~ Live music Mon and Sat evenings ~ Open 11-11; 12-10.30 Sun

Ship 🍷 (Wandsworth) Map 12

41 Jews Row, SW18; ⇌ Wandsworth Town

With a Thames barge moored alongside, the extensive two-level riverside terrace of this smartly bustling pub really comes into its own in summer, when it has picnic tables, pretty hanging baskets and brightly coloured flower-beds, small trees, and its own bar. Inside, only a small part of the original ceiling is left in the main bar – the rest is in a light and airy conservatory style; wooden tables, a medley of stools, and old church chairs on the wooden floorboards, and a relaxed, chatty atmosphere. One part has a Victorian fireplace, a huge clock surrounded by barge prints, and part of a milking machine on a table, and there's a rather battered harmonium, old-fashioned bagatelle, and jugs of flowers around the window sills. The basic public bar has plain wooden furniture, a black kitchen range in the fireplace and darts, pinball and a juke box. Youngs Bitter, Special and Winter Warmer on handpump, freshly squeezed orange juice, and a wide choice of wines, a dozen by the glass. A sensibly short range of very good, unusual bar food (made with mostly free-range produce), might include sandwiches, luberon bouillabaisse (£3.50), New Zealand mussel salad (£4.50), Chinese spare ribs on a beansprout and fruit salad (£6) and duck kebabs with a quince and red onion sauce (£7); there's an al fresco restaurant on the terrace. Service is friendly and helpful – one couple was delighted when they happily made sandwiches specially and offered to heat their baby's bottle. The pub's annual firework display draws huge crowds of young people. The adjacent car park can get full pretty quickly in the summer. *(Recommended by Bob and Maggie Atherton, R Vernon, P Gillbe, James Macrae)*

Youngs ~ Licensees Charles Gotto and D N Haworth ~ Real ale ~ Meals (12-3, 7-10) and snacks (all day) ~ Restaurant ~ 0181-870 9667 ~ Children in eating area of bar and restaurant ~ Open 11-11

White Cross 🍷 (Richmond) Map 12

Cholmondeley Walk; ⊖ ⇌ Richmond

Make sure when leaving your car outside this imposing riverside pub you know the tide times – it's not unusual for the water to rise right up the steps into the bar, completely covering anything that gets in its way. There may even be occasions when however you've arrived you could be cut off altogether – though it's not a bad place to be marooned in. Very cosy in the winter, the pub really comes into its own in summer, when the whole area takes on the flavour of a civilised and rather cosmopolitan seaside resort. A big paved front garden has its own summer bar, and plenty of seats and picnic tables, many of them sheltered by a big tree, prettily fairy-lit in the evening. Inside, the two chatty main rooms still have something of the feel of the hotel this once was, as well as comfortable long red banquettes curving round the tables in the deep bay windows, local prints and photographs, three log fires (one with a big mirror over the fireplace), and a good mix of variously aged customers; the old-fashioned wooden island servery is on the right. The views of the river from here are some of the nicest along the Thames, though they're better still from the balcony of a big bright and airy room upstairs, which has lots more tables and a number of plates on a shelf running round the walls. From a servery at the foot of the stairs, good bar food – all home-made – includes celery and almond soup (£1.95), sandwiches (from £2.25), ploughman's (£3.95), salads (from £5, with home-cooked meats), and several daily changing hot dishes like spinach terrine or asparagus, butter bean and tomato bake (£4.95), beef and marrow curry, pasta with herbs, squid and tomatoes, or turkey, vegetable and bacon pie (around £5.25), and puddings such as summer fruit bavarois or apple crumble (£2.50); they generally do sandwiches or pasties up to 7 o'clock. Youngs Bitter and Special on handpump, and a good range of thirty or so carefully chosen wines by the glass; efficient, friendly service. No music or machines – the only games are chess and backgammon. Bonzo the flat coat retriever loves fetching sticks thrown by customers – even if that means taking a dip in the river. Boats leave from immediately outside to Kingston or Hampton Court. *(Recommended by Nigel Williamson and others)*

Youngs ~ Managers Quentin and Denise Thwaites ~ Real ale ~ Lunchtime meals and snacks ~ 0181-940 6844 ~ Children in big upstairs room (high chairs and changing facilities) ~ Very occasional live music (jazz or a harpist on the balcony for example) ~ Open 11-11

Please let us know of any pubs where the wine is particularly good.

Windmill 🍷 (Clapham) Map 12

Clapham Common South Side, SW4; ⊖ Clapham Common/Clapham South

One reader called at this fine old Victorian inn after an interval of ten years and came away convinced all the customers were the same as on his last visit. That wouldn't be surprising – smartly civilised, busy and bustling, it's the kind of place that once discovered you can happily return to time and time again. Drawing particular acclaim over the past year or so have been the entertaining Monday opera evenings in the no-smoking conservatory, when the genre's rising stars perform various solos and arias (proof, if it were needed, that opera isn't just for toffs); they also have good jazz in here, all nicely segregated from the comfortable domed main bar. Spacious and airy, this has as its centrepiece an illuminated aquarium, surrounded by colourfully upholstered L-shaped banquettes, and plenty of prints and pictures on the walls, including several of Dutch windmills. It's a big place, so though it often gets lively, you should usually be able to find a quiet corner. Bar food such as sandwiches and baguettes (from £1.50), soup (£1.75), ploughman's (from £3.50), vegetable lasagne or kedgeree (£3.75), salads (from £4.45), chicken satay (£5.25), barbecue spare ribs (£6.50), steak (£9.75) and home-made daily specials; service is friendly and cheerful. Youngs Bitter and Special on handpump, a good choice of wines by the glass and plenty more by the bottle; fruit machine and video game. There's a barbecue area in the secluded front courtyard with tubs of shrubs. The inn can get packed in summer, when it seems to serve not just the pub but half of neighbouring Clapham Common too. A painting in the Tate by J P Herring has the Windmill in the background, shown behind local turn-of-the-century characters returning from the Derby Day festivities. It's a particularly nice play to stay – they've spent a good deal of time and effort upgrading the accommodation side over the last couple of years. *(Recommended by Christopher Gallop, James Macrae, Angeline Chan and others)*

Youngs ~ Managers J R and H A Williamson ~ Real ale ~ Meals and snacks (till 10) ~ Restaurant (not Sun evening) ~ 0181-673 4578 ~ Children in no-smoking conservatory ~ Live opera by up-and-coming artists Mon evening, jazz Thurs pm and Sat lunch ~ Open 11-11 ~ Bedrooms: £75B/£85B, around £20 less at weekends

WEST LONDON

During weekday or Saturday daytime you may not be able to find a meter very close to the Anglesea Arms or the Windsor Castle, and parking very near in the evening may sometimes be tricky with both of these, but there shouldn't otherwise be problems in this area

Anglesea Arms (Chelsea) Map 13

15 Selwood Terrace, SW7; ⊖ South Kensington

Often so busy in the evenings that the customers spill out onto the terrace and pavement, this cheerily chatty pub manages the rare feat of being smart and cosy at the same time. The bar has central elbow tables, leather chesterfields, faded Turkey carpets on the bare wood-strip floor, wood panelling, and big windows with attractive swagged curtains; at one end several booths with partly glazed screens have cushioned pews and spindleback chairs, and down some steps there's a small carpeted room with captain's chairs, high stools and a Victorian fireplace. The genuinely old-fashioned mood is heightened by some heavy portraits, prints of London, a big station clock, bits of brass and pottery, and large brass chandeliers. Well kept Adnams, Boddingtons, Brakspears SB, Flowers Original, Fullers London Pride, Harveys, and Youngs Special on handpump, and several malt and Irish whiskies. Food from a glass cabinet includes doorstep sandwiches (from £1.50), ploughman's (£2.75), broccoli and cheese bake or pies such as turkey and ham or steak and mushroom (£3.90), sirloin steak (£6), and a Sunday roast (£4.95); in the late evening, you may get sandwiches for £1 or less. Good, quick service. The pub is very popular with well-heeled young people, but is well liked by locals too (though admittedly that could be because many of the locals are well-heeled young people). *(Recommended by Andy Thwaites, Yolanda Henry, John Fazakerley, Michael J Lumia, Quentin Williamson, Sue Demont, Tim Barrow; more reports please)*

Free house ~ Licensee Patrick Timmons ~ Real ale ~ Meals and snacks (not Sun evening) ~ 0171-373 7960 ~ Children welcome till 7pm ~ Daytime parking metered ~ Open 11-3, 5(7 Sat)-11; closed Dec 25/26

Churchill Arms £ (Kensington) Map 12

119 Kensington Church St; ⊖ Notting Hill Gate/Kensington High St

Full of character and characters, this wonderfully friendly pub feels very much like a bustling village local, something that owes a lot to the enthusiasm of the good-natured Irish landlord, who has just celebrated his tenth year here. He obviously really cares about the pub and the people that come in it, going out of his way to offer an individual welcome, remembering faces after only a couple of visits, and putting a great deal of effort into organising special events and activities. They really go to town around Halloween or the week leading up to Churchill's birthday (November 30th), decorating the place with balloons, candles and appropriate oddities, serving special drinks and generally just creating a lively carefree atmosphere. One of the landlord's hobbies is collecting butterflies, and you'll see a variety of prints and books on the subject dotted around the bar. There are also lamps, miners' lights, horse tack, bedpans and brasses hanging from the ceiling, a couple of interesting carved figures and statuettes behind the central bar counter, prints of American presidents, and lots of Churchill memorabilia. The spacious and rather smart plant-filled dining conservatory may be used for hatching butterflies, but is better known for its big choice of really excellent Thai food: chicken and cashew nuts (£4.75) or Thai noodles, roast duck curry or beef curry (£4.95). They also do things like sandwiches (from £1.75), ploughman's (£2.75) or home-made steak and kidney (£2.95), and Sunday lunch (£4.95). Well kept (and nicely priced) Fullers ESB, London Pride, Chiswick and Hock Mild on handpump; cheerful service. Shove-ha'penny, fruit machine, and unobtrusive piped music; they have their own cricket and football teams. *(Recommended by LM, Ian Phillips, Bob Shearer, Mimi O'Connor, David Peakall, Stephen R Holman, Tony and Lynne Stark, Susan and John Douglas and others)*

Fullers ~ Manager Gerry O'Brien ~ Real ale ~ Meals and snacks (12-2.30, 6-9.30; not Sun evening) ~ Restaurant (not Sun evening) ~ 0171-727 4242 ~ Children welcome ~ Open 11-11; closed evening Dec 25

Dove ★ (Hammersmith) Map 12

19 Upper Mall, W6; ⊖ Ravenscourt Park

Ask any group of Londoners to name their favourite Thamesside pub and chances are most of then will come up with this old favourite. In summer most people head for the the tiny river view terrace at the back, where the main flagstoned area, down some steps, has a few teak tables and white metal and teak chairs looking over the low river wall to the Thames reach just above Hammersmith Bridge; a very civilised spot. In the evenings you'll often see rowing crews practising along this stretch of the water. By the entrance from the quiet alley, the main bar has black wood panelling, red leatherette cushioned built-in wall settles and stools around dimpled copper tables, old framed advertisements, and photographs of the pub; very well kept Fullers London Pride and ESB on handpump. Up some steps, a room with small settles and solid wooden furniture has a big, clean and efficiently served glass food cabinet, offering sandwiches, filled baked potatoes (£3.50), salads (£3.95), cottage pie (£4.50), steak and kidney pie or smoked haddock pasta (£4.95), and lots of changing daily specials; they also do a range of Thai meals, particularly in the evening (from £5.50). No noisy games machines or piped music. Perhaps the best time to visit is at lunchtime when it's not quite so crowded, but even at its busiest, the staff remain briskly efficient. There's a manuscript of 'Rule Britannia' on the wall in one of the bars: James Thomson is said to have composed it here, and he also wrote the final part of his less well-known 'The Seasons' in an upper room, whilst dying of a fever he'd caught travelling to Kew in bad weather. Elsewhere a plaque marks the level of the highest-ever tide in 1928. Several pubs punctuate this part of the river – this is the best. *(Recommended by Dave Irving, Ewan McCall, Roger Huggins, Tom McLean, A W Dickinson, James Macrae, Stephen George Brown, Ian Phillips, Gordon, Martin Kay, Andrea Fowler, Andy Thwaites, Stephen and Julie Brown, Simon Collett-Jones, L Grant, Jenny and Brian Seller)*

Fullers ~ Tenant Brian Lovrey ~ Real ale ~ Meals and snacks (12-3, 6-10) ~ 0181-748 5405 ~ Open 11-11

Eel Pie (Twickenham) Map 12

9 Church Street; ⇌ Twickenham

Busy and unpretentious, this friendly pub is well liked for its range of well kept real ales on handpump, generally including Badger Best, Hard Tackle and Tanglefoot, Gribble Black Adder, Smiles Best and Wadworths 6X; they also keep around 14 malt whiskies. Sandwiches are served all day (from £1.20, not Sunday), and at lunchtime there might be ploughman's (£2.85), salads, and three or four changing hot dishes like steak in ale, lamb chops in mint gravy, chicken and broccoli bake, or vegetable curry (all £3.95). Seats at the front window of the simply furnished downstairs bar, decorated in Laura Ashley style, look out to the quiet village street; bar billiards, fruit machine, jukebox, pinball, maybe Brady, the Irish wolfhound. There are benches outside on the cobbles. It can be very popular at weekends, especially if there's a rugby match taking place. *(Recommended by Liz and Benton Jennings, James Macrae, M Clarke and others, Lynne Stark)*

Badger ~ Manager Colin Clark ~ Real ale ~ Meals (not evening or Sun) and snacks (not Sun) ~ 0181-891 1717 ~ Children welcome till 7 or 8pm ~ Open 11-11; 12-10.30 Sun

Ferret & Firkin (Fulham) Map 12

Lots Road, SW10; ⊖ Fulham Broadway, but some distance away

As infectiously cheery as most of the other Firkin pubs, this is a determinedly basic place, popular with a good mix of mostly young, easy-going customers. A small, unusually curved corner-house, it has traditional furnishings well made from good wood on the unsealed bare floorboards, slowly circulating colonial-style ceiling fans, a log-effect gas fire, tall airy windows, and plenty of standing room in front of the long bar counter – which is also curved. Several readers feel it looks like a sort of anglicised Wild-West saloon. Well kept beers brewed in the cellar downstairs include the notoriously strong Dogbolter, Balloonastic, Ferret, and Golden Glory; with 24 hours' notice you may be able to collect a bulk supply of these beers. Good friendly service. A food counter serves heftily filled giant meat-and-salad rolls (from £2.75) and salads all afternoon, and at lunchtime they do three hot dishes like chilli con carne, steak and kidney pie or casseroles (£3.75); Sunday roast (£4.75). Good – and popular – juke box, bar billiards, dominoes, fruit machine. It's handy for Chelsea Harbour, which, to continue the Western analogies, at times feels rather like a ghost town. *(Recommended by Richard Houghton, Dr and Mrs A K Clarke, Simon Collett-Jones, Gordon, Dave Carter, Graham Reeve)*

Own brew ~ Manager Fergal Bolger ~ Real ale ~ Meals and snacks (12-7) ~ 0171-352 6645 ~ Daytime parking is metered and may be difficult ~ Pianist Fri evening, guitarist Sat, blues/jazz Sun ~ Open 11-11

Kings Arms (Hampton Court) Map 12

Hampton Court Rd; next to Lion Gate; ⇌ Hampton Court

Cosy, comfortable and notably welcoming, this imposing, white-painted pub is right on the edge of the grounds of Hampton Court. The bar leading off to the right has black panelling, some seats and tables made from casks, and fine stained glass around the serving counter, while the lounge bar on the left, mainly given over to food, has one or two settles, bunches of dried flowers over an old cooking range and walls stripped back to the brick. From an efficient servery, the well liked bar food includes sandwiches, good soup (£2.25), popular ploughman's (£3.95), smoked haddock and poached egg (£4.40), battered cod and chips (£4.95) and steak, mushroom and ale pie (£5.95). Well kept Badger Best, Hard Tackle and Tanglefoot, Eagle IPA, Gribble Black Adder, and Wadworths 6X on handpump; service is friendly and efficient. They also have a little tea shop, with several unusual varieties of the brew and light snacks. The public bar at the end is properly old-fashioned and very relaxed, with good games – an old pin-ball machine that takes two-pence pieces (proceeds to the RNLI), and a decent darts area; sawdust on the floor, dried hops hanging from the beams, a few casks, a fireplace with a stuffed pheasant above it, unobtrusive piped music, and some enamel adverts, one for Camp coffee. They can be busy in summer. There are several picnic tables outside by the road. Dogs welcome (free biscuits for them). Parking is metered nearby. *(Recommended by Peter Burton, John Ames, Jamie and Ruth Lyons, Susan and John Douglas, Yolanda Henry, Ralf Zeyssig, Gill Earle, Andrew Burton, Ian Phillips)*

Badger ~ Manager Niall Williams ~ Real ale ~ Meals and snacks (11-10) ~ Upstairs restaurant; closed Sun evening, Mon ~ 0181-977 1729 ~ Children welcome till 8pm ~ Open 11-11, 12-10.30 Sun; closed evening Dec 25

Ladbroke Arms (Holland Park) Map 12

54 Ladbroke Rd, W11; ⊖ Holland Park

Describing the food at this stylish place as good would be like saying Holland Park has some nice-looking houses. Few London pubs offer meals this impressive, and it comes as quite a bonus that the pub itself would still be worth a stop even if the only food was a packet of crisps. Chalked up on a couple of blackboards on the right hand side of the central servery, the imaginative range of home-made dishes might typically include grilled goat's cheese and bacon salad (£4.25), pasta with pesto and sun-dried tomatoes (£5.50), beef goulash (£6.95), salmon fishcakes with hollandaise sauce or chicken breast stuffed with avocado and garlic (£7.95), escalope of turkey filled with mozzarella and bacon on a bed of noodles (£8.95), rack of lamb with barlotti beans (£9.50), steak in a pink peppercorn sauce (£9.95), and freshly delivered fish such as baked cod with coriander; friendly staff bring French bread to the table, and even the mustards and other accompaniments are better quality than average. There's a warm red hue to some parts of the immaculate bar (especially up in a slightly raised area with a fireplace), as well as simple wooden tables and chairs, comfortable red-cushioned wall-seats, several colonial-style fans on the ceiling, some striking moulding on the dado, colourful flowers on the bar, newspapers and *Country Life* back numbers to read, and a broad mix of customers and age-groups; soft piped jazz blends in with the smartly chatty atmosphere. The landlord deals in art so the interesting prints can change on each visit. Courage Best and Directors, John Smiths, Shepherd Neame Spitfire (replaced by Eldridge Pope Royal Oak in winter) and Wadworths 6X on handpump, and over a dozen malt whiskies. Lots of picnic-table sets in front, overlooking the quiet street. *(Recommended by Mrs J A Blanks, Mrs Wyn Churchill, Elizabeth Ibbott)*

Courage ~ Lease: Ian McKenzie ~ Real ale ~ Meals and snacks (till 10) ~ 0171-727 6648 ~ Children welcome ~ Open 11-11; 11-3, 5.30-11 winter; closed evening 25 Dec

Popes Grotto (Twickenham) Map 12

Cross Deep; ⇌ Strawberry Hill

Opposite some pretty public gardens sloping down to the Thames (closed at night), this well-run and spacious pub has a very relaxed and comfortable feel in the stroll-around main bar. There are lots of little round seats and armed chairs, and a quieter, more intimate fringe behind a balustrade at the back. Also, a snug and rather stylish bow-windowed front bar, and a public bar with darts, shove-ha'penny, dominoes, cribbage, fruit machine and video game. Good bar food includes soup (£1.70), sandwiches (from £2), filled baked potatoes (from £2.85), salads (from £3.80), chicken curry (£4), spinach and mushroom lasagne (£4.50), gammon (£5), sirloin steak (£8.30), puddings, daily specials and Sunday lunch (£4.95). Well kept Youngs Bitter and Special on handpump, with the brewery's seasonal brews like their Winter Warmer; also a good range of malt and other whiskies. The back terraced garden has seats and tables under trees, with more on the front terrace. The pub is named after the poet Alexander Pope who had a villa nearby. *(Recommended by P Gillbe; more reports please)*

Youngs ~ Manager Stephen Brough ~ Real ale ~ Meals and snacks (not Sun evening) ~ 0181-892 3050 ~ Well-behaved children in eating area of bar till 9pm (no noisy babies or toddlers) ~ Open 11-3, 5.30-11, all day Sat; closed evening 25 Dec

White Horse (Fulham) Map 12

1 Parsons Green, SW6; ⊖ Parsons Green

One of the highlights of this all-round-excellent pub has long been the eclectic and well chosen selection of drinks, and they now plan to pass on their expertise with a series of tutored wine and beer tastings. The food, atmosphere and smiling service all stand out too, so it's odd we don't hear more from readers about the place – to our minds undoubtedly one of the very best pubs in London. Particularly well kept and often unusual beers might include Adnams Extra, Bass, Harveys Sussex, Highgate Mild and a guest on handpump, with some helpful tasting notes; they also have 15 Trappist beers, a guest foreign lager on draught, a dozen malt whiskies, and good, interesting and not overpriced wines (a new Cruover machine should increase the choice by the glass). Well-liked weekday lunches might include sandwiches, soup (£2.50), pasta with artichokes, peppers and mushrooms (£4.25), braised sausages in beer and onion gravy (£4.50), and Chinese spiced pork (£5.25), with evening dishes like spaghetti with sun-dried tomatoes, coriander, roasted peppers and black olives (£5.95), and Thai stir-fried monkfish or warm chicken salad with satay sauce (£6.50). They also do a very good Sunday lunch served in the old billiard room upstairs. The main part of the spacious and tastefully refurbished U-shaped bar has big leather chesterfields and huge windows with slatted wooden blinds; to one side is a plainer area with leatherette wall banquettes on the wood plank floor, and a tiled Victorian fireplace; several of the high-backed pews on the right hand side may be reserved for eating; dominoes, cribbage, chess, cards, fruit machine. It's a favourite with smart young people, who on summer evenings relax at the white cast-iron tables and chairs on the rather continental front terrace overlooking the green, so earning the pub its well-known soubriquet 'the Sloaney Pony'. They organise several themed beer evenings and weekends (often spotlighting regional breweries) – the best known is for strong old ale held on the last Saturday in November; lively celebrations too on American Independence Day or Thanksgiving. They tell us the former manageress has retired to the golf course, but the other half of the partnership is keeping standards as high as ever; they plan slight changes to the decor and furnishings early this year. *(Recommended by Sue Demont, Tim Barrow, Bob and Maggie Atherton; more reports please)*

Bass ~ Managers Mark Dorber, Rupert Reeves ~ Real ale ~ Meals and snacks (12-2.45, 5.30-10) ~ 0171-736 2115 ~ Children in eating area ~ Occasional jazz nights ~ Open 11-11; closed 25-28 Dec

Windsor Castle (Holland Park/Kensington) Map 12

114 Campden Hill Road, W8; ⊖ Holland Park/Notting Hill Gate

It only takes one visit to be smitten by this charming pub, reckoned by several readers to be the nicest in London. It's said that when it was built in the early 19th c you could see the real Windsor Castle from the top of this hill, and though the surroundings and view have changed almost beyond recognition since then, the pub has stayed very much the same, a relaxing country-style tavern with a great deal of character and atmosphere. The series of little dark-panelled, old-fashioned rooms have time-smoked ceilings, soft lighting, and on first acquaintance what seems to be a bewildering number of snug little areas and doors leading out into the street – you can easily miss seeing the people you're meeting, particularly if they're hidden away behind the sturdy built-in elm benches. A cosy little pre-war-style dining room opens off the bar. The distinctive choice of good bar food typically includes sandwiches (from £2.25), seafood chowder (£2.95), salads such as spinach, stilton and walnut or riccotta and aubergine (from £3.25), grilled goat's cheese (£3.95), vegetable couscous (£4.75), tuna steak, salmon fishcakes or moules marinières (£4.95), half a dozen oysters (£5), steak and kidney pudding, rack of lamb, game pie or rabbit pie (all £5.95), and steaks; the Sunday lunch is popular. Over the bar they sell sausages made by the landlord's brother (75p); he has a sausage shop nearby. Adnams Extra, Bass, Charringtons IPA, and a monthly guest like Stones on handpump; decent house wines, various malt whiskies, maybe mulled wine in winter. Helpful, enthusiastic staff. No fruit machines or piped music. An attractive summer feature is the busy tree-shaded back garden, which has lots of sturdy teak seats and tables on flagstones, knee-high stone walls (eminently sittable-on) dividing them, high ivy-covered sheltering walls, and soft shade from a sweeping, low-branched plane tree, a lime and a flowering cherry. There's a brick garden bar out here too. Usually fairly quiet at lunchtime, the pub can be packed some evenings, often with smart young people. The Camden bar is no-smoking at lunchtimes. ***(Recommended by Sue Demont, Tim Barrow, Adrian Carter, Andy Thwaites, Annie Rolfe, Gordon, Ian Phillips, Nick Dowson, B Brown, David Quirk, and others)***

Charringtons (Bass) ~ Manager Matthew O'Keefe ~ Real ale ~ Meals and snacks (11-11) ~ (0171) 727 8491 ~ Children in eating area of bar ~ Daytime parking metered ~ Open 11-11

EAST LONDON

Grapes (Limehouse) Map 12

76 Narrow Street, E14; ⊖ Shadwell (some distance away) or Westferry on the Docklands Light Railway; the Limehouse link has made it hard to find by car – turn off Commercial Rd at signs for Rotherhithe tunnel, from Tunnel Approach slip-road on left leads to Branch Rd then Narrow St

'A tavern of dropsical appearance' was how Dickens described this characterful 16th c pub when he used it as the basis of his 'Six Jolly Fellowship Porters' in *Our Mutual Friend:* 'It had not a straight floor and hardly a straight line, but it had outlasted and would yet outlast many a better-trimmed building, many a sprucer public house.' Not much has changed since, though as far as we know watermen no longer row out drunks from here, drown them, and sell the salvaged bodies to the anatomists as they did in Dickens' day. Nicely off the tourist track, it was a favourite with Rex Whistler who came here to paint the river (the results are really quite special). The back part is the oldest, with the recently refurbished back balcony a fine place for a sheltered waterside drink; steps lead down to the foreshore. The partly-panelled bar has lots of prints, mainly of actors, and some elaborately etched windows. Friary Meux, Ind Coope Burton, Tetleys and a guest beer on handpump, and a dozen malt whiskies. Bar food such as sandwiches, moules marinières or a pint of prawns (£3.75), bangers and mash with a thick onion gravy (£4.35), daily fresh fish like plaice or cod (£4.50), and a Sunday roast; the upstairs fish restaurant (with fine views of the river) is highly praised. Shove ha'penny, table skittles, cribbage, dominoes, backgammon, maybe piped music; no under 12s. ***(Recommended by Eddie Edwards, Andy Thwaites; more reports please)***

Taylor-Walker (Allied) ~ Manager Barbara Haigh ~ Real ale ~ Meals and snacks (not Sun evening) ~ Restaurant (closed Sun) ~ 0171-987 4396 ~ Open 12-3, 5.30(7 Sat)-11

Pubs staying open all afternoon are listed at the back of the book.

Lucky Dip

Besides the fully inspected pubs, you might like to try these Lucky Dips recommended to us and described by readers (if you do, please send us reports). We have split them into the main areas used for the full reports – Central, North, and so on. Within each area the Lucky Dips are listed by postal district, ending with Greater London suburbs on the edge of that area.

CENTRAL LONDON

EC1

[W Smithfield], *Bishops Finger*: Single room with wooden floorboards, full Shepherd Neame range and a guest beer, separate food servery, efficient busy and friendly staff; popular *(Chris Westmoreland)*

[43 Clerkenwell Green], *Crown*: Smart friendly pub, good range of real ales *(Chris Westmoreland)*

☆ [115 Charterhouse St], *Fox & Anchor*: Good food esp tender meat in long, narrow bar with narrow tables, interesting paintings, period prints and Edwardian photographs, well kept Greene King Abbot, Tetleys and other ales; opens early for Smithfield workers' breakfasts *(Ian Phillips)*

☆ [1 Middle St], *Hand & Shears*: Traditional Smithfield pub with three rooms around central servery, lively mixed clientele, Courage and Theakstons Best, quick friendly service, interesting bric-a-brac, reasonably priced food – evening too; open all day exc weekends, cl Sun *(Ian Phillips, Gordon, BB)*

[33 Seward St], *Leopard*: Big pleasant walled garden with picnic tables, reasonably priced well prepared food served promptly; Courage-related ales *(Ian Phillips)*

☆ [166 Goswell Rd], *Pheasant & Firkin*: Own cheap light Pluckers, also good value Pheasant and powerful Dogbolter brewed here, and basic range of food; bare boards, pleasant atmosphere (esp midweek evenings), congenial staff, daily papers, good cheap CD juke box, cheerful Fri night guitarist *(Ian Phillips, Sue Demont, Tim Barrow, LYM)*

[Rising Sun Ct; Cloth Fair], *Rising Sun*: Recent major refit, elaborate carved dark woodwork, lots of little tables, stools and benches, books in ornate carved bookcase, friendly staff and youngish atmosphere, piped music, good value Sam Smiths, chess, dominoes, cribbage; music and Sky TV may be loud, quieter upstairs (not always open) *(Christopher Gallop, Tim Heywood, Sophie Wilne)*

[Sekforde St], *Sekforde Arms*: Attractive Youngs pub with friendly welcome and well kept beers *(Chris Westmoreland)*

[4 Leather Lane], *Sir Christopher Hatton*: Newish pub at base of new office block, in wide pedestrian area festooned with tables and chairs; big cellar bar sensibly split into separate areas by pillars and changes of floor level, well kept Bass, Worthington BB and other ales, popular lunchtime bar food; has been cl Sat evening and Sun *(Dr and Mrs A K Clarke, Chris Westmoreland)*

[Carthusian St], *Sutton Arms*: Friendly and comfortable, long and narrow, reasonably priced food *(Ian Phillips)*

EC3

☆ [St Michaels Alley, Cornhill], *Jamaica Wine House*: Long upstairs bare-boards bar known as the Jampot, benches and partitions, wine bottles and intriguing collection of copper vessels behind bar; downstairs livelier with young city gents, on hot days spilling into alleys and adjacent St Michaels churchyard; good lunchtime sandwiches esp beef and hot dishes, champagne by the glass, friendly atmosphere *(Ian Phillips, Eddie Edwards, Christopher Gallop)*

[10 Leadenhall Market], *Lamb*: Occupies one side of the arcade, on three floors inc basement, changed little since turn of the century *(Ian Phillips)*

EC4

[Charterhouse St], *Fox & Anchor*: Friendly, small and cosy, well refurbished, with tiled facade, all-wood interior with small snugs at the back; good reasonably priced food, good range of well kept beers *(Chris Westmoreland)*

[29 Knightrider St], *Horn*: Lots of little booths, well kept Eldridge Pope; said to be associated with Guy Fawkes *(Dr and Mrs A K Clarke)*

☆ [194 Fleet St], *Old Bank of England*: Sumptuous conversion of austere Italianate building, enormous lofty bar like a cross between marble ballroom and pub, lots of other areas off inc balcony, dining room specialising in fish, full Fullers range, decent wines, already very popular *(BB)*

☆ [Fleet St, nr Ludgate Circus], *Old Bell*: Unusually small and cosy for a City pub, largely unspoilt flagstoned front bar with trap door to cellar, stained-glass window, nice window seat; back bar with cast-iron tables and three-legged triangular stools on sloping bare boards; particularly well kept beer; rebuilt by Wren as commissariat for his workers on former church behind *(Andy Thwaites, Gordon)*

☆ [Ludgate Circus], *Old King Lud*: 10 to 15 changing reasonably priced real ales in busy beams-and-sawdust style pub, no music, knowledgeable and helpful staff; yesterday's sports page from *The Times* framed in the gents' *(Tim Heywood, Carl Stevenage)*

☆ [99 Fleet St], *Punch*: Warm, comfortable, softly lit Victorian pub, not too smart, fine mirrors, dozens of Punch cartoons, ornate plaster ceiling with unusual domed skylight, good bar food, Tetleys-related and other ales such as Marstons and Wadworths *(Gordon, Chris Westmoreland)*

SW1

☆ [Eaton Terr], *Antelope*: Cheery upmarket panelled local, well kept Tetleys-related and guest ales, decent wines, decent food – quiet and relaxed upstairs weekday lunchtimes, can get crowded evenings; open all day, children in eating area *(Gordon, TBB, LYM)*

[6 Buckingham Palace Rd, corner Lower Grosvenor Pl], *Bag o' Nails*: Small local with well kept real ales, simple food such as pie or fish and chips, a real welcome for strangers *(Richard Helmbrecht)*

[53 Whitehall], *Clarence*: Olde-worlde, with scrubbed wooden tables and floorboards, old oak beams and gas lamps; food all day into evening, at least four real ales, good welcoming service, pavement tables; very busy Fri evening *(Mark Walker)*

[20 The Broadway], *Feathers*: Large comfortable pub, a Scotland Yard local, bar food downstairs, restaurant up, well kept Bass and Charrington IPA *(Robert Lester, LYM)*

[29 Passmore St], *Fox & Hounds*: Small cosy single bar, wall benches, big hunting paintings, piano tucked in so that you can't reach the bottom notes; pleasant landlord *(Gordon)*

☆ [14 Little Chester St], *Grouse & Claret*: Solidly built pastiche of discreetly old-fashioned tavern just off Belgrave Sq, smart but welcoming and very well run, with attractive furnishings, well kept ales such as Boddingtons, Brakspears, Greene King IPA, Wadworths 6X and Youngs Special, games area, decent bar food; basement wine bar with three-course lunches, swish upstairs restaurant; children in eating area, open all day weekdays, cl Sun evening and bank hols *(John Scarisbrick, Richard Waller, Susan and John Douglas, LYM)*

☆ [58 Millbank], *Morpeth Arms:* Roomy Victorian Youngs pub handy for the Tate, old books and prints, photographs, earthenware jars and bottles; busy lunchtimes, quieter evenings – well kept ales, good choice of wines, food, helpful staff; seats outside (a lot of traffic) *(Dr J R G Beavon, Quentin Williamson, BB)*

☆ [153 Knightsbridge], *Paxtons Head*: Peaceful Victorian pub, attractive period decor and furnishings (the glass and mirrors came from Paxton's Crystal Palace), decent steaks and so forth upstairs, nice little cellar overflow bar *(Ian Phillips)*

☆ [23 Crown Passage; behind St James's St, off Pall Mall], *Red Lion*: Small cosy local, one of West End's oldest, tucked down narrow pedestrian alley nr Christies; friendly relaxed atmosphere, panelling and leaded lights, decent lunchtime food, unobtrusive piped music, real ales such as Fullers and Ruddles *(Walter Reid, Gordon, BB)*

☆ [D of York St], *Red Lion*: Busy little pub notable for dazzling mirrors, crystal chandeliers and cut and etched windows, splendid mahogany, ornamental plaster ceiling – architecturally, central London's most perfect small Victorian pub; decent sandwiches, snacks and hot dishes, well kept Tetleys-related ales *(LYM)*

[33 Whitehall], *Silver Cross:* Small maybe crowded pub with suprising Italian waggon-vaulted ceiling; good lunchtime food from servery by entrance, pleasant atmosphere, Courage-related beers; said to have been a tavern since 1674, and to date back to 13th century *(Mark Walker, BB)*

[Allington St], *Stage Door*: Raised seating area nr windows opp Victoria Palace stage door; Courage-related and other real ales, lots of bottled beers, reasonably priced tasty food inc fairly big home-made pies with lots of veg, pleasant service, good cup of tea; tables on pavement under pretty window-boxes *(John Wooll)*

☆ [Victoria Stn], *Wetherspoons*: Warm, comfortable and individual, with cheap real ale, reasonably priced food all day, good furnishings, staff and housekeeping *(Comus Elliott, Neil Barker, Sue Demont, Tim Barrow)*

[Horseferry Rd, corner Monck St], *White Horse & Bower*: Recently well refurbished in ancient style, food at lunchtime (busy then), Fullers London Pride, Worthington BB, darts, TV, some seats outside *(Dr J R G Beavon)*

SW3

☆ [87 Flood St], *Coopers Arms*: Relaxed atmosphere, interesting style with country furnishings and lots of stuffed creatures, food (not Sat/Sun evenings) inc some inventive hot dishes and attractive show of cheeses and cold pies on chunky deal table; well kept Youngs Bitter and Special, good choice of wines by the glass; under same management as Alma and Ship in South London (see main entries) *(George Atkinson, LYM)*

[43 Beauchamp Pl], *Grove:* Something of an oasis, with reasonably priced bar food inc good value big brown baps and baked potatoes, decent house wines *(Jan and Colin Roe, Dave Braisted)*

☆ [50 Cheyne Walk], *Kings Head & Eight Bells*: Attractive location by gardens across (busy) road from Thames, some tables outside; particularly welcoming local feel, clean and comfortable, with decent food at reasonable prices in bar and restaurant, three well kept ales inc Brakspears; well behaved dogs allowed *(Mark Walker, David Dimock, George Atkinson, Robert E Jankowski, Gordon, Paul Bowden, BB)*

[392 Kings Road], *Man in the Moon*: Inexpensive pub theatre with well done low-budget productions; attractive frieze above bar *(Larry Miller, BB)*

W1

☆ [54 Old Compton St], *Admiral Duncan*: Friendly drinking pub, a bit bright nowadays, with well kept Theakstons Best and Old Peculier, quick service, bare bricks and boards, good busy atmosphere, piped music, fruit machine *(Mark Walker)*

☆ [41 Mount St], *Audley*: Roomy and solid, with fine woodwork and panelling, clock hanging from ornate ceiling in lovely carved wood bracket, well kept Courage Best and

Theakstons, good service; upstairs dining room *(Gordon, LYM)*

☆ [Shepherd Mkt], *Bunch of Grapes*: Old-fashioned traditional pub, softly lit friendly bar, good range of well kept ales, simple bar food, roaring fire; often packed with smartly dressed people evenings, surrounded by the bustle of this lively enclave; open all day, children welcome *(Ian Phillips, Gordon, LYM)*

[Poland St], *Coach & Horses*: Small *Private Eye* local, with friendly staff, good choice of real ales such as Greene King Abbot, Marstons Pedigree, Morlands Old Speckled Hen and three or four others, good coffee and house wines *(G Atkinson, Walter Reid, Nigel Woolliscroft)*

[27 Great Portland St], *Cock*: Large Sam Smiths local with Victorian tiled floor, lots of wood inc good carving, some cut and etched glass, ornate plasterwork, velvet curtains, coal-effect gas fire; lunchtime food such as breaded haddock upstairs *(Walter Reid, Ian Phillips)*

[17 Denman St], *Devonshire Arms*: Small wood-and-sawdust bar downstairs, small lounge up, food all day, welcoming friendly staff, Courage Best and Directors *(Mark Walker)*

[43 Weymouth Mews], *Dover Castle*: Well kept ales such as Adnams, Boddingtons and Wadworths 6X, relaxing and friendly, some panelling and old prints, cosy back area *(Gordon, Sue Demont, Tim Barrow)*

[94a Crawford St], *Duke of Wellington*: Friendly little pub with lots of pictures, jugs and Wellington memorabilia, warm and comfortable; salt beef speciality, well kept beers inc guest; tables out on pavement *(Gordon, Peter and Jenny Quine)*

[47 Rathbone St], *Duke of York*: Small and cosy, lots of caricatures from *The Statesman* and other Victorian prints, Greene King ales, odd advertisements eg 'Noggin of Bragget ¼d', tables outside with hanging baskets; shame about the piped music *(Gordon)*

☆ [30 Bruton Pl], *Guinea*: Well kept Young beers, amazing meal-price sandwiches such as steak and anchovy or chargrilled chicken with bacon, olives and mascarpone, both in ciabata bread; summer overflow into mews off Berkeley Sq *(Adrian Zambardino, Debbie Chaplin, LYM)*

[118 Marylebone High St], *Prince Alfred*: Smallish old-fashioned bar, comfortable and friendly, in typical Victorian pub with well worn cushioned seats, polished wood floor, dark green walls; Theakstons ale, jazz nights *(Gordon)*

[41 Farm St], *Punch Bowl*: Quiet tucked-away Mayfair local with bar and dining room off panelled corridor, reliable lunchtime food changing daily inc a vegetarian dish, well kept real ale, decent wine *(Mark Johnson)*

☆ [Kingly St], *Red Lion*: Friendly, solidly modernised without being spoilt, with well kept Sam Smiths OB and Museum at sensible prices, reasonably priced good food upstairs; video juke box (may be loud evening) *(Mark Walker, Susan and Nigel Wilson)*

[1 Portman Mews S], *Three Tuns*: Several busy interconnecting rooms, decent food, bare boards, beams with foreign banknotes and coins; handy for Oxford St *(Gordon, Jim Merrett)*

W2

[Bathurst St; opp Royal Lancaster Hotel], *Archery*: Well kept Badger and other ales and good helpings of decent food in homely early Georgian three-room pub with pots and hanging baskets of dried flowers and herbs in pleasant front rooms, darts etc in back room, horses stabled in the yard behind; tables outside *(Gordon, Stephen and Jean Curtis)*

☆ [66 Bayswater Rd], *Swan*: Pleasant tree-shaded courtyard looking across busy road to Kensington Gardens, old London prints, well kept Courage-related ales, busy food bar, quiet upper room at back *(Frank W Gadbois, LYM)*

[10a Strathearn Pl], *Victoria*: Unusual corner pub, lots of Victorian royal and other memorabilia, interesting little military paintings, two cast-iron fireplaces, mahogany panelling, Bass and Charrington IPA, picnic tables on pavement; upstairs (not always open) replica of Gaiety Theatre bar, all gilt and red plush *(Gordon, LYM)*

WC1

☆ [1 Pakenham St], *Pakenham Arms*: Informal unspoilt split-level bar, largely local customers and generally quiet at lunchtime; well kept ales such as Adnams, Brakspears and unusual guest beers, big helpings of good value food *(Sue Demont, Tim Barrow)*

WC2

[91 Strand], *Coal Hole*: Pleasant and comfortable, esp downstairs bar with carefully revamped high ceiling; good range of beers, good well priced sandwiches, baked potatoes etc; handy for theatre *(Mr and Mrs Fyall, BB)*

☆ [31 Endell St], *Cross Keys*: Lovely little pub festooned with hanging baskets and window-boxes, friendly and cosy, with lots of photographs, posters, brasses and bric-a-brac, good comfortable feel; basic lunchtime food, fruit machine, small upstairs bar, tables outside *(Gordon, Dr and Mrs A K Clarke, Ian Phillips)*

[22 Neal St], *Crown & Anchor*: Welcoming, furnishings old but spotless, service with finesse by barman and long-serving landlord; morning papers, pies etc *(Janet Lee)*

[Betterton St/Drury Lane], *Hogshead*: Good range of well kept Whitbreads-related and other ales, very basic cheap food, pleasant bustling atmosphere *(Sue Demont, Tim Barrow, Alastair Campbell)*

☆ [39 Bow St], *Marquis of Anglesea*: Well kept Youngs, reasonable choice of food inc vegetarian upstairs where bar-style seating looks over window-boxes to street below; good service even when busy – they try to

serve quickly if you're going to the theatre (opp Royal Opera House); no loud music *(Gill Earle, Andrew Burton, Mark Walker)*
[Chandos Pl], *Marquis of Granby:* Small and cosy, with small parlour-like areas each end through arched wood-and-glass partitions *(Gordon)*
[Bedford St/King St], *Roundhouse*: Interesting changing ales inc guests such as Clarks Burglar Bill, serviceable basic food, few tables *(Thomas Nott, BB)*
☆ [90 St Martins Lane], *Salisbury*: Sumptuous Victorian pub with sweeps of red velvet, huge sparkling mirrors and cut glass, glossy brass and mahogany; decent food (confined to right-hand side evening; even doing Sun lunches over Christmas/New Year), well kept Tetleys-related ales, decent house wines, no-smoking back room, acceptable piped music, friendly service *(Wayne Brindle, Martin Hickes, BB)*
[Strand], *Savoy*: The American Bar has stood out for decades as a beautifully designed setting for a perfectly prepared cocktail – though such surroundings come at a price; bedrooms *(Walter Reid, BB)*
[10 Northumberland St/Craven Pl], *Sherlock Holmes*: Well appointed pub decorated with Sherlock Holmes memorabilia, inc complete model of Mr Holmes' den; real ales, comfortable plush booths, upstairs restaurant; busy lunchtime *(Rob Swain, BB)*
☆ [66 Long Acre], *Sun*: Well kept Courage-related ales, several dozen malt whiskies and a good many blends, chatty landlady, decent food inc Sun lunches, good old photographs of Covent Gdn market, first-floor wine bar; not as smart as many pubs round here, but less touristy and more enjoyable *(Andy Thwaites, David Wright, BB)*

NORTH LONDON
N1
☆ [10 Thornhill Rd], *Albion*: Rather countrified and unspoilt (despite the Front Bench faces), horse brasses and tack recalling the long-distance coach which was named after it; low ceilings, various snug nooks and crannies inc room behind bar furnished like someone's drawing room, cosy back hideaway on the right, some old photographs of the pub, open fires, some gas lighting, real ales, food, very friendly landlord; big back terrace with vine canopy, interesting Victorian gents' *(Adam Nell, Gordon, BB)*
[116 Cloudesley St], *Crown*: Genuinely friendly old-fashioned local with welcoming tenants, well kept Fullers ales, limited but expanding choice of truly freshly prepared food inc good Sun lunch in eating area with fresh flowers, superb barbecues on small forecourt *(Edward Simmons)*
☆ [87 Noel Rd], *Island Queen*: Good freshly made and often unusual food in amiable character pub with eccentric life-size caricature fancy-dress figures floating from ceiling, well kept Bass and Worthington BB, upstairs restaurant; lively youngish welcoming atmosphere, good juke box; handy for Camden Passage antiques area; children welcome *(Sue Demont, Tim Barrow, LYM)*

N4
☆ [Stroud Green Rd], *White Lion of Mortimer*: One of the first Wetherspoons pubs, and still the same good value for all-day food and drink, with good choice of both inc well kept real ales, country wines and farm cider, pleasantly solid frnishings, restful back conservatory; part no smoking *(Russell and Margaret Bathie, LYM)*

N5
[26 Highbury Pk], *Highbury Barn*: Recently refurbished, with well kept beer, good value food; very popular with Arsenal supporters on match nights *(Nigel Woolliscroft)*

N6
☆ [77 Highgate West Hill], *Flask*: Villagey Georgian pub, largely modernised but still has intriguing up-and-down layout, sash-windowed bar hatch, panelling and high-backed carved settle tucked away in snug lower area; usual food inc salad bar, Tetleys-related and Youngs ales, well behaved children allowed, tables out in attractive front courtyard *(Dave Braisted, Gordon, LYM)*
[1 North Hill], *Gate House*: Reliable Wetherspoons pub with good staff, good value beer, no-smoking area, tables in back yard *(Neil Barker, Don Kellaway, Angie Coles)*

N14
[Arnos Grove], *Bankers Draft*: What a tourist pictures an English pub to be: good lunches, friendly management, well kept beers *(Edward Hoban, Comus Elliott)*

N16
[Allan Rd], *Shakespeare*: Pleasant friendly local with theatrical element – classical figures dancing on walls, central Victorian bar with Flowers, Ind Coope Burton and wide choice of bottled beers; good juke box, lots of young people *(Jan Pancheri)*

N17
[Ferry Lane], *Ferry Boat*: Popular fishermen's local, small friendly public bar, log fire in lounge, good food inc interesting sandwiches; Bass and Fullers London Pride, long-serving local staff; well behaved children allowed, climbing frame in lovely garden by river Lea with swans, geese and ducks *(Thomas Weber)*

N20
[Totteridge Village], *Orange Tree*: Nice sitting out by the duckpond; spacious and plush inside, with restaurant *(GB, BB)*

NW1
[65 Gloucester Ave], *Engineer*: Relaxed pub signed from Regents Canal nr Camden Lock,

transformed by recent redecoration with lots of light wood; American chef doing notable modernist food, real ales such as Adnams and Fullers, tables outside *(Walter Reid)*

NW3

☆ [14 Flask Walk], *Flask*: Well kept Youngs, decent coffee, friendly staff, good value food inc baked potatoes and several hot dishes more interesting than usual, in bustling and relatively unspoiled Hampstead local with carved wooden archway and stained glass panels dividing the two front bars, interesting back part, partly arched and vaulted stone; popular with actors and artists as it has been for 300 years; friendly helpful service *(Ian Phillips, Wayne Brindle, Gordon, LYM)*

☆ [32 Downshire Hill], *Freemasons Arms*: Big pub with spacious but busy garden right by Hampstead Heath, good arrangements for serving food and drink outside; several comfortable rooms inside, well spaced variously sized tables, leather chesterfield in front of log fire; usual bar food inc Sun roast beef (no-smoking eating area, at lunchtime), Bass and Charrington IPA; children allowed in dining room, dogs in bar, open all day summer *(Ben Grose, Don Kellaway, Angie Coles, Wayne Brindle, LYM)*

☆ [North End Way], *Old Bull & Bush*: Family-oriented pub attractively refurbished in Victorian style, comfortable sofa and easy chairs, nooks and crannies, side library bar with lots of bookshelves and pictures and mementoes of Florrie Ford who made the song about the pub famous; friendly landlord, efficient staff, good food bar inc good Sun specials, decent wines and mulled wine *(Gordon, Nigel Gursu)*

[97 Haverstock Hill], *Sir Richard Steele*: Relaxed local feel, well kept beers, laid-back staff, characterful snug rooms, good music (esp Sun) *(Julian Woodward, BB)*

[30 Well Walk], *Wells Tavern*: Cosy and villagey Hampstead local handy for the Heath, great atmosphere with roaring fires; can sometimes be a bit smoky; tables outside great for watching people make a mess of parking *(Don Kellaway, Angie Coles, BB)*

NW4

[56 The Burroughs (A504)], *White Bear*: Useful for baguettes, filled baked potatoes and half a dozen generous changing reasonably priced main dishes, willing service *(A C Morrison, Keith Hollingworth)*

NW8

☆ [24 Aberdeen Pl], *Crockers*: Ostentatious marble, decorated plaster and opulent woodwork in showy Victorian pub, relaxing and comfortable, with Vaux, Wards and a wide range of other ales, friendly service, decent food inc vegetarian *(Gordon, Dr and Mrs A K Clarke, LYM)*

Barnet

[St Albans Rd (A1081); nr M25], *Green Dragon*: Fairly limited but good reasonably priced choice of food, good choice of well kept ales inc Flowers and changing guests, pleasant back conservatory overlooking fields, never seems overcrowded *(A C Morrison, Gareth Edwards)*

☆ [18 Hadley Highstone, towards Potters Bar], *King William IV*: Cosy and well tended old local with real fires, nooks and corners, some antique Wedgwood plates over fireplaces, home-cooked food inc good fresh fish Fri, friendly staff, flower-framed front terrace *(Prof John White, Patricia White, GB, CH)*

☆ [58 High St], *Olde Mitre*: Small early 17th-c local, bay windows in low-ceilinged panelled front bar with fruit machines, three-quarter panelled back area on two slightly different levels, lots of dark wood, dark floral wallpaper, pleasant atmosphere, friendly service, well kept Wadworths 6X and Tetleys-related ales *(Brian Jones, BB)*

Edgware

[122 High St], *Blacking Bottle*: Attractively converted Wetherspoons pub with good food, sensible prices, bargain beer, good staff, no-smoking area *(Neil Barker, Russell and Margaret Bathie)*

Harrow

[19 The Broadwalk; Pinner Rd, N Harrow], *J J Moons*: Good Wetherspoons pub, well kept sensibly priced beer, among the best of the chain for food; no-smoking area, occasional beer festivals *(Neil Barker, Barbara Hatfield)*

Hatch End

☆ [250 Uxbridge Rd], *Moon & Sixpence*: Converted from a bank to comfortable Wetherspoons pub, good service, well kept beers, good value food, sensible prices *(Russell and Margaret Bathie, Neil Barker)*

Pinner

[Waxwell Lane], *Oddfellows Arms*: Friendly management, relaxed atmosphere, well prepared appetising food; lovely garden *(Angela Wood)*

Southgate

☆ [115 Chase Side], *Moon Under Water*: Wetherspoons pub in lovely old converted chapel, with sensible prices, good food, service and beer; big barn of a place with some slightly surreal decor inc a landau in the lounge and unreachable library; separate smoking and no-smoking areas *(Neil Barker, Philip O'Loughlin)*

SOUTH LONDON

SE1

[Waterloo Stn], *Coopers*: Grand staircase to below the main station concourse, Victorian-style decor with cast iron, polished wood, ferns and mirrors; inside lots of sepia paint on walls and ceilings, pastel carpet, prints, brass and light washed wood; one big spacious room, lively and noisy, nine wines by the glass *(Christopher Gallop)*

[Upper Ground, by Blackfriars Bridge],

Doggetts Coat & Badge: Well run modern pub on several floors, good Thames views, pleasant outside drinking area, well kept range of real ales *(Dr and Mrs A K Clarke, BB)*
[27 Clenham St], *Lord Clyde:* Good lunchtime food, well kept real ales, good local atmosphere *(Dr and Mrs A K Clarke)*
☆ [St Mary Overy Wharf; off Clink St], *Old Thameside*: Good pastiche of ancient tavern, two floors – hefty beams and timbers, pews, flagstones, candles; splendid river view upstairs and from charming waterside terrace by schooner docked in landlocked inlet; well kept Tetleys, Wadworths 6X and Nicholsons Best, all-day salad bar, lunchtime hot buffet *(Dr and Mrs A K Clarke, LYM)*
[81 Waterloo Rd], *Wellington*: Good Irish pub with good facilities, deaf people's night every other Fri, very friendly atmosphere, great service, good food *(Christof Niklaus)*
[6 Stoney St], *Wheatsheaf*: Early Victorian house close to market; interesting prints and glass *(Dr and Mrs A K Clarke)*

SE3
☆ [1a Eliot Cottages], *Hare & Billet*: Nicely matured Victorian refurbishment, good solid furniture and open fire, view over Blackheath, popular food, well kept Whitbreads-related and other ales inc Fullers, good atmosphere esp weekends *(Andy Thwaites, Richard Stokes, BB)*
☆ [1 Montpellier Row], *Princess of Wales*: Roomy pub with pleasant front prospect of Blackheath, well kept Bass, Fullers London Pride, Harveys, Wadworths 6X and Worthingtons, occasional beer festivals, good basic snacks and hot meals, brisk service, back conservatory and sheltered garden *(Tony Gayfer)*

SE5
[149 Denmark Hill], *Fox on the Hill*: Wetherspoons pub with tables in extensive grounds; usual high standards, food always available, low prices, good staff *(Neil Barker, Dr and Mrs A K Clarke)*

SE6
☆ [Bromley Rd/Southend Ln], *Tigers Head*: Pleasant Wetherspoons pub festooned with hanging baskets in summer, good inexpensive bar meals, impressive choice of ales (one very cheap), roomy inside with good layout and no music or machines, picnic tables on forecourt; can get loud at weekends, but pleasant staff stay well in control *(AT, E G Parish, A M Pring)*

SE10
[opp Cutty Sark], *Gypsy Moth*: Comfortable split-level dining lounge, simple bar menu, well kept Adnams and Tetleys-related ales, polite efficient staff; not too crowded, picnic tables in good garden *(S R Howe, Mark Walker)*
[Park Row], *Trafalgar*: Splendid river view, fine panelled rooms – some 200 years old; friendly staff *(Dave Braisted)*

SE16
☆ [117 Rotherhithe St], *Mayflower*: Friendly and cosy riverside local with black beams, high-backed settles and open fire, good views from upstairs and atmospheric wooden jetty, well kept Bass and Greene King IPA, Abbot and Rayments, decent bar food (not Sun night), friendly staff; children welcome, open all day; in unusual street with beautiful church *(Jon Lyons, Nigel and Sue Foster, Joanna Whitehouse, LYM)*

SE21
[Park Hall Rd], *Alleyns Head*: Comfortable well spaced seating, book-lined walls giving the saloon a collegey touch, bargain two and three-course meals, accommodating service *(E G Parish)*

SE22
☆ [Dartmouth Rd, Forest Hl], *Bird in Hand*: Civilised Wetherspoons pub, attractive glass-topped panelled recesses, marble-topped tables in no-smoking food area, spotless throughout; very pleasant staff, good moderately priced food all day, four real ales *(E G Parish)*
[Crystal Palace Rd], *Crystal Palace Tavern*: Good cheerful mix (children welcome too), well kept beer, quiz nights *(James Ball)*

SE23
[35 Dartmouth Rd], *Bird in Hand*: Nice clean Wetherspoons pub with food all day, real ales, friendly service; quite a few OAP regulars *(Neil Barker, AMP)*

SE26
☆ [39 Sydenham Hill], *Dulwich Wood House*: Consistently welcoming Youngs pub in Victorian lodge gatehouse complete with turret, well kept ales, food popular at lunchtime with local retired people, lots of tables in big pleasant back garden with barbecues *(E G Parish, Andy Thwaites)*
[Sydenham Rd (A212)], *Golden Lion:* Very decorative, with flower tubs, white latticed seats on terrace; good food pleasantly served in roomy and well carpeted lounge and bars (Anon)

SW2
☆ [2 Streatham Hill, on South Circular], *Crown & Sceptre*: Ornate and substantial Wetherspoons pub, good traditional decor, sensible-sized areas inc no smoking, well kept reasonably priced ales inc some unusual ones, good value well organised food, good service *(Sue Demont, Tim Barrow, E G Parish, Neil Barker)*
[Acre Lane], *Hope & Anchor*: Large Youngs pub with big colourful garden, good food inc well priced daily pie and salads, friendly landlord, games machines; often live busking-style music *(Charles Davey, Sue Demont, Tim Barrow)*

SW8
[43 St Stephens Terr, off S Lambeth Rd],

Royal Albert: In handsome Regency square in unpropitious area, well kept beer, good friendly staff, friendly and relaxed old-fashioned atmosphere, lunchtime bar food, pool room; garden *(Dave Urwin, Sue Demont, Tim Barrow, BB)*

☆ [16 Southville], *Surprise*: Quintessential small London local, friendly to all; big collection of framed caricatures, well kept Youngs and cheap wholesome food in two cosy rooms decorated in colourful Liberty prints; dried flowers, real fire, friendly dog and cat, pin table, tables out under leafy arbour overlooking small park *(Christopher Gallop, John Douglas, BB)*

SW11

[St Johns Hill], *Falcon*: Comfortable lounge, more spartan public area with different customers, welcoming staff, honest basic lunchtime food till 3, good range of real ales such as Bass, Fullers London Pride, Morlands Old Speckled Hen, Worthington BB and Youngs Special; cheap tea or coffee *(CN, Graham Reeve)*

[339 Battersea Pk Rd], *Legless Ladder*: Friendly well run local with decent food inc popular Sun lunch, big-screen TVs for sports events, well kept real ales, splendid array of optics *(Michael Synnott)*

☆ [60 Battersea High St], *Woodman*: Busy, friendly and individual young people's local, with little panelled front bar, long main room, log-effect gas fires, lots of enamel advertising signs; tied to Badger, with their beers and those from their own-brew pub at Oving in Sussex, also several guests such as Wadworths 6X, at fair prices, cappuccino coffee; food inc Sun breakfast from 9.30, bar billiards, darts and games machines at one end, picnic tables on partly covered back terrace with barbecue; they're good with children *(James Macrae, Sue Demont, Tim Barrow, Ted Burden, BB)*

SW12

[194 Balham High Rd], *Moon Under Water*: Wetherspoons pub with food always available, low prices, good staff *(Neil Barker, Sue Demont, Tim Barrow)*

☆ [97 Nightingale Lane], *Nightingale*: Welcoming, comfortable and civilised local, good bar food, well kept Youngs, sensible prices, very friendly staff, timeless cream and brown decor with gallery of sponsored guide-dog pictures on one wall, attractive back family conservatory; children in useful small family area *(L G Milligan, BB)*

SW13

☆ [2 Castelnau], *Red Lion*: Big smartly restored Fullers pub with impressive Victorian woodwork, three separate areas, good service, well kept Fullers Chiswick, London Pride and ESB, nice atmosphere, good choice of lunchtime food inc children's helpings; big garden with good play area, barbecue and pets' corner *(Martin Kay, Andrea Fowler, BB)*

☆ [7 Church Rd], *Sun*: Several spacious solidly renovated areas around central servery, pleasant atmosphere, Tetleys-related and a guest ale, usual food, benches and tables over road overlooking duckpond; very popular in summer *(Susan and John Douglas, Ian Phillips)*

SW14

☆ [10 West Temple Sheen], *Victoria*: Large friendly pub, often crowded, with generous reasonably priced food, all home-made, well kept Courage-related beers, helpful staff, good conservatory and garden *(P Gillbe)*

SW15

☆ [8 Lower Richmond Rd], *Dukes Head*: Classic Youngs pub, spacious and grand yet friendly, in great spot by Thames, well kept ales, 20 wines by the glass; main bar light and airy with big ceiling fans, very civilised feel, tables by window with great Thames view, smaller more basic locals' bar, good fresh lunchtime food; plastic glasses for outside, service can slow right down on sunny days *(BB)*

☆ [Wildcroft Rd], *Green Man*: Friendly old local on the edge of Putney Heath, with cosy main bar, quiet sitting room, attractive garden with barbecues most days, straightforward food (not winter evenings), well kept Youngs; open all day; has lost its main-entry place this year only through lack of reports *(LYM)*

[61 Lacy Rd], *Jolly Gardeners*: Small warmly furnished Fullers pub with basic bar food, fair prices, interesting prints and decorative objects on the walls *(Brad and Joni Nelson, Martin Kay, Andrea Fowler)*

☆ [14 Putney High St], *Slug & Lettuce*: Bright, spacious, smart and tasteful, delicious food esp rissottos, home-baked bread, chatty staff, piped classical music lunchtime, quiet pop evenings; others recommended in this useful chain in Warwick Way (SW1), Islington Green (N1), Alma Lane (SW18), Water Lane (Richmond) and Fulham Rd (SW6) *(BB)*

SW16

☆ [151 Greyhound Lane], *Greyhound*: Fine three-bar Victorian local with several beers brewed on the premises, food all day, efficient staff, well equipped games bar, spacious and attractive family conservatory, sizeable garden *(L G Milligan, Richard Houghton, LYM)*

SW18

[345 Trinity Rd], *County Arms*: Character three-room Youngs local, younger in front, wider mix in back, from grannies with dogs to families; back grand piano for customers – Scott Joplin to Mozart; decor doesn't jump out at visitors but has gently relaxed aura, with original fittings; summer spills out on to nearby grass *(Dana Tatlock, BB)*

[35 Putney Bridge Rd], *Queen Adelaide*: Friendly atmosphere, helpful staff, roomy garden with great summer barbecues *(Matthew Gordon)*

SW19

☆ [6 Crooked Billet], *Hand in Hand*: Very well kept Youngs inc seasonal Winter Warmer, good straightforward food inc home-made pizzas and burgers, relaxed and cheerful U-shaped bar serving several small areas, some tiled, others carpeted, log fire, simple no-smoking family room with bar billiards, darts etc; tables out in courtyard with vine and hanging baskets, benches out by common; can get very crowded with young people esp summer evenings *(Christopher Gallop, David Peakall, Ted Burden, BB)*

[The Broadway], *Prince of Wales*: Large handsomely furnished pub with good reasonably priced food inc buffet, Theakstons and other real ales, German beer on draught, wide range of bottled beers *(Per Ness)*

☆ [55 Wimbledon High St], *Rose & Crown*: Comfortably modernised old local, can get very busy, with well kept Youngs, friendly service, decent generous food from back servery at sensible prices, open fires, set of Hogarth's proverb engravings, green plush seats in alcoves; tables in former coachyard *(IP, LYM)*

Beckenham

[Chancery Lane], *Jolly Woodman*: Cosy little local, very friendly, cheap beer; seats out in cosy garden and tiny street *(Alan Skull)*

Bexley

[North Cray Rd], *White Cross*: Friendly welcome, good choice of bar food *(David Webb)*

Coulsdon

[Old Coulsdon; Coulsdon Rd (B2030) on the edge of the Common], *Fox*: Attractive pub in unusual setting, well kept real ale, good ploughman's inc ham and turkey, interesting displays, nice garden, engagingly wild bunch of antipodean barmen; popular with ramblers and footballers weekends *(Brian and Jenny Seller)*

Cudham

☆ [Cudham Lane], *Blacksmiths Arms*: Decent reasonably priced food inc interesting soups, huge helpings, well kept ales such as Courage, King & Barnes and Morlands Old Speckled Hen, good coffee, friendly service; nearly always busy yet plenty of tables, with cheerful cottagey atmosphere, soft lighting, blazing log fires, low ceiling; big garden, pretty window-boxes, handy for good walks *(Jenny and Brian Seller, John and Elspeth Howell, Mrs R D Knight)*

Kingston

☆ [Canbury Gdns; park in Lower Ham Rd if you can], *Boaters*: Good Thames views, very wide choice of generous good value food inc Sun lunch, comfortable banquettes in quiet charming bar, floodlit tables in garden, Courage-related and guest ales, friendly welcoming service, unobtrusive piped jazz (live Sun evening); in small park, ideal for children in summer *(Martin Jones)*

[88 London Rd, corner Albert Rd], *Flamingo Brewery*: Large Edwardian pub, bare boards, back room dominated by enormous brass chandelier, snugs and corners but lots of standing room too; three good real ales brewed here, good value bar food, family room with adventure playground and view into brewery *(Marc Bradfield)*

[13 Bloomfield Rd, just S of Polytechnic, E of B3363], *Spring Grove*: Friendly local redecorated in casual style, decent food, well kept beer, darts and golf teams *(Leo)*

New Malden

[Coombe Rd], *Royal Oak*: Large pub popular lunchtime for wide range of reliably good home-made food inc big helpings of fresh veg; good choice of well kept Tetleys-related ales, big garden *(G W and I L Edwards, P Gillbe)*

Richmond

[345 Petersham Rd, Ham Common], *New Inn*: Bright and clean, welcoming even to young women on their own, with good choice of good hot and cold lunchtime bar food, friendly atmosphere, pleasant evening dining area; attractive spot *(Jill Bickerton, Brig T I G Gray)*

☆ [45 Kew Rd], *Orange Tree*: Interesting main bar with fine plasterwork, big coaching and Dickens prints, fine set of 1920s paintings; open all day, with theatre club upstairs, well kept Youngs, friendly service, decent food all day (not Sun evening) in civilised and spacious cellar bar; pleasant tables outside *(Liz and Benton Jennings, BKA, LYM)*

☆ [Petersham Rd], *Rose of York*: Comfortable seats inc leather chesterfields, Turner prints on stripped pine panelling, old photographs, attractive layout inc no-smoking area; good choice of reasonably priced Sam Smiths ales, pleasant helpful service; high chairs, bar billiards, fruit machines, TV, piped pop music; lighting perhaps a bit bright; bedrooms *(G W Stevenson, Susan and John Douglas)*

[17 Parkshot], *Sun*: Rows of cased rugby shirts around walls just below ceilings, also rugby posters, cartoons and photographs – even the day's rugby reports from *The Telegraph* as well as the front page in the gents'; pleasant atmosphere, Fullers Chiswick, London Pride and ESB, reasonably priced food *(Ian Phillips)*

☆ [25 Old Palace Lane], *White Swan*: Pleasant setting for little rose-covered cottage with pretty paved garden, barbecues, easy welcoming feel in dark-beamed open-plan bar, well kept Courage beers, good coal fires, usual bar food; children allowed in conservatory *(Susan and John Douglas, Ian Phillips, LYM)*

South Norwood

☆ *Goat House*: Wonderful art deco pub, not too noisy, with full range of Fullers ales kept well, snugs, real fires, public bar with public-bar prices, pair of goats out behind *(Andy Barber, Martin Kay, Andrea Fowler)*

Sutton
[5 Hill Rd], *Moon on the Hill*: Huge Wetherspoons pub with superb choice of beer, reasonably priced food; absolutely packed some nights eg Fri *(Neil Barker, JS, BS)*

Wallington
☆ [25 Ross Parade, Woodmancote Rd], *Whispering Moon*: Civilised Wetherspoons pub with lots of well spaced tables in cosily divided area, good solid furnishings and pleasant decor, no music or machines, well kept ales such as Courage Directors, Greene King, Wadworths 6X and Youngers Scotch, decent generous wines, good staff, good value unpretentious food all day served quickly; no-smoking area *(Neil Barker, BB)*

West Wickham
☆ [Pickhurst Lane], *Pickhurst*: Big dining pub with good value Sun lunches (two sittings), double-sitting evening meals too, worth booking Apr-Oct; food and service good *(E G Parish)*

WEST LONDON
SW7
[2 Ennismore Mews], *Ennismore Arms*: Pleasant cosy one-bar pub with big open fire, simple furniture (mainly wooden tables and chairs), well kept Courage and Theakstons, friendly service, interesting bar food inc Sun lunches *(Paul Randall)*
[Gloucester Rd], *Harrington*: Renovated Chef & Brewer pub, high ceiling, mezzanine hayloft with extra seats, lots of wood and posters; food all day, Courage-related beers; fruit machines *(Sean Morrissey)*

SW10
[1 Billing Rd], *Fox & Pheasant*: Cosy charmingly old-fashioned back-street local, feels like a country pub in middle of town; particularly well kept beer at sensible prices, decent food *(Mark Whelan, BB)*
[Burnaby St], *Ram*: Youngs pub spruced up under new tenants, quiet back part, decent lunches *(Lizzie Broadbent, BB)*
☆ [6 Camera Pl], *Sporting Page*: Unusual civilised and upmarket pub off Kings Rd, one of the few in London to have genuinely good interesting food; well kept Courage-related and a guest ale, decent house wines, one or two seats outside *(LYM)*
[Kings Rd], *Worlds End*: Remarkable architecture, a sharp contrast to the Worlds End housing estate behind it; good range of well kept Courage-related and other ales, plush seats, bar food *(Dr and Mrs A K Clarke, BB)*

W4
☆ [72 Strand on the Green], *Bell & Crown*: Big busy pub with lovely river-view terrace, very friendly feel, local paintings and photographs, simple good value food inc sandwiches and lunchtime hot dishes, well kept Fullers, log fire, no piped music or machines; good towpath walks *(Steven Tait, Susie Lonie, P A Chodzko-Zajko)*
☆ [15 Strand on the Green], *Bulls Head*: Lovely Thames-side spot for this unpretentious well worn-in old pub with little rambling rooms, black-panelled alcoves, simple traditional furnishings, Courage-related ales, no-smoking eating area (not Sun or Mon evenings), no piped music, back games bar; picnic tables by river, children allowed in back conservatory *(Gordon, LYM)*
☆ [185 Chiswick High St], *George IV*: Pleasant staff, good food esp well filled pies, well kept Fullers ales inc Chiswick, good friendly atmosphere; clean and comfortable *(Mrs S Jones, Martin Kay, Andrea Fowler)*

W5
☆ [124 Pitshanger Lane], *Duffys*: Attractive and civilised, soft lighting, stripped floor, chessboard tables, well kept Brakspears, Fullers London Pride and Wadworths 6X, reasonably priced bar food, friendly staff, slightly separate small restaurant – appetising aromas *(Andrew Stephenson, Mark Percy)*
☆ [Church Gdns; off St Marys Rd], *Rose & Crown*: Good food and atmosphere in 1920s/30s pub with small public bar, fairly big lounge and conservatory, well kept Fullers ales, smart efficient staff; games machines, unobtrusive piped country music; tables in back garden *(P A Chodzko-Zajko)*

W6
☆ [2 South Black Lion Lane], *Black Lion*: Chef & Brewer with cosy and welcoming local atmosphere, helpful staff, food reasonably priced and quite imaginative, served evenings too; big log-effect gas fire separating off area with pool tables, machines etc *(Ian Phillips, Helen Pickering, James Owen, BB)*

W8
☆ [40 Holland St], *Elephant & Castle*: Basic two-bar open-plan pub, bigger than it looks, with friendly staff, well kept Bass and Worthington BB, good food inc pizzas (busy at lunchtime); good seats on small suntrap terrace with very pretty hanging baskets *(George Schaff)*
☆ [23a Edwardes Sq], *Scarsdale Arms*: Busy Chef & Brewer (not the local it used to be) in lovely leafy square, stripped wooden floors, two or three fireplaces with good coal-effect gas fires, lots of nick-nacks, ornate bar counter; Courage-related ales, decent wines, back food servery with reasonably priced food; tree-shaded front courtyard with impressive show of flower tubs and baskets *(Susan and John Douglas, Gordon, LYM)*

W9
☆ [93 Warrington Cres], *Warrington*: Ornate superbly decorated Victorian pub, well kept real ale, good pub food *(Dr and Mrs A K Clarke)*

☆ [6 Warwick Pl], *Warwick Castle*: Busy high-ceilinged Victorian local, good unspoilt atmosphere (dogs allowed), decent bar snacks, well kept real ales, saucy murals, good value Thai food upstairs; benches out by quiet lane nr Little Venice *(Gary Gibbon, Sue Demont, Tim Barrow, S J Elliott, BB)*

W12

[80 Chiswick High Rd], *J J Moons*: Good well run Wetherspoons pub, usual virtues, also interesting local history *(Helen Pickering, James Owen)*

Hampton

[122 High St], *Dukes Head*: Friendly traditional local doing well under new licensees – he's a former restaurant chef and the food is unusually good *(Trevor Meacham)*

[Station Approach], *Railway Bell*: Small friendly beamed local, good lunchtime food; present landlord is third generation to run this classic pub *(Trevor Meacham)*

☆ [70 High St], *White Hart*: Eight well kept interesting changing ales, good log fire and quiet relaxed atmosphere; subdued lighting, good staff, small front terrace *(Alain and Rose Foote, Debby Hawkins, Mark Johnson)*

Hampton Court

[Hampton Court Rd], *Mitre*: Comfortable riverside bar opp palace and gardens, a bit like a licensed conservatory, with flagstoned terrace (and landing stage), Thames view, traditional dark wood tables and chairs, simple bar food, well kept Courage-related ales; piped music; bedrooms *(E G Parish, PR)*

Harefield

☆ [Shrubs Rd/Harefield Rd; Woodcock Hill, off A404 E of Rickmansworth at Batchworth], *Rose & Crown*: Warm welcoming staff, well kept Tetleys-related and Youngs ales and good choice of efficiently served food in attractively refurbished low-ceilinged country local; beautiful garden *(J S M Sheldon)*

Hillingdon

[Pield Heath Rd], *Prince Albert*: Well run friendly local with good pub food, generous carvery Fri/Sat night, three real ales inc a changing guest beer *(Phil Moore)*

Norwood Green

☆ [Tentelow Lane (A4127)], *Plough*: Attractive old-fashioned low-beamed decor, cheerful villagey feel, well kept Fullers ales inc Chiswick, congenial attentive service, cosy family room, even a bowling green dating to 14th century; decent if limited straightforward lunchtime food, flame-effect gas fire; fairly compact and does get crowded weekends; occasional barbecues in lovely garden with play area, open all day, lavatories for the disabled *(Jenny and Brian Seller, Martin Kay, Andrea Fowler, Annabel and Chris Holmes)*

Osterley

☆ [Windmill Lane; B454, off A4], *Hare & Hounds*: Large comfortable open-plan suburban Fullers pub in nice rural setting opp beautiful Osterley Park, lots of tables under big oriental umbrellas in good mature garden; soft lighting, reasonably priced straightforward bar lunches, prompt friendly service; darts, piped music *(Martin Kay, Andrea Fowler, Ian Phillips)*

Ruislip

☆ [12 Victoria Rd; opp Ruislip Manor tube], *J J Moons*: Big but cosily divided Wetherspoons pub, good traditional style and atmosphere (you'd never guess it was a Woolworths quite recently), good value food all day and beer of consistently high standard yet prices very attractive *(Neil Barker)*

Twickenham

☆ [Riverside], *White Swan*: Relaxed country-style pub tucked away in very quiet spot by the Thames, pleasant balcony overlooking it and tables outside right down to the water's edge; attractive lunchtime buffet with reasonably priced hot food, real ales, big rustic tables, walls packed with Rugby memorabilia (other sports banned on TV), blazing fire; very busy Sun lunchtime and for events such as barbecues, raft races *(Ian Phillips, Sue Demont, Liz and Benton Jennings, LYM)*

Uxbridge

☆ [Villiers St; off Clevedon Rd opp Brunel University], *Load of Hay*: Good value generous food, friendly staff, well kept Courage-related and genuine guest beers, choice of teas inc Earl Grey and Darjeeling, impressive fireplace in no-smoking back lounge-area part used by diners, more public-bar atmosphere nearer serving bar, another separate bar, local paintings, back garden *(R Houghton, John Barker, TBB)*

EAST LONDON

E1

[Wapping High St], *Captain Kidd*: Well done pub on the theme of the pirate Captain Kidd who was hanged nearby *(RL)*

☆ [9 Exmouth St], *Hollands*: Worth penetrating the surrounding estates for this unspoilt Victorian gem, lots of original fittings inc bar snob-screens and fine mirrors, interesting bric-a-brac, Youngs ales, simple bar food, darts; open all day; loses its main entry only through absence of recent reports *(LYM)*

[285 Whitechapel Rd], *Lord Rodneys Head*: Lively East End pub with good beer, regular live music and wide mix of customers; tables out in front *(Mark Wakeling)*

[1 Little Somerset St], *Still & Star*: Friendly little local, interesting mix of horse brasses, jugs, teapots, plates and pictures, homely atmosphere *(Gordon)*

☆ [62 Wapping High St], *Town of Ramsgate*: Interesting old-London Thames-side setting, with restricted but evocative river view from terrace; long narrow bar with squared oak panelling, bric-a-brac, old Limehouse prints, fine etched mirror of Ramsgate harbour, well kept ales inc Fullers London Pride, good choice of usual bar food, friendly service, good sociable mix of customers, open all day *(Dave Kitchenham)*

E8

[Forest Road], *Lady Diana*: Useful find for the area, comfortable and friendly local with good choice of well kept ales, good home-made pizzas, tables out on sheltered back terrace *(NHB)*

E11

☆ [off Whipps Cross Rd], *Alfred Hitchcock*: More atmosphere than usual round here, rather countrified, with well kept ales such as Boddingtons, Courage Best and Directors, Felinfoel Double Dragon, Wadworths 6X; useful Chinese restaurant *(Caroline Shearer)*

☆ [36 High St], *Clutterbucks*: Long narrow bar with lots of panelling and character, friendly service, good range of ales such as Eldridge Pope Thomas Hardy, Tetleys; several board games, lovely old black and white photographs; one of Jack the Ripper's victims said to have been murdered in a next-door yard *(Gordon, Robert Lester)*

[Wanstead High St], *George*: Nice atmosphere in Wetherspoons pub with wide choice of well kept beer, good value food, no-smoking area; popular with older people at lunchtime *(Caroline Wright, Neil Barker)*

E14

☆ [44 Narrow St], *Barley Mow*: Spacious if breezy terrace overlooking Limehouse Basin, mouth of Regents Canal and two Thames reaches; clean and comfortable pump-house conversion, lots of sepia Whitby photographs, food, Tetleys-related ales, conservatory *(Paul Haworth, Andy Thwaites)*

[114 Glengall Gr], *George*: Cheery and pleasant East End pub, good food in bar and restaurant inc good value specials and market-fresh fish, real ales such as Ruddles, conservatory dining room *(Ian Phillips)*

Barking

[61 Station Par], *Barking Dog*: Roomy Wetherspoons pub with booth seating, Theakstons XB, Wadworths 6X and Youngers Scotch on handpump, food all day, good dining area – part no smoking *(Robert Lester, Neil Barker)*

Ilford

[308 Ley St; nr A123], *Bell*: Courage Best and Hunters on handpump, recent smart bright refurbishment not unlike the Wetherspoons style, old local photographs in saloon; occasional live music *(Robert Lester)*

☆ [553 Ilford High Rd; A118], *Cauliflower*: Massive Victorian open-plan pub, good friendly atmosphere, regular live music, Courage-related ales *(Robert Lester)*

Romford

[South St], *Moon & Stars*: Comfortable and roomy Wetherspoons pub with booths down one side, raised end area, usual range of beers with a regular guest, decent food all day *(D Cox, Eddie Edwards)*

Anyone claiming to arrange or prevent inclusion of a pub in the *Guide* is a fraud. Pubs are included only if recommended by genuine readers and if our own anonymous inspection confirms that they are suitable.

Scotland

Several of our main entry inns and hotels up here have cut their bedroom prices this year, and many others have held them steady, making the country increasingly good value for a touring holiday. Places we'd recommend for enjoyable meals out include the Applecross Inn in its wonderful position at Applecross (it gains one of our Food Awards this year), the Riverside Inn in Canonbie, the Creebridge House at Creebridge, the Crinan Hotel at Crinan (our dining recommendation here is for its smart top-floor restaurant, with a terrific sea view), the Kilberry Inn at Kilberry (like the Applecross Inn a tremendous expedition – but well worth while), Burts Hotel in Melrose, the Killiecrankie Hotel just outside Pitlochry, the Crown at Portpatrick (especially on Thursdays when the fishing fleet's brought a new catch in), the Wheatsheaf at Swinton (unusual attention to detail in the cooking here), the simple Tayvallich Inn at Tayvallich (excellent seafood) and the Lion & Unicorn at Thornhill (ringing the changes on the menu much more than most Scottish places). Despite its small size (and relative inaccessibility), our choice as Scottish Dining Pub of the Year is the Kilberry Inn at Kilberry. Outside the biggest towns, genuinely pubby pubs are at a real premium in Scotland: among them we'd include the Fishermans Tavern in Broughty Ferry, the Old Inn at Carbost, the Cawdor Tavern at Cawdor, the Tigh an Truish at Clachan Seil, the Ship at Elie, one of our new entries the Lock in Fort Augustus, the Eilean Iarmain at Isle Ornsay, the Four Marys in Linlithgow, the Gordon Arms at Mountbenger, the Crown at Portpatrick, the Lairhillock near Stonehaven and the Ferry Boat in Ullapool. Although malt whisky is often cheaper than in England, with generally a much better choice, wine choice and quality still lag behind in most Scottish pubs (ironic, as wine was a popular drink in Scotland in the days when it was confined to the tables of the gentry in England). Though real ales have spread widely and well in the last few years, beer prices too tend to be higher in Scotland than in England; the cheapest places we found were the Guildford Arms in Edinburgh, the Riverside at Canonbie and the Fishermans Tavern in Broughty Ferry. In the Lucky Dip section at the end of the chapter, pubs and inns currently showing well, on which we'd be particularly grateful for more reports, include the Queens Head in Kelso (Borders), Clachan at Drymen, Inverarnan Drovers Inn at Inverarnan and Birds & the Bees on the edge of Stirling (Central), Old Smugglers at Auchencairn and Masonic Arms at Gatehouse of Fleet (Dumfries and Galloway), Ferryhill House in Aberdeen and Marine in Stonehaven (Grampian), Dores Inn at Dores, Cluanie at Glen Shiel, Clachaig in Glencoe and Glenelg in Glenelg (Highland), Wagon in Aberlady and Hawes in Queensferry (Lothian), Ardentinny Hotel at Ardentinny, Cuilfail at Kilmelford and Wheatsheaf at Symington (Strathclyde), Old Smiddy at Errol, Kenmore Hotel at Kenmore and Muirs in Kinross (Tayside), and the Sligachan Hotel on Skye. There's a magnificent choice of interesting pubs and bars in Edinburgh.

ABERDEEN (Grampian) NJ9305 Map 11

Prince of Wales £

7 St Nicholas Lane

Standing in the narrow cobbled lane outside this individual old tavern, you easily forget that this is the very heart of Aberdeen's shopping centre, with Union Street almost literally overhead. A bustlingly cosy flagstoned area has the city's longest bar counter and is furnished with pews and other wooden furniture in screened booths, while a smarter main lounge has sensibly placed darts and fruit machine. Popular, good value and generously served lunchtime food includes soup (£1), chicken in cider sauce (£3.30) and home-made pies (£3.50). A superb range of excellently kept beers includes Bass, Caledonian 80/-, Courage Directors, Orkney Dark Island, Theakstons Old Peculier, Youngers No 3 and several guests on handpump and tall fount air pressure. *(Recommended by Duncan and Vi Glennig, Les Mackay, Mark Walker, Julian Bessa)*

Free house ~ Licensee Peter Birnie ~ Real ale ~ Lunchtime meals and snacks (not Sun) ~ (01224) 640597 ~ Children in eating area of bar ~ No nearby parking ~ Open 11am-12pm

APPLECROSS (Highland) NG7144 Map 11

Applecross Inn

Off A896 S of Shieldaig

In a lonely setting against a breathtaking backdrop towards Raasay and Skye this refreshingly jolly and decidedly unsmart inn is doing very well at the moment, particularly for popular fresh local seafood and bar food such as soup (£1.50), burger (from £1.95, venison £2.15), toasties (£1.80), fresh haddock or cod (£4.75), beef chilli, half a pint of prawn tails or chicken with herbs and garlic (£4.95), fresh local crab salad or local queen scallops in mushroom and wine sauce (£6.50), half a dozen local oysters (£6.95), sirloin steak (£9.50), a couple of vegetarian dishes, and puddings like blackberry and apple crumble (from £1.95). The simple bar is friendly and quite comfortable, with quite a lot of cheery regulars – especially as the evening wears on. The lively landlord is from Yorkshire. Musicians particularly are welcomed, and in the background there's usually piped folk music; darts, pool, dominoes and trivia; decent coffee, a good choice of around fifty malt whiskies, efficient service. There is a nice garden by the shore with tables. Bedrooms are small and simple but adequate, all with a sea view; booking for the seafood restaurant is essential. *(Recommended by Tony and Joan Walker, Dr and Mrs Peter Kemp, Lee Goulding, N C Walker, Dave Braisted, Ian and Deborah Carrington, Christine and Malcolm Ingram, A J and J A Hartigan)*

Free house ~ Licensee Judith Fish ~ Meals and snacks (12-9 in summer; 12-2, 7-9 in winter) ~ Restaurant ~ (01520) 744262 ~ Children welcome until 8.30pm ~ Open 11-11(11.30 Sat); winter weekdays 11-2.30, 5-11 (closed 1 Jan) ~ Bedrooms: £22.50/£45

ARDFERN (Strathclyde) NM8004 Map 11

Galley of Lorne

B8002; village and inn signposted off A816 Lochgilphead—Oban

There are marvellously peaceful views of the sea loch and yacht anchorage from the sheltered terrace and the big windows here. The cosy main bar, refurbished since last year's edition, has a log fire and is decorated with old Highland dress prints and other pictures, big navigation lamps by the bar counter, and an unfussy assortment of furniture, including little winged settles and upholstered window-seats on its lino tiles. Very good bar food includes venison burgers (£3.95), haggis and neeps (£4.95), fresh squid in white wine and tomato or salmon in herb butter (£8.75) and large prawns (£11.50); puddings like sticky ginger pudding or chocolate cheesecake (from £2.50); children's helpings; spacious restaurant. A wide choice of malt whiskies and bin-end wines; darts, pool, dominoes, fruit machine and piped music; no credit cards for meals. *(Recommended by Margaret and Fred Punter, Capt E P Gray; more reports please)*

Free house ~ Licensee Susana Garland ~ Meals and snacks ~ Restaurant ~ (01852) 500284 ~ Children in eating area of bar ~ Open 11-2.30, 5-11; 11-12 Sat in summer; closed February ~ Bedrooms: £27(£32B)/£54(£64B)

ARDUAINE (Strathclyde) NM7910 Map 11

Loch Melfort Hotel

On A816 S of Oban and beside Luing

This comfortable hotel is very popular with passing yachtsmen who are welcome to use their mooring facilities. There's a magnificent view over the wilderness of the loch and its islands from the wooden seats on the front terrace, and it's only a short stroll through grass and wild flowers to the rocky foreshore, where the licensees keep their own lobsters pots and nets, serving up the catch for dinner that evening. The airy and modern bar has a pair of powerful marine glasses which you can use to search for birds and seals on the islets and on the coasts of the bigger islands beyond. The walls are papered with nautical charts, and there's a freestanding woodburning stove and dark brown fabric-and-wood easy chairs around light oak tables. With quite an emphasis on seafood the bar menu might include local mussels with cider, cream and herbs or haggis parcels with creamed leeks (£5.75), local venison sausages (£5.95) and grilled langoustine (£8.75); no-smoking restaurant; good wine list and selection of malt whiskies. Darts and piped music. From late April to early June the walks through the neighbouring Arduaine woodland gardens are lovely. Comfortable well equipped bedrooms with sea views. *(Recommended by Martin, June, Simon and Laura Bailey, Christine and Malcolm Ingram, Walter Reid, L Walter)*

Free house ~ Licensee Philip Lewis ~ Meals and snacks ~ Restaurant ~ (01852) 200233 ~ Children welcome ~ Open 9.30-11(11.30 Fri and Sat); between Jan 5 and Feb 24 open 11-2 only ~ Bedrooms: £59B/£93B

ARDVASAR (Isle of Skye) NG6203 Map 11

Ardvasar Hotel

A851 at S of island; just past Armadale pier where the summer car ferries from Mallaig dock

This comfortably modernised 18th-c white stone coaching inn commands fine views across the Sound of Sleat – an area often referred to as the Island's garden – and to the dramatic mountains of Knoydart. It can get busy in the evening with locals gathering in the simple public bar which has stripped pews and kitchen chairs. The recently extended cocktail bar is furnished with plush wall seats and stools around dimpled copper coffee tables on the patterned carpet and Highland dress prints on the cream hessian-and-wood walls. In a room off the comfortable hotel lounge there are armchairs around the open fire (and a large TV); darts, dominoes, bar billiards, pool table, pinball, video game, juke box and fruit machine. Excellent home-made bar food and high tea include pea and ham soup (£2), local mussels in leek and wine sauce (£3.75), spiced lamb babotie (£4.50), vegetarian nut and vegetable roast provencale (£5.50), Highland game casserole with herb doughballs (£5.80) or crab salad (£7.50). Handy for the Clan Donald centre. *(Recommended by Capt E P Gray, Eric and Jackie Robinson, N H and B Ellis, G C Brown, James Nunns)*

Free house ~ Licensees Bill and Gretta Fowler ~ Meals and snacks (12-2, 5-7) ~ Restaurant ~ (01471) 844223 ~ Open 11-11; closed afternoon in winter and Mon in Jan and Feb ~ Bedrooms: £35B/£60B

Pubs with particularly interesting histories, or in unusually interesting buildings, are listed at the back of the book.

BLANEFIELD (Central) NS5579 Map 11

Carbeth Inn

West Carbeth; A809 Glasgow—Drymen, just S of junction with B821

The cheerfully old-fashioned bar at this relaxed and well kept old country pub has heavy cast-iron-framed tables on the stone and tile floor, cushioned booths built from pine planking under a high frieze of tartan curtain (with a big colour TV peeping out) and a high ceiling of the same brown wood. At one end, under the mounted stag's head, there's an open fire and at the other end, a woodburning stove. Generous helpings of good value bar food include home-made soup (£1.40), breaded mushrooms (£1.80), chicken liver pâté (£2.10), prawn cocktail (£2.45), macaroni cheese (£3.95), deep fried haddock (£4.50), lasagne, country vegetable and cheese pie (£4.25), steak pie (£4.75), haggis with filo pasty and whisky and onion sauce or scampi (£4.75), gammon steak (£5.95), rib eye steak (£6.95); home-made puddings like fruit crumbles (£2.45), usual children's menu (from £1.75). Well kept Belhaven 80/- under light blanket pressure, and quite a few malt whiskies; fruit machine and piped music. On the front terrace outside there are lots of rustic benches and tables, and in summer they may have children's pony rides. *(Recommended by Ian Rorison, Andy and Jill Kassube)*

Belhaven ~ Lease: Brian and Kate McDade ~ Real ale ~ Meals ~ Restaurant ~ (01360) 770002 ~ Children welcome till 9pm ~ Folk music Fri and Sat night ~ Open 12-12(1am Sat) ~ Bedrooms £15/£30

BRIG O TURK (Central) NN5001 Map 11

Byre 🍷

A821 Callander—Trossachs

There is some emphasis on dining at this carefully converted 18th-century cowshed (or byre in Scots) which is in a lovely setting on the edge of a network of forest and lochside tracks in the Queen Elizabeth Forest Park on the Killin—Loch Lomond cycle way – also much loved by walkers. The cosy, spotless beamed bar has comfortable brass-studded black dining chairs, an open fire, stuffed wildlife, some decorative plates, and rugs on the stone and composition floor. There's a stylish no-smoking dining room. Interesting bar food includes lunchtime dishes like soup (£1.95), pâté (£3.55), warm chicken and prawn salad with blue cheese dressing (£4.20), mushroom stroganoff (£5.45), beef steak and oyster pie (£5.75), chicken, bacon and haggis in a mustard sauce (£5.85); in the evening a few more elaborate dishes are added like warm goat's cheese salad (£4.25), calf's liver, bacon, shallots and garlic (£9.95) and roast guinea fowl with fresh tarragon and Dijon mustard gravy (£10.95); pleasant, friendly service. Well kept Broughton Special Bitter and Greenmantle on handpump, several local and rare malt whiskies, and very good wines; piped music. The lovable cat is called Soda. There are tables and parasols outside. *(Recommended by Dave Davey, John Hazel, Ian Rorison)*

Free house ~ Licensee John Park ~ Real ale ~ Meals and snacks ~ Restaurant ~ (01877) 376292 ~ Children in eating area of bar till 8pm ~ Open 12-2, 6-11; 12-11 Sat, closed Wed in winter

BROUGHTY FERRY (Tayside) NO4630 Map 11

Fishermans Tavern

12 Fort St; turning off shore road

There's an unusually good range of extremely well kept real ales at this friendly town pub, including Belhaven 60/-, 80/- and St Andrews, Boddingtons, Maclays 80/- and lots of quickly rotating guests like Marstons Pedigree on handpump and tall fount air pressure; there's also a choice of around 30 malt whiskies, some local fruit wines by the glass and quite a few Belgian and German beers. The little brown carpeted no-smoking snug has light pink soft fabric seating, basket-weave wall panels and beige lamps. The carpeted back bar which is popular with diners has a Victorian fireplace and brass wall lights; dominoes and fruit machine. Straightforward lunchtime bar food includes filled rolls (from £1), soup (£1.10), steak mince roll (£2), steak pie, lasagne, chicken curry or vegetable nut roast (£4), fisherman's pie or liver, bacon and onions (£4.10). The nearby seafront gives a good view of the two long, low Tay bridges. Bedrooms are comfortable. It can get very busy on weekend evenings; efficient service. *(Recommended by Bill and Lydia Ryan, Iain High, Julian Bessa)*

Free house ~ Licensee Jonathan Stewart ~ Real ale ~ Lunchtime meals and snacks (snacks only evenings and Sun) ~ Restaurant (not Sun) ~ (01382) 775941 ~ Children welcome ~ Folk music Thurs evening ~ Open 11-midnight ~ Bedrooms: £18/£32

CANONBIE (Dumfries and Galloway) NY3976 Map 9

Riverside

Village signposted from A7

There's a peaceful atmosphere in the comfortable communicating rooms of the bar here which is decorated with some stuffed wildlife and local pictures and a mix of chintzy furnishings and dining chairs. Half of the bar and the dining room are no smoking. Tables are usually laid for dining and the seasonal bar menu is chalked up on two blackboards and might include potted wild salmon and dill (£4.25), leek and tomato croustade (£5.25), pork and venison pie or beef loaf (£5.55), char-grilled red snapper (£7.25), and puddings like toffee apple pudding (£2.95). There are careful small touches like virgin olive oil for the salad dressings, bread baked on the premises or at the local bakery in Melmerby, and a concentration on "organic" foods such as undyed smoked fish, wild salmon and naturally-fed chickens. Lunchtime service can stop quite promptly. Well kept Black Sheep, Boddingtons, Butterknowle, Yates and regularly changing guest beers on handpump; a good range of properly kept and served wines; about twelve malt whiskies; organic wines and farm ciders; dominoes. In summer – when it can get very busy – there are tables under the trees on the front grass. Bedrooms are notably comfortable and well decorated. Over the quiet road, a public playground runs down to the Border Esk (the inn can arrange fishing permits), and there are lovely walks in the area. *(Recommended by John Fazakerley, M A Robinson, F A Noble, Mrs Guyneth Holland, Lucy Herring, Roger Berry, Nick and Meriel Cox, R M MacNaughton, John and Elspeth Howell, Dr and Mrs and Hilary Forrest, L Grant, Brian and Anna Marsden, John Watson, Mike and Wendy Proctor, Leith Stuart, Richard Davies, Jack Hill, George and Chris Miller, Capt E P Gray, Andy and Jill Kassube, W J Uzielli)*

Free house ~ Licensee Robert Phillips ~ Real ale ~ Meals and snacks (not Sun lunchtime) ~ Children welcome ~ Restaurant (closed Sun) ~ (013873) 71512/71295 ~ Open 11-2.30, 6.30-11(12 Sat); closed Sun lunchtime, 2 weeks in Feb and Nov, Dec 25,26 and Jan 1,2 ~ Bedrooms: £55B/£72B

CARBOST (Isle of Skye) NG3732 Map 11

Old Inn

This is the Carbost on the B8009, in the W of the central part of the island

This basically furnished stone house beside Loch Harport is one of the most traditionally pubby places on the island. It's popular with climbers down from the harshly craggy peaks of the Cuillin Hills, which you can see from the lochside terrace, and it's handy too for the Talisker distillery – where there are guided tours, with free samples, most days in summer. The pub stocks the whisky from here, plus a good few more malts. The three straightforward areas of the main, bare-board bar are knocked through into one, and furnished with red leatherette settles, benches, and seats, part-whitewashed and part-stripped stone walls, and a peat fire; darts, pool, cribbage, dominoes, and piped traditional music. A small selection of sustaining and quickly served bar meals includes cod bites with a dip (£2.30), beef curry (£5.20), fillet of salmon (£5.95) and puddings like chocolate cream and fudge gateaux (£2.25); children's play area. Non-residents can come for the breakfasts if they book the night before. Well equipped new bedrooms in a separate annexe have sea views. ***(Recommended by Mark Gillis, David Atkinson, Mr and Mrs G Hart, Nigel Woolliscroft; more reports please)***

Free house ~ Licensee Deirdre Cooper ~ Meals and snacks (12-2, 5.30-10) ~ (01478) 640205 ~ Children welcome till 8pm ~ Occasional live music ~ Open 11-midnight(11.30 Sat); winter 11-2.30, 5-11 ~ Bedrooms: £22.50B/£45B

CAWDOR (Highland) NH8450 Map 11

Cawdor Tavern

Just off B9090; Cawdor Castle signposted from A96 Inverness—Nairn

The exterior of this little Highland village pub with its concrete terrace looks modern but there's a surprisingly eclectic and stately appearance to the substantial lounge and furnishings, largely due to the oak panelling and chimney breast salvaged from the nearby castle. The public bar on the right has surprising elaborate wrought-iron wall lamps, chandeliers laced with bric-a-brac, banknotes pinned to joists, a substantial alabaster figurine, and imposing pillared serving counter. Darts, pool, cribbage, dominoes, juke box and video game. The lounge has green plush button-back built-in wall banquettes and bucket chairs, a delft shelf with toby jugs and decorative plates (chiefly game), small tapestries, attractive sporting pictures and a log fire. Bar food under the new licensee includes sandwiches (from £1.65), chicken liver pâté with apple jelly (£2.95), ham and haddock in white wine sauce (£2.95), mini cold seafood platter (£3.75), venison burgers with rowan berry jelly (£5.25), double loin lamb chops grilled with rosemary (£6.50), breast of chicken coated in Drambuie and mushroom sauce (£7.65), and a specials board with possibly gammon steak with pineapple (£5.95), sole fillet with lemon and herb butter (£6.50) and vegetarian pasta with cream and garlic sauce (£5.25). Well kept Tetleys and a guest like Maclays 80/- on handpump, and well over a hundred malt whiskies and some rare blends, and a good choice of wines. There are tables on the front terrace, with tubs of flowers, roses, and creepers climbing the supports of a big awning; no dogs; no-smoking area in restaurant. ***(Recommended by R M Macnaughton, G Washington, Tony and Joan Walker, Spider Newth, Mr and Mrs G Arbib, Peter and Lynn Brueton, R H Rowley)***

Free house ~ Licensee Norman Sinclair ~ Real ale ~ Meals and snacks (12-2, 5.30-9) ~ Restaurant ~ (01667) 404316 ~ Children welcome away from public bar until 9.30 ~ Open 11-2.30, 5-11

CLACHAN SEIL (Highland) NM7718 Map 11

Tigh an Truish

This island is linked by a bridge via B844, off A816 S of Oban

Off the beaten track, this traditional 18th-century inn is well worth a visit just for its lovely setting near an attractive anchorage, and next to the handsome old bridge which joins Seil Island to the mainland of Scotland. There is a thriving local pubby atmosphere in its unpretentious and informal L-shaped bar which has a solid wood feel, with pine-clad walls and ceiling, some fixed wall benches along with the wheelback and other chairs, tartan curtains for the bay windows overlooking the inlet, prints and oil paintings, a woodburning stove in one room, and open fires in the others. Tasty good value bar food includes home-made soup (£1.50), chicken liver pâté (£2.15), beef burger (£2.95), moules marinières (£3.95), spicy bean casserole (£3.95), lasagne (£4.50), pork chops in coarse grain mustard sauce (£4.75), steak and ale pie (£6.50), venison in Drambuie and pepper cream sauce (£6.75), scallops in lemon chive sauce or local prawns (£6.95), and other local seafood; puddings like sticky toffee pudding or rhubarb crumble (from £1.50). Well kept

McEwans 80/- on handpump, and a good choice of malt whiskies; darts, dominoes and piped music. There are some seats in the small garden, and they have their own filling station just opposite. *(Recommended by Capt E P Gray, S R and A J Ashcroft, G C Brown; more reports please)*

Free house ~ Licensee Miranda Brunner ~ Real ale ~ Meals and snacks (12-2, 6-8.30) ~ (01852) 300242 ~ Children in family room ~ Open 11-11(12 Sat); 11-2.30, 5-11 Mon-Thurs in winter ~ Self catering flats: £40B

CLEISH (Tayside) NT0998 Map 11

Nivingston House

1½ miles from M90 junction 5; follow B9097 W until village signpost, then almost immediately inn is signposted

The atmosphere at this smartly plush and comfortable country house hotel is relaxed and friendly, and the service exceptionally welcoming and efficient. It's set in twelve acres of landscaped gardens with benches looking out over a lawn sweeping down to shrubs and trees, with hills in the distance. There's a restful warmly decorated, mainly modern L-shaped bar with bold wallpaper and a log fire, and a library. Well-presented, interesting and tasty bar lunches might include tomato and orange soup (£1.95), home-made pâté with oatcakes (£3.95), venison burger (£4.95), tagliatelle carbonara (£4.95), hot smoked trout (£5.35), chicken tikka or croque madame (£5.45), Scotch smoked salmon and prawn platter (£5.95), minute steak (£5.95) and daily specials; home-made puddings (from £2). No bar snacks in the evening when meals are a bit more formal. Carlsberg-Tetley Alloa Calders on tap and a good choice of malt whiskies and an extensive wine list. *(Recommended by Tony and Joan Walker, Christine and Malcolm Ingram, June and Tony Baldwin, Susan and John Douglas, Capt E P Gray)*

Free house ~ Licensee Allan Deeson ~ Real ale ~ Meals and snacks ~ Restaurant ~ (01577) 850216 ~ Children welcome ~ Open 12-2.30, 5.30-11(11.45 Sat) ~ Bedrooms: £75B/£95B

CREEBRIDGE (Dumfries and Galloway) NX4165 Map 9

Creebridge House

Minnigaff, just E of Newton Stewart

The welcoming and neatly kept carpeted bar at this sizeable country house hotel has that great rarity for Scotland, a bar billiards table as well as Boddingtons, Ind Coope Burton and Orkney Dark Island on handpump, about 30 malt whiskies, darts, dominoes, and comfortably pubby furniture; maybe unobtrusive piped music. The main draw is the good food, which includes soup (£1.95), fried potato skins (£2.75), smoked haddock pâté (£3.45), hot beef roll or open sandwiches (£3.75), local smoked salmon (£5.40), vegetable stroganoff or broccoli and cream cheese bake (£5.95), fish and chips (£6.10), lasagne (£6.50), breaded scampi (£6.75), chicken korma or home-made sausages (£6.95), chicken supreme with sweet pepper sauce or prawn stir fry (£7.10), poached fillet of salmon (£7.75), grilled lamb cutlets with rosemary (£7.95), and blackboard specials with excellent fresh fish on Fridays and game in season; Sunday lunch carvery (£9.50). Meats are local and well hung, presentation is careful with good attention to detail; home-made puddings might include chocolate roulade with coffee sauce and passionfruit pavlova (£2.10). Airy and comfortable no-smoking restaurant. In fine weather, tables under cocktail parasols out on the front terrace look across a pleasantly planted lawn. *(Recommended by MKP, JLP, MJVK, John Watson, Neil Townend; more reports please)*

Free house ~ Licensees Susan and Chris Walker ~ Real ale ~ Meals and snacks (12.30-2, 7-8.30) ~ Restaurant ~ (01671) 402121 ~ Children welcome ~ Open 12-2.30, 6-11(11.30 Sun) ~ Bedrooms:£40B/£75B

CRINAN (Strathclyde) NR7894 Map 11

Crinan Hotel

A816 NE from Lochgilphead, then left on to B841, which terminates at the village

There's quite a warren of bars and restaurants at this beautifully positioned large hotel but the simpler ground floor wooden floored public bar, which opens onto a side terrace with seating, has a cosy stove and kilims on the seats, as well as marvellous views of the village, lighthouse and busy entrance basin of the Crinan Canal, with its fishing boats and yachts wandering out towards the Hebrides. Popular lunchtime only bar food includes soup (£2.20), smoked haddock (£5.95), local sea loch mussels (£6.25), fillet of local trout (£6.95), Loch Fyne clams (£9.50), and some local fresh fish on a blackboard, pudding of the day (£2.95), and you can get sandwiches from their coffee shop. There's a good wine list, and about 20 malt whiskies and freshly squeezed orange juice. Upstairs there are two stylish and much smarter glass enclosed roof bars both with stunning panoramic views of the loch. The cocktail bar has a nautical theme with wooden floors, oak and walnut panelling, antique tables and chairs, sailing pictures and classic yachts framed in walnut on a paper background of rust and green paisley, matching the tartan upholstery. The recently opened Gallery bar, done in pale terracotta and creams, has a central bar with stools, Lloyd Loom tables and chairs and lots of plants. The restaurants where very popular seafood is served are very formal and no smoking until after dinner. *(Recommended by Walter Reid, Nigel Wikeley, Capt E P Gray; more reports please)*

Free house ~ Licensee Nicholas Ryan ~ Lunchtime meals ~ Children welcome ~ Restaurant ~ (01546) 830261 ~ Open 11-11 (winter 11-2.30, 5-11) ~ Bedrooms: £75B/£115B

CROOK OF ALVES (Grampian) NJ1362 Map 11

Crooked Inn

Burghead Rd, just off A96 Elgin—Forres

The new owners have made this village inn a most inviting stop-off. As you go in, the first room has traditional settles, walls crowded with old posters, farm tools and some nautical bric-a-brac, beams painted with snappy sayings and hung with a good collection of whisky-water jugs, and a central open fire; beyond, a lower room has more dining tables, and blackboards listing good value food. The starters are big enough to serve people with light appetites as main courses, and puddings are very generously served too, as are Sunday roasts. Well kept Theakstons Best on handpump, decent wines, friendly service; unfortunately the landlord refused to give us any information about prices and so forth – the first time we've come across this lack of cooperation in Scotland – so please take the details below with a pinch of salt. *(Recommended by Spider Newth, RLW, Dizzy, Mr and Mrs M V Wright)*

Free house ~ Real ale ~ Meals and snacks ~ Open 11-3, 6-11; may be open all day in summer

EDINBURGH (Lothian) NT2574 Map 11

The two main areas here for finding good pubs, both main entries and Lucky Dips, are around Rose St (just behind Princes St in the New Town) and along or just off the top part of the Royal Mile in the Old Town. In both areas parking can be difficult at lunchtime, but is not such a problem in the evenings.

Abbotsford

Rose St; E end, beside South St David St

An eclectic mix of business people and locals gather at lunchtime in this small gently formal single bar pub that's long been an old favourite of the city folk. Soft orange lighting and a welcoming log effect gas fire cast a warm glow on the dark wooden half panelled walls and highly polished Victorian island bar counter with, long wooden tables and leatherette benches. There are prints on the walls and a notably handsome ornate plaster moulded high ceiling. Well kept R & D Deuchars IPA, Flowers IPA, McEwans 80/-, S & N Newcastle Exhibition, Theakstons and a guest on handpump, about 50 malt whiskies; the fruit machine is tucked well away. Good, reasonably priced food includes soup (90p), ploughman's (£3.50), haggis and mashed turnip (£3.50), roast pork and apple sauce, vegetarian spaghetti or granary crumble (£3.90), lamb goulash or chicken in white wine (£4), roast leg of lamb and mint sauce or roast beef and yorkshire pudding (£4.25), mixed grill (£5.50) and puddings like apple crumble or hot chocolate fudge cake (£1.75); efficient service from dark-uniformed or white shirted staff, although it can be slower in the restaurant (where you can eat in the evening) when they are busy. *(Recommended by Liz and Benton Jennings, Mark Walker, Capt E P Gray, John Fazakerley, Ian Phillips, Chris and Anne Fluck)*

Free house ~ Licensee Colin Grant ~ Real ale ~ Lunchtime meals and snacks ~ Restaurant ~ (0131) 225 5276 ~ Children in eating area of bar and restaurant ~ Open 11-2.30, 5-11; Sat 11-11; closed Sun, 25, 26 Dec and 1, 2 Jan

Athletic Arms £

Angle Park Terr; on corner of Kilmarnock Rd (A71)

Also known as the Diggers, thanks to its earlier popularity with workers from the nearby cemetery, this thoroughly unpretentious, old fashioned, plain but bustling pub is at its busiest when football or rugby matches are being played at Tynecastle or Murrayfield, when they may have a team of up to 15 red-jacketed barmen serving. It's the official home of McEwans 80/-, so you'll find it exceptionlly well kept, and dispensed from a gleaming row of eleven tall air-pressure fonts which also serve S & N Exhibition and guests like Black Bull Bitter, Charles Wells Bombardier and Gales HSB. Opening off the central island servery there are some cubicles partitioned in glossy grey wood with photographs of Hearts and Scotland football teams – a side room is crowded with keen dominoes players; fruit machine, cribbage and darts; predominantly young customers. Good value toasties (75p), pies (80p), stovies (£1.20), filled baked potatoes (£1.30) and steak and onion baguettes (£1.50) are served all day. *(Recommended by Mark Walker, Lawrence Eckhardt)*

S & N ~ Manager Scott Martin ~ Real ale ~ Snacks all day ~ 0131 337 3822 ~ Live folk most Wed nights ~ Open 11-11(midnight Thurs-Sat); 12.30-6 Sun

Bannermans Bar £

212 Cowgate

Set in the heart of the city, there's loads of atmosphere in this unique warren of simple crypt-like flagstoned rooms which have barrel-vaulted ceilings, bare stone walls and bright strip lighting, wood panelling and pillars at the front, and theatrical posters and handbills in the rooms leading off. A huge mixture of purely functional furnishings includes old settles, pews and settees around barrels, red-painted tables and a long mahogany table. A no-smoking back area, with tables and waitress service, is open when they're busy. It's popular with students, and one of the best times to visit is during the Festival when it seems to hum with suppressed excitement and arty-looking characters constantly flow in and out. A very good choice of well kept beers includes Boddingtons, Caledonian 80/- and IPA, McEwans 80/-, Theakstons Best, and Youngers No 3, all on handpump, with plenty of malt whiskies and Belgian fruit beers. Good value, straightforward food includes filled rolls (served all day, 90p), soup (95p), filled baked potatoes (£2.75), a budget special (£2.65), ploughman's (£2.95), vegetarian specials (£2.50-£3) and a meat dish (£2.20-£3). Dominoes, cribbage, chess, draughts and backgammon. *(Recommended by Capt E P Gray, Ian Phillips, Terry Barlow, John A Baker; more reports please)*

Free house ~ Licensee Douglas Smith ~ Real ale ~ Lunchtime meals and snacks, evening snacks ~ (0131) 556 3254 ~ Children in eating area of bar daytime only

~ Folk bands Sun-Thurs evenings ~ Open 11-midnight (Sat till 1am); closed 25 Dec and 1 Jan

Bow Bar ★ £

80 West Bow

At any time this stongly traditional town drinking pub has 12 perfectly-kept real ales rotated from a range of about 80 such as Bass, Caledonian 70/-, 80/-, Deuchars IPA, Courage Directors, Exmoor Gold, their own Edinburgh Real Ale, Greenmantle, Ind Coope Burton, Mitchells Mild, ESB and Bitter, Orkney Dark Island and Raven, Tetleys, and Timothy Taylors Best and Landlord – all served on impressive tall founts made by Aitkens, Mackie & Carnegie, Gaskell & Chambers, and McGlashan, dating from the 1920s. The grand carved mahogany gantry holds an impressive array of malts (over 140) including lots of Macallan variants and 'cask strength' whiskies. The pub is an exclusive supplier of Scottish Still Spirit, with a good collection of vodkas (nine), gins (eight), and rums (24). Splendidly redesigned a few years ago to catch the essence of the traditional Edinburgh bar, the spartan rectangular room has a fine collection of appropriate enamel advertising signs and handsome antique trade mirrors, sturdy leatherette wall seats and heavy narrow tables on its lino floor, cafe-style bar seats, an umbrella stand by the period gas fire, a (silent) prewar radio, a big pendulum clock, and a working barograph. Look out for the antiqued photograph of the present bar staff in old-fashioned clothes (and moustaches). Simple, cheap bar snacks – filled rolls (90p), mince and steak pies (from 80p-90p), and forfar bridies (£1.05); no games or music – just relaxed chat, and the clink of glasses; quick and helpful service and friendly landlord. It's conveniently located just below the Castle. *(Recommended by John A Baker, John Fazakerley, Chris and Anne Fluck, Thomas Nott, Andy and Jill Kassube; more reports please)*

Free house ~ Licensee Bill Strachan ~ Real ale ~ Lunchtime snacks ~ (0131) 226 7667 ~ Open 11a.m.-11.15p.m.

Cafe Royal Circle Bar

West Register St

Originally built with great pride as a flagship for the latest in Victorian gas and plumbing fittings, this attractively refurbished bar features a series of highly detailed Doulton tilework portraits (although sadly they are partly obscured by the fruit machines) of historical innovators Watt, Faraday, Stephenson, Caxton, Benjamin Franklin and Robert Peel (famous as the introducer of calico printing). There's quite a stylish and sophisticated feel in the interesting cafe style rooms which soon fill up when the shops and offices close. The gantry over the big island bar counter is similar to the one that was here initially, the floor and stairway are laid with marble and there are leather covered seats; Victorian-style chandeliers hang from the fine ceilings. Well kept McEwans 80/-, Theakstons Best, Youngers No 3 and a weekly guest beer on handpump (some kept under light blanket pressure); about 25 malt whiskies. There is a lunchtime carvery in the bar with hot roast beef, pork and lamb rolls carved to order. Good choice of daily newspapers; fringe productions in the building during festival week. *(Recommended by Stephen and Jean Curtis, Ian Phillips, John A Baker, Walter Reid, Mark Walker, Capt E P Gray, Susan and John Douglas, R L W and Dizzy)*

S & N ~ Manager Graeme Bell ~ Real ale ~ Lunchtime snacks (no carvery Sunday) ~ Restaurant ~ (0131) 556 1884 ~ Children in restaurant ~ Open 11-11(till 12 Thurs and Fri, and 1am Sat; 12.30-11.30 Sun)

Guildford Arms

West Register St

This year they've really smartened up the unique and breathtaking bar of this well preserved high Victorian city pub with new carpets, upholstery and wallpaper, but its architectural grandeur remains completely intact with lots of mahogany, glorious colourfully painted plasterwork and ceilings, big original advertising mirrors, and heavy swagged velvet curtains at the arched windows. The snug little upstairs gallery restaurant gives a dress-circle view of the main bar (notice the lovely old mirror decorated with two tigers on the way up), and under this gallery a little cavern of arched alcoves leads off the bar. The bustling atmosphere is welcoming and friendly and there's a good mix of customers. There's always an extremely good choice of real ales on handpump, six of which are usually Scottish: Bass, Belhaven 60/-, Caledonian R & D Deuchers IPA and 80/-, Orkney Dark Island, one Scottish and three English guest ales. During the Edinburgh festival they may hold a beer and folk festival. Good choice of malt whiskies; fruit machine, lunchtime piped jazz and classical music. Lunchtime only bar food includes soup (£1.15), fresh mussels steamed in tomato and basil (£1.85), local salmon, cheese tortellini with spinach and mushroom sauce or burgers (£3.95), steak and Guinness pie (£4.05), fresh breaded haddock (£4.45) and 8oz sirloin steak (£7.55). It is very popular, but even at its busiest you shouldn't have to wait to be served. *(Recommended by Susan and John Douglas, Richard Lewis, Andy and Jill Kassube, Stephen and Jean Curtis, John A Baker, Mark Walker, Chris and Anne Fluck, Mr and Mrs S Ashcroft, Ian Phillips, John Fazakerley, George Atkinson)*

Free house ~ Licensee John Durnan ~ Real ale ~ Lunchtime snacks and meals ~ (0131) 556 4312 ~ Open 11-11(12 Sat); 12.30-11 Sun

Kays Bar £

39 Jamaica St West; off India St

They keep a very good range of constantly changing and interesting real ales at this comfortable reproduction Victorian tavern which might include well kept Belhaven 80/-, Boddingtons, Theakstons BB, McEwans 80/-, Theakstons Best and XB, Tomintoul Wild Cat, Exmoor Ale, Exe Valley Devon Glory and Youngers No 3; up to 70 malts between eight and 40 years old, and 10 blended whiskies – they tell us they keep lager for visitors. The cosy little bar is bigger than the exterior suggests and has casks, vats and old wine and spirits merchant notices, gas-type lamps, well worn red plush wall banquettes and stools around cast-iron tables, and red pillars supporting a red ceiling. A quiet panelled back room leads off, with a narrow plank-panelled pitched ceiling; very warm open coal fire in winter. Simple lunchtime bar food includes soup (85p), haggis, neaps and tatties, chilli or steak pie (£2.60), filled baked potatoes (£2.75) and chicken balti, lasagne or mince and tatties (£3); cribbage and dominoes. *(Recommended by Ian Phillips, John Fazakerley, Capt E P Gray; more reports please)*

S & N ~ Tenant David W L Mackenzie ~ Real ale ~ Lunchtime meals and snacks ~ (0131) 225 1858 ~ Children in back room until 5pm ~ Open 11(12.30 Sun)-11.45

Starbank 🍷

67 Laverockbank Road, off Starbank Road

Like most of our main entries in the city this comfortably elegant pub is an excellent place for a wide range of rotating beers, with around ten well kept real ales on handpump that might include a combination from the brewers Belhaven, Broughton, Caledonian, Harviestoun, Maclays, Orkney and Tomintoul and a range from south of the border. A good choice of wines too, with usually around 12 by the glass, and 25 malt whiskies. There are marvellous views over the Firth of Forth from the picture windows in the neat and airy bar. Well-presented good bar food such as soup (£1.20), marinated herring in madeira (£2.50), a vegetarian dish (£4.25), chilli or roast beef with yorkshire pudding (£4.50), ploughman's (£4.75), baked haddock mornay or casserole of lamb with garlic and baby onions in a vol-au-vent (£5) and poached salmon fillet with dill and white wine (£6.25); puddings (£2.50). Service is helpful and friendly; sheltered back terrace. *(Recommended by R M Macnaughton, Keith Steven, Capt E P Gray, Gerry Z Pearson; more reports please)*

Free house ~ Licensee: Valerie West ~ Real ale ~ Meals and snacks ~ Restaurant ~ (0131) 552 4141 ~ Children welcome till 8pm ~ Open 11-11(till midnight Thurs-Sat); Sun 12.30-11

ELIE (Fife) NO4900 Map 11

Ship

Harbour

This welcoming and cosily old-fashioned harbourside pub and its garden are prettily set above the beach which at low tide is mostly sand and on summer Sundays provides a pitch for the pub's cricket team. There are views across the water to the grassy headland which swings round the bay, to the pier and the old stone fish granary on the left, and to the little town on the right – or you can look more closely through a telescope positioned on the balcony of the restaurant. In summer there's a bar and barbecues in the garden, both lunchtime and evening (not Sunday evening). The villagey, unspoilt beamed bar with friendly locals and staff still has its lively nautical feel, as well as coal fires and winged high-backed button-back leather seats against the partly panelled walls, now studded with old maps; there's a simple carpeted back room. Good bar food includes dishes such as soup (£1.35), chicken liver pâté (£3.25), haddock and chips (£4.30), seafood crêpes (£4.90), mushroom stroganoff (£4.95), steak and Guinness pie (£4.95), sole fillets rolled with smoked salmon in white wine sauce (£7.80), scampi tails in cream and mustard with brandy (£9.25), and daily specials. The Belhaven 80/-, Boddingtons and Theakstons Best on handpump are well kept, various wines and malt whiskies; darts, dominoes, captain's mistress, cribbage and shut-the-box. *(Recommended by Dennis Dickinson, M Carey, A Groocock, Paul and Ursula Randall, Eric Locker, Susan and John Douglas)*

Free house ~ Licensees Richard and Jill Philip ~ Real ale ~ Meals and snacks 12-2.30(3 Sun), 6-9.30(9 Sun) ~ Restaurant (not Sun eve) ~ (01333) 330 246 ~ Children in restaurants and lounge bar ~ Occasional jazz in beer garden ~ Open 11-midnight; 12.30-11 Sun; closed 25 Dec

FORT AUGUSTUS (Highland) NH3709 Map 11

Lock

At the foot of Loch Ness, and right by the first lock of the flight of five that start the Caledonian Canal's climb to Loch Oich, this is a real pub – a striking contrast to the hotel bars that tend to do duty for pubs in this area, and with the advantage over many of them that it's open in winter as well as summer. Homely and comfortable in a thoroughly unpretentious way, with a gently faded decor and some stripped stone, it was once the village post office. It's really come into its own under its present ex-Merchant sailor landlord, a real character and very hospitable. The atmosphere is lively and cheerful – crowded in summer, when it can be packed in the evenings with a good mix of locals and boating people (it can get a bit smoky then). Good value plain substantial food, with good helpings of chips, includes fresh local haddock (£4.95), venison hot pot or steak pie (£5.80), fresh salmon salad (£5.95) and a few blackboard specials; quite a bit of the space is set aside for people eating. A good choice of about 70 malt whiskies, big open fire; there's often unobtrusive piped traditional Scottish music. Upstairs the restaurant is no smoking. *(Recommended by Mark Gillis, Liz and Benton Jennings, June and Tony Baldwin, R M Watt, Ann and Bob Westbrook)*

Free house ~ James MacLennen ~ Real ale ~ Meals and snacks (12-3, 6-9) ~ Evening restaurant ~ (01320) 366302 ~ Live music three or four nights a week ~ Open 11-12(11.45 Sat and 1am Thurs and Fri); closed 25 Dec, 1 Jan

The ■ symbol shows pubs which keep their beer unusually well or have a particularly good range.

GIFFORD (Lothian) NT5368 Map 11

Tweeddale Arms

High St

This civilised old inn looks across the peaceful village green to the 300-year-old avenue of lime trees leading to the former home of the Marquesses of Tweeddale. The comfortably relaxed lounge has big Impressionist prints on the apricot coloured walls (there are matching curtains to divide the seats), modern stools on a muted red patterned carpet and brass lamps. The gracious dining room has unusual antique wallpaper. The tranquil hotel lounge has antique tables and paintings, chinoiserie chairs and chintzy easy chairs, an oriental rug on one wall, a splendid corner sofa and magazines on a table. Sandwiches are available all day, and the lunchtime bar food consists of a dish of the day, and starters and snacks like soup (£1.30), creamed smoked haddock in puff pastry (£3.25), smoked salmon (£4.75), haddock in batter (£5.25), poached fillet of salmon with smoked salmon sauce, lasagne, beef, kidney and ale pie, cold meat platter or creamed chicken and mushroom in puff pastry (£5.50), and puddings like layer cheesecake or Amaretto and almond cream bar (£2.30). In the evening you may be able to order dishes in the bar from the restaurant. Broughton River Tweed, Caledonian 125 and Golden Promise, Courage Directors, Eldridge Pope Royal Oak, Greene King Abbot, Greenmantle, Inde Coope Burton, Robinsons Best Bitter on hand pump or air pressure; lots of malt whiskies; charming, efficient service; dominoes, fruit machine, darts and piped music. ***(Recommened by Christopher Turner, Roger A Bellingham, Mr and Mrs R M Macnaughton, Frank Davidson, Mrs W E Darlaston)***

Free house ~ Licensee Chris Crook ~ Real ale ~ Meals and snacks ~ Restaurant ~ (01620) 810240 ~ Open 11-11(midnight Sat) ~ Bedrooms: £47.50B/£65B

GLASGOW (Strathclyde) NS5865 Map 11

Babbity Bowster

16-18 Blackfriars St

This recently restored 18th-c town house which is attributed to Robert Adam is set down a quiet pedestrian-only street and takes its name from Bab at the Bowster, a folk song illustrated in the bar by a big ceramic of a kilted dancer and piper. Opening at 8am for breakfast and coffee it's rather more like a cafe than a traditional British pub, with a chatty atmosphere and varied clientele from tea drinking old ladies to journalists drinking anything but tea. The simply decorated light interior has dark grey stools and wall seats around dark grey tables on the stripped wooden boards, an open peat fire, fine tall windows, and well lit photographs and big pen-and-wash drawings in modern frames of Glasgow and its people and musicians. The bar opens onto a small terrace which has tables under cocktail parasols and boules; dominoes. Simple but tasty bar food includes soup (£1.50), mixed bean casserole (£2.95), haggis, neeps and tatties (£3.65), bacon and garlic stovies or cassoulet (£3.95) and mussels in white wine and cream or six local oysters (£4.50). There are more elaborate meals in the airy upstairs restaurant. Well kept Maclays 70/-, 80/-, Babbity Thistle beer (brewed for the pub by Maclays) and several guest beers on air pressure tall fount, a remarkably sound collection of wines, freshly squeezed orange juice and good tea and coffee. Enthusiastic service is consistently efficient and friendly, taking its example from the energetic landlord. Piped Celtic music in the restaurant. Car park. ***(Recommended by Ian Phillips, Walter Reid, Alan and Paula McCully, Leith Stuart, Stephen R Holman, John Scarisbrick, Mark Bradley, Mark Walker, Calum and Susan Maclean, Mike and Penny Sanders, RLW and Dizzy, E Carter)***

Free house ~ Licensee Fraser Laurie ~ Real ale ~ Meals and snacks (12-11) ~ Restaurant ~ 0141 552 5055 ~ Children in restaurant ~ Folk Sun evenings ~ Open 8a.m.-midnight; closed 25 Dec and 1 Jan ~ Bedrooms: £40B/£60B

Bon Accord

153 North St

Recently refurbished in the style of a Victorian kitchen, this busy friendly and basic traditional pub is well known for its outstanding choice of about a dozen well kept real ales served from tall founts that might include Marstons Pedigree, McEwans 80/-, Theakstons Best and Old Peculier, Youngers No 3, and a good few guest beers on handpump; a good selection of malt whiskies. Tasty well priced bar food includes snacks like soup (95p), filled baguettes (£1.95), filled baked potatoes (£2.50), ploughman's (£2.60), sausage, chips and beans (£2.95), breaded haddock, gammon steak or shepherd's pie (£3.35), traditional pies (from £2.25), two daily specials and puddings (£1.50). There may only be light snacks weekday evenings; piped music. *(Recommended by Alastair Campbell, Michael Hanna, John Scarisbrick, Mike and Penny Sanders; more reports please)*

S & N ~ Manageress Anne Kerr ~ Real ale ~ Meals and snacks (till 9) ~ Restaurant ~ (0141) 248 4427 ~ Daytime parking restricted ~ Open 11-11.45

Horseshoe £

17-19 Drury Street

Full of beautiful Victoriana, this bustling friendly city pub is listed in the *Guinness Book of Records* as having the longest bar counter in Britain. Still in authentic condition the bar has old-fashioned brass water taps and pillared snob-screens. The horseshoe motif spreads through the place from the apposite promontories of the bar itself to the horseshoe wall clock and horseshoe-shaped fireplaces (most blocked by mirrors now); there's a great deal of glistening mahogany and darkly varnished panelled dado, a mosaic tiled floor, a lustrous pink and maroon ceiling, standing height lean-on tables, lots of old photographs of Glasgow and its people, antique magazine colour plates, pictorial tile inserts of decorous ladies, and curly brass and glass wall lamps. Bass, Belhaven Best, Broughton Greenmantle, Caledonian 80/- and Aitkens 80/- on handpump, large selection of malts; fruit machines, trivia and three televisions. Amazingly cheap food is served in the upstairs bar which is less special with seating in rows, though popular with young people: filled rolls (from 50p), Scotch pie and peas (80p), lasagne (£1.80), and a three-course lunch with a choice of dishes such as haddock, roast beef or macaroni cheese (£2.40); part of the lounge is no smoking and may have piped music. Not far from Central Station. *(Recommended by Walter Reid, Calum and Susan Maclean; more reports please)*

Tennents (Bass Taverns) ~ Manager David Smith ~ Real ale ~ Meals and snacks (11-7; not Sun) ~ 0141 221 3051 ~ Children welcome in lounge until 7 ~ Karaoke every eve and Sun afternoon ~ Open 11-midnight; Sun 12.30-12; closed Jan 1

GLENDEVON Tayside NN9904 Map 11

Tormaukin

A823

This smallish hotel is fairly remotely set in beautiful countryside with good walks over the nearby Ochils or along the River Devon, and there are said to be over 100 golf courses (including St Andrews) within an hour's drive of this comfortable and neatly kept place. The softly lit bar has plush seats against stripped stone and partly panelled walls with gentle piped music. Bar food includes soup (£1.80), chicken liver pâté (£3.25), deep fried haddock with home-made tartare sauce or spicy lentil burger (£5.75), venison sausages with red wine and redcurrant jelly (£5.95), baked trout or chilli (£6.25), mushroom stroganoff (£6.45), chicken cooked with tarragon and cream (£6.50), rolled beef stuffed with haggis (£6.75), local game pie (£7.45), chargrilled rump steak (£8.25), daily specials like fresh fillet of plaice with ginger and spring onion (£7.45) and braised rump steak with red wine and mushrooms (£7.65), puddings like sticky toffee pudding or deep crust apple and banana pie (from £2.85);

children's menu (from £2.65); good breakfasts. Well kept Harviestoun 80/-, Waverley 70/- and Ptarmigan 85/- and Ind Coope Burton on handpump, around 80 wines, and some 30 malt whiskies. Some of the bedrooms are in a converted stable block. Loch and river fishing can be arranged. *(Recommended by R M MacNaughton, John T Ames, Neville Kenyon, Susan and John Douglas, Gerry Z Pearson, Mark Hydes, Katie Tyler)*

Free house ~ Licensee Marianne Worthy ~ Real ale ~ Meals and snacks (12-2, 5.30-9.30; all day Sun) ~ (01259) 781252 ~ Restaurant (not Sun lunch) ~ Children welcome ~ Open 11-11; closed 25 Dec, two weeks in Jan after New Year ~ Bedrooms: £49B/£68.50B

INNERLEITHEN (Borders) NT3336 Map 9

Traquair Arms

Traquair Rd (B709, just off A72 Peebles—Galashiels; follow signs for Traquair House)

There's a bustling welcoming feel in the pleasantly modernised and simple little bar with a warm open fire, and Traquair House Ale (very rare on handpump, as it's usually all bottled) from the fine brewhouse at nearby Traquair House, as well as well kept Greenmantle, Theakstons Best and maybe Traquair Bear. House wines are above average, and there's an interesting selection of bottled beers. Good well served bar food includes sandwiches (from £1), home-made soup (£1.45), filled baked potatoes (from £2.60), omelettes (from £3.50), mushroom and leek lasagne (£3.95), lamb's liver ragout (£4.25), chicken pesto or babotie (£4.50), fried haddock fillet (£5.10), 8oz sirloin (£11.50), and puddings (from £1.95); there's usually a good choice of vegetarian dishes. They are particuarly well known for their extremely good breakfasts. A pleasant roomy no-smoking dining room has an open fire and high chairs for children if needed. Good quick service, welcoming licensees, no music or machines. *(Recommended by J M Potter, I S Thomson, Mark Walker, David Dolman, Brian and Anna Marsden, Roger Berry, Mike and Wendy Proctor, Cathryn and Richard Hicks)*

Free house ~ Licensee Hugh Anderson ~ Real ale ~ Meals and snacks (12-9) ~ Restaurant ~ (01896) 830229 ~ Children welcome ~ Story telling and singing 1st Sun evening of month ~ Open 11-midnight, closed 25, 26 Dec and 1, 2 Jan ~ Bedrooms: £42B/£64B

ISLE OF WHITHORN (Dumfries and Galloway) NX4736 Map 9

Steam Packet £

A bit off the beaten track, the big picture windows of this wonderfully positioned and comfortably modernised inn look out on to a picturesque natural working harbour with yachts, inshore fishing boats, fishermen mending their nets, and boys fishing from the end of the pier. Inside, the cheery low-ceilinged, grey carpeted bar is split into two: on the right, plush button-back banquettes, brown carpet, and boat pictures; on the left, green leatherette stools around cast-iron-framed tables on big stone tiles, and a wood-burning stove in the bare stone wall. Bar food can be served in the lower beamed dining room, which has a big model steam packet boat on the white wall, excellent colour wildlife photographs, rugs on its wooden floor, and a solid fuel stove, and there's also a small eating area off the lounge bar; dominoes, pool and piped music; friendly, welcoming service. Bar food includes home-made soup (95p), venison pâté (£1.85), beefburger (£2.05), pork schnitzel (£2.40), blackboard dish of the day (£3.25), fried chicken and bacon (£3.95), fried scampi (£4.40) and fresh local mussels (£4.50), and in the evening a few additional dishes like salmon and broccoli cutlet (£5.20) and chicken breast with coriander and garlic (£7.35); fresh lobster is usually available from tanks at the back of the hotel – prices vary according to the market price and it's helpful if you can order in advance. Well kept Boddingtons and Theakstons XB on handpump. Good range of malt whiskies, and reasonably priced wine by the glass or bottle. White tables and chairs in the garden. Every 1½ to 4 hours there are boat trips from the harbour, and in the rocky grass by its mouth are the remains of St Ninian's Kirk. *(Recommended by Capt E P Gray, Geoffrey and Brenda Wilson, James and Patricia Halfyard, David Bloomfield, MJVK, J L Phillips)*

Free house ~ Licensee John Scoular ~ Real ale ~ Meals and snacks ~ Restaurant ~ (01988) 500334 ~ Children welcome except in public bar ~ Occasional live folk music Fri evenings ~ Open 11-11(12 Sat); winter 12-3, 5-11 ~ Bedrooms: £22.50B/£45B

ISLE ORNSAY (Isle of Skye) NG6912 Map 11

Tigh Osda Eilean Iarmain

Signposted off A851 Broadford—Armadale

Gaelic is truly the first language of the staff (even the menus are bilingual) at this 19th-c inn by the sea overlooking the harbour in this picturesque part of Skye. Currently winning many prestigeous awards, and no wonder – this civilised, carefully managed and extremely welcoming hotel is a delightful place to stay. The big and cheerfully busy bar in this white inn has a swooping stable-stall-like wooden divider that gives a two-room feel: good tongue-and-groove panelling on the walls and ceiling, leatherette wall seats, brass lamps, a brass-mounted ceiling fan, and a huge mirror over the open fire. There are about 34 local brands of blended and vatted malt whisky (including their own blend, Te Bheag, and a splendid vatted malt, Poit Dhubh Green Label, bottled for them but available elsewhere), and an excellent wine list; darts, dominoes, and piped music. With emphasis on seafood and game from the hills, bar food includes lunchtime sandwiches (from £1.50), soup (£1.50), smoked venison or duck or vegetable burger (£3.50), potato, cheese and onion pasty (£4.50), cheese and vegetable country bake (£5), deep fried chicken (£5.50), herring in oatmeal (£5.95), roast venison with barley risotto (£6.50), salmon steak (£8.50), a daily special, and puddings such as home-made apple pie (£1.75). The pretty no-smoking dining room has a lovely sea view past the little island of Ornsay itself and the lighthouse on Sionnach (you can walk over the sands at low tide). Some of the bedrooms are in a cottage opposite. The most popular room has a canopied bed from Armadale Castle. *(Recommended by John and Elspeth Howell, Annette Moore, Chris Pearson, Christine and Malcolm Ingram, Bill Bailey, Tom Espley, N H and B Ellis, James Nunns, Simon J Barber, Richard Dyson)*

Free house ~ Licensee: Sir Ian Noble ~ Meals and snacks ~ Restaurant ~ (01471) 833332 ~ Children welcome but only till 8.30 in the bar ~ Folk and Scottish music some Fri and Sat evenings; quiz night Weds evening ~ Open 12-3, 5-12 (11.30 Sat) ~ Bedrooms: £55B/£79B

KILBERRY (Strathclyde) NR7164 Map 11

Kilberry Inn

B8024

Scottish Dining Pub of the Year

The remarkably varied and individually cooked country food prepared from fresh ingredients at this white painted croft post office might include ploughman's served with home-baked bread (£4.95), country sausage pie (£7.95), pheasant breast with a calvados sauce or rump steak cooked in red wine and topped with stilton (£13.95), and tempting puddings like home-made vanilla ice cream with hot butterscotch sauce. They appreciate booking if you want an evening meal. The small relaxed dining bar is tastefully and simply furnished but warmly welcoming, with a good log fire. No real ale, but bottled beers and plenty of malt whiskies. The pub is on a delightful slow winding and hilly circular drive over Knapdale, from the A83 south of Lochgilphead, with breathtaking views over the rich coastal pastures to the sea and the island of Gigha beyond. *(Recommended by Geoff and Marjorie Cowley, Mr and Mrs J Tyrer, Mrs Pat Crabb, Nicky Bennison, Mark Jobling, L Walker)*

Free house ~ Licensee John Leadbeater ~ Meals and snacks ~ (01880) 770223 ~ Well behaved children in family room ~ Open 11-2 ,5-11; closed Sun and mid Oct to Easter ~ No-smoking bedrooms: £32.50B/£55B

KIPPEN (Central) NS6594 Map 11

Cross Keys

Main Street; village signposted off A811 W of Stirling

There's a good log fire in the relaxed and straightforward lounge of this warmly welcoming little family run 18th-c hotel, with a coal fire in the painted stone walled family dining room, and a separate public bar decorated with militaria. Decent waitress-served home-made bar food from fresh produce includes soup (£1.30), deep fried brie with fresh fruit coulis (£2.25), bramble and port liver pâté (£2.25), ploughman's (£3.50), lasagne (£4.25), fillet of haddock (£4.85), steak pie (£5.30), scottish salmon poached with a light salmon sauce (£5.35), chicken breast with lemon and tarragon sauce (£5.75), sirloin steak (£10.25); a vegetarian dish (£4); smaller portions for children; puddings like apple pie or cloutie dumpling (from £2.10). Readers have been impressed by the nappy-changing facilities in the ladies'. Well kept Greenmantle and Youngers No 3 on electric and handpump, lots of malt whiskies, good tea or coffee; pool, darts, dominoes, fruit machine and juke box. The garden with tables and a play area has recently been landscaped; simple bedrooms. *(Recommended by R M McNaughton, Andy and Jill Kassube, R H Rowley, J M Hill, Peter J Moore)*

Free house ~ Licensees Angus and Sandra Watt ~ Real ale ~ Meals (12-2, 5.30-9.30 ~ Restaurant ~ (01786) 870293 ~ Children in restaurant ~ Open 12-2.30, 5.30-12; closed 1 Jan ~ Bedrooms £19.50/£39

KIRKTON OF GLENISLA (Tayside) NO2160 Map 11

Glenisla Hotel

B951 N of Kirriemuir and Alyth

The new licensees have done only good things at this lively 17th-century former posting inn which is up one of the prettiest of the Angus Glens and very much at the centre of local life. It's been cheerfully and attractively refurbished with a lot of stripped wood – both in the building and in its furniture. The simple but cosy carpeted pubby bar has an open fire, decent prints, and a rather jolly thriving atmosphere, especially towards the end of the week. Very carefully prepared and imaginative bar food using fresh local ingredients includes soup (£1.75), Orkney scallops in white wine and shallots (£3.95), macaroni cheese (£5.50), mushroom and artichoke crêpe or lamb's liver with bacon (£6.35), three lamb chops with mint sauce (£7.40), duck breast with morello sauce (£9.35), and puddings like sticky toffee and bread and butter pudding (£2.50), and cream teas in a sunny and comfortable lounge. No-smoking dining room. Boddingtons, McEwans 80/- and Theakstons Best on handpump, a good range of island malt whiskies; caring and attentive service. A refurbished stable block has skittles, also darts and pool. The bedrooms are attractively individual, and the hotel has fishing and skeet shooting. *(Recommended by J F M West, John and Kathleen Potter, Johanna King, Bruce Lawrence, Susan and John Douglas, SRP, Stephen King)*

Free house ~ Licensees Simon and Lyndy Blake ~ Real ale ~ Meals and snacks ~ Restaurant ~(01575) 582223 ~ Children welcome ~ Open 11-11(12 Sat); closed 24-27 Dec ~ Bedrooms £35B/£60B

People don't usually tip bar staff (different in a really smart hotel, say). If you want to thank them – for dealing with a really large party say, or special friendliness – offer them a drink.

LINLITHGOW (Lothian) NS9976 Map 11

Four Marys

65 High St; 2 miles from M9 junction 3 (and little further from junction 4) – town signposted

Named after the Maids of Honour of Mary Queen of Scots who was born at nearby Linlithgow Palace, the L-shaped, comfortable and friendly bar of this atmospheric pub has masses of mementoes of the ill-fated queen. As well as pictures and written records there's a piece of bed curtain said to be hers, part of a 16th-century cloth and swansdown vest of the type she'd be likely to have worn and a facsimile of her death-mask. Seats are mostly green velvet and mahogany dining chairs around stripped period and antique tables, there are a couple of attractive antique corner cupboards, and an elaborate Victorian dresser serves as a bar gantry, housing several dozen malt whiskies (they stock around 100 altogether). The walls are mainly stripped stone, including some remarkable masonry in the inner area. A very good choice of ten constantly changing, very reasonably priced well kept real ales includes Batemans Mild, Belhaven 70/-, 80/- and St Andrews, Black Sheep Bitter, Caledonian R & D Deuchars IPA, Courage Directors, Harviestoun Schiehallion and Theakston Black Bull on handpump, with a twice-yearly beer festival and 80 malt whiskies; friendly and helpful staff; maybe piped pop music. Enjoyable waitress-served bar food, changing daily, includes spicy beetroot soup (£1.30), Arbroath smokie mousse (£2.65), creamy smoked haddock omelette (£3.50), lamb's liver and bacon (£4) and beef goulash or battered cod fillet (£4.50); good value Sunday lunch. When the building was an apothecary's shop David Waldie experimented in it with chloroform – its first use as an anaesthetic; parking difficult. *(Recommended by Dave Braisted, Duncan Small, Capt E P Gray, Ian Phillips, Brian Jones, JJW, CMW)*

Free house ~ Licensee Gordon Scott ~ Real ale ~ Meals and snacks (not Sun evening) ~ (01506) 842171 ~ Children in eating area of bar ~ Open 12-2.30, 5-11.30; Sat 12-11.30

LYBSTER (Highland) ND2436 Map 11

Portland Arms

A9 S of Wick

They've recently completed some fairly extensive refurbishments at this staunch old granite hotel – our most northerly main entry – which was built as a staging post on the early 19th-c Parliamentary Road. The newly knocked through open plan bar has been considerably smartened up and now has comfortable new upholstery, carpets and furniture, darts, pool and a fruit machine. There's also a small but cosy and comfortable panelled cocktail bar; maybe unobtrusive piped music. Friendly and obliging staff serve a wide choice of very generous bar food including fish soup or egg mayonnaise (£1.80), sandwiches (from £1.50), game terrine (£1.90), roast beef or scampi (£4.95) and seafood platter (£6.50); the same dishes are served for high tea at slightly higher prices in the dining room. They keep 40 or more malt whiskies (beers are keg) and squeeze fresh orange juice. They can arrange fishing and so forth, and the inn is a good base for the area with its spectacular cliffs and stacks; pets in bedrooms but not public rooms. *(Recommended by Alan Wilcock, Christine Davidson, Karen Eliot, Stephen R Holman)*

Free house ~ Licensee Gerald Henderson ~ Meals and snacks (11-2.30, 5-9) ~ Restaurant ~ (01593) 721208 ~ Children welcome ~ Open 11-11(11.45 Sat) ~ Bedrooms: £38.50B/£58B

MELROSE (Borders) NT5434 Map 9

Burts Hotel

A6091

Set in a picturesque 18th-c market square of probably the most villagey of the

Border towns, this quite smart and comfortable 200-year-old listed hotel is both an ideal place to stay and an excellent stop for an imaginative and good value bar meal. Well presented and promptly served dishes from the changing menu might include chicken liver pâté (£2.80), parfait of guinea fowl (£3.45), fried brie on cumberland sauce (£4.25), vegetable lasagne (£4.95), ragout of kidneys and button mushrooms with red wine sauce or fried crab cakes with tomato and herb sauce (£5.50), fillet of trout coated in breadcrumbs and almonds (£6.50), escalope of liver on garlic mash potato or grilled plaice with shredded smoked salmon and orange hollandaise (£6.75), breaded envelope of pork stuffed with apple and prune (£6.95), 8oz sirloin (£11.75) and puddings like apple pie or summer pudding or layered chocolate terrine with elderflower and mint syrup (£2.50-£3.45); extremely good breakfasts. Try and get there early, as the food's popularity means tables will go quickly. The comfortable and friendly L-shaped lounge bar has lots of cushioned wall seats and windsor armchairs on its turkey carpet, and Scottish prints on the walls; Belhaven 80/-, Festival and St Andrews and Courage Directors on handpump; about 80 malt whiskies, and a good wine list. There's a well tended garden (with tables in summer). An alternative way to view the abbey ruins is from the top of the tower at Smailholm. *(Recommended by Richard Davies, Mrs J M Deale, Mrs Gwyneth Holland, Neville Kenyon, Nick and Meriel Cox, Anne and Sverre Hagen, Eric and Jackie Robinson, Brian and Anna Marsden, Wayne A Wheeler, David Gittins, Richard Davies, Capt E P Gray, RJH, Mark Walker, J M Potter, Thomas Nott, LB, CB, R M Macnaughton, J R Whetton)*

Free house ~ Licensee Graham Henderson ~ Real ale ~ Meals and snacks ~ Restaurant ~ (01896) 822285 ~ Children welcome till 8pm ~ Open 11-2.30, 5-11; closed 26 Dec ~ Bedrooms: £43B/£74B

MOUNTBENGER (Borders) NT3125 Map 9

Gordon Arms

Junction A708/B709

The very friendly landlord at this welcoming little inn remotely set among splendid empty moorlands has started running weekend residential outdoor pursuits courses in hill navigation, rock climbing, rafting and much more – it's already known as a walker's haven. The warmly welcoming and comfortable public bar has an interesting set of period photographs of the neighbourhood, one dated 1865, there's a fire in cold weather and some well illustrated poems including a local 'shepherd song' and 'A Glorious Glout' on Scotland's 1990 Rugby Grand Slam are pinned on the wall. The literary traditions reach far back, as the inn was known to both Sir Walter Scott and James Hogg, the 'Ettrick Shepherd', and is said to be the last place they met. Well kept Greenmantle and a changing guest ale on handpump as well as Broughton Brewery's Scottish oatmeal stout and a choice of about 55 malt whiskies. Good home-made bar food includes soup (£1.65), lunchtime sandwiches (£2.15), pâté and oakcakes (£3.50), filled baked potatoes (from £3.75), crispy garlic mushrooms (£3.95), all day breakfast (£4.75), breaded haddock or chicken portions (£5.50), steak pie (£5.95) grilled lamb chops or breaded scampi (£6.50), fresh local trout (£6.70), various vegetarian dishes, and favourite Scottish puddings like clootie dumpling, crannachan, Scotch trifle and border tart; usual children's dishes and smaller helpings at reduced prices for pensioners. The lounge bar serves high teas in summer – a speciality here. In addition to the hotel bedrooms, there's a bunkhouse which provides cheap accommodation for hill walkers, cyclists and fishermen, all of whom should find this area particularly appealing. The resident family of bearded collies are called Jura, Misty and Morah. *(Recommended by Nick and Meriel Cox, Andy and Jill Kassube; more reports please)*

Free house ~ Licensee Harry Mitchell ~ Real ale ~ Meals and snacks (and high teas 4-6 Easter-Oct) ~ Restaurant (not Sun eve) ~ (01750) 82232 ~ Children in eating area of bar until 8pm ~ Accordion and fiddle club third Weds every month ~ Open 11-11(midnight Sat); 11-3, 6.30-11 in winter; closed Tues mid Oct-Easter ~ Bedrooms: £25/£40; bunkhouse £4.50

OBAN (Strathclyde) NM8630 Map 11

Oban Inn

North Pier, between Stafford St and Oban

Both bars of this late 18th-c inn overlook the harbour. The beamed downstairs bar with small stools, pews and black-winged modern settles on its uneven slate floor, blow-ups of old Oban postcards on the cream walls, and unusual brass-shaded wall lamps is popular with lively young locals. The smarter, partly panelled upstairs bar has button-back banquettes around cast-iron-framed tables, a coffered woodwork ceiling, and little backlit arched false windows with heraldic roundels in aged stained glass. Well kept McEwans 80/-, a large selection of whiskies. Good straightforward lunchtime bar food includes home-made soup (£1.20), garlic mushrooms (£1.60), smoked mackerel (£1.95), vegetarian sausage or macaroni cheese (£3.75), lasagne and vegetable lasagne (£3.95), steak and ale pie (£4.20), haddock in batter (£4.25), breaded scampi or chicken kiev (£4.75) and a dish of the day on the blackboard, and puddings (from £1.85); high tea (£5.75); juke box or piped music can be loud; trivia, fruit machine, dominoes and chess. *(Recommended by Mark Gillis, S R and A J Ashcroft, John Atherton, David Warrellow; more reports please)*

S & N ~ Manageress Jeanette McLean ~ Real ale ~ Meals and snacks (12-2.30, 5-8) ~ (01631) 562484 ~ Children in small area of lounge at mealtimes only ~ Open 11-12.45

nr PITLOCHRY (Tayside) NN9162 Map 11

Killiecrankie Hotel

Killiecrankie signposted from A9 N of Pitlochry

An ideal halfway stop for lunch off the tourist route between Edinburgh and Inverness, this pleasant and comfortable country hotel is splendidly set in lovely peaceful grounds with dramatic views of the mountain pass, a putting course, a croquet lawn – and sometimes roe deer and red squirrels. The home-made food is still deservedly popular, with a typical choice of soup (£1.95), chicken liver pâté (£2.95), terrine of hare and rabbit (£3.50), fresh salmon cocktail (£3.75), stilton ploughman's (£4.95), home-baked ham (£6.95), venison burger (£5.50), lamb kofta kebab or oak smoked chicken breast (£5.95), rainbow trout (£6.25), Cajun spiced pork steak (£6.95), fried breaded goujons of sole (£7.60), 8oz sirloin steak (£11.25) and puddings like chocolate orange mousse with shortbread or syrup sponge pudding (from £2.75). Helpful service. Decent wines and about 20 malt whiskies, coffee and a choice of teas. The well furnished bar has mahogany panelling, upholstered seating and mahogany tables and chairs, as well as stuffed animals and some rather fine wildlife paintings; in the airy conservatory extension there are light beech tables and upholstered chairs, with discreetly placed plants and flowers. *(Recommended by Robin and Anne Denness, Ralph A Raimi, Paul and Ursula Randall; more reports please)*

Free house ~ Licensees Colin and Carole Anderson ~ Meals and snacks ~ Evening restaurant ~ (01796) 473220 ~ Children welcome ~ Open 11-11 ~ Bedrooms: £50.50B/£101B

PLOCKTON (Highland) NG8033 Map 11

Plockton Hotel

Village signposted from A87 near Kyle of Lochalsh

After a long drive across the hills this National Trust village is a delightful surprise. With its dramatic mountainous backdrop, the hotel is set in a row of elegant but pretty houses with a delightful outlook across the palm tree and colourful flowering shrub lined shore and sheltered anchorage across to the rugged mountainous surrounds of Loch Carron. The welcome and service are notably friendly, and the licensees go to great trouble to make sure things are right. The recently refurbished comfortably furnished and lively lounge bar has window seats looking out to the boats on the water, as well antiqued dark red leather seating around neat Regency-style tables on a tartan carpet, three model ships set into the woodwork, and partly panelled and partly bare stone walls. The separate public bar has darts, pool, shove-ha'penny, dominoes, cribbage, and piped music; dogs welcome (except in lounge at mealtimes). Very well liked bar food includes home-made soup (£1.50), cream of fish soup (£2.50), home-made chicken liver and whisky pâté (£2.95), burger (£4.75), smoked fish platter (£4.95), Plockton Bay prawns (£5.65/£10.95, home-made lasagne (£5.75), local venison (£5.95), smoked fillet of haddock (£6.25), crab salad (£7.75), local scallops (£9.65), monkfish and prawn thermidor (£9.85); usual children's menu (£1.95); good breakfasts; small no-smoking restaurant. Caledonian and Tennents Aitkens 70/- and 80/- on tall fount air pressure, a good collection of whiskies and a short wine list. *(Recommended by Alan Reid, Dr and Mrs Peter Kemp, Darren Ford, Karen Eliot, David and Margaret Bloomfield, Capt E P Gray, G Washington, Mark Gillis, N C Walker, Joan and Tony Walker, Mr and Mrs G Arbib)*

Free house ~ Licensee Tom Pearson ~ Real ale ~ Meals and snacks (12-2, 6-10) ~ Restaurant ~ (01599) 544 274 ~ Children in eating area of bar and restaurant till 9.30 ~ Local traditional band Thurs night ~ Open 11-2.30, 5-12(11.30 Sat); closed 1 Jan ~ Bedrooms: £27.50B/£45B

PORTPATRICK (Dumfries and Galloway) NX0154 Map 9

Crown ★

Perhaps the best day to visit this traditionally atmospheric harbourside inn is Thursday, when the fishing fleet comes in and you can sit outside on seats served by a hatch in the front lobby and make the most of the evening sun. Inside the bustling characterful old-fashioned bar has lots of rambling and dim little nooks, crannies and alcoves, and interesting old furnishings such as a carved settle with barking dogs as its arms, an antique wicker-backed armchair, a stag's head over the coal fire, and shelves of old bottles above the bar counter. The partly panelled butter-coloured walls are decorated with old mirrors with landscapes painted in their side panels. Bar food still has an emphasis on very fresh and beautifully cooked local seafood which is really popular with lots of our readers: moules marinierès or fish kebab (£4.95), grilled scallops wrapped in bacon with garlic butter sauce (£4.45), crab salad (£7), whole grilled jumbo prawns (£12), lobster (from £20), as well as sandwiches (from £1.55, open sandwiches from £1.95), chicken (£4.25), haddock (£4.95) and roast beef salad (£6.95); puddings such as apple tart or brandy snaps (£2.20); excellent big breakfasts. Carefully chosen wine list, and quite a few malt whiskies. Piped music; fruit machine. An airy and very attractively decorated early 20th-century dining room opens through a quiet no-smoking conservatory area into a sheltered back garden. Even when it's busy there still seems to be enough space. Unusually attractive bedrooms have individual touches such as uncommon Munch prints. *(Recommended by M A Cameron, Eric and Jackie Robinson, Geoffrey and Brenda Wilson, S H Godsell, Neil Townend, Walter and Susan Rimaldi-Butcher, Nigel Woolliscroft)*

Free house ~ Licensee Bernard Wilson ~ Meals and snacks (till 10) ~ No-smoking conservatory restaurant ~ (01776) 810261 ~ Children welcome ~ Open 11-11.30 ~ Bedrooms: £35B/£70B

SHERIFFMUIR (Central) NN8202 Map 11

Sheriffmuir Inn

Signposted off A9 just S of Blackford; and off A9 at Dunblane roundabout, just N of end of M9; also signposted from Bridge of Allan; OS Sheet 57 map reference 827022

This remotely placed white house, by a single-track road with spectacular views over a sweep of moorland uninhabited except for the sheep, cattle and birds, was built in the same year as the Battle of Sheriffmuir (1715) – making it one of the oldest inns in

Scotland. The welcoming and neat family run L-shaped bar is surprisingly popular for such an isolated spot. Basic but comfortable, there are pink plush stools and button-back built-in wall banquettes on a smart pink patterned carpet, polished tables, olde-worlde coaching prints on its white walls, and a woodburning stove in a stone fireplace. Well kept Arrols 80/-, Ind Coope Burton, Marstons Pedigree and a weekly guest on handpump under light blanket pressure, good choice of whiskies, a range of wines, decent coffee; friendly, neatly uniformed staff, unobtrusive well reproduced piped 1960s music. Promptly-served lunchtime bar food includes steak pie (£4.65) and haddock or nacho chicken (£4.95). There are tables and a children's play area outside. *(Recommended by Capt E P Gray, Julian Holland, Graham Bush, L Grant, J F M West, Susan and John Douglas)*

Free house ~ Licensee Roger Lee ~ Real ale ~ Lunchtime snacks ~ Restaurant ~ (01786) 823285 ~ Children welcome ~ Open 11.30-2.30; 5.30-11 (Sat 11.30-11)

SHIELDAIG (Highland) NG8154 Map 11

Tigh an Eilean

Village signposted just off A896 Lochcarron—Gairloch

This friendly hotel is well positioned in a 19th-century village looking over the Shieldaig Island – a sanctuary for a stand of ancient Caledonian pines – to Loch Torridon and then out to the sea beyond. It's a usefully comfortable place to stay with easy chairs, books and a well stocked help-yourself bar in the neat and prettily decorated two-room lounge, and an attractively modern comfortable dining room specialising in good value local shellfish, fish and game. Quickly served, simple well priced bar food includes toasted sandwiches (£1.35), local crab cocktail (£2.25), macaroni cheese (£3.85), roast lamb or lamb and mushroom stew (£4.15), lasagne (£4.25), chicken in cream sauce (£4.75), roast duck salad, roast beef and yorkshire pudding or venison salad (£4.95), fresh turbot in butter (£5.95), and puddings like pineapple sponge cake and crème caramel (£1.50). In contrast, the smallish bar which is popular with locals is very simple with red brocaded button-back banquettes in little bays, picture windows looking out to sea and three picnic tables outside in a sheltered front courtyard. Winter darts, and dominoes. They have private fishing and can arrange sea fishing, while the National Trust Torridon estate or the Beinn Eighe nature reserve aren't too far away. *(Recommended by Mark Gillis, Christine and Malcolm Ingram, David and Margaret Bloomfield, Jeanne and Tom Barnes)*

Free house ~ Licensee Mrs E Stewart ~ Meals and snacks (12-2.15, 6-8.30) ~ Evening restaurant summer only with advance booking ~ (01520) 755251 ~ Children welcome till 8 ~ Open 11-11 (closed Sun night); winter 11-2.30, 5-11 ~ Bedrooms: £39.50B/£87B

SKEABOST (Isle of Skye) NG4148 Map 11

Skeabost House Hotel ★

A850 NW of Portree, 1½ miles past junction with A856

This very civilised and friendly family run late Victorian hotel is magnificently set in 12 acres of secluded woodland and gardens with glorious views over Loch Snizort. The bustling high-ceilinged bar has a pine counter and red brocade seats on its thick red carpet, and a fine panelled billiards room leads off the stately hall; there's a wholly separate public bar with darts, pool, fruit machine, trivia and juke box (and even its own car park). Popular lunchtime bar food includes good filled baked potato (£1.95), home-made soup (£1.50), haggis and oatcakes (£1.50), minute steak with a French stick (£4.70), home-made pizza (£4.75), smoked salmon platter (£7), battered scampi (£6.25), and a good cold buffet lunch (from £4.80); assorted cold puddings; the spacious and airy no-smoking conservatory has an attractively laid out buffet table with lots of salads and an evening menu; good selection of over 85 single malt whiskies, including their own. Note that the hotel side is closed in winter. The loch has some of the best salmon fishing on the island. *(Recommended by Dr and Mrs*

Peter Kemp, Lee Goulding, Mark Gillis, Eric and Jackie Robinson, Richard Dyson)

Free house ~ Licensee Iain McNab ~ Meals and snacks (not Sun) ~ No-smoking evening restaurant ~ (01470) 532202 ~ Open 11-2.30, 5-11; public bar closed Sun ~ Bedrooms: £44B/£92B

ST MARY'S LOCH (Borders) NT2422 Map 9

Tibbie Shiels Inn

In a perfectly tranquil setting beside a beautiful loch, this down to earth and unchanged old inn is named after the redoubtable woman who kept house here for 75 years until she died in 1878, aged 96. The wife of the local mole-catcher, she was a favourite character of Edinburgh literary society during the Age of Enlightenment. Her photograph hangs in the cosy stone back bar with its well cushioned wall benches or leatherette armed chairs. Good value straightforward waitress-served lunchtime bar food includes home-made soup (£1.50), beefburger (£2.35), ploughman's (£3.10), spicy chicken (£3.90), chilli or Yarrow trout (£4.60), vegetarian dishes including cashew nut loaf, mushroom and hazelnut crumble or vegetable strudel (£3.85), and puddings like home-made clootie dumpling, chocolate fudge gateau and treacle sponge (£2). The lounge bar is no smoking. Well kept Belhaven 80/- and Broughton Greenmantle on handpump; and about 50 malt whiskies, a choice of wines; darts, shove-ha'penny, cribbage and dominoes. The Southern Upland Way – a long-distance foot path – passes close by, and the Grey Mare's Tail waterfall is just down the glen. Day members are welcome at the sailing club on the loch, with fishing free to the inn's residents; it's very peaceful – except when low-flying jets explode across the sky. *(Recommended by June and Tony Baldwin, Mike and Wendy Proctor, J and M Falcus, Mike and Penny Sanders, Dr S W Tham, Jean and Douglas Troup, Nigel Woolliscroft, Nick and Meriel Cox, Mrs J M Deale, Andy and Jill Kassube, Capt E P Gray, Brian and Anna Marsden, Thomas Nott, Mrs and Mrs I B White, D T Deas)*

Free house ~ Licensee Jack Brown ~ Real ale ~ Meals and snacks (12.30-2.30, 6.30-8.30) ~ Restaurant ~ (01750) 42231 ~ Children welcome ~ Open 11-11(12 Sat); closed Mon in winter ~ Bedrooms: £26B/£46B

nr STONEHAVEN (Grampian) NO8493 Map 11

Lairhillock

Netherley; 6 miles N of Stonehaven, 6 miles S of Aberdeen, take the Durris turn-off from the A90 (old A92)

This smart but very relaxed and friendly 18th-century country pub (much extended) is a very popular place for very good and unusual home-cooked bar food, freshly prepared and heavily influenced by the imaginative French and German chefs: soup (£1.80), cullen skink (£2.95), terrine or pâté or filled baguette (£3.95), seafood filled pancakes with burgundy sauce and cheese (£4.35/£7.25), ploughman's (£5.15), curry of the day (£6.50), chicken and chestnut lasagne, fish of the day or Hungarian deer goulash (£6.95), grilled chicken breast with paprika cream sauce (£7.50), Aberdeen Angus steak (from £11.50), and about four vegetarian dishes like spinach and mushroom lasagne (£6.75) and pasta with wild mushroom cream sauce (£5.95); puddings on the blackboard (£2.75); Sunday bar lunch is a cold buffet. There are countryside views from the bay window in the cheerfully atmospheric beamed bar, as well as panelled wall benches and a mixture of old seats, dark woodwork, harness and brass lamps on the walls, and a good open fire. The spacious separate lounge has a central fire; the traditional atmosphere is always welcoming, even at its busiest. Well kept Boddingtons, Flowers IPA, Thwaites Craftsman and a changing guest ale all on handpump, over forty malt whiskies and an extensive wine list; friendly efficient staff; darts, cribbage, dominoes, a trivia game and maybe piped music. The restaurant in a converted raftered barn behind is cosy, with another log fire. Panoramic southerly views from the conservatory. *(Recommended by C Moncreiffe, Julian Bessa, Mark Walker)*

Free house ~ Licensee Frank Budd ~ Real ale ~ Meals and snacks (12-2, 6-9.30; till 10 Fri, Sat) ~ Restaurant ~ (01569) 730001 ~ Children in eating area of bar, dining room or conservatory ~ Occasional live music in snug Fri nights ~ Open 11-2.30, 5-11(12 Fri, Sat)

STRACHUR (Strathclyde) NN0901 Map 11

Creggans

A815 N of village

You can walk for hours from this smartly charming little hotel through beautiful countryside, and deerstalking as well as fishing and ponytrekking may be arranged for residents. The cosy and attractively tweedy cocktail bar with wooden ceilings and signed showbiz photos has panoramic views overlooking the loch to the hills on the far side, and there are more seats in a conservatory; this and part of the cocktail bar are no smoking. The public bar, lively with locals, has a central stove, and pool in separate room; darts, fruit machine, dominoes, and piped music. There's a good selection of malt whiskies, including their own vatted malt, as well as coffee and tea, a cappuccino bar and gift shop with home baked goodies. Popular, quite restauranty and very good value bar food with emphasis on local seafood includes home-made soup (£1.55), filled rolls and toasties (from £1.80), home-made game pâté (£3.65), vegetarian stroganoff with cream and paprika (£4.25), lasagne (£4.35), local moules marinières (£4.55), beef or venison burgers (£4.85), half-a-dozen local oysters (£5.40), trout pan-fried in oatmeal (£5.75), seafood selection (£6.75), Aberdeen Angus steak (£8.95), and puddings (from £2.25); no-smoking restaurant. In front are some white tables. ***(Recommended by Duncan and Sheila McLaren, Capt E P Gray, Dorothy and David Young, J Roy Smylie, Michael and Harriet Robinson, Walter Reid, Mrs S Woodburn, John G Bockstoce)***

Free house ~ Licensee Sir Fitzroy Maclean ~ Meals and snacks (till 10) ~ Restaurant ~ (0136 986) 279 ~ Children welcome ~ Occasional live entertainment Sat ~ Open 11-12 ~ Bedrooms: £35B/£70B

SWINTON (Borders) NT8448 Map 10

Wheatsheaf

A6112 N of Coldstream

The emphasis at this smart and very well run restauranty sandstone hotel is very much on the superb, extremely good value food which is prepared by the charming landlord who is also the head chef and includes soup (£1.95), deep fried aubergine with curry and mango mayonnaise (£3.65), baked avocado with seafood topped with cream and cheese (£4.35), vegetable and nut fricassée in filo pastry baskets (£5.80), smoked ham and haddock pancake (£6.20), roast breast of chicken with Madeira jus (£8.95), escalope of pork filled with a duxelle of mushrooms and shallots with an Orkney mustard sauce (£9.45), roast Gressingham duckling in orange liqueur sauce with julienne of aprcots (£11.45), and blackboard specials like moules marinières (£3.70), crab cocktail (£3.90), sautéed lamb's liver and bacon (£5.40), braised oxtail and root vegetables (£5.80), and fresh game and lobster in season. Delicious puddings like sticky toffee pudding (£2.90) and hot baked chocolate cheese cake with warm coffee bean sauce (from £2.80). Booking is advisable, particularly from Thursday to Saturday evening. Well kept Greenmantle and a monthly changing guest like Greene King IPA or Hardy Country on handpump; decent range of malt whiskies, good choice of wines. The friendly service and careful decor all indicate tremendous attention to detail. The main area has an attractive long oak settle and some green-cushioned window seats as well as the wheelback chairs around the tables, a stuffed pheasant and partridge over the log fire, and sporting prints and plates on the bottle-green wall covering; a small lower-ceilinged part by the counter has pubbier furnishings, and small agricultural prints on the walls – especially sheep. At the side is a separate locals' bar; no-smoking front conservatory with a vaulted pine ceiling and walls of local stone; cribbage, dominoes. The garden has a play area for children. *(Recommended by June and Tony Baldwin, Arthur and Lliz Burt, RJH, Heather Couper, G W Lindley, R C Hopton, Thomas Nott)*

Free house ~ Licensee Alan Reid ~ Real ale ~ Meals and snacks (12-2, 6-9.30) ~ Restaurant ~ (01890) 860257 ~ Children welcome till 8pm ~ Open 11-2.30, 6-11; closed Mon, Sun evening Nov-Mar; closed last two weeks Feb and last week Oct ~ Bedrooms: £28(£42S)/£42(£60S)

TAYVALLICH (Strathclyde) NR7386 Map 11

Tayvallich Inn

B8025, off A816 1 mile S of Kilmartin; or take B841 turn-off from A816 two miles N of Lochgilphead

There's a chance that local fishermen will have delivered fresh fish to this pleasant and simply refurbished pub, across the lane from the sheltered yacht anchorage and bay of Loch Sween, minutes before you order. Understandably there's some emphasis on very good local seafood: soup (£1.50), moules marinières (£3), fillet of haddock or sweet and sour vegetables (£4), spicy bean casserole (£4.20), steak burger (£4.25), warm salad of smoked haddock and prawns (£5), beef curry (£5.10), Cajun chicken (£5.50), six Loch Sween oysters (£6), fried Sound of Jura scallops (£9.95) and seafood platter (£12.50), half portions for children, and home-made puddings (£3); decent house wines, coffee in cafetiere, several Islay malts. Service is friendly and helpful and people with children are very much at home here. The small bar has cigarette cards and local nautical charts on brown hessian walls, exposed ceiling joists, and pale pine upright chairs, benches and tables on its quarry-tiled floor; sliding glass doors open on to lovely views from a concrete terrace furnished with picnic tables, and a garden. There's a no-smoking dining conservatory. *(Recommended by Michael and Harriet Robinson, Karen Kalaway, L Walker, Vicky and David Sarti, Mr and Mrs G Hart, Andrew and Helen Latchem)*

Free house ~ Licensee John Grafton ~ Meals and snacks (12-2, 6-8) ~ Restaurant ~ (01546) 870282 ~ Children welcome ~ Open 11-11(1am Sat); Nov-March 11-2.30, 6-11, closed Mon

THORNHILL (Central) NS6699 Map 11

Lion & Unicorn

A873

There's a fairly extensive changing blackboard menu at this pleasant friendly inn. Very tasty bar food includes starters like soup (£1.50), mushrooms stuffed with cream cheese in a garlic and chive batter (£3.50), sautéed breast of local pigeon in claret sauce or local mussels in whisky, oatmeal and cream (£4) and medallions of ostrich in Madeira sauce (£5.50), and main courses like steak and Guinness pie or haddock in real ale batter (£5.50), daily roast (£6), breast of chicken with asparagus or wild mushroom stroganoff (£6.50), local salmon with citrus fruit or venison in cranberry and claret sauce (£8.50), wild boar in apple gravy or breast of duck with melon and basil sauce (£9), smaller portions available for children, or the usual children's dishes; puddings like spicy bread and butter pudding or white chocolate and Drambuie mousse (from £2.50). There are new wood floors in the open plan beamed and stone walled bar which is divided by a two sided log fire. The beamed public bar with stone walls and floors has a parrot, darts, pool, cribbage, dominoes and a fruit machine. A changing range of three well kept real ales might include Bass, Broughton Merlin, Caledonian 80/- and R & D Deuchars IPA, Ind Coope Burton, Morlands Old Speckled Hen on handpump, with a decent range of changing malt whiskies, and a good choice of wines. The no-smoking restaurant is in the original part of the building which dates from 1635 and contains the original massive fireplace (six feet high and five feet wide). Dogs welcome; piped music. In summer it's pleasant to sit in the garden (where they have summer barbecues) and watch the bowling on the pub's own bowling green – it can be used by non-residents. *(Recommended by Michael and Harriet Robinson, J M Hill, Martin, Jane, Simon and Laura Bailey, R H Rowley)*

Free house ~ Licensees Walter and Ariane MacAulay ~ Real ales ~ Meals and snacks (12-10pm) ~ Restaurant ~ (01786) 850204 ~ Children welcome ~ Monthly live music ~ Open 12-12 (1am Fri and Sat) ~ Bedrooms: £25/£37.50

TURRIFF (Grampian) NJ7250 Map 11

Towie

Auchterless; A947, 5 miles S

This extended white pebble-dash dining pub has a carefully and comfortably furnished series of warmly welcoming rooms, including an elegant no-smoking dining room. Good, reasonably priced seasonal home-made food from monthly changing menu using local produce includes starters like soup (£1.65), cullen skink (£2.50), guacamole with nachos (£3.50), seafood platter with dill mayonnaise (£4.50), deep fried crumbed haddock (£4.95), supreme of chicken, venison and mushroom pie or local scampi tails (£6.50) and roast rib of beef with onion, mushroom and wine sauce (£6.95). Well kept Theakstons and a weekly changing guest on handpump, decent wine list and over 60 malt whiskies; darts, fruit machine, pool, dominoes and piped music. Handy for Fyvie Castle (Scottish National Trust) and Delgatie Castle. *(Recommended by John and Christine Deacon; more reports please)*

Free house ~ Licensee Douglas Pearson ~ Real ale ~ Meals and snacks (all day Sun) ~ Restaurant (12-8.30 Sun) ~ (01888) 511201 ~ Children welcome ~ Open 11-2.30, 6-12

TUSHIELAW (Borders) NT3018 Map 9

Tushielaw

Ettrick Valley, B709/B7009 Lockerbie—Selkirk

This very small country hotel is in a lovely spot, with pretty views over Ettrick Water; a good base for walkers or for touring, with its own fishing on Clearburn Loch up the B711. The unpretentious but comfortable little bar has decent house wines, a good few malts, and an open fire, and opens on to a terrace with tables for those who are lucky with the weather; darts, shove-ha'penny, dominoes and piped music. Welcoming young owners, and a very good range of home-cooked food such as home-made soup (£1.95), toasties (from £1.95), mushrooms stuffed with stilton and served with garlic mayonnaise or filled baked potatoes (£2.95), ploughman's (from £3.50), lasagne (£4.75), steak and stout pie (£4.95), fresh fish such as sole, trout or salmon (from £7), fillet of pork en croute with hazelnut and orange sauce (£8.95), steaks (from £8.95), and home-made puddings (from £2); Sunday roast; no-smoking restaurant; Broughton ale on air pressure. *(Recommended by Gen and Dry, John and Molly Knowles, T G Brierly, Andrea and Peter Peirson, Ian Parsons)*

Free house ~ Licensees Steve and Jessica Osbourne ~ Real ale ~ Meals and snacks (all day Sun) ~ Restaurant ~ (01750) 62205 ~ Children in eating areas ~ Open 12-2.30, 6(7 winter)-11; all day Sun; closed Mon, Tues, Wed lunchtime in winter ~ Bedrooms: £22B/£38B

TWEEDSMUIR (Borders) NT0924 Map 9

Crook

A701 a mile N of village

Though this early 17th-c inn has been extended and modernised there's still a cosy, old-fashioned look and feel to the place. The flagstoned back bar is simply furnished, with local photographs on its walls; one very thick wall, partly knocked through, has a big hearth, and opens into a large airy lounge with comfortable chairs around low tables and an open log fire; beyond is a sun lounge. The pub's various art-deco features are most notable in the lavatories – superb 1930s tiling and cut design mirrors. Well kept Broughton Greenmantle on handpump and a good choice of malt whiskies. Bar food includes home-made soup (£1.50), filled baked potatoes (from £2.95), ploughman's (£3.95), deep fried breaded haddock (£4.50), chilli (£4.75), mushroom stroganoff or grilled lamb's liver with bacon, onion and tomato (£4.95), local trout with almonds and lemon (£5.75), cashew and pinenut roast with tomato sauce or scampi (£5.95), grilled lamb chops with gooseberry and mint sauce or poached salmon steak with dill sauce (£6.95), rump steak (£8.95), mixed grill (£11.95), and puddings like apple pie or hot chocolate fudge cake (£2.95); high tea (£6.95); friendly service. A separate room has darts, dominoes, cribbage, shove-ha'penny, fruit machine and video game. There are tables on the grass outside, with a climbing frame and slide, and across the road the inn has an attractive garden, sheltered by oak trees; maybe pétanque here in summer. Trout fishing permits for about 30 miles, fishing on the Tweed and its tributaries are available from the pub at about £5 a day. They've just added a craft centre to the old stable block with displays and demonstrations of glassblowing. *(More reports please)*

Free house ~ Licensee Stuart Reid ~ Real ale ~ Meals and snacks (12-9) ~ Restaurant ~ (0189 97) 272 ~ Children welcome ~ Open 11-12 ~ Bedrooms: £36B/£52B

ULLAPOOL (Highland) NH1294 Map 11

Ceilidh Place

West Argyle St

Wonderfully unusual for this part of Scotland, the atmosphere in this pretty rose draped white house is rather like that of a stylish arty cafe-bar, but with a distinctly Celtic character. There's an art gallery, lots of live jazz, classical and folk music, dance and some experimental theatre in the auditorium, a bookshop and a coffee shop. It's set in a quiet side street above Shore Street, there are tables on a terrace looking over the other houses to the distant hills beyond the natural harbour. Inside there are bentwood chairs and one or two cushioned wall benches among the rugs on its varnished concrete floor, spotlighting from the dark planked ceiling, attractive modern prints and a big sampler on the textured white walls, piped classical or folk music, magazines to read, Venetian blinds, houseplants, and mainly young upmarket customers, many from overseas. There's a woodburning stove and dominoes. The side food bar – you queue for service at lunchtime – does good hot dishes from fresh ingredients – there's always a good choice for vegetarians – serves soup (£2.25), mushroon and walnut pâté, falafels (£2.75), seafood terrine (£4.50), smoked salmon or local venison (£6.95), bouillabaisse or beef stroganoff (£7.95), lemon chicken (£8.30), local scallops (£13.50), and puddings like fruit pie or fresh fruit salad (from £2.75), served by efficient waitresses. Though the beers are keg they have decent wines by the glass (and pineau de charentes), some uncommon European bottled beers and Orkney bottled real ales, an interesting range of high-proof malt whiskies and a choice of cognacs that's unmatched around here. There's an attractive conservatory dining room and the bedrooms are comfortable and pleasantly decorated. *(Recommended by Andrew Low, Monica Shelley, Ian and Deborah Carrington, Eric Locker, Anthony Marriott)*

Free house ~ Mrs Jean Urquhart ~ Meals and snacks (12-9.30pm) ~ No-smoking restaurant (Wed – Sun, 7-9) and conservatory ~ Ullapool (01854) 612103 ~ Children in eating area of bar and restaurant ~ Regular ceilidhs, folk, jazz and classical music ~ Open 11-11 ~ Bedrooms: £37(£50B)/£74.50(£100B)

Please let us know what you think of a pub's bedrooms. No stamp needed: *The Good Pub Guide*, FREEPOST TN1569, Wadhurst, E Sussex TN5 7BR.

Ferry Boat

Shore St

In summer it's incredibly popular to sit on the wall across the road, with a beer from this traditional pub, and take in the fine views to the tall hills beyond the attractive fishing port with its bustle of yachts, ferry boats, fishing boats and tour boats for the Summer Isles. Equally popular, the simple genuine two-roomed pubby bar has brocade-cushioned seats around plain wooden tables, quarry tiles by the corner serving counter and patterned carpet elsewhere, big windows with similar views as outside, and a stained glass door hanging from the ceiling. The quieter inner room has a coal fire, a delft shelf of copper measures and willow-pattern plates. Well kept constantly changing real ales that might include Belhaven 80/- or Best, Boddingtons or McEwans 80/- on air-pressure tall fount, a decent choice of whiskies. Straighforward but very tasty home-made bar lunches include soup (£1.35), sandwiches (from £1.80), ploughman's (£3.60), venison pâté (£3.75), chilli (£5.25), pork in ginger and orange or aubergine, pepper and mushroom lasagne (£5.75), fish cakes with dill sauce (£5.95), grilled hake with lemon butter (£6.25), and puddings (from £1.90). They do a wonderful afternoon tea with lots of scones, cakes and tea. Unobtrusive piped pop music; fruit machine. *(Recommended by Jeanne and Tom Barnes, Mark Gillis, Karen Eliot, Ian, Kathleen and Helen Corsie, Mike and Penny Sanders, Anthony Marriott, Erick Locker)*

Free house ~ Licensee Richard Smith ~ Real ale ~ Lunchtime meals and snacks ~ Evening restaurant ~ (01854) 612366 ~ Children in eating area of bar and restaurant ~ Sometimes live music Thurs eve ~ Open 11-11; closed 1 Jan ~ Bedrooms: £32B/£58B

Morefield Motel

North Rd

The superbly fresh seafood and fish served here for over fourteen years has built them a tremendous reputation. The owners (themselves ex-fishermen and divers) have a ship to shore radio in the office which they use to corner the best of the day's catch before the boats have even come off the sea, and they've recently installed a lobster tank in the cellar from which customers are urged to take their pick. Served in large helpings and changing seasonally, the choice in the bar might include soup (£2.35), salmon pâté (£2.95), sesame prawn toasts or mussels (£3.75), prawn cocktail or butterfly wings (£4.50), mushroom and courgette tikka or brie and broccoli bake (£5.95), pork and mushroom stroganoff or haddock bake (£6.25), steak and kidney pie, scampi or fresh dressed crab (£6.50), mussels (£6.75), chicken breast with white wine, herbs, cream and mushrooms on flaky pastry (£6.95), venison saddle chops, salmon or scallops (£7.25), seafood thermidor (£7.50), half a lobster (£8.50) and salmon and langoustine (£8.95). You can also eat in the smarter Mariners restaurant which has a slightly more elaborate menu. In winter (from November to March) the diners tend to yield to local people playing darts or pool, though there's bargain food then, including a very cheap three-course meal. They now have well kept Whitbread Castle Eden and a guest on handpump, and a very good range of over 90 malt whiskies, some nearly 30 years old; decent wines and friendly tartan-skirted waitresses; piped pop music, fruit machine. The L-shaped lounge, newly refurbished, is partly no-smoking. There are tables on the terrace. The bedrooms are functional. *(Recommended by Lee Goulding, Ian and Deborah Carrington, Anthony Marriott, Joan and Tony Walker, Monica Shelley, E J Wilde, Karen Eliot)*

Free house ~ Licensee David Smyrl ~ Real Ale ~ Meals and snacks ~ Evening restaurant ~ (01854) 612161 ~ Children welcome ~ Occasional live music winter Fri ~ Open 11-11 (11-2.30, 5-11 winter) ~ Bedrooms: £30B/£45B

All *Guide* inspections are anonymous. Anyone claiming to be a *Good Pub Guide* inspector is a fraud, and should be reported to us with name and description.

WEEM (Tayside) NN8449 Map 11

AileAn Chraggan

B846

This comfortably friendly inn is another of those Scottish places that's highly recommended for its fish dishes. The well presented bar food includes soup (£1.95), chicken liver pâté (£3.25), seafood soup (£3.75), vegetable tagliatelle (£6.25), breaded scampi (£6.95), moules marinières (£7), salmon fillet or venison casserole (£7.50), sirloin steak (£10.50), seafood platter (£12.50), and puddings like sticky toffee pudding or blackberry cheesecake (from £3.25). The menu is the same in the restaurant. The modern lounge has long plump plum-coloured banquettes, and Bruce Bairnsfather First World War cartoons on the red and gold Regency striped wallpaper; piped music; winter darts and dominoes; a good wine list and about eighty malt whiskies. It's in a lovely spot with an excellent view from the tables on the large terrace outside, across the flat ground between here and the Tay to the mountains beyond, sweeping up Ben Lawers (the highest in this part of Scotland). Bedrooms are described by readers as spacious and comfortable. *(Recommended by Susan and John Douglas, Pat and Derek Westcott, Paul and Ursula Randall, C Moncreiffe, Bob Ellis, A N Ellis)*

Free house ~ Licensee Alastair Gillespie ~ Meals and snacks ~ Restaurant ~ (01887) 820346 ~ Children welcome ~ Open 11-11 ~ Bedrooms: £28B/£56B

WESTRUTHER (Borders) NT6450 Map 10

Old Thistle

B6456 – off A697 just SE of the A6089 Kelso fork

During the week this unpretentious local is only open in the evenings when local farmers, fishermen, gamekeepers and shepherds all come down from the hills – and may even break into song when Andrew strikes up on the accordion. There's a tiny, quaint bar on the right with some furnishings that look as if they date back to the inn's 1721 foundation – the elaborately carved chimney piece, an oak corner cupboard, the little bottom-polished seat by the coal fire; some fine local horsebrasses. A simple back room with whisky-water jugs on its black beams has darts, pool, dominoes, fruit machine and video game, and doors from here lead out onto their terrace; there's a small, plain room with one or two tables on the left. On the food front, what really stands out is the quality of the evening steaks – fine local Aberdeen Angus, hung and cooked to perfection (8oz sirloin £8.50, 8oz fillet £10, 20oz T-bone £13). The weekend lunchtime menu is otherwise very simple, with soup (£1.30), sandwiches (£1.50) sausage (£3), haddock (£4.50) and lasagne (£5.50). A more conventionally comfortable two-roomed lounge has flowery brocaded seats, neat tables and a small coal fire, leading into the restaurant; piped music. *(Recommended by R M Tudor, Stephen R Holman, Gerry Pearson; more reports please)*

Free house ~ Licensee David Silk ~ Meals and snacks (5-9 Mon-Fri, 12-9 Sat, Sun) ~ Restaurant ~ (01578) 740275 ~ Children welcome ~ Open 5-11; 12-11 Sat-Sun ~ Bedrooms: £22.50B/£45B

Lucky Dip

Besides the fully inspected pubs, you might like to try these Lucky Dips recommended to us and described by readers (if you do, please send us reports):

BORDERS

Allanton [B6347; NT8755], *Allanton Inn*: Unassuming but very welcoming, in stone village terrace; outstanding food, interesting perceptive wine list; open all day weekends; bedrooms *(Jan and Colin Roe)*

☆ **Bonchester Bridge** [A6088; NT5812], *Horse & Hound*: Wide range of good home cooking, well kept changing ales such as Ansells Mild and Orkney Dark Island, interesting building, splendid open fire in each bar, welcoming landlord, evening restaurant, children's area; bedrooms; cl Tues in winter *(Alison Bell, Michael Patterson,*

Wayne A Wheeler, Mr Robbins)
Eddleston [A703 Peebles—Penicuik; NT2447], *Horseshoe*: Civilised old stone pub, soft lighting, gentle music, comfortable seats, well kept S & N ales *(G Washington, LYM)*
Eyemouth [NT9564], *Ship*: Straightforward pub in interesting position in pretty fishing village, harbour view from upstairs dining room, Caledonian 70/- and Tetleys, friendly service *(Brian and Anna Marsden, Thomas Nott)*
☆ **Greenlaw** [NT7146], *Castle*: Lovely outside, straightforward in, with decent food inc good value Sun lunch; well kept Greenmantle, friendly landlords and dogs *(Heather Couper)*
Jedburgh [NT6521], *Pheasant*: Very warm welcome, friendly efficient service, fair choice of wine and whiskies, good range of generous food inc amazing value pheasant in season, S&N ales, decent wines *(Jonathan Mann, Abigail Regan, Mike and Penny Sanders)*
☆ **Kelso** [Bridge St (A699); NT7334], *Queens Head*: Old coaching inn with good mix of modern and traditional, pleasant big back lounge, small front locals' bar with pool, efficient courteous staff, wide choice of good generous imaginative food, reasonable prices, well kept ales such as Boddingtons, Greenmantle, McEwans 70/- and Theakstons; children welcome; good value bedrooms, bright and clean *(Gerry McGarry, Nigel Woolliscroft, P Woodward, Neville Kenyon, Thomas Nott, Mrs W E Darlaston, Brian and Anna Marsden, A D Lealan)*
Leitholm [B6461 Kelso—Berwick; NT7944], *Plough*: Redecorated by friendly new licensees, nice open fire, good value bar food, well kept Arrolls 80/- *(Wayne A Wheeler)*
Melrose [High St; NT5434], *Kings Arms*: Late 18th-c inn with old chairs, interesting ornaments and cosy log fire in warmly welcoming beamed bar, well kept Calders 70/-, Ind Coope Burton and Tetleys on handpump, good choice of malt whiskies, good varied reasonably priced largely home-made food inc fine Aberdeen Angus steaks and good children's menu; can get busy Sat; bedrooms *(Mike and Penny Sanders)*
Newcastleton [NY4887], *Liddesdale*: Limited choice of attractively served palatable lunchtime food; bedrooms *(S H Godsell)*
Newmill [A7 S of Hawick; NT4510], *Newmill*: Pleasant and friendly, with small but varied reasonably priced wine list, good value food *(R H and M I Gilbert)*
Peebles [S of Tweed bridge; NT2540], *Kingsmuir*: Popular for bar food inc local dishes, handsome Edwardian lounge, Greenmantle beer; bedrooms *(Mr and Mrs I B White)*
Selkirk [Market Pl; NT4728], *Cross Keys*: Well kept Caledonian 80/- and Tetleys, small bar area with US number plates, larger lounge area behind, attentive helpful licensees; can get packed Sat evening *(Brian and Anna Marsden, Mr Robbins)*
☆ **St Boswells** [A68 just S of Newtown St Boswells; NT5931], *Buccleuch Arms*: Civilised and spacious Georgian-style plush panelled bar in well established sandstone inn, wide choice of imaginative well prepared bar food (not Sun), sandwiches all day, no-smoking alcove, restaurant, tables in garden behind; children welcome; bedrooms *(Susan and John Douglas, Gordon Smith, LYM)*

CENTRAL

☆ **Callander** [Stirling Rd (A84 a mile outside); NN6507], *Myrtle*: Interesting food inc good vegetarian choice and outstanding puddings in attractive old dining pub; small front bar leading to two cosy prettily decorated restaurant rooms inc no-smoking area, keg beer but sensibly priced wine, herbal tea, decaf coffee, obliging service; can get very busy – may have to book *(Gerry Z Pearson, Bob and Moira Tildsley)*
Callander [Main St], *Waverley*: Good range of beers, coffee, friendly service *(Bob and Moira Tildsley)*
Camelon [Main St; NS8680], *Copper Top*: Lots of copper in lounge, food inc home-made chips, vegetarian choice; high chairs *(Ian and Freda Millar)*; [Main St], *Rosebank*: Reliable Beefeater in converted maltings by canal, usual food, good range of Whitbreads-related beers, lots of local photographs *(Ian Phillips)*
☆ **Castlecary** [village signed off A80 Glasgow—Stirling; NS7878], *Castlecary House*: Generous quick low-priced decent food till 10 in handily placed cheerful pub, open all day, with well kept Bass, Belhaven 80/-, Jennings Cumberland, John Smiths Magnet and Stones on handpump, very friendly staff; restaurant specialising in steaks on hot metal platters; comfortable well equipped bedrooms, generous breakfast *(Karen Phillips, LYM)*
☆ **Dollar** [Chapel Pl; NS9796], *Strathallan*: Good bar food esp fresh fish in pleasant, clean and welcoming pub with well kept local Harviestoun 70/-, 80/-, 85/- and Strong, also Belhaven 80/- and lots of malt whiskies inc bargain malt of the month; good service, thriving friendly atmosphere; bedrooms *(Jean and Douglas Troup, Gerry Z Pearson)*
Dollar, *Kings Seat*: Friendly family-run pub with comfortable lounge, good home-made food inc vegetarian, Harviestoun and Orkney Dark Island ales *(Carol Whittaker, John Crompton)*
☆ **Drymen** [The Square; NS4788], *Clachan*: Great atmosphere in small cottagey pub, licensed since 1734, friendly and welcoming; original fireplace with side salt larder, tables made from former bar tops, former Wee Free pews along one wall; good fresh food, well kept beer, friendly service; on square of attractive village *(Ian Phillips, Dr and Mrs Peter Kemp)*
Dunblane [NN7801], *Stirling Arms*: Relaxed and friendly, with good range of good value bar food, generous glasses of wine; good

panelled restaurant downstairs with river views *(Heidi Williamson)*

Falkirk [14 Melville St, opp Grahamston Stn; NS8880], *Behind the Wall*: Attractive pub with real ale and even Belgian Leffe Blond on tap; large conservatory allows children, decent food *(Paddy Moindrot)*; [Baxters Wynd], *Wheatsheaf*: Traditional old Scots pub, friendly staff, good choice of ales inc Wallaces Folly named for the owner *(Bob Maxwell)*

Fintry [23 Main St; NS6186], *Fintry*: Friendly pub with island bar dividing cosy public bar from games room; lots of beams and exposed stonework, big plusher lounge and upstairs restaurant, straightforward bar food inc fresh pizza, Belhaven and Boddingtons *(Angus Lyon)*

☆ **Inverarnan** [A82 N of Loch Lomond; NN3118], *Inverarnan Drovers Inn*: Real oddity, with sporting trophies, other stuffed animals, armour, deerskins slung over the settles, haphazard decaying fabric and furnishings, Hogarthian candlelight, peat or log fires, some very stray customers and animals; readers with a taste for the unusual (and a blind eye to the niceties of housekeeping) like it a lot, probably much closer to what inns were really like 200 years ago than the usual anaemic imitations; Scots music, great collection of malt whiskies, well kept Caledonian 80/-, farm cider, well behaved children allowed, open all day; creaky ageing bedrooms (look before you sleep), late breakfast *(Susan and John Douglas, Barry A Lynch, Peter and Lynn Brueton, Annette Moore, Chris Pearson, Mary Moore, Tom Espley, LYM)*

☆ **Kilmahog** [A821/A84 just N of Callander; NN6108], *Lade*: Proper well run pub with wide range of straightforward food inc help-yourself salad, vegetarian and children's, efficient casual service, good range of wines by the glass, real ales, no-smoking area, pleasant garden with summer evening barbecues; bedrooms *(Dave Davey, A J Netherton, James Nunns)*

☆ **Stirling** [91 St Mary's Wynd; from Wallace Memorial in centre go up Baker St, keep right at top; NS7993], *Settle*: Early 18th-century, restored to show beams, stonework, great arched fireplace and barrel-vaulted upper room; bar games, snacks till 7, Belhaven 70/- and 80/- and Maclays on handpump, friendly staff; piped music, open all day *(Julian Holland, LYM)*

Stirling [Baker St], *Hogs Head*: Traditionally done out by Whitbreads with stripped wood and mock gaslamps, eight real ales on handpump, more tapped from the cask, usual lunchtime food *(Julian Holland)*

☆ *nr* **Stirling** [Easter Cornton Rd, Causewayhead; off A9 N], *Birds & the Bees*: Convivial and interestingly furnished dim-lit ex-byre, Caledonian 80/-, Tennents Special and 80/-, guests such as Alloa 80/-, Harviestoun, Marstons Pedigree, good range of food, helpful staff; decor includes milk churns, iron sculptures and re-fleeced sheep; live bands most weekends, open all day till 1am – very popular with young people, reliably well run; children welcome *(Julian Holland, Heidi Williamson, LYM)*

DUMFRIES AND GALLOWAY

Annan [41 Scotts St; NY1966], *Firth*: Part of sandstone hotel, welcoming local atmosphere, real ales, exotic beers, hundreds of whiskies, food inc local meat and seafood; comfortable bedrooms *(Stuart Vivers)*

☆ **Auchencairn** [about 2½ miles off A711; NX7951], *Old Smugglers*: Warmly welcoming popular 18th-c inn, comfortable and attractive with clean white woodwork, good pub food at sensible prices inc outstanding puddings and cakes, quick competent all-female staff, pretty garden and terrace; children welcome *(Dr M I Crichton, J L Phillips)*

☆ **Auchencairn**, *Balcary Bay*: Well ordered and comfortable hotel, lovely spot for eating outside with terrace and gardens in peaceful surroundings, magnificent sea views, civilised but friendly bar, well presented food from soup and open sandwiches up (inc huge child's helpings); reasonable prices, pleasant service; bedrooms *(P and J Coombs, Ian Rorison)*

Canonbie [NY3976], *Cross Keys*: Attractive old coaching inn with fishing in River Esk; wide choice of good food in spacious and comfortable lounge bar, good weekend carvery, staff courteous and friendly even when very busy, friendly locals; bedrooms *(DMT)*

☆ **Dalbeattie** [1 Maxwell St; NX8361], *Pheasant*: Good choice of bar food till 10 in simply modernised but comfortable upstairs lounge/restaurant; lively downstairs bar, children welcome till 6, open all day; bedrooms *(Paul and Ursula Roberts, LYM)*

Dunscore [B729 9 miles NW of Dumfries; NX8684], *George*: Good well presented food, wider choice in evening, Bass and Greenmantle beers; bedrooms *(DAV)*

☆ **Gatehouse of Fleet** [NX5956], *Murray Arms*: Small hotel with well kept ale such as Theakstons XB, lots of malt whiskies, interesting layout of mainly old-fashioned comfortable seating areas, friendly staff, games in quite separate public bar, rather upmarket restaurant; one part with soft easy chairs open all day for food in summer, children welcome; bedrooms *(R E and P Pearce, James and Patricia Halfyard, Ian Phillips, John Watson, LYM)*

☆ **Gatehouse of Fleet** [Ann St], *Masonic Arms*: Welcoming comfortably refurbished bar with friendly helpful staff, varied plentiful reasonably priced good food served quickly even when busy; conservatory and garden *(MKP, JLP, MJVK, C Philip)*

☆ **Gatehouse of Fleet** [High St], *Angel*: Warm and cosy hotel lounge bar, good friendly service, popular bar food, sensibly priced restaurant, McEwans ales; bedrooms comfortable and good value *(Maysie Thompson)*

Gretna [NY3267], *Gretna Chase*: Only a few yards from the border, under new management, imaginative good value food, quick friendly service, spotless housekeeping; lovely garden inc formal roses; bedrooms *(Fred and Cynthia Sealey)*

☆ **Kippford** [NX8355], *Anchor*: Wide range of generous bar food inc children's (served all day in summer) in waterside inn facing quiet yacht anchorage, traditional back bar with lots of varnished woodwork, plush front dining bar with lots of prints on stripped stone walls, log fire, S & N real ales; games room, seats out facing water; open all day summer *(John Watson, Geoffrey and Brenda Wilson, Nigel and Sara Walker, LYM)*

☆ **Kirkcudbright** [Old High St; NX6851], *Selkirk Arms*: Quiet modern decor in cosy and comfortable partly panelled lounge with good local flavour; good food in bar and restaurant, friendly efficient service, tables in good spacious garden; fishing; children in restaurant and lounge; good value bedrooms *(Maysie Thompson, LYM)*

Lockerbie [NY1381], *Dryfesdale*: Stunning setting, good fresh food in hotel bar, separate restaurant, very friendly staff; comfortable bedrooms *(DMT)*

☆ **Moffat** [44 High St; NT0905], *Star*: Amazingly narrow building yet has two surprisingly capacious bars inc quiet, comfortable and relaxing lounge; warm friendly atmosphere, swift service, reasonably priced interesting food, well kept S & N beers on tall fount, good coffee, moderately priced wine by the bottle; bedrooms *(TBB)*

☆ **Moffat** [High St], *Balmoral*: Well kept ale, good simple food, quick cheerful service, comfortable peaceful bar *(Stephen R Holman)*

☆ **Moffat** [1 Churchgate], *Black Bull*: Quick friendly service, generous hearty food, friendly public bar with railway memorabilia and good open fire (may be only bar open out of season), plush softly lit cocktail bar, simply furnished tiled-floor dining room, side games bar with juke box; children welcome, open all day; bedrooms comfortable *(Cyril Burton, LYM)*

☆ **Moffat** [High St], *Moffat House*: Friendly well run extended Adam-style hotel with good range of good value food in big comfortable lounge bar, good service, real ale (not always in winter); comfortable bedrooms with good breakfast *(Norman Ellis, G P Fogelman)*

☆ *nr* **Moffat** [hotel signed off A74], *Auchen Castle*: Beautifully appointed country-house hotel (so dress appropriately) in lovely quiet spot with spectacular hill views, imaginative food in peaceful and comfortable bar, decent wines, good choice of malt whiskies, friendly service; trout loch in good-sized grounds; bedrooms superbly decorated, wonderful views *(Rev J E Cooper)*

FIFE

☆ **Anstruther** [Bankwell Rd; NO5704], *Craws Nest*: Well run popular hotel with good variety of reliably good generous food inc outstanding haddock and other fresh fish in straightforward lounge; good service, keg beer; bedrooms *(Paul and Ursual Randall)*

Anstruther [Cellardyke], *Haven*: Welcoming pub/restaurant with charming garden, plenty of atmosphere, varied well prepared generous food, reasonable prices, interesting old local photographs *(Eric Locker)*

☆ **Crail** [4 High St; NO6108], *Golf*: Welcoming landlord, small unpretentious bar, restrained lounge, restaurant with views over Firth of Forth, well kept S & N ales, good range of malt whiskies, good service, coal fire, above-average food, quaint fishing-village atmosphere; simple comfortable bedrooms, good breakfast *(H Bramwell)*

Kingsbarns [NO5912], *Cambo Arms*: Good food *(Sandy Fyfe)*

☆ **Lower Largo** [The Harbour; NO4102], *Crusoe*: Comfortable friendly harbourside inn with good food from servery in beamed family bar, stripped stonework, settees in bays, open fire, S & N beers, quick service; separate lounge bar with Crusoe/Alexander Selkirk mementoes, restaurant; bedrooms spacious and comfortable, with good sea views *(Christine and Malcolm Ingram)*

☆ **North Queensferry** [NT1380], *Queensferry Lodge*: Useful motorway break with good views of Forth bridges and the Firth from light and airy hotel lounge, tastefully decorated with lots of wood and plants; McEwans real ale, good value bar food running up to decent steaks 12-2.30, 5-10; bedrooms good, buffet breakfast *(Norman Ellis)*

North Queensferry [1 Main St], *Ferrybridge*: Comfortable and cosy hotel prettily snuggled under Forth Bridge, good varied well cooked food inc popular Sun lunch, attractive prices, Tennents beer, good choice of wine, courteous service; good bedrooms *(Margaret and Alan Critchley)*

☆ *nr* **St Andrews** [Grange Rd – a mile S], *Grange*: More restaurant than pub, good choice of food in spotless small bar too, friendly service, good range of malt whiskies, decent wines (but keg beers), furniture in keeping with the age of the building, attractive setting *(Brian Bannatyne-Scott)*

Wormit [NO4026], *Sandford*: Elegant and comfortable yet friendly bar of country house hotel, cushioned window seat overlooks pretty garden as does the terrace, friendly waitresses in Highland dress; bedrooms good *(Susan and John Douglas)*

GRAMPIAN

☆ **Aberdeen** [Bon Accord St], *Ferryhill House*: Half a dozen well kept real ales and well over 100 malt whiskies in well run small hotel's comfortable communicating spacious and airy bar areas, friendly staff, wide range of generous bar food, cheap set lunches; lots of well spaced tables on neat sheltered lawns; open all day, children allowed in restaurant; bedrooms comfortable *(P Corris, Mark Walker, LYM)*

Aberdeen [45 Langstane Pl], *Betty Burkes*: Popular and welcoming, polite efficient service, Caledonian and other real ales, on-going Drink the World competition with 30 bottled beers from around the world *(Mark Walker)*; [121 Gallowgate], *Blue Lamp*: Dark modern flagstoned lounge, good friendly staff, S & N real ales, free juke box, fruit machine, occasional band *(Mark Walker)*; [Netherkirkgate], *Bond Bar*: Good variety of entertainment, pleasant for a relaxing drink or for a night out *(L Gray)*; [1 Backwynd], *Booths*: Good choice of tasty inexpensive food, well kept beers *(John Howard, Stephen and Jean Curtis)*; [504 Union St], *Cocky Hunters*: Traditional bare-boards pub, lively in evenings when usually entertainment, friendly staff, decent food, big-screen sports TV, OAPs' happy hour *(Mark Walker, J Randy Davis)*; [Castle St], *Tilted Wig*: Comfortable open-plan pub with Caledonian 80/ and Tetleys-related ales *(Julian Bessa, Mark Walker)*; *Under the Hammer*: Decent food in enjoyable local *(Paul Gayton)*

☆ **Braemar** [NO1491], *Fife Arms*: Welcoming and elegantly refurbished big Victorian hotel, comfortable sofas and tartan cushions, reasonably priced pub food, decent staff; children and dogs welcome (and on the coach routes); bedrooms warm and comfortable *(Susan and John Douglas, Julian Bessa, Liz and Benton Jennings, R M Macnaughton)*

☆ **Catterline** [NO8778], *Creel*: Cosy bar with real fire, big lounge with friendly cat and plenty of tables, good generous food in bar and seaview restaurant, well kept Maclays 70/- and Tennents 80/-, welcoming landladies; bedrooms *(Roger and Sheila Thompson, M D Farman)*

Crathie [NO3695], *Inver*: 18th-c inn with pleasant bar, quiet lounge with open fire, decent food with fresh veg, well kept Tennents 80/-; bedrooms *(anon)*

Fettercairn [NO6473], *Ramsay Arms*: Substantial small hotel useful for reasonably priced bar food *(Ian Rorison)*

Findhorn [NJ0464], *Crown & Anchor*: Useful family pub with usual food all day inc children's dishes, up to six changing real ales, big fireplace in lively public bar, separate lounge; bedrooms, good boating in Findhorn Bay (boats for residents) *(Spider Newth, LYM)*; *Kimberley*: Unpretentious, with friendly staff, weekly changing guest beers, good generous food esp chicken tikka *(G Hooper, Mr and Mrs M V Wright)*

Monymusk [signed from B993 SW of Kemnay; NJ6815], *Grant Arms*: Comfortable well kept inn with good fishing on the Don, log fire dividing dark-panelled lounge bar, lots of malt whiskies, S & N real ales, games in simpler public bar, wide choice of bar food, restaurant; children welcome, open all day weekends; bedrooms *(John Howard, LYM)*

☆ **Stonehaven** [Shorehead; NO8786], *Marine*: Welcoming basic harbourside pub with good cheap food, five real ales inc McEwans 80/- and guests, coffee and tea, polite service, upstairs lounge and restaurant, superb view – in summer people drink out on the harbour wall; lively downstairs, piped music may compete with TV, dogs allowed here; juke box, games machines and pool table in room past bar; open all day; bedrooms *(Mark Walker, Sandy Henderson, JJW, CMW)*

Strachan [NO6792], *Feughside*: Friendly family service, wide choice of generous food, riverside gardens; can arrange fishing and shooting, trout lake in sight 200 yds away; bedrooms *(David and Julie Glover)*

HIGHLAND

☆ **Ardelve** [A87 8 miles E of Kyle of Lochalsh; NG8727], *Loch Duich*: Friendly hotel set in magnificent scenery overlooking Eilean Donan castle, above-average bar meals using local produce inc wild salmon, venison, lamb, good restaurant, live bar music Sat, Bass, Tennents 80/-, good wine list; comfortable bedrooms *(A Dyson, Joan and Tony Walker)*

Aultbea [NG8689], *Drumchork Lodge*: Good food and drink *(G Washington)*

Aultguish [NH3570], *Aultguish*: Isolated highland inn nr Loch Glascarnoch with friendly licensees and staff, decent food, a welcome for children and walkers; bedrooms inexpensive, simple but good *(Tim Galligan, LYM)*

Aviemore [Coylumbridge Rd; NH8912], *Olde Bridge*: Well kept friendly inn in pleasant surroundings, small but busy, with good bar food inc four-course meals (with whisky for the haggis), some live entertainment *(P G Topp, G Washington, TBB, Dono and Carol Leaman)*; [Main Road], *Winking Owl*: Decent food in clean pub with pleasant service *(TBB)*

Beauly [The Square; NH5246], *Priory*: Always busy; good cheap set lunch, quite restauranty, popular with locals; bedrooms *(Christine and Malcolm Ingram)*

☆ **Carrbridge** [NH9022], *Dalrachney Lodge*: Good menu, friendly staff, pleasant shooting-lodge-type hotel with simply furnished bar, quiet and comfortable lounge with books and log fire in ornate inglenook, decent malt whiskies, old-fashioned dining room; bedrooms, most with mountain and river views *(E J Wilde)*

Cromarty [Marine Terr; NH7867], *Royal*: Good value food inc huge pieces of home-made shortbread, beautiful view across Cromarty Firth to Ben Wyvis; bedrooms *(L Grant, Christine and Malcolm Ingram)*

☆ **Dores** [B852 SW of Inverness; NH5934], *Dores Inn*: Reasonably priced popular bar food inc good seafood, well kept beer and friendly staff in attractive traditional country inn; stripped stone, low ceilings, basic public bar, more comfortable lounge with open fire; beautiful views over Loch Ness, front garden and tables out behind *(Alan Wilcock, Christine Davidson, Peter and Lynn Brueton)*

Gairloch [just off A832 nr bridge; NG8077], *Old Inn*: Usefully placed over rd from small harbour, nr splendid beach; dimpled copper tables and so forth in two small and rather dark rooms of comfortable lounge, a good few malts, Youngers No 3 and maybe Bass, popular bar food, games in public bar; piped music may be loud, and does catch the tourist coaches; picnic tables out by stream, open all day; bedrooms *(BB)*

☆ **Glen Shiel** [A87 Invergarry—Kyle of Lochalsh, on Loch Cluanie – OS Sheet 33 map ref 076117; NH0711], *Cluanie*: Nice place in wild setting by Loch Cluanie (good walks), big helpings of good simple freshly prepared bar food in three knocked-together rooms with dining chairs around polished tables, overspill into restaurant; friendly and efficient staff, good fire, real ale such as Orkney, no pool or juke box; children welcome; interesting gift shop, big comfortable modern bedrooms nicely furnished in pine, stunning views and good bathrooms – great breakfasts for non-residents too *(Nigel Woolliscroft, Mr and Mrs C Nethercott, Derek and Maggie Washington, A P Jeffreys)*

☆ **Glencoe** [on old Glencoe rd, behind NTS Visitor Centre; NN1256], *Clachaig*: Tremendous setting, surrounded by soaring mountains, inn doubling as mountain rescue post and very popular indeed with outdoor people (service can slow when it's crowded); cheery walkers' bar with two woodburners and pool, pine-panelled snug, big modern-feeling lounge bar; simple snacks all day, wider evening choice, lots of malt whiskies, half a dozen well kept ales such as Arrols 80/-, Caledonian, Heather, Maclays 80/-, Theakstons Old Peculier and Youngers No 3; children in no-smoking restaurant; frequent live music, service not always ideal; bedrooms, good breakfast *(Capt E P Gray, John Hazel, Calum and Susan Maclean, Barry A Lynch, D J Atkinson, Dave Braisted, Tom Espley, S R and A J Ashcroft, LYM)*

☆ **Glencoe** [off A82 E of Pass; NN1058], *Kings House*: Alone in a stupendous mountain landscape, with simple bar food inc children's, well kept McEwans 80/- and a guest such as Orkney Dark Island or Shipstones; basic back climbers' bar with loud pop music, pool and darts, central cocktail bar with cloth banquettes and other seats around wood-effect tables, suntrap lounge with scenic windows and log fire; open all day; bedrooms in inn itself, and in cheaper dormitory-style bunkhouse *(Karen Eliot, D J Atkinson, John Hazel, LYM)*

☆ **Glenelg** [unmarked rd from Shiel Bridge (A87) towards Skye; NG8119], *Glenelg*: Overlooking Skye across own beach and sea loch; bright cheery public bar/snack bar with blazing fire even in summer, plain solid furnishings, pool table, piped music, homely pictures; good simple fresh food, lots of whiskies, decent wine list, fine set menu in nice restaurant, tables on terrace; steep, narrow road to inn has spectacular views of Loch Duich – there's a short summer ferry crossing from Skye, too; bedrooms good, superb views *(Peter Watkins, Pam Stanley, J G Wilkinson, Mr and Mrs C Nethercott)*

Grantown on Spey [NJ0328], *Strathspey*: Warm and friendly, with log fire, pleasant food, efficient friendly service, good mix of tourists and locals; keg beer *(A P Jeffreys)*

Inverness [Academy St; NH6645], *Blackfriars*: Pleasant local atmosphere, good service *(Dr Paul McGowan)*; [Ness Bank Rd], *Nicky Tams*: Part of hotel, McEwans 80/- and guests such as Crown Buckleys and Ushers Foundation, tasty bar food, good restaurant *(Gerry Z Pearson)*

Kilchoan [W Ardnamurchan; NM4864], *Sonachan*: Plain but spotless bar and lounge, cheerful prompt service, wide choice of well cooked food, well stocked bar; most westerly point on mainland; bedrooms *(I S Thomson)*

☆ **Kinlochewe** [NH0262], *Kinlochewe*: Welcoming public bar and lounge, good food from toasties and ploughman's up, open fire, piped classical music, Tennents 80/-; stupendous scenery all around, especially Loch Maree and Torridon mountains; attractive bedrooms *(N C Walker, Jeanne and Tom Barnes)*

☆ **Kylesku** [A894; S side of former ferry crossing; NC2234], *Kylesku*: Useful for this remote NW coast (but in winter open only weekends, just for drinks), rather spartan but pleasant local bar (unusual in facing the glorious view), helpful service, short choice of reasonably priced good local seafood, also sandwiches and soup; restaurant, five comfortable and peaceful if basic bedrooms, good breakfast; boatman does good loch trips *(Jeanne and Tom Barnes, MS, G Washington, Christopher Beadle)*

☆ **Melvich** [A836; NC8765], *Melvich*: Good food inc fresh wild salmon in civilised lounge bar or restaurant, relaxed atmosphere, friendly staff, peat or log fire; lovely spot, beautiful sea and coast views; bedrooms *(Alan Wilcock, Christine Davidson)*

☆ **Plockton** [Innes St; NG8033], *Creag Nan Darach*: Fresh well cooked food with real chips and veg done just right, McEwans 80/-, good service; comfortable bedrooms *(John and Molly Knowles, David and Margaret Bloomfield)*

☆ **Spean Bridge** [A82 7 miles N; NN2491], *Letterfinlay Lodge*: Well established hotel, extensive comfortably modern main bar with popular lunchtime buffet and usual games, small smart cocktail bar, no-smoking restaurant; good malt whiskies, friendly service, children and dogs welcome, pleasant lochside grounds, own boats for fishing; clean and comfortable bedrooms, good breakfasts; gents' have good showers and hairdryers – handy for Caledonian Canal sailors *(P G Topp, Christine and Malcolm Ingram, Jeanne and Tom Barnes, Tony and Joan Walker)*

Strathcarron [NG9442], *Strathcarron*: Reasonably priced traditional bar food, well kept real ales introduced by English owner;

bedrooms *(N C Walker)*

Strathy [A836 Trugue—Thurso; NC8365], *Strathy*: Simple but pleasant and welcoming small bars, Tennents 80/-, decent if limited freshly prepared bar food, restaurant, reasonable prices; bedrooms small but comfortable and clean *(E A George, Paul and Ursula Randall)*

Tongue [A836; NC5957], *Ben Loyal*: Lovely views up to Ben Loyal and out over Kyle of Tongue, good value bar meals (stop 2 prompt), Tennents 80/-, fresh local (even home-grown) food in restaurant; traditional live music in lounge bar in summer; comfortable good value bedrooms *(Alan Wilcock, Christine Davidson, E A George)*

LOTHIAN

☆ **Aberlady** [Main St; A198 towards Edinburgh; NT4679], *Wagon*: Very attractive friendly and well run bar and restaurant, distant sea and Fife views from airy high-ceilinged back extension and tables in clematis-sheltered yard, wide range of decent food in bar and restaurant, well kept McEwans 80/-, reasonable wine list *(Ian Phillips, LYM)*

Aberlady [off A198 E], *Green Craigh*: Very pleasant surroundings and staff, good food inc venison casserole, tasty puddings and cheese; bedrooms *(John Dunford)*

Champany [NT0279], *Champany*: Group of converted farm buildings, more restaurant than pub (and packed every night), but does have Belhaven real ales as well as good food (inc delectable puddings); good service *(Gerry Z Pearson)*

☆ **Cramond** [Cramond Glebe Rd; NT1876], *Cramond*: Reopened by Sam Smiths with emphasis on dining, traditional English furnishing and Scottish artefacts, little rooms with bric-a-brac, good coal and log fires, good well priced food, service and atmosphere; very popular with retired couples at lunchtime *(EPG, LYM)*

☆ **Cramond Bridge** [A90 N of Edinburgh; NT1875], *Cramond Brig*: Well run family stop done out in neo-Victorian books style, with family rooms, play area, video and children's menu; bar food all day, well kept McEwans 80/-, restaurant, helpful staff; bedrooms *(Robert and Gladys Flux, Brian and Louisa Routledge, LYM)*

☆ **Dirleton** [village green; NT5184], *Castle*: Good helpings of imaginative reasonably priced food esp fish and well filled sandwiches, well kept ales such as Belhaven or McEwans 80/-, pleasant unpretentious but comfortable lounge; friendly service, restaurant; attractive spot in pretty village on green opp castle, tables in garden; bedrooms *(Ian Phillips)*

☆ **Dirleton**, *Open Arms*: Small comfortable hotel, not a place for just a drink, but good for bar food inc huge open sandwiches and well presented hot dishes such as tender venison casserole with good fresh veg; welcoming service, lovely little sitting room with good open fire, fine position facing castle; comfortable bedrooms *(Ian Phillips)*

Dunbar [NT6878], *Eagle*: Cheap and civil pub, popular basic food, well priced wine *(Frank Davidson)*

☆ **East Linton** [5 Bridge St; NT5977], *Drovers*: Friendly helpful service and good imaginative bistro-style food inc fresh local fish and well cooked veg in small and attractive cleanly renovated pub dating back to 18th century; interesting changing well kept real ales, unusual decor, upstairs restaurant *(R J Archbold, W F Coghill)*

☆ **Edinburgh** [James Ct; by 495 Lawnmarket], *Jolly Judge*: Good atmosphere in interesting and comfortable basement of 16th-c tenement, traditional fruit-and-flower-painted wooden ceiling, quickly served lunchtime bar meals and afternoon snacks, Caledonian 80/- and Ind Coope Burton on handpump, changing malt whiskies, hot drinks, friendly service, lovely fire; piped music, games machine; children allowed at lunchtime in eating area; cl Sun lunchtime; space outside in summer *(Mr and Mrs S Ashcroft, Ian Phillips, Mark Walker, LYM)*

☆ **Edinburgh** [The Causeway, out below Arthurs Seat at Duddingston], *Sheep Heid*: Old-fashioned rather upmarket ex-coaching inn in lovely spot beyond Holyroodhouse, relaxed pubby atmosphere, interesting pictures and fine rounded bar counter in main room, well kept Caledonian 80/-, Bass and Worthington BB, newspapers, children allowed; piped music; restaurant, pretty garden with summer barbecues, skittle alley; open all day, can get crowded *(Ian Phillips, Mark Walker, Brian and Anna Marsden, LYM)*

☆ **Edinburgh** [8 Leven St], *Bennets*: Elaborate Victorian bar with lots of ornate ornamentation to admire, well kept Caledonian 70/-, S & N and other ales from tall founts, bar snacks and simple lunchtime hot dishes, children allowed in eating area lunchtime; open all day, cl Sun lunchtime *(Jon Wood, LYM)*

☆ **Edinburgh** [Rose St, corner of Hanover St], *Milnes*: Large bar with another downstairs, dark wood, bare floorboards, cask tables and old-fashioned decor; lots of S & N real ales with a guest or two such as Burton Bridge and Marstons Pedigree, good range of snacks and hot food (not Sun evening) inc various pies charged by size; very busy but cheerful quick aproned staff; mixed customers, lively atmosphere *(Jim Penman, Spider Newth)*

☆ **Edinburgh** [Lindsay Rd, Newhaven], *Peacock*: Good food esp fresh seafood in smart, stylish and plushly comfortable pub with conservatory-style back room leading to garden, well kept McEwans 80/-; very popular, best to book evenings and Sun lunchtime; open all day; children welcome *(David Logan, LYM)*

☆ **Edinburgh** [55 Rose St], *Rose Street Brewery*: Malt-extract beer brewed on the premises, mild-flavoured though quite potent Auld Reekie 80/- and stronger Sticky 90/- ; tiny brewery can be seen from upstairs lounge (cl at quiet times); back-to-basics downstairs bar open all day, with well reproduced pop music from its CD juke box, machines; usual bar food, good service, tea and coffee, live music some evenings *(Nick and Meriel Cox, Liz and Benton Jennings, Walter Reid, Mark Walker, Bill and Lydia Ryan, David Warrellow, BB)*

Edinburgh [1 Princes St], *Balmoral*: By no means a pub, but this corner lobby of the former North British Hotel is a relaxing refuge, with deep armchairs, welcoming staff, good hot rolls filled with daily roast (not cheap); piped music a bit redundant; bedrooms *(Walter M Reid, Mark Walker, Jim Penman)*; [18-20 Grassmarket], *Beehive*: Civilised comfortable lounge with good range of well kept ales, cheerful atmosphere, good value food noon-6pm, upstairs restaurant *(John Fazakerley, Bill and Lydia Ryan, P Woodward, LYM)*; [27 William St], *Berts Bar*: Well kept ales such as Caledonian 80/-, Timothy Taylors, good range of tasty straightforward food inc vegetarian *(Jon Wood)*; [96 Grassmarket], *Biddy Milligans*: Busy Irish bar with well kept Caledonian 80/- and Deuchars (also Kilkenny Irish), interesting tasty bar food, pleasant staff, quaint decor, piped Irish jokes in lavatories (wonderful tiles in gents'); live music Sun *(Arthur Mustard, W D Christian)*; [50 West Port], *Braidwoods*: Site of first organised fire service, name commemorates first chief officer, lots of fire brigade memorabilia, good generous hot bar food, well kept McEwans 80/-; plenty of room downstairs, verandah bar upstairs *(W D Christian)*; [Young St], *Cambridge*: Small quiet rooms, Caledonian Deuchars and Tetleys-related ales, decent snacks, daily papers, dominoes *(Walter Reid, Ian Phillips)*; [Cumberland St], *Cumberland*: Charming old-fashioned pubby decor, good range of well kept real ales, decent malt whiskies, friendly staff, pleasant atmosphere *(John Wallace)*; [435 Lawnmarket], *Deacon Brodies*: Entertainingly commemorating the notorious highwayman town councillor who was eventually hanged on the scaffold he'd designed; limited decent food inc some unusual home-made dishes, Arrols 80/-, comfortable leather-chair upstairs lounge *(Thomas Nott, Mark Walker, BB)*; [19 Cockburn St], *Drew Nicols*: Well kept Caledonian Deuchars and other changing ales, genial ex-chef landlord, decent food, small bar with horse-racing theme *(Tim Steward)*; [Royal Mile], *Ensign Ewart*: Comfortable old-world pub handy for Castle, lots of interesting memorabilia relating to Ewart and Waterloo, Alloa, Caledonian 80/-, Deuchars IPA, Orkney Dark Island, wide range of whiskies, usual food lunchtime and some summer evenings; juke box, fruit machine, folk music Thurs/Sun *(Mark Walker, Liz and Benton Jennings)*; [3 The Shore, Leith], *Fishers*: Decent food, good atmosphere *(Sena Benson-Arb)*; [31 Wrights Houses], *Golf*: Dating from 1456 though does not seem old, on edge of Bruntisfield Links (where golf first played here); good atmosphere, consistently good food all day, Theakstons Best, McEwans 80/- and two other beers on handpump, leather chesterfields, newspapers, moderate prices, prompt friendly service, upstairs restaurant *(Christine and Malcolm Ingram, Mark Walker, BB)*; [Rose St], *Gordon Arms*: Popular basic small local, friendly attentive staff, Caledonian 80/-, snacks such as pies, two TVs on different stations *(Mark Walker)*; [152 Rose St], *Kenilworth*: Friendly Edwardian pub with ornate high ceiling, carved woodwork, etched mirrors and windows, not many seats; central bar with Tetleys-related and a guest ale, hot drinks inc espresso, good generous bar food lunchtime and evening, quick friendly service, back family room; piped music may obtrude, games machine, TV; space outside in summer, open all day *(Ian Phillips, John Fazakerley, Mark Walker, Spider Newth, LYM)*; [74 Grassmarket], *Last Drop*: Lots of atmosphere, limited evening food, well kept beer, good staff *(Ian Phillips)*; [Cockburn St], *Malt Shovel*: Refurbished with lots of panelling, long serving bar (less seating), Caledonian 60/-, 70/- and 80/-, Broughton Greenmantle, Orkney Dark Island and Tetleys, good value basic food popular with students; piped music, machines, TV, occasional folk music *(Bill and Lydia Ryan, Richard Lewis)*; [8 Young St], *Oxford*: Unspoiled town pub with great landlady, busy friendly front bar, quieter back room, lino floor, Belhaven, Courage and St Andrews real ales, mutton pies, pickled eggs, Forfar bridies, lots of interesting characters; not unlike the nearby Cambridge – see above *(John A Baker, Walter Reid)*; [Rose St], *Paddys*: Fair-sized open-plan pub with friendly service and locals, lunchtime food, Arrols 80/- *(Jim Penman, Mark Walker)*; [Dalkeith Rd], *Physician & Firkin*: Big rooms with old medical charts and posters, brewing its own good Dogbolter and two other beers in brewhouse visible from bar; friendly staff, reasonably priced wholesome straightforward food; popular with students *(Ian Abernethy)*; [Royal Mile], *Royal Mile Tavern*: Plush comfortable lounge bar, friendly service, McEwans 80/- on tall fount and a guest ale, good reasonably priced food in upstairs restaurant, snacks in bar; piped music, fruit machine *(Mark Walker)*; [26 The Shore, Leith], *Ship on the Shore*: Good slightly bohemian unpretentious atmosphere, friendly staff, innovative rather Franco-Scottish food; on docks close to water *(Bryan Phillips, John Whitley)*

Fala [Blackshiels, A68 S of Edinburgh; NT4461], *Juniperlea*: Spacious old inn with mainly orange/brown decor (makes a change from red), well priced good home-cooked bar food, restaurant *(Dorothy and David Young)*

North Berwick [Westgate; NT5485], *Quarter Deck*: Good home-made food with succulent veg, lots of foreign bottled beers, nautical charts and brass diver's helmet in back lounge; front dominated by pool table, TV and juke box *(Ian Phillips)*

North Middleton [off A7 S of Gorebridge; NT3659], *Middleton*: Good welcoming atmosphere, wide choice of good sensibly priced food, concerned management; tables in garden *(Mr and Mrs G Arbib)*

☆ **Queensferry** [South Queensferry; NT1278], *Hawes*: Comfortably modernised lounge bar with fine views of the Forth bridges, featured famously in *Kidnapped*; good choice of good value standard food from efficient food counter, well kept Arrols 80/-, Ind Coope Burton and guest beers such as Caledonian 80/- from tall founts, games in small public bar, no-smoking family room, restaurant, children welcome; tables on back lawn with play area; bedrooms *(Ian Phillips, Robert and Gladys Flux, Mark Walker, LYM)*

☆ **Ratho** [NT1370], *Bridge*: Extended 18th-c pub open all day from noon, enjoyed by all ages, decent range of food inc vegetarian, good children's dishes and tactful choice of food for those with smaller appetites, well kept Belhaven, pleasant helpful and chatty staff; garden by partly restored Union Canal, good well stocked play area, own canal boats (doing trips for the disabled, among others) *(Dave Irving, Roger Bellingham)*

STRATHCLYDE

☆ **Ardentinny** [NS1887], *Ardentinny Hotel*: Comfortable family hotel with lovely views of Loch Long from waterside bars and garden (dogs allowed out here), friendly helpful staff, consistently good often inventive home-made bar food inc local seafood, Belhaven ale, own moorings, Harry Lauder bar with appropriate memorabilia; no-smoking evening restaurant, children allowed in eating area; decent bedrooms, cl winter *(Michael and Harriet Robinson, Walter Reid, Karen Kalaway, Ian and Deborah Carrington, LYM)*

Ballantrae [NX0882], *Kings Arms*: Friendly pub with well kept Tetleys-related ales, tasty well priced food in restaurant *(Dr Brian Hamilton)*

Balloch [Balloch Rd, just N of A811; NS3881], *Balloch Hotel*: Very pleasant atmosphere, helpful barman, wide choice of decent ales inc well kept Caledonian 80/-; big bar broken up by pillars and many small tables, scattering of fish tackle on walls; bedrooms *(Dave Irving)*

Barrhead [Glasgow Rd, The Hurlet; NS5058], *Waterside*: Tastefully redecorated, with good value-for-money food in bar and restaurant *(Rona and Eric Walker)*

Bellshill [Main St; NS7360], *Gates*: Enjoyable local *(Paul McKeen)*

Bishopton [Main St (A8); NS4371], *Golf*: Adventurous and unusual range of beers inc Schiehallion (new to us), good atmosphere, welcoming landlord *(Walter Reid)*

☆ **Bothwell** [27 Hamilton Rd (B7071); a mile from M74 junction 5, via A725; NS7058], *Cricklewood*: Smartly refurbished dining pub with good bar food, S & N real ale, pleasant restful atmosphere, neat decorations inc old carved wooden trade signs on stairway, complete sets of cigarette cards in gents'; open all day; bedrooms *(G Washington)*

Cairnbaan [NR8390], *Cairnbaan*: Much extended old canalside inn, lots of maritime activity to be observed; redecoration gives a slightly urban feel, though still has attractive bare boards and restful green walls *(Walter Reid)*

Cairndow [NN1810], *Cairndow*: Nice setting, friendly locals, good food, lochside garden on loch shore; bedrooms *(Dr Pete Crawshaw)*

Carnwath [A721 E of Carstairs; NS9846], *Wee Bush*: Old thatched inn with stone floors, good food such as herring in mustard sauce or venison and chicken, Tennents 70/-; Burns wrote Better a Wee Buss Than Nae Bield outside *(Dave Braisted)*

☆ **Connel** [North Connel; NM9134], *Lochnell Arms*: Attractive hotel with cosy public bar, small lounge, conservatory extension; decent straightforward food inc good seafood, friendly service, bric-a-brac, plants, beautiful view over Loch Etive; waterside garden; bedrooms *(Jean and Douglas Troup)*

Dalry [NS2949], *Clachan*: Very welcoming licensees, decent food *(Wendy R Crutsinger)*

East Kilbride [Strathaven Rd; NS6354], *New Farm*: Good atmosphere, good choice of real ales, decent food, friendly staff, no piped music; warm, roomy and clean *(George Moody)*

Ford [B840, end of Loch Awe; NM8603], *Ford*: Anglers' pub in tiny village, good atmosphere and lots of photographs of customers with prize catches in traditional bar, snug bar with piped fiddle music, food esp fresh trout, tea; fishing permits; bedrooms *(Vicky and David Sarti)*

Gateside [the one nr Beith; NS3653], *Gateside*: Cosy village inn with banquette seating, exposed stone and panelling, Aitkens and Greenmantle beers *(Walter Reid)*

☆ **Glasgow** [12 Ashton Lane], *Ubiquitous Chip*: Great atmosphere, minimal decoration apart from some stained glass, real ale, wide choice of malt whiskies, some decent wines by the glass, daily changing home-cooked lunchtime food in upstairs dining area inc vegetarian dishes, peat fire; wider choice in downstairs restaurant opening on to courtyard, with outstanding wines; often packed with lots of university staff and students *(Walter Reid, Ian Phillips)*

Glasgow [Byres Rd], *Aragon*: Very pubby, pleasant decor, lots of well kept S & N ales with a guest beer; quite small and friendly, pleasant and unintimidating *(S Crosier)*; [445 Gt Western Rd], *Big Blue*: Relatively new, friendly atmosphere, good up-to-date decor, decent food, nice choice of music *(Mark Billington)*; [154 Hope St], *Cask & Still*: Formerly the Pot Still, popular lunchtime dining pub (menu limited evenings) with well kept beers inc unusual guests such as Adnams Mayday, Chatterley Wheat Beer and Hambleton Goldfields; huge range of malt whiskies *(Mike and Penny Sanders, LYM)*; [16 Algie St], *Church on the Hill*: Converted church now a busy bar; good food, fast efficient service *(Calum and Susan Maclean)*; [93 St Vincent St], *Drum & Monkey*: Great atmosphere esp lunchtime, good quick friendly and helpful food service, magnificent home-made smoked fish soup and great mince and tatties – cheap and very filling; former bank *(Mike Beiley)*; [Woodlands Rd], *Halt*: Poised between Sauchiehall St and University, unpretentious mix of Glasgow's old and new, good choice of malt whiskies, local beers, nightly live music from traditional to classical *(Dave Sobel)*; [Dumbarton Rd, by Kelvin Hall arena], *Hogshead*: Wide choice of well kept ales on handpump or tapped from cask, friendly service, well reproduced piped blues music, games machines; can get busy *(Alastair Campbell)*; [23 Ashton Lane], *Jinty McGuintys*: Very Irish, with live traditional music, Irish poet decorations, Guinness of course, friendly staff, great atmosphere; good small unusual restaurant upstairs *(John Lynch)*; [Gt Western Rd/Kelvin Way], *Ma Hubbards*: Converted bakery with bare boards, lots of little nooks and crannies, pleasant chatty atmosphere, good choice of well kept guest beers such as Titanic Lifeboat *(Alan and Paula McCully)*; [12 Brunswick St], *Mitre*: Unspoilt, a genuine free house, tiny bar with real ales and unusual Belgian and other bottled beers; cl Sun *(Ross Hunter)*; [11 Exchange Pl], *Rogano*: Not a pub, but a fine drinking place, lovingly restored and preserved 1930s art deco interior, good cocktails in ground-floor oyster bar (Guinness too), good well priced wines; good if slightly pricy restaurant, downstairs cafe cheaper but good too – emphasis on fish *(Walter Reid)*; [Sauchiehall St], *Shennanigans*: Wide choice of food all day, wide choice of beers and whisky, welcoming staff, very enjoyable watching the world go by; gets very busy evening *(Calum and Susan Maclean)*; [Airport], *Tap & Spile*: Outstanding as an airport bar, traditional pub elements blended with good use of space and light to create bright yet peaceful atmosphere; well kept Arrols 80/- and several changing guest beers such as Caledonian, Greenmantle and Ind Coope Burton, decent malt whiskies inc regular promotions, good snacks inc fresh tasty sandwiches, no-smoking area *(Walter Reid, Alan and Paula McCully, Mike and Penny Sanders)*; [Byres Rd], *Tennents*: Big busy high-ceilinged pub with Caledonian 70/- or 80/-, Greenmantle, Theakstons Best and lots of interesting changing guest ales, also plenty of good malt whiskies; cheerful atmosphere, usual bar food *(S Crosier, Michael Hanna)*; [63 Trongate], *Tron*: Good theatre bar with decent food *(Stewart Steel)*; [232 Woodlands Rd], *Uisge Beatha*: Pleasant dimly lit bar with fine choice of malt whiskies *(Stuart McCulloch)*; [Bridgegate], *Victoria*: Well worn long narrow bar, very warm and friendly, with plenty of old panelling and theatrical connections; Maclays 70/-, cheap snacks *(Alan and Paula McCully)*

Glendaruel [NR9985], *Glendaruel*: Plain but friendly, in lovely countryside; bar meals, small lounge, separate bar with darts; outside seats *(Diane Devine, Walter Reid)*

☆ **Houston** [Main St; NS4166], *Fox & Hounds*: Comfortable village pub with exceptional quick friendly service, good atmosphere (busy evening, quieter daytime), well kept Greenmantle and McEwans 70/-, clean plush hunting-theme lounge, comfortable seats by fire, wide range of food upstairs, good filled rolls downstairs, also sophisticated restaurant; separate livelier bar with video juke box and pool; open all day *(Walter Reid, Angus Lyon, Calum and Susan Maclean)*

☆ **Inveraray** [Main St E; NN0908], *George*: Pleasant old-fashioned pub, very popular locally, interesting old Highland feel to friendly low-beamed public bar with real fires, stone walls and fine flagstones; Tennents 80/-, good choice of whiskies, bar games, good value pub food served noon to 9pm; children welcome; bedrooms reasonably priced *(Capt E P Gray, Dr and Mrs Peter Kemp)*

Inveraray, *Great Inn*: Stately old-fashioned hotel overlooking Loch Fyne (especially spacious front conservatory), good choice of bar food and malts, maybe one or two real ales, games in public bar, restaurant; well run, a nice place to stay; open all day *(Liz and Benton Jennings, LYM)*

Irvine [Harbour St; NS3739], *Keys*: Recently modernised, overlooking harbour; good atmosphere, warmly welcoming staff, good food (all day Sat/Sun) *(Calum and Susan Maclean)*; [Harbour St], *Ship*: Modernised 1800s pub keeping character, old beams, flagstones, wooden tables, good food and service; charcoal impression of how the pub and harbour used to look on ceiling *(Calum and Susan Maclean)*; [32 Eglinton St], *Turf*: Welcoming, with blazing coal fires, good value bar snacks; pool room *(Calum and Susan Maclean)*

☆ **Johnstone** [High St; NS4263], *Coanes*: Thriving atmosphere in old-fashioned oak-balustered bar with enterprising range of well kept real ales, good malt whiskies inc malt of the month, good friendly staff, above-average food; larger plush lounge popular with young *(Walter Reid)*

Kames [NR9671], *Kames*: Attractive and well done up, food all day, real ale, pleasant games area with darts, pool etc; beautiful view over Kyles of Bute; bedrooms *(Diane Devine)*

Kilchrenan [B845 7 miles S of Taynuilt; NN0322], *Taychreggan*: Smart and airy hotel bar with easy chairs and banquettes around low glass-topped tables, stuffed birds and fish and good local photographs; wide range of reasonably priced and well served lunchtime bar food inc local fish, well kept beers (bar service stops 2), polite efficient staff, Sun lunch in no-smoking dining room, unusual lochside garden (good fishing), pretty inner courtyard, children welcome; cl Nov-March, comfortable bedrooms *(Revd A Nunnerley, LYM)*

☆ **Kilmelford** [NM8412], *Cuilfail*: Enthusiastically and ably run attractice former coaching inn in attractive setting, cheerful stripped-stone pubby bar, welcoming family service, good value often imaginative food in inner eating room with light wood furnishings, well kept McEwans and Youngers No 3, good range of malt whiskies, charming garden across road; comfortable bedrooms *(Walter Reid, LYM)*

Langbank [NS3873], *Langbank Lodge*: Incredible Clyde views from well designed split-level place with wide range of food, lots of modern wooden beams – rather Austrian/Swiss in feel; keen young staff *(Ian Phillips)*

Lochwinnoch [Main St; NS3558], *Brown Bull*: Traditional village inn restored with restraint, good range of weekly changing real ales, decent wines and whiskies, exposed stonework *(Walter Reid)*; [Lares Rd], *Mossend*: Brewers Fayre family dining pub with reliable efficiently served food, four well kept changing ales from the Whitbreads portfolio, periodic beer festivals; playground, good walking area *(Tom McEwan, Walter Reid)*

Luss [A82 about 3 miles N; NS3593], *Inverbeg*: Across road from Loch Lomond, lounge often crowded for decent straightforward waitress-served food (also restaurant), well kept real ales, games in simple public bar; bedrooms *(D J Atkinson, LYM)*

Paisley [Glasgow Rd; NS4864], *Anchor*: Good lunchtime food (till 3), friendly staff; busy *(Calum and Susan Maclean)*; [New St], *Bull*: Noted Art Nouveau facade, pleasant if lively inside, old local photographs, real ale *(Leith Stuart)*; [4 Causewayside St], *Hamiltons*: Reasonably priced good food and good atmosphere in bar-style diner *(Calum and Susan Maclean)*

Sorn [NS5526], *Sorn*: Very friendly family-run inn in conservation village, good food, helpful staff; bedrooms comfortable *(A N Ellis)*

☆ **Symington** [Main St; just off A77 Ayr—Kilmarnock; NS3831], *Wheatsheaf*: Charming and cosy 18th-c pub in pretty village, consistently good original food esp fish and local produce, Belhaven beers, friendly quick service; tables in garden *(Christine and Malcolm Ingram, Walter Reid, DMT)*

Tarbert [A82/A83; NR8467], *Tarbert Hotel*: Good atmosphere and coal fires in warm welcoming public bar, atmospheric and quaint; good basic bar food, lovely harbour view; bedrooms comfortable, with good breakfast *(Calum and Susan Maclean)*; [Bardmore Rd], *Victoria*: Friendly and efficient pub overlooking harbour, imaginative well prepared food *(Mrs Pat Crabb, Calum and Susan Maclean)*; [A83 a mile S], *West Loch*: Enthusiastically decorated and immaculately kept old inn overlooking sea loch, convenient for Islay ferry; McEwans beers, good choice of reasonably priced food in bar and restaurant inc interesting dishes and emphasis on local seafood, friendly service; bedrooms *(Deborah and Ian Carrington, Walter Reid, LYM)*

☆ **Taynuilt** [a mile past village, which is signed off A85; NN0030], *Polfearn*: Pleasant lounge bar with picture windows making most of setting by loch with Ben Cruachan towering over, well kept beers, relaxed atmosphere, welcoming landlord, good food esp local mussels and fish soup; bedrooms *(Revd A Nunnerley)*

TAYSIDE

Alyth [NO2548], *Alyth*: Family run 18th-c hotel overlooking river, decent food, obliging owners, good range of malt whiskies, home-cooked food in bar and restaurant inc wild salmon, teas and high teas (home-baked bread); folk music last Fri of month; bedrooms *(Anon)*

☆ **Bridge of Cally** [NO1451], *Bridge of Cally*: Good atmosphere in straightforward friendly and comfortable bar, sensible choice of good value food inc outstanding ploughman's; bedrooms, attractive area *(Ian Rorison)*

☆ **Broughty Ferry** [behind lifeboat stn; NO4630], *Ship*: Consistently good generous food in pretty nautical-theme upstairs dining room with fantastic view; downstairs bar handsomely refurbished in burgundy and dark wood, stately model sailing ship; very friendly *(Susan and John Douglas)*

Crieff [N, signed off A85, A822; NN8562], *Glenturret Distillery*: Not a pub, but good adjunct to one of the best whisky-distillery tours; good value whiskies in big country-style bar/dining area overlooking countryside, with tasty sandwiches, good generous Highland soups, stews, pies and knock-out Glenturret ice cream from self-service food counter – alas, has been known to slow to a crawl *(R M Macnaughton, Susan and John Douglas, Joyce and Stephen Stackhouse)*

☆ **Dundee** [Brook St; NO4030], *Royal Oak*: Friendly and unusual, with sombre dark green decor and surprising range of interesting reasonably priced food esp curries in bar and restaurant; well kept Tetleys-related ales, courteous friendly staff *(Neil Townend, Paul and Ursula Randall)*

Dundee [Westport], *Mickey Coyles*: Student-type pub, less busy out of term, good value bar food, good range of beers inc well kept Greenmantle *(Mr and Mrs Fyall)*; [10 South Tay St], *Number Ten Lounge*: Fresh stylish dark green decor, attractive framed prints, smart lively meeting place, popular with young people – crowded Fri evening; now has adjoining restaurant *(Susan and John Douglas)*

Dunkeld [NO0243], *Atholl Arms*: Nice old-fashioned country hotel with decent food in relaxing lounge bar, welcoming owners; keg beer; bedrooms *(Walter Reid)*

Dunkeld [NO0243], *Royal Dunkeld*: Ancient fishermen's/coaching hotel, extensively modernised in last decade, with changing real ales, good bar food, and well cooked and imaginative affordable food in restaurant/carvery; delightful small historic town; 35 comfortable well equipped bedrooms *(Paul Randall)*

☆ **Errol** [The Cross; NO2523], *Old Smiddy*: Unusual food putting an interesting twist on fresh local ingredients, well kept Belhaven 80/-, lots of country wines, attractive heavy-beamed bar with assorted old country furniture, lots of farm and smithy tools inc massive bellows; open all day Sun, cl Mon/Tues lunchtime *(Susan and John Douglas)*

Glen Clova [NO3373], *Clova*: Very remote basic public bar popular with walkers and climbers; welcoming staff, well kept beers, popular food *(Nick and Meriel Cox)*

☆ **Kenmore** [NN7745], *Kenmore Hotel*: Civilised and quietly old-fashioned small hotel beautifully set in very pretty 18th-c village by Loch Tay, long landscape poem composed here written in Burns' own handwriting on residents' lounge chimneybreast, clean, friendly and smart back bar, lively separate barn bar, lovely views from back terrace; good bar food, helpful staff, restaurant, Tay fishing, fine walks; comfortable bedrooms *(Susan and John Douglas, Walter Reid, M E and G R Keene, LYM)*

Kinnesswood [NO1703], *Lomond*: Good value set menu strong on fresh local produce, well kept Belhaven and Jennings beers; bedrooms comfortable *(Andy and Jill Kassube)*

☆ **Kinross** [49 The Muirs; NO1102], *Muirs*: Extended and refurbished in restrained traditional manner, small plain standing bar with rare original Edwardian bar fittings and mirrors, second panelled bar with small pot still, lounge and supper room with banquettes; good traditional Scottish food and up to eight well kept ales such as Belhaven, Caledonian, Greenmantle and Orkney Dark Island, superb choice of malt whiskies, interesting bottled beers; lavatory for the disabled; bedrooms *(Andy and Jill Kassube)*

Kinross [20 High St], *Kirklands*: Friendly welcome, good value basic bar food, well kept Maclays 70/- and 80/- and a guest beer; bedrooms comfortable and reasonably priced *(Andy and Jill Kassube)*

Meikleour [on A984; NO1539], *Meikleour*: Two lounges, one with stripped stone, flagstones and armour, another more chintzy, both with open fires (shame about the fruit machines); good bar food inc fine range of open sandwiches, well kept Maclays 70/-, back public bar; charming garden with tall pines and distant Highland view; nr famous 100ft beech hedge planted in 1746 *(Walter Reid, Susan and John Douglas)*

☆ **Memus** [NO4259], *Drovers*: Small friendly pub with Maclays IPA, McEwans 80/- and Oatmeal Stout on tall fount, choice of wines and whiskies, roaring old-fashioned fire, good well balanced menu with imaginative starters and puddings, also fish, game, meat and daily vegetarian dish, pleasant service in small dining area which can be busy *(P Burvill, Nick and Meriel Cox)*

Montrose [George St; NO7157], *George*: Plush comfortable lounge, open fire, Whitbreads-related ales, good value generous food, back no-smoking area, adjoining restaurant; piped music, TV; bedrooms *(Mark Walker)*

☆ **Perth** [15 South St; NO1123], *Greyfriars*: Welcoming simply decorated bar with unusual guest beers on handpump, reasonably priced bar food, daily papers, prints of Perth; small restaurant upstairs *(Julian Holland, Walter Reid)*

Stanley [NO1033], *Tayside*: Welcoming fishing hotel with photographs of remarkable catches in banquette-lined bar, remarkable stuffed fish in the hall, decent food *(Walter Reid)*

THE ISLANDS

Gigha

Gigha [NR6450], *Gigha Hotel*: Well kept, nicely furnished and clean, in lovely spot overlooking the Sound and Kintyre; pine-decor public bar, sofas in drawing-room bar, good service; bedrooms *(Margaret and Fred Punter, Mrs Pat Crabb)*

Islay

Ballygrant [A846 Port Askaig—Bridgend; NR3966], *Ballygrant*: Family run with real enthusiasm, good views, good home cooking, maybe a real ale *(Walter Reid)*

Bridgend [NR3362], *Bridgend*: Country house hotel with comfortable tartan-carpet cocktail bar, interesting prints and maps, open fire; fine range of food with commendable emphasis on Scottish dishes; bedrooms *(Walter Reid)*

☆ **Port Askaig** [NR4268], *Port Askaig Hotel*: Glorious sea views, buzz of ferry activity, two basic bars, one a cosy snug, with full range of the island's malt whiskies, good food inc local dishes and produce from the garden, tables out on big stretch of grass; bedrooms, self-catering across road *(Mrs A Storm, Walter Reid)*

Jura

Craighouse [NR5267], *Jura Hotel*: The only licensed premises on Jura but good by any standards, attractive bar with good food, magnificent views to the Small Isles; bedrooms *(Walter Reid)*

North Uist

☆ **Claddach Kirkibost** [NF7766], *Westford*: Very old inn in windswept desolate spot, good original home-made food inc local seafood in two small pine-fitted rooms, enterprising dinner menu; big back public bar, local, traditional music; handy for RSPB reserve at Dalranald, landlord helpful about local walks and archaeology; bedrooms *(Mr MacGwire, Hayes Durlston, Nigel Woolliscroft)*

Orkney

☆ Stromness [HY2509], *Ferry*: Busiest pub here, very popular with locals and diving groups exploring the German fleet in Scapa Flow – so bar can be rather noisy and smoky; wide choice of good fast reasonably piced food inc good fish and steak, adjoining restaurant, McEwans 80/- and Orkney Dark Island, friendly staff and atmosphere; very handy for Scrabster ferry; bedrooms *(Ian, Kathleen and Helen Corsie)*

Skye

Ardvasar [Armadale Pier; NG6203], *Ferry*: Don't be put off by the fact that this looks like a scout hut; music three nights per week, decent straightforward food, S & N real ales *(Dave Braisted)*

Kyleakin [NG7426], *Kyleakin*: Fantastic collection of miniatures in Marine Bar, rowdy set of semi-residents that seem to grow on you; bedrooms *(Dave Braisted)*

Portree [harbourside; NG4843], *Pier*: Down-to-earth fishermen's bar, language to match sometimes, keg beers, restaurant meals fish-based and served in huge helpings; very welcoming landlord, occasional live music, pipers during Skye games week; bedrooms good value *(Nigel Woolliscroft)*

☆ Sligachan [A850 Broadford—Portree, junction with A863; NG4830], *Sligachan Hotel*: Remote inn, capacious, welcoming and comfortable, with well laid-out huge modern bar (children's play area, games room, red telephone box) separating the original basic climbers' and walkers' bar from the plusher more sedate hotel side; well kept McEwans 80/-, quickly served food inc particularly fresh seafood, friendly staff, restaurant; very lively some nights; big campsite opp; bedrooms good value; cl winter *(Ian and Deborah Carrington, Nigel Woolliscroft, James Nunns, David Atkinson, Tom Espley, Peter and Lynn Brueton, John and Elspheth Howell, LYM)*

Uig [Sgitheanach, by ferry terminal; NG3963], *Bacabar*: Unlikely-looking bungalow-style building with pleasant staff, well cooked good value simple food inc fresh local seafood lunchtime and early evening, good choice of whiskies; pool, darts *(Mr and Mrs Craig)*; *Ferry*: Tiny but friendly saloon bar with very comfortable atmosphere, reasonably priced varied food inc good fresh fish; good value bedrooms, comfortable and bright, overlooking pier and water *(Mrs W E Darlaston, John and Elspeth Howell, Nigel Woolliscroft)*

South Uist

Lochboisdale [nr ferry dock; NF7919], *Lochboisdale Hotel*: Good views over sea loch, tasty reasonably priced bar food, good decor, competent friendly staff *(Mr and Mrs Craig)*

Please keep sending us reports. We rely on readers for news of new discoveries, and particularly for news of changes – however slight – at the fully described pubs. No stamp needed: *The Good Pub Guide*, FREEPOST TN1569, Wadhurst, E Sussex TN5 7BR.

Wales

Food in Welsh pubs has taken tremendous strides recently. We have found much more use of fresh ingredients, particularly fish, with ample opportunity to assess the superiority of wild salmon over the farmed sort, brown trout over the usual more corpulent rainbow trout, and fresh local mountain lamb and occasionally even mutton over frozen New Zealand meat. Genuinely Welsh specialities crop up more and more, too, especially cawl, the nourishing national broth, and interesting local cheeses. Imaginative pub cooking has become more widespread, too. For many years the Walnut Tree at Llandewi Skirrid has shown just how far the boundaries of pub food can be pushed. Until recently it was a very lonely outpost of excellence. Though the Walnut Tree is still in a class of its own, and our choice as Welsh Dining Pub of the Year, we can now confidently recommend quite a few other Welsh pubs for really enjoyable meals out, including the Penhelig Arms in Aberdovey, the Olde Bulls Head in Beaumaris, the Ty Gwyn at Betws-y-Coed, the Bear at Crickhowell, the Nantyffin Cider Mill just outside, the Olde Bull at Llanbedr-y-Cennin (excellent specials), the Queens Head near Llandudno Junction, the Griffin at Llyswen, the Clytha Arms near Raglan and the Ship on Red Wharf Bay. A special point for families is that in the Dinorben Arms at Bodfari children eat free if their parents are dining. Another good point is that many Welsh pubs have pegged their food prices in the last year: a shining example is the Parciau Arms at Marianglas, which has actually knocked 20% or so off its food prices. Besides the pubs we've mentioned, ones currently doing specially well include the Halfway Inn on the road to Aberystwyth, the Aleppo Merchant at Carno, the White Horse at Cilcain, the Blue Anchor at East Aberthaw, the Prince of Wales at Kenfig, the Pen-y-Gwryd up above Llanberis, the White Swan at Llanfrynach, the Vine Tree at Llangattock, the Grapes at Maentwrog, the Harp at Old Radnor, the Open Hearth at Pontypool, the Bush at St Hilary, and four places new to this edition (or back among the main entries after a break): the ancient and very friendly Pendre at Cilgerran, the civilised Mountain View near Colwyn Bay, the interesting old Druid in its fine position at Llanferres and (for its unusual range of real ales) the basic Star at Talybont-on-Usk. It's certainly become easier to find interesting well kept ales in Wales, and drinks prices are now a little below the English average. Though pubs tied to small breweries tended to have particularly low prices, we found that pubs here tied to or getting their beers from national combines have held their prices steadier over the last year than other pubs – showing that in Wales price competition is now working well for pubgoers. The Lucky Dip section at the end of the chapter includes a great many pubs particularly worth visiting – too many for us to shortlist here; but we would be particularly grateful for readers' feedback on which deserve most consideration as potential main entries (in helping us to weigh up readers' comments, we should perhaps note that an ounce of factual description is often worth several pounds of 'very goods'!)

ABERDOVEY (Gwynedd) SN6296 Map 6

Penhelig Arms

Opp Penhelig railway station

Most people seem to come to this mainly 18th-c hotel in the summer, when you can sit outside by the harbour wall, and while this is quite understandable, it's a shame more people don't visit in winter too, when the views across the Dyfi estuary are just as dramatic, but the atmosphere is altogether snugger. The small original beamed bar has a warmly cosy feel, cheery locals and winter fires, and changing real ales such as Dartmoor Legend, Greenalls Original, Ind Coope Burton, Tetleys (nicely priced below the Welsh average) or Youngers Scotch on handpump. Food, both in the bar and restaurant, plays a big part here, and you can eat the lunchtime bar food in the restaurant if you prefer: sandwiches (from £1.75), soup (£1.95), smoked chicken roulade (£3.95), omelettes (from £4.50), tortellini with a tomato and basil sauce (£4.95), fresh dressed crab, steak and mushroom pie or home baked ham and eggs (£5.95), fresh salmon (£6.50), plenty of specials such as loin of Welsh lamb (£6.50), brochettes of monkfish with king prawns and garlic mayonnaise (£7.50), or lots more fresh fish, and puddings like chocolate brandy truffle cake or apricot frangipane tart (£2.20); children's helpings. Three-course Sunday lunch (£11.50) in the restaurant. An excellent wine list with over 40 half bottles, two dozen malt whiskies, fruit or peppermint teas, and coffee; friendly, helpful service. *(Recommended by David Wallington, Sue and Bob Ward, Pearl Williams, Christopher Turner, J S M Sheldon)*

Free house ~ Licensees Robert and Sally Hughes ~ Real ale ~ Meals and snacks (no bar food Sun lunchtime or maybe summer evenings, depending on how busy the restaurant is) ~ Restaurant (not Sun evening) ~ (01654) 767215 ~ Children in eating area of bar and restaurant ~ Open 11.30-3, 6-11; closed 25 Dec ~ Bedrooms: £39B/£68B

ABERGORLECH (Dyfed) SN5833 Map 6

Black Lion

B4310 (a pretty road roughly NE of Carmarthen)

Deep in the heart of Wales with accents in the bar to match, this pleasant old black and white pub is well-placed in the beautiful Cothi Valley with the Brechfa Forest around; picnic table sets and wooden seats and benches across the quiet road take in the view. The garden slopes down towards the River Cothi where there's a Roman triple-arched bridge; the licensee has fishing rights and the river is good for trout, salmon and sea trout fishing. The atmospheric stripped-stone bar is traditionally furnished with plain oak tables and chairs, high-backed black settles facing each other across the flagstones by the log-effect gas fire, horsebrasses on the black beams, and some sporting prints; a restaurant extension has light-oak woodwork. Bar food includes sandwiches, soup (£1.75), ploughman's (from £3.25), chicken balti (£4.75), 10oz gammon steak (£5.20), chicken in cranberry and whisky sauce (£5.50), salmon fillet in lobster and brandy sauce (£5.65), steaks (from £6), daily specials, and children's meals; in summer there may be afternoon teas with a selection of home-made cakes, and Saturday barbecues. Well kept Flowers Original and Worthingtons Best on handpump, and Addlestone's cider; good service from friendly licensees and staff. Sensibly placed darts, cribbage, dominoes, trivia, and unobtrusive piped music. Remy the Jack Russell loves to chew up beer mats. Lots of good walks nearby. *(Recommended by John and Joan Nash, Mr and Mrs Bryn Gardner, Patrick Freeman, Helen Crookston, Martin and Pauline Richardson)*

Free house ~ Licensee Mrs Brenda Entwhistle ~ Real ale ~ Meals and snacks (not Mon evenings, and limited Mon lunch) ~ Restaurant (not evening Sun/Mon) ~ (01558) 685271 ~ Children welcome ~ Open 11.30-11; 12-3, 7-10 in winter

Planning a day in the country? We list pubs in really attractive scenery at the back of the book.

nr ABERYSTWYTH (Dyfed) SN6777 Map 6

Halfway Inn ★

Pisgah (NOT the Pisgah near Cardigan); A4120 towards Devil's Bridge, 5¾ miles E of junction with A487

Several hundred feet above sea level, with panoramic views down over the Rheidol Valley, this enchanting old place is full of genuine old-fashioned charm. Unusually, they still let you tap beers such as Charles Wells Bombardier or Shepherd Neame Spitfire from the cask, though they also keep Felinfoel Double Dragon, Flowers Original and Whitbreads Castle Eden on handpump for those who prefer their pints professionally pulled; also, five draught ciders, including Westons Old Rosie, and Welsh wines. Good generously served bar food includes soup (£1.50), filled baked potatoes (from £1.75), sandwiches (from £2.25), leek and double gloucester filo tartlet in a mustard sauce or chicken liver pâté with Cointreau and orange (£3.45), ploughman's (£4.25), spaghetti bolognaise (£4.50), breaded plaice (£4.95), brie and broccoli pithivier (£5.50), home-made chicken, ham and mushroom pie (£6.95), char-grilled Scotch steaks (from £8.50), daily specials like dressed Cardigan bay crab (£4.95) or steak in ale pie (£6.95), home-made puddings such as treacle tart (£2), and children's meals (£2.75); efficient friendly service. The beamed and flagstoned bar has stripped deal tables and settles, bare stone walls, and a dining room/restaurant area where tables can be reserved. Darts, pool and piped music (classical at lunchtimes, popular folk and country in the evenings). Outside, picnic tables under cocktail parasols have fine views of wooded hills and pastures; there's a play area, free overnight camping for customers and a paddock for pony-trekkers. The Friday night live music is good. Bedrooms are comfortable, but watch your head. It's particularly busy in summer, when there may be special events such as sheep shearing contests and Welsh choirs. *(Recommended by Jed and Virginia Brown, John Hazel, John and Joan Nash, Liz and Roger Morgan, Tim and Tina Banks, LD, JD, Gwyneth and Salvo Spadaro-Dutturi, M Joyner)*

Free house ~ Licensees Raywood and Sally Roger ~ Real ale ~ Meals and snacks ~ Restaurant ~ (01970) 880631 ~ Children welcome except in serving bar ~ Live music Fri – jazz, pop or Celtic folk ~ Open 11-11; 11.30-2.30, 6.30-11 winter weekdays ~ Bedrooms: £28B/£38B

BEAUMARIS (Anglesey) SH6076 Map 6

Olde Bulls Head ★

Castle Street

All sorts of people have visited this smartly cosy old inn since it was built in 1472, from the Cromwellian forces who commandeered it during the Civil War, to more genteel figures like Samuel Johnson and Charles Dickens, neither of whom would look particularly out of place here today. The quaintly old-fashioned rambling bar is full of reminders of its long and illustrious past: a rare 17th-c brass water clock, a bloodthirsty crew of cutlasses, even the town's oak ducking stool. There's also lots of copper and china jugs, snug alcoves, low beams, low-seated settles, leather-cushioned window seats and a good open fire. The entrance to the pretty courtyard is closed by the biggest simple hinged door in Britain. Very good daily changing lunchtime bar food might include sandwiches (from £1.60), home-made mushroom and fennel soup (£1.85), good ploughman's with Welsh cheeses (£3.10), smoked chicken and tarragon omelette (£3.95), beef and Guinness casserole or braised pork in a sweet and sour sauce (£4.50), steamed fillet of hake with a prawn and chervil cream sauce or rare roast sirloin salad with pickled walnuts (£4.70), and puddings such as spicy raisin tart or apple flan (£1.75). The no-smoking restaurant does a splendid three-course Sunday lunch (£14.75). Very well kept Bass, Worthington Best and a guest on handpump, a good comprehensive list of over 180 wines (with plenty of half bottles), and freshly squeezed orange juice; cheerful, friendly service. Dominoes, chess, draughts and cards. The charming bedrooms (with lots of nice little extras) are named after characters in Dickens' novels; they've recently added four more.

(Recommended by Andy and Jill Kassube, J R Whetton, J Roy Smylie, Martin and Penny Fletcher, David and Ruth Hollands)

Free house ~ Licensee David Robertson ~ Real ale ~ Lunchtime meals and snacks (not Sun – but restaurant open then) ~ Restaurant ~ (01248) 810329 ~ Children in eating area and restaurant, no under 7s in dining room in evening ~ Open 11-11; closed evening 25 Dec ~ Bedrooms: £43B/£73B

BETWS-Y-COED (Gwynedd) SH7956 Map 6

Ty Gwyn

A5 just S of bridge to village

The atmosphere at this cottagey family-run former coaching inn is very much like that of a private house, and people who come here often do end up feeling like welcome personal guests. The license is such that you can only have a drink if you're eating or staying, but that shouldn't be a problem: the food is imaginative and well presented and it's a delightful place to spend a night or two, well placed for all the area's attractions, but without a touristy feel. Highly regarded by readers, the promptly served dishes from the daily changing menu might include good soup (£1.95), sandwiches (lunchtime only, from £1.95), black pudding with mustard (£2.95), frogs' legs in garlic butter (£3.50), aubergine and mushroom stroganoff or spicy bean tortilla (£5.50), home-made curry or Welsh lamb kebab (£5.95), dressed crab salad (£6.25), chicken stuffed with lobster and prawns or fresh skate (£6.95), fresh Conwy salmon with a dill and dubonnet sauce (£7.95), local pheasant in a beaujolais and wild mushroom sauce (£8.50), and whole fresh lobster thermidor (£15.50); children's menu (highchair and toys available), excellent three-course Sunday lunch (£11.50) and well-liked daily set three-course menu (£16.95). Helpings are generous, and service efficient and unhurried. The bar has an ancient cooking range worked in well at one end and rugs and comfortable chintz easy chairs on its oak parquet floor; Theakstons Best on handpump, maybe two friendly cats. The interesting clutter of unusual old prints and bric-a-brac in the beamed lounge bar reflects the fact that the owners run an antique shop next door. *(Recommended by Barbara and Denis Melling, Mike and Penny Sanders, Phil and Heidi Cook, John and Christine Vittoe, C Smith, KC, Basil J S Minson, Michael J Boniface, Gordon Theaker, Dave and Jules Tuckett, David Heath, Peter and Jenny Quine, J L Moore, Nick Haslewood, Tina and David Woods-Taylor)*

Free house ~ Licensees Jim and Shelagh Ratcliffe ~ Real ale ~ Meals and snacks ~ Restaurant ~ (01690) 710383/710787 ~ Children welcome ~ Open 12-3, 7-11 ~ Bedrooms: £19/£35(£54B)

BODFARI (Clwyd) SJ0970 Map 6

Dinorben Arms ★

From A541 in village, follow Tremeirchion 3 signpost

The ancient well in the bar of this characterful and warmly welcoming place could be the one that, according to local legend, possessed magical qualities. Mothers would dip their babies in the water in the belief that this would stop them from crying at night ever again – though those hoping this trick still works today will find the well has been glassed over. There's an impressive range of drinks: as well as the John Smiths, Ruddles County and Websters Yorkshire on handpump, they keep around 150 whiskies (including the full Macallan range and a good few from the Islay distilleries), plenty of good wines (with several classed growth clarets), vintage ports and cognacs, and a few unusual coffee liqueurs. The good-value eat-as-much-as-you-like smorgasbord counter is still the main draw at lunchtimes (£8.50); other snacks then include home-made vegetable soup, filled rolls, ploughman's, or their popular Chicken Rough (£4.45), with evening meals such as home-made steak and kidney pie (£4.45), vegetarian lasagne (£4.95), salads (from £4.95), fresh grilled salmon or gammon (£5.95), steaks (from £6.95) and specials like welsh-style chicken

(£7.95) or local trout (£8.50). Children eat free if both parents are dining (except on Saturdays). Upstairs, there's a carvery on Friday and Saturday evenings (£12.95) and a good help-yourself hot and cold buffet on Wednesday and Thursday evenings (£8.95). There may be delays at busy times. The three rooms which open off the heart of the carefully extended building have beams hung with tankards and flagons, high shelves of china, old-fashioned settles and other seats, and three open fires; there's also a light and airy garden room. Two parts of the restaurant are no-smoking; piped music. Lots of tables outside on the prettily-landscaped and planted brick-floored terraces, with attractive sheltered corners and charming views, and there's a grassy play area which – like the car park – is neatly sculpted into the slope of the hills. *(Recommended by Mrs J Oakes, David Peakall, KC, Michael and Janet Hepworth, Brian and Jill Bond)*

Free house ~ Licensee David Rowlands ~ Real ale ~ Meals and snacks (12-2.30, 6-10.30, Sun lunchtime only smorgasbord) ~ Restaurant ~ (01745) 710309 ~ Children welcome ~ Open 12-3.30, 6-11

BURTON GREEN (Clwyd) SJ3458 Map6

Golden Grove

Off A483 N of Wrexham: heading N, turn left into B5102 from roundabout, then first right, through Burton, and at T-junction after a little over a mile turn right into Lydir Lane; OS sheet 117 map reference SJ354587

As the directions above indicate, this peaceful and old-fashioned half-timbered 13th-c coaching inn is quite hard to track down, but is well worth the effort; it's the kind of place where everyone is welcomed as though they were a familiar local. Standing timbers and plaster separate the knocked-together rooms, which have two open fires, comfortable settees, settles and copper-topped tables, collections of plates and horsebrasses, figures carved in the beams, and a friendly, relaxed atmosphere. Decent home made bar food might include soup, sandwiches (from £2.25), pies such as steak and kidney or chicken and leek (£5.95), a big mixed grill (£7.95), daily specials, fresh fish, and a Sunday roast (£5.95). A separate restaurant is open Friday and Saturday evenings, though you can generally book a table here and eat the bar food at other times. Well kept Marstons Best and Pedigree on handpump, and quite a few malt whiskies; fruit machine, piped music. Obliging service. The big back streamside garden has a barbecue area and children's adventure playground with lifesize plane, train and ship, climbing frame and bouncy castle. *(Recommended by J R Smylie, Brian and Anna Marsden and others; more reports please)*

Marstons ~ Tenant Christine Morris ~ Real ale ~ Meals and snacks (till 10pm) ~ Restaurant ~ (01244) 570445 ~ Children in eating area ~ Open 12-3, 6-11; 12-11 summer Sats

CAERPHILLY (Mid Glam) ST1484 Map 6

Courthouse

Cardiff Road; one-way system heading N, snugged in by National Westminster Bank – best to park before you get to it

This venerable place has its own dairy, producing the caerphilly you may find in the ploughman's and other dishes. Originally built as a longhouse in the 14th c, the Courthouse still has much of its old character, with the stone walls and roof and the raftered gallery at one end all bearing witness to its age. There are splendid views of the adjacent Castle and its peaceful lake from the tables out on the grassy terrace behind, or from the light and airy modern cafe/bar at the back. The long bar has pews, comfortable cloth-upholstered chairs and window seats, rugs on ancient flagstones, shutters and curtains on thick wooden rails for the small windows and a formidably large stone fireplace. Lunchtime bar food includes home-made soup (£1.40), big filled baguettes (the hot beef is good, £2.20), omelettes or cod (£4.25), tuna and pasta bake, vegetarian nut cutlets or cheese and lentil rissoles (£4.45), chicken with leek and stilton sauce or steak and onion pie (£4.95), a daily lunchtime carvery (from £4.45), and children's meals (from £1.30); on the evenings when they serve food they add dishes like whole trout with almonds and prawns (£5.45) and beef Wellington (£7.95). Part of the eating area is no smoking. Well kept Brains Best, Ruddles Best, Shepherd Neame Spitfire and Wadworths 6X on handpump, good coffee; cribbage, fruit machine and piped pop music (even outside). Note that children may not be allowed even in the garden in the evening. *(Recommended by Barbara Ann Mayer, Rachael Pole, Y M Rees, M J Laing; more reports please)*

Courage ~ Lease: James Jenkins ~ Real ale ~ Meals and snacks (till 9.30 Tues-Thurs, 5.30 Mon/Fri/Sat, and 3 Sun) ~ Restaurant (Tues-Thurs evenings only) ~ (01222) 888120 ~ Children in restaurant only (see above) ~ Open 11-11; closed 25 Dec

CAREW (Dyfed) SN0403 Map 6

Carew Inn

A4075 just off A477

In a good setting opposite the imposing ruins of Carew Castle, this simple old inn is a friendly place with a good deal of character. The snug little panelled public bar and comfortable lounge both have old-fashioned settles and scrubbed pine furniture, and interesting prints and china hanging from the beams, while a no-smoking upstairs dining room has an elegant china cabinet, a mirror over the tiled fireplace and sturdy chairs around the well-spaced tables. Generously served home-made bar food includes sandwiches, soup (£1.50), pâté (£2.25), mussels provencale (£3.50), spaghetti bolognaise or chilli (£3.95), salads (from £4.50 – the crab is recommended), steak and mushroom pie (£4.95), potato, leek and mushroom pie (£5.50), specials such as half a dozen oysters from a farm down the road (£3.50), Welsh lamb, duck breast in orange sauce (£9.50) and local sea bass (£9.95), puddings (from £1.95) and children's meals; two-course Sunday lunch (£5.95). The local mackerel can be caught and served within two hours. Well kept Crown Buckley Best and Reverend James, Worthington Best (£1 a pint during their 4.30-7 pm happy hour), and locally-brewed Main Street Bitter on handpump, as well as local wines and mineral waters; sensibly placed darts, dominoes, cribbage, piped music. Efficient friendly service. Dogs in the public bar only. In summer there may be barbecues on Thursday evenings. There's a remarkable 9th-c Celtic cross in view of the sunny back courtyard (now partly covered), and more seats in the little flowery front garden look down to the river, where a tidal watermill is open for afternoon summer visits. *(Recommended by Stuart Earle, S Watkins, P A Taylor, Bob and Hilary Gaskin, M E Hughes, Patrick Freeman, David Wallington; more reports please)*

Free house ~ Licensees Rob and Mandy Hinchliffe ~ Real ale ~ Snacks (not Sun lunch) and meals ~ Restaurants ~ (01646) 651267 ~ Children in eating area ~ Live music Thurs evening ~ Open 11-11; 12-2.30, 4.30-11 wkdys Sept-Jun ~ Bedrooms: £15/£25

CARNO (Powys) SN9697 Map 6

Aleppo Merchant

A470 Newtown—Machynlleth

Notably friendly and welcoming, this reliably hospitable place was named after the sea captain who retired to open it in 1632. The beamed lounge bar is comfortably modernised with red plush button-back banquettes around its low wooden tables and plenty of tapestries on the partly stripped stone walls; more tapestries in the small adjoining lounge, which also has dining tables and an open fire in winter. Part of this area is no smoking. A wide choice of well liked bar food includes onion bhajees (£1.75), home-made sandwiches (from £1.45), stockpot soup (£1.75), ploughman's (from £2.55), vegetable balti or broccoli and cream cheese bake (£4.95), smoked haddock and vegetables au gratin (£5.15), steak and kidney pie

(£5.45), whole rack of ribs (£5.95), Welsh lamb chops (£6.35), steaks (from £7.95), and puddings like treacle and walnut tart (£2.25). Pool, darts, dominoes, fruit machine, trivia, and juke box in the public bar. Well kept Boddingtons, Brains SA and an occasional guest on handpump, and Welsh spirits, wines, and waters; piped music. Local girl Laura Ashley was in here the night before she died and is buried in the churchyard immediately opposite. *(Recommended by W H and E Thomas, Miles and Deborah Protter, G Washington, I M Kirk, Mike and Wendy Proctor, Thorstein Moen, Dr M V Jones, P Appleby, Derek and Cerys Williams, Ian Phillips)*

Free house ~ Licensee John Carroll ~ Real ale ~ Meals and snacks (not 25 Dec) ~ Restaurant ~ (01686) 420210 ~ Children in restaurant and garden only ~ Open 11.30-2.30, 6(7 winter Mon and Tues)-11 ~ Bedrooms;£20/£35

CILCAIN (Clwyd) SJ1865 Map 7

White Horse

Village signposted from A494 W of Mold; OS Sheet 116 map reference 177652

Part of an idyllic cluster of stone houses and marked out by its attractively naive inn-sign, this creeper-covered flower-decked pub is the sort of homely place where everything comes with a smile. The cosy parlour by the bar has exposed joists in the low ochre ceiling, mahogany and oak settles, a shelf of china and copper, and a snug inglenook fireplace; there are Lloyd Loom chairs, old local photographs and a goldfish tank in the room on the right, and beyond a further little room with a piano and a grandfather clock. A separate quarry-tiled bar at the back allows dogs, and the whole place can fill up very quickly in the evening. Well presented home-made food includes lunchtime filled rolls, home-made steak and kidney pie, bacon cassoulet, various curries or cannelloni (all £5.80), chicken and herb pie (£6.40), and home-baked ham and eggs (£6.50), with plenty of seasonal game dishes like venison casserole or devilled pheasant, and puddings like raspberry pie (£2.10); they rely a lot on local produce, using organically grown vegetables and free range eggs. Three well kept changing real ales on handpump such as Fullers London Pride, Greene King Abbot, Marstons Pedigree, Wadworths 6X and Youngs Special; Addlestones cider, varied range of wines. Darts, dominoes, cribbage and fruit machine. There are picnic tables at the side. Note they don't allow children inside. *(Recommended by Graham and Lynn Mason, Elizabeth Kew, Peter Lewis)*

Free house ~ Licensee Peter Jeory ~ Real ale ~ Meals and snacks (till 10pm Fri and Sat) ~ (01352) 740142 ~ Open 12-3.30, 7-11, 12-11 Sat

CILGERRAN (Dyfed) SN1943 Map 6

Pendre

Village signposted from A478

The massive walls in this ancient place – one of the oldest pubs in West Wales – are stripped back to show 14th-c stonework above a panelled dado, and there's a beautiful polished slate floor. The comfortable bar also has armchairs and antique high-backed settles on the broad flagstones, and a cheery, old-fashioned atmosphere. Good bar food includes filled rolls, home-made soup (£1.95), filled baked potatoes, vegetable and cheese crumble, home-made steak and kidney pie (£5.65), local Welsh meats, fresh local sewin (sea trout, £6), and steaks (from £7, evening only); on Sunday lunchtimes they only do filled rolls. Bass and Worthington BB on handpump, personal service from the friendly licensees and staff. The public bar has a juke box, darts, pool, and a fruit machine; part of the restaurant is no-smoking. There are seats outside, with an enclosed play area for small children. The other end of the town leads down to the River Teifi, with a romantic ruined castle on a crag nearby, where coracle races are held on the Saturday before the August Bank holiday. There's a good local wildlife park nearby, and this is a good area for fishing. *(Recommended by David Wallington, D M Wilkins, Malcolm Taylor, S P Bobeldijk, Patrick Freeman, Barbara Ann Mayer)*

Free house ~ Licensees P T and M O McGovern ~ Real ale ~ Meals and snacks (12-3, 6-9) ~ Restaurant (not Sun lunchtime) ~ (01239) 614223 ~ Children welcome ~ Open 11.30-11

COLWYN BAY (Clwyd) SH8578 Map 6

Mountain View

Mochdre; take service-road into village off link road to A470, S from roundabout at start of new A55 dual carriageway to Conwy; OS Sheet 116 map reference 825785

Not the easiest place to find but unexpectedly plush and spacious once you get there, this neatly kept pub is very well regarded in the area for its wide range of good value bar food. Promptly served dishes might include good soup (£1.95), lunchtime filled rolls (from £2.45), filled baked potatoes (from £2.95), asparagus prawn gratin (£3.45), tagliatelli carbonara or steak and kidney pie (£4.95), beef burgundy (or chicken curry £5.95), fresh fish, daily specials, and children's meals (£2.50); pleasant and efficient service. Near the entrance is a big picture of the Aberglaslyn Pass, and several others of Conwy Castle are hung throughout the spreading carpeted areas; there are also plush seats, arched dividing walls, and quite a few houseplants (and bright window-boxes in the large windows). Well kept Burtonwood on handpump, and a good few malt whiskies; darts, pool, pinball, dominoes, fruit machine, table football, juke box and unobtrusive piped music (in the lounge). A couple of readers have mourned the passing of the no-smoking area. *(Recommended by KC, Mr and Mrs Hobden; more reports please)*

Burtonwood ~ Tenant Paul Andrew Sutherland ~ Real ale ~ Meals and snacks (not Sun evening) ~ (01492) 544724 ~ Children welcome ~ Open 11.30-3, 6-11; 11.30-11 Sat; closed evening 25 Dec

CRESSWELL QUAY (Dyfed) SN0406 Map 6

Cresselly Arms

Village signposted from A4075

Pubs rarely come as traditional as this unpretentious place. Covered in creepers and facing the tidal creek of the Cresswell River, it's simple and thoroughly old-fashioned – no food, children or dogs, just a good honest atmosphere and friendly welcome. There are seats out by the water, and, if the tides are right, you can get here by boat. Inside, the two comfortably unchanging communicating rooms have red-and-black flooring tiles, built-in wall benches, kitchen chairs and plain tables. There's an open fire in one room, and a working Aga in the other, a high beam-and-plank ceiling hung with lots of pictorial china, and a relaxed and jaunty feel. A third red-carpeted room is more conventionally furnished, with red-cushioned mate's chairs around neat tables. Well kept Flowers Original is tapped straight from the cask into glass jugs; helpful service, fruit machine and darts. *(Recommended by Martin Pritchard, Pete Baker, Stuart Earle, Mr and Mrs Steve Thomas, David Wallington, Simon and Amanda Southwell, Pete Baker)*

Free house ~ Licensees Maurice and Janet Cole ~ Real ale ~ (01646) 651210 ~ Open 11-3, 5-11

CRICKHOWELL (Powys) SO2118 Map 6

Bear ★

Brecon Road; A40

A good many people really do rate this exceptional old coaching inn very highly indeed, and no wonder – the food, service, drinks and atmosphere all blend together in a way so natural it seems effortless. Beautifully presented bar meals might include substantial sandwiches (from £1.95), home-made soup (£2.10), chicken liver and pink peppercorn pâté (£3.25), filo parcels of brie with cranberry marmalade or deep fried laverbread, cockle and bacon balls (£3.95), home-made faggots (£4.95), fish stew (£5.95), duck confit or parcel of Thai minced pork with peanuts and garlic (£6.95), liver and bacon on a bed of fried onions with sautéed apple wedges (£7.25), chicken supreme in cider with peaches and pineapple (£7.50), and very good puddings like an elaborate rum-flavoured bread and butter pudding, or lemon crunch pie (£2.95). The partly no-smoking restaurant has an à la carte menu specialising in Welsh produce, though readers seem to prefer the bar food. Well kept John Smiths, Ruddles Best and County and Websters Yorkshire on handpump; malt whiskies, vintage and late-bottled ports, and unusual wines and liqueurs, with some hops tucked in amongst the bottles. The fascinating heavily beamed lounge has lots of little plush-seated bentwood armchairs and handsome cushioned antique settles and, up by the great roaring log fire, a big sofa and leather easy chairs are spread among the rugs on the oak parquet floor; antiques include a fine oak dresser filled with pewter and brass, a longcase clock and interesting prints. A window seat looks down on the market square. It can get terribly busy, but service remains welcoming and friendly. The back bedrooms – particularly in the quieter new block – are the most highly recommended, though there are three more bedrooms in the pretty cottage at the end of the garden. Lovely window boxes, and you can eat in the garden in summer. *(Recommended by J Honnor, Graham and Glenis Watkins, William Russell, G Washington, Rob Holt, Howard James, TBB, Gwen and Peter Andrews, John Hibberd, James House, Pat and John Millward, David Shillitoe, E Carter, Adam Neil, Mike Pugh, Roy Y Bromell, John Cox, Dr and Mrs Richard Neville, A R and B E Sayer, Gwynne Harper, Alan and Heather Jacques, Brian and Jill Bond, Simon Collett-Jones, Mr and Mrs J Brown, Mrs S Segrove, Jenny and Brian Seller, Barry and Anne, Rita Horridge, A P Jeffreys, Julia Stone, Andrew Latchem, Helen Reed, D J and J R Tapper, Jonathan and Rachel Marsh, Maureen and Keith Ginson, Mr and Mrs H S Hill)*

Free house ~ Licensee Mrs Judy Hindmarsh ~ Real ale ~ Meals and snacks (till 10pm) ~ Restaurant (not Sun evening) ~ (01873) 810408 ~ Children in separate family bar (no smoking at lunchtime) and in restaurant ~ Open 11-3, 5-11 ~ Bedrooms: £42B/£54B

nr CRICKHOWELL (Powys) SO2118 Map 6

Nantyffin Cider Mill

1½ miles NW, by junction A40/A479

In beautiful countryside, this rather handsome L-shaped pink-washed tiled stone dining pub faces an attractive stretch of the River Usk, and has charming views from the tables out on the lawn above its neat car park. Highly praised by readers, the beautifully presented food is easily restaurant standard, but the smartly traditional pubby atmosphere leaves the place feeling more like a brasserie. Relying heavily on local produce and with fresh fish and seafood from Cornwall, the changing range of meals might include home-made soup (£2.25), sautéed flat mushrooms on chargrilled polenta with pesto and pecorino cheese (£3.80), fresh crab meat with lemon and coriander and avocado slices (£4.50), lunchtime open sandwiches (£4.95) or ploughman's (£5.95), grilled black pudding with welsh whisky sauce and braised red cabbage (£5.25), very good steak and kidney pie (£6.20), slow-roasted aubergine filled with cous-cous on a light Thai curry (£6.95), grilled trout with tomato and dill rissoto (£8.70), char-grilled wood pigeon with bubble and squeak and wild mushroom (£8.95), daily specials such as baked hake steak with fresh spinach and nutmeg sauce (£9.95), and escalope of local venision with celeriac and horseradish purée or king scallop and bacon kebab on minted feta tabboulah (£10.90), puddings like caramelised raisin and honey bread and butter pudding or white chocolate and hazelnut cheesecake (£3.25), and children's meals or helpings. Given the individual cooking, it's no surprise that there can be a wait for food. The bar at one end of the main open-plan area has several real ales on handpump, drawn in rotation from a pool of Bass, Crown Buckley Reverend James, Felinfoel Double Dragon, Gibbs Mew Bishops Tipple, Marstons Pedigree, Mitchells Fortress, Morlands Old Speckled Hen and Smiles Best, with other guest beers, several farm ciders, and good wines, several by the glass or half bottle. The look of the place is smartly traditional, with a woodburner in a fine broad fireplace, warm grey stonework, cheerful bunches of fresh and dried flowers, and good solid comfortable tables and chairs. A raftered barn with a big cider press has been converted into quite a striking restaurant; the same menu is served throughout the pub. A ramp makes disabled access easy. *(Recommended by Dr and Mrs A K Clarke, Mrs Brenda Calver, Colin McKerrow, R C Morgan, W Marsh, Anne Morris, M Stroud, N H E Lewis)*

Free house ~ Licensees Glyn Bridgeman, Sean Gerrard ~ Real ale ~ Meals and snacks (12-2.30, 6.30-10) ~ Restaurant (not Sun evening) ~ (01873) 810775 ~ Children welcome ~ Open 12-2.30, 6(6.30 winter)-11; cl Mon during Oct/Nov and Jan-Apr, and cl 2 weeks Jan

EAST ABERTHAW (South Glamorgan) ST0367 Map 6

Blue Anchor ★

B4265

Delightfully unspoilt, this lovely creeper-covered thatched pub can barely have changed since it was built in the late 14th c – which makes the power station on the distant skyline seem all the more incongruous. Low-beamed cosy rooms still wriggle through massive stone walls and tiny doorways (watch your head!), and there are open fires everywhere, including one in an inglenook with antique oak seats built into its stripped stonework. Other seats and tables are worked into a series of chatty little alcoves, and in the more open front bar is an old lime-ash floor; darts, dominoes, fruit machine. Good value bar food includes sandwiches (from £1.65), soup (£1.95), filled baked potatoes (from £2.50), fresh crab salad, lamb stew, or steak and kidney pie (£4.50), fish pie (£4.70), a daily roast, puddings (£1.75), and children's meals (£1.75), with evening dishes such as tenderloin of pork with black pudding and cider, apple and stilton sauce (£9.95), or roast fillet of monkfish wrapped in bacon (£10.65); Sunday lunchtime they just do a three-course roast lunch (£9.45), for which it's best to book. Carefully kept Boddingtons, Buckleys Best, Flowers IPA, Marstons Pedigree, Theakstons Old Peculier, and Wadworths 6X on handpump, along with a guest beer that changes up to four times a week. Rustic seats shelter peacefully among tubs and troughs of flowers outside, with more stone tables on a newer terrace. From here a path leads to the shingly flats of the estuary. The pub can get packed in the evenings and on summer weekends, and it's a shame the front seats are right beside the car park. *(Recommended by Risha Stapleton, Howard James, Nigel Clifton, Mr and Mrs Steve Thomas, Patrick and Mary McDermott, L P Thomas, Gwynne Harper, David Lewis, Chris and Anne Fluck)*

Free house ~ Licensee Jeremy Coleman ~ Real ale ~ Meals and snacks (not Sun) ~ Evening restaurant (not Sun) ~ (01446) 750329 ~ Children in eating areas of bar till 8pm ~ Open 11-11

HALKYN (Clwyd) SJ2172 Map 6

Britannia

Pentre Rd, off A55 for Rhosesmor

Handy for a lunchtime stop whilst driving along the North Wales coast, this cosy and friendly place dates back in part to the 15th-c, when it was a farm. It's been extended many times since then, most recently with the dining conservatory and terrace that make the most of the great views right over the Dee estuary to the Wirral, but the old and new parts blend together very comfortably. The cosy unspoilt lounge bar has some very heavy beams, with horsebrasses, harness, jugs, plates and other bric-a-brac; there's also a games room with darts, pool, dominoes, and fruit machine. Reliable bar food includes sandwiches (from £1.55), home-made soups with rhes-y-cac bread (£1.85), burgers (from £2.95, including vegetarian), filled baked potatoes (£2.95), ploughman's (£4.20), all-day brunch (£4.60), steak and kidney pie (£5.80), vegetarian stir-fry (£5.95), chicken madras or gammon steak with their own fresh eggs (£6.20), grilled Welsh lamb chops with honey and rosemary sauce (£6.40), steaks (from £7.85), daily specials, puddings (from £2.25), and children's meals (£1.95); helpings are good and vegetables and butter generally come in little dishes. Best to book if you want the view. Part of the restaurant is no-smoking. Service can slow down a little when busy but is always friendly and attentive, and the licensees really take pride in what they're doing. Lees Bitter on handpump, a dozen or so malt whiskies, and a choice of coffees. *(Recommended by KC, Andy and Jill Kassube, Mr and Mrs A E McCully, B A and R Davies, L G Milligan, Andy and Jill Kassube, David Heath, Nick Haslewood)*

J W Lees ~ Tenant Terry O'Neill ~ Real ale ~ Meals and snacks (till 10pm) ~ Restaurant ~ (01352) 780272 ~ Children welcome ~ Open 11-11; 11-3, 5.30-11 winter

KENFIG (Mid Glamorgan) SS8383 Map 6

Prince of Wales £

2¼ miles from M4 junction 37; A4229 towards Porthcawl, then right when dual carriageway narrows on bend, signposted Maudlam, Kenfig

This unspoilt and unpretentious old place still has a few reminders of the days when Kenfig was an important medieval port: the aldermen's mace kept upstairs (where, uniquely, they also hold Sunday school), and ghostly voices from the old town said to have become embedded in the walls. The town has long since become a victim of the relentless shifting sands, with the busy pub just about the only survivor. It's well liked for its good range of well kept real ales, probably the best in the area. These might include brews like Bass, Camerons Strong Arm, Felinfoel Double Dragon, Fullers London Pride and ESP, Hancocks HB, Marstons Pedigree, Mitchells ESB, Morrells Varsity and Wadworths 6X on tap/gravity and Worthington BB on handpump. Its walls stripped back to the stone, the friendly main bar has heavy settles and red leatherette seats around a double row of close-set cast-iron-framed tables, an open fire, and small storm windows. The simple home-made bar food is very popular, and quickly served, with large filled baps (from £1 – the home-roasted meat is well done), and very good value dishes such as cheese and potato pie or cottage pie (£1.50), and lasagne (£2.95) – vegetables are extra, but even then the meals are a good deal cheaper than you'll find elsewhere. There's also a wide range of lunchtime daily specials such as bacon and laver bread, braised steak and gravy, or rabbit pie (around £4.50), and they've started doing a lot of fresh fish such as cod fillet or skate wing; 3-course Sunday lunch (£4.95). In summer all the vegetables and potatoes come from the garden, and the eggs are from their own hens. Dominoes, cribbage and card games. There's a nature reserve just across the road, and plenty of rewarding walks nearby. *(Recommended by John and Joan Nash, Mr and Mrs A Plumb, Eddy Street, Anna McGroary, Barbara Ann Mayer, Malcolm Davies, John and Helen Thompson)*

Free house ~ Licensee Jeremy Evans ~ Real ale ~ Meals and snacks (all day) ~ Restaurant ~ (01656) 740356 ~ Children welcome ~ Open 11.30-4, 6-11; closed evening 25 Dec

LITTLE HAVEN (Dyfed) SM8512 Map 6

Swan

A welcoming place really making the best of the lovely views across the broad and sandy hill-sheltered cove – both from seats in the bay window or from the sea wall outside (just the right height for sitting on). The two communicating rooms have quite a cosily intimate feel, as well as comfortable high-backed settles and windsor chairs, a winter open fire, and old prints on the walls that are partly stripped back to the original stonework. Cooked by the landlord, the compact choice of well-liked lunchtime bar food includes home-made soup (£1.75), sandwiches (from £1.25), ploughman's (from £3.50), crab bake or sardines grilled with spinach, egg and mozzarella (£4.25), chicken or beef curry (£4.50), ham salad (£5.50), locally smoked salmon or fresh local crab (£6.75), lobster in season, and home-made puddings (£2.25); this is another place where you won't often see plastic packets of butter, milk or sugar – the good coffee may come with a little jug of cream. No credit cards. Well kept Wadworths 6X and Worthington BB on handpump from the heavily panelled bar counter, and a good range of wines and whiskies; pleasant, efficient service. Little Haven is one of the prettiest coastal villages in west Wales, and a footpath from the pub takes you down to the cove itself. *(Recommended by Professor I H Rorison, David Wallington, Gwynne Harper, Ewan and Moira McCall, Barbara Ann Mayer; more reports please)*

James Williams (who no longer brew) ~ Tenants Glyn and Beryl Davies ~ Real ale ~ Lunchtime meals and snacks (not Dec 25) ~ Tiny evening restaurant Weds-Sat in summer, bookings only in winter (and advisable in summer) ~ (01437) 781256 ~ Open 11-3, 6(7 winter)-11; closed evening Dec 25

LLANBEDR-Y-CENNIN (Gwynedd) SH7669 Map 6

Olde Bull

Village signposted from B5106

A lovely spot, this 16th-c drovers' inn has splendid views down over the Vale of Conwy to the mountains beyond, and a big wild garden with a waterfall and orchard, a fishpond, and plenty of seats. It's doing well under the current licensee, certainly no local, and indeed one of the only Scandinavian landlords we've ever heard of. Inside, the knocked-through rooms are full of massive low beams (some salvaged from a wrecked Spanish Armada ship), elaborately carved antique settles, a close crowd of cheerfully striped stools, brassware, photographs, Prussian spiked helmets, and good open fires (one in an inglenook); there might be some subdued Sibelius in the background. Well kept Lees Bitter and Mild on handpump from wooden barrels, and several malt whiskies; friendly service. The very good changing bar food might include soup (£1.50), sandwiches (from £1.95), smoked trout on a rhubarb and ginger coulis, filled baked potatoes (from £2.80), sausage, egg and black pudding (£3.45), an elaborate Danish open sandwich (£3.75), ploughman's (£3.95), steak, kidney and Guinness pie (£4.95), mushroom tagliatelli (£5.75), fresh fish, imaginative changing specials such as creole jambalaya, scampi flamed in apricot brandy, simmered in cream and mushrooms and topped with toasted almonds, or chicken topped with banana and hot honey, and maybe a couple of the licensee's native dishes such as Finnish meatballs with the traditional accompaniments (£5.75); on Sunday they do a three-course lunch (£6.50), other meals may be limited then. It's worth arriving early for food – one reader wasn't able to order as the chef already had too many meals to cook. The pub is popular with walkers. Darts, dominoes, cribbage. Lavatories are outside. *(Recommended by A and J Tierney-Jones, Paul Bailey, J Roy Smylie, Liz and Roger Morgan, Tim and Tina Banks, Dave Thompson, Margaret Mason, Beryl and Bill Farmer, John A Barker, Roger Byrne, Dave Braisted)*

Lees ~ Tenant Paavo Alexander Salminen ~ Real ale ~ Meals and snacks (not winter Mons) ~ Restaurant ~ (01492) 660508 ~ Children welcome ~ Open 12-3, 6.30-11; closed Sun evening

nr LLANBERIS (Gwynedd) SH6655 Map 6

Pen-y-Gwryd

Nant Gwynant; at junction of A498 and A4086, ie across mountains from Llanberis – OS Sheet 115 map reference 660558

Apart from its magnificent setting the main draw of this jovial climbers' inn must be the wonderful atmospere – simple, cheery and welcoming. The rugged slate-floored climbers' bar is like a log-cabin and doubles as a mountain rescue post; there's also a smaller room with a collection of boots that have done famous climbs, and a cosy panelled smoke room with more climbing mementoes and equipment. Like many other mountaineers, the team that first climbed Everest in 1953 used the inn as a training base, leaving their fading signatures scrawled on the ceiling. A snug little room with built-in wall benches and sturdy country chairs lets you contemplate the majestic surrounding mountain countryside – like precipitous Moel-siabod beyond the lake opposite. There's a hatch where you order lunchtime bar meals: good robust helpings of home-made food such as soup, sandwiches, ploughman's using home-baked french bread, quiche Lorraine or pâté (£2.50) and a home-made pie of the day (£3), with casseroles in winter. In the evening residents sit down together for the hearty and promptly served dinner (check on the time when you book); the dining room is no smoking. As well as Bass, and mulled wine in winter, they serve sherry from their own solera in Puerto Santa Maria; friendly, obliging service. This is a particularly enjoyable place to stay: residents have their own charmingly furnished, panelled sitting room, a new sauna in the trees, and table tennis, darts, pool, bar billiards, table skittles, dominoes, and shove-ha'penny. Bedrooms are clean and sensible rather than luxurious; one has an unusual Edwardian bath in it, and another an older Victorian one colourfully decked out with raised fruit and flowers – the V & A apparently say they've never seen anything like it. Not so long ago press reports described this as one of the most romantic settings in the country, so it might be best to book ahead. *(Recommended by Jenny and Brian Seller, Martin Howard Pritchard, Nigel Woolliscroft, John and Joan Nash, Andrew Stephenson, John Le Sage, Dave and Jules Tuckett, Lorrie and Mick Marchington, Dr M G Yates)*

Free house ~ Licensee Jane Pullee ~ Real ale ~ Lunchtime meals and snacks ~ Evening restaurant ~ (01286) 870211 ~ Well behaved children welcome, except residents bar ~ Open 11-11; no drinks on Sun except to residents; closed early Nov to New Year, open weekends only Jan and Feb ~ Bedrooms: £20(£24B)/£40(£48B)

LLANCARFAN (South Glamorgan) ST0570 Map 6

Fox & Hounds

Village signposted from A4226; also reached from B4265 via Llancadle or A48 from Bonvilston

A comfortably modernised old pub in a nice setting, blending in very well with the rest of the lovely village. Rambling through arches in thick Tudor walls the neatly kept carpeted bar has high-backed traditional settles as well as the plush banquettes around its copper-topped cast-iron tables, a coal fire in winter, and a weekly changing real ale such as Fullers London Pride. Under the new licensees, bar food includes things like sandwiches (from £1.75), soup (£1.75), pork and liver pâté laced with port and brandy (£2.95), fresh battered cod (£4.50), fresh local salmon with hollandaise sauce (£4.95), and steaks; by the time this edition of the Guide hits bookshops they should have a new candle-lit bistro area serving full meals. Darts, fruit machine, unobtrusive piped music. The crazy-paved terrace and garden at the back have been tidied up and refurnished with hand-made wooden seats and tables; there are more tables under flowering trees beside a little stream overhung by a thicket of honeysuckle. The nearby churchyard is interesting. *(Recommended by Nigel Clifton, Richard Mattick, Gareth and Kay Jones, Steve Thomas, David Lewis; reports on the new regime please)*

Free house ~ Licensee Mr M J Ashmoor ~ Real ale ~ Meals and snacks ~ (01446) 781297 ~ Children welcome ~ Open 11-3, 5.30-11; all day Thurs-Sat

LLANDEWI SKIRRID (Gwent) SO3416 Map 6

Walnut Tree ★ Ⓜ 🍷

B4521

Welsh Dining pub of the Year

Quite different from most of the places we recommend, this excellent establishment is now pretty much a restaurant, but the atmosphere doesn't have the formality that

that suggests – they still have a pub licence, and they're quite happy for people to come for just one course, or even a drink and a pudding. In fact the food is significantly better than in most restaurants, and cooked with considerable skill; readers who come here often (one has visited every year since 1968) consider them pretty much faultless. As usual however, quality doesn't come cheap, so you'll probably need your cheque book (they don't take credit cards). A typical menu might include gazpacho soup (£4.25), crab pancake (£5.75), bruschetta with seafood (£7), tagliolini with courgette flowers and truffle paste or griddled squid (£7.25), half-a-dozen oysters (£9), vegetarian platter (£10.25), calf's liver with sweet and sour onions (£11.25), escalope of salmon with rhubarb and ginger or roast guinea fowl with spinach, mushrooms and vin santo (£13.25), roast duck with figs and strawberries (£14.25), fricassée of lobster and monkfish (£15.25), and puddings such as coconut parfait with mango sauce (£4.50). The attractive choice of wines is particularly strong in Italian ones (they import their own), and the house wines by the glass are good value, as is the coffee. Service is efficient and friendly. The small white-walled bar has some polished settles and country chairs around the tables on its flagstones, and a log-effect gas fire. It opens into an airy and relaxed dining lounge with rush-seat Italianate chairs around gilt cast-iron-framed tables. There are a few white cast-iron tables outside in front. *(Recommended by R W Saunders, B W and S J, Mike and Ruth Dooley, A J Bowen, SRP, Andrew Stephenson, Nigel Wilkinson, Rita Horridge, the Monday Club)*

Free house ~ Licensee Ann Taruschio ~ Meals and snacks (12-3, 7-10.15, not Sun or Mon) ~ Restaurant (not Sun or Mon) ~ Abergavenny (01873) 852797 ~ Children welcome ~ Open 12-3, 7-12; closed Sun and Mon

LLANDRINDOD WELLS (Powys) SO0561 Map 6

Llanerch £

Waterloo Road; from centre, head for station

A cheerful 16th-c local with peaceful mountain views from its back terrace; it feels very much like a country pub but is in fact in the middle of town. Like the atmosphere the food is decidedly no-frills, but for value it's hard to beat, with popular lunchtime dishes like soup (£1.75), sandwiches (from £1.75), filled baked potatoes or Welsh rarebit (from £2.25), vegetable pancake rolls (£2.95), fisherman's pie, lasagne, or gammon casserole (£3.25), salads (from £4.50), steak and kidney pie (£4.75), mixed grill (£7.95), and children's meals (from £1.75), and evening extras like chicken bonne femme or beef bourguignon (£5.50). The squarish beamed main bar has old-fashioned settles snugly divided by partly glazed partitions and a big stone fireplace that's richly decorated with copper and glass; there are more orthodox button-back banquettes in communicating lounges (one of which is no smoking at lunchtimes and early evenings). Well kept Hancocks HB, Worthingtons Best and a guest beer on handpump; there may be up to 20 real ales during their late August Victorian Festival. Service is prompt and generally friendly, though visitors won't be treated as anything special; fruit machine, video game, trivia and piped music, while a separate pool room has darts, cribbage and dominoes. The back terrace has tables and a summer bar and leads on to a garden (with boules), looking over the Ithon Valley; also, a play area and front orchard. *(Recommended by Joan and Michel Hooper-Immins, N J Clifton, Howard James, George Atkinson, M Joyner)*

Free house ~ Licensee John Leach ~ Real ale ~ Meals and snacks ~ Restaurant ~ (01597) 822086 ~ Children in eating area and games room ~ Occasional live entertainment last Thurs of month ~ Open 11.30-3(2.30 winter weekdays), 6-11 ~ Bedrooms: £32.50B/£49B

nr LLANDUDNO JUNCTION (Gwynedd) SH8180 Map 6

Queens Head

Glanwydden; heading towards Llandudno on A546 from Colwyn Bay, turn left into Llanrhos Road as you enter the Penrhyn Bay speed limit; Glanwydden is signposted as the first left turn off this

The thoughtfully prepared food at this modest village pub is excellent – no wonder so many people make major detours just to have a meal here. When choosing what to have, fish or seafood is always a good bet, as are the puddings – a huge range, from traditional bread and butter pudding or treacle tart to more exotic orange and coffee liqueur trifle or lemon and wine syllabub (£2.50). Other carefully prepared and generously served home-made food might include soup such as fresh pea and mint (£1.95), open rolls (£2.95), home-made pâtés such as smoked trout (£3.75), smoked breast of goose with kiwi fruit (£4.35), baked black pudding with apple and brandy (£4.50), lovely fat Conway mussels in garlic butter topped with smoked cheese (£5.25), salads (from £5.75), vegetarian pancake with mushrooms and asparagus (£5.95), and daily specials like steak and mushroom pie (£6.25), local grey mullet wrapped in smoked bacon in a tomato and basil sauce (£6.75), braised pork with apricots and brandy or fresh dressed Conway crab (£6.95), grilled Welsh lamb cutlets in a plum and port wine sauce (£7.50), or fresh dressed Conway crab (£6.95). Fresh local produce is firmly in evidence, and even the mints with the coffee might be home-made. Best to get there early to be sure of a table – it's very popular indeed. Service stands out too: drop a knife and you may find they've brought another before you've finished bending down for the original. Well kept Benskins, Ind Coope Burton, Tetleys and maybe a guest like Youngs Bitter on handpump, decent wine list, several malts, and good coffee, maybe served with a bowl of whipped cream. The spacious and comfortably modern lounge bar has brown plush wall banquettes and windsor chairs around neat black tables and is partly divided by a white wall of broad arches and wrought-iron screens; there's also a little public bar. There are some tables out by the car park. No dogs. *(Recommended by J R Whetton, Chris Walling, Maysie Thompson, KC, Mr and Mrs Jones, A and J Tierney-Jones, J E Hilditch, Roy Smylie, W C M Jones, Mark Bradley, Mr and Mrs B Hobden and others)*

Ansells ~ Lease: Robert and Sally Cureton ~ Real ale ~ Meals and snacks ~ (01492) 546570 ~ Children over 7 only ~ Open 11-3, 6.30-11; closed 25 Dec

7

LLANFERRES (Clwyd) SJ1961 Map 6

Druid

A494 Mold—Ruthin

On a popular tourist route, this extended 17th-c inn stands on a slight rise by the churchyard, looking down over the road to the Alyn valley and the Craig Harris mountains beyond; this is good walking country. Tables outside sheltered in a corner of the building by a low wall with rock-plant pockets make the most of the view, as does the bay window in the civilised and sympathetically refurbished smallish plush lounge. You can also see the hills from the bigger beamed back bar, also carpeted (with quarry tiles by the log fire), with its two handsome antique oak settles as well as a pleasant mix of more modern furnishings. The attractive dining room is relatively smoke-free. Warmly welcoming licensees who took over in 1994 are doing consistently good food: besides sandwiches, dishes finding special favour with readers in recent months have included soups such as asparagus, watercress or chicken and mushroom (£1.95), black pudding with redcurrant jelly or apple sauce (£1.95), stilton-stuffed mushrooms or mussels and mozzarella cheese in a creamy pesto sauce with garlic bread (£2.95), steak and mushroom pie with good pastry (£5.25) and tagliatelle with lots of prawns (£5.55); other main courses run from good vegetarian dishes such as baked mushrooms and sweet peppers with mozzarella to duck breast with oyster sauce (£8.25) and fillet steak with bearnaise sauce (£11.50); vegetables are fresh and generous. Well kept Burtonwood Best and Forshaws on handpump, decent malt whiskies; games area with darts and pool, also dominoes, bagatelle, Jenga and other board games; maybe unobtrusive piped music. *(Recommended by KC, J S M Sheldon, Mrs J Jones, Mr and Mrs M St-Amour, Paul McPherson, Dr Bill Baker, J S Green)*

Burtonwood ~ Licensee James Dolan ~ Real ale ~ Meals and snacks (12-3, 5.30-11; all day Sat) ~ Restaurant ~ (01352) 810225 ~ Children welcome ~ Open 12-3, 5.30-11 (12-11 Sat) ~ Bedrooms: £18.75/£34.50

LLANFIHANGEL CRUCORNEY (Gwent) SO3321 Map 6

Skirrid

Village signposted off A465

The oldest pub in Wales (and up there amongst the oldest in Britain), this dark brown stone inn has a number of medieval windows, oak beams made from ships' timbers, and panelling in the dining room said to be from a British man o' war. The high-ceilinged bar has settles and wooden tables on its flagstones, walls stripped back to show ancient stonework, and a big open fire in the stone hearth. For many years the pub served as the area's courthouse, and between 1110 and the 17th c nearly 200 people were hanged here; you can still see the scorch and drag marks of the rope on the beam above the foot of the stairs which served as the traditional scaffold. Good popular bar food includes sandwiches, home-made soup, ploughman's with a range of Welsh cheeses, vegetarian loaf (£5.95), venison sausages with warm home-made apricot and raisin chutney (£6.50), local lamb chops glazed with an apple and rosemary jelly (£6.95), and whole fresh Crucorney trout stuffed with smoky bacon, apple and celery (£8.95). Well kept Ushers Best, Founders and four seasonal brews on handpump, a range of malt whiskies; darts, pool, and juke box. The generally friendly welcome can be a little variable if they're expecting big groups or coach parties. A crazy-paved back terrace has white seats and tables, and there are more rustic ones on a small sloping back lawn. *(Recommended by Mike and Ruth Dooley, Rick and Vicki Blechta, Nigel Clifton, Mr and Mrs E H Warner, Mike and Wendy Proctor, Chamberlain, R C Morgan, Gwynne Harper, Ian Jones)*

Ushers ~ Lease: Steven and Heather Gant ~ Real ale ~ Meals and snacks (not Tues evening) ~ Restaurant (not Sun evening) ~ (01873) 89058 ~ Children welcome ~ Occasional folk or other live entertainment ~ Open 11-3, 6-11, all day Sat ~ Bedrooms: £25B/£50B

LLANFRYNACH (Powys) SO0725 Map 6

White Swan

Village signposted from B4558, just off A40 E of Brecon bypass

The secluded terrace behind this well-run and pretty black and white pub is attractively divided into sections by roses and climbing shrubs, and overlooks peaceful paddocks; there are plenty of stone and other tables out here. Inside all is friendly and relaxed, and the lounge bar rambles back into a series of softly lit alcoves, with plenty of well spaced tables on the flagstones, a big log fire, and partly stripped stone walls; there may be piped classical music. Very good bar food includes French onion soup (£2.50), ploughman's (from £4), snails in garlic butter, lasagne or macaroni and broccoli cheese (£4.50), two eggs on garlic sausage with ham, peppers and green beans (£4.75), chicken curry or haddock and prawn pie (£6), lamb chops marinated in garlic and herbs (£8.75), welsh-style grilled trout with bacon (£8), beef and mushroom pie (£9.25), well hung steaks (from £9.50), puddings such as sherry trifle (£2.25), children's dishes (£3.75), and maybe weekend specials; well-cooked vegetables. Service is courteous and efficient; well kept Brains Bitter and Flowers IPA on handpump. The churchyard is across the very quiet village lane. *(Recommended by A J Bowen, Mrs Brenda Calver, Tony and Sarah Thomas, Michel Sargent, R C Morgan, R T and J C Moggridge, TBB, D J and J R Tapper, P J Howell)*

Free house ~ Licensee David Bell ~ Real ale ~ Meals and snacks (until lunches stop – 1.30 Sun) ~ (01874) 665276 ~ Children welcome ~ Open 12-2.30, 7-11; closed Mon (except Bank Holidays), and last three weeks of Jan

LLANGATTOCK (Powys) SO2117 Map 6

Vine Tree

A4077; village signposted from Crickhowell

All the meals at this friendly dining pub seem to come with that little bit extra attention; they bake their own bread, most of their produce is carefully selected locally, and they even arrange children's meals to look like a funny face. Popular and generously-served dishes include lunchtime ploughman's (£4.50) and cottage pie (£4.75), stockpot soup (£1.75), home-made pâté (£3.25), garlic mushrooms with chilli butter (£3.25), steak and kidney pie, vegetable bake or nut roast (£5.75), pork chop in almond and cheese sauce (£6.90), chicken in a spicy honey and tomato sauce (£6.95), fresh salmon, lamb chop with rosemary and garlic or trout in a chive sauce (£7.95), steaks (from £8.95), lots of puddings, and a choice of Sunday roasts (£4.75); their fish comes twice a week from Cornwall, and they use local meat and vegetables. The front part of the bar has soft seats, some stripped stone masonry, and brass ornaments around its open fireplace. The back is set aside as a dining area with windsor chairs, scrubbed deal tables, and decorative plates and Highland cattle engravings on the walls; most of the tables are set out for eating. Well kept Boddingtons, Flowers Original, and Whitbreads West Country PA on handpump. Tables under cocktail parasols give a view of the splendid medieval stone bridge over the River Usk, and a short stroll takes you to our Crickhowell main entry, the Bear. *(Recommended by Mr and Mrs A Plumb, Mrs Brenda Calver, Nigel Clifton, Ian Phillips, Neil and Jenny Jackson, Barry and Anne, P J Howell)*

Free house ~ Licensee I S Lennox ~ Real ale ~ Meals ~ Restaurant (not Sun evening) ~ (01873) 810514 ~ Children welcome ~ Open 12-3, 6-11

LLANGYNWYD (Mid Glamorgan) SS8588 Map 6

Old House

From A4063 S of Maesteg follow signpost Llan ¾ at Maesteg end of village; pub behind church

Known locally as Yr Hen Dy, this friendly thatched and thick-walled pub dates back in part to 1147, making it among the oldest in Wales. It has quite a history – Wil Hopkin is said to have written Bugeilio'r Gwenith Gwyn here, and what's now the restaurant was originally the first nonconformist chapel in the Valleys. It's been much modernised, but there are still comfortably traditional touches in the two cosy rooms of its busy bar, which have high-backed black built-in settles, lots of china and brass around the huge fireplace, shelves of bric-a-brac, and decorative jugs hanging from the beams. Good generously served bar food includes soup (£1.75), sausages (£2.75), omelettes (£3.75), aubergine lasagne (£3.80), home-made steak and kidney pie or beef curry (£4.20), salads (from £4.25), gammon and eggs (£6.10), trout and almonds (£6.50), poached salmon (£7.90), steaks (from £10.10), puddings such as raspberry charlotte (£1.95), daily specials, and children's meals (from £1.25). Well kept Bass, Brains SA and Flowers IPA and Original, good range of whiskies, and a choice of wines by the glass. An attractive conservatory extension (half no smoking) leads on to the garden with good views, play area, and a soft-ice-cream machine for children. At Christmas they still go in for the ancient Mari Lwyd tradition, which involves parading around a horse's skull on a stick decorated with ribbons, calling at each house and singing impromptu verses about the people in them. It's a shame this has died out elsewhere – abusing your neighbours using the excuse of an ancient custom strikes us as eminently enjoyable. *(Recommended by R Michael Richards; more reports please)*

Whitbreads ~ Lease: R T and P C David ~ Real ale ~ Meals and snacks (11-2.30, 5.30-10) ~ Restaurant ~ (01656) 733310 ~ Children welcome ~ Open 11-11

LLANNEFYDD (Clwyd) SH9871 Map 6

Hawk & Buckle

Village well signposted from surrounding main roads; one of the least taxing routes is from Henllan at junction of B5382 and B5429 NW of Denbigh

Seven hundred feet up in the hills, this welcoming village inn has remarkable views over Rhyl and Prestatyn to the Irish Sea from almost all its bedrooms (and its car park). In very clear weather you can see as far as the Lancashire coast, and on autumn evenings those with very keen sight may be able to pick out Blackpool Tower, 40 miles away. The bar food is well above average, with a choice of home-made dishes like toasted sandwiches (from £1.85), soup (£1.95), ploughman's (£3.95), steak and kidney pie or various vegetarian dishes like mushroom and nut fettuccini (£4.95), chicken madras (£5.25), lemon sole (£6.95) and sirloin steak (from £8.45); the dining room is no-smoking. The long knocked-through black-beamed lounge bar has comfortable modern upholstered settles around its walls and facing each other across the open fire, and a neat red carpet in the centre of its tiled floor, while a lively locals' side bar has darts, pool and piped music; good house wines. The landlord is friendly, as are the two cats and dog. There's an attractive mosaic mural on the way through into the back bedroom extension; the modern rooms here are comfortable and well equipped. *(Recommended by Anne and Sverre Hagen, Maysie Thompson, Daniel and Patricia Neukom; more reports please)*

Free house ~ Licensees Bob and Barbara Pearson ~ Meals and snacks (lunch service stops 1.30; no lunch Mon or winter weekdays) ~ Restaurant (closed Sun) ~ (01745) 540249 ~ Children in eating area till 8.30 ~ Open 12-2, 7-11; closed lunchtimes Mon/Tues/Thurs/Fri in winter, all day Dec 25 ~ Bedrooms: £38B/£50B

LLANTHONY (Gwent) SO2928 Map 6

Abbey Hotel

Shortly after the abbey was founded here in the 12th c the site was described as 'a place truly fitted for contemplation', and despite the passing of time that's just as apt today. The pub, originally part of the prior's house, is lifted out of the ordinary by this lovely setting, one of the most unusual and atmospheric you're likely to come across; it's surrounded by and indeed really part of the abbey's graceful ruins, with lawns among the lofty arches and tranquil views towards the border hills. The dimly-lit, vaulted crypt bar still has some of the atmosphere of its contemplative past – you can almost imagine the monks going about their daily business (if that's the right word). The main bar is basic and simply furnished with half-a-dozen wooden tables, spindleback chairs and wooden benches on the flagstone floor, and serves well kept Bass, Flowers Original, Ruddles County, and Wadworths 6X on handpump or tapped from the cask, and farm cider in summer. Lunchtime bar food is simple too, with toasted sandwiches, good home-made soups (£2.25), decent ploughman's (£3.95), and home-made meat and vegetarian burgers (£3.95), with evening dishes like spicy bean goulash (£5.75), and nut roast with chestnut stuffing and wine sauce or local lamb with garlic, wine and mushrooms (£6.25). Service can be a little indifferent at times, and the outside lavatories could perhaps do with a tidy-up. Note they don't allow children inside. *(Recommended by John and Joan Nash, Guyneth and Salvo Spadaro-Dutturi, Nigel Clifton, Leslie and Dorothy Pilson, Anthony Barnes, Patrick Freeman, Sue Demont, Tim Barrow, Gwynne Harper, Barry and Anne)*

Free house ~ Licensee Ivor Prentice ~ Real ale ~ Meals and lunchtime snacks ~ (01873) 890487 ~ Occasional live music ~ Open 11-3, 6-11; 11-11 Sat and summer holidays; closed weekdays end Nov-end Mar except Christmas and New Year week ~ Bedrooms: £21(Sun-Thurs)/£41)

LLANYNYS (Clwyd) SJ1063 Map 6

Cerrigllwydion Arms

Village signposted from A525 by Drovers Arms just out of Ruthin, and by garage in Pentre further towards Denbigh

A happy place in a wonderfully remote setting, this characterful old pub dates back in part some 600 years. The vicar of the parish at that time allowed construction of the pub partly within the churchyard, so it wouldn't spoil his view of Denbigh

Castle. It looks quite small from the outside but once through the door you find it rambles about delightfully, the maze of atmospheric little rooms filled with dark oak beams and panelling, a good mix of seats, old stonework, interesting brasses, and a collection of teapots. Well kept Bass and Tetleys on handpump, and a good choice of malt whiskies and liqueurs; darts, dominoes and unobtrusive piped music. Using fresh local ingredients, bar food includes home-made soup (£1.70), sandwiches, standard bar snacks, and changing specials such as baked pork chops in apple and cider sauce (£5.90), lamb cutlets in honey and mustard (£6.45), duck in port and brandy sauce (£7.45), local venison in red wine and shallot sauce (£7.60), and a big mixed grill (£9.25); the restaurant is no-smoking. Dogs welcome. Across the quiet lane is a neat garden with teak tables among fruit trees looking across the fields to wooded hills; the church is interesting. *(Recommended by KC, R W Abel, G Richardson, E G Parish, G Hallett, Brian Kneale, Paul Boot, Jeanne and Tom Barnes)*

Free house ~ Licensee Brian Pearson ~ Real ale ~ Meals and snacks ~ Restaurant ~ (01745) 890247 ~ Children welcome ~ Open 11.30-3, 7-11

LLWYNDAFYDD (Dyfed) SN3755 Map 6

Crown

Coming S from New Quay on A486, both the first two right turns eventually lead to the village; the side roads N from A487 between junctions with B4321 and A486 also come within signpost distance; OS Sheet 145 map reference 371555

Standing out in an otherwise undistinguished area for pubs, this is a popular choice for a family lunch, and even out of season it can get busy. The pretty tree-sheltered garden has won several awards, and there are picnic tables on a terrace above a small pond among shrubs and flowers, as well as a good play area for children. Home-made bar food includes decent lunchtime sandwiches, as well as soup (£2.30), garlic mushrooms (£2.95), deep-fried haddock (£4.95), pizzas (from £5.25), vegetarian stuffed peppers or pies such as lamb or steak and kidney (£5.45), salads (from £5.50), local trout (£5.95), steaks (from £7.55), fresh fish, daily specials, and children's meals (from £2); the choice may be limited at Sunday lunchtime when they do a traditional roast. Notably well kept Boddingtons, Flowers IPA, Fuggles Imperial IPA and guests on handpump, a range of wines, and good choice of malt whiskies. The friendly, partly stripped-stone bar has red plush button-back banquettes around its copper-topped tables, and a big woodburning stove; darts, piped music. It's best to get there early if you want a seat at the weekend. The side lane leads down to a cove with caves by National Trust cliffs. *(Recommended by Ian Phillips, Stella Knight, Mike and Wendy Proctor, H D Spottiswoode, G W and M C Brooke-Williams)*

Free house ~ Licensee Keith Soar ~ Real ale ~ Meals and lunchtime snacks ~ Restaurant ~ (01545) 560396 ~ Children in eating area and long room without bar ~ Open 12-3, 6(7 Sat)-11; closed Sun evening Jan-March

LLYSWEN (Powys) SO1337 Map 6

Griffin ★

A470, village centre

It's easy to see that the welcoming licensees of this attractive ivy-covered inn really enjoy running the place and organising its varied activities, and their enthusiasm immediately rubs off onto customers. It's quite a favourite with some readers for its warmly old-fashioned character and good range of hearty country cooking, which relies firmly on local produce, some from their own gardens. Excellent lunchtime meals might include delicious home-made soup such as carrot and sweetcorn (£2.95), warm sausage, bacon and kidney salad or stilton, celery and port terrine (£3.50), a selection of Welsh cheeses, tagliatelli and walnuts in mushroom mornay or fresh salmon in turmeric sauce (£5.75), wild rabbit stew or chicken and mushroom pancakes (£7.85), evening dishes like braised oxtail in beer (£8.90) or roast duckling with apple sauce (£10.95), and home-made puddings like lemon crunch or banana and rum trifle. Most days after Easter they serve brook trout and salmon, caught by the family or by customers in the River Wye just over the road, and they're well known for very good seasonal game dishes such as jugged hare or pheasant (around £8.50). In the evenings you may find a range of tapas, and they do regular theme nights and menus. Boddingtons, Flowers IPA and Hook Norton Best on handpump, and a good varied wine list with several half bottles. The Fishermen's Bar is decorated with old fishing tackle and has a big stone fireplace with a good log fire, and large windsor armchairs and padded stools around its low tables; at lunchtime there's extra seating in the no-smoking dining room for bar meals. Quoits, a friendly cat, and huge dog, Amber; others are allowed. You can shoot or fish here – they have a full-time ghillie and keeper. It's a particularly pleasant place to stay. Service is friendly and helpful, though can slow down at busy times. *(Recommended by Frank Cummins, Karen Eliot, Dr Paul Kitchener, Norma Farris, Andrew Stephenson, Mrs J Jones, John and Joan Nash, Chamberlain, Martin and Pauline Richardson, Sue Demont, Tim Barrow, Patrick Freeman, David J B Lewis, Dave and Jules Tuckett, Dr and Mrs A K Clarke, A K Thorlby, Wyn Churchill, Pat and John Millward)*

Free house ~ Licensees Richard and Di Stockton ~ Real ale ~ Meals and snacks (roast only Sun lunchtime, no food Sun evening except for residents) ~ Restaurant (not Sun evening) ~ (01874) 754241 ~ Children welcome ~ Open 12-3, 7-11 ~ Bedrooms: £28.50B/£50B

MAENTWROG (Gwynedd) SH6741 Map 6

Grapes ★

A496; village signposted from A470

George Burrows wrote in his book *Wild Wales* of taking brandy and water in the 'magnificent parlour' of this warmly welcoming and atmospheric coaching inn. Well geared up for families, it's quite a favourite with locals (always a good sign), and you'll often hear Welsh speakers mixed up with the visitors come to eat the consistently tasty bar food. Home-made, wholesome, and served in hearty helpings, the choice at lunchtime includes sandwiches (not Sun, from £1.50) and ploughman's, notably good soup (£1.75), deep-fried potato wedges (£3), burgers or salads (from £5), several vegetarian (and vegan) dishes like stilton and mushroom bake or hot chilli with jalapenas (£5.25), steak and kidney pie or leek and ham bake (£5.50), rack of Welsh lamb (£7.50), 10oz steaks (from £8.50), children's meals (from £2.25), and good specials tending to concentrate on fresh fish, like a very good fish pie, monkfish tails in orange sauce, grilled turbot with anchovy butter or john dory with a wine and asparagus sauce (£7.75). Unusually, they also do snacks like omelettes (£3.25) or savoury pancakes (from £3.50) between 2.15 and 6pm. Big breakfasts. Quick, friendly service even at the busiest times, reliably well kept Bass, Eldridge Pope Royal Oak, Worthingtons Best and a rotated guest beer on handpump, varied wine list (especially in the restaurant), decent selection of malts, and good coffee. All three bars are full of stripped pitch-pine usually salvaged from chapels – pews, settles, pillars and carvings – and the effect is very attractive and characterful. Good log fires – there's one in the great hearth of the restaurant where there may be spit-roasts. Dominoes, cribbage and interesting juke box in the public bar, where there's also an intriguing collection of brass blowlamps. The good-sized, sheltered verandah (with a shellfish counter at one end) catches the evening sunshine and has lovely views over a pleasant back terrace and walled garden; there's a fountain on the lawn, and magnificent further views. The dining room is no smoking. *(Recommended by Gordon Theaker, Martin and Penny Fletcher, Roger Byrne, Peter and Audrey Dowsett, Basil J S Minson, David Atkinson, the Mair family, David Rogers, Gordon Theaker, Mr and Mrs H Hobden, Michael and Janet Hepworth, Dave and Jules Tuckett, David J B Lewis, John Nash, Phil and Heidi Cook, P Jay Voss, G Richardson, J E Hilditch)*

Free house ~ Licensees Brian and Gill Tarbox ~ Real ale ~ Meals and snacks (12-2.15, 6-9.30) ~ Restaurant (not Sun evening) ~ (01766) 590208/365 ~ Children in dining room and verandah (with baby changing facilities) ~ Open 11-11 ~ Bedrooms: £25B/£50B

MARIANGLAS (Anglesey) SH5084 Map 6

Parciau Arms

B5110

A well liked lunchtime food stop, this warmly cosy and welcoming pub is one of the few places we know of that has significantly reduced its prices for food and drink over the last year. There's plenty to look at around its gleaming bar, with local colour photographs on the dark red hessian walls of the inner area, and miner's lamps, horse bits, lots of brass (especially car horns), a mounted jungle fowl and other bric-a-brac dotted around. The main seating area has comfortable built-in wall banquettes and stools around elm tables, a big settee matching the flowery curtains, spears, rapiers and so forth on the elaborate chimney-breast over the coal fire, and antique coaching prints. An airy family dining room with little bunches of flowers on the tables has a series of prints illustrating the rules of golf. Decent bar food includes sandwiches (from £1.65), home-made soup (£2), lots of pizzas (from £2.50), filled baked potatoes or vegetable curry (£3.50), ploughman's (from £3.95), turkey rogan josh (£4.25), local plaice with parsley sauce or home-made steak and kidney pie (£5.25), gammon and egg (£5.50), fresh poached salmon (£6.95), 8oz sirloin steak (£8.95), puddings like sherry trifle (£1.95), children's meals (from £1.95), and specials such as chicken provençale, fresh trout, or lamb in cider (all £5.50); they may offer a choice of vegetables. Also morning coffee and afternoon tea. Well kept Bass, Tetleys and Boddingtons or a changing guest on handpump, various wines and whiskies, freshly squeezed orange juice, milk shakes; obliging, cheery service. Darts, pool, cribbage, shove ha'penny, dominoes, fruit machine, video game, satellite TV, juke box and piped music; boules area. There are picnic tables on a terrace, with pews and other tables under cocktail parasols in a good-sized garden; it also has a good play area including a pensioned-off tractor, a camel-slide, a climber and a children's cabin with video game. *(Recommended by Andy and Jill Kassube, Roger Byrne, Mr and Mrs A E McCully, M Joyner, Mr and Mrs D C Shenton, Richard Houghton)*

Free house ~ Licensee Philip Moore ~ Real ale ~ Meals and snacks (all day) ~ Restaurant ~ (01248) 853766 ~ Well behaved children in eating area of bar till 9 ~ Open 11-11; only open 2 hours lunchtime 25 Dec

MOLD (Clwyd) SJ1962 Map 7

We Three Loggerheads

Loggerheads; A494 3 miles towards Ruthin

Though there's still quite a pubby feel to this carefully refurbished old pub the emphasis is very much on the food, with the menu featuring a good number of rather unusual dishes and flavours. As well as sandwiches (£2.45), you might find well-presented dishes such as spicy Greek sausages with yoghurt and mint dip (£3.25), a choice of ploughman's (£4.45), home-made chicken and mango curry (£4.95), pies like steak and kidney with Guinness or pumpkin and cheese (£5.25), and a huge range of interesting daily specials like lamb samosas (£3.25), green-lipped mussels in garlic and lemon (£3.95), sizzling teriyaki-style beef (£5.95), and their popular spicy Mexican feast (nachos in melted cheese with jalapenos, sour cream, chillis, salsa and taco dips, £6.95 for two); home-made puddings such as spice and cinnamon rice pudding or a brandy snap basket with fresh berries, fruit coulis and creme anglais (from £2.45). Under 14s can eat for just £1. It's on two levels, with on the right owl prints and other country pictures, stuffed birds and a stuffed fox, and lighting by pretty converted paraffin lamps. On the left a tiled-floor locals' bar has pool, dominoes, shove-ha'penny and table skittles. The arched windows came from a former colliery winding house. Up steps at the back is a very spacious area with high rafters, pillars, a false ceiling holding farm machinery and carts, and comfortable green cloth banquettes set around tables in stripped-wood stalls. Well kept Bass tapped from the cask and maybe a guest beer or two; friendly, chatty service. Loudish juke box, fruit machine and trivia, popular Sunday night quiz. There are white tables and chairs on a side terrace. The sign outside only has two faces – ask about the other and they point back at you as the third. *(Recommended by KC, David and Ruth Shillitoe, Simon and Louise Chappell, Paul McPherson)*

Bass ~ Manager Tim Astall ~ Real ale ~ Meals and snacks (till 10, 9 Sun) ~ Restaurant ~ (01352) 810337 ~ Children welcome ~ Open 12-3, 5.30-11, all day Fri, Sat, Sun; closed evening 25 Dec

MONMOUTH (Gwent) SO5113 Map 6

Punch House

Agincourt Square

A good traditional market-town pub, this is a handsome place, the 17th c building decked out with colourful hanging baskets. There are tables outside on the cobblestones overlooking the square. Inside, the spreading open-plan beamed bar has a chatty, relaxed atmosphere, red leatherette settles, lots of copper, brass and horse-tack, bound copies of early issues of *Punch* (even the dog is called Punch), a big fireplace, and the original oak gate from the town gaol; one area is no smoking. Big helpings of straightforward lunchtime bar food such as sandwiches, home-made soup (£1.90), steak and kidney pie (£4.75), grilled trout (£6) and roast pork with apple sauce (£6.75); the restaurant has a wide range of elaborate dishes prepared by their Italian chef. Prompt, friendly service. Well kept Bass, Hancocks HB, Wadworths 6X and Worthington Best on handpump, decent range of wines; fruit machine, piped music. *(Recommended by George Atkinson, Piotr Chodzko-Zajko)*

Free house ~ Licensee John Wills ~ Real ale ~ Meals and snacks ~ Restaurant ~ (01600) 713855 ~ Children welcome ~ Occasional live entertainment ~ Open 11-11; 11-3, 5-11 Mon-Thurs in winter; closed 25 Dec

MONTGOMERY (Powys) SO2296 Map 6

Dragon

The Square

A strikingly timbered characterful 17th-c hotel right in the centre of this peaceful county town, well-placed for splendid walks and views. Many of the beams and much of the masonry are reputed to have come from the castle just up the hill after it was destroyed by Cromwell. Other interesting old features include a window in the restaurant signed by the hangman at his last public hanging in the market square, and an arch from the pub's days as a coaching inn now converted to an inside patio. It's a popular place for eating, with bar meals such as sandwiches and toasties (from £1.85), soup (£1.95), grilled half orange with sherry and brown sugar (£2.25), fresh pasta with tomato sauce (£2.50), ploughman's (from £3.50), battered cod (£4.25), grilled lamb cutlets with cranberry gravy, steak and kidney pie, or sautéed lamb's liver in an onion and stilton sauce (£6.25), roast duck with a cherry and cinnamon sauce (£7.95), mixed grill (£8.95), and children's meals (£2.75); three course Sunday lunch (£7.50, more in restaurant). Non-residents can have free use of the hotel swimming pool by ordering a full meal in the bar or partly no-smoking restaurant; the food will be ready when you come out. The carpeted lounge bar has a window seat looking down to the market square and the old town hall (which has a very sweet-toned clock bell), tapestried stools and wall benches around dimpled copper tables, game bird and old England prints, and willow-pattern plates on a high shelf, up by the colonial ceiling fan. Efficient licensees. Very well kept Felinfoel Double Dragon, Powells Old Sam and a weekly changing guest on handpump, and good coffee; jigsaws in winter, and maybe unobtrusive piped music. *(Recommended by G Washington, R Ward, Joan and Michel Hooper-Immins, Margaret and Arthur Dickinson, G A and J E Gibbs)*

Free house ~ Licensees Mark and Sue Michaels ~ Real ale ~ Meals and snacks (limited choice after 7.30pm Sat) ~ Restaurant (lunchtime bookings essential) ~ (01686) 668359/287 ~ Children in eating areas and separate room till 9.30 ~ Open 11-11 ~ Bedrooms: £42B/£69B

NEVERN (Dyfed) SN0840 Map 6

Trewern Arms

B4582 – a useful short-cut alternative to most of the A487 Newport—Cardigan

The setting of this cosily extended inn is lovely, just round a bend from a medieval bridge crossing the River Nyfer. It's the stripped-stone slate-floored bar that most people head for, its high rafters strung with nets, ships' lamps, ancient farm and household equipment, shepherds' crooks and cauldrons, and with a couple of high-backed traditional settles, and comfortable plush banquettes. Well kept Boddingtons, Flowers Original and Whitbreads Castle Eden and Pompey Royal on handpump; service is efficient, but can slow down in the bar. A games room has sensibly placed darts, pool, fruit machine, video game, trivia, and a loudish juke box; beyond is a more spacious lounge. The lawn has tables set among shrubs and trees. Bar food such as sandwiches, ploughman's (£3.70), quarter chicken (£4.80), vegetarian dishes (£5.70), steak and kidney pie or lasagne (£5.90), trout and almonds or gammon (£6.90) and steaks (from £9), with children's dishes (from £2.80), and puddings; huge breakfasts. The pilgrims' church over the river has a notable Celtic cross and pre-Christian stones set into its windows, and is sheltered by fat yew trees which are said to weep tears of what local people say is blood if the priest is not Welsh-speaking. *(Recommended by G Washington, Ron and Sheila Corbett, Patrick Freeman, S P Bobeldijk, Roy and Bettie Derbyshire, Jed and Virginia Brown, Mac Tennick; more reports please)*

Free house ~ Licensee Mrs E A Jones ~ Real ale ~ Meals and snacks ~ Restaurant (evenings Thurs-Sat and Sunday lunch) ~ (01239) 820395 ~ Children welcome ~ Open 11-3, 6-11 ~ Bedrooms: £30S/£45S

OLD RADNOR (Powys) SO2559 Map 6

Harp

Village signposted from A44 Kington—New Radnor just W of B4362 junction

Charles I was one of the few people left unmoved by this idyllically set old hilltop inn – he complained about the food during his visit. Others are generally won over straight away, with the licensees notable examples. They came here for their honeymoon two decades ago and liked it so much that when they heard it was on the market a couple of years back they bought it straight away, and it's been going from strength to strength ever since. The pub guards the village green from its nice position beside the 15th-c turreted church (worth a look for its early organ screen), and has splendid views over the Marches; there's plenty of outside seating, either under the big sycamore tree, or on the side grass, where there's a play area. Out here you may come across Hattie the goat, Pilsner the peacock, and Sweetie Pie the donkey. Inside, it's full of character, and the old-fashioned brownstone public bar has high-backed settles, an antique reader's chair and other elderly chairs around a log fire, as well as friendly locals. In addition to darts and dominoes they play table quoits (Monday evenings) and cribbage (Fridays). The cosy slate-floored lounge has a handsome curved antique settle and a fine inglenook log fire, and there are lots of local books and guides for residents. Well kept Woods Special, Wye Valley Hereford and guests on handpump. Simple bar food might include sandwiches (from £1.75), very good home-made soup (£1.95), sautéed garlic mushrooms on toast (£2.95), ploughman's (from £3), a pasta special or deep pan pizza (£3.95), lasagne (£5.75), beef curry (£6.95), and daily specials. Well behaved dogs allowed. Lots of good walks nearby. *(Recommended by T R and B C Jenkins, Liz and Roger Morgan, Tim and Tina Banks, Sarah and Peter Gooderham, Lynn Sharpless, Bob Eardley, A E and P McCully, Margaret and Arthur Dickinson, John MacLean, James Skinner, Anthony Barnes)*

Free house ~ Licensees Stephen and Dee Cope ~ Real ale ~ Meals and snacks (not Mon) ~ Restaurant ~ (01544) 350655 ~ Well behaved children welcome ~ Live entertainment Sat lunchtime ~ Open 11.30-11, maybe less in winter ~ Bedrooms: £30/£40

PEMBROKE FERRY (Dyfed) SM9603 Map 6

Ferry

Nestled below A477 toll bridge, N of Pembroke

This former sailors' haunt has a nautical decor to suit its past, and its attractive setting right on the water can make for fascinating views. It has a very rewarding combination of a fine relaxed yet buoyantly pubby atmosphere with a good range of drinks and good tasty food that makes full use of local produce – particularly from the sea. Fish is cooked simply, so as not to mask the delicacy of its freshness: between cod and plaice (£4.50) and lobster (from £8.95), there may be crab thermidor (£4.50), brill or turbot (£6.95), Dover sole, local Carew oysters (£3.60), crayfish and salmon. The choice depends on market supplies so some dishes may quickly sell out. Other meals could include vegetable kiev or leek and bacon pie (£3.50), garlic tiger prawns (£3.95), schnitzel with a creamy mushroom sauce (£4.95) and steak (£7.95). Booking is virtually essential for Sunday lunch. Well kept Bass and Hancocks HB on handpump, and a decent choice of malt whiskies. Efficient service, fruit machine, unobtrusive piped music. There are tables out on the waterside terrace. *(Recommended by A J nd M Thomasson, Howard and Lynda Dix, Ian Jones, R and M Jones, Mr and Mrs R Franklin, R.T and J C Moggridge, Linda and Brian Davis)*

Free house ~ Licensee David Henderson ~ Real ale ~ Meals and snacks (till 10) ~ Restaurant (Sunday lunch only) ~ (01646) 682947 ~ Children in restaurant ~ Open 11.30-2.45, 6.30(7 Mon)-11

PONTYPOOL (Gwent) ST2998 Map 6

Open Hearth

The Wern, Griffithstown; Griffithstown signposted off A4051 S – opposite British Steel main entrance turn up hill, then first right

The stretch of the Monmouthshire & Brecon Canal which runs above this cheery and welcoming pub has recently reopened, and you can watch the comings and goings from the comfortable lounge bar. But the main attraction here is the excellent range of changing real ales, much better than you'll find anywhere else in the area, with usually Archers Best and Golden, Brains SA, Boddingtons, Bull Mastiff Best, Butcombe, Hancocks HB, and three guests on handpump; they also have a good choice of wines and malt whiskies. Reliably tasty and good value bar food (with some prices down on last year) includes filled rolls (from £1.20), soup (£1.50), filled baked potatoes (from £2.75), various curries (from £3.95), vegetable stir fry (£4.25), steak and Guinness pie, rainbow trout with almonds or cheese filled tortellini with baby sweetcorn and mixed peppers (£4.95), and specials such as chicken napoleon (£6.50) or various steaks (from £7.95); three-course Sunday lunch. They do their best to suit you if you want something not on the menu, and the downstairs restaurant is something of a local landmark; decent coffee, cheap tea, very friendly and efficient service. The smallish, comfortably modernised lounge has a turkey carpet and big stone fireplace; a back bar has more space and leatherette seating. Cribbage, dominoes, and piped music; boules in summer. There are picnic tables, swings, and shrubs in the recently tidied-up garden. *(Recommended by Gwyneth and Salvo Spadaro-Dutturi, Nigel Clifton, Nick and Helen Hilton, the Monday Club, Graham Reeve)*

Free house ~ Licensees Gwyn Philips and Joeanne Lawrence ~ Real ale ~ Meals and snacks (till 10) ~ Restaurant (not Sun evening) ~ (01495) 763752 ~ Children in eating area and restaurant ~ Open 11.30-3(4.30 Sat), 6-11

PRESTEIGNE (Powys) SO3265 Map 6

Radnorshire Arms

High Street; B4355 N of centre

Renovations at this rambling timbered Forte inn have revealed secret passages and priest's holes, with one priest's diary showing he was walled up here for two years. It's now a good deal more comfortable than he'd remember, though he might recognise the venerable dark oak panelling, latticed windows and elegantly moulded black oak beams, now decorated with horse brasses; the old-fashioned charm and atmosphere never seem to change. Reasonably priced bar food might include good sandwiches (from £1.80) or filled baguettes (from £3.50), home-made soup (£1.95), cumberland sausage and mash (£4.20), popular ploughman's (£3.65), vegetable lasagne (£4.95), steak, kidney and mushroom pie (£5.50), gammon steak with fried egg (£5.95) and puddings (£2.95); children's helpings (about £2.10), morning coffee, afternoon tea. Bass and Ruddles County on handpump, English wines by the glass, several malt whiskies, and welcoming, attentive service; separate no-smoking restaurant. Furnishings are discreetly modern. There are some well-spaced tables on the sheltered flower-bordered lawn, which used to be a bowling green. The building was constructed by the brother of one of the men who signed Charles I's death warrant, though it wasn't actually licensed until 1792. This is a nice area for a quiet weekend. *(Recommended by Barbara and Denis Melling, David and Brenda Tew, Sarah and Peter Gooderham, the Monday Club, Neville Kenyon, Pat and John Millward, A P Jeffreys)*

Free house ~ Manager Aidan Treacy ~ Real ale ~ Meals and snacks ~ Restaurant ~ (01544) 267406 ~ Children welcome ~ Open 11-11 ~ Bedrooms: £73.50B/£92B

nr RAGLAN (Gwent) SO3608 Map 6

Clytha Arms

Clytha, off Abergavenny road – former A40, now declassified

The excellent food at this fine old building never disappoints, but it stands out too for the way the licensees obviously put just as much effort into the pub side of the business. The tastefully refurbished bar has a good traditional atmosphere, and half a dozen well kept and often unusual ales on handpump such as Archers Golden, Badger Tanglefoot, Bass, Felinfoel Double Dragon, Nethergate Old Growler, and Theakstons XB; also Weston's farm ciders and freshly squeezed orange juice. Furnishings are solidly comfortable, there are a couple of log fires, and there's a warm welcome from the cheerful helpful staff (and maybe quietly friendly dogs); darts, shove ha'penny, boules, table skittles, cribbage, draughts and chess – no music or machines. The changing choice of fresh food, well prepared and presented, is increasingly the main draw, and besides sandwiches (from £1.60, open sandwiches from £2.75) and ploughman's (£4.35), the menu chalked on the beams might include faggot and mushy peas (£3.20), black pudding with apple and mustard sauce (£3.80), bacon, laverbread and cockles or venison sausages with potato pancakes (£3.95), oysters with leeks and caerphilly (£4.95), Caribbean fruit curry or Spanish meatballs (£7.95), asparagus and goat's cheese soufflé (£8.50), fillet of turbot with crab and calvados sauce (£9.70), monkfish with wild mushrooms (£9.90), roast duck with orange and turnip brûlée (£10.50), delicious home-made puddings (£3) and a good value three-course Sunday lunch (£9.50). There is a roomy no-smoking dining room. The well cared-for grounds are a mass of colour in spring. *(Recommended by Gwyneth and Salvo Spadaro-Dutturi, Mike Pugh, A R and B E Sayer, R and M Jones, Julia Stone)*

Free house ~ Licensees Andrew and Beverley Canning ~ Real ale ~ Meals and snacks (not Sun evening or Mon) ~ Restaurant (not Sun evening) ~ (01873) 840206 ~ Children welcome ~ Open 11.30-3.30, 6-11; all day Sat; cl Mon lunchtime exc bank holidays ~ Bedrooms: £45B/£65B

RED WHARF BAY (Anglesey) SH5281 Map 6

Ship

Village signposted off B5025 N of Pentraeth

Lovely fresh sea views from this solid, slate-roofed 16th-c house: tables on the front terrace look down over ten square miles of treacherous tidal cockle-sands, with low wooded hills sloping down to the broad bay. Inside is characterful and old-fashioned, with a big room on each side of the busy stone-built bar counter, both with long cushioned varnished pews built around the walls, glossily varnished cast-iron-framed tables, and quite a restrained decor including toby jugs, local photographs, attractive antique foxhunting cartoons and coal fires. Enterprising and well-presented daily changing bar food might typically include sandwiches, deep-fried cockles or spicy avocado with mozzarella (£3.95), chicken and ham pie with home-made chutney (£4.40), Welsh sausages with a leek sauce (£5.10), braised meatballs with peppers and tomato (£5.20), parsnip and walnut tatin (£5.30), pepperpot beef and ginger (£6.50), salmon steak with horseradish crust (£6.90), and puddings like rhubarb and ginger crumble (£2.60). Lunchtime service can stop promptly. There may be delays at busy times (it can be quite crowded on Sundays), but service is always friendly and smiling; the cheery licensees have been here now for over 20 years. The dining room is no-smoking. Well kept Tetleys, Benskins, Ind Coope Burton, and summer guests are drawn by handpump with a tight spray to give a northern-style creamy head; a wider choice of wines than usual for the area, and quite a few malt whiskies. Pool, darts and dominoes in the back room, and a family room; piped music. There are rustic tables and picnic tables by an ash tree on grass by the side. *(Recommended by R A Hobbs, A and J Tierney-Jones, D Goodger, J R Whetton, Julie Peters, Wayne Brindle, Mark Bradley, Philip Putwain, Brian and Jill Bond, L G Milligan)*

Free house ~ Licensee Andrew Kenneally ~ Real ale ~ Meals and snacks ~ (01248) 852568 ~ Restaurant ~ Children in family room ~ Open 11-11 Jul-Sept, otherwise 11-3, 7-11 weekdays and bank holidays

ST HILARY (South Glamorgan) ST0173 Map 6

Bush

Village signposted from A48 E of Cowbridge

Genuinely old-fashioned and friendly, this is a lovely 16th-c thatched pub tucked away behind the village church, still said to be haunted by a notorious local highwayman, and very close to Stalling Down, a hill rich in Welsh history. The comfortable and snugly cosy low-beamed lounge bar has walls stripped to the old stone, and windsor chairs around copper-topped tables on the carpet, while the public bar has old settles and pews on aged flagstones, and darts, bar billiards, table skittles, cribbage and dominoes in a room leading off; subdued piped music. Good bar food, using fresh ingredients, includes sandwiches (from £1.50), French onion soup (£1.95), laverbread and bacon (£2.35), Welsh rarebit (£2.95), spinach and cheese pancake (£3.35), ploughman's (£3.60), liver or sausages with onion gravy (£3.95), salads (from £3.95), steak and ale pie (£4.75), gammon (£5.25), mixed grill (£6.75) and good daily specials; the restaurant menu is available in the bar in the evenings, with meals like trout panfried in sherry with toasted almonds (£7.95) or medallions of pork Normandy (£8.50). A three-course set meal is £5.50 at lunch, £7.95 in the evening. Well kept Bass, and Morlands Old Speckled Hen on handpump, with a range of malt whiskies; friendly and efficient service. There are tables and chairs in front, and more in the back garden. *(Recommended by M Joyner, Mr and Mrs Steve Thomas, Nigel Clifton, Michael Richards, Gwynne Harper, Patrick and Mary McDermott)*

Bass ~ Lease: Sylvia Murphy ~ Real ale ~ Meals and snacks (till 10; not winter Sun evenings) ~ Restaurant (not Sun evening) ~ (01446) 772745 ~ Children welcome ~ Open 11-11

STACKPOLE (Dyfed) SR9896 Map 6

Armstrong Arms

Village signposted off B4319 S of Pembroke

Though this rather Swiss-looking building on the Stackpole estate was converted some time ago, it was opened as a pub only three or four years ago. In that time it's built up an enviable reputation for its food, and besides sandwiches (from £1.35) and ploughman's (from £3.45), cheerful black-and-white uniformed waitresses serve dishes such as broccoli and stilton soup (£2.25), gravadlax with grand marnier and caper sauce (£4.50), baked hock of ham with spiced lentils (£5.25), cashew nut and mushroom rissotto (£5.45), beef casseroled in red wine with bacon, shallots and mushroom (£6.45), grilled chicken supreme wrapped in parma ham or tenderloin of pork with an apricot and brandy cream (£7.45), a good choice of fresh fish, and excellent home-made puddings such as dark chocolate and rum torte with raspberry coulis (from £1.50); vegetables are first-class, there's a choice of potatoes, and coffee is good. Well kept Bass, Greenalls Original, Worthingtons Best and guests like Caledonian 80/-, Fullers London Pride and Greene King Abbot. One spacious area has darts, pool, fruit machine and juke box (the beers may be cheaper in here), but the major part of the pub, L-shaped on four different levels, is given over to diners, with neat light oak furnishings, and glossy beams and ceilings to match. There are tables out in the attractive gardens, with colourful flower beds and mature trees around the car park. *(Recommended by A J Miller, Arthur Mole, David Wallington, Miss L Kassam, D Bruford)*

Free house ~ Licensees Senga and Peter Waddilove ~ Real ale ~ Meals (not Sun evening) and lunchtime snacks ~ (01646) 672324 ~ Children welcome ~ Open 11-3, 6-11

TALYBONT-ON-USK (Powys) SO1122 Map 6

Star

B4558

The highlight here is the excellent changing range of a dozen real ales, the names chalked up by the central servery including familiar brews such as Bass, Boddingtons, Felinfoel Double Dragon, and Marstons Pedigree, and more unusual flavours like Bullmastiff, Freeminers and Reckless Erics; they keep two or three farm ciders such as Wilkin's on handpump too. Several plainly furnished rooms – unashamedly stronger on character than on creature comforts – radiate from this heart, including a brightly lit games area with pool table, fruit machine and juke box; cosy winter fires, one in a splendid stone fireplace. Good value bar food includes sandwiches (from £1.50), soup (£2.25), sausage, beans and chips (£2.50), ploughman's (£3), chicken curry (£4.50), lamb's liver casserole or broccoli, cheese and potato pie (£4.95), chicken in leek and stilton sauce or carbonnade of beef (£5.50), and children's meals (£1.80). Friendly service. You can sit outside at picnic tables with parasols in the sizeable tree-ringed garden, and the village, with both the Usk and the Monmouth & Brecon Canal running through, is surrounded by the Brecon Beacons national park. *(Recommended by Mr and Mrs A Plumb, Phil Putwain, John and Joan Nash, John and Joan Wyatt, A P Jeffreys, David and Kate Jones, M Joyner)*

Free house ~ Licensee Mrs Joan Coakham ~ Real ale ~ Meals and snacks (12-2.15, 6.30-9.45) ~ (01874) 676635 ~ Children welcome ~ Live blues/rock Weds evening ~ Open 11-3, 6-11, all day Sat ~ Bedrooms: £20B/£35B

TY'N Y GROES (Gwynedd) SH7672 Map 6

Groes

B5106 N of village

Apparently the first Welsh pub to be properly licensed in 1573, this neat old family-run pub really is a charming spot, especially in summer when it's decked out with colourful plants and flowers. Seats by the road in front have a good view of the River Conwy, and there are more in the pretty back garden with its flower-filled hayricks; an ideal spot for sampling one of their good afternoon teas (not winter weekdays). Inside is a homely series of rambling, low-beamed and thick-walled rooms with antique settles and an old sofa, old clocks, portraits, hats and tins hanging from the walls and a good welcoming atmosphere. A fine antique fireback is built into one wall, perhaps originally from the formidable fireplace which houses a collection of stone cats as well as winter log fires. A no-smoking conservatory has lovely mountain views. Well liked, imaginative bar food – even better since the arrival of their new chef – might include sandwiches, unusual soups (£2), home-baked gammon with apricot sauce (£5.25), lavender chicken (£5.50), good pies (£6.25), poached fresh Conwy salmon (£6.50), Aga-baked whole baby sea bass, local Welsh lamb, lots of seasonal game dishes, half-boned roast duckling (£7.50), and splendid puddings; Sunday lunch (£12.50, including coffee). They do various theme nights (usually on the last Friday of the month, September-April) such as fish or game – the menus are up well in advance and booking is pretty much essential. Well kept (though not cheap for the area) Ind Coope Burton and Tetleys on handpump, a good few malt whiskies, and a fruity fresh Pimms in summer; cribbage, dominoes and light classical piped music at lunchtimes (music from the 1930s-1950s at other times). It can get busy, but this shouldn't cause any problems with the efficient, friendly service. They hope bedrooms will be ready by this summer. It's only a couple of miles from here to Conwy. *(Recommended by Roger and Christine Mash, Roger Byrne, John Evans, Paul Bailey, Pearl Williams, Martin and Penny Fletcher, Mrs J Oakes, Gordon Theaker, M G Lavery, John Roberts, David J B Lewis, D W Jones-Williams, G R Sunderland, J E Hilditch)*

Free house ~ Licensees Dawn, Tony and Justin Humphreys ~ Real ale ~ Meals and snacks ~ Restaurant ~ (01492) 650545 ~ Children in eating areas; in restaurant if over 10 ~ Open 12-11.30; closed winter Sun evenings

USK (Gwent) SO3801 Map 6

Royal

New Market Street (off A472 by Usk bridge)

Locals and visitors agree that when in Usk this characterful Georgian country-town pub is the place to head for, and there's usually a good mix of people filling up the two open-plan rooms of the homely and old-fashioned bar. Many of them are enjoying the tasty bar meals, served in big helpings from a range that might include ploughman's (£2.50), an elaborate vegetarian bake (£6), chicken kiev (£6.20), seafood pasta or deep-fried ricotta parcels (£6.25), beef in red wine (£6.75), grilled lamb chops (£7.20), grilled fresh bream with prawns (£7.25), and lovely tender steaks; you'll generally find some cheaper dishes too, and they do a popular Sunday lunch (when the ordinary menu isn't available). Service can slow down at busy times. The left-hand room is the nicer, with a cream-tiled kitchen range flush with the pale ochre back wall, a comfortable mix of tables and chairs, a rug on neat slate flagstones, plates and old pictures on the walls, china cabinets, and a tall longcase clock. Particularly well kept Bass, Felinfoel Double Dragon, Hancocks HB and a guest on handpump; open fires, dominoes, cribbage, cards, and piped music. Seats out in front face a cedar tree, and readers visiting recently have also come across canaries in cages hanging out here. *(Recommended by Mrs S Jones, Graham Reeve, Mike Pugh, A R and B E Sayer, Peter and Audrey Dowsett; more reports please)*

Free house ~ Licensees Anthony Lyons and Michael Corbett ~ Real ale ~ Meals and snacks (not Sun evening or Mon lunchtime, roasts only Sun lunch) ~ (01291) 672931 ~ Children welcome ~ Open 11-3, 7-11; closed Mon lunchtime

Post Office address codings confusingly give the impression that some pubs are in Gwent or Powys, Wales when they're really in Gloucestershire or Shropshire (which is where we list them).

Lucky Dip

Besides the fully inspected pubs, you might like to try these Lucky Dips recommended to us and described by readers (if you do, please send us reports):

ANGLESEY

Beaumaris [off main st; SH6076], *George & Dragon*: Tudor, with many original beams, welcoming landlord happy to show rare bits of wall paintings and painted beams upstairs, original fireplace and section of wattle and daub wall; good value bar food, Robinsons, friendly staff, nice atmosphere *(Jeanne Cross, Paul Silvestri)*; [Castle St], *Liverpool Arms*: Friendly staff in plushly refurbished pub with nautical atmosphere; bedrooms *(John and Pam Smith)*

☆ **Bodedern** [SH3281], *Crown*: Recently repainted quiet local, very pretty; friendly staff, well kept beer, good well served basic food; bedrooms *(Margaret Mason, David Thompson, L G Milligan)*

Cemaes Bay [High St; SH3793], *Stag*: Popular straightforward village local, small, warm and cosy; good value bar food, well kept Burtonwood, real fire; lounge, bar and pool room *(Jeanne Cross, Paul Silvestri)*

☆ **Menai Bridge** [St Georges Pier, by Straits; SH5572], *Liverpool Arms*: Unpretentious old-fashioned four-roomed local with cheerful relaxed atmosphere, low beams, interesting mostly maritime photographs and prints, conservatory with plastic terrace furniture, tasty straightforward good value bar food inc fresh home cooking, panelled dining room, well kept Greenalls Special and Best on handpump, welcoming landlord, good service; no music *(Jeanne Cross, Paul Silvestri, G Roberts, Dennis Dickinson, David Lewis, Andy and Jill Kassube, Richard Houghton)*

Menai Bridge, *Anglesey Arms*: By suspension bridge, pleasant lounge with wide choice of food inc vegetarian and children's, conservatory restaurant, good service, well kept beers, locals' bar, tables outside; comfortable bedrooms *(Andy and Jill Kassube)*

Valley [A5; SH2979], *Bull*: Wide choice of good value food in bar and popular restaurant, well kept Greenalls, very busy (and can be smoky) despite plenty of space; big garden *(L G Milligan, B A Hobbs, Roger Byrne)*

CLWYD

Bangor Is Y Coed [SJ3945], *Bucks Head*: Genuine food inc good sandwiches and puddings such as feather-light blackberry and raspberry flan with fresh whipped farm cream *(Ann and Stan Webber)*

☆ **Bylchau** [A543 3 miles S; SH9863], *Sportsmans Arms*: Wide views from highest pub in Wales, reliable straightforward food with all fresh veg and vegetarian dishes, well kept Lees Traditional and Best Dark Mild, drinks cheaper than usual; Welsh-speaking locals, cheerful and welcoming prompt service, good log fire, old-fashioned high-backed settles among more modern seats, darts and pool, no piped music, harmonium and Welsh singing Sat evening; children allowed in eating area, cl Mon/Tues lunchtimes in winter (and maybe other lunchtimes then) *(Mr and Mrs B Hobden, KC, B A and R Davies, LYM)*

Carrog [off A5 Llangollen—Corwen; SJ1144], *Grouse*: Terrace and walled garden with sweet peas and honeysuckle and tables overlooking Dee bridge, pleasantly chatty landlord, Lees Bitter, good menu, pool room; Rum and Coke are two goats, Thomas the old cat; dogs allowed on lead; bedrooms *(T G Thomas)*

Cerrigydrudion [SH9549], *Saracens Head*: A hotel, but useful stop for bar food; low-cost bedrooms *(K H Frostick)*

☆ **Chirk** [Chirk Bank, S; SJ3028], *Bridge*: Varied and interesting range of reasonably priced home-made food in big helpings, well kept beer, friendly staff; handy for canal *(A D Marsh, Roger Berry)*

Corwen [SJ0843], *Crown*: Welcoming, with good food esp good value Sun lunch; bedrooms *(DC)*

Denbigh [Old Ruthin Rd; SJ0666], *Brookhouse Mill*: Friendly pub/restaurant by River Ystrad, well kept beer, good choice of other drinks, decent food in bar and restaurant; play area outside *(GF)*

☆ **Erbistock** [village signed off A539 W of Overton; SJ3542], *Boat*: Idyllic spot, tables in a pretty partly terraced garden sharing a sleepy bend of the River Dee with a country church; has closed and reopened a couple of times in the last two years, but by summer 1995 was thriving again as a dining pub (not cheap), with an attractive small flagstoned bar, comfortably plush beamed dining room, roomy annexe (with sandwiches even on Sun, when the main pub does set meals) *(GM, LYM)*

Ffrith [B5101, just off A541 Wrexham—Mold; SJ2855], *Poachers Cottage*: Pleasant 18th-c pub, two bars and restaurant, real ales, decent changing wines, good reasonably priced home-cooked food inc good vegetarian dishes and some Danish specialities; cl lunchtime exc Sun *(David Parry)*

Graianrhyd [B5430, signed off A494 and A5104; SJ2156], *Rose & Crown*: Isolated in Clwydian Hills, roaring fire, good choice of home-cooked food inc swordfish steak and heaped mixed grill, Whitbreads-related ales, efficient service; cl 2.30 sharp *(Joan and Michel Hooper-Immins)*

☆ **Gresford** [Old Wrexham Rd; SJ3555], *Pant-yr-Ochain*: Roomy and attractive, with masses of pictures and bric-a-brac, big dining area with floor-to-ceiling books, polite staff, well kept beers, good food *(Dr Andrew Schuman, Anna Brewer)*

☆ **Gwaenysgor** [just S of Prestatyn; SJ0881], *Eagle & Child*: Welcoming and spotless early 19th-c pub, shining brasses and plates, generous freshly cooked good value food, Bass, good service; well kept floodlit gardens, in hilltop village with fine views *(Derek and Cerys Williams, J E Hilditch)*

☆ **Hanmer** [SJ4639], *Hanmer Arms*: Good range of reasonably priced straightforward food inc vegetarian in relaxed and pleasantly uncrowded country inn with well kept bar, Tetleys-related ales, big family dining room upstairs – good for Sun lunch; no music, neat and attractive garden, with church nearby making a pleasant backdrop; pretty village; comfortable good value bedrooms in former courtyard stable block *(G Hallett)*

Hawarden [SJ3266], *Gwynne Arms*: Small hotel with decent bar food inc good ploughman's and well kept Theakstons Best, XB and Old Peculier in attractive bar, brass ornaments and circular trays, friendly service; bedrooms *(David Shillitoe)*

Henllan [B5382 nr Denbigh; SJ0268], *Llindir*: Well run and friendly ancient thatched and stone-built local with well kept ales inc Bass, simple food at reasonable prices; very popular, esp with farmers *(Mr and Mrs M St-Amour)*

☆ **Llanarmon D C** [SJ1633], *West Arms*: Warm welcome and roaring log fires in extended 16th-c beamed and timbered inn, good base for walking; picturesque upmarket lounge bar full of antique settles, sofas, even an elaborately carved confessional stall, well kept Boddingtons, good range of wines and malt whiskies, more sofas in old-fashioned entrance hall, comfortable back bar too; food, not cheap, inc good fresh fish; pretty lawn running down to River Ceiriog (fishing for residents); children welcome; bedrooms comfortable *(Sue and Bob Ward, BJSM, T A Smith, Paul McPherson, LYM)*

☆ **Llanarmon D C**, *Hand*: Civilised inn tucked away in lovely countryside, good value food in spacious side room next to bar and in restaurant, pleasant afternoon teas, helpful attentive staff, good log fires; children welcome, comfortable bedrooms *(Tom Linton, Paul McPherson, LYM)*

Llanasa [SJ1082], *Red Lion*: Tucked away in the hills above Prestatyn, well kept beer, good bar food, lovely atmosphere, welcoming licensees and log fire *(M A Cameron)*

☆ **Llanelian Yn Rhos** [S of Colwyn Bay; signed off A5830 (shown as B5383 on some maps) and B5381; SH8676], *White Lion*: Very well run old inn, wide choice of good reasonably priced bar food from sandwiches up in neat and spacious dining area, broad steps down to traditional flagstoned snug bar with antique settles and big fire; well kept Courage-related beers, good wine list, lots of malt whiskies; can get busy with tourists in summer; dominoes, cribbage, piped music; rustic tables outside, good walking nearby; children in eating area; bedrooms *(F M Bunbury, LYM)*

Llanelidan [B5429 just E of village; signed off A494 S of Ruthin; OS Sheet 116 map ref 110505; SJ1150], *Leyland Arms*: We've heard that this beautifully set interesting old pub, closed since 1991, has now reopened, but have no detailed reports yet *(News please)*

☆ **Llangedwyn** [B4396; SJ1924], *Green*: Very old country dining pub, clean and well run, with lots of nooks and crannies, oak settles, roaring log fire, pleasant helpful service, good quickly served home-cooked food esp fish in bar and upstairs evening restaurant, well kept Whitbreads-related and guest ales, good choice of malt whiskies and wines; lots of tables in beautiful garden over rd, lovely Tanat Valley surroundings, own fishing *(Nigel Woolliscroft, Basil Minson, Paddy Moindrot, Paul McPherson)*

Llangollen [A542 1½ miles W; SJ2142], *Abbey Grange*: More hotel than pub, but welcoming with good service, moderately priced food all day (at least in summer) inc good Sun lunch, ales inc Theakstons, picnic tables outside, shire horses in the grounds; beautiful spot with superb views nr Valle Crucis Abbey; comfortable bedrooms *(Bill Sykes, Derek and Cerys Williams)*; [Regent St (A5 W)], *Wild Pheasant*: Hotel with friendly pubby atmosphere in bar, friendly staff, good food and beer; spacious grounds; bedrooms *(Gordon Theaker)*

☆ nr **Llangollen** [Trevor Uchaf, off A539; SJ2442], *Sun Trevor*: High up over Dee Valley with spectacular views, good food in bar and restaurant, friendly staff, well kept Courage-related ales *(P G Topp)*

nr **Llangollen** [Horseshoe Pass; A542 N – extreme bottom right corner of OS Sheet 116 at overlap with OS Sheet 117, map ref 200454], *Britannia*: Lovely Dee Valley views from picturesque though much extended inn, two quiet bars and brightly cheerful dining area, Whitbreads-related ales; usual food inc OAP bargains, piped music; well kept garden; good value attractive bedrooms *(Joan and Michel Hooper-Immins, D W Jones-Williams, KC)*

☆ **Llanrhaeadr** [just off A525 Ruthin—Denbigh; SJ0863], *Kings Head*: Good value food, well kept beer, pleasant atmosphere; nice village – good Jesse window in church; bedrooms *(D W Jones-Williams)*

☆ **Llansannan** [A544 Abergele—Bylchau; SH9466], *Red Lion*: Charming little old-fashioned front parlour in friendly Welsh-speaking 13th-c hill-village local, other more straightforward bars; well kept Lees, obliging service, roaring fire, simple food inc children's dishes; cl Mon; seats in garden, bedrooms *(Derek and Cerys Williams, LYM)*

Llay [SJ3356], *Holly Bush*: Tastefully modernised lounge in olde-worlde civilised local, good food inc very popular Sun lunch *(Miss R M Tudor)*

Northop [SJ2569], *Boot*: Doing well under friendly new management, wide choice of reasonably priced food cooked fresh by Spanish chef *(Mr and Mrs M St-Amour)*

☆ **Overton Bridge** [A539; SJ3643], *Cross Foxes*: Warm and friendly 17th-c coaching inn in attractive setting on Dee, lots of little rooms, one with river views, good value generous straightforward home cooking with some interesting specials *(E G Parish, Graham and Lynn Mason)*

☆ **Pontblyddyn** [A5104/A541, 3 miles SE of Mold; SJ2761], *Bridge*: Cosy old traditional bar, sympathetically restored, with good log fire, bar food cooked to order inc some interesting dishes, attractive dim-lit dining area with sensible tables and chairs and another big open fire, good Sun lunches, real ales, attentive staff; tables on roadside terrace, pleasant gardens by River Alyn with ducks and geese – good for children *(KC)*

Pontblyddyn [Wrexham Rd (A541)], *Druid*: Good choice of popular generous good value food in dark, warm and friendly pub, good service, picnic tables and good play area out in flower garden *(Graham and Lynn Mason, KC)*

Prestatyn [A548 4 miles E; SJ0783], *Bells of St Marys*: Useful Brewers Fayre pub, open all day, with Whitbreads-related ales, nooks and crannies in big dining areas, pithy sayings on beams, rendered brickwork, leaded lights, prints, bric-a-brac and tools; piped music, fruit machine; play areas inside and out *(D Hanley)*

☆ **Rhewl** [the one on A525 Ruthin—Denbigh; SJ1160], *Drovers Arms*: Good value food inc children's in three roomy and spotless eating areas of old-fashioned low-beamed pub, reasonable prices, good service, friendly locals, well kept beer, no piped music, pool room; attractive garden *(KC)*

☆ **Rhewl** [the one off A5 W of Llangollen; OS Sheet 125 map ref 176448; SJ1744], *Sun*: Friendly and unpretentious little cottage in good walking country just off Horseshoe Pass, with relaxing views from terrace and garden; simple good value food from sandwiches to good Sun lunch, well kept Felinfoel Double Dragon and cheap Worthington BB, malt whiskies, old-fashioned hatch service to back room, dark little lounge, portakabin games room – children allowed here and in eating area *(Andy and Jill Kassube, Dave Thompson, Margaret Mason, J and B Gibson, David Atkinson, LYM)*

Rhos on Sea [Rhos Rd; SH8481], *Rhos Fynach*: Stonebuilt with big lounge, two open fires, prints, brassware, Ind Coope Burton and Tetleys, bar food from noon, upstairs evening restaurant, separate bar; piped music *(D Hanley)*

Ruthin [Rhos St; SJ1258], *Olde Anchor*: Friendly landlord, good food in bar and restaurant, well kept Bass and Worthington, colourful window-boxes; bedrooms good and inexpensive *(Mrs A Taylor, Norman and Barbara Ellis)*

St George [off A55 nr Abergele; SH9576], *Kinmel Arms*: Doing well under new owners, good range of real ales with weekly guest, interesting food inc lovely salads in bar and restaurant, reasonable prices; bedrooms, attractive village *(Colin Francis, Nathan Bird)*

Towyn [Towyn Rd, off A548 Rhyl—Abergele; SH9779], *Farmhouse*: Large L-shaped room with plates above bar, open fire, heavy woodwork; John Smiths, bar food, seats outside *(D Hanley)*

☆ **Tremeirchion** [off B5429 up lane towards church; SJ0873], *Salusbury Arms*: Lovely log fires in beamed pub with some 14th-c panelling, comfortable attractive furnishings, well kept Marstons Pedigree, Morlands Old Speckled Hen and several changing guest beers, well equipped games room, children welcome, pretty garden with under-cover barbecue; usual food (not Sun evening), open all day summer *(Mr and Mrs R F Wright, KC, Martin and Penny Fletcher, John and Avian Withinshaw, LYM)*

☆ **Trofarth** [B5113 S of Colwyn Bay; SH8470], *Holland Arms*: Good value food inc lunchtime bargains in old-fashioned 17th-c former coaching inn, warm cosy atmosphere, prompt friendly service, Tetleys and Ansells Mild, farm tools in one room, stuffed owls in the other, raised dining area open when busy; some tables outside with valley and mountain views; handy for Bodnant *(Roger Byrne, David Wynne Hughes)*

Wrexham [Yorke St; SJ3450], *Wynnstay Arms*: Lively bar with very good value generous food, pleasant staff *(W L G Watkins)*

DYFED

Aberaeron [Queen St; SN4462], *Prince of Wales*: Cosy backstreet pub with open fires, friendly ex-butcher landlord, good steaks, real ale *(J Honnor)*; [High St], *Royal Oak*: Clean and pleasant, with big but invitingly cosy front lounge, nicely cooked well presented food, friendly prompt service, Ansells on handpump; back games area with pool, machines *(Ian Phillips, Mike and Wendy Proctor, Madeline and Ernest Knight)*

Abercych [follow Boncath signs; SN2441], *Nags Head*: Restored after two-year closure, flagstones, stripped stone, leather chesterfields, old tables and chairs, woodburner, Whitbreads-related ales, decent bar food till 7 then restaurant meals (must book weekend); children's dishes *(Dr D Radley)*

Aberystwyth [Mill St; SN6777], *Mill*: Friendly local open all day, several well kept Tetleys-related ales with a couple of guests such as local Dinas and Felinfoel Double Dragon, good simple lunchtime cold snacks, pool table, friendly staff *(Joan and Michel Hooper-Immins, Richard Lewis)*

☆ **Amroth** [SN1607], *New Inn*: Traditional beamed local by lovely beach, wide choice of good generous home cooking inc good soups, local seafood, real chips and children's dishes; three small rooms with open fires, no music and good atmosphere, upstairs lounge bar, games room with pool tables and machines (children allowed); well kept real ales inc Ind Coope Burton, friendly staff; picnic tables in good garden, holiday flat to let *(David Wallington, Gwyneth and Salvo Spadaro-Dutturi, A J Bowen)*

Angle [B4320; SM8603], *Hibernia*: Lively village local with cheap well kept Worthington BB, wide choice of generous food, obliging landlord *(Stuart Earle)*; [East Angle Bay, signed off B4320 in village], *Old Point House*: Idyllic spot overlooking Milford Haven, dating from 14th century, unspoilt but comfortable, with Hancocks HB and Worthington, basic food strong on local seafood; run by local lifeboat coxswain, many photographs; plenty of benches and ancient slate seats outside *(Stuart Earle)*

Bosherston [SR9694], *St Govans*: Welcoming open-plan bar, useful food (all day Sun in summer), Worthington BB on handpump, piped music, bar billiards, bedrooms; the eponymous hermit's chapel overlooking the sea is worth getting to, as are the nearby lilyponds *(Mr and Mrs Steve Thomas, LYM)*

☆ *nr* **Broad Haven** [N of village on coast rd, bear L for about 1½ miles then follow sign L to Druidstone Haven – inn a sharp left turn after another ½ mile; OS Sheet 157 map ref 862168, marked as Druidston Villa], *Druidstone*: A great favourite with many readers (and the Editor), very unusual and – if it suits you – a marvellous place to stay; its club licence means you can't go for just a drink and have to book to eat there (the food is inventively individual home cooking, with fresh ingredients and a leaning towards the organic; restaurant cl Sun evening); a very individual, lived-in and informal house alone in a grand spot above the sea, with terrific views, spacious homely bedrooms, erratic plumbing, a cellar bar (good food here too) with a strong 1960s folk-club feel, Worthington BB and good wines, country wines and other drinks, ceilidhs and folk jamborees, chummy dogs (dogs welcomed), all sorts of sporting activities from boules to sand-yachting; cl Nov and Jan; bedrooms *(Jed and Virginia Brown, Mrs Cynthia Archer, Mrs Heather Martin, Bob Riley, Paula Harrison, LYM)*

Caio [off A482 Llanwrda—Lampeter; SN6739], *Brunant Arms*: Unspoilt village pub, well kept Boddingtons, Greenalls and Morlands Old Speckled Hen *(R C Morgan)*

☆ **Cardigan** [leaving centre southwards on right after bridge; SN1846], *Eagle*: Very popular llively local, bright and cheerful, rugs on tiled floor, hop-festooned beams, thousands of beer mats on ceiling, lots of bric-a-brac, entertaining verses in poet's corner, well kept Crown Buckley, good straightforward food from outstanding ham rolls to real blowouts *(Federico and Mario Cristini, David Wallington)*

Carmarthen [Lammas St; SN4120], *Drovers Arms*: Small family-run hotel with homely bar where women feel happy, plenty of character, decent food, well kept Felinfoel Double Dragon; comfortable bedrooms *(Sian Thomas)*; [Queen St], *Queens*: Two rooms either side of bar, efficient friendly service, good range of beers such as Worthington, generous bar food inc tempting sandwiches and good value cawl; separate wine bar and restaurant *(Anne Morris)*

Cenarth [A484 Cardigan—Newcastle Emlyn; SN2641], *Three Horseshoes*: Welcoming family-run village pub with friendly attentive staff, good choice of generous reasonably priced food – most people here to eat; medieval alehouse at the back *(P and J Daggett)*

☆ **Cwm Gwaun** [Pontfaen; Cwm Gwaun and Pontfaen signed off B4313 E of Fishguard; SN0035], *Dyffryn Arms*: Very basic and idiosyncratic Welsh-speaking country tavern known locally as Bessie's, run by same family since 1840; plain deal furniture, well kept Bass and Ind Coope Burton served by jug through a hatch, good sandwiches if you're lucky, Great War prints, draughts-boards inlaid into tables, very relaxed atmosphere; pretty countryside *(Patrick Freeman, Paul McPherson, LYM)*

Dinas [A487; SN0139], *Ship Aground*: 18th-c smugglers' pub done up with nautical trappings, some interesting ropework; friendly staff and locals, good value limited lunchtime bar food, wide evening choice inc local fish and seafood, well kept Crown Buckley; open all day in summer *(John Allsopp, BB)*

☆ **Dreenhill** [Dale Rd (B4327); SM9214], *Denant Mill*: 16th-c converted watermill with well kept ales, inexpensive wines, decent coffee, good informal stripped-stone restaurant with often exotic freshly cooked food inc authentic Goan dishes; remote setting down narrow lane, big safe garden with ducks on millpond, extensive wood behind; bedrooms clean and reasonably priced *(R T and J C Moggridge, Paul Bachelor, Wendy Trineman)*

☆ **Fishguard** [Lower Town; SM9537], *Ship*: Cheery landlord and lots of atmosphere in dimly lit red-painted fishermen's local nr old harbour, well kept Worthington BB and Dark Mild tapped from the cask, homely bar food (not weekends), coal fire, lots of boat pictures, model ships; children welcome, toys provided *(Ian Phillips, Patrick Freeman, LYM)*

☆ **Fishguard** [The Square, Upper Town], *Royal Oak*: Decent standard food inc good fish pie in bar and back restaurant, coal fire, Bass, Hancocks HB and Worthington BB; military prints and pictures commemorating defeat here of second-last attempted French invasion, long narrow bar stepping down to picture-window dining area *(R Michael Richards, Prof I H Rorison, Ian Phillips)*

☆ **Haverfordwest** [24 Market St; SM9515], *Georges*: Unusually wide choice of generous home-made food using fresh veg and good meat in attractive bar with character stable-like furnishings, informal relaxed atmosphere and good choice of well kept ales such as Bass, Ind Coope Burton and Marstons Pedigree; more sophisticated evening restaurant, good friendly service; no dogs *(Carole Fletcher, Howard and Lynda Dix, Jane Byrski, Michael Hunt, Gareth Coombe)*

☆ **Haverfordwest** [Old Quay, Quay St; from A40 E, keep left after crossing river, then first left], *Bristol Trader*: Much modernised old pub in lovely waterside setting, friendly service, cheap generous home-made lunchtime food, well kept Ind Coope Burton, decent malt whiskies, CD juke box, maybe entertainment; children allowed if well behaved, tables out overlooking water; open all day Fri, Sat *(Barbara Ann Mayer, LYM)*

Lampeter [SN5748], *Ram*: Good food, well kept beer *(G Washington)*

Lamphey [SN0100], *Dial*: Good helpings of well presented home-made food inc interesting changing specials and good puddings, Bass, Hancocks HB and guest beer on handpump, big public bar, family room, games room and eating area, friendly fast service by attentive staff *(Stuart Earle)*

☆ **Landshipping** [SN0111], *Stanley Arms*: Friendly ex-farmhouse local on lovely estuary (moorings), good imaginative food inc vegetarian and children's, well kept Crown Buckley Reverend James and Worthington BB, farm cider, two cats; weekend live music; tables on lawn under ancient chestnut, colourful window boxes and flower baskets, afternoon cream teas *(S Watkin, S A and L M Taylor)*

☆ **Little Haven** [SM8512], *Castle*: Good fresh local fish (though not many snacks or vegetarian dishes) quickly served in friendly well placed pub by green, view over sandy bay, Worthington BB, good service; big oak tables, stone walls, oak beams in bar lounge and restaurant area, collection of castle prints, outside seating; children welcome, good facilities for them; the village has a paying car park *(Madeline and Ernest Knight, R T and J C Moggridge, Barbara Ann Mayer)*

☆ **Little Haven** [in village itself, not St Brides hamlet further W], *St Brides*: A short stroll from the sea, with Worthington BB and guest beers such as Theakstons Old Peculier, pews in stripped-stone bar and communicating dining area (children allowed here), quite a wide choice of food, piped music; interesting well in back corner may be partly Roman; big comfortable bedrooms, some in annexe over rd *(Mrs K F Gogerty, Mr Evans, David and Helen Wilkins, LYM)*

☆ **Llanarthne** [B4300 E of Carmarthen; SN5320], *Golden Grove Arms*: Interestingly laid-out inn with roomy lounge, open fire, well kept ales inc Boddingtons and local Crown Buckley BB and Reverend James, huge choice of good food, very pleasant prompt service, children's play area; many Welsh-speaking customers, Tues folk night; bedrooms *(Anne Morris, LYM)*

☆ **Llanarthne** [B4300], *Paxton*: Extraordinary profusion of bric-a-brac, balloons, flashing lights, more restrained restaurant, most obliging friendly service (chatty landlord may wear Victorian dress), wide choice of generous bar food and good value lunch, well kept Worthington BB and a guest such as Theakstons, good local farm cider, decent malt whiskies; very music-oriented – jazz, folk, blues and poetry, with occasional beer and music festivals; opp wood leading to Paxtons Tower (NT) *(Anne Morris, Pete Baker)*

☆ **Llanddarog** [SN5016], *Butchers Arms*: Good generous home cooking from sandwiches up inc quite sophisticated daily specials, well kept Felinfoel Double Dragon and other ales tapped from the cask, tiny low-beamed central bar with woodburner, brasses and old photographs, two mainly dining areas off, friendly very helpful staff; tables outside *(Ian Phillips, A J Bowen, Anne Morris)*

Llanddarog [just off A48], *White Hart*: Stonebuilt thatched pub, new management doing good food *(Howard James)*

Llandissilio [A478, 3 miles N of A40; SN1221], *Bush*: Doing well under friendly new management, smart and clean, with efficient service, good standard food *(Ron and Sheila Corbett)*

Llandovery [Market Sq; SN7634], *Red Lion*: One basic but welcoming room with no bar, well kept Crown Buckley tapped from the cask, friendly and individual landlord; cl Sun, may close early evening if no customers *(Pete Baker, BB)*

☆ **Llandybie** [6 Llandeilo Rd; SN6115], *Red Lion*: Wide choice of generous reasonably priced good fresh food in attractive inn's tastefully modernised, spacious and comfortable bar and restaurant; several well kept Whitbreads-related ales, welcoming efficient service, local pictures for sale; bedrooms, new upstairs function room *(Wyn Churchill, Howard James)*

☆ **Llangranog**, *Ship*: In pretty fishing village, with tables under canopy by beachside car park giving continental feel in summer; interesting varied home-cooked food inc vegetarian, good Sun carvery, well kept Whitbreads-related ales, open fire; can get busy summer, may be cl Mon in winter; bedrooms *(David Wallington)*

☆ **Llanwnnen** [A475 Lampeter—Newcastle Emlyn; SN5346], *Grannel*: Roomy and comfortably refurbished, with good personal service, well kept Worthington BB, good value largely home-made straightforward food in bar and restaurant; good value bedrooms *(R T and J C Moggridge)*

Lydstep [SS0898], *Lydstep*: Warm, appealing and well decorated main bar and clean, tidy family room; good home-made food, friendly service, well kept Tetleys and Worthington *(Tim and Tracy Clark)*

Manorbier [SS0697], *Castle*: Friendly, special little place useful for coast path – open all day in summer; good home-made food inc vegetarian, seafood and children's, Theakstons *(Shirley Pielou)*

Marloes [OS Sheet 157 map ref 793083; SM7908], *Lobster Pot*: Clean, pleasant and friendly, decent sandwiches, well kept beer *(D C Pressey)*

☆ **Mathry** [off A487 Fishguard—St Davids; SM8732], *Farmers Arms*: Welcoming local with happy atmosphere, unusually good generous home-cooked food inc local fish and seafood, well kept Bass and Worthington BB, small garden; has been open all day, at least in summer *(C Driver, James and Linda Skinner)*

Meidrim [off B4298/A299, ¾ mile W; SN2820], *Maenllwyd*: Old-fashioned unspoilt pub with lounge like 1940s parlour, games room with darts and cards, no bar counter – well kept Crown Buckley on handpump in back room, friendly landlord; cl lunchtime and Sun *(Pete Baker)*

Mynydd y Garreg [2 km NE Kidwelly, follow signs to Industrial Museum; SN4308], *Gwenllian Court*: Riverside hotel with popular bar food, carvery and restaurant meals, good choice of beers, big bar with cane furniture; by old tin-working museum, tables out by water, good walks; good value bedrooms *(Steve Thomas)*

Narberth [High St; SN1114], *Angel*: Good food, well kept beer *(G Washington)*

☆ **Newcastle Emlyn** [Sycamore St (A475)], *Pelican*: Friendly 17th-c inn with reasonable choice of well priced bar food, real ales, helpful service, pews and panelling, and fireplace with bread oven still recognisable as the one where Rowlandson in 1797 sketched a dog driving the roasting spit; tables in garden, children welcome; bedrooms in adjoining cottage *(S P Bobeldijk, Mike and Wendy Proctor, LYM)*

Newcastle Emlyn [Bridge St; SN3040], *Bunch of Grapes*: Solid oak round tables and chairs in roomy and welcoming bar, well kept Bass and other beers, food inc good cawl (and takeaways or delivered lunches), conservatory with grape vines; in attractive main street leading to bridge *(Anne Morris, J Honnor, S P Bobeldijk)*

Newgale [A487 S of St Davids; SM8422], *Duke of Edinburgh*: Simple pub just over shingle bank from splendid beach, lounge, public bar and pool room; decent straightforward food all day, well kept real ale, obliging service *(BB)*

Newport [East St; SN0539], *Llwyngwair Arms*: Friendly local with good food inc genuine Indian dishes (takeaways too), well kept Worthington, coal fire *(Michael Richards)*

☆ **Pont ar Gothi** [A40 6 miles E of Carmarthen; SN5021], *Cresselly Arms*: Doing well under welcoming new licensees, cosy low-beamed restaurant overlooking river, step up to tiled bar area with fishing memorabilia and copper-topped tables around the edges, another step to relaxing lounge area with woodburner and TV; good value bar food, Whitbreads-related ales, riverside walks *(Peter Churchill, Michael Richards, Mr and Mrs S Thomas, Howard James)*

☆ **Pont ar Gothi**, *Salutation*: Good friendly atmosphere in traditional pub with promptly served plentiful bar food, well kept Felinfoel Double Dragon, log fire, big settles in small flagstone-floored rooms, restaurant; bedrooms *(A J Bowen, Huw and Carolyn Lewis)*

☆ **Pontarsais** [A485 Carmarthen—Lampeter; SN4428], *Stag & Pheasant*: Welcoming and unpretentious, with good range of reasonably priced food from cawl to more substantial meals, decent choice of real ales, pleasant decor *(I H Rorison, Kathryn and Brian Heathcote, Dave and Judith Risley)*

☆ *nr* **Ponterwyd** [A44 nearly 2 miles E; SN7781], *Dyffryn Castell*: Homely friendly atmosphere, good value bar food and well kept Marstons Pedigree, John Smiths and Worthington BB in unpretentious but comfortable inn dwarfed by the mountain slopes sweeping up from it; bedrooms clean, comfortable and good value *(D Jones-Williams, LYM)*

Pontrhydygroes [SN7472], *Miners Arms*: Friendly, good genuine country cooking inc super vegetarian range; mix of locals and visitors; live music Sun *(Jennie Munro, Jim Wingate)*

☆ **Porthgain** [SM8132], *Sloop*: Largely unspoilt old pub in interesting village, close to old harbour; friendly relaxing local atmosphere, dark bare stone, lots of alcoves, character old furniture, nautical and wreck memorabilia, newer family/eating extension; well kept Felinfoel Double Dragon and Hancocks HB, wide range of good value food inc nice full crab sandwiches, afternoon teas, small seating area outside *(Patrick Freeman, S Hassrip, A A Turnbull, John Allsopp, Paul McPherson, Mike and Wendy Proctor)*

Pwll [Bassett Terr; A484 W of Llanelli; SN4801], *Tafarn y Sospan*: Wide range of bar food inc good Welsh dishes, popular restaurant, welcoming service, pool room, good choice of beers *(Mr and Mrs Steve Thomas)*

☆ **Rhosmaen** [SN6424], *Plough*: Deep-cushioned comfort and good value fresh bar food inc good puddings in smart lounge with picture-window views, well kept Bass, tiled front bar, separate less cheap popular restaurant; long-serving friendly licensees *(Mrs S Wright, Howard James, Wyn Churchill, LYM)*

Rosebush [aka Tafarn Newydd; SN0729], *New Inn*: Cottagey pub with three fireplaces (one huge), wonderful stone walls and floor, artisan furniture, unusual real ales, interesting wines, good food *(Ian Phillips)*

☆ **Saundersfoot** [Wogan Terr; SN1304], *Royal Oak*: Very popular friendly and unspoilt local, well kept Bass, Boddingtons and Flowers Original, no music or machines, tasty food esp fresh fish, tables outside *(Simon and Amanda Southwell, Colin and Ann Hunt)*

Solva [Lower Solva; SM8024], *Cambrian Arms*: Attractive dining pub with pleasant atmosphere, popular bar food esp prawn and mushroom pancake and home-made pasta, decent Italian wines, well kept Tetleys-related ales, log fires; no dogs or children *(Gwynne Harper, Dave Braisted, H D Spottiswoode)*;

[High St, Upper Solva], *Royal George*: Cosy and comfortable with relaxed atmosphere, friendly service, good sea views esp from terrace; imaginative food using fresh local produce, good vegetarian specials *(R S Kular)*
St Davids [Goat St; SM7525], *Farmers Arms*: Cheap and cheerful genuine pub, busy and well patronised, with good food, well kept Worthington BB, cathedral view from tables in tidy back garden *(Prof I H Rorison, Patrick Freeman)*
St Dogmaels [SN1645], *Ferry*: Old stone building with various modern additions overlooking Teifi estuary, friendly character bar, pine tables, nice clutter of bric-a-brac inc many old advertising signs; Wadworths 6X, generous bar food, children welcome, tables out on terrace *(Michael Sargent, D M Wilkins, BB)*; *Teifi Netpool*: Run by Rugby enthusiast, well kept Llanelli real ale, food inc outstanding dressed crab, spotless oak tables; lovely walk to Poppitt sands *(Patrick Freeman)*
Talybont [SN6589], *Black Lion*: Substantial stone village inn with comfortably modernised back lounge, games in and off front public bar, decent bar food inc vegetarian, friendly staff, Bass real ale, restaurant; seats in sheltered back garden *(Kathy Newens, LYM)*
☆ **Tenby** [Upper Frog St; SN1300], *Coach & Horses*: Comfortable lounge with wide choice of home-made food inc at least two fresh locally caught fish dishes, three well kept Whitbreads-related ales, good choice of bottled beers, good service, lively separate bar with games machines and CD juke box; open all day *(Martin Bevan, Ian Phillips)*
Tenby, *Plantagenet*: Unusual interior in ancient building with marvellous old chimney, four rooms on two levels, unusual not cheap food inc fine soups and crab sandwiches, choice of Welsh cheeses and salad *(Shirley Pielou)*
☆ **Wolfs Castle** [A40 Haverfordwest—Fishguard; SM9526], *Wolfe*: Wide choice of good popular home-made food (not Sun or Mon evenings in winter) in comfortable lounge, garden room and conservatory, well kept Ind Coope Burton and Tetleys, decent wines, attractively laid-out garden; simpler public bar with darts; restaurant; children welcome; bedrooms *(Gwynne Harper, Gary Roberts, Ann Stubbs, Howard and Lynda Dix, H and A McFarlane, LYM)*

GLAMORGAN – MID

Caerphilly [Groeswen, NW of town – OS Sheet 171 map ref 128869; ST1286], *White Cross*: Good atmosphere, full range of well kept Theakstons ales and guests such as Hook Norton Old Hookey and Greene King Abbot and Morlands Old Specked Hen, good range of cheap bar food; separate dining room, children welcome; weekend evening barbecues in summer, play area *(Ian Fairweather, Miss E Kingdon)*
☆ *nr* **Caerphilly** [Watford; Tongwynlais exit from M4 junction 32, then right just after church; ST1484], *Black Cock*: Wide range of good value food from cheap snacks up in neat blue-plush bar with open fire in pretty tiled fireplace, and interesting brass-tabled public bar where children allowed; well kept Bass, sizeable terraced garden among trees with play area and barbecue, restaurant extension; up in the hills, just below Caerphilly Common *(the Sandy family, BB)*
☆ **Llangeinor** [nr Blackmill; SS9187], *Llangeinor Arms*: Partly 15th-c beamed pub with terrific views from front conservatory (children allowed here), lounge with old Welsh china and bygones, coal fire, friendly helpful staff, decent usual bar food, well kept Bass, Hancocks HB and Brains SA, evening restaurant *(R Michael Richards, John and Joan Nash, Nigel Clifton, Peter Douglas, LYM)*
Nant y Moel [Ogwy St, off A4061 – OS Sheet 170 map ref 930934; SS9393], *Blaenogwr*: Comfortable and well maintained, welcoming staff, good reasonably priced bar food, well kept Worthington, no music; well behaved children allowed *(J Lloyd)*
☆ **Nottage** [Heol y Capel (off A4229); handy for M4 junction 37; SS8178], *Rose & Crown*: Useful Chef & Brewer family dining pub in comfortably modernised old inn not far from coast, flagstones and beams, good choice of usual food in bar and restaurant, friendly service, well kept Courage-related ales, unobtrusive piped music, fruit machine; open all day Sat; children in eating area and restaurant; comfortable well equipped bedrooms *(Judith and Stephen Gregory, Dr and Mrs A K Clarke, LYM)*
Nottage, *Swan*: Attractive old pub with well kept Courage Directors and Wadworths 6X, good service, cheerful atmosphere; lunchtime food *(John and Joan Nash)*
☆ **Ogmore** [B4524; SS8674], *Pelican*: Friendly and comfortable old country local above ruined castle, functional main bar leading back to snug, cosy side area and pretty little bistro, cheap popular bar food inc fresh fish, welcoming staff, well kept Courage-related ales; side terrace with swings beside, quite handy for the beaches *(Steve Thomas, Nigel Clifton, LYM)*
Pontsticill [above A465 N of Merthyr Tydfil; SO0511], *Butchers Arms*: Reasonably priced genuine home cooking inc local game and home-cured gammon, choice of real ales, raised dining area and hidden-away pool and games room, tables outside with stunning views inc mountain railway *(Ian Phillips)*
Pontypridd [Ynysangharad Rd, off A4054; ST0690], *Bunch of Grapes*: Comfortable pub with efficient food service and well kept real ale *(Nigel Clifton)*; [Upper Church Village], *Farmers Arms*: Very busy free house with well kept good Bass and Hancocks HB, decent food *(Barbara Davies)*
Taffs Well [ST1283], *Fagins*: Wide changing range of real ales from handpump or tapped from the cask, friendly olde-worlde atmosphere, flagstone floor, bare wooden

benches and tables, good bar meals, reasonably priced restaurant, live music *(S P Bobeldijk, R Collis, Nigel Clifton)*

GLAMORGAN – SOUTH

☆ **Cardiff** [St Marys St; nr Howells], *Cottage*: Popular for well kept Brains SA, Bitter and Dark Mild and good value home-cooked lunches, long bar with narrow frontage and back eating area, lots of polished wood and glass, good cheerful service, decent choice of wines; open all day *(Mike Pugh, Steve Thomas, Joan and Michel Hooper-Immins)*

Cardiff [Harrowby St, Butetown], *New Sea Lock*: This popular unspoilt pub closed in 1995 *(PB)*; [Thornhill Rd, Llanishen; ST1781], *Nine Giants*: Pleasant surroundings, friendly staff, good food, lots of tables in big garden *(Judith and Stephen Gregory)*; [Atlantic Wharf], *Wharf*: Big newish Victorian-look pub in pleasant setting, now largely residential, on edge of old dock, lunchtime bar food, Brains and changing guest ales, nautical theme and old prints and local photographs downstairs, small lounge bar and restaurant upstairs; local bands Fri/Sat, sometimes Thurs *(Gwynne Harper, M G Hart)*

Colwinston [SS9475], *Sycamore*: Comfortable place with well kept ale *(Nigel Clifton)*

☆ **Cowbridge** [High St, signed off A48; SS9974], *Bear*: Neatly kept old coaching inn with Brains Bitter and SA, Hancocks HB, Worthington BB and a guest beer, decent house wines, friendly young bar staff, flagstones, panelling and big log fire in beamed bar on left, pool and good pin table in back games area, quieter room with plush armchairs on right, log-effect gas fires, usual lunchtime bar food from sandwiches up; children welcome; bedrooms quiet and comfortable, good breakfast *(Chris and Anne Fluck, Shelton Little, LYM)*

☆ **Craig Penllyn** [SS9777], *Barley Mow*: Welcoming, with good value food and well kept varied real ales; bedrooms comfortable *(Nigel Clifton, Chris Morgan, Barbara Davies)*

Dinas Powis [ST1571], *Cross Keys*: Well presented good cheap food, good atmosphere, no-smoking room *(Michael and Sarah McCrum)*; [Station Rd], *Star*: Well kept Brains and good quick cheap food in spacious well run four-room village pub, stripped stonework and attractive panelling, heavy Elizabethan beams, two open fires, plainer no-smoking room, Sky TV and juke box elsewhere; friendly licensees, cheerful locals, decent wines by the glass; best to book Sun lunch *(Mr and Mrs Steve Thomas, LYM)*; [Twyn], *Three Horseshoes*: Pretty floral displays in summer, efficient service; pleasant family pub *(Mr and Mr S Thomas)*

Lisvane [follow Mill Rd into Graig Rd, then keep on – OS Sheet 171 map ref 183842; ST1883], *Ty Mawr Arms*: Country pub with attractive garden looking down over Cardiff, changing real ales, several comfortable rooms one with big open fire *(Gwynne Harper, LYM)*

☆ **Monknash** [Marcross, Broughton sign off B4265 St Brides Major—Llantwit Major, then left at end of Water St – OS Sheet 170 map ref 920706; SS9270], *Plough & Harrow*: Unspoilt and untouched isolated country pub, welcoming and very basic – flagstones, old-fashioned stripped settles, logs burning in cavernous fireplace with huge side bread oven, simple choice of good value food inc vegetarian, up to six ales such as Bass, Hancocks HB, Worthington and maybe some from the Whitbreads family tapped from the cask, daily papers, children welcome; pool, juke box and fruit machine in room on left, picnic tables on grass outside the white cottage *(David Lewis, Mr and Mr S Thomas, Stuart Joy, BB)*

Morriston [Woodfield St; SS6698], *Red Lion*: Good food, Welsh beers *(Martyn Heard)*

Penarth [Sea Front; ST1871], *Inn at the Deep End*: Converted seafront swimming bath opp pier with two-tier bar, good choice of bar food and of beers, teas and coffees too, upstairs restaurant (fish specialities), children welcome, some live music; seaview terrace with barbecues, open all day *(Mr and Mrs Steve Thomas)*

☆ *nr* **Penarth** [Beach Rd, Swanbridge – signed off B4267 at Penarth end of Sully], *Captains Wife*: Recently refitted by Whitbreads as extensive and popular family dining pub, fine spot right by shore opp Sully Island *(Mr and Mrs Steve Thomas, LYM)*

Penllyn [village signed off A48 Cowbridge—Bridgend; SS9776], *Red Fox*: Good choice of real ales, bargain pub lunches, obliging service, evening restaurant *(Christopher Morgan, BB)*

Penmark [ST0568], *Six Bells*: Pleasant village local, interesting relics of Hancocks Brewery in public bar, decent food *(Clive Dumas)*

☆ **Sigingstone** [SS9771], *Victoria*: Quickly served good food inc good veg, not cheap but beautifully presented and good value, in welcoming and spotless neo-Victorian country pub/restaurant; well kept Bass (though not the sort of place to go to for just a drink), pleasant surroundings, excellent service *(Patrick and Mary McDermott, John and Joan Nash, C A and B Bristow)*

GLAMORGAN – WEST

Alltwen [Alltwen Hill; Rhos rd; SN7203], *Butchers Arms*: Open-plan, good imaginative menu inc vegetarian, well kept Everards Old Original *(Nigel Clifton, G Reeve)*

☆ **Bishopston** [50 Bishopston Rd, off B4436; SS5789], *Joiners Arms*: Thriving local, clean and welcoming, with quarry-tiled floor, traditional furnishings, local paintings and massive solid fuel stove; cheap simple food lunchtime and early evening, particularly well kept Courage-related ales with guests such as Brains Dark Mild and Marstons Pedigree, children welcome, open all day Thurs-Sat – the Rugby club's local on Sat nights; parking can be difficult *(HK, Michael Launder, John and Joan Nash, Dave and Jules Tuckett, Graham Reeve, J S M Sheldon, LYM)*

Blaengwynfi [off A4107; SS8996], *Great Western*: Amazingly posh pub in small village, with well kept Brains *(Dr and Mrs A K Clarke)*

Glais [625 Birchgrove Rd; off A4067, 1 m from M4 junction 45; SN7000], *Old Glais*: Traditional old two-bar pub in lovely surroundings, warm welcome, good atmosphere, good range of well kept beers, interesting varied reasonably priced food, quite a few antiques *(Andrew Lindell, Graham Reeve)*

☆ **Kittle** [18 Pennard Rd; SS5789], *Beaufort Arms*: Lovely old pub sheltering below ancient chestnut tree, plenty of character in carefully renovated saloon with stripped beams and stonework, comfortably cushioned settles, shortish choice of good food esp fresh fish, also sandwiches, quick friendly service, well kept Crown Buckley Reverend James, similar public bar though with less seating *(Anthony Marriott, J S M Sheldon)*

Mumbles [Park Rd; SS6287], *Park*: Cosy little pub in terraced street, well kept beers and good home-cooked food *(Brian Thomas)*; [Mumbles Rd], *Vincents*: Good local atmosphere in genuine ale-house with sawdust on floor and very extensive range of beers inc good Bass and different guest beer each week or so; Spanish landlord cooks good tapas *(Brian Thomas)*

☆ **Oldwalls** [SS4891], *Greyhound*: Reasonably priced popular bar food inc good local fish and ploughman's with choice of Welsh cheeses in busy but spacious and comfortable beamed and dark-panelled lounge bar, well kept Bass, Hancocks HB and a guest beer, good coffee inc decaf, coal fire, friendly service; back bar with display cases; restaurant popular at weekends; big tree-shaded garden with play area *(John and Joan Nash, the Sandy family, Mr and Mrs S Thomas)*

Parkmill [A4118; SS5489], *Gower*: Roomy beamed pub with walkers' bar, no-smoking restaurant, good quick service, good range of bar food inc vegetarian; Bass-related ales with a guest such as Mitchells *(Deborah and Ian Carrington)*

☆ **Reynoldston** [SS4789], *King Arthur*: Prettily set overlooking green and common, in good walking country (discounts for YHA members), spacious and airy bar with big log fire, rugs on floorboards, prints, warming pans, interesting displays eg bullets, delft shelf; plusher dining lounge, back games bar; good bar food changing daily inc fresh fish, well kept Bass and Felinfoel Double Dragon, cheerful staff; back garden with play area, bedrooms *(J S M Sheldon, Nigel Clifton, Graham Reeve, John and Joan Nash, A J Madel, Dave Braisted, A J Bowen)*

Swansea [Vivian Rd; SS6593], *Vivian Arms*: Popular local, one of only two here to sell Brains real ales; good bar lunches cooked by landlady *(Eric Jones)*

Taibach [Commercial Rd, handy for M4 junction 40; SS7789], *Somerset Arms*: Large, with lots of small rooms, carefully modernised restaurant *(Dr and Mrs A K Clarke)*

West Cross [A4067 Mumbles—Swansea; SS6089], *West Cross*: Unrivalled clear view over the sweep of Mumbles Bay, comfortably refurbished with steps up to glassed back extension and garden below by pedestrian/cycle way around bay; good choice of usual pub food, decent range of beers *(Anne Morris)*

GWENT

☆ **Abergavenny** [Mkt St; SO3014], *Greyhound*: Good interesting reasonably priced food, Boddingtons real ale, decent wines, good service, comfortable and enjoyable; good evening meals – more restauranty then *(Peter Yearsley, I H Rorison)*

☆ **Abergavenny** [Flannel St], *Hen & Chickens*: Welcoming local with tidy bar and cosy back room, good choice of wholesome cheap home-cooked food and thick lunchtime sandwiches, well kept ales inc Bass, friendly staff *(Ted George, Mike Pugh)*

Abergavenny [3 miles out on Brecon Rd (A40)], *Lamb & Flag*: Good straightforward pub with big helpings of good value food in bar or two dining rooms, well kept Brains Bitter and SA in big bar, good service; children welcome, high chairs; open all day in summer, looks out to Brecon Beacons – tables outside; comfortable bedrooms *(Joan and Michel Hooper-Immins)*

Blackwood [Tredegar Rd; ST1797], *Rock*: Friendly olde-worlde pub with good choice of real ales, good reasonably priced food *(Ken Orger)*

Caerleon [Llanhennock; ST3592], *Wheatsheaf*: Cosy, friendly country pub, three well kept beers inc Bass, good value food; children welcome *(Mike Pugh)*

☆ **Chepstow** [ST5394], *Bridge*: Civilised low-ceilinged pub beautifully placed opp Wye bridge, flagstoned entrance, carpeted main room with light pine tables and chairs, prints on walls, open fire; attractively served bar food, quietly friendly staff, well kept real ales; tables out in delightful garden with castle view *(Mike Pugh)*

Chepstow [16 Bridge St], *Castle View*: Civilised, with splendid views to castle and beyond, small comfortable bar with magazines and papers, soft piped classical music, good coffee, Tetleys, wide range of unusual bar food inc vegetarian, attractive garden; bedrooms *(George Atkinson)*; [Welsh St, just outside Town Arch], *Coach & Horses*: Well kept Bass, Brains, Crown Buckley Reverend James and other ales, comfortable and well appointed split-level rooms, fine old etched windows, open fire, prints *(Andrew and Liz Roberts)*

Cross Ash [B4521 E of Abergavenny; SO4119], *Three Salmons*: Small, warm and friendly, with good varied menu, changing

real ales *(Paul and Heather Bettesworth)*
Cwmbran [Llanyrafon; ST3094], *Crows Nest*: New Bass pub in residential area nr boating lake and golf club, welcoming and obliging staff, very well priced food, tables outside *(Gwyneth and Salvo Spadaro-Dutturi)*

☆ **Gilwern** [High St; SO2414], *Bridgend*: Good range of well kept changing beers and of nicely presented food inc unusual burgers in small welcoming canalside pub with canal-related prints, friendly staff, sleepy red setter; children welcome; tiled terrace on grassy rise above towpath and moored boats *(C H Stride, Nigel Clifton, Mike Dickerson)*

Grosmont [SO4024], *Angel*: Simple friendly 17th-c village pub on attractive steep single street – nice to sit out, next to ancient market hall and not far from castle and 13th-c church; welcoming atmosphere, usual bar food, well kept Crown Buckley; bedrooms *(R T and J C Moggridge, BB)*; [B4347 N], *Cupids Hill*: A real throwback to prewar pubs, tiny homely cottage bar on very steep hill in pretty countryside, old settles by fire, low white ceiling, one keg beer, table skittles, dominoes, cribbage; in same family for 80-odd years *(Gordon, BB)*

Kemeys Commander [B4598 Usk—Abergavenny; SO3505], *Chainbridge*: Splendid riverside setting, spacious bar area with open fire at top level and views of river and hills from lower level; good range of beers, extensive menu; service could sometimes be quicker *(Anne Morris)*

☆ **Llangattock Lingoed** [SO3620], *Hunters Moon*: Attractive beamed and flagstoned country pub nr Offa's Dyke, two character bars dating from 13th century, very friendly atmosphere, good straightforward reasonably priced food, well kept Bass; landlord plays the bagpipes, wife does the cooking, dog's very welcoming *(R G Stephenson, Gwyneth and Salvo Spadaro-Dutturi, BB)*

☆ **Llantarnam** [Newport Rd (A4042 N of M4 junction 26); ST3093], *Greenhouse*: Welcoming and roomy old pub, wide choice of good value popular food from good sandwiches up, well kept Courage-related ales, beautiful big garden; folk nights *(John and Joan Nash)*

Llanthony [SO2928], *Half Moon*: Basic country inn suiting this unspoilt valley with its great walks and pony-trekking centres, decent plain food, real ales such as Bull Mastiff Son-of-a-Bitch and Flowers Original; bedrooms not luxurious but clean and comfortable *(John Cox, John Nash)*

Llantilio Crosseny [SO3915], *Halfway House*: Simple bar with comfortable furnishings, well kept Bass and Felinfoel Double Dragon, friendly staff, good food inc some unusual specials and good veg, well kept cricket field *(Paul and Heather Bettesworth)*

☆ **Llantrisant** [off A449; ST3997], *Greyhound*: Good hill views from attractive country pub with well presented reasonably priced reliable home-cooked bar food inc vegetarian, spacious open-plan rooms, friendly service; bedrooms in small attached motel – lovely setting *(R Michael Richards, M E Tennick, the Monday Club)*

Llanvetherine [SO3617], *Kings Arms*: This former inn, popular for good value food and well kept beers, has closed *(GSD)*

Magor [a mile from M4 junction 23; B4245; ST4287], *Wheatsheaf*: Traditional pub with well kept beers *(Dr and Mrs A K Clarke)*

☆ **Monmouth** [Lydart; B4293 towards Trelleck; SO5009], *Gockett*: Old carefully extended pub, pleasant lounge bar with eating areas and small restaurant, good range of generous hot food inc good Sun lunch and puddings, real ales such as Bass and Hardington, cheerful efficient service; tables in attractive garden; children welcome; bedrooms with own bathrooms *(Mr and Mrs A R Hawkins, Mrs S Thursfield, Richard and Alison Evans, A Y Drummond, John Champion)*

Monmouth [St Thomas Sq], *Green Dragon*: Well kept real ales, interesting varied home-cooked food, friendly welcome, comfortable atmosphere; tables in new garden with play area *(J F Risbey)*; [centre], *Vine Tree*: Welcoming town pub with pleasant garden, small cosy bar *(Gwen and Peter Andrews)*

Nantyderry [between A4042 and B4598 (former A471), N of Pontypool and Usk – OS Sheet 161 map ref 332061; SO3306], *Foxhunter*: Comfortable and very popular country pub with wide range of good bar food inc vegetarian, well kept Bass, spotless housekeeping and quick service; good garden with fountain, lawn and swing *(Sylvia Jones)*

New Inn [The Highway; SO4800], *Sun*: Friendly local atmosphere, quiet and relaxed; reasonable prices *(Tom Davies)*

☆ **Rhyd y Meirch** [up cul-de-sac off A4042 S of Abergavenny – OS Sheet 161 map ref 289073; SO2807], *Goose & Cuckoo*: Tiny unspoilt country pub run by very friendly Scottish couple, lots of malt and blended whiskies, good home-cooked food esp vegetarian, well kept Bullmastiff, Wadworths 6X and more esoteric ales; near hill walks, Vietnamese pot-bellied pigs in field behind; dogs allowed if on lead *(Mike Pugh, Anne Morris, Gwyneth and Salvo Spadaro-Dutturi)*

Rhymney [Hill St; SO1107], *Tredegar Arms*: Good atmosphere in hospitable Valleys local *(David Evans)*

☆ **Shirenewton** [B4235 Chepstow—Usk; ST4893], *Carpenters Arms*: Four small well refurbished rooms off central bar, flagstone floors, two good log fires, welcoming staff, seven well kept ales inc guests such as Bass, Hook Norton Best, Theakstons XB, wide choice of good reasonably priced food from sandwiches up; still has the huge bellows used when this was a smithy; beautiful hanging baskets and little flowerbeds in summer; children may be allowed *(A R and B E Sayer, Peter Hesketh, Nigel Clifton)*

☆ **Talycoed** [B4233 Monmouth—Abergavenny; SO4115], *Halfway House*: Well run unspoilt

16th-c character inn in pleasant countryside, good fresh home-cooked food (not Sun evening), pleasant service, well kept real ale, log fires, timbers and stripped stone; tables in well kept garden, charming views; bedrooms *(W W Swait)*

Tintern [Devauden Rd; off A446; SO5301], *Cherry Tree*: Quaint unspoilt country pub, well kept Hancocks PA and farm cider, charming garden; children welcome *(Paul and Heather Bettesworth)*

☆ **Trelleck** [B4293 6 miles S of Monmouth; SO5005], *Lion*: Good interesting food with proper veg in quiet and unpretentious country pub's pleasant lounge bar; cl weekday lunchtimes *(Terry and Pat Scott)*

☆ **Trelleck**, *Village Green*: Sensitively preserved old building, really a restaurant/bistro, but a cosy little bar too, with well kept Bass and Worthington, and good wines; comfortable, with prints, lots of dried flowers on beams, welcoming service, good changing food using local produce; piped Radio 1 a bit de trop; bedrooms in well converted former stables *(R G and M P Lumley, Kevin Gray, Paul Weedon, R C Morgan)*

☆ **Trelleck Grange** [minor rd St Arvans—Trelleck; SO4902], *Fountain*: Welcoming atmosphere, cheerful landlord, good food, well kept beers, interesting range of malt whiskies, lovely location; bedrooms simple but comfortable *(Mrs S Thursfield, Richard and Alison Evans)*

Usk [SO3801], *Greyhound*: Pleasant staff, reasonably priced good food *(M E Tennick, Mike Pugh)*; [The Square], *Nags Head*: Relaxed and pleasant, unusual food esp home-made pies and game in season, interesting decor *(Mike Pugh)*

GWYNEDD

Bangor [SH5973], *Antelope*: Superb views over Menai Bridge, good atmosphere and service, wide range of consistent well priced home-cooked food *(Dr and Mrs D Elliott)*; [Garth Rd, nr pier], *Union*: Several friendly rooms with lots of entertaining bric-a-brac, atmospheric sound of yards rattling against masts, well kept Ind Coope Burton, reasonably priced basic food inc delicious home-cooked ham *(Dave Thompson, Margaret Mason)*

☆ **Barmouth** [Church St; SH6116], *Last*: Glassy new frontage for darkly low-beamed harbourside local with flagstones, ship's lamps, little waterfall down back bar's natural rock wall, wide choice of good cheap bar lunches inc local crab, well kept Marstons Pedigree, friendly service *(Richard Houghton, Joan and Michel Hooper-Immins)*

Barmouth [St Annes Pl], *Tal-y-Don*: Welcoming two-bar Burtonwood pub, well kept Bitter and Mild, good value restaurant inc speciality steaks; open all day in summer; bedrooms good value *(Joan and Michel Hooper-Immins)*

Beddgelert [SH5948], *Prince Llewelyn*: Plush hotel bar with log fire and raised dining area, simpler summer bar, wide choice of good value generous bar food, Robinsons, rustic seats on verandah overlooking village stream and hills – great walking country; busy at peak holiday times, children allowed at quiet times; bedrooms pleasant, with good breakfast *(PD, BB)*; *Tanronen*: No reports on this since massive new refurbishment; has been good, with friendly bar and bedrooms overlooking river across road, or fields and mountains behind *(GT, BB; news please)*

Betws-y-Coed [SH7956], *Royal Oak*: Much more hotel than pub, but good range of food esp local fish in civilised grill bar or more upmarket restaurant, also big side stables bar with pool, juke box and TV one end, eating area the other, reasonably priced menu, Whitbreads-related ales, lots of tables out in courtyard; friendly staff, open all day, live jazz Thurs; bedrooms *(Phil and Heidi Cook, John A Barker, Roger Byrne)*; [A5 next to BP garage and Little Chef], *Waterloo*: Wide choice of generous food inc interesting soups and hot dishes, even mountain mutton sometimes; pleasant efficient service, no smokers; bedrooms *(KC)*

Betwys Garmon [A4085 at N end of Llyn Cwellyn; SH5458], *Castell Cidwm*: Good food, peaceful location, friendly licensees; comfortable bedrooms *(D W Jones-Williams)*

Bontnewydd [SH4860], *Newborough Arms*: Welcoming comfortable local with well kept Burtonwood and other ales, fair range of decent food, dining room; juke box can be loud; bedrooms *(Dave Thompson, Margaret Mason)*

Caernarfon [Northgate St; SH4863], *Black Boy*: Bustling local by castle walls, beams from ships wrecked here in 16th c, bare floors, cheery fire, homely and cosy atmosphere, good choice of real ales inc Bass, good value well presented food in bar and restaurant, pleasant service; TV in main bar *(M G Lavery, Richard Houghton, W A D Hoyle)*

☆ **Capel Curig** [SH7258], *Bryn Tyrch*: Good choice of interesting food esp vegetarian dishes, well kept ales such as Marstons Pedigree and Whitbreads Castle Eden, friendly obliging service, homely and pleasantly informal bar with old pews, big restaurant, good summer mix of walkers and holiday people; simple good value bedrooms, good breakfast *(C M Charlton, N K Musgrave, Ron Leigh, Neal Marsden, John A Barker, Dave Thompson, Margaret Mason)*

☆ **Capel Curig**, *Cobdens*: Civilised feel, with good varied satisfying food inc home-made bread and interesting vegetarian dishes, well kept Courage-related beers, good pleasant service, friendly old english sheepdog and border collie cross; so close to mountain that back bar has bare rockface, lovely river scene across road, good walks all around; bedrooms *(Mr and Mrs D J Tapper, KC, Nick Haslewood)*

☆ **Capel Garmon** [signed from A470 just outside Betws-y-Coed, towards Llanrwst; SH8255], *White Horse*: Low-beamed inn dating from 16th century, comfortable and homely, with welcoming licensees, log fires, well kept Bass, Stones and Worthington BB, wide choice of food inc local salmon and game, prettily refurbished cottage restaurant, games in public bar; bedrooms simple but comfortable (quietest in new part), fine countryside with magnificent views *(D A Hasprey, John A Barker, Peter Burridge, Peter Titchmarsh, Mr and Mrs D Tapper, Dave Thompson, Margaret Mason, D W Jones-Williams, K H Frostick)*

☆ **Dinas Mawddwy** [just off A470; SH8615], *Llew Coch*: Genuine country local with charming timbered front bar dripping with sparkling brasses, well kept Bass, friendly staff, food inc trout or salmon from River Dovey just behind; plainer inner family room lively with video games, pool and Sat evening live music, tables out on quiet street; surrounded by steep fir forests, good walks *(Paul McPherson, Dave Thompson, Margaret Mason, John Hazel, BB)*

Dinas Mawddwy [set back from A470], *Dolbrodmaeth*: 19th-c farm building lovingly restored by present owners, two smart bars overlooking River Dovey, Ind Coope Burton, interesting choice of food from good value sandwiches and home-cooked ham ploughman's up, also restaurant; tables in garden, riverside walk from pub; bedrooms *(Jenny and Brian Seller)*

☆ **Ganllwyd** [SH7224], *Tyn-y-Groes*: Old inn owned by NT in lovely Snowdonia setting, fine forest views, old-fashioned furnishings in partly panelled lounge, Boddingtons, Felinfoel Double Dragon and Flowers IPA, quite a few malt whiskies, usual bar food and (not Sun evening) no-smoking restaurant, public bar with games; comfortable well equipped bedrooms, salmon and seatrout fishing *(K H Frostick, J S Green, LYM)*

☆ **Llandudno** [Old St, behind tram stn; SH7883], *Kings Head*: Rambling pub, much extended around 16th-c core, spaciously open-plan, with comfortable traditional furnishings, red wallpaper, dark pine, wide range of generous food, changing Tetleys-related real ales; children allowed, open all day in summer *(Mike and Penny Sanders, Mike and Wendy Proctor, LYM)*

☆ **Llandwrog** [SH4456], *Harp*: Warmly welcoming and attractive, with good value food, well kept Whitbreads-related real ales, comfortable straightforward furnishings; good bedrooms, pretty village *(Dave Thompson, Margaret Mason, B A and R Davies, D W Jones-Williams)*

☆ **Llanengan** [Lleyn Peninsula; SH2927], *Sun*: Good pub in small village near spectacular Hells Mouth beach, wide range of drinks inc well kept Ind Coope Burton and Tetleys on handpump, good food inc wholesome ploughman's, friendly service; bedrooms *(Ian J Clay)*

☆ *nr* **Llanrwst** [Maenan (A470 N); SH7965], *Priory*: Steep-gabled substantial Victorian building with battlemented tower in charming stately grounds, lots of tables outside and good play area; bar food in elegant and airy back dining lounge, small front bar with Websters Choice and Yorkshire, unobtrusive piped music and Welsh singing Sat night; partly no-smoking restaurant, children welcome; comfortable bedrooms *(Mrs Thomas, Dave and Jules Tuckett, KC, Eric and Jackie Robinson, Brian and Jill Bond, LYM)*

☆ **Llanwnda** [signed off A499 S of Caernarfon; SH4758], *Goat*: Friendly village local with back bar divided by traditional small-paned hatch servery, coal fire, games room with pool, genteel front room; the good help-yourself lunchtime cold table which up to last year made this pub a regular main entry has sadly been suspended because of ill health, and as we went to press there was no bar food; tables outside, children welcome, cheap good value bedrooms *(LYM)*

☆ **Morfa Nefyn** [A497/B4412; SH2840], *Bryncynan*: Modernised pub concentrating (particularly in summer) on quickly served well presented good value bar food inc vegetarian and local fish and seafood; quiet in winter with good log fire; above-average summer choice of well kept Tetleys-related ales, restaurant, rustic seats outside, children allowed; cl Sun *(Michael and Janet Hepworth, LYM)*

☆ **Morfa Nefyn**, *Cliff*: Good choice of reasonably priced bar food and friendly service in tastefully furnished pub, popular with locals; attractive conservatory dining area in lovely setting overlooking sea *(D Jones-Williams, Mrs D M Everard)*

☆ **Penmaenpool** [SH6918], *George III*: Attractive inn with cheery 17th-c beamed and flagstoned bottom bar and civilised partly panelled upstairs bar opening into cosy and chintzy inglenook lounge; lovely setting on Mawddach estuary, sheltered terrace, good walks; home-cooked food in bar and restaurant inc some interesting dishes esp good lamb and seafood, Courage-related ales under light CO2 blanket, children in eating area, open all day; good bedrooms inc some in interesting conversion of former station on disused line *(Mr and Mrs R F Wright, Sarah and Peter Gooderham, Monica Shelley, F C Johnston, Mrs C Watkinson, LYM)*

Pentir [SH5767], *Vaynol Arms*: Plushy pub with good food inc children's helpings in bar and new extension restaurant, friendly service, children very welcome; Theakstons Old Peculier and a guest ale *(MM, DT, Alan Ashcroft)*

☆ **Porth Dinllaen** [beach car park signed from Morfa Nefyn, then a good 15-min walk – which is part of the attraction; SH2741], *Ty Coch*: Right on curving beach, far from the roads, with stunning view along coast to mountains; pub itself full of attractive salvage and RNLI memorabilia; beach drinks in plastic glasses, service may be slow, beer keg and food ordinary – so it's the position which appeals, and the coffee's decent; may be closed much of winter, but open all day summer *(Neil and Elaine Piper, John Evans, LYM)*

☆ **Porthmadog** [Lombard St; SH5639], *Ship*: Peaceful welcoming backstreet local with wide choice of mostly fresh generous nicely cooked food, popular upstairs evening Cantonese restaurant, well kept Ind Coope Burton, Tetleys and a weekly guest beer; huge open fireplace in lounge (mainly eating in here), long comfortable public bar; children may be allowed in small back room with video games/fruit machines, beyond pool room *(A P Jeffreys, David Lewis, Richard Houghton, Joan and Michel Hooper-Immins)*

☆ **Rhyd Ddu** [A4085 N of Beddgelert; SH5753], *Cwellyn Arms*: Cosy stone-built pub popular for good generous sensibly priced food inc vegetarian; Bass, Worthington, flagstones, log fire in huge ancient fireplace, small games bar with pool, darts and TV, restaurant; children and walkers welcome, fine Snowdon views from garden tables with barbecue, big adventure playground; open all day Sun at least in summer *(Lorrie and Mick Marchington, Gordon Theaker, Mike and Ruth Dooley, Richard Houghton)*

Tal y Bont [SH7669], *Lodge*: Good value food esp fish and seafood, some veg grown by the pub; very friendly staff *(D W Jones-Williams)*

Tal y Cafn [A470 Conway—Llanwrst; SH7972], *Tal y Cafn*: Good reasonably priced bar food worth the wait in cheerful and comfortable lounge bar with big inglenook, friendly staff, Greenalls, spacious garden; children welcome; handy for Bodnant *(M A Cameron, LYM)*

☆ **Tremadog** [SH5640], *Golden Fleece*: Busy stonebuilt inn on attractive square, friendly attentive staff, good value standard bar food inc vegetarian, well kept Bass, Mild and Marstons Pedigree, cosy partly partitioned rambling beamed lounge with open fire, nice little snug, separate bistro (children allowed here and in small family room), games room, intriguing cellar bar, tables in sheltered inner courtyard; cl Sun *(A P Jeffreys, Gordon Theaker, LYM)*

☆ **Tudweiliog** [Nefyn Rd; B4417, Lleyn Peninsula; SH2437], *Lion*: Friendly and cheery unpretentious village inn, handy for the area, with wide choice of decent straightforward food in bar and no-smoking extension family dining room (small helpings for children), well kept Boddingtons, Marstons Pedigree, Ruddles Best and Theakstons Best and Mild, games and juke box in lively public bar; bedrooms *(Nick Haslewood, Roger Byrne, LYM)*

POWYS

Berriew [A483 S of Welshpool; SJ1801], *Horseshoes*: Pleasant and relaxing, good food inc homemade soups and wide-ranging puddings, tasteful decor with copper and brass *(T and M E Mahoney)*; *Lion*: Friendly black and white timber-framed country inn, good home-cooked food in bar and restaurant, Bass and Worthington with guest beers such as Greene King and Shepherd Neame, separate public bar; a pleasant place to stay *(Paul and Maggie Baker, D Jones-Williams)*

☆ **Beulah** [A483 Llanwrtyd Wells—Builth Wells; SN9351], *Trout*: Friendly, well kept nicely refurbished front lounge, spacious well lit dining area with wide choice of reasonably priced home-cooked food (limited Mon/Tues) inc good puddings, public bar and pool, Hancocks HB, Youngers IPA and Worthington BB; very busy at weekends; six comfortable bedrooms *(M and J Back)*

☆ **Bleddfa** [A488 Knighton—Penybont; SO2168], *Hundred House*: Friendly country local with comfortable and attractively furnished stripped-stone lounge bar, good log fire in very fine fireplace, good home cooking, well kept Flowers Original and Worthington Best, big separate bar and games room – walkers welcome; tables in garden with barbecue, lovely countryside; bedrooms *(Lyn Juffernholz, Alan Ruttley, Dorsan Baker)*

Brecon [nr R Usk Bridge; SO0428], *Olde Boars Head*: Recently refurbished and welcoming, with several well kept ales such as Fullers London Pride and Thwaites, pool table *(Gwyneth and Salvo Spadaro-Dutturi)*

☆ **Coedway** [B4393 W of Shrewsbury; SJ3415], *Old Hand & Diamond*: Roomy and pleasant, with well kept beers, log fire, good reasonably priced food in dining area and restaurant, smaller back bar, friendly service, no music *(D E P and I D Hughes)*

☆ **Crickhowell** [New Rd; SO2118], *Bridge End*: Chatty and attractive roomy local in good spot by many-arched bridge over weir of river Usk, good straightforward food, gleaming furniture, well kept Bass and Worthington BB on handpump; open all day *(Barry and Anne)*

Defynnog [SN9228], *Tanners Arms*: Lounge, public bar and restaurant, friendly licensees, wide choice of good value food inc home-made, seats outside overlooking fields and mountains *(Mrs S Wright)*

☆ **Derwenlas** [A487 Machynlleth—Aberystwyth; SN7299], *Black Lion*: Quaint 450-year-old pub, huge log fire in low-beamed cottagey bar divided by oak posts and cartwheels, good home-cooked food in dining area, well kept Marstons Pedigree on handpump, decent wines, unobtrusive piped music; garden up behind with adventure playground and steps up into woods *(Derek and Cerys Williams, David Wallington)*

☆ **Dolfor** [inn sign up hill off A483 about 4 miles S of Newtown; SO1187], *Dolfor Inn*: Generous good value above-average bar food and friendly service in much modernised hillside inn with easy chairs in beamed lounge opening into neatly modern dining area, well kept ales, unobtrusive piped music, good views from behind; bedrooms comfortable and good value *(W F C Phillips, M Owton, LYM)*

Erwood [SO0942], *Erwood*: Friendly village local, generous helpings of reasonably priced traditional food from bar snacks to full meals; looks out towards Wye behind *(Tony and Sarah Thomas)*

☆ **Garthmyl** [SO1999], *Nags Head*: Welcoming oasis, with good choice of generous home-cooked food (even properly cured home-cooked ham for the sandwiches), real effort made in presentation and service, well kept beers, open fire in lounge; handy for Montgomery Canal, good towpath walks *(Col A H N Reade, Pete Yearsley)*

☆ **Gladestry** [SO2355], *Royal Oak*: Relaxing unpretentious beamed and flagstoned inn handy for Offa's Dyke Path, friendly service, well kept Bass and Felinfoel Double Dragon, good simple bar food inc home-cooked ham, gammon and fish, reasonable prices – lunch opening 12-2; refurbished lounge, separate bar, children allowed, picnic tables in lovely secluded garden behind, safe for children; bedrooms clean, well equipped and good value, with good breakfast *(Mrs B Sugarman, Ian Jones, C J Parsons)*

Glyntawe [A4067 Swansea—Sennybridge just N of Dan yr Ogof caves; SN8416], *Tafarn y Garreg*: Beautifully set pub with lovely garden, three small bars, real ale, evening meals *(Mr and Mrs A Plumb)*

☆ **Guilsfield** [3 miles N of Welshpool; SJ2212], *Kings Head*: Clean and shiny old pub with well kept Boddingtons and Flowers IPA, wide choice of genuine home cooking inc vegetarian, chatty landlady, beautiful big garden with tubs and hanging baskets; walkers welcome *(Brenda and Derrick Swift, Pete Yearsley)*

☆ **Hay on Wye** [26 Lion St; SO2342], *Old Black Lion*: Friendly low-beamed partly black-panelled traditional bar, particularly atmospheric in autumn or winter with candles and soft lighting, wide choice of bar food, often excellent, inc some interesting cooking and a lot for vegetarians, candlelit restaurant, well kept Flowers Original or Worthington BB and Fullers London Pride, decent wines; children welcome in eating areas; comfortable good value bedrooms, Wye fishing rights *(Nigel Clifton, Karen Eliot, Dorothy Pilson, Sue Demont, Tim Barrow, Geoff and Angela Jaques, John Gorman, DAV, David J B Lewis, LYM)*

☆ **Hay on Wye** [Bull Ring], *Kilvert Court*: Small well furnished hotel bar with flagstones and candles, friendly staff, well kept Bass on handpump, good range of good food in bar and restaurant; live music Thurs; outside tables overlooking small town square; bedrooms immaculate and well equipped *(Katie and Steve Newby, Mrs C Watkinson)*

Hay on Wye, *Swan*: Pleasant bars, varied good value bar food, helpful staff *(W H and E Thomas)*

☆ **Hundred House** [SO1154], *Hundred House*: Good friendly licensees in attractive, clean and interesting pub full of curios, well kept Bass and Hancocks HB with interesting guest beers such as Woods Christmas Cracker in season, good wine list, decent food in small dining room, big garden with play area; children welcome *(Mrs J Holding, Pat and John Millward)*

Libanus [Tai'r-Bull; A470 SW of Brecon; SN9925], *Bull*: Reopened after long time, good Welsh Bitter, decent fairly cheap plain food, very friendly staff; well liked by locals *(Dick Brown)*

Llandrindod Wells [Temple St (A470); SO0561], *Metropole*: Comfortable front bar of big hotel useful for serving straightforward food all day; well kept Whitbreads-related ales; bedrooms *(Joan and Michel Hooper-Immins, E H and R F Warner)*

Llanfyllin [High St (A490); SJ1419], *Cain Valley*: Old coaching inn with welcoming helpful staff, good food inc fresh veg and well kept beers in hotelish panelled lounge bar; handsome Jacobean staircase to comfortable bedrooms, good breakfasts *(A N Ellis, Richard Houghton)*; [High St], *Old New Inn*: Pleasant central pub with reasonably priced bar food, real ales inc Marstons Pedigree, log fire, large back reception room; wheelchair access *(Paddy Moindrot)*

☆ **Llangenny** [off A40 Abergavenny—Crickhowell; SO2417], *Dragons Head*: Well kept beer, good food and pleasant staff in low-beamed bar with big log fire, pews, housekeeper's chairs and a high-backed settle among other seats, restaurant, tables outside; lovely spot in little riverside hamlet tucked below the Black Mountains *(P J S Goward, LYM)*

☆ **Llangorse** [SO1327], *Red Lion*: Efficient friendly service, wide range of well kept Welsh and other beers, good farm cider, good straightforward food at sensible prices, attractive position by stream through village; bedrooms *(Anne Morris, P J S Goward, BB)*

Llangorse, *Castle*: Hearty bar snacks, well kept Brains Bitter, very welcoming atmosphere *(W H and E Thomas)*

☆ **Llangurig** [Pant Mawr; A44 Aberystwyth rd, 4½ miles W; SN8482], *Glansevern Arms*: Very civilised, with cushioned antique settles and log fire in high-beamed bar, yet manages to preserve something of a local atmosphere; well kept Bass and Worthington Dark Mild, decent malt whiskies and wines, lunchtime sandwiches and hot soup (not Sun) with maybe cold wild salmon in season; good value seven-course dinners (not Sun evening; must book, and courses served to fairly strict timing); by main road, but over 1,000 ft up with mountains all around; big bedrooms, warm and clean *(Philip Moses, N J Clifton, Roger Entwistle, D W Jones-Williams, LYM)*

Llangurig [A44; SN9179], *Black Lion*: Good well presented food at reasonable prices *(R P Rees)*; *Blue Bell*: Cheerful country inn, decent food and well kept beer; bedrooms *(G Washington, LYM)*

☆ **Llangynidr** [B4558, Cwm Crawnon; SO1519], *Coach & Horses*: Friendly and spacious, with wide choice of generous well presented straightforward bar food, well kept changing Courage-related ales, open fire, pub games, restaurant; children welcome, safely fenced pretty sloping waterside garden by Brecon—Monmouth Canal across road, lovely views and walks *(M B Crump, K W J Wood , Mike Dickerson, Steve Thomas, LYM)*

☆ **Llangynidr** [off B4558], *Red Lion*: Creeper-covered 16th-c inn, attractively furnished bow-windowed bar with good range of real ales inc Theakstons Best and XB on handpump, good sandwiches and interesting range of unusual hot dishes, lively games room, sheltered pretty garden; comfortable bedrooms *(Jenny and Brian Seller, Mr and Mrs A Plumb, LYM)*

Llanidloes [Long Bridge St; SN9584], *Red Lion*: Well kept beer, good food, excellent service; comfortable bedrooms *(B Crowther)*

☆ **Llanwddyn** [SJ0219], *Lake Vyrnwy*: Comfortable old-feeling well done newish pub extension alongside smart country hotel overlooking lake; friendly staff, two real ales, good food, darts, great view from big windows or balcony; bedrooms *(Dr and Mrs A K Clarke, W F C Phillips)*

☆ **Llanyre** [SO0462], *Bell*: Old but modernised inn, very comfortable and well kept, with wide choice of particularly good food well presented by efficient staff in stylish restaurant; bedrooms *(C E Power, Frank Cummins)*

☆ **Machynlleth** [Heol Pentrerhedyn; A489, nr junction with A487; SH7501], *White Lion*: Welcoming atmosphere, dark oak and copper-topped tables, dark pink plush seats, well kept Banks's Bitter and Mild and Marstons Pedigree, big log fire, wide range of food inc good vegetarian choice, adjacent dining area, service brisk and pleasant; best to book for 3-course Sun lunch; pretty views from picnic tables in garden; neatly modernised stripped pine bedrooms *(Mervyn and Zilpha Reed)*

Montgomery [B4386; SO2296], *Bricklayers Arms*: Smallish lively bar with cheery locals and Boddingtons and Worthington, wide choice of good value food in dining area with pine tables, linen-set restaurant *(M and J Back)*

☆ **Newbridge on Wye** [SO0158], *New Inn*: Good home cooking in friendly Upper Wye village inn, well kept Flowers IPA, spacious carpeted back lounge with button-back banquettes in big bays, good local atmosphere in straightforward public bar with darts and pool, third snug with cushioned wall benches, restaurant; clean fresh well equipped bedrooms, good breakfasts *(J S M Sheldon, BB)*

Rhayader [West St; SN9668], *Cornhill*: Only a small pub, but wonderfully welcoming, with interesting guest beers, ample good cheap food *(Phil Shulkind)*

☆ **Talybont on Usk**, *Usk*: Unspoilt traditional character inn, one bar with log fire, flagstones with scattered rugs, panelling and sporting prints, another with fishing prints and memorabilia – fishing available; varied adventurous food inc game, friendly staff, antiques shop; good value well equipped bedrooms, big breakfast *(Peter Bond, Mrs Rhian Oliver)*

Welshpool [Raven Sq – OS Sheet 126 map ref 223081; SJ2207], *Raven*: Cheerful welcome, wide choice of food in lounge bar/restaurant inc good vegetarian choice, well kept Banks's; handy for steam railway *(R C Morgan, Pete Yearsley, Paul McPherson)*

People don't usually tip bar staff (different in a really smart hotel, say). If you want to thank a barman – dealing with a really large party say, or special friendliness – offer him a drink. Common expressions are: 'And what's yours?' or 'And won't you have something for yourself?'.

Channel Islands

Two new Jersey entries this year are the Old Smugglers on Ouaisne Bay in St Brelade, Jersey, extended but with lots of atmosphere, and the stylish new Tipsy Toad Town House in St Helier, brewing its own real ale – like its slightly longer-established but smaller sister pub the Star & Tipsy Toad at St Peter. Other outstanding Jersey pubs are the cosy Greve de Lecq at Moulin de Lecq (very good play area for children), the Rozel Bay Inn (smartened up under a new landlady, very good food now – it's our choice as Channel Islands Dining Pub of the Year), and the Old Portelet Inn in St Brelade (another fine family pub). On Guernsey, the Fleur du Jardin at Kings Mills goes from strength to strength; and the new licensee at the Hougue du Pommier (Castel) is doing a good carvery. In the Lucky Dip section at the end of the chapter we'd particularly pick out the Harbour Lights on Alderney and the Rocquaine Bistro (Rocquaine Bay) on Guernsey for their marvellous fresh fish and shellfish; and the Ship & Crown in St Peter Port (Guernsey), Chambers in St Helier (Jersey) and Stocks Hotel (Sark). Drinks prices are still way below the mainland average, but have again risen rather more than the national average in the last year, so that the gap is perceptibly closing. Food prices are relatively low too – especially for the finest fish and seafood.

Pubs on Guernsey close on Sundays; those on Jersey have a break between 1 and 4.30 that day (but pub/restaurants can serve drinks with meals). Sunday is a real family day for the islands' residents, with pub/restaurants pretty much booked out for lunch.

CASTEL (Guernsey) Map 1

Hougue du Pommier ⇦

Route de Hougue du Pommier, off Route de Carteret; just inland from Cobo Bay and Grandes Rocques

This pleasantly set friendly and well equipped hotel – called 'Apple Tree Hill' – was a cider mill in the 18th c, and plenty of fruit trees still stand shading the tables on its neatly trimmed lawn, as well as by the swimming pool in the sheltered walled garden, and in a shady flower-filled courtyard. Inside, the most prized seats are perhaps those in the snug area by the big stone fireplace with its attendant bellows and copper fire-irons. The rest of the oak-beamed bar is quite roomy, with leatherette armed chairs around wood tables, old game and sporting prints, guns, sporting trophies and so forth. As well as a wide variety of daily specials, under the new licensee good bar food includes burgers (£4.50), steak and kidney pie or lasagne (£4.95), fresh fish of the day, good carvery and a vegetarian dish; decent wines. Pool, darts, dominoes, cribbage and maybe unobtrusive piped music; no-smoking areas in the bar and restaurant. Good leisure facilities include a pitch-and-putt golf course and a putting green (for visitors as well as residents). For residents there's free temporary membership to the Guernsey Indoor Green Bowling Association, the stadium is next door and rated as one of the best in Europe, and a daily courtesy bus into town. No dogs. *(Recommended by Mike Dickerson, Mike and Pam Simpson, Sharon and Laurie Gepheart, John Evans, Major and Mrs E M Warrick)*

Free house ~ Licensee Diane Thompson ~ Meals and snacks 12-2; 6.30-8.30 (not Sun eve) ~ Restaurant ~ (01481) 56531 ~ Children welcome ~ Open 11-2.30, 6-11.45 ~ Bedrooms: £43B/£86B

GREVE DE LECQ (Jersey) OS583552 Map 1

Moulin de Lecq

It's well worth a visit to this serenely placed black-shuttered old mill here just to see the massive reconstructed waterwheel turning outside, with its formidable gears remorselessly meshing in their stone housing behind the bar. But far from being a touristy gimmick, this is a very proper pub, with plenty of local custom and a warm and pleasant atmosphere. Well kept Ann Street Ann's Treat and Old Jersey and Guernsey Bitter on handpump. There's a good log fire, toasting you as you come down the four steps into the cosy bar, as well as plush-cushioned black wooden seats against the white-painted walls; piped music. Good bar food is from the daily specials board or menu and includes soup (£1.20), filled baked potatoes (from £2.75), ploughman's (£3.50), lasagne (£4.50), steak and kidney pie or breaded scampi (£4.75), vegetarian dishes like stir-fry vegetables or lasagne (from £4.25); summer barbecue from May to September. In winter they serve traditional Jersey dishes such as bean crock, rabbit casserole and beef in red wine. Service is welcoming and helpful. The terrace has picnic tables under cocktail parasols, and there's a good children's adventure playground. The road past here leads down to pleasant walks on one of the only north-coast beaches. *(Recommended by Wayne Brindle, Steve and Carolyn Harvey, Richard Dolphin, Stephen and Julie Brown)*

Ann Street ~ Manager Shaun Lynch ~ Real ale ~ Meals and snacks 12-2.30, 6-8.30 (not Sun eve) ~ (01534) 482818 ~ Children welcome till 9pm ~ Open 11-11

KINGS MILLS (Guernsey) Map 1

Fleur du Jardin

Kings Mills Rd

Set in one of the prettiest spots on the island, this stone house stands in its own two acres of beautiful gardens in the centre of a delightful conservation village. Sensitive refurbishments which aimed at taking the steep-tiled inn's character and appearance closer to its origins have exposed the low-beamed ceilings and thick granite walls, and there's a nice cosy old fashioned feel to the place. The friendly public bar has cushioned pews and a good log fire, and the lounge bar on the hotel side has individual country furnishings. Very good bar food includes sandwiches (from £1.75, hot char-grillled steak £4.95), chilli con carne (£3.95), steak and kidney pie (£4.45), mushroom stroganoff (£4.60), grilled rainbow trout, and quite a few imaginative daily specials like seafood pâté with lemon mayonnaise (£3.95), smoked salmon and halibut cones filled with dill cream cheese (£4.50), pasta with sweet pepper and aubergine sauce (£4.25), swordfish steak with tomato and mozzarella cheese (£6.50), fried medallions of pork fillet with stilton sauce (£6.95) and venison casserole (£7.85). Well kept Guernsey Sunbeam and their winter or summer ale on handpump, and maybe other guest beers, decent wines by the glass or bottle; friendly efficient service; unobtrusive piped music; darts. Part of the restaurant is no smoking. Outside picnic tables are surrounded by flowering cherries, shrubs, colourful borders, bright hanging baskets, and unusual flower barrels cut lengthwise rather than across; play area. *(Recommended by Spider Newth, Mike and Pam Simpson, Julian Charman, Tina and David Woods-Taylor, Mr and Mrs Box, J S Rutter, Mike Dickerson)*

Free house ~ Licensee Keith Read ~ Real ale ~ Meals and snacks ~ Restaurant ~ (01481) 57996 ~ Children welcome ~ Open 11-11.45 ~ Bedrooms:37.75B/£75.50B

Pubs in outstandingly attractive surroundings are listed at the back of the book.

ROZEL (Jersey) Map 1

Rozel Bay

Channel Islands Dining Pub of the Year

A dynamic and friendly new licensee has taken over this idyllic little pub on the edge of a sleepy little fishing village, just out of sight of the sea and the delightful harbour. Mrs Bouchet has really boosted the food side of the business and from Wednesday to Saturday evening it's almost essential to book a table for the delightful new French food. Served at gingham covered tables with french bread, the imaginative menu usually includes lots of fresh fish and might comprise starters like gateau of crab with pink grapefruit (£4.25), warm salad of scallops on caramelised orange on pesto or local oysters poached in chive butter (£4.25), and main courses like scallops provençale with bordelaise sauce (£6.50), braised turbot with ginger butter sauce or roast duck with tartlets of shallots and port wine or herb encrusted rump of lamb (£6.75), lobster or fruits de mer can be ordered in advance. At lunchtime when they're still concentrating on more usual pub fare the menu isn't quite as exciting: sandwiches (from £1.30), ploughman's (£2.75), sausage, egg and chips (£3), chicken and chips (£3.25) and scampi (£3.50). There is a genuinely snug and cosy feel to the interior of the small dark-beamed back bar which has an open fire, old prints and local pictures on its cream walls, dark plush wall seats and stools around tables. Leading off is a newly carpeted and decorated area with flowers on big solid square tables; pool, darts and juke box in the games room; piped music. Well kept Bass on handpump. Set among award winning flower displays, there are tables under cocktail parasols by the quiet lane past the pub, and more behind in the attractive big gardens steeply terraced up the hillside. *(Recommended by Georgina Cole; more reports please)*

Randalls ~ Tenant Mrs Eve Bouchet ~ Real ale ~ Lunchtime meals and snacks (not Sun) ~ (01534) 863438 ~ Children welcome ~ Open 10-11.30

ST AUBIN (Jersey) OS 607486 Map 1

Old Court House Inn ⇦

Fine sea views from this charming 15th-c inn across the tranquil harbour to St Aubin's fort, and right across the bay to St Helier. The restaurant still shows signs of its time as a courtroom and the front part of the building used to be the home of a wealthy merchant, whose cellars stored privateers' plunder alongside more legitimate cargo. The upstairs cocktail bar is elegantly (and cleverly) crafted as the aft cabin of a galleon, with a transom window and bowed varnished decking planks on the ceiling. The atmospheric main basement bar which can get crowded and smoky has cushioned pale wooden seats built against its stripped granite walls, low black beams and joists in a white ceiling, heavy marble-topped tables on a turkey carpet and an open fire, a dimly lantern-lit inner room with an illuminated rather brackish-looking deep well, and beyond that a spacious cellar room open in summer. Bar food includes plenty of fish such as excellent moules marinières, grilled prawns, crab, lobster mayonnaise and fisherman's platter as well as soup, ploughman's, sausage and mash, lasagne or spare ribs and steaks; Marstons Pedigree and two guests on handpump; darts and bar billiards in winter. The bedrooms, individually decorated and furnished, are small but comfortable, and you might get one on the harbour front. *(Recommended by Wayne Brindle, Steve and Carolyn Harvey, Beverley James, Martin Wight, Stephen and Julie Brown)*

Free house ~ Licensee Jonty Sharp ~ Meals and snacks (not Sun evening) ~ Restaurant ~ (01534) 46433 ~ Children welcome ~ Open 11-11.30 ~ Bedrooms: £40B/£80B

ST BRELADE (Jersey) OS 603472 Map 1

Old Portelet Inn

Portelet Bay

They've recently modified this characterful 17th-c clifftop farmhouse as a really good

place for a family visit. Children are welcome in the atmospheric low ceilinged, beamed downstairs bar with a stone bar counter on bare oak boards and quarry tiles, a huge open fire, gas lamps, old pictures, etched glass panels from France and a nice mixture of old wooden chairs. This bar has been opened up into the big timber ceilinged restaurant with standing timbers and plenty of highchairs. They've also added a terrific play area (entrance £1). The upstairs wooden floored loft bar commands magnificent views across Portelet, Jersey's most southerly bay. Outside there are picnic tables on the partly covered flower-bower terrace by a wishing well, with more in a sizeable landscaped garden with lots of scented stocks and other flowers (the piped music may follow you out here). Right below, there's a sheltered cove, reached by a long flight of steps with glorious views on the way down. Decent well priced bar food (the same menu is available in the restaurant) includes potato skin and garlic dip (£1.50), moules marinières (£4.50), steak and mushroom pie or devilled chicken marinated and roasted in garlic and rosemary (£4.80), children's menu (£2), and Sunday cream teas; friendly neatly dressed staff are quick and well drilled. Well kept Boddingtons and guest on handpump, and reasonably priced house wine; darts, pool, cribbage, dominoes, video games, fruit machine, piped music and plenty of board games in the loft bar; no-smoking area; baby changing room.
(Recommended by Steve and Carolyn Harvey, Wayne Brindle, Mark Hydes, Richard Dolphin)

Randalls ~ Manageress Tina Lister ~ Real ale ~ Meals and snacks 12-2.15, 6-9 (12-9 in summer) ~ Restaurant ~ (01534) 41899 ~ Children welcome, over ten only in Loft bar ~ Irish folk five nights a week in summer ~ Open 10-11.30

Old Smugglers

Ouaisne Bay; OS map reference 595476

Once old fishermen's cottages, this friendly, extended place then became a small residential hotel until after World War II when it emerged as a popular pub. It's in a pretty position overlooking Ouaisne Bay and Common – and a little further along are some attractive public gardens. Inside, there are thick walls and black beams, open fires, cosy black built-in settles, and a genuinely relaxed, pubby atmosphere. Promptly served, the bar food includes home-made soup (£1.20; local seafood chowder £1.95), home-made pâté (£2.50), lunchtime filled baked potatoes (from £2.75) and ploughman's (£3.25), burgers (from £3.95), dressed crab claws with spicy dip (£4.25), steak and mushroom pie or cod in beer batter (£4.50), oriental vegetables (£4.95), ragout of seafood with a herb and lemon sauce (£5.95), king prawns in black bean sauce (£6.25), steaks (from £6.75), and daily specials like Thai beef (£5.95), Cantonese prawns (£6.25) or half local lobster and prawn salad (£8.50). Well kept Bass, Crouch Vale, Gibbs Mew, Shepherd Neame, and Wadworths on handpump; sensibly placed darts as well as cribbage and dominoes.
(Recommended by E D Bailey, P A Legon, Wayne Brindle)

Free house ~ Licensee Nigel Godfrey ~ Real ale ~ Meals and snacks 12-2, 6-8.45 (not winter Sun evening) ~ Restaurant ~ (01534) 41510 ~ Children welcome ~ Open 11-11.30; 11-1, 4.30-11.30 Sun

ST HELIER (Jersey) Map 1

Admiral £

St James St

This big and atmospheric candlelit pub has been carefully renovated with dark wood panelling, attractive and solid country furniture, heavy beams (some of which are inscribed with famous quotations), interesting decorations such as old telephones, a clocking-in machine, copper milk churn, enamel advertising signs (many more in the small back courtyard which also has lots of old pub signs), and nice touches such as the daily papers to read and an old penny 'What the Butler Saw' machine. Extremely good value tasty bar food which changes daily includes filled baked potatoes (£2.75), a pasta dish (£3.25), a curry and a vegetarian dish (£3.50), sausage and mash (£3.90) and steak pie (£3.95); three course Sunday lunch (£6.50). Well kept

Boddingtons and Theakstons XB on electric pump; efficient, friendly staff; dominoes, cribbage and chess; plastic tables outside on flagged terrace. *(Recommended by Steve and Carolyn Harvey, Mark Percy, Stephen and Julie Brown, Wayne Brindle)*

Randalls ~ Licensee Les de la Haye (Manager: Carolin Reay) ~ Real ale ~ Meals and snacks 12-2, 6-8 (not Fri, Sat, Sun evening) ~ (01534) 30095 ~ Children welcome until 6pm ~ Open 11-11; closed 25 Dec evening

Tipsy Toad Town House

New Street

This attractively converted 1930s corner building now includes a monster microbrewery, very much the centrepiece, its gleaming copperwork highly visible through glass panels in the various rooms built around it. It's on two floors, and downstairs is mostly quite traditional, with old photographs on the walls, solid furnishings, some attractive panelling and stained glass, and heavy brass doors between its two main parts; there's wheelchair access. Every table's laid for food, as the licence prevents alcohol being sold after 9pm unless it's to accompany a meal: the very wide choice of decent food includes filled baguetttes (from £1.85), macaroni cheese, local sausages and mash or warm salads such as chicken liver or bacon lardons (£4.95), haggis (£5.95), fajitas with salsa, guacamole and cream dips (from £6.50), char-grilled steaks (from £8.95), lots of fresh fish on the blackboard, and a very good value daily special dish like steak and ale pie or chicken and mango in curry sauce (£2.95), with children's dishes (from £2). But the main point is the beer: Cyrils, Summer Ale and Black Tadger in winter, with up to half a dozen changing well kept mainland guest beers such as Ringwoods Best and Old Thumper and Wadworths Farmer's Glory. The house wines are sound, and the whole place is immaculate, running like clockwork. Upstairs has at least as much space again as downstairs, very well planned with a lot of attention to detail, rather more toadery and a garden room. An adjoining shop sells bottled beers and toady or pub-related things. *(Recommended by Steve and Carolyn Harvey)*

Own brew ~ Licensees Steve and Sarah Skinner ~ Real ale ~ Meals and snacks 12.30-2.30, 6.30-10 (Sun in summer 6.30-8.30) ~ Restaurant ~ Children welcome ~ Live music most nights ~ Open 11-11

ST LAWRENCE (Jersey) Map 1

British Union

Main Rd

In the centre of the island, this bustling lively roadside pub is opposite St Lawrence church. The busy friendly lounge bar is decorated in a cottagey style with pretty wallpaper, beams and panelling, *Punch*-style cartoons, and royal prints, and a large ceiling fan; leading off here is an interconnecting snug, largely set out for diners, with a wood-burning stove, and toy cupboard full of well loved toys, books and games. Locals tend to favour the quieter little bar with cigarette card collections, gun cartridges, and brass beer spigots on the walls, and darts. Children are welcome in the plainly furnished games room with pool, trivia and video games, cribbage and dominoes and juke box and there is even a child-sized cat flap leading out to a small enclosed terrace with a playhouse. Good bar food includes soup (£1.35), filled baked potatoes (from £2.75), ploughman's (£3), steak sandwich or scampi (£3.50), lasagne (£4.50), spicy chicken breast (£4.75), steak and ale pie or beef stir fry (£5), 9oz rump steak (£6), and children's meals (£1.60). Well kept Ann Street Sunbeam on handpump; efficient, thoughtful service; piped music. *(Recommended by Steve and Carolyn Harvey; more reports please)*

Ann Street ~ Manager: Mary Boschat ~ Real ale ~ Meals and snacks 12-2, 6-8.15 ~ (01534) 861070 ~ Children welcome ~ Live entertainment Sun eve ~ Open 9.30-11.30

ST PETER (Jersey) OS 595519 Map 1

Star & Tipsy Toad

In village centre

There are tours and tastings every day at this pub's own brewery – the only one on the island – and if it's closed you can see the workings through a window in the pub. As well as their own brews, Horny Toad and JB Bitter, they serve a mainland guest beer like Bass, Fullers, Morlands Old Speckled Hen, Theakstons Old Peculiar or Worthington on handpump. You'll find the licensees and their staff are very welcoming. It's a popular place, sensitively refurbished, with cottagey decor, panelling, exposed stone walls, tiled and wood-panelled floors, a good family conservatory, and children's playground and terraces. Good bar food includes home-made soup (£1.60), filled rolls (from £2), home-made pâté with cumberland sauce (£3), ploughman's (£3.85), vegetarian cutlet (£4.40), burgers (from £4.35), home-cooked ham and egg (£4.40), chicken in port wine sauce or steak and ale pie (£4.95), fresh cod in their own beer batter (£5.50), salads (£5.50), seafood pancakes (£5.50), melon with prawns (£6), grilled tuna steak (£6.50), steaks (from £6.50), and children's dishes (£1.85). A small games room has darts, pool, bar billiards, cribbage, dominoes, video game, football table and piped music; wheelchair access and disabled lavatories. *(Recommended by Steve and Carolyn Harvey, Stephen, Julie and Hayley Brown)*

Own brew ~ Licensees Steve and Sarah Skinner ~ Real ale ~ Meals and snacks 12-2.15, 6-8.15 (not Sun) ~ (01534) 485556 ~ Children welcome ~ karaoke Wed night; blues, jazz and folk Fri, Sat and Sun ~ Open 10am-11.30pm

Lucky Dip

Besides the fully inspected pubs, you might like to try these Lucky Dips recommended to us and described by readers (if you do, please send us reports):

ALDERNEY

☆ Newtown, *Harbour Lights*: Varied good bar food esp fresh local fish and seafood at (for mainlanders) ridiculously low prices, in welcoming, clean and well run hotel/pub in a quieter part of this quiet island; pleasant garden; caters particularly for families with children; well kept Guernsey Bitter, terrace; children welcome; bedrooms *(D Godden)*

☆ St Anne [Victoria St], *Georgian House*: Small civilised hotel bar, relaxing and welcoming, with Ringwood Best and Old Thumper, good interesting food in bar and restaurant, charming staff; nice back garden with barbecue and summer food servery; comfortable bedrooms *(Steve and Carolyn Harvey)*

☆ St Anne [Le Huret], *Rose & Crown*: Wide choice of home-cooked food from straightforward dishes to interesting slow-cooked South African potjiekos, well kept Wadworths 6X, friendly staff, excellent choice of wines (doubles as specialist off licence); nice back garden; comfortable bedrooms *(Steve and Carolyn Harvey, Mark Bristow)*

GUERNSEY

Forest [Le Bourg, main airport rd], *Deerhound*: Stonebuilt pub with good bar snacks and evening restaurant dishes, Guernsey real ale, big garden with play area *(Mike Dickerson)*

Grande Havre [Rte de Picquerel (part of Houmet du Nord Hotel)], *Houmet*: Good value straightforward bar meals, friendly atmosphere, well kept Guernsey real ale, big picture windows overlooking rock and sand beach; bedrooms *(Mike and Pam Simpson, BB)*

☆ Rocquaine Bay, *Rocquaine Bistro*: Good if not cheap fresh well presented fish and seafood (they have their own outdoor live tanks) in cool, quietly stylish and civilised bar/bistro with decent wines, welcoming service; superb views of islet-dotted sea from terrace tables with cocktail parasols; part no smoking, children welcome, cl winter *(P J Caunt, LYM)*

☆ St Martin [Jerbourg, nr SE tip of island], *Auberge Divette*: Glorious view of coast and Herm from fairy-lit garden high above sea; unpretentious picture-window saloon and lounge both with button-back banquettes, sensibly placed darts and bar billiards in back public bar; well kept Guernsey Bitter and Mild, basic food inc children's (may be a wait); good cliff walks *(Barrie and Pat Noonan, Spider Newth)*

St Martin [La Fosse], *Bella Luce*: Former 12th-c manor, more hotel than pub, but has a super small bar, old-world atmosphere and reasonably priced bar food; keg beer only; lovely gardens; bedrooms *(Mike Dickerson)*

☆ St Peter Port [North Esplanade], *Ship &*

Crown: Busy popular town pub with good harbour view from bay windows and sharing building with Royal Guernsey Yacht Club; interesting ship and boat photographs, fair-priced bar food from sandwiches to steak, well kept Guernsey Bitter, welcoming service *(FWG, Spider Newth, LYM)*

St Peter Port [Le Charroterie], *Drunken Duck*: Well kept beer from several breweries, cheerful licensees, live music *(Matthew Parker)*; [Lower Pollet], *Thomas De La Rue*: Recently renovated, nautical bric-a-brac, good furnishings, locally popular food, well kept Guernsey real ales; music gets louder after 8pm *(Spider Newth)*

St Peters [Rue de Longfrie; SO8439], *Longfrie*: Useful children-oriented pub, service good even when busy, well kept Guernsey beer, straightforward food *(Mike Dickerson)*

☆ **St Sampsons** [Grand Fort Rd, Les Capelles], *Pony*: Very cheap straightforward food in friendly modern local, lounge done up in shades of brown, with russet plush armchairs and booth seats; well kept Guernsey Mild and Bitter; public bar with games and juke box; tables out by front car park *(Mike and Pam Simpson, Mike Dickerson, P J Caunt, A Craig, LYM)*

St Saviour [Sous l'Eglise], *Auberge du Val*: Newly refurbished restaurant, very attractively decorated and situated, good tagliatelle and puddings *(J S Rutter)*

HERM

Mermaid: Lovely spot on idyllic island, tables outside by the birds, good barbecued food and beer; best at peaceful times, can be busy on fine days *(J S Rutter)*; *Ship*: Excellent local seafood, attractive wines and friendly service; charming surroundings, distant sea view if you choose your viewpoint carefully; bedrooms *(A Craig, J S Rutter)*

JERSEY

☆ **Gorey** [The Harbour; map ref 714503], *Dolphin*: Basic fishing theme (nets etc), unpretentious pubby atmosphere, good fish and seafood inc scallops, big prawns, grilled sardines, seafood platter; restaurant, children in eating area; very busy indeed Sun lunchtime; piped music, Iberian waiters; comfortable bedrooms *(Georgina Cole)*

Jersey Airport [take lift up from Departures building], *Aviator Bar*: Helpful service, decent food, entertaining runway view, very wide choice of spirits *(John Evans, BB)*

☆ **St Helier** [Mulcaster St], *Chambers*: Huge new pub, well designed around law-court theme, lots of imposing paintings and prints, some good quotes on the heavy authentic beams, a library just inside the front door, old 1d slot machines and some impressive pieces of furniture; Boddingtons and Theakstons, quickly served bar food, back restaurant, good wine list; evenings is a place for smart young people and packed with them, no trainers allowed after 7pm and bouncers on door so feels like a club *(Steve and Carolyn Harvey, Mark Percy)*

☆ **St Helier** [Mulcaster St], *Lamplighter*: Good gas-lit atmosphere in atmospheric pub with heavy timbers, rough panelling and scrubbed pine tables; good value simple food, well kept Bass, open 14 hours a day *(Steve and Carolyn Harvey, LYM)*

☆ **St Helier** [Halkett Pl], *Cock & Bottle*: Period-feel pub, lively but smart, with lots of woodwork; bars upstairs (with zinc-topped counter) and downstairs, good range of beers inc Old Jersey Ale, good value bar food, fast friendly service; well placed on distinguished old leafy square *(Wayne Brindle)*

St Helier [Grenville St], *Exchange*: Smart and classy, with lots of etched glass, ornate ceiling, fine panelling, pillared entrance, smart staff, Bass and Marstons Pedigree, bar food; lively young atmosphere downstairs, expensive seafood restaurant up *(Wayne Brindle)*; [4 Market St, off Halkett St], *Lidos*: Cheerful busy atmosphere, very friendly, relaxed and buzzing, popular with office workers; good choice of wines and draught beers, tempting food *(Georgina Cole)*

☆ **St John** [Le Grand Mourier, map ref 620565], *Les Fontaines*: Original core is the back bar, genuine traditional tavern with old-fashioned local atmosphere in ancient surroundings; separate large extended lounge with modern furnishings, games room etc *(Stephen and Julie Brown, LYM; more reports on new management please)*

St Ouens Bay [S end, Five Mile Rd – map ref 562488], *La Pulente*: Across road from the island's longest beach; popular with older local people for lunch, with reasonably priced food, well kept ales inc Fullers London Pride, green leatherette armchairs in smallish lounge, sailing ship prints, leatherette-topped tables; fairy-lit side terrace *(P A Legon, BB)*

Trinity [map ref 663539], *Trinity Arms*: Large cheap basic meals and well kept Guernsey and Old Jersey ale in cheery Jersey country local, spacious and comfortable turkey-carpeted lounge and rambling quarry-tiled public bar with pool, video game and juke box or piped music; tables outside *(Mike Dickerson, BB)*

SARK

☆ *Stocks*: Welcoming family-run hotel with wide choice of pleasant food served quickly in good conservatory cafe/bistro, in sheltered courtyard and on poolside terrace; comfortably snug and friendly stone-and-beams bar with stormy sailing-ship prints; good cream teas, good value fresh set evening meals in candlelit partly no smoking restaurant; comfortable bedrooms in elegant old extended country house *(Melinda Pople, Mike Dickerson, LYM)*

Overseas Lucky Dip

We're always interested to hear of good bars and pubs overseas – or, more desirably, their genuine local equivalents. These are ones recently recommended by readers. We start with ones in the British Isles, then work alphabetically through other countries. We mark with a star the few pubs that we can be confident would qualify as main entries.

IRELAND

☆ Belfast [Gt Victoria St; opp Europa Hotel], *Crown*: 19th-c gin palace with pillared entrance, opulent tiles outside and in, elaborately coloured windows, almost church-like ceiling, handsome mirrors, individual snug booths with little doors and bells for waiter service, gas lighting, mosaic floor – wonderful atmosphere; good lunchtime meals inc oysters, Hilden real ale, open all day; National Trust *(I MacG Binnie)*

Belfast [192 Cavehill Rd], *Ben Madigan*: Decent food, great atmosphere *(David Taggart)*; [Docks], *Pats Bar*: Old-style men's pub, famous among dock workers for its stout and its crack; staff are friendly if gruff, atmosphere great *(James S Noble)*

Boyle, *Lavins*: Collection of tiny intimate snugs with roaring peat fires, great Irish hospitality; warm, cosy atmosphere *(Graham Bush)*; *Maloneys*: Good food, young atmosphere, Creightons beer *(Graham Bush)*

Bushmills, *Bushmills*: Genteel atmosphere, perfect place for Guinness *(M A Cameron)*

Cork [15 Princes St], *Clancys*: Very clean long bar, first-class service, good food *(Douglas Allen)*

Dalkey, *Kings*: Front conservatory bar with cane seats, sofas and garden-style tables, comfortable for tea or coffee; darker, smokier locals' back bar with TV; bar snacks *(Alan and Paula McCully)*; [just S of Dublin], *Queens*: Startling yellow building in charming coastal village; very welcoming scrubbed wood interior with plenty of small seating areas off main bar *(Alan and Paula McCully)*

Dingle [aka The Small Bridge], *An Droichead Beag*: Very popular with the area's young people, with good resident Irish band, guest bands eg Cajun, cool bar staff, nice atmosphere *(Mel)*

Dublin [Crown Alley], *Bad Ass Cafe*: Great atmosphere, good food, cold beers *(Martin Reid)*; *Lanagans*: Super lively atmosphere *(Wayne Brindle)*; [Merrion Sq, part of Mont Clare Hotel], *Merrion*: Pubby hotel bar with pleasant atmosphere, dark wood and stained glass, friendly efficient staff, good Guinness; open all day; bedrooms *(Alan and Paula McCully)*; [Lower Baggot St], *O'Donoghues*: Small traditional bar popular with musicians – maybe an impromptu riot of Celtic tunes played on anything from spoons to banjo or pipes; gets packed but long-armed owner ensures quick service; open all day *(Alan and Paula McCully)*

Hillsborough [Main St], *Plough*: Atmospheric local of considerable age, tasteful decor, good food in popular restaurant *(Alan McCullough, Mike Hobbs)*

Killyleagh, *Dufferin Arms*: Very atmospheric, with two rooms upstairs, two more down a small stairway; superb Guinness, generous helpings of well priced food, well cooked using fresh produce; in the castle's shadow, with two self-catering flats *(Stephen George Brown)*

Kilmore, *Marys Old Thatched Cabin*: Tiny ancient thatched pub which appears to be collapsing at the back, walls covered with poems, antique nick-nacks etc; one small snug/bar room with room for few more than a dozen *(Graham Bush)*

Roundstone, *O'Dowds Seafood Bar*: Friendly oak-panelled bar in beautiful Connemara fishing village, popular with sea-encrusted locals; homely peat fire, outstanding seafood chowder etc in seafood restaurant *(Robert Bland)*

Shannon [Shannon Airport], *Hotel Great Southern*: Good atmosphere and service in this hotel's bar, very popular with flight crews; comfortable bedrooms *(Richard Boso)*

ISLE OF MAN

☆ Laxey [Tram Station – OS Sheet 95 map ref 433846; SC4484], *Mines Tavern*: Beamed pub in lovely woodland clearing where Manx electric railway and Snaefell mountain railway connect, just below the Lady Isabella wheel (largest working water wheel in the world); splendid old tram photographs, advertisements and other memorabilia in one bar with counter salvaged from former tram, other bar dedicated to mining; fresh sandwiches and reasonably priced home cooking, well kept Bass Mild, Okells and Tetleys ales; piped music, darts, fruit machines (public bar not lounge); can sit outside and watch Victorian trams *(W F C Phillips, David Campbell, Vicki McLean, Barry and Lindsey*

Blackburn, Bill Sykes, A Craig)
Peel [Station Pl/North Quay; NX2484], *Creek*: Worth knowing for its lovely setting on the ancient quayside, may have fish fresh from the boats *(Charles Cain)*
Port Soderick [off A25 Douglas—Castletown; SC3472], *Anchor*: In former smugglers' cove with expansive sea views, spacious lounge, bar with nautical feel, seafront tables, Cains, Okells and Tetleys, barbecue parties; piped music, live weekends *(D Craine, D Williams, A Kelly)*
Sulby Glen [A14 below Snaefell; NX3793], *Tholt-e Will*: Attractive and welcoming Swiss chalet by stream in richly wooded glen below Snaefell, good choice of local and other beers inc Smithwicks, good bar food inc good generous Manx cheese with the ploughman's; very popular with the locals *(Stephen R Holman, Rosemarie Johnson, Daniel Travis)*

LUNDY
☆ [SS1345], *Marisco*: One of England's most isolated pubs, great setting, atmospheric roomy interior decorated with shipwreck relics, obviously the focal point for island life; brews its own beer, also others and Lundy spring water on tap, good value house wines, welcoming staff, food based around island produce; souvenir shop, and doubles as general store for the island's few residents *(B M Eldridge, Ian Christie, Judy Jones)*

AUSTRALIA
Adelaide [O'Connel St, N Adelaide], *Oxford*: Pub/restaurant with imaginative menu inc amazing Caesar salads the size and shape of an iceberg lettuce, lovely fruit puddings eg crème brûlée with mixed fruits as well as resurrection chocolate (typically optimistic Oz version of death by chocolate); covered back yard *(Jane Kingsbury)*
Adelaide Hills [Norton Summit], *Scenic Hotel*: Amazing views from terrace of lovely 19th-c inn protected by National Heritage Trust *(Jane Kingsbury)*
Atherton Tablelands [nr Yungaburra; N Queensland], *Peeramon*: Classic Australian hotel built 1908 with tin roof and deep verandahs upstairs and down, palms and shade trees around; cold Powers beer, quiet and friendly by day, lively at night with great atmosphere and food *(E V Walder, Martyn and Mary Mullins)*
Auburn [Main North Rd; S Australia], *Rising Sun*: Log fire, good choice of bar food with well cooked chips and interesting salads, lovely old-fashioned long hall, nice dining room, separate bar with darts etc, garden; handy for Clare Valley wineries (book at least a year ahead for the Clare Gourmet Weekend), and for the Coca-Cola Memorabilia Museum; bedrooms in comfortably converted mews; historic town *(Jane Kingsbury)*
Brisbane [Margaret St; Queensland], *Port Office*: Great atmosphere, two bars, tables in yard, superb changing lunchtime food inc good meat and fish as well as vegetarian; waitresses top up your drinks *(E J and M W Corrin)*
Hahndorf [69 Main St; S Australia], *German Arms*: Locals' bar with something of the atmosphere of a German pub, Dortmunder and Guinness in pints and 300ml schooners as well as Coopers from Adelaide, bistro in modern back extension with good hearty food inc sausage and sauerkraut, fine fish and chips, fresh hot dampers and garlic bread, huge helpings of great chips for children – big helpings, reasonable prices, good service *(Jane Kingsbury)*
Kangaroo Island [Penneshaw; S Australia], *Old Post House*: Imaginative food such as shark steaks in peppercorn cream sauce, home-baked rolls and a singing chef in covered backyard with central stove; sensible prices, and interesting puddings such as banana crumble with liqueur *(Jane Kingsbury)*; *Tandanya Farm Kitchen*: Wonderful oasis after miles of dirt tracks; decent food inc well cooked fish and chips, big room with benches, enormous barbecue, garden with not only gnomes and goldfish pond but also palm trees and even an elephant; helicopter rides to see the remarkable rocks and Admiral's Arch *(Jane Kingsbury)*
Leitchville [Main St], *Royal*: Cheap beer, esp Fri night – has even been known to be free Sat night *(Michael Hore)*
New Norfolk [Montagu St; Tasmania], *Bush*: Oldest continually licensed pub in Australia, atmospheric and really pub-like, with lovely terrace overlooking river and hills, restaurant named for Dame Nellie Melba who in 1932 broadcast from here music from the opera Montana written here; wide choice of food, Irish landlord, Guinness; folk song evenings; bedrooms wonderfully old-fashioned, a memorable place to stay *(Jane Kingsbury)*
☆ **Sydney** [Argyle Pl, The Rocks], *Lord Nelson*: Solid stone, with beams and bare floorboards – the city's oldest pub; brews its own Nelsons Revenge, Three Sheets, Trafalgar and Victory, and has tastings first Weds of month (not Jan); good choice of other Australian beers, nautical theme, upmarket atmosphere, pine furniture; open all day, gets touristy *(Tina Hammond)*
Sydney, *Harts*: Recently refurbished English-type pub with good local beers, free popcorn; slightly off the beaten track on the edge of the business district *(Dr and Mrs A K Clarke)*; *Pumphouse Brewery*: Brews its own six beers; part of the jolly Darling Harbour development, nr Chinese Friendship Garden; tables outside *(Dr and Mrs A K Clarke)*; *Pyrmont Bridge*: Large hotel bar in the old style, nr National Maritime Museum; range of local beers, very friendly, interesting decor *(Dr and Mrs A K Clarke)*

AUSTRIA
Seefeld [on plateau above; short bus ride from centre], *Wildmoosalm*: Typically picturesque, with wooden tables and benches, wildlife pictures, stuffed birds of prey, flowers on tables; good atmosphere, two big rooms packed in the cross-country skiing season (it's a centre), free glass of schnapps on way in *(John and Joan Nash)*

BARBADOS

☆ **St Philip**, *Lantern*: Just outside Sam Lords Castle, friendly and relaxed informal atmosphere in small bar on the right, and further drinking area past the restaurant; good local Banks beer, great martinis and rum-based cocktails, modest but good snack menu such as flying-fish sandwiches, good English or continental breakfasts, evening meals with fresh-caught king fish, grilled chub and so forth, lots of lovely puddings inc home-made apple pie; great cocktails; good service, wide windows, bright colours and fans make it seem cool; small drinking area outside *(Fiona Sellors)*

BELGIUM

Brussels [R Montagne aux Herbes Potageres], *Mort Subite*: A local institution, producing its own good traditional Gueuze, sweet Faro and fruit Kriek and Framboise ales; long room with mirrors on all sides, host of small tables with leather seats, swift waiters and waitresses; good snacks such as omelettes and croques monsieur *(Joan and Michel Hooper)*

BERMUDA

Hamilton [Hamilton Princess Hotel], *Colony*: English-style panelled hotel theme bar useful for decent snacks and food inc pasties and very good steaks; evening pianist; not cheap, service charge added to food orders and drinkers expected to tip barman *(John Evans)*; [Burnaby Hill, off Front St], *Hog Penny*: Probably the nearest thing to an English pub here – nice atmosphere, friendly service, food from English pub and US bar standbys to local fish and grills; more formal evenings – but that's relative; live entertainment till 1am *(J S Evans)*
Somerset [Mangrove Bay Rd], *Loyalty*: Tables out overlooking bay, huge interesting menu inc amazing Sunday brunch, friendly local staff *(June and Malcolm Farmer)*; [Mangrove Bay Rd], *Somerset Country Squire*: Very English, dark, with old prints, long bar, piano; wide choice of food inc sandwiches, also fish chowder and wahoo; reasonable prices, seats outside *(June and Malcolm Farmer)*
St Georges [Kings Sq], *Murphys Bar*: Guinness and Murphys, Watneys and Heineken; more bar than pub *(June and Malcolm Farmer)*; [Kings Sq], *White Horse*: Good atmosphere in very large popular pub right on the waterfront in beautiful old square, Bermudan/American tilt to food and service ('please wait to be seated'), many local seafood specialities, not too expensive, Watneys and other beers; nice to feed the fish from the verandah – and watch the local lads fishing *(John Evans, June and Malcolm Farmer)*

CANADA

Ashton [Ottawa], *Old Mill*: Very pleasant if a little self-consciously British, good fish and chips, steak and kidney pie, Cornish pasties, ploughman's and salads; cl Tues *(John Roue)*
Banff [Banff Springs Hotel; Alberta], *King Henry VIII*: Away from the main hotel, just above the Bow Falls, with good views over golf course and river; done up with arms, armour, heraldic shields, with reasonable range of bar food, Kokanee Gold dark lager on tap, intimate stable-style stalls each with a couple of British pub and topographical prints; shame about the TV *(Ian Phillips)*
Brandon [10th St; Manitoba], *Triple Decker*: A genuine pub, the first in this prairie town; dedicated group of enthusiastic regulars *(M J Thornington)*
Carp [2193 Richardson Side Rd], *Cheshire Cat*: Formerly small rural school, now a good try at reproducing the ambience of a small English village pub *(John Roue)*; [108 Falldown Lane; Ontario], *Swan*: Ex-Wigan landlord makes great atmosphere in three-room Northern-style pub with food inc mushy peas; seats out on terrace; well kept real ale from local brewer Hart of Carleton Place *(Jamie McDonell, Roger Britton)*
Lake Louise [109 Lake Louise Dr; Alberta], *Deer Lodge*: Log-cabin-style inn with blazing log fire in super fireplace by deep armchairs, comfortable bamboo furniture, elk heads, friendly and personal atmosphere, discreet piped classical music, Red Rock on tap, lots of bottled beers, good bar food, restaurant *(Ian Phillips)*
Niagara on the Lake [224 Regent St; Ontario], *Olde Angel*: Built 1815 after town burnt in 1812 War, open fires, heavy beams, British pub style; good well priced food, well kept local Bitter; bedrooms with beams, bare boards, Colonial-style furnishings *(Stephen, Julie and Hayley Brown)*
Orangeville [63 Broadway Ave; Ontario], *Greystones*: Good food, classic decor, good range of wines, very reasonable prices – great value *(R Gaunt)*
Toronto [962 Kingston Rd; Ontario], *Feathers*: Victorian-style local twinned with the Feathers in Ludlow (Shrops), good food, British beers inc a real ale, convivial atmosphere *(Howard)*; [75 Victoria St; Ontario], *Growlers*: Good food and atmosphere, and particularly good rich dark lager brewed here – Royal Dunkel *(Jamie McDonell, Barry A Lynch)*; [263 Gerrard St E; Ontario], *Pimblets*: Charming unpretentious local where the cat greets you like an old friend, beers listed on board alongside specials, shepherd's pie, daily roasts etc, wide choice of malt whiskies, open fire, friendly people, great music *(Ian G Thomson)*
Vancouver [Pacific Centre; British Columbia], *Elephant & Castle*: Authentic British pub food inc great shepherd's pie *(Arlene Spiegel)*; [828 W Hastings], *Jolly Taxpayer*: Great food and location, drink special offers, warm and pleasant environment, CD juke box, perky waitresses *(Robert Skelly)*
Winnipeg [Portage Ave; Manitoba], *Keg*: Popular pub/restaurant *(David)*

FIJI

☆ **Levuka**, *Ovalau Club*: Welcoming former colonial haunt, Victorian snooker table, Fiji

Bitter brewed under licence from VB in Melbourne *(Tony and Lynne Stark)*

FRANCE

Paris [116 rue St Denis], *Frog & Rosbif*: Panelled English-style pub with real ales, bare boards, rugby shirts, English dailies; beer extraordinarily expensive *(Anon)*

Val Thorens [Les Neves], *Frog & Roastbeef*: Said to be the highest pub in Europe – pleasant well decorated little ski-resort bar with live music, reasonable range of food, Amstel and Murphys on tap at a price, plenty of atmosphere; may close outside season *(Ian Phillips)*

GERMANY

Bad Essen [Auf dem Kampe 2], *Auf dem Kampe*: Well kept family-owned 18th-c Lower Saxon farmhouse-style gasthaus, cosy atmosphere, good choice of tasty inexpensive local food, tables outside; very well run, English spoken; busy in summer; bedrooms affordable, quiet and modern; cl Weds *(S H von Pannwitz)*

Dortmund, *Nachrichten Treff*: Good cheap beer, good strong wooden tables, great lederhosen, good Bavarian/Black Forest style music *(Rob Hunter)*

Frankfurt [1 Rosenberger Str], *12 Aposteln*: Beautiful old beer cellar with delicious beer, fresh and hoppy, brewed on premises, good meaty food with Balkan tendencies; always packed *(Ed Herrmann)*

Osnabruck [Kamp 42], *Neumarkt-Muhle*: Popular central pub/restaurant nr shops and parking, barn-type decor, good range of German Pilsner and Bavarian beers, delicious food at average prices inc good baked potatoes with quark (cottage cheese sauce) *(S H von Pannwitz)*

☆ **Trier** [Fleischstrasse 12], *St Gangolfstubchen*: Very well appointed part pavement cafe, part Viennese Konditorei, part Anglo-French brasserie, part good German Hofbrauhaus – owned by Bitburger brewery, good Pils in all sizes from 20 ml to one-litre stone tankards; good moderately priced food sometimes inc Eiffel area specialities; named after nearby church *(John C Baker)*

GRENADA

Grand Anse, *Prime Lime*: Unusual pub with Carib lager and locally brewed Guinness (stronger and more bitter than UK version), fish and chips served in newspaper, ploughman's, good reasonably priced restaurant – even lobster is served with British-style brussels sprouts, peas and carrots; a few mins' walk from the beautiful beach, cheap minibus from St Georges; see the land crabs in the nearby grass verges *(Jenny and Brian Seller)*

KENYA

Mombasa [6 miles N], *Pirates Bar*: Newly opened, with great atmosphere, adjoining restaurant; close to public beach *(Georgina Cole)*; [8 miles N], *Yuls Bar*: One of few privately run bars along this coast; good food, music loud but very trendy and lively *(Georgina Cole)*

Mtwapa Creek [N Mombasa, just off Malindi rd], *Moorings*: Newly opened floating bar/restaurant, great place to watch sunset; popular with English expats *(Georgina Cole)*

LUXEMBOURG

Luxembourg [Rue Albert Unden], *George & Dragon*: A British pub so genuine that (confusingly for locals) one goes to the bar to order drinks, and pays for pub-style lunches before eating them; fair range of British and Irish keg beers and ciders, English (and often little else) spoken *(Dominic and Sue Dunlop)*; *Pub in the Grund*: Fine pub in picturesque old town's river gorge, British and Irish beers and ciders; no food to speak of, packed and noisy on summer nights; cl winter lunchtimes *(Dominic and Sue Dunlop)*

MADEIRA

Funchal [Old Town], *Hotel Monte Carlo*: Well worth knowing for the harbour view from its terrace, which repays quite a climb – and the Manuel look-alike mixes a delicious Ponche *(Beryl and Bill Farmer)*

NETHERLANDS

☆ **Amsterdam** [Spuistraat 18], *Cafe Hoppe*: Probably Amsterdam's most famous 'brown cafe', its huge old-fashioned bar busy from early morning till late at night, with staggering range of gins and whiskies as well as fine beers from Delft handpumps; one part traditional, with sand on floor, heavy leather portière and standing only, the other with tables and chairs; in good weather most customers are out on pavement *(Anon)*

AmsterdamWesterstraat, Jordaan], *Cafe de Blaffende*: In old quarter, with wooden floorboards, wooden steps up to floor above, prints behind bar, good choice of beers on tap, open sandwiches, laid-back brown-cafe atmosphere, jazz or hip/hop piped music, tables outside *(Terry Barlow)*; [Nieuwe Zijdskolk 5], *In De Wildeman*: 17 draught beers, 150 or more bottled, in former gin distillery, run by same firm for over 300 years; two bars, one no smoking, with no music or machines – plain drinking house with very welcoming managers; cl Sun *(Colin West)*; [Jordaan], *Smalle*: Typical Dutch pub nr Westertoren; small and often crowded, streetside summer tables, friendly owners and staff, lots of regulars *(H Nicolai)*

Valkenburg [Daalhermer Weg 2], *Bar't Pumpke*: Opp castle ruins in popular tourist town; old musical instruments, old lamps and brassware, 7 well kept draught beers and three dozen bottled served in own glasses and priced on board outside; limited but good food, seats on terrace, welcoming landlord *(Colin West)*

NORWAY

Bodo [Glasshouse Shopping Arcade], *Cinema*: Basement room with film posters etc, friendly English-speaking staff, beer good value for Norway (prices up after 10pm); useful for the area *(P R Morley)*

OMAN

Muscat [Al Bustan Palace Hotel], *Al Bustan Bar*: Friendly, welcoming and relaxing bar with imported beers, free nibbles and local fish caught by staff's families, in sumptuous and exotic surroundings of national guest palace, run as hotel when not needed for visiting heads of state; breathtakingly opulent central domed area with national treasures around main fountain, several good restaurants; bedrooms sumptuously comfortable *(Bill Bailey)*; [Intercontinental Hotel], *Al Ghazal*: Two pool tables, lots of little booths, Guinness and various keg beers, good friendly service; this is not a strictly Moslem country, so there's the unusual sight of men in full Arab dress downing pints of lager *(Dr and Mrs A K Clarke)*

SINGAPORE

☆ **Singapore** [Beach Rd], *Raffles*: Magnificent, truly a national monument, lavishly restored: Long Bar well worth a visit for its atmosphere, Singapore slings and underfoot peanut shells, sedate Billiards Bar, Tiffin Room with elaborate changing buffets, more expensive meals in the Writer's Room, and five other food outlets each with its own style of cooking; cultural and Raffles displays; prices can be astronomical if you stay *(Dr and Mrs A K Clarke)*

SPAIN

Aeri De Montserrat [base station for monastery cable car], *Bar Rincon*: From station (below which pre-WWI German cable car takes one most of way up to monastery) sign down woodland track leads here for good omelettes, plates of various sausages or local smoked ham; Estrella beer *(John C Baker)*
Barcelona [La Rambla], *Cafe Opera*: Busy bar with complete cross-section of Barcelona society, most Spanish beers – worth asking for the brand you want; cafe upstairs *(John C Baker)*; [Placa Cataluna], *Lemans*: Waiters dash about expertly keeping it spotless and serving successive waves of customers; full range of beers from the nearby Damm brewery inc Estrella (full-bodied Pilsner), Voll Damm (delicious strong), Bock Damm (like a strongish Mild), also good choice of Belgian beers; perfect refined tapas-style food inc all manner of delicious shellfish (even razor shells), as well as squid, octopus, spicy little sausage *(John C Baker)*; [La Rambla], *Viena*: Thoroughly Catalonian – lots of stools in big cheerful horseshoe bar, good local Estrella beer, pleasant very speedy service, speciality tapas sampler (croissants cut up and topped with multitude of different toppings from chorizo to very well matured cheese) *(John C Baker)*
Nerja, *Irish Pub*: Friendly Irish landlady and expertly served Guinness – warm and cosy haven for homesick Irish folk, escape from the frantic crowded streets *(Mrs C Blake)*; [Los Huerros 33], *Viejo Sotano*: A bit off the tourist track, often with a good young pianist *(Mrs C Blake)*

SWITZERLAND

Cery, *Fleur de Lys*: Good food inc Swiss specialities esp croûte au fromage, fine local Boxer aged lager; narrow-gauge trains from Lausanne twice an hour *(John C Baker)*

THAILAND

Bangkok [Silom Rd], *El Gordos Cantina*: Small bar just outside 'naughty' district, great guitar music, good mexican-style food, very friendly owner, warm atmosphere; children welcome *(E J and M W Corrin)*

USA

☆ **Alexandria** [121 S Union St; on Potomac River just S of Washington DC; Virginia], *Union Street*: Airy and high-ceilinged, with lots of character, dark wood and wide range of interesting beers inc several brewed specially for it, others from US microbreweries, maybe some from UK; reasonably priced sandwiches, pastas and salads *(Wayne Brindle)*
Berkley [Oakland], *Berkley Front*: Newish, with 30 beers on tap, none from big US breweries, and lots of bottled beers; smoke free, with leather chesterfields, limited good food; Mon happy hour usually sponsored by a local distributor who offers all you can drink of a particular beer style, snacks included; weekend jazz upstairs *(Brian Dubrinsky)*
Boca Raton [Florida], *English Pub*: Ambience gets seal of approval from local displaced Brits; decent food *(Terry Richards)*
Boulder Creek [18025 Highway 9, 4 miles N; California], *White Cockade*: Scottish-style country pub, open Tues-Sun 3.30 till midnight *(Anon)*
Bradenton [4921 Cortez Rd; Florida], *Crown & Anchor*: Good food and atmosphere *(Eric J Keifer)*
Chapel Hill [149 ½ E Franklin St; N Carolina], *Groundhog*: Small cellar bar specialising in changing range of microbrewery products, also Anchor Steam on tap, Canadian and even bottled British beers – very worthy considering N Carolina's alcohol import rules; reasonably priced food *(Jonathan and Helen Palmer)*
Columbus [1311 Clydesdale Ct; Ohio], *Karens Pub*: Blowing my own trumpet! *(Karen Aneshansley)*
Fort Lauderdale [Commercial Blvd; Florida], *Rose & Crown*: Good food inc Scotch eggs etc, darts, convivial atmosphere, ample choice of ale *(Larry Gretzinger)*
Germantown, *Boscos*: Brews its own beer, friendly staff, good pub food *(Avinash Patel)*
Hollywood [Sunset Blvd; California], *Cat & Fiddle*: Good food, well leaned-upon bar, clientele leaning heavily on the entertainment side (inc Brits); good food inc ploughman's, fish and chips, chicken pie, fresh fruit crumble; Newcastle Brown, Bass, Watneys and Stout on

tap, several single malts *(Joe Seta)*
Larkspur [Larkspur Landing, mall next to Larkspur/San Francisco ferry terminal; California], *Marin Brewery*: Welcoming microbrewery with good, interesting and even eccentric beers; good restaurant with standbys like ploughman's, bangers and mash, outstanding burgers, two dartboards, young friendly staff; worthwhile 50-min ferry trip past Alcatraz and San Quentin, footbridge from ferry – the mall is lovely *(Jones o' the Outback, Stephen R Holman)*
Littleton [Parkers Marketplace; 127 Main St; New Hampshire], *Italian Oasis*: Family-run Italian bar/restaurant with microbrewery producing pale ale, wheat beer, stout and porter; two hours N of Boston in ski country *(Keith Stevens)*
Minneapolis [Minnesota], *Rock Bottom Brewery*: Outstanding service and good food and beer in distinctive brewpub; other branches in this useful small chain in Boulder, Denver, Houston, Portland, Addison (nr Dallas), Cleveland and now Chicago *(Gary Rasmusson)*
Muir Beach [from Highway 101 take Stinson Beach/Highway 1 exit; California], *Pelican*: May be synthetic, but hits off the Tudor style well enough if you've been hiking strenuously through Muir Woods or up the mountain (or are very homesick) – beautiful beach/mountain location, more English than England itself, with inglenook, Bass and Courage, bangers and mash etc; olde-worlde-style bedrooms *(Nigel Flook, Betsy Brown)*
Naranga [Florida], *Kegs South*: Very good choice of beers, good choice of food, friendly atmosphere; pool tables, clean, nice people *(Dick Jacob)*
New York [3 West 18th St], *Zip City Brewing Co*: Very beautiful architecturally; brews its own good beers inc classic wheat beer; decent choice of bottled beers, some malt whiskies, piped rock music, mellow early-evening crowd *(Joel Dobris)*
Portland [1629 SE Hawthorne St; Oregon], *Barley Mill*: 35 taps feature McMenamin beers and seasonal favourites from other brewers, inc real ales – quick enough turnover to keep them fresh; worth trying Terminator Stout or Black Rabbit Porter; families welcome, food mainly hot sandwiches and mounds of home-fries *(Peter Morris)*; [65 SW Yamhill], *Paddys*: Concept bar for Yamhill Historic District – seems old; six beers on tap, some malt whiskies, mixed crowd *(Joel Dobris)*
Roseberg [Cass/Rose; Oregon], *Timber Room*: Great local, straight-speaking folks *(Joel Dobris)*
Rosslyn [3 miles from central Washington DC, tho' in W Virginia], *Lighthouse*: Friendly local pub and restaurant with good value lobster dinners and Samuel Adams beer; by Metro stn *(Anne and Iain Shute)*
San Diego [1157 Columbia St; California], *Old Columbia*: Working brewery – from bar seats you can see vats where they brew Downtown After Dark (rich, nutty and dark) and Berliner (light wheat beer served with drop of raspberry puree in bottom of glass – delicious); good reasonably priced food inc huge main courses, very friendly atmosphere; brewery tours *(Anne and Iain Shute)*; [Kettener St; California], *Princess of Wales*: Long-standing British-style pub with Bass, Watneys, Guinness etc, ciders, decent food; weekday happy hour 4-7, satellite TV UK football matches *(Marko)*
☆ **San Francisco** [155 Columbus Ave; California], *San Francisco Brewing Co*: Unusual for brewing lagers as well as top-fermented beers such as great Barbary Coast ESB; good food such as hot Louisiana sausage and pepper sandwich, turn-of-the-c stained glass, mahogany and brass; hums with activity lunchtime and early evening; facing one of the few old wooden buildings left here (dwarfed by Trans-Am Pyramid), handy for Chinatown *(Tony and Lynne Stark)*
San Luis Obispo [1119 Gordon St; California], *SLO Brewing Co*: Good lively atmosphere in brewpub/restaurant with wide range of good fresh food, own Pale Ale, Garden Alley Amber Ale and Cole Porter, live music Thurs-Sat, huge light and airy bar, antique-looking pool room; brewery tours can be arranged *(Dan Neukom, M G Wilkes)*
Sanibel Island [Periwinkle Way; Florida], *Wils Landing*: Alligator-view restaurant with local speciality stone crab claws and good Caesar salad, cocktail bar really welcoming to children (free popcorn, baseball caps etc) *(Mrs C Blake)*
St Augustine [6460 US1 N; Florida], *Kings Head*: Good food and drink *(Damon Landry)*
St Louis [Airport; Missouri], *Cheers*: Airport bar themed on the TV series (inc programme reruns), with super-friendly staff and appropriately named cocktails and snacks *(Mrs C Blake)*
Troutdale [2126 SW Halsey St; Massachussetts], *Edgefield*: Beautiful old mansion, paintings throughout, now has its own microbrewery, also good wine cellar and good food; comfortable bedrooms *(Josh)*
Troy [217 River St; New York], *Brown & Morans*: Brewpub on the banks of the Hudson River, in very pretty old mill town; half a dozen own brews inc great rye beer, good choice of bottled beers, bar food, lots of beer memorabilia; huge former warehouse *(Joel Dobris)*
Vermont [Vermont], *Long Trail*: Irish pub welcoming walkers from Appalachian Trail, one of continent's longest footpaths; good food inc Irish stew, comfortable lounge, TV room, good beers on handpump inc local Long Trail Ale; bedrooms comfortable and reasonably priced *(Nick and Meriel Cox)*
☆ **Washington** [1523 22nd St, NW; DC], *Brickskeller*: Marvellous collection of over 550 beers from all over the world, the more obscure and distant microbrews not priced appreciably higher than national US brands; good cosy atmosphere, friendly service, quick good value food and gingham tablecloths in stripped-brick and flagstone dining room, smartly informal games bar *(Wayne Brindle)*

Special Interest Lists

OPEN ALL DAY (AT LEAST IN SUMMER)

We list here all the pubs that have told us they plan to stay open all day, even if it's only on a Saturday. We've included the few pubs which close just for half an hour to an hour, and the many more, chiefly in holiday areas, which open all day only in summer. The individual entries for the pubs themselves show the actual details. A few pubs in England and Wales, allowed to stay open only in the last two or three years, are still changing their opening hours – let us know if you find anything different.

Berkshire
Chaddleworth, Ibex
Great Shefford, Swan
Sonning, Bull
Yattendon, Royal Oak

Buckinghamshire
Brill, Pheasant
Cheddington, Old Swan
Great Missenden, George
Ley Hill, Swan
Littleworth Common, Blackwood Arms
West Wycombe, George & Dragon

Cambridgeshire and Bedfordshire
Cambridge, Anchor
Cambridge, Eagle
Cambridge, Mill
Duxford, John Barleycorn
Etton, Golden Pheasant
Stretham, Lazy Otter
Wansford, Haycock

Cheshire
Aldford, Grosvenor Arms
Barbridge, Barbridge Inn
Barthomley, White Lion
Burleydam, Combermere Arms
Great Budworth, George & Dragon
Macclesfield, Sutton Hall
Mobberley, Bird in Hand
Swettenham, Swettenham Arms
Wrenbury, Dusty Miller

Cornwall
Boscastle, Cobweb
Crows Nest, Crows Nest
Falmouth, Quayside Inn & Old Ale House
Helford Passage, Ferryboat
Helston, Blue Anchor
Lanner, Fox & Hounds
Lostwithiel, Royal Oak
Mousehole, Ship
Mylor Bridge, Pandora
Polruan, Lugger
Port Isaac, Golden Lion
Port Isaac, Port Gaverne
St Agnes, Railway
St Agnes, Turks Head
St Just in Penwith, Star
Trebarwith, Port William
Treen, Logan Rock
Tresco, New Inn
Truro, Old Ale House

Cumbria
Ambleside, Golden Rule
Bowness on Windermere, Hole in t' Wall
Braithwaite, Coledale
Buttermere, Bridge
Cartmel, Cavendish Arms
Chapel Stile, Wainwrights
Dent, Sun
Dockray, Royal
Elterwater, Britannia
Eskdale Green, Bower House
Eskdale Green, King George IV
Grasmere, Travellers Rest
Hawkshead, Kings Arms
Hawkshead, Queens Head
Heversham, Blue Bell
Kirkby Lonsdale, Snooty Fox
Kirkby Lonsdale, Sun
Langdale, Old Dungeon Ghyll
Little Langdale, Three Shires
Loweswater, Kirkstile
Seathwaite, Newfield
Sedbergh, Dalesman
Troutbeck, Queens Head
Ulverston, Bay Horse

Derbyshire and Staffordshire
Acton Trussell, Moat House
Ashbourne, Smiths Tavern
Ashford in the Water, Ashford
Castleton, Olde Nags Head
Derby, Brunswick
Foolow, Barrel
Grindleford, Maynard Arms
Hardwick Hall, Hardwick
Hayfield, Lantern Pike
Monsal Head, Monsal Head Hotel
Onecote, Jervis Arms
Shardlow, Hoskins Wharf
Shraleybrook, Rising Sun
Tatenhill, Horseshoe
Wardlow, Three Stags Heads

Devon
Abbotskerswell, Court Farm
Bishops Tawton, Chichester Arms
Branscombe, Masons Arms
Budleigh Salterton, Salterton Arms
Cockwood, Anchor
Combeinteignhead, Coombe Cellars
Dartmouth, Cherub
Dartmouth, Royal Castle
Exeter, Double Locks
Exeter, White Hart
Exminster, Turf
Hatherleigh, George
Haytor Vale, Rock
Lustleigh, Cleave
Moretonhampstead, White Hart
Newton St Cyres, Beer Engine
Postbridge, Warren House
Stoke Gabriel, Church House
Topsham, Passage
Torcross, Start Bay
Welcombe, Old Smithy
Wonson, Northmore Arms

Dorset
Abbotsbury, Ilchester Arms
Bridport, George
Chideock, Anchor
Corfe Castle, Greyhound
Corscombe, Fox
Dorchester, Kings Arms
Osmington Mills, Smugglers
Tarrant Monkton, Langton Arms
West Bexington, Manor
Worth Matravers, Square & Compass

Essex
Dedham, Marlborough Head
Lamarsh, Red Lion
Leigh on Sea, Crooked Billet
Littlebury, Queens Head
Rickling Green, Cricketers Arms
Stock, Hoop

Gloucestershire
Amberley, Black Horse
Ampney Crucis, Crown of Crucis
Bibury, Catherine Wheel
Broad Campden, Bakers Arms
Chipping Campden, Kings Arms
Chipping Campden, Noel Arms
Clearwell, Wyndham Arms
Coln St Aldwyns, New Inn
Ewen, Wild Duck
Ford, Plough
Great Barrington, Fox
Kingscote, Hunters Hall

Lechlade, Trout
Littleton upon Severn, White Hart
Old Sodbury, Dog
Parkend, Woodman
Redbrook, Boat
Sheepscombe, Butchers Arms
South Cerney, Eliot Arms
Stanton, Mount
Woodchester, Ram

Hampshire
Alresford, Horse & Groom
Bentley, Bull
Bursledon, Jolly Sailor
Droxford, White Horse
Langstone, Royal Oak
Locks Heath, Jolly Farmer
Pilley, Fleur de Lys
Portsmouth, Still & West
Rotherwick, Coach & Horses
Sopley, Woolpack
Southsea, Wine Vaults
Wherwell, Mayfly
Winchester, Wykeham Arms

Hereford and Worcester
Bewdley, Little Pack Horse
Broadway, Crown & Trumpet
Defford, Monkey House
Knightwick, Talbot
Ledbury, Feathers
Lugwardine, Crown & Anchor
Ombersley, Kings Arms

Hertfordshire
Aldbury, Valiant Trooper
Ayot St Lawrence, Brocket Arms
Barley, Fox & Hounds
Bourne End, Three Horseshoes
Great Offley, Green Man
Knebworth, Lytton Arms
St Albans, Fighting Cocks
St Albans, Garibaldi
Watton at Stone, George & Dragon

Isle of Wight
Chale, Clarendon (Wight Mouse)
Cowes, Folly
Niton, Buddle
Shorwell, Crown
Ventnor, Spyglass

Kent
Bough Beech, Wheatsheaf
Boughton Aluph, Flying Horse
Chiddingstone, Castle
Groombridge, Crown
Oare, Shipwrights Arms
Speldhurst, George & Dragon
Tunbridge Wells, Sankeys

Lancashire
Bilsborrow, Owd Nells
Croston, Black Horse
Darwen, Old Rosins
Liverpool, Philharmonic Dining Rooms
Lytham, Taps
Manchester, Dukes 92
Manchester, Lass o' Gowrie
Manchester, Marble Arch
Manchester, Royal Oak
Manchester, Sinclairs Oyster Bar
Marple, Romper
Newton, Parkers Arms
Uppermill, Cross Keys
Yealand Conyers, New Inn

Leicestershire, Lincolnshire and Nottinghamshire
Dyke, Wishing Well
Empingham, White Horse
Grantham, Beehive
Kimberley, Nelson & Railway
Lincoln, Wig & Mitre
Loughborough, Swan in the Rushes
Loughborough, Swan in the Rushes
Normanton on Trent, Square & Compass
Nottingham, Fellows Morton & Clayton
Nottingham, Lincolnshire Poacher
Nottingham, Olde Trip to Jerusalem
Redmile, Peacock
Retford, Market
Stamford, George of Stamford
Stretton, Ram Jam
Wellow, Olde Red Lion

Midlands (including Warwickshire and Northants)
Ashby St Ledgers, Olde Coach House
Badby, Windmill
Brierley Hill, Vine
Coventry, Old Windmill
Himley, Crooked House
Kenilworth, Virgins & Castle
Lapworth, Navigation
Lowsonford, Fleur de Lys
Netherton, Little Dry Dock
Oundle, Ship
Stratford upon Avon, Slug & Lettuce
Twywell, Old Friar

Norfolk
Aldborough, Black Boys
Blakeney, Kings Arms
Burnham Market, Hoste Arms
Holkham, Victoria
Kings Lynn, Tudor Rose
Letheringsett, Kings Head
Mundford, Crown
Norwich, Adam & Eve
Scole, Scole Inn
Snettisham, Rose & Crown
Swanton Morley, Darbys
Thornham, Lifeboat
Tivetshall St Mary, Old Ram
Winterton-on-Sea, Fishermans Return

Northumbria (including Northumberland, Durham, etc)
Corbridge, Wheatsheaf
Cotherstone, Fox & Hounds
Craster, Jolly Fisherman
Matfen, Black Bull
New York, Shiremoor House Farm
Newcastle upon Tyne, Bridge
Newcastle upon Tyne, Cooperage
Newcastle upon Tyne, Crown Posada
North Shields, Chain Locker
North Shields, Wooden Doll
Piercebridge, George

Oxfordshire
Bampton, Romany
Barford St Michael, George
Blewbury, Red Lion
Clifton Hampden, Plough
Cropredy, Red Lion
Deddington, Kings Arms
Faringdon, Bell
Finstock, Plough
Kelmscot, Plough
Oxford, Turf Tavern
Tadpole Bridge, Trout
Wytham, White Hart

Shropshire
Llanyblodwel, Horse Shoe

Somerset
Ashcott, Ashcott Inn
Bath, Old Green Tree
Bristol, Highbury Vaults
Clapton in Gordano, Black Horse
Easton in Gordano, Rudgleigh
Huish Episcopi, Rose & Crown
Norton St Philip, George
South Stoke, Pack Horse
Stanton Wick, Carpenters Arms
Wellow, Fox & Badger
West Harptree, Blue Bowl

Suffolk
Aldeburgh, Cross Keys
Bildeston, Crown
Chelmondiston, Butt & Oyster
Clare, Bell
Cotton, Trowel & Hammer
Ipswich, Brewery Tap
Lavenham, Angel
Walberswick, Bell

Surrey
Coldharbour, Plough
Effingham, Sir Douglas Haig
Laleham, Three Horseshoes
Oxted, George
Pirbright, Royal Oak
Pyrford Lock, Anchor
Shamley Green, Red Lion
Warlingham, White Lion

Sussex
Brighton, Cricketers
Ditchling, Bull
Eartham, George
Fletching, Griffin
Fulking, Shepherd & Dog
Gun Hill, Gun

Hartfield, Anchor
Lewes, Snowdrop
Mayfield, Middle House
Mayfield, Rose & Crown
Normans Bay, Star
Oving, Gribble
Rye, Mermaid
West Ashling, Richmond Arms

Wiltshire
Barford St Martin, Barford
Box, Quarrymans Arms
Devizes, Bear
Hindon, Lamb
Lacock, George
Lacock, Red Lion
Salisbury, Haunch of Venison
Sherston, Rattlebone
Wootton Rivers, Royal Oak

Yorkshire
Beverley, White Horse
Blakey Ridge, Lion
Buckden, Buck
Cray, White Lion
Crayke, Durham Ox
Cropton, New Inn
East Witton, Blue Lion
Elslack, Tempest Arms
Goathland, Mallyan Spout
Harden, Malt Shovel
Harrogate, Squinting Cat
Helmsley, Feathers
Hubberholme, George
Hull, Minerva
Hull, Olde White Harte
Knaresborough, Blind Jacks
Lastingham, Blacksmiths Arms
Ledsham, Chequers
Leeds, Whitelocks
Low Catton, Gold Cup
Masham, Kings Head
Masham, White Bear
Muker, Farmers Arms
Newton on Ouse, Dawnay Arms
Otley, Spite
Pickhill, Nags Head
Pool, White Hart
Ramsgill, Yorke Arms
Ripponden, Old Bridge
Robin Hoods Bay, Laurel
Saxton, Greyhound
Settle, Royal Oak
Sicklinghall, Scotts Arms
Skidby, Half Moon
Sowerby Bridge, Moorings
Thornton Watlass, Buck
Wakefield, Tap & Spile
York, Black Swan
York, Olde Starre
York, Spread Eagle
York, Tap & Spile

London, Central
London EC1, Eagle
London EC1, Olde Mitre
London EC2, Hamilton Hall
London EC4, Black Friar
London EC4, Olde Cheshire Cheese
London SW1, Nags Head
London SW1, Albert
London SW1, Orange Brewery
London SW1, Star
London SW1, Westminster Arms
London W1, Argyll Arms
London W1, Dog & Duck
London W1, Glassblower
London W1, Old Coffee House
London W1, Red Lion
London WC1, Cittie of Yorke
London WC1, Lamb
London WC1, Museum Tavern
London WC1, Princess Louise
London WC2, Chandos
London WC2, Lamb & Flag
London WC1, Sun
London WC2, Seven Stars

London, North
London N1, Compton Arms
London N1, Waterside
London NW3, Olde White Bear
London NW3, Spaniards

London, South
London SE1, Anchor
London SE1, George
London SE1, Hole in the Wall
London SE1, Horniman
London SE1, Market Porter
London SE5, Phoenix & Firkin
London SE10, Cutty Sark
London SE21, Crown & Greyhound
London SW4, Olde Windmill
London SW13, Bulls Head
London SW18, Alma
London SW18, Ship
London SW19, Fox & Grapes
Richmond, White Cross

London, West
Hampton Court, Kings Arms
London SW6, White Horse
London SW10, Ferret & Firkin
London W6, Dove
London W8, Windsor Castle
London W11, Ladbroke Arms
Twickenham, Eel Pie
Twickenham, Popes Grotto

Scotland
Aberdeen, Prince of Wales
Applecross, Applecross Inn
Ardfern, Galley of Lorne
Arduaine, Loch Melfort
Ardvasar, Ardvasar Hotel
Blanefield, Carbeth
Brig o Turk, Byre
Broughty Ferry, Fishermans Tavern
Carbost, Old Inn
Clachan Seil, Tigh an Truish
Crinan, Crinan Hotel
Edinburgh, Abbotsford
Edinburgh, Athletic Arms
Edinburgh, Bannermans Bar
Edinburgh, Bow Bar
Edinburgh, Cafe Royal
Edinburgh, Guildford Arms
Edinburgh, Kays Bar
Edinburgh, Starbank
Elie, Ship
Fort Augustus, Lock
Gifford, Tweeddale Arms
Glasgow, Babbity Bowster
Glasgow, Bon Accord
Glasgow, Horseshoe
Glendevon, Tormaukin
Innerleithen, Traquair Arms
Isle of Whithorn, Steam Packet
Kirkton of Glenisla, Glenisla Hotel
Linlithgow, Four Marys
Lybster, Portland Arms
Mountbenger, Gordon Arms
Oban, Oban Inn
Pitlochry, Killiecrankie
Portpatrick, Crown
Sheriffmuir, Sheriffmuir Inn
Shieldaig, Tigh an Eilean
St Mary's Loch, Tibbie Shiels
Strachur, Creggans
Tayvallich, Tayvallich Inn
Thornhill, Lion & Unicorn
Turriff, Towie Tavern
Tweedsmuir, Crook
Ullapool, Ceilidh Place
Ullapool, Ferry Boat
Ullapool, Morefield Motel
Weem, Ailean Chraggan
Westruther, Old Thistle

Wales
Abergorlech, Black Lion
Aberystwyth, Halfway
Beaumaris, Olde Bulls Head
Burton Green, Golden Grove
Caerphilly, Courthouse
Carew, Carew Inn
Cilcain, White Horse
Cilgerran, Pendre
Colwyn Bay, Mountain View
East Aberthaw, Blue Anchor
Halkyn, Britannia
Llanberis, Pen-y-Gwryd
Llancarfan, Fox & Hounds
Llanferres, Druid
Llanfihangel Crucorney, Skirrid
Llangynwyd, Old House
Llanthony, Abbey
Maentwrog, Grapes
Marianglas, Parciau Arms
Mold, We Three Loggerheads
Monmouth, Punch House
Montgomery, Dragon
Old Radnor, Harp
Presteigne, Radnorshire Arms
Raglan, Clytha Arms
Red Wharf Bay, Ship
St Hilary, Bush
Talybont-on-Usk, Star
Tyn y Groes, Groes

Channel Islands
Greve de Lecq, Moulin de Lecq
Kings Mills, Fleur du Jardin

St Aubin, Old Court House
St Brelade, Old Portelet
St Brelade, Old Smugglers
St Helier, Admiral
St Helier, Tipsy Toad Town House
St Lawrence, British Union
St Peter, Star & Tipsy Toad

NO-SMOKING AREAS

Most pubs in this book now make some provision for the majority of their customers – that's to say non-smokers. We list here all that have told us they do set aside at least some part of the pub as a no-smoking area. Look at the individual entries for the pubs themselves to see just what they do: provision is much more generous in some pubs than in others.

Berkshire
Cookham, Bel & the Dragon
Frilsham, Pot Kiln
Hamstead Marshall, White Hart
Hare Hatch, Queen Victoria
Marsh Benham, Water Rat
Waltham St Lawrence, Bell
West Ilsley, Harrow
Woolhampton, Rowbarge

Buckinghamshire
Amersham, Queens Head
Bolter End, Peacock
Cheddington, Old Swan
Fawley, Walnut Tree
Fingest, Chequers
Forty Green, Royal Standard of England
Great Missenden, George
Ley Hill, Swan
Marlow, Hare & Hounds
Skirmett, Old Crown
West Wycombe, George & Dragon

Cambridgeshire and Bedfordshire
Barnack, Millstone
Bythorn, White Hart
Cambridge, Anchor
Cambridge, Free Press
Cambridge, Live & Let Live
Dullingham, Kings Head
Etton, Golden Pheasant
Gorefield, Woodmans Cottage
Hinxton, Red Lion
Holywell, Old Ferry Boat
Horningsea, Plough & Fleece
Keysoe, Chequers
Keyston, Pheasant
Stretham, Lazy Otter
Sutton Gault, Anchor
Swavesey, Trinity Foot
Wansford, Haycock
Woodditton, Three Blackbirds

Cheshire
Barbridge, Barbridge Inn
Cotebrook, Alvanley Arms
Great Budworth, George & Dragon
Higher Burwardsley, Pheasant
Langley, Leathers Smithy
Marbury, Swan
Mobberley, Bird in Hand
Peover Heath, Dog
Plumley, Smoker
Pott Shrigley, Cheshire Hunt
Sutton, Ryles Arms
Swettenham, Swettenham Arms
Weston, White Lion
Wrenbury, Dusty Miller

Cornwall
Chapel Amble, Maltsters Arms
Constantine, Trengilly Wartha
Helston, Halzephron
Lanner, Fox & Hounds
Lerryn, Ship
Mithian, Miners Arms
Mylor Bridge, Pandora
Pillaton, Weary Friar
Polruan, Lugger
Port Isaac, Port Gaverne
Scorrier, Fox & Hounds
St Agnes, Turks Head
St Mawgan, Falcon
St Teath, White Hart
Trebarwith, Port William
Tresco, New Inn

Cumbria
Appleby, Royal Oak
Bassenthwaite, Pheasant
Beetham, Wheatsheaf
Braithwaite, Coledale
Cartmel, Cavendish Arms
Casterton, Pheasant
Chapel Stile, Wainwrights
Cockermouth, Trout
Dent, Sun
Elterwater, Britannia
Eskdale Green, Bower House
Eskdale Green, King George IV
Grasmere, Travellers Rest
Hawkshead, Drunken Duck
Hawkshead, Kings Arms
Hawkshead, Queens Head
Heversham, Blue Bell
Ings, Watermill
Lanercost, Abbey Bridge
Little Langdale, Three Shires
Melmerby, Shepherds
Seathwaite, Newfield
Sedbergh, Dalesman
Troutbeck, Mortal Man
Ulverston, Bay Horse
Yanwath, Gate

Derbyshire and Staffordshire
Acton Trussell, Moat House
Ashford in the Water, Ashford
Birchover, Druid
Brassington, Olde Gate
Cresswell, Izaak Walton
Derby, Brunswick
Fenny Bentley, Coach & Horses
Froggatt Edge, Chequers
Grindleford, Maynard Arms
Kirk Ireton, Barley Mow
Melbourne, John Thompson
Monsal Head, Monsal Head Hotel
Over Haddon, Lathkil
Shardlow, Hoskins Wharf
Tatenhill, Horseshoe
Tutbury, Olde Dog & Partridge
Woolley Moor, White Horse

Devon
Ashprington, Watermans Arms
Berrynarbor, Olde Globe
Branscombe, Fountain Head
Branscombe, Masons Arms
Churchstow, Church House
Cockwood, Anchor
Combeinteignhead, Coombe Cellars
Dartington, Cott
Dartmouth, Royal Castle
Doddiscombsleigh, Nobody
East Down, Pyne Arms
Exminster, Turf
Harberton, Church House
Hatherleigh, Tally Ho
Haytor Vale, Rock
Holne, Church House
Kilmington, Old Inn
Kingston, Dolphin
Knowstone, Masons Arms
Lustleigh, Cleave
Lydford, Castle
Lynmouth, Rising Sun
Miltoncombe, Who'd Have Thought It
Moretonhampstead, White Hart
Noss Mayo, Old Ship
Peter Tavy, Peter Tavy
Sidford, Blue Ball
Tipton St John, Golden Lion
Torcross, Start Bay
Totnes, Kingsbridge
Trusham, Cridford

Dorset
Abbotsbury, Ilchester Arms
Askerswell, Spyway
Bishops Caundle, White Hart
Bridport, George
Burton Bradstock, Three Horseshoes
Chideock, Anchor
Christchurch, Fishermans Haunt
Church Knowle, New Inn
Corfe Castle, Greyhound
East Chaldon, Sailors Return
East Knighton, Countryman
Kingston, Scott Arms
Nettlecombe, Marquis of Lorne
Osmington Mills, Smugglers
Plush, Brace of Pheasants
Powerstock, Three Horseshoes
Stoke Abbott, New Inn
Symondsbury, Ilchester Arms
Tarrant Monkton, Langton Arms

West Bexington, Manor

Essex
Castle Hedingham, Bell
Chappel, Swan
Clavering, Cricketers
Gosfield, Green Man
Great Yeldham, White Hart
Hatfield Broad Oak, Cock
Lamarsh, Red Lion
Littlebury, Queens Head
Peldon, Rose
Rickling Green, Cricketers Arms
Tillingham, Cap & Feathers

Gloucestershire
Amberley, Black Horse
Ampney Crucis, Crown of Crucis
Aust, Boars Head
Bledington, Kings Head
Brimpsfield, Golden Heart
Edge, Edgemoor
Great Rissington, Lamb
Greet, Harvest Home
Gretton, Royal Oak
Hyde, Ragged Cot
Kilkenny, Kilkeney Inn
Kingscote, Hunters Hall
Lechlade, Trout
Little Washbourne, Hobnails
Littleton upon Severn, White Hart
Minchinhampton, Old Lodge
Old Sodbury, Dog
Oldbury-on-Severn, Anchor
Sapperton, Daneway
Sheepscombe, Butchers Arms
South Cerney, Eliot Arms
Southrop, Swan
St Briavels, George
Stow on the Wold, Coach & Horses

Hampshire
Boldre, Red Lion
Bramdean, Fox
Bursledon, Jolly Sailor
Chalton, Red Lion
Droxford, White Horse
Ibsley, Old Beams
Locks Heath, Jolly Farmer
Micheldever, Dever Arms
Portsmouth, Still & West
Rockbourne, Rose & Thistle
Sparsholt, Plough
Vernham Dean, George

Hereford and Worcester
Berrow, Duke of York
Bransford, Bear & Ragged Staff
Bredon, Fox & Hounds
Bretforton, Fleece
Dorstone, Pandy
Fownhope, Green Man
Michaelchurch Escley, Bridge
Ombersley, Crown & Sandys Arms
Ombersley, Kings Arms
Ruckhall, Ancient Camp
Weobley, Olde Salutation
Woolhope, Butchers Arms
Woolhope, Crown

Hertfordshire
Aldbury, Valiant Trooper
Ashwell, Bushel & Strike
Ayot St Lawrence, Brocket Arms
Barley, Fox & Hounds
Burnham Green, White Horse
Knebworth, Lytton Arms
Rushden, Moon & Stars
St Albans, Garibaldi
Watton at Stone, George & Dragon

Isle of Wight
Niton, Buddle
Seaview, Seaview Hotel
Shorwell, Crown
Ventnor, Spyglass

Kent
Boyden Gate, Gate
Hernhill, Red Lion
Oare, Shipwrights Arms
Smarden, Bell
Tunbridge Wells, Sankeys

Lancashire
Balderstone, Myerscough
Bilsborrow, Owd Nells
Darwen, Old Rosins
Goosnargh, Bushells Arms
Liverpool, Philharmonic Dining Rooms
Manchester, Sinclairs Oyster Bar

Leicestershire, Lincolnshire and Nottinghamshire
Braunston, Blue Ball
Braunston, Old Plough
Donington on Bain, Black Horse
Drakeholes, Griff
Empingham, White Horse
Hose, Rose & Crown
Knipton, Red House
Nottingham, Sir John Borlase Warren
Old Dalby, Crown
Old Somerby, Fox & Hounds
Redmile, Peacock
Sibson, Cock
Snaith, Brewers Arms
Stretton, Ram Jam
Wellow, Olde Red Lion

Midlands (including Warwickshire and Northants)
Alderminster, Bell
Ashby St Ledgers, Olde Coach House
Fotheringhay, Falcon
Himley, Crooked House
Ilmington, Howard Arms
Oundle, Mill
Oundle, Ship
Priors Marston, Falcon
Sudborough, Vane Arms
Sulgrave, Star
Twywell, Old Friar

Norfolk
Blakeney, Kings Arms
Blickling, Buckinghamshire Arms
Burnham Market, Hoste Arms
Burnham Thorpe, Lord Nelson
Cawston, Ratcatchers
Colkirk, Crown
Hunworth, Hunny Bell
Kings Lynn, Tudor Rose
Norwich, Adam & Eve
Reedham, Ferry
Ringstead, Gin Trap
Snettisham, Rose & Crown
Stow Bardolph, Hare Arms
Swanton Morley, Darbys
Titchwell, Manor
Tivetshall St Mary, Old Ram
Upper Sheringham, Red Lion
Warham, Three Horseshoes
Woodbastwick, Fur & Feather

Northumbria (including Northumberland, Durham, etc)
Carterway Heads, Manor House
Cotherstone, Fox & Hounds
Great Whittington, Queens Head
Matfen, Black Bull
Newton on the Moor, Cook & Barker Arms
North Shields, Wooden Doll
Romaldkirk, Rose & Crown
Stannersburn, Pheasant

Oxfordshire
Adderbury, Red Lion
Bampton, Romany
Barnard Gate, Boot
Blewbury, Red Lion
Burcot, Chequers
Burford, Angel
Burford, Lamb
Church Enstone, Crown
Clanfield, Clanfield Tavern
Clifton, Duke of Cumberlands Head
Clifton Hampden, Plough
East Hendred, Wheatsheaf
Fyfield, White Hart
Lewknor, Olde Leathern Bottle
Moulsford, Beetle & Wedge
Shipton-under-Wychwood, Lamb
Shipton-under-Wychwood, Shaven Crown
Stanton St John, Star
Tadpole Bridge, Trout

Shropshire
Bridges, Horseshoe
Brockton, Feathers
Hope, Stables
Ludlow, Unicorn
Much Wenlock, Talbot
Upper Farmcote, Lion of Morfe
Wenlock Edge, Wenlock Edge Inn

Somerset
Appley, Globe
Ashcott, Ashcott Inn
Bath, Old Green Tree
Compton Martin, Ring o' Bells
Croscombe, Bull Terrier
Dowlish Wake, New Inn
East Woodlands, Horse & Groom
Freshford, Inn at Freshford
Haselbury Plucknett, Haselbury
Kilve, Hood Arms
Langley Marsh, Three Horseshoes
Montacute, Kings Arms
Over Stratton, Royal Oak
Stoke St Gregory, Rose & Crown
Stoke St Mary, Half Moon
Triscombe, Blue Ball
Wambrook, Cotley
West Huntspill, Crossways

Suffolk
Bildeston, Crown
Blyford, Queens Head
Clare, Bell
Great Glemham, Crown
Hundon, Plough
Ipswich, Brewery Tap
Lavenham, Angel
Lavenham, Swan
Levington, Ship
Long Melford, Bull
Orford, Jolly Sailor
Southwold, Crown
Thornham Magna, Four Horseshoes
Walberswick, Bell

Surrey
Blackbrook, Plough
Charleshill, Donkey
Coldharbour, Plough
Laleham, Three Horseshoes
Warlingham, White Lion
West Clandon, Onslow Arms

Sussex
Alciston, Rose Cottage
Alfriston, Star
Cowbeech, Merrie Harriers
Ditchling, Bull
Eartham, George
Firle, Ram
Gun Hill, Gun
Kingston near Lewes, Juggs
Kirdford, Half Moon
Lodsworth, Halfway Bridge
Lower Beeding, Crabtree
Midhurst, Spread Eagle
Nuthurst, Black Horse
Oving, Gribble
Punnetts Town, Three Cups
Seaford, Golden Galleon
Stopham, White Hart

Wiltshire
Axford, Red Lion
Box, Quarrymans Arms
Brinkworth, Three Crowns
Devizes, Bear
Ebbesbourne Wake, Horseshoe
Hindon, Lamb
Kilmington, Red Lion
Lacock, Red Lion
Little Bedwyn, Harrow
Lower Woodford, Wheatsheaf
Malmesbury, Suffolk Arms
Potterne, George & Dragon
Ramsbury, Bell
Seend, Barge
Semington, Lamb
Sherston, Rattlebone
Wylye, Bell

Yorkshire
Askrigg, Kings Arms
Beverley, White Horse
Bilbrough, Three Hares
Bingley, Brown Cow
Blakey Ridge, Lion
Buckden, Buck
Burnsall, Red Lion
Carlton, Foresters Arms
Carthorpe, Fox & Hounds
Cray, White Lion
Cropton, New Inn
Goathland, Mallyan Spout
Goose Eye, Turkey
Harden, Malt Shovel
Harrogate, Squinting Cat
Hatfield Woodhouse, Green Tree
Hetton, Angel
Hull, Minerva
Kirkbymoorside, George & Dragon
Kirkham, Stone Trough
Lastingham, Blacksmiths Arms
Levisham, Horseshoe
Linthwaite, Sair
Linton in Craven, Fountaine
Meltham, Will's o' Nat's
Penistone, Cubley Hall
Pickhill, Nags Head
Pool, White Hart
Ramsgill, Yorke Arms
Redmire, Kings Arms
Rosedale Abbey, Milburn Arms
Sawley, Sawley Arms
Sheffield, Fat Cat
Skidby, Half Moon
Sowerby Bridge, Moorings
Starbotton, Fox & Hounds
Sutton upon Derwent, St Vincent Arms
Wath-in-Nidderdale, Sportsmans Arms
Wigglesworth, Plough
Wormald Green, Cragg Lodge
York, Olde Starre

London, Central
London EC2, Hamilton Hall
London W1, Argyll Arms
London WC1, Lamb

London, North
London N1, Waterside
London NW3, Spaniards

London, South
London SE21, Crown & Greyhound
London SW4, Olde Windmill

London, West
London W8, Windsor Castle

Scotland
Applecross, Applecross Inn
Arduaine, Loch Melfort
Brig o Turk, Byre
Broughty Ferry, Fishermans Tavern
Canonbie, Riverside
Cawdor, Cawdor Tavern
Creebridge, Creebridge House
Edinburgh, Starbank
Glasgow, Horseshoe
Innerleithen, Traquair Arms
Isle Ornsay, Tigh Osda Eilean Iarmain
Kilberry, Kilberry Inn
Kirkton of Glenisla, Glenisla Hotel
Pitlochry, Killiecrankie
Plockton, Plockton Hotel
Portpatrick, Crown
Skeabost, Skeabost House
St Mary's Loch, Tibbie Shiels
Strachur, Creggans
Swinton, Wheatsheaf
Tayvallich, Tayvallich Inn
Thornhill, Lion & Unicorn
Turriff, Towie Tavern
Tushielaw, Tushielaw Inn
Ullapool, Ferry Boat
Ullapool, Morefield Motel

Wales
Bodfari, Dinorben Arms
Caerphilly, Courthouse
Carew, Carew Inn
Carno, Aleppo Merchant
Cilgerran, Pendre
Halkyn, Britannia
Llanberis, Pen-y-Gwryd
Llandrindod Wells, Llanerch
Llangynwyd, Old House
Llannefydd, Hawk & Buckle
Llanynys, Cerrigllwydion Arms
Llyswen, Griffin
Maentwrog, Grapes
Monmouth, Punch House
Montgomery, Dragon
Presteigne, Radnorshire Arms
Raglan, Clytha Arms
Tyn y Groes, Groes

Channel Islands
Castel, Hougue du Pommier
Greve de Lecq, Moulin de Lecq
St Brelade, Old Portelet
St Brelade, Old Smugglers

PUBS WITH GOOD GARDENS

The pubs listed here have bigger or more beautiful gardens, grounds or terraces than are usual for their areas.

Note that in a town or city this might be very much more modest than the sort of garden that would deserve a listing in the countryside.

Berkshire
Aldworth, Bell
Chaddleworth, Ibex
Cookham Dean, Jolly Farmer
Hamstead Marshall, White Hart
Holyport, Belgian Arms
Hurley, Dew Drop
Marsh Benham, Water Rat
West Ilsley, Harrow
Winterbourne, Winterbourne Arms
Woolhampton, Rowbarge

Buckinghamshire
Amersham, Queens Head
Bledlow, Lions of Bledlow
Bolter End, Peacock
Fawley, Walnut Tree
Fingest, Chequers
Ford, Dinton Hermit
Hambleden, Stag & Huntsman
Lacey Green, Pink & Lily
Little Horwood, Shoulder of Mutton
Marsh Gibbon, Greyhound
Northend, White Hart
Skirmett, Old Crown
Waddesdon, Five Arrows
West Wycombe, George & Dragon
Worminghall, Clifden Arms

Cambridgeshire and Bedfordshire
Bolnhurst, Olde Plough
Eltisley, Leeds Arms
Fowlmere, Chequers
Horningsea, Plough & Fleece
Madingley, Three Horseshoes
Riseley, Fox & Hounds
Stretham, Lazy Otter
Swavesey, Trinity Foot
Ufford, Olde White Hart
Wansford, Haycock

Cheshire
Aldford, Grosvenor Arms
Barbridge, Barbridge Inn
Brereton Green, Bears Head
Broomedge, Jolly Thresher
Lower Peover, Bells of Peover
Macclesfield, Sutton Hall
Swettenham, Swettenham Arms
Weston, White Lion

Cornwall
Helford, Shipwrights Arms
Philleigh, Roseland
St Agnes, Turks Head
St Mawgan, Falcon
Tresco, New Inn

Cumbria
Bassenthwaite, Pheasant
Cockermouth, Trout
Eskdale Green, Bower House

Derbyshire and Staffordshire
Acton Trussell, Moat House
Birch Vale, Waltzing Weasel
Buxton, Bull i' th' Thorn
Grindleford, Maynard Arms
Little Longstone, Packhorse
Melbourne, John Thompson
Onecote, Jervis Arms
Shardlow, Hoskins Wharf
Tatenhill, Horseshoe
Tutbury, Olde Dog & Partridge
Woolley Moor, White Horse

Devon
Berrynarbor, Olde Globe
Broadhembury, Drewe Arms
Clyst Hydon, Five Bells
Cornworthy, Hunters Lodge
Dartington, Cott
Doddiscombsleigh, Nobody
Exminster, Turf
Haytor Vale, Rock
Lower Ashton, Manor
Poundsgate, Tavistock
Sidford, Blue Ball
South Zeal, Oxenham Arms
Torbryan, Old Church House
Welcombe, Old Smithy
Weston, Otter

Dorset
Child Okeford, Saxon
Christchurch, Fishermans Haunt
Corfe Castle, Fox
Farnham, Museum
Kingston, Scott Arms
Nettlecombe, Marquis of Lorne
Osmington Mills, Smugglers
Plush, Brace of Pheasants
Shave Cross, Shave Cross Inn
Stoke Abbott, New Inn
Tarrant Monkton, Langton Arms
West Bexington, Manor
West Lulworth, Castle

Essex
Castle Hedingham, Bell
Chappel, Swan
Coggeshall, Compasses
Great Yeldham, White Hart
Littlebury, Queens Head
Mill Green, Viper
Peldon, Rose
Stock, Hoop
Wendens Ambo, Bell
Woodham Walter, Cats

Gloucestershire
Amberley, Black Horse
Ampney Crucis, Crown of Crucis
Bibury, Catherine Wheel
Brockhampton, Craven Arms
Chipping Campden, Kings Arms
Ewen, Wild Duck
Great Rissington, Lamb
Greet, Harvest Home
Gretton, Royal Oak
Kilkenny, Kilkeney Inn
Kingscote, Hunters Hall
Lechlade, Trout
Minchinhampton, Old Lodge
North Nibley, New Inn
Oddington, Horse & Groom
Old Sodbury, Dog
Redbrook, Boat
Sapperton, Daneway
Southrop, Swan

Hampshire
Battramsley, Hobler
Bramdean, Fox
Lymington, Chequers
Ovington, Bush
Petersfield, White Horse
Steep, Harrow
Stockbridge, Vine
Tichborne, Tichborne Arms

Hereford and Worcester
Berrow, Duke of York
Bretforton, Fleece
Fownhope, Green Man
Much Marcle, Slip Tavern
Sellack, Lough Pool
Woolhope, Butchers Arms

Hertfordshire
Ayot St Lawrence, Brocket Arms
Great Offley, Green Man
Tewin, Plume of Feathers

Isle of Wight
Chale, Clarendon (Wight Mouse)
Niton, Buddle
Shorwell, Crown

Kent
Biddenden, Three Chimneys
Bough Beech, Wheatsheaf
Chiddingstone, Castle
Dargate, Dove
Groombridge, Crown
Newnham, George
Penshurst, Bottle House
Ringlestone, Ringlestone
Smarden, Bell
Sole Street, Compasses
Toys Hill, Fox & Hounds
Ulcombe, Pepper Box

Lancashire
Darwen, Old Rosins
Newton, Parkers Arms
Uppermill, Cross Keys
Whitewell, Inn at Whitewell

Leicestershire, Lincolnshire and Nottinghamshire
Braunston, Old Plough
Colston Bassett, Martins Arms
Drakeholes, Griff
Exton, Fox & Hounds
Kimberley, Nelson & Railway
Medbourne, Nevill Arms
Newton, Red Lion
Old Dalby, Crown
Stamford, George of Stamford
Upton, French Horn

Midlands (including Warwickshire and Northants)
Ashby St Ledgers, Olde Coach House
East Haddon, Red Lion
Ettington, Chequers
Farnborough, Butchers Arms
Ilmington, Howard Arms
Lower Brailes, George
Lowsonford, Fleur de Lys
Priors Marston, Holly Bush
Stratford upon Avon, Slug & Lettuce
West Bromwich, Manor House

Norfolk
Castle Acre, Ostrich
Letheringsett, Kings Head
Reedham, Ferry
Stow Bardolph, Hare Arms
Titchwell, Manor
Woodbastwick, Fur & Feather

Northumbria (including Northumberland, Durham, etc)
Blanchland, Lord Crewe Arms
Diptonmill, Dipton Mill
Piercebridge, George

Oxfordshire
Beckley, Abingdon Arms
Binfield Heath, Bottle & Glass
Brightwell Baldwin, Lord Nelson
Broadwell, Five Bells
Burford, Lamb
Chinnor, Sir Charles Napier
Clifton, Duke of Cumberlands Head
Finstock, Plough
Fyfield, White Hart
Hook Norton, Gate Hangs High
Hook Norton, Pear Tree
Kelmscot, Plough
Maidensgrove, Five Horseshoes
Moulsford, Beetle & Wedge
Shipton-under-Wychwood, Shaven Crown
South Leigh, Mason Arms
South Stoke, Perch & Pike
Stanton St John, Star
Tadpole Bridge, Trout
Watlington, Chequers
Woodstock, Feathers

Shropshire
Bishops Castle, Three Tuns
Norton, Hundred House
Upper Farmcote, Lion of Morfe

Somerset
Ashcott, Ashcott Inn
Bristol, Highbury Vaults
Combe Hay, Wheatsheaf
Compton Martin, Ring o' Bells
Dunster, Luttrell Arms
Exebridge, Anchor
Freshford, Inn at Freshford
Litton, Olde Kings Arms
Monksilver, Notley Arms
Over Stratton, Royal Oak
South Stoke, Pack Horse
West Huntspill, Crossways

Suffolk
Bildeston, Crown
Brandeston, Queens Head
Dennington, Queens Head
Hoxne, Swan
Lavenham, Angel
Lavenham, Swan
Laxfield, Kings Head
Rede, Plough
Walberswick, Bell

Surrey
Albury, Drummond Arms
Charleshill, Donkey
Coldharbour, Plough
Compton, Withies
Hascombe, White Horse
Laleham, Three Horseshoes
Mickleham, King William IV
Pirbright, Royal Oak
Pyrford Lock, Anchor
Warlingham, White Lion

Sussex
Ashurst, Fountain
Blackboys, Blackboys
Byworth, Black Horse
Eartham, George
Elsted, Three Horseshoes
Firle, Ram
Fletching, Griffin
Fulking, Shepherd & Dog
Gun Hill, Gun
Heathfield, Star
Kirdford, Half Moon
Lickfold, Lickfold Inn
Oving, Gribble
Rowhook, Chequers
Seaford, Golden Galleon
Stopham, White Hart
Wineham, Royal Oak

Wiltshire
Bradford-on-Avon, Cross Guns
Brinkworth, Three Crowns
Chicksgrove, Compasses
Lacock, George
Lacock, Rising Sun
Lower Woodford, Wheatsheaf
Norton, Vine Tree
Salisbury, Old Mill
Seend, Barge

Yorkshire
East Witton, Blue Lion
Egton Bridge, Horse Shoe
Harrogate, Squinting Cat
Heath, Kings Arms
Penistone, Cubley Hall
Sutton upon Derwent, St Vincent Arms
Threshfield, Old Hall

London, Central
London W1, Red Lion

London, North
London N1, Waterside
London NW3, Spaniards

London, South
London SE21, Crown & Greyhound
London SW18, Ship

London, West
London W6, Dove
London W8, Windsor Castle

Scotland
Ardfern, Galley of Lorne
Arduaine, Loch Melfort
Cleish, Nivingston House
Creebridge, Creebridge House
Edinburgh, Starbank
Gifford, Tweeddale Arms
Pitlochry, Killiecrankie
Skeabost, Skeabost House
Strachur, Creggans
Thornhill, Lion & Unicorn
Tweedsmuir, Crook

Wales
Aberystwyth, Halfway
Bodfari, Dinorben Arms
Burton Green, Golden Grove
Caerphilly, Courthouse
Crickhowell, Bear
Crickhowell, Nantyffin Cider Mill
Llancarfan, Fox & Hounds
Llandrindod Wells, Llanerch
Llanfrynach, White Swan
Llanthony, Abbey
Llwyndafydd, Crown
Marianglas, Parciau Arms
Nevern, Trewern Arms
Old Radnor, Harp
Presteigne, Radnorshire Arms
St Hilary, Bush
Stackpole, Armstrong Arms
Tyn y Groes, Groes

Channel Islands
Castel, Hougue du Pommier
Kings Mills, Fleur du Jardin
Rozel, Rozel Bay

WATERSIDE PUBS

The pubs listed here are right beside the sea, a sizeable river, canal, lake or loch that contributes significantly to their attraction.

Berkshire
Great Shefford, Swan
Woolhampton, Rowbarge

Cambridgeshire and Bedfordshire
Cambridge, Anchor
Cambridge, Mill
Holywell, Old Ferry Boat
Odell, Bell
Stretham, Lazy Otter
Sutton Gault, Anchor
Wansford, Haycock

Cheshire
Barbridge, Barbridge Inn

Wrenbury, Dusty Miller

Cornwall
Falmouth, Quayside Inn & Old Ale House
Helford, Shipwrights Arms
Helford Passage, Ferryboat
Mousehole, Ship
Mylor Bridge, Pandora
Polkerris, Rashleigh
Polruan, Lugger
Port Isaac, Port Gaverne
Porthallow, Five Pilchards
Porthleven, Ship
St Agnes, Turks Head
Trebarwith, Port William
Tresco, New Inn

Cumbria
Cockermouth, Trout
Ulverston, Bay Horse

Derbyshire and Staffordshire
Onecote, Jervis Arms
Shardlow, Hoskins Wharf
Shardlow, Old Crown

Devon
Ashprington, Watermans Arms
Brendon, Rockford
Combeinteignhead, Coombe Cellars
Dartmouth, Royal Castle
Exeter, Double Locks
Exminster, Turf
Lynmouth, Rising Sun
Noss Mayo, Old Ship
Plymouth, China House
Topsham, Passage
Torcross, Start Bay
Weston, Otter

Dorset
Chideock, Anchor
Lyme Regis, Pilot Boat

Essex
Chappel, Swan
Leigh on Sea, Crooked Billet

Gloucestershire
Ashleworth Quay, Boat
Great Barrington, Fox
Lechlade, Trout
Redbrook, Boat

Hampshire
Bursledon, Jolly Sailor
Langstone, Royal Oak
Ovington, Bush
Portsmouth, Still & West
Wherwell, Mayfly

Hereford and Worcester
Knightwick, Talbot
Michaelchurch Escley, Bridge
Wyre Piddle, Anchor

Hertfordshire
Bourne End, Three Horseshoes

Isle of Wight
Cowes, Folly
Seaview, Seaview Hotel
Shanklin, Fishermans Cottage
Ventnor, Spyglass

Kent
Faversham, Albion
Oare, Shipwrights Arms

Lancashire
Bilsborrow, Owd Nells
Garstang, Th'Owd Tithebarn
Manchester, Dukes 92
Manchester, Mark Addy
Whitewell, Inn at Whitewell

Midlands (including Warwickshire and Northants)
Lapworth, Navigation
Lowsonford, Fleur de Lys
Netherton, Little Dry Dock
Oundle, Mill

Norfolk
Reedham, Ferry

Northumbria (including Northumberland, Durham, etc)
North Shields, Chain Locker
Piercebridge, George

Oxfordshire
Moulsford, Beetle & Wedge
Tadpole Bridge, Trout

Shropshire
Llanyblodwel, Horse Shoe
Ludlow, Unicorn
Whitchurch, Willey Moor Lock

Somerset
Exebridge, Anchor
Freshford, Inn at Freshford

Suffolk
Aldeburgh, Cross Keys
Chelmondiston, Butt & Oyster
Ipswich, Brewery Tap

Surrey
Pyrford Lock, Anchor

Sussex
Stopham, White Hart

Wiltshire
Bradford-on-Avon, Cross Guns
Salisbury, Old Mill
Seend, Barge

Yorkshire
Hull, Minerva
Newton on Ouse, Dawnay Arms
Pool White Hart
Sowerby Bridge, Moorings

London, North
London N1, Waterside

London, South
London SE1, Anchor
London SE1, Horniman
London SE10, Cutty Sark
London SW13, Bulls Head
London SW18, Ship
Richmond, White Cross

London, West
London W6, Dove

London, East
London E14, Grapes

SCOTLAND
Ardfern, Galley of Lorne
Arduaine, Loch Melfort
Carbost, Old Inn
Clachan Seil, Tigh an Truish
Crinan, Crinan Hotel
Edinburgh, Starbank
Elie, Ship
Fort Augustus, Lock
Isle Ornsay, Tigh Osda Eilean Iarmain
Isle of Whithorn, Steam Packet
Plockton, Plockton Hotel
Portpatrick, Crown
Shieldaig, Tigh an Eilean
Skeabost, Skeabost House
St Mary's Loch, Tibbie Shiels
Strachur, Creggans
Tayvallich, Tayvallich Inn
Ullapool, Ferry Boat

Wales
Aberdovey, Penhelig Arms
Abergorlech, Black Lion
Cresswell Quay, Cresselly Arms
Little Haven, Swan
Nevern, Trewern Arms
Pembroke Ferry, Ferry
Pontypool, Open Hearth
Red Wharf Bay, Ship

Channel Islands
St Aubin, Old Court House

PUBS IN ATTRACTIVE SURROUNDINGS

These pubs are in unusually attractive or interesting places – lovely countryside, charming villages, occasionally notable town surroundings. Waterside pubs are listed again here only if their other surroundings are special, too.

Berkshire
Aldworth, Bell
Frilsham, Pot Kiln
Hurley, Dew Drop
Waltham St Lawrence, Bell

Buckinghamshire
Bledlow, Lions of Bledlow
Brill, Pheasant
Frieth, Prince Albert
Hambleden, Stag & Huntsman
Littleworth Common, Blackwood Arms
Northend, White Hart
Turville, Bull & Butcher

Cambridgeshire and Bedfordshire
Dullingham, Kings Head

Cheshire
Barthomley, White Lion
Bottom of the Oven, Stanley Arms
Great Budworth, George &

Dragon
Langley, Leathers Smithy
Lower Peover, Bells of Peover
Marbury, Swan
Sutton, Ryles Arms
Swettenham, Swettenham Arms

Cornwall
Boscastle, Cobweb
Chapel Amble, Maltsters Arms
Helston, Halzephron
Lerryn, Ship
Morwenstow, Bush
Penelewey, Punch Bowl & Ladle
Pillaton, Weary Friar
Porthallow, Five Pilchards
St Agnes, Turks Head
St Breward, Old Inn
St Kew, St Kew Inn
St Mawgan, Falcon
Tresco, New Inn

Cumbria
Alston, Angel
Askham, Punch Bowl
Bassenthwaite, Pheasant
Boot, Burnmoor
Braithwaite, Coledale
Cartmel, Cavendish Arms
Chapel Stile, Wainwrights
Dent, Sun
Dockray, Royal
Elterwater, Britannia
Eskdale Green, King George IV
Garrigill, George & Dragon
Grasmere, Travellers Rest
Hawkshead, Drunken Duck
Hawkshead, Kings Arms
Ings, Watermill
Lanercost, Abbey Bridge
Langdale, Old Dungeon Ghyll
Little Langdale, Three Shires
Loweswater, Kirkstile
Melmerby, Shepherds
Seathwaite, Newfield
Troutbeck, Mortal Man
Troutbeck, Queens Head
Ulverston, Bay Horse

Derbyshire and Staffordshire
Alstonefield, George
Ashford in the Water, Ashford
Brassington, Olde Gate
Castleton, Olde Nags Head
Froggatt Edge, Chequers
Hardwick Hall, Hardwick
Hayfield, Lantern Pike
Holmesfield, Robin Hood
Kirk Ireton, Barley Mow
Little Hucklow, Old Bulls Head
Little Longstone, Packhorse
Monsal Head, Monsal Head
Over Haddon, Lathkil
Woolley Moor, White Horse

Devon
Blackawton, Normandy Arms
Branscombe, Fountain Head
Brendon, Rockford
Broadclyst, Red Lion
Chagford, Ring o' Bells
Exminster, Turf
Haytor Vale, Rock
Holbeton, Mildmay Colours
Holne, Church House
Horndon, Elephants Nest
Horsebridge, Royal
Iddesleigh, Duke of York
Kingston, Dolphin
Knowstone, Masons Arms
Lower Ashton, Manor
Lustleigh, Cleave
Lydford, Castle
Lynmouth, Rising Sun
Meavy, Royal Oak
Peter Tavy, Peter Tavy
Postbridge, Warren House
Rattery, Church House
Wonson, Northmore Arms

Dorset
Abbotsbury, Ilchester Arms
Askerswell, Spyway
Burton Bradstock, Three Horseshoes
Corfe Castle, Fox
Corscombe, Fox
East Chaldon, Sailors Return
Farnham, Museum
Kingston, Scott Arms
Milton Abbas, Hambro Arms
Osmington Mills, Smugglers
Plush, Brace of Pheasants
Powerstock, Three Horseshoes
West Lulworth, Castle
Worth Matravers, Square & Compass

Essex
Leigh on Sea, Crooked Billet
Little Dunmow, Flitch of Bacon
Mill Green, Viper
North Fambridge, Ferryboat

Gloucestershire
Amberley, Black Horse
Ashleworth Quay, Boat
Bibury, Catherine Wheel
Bisley, Bear
Bledington, Kings Head
Brockhampton, Craven Arms
Brockweir, Brockweir Inn
Chedworth, Seven Tuns
Cold Aston, Plough
Coln St Aldwyns, New Inn
Great Rissington, Lamb
Guiting Power, Olde Inne
Minchinhampton, Old Lodge
Nailsworth, Weighbridge
Newland, Ostrich
North Nibley, New Inn
Sapperton, Bell
Sapperton, Daneway
St Briavels, George
Stanton, Mount
Stow on the Wold, Queens Head

Hampshire
Crawley, Fox & Hounds
Lymington, Chequers
Micheldever, Dever Arms
Ovington, Bush
Petersfield, White Horse
Tichborne, Tichborne Arms

Hereford and Worcester
Broadway, Crown & Trumpet
Hanley Castle, Three Kings
Knightwick, Talbot
Michaelchurch Escley, Bridge
Much Marcle, Slip Tavern
Ruckhall, Ancient Camp
Sellack, Lough Pool
Weobley, Olde Salutation
Woolhope, Butchers Arms

Hertfordshire
Ashwell, Bushel & Strike
St Albans, Fighting Cocks
Westmill, Sword in Hand

Isle of Wight
Chale, Clarendon (Wight Mouse)

Kent
Boughton Aluph, Flying Horse
Brookland, Woolpack
Chiddingstone, Castle
Groombridge, Crown
Lamberhurst, Brown Trout
Newnham, George
Sole Street, Compasses
Toys Hill, Fox & Hounds

Lancashire
Blacko, Moorcock
Blackstone Edge, White House
Downham, Assheton Arms
Marple, Romper
Newton, Parkers Arms
Uppermill, Cross Keys
Whitewell, Inn at Whitewell

Leicestershire, Lincolnshire and Nottinghamshire
Exton, Fox & Hounds
Glooston, Old Barn
Hallaton, Bewicke Arms
Harringworth, White Swan
Laxton, Dovecote
Lyddington, Marquess of Exeter

Midlands (including Warwickshire and Northants)
Himley, Crooked House
Priors Marston, Holly Bush

Norfolk
Blakeney, White Horse
Blickling, Buckinghamshire Arms
Burnham Market, Hoste Arms
Castle Acre, Ostrich
Cley Next the Sea, George & Dragon
Thornham, Lifeboat
Woodbastwick, Fur & Feather

Northumbria (including Northumberland, Durham, etc)
Blanchland, Lord Crewe Arms
Craster, Jolly Fisherman
Diptonmill, Dipton Mill

Great Whittington, Queens Head
Haltwhistle, Milecastle
Matfen, Black Bull
Romaldkirk, Rose & Crown
Stannersburn, Pheasant

Oxfordshire
Ardington, Boars Head
Brightwell Baldwin, Lord Nelson
Burford, Angel
Chinnor, Sir Charles Napier
Christmas Common, Fox & Hounds
Cropredy, Red Lion
Great Tew, Falkland Arms
Hailey, King William IV
Kelmscot, Plough
Maidensgrove, Five Horseshoes
Oxford, Turf Tavern
Shenington, Bell
Shipton-under-Wychwood, Shaven Crown
Swinbrook, Swan

Shropshire
Bridges, Horseshoe
Cardington, Royal Oak
Hope, Stables
Llanfair Waterdine, Red Lion
Wenlock Edge, Wenlock Edge

Somerset
Appley, Globe
Blagdon, New Inn
Combe Hay, Wheatsheaf
Cranmore, Strode Arms
Luxborough, Royal Oak
Stogumber, White Horse
Triscombe, Blue Ball
Wambrook, Cotley
Winsford, Royal Oak

Suffolk
Dennington, Queens Head
Dunwich, Ship
Lavenham, Angel
Levington, Ship
Long Melford, Bull
Snape, Plough & Sail
Walberswick, Bell

Surrey
Albury, Drummond Arms
Blackbrook, Plough
Cobham, Cricketers
Englefield Green, Fox & Hounds
Mickleham, King William IV

Sussex
Billingshurst, Blue Ship
Brownbread Street, Ash Tree
Burpham, George & Dragon
Burwash, Bell
Ditchling, Bull
Eartham, George
Eastdean, Tiger
Fletching, Griffin
Fulking, Shepherd & Dog
Heathfield, Star
Kirdford, Half Moon
Lickfold, Lickfold Inn
Lurgashall, Noahs Ark
Mayfield, Middle House
Seaford, Golden Galleon
Wineham, Royal Oak

Wiltshire
Axford, Red Lion
Bradford-on-Avon, Cross Guns
Ebbesbourne Wake, Horseshoe
Lacock, Rising Sun
Wootton Rivers, Royal Oak

Yorkshire
Appletreewick, Craven Arms
Askrigg, Kings Arms
Blakey Ridge, Lion
Buckden, Buck
Burnsall, Red Lion
Byland Abbey, Abbey
Cray, White Lion
East Witton, Blue Lion
Heath, Kings Arms
Hubberholme, George
Kirby Hill, Shoulder of Mutton
Lastingham, Blacksmiths Arms
Levisham, Horseshoe
Linton in Craven, Fountaine
Litton, Queens Arms
Masham, Kings Head
Meltham, Will's o' Nat's
Muker, Farmers Arms
Ramsgill, Yorke Arms
Robin Hoods Bay, Laurel
Rosedale Abbey, Milburn Arms
Shelley, Three Acres
Starbotton, Fox & Hounds
Terrington, Bay Horse
Thornton Watlass, Buck
Wath-in-Nidderdale, Sportsmans Arms
Widdop, Pack Horse
Wigglesworth, Plough

London, Central
London EC1, Olde Mitre

London, North
London NW3, Spaniards

London, South
London SE1, Horniman
London SE21, Crown & Greyhound
London SW4, Olde Windmill
London SW19, Fox & Grapes

London, West
Hampton Court, Kings Arms

Scotland
Applecross, Applecross Inn
Arduaine, Loch Melfort
Brig o Turk, Byre
Clachan Seil, Tigh an Truish
Crinan, Crinan Hotel
Kilberry, Kilberry Inn
Mountbenger, Gordon Arms
Pitlochry, Killiecrankie
Sheriffmuir, Sheriffmuir Inn
St Mary's Loch, Tibbie Shiels
Strachur, Creggans
Tushielaw, Tushielaw Inn
Tweedsmuir, Crook

Wales
Abergorlech, Black Lion
Aberystwyth, Halfway
Caerphilly, Courthouse
Carew, Carew Inn
Cilcain, White Horse
Crickhowell, Nantyffin Cider Mill
Kenfig, Prince of Wales
Llanbedr-y-Cennin, Olde Bull
Llanberis, Pen-y-Gwryd
Llanthony, Abbey
Maentwrog, Grapes
Monmouth, Punch House
Old Radnor, Harp
Red Wharf Bay, Ship

Channel Islands
St Brelade, Old Portelet
St Brelade, Old Smugglers

PUBS WITH GOOD VIEWS

These pubs are listed for their particularly good views, either from inside or from a garden or terrace. Waterside pubs are listed again here only if their view is exceptional in its own right – not just a straightforward sea view, for example.

Berkshire
Chieveley, Blue Boar

Buckinghamshire
Brill, Pheasant

Cheshire
Higher Burwardsley, Pheasant
Langley, Hanging Gate
Langley, Leathers Smithy
Overton, Ring o' Bells

Cornwall
Polruan, Lugger
St Agnes, Turks Head

Cumbria
Braithwaite, Coledale
Cartmel Fell, Masons Arms
Eskdale Green, King George IV
Hawkshead, Drunken Duck
Langdale, Old Dungeon Ghyll
Loweswater, Kirkstile
Troutbeck, Queens Head
Ulverston, Bay Horse

Derbyshire and Staffordshire
Foolow, Barrel
Monsal Head, Monsal Head Hotel
Over Haddon, Lathkil

Devon
Postbridge, Warren House

Dorset
Kingston, Scott Arms
West Bexington, Manor
Worth Matravers, Square & Compass

Gloucestershire
Amberley, Black Horse
Cranham, Black Horse
Edge, Edgemoor
Gretton, Royal Oak
Kilkenny, Kilkeney Inn
Sheepscombe, Butchers Arms
Stanton, Mount
Woodchester, Ram

Hampshire
Beauworth, Milbury's

Hereford and Worcester
Ruckhall, Ancient Camp
Wyre Piddle, Anchor

Hertfordshire
Great Offley, Green Man

Isle of Wight
Niton, Buddle
Ventnor, Spyglass

Kent
Penshurst, Spotted Dog
Ulcombe, Pepper Box

Lancashire
Blacko, Moorcock
Blackstone Edge, White House
Darwen, Old Rosins
Marple, Romper
Tockholes, Rock
Uppermill, Cross Keys

Leicestershire, Lincolnshire and Nottinghamshire
Knipton, Red House

Northumbria (including Northumberland, Durham, etc)
North Shields, Wooden Doll
Seahouses, Olde Ship

Shropshire
Hope, Stables

Somerset
Blagdon, New Inn

Suffolk
Erwarton, Queens Head
Hundon, Plough
Levington, Ship

Sussex
Burpham, George & Dragon
Byworth, Black Horse
Elsted, Three Horseshoes
Fletching, Griffin

Wiltshire
Axford, Red Lion
Box, Quarrymans Arms
Lacock, Rising Sun

Yorkshire
Appletreewick, Craven Arms
Blakey Ridge, Lion
Kirby Hill, Shoulder of Mutton
Kirkham, Stone Trough
Litton, Queens Arms
Meltham, Will's o' Nat's
Shelley, Three Acres

Scotland
Applecross, Applecross Inn
Ardvasar, Ardvasar Hotel
Crinan, Crinan Hotel
Edinburgh, Starbank
Isle Ornsay, Tigh Osda Eilean Iarmain
Kilberry, Kilberry Inn
Pitlochry, Killiecrankie
Sheriffmuir, Sheriffmuir Inn
Shieldaig, Tigh an Eilean
St Mary's Loch, Tibbie Shiels
Strachur, Creggans
Tushielaw, Tushielaw Inn
Ullapool, Ferry Boat
Weem, Ailean Chraggan

Wales
Aberdovey, Penhelig Arms
Aberystwyth, Halfway
Bodfari, Dinorben Arms
Caerphilly, Courthouse
Halkyn, Britannia
Llanbedr-y-Cennin, Olde Bull
Llanberis, Pen-y-Gwryd
Llanferres, Druid
Llangynwyd, Old House
Llannefydd, Hawk & Buckle
Old Radnor, Harp
Tyn y Groes, Groes

Channel Islands
St Aubin, Old Court House

PUBS IN INTERESTING BUILDINGS

Pubs and inns are listed here for the particular interest of their building – something really out of the ordinary to look at, or occasionally a building that has an outstandingly interesting historical background.

Berkshire
Cookham, Bel & the Dragon

Buckinghamshire
Forty Green, Royal Standard of England

Cornwall
Morwenstow, Bush

Derbyshire and Staffordshire
Buxton, Bull i' th' Thorn

Devon
Dartmouth, Cherub
Harberton, Church House
Rattery, Church House
Sourton, Highwayman
South Zeal, Oxenham Arms

Hampshire
Beauworth, Milbury's

Hereford and Worcester
Bretforton, Fleece

Lancashire
Garstang, Th'Owd Tithebarn
Liverpool, Philharmonic Dining Rooms

Leicestershire, Lincolnshire and Nottinghamshire
Nottingham, Olde Trip to Jerusalem
Stamford, George of Stamford

Midlands (including Warwickshire and Northants)
Himley, Crooked House
West Bromwich, Manor House

Norfolk
Scole, Scole Inn

Northumbria (including Northumberland, Durham, etc)
Blanchland, Lord Crewe Arms

Oxfordshire
Fyfield, White Hart

Somerset
Norton St Philip, George

Suffolk
Lavenham, Swan
Long Melford, Bull

Sussex
Alfriston, Star
Rye, Mermaid

Wiltshire
Salisbury, Haunch of Venison

Yorkshire
Hull, Olde White Harte

London, Central
London EC2, Hamilton Hall
London EC4, Black Friar
London WC1, Cittie of Yorke

London, South
London SE1, George
London SE5, Phoenix & Firkin

Scotland
Edinburgh, Cafe Royal
Edinburgh, Guildford Arms
Glasgow, Horseshoe

Wales
Llanfihangel Crucorney, Skirrid
Llanthony, Abbey

PUBS THAT BREW THEIR OWN BEER

The pubs listed here brew their own beer on the premises; many others not listed have beers brewed for them specially, sometimes to an individual recipe (but by a separate brewer). We mention these in the text.

Cornwall
Helston, Blue Anchor

Cumbria
Cartmel Fell, Masons Arms
Dent, Sun

Derbyshire and Staffordshire
Burton on Trent, Burton Bridge
Derby, Brunswick
Melbourne, John Thompson
Shraleybrook, Rising Sun

Devon
Ashburton, London
Hatherleigh, Tally Ho
Holbeton, Mildmay Colours
Horsebridge, Royal
Newton St Cyres, Beer Engine

Hertfordshire
Barley, Fox & Hounds

Lancashire
Manchester, Lass o' Gowrie

Leicestershire, Lincolnshire and Nottinghamshire
Burrough on the Hill, Stag & Hounds
Nottingham, Fellows Morton & Clayton
Snaith, Brewers Arms

Midlands (including Warwickshire and Northants)
Brierley Hill, Vine
Langley, Brewery

Norfolk
Woodbastwick, Fur & Feather

Shropshire
Bishops Castle, Three Tuns
Wistanstow, Plough

Somerset
Trudoxhill, White Hart

Suffolk
Earl Soham, Victoria

Sussex
Chidham, Old House At Home
Seaford, Golden Galleon

Yorkshire
Cropton, New Inn
Hull, Minerva
Linthwaite, Sair
Sheffield, Fat Cat

London, Central
London SW1, Orange Brewery

London, South
London SE5, Phoenix & Firkin

London, West
London SW10, Ferret & Firkin

Channel Islands
Star & Tipsy Toad, St Peter
Tipsy Toad Town House, St Helier

PUBS CLOSE TO MOTORWAY JUNCTIONS

The number at the start of each line is the number of the junction. Detailed directions are given in the main entry for each pub. In this section, to help you find the pubs quickly before you're past the junction, we give in abbreviated form the name of the chapter where you'll find them in the text.

M1
18: Crick (Midlands) 1 mile; Ashby St Ledgers (Midlands) 4 miles
24: Kegworth (Leics/Lincs/Notts) under a mile; Shardlow (Derbys/Staffs) 3¼ miles
26: Kimberley (Leics/Lincs/Notts) 2 miles
29: Hardwick Hall (Derbys/Staffs) 4 miles

M2
7: Selling (Kent) 3½ miles

M3
5: Mattingley (Hants) 3 miles; Rotherwick (Hants) 4 miles
7: Dummer (Hants) ½ mile

M4
9: Holyport (Berks) 1½ miles
12: Stanford Dingley (Berks) 4 miles
13: Chieveley (Berks) 3½ miles; Winterbourne (Berks) 3½ miles
14: Great Shefford (Berks) 2 miles
18: Old Sodbury (Somerset) 2 miles
21: Aust (Somerset) ½ mile; Littleton upon Severn (Somerset) 3½ miles
37: Kenfig (Wales) 2¼ miles

M5
2: Langley (Midlands) 1½ miles
9: Bredon (Herefs & Worcs) 4½ miles
16: Almondsbury (Somerset) 1¼ miles
19: Easton in Gordano (Somerset) 1 mile; Clapton in Gordano (Somerset) 4 miles
23: West Huntspill (Somerset) 2¾ miles
25: Stoke St Mary (Somerset) 2¾ miles
28: Broadhembury (Devon) 5 miles
30: Woodbury Salterton (Devon) 3½ miles; Topsham (Devon) 2 miles and 2¼ miles; Exeter (Devon) 4 miles

M6
2: Withybrook (Midlands) 4 miles
9: West Bromwich (Midlands) 2 miles
13: Acton Trussell (Derbys/Staffs) 2 miles
16: Barthomley (Cheshire) 1 mile; Shraleybrook (Derbys/Staffs) 3 miles; Weston (Cheshire) 3½ miles
17: Brereton Green (Cheshire) 2 miles
19: Plumley (Cheshire) 2½ miles; Great Budworth (Cheshire) 4½ miles
29: Brindle (Lancs etc) 3 miles
31: Balderstone (Lancs etc) 2 miles
32: Goosnargh (Lancs etc) 4 miles
35: Yealand Conyers (Lancs etc) 3 miles
40: Stainton (Cumbria) 3 miles; Yanwath (Cumbria) 2¼ miles; Tirril (Cumbria) 3½ miles; Askham (Cumbria) 4½ miles

M9
3: Linlithgow (Scotland) 2 miles

M11
10: Hinxton (Cambs/Beds) 2 miles

M18
5: Hatfield Woodhouse (Yorks) 2 miles

M25
8: Betchworth (Surrey) 4 miles
10: Pyrford Lock (Surrey) 3¼ miles; Cobham (Surrey) 3¾ miles
18: Chenies (Bucks) 2 miles; Flaunden (Herts) 4 miles

M27
1: Cadnam (Hants) ½ mile
8: Bursledon (Hants) 2 miles
9: Locks Heath (Hants) 2½ miles

M40
2: Beaconsfield (Bucks) 1 mile; Forty Green (Bucks) 3½ miles
5: Bolter End (Bucks) 4 miles
6: Lewknor (Oxon) ½ mile; Watlington (Oxon) 2¼ miles; Cuxham (Oxon) 4 miles
7: Little Milton (Oxon) 2½ miles
8: Worminghall (Bucks) 4½ miles

M56
12: Overton (Cheshire) 2 miles

M90
5: Cleish (Scotland) 1½ miles

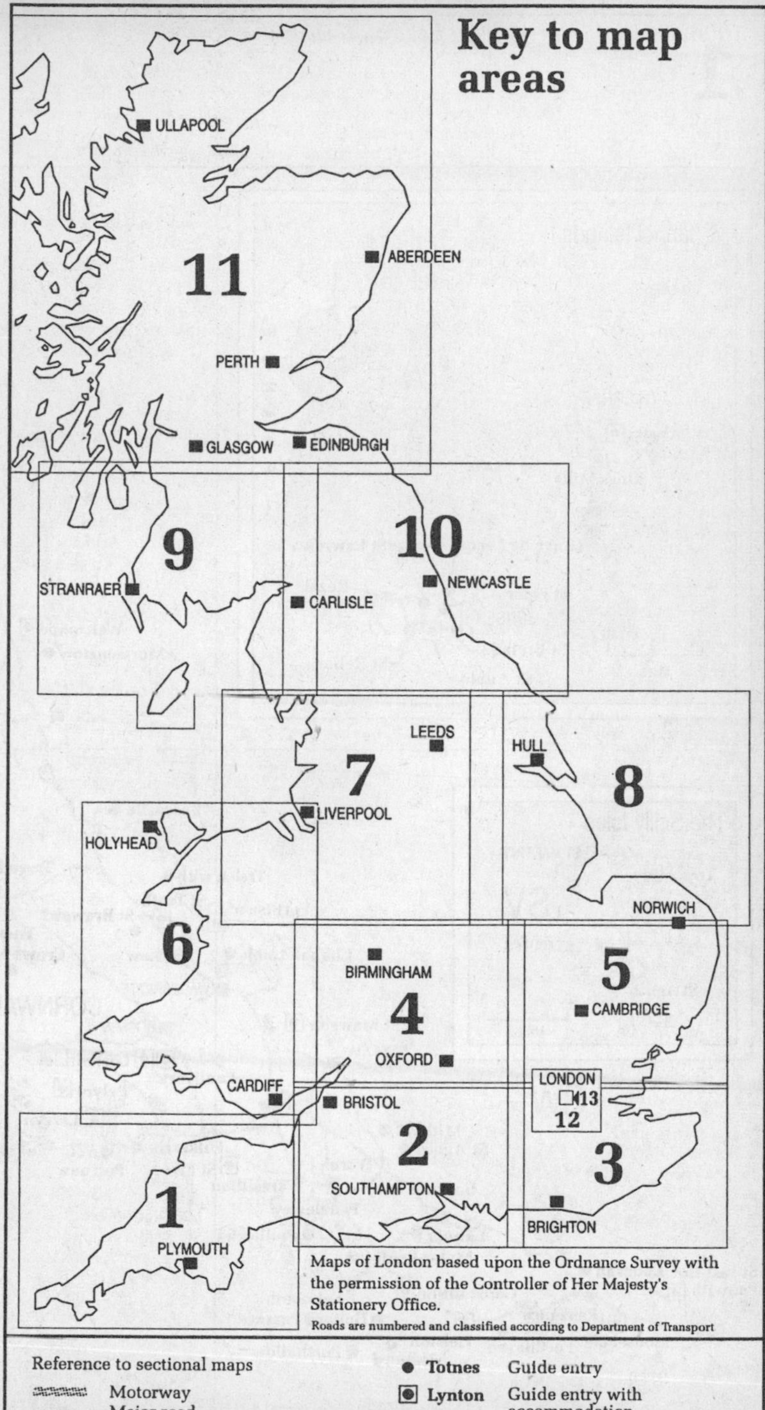

Maps of London based upon the Ordnance Survey with the permission of the Controller of Her Majesty's Stationery Office.

Roads are numbered and classified according to Department of Transport

Reference to sectional maps

Motorway	
Major road	
County boundary	

● **Totnes**	Guide entry
Lynton	Guide entry with accommodation
■ BODMIN	Place name to assist location

1

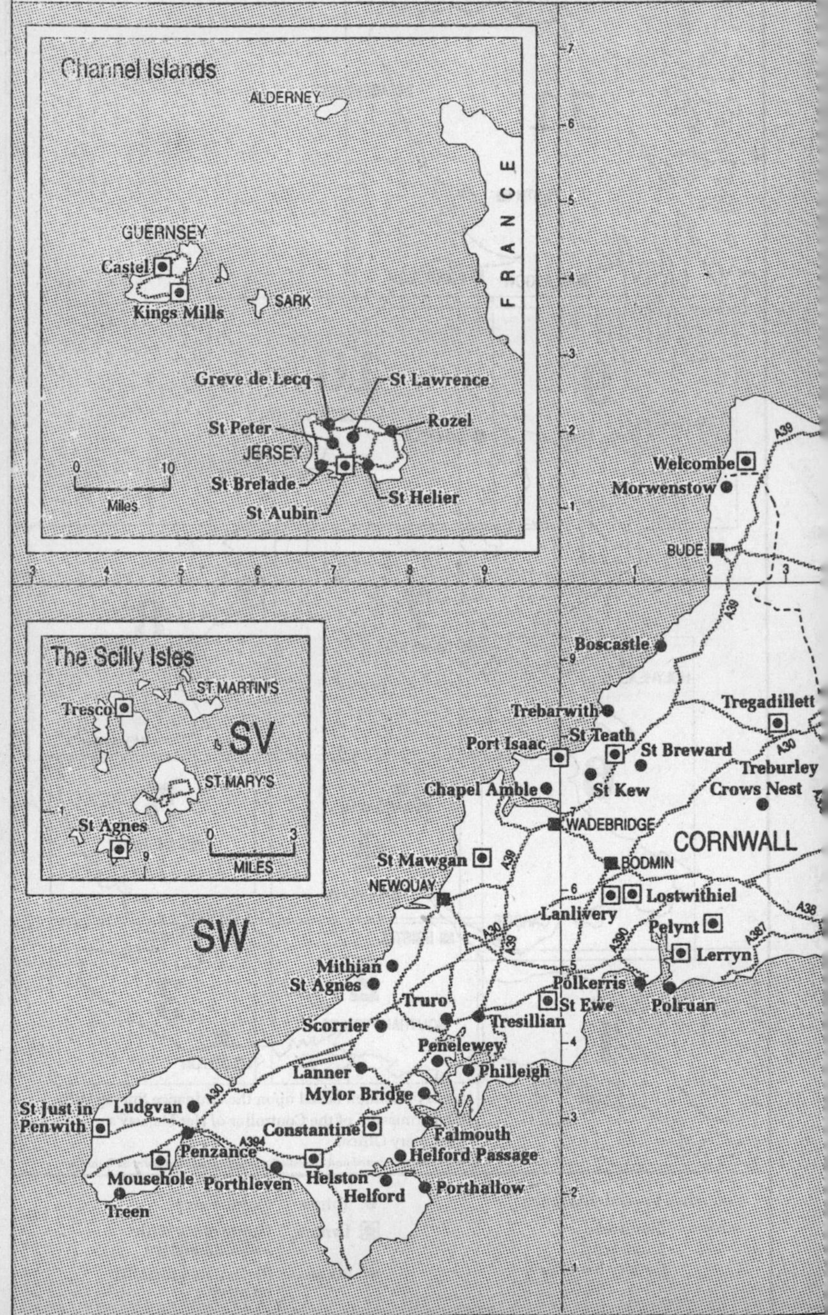

Channel Islands
ALDERNEY
FRANCE
GUERNSEY
Castel
Kings Mills
SARK
Greve de Lecq
St Lawrence
St Peter
Rozel
JERSEY
St Brelade
St Helier
St Aubin
0 10 Miles
The Scilly Isles
ST MARTIN'S
Tresco
SV
ST MARY'S
St Agnes
0 3 MILES
SW
Welcombe
Morwenstow
BUDE
Boscastle
Trebarwith
Tregadillett
Port Isaac
St Teath
St Breward
Treburley
Chapel Amble
St Kew
Crows Nest
WADEBRIDGE
CORNWALL
St Mawgan
BODMIN
NEWQUAY
Lostwithiel
Lanlivery
Pelynt
Lerryn
Mithian
St Agnes
Polkerris
Truro
St Ewe
Polruan
Scorrier
Tresillian
Penelewey
Lanner
Philleigh
Mylor Bridge
St Just in Penwith
Ludgvan
Constantine
Falmouth
Penzance
Helford Passage
Mousehole
Porthleven
Helston
Helford
Porthallow
Treen
A39
A30
A38
A390
A387
A394

SS
ST
SX
SY
AVON
SOMERSET
DEVON
Clapton in Gordano
WESTON SUPER MARE
Churchill
M5
A38
West Huntspill
Catcott
Bradley Green
Ashcott
2
Lynmouth
Berrynarbor
Brendon
A39
East Down
Brayford
Dunster
Luxborough
Kilve
Stogumber
Monksilver
Withypool
Triscombe
Winsford
A396
BARNSTAPLE
Bishops Tawton
Langley Marsh
East Lyng
Stoke St Gregory
Knowstone
Appley
TAUNTON
Knapp
Huish Episcopi
Buckland Brewer
A361
Exebridge
Stoke St Mary
Chittlehamholt
Torrington
A388
A377
Ashill
Over Stratton
A386
Dowlish Wake
Sheepwash
Iddesleigh
Butterleigh
Wambrook
Hinton St George
Hatherleigh
Broadhembury
Stockland
Chardstock
A3072
Clyst Hydon
A30
Haselbury Plucknett
Coleford
Broadclyst
Weston
Dalwood
Shave Cross
South Zeal
Cheriton Bishop
Newton St Cyres
Exeter
Tipton St John
Kilmington
Symondsbury
Sourton
Wonson
Woodbury Salterton
Colyton
Drewsteignton
Doddiscombsleigh
Sidford
Branscombe
Axmouth
Lyme Regis
Chideock
Lydford
Chagford
Lower Ashton
Topsham
Moretonhampstead
Exminster
Horndon
Trusham
Lustleigh
Peter Tavy
Budleigh Salterton
Haytor Vale
Postbridge
Cockwood
Horsebridge
Ashburton
Kingsteignton
Poundsgate
Combeinteignhead
Holne
Torbryan
Abbotskerswell
Meavy
Staverton
Dartington
Kingskerswell
Miltoncombe
Pillaton
Littlehempston
Rattery
Totnes
Harberton
Lutton
Ashprington
Stoke Gabriel
Cornworthy
Plymouth
A379
Kingston
Dartmouth
Holbeton
Blackawton
Stoke Fleming
Noss Mayo
Churchstow
Ringmore
Bantham
Torcross
South Pool
0
10
20
MILES

2

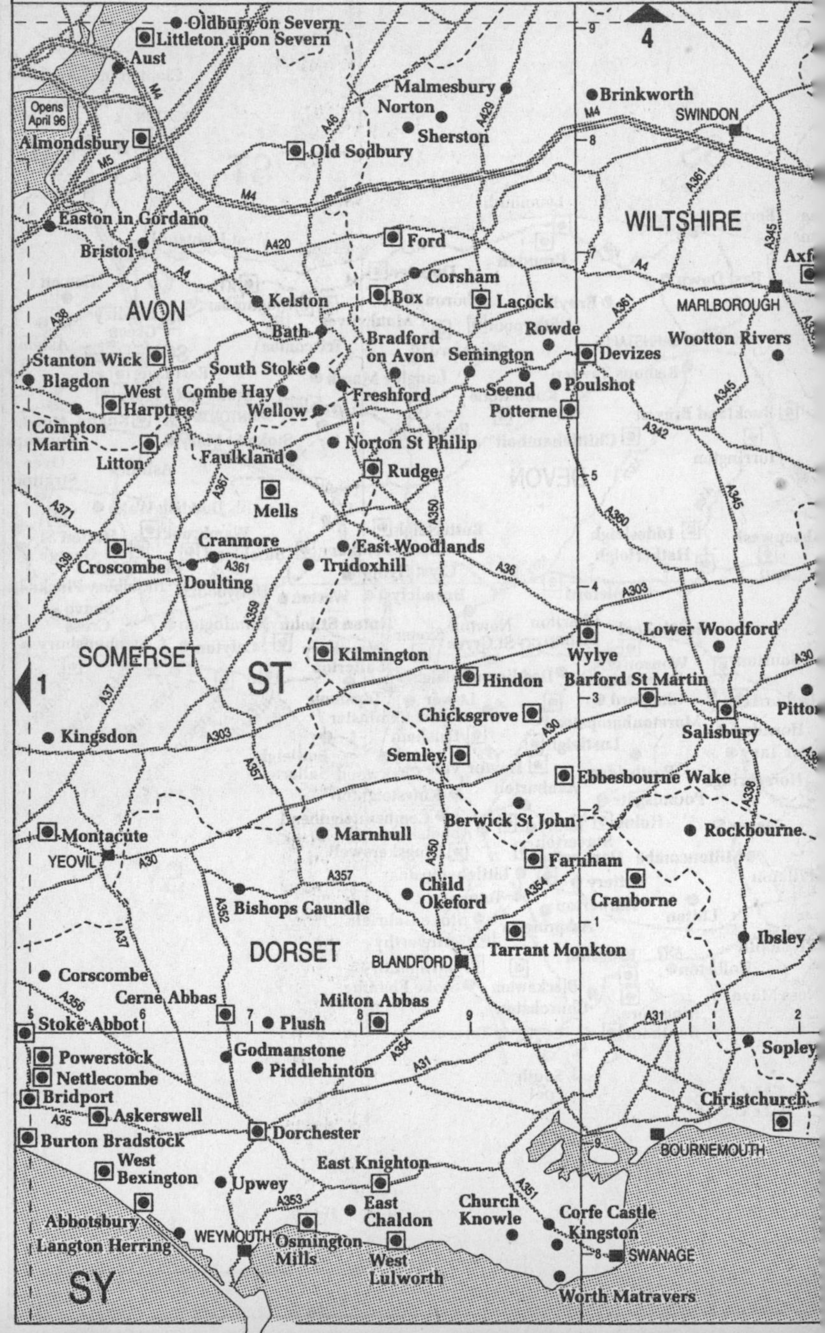

Oldbury on Severn
Littleton upon Severn
Aust
Opens April 96
M4
Almondsbury
M5
Malmesbury
Norton
Sherston
A46
A429
Old Sodbury
Brinkworth
SWINDON
M4
A361
Easton in Gordano
Bristol
A420
Ford
WILTSHIRE
A345
Axf
A4
Corsham
AVON
Kelston
Box
Lacock
MARLBOROUGH
A38
Bath
Bradford on Avon
Rowde
A361
Wootton Rivers
Stanton Wick
South Stoke
Semington
Devizes
Blagdon
West Harptree
Combe Hay
Freshford
Seend
Poulshot
A345
Wellow
Potterne
Compton Martin
A342
Litton
Norton St Philip
Faulkland
Rudge
A367
Mells
A371
A350
A360
A345
Cranmore
East Woodlands
A39
Croscombe
Doulting
A361
Trudoxhill
A36
A303
A359
Lower Woodford
Wylye
SOMERSET
Kilmington
ST
1
Hindon
Barford St Martin
A30
A37
Pittor
Chicksgrove
Salisbury
Kingsdon
A303
A30
A357
Semley
Ebbesbourne Wake
A338
Berwick St John
Rockbourne
Marnhull
Montacute
YEOVIL
A30
A350
Farnham
A357
Child Okeford
A354
Cranborne
Bishops Caundle
A352
A37
Ibsley
DORSET
Tarrant Monkton
BLANDFORD
Corscombe
A356
Cerne Abbas
Milton Abbas
Stoke Abbot
Plush
A31
Sopley
Godmanstone
A354
Powerstock
Piddlehinton
A31
Nettlecombe
Bridport
Christchurch
Askerswell
A35
Dorchester
Burton Bradstock
BOURNEMOUTH
West Bexington
East Knighton
Upwey
A351
A353
Church Knowle
Corfe Castle
Abbotsbury
East Chaldon
Kingston
WEYMOUTH
Osmington Mills
Langton Herring
SWANAGE
West Lulworth
SY
Worth Matravers

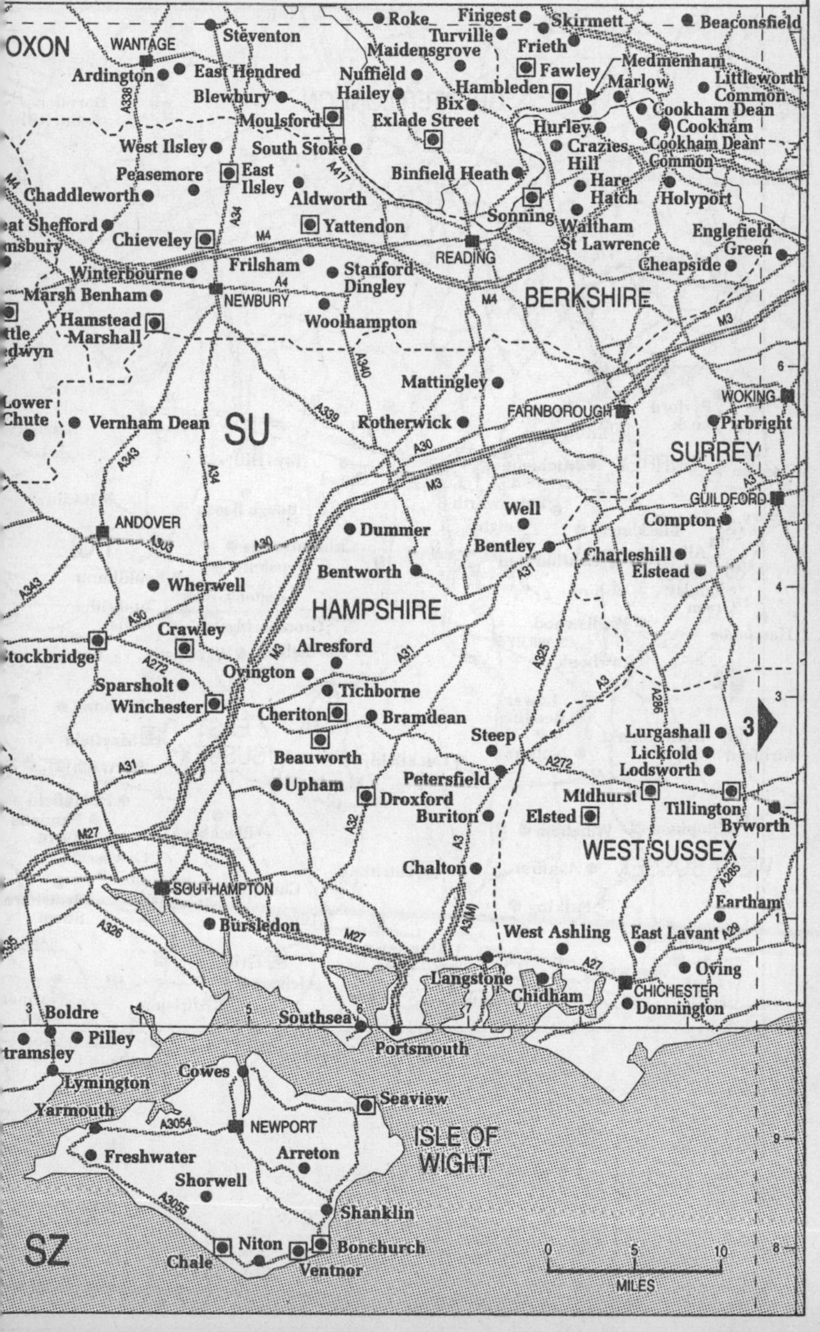

OXON
WANTAGE
Steventon
Roke
Fingest
Skirmett
Beaconsfield
Turville
Frieth
Maidensgrove
Medmenham
Ardington
East Hendred
Nuffield
Fawley
Littleworth Common
Blewbury
Hailey
Hambleden
Marlow
Bix
Cookham Dean
Moulsford
Exlade Street
Hurley
Cookham
West Ilsley
South Stoke
Crazies Hill
Cookham Dean Common
Peasemore
East Ilsley
Binfield Heath
Hare Hatch
Chaddleworth
Aldworth
Holyport
Sonning
Waltham St Lawrence
Great Shefford
Yattendon
Englefield Green
Chieveley
READING
Cheapside
Winterbourne
Frilsham
Stanford Dingley
Marsh Benham
NEWBURY
BERKSHIRE
Hamstead Marshall
Woolhampton
Mattingley
WOKING
Lower Chute
Vernham Dean
SU
FARNBOROUGH
Rotherwick
Pirbright
SURREY
GUILDFORD
Well
Compton
ANDOVER
Dummer
Bentley
Charleshill
Bentworth
Elstead
Wherwell
HAMPSHIRE
Crawley
Stockbridge
Alresford
Ovington
Sparsholt
Tichborne
Winchester
Cheriton
Bramdean
Lurgashall
Steep
3
Beauworth
Lickfold
Lodsworth
Petersfield
Upham
Droxford
Midhurst
Tillington
Buriton
Elsted
Byworth
WEST SUSSEX
Chalton
SOUTHAMPTON
Eartham
Bursledon
West Ashling
East Lavant
Oving
Langstone
Chidham
CHICHESTER
Donnington
Boldre
Southsea
Pilley
Portsmouth
Lymington
Cowes
Seaview
Yarmouth
NEWPORT
ISLE OF WIGHT
Freshwater
Arreton
Shorwell
Shanklin
SZ
Niton
Bonchurch
Chale
Ventnor
0
5
10
MILES

3

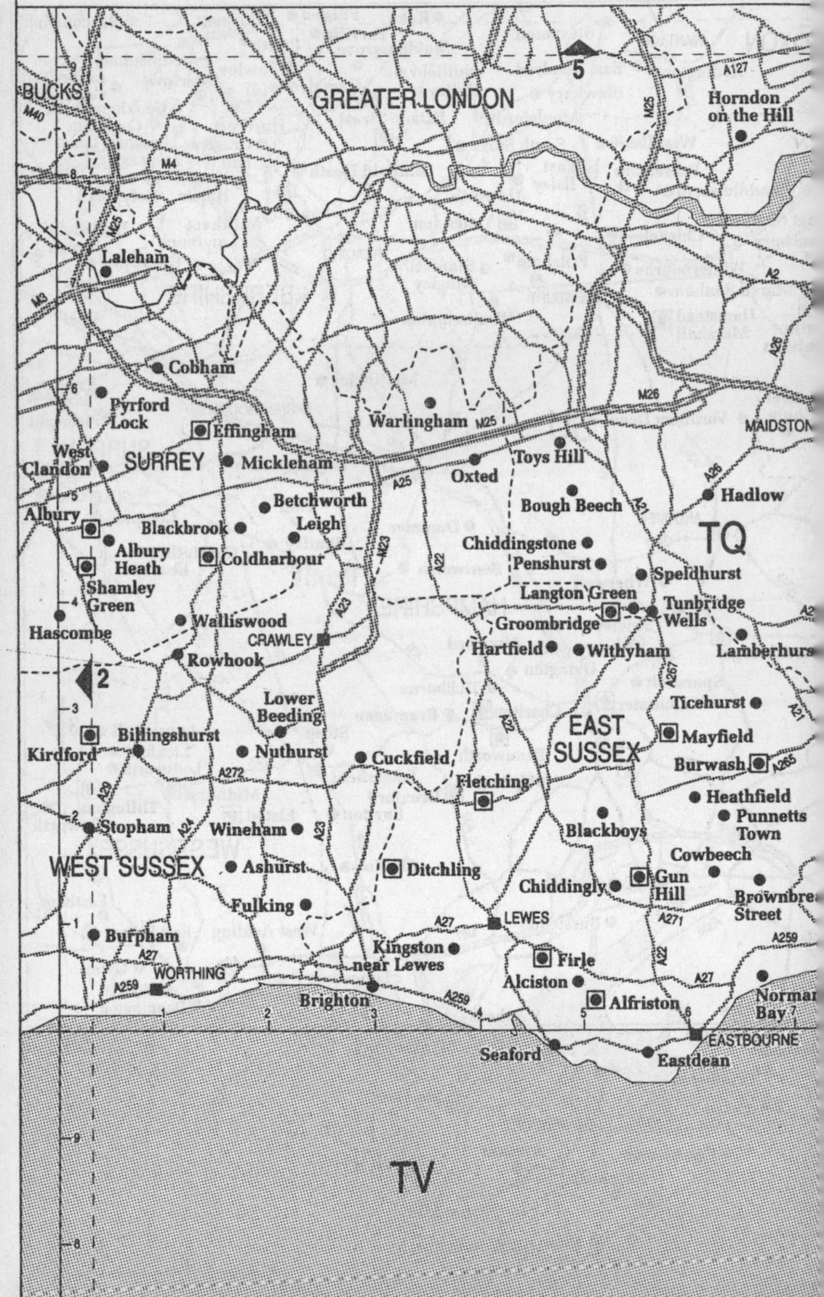

BUCKS
M40
GREATER LONDON
5
M4
M25
A127
Horndon on the Hill
Laleham
M3
A2
A26
Cobham
M26
Pyrford Lock
Effingham
Warlingham
M25
MAIDSTON
West Clandon
SURREY
Mickleham
Toys Hill
Oxted
A25
A26
Hadlow
Albury
Betchworth
Bough Beech
A21
Blackbrook
Leigh
TQ
Albury Heath
Coldharbour
Chiddingstone
M23
A22
Penshurst
Shamley Green
Speldhurst
Langton Green
Tunbridge Wells
Walliswood
A23
Groombridge
Hascombe
CRAWLEY
Hartfield
Withyham
Lamberhurs
Rowhook
A267
2
Lower Beeding
Ticehurst
A21
EAST SUSSEX
Billingshurst
Mayfield
Kirdford
Nuthurst
Cuckfield
A272
Burwash
A265
Fletching
A29
Heathfield
Punnetts Town
Stopham
A24
Wineham
A23
Blackboys
Cowbeech
WEST SUSSEX
Ashurst
Ditchling
Chiddingly
Gun Hill
Fulking
Brownbre
Street
A27
LEWES
A271
Burpham
A259
Kingston near Lewes
Firle
A22
A27
WORTHING
A259
Alciston
A27
Alfriston
Norman Bay
Brighton
A259
EASTBOURNE
Seaford
Eastdean
TV

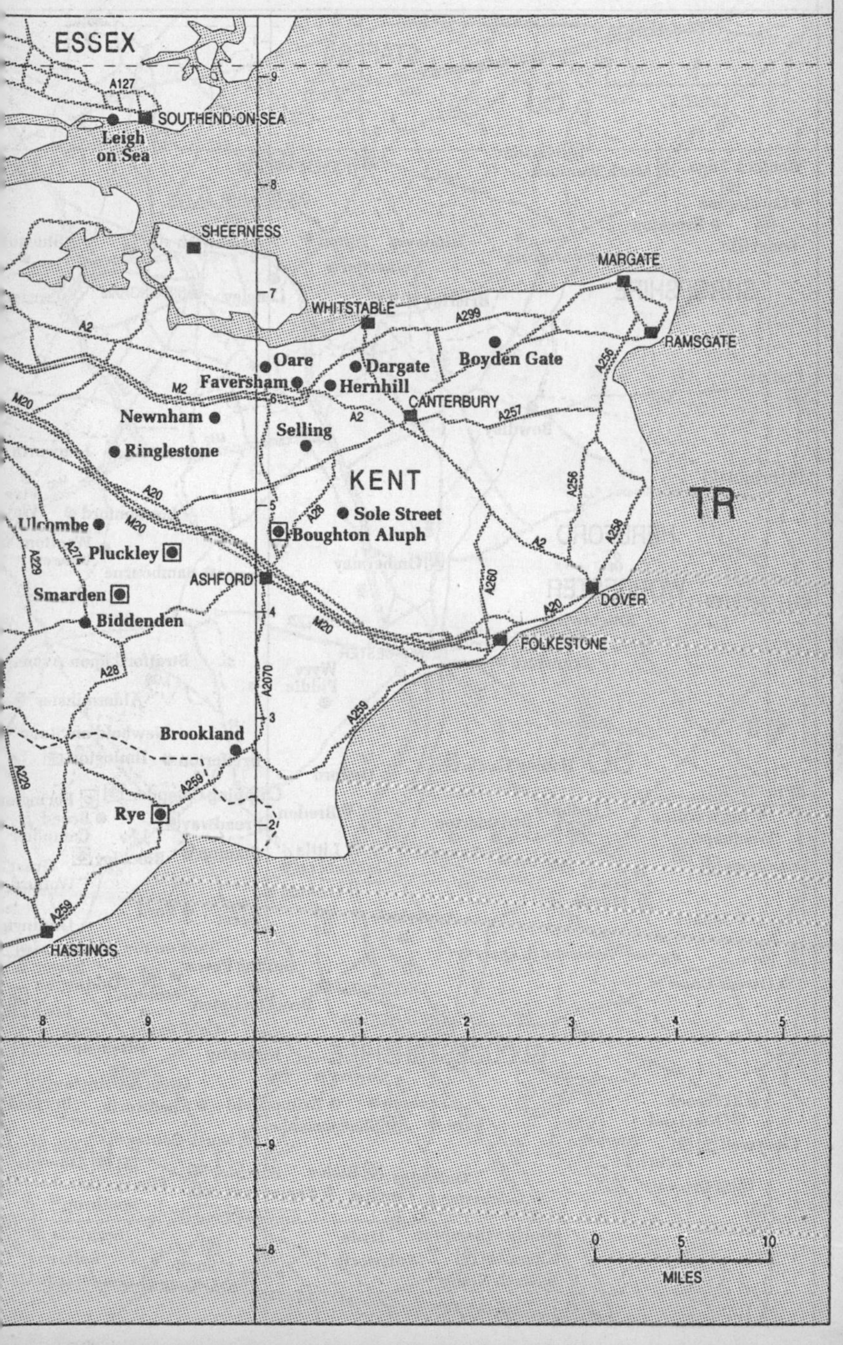
ESSEX
A127
SOUTHEND-ON-SEA
Leigh on Sea
SHEERNESS
MARGATE
RAMSGATE
WHITSTABLE
A299
A2
Boyden Gate
A256
Oare
Dargate
Faversham
Hernhill
M2
M20
CANTERBURY
A257
Newnham
Selling
Ringlestone
KENT
A20
A256
TR
Sole Street
Ulcombe
M20
A28
Boughton Aluph
A229
A274
Pluckley
A2
A258
ASHFORD
A260
Smarden
DOVER
A20
Biddenden
M20
FOLKESTONE
A28
A2070
A259
Brookland
A229
A259
Rye
A259
HASTINGS
MILES
0
5
10

4

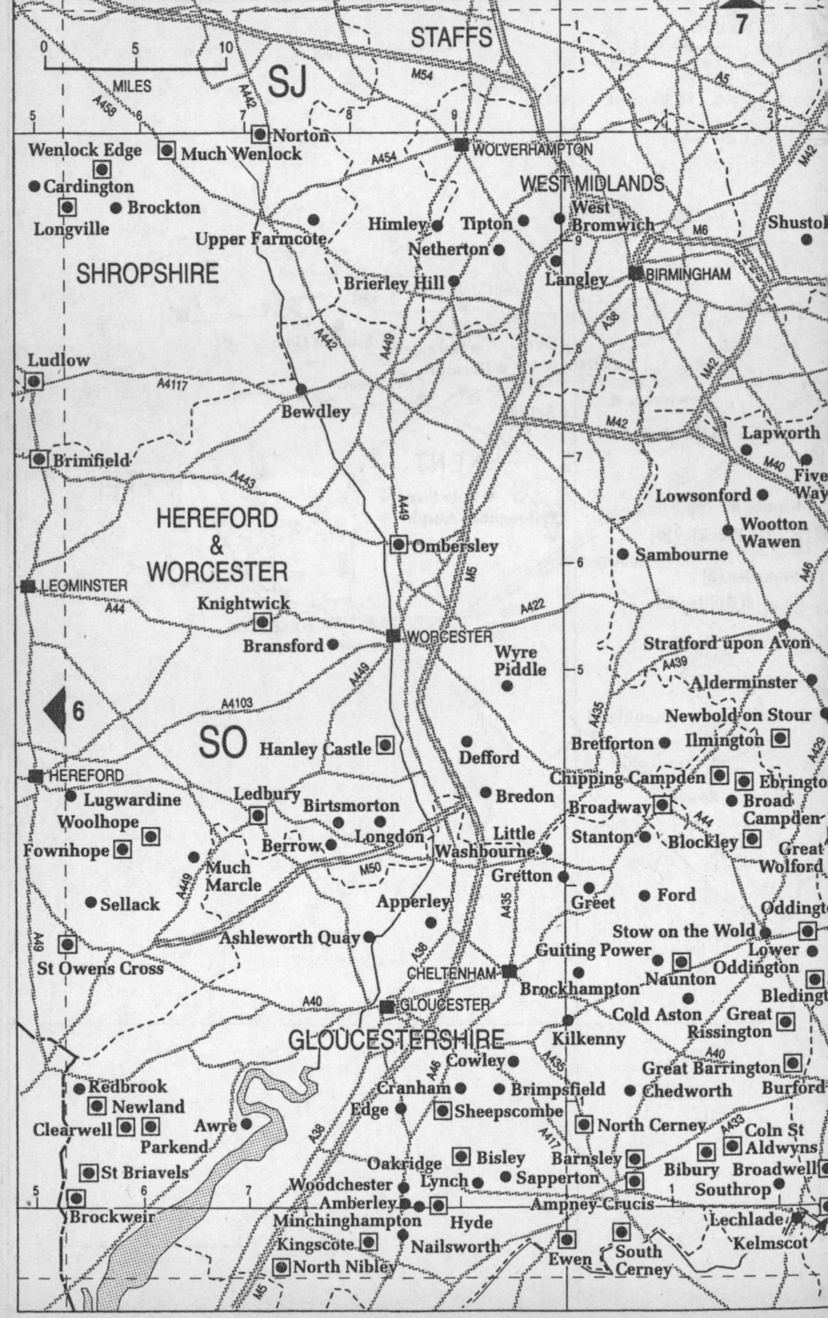

STAFFS
7
0
5
10
MILES
SJ
M54
A5
A458
A442
5
6
7
8
9
1
2
Norton
Wenlock Edge
Much Wenlock
A454
WOLVERHAMPTON
M42
Cardington
WEST MIDLANDS
Brockton
Longville
Upper Farmcote
Himley
Tipton
West
Bromwich
M6
Shustoke
Netherton
SHROPSHIRE
Brierley Hill
Langley
BIRMINGHAM
A442
A449
A38
M42
Ludlow
A4117
Bewdley
M42
Lapworth
Brimfield
M40
Five
Ways
A443
Lowsonford
A449
HEREFORD
&
WORCESTER
Wootton
Wawen
Ombersley
Sambourne
M5
A46
LEOMINSTER
A44
Knightwick
A422
Bransford
WORCESTER
Wyre
Piddle
Stratford upon Avon
A449
A439
Alderminster
6
A4103
A435
Newbold on Stour
SO
Hanley Castle
Defford
Bretforton
Ilmington
A429
HEREFORD
Chipping Campden
Ebrington
Lugwardine
Ledbury
Bredon
Broadway
Broad
Campden
Woolhope
Birtsmorton
A44
Berrow
Longdon
Little
Washbourne
Stanton
Blockley
Great
Wolford
Fownhope
Much
Marcle
M50
Gretton
A449
Ford
Sellack
Apperley
A435
Greet
Oddington
Stow on the Wold
A49
Ashleworth Quay
Lower
Oddington
A38
Guiting Power
St Owens Cross
CHELTENHAM
Naunton
Brockhampton
Bledington
A40
GLOUCESTER
Cold Aston
Great
Rissington
GLOUCESTERSHIRE
Kilkenny
A40
Cowley
A435
Great Barrington
A46
Redbrook
Cranham
Brimpsfield
Chedworth
Burford
Newland
Edge
Sheepscombe
Clearwell
Awre
A417
North Cerney
Parkend
A38
A433
Coln St
Aldwyns
Bisley
Barnsley
Oakridge
Bibury
Broadwell
St Briavels
Sapperton
Lynch
Woodchester
Southrop
5
6
7
1
Brockweir
Amberley
Ampney Crucis
Minchinghampton
Hyde
Lechlade
Kingscote
Nailsworth
Kelmscot
Ewen
South
Cerney
North Nibley
M5

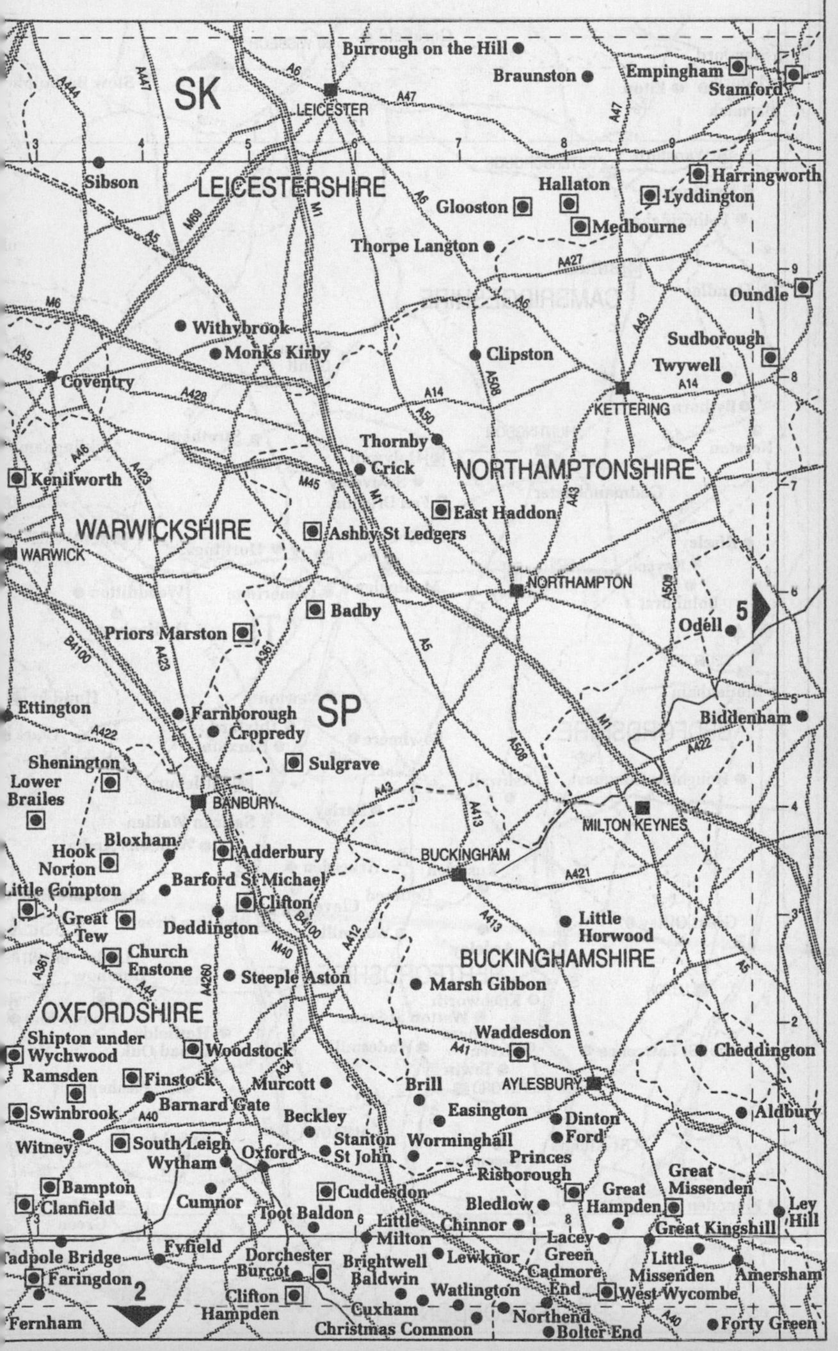
SK
SP
LEICESTER
LEICESTERSHIRE
WARWICKSHIRE
NORTHAMPTONSHIRE
BUCKINGHAMSHIRE
OXFORDSHIRE
KETTERING
NORTHAMPTON
MILTON KEYNES
BUCKINGHAM
BANBURY
AYLESBURY
WARWICK
Burrough on the Hill
Braunston
Empingham
Stamford
Sibson
Hallaton
Harringworth
Lyddington
Glooston
Medbourne
Thorpe Langton
Oundle
Withybrook
Monks Kirby
Clipston
Sudborough
Twywell
Coventry
Thornby
Crick
Kenilworth
East Haddon
Ashby St Ledgers
Badby
Priors Marston
Odell
5
Ettington
Farnborough
Cropredy
Biddenham
Shenington
Sulgrave
Lower Brailes
Bloxham
Hook Norton
Adderbury
Barford St Michael
Little Compton
Clifton
Great Tew
Deddington
Little Horwood
Church Enstone
Steeple Aston
Marsh Gibbon
Shipton under Wychwood
Woodstock
Waddesdon
Cheddington
Ramsden
Finstock
Murcott
Brill
Swinbrook
Barnard Gate
Easington
Dinton
Aldbury
Beckley
Ford
Witney
South Leigh
Stanton St John
Worminghall
Wytham
Oxford
Princes Risborough
Great Missenden
Bampton
Clanfield
Cumnor
Cuddesdon
Great Hampden
Bledlow
Ley Hill
Toot Baldon
Little Milton
Chinnor
Great Kingshill
Fyfield
Lacey Green
Tadpole Bridge
Dorchester
Burcot
Brightwell Baldwin
Lewknor
Little Missenden
Amersham
Faringdon
2
Clifton Hampden
Cadmore End
Watlington
West Wycombe
Cuxham
Northend
Fernham
Christmas Common
Bolter End
Forty Green
A6
A47
A444
A447
M69
M1
A5
M6
A45
A428
A14
A50
A508
A427
A43
A46
A423
M45
A509
B4100
A361
A422
A413
A421
A412
M40
A4260
A44
A34
A41
A40
1
2
3
4
5
6
7
8
9

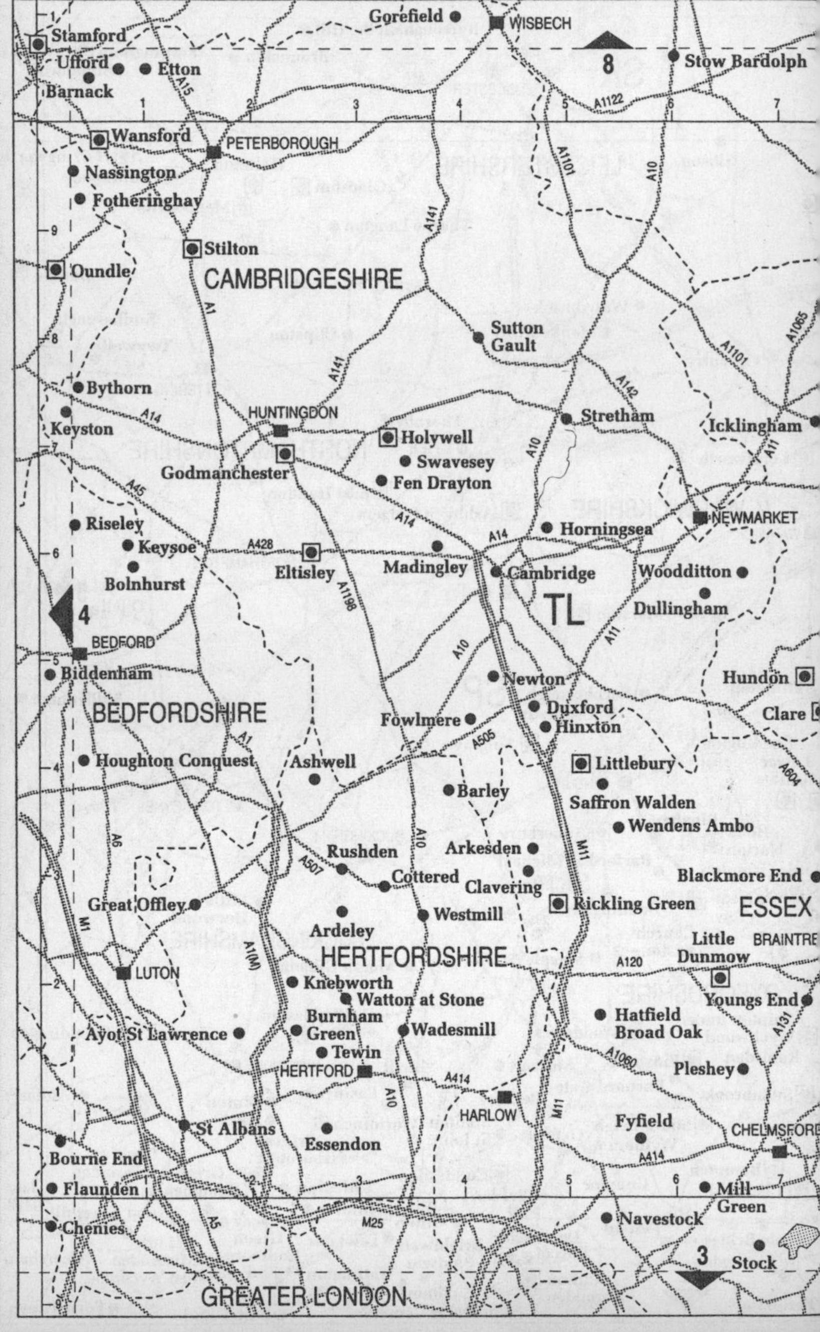
5
Gorefield
WISBECH
Stamford
Ufford
Etton
Barnack
8
Stow Bardolph
A1122
A15
Wansford
PETERBOROUGH
Nassington
Fotheringhay
A1101
A10
A141
Stilton
Oundle
CAMBRIDGESHIRE
A1
Sutton
Gault
A1065
A141
A1101
A142
Bythorn
A14
HUNTINGDON
Stretham
Keyston
Holywell
Icklingham
Swavesey
A10
A11
Godmanchester
Fen Drayton
A45
A14
NEWMARKET
Riseley
A14
Horningsea
Keysoe
A428
Eltisley
Madingley
Cambridge
Woodditton
Bolnhurst
A1198
TL
Dullingham
4
BEDFORD
A10
A11
Biddenham
Newton
Hundon
BEDFORDSHIRE
Duxford
Fowlmere
Hinxton
Clare
A1
A505
Houghton Conquest
Ashwell
Littlebury
A604
Barley
Saffron Walden
Wendens Ambo
A6
A10
M11
Rushden
Arkesden
A507
Cottered
Clavering
Blackmore End
Great Offley
Rickling Green
ESSEX
Westmill
Ardeley
M1
A1(M)
HERTFORDSHIRE
Little
Dunmow
BRAINTREE
LUTON
A120
Knebworth
Watton at Stone
Youngs End
Burnham
Hatfield
Green
Broad Oak
Ayot St Lawrence
Wadesmill
A131
Tewin
A1060
HERTFORD
Pleshey
A414
A10
HARLOW
M11
St Albans
Fyfield
Essendon
CHELMSFORD
Bourne End
A414
Flaunden
Mill
Green
M25
Navestock
Chenies
A5
3
Stock
GREATER LONDON

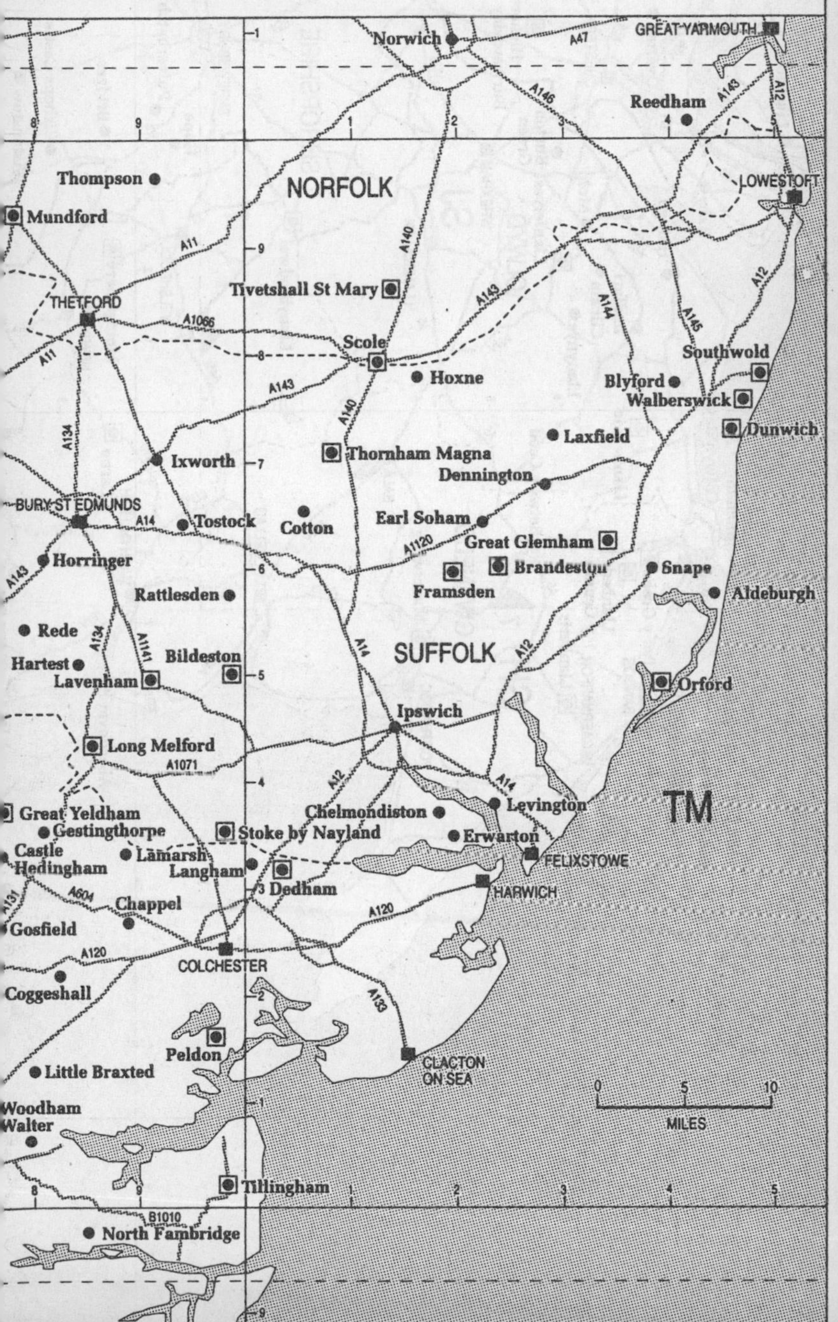
NORFOLK
SUFFOLK
TM
Norwich
GREAT YARMOUTH
Reedham
LOWESTOFT
Thompson
Mundford
THETFORD
Tivetshall St Mary
Scole
Hoxne
Southwold
Blyford
Walberswick
Dunwich
Laxfield
Ixworth
Thornham Magna
Dennington
BURY ST EDMUNDS
Tostock
Cotton
Earl Soham
Great Glemham
Horringer
Brandeston
Snape
Framsden
Aldeburgh
Rattlesden
Rede
Hartest
Lavenham
Bildeston
Orford
Ipswich
Long Melford
Great Yeldham
Gestingthorpe
Chelmondiston
Levington
Stoke by Nayland
Erwarton
Castle Hedingham
Lamarsh
Langham
FELIXSTOWE
Dedham
HARWICH
Chappel
Gosfield
COLCHESTER
Coggeshall
Peldon
CLACTON ON SEA
Little Braxted
Woodham Walter
Tillingham
North Fambridge
A47
A146
A143
A12
A11
A140
A1066
A144
A145
A14
A1120
A134
A1141
A1071
A604
A131
A120
A133
B1010
0 5 10
MILES

6

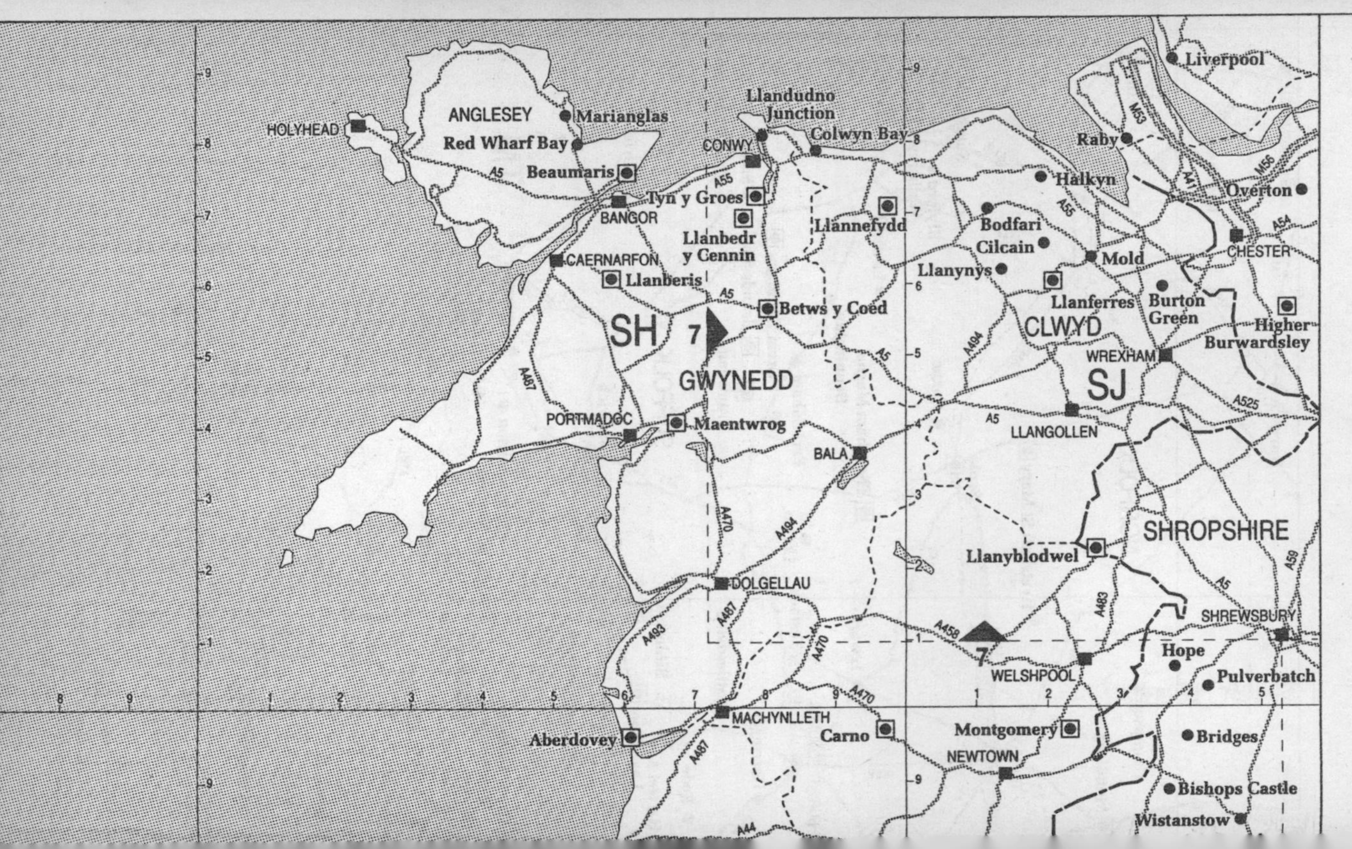

ANGLESEY
HOLYHEAD
Marianglas
Red Wharf Bay
Beaumaris
A5
BANGOR
Tyn y Groes
A55
CONWY
Llandudno Junction
Colwyn Bay
Llannefydd
Llanbedr y Cennin
CAERNARFON
Llanberis
Betws y Coed
SH
7
GWYNEDD
A487
PORTMADOC
Maentwrog
BALA
A470
A494
DOLGELLAU
A493
A487
MACHYNLLETH
Aberdovey
Carno
A470
A458
7
WELSHPOOL
Montgomery
NEWTOWN
A44
Halkyn
Bodfari
Cilcain
Llanynys
Mold
Llanferres
CLWYD
Burton Green
WREXHAM
SJ
LLANGOLLEN
A5
A525
Raby
M53
Liverpool
M56
A41
Overton
CHESTER
A54
Higher Burwardsley
SHROPSHIRE
Llanyblodwel
A483
A5
A59
SHREWSBURY
Hope
Pulverbatch
Bridges
Bishops Castle
Wistanstow

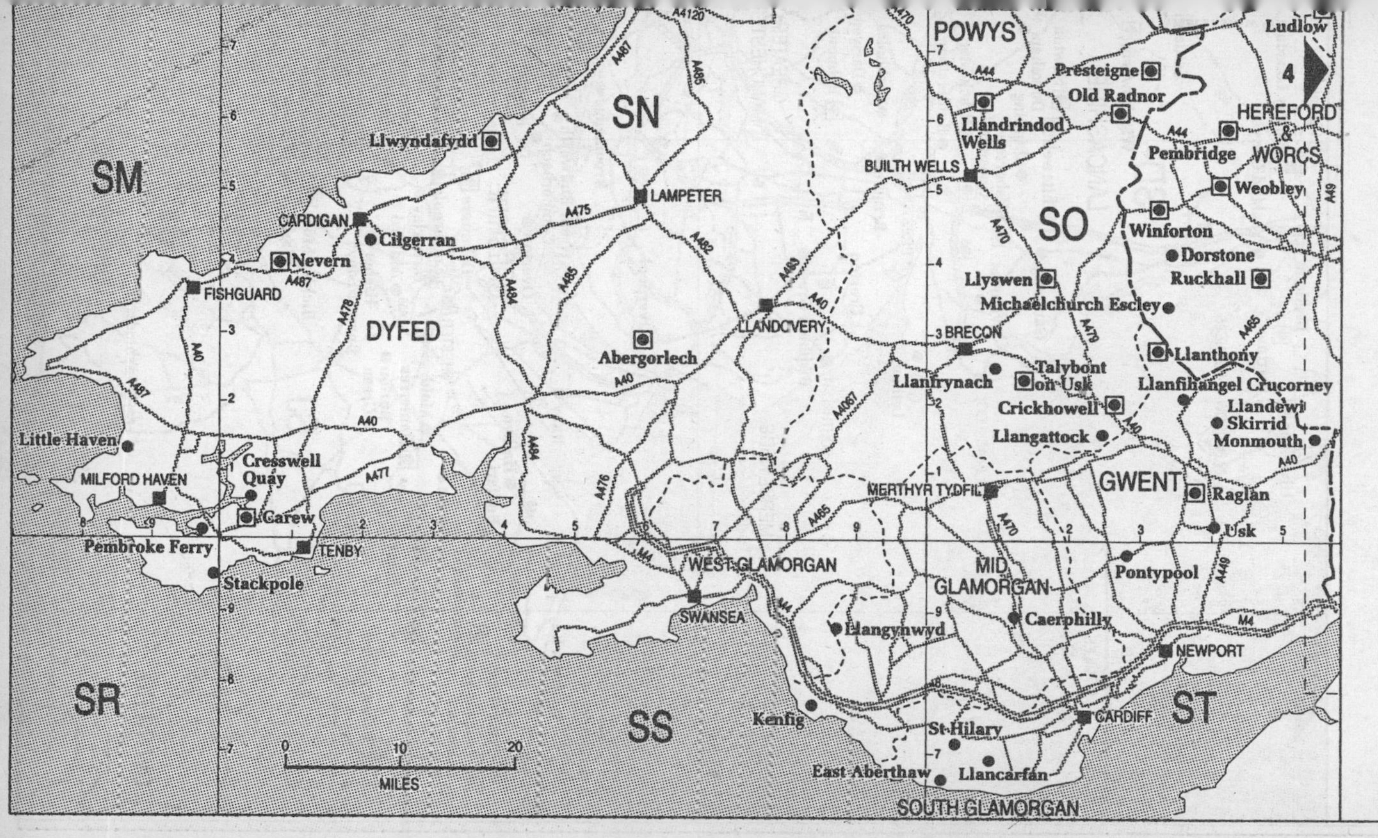
6
SM
SN
SO
SR
SS
ST
POWYS
DYFED
HEREFORD & WORCS
GWENT
MID GLAMORGAN
WEST GLAMORGAN
SOUTH GLAMORGAN
4
Ludlow
Presteigne
Old Radnor
Llandrindod Wells
BUILTH WELLS
Pembridge
Weobley
Winforton
Dorstone
Ruckhall
Llyswen
Michaelchurch Escley
BRECON
Llanthony
Talybont on Usk
Llanfrynach
Llanfihangel Crucorney
Llandewi Skirrid
Monmouth
Crickhowell
Llangattock
Raglan
Usk
MERTHYR TYDFIL
Pontypool
Caerphilly
NEWPORT
CARDIFF
St Hilary
Llancarfan
East Aberthaw
Kenfig
Llangynwyd
SWANSEA
LLANDOVERY
Abergorlech
LAMPETER
Llwyndafydd
CARDIGAN
Cilgerran
Nevern
FISHGUARD
Little Haven
MILFORD HAVEN
Cresswell Quay
Carew
Pembroke Ferry
TENBY
Stackpole
MILES
0
10
20

7

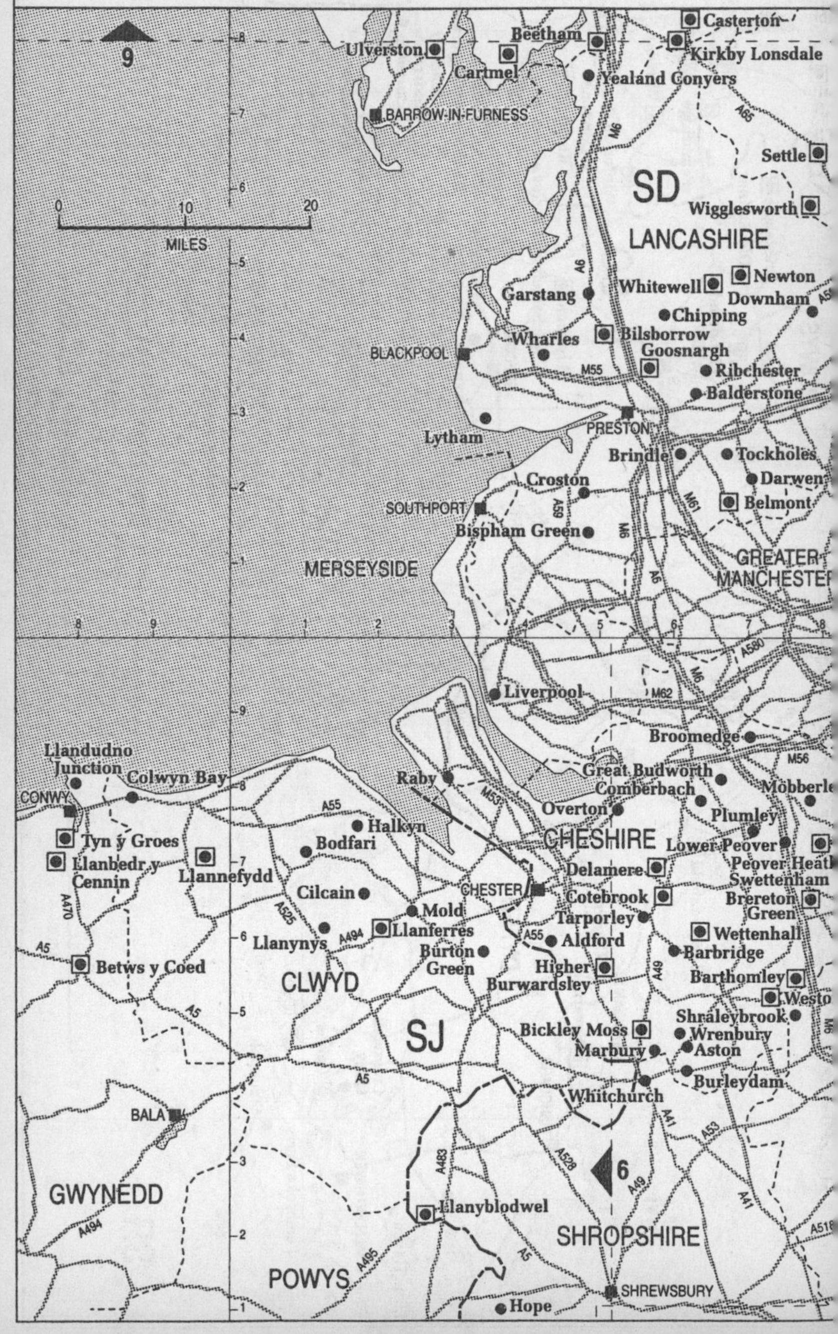
9
0 10 20
MILES
Ulverston
Cartmel
Beetham
Casterton
Kirkby Lonsdale
Yealand Conyers
BARROW-IN-FURNESS
M6
A65
Settle
SD
Wigglesworth
LANCASHIRE
A6
Whitewell
Newton
Downham
Garstang
Chipping
Wharles
Bilsborrow
Goosnargh
BLACKPOOL
M55
Ribchester
Balderstone
PRESTON
Lytham
Brindle
Tockholes
Darwen
Croston
Belmont
M61
SOUTHPORT
A59
Bispham Green
M6
MERSEYSIDE
GREATER MANCHESTER
A6
A580
M6
Liverpool
M62
Broomedge
M56
Llandudno Junction
Colwyn Bay
CONWY
Raby
Great Budworth
Comberbach
Mobberley
Overton
Plumley
A55
Halkyn
M53
CHESHIRE
Lower Peover
Tyn y Groes
Bodfari
Peover Heath
Llanbedr y Cennin
Llannefydd
Delamere
Swettenham
A470
Cilcain
CHESTER
Cotebrook
Brereton Green
A525
Mold
Tarporley
Wettenhall
A5
Llanynys
A494
Llanferres
A55
Aldford
Barbridge
Burton Green
Betws y Coed
Higher Burwardsley
A49
Barthomley
CLWYD
Weston
A5
Shraleybrook
SJ
Bickley Moss
Wrenbury
Marbury
Aston
A5
Burleydam
Whitchurch
BALA
A41
A53
A483
A528
6
A49
A41
GWYNEDD
A494
Llanyblodwel
SHROPSHIRE
A518
A5
POWYS
A495
SHREWSBURY
Hope

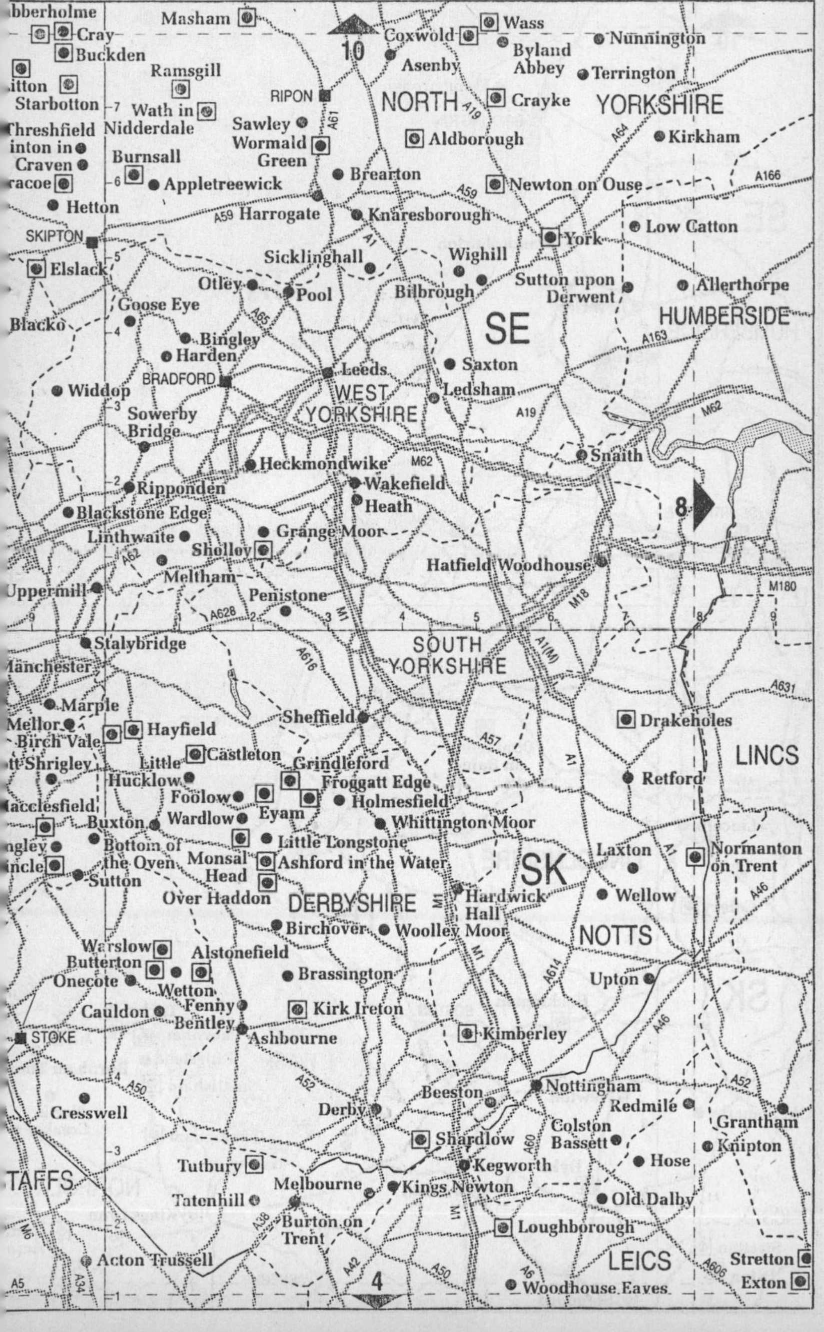
Masham
Cray
Buckden
Ramsgill
Starbotton
Wath in Nidderdale
Sawley
Wormald Green
Burnsall
Appletreewick
Hetton
SKIPTON
Elslack
RIPON
Coxwold
Wass
Byland Abbey
Nunnington
Asenby
Terrington
NORTH
YORKSHIRE
Crayke
Aldborough
Kirkham
Brearton
Newton on Ouse
Harrogate
Knaresborough
York
Low Catton
Sicklinghall
Wighill
Otley
Pool
Bilbrough
Sutton upon Derwent
Allerthorpe
HUMBERSIDE
Goose Eye
Blacko
SE
Bingley
Harden
BRADFORD
Leeds
Saxton
WEST YORKSHIRE
Ledsham
Widdop
Sowerby Bridge
Snaith
Heckmondwike
Wakefield
Heath
Ripponden
Blackstone Edge
Grange Moor
Linthwaite
Sholley
Meltham
Hatfield Woodhouse
Uppermill
Penistone
Stalybridge
SOUTH YORKSHIRE
Manchester
Marple
Mellor
Birch Vale
Hayfield
Sheffield
Drakeholes
Castleton
Little Hucklow
Grindleford
Froggatt Edge
Holmesfield
LINCS
Retford
Foolow
Eyam
Buxton
Wardlow
Whittington Moor
Bottom of the Oven
Little Longstone
Laxton
Normanton on Trent
Sutton
Monsal Head
Ashford in the Water
SK
Over Haddon
DERBYSHIRE
Hardwick Hall
Wellow
Birchover
Woolley Moor
NOTTS
Warslow
Alstonefield
Butterton
Onecote
Brassington
Wetton
Upton
Fenny Bentley
Cauldon
Kirk Ireton
STOKE
Ashbourne
Kimberley
Nottingham
Beeston
Cresswell
Redmile
Derby
Grantham
Colston Bassett
Shardlow
Knipton
Tutbury
Kegworth
Hose
STAFFS
Melbourne
Kings Newton
Tatenhill
Old Dalby
Burton on Trent
Loughborough
Acton Trussell
LEICS
Stretton
Exton
Woodhouse Eaves
10
8
4
A61
A19
A64
A166
A59
A1
A65
A163
M62
A62
A628
M1
A616
M18
A1(M)
M180
A631
A57
A614
A46
A52
A50
A60
A38
A42
A6
A606
A5
A34
M6

8

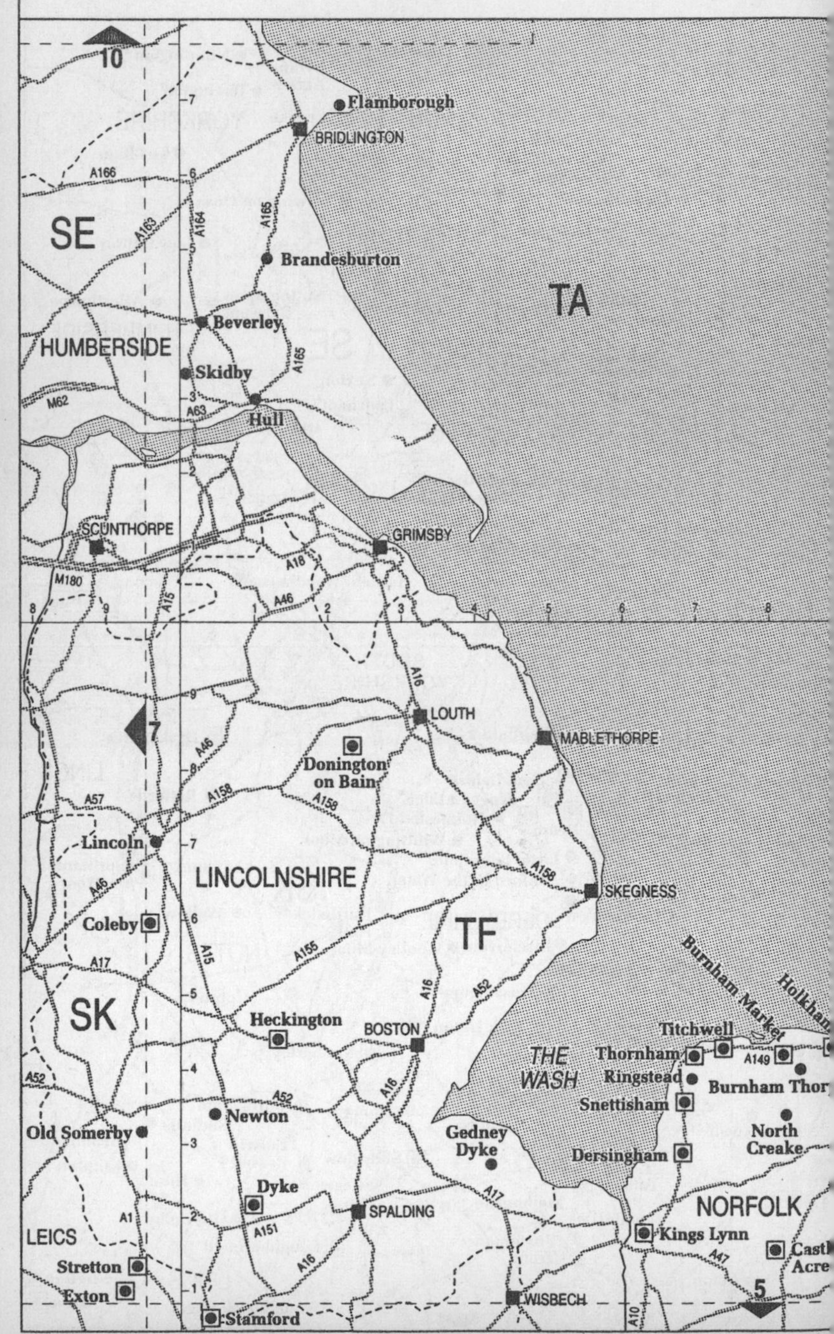

10
SE
HUMBERSIDE
Flamborough
BRIDLINGTON
A166
A163
A164
A165
Brandesburton
TA
Beverley
Skidby
M62
A63
Hull
SCUNTHORPE
GRIMSBY
A18
M180
A15
A46
LOUTH
A16
MABLETHORPE
Donington on Bain
A57
A158
Lincoln
LINCOLNSHIRE
SKEGNESS
Coleby
TF
A17
A155
A52
SK
Heckington
BOSTON
THE WASH
Newton
Old Somerby
Gedney Dyke
Dyke
SPALDING
A151
A1
LEICS
Stretton
Exton
Stamford
WISBECH
A10
Burnham Market
Holkham
Titchwell
Thornham
A149
Ringstead
Burnham Thor
Snettisham
North Creake
Dersingham
NORFOLK
Kings Lynn
A47
Castl Acre
5

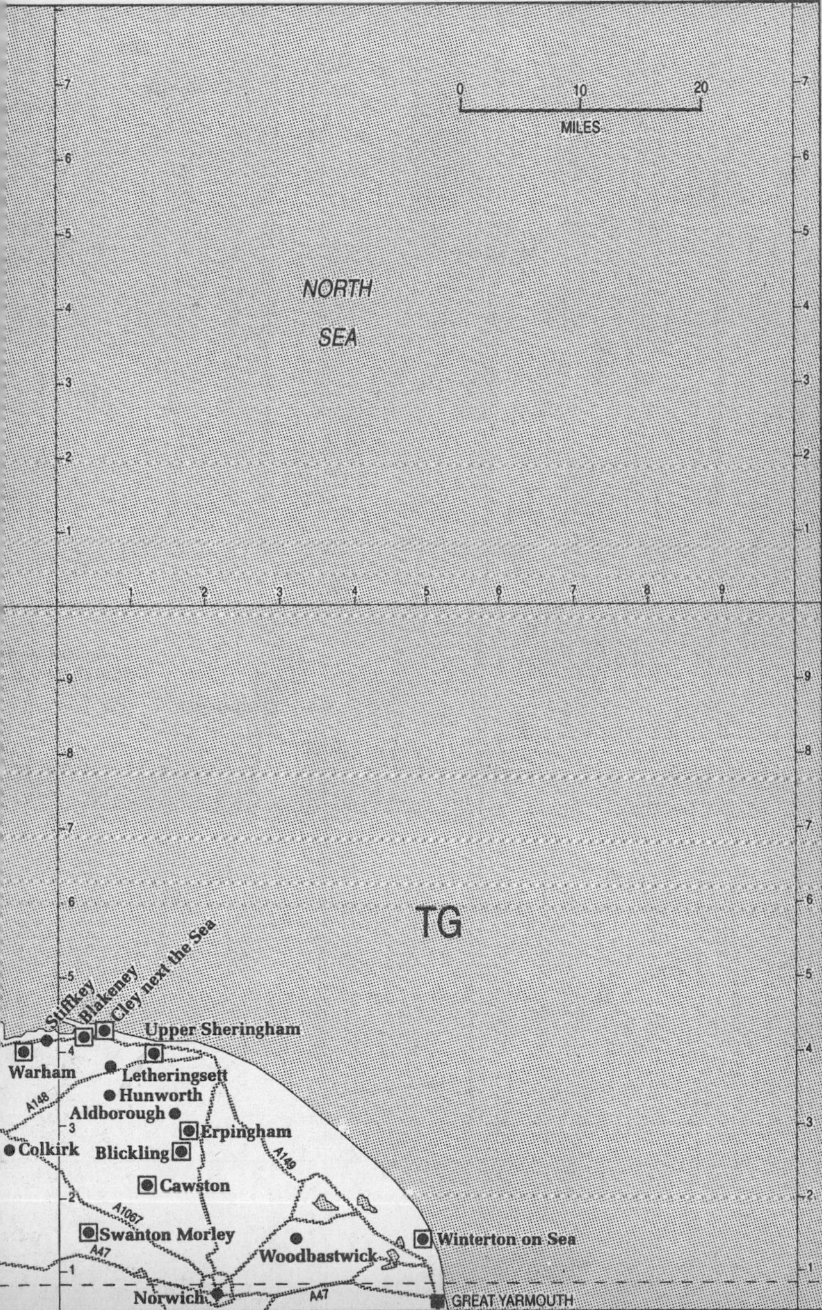
0
10
20
MILES
NORTH
SEA
TG
Stiffkey
Blakeney
Cley next the Sea
Upper Sheringham
Warham
Letheringsett
Hunworth
Aldborough
Erpingham
Colkirk
Blickling
Cawston
Swanton Morley
Woodbastwick
Winterton on Sea
Norwich
GREAT YARMOUTH
A148
A149
A1067
A47

9

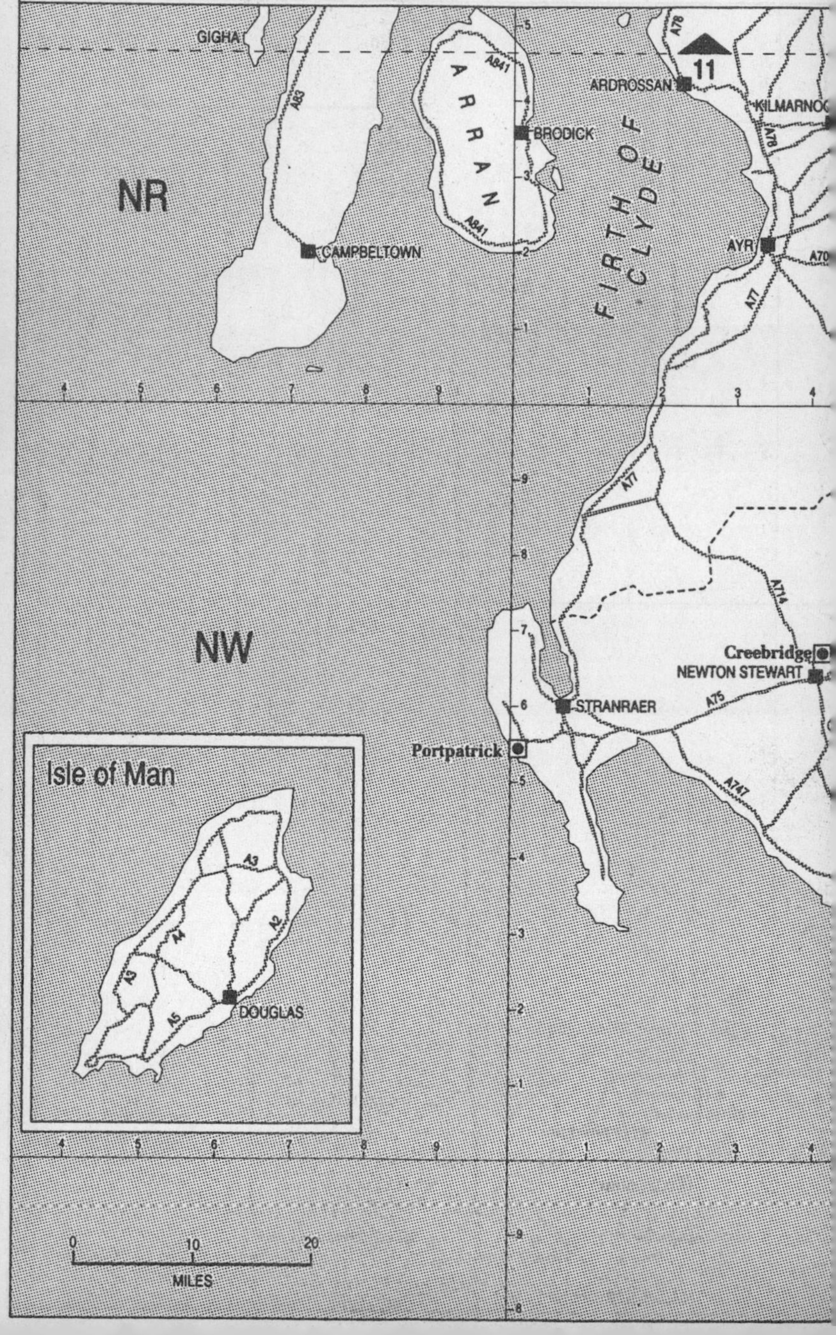

GIGHA
A83
ARRAN
A841
BRODICK
11
ARDROSSAN
A78
KILMARNOC
FIRTH OF CLYDE
NR
CAMPBELTOWN
AYR
A70
A77
NW
A714
Creebridge
NEWTON STEWART
STRANRAER
A75
Portpatrick
A747
Isle of Man
A3
A2
A4
A5
DOUGLAS
0
10
20
MILES

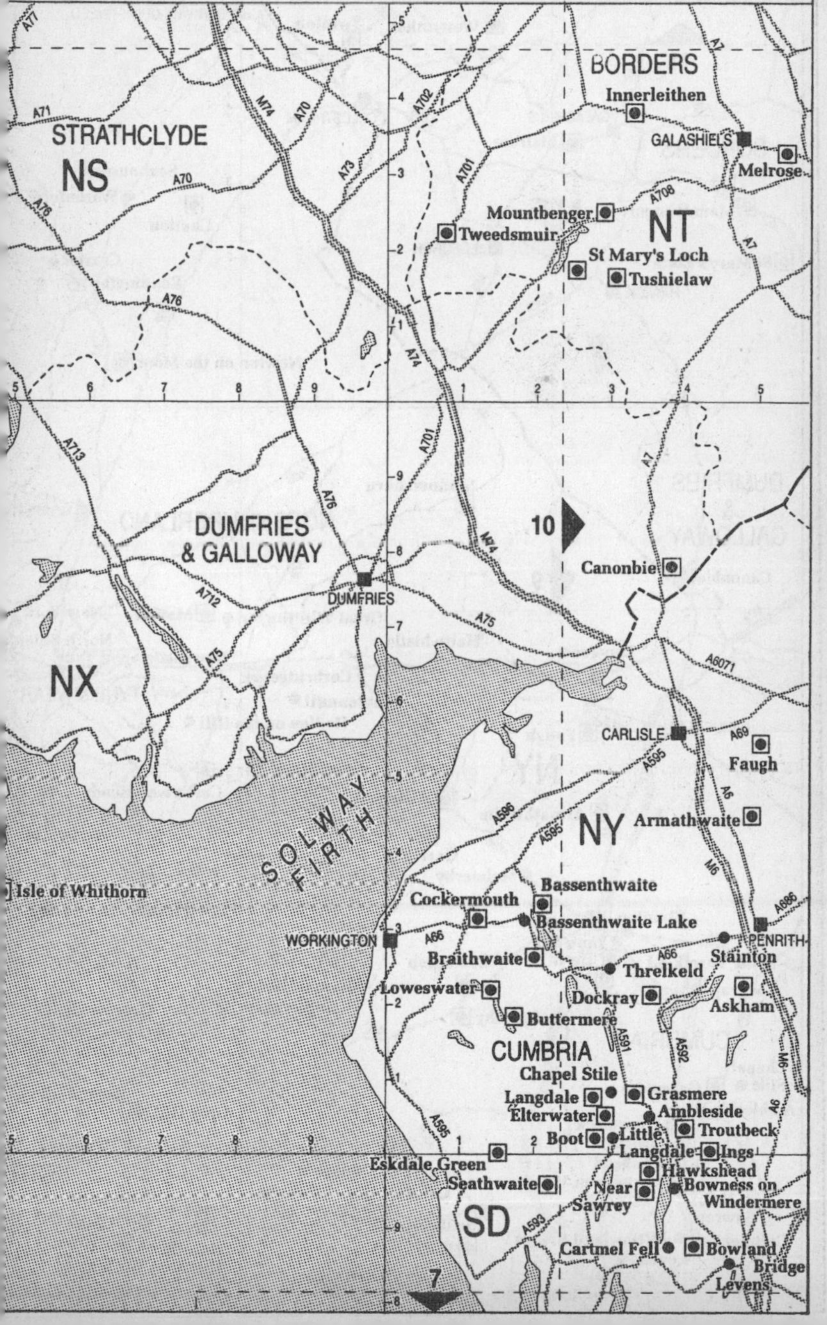

STRATHCLYDE
NS
BORDERS
Innerleithen
GALASHIELS
Melrose
Mountbenger
NT
Tweedsmuir
St Mary's Loch
Tushielaw
DUMFRIES
& GALLOWAY
DUMFRIES
10
Canonbie
NX
CARLISLE
Faugh
SOLWAY
FIRTH
NY
Armathwaite
Isle of Whithorn
Bassenthwaite
Cockermouth
Bassenthwaite Lake
WORKINGTON
PENRITH
Stainton
Braithwaite
Threlkeld
Loweswater
Dockray
Askham
Buttermere
CUMBRIA
Chapel Stile
Langdale
Grasmere
Elterwater
Ambleside
Boot
Little
Langdale
Troutbeck
Ings
Eskdale Green
Hawkshead
Seathwaite
Near
Sawrey
Bowness on
Windermere
SD
Cartmel Fell
Bowland
Bridge
Levens
7
A77
A71
A70
A76
M74
A702
A73
A701
A74
A7
A708
A713
A712
A75
A6071
A69
A595
A596
A6
M6
A686
A66
A591
A592
A593

10

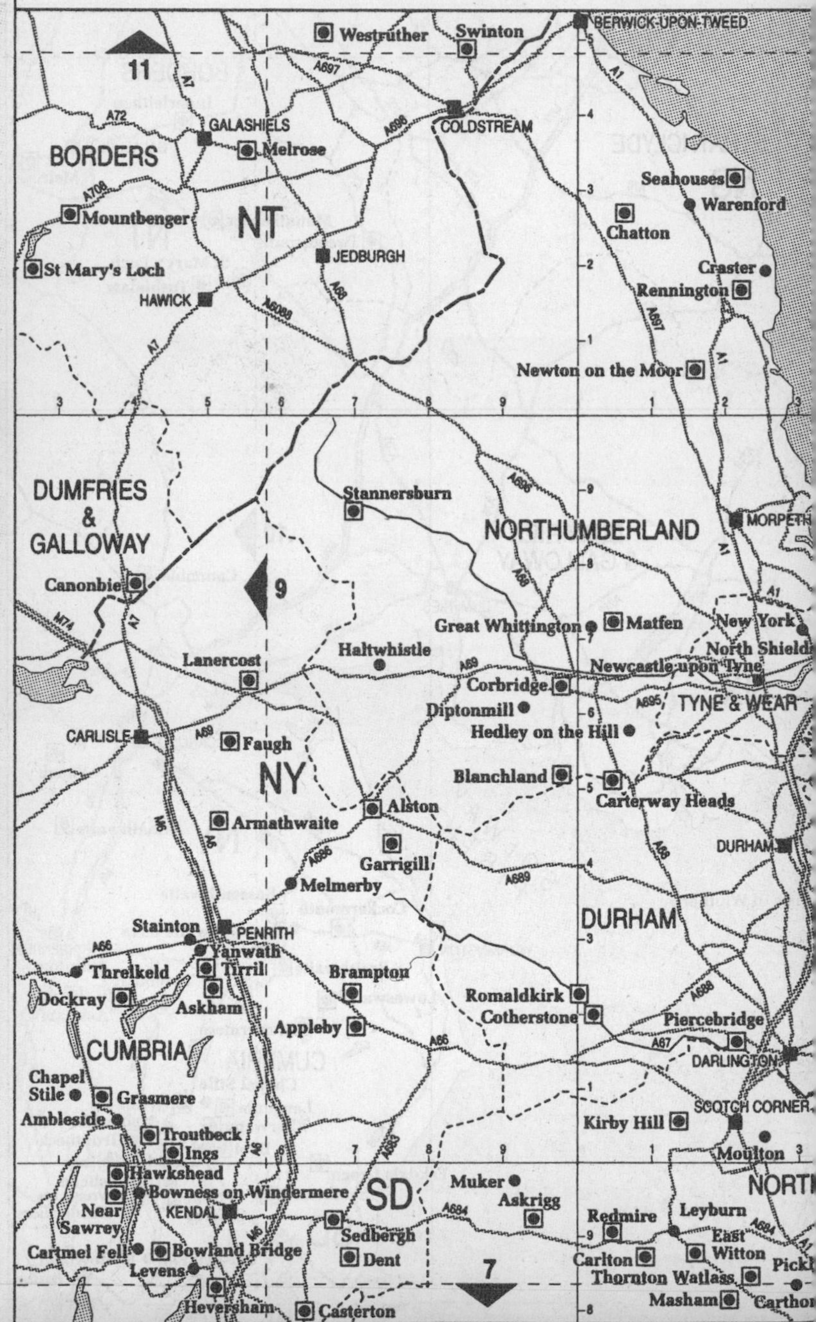
11
Westruther
Swinton
BERWICK-UPON-TWEED
GALASHIELS
COLDSTREAM
BORDERS
Melrose
Seahouses
Warenford
Mountbenger
NT
Chatton
JEDBURGH
St Mary's Loch
Craster
Rennington
HAWICK
Newton on the Moor
DUMFRIES & GALLOWAY
Stannersburn
NORTHUMBERLAND
MORPETH
Canonbie
9
Great Whittington
Matfen
New York
North Shields
Haltwhistle
Lanercost
Newcastle upon Tyne
Corbridge
Diptonmill
TYNE & WEAR
CARLISLE
Faugh
Hedley on the Hill
NY
Blanchland
Carterway Heads
Alston
Armathwaite
DURHAM
Garrigill
Melmerby
Stainton
PENRITH
DURHAM
Yanwath
Threlkeld
Tirril
Brampton
Dockray
Askham
Romaldkirk
Cotherstone
Piercebridge
Appleby
CUMBRIA
DARLINGTON
Chapel Stile
Grasmere
Ambleside
SCOTCH CORNER
Kirby Hill
Troutbeck
Ings
Moulton
Hawkshead
Muker
Bowness on Windermere
SD
Askrigg
Near Sawrey
KENDAL
Redmire
Leyburn
Sedbergh
East Witton
Cartmel Fell
Bowland Bridge
Carlton
Dent
Levens
Thornton Watlass
7
Masham
Heversham
Casterton

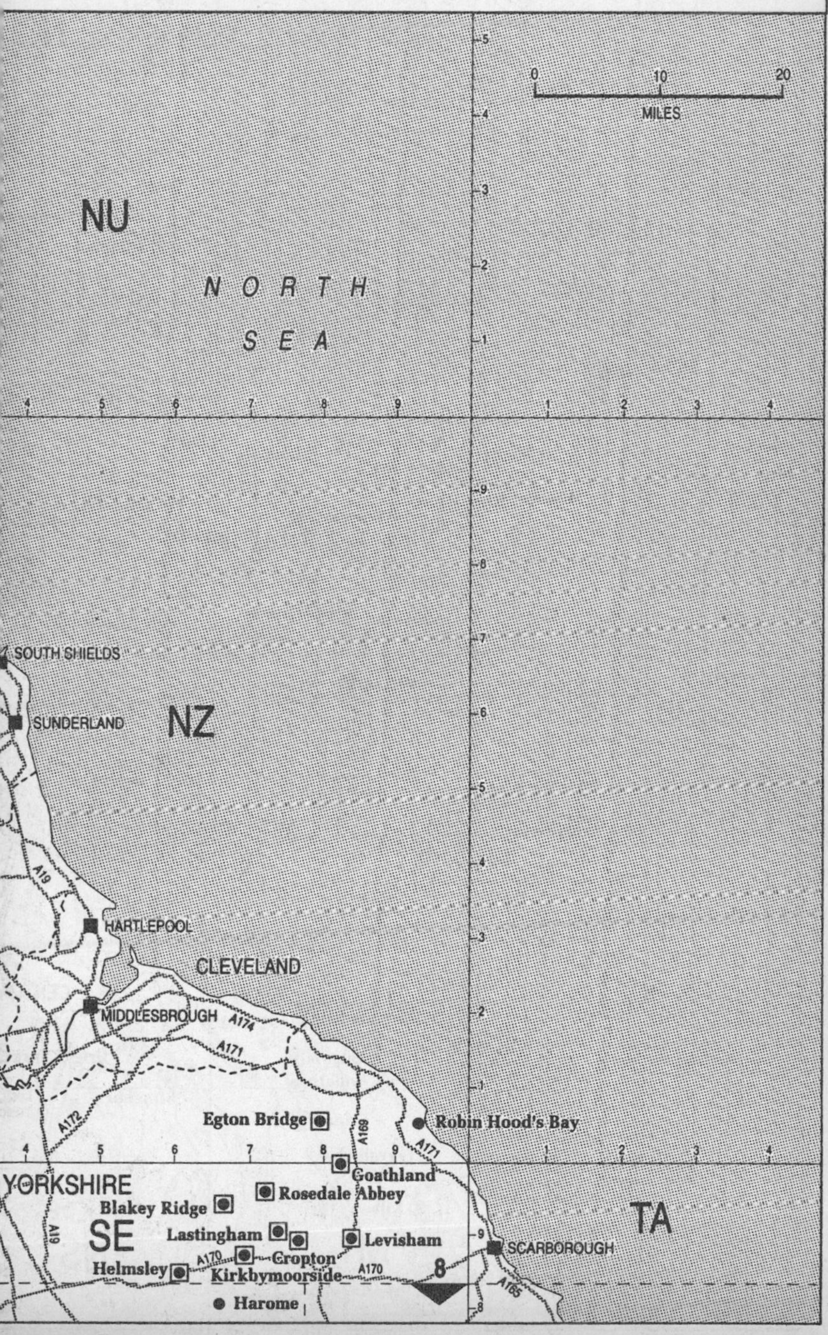
0
10
20
MILES
NU
NORTH
SEA
SOUTH SHIELDS
SUNDERLAND
NZ
A19
HARTLEPOOL
CLEVELAND
MIDDLESBROUGH
A174
A171
A172
Egton Bridge
A169
Robin Hood's Bay
A171
YORKSHIRE
Goathland
Rosedale Abbey
Blakey Ridge
SE
A19
Lastingham
Levisham
Cropton
Kirkbymoorside
A170
Helmsley
A170
8
Harome
SCARBOROUGH
A165
TA

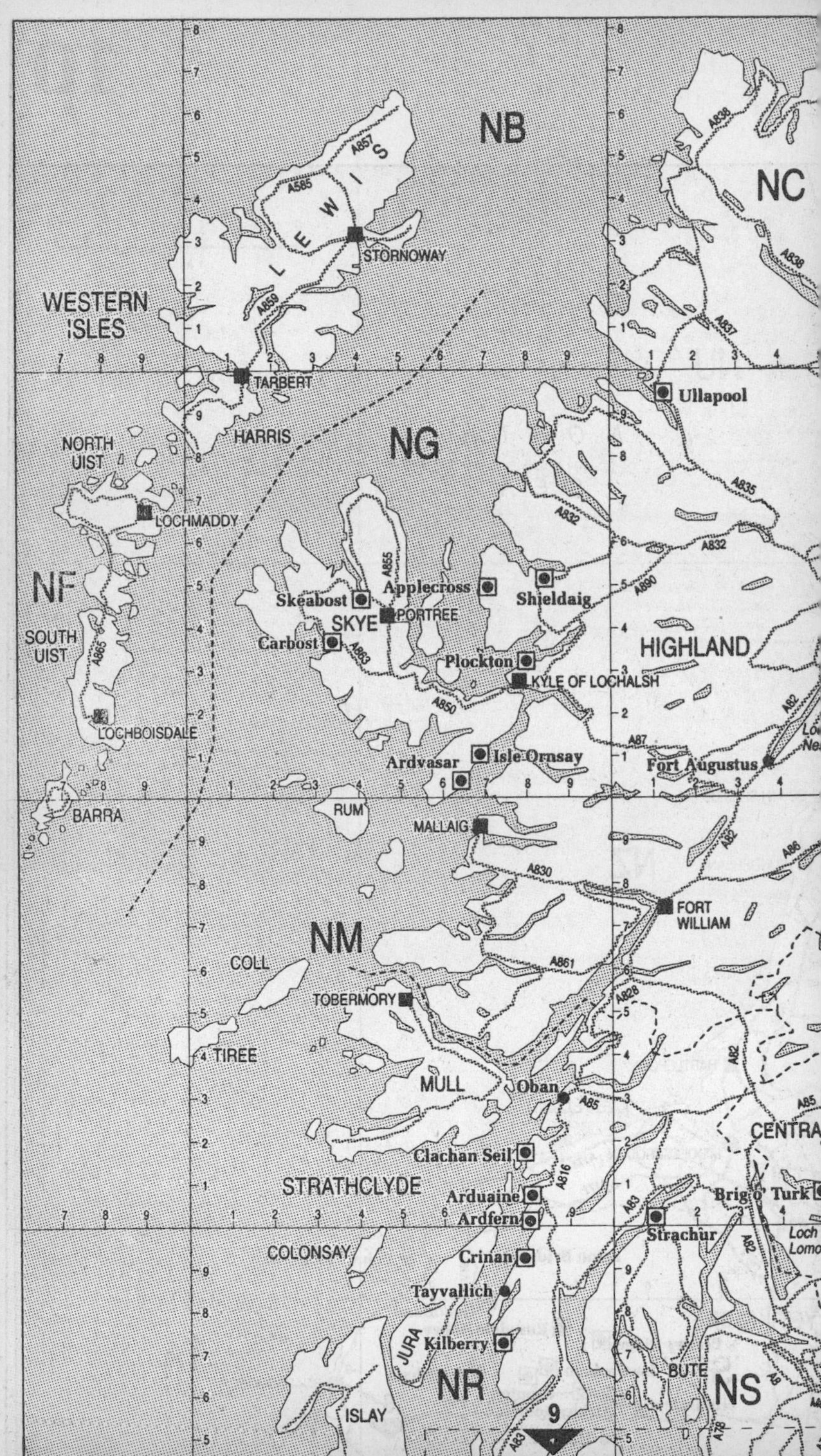

NB
NC
NG
NF
NM
NR
NS
WESTERN ISLES
LEWIS
STORNOWAY
A857
A585
A859
A838
A837
TARBERT
HARRIS
Ullapool
NORTH UIST
LOCHMADDY
SOUTH UIST
A865
LOCHBOISDALE
BARRA
A835
A832
A890
A855
Applecross
Shieldaig
Skeabost
SKYE
PORTREE
Carbost
A863
Plockton
KYLE OF LOCHALSH
HIGHLAND
A850
A87
A82
Isle Ornsay
Ardvasar
Fort Augustus
RUM
MALLAIG
A830
A86
FORT WILLIAM
COLL
A861
A828
TOBERMORY
TIREE
MULL
Oban
A85
CENTRA
Clachan Seil
A816
STRATHCLYDE
Arduaine
Ardfern
A83
Strachur
Brig o' Turk
Crinan
Tayvallich
COLONSAY
JURA
Kilberry
BUTE
ISLAY
A78
9

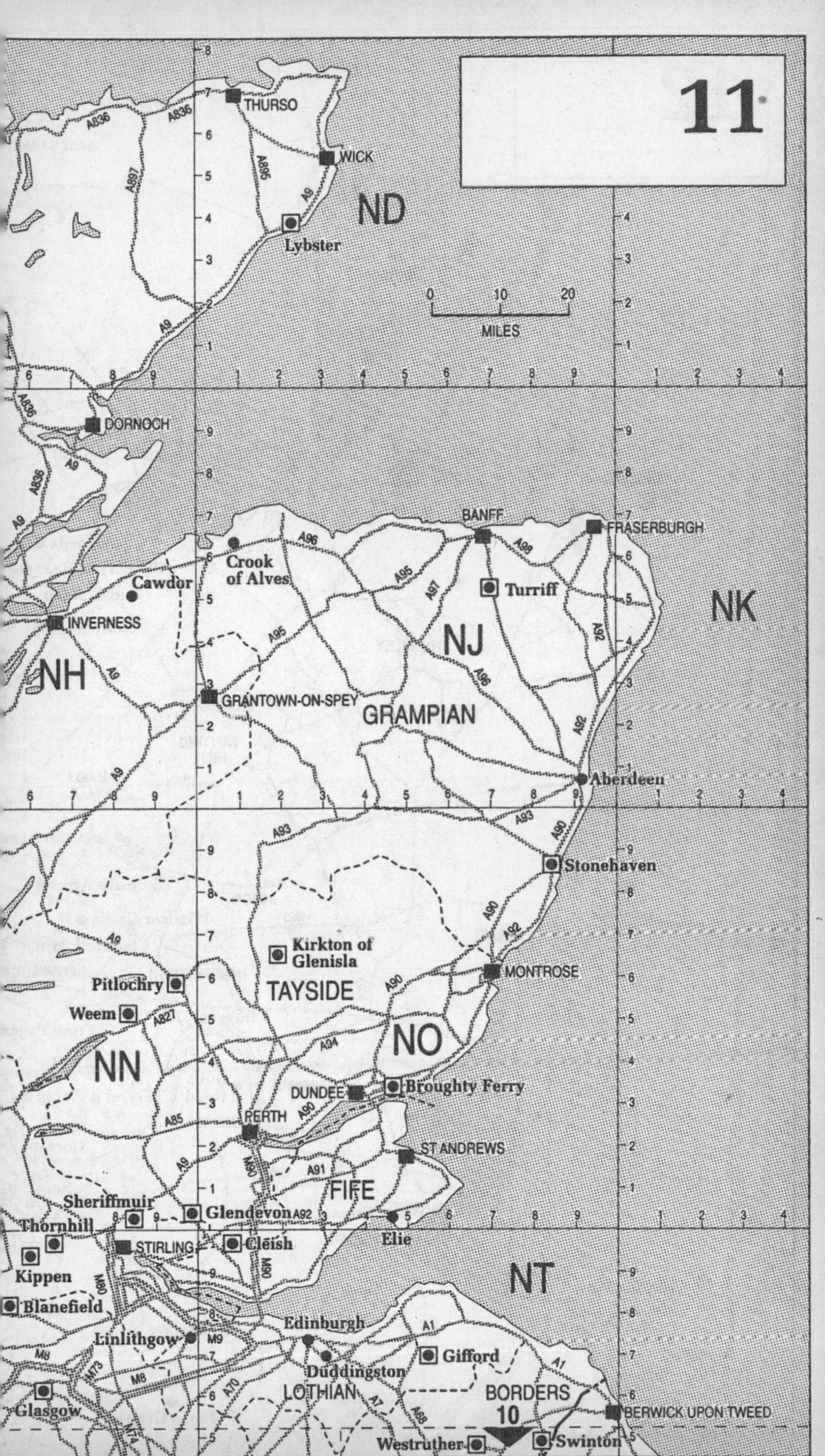

11
THURSO
WICK
Lybster
ND
A836
A897
A895
A9
0 10 20
MILES
DORNOCH
BANFF
FRASERBURGH
Crook of Alves
Cawdor
Turriff
INVERNESS
NJ
NK
NH
GRANTOWN-ON-SPEY
GRAMPIAN
A96
A95
A97
A98
A92
Aberdeen
A93
A90
Stonehaven
Kirkton of Glenisla
MONTROSE
Pitlochry
TAYSIDE
Weem
A827
NO
NN
A94
DUNDEE
Broughty Ferry
PERTH
A85
ST ANDREWS
A91
FIFE
Sheriffmuir
Glendevon
A92
Thornhill
STIRLING
Cleish
Elie
Kippen
NT
Blanefield
M90
M80
Edinburgh
Linlithgow
M9
A1
Gifford
M8
M73
Duddingston
Glasgow
A70
LOTHIAN
A7
A68
BORDERS
10
BERWICK UPON TWEED
Westruther
Swinton
M74

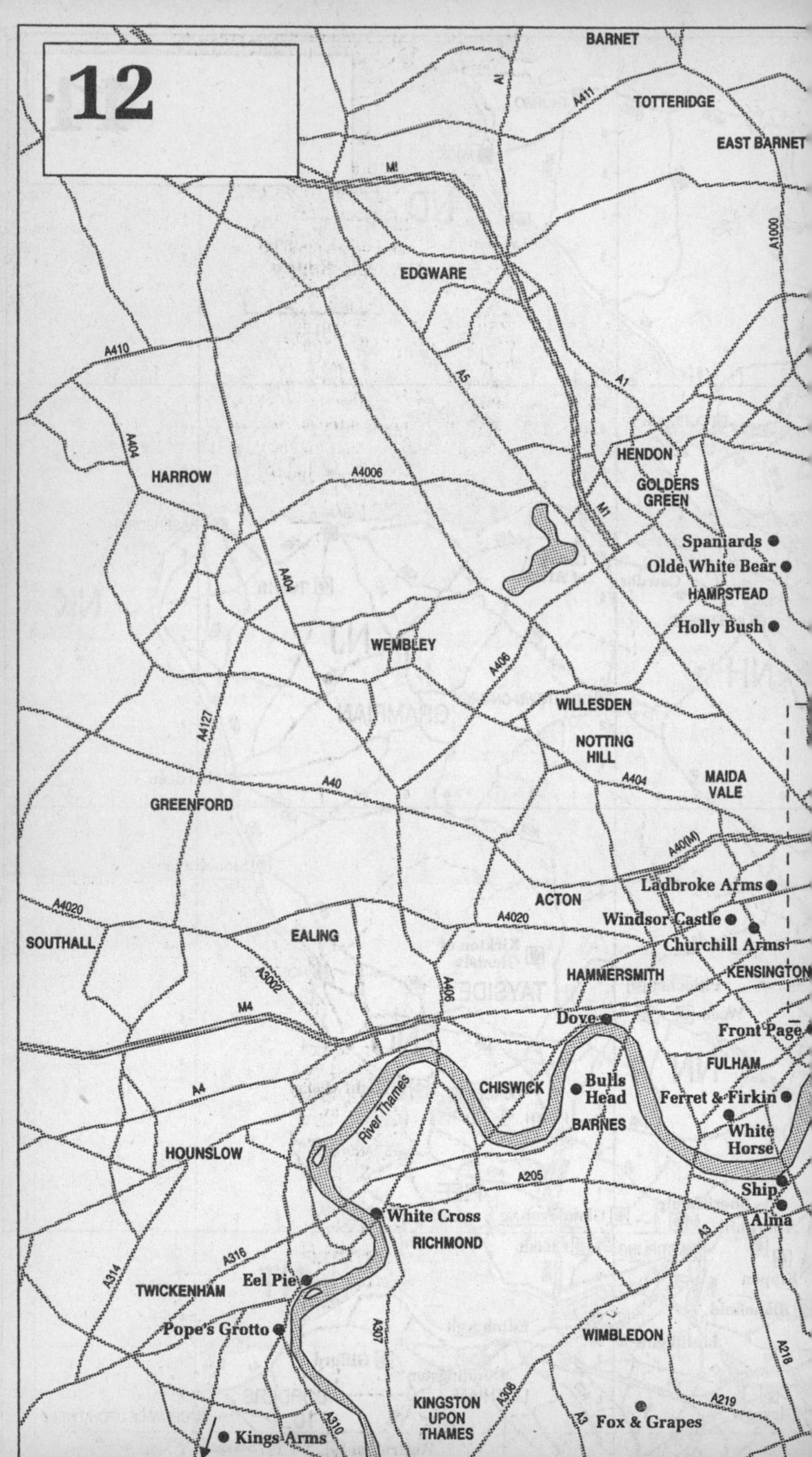
12
BARNET
TOTTERIDGE
EAST BARNET
M1
A1
A411
A1000
EDGWARE
A410
A5
A1
A404
HARROW
A4006
HENDON
GOLDERS GREEN
M1
Spaniards
Olde White Bear
HAMPSTEAD
Holly Bush
A404
WEMBLEY
A406
WILLESDEN
A4127
NOTTING HILL
MAIDA VALE
A40
A404
GREENFORD
A40(M)
Ladbroke Arms
ACTON
Windsor Castle
Churchill Arms
A4020
A4020
SOUTHALL
EALING
A3002
A406
HAMMERSMITH
KENSINGTON
M4
Dove
Front Page
FULHAM
A4
River Thames
CHISWICK
Bulls Head
Ferret & Firkin
BARNES
White Horse
HOUNSLOW
A205
Ship
Alma
White Cross
A3
RICHMOND
A316
A314
Eel Pie
TWICKENHAM
Pope's Grotto
A307
WIMBLEDON
A218
A308
A219
KINGSTON UPON THAMES
A3
Fox & Grapes
A310
Kings Arms

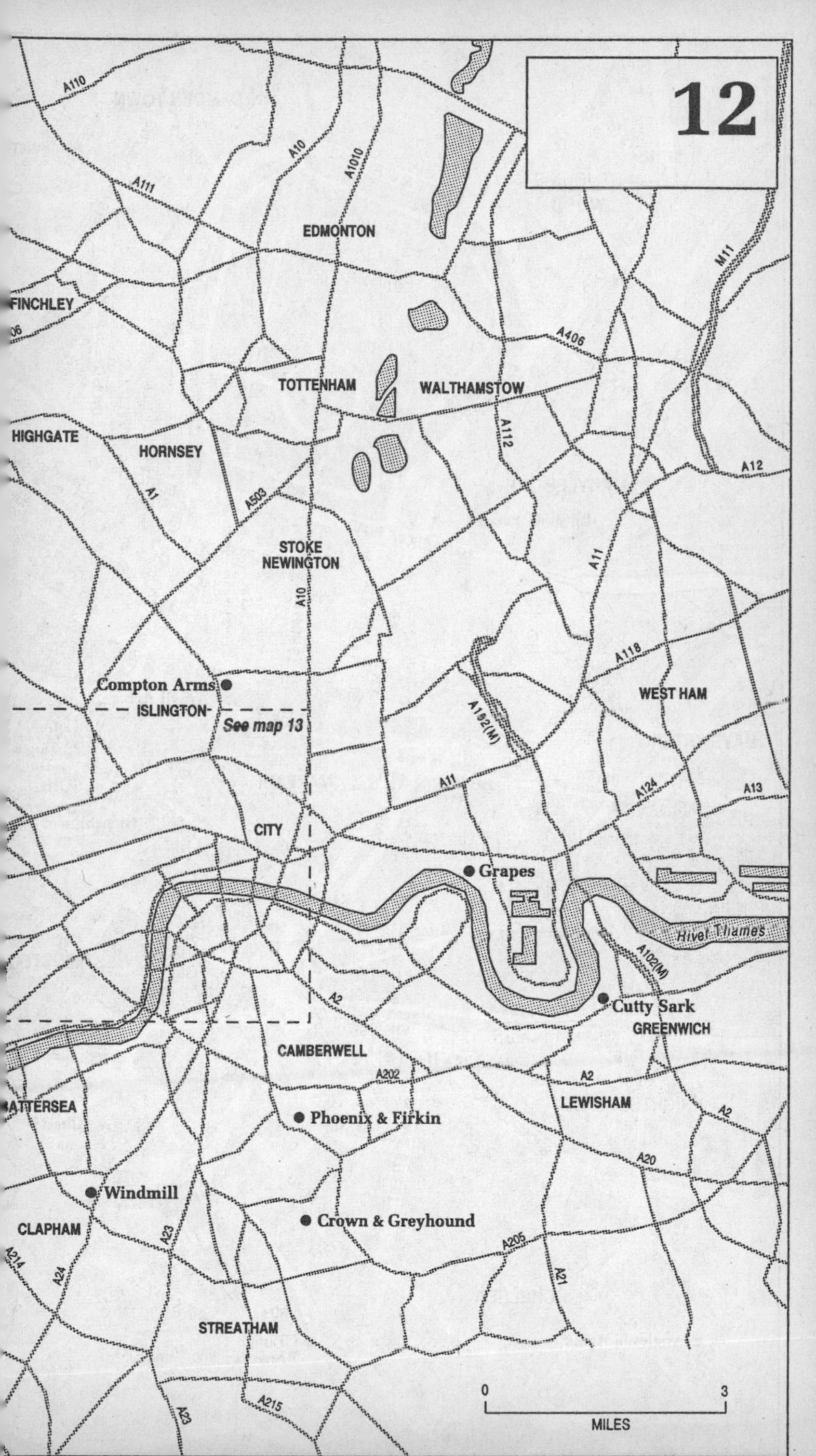
12
A110
A10
A1010
A111
EDMONTON
M11
FINCHLEY
A406
TOTTENHAM
WALTHAMSTOW
HIGHGATE
HORNSEY
A112
A12
A1
A503
STOKE
NEWINGTON
A11
A10
A118
Compton Arms
WEST HAM
ISLINGTON
See map 13
A102(M)
A11
A124
A13
CITY
Grapes
River Thames
A102(M)
A2
Cutty Sark
GREENWICH
CAMBERWELL
A202
A2
LEWISHAM
ATTERSEA
Phoenix & Firkin
A2
A20
Windmill
Crown & Greyhound
CLAPHAM
A23
A205
A214
A24
A21
STREATHAM
A215
A23
0
3
MILES

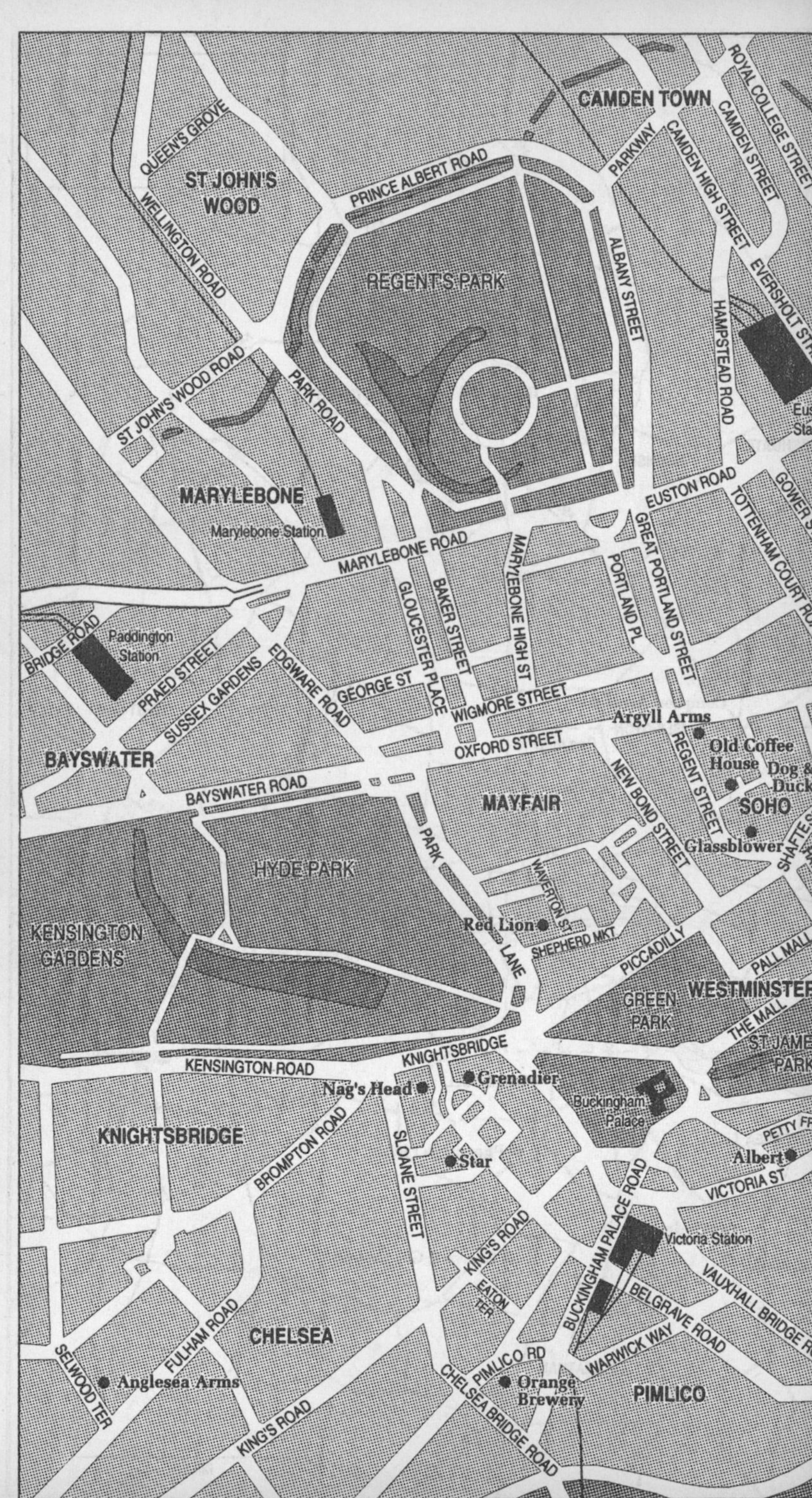

CAMDEN TOWN
ROYAL COLLEGE STREET
CAMDEN STREET
CAMDEN HIGH STREET
PARKWAY
QUEEN'S GROVE
ST JOHN'S WOOD
WELLINGTON ROAD
PRINCE ALBERT ROAD
REGENT'S PARK
ALBANY STREET
HAMPSTEAD ROAD
EVERSHOLT STREET
ST JOHN'S WOOD ROAD
PARK ROAD
MARYLEBONE
Marylebone Station
EUSTON ROAD
TOTTENHAM COURT ROAD
GOWER ST
MARYLEBONE ROAD
GLOUCESTER PLACE
BAKER STREET
MARYLEBONE HIGH ST
PORTLAND PL
GREAT PORTLAND STREET
BRIDGE ROAD
Paddington Station
PRAED STREET
SUSSEX GARDENS
EDGWARE ROAD
GEORGE ST
WIGMORE STREET
Argyll Arms
Old Coffee House
Dog & Duck
BAYSWATER
OXFORD STREET
BAYSWATER ROAD
MAYFAIR
NEW BOND STREET
REGENT STREET
SOHO
Glassblower
PARK
HYDE PARK
WAVERTON ST
KENSINGTON GARDENS
Red Lion
SHEPHERD MKT
LANE
PICCADILLY
PALL MALL
GREEN PARK
WESTMINSTER
THE MALL
ST JAMES PARK
KNIGHTSBRIDGE
KENSINGTON ROAD
Grenadier
Nag's Head
Buckingham Palace
KNIGHTSBRIDGE
BROMPTON ROAD
SLOANE STREET
Star
Albert
VICTORIA ST
BUCKINGHAM PALACE ROAD
Victoria Station
KING'S ROAD
EATON TER
VAUXHALL BRIDGE ROAD
BELGRAVE ROAD
FULHAM ROAD
CHELSEA
WARWICK WAY
SELWOOD TER
Anglesea Arms
PIMLICO RD
Orange Brewery
PIMLICO
KING'S ROAD
CHELSEA BRIDGE ROAD

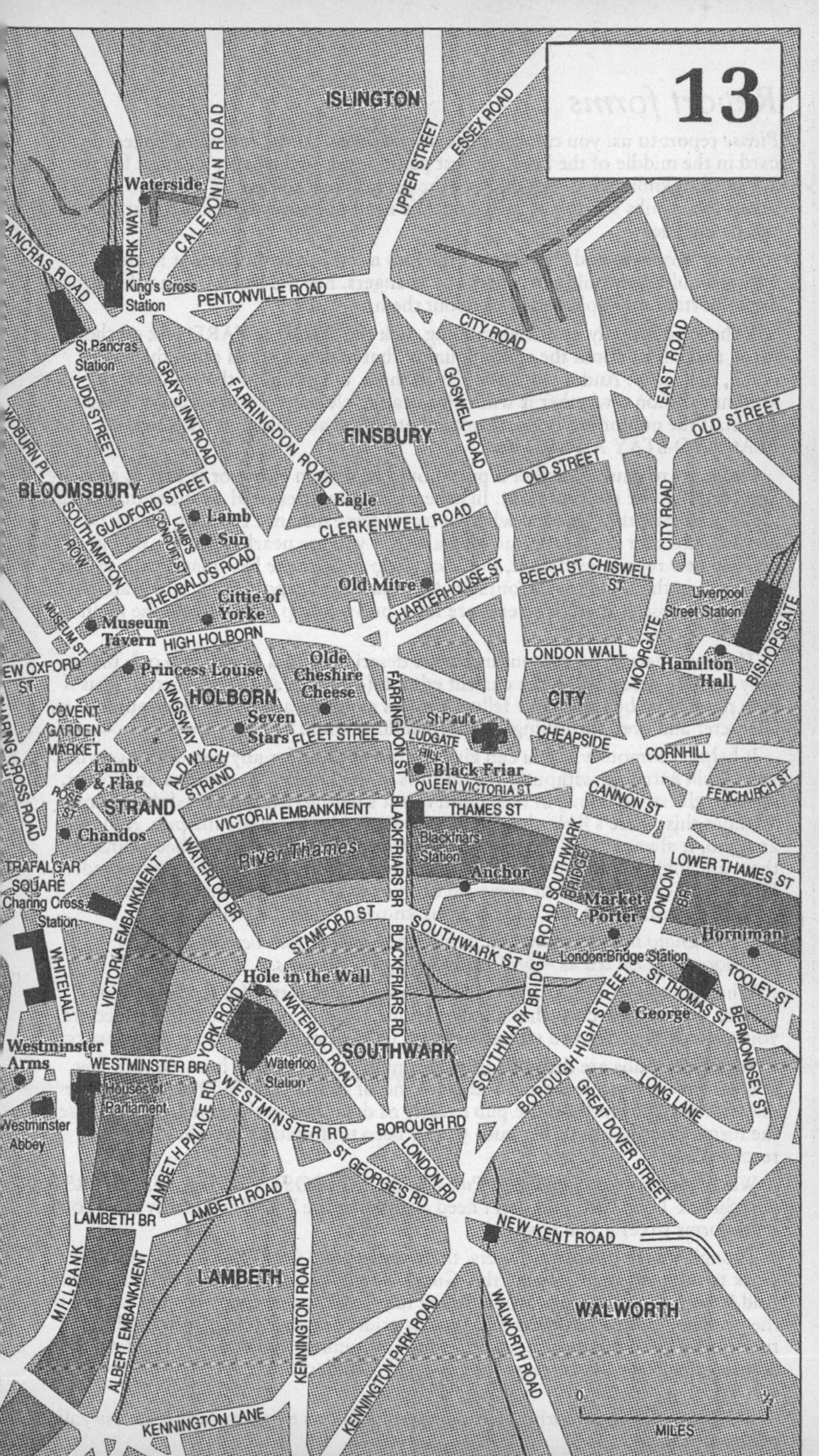

13
ISLINGTON
ESSEX ROAD
UPPER STREET
CALEDONIAN ROAD
Waterside
YORK WAY
PANCRAS ROAD
King's Cross Station
PENTONVILLE ROAD
St Pancras Station
CITY ROAD
EAST ROAD
JUDD STREET
GRAY'S INN ROAD
FARRINGDON ROAD
FINSBURY
GOSWELL ROAD
OLD STREET
WOBURN PL
BLOOMSBURY
SOUTHAMPTON ROW
GULFORD STREET
LAMB'S CONDUIT ST
Lamb
Sun
Eagle
CLERKENWELL ROAD
THEOBALD'S ROAD
Cittie of Yorke
Old Mitre
CHARTERHOUSE ST
BEECH ST
CHISWELL ST
CITY ROAD
Liverpool Street Station
MUSEUM ST
Museum Tavern
HIGH HOLBORN
NEW OXFORD ST
Princess Louise
Olde Cheshire Cheese
LONDON WALL
MOORGATE
Hamilton Hall
BISHOPSGATE
HOLBORN
KINGSWAY
COVENT GARDEN MARKET
Seven Stars
FLEET STREET
FARRINGDON ST
St Paul's
LUDGATE HILL
CITY
CHEAPSIDE
CORNHILL
CHARING CROSS ROAD
Lamb & Flag
ROSE ST
ALDWYCH
STRAND
Black Friar
QUEEN VICTORIA ST
CANNON ST
FENCHURCH ST
STRAND
VICTORIA EMBANKMENT
THAMES ST
Chandos
Blackfriars Station
River Thames
WATERLOO BR
BLACKFRIARS BR
Anchor
SOUTHWARK BRIDGE
LOWER THAMES ST
TRAFALGAR SQUARE
Charing Cross Station
Market Porter
LONDON BR
STAMFORD ST
SOUTHWARK ST
Horniman
WHITEHALL
VICTORIA EMBANKMENT
BLACKFRIARS RD
London Bridge Station
TOOLEY ST
Hole in the Wall
WATERLOO ROAD
SOUTHWARK BRIDGE ROAD
ST THOMAS ST
George
YORK ROAD
BOROUGH HIGH STREET
BERMONDSEY ST
Westminster Arms
WESTMINSTER BR
SOUTHWARK
Waterloo Station
Houses of Parliament
WESTMINSTER RD
GREAT DOVER STREET
LONG LANE
Westminster Abbey
LAMBETH PALACE RD
BOROUGH RD
LONDON RD
ST GEORGE'S RD
LAMBETH ROAD
LAMBETH BR
NEW KENT ROAD
MILLBANK
ALBERT EMBANKMENT
LAMBETH
KENNINGTON ROAD
KENNINGTON PARK ROAD
WALWORTH ROAD
WALWORTH
0
½
MILES
KENNINGTON LANE

Report forms

Please report to us: you can use the tear-out forms on the following pages, the card in the middle of the book, or just plain paper – whichever's easiest for you. We need to know what you think of the pubs in this edition. We need to know about other pubs worthy of inclusion. We need to know about ones that should not be included.

The atmosphere and character of the pub are the most important features – why it would, or would not, appeal to strangers. But the bar food and the drink are important too – please tell us about them.

If the food is really quite outstanding, tick the FOOD AWARD box on the form, and tell us about the special quality that makes it stand out – the more detail, the better. And if you have stayed there, tell us about the standard of accommodation – whether it was comfortable, pleasant, good value for money. Again, if the pub or inn is worth special attention as a place to stay, tick the PLACE-TO-STAY AWARD box.

Please try to gauge whether a pub should be a main entry, or is best as a Lucky Dip (and tick the relevant box). In general, main entries need qualities that would make it worth other readers' while to travel some distance to them; Lucky Dips are the pubs that are worth knowing about if you are nearby. But if a pub is an entirely new recommendation, the Lucky Dip may be the best place for it to start its career in the *Guide* to encourage other readers to report on it, and gradually build up a dossier on it; it's very rare for a pub to jump straight into the main entries.

The more detail you can put into your description of a Lucky Dip pub that's only scantily described in the current edition (or not in at all), the better. This'll help not just us but also your fellow readers gauge its appeal. A description of its character and even furnishings is a tremendous boon.

It helps enormously if you can give the full address for any new pub – one not yet a main entry, or without a full address in the Lucky Dip sections. In a town, we need the street name; in the country, if it's hard to find, we need directions. Without this, there's little chance of our being able to include the pub. And with any pub, it always helps to let us know about prices of food (and bedrooms, if there are any), and about any lunchtimes or evenings when food is not served. We'd also like to have your views on drinks quality – beer, wine, cider and so forth, even coffee and tea; and do let us know if a pub has bedrooms.

If you know that a Lucky Dip pub is open all day (or even late into the afternoon), please tell us – preferably saying which days.

When you go to a pub, don't tell them you're a reporter for the *Good Pub Guide;* we do make clear that all inspections are anonymous, and if you declare yourself as a reporter you risk getting special treatment – for better or for worse!

Sometimes pubs are dropped from the main entries simply because very few readers have written to us about them – and of course there's a risk that people may not write if they find the pub exactly as described in the entry. You can use the form opposite just to list pubs you've been to, found as described, and can recommend.

When you write to *The Good Pub Guide*, FREEPOST TN1569, WADHURST, East Sussex TN5 7BR, you don't need a stamp in the UK. We'll gladly send you more forms (free) if you wish.

Though we try to answer letters, there are just the four of us – and with other work to do, besides producing this *Guide.* So please understand if there's a delay. And from June till August, when we are fully extended getting the next edition to the printers, we put all letters and reports aside, not answering them until the rush is over (and after our post-press-day late summer holiday). The end of May is pretty much the cut-off date for reasoned consideration of reports for the next edition.

We'll assume we can print your name or initials as a recommender unless you tell us otherwise.

I have been to the following pubs in *The 1996 Good Pub Guide* in the last few months, found them as described, and confirm that they deserve continued inclusion:

Continued overleaf

PLEASE GIVE YOUR NAME AND ADDRESS ON THE BACK OF THIS FORM

Pubs visited continued...

Your own name and address *(block capitals please)*

Please return to
The Good Pub Guide,
FREEPOST TN1569,
WADHURST,
East Sussex
TN5 7BR

REPORT ON (*pub's name*)

Pub's address

☐ YES MAIN ENTRY ☐ YES *Lucky Dip* ☐ NO don't include

Please tick one of these boxes to show your verdict, and give reasons and descriptive comments, prices etc

☐ Deserves FOOD award ☐ Deserves PLACE-TO-STAY award 96:1

PLEASE GIVE YOUR NAME AND ADDRESS ON THE BACK OF THIS FORM

REPORT ON (*pub's name*)

Pub's address

☐ YES MAIN ENTRY ☐ YES *Lucky Dip* ☐ NO don't include

Please tick one of these boxes to show your verdict, and give reasons and descriptive comments, prices etc

☐ Deserves FOOD award ☐ Deserves PLACE-TO-STAY award 96:2

PLEASE GIVE YOUR NAME AND ADDRESS ON THE BACK OF THIS FORM

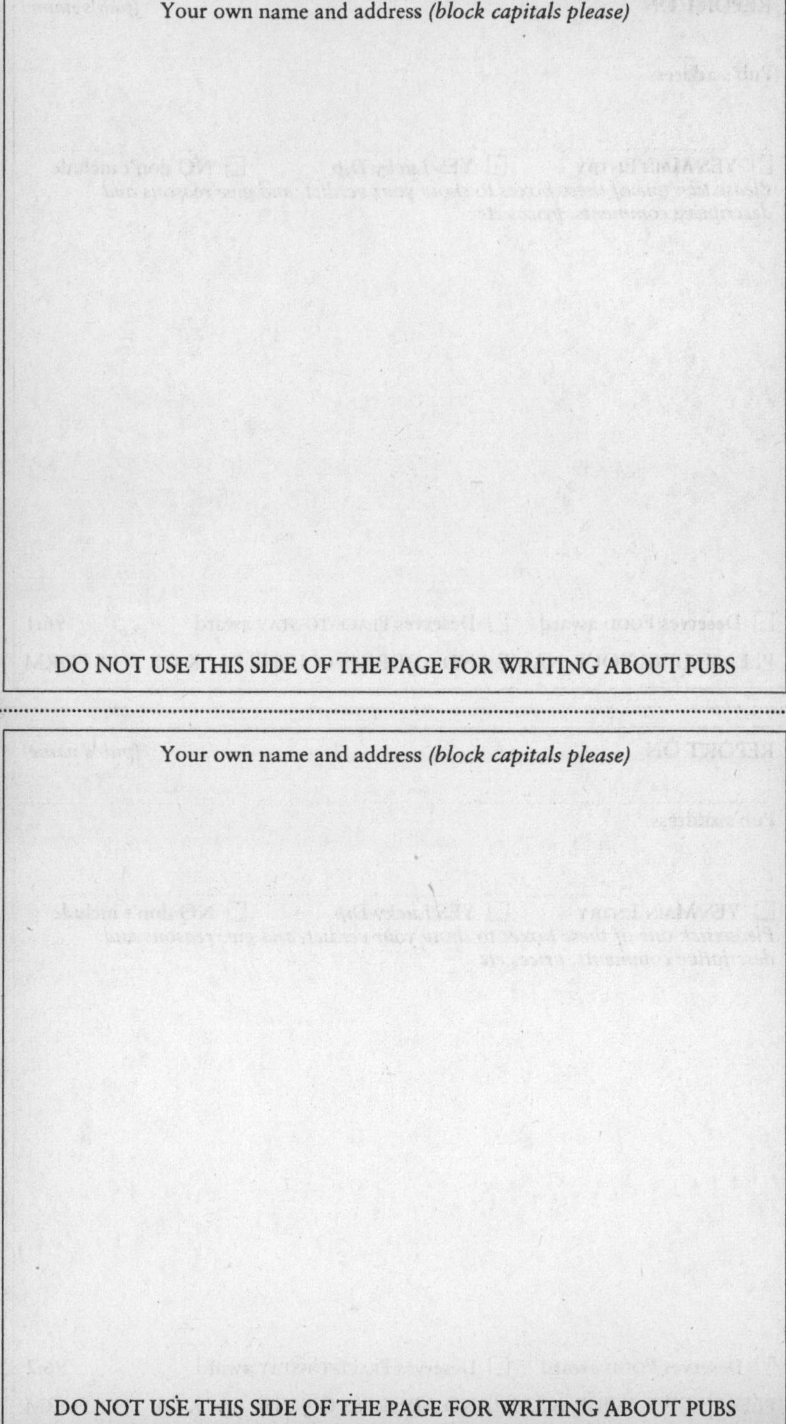
Your own name and address *(block capitals please)*

DO NOT USE THIS SIDE OF THE PAGE FOR WRITING ABOUT PUBS

Your own name and address *(block capitals please)*

DO NOT USE THIS SIDE OF THE PAGE FOR WRITING ABOUT PUBS

REPORT ON *(pub's name)*

Pub's address

☐ **YES** **MAIN ENTRY** ☐ **YES** ***Lucky Dip*** ☐ **NO don't include**

Please tick one of these boxes to show your verdict, and give reasons and descriptive comments, prices etc

☐ **Deserves FOOD award** ☐ **Deserves PLACE-TO-STAY award** **96:3**

PLEASE SUPPLY YOUR NAME AND ADDRESS

REPORT ON *(pub's name)*

Pub's address

☐ **YES** **MAIN ENTRY** ☐ **YES** ***Lucky Dip*** ☐ **NO don't include**

Please tick one of these boxes to show your verdict, and give reasons and descriptive comments, prices etc

☐ **Deserves FOOD award** ☐ **Deserves PLACE-TO-STAY award** **96:4**

PLEASE SUPPLY YOUR NAME AND ADDRESS

Also from *The Good Pub Guide* team...

The 1996 Good Weekend Guide

'Excellent if you are planning day trips or short breaks' *Daily Mail*

When time is short you need a reliable guide to help you decide where to go and what to see. Perfect for weekend breaks, days away or as a holiday guide, *The Good Weekend Guide* is *packed* with useful information and is essential reading for everyone who wants to make the most of what Britain has to offer.

★ A thoroughly practical guide, with up-to-date, reliable and timely advice for every kind of weekend or day out in Britain

★ Includes over 10,000 places to visit and things to do

★ Recommends places to eat and stay

★ Includes detailed maps, symbols and calendars

★ An entirely independent publication from the bestselling *Good Pub Guide* team – no advertising, no paid entries, no sponsorship and all inspections are anonymous

The 1996 Good Weekend Guide will be available from 4th January 1996. To order your copy direct from Vermilion (p&p free), use the form overleaf or call our credit-card hotline on:

01279 427203

Available now...

The 1996 Good Hotel Guide

'An invaluable publication, the best' *Daily Telegraph*

★ *The 1996 Good Hotel Guide* contains over 1400 town and country hotels in Britain and Europe

★ An entirely independent publication – no advertising, no paid entries, no sponsorship and all inspections are anonymous

★ Includes hotels which welcome children and dogs, and those with smoking restrictions

★ Gives details of facilities available, parking, suitability for the disabled, atmosphere, decor, food, drink and service you can expect

★ Completely revised and updated every year

To order your copy of *The 1996 Good Hotel Guide* direct from Vermilion (p&p free), use the form overleaf or call our credit-card hotline on:

01279 427203